$$AR_v + MR = C \overset{relates}{\underset{to}{\rightleftharpoons}} P$$

Actus
Reus

Mens
Rea

culpability

Actus Reus - culpable conduct

Men Rea - culpable mental state PLUS

The amount of culpability depends on the degree
of AR + MR (which is the crime committed). AR + MR
can change the degree of culpability to which the
crime is committed because the degree of AR + MR
may be less, more severe, or equal to the crime
committed.

$$\underbrace{ME}_{AR_v + MR} \text{ material}_{element}$$

Benthams rule of proportionality

SI specific intent	GI general intent	SL strict liability
intentionally knowingly	reckless negligence	strict culpability

MALA INSE - crimes do for themselves
(You should know the wrongs)

MALA Prohibitum - crosses between
civil $\rightarrow$ Torts / crimes
wrongs   punishment

(MANL laws
tough to know them all)
ignorance

CRIMINAL LAW AND ITS PROCESSES

CASES AND MATERIALS

CRIMINAL LAW AND ITS PROCESSES

CASES AND MATERIALS

SIXTH EDITION

Sanford H. Kadish

Alexander F. and May T. Morrison
Professor of Law, Emeritus
University of California, Berkeley

Stephen J. Schulhofer

Julius Kreeger Professor of Law and Criminology
University of Chicago

Little, Brown and Company
Boston   New York   Toronto   London

Library of Congress Catalog Card No. 94-79722
ISBN 0-316-47818-0

Sixth edition

Second Printing

KP

*Published simultaneously in Canada
by Little, Brown & Company (Canada) Limited*

Printed in the United States of America

SUMMARY OF CONTENTS

CONTENTS

CHAPTER 2

CHAPTER 3

DEFINING CRIMINAL CONDUCT —
THE ELEMENTS OF JUST PUNISHMENT   171

CHAPTER 5

HOMICIDE   385

CHAPTER 6

THE SIGNIFICANCE OF RESULTING HARM   547

CHAPTER 7

GROUP CRIMINALITY   641

CHAPTER 8

EXCULPATION   801

CHAPTER 9

THEFT OFFENSES   1039

PREFACE

We have tried in this edition to freshen the material in the previous edition while at the same time maintaining close continuity with it. Thus we have left unaltered the basic organization, tone, and perspective of the book. We have replaced relatively few of the major cases, only doing so to improve teachability or to introduce new developments. Most of the changes have been in the notes and problems, in which we try to present the most interesting ideas in the non-case literature, in the presentation of new topics, and in the organization of some of the chapters.

Why substantive criminal law? We conceive of a criminal law course as serving the ends of both general legal education and training in the criminal law in particular. There are, as we see it, three chief ways the course can contribute to the general legal education of the law student. One way is to provide a vehicle for the close reading of statutory texts — primarily the Model Penal Code, but also state statutory formulations — to help balance the emphasis on case law in the first-year curriculum.

The second way is to introduce the student to the operation of a system of rules and principles designed to apportion blame and responsibility in accordance with our moral norms. While the criminal law is the primary institution serving this function, fault and wrongdoing play a role in determining liability throughout the law. Hence some understanding of the analytical elements in assessing blame for a person's conduct or for the conduct of another, and of the concepts of excuse and justification, is an important element in a lawyer's legal education.

The other way the criminal law course serves the purposes of general legal education is by enlarging insight into and understanding of the potentialities and limitations of the law as an instrument of social control. We have in mind the hard problems encountered in using the law for this purpose: the difficulty of giving legal form to the compromises made necessary when goals conflict; the creation of institutional arrangements — judicial and administrative — appropriate to the goals sought; the limitations — moral and practical — on the use of the law as a means of social control; the relation of legal controls to other social processes. The substantive criminal law is an unusually suitable introduction to these pervasive problems of the law. The ends criminal law serves involve social and human values of the highest order. Its means, entailing the imposition of brute force on the lives of individuals, are potentially the most destructive and abusive to be found within the legal system. The issues it raises and the setting in which it raises them are compelling and vivid. Its institutions are acutely controversial and often controverted. And one of its underlying themes is the momentous issue of the reconciliation of authority and the individual. As Professor

Herbert Wechsler has written: "Whatever views one holds about the penal law, no one will question its importance in society. This is the law on which men place their ultimate reliance for protection against all the deepest injuries that human conduct can inflict on individuals and institutions. By the same token penal law governs the strongest force that we permit official agencies to bring to bear on individuals. Its promise as an instrument of safety is matched only by its power to destroy. If penal law is weak or ineffective, basic human interests are in jeopardy. If it is harsh or arbitrary in its impact, it works a gross injustice on those caught within its toils. The law that carries such responsibilities should surely be as rational and just as law can be. Nowhere in the entire legal field is more at stake for the community or for the individual."[1]

What of the course's narrower purpose of training students in the criminal law in particular? Here there are two main pedagogic objectives. One is to furnish a solid foundation for those who will, in greater or lesser degree, participate directly in the processes of the criminal law. This foundation does not require mastery of the full range of technical skills and information held by the practicing criminal lawyer or administrator, but rather the development of confidence in handling principles and rules — judge-made or statutory — through knowledge about the larger implications of the doctrines and institutions of the criminal law. The second purpose is to create in law school graduates who will have little occasion to practice criminal law an understanding of the problems of the criminal law. As influential members of their communities — and more directly as judges, legislators, or teachers — lawyers versed in the principles of criminal law can bring an informed intelligence to the challenge of solving some of the most vexing problems of our times.[2]

Revisions for the sixth edition. In the procedural sections (Chapter 1), we have streamlined the materials but have retained those fundamentals of criminal trial procedure that we consider essential for understanding the issues in substantive criminal law (rules of evidence, burden of proof, presumptions, and the role of the jury). These topics can now be covered in two to three classes. We believe that a brief but intensive treatment of this material at the outset of the course adds immeasurably to the student's appreciation of the concrete setting in which substantive law issues arise and the practical considerations that so often influence those debates. We have retained in Chapter 1 a substantial but more tightly edited section dealing with the ethical responsibilities of the criminal defense attorney. The themes of this section are central to the study and practice of law, and we believe that students can profit from exposure to these themes early and often in their legal education.

The growing complexity and importance of sentencing procedure and sentencing guidelines pose a dilemma for an introductory criminal law course. The subject is too important to be ignored but too complex to be covered comprehensively. We have sought to strike an appropriate balance by providing in Chapter 2 both a textual summary of current sentencing procedures and a principal case (United States v. Johnson) that can serve as a focal point for discussion in

---

1. Herbert Wechsler, The Challenge of a Model Penal Code, 65 Harv. L. Rev. 1097, 1097-1099 (1952).
2. For a fuller discussion of the role of the criminal law course in the law school curriculum, see Sanford H. Kadish, Why Substantive Criminal Law — A Dialogue, 29 Clev. St. L. Rev. 1 (1980).

class. Though brief and tightly edited, the material is sufficient to illustrate for students the mechanics of how guidelines work, as well as the tough jurisprudential issues underlying them.

In the substantive sections we have updated the cases, added Notes and Problems dealing with issues of current concern, and modestly reorganized several sections (most notably, those on conspiracy, complicity, causation, and insanity) to permit a more succinct treatment. Among the new principal cases are Staples v. United States (the latest mens rea decision of the Supreme Court), Harmelin v. Michigan (on cruel and unusual punishment), Commonwealth v. Berkowitz and In re M.T.S. (two significant recent rape cases), Cheek v. United States (the latest venture of the Supreme Court into the mistake of law issue), and State v. Korell (legal insanity). The major new topics introduced in the new edition include blackmail, suicide and euthanasia (the *Cruzan* case and the recent Michigan case involving Dr. Kevorkian), and the nature of prison punishment in America.

In addition, we now provide expanded coverage of issues that have grown in importance since publication of the Fifth Edition. The topics now treated in more detail include RICO, the law of rape, self-defense, gender issues generally, and the federal sentencing guidelines. In treating these new and expanded topics, we continue to select materials that will highlight the importance of the social context in which these legal issues arise.

As in previous editions, the substantive materials continue to focus on imparting an understanding of what is often called the "general part" of the criminal law — that is, those basic principles and doctrines that come into play across the range of specific offenses (for example, actus reus, mens rea, and the various justifications and excuses). We believe that mastery of the detailed elements of many particular crimes is a goal that is inappropriate for a basic criminal law course. Nevertheless, we have found that understanding of the basic principles is enhanced by testing their applications and interactions in the context of particular offenses. Accordingly, we examine in detail three offense categories: rape (Chapter 4), homicide (Chapter 5), and theft (Chapter 9). The chapter on rape provides an opportunity to focus on the definitional elements of a major crime in a context that has become the focus of acute controversy because of changing perceptions and changing social values. The theme of the homicide chapter is the task of legislative grading of punishment in a particularly challenging area. The theft chapter explores the significance of history and the continued impact of old doctrinal categories on the resolution of thoroughly modern difficulties in defining the boundaries of the criminal law.

Use of the materials in diverse teaching formats. Over the past decade, law schools have begun experimenting with a variety of formats for the basic criminal law course. Although the year-long five- or six-hour course remains common, some schools offer criminal law as a four- or even three-hour course, and some schedule the course in the first or second semester or even in the second or third years. Under these circumstances, a short book designed to be taught straight through, without adjustments or deletions, is bound to prove unsatisfactory for many users. In preparing the sixth edition we have sought to edit the materials tightly enough to avoid significant surplusage for the average course, but we have not attempted to preempt all possible judgments about inclusion and exclusion. Rather, we thought it essential to preserve some freedom for teachers to select topics that accord with their own interests and with the curricular arrangements at their own schools. Thus, we have aspired to create a flexible teaching tool, one that reflects the rich diversity of the subject.

For the five- or six-hour, year-long course, the book can be taught straight through, perhaps with some minor deletions. For a four-hour course, and especially in the case of a three-hour course, substantial ommissions will be necessary. Many teachers will have their own preferences, of course. We present here our own thoughts, based on our experience in structuring the material for use in shorter courses, both in the first semester and in the second and third years.

Chapter 1 (How Guilt is Established). Part A of this chapter (The Structure of the Criminal Justice System) consists of textual material that lends itself either to class discussion or to reading outside of class. In a shorter course it should be assigned as background reading, and the first class can begin with a discussion of the material in Part B (The Process of Proof).

In schools that require a criminal procedure course before the study of criminal law, Part B of Chapter 1 can be largely omitted. It may be appropriate, however, to take up Section B3 (Proof Beyond a Reasonable Doubt).

For students taking criminal law in the first semester of their first year, Part B of Chapter 1 provides basic grounding in process. The teacher who is unable to cover the entire Part can consider assigning Section B1 (overview), and Sections B2 (evidence) and B3 (assigning the burden-of-proof materials but omitting the material on presumptions). We believe that this material, which can be covered in roughly two or three classes, provides a solid foundation for the subsequent study of substantive law. Teachers who skip Section B5 (role of counsel) at the beginning of the course may wish to return to it later. This material raises provocative issues of pervasive importance for the study and practice of law; its themes can provide an appropriate and effective concluding topic for the course.

Chapter 2 (The Justification of Punishment) is basic to the substantive part of the course. Part A (What Is Punishment?) provides descriptive material, both legal and sociological, that affords a sense of the character of imprisonment and other punitive sanctions as they work in actual practice in contemporary American society. Whether simply assigned as background reading or used to stimulate class discussion, this material can help make vivid and concrete the pains of "punishment" and can thus help to give some immediacy to the otherwise abstract jurisprudential debates about when punishment is justified. Part B (Why Punish?) presents material that many teachers will wish to discuss directly and in depth in class. Others have found it preferable, either because of time pressure or pedagogical taste, to deal with the purposes of punishment in the context of particular substantive subjects, such as mens rea, actus reus, causation attempt, justification, or excuse. Part C (What to Punish?) raises basic problems that can be examined usefully either at this point or toward the end of the course.

Chapters 3 (Elements of Just Punishment), 5 (Homicide), 6 (Harm), 7 (Group Criminality), and *8 (Justification and Excuse)* will constitute the core of the typical substantive criminal law course, and, generally, teachers will want to cover them in depth.

Chapter 4 (Rape) is important in its own right and as a complement to the materials on mens rea. Part D of the chapter on rape (Problems of Proof) ca be used to pursue in more detail the themes studied in Chapter 1, or it can be used to introduce those themes when time does not permit full consideration of Chapter 1.

Chapter 9 (Theft) pursues the general themes of the course in the context of a specific crime heavily influenced by historical tradition and by the common law method. In the typical three-hour course, either this chapter or a substantial segment of other material (such as conspiracy) often has to be omitted. In a four-hour course, a detailed treatment of this chapter affords an occasion to explore the problems of defining actus reus and mens rea and determining the appropriate reach of criminalization in a setting of continuing practical importance.

Collateral Reading. There are a number of useful readings for students interested in pursuing further the questions developed in this casebook.

Comprehensive Works: The following publications should be of considerable use to the student:

American Law Institute, Model Penal Code and Commentaries (1980–1985). This is a 6-volume set containing the text and supporting commentaries of the Model Penal Code. The commentaries constitute the most comprehensive available examination of the American substantive criminal law.

Encyclopedia of Crime and Justice (S. H. Kadish ed., Macmillan and Free Press, 1983). This work contains relatively short treatments, written by experts for the general lay reader, on virtually all the subjects covered in this casebook. It should prove particularly helpful for orientation and perspective.

Textbooks: There are several conventional textbooks that are useful for review purposes:

Wayne LaFave and Austin Scott, Jr., Criminal Law (West Publishing Co. 2d ed. 1987). A widely used hornbook; comprehensive and heavily footnoted.

Joshua Dressler, Understanding Criminal Law (Matthew Bender, 1987). A shorter textbook, available in paperback; its coverage largely focuses on the subjects covered in this casebook.

In addition, students may wish to consult the English materials. Professor Glanville Williams has written two outstanding accounts of the criminal law: Criminal Law: The General Part (2d ed. 1961) and a more recent book addressed to law students, Textbook of Criminal Law (2d ed. 1983).

Monographs: There are four works that deal selectively with aspects of the criminal law:

George Fletcher, Rethinking Criminal Law (Little, Brown, 1978): A comparative and theoretical treatment of the criminal law that is highly critical of dominant thinking in the field.

H. L. A. Hart, Punishment and Responsibility (Oxford University Press, 1968): A collection of powerfully argued essays that have had a great influence on contemporary thinking concerning issues of punishment and excuse.

Sanford H. Kadish, Blame and Punishment — Essays in the Criminal Law (Macmillan, 1987): Authored by one of the editors of this casebook, a collection of essays, most of which grew out of the experience of teaching prior editions.

Herbert Packer, The Limits of the Criminal Sanction (Stanford, 1968): A classic treatment of the problems of criminalization and the theory of punishment.

Style. Citations in the footnotes and text of extracted material have been omitted when they did not seem useful for pedagogical purposes, and we have not used ellipses or other signals to indicate such deletions. Ellipses are used, however, to indicate omitted text material. Where we have retained footnotes in readings and quotations, the original footnote numbers are preserved. Our own footnotes to excerpts and quotations from other works are designated by letter while footnotes to our own Notes are numbered consecutively throughout each chapter.

Acknowledgments: Sanford Kadish gratefully acknowledges the support provided for his research by Dean Herma Hill Kay through the Alexander F. and May T. Morrison Chair at Boalt Hall. Stephen Schulhofer gratefully acknowledges the support provided for his research by the Russell J. Parsons Faculty Research Fund and the Sonnenschein Fund at the University of Chicago Law School. In addition, we wish to express our thanks to a number of people who have provided invaluable assistance to each of us:

To Ms. Kristin Largent-Moyes (Berkeley) and Ms. Brenda Huffman (Chicago) for their excellent secretarial support.

To our students, Michael von Loewenfeldt (Berkeley) and Kimberly Dunn, Adam Goodman, and Katherine Moir (Chicago) for their research assistance.

To our wives, June (Berkeley) and Laurie Wohl (Chicago), again, for their cheerful forbearance.

SHK
SJS

February 1995

ACKNOWLEDGMENTS

The authors would like to acknowledge the permission of the authors, publishers, and copyright holders of the following publications for permission to reproduce excerpts herein:

Allen, Francis, The Erosion of Legality in American Criminal Justice: Some Latter-Day Adventures of the Nulla Poena Principle, 29 Arizona Law Review 387 (1987). Copyright © 1987 by the Arizona Board of Regents. Reprinted by permission of the author and publisher.

Alschuler, Albert W., The Prosecutor's Role in Plea Bargaining, 36 University of Chicago Law Review 50 (1968). Reprinted by permission.

American Bar Association, Model Code of Professional Responsibility and Model Rules of Professional Conduct. Copyright © by the American Bar Association. All rights reserved. Reprinted with permission.

American Law Institute, Model Penal Code and Commentaries (Tentative Drafts No. 4, 1955, No. 10, 1960). Copyright © 1955, 1960 by the American Law Institute. Reprinted by permission of the American Law Institute.

American Law Institute, Model Penal Code and Commentaries (1985). Copyright © 1955, 1960, 1962, 1980, 1985 by the American Law Institute. Reprinted by permission of the American Law Institute.

Andenaes, Johannes, General Prevention — Illusion or Reality?, 43 Journal of Criminal Law, Criminology & Police Science 176 (1952). Reprinted by special permission of Northwestern University School of Law.

Andenaes, Johannes, The General Preventive Effects of Punishment, 114 University of Pennsylvania Law Review 949 (1966). Copyright © by the University of Pennsylvania Law Review and reprinted with their permission and that of Fred B. Rothman & Co.

Appel, Brent, *Nix v. Whiteside:* The Role of Apples, Oranges and the Great Houdini in Constitutional Adjudication, 23 Criminal Law Bulletin 5 (1987). Reprinted with permission from Criminal Law Bulletin. Copyright © 1987, Warren, Gorham and Lamont Inc., 210 South Street, Boston MA 02111. All rights reserved.

Arenella, Peter, The Diminished Capacity and Diminished Responsibility Defenses: Two Children of a Doomed Marriage, 77 Columbia Law Review 827 (1977). Copyright © 1977 by the Directors of the Columbia Law Review Association, Inc. All rights reserved. Reprinted by permission.

Arlen, Jennifer, The Potentially Perverse Effects of Corporate Criminal Liability, 23 Journal Legal Studies 833 (1994). Copyright © 1994 by University of Chicago Press. Reprinted by permission.

Armour, Jody D., Race Ipsa Loquitur, 46 Stanford Law Review 781 (1994). Copyright © 1994 by the Board of Trustees of the Leland Stanford Junior University and reprinted with their permission and that of Fred B. Rothman & Co.

Ashley, Jack, Letter to The Times, May 12, 1975. Reprinted by permission of the author.

Ashworth, A. J., The Doctrine of Provocation, 35 Cambridge Law Journal 292 (1976). Copyright © 1976 by Cambridge University Press. Reprinted with the permission of Cambridge University Press.

Austin, J. L., A Plea for Excuses, 57 Proceedings of the Aristotelian Society (1956-1957). Copyright © 1956 by The Aristotelian Society. Reprinted by permission.

Barzun, Jacques, In Favor of Capital Punishment. Reprinted from The American Scholar, Volume 31, Number 2, Spring, 1962. Copyright © 1962 by the publisher. Reprinted by the permission of the publisher.

Bedau, Hugo, Death as a Punishment, from the book The Death Penalty in America (H. Bedau ed. (1964)). Copyright © 1964 by Hugo Adam Bedau. Reprinted by permission of Doubleday, a division of Bantam, Doubleday, Dell Publishing Group, Inc.

Bedau, Hugo & Michael L. Radelet, Miscarriages of Justice in Potentially Capital Cases, 40 Stanford Law Review 21 (1987). Copyright © 1987 by the Board of Trustees of the Leland Stanford Junior University. Reprinted by permission.

Berger, Joseph, Goetz Case: Commentary on Nature of Urban Life, The New York Times, June 18, 1987. Copyright © 1987 by the New York Times Company. Reprinted by permission.

Berger, Vivian O., Not So Simple Rape, 7 Criminal Justice Ethics 69 (1988). Reprinted by permission of The Institute for Criminal Justice Ethics, 899 Tenth Avenue, New York, NY, 10019.

Bishop, Katherine, Asian Tradition at War with American Laws, The New York Times, February 10, 1988, p. 10. Copyright © 1988 by the New York Times Company. Reprinted by permission.

Black, Charles L., Jr., Capital Punishment: The Inevitability of Caprice and Mistake, Second Edition, Augmented. Reprinted by permission of W. W. Norton & Company, Inc. Copyright © 1981, 1974 by W. W. Norton & Company Inc. Copyright © 1977, 1978 by Charles L. Black, Jr.

Blackman, Julie, Potential Uses for Expert Testimony: Ideas Towards the Representation of Battered Women Who Kill, 9 Women's Rights Law Reporter 22' (1986). Reprinted by permission.

Boldt, Richard, The Construction of Responsibility in the Criminal Law, 14(University of Pennsylvania Law Review 2245 (1992). Copyright © by the University of Pennsylvania Law Review and reprinted by their permissio and that of Fred B. Rothman & Co.

Boorse, Christopher & Roy A. Sorensen, Ducking Harm, 85 Journal of Philosc phy 115 (1988). Reprinted by permission.

Bress, David G., Professional Ethics in Criminal Trials: A View of Defense Cour sel's Responsibility, 64 Michigan Law Review 1493 (1966). Reprinted b permission.

Brickey, Kathleen, Rethinking Corporate Liability Under the Model Penal Cod 19 Rutgers Law Journal 593 (1988). Reprinted by permission.

Broeder, Dale W., The Function of the Jury — Facts or Fictions?, 21 Universi of Chicago Law Review 386 (1947). Reprinted by permission.

Brown, Sharon Morey & Andrian Lynch, Voluntariness, Causation and Strict I ability, [1978] Criminal Law Review 74. Reprinted by permission of Sweet & Maxwell Ltd.

Brown, Sharon Morey & Nicholas J. Wittner, Criminal Law (1978 Annual Survey of Michigan Law), 25 Wayne Law Review 335 (1979). Reprinted by permission.

Busy, Pamela H., Corporate Ethos: A Standard for Imposing Corporate Criminal Liability, 75 Minnesota Law Review 1095 (1991). Reprinted by permission.

Chicago Tribune, excerpts from the articles appearing on May 20, 1987 and September 9, 1987. Copyrighted 1987, Chicago Tribune Corporation. All rights reserved. Used with permission.

Cipparone, Rocco C., The Defense of Battered Women Who Kill, 135 University of Pennsylvania Law Review 427 (1987) Copyright © 1987 University of Pennsylvania Law Review. Reprinted by permission.

Cohen, Morris, Moral Aspects of the Criminal Law, 49 Yale Law Journal 987, 1012-1014 (1940). Reprinted by permission of Yale Law Journal and Fred B. Rothman & Co.

Comment, 43 University of Chicago Law Review 613 (1976). Reprinted by permission.

Comment, The Law of Necessity as Applied in the *Bisbee* Deportation Case, 3 Arizona Law Review 264 (1961). Copyright © 1961 by the Arizona Board of Regents. Reprinted by permission.

Comment (on Stephenson), 31 Michigan Law Review 659 (1933). Reprinted by permission.

Commentary on the *Anderson and Morris* Case, [1966] Criminal Law Review 385. Reprinted by permission of Sweet & Maxwell Ltd.

Conley, John, Will O'Barr, E. Allen Lind, The Power of Language [1978] Duke Law Journal 1375. Copyright © 1978 by Duke University School of Law. Reprinted by permission.

Cook, Phillip, The Use of Criminal Sanctions to Regulate Product Safety: Comment on *Wheeler*, 13 Journal of Legal Studies 619 (1984). Copyright © 1984 by University of Chicago Press. Reprinted by permission.

Coughlin, Anne M., Excusing Women, 82 California Law Review 4 (1994). Copyright © 1994 by California Law Review Inc. Reprinted by permission.

Cross, Rupert, Reflections on *Bratty's Case*, 78 Law Quarterly Review 236 (1962). Reprinted with permission of Sweet & Maxwell Ltd.

Crump, David & Susan W. Crump, In Defense of the Felony-Murder Doctrine, 8 Harvard Journal of Law and Public Policy 359 (1985). Reprinted by permission of the publishers and authors.

Dan-Cohen, Meir, Actus Reus, in 1 Encyclopedia of Crime and Justice 15 (1983). Copyright © 1983 by The Free Press. Reprinted by permission of Simon & Schuster Macmillan.

Dan-Cohen, Meir, Causation, in 1 Encyclopedia of Crime and Justice 165 (1983). Copyright © 1983 by The Free Press. Reprinted by permission of Simon & Schuster Macmillan.

Delgado, Richard, "Rotten Social Background": Should the Criminal Law Recognize a Defense of Severe Environmental Deprivation?, 3 Law and Inequality 9 (1985). Reprinted by permission.

Denning, Alfred T., Freedom Under the Law (1949). Reprinted by permission of Sweet & Maxwell Ltd.

Denzer, R. G. & P. McQuillan, Supplementary Practice Commentary (McKinney's Consolidation Laws N.Y., bk. 39 §35.20, Cum. Ann. Pkt. Part (1973-1974)). Reprinted with permission of West Publishing Co.

Devlin, Sir Patrick, Criminal Responsibility and Punishment: Functions of Judge and Jury, [1954] Criminal Law Review 661. Reprinted with permission of Sweet & Maxwell Ltd.

Devlin, Sir Patrick, The Enforcement of Morals (1959). Copyright © 1959 by Oxford University Press. Reprinted by permission of Oxford University Press.

Dressler, Joshua, Rethinking Heat of Passion: A Defense in Search of a Rationale, 73 Journal of Criminal Law and Criminology 421 (1982). Reprinted by permission of Northwestern University School of Law.

Durkheim, Emile, The Division of Labor in Society (George Simpson translator 1964). Reprinted by permission of The Free Press, New York.

Dworkin, G. & G. Blumenfeld, Punishments for Intentions, 75 Mind 396 (1966). Copyright © 1966 by Oxford University Press.

Edgar, Harold, Mens Rea, in 3 Encyclopedia of Crime and Justice, Copyright © 1983 by The Free Press. Reprinted by permission of Simon & Schuster/Macmillan.

Erlinder, Peter C., Paying the Price for Vietnam, 25 Boston College Law Review 305 (1984). Reprinted by permission.

Estrich, Susan, Defending Women, 88 Michigan Law Review 1430 (1990). Reprinted by permission.

Estrich, Susan R., Palm Beach Stories, 11 Law & Philosophy 5 (1992). Reprinted by permission of Kluwer Academic Publishers.

Estrich, Susan R., Real Rape (1987). Reprinted by permission of the publishers Cambridge, Mass: Harvard University Press. Copyright © 1987 by the President and Fellows of Harvard College.

Estrich, Susan, R., Teaching Rape Law, 102 Yale Law Journal 509 (1992). Reprinted by permission of The Yale Law Journal Company and Fred B. Rothman & Company from The Yale Law Journal, Vol. 102, pages 509-520.

Ewing, A. C., A Study of Punishment II: Punishment as Viewed by the Philosopher, 21 Canadian Bar Review 102 (1943). Reprinted by permission.

Faigman, David, The Battered Women Syndrome and Self-Defense, 72 Virginia Law Review 619 (1986). Reprinted with permission of the Virginia Law Review and Fred B. Rothman & Co.

Fingarette, Herbert, The Meaning of Criminal Insanity (1972). Copyright © 1972 The Regents of the University of California. Reprinted by permission of University of California Press.

Fischel, Daniel R. & Alan O. Sykes, Civil RICO After *Reves:* An Economic Commentary, [1993] Supreme Court Review 157 —. © 1995 by The University of Chicago. All Rights Reserved. Published 1995. Reprinted by permission.

Fletcher, George P., Blackmail: The Paradigmatic Crime, 141 University of Pennsylvania Law Review 1617 (1993). Copyright © by the University of Pennsylvania Law Review and reprinted by their permission and that of Fred B. Rothman & Co.

Fletcher, George P., A Crime of Self-Defense: Bernhard Goetz and the Law of Trial (1988). Reprinted by permission.

Fletcher, George P., Reflections on Felony-Murder, 12 Southwestern University Law Review 413 (1981). Reprinted by permission.

Fletcher, George P., Rethinking Criminal Law (1978). Copyright © 1978 by George P. Fletcher. Reprinted by permission of Little, Brown and Company and the author.

Foot, Phillipa, Life and Death, London Review of Books, August 7, 1986. Reprinted by permission.

Frankel, Marvin, Criminal Sentences: Law Without Order (1973). Copyright © 1973 by Farrar, Straus & Giroux. Reprinted by permission.

Freedman, Monroe H., Lawyers' Ethics in an Adversary System (1975). Published by The Michie Company, a subsidiary of Macmillan Publishing Co. Reprinted by permission of the author.

Gilligan, Matthew J., Note, Stalking the Stalker: Developing New Laws to Thwart Those Who Terrorize Others, 27 Georgia Law Review 285 (1992). This article was originally published at 27 Georgia Law Review 285 (1992) and is reprinted with permission.

Ginsburg, Douglas and Paul Schechtman, Blackmail: An Economic Analysis of the Law, 141 University of Pennsylvania Law Review 1873 (1993). Copyright © by the University of Pennsylvania Law Review. Reprinted by permission of University of Pennsylvania Press and Fred B. Rothman & Co.

Glazebrook, Peter, How Long, Then, Is the Arm of the Law to Be?, 25 Modern Law Review 301 (1962). Reprinted by permission.

Glazebrook, Peter, The Necessity Plea in English Criminal Law, 30 Cambridge Law Journal 87 (1972). Copyright © 1972 by Cambridge University Press. Reprinted by permission.

Goff, Robert, The Mental Element in Murder, 104 Law Quarterly Review 30 (1988). Reprinted with permission of Sweet & Maxwell Ltd.

Goldstein, Abraham, Conspiracy to Defraud the United States, 68 Yale Law Journal 4095 (1959). Reprinted by permission of The Yale Law Journal Company and the author.

Goldstein, Abraham, The Insanity Defense (1967). Reprinted by permission of the author and Yale University Press.

Goodhart, Arthur, Possession of Drugs and Absolute Liability, 84 Law Quarterly Review 382 (1968). Reprinted by permission of Stevens & Sons, Ltd.

Gordon, Margaret T. and Stephanie Riger, The Female Fear: The Social Cost of Rape (1991). Reprinted with the permission of The Free Press, a Division of Simon & Schuster. Copyright © 1989 by the authors.

Gordon, Wendy J., Truth and Consequences: The Force of Blackmail's Central Case, 141 University of Pennsylvania Law Review 1741 (1993). Copyright © by the author and reprinted with her permission and that of University of Pennsylvania Law Review and Fred B. Rothman & Co.

Greenawalt, Kent, "Uncontrollable" Actions and the Eighth Amendment, 69 Columbia Law Review 927 (1969). Copyright © 1969 by the Directors of the Columbia Law Review Association, Inc. All rights reserved. Reprinted by permission.

Gusfield, Joseph, On Legislating Morals: The Symbolic Process of Designating Deviancy, 56 California Law Review 54 (1968). Copyright © 1967 by the Society for the Study of Social Problems. Reprinted by permission.

Hall, Jerome, General Principles of Criminal Law (1960). Reprinted by permission.

Hall, Jerome, Theft, Law and Society (2d ed. 1952). Published by Michie, Bobbs-Merrill, Inc. Reprinted by permission of the publisher and the author.

Hans, Valerie P. & Neil Vidmar, Judging the Jury (1986). Reprinted with permission of Plenum Publishing Corp. and the authors.

Hart, H. L. A., Book Review (Wootton, Crime and the Criminal Law (163)), 74 Yale Law Journal 135 (1965). Reprinted by permission of The Yale Law Journal Company, Fred B. Rothman & Company, and the author from the Yale Law Journal.

Hart, H. L. A., Law, Liberty and Morality (1963). Reprinted by permission of Stanford University Press.

Hart, H. L. A., The Morality of the Criminal Law (1965). Published by Magnes Press. Reprinted by permission.

Hart, H. L. A., Punishment and Responsibility (1968). Copyright © 1968 by Oxford University Press. Reprinted by permission of Oxford University Press.

Hart, H. L. A. & A. Honoré, Causation in the Law (1958). Reprinted by permission.

Hart, H. L. A. & A. Honoré, Causation in the Law (1959). Reprinted by permission.

Hassett, Patricia, Absolutism in Causation, 38 Syracuse Law Review 683 (1987). Reprinted by permission.

Hawkins, Gordon, Deterrence: The Legal Threat in Crime Control (1973). Reprinted by permission.

Hazard, Geoffrey C., Jr., Criminal Justice System: Overview, in 2 Encyclopedia of Crime and Justice 450 (1983). Copyright © 1983 by The Free Press. Reprinted by permission of Simon & Schuster Macmillan.

Holtzman, Elizabeth, Premenstrual Symptoms: No Legal Defense, 60 St. Johns Law Review 712 (1986). Reprinted by permission.

Hughes, Graham, Criminal Responsibility, 16 Stanford Law Review 470 (1964). Copyright © 1964 by the Board of Trustees of the Leland Stanford Junior University and reprinted with their permission and that of Fred B. Rothman & Co.

Husak, Douglas N. & George C. Thomas, III, Date Rape, Social Convention and Reasonable Mistakes, 11 Law & Philosophy 95 (1992). Reprinted by permission of Kluwer Academic Publishers.

Isenbergh, Joseph, Blackmail from A to C, 141 University of Pennsylvania Law Review 1905 (1993). Copyright © by the University of Pennsylvania Law Review and reprinted by their permission and that of Fred B. Rothman & Co

Jeffries, John Calvin, Jr. & Paul B. Stephan, Defense, Presumptions and Burdens of Proof in the Criminal Law, 88 Yale Law Journal 1325 (1979) Reprinted by permission of the Yale Law Journal Company, Fred B. Rothman & Company, and the authors from the Yale Law Journal, Volume 88 pages 1345-1347, 1389.

Johnson, Phillip E., Strict Liability: The Prevalent View, in 4 Encyclopedia o Crime and Justice 1518 (1983). Copyright © 1983 by The Free Press. Reprinted by permission of Simon & Schuster Macmillan.

Johnson, Phillip E., The Unnecessary Crime of Conspiracy, 61 California Law Review 1137 (1973). Copyright © 1973 by the California Law Review, Inc Reprinted by permission of Fred B. Rothman & Company.

Junker, John M., Criminalization and Criminogenesis, 19 U.C.L.A. Law Review 697 (1972). Reprinted by permission of U.C.L.A. Law Review and Fred B. Rothman & Company.

Law Review 661 (1987). Copyright © 1987 by the Directors of the Columbia Law Review Association, Inc. All rights reserved. Reprinted by permission.

Mackie, J. L., Retributivism: A Test Case for Ethical Objectivity. Published by permission of Mrs. Joan Mackie. All rights to further publication reserved.

MacKinnon, Catherine A., Feminism, Marxism, Method, and the State: Toward a Feminist Jurisprudence, 8 Signs 635 (1983). Copyright © 1983 by the University of Chicago. All rights reserved. Reprinted with permission.

MacKinnon, Catherine A., Feminism Unmodified (1987). Reprinted with permission of Harvard University Press.

Marcus, Paul, Criminal Conspiracy Law: Time to Turn Back From an Ever Expanding, Ever More Troubling Area, 1 William & Mary Bill of Rights Journal 1 (1992). Reprinted by permission.

Markus, Richard, A Theory of Trial Advocacy, 56 Tulane Law Review 95 (1981). Reprinted by permission.

Martinson, Robert, New Findings, New Views: A Note of Caution Regarding Sentencing Reform, 7 Hofstra Law Review 243 (1979). Reprinted by permission.

McCord, David and Sandra Lyons, Moral Reasoning and the Criminal Law: The Example of Self Defense, 30 American Criminal Law Review 97 (1992). Reprinted by permission.

Michael, Jerome & Herbert Wechsler, A Rationale of the Law of Homicide, 37 Columbia Law Review 701 (1937). Copyright © 1937 by the Directors of the Columbia Law Review Association, Inc. All rights reserved. Reprinted by permission.

Milgram, Stanley, Obedience to Authority (1974). Reprinted with permission of Harper & Row Publishers, Inc.

Moore, Jennifer, Corporate Culpability and the Federal Sentencing Guidelines, 34 Ariz. L. Rev. 744 (1992). Copyright © 1992 by the Arizona Board of Regents. Reprinted by permission.

Moore, Michael S., Law and Psychiatry (1984). Copyright © 1984 by Cambridge University Press. Reprinted with the permission of Cambridge University Press.

Moore, Michael S., The Moral Worth of Retribution, Responsibility, Character and Emotions 179 (F. Schoeman, ed., 1987). Copyright © 1987 by Cambridge University Press. Reprinted by permission.

Moore, Robert A., Legal Responsibility and Chronic Alcoholism, 122 American Journal of Psychiatry 748 (1966). Copyright © 1966, The American Psychiatric Association. Reprinted by permission.

Morris, Herbert, On Guilt and Innocence (1976). Copyright © 1976 by The Regents of the University of California. Reprinted by permission of the University of California Press and The Hegler Institute.

Morris, Norval R., An Australian Newsletter, [1955] Criminal Law Review 290 Reprinted with permission of Sweet & Maxwell Ltd.

Morris, Norval R., Somnambulistic Homicide: Ghosts, Spiders and North Koreans, 5 Res Judicatae 29 (1951). Reprinted by permission of the publisher.

Morse, Stephen J., Undiminished Confusion in Diminished Capacity, 75 Journal of Criminal Law and Criminology 1 (1984). Reprinted by permission of Northwestern University School of Law and the author.

Murphy, Jeffrie, Involuntary Acts and Criminal Liability, 51 Ethics 332 (1971) Copyright © 1971 University of Chicago Press. Reprinted by permission.

Murphy, Jeffrie, Marxism and Retribution, 2 Philosophy & Public Affairs 21

(Spring 1973). Copyright © 1973 Princeton University Press. Reprinted with permission.

Newman, D., Conviction (1966). Reprinted by permission of Little, Brown & Company.

New York Times, excerpt from article appearing February 7, 1968. Copyright © 1968 by The New York Times Company. Reprinted by permission.

1971 Sentencing Institute for California Superior Court Judges, 100 California Reporter 32 (1971). Reprinted by permission of West Publishing Company.

Noonan, John T., Book Review, 29 Stanford Law Review 363 (1977). Copyright © 1977 by the Board of Trustees of Leland Stanford Junior University. Reprinted by permission.

Note, A Rationale of the Law Aggravated Theft, 54 Columbia Law Review 84 (1954). Copyright © 1954 by the Directors of the Columbia Law Review Association. All rights reserved. Reprinted by permission.

Note, Corporate Homicide: A New Assault on Corporate Decision-Making, 54 Notre Dame Lawyer 911 (1979). Copyright © 1979 by the Notre Dame Lawyer, University of Notre Dame.

Note, Developments in the Law — Corporate Crime: Regulating Corporate Behavior through Criminal Sanction, 92 Harvard Law Review 1227 (1979). Copyright © 1979 by the Harvard Law Review Association. Reprinted by permission.

Note, Developments in the Law — Criminal Conspiracy, 72 Harvard Law Review 920 (1959). Copyright © 1959 by the Harvard Law Review Association. Reprinted by permission.

Note, Does Plight Make Right: The Battered Woman Syndrome, Expert Testimony and the Law of Self-Defense, 62 Indiana Law Journal 1253 (1987). Reprinted by permission of the Indiana Law Journal and Fred B. Rothman & Co.

Note, Individual Liability of Agents for Corporate Crimes Under the Proposed Federal Criminal Code, 31 Vanderbilt Law Review 965 (1978). Copyright © 1978 by Vanderbilt Law Review. Reprinted by permission.

Note, Leading Cases, 101 Harvard Law Review 119 (1987). Copyright © 1987 by the Harvard Law Review Association. Reprinted by permission of the Harvard Law Review Association.

Note on the *McNally Case,* 11 Harvard Journal of Law and Public Policy 286 (1988). Reprinted by permission.

Note, The Battered Woman Syndrome and Self-Defense: A Legal and Empirical Dissent, 72 Virginia Law Review 619 (1986). Reprinted by permission of the Virginia Law Review Association and Fred B. Rothman & Co.

Nozick, Robert, Anarchy, State and Utopia (1974). Copyright © 1974 by Basic Books Inc. Reprinted by permission of Basic Books Inc., Publishers.

Orkin, Mark M., Defence of One Known to Be Guilty, 1 Criminal Law Quarterly 170 (1958). Reprinted by permission of Canada Law Books, Ltd.

Orne, M., Reiter, Antisocial or Criminal Acts and Hypnosis: A Case Study, 46 American Bar Association Journal 81 (1960). Reprinted with permission from the ABA Journal, The Lawyer's Magazine, published by the American Bar Association.

Packer, Herbert, The Limits of Criminal Sanction (1968). Reprinted by permission of Stanford University Press.

Pearce, Jack, Theft by False Promises, 101 University of Pennsylvania Law Review

967 (1953). Copyright © 1953 by the University of Pennsylvania Law Review. Reprinted by permission.

Perry, Samuel, Allen Frances & John Clarkin, A DSM-III Casebook of Differential Therapeutics (1985). Reprinted with permission of Brunner-Mazel, Inc.

Rachels, James, Active and Passive Euthanasia, excerpted from material originally appearing in 292 New England Journal of Medicine 78 (1975). Reprinted by permission.

Radzinowicz, Leon & J. W. C. Turner, A Study of Punishment I: Introductory Essay, 21 Canadian Bar Review 91 (1943). Reprinted by permission.

Rapaport, Elizabeth, The Death Penalty and Gender Discrimination, 25 Law & Society Review 367 (1991). Reprinted by permission of the Law and Society Association.

Raspberry, William, In the Goetz Case, Whites and Blacks Are Both Wrong, Chicago Tribune, June 22, 1987. Copyright © 1987 Washington Post Writers Group. Reprinted with permission.

Report of the Royal Commission on Capital Punishment, 1949-1953, 25-28, (1953), Cmd. 8932, para. 143. Crown copyright is reproduced with the permission of the Controller of HMSO.

Restak, Richard, The Fiction of the "Reasonable Man," Washington Post, May 17, 1983. Reprinted by permission of the author.

Russell, Diana E. H., Rape in Marriage (1982). Reprinted with the permission of Indiana University Press.

San Francisco Chronicle, excerpts from article appearing on September 7, 1974, page 2. Reprinted by permission of the San Francisco Chronicle.

San Francisco Chronicle, excerpts from article appearing on November 14, 1964, page 4. Reprinted by permission of the San Francisco Chronicle.

Sayre, Francis, Criminal Responsibility for the Acts of Another, 43 Harvard Law Review 689 (1930). Copyright © 1930 by the Harvard Law Review Association.

Schneider, Elizabeth, Describing and Changing: Women's Self-Defense Work and the Problem of Expert Testimony on Battering, 9 Women's Rights Law Reporter 195 (1986). Reprinted with permission of the author.

Schulhofer, Stephen J., Attempt, in Encyclopedia of Crime and Justice 97 (1983) Copyright © by The Free Press. Reprinted by permission of Simon & Schuster Macmillan.

Schulhofer, Stephen J., Due Process of Sentencing, 128 University of Pennsylvania Law Review 733 (1980). Copyright © 1980 by the University of Pennsylvania Law Review. Reprinted by permission of the publisher and the author.

Schulhofer, Stephen J., The Gender Question in Criminal Law, 7 Social Philosophy and Public Policy 105 (1990). © Social Philosophy & Policy 1990. Reprinted with permission of Blackwell Publishers.

Schulhofer, Stephen J., Harm and Punishment: A Critique of Emphasis on the Results of Conduct in the Criminal Law, 122 University of Pennsylvania Law Review 1497 (174). Copyright © 1974 University of Pennsylvania Law Review. Reprinted by permission of the publisher and Fred B. Rothman and Company.

Sellin, Johan Thorsten, The Death Penalty (1959). Copyright © 1959 by The American Law Institute. Reprinted by permission of The American Law Institute.

Sentelle, David B., RICO: The Monster That Ate Jurisprudence, pp. 5-13 of the Lecture to the CATO Institute, Oct. 18, 1989. Reprinted by permission.

Simon, William, Homo Psychologicus: Notes on a New Legal Formalism, 32 Stanford Law Review 487 (1980). Copyright © 1980 by the Board of Trustees of the Leland Stanford Junior University. Reprinted by permission.

Singer, Richard, The Resurgence of Mens Rea: I — Provocation, Emotional Disturbance and the Model Code, 27 Boston College Law Review 243 (1986). Reprinted by permission.

Smith, J. C., Comment, [1987] Criminal Law Review 480. Reprinted by Sweet & Maxwell Ltd.

Smith, J. C., Comment on *Howe*, [1987] Criminal Law Review 480. Reprinted with permission of Sweet & Maxwell Ltd.

Smith, J. C., A Criticism of the *Kingston Case*, [1994] Criminal Law Review 784. Reprinted with permission of Sweet & Maxwell Ltd.

Smith, J. C., The Element of Chance in Criminal Liability, [1971] Criminal Law Review 63. Reprinted with permission of Sweet & Maxwell Ltd.

Smith, J. C., Justification and Excuse in the Criminal Law (1989). Reprinted with permission of Sweet & Maxwell Ltd.

Smith, J. C., The Law of Rape: The Heilbron Report, [1976] Criminal Law Review 97. Reprinted by permission of Sweet & Maxwell Ltd.

Smith, J. C., Letter to the Times, May 7, 1975. Reprinted by permission of the author.

Smith, J. C., Liability for Omission in Criminal Law, 14 Legal Studies 88 (1984). Copyright Butterworth's & Co. Ltd. Reprinted by permission.

Stanko, Elizabeth A., Intimate Intrusions (1985). Reprinted by permission of Thomson Publishing Services Ltd.

Stone, Alan A., Law, Psychiatry and Morality (1984). Reprinted by permission of the author and the American Psychiatric Press, Inc.

Sykes, Gresham M., The Society of Captives (1971). Copyright © 1971 by Princeton University Press. Reprinted by permission of Princeton University Press.

Tarlow, Barry, RICO: The New Darling of the Prosecutor's Nursery, 49 Fordham Law Review 165 (1980). Reprinted by permission.

Thomas, Clarence, Crime and Punishment — and Personal Responsibility. Reprinted with permission.

Thornton, Mark, The Intention in Criminal Law, 5 Can. J. of L. and Juris. 177 (1992). Reprinted by permission.

Tiffany, Lawrence & Carl Anderson, Legislating the Necessity Defense in Criminal Law, 52 Denver Law Journal 839 (1975). Reprinted by permission.

Underwood, Barbara D., The Thumb on the Scales of Justice: Burdens of persuasion in Criminal Cases, 86 Yale Law Journal 1299 (1977). Reprinted by permission of The Yale Law Journal Company and Fred B. Rothman & Company from The Yale Law Journal, Vol. 86, pages 1299-1348.

van den Haag, Ernest, On Deterrence and the Death Penalty, 60 Journal of Criminal Law, Criminology & Political Science 141 (1969). Copyright © 1969 by Northwestern University School of Law. Reprinted by permission.

van den Haag, Ernest, Punishing Criminals: Concerning a Very Old and Painful Question (1975). Copyright © 1975 by Basic Books, Inc. By permission of Basic Books, Inc., Publishers, New York, N.Y.

Vitiello, Michael, Reconsidering Rehabilitation, 65 Tulane Law Review 1011 (1991). Reprinted with permission.

Wasserstrom, Richard, Lawyers as Professionals: Some Moral Issues, 5 Human Rights 1 (1975). Reprinted by permission.

Wechsler, Herbert, The Challenge of a Model Penal Code, 65 Harvard Law Review 1097 (1952). Copyright © 1952 by the Harvard Law Review Association. Reprinted by permission of the Harvard Law Review Association and the author.

Weiner, Robin D. Shifting the Communication Burden: A Meaningful Consent Standard in Rape, 6 Harvard Women's Law Journal 143 (1983). Copyright © 1983 by the Harvard Women's Law Journal. Reprinted by permission.

Wharton, Francis, Wharton's Criminal Law (12th ed. 1932). Copyright Lawyer's Cooperative Publishing Co. Reprinted by permission.

Wheeler, Malcolm E., Products Liability: Manufacturers, Wrong Targets for Threat of Criminal Sanctions?, National Law Journal (December 22, 1980). Reprinted by permission of New York Law Publishing Company.

Wheeler, Malcolm E., The Use of Criminal Statutes to Regulate Product Safety, 13 Journal of Legal Studies 593 (1984). Copyright © 1984 by the Chicago University Press. Reprinted by permission.

Williams, Glanville, Blackmail, [1954] Criminal Law Review 162. Reprinted with permission of Sweet & Maxwell Ltd.

Williams, Glanville, Criminal Law: The General Part (2d edition 1961). Reprinted by permission of Sweet & Maxwell Ltd.

Williams, Glanville, Euthanasia, 41 Medico-Legal Journal 14 (1973). Reprinted by permission of the publisher and the author.

Williams, Glanville, Letter to The Times, May 8, 1975. Reprinted by permission of the author.

Williams, Glanville, The Mental Element in Crime (1965). Copyright © The Magnes Press. Reprinted by permission.

Williams, Glanville, Oblique Intention, Cambridge Law Journal 417 (1987). Reprinted by permission of Cambridge University Press.

Williams, Glanville, Police Control of Intending Criminals, [1955] Criminal Law Review 6. Reprinted by permission of Sweet & Maxwell Ltd. and the author.

Williams, Glanville, The Proof of Guilt (3d edition 1963). Reprinted by permission of Sweet & Maxwell Ltd. and the author.

Williams, Glanville, Provocation and the Reasonable Man, [1954] Criminal Law Review 740. Reprinted by permission of Sweet & Maxwell Ltd. and the author.

Williams, Glanville, Textbook of the Criminal Law (2d ed. 1983). Reprinted with permission of Sweet & Maxwell Ltd.

Williams, Glanville, The Unresolved Problem of Recklessness, 8 Legal Studies 74 (1988). Copyright Butterworth's & Co. Ltd. Reprinted by permission.

Wootton, Lady Barbara, Crime and the Criminal Law (1963). Reprinted by permission of Sweet & Maxwell Ltd.

Yaeger, Daniel B., A Radical Community of Aid: A Rejoinder to Opponents of Affirmative Duties to Help Strangers, 71 Washington University Law Quarterly 1 (1993). Reprinted with permission.

Younger, Irving, The Facts of a Cases, 3 University of Arkansas at Little Rock Law Review 345 (1980). Reprinted by permission.

CRIMINAL LAW AND ITS PROCESSES

CASES AND MATERIALS

CHAPTER

1

HOW GUILT IS ESTABLISHED

A. THE STRUCTURE OF THE CRIMINAL JUSTICE SYSTEM

PRESIDENT'S COMMISSION ON LAW ENFORCEMENT
AND THE ADMINISTRATION OF JUSTICE,
THE CHALLENGE OF CRIME IN A FREE SOCIETY

7-12, 91-107, 127-137, 141-150 (1967)[1]

Any criminal justice system is an apparatus society uses to enforce the standards of conduct necessary to protect individuals and the community. It operates by apprehending, prosecuting, convicting, and sentencing those members of the community who violate the basic rules of group existence. The action taken against lawbreakers is designed to serve three purposes beyond the immediately punitive one. It removes dangerous people from the community; it deters others from criminal behavior; and it gives society an opportunity to attempt to transform lawbreakers into law-abiding citizens. What most significantly distinguishes the system of one country from that of another is the extent and the form of the protections it offers individuals in the process of determining guilt and imposing punishment. Our system of justice deliberately sacrifices much in efficiency and even in effectiveness in order to preserve local autonomy and to protect the individual. . . .

The criminal justice system has three separately organized parts — the police, the courts, and corrections — and each has distinct tasks. However, these parts are by no means independent of each other. What each one does and how it does it has a direct effect on the work of the others. The courts must deal, and can only deal, with those whom the police arrest; the business of corrections is with those delivered to it by the courts. How successfully corrections reforms

1. For convenience of exposition, we have added some headings and altered the sequence of certain paragraphs in this excerpt. Though criminal justice problems have changed in many respects since the publication of this report, it provides a useful overview of the organization and functioning of the criminal justice system, and the passages excerpted here are still accurate as descriptions of current conditions. Where appropriate, we have provided more recent information brackets and in the footnotes. Except as otherwise noted, current statistics were drawn from U.S. Dept. of Justice, Bureau of Justice Statistics, Sourcebook of Criminal Justice Statistics — 1992 993), and Federal Bureau of Investigation, Uniform Crime Reports — 1992 (1993).

convicts determines whether they will once again become police business and influences the sentences the judges pass; police activities are subject to court scrutiny and are often determined by court decisions. And so reforming or re-organizing any part or procedure of the system changes other parts or proce-dures. . . . A study of the system must begin by examining it as a whole. . . .

I.   AGENCIES AND OFFICIALS OF THE CRIMINAL JUSTICE SYSTEM

A.   THE POLICE

At the very beginning of the process — or, more properly, before the process begins at all — something happens that is . . . seldom recognized by the public: law enforcement policy is made by the policeman. For policemen cannot and do not arrest all the offenders they encounter. It is doubtful that they arrest most of them. A criminal code, in practice, is not a set of specific instructions to po-licemen but a more or less rough map of the territory in which policemen work. How an individual policeman moves around that territory depends largely on his personal discretion.

That a policeman's duties compel him to exercise personal discretion many times every day is evident. Crime does not look the same on the street as it does in a legislative chamber. How much noise or profanity makes conduct "disor-derly" within the meaning of the law? When must a quarrel be treated as a crimi-nal assault: at the first threat or at the first shove or at the first blow, or after blood is drawn, or when a serious injury is inflicted? How suspicious must con-duct be before there is "probable cause," the constitutional basis for an arrest? Every policeman, however complete or sketchy his education, is an interpreter of the law.

Every policeman, too, is an arbiter of social values, for he meets situation after situation in which invoking criminal sanctions is a questionable line of action. It is obvious that a boy throwing rocks at a school's windows is committing the statutory offense of vandalism, but it is often not at all obvious whether a police-man will better serve the interests of the community and of the boy by taking the boy home to his parents or by arresting him. Who are the boy's parents? Can they control him? Is he a frequent offender who has responded badly to leniency? Is vandalism so epidemic in the neighborhood that he should be made a cautionary example? With juveniles especially, the police exercise great discretion.

Finally, the manner in which a policeman works is influenced by practical matters: the legal strength of the available evidence, the willingness of victims to press charges and of witnesses to testify, the temper of the community, the time and information at the policeman's disposal. Much is at stake in how the police-man exercises this discretion. If he judges conduct not suspicious enough to justify intervention, the chance to prevent a robbery, rape, or murder may be lost. If he overestimates the seriousness of a situation or his actions are con-trolled by panic or prejudice, he may hurt or kill someone unnecessarily. His actions may even touch off a riot.

It is in the cities that . . . social tensions are the most acute, that riots occur, that crime rates are the highest, that the fear of crime and the demand for effec-tive action against it are the strongest. It is in the cities that a large proportioof American policemen work and that a large proportion of police money is spent. Though there are 40,000 separate law enforcement agencies in the Nation, 55 of them, the police departments of the cities of more than 250,000 population, employ almost one-third of all police personnel. Policing a city of more than one million population costs $27.31 per resident per year; policing a city of less than 50,000 costs less than one-third as much, or $8.74. . . .

The current police-population ratio of 1.7 policemen per thousand citizens obscures the many differences from city to city and region to region. Even the big-city ratio of 2.3 per thousand is misleading, for in San Diego there are 1.07 policemen per thousand citizens and in Boston 4.04.

There appears to be no correlation between the differing concentrations of police and the amount of crime committed, or the percentage of known crimes solved, in the various cities.[a]

At the same time it is apparent that, nationwide, the number of police has not kept pace with the relocation of the population and the attendant increases in crime and police responsibility. . . .

[By 1991 the national police-population ratio had risen to 2.1 police officers per thousand citizens and a total of 2.8 police employees, including civilian employees, per thousand. But there were still wide variations from city to city and from region to region.] . . .

B. PROSECUTORS

The key administrative officer in the processing of cases is the prosecutor. Theoretically the examination of the evidence against a defendant by a judge at a preliminary hearing, and its reexamination by a grand jury, are important parts of the process. Practically they seldom are because a prosecutor seldom has any difficulty in making a prima facie case against a defendant. [M]uch more often than not grand juries indict precisely as prosecutors ask them to. The prosecutor wields almost undisputed sway over the pretrial progress of most cases. He decides whether to press a case or drop it. He determines the specific charge against a defendant. When the charge is reduced, as it is in as many as two-thirds of all cases in some cities, the prosecutor is usually the official who reduces it. . . .

The prosecutor's discretion to decide what charge to bring against, and what disposition to recommend for, an offender is indicative of his crucial position in the law enforcement system. . . . Except for the judge he is the most influential court official.

Yet many prosecutors in this country are part-time officers. They generally are elected or selected on a partisan political basis and serve for relatively short terms.[b] In many places the office traditionally has been a stepping-stone to higher political office or the bench. Prosecutors in most places are so poorly

---

a. An important study, based on experimental variations in Kansas City police patrol patterns, as provided substantial support for this hypothesis. See G. Kelling et al., The Kansas City Preventive Patrol Experiment: A Technical Report (1974). — EDS.

b. As of 1990, 97 percent of all chief prosecutors were elected officials; only the federal government and four states (Alaska, Connecticut, Delaware, and New Jersey) chose their chief prosecutors by appointment. Large cities always have a chief prosecutor employed full-time and a large staff of full-time assistants, but overall only 53 percent of American jurisdictions have a full-time chief prosecutor, and 50 percent of the chief prosecutors have no legal assistants. See U.S. Dept. of Justice, Bureau of Justice Statistics, Prosecutors in State Courts, 1990, pp. 1-3 (Mar. 1992). — EDS.

paid that they must, and are expected to, engage in private law practice. This creates inevitable conflicts between the demands of the office and of private practice. It can lead to undesirable potential conflicts of interest in dealings with other attorneys, judges, and members of the community. As the participation of defense counsel in criminal cases grows, the need to improve the quality of the prosecution becomes increasingly urgent. . . .

C.   THE JUDICIARY

The Magistrate

In direct contrast to the policeman, the magistrate before whom a suspect is first brought usually exercises less discretion than the law allows him. He is entitled to inquire into the facts of the case, into whether there are grounds for holding the accused. He seldom does. He seldom can. The more promptly an arrested suspect is brought into magistrate's court, the less likelihood there is that much information about the arrest other than the arresting officer's statement will be available to the magistrate. Moreover many magistrates, especially in big cities, have such congested calendars that it is almost impossible for them to subject any case but an extraordinary one to prolonged scrutiny. . . .

Judges

The quality of the judiciary in large measure determines the quality of justice. It is the judge who tries disputed cases and who supervises and reviews negotiated dispositions. Through sentencing the judge determines the treatment given to an offender. Through the exercise of his administrative power over his court he determines its efficiency, fairness, and effectiveness. No procedural or administrative reforms will help the courts, and no reorganizational plan will avail unless judges have the highest qualifications, are fully trained and competent, and have high standards of performance.

Selection of Judges. Methods for the selection of judges vary from jurisdiction to jurisdiction, and some States use different methods of selection for upper court judges than for lower court judges. In 11 States judges are appointed either by the Governor or the legislature; in some of these States they are first appointed and then must run for election on their records; in 15 States they are elected without party labels, and in 19 States they are elected on a partisan basis. In a number of States there is a professional or nonpartisan screening process that develops an identified group of professionally qualified persons from which all nominations or appointments are made, or that reviews proposed nominations or appointments for professional competence. Sometimes this process is required by State constitution or statute; sometimes it is informal. Sometimes it is employed for all judges, sometimes only for certain kinds of judges. It is employed least often in the States in which judges are elected in partisan contests. . . .

The Lower Courts

In many big cities the congestion that produces both undue delay and unseemly haste is vividly exemplified in the lower courts — the courts that dispose of cases that are typically called "misdemeanors" or "petty offenses," and that process the first stages of felony cases. The importance of these courts in the prevention or deterrence of crime is incalculably great, for these are the courts that process the overwhelming majority of offenders. . . .

The Nation's court system was designed originally for small, rural communities. The basic unit of court organization in most States remains the county, and about two-thirds of the counties in this country still are predominantly rural in nature. But most Americans live in an urban environment, in large communities with highly mobile populations that are being subjected to particular stress. It is the urban courts that particularly need reform.

In a rural community the parties involved in a criminal case, the offender, the victim, the attorneys, the judge, and the jury, often know each other. What the trial does is to develop specific facts about the offense. In a city or large suburban community the parties in a case are likely to be strangers. One result is that prosecutors and judges seldom know anything at all about a defendant's background, character, or way of life either at first hand or by hearsay. Moreover, information of crucial importance to a magistrate when he fixes bail, to a prosecutor when he decides upon a charge, to a trial judge when he passes sentence is not always easy to obtain. Gathering such data requires trained personnel using time-consuming procedures. In city and suburban courts today these personnel and procedures are not adequate. [In many urban jurisdictions, computerized systems for storing and retrieving information, together with improvements in organization and staffing, now provide much better access to at least some kinds of data. Nevertheless, the procedures and personnel available in city and suburban courts frequently remain inadequate.]

[U]ntil legislation [in 1966] increased the number of judges, the District of Columbia Court of General Sessions had four judges to process the preliminary stages of more than 1,500 felony cases, 7,500 serious misdemeanor cases, and 38,000 petty offenses and an equal number of traffic offenses per year. An inevitable consequence of volume that large is the almost total preoccupation in such a court with the movement of cases. The calendar is long, speed often is substituted for care, and casually arranged out-of-court compromise too often is substituted for adjudication. Inadequate attention tends to be given to the individual defendant, whether in protecting his rights, sifting the facts at trial, deciding the social risk he presents, or determining how to deal with him after conviction. . . .

7.   CORRECTIONS

The correctional apparatus to which guilty defendants are delivered is in every respect the most isolated part of the criminal justice system. Much of it is physically isolated . . . in rural areas, remote from the courts where the institutions' inmates were tried and from the communities where they lived. The correctional apparatus is isolated in the sense that its officials do not have everyday working relationships with officials from the system's other branches, like those that commonly exist between policemen and prosecutors, or prosecutors and judges. . . . Finally, it is isolated from the public partly by its invisibility and physical remoteness; partly by the inherent lack of drama in most of its activities, but perhaps most importantly by the fact that the correctional apparatus is often used — or misused — by both the criminal justice system and the public as a rug under which disturbing problems and people can be swept.

The most striking fact about the correctional apparatus today is that, although the rehabilitation of criminals is presumably its major purpose, the custody of criminals is actually its major task. On any given day there are well over a million people being "corrected" in America, two-thirds of them on probation or parole and one-third of them in prisons or jails. However, prisons and jails are where four-fifths of correctional money is spent and where nine-tenths of correctional employees work.

[This situation has persisted. There are now roughly a million prisoners in federal and state custody at any given time, but these account for only 20 percent of the total offenders subject to "correction"; more than 3.2 million offenders are on probation or parole.

[The population subject to criminal justice correction has grown at a striking rate. At the end of 1992, more than 4.5 million people (one of every 41 American adults) were subject to some form of criminal justice system control, including 2.7 million offenders on probation (a 13 percent increase since 1988) and over 500,000 offenders on parole (a 30 percent increase since 1988).[c] The growth in prison populations has been especially striking. There were 883,593 offenders in state or federal prisons, an increase of 40 percent since 1988 and 168 percent since 1980;[d] prison populations are projected to pass the one million mark before the end of 1994. In addition, at mid-year 1991 there were a record 425,000 inmates held in local jails, an increase of 24 percent since 1988 and 169 percent since 1978. Growing use of incarceration for drug offenders accounts for about 40 percent of the total increase in prison populations; there are large increases in imprisonment for the other major offense categories as well.[e]

[The precipitous growth of the corrections system has had a particularly severe impact on young black males. Recent studies in the District of Columbia suggest that at any one time, 42 percent of the city's black males aged 18 to 35 are subject to some form of criminal justice system control (incarceration, probation, parole, or bond for release pending disposition of criminal charges). For Baltimore the corresponding figure is 56 percent.[g] For an inner city black male, the lifetime risk of arrest and incarceration may approach 90 percent.[h]]

[F]ewer than one-fifth of the people who work in State prisons and local jails have jobs that are not essentially either custodial or administrative in character. Many jails have nothing but custodial and administrative personnel. Of course, many jails are crowded with defendants who have not been able to furnish bail and who are not considered by the law to be appropriate objects of rehabilitation because it has not yet been determined that they are criminals who need it.

What this emphasis on custody means in practice is that the enormous potential of the correctional apparatus for making creative decisions about its treatment of convicts is largely unfulfilled. This is true not only of offenders in

---

c. Probation and parole figures reflect the status at the end of 1990, the most recent year for which data is available. — EDS.

d. See U.S. Dept. of Justice, Bureau of Justice Statistics, Prisoners in 1992, p. 1 (May 1993). — EDS.

e. Id. at 7. — EDS.

f. See Jerome G. Miller, Hobbling a Generation: Young African American Males in D.C.'s Criminal Justice System (Natl. Center on Institutions & Alternatives 1992); Mark Mauer, Young Black Men and the Criminal Justice System: A Growing National Problem 8 (The Sentencing Project 1990). — EDS.

g. Jerome G. Miller, Hobbling a Generation: Young African American Males in the Criminal Justice System of America's Cities: Baltimore, Maryland (Natl. Center on Institutions & Alternatives 1992). — EDS.

h. Miller, supra footnote f. — EDS.

custody but of offenders on probation and parole. Most authorities agree that while probationers and parolees need varying degrees and kinds of supervision, an average of no more than 35 cases per officer is necessary for effective attention; 97 percent of all officers handling adults have larger caseloads than that. . . .

II. Criminal Justice Procedures

A. OVERVIEW OF THE STEPS IN THE CRIMINAL JUSTICE PROCESS

The popular, or even the lawbook, theory of everyday criminal process oversimplifies in some respects and overcomplicates in others what usually happens. That theory is that when an infraction of the law occurs, a policeman finds, if he can, the probable offender, arrests him and brings him promptly before a magistrate. If the offense is minor, the magistrate disposes of it forthwith; if it is serious, he holds the defendant for further action and admits him to bail. The case then is turned over to a prosecuting attorney who charges the defendant with a specific statutory crime. This charge is subject to review by a judge at a preliminary hearing of the evidence and in many places if the offense charged is a felony, by a grand jury that can dismiss the charge, or affirm it by delivering it to a judge in the form of an indictment. If the defendant pleads "not guilty" to the charge he comes to trial; the facts of his case are marshaled by prosecuting and defense attorneys and presented, under the supervision of a judge, through witnesses, to a jury. If the jury finds the defendant guilty, he is sentenced by the judge to a term in prison, where a systematic attempt to convert him into a law-abiding citizen is made, or to a term of probation, under which he is permitted to live in the community as long as he behaves himself.

Some cases do proceed much like that, especially those involving offenses that are generally considered "major": serious acts of violence or thefts of large amounts of property. However, not all major cases follow this course, and, in any event, the bulk of the daily business of the criminal justice system consists of offenses that are not major — of breaches of the peace, crimes of vice, petty thefts, assaults arising from domestic or street-corner or barroom disputes. These and most other cases are disposed of in much less formal and much less deliberate ways. . . .

B. THE INITIAL STAGES OF A CRIMINAL CASE

Investigation

When patrol fails to prevent a crime or apprehend the criminal while he is committing it, the police must rely upon investigation. Every sizable department has a corps of investigative specialists — detectives — whose job is to solve crimes by questioning victims, suspects, and witnesses, by accumulating physical evidence at the scene of the crime, and by tracing stolen property or vehicles associated with the crime. In practically every department the caseloads carried by detectives are too heavy to allow them to follow up thoroughly more than a small percentage of the cases assigned them. In other words, a great many cases are unsolved by default — or, at least, time will not permit a determination of whether or not they are solvable. . . .

In the present state of police knowledge and organization many crimes are, in fact, not solvable. In the great majority of cases, personal identification by a victim or witness is the *only* clue to the identity of the criminal. The Commission analyzed 1,905 crimes reported during January of 1966 in Los Angeles, which has a notably well-trained and efficient police department. The police were furnished a suspect's name in 349 of these cases, and 301 were resolved either by arrest or in some other way — either the victim would not prosecute, subsequent investigation disclosed that the reported crime was not actually a crime, or a prosecutor declined to press the case. Of the 1,375 crimes for which no suspect was named, only 181 cases were cleared. Since crimes against the person are more likely to be named-suspect crimes than crimes against property, it is natural that a much higher proportion of them are solved. In 1965, 78 percent of reported serious crimes against property were never solved. . . .

[FBI statistics for 1992 indicate that of the violent crimes (murder, aggravated assault, forcible rape, and robbery) reported or otherwise known to the police, 45 percent were cleared by an arrest. Of the serious property crimes (burglary, motor vehicle theft, and other larceny-theft), only 18 percent of the offenses known to the police were cleared by an arrest. For cities over 250,000 population, only 38 percent of violent offenses and 14 percent of serous property offenses were cleared.] . . .

The Diversion of Cases before Charge

The limited statistics available indicate that approximately one-half of those arrested are dismissed by the police, a prosecutor, or a magistrate at an early stage of the case. Some of these persons are released because they did not commit the acts they were originally suspected of having committed, or cannot be proved to have committed them, or committed them on legally defensible grounds. The police can arrest on "probable cause," while conviction requires proof "beyond a reasonable doubt." Therefore, some justified arrests canno lead to prosecution and conviction.

However, others who are released probably did commit the offenses for which they were arrested. In some instances offenders who could and should be convicted are released simply because of an overload of work, or inadequate investigation in the prosecutor's office. In other cases the police, or more often prosecutors, have exercised [discretion] to decline to prosecute offenders . . . who present clear medical, mental, or social problems that can be better dealt with outside the criminal process. . . . First offenders are often dealt with in this way. So are persons whose offenses arise from drinking or mental problems, if the offenses are minor. So are many cases of assault or theft within families or among friends, of passing checks with insufficient funds, of shoplifting when restitution is made, of statutory rape when both boy and girl are young, of automobile theft by teenagers for the purpose of joyriding. . . .

Pretrial Release

One-half or more of the defendants who are brought into a police or magistrate's court are released or convicted and sentenced within 24 hours of the arrest. The cases of the remainder, including all those against whom the accusation of a serious crime can be maintained, await final disposition for days or weeks or sometimes months, depending on the prosecutor's caseload, the gravity and complexity of the case, and the condition of the calendar in the court that will hear it.

The magistrate is empowered to decide whether or not such defendants will be released pending trial. . . .

[Traditionally, the device most often used to free an untried defendant and at the same time assure his or her appearance for trial was money bail. In this system, still in use in many areas, the court fixes the amount of an bond to be posted in cash or by a secured pledge; defendants able to post the required amount win their release and recover the sum upon appearance for trial. Defendants unable to raise the required amount usually attempt to secure the services of a bail-bond agency, which posts the necessary bond in return for a fixed fee, typically 10 percent of the total bail. In this system the bondsman's obligations are satisfied upon the defendant's appearance, but the 10 percent charge has to be paid by the defendant in any event.

[The money bail system is unsatisfactory in many respects. It results in confinement of large numbers of untried defendants, solely on account of inability to raise the required amounts. The bail figure often is set by a fixed schedule, without regard to the defendant's means, ties to the community, or likelihood of flight. For those who can raise funds to pay the bondsman's fee, the system provides release but no financial incentive to appear. And in many localities the relationships between bail-bond agencies and court officials have been a source of malfeasance and corruption.

[During the 1960s and 1970s bail-reform projects were initiated in numerous cities around the country. The principal aims of these projects were to ascertain the kinds of community ties that would make defendants safe candidates for release without financial guarantees, to establish procedures for expeditiously collecting the background information necessary to identify such defendants, and to develop a better system of financial guarantees for defendants who could not qualify for release on any other basis. The success of these projects in demonstrating the value of alternatives to money bail led to widespread changes. Pretrial release projects now functioning in more than 100 cities assist the local magistrates in identifying defendants who can be released without money bail and often provide follow-up to help insure that the defendant returns for any scheduled appearances. Often defendants will simply be released "on recognizance" ("ROR"), that is, on their personal, unsecured promise to appear when scheduled. In many states (and in the federal system) when a defendant does not qualify for ROR, the magistrate is required to explore a variety of alternatives to money bail and to select the least restrictive option that will be adequate to assure the defendant's appearance. When money bail is used, many jurisdictions now follow a "10 percent plan," under which the defendant is permitted to post directly with the court 10 percent of the face amount of the bail bond, and most or all of this sum is refundable when the defendant appears for trial. This system eliminates the potential for corruption associated with bail-bond agencies, restores the financial incentive for appearance, and (because the sum to be raised is recuperable) makes it easier for many defendants to obtain the necessary amounts.[i]

i. One such 10 percent plan is discussed (and its constitutionality upheld) in Schilb v. Kuebel, 404 U.S. 357 (1971). As of 1978, 24 states had established a statutory preference for using ROR where feasible, and 22 states had mandated release on the least restrictive conditions possible. At least 18 states had adopted 10 percent plans. See J. Goldkamp, Two Classes of Accused: A Study of Bail and Detention in American Justice (1979). — EDS.

[These reforms led to dramatic increases in the proportion of defendants released rather than detained for trial.[j] Nevertheless, traditional money bail survives in many localities as the primary avenue of pretrial release. In addition, even where a strong preference for other nonfinancial release has been established, the ultimate decision about a defendant's eligibility for these programs remains in the hands of a magistrate, who must balance a variety of subjective factors in determining the risk of flight in a particular case. Concern persists about the fairness and accuracy of these judgments and particularly about the extent to which they are used as a screen for impermissible objectives. Defendants denied ROR and offered only a bail figure much higher than they can meet may be told that the decision is based on risk of flight, but the judgment often stems primarily from the magistrate's desire to insure immediate confinement for defendants perceived as dangerous to the community. In practice, this indirect form of preventive detention is very difficult to challenge.

[The Bail Reform Act of 1984, 18 U.S.C. §§1341-1350, expressly authorizes preventive detention prior to trial in federal criminal prosecutions, on a finding that "no condition or conditions [of release] will reasonably assure the appearance of the [defendant] as required and the safety of any other person and the community." §3142(e). Unlike earlier D.C. legislation, the federal statute does not permit judges to insure detention by setting high money bail on the pretext of "risk of flight"; §3142(c) specifies that the "judicial officer may not impose a financial condition that results in the pretrial detention of the person." The statute thus appears to contemplate that detention prior to trial will occur only after compliance with the specific procedural requirements of the preventive detention hearing, and as a result such hearings have been held with some frequency. The Supreme Court upheld the constitutionality of the preventive detention provisions in United States v. Salerno, 481 U.S. 739 (1987).]

C.   THE GUILTY PLEA

Most defendants who are convicted — as many as 90 percent in some jurisdictions — are not tried. They plead guilty, often as the result of negotiations about the charge or the sentence. . . . A plea negotiation can be, and often is in a minor case, a hurried conversation in a courthouse hallway. In grave cases it can be a series of elaborate conferences over the course of weeks in which facts are thoroughly discussed and alternatives carefully explored. Most often the negotiations are between a prosecutor and defense counsel, but sometimes a magistrate or a police officer or the defendant himself is involved. In some court there are no plea negotiations at all. There almost never are negotiations in the cases of petty offenders. And, of course, many guilty pleas are not the result of negotiations. . . .

D.   THE TRIAL

. . . The cases decided at trial are only a small fraction of the total of cases, but they are most important to the process because they set standards for the con

---

j. For example, from 1962 to 1971, the percentage of defendants who were detained throughout the period prior to trial dropped from 52 percent to 33 percent in felony cases and from 21 percent to only 12 percent in major misdemeanor cases. See W. Thomas, Bail Reform in America (1976 — Eds.

duct of all cases. The trial decides the hard legal issues, and reviews and rules on claims of official abuse. . . .

E.   SENTENCING

There is no decision in the criminal process that is as complicated and difficult as the one made by the sentencing judge. A sentence prescribes punishment, but it also should be the foundation of an attempt to rehabilitate the offender, to insure that he does not endanger the community, and to deter others from similar crimes in the future. Often these objectives are mutually inconsistent, and the sentencing judge must choose one at the expense of the others. A man who has committed murder in a moment of extreme emotion may require no correctional program and may present no significant threat to the general safety, but few judges would be likely to respond to an offense so heinous by suspending the offender's sentence or granting him probation. . . .

Sentencing Procedures

Although the criminal trial on the issue of guilt is a strictly formal procedure, the determination of what is to be done with a convicted offender is often a rather informal one. A judge, when he sentences, needs facts about the offender and his offense. Both will be absent in those many instances when conviction has resulted from a plea of guilty and the court lacks, or has inadequate facilities for preparing, presentence reports. The judge then must rely on the necessarily incomplete and biased oral statements of the prosecutor, defense counsel, and defendant. Such statements may be supplemented by a "rapsheet," a 1-page record of the offender's prior criminal involvements. . . .

III.   THE FLOW OF CASES THROUGH THE SYSTEM

[The chart presented on the next page, taken from the report of the President's Commission at page 8, sets forth in simplified form the flow of cases through the criminal justice system and dramatically illustrates the filtering process through which the vast majority of all cases are winnowed out prior to trial.]

GEOFFREY C. HAZARD, JR., CRIMINAL JUSTICE SYSTEM: OVERVIEW, in 2 Encyclopedia of Crime and Justice 450, 454-456 (S. H. Kadish ed. 1983): [In this essay, the author identifies four significant characteristics of the criminal justice system.] First, [the system] is required to deal with a large and never-ending flow of cases. Even though the system attempts to individualize its response to each offender, and in theory is supposed to treat each case as though it stood alone under the law, the process is in fact one of mass production. This is not to say that the system was planned as a mass-production system. Quite the contrary, many difficulties with it arise from the discrepancy between the fact of mass production and the ideal that each case can be considered on its own merit.

A second general observation is that the system is pervaded by exercise of loosely controlled discretion, which is both systemic and particular. Systemically, discretion is exercised to mediate between the high incidence of crime and the modest resources available to respond to it. Decisions must be made as to the allocation of the system's resources. These decisions . . . often . . . are not based

A general view of The Criminal Justice System

This chart seeks to present a simple yet comprehensive view of the movement of cases through the criminal justice system. Procedures in individual jurisdictions may vary from the pattern shown here. The differing weights of line indicate the relative volumes of cases disposed of at various points in the system, but this is only suggestive since no nationwide data of this sort exists.

1. May continue until trial.

2. Administrative record of arrest. First step at which temporary release on bail may be available.

3. Before magistrate, commissioner, or justice of peace. Formal notice of charge, advice of rights. Bail set. Summary trials for petty offenses usually conducted here without further processing.

4. Preliminary testing of evidence against defendant. Charge may be reduced. No separate preliminary hearing for misdemeanors.

5. Charge filed by prosecutor on basis of information submitted by police or citizens. Alternative to grand jury indictment; often used in felonies, almost always in misdemeanors.

6. Reviews whether Government evidence sufficient to justify trial. Some States have no grand jury system; others seldom use it.

7. Appearance for plea; defendant elects trial by judge or jury (if available); counsel for indigent usually appointed here in felonies. Often not at all in other cases.

8. Charge may be reduced at any time prior to trial in return for plea of guilty or for other reasons.

9. Challenge on constitutional grounds to legality of detention. May be sought at any point in process.

10. Police often hold informal hearings, dismiss or adjust many cases without further processing.

11. Probation officer decides desirability of further court action.

12. Welfare agency, social services, counselling, medical care, etc., for cases where adjudicatory handling not needed.

upon open deliberation. Thus, for example, no legislative act or mayoral directive says that the police shall devote intensive effort to investigating crimes
against police officers, or that they shall deal with rape only where the victim is
willing to carry the prosecution all the way through, but such policies in fact exist
in most communities. . . .

Exercise of discretion is particular in that subsystems and individual officials
within the system have a high degree of autonomy in performing their functions. A policeman is assigned a beat, but the patrol of the beat is usually under
minimal supervision from superior police officers; the patrolman's allocation of
time and effort is not subject to anything like the direction given an ordinary
office or production-line worker, for example. In prosecutor's offices, individual
deputy prosecutors generally have considerable discretion in deciding on the
types and quality of cases that should be fully prosecuted. . . . [J]udges . . . have
broad professional discretion in the exercise of their functions, particularly in
sentencing. . . .

Taken as a whole, the system is subject to pervasive formal legal controls, but
it is also characterized by the pervasive exercise of unsupervised discretion.
There are dynamic relationships between these two phenomena: because legal
rules so thoroughly govern official action, it is assumed that the official actions
are under control and that higher administrative controls are unnecessary; and
the rigidity of legal controls creates incentives to seek waivers, a fact that in turn
entails exercise of discretion.

[A third point concerns balkanization.] The administrative structure of the
criminal justice system is extremely decentralized. There are about forty thousand different public police forces in the United States, one for almost every city
and for many villages, and usually a separate one in every county. In some large
cities there are several different police agencies, such as transit police or housing
police, in addition to the municipal police as such. In virtually all states, the
prosecutorial function is centered at the county level in the office of the district
attorney. Many large cities have a further division of prosecutorial authority in
that municipal legal departments prosecute misdemeanors. The judiciary is usually organized along county lines. . . . In any case, the work load of judges and
supporting court staff is unbalanced and poorly managed in many jurisdictions.

The correctional system is sharply divided in almost all states between local
authorities and state authorities. . . .

The foregoing description if anything understates the lack of administrative
coordination in criminal justice. A complete account would require describing
the separation between various federal criminal justice agencies and their state
counterparts, and between state-level criminal justice agencies, such as the state
police and the state attorney general's office, and their local counterparts. It
would also describe how these separations impede vital routines, such as controlling the flow of cases from one subsystem to another, coordinating allocation
of resources, and using common terminology and comparable statistics. . . .

[A fourth] generalization is that the degree of professionalism and competence in the broadest sense varies considerably throughout the country. The
variance is probably much less than it was around 1960, and certainly less
than it was in 1930. The day of the bumpkin sheriff or of the judge who is law
unto himself has virtually passed. Modern communication and interaction
disseminate techniques and standards of performance despite administrative

boundaries. Nevertheless, variance remains and has important consequences. "Professionalism" implies certain values, particularly impersonality, neutrality, and formal rationality in goals and techniques. The fact that professionalism is unevenly distributed among various elements in the system indicates, among other things, that there are corresponding differences of public opinion on the underlying issues of value.

B.   THE PROCESS OF PROOF

1.   *An Overview of Criminal Trial Procedure*

IRVING YOUNGER, THE FACTS OF A CASE, 3 U. Ark. L. Rev. 345, 345-347 (1980): The phrase is "the facts of a case." In that or some variant form each of us heard it during the first class we attended on the first day of our first term at law school. "Mr. Smith," the instructor in torts may have said, "what were the facts in Brown v. Kendall?" Or in property, "Miss Jones, state the facts of Armory v. Delamirie." And we palpitatingly did. . . . "The facts were," recites Mr. Smith, "that Kendall tried to separate two fighting dogs by beating them with a stick. He raised the stick over his shoulder and struck Brown in the eye. Brown sued Kendall for the resulting damages." "In the *Armory* case," says Miss Jones, "a chimney sweep found a jewel in the dust. He took it to a jeweler to be examined and when the jeweler refused to return it, sued for it in King's Bench." Mr. Smith and Miss Jones know that these are the facts of the case because the opinion in the casebook says they are. How the author of the opinion came by those facts is a question beyond their fathoming on that first day of law school, and understandably. . . . The facts, we tend to think at the beginning, are like acorns on an oak tree. When they are ripe, they drop to the ground. If you want some, just bend down and pick them up. Observe how they are arranged. Should they fall into the pattern we designate "negligence," Brown wins his suit against Kendall. If the pattern is that of one of the bundle of rights called "property," Armory prevails over Delamirie. Why, there's nothing to it but learning the patterns. That, I repeat, is what we tend to think at the beginning. It is what teachers of the law seem to have thought for a very long time.

   With experience and reflection comes a deeper comprehension. Facts do not grow on trees, we learn. They must be investigated and proved. Cases are more often won before a jury than in the appellate courtroom. Sometimes the facts fall into a preexisting pattern, but sometimes a pattern is devised to their con figuration, in accordance with whatever their arrangement happens to be. The facts, in short, are just as obscure as the law, just as malleable, just as controver sial, and in determining the outcome of a lawsuit or the elaboration of a rule more important than paltry logic.

RICHARD M. MARKUS, A THEORY OF TRIAL ADVOCACY, 56 Tulane L. Rev 95, 97-99 (1981): Commentators have variously described a trial as an attemp to transport jurors to the time and place of the disputed event, to recreate th disputed event or at least to explain that event with maximum accuracy. All o these descriptions are more metaphorical than material. A trial presents se lected witnesses who recite selected portions of their respective memories, concerning selected observations of the disputed event. These multiple selections are referred to here as the abstraction process. At each stage of the abstraction process, the tale is blurred or altered by inadvertent or deliberate errors. . . .

The event itself comprises unlimited detail. . . . No witness can perceive all of those characteristics at any instant, for any action, for any participant, or for any locale. Using his senses the witness abstracts a mental impression from that unfathomable array of detail. . . .

At the trial the witness recites part of the then-remembered data. The extent of uncommunicated retained data at this level of abstraction depends upon the selective inquiry of counsel and the selective disclosure by the witness. Counsel's selections result from strategy considerations and judicial limits on permitted recitations. . . . Manifestly, the recited data are a fraction of the remembered data, which is a fraction of the observed data, which is a fraction of the total data for the event.

NOTE ON CREDIBILITY PROBLEMS

Guilt probably turns more frequently on the resolution of disputes about the facts than it turns on the resolution of subtle legal questions about the meaning or scope of a penal prohibition. Accordingly, a major aspect of the jury's factfinding function is to decide which witnesses are telling the truth. But how does the jury make these credibility determinations? In the classic courtroom dramas of stage and screen, the false witness gives himself away by shifty eyes, a sweaty brow, or a mass of obvious contradictions; if not, cross-examination brilliantly exposes the lie. In everyday trials, the need to choose among conflicting stories is just as pressing, but the clues to truth are more elusive. The jury's crucial credibility findings become problematic. Consider the following studies.

New York Task Force on Women in the Courts, Report 183-186 (N.Y. Office of Court Administration 1986): Witnesses' testimony is the principal ingredient of the factfinding process. To be credited, the witness must be credible. Credibility, in turn, may not always depend on the witness's objective candor and reliability for, as Justice Benjamin N. Cardozo once observed: "The forces of which Judges . . . avail to shape the form and the content of their judgments" include "the likes and dislikes, the predilections and the prejudices, the complex of instincts and emotions and habits and convictions, which make the man, whether he be litigant or judge."[290]

Women have long been stereotyped by society as impulsive, emotional, irrational, and unpredictable. In a courtroom setting this may translate into women being presumptively viewed as incredible witnesses. Indeed, two notable trial practitioners advised their colleagues in a practice guide that:

Women, like children, are prone to exaggeration; they generally have poor memories as to previous fabrications and exaggerations. They are also stubborn. You will have difficulty trying to induce them to qualify their testimony. Rather, it might be

290. B. Cardozo, The Nature of the Judicial Process at p. 167 (Yale Univ. 1921). . . .

easier to induce them to exaggerate and cause their testimony to appear incredible. An intelligent woman will very often be evasive. She will avoid making a direct answer to a damaging question. Keep after her until you get a direct answer — but always be the gentleman.[292]

The Task Force heard compelling testimony at the public hearings from lawyers, legislators, lay advocates and scholars that women litigants' claims are subject to undue skepticism in New York's Courts. [Elsewhere in its report (at 183 n. 289) the Task Force noted:] There is a substantial body of social science research showing that in a variety of contexts, both women and men perceive women as being less credible than men in all of the senses of the term as defined here, and that recent years have by no means eliminated these attitudes despite the many other advances towards equality. A Kent State University Professor in 1985 [conducted an] experiment in which 150 male and 150 female subjects were randomly assigned to read an essay with the author's name indicated as either John T. McKay, J. T. McKay or Joan T. McKay and asked to rate it on such qualities as persuasiveness, intellectual depth and style. Although the essays were identical, those believed to have been written by "Joan" consistently received lower ratings from male and female readers than those believed to have been written by "John" or "J. T."

John M. Conley, William M. O'Barr & E. Allan Lind, The Power of Language: Presentational Style in the Courtroom, [1978] Duke L.J. 1375, 1375-1386: The rules of evidence control the content of testimony that may be introduced at trial. Those same rules, however, place relatively few constraints on *how* testimony is presented once it is deemed admissible. This freedom in testimonial style, together with the impact that a witness' demeanor has upon the reception of his testimony, makes the prediction and control of the witness' presentational style issues of importance to the practicing attorney. . . .

In order to discover the various testimony styles that occur frequently in trials the authors conducted an extensive study of the speaking styles of actual courtroom witnesses. With the permission of the court, all criminal trials in the Superior Court of Durham County, North Carolina during the summer of 197 were tape recorded. . . .

One empirically derived "style" of courtroom speech was . . . characterized b the frequent use of words and expressions that convey a lack of forcefulness i speaking. Among the specific features of this style is the abundant use of *hedge* (prefatory remarks such as "I think" and "It seems like"; appended remarks lik "you know"; and modifiers such as "kinda" and "sort of"); *hesitation form* (words and sounds that carry no substantive meaning but only fill possib! speech pauses, such as "uh" "um" and "well"); *polite forms* (for example, th use of "sir" and "please"); and *question intonation* (making a declarative stat ment with rising intonation so as to convey uncertainty). An additional featu of this style is the frequent use of *intensifiers* (for example, "very," "definitel and "surely") — words that, though they normally increase the force of an a sertion, may be so overused that they suggest that the speaker is not to be tak

---

292. F. Lee Bailey and Henry B. Rothblatt, Successful Techniques for Criminal Trials §205, pp. 190-191 (1971). This text was not deleted until the 1985 edition.

seriously in their absence. These features tended to occur together in the taped testimony, comprising a definite style in the delivery of testimony.

. . . A review of the tapes and notes of the trials revealed that witnesses of low social status — the poor and uneducated — were most likely to use this style of testimony. Female witnesses used the style more frequently than men. Because the incidence of use of this style was more common among those with little social power, it was termed the "powerless" style of testimony.

In marked contrast to the powerless style is a more straightforward manner of testifying. Those witnesses in the taped trials whose social status in court was higher — for example, well-educated, white collar men and expert witnesses of both sexes — tended to use a style that exhibited relatively few features of the powerless style. The difference between the testimony used by witnesses testifying in a "powerful" style as opposed to the "powerless" style is best illustrated by examples of the same substantive testimony given by witnesses speaking in the two different styles:

Q.   Approximately how long did you stay there before the ambulance arrived?
A.   (Powerless): Oh, it seems like it was about, uh, twenty minutes. Just long enough to help my friend, Mrs. Davis, you know, get straightened out.
     (Powerful): Twenty minutes. Long enough to help get Mrs. Davis straightened out. . . .
Q.   You know your way around?
A.   (Powerless): Yes, I guess I do.
A.   (Powerful): Yes.

[T]he next step was to determine whether witnesses using one style were in fact perceived differently than witnesses using the other style. [The authors chose an example of the "powerless" speech style in one of the original trial tapes and recorded it twice — once by a male and once by a female actor-"witness." The authors then rewrote the testimony to omit the features characteristic of the "powerless" speech style and recorded the modified ("powerful") testimony by the same two actor-"witnesses." The authors played one of the four versions of the testimony (all identical in content) to randomly selected groups of participant-jurors and tabulated the participants' reactions.]

Table 2 shows the average rating-scale responses compiled from five questions about the witness. For each of these questions, a rating of "+5" indicates a very

Table 2
Average Rating of Witnesses Using Powerful Versus Powerless Testimony Styles

Question Asked	Female Witness		Male Witness	
	Powerful	Powerless	Powerful	Powerless
"How convincing in general was this witness?"	3.00	1.65	3.52	2.09
"To what extent did you believe the witness was telling the truth?"	3.70	1.88	4.24	2.86
"To what extent do you feel that the witness was competent?"	2.61	0.85	2.44	0.18
"To what extent do you feel that the witness was intelligent?"	2.57	−0.23	1.80	0.18
"To what extent do you feel that the witness was trustworthy?"	3.04	1.65	3.48	2.00

strong positive response to the question, while a rating of "−5" indicates a strong negative response. The effects of the testimonial style of the female witness may be seen by contrasting the first and second columns of the table. The results for the male witness are presented in the third and fourth columns of the table.

. . . These analyses indicate, with a generally high degree of certainty, that in comparison to those who heard the female witness give her testimony in the powerless style, those who heard her use the powerful style indicated that they believed the witness more . . . and thought that she was more competent, more intelligent and more trustworthy. . . . The same pattern of results was found in the comparison of the male witness' powerful and powerless testimony.[a]

NOTE ON "NEGOTIATING" THE FACTS

The great majority of criminal convictions are the result of guilty pleas entered without any formal factfinding. Does the guilty plea system produce results different from those that would occur at trial? To be more specific, does it convict defendants who are in fact innocent (*and* would be acquitted) or convict defendants who committed the offense but could not be found guilty beyond a reasonable doubt at trial? Does the plea negotiation process produce convictions for offenses significantly different from the crimes a defendant may actually have committed? For the many observers who are inclined to give affirmative answers to these questions, the entire body of substantive criminal law may seem a supreme irrelevance; up to 90 percent of all convictions are obtained by guilty pleas, and these convictions are seen as the outcome of hurried horsetrading rather than the thoughtful application of complex legal principles to the known facts. What is the practical significance of substantive law in a world dominated by plea bargaining? Consider the following comments.

Donald Newman, Conviction 216 (1966): A charge reduction or sentence promise is not ordinarily a result of personal influence of the lawyer with the prosecutor or judge. The strength of a lawyer's argument for a charge reduction depends in good part on how strong a professional case he can make for the appropriateness of the lesser charge and doubtful convictability on the higher count. . . . In short, the full-blown negotiated plea is not merely an appeal for mercy; it is an adversary process and the lawyer serves the function of the guilty defendant's advocate.

Arnold Enker, Perspectives on Plea Bargaining, in President's Commission on Law Enforcement and the Administration of Justice, Task Force Report: The Courts 113-11 (1967): [C]oncern over the possibility that a negotiated plea can result in an erroneous judgment of conviction assumes a frame of reference by which the accuracy of the judgment is to be evaluated. It assumes an objective truth existing in a realm of objective historical fact which it is the sole function of ou

a. Note also in the Table that for *either* testimonial style ("powerful" or "powerless"), the mal witness generally (though not uniformly) receives a higher credibility rating than the female wi ness presenting the identical testimony — Ens process to discover. Some, but by no means all, criminal cases fit this image. For example, this is a relatively accurate description of the issues at stake in a case in which the defendant asserts a defense of mistaken identity. . . .

But not all criminal cases fit the above picture. . . . Much criminal adjudication concerns the passing of value judgments on the accused's conduct as is obvious where negligence, recklessness, reasonable apprehension of attack, use of unnecessary force, and the like are at issue. Although intent is thought of as a question of fact, it too can represent a judgment of degrees of fault, for example, in cases where the issue is whether the defendants entertained intent to defraud or intent to kill. In many of these cases, objective truth is more ambiguous, if it exists at all. Such truth exists only as it emerges from the fact-determining process, and accuracy in this context really means relative equality of results as between defendants similarly situated and relative congruence between the formal verdict and our understanding of society's less formally expressed evaluation of such conduct.

The negotiated plea can, then, be an accurate process in this sense. So long as the judgment of experienced counsel as to the likely jury result is the key element entering into the bargain, substantial congruence is likely to result. Once we recognize that what lends rationality to the factfinding process in these instances lies not in an attempt to discover objective truth but in the devising of a process to express intelligent judgment, there is no inherent reason why plea negotiation need be regarded any the less rational or intelligent in its results.

Indeed, it may be that in some instances plea negotiation leads to more "intelligent" results. A jury can be left with the extreme alternatives of guilty of a crime of the highest degree or not guilty of any crime, with no room for any intermediate judgment. And this is likely to occur in just those cases where an intermediate judgment is the fairest and most "accurate" (or most congruent).

Clearly, the line between responsibility and irresponsibility due to insanity is not as sharp as the alternatives posed to a jury would suggest. . . . The very visibility of a trial process may be one factor that prevents us from offering the jury [a] compromise in order to preserve the symbolism of uniform rules evenly applied. The low visibility of the negotiated plea allows this compromise which may be more rational and congruent than the result we are likely to arrive at after a trial. While the desire to protect the symbolism of legality and the concern over jury compromises may warrant limiting the jury to extreme alternative[s], it does not follow that to allow the defendant to choose such a compromise is an irrational or even a less rational procedure.

Albert W. Alschuler, The Prosecutor's Role in Plea Bargaining, 36 U. Chi. L. Rev. 50, 1-79 (1968): Professor Enker suggests that the insanity defense raises problems that frequently merit a compromise solution. Such a solution was provided in the publicized case of William Heirens, a seventeen-year-old college student who pleaded guilty to three separate murders and was sentenced to three consecutive life terms. . . .

William Heirens' culpability under traditional legal standards was doubtful, yet both the defendant and society were deprived of an authoritative resolution of this issue. Heirens is today an inmate of the Stateville Penitentiary, although no one has determined on the basis of the evidence that a prison is where Heirens belongs. Society devised the insanity defense precisely to avoid such distressing spectacles. Like other legal issues, the defense was designed to be tried, not compromised. . . .

Finally, consider the case that District Attorney [Arlen] Specter advances to illustrate his concept of "variable guilt." . . . :

> The dictum that "justice and liberty are not the subjects of bargaining and barter" does not fit the realities of a typical barroom killing. . . .
>
> There is ordinarily sufficient evidence of malice and deliberation in such cases for the jury to find the defendant guilty of murder in the first degree, which [in Pennsylvania] carries either life imprisonment or death in the electric chair. Or, the conceded drinking by the defendant may be sufficient to nullify specific intent . . . to make the case second degree murder, which calls for a maximum of 10 to 20 years in jail. From all the prosecutor knows by the time the cold carbon copies of the police reports reach the District Attorney's office, the defendant may have acted in "hot blood," which makes the offense only voluntary manslaughter with a maximum penalty of 6 to 12 years. And, the defense invariably produces testimony showing that the killing was pure self-defense.
>
> When such cases are submitted to juries, a variety of verdicts are returned, which leads to the inescapable conclusion of variable guilt. Most of those trials result in convictions for second degree murder or voluntary manslaughter. The judges generally impose sentences with a minimum range of 5 to 8 years and a maximum of 10 to 20 years. That distilled experience enables the assistant district attorney and the defense lawyer to bargain on the middle ground of what experience has shown to be "justice" without the defense running the risk of the occasional first degree conviction . . . and without the Commonwealth tying up a jury room for 3 to 5 days and running the risk of acquittal.[62]

This argument seems to rest on the notion that when a man has seen one barroom killing, he has seen them all. [Yet] Specter's argument is a forceful one In the homicide area particularly, . . . the distinctions drawn by the crimina code . . . sometimes prove too fine for workable, everyday application.

. . . If the perspective of these practitioners is sound, the best solution to the defects they perceive in the trial system does not lie in a shift from trial proce dures to off-stage compromises. It lies instead in a simplification of the crim nal code to reflect "everyday reality" rather than common-law refinemen [Moreover,] it seems doubtful that plea negotiation can eliminate the irration alities of the criminal code without substituting more serious irrationalities of i own. . . . Most barroom killings seem to end in bargained pleas to voluntar manslaughter; but some end in bargained pleas to second degree murder; som end in bargained pleas to various categories of felonious assault; and I know (one barroom shooting that was resolved by a guilty plea to the crime of invc untary manslaughter, which, under the circumstances, seemed to be the la crime in the code of which the defendant might be guilty. It is therefore ne clear that plea negotiation leads to greater uniformity of result than trial by jur

Juries, of course, have biases, but the rules of evidence attempt to direct the attention to relevant issues. There are no rules of evidence in plea negotiatio individual prosecutors may be influenced not only by a desire to smooth out th irrationalities of the criminal code but by thoroughly improper consideratio

---

62. Specter, Book Review, 76 Yale L.J. 604, 606-07 (1967) (D. Newman, Conviction).

that no serious reformer of the penal code would suggest. . . . Juries may react differently to the circumstances of indistinguishable crimes, but at least they react to the circumstances of the crimes. A jury is unlikely to seek conviction for the sake of conviction, to respond to a defense attorney's tactical pressures, to penalize a defendant because he has taken an inordinate share of the court's and the prosecutor's time, to do favors for particular defense attorneys in the hope of future cooperation, or to attempt to please victims and policemen for political reasons.

NOTE ON FORMAL TRIAL PROCEDURE

Section A of this Chapter describes the organization of the criminal justice system and typical pretrial procedures. To introduce our examination of the trial stage itself, the present Note briefly summarizes the typical course of a formal criminal trial. Naturally, the procedure followed in some jurisdictions or in particular cases may differ in points of detail from that set out in this preliminary overview.

A formal trial typically begins with the selection of the jury. A panel of prospective jurors (called a *venire*) enters the courtroom, and the judge describes the nature of the case and the identity of the parties so that any prospective jurors who are personally involved may be excused. Prospective jurors are then questioned individually by the judge or by opposing counsel to determine possible bias. On the basis of this questioning (called *voir dire*) prospective jurors may be excused *for cause,* and both prosecution and defense may remove a certain number of the panel, without showing cause, by exercising *peremptory challenges.* When the requisite number of acceptable jurors (usually 12) has been obtained by this procedure, the panel is sworn.

Now the presentation of the case begins. Usually the indictment is read to the jury; the prosecutor then makes an opening statement outlining the facts she plans to prove. Defense counsel also may make an opening statement. Claims made in these statements do not constitute *evidence;* they serve only to help the jury understand the testimony about to be presented. In many jurisdictions, motions relating to the scope or validity of the indictment and motions to suppress evidence must be made a certain number of days prior to trial. In others, such motions can be made at the outset of the trial. If the judge grants a motion to dismiss the indictment, the case will terminate at this point. Otherwise the trial goes forward, although motions may be made or renewed as the trial proceeds.

Next the prosecution calls its witnesses. The presentation of their testimony often evokes objections from counsel, and the judge must decide the bounds of permissible testimony under complex rules of evidence. We examine some of these rules in the sections to follow. When the prosecution has completed the presentation of its evidence, the defense may choose to stand on the *presumption of innocence* and move for a *directed verdict* or *judgment of acquittal* on the ground that the charges have not been proved beyond a reasonable doubt. If such a motion is not made, or if the motion is made and denied, the defense may decide to offer its own evidence (through the defendant or other witnesses). The prosecution then will have an opportunity to present further evidence in rebuttal. When both sides have rested, having completed the presentation of their evidence, opposing counsel may make a closing argument to the jury. Ordinarily the prosecution's closing argument is presented first (because it bears the burden of proof), and the prosecutor is usually allowed an opportunity for rebuttal after the closing argument of the defense.

At this point the work of the opposing parties has been completed. The judge now intercedes with his most important contribution to the proceedings — the instructions to the jury. The judge may begin with a summary of the evidence; ordinarily, however, judicial comment on the evidence tends to be cautious and limited. Formal instructions on the law, however, are always given, and they are typically quite detailed. The instructions serve both as a guide for the jury's deliberations and as a focal point for challenges on appeal in the event of a conviction. Usually the instructions cover formal procedures and responsibilities of the jurors (for example, how to elect a foreperson, when to refrain from discussing the case with other jurors or outsiders), matters related to the weight or relevance of particular kinds of testimony, and, above all, detailed explanations of the substantive criminal law applicable to the case, including specification of the facts necessary to establish the offense and definitions of legal concepts that the jury is called on to apply.

The jury at last retires to deliberate. Its verdict of guilty or not guilty on each charge must be reached by a substantial majority (and usually by unanimity). After a verdict of guilty and the imposition of sentence (usually by the judge), the trial terminates. There may of course be an appeal. If it finds trial errors, the reviewing court may reverse the conviction and order another trial, since American double jeopardy principles generally do not bar the retrial of a defendant who has successfully appealed her conviction.[2] A verdict of not guilty terminates the proceedings and is not subject to appeal or review of any kind, regardless of whether flagrant errors prejudicial to the prosecution occurred at trial.[3] When the jury is unable to agree by the requisite majority on a verdict of either guilty or not guilty (a hung jury case), a *mistrial* is declared, and the defendant then may be retried at the prosecutor's discretion.

Such, in rough outline, is the procedure by which guilt must be established when a criminal case is fully litigated through the formal trial stage. Of course as we have already seen, guilt can be (and often is) established by entry of a guilt plea before the trial stage is ever reached.

Comprehensive treatment of all important aspects of trial procedure lies beyond the province of this book. Nevertheless, a book devoted primarily to the substantive law should provide an introduction to some of the central features of the process of proof, in order to illuminate the actual context in which criminal law is applied and the ways in which the procedural system shapes (and in turn is shaped by) the substantive content of the criminal law. In the remaining sections of this chapter we undertake such an exploration.

---

2. Burks v. United States, 437 U.S. 1 (1978). The English rule is to the contrary on this important issue. In that country, when a reviewing court finds prejudicial error, the conviction is "quashed" and no retrial is permitted, except in certain circumstances. Criminal Appeal Act, 1968, ch. §2(2)-(3); see M. Friedland, Double Jeopardy 221-228 (1969).

3. To avoid this difficulty many states provide for rulings prior to the start of trial on significant issues of law and permit the prosecutor to appeal an adverse ruling at that point.

2. *The Presentation of Evidence*

INTRODUCTORY NOTES

1. The order of proof. At trial the evidence is presented in accordance with a formally prescribed order. The prosecution first calls witnesses in an effort to prove the elements of the offense charged. As we have just seen, page 21 supra, the case may terminate at this point if the prosecution fails to sustain its preliminary burden of proof. If not, the defense may then call witnesses in an effort to refute the prosecution's *case-in-chief* or to establish some *affirmative defense.* The prosecution then has an opportunity to recall witnesses or to call new witnesses solely for purposes of *rebuttal,* that is, to refute evidence offered by the defense. The defense in turn is afforded a chance to meet by *rejoinder* any matters introduced in the prosecutor's rebuttal.

Within these stages the examination of each witness follows a similar pattern. The witness is first questioned by the party that called the witness (*direct examination*), and afterward the opposing party has an opportunity to question that witness (*cross-examination*). Further questioning by the first party (*re-direct*) and by the opposing side (*re-cross*) may follow.

2. Relevance. The rules governing the admissibility of evidence are extremely detailed and complex. For present purposes, it will be useful to begin by focusing on one obvious but deceptively simple requirement that has pervasive importance, the rule of relevancy. First, evidence is *never* admissible if it is irrelevant. The converse cannot be stated so categorically. Relevant evidence is *generally* admissible, but there are many exceptions to this principle. Before turning to these exceptions, we must first be clear about the meaning of *relevancy.*

Evidence is considered relevant for purposes of the rules of evidence only if it both *probative* and *material,* and these are precise terms of art. Evidence is probative only if it tends to establish the proposition for which it is offered or — to be precise — if the proposition is more likely to be true given the evidence than it would be without the evidence. Thus, if the proposition to be proved is that *H* was the person who killed his wife *W,* evidence of a motive (that is, that *H* stood to inherit a substantial estate on *W*'s death) is probative. Of course, the existence of the motive does not, by itself, make it probable that *H* is the killer, but *H* is more likely to be the killer if he had a motive than if he did not; this greater likelihood is all that is required to establish probative value.

Probative value alone is often thought of as synonymous with relevancy. But relevancy for purposes of the rules of evidence requires in addition that the proposition that the evidence tends to prove be one that will affect the outcome of the case under applicable law. So, for example, evidence in a homicide prosecution that defendant acted in self-defense is material because under the substantive law self-defense is a defense. But evidence that the deceased consented to be killed is not material, because under the substantive law consent by the victim is not a defense to a homicide charge. Thus, evidence may be excluded as irrelevant for one of two distinct reasons — either because the evidence does not tend to establish the proposition in question or because that proposition is not material to the outcome of the case. The materiality requirement means that the first prerequisite for determining the relevancy and hence the admissibility of evidence is a command of the substantive law of crimes.

We may sum up what we have so far said about relevancy by quoting the formulation used in the Federal Rules of Evidence:

RULE 401

"Relevant evidence" means evidence having any tendency to make the existence of any fact that is of consequence to the determination of the action more probable or less probable than it would be without the evidence.

RULE 402

All relevant evidence is admissible, except as otherwise provided. . . . Evidence which is not relevant is not admissible.

3. Privilege. Under what circumstances is relevant evidence *not* admissible? The law of evidence embodies dozens of distinct rules requiring the exclusion of relevant evidence. For example, the various rules relating to *privilege* give individuals the right to withhold certain kinds of testimony, often in order to protect particular interests of a witness or specially important relationships with others.

One of the most important privileges is the privilege against self-incrimination. The Fifth Amendment provides: "[N]or shall [any person] be compelled in any criminal case to be a witness against himself." The Supreme Court has construed this provision to imply that the government cannot require a criminal defendant to take the witness stand, cannot invite a jury to draw adverse inferences from a defendant's refusal to testify, and cannot in any other way compel the defendant to disclose potentially incriminating facts about the case. These principles are of great significance for the substantive criminal law. They not only make the prosecutor's task more difficult than it otherwise would be, but they pose an especially difficult barrier when the defendant's own frame of mind is an essential part of what the prosecutor must prove. The effect of the privilege against self-incrimination is to place largely beyond the government's reach the best (and sometimes the only) source of information about these especially elusive state-of-mind facts. As a result, substantive criminal law must constantly confront the questions whether government should be obliged to prove state-of-mind facts, and if so, what kinds of evidence will satisfy that obligation.

4. Other exclusionary rules: prejudice. Like the rules of privilege, many other rules of evidence operate to exclude relevant evidence. We will consider some of these rules in connection with the substantive crimes for which they have the greatest significance.[4] The balance of the present section is devoted to exploring one rather open-ended rule — the rule that evidence must be excluded whenever its probative value is outweighed by its *prejudicial effect.* This exclusionary rule is of pervasive importance in the substantive criminal law, and we will encounter it repeatedly in the chapters that follow. The principle of weighing

4. The hearsay rule and one of its important exceptions are explored in connection with conspiracy law, pages 725-727 infra. Special restrictions intended to protect the privacy of a witness are examined in connection with the materials on rape, pages 372-384 infra.

probative value against prejudicial effect is particularly central to developing doctrines in such areas as rape shield laws, the adequacy of victim provocation in homicide, battered spouse evidence, and testimony concerning intoxication, diminished capacity, and the insanity defense. As a foundation for the study of such topics throughout this book, the present section considers the problem of prejudicial effect in depth, in a context of recurring importance for criminal prosecutions — the rules concerning use of evidence of other crimes.

The term *prejudicial effect* has a rather technical meaning. To pursue the example previously mentioned, suppose that in *H*'s murder prosecution testimony is offered to the effect that shortly before the discovery of *W*'s bullet-ridden body, *H* was seen running from the scene carrying a smoking revolver. This testimony will undoubtedly be quite harmful to *H*'s chances for acquittal, but it will not be prejudicial, in the technical sense, because its harmfulness flows solely from its legitimate probative value. Evidence is considered prejudicial only when it is likely to affect the result in some *improper* way. Thus, prejudice is involved if the jury is likely to overestimate the probative value of the evidence or if the evidence will arouse undue hostility toward one of the parties.

The next case illustrates the application of these principles and their relationship to basic conceptions of criminal responsibility.

PEOPLE v. ZACKOWITZ

New York Court of Appeals
254 N.Y. 192, 172 N.E. 466 (1930)

[Defendant was convicted of first-degree murder and sentenced to death.] CARDOZO, C.J. On November 10, 1929, shortly after midnight, the defendant in Kings county shot Frank Coppola and killed him without justification or excuse. A crime is admitted. What is doubtful is the degree only.

Four young men, of whom Coppola was one, were at work repairing an automobile in a Brooklyn street. A woman, the defendant's wife, walked by on the opposite side. One of the men spoke to her insultingly, or so at least she understood him. The defendant, who had dropped behind to buy a newspaper, came up to find his wife in tears. He was told she had been insulted, though she did not then repeat the words. Enraged, he stepped across the street and upbraided the offenders with words of coarse profanity. He informed them, so the survivors testify, that "if they did not get out of there in five minutes, he would come back and bump them all off." Rejoining his wife, he walked with her to their apartment house located close at hand. He was heated with liquor which he had been drinking at a dance. Within the apartment he induced her to tell him what the insulting words had been. A youth had asked her to lie with him, and had offered her two dollars. With rage aroused again, the defendant went back to the scene of the insult and found the four young men still working at the car. In a statement to the police, he said that he had armed himself at the apartment with a twenty-five calibre automatic pistol. In his testimony at the trial he said that his pistol had been in his pocket all the evening. Words and blows followed, and then a shot. The defendant kicked Coppola in the stomach. There is evidence that Coppola went for him with a wrench. The pistol came from the pocket, and from the pistol a single shot, which did its deadly work. . . .

At the trial the vital question was the defendant's state of mind at the moment of the homicide. Did he shoot with a deliberate and premeditated design to kill? Was he so inflamed by drink or by anger or by both combined that, though he knew the nature of his act, he was the prey to sudden impulse, the fury of the fleeting moment?[a] If he went forth from his apartment with a preconceived design to kill, how is it that he failed to shoot at once? How reconcile such a design with the drawing of the pistol later in the heat and rage of an affray? These and like questions the jurors were to ask themselves and answer before measuring the defendant's guilt. Answers consistent with guilt in its highest grade can reasonably be made. Even so, the line between impulse and deliberation is too narrow and elusive to make the answers wholly clear. The sphygmograph records with graphic certainty the fluctuations of the pulse. There is no instrument yet invented that records with equal certainty the fluctuations of the mind. At least, if such an instrument exists, it was not working at midnight in the Brooklyn street when Coppola and the defendant came together in a chance affray. With only the rough and ready tests supplied by their experience of life, the jurors were to look into the workings of another's mind, and discover its capacities and disabilities, its urges and inhibitions, in moments of intense excitement. Delicate enough and subtle is the inquiry, even in the most favorable conditions, with every warping influence excluded. There must be no blurring of the issues by evidence illegally admitted and carrying with it in its admission an appeal to prejudice and passion.

Evidence charged with that appeal was, we think, admitted here. . . . Almost at the opening of the trial the People began the endeavor to load the defendant down with the burden of an evil character. He was to be put before the jury as a man of murderous disposition. To that end they were allowed to prove that at the time of the encounter and at that of his arrest he had in his apartment, kept there in a radio box, three pistols and a teargas gun. There was no claim that he had brought these weapons out at the time of the affray, no claim that with any of them he had discharged the fatal shot. He could not have done so, for they were all of different calibre. The end to be served by laying the weapons before the jury was something very different. The end was to bring persuasion that here was a man of vicious and dangerous propensities, who because of those propensities was more likely to kill with deliberate and premeditated design than a man of irreproachable life and amiable manners. Indeed, this is the very ground on which the introduction of the evidence is now explained and defended. The District Attorney tells us in his brief that the possession of the weapons characterized the defendant as "a desperate type of criminal," a "person criminally inclined." The dissenting opinion, if it puts the argument less bluntly, leaves the substance of the thought unchanged. "Defendant was presented to the jury as a man having dangerous weapons in his possession, making a selection therefrom and going forth to put into execution his threats to kill." The weapons were not brought by the defendant to the scene of the encounter. They were left in his

a. Under New York law, a deliberate and premeditated killing would be first-degree murder while a killing in "the fury of the fleeting moment" would be second-degree murder. At the time of the *Zackowitz* decision the former offense was punishable by death and the latter by imprisonment from a minimum of 20 years to a maximum of life. N.Y. Penal Law §§1045, 1048 (Penal Code of 1909, as amended 1928). For current penalty provisions in New York and other representative states, see pages 388-393 infra. — EDS.

apartment where they were incapable of harm. In such circumstances, owner-ship of the weapons, if it has any relevance at all, has relevance only as indicating a general disposition to make use of them thereafter, and a general disposition to make use of them thereafter is without relevance except as indicating a "des-perate type of criminal," a criminal affected with a murderous propensity. . . .

If a murderous propensity may be proved against a defendant as one of the tokens of his guilt, a rule of criminal evidence, long believed to be of fundamen-tal importance for the protection of the innocent, must be first declared away. Fundamental hitherto has been the rule that character is never an issue in a criminal prosecution unless the defendant chooses to make it one (Wigmore, Evidence, vol. 1, §§55, 192). In a very real sense a defendant starts his life afresh when he stands before a jury, a prisoner at the bar. There has been a homicide in a public place. The killer admits the killing, but urges self-defense and sud-den impulse. Inflexibly the law has set its face against the endeavor to fasten guilt upon him by proof of character or experience predisposing to an act of crime. . . . The principle back of the exclusion is one, not of logic, but of policy. There may be cogency in the argument that a quarrelsome defendant is more likely to start a quarrel than one of milder type, a man of dangerous mode of life more likely than a shy recluse. The law is not blind to this, but equally it is not blind to the peril to the innocent if character is accepted as probative of crime. "The natural and inevitable tendency of the tribunal — whether judge or jury — is to give excessive weight to the vicious record of crime thus exhibited, and either to allow it to bear too strongly on the present charge, or to take the proof of it as justifying a condemnation irrespective of guilt of the present charge" (Wigmore, Evidence, vol. 1, §194, and cases cited).

A different question would be here if the pistols had been bought in expecta-tion of this particular encounter. They would then have been admissible as evi-dence of preparation and design. A different question would be here if they were so connected with the crime as to identify the perpetrator, if he had dropped them, for example, at the scene of the affray. They would then have been admissible as tending to implicate the possessor (if identity was disputed), no matter what the opprobrium attached to his possession. Different, also, would be the question if the defendant had been shown to have gone forth from the apartment with all the weapons on his person. To be armed from head to foot at the very moment of an encounter may be a circumstance worthy to be considered, like acts of preparation generally, as a proof of preconceived design. There can be no such implication from the ownership of weapons which one leaves behind at home.

The endeavor was to generate an atmosphere of professional criminality. It was an endeavor the more unfair in that, apart from the suspicion attaching to the possession of these weapons, there is nothing to mark the defendant as a man of evil life. . . . If his own testimony be true, he had gathered these weapons together as curios, a collection that interested and amused him. Perhaps his explanation of their ownership is false. There is nothing stronger than mere suspicion to guide us to an answer. Whether the explanation be false or true, he should not have been driven by the People to the necessity of offering it. Brought to answer a specific charge, and to defend himself against it, he was placed in a position where he had to defend himself against another, more gen-eral and sweeping. He was made to answer to the charge, pervasive and poisonous even if insidious and covert, that he was a man of murderous heart, of criminal disposition. . . .

The judgment of conviction should be reversed, and a new trial ordered.

POUND, J. (dissenting). . . .

The People may not prove against a defendant crimes not alleged in the indictment committed on other occasions than the crime charged as aiding the proofs that he is guilty of the crime charged unless such proof tends to establish (1) motive; (2) intent; (3) absence of mistake or accident; (4) a common scheme or plan embracing the commission of two or more crimes so related to each other that proof of the one tends to establish the other; (5) the identity of the person charged with the commission of the crime on trial. These exceptions are stated generally and not with categorical precision and may not be all-inclusive. None of them apply here nor were the weapons offered under an exception to the general rule. They were offered as a part of the transaction itself. The accused was tried only for the crime charged. The real question is whether the matter relied on has such a connection with the crime charged as to be admissible on any ground. If so, the fact that it constitutes another distinct crime does not render it inadmissible. . . .

As the District Attorney argues in his brief, if defendant had been arrested at the time of the killing and these weapons had been found on his person, the People would not have been barred from proving the fact, and the further fact that they were nearby in his apartment should not preclude the proof as bearing on the entire deed of which the act charged forms a part. Defendant was presented to the jury as a man having dangerous weapons in his possession, making a selection therefrom and going forth to put into execution his threats to kill; not as a man of a dangerous disposition in general, but as one who, having an opportunity to select a weapon to carry out his threats, proceeded to do so. . . .

The judgment of conviction should be affirmed.

NOTES ON ZACKOWITZ

1. On the facts of *Zackowitz*, we may assume that the killing was intentional. The principal issue at trial was whether the killing was "deliberate" (that is, whether the intent to kill was formulated before the shot, making the crime first-degree murder) or whether the killing was instead "impulsive" (that is, whether the intent to kill was formulated during the final scuffle, making the crime second-degree murder). Does defendant's possession of the weapons have some bearing on this issue? Recall that very slight probative value is usually sufficient to render evidence admissible; for example, evidence that Zackowitz stood to inherit money from the victim would undoubtedly be admissible as tending to show a motive for a deliberate killing. Does the evidence of weapons possession have at least that much probative value?

2. If the weapons evidence was relevant, as Judge (later Justice) Cardozo seems to assume, are there convincing reasons for excluding it? Cardozo stresses that the issue in the case was a "delicate" and "subtle" one. Under these circumstances was it not particularly important for the jury to have access to as much relevant evidence as possible? In which case will the trier of fact be better able to evaluate what actually happened: when it knows about the weapons, knows the defendant's explanation for them, and has a chance to judge the credibility of that explanation or when — as *Zackowitz* requires — all of this information is withheld?

NOTES ON "OTHER-CRIMES" EVIDENCE UNDER CURRENT LAW

1. The general rule and its foundations. Subject to certain exceptions to be explored below, the basic principle invoked by the majority in *Zackowitz* appears to enjoy universal acceptance: Other crimes (and indeed any other kind of evidence designed to show "bad character") may not be introduced in order to show that the accused had an evil disposition and thus was more likely to have committed the offense charged.

Rules 403 and 404(b) of the Federal Rules of Evidence illustrate one rigorous statement of these principles:

RULE 403 . . .

Although relevant, evidence may be excluded if its probative value is substantially outweighed by the danger of unfair prejudice, confusion of the issues, or misleading the jury, or by considerations of undue delay, waste of time, or needless presentation of cumulative evidence.

RULE 404 . . .

(b) Other crimes, wrongs, or acts. Evidence of other crimes, wrongs, or acts is not admissible to prove the character of a person in order to show action in conformity therewith. It may, however, be admissible for other purposes, such as proof of motive, opportunity, intent, preparation, plan, knowledge, identity, or absence of mistake or accident. . . .

What is the justification for these principles? McCormick states that such evidence "is not irrelevant, but in the setting of jury trial the danger of prejudice outweighs the probative value." C. McCormick, Evidence §190, at 447 (2d ed. 1972). See also Michelson v. United States, 335 U.S. 469, 475-476 (1948): "The inquiry is not rejected because character is irrelevant; on the contrary it is said to weigh too much with the jury and to so overpersuade them as to prejudge one with a bad general record and deny him a fair opportunity to defend against a particular charge." Undoubtedly, this statement holds true in a very wide range of contexts. But there can be situations in which the danger of prejudice is arguably insufficient to justify the exclusion. And when a judge tries the case without a jury, the danger that the evidence will exert improper influence on the result seems considerably less. Should the rule of inadmissibility be abandoned when the case is tried to a judge?[5] Or are there other, perhaps more basic, reasons for restricting the admissibility of other-crimes evidence?

---

5. Courts have differed in their treatment of other-crimes evidence in nonjury trials. A. Leo Levin & Harold K. Cohen, The Exclusionary Rules in Nonjury Criminal Cases, 119 U. Pa. L. Rev. 905 (1971).

Consider how the criminal process would be affected if the prosecution were free to support its case by proving previous instances of criminal conduct by the accused. The defendant, who of course is contesting the charges of the present indictment, may deny having committed the other crimes as well. In particular, if the prosecution has not already obtained a formal conviction for the other crimes (that was the case in *Zackowitz*, for example), the entire focus of the trial could be diverted by the dispute about whether the other crimes were in fact committed.

Even if the defendant admits to committing other crimes or the other crimes are easily proved by a record of prior convictions, the defendant may feel called upon to explain the background of the other offenses or to claim extenuating circumstances. (This too happened in *Zackowitz*.) The vice here is not simply that time and attention may be diverted from the main issue in the case. It is also that a defendant should not be forever obliged to explain prior transgressions in order to dispel suspicions of further misconduct. Thus, a person who has suffered conviction and sentence is said to have "paid his debt to society"; the slate should be wiped clean. Cardozo alludes to these concerns when he states: "In a very real sense a defendant starts his life afresh when he stands before a jury, a prisoner at the bar. . . . Whether the explanation [for Zackowitz's possession of the weapons] be true or false, he should not have been driven by the People to the necessity of offering it."

Whether or not a defendant has already "paid his debt" for the prior offense, basic assumptions about criminal responsibility are tested when the focus of the trial becomes centered on the defendant's general character rather than on his behavior in a discrete situation. To be sure, a trial designed to determine a defendant's responsibility for particular events often must explore many circumstances of his life, but ultimately the events themselves are at issue, the concrete behavior precisely specified in the charges. The criminal trial usually is not viewed as a vehicle for passing judgment on the whole person. Again, Cardozo alludes to this principle: "Brought to answer a specific charge, [the defendant] had to defend himself against another, more general and sweeping[,] . . . pervasive and poisonous even if insidious and covert, that he was a man of murderous heart, or criminal disposition."

The Supreme Court has not yet been forced to reach the question whether it is unconstitutional for a state to rely on prior-crimes evidence to suggest a defendant's criminal propensity. See Estelle v. McGuire, 502 U.S. 62 (1991). The issue arose in McKinney v. Rees, 993 F.2d 1378 (9th Cir. 1993), where the defendant had been charged with killing his mother by slitting her throat. Following a strategy strikingly similar to that in *Zackowitz*, prosecutors introduced extensive evidence of the defendant's fascination with knives and his possession of numerous weapons, including one knife that could not possibly have been used to commit the crime. The defendant was convicted of murder in the California state courts, but in federal habeas corpus proceedings the Ninth Circuit set aside the conviction, holding that the state's use of character evidence to prove propensity had rendered the trial so fundamentally unfair as to violate due process.

Consider Gerard E. Lynch, RICO: The Crime of Being a Criminal, Parts III & IV, 87 Colum. L. Rev. 920, 934-936 (1987):

> [T]he model of crime based on specific incidents or acts [is] associated with a particular conception of the individual as a moral actor. . . . The individual is im-

plicitly conceived not only as free in principle to act in accordance with or in violation of defined norms, but also as free at any given moment to make choices at odds with any consistent character that may be deduced from his prior acts. To infer that a defendant committed the particular offense for which he is being tried from the fact that he has previously committed other crimes of a generally similar nature — or, worse still, other crimes of an entirely different nature — is not only unfair, but inconsistent with a fundamental supposition that criminal behavior is punishable because it represents a free choice at a particular moment in time to commit an immoral act.

Questions: To what extent are the values described fundamental to a just system of criminal law? Are they, for example, more important than the most accurate possible determination of the truth? Should they apply with as much force in proceedings to determine sentence (or the *degree* of the offense in *Zackowitz*) as they do when the issue is guilt versus innocence?[6] Consider the extent to which these values in fact *are* respected, or flouted, by the doctrines of criminal law examined in the remainder of this section and throughout this book.

2. Exceptions to the rule. Situations in which other-crimes evidence might be admissible are mentioned by the court in *Zackowitz,* and the dissenting opinion presents five specific "exceptions" to the rule of exclusion. Thus, for example, if a defendant is prosecuted for the murder of *V,* evidence that the defendant previously committed a robbery witnessed by *V* will be admissible — not to show that the defendant was generally disposed to violence but rather to show his *motive* for this particular killing. Similarly, evidence that the defendant had previously stolen the pistol with which *V* was shot will be admissible — not to show the defendant's disposition to crime but to help *identify* him as the killer. Many other exceptions could be given.

Technically speaking, these situations do not involve exceptions to the rule of exclusion because, properly stated, that rule renders other-crimes evidence inadmissible only when offered "to prove the character of a person in order to show that he acted in conformity therewith." Fed. R. Evid. 404(b). In other words, the rule itself does not bar the use of other-crimes evidence for some purpose *other than* that of suggesting that he acted in conformity with a bad character. See Estelle v. McGuire, 502 U.S. 62 (1991); People v. Vandervliet, 444 Mich. 52, 508 N.W.2d 114 (1993).

Treatises on evidence discuss the various possible uses of other-crimes evidence, and the categories themselves probably are not firm or all-inclusive. The central point is that other-crimes evidence may be admissible if it is offered for some specific purpose *other than* that of suggesting that the defendant may have committed the crime because he or she has a bad character. Nevertheless it is not always easy to tell whether the evidence links the defendant to the crime in some legitimate way or whether it simply suggests a criminal propensity. The problem consistently provides a large volume of litigation, and Rule 404(b) has become one of the most-often cited provisions in the Federal Rules of Evidence. For helpful discussions, see Miguel Angel Mendez, California's New Law on Character Evidence: Evidence Code Section 352 and the Impact of Recent Psychological Studies, 31 U.C.L.A.L. Rev. 1003 (1984); Richard Uviller, Evidence of

---

6. For exploration of the question whether punishment should be tailored to the character of the offender rather than the seriousness of the offense, see Chapter 2 infra.

Character to Prove Conduct: Illusion, Illogic and Injustice in the Courtroom, 130 U. Pa. L. Rev. 845 (1982). Consider the following important exceptions.

(a) *The signature exception.* Evidence of other crimes committed by the defendant is admissible when the other crimes are "so nearly identical in method as to earmark them as the handiwork of the accused. . . . The device used must be so unusual and distinctive as to be like a signature." McCormick, page 32 supra, §190, at 449. The most famous illustration of this rule is the "brides in the bath" case, Rex v. Smith, 84 Cr. App. (K.B.) 137 (1915). The defendant's wife was found drowned in her bathtub shortly after she had executed a will in his favor. At his trial for her murder, the prosecution was allowed to prove that after this wife's death the defendant made two subsequent marriages, both of which had ended when the new bride, shortly after making a will in the defendant's favor, was found drowned in her bath. Here the uniqueness of the modus operandi gave the other crimes strong probative value in helping to identify Smith as the cause of his first wife's death.

Notice the assumption that the two other incidents *were* crimes. In *Smith* the prosecution probably could not prove guilt beyond a reasonable doubt in any one incident taken by itself. But in order for evidence to be admissible, the facts necessary to make that evidence relevant need not be proved beyond a reasonable doubt; proof of those facts by a preponderance of the evidence is sufficient. Thus, in *Smith,* if there is a likelihood of guilt (that is, a 51 percent chance) in each instance considered separately, and if the incidents can then be considered together, the jury might be convinced beyond a reasonable doubt of the defendant's guilt in all three incidents.

Should the prosecution be permitted to present as "other crimes," under any of the various exceptions, evidence concerning charges for which the defendant has been *acquitted*? Applying the principle that admissibility requires only proof by a preponderance that other crimes occurred, the Supreme Court held in Dowling v. United States, 493 U.S. 342, 348-349 (1990), that an acquittal (which implied only a reasonable doubt) did not bar subsequent prosecutors from offering evidence that the defendant was guilty of the prior charges. Thus, so long as the other crimes can be offered for some purpose other than proving propensity, the defendant is in effect forced to relitigate his guilt in the prior incidents. Cardozo's rule that a defendant on trial "starts his life afresh" can be nullified.

Because the various exceptions can so easily defeat the values that the other-crimes rule serves, it becomes critical to assure that other-crimes evidence is being used for some purpose *other than* that of suggesting a criminal propensity. In "signature" cases, courts often have difficulty determining whether the pattern of criminality is sufficiently unusual. In State v. Laureano, 682 P.2d 889, 901 (Wash. 1984), the court said the test was that "[t]he method employed in the commission of both crimes must be so unique that mere proof that an accused committed one of them creates high probability that he also committed the act charged." Consider the following cases, in all of which the trial judges admitted the other-crimes evidence. Does that evidence suggest a distinctive signature or at most only a propensity to commit offenses of some general type?

(i) *H* and *M* are charged with committing a series of three robberies over a five-month period. In all three cases two armed men, wearing handkerchiefs over their faces, used an employees' entrance to enter stores shortly after closing time, forced some of the employees to lie down on the floor, and fled with large amounts of cash. Should the prosecution be permitted to prove that two years earlier *H* and *M* had robbed two restaurants in the same fashion? See People v. Haston, 69 Cal. 2d 233, 444 P.2d 91 (1969).

(*ii*) *L* is charged with picking up a woman in a bar, asking her for a ride home, and then raping her in her car. His defense is consent. Should the prosecution be permitted to prove that nine days earlier, *L* had met another woman in the same bar, asked her for a ride home, and then attempted to rape her in her car? See State v. Lamoureux, 623 A.2d 9 (R.I. 1993).

(*iii*) The defendant was convicted of burglary and murder and sentenced to death. The charge involved a midnight break-in at the home of a 74-year-old woman. The house was ransacked, and a TV set, a radio, and a ring were stolen; the woman, brutally beaten about the face and body, later died. Four weeks after the crime a search at the defendant's home turned up the three stolen items, but there was little other evidence to connect him to the crime. Two months before this crime, at a location four blocks away, there was a break-in, near midnight, at the home of an 84-year-old woman. The house was ransacked; the woman was severely beaten about the face but recovered. In that offense, the defendant was identified as the perpetrator, his palm print was found in the victim's house, and he was convicted of the crime. Should the prosecution be permitted to prove this earlier offense for purposes of identifying the defendant as the perpetrator of the later one? One of the appellate court judges considered this a case where the "similarities are confined to relatively insignificant details that would likely be common elements regardless of who had committed the crimes." Another judge concluded that the crimes were "so close in time and geographic proximity and so similar in gratuitous brutality . . . as to naturally show that the person who committed one also committed the other." A third said that "[t]he two incidents here were as nearly similar as human events will allow." Who was right? See Commonwealth v. Bryant, 530 A.2d 83, 86, 88-89 (Pa. 1987).

(*b*) *Sex offenses.* The Violent Crime Control and Law Enforcement Act of 1994 amends the Federal Rules of Evidence by adding the following provision (Fed. R. Evid. 413(a)):

> In a criminal case in which the defendant is accused of an offense of sexual assault, evidence of the defendant's commission of another offense or offenses of sexual assault is admissible, and may be considered for its bearing on any matter to which it is relevant.

The Act adds an analogous provision (Fed. R. Evid. 414(a)) rendering the defendant's commission of child molestation admissible in a prosecution for other acts of child molestation. See 55 Crim. L. Rptr. 2411-2412 (1994).

What is the basis for treating prior sexual acts differently from other evidence of bad character or criminal propensity? Can an exception to the rule of exclusion be justified on the ground that sexual misconduct has greater value than other misconduct in predicting future behavior? Or should the rule of exclusion be applied even *more* strictly, on the ground that evidence of prior sexual misconduct has especially strong prejudicial effects? A few state courts have been willing in sex offense cases to admit evidence of a defendant's prior sex offenses, but in most jurisdictions the prior-misconduct rule is applied just as strictly in rape trials as in other kinds of prosecutions. E.g., Lannan v. State, 600 N.E.2d 1334 (Ind. 1992). See David P. Bryden & Roger C. Park, "Other Crimes" Evidence in Sex Offense Cases, 78 Minn. L. Rev. 529 (1994); Sara Sun Beale, Prior Similar Acts in Prosecutions for Rape and Child Sex Abuse, 4 Crim. L. Forum 307 (1993).

Congress was sufficiently troubled by the issue to include in the 1994 Act an unusual provision requiring a committee of federal judges to submit a report on the new rules, after which Congress will have an opportunity to reconsider them. See Violent Crime Control and Law Enforcement Act of 1994, §320935(c), 55 Crim. L. Rptr. 2412 (1994). How should the judges respond?

(c) *The impeachment exception.* In all of the situations so far discussed, the question has been whether the prosecution can use evidence of other crimes as part of its case-in-chief. Even when the other-crimes evidence is clearly inadmissible for this purpose, if the accused chooses to testify in his own defense, then the prosecution generally will be permitted to ask about the other crimes in its cross-examination of the accused and to introduce other-crimes evidence in its rebuttal for purposes of impeaching the defendant's testimony. In theory, the other-crimes evidence may not be used to provide affirmative support for the prosecution's case. It may be considered only for purposes of judging the credibility of the defendant's testimony, and the jury will be so instructed.

The rationale of the impeachment exception appears to be that a person convicted of crime may be less trustworthy and more likely to give false testimony than a citizen with a "clean" record.[7] Whatever the soundness of this rationale when the previous misconduct involves perjury or similar crimes of dishonesty, its invocation in the case of other crimes can border on the absurd. In a prosecution for burglary, previous burglary convictions are clearly inadmissible for the purpose of showing the defendant's disposition to commit this crime, but if the defendant claims to have been elsewhere at the time, the burglary convictions will generally be held admissible to show a possibility that the defendant may be disposed to perjury!

In recent years an increasing number of courts have recognized the injustice of this unqualified exception for impeachment use of prior offenses; these courts require admissibility to be determined on a case-by-case basis, weighing such factors as the recency of the prior offense, whether the crime involved dishonesty, and whether the crime was so similar to that charged as to enhance the danger of prejudice.[8] Even in these limited terms, the impeachment exception presents a striking anomaly. If the defendant is prosecuted for perjury, previous convictions for perjury or other dishonest behavior cannot be introduced as part of the prosecution's case-in-chief in order to show the defendant's propensity to lie under oath. But whenever a defendant chooses to testify, the prior convictions become admissible precisely for that purpose.

To what extent does the impeachment exception impair the values reflected

---

7. At common law a person convicted of treason, felony, or other crime of infamy or dishonesty (crimen falsi) was disqualified from testifying as a witness. In the mid-1800s, when common law jurisdictions moved to remove the absolute disqualification, they generally provided by statute that prior convictions of the witness could be introduced for purposes of impeachment. See 2 J. Wigmore §§519-520 (3d ed. 1940); 3A J. Wigmore §§986-987 (Chadbourn rev. 1970).

8. See Gordon v. United States, 383 F.2d 936 (D.C. Cir. 1967) (Burger, J.). See also Fed. R. Evid. 609.

in the general rule against use of other-crimes evidence? Does it matter whether these values are preserved only when the defendant chooses not to testify?[9]

The impeachment exception is premised on the assumption that the jury will consider the other crimes *only* for the limited purpose of judging credibility and will not treat the other crimes as affirmative evidence of guilt. Is this a plausible assumption? Lawyers and social scientists have studied the question but have not reached definitive conclusions. The Note that follows explores the effectiveness of cautionary instructions and collects some of the available findings. The problem immediately at hand is to understand how the rules concerning other-crimes evidence actually function, but questions about the effectiveness of jury instructions are central to understanding the actual impact of all the elaborately crafted rules of criminal law and evidence that the jury is called upon to apply.

NOTE ON THE EFFECTIVENESS OF JURY INSTRUCTIONS

When other-crimes evidence has been introduced for impeachment purposes, a typical instruction to the jury might read as follows (1 E. Devitt & C. Blackmar, Federal Jury Practice and Instructions §11.12 (4th ed. 1992)):

> Evidence of a defendant's previous conviction of a crime may be considered by the jury only insofar as it may affect the credibility of the defendant as a witness and must never be considered as any evidence of [his] [her] guilt of the crime for which the defendant is now on trial.

Such an instruction calls on the jury to perform an intellectual task that is bound to run counter to the jury's natural inclinations. Indeed the rule generally excluding other-crimes evidence is premised on the assumption that such evidence *is* relevant to guilt and is very difficult for the jury to keep in perspective once it becomes known. Thus jurors may be strongly tempted to disregard the instruction, even if they are able to grasp the subtle distinction it asks them to draw. The problem arises over and over in the administration of the complex body of rules that ostensibly govern the criminal process. Yet just as the jury creates the need for many of these complicated rules, the nature of the jury raises doubts about whether subtle or counter-intuitive instructions actually affect the outcome of the case.

Experienced judges confronting this question have expressed sharply divergent views about the effectiveness of jury instructions. Sometimes the courts suggest that there is no practical alternative to reliance on instructions and therefore that the effectiveness of such instructions must be assumed. In Spencer v. Texas, 385 U.S. 554, 565 (1967), the Supreme Court expressed its faith in "the ability of juries to approach their task responsibly and to sort out discrete issues given to them under proper instructions. . . ."[10] Others have been more

9. It is sometimes said that, by deciding to testify, a defendant *chooses* to put his character in issue. Is this convincing? See State v. Santiago, 53 Hawaii 254, 492 P.2d 657 (1971).

10. *Spencer* involved a challenge to the procedure followed under Texas habitual criminal statutes. The statutes provided for enhanced punishment for those convicted of crime who were shown to have been convicted of other crimes in the past. When the prosecution sought to invoke the enhanced-punishment provisions, the prior offenses would be alleged in the indictment and

skeptical. Chief Justice Warren once wrote that "it flouts human nature to suppose that a jury would not consider a defendant's previous trouble with the law in deciding whether he has committed the crime charged against him." Id. at 575 (dissenting opinion). Justice Jackson warned: "The naive assumption that prejudicial effects can be overcome by instructions to the jury . . . all practicing lawyers know to be unmitigated fiction." Krulewitch v. United States, 336 U.S. 440, 453 (1949) (concurring opinion), reprinted at pages 720-724 infra. In Dunn v. United States, 307 F.2d 883, 886 (5th Cir. 1962), the court was even more pessimistic:

> [O]ne cannot unring a bell; after the thrust of the saber it is difficult to say forget the wound; and finally, if you throw a skunk into the jury box, you can't instruct the jury not to smell it.

In recent years social scientists have undertaken studies to determine where the truth lies, but the results have been inconclusive. One problem is that the experimental method cannot be applied directly to actual juries deciding actual cases. Often the "case" is not presented in realistic courtroom fashion, the "jurors" may not be representative of those likely to serve on an actual jury, and the research subjects often cast their votes without the group deliberations that can affect the final ballot of jurors in real cases.[11]

Such studies in any event have failed to produce a clear picture with regard to the impact of jury instructions. A 1968 study of pretrial publicity found that volunteer "jurors" exposed to a sensational newspaper account of the case were much more likely to convict, but among jurors instructed to disregard the newspaper accounts, the difference in conviction rates disappeared.[12]

In contrast, in a 1973 experiment, researchers found that exposure to a legally inadmissible confession significantly increased the likelihood of a guilty verdict when other evidence was weak and that instructions to disregard the confession had no significant effect on the likelihood of conviction.[13]

---

proved at trial. Thus the jurors trying the current charge would learn of the prior offenses, even though they would be instructed that those offenses could not be considered in determining the defendant's guilt for the present offense. The Court held that the Texas procedure was consistent with due process, rejecting the defendant's argument that the state should be required to postpone all reference to the prior offenses until after a verdict of conviction is rendered. *Spencer* was explicitly reaffirmed in Marshall v. Lonberger, 459 U.S. 422, 438 n. 6 (1983). Four justices argued that *Spencer* should be reexamined.

In a few discrete areas, the Court has held that cautionary instructions are inadequate to eliminate particularly severe prejudicial effects. For example, in Jackson v. Denno, 378 U.S. 368 (1964), the Court held unconstitutional a New York procedure under which juries were required to determine the voluntariness of a confession and instructed that in passing on the question of guilt they should disregard the confession if it was found involuntary. The Court held that in order to insure that an involuntary confession did not contribute to the verdict, the trial judge must make a preliminary determination outside the jury's presence and exclude any confession found involuntary.

11. There is evidence, however, that jury verdicts tend to reflect the position favored by a majority on the first ballot. See Harry Kalven & Hans Zeisel, The American Jury 487-488 (1966).

12. Rita James Simon, The Effects of Newspapers on the Verdicts of Potential Jurors, in R Simon, The Sociology of Law 617-627 (1968). To the same effect, see Robin Reed, Jury Simulation The Impact of Judge's Instructions and Attorney Tactics on Decisionmaking, 71 J. Crim. L. & Crimi nology 68 (1980).

13. Stanley Sue, Ronald Smith, & Cathy Caldwell, Effects of Inadmissible Evidence on the Deci sions of Simulated Jurors: A Moral Dilemma, 3 J. Applied Soc. Psych. 345 (1973). For comparable

A 1973 English study[14] focused on the impact of juror exposure to a defendant's record of prior convictions. The researchers found that evidence of previous similar offenses significantly increased the likelihood of conviction, but that a cautionary instruction removed most (though not all) of the prejudicial effect: Defendants afforded the cautionary instruction were still more likely to be convicted than those whose prior record had not been mentioned at all.

To the extent that cautionary instructions fail to eradicate prejudicial effects, the result could be due, in part, to jurors' inability to *understand* the subtle distinctions that such instructions sometimes require. Several studies have produced disturbing evidence that jurors often do not grasp the judge's explanations of legal concepts. One study found that the average juror understands only about one-half of the judge's instructions on the law.[15] Part of this problem may lie in the phraseology used, rather than in the intrinsic complexity of the concepts.

QUESTIONS ON JURY INSTRUCTIONS

Whatever the available evidence may suggest about the usefulness of jury instructions, there clearly remain substantial doubts about whether instructions are as fully effective in practice as they are assumed to be in theory. What are the implications of this situation? Granted that jury instructions function imperfectly (at best), what is the alternative?

One pragmatic approach has been to consider changes in trial procedure that might enhance the effectiveness of instructions. For example, the wording of instructions could be improved so that their meaning is more clearly explained to the jury.[16] Beyond this, when a judge tells a jury to disregard evidence, should she explain *why* the law considers the evidence misleading? The standard cautionary instructions tend to be rather perfunctory. For ways to convey a more forceful message, see Albert W. Alschuler, Courtroom Misconduct by Prosecutors and Trial Judges, 50 Tex. L. Rev. 629, 652-654 (1972).

Can ameliorative reforms cure the difficulties of overly cumbersome jury instructions, or is the basic problem more fundamental? Note that jury instructions are necessary in the first place only because we want citizens without special training to participate and at the same time we want their decisions to conform

---

findings, see Sarah Tanford & Steven Penrod, Social Inference Processes in Juror Judgments of Multiple Offense Trials, 47 J. Personality & Soc. Psych. 749 (1984); Saul M. Kassin & Lawrence S. Wrightsman, Coerced Confessions, Judicial Instruction and Mock Juror Verdicts, 11 J. Applied Soc. Psych. 489 (1981).

14. W. R. Cornish & A. P. Sealy, Juries and the Rules of Evidence (London School of Economics Jury Project), [1973] Crim. L. Rev. 208.

15. Amiram Elwork, Bruce D. Sales, & James J. Alfini, Making Jury Instructions Understandable 2 (1982).

16. A proposal for clarifying jury instructions and translating them into plain English is developed in William E. Schwartzer, Communicating with Juries: Problems and Remedies, 69 Cal. L. Rev. 731 (1981). See also Larry Heuer & Steven D. Penrod, Instructing Jurors: A Field Experiment with Written and Preliminary Instructions, 13 L. & Human Behavior 409 (1989); Elwork, et al., supra note 15; Lawrence J. Severance, Edith Greene, & Elizabeth F. Loftus, Toward Criminal Jury Instructions that Jurors Can Understand, 75 J. Crim. L. & C. 198 (1984). The last two sources include empirical tests showing that linguistically simplified instructions improve juror comprehension of legal concepts.

to law. Do these partially inconsistent desires require a system that is simply too complex to function properly? This problem can be reconsidered in connection with the materials on other countries' approaches to lay participation. See pages 64-65 infra.

3.   Proof Beyond a Reasonable Doubt

INTRODUCTORY NOTES

1. *The constitutional rule and its foundations.* In In re Winship, 397 U.S. 358, 364 (1970), the Supreme Court held that "the Due Process Clause protects the accused against conviction except upon proof beyond a reasonable doubt of every fact necessary to constitute the crime charged." The Court explained the fundamental importance of this standard of proof as follows (id. at 363-364).

> The reasonable-doubt standard . . . is a prime instrument for reducing the risk of convictions resting on factual error. The standard provides concrete substance for the presumption of innocence — that bedrock "axiomatic and elementary" principle whose "enforcement lies at the foundation of the administration of our criminal law." . . .
>
> The accused during a criminal prosecution has at stake interests of immense importance, both because of the possibility that he may lose his liberty upon conviction and because of the certainty that he would be stigmatized by the conviction. Accordingly, a society that values the good name and freedom of every individual should not condemn a man for commission of a crime when there is reasonable doubt about his guilt. . . .
>
> Moreover, use of the reasonable-doubt standard is indispensable to command the respect and confidence of the community in applications of the criminal law. It is critical that the moral force of the criminal law not be diluted by a standard of proof that leaves people in doubt whether innocent men are being condemned. It is also important in our free society that every individual going about his ordinary affairs have confidence that his government cannot adjudge him guilty of a criminal offense without convincing a proper factfinder of his guilt with utmost certainty.

In a concurring opinion Mr. Justice Harlan added (id. at 371-372):

> If . . . the standard of proof for a criminal trial were a preponderance of the evidence rather than proof beyond a reasonable doubt, there would be a smaller risk of factual errors that result in freeing guilty persons, but a far greater risk of factual errors that result in convicting the innocent. Because the standard of proof affects the comparative frequency of these two types of erroneous outcomes, the choice of the standard to be applied in a particular kind of litigation should, in a rational world, reflect an assessment of the comparative social disutility of each.
>
> When one makes such an assessment, the reason for different standards of proof in civil as opposed to criminal litigation becomes apparent. In a civil suit between two private parties for money damages, for example, we view it as no more serious in general for there to be an erroneous verdict in the defendant's favor than for there to be an erroneous verdict in the plaintiff's favor. . . .
>
> In a criminal case, on the other hand, we do not view the social disutility of convicting an innocent man as equivalent to the disutility of acquitting someone

who is guilty. . . . In this context, I view the requirement of proof beyond a reasonable doubt in a criminal case as bottomed on a fundamental value determination of our society that it is far worse to convict an innocent man than to let a guilty man go free.

2. *How burden-of-proof problems arise.* Problems relating to the reasonable-doubt standard can surface in many different ways. The issue normally arises first at the close of the prosecution's case. If the judge decides that the evidence raises a reasonable doubt about guilt *as a matter of law* (an elusive concept explored in the next note), the judge must direct a verdict for the defendant. The same problem of assessing the sufficiency of the evidence may be presented to the judge again at the close of all the evidence (when the defendant may again move for a directed verdict); it will be a central concern of the jurors in their deliberations; and it may arise again on appeal (when the defendant may seek reversal on the basis of insufficient evidence).

3. *Legal sufficiency: reasonable doubt as a matter of law.* Courts often have difficulty articulating the standard that judges should apply in determining whether the evidence is insufficient as a matter of law. In a sense the judges must give the defendant the *benefit of the doubt.* If there is a reasonable doubt, then a guilty verdict would seem improper. On the other hand, before taking a case away from the jury (or reversing a jury's verdict), judges must resolve all evidentiary doubts against the proponent of the motion; in this sense the courts must give the *prosecution* the benefit of the doubt on the question whether its evidence does prove guilt beyond a reasonable doubt. The following comment from the opinion in Curley v. United States, 160 F.2d 229, 232-233 (D.C. Cir. 1947), helps clarify this elusive problem and provides a relatively precise statement of the test that judges apply in passing on questions of evidentiary sufficiency:

> [It is sometimes said] that unless the evidence excludes the hypothesis of innocence, the judge must direct a verdict . . . [and] that if the evidence is such that a reasonable mind might fairly conclude either guilt or innocence, a verdict of guilt must be reversed on appeal. But obviously neither of those translations is the law. Logically the ultimate premise of that thesis is that if a reasonable mind might have a reasonable doubt, there is, therefore, a reasonable doubt. That is not true. . . .
>
> The functions of the jury include the determination of the credibility of witnesses, the weighing of the evidence, and the drawing of justifiable inferences of fact from proven facts. It is the function of the judge to deny the jury any opportunity to operate beyond its province: The jury may not be permitted to conjecture merely, or to conclude upon pure speculation or from passion, prejudice or sympathy. The critical point in this boundary is the existence or non-existence of a reasonable doubt as to guilt. If the evidence is such that reasonable jurymen must necessarily have such a doubt, the judge must require acquittal, because no other result is permissible within the fixed bounds of jury consideration. But if a reasonable mind might fairly have a reasonable doubt or might fairly not have one, the case is for the jury, and the decision is for the jurors to make. . . .
>
> The true rule, therefore, is that a trial judge, in passing upon a motion for directed verdict of acquittal, must determine whether upon the evidence, giving full play to the right of the jury to determine credibility, weigh the evidence, and draw justifiable inferences of fact, a reasonable mind might fairly conclude guilt beyond a reasonable doubt. . . . If he concludes that either of the two results, a reasonable doubt or no reasonable doubt, is fairly possible, he must let the jury decide the matter. In a given case, particularly one of circumstantial evidence, that determi-

nation may depend upon the difference between pure speculation and legitimate inference from proven facts. The task of the judge in such [a] case is not easy, for the rule of reason is frequently difficult to apply, but we know of no way to avoid that difficulty.

4. *Factual sufficiency: explaining reasonable doubt.* The problem of evidentiary sufficiency arises not only for judges but for the jury, and the instructions accordingly must tell the jury how it should evaluate the evidence. Empirical studies tend to confirm that jurors convict more readily when instructed under a more-likely-than-not standard than when instructed under the reasonable doubt standard,[17] and courts must protect the jury against any instruction that might dilute the latter standard. Accordingly, a conviction must be reversed for error in explaining the reasonable doubt standard to the jury, even when the appellate court does not find the evidence insufficient as a matter of law.

(*a*) In McCullough v. State, 657 P.2d 1157 (Nev. 1983), the trial judge had explained degrees of proof to the jury in terms of "a scale of zero to ten." He placed the preliminary hearing standard of probable cause at one and the burden of persuasion in civil trials at just over five. He then described beyond a reasonable doubt as "seven and a half, if you had to put it on a scale." The Nevada Supreme Court reversed, stating (id. at 1159): "The concept of reasonable doubt is inherently qualitative. Any attempt to quantify it may impermissibly lower the prosecution's burden of proof, and is likely to confuse rather than clarify."

(*b*) Courts often get into trouble when attempting to explain "reasonable doubt" in qualitative terms. In Cage v. Louisiana, 498 U.S. 39 (1990), the trial judge in a first-degree murder prosecution had instructed the jury that "a reasonable doubt [must be] founded upon a real tangible substantial basis and not upon mere caprice and conjecture. It must be such doubt as would give rise to a grave uncertainty. . . . A reasonable doubt is not a mere possible doubt. It is an actual substantial doubt. . . . What is required is not an absolute or mathematical certainty, but a moral certainty." The Supreme Court reversed the conviction, holding that the references to "grave uncertainty," "substantial doubt," and "moral certainty" improperly diluted the *Winship* standard.

(*c*) A traditionally accepted definition of reasonable doubt is the following, which is required by Cal. Penal Code §1096:

> Reasonable doubt is . . . not a mere possible doubt; because everything relating to human affairs, and depending on moral evidence, is open to some possible or imaginary doubt. It is that state of the case which, after the entire comparison and consideration of all the evidence, leaves the minds of the jurors in that condition that they cannot say they feel an abiding conviction, to a moral certainty, of the truth of the charge.

This language is drawn verbatim from an 1850 jury instruction given by Massachusetts Chief Justice Lemuel Shaw, see Commonwealth v. Webster, 59 Mass 295, 320 (1850), and it is still in widespread use today. What is the meaning, to a

17. See Barbara D. Underwood, The Thumb on the Scales of Justice: Burdens of Persuasion in Criminal Cases, 86 Yale L.J. 1299, 1309-1311 (1977); W. R. Cornish & A. P. Sealy, Juries and the Rules of Evidence, [1973] Crim. L. Rev. 208; Rita James Simon & Linda Mahan, Quantifying Burdens of Proof, 5 L. & Soc. Rev. 319 (1971). For exploration of the impact of jury instructions generally, see pages 35-37 supra.

modern juror, of "moral evidence" and "moral certainty"? Does the instruction meet the requirements of *Winship* and Cage v. Louisiana?

In Sandoval v. California, 114 S. Ct. 1239 (1994), the Court distinguished *Cage* and upheld the constitutionality of the California instruction. The court conceded that "the phrase 'moral evidence' is not a mainstay of the modern lexicon," and that "moral certainty is ambiguous" but concluded that the instruction as a whole gave sufficient content to the reasonable doubt requirement. Several concurring justices agreed that use of the nineteenth century phrases was not unconstitutional, but they urged states to choose more comprehensible modern language.

(*d*) In Victor v. Nebraska, 114 S. Ct. 1239 (1994), the trial judge had defined reasonable doubt as "an actual and substantial doubt, arising from the evidence . . . as distinguished from a doubt arising from mere possibility, from bare imagination, or from fanciful conjecture." The Court said that "this construction is somewhere problematic," because "substantial," if interpreted to mean doubt "to a large degree," would overstate the degree of doubt required for acquittal under *Winship*. Nonetheless, the Court found *Cage* inapplicable and upheld the conviction, on the ground that "the context makes clear that 'substantial' is used in the sense of existence rather than magnitude of the doubt."

(*e*) Because reasonable doubt is difficult to explain correctly, several courts consider it preferable to give the jury no explanation at all. In United States v. Reives, 15 F.3d 42 (4th Cir. 1994), a jury that had received no explanation of reasonable doubt sent the judge a note asking him to define it. After the judge refused, the jury convicted. The Fourth Circuit affirmed, stating that "trying to explain things will confuse matters." Is this an appropriate solution to the problem?

5. *Subsidiary issues.* An important aspect of the overall sufficiency of the evidence is the burden of proof on particular subsidiary issues in the case. Even though the prosecution must prove guilt beyond a reasonable doubt, the state is sometimes permitted to allocate the burden of persuasion on these subsidiary issues to the defense. In addition, the prosecution may, while retaining the burden of proof, seek to invoke a *presumption*. Through this device the burden of establishing some essential fact can be met through proof of some other fact (from which the existence of the essential fact can be "presumed"). In situations involving allocation issues or presumptions, the prosecution normally will concede that it has not proved a particular point beyond a reasonable doubt; the question will be whether it must do so.

The remaining materials in this section explore these aspects of the burden of proof — the allocation of the burden and the use of presumptions.

a.   Allocating the Burden of Proof

PATTERSON v. NEW YORK

Supreme Court of the United States
432 U.S. 197 (1977)

JUSTICE WHITE delivered the opinion of the Court. . . .

After a brief and unstable marriage, the appellant, Gordon Patterson, Jr., became estranged from his wife, Roberta. Roberta resumed an association with John Northrup, a neighbor to whom she had been engaged prior to her marriage to appellant. On December 27, 1970, Patterson borrowed a rifle from an acquaintance and went to the residence of his father-in-law. There, he observed his wife through a window in a state of semiundress in the presence of John Northrup. He entered the house and killed Northrup by shooting him in the head.

Patterson was charged with second-degree murder. In New York there are two elements of this crime: (1) "intent to cause the death of another person"; and (2) "caus[ing] the death of such person or of a third person." Malice aforethought is not an element of the crime. In addition, the State permits a person accused of murder to raise an affirmative defense that he "acted under the influence of extreme emotional disturbance for which there was a reasonable explanation or excuse."[a]

New York also recognizes the crime of manslaughter. A person is guilty of manslaughter if he intentionally kills another person "under circumstances which do not constitute murder because he acts under the influence of extreme emotional disturbance." Appellant confessed before trial to killing Northrup, but at trial he raised the defense of extreme emotional disturbance.

The jury was instructed as to the elements of the crime of murder. Focusing on the element of intent, the trial court charged:

> [Y]ou must not expect or require the defendant to prove to your satisfaction that his acts were done without the intent to kill. Whatever proof he may have attempted, however far he may have gone in an effort to convince you of his innocence or guiltlessness, he is not obliged, he is not obligated to prove anything. It is always the People's burden to prove his guilt, and to prove that he intended to kill in this instance beyond a reasonable doubt.

The jury was further instructed, consistently with New York law, that the defendant had the burden of proving his affirmative defense by a preponderance of the evidence. The jury was told that if it found beyond a reasonable doubt that appellant had intentionally killed Northrup but that appellant had demonstrated by a preponderance of the evidence that he had acted under the influence of extreme emotional disturbance, it had to find appellant guilty of manslaughter instead of murder.

The jury found appellant guilty of murder. Judgment was entered on the verdict, and the Appellate Division affirmed. While appeal to the New York Court of Appeals was pending, this Court decided Mullaney v. Wilbur, 421 U.S. 684 (1975), in which the Court declared Maine's murder statute unconstitutional. Under the Maine statute, a person accused of murder could rebut the statutory presumption that he committed the offense with "malice aforethought" by proving that he acted in the heat of passion on sudden provocation. The Court held that this scheme improperly shifted the burden of persuasion from the prosecutor to the defendant and was therefore a violation of due process. In the Court of Appeals appellant urged that New York's murder statute is functionally equivalent to the one struck down in *Mullaney* and that therefore his conviction should be reversed.

a. The relevant provisions of the New York Penal Code may be found at pages 391-392 infra. — EDS.

The Court of Appeals rejected appellant's argument. . . . This appeal ensued. . . .

In determining whether New York's allocation to the defendant of proving the mitigating circumstances of severe emotional disturbance is consistent with due process, it is . . . relevant to note that this defense is a considerably expanded version of the common-law defense of heat of passion on sudden provocation and that at common law the burden of proving the latter, as well as other affirmative defenses — indeed, "all . . . circumstances of justification, excuse or alleviation" — rested on the defendant. 4 W. Blackstone, Commentaries *201. This was the rule when the Fifth Amendment was adopted, and it was the American rule when the Fourteenth Amendment was ratified.

In 1895 the common-law view was abandoned with respect to the insanity defense in federal prosecutions. Davis v. United States, 160 U.S. 469 (1895). This ruling had wide impact on the practice in the federal courts with respect to the burden of proving various affirmative defenses, and the prosecution in a majority of jurisdictions in this country sooner or later came to shoulder the burden of proving the sanity of the accused and of disproving the facts constituting other affirmative defenses, including provocation. Davis was not a constitutional ruling, however, as Leland v. Oregon, [343 U.S. 790 (1952)], made clear.

At issue in Leland v. Oregon was the constitutionality under the Due Process Clause of the Oregon rule that the defense of insanity must be proved by the defendant beyond a reasonable doubt. Noting that Davis "obviously establish[ed] no constitutional doctrine," the Court refused to strike down the Oregon scheme, saying that the burden of proving all elements of the crime beyond reasonable doubt, including the elements of premeditation and deliberation, was placed on the State under Oregon procedures and remained there throughout the trial. To convict, the jury was required to find each element of the crime beyond a reasonable doubt, based on all the evidence, including the evidence going to the issue of insanity. Only then was the jury "to consider separately the issue of legal sanity per se. . . ." This practice did not offend the Due Process Clause even though among the 20 States then placing the burden of proving his insanity on the defendant, Oregon was alone in requiring him to convince the jury beyond a reasonable doubt. . . .

[After the decision in Mullaney, supra,] the Court confirmed that it remained constitutional to burden the defendant with proving his insanity defense when it dismissed, as not raising a substantial federal question, a case in which the appellant specifically challenged the continuing validity of Leland v. Oregon. . . . Rivera v. Delaware, 429 U.S. 877 (1976). . . .

We cannot conclude that Patterson's conviction under the New York law derived him of due process of law. The crime of murder is defined by the statute, which represents a recent revision of the state criminal code, as causing the death of another person with intent to do so. The death, the intent to kill, and causation are the facts that the State is required to prove beyond a reasonable doubt if a person is to be convicted of murder. No further facts are either presumed or inferred in order to constitute the crime. . . . It seems to us that the State satisfied the mandate of Winship [page 38 supra,] that it prove beyond a reasonable doubt "every fact necessary to constitute the crime with which [Patterson was] charged."

. . . New York did no more than Leland and Rivera permitted it to do. . . . Under those cases, once the facts constituting a crime are established beyond a reasonable doubt, based on all the evidence including the evidence of the defendant's mental state, the State may refuse to sustain the affirmative defense of insanity unless demonstrated by a preponderance of the evidence. . . .

We are unwilling to reconsider *Leland* and *Rivera*. But even if we were to hold that a State must prove sanity to convict once that fact is put in issue, it would not necessarily follow that a State must prove beyond a reasonable doubt every fact, the existence or nonexistence of which it is willing to recognize as an exculpatory or mitigating circumstance affecting the degree of culpability or the severity of the punishment. Here, in revising its criminal code, New York provided the affirmative defense of extreme emotional disturbance, a substantially expanded version of the older heat-of-passion concept; but it was willing to do so only if the facts making out the defense were established by the defendant with sufficient certainty. The State was itself unwilling to undertake to establish the absence of those facts beyond a reasonable doubt, perhaps fearing that proof would be too difficult and that too many persons deserving treatment as murderers would escape that punishment if the evidence need merely raise a reasonable doubt about the defendant's emotional state. It has been said that the new criminal code of New York contains some 25 affirmative defenses which exculpate or mitigate but which must be established by the defendant to be operative.[10] The Due Process Clause, as we see it, does not put New York to the choice of abandoning those defenses or undertaking to disprove their existence in order to convict of a crime which otherwise is within its constitutional power to sanction by substantial punishment.

The requirement of proof beyond a reasonable doubt in a criminal case is "bottomed on a fundamental value determination of our society that it is far worse to convict an innocent man than to let a guilty man go free." *Winship*, 39 U.S., at 372 (Harlan, J., concurring). . . . While it is clear that our society has willingly chosen to bear a substantial burden in order to protect the innocent, it is equally clear that the risk it must bear is not without limits. . . . Due process does not require that every conceivable step be taken, at whatever cost, to eliminate the possibility of convicting an innocent person. . . .

It is . . . very likely true that fewer convictions of murder would occur if New York were required to negative the affirmative defense at issue here. But in each instance of a murder conviction under the present law, New York will have proved beyond a reasonable doubt that the defendant has intentionally killed another person, an act which it is not disputed the State may constitutionally criminalize and punish. If the State nevertheless chooses to recognize a factor that mitigates the degree of criminality or punishment, we think the State may assure itself that the fact has been established with reasonable certainty. To recognize at all a mitigating circumstance does not require the State to prove its

10. The State of New York is not alone in this result: "Since the Model Penal Code was completed in 1962, some 22 states have codified and reformed their criminal laws. At least 12 of the jurisdictions have used the concept of an 'affirmative defense' and have defined that phrase require that the defendant prove the existence of an 'affirmative defense' by a preponderance the evidence. . . ." Low & Jeffries, DICTA: Constitutionalizing the Criminal Law?, 29 Va. Law Week No. 18, p. 1 (1977). Even so, the trend over the years appears to have been to require the prosecution to disprove affirmative defenses beyond a reasonable doubt. The split among the various jurisdictions varies for any given defense. . . .

nonexistence in each case in which the fact is put in issue, if in its judgment this would be too cumbersome, too expensive, and too inaccurate.[11] . . .

This view may seem to permit state legislatures to reallocate burdens of proof by labeling as affirmative defenses at least some elements of the crimes now defined in their statutes. But there are obviously constitutional limits beyond which the States may not go in this regard. "[I]t is not within the province of a legislature to declare an individual guilty or presumptively guilty of a crime." McFarland v. American Sugar Rfg. Co., 241 U.S. 79, 86 (1916). The legislature cannot "validly command that the finding of an indictment, or mere proof of the identity of the accused, should create a presumption of the existence of all the facts essential to guilt." Tot v. United States, 319 U.S. 463, 469 (1943). . . .

It is urged that Mullaney v. Wilbur necessarily invalidates Patterson's conviction. In *Mullaney* the charge was murder, which the Maine statute defined as the unlawful killing of a human being "with malice aforethought, either express or implied." The trial court instructed the jury that the words "malice aforethought" were most important because "malice aforethought is an essential and indispensable element of the crime of murder." Malice, as the statute indicated and as the court instructed, could be implied and was to be implied from "any deliberate, cruel act committed by one person against another suddenly . . . or without a considerable provocation," in which event an intentional killing was murder unless by a preponderance of the evidence it was shown that the act was committed "in the heat of passion, on sudden provocation." The instructions emphasized that "'malice aforethought and heat of passion on sudden provocation are two inconsistent things'; thus, by proving the latter the defendant would negate the former." . . . This Court . . . unanimously [held] that Wilbur's due process rights had been invaded by the presumption casting upon him the burden of proving by a preponderance of the evidence that he had acted in the heat of passion upon sudden provocation.

Mullaney's holding, it is argued, is that the State may not permit the blameworthiness of an act or the severity of punishment authorized for its commission to depend on the presence or absence of an identified fact without assuming the burden of proving the presence or absence of that fact, as the case may be, beyond a reasonable doubt. In our view, the *Mullaney* holding should not be so broadly read. . . . The Maine Supreme Judicial Court made it clear that . . . malice, in the sense of the absence of provocation, was part of the definition of that crime. Yet malice, i.e., lack of provocation, was presumed and could be rebutted by the defendant only by proving by a preponderance of the evidence that he acted with heat of passion upon sudden provocation. . . .

---

11. The drafters of the Model Penal Code would, as a matter of policy, place the burden of proving the nonexistence of most affirmative defenses, including the defense involved in this case, on the prosecution once the defendant has come forward with some evidence that the defense is present. The drafters recognize the need for flexibility, however, and would, in "some exceptional situations," place the burden of persuasion on the accused. "Characteristically these are situations where the defense does not obtain at all under existing law and the Code seeks to introduce a mitigation. Resistance to the mitigation, based upon the prosecution's difficulty in obtaining evidence, ought to be lowered if the burden of persuasion is imposed on the defendant. Where that difficulty appears genuine and there is something to be said against allowing the defense at all, we consider it defensible to shift the burden in this way." ALI, Model Penal Code §1.13, Comment, 113 (Tent. Draft No. 4, 1955). . . .

As we have explained, nothing was presumed or implied against Patterson. . . . The judgment of the New York Court of Appeals is affirmed.

JUSTICE POWELL, with whom JUSTICE BRENNAN and JUSTICE MARSHALL join, dissenting. . . .

Mullaney held invalid Maine's requirement that the defendant prove heat of passion. The Court today, without disavowing the unanimous holding of *Mullaney,* approves New York's requirement that the defendant prove extreme emotional disturbance. The Court manages to run a constitutional boundary line through the barely visible space that separates Maine's law from New York's. It does so on the basis of distinctions in language that are formalistic rather than substantive. . . .

Maine's statute was invalid, the Court reasons, because it "defined [murder] as the unlawful killing of a human being 'with malice aforethought, either express or implied.'" . . . *Winship* was violated only because this "fact" — malice — was "presumed" unless the defendant persuaded the jury otherwise by showing that he acted in the heat of passion. New York, in form presuming no affirmative "fact" against Patterson, and blessed with a statute drafted in the leaner language of the 20th century, escapes constitutional scrutiny unscathed even though the effect on the defendant of New York's placement of the burden of persuasion is exactly the same as Maine's.

This explanation of the *Mullaney* holding bears little resemblance to the basic rationale of that decision. . . . The test the Court today establishes allows a legislature to shift, virtually at will, the burden of persuasion with respect to any factor in a criminal case, so long as it is careful not to mention the nonexistence of that factor in the statutory language that defines the crime. . . .

With all respect, this type of constitutional adjudication is indefensibly formalistic. . . . What *Winship* and *Mullaney* had sought to teach about the limits a free society places on its procedures to safeguard the liberty of its citizens becomes a rather simplistic lesson in statutory draftsmanship. Nothing in the Court's opinion prevents a legislature from applying this new learning to many of the classical elements of the crimes it punishes. . . .[8]

The Court understandably manifests some uneasiness that its formalistic approach will give legislatures too much latitude in shifting the burden of persuasion. And so it issues a warning that "there are obviously constitutional limits beyond which the States may not go in this regard." . . . But if the State is careful to conform to the drafting formulas articulated today, the constitutional limits are anything but "obvious." This decision simply leaves us without a conceptual framework for distinguishing abuses from legitimate legislative adjustments of the burden of persuasion in criminal cases.

It is unnecessary for the Court to retreat to a formalistic test for applying *Winship.* Careful attention to the *Mullaney* decision reveals the principles that should control in this and like cases. *Winship* held that the prosecution must

---

8. For example, a state statute could pass muster under the only solid standard that appears in the Court's opinion if it defined murder as mere physical contact between the defendant and the victim leading to the victim's death, but then set up an affirmative defense leaving it to the defendant to prove that he acted without culpable mens rea. The State, in other words, could be relieved altogether of responsibility for proving *anything* regarding the defendant's state of mind, provided only that the face of the statute meets the Court's drafting formulas. . . .

bear the burden of proving beyond a reasonable doubt "the existence of every fact necessary to constitute the crime charged." In *Mullaney* we concluded that heat of passion was one of the "facts" described in *Winship* — that is, a factor as to which the prosecution must bear the burden of persuasion beyond a reasonable doubt. We reached that result only after making two careful inquiries. First, we noted that the presence or absence of heat of passion made a substantial difference in punishment of the offender and in the stigma associated with the conviction. Second, we reviewed the history, in England and this country, of the factor at issue. Central to the holding in *Mullaney* was our conclusion that heat of passion "has been, almost from the inception of the common law of homicide, the single most important factor in determining the degree of culpability attaching to an unlawful homicide."

Implicit in these two inquiries are the principles that should govern this case. The Due Process Clause requires that the prosecutor bear the burden of persuasion beyond a reasonable doubt only if the factor at issue makes a substantial difference in punishment and stigma. The requirement of course applies a fortiori if the factor makes the difference between guilt and innocence. But a substantial difference in punishment alone is not enough. It also must be shown that in the Anglo-American legal tradition the factor in question historically has held that level of importance. If either branch of the test is not met, then the legislature retains its traditional authority over matters of proof. . . .

I hardly need add that New York's provisions allocating the burden of persuasion as to "extreme emotional disturbance" are unconstitutional when judged by these standards. "Extreme emotional disturbance" is, as the Court of Appeals recognized, the direct descendant of the "heat of passion" factor considered at length in *Mullaney*. . . . The presence or absence of extreme emotional disturbance makes a critical difference in punishment and stigma, and throughout our history the resolution of this issue in fact, although expressed in somewhat different terms, has distinguished manslaughter from murder. See 4 W. Blackstone, Commentaries *190-193, 198-201.

The Court beats its retreat from *Winship* apparently because of a concern that otherwise the federal judiciary will intrude too far into substantive choices concerning the content of a State's criminal law. The concern is legitimate, but misplaced. . . . [W]here a State has chosen to retain the traditional distinction between murder and manslaughter, as have New York and Maine, the burden of persuasion must remain on the prosecution with respect to the distinguishing factor, in view of its decisive historical importance. But nothing in *Mullaney* or *Winship* precludes a State from abolishing the distinction between murder and manslaughter and treating all unjustifiable homicide as murder.[13] In this signifi-

---

13. Perhaps under other principles of due process jurisprudence, certain factors are so fundamental that a State could not, as a substantive matter, refrain from recognizing them so long as it chooses to punish given conduct as a crime. . . . But substantive limits were not at issue in *Winship* or *Mullaney*, and they are not at issue here.

Even if there are no constitutional limits preventing the State, for example, from treating all homicides as murders punishable equally regardless of mitigating factors like heat of passion or extreme emotional disturbance, the *Winship/Mullaney* rule still plays an important role. The State then obliged to make its choices concerning the substantive content of its criminal laws with full awareness of the consequences, unable to mask substantive policy choices by shifts in the burden cant respect, neither *Winship* nor *Mullaney* eliminates the substantive flexibility that should remain in legislative hands.

Moreover, it is unlikely that more than a few factors — although important ones — for which a shift in the burden of persuasion seriously would be considered will come within the *Mullaney* holding. . . . New ameliorative affirmative defenses, about which the Court expresses concern, generally remain undisturbed by the holdings in *Winship* and *Mullaney* — and need not be disturbed by a sound holding reversing Patterson's conviction.

Furthermore, as we indicated in *Mullaney*, even as to those factors upon which the prosecution must bear the burden of persuasion, the State retains an important procedural device to avoid jury confusion and prevent the prosecution from being unduly hampered. The State normally may shift to the defendant the burden of production, that is, the burden of going forward with sufficient evidence "to justify [a reasonable] doubt upon the issue." If the defendant's evidence does not cross this threshold, the issue — be it malice, extreme emotional disturbance, self-defense, or whatever — will not be submitted to the jury. . . .

NOTES AND QUESTIONS

1. The burden of production versus the burden of persuasion. Rules allocating the burden of proof deal with two distinct problems. The first concerns allocating the burden of coming forward with enough evidence to put a certain fact in issue. This is commonly referred to as the burden of *production*. The second problem concerns allocating the burden of convincing the trier of fact. This is commonly referred to as the burden of *persuasion*. With respect to most elements of most crimes, the prosecution bears *both* burdens. That is, the prosecution must introduce enough evidence not only to put the facts in issue but also to persuade the trier of fact beyond a reasonable doubt. In some instances state law may require the defense to bear both burdens, and *Patterson* deals with the question of when this is constitutionally permissible. But note that an intermediate position is possible: State law might allocate the burden of *production* to the defense but the burden of *persuasion* to the prosecution. For example, the state might provide that a defendant seeking acquittal on grounds of duress must introduce some evidence of duress,[18] but that once this is done, the prosecution must prove the absence of duress beyond a reasonable doubt. In this situation it is sometimes said (confusingly) that the defendant bears the initial burden of proof and that, once duress is at issue, the burden *shifts* to the prosecution. O

---

of persuasion. See Fletcher, Two Kinds of Legal Rules: A Comparative Study of Burden-of-Persuasion Practices in Criminal Cases, 77 Yale L.J. 880, 894 (1968). . . .

18. With respect to certain special defenses, notably alibi and insanity, states sometimes require that the defendant give notice of the claim by pleading it prior to trial. Typically, however, the defendant need not raise the defense by a formal pleading, even when he has the burden of production. Note also that the prosecutor's case may itself contain evidence sufficient to put some defense in issue. For example, testimony that defendant shot the deceased during a quarrel may include at least some evidence supportive of a self-defense claim. The burden of production is thereby satisfied even if the evidence is not offered by the defense itself. When we say that the defendant bears the burden of production we mean not that defense witnesses must produce the evidence directly but only that the defense will lose on the issue if some evidence is not produced.

it may be said that absence of duress is *presumed,* but that when evidence of duress is introduced the presumption is *rebutted* or simply *disappears.* All these expressions are equivalent to the more straightforward statement that the defendant bears the burden of production and the prosecution the burden of persuasion.

When the defendant bears the burden of production on an issue, the issue is commonly referred to as an *affirmative defense.* In some states, when an issue is designated an affirmative defense, the defendant must bear the burdens of both production and persuasion, but it is common practice to treat burdens of production and persuasion as separate issues. Thus, the defendant may bear the burden of persuasion on *some* affirmative defenses, but with respect to others he may bear *only* the burden of production. Under the Model Penal Code, the defendant generally bears only the burden of production, and once an affirmative defense is raised, the prosecution must disprove it beyond a reasonable doubt. See Model Penal Code §1.12(2)(a), Appendix.

Under what circumstances should the burden of production be placed upon the defendant? There appears to be relatively little case law concerning the constitutionality of assigning this burden (as distinguished from the burden of persuasion) to the defense, and in practice the essential considerations are largely pragmatic (Model Penal Code and Commentaries, Comment to §1.12 at 193-194 (1985)):

> No single principle can be conscripted to explain when such shifts of burden to defendants are justified, even where the burden goes no further than to call for the production of some evidence. [A] defendant ought not to be required to defend until some solid substance is presented to support the accusation, but beyond this [there is] a point where the need for narrowing the issues coupled with the relative accessibility of evidence to the defendant warrants calling upon him to present his defensive claim. No doubt this point is reached more quickly if, taking the facts the prosecution must establish, the normal probabilities are against the defense, but this is hardly an essential factor. Given the mere fact of an intentional homicide, no one can estimate the a priori probability that it was or was not committed in self-defense. The point is rather that purposeful homicide is an event of such gravity to society, and the basis for a claim of self-defense is so specially within the cognizance of the defendant, that it is fair to call on him to offer evidence if the defense is claimed.

When the defendant does bear the burden of production, how much evidence is necessary to satisfy that burden so that the prosecution will be required to disprove the claim beyond a reasonable doubt? One court has said "some" evidence is required but "more than a mere scintilla." Kadis v. United States, 373 F.2d 370, 374 (1st Cir. 1967). There appears to be a trend toward requiring that the evidence be sufficient to raise at least a reasonable doubt on the matter. See Frazier v. Weatherholtz, 572 F.2d 994 (4th Cir. 1978). When the defense produces evidence sufficient to satisfy the threshold requirements, it becomes necessary to determine which party must bear the burden of persuading the trier of fact.

2. *Allocating the burden of persuasion: the basis of* Patterson. Are states free to allocate the burden of persuasion however they choose, or does the reasoning of *Patterson* suggest some limits? Consider the following problems.

(*a*) *The formal structure of the statute.* Suppose that (as is commonly the case) state law defines murder as an "unlawful killing with malice aforethought." Under such a statute a justification like self-defense presumably renders a killing lawful and thus negates one of the definitional elements of murder. Does this mean that the constitution forbids imposing the burden of persuasion on the defendant on the self-defense issue? Should the result be different if state law explicitly describes self-defense as an affirmative defense; if state law expressly imposes the burden of persuasion on the defendant, or only if the word *unlawful* is absent from the language defining murder? Why should constitutional requirements turn on distinctions of this kind? Compare Wynn v. Mahoney, 600 F.2d 448 (4th Cir. 1979) (placing burden on defendant is unconstitutional because in North Carolina "unlawfulness" is an element of murder), with Williams v. Mohn, 462 F. Supp. 756 (N.D. W. Va. 1978) (opposite result because in West Virginia "unlawfulness" not an element of murder).

(*b*) *The alibi defense.* Suppose that a judge charges the jury that (1) the state must prove beyond a reasonable doubt all the elements of robbery and must prove beyond a reasonable doubt that the robbery was committed by this defendant, and (2) as for the defendant's claim "that he was not present at the time . . . this is known as the affirmative defense of alibi. [I]t is the defendant's burden to prove to your satisfaction the defense of alibi . . . by a preponderance of the evidence. . . ." Does this charge fit the pattern of cases like *Rivera* and *Patterson,* or is it impermissible under *Mullaney*? See Rogers v. Redman, 457 F. Supp. 929 (D. Del. 1978).

(*c*) *Liberalizing and nonliberalizing changes in the law.* In *Patterson* the affirmative defense involved "a substantially expanded version of the older heat-of-passion concept," and the Court stressed the need for permitting the states flexibility in this situation. But what if, after *Patterson,* a state shifts to the defendant a burden of persuasion previously imposed on the prosecution and does not enlarge the scope of the defense? See State v. King, 39 Wash. 2d 541, 599 P.2d 522 (1979) (self-defense); Novosel v. Helgemore, 384 A.2d 124 (N.H. 1978) (insanity) Should it matter whether the traditional defense might otherwise have been restricted or repealed?

3. *Should the greater power include the lesser?* The *Patterson* majority assumed that New York could eliminate the "extreme emotional disturbance" defense altogether, a point conceded by Justice Powell's dissent. If this is so, how can there be any serious challenge to the constitutionality of recognizing the defense only in diluted form, that is, when the defendant can prove it? Several commentators argue that "the greater power should include the lesser."[19] Under this analysis the constitutionality of imposing a burden of persuasion on the defendant would not depend on either the formal structure of the statute or the kind of historical analysis emphasized in the dissent. Rather, states would be free to reallocate burdens of persuasion relating to any fact that is not a constitutionally mandated prerequisite to just punishment, but conversely, states would be required to prove a fact beyond a reasonable doubt if punishment would be impermissible (or excessive, violating Eighth Amendment proportionality re-

19. The originator of the greater-includes-the-lesser argument in this context is generally thought to be Justice Holmes, who advanced it in his opinion for the Court in Ferry v. Ramsey, 277 U.S. 88 (1928).

quirements) as applied to conduct not involving that fact. See, e.g., Ronald Allen, The Restoration of *In re Winship:* A Comment on Burdens of Persuasion in Criminal Cases after Patterson v. New York, 76 Mich. L. Rev. 30 (1977). Consider the following comments.

John C. Jeffries Jr. & Paul B. Stephan, Defenses, Presumptions and Burdens of Proof in the Criminal Law, 88 Yale L.J. 1325, 1345-1347 (1979): [A] purely procedural interpretation of *Winship* — one that is wholly illogical as a statement of substantive policy — must find its justification in an exclusively procedural concern. . . . The chief justification for proof beyond a reasonable doubt in general has always been thought to be that it enhances the certainty of the factual findings needed for criminal conviction. . . . The trouble is that this rationale does not justify the rule for which it is offered. Implementing the presumption of innocence — whether on an actual or a symbolic level — requires that *something* be proved beyond a reasonable doubt. It does not, however, speak to the question of *what* that something must be. . . . In our view, these rationales extend only so far as the substantive issue at stake is thought to be an essential ingredient of the state's case. When, in contrast, the state considers a gratuitous defense, that is, one that it may grant or deny as it sees fit, a constitutional insistence on proof beyond a reasonable doubt no longer makes sense. Such a rule would purport to preserve individual liberty and the societal sense of commitment to it by forcing the government *either* to disprove the defense beyond a reasonable doubt *or* to eliminate the defense altogether. The latter solution results in an extension of penal liability despite the presence of mitigating or exculpatory facts. It is difficult to see this result as constitutionally compelled and harder still to believe that it flows from a general policy, whether actual or symbolic, in favor of individual liberty. . . .

The trouble lies in trying to define justice in exclusively procedural terms. *Winship*'s insistence on the reasonable doubt standard is thought to express a preference for letting the guilty go free rather than risking conviction of the innocent. This value choice, however, cannot be implemented by a purely procedural concern with burden of proof. Guilt and innocence are substantive concepts. Their content depends on the choice of facts determinative of liability. If this choice is remitted to unconstrained legislative discretion, no rule of constitutional procedure can restrain the potential for injustice. . . .

Barbara D. Underwood, The Thumb on the Scales of Justice: Burdens of Persuasion in Criminal Cases, 86 Yale L.J. 1299, 1312-1313, 1321-1324 (1977): [The author challenges the "greater includes the lesser" argument on several grounds. Two are particularly relevant for present purposes. First, she argues that adjusting burdens of proof is an inappropriate way of compromising disputes over the proper reach of substantive law. Second, this approach tends to obscure the substantive commands of the law. Excerpts from the discussion of these two points follow.]
[First, s]uppose that a legislature has decided to prohibit the possession of certain narcotic drugs. Suppose further that there is a controversy over a proposal to exempt from punishment those who possess narcotics solely for their personal use. Proponents and opponents of the defense might well seek an intermediate position that would recognize a defense for some, but not all, of those who possess for personal use. One possibility for substantive compromise

would be to exempt from punishment only those who possess specified small quantities for personal use. Another possibility would be to exempt only those who possess for personal use in the privacy of their homes. Each of these compromises, by redefining the prohibited conduct, seeks to accommodate differing views about the harm caused, or the harm threatened, or the culpability of the actor in various situations. . . .[77]

A substantive disagreement about whether to recognize a defense [of possession solely for personal use] amounts to a disagreement about whether the person with the proposed defense is less suitable than other offenders for specified criminal sanctions. By shifting the burden of persuasion [on the personal-use issue] to the defendant, a legislature limits the defense to those for whom the evidence is most abundant. That group, however, is not necessarily the least culpable, least harmful, or least deterrable. . . . An exception [to the reasonable-doubt rule] designed solely for the purpose of compromise would subvert the policies of the rule, without accomplishing an appropriate compromise of substantive disagreements. . . .

[Second, a]lthough popular understanding of the substantive law is notoriously deficient, rules about proof at trial are even less accessible to popular understanding than rules about conduct in society. One consequence of that fact is that . . . unusual rules of proof, even more than unusual substantive laws, are likely to trap an unsuspecting public into reliance on a false idea of the law. . . . This is an argument for truth-in-labeling.

For recent scholarship critical of *Patterson*'s "greater includes the lesser" approach, see Scott E. Sunby, The Reasonable Doubt Rule and the Meaning of Innocence, 40 Hastings L.J. 457 (1989); Donald A. Dripps, The Constitutional Status of the Reasonable Doubt Rule, 75 Cal. L. Rev. 1665 (1987). Both authors argue that the due process clause should be construed to require proof beyond a reasonable doubt for any fact that makes a significant difference in the authorized range of punishment. See also Note, *Winship* on Rough Waters, The Erosion of the Reasonable Doubt Standard, 106 Harv. L. Rev. 1093 (1993).

4. *Nongratuitous defenses.* In *Patterson* the affirmative defense was "gratuitous," in the sense that the state could have eliminated the defense completely. Should the state's freedom to shift the burden of proof extend to defenses that are *no* gratuitous? Consider, for example, the insanity defense. There is a long-standing debate (see pages 966-973 infra) over the question whether some form of an insanity defense is constitutionally mandated. Yet in Rivera v. Delaware (discussed in *Patterson,* page 43 supra), the court summarily dismissed a challenge to a Delaware law that required the defendant to bear the burden of proving insanity. Should *Rivera* be read as holding, by implication, that states are free to eliminate the insanity defense completely? If not, what is the justification for permitting states to avoid the reasonable doubt requirement and to "dilute" defense that may be constitutionally mandated?

---

77. A compromise that takes the form of redefining the crime may of course be motivated by evidentiary considerations. In each of the examples in text, the group might be singled out for the defense precisely because their claim of possession for personal use is thought most likely to be true. Nevertheless, if the compromise is forced into the form of an intermediate position on substantive liability, then it avoids two of the principal targets of the reasonable doubt rule: the opportunity for arbitrariness in the decision of individual cases by prosecutor or factfinder, and the low visibility of a compromise framed in procedural terms.

In connection with these questions consider Martin v. Ohio, 480 U.S. 228 (1987). The defendant shot her husband in what she claimed was an act of self-defense. She was charged with aggravated murder, which is defined under Ohio law as a killing "purposely, and with prior calculation and design." Ohio law also provides that self-defense is a complete defense when three elements are present: "(1) that the defendant was not at fault in creating the situation giving rise to the argument; (2) the defendant had an honest belief that she was in imminent danger of death or great bodily harm and that her only means of escape from such danger was in the use of such force; and (3) the defendant must not have violated any duty to retreat or avoid danger." At trial, the jury was instructed that the prosecution had to prove beyond a reasonable doubt all the elements of aggravated murder, but that the defendant was required to prove her self-defense claim by a preponderance of the evidence. The defendant's aggravated murder conviction was upheld by the Supreme Court. Writing for the majority, Justice White said (id. at 233-235):

> As in *Patterson*, the jury was here instructed that to convict it must find . . . that none of the evidence, whether offered by the State or by Martin in connection with her plea of self-defense, raised a reasonable doubt that Martin had killed her husband, that she had the specific purpose and intent to cause his death, or that she had done so with prior calculation and design.
>
> [T]his conviction did not violate the Due Process Clause. The State did not exceed its authority in defining the crime of murder as purposely causing the death of another with prior calculation or design. It did not seek to shift to Martin the burden of proving any of those elements, and the jury's verdict reflects that none of her self-defense evidence raised a reasonable doubt about the state's proof that she purposefully killed with prior calculation and design. . . .
>
> Petitioner submits that there can be no conviction under Ohio law unless the defendant's conduct is unlawful and that because self-defense renders lawful what would otherwise be a crime, unlawfulness is an element of the offense that the state must prove by disproving self-defense. [B]ut the Ohio courts hold that the unlawfulness in cases like this is the conduct satisfying the elements of aggravated murder — an interpretation of state law that we are not in a position to dispute. The same is true of the claim that it is necessary to prove a "criminal" intent to convict for serious crimes, which cannot occur if self-defense is shown: the necessary mental state for aggravated murder under Ohio law is the specific purpose to take life pursuant to prior calculation and design.

Justice Powell, writing for the four dissenters, argued that the defense claim of imminently necessary self-defense was inherently inconsistent with the prosecution claim of killing "by prior calculation and design." As a result, he argued, the instruction requiring the defendant to prove self-defense was in direct conflict with the instruction requiring the prosecution to prove aggravated murder beyond a reasonable doubt. As to this point, the majority asserted (id. at 235) that "the instructions were sufficiently clear to convey to the jury that the state's burden of proving prior calculation did not shift."

Note that no problem of conflicting instructions would be present if murder were simply defined as an intentional killing (without prior calculation or design). Yet no member of the Court challenged Justice White's assertion, supra, that "[t]he State did not exceed its authority in defining the crime of murder as purposely causing the death of another. . . ." Is this so clear? Could a state con-

stitutionally abolish the defense of self-defense altogether? Could the state condemn as a murderer, and sentence to long-term imprisonment, a person who
kills when such an act is the only available means to avoid an unlawful threat of
imminent death? [20]

5. *How should a state exercise its discretion?* Even where *Patterson* leaves a state
free to impose a burden of persuasion on the defendant, the decision does
not of course imply that the state must do so or should do so. State legislatures
(or state courts, when statutes do not control) must decide what is desirable
with respect to each defense of this kind. Those making the choice usually consider whether the defendant would have more access to the relevant evidence,
whether a defendant's claim would be difficult to refute beyond a reasonable
doubt, and whether placing the burden of persuasion on the prosecution would
prevent recognition of a new or expanded substantive defense. Burden-of-proof
questions therefore should be reconsidered in light of problems associated with
particular substantive law doctrines.

6. *Further reading.* For a useful analysis of the early American decisions and a
comparison to French and German approaches, see George Fletcher, Two Kinds
of Legal Rules: A Comparative Study of Burden-of-Persuasion Practices in Crimi-
nal Cases, 77 Yale L.J. 880 (1968). See also Fernand N. Dutile, The Burden of
Proof in Criminal Cases: A Comment on the *Mullaney-Patterson* Doctrine, 55
Notre Dame Law. 380 (1980); Marina Angel, Substantive Due Process and the
Criminal Law, 9 Loy. Chi. L.J. 61, 93-111 (1977); Harold A. Ashford & D. Michael
Risinger, Presumptions, Assumptions, and Due Process in Criminal Cases: A
Theoretical Overview, 79 Yale L.J. 165 (1969).

b. Presumptions

As the preceding section shows, the prosecution's burden of proof often can
be eased by defining an offense in such a way that the burden of proving certain
facts can be assigned to the defense. Another device that can ease the prosecutor's burden is the *presumption*. The presumption can come into play even when
the state has not (or cannot) exercise the *Patterson* option of reallocating the
burden of proof. Suppose, for example, that murder is defined as an *intentional*
killing. The state might hesitate to redefine murder as including all killing (with
lack of intent relevant only as an affirmative defense). Can the state instead
choose to retain intent as a required element of murder, but then provide that
the existence of the necessary intent will be *presumed* from some other fact (for
example, from the use of a deadly weapon)? This section considers the functional significance of such "presumptions" and the constitutional limitations on
their use.

---

20. The issue was raised in Rowe v. Debruyn, 17 F.3d 1047 (7th Cir. 1994), where, under Indiana prison regulations, a prisoner was disciplined notwithstanding that his assault on another prisoner was necessary to resist being raped. A majority held that even if a person has a constitutional
right to use physical force in self-defense, that right does not extend to prisons, where the use of
violence against violence would disserve order and safety in prison life. The dissent advanced a
right of self-defense so fundamental that it must extend to all contexts, within as well as outside
prisons.

NOTES ON PRESUMPTIONS

1. The terminology of presumptions. Professor Charles McCormick wrote (Evidence §342, at 802-803 (2d ed. 1972)): "One ventures the assertion that 'presumption' is the slipperiest member of the family of legal terms, except its first cousin, 'burden of proof.' One author has listed no less than eight senses in which the term has been used by the courts." To understand the significance of a presumption, one cannot simply resort to a dictionary but must focus on the precise effect of the presumption at trial. True presumptions concern an inference of fact to be drawn from some other fact in evidence. Normally there must, at a minimum, be some rational connection between the fact proved and the other fact to be inferred from it. But such common presumptions as the *presumption of innocence* do not function in this evidentiary sense at all. We shall call them *misnamed presumptions.*

(*a*) *Misnamed presumptions.* It is commonly said that a defendant in a criminal case is "presumed innocent until proven guilty." Is this because there is some "rational connection," a "more-often-than-not" relationship between being charged as defendant and being innocent? Obviously not: The vast majority of criminal defendants are ultimately found guilty, and indeed the filing of an indictment requires a formal finding of probable guilt. The presumption of innocence does not concern the drawing of rational inferences from facts in evidence but rather is simply a traditional way of stating that the prosecution bears the burden of proving guilt beyond a reasonable doubt. Similarly, it is common to state that an intentional killing is "presumed to be unlawful," unless the defendant produces evidence of some justification. What is normally meant is that the defendant has the burden of production (and possibly the burden of persuasion) on the issue of justification. As we have seen earlier in this chapter, pages 41-54 supra, there are constitutional limitations applicable here, but the applicable tests do not involve the requirement of some "rational connection." It could be that intentional killings are often, even half the time, committed in self-defense: A true presumption — an evidentiary inference of no self-defense — would surely be unconstitutional, but a presumption that serves only to allocate the burden of production almost surely is constitutional.

(*b*) *True presumptions.* True presumptions deal with inferences drawn from a fact actually proved (the *basic fact*) to some other critical fact (the *presumed fact*). Typically the presumed fact is one on which the prosecution bears the burden of persuasion. The presumption makes this burden easier to carry.

A presumption may ease the prosecution's burden in several distinct ways. For example, a presumption might allow the jury to draw the inference from basic to presumed fact, or instead the presumption might *require* the jury to draw the inference. The former are often called *permissive* presumptions or permissive inferences; the latter are often called *mandatory* presumptions. Presumptions may also differ in the extent to which they remain effective after the defense offers rebuttal evidence to negate the presumed fact.[21] At one extreme a pre-

---

21. Note that the defense also may offer evidence to challenge the existence of the basic fact. Since the presumption cannot come into play until the trier of fact is satisfied that the *basic* fact exists, refuting the basic fact will always render the presumption inoperative.

sumption requiring an inference to be drawn might remain in effect no matter how much evidence was offered to refute the presumed fact. A presumption of this kind is often called a *conclusive presumption:* In effect it is not a presumption at all because it establishes a substantive rule rendering the basic fact determinative and the presumed fact legally irrelevant. (Do you see why?) At the other extreme, the effect of a presumption might be entirely eliminated once the defense produces a rather small quantum of evidence. A presumption of this kind has precisely the same effect as a rule allocating the burden of production (do you see why?), and once that production burden is satisfied, the so-called presumption has no impact at all on the burden of persuasion.

Other presumptions retain some force even after rebuttal evidence is introduced, but the range of possible variations is wide. For the sake of convenience we will divide the true presumptions into two major categories: First are the *mandatory-but-rebuttable* presumptions. Here the jury will be told that upon proof of the basic fact, it *must* find the presumed fact, unless a given quantum of rebuttal evidence is forthcoming. Second, we have *permissive inferences.* Here the jury will be told that upon proof of the basic fact it *may* (but is not required) to find the presumed fact. Thus, the jury may reject the presumed fact even if no rebuttal is offered, and it may find the presumed fact even if extensive rebuttal is offered.

2. *Constitutional limitations.* The Supreme Court has developed standards governing the constitutionality of conclusive presumptions, mandatory-but-rebuttable presumptions, and permissive inferences.

(*a*) Because a conclusive presumption in effect renders the presumed fact legally immaterial, such a presumption will be unconstitutional whenever the presumed fact is constitutionally required for conviction. A related principle applies when the presumed fact, though not constitutionally mandated, has been made relevant by the state's own definition of an offense. *Patterson* appears to prohibit states from identifying a fact as a required element and then evading its responsibility to prove the fact beyond a reasonable doubt. Thus a conclusive presumption of intent would be unconstitutional, even though the state presumably could replace the intent element with whatever lesser facts were thought sufficient to justify the conclusive presumption.

(*b*) In County Court v. Allen, 442 U.S. 140 (1979), the Supreme Court developed rules applicable to mandatory presumptions and permissive inferences. The Court said that a mandatory presumption (one that the jury is required to accept in the absence of defense rebuttal) would pass muster only if, over the generality of cases, it held true beyond a reasonable doubt. In contrast, a permissive inference would pass muster if it was "more likely than not" to hold true on the facts of the particular case.

3. Is the standard applied to permissive inferences consistent with the requirement of proof beyond a reasonable doubt? The question is important because crucial elements of an offense are often established with the aid of such inferences. For example, courts often instruct that knowledge of the stolen character of goods can be inferred from unexplained possession, or that possession and control of an illegal substance can be inferred from the defendant's presence on the premises where it is found. Consider the facts of *County Court:* Four persons, three adult males and a 16-year-old girl, riding in a Chevrolet, were stopped for speeding on the New York Thruway. Two large-caliber handguns

were seen through the window of the car by the investigating police officer. The weapons were in an open handbag on either the front floor or the front seat of the car on the passenger side where the girl was sitting, and she admitted that the handbag was hers. All four people in the car were charged with illegal possession of the handguns, and at trial the judge instructed the jurors that upon proof of the presence of a firearm in an automobile, they were permitted to infer possession by all persons then occupying the vehicle. All four defendants were convicted, and the Supreme Court affirmed.

Question: If the inference in *County Court* is no better than rational (more likely than not), then is the jury in effect permitted to find the presumed fact (that is, possession) on a mere preponderance of the evidence? How can such a permissive inference be reconciled with *Winship* and *Mullaney?* In *County Court,* Justice Stevens wrote for the majority (442 U.S. at 167):

> There is no more reason to require a permissive statutory presumption to meet a reasonable doubt standard before it may be permitted to play any part in a trial than there is to require that degree of probative force for other relevant evidence before it may be admitted. As long as it is clear that the presumption is not the sole and sufficient basis for a finding of guilt, it need only satisfy the [more likely than not] test. . . .

4. Sandstrom v. Montana, 442 U.S. 510 (1979), involved a prosecution for "deliberate homicide." Under Montana law one element of the offense was an intent to kill. The defendant admitted the act of killing but introduced evidence suggesting that the act was not intentional. The jury was instructed that "[t]he law presumes that a person intends the ordinary consequences of his voluntary acts." On appeal from the conviction, the prosecution contended that the quoted language (which was not otherwise explained to the jury) established either a permissive inference or at most only a mandatory presumption rebuttable by "some" evidence and that under either interpretation the presumption satisfied applicable standards. The Supreme Court unanimously reversed. The Court held that the jurors might have understood the instruction either as establishing a conclusive presumption (that is, that intent was deemed to be established regardless of the defendant's proof) or as shifting the burden of persuasion (that is, requiring the defendant to prove the lack of intent by at least a preponderance of the evidence). In either event the presumption violated *Winship,* page 38 supra, and *Mullaney,* page 42 supra, because state law specifically made intent an element of the offense. The Court accordingly did not reach the question whether the instruction would pass muster if it were coupled with language clearly rendering its effect permissive or mandatory-but-rebuttable.

PROBLEMS

1. Leverett was prosecuted for negligent homicide after his vehicle struck and killed a pedestrian. The judge instructed the jury that "[i]f there was at that time [a blood-alcohol] concentration of 0.10 or more, it shall be presumed that the person was under the influence of alcohol. Such presumption is rebuttable."

Was the instruction constitutionally permissible? See State v. Leverett, 245 Mont. 124, 799 P.2d 119 (1990).

2. Consider the facts of Francis v. Franklin, 471 U.S. 307, 309-312 (1985):

Raymond Lee Franklin, then 21 years old and imprisoned for offenses unrelated to this case, sought to escape custody on January 17, 1979, while he and three other prisoners were receiving dental care at a local dentist's office. The four prisoners were secured by handcuffs to the same 8-foot length of chain as they sat in the dentist's waiting room. At some point Franklin was released from the chain, taken into the dentist's office and given preliminary treatment, and then escorted back to the waiting room. As another prisoner was being released, Franklin, who had not been reshackled, seized a pistol from one of the two officers and managed to escape. He forced the dentist's assistant to accompany him as a hostage.

. . . They came to the home of the victim, one Collie. Franklin pounded on the heavy wooden front door of the home and Collie, a retired 72-year-old carpenter, answered. Franklin was pointing the stolen pistol at the door when Collie arrived. As Franklin demanded his car keys, Collie slammed the door. At this moment Franklin's gun went off. The bullet traveled through the wooden door and into Collie's chest killing him. Seconds later the gun fired again. The second bullet traveled upward through the door and into the ceiling of the residence.

Hearing the shots, the victim's wife entered the front room. In the confusion accompanying the shooting, the dental assistant fled and Franklin did not attempt to stop her. Franklin entered the house, demanded the car keys from the victim's wife, and added the threat "I might as well kill you." When she did not provide the keys, however, he made no effort to thwart her escape. . . . Failing to obtain a car, Franklin left and remained at large until nightfall.

Shortly after being captured, Franklin made a formal statement to the authorities in which he admitted that he had shot the victim but emphatically denied that he did so voluntarily or intentionally. He claimed that the shots were fired in accidental response to the slamming of the door. He was tried in the Superior Court of Bibb County, Georgia, on charges of malice murder[1] — a capital offense in Georgia — and kidnapping. His sole defense to the malice murder charge was a lack of the requisite intent to kill. To support his version of the events Franklin offered substantial circumstantial evidence tending to show a lack of intent. He claimed that the circumstances surrounding the firing of the gun, particularly the slamming of the door and the trajectory of the second bullet, supported the hypothesis of accident, and that his immediate confession to that effect buttressed the assertion. He also argued that his treatment of every other person encountered during the escape indicated a lack of disposition to use force.

[The trial judge instructed the jury that "the defendant enters upon his trial with the presumption of innocence in his favor and this presumption . . . remains with him throughout the trial, unless it is overcome by evidence sufficiently strong to satisfy you of his guilt . . . beyond a reasonable doubt."] On the dispositive issue of intent, the trial judge instructed the jury as follows:

. . . A person shall not be found guilty of any crime committed by misfortune or accident where it satisfactorily appears there was no criminal scheme or undertaking or intention or criminal negligence. The acts of a person of

---

1. The malice murder statute at the time in question provided: "A person commits murde when he unlawfully and with malice aforethought, either express or implied, causes the death c another human being. . . . Malice shall be implied where no considerable provocation appears an where all the circumstances of the killing show an abandoned and malignant heart."

sound mind and discretion are presumed to be the product of the person's will, but the presumption may be rebutted. A person of sound mind and discretion is presumed to intend the natural and probable consequences of his acts, but the presumption may be rebutted. A person will not be presumed to act with criminal intention but the trier of facts, that is, the Jury, may find criminal intention upon a consideration of the words, conduct, demeanor, motive and all other circumstances connected with the act for which the accused is prosecuted.

[The jury] returned a verdict of guilty. The next day Franklin was sentenced to death for the murder conviction.

On appeal, what should be the result?

4. The Role of the Jury

DUNCAN v. LOUISIANA

Supreme Court of the United States
391 U.S. 145 (1968)

JUSTICE WHITE delivered the opinion of the Court.

Appellant, Gary Duncan, was convicted of simple battery in the Twenty-fifth Judicial District Court of Louisiana. Under Louisiana law simple battery is a misdemeanor, punishable by two years' imprisonment and a $300 fine. Appellant sought trial by jury, but because the Louisiana Constitution grants jury trials only in cases in which capital punishment or imprisonment at hard labor may be imposed, the trial judge denied the request. Appellant was convicted and sentenced to serve 60 days in the parish prison and pay a fine of $150. Appellant sought review in the Supreme Court of Louisiana, asserting that the denial of jury trial violated rights guaranteed to him by the United States Constitution. The Supreme Court [of Louisiana denied review.] We noted probable jurisdiction. . . .

While driving on Highway 23 in Plaquemines Parish on October 19, 1966, [appellant] saw two younger cousins engaged in a conversation by the side of the road with four white boys. Knowing his cousins, Negroes who had recently transferred to a formerly all-white high school, had reported the occurrence of racial incidents at the school, Duncan stopped the car, got out, and approached the six boys. . . . The testimony was in dispute on many points, but the witnesses agreed that appellant and the white boys spoke to each other, that appellant encouraged his cousins to break off the encounter and enter his car, and that appellant was about to enter the car himself for the purpose of driving away with his cousins. The whites testified that just before getting in the car appellant slapped Herman Landry, one of the white boys, on the elbow. The Negroes testified that appellant had not slapped Landry, but had merely touched him. The trial judge concluded that the State had proved beyond a reasonable doubt that Duncan had committed simple battery, and found him guilty.

. . . Because we believe that trial by jury in criminal cases is fundamental to the American scheme of justice, we hold that the Fourteenth Amendment guarantees a right of jury trial in all criminal cases which — were they to be tried in a federal court — would come within the Sixth Amendment's guarantee. Since we consider the appeal before us to be such a case, we hold that the Constitution was violated when appellant's demand for jury trial was refused.

The history of trial by jury in criminal cases has been frequently told. It is sufficient for present purposes to say that by the time our Constitution was written, jury trial in criminal cases had been in existence in England for several centuries and carried impressive credentials traced by many to Magna Carta. Its preservation and proper operation as a protection against arbitrary rule were among the major objectives of the revolutionary settlement which was expressed in the Declaration and Bill of Rights of 1689. . . .

The guarantees of jury trial in the Federal and State Constitutions reflect a profound judgment about the way in which law should be enforced and justice administered. A right to jury trial is granted to criminal defendants in order to prevent oppression by the Government. Those who wrote our constitutions knew from history and experience that it was necessary to protect against unfounded criminal charges brought to eliminate enemies and against judges too responsive to the voice of higher authority. The framers of the constitutions strove to create an independent judiciary but insisted upon further protection against arbitrary action. Providing an accused with the right to be tried by a jury of his peers gave him an inestimable safeguard against the corrupt or overzealous prosecutor and against the compliant, biased, or eccentric judge. If the defendant preferred the common-sense judgment of a jury to the more tutored but perhaps less sympathetic reaction of the single judge, he was to have it. Beyond this, the jury trial provisions in the Federal and State Constitutions reflect a fundamental decision about the exercise of official power — a reluctance to entrust plenary powers over the life and liberty of the citizen to one judge or to a group of judges. . . . The deep commitment of the Nation to the right of jury trial in serious criminal cases as a defense against arbitrary law enforcement qualifies for protection under the Due Process Clause of the Fourteenth Amendment, and must therefore be respected by the States. . . .

We are aware of the long debate, especially in this century, among those who write about the administration of justice, as to the wisdom of permitting untrained laymen to determine the facts in civil and criminal proceedings. [M]ost of the controversy has centered on the jury in civil cases. [A]t the heart of the dispute have been express or implicit assertions that juries are incapable of adequately understanding evidence or determining issues of fact and that they are . . . little better than a roll of dice. Yet, the most recent and exhaustive study of the jury in criminal cases concluded that juries do understand the evidence and come to sound conclusions in most of the cases presented to them and that when juries differ with the result at which the judge would have arrived, it is usually because they are serving some of the very purposes for which they were created and for which they are now employed.[26]

The State of Louisiana urges that holding that the Fourteenth Amendment assures a right to jury trial will cast doubt on the integrity of every trial conducted without a jury. . . . We would not assert, however, that every criminal trial — or any particular trial — held before a judge alone is unfair or that a defendant may never be as fairly treated by a judge as he would be by a jury. Thus we hold no constitutional doubts about the practices, common in both federal and state

26. Kalven & Zeisel, [The American Jury (1966)].

courts, of accepting waivers of jury trial and prosecuting petty crimes without extending a right to jury trial. However, the fact is that in most places more trials for serious crimes are to juries than to a court alone; a great many defendants prefer the judgment of a jury to that of a court. Even where defendants are satisfied with bench trials, the right to a jury trial very likely serves its intended purpose of making judicial or prosecutorial unfairness less likely.

Louisiana's final contention is that even if it must grant jury trials in serious criminal cases, the conviction before us is valid and constitutional because here the petitioner was tried for simple battery and was sentenced to only 60 days in the parish prison. We are not persuaded. It is doubtless true that there is a category of petty crimes or offenses which is not subject to the Sixth Amendment jury trial provision and should not be subject to the Fourteenth Amendment jury trial requirement here applied to the States. . . .

We need not, however, settle in this case the exact location of the line between petty offenses and serious crimes. It is sufficient for our purpose to hold that a crime punishable by two years in prison is, based on past and contemporary standards in this country, a serious crime and not a petty offense. Consequently, appellant was entitled to a jury trial and it was error to deny it. . . .

Reversed and remanded.

JUSTICE HARLAN, with whom JUSTICE STEWART joins, dissenting. . . .

[There] is a wide range of views on the desirability of trial by jury, and on the ways to make it most effective when it is used; there is also considerable variation from State to State in local conditions such as the size of the criminal caseload, the ease or difficulty of summoning jurors, and other trial conditions bearing on fairness. We have before us, therefore, an almost perfect example of a situation in which the celebrated dictum of Mr. Justice Brandeis should be invoked. It is, he said, "one of the happy incidents of the federal system that a single courageous state may, if its citizens choose, serve as a laboratory. . . ." New State Ice Co. v. Liebmann, 285 U.S. 262, 280, 311 (dissenting opinion). This Court, other courts, and the political process are available to correct any experiments in criminal procedure that prove fundamentally unfair to defendants.

NOTES

1. The scope of the right to jury trial. Mr. Justice Frankfurter once wrote that "[n]o changes or chances can alter the content of the verbal symbol of 'jury' — a body of twelve men who must reach a unanimous conclusion if the verdict is to go against the defendant." Rochin v. California, 342 U.S. 165, 170 (1952). Except for the limitation to males, which had passed away long before Frankfurter reiterated it, this statement expressed a nearly universal view about what was meant by a jury. Nevertheless, in Williams v. Florida, 399 U.S. 78, 86 (1970), the Court said that the decision to fix the size of the jury at 12 "appears to have been a historical accident, unrelated to the great purposes that gave rise to the jury" and held that a 6-member jury satisfied the constitutional requirement.[22] In Apodaca v. Oregon, 406 U.S. 404 (1972), the Court held that unanimity was not required in state criminal trials, so long as a substantial majority

---

22. In Ballew v. Georgia, 435 U.S. 223 (1978), the Court held that a 5-person jury did not fulfill the constitutional jury trial requirement.

of the jury supports the verdict. The Court in that case upheld guilty verdicts obtained by 11–1 and 10–2 votes, without ruling explicitly on whether a smaller majority could also be sufficiently substantial.[23]

Duncan had raised, but not resolved, the question of what may be deemed a "petty offense," for which the Sixth Amendment jury trial guarantee would be inapplicable. In Baldwin v. New York, 399 U.S. 66 (1970), the Court held that no offense may be deemed petty where imprisonment for more than 6 months is authorized. In such cases a defendant has a constitutional right to jury trial, whether or not imprisonment is in fact likely to be imposed.

2. *The effect of jury trial on the criminal justice system.* The existence of the jury has a profound effect on the administration of American criminal law.

(*a*) Because lay people may not assess items of proof as carefully as the law-trained, the Anglo-American law includes an elaborate structure of rules providing for the exclusion of certain evidence at the trial.

(*b*) The existence of the jury creates a great range of legal issues:

> (i) The judge is judge of the law; the jury decides questions of fact. The legal system must characterize the nature of a given question: Is it a question of law or of fact?
>
> (ii) The judge and the jury may take different views of a case, thus putting them into a kind of contest resolved in the common law by rules respecting directed verdicts, motions to set aside verdicts, and judgments notwithstanding verdicts.
>
> (iii) The very presence of 12 lay people participating in a trial gives rise to a great many possible errors in respect to their conduct or in respect to their mode of reaching a decision.
>
> (iv) Judges must formulate for jurors' use an acceptable statement of applicable legal rules, though these rules may be the most difficult imaginable. Obviously a great many errors in statements are made that require reversal.

(*c*) The entire texture and coloration of the trial is influenced by the existence of the jury. Instead of addressing arguments to one law-trained person, the lawyers address themselves to 12 lay people. Obviously lawyers believe that nonlegal factors will influence a jury and attempt, with some success, to put such matters before it.

3. *The policies served (and disserved) by jury trial.* The Court in *Duncan* summarizes the principal reasons why it regards the availability of trial by jury as an essential component of fair procedure. Is it clear that the advantages of jury trial outweigh its costs or that experimentation with different kinds of fact-finding procedures should be considered intolerable? Consider the following comments.

Glanville Williams, The Proof of Guilt 271-272 (3d ed. 1963): [I]t is an understatement to describe a jury, with Herbert Spencer, as a group of twelve people o*

---

23. In Burch v. Louisiana, 441 U.S. 130 (1979), the Court held that a 5-1 vote did not satisf* constitutional requirements. Thus, where states elect to use a 6-person jury, the verdict must b* unanimous. The opinions in *Apodaca* suggest that for *federal* criminal trials, a majority of the Cour* would continue to view unanimity as constitutionally mandated. In any event, Rule 31(a) of the* Federal Rules of Criminal Procedure requires a unanimous verdict in federal prosecutions.

average ignorance. There is no guarantee that members of a particular jury may not be quite unusually ignorant, credulous, slow-witted, narrow-minded, biased or temperamental. The danger of this happening is not one that can be removed by some minor procedural adjustment; it is inherent in the English notion of a jury as a body chosen from the general population at random.

Dale W. Broeder, The Functions of the Jury — Facts or Fictions?, 21 U. Chi. L. Rev. 386, 413-417 (1947): From the time of the Alien and Sedition Acts, the government's attempted inroads on civil rights seem to have received the enthusiastic support of jurors. . . .

But the case against the criminal jury as a protector of individual liberty extends further than to contests between government and citizens opposed to its policies. Minority groups have often suffered at the hands of jurymen. Wholesale acquittals of lynch-law violators, convictions of Negroes on the slightest evidence, and numerous other occurrences which have now almost become a part of the jury tradition might be instanced as examples. . . .

Aside from the incidental psychological functions which the criminal jury is alleged to perform, the sole remaining virtue claimed for it lies in its ability to make allowances for the circumstances of the particular case — to dispense with a rule of law. As noted previously, however, law-dispensing is a two-edged sword, and there is no current means of ascertaining which way it more often swings. It may seriously be doubted whether entrusting the jury with law-dispensing powers is justified. While flexibility of legal administration is desirable, it would seem that the necessary exceptions to the normal rules could with better reason be fashioned by the legislature or court.

Harry Kalven & Hans Zeisel, The American Jury 7-9 (1966): The [jury] controversy centers around three large issues. First, there is a series of collateral advantages and disadvantages that are often charged against, or pointed to on behalf of, the jury as an institution. In this realm fall such positive points as that the jury provides an important civic experience for the citizen; that, because of popular participation, the jury makes tolerable the stringency of certain decisions; that, because of its transient personnel, the jury acts as a sort of lightning rod for animosity and suspicion which otherwise might center on the more permanent judge; and that the jury is a guarantor of integrity, since it is said to be more difficult to reach twelve men than one. Against such affirmative claims, serious collateral disadvantages have been urged, chiefly that the jury is expensive; that it contributes to delay in civil litigation; that jury service imposes an unfair tax and social cost on those forced to serve; and that, in general, exposure to jury duty disenchants the citizen and causes him to lose confidence in the administration of justice.

Second, there is a group of issues that touch directly on the competence of the jury. Here the debate has been fascinating but bitter. On the one hand, it is urged that the judge, as a result of training, discipline, recurrent experience, and superior intelligence, will be better able to understand the law and analyze the facts than laymen, selected from a wide range of intelligence levels, who have no particular experience with matters of this sort, and who have no durable official responsibility. On the other hand, it is argued that twelve heads are inevitably better than one; that the jury as a group has wisdom and strength which need not characterize any of its individual members; that it makes up in common sense and common experience what it may lack in professional training, and that its very inexperience is an asset because it secures a fresh perception of each trial, avoiding the stereotypes said to infect the judicial eye.

The third group of issues about the jury goes to what is perhaps the most interesting point. The critics complain that the jury will not follow the law, either because it does not understand it or because it does not like it, and that thus only a very uneven and unequal administration of justice can result from reliance on the jury; indeed, it is said that the jury is likely to produce that government by man, and not by rule of law, against which Anglo-American political tradition is so steadfastly set.

This same flexibility of the jury is offered by its champions as its most endearing and most important characteristic. The jury, it is said, is a remarkable device for insuring that we are governed by the spirit of the law and not by its letter; for insuring that rigidity of any general rule of law can be shaped to justice in the particular case. One is tempted to say that what is one man's equity is another man's anarchy.

4. Lay adjudicators in other countries. Other legal systems use different means to provide for lay participation. Consider the following comment.

Glanville Williams, The Proof of Guilt 254-256, 307 (3d ed. 1963): So great was the prestige of the British jury that it was transplanted to one Continental country after another as a symbol of new-found political freedom. . . .

[E]fforts to acclimatise jury trial have generally met with indifferent success, partly because of a failure to settle satisfactorily the relative provinces of judge and jury. Perhaps another contributing factor was the failure to apply the restrictive rules of the law of evidence (particularly in respect of the character of the accused) which English experience had shown to be necessary. . . . The strong tendency on the Continent of late years has been to replace the jury by lay justices or assessors, sitting with the judges and sharing with them the responsibility of deciding both fact and law and determining sentence. These lay justices may, as in France since 1941, bear the name of a jury and be very close to the English jury in being chosen at random from the community, differing, however, in that they sit on the Bench for a whole session and constitute a joint tribunal with the professional judges; or they may, as in Sweden, be somewhat similar to the English justices of the peace, being lay magistrates specially chosen to serve for a period of office and not merely for a particular case or short series of cases; in Sweden the choice of magistrates is made by election. . . .

Looking at these strains and stresses of the jury system in other countries, we may find the comparative success of the English jury is not in its ability to nullify unpopular laws, nor in its superior ability to ascertain facts, but in the fact that our system of summing up enables the judge to give the jury a lead,[a] which the jury follow sufficiently often to give an appearance of reliability to the mode of

---

a. This role for the judge is generally not seen in the United States. Judicial commentary of the kind described by Prof. Williams is often viewed as a violation of state constitutional provisions making the jury the exclusive trier of fact. See Harry Kalven & Hans Zeisel, The American Jury 418-425 (1966); Stephen Saltzburg, The Unnecessarily Expanding Role of the American Trial Judge 64 Va. L. Rev. 1, 22-52 (1978) — Eds.

trial. It need hardly be pointed out that this explanation of the jury's success is not one that yields any very strong argument for a continuation of the system.

5. *The behavior of the jury in the United States.* The empirical study referred to by the Court in *Duncan,* Harry Kalven & Hans Zeisel, The American Jury (1966), represents an effort to determine the extent to which juries decide cases differently from the way judges would and to determine the sources of such differences. The entire book warrants careful reading in connection with efforts to understand the impact of jury trial in American criminal cases.[24] The authors find that judges and juries disagree in roughly 25 percent of jury trial cases. In a small portion of these (2 percent of the total cases), the jury convicts when the judge would acquit; in 17 percent of all cases the jury acquits when the judge would convict; in roughly 6 percent of the cases the jury "hangs" (fails to agree on a verdict). Id. at 56-57.

The authors examine in great depth the possible reasons for judge-jury disagreement. They conclude that of the various factors apparently involved, differences in assessing the evidence in close cases played a significant role. They attributed 79 percent of the disagreements to this source. The other major factors that helped account for disagreement were jury sentiments about the law (50 percent of the cases), jury sentiments about the defendant (22 percent), facts only the judge knew (5 percent), and disparity of counsel (8 percent). Id. at 111. Often there was more than one reason for disagreement in a case. In fact, the closeness of the evidence usually appeared with one of the other reasons, so that this factor apparently "liberated the jury to respond to non-evidentiary factors." Id. at 106. It thus appeared that jury sentiment about the law was one of the most significant considerations, and this factor of course lies close to the heart of the jury's function as a guarantor of lenity and equity in dispensing criminal justice. The study suggests that "in cases having a de minimus cast or a note of contributory fault or provocation . . . the jury will exercise its de facto powers to write these equities into the criminal law." Id. at 285. Other sentiments about the law that appeared to have significant impact included "impatience with the nicety of the law's boundaries hedging the privilege of self-defense" (id. at 241) and resistance to the enforcement of a few unpopular laws, primarily hunting, liquor, gambling, and drunken-driving laws. While the study provides extensive evidence of jury nullification, it also should be noted that judge and jury *agreed* in 75 percent of the cases, that only half the disagreement cases involved jury sentiments about the law, and that these sentiments usually (78 percent of the time, id. at 113) emerged in combination with other factors, principally the closeness of the evidence. The authors thus observe that the "jury's war with the law is now a polite one" (id. at 76) and conclude (at 498):

> The jury thus represents a uniquely subtle distribution of official power, an unusual arrangement of checks and balances. It represents also an impressive way of building discretion, equity and flexibility into a legal system. Not the least of the advantages is that the jury, relieved of the burdens of creating precedent, can bend the law without breaking it.

---

24. For a critique of the methodology employed in this ground-breaking study, see Michael H. Walsh, The American Jury: A Reassessment, 79 Yale L.J. 142 (1969).

Notice that in *Duncan* the Court, referring to Kalven and Zeisel, says that when juries differ from the judge "it is usually because they are serving some of the very purposes for which they were created." Does this mean that the jury's equity-dispensing function is constitutionally protected and that procedures designed to minimize nullification would be unconstitutional?

UNITED STATES v. DOUGHERTY

United States Court of Appeals, District of Columbia Circuit
473 F.2d 1113 (1972)

LEVENTHAL, J. Seven of the so-called "D.C. Nine" bring this joint appeal from convictions arising out of their unconsented entry into the Washington office of the Dow Chemical Company, and their destruction of certain property therein.[a] . . . [A]fter a six-day trial, the seven were each convicted of two counts of malicious destruction. . . .

Appellants urge [that] the judge erroneously refused to instruct the jury of its right to acquit appellants without regard to the law and the evidence, and refused to permit appellants to argue that issue to the jury. . . .

[Appellants] say that the jury has a well-recognized prerogative to disregard the instructions of the court even as to matters of law, and that they accordingly have the legal right that the jury be informed of its power. . . .

There has evolved in the Anglo-American system an undoubted jury prerogative-in-fact, derived from its power to bring in a general verdict of not guilty in a criminal case, that is not reversible by the court. The power of the courts to punish jurors for corrupt or incorrect verdicts, which persisted after the medieval system of attaint by another jury became obsolete, was repudiated in 1670 when Bushell's Case, 124 Eng. Rep. 1006 (C.P. 1670), discharged the jurors who had acquitted William Penn of unlawful assembly. Juries in civil cases became subject to the control of ordering a new trial; no comparable control evolved for acquittals in criminal cases.

The pages of history shine on instances of the jury's exercise of its prerogative to disregard uncontradicted evidence and instructions of the judge. Most often commended are the 18th century acquittal of Peter Zenger of seditious libel, on the plea of Andrew Hamilton, and the 19th century acquittals in prosecutions under the fugitive slave law. The values involved drop a notch when the liberty vindicated by the verdict relates to the defendant's shooting of his wife's paramour, or purchase during Prohibition of alcoholic beverages. . . .

The existence of an unreviewable and unreversible power in the jury, to acquit in disregard of the instructions on the law given by the trial judge, has for many

---

a. The background of the case is capsulated in the separate opinion of Judge Adams: "Here, the defendants, by interrupting the business of a large chemical company, attempted to publicize their dissenting views regarding the morality of the American involvement in the Vietnam War. It is apparent that the defendants attempted to exploit their criminal trial by using it as a platform for further exposition of their beliefs. . . . In furtherance of their efforts to transform what would otherwise be an ordinary criminal trial into a 'political' fray, defendants wished to represent themselves, to deviate from the usual mode of conducting a criminal trial, and to argue to the jury that although they were in violation of the applicable statutes, they should be acquitted because their actions were morally justified." — EDS.

years co-existed with legal practice and precedent upholding instructions to the jury that they are required to follow the instructions of the court on all matters of law. . . .

The rulings [in the early cases] did not run all one way, but rather precipitated "a number of classic exchanges on the freedom and obligations of the criminal jury."[36] This was, indeed, one of the points of clash between the contending forces staking out the direction of the government of the newly established Republic, a direction resolved in political terms by reforming but sustaining the status of the courts, without radical change. As the distrust of judges appointed and removable by the king receded, there came increasing acceptance that under a republic the protection of citizens lay not in recognizing the right of each jury to make its own law, but in following democratic processes for changing the law. . . .

Since the jury's prerogative of lenity . . . introduces a "slack into the enforcement of law, tempering its rigor by the mollifying influence of current ethical conventions," it is only just, say appellants, that the jurors be so told. It is unjust to withhold information on the jury power of "nullification," since conscientious jurors may come, ironically, to abide by their oath as jurors to render verdicts offensive to their individual conscience, to defer to an assumption of necessity that is contrary to reality.

This so-called right of jury nullification is put forward in the name of liberty and democracy, but its explicit avowal risks the ultimate logic of anarchy. This is the concern voiced by Judge Sobeloff in United States v. Moylan, 417 F.2d 1002, 1009 (4th Cir. 1969): "To encourage individuals to make their own determinations as to which laws they will obey and which they will permit themselves as a matter of conscience to disobey is to invite chaos. No legal system could long survive if it gave every individual the option of disregarding with impunity any law which by his personal standard was judged morally untenable. . . ." [T]he advocates of jury "nullification" apparently assume that the articulation of the jury's power will not extend its use or extent, or will not do so significantly or obnoxiously. Can this assumption fairly be made? . . .

The way the jury operates may be radically altered if there is alteration in the way it is told to operate. The jury knows well enough that its prerogative is not limited to the choices articulated in the formal instructions of the court. The jury gets its understanding as to the arrangements in the legal system from more than one voice. . . .

When the legal system relegates the information of the jury's prerogative to an essentially informal input, it is not being duplicitous, chargeable with chicane and intent to deceive. The limitation to informal input is, rather, a governor to avoid excess: the prerogative is reserved for the exceptional case, and the judge's instruction is retained as a generally effective constraint. We "recognize a constraint as obligatory upon us when we require not merely reason to defend our rule departures, but damn good reason."[49] The practicalities of men, machinery

---

36. M. R. Kadish and S. H. Kadish, On Justified Rule Departures by Officials, 59 Calif. L. Rev. 905, 914 (1971).

49. Kadish and Kadish, supra, note 36, 59 Calif. L. Rev. at 926. [The "damn-good-reason" position is criticized in Alan Scheflin & Jon Van Dyke, Jury Nullification: The Contours of a Controversy, 3 L. & Contemp. Prob. 51, 98-108 (1980). — Eds.]

and rules point up the danger of articulating discretion to depart from a rule, that the breach will be more often and casually invoked. We cannot gainsay that occasionally jurors uninstructed as to the prerogative may feel themselves compelled to the point of rigidity. The danger of the excess rigidity that may now occasionally exist is not as great as the danger of removing the boundaries of constraint provided by the announced rules. . . .

Moreover, to compel a juror involuntarily assigned to jury duty to assume the burdens of mini-legislator or judge, as is implicit in the doctrine of nullification, is to put untoward strains on the jury system. It is one thing for a juror to know that the law condemns, but he has a factual power of lenity. To tell him expressly of a nullification prerogative, however, is to inform him, in effect, that it is he who fashions the rule that condemns. That is an overwhelming responsibility, an extreme burden for the jurors' psyche. And it is not inappropriate to add that a juror called upon for an involuntary public service is entitled to the protection, when he takes action that he knows is right, but also knows is unpopular, either in the community at large or in his own particular grouping, that he can fairly put it to friends and neighbors that the was merely following the instructions of the court. . . .

[W]hat is tolerable or even desirable as an informal, self-initiated exception, harbors grave dangers to the system if it is opened to expansion and intensification through incorporation in the judge's instruction. . . .

BAZELON, C.J., concurring in part and dissenting in part. . . .

[T]he Court apparently concedes — although in somewhat grudging terms — that the power of nullification is a "necessary counter to case-hardened judges and arbitrary prosecutors," and that exercise of the power may, in at least some instances, "enhance the over-all normative effect of the rule of law." We could not withhold that concession without scoffing at the rationale that underlies the right to jury trial in criminal cases, and belittling some of the most legendary episodes in our political and jurisprudential history.

The sticking point, however, is whether or not the jury should be told of its power to nullify the law in a particular case. Here, the trial judge not only denied a requested instruction on nullification, but also barred defense counsel from raising the issue in argument before the jury. The majority affirms that ruling. I see no justification for, and considerable harm in, this deliberate lack of candor.

[T]he justification for this sleight-of-hand lies in a fear that an occasionally noble doctrine will, if acknowledged, often be put to ignoble and abusive purposes — or, to borrow the Court's phrase, will "run the risk of anarchy." . . . The Court assumes that these abuses are most likely to occur if the doctrine is formally described to the jury by argument or instruction. . . . It seems substantially more plausible to me to assume that the very opposite is true. . . .

[T]he Court takes comfort in the fact that informal communication to the jury "generally convey[s] adequately enough the idea of prerogative, of freedom in an occasional case to depart from what the judge says." . . . [But if] awareness is preferable to ignorance, then I simply do not understand the justification for relying on a haphazard process of informal communication whose effectiveness is likely to depend, to a large extent, on whether or not any of the jurors are so well-educated and astute that they are able to receive the message. If the jury should know of its power to disregard the law, then the power should be explicitly described by instruction of the court or argument of counsel. . . .

NOTES AND QUESTIONS ON NULLIFICATION INSTRUCTIONS

1. In State v. McClanahan, 212 Kan. 208, 510 P.2d 153, 154-155 (1973), the court held the following instruction improper:

> [J]udges are presumed to be the best judges of the law. Accordingly, you must accept my instructions as being correct statements of the generally accepted legal principles that apply in a case of the type you have heard. . . .
>
> Even so, it is difficult to draft legal statements that are so exact that they are right for all conceivable circumstances. Accordingly, you are entitled to act upon your conscientious feeling about what is a fair result in this case and acquit the defendant if you believe that justice requires such a result.
>
> Exercise your judgment without passion or prejudice, but with honesty and understanding. Give respectful regard to my statements of the law for what help they may be in arriving at a conscientious determination of justice in this case.

Do the *Dougherty* court's concerns apply to this cautiously worded instruction?

2. The federal courts and nearly all the states follow *Dougherty* and refuse to permit instructions informing the jury of its nullification power. See, e.g., United States v. Krzyske, 836 F.2d 1013 (6th Cir. 1988); Commonwealth v. Leno, 415 Mass. 835, 616 N.E.2d 453 (1993). Consider State v. Ragland, 105 N.J. 189, 519 A.2d 1361, 1371-1372 (1986):

> The fundamental defect in jury nullification is obvious. It is a power that is absolutely inconsistent with the most important value of Western democracy, that we should live under a government of laws and not of men. . . . With jury nullification, these free people [the jurors] are told, either explicitly or implicitly, that *they* are the law, that what the sovereign has pronounced ahead of time either may or may not be followed, and that if they want to, they may convict every poor man and acquit every rich man; convict the political opponent but free the crony; put the long-haired in jail but the crew-cut on the street; imprison the black and free the white; or, even more arbitrarily, just do what they please whenever they please.
>
> One of the biggest problems in the administration of criminal justice is the inequality of its enforcement. . . . Absolutely nowhere in the system is there some notion that someone should have the power, arbitrarily, to pick and choose who shall live and who shall die. But that is precisely what jury nullification is: the power to undo everything that is precious in our system of criminal justice, the power to act arbitrarily to convict one and acquit another where there is absolutely no apparent difference between the two. It is a power, unfortunately, that is there, that this Court cannot terminate, but a power that should be restricted as much as possible.
>
> . . . The lengths to which we go to exclude irrelevant evidence, the expenditures made to protect defendants from juror prejudice, the energy, study, and work devoted to a particular prosecution, all of these are prodigious. Having gone through that process, admired by us both for its thoroughness and its goals, astonishing to others for its devotion to fairness and reason, it is incomprehensible that at the very end we should tell those who are to make the judgment that they may do so without regard to anything that went before and without guidance as to why they should disregard what went on before, and without the obligation of explaining why they so disregarded everything. . . .
>
> Jury nullification is an unfortunate but unavoidable power. It should not be advertised, and, to the extent constitutionally permissible, it should be limited. Ef-

forts to protect and expand it are inconsistent with the real values of our system of criminal justice.

3. In People v. Fernandez, 31 Cal. Rptr. 677 (Ct. App. 1994), the jurors interrupted their deliberations to send the judge a note in which they stated their belief that the defendant had committed battery with serious bodily injury and then asked whether they nonetheless had the power to acquit on that charge and instead return a verdict of guilty on the lesser offense of assault. The trial judge simply replied, "No." The court of appeal held that this response was not error.

4. In three states the approach rejected in *Dougherty* still survives through constitutional provisions that the jury shall be the judge of the law as well as the fact. Ga. Const. art. 1, §1, ¶11(a); Ind. Const. art. 1, §19; Md. Const., Decl. of Rights, art. 23. In Georgia, however, courts have tended to confine the effect of the provision, for example by upholding a charge that the jurors are the judges of the law but are obliged to apply the court's instructions to the facts and by forbidding defense counsel to argue to the jury that it should disregard the law. See Drummond v. State, 326 S.E.2d 787 (Ga. App. 1985); Jones v. State, 235 Ga. 103, 218 S.E.2d 899 (1975). Current practice in Indiana and Maryland is summarized in Alan Scheflin & Jon Van Dyke, Jury Nullification: The Contours of a Controversy, 43 L. & Contemp. Prob. 51, 79-85 (1980).

5. Does it follow from *Dougherty* that a judge not only may refuse to inform the jury of its nullification power but also may refuse to inform the jury about the severity of the sentence that a defendant faces upon conviction? The question has become increasingly important with the proliferation of mandatory minimum sentencing laws, which often dictate long terms of imprisonment for possession of small quantities of drugs, even when the defendant is a first offender. Nearly all courts hold that because the jury's role is solely to determine the facts relevant to guilt, the jury has no legitimate concern with the consequences of a conviction. E.g., United States v. Broxton, 926 F.2d 1180, 1183 (D.C. Cir. 1991). Compare United States v. Datcher, 830 F. Supp. 411, 414-418 (M.D. Tenn. 1993):

> [R]espect for nullification flows from the role of the jury as the "conscience of the community" in our criminal justice system. Witherspoon v. Illinois, 391 U.S. 510, 519 & n. 15 (1968). [T]he essential purpose of the jury trial [is] "to prevent oppression by the Government." And it is this essential purpose that is to be used in determining the constitutional requirements of a jury trial.
>
> When measured by this standard, a defendant's right to inform the jury of that information essential "to prevent oppression by the Government" is clearly of constitutional magnitude. [T]o deny a jury information necessary to such oversight is to deny a defendant the full protection to be afforded by jury trial. Indeed, to deny a defendant the possibility of jury nullification would be to defeat the central purpose of the jury system.
>
> Argument against allowing the jury to hear information that might lead to nullification evinces a fear that the jury might actually serve its primary purpose, that is, it evinces a fear that the community might in fact think a law unjust. The government, whose duty it is to seek justice and not merely conviction, should not shy away from having a jury know the full facts and law of a case. . . .
>
> Overly harsh punishments were the impetus to development of jury nullifica-

tion. Institution of the jury system was meant to protect against unjust punishment perpetrated by government, not merely unjust conviction. . . .

No instruction on jury nullification was requested by the defendant, and none would be given if it were requested. The defendant may, however, put that information before the jury that allows it to decide, independently, whether the law under which the defendant could be convicted is just or unjust. The prosecution, of course, may also discuss this law and argue for its propriety. Mr. Datcher may not be particularly sympathetic to the jurors, and the possible penalties may not seem harsh at all in today's anti-drug environment. But Mr. Datcher is entitled to have the jury perform its full oversight function, and informing the jury of possible punishment is essential to this function. The court finds no good reason for opposing candor.

6. Suppose that the jurors are instructed, over the defendant's *objection*, that they are the judges of the law as well as the facts. Does such an instruction subject the defendant to capricious judgment and violate his right to be tried in accordance with ascertainable law? See Wyley v. Warden, 372 F.2d 742 (4th Cir. 1967); Isaacs v. State, 31 Md. App. 604, 358 A.2d 273 (1976).

7. For further exploration of the issues posed by *Dougherty,* see Mortimer Kadish & Sanford Kadish, Discretion to Disobey 37-94 (1973); Gary J. Simpson, Jury Nullification in the American System: A Skeptical View, 54 Tex. L. Rev. 488 (1976); Alan Scheflin, Jury Nullification: The Right to Say "No," 45 S. Cal. L. Rev. 168 (1972). See also Scheflin & Van Dyke, Note 4 supra.

NOTES AND QUESTIONS ON SPECIAL VERDICTS

1. *The* Spock *case.* United States v. Spock, 416 F.2d 165 (1st Cir. 1969), involved the prosecution of Dr. Benjamin Spock, Reverend William Sloane Coffin, Jr., and several others who had helped organize protests against the Vietnam war and the draft to support it. The defendants were charged with conspiring to "counsel, aid and abet diverse Selective Service registrants to . . . neglect, fail, refuse and evade service in the armed forces." Over defendants' objections, the trial judge put to the jury, in addition to the general issue of guilt, ten special questions to be answered yes or no. One question, for example, asked the jury to consider whether the defendants had conspired to "counsel" draft evasion; a second question substituted for the word *counsel* the word *aid;* a third substituted the word *abet.* Four defendants were convicted, but the United States Court of Appeals held that the submission of these special questions required reversal. The court noted that although such special verdicts are an everyday occurrence in civil cases, they pose special dangers in a criminal case (id. at 181-182):

> [N]ot only must the jury be free from direct control in its verdict, but it must be free from judicial pressure, both contemporaneous and subsequent. . . . There is no easier way to reach, and perhaps force, a verdict of guilty than to approach it step by step. A juror, wishing to acquit, may be formally catechized . . . [and] led to vote for a conviction which, in the large, he would have resisted. . . . The constitutional guarantees of due process and trial by jury require that a criminal defendant be afforded the full protection of a jury unfettered, directly or indirectly.

The court added that although some courts had upheld convictions where the use of a special verdict did not appear prejudicial, "we do not think it desirable to treat this issue by weighing subjective prejudice; to some extent the pressure is always present." Id. at 183 n. 41½.

Questions: If the questions put to the *Spock* jurors fairly focused their attention on the proper issues, then didn't the questions serve to enhance the probability that the jury would follow the judge's instructions on the law? Was the court saying that this is undesirable? Can the approach to special verdicts taken in *Spock* be reconciled with the approach to nullification instructions taken in *Dougherty?*

2. *Current status of the* Spock *rule.* Although the *Spock* decision appeared to treat the use of special verdicts as erroneous per se, regardless of whether they would tend to "lead" the jury to a particular result, most of the recent decisions appear to uphold the use of special verdicts where the appellate court concludes that under all the circumstances there is "no indication that judicial pressure was brought to bear." United States v. Looney, 544 F.2d 385, 392 (9th Cir. 1976).[25] Can such decisions be reconciled with *Spock?* Will even a noncoercive special verdict tend to constrain the jury in exercising its privilege to acquit against the weight of the evidence? Compare the comments of Judge Jon Newman, concurring and dissenting in United States v. Ruggiero, 726 F.2d 913, 927-928 (2d Cir. 1984):

> On balance, I am persuaded that a District Court should have the discretion to use a jury interrogatory in cases where risk of prejudice to the defendant is slight and the advantage of securing particularized factfinding is substantial. Ascertainment of predicate acts in a complex RICO trial is an example where the balance tips decidedly in favor of using an interrogatory. The concerns that have prompted disapproval of interrogatories in other contexts are either totally lacking or at best insignificant in this type of case, and such use might avoid the time and cost of a long retrial. I therefore agree that we should join with the Third Circuit [United States v. Palmeri, 630 F.2d 192 (3d Cir. 1980)] in approving the use of an interrogatory to identify proven predicate acts in complex RICO trials.[a]

3. *Defense requests for a special verdict.* Suppose that a defendant seeks to clarify the issues in a complex case by asking the jury to return a special verdict. In United States v. Coonan, 839 F.2d 886 (2d Cir. 1988), the court held that a trial judge could submit special interrogatories to the jury, over the prosecutor's objections, where the judge felt that this procedure would help prevent prejudicial spillover effects in a complex case. But most courts appear to uphold the denial of such defense requests, often with broad statements about the impropriety of special verdicts.[26] Is the rationale of *Spock* really applicable when the defendant *wants* a special verdict? Is there any good reason for restricting *defense* efforts to insure that the jury faithfully follows judicial instructions on the law?

25. See also Heald v. Mullaney 505 F.2d 1241, 1246 (1st Cir. 1974) (special verdict did not "coerce the jury's decision-making"); Commonwealth v. Beneficial Finance Co., 360 Mass. 188, 275 N.E.2d 33, 97 (1971) (special verdict did not "lead the jurors down the guilty trail").

a. RICO prosecutions are discussed in Chapter 7, page 781 infra. — EDS.

26. See, e.g., United States v. McCracken, 488 U.S. 406 (5th Cir. 1974); United States v. Frezze Bros., Inc., 602 F.2d 1123 (3d Cir. 1979).

NOTES AND QUESTIONS ON INCONSISTENT VERDICTS

1. The problem and the prevailing solutions. When a prosecution involves several separate counts, it sometimes happens that the jury's verdict on one count will be irreconcilably in conflict with its verdict on another count. Consider, for example, DeSacia v. State, 469 P.2d 369 (Alaska 1970). The defendant's reckless driving forced another vehicle off the road, and both the driver (Hogan) and passenger (Evangelista) in the other vehicle were killed. The defendant was prosecuted on two counts of manslaughter; the jury convicted on the count charging manslaughter of Evangelista but acquitted on the count charging manslaughter of Hogan. Because the defendant's conduct had endangered the two victims in precisely the same way, he was in principle guilty of manslaughter either in both cases or in neither. Should the inconsistent verdicts nevertheless be allowed to stand?

In the *DeSacia* case, the court noted that the verdict of acquittal was final; any relitigation of that count would violate the double jeopardy clause. But the court set aside the conviction on the other count, explaining that such action was necessary to assure that the conviction was not the product of jury confusion or irrationality. The court therefore remanded for a new trial on the count relating to the death of Evangelista. Only a minority of American jurisdictions appear to follow this approach, however. The federal courts and most of the states would allow the inconsistent conviction to stand. See, e.g., United States v. Zuniga-Salinas, 952 F.2d 876 (5th Cir. 1992).

Which approach seems more faithful to the premises of jury trial? If the jury is expected to give voice to the rough common sense of the community, isn't the *DeSacia* court's desire for logic out of place?[27] Consider whether inconsistent verdicts facilitate the exercise of the jury's leniency or whether they encourage compromise *convictions* on counts about which the jury may not really be persuaded beyond a reasonable doubt.

The federal rule, which precludes an attack on inconsistent jury verdicts, was reaffirmed in United States v. Powell, 469 U.S. 57 (1984). Justice Rehnquist, speaking for a unanimous Court, noted (id. at 65):

> Inconsistent verdicts . . . present a situation where "error," in the sense that the jury has not followed the court's instructions, most certainly has occurred, but it is unclear whose ox has been gored. Given this uncertainty, and the fact that the Government is precluded from challenging the acquittal, it is hardly satisfactory to allow the defendant to receive a new trial on the conviction as a matter of course. . . . For us, the possibility that the inconsistent verdicts may favor the criminal defendant as well as the Government militates against review of such convictions at the defendant's behest.

2. Constitutional implications. Do decisions like *DeSacia,* which bar inconsistent verdicts, violate the constitutional right to jury trial, by impairing the jury's func-

---

27. "The verdict of the jurors is not just the verdict of twelve men; it is the verdict of a *pays,* a 'country,' a neighborhood, a community. . . . The justices seem to feel that if they analyzed the verdict they would miss the very thing for which they are looking, the opinion of the country." 2 F. Pollock & F. Maitland, History of English Law 624, 626 (2d ed. 1952).

tion as a safety valve for tempering the law's rigid logic? One answer may simply be that the defendant will not complain, because the rule leads only to reversal of the illogical conviction. But what if the prosecution seeks an instruction, in a case like *DeSacia,* that the jury must either acquit on both counts or convict on both counts? The result in *DeSacia* in effect requires such an instruction in future cases, does it not? If so, would the defendant then be justified in claiming that the instruction improperly constrained the jury's equity-dispensing function?

In connection with the constitutional problems, consider whether it was entirely a coincidence that the *DeSacia* jury convicted for the death of Evangelista, who was a passenger, but acquitted for the death of Hogan, the other driver. As we shall see, contributory negligence ordinarily is not a defense in a criminal prosecution, see page 443 infra, but the Kalven and Zeisel study, page 65 supra, at 242-257, showed that jury nullification often occurred when contributory fault by the victim was involved. If this factor played a role in the acquittal with respect to Hogan, then wasn't the jury — to quote from Duncan v. Louisiana, page 60 supra — "serving some of the very purposes for which [it was] created"?

3. *Inconsistency in nonjury trials.* Jurisdictions that permit inconsistent verdicts in jury trials must decide whether to follow the same approach when an inconsistent acquittal and conviction are rendered in a bench trial. In United States v. Maybury, 274 F.2d 899 (2d Cir. 1960), the court, in an opinion by Judge Friendly, held such inconsistency unacceptable in a bench trial and reversed the conviction. See also People v. O'Neil, 550 N.E.2d 1090 (Ill. App. 1990). But several other state and federal courts have rejected *Maybury.*[28] Are the reasons for tolerating inconsistent jury verdicts applicable in trials before a judge? If it is sound to protect the jury's equity-dispensing power, why should a judge not have the same power?

5. The Role of Counsel

MONROE FREEDMAN, LAWYERS' ETHICS
IN AN ADVERSARY SYSTEM

3-4, 27-42 (1975)

[T]he adversary process has its foundations in respect for human dignity, even at the expense of the search for truth[.] I do not mean to deprecate the search for truth or to suggest that the adversary system is not concerned with it. On the contrary, truth is a basic value, and the adversary system is one of the most efficient and fair methods designed for determining it. . . . Nevertheless, the point that I now emphasize is that in a society that honors the dignity of the individual the high value that we assign to truth-seeking is not an absolute, but may on occasion by subordinated to even higher values. . . .

---

28. See, e.g., United States v. West, 549 F.2d 545 (8th Cir. 1977). The Supreme Court has held that the due process clause does not bar inconsistency in state bench trials, nor does the constitution require state judges to give reasons for rendering facially inconsistent judgments. See Harris v. Rivera, 454 U.S. 339 (1981).

Is it ever proper for a criminal defense lawyer to present perjured testimony?

One's instinctive response is in the negative. On analysis, however, it becomes apparent that the question is an exceedingly perplexing one. My own answer is in the affirmative.

At the outset, we should dispose of some common question-begging responses. The attorney, we are told, is an officer of the court, and participates in a search for truth. Those propositions, however, merely serve to state the problem in different words: As an officer of the court, participating in a search for truth, what is the attorney obligated to do when faced with perjured testimony? That question cannot be answered properly without an appreciation of the fact that the attorney functions in an adversary system of criminal justice which . . . imposes special responsibilities upon the advocate.

First, the lawyer is required to determine "all relevant facts known to the accused," because "counsel cannot properly perform their duties without knowing the truth." The lawyer who is ignorant of any potentially relevant fact "incapacitates himself to serve his client effectively," because "an adequate defense cannot be framed if the lawyer does not know what is likely to develop at trial."

Second, the lawyer must hold in strictest confidence the disclosures made by the client in the course of the professional relationship. . . . If this were not so, the client would not feel free to confide fully, and the lawyer would not be able to fulfill the obligation to ascertain all relevant facts. . . .

Third, the lawyer is an officer of the court, and his or her conduct before the court "should be characterized by candor."

As soon as one begins to think about those responsibilities, it becomes apparent that the conscientious attorney is faced with what we may call a trilemma — that is, the lawyer is required to know everything, to keep it in confidence, and to reveal it to the court. . . .

If we recognize that professional responsibility requires that an advocate have full knowledge of every pertinent fact, then the lawyer must seek the truth from the client, not shun it. That means that the attorney will have to dig and pry and cajole, and, even then, the lawyer will not be successful without convincing the client that full disclosure to the lawyer will never result in prejudice to the client by any word or action of the attorney. That is particularly true in the case of the indigent defendant, who meets the lawyer for the first time in the cell block or the rotunda of the jail. The client did not choose the lawyer, who comes as a stranger sent by the judge, and who therefore appears to be part of the system that is attempting to punish the defendant. It is no easy task to persuade that client to talk freely without fear of harm. [T]he truth can be obtained only by persuading the client that it would be a violation of a sacred obligation for the lawyer ever to reveal a client's confidence. Of course, once the lawyer has thus persuaded the client of the obligation of confidentiality, that obligation must be respected scrupulously.

Assume the following situation. Your client has been falsely accused of a robbery committed at 16th and P Streets at 11:00 P.M. He tells you at first that at no time on the evening of the crime was he within six blocks of that location. However, you are able to persuade him that he must tell you the truth and that doing so will in no way prejudice him. He then reveals to you that he was at 15th and P Streets at 10:55 that evening, but that he was walking east, away from the scene of the crime, and that, by 11:00 P.M., he was six blocks away. At the trial, there are two prosecution witnesses. The first mistakenly, but with some degree of persuasiveness, identifies your client as the criminal. At that point the prosecution's case depends upon that single witness, who might or might not be believed. The second prosecution witness is an elderly woman who is somewhat nervous and who wears glasses. She testifies truthfully and accurately that she saw your client at 15th and P Streets at 10:55 P.M. She has corroborated the erroneous testimony of the first witness and made conviction extremely likely. However, on cross-examination her reliability is thrown into doubt through demonstration that she is easily confused and has poor eyesight. Thus, the corroboration has been eliminated, and doubt has been established in the minds of the jurors as to the prosecution's entire case.

The client then insists upon taking the stand in his own defense, not only to deny the erroneous evidence identifying him as the criminal, but also to deny the truthful, but highly damaging, testimony of the corroborating witness who placed him one block away from the intersection five minutes prior to the crime. Of course, if he tells the truth and thus verifies the corroborating witness, the jury will be more inclined to accept the inaccurate testimony of the principal witness, who specifically identified him as the criminal. . . .

The most obvious way to avoid the ethical difficulty is for the lawyer to withdraw from the case, at least if there is sufficient time before trial for the client to retain another attorney. The client will then go to the nearest law office, realizing that the obligation of confidentiality is not what it has been represented to be, and withhold incriminating information or the fact of guilt from the new attorney. In terms of professional ethics, the practice of withdrawing from a case under such circumstances is difficult to defend, since the identical perjured testimony will ultimately be presented. Moreover, the new attorney will be ignorant of the perjury and therefore will be in no position to attempt to discourage the client from presenting it. Only the original attorney, who knows the truth, has that opportunity, but loses it in the very act of evading the ethical problem.

The difficulty is all the more severe when the client is indigent. In that event, the client cannot retain other counsel, and in many jurisdictions it is impossible for appointed counsel or a public defender to withdraw from a case except for extraordinary reasons. Thus, the attorney can successfully withdraw only by revealing to the judge that the attorney has received knowledge of the client's guilt,* or by giving the judge a false or misleading reason for moving for leave to withdraw. However, for the attorney to reveal knowledge of the client's guilt would be a gross violation of the obligation of confidentiality, particularly since it is entirely possible in many jurisdictions that the same judge who permits the attorney to withdraw will subsequently hear the case and sentence the defendant. Not only will the judge then have personal knowledge of the defendant's guilt before the trial begins, but it will be knowledge of which the newly appointed counsel for the defendant will very likely be ignorant. . . .

Another solution that has been suggested is that the attorney move for leave

---

* The typical formula is for the attorney to advise the judge of "an ethical problem." The judge understands that to mean that the client is insisting upon a perjured alibi over the lawyer's objections. In one case, the judge incorrectly drew that inference when the lawyer's ethical concern was with the fact that the client wanted to enter a guilty plea despite the fact that he was innocent.

to withdraw and that, when the request is denied, the attorney then proceed with the case, eliciting the defendant's testimony and arguing the case to the jury in the ordinary fashion. Since that proposal proceeds on the assumption that the motion will be denied, it seems to me to be disingenuous. If the attorney avoids the ethical problem, it is only by passing it on to the judge. Moreover, the client in such a case would then have grounds for appeal on the basis of deprivation of due process and denial of the right to counsel, since the defendant would have been tried before, and sentenced by, a judge who had been informed by the defendant's own lawyer that the defendant is guilty both of the crime charged and of perjury. . . .

Another unsuccessful effort to deal with the problem appears in the ABA Standards Relating to the Defense Function. . . . Section 7.7 of the Standards requires that the lawyer "must confine his examination to identifying the witness as the defendant and permitting him to make his statement." That is, the lawyer "may not engage in direct examination of the defendant . . . in the conventional manner." Thus, the client's story will become part of the record, although without the attorney's assistance through direct examination. The general rule, of course, is that in closing argument to the jury "the lawyer may argue all reasonable inferences from the evidence in the record." Section 7.7 also provides, however, that the defense lawyer is forbidden to make any reference in closing argument to the client's testimony.

There are . . . critical flaws in that proposal. [E]xperienced trial attorneys have often noted that jurors assume that the defendant's lawyer knows the truth about the case, and that the jury will frequently judge the defendant by drawing inferences from the attorney's conduct in the case. There is, of course, only one inference that can be drawn if the defendant's own attorney turns his or her back on the defendant at the most critical point in the trial, and then, in closing argument, sums up the case with no reference to the fact that the defendant has given exculpatory testimony. . . . Ironically, the Standards reject any solution that would involve informing the judge, but then propose a solution that, as a practical matter, succeeds in informing not only the judge but the jury as well.

It would appear that the ABA Standards have chosen to resolve the trilemma by maintaining the requirements of complete knowledge and of candor to the court, and sacrificing confidentiality. Interestingly, however, that may not in fact be the case. I say that because the Standards fail to answer a critically important question: Should the client be told about the obligation imposed by Section 7.7? That is, the Standards ignore the issue of whether the lawyer should say to the client at the outset of their relationship: "I think it's only fair that I warn you: If you should tell me anything incriminating and subsequently decide to deny the incriminating facts at trial, I would not be able to examine you in the ordinary manner or to argue your untrue testimony to the jury." . . . Obviously, any other course would be a betrayal of the client's trust, since everything else said by the attorney in attempting to obtain complete information about the case would indicate to the client that no information thus obtained would be used to the client's disadvantage. On the other hand, the inevitable result of [this] position would be to caution the client not to be completely candid with the attorney. That, of course, returns us to resolving the trilemma by maintaining confidentiality and candor, but sacrificing complete knowledge. . . . I continue to stand with those lawyers who hold that "the lawyer's obligation of confidentiality does not permit him to disclose the facts he has learned from his client which form the basis for his conclusion that the client intends to perjure himself." What that means — necessarily, it seems to me — is that the criminal defense attorney, however unwillingly in terms of personal morality, has a professional responsibility as an advocate in an adversary system to examine the perjurious client in the ordinary way and to argue to the jury, as evidence in the case, the testimony presented by the defendant.

JOHN NOONAN, BOOK REVIEW, 29 Stan. L. Rev. 363-366 (1977): Can an honest person practice regularly as a criminal defense lawyer in the United States? . . . Dean Freedman's implicit answer to [this question] is "no." . . .

Under our constitutional system, the right to counsel in a criminal case cannot be denied. The right to counsel includes the right to give one's lawyer in confidence all of the facts that one subjectively believes are relevant to one's defense. These two propositions are incontestable. From them, Dean Freedman concludes that one has a right to appear as a witness for oneself and to be examined by one's counsel, whether the story one is telling is true or false. The attorney who is unable to dissuade his client from perjury must proceed by presenting the testimony and arguing the case to the jury in the normal fashion. To say that counsel must or even may withdraw or not conduct the examination if his client insists on perjuring himself is, Dean Freedman contends, to deny the constitutional right. To support his contention he has the . . . proclaimed practice of 90 percent of the lawyers answering a survey in the District of Columbia.

Dean Freedman is very American in implying that what is required by the Constitution of the United States must be morally good, and his use of common practice to establish morality only transfers to the field of legal ethics an argument frequently used as to sexual morality. Both standards, however, are parochial. The Constitution of the United States once required the return of fugitive slaves. Dean Freedman himself is not at all happy with common practice as the criterion when he discusses the practices of prosecutors. . . . Rejecting the criteria Dean Freedman uses here, I continue to believe that the presentation of perjury to a court is fraud whether it is done by concocting a document, hiring a witness, or presenting one's own lying client as a truthteller. If, as Dean Freedman maintains, criminal law practice cannot be carried on otherwise, then honest persons cannot engage in it.

Yet ours, Dean Freedman might point out, is not an ordinary trade. It is socially indispensable. Moreover, it is indispensable to the defense of human dignity. Without counsel, the defendant in a criminal case stands naked before the power of the state. Is not the object of criminal trial procedure as much the preservation of the dignity of the defendant as the discovery of the truth? If it is, counsel performs a noble role, and if those who do in fact perform this role assert that only by cooperating in perjury can they accomplish it, should not their noble role justify their aid to falsehood?

The importance of preserving human dignity . . . I willingly grant. But it seems strange to me to build on this foundation a defense of lying. "Only if I can tell my shabby falsehood with your help can I retain my sense of human worth" is what we must take to be the plea of each incriminated defendant who wants to testify falsely. I have difficulty grasping how accepting such an appeal preserves the dignity of the accused. . . .

Dean Freedman rightly points out that the attorney's difficulty is particularly acute when the client is indigent, since he cannot retain other counsel. Moreover, in many jurisdictions appointed counsel or the public defender may only withdraw from a case for extraordinary reasons, which would necessarily require revealing the client's perjurious intent to the very judge before whom he will be tried and sentenced. But Dean Freedman ignores an alternative to the problem: allow the attorney to withdraw without breaching the confidence and if prejudicial inferences are likely to be drawn, assign both a new judge and a new attorney. . . .

Yet the problem remains, says Freedman, since the client, "realizing that the obligation of confidentiality is not what it has been represented to be," will withhold incriminating information or the fact of guilt from the new attorney and perjured testimony will be presented by an unwitting attorney. This may be true, but there is a crucial difference this time around: neither the first nor the second attorney has knowingly acquiesced in perjury, a result of no small importance in preserving the integrity of a truth-seeking system. . . .

The principle I espouse excludes the use of perjury even in the "hard cases" that Dean Freedman has appealingly constructed. Consequently I answer the first question in this review differently from the answer implicit in Lawyers' Ethics in an Adversary System.

NOTES

1. The American Bar Association has adopted Model Rules of Professional Conduct to prescribe standards for lawyers in matters related to ethics and professional responsibility. Many states have enacted the Model Rules (along with various local amendments) as legally enforceable rules of conduct. See ABA, Annotated Model Rules of Professional Conduct (2d ed. 1992). Rules 1.6 and 3.3 of the Model Rules resolve the problems of candor, honesty, and confidentiality as follows:

RULE 1.6   CONFIDENTIALITY OF INFORMATION

(a) A lawyer shall not reveal information relating to representation of a client unless the client consents after consultation, . . . except as stated in paragraph (b).

(b) A lawyer may reveal such information to the extent the lawyer reasonably believes necessary:

(1) to prevent the client from committing a criminal act that the lawyer believes is likely to result in imminent death of substantial bodily harm; or

(2) to establish a claim or defense on behalf of the lawyer in a controversy between the lawyer and the client. . . .

RULE 3.3   CANDOR TOWARD THE TRIBUNAL

(a) A lawyer shall not knowingly:

(1) make a false statement of material fact or law to a tribunal;

(2) fail to disclose a material fact to a tribunal when disclosure is necessary to avoid assisting a criminal or fraudulent act by the client; . . . or

(4) offer evidence that the lawyer knows to be false. If a lawyer has offered material evidence and comes to know of its falsity, the lawyer shall take reasonable remedial measures.

(b) The duties stated in paragraph (a) continue to the conclusion of the proceeding, and apply even if compliance requires disclosure of information otherwise protected by Rule 1.6. . . .

The Commentary to Rule 3.3[29] states:

While it is agreed that the lawyer should seek to persuade the client to refrain from perjurious testimony, there has been dispute concerning the lawyer's duty when that persuasion fails [and when withdrawal is not possible.]

Three resolutions of this dilemma have been proposed. One is to permit the accused to testify by a narrative without guidance through the lawyer's questioning. This compromises both contending principles; it exempts the lawyer from the duty to disclose false evidence but subjects the client to an implicit disclosure of information imparted to counsel. Another suggested resolution, of relatively recent origin, is that the advocate be entirely excused from the duty to reveal perjury if the perjury is that of the client. This is a coherent solution but makes the advocate a knowing instrument of perjury.

The other resolution of the dilemma is that the lawyer must reveal the client's perjury if necessary to rectify the situation. A criminal accused has a right to the assistance of an advocate, a right to testify and a right of confidential communication with counsel. However, an accused should not have a right to assistance of counsel in committing perjury. Furthermore, an advocate has an obligation, not only in professional ethics but under the law as well, to avoid implication in the commission of perjury or other falsification of evidence. . . .

If withdrawal will not remedy the situation or is impossible, the advocate should make disclosure to the court. It is for the court then to determine what should be done — making a statement about the matter to the trier of fact, ordering a mistrial or perhaps nothing. If the false testimony was that of the client, the client may controvert the lawyer's version of their communication when the lawyer discloses the situation to the court. If there is an issue whether the client has committed perjury, the lawyer cannot represent the client in resolution of the issue and a mistrial may be unavoidable. . . .

The general rule — that an advocate must disclose the existence of perjury with respect to a material fact, even that of a client — applies to defense counsel in criminal cases, as well as in other instances. However, the definition of the lawyer's ethical duty in such a situation may be qualified by constitutional provisions for due process and the right to counsel in criminal cases. In some jurisdictions these provisions have been construed to require that counsel present an accused as a witness if the accused wishes to testify, even if counsel knows the testimony will be false. The obligation of the advocate under these Rules is subordinate to such a constitutional requirement.

2. Should it follow under the Model Code that the attorney must, at the ou[t]set of the representation, advise the client of the limitation on the confidentia[l]ity of attorney-client communications? Professor Norman Lefstein, the reporte[r] for a related ABA Committee on Standards Relating to the Defense Functio[n]

---

29. ABA, Model Rules of Professional Conduct, Rule 3.3, Comment at 330-332 (2d ed. 199[2]

urges that such advice be given. See Lefstein, The Criminal Defendant Who Proposes Perjury, 6 Hofstra L. Rev. 665, 687-691 (1978). Could such a warning inhibit full disclosure and effective defense planning for the defendant who may have a legitimate defense? Compare ABA Formal Opinion No. 87-353 (April 20, 1987), holding that disclosure of the client's intent to commit perjury is not inconsistent with the attorney's commitment to preserve client confidences (id. at 6): "Implicit in the promise of confidentiality is its nonapplicability where the client seeks the unlawful end of corrupting the judicial process by false evidence."

3. What is the significance of the last paragraph of the ABA Commentary? Consider the case that follows.

NIX v. WHITESIDE

Supreme Court of the United States
475 U.S. 157 (1986)

CHIEF JUSTICE BURGER delivered the opinion of the Court.
. . . Whiteside and two others went to one Calvin Love's apartment seeking marihuana. [An argument] ensued. At one point, Love directed his girlfriend to get his "piece," and at another point got up, then returned to his bed. According to Whiteside's testimony, Love then started to reach under his pillow and moved toward Whiteside. Whiteside stabbed Love in the chest, inflicting a fatal wound.

Whiteside was charged with murder. [He gave Robinson, his appointed counsel,] a statement that he had stabbed Love as the latter "was pulling a pistol from underneath the pillow on the bed." Upon questioning by Robinson, however, Whiteside indicated that he had not actually seen a gun, but that he was convinced that Love had a gun. No pistol was found on the premises. . . . Robinson interviewed Whiteside's companions who were present during the stabbing and none had seen a gun during the incident. Robinson advised Whiteside that the existence of a gun was not necessary to establish the claim of self defense, and that only a reasonable belief that the victim had a gun nearby was necessary. . . .

About a week before trial, during preparation for direct examination, Whiteside for the first time told Robinson . . . that he had seen something "metallic" in Love's hand. When asked about this, Whiteside responded that "in Howard Cook's case there was a gun. If I don't say I saw a gun I'm dead." Robinson told Whiteside that such testimony would be perjury and repeated that it was not necessary to prove that a gun was available but only that Whiteside reasonably believed that he was in danger. On Whiteside's insisting that he would testify that he saw "something metallic" Robinson told him, according to Robinson's testimony,

we could not allow him to [testify falsely] because that would be perjury, and as officers of the court we would be suborning perjury if we allowed him to do it; . . . I advised him that if he did do that it would be my duty to advise the Court of what he was doing and that I felt he was committing perjury; also, that I probably would be allowed to attempt to impeach that particular testimony.

Robinson also indicated he would seek to withdraw from the representation if Whiteside insisted on committing perjury.

Whiteside testified in his own defense at trial and stated that he "knew" that Love had a gun and that he believed Love was reaching for a gun and he had acted swiftly in self defense. On cross examination, he admitted that he had not actually seen a gun in Love's hand. Robinson presented evidence that Love had been seen with a sawed-off shotgun on other occasions, that the police search of the apartment may have been careless, and that the victim's family had removed everything from the apartment shortly after the crime. Robinson presented this evidence to show a basis for Whiteside's asserted fear that Love had a gun.

The jury returned a verdict of second-degree murder and Whiteside moved for a new trial, claiming that he had been deprived of a fair trial by Robinson's admonitions not to state that he saw a gun or "something metallic.". . .

The Supreme Court of Iowa affirmed respondent's conviction. That court held that the right to have counsel present all appropriate defenses does not extend to using perjury, and that an attorney's duty to a client does not extend to assisting a client in committing perjury. [T]he Iowa court concluded that not only were Robinson's actions permissible, but were required. The court commended [Robinson] "for the high ethical manner in which this matter was handled."

Whiteside then petitioned for a writ of habeas corpus. . . .

The United States Court of Appeals for the Eighth Circuit . . . directed that the writ of habeas corpus be granted. The Court of Appeals accepted the findings of the trial judge, affirmed by the Iowa Supreme Court, that trial counsel believed with good cause that Whiteside would testify falsely. . . . Nevertheless the court reasoned that an intent to commit perjury, communicated to counsel does not alter a defendant's right to effective assistance of counsel and that Robinson's admonition to Whiteside that he would inform the court of Whiteside's perjury constituted a threat to violate the attorney's duty to preserve client confidences. According to the Court of Appeals, this threatened violation of client confidences breached the standards of effective representation set down in Strickland v. Washington, 466 U.S. 668 (1984). . . .

In *Strickland* we held that to obtain relief . . . on a claim of a deprivation of effective assistance of counsel under the Sixth Amendment, the movant must establish both serious attorney error and prejudice. To show such error, it must be established that . . . "counsel made errors so serious that counsel was not functioning as 'counsel' guaranteed the defendant by the Sixth Amendment. To show prejudice, it must be established that the claimed lapses in counsel performance rendered the trial unfair so as to "undermine confidence in the outcome" of the trial. . . .

In *Strickland,* we recognized counsel's duty of loyalty and his "overarching duty to advocate the defendant's cause." Plainly, that duty is limited to legitimate, lawful conduct compatible with the very nature of a trial as a search for truth. Although counsel must take all reasonable lawful means to attain the objectives of the client, counsel is precluded from taking steps or in any way assisting the client in presenting false evidence or otherwise violating the law. This principle has consistently been recognized in most unequivocal terms by expositors of the norms of professional conduct since the first Canons of Professional Ethics were adopted by the American Bar Association in 1908. . . .

These principles have been carried through to contemporary codifications[4] of an attorney's professional responsibility. Disciplinary Rule 7-102 of the Model Code of Professional Responsibility (1980), entitled "Representing a Client Within the Bounds of the Law," provides that

(A) In his representation of a client, a lawyer shall not: . . .
    (4) Knowingly use perjured testimony or false evidence. . . .
    (7) Counsel or assist his client in conduct that the lawyer knows to be illegal or fraudulent.

This provision has been adopted by Iowa, and is binding on all lawyers who appear in its courts. The more recent Model Rules of Professional Conduct (1983) similarly admonish attorneys to obey all laws in the course of representing a client:

RULE 1.2   SCOPE OF REPRESENTATION . . .

(d) A lawyer shall not counsel a client to engage, or assist a client, in conduct that the lawyer knows is criminal or fraudulent. . . .

Both the Model Code of Professional Conduct and the Model Rules of Professional Conduct also adopt the specific exception from the attorney-client privilege for disclosure of perjury that his client intends to commit or has committed. DR 4-101(C)(3) (intention of client to commit a crime); Rule 3.3 (lawyer has duty to disclose falsity of evidence even if disclosure compromises client confidences). Indeed, both the Model Code and the Model Rules do not merely *authorize* disclosure by counsel of client perjury; they *require* such disclosure. See Rule 3.3(a)(4); DR 7-102(B)(1). . . . This special duty of an attorney to prevent and disclose frauds upon the court derives from the recognition that perjury is as much a crime as tampering with witnesses or jurors by way of promises and threats, and undermines the administration of justice. . . .

It is universally agreed that at a minimum the attorney's first duty when confronted with a proposal for perjurious testimony is to attempt to dissuade the client from the unlawful course of conduct. . . . Similarly, the Model Rules and the commentary, as well as the Code of Professional Responsibility adopted in Iowa expressly permit withdrawal from representation as an appropriate response of an attorney when the client threatens to commit perjury. . . .[6]

4. There currently exist two different codifications of uniform standards of professional conduct. The Model Code of Professional Responsibility was originally adopted by the American Bar Association in 1969, and was subsequently adopted (in many cases with modification) by nearly every state. The more recent Model Rules of Professional Conduct were adopted by the American Bar Association in 1983. Since their promulgation by the American Bar Association, the Model Rules have been adopted by 11 States. . . . Iowa is one of the States that adopted a form of the Model Code of Professional Responsibility, but has yet to adopt the Model Rules.

[The 1969 Model Code remains in force in many states. More than half the states have now adopted the Model Rules of Professional Conduct, though often with significant amendments. See John M. Burkoff, Criminal Defense Ethics, pp. 1-3, 1-5 (rev. ed. 1991). — EDS.]

6. In the evolution of the contemporary standards promulgated by the American Bar Association, an early draft reflects a compromise suggesting that when the disclosure of intended perjury is made during the course of trial, when withdrawal of counsel would raise difficult questions of a mistrial holding, counsel had the option to let the defendant take the stand but decline to affir-

The essence of the brief amicus of the American Bar Association reviewing practices long accepted by ethical lawyers, is that under no circumstances may a lawyer either advocate or passively tolerate a client's giving false testimony. . . . The suggestion sometimes made that "a lawyer must believe his client not judge him" in no sense means a lawyer can honorably be a party to or in any way give aid to presenting known perjury.

Considering Robinson's representation of respondent in light of these accepted norms of professional conduct, we discern no failure to adhere to reasonable professional standards that would in any sense make out a deprivation of the Sixth Amendment right to counsel. . . . Nothing counsel did in any way undermined Whiteside's claim that he believed the victim was reaching for a gun. . . . Whiteside did testify, and he was "restricted" or restrained only from testifying falsely. . . . Robinson divulged no client communications until he was compelled to do so in response to Whiteside's post-trial challenge to the quality of his performance. We see this as a case in which the attorney successfully dissuaded the client from committing the crime of perjury.

Paradoxically, even while accepting the conclusion of the Iowa trial court that Whiteside's proposed testimony would have been a criminal act, the Court of Appeals held that Robinson's efforts to persuade Whiteside not to commit that crime were improper, *first,* as forcing an impermissible choice between the right to counsel and the right to testify; and *second,* as compromising client confidences because of Robinson's threat to disclose the contemplated perjury.

Whatever the scope of a constitutional right to testify, it is elementary that such a right does not extend to testifying *falsely.* . . . Robinson's admonitions to his client can in no sense be said to have forced respondent into an *impermissible* choice . . . for there was no *permissible* choice to testify falsely. . . . When an accused proposes to resort to perjury or to produce false evidence, one consequence is the risk of withdrawal of counsel.

. . . Similarly, we can discern no breach of professional duty in Robinson's admonition to respondent that he would disclose respondent's perjury to the court. An attorney's duty of confidentiality, which totally covers the client's admission of guilt, does not extend to a client's announced plans to engage in future criminal conduct. In short, the responsibility of an ethical lawyer, as an officer of the court and a key component of a system of justice, dedicated to a search for truth, is essentially the same whether the client announces an intention to bribe or threaten witnesses or jurors or to commit or procure perjury. No system of justice worthy of the name can tolerate a lesser standard. . . . Since

---

matively assist the presentation of perjury by traditional direct examination. Instead, counsel would stand mute while the defendant undertook to present the false version in narrative form in his own words unaided by any direct examination. This conduct was thought to be a signal at least to the presiding judge that the attorney considered the testimony to be false and was seeking to disassociate himself from that course. Additionally, counsel would not be permitted to discuss the known false testimony in closing arguments. See ABA Standards for Criminal Justice, 4-7.7 (2d ed. 1980). Most courts treating the subject rejected this approach and insisted on a more rigorous standard. The Eighth Circuit in this case and the Ninth Circuit have expressed approval of the "free narrative" standards.

The Rule finally promulgated in the current Model Rules of Professional Conduct rejects any participation or passive role whatever by counsel in allowing perjury to be presented without challenge.

there has been no breach of any recognized professional duty, it follows that there can be no deprivation of the right to assistance of counsel under the *Strickland* standard. . . .

Reversed.

JUSTICE BRENNAN, concurring in the judgment.

This Court has no constitutional authority to establish rules of ethical conduct for lawyers practicing in the state courts. . . .

Unfortunately, the Court seems unable to resist the temptation of sharing with the legal community its vision of ethical conduct. But let there be no mistake; the Court's essay regarding what constitutes the correct response to a criminal client's suggestion that he will perjure himself is pure discourse without force of law. . . . Lawyers, judges, bar associations, students and others should understand that the problem has not now been "decided."

JUSTICE BLACKMUN, with whom JUSTICE BRENNAN, JUSTICE MARSHALL, and Justice Stevens join, concurring in the judgment. . . .

The only federal issue in this case is whether Robinson's behavior deprived Whiteside of the effective assistance of counsel; it is not whether Robinson's behavior conformed to any particular code of legal ethics.

Whether an attorney's response to what he sees as a client's plan to commit perjury violates a defendant's Sixth Amendment rights may depend on many factors: how certain the attorney is that the proposed testimony is false, the stage of the proceedings at which the attorney discovers the plan, or the ways in which the attorney may be able to dissuade his client, to name just three. The complex interaction of factors, which is likely to vary from case to case, makes inappropriate a blanket rule that defense attorneys must reveal, or threaten to reveal, a client's anticipated perjury to the court. Except in the rarest of cases, attorneys who adopt "the role of the judge or jury to determine the facts," pose a danger of depriving their clients of the zealous and loyal advocacy required by the Sixth Amendment.

I therefore am troubled by the Court's implicit adoption of a set of standards of professional responsibility for attorneys in state criminal proceedings. [T]his Court's responsibility extends only to ensuring that the restrictions a State enacts do not infringe a defendant's federal constitutional rights. . . . Because I conclude that the respondent in this case failed to show such an effect, I join the Court's judgment that he is not entitled to federal habeas relief.

JUSTICE STEVENS, concurring in the judgment.

Justice Holmes taught us that a word is but the skin of a living thought. A "fact" may also have a life of its own. From the perspective of an appellate judge, after a case has been tried and the evidence has been sifted by another judge, a particular fact may be as clear and certain as a piece of crystal or a small diamond. A trial lawyer, however, must often deal with mixtures of sand and clay. . . .

As we view this case, it appears perfectly clear that respondent intended to commit perjury, that his lawyer knew it, and that the lawyer had a duty — both to the court and to his client, for perjured testimony can ruin an otherwise meritorious case — to take extreme measures to prevent the perjury from occurring. The lawyer was successful and, from our unanimous and remote perspective, it is now pellucidly clear that the client suffered no "legally cognizable prejudice."

Nevertheless, beneath the surface of this case there are areas of uncertainty that cannot be resolved today. A lawyer's certainty that a change in his client's recollection is a harbinger of intended perjury — as well as judicial review of such apparent certainty — should be tempered by the realization that, after reflection, the most honest witness may recall (or sincerely believe he recalls) details that he previously overlooked. Similarly, the post-trial review of a lawyer's pre-trial threat to expose perjury that had not yet been committed — and, indeed, may have been prevented by the threat — is by no means the same as review of the way in which such a threat may actually have been carried out. Thus, one can be convinced — as I am — that this lawyer's actions were a proper way to provide his client with effective representation without confronting the much more difficult questions of what a lawyer must, should, or may do after his client has given testimony that the lawyer does not believe.

NORMAN LEFSTEIN, LEGAL ETHICS, 1 Crim. Justice 27, 28-30 (ABA 1986): The majority opinion's "essay" [in *Nix*] contains a shocking misstatement of the law pertaining to client perjury. In its zeal to advise the nation's defense attorneys that they should inform judges whenever their clients propose to commit perjury, the Court did not seriously consider the ABA's former policy on the subject, i.e., permitting the defendant to testify by making a narrative statement and prohibiting counsel from arguing the defendant's testimony to the jury. The only reference to standard 7.7 is in a footnote, in which it is said that "[m]ost courts treating the subject rejected this approach and insisted on a more rigorous standard. . . ." This statement is not accurate.

Three cases are cited by the Court in support of its observation that standard 7.7 was rejected by most courts. Remarkably, [none] of the cases [is on point]. . . .

Even more startling than the Court's use of [these] cases is its failure to cite any of the numerous appellate decisions that have endorsed standard 7.7's free narrative approach. . . .

In the wake of the *Nix* decision, what should defense counsel do when confronted by a client determined to lie under oath? Obviously, counsel must try to dissuade the client from seeking to present false testimony. If this effort fails, an appropriate next step is for counsel to seek to withdraw from the case. But if withdrawal from the case is not feasible because, for example, the perjury dilemma arises during the midst of trial or if withdrawal is denied by the judge counsel must decide on another approach.

Regardless of the precise course finally adopted, counsel should not under any circumstances aid the defendant in presenting testimony that counsel knows to be false. . . .

It does not necessarily follow, however, that a defendant's proposed perjury should be expressly revealed to the judge. If disclosure of a defendant's intent to commit perjury will not violate the Sixth Amendment, as the Court holds in *Nix*, permitting defendant to present his or her story in a narrative fashion will not do so either. . . . Admittedly, [the free narrative approach] implicitly informs the judge and perhaps the jury that the client's testimony is untrue. The defendant especially may be disadvantaged when the attorney fails to argue the defendant's version of the case to the jury. . . . But if this is a problem for the defendant, it is one for which the defendant clearly is responsible by insisting on presenting perjury.

Furthermore, compared to the alternative of advising the judge that defendant proposes to commit perjury, the free narrative approach has much to commend it. Most importantly, it avoids the confusion and confrontation that arise when an attorney informs a judge that the defendant plans to testify perjuriously. If, for example, counsel tells the judge that defendant's testimony will be false, the defendant will most likely deny counsel's allegation. How should the judge and defense attorney then respond? One possibility would be for the judge, relying on defense counsel's statements, to deny defendant the opportunity to be sworn as a witness — a solution seemingly endorsed in the *Nix* opinion. . . . However, if despite defense counsel's statements, the judge permits defendant to testify, counsel is faced with the dilemma of deciding how to conduct direct examination. If defendant is examined like any other witness, defense counsel conceivably could be charged with suborning perjury in light of counsel's earlier announcement to the judge that defendant's testimony would be false. An alternative would be for counsel to invite the defendant to make a narrative statement, which is probably what counsel should have done in the first place. Finally, no matter what happens after defense counsel informs the judge that the client plans to testify falsely, all trust and confidence between counsel and client will be destroyed.

NOTES AND QUESTIONS ON CLIENT PERJURY

1. *Disclosure: when and how.* Both *Nix* and Model Rule 3.3 stress that the attorney whose client is about to commit perjury *must* disclose that fact to the court. How should the lawyer fulfill this obligation? Can the attorney stand up during the trial and state, in front of the jury: "The testimony you are about to hear is false"? Why not?

(*a*) Consider Lowery v. Cardwell, 575 F.2d 727 (9th Cir. 1978). During a murder trial before a judge sitting without a jury, the defendant flatly denied shooting the deceased. Defense counsel then requested a recess and in chambers, without the defendant present, moved to withdraw. When counsel refused to state the reason for the motion, the trial judge denied it. Back in court, defense counsel asked defendant no further questions, and in closing argument he made no reference to her denial of having fired the fatal shots. The court of appeals found that counsel's actions amounted to "an unequivocal announcement" that the defendant had committed perjury. The court then ruled that because the announcement had placed counsel in open opposition to his client and had disabled the fact finder from ruling on the merits of the case, the defendant had been deprived of a fair trial. The court added (id. at 730): "If in truth the defendant has committed perjury (a fact we do not know in this case) she does not by that falsehood forfeit her right to a fair trial."

Questions: Does the result in *Lowery* remain sound after *Nix*? Could defense counsel now argue that his "unequivocal announcement" of perjury was precisely the step that *Nix* approved? If not, what action would *Nix* permit or require under the circumstances of *Lowery*?

(*b*) When the trier of fact is a jury, can defense counsel avoid the *Lowery* problem by making the disclosure to the judge outside the presence of the jury? Note that the judge not only makes important evidentiary rulings at trial but also imposes sentence after conviction. Moreover, under United States v. Grayson, 438 U.S. 41 (1978), a sentencing judge is permitted to impose a higher punishment on the basis of her belief that the defendant testified falsely at trial. If disclosure of perjury to the trier of fact is unduly prejudicial, isn't there a similar problem in disclosing perjury to the judge even in a jury trial?

(*c*) *Nix* offers some support for the argument that disclosure does not impair a fair trial because there is nothing unfair about penalizing the defendant who commits perjury. On this view, it might be argued that the defendant in *Lowery* received a fair trial, even though the disclosure was made to a judge who was sitting as the trier of fact. But how do we know that the defendant in *Lowery* did commit perjury? Should defense counsel have the power to make this determination unilaterally? Consider United States v. Scott, 909 F.2d 488 (11th Cir. 1990). Scott was on trial for unlawful possession of a firearm. After the government had presented its case, defense counsel moved to withdraw, stating that she could not disclose her reasons. The trial judge held a conference and advised Scott that he had two options: he could proceed with counsel, in which case counsel could refuse to let him testify, or he could discharge his counsel and represent himself. Scott chose the latter option and was convicted. The court of appeals reversed, holding that the judge could not force Scott to choose between his right to counsel and his right to testify, in the absence of proof that his intended testimony would be false. The court left open the question of what would be the appropriate course of action when the record affirmatively establishes an intent to commit perjury.

The court took a different approach in United States v. Long, 857 F.2d 436 (8th Cir. 1988). Co-defendant Jackson, facing forgery charges, decided not to testify, after his counsel informed the judge that Jackson might perjure himself. The court held (id. at 446) that such a disclosure was improper unless the defense attorney had a "firm factual basis" for concluding that the testimony would be false. The court therefore called for an evidentiary hearing to determine the basis for defense counsel's concern. (In subsequent proceedings, the courts found that counsel did have a sufficient basis for his conclusion and therefore held that he did not act improperly in preventing Jackson from testifying. United States v. Jackson, 928 F.2d 245 (8th Cir. 1991).)

If a defendant insists on testifying and counsel seeks to withdraw, the trial judge will need to know whether the defense attorney has a "firm factual basis" for his concern. How should the trial judge proceed? If a hearing is held, who should represent the defendant at the hearing? Who should preside at the hearing?

2. *After disclosure.* When the relationship between defense counsel and client breaks down prior to trial, the judge will often permit counsel to withdraw. But when a conflict arises during trial, withdrawal will seldom be permitted. How should the ethical defense attorney proceed if she fails to dissuade her client from perjury and fails to obtain leave to withdraw? *Nix*, which presented the perjury problem in a different context, has not settled the matter. Several competing approaches are being advanced.

(*a*) The National Association of Criminal Defense Lawyers, endorsing the position of Professor Monroe Freedman, argues that when the defense attorney fails to dissuade his client from committing perjury, the Sixth Amendment right to effective assistance of counsel requires the attorney to elicit the false testimony and argue it to the jury in the usual way.[30] Can this approach be reconciled with the *Nix* court's reading of the Sixth Amendment?

(*b*) An alternative is the so-called free narrative approach — the client testifies without his attorney's aid and the attorney does not argue the testimony to the jury. Jurisdictions are widely split on the propriety of this approach. Florida explicitly prohibits it.[31] The California courts have held that the free narrative approach, while not ideal, does not deny the constitutional right to effective assistance of counsel.[32] The District of Columbia bar has adopted the ABA's 1983 Model Rules, including Rule 3.3, but has added an amendment stating that when counsel cannot withdraw or dissuade the client from testifying, the free narrative approach is permissible.[33]

(*c*) *Nix* condemns the free narrative approach and insists on a "more rigorous standard" (supra page 83-84 n. 6). What would the more rigorous approach be? Should the attorney simply refuse to participate at all? Compare Matter of Goodwin, 305 S.E.2d 578 (S.C. 1983), where after denial of motions to withdraw, defense counsel was held in contempt for continued refusal to represent a client who intended to commit perjury at trial. The court said that by following the free narrative approach, the attorney would fulfill his ethical obligations.

In Florida Bar v. Rubin, 549 So. 2d 1000 (Fla. 1989), defense counsel had refused to proceed on a free narrative basis after his withdrawal motion was denied, and he served 30 days for contempt of court. Subsequently, the Florida Supreme Court reprimanded him for unethical conduct. The court said that even though the free narrative approach was prohibited under the Florida Code of Professional Responsibility, defense counsel should have proceeded on that basis when the trial court ordered him to do so; the trial court's order would have afforded him a defense if an effort had been made to discipline him for participating on a free narrative basis.

Questions: Was the trial court justified in ordering Rubin to proceed? If not, what steps would be proper in a jurisdiction that outlaws the free narrative approach?

3. *Further reading.* A detailed procedure for responding to client perjury situations is developed in Carol T. Rieger, Client Perjury: A Proposed Resolution of the Constitutional and Ethical Issues, 70 Minn. L. Rev. 121 (1985). See also Monroe H. Freedman, Understanding Lawyers' Ethics 109-141 (1990).

NOTE ON PROBLEMS ARISING "WITHIN THE BOUNDS OF THE LAW"

Despite the wide range of disagreement reflected in the preceding materials, all participants in the debate accept that in principle an attorney should not use

---

30. Natl. Assn. of Criminal Defense Lawyers, Formal Op. 92-2 (1992), quoted in John Wesley Hall, Jr., Professional Responsibility of the Criminal Lawyer §24.17, at 223-239 (Cum. Supp. 1993).
31. See Re Rules Regulating the Fla. Bar, 494 So. 2d 977 (Fla. 1986) (Rule 4-3.3 and Comment).
32. People v. Guzman, 45 Cal. 3d 915, 755 P.2d 917 (1988).
33. D.C. Rules Ann., Rules of Prof. Conduct, §3.3(b) (Michie 1993).

illegal means to further a client's interests. No one would argue that a zealous defense attorney should attempt to shoot (or even bribe) the prosecution's chief witness. Professor Freedman stresses that defense counsel should always attempt to dissuade her client from perjury. Disagreement arises when the attorney can avoid illegality only by compromising some other contending principle; putting this somewhat special problem to one side, all agree that zealous representation must remain "within the bounds of the law."[34]

Does it follow that ethical counsel may (and indeed *must,* to be truly effective) use all helpful tactics that *are* within the bounds of the law? Even after we have ruled out illegal means, is it not still troublesome for an attorney to exercise her special training and skills, to use all of her best effort, in order to promote a result that she knows to be socially harmful? Consider the following comments.

MARK M. ORKIN, DEFENCE OF ONE KNOWN TO BE GUILTY
1 Crim. L.Q. 170, 172-175 (1958)

Dr. Johnson, as usual, resumed the question with judicial finality: "We asked of the practice of law. Sir William Forbes said he thought an honest lawyer should never undertake a cause which he was satisfied was not a just one. Sir (said Mr. Johnson), a lawyer has no business with the justice or injustice of the cause which he undertakes, unless his client asks his opinion and then he is bound to give it honestly. The justice or injustice of the cause is to be decided by the judge. Consider, Sir, what is the purpose of courts of justice? It is, that every man may have his cause fairly tried, by men appointed to try causes. A lawyer is not to tell what he knows to be a lie: he is not to produce what he knows to be a false deed; but he is not to usurp the province of the jury and of the judge, and determine what shall be the effect of evidence — what shall be the result of legal argument. . . . If lawyers were to undertake no causes till they were sure they were just, a man might be precluded altogether from a trial of his claim, though, were it judicially examined, it might be found a very just claim."[1] . . .

MONROE FREEDMAN, LAWYERS' ETHICS IN AN ADVERSARY SYSTEM
43-49 (1975)

More difficult than the question of whether the criminal defense lawyer should present known perjury, is the question of whether the attorney should cross-examine a witness who is testifying accurately and truthfully, in order to make the witness appear to be mistaken or lying. The issue was raised effectively in a symposium on legal ethics through the following hypothetical case.

---

34. The 1969 Model Rules state (EC 7-1) that "[t]he duty of a lawyer . . . is to represent his client zealously within the bounds of the law." In the 1983 Model Code, Rule 1.3 provides that "[a] lawyer shall act with reasonable diligence . . . ," and the Comment (ABA Model Rules, supra page 80 n. 29, at 41) states that "[a] lawyer should act with commitment and dedication to the interests of the client and with zeal in advocacy. . . ."

1. Boswell's Life of Johnson, vol. 5, pp. 28-29.

The accused . . . is charged with rape. . . . The alleged victim is the twenty-two-year-old daughter of a local bank president. She is engaged to a promising young minister in town. The alleged rape occurred in the early morning hours at a service station some distance from town, where the accused was employed as an attendant. That is all you know about the case when you have your first interview with your client.

At first the accused will not talk at all. You assure him that you cannot help him unless you know the truth and that he can trust you to treat what he says as confidential. He then says that he had intercourse with the young woman, but that she "consented in every way." . . . He says that on the night in question she came in for gas; they talked; and she invited him into the car. One thing led to another and, finally, to sexual intercourse. . . .

The accused tells you he was tried for rape in California four years ago and acquitted. He has no previous convictions. . . .

You learn that the victim has had affairs with two local men from good families. . . . Jones, apparently a bitterly disappointed and jealous suitor, readily states that he frequently had intercourse with the victim, and describes her behavior toward strange men as scandalous. He once took her to a fraternity dance, he says, and, having noticed she had been gone for some time, discovered her upstairs with Smith, a fraternity brother, on a bed in a state of semi-undress. He appears eager to testify and he states that the girl got what she'd always been asking for. You believe Jones, but are somewhat repelled by the disappointed suitor's apparent willingness to smear the young woman's reputation.

Suppose the accused, after you press him, admits that he forced himself on the victim and admits that his first story was a lie. He refuses to plead guilty to the charge or any lesser charge. He says that he can get away with his story, because he did once before in California.

Should the defense lawyer use the information supplied by Jones to impeach the young woman and, if necessary, call Jones as a witness?

One of the panelists who spoke to that question was Chief Justice (then Judge) Burger. The Chief Justice first discussed the question in terms of "basic and fundamental rules." One of those rules, which he characterized as "clear-cut and unambiguous," is that "a lawyer may never, under any circumstances, knowingly . . . participate in a fraud on the court." That rule, he said, "can never admit of any exception, under any circumstances," and no other consideration "can ever justify a knowing and conscious departure" from it. . . .

After that powerful rhetoric, Chief Justice Burger's response to the question posed is a matter of some astonishment. The function of an advocate, and "particularly the defense advocate in the adversary system," is to use "all the legitimate tools available to test the truth of the prosecution's case." Therefore, he concluded, "the testimony of bad repute of the complaining witness, being recent and not remote in point of time, is relevant to her credibility." The Chief Justice was even more explicit in the question period following the panel discussion: he considers it ethical to cast doubt on the woman's credibility by destroying her reputation, even though the lawyer knows that she is telling the truth.

That, of course, is sanction for nothing less than a deliberate attempt to perpetrate a fraud upon the finder of fact. The lawyer knows that the client is guilty and that the prosecutrix is truthful. In cross-examining, the lawyer has one purpose, and one purpose only: to make it appear, contrary to fact, that the prosecutrix is lying in testifying that she was raped.

There is only one difference in practical effect between presenting the defendant's perjured alibi — which the Chief Justice considers to be clearly improper — and impeaching the truthful prosecutrix. In both cases, the lawyer participates in an attempt to free a guilty defendant. In both cases, the lawyer participates in misleading the finder of fact. In the case of the perjured witness, however, the attorney asks only nonleading questions, while in the case of impeachment, the lawyer takes an active, aggressive role, using professional training and skills, including leading questions, in a one-on-one attack upon the client's victim. The lawyer thereby personally and directly adds to the suffering of the prosecutrix, her family, and the minister to whom she is engaged. In short, under the euphemism of "testing the truth of the prosecution's case," the lawyer communicates, to the jury and to the community, the most vicious of lies.

That case takes us to the heart of my disagreement with the traditional approach to dealing with difficult questions of professional responsibility. That approach has two characteristics. First, in a rhetorical flourish, the profession is committed in general terms to all that is good and true. Then, specific questions are answered by uncritical reliance upon legalistic norms, regardless of the context in which the lawyer may be acting, and regardless of the motive and the consequences of the act. Perjury is wrong, and therefore no lawyer, in any circumstance, should knowingly present perjury. Cross-examination, however, is good, and therefore any lawyer, under any circumstances and regardless of the consequences, can properly impeach a witness through cross-examination. The system of professional responsibility that I have been advancing, on the other hand, is one that attempts to deal with ethical problems in context.

Let us return, then, to the case involving the street robbery at 16th and P Streets, in which the defendant has been wrongly identified as the criminal, but correctly identified by the nervous, elderly woman who wears eyeglasses, as having been only a block away five minutes before the crime took place.[a] [T]he lawyer could take the position that since the woman is testifying truthfully and accurately, she should not be made to appear to be mistaken or lying. But if a similar course were to be adopted by every lawyer who learned the truth through confidential disclosures from the client, such disclosures would soon cease to be made. . . .

Obviously, however, the rape case is a much harder one, because the injury done to the prosecutrix is far more severe than the more limited humiliation of the public-spirited and truthful witness in the case of the street robbery. In addition, in the rape case, the lawyer is acting pursuant to a manifestly irrational rule, that is, one that permits the defense to argue that the prosecutrix is the kind of person who would have sexual intercourse with a stranger because she has had sexual relations with two men whom she knew in wholly different social circumstances. Irrational or not, however, in those jurisdictions in which the defense of unchastity is still the law, the attorney is bound to provide it on the client's behalf. For the lawyer who finds the presentation of that defense, and perhaps others in rape cases, to go beyond what he or she can in good conscience do, there are two courses that should be followed. The first is to be active in efforts to reform the law in that regard; the second is to decline to accept the defense of rape cases, on the grounds of a conflict of interest (a strong persona

a. See page 75 supra. — Eds.

view) that would interfere with providing the defendant with his constitutional right to effective assistance of counsel.

RICHARD WASSERSTROM, LAWYERS AS PROFESSIONALS: SOME MORAL ISSUES

5 Human Rights 1, 5-15 (1975)

Conventional wisdom has it that where the attorney-client relationship exists, . . . it is often appropriate and many times even obligatory for the attorney to do things that, all other things being equal, an ordinary person need not, and should not do. What is characteristic of this role of a lawyer is the lawyer's required indifference to a wide variety of ends and consequences that in other contexts would be of undeniable moral significance. . . . Provided that the end sought is not illegal, the lawyer is, in essence, an amoral technician whose peculiar skills and knowledge in respect to the law are available to those with whom the relationship of client is established. The question . . . is whether this particular and pervasive feature of professionalism is itself justifiable. At a minimum, I do not think any of the typical, simple answers will suffice.

. . . The received view within the profession (and to a lesser degree within the society at large) is that having once agreed to represent the client, the lawyer is under an obligation to do his or her best to defend that person at trial, irrespective, for instance, even of the lawyer's belief in the client's innocence. [I]t is thought both appropriate and obligatory for the attorney to put on as vigorous and persuasive a defense of a client believed to be guilty as would have been mounted by the lawyer thoroughly convinced of the client's innocence. I suspect that many persons find this an attractive and admirable feature of the life of a legal professional. . . .

But part of the difficulty is that the irrelevance of the guilt or innocence of an accused client by no means exhausts the altered perspective of the lawyer's conscience, even in criminal cases. For in the course of defending an accused, an attorney may have, as a part of his or her duty of representation, the obligation to invoke procedures and practices which are themselves morally objectionable and of which the lawyer in other contexts might thoroughly disapprove. . . . For example, in California, the case law permits a defendant in a rape case to secure in some circumstances an order from the court requiring the complaining witness, that is the rape victim, to submit to a psychiatric examination before trial. For no other crime is such a pretrial remedy available. . . . I think such a rule is wrong and is reflective of the sexist bias of the law in respect to rape. . . . Nonetheless, it appears to be part of the role-differentiated obligation of a lawyer for a defendant charged with rape to seek to take advantage of this particular rule of law — irrespective of the independent moral view he or she may have of the rightness or wrongness of such a rule.

Nor, it is important to point out, is this peculiar, strikingly amoral behavior limited to the lawyer involved with the workings of the criminal law. . . . Suppose that a client desires to make a will disinheriting her children because they opposed the war in Vietnam. Should the lawyer refuse to draft the will because the lawyer thinks this a bad reason to disinherit one's children? [T]he accepted view within the profession is that these matters are just of no concern to the lawyer qua lawyer. The lawyer need not of course agree to represent the client (and that is equally true for the unpopular client accused of a heinous crime), but there is nothing wrong with representing a client whose aims and purposes are quite immoral. And having agreed to do so, the lawyer is required to provide the best possible assistance, without regard to his or her disapproval of the objective that is sought.

. . . In this way, the lawyer as professional comes to inhabit a simplified universe which is strikingly amoral — which regards as morally irrelevant any number of factors which nonprofessional citizens might take to be important, if not decisive, in their everyday lives. And the difficulty I have with all of this is that the arguments for such a way of life seem to be not quite so convincing to me as they do to many lawyers. . . .

[O]ne feature of this simplified, intellectual world is that it is often a very comfortable one to inhabit. To be sure, on occasion, a lawyer may find it uncomfortable to represent an extremely unpopular client. On occasion, too, a lawyer may feel ill at ease invoking a rule of law or practice which he or she thinks to be an unfair or undesirable one. Nonetheless, for most lawyers, most of the time, pursuing the interests of one's clients is an attractive and satisfying way to live in part just because the moral world of the lawyer is a simpler, less complicated, and less ambiguous world than the moral world of ordinary life. There is, I think, something quite seductive about being able to turn aside so many ostensibly difficult moral dilemmas and decisions with the reply: but that is not my concern; my job as a lawyer is not to judge the rights and wrong of the client or the cause; it is to defend as best I can my client's interests. . . .

But there is, of course, also an argument which seeks to demonstrate that it is good and not merely comfortable for lawyers to behave this way.

It is good, so the argument goes, that the lawyer's behavior and concomitant point of view are role-differentiated because the lawyer qua lawyer participates in a complex institution which functions well only if the individuals adhere to their institutional roles. . . .

When an individual is charged with having committed a crime, the trial is the mechanism by which we determine in our society whether or not the person is in fact guilty. Just imagine what would happen if lawyers were to refuse, for instance, to represent persons whom they thought to be guilty. . . . The private judgment of individual lawyers would in effect be substituted for the public, institutional judgment of the judge and jury. The amorality of lawyers helps to guarantee that every criminal defendant will have his or her day in court. . . .

[A]rguments that support the role-differentiated amorality of the lawyer on institutional grounds can succeed only if the enormous degree of trust and confidence in the institutions themselves is itself justified. . . . But the less certain we are entitled to be of either the rightness or the self-corrective nature of the larger institutions of which the professional is a part, the less apparent it is that we should encourage the professional to avoid direct engagement with the moral issues as they arise. And we are, today, I believe, certainly entitled to be quite skeptical both of the fairness and of the capacity for self-correction of our larger institutional mechanisms, including the legal system. . . .

Second, it is clear that there are definite character traits that the professional such as the lawyer must take on if the system is to work. What is less clear is that

they are admirable ones. Even if the role-differentiated amorality of the professional lawyer is justified by the virtues of the adversary system, this also means
that the lawyer qua lawyer will be encouraged to be competitive rather than
cooperative; aggressive rather than accommodating; ruthless rather than compassionate; and pragmatic rather than principled. This is, I think, part of the
logic of the role-differentiated behavior of lawyers in particular, and to a lesser
degree of professionals in general. . . .

Third, there is a special feature of the role-differentiated behavior of the lawyer that distinguishes it from the comparable behavior of other professionals.
What I have in mind can be brought out through the following question: Why is
it that it seems far less plausible to talk critically about the amorality of the doctor, for instance, who treats all patients irrespective of their moral character than
it does to talk critically about the comparable amorality of the lawyer? Why is it
that it seems so obviously sensible, simple and right for the doctor's behavior to
be narrowly and rigidly role-differentiated, i.e., just to try to cure those who are
ill? And why is it that at the very least it seems so complicated, uncertain, and
troublesome to decide whether it is right for the lawyer's behavior to be similarly
role-differentiated?[a]

The answer, I think, is twofold. To begin with . . . it is, so to speak, intrinsically
good to try to cure disease, but in no comparable way is it intrinsically good to
try to win every lawsuit or help every client realize his or her objective.[b] In
addition . . . , the lawyer's behavior is different in kind from the doctor's. The
lawyer — and especially the lawyer as advocate — directly says and affirms
things. The lawyer makes the case for the client. He or she tries to explain, persuade and convince others that the client's cause should prevail. . . . If the lawyer
actually believes everything that he or she asserts on behalf of the client, then it
appears to be proper to regard the lawyer as in fact embracing and endorsing
the points of view that he or she articulates. If the lawyer does not in fact believe
what is urged by way of argument, if the lawyer is only playing a role, then it
appears to be proper to tax the lawyer with hypocrisy and insincerity. To be sure,
actors in a play take on roles and say things that the characters, not the actors,
believe. But we know it is a play and that they are actors. The law courts are not,
however, theaters, and the lawyers both talk about justice and they genuinely
seek to persuade. . . . [T]he lawyer's words, thoughts, and convictions are, appar-

---

a. Consider John Kaplan & Jon R. Waltz, The Trial of Jack Ruby 5 (1965): "Oswald slumped,
moaning, to the floor while policemen piled in from all sides to drag down his assailant. . . . Within
four minutes of the shooting an ambulance arrived, and . . . rushed Oswald to the Parkland Memorial Hospital. There, in an emergency room just across the hall from the one in which President
Kennedy had been pronounced dead two days before, a twelve-man surgical team — the majority
of whom would probably have considered as somehow immoral any lawyer who attempted to save
Oswald's life by defending him in court — opened Oswald's chest and massaged his heart in
relays. . . . Two of the doctors who struggled to preserve Oswald's life had rendered similar service
to the expiring President." — Eds.

b. See also William Simon, Homo Psychologicus: Notes on a New Legal Formalism, 32 Stan. L.
Rev. 487, 501-502 (1980): "The analogies to such roles as doctor and priest are fundamentally
misleading. For unlike the relations defined by these roles, the lawyer-client relation is fundamentally impersonal and other-regarding. . . . In the case of doctors and priests, the principal impact
of the professional's activity occurs within the professional relation in the form of the change which
the patient or penitent undergoes. But in the case of lawyers, the principal impact occurs *outside*
the professional relation. The client benefits only to the extent that outsiders are affected." — Eds.

ently, for sale. . . . The verbal, role-differentiated behavior of the lawyer qua advocate puts the lawyer's integrity into question in a way that distinguishes the lawyer from the other professionals.

Fourth, . . . even if on balance the role-differentiated character of the lawyer's way of thinking and acting is ultimately deemed to be justifiable within the system on systemic instrumental grounds, it still remains the case that we do pay a social price for that way of thought and action. For to become and to be a professional, such as a lawyer, is to incorporate within oneself ways of behaving and ways of thinking that shape the whole person. . . .

NOTE

The questions raised by Wasserstrom are central to the work of all lawyers. The issues remain extremely controversial among academics and within the legal profession generally. For commentary that is critical of the highly role-differentiated standards of prevailing legal ethics, see Alan H. Goldman, The Moral Foundations of Professional Ethics (1980); William H. Simon, The Ethics of Criminal Defense, 91 Mich. L. Rev. 1703 (1993); William H. Simon, The Ideology of Advocacy, [1978] Wis. L. Rev. 29. Prominent discussions that largely support a role-differentiated standard and zealous advocacy on behalf of criminal defendants (including those who are guilty) include David Luban, Are Criminal Defenders Different?, 91 Mich. L. Rev. 1729 (1993); Charles J. Ogletree, Jr., Beyond Justifications: Seeking Motivations to Sustain Public Defenders, 106 Harv. L. Rev. 1239 (1993); Charles Fried, The Lawyer as Friend: The Moral Foundations of the Lawyer-Client Relation, 85 Yale L.J. 1060 (1976). A comprehensive treatment of the issues appears in David Luban, Lawyers and Justice (1988).

CHAPTER
2

THE JUSTIFICATION
OF PUNISHMENT

A. WHAT IS PUNISHMENT?

INTRODUCTORY NOTE

The proper justification for criminal punishment is a subject of continuing controversy in jurisprudence and criminal law. In Section B below we examine the issues in detail. But before exploring the terms of that debate, which can occasionally seem a bit abstract, we believe it necessary for students to have clearly in mind a concrete conception of what criminal punishment *is*. For example, we will want to consider whether it is justified, in order to promote effective deterrence, to impose "criminal punishment" on those who cause certain kinds of serious harm, even when we cannot prove that they caused the harm deliberately or negligently. In examining that question, it is essential to keep in mind exactly what that "criminal punishment" will consist of.

In broad outline, the principal forms of criminal punishment are familiar. Punishment may consist of a fine, probation, imprisonment, or some combination of these three. Some especially heinous crimes may be subject to the death penalty. Less obviously, the conviction itself is a form of punishment, carrying with it a social stigma, a barrier to future employment, and a risk of enhanced punishment in the event of a future offense.

Fines entail the payment of a money penalty to the court; failure to pay the fine can lead to imprisonment. Probation ordinarily entails certain restrictions on travel and behavior (for example, no use of drugs or association with former gang cohorts). Probation may also involve an obligation to report periodically to a probation officer, but "nonreporting" probation is not uncommon. In practice, the most important consequence of probation is that if probation conditions are violated or if a subsequent offense is committed, probation can be revoked, and the offender then faces imprisonment for the original offense.

Contemporary courts are now actively developing "intermediate sanctions" less harsh than imprisonment but more severe than probation. These include weeks or months of home detention, mandated community service, or "intensive-supervision" probation (which often includes mandatory counseling or drug treatment). Again, failure to satisfy the conditions of an intermediate sanction exposes the offender to imprisonment.

In a sense, then, imprisonment represents the quintessential criminal punishment. Though not inflicted in every case, it is almost always an option that the judge has discretion to impose. And even when not imposed, imprisonment remains in the background as a possible consequence of any failure to meet conditions of a fine, probation, or intermediate sanction.

The meaning of imprisonment is obvious and yet, for most of us, unfamiliar. The remaining materials in this section present some aspects of what incarceration entails in contemporary America, with a particular focus on the large, medium- to high-security prison that is now typical. A sense of what imprisonment means in practice can serve as a preface to a discussion of the circumstances under which it is ever justified to inflict this kind of sanction.

GRESHAM M. SYKES, THE SOCIETY OF CAPTIVES
65-75 (1971)

THE DEPRIVATION OF GOODS AND SERVICES . . .

[T]here are a number of prison officials who will argue that some inmates are better off in prison, in strictly material terms, than they could ever hope to be in the rough-and-tumble economic life of the free community. Possibly this is so, but . . . [t]he average inmate finds himself in a harshly Spartan environment which he defines as painfully depriving. . . . In modern Western culture, material possessions are so large a part of the individual's conception of himself that to be stripped of them is to be attacked at the deepest layers of personality. . . .

THE DEPRIVATION OF HETEROSEXUAL RELATIONSHIPS

Unlike the prisoner in many Latin-American countries, the inmate of the maximum security prison in New Jersey does not enjoy the privilege of so-called conjugal visits. And in those brief times when the prisoner is allowed to see his wife, mistress, or "female friend," the women must sit on one side of a plate glass window and the prisoner on the other, communicating by means of a phone under the scrutiny of a guard. . . . [I]t is clear that the lack of heterosexual intercourse is a frustrating experience for the imprisoned criminal and that it is a frustration which weighs heavily and painfully on his mind during his prolonged confinement. . . .[a]

THE DEPRIVATION OF SECURITY

However strange it may appear that society has chosen to reduce the criminality of the offender by forcing him to associate with more than a thousand other

---

a. Although Sykes' discussion focuses on the plight of the heterosexual prisoner, gay men often suffer serious problems as well. In some prisons, gays are especially likely to become targets for rape and other abuses. — EDS.

criminals for years on end, there is one meaning of this involuntary union which is obvious — the individual prisoner is thrown into prolonged intimacy with other men who in many cases have a long history of violent, aggressive behavior. It is a situation which can prove to be anxiety-provoking even for the hardened recidivist and it is in this light that we can understand the comment of an inmate of the New Jersey State Prison who said, "The worst thing about prison is you have to live with other prisoners."

The fact that the imprisoned criminal sometimes views his fellow prisoners as "vicious" or "dangerous" may seem a trifle unreasonable. Other inmates, after all, are men like himself, bearing the legal stigma of conviction. But even if the individual prisoner believes that he himself is not the sort of person who is likely to attack or exploit weaker and less resourceful fellow captives, he is apt to view others with more suspicion. And . . . regardless of the patterns of mutual aid and support which may flourish in the inmate population, there are a sufficient number of outlaws within this group of outlaws to deprive the average prisoner of that sense of security which comes from living among men who can be reasonably expected to abide by the rules of society. . . .

An important aspect of this disturbingly problematical world is the fact that the inmate is acutely aware that sooner or later he will be "tested" — that someone will "push" him to see how far they can go and that he must be prepared to fight for the safety of his person and his possessions. If he should fail, he will thereafter be an object of contempt, constantly in danger of being attacked by other inmates who view him as an obvious victim, as a man who cannot or will not defend his rights. And yet if he succeeds, he may well become a target for the prisoner who wishes to prove himself, who seeks to enhance his own prestige by defeating the man with a reputation for toughness. Thus both success and failure in defending one's self against the aggressions of fellow captives may serve to provoke fresh attacks and no man stands assured of the future.

The prisoner's loss of security arouses acute anxiety, in short, not just because violent acts of aggression and exploitation occur but also because such behavior constantly calls into question the individual's ability to cope with it. . . . These uncertainties constitute an ego threat for the individual forced to live in prolonged intimacy with criminals, regardless of the nature or extent of his own criminality; . . . the prison inmate can never feel safe.

NOTES

1. Prison violence. Accurate estimates of the prevalence of rape and other serious assaults in prisons are difficult to obtain, and informed observers are to some extent divided in their opinions. The situation undoubtedly varies from prison to prison. Overall there seems little question that the threat of violent attack is a significant, and sometimes extremely serious, problem for the American prisoner. Some observers are especially pessimistic. See, e.g., Kathleen Engel & Stanley Rothman, Prison Violence and the Paradox of Reform, 73 The Public Interest 91 (Fall 1983): "Men's prisons across the country are besieged by violence. . . . The realities of today's prisons are grim indeed." Similarly, in United States v. Bailey, 444 U.S. 394, 420-422 (1980), Justice Blackmun, dissenting, commented:

The complaints that this Court, and every other American appellate court, receives almost daily from prisoners about conditions of incarceration, about filth, about homosexual rape, and about brutality are not always the mouthings of the purely malcontent. The Court itself acknowledges that the conditions these respondents complained about do exist. . . . And the Government concedes: "In light of prison conditions that even now prevail in the United States, it would be the rare inmate who could not convince himself that continued incarceration would be harmful to his health or safety." Brief for United States 27.

One factor contributing to the prevalence of prison violence is that when constitutional litigation in the 1960s and 1970s restricted the ability of prison guards to discipline inmates through summary corporal punishments, prisoners became harder to control, and in many prisons the reduction in brutality perpetrated by guards was more than offset by the increase in abuses perpetrated by inmates. See James B. Jacobs, New Perspectives on Prisons and Imprisonment 57 (1983); Engel & Rothman, supra at 91. Few prison administrators or reformers advocate a return to the days of freewheeling, unrestricted disciplinary powers for prison guards. But to have both a safe prison and due process restrictions on official discipline requires improvements in prison design and significantly higher ratios of guards to prisoners; these steps imply substantial increases in per-prisoner expenditures that legislatures hesitate to authorize and that courts cannot easily enforce. As a result, inmate violence persists in many prisons, despite court decrees and conscientious efforts by prison administrators to control it.

Nonetheless, a number of knowledgeable observers suggest that the problem of violence may no longer be so acute, at least in many prisons.[1] One long-term Louisiana inmate has written:[2]

While [rapes] used to be a regular feature of life here at the Louisiana State Penitentiary, they are now a rare occurrence. . . . In 1976, Federal District Court Judge E. Gordon West ordered a massive crackdown on overall violence at the prison, which paved the way for the allocation of money, manpower, and sophisticated electronic equipment to do the job. Since then, *any* kind of violence at all between inmates elicits swift administrative reprisal and certain prosecution. This, more than anything else, has made Angola [prison] safe for the average youngster coming into the prison today.

2. Crowding. One characteristic of American prisons that is important both as a cause of prison violence and as a serious problem in its own right is pervasive overcrowding. Overcrowded conditions have proved highly resistant to reform efforts because rising rates of incarceration and lengthening sentences have far outstripped the willingness and ability of states to build new prisons. Although efficient prison management requires prisons to operate significantly below their full capacity levels,[3] at year end 1992 the federal system was operating at 37 percent above capacity, and 43 states were likewise operating well above their capacity levels.[4] Many states are under court orders to reduce overcrowding, but

1. See, e.g, Norval Morris, The Modern Prison, in David Rothman & Norval Morris, eds., The History of Imprisonment (1995).
2. Walter Rideau, The Sexual Jungle, quoted in Morris, supra footnote 1.
3. See U.S. Dept. of Justice, Bureau of Justice Statistics, Prisoners in 1992, at 6 (1993).
4. Id. On the ambiguities in the concept of prison "capacity" and the difficulties in measuring it accurately, see Franklin E. Zimring, Are State Prisons Undercrowded?, 4 Fed. Sent. Rptr. 34 (May/June 1992).

as inmate admissions rise and construction lags, courts are often reluctant to
order the release of violent offenders. As a result, severely overcrowded conditions have persisted on a "temporary" basis in most states since the 1970s and
show no signs of abating. See Stephen D. Gottfredson, Institutional Responses
to Prison Crowding, 12 N.Y.U. Rev. L. & Soc. Change 259 (1983).

3. *Women in prison.* During the past decade the number of women in prison
has grown almost twice as fast as the number of men, but women still represent
less than 6 percent of the total prison population.[5] Physical danger, though occasionally a concern in women's prisons, is generally a less serious problem than
it is in men's prisons. But women inmates face other difficulties. Because most
states have few women's prisons, female prisoners are likely to be sent much
farther from their homes and families than male prisoners are. And women's
prisons typically afford far fewer educational and vocational programs than
men's prisons do. For a discussion of the problems, see Nicole Hahn Rafter,
Partial Justice: Women, Prisons, and Social Control (2d ed. 1990).

4. *Different kinds of prisons.* The foregoing descriptions of prison life focus primarily on conditions in medium- and high-security institutions. Although these
kinds of prisons are now the most common destination for the incarcerated offender, other types of custodial institutions remain important. Some minimum-
security prisons and "prison camps" operate without guard towers or walls, and
afford dormitory-type rooms along with modestly good recreational facilities. In
contrast, prisons in the maximum-security category typically feature high walls,
long blocks of barred cells, and highly overcrowded conditions. Although many
minimum-security prisoners avoid the worst forms of violence and degradation,
some of the other consequences of imprisonment described by Sykes are probably inherent in any form of incarceration. To some extent, of course, imprisonment is *supposed to be* unpleasant. To what extent should society seek to moderate
or reinforce the pains that are intrinsic to penal confinement?

B. WHY PUNISH?

INTRODUCTORY NOTE

The material in this section addresses the question of the justification of the
social practice of punishing criminal offenders. The first subsection presents a
variety of viewpoints organized according to what are conventionally taken to be
the major purposes of punishment. The second subsection presents a number
of case studies designed to provide concrete settings for examining the general
ideas in the first subsection.

As a framework for both subsections, consider the following statutory statements concerning the purposes of punishment.

MODEL PENAL CODE: *Section 1.02.* (1) The general purposes of the provisions governing the definition of offenses are: (a) to forbid and prevent conduct
that unjustifiably and inexcusably inflicts or threatens substantial harm to indi-

---

5. See U.S. Dept. of Justice, Bureau of Justice Statistics, Women in Prison 1, 2 (1991).

vidual or public interests; (b) to subject to public control persons whose conduct indicates that they are disposed to commit crimes; . . . (e) to differentiate on reasonable grounds between serious and minor offenses.

(2) The general purposes of the provisions governing the sentencing and treatment of offenders are: (a) to prevent the commission of offenses; (b) to promote the correction and rehabilitation of offenders; (c) to safeguard offenders against excessive, disproportionate or arbitrary punishment. . . .

NEW YORK PENAL LAW: *Section 1.05.* The general purposes of the provisions of this chapter are: . . .

5. To insure the public safety by preventing the commission of offenses through the deterrent influence of the sentences authorized, the rehabilitation of those convicted, and their confinement when required in the interests of public protection.

CALIFORNIA PENAL CODE: *Section 1170.* The Legislature finds and declares that the purpose of imprisonment for crime is punishment. This purpose is best served by terms proportionate to the seriousness of the offense with provision for uniformity in the sentences of offenders committing the same offense under similar circumstances. The Legislature further finds and declares that the elimination of disparity and the provision of uniformity of sentences can best be achieved by determinate sentences fixed by statute in proportion to the seriousness of the offense as determined by the Legislature to be imposed by the court with specified discretion.

1.   Perspectives on Punishment

INTRODUCTORY NOTE

There is a large literature on the subject of punishment. For a valuable introductory treatment, see the article by Kent Greenawalt, Punishment, in Encyclopedia of Crime and Justice 1336 (1983). Bibliographies may be found in Edward Pincoffs, The Rationale of Legal Punishment 139 et seq. (1966); Herbert Morris, Freedom and Responsibility 546-547 (1961) (the bibliography is brought up-to-date in K. Pecarovich, Bibliography of Responsibility, 49 L. & Contemp. Prob. 277 (1986)). The ideas of Professor H. L. A. Hart have been highly influential in recent years. His essays on punishment are contained in Punishment and Responsibility (1968), available in paperback.

a.   Retribution

i.   What Is Retribution?

IMMANUEL KANT, THE PHILOSOPHY OF LAW (W. Hastie tr. 1887): The right of administering punishment is the right of the sovereign as the supreme power to inflict pain upon a subject on account of a crime committed by him. . . .

Judicial or juridical punishment (*poena forensis*) is to be distinguished from natural punishment (*poena naturalis*), in which crime as vice punishes itself, and does not as such come within the cognizance of the legislator. Juridical punishment can never be administered merely as a means of promoting another good either with regard to the criminal himself or to civil society, but must in all cases be imposed only because the individual on whom it is inflicted *has committed a crime*. For one man ought never to be dealt with merely as a means subservient to the purpose of another, nor be [treated as though he were subject to the law of property.] Against such treatment his inborn personality has a right to protect him, even although he may be condemned to lose his civil personality. He must first be found guilty and *punishable*, before there can be any thought of drawing from his punishment any benefit for himself or his fellow-citizens. The penal law is a categorical imperative; and woe to him who creeps through the serpent-windings of utilitarianism to discover some advantage that may discharge him from the justice of punishment, or even from the due measure of it, according to the Pharisaic maxim: "It is better that *one* man should die than that the whole people should perish." For if justice and righteousness perish, human life would no longer have any value in the world. What, then, is to be said of such a proposal as to keep a criminal alive who has been condemned to death, on his being given to understand that if he agreed to certain dangerous experiments being performed upon him, he would be allowed to survive if he came happily through them? It is argued that physicians might thus obtain new information that would be of value to the commonweal. But a court of justice would repudiate with scorn any proposal of this kind if made to it by the medical faculty; for justice would cease to be justice if it were bartered away for any consideration whatever.

But what is the mode and measure of punishment which public justice takes as its principle and standard? It is just the principle of equality, by which the pointer of the scale of justice is made to incline no more to the one side than the other. It may be rendered by saying that the undeserved evil which any one commits on another is to be regarded as perpetrated on himself. Hence it may be said: "If you slander another, you slander yourself; if you steal from another, you steal from yourself; if you strike another, you strike yourself; if you kill another, you kill yourself." This is the right of retaliation (*jus talionis*); and properly understood, it is the only principle which in regulating a public court, as distinguished from mere private judgment, can definitely assign both the quality and the quantity of a just penalty. All other standards are wavering and uncertain; and on account of other considerations involved in them, they contain no principle conformable to the sentence of pure and strict justice. . . .

But how then would we render the statement: "If you *steal* from another, you steal from yourself"? In this way, that whoever steals anything makes the property of all insecure; he therefore robs himself of all security in property, according to the right of retaliation. Such a one has nothing, and can acquire nothing, but he has the will to live; and this is only possible by others supporting him. But as the state should not do this gratuitously, he must for this purpose yield his powers to the state to be used in penal labour; and thus he falls for a time, or it may be life, into a condition of slavery. But whoever has committed murder must *die*. There is, in this case, no juridical substitute or surrogate that can be given or taken for the satisfaction of justice. There is no *likeness* or proportion between life, however painful, and death; and therefore there is no equality between the crime of murder and the retaliation of it but what is judicially accomplished by the execution of the criminal. His death, however, must be kept free from all maltreatment that would make the humanity suffering in his person loathsome or abominable. Even if a civil society resolved to dissolve itself with the consent of all its members — as might be supposed in the case of a people inhabiting an island resolving to separate and scatter themselves through the whole world — the last murderer lying in the prison ought to be executed before the resolution was carried out. This ought to be done in order that every one may realize the desert of his deeds, and that bloodguiltiness may not remain upon the people; for otherwise they might all be regarded as participators in the murder as a public violation of justice.

2 JAMES FITZJAMES STEPHEN, A HISTORY OF THE CRIMINAL LAW OF ENGLAND 81-82 (1883 ed.): [T]he sentence of the law is to the moral sentiment of the public in relation to any offence what a seal is to hot wax. It converts into a permanent final judgment what might otherwise be a transient sentiment. The mere general suspicion or knowledge that a man has done something dishonest may never be brought to a point, and the disapprobation excited by it may in time pass away, but the fact that he has been convicted and punished as a thief stamps a mark upon him for life. In short, the infliction of punishment by law gives definite expression and a solemn ratification and justification to the hatred which is excited by the commission of the offence, and which constitutes the moral or popular as distinguished from the conscientious sanction of that part of morality which is also sanctioned by the criminal law. The criminal law thus proceeds upon the principle that it is morally right to hate criminals, and it confirms and justifies that sentiment by inflicting upon criminals punishments which express it. . . . I am also of opinion that this close alliance between criminal law and moral sentiment is in all ways healthy and advantageous to the community. I think it highly desirable that criminals should be hated, that the punishments inflicted upon them should be so contrived as to give expression to that hatred, and to justify it so far as the public provision of means for expressing and gratifying a healthy natural sentiment can justify and encourage it. . . . No doubt they are peculiarly liable to abuse, and in some states of society are commonly in excess of what is desirable, and so require restraint rather than excitement, but unqualified denunciations of them are as ill-judged as unqualified denunciations of sexual passion. The forms in which deliberate anger and righteous disapprobation are expressed, and the execution of criminal justice is the most emphatic of such forms, stand to the one set of passions in the same relation in which marriage stands to the other.[a]

ROYAL COMMISSION ON CAPITAL PUNISHMENT, Minutes of Evidence, Ninth Day, Dec. 1, 1949, Memorandum Submitted by the Rt. Hon. Lord Justice Denning, 207: Whilst everyone agrees that crimes must be punished, there is

a. Stephen put this idea more pointedly in the first, 1863, edition of A History of the Criminal Law of England, Volume 2, p. 99: "The criminal law stands to the passion of revenge in much the same relation as marriage to the sexual appetite." There is a story that on an examination a student (one presumes English) once put the idea as follows: "Stephen maintains that marriage is to love what punishment is to crime." See Cross, The Making of English Criminal Law, (6) Sir James Fitzjames Stephen [1976] Crim. L. Rev. 652, 654. — EDS.

profound disagreement as to the form which punishment should take. Many are inclined to test the efficacy of punishment solely by its value as a deterrent: but this is too narrow a view. Punishment is the way in which society expresses its denunciation of wrong doing: and, in order to maintain respect for law, it is essential that the punishment inflicted for grave crimes should adequately reflect the revulsion felt by the great majority of citizens for them. It is a mistake to consider the objects of punishment as being deterrent or reformative or preventive and nothing else. If that were so, we should not send to prison a man who was guilty of motor manslaughter, but only disqualify him from driving; but would public opinion be content with this? The truth is that some crimes are so outrageous that society insists on adequate punishment, because the wrong-doer deserves it, irrespective of whether it is a deterrent or not. . . . Some cases are so outrageous that, irrespective of the value of the death penalty as a deterrent, the great bulk of the community consider that the only fitting penalty is death. In my view the ultimate justification of any punishment is, not that it is a deterrent, but that it is the emphatic denunciation by the community of a crime: and from this point of view, there are some murders which, in the present state of public opinion, demand the most emphatic denunciation of all, namely the death penalty.

EMILE DURKHEIM, THE DIVISION OF LABOR IN SOCIETY 108-109 (Simpson trans. 1964): Although [punishment] proceeds from a quite mechanical reaction, from movements which are passionate and in great part non-reflective, it does play a useful role. Only this role is not where we ordinarily look for it. It does not serve, or else only serves quite secondarily, in correcting the culpable or in intimidating possible followers. From this point of view, its efficacy is justly doubtful and, in any case, mediocre. Its true function is to maintain social cohesion intact, while maintaining all its vitality in the common conscience. Denied so categorically, it would necessarily lose its energy, if an emotional reaction of the community did not come to compensate its loss, and it would result in a breakdown of social solidarity. It is necessary, then, that it be affirmed forcibly at the very moment when it is contradicted, and the only means of affirming it is to express the unanimous aversion which the crime continues to inspire, by an authentic act which can consist only in suffering inflicted upon the agent. Thus, while being the necessary product of the causes which engender it, this suffering is not a gratuitous cruelty. It is the sign which witnesses that collective sentiments are always collective, that the communion of spirits in the same faith rests on a solid foundation, and accordingly, that it is repairing the evil which the crime inflicted upon society. That is why we are right in saying that the criminal must suffer in proportion to his crime, why theories which refuse to punishment any expiatory character appear as so many spirits subversive of the social order. It is because these doctrines could be practiced only in a society where the whole common conscience would be nearly gone. Without this necessary satisfaction, what we call the moral conscience could not be conserved. We can thus say without paradox that punishment is above all designed to act upon upright people, for, since it serves to heal the wounds made upon collective sentiments, it can fill this role only where these sentiments exist, and commensurately with their vivacity. Of course, by warning already disturbed spirits of a new enfeeblement of the collective soul, it can even stop attacks from multiplying, but this result, however useful, is only a particular counter blow. In short, in order to form an exact idea of punishment, we must reconcile the two contradictory theories which deal with it: that which sees it as expiation, and that which makes it a weapon for social defense. It is certain that it functions for the protection of society, but that is because it is expiatory. Moreover, if it must be expiatory, that does not mean that by some mystical virtue pain compensates for the error, but rather that it can produce a socially useful effect only under this condition.

MICHAEL S. MOORE, THE MORAL WORTH OF RETRIBUTION, in F. Schoeman, ed., Responsibility, Character and Emotions 179 (1987): *Retributivism* is the view that punishment is justified by the moral culpability of those who receive it. A retributivist punishes because, and only because, the offender deserves it. Retributivism thus stands in stark contrast to utilitarian views that justify punishment of past offenses by the greater good of preventing future offenses. It also contrasts sharply with rehabilitative views, according to which punishment is justified by the reforming good it does the criminal.

Less clearly, retributivism also differs from a variety of views that are often paraded as retributivist, but that in fact are not. . . . The leading confusions seem to me to be [several].

1. First, retributivism is sometimes identified with a particular measure of punishment such as *lex talionis,* an eye for an eye, or with a kind of punishment such as the death penalty. Yet retributivism answers a question prior to the questions to which these could be answers. True enough, retributivists at some point have to answer the "how much" and "what type" questions for specific offenses, and they are committed to the principle that punishment should be graded in proportion to desert; but they are not committed to any particular penalty scheme nor to any particular penalty as being deserved. Separate argument is needed to answer these "how much" and "what type" questions, *after* one has described why one is punishing at all. It is quite possible to be a retributivist and to be against both the death penalty and *lex talionis,* the idea that crimes should be punished by like acts being done to the criminal.

2. . . . [R]etributivism is *not* "the view that only the guilty are to be punished." A retributivist will subscribe to such a view, but that is not what is distinctive about retributivism. The distinctive aspect of retributivism is that the moral desert of an offender is a *sufficient* reason to punish him or her; the principle [that only the guilty may be punished makes] such moral desert only a *necessary* condition of punishment. Other reasons — typically, crime prevention reasons — must be added to moral desert, in this view, for punishment to be justified. Retributivism has no room for such additional reasons. That future crime might also be prevented by punishment is a happy surplus for a retributivist, but no part of the justification for punishing.

3. Retributivism is not the view that punishment of offenders satisfies the desires for vengeance of their victims. . . . A retributivist can justify punishment as deserved even if the criminal's victims are indifferent (or even opposed) to punishing the one who hurt them. Indeed, a retributivist should urge punishment on all offenders who deserve it, even if *no* victims wanted it.

4. [R]etributivism is not the view that the preferences of all citizens (not just crime victims) should be satisfied. A preference utilitarian might well believe, as did Sir James Fitzjames Stephen, that punishment should be exacted "for th

sake of gratifying the feeling of hatred — call it revenge, resentment, or what you will — which the contemplation of such [criminal] conduct excites in healthily constituted minds . . . ," or that "the feeling of hatred and the desire of vengeance . . . are important elements of human nature which ought . . . to be satisfied in a regular public and legal manner." Yet a retributivist need not believe such things, but only that morally culpable persons should be punished, irrespective of what other citizens feel, desire, or prefer.

5. [R]etributivism is not the view that punishment is justified because without it vengeful citizens would take the law into their own hands. . . . Punishment for a retributivist is not justified by the need to prevent private violence, which is an essentially utilitarian justification. Even in the most well-mannered state, those criminals who deserve punishment should get it, according to retributivism.

6. Nor is retributivism to be confused with denunciatory theories of punishment. In this latter view punishment is justified because punishment is the vehicle through which society can express its condemnation of the criminal's behavior. This is a utilitarian theory, not a retributive one, for punishment is in this view to be justified by the good consequences it achieves — either the psychological satisfactions denunciation achieves, or the prevention of private violence, or the prevention of future crimes through the education benefits of such denunciation. A retributivist justifies punishment by none of these supposed good consequences of punishing. . . .

Retributivism is a very straightforward theory of punishment: We are justified in punishing because and only because offenders deserve it. Moral culpability ("desert") is in such a view both a sufficient as well as a necessary condition of liability to punitive sanctions. Such justification gives society more than merely a right to punish culpable offenders. It does this, making it not unfair to punish them, but retributivism justifies more than this. For a retributivist, the moral culpability of an offender also gives society the *duty* to punish. Retributivism, in other words, is truly a theory of justice such that, if it is true, we have an obligation to set up institutions so that retribution is achieved.

ii. Views on Retribution

HERBERT MORRIS, ON GUILT AND INNOCENCE 33-34 (1976): I want to . . . set . . . out two complex types of institutions both of which are designed to maintain some degree of social control. In the one a central concept is punishment for wrongdoing and in the other the central concepts are control of dangerous individuals and treatment of disease.

Let us first turn attention to the institutions in which punishment is involved. The institutions I describe will resemble those we ordinarily think of as institutions of punishment; they will have, however, additional features we associate with a system of just punishment.

Let us suppose that men are constituted roughly as they now are, with a rough equivalence in strength and abilities, a capacity to be injured by each other and to make judgments that such injury is undesirable, a limited strength of will, and a capacity to reason and to conform conduct to rules. Applying to the conduct of these men are a group of rules, ones I shall label "primary," which closely resemble the core rules of our criminal law, rules that prohibit violence and deception and compliance with which provides benefits for all persons. These benefits consist of noninterference by others with what each person values, such matters as continuance of life and bodily security. The rules define a sphere for each person then, which is immune from interference by others. Making possible this mutual benefit is the assumption by individuals of a burden. The burden consists in the exercise of self-restraint by individuals over inclinations that would, if satisfied, directly interfere or create a substantial risk of interference with others in proscribed ways. If a person fails to exercise self-restraint even though he might have and gives in to such inclinations, he renounces a burden which others have voluntarily assumed and thus gains an advantage which others, who have restrained themselves, do not possess. This system, then, is one in which the rules establish a mutuality of benefit and burden and in which the benefits of noninterference are conditional upon the assumption of burdens.

Connecting punishment with the violation of these primary rules, and making public the provision for punishment, is both reasonable and just. First, it is only reasonable that those who voluntarily comply with the rules be provided some assurance that they will not be assuming burdens which others are unprepared to assume. Their disposition to comply voluntarily will diminish as they learn that others are with impunity renouncing burdens they are assuming. Second, fairness dictates that a system in which benefits and burdens are equally distributed have a mechanism designed to prevent a maldistribution in the benefits and burdens. Thus, sanctions are attached to noncompliance with the primary rules so as to induce compliance with the primary rules among those who may be disinclined to obey. In this way the likelihood of an unfair distribution is diminished.

Third, it is just to punish those who have violated the rules and caused the unfair distribution of benefits and burdens. A person who violates the rules has something others have — the benefits of the system — but by renouncing what others have assumed, the burdens of self-restraint, he has acquired an unfair advantage. Matters are not even until this advantage is in some way erased. Another way of putting it is that he owes something to others, for he has something that does not rightfully belong to him. Justice — that is punishing such individuals — restores the equilibrium of benefits and burdens by taking from the individual what he owes, that is, exacting the debt. It is important to see that the equilibrium may be restored in another way. Forgiveness — with its legal analogue of a pardon — while not the righting of an unfair distribution by making one pay his debt is, nevertheless, a restoring of the equilibrium by forgiving the debt. Forgiveness may be viewed, at least in some types of cases, as a gift after the fact, erasing a debt, which had the gift been given before the fact, would not have created a debt. But the practice of pardoning has to proceed sensitively, for it may endanger in a way the practice of justice does not, the maintenance of an equilibrium of benefits and burdens. If all are indiscriminately pardoned less incentive is provided individuals to restrain their inclinations, thus increasing the incidence of persons taking what they do not deserve.

MICHAEL S. MOORE, LAW AND PSYCHIATRY 238-243 (1984): Once one grants that there are two sorts of prima facie justifications of punishment — effecting a net social gain (utilitarian) and giving just deserts (retributivist) — one can also see that in addition to the two pure theories of punishment there

1. Where it is *groundless:* where there is no mischief for it to prevent; the act not being mischievous upon the whole.   ~adultum ~prostitution, consuled sodomy~

2. Where it must be *inefficacious:* where it cannot act so as to prevent the mischief.   ~post facto~

3. Where it is *unprofitable;* or too expensive: where the mischief it would produce would be greater than what it prevented.

4. Where it is *needless:* where the mischief may be prevented, or cease of itself, without it: that is, at a cheaper rate. . . .   ~juvenile mischief~

JOHN L. MACKIE, RETRIBUTION: A TEST CASE FOR ETHICAL OBJECTIVITY, in Joel Feinberg & Hyman Gross, eds., Philosophy of Law 677 (1991):

[R]etribuo in Latin means "I pay back." But surely the central notion is not that the criminal repays a debt, pays something back to society, but that someone else pays the criminal back for what he has done. Punitive retribution is the repaying of harm with harm, as reward is the repaying of benefit with benefit. We can class as an essentially retributivist approach any that sees at least some prima facie rightness in the repaying of evil with evil, especially a proportionate evil.

. . . But this is a very dark saying. *Why* should it be so? Is there any way in which we can make sense of this curious principle, at least by relating it to [a] network of other moral ideas? . . .

Repayment: How does the criminal's suffering or deprivation pay anything to society? No doubt repaying a debt often hurts the person who pays it, but it does not follow that anything that hurts someone amounts to his repaying a debt. . . . So this account is simply incoherent unless it is transformed into a theory of reparations, which are not punishment, or into the satisfaction theory which . . . is consequentialist and will not explain retributivism.

Annulment: This notion . . . goes back at least to Hegel. . . . Hegel's idea seems to be that as long as a criminal goes scot-free, the crime itself still exists, still flourishes, but when the criminal is adequately punished the crime itself is somehow wiped out. It is not, therefore, by any sort of repayment or restitution that "right is restored," but just by trampling on the previously flourishing crime. But this notion is simply incoherent: there is no comprehensible way in which a penalty wipes out an otherwise still-existing crime. . . .

Kant's remark that if the "last murderer" is not executed blood-guilt will adhere to the people . . . might be . . . understood as something like an anticipation of Hegel's notion of annulment. The guilt, the badness, of the crime is still floating around as long as the criminal is unpunished, and by letting him go free the people would share in this guilt as accessories after the act. But to suppose that this guilt is extinguished by the carrying out of the penalty requires the incomprehensible Hegelian notion of annulment, and to say that the people would be accessories if they did not punish the criminal presupposes, and therefore cannot explain, the principle that the crime in itself morally requires the penalty.

Fair play: Here the suggestion is that the various members of society are all in competition with one another, a competition governed by rules. The criminal has gained an unfair advantage by breaking the rules; to restore fairness this advantage must be taken away from him. Unlike our last two approaches, this one is not incoherent; it makes perfectly good sense in certain contexts. It has its clearest exemplification in the award of a penalty in football . . . when there has been a foul. . . . It is also retributivist in our basic sense of being retrospective; the justification is complete when the penalty has been imposed; fairness has (roughly at least) been restored, irrespective of whether there are or are not any further desirable consequences. The trouble with this approach, however, is that it has little relation to most cases of punishment. Any serious attempt to apply it would lead to bizarre results, not at all well correlated with what is thought of as desert or degree of wrongness or guilt. It implies that penalties should as far as possible be proportional to the advantage that the criminal has gained. . . . Thus if a businessman has secured a contract worth $100,000, but has exceeded the speed limit in order to get to the relevant appointment on time, he should presumably be fined $100,000, whereas a fine of $1 would be enough for someone who murders a blind cripple to rob him of $1. And so on. Unsuccessful attempts at murder (or anything else) should not be punished at all. . . .

What is basically wrong with the fair play approach . . . is that it focuses on the advantage that may have been gained by the criminal in some sort of social competition, whereas the point of punishment surely lies not in this but in wrongness of his act and the harm that he has done or tried to do. We can agree that he has acted unfairly, and that this implies that he cannot say that it is unfair if he suffers some proportionate penalty. . . . But [it] is still quite unclear how fairness *to the law abiding* is secured by the punishing of the law-breaker in itself, that is, unless this punishment secures some benefit for the law-abiding. So the fair play theory still fails to yield any defence of the principle of positive retributivism. . . .

Every one of these approaches fails completely to supply any coherent expansion or explanation of the retributivist principle, and, as far as I know, there are no others on offer. On the other hand it is plain that a considerable number of people have what would be called an intuition that a wrong action in itself calls for the infliction of suffering or deprivation on the agent. . . .

In conclusion, therefore, I maintain that it is easy to understand why we have a deeply ingrained tendency to see wrong actions as calling for penalties and some sorts of good actions as calling for reward. Though retributive principles cannot be defended, with any plausibility, as allegedly objective moral truths, retributive attitudes can be readily understood and explained as sentiments that have grown up and are sustained partly through biological processes, and partly through analogous sociological ones.

JEFFRIE MURPHY, MARXISM AND RETRIBUTION

2 Phil. & Pub. Aff. 217 (1973)

Is it not a delusion to substitute for the individual with his real motives, with multifarious social circumstances pressing upon him, the abstraction of "free will" — one among the many qualities of man for man himself? . . . Is there not a necessity for deeply reflecting upon an alteration of the system that breeds these crimes, instead of glorifying the hangman who executes a lot of criminals to make room only for the supply of new ones?

> Karl Marx, Capital Punishment,
> N.Y. Daily Tribune, Feb. 18, 1853

In outline . . . I want to argue that when Marx challenges the material adequacy of the retributive theory of punishment, he is suggesting that it presupposes a certain view of man and society that is false. . . .

In trying to develop this case, I shall draw primarily upon Willem Bonger's Criminality and Economic Conditions (1916), one of the few sustained Marxist analyses of crime and punishment. . . .

Put bluntly, his theory is as follows. Criminality has two primary sources: (1) need and deprivation on the part of disadvantaged members of society, and (2) motives of greed and selfishness that are generated and reinforced in competitive capitalistic societies. Thus criminality is economically based — either directly in the case of crimes from need, or indirectly in the case of crimes growing out of motives or psychological states that are encouraged and developed in capitalistic society. In Marx's own language, such an economic system alienates men from themselves and from each other. It alienates men from themselves by creating motives and needs that are not "truly human." It alienates men from their fellows by encouraging a kind of competitiveness that forms an obstacle to the development of genuine communities to replace mere social aggregates. And in Bonger's thought, the concept of community is central. He argues that moral relations and moral restraint are possible only in genuine communities characterized by bonds of sympathetic identification and mutual aid resting upon a perception of common humanity. All this he includes under the general rubric of reciprocity. In the absence of reciprocity in this rich sense, moral relations among men will break down and criminality will increase. Within bourgeois society, then, crimes are to be regarded as normal, and not psychopathological, acts. That is, they grow out of need, greed, indifference to others, and sometimes even a sense of indignation — all, alas, perfectly typical human motives. . . .

No doubt this claim will strike many as extreme and intemperate — a sample of the old-fashioned Marxist rhetoric that sophisticated intellectuals have outgrown. Those who are inclined to react in this way might consider just one sobering fact: of the 1.3 million criminal offenders handled each day by some agency of the United States correctional system, the vast majority (80 percent on some estimates) are members of the lowest 15-percent income level — that percent which is below the "poverty level" as defined by the Social Security Administration. Unless one wants to embrace the belief that all these people are poor because they are bad, it might be well to reconsider Bonger's suggestion that many of them are "bad" because they are poor. At any rate, let us suppose for purposes of discussion that Bonger's picture of the relation between crime and economic conditions is generally accurate. At what points will this challenge the credentials of the contractarian retributive theory . . . ?

The retributive theory claims to be grounded on justice; but is it just to punish people who act out of those very motives that society encourages and reinforces? If Bonger is correct, much criminality is motivated by greed, selfishness, and indifference to one's fellows; but does not the whole society encourage motives of greed and selfishness ("making it," "getting ahead"), and does not the competitive nature of the society alienate men from each other and thereby encourage indifference — even, perhaps, what psychiatrists call psychopathy? . . . There is something perverse in applying principles that presuppose a sense of community in a society which is structured to destroy genuine community.

Related to this is the whole allocation of benefits in contemporary society. The retributive theory really presupposes what might be called a "gentlemen's club" picture of the relation between man and society — i.e., men are viewed as being part of a community of shared values and rules. The rules benefit all concerned and, as a kind of debt for the benefits derived, each man owes obedience to the rules. In the absence of such obedience, he deserves punishment in the sense that he owes payment for the benefits. For, as a rational man, he can see that the rules benefit everyone (himself included) and that he would have selected them in the original position of choice. . . .

But to think that [this] applies to the typical criminal, from the poorer classes, is to live in a world of social and political fantasy. [T]hey certainly would be hard-pressed to name the benefits for which they are supposed to owe obedience. If justice, as both Kant and Rawls suggests, is based on reciprocity, it is hard to see what these persons are supposed to reciprocate for. . . .

Consider one example: a man has been convicted of armed robbery. On investigation, we learn that he is an impoverished black whose whole life has been one of frustrating alienation from the prevailing socio-economic structure — no job, no transportation if he could get a job, substandard education for his children, terrible housing and inadequate health care for his whole family, condescending-tardy-inadequate welfare payments, harassment by the police but no real protection by them against the dangers in his community, and near total exclusion from the political process. Learning all this, would we still want to talk — as many do — of his suffering punishment under the rubric of "paying a debt to society"? Surely not. Debt for what? I do not, of course, pretend that all criminals can be so described. But I do think that this is a closer picture of the typical criminal than the picture that is presupposed in the retributive theory — i.e., the picture of an evil person who, of his own free will, intentionally acts against those just rules of society which he knows, as a rational man, benefit everyone including himself.

But what practical help does all this offer, one may ask. How should we design our punitive practices in the society in which we now live? This is the question we want to ask, and it does not seem to help simply to say that our society is built on deception and inequity. How can Marx help us with our real practical problem? The answer, I think, is that he cannot and obviously does not desire to do so. For Marx would say that we have not focused (as all piecemeal reform fails to focus) on what is truly the real problem. And this is changing the basic social relations. Marx is the last person from whom we can expect advice on how to make our intellectual and moral peace with bourgeois society. And this is surely his attraction and his value.

What does Bonger offer? He suggests, near the end of his book, that in a properly designed society all criminality would be a problem "for the physician rather than the judge." But this surely will not do. The therapeutic state, where prisons are called hospitals and jailers are called psychiatrists, simply raises again all the old problems about the justification of coercion and its reconciliation with autonomy that we faced in worrying about punishment. The only difference is that our coercive practices are now surrounded with a benevolent rhetoric which makes it even harder to raise the important issues. Thus the move to therapy, in my judgment, is only an illusory solution — alienation remains and the problem of reconciling coercion with autonomy remains unsolved. Indeed if the alternative is having our personalities involuntarily restructured by some state psychiatrist, we might well want to claim the "right to be punished" that Hegel spoke of.

Perhaps, then, we may really be forced seriously to consider a radical proposal

B. Why Punish?

If we think that institutions of punishment are necessary and desirable, ar we are morally sensitive enough to want to be sure that we have the moral ri to punish before we inflict it, then we had better first make sure that we ha restructured society in such a way that criminals genuinely do correspond to the only model that will render punishment permissible — i.e., make sure that they are autonomous and that they do benefit in the requisite sense. Of course, if we did this then — if Marx and Bonger are right — crime itself and the need to punish would radically decrease if not disappear entirely.

NOTE

For other inquiries into Marxist criminal theory, see Jeffrey Reiman, the Marxian Critique of Criminal Justice, 6 Crim. Just. Ethics 30 (1987); Luigi Ferrajoli & Daniel Zolo, Marxism and the Criminal Question, 4 L. & Phil. 71 (1985).

b. Deterrence

INTRODUCTORY NOTE

Deterrence theories furnish a widely accepted rationale of the practice of punishment. According to these theories, punishment should not be designed to exact retribution on convicted offenders but to deter the commission of future offenses. Deterrence theorists distinguish between the effect of punishment as a general deterrent and its effect as a special deterrent. Punishment acts as a *general deterrent* insofar as the threat of punishment deters potential offenders in the general community. It acts as a *specific deterrent* insofar as the infliction of punishment on convicted defendants leaves *them* less likely to engage in the crime. For a study of the extent to which the doctrines of the criminal law (e.g., intent, attempt, justification, and excuse) are explainable on deterrence theories, see Steven Shavell, Criminal Law and the Optimal Use of Nonmonetary Sanctions as a Deterrent, 85 Colum. L. Rev. 1232 (1985), especially pp. 1247-1259. See also Richard Posner, An Economic Theory of the Criminal Law, 85 Colum. L. Rev. 1193 (1985).

Debate about deterrence theories has usually concentrated on the empirical question whether criminals and would-be criminals are dissuaded from crime by their assessment of the risks of conviction and the unpleasantness of imprisonment. Modern deterrence theories also emphasize the broader effects of punishment in inculcating and maintaining a habit of law-abiding conduct in the general population. Another issue in the deterrence debate is the morality of punishing some offenders in order to deter others.

The following selections exhibit aspects of these themes.

JEREMY BENTHAM, PRINCIPLES OF PENAL LAW, Pt. II, bk. 1, ch. 3, in J. Bentham's Works 396, 402 (J. Bowring ed. 1843): Pain and pleasure are the great springs of human action. When a man perceives or supposes pain to be the consequence of an act, he is acted upon in such a manner as tends, with a certain force, to withdraw him, as it were, from the commission of that act. If the apparent magnitude, or rather value of that pain be greater than the apparent magnitude or value of the pleasure or good he expects to be the consequence of the act, he will be absolutely prevented from performing it. The mischief which would have ensued from the act, if performed, will also by that means be prevented. . . .

The observation of rules of proportion between crimes and punishments has been objected to as useless, because they seem to suppose, that a spirit of calculation has place among the passions of men, who, it is said, never calculate. But dogmatic as this proposition is, it is altogether false. In matters of importance every one calculates. Each individual calculates with more or less correctness, according to the degrees of his information, and the power of the motives which actuate him, but all calculate. It would be hard to say that a madman does not calculate. Happily, the passion of cupidity, which on account of its power, its constancy, and its extent, is most formidable to society, is the passion which is most given to calculation. This, therefore, will be more successfully combated, the more carefully the law turns the balance of profit against it.

JOHANNES ANDENAES, GENERAL PREVENTION — ILLUSION OR REALITY?, 43 J. Crim. L., Criminology & Police Science 176, 179-180 (1952): By general prevention we mean the ability of criminal law and its enforcement to make citizens law-abiding. If general prevention were 100 percent effective there would be no crime at all. General prevention may depend on the mere frightening or deterrent effect of punishment — the risk of discovery and punishment outweighing the temptation to commit crime. This was what Feuerbach had in mind when he designed his famous theory of punishment as psychological coercion directed against the citizen. Later theory puts much stress on the ability of penal law to arouse or strengthen inhibitions of another sort. In Swedish discussion the *moralizing* — in other words the *educational* — function has been greatly stressed. The idea is that punishment as a concrete expression of society's disapproval of an act helps to form and to strengthen the public's moral code and thereby creates conscious and unconscious inhibitions against committing crime. Unconscious inhibitions against committing forbidden acts can also be aroused without appealing to the individual's concepts of morality. Purely as a matter of habit, with fear, respect for authority or social imitation as connecting links, it is possible to induce favorable attitudes toward this or that action and unfavorable attitudes toward another action. . . .

We can say that punishment has three sorts of general-preventive effects: it may have a *deterrent* effect, it may strengthen *moral inhibitions* (a *moralizing* effect), and it may stimulate habitual *law-abiding conduct*. I have reason to emphasize this, since many of those who are most skeptical of general prevention think only of the deterrent effect. Even if it can be shown that conscious fear of punishment is not present in certain cases, this is by no means the same as showing that the secondary effects of punishment are without importance. To the lawmaker, the achievement of inhibition and habit is of greater value than mere deterrence. For these apply in cases where a person need not fear detection and punishment, and they can apply without the person even having knowledge of the legal prohibition.

law becomes an habit

NOTE

For a critique of utilitarian approaches to deterrence and a thoughtful exploration of the relationship between retributive conceptions and the deterrence problem, see Louis M. Seidman, Soldiers, Martyrs, and Criminals: Utilitarian Theory and the Problem of Crime Control, 94 Yale L.J. 315 (1984).

NOTE AND QUESTIONS ON CERTAINTY
AND SEVERITY OF PUNISHMENT

The two plausible ways to increase the deterrent effect of punishment are, first, to increase the risk of conviction, and second, to increase the severity of punishment. The first of these alternatives appears to be the more effective, although it is also the more difficult to implement.

The evidence supporting a correlation between effective enforcement and deterrence is anecdotal. See Franklin Zimring & Gordon Hawkins, Deterrence: The Legal Threat in Crime Control 158-172 (1973). Where enforcement has been weak or nonexistent, certain crime has increased dramatically. In Liverpool in 1919, a police strike preceded widespread looting; in Copenhagen in 1944, arrest of the police by the German occupying forces was followed by a tenfold increase in robberies and larcenies. Conversely, where the likelihood of conviction has increased, the crime rate has dropped. Improvements in chemical and toxicological techniques for investigating poisoning were followed by a decrease in this type of crime. Likewise, bank robberies and kidnappings decreased following enactment of legislation making these offenses federal crimes. See Johannes Andenaes, The General Preventive Effects of Punishment, 114 U. Pa. L. Rev. 949, 961-962 (1960). A study in New York reports that the crime rate in one precinct fell sharply after the number of police stationed there was more than doubled. Thorsten Sellin, The Law and Some Aspects of Criminal Conduct, in Aims and Methods of Legal Research 113, 119-120 (A. Conard ed. 1955).

It is important to note, however, that increased enforcement does not by itself result directly in increased general deterrence. Since the effectiveness of the threat of punishment must be judged from the viewpoint of the potential criminal, certainty of punishment is important only as it contributes to the appearance of certainty.

Increased severity of punishment has a more doubtful deterrent effect. Some studies have gone so far as to question whether increased severity has any correlation at all with increased deterrence. A California study, for instance, concludes (California Assembly Committee on Criminal Procedure, Progress Report, Deterrent Effects of Criminal Sanctions 7 (May 1968)):

> [A]dult prison inmates had the highest degree of knowledge of penalties, yet at least half had not been restrained in their actions because of this knowledge. Furthermore, it was known that California ranked fifth among all states in the length of time it held people in prison — almost 10 times longer than the national average. Yet our crime rate is higher and as many men fail on parole here as in other states where prison time was considerably less.

Question: What problems do you see in this reasoning? Other studies have been more equivocal, largely because of the absence of extensive empirical evidence. See Franklin Zimring & Gordon Hawkins, Deterrence: The Legal Threat in Crime Control 194-208 (1973).

Consider Johannes Andenaes, The General Preventive Effects of Punishment, 114 U. Pa. L. Rev. 949, 965-970 (1966):

> It seems reasonable to conclude that as a general rule, though not without exceptions, the general preventive effect of the criminal law increases with the growing severity of penalties. Contemporary dictatorships display with almost frightening clarity the conformity that can be produced by a ruthlessly severe justice.[a]
>
> However, it is necessary to make two important reservations. In the first place, as we indicated when discussing the risk of detection, what is decisive is not the actual practice but how this practice is conceived by the public. Although little research has been done to find out how much the general public knows about the penal system, presumably most people have only vague and unspecified notions. Therefore, only quite substantial changes will be noticed. Only rarely does a single sentence bring about significant preventive effects.
>
> In the second place, the prerequisite of general prevention is that the law be enforced. Experience seems to show that excessively severe penalties may actually reduce the risk of conviction, thereby leading to results contrary to their purpose.

FRANKLIN ZIMRING & GORDON HAWKINS, DETERRENCE: THE LEGAL THREAT IN CRIME CONTROL 35-37 (1973): One of the most familiar and influential statements of objection [to punishment for deterrent purposes] is contained in a passage from Immanuel Kant's Philosophy of Law. "Punishment," says Kant, "can never be administered merely as a means for promoting another good. . . . For one man ought never be dealt with merely as a means subservient to the purpose of another." Now Professor Andenaes in a recent article on The Morality of Deterrence[44] deals with this objection, and what we have to say on this point can conveniently be stated by reference to his treatment of it.

Andenaes states Kant's principle as being "that man should always be treated as an end in himself, not only as a means for some other end." He goes on to say that "realistically, societies often treat people in ways designed to promote the good of society at the expense of the individual concerned." By way of example he cites military conscription, quarantine regulations, the confinement of dangerous mentally ill patients and the detention of enemy citizens in wartime. And he concludes that "the Kantian principle, in practical application, is of doubtful value."

Nevertheless, Professor Andenaes admits that the Kantian principle "lends itself to different interpretations." And it seems to us that a different interpretation both preserves what is valuable in the Kantian position and at the same time does not constitute an irrebuttable objection to deterrence. The point is a very simple one. It is that Kant did not say we must never treat men as means. He said that men should never be treated *merely as a means* or, as Andenaes put:

---

a. The lower crime rates in dictatorships might also be attributed to the unusually large police forces maintained by such governments. Hence the risk of apprehension and conviction is also higher in dictatorships than in democracies. See MacNamara, Crime Patterns in Democratic and Totalitarian Society, 1 J.A. Psych. Treatment Offenders 4 (Oct. 1957). — Eds.

44. [1970] U. Chi. L. Rev. 649.

it, *only as a means*. This interpretation is favored by Professor H. L. A. Hart in his discussion of Chief Justice Holmes's theory of objective liability.[48]

Kant, Hart maintains, insisted that we should never treat men *only* as means "but in every case as ends also." Hart goes on to say that this means "we are justified in requiring sacrifices from some men for the good of others only in a social system which also recognizes their rights and their interests. In the case of punishment, the right in question is the right of men to be left free and not punished for the good of others, unless they have broken the law where they had the capacity and a fair opportunity to conform to its requirements." Insofar as this interpretation is valid, the Kantian principle does not necessarily imply the rejection of punishment based on deterrence; but it manifestly implies some limitations upon its use.

QUESTIONS

Would one of the limitations of the Kantian principle suggested by Zimring and Hawkins have to do with the effectiveness of deterrence? If punishment of offenders had no deterrent effect in fact, would it then not only be futile but also unjust as a gratuitous infliction of suffering? How much proof is needed to establish the injustice? Who should bear the burden of proof, the proponents or opponents? What is the moral case for punishment in a situation of uncertainty?

Consider, as well, the implications of (1) punishment in excess of what is needed to deter; (2) punishment that is more severe than usual in periods in which the crimes offenders commit are sharply increasing in frequency; (3) singling out for exemplary punishment only offenders of a particular kind, for example, those whose offenses are most likely to capture public attention because they involve public figures or newsworthy circumstances, thus enabling the criminal justice system to minimize the amount of total punishment while attaining the maximum deterrent impact. See Zimring & Hawkins, supra, at 37-50.

c. Reform

LEON RADZINOWICZ & J. W. CECIL TURNER, A STUDY OF PUNISHMENT I: INTRODUCTORY ESSAY

21 Canadian B. Rev. 91, 91-97 (1943)

[I]n the past 150 years . . . our penal policy is seen to move in three main stages. In the earliest the salient feature is a crude utilitarianism aiming at the reduction of crime through the weapon of terror. The following passage indicates how this doctrine inspired the legislator.

"If a man injured Westminster Bridge, he was hanged. If he appeared disguised on a public road, he was hanged. If he cut down young trees; if he shot rabbits; if he stole property valued at five shillings; if he stole anything at all from a bleach field; if he wrote threatening letters to extort money; if he returned

---

48. H. L. A. Hart, Punishment and Responsibility (1968) 242-244.

prematurely from transportation; for any of these offenses he was immediately hanged."

The attitude of the contemporary moralist is well illustrated by the views expressed by the Reverend Sydney Smith, Editor of the Edinburgh Review in the eighteen-thirties, in the following quotations:

"The real and only test, in short, of a good prison system is the diminution of offences by the terror of the punishment.

"Mrs. Fry is an amiable excellent woman, and a thousand times better than the infamous neglect that preceded her; but hers is not the method to stop crimes. In prisons which are really meant to keep the multitude in order, and to be a terror to evil-doers, there must be no sharing of profits — no visiting friends — no education but religious education — no freedom of diet — no weavers' looms or carpenters' benches. There must be a great deal of solitude; coarse food; a dress of shame; hard, incessant, irksome, eternal labour; a planned and regulated and unrelenting exclusion of happiness and comforts." . . .

Speaking generally, the study of this first stage of our criminal policy establishes the conclusion that there was no acceptance of any principle that the severity of punishment should be equated to the gravity of the offence. This principle became prominent in the second stage, when the doctrine of retribution took a leading place in contemporary thought on penal questions and therefore the crimes have to be graded according to their gravity and the punishments correspondingly graded so as to fit the crime in each case. The major assumption on which this conception rests is that every individual in the State has certain fundamental rights as a human being, which should not be forfeited by the fact that he may have committed a crime.

Certain thinkers in Europe had drawn attention to the evils which resulted from the policy of terror, especially when, as often, it allowed too great a discretion to the tribunals and also too great freedom to those who carried out the sentences of the tribunals. As a safeguard against this danger it was felt that the individual should be protected by the establishment of legal rules which would closely define the nature and the amount of punishment which should be administered for each crime. . . .

If it is to be granted that all individuals have equal fundamental rights it seemed naturally to follow that they all must bear equal responsibilities; and the result was that whereas the liberal doctrine of equality protected the individual against the arbitrary cruelties of the policy of terror, it tended to assume that all individuals have the same powers of resistance to temptation and that each will deserve the same punishment for the same crime, and moreover will react in the same way to that punishment. Thus it may be said that the liberal theory standardised individuals and concerned itself little or not at all with what at the present day is so closely studied, namely the variations of individual personality. According to this idea the primary consideration in determining the punishment to be imposed is the intrinsic nature of the particular crime which the delinquent has committed.

This development marks a revulsion against the defects which were detected in the brutality of the earlier period but in its turn it was found to be insufficiently effective to reduce adequately the volume of crime. The volume of crime was a fact to cause concern to the least speculative observer but there were other forces at work in the second half of the nineteenth century which helped to create a general consciousness that our penal system needed overhauling. In all branches of science there arose a desire to enquire into origins, and this tendency affected those thinkers who were interested in the problem of crime. Investigations (largely stimulated by the writers of the Italian school) into the social and biological causes of crime produced results which cast doubts on many of the established theories concerning free will, and the efficacy of basing criminal policy on deterrence and retribution. Advances in medical science drew attention to varieties of mental abnormality hitherto not properly appreciated. Developments in educational science also brought about a realisation that children and adolescents have their own special difficulties in life and that there was needed a new approach to their problems. Again, more attention was paid to the publication of the official criminal statistics which, to take only two features, revealed the very large percentage of juvenile offenders and recidivists. Investigations showed the ineffectiveness of the practice of short term detention, and on the other hand the corruptive effect of unscientific and antiquated prison organization. . . .

The new approach which characterises the third period involved a fuller appreciation of the necessity of studying the personality of the offender if the disease of crime was to be successfully attacked. This led to the introduction of measures which adopted and regulated the punishment deemed appropriate for defined groups of offenders, in general without any special regard to the particular character of the crimes which they might commit. This appreciation is shown in the Report from the Departmental Committee on Prisons which, speaking of persistent offenders states: "To punish them for the particular offence in which they are detected is almost useless . . . the real offence is the willful persistence in the deliberately acquired habit of crime. We venture to offer the opinion formed during the inquiry that a new form of sentence should be placed at the disposal of the judges by which those offenders might be segregated for long periods of detention." In 1908 an Act of Parliament singled out two special groups of delinquents for one of which, now known as the "Young Adults," is prescribed a special treatment, namely, the Borstal sanction, and for the other groups, being adult habitual offenders, the sanction of prolonged detention. It is significant that this statute was called the "Prevention of Crime Act." The same idea of prevention had inspired the Probation Act of 1907, which in its main provisions, rejecting the doctrine that a retributory punishment must follow crime, has concentrated on the personality of the delinquent and on the external circumstances affecting his past and future conduct. When it is remembered that in the period immediately preceding the present war out of every ten offenders found guilty of indictable offences more than five were dealt with under the provisions of this Act it will be realized how far our criminal policy has moved away from the position it had taken up in the nineteenth century.

NOTE ON THE REHABILITATIVE IDEAL

The development of the rehabilitative ideal had great influence on American penology and corrections policies. In recent years, however, its influence has gone into eclipse, an eclipse exemplified most dramatically by what has happened in California. California pioneered with an indeterminate-sentence law in 1917. This law was grounded on a commitment to individualized correction, with prison sentences statutorily set over a broad span of years and the time and conditions of release administratively determined by the progress of the prisoner. In 1976, however, the state rejected this arrangement by enacting a determinate-sentence law that declared that "the purpose of imprisonment for crime is punishment" and that accordingly set the punishment for each crime at a fixed number of years of imprisonment, with only narrow judicial authority to vary the statutory sentence. For an analysis of the forces that produced this situation, see F. A. Allen, The Decline of the Rehabilitative Ideal — Penal Policy and Social Policy (1981).

H. L. A. HART, PUNISHMENT AND RESPONSIBILITY 25-27 (1968): It is . . . important to see precisely what the relation of Reform to punishment is because its advocates too often misstate it. "Reform" as an objective is no doubt very vague; it now embraces any strengthening of the offender's disposition and capacity to keep within the law, which is intentionally brought about by human effort otherwise than through fear of punishment. Reforming methods include the inducement of states of repentance, or recognition of moral guilt, or greater awareness of the character and demands of society, the provision of education in a broad sense, vocational training and psychological treatment. Many, seeing the futility and indeed harmful character of much traditional punishment, speak as if Reform could and should be the General Aim of the whole practice of punishment or the dominant objective of the criminal law:

> The *corrective theory* based upon a conception of multiple causation and curative-rehabilitative treatment, should clearly predominate in legislation and in judicial and administrative practices.[26]

Of course this is a possible ideal but is not an ideal for punishment. Reform can only have a place within a system of punishment as an exploitation of the opportunities presented by the conviction or compulsory detention of offenders. It is not an alternative General Justifying Aim of the practice of punishment but something the pursuit of which within a system of punishment qualifies or displaces altogether recourse to principles of justice or proportion in determining the amount of punishment. This is where both reform and individualized punishment have run counter to the customary morality of punishment.

There is indeed a paradox in asserting that Reform should "predominate" in a system of Criminal Law, as if the main purpose of providing punishment for murder was to reform the murderer not to prevent murder; and the paradox is greater where the legal offence is not a serious moral one: e.g., infringing a state monopoly of transport. The objection to assigning to Reform this place in punishment is not merely that punishment entails suffering and Reform does not; but that Reform is essentially a remedial step for which ex hypothesi there is an opportunity only at the point where the criminal law has failed in its primary task of securing society from the evil which breach of the law involves. Society is divisible at any moment into two classes (i) those who have actually broken a

26. Hall and Glueck, Cases on Criminal Law and Its Enforcement (1951), p. 14.

given law and (ii) those who have not yet broken it but may. To take Reform as the dominant objective would be to forgo the hope of influencing the second and — in relation to the more serious offences — numerically much greater class. We should thus subordinate the prevention of first offences to the prevention of recidivism.

Consideration of what conditions or beliefs would make this appear a reasonable policy brings us to the topic to which this paper is a mere prolegomenon: modern sceptical doubt about the whole institution of punishment. If we believed that nothing was achieved by announcing penalties or by the example of their infliction, either because those who do not commit crimes would not commit them in any event or because the penalties announced or inflicted on others are not among the factors which influence them in keeping the law, then some dramatic change concentrating wholly on actual offenders, would be necessary. Just because at present we do not entirely believe this, we have a dilemma and an uneasy compromise. Penalties which we believe are required as a threat to maintain conformity to law at its maximum may convert the offender to whom they are applied into a hardened enemy of society; while the use of measures of Reform may lower the efficacy and example of punishment on others. At present we compromise on this relatively new aspect of punishment as we do over its main elements. What makes this compromise seem tolerable is the belief that the influence which the threat and example of punishment extracts is often independent of the severity of the punishment, and is due more to the disgrace attached to conviction for crime or to the deprivation of freedom which many reforming measures at present used in any case involve.

MICHAEL MOORE, LAW AND PSYCHIATRY 234-235 (1984): Rehabilitation is perhaps the most complex of the theories of punishment, because it involves two quite different ideals of rehabilitation that are usually confused. These two rehabilitative ideals can best be separated by thinking about two different ways of rendering offenders nondangerous. First, imagine that what is done is to place offenders in extraordinarily awful places of detention, with harsh treatment by inmates and guards. Here, nondangerousness is achieved because such offenders either become "penitent," or they are no longer willing to commit crimes because they are unwilling to risk again such awful treatment. For comparison, imagine that the same level of nondangerousness can be achieved if prisoners are placed in much nicer facilities, with kinder personnel (all of them soft-spoken, in white coats, and manifesting sincere concern), a place in which extensive therapy programs are undertaken. Imagine further that the second such program, although much more expensive than the first, not only makes offenders nondangerous, but also makes them flourishing, happy, and self-actualizing members of our society.

The first sort of rehabilitative ideal is one that is achieved when we make criminals safe to return to the streets. This sort of rehabilitative theory justifies punishment, not by appeal to how much better off criminals will be at the end of the process, but rather by how much better off all of us will be if "treatment" is completed because the streets will be that much safer. Such a theory seeks to rehabilitate criminals only as a cost effective means of shortening the expensive incarceration that would otherwise be necessary to protect us all against crime. The second sort of rehabilitative ideal, by way of contrast, is a paternalistic theory. it seeks to rehabilitate offenders not just so they can be returned safely to the streets, but so they can lead flourishing and successful lives. Such a theory justifies punishment, not in the name of all of us, but rather in the offenders' own name; since it does so in their name, but contrary to their own expressed wishes (few offenders want to be punished), this kind of rehabilitative theory is paternalistic in character.

This paternalistic type of rehabilitative theory has no proper part to play in any theory of punishment, even in the minimal sense of constituting a prima facie justification of punishment. There are three reasons why this is so. First, such a paternalistic reform theory allocates scarce societal resources away from other, more deserving groups that want them (such as retarded and autistic children or the poor), to a group that hardly can be said to deserve such favored status and, moreover, does not want such "benefits." As a simple matter of distributive justice it is difficult to argue that criminals should be favored in the allocation of scarce social resources in these ways. Second, in any political theory according high value to liberty, paternalistic justifications are themselves to be regarded with suspicion. Criminals are not in the standard classes in society for which paternalistic state intervention is appropriate, such as the severely disordered, the young, or others whose capacity for rational choice is diminished; such a paternalistic theory is suspect on this ground alone. Third, such recasting of punishment in terms of "treatment" for the good of the criminal makes possible a kind of moral blindness that is dangerous in itself. As C. S. Lewis pointed out some years ago, adopting a "humanitarian" conceptualization of punishment makes it easy to inflict treatments and sentences that need bear no relation to the desert of the offender. We may do more to others "for their own good" than we ever allow ourselves to do when we see that it is really for our good that we act.

MORRIS R. COHEN, MORAL ASPECTS OF THE CRIMINAL LAW, 49 Yale L.J. 987, 1012-1014 (1940): The most popular theory today is that the proper aim of criminal procedure is to reform the criminal so that he may become adjusted to the social order. A mixture of sentimental and utilitarian motives gives this view its great vogue. With the spread of humane feeling and the waning of faith in the old conception of the necessity for inflicting pain in the treatment of children and those suffering from mental disease, there has come a revulsion at the hardheartedness of the old retributive theory. The growing belief in education and in the healing powers of medicine encourages people to suppose that the delinquent may be reeducated to become a useful member of society. Even from the strictest economic point of view, individual men and women are the most valuable assets of any society. Is it not better to save them for a life of usefulness rather than punish them by imprisonment which generally makes them worse after they leave than before they entered?

There are, however, a number of highly questionable assumptions back of this theory which need to be critically examined.

We have already had occasion to question the assumption that crime is a physical or mental disease. We may now raise the question whether it is curable and if so at what cost to society? Benevolent social reformers are apt to ignore the amount of cold calculating business shrewdness among criminals. Some hot-blooded ones may respond to emotional appeal; but they are also likely to backslide when opportunity or temptation comes along. Human beings are not putty that can be remolded at will by benevolent intentions. The overwhelming majority of our criminals have been exposed to the influence of our school system which we have at great cost tried to make as efficient as possible. Most criminals are also religious, as prison chaplains can testify. Yet with all our efforts school education and religion do not eliminate crime. It has not even been demonstrated that they are progressively minimizing it. Nor does the record of our special reformatories for young offenders prove that it is always possible to reform even young people so that they will stay reformed for any length of time. The analogy of the criminal law to medicine breaks down. The surgeon can determine with a fair degree of accuracy when there is an inflamed appendix or cancerous growth, so that by cutting it out he can remove a definite cause of distress. Is there in the complex of our social system any one cause of crime which any social physician can as readily remove on the basis of similarly verifiable knowledge?

Let us abandon the light-hearted pretension that any of us know how all cases of criminality can be readily cured, and ask the more modest and serious question: to what extent *can* criminals be re-educated or reconditioned so that they can live useful lives? It would indeed be illiberal dogmatism to deny all possibility and desirability of effort along this line. Yet we must keep in mind our human limitations.

If the causes of crime are determined by the life of certain groups, it is foolish to deal with the individual as if he were a self-sufficient and self-determining system. We must deal with the whole group to which he naturally belongs or gravitates and which determines his morale. Otherwise we have to adapt him completely to some other group or social condition, which is indeed a very difficult problem in social engineering.

And here we must not neglect the question of cost. When we refer to any measure as impracticable, we generally mean that the cost is too great. There is doubtless a tremendous expense in maintaining our present system of punishment. But this expense is not unlimited. Suppose that fiendish perpetrators of horrible crimes on children could be reformed by being sent first for several years to a special hospital. Will people vote large funds for such purposes when honest law-abiding citizens so often cannot get adequate hospital facilities? Suppose that we find that a certain social environment or that an elaborate college course will reform a burglar or gunman, would our community stand for the expense when so many worthy young people cannot afford to go to college because they have to go to work? We certainly should not give even the appearance of reward for criminality. Let us not forget that there is always a natural resentment in any society against those who have attacked it. Will people be satisfied to see one who is guilty of horrible crimes simply reformed, and not give vent to the social horror and resentment against the miscreant?

NOTE

The actual effects of reformative penal regimens have been questioned. In an important 1974 paper (Robert Martinson, What Works? — Questions and Answers About Prison Reform, 36 Pub. Interest 22 (1974)), the author concluded: "With few and isolated exceptions, the rehabilitative efforts that have been reported so far have no appreciable effect on recidivism" (p. 25). In a later study, New Findings, New Views: A Note of Caution Regarding Sentencing Reform, 7 Hofstra. L. Rev. 243 (1979), he withdrew that conclusion, having found evidence that different programs worked differently in different settings and circumstances, and that some programs do reduce recidivism for particular types of offenders in particular treatment settings. Subsequent research has reinforced this cautiously optimistic view. For a thorough reassessment of the moral and empirical issues, see Michael Vitiello, Reconsidering Rehabilitation, 65 Tulane L. Rev. 1011 (1991). With respect to the effectiveness of rehabilitative programs, Professor Vitiello concludes (id. at 1037):

> In the early and middle 1970s, based on then-current studies, one might have argued that rehabilitation was ineffective. Efforts at sentencing reform, underway since the 1970s, proceeded on that assumption. Ironically, by the time Congress enacted sentencing reform, new studies were available that should have made reformers rethink their attack on rehabilitation. . . . More sophisticated research techniques demonstrate that some offenders are amenable to rehabilitation and that social scientists can identify those offenders by use of objective criteria, at least some of which relate to post-conviction behavior.

d. Incapacitation

JACQUELINE COHEN, INCAPACITATING CRIMINALS: RECENT RESEARCH FINDINGS [a]

U.S. Department of Justice, National Institute of Justice, Research in Brief (December 1983)

Increased attention given in recent years to incapacitation as a crime control strategy, and as a purpose of sentencing, stems from a number of factors:

* confidence has waned in the ability of correctional programs to rehabilitate offenders
* public attitudes toward crime and criminals have become more punitive
* prisons throughout the United States are crowded, having reached an all-time peak population of 431,829 on June 30, 1983 [b]
* recent research efforts suggest that it may be possible to identify and incarcerate high-rate offenders, thereby promising an eventual ability to reduce crime without crowding the prisons.

Researchers and public policy advocates distinguish between *collective incapacitation* and *selective incapacitation*. Under *collective* strategies, all persons convicted of a designated offense, say robbery or any second felony conviction, would receive the same sentence, say 5 years. Research has shown that the reduction in

a. This report summarizes J. Cohen, Incapacitation as a Strategy for Crime Control: Possibilities and Pitfalls, in Crime and Justice: An Annual Review of Research, Volume 5, pp. 1-84 (M. Tonry & N. Morris eds. 1983). — Eds.

b. The number rose to 883,593 as of December 31, 1992. U.S. Dept. Justice, Bureau of Justice Statistics, Prisoners in 1992, p. 1 (May 1993) — Eds.

crime that would result from such policies is limited and that prison populations would increase dramatically if such policies were systematically pursued.

Selective strategies would involve individualized sentences based on predictions that particular offenders would commit serious offenses at a high rate if not incarcerated. A recent RAND Corporation report[c] concludes that use of such predictions could reduce crime with little or no increase in prison populations. However, other major researchers assert that the Greenwood work has serious limitations and that the best available prediction methods are simply not good enough to serve as the basis of a system of selective incapacitation. . . .

COLLECTIVE INCAPACITATION

. . . Offenders who are imprisoned are unable to commit crimes in the free community. Thus, all imprisonment is incapacitative and should result in the commission of fewer crimes. . . .

By checking the past criminal records of persons currently convicted of crimes, it is possible to determine which current offenders would have been imprisoned under, say, a mandatory 5-year sentencing policy for all violent felonies, and to conclude that the current offense would not have been committed. . . .

[In the studies cited by Cohen the crime-reduction effect on incapacitation strategies was less than 10 percent in two studies and varied from 14 to 17 percent in four others. But the Rand study estimated a 31 percent reduction in violent crime and a 42 percent reduction in burglary.]

The most striking finding of the major published research is that incapacitation does not appear to achieve large reductions in crime. . . . [T]he estimated crime reduction effect is in the 10-20 percent range. This is not insubstantial, representing from 131,000 to 262,000 reported violent index offenses in the United States during 1980. Nonetheless, incapacitation does not make the dent in crime that might have been expected from a "lock-em-up" strategy.

In part, this is because incapacitation policies can prevent only the subsequent crimes of convicted offenders who are eligible for incarceration. Many people charged with crimes, however, have not been convicted before. In Cohen's District of Columbia study, for example, 76 percent of adult arrestees had not previously been convicted of the offenses studied. Thus, at most, only 24 percent of the current adult arrests could have been prevented by imposing lengthy prison terms at the time of the earlier conviction.

. . . Although the effects of collective incapacitation on crime reduction are low, the effects on prison populations are likely to be substantial. Table 3 [omitted] shows the probable impact on prison populations of 5-year mandatory prison sentences for selected offenses for several . . . jurisdictions. . . . Prison populations would be doubled, tripled, or even more dramatically increased. [The RAND study, which predicted large crime reduction effects, also predicted a 450 percent increase in prison population.]

Thus, the research demonstrates that broadly based collective incapacitation policies involving lengthy prison sentences for serious crimes are not feasible. . . .

c. P. Greenwood, with A. Abrahams, Selective Incapacitation: Report to the National Institute of Justice (1982). — EDS.

SELECTIVE INCAPACITATION

It is frequently observed that a small number of offenders commits a disproportionately large number of offenses. If prison resources can be effectively targeted
to high-rate offenders, it should be possible to achieve current, or improved,
levels of crime control with reduced numbers in prison. The key to such a policy
rests on an ability to identify high-rate offenders prospectively, and at relatively
early stages in their careers.

Recent selective incapacitation research has stimulated considerable controversy. Some of the debate has focused on ethical implications of selective incapacitation and some has focused on limitations of the existing research.

ETHICAL CONCERNS

A key element of selective incapacitation is that some offenders would be imprisoned for a longer period than others convicted of the same offense, because
of predictions about their *future* criminality. Reactions to selective incapacitation
proposals are influenced by differing views about the purposes of criminal punishments. Proponents argue that persons convicted of crimes can justly receive
any lawful sentence (unless, perhaps, it is so disproportionately severe as to be
unjust), and that holding some offenders longer than others for predictive reasons raises no significant ethical problems. Moreover, proponents point out that
existing sentencing is implicitly incapacitative: presumably, most judges and
other officials base their decisions in part on their beliefs about an offender's
future dangerousness. From this perspective, selective incapacitation policies
are preferable to existing practice because predictions of future crime would no
longer be ad hoc and idiosyncratic, but would be based upon the best available
scientific evidence.

Some critics argue against selective incapacitation in principle: punishment
should be *deserved* and two persons who have committed the same offense deserve equal punishment. If selective incapacitation means that one person will
be held longer than another because of predictions of future crimes, it is unjust.

Other critics — including people who in principle do not object to unequal
punishments — offer other objections:

1. It is *unfair* to punish people for crimes they have not yet committed,
   and might not commit if released.
2. It is unjust to incarcerate (or further incarcerate) people on the basis
   of predictions of future crime because those predictions are too often
   wrong — typically two out of three persons so identified are "false positives," people who would not have committed future crimes even if
   released.
3. Many of the variables in prediction formulas raise other policy or ethical questions. For example, several of the RAND variables involved
   juvenile records, which many believe should not be admissible in relation to adult prosecutions. For another example, the RAND formula
   includes employment information, which many would exclude from
   consideration at sentencing, along with education and similar factors,
   as class-based variables that, in effect, discriminate against the poor.

4. Many prediction variables, like education, employment, and residential stability, are associated with race: some minorities are on average less well educated and less stably employed than the white majority. Building such variables into sentencing standards, while not intended to punish minorities more severely, would have that effect. . . .

EMPIRICAL PROBLEMS IN PREDICTION

Efforts at predicting future crimes have not been very successful. In recent review of efforts to predict violence, John Monahan (1981) reports that the best predictions have false-positive rates of over 60 percent; of every three individuals predicted to be violent in the future, two were *not* observed to be violent.

Greenwood's selective incapacitation research focused on inmates currently convicted for robbery or burglary. The inmates were divided into low-, medium-, and high-rate offenders for robbery and burglary on the basis of armed robberies and burglaries they admitted committing during the time they were free in the 2 years preceding the current incarceration. Using one variable at a time, a variety of other characteristics were then examined for their association with individual crime rates. Seven variables[d] were selected to form a simple additive scale for distinguishing offenders. Using this scale as a basis for imposing long prison terms for predicted high-rate offenders, Greenwood estimated that the number of robberies by adults in California could be reduced by 20 percent with only 2.5 percent increase in total prison population.

These results are an important illustration of the *potential* of selective incapacitation policies. The research, however, has a number of serious methodological and practical shortcomings.

. . . Given the crucial issues of low predictive accuracy and the tentativeness of the estimated impacts characterizing this research, there is as yet no sound basis for implementing selective incapacitation policies.

CRIMINAL CAREER INCAPACITATION

A different approach to incapacitation, based on criminal career patterns, may avoid some of the problems associated with selective incapacitation. This approach relies on recent empirical research on criminal careers. . . .

The goal is to identify classes of offenders who, on average, would remain active at high rates. In Blumstein and Cohen's analysis of criminal career patterns for arrestees in Washington, D.C.,[e] convicted robbery and burglary de-

---

d. The variables used to distinguish inmates by individual crime rates were:

1. Prior conviction for same charge
2. Incarcerated more than 50 percent of preceding two years
3. Convicted before age sixteen
4. Served time in state juvenile facility
5. Drug use in preceding two years
6. Drug use as juvenile
7. Employed less than 50 percent of preceding two years. — EDS.

e. Alfred Blumstein & Jacqueline Cohen, Estimation of Individual Crime Rates from Arrest Records, 70 J. Crim. L. & C. 561 (1979). — EDS.

fendants emerged as prime candidates for incapacitation. They commit these offenses, on average, at relatively high rates, and have relatively short careers. Short prison terms for these offenders have the potential to avert large portions of their expected careers and thereby to reduce robbery and burglary rates. . . .

Minimum 2-year terms imposed on all adult defendants convicted of robbery would result in an 8 percent reduction in robberies by adults, while increasing the total prison population by 7 percent.

Like Greenwood's selective incapacitation research, this alternative approach is at an early stage. However, if it can be perfected, it may avoid some of the ethical pitfalls of selective incapacitation. Being based solely on present and past criminal records, it is less susceptible to attack for reliance on controversial personal variables, and since sentencing policies would apply uniformly to groups of similar offenders — a form of targeted collective incapacitation — objections of unjust, unequal punishment have less force. . . .

NOTES

1. *Franklin Zimring & Gordon Hawkins, Incapacitation: Penal Confinement and the Restraint of Crime (forthcoming 1995):* [T]he gulf between what is known about incapacitation and what is claimed for it has never been greater than in the early 1990s. Policy debates on incapacitation are infected with impossible claims. In the summer of 1993, United States Senator Phil Gramm asserted that each year of confinement in the United States saved $230,000 in crime. With 700,000 additional persons confined in the United States since 1980, Senator Gramm's calculations should have produced a $300 billion savings in the cost of crime, an amount greater than the federal deficit or the national defense budget. The Senator did not mention where these savings could be found. In the current debate, the expert on penal policy often seems to be the one who shouts the loudest.

. . . If the criminal justice system locks up 10,000 convicted offenders, it follows as a matter of course that some offenses will be prevented as a consequence of incarceration. The only significant question relates to the amount of crime that will be avoided. . . .

Conspicuously lacking . . . are global estimates of the amount of crime prevention attributable to incapacitation. . . . The amount of crime prevented by incapacitation is both variable and contingent. It will vary in relation to different social circumstances and under different criminal justice policies. . . .

Moreover, the topic is not well suited to either unqualified acceptance or total rejection as a purpose of penal confinement. To use imprisonment at all and exclude incapacitation as one of its purposes would be absurd. If prisons are good for anything it is as institutions of restraint. Yet incapacitation is impossibly open-ended as a general principle of criminal punishment. If those who present some threat of future crime are to be confined, why not confine all of them indefinitely. The balance of desert and proportionality with preventive potential, as well as rough calculations of cost and benefit, are the inescapable elements of decision regarding the scope of preventive confinement in modern criminal justice.

2. Would a "collective incapacitation" strategy be acceptable if it could in fact achieve a very substantial reduction in crime rates? (Consider, for example, the estimated 42 percent reduction in burglary rates claimed in the RAND study.) Is society unwilling to pay the cost (in terms of increased prison populations) of achieving such a reduction in crime? Or is such a strategy unacceptable for reasons unrelated to cost?

3. Is Cohen's proposal for a strategy of "criminal career incapacitation" also subject to ethical objections relating either to the proportion of false positives or to the requirement that punishment be *deserved*?

4. An argument defending the fairness of "selective incapacitation" is developed in Note, Selective Incapacitation: Reducing Crime through Prediction of Recidivism, 96 Harv. L. Rev. 511 (1982). The author stresses, with respect to the problem of false positives, that "[a]n offender who would be mistakenly singled out by a selective incapacitation policy could easily receive an unnecessarily long sentence under the present informal consideration of these same factors." Id. at 529. Similarly, the author argues that the potentially invidious social and economic variables used in selective incapacitation proposals "are already used by both judges and parole boards in setting sentence lengths." Id. For an opposing view that develops ethical and empirical objections in depth, see Jacqueline Cohen, Selective Incapacitation: An Assessment, 1984 U. Ill. L. Rev. 253, and Leonard J. Long, Rethinking Selective Incapacitation: More at Stake than Controlling Violent Crime, 62 U.M.K.C.L. Rev. 107 (1993). For later reservations of one of the early advocates of selective incapacitation, see Peter W. Greenwood & Susan Turner, Selective Incapacitation Revisited: Why the High-Rate Offenders Are Hard to Predict (RAND Corp. 1987).

5. For further review of empirical data, see Jacqueline Cohen & Jose A. Canela-Cacho, Incapacitation and Violent Crime (Natl. Academy of Sciences 1994); Jacqueline Cohen, Research on Criminal Careers: Individual Frequency Rates and Offense Seriousness, in Alfred Blumstein et al. (eds.), Criminal Careers and "Career Criminals," Volume 1 (Natl. Academy of Sciences 1986).

2.   Case Studies

REGINA v. DUDLEY AND STEPHENS

Queen's Bench Division
14 Q.B.D. 273 (1884)

LORD COLERIDGE, C.J. The two prisoners, Thomas Dudley and Edwin Stephens, were indicted for the murder of Richard Parker on the high seas on the 25th of July in the present year. They were tried before my Brother Huddleston at Exeter on the 6th of November, and, under the direction of my learned Brother, the jury returned a special verdict, the legal effect of which has been argued before us, and on which we are now to pronounce judgment. The special verdict . . . is as follows.

That on July 5, 1884, the prisoners, Thomas Dudley and Edward [sic] Stephens, with one Brooks, all able-bodied English seamen, and the deceased also an English boy, between seventeen and eighteen years of age, the crew of an English yacht, a registered English vessel, were cast away in a storm on the high seas 1,600 miles from the Cape of Good Hope, and were compelled to put into an open boat belonging to the said yacht. That in this boat they had no supply of water and no supply of food, except two 1 lb. tins of turnips, and for three days they had nothing else to subsist upon. That on the fourth day they caught a small turtle, upon which they subsisted for a few days, and this was the only food they had up to the twentieth day when the act now in question was committed. That on the twelfth day the remains of the turtle were entirely consumed, and for the next eight days they had nothing to eat. That they had no fresh water, except such rain as they from time to time caught in their oilskin capes. That the boat was drifting on the ocean, and was probably more than 1,000 miles away from land. That on the eighteenth day, when they had been seven days without food and five without water, the prisoners spoke to Brooks as to what should be done if no succour came, and suggested that some one should be sacrificed to save the rest, but Brooks dissented, and the boy, to whom they were understood to refer, was not consulted. That on the 24th of July, the day before the act now in question, the prisoner Dudley proposed to Stephens and Brooks that lots should be cast who should be put to death to save the rest, but Brooks refused to consent, and it was not put to the boy, and in point of fact there was no drawing of lots. That on the day the prisoners spoke of their families, and suggested it would be better to kill the boy that their lives should be saved, and Dudley proposed that if there was no vessel in sight by the morrow morning the boy should be killed. That next day, the 25th of July, no vessel appearing, Dudley told Brooks that he had better go and have a sleep, and made signs to Stephens and Brooks that the boy had better be killed. The prisoner Stephens agreed to the act, but Brooks dissented from it. That the boy was then lying at the bottom of the boat quite helpless and extremely weakened by famine and by drinking sea water, and unable to make any resistance, nor did he ever assent to his being killed. The prisoner Dudley offered a prayer asking forgiveness for them all if either of them should be tempted to commit a rash act, and that their souls might be saved. That Dudley, with the assent of Stephens, went to the boy, and telling him that his time was come, put a knife into his throat and killed him then and there; that the three men fed upon the body and blood of the boy for four days; that on the fourth day after the act had been committed the boat was picked up by a passing vessel, and the prisoners were rescued, still alive, but in the lowest state of prostration. That they were carried to the port of Falmouth, and committed for trial at Exeter. That if the men had not fed upon the body of the boy they would probably not have survived to be so picked up and rescued, but would within four days have died of famine. That the boy, being in a much weaker condition, was likely to have died before them. That at the time of the act in question there was no sail in sight, nor any reasonable prospect of relief. That under these circumstances there appeared to the prisoners every probability that unless they then fed or very soon fed upon the boy or one of themselves they would die of starvation. That there was no appreciable chance of saving life except by killing some one for the others to eat. That assuming any necessity to kill anybody, there was no greater necessity for killing the boy than any of the other three men. But whether upon the whole matter by the jurors found the killing of Richard Parker by Dudley and Stephens be felony and murder the jurors are ignorant, and pray the advice of the Court thereupon, and if upon the whole matter the Court shall be of opinion that the killing of Richard Parker be felony and murder, then the jurors say that Dudley and Stephens were each guilty of felony and murder as alleged in the indictment. . . .

From these facts, stated with the cold precision of a special verdict, it appears sufficiently that the prisoners were subject to terrible temptation, to sufferings which might break down the bodily power of the strongest man, and try the conscience of the best. Other details yet more harrowing, facts still more loathsome and appalling, were presented to the jury, and are to be found recorded in my learned Brother's notes. But nevertheless this is clear, that the prisoners put to death a weak and unoffending boy upon the chance of preserving their own lives by feeding upon his flesh and blood after he was killed, and with the certainty of depriving *him* of any possible chance of survival. The verdict finds in terms that "if the men had not fed upon the body of the boy they would *probably* not have survived," and that "the boy being in a much weaker condition was *likely* to have died before them." They might possibly have been picked up next day by a passing ship; they might possibly not have been picked up at all; in either case it is obvious that the killing of the boy would have been an unnecessary and profitless act. It is found by the verdict that the boy was incapable of resistance, and, in fact, made none; and it is not even suggested that his death was due to any violence on his part attempted against, or even so much as feared by, those who killed him. Under these circumstances the jury say that they are ignorant whether those who killed him were guilty of murder, and have referred it to this Court to determine what is the legal consequence which follows from the facts which they have found. . . .

[T]he real question in the case [is] whether killing under the circumstances set forth in the verdict be or not be murder. The contention that it could be anything else was, to the minds of us all, both new and strange, and we stopped the Attorney General in his negative argument in order that we might hear what could be said in support of a proposition which appeared to us to be at once dangerous, immoral, and opposed to all legal principle and analogy. . . . First it is said that it follows from various definitions of murder in books of authority, which definitions imply, if they do not state, the doctrine, that in order to save your own life you may lawfully take away the life of another, when that other is neither attempting nor threatening yours, nor is guilty of any illegal act whatever towards you or any one else. But if these definitions be looked at they will not be found to sustain this contention. . . .

It is . . . clear . . . that the doctrine contended for receives no support from the great authority of Lord Hale. It is plain that in his view the necessity which justified homicide is that only which has always been and is now considered a justification. . . . Lord Hale regarded the private necessity which justified, and alone justified, the taking the life of another for the safeguard of one's own to be what is commonly called "self-defence." (Hale's Pleas of the Crown, i. 478.)

But if this could be even doubtful upon Lord Hale's words, Lord Hale himself has made it clear. For in the chapter in which he deals with the exemption created by compulsion or necessity he thus expresses himself: — "If a man be desperately assaulted and in peril of death, and cannot otherwise escape unless, to satisfy his assailant's fury, he will kill an innocent person then present, the fear and actual force will not acquit him of the crime and punishment of murder, if he commit the fact [sic], for he ought rather to die himself than kill an innocent; but if he cannot otherwise save his own life the law permits him in his own defence to kill the assailant, for by the violence of the assault, and the offence committed upon him by the assailant himself, the law of nature, and necessity, hath made him his own protector. . . ." (Hale's Pleas of the Crown, vol. i. 51.)

But, further still, Lord Hale in the following chapter deals with the position asserted by the casuists, and sanctioned, as he says, by Grotius and Puffendorf, that in a case of extreme necessity, either of hunger or clothing; "theft is no theft, or at least not punishable as theft, as some even of our own lawyers have asserted the same." "But," says Lord Hale, "I take it that here in England, that rule, at least by the laws of England, is false; and therefore, if a person, being under necessity for want of victuals or clothes, shall upon that account clandestinely and animo furandi steal another man's goods, it is felony, and a crime by the laws of England punishable with death." (Hale, Pleas of the Crown, i. 54.) If, therefore, Lord Hale is clear — as he is — that extreme necessity of hunger does not justify larceny, what would he have said to the doctrine that it justified murder? [The opinion then reviewed other early text writers and found that none of them supported the defendants' contentions.]

Is there, then, any authority for the proposition which has been presented to us? Decided cases there are none. . . . The American case cited by my Brother Stephen in his Digest, from Wharton on Homicide, in which it was decided, correctly indeed, that sailors had no right to throw passengers overboard to save themselves, but on the somewhat strange ground that the proper mode of determining who was to be sacrificed was to vote upon the subject by ballot, can hardly, as my Brother Stephen says, be an authority satisfactory to a court in this country.[a] . . .

The one real authority of former time is Lord Bacon, who . . . lays down the law as follows: — "Necessity carrieth a privilege in itself. Necessity is of three sorts — necessity of conservation of life, necessity of obedience, and necessity of the act of God or of a stranger. First of conservation of life; if a man steals viands to satisfy his present hunger, this is no felony nor larceny. So if divers be in danger of drowning by the casting away of some boat or barge, and one of them get to some plank, or on the boat's side to keep himself above water, and another to save his life thrust him from it, whereby he is drowned, this is neither se defendendo nor by misadventure, but justifiable."[b] . . . Lord Bacon was great even as a lawyer; but it is permissible to much smaller men, relying upon principle and on the authority of others, the equals and even the superiors of Lord Bacon as lawyers, to question the soundness of his dictum. There are many conceivable states of things in which it might possibly be true, but if Lord Bacon meant to lay down the broad proposition that man may save his life by killing, if necessary, an innocent and unoffending neighbour, it certainly is not law at the present day. . . .

Now it is admitted that the deliberate killing of this unoffending and unresisting boy was clearly murder, unless the killing can be justified by some well-recognised excuse admitted by the law. It is further admitted that there was in this case no such excuse, unless the killing was justified by what has been called

a. Lord Coleridge is referring to United States v. Holmes, 26 F. Cas. 360, 1 Wall. Jr. 1 (C.C.E.D. Pa. 1842), which is summarized at page 876 infra.

b. The omitted first sentence with which Bacon introduced the passage quoted read as follows:

The law chargeth no man with default where the act is compulsory and not voluntary, and where there is not a consent and election: and therefore, if either there be an impossibility for a man to do otherwise, or so great a perturbation of the judgment and reason as in presumption of law man's nature cannot overcome, such necessity carrieth a privilege in itself.

Shedding, Ellis & Heath, The Works of Francis Bacon 343 (1859). — Eds.

"necessity." But the temptation to the act which existed here was not what the law has ever called necessity. Nor is this to be regretted. Though law and morality are not the same, and many things may be immoral which are not necessarily illegal, yet the absolute divorce of law from morality would be of fatal consequence; and such divorce would follow if the temptation to murder in this case were to be held by law an absolute defence of it. It is not so. To preserve one's life is generally speaking a duty, but it may be the plainest and the highest duty to sacrifice it. War is full of instances in which it is a man's duty not to live, but to die. The duty, in case of shipwreck, of a captain to his crew, of the crew to the passengers, of soldiers to women and children, as in the noble case of the *Birkenhead;* these duties impose on men the moral necessity, not of the preservation, but of the sacrifice of their lives for others, from which in no country, least of all, it is to be hoped, in England, will men ever shrink, as indeed, they have not shrunk. It is not correct, therefore, to say that there is any absolute or unqualified necessity to preserve one's life. *Necesse est ut eam, non ut vivam,*[c] is a saying of a Roman officer quoted by Lord Bacon himself with high eulogy in the very chapter on necessity to which so much reference has been made. It would be a very easy and cheap display of commonplace learning to quote from Greek and Latin authors, from Horace, from Juvenal, from Cicero, from Euripides, passage after passage, in which the duty of dying for others has been laid down in glowing and emphatic language as resulting from the principles of heathen ethics; it is enough in a Christian country to remind ourselves of the Great Example whom we profess to follow. It is not needful to point out the awful danger of admitting the principle which has been contended for. Who is to be the judge of this sort of necessity? By what measure is the comparative value of lives to be measured? Is it to be strength, or intellect, or what? It is plain that the principle leaves to him who is to profit by it to determine the necessity which will justify him in deliberately taking another's life to save his own. In this case the weakest, the youngest, the most unresisting, was chosen. Was it more necessary to kill him than one of the grown men? The answer must be "No" —

> So spake the Fiend, and with necessity,
> The tyrant's plea, excused his devilish deeds.

It is not suggested that in this particular case the deeds were "devilish," but it is quite plain that such a principle once admitted might be made the legal cloak for unbridled passion and atrocious crime. There is no safe path for judges to tread but to ascertain the law to the best of their ability and to declare it according to their judgment; and if in any case the law appears to be too severe on individuals, to leave it to the Sovereign to exercise that prerogative of mercy which the Constitution has intrusted to the hands fittest to dispense it.

It must not be supposed that in refusing to admit temptation to be an excuse for crime it is forgotten how terrible the temptation was; how awful the suffering; how hard in such trials to keep the judgment straight and the conduct pure. We are often compelled to set up standards we cannot reach ourselves, and to lay down rules which we could not ourselves satisfy. But a man has no right to declare temptation to be an excuse, though he might himself have yielded to it,

---

c. "It is necessary to go [to war], not to live." — EDS.

nor allow compassion for the criminal to change or weaken in any manner the legal definition of the crime. It is therefore our duty to declare that the prisoners' act in this case was wilful murder, that the facts as stated in the verdict are no legal justification of the homicide; and to say that in our unanimous opinion the prisoners are upon this special verdict guilty of murder.[1]

The Court then proceeded to pass sentence of death upon the prisoners.[2]

NOTE

For discussions of the historical background of the principal case, see A. W. B. Simpson, Cannibalism and the Common Law: The Story of the Tragic Last Voyage of the Mignonette and the Strange Legal Proceedings to Which It Gave Rise (1984); Mallin, In Warm Blood: Some Historical and Procedural Aspects of *Regina v. Dudley and Stephens,* 34 U. Chi. L. Rev. 387 (1967). See also Allen D. Boyer, Crime, Cannibalism and Joseph Conrad: The Influence of *Regina v. Dudley and Stephens* on Lord Jim, 20 Loy. L.A. L. Rev. 9 (1986).

UNITED STATES v. BERGMAN

United States District Court, S.D.N.Y.
416 F. Supp. 496 (1976)

FRANKEL, J. Defendant is being sentenced upon his plea of guilty to two counts of an 11-count indictment. . . . It seems fitting now to report in writing the reasons upon which the court concludes that defendant must be sentenced to a term of four months in prison.

Defendant appeared until the last couple of years to be a man of unimpeachably high character, attainments, and distinction. A doctor of divinity and an ordained rabbi, he has been acclaimed by people around the world for his works of public philanthropy, private charity, and leadership in educational enterprises. Scores of letters have come to the court from across this and other countries reporting debts of personal gratitude to him for numerous acts of extraordinary generosity. . . . In addition to his good works, defendant has managed to amass considerable wealth in the ownership and operation of nursing homes, in real estate ventures, and in a course of substantial investments.

Beginning about two years ago, investigations of nursing homes in this area, including questions of fraudulent claims for Medicaid funds, drew to a focus upon this defendant among several others. The results that concern us were the present indictment and two state indictments. After extensive pretrial proceedings defendant embarked upon elaborate plea negotiations with both state and federal prosecutors. A state guilty plea and the instant plea were entered in March of this year. . . . As part of the detailed plea arrangements, it is expected

1. My brother Grove has furnished me with the following suggestion, too late to be embodied in the judgment but well worth preserving: "If the two accused men were justified in killing Parker, then if not rescued in time, two of the three survivors would be justified in killing the third, and of the two who remained the stronger would be justified in killing the weaker, so that three men might be justifiably killed to give the fourth a chance of surviving." — C.

2. This sentence was afterwards commuted by the Crown to six months' imprisonment.

that the prison sentence imposed by this court will comprise the total covering the state as well as the federal convictions.

For purposes of the sentence now imposed, the precise details of the charges, and of defendant's carefully phrased admissions of guilt, are not matters of prime importance. Suffice it to say that the plea on Count One (carrying a maximum of five years in prison and a $10,000 fine) confesses defendant's knowing and wilful participation in a scheme to defraud the United States in various ways, including the presentation of wrongfully padded claims for payments under the Medicaid program to defendant's nursing homes. Count Three, for which the guilty plea carries a theoretical maximum of three more years in prison and another $5,000 fine, is a somewhat more "technical" charge. Here, defendant admits to having participated in the filing of a partnership return which was false and fraudulent in failing to list people who had bought partnership interests from him in one of his nursing homes, had paid for such interests, and had made certain capital withdrawals.

The conspiracy to defraud, as defendant has admitted it, is by no means the worst of its kind. . . . At the same time, the sentence, as defendant has acknowledged, is imposed for two federal felonies including, as the more important, a knowing and purposeful conspiracy to mislead and defraud the Federal Government.

[D]efense counsel urge that no licit purpose could be served by defendant's incarceration. Some of these arguments are plainly sound; others are not.

The court agrees that this defendant should not be sent to prison for "rehabilitation." Apart from the patent inappositeness of the concept to this individual, this court shares the growing understanding that no one should ever be sent to prison *for rehabilitation*. That is to say, nobody who would not otherwise be locked up should suffer that fate on the incongruous premise that it will be good for him or her. Imprisonment is punishment. . . . If someone must be imprisoned — for other, valid reasons — we should seek to make rehabilitative resources available to him or her. But the goal of rehabilitation cannot fairly serve in itself as grounds for the sentence to confinement.

Equally clearly, this defendant should not be confined to incapacitate him. He is not dangerous. It is most improbable that he will commit similar, or any, offenses in the future. There is no need for "specific deterrence."

Contrary to counsel's submissions, however, two sentencing considerations demand a prison sentence in this case:

First, the aim of *general deterrence,* the effort to discourage similar wrongdoing by others through a reminder that the law's warnings are real and that the grim consequence of imprisonment is likely to follow from crimes of deception for gain like those defendant has admitted.

Second, the related, but not identical, concern that any lesser penalty would, in the words of the Model Penal Code, §7.01(1)(c), "depreciate the seriousness of the defendant's crime."

Resisting the first of these propositions, defense counsel invoke Immanuel Kant's axiom that "one man ought never to be dealt with merely as a means subservient to the purposes of another." . . .

[We] take the widely accepted stance that a criminal punished in the interest of general deterrence is not being employed "*merely* as a means. . . ." Reading Kant to mean that every man must be deemed *more* than the instrument of others, and must "always be treated as an end in himself," the humane principle is not offended here. Each of us is served by the enforcement of the law — not least a person like the defendant in this case, whose wealth and privileges, so long enjoyed, are so much founded upon law. . . .

But the whole business, defendant argues further, is guesswork; we are by no means certain that deterrence "works." . . . It would be better, to be sure, if we had more certainty and precision. Lacking these comforts, we continue to include among our working hypotheses a belief (with some concrete evidence in its support) that crimes like those in this case — deliberate, purposeful, continuing, non-impulsive, and committed for profit — are among those most likely to be generally deterrable by sanctions most shunned by those exposed to temptation.

The idea of avoiding depreciation of the seriousness of the offense implicates two or three thoughts, not always perfectly clear or universally agreed upon, beyond the idea of deterrence. It should be proclaimed by the court's judgment that the offenses are grave, not minor or purely technical. Some attention must be paid to the demand for equal justice; it will not do to leave the penalty of imprisonment a dead letter as against "privileged" violators while it is employed regularly, and with vigor, against others. There probably is in these conceptions an element of retributiveness, as counsel urge. And retribution, so denominated, . . . remains a factor. . . . [W]e have not yet reached a state, supposing we ever should, in which the infliction of punishments for crime may be divorced generally from ideas of blameworthiness, recompense, and proportionality.

Resisting prison above all else, defense counsel included in their thorough memorandum on sentencing two proposals for what they call a "constructive," and therefore a "preferable" form of "behavioral sanction." One is a plan for Dr. Bergman to create and run a program of Jewish vocational and religious high school training. The other is for him to take charge of a "Committee on Holocaust Studies," again concerned with education at the secondary school level. . . .

[Both] of the carefully formulated "sanctions" in the memorandum involve work of an honorific nature, not unlike that done in other projects to which the defendant has devoted himself in the past. It is difficult to conceive of them as "punishments" at all. . . . The seriousness of the crimes to which Dr. Bergman has pled guilty demands something more than "requiring" him to lend his talents and efforts to further philanthropic enterprises. . . .

The criminal behavior, as has been noted, is blatant in character and unmitigated by any suggestion of necessitous circumstance or other pressures difficult to resist. . . . Viewed against the maxima Congress ordained, and against the run of sentences in other federal criminal cases, it calls for more than a token sentence.

On the other side are factors that take longer to enumerate. Defendant's illustrious public life and works are in his favor, though diminished, of course, by what this case discloses. This is a first, probably a last, conviction. Defendant is 64 years old and in imperfect health, though by no means so ill, from what the court is told, that he could be expected to suffer inordinately more than many others of advanced years who go to prison. . . .

Given . . . that this is a first offense, by a man no longer young and not perfectly well, where danger of recidivism is not a concern — it verges on cruelty to think of confinement for a term of years. We sit, to be sure, in a nation where prison sentences of extravagant length are more common than they are almost anywhere else. By that light, the term imposed today is not notably long. For this sentencing court, however, for a nonviolent first offense involving no direct assaults or invasions of others' security (as in bank robbery, narcotics, etc.), it is a stern sentence. For people like Dr. Bergman, who might be disposed to engage in similar wrongdoing, it should be sufficiently frightening to serve the major end of general deterrence. For all but the profoundly vengeful, it should not depreciate the seriousness of his offenses.

Much of defendant's sentencing memorandum is devoted to the extensive barrage of hostile publicity to which he has been subjected during the years before and since his indictment. . . .

Defendant's . . . point about his public humiliation is the frequently heard contention that he should not be incarcerated because he "has been punished enough." . . . Defendant's notoriety should not in the last analysis serve to lighten, any more than it may be permitted to aggravate, his sentence. The fact that he has been pilloried by journalists is essentially a consequence of the prestige and privileges he enjoyed before he was exposed as a wrongdoer. . . . It is not possible to justify the notion that this mode of nonjudicial punishment should be an occasion for leniency not given to a defendant who never basked in such an admiring light at all. The quest for both the appearance and the substance of equal justice prompts the court to discount the thought that the public humiliation serves the function of imprisonment. . . .

[The court imposed a sentence of four months' imprisonment.]

NOTE

Compare the *Bergman* case with that of former Reagan White House deputy chief of staff Michael K. Deaver. On September 23, 1988, Deaver received a 3-year suspended prison sentence for three counts of lying under oath to a congressional committee and a grand jury that were investigating his lobbying activities. He could have been sentenced to 15 years' imprisonment. Deaver was also fined $100,000, placed on probation, and ordered to perform 1,500 hours of community service. The judge acknowledged that Deaver knew his testimony was false but noted that Deaver's alcoholism was a "distraction from exercising the judgment required" to tell the truth to Congress. Philip Shenon, Deaver Gets Fine of $100,000 and a Suspended Sentence, N.Y. Times, Sept. 24, 1988, at A1, A9. Before he was sentenced, Deaver pled for mercy: "This entire matter . . . has taken a terrible toll on me, my family, my friends and my business. . . . I would only ask that you offer me a chance to contribute to my community and to my country." "Calling Mr. Deaver's false statements a 'crime of circumstance and opportunity,' the judge said a prison term would probably not deter other perjurers. 'Nor would a prison term serve to rehabilitate Michael Deaver.'" Id.

Representative John Dingell (D-Michigan), who was heading the committee Deaver lied to, criticized the lenient sentence: "An ordinary citizen who steals a Social Security check . . . goes to jail, but someone of wealth and influence who lies to a grand jury and Congress has little to fear." Id. President Reagan defended Deaver: "I still believe that he didn't do anything wrong. . . . This is a sad day. . . . Michael Deaver has been our friend for more than 20 years and has served us and his country with uncommon dedication." Deaver Given Probation, Fined $100,000, S.F. Chron., Sept. 24, 1988, at A1.

STATE v. CHANEY

Supreme Court of Alaska
477 P.2d. 441 (1970)

RABINOWITZ, J. Appellee Donald Scott Chaney was indicted on two counts of forcible rape and one count of robbery. After trial by jury, appellee was found guilty on all three counts. The superior court imposed concurrent one-year terms of imprisonment and provided for parole in the discretion of the parole board. The State of Alaska has appealed from the judgment and commitment which was entered by the trial court. . . . In such circumstances, the [law] prohibit[s] any increase in the sentence which was passed by the trial court although this court may express its approval or disapproval of the sentence in a written opinion. . . .

In the case at bar, appellant, the State of Alaska, claims that the one-year concurrent sentences were too lenient in view of the severity of the crimes of forcible rape and robbery, the need to deter others from such brutal behavior, and in view of the presentence recommendations, all of which called for significantly greater sentences than those which were imposed by the superior court. . . .

Under Alaska's Constitution, the principles of reformation and necessity of protecting the public constitute the touchstones of penal administration. Multiple goals are encompassed within these broad constitutional standards. Within the ambit of this constitutional phraseology are found the objectives of rehabilitation of the offender into a noncriminal member of society, isolation of the offender from society to prevent criminal conduct during the period of confinement, deterrence of the offender himself after his release from confinement or other penological treatment, as well as deterrence of other members of the community who might possess tendencies toward criminal conduct similar to that of the offender, and community condemnation of the individual offender, or in other words, reaffirmation of societal norms for the purpose of maintaining respect for the norms themselves. . . .

We now turn to the facts of the case at bar. At the time appellee committed the crimes of forcible rape and robbery, he was an unmarried member of the United States Armed Forces stationed at Fort Richardson, near Anchorage, Alaska. Appellee was born in 1948, the youngest of eight children. His youth was spent on the family's dairy farm in Washington County, Maryland. He played basketball on the Boonsboro High School team, was a member of Future Farmers of America and the Boy Scouts. Appellee did not complete high school, having dropped out one month prior to graduation. After a series of varying types of employment, appellee was drafted into the United States Army in 1968. At sentencing, it was disclosed that appellee did not have any prior criminal record, was not a user of drugs, and was only a social drinker.

From the record that has been furnished, it appears that appellee and a companion picked up the prosecutrix at a downtown location in Anchorage. After driving the victim around in their car, appellee and his companion beat her and forcibly raped her four times. During this same period of time, the victim's money was removed from her purse. Upon completion of these events, the prosecutrix was permitted to leave the vehicle to the accompaniment of dire threats of reprisals if she attempted to report the incident to the police.

The presentence report which was furnished to the trial court prior to sentencing contains appellee's version of the rapes. According to appellee, he felt "that it wasn't rape as forcible and against her will on my part." As to his conviction of robbery, appellee states: "I found the money on the floor of the car afterwards and was planning on giving it back, but didn't get to see the girl." At the time of sentencing, appellee told the court that he "didn't direct any violence against the girl."

The Division of Corrections, in its presentence report, recommended appellee be incarcerated and parole be denied. The assistant district attorney who appeared for the state at the time of sentencing recommended that appellee receive concurrent seven-year sentences with two years suspended on the two rape convictions, and that the appellee be sentenced to a consecutive five-year term of imprisonment on the robbery conviction, and that this sentence be suspended and appellee be placed on probation during this period of time. At the time of sentencing, a representative of the Division of Corrections recommended that appellee serve two years on each of the rape convictions and that appellee be sentenced to two years suspended with probation as to the robbery conviction. In his opinion, there was "an excellent possibility of . . . early parole." Counsel for appellee concurred in the Division of Corrections' recommendation. As was indicated at the outset, the trial court imposed concurrent one-year terms of imprisonment and provided for parole at the discretion of the parole board.[21] The trial judge further recommended that appellee be placed in a minimum security facility. . . .

In imposing this sentence, the trial judge remarked that he was "sorry that the [military] regulations would not permit keeping [appellee] . . . in the service if he wanted to stay because it seems to me that is . . . a better setup for everybody concerned than putting him in the penitentiary." At a later point in his remarks, the trial judge said:

> Now as a matter of fact, I have sentenced you to a minimum on all 3 counts here but there will be no problem as far as I'm concerned for you to be paroled at the first day the Parole Board says that you're eligible for parole. . . . [If] the Parole Board should decide 10 days from now that you're eligible for parole and parole you, it's entirely satisfactory with the court.

[W]e express our disapproval of the sentence which was imposed by the trial court in the case at bar. In our opinion, the sentence was too lenient considering the circumstances surrounding the commission of these crimes. It further appears that several significant goals of our system of penal justice were accorded little or no weight by the sentencing court.

Forcible rape and robbery rank among the most serious crimes. In the case at bar, the record reflects that the trial judge explicitly stated, on several occasions,

---

21. These were minimum sentences under the applicable statutes. Rape carries a potential range of imprisonment from 1 to 20 years while a conviction of robbery can result in imprisonment from 1 to 15 years.

that he disbelieved appellee and believed the prosecutrix's version of what happened after she entered the vehicle which was occupied by appellee and his companion. Considering both the jury's and the trial judge's resolution of this issue of credibility, and the violent circumstances surrounding the commission of these dangerous crimes, we have difficulty in understanding why one-year concurrent sentences were thought appropriate.

Review of the sentencing proceedings leads to the impression that the trial judge was apologetic in regard to his decision to impose a sanction of incarceration. Much was made of appellee's fine military record and his potential eligibility for early parole. On the one hand, the record is devoid of any trace of remorse on appellee's part. Seemingly all but forgotten in the sentencing proceedings is the victim of appellee's rapes and robbery. On the other hand, the record discloses that the trial judge properly considered the mitigating circumstance that the prosecutrix, who at the time did not know either appellee or his companion, voluntarily entered appellee's car. But the crux of our disapproval of the sentence stems from what we consider to be the trial judge's de-emphasis of several important goals of criminal justice.

In view of the circumstances of this record, we think the sentence imposed is not well calculated to achieve the objective of reformation of the accused. Considering the apologetic tone of the sentencing proceedings, the court's endorsement of an extremely early parole, and the concurrent minimum sentences which were imposed for these three serious felonies, we fail to discern how the objective of reformation was effectuated. At most, appellee was told that he was only technically guilty and minimally blameworthy, all of which minimized the possibility of appellee's comprehending the wrongfulness of his conduct.

We also think that the sentence imposed falls short of effectuating the goal of community condemnation, or the reaffirmation of societal norms for the purpose of maintaining respect for the norms themselves. In short, knowledge of the calculated circumstances involved in the commission of these felonies and the sentence imposed could lead to the conclusion that forcible rape and robbery are not reflective of serious antisocial conduct. Thus, respect for society's condemnation of forcible rape and robbery is eroded and reaffirmation of these societal norms negated.

We believe that a . . . sentence of imprisonment for a substantially longer period of imprisonment than the one-year sentence which was imposed would unequivocally bring home to appellee the seriousness of his dangerously unlawful conduct, would reaffirm society's condemnation of forcible rape and robbery, and would provide the Division of Corrections of the State of Alaska with the opportunity of determining whether appellee required any special treatment prior to his return to society.

UNITED STATES v. JACKSON

United States Court of Appeals, 7th Circuit
835 F.2d 1195 (1987)

EASTERBROOK, J. Thirty minutes after being released from prison, to which he had been sent on conviction of two bank robberies, Dwight Jackson robbed another bank. He was let out as part of a "work release program" and returned to his old line of work. Told to get a job, he decided to do a bank job. A passer-by saw a suspicious person flee the bank and noted the license plate of the car. . . . Jackson was back in prison before the sun set on the day of his release. His principal sentence — life in prison without possibility of parole — came under a statute forbidding possession of weapons by career criminals, 18 U.S.C. App. §1202. . . .

Section 1202 provided that anyone "who . . . possesses . . . any firearm and who has three previous [felony] convictions for robbery or burglary, or both, . . . shall be fined not more than $25,000 and imprisoned not less than fifteen years, and, notwithstanding any other provision of law, the court shall not suspend the sentence of, or grant a probationary sentence to, such person . . . , and such person shall not be eligible for parole with respect to the sentence imposed under this subsection." Jackson, who had been convicted of four armed bank robberies and one armed robbery, brandished his revolver and robbed the Continental Bank of Oakbrook Terrace, Illinois, on May 30, 1986, while this statute was in force. . . .

Jackson . . . concedes that the statute permitted the imposition of any term of years but insists that it allowed only determinate numbers of years and therefore did not authorize a life sentence. When parole is forbidden, however, a judge may use either method to reach the same result. Jackson was 35 when he committed the crime. Unless there are startling advances in geriatric medicine, a long term of imprisonment (say, 60 years) and life are the same sentence; it would be silly to read the statute as authorizing one but not the other. . . .

The imposition of life in prison on Jackson was permissible. The selection of a sentence within the statutory range is essentially free of appellate review. Armed bank robbery on the day of release — following earlier armed robbery convictions back to 1973 — marked Jackson as a career criminal. Specific deterrence had failed. The court was entitled to consider general deterrence and incapacitation. Although life without possibility of parole is the upper end of the scale of sanctions (short of capital punishment), the statute reflects a judgment that career criminals who persist in possessing weapons should be dealt with most severely. . . . If this sentence is unduly harsh, the holder of the clemency power may supply a remedy. . . . Affirmed.

POSNER J., concurring. I join the opinion and judgment of the court; but I think the sentence Jackson received is too harsh and I think it appropriate to point this out even though he presents no ground on which we are authorized to set aside an excessively severe sentence.

Jackson is unquestionably a dangerous and hardened criminal. He has been convicted of armed robbery four times (three were bank robberies — all of the same bank!); in each robbery he was carrying a loaded gun. I do not mean to denigrate the gravity of his offenses by pointing out that he has never inflicted a physical injury; but that fact is relevant to deciding whether the sheer enormity of his conduct warrants imprisonment for the rest of his life as a matter of retributive justice. It does not. Few murderers, traitors, or rapists are punished so severely. . . . The grounds for the sentence in this case must be sought elsewhere.

One ground, the one articulated by the district judge, is the need to prevent Jackson from committing further crimes. There is little doubt that if he were released tomorrow he would commit a bank robbery, perhaps on the same day. But it is extremely unlikely that if he were released 25 or 30 years from now (he is 35 years old) he would resume his career as a bank robber. We know that criminal careers taper off with age, although with the aging of the population and the improvements in the health of the aged the fraction of crimes committed by the elderly is rising. Crimes that involve a risk of physical injury to the criminal are especially a young man's game. In 1986 more than 62 percent of all persons arrested for robbery . . . were below the age of 25, and only 3.4 percent were 60 years old or older. . . . Bank robbery in particular, I suspect, is a young man's crime. A bank robber must be willing to confront armed guards and able to make a quick getaway. To suppose that if Jackson is fortunate enough to live on in prison into his seventies or eighties it would still be necessary to detain him lest he resume his life of crime after almost a lifetime in prison is too speculative to warrant imprisoning him until he dies of old age. . . .

The remaining possibility is that this savage sentence is proper *pour encourager les autres*. Indeed, deterrence is the surest ground for punishment, since retributive norms are so unsettled and since incapacitation may, by removing one offender from the pool of offenders, simply make a career in crime more attractive to someone else. . . . Thus, even if one were sure that Jackson would be as harmless as a mouse in the last 10, or 15, or 20 years of his life, his sentence might be justified if the example of it were likely to deter other people, similarly situated, from committing such crimes. This is possible, but speculative; it was not mentioned by the district judge.

We should ask how many 35 year olds would rob a bank if they knew that if they were caught it would mean 20 years in prison with no possibility of parole (the sentence I would have given Jackson if I had been the sentencing judge), compared to the number who would do so if it would mean life in prison. Probably very few would be deterred by the incremental sentence. Bank robbery is a crime of acquisition, not of passion; the only gains are financial — and are slight (in 1986 the average "take" from a bank robbery was $2,664). The net gains, when the expected cost of punishment is figured in, must be very small indeed. Clearance rates for bank robbery are very high; of all bank robberies investigated by the FBI during 1978 and 1979 . . . , 69 percent had been cleared by arrest by 1982. Conviction rates are high (90 percent in federal prosecutions for bank robbery) and average punishments severe (more than 13 years for federal defendants). It's a losers' game at best. Persons who would go ahead and rob a bank in the face of my hypothetical 20-year sentence are unlikely to be deterred by tightening the punishment screws still further. A civilized society locks up such people until age makes them harmless but it does not keep them in prison until they die.

NOTES AND QUESTIONS

1. In a subsequent proceeding the sentencing judge denied a motion for reduction of sentence, stating that Judge Posner's concerns had not persuaded him to reconsider. The sentencing judge mentioned, among other factors, that Jackson had persisted in denying his guilt; that his prior record, in addition to seven armed robbery convictions, included an attempt to murder his army colonel in Vietnam and an assault on a sergeant; and that the possession of firearm by this "incorrigible and hostile recidivist" created a distinct possibility that se vere injury or death could result from any future criminal conduct. See United States v. Jackson, 780 F. Supp. 1508 (N.D. Ill. 1991).

2. What sentence *should* be imposed on Jackson? For what purpose?

3. *"Three strikes and you're out."* Several states have enacted or considered legislation providing that upon conviction of a felony (or *violent* felony) after two prior felony convictions, a defendant must be sentenced to life imprisonment without possibility of parole. What purpose is such a sentence intended to serve? Do the additional benefits of a life sentence in such cases (compared, for example, to a 15-year or 20-year sentence) justify the additional costs?

4. *Problem.* Consider the following presentence report adapted from 93 Cal. Rptr., Appendix at 25-26 (1970):

OFFENSE: BURGLARY SECOND

Defendant broke into a pharmacy and removed several containers of drugs from a locked cabinet. He was apprehended shortly thereafter and readily admitted the offense, and two others of a similar nature.

Prior Criminal History

1975-77	County X	Juvenile offenses	Probation
8/79	County X	Battery	5 days county jail
3/81	County X	Burglary	2 years probation
4/82	County X	Burglary	60 days county jail
1/83	County X	Sale of narcotics	Sent to California Rehabilitation Center
4/84	CRC	Released on parole	Discharged from parole in April 1987
3/89	County X	Present offense	

CASE HISTORY INFORMATION

This 29-year-old man of Latin-American laboring class ancestry was born and raised in a large urban community in Southern California, the oldest of three children. He was 12 years old when his father died, and his mother subsequently supported the family by performing domestic labor, unskilled factory work and by welfare. One sister had been institutionalized in a mental hospital, while his youngest sister, now age 24, has become a nurse.

Defendant has an exceptionally high IQ and has done very well in high school and in college which he is currently attending during the day. As a youngster, he had a series of offenses as part of a juvenile gang including petty theft and burglary, for which he was made a ward of the court. He began using marijuana at the age of 15 and later graduated to using heroin. His offenses as a young adult were related to his narcotic addiction since he was stealing to try to finance his drug habit. Finally in 1983, he was committed to the California Rehabilitation Center where he spent the ensuing 15 months in treatment. Institutional officials at CRC commented favorably about his active involvement in the treatment program and he was paroled to a job in Northern California. Significantly he managed to refrain from the use of drugs for a three-year period, which led to his successful discharge from parole in 1987. Furthermore, in the almost two years since his discharge from parole there was no record of any offenses except the present ones.

He was married at the age of 19 and one child was born to that union. The marriage was dissolved after his son was born and he assumes full responsibility for not having sufficient maturity at the time to adequately act as a husband and father. When he has not been institutionalized, he has made efforts to contribute to the support of his child.

For the past three years, he has been working nights at a semiskilled job while attending college during the daytime. He has completed three and one-half years of college in business administration and his verified academic record is excellent. He hopes to become a business executive.

CASE EVALUATION

This is a young adult who, despite a poor start, has striven in recent years to assume a productive role in society. His present offense is related to narcotics which he started using again approximately three months ago. He is very bright and verbal and attributes his present predicament to an exceptionally stressful situation caused by the pressures of working full time coupled with keeping up with a demanding college program. He does not have a heavy drug habit at this time since he attempted to limit his drug use in his most recent encounter. His return to the CRC program[a] is not recommended by the probation officer who prepared the court report on the grounds that he has derived all the benefits that their program has to offer. The District Attorney and arresting narcotics officer feel he is a menace to society and should be sent to prison. They note that he committed several offenses and would have committed more if he hadn't been caught.

In most states the sentencing options available in a case of this sort would include fine or probation, short-term imprisonment in a county jail (with little or no facilities for vocational training, drug treatment, or other rehabilitation), or longer term confinement in state prison (where facilities and rehabilitation programs are normally better). Also available in most jurisdictions are special drug rehabilitation programs involving a mixture of confinement, probation, and medical and psychological treatment.

Question: What sentence should be imposed in this case? For what purpose?

NOTES ON THE ALLOCATION OF SENTENCING AUTHORITY

Until recently, the punishment decision was entrusted largely to the discretion of the trial judge. Statutory limits on sentences, the charging authority of the prosecutor, and the releasing authority of the parole board qualified the trial judge's power, but the individual judge formally controlled the penalty. That situation probably still prevails today in a majority of the states, but a growing minority have moved to limit the trial judge's power (1) by narrowing the range of penalties authorized by statute or by mandating specified punishments, (2) by establishing an administrative agency to promulgate guidelines channeling the choice of sentence in particular cases, (3) by providing for appellate review of trial court sentencing, or (4) by some combination of these measures. Authority

---

a. The CRC (California Rehabilitation Center) program provided for confinement in a special facility oriented toward intensive treatment of offenders with drug-related problems. Similar programs exist in many other states. — EDS.

to determine the actual punishment has always been divided to some degree, and today the divisions are perhaps more complex and less uniform among the states than in the past. The present Notes provide a brief introduction to these important and controversial developments.

1. The traditional sentencing system. The organization of sentencing authority that was found in virtually all jurisdictions until recently is described in Franklin Zimring, Making the Punishment Fit the Crime: A Consumer's Guide to Sentencing Reform, Hastings Center Rep. 13-14 (Dec. 1976):

> The best single phrase to describe the allocation of sentencing power in state and federal criminal justice is "multiple discretion." Putting aside the enormous power of the police to decide whether to arrest, and to select initial charges, there are four separate institutions that have the power to determine criminal sentences — the legislature, the prosecutor, the judge, and the parole board or its equivalent.
>
> The *legislature* sets the range of sentences legally authorized after conviction for a particular criminal charge. Criminal law in the United States is noted for extremely wide ranges of sentencing power, . . . with extremely high maximum penalties and very few limits on how much less than the maximum can be imposed. In practice, then, most legislatures delegate their sentencing powers to other institutions. . . .
>
> The *prosecutor* is not normally thought of as an official who has, or exercises, the power to determine punishment. In practice, however, the prosecutor is the most important institutional determinant of a criminal sentence. . . . He has the legal authority in most systems to determine the specific offense for which a person is to be prosecuted, and this ability to select a charge can also broaden or narrow the range of sentences that can be imposed upon conviction. In congested urban court systems (and elsewhere) he has the absolute power to reduce charges in exchange for guilty pleas and to recommend particular sentences to the court as part of a "plea bargain"; rarely will his recommendation for a lenient sentence be refused in an adversary system in which he is supposed to represent the punitive interests of the state.
>
> The *judge* has the power to select a sentence from the wide range made available by the legislature for any charge that produces a conviction. His powers are discretionary — within this range of legally authorized sanctions his selection cannot be appealed, and is not reviewed. . . . On occasion, the legislature will provide a mandatory minimum sentence, such as life imprisonment for first-degree murder, that reduces the judge's options once a defendant has been convicted of that particular offense. In such cases the prosecutor and judge retain the option to charge or convict a defendant for a lesser offense in order to retain their discretionary power. More often the judge has a wide range of sentencing choices and, influenced by the prosecutor's recommendation, will select either a single sentence (such as two years) or a minimum and maximum sentence (not less than two nor more than five years) for a particular offender.
>
> The *parole* or *correctional authority* normally has the power to modify judicial sentences to a considerable degree. When the judge pronounces a single sentence, such as two years, usually legislation authorizes release from prison to parole after a specified proportion of the sentence has been served. When the judge has provided for a minimum and maximum sentence, such as two to five years, the relative power of the correctional or parole authority is increased, because it has the responsibility to determine at what point in a prison sentence the offender is to be released. The parole board's decision is a discretionary one, traditionally made without guidelines or principles of decision.

2. Disaffection with the traditional approach. The system of broad, unstructured sentencing discretion has come under attack from diverse perspectives. Some object that the inconsistencies and uncertainties associated with discretion undermine deterrence and permit undue leniency. Others see discretion as permitting vindictively harsh punishments and invidious discrimination among offenders. A particularly influential critique of the traditional sentencing structure is that of then-Judge Marvin Frankel, Criminal Sentences: Law Without Order 5, 9-11, 17-23 (1973):

> [T]he almost wholly unchecked and sweeping powers we give to judges in the fashioning of sentences are terrifying and intolerable for a society that professes devotion to the rule of law. . . .
>
> The . . . problem of excessive judicial power reflects a congeries of causes, advertent and accidental. To look only at the most important and positive of these, the prevalent thesis of the last hundred years or so has been that the treatment of criminals must be "individualized." The Mikado's boast, we have proudly thought, was silly; the punishment in a civilized society must fit the unique criminal, not the crime. . . . The ideal of individualized justice is by no means an unmitigated evil, but it must be an ideal of justice *according to law.* This means we just reject individual distinctions — discriminations, that is — unless they can be justified by relevant tests capable of formulation and application with sufficient objectivity to ensure that the results will be more than the idiosyncratic ukases of particular officials, judges or others. . . . The judges simply are not good enough — nobody could be — to redress the fundamental absurdities of the system. . . .
>
> [S]weeping penalty statutes allow sentences to be "individualized" not so much in terms of defendants but mainly in terms of the wide spectrums of character, bias, neurosis, and daily vagary encountered among occupants of the trial bench. It is no wonder that wherever supposed professionals in the field — criminologists, penologists, probation officers, and, yes, lawyers and judges — discuss sentencing, the talk inevitably dwells upon the problem of "disparity." . . . The evidence is conclusive that judges of widely varying attitudes on sentencing, administering statutes that confer huge measures of discretion, mete out widely divergent sentences where the divergences are explainable only by the variations among the judges, not by material differences in the defendants or their crimes. . . .
>
> [T]he tragic state of disorder in our sentencing practices is not attributable to any unique endowments of sadism or bestiality among judges as a species. [Judges] may be somewhat calmer, more dispassionate, and more humane than the average of people across the board. But nobody has the experience of being sentenced by "judges in general." The particular defendant on some existential day confronts a specific judge. The occupant of the bench on that day may be punitive, patriotic, self-righteous, guilt-ridden, and more than customarily dyspeptic. The vice in our system is that all such qualities have free rein as well as potentially fatal impact upon the defendant's finite life.
>
> Such individual, personal powers are not evil only, or mainly, because evil people may come to hold positions of authority. The more pervasive wrong is that a regime of substantially limitless discretion is by definition arbitrary, capricious, and antithetical to the rule of law. . . .

3. The "determinate sentencing" alternative. In response to the problems just described and to public demand for harsher, more consistent punishments, many jurisdictions have replaced the traditional, discretionary systems with some form of "determinate" sentencing, in which possibilities for release on parole are reduced or eliminated, and the range of sentences authorized after conviction is greatly narrowed, either by statutory categories or by guidelines promulgated by an administrative agency. The developments are reviewed in Michael Tonry, Sentencing Reform Impacts (1987).

4. Federal sentencing guidelines. One of the most important of the new approaches to sentencing is the one that Congress adopted for federal criminal prosecutions in the Crime Control Act of 1984. The Act abolished parole and created a United States Sentencing Commission charged with promulgating guidelines for judges to use in federal sentencing decisions. See 28 U.S.C. §§991-998. The Act required the Commission to establish sentencing categories based on specific combinations of offense and offender characteristics and to identify a narrow range of authorized sentences (with no more than a 25 percent spread between minimum and maximum terms of imprisonment) for each category. See 28 U.S.C. §994(b). Judges normally must impose a sentence within the authorized range. See 18 U.S.C. §3553:

> (a) *Factors To Be Considered in Imposing a Sentence.* — The court shall impose a sentence sufficient, but not greater than necessary, to comply with the purposes set forth in paragraph (2) of this subsection. The court, in determining the particular sentence to be imposed, shall consider —
> (1) the nature and circumstances of the offense and the history and characteristics of the defendant;
> (2) the need for the sentence imposed —
> (A) to reflect the seriousness of the offense, to promote respect for the law, and to provide just punishment for the offense;
> (B) to afford adequate deterrence to criminal conduct;
> (C) to protect the public from further crimes of the defendant; and
> (D) to provide the defendant with needed educational or vocational training, medical care, or other correctional treatment in the most effective manner; . . .
> (4) the kinds of sentence and the sentencing range established for the applicable category of offense committed by the applicable category of defendant as set forth in the guidelines that are issued by the Sentencing Commission. . . .
> (b) *Application of Guidelines in Imposing a Sentence.* — The court shall impose a sentence of the kind, and within the range, referred to in subsection (a)(4) unless the court finds that there exists an aggravating or mitigating circumstance of a kind, or to a degree, not adequately taken into consideration by the Sentencing Commission in formulating the guidelines that should result in a sentence different from that described. . . .

The guidelines promulgated by the Commission took effect in 1987. This complex set of rules for calculating federal sentences runs over 400 pages and has been amended annually. For a useful introduction, see Stephen Breyer, The Federal Sentencing Guidelines and the Key Compromises upon which They Rest, 17 Hofstra L. Rev. 1 (1988). Although the guidelines probably have reduced unwarranted disparities in punishment, at least for certain kinds of cases, they remain controversial. Prominent concerns are that the guidelines arguably: (1) create new kinds of disparity in the process of eliminating the old ones, (2) can be overly rigid and thus prevent appropriate individualization of sentences, and (3) can overly restrict the use of probation and require sentences that many critics consider too severe. The issues are explored in Daniel J. Freed,

Federal Sentencing in the Wake of Guidelines: Unacceptable Limits on the Discretion of Sentencers, 101 Yale L.J. 1681 (1992); Stephen J. Schulhofer, Assessing the Federal Sentencing Process: The Problem Is Uniformity, Not Disparity, 29 Am. Crim. L. Rev. 833 (1992).

The next case illustrates one kind of problem that arises under the guidelines, and the complex relationship between penal theories and their implementation in actual cases.

UNITED STATES v. JOHNSON

United States Court of Appeals, 2d Circuit
964 F.2d 124 (1992)

OAKES, J. . . . In the spring of 1989, Cheryl Purvis, a payroll clerk at the Bronx V.A. Hospital, told her co-worker Cynthia Johnson and two others about a scheme Purvis had concocted to steal money by inflating paychecks. By writing pay increases for herself and others on a standard pay adjustment form . . . Purvis was able to secure inflated paychecks. Johnson and the others accepted Purvis's offer to inflate their paychecks, and shortly thereafter Johnson began offering the same to other hospital employees. In return, Purvis and Johnson received fifty percent kickbacks from the employees whose paychecks they inflated. In all, fifteen employees participated in the scheme, receiving a total of approximately $89,222.

The criminal complaint against Purvis and Johnson charged them with stealing money from the government in violation of 18 U.S.C. §641 (1988). The indictment added a charge of bribery in violation of 18 U.S.C. §201 (1988), because the defendants' conduct, while at essence a theft, insofar as it involved the acceptance of kickbacks fitted within the statutory definition of bribery. After a jury trial, the defendants were convicted on all counts. . . .

Judge Patterson calculated Johnson's sentence as follows. The base offense level for the bribery counts, under U.S.S.G. [U.S. Sentencing Guidelines] §2C1.1(a), was ten. The judge then added two levels because Johnson committed more than one bribe, id. §2C1.1(b)(1); added five levels because the total amount of the bribes exceeded $40,000, id. §§2C1.1(b)(2)(A), 2F1.1(b)(1) (F); added four levels for Johnson's role as an organizer of the criminal activity, id. §3B1.1(a); and added two levels for obstruction of justice, id. §3C1.1. These adjustments increased the offense level by thirteen levels, from ten to twenty-three.[a]

The court then proceeded to decrease the offense level. Because Johnson's crime, though technically classifiable as a bribery, "more closely resembl[ed] theft than bribery," the court subtracted two levels. The court deducted one

---

a. The guidelines specify that the authorized sentencing range (in months of imprisonment) is 6-12 months at level 10, 33-41 months at level 20, and 46-57 months at level 23. Where the guideline range is 0-6 months, a judge is permitted to grant probation; where the range is 6-12 months, the judge may grant probation only on condition that the offender serve the minimum term in home detention, community confinement (such as a halfway house or drug treatment center), or intermittent confinement (e.g., spending weekends in jail); where the guideline range is 12-18 months or higher, the entire sentence must be served in prison. See U.S.S.G. §5C1.1. — EDS.

more level because the proceeds of the crime were divided with Purvis. Turning to Johnson's family circumstances, Judge Patterson made the following findings:

> The defendant is a single mother. . . . Her [institutionalized] daughter, age 21 is . . . the mother of a six-year-old child who currently resides with the defendant. Also residing with the defendant in Florida is her son, Lamont, and two children aged six and five, as well as her youngest child, who is five months old. The father of this child is unemployed and resides in Queens, New York. . . . There are no signs of use [of] drugs or alcohol, and she apparently has no mental or emotional health problems.

Concluding that Johnson was solely responsible for the upbringing of four young children, Judge Patterson deducted ten levels. Thus, a total downward departure of thirteen levels yielded a final offense level of ten. The court sentenced Johnson to six months of home detention, followed by three years of supervised release, and restitution of $27,973.

The government would have us hold that family circumstances, taken alone, can never justify a downward departure. . . . The government's argument relies almost entirely on a policy statement issued by the Sentencing Commission, which provides that "[f]amily ties and responsibilities . . . are not ordinarily relevant in determining whether a sentence should be outside the applicable guideline range." U.S.S.G. §5H1.6, p.s. . . .

Congress explicitly provided for sentencing departures in the Sentencing Reform Act of 1984. A district court, according to the statute, may depart from the applicable guideline range if it finds a circumstance "not adequately taken into consideration by the Sentencing Commission in formulating the guidelines." 18 U.S.C. §3553(b) (1988). Policy statements, inasmuch as they are issued by the Commission itself, give a strong indication of what the Commission has, in fact, considered. . . .

The policy statement of U.S.S.G. §5H1.6 . . . leads us to the unsurprising conclusion that the Commission took ordinary family responsibilities into account when formulating the Guidelines. The Sentencing Commission understood that many defendants shoulder responsibilities to their families, their employers, and their communities. Disruption of the defendant's life, and the concomitant difficulties for those who depend on the defendant, are inherent in the punishment of incarceration. The Commission made this clear by explaining that such disruption of the defendant's exercise of responsibility, as a general matter, should not be cause for downward departure. . . .

Extraordinary circumstances, however, are by their nature not capable of adequate consideration. They therefore may constitute proper grounds for departure. Policy statement 5H1.6 does not alter this conclusion, but simply reinforces what we would have expected in any case: . . . ordinary family circumstances do not justify departure, but *extraordinary* family circumstances may. . . .

Such extraordinary family circumstances were present in United States v. Alba, 933 F.2d 1117 (2d Cir. 1991). There, the defendant and his wife cared for their four- and eleven-year-old daughters and the defendant's disabled father and paternal grandmother. Noting the special situation of this "close-knit family whose stability depends on [the defendant's] continued presence," we let stand the sentencing court's finding that "incarceration in accordance with the Guidelines might well result in the destruction of an otherwise strong family unit" and its conclusion "that these circumstances were sufficiently extraordinary in this case to support a downward departure." . . .

To confirm that parental responsibilities can be extraordinary, we need look no further than the circumstances faced by Cynthia Johnson. She faced more than the responsibilities of an ordinary parent, more even than those of an ordinary single parent. Johnson was solely responsible for the upbringing of her three young children, including an infant, and of the young child of her institutionalized daughter. The number, age and circumstances of these children all support the finding that Johnson faced extraordinary parental responsibilities. Johnson's situation, in fact, is substantially more compelling than that of the defendant in *Alba*, whose children were ages four and eleven, and whose spouse could care for their children and elderly dependents.

The rationale for a downward departure here is not that Johnson's family circumstances decrease her culpability, but that we are reluctant to wreak extraordinary destruction on dependents who rely solely on the defendant for their upbringing. Judge Patterson made it clear that the departure was not on behalf of the defendant herself, but on behalf of her family:

> In view of the special circumstances of the defendant — I shouldn't say "defendant," I should say of the "defendant's family," which, as the court sees it, is a family in which the mother is the sole link between the children, the six-month-old child . . . and having the father in Queens who does not contribute to the support of the five- and six-year-old children, . . . a 17-year-old boy having a father who does not contribute to his support, and a six-year-old grandchild whom the mother is unable to keep because of the circumstances of her having another child, at the age of 21, and living in an institution . . . I'm going to reduce the level.

A week later, at Purvis's sentencing, the court explained the Johnson departure: "I did feel that those children being without a mother for an extended period of time was a hardship on them, not on her, hardship on them, and that was extraordinary grounds for a departure."

. . . [W]e are satisfied that Judge Patterson's departure was reasonable.

Accordingly, the judgment of the district court is affirmed.

NOTES

1. According to what theory of punishment does Johnson's family situation warrant a reduction in her sentence?

2. Johnson's co-defendant, Cheryl Purvis, was also a first offender. Judge Patterson placed her at guideline level 18 (which specifies a sentence range of 27-33 months), and he sentenced her to 27 months in prison, followed by supervised release for 2 years, and restitution of $20,183. Was Purvis a victim of sentencing "disparity"?

3. In United States v. Alba, 933 F.2d 1117 (2d Cir. 1991), defendant, a first offender, pled guilty to a charge of conspiracy to distribute two kilograms of cocaine. The authorized sentence range under the guidelines was 41-51 months' imprisonment. The district judge departed downward and sentenced the defendant to 6 months in a halfway house. One of the principal justifications for the departure was the defendant's family situation: He had been married for 12 years, had held a steady job and was responsible for the support of his wife, his 2 children (aged 4 and 11), his disabled father, and his grandmother. The court of appeals noted (id. at 1122) that defendant "was aptly described as a man who works hard to provide for his family," and that "his is a close-knit family whose stability depends on [his] continued presence." Do these family circumstances warrant a below-guideline sentence? If so, how much of a downward departure is appropriate?

4. *Problems.* (a) Smith is a lawyer convicted of helping a client "launder" money and perpetrate a tax fraud. Based on the dollar amounts involved and other factors, Smith's guideline range is 51-63 months. Smith is currently supporting his 2 children, aged 2 and 9, and his wife, who is unable to work because of a back ailment. All of Smith's assets have been exhausted defending against the charges. If he is sent to prison, his wife and children will probably have to go on welfare. Does Smith's family situation warrant a reduction in his sentence?

(b) Jones carries a quantity of cocaine from New Jersey to New York, where she is arrested by federal agents. Based on the quantity of the drug and other factors, the guideline range is 33-41 months' imprisonment. While awaiting trial Jones gets pregnant, and when she appears before the judge for sentencing, she is due to deliver her baby in 6 months. Guideline §5H1.4 states that a defendant's physical condition is "not ordinarily relevant," but it does not refer explicitly to pregnancy. Should Jones's pregnancy affect the length of her sentence? Alternatively, should Jones be permitted to defer the start of her imprisonment until after the baby is born? Note that after the birth, if no member of Jones's family is able to care for her baby, it may be necessary to place the baby in foster care or an institution. In that event, should Jones qualify for a reduction in sentence on the basis of her family responsibilities? See United States v. Pozzy, 902 F.2d 133, 138-139 (1st Cir. 1990); Myrna C. Raeder, Gender and Sentencing: Single Moms, Battered Women and Other Sex-Based Anomalies in the Gender-Free World of the Federal Sentencing Guidelines, 20 Pepp. L. Rev. 905, 945-962 (1993).

C.   WHAT TO PUNISH?

INTRODUCTORY NOTE

It is obvious that our society does not subject to criminal punishment all conduct that is antisocial or otherwise undesirable. Criminal punishment is only one of many sanctions available to induce compliance with preferred norms of conduct. A society may attempt to discourage undesired conduct by taxing it; it may provide for civil liability, including injunctive relief at the behest of a public agency or an injured party; it may establish an agency to govern such behavior through licenses, rules, and regulations; or, for, reasons practical or principled, it may leave it to be dealt with by private social pressures.

When, then, is criminal punishment the appropriate choice? What is there about the nature of punishment that may make it improper or unsuitable for certain kinds of conduct? At least when we pass beyond the major forms of invasion of personal security and property and community security to the numerous and varied lesser forms of conduct that are thought to be undesirable, the issues are of great consequence.

For an introduction to the problems of the reach of the criminal law, we have chosen as a principal example the use of the criminal law to deal with sexual misconduct. This area has witnessed revolutionary changes in the last generation. Criminal prohibitions long imbedded in American laws — on sex outside of marriage, unconventional sex practices, and homosexuality (though not prostitution) — have been lifted in many jurisdictions. Following the lead of the Model Penal Code §17, recently revised state penal codes have omitted adultery and fornication statutes. Model Penal Code and Commentaries, Note to Article 213 at 439 (1980). More than one-half of the states now exclude criminal sanctions for any form of sexual intimacy between husband and wife. Id., Comment to §213.2 at 364. Laws prohibiting adult consensual homosexuality have also changed, though more slowly. The Model Penal Code Commentary states (id. at 372-373):

> As of that date [1955], the Model Penal Code exclusion of criminal penalties for consensual sodomy was without precedent in this country.
>
> Many European nations had excepted private sexual behavior from their penal laws and Great Britain has since followed suit by enacting the recommendations of the Wolfenden Commission in 1967. In 1961, Illinois became the first American jurisdiction to adopt the Model Code position. A number of other states have taken this step in recent revisions, and . . . even though many states still punish consensual sodomy, most modern revision efforts effect a substantial reduction in the gravity of sanctions authorized for such behavior.

[For a survey of state law, see Note, Survey on the Constitutional Right to Privacy in the Context of Homosexual Activity, 40 Miami U. L. Rev. 521 (1986).]

NEW YORK REVISED PENAL LAW: *Section 1.05*. The general purposes of the provisions of this chapter: 1. To proscribe conduct which unjustifiably and inexcusably causes or threatens substantial harm to individual or public interests.

CRIMINAL JUSTICE REFORM ACT OF 1973, S. 1, 93d Cong., 1st Sess.: *Section 1-1A.2*. General Purposes: The purpose of this code is to establish order with justice so that the nation and its people may be secure in their persons, property, relationships, and other interests. This code aims at the articulation of the nation's fundamental system of values and its vindication through the imposition of merited punishment.

LOUIS B. SCHWARTZ, THE PROPOSED FEDERAL CRIMINAL CODE, COMPARISON OF S. 1 AND THE RECOMMENDATIONS OF THE NATIONAL COMMISSION ON REFORM OF FEDERAL CRIMINAL LAWS 10 (Feb. 19, 1973) (mimeo): S. 1 injects a new, false, and dangerous notion that the criminal code "aims at the articulation of the nation's fundamental system of public values" and its vindication through punishment. A criminal code necessarily falls far short of expressing the nation's morality. Many things are evil or undesirable without being at all appropriate for imprisonment: lying, overcharging for goods and services, marital infidelity, lack of charity or patriotism. Nothing has been more widely recognized in modern criminal law scholarship than the danger of creating more evil by ill-considered use of the criminal law than is caused by the target misconduct. Accordingly, the failure to put something under the ban of the penal code is not an expression of a favorable "value" of the nonpenalized behavior. It is a fatal confusion of values to see the Criminal Code as anything but a list of those most egregious misbehaviors, which, according to a broad community consensus, can be usefully dealt with by social force.

BOWERS v. HARDWICK

Supreme Court of the United States
478 U.S. 186 (1986)

JUSTICE WHITE delivered the opinion of the Court.

In August 1982, respondent was charged with violating the Georgia statute criminalizing sodomy[1] by committing that act with another adult male in the bedroom of respondent's home. After a preliminary hearing, the District Attorney decided not to present the matter to the grand jury unless further evidence developed.

Respondent then brought suit in the Federal District Court, challenging the constitutionality of the statute insofar as it criminalized consensual sodomy. He asserted that he was a practicing homosexual, that the Georgia sodomy statute, as administered by the defendants, placed him in imminent danger of arrest, and that the statute for several reasons violates the Federal Constitution. . . .

A divided panel of the Court of Appeals for the Eleventh Circuit [held] that the Georgia statute violated respondent's fundamental rights because his homosexual activity is a private and intimate association that is beyond the reach of state regulation by reason of the Ninth Amendment and the Due process Clause of the Fourteenth Amendment. . . . We agree with the State that the Court of Appeals erred. . . .

This case does not require a judgment on whether laws against sodomy between consenting adults in general, or between homosexuals in particular, are wise or desirable. It raises no question about the right or propriety of state legislative decisions to repeal their laws that criminalize homosexual sodomy, or of state court decisions invalidating those laws on state constitutional grounds. The issue presented is whether the Federal Constitution confers a fundamental right upon homosexuals to engage in sodomy and hence invalidates the laws of the many states that still make such conduct illegal and have done so for a very long time. . . .

[R]espondent would have us announce, as the Court of Appeals did, a fundamental right to engage in homosexual sodomy. This we are quite unwilling to do. . . . It is true that despite the language of the Due Process Clauses of the Fifth

---

1. Ga. Code Ann. §16-6-2 (1984) provides, in pertinent part, as follows:

(a) A person commits the offense of sodomy when he performs or submits to any sexual act involving the sex organs of one person and the mouth or anus of another. . . .

(b) A person convicted of the offense of sodomy shall be punished by imprisonment for not less than one nor more than 20 years. . . .

and Fourteenth Amendments, which appears to focus only on the processes by which life, liberty, or property is taken, the cases are legion in which those Clauses have been interpreted to have substantive content, subsuming rights that to a great extent are immune from federal or state regulation or proscription. Among such cases are those recognizing rights that have little or no textual support in the constitutional language. [As examples, the Court here mentioned, among other cases, Meyer v. Nebraska, 262 U.S. 390 (1923) (dealing with child rearing and education); Loving v. Virginia, 388 U.S. 1 (1967) (right to marry); and Roe v. Wade, 410 U.S. 113 (1973) (right to abortion).] . . .

In Palko v. Connecticut, 302 U.S. 319, 325, 326 (1937), it was said that this category includes those fundamental liberties that are "implicit in the concept of ordered liberty," such that "neither liberty nor justice would exist if [they] were sacrificed." A different description of fundamental liberties appeared in Moore v. East Cleveland, 431 U.S. 494, 503, (1977) (opinion of Powell, J.), where they are characterized as those liberties that are "deeply rooted in this Nation's history and tradition."

It is obvious to us that neither of these formulations would extend a fundamental right to homosexuals to engage in acts of consensual sodomy. Proscriptions against that conduct have ancient roots. Sodomy was a criminal offense at common law and was forbidden by the laws of the original thirteen States when they ratified the Bill of Rights. In 1868, when the Fourteenth Amendment was ratified, all but 5 of the 37 States in the Union had criminal sodomy laws. In fact, until 1961, all 50 States outlawed sodomy, and today, 24 States and the District of Columbia continue to provide criminal penalties for sodomy performed in private and between consenting adults. Against this background, to claim that a right to engage in such conduct is "deeply rooted in this Nation's history and tradition" or "implicit in the concept of ordered liberty" is, at best, facetious. . . .

Even if the conduct at issue here is not a fundamental right, respondent asserts that there must be a rational basis for the law and that there is none in this case other than the presumed belief of a majority of the electorate in Georgia that homosexual sodomy is immoral and unacceptable. This is said to be an inadequate rationale to support the law. The law, however, is constantly based on notions of morality, and if all laws representing essentially moral choices are to be invalidated under the Due Process Clause, the courts will be very busy indeed. Even respondent makes no such claim, but insists that majority sentiments about the morality of homosexuality should be declared inadequate. We do not agree, and are unpersuaded that the sodomy laws of some 25 States should be invalidated on this basis.

Reversed.

CHIEF JUSTICE BURGER, concurring.

I join the Court's opinion, but I write separately to underscore my view that in constitutional terms there is no such thing as a fundamental right to commit homosexual sodomy.

. . . Decisions of individuals relating to homosexual conduct have been subject to state intervention throughout the history of Western civilization. Condemnation of those practices is firmly rooted in Judaeo-Christian moral and ethical standards. . . . To hold that the act of homosexual sodomy is somehow protected as a fundamental right would be to cast aside millennia of moral teaching. . . .

JUSTICE BLACKMUN, with whom JUSTICE BRENNAN, JUSTICE MARSHALL, and JUSTICE STEVENS join, dissenting.

This case is [not] about "a fundamental right to engage in homosexual sodomy," as the Court purports to declare. . . . Rather, this case is about "the most comprehensive of rights and the right most valued by civilized men," namely, "the right to be let alone." Olmstead v. United States, 277 U.S. 438, 478 (1928) (Brandeis, J., dissenting).

The statute at issue, Ga. Code Ann. §16-6-2 (1984), denies individuals the right to decide for themselves whether to engage in particular forms of private, consensual sexual activity. . . . I believe we must analyze respondent's claim in the light of the values that underlie the constitutional right to privacy. If that right means anything, it means that, before Georgia can prosecute its citizens for making choices about the most intimate aspects of their lives, it must do more than assert that the choice they have made is an " 'abominable crime not fit to be named among Christians,' " Herring v. State, 119 Ga. 709, 721, 46 S.E. 876, 882 (1904).

[T]he Court's almost obsessive focus on homosexual activity is particularly hard to justify in light of the broad language Georgia has used. Unlike the Court, the Georgia Legislature has not proceeded on the assumption that homosexuals are so different from other citizens that their lives may be controlled in a way that would not be tolerated if it limited the choices of those other citizens. Rather, Georgia has provided that "[a] person commits the offense of sodomy when he performs or submits to any sexual act involving the sex organs of one person and the mouth or anus of another." The sex or status of the persons who engage in the act is irrelevant as a matter of state law. . . . Michael Hardwick's standing may rest in significant part on Georgia's apparent willingness to enforce against homosexuals a law it seems not to have any desire to enforce against heterosexuals. But his claim that §16-6-2 involves an unconstitutional intrusion into his privacy and his right of intimate association does not depend in any way on his sexual orientation. . . . "Our cases long have recognized that the Constitution embodies a promise that a certain private sphere of individual liberty will be kept largely beyond the reach of government." Thornburgh v. American Coll. of Obst. & Gyn., 106 S. Ct. 2169 (1986). . . .

Only the most willful blindness could obscure the fact that sexual intimacy is "a sensitive, key relationship of human existence, central to family life, community welfare, and the development of human personality." The fact that individuals define themselves in a significant way through their intimate sexual relationships with others suggests, in a Nation as diverse as ours, that there may be many "right" ways of conducting those relationships, and that much of the richness of a relationship will come from the freedom an individual has to *choose* the form and nature of these intensely personal bonds. . . .

[N]either of the two general justifications for §16-6-2 that petitioner has advanced warrants dismissing respondent's challenge for failure to state a claim.

First, petitioner asserts that the acts made criminal by the statute may have serious adverse consequences for "the general public health and welfare," such as spreading communicable diseases or fostering other criminal activity. Inasmuch as this case was dismissed by the District Court on the pleadings, it is not surprising that the record before us is barren of any evidence to support petitioner's claim. In light of the state of the record, I see no justification for the Court's attempt to equate the private, consensual sexual activity at issue here with the "possession in the home of drugs, firearms, or stolen goods," to which [this Court] refused to extend its protection. None of the behavior so mentioned . . . can properly be viewed as "[v]ictimless": drugs and weapons are inherently dangerous, and for property to be "stolen," someone must have been wrongfully deprived of it. Nothing in the record before the Court provides any justification for finding the activity forbidden by §16-6-2 to be physically danger-ous, either to the persons engaged in it or to others.[4]

The core of petitioner's defense of §16-6-2, however, is that respondent and others who engage in the conduct prohibited by §16-6-2 interfere with Georgia's exercise of the "right of the Nation and of the States to maintain a decent soci-ety." Essentially, petitioner argues, and the Court agrees, that the fact that the acts described in §16-6-2 "for hundreds of years, if not thousands, have been uniformly condemned as immoral" is a sufficient reason to permit a State to ban them today.

I cannot agree that either the length of time a majority has held its convictions or the passions with which it defends them can withdraw legislation from this Court's scrutiny. . . .

The assertion that "traditional Judeo-Christian values proscribe" the conduct involved cannot provide an adequate justification for §16-6-2. That certain, but by no means all, religious groups condemn the behavior at issue gives the State no license to impose their judgments on the entire citizenry. The legitimacy of secular legislation depends instead on whether the State can advance some jus-tification for its law beyond its conformity to religious doctrine. Thus, far from buttressing his case, petitioner's invocation of Leviticus, Romans, St. Thomas Aquinas, and sodomy's heretical status during the Middle Ages undermines his suggestion that §16-6-2 represents a legitimate use of secular coercive power.[6] A State can no more punish private behavior because of religious intolerance than it can punish such behavior because of racial animus. "The Constitution cannot control such prejudices, but neither can it tolerate them. Private biases may be outside the reach of the law, but the law cannot, directly or indirectly, give them effect." Palmore v. Sidoti, 466 U.S. 429, 433 (1984). . . .

Nor can §16-6-2 be justified as a "morally neutral" exercise of Georgia's power to "protect the public environment," [Paris Adult Theatre Slaton, 413 U.S. 49, 68-69 (1973)]. 413 U.S., at 68-69. Petitioner and the Court fail to see the differ-

---

4. Although I do not think it necessary to decide today issues that are not even remotely before us, it does seem to me that a court could find simple, analytically sound distinctions between certain private, consensual sexual conduct, on the one hand, and adultery and incest (the only two vaguely specific "sexual crimes" to which the majority points), on the other. For example, marriage, in addition to its spiritual aspects, is a civil contract that entitles the contracting parties to a variety of governmentally provided benefits. A State might define the contractual commitment necessary to become eligible for these benefits to include a commitment of fidelity and then punish individuals for breaching that contract. Moreover, a State might conclude that adultery is likely to injure third persons, in particular, spouses and children of persons who engage in extramarital affairs. With respect to incest, a court might well agree with respondent that the nature of familial relationships renders true consent to incestuous activity sufficiently problematical that a blanket prohibition of such activity is warranted. Notably, the Court makes no effort to explain why it has chosen to group private, consensual homosexual activity with adultery and incest rather than with private, consen-sual heterosexual activity by unmarried persons or, indeed, with oral or anal sex within marriage.

6. The theological nature of the origin of Anglo-American antisodomy statutes is patent. It was not until 1533 that sodomy was made a secular offense in England. Until that time, the offense was, in Sir James Stephen's words, "merely ecclesiastical." . . . The transfer of jurisdiction over prosecu-tions for sodomy to the secular courts seems primarily due to the alteration of ecclesiastical juris-diction attendant on England's break with the Roman Catholic Church, rather than to any new understanding of the sovereign's interest in preventing or punishing the behavior involved.

ence between laws that protect public sensibilities and those that enforce private morality. . . . [T]he mere fact that intimate behavior may be punished when it takes place in public cannot dictate how States can regulate intimate behavior that occurs in intimate places.

This case involves no real interference with the rights of others, for the mere knowledge that other individuals do not adhere to one's value system cannot be a legally cognizable interest, let alone an interest that can justify invading the houses, hearts, and minds of citizens who choose to live their lives differently.

NOTE

Although the majority in *Bowers* found that the federal constitution does not create a right to engage in homosexual sex, a few state courts have ruled that their own constitutions do. For example, the Kentucky Supreme Court held that Kentucky's homosexual sodomy law violated the privacy and equal protection guarantees of the Kentucky state constitution. Wasson v. Kentucky, 842 S.W.2d 487 (1992); see also Texas v. Morales, 826 S.W.2d 201 (Text. Ct. App. 1992).

HOME OFFICE, SCOTTISH HOME DEPARTMENT, REPORT OF THE COMMITTEE ON HOMOSEXUAL OFFENSES AND PROSTITUTION (WOLFENDEN REPORT)
9-10, 20-21, 79-80 (1957)

48. [W]e have reviewed the existing provisions of the law in relation to homosexual behaviour between male persons. We have found that with the great majority of these provisions we are in complete agreement. We believe that it is part of the function of the law to safeguard those who need protection by reason of their youth or some mental defect, and we do not wish to see any change in the law that would weaken this protection. Men who commit offences against such persons should be treated as criminal offenders. Whatever may be the causes of their disposition or the proper treatment for it, the law must assume that the responsibility for the overt acts remains theirs, except where there are circumstances which it accepts as exempting from accountability. Offences of this kind are particularly reprehensible when the men who commit them are in positions of special responsibility or trust. We have been made aware that where a man is involved in an offence with a boy or youth the invitation to the commission of the act sometimes comes from him rather than from the man. But we believe that even when this is so that fact does not serve to exculpate the man.

49. It is also part of the function of the law to preserve public order and decency. We therefore hold that when homosexual behavior between males takes place in public it should continue to be dealt with by the criminal law. . . .

52. [W]e have reached the conclusion that legislation which covers acts [committed between adults in private] goes beyond the proper sphere of the law's concern. We do not think that it is proper for the law to concern itself with what a man does in private unless it can be shown to be so contrary to the public good that the law ought to intervene in its function as the guardian of that public good. . . .

61. . . . There remains one additional . . . argument which we believe to be decisive, namely, the importance which society and the law ought to give to individual freedom of choice and action in matters of private morality. Unless a deliberate attempt is to be made by society, acting through the agency of the law, to equate the sphere of crime with that of sin, there must remain a realm of private morality and immorality which is, in brief and crude terms, not the law's business. To say this is not to condone or encourage private immorality. On the contrary, to emphasise the personal and private nature of moral or immoral conduct is to emphasise the personal and private responsibility of the individual for his own actions, and that is a responsibility which a mature agent can properly be expected to carry for himself without the threat of punishment from the law. . . .[a]

PATRICK DEVLIN, THE ENFORCEMENT OF MORALS
2, 4, 6-10, 13-14, 17 (1965)

What is the connection between crime and sin and to what extent, if at all, should the criminal law of England concern itself with the enforcement of morals and punish sin or immorality as such?

The statements of principle in the Wolfenden Report provide an admirable and modern starting-point for such an inquiry. . . .

I must admit that I begin with a feeling that a complete separation of crime from sin . . . would not be good for the moral law and might be disastrous for the criminal. But can this sort of feeling be justified as a matter of jurisprudence? And if it be a right feeling how should the relationship between the criminal and the moral law be stated? Is there a good theoretical basis for it, or is it just a practical working alliance, or is it a bit of both? That is the problem which I want to examine. . . .

The criminal law of England has from the very first concerned itself with moral principles. A simple way of testing this point is to consider the attitude which the criminal law adopts towards consent.

Subject to certain exceptions inherent in the nature of particular crimes, the criminal law has never permitted consent of the victim to be used as a defence. In rape, for example, consent negatives an essential element. But consent of the victim is no defence to a charge of murder. It is not a defence to any form of assault that the victim thought his punishment well deserved and submitted to it; to make a good defence the accused must prove that the law gave him the right to chastise and that he exercised it reasonably. Likewise, the victim may not forgive the aggressor and require the prosecution to desist; the right to enter a nolle prosequi belongs to the Attorney-General alone.

Now, if the law existed for the protection of the individual, there would be no reason why he should avail himself of it if he did not want it. The reason why a

---

a. Ten years after the publication of the recommendations of the Wolfenden Report, Parliament repealed criminal penalties for homosexual acts committed in private by consenting adults in England. Sexual Offenses Act, Pt. II, ch. 60 (1967). A later study of related issues is contained in the Working Party Report of the Sexual Law Reform Society. A shortened version of this report may be found in [1975] Crim. L. Rev. 323 — Eds.

man may not consent to the commission of an offence against himself before-hand or forgive it afterwards is because it is an offence against society. . . .

Thus, if the criminal law were to be reformed so as to eliminate from it every-thing that was not designed to preserve order and decency or to protect citizens (including the protection of youth from corruption), it would overturn a fun-damental principle. It would also end a number of specific crimes. Euthanasia, or the killing of another at his own request, suicide, attempted suicide and sui-cide pacts, dueling, abortion, incest between brother and sister, are all acts which can be done in private and without offence to others and need not involve the corruption or exploitation of others. . . .

I think it is clear that the criminal law as we know it is based upon moral principle. In a number of crimes its function is simply to enforce a moral prin-ciple and nothing else. . . .

In jurisprudence, as I have said, everything is thrown open to discussion and, in the belief that they cover the whole field, I have framed three interrogatories addressed to myself to answer:

1. Has society the right to pass judgement at all on matters of morals? Ought there, in other words, to be a public morality, or are morals always a matter for private judgment?
2. If society has the right to pass judgment, has it also the right to use the weapon of the law to enforce it?
3. If so, ought it to use that weapon in all cases or only in some; and if only in some, on what principles should it distinguish? . . .

The language used in . . . the Wolfenden Report suggest[s] the view that there ought not to be a collective judgment about immorality per se. Is this what is meant by "private morality" and "individual freedom of choice and action"? . . . In truth, the Report takes it for granted that there is in existence a public mo-rality which condemns homosexuality and prostitution. What the Report seems to mean by private morality might perhaps be better described as private behav-iour in matters of morals.

This view — that there is such a thing as public morality — can also be justi-fied by a priori argument. What makes a society of any sort is community of ideas, not only political ideas but also ideas about the way its members should behave and govern their lives; these latter ideas are its morals. Every society has a moral structure as well as a political one: or rather, since that might suggest two independent systems, I should say that the structure of every society is made up both of politics and morals. . . .

[W]ithout shared ideas on politics, morals, and ethics no society can exist. Each one of us has ideas about what is good and what is evil; they cannot be kept private from the society in which we live. If men and women try to create a society in which there is no fundamental agreement about good and evil they will fail; if having based it on common agreement, the agreement goes, the so-ciety will disintegrate. For society is not something that is kept together physi-cally; it is held by the invisible bonds of common thought. If the bonds were too far relaxed the members would drift apart. A common morality is part of the bondage. The bondage is part of the price of society; and mankind, which needs society, must pay its price. . . .

Society is entitled by means of its laws to protect itself from dangers, whether from within or without. Here again I think that the political parallel is legitimate. The law of treason is directed against aiding the king's enemies and against sedition from within. The justification for this is that established government is necessary for the existence of society and therefore its safety against violent overthrow must be secured. But an established morality is as necessary as good government to the welfare of society. Societies disintegrate from within more frequently than they are broken up by external pressures. There is disintegration when no common morality is observed and history shows that the loosening of moral bonds is often the first state of disintegration, so that society is justified in taking the same steps to preserve its moral code as it does to preserve its government and other essential institutions. The suppression of vice is as much the law's business as the suppression of subversive activities; it is no more possible to define a sphere of private morality than it is to define one of private subversive activity. . . .

Nothing should be punished by the law that does not lie beyond the limits of tolerance. It is not nearly enough to say that a majority dislike a practice; there must be a real feeling of reprobation. Those who are dissatisfied with the present law on homosexuality often say that the opponents of reform are swayed simply by disgust. If that were so it would be wrong, but I do not think one can ignore disgust if it is deeply felt and not manufactured. Its presence is a good indication that the bounds of toleration are being reached. Not everything is to be tolerated. No society can do without tolerance, indignation, and disgust; they are the forces behind the moral law, and indeed it can be argued that if they or something like them are not present the feelings of society cannot be weighty enough to deprive the individual of freedom of choice. . . . Every moral judgment, unless it claims a divine source, is simply a feeling that no right-minded man could behave in any other way without admitting that he was doing wrong. . . . There is, for example, a general abhorrence of homosexuality. We should ask ourselves in the first instance whether looking at it calmly and dispassionately, we regard it as a vice so abominable that its mere presence is an offence. If that is the genuine feeling of the society in which we live, I do not see how society can be denied the right to eradicate it. . . .[b]

NOTES

1. In the course of his argument, Lord Devlin observes (at 176) that if the law were to be reformed along the lines of the Wolfenden Report "it would overturn

b. For a similar view from a sociologist, see Emile Durkheim, The Division of Labor in Society 93-107 (Simpson trans. 1933).

> Thus we see what type of solidarity penal law symbolizes. Everybody knows that there is a social cohesion whose cause lies in a certain conformity of all particular consciences to a common type which is none other than the psychic type of society. In these conditions, not only are all the members of the group individually attracted to one another because they resemble one another, but also because they are joined to what is the condition of existence of this collective type; that is to say, to the society that they form by their union. Not only do citizens love each other and seek each other out in preference to strangers, but they love their country. . . . It is this solidarity which repressive law expresses, at least whatever there is vital in it. . . ."

Id. at 105-106. — EDS.

a fundamental principle" and "would also end a number of specific crimes," including "euthanasia, or the killing of another at his request, suicide, attempted suicide and suicide pacts, dueling, abortion, incest between brother and sister." In the United States, while the Supreme Court has declined to hold sodomy laws unconstitutional (Bowers v. Hardwick, supra), homosexual practices are no longer a crime in many states. Moreover, even where they are still criminal, enforcement practices have produced a substantial informal decriminalization. And, indeed, some of the consequences Lord Devlin predicted would follow a decriminalization of homosexual practices have occurred in the years since his lecture. Some practices that would have been condemned as euthanasia have been decriminalized by judicial decision. Further, a more accepting attitude to suicide has emerged: Attempted suicide has long ceased to be criminal in virtually all jurisdictions, and laws against helping another to commit suicide, while still on the books of half the states, have been increasingly subject to constitutional attack. (These issues are explored infra pages 197, 880.) In addition, abortion is now constitutionally protected in the United States. Roe v. Wade, 410 U.S. 113 (1973). What relevance does all this have to Lord Devlin's thesis? Does it strengthen it, weaken it, or leave it unaffected?

2. Consent to serious physical assault is uniformly held to constitute no defense. See the recent House of Lords decision in Regina v. Brown, [1993] 2 All E.R. 75, reviewing the common law history and declining to make an exception for voluntary sadomasochistic wounding, on the ground that consent is a defense to assault only in a restricted class of cases, such as necessary surgery and regulated sports. See Law Commission Consultation Paper No. 134, Consent and Offences Against the Person (H.M.S.O. 1994). The same is true in the United States. See, e.g., People v. Samuels, 250 Cal. App. 2d 501 (Ct. App. 1967). A comment on this case in 81 Harv. L. Rev. 1339, 1340 (1968), observes:

> Surgeons who perform an operation at the request of a patient as well as sports participants who injure opponents in the course of competition appear to be in no danger of conviction. On the other hand, assaults involving aberrant behavior or conduct with no apparent social utility are often held to be criminal without regard to the consent of the victim if the force used has as its probable result bodily injury.

Question: Is the distinction between boxing and consensual sadomasochistic beatings a tenable one?

3. Professor H. L. A. Hart in Law, Liberty, and Morality (1963), replies to Devlin's argument founded on the law's acceptance of the principle that consent of the victim is no defense. Devlin argued that the function of disallowing this defense is "to enforce a moral principle and nothing else" — the moral principle being the sanctity of human life and physical integrity of the person. Hart disagrees, stating (id. at 31) that the

> rules excluding the victim's consent as a defense to charges of murder or assault may perfectly well be explained as a piece of paternalism, designed to protect individuals against themselves. Mill no doubt might have protested against a paternalistic policy of using the law to protect even a consenting victim from bodily harm nearly as much as he protested against laws used merely to enforce positive morality; but this does not mean that these two policies are identical.

To what extent can the distinctions that courts have made as to when to recognize consent as a defense (discussed in the preceding note) be explained on grounds of paternalism rather than legal moralism? Is it physical injury to persons, even consenting persons, that the courts are protecting against or physical harm in the course of immoral behavior?[6]

4. On the issue of the consensus on moral standards, which Lord Devlin argues is legitimately expressed by criminal prohibitions, Professor Gusfield contributes the insight that in many situations it is not consensus that is expressed but rather the symbolic interim victory of one set of contending forces or interests over another. See Joseph Gusfield, On Legislating Morals: The Symbolic Process of Designating Deviancy, 56 Cal. L. Rev. 54, 58-59 (1968):

> Affirmation through law and governmental acts expresses the public worth of one subculture's norms relative to those of others, demonstrating which cultures have legitimacy and public domination. Accordingly it enhances the social status of groups carrying the affirmed culture and degrades groups carrying that which is condemned as deviant. . . . My analysis of the American temperance movement has shown how the issue of drinking and abstinence became a politically significant focus for the conflicts between Protestant and Catholic, rural and urban, native and immigrant, middle class and lower class in American society, as an abstinent Protestant middle class attempted to control the public affirmation of morality in drinking. Victory or defeat thus symbolized the status and power of the opposing cultures, indicating that legal affirmation or rejection can have symbolic as well as instrumental importance.

5. Professor Joel Feinberg has produced a comprehensive treatment of the issues of the proper limits of the criminal sanction in a multi-volumed treatise entitled The Moral Limits of the Criminal Law, comprising the following: Volume 1, Harm to Others (1984); Volume 2, Offense to Others (1985); Volume 3, Harm to Self (1986); Volume 4, Harmless Wrongdoing (1988). The last deals most directly with the issues here raised, issues that Professor Feinberg brings together under the heading "legal moralism."

SANFORD H. KADISH, THE CRISIS OF OVERCRIMINALIZATION, 374 The Annals 157 (1967): My objective is to call attention to matters of the hardest concreteness and practicality, which should be of as much concern in reaching final judgment to a Devlin as to the staunchest libertarian; namely, the adverse consequences to effective law enforcement of attempting to achieve conformity with private moral standards through use of the criminal law.

The classic instance of the use of the criminal law purely to enforce a moral code is the laws prohibiting extra-marital and abnormal sexual intercourse between a man and a woman. [It is not] disputed that there is no effort to enforce these laws. The traditional function of the criminal law, therefore — to curtail socially threatening behavior through the threat of punishment and the incapacitation and rehabilitation of offenders — is quite beside the point. Thurman Arnold surely had it right when he observed that these laws "are unenforced

---

6. Professor Hart develops a full-dress reply to Devlin in his Law, Liberty, and Morality (1962). See also his later article, Social Solidarity and the Enforcement of Morality, 35 U. Chi. L. Rev. 1 (1967). For other treatment of the issues, see D. Don Welch, Legitimate Government Purposes and State Enforcement of Morality, 1993 Univ. Ill. L. Rev. 67; Ronald Dworkin, Lord Devlin and the Enforcement of Morals, 75 Yale L.J. 986 (1966); Graham Hughes, Morals and the Criminal Law, 71 Yale L.J. 662 (1962).

because we want to continue our conduct, and unrepealed because we want to preserve our morals."

But law enforcement pays a price for using the criminal law in this way. First, the moral message communicated by the law is contradicted by the total absence of enforcement; for while the public sees the conduct condemned in words, it also sees in the dramatic absence of prosecutions that it is not condemned in deed. Moral adjurations vulnerable to a charge of hypocrisy are self-defeating no less in law than elsewhere. Second, the spectacle of nullification of the legislature's solemn commands is an unhealthy influence on law enforcement generally. It tends to breed a cynicism and an indifference to the criminal-law processes which augment tendencies toward disrespect for those who make and enforce the law, a disrespect which is already widely in evidence. . . .

Finally, these laws invite discriminatory enforcement against persons selected for prosecution on grounds unrelated to the evil against which these laws are purportedly addressed, whether those grounds be "the prodding of some reform group, a newspaper-generated hysteria over some local sex crime, a vice drive which is put on by the local authorities to distract attention from defects in their administration of the city government." . . .

The criminalization of consensual adult homosexuality represents another attempt to legislate private morality. . . . One major reason for the ineffectiveness of these laws is that the private and consensual nature of the conduct precludes the attainment of any substantial deterrent efficacy through law enforcement. There are no complainants, and only the indiscreet have reasons for fear. Another reason is the irrelevance of the threat of punishment. Homosexuality involves not so much a choice to act wickedly as the seeking of normal sexual fulfillment in abnormal ways (though not abnormal to the individual) preferred by the individual for reasons deeply rooted in his development as a personality. . . .

On the other hand, the use of the criminal law has been attended by grave consequences. . . . [E]nforcement efforts by police have created problems both for them and for the community. Opportunities for enforcement are limited by the private and consensual character of the behavior. . . . To obtain evidence, police are obliged to resort to behavior which tends to degrade and demean both themselves personally and law enforcement as an institution. However one may deplore homosexual conduct, no one can lightly accept a criminal law which requires for its enforcement that officers of the law sit concealed in ceilings, their eyes fixed to "peepholes," searching for criminal sexuality in the lavatories below, or that they loiter suggestively around public toilets or in corridors hopefully awaiting a sexual advance. Such conduct corrupts both citizenry and police and reduces the moral authority of the criminal law, especially among those liable to be treated in an arbitrary fashion. The complaint of the critical that the police have more important things to do with their time is amply attested by the several volumes of the National Crime Commission's reports.

The offense of prostitution creates similar problems. Although there are social harms beyond private immorality in commercialized sex — spread of venereal disease, exploitation of the young, and the affront of public solicitation, for example — the blunt use of the criminal prohibition has proven ineffective and costly. Prostitution has perdured in all civilizations; indeed, few institutions have proven as hardy. The inevitable conditions of social life unfailingly produce the supply to meet the ever-present demand. As the Wolfenden Report observed: "There are limits to the degree of discouragement which the criminal law can properly exercise towards a woman who has deliberately decided to live her life in this way, or a man who has deliberately chosen to use her services." The more so, one may add, in a country where it has been estimated that over two-thirds of white males alone will have experience with prostitutes during their lives. The costs, on the other hand, . . . are similar to those entailed in enforcing the homosexual laws — diversion of police resources; encouragement of use of illegal means of police control (which, in the case of prostitution, take the form of knowingly unlawful harassment arrests to remove suspected prostitutes from the streets; and various entrapment devices, usually the only means of obtaining convictions); degradation of the image of law enforcement; discriminatory enforcement against the poor; and official corruption.

To the extent that spread of venereal disease, corruption of the young, and public affront are the objects of prostitution controls, it would require little ingenuity to devise modes of social control short of the blanket criminalization of prostitution which would at the same time prove more effective and less costly for law enforcement. Apparently, the driving force behind prostitution laws is principally the conviction that prostitution is immoral. Only the judgment that the use of the criminal law for verbal vindication of our morals is more important than its use to protect life and property can support the preservation of these laws as they are. . . .

Laws against gambling and narcotics present serious problems for law enforcement. Despite arrests, prosecutions and convictions, and increasingly severe penalties, the conduct seems only to flourish. The irrepressible demand for gambling and drugs, like the demand for alcohol during Prohibition days, survives the condemnation of the criminal law. Whether or not the criminal restriction operates paradoxically, as some have thought, to make the conduct more attractive, it is clear that the prohibitions have not substantially eliminated the demand.

Nor have the laws and enforcement efforts suppressed sources of supply. No one with an urge to gamble in any fair-sized city of this country has far to go to place an illegal bet. And in the case of narcotics, illicit suppliers enter the market to seek the profits made available by the persistence of the demand and the criminal law's reduction of legitimate sources of supply, while "pusher"-addicts distribute narcotics as a means of fulfilling their own needs. Risk of conviction, even of long terms of imprisonment, appears to have little effect. Partly, this is because the immediate and compelling need of the "pusher"-addict for narcotics precludes any real attention to the distant prospect of conviction and imprisonment. For large-scale suppliers, who may not be addicts, the very process of criminalization and punishment serves to raise the stakes — while the risk becomes greater, so do the prospects of reward.[31] . . .

Our indiscriminate policy of using the criminal law against selling what people insist on buying has spawned large-scale, organized systems, often of national scope, comprising an integration of the stages of production and distribution of

31. Herbert Packer, The Crime Tariff, 33 American Scholar 551 (1964). [For the case for legalizing narcotics, see Ethan Nadelman, Drug Prohibition in the United States: Costs, Consequences, and Alternatives, 245 Science 939 (Sept. 1989). Compare John Kaplan, The Hardest Drug: Heroin and Public Policy (1983). — EDS.]

the illicit product on a continuous and thoroughly businesslike basis. Not only are these organizations especially difficult for law enforcement to deal with; they have the unpleasant quality of producing other crimes as well. . . . To enhance their effectiveness, these organized systems engage in satellite forms of crime, of which bribery and corruption of local government are the most far-reaching in their consequences. Hence the irony that, in some measure, crime is encouraged and successful modes of criminality are produced by the criminal law itself. . . .

There is, finally, a cost of inestimable importance, one which tends to be a product of virtually all the misuses of the criminal law discussed in this paper. That is the substantial diversion of police, prosecutorial, and judicial time, personnel, and resources. At a time when the volume of crime is steadily increasing, the burden on law-enforcement agencies is becoming more and more onerous, and massive efforts are being considered to deal more effectively with threats to the public of dangerous and threatening conduct, releasing enforcement resources from the obligation to enforce the vice laws must be taken seriously. Indeed, in view of the minimal effectiveness of enforcement measures in dealing with vice crimes and the tangible costs and disadvantages of that effort, the case for this rediversion of resources to more profitable purposes becomes commanding. It seems fair to say that in few areas of the criminal law have we paid so much for so little.

NOTES ON OTHER PROBLEMS OF CRIMINALIZATION

The materials just presented provide some examples of the complexity of judging whether certain conduct is criminal. The minimum lesson they teach is that the undesirability of certain conduct, even in the eyes of most people, is not alone a sufficient reason to criminalize it. The kinds of conduct on which we focused above are just examples. Some other important current problems of criminalization include the following, some of which are discussed later in this book.

1. *Suicide.* Statutes making suicide (or attempted suicide) criminal have disappeared. Indeed, there is increasing authority that it is unconstitutional to inflict life-saving treatment on a person who prefers to die rather than receive the treatment. See Cruzan v. Director, Missouri Department of Health, 497 U.S. 261 (1990). But Model Penal Code §210.5 and about half the states prohibit assisting another to commit suicide. Can this legislation be defended? Are there special concerns that arise where one person helps another to commit suicide that do not arise where a physician aborts treatment at the request of the patient? Is the threat of a criminal sanction an appropriate response to such concerns? These issues are explored in connection with the issue of justification, page 880 infra.

2. *Maternal fetal abuse.* In December 1988, Jennifer Johnson was hospitalized after overdosing on crack cocaine. She was pregnant at the time and admitted using cocaine and marijuana throughout her pregnancy. In January she informed her doctor that she had used cocaine that morning while she was in labor. She was arrested and convicted of delivering cocaine to her daughter during the 60 to 90 seconds after her birth before the umbilical cord was detached. Her conviction was overturned by the Florida Supreme Court, which held that the legislature had not intended "delivery" to include drugs passed through the umbilical cord. Johnson v. State, 602 S. 2d 1288 (Fla. 1992).

The woman in such a case already commits a crime in ingesting the drug. But should we make it an additional crime with further penalties where the woman is pregnant or the fetus is born damaged or stillborn? Of course, the harm the drug inflicts on infants is clear. But are there considerations that might militate against choosing the criminal sanction to address this problem? Consider the relevance of such questions as the following: Is it likely that the threat of additional penalties would add to the deterrent threat of the drug laws already in existence? Can we fairly criminalize a pregnant woman ingesting illegal drugs without also criminalizing other forms of fetal neglect, like excessive consumption of alcohol, aspirin or caffeine, or inadequate diet or improper activities? Does the focus on abuse of certain drugs have a unfairly disparate impact on those who are poor and socially marginal? If we criminalize all forms of fetal neglect, what would the enforcement costs be? Would a campaign of criminalization discourage drug-addicted women from seeking prenatal care? See Dorothy E. Roberts, Punishing Drug Addicts Who Have Babies: Women of Color, Equality, and the Right of Privacy, 104 Harv. L. Rev. 1419 (1991).

3. Products liability. Should the criminal law enforce standards of product liability, or should issues of defective products be delegated to tort law?

Consider first the argument in favor of the criminal sanction: Consumers have a right to be free from hazardous products. This right is not adequately protected by the tort law, which allows manufacturers to estimate the financial cost to them if the harm should materialize and to choose to make a defective product anyway if paying off the victims is cheaper than fixing the problem. Such transactions are improper because we can put no price on human safety; society must express that judgment by punishing as criminals corporations that violate their basic duty of producing safe products.

Now consider the arguments against: Any fine levied by statute would be far smaller than the potential tort liability for each accident. Therefore, fear of monetary penalties would not add a significant deterrent. The deterrent effect of criminal sanction would therefore rest on the stigma involved. That stigma will unfairly fall on all persons associated with the corporation, and furthermore, a judge cannot vary the degree of stigma based on the culpability or deterrability of the offense. Stigma is therefore not likely to be an effective tool. Furthermore, the complicated issues involved in such prosecutions guarantee trials that last for months and cost millions of dollars, resources that might be better used combatting other crimes. Finally, there is a more basic problem with criminalization: Consumers do not want safety at any cost. A car must still be affordable, and consumers may prefer not to pay for the extra safety, obliging manufacturers to engage in a cost-benefit analysis when confronted with each incremental addition to safety.

These problems are explored infra, pages 698-705, in connection with corporate liability.

4. Theft. The chapter on theft, Chapter 9, raises a number of criminalization issues. Issues that arise in connection with the mail and wire fraud statutes are explored at pages 1102-1114 infra. The basic issue is how to interpret the term "fraud" in these criminal statutes. Should it be given its traditional criminal law meaning, which confines it to deception of various kinds in the acquisition of another's property? Or should it be read more expansively to include abuses of power by governmental officials on the theory that they defraud citizens of their right to honest government? Section A4 on blackmail explores the task of determining when threats (which, after all, are pervasively used in our society, along with promises and persuasion, to get people to do as one wants) should be made criminal and when not. Other criminalization issues explored in Chapter 9 include the treatment of the appropriation of confidential information, page 1094, and appropriation by a partner of partnership property, page 1100.

CHAPTER

3

DEFINING CRIMINAL CONDUCT — THE ELEMENTS OF JUST PUNISHMENT

A. INTRODUCTION

The material in this section is informed by the view that our law reflects three principles that function to limit the distribution of punishment: culpability, proportionality, and legality. These principles correspond to three of the general purposes stated in §1.02(1) of the Model Penal Code governing the definition of offenses: "to safeguard conduct that is without fault from condemnation as criminal" (culpability), "to give fair warning of the nature of the conduct declared to constitute an offense" (legality), and "to differentiate on reasonable grounds between serious and minor offenses" (proportionality).

How faithful is the system of justice in the United States to the three principles identified here? When departures from them occur, what are the circumstances that are said to justify them and are they adequate?

B. CULPABILITY

1. *Actus Reus — Culpable Conduct*

a. **Positive Actions**

MARTIN v. STATE

Alabama Court of Appeals
31 Ala. App. 334, 17 So. 2d 427 (1944)

SIMPSON, J. Appellant was convicted of being drunk on a public highway, and appeals. Officers of the law arrested him at his home and took him onto the highway, where he allegedly committed the proscribed acts, viz., manifested a drunken condition by using loud and profane language.

The pertinent provisions of our statute are: "Any person who, while intoxicated or drunk, appears in any public place where one or more persons are present, . . . and manifests a drunken condition by boisterous or indecent conduct, or loud and profane discourse, shall, on conviction, be fined," etc. Code 1940, Title 14, Section 120.

Under the plain terms of this statute, a voluntary appearance is presupposed. The rule has been declared, and we think it sound, that an accusation of drunkenness in a designated public place cannot be established by proof that the accused, while in an intoxicated condition, was involuntarily and forcibly carried to that place by the arresting officer. . . .

Conviction of appellant was contrary to this announced principle and, in our view, erroneous. . . .

Reversed and rendered.

NOTES

1. What was the basis for the decision in the *Martin* case? Was it simply the language of the statute, or was it a more general principle? Suppose the statute had provided: "Any person who manifests a drunken condition by boisterous or indecent conduct, or loud and profane discourse in a public place where one or more persons are present, shall, on conviction, be fined," etc. Could Martin have been convicted under this statute?

2. Suppose a statute had made it criminal simply to be (or to be found) in a public place in a drunken condition. Would a defendant in Martin's situation have a defense? What would it be? Consider what bearing the following variations would have:

    (a) A bartender gently but firmly ejects Martin because of his obstreperous behavior.

    (b) A bully assaults Martin without justification and throws him out of the bar into the street.

Questions: What result under the principle of the *Martin* case? Are (a) and (b) distinguishable? One court so held, finding, in effect, that Martin would have a defense in situation (b), but not in (a). O'Sullivan v. Fisher, [1954] S.A.S.R. 33 (S. Ct. So. Australia). Can this distinction be justified? If not, is there a defense in both cases, or in neither?

3. Consider Norval Morris, An Australian News Letter, [1955] Crim. L. Rev. 290, 295:

> Since first reading criminal law I have had the greatest sympathy with Miss Larsonneur who, in 1933, was held by the Court of Criminal Appeal to have offended against Article 18(1)(b) of the Aliens Order, 1920, by being an alien who was "found" in the United Kingdom without permission. Miss Larsonneur was a French woman who, it is said, worked more by night than by day. She decided to come to England, possibly in an endeavour to acquire a sufficient dowry to return to a happy Continental marriage. She was given permission to land in England. Later, the propriety of her means of livelihood being doubted, she was required to leave. Anxious not to commit an offence, she promptly travelled to the Irish Free State. Far from being welcomed there, she was arrested and handed back in cus

tody to the English police. She was then, by skilful detection, "found" in the United Kingdom — in a cell. The Court of Appeal held her offense to be complete. How far must one go to avoid a crime?

4. The implication in *Martin* is that after arresting him the police officers *physically* "took him onto the highway." Suppose instead they had instructed him to accompany them out onto the highway and that he did so. Would this also be a case where Martin did not act, or a case where Martin merely had a very difficult choice to make? Would the defense available in the *Martin* case still be available to him? If not, would he have any other defense? See the section on duress, page 897 infra.

PEOPLE v. NEWTON

California District Court of Appeal
8 Cal. App. 3d 359, 87 Cal. Rptr. 394 (1970)

RATTIGAN, J. Huey P. Newton appeals from a judgment convicting him of voluntary manslaughter.

[Newton was charged with the murder of John Frey, a police officer who died of bullet wounds received in a struggle with defendant. A jury found him guilty of voluntary manslaughter.

[Frey stopped a car driven by Newton and ordered him out of the car, and an altercation ensued. From the testimony of the prosecution's witnesses, it appeared that Newton had drawn a gun, and, in the struggle for its possession, the gun went off and wounded Heanes, another police officer. The struggle continued, and Heanes fired a shot at Newton's midsection. At some point, Newton wrested the gun away and fired several fatal shots point-blank at Frey. He then ran away. Shortly afterward, Newton appeared at a hospital emergency room, seeking treatment for a bullet wound in the abdomen.

[Newton testified that he had carried no gun. According to his account, the struggle began when Frey struck him for protesting his arrest. As he stumbled backwards, Frey drew a revolver. At this point, he felt a "sensation like . . . boiling hot soup had been spilled on my stomach," and heard an "explosion," then a "volley of shots." He remembered "crawling . . . a moving sensation," but nothing else until he found himself at the entrance of Kaiser Hospital with no knowledge of how he arrived there. He expressly testified that he was "unconscious or semiconscious" during this interval, that he was "still only semiconscious" at the hospital entrance, and that — after recalling some events at Kaiser Hospital — he later "regained consciousness" at another hospital.]

The defense called Bernard Diamond, M.D., who testified that defendant's recollections were "compatible" with the gunshot wound he had received; and that

[a] gunshot wound which penetrates in a body cavity, the abdominal cavity or the thoracic cavity is very likely to produce a profound reflex shock reaction, that is quite different than a gunshot wound which penetrates only skin and muscle and it is not at all uncommon for a person shot in the abdomen to lose consciousness and go into this reflex shock condition for short periods of time up to half an hour or so.

Defendant asserts prejudicial error in the trial court's failure to instruct the jury on the subject of *unconsciousness* as a defense to a charge of criminal homicide. . . .

Although the evidence of the fatal affray is both conflicting and confused as to who shot whom and when, some of it supported the inference that defendant had been shot in the abdomen before he fired any shots himself. Given this sequence, defendant's testimony of his sensations when shot — supplemented to a degree, as it was, by Dr. Diamond's opinion based upon the nature of the abdominal wound — supported the further inference that defendant was in a state of unconsciousness when Officer Frey was shot.

Where not self-induced, as by voluntary intoxication or the equivalent (of which there is no evidence here . . .), unconsciousness is a complete defense to a charge of criminal homicide. (Pen. Code, §26, subd. 5; . . .) "Unconsciousness," as the term is used in the rule just cited, need not reach the physical dimensions commonly associated with the term (coma, inertia, incapability of locomotion or manual action, and so on); it can exist — and the above-stated rule can apply — where the subject physically acts in fact but is not, at the time, conscious of acting. The statute underlying the rule makes this clear,[11] as does one of the unconsciousness instructions originally requested by defendant.[12] Thus, the rule has been invoked in many cases where the actor fired multiple gunshots while inferably in a state of such "unconsciousness" . . . including some in which the only evidence of "unconsciousness" was the actor's own testimony that he did not recall the shooting. . . .

Where evidence of involuntary unconsciousness has been produced in a homicide prosecution, the refusal of a requested instruction on the subject, and its effect as a complete defense if found to have existed, is prejudicial error. . . .

NOTES AND QUESTIONS

1. The Model Penal Code approach. Consider at this point Model Penal Code §2.01(1), Appendix. The Code excludes liability in the absence of a voluntary act, but does the Code define what voluntary action is? How would the *Martin* and *Newton* cases be decided under the Code?

The theory behind excluding liability in the absence of a voluntary action is explained as follows (Model Penal Code and Commentaries, Comment to §2.01 at 214-215 (1985)):

> That penal sanctions cannot be employed with justice unless these requirements are satisfied seems wholly clear. It is fundamental that a civilized society does not punish for thoughts alone. Beyond this, the law cannot hope to deter involuntary movement or to stimulate action that cannot physically be performed; the sense of personal security would be undermined in a society where such movement or in-

---

11. Penal Code section 26 provides in pertinent part that "All persons are capable of committing crimes except those belonging to the following classes: . . . Five — Persons who *committed the act charged without being conscious thereof.*" (Italics added.)

12. CALJIC 71-C, which read in pertinent part as follows:

"Where a person *commits an act without being conscious thereof,* such act is not criminal even though, if committed by a person who was conscious, it would be a crime. . . ." (Italics added.)

activity could lead to formal social condemnation of the sort that a conviction necessarily entails. People whose involuntary movements threaten harm to others may present a public health or safety problem, calling for therapy or even for custodial commitment; they do not present a problem of correction.

2. *Distinguishing between voluntary and involuntary acts.* What does it mean to say that an act is involuntary, in situations other than the paradigmatic ones in which a person physically forces the movements of another or in which one's body is in the grip of a spasm or reflex? In Bratty v. Attorney-General [1963] A.C. 386, 409-410 (H.L. 1961), Lord Denning stated as follows:

> No act is punishable if it is done involuntarily: and an involuntary act in this context — some people nowadays prefer to speak of it as "automatism" — means an act which is done by the muscles without any control by the mind such as a spasm, a reflex action or a convulsion; or an act done by a person who is not conscious of what he is doing such as an act done whilst suffering from concussion or whilst sleep-walking. The point was well put by Stephen J., in 1889: "Can anyone doubt that a man who, though he might be perfectly sane, committed what would otherwise be a crime in a state of somnambulism, would be entitled to be acquitted? And why is this? Simply because he would not know what he was doing." . . . The term "involuntary act" is, however, capable of wider connotations: and to prevent confusion it is to be observed that in the criminal law an act is not to be regarded as an involuntary act simply because the doer does not remember it. . . . Nor is an act to be regarded as an involuntary act simply because the doer could not control his impulse to do it. When a man is charged with murder, and it appears that he knew what he was doing, but he could not resist it, then his assertion "I couldn't help myself" is no defence in itself. . . . Nor is an act to be regarded as an involuntary act simply because it is unintentional or its consequences are unforeseen. When a man is charged with dangerous driving, it is no defence for him to say, however truly, "I did not mean to drive dangerously."

Consider the following problems.

(a) Habit. The Model Penal Code expressly declares that a habitual action done without thought is to be treated as a voluntary action. Why should this be so? Consider, for example, a person who, immediately after announcing to her husband that she plans to drive downtown before going to her office, gets into her car and starts driving her habitual route to the office instead of heading downtown. Or consider a person who continues to say "You know" before every other sentence, despite having firmly resolved never again to use that abominable locution. Why should these habits be treated as voluntary acts?

(b) Possession. Suppose a smuggler surreptitiously places a packet of heroin into the baggage of a respectable looking traveler, in the expectation that the latter will not be searched and that he, the smuggler, will later retrieve the drugs through some ruse. Suppose further that the respectable traveler is searched, the drugs are discovered, and she is charged with illegal possession. Model Penal Code §2.01(4) provides that possession is an act only if the person is aware she has the thing she is charged with possessing. The majority of courts also treat possession as requiring knowledge, even where the statute prohibiting possession is silent on the issue of scienter. See United States v. Anderson, 885 F.2d 1248 (5th Cir. 1989); Dawkins v. State, 313 Md. 638, 547 A.2d 1041 (1988). Some

courts hold, particularly where the penalty is not severe, that it is sufficient that the defendant should have known. See United States v. Garrett, 984 F.2d 1402 (5th Cir. 1993), where the court observed:

> Like many people trying to catch a plane around the holidays, [defendant] was in a hurry. Unlike most, she forgot that she had a gun in her purse, or so she says. The principal question . . . is whether the federal statute that criminalizes this conduct requires any degree of mens rea as an element of the offense. We hold that a "should have known" standard applies.

In a few jurisdictions, however, drug possession statutes are interpreted as dispensing with any need to show that the defendant knew or should have known of the presence of the drugs. See, e.g., State v. Cleppe, 96 Wash. 2d 393, 635 P.2d 435 (1981).

(c) Hypnosis. Are actions taken while a person is in a hypnotic trance voluntary actions? There are few decisions on the subject. See People v. Marsh, 170 Cal. App. 2d 284, 338 P.2d 495 (1959), where the defense was rejected by the jury.

The Model Penal Code took the position that the acts of a hypnotized subject are not voluntary, stating (Model Penal Code and Commentaries, Comment to §2.01 at 221 (1985)):

> The widely held view that the hypnotized subject will not follow suggestions which are repugnant to him was deemed insufficient to warrant treating his conduct while hypnotized as voluntary; his dependency and helplessness are too pronounced.

Consider the following observations of Dr. Martin Orne in his review of Reiter, Antisocial or Criminal Acts and Hypnosis: A Case Study, 46 A.B.A.J. 81, 83 (1960). The book describes a prolonged personal relationship between two cellmates in which one, the hypnotist, established an ability to control the actions of the other, the subject, to a surprising extent. After his release, the hypnotist suggested to the subject who was in a hypnotic state that he rob a bank to obtain funds for some fantastic political movement. The subject did so and in the process killed several people. To the conclusion of Dr. Reiter that this demonstrated that a person can be impelled to perform criminal acts in hypnosis, Dr. Orne retorts:

> As in any intense relationship the motivations of the individuals involved are extremely complex and the behavior of each with regard to the other must be understood in the context of the total relationship. An explanation which purports to account for such behavior by singling out one aspect of the relationship — i.e., hypnosis — must be viewed with skepticism.
>
> With regard to criminal behavior it is not extraordinary for one individual to perform antisocial behavior which benefits another. The only unusual feature of the *Reiter* case is that hypnosis played some role. We would not ascribe the subject's motivation to hypnotic influence, as Dr. Reiter seems to do, but would relate it to the kind of relationship which existed between *H* and *N*. In this case the relationship seems to have been characterized by a shared psychotic system and there are some indications of latent homosexuality. The role that hypnosis plays is to disguise for the subject his own motivation and to create a situation which allows the subject to, at some level, disclaim responsibility for his actions. We will refrain from committing ourselves on the question of legal or moral responsibility which, in any

case, is not for a psychiatrist to settle. In our view antisocial behavior such as *H*'s could have been performed without the introduction of hypnosis.

See Comment (Mary C. Bonnema), "Trance on Trial": An Exegesis of Hypnotism and Criminal Responsibility, 39 Wayne L. Rev. 1299 (1993).

(d) Somnambulism. Should acts done during sleepwalking be treated as involuntary? Consider Norval Morris, Somnambulistic Homicide: Ghosts, Spiders, and North Koreans, 5 Res Judicatae 29, 29-30 (1951):

Mrs. Cogdon was charged with the murder of her only child, a daughter called Pat, aged nineteen. . . . Describing the relationship between Pat and her mother, Mr. Cogdon testified: "I don't think a mother could have thought any more of her daughter. I think she absolutely adored her." On the conscious level, at least, there was no reason to doubt Mrs. Cogdon's deep attachment to her daughter.

To the charge of murdering Pat, Mrs. Cogdon pleaded not guilty. Her story, though somewhat bizarre, was not seriously challenged by the Crown, and led to her acquittal. She told how, on the night before her daughter's death she had dreamt that their house was full of spiders and that these spiders were crawling all over Pat. In her sleep, Mrs. Cogdon left the bed she shared with her husband, went into Pat's room and awakened to find herself violently brushing at Pat's face, presumably to remove the spiders. This woke Pat. Mrs. Cogdon told her she was just tucking her in. At the trial, she testified that she still believed, as she had been told, that the occupants of a nearby house bred spiders as a hobby, preparing nests for them behind the pictures on their walls. It was these spiders which in her dreams had invaded their home and attacked Pat. There had also been a previous dream in which ghosts had sat at the end of Mrs. Cogdon's bed and she had said to them, "Well, you have come to take Pattie." It does not seem fanciful to accept the psychological explanation of these spiders and ghosts as the projections of Mrs. Cogdon's subconscious hostility towards her daughter; a hostility which was itself rooted in Mrs. Cogdon's own early life and marital relationship.

The morning after the spider dream she told her doctor of it. He gave her a sedative and, because of the dream and certain previous difficulties she had reported, discussed the possibility of psychiatric treatment. That evening Mrs. Cogdon suggested to her husband that he attend his lodge meeting, and asked Pat to come with her to the cinema. After he had gone Pat looked through the paper, not unusually found no tolerable programme, and said that as she was going out the next evening she thought she would rather go to bed early. Later while Pat was having a bath preparatory to retiring, Mrs. Cogdon went into her room, put a hot water bottle in the bed, turned back the bedclothes, and placed a glass of hot milk beside the bed ready for Pat. She then went to bed herself. There was some desultory conversation between them about the war in Korea, and just before she put out her light Pat called out to her mother, "Mum, don't be so silly worrying about the war, it's not on our front door step yet."

Mrs. Cogdon went to sleep. She dreamt that "the war was all around the house," that the soldiers were in Pat's room, and that one soldier was on the bed attacking Pat. This was all of the dream that she could later recapture. Her first "waking" memory was of running from Pat's room, out of the house to the home of her sister who lived next door. When her sister opened the front door Mrs. Cogdon fell into her arms crying, "I think I've hurt Pattie."

In fact Mrs. Cogdon had, in her somnambulistic state, left her bed, fetched an axe from the woodheap, entered Pat's room, and struck her two accurate forceful blows on the head with the blade of the axe, thus killing her.

Mrs. Cogdon's story was supported by the evidence of her physician, a psychiatrist, and a psychologist. The burden of the evidence of all three, which was not contested by the prosecution, was that Mrs. Cogdon was suffering from a form of hysteria with an overlay of depression, and that she was of a personality in which such dissociated states as fugues, amnesias, and somnambulistic acts are to be expected. They agreed that she was not psychotic, and that if she had been awake at the time of the killing no defence could have been spelt out under the *M'Naughten Rules* [governing the defense of legal insanity]. They hazarded no statement as to her motives, the idea of defence of the daughter being transparently insufficient. However, the psychologist and the psychiatrist concurred in hinting that the emotional motivation lay in an acute conflict situation in her relations with her own parents; that during marital life she suffered very great sexual frustration; and that she over-compensated for her own frustration by over-protection of her daughter. Her exaggerated solicitude for her daughter was a conscious expression of her subconscious emotional hostility to her, and the dream ghosts, spiders, and Korean soldiers were projections of that aggression. . . .

At all events the jury believed Mrs. Cogdon's story. [S]he was acquitted because the act of killing itself was not, in law, regarded as her act at all.

A recent sleepwalking case is Regina v. Parks, 95 D.L.R.4th 27, 77 C.C.C.3d 287 (1992), which involved the acquittal of a man who drove to his mother-in-law's house and killed her in a state the jury found to be somnambulatory.

Note that the effect of the acquittals of Mrs. Cogdon and Mr. Parks is that they are immediately discharged without further supervision over their conduct. If they had been acquitted on grounds of legal insanity, however, a variety of protective procedures would have been available, if not mandatory, including institutionalization. The difference turns on whether the case is determined to be one of sane or insane automatism. This matter is further pursued infra page 994.

3. *Problem.* Can there be situations in which the defendant may be held criminally liable even though the action immediately causing the harm was clearly involuntary — for example, epileptic reflexes? Consider People v. Decina, 2 N.Y.2d 133, 139-140, 138 N.E.2d 799, 803-804 (1956):

The indictment states essentially that defendant, *knowing* "that he was subject to epileptic attacks or other disorder rendering him likely to lose consciousness for a considerable period of time," was culpably negligent "in that he consciously undertook to and *did operate* his Buick sedan on a public highway" (emphasis supplied) and "while so doing" suffered such an attack which caused said automobile "to travel at a fast and reckless rate of speed, jumping the curb and driving over the sidewalk" causing the death of 4 persons. In our opinion, this clearly states a violation of section 1053-a of the Penal Law. . . . ["A person who operates or drives any vehicle of any kind in a reckless or culpably negligent manner, whereby a human being is killed is guilty of criminal negligence in the operation of a vehicle resulting in death."]

Assuming the truth of the indictment, as we must on a demurrer, this defendant knew he was subject to epileptic attacks and seizures that might strike at any time. He also knew that a moving motor vehicle uncontrolled on a public highway is a highly dangerous instrumentality capable of unrestrained destruction. With this *knowledge,* and without anyone accompanying him, he deliberately took a chance by making a conscious choice of a course of action, in disregard of the consequences which he knew might follow from his conscious act, and which in this case did ensue. How can we say as a matter of law that this did not amount to culpable negligence within the meaning of section 1053-a?

To hold otherwise would be to say that a man may freely indulge himself in liquor in the same hope that it will not affect his driving, and if it later develops that ensuing intoxication causes dangerous and reckless driving resulting in death, his unconsciousness or involuntariness at that time would relieve him from prosecution under the statute. His awareness of a condition which he knows may produce such consequences as here, and his disregard of the consequences, renders him liable for culpable negligence, as the courts below have properly held. To have a sudden sleeping spell, an unexpected heart or other disabling attack, without any prior knowledge or warning thereof, is an altogether different situation.

4. Why does the law distinguish between nonactions and excused actions? Professor J. G. Murphy, in Involuntary Acts and Criminal Liability, 51 Ethics 332 (1971), points out that there are two basic situations in which human actions "misfire." One is where actions are done mistakenly, accidentally, compulsorily, or under duress. The other is where the action misfires in a more basic way — such as in cases of seizures, convulsions, reflex movements, and somnambulism. In the first group of cases, we speak of mitigating the actor's responsibility or of excusing the act. In the second group of cases, however, we do not think of excuse but rather that no human action occurred at all — "talk of excuse here seems to make no more sense than would talk of excusing a rock for falling on one's head." Indeed, this dichotomy is reflected in the organization of this casebook. The second group of cases is at issue here; problems of mistake and accident are dealt with in the section on mens rea that follows, and problems of excuse generally are dealt with in Chapter 8, Section B.

The distinction between these two categories of actions misfiring can have important legal consequences. As we shall see, it may make a difference in cases of strict liability, where ignorance or accident is ruled out as a defense but where the defense of no action (or no voluntary action) may serve as a defense. See page 249 infra. The distinction may also matter in cases involving the defenses based on severe mental disturbance. As was just indicated, the legal consequences of a finding that the disturbance produced an involuntary action are radically different from a finding that it produced legal insanity.

Question: Is there a rational justification for distinguishing these two classes of cases? Compare the views of Professor Murphy in the article just cited with those of Professor Hart in Punishment and Responsibility 90-112 (1968).

5. The foregoing and other problems of the criminal law with respect to the requirement of an action are comprehensively dealt with in Michael S. Moore, Act and Crime — The Philosophy of Action and its Implications for the Criminal Law (1993).

NOTE ON INNOCENT ACTS AND CULPABLE THOUGHTS

As we have seen, the absence of an *act* precludes culpability. In such a case, there is physical action, but it is discounted because there is no mental disposition to take such action, let alone a criminal disposition. Now consider two similar, but actually distinguishable, situations in which the absence of an appropriate action is sometimes said to preclude criminality.

1. First, consider the case in which there is external behavior accompanied by a criminal disposition, but the external behavior is, looked at from an objective view, wholly innocent. Consider these examples:

A soldier during battle shoots and kills an enemy soldier believing that his victim is his own sergeant.

A man has sexual intercourse with a woman over the age of consent, though he believes that she is underage.

Defendant deliberately shoots and kills victim, unaware that at that very instant victim was about to kill him.

Does the principle that requires a voluntary act or any other principle preclude imposing punishment in these cases? These problems are discussed more fully at page 623 infra in connection with the defense of impossibility to a charge of an attempt to commit a crime.

For a discussion of these and related questions, see G. Williams, Criminal Law: The General Part 22-27 (2d ed. 1961).

2. Second, consider the case in which there is no external behavior, but there is a criminal disposition. An example is the situation in which a person, who conceives a criminal plot in his or her mind, takes no action to further the plot. In such a case, is it the principle that conditions criminality on a voluntary act that precludes criminality, or is it some other principle? Criminality is said to be precluded in this case by the maxim *cogitationis poenam nemo patitur* (no one is punishable solely for his thoughts). What is the root justification of this principle? Consider the following comments.

4 William Blackstone, Commentaries *21: Indeed, to make a complete crime, cognizable by human laws, there must be both a will and an act. For though, in *foro conscientiae,* a fixed design or will to do an unlawful act is almost as heinous as the commission of it, yet, as no temporal tribunal can search the heart, or fathom the intentions of the mind, otherwise than as they are demonstrated by outward actions, it therefore cannot punish for what it cannot know. For which reason in all temporal jurisdictions an overt act, or some open evidence of an intended crime, is necessary, in order to demonstrate the depravity of the will, before the man is liable to punishment.

2 James Fitzjames Stephen, A History of the Criminal Law of England 78 (1833): Sinful thoughts and dispositions of mind might be the subject of confession and of penance, but they were never punished in this country by ecclesiastical criminal proceedings. The reasons for imposing this great leading restriction upon the sphere of criminal law are obvious. If it were not so restricted it would be utterly intolerable; all mankind would be criminals, and most of their lives would be passed in trying and punishing each other for offences which could never be proved.

G. Dworkin & G. Blumenfeld, Punishments for Intentions, 75 Mind 396, 401 (1966): What would a system of laws embodying a rule providing for the punishment of intentions look like? When would punishment be administered? As soon as we find out the agent's intentions? But how do we know he will not change his mind? Furthermore, isn't the series — fantasying, wishing, desiring, wanting, intending — a continuum, making it a rather hazy matter to know just when a person is intending rather than wishing? This last objection has two aspects, the difficulty of the authorities distinguishing between fantasying, wishing, etc. and even more importantly the difficulties the individual would have in identifying the nature of his emotional and mental set. Would we not be constantly worried about the nature of our mental life? Am I only wishing my mother-in-law were dead? Perhaps I have gone further. The resultant guilt would tend to impoverish and stultify the emotional life.

Glanville Williams, Criminal Law: The General Part 2 (2d ed. 1961): Better reasons for the rule would be (1) the difficulty of distinguishing between daydream and fixed intention in the absence of behavior tending towards the crime intended, and (2) the undesirability of spreading the criminal law so wide as to cover a mental state that the accused might be too irresolute even to begin to translate into action.

Abraham Goldstein, Conspiracy to Defraud the United States, 68 Yale L.J. 405, 405-406 (1959): It [the maxim that we do not punish an evil intent alone] expresses today, as it did three centuries ago, the feeling that the individual thinking evil thoughts must be protected from a state which may class him as a threat to its security. Rooted in skepticism about the ability either to know what passes through the minds of men or to predict whether antisocial behavior will follow from antisocial thoughts, the act requirement serves a number of closely-related objectives: it seeks to assure that the evil intent of the man branded a criminal has been expressed in a manner signifying harm to society; that there is no longer any substantial likelihood that he will be deterred by the threat of sanction; and that there has been an identifiable occurrence so that multiple prosecution and punishment may be minimized.

3. It should be remembered that while the common law requires an act as well as an accompanying state of mind (mens rea) and does not generally consider a verbal declaration of the mens rea a sufficient act in itself, words are a kind of act and are treated as such for some purposes. In cases of treason, seditious utterance, solicitation, conspiracy, or aiding and abetting another to commit a crime through instruction or encouragement, for example, words are sufficient to constitute the actus reus of the crime. Is this consistent with the doctrine that a person is not criminally liable for his or her thoughts alone?

4. This Note has addressed the problem of punishing people solely for their evil thoughts. Compare the problem of punishment for a failure to act. Are the two problems the same? Do the reasons for not punishing for evil thoughts also support the policy of not punishing for failing to act? Are there other reasons why punishing for failing to act may be problematic? Consider the following material in this connection.

b. Omissions

POPE v. STATE

Maryland Court of Appeals
284 Md. 309, 396 A.2d 1054 (1979)

ORTH, J. Joyce Lillian Pope was found guilty by the court in the Circuit Court for Montgomery County under the 3rd and 5th counts of a nine count indictment, no. 18666. The 3rd count charged child abuse, presenting that "on or about April 11, 1976, . . . while having the temporary care, custody and responsibility for the supervision of Demiko Lee Norris, a minor child under the age of eighteen years [she] did unlawfully and feloniously cause abuse to said minor child in violation of Article 27, Section 35A of the Annotated Code of Maryland. . . ." The 5th count charged misprision of felony under the common law, alleging that on the same date she "did unlawfully and willfully conceal and fail to disclose a felony to wit: the murder of Demiko Lee Norris committed by Melissa Vera Norris on April 11, 1976, having actual knowledge of the commission of the felony and the identity of the felon, with the intent to obstruct and hinder the due course of justice and to cause the felon to escape unpunished. . . ."

[Melissa Norris, a young mother with a three-month-old infant, was suffering from a serious mental illness and given to episodes of violent religious frenzy. The defendant (Mrs. Pope) took Norris and her child into her house one Friday night after church services because they had no other place to go. During the weekend Mrs. Pope fed them both and looked after the child in a variety of ways. On Sunday afternoon Melissa went into a frenzy, claiming she was God and that Satan had hidden himself in the body of her child. In Mrs. Pope's presence she savagely beat and ripped and tore at the infant, doing it violent and serious injury. During this prolonged period Mrs. Pope did nothing to try to protect the child, to call the authorities, or to seek medical assistance. She went to church with Melissa and later brought her back to her home where she spent the night. At some point in the evening the infant died from the beating.]

[A] person may be convicted of the felony of child abuse created by §35A[a] as a principal in the first degree upon evidence legally sufficient to establish that the person

(1) was (a) the parent of, or (b) the adoptive parent of, or (c) in loco parentis to, or (d) responsible for the supervision of a minor child under the age of eighteen years, AND
(2) caused, by being in some manner accountable for, by act of commission or omission, abuse to the child in the form of (a) physical injury or injuries sustained by the child as the result of (i) cruel or inhumane treatment, or (ii) malicious act or acts by such person, . . .

. . . Pope's lack of any attempt to prevent the numerous acts of abuse committed by the mother over a relatively protracted period and her failure to seek medical assistance for the child, although the need therefor was obviously compelling and urgent, could constitute a cause for the further progression and worsening of the injuries which led to the child's death. In such circumstances,

---

a. Article 27, Section 35A, insofar as it is relevant to this case, reads as follows:
"(a) *Penalty.* Any parent, adoptive parent or other person who has the permanent or temporary care or custody or responsibility for the supervision of a minor child under the age of eighteen years who causes abuse to such minor child shall be guilty of a felony and upon conviction shall be sentenced to not more than fifteen years in the penitentiary.
"(b) *Definitions.* Wherever used in this section, unless the context clearly indicates otherwise . . . 7. '*Abuse*' shall mean any . . . physical injury or injuries sustained by a child as a result of cruel or inhumane treatment or as a result of malicious act or acts by any parent, adoptive parent or other person who has the permanent or temporary care or custody or responsibility for the supervision of a minor child. . . ." Eds.

Pope's omissions constituted in themselves cruel and inhumane treatment within the meaning of the statute. See State v. Fabritz, 276 Md. 416, 348 A.2d 275 (1975).[b] It follows that Pope would be guilty of child abuse *if her status brought her within the class of persons specified by the statute.* It being clear that she was neither the child's parent nor adoptive parent, and there being no evidence sufficient to support a finding that she had "the permanent or temporary care or custody" of the child so as to be in loco parentis to the child, the sole question is whether she had "responsibility for the supervision of" the child in the circumstances. If she had such responsibility the evidence was legally sufficient to find her guilty of child abuse as a principal in the first degree.

The State would have us translate compassion and concern, acts of kindness and care, performance of maternal functions, and general help and aid with respect to the child into responsibility for the supervision of the child. The crux of its argument is that although Pope was not under any obligation to assume responsibility for the supervision of the child at the outset, "once she undertook to house, feed, and care for [the mother and child], she did accept the responsibility and came within the coverage of the statute." But the mother was always present. Pope had no right to usurp the role of the mother even to the extent of responsibility for the child's supervision. . . . It would be most incongruous that acts of hospitality and kindness, made out of common decency and prompted by sincere concern for the well-being of a mother and her child, subjected the Good Samaritan to criminal prosecution for abusing the very child he sought to look after. And it would be especially ironic were such criminal prosecution to be predicated upon an obligation to take affirmative action with regard to abuse of the child by its mother, when such obligation arises solely from those acts of hospitality and kindness.

The evidence does not show why Pope did not intervene when the mother abused the child or why she did not, at least, timely seek medical assistance, when it was obvious that the child was seriously injured. Whether her lack of action was from fear or religious fervor or some other reason is not clearly indicated. . . . But Pope's conduct, during and after the acts of abuse, must be evaluated with regard for the rule that although she may have had a strong moral obligation to help the child, she was under no legal obligation to do so unless she then had responsibility for the supervision of the child as contemplated by the child abuse statute. She may not be punished as a felon under our system of justice for failing to fulfill a moral obligation, and the short of it is that she was

---

b. This case held that the failure of a mother to seek needed medical assistance for her child, who had been severely beaten by a babysitter, "caused" the child to sustain bodily injury beyond that inflicted by the babysitter's assault. Referring to the Maryland child abuse statute, the court stated: "In making it an offense for a person having custody of a minor child to 'cause' the child to suffer a 'physical injury,' the Legislature did not require that the injury result from a physical assault upon the child or from any physical force initially applied by the accused individual; it provided instead, in a more encompassing manner, that the offense was committed if physical injury to the child resulted either from a course of conduct constituting 'cruel or inhumane treatment' or by malicious act or acts.'" The court concluded that the omission by the mother "constituted a cause of the further progression and worsening of the injuries which led to [the child's] death; and that in these circumstances [the mother's] treatment of [the child] was 'cruel or inhumane' within the meaning of the statute as those terms are commonly understood. . . ." A federal court later set aside the conviction because there was no evidence that the child's mother knew the babysitter would abuse the child, or that she was risking the child's life in not seeking medical assistance. Fabritz v. Traurig, 583 F.2d 697 (4th Cir. 1978). — Eds.

under no legal obligation. In the circumstances, the mother's acquiescence in Pope's conduct was not a grant of responsibility to Pope for the supervision of the child, nor was Pope's conduct an acceptance of such responsibility. . . . We hold that the evidence was not sufficient in law to prove that Pope fell within that class of persons to whom the child abuse statute applies. Thus it is that the judgment of the trial court that she was a principal in the first degree in the commission of the crime of child abuse was clearly erroneous and must be set aside.

The mental or emotional state of the mother, whereby at times she held herself out as God, does not change the result. We see no basis in the statute for an interpretation that a person "has" responsibility for the supervision of a child, if that person believes or may have reason to believe that a parent is not capable of caring for the child. There is no right to make such a subjective judgment in order to divest parents of their rights and obligations with respect to their minor children, and therefore, no obligation to do so. . . .

There is an understandable feeling of outrage at what occurred, intensified by the fact that the mother, who actually beat the child to death, was held to be not responsible for her criminal acts. But it is the law, not indignation, which governs. The law requires that Pope's conviction of the felony of child abuse be set aside as clearly erroneous due to evidentiary insufficiency. . . .

We assume, *arguendo,* that misprision of felony was a crime under the common law of England, and that it became the law of this State pursuant to Art. 5 of the Declaration of Rights. The question is whether it is to be deemed an indictable offense in Maryland today. . . .

We are satisfied, considering its origin, the impractical and indiscriminate width of its scope, its other obvious deficiencies, and its long non-use, that it is not now compatible with our local circumstances and situation and our general code of laws and jurisprudence. Maintenance of law and order does not demand its application, and, overall, the welfare of the inhabitants of Maryland and society as enjoyed by us today, would not be served by it. If the Legislature finds it advisable that the people be obligated under peril of criminal penalty to disclose knowledge of criminal acts, it is, of course, free to create an offense to that end, within constitutional limitations, and, hopefully, with adequate safeguards. We believe that the common law offense is not acceptable by today's standards, and we are not free to usurp the power of the General Assembly by attempting to fashion one that would be. We hold that misprision of felony is not a chargeable offense in Maryland.

We have reversed Pope's conviction of the felony of child abuse because the evidence was insufficient to sustain the verdict. She may not be tried again for that crime.

As we have held that the crime of misprision of felony does not now exist in Maryland, Pope may not, of course, be retried on a charge of that crime.

Pope moved that we strike from the State's brief and appendix a selection from the Year Book of 1484 written in Medieval Latin and references thereto. The State provided no translation and conceded a total lack of knowledge of what it meant. The motion is granted.

DIANE KIESEL, WHO SAW THIS HAPPEN — STATES MOVE TO MAKE CRIME BYSTANDERS RESPONSIBLE, 69 A.B.A.J. 1208 (1983): Shocking news accounts of the alleged gang rape of a woman in a Massachusetts tavern, while patrons gaped and cheered, have caused some state legislatures to consider making it a crime for witnesses to rapes and other felonies not to report them to police.

Although 48 states and the District of Columbia have "Good Samaritan" statutes absolving bystanders from most civil liability when they help persons in danger, Vermont and Minnesota mandate such rescue actions under penalty of a criminal fine.

In May, Rhode Island enacted a law making it a misdemeanor punishable by up to one year in jail, a $500 fine or both for anyone, other than the victim, to fail to report to police a rape that takes place in his or her presence. But the law does not require a bystander to try to stop the assault. Massachusetts and Pennsylvania legislators are considering similar proposals that would apply to rape and other serious felonies.

If the gang rape in March at the New Bedford, Mass., tavern happened as the witnesses said, it was unquestionably heinous and revolting. But some say the answer does not lie in laws like the one passed in Rhode Island. That measure was opposed by, surprisingly enough, the Rhode Island Rape Crisis Center, which raised questions about rape victims' privacy. The Rhode Island chapter of the American Civil Liberties Union also opposed it, citing constitutional and practical objections.

Others think such statutes may be valid but ineffective.

"These statutes will be no more effective than jaywalking laws," said Arthur Miller, Harvard law professor and television law commentator. "But that doesn't mean we shouldn't legislate in this area. It would give legal effect to a moral principle that we are our brother's keeper."

The public outcry in the New Bedford situation recalled the uproar that followed the 1964 murder of Catherine "Kitty" Genovese in Queens, N.Y. The young bar manager was stabbed to death on the street in her middle-class neighborhood in an attack that lasted some 35 minutes. Witnesses peered through their curtains and did nothing.

The assailant followed Genovese from her parking lot toward her apartment building as she came home from work about 3:20 A.M. He started stabbing her, then fled when she screamed for help. But when her calls went unheeded, he returned to strike again. After the second assault he headed for his car and drove away while Genovese slowly crawled to her apartment doorway. Amazingly, the killer returned a third time, repeated his attack, and Genovese died. The first call to police was not made until 3:40 A.M. The man who finally called said he waited because he "didn't want to get involved."

Genovese, whose death made headlines around the world, became for many the symbol for a society that had somehow lost its sense of humanity. "Who can explain such shocking indifference on the part of a cross-section of our fellow New Yorkers?" lamented the *New York Times* in a March 28, 1964, editorial. "We regretfully admit that we do not know the answers."

Rhode Island State Sen. Gloria Kennedy Fleck, author of the sex crime reporting bill, thinks she has found a way to overcome such bystander indifference.

"It's too bad that this poor woman has to be the brunt of it, but the New Bedford incident has raised our consciousness again," said Fleck. . . .

DANIEL B. YEAGER, A RADICAL COMMUNITY OF AID: A REJOINDER TO
OPPONENTS OF AFFIRMATIVE DUTIES TO HELP STRANGERS, 71 Wash.
U.L.Q. 1, 15 (1993): Why those who see others in danger so often do nothing is
unclear. In the case of witnesses to crimes, danger — real or imagined — and
fear of retaliation account for some failures to intervene or notify authorities. In
addition, because emergencies are, for most of us, exotic, a bystander's lack of
opportunity for planning and rehearsal and the difficulty of quickly selecting
the appropriate type of intervention might make her assistance less likely. . . .

The presence of other bystanders may reduce each potential rescuer's individual sense of responsibility to the imperiled, and increase the probability of
free-riding. Each is lulled into a state of "pluralistic ignorance," which induces
multiple bystanders to interpret others' nonaction as a sign of no danger. Despite the apparent incentive that risk-sharing would provide to potential co-
intervenors, because of social inhibitions that arise in groups, people are more
prone to respond to another's distress when alone than when accompanied by
other witnesses.

Bystanders thus face a "choice of nightmares": fail to intervene and experience the empathic distress of watching another human being suffer, the guilt of
failing to live up to a minimal threshold of decency, and the shame of having
that failure witnessed by others; or, intervene and risk retaliation by an assailant,
the ridicule and derision of nonintervening bystanders, and the threat of being
mistaken for the cause of the harm. Moreover, the victim may spurn, attack, or
become completely dependent on the rescuer, while the legal system may enlist
the rescuer as a witness subject to innumerable encounters with police, lawyers
and judges. The nightmare then may be most easily resolved by convincing oneself that the victim is not imperiled.

NOTE ON MISPRISION OF FELONY

As Judge Orth notes in *Pope*, the common law offense of misprision of felony
is not a crime in American jurisdictions. No state court has upheld a conviction
for misprision of felony since 1878. See Lionel H. Frankel, Criminal Omissions:
A Legal Microcosm, 11 Wayne L. Rev. 367, 417 n. 170 (1965) (finding only one
reported state conviction for misprision of felony: State v. Hahn, 40 N.J.L. 228
(Sup. Ct. 1878)). Congress enacted a misprision of felony statute in 1909, 18
U.S.C. §4[1]. However, the federal courts have interpreted this statute as requiring
active concealment of the felony; mere failure to report is not sufficient. United
States v. Johnson, 546 F.2d 1225 (5th Cir. 1977).

Although the *Pope* case denounced misprision of felony as "not acceptable by
today's standards," the offense is quite common in European jurisdictions. Consider, e.g., article 62 of the French Penal Code: "When it was possible to limit
the effects of the pending felony, or when by a denunciation it might have been
possible to prevent the perpetrators, or any of them from committing a further
felony, it shall be unlawful for anybody who has gained knowledge of such an
attempted or perpetrated felony, not to notify administrative or judicial authori-

---

1. "Whoever, having knowledge of the actual commission of a felony cognizable by a court of
the United States, conceals and does not as soon as possible make known the same to some judge
or other person in civil or military authority under the United States, shall be fined not more than
$500 or imprisoned not more than three years, or both."

ties immediately." [2] See also German Penal Code Article 138 (28 The American Series of Foreign Penal Codes (Germany) (Joseph J. Darby, trans. 1987)).

Some states have recently adopted statutes that revive misprision of felony, at least for serious crimes. Florida punishes the failure to report a sexual battery.[3] Massachusetts[4] and Rhode Island[5] punish the failure to report a rape, homicide, or robbery. Washington punishes failure to report all crimes involving violence,[6] Wisconsin all crimes involving bodily harm.[7] Ohio requires citizens to report all felonies.[8] Failure to comply with the above laws is a misdemeanor in all states except Massachusetts (which imposes only a $500-$1,000 fine), with possible sentences ranging from one month to one year in county jail. Additionally, all American jurisdictions require physicians and members of other designated professions to report child abuse; the vast majority of jurisdictions make failure to do so a misdemeanor.[9]

JOHN KLEINIG, GOOD SAMARITANISM

5 Phil. & Pub. Aff. 382 (1976)

The parable of the Good Samaritan was originally told in part-answer to the question, What shall I do to inherit eternal life? But the Samaritan's example has now been absorbed into the general moral traditions of our culture. Over the past 130 years it has increasingly been made a legal requirement. In the Russian Criminal Code of 1845 and, since then, in almost every continental European country, the failure to be a Good Samaritan has been declared a criminal offense. The glaring exceptions to this trend have been those countries within the Anglo-American legal tradition. This has been no mere oversight, but a matter of policy. In the words of C. J. Carpenter:

> With purely moral obligations, the law does not deal. For example, the priest and the Levite who passed by on the other side were not, it is supposed, liable at law for the continued suffering of the man who fell among thieves, which they might and morally ought to have prevented or relieved. Suppose *A,* standing close by a railroad, sees a two-year old babe on the track and a car approaching. He can easily rescue the child with entire safety to himself. And the instincts of humanity require him to do so. If he does not, he may perhaps justly be styled a ruthless savage and a moral monster, but he is not liable in damages for the child's injury or indictable under the statute for its death.

Though the position is slowly changing in torts, the criminal law situation remains substantially the same. "The law does not compel active benevolence between man and man. It is left to one's conscience whether he shall be the Good Samaritan or not." . . . In attempting to understand the current Anglo-American

---

2. 1 The American Series of Foreign Penal Codes (The French Penal Code) 38 (Gerhard O. W. Mueller & Jean F. Moreau trans. 1960).
3. Fla. Stat. Ann. §794.027 (West 1992).
4. Mass. Gen. Laws Ann. ch. 268, §40 (West 1990).
5. R.I. Gen. Laws §11-37-3.1 (Supp. 1993).
6. Wash. Rev. Code Ann. §9.69.100 (West 1988).
7. Wis. Stat. Ann. §940.34(2) (West Supp. 1993).
8. Ohio Rev. Stat. Ann. §2921.22(A) (Anderson 1993).
9. Irving Sloan, Child Abuse: Governing Law and Legislation 22-23, 43-45 (1983).

position with regard to Good Samaritan legislation, it is instructive to look at some of the debate which has led to it, since it has not come about without opposition.

Even in the eighteenth century, before Russia became the first continental European country to incorporate Good Samaritanism into its criminal code, there was some effort made to persuade the legislatures of England and the United States of the propriety of requiring Good Samaritanism. Bentham, for example, in his Introduction to the Principles of Morals and Legislation, asked the question: "In cases where the person is in danger, why should it not be made the duty of every man to save another from mischief, when it can be done without prejudicing himself, as well as abstain from bringing it on him?" Undoubtedly, he felt that no satisfactory answer could be given:

> A woman's head-dress catches fire, water is at hand: a man, instead of assisting to quench the fire, looks on, and laughs at it. A drunken man, falling with his face downwards into a puddle, is in danger of suffocation: lifting his head a little to one side would save him: another man sees this and lets him lie. A quantity of gunpowder lies scattered about a room: a man is going into it with a lighted candle: another, knowing this, lets him go in without warning. Who is there that in any of these cases would think punishment misapplied? . . .

Mill, who on matters of social policy remained close to Bentham, . . . points out that there are also "many positive acts for the benefit of others" which a person may "rightly be compelled to perform." Among these he includes

> certain acts of individual beneficence, such as saving a fellow creature's life, or interposing to protect the defenceless against ill-usage, things which whenever it is obviously a man's duty to do, he may rightfully be made responsible to society for not doing. A person may cause evil to others not only by his actions but by his inaction, and in either case he is justly accountable to them for the injury.

On Mill's view, it is our duty to render aid because, by not doing so, we *harm another.* . . .

The most influential reaction came from Lord Macaulay et al. In their *Notes on the Indian Penal Code,* . . . Macaulay criticized the proposal of an offense of homicide by omission. . . . The problem as Macaulay sees it is to draw the line between harm-producing omissions which ought to be legally proscribed, and those which ought not. He has no doubt that there are cases of each, even where the imperiled person dies. If a gaoler omits to supply a prisoner with food; if an official omits to warn travelers that the river is too high to ford; if the owner of a dog which is attacking someone omits to call it off; and death results, the person who failed to act is guilty of murder. But, if a man omits to give alms to a starving beggar; if a surgeon refuses to go from Calcutta to Meerut to perform a life-saving operation; if one traveler omits to warn others that the river is too high to ford; if a passer-by omits to call off the attacking dog; and death results, the person who failed to act is not guilty of murder. Macaulay . . . [is] prepared to grant that a rich man who lets a beggar die at his feet is morally worse than some for whom severe punishment was prescribed. "But we are unable to see where, if we make such a man legally punishable, we can draw the line." How rich is rich enough, and how much can be required? If it takes a thousand rupees to save the beggar's life, should the rich man be required to provide it? If not, where is the line to be drawn? And if the potential Good Samaritan is not a rich man, how much should he be required to give? Macaulay therefore proposes that omissions which cause or threaten harm be punishable only where they are, "on other grounds, illegal." In other words, only where there are already existing legal duties to aid should the failure to aid be indictable!

The bulk of Macaulay's argument seems to be directed to the impracticability of Good Samaritan legislation. But in his final remarks new considerations are smuggled in:

> It is, indeed, most highly desirable that men should not merely abstain from doing harm to their neighbours, but should render active services to their neighbours. In general, however, the penal law must content itself with keeping men from doing positive harm, and must leave to public opinion, and to the teachers of morality and religion, the office of furnishing men with motives for doing positive good. It is evident that to attempt to punish men by law for not rendering to others all the services which it is their duty to render others would be preposterous. We must grant impunity to the vast majority of those omissions which a benevolent morality would pronounce reprehensible, and must content ourselves with punishing such omissions only when they are distinguished from the rest by some circumstance which marks them out as peculiarly fit objects of penal legislation.

There is a suggestion here, contrary to earlier statements, that Bad Samaritanism does not constitute the causing of harm, but only the withholding of a positive good. And therefore, since the function of law is to prevent harm and not to enforce benevolence, it would be improper for the law to require Good Samaritanism, . . .

What are the consequences of Good Samaritan legislation so feared by Macaulay and other opponents? On the surface it looks like a problem of legal draftsmanship. Such are the differences between men and circumstances that no workable formula for specifying those occasions on which a Samaritan ought to be legally required to render aid can be produced. . . . Livingston's criterion, that aid ought to be mandatory when it can be given "without personal danger or pecuniary loss," is considered to be open to serious objection. The surgeon summoned from Calcutta to Meerut might profit financially, and the trip might present no greater dangers than staying in Bengal, but it might still be extremely inconvenient for him: "He is about to proceed to Europe immediately, or he expects some members of his family by the next ship, and wishes to be at the presidency to receive them." If he refuses to go, he is no "murderer," and a good sight better than another who, "enjoying ample wealth, should refuse to disburse an anna to save the life of another." On Livingston's criterion, the latter but not the former should go free.

About the best that could be said for this argument is that it shows the inadequacy of Livingston's criterion. But it does not do much more. It does nothing to show that if Good Samaritan legislation is introduced, unreasonable sacrifices of welfare and interests will be demanded of Samaritans. As is the case with Good Samaritan provisions in those countries that already have them, the Samaritan will be required only to take reasonable steps to give or procure aid for the imperiled person. Judgments of reasonableness are not impossible of determination, and are the bread and butter of the courts. . . .

However, I think another, rather different fear underlies Macaulay's opposition to Good Samaritan legislation. Made explicit by later writers, it is basically the fear that Good Samaritan legislation will substantially diminish freedom. In a culture steeped in individualism, nothing produces more hysteria than measures which encroach on individual liberty. "You owe me nothing; I owe you nothing. You stay out of my way, and I'll stay out of yours." That is an extreme expression, but it constitutes an important thread within the Anglo-American sociomoral fabric. . . .

The freedom to pursue one's interests is not, as Mill and Bentham clearly saw, unlimited. Where the pursuit of one's interests is a causal factor in another's harm, or threatens additional harm, as in Bad Samaritanism, we have the important beginnings of a case for justifiable state interference. . . .

NOTE

A handful of states, including Minnesota, Rhode Island, Vermont, and Wisconsin, have enacted Good Samaritan statutes, which make it criminal to refuse to rescue a person in emergency situations. See, e.g., Vt. Stat. Ann. tit. 12, §519:

> A person who knows that another is exposed to grave physical harm shall, to the extent that the same can be rendered without danger or peril to himself or without interference with important duties owed to others, give reasonable assistance to the exposed person unless that assistance or care is being provided by others.

European countries have long used the criminal law to enforce a duty to aid another in distress. An example is Article 323c of the German Criminal Code:

> Whoever does not render help in cases of accident, common danger or necessity although help is needed and can be provided in the circumstances without danger of serious injury to the person and without violation of other important duties, will be punished by imprisonment up to one year or by fine.

Another example is the French Criminal Code, Article 63. See Andrew Ashworth & Eva Steiner, Criminal Omissions and Public Duties: The French Experience, 10 Leg. Stud. 153 (1990).

The issue has been controversial in this country. See, e.g., Daniel B. Yeager, A Radical Community of Aid: A Rejoinder to Opponents of Affirmative Duties to Help Strangers, 71 Wash. U.L.Q. 1 (1993); F. R. Denton, The Case Against a Duty to Rescue, 4 Canadian J. L. & Juris. 101 (1991). A comprehensive examination of this and related issues is Steven J. Heyman, Foundations of the Duty to Rescue, 47 Vand. L. Rev. 673 (1994).

Statutes in most states make it a crime to fail to obey police officers who command bystanders to assist them. This is, as we have seen, in striking contrast to the rarity of criminal sanctions to compel persons to help another in distress or to take steps to enlist the assistance of the police when they witness a crime being committed. In High Noon Revisited: Commands of Assistance by Peace Officers in the Age of the Fourth Amendment, 101 Yale L.J. 1475 (1992), Judge Jon C. Blue reviews the law and practice of compelled assistance and concludes: "It is a misuse of power in modern society for an agent of the state to summarily draft a citizen off the street and impress him into hazardous police duty." Id. at 1490.

JONES v. UNITED STATES

United States Court of Appeals, District of Columbia Circuit
308 F.2d 307 (1962)

WRIGHT, J. [Defendant was found guilty of involuntary manslaughter through failure to provide for Anthony Lee Green, which failure resulted in his death. The deceased was the 10-month-old illegitimate baby of Shirley Green. He was placed with the defendant, a family friend. Shirley Green lived in the house with defendant for some of the time, but there was conflict in the evidence as to how long. There was also conflict as to whether or not the defendant was paid for taking care of the baby. The medical evidence was uncontested that the defendant had ample means to provide food and medical care.]

Appellant . . . takes exception to the failure of the trial court to charge that the jury must find beyond a reasonable doubt, as an element of the crime, that appellant was under a legal duty to supply food and necessities to Anthony Lee. . . .

The problem of establishing the duty to take action which would preserve the life of another has not often arisen in the case law of this country. The most commonly cited statement of the rule is found in People v. Beardsley, 150 Mich. 206, 113 N.W. 1128, 1129:

> The law recognizes that under some circumstances the omission of a duty owed by one individual to another, where such omission results in the death of the one to whom the duty is owing, will make the other chargeable with manslaughter. . . . This rule of law is always based upon the proposition that the duty neglected must be a legal duty, and not a mere moral obligation. It must be a duty imposed by law or by contract, and the omission to perform the duty must be the immediate and direct cause of death. . . .

There are at least four situations in which the failure to act may constitute breach of a legal duty. One can be held criminally liable: first, where a statute imposes a duty to care for another; second, where one stands in a certain status relationship to another;[9] third, where one has assumed a contractual duty to care for another; and fourth, where one has voluntarily assumed the care of another and so secluded the helpless person as to prevent others from rendering aid.

It is the contention of the Government that either the third or the fourth ground is applicable here. However, it is obvious that in any of the four situations, there are critical issues of fact which must be passed on by the jury — specifically in this case, whether appellant had entered into a contract with the mother for the care of Anthony Lee or, alternatively, whether she assumed the

---

9. 10 A.L.R. 1137 (1921) (parent to child); Territory v. Manton, 8 Mont. 95, 19 P. 387 (husband to wife); Regina v. Smith, 8 Carr. & P. 153 (Eng. 1837) (master to apprentice); United States v. Knowles, 26 Fed. Cas. 800 (No. 15,540) (ship's master to crew and passengers); cf. State v. Reitze, 86 N.J.L. 407, 92 A. 576 (innkeeper to inebriated customers).

care of the child and secluded him from the care of his mother, his natural protector. On both of these issues, the evidence is in direct conflict, appellant insisting that the mother was actually living with appellant and Anthony Lee, and hence should have been taking care of the child herself, while Shirley Green testified she was living with her parents and was paying appellant to care for both children.

In spite of this conflict, the instructions given in the case failed even to suggest the necessity for finding a legal duty of care. The only reference to duty in the instructions was the reading of the indictment which charged, inter alia, that the [defendant] "failed to perform [her] legal duty." A finding of legal duty is the critical element of the crime charged and failure to instruct the jury concerning it was plain error. . . .

Reversed and remanded.

NOTES

1. There is nothing conceptually problematic in a statute making it criminal to fail to act in certain situations. Indeed such statutes are common. The issue is only the desirability of imposing such obligations, as in the example of the Good Samaritan laws just considered. The *Jones* case, however, presents a different issue: Where a crime is defined in terms of producing a result (like homicide, which prohibits "killing" another person, or child abuse laws, which prohibit abusing a child), when may a person who fails to act to avert the prohibited result be said to have produced it?

Jones reflects the general Anglo-American position that unless a penal statute specifically requires a particular action to be performed, criminal liability for omission arises only when the law of torts or some other law concerning civil liability imposes a duty to act in the circumstances. This is a position also taken by the Model Penal Code in §2.01(3) (liability for an omission only when "a duty to perform the omitted act is otherwise imposed by law").

2. Most cases where liability for homicide is imposed for a failure to act are, like the *Jones* case, cases of involuntary manslaughter. Such a case, however, might be murder if the defendant intentionally refused aid with the intention of achieving the death of the decedent, or with full knowledge of a great risk that the decedent would die as a result. For example, in Commonwealth v. Pestinikas, 617 A.2d 1339 (Pa. Super. Ct. 1992), defendant permitted a 92-year-old person to die of starvation after agreeing to feed him and knowing there was no other way for him to obtain food. He was convicted of murder in the third degree.

3. As *Pope* and *Jones* illustrate, a person who is not a child's parent, guardian, or caretaker ordinarily cannot be convicted on the basis of a failure to protect the child from abuse by a third party. But the child's *mother* can be, and often is, convicted of child abuse or homicide when she fails to protect her child from battering or sexual assault inflicted by a male member of the household. See Dorothy E. Roberts, Motherhood and Crime, 79 Iowa L. Rev. 95 (1993). Because the duty of parent to child is well established, convictions of this sort pose no novel conceptual problems. But such convictions can sometimes pose a practical problem. Consider Commonwealth v. Cardwell, 515 A.2d 311 (Pa. Super. 1986)

Defendant Julia Cardwell lived with her daughter Alicia and Clyde Cardwell, who was Julia's husband and Alicia's stepfather. For 4 years, beginning in 1979 (when Alicia was about 11 years old), Clyde sexually abused Alicia. In October 1983 Alicia told her mother Julia about the assaults. Ten months later Alicia ran away from home. Julia was convicted of child abuse for failing to take sufficient steps in the interim to protect her daughter:

> In those ten months, Julia's only actions directed at protecting her daughter consisted of: writing two letters to Clyde that did little more than express her knowledge of and anger at his abuse of Alicia; applying for Alicia to transfer schools; and moving some of her and Alicia's clothing to Julia's mother's house. We note that the remedy of moving to Julia's mother's house was tragically frustrated by the destruction by fire of that house in May 1984, but the fact remains that Julia took no further steps to relieve her daughter's desperate situation in the four months that ensued from May 1984 until Alicia ran away from home in September 1984.

The court's opinion mentioned, without comment, several further details:

> Alicia testified that she and Julia were afraid of Clyde, that Clyde beat up Julia on one occasion, that he threw and broke things in the house, that he had punched a number of holes in the walls of the house, and that he carried a .357 magnum pistol, which he kept on the mantelpiece.

Nonetheless the court upheld the conviction, noting:

> The affirmative performance required . . . cannot be met simply by showing any step at all toward preventing harm, however incomplete or ineffectual. An act which will negate intent is not necessarily one which will provide a successful outcome. However, the person charged with the duty of care is required to take steps that are reasonably calculated to achieve success. Otherwise, the meaning of "duty of care" is eviscerated.

A concurring judge conceded that "Julia's real choices in view of her not unreasonable fear of her husband were limited and difficult — she could report her husband to the authorities, she could take her daughter and leave the marital home, or she could send her daughter away." The judge nonetheless concurred in affirming the conviction because Julia "unquestionably endangered her daughter's welfare by doing nothing to prevent the child's continued abuse."

Questions: How should Clyde's violence toward Julia affect the extent of her duty to prevent him from harming her child? The strict requirements for a duress defense are not met, as we shall see, infra page 897. To what extent should a mother be forced to risk her own life in order to avoid criminal liability for injuries inflicted intentionally by her spouse or boyfriend? Consider Roberts, supra, at 111-113:

> Women who fail to protect their children from violence are often victims of violence themselves. . . .
>
> Courts, however, have not asked how this web of violence affects the mother's liability. They presume that a woman's obligation to her children always takes precedence over her own interest in independence and physical safety. Feminists have criticized people who ask battered women "Why didn't you leave?" because this

question fails to recognize the physical, social, and legal constraints that keep women in violent homes. Courts slowly are beginning to acknowledge these constraints in self-defense cases.

These impediments do not seem to matter, however, when mothers [fail to protect] abused children. Judges assume that a woman's maternal instinct to protect her children from harm overcomes any barriers to escape.

PROBLEMS

How can we explain the recourse to the law of civil liability to determine criminal liability? What are the circumstances in which a duty to act has been held to exist? On what criteria should such determinations be made? Consider the following cases.

1. *People v. Beardsley, 150 Mich. 206, 113 N.W. 1128 (1907).* Beardsley spent a weekend at his home with a woman he was not married to. During this period, the woman took a fatal dose of morphine tablets. Beardsley failed to call a physician to help her. She died, and he was charged and convicted of manslaughter. The supreme court reversed the conviction on the ground that defendant owed deceased no legal duty, whatever his moral duty. The court stated (113 N.W. at 1131):

> It is urged by the prosecutor that the respondent "stood towards this woman for the time being in the place of her natural guardian and protector, and as such owed her a clear legal duty which he completely failed to perform." The fact that this woman was in his house created no such legal duty as exists in law and is due from a husband towards his wife, as seems to be intimated by the prosecutor's brief. Such an inference would be very repugnant to our moral sense.

Questions: What if the relationship between defendant and deceased had been more permanent? Suppose she was his mistress of long standing instead of a weekend guest? Would it depend on whether a common law marriage could be made out and whether the common law marriage were recognized in the jurisdiction? Is there any sound reason why defendant should not have been held responsible?

2. *Regina v. Stone and Dobinson, [1977] Q.B. 354, 357-358.* The two defendants were Stone, a 67-year-old ex-miner, and Dobinson, his 43-year-old housekeeper and mistress. In 1972, Stone's 61-year-old sister, Fanny, came to live with the defendants, paying them a small amount each week for rent. She had been living with her sister, Rosy, but "[f]or some reason, probably because Rosy could not tolerate her any longer, she had decided to leave." Fanny constantly worried about her weight and would often hide in her room for days. In 1975, she developed severe *anorexia nervosa* and stopped eating anything but "biscuits and pop." She refused to tell the defendants the name of her doctor, fearing she would be "put away." Stone and Dobinson tried to find her doctor but were unsuccessful. They also tried once to find another doctor. However, once that attempt failed, they took no other steps to help Fanny, not even mentioning her condition to the social worker who came periodically to help with Stone's mentally retarded son. Meanwhile Fanny had retired permanently to her bed. Several weeks later she died in terrible degradation from the lack of nursing care.

The defendants were both convicted of manslaughter, and their conviction was affirmed on appeal. The court held that the defendants had assumed a duty of care: "Whether Fanny was a lodger or not she was a blood relative of the appellant Stone; she was occupying a room in his house; Mrs. Dobinson had undertaken the duty of trying to wash her. . . . They tried to get a doctor; they tried to discover the previous doctor."

Questions: On what basis is *Stone and Dobinson* distinguishable from *Beardsley?* Did Stone's duty come from being a blood relative,[10] or from the fact that Fanny was a lodger rather than a guest? Is Dobinson liable because, by washing the deceased and once trying to contact a doctor, she assumed a duty of care? Would she not have been liable if she had never tried to help at all? Professor Glanville Williams has criticized the reasoning in this case while defending its holding. He argues that the decision should be grounded on a rule of law that an occupier of a house must take reasonable steps to save the life of a fellow occupant. Textbook of the Criminal Law 264-265 (2d ed. 1983).

3. *People v. Oliver, 210 Cal. App. 3d 138, 258 Cal. Rptr. 138 (1989).* Defendant Oliver met Cornejo, already intoxicated, at a bar. She invited Cornejo to her house where he asked for a spoon to ingest some heroin. She gave it to him, and he repaired to the bathroom and ingested the drug. Immediately thereafter he passed out in her living room. Unable to rouse him, she returned to the bar. When her daughter later discovered Cornejo and telephoned her mother for instructions, Oliver told her to drag him outside and put him behind a shed where he wouldn't be seen by neighbors. When Oliver returned later with a boyfriend she saw Cornejo still lying there. The next morning, seeing he was still there and now thinking he might be dead, she left instructions for her daughter to call the police. The police found Cornejo dead, the result of morphine poisoning. Oliver was then charged and convicted of involuntary manslaughter under an instruction that allowed the jury to find guilt on a criminal negligence theory. The court of appeal affirmed, rejecting defendant's argument that as a matter of law she did not owe decedent any duty to seek medical care, and stating (210 Cal. App. 3d at 149):

> We conclude that the evidence of the combination of events which occurred between the time appellant left the bar with Cornejo through the time he fell to the floor unconscious, established as a matter of law a relationship which imposed upon appellant a duty to seek medical aid. At the time appellant left the bar with Cornejo, she observed that he was extremely drunk, and drove him to her home. In so doing, she took him from a public place where others might have taken care to prevent him from injuring himself, to a private place — her home — where she alone could provide such care. To a certain, if limited, extent, therefore, she took charge of a person unable to prevent harm to himself. (Rest. 2d Torts §324.)[a] She then allowed Cornejo to use her bathroom, without any objection on her part, to inject himself with narcotics, an act involving the definite potential for fatal con-

---

10. The only familial relationships that create a legal duty of care are parent to minor child and spouse to spouse. LaFave & Scott, Criminal Law §3.3(a)(1), at 203-204 (2d ed. 1986).

a. Section 324 of the Restatement (Second) of Torts provides in part: "One who, being under no duty to do so, takes charge of another who is helpless adequately to aid or protect himself is subject to liability to the other for any bodily harm caused to him by (a) the failure of the actor to exercise reasonable care to secure the safety of the other while within the actor's charge. . . ." — Eds.

sequences. When Cornejo collapsed to the floor, appellant should have known that her conduct had contributed to creating an unreasonable risk of harm for Cornejo — death. At that point, she owed Cornejo a duty to prevent that risk from occurring by summoning aid, even if she had not previously realized that her actions would lead to such risk. (Rest. 2d Torts §321.)[b] Her failure to summon any medical assistance whatsoever and to leave him abandoned outside her house warranted the jury finding a breach of that duty.

Questions: Do the sections of the Restatement of Torts relied on by the court really support the court's conclusion? What if the facts were the same except that the decedent used the spoon without asking Oliver's permission? Except that he had a heart seizure while visiting her? How do you account for the differing results in *Beardsley* and this case?

4. *Jones v. State, 220 Ind. 384, 43 N.E.2d 1017 (1942).* The defendant raped a child of 12, who, "distracted by pain and grief," fell or jumped into a creek where she drowned. The defendant intentionally abstained from rescuing her although able to do so without risk to himself. The supreme court affirmed a conviction of second-degree murder, stating: "Can it be doubted that one who by his own overpowering criminal act has put another in danger of drowning has the duty to preserve her life?" 220 Ind. at 387, 43 N.E.2d at 1018.

Questions: Is there criminal responsibility because there is a legal duty, or a legal duty because there is criminal responsibility? Would a duty to rescue have arisen even if the defendant's action were wholly innocent? Suppose a defendant wounds an assailant in perfect self-defense. Is she obliged to seek aid or otherwise try to save her assailant's life? The issue is touched on in King v. Commonwealth, 285 Ky. 654, 148 S.W.2d 1044 (1941).

5. *A, B, C,* and *D* watch a child drowning in a pool but take no steps to save her. *A* is her father. *B, C,* and *D* are all strangers. *B,* intending to drown the child, had knocked her into the pool by pushing *C* into her. *D* just happened to be there. The child drowns.

Question: *A* presents a classic omission case in which liability would rest on a duty to the child. Would this be so even if *A* did not realize she was his own child?

B would not be thought of as presenting an omission case at all; it would be said that *B* killed the child by his act of pushing her in. *Questions:* Are *A* and *B* in wholly different kinds of situations, or is it possible to adduce a general principle sufficient to account for both *A*'s and *B*'s liability? May we do so by saying that *B*'s act in pushing the child into the pool creates a duty to rescue her, which duty is supplied in *A*'s case by his being her father? Or is it preferable to say that *A*'s being her father is in the nature of acts making him responsible for the deceased's predicament to the same degree as *B*'s act of pushing her in?

D, of course, presents the classic omission case where, under common law doctrine, there is no duty and hence no liability. But how about *C*? Is *C* in the same position as *D,* or does he have a duty to act because it was his body that propelled the child into the pool? Does it matter that he was pushed, so that he

b. Section 321 of the Restatement (Second) of Torts provides: "(1) If the actor does an act, and subsequently realizes or should realize that it has created an unreasonable risk of causing physical harm to another, he is under a duty to exercise reasonable care to prevent the risk from taking effect. (2) The rule stated in Subsection (1) applies even though at the time of the act the actor has no reason to believe that it will involve such a risk." — Eds.

did not act at all? Suppose, then, that *C* walked into the child because he didn't see her (perhaps through no fault of his own)? Would he then have a duty on the ground that his act, even though innocent, caused the child's peril?

Consider the observations of Professor J. C. Smith in Liability for Omissions in Criminal Law, 14 Leg. Stud. 88, 94 (1984):

> [I]n Green v. Cross [(1910) 103 L.T. 279] . . . the defendant inadvertently caught a dog in a trap. At the time when he found the animal trapped and in pain, he had committed no offence. But if he then failed to take steps which he might reasonably have been expected to take to release it from its misery, he was guilty of causing it to be ill-treated, abused and tortured, contrary to the Cruelty to Animals Act 1849. Other interests call, *a fortiori*, for similar protection. . . .
>
> Suppose that, on leaving my office on Friday evening, I lock the storeroom door, reasonably believing the room to be empty. I then hear movement inside and realize that I have locked in a colleague and that he will be imprisoned there for the weekend unless I unlock the door and let him out. Surely my omission to do so would render me liable for false imprisonment (in criminal as well as civil law); and it should be no answer that locking the door was an entirely lawful and reasonable act.
>
> Suppose, again, that without any fault on my part, I were to knock a small child into the notorious shallow pool — he was careering along not looking where he was going until we collided. Surely the lenience of the common law does not extend so far as to permit me to walk off, leaving him to drown when I could easily have saved him.
>
> I venture, therefore, to suggest a general principle: . . . Whenever the defendant's act, though without his knowledge, imperils the person, liberty or property of another, or any other interest protected by the criminal law, and the defendant becomes aware of the events creating the peril, he has a duty to take reasonable steps to prevent the peril from resulting in the harm in question.

Do you agree with Professor Smith? Why should a wholly innocent accident serve to create a duty to help another where none would exist in the absence of the accident?

BARBER v. SUPERIOR COURT

California District Court of Appeal
147 Cal. App. 3d 1006, 195 Cal. Rptr. 484 (1983)

[After a preliminary hearing, the magistrate dismissed murder and conspiracy charges against two physicians. The superior court set aside the magistrate's order and reinstated the complaint. The physicians then petitioned the court of appeal for review of the decision of the superior court.]

COMPTON, A. J. . . . Deceased Clarence Herbert underwent surgery. [W]hile in the recovery room, Mr. Herbert suffered a cardio-respiratory arrest. He was revived by a team of physicians and nurses and immediately placed on life support equipment.

Within the following three days, it was determined that Mr. Herbert was in a deeply comatose state. [Tests] indicated that Mr. Herbert had suffered severe brain damage, leaving him in a vegetative state, which was likely to be permanent.

At that time petitioners [his physicians] informed Mr. Herbert's family of their opinion as to his condition and chances for recovery. While there is some dispute as to the precise terminology used by the doctors, it is clear that they communicated to the family that the prognosis for recovery was extremely poor. At that point, the family convened and drafted a written request to the hospital personnel stating that they wanted "all machines taken off that are sustaining life" (sic). As a result, petitioners, either directly or as a result of orders given by them, caused the respirator and other life-sustaining equipment to be removed. Mr. Herbert continued to breathe without the equipment but showed no signs of improvement. . . . After two more days had elapsed, petitioners, after consulting with the family, ordered removal of the intravenous tubes which provided hydration and nourishment. From that point until his death, Mr. Herbert received nursing care which preserved his dignity and provided a clean and hygienic environment.

The precise issue for determination by this court is whether the evidence presented before the magistrate was sufficient to support his determination that petitioners should not be held to answer to the charges of murder, and conspiracy to commit murder. . . .

"Murder is the *unlawful* killing of a human being, . . . with malice aforethought." . . .

[W]e accept the superior court judge's analysis that if petitioners unlawfully and intentionally killed Mr. Herbert, the malice could be presumed regardless of their motive.

The use of the term "unlawful" in defining a criminal homicide is generally to distinguish a criminal homicide from those homicides which society has determined to be "justifiable" or "excusable." Euthanasia, of course, is neither justifiable nor excusable in California. . . .

Historically, death has been defined in terms of cessation of heart and respiratory function. Health and Safety Code section 7180(a)(2) now provides for an alternative definition in terms of irreversible cessation of all brain function. . . .

Of course it is conceded by all that at the time petitioners terminated further treatment, Mr. Herbert was not "dead" by either statutory or historical standards since there was still some minimal brain activity. . . .

We thus turn to an analysis of the superior court's determination that petitioners' conduct was "unlawful" as a matter of law. . . .

As a predicate to our analysis of whether the petitioners' conduct amounted to an "unlawful killing," we conclude that the cessation of "heroic" life support measures is not an affirmative act but rather a withdrawal or omission of further treatment.

Even though these life support devices are, to a degree, "self-propelled," each pulsation of the respirator or each drop of fluid introduced into the patient's body by intravenous feeding devices is comparable to a manually administered injection or item of medication. Hence "disconnecting" of the mechanical devices is comparable to withholding the manually administered injection or medication.

Further we view the use of an intravenous administration of nourishment and fluid, under the circumstances, as being the same as the use of the respirator or other form of life support equipment. . . .

Medical nutrition and hydration may not always provide net benefits to patients. Medical procedures to provide nutrition and hydration are more similar to other medical procedures than to typical human ways of providing nutrition and hydration. Their benefits and burdens ought to be evaluated in the same manner as any other medical procedure. . . .

There is no criminal liability for failure to act unless there is a legal duty to act. Thus the critical issue becomes one of determining the duties owed by a physician to a patient who has been reliably diagnosed as in a comatose state from which any meaningful recovery of cognitive brain function is exceedingly unlikely. . . .

A physician has no duty to continue treatment, once it has proved to be ineffective. Although there may be a duty to provide life-sustaining machinery in the *immediate* aftermath of a cardio-respiratory arrest, there is no duty to continue its use once it has become futile in the opinion of qualified medical personnel. . . .

Of course, the difficult determinations that must be made under these principles [are] the point at which further treatment will be of no reasonable benefit to the patient, who should have the power to make that decision and who should have the authority to direct termination of treatment.

No precise guidelines as to when or how these decisions should be made can be provided by this court since this determination is essentially a medical one to be made at a time and on the basis of facts which will be unique to each case. . . .

Several authorities have discussed the issue of which life-sustaining procedures must be used and for how long their use must be maintained in terms of "ordinary" and "extraordinary" means of treatment. The use of these terms begs the question. A more rational approach involves the determination of whether the proposed treatment is proportionate or disproportionate in terms of the benefits to be gained versus the burdens caused.

Under this approach, proportionate treatment is that which, in the view of the patient, has at least a reasonable chance of providing benefits to the patient, which benefits outweigh the burdens attendant to the treatment. [A] treatment course which is only minimally painful or intrusive may nonetheless be considered disproportionate to the potential benefits if the prognosis is virtually hopeless for any significant improvement in condition. . . .

Of course the patient's interests and desires are the key ingredients of the decision making process. . . .

When the patient, however, is incapable of deciding for himself, because of his medical condition or for other reasons, there is no clear authority on the issue of who and under what procedure is to make the final decision. . . .

Under the circumstances of this case, the wife was the proper person to act as a surrogate for the patient with the authority to decide issues regarding further treatment, and would have so qualified had judicial approval been sought. There is no evidence that there was any disagreement among the wife and children. Nor was there any evidence that they were motivated in their decision by anything other than love and concern for the dignity of their husband and father.

Furthermore, in the absence of legislative guidance, we find no legal requirement that prior judicial approval is necessary before any decision to withdraw treatment can be made. . . .

In summary we conclude that the petitioners' omission to continue treatment under the circumstances, though intentional and with knowledge that the patient would die, was not an unlawful failure to perform a legal duty. . . .

The superior court erred in determining that as a matter of law the evidence required the magistrate to hold petitioners to answer.

AIREDALE NHS TRUST v. BLAND, [1993] All E.R. 821 (H.L.): [In this case, the House of Lords faced the question whether artificial feeding and antibiotic drugs may lawfully be withheld from an insensate patient with no hope of recovery, when it is known that without the treatment the patient will shortly die. The House of Lords answered the question in the affirmative. Lord Goff stated in his address:]

[T]he law draws a crucial distinction between cases in which a doctor decides not to provide, or to continue to provide, for his patient treatment or care which could or might prolong his life and those in which he decides, for example by administering a lethal drug, actively to bring his patient's life to an end. . . . [T]he former may be lawful, either because the doctor is giving effect to his patient's wishes by withholding the treatment or care, or even in certain circumstances in which . . . the patient is incapacitated from stating whether or not he gives his consent. But it is not lawful for a doctor to administer a drug to his patient to bring about his death, even though that course is prompted by a humanitarian desire to end his suffering, however great that suffering may be. So to act is to cross the Rubicon which runs between on the one hand the care of the living patient and on the other hand euthanasia — actively causing his death to avoid or to end his suffering. Euthanasia is not lawful at common law. It is of course well known that there are many responsible members of our society who believe that euthanasia should be made lawful; but that result could, I believe, only be achieved by legislation which expresses the democratic will that so fundamental a change should be made in our law, and can, if enacted, ensure that such legalized killing can only be carried out subject to appropriate supervision and control. It is true that the drawing of this distinction may lead to a charge of hypocrisy, because it can be asked why, if the doctor, by discontinuing treatment, is entitled in consequence to let his patient die, it should not be lawful to put him out of his misery straight away, in a more humane manner, by a lethal injection, rather than let him linger on in pain until he dies. But the law does not feel able to authorize euthanasia, even in circumstances such as these, for, once euthanasia is recognized as lawful in these circumstances, it is difficult to see any logical basis for excluding it in others.

At the heart of this distinction lies a theoretical question. Why is it that the doctor who gives his patient a lethal injection which kills him commits an unlawful act and indeed is guilty of murder, whereas a doctor who, by discontinuing life support, allows his patient to die may not act unlawfully and will not do so if he commits no breach of duty to his patient? Professor Glanville Williams has suggested (see Textbook of Criminal Law (2nd edn, 1983), p. 282) that the reason is that what the doctor does when he switches off a life support machine 'is in substance not an act but an omission to struggle' and that 'the omission is not a breach of duty by the doctor, because he is not obliged to continue in a hopeless case'.

I agree that the doctor's conduct in discontinuing life support can properly be categorized as an omission. It is true that it may be difficult to describe what the doctor actually does as an omission, for example where he takes some positive step to bring the life support to an end. But discontinuation of life support is, for present purposes, no different from not initiating life support in the first place. In each case, the doctor is simply allowing his patient to die in the sense that he is desisting from taking a step which might, in certain circumstances, prevent his patient from dying as a result of his pre-existing condition; and as a matter of general principle an omission such as this will not be unlawful unless it constitutes a breach of duty to the patient. I also agree that the doctor's conduct is to be differentiated from that of, for example, an interloper who maliciously switches off a life support machine because, although the interloper may perform exactly the same act as the doctor who discontinues life support, his doing so constitutes interference with the life-prolonging treatment then being administered by the doctor. Accordingly, whereas the doctor, in discontinuing life support, is simply allowing his patient to die of his pre-existing condition, the interloper is actively intervening to stop the doctor from prolonging the patient's life, and such conduct cannot possibly be categorized as an omission.

The distinction appears, therefore, to be useful in the present context in that it can be invoked to explain how discontinuance of life support can be differentiated from ending a patient's life by a lethal injection. But in the end the reason for that difference is that, whereas the law considers that discontinuance of life support may be consistent with the doctor's duty to care for his patient, it does not, for reasons of policy, consider that it forms any part of his duty to give his patient a lethal injection to put him out of his agony.

GLANVILLE WILLIAMS, EUTHANASIA, 41 Med.-Legal J. 14, 21 (1973): The proposition that switching off the respirator should be regarded as an omission may be proved as follows. Suppose that the respirator worked only as long as the doctor turned a handle. Then, if he stopped turning, he would thereafter be regarded merely as omitting. Suppose, alternatively, that the respirator worked electrically but was made to shut itself off every 24 hours. Then the deliberate failure to restart it would again be an omission. It can make no moral difference that the respirator is constructed to run continuously and has to be stopped. Stopping the respirator is not a positive act of killing the patient, but a decision not to strive any longer to save him.

If this distinction between an act and an omission is thought to be artificial, its artificiality is imposed on us by our refusal to accord the same moral freedom for action as we do for inaction. Pending a change of thought, the concept of an omission is a useful way of freeing us from some of the consequences of over-rigid moral attitudes.

JAMES RACHELS, ACTIVE AND PASSIVE EUTHANASIA, 292 New Eng. J. of Med. 78 (1975): The distinction between active and passive euthanasia is thought to be crucial for medical ethics. The idea is that it is permissible, at least in some cases, to withhold treatment and allow a patient to die, but it is never permissible to take any direct action designed to kill the patient. This doctrine seems to be accepted by most doctors, and it is endorsed in a statement adopted by the House of Delegates of the American Medical Association on December 4, 1973. . . . However, a strong case can be made against this doctrine. . . .

One reason why so many people think that there is an important moral difference between active and passive euthanasia is that they think killing someone is morally worse than letting someone die. But is it? . . . To investigate this issue, two cases may be considered that are exactly alike except that one involves killing whereas the other involves letting someone die. . . .

In the first, Smith stands to gain a large inheritance if anything should happen to his six-year-old cousin. One evening while the child is taking his bath, Smith sneaks into the bathroom and drowns the child, and then arranges things so that it will look like an accident.

In the second, Jones also stands to gain if anything should happen to his six-year-old cousin. Like Smith, Jones sneaks in planning to drown the child in his bath. However, just as he enters the bathroom Jones sees the child slip and hit his head, and fall face down in the water. Jones is delighted; he stands by, ready to push the child's head back under if it is necessary, but it is not necessary. With only a little thrashing about, the child drowns all by himself, "accidentally," as Jones watches and does nothing.

Now Smith killed the child, whereas Jones "merely" let the child die. That is the only difference between them. Did either man behave better, from a moral point of view? . . . I think not. In the first place, both men acted from the same motive, personal gain, and both had exactly the same end in view when they acted. It may be inferred from Smith's conduct that he is a bad man. . . . But would not the very same thing be inferred about Jones from his conduct? . . .

[T]he bare difference between killing and letting die does not, in itself, make a moral difference. If a doctor lets a patient die, for humane reasons, he is in the same moral position as if he had given the patient a lethal injection for humane reasons. If his decision was wrong — if, for example, the patient's illness was in fact curable — the decision would be equally regrettable no matter which method was used to carry it out. And if the doctor's decision was the right one, the method used is not in itself important. . . .

[I]t is very easy to conflate the question of whether killing is, in itself, worse than letting die, with the very different question of whether most actual cases of killing are more reprehensible than most actual cases of letting die. [O]ne learns to think of killing in a much worse light than of letting die. But this does not mean that there is something about killing that makes it in itself worse than letting die, for it is not the bare difference between killing and letting die that makes the difference in these cases. Rather, the other factors — the murderer's motive of personal gain, for example, contrasted with the doctor's humanitarian motivation — account for different reactions to the different cases.

[I]t follows that active euthanasia is not any worse than passive euthanasia. What arguments can be given on the other side? The most common, I believe, is the following:

The important difference between active and passive euthanasia is that, in passive euthanasia, the doctor does not do anything to bring about the patient's death. The doctor does nothing, and the patient dies of whatever ills already afflict him. In active euthanasia, however, the doctor does something to bring about the patient's death: he kills him. The doctor who gives the patient with cancer a lethal injection has himself caused his patient's death; whereas if he merely ceases treatment, the cancer is the cause of the death.

A number of points need to be made here. The first is that it is not exactly correct to say that in passive euthanasia the doctor does nothing, for he does do one thing that is very important: he lets the patient die. . . . The decision to let a patient die is subject to moral appraisal in the same way that a decision to kill him would be subject to moral appraisal: it may be assessed as wise or unwise, compassionate or sadistic, right or wrong. If a doctor deliberately let a patient die who was suffering from a routinely curable illness, the doctor would certainly be to blame for what he had done, just as he would be to blame if he had needlessly killed the patient. Charges against him would then be appropriate. If so, it would be no defense at all for him to insist that he didn't "do anything." He would have done something very serious indeed, for he let his patient die. . . .

PHILIPPA FOOT, LIFE AND DEATH, Lond. Rev. of Books, Aug. 7, 1986: Rachels insists . . . that we cannot make a moral distinction between killing someone and allowing him to die. Apart from differences of motive or of side-effect the two are simply morally equivalent. This Rachels thinks he can show by his favorite example of a baby who is either deliberately drowned in the bath or else deliberately allowed to die. (In both cases by a villain who wants him dead.) From the fact that one action seems as bad as the other Rachels concludes that there is no "intrinsic" difference between killing and allowing to die. What he has failed to notice is that we can construct another example in which again we hold motive and outcome constant but where it is permissible to allow the child to die but not to push him underwater. We only have to imagine that the lives of our children are at stake to see that while we could indeed leave one to drown while hurrying to save the others, we would very properly be had up for murder if we held him under the water as part of a plan to save them. Rachels and others like him who insist on the moral irrelevance of the distinction between killing and letting die do so partly because they do not discuss the right distinction, which should be seen as separating not act and omission as such but rather the origination of harm from the failure to bring aid. The deeper root of the mistake lies, however, in the belief that a decent moral code can be constructed without bringing in the concept of *rights* at an early stage. All sorts of absurdities follow from the failure to recognize that the right human beings have not to be interfered with carries much further than their right to be rescued from trouble.

NOTE

For further exploration of these issues, see James Lindgren, Death by Default, 56 Law & Contemp. Prob. 185 (1993). The use of the omission doctrine to legalize decisions not to employ life-sustaining medical measures does not, as the decisions in this area are quick to point out, necessarily serve to justify assisted suicides or killings in euthanasia situations. That further step is considered in the section on Justification, infra page 880.

2. *Mens Rea — Culpable Mental States*

a. **Basic Conceptions**

INTRODUCTORY NOTE

The criminal law constitutes a description of harms that society seeks to pro-hibit by threat of criminal punishment. At the same time, the criminal law in-cludes an elaborate body of qualifications to these prohibitions and threats, based on the absence of fault. A common usage is to express all of these qualifi-cations to liability in terms of the requirement of mens rea. This usage is the thought behind the classic maxim, *actus non facit reum, nisi mens sit rea.* Or in Blackstone's translation, "an unwarrantable act without a vicious will is no crime at all." The vicious will was the mens rea. And reduced to its essence, "vicious will" refers to the blameworthiness entailed in choosing to commit a criminal wrong. One way the requirement of mens rea may be rationalized is on the com-mon sense view of justice that blame and punishment are inappropriate and unjust in the absence of choice.[11] So viewed, a great variety of defenses to crimi-nal liability may be characterized as presenting mens rea defenses — involuntary act, duress, legal insanity, accident, mistake, for example.

This all-encompassing usage of mens rea may be referred to as mens rea in its general sense. For present purposes we propose to identify a narrower usage of mens rea, which may be referred to as mens rea in its special sense. In this special sense, mens rea refers only to the mental state required by the definition of the offense to accompany the act that produces or threatens the harm.

Not all possible mental states are relevant to the law's purposes. Whether the defendant acted regretfully, arrogantly, eagerly, hopefully, and so forth may be relevant for a judge contemplating the sentence to be imposed. But the mental states relevant to defining criminal conduct and differentiating degrees of cul-pability are much more limited in our legal system. Indeed, mental state is something of a misnomer. The concern of the criminal law is with the level of intentionality with which the defendant acted, in other words, with what the defendant intended, knew, or should have known when he acted.

Consider some examples: an attempt to commit a crime consists of an act that comes close to its commission done with the *purpose* that the acts constituting the crime be committed. Unlawful assembly is the act of joining with a group in a public place with *intent* to commit unlawful acts. Larceny consists of the appro-priation of another's property, *knowing* that it is not your own, with *intent* to deprive the owner or possessor of it permanently. Receiving stolen goods is a crime when one receives stolen goods *knowing* they are stolen. Manslaughter is the killing of another by an act done with the *awareness* of a substantial and unjustifiable risk of doing so.

That the absence of the mens rea, in this special sense of the required mental state, precludes liability in all of these cases is of course the merest tautology. This is the way these crimes are defined. But it is important to see that they are

---

11. This view, of course, is only one way of looking at the problem. H. L. A. Hart has given it its clearest expression. See his Punishment and Responsibility 28 (1968).

so defined because the special mens rea element is crucial to the description of the conduct we want to make criminal. And description is crucial insofar as it is regarded as important to exclude from the definition of criminality what we do not want to punish as criminal. To revert to the examples just given, it would not be regarded as appropriate to make criminal the taking of another's property when the taker believed honestly that he or she was taking his or her own property. Neither would it make sense to make persons guilty of receiving stolen goods when they neither knew nor had occasion to know that the goods were stolen. And surely we should see nothing criminal in joining a group in a public place, apart from the intent to commit unlawful acts.

The mental element required by the definition of any crime, therefore, is of central concern. This subsection on basic conceptions and terminology is designed to help the student identify and distinguish the various kinds of mental states that may be used in the definition of crimes. In the subsections that follow, we explore the issue of mistake, which, though logically related to the definition of the mental element, has to some degree produced its own body of doctrine.

Of course, these subsections will not conclude our considerations of mens rea in the special sense of levels of intentionality. The issue will be encountered at many points in this course — notably in the definition of specific crimes (for example, culpable homicides, attempt, conspiracy, rape, theft) and in some of the defenses to criminal liability, such as voluntary intoxication. It will be apparent as we encounter the issue of mens rea in these various contexts that legislatures have often left the mental element undefined or have treated it ambiguously, while courts have as often failed to analyze it with precision. This subsection on terminology should help provide a vocabulary and an analytic framework for understanding and assessing what Justice Jackson has called "the variety, disparity and confusion of [the courts'] definitions of the requisite but elusive mental element." Morissette v. United States, 342 U.S. 246, 252 (1952).

REGINA v. CUNNINGHAM

Court of Criminal Appeal
[1957] 2 Q.B. 396

BYRNE, J., read the following judgment. The appellant was convicted at Leeds Assizes upon an indictment framed under section 23 of the Offences against the Person Act, 1861, which charged that he unlawfully and maliciously caused to be taken by Sarah Wade a certain noxious thing, namely, coal gas, so as thereby to endanger the life of the said Sarah Wade.

The facts were that the appellant was engaged to be married and his prospective mother-in-law was the tenant of a house, No. 7A, Bakes Street, Bradford, which was unoccupied, but which was to be occupied by the appellant after his marriage. Mrs. Wade and her husband, an elderly couple, lived in the house next door. At one time the two houses had been one, but when the building was converted into two houses a wall had been erected to divide the cellars of the two houses, and that wall was composed of rubble loosely cemented.

On the evening of January 17, 1957, the appellant went to the cellar of No. 7A, Bakes Street, wrenched the gas meter from the gas pipes and stole it, together with its contents, and in a second indictment he was charged with the larceny of the gas meter and its contents. To that indictment he pleaded guilty and was sentenced to six months' imprisonment. In respect of that matter he does not appeal.

The facts were not really in dispute, and in a statement to a police officer the appellant said: "All right, I will tell you. I was short of money. I had been off work for three days, I got eight shillings from the gas meter. I tore it off the wall and threw it away." Although there was a stop tap within two feet of the meter the appellant did not turn off the gas, with the result that a very considerable volume of gas escaped, some of which seeped through the wall of the cellar and partially asphyxiated Mrs. Wade, who was asleep in her bedroom next door, with the result that her life was endangered.

At the close of the case for the prosecution, Mr. Brodie, who appeared for the appellant at the trial and who has appeared for him again in this court, submitted that there was no case to go to the jury, but the judge, quite rightly in our opinion, rejected this submission. The appellant did not give evidence.

The act of the appellant was clearly unlawful and therefore the real question for the jury was whether it was also malicious within the meaning of section 23 of the Offences against the Person Act, 1861.

Before this court, Mr. Brodie has taken three points, all dependent upon the construction of that section. Section 23 provides:

> Whosoever shall unlawfully and maliciously administer to or cause to be administered to or taken by any other person any poison or other destructive or noxious thing, so as thereby to endanger the life of such person, or so as thereby to inflict upon such person any grievous bodily harm, shall be guilty of felony. . . .

Mr. Brodie argued, first, that mens rea of some kind is necessary. Secondly, that the nature of the mens rea required is that the appellant must intend to do the particular kind of harm that was done, or, alternatively, that he must foresee that that harm may occur yet nevertheless continue recklessly to do the act. Thirdly, that the judge misdirected the jury as to the meaning of the word "maliciously." . . .

[T]he following principle was propounded by the late Professor C. S. Kenny in the first edition of his Outlines of Criminal Law published in 1902; . . .

> In any statutory definition of a crime, malice must be taken not in the old vague sense of wickedness in general but as requiring either (1) An actual intention to do the particular kind of harm that in fact was done; or (2) recklessness as to whether such harm should occur or not (i.e., the accused has foreseen that the particular kind of harm might be done and yet has gone on to take the risk of it). It is neither limited to nor does it indeed require any ill will towards the person injured. . . .

We think that this is an accurate statement of the law. . . . In our opinion the word "maliciously" in a statutory crime postulates foresight of consequence.

In his summing-up Oliver, J., directed the jury as follows:

> You will observe that there is nothing there about "with intention that that person should take it." He has not got to intend that it should be taken; it is sufficient that

by his unlawful and malicious act he causes it to be taken. What you have to decide here, then, is whether, when he loosed that frightful cloud of coal gas into the house which he shared with this old lady, he caused her to take it by his unlawful and malicious action. "Unlawful" does not need any definition. It is something forbidden by law. What about "malicious"? "Malicious" for this purpose means wicked — something which he has no business to do and perfectly well knows it. "Wicked" is as good a definition as any other which you would get.

The facts . . . are these. . . . [T]he prisoner quite deliberately intended to steal the money that was in the meter . . . broke the gas meter away from the supply pipes and thus released the main supply of gas at large into that house. When he did that he knew that this old lady and her husband were living next door to him. The gas meter was in a cellar. The wall which divided his cellar from the cellar next door was a kind of honeycomb wall through which gas could very well go, so that when he loosed that cloud of gas into that place he must have known perfectly well that gas would percolate all over the house. If it were part of this offense — which it is not — that he intended to poison the old lady, I should have left it to you to decide, and I should have told you that there was evidence on which you could find that he intended that, since he did an action which he must have known would result in that. As I have already told you, it is not necessary to prove that he intended to do it; it is quite enough that what he did was done unlawfully and maliciously.

With the utmost respect to the judge, we think it is incorrect to say that the word "malicious" in a statutory offence merely means wicked. We think the judge was, in effect, telling the jury that if they were satisfied that the appellant acted wickedly — and he had clearly acted wickedly in stealing the gas meter and its contents — they ought to find that he had acted maliciously in causing the gas to be taken by Mrs. Wade so as thereby to endanger her life.

In our view, it should have been left to the jury to decide whether, even if the appellant did not intend the injury to Mrs. Wade, he foresaw that the removal of the gas meter might cause injury to someone but nevertheless removed it. We are unable to say that a reasonable jury, properly directed as to the meaning of the word "maliciously" in the context of section 23, would without doubt have convicted.

In these circumstances this court has no alternative but to allow the appeal and quash the conviction.

Conviction quashed.[a]

REGINA v. FAULKNER, 13 Cox Crim. Cas. 550, 555, 557 (1877): [Defendant was a sailor aboard the ship *Zemindar*. While on the high seas he went to the forecastle hold to steal some rum and lit a match in order to see better in the dark hold. Some of the rum caught fire and the fire spread, injuring him and completely destroying the ship. He was convicted by a jury of violating the Malicious Damage Act by maliciously setting fire to the ship (arson) upon an instruction by the judge that "although the prisoner had no actual intention of burning

a. The clarity of the analysis of recklessness in *Cunningham* has since been obscured by the decision of the House of Lords in Regina v. Caldwell, [1982] A.C. 341, a decision that has drawn great academic criticism. See, e.g., Glanville Williams, The Unresolved Problem of Recklessness, 8 eg. Stud. 74 (1988). — EDS.

the vessel, still, if they found he was engaged in stealing the rum, and that the fire took place in the manner above stated, they ought to find him guilty." In stating the case for the Court for Crown Cases Reserved, the judge observed: "It was conceded that the prisoner had no actual intention of burning the vessel, and I was not asked to leave any question to the jury as to the prisoner's knowing the probable consequences of his act, or as to his reckless conduct." The conviction for arson of the ship was quashed:

BARRY, J. A broad proposition has been contended for by the Crown, namely, that if, while a person is engaged in committing a felony, or, having committed it, is endeavoring to conceal his act, or prevent or spoil waste consequent on that act, he accidentally does some collateral act, which if done wilfully would be another felony either at common law or by statute, he is guilty of the latter felony. I am by no means anxious to throw any doubt upon, or limit in any way, the legal responsibility of those who engage in the commission of felony, or acts mala in se; but I am not prepared without more consideration to give my assent to so wide a proposition. I shall not pronounce any opinion, as I shall consider myself bound for the purpose of this case by the authority of Reg. v. Pembliton (12 Cox C.C. 607).[b] That case must be taken as deciding that to constitute an offence under the Malicious Injuries to Property Act, sect. 51, the act done must be in fact intentional and wilful, although the intention and will may (perhaps) be held to exist in, or be proved by, the fact that the accused knew that the injury would be the probable result of his unlawful act, and yet did the act reckless of such consequences. The present indictment charges the offence to be under the 42nd section of the same Act, and it is not disputed that the same construction must be applied to both sections. The jury were, in fact, directed to give a verdict of guilty upon the simple ground that the firing of the ship, though accidental, was caused by an act done in the course of, or immediately consequent upon, a felonious operation, and no question of the prisoner's malice, constructive or otherwise, was left to the jury. I am of opinion that, according to Reg. v. Pembliton, that direction was erroneous, and that the conviction should be quashed.

FITZGERALD, J. I concur in opinion with my brother Barry, and for the reasons he has given, that the direction of the learned judge cannot be sustained in law, and that therefore the conviction should be quashed. Counsel for the prosecution in effect insisted that the defendant, being engaged in the commission of or in an attempt to commit a felony, was criminally responsible for every result that was occasioned thereby, even though it was not a probable consequence of his act or such as he could have reasonably foreseen or intended. No authority has been cited for a proposition so extensive, and I am of opinion that it is no warranted by law.

b. Defendant was convicted under §51 of the Malicious Damage Act for unlawfully and mal ciously breaking a window. It appeared that defendant resumed a running fight with his opponent after they had been thrown out of a public house, by throwing a stone at them from across th street. The stone missed and broke a window of the public house. The jury convicted despite finding that he did not intend to break the window. Conviction was quashed by the Court for Crow Cases Reserved on the ground that intention or at least recklessness as to the window breaking ha to be established. — EDS.

SANTILLANES V. NEW MEXICO

Supreme Court of New Mexico
115 N.M. 215, 849 P.2d 358 (1993)

FROST, J. . . . Santillanes cut his 7-year-old nephew's neck with a knife during an altercation. The jury convicted him of child abuse [under a statute defining child abuse as including] "negligently, . . . causing . . . a child to be . . . placed in a situation that may endanger the child's life or health. . . ."

After the close of all evidence, defense counsel submitted a requested jury instruction . . . patterned after the definition of criminal negligence in Model Penal Code Section 2.02(2)(d) (1985). The trial court refused Santillanes' instruction and instead instructed the jury on a civil negligence standard, [stating] "An act, to be 'negligence,' must be one which a reasonably prudent person would foresee as involving an unreasonable risk of injury to himself or to another and which such a person, in the exercise of ordinary care, would not do."

In this Court, Santillanes maintains that felony punishment should attach only to criminal behavior, in this case criminal negligence, not to ordinary civil negligence. . . .

At common law, the conviction of a crime required satisfaction of the element of intent. The legislature, however, may define certain conduct as criminal without the element of intent. When a criminal statute is silent about whether a mens rea element is required, we do not assume that the legislature intended to enact a no-fault or strict liability crime. Instead, it is well settled that we presume criminal intent as an essential element of the crime unless it is clear from the statute that the legislature intended to omit the mens rea element. This determination is one of statutory construction in light of what the common law required.

It is also well settled that the legislature has the authority to make negligent conduct a crime. The issue in this case . . . is when the legislature has included but not defined the mens rea element in a criminal statute, here the term "negligently," what degree of negligence is required.

[O]ur interpretation of this criminal statute requires that the term "negligently" be interpreted to require a showing of criminal negligence instead of ordinary civil negligence. . . . [W]hen moral condemnation and social opprobrium attach to the conviction of a crime, the crime should typically reflect a mental state warranting such contempt.

We believe that there is a reasonable doubt as to the intended scope of proscribed conduct under the child abuse statute. Strictly construing the statutory language in favor of lenity, and in the absence of a clear legislative intention that ordinary civil negligence is a sufficient predicate for a felony, we conclude that the civil negligence standard, as applied to the child abuse statute, improperly goes beyond its intended scope and criminalizes conduct that is not morally contemptible. . . . We construe the intended scope of the statute as aiming to punish conduct that is morally culpable, not merely inadvertent. We interpret the mens rea element of negligence in the child abuse statute, therefore, to require a showing of criminal negligence instead of ordinary civil negligence. . . .

[The Court affirmed the conviction despite the erroneous instruction because it found that on the facts of the case the error was harmless.]

NOTE

The following text and commentary of the Model Penal Code on culpability requirements (mental elements) is of great importance and should be studied with care. The significance of the commentary will be increasingly apparent as the student progresses through the materials. It should be reviewed as the need arises.

MODEL PENAL CODE

SECTION 2.02.   General Requirements of Culpability

[See Appendix.]

MODEL PENAL CODE AND COMMENTARIES, COMMENT TO §2.02 AT 229-241 (1985):
1. *Objective.* This section expresses the Code's basic requirement that unless some element of mental culpability is proved with respect to each material element of the offense, no valid criminal conviction may be obtained. . . .

The section further attempts the extremely difficult task of articulating the kinds of culpability that may be required for the establishment of liability. It delineates four levels of culpability: purpose, knowledge, recklessness and negligence. It requires that one of these levels of culpability must be proved with respect to each "material element" of the offense, which may involve (1) the nature of the forbidden conduct, (2) the attendant circumstances, or (3) the result of conduct.[1] The question of which level of culpability suffices to establish liability must be addressed separately with respect to each material element, and will be resolved either by the particular definition of the offense or the general provision of this section.

The purpose of articulating these distinctions in detail is to . . . dispel the obscurity with which the culpability requirement is often treated when such concepts as "general criminal intent," "mens rea," "presumed intent," "malice," "wilfulness," "scienter" and the like have been employed. What Justice Jackson called "the variety, disparity and confusion" of judicial definitions of "the requisite but elusive mental element" in crime should, insofar as possible, be rationalized by a criminal code.

The Model Code's approach is based upon the view that clear analysis requires that the question of the kind of culpability required to establish the commission of the offense be faced separately with respect to each material element of the crime. The Code provision on rape will afford an illustration. Under Section 213.1(1), a purpose to effect the sexual relation is clearly required. But

---

1. Section 1.13(9) defines an "element of an offense" to include conduct, attendant circumstances or results that are included in the description of the offense, that negative an excuse or justification for an offense, or that negative a defense under the statute of limitations or establish jurisdiction or venue. Section 1.13(10) defines the concept of "material element" to include all elements except those that relate exclusively to statutes of limitation, jurisdiction, venue, and the like. The "material elements" of offenses are thus those characteristics (conduct, circumstances, result) of the actor's behavior that, when combined with the appropriate level of culpability, will constitute the offense.

other circumstances are also made relevant by the definition of the offense. The victim['s] consent to sexual relations would, of course, preclude the crime. Must the defendant's purpose have encompassed the [fact that] she opposed his will? [This is an] entirely different [question]. Recklessness may be sufficient for [this circumstance] of the offense, although purpose is required with respect to the sexual result that is an element of the offense.

It should also be noted that, as indicated in Section 1.13, the concept of "material element" to which these requirements adhere includes facts that negative an excuse or justification as well as the facts included in the definition of the crime. Thus, in a charge of murder, the level of culpability required to be proved normally focuses upon that element of the crime that involves the result of the defendant's conduct, namely the death of the victim. The law requires knowledge or purpose, as the case may be, usually with that element in view. However, when one considers the defense of self-defense, it is not unusual to provide that the defendant's belief in the necessity to save himself must have rested upon reasonable grounds. As to the element of death of the victim, in short, purpose or knowledge will suffice for conviction; as to the elements of self-defense, negligence will deprive the defendant of his defense.

Failure to face the question of culpability separately with respect to each of these ingredients of the offense results in obvious confusion, as does the failure to consider the defense as a "material element" in the total description of the crime. To call murder a "specific intent" crime or to say that it requires an "intent to kill" does not speak with clarity to the issue of what the defendant must have believed, and how carefully he must have formed his belief, in order to successfully claim self-defense. Considering facts that negative an excuse or justification as material elements of the offense, moreover, focuses attention on an obviously relevant grading factor when it comes to assessment of the seriousness of the crime the defendant has committed. . . .

2. *Purpose and Knowledge.* In defining the kinds of culpability, the Code draws a narrow distinction between acting purposely and knowingly, one of the elements of ambiguity in legal usage of the term "intent." Knowledge that the requisite external circumstances exist is a common element in both conceptions. But action is not purposive with respect to the nature or result of the actor's conduct unless it was his conscious object to perform an action of that nature or to cause such a result. It is meaningful to think of the actor's attitude as different if he is simply aware that his conduct is of the required nature or that the prohibited result is practically certain to follow from his conduct.[6]

It is true, of course, that this distinction is inconsequential for most purposes of liability: acting knowingly is ordinarily sufficient. But there are areas where the discrimination is required and is made under traditional law, which uses the awkward concept of "specific intent." This is true in treason, for example, insofar as a purpose to aid the enemy is an ingredient of the offense, and in attempts, complicity and conspiracy, where a true purpose to effect the criminal result is requisite for liability.[a] . . .

6. As pointed out in the preliminary study of the subject for the Brown Commission, the distinction is "between a man who wills that a particular act or result takes place and another who is merely willing that it should take place." 1 Brown Commn. Working Papers 124.

a. Consider United States v. Bennie Stewart, 19 C.M.R. 58 (1969), where the Court of Military

3. *Recklessness.* An important discrimination is drawn between acting either purposely or knowingly and acting recklessly. As the Code uses the term, recklessness involves conscious risk creation. It resembles acting knowingly in that a state of awareness is involved, but the awareness is of risk, that is of a probability less than substantial certainty; the matter is contingent from the actor's point of view.[13] Whether the risk relates to the nature of the actor's conduct, or to the existence of the requisite attendant circumstances, or to the result that may ensue, is immaterial; the concept is the same, and is thus defined to apply to any material element.

The risk of which the actor is aware must of course be substantial in order for the recklessness judgment to be made. The risk must also be unjustifiable. Even substantial risks, it is clear, may be created without recklessness when the actor is seeking to serve a proper purpose, as when a surgeon performs an operation that he knows is very likely to be fatal but reasonably thinks to be necessary because the patient has no other, safer chance. Some principle must, therefore, be articulated to indicate the nature of the final judgment to be made after everything has been weighed. Describing the risk as "substantial" and "unjustifiable" is useful but not sufficient, for these are terms of degree, and the acceptability of a risk in a given case depends on a great many variables. Some standard is needed for determining *how* substantial and *how* unjustifiable the risk must be in order to warrant a finding of culpability. There is no way to state this value judgment that does not beg the question in the last analysis; the point is that the jury must evaluate the actor's conduct and determine whether it should be condemned. . . .

4. *Negligence.* The fourth kind of culpability is negligence. It is distinguished from purposeful, knowing or reckless action in that it does not involve a state of awareness. A person acts negligently under this subsection when he inadvertently creates a substantial and unjustifiable risk of which he ought to be aware. He is liable if given the nature and degree of the risk, his failure to perceive it is, considering the nature and purpose of the actor's conduct and the circumstances known to him, a gross deviation from the care that would be exercised by a reasonable person in his situation. As in the case of recklessness, both the substantiality of the risk and the elements of justification in the situation form the relevant standards of judgment. And again it is quite impossible to avoid tautological articulation of the final question. The tribunal must evaluate the actor's failure of perception and determine whether, under all the circumstances, it was serious enough to be condemned. The jury must find fault, and must find that

---

Appeals set aside a plea of guilty to desertion with intent to avoid hazardous duty. The court found the plea improvident on the ground that the defendant's statements to the court-martial suggested that while he knew he would miss hazardous duty by his unauthorized absence, he did not absent himself for that reason (at 59): "In our opinion, there is a fundamental difference between pleading guilty to such a desertion charge because one intends to avoid hazardous duty and pursuing the same course only because one believes that a consequence of his act was the avoidance of hazardous duty, regardless of intent." But see United States v. Johnson, 24 M.J. 101 (Ct. Mil. App. 1987) where "intent" to injure or interfere with national defense was construed to mean "knowing that the result is practically certain to follow." — Eds.

13. With respect to result elements, one cannot of course "know" infallibly that a certain result will follow from engaging in conduct, and thus to some extent "knowledge," when applied to result elements, includes a contingency factor as well. This is expressed definitionally in terms of whether the actor is "practically certain" that the result will follow.

it was substantial and unjustified; that is the heart of what can be said in legislative terms. . . .

NOTES

1. Exercises: There follow some non-Model Penal Code definitions of crimes. As an exercise, it is suggested that the student identify the material elements of each crime (nature of the conduct, attendant circumstances, and result), determine the mens rea required by the definition, and determine the mens rea that would be required if the Model Penal Code's general principles of interpretation were applicable (for example, §2.02(2)-(4)).

BURGLARY (N.Y. PENAL LAW §140.25):

double   specific   Intent crime

A person is guilty of burglary in the second degree when he knowingly enters or remains unlawfully in a building with intent to commit a crime therein, and when . . . [t]he building is a dwelling and the entering or remaining occurs at night.

BURGLARY (CAL. PENAL CODE §§459-460):

Every person who enters any house, room, apartment . . . or other building . . . with intent to commit grand or petit larceny or any felony is guilty of burglary.
. . . Every burglary of an inhabited dwelling house . . . committed in the nighttime . . . is burglary of the first degree.
. . . All other kinds of burglary are burglary of the second degree.

DESTRUCTION OF PROPERTY (D.C. CODE ANN. §22-3108):

Whoever maliciously cuts down or destroys by girding or otherwise, any standing or growing vine, bush, shrub, sapling, or tree on the land of another, . . . shall, if the value of the thing destroyed or the amount of the damage done . . . is fifty dollars or more, be imprisoned for not less than one year nor more than three years. . . .

DESTRUCTION OF PROPERTY (N.Y. PENAL LAW §145.10):

A person is guilty of criminal mischief in the second degree when with intent to damage property of another person, and having no right to do so nor any reasonable ground to believe that he has such right, he damages property of another person in an amount exceeding one thousand five hundred dollars.

ASSAULT ON AN OFFICER (ME. REV. STAT. ANN. TIT. 17-A, §752-A):

A person is guilty of assault on an officer if:
A. He intentionally, knowingly or recklessly causes bodily injury to a law enforcement officer while the officer is in the performance of his official duties; or

B. While in the custody in a penal institution or other facility pursuant to an arrest or pursuant to a court order, he commits an assault on a member of the staff of the institution or facility.

2. *Influence of the Code.* The mens rea proposals of the Model Penal Code have had considerable influence on criminal law reform. Paul Robinson, A Brief History of Distinctions in Criminal Culpability, 31 Hastings L. Rev. 815, 816 (1980), concludes:

> Since the drafting of the Model Penal Code, nearly three-fourths of the states have revised their criminal codes. Recognizing the value of the Code's culpability structure, approximately seventy percent of those states . . . have adopted an essentially identical system.

Some of the variations enacted by states include (1) omitting the notion of acting purposely, as distinguished from knowingly, with respect to attendant circumstances (*question:* what can it mean to act purposely with regard to an attendant circumstance?), and (2) omitting the notion of acting recklessly or negligently with respect to the nature of the conduct.

Question: Is this an improvement? See Model Penal Code and Commentaries, Comment to §2.02 at 238-240 (1985). Two probing critiques of the sufficiency of the Model Penal Code mens rea provisions are Kenneth W. Simons, Rethinking Mental States, 72 B.U.L. Rev. 463 (1992); Paul Robinson & Jane Grall, Element Analysis in Defining Criminal Liability: The Model Penal Code and Beyond, 35 Stan. L. Rev. 681 (1983).

3. *Purpose, knowledge, intention, and motive: (a)* What is the significance of the actor's motive? Does it differ from the Model Penal Code's concept of purpose? Consider Glanville Williams, The Mental Element in Crime 10, 14 (1965). The author defines intention in terms of desiring a consequence: "A consequence is intended when it is desired to follow as the result of the actor's conduct." He then cautions:

> [T]he consequence need not be desired as an end in itself; it may be desired as a means to another end. . . . There may be a series of ends, each a link in a chain of purpose. Every link in the chain, when it happens, is an intended consequence of the original act. Suppose that a burglar is arrested when breaking into premises. It would obviously be no defence for him to say that his sole intention was to provide a nurse for his sick daughter, and for that purpose to take money from the premises, but that he had no desire or intention to deprive anyone of anything. Such an argument would be fatuous. He intended (1) to steal money (2) in order to help his daughter. These are two intentions, and the one does not displace the other. English lawyers call the first an "intent" and the second a "motive"; this is because the first (the intent to steal) enters into the definition of burglary and is legally relevant, while the second (the motive of helping the daughter) is legally irrelevant, except perhaps in relation to sentence. Although the verbal distinction between "intention" and "motive" is convenient, it must be realized that the remoter intention called motive is still an intention.

(b) It is generally agreed that "hardly any part of the penal law is more definitely stated than that motive is irrelevant to criminal liability." Jerome Hall, Principles of Criminal Law 88 (2d ed. 1960). Yet motive is commonly regarded

as highly relevant to sentence. Why should it be that motive is regarded as relevant to sentencing but not to liability? A common response is that "it is impracticable to make allowance for individual, idiosyncratic motives" in defining criminal liability. Mark Thornton, Intention in Criminal Law, 5 Can. J. L. & Juris. 177, 180-181 (1992). But consider Douglas Husak, Motive and Criminal Liability, 8 Crim. Just. Ethics 3-14 (1989). The author offers several examples of situations in which the law actually does make motive relevant to criminal liability. Crimes defined in terms of doing an act with some further intention (specific intent) turn on the motive of the action. So do defenses based on the rationale of justification insofar as they require that the defendant have acted with a proper motive, for example, self-defense. Motive is also relevant to determine the liability of a person who disconnects a terminal patient from a life support system — if the motive is beneficent the behavior will often be treated as an omission to continue preserving life and, in the absence of a duty to do so, not criminal. But if the motive is otherwise (an heir seeking her inheritance, a burglar, and so on), the behavior will be treated as culpable homicide. See Barber v. Superior Court, supra page 197 and notes following. In addition, particular statutes may make motive determinative of criminality or punishment. An example of the latter is so-called "hate crimes" statutes that make a crime of violence against a person subject to greater punishment if it is invidiously motivated against certain classes of persons. See Paul H. Robinson, Hate Crimes: Crimes of Motive, Character, or Group Terror?, 1992/1993 Annual Survey of American Law 605.

For further discussion of motive see Martin Gardner, The Mens Rea Enigma: Observations on the Role of Motive in the Criminal Law Past and Present, 1993 Utah L. Rev. 635.

(c) Suppose a desperate husband finally, after long resistance, yields to the pleas of his bed-ridden and incurably ill wife to leave poison by her bedside so that she might take her life. Assume he wants her to live and prays she does not drink the poison, but is moved to leave it for her out of respect for her dignity as a person. Is he guilty of violating §210.5 of the Model Penal Code, which provides: "A person who purposely aids or solicits another to commit suicide is guilty of a felony. . . ."? Was it the husband's purpose (his "conscious object," as the Model Penal Code defines the term, §2.02(2)(a)) to aid his wife to commit suicide? Or was his conscious object to please his wife, though knowing it would (or might) help her to commit suicide. Or is it more accurate to say his conscious object was to please his wife *by* helping her to commit suicide? Suppose he had poured the poison down her throat in response to the identical pleas and for the identical reasons — would he have poisoned her purposely, or only knowingly?

4. Purpose, intention, and "wishing." Is there a difference between wishing and intending? Suppose a person makes a gift of an airplane ticket to someone, hoping that the plane will crash and kill her. Assume it does, and the traveler is killed. Could it be said that defendant intentionally (or purposely) killed her?

Consider what difference it would make, if any, to your answer if:

(a) the defendant knew that the chances of the plane's crashing were exceedingly remote, but he was given to taking long shots; or
(b) the defendant believed the plane would crash because his astrologer predicted it would; or

(c) the defendant believed it would crash because he knew that a group
of terrorists had targeted it.

Consider the following observations of Lord Goff, The Mental Element in
Murder, 104 Law Q. Rev. 30, 43-44 (1988):

> [T]here can be intention to achieve the relevant result even though that is most
> unlikely to occur and so cannot be said to have been foreseen. To take an example
> from the Bible (First Book of Kings, Chap. 22 v. 34), the man who drew a bow as a
> venture must have been astonished when he found out he had killed King Ahab;[a]
> yet, if there had been no war, he would have been guilty of murder. The idea that
> intention and foresight of consequences, or probability, necessarily coexist was
> [debunked] by Lord Reid when he said (in Gollins v. Gollins).
>
> > In fact people often intend something quite different from what they know
> > to be the natural and probable result of what they are doing. To take a trivial
> > example, if I say I intend to reach the green, people will believe me although
> > we all know that the odds are ten to one against my succeeding; and no
> > one but a lawyer would say that I must be presumed to have intended to put
> > my ball in the bunker because that was the natural and probable result of
> > my shot.
>
> So there can be intention without foresight that the relevant consequence was
> likely to occur. Conversely, there can be foresight of consequences without
> intention.

5. *Recklessness and awareness.* The Model Penal Code distinguishes two kinds
of culpable unintentional actions, those that are reckless and those that are negligent. Negligence is less culpable because the actor only acts inadvertently;
though she should have been aware of the danger of her action, she was not.
Her fault is inattentiveness. Recklessness is more culpable because the actor was
aware of the danger of her action but acted anyway. Her fault is indifference.

So the crucial factor distinguishing these levels of culpability is awareness. But
awareness of precisely what? The Model Penal Code requires for reckless conduct that the person "consciously disregards a substantial and unjustifiable risk"
that some circumstance exists or that some result will follow from his conduct.
Does this mean that the actor must be aware (i) that there is a risk, (ii) that the
risk is substantial, *and* (iii) that the risk is unjustifiable? Or does it mean only
that the actor must be aware that there is some risk, which the jury finds to be
substantial and unjustifiable? Or could it mean that the actor must be aware that
there is a substantial risk, which the jury finds to be unjustifiable?

Grammatically, the Model Penal Code appears to require conscious awareness
as to all three of the crucial factors. But is this interpretation tenable in practice?
Consider a person who regards himself as an extraordinarily skillful driver. Finding himself in a hurry, he drives in a manner that creates an outrageously high
risk of killing someone. He believes, however, that there is little risk because of
his expertise as a driver. He drove negligently, but did he drive recklessly? See

a. The reference is to an incident in which, during a battle, King Ahab, knowing he was the
target of the attack, sought to defend himself by disguising his appearance. Apparently his disguise
was effective, "But one man drew his bow at random and hit the King of Israel, fatally injuring
him " The New English Bible, Oxford Study Edition 383 (1976). — Eds.

David Trieman, Recklessness and the Model Penal Code, 9 Am. J. Crim. L. 283, 361-371 (1981), for a helpful analysis of this issue.

Consider the observations of Glanville Williams on these issues in The Unresolved Problem of Recklessness, 8 Legal Stud. 74, 77 (1988):

> [The subjective] theory [of recklessness] has to deal with the awkward customer who undertook a course of conduct that he knew would involve serious risks if performed by someone not highly skilled, but thought that he himself possessed sufficient skill to eliminate danger. One's reaction to this general situation depends upon the specific facts. If the defendant is a doctor who acted in good faith but lacked sufficient skill, one would not want to characterize him as subjectively reckless. But, in contrast, take *Shimmen*'s case [84 Cr. App. R. 7 (1986)]. The defendant, who held a green belt and yellow belt in the Korean art of self-defence, was demonstrating his skill to his friends. To do this, he made as if to strike a plate-glass window with his foot; however, his kick broke the window. A Divisional Court held that he was guilty of criminal damage by recklessness, since he 'was aware of the kind of risk which would attend his act if he did not take adequate precautions,' even though he believed he had taken enough precautions to eliminate or minimise risk. . . .
>
> On subjective principles the court was wrong in saying that a person who believes he has taken enough precautions to eliminate risk is to be held guilty of recklessness merely because he perceived a risk before taking the precautions. If Shimmen thought he had eliminated risk, he was not subjectively reckless, but the court might have remitted the case to the magistrates with an instruction to decide whether he thought he had eliminated or merely mitigated the risk. This was a case where the defendant needed to be cross-examined. 'Would you have kicked with such force towards your girl friend's or wife's or your baby's head, relying on your ability to stop within an inch of it? No? Then you knew that there was some risk of your boot travelling further than you intended.' A person may be convinced of his own skill, and yet know that on rare (perhaps very rare) occasions it may fail him. In the case at bar, the victim, the owner of the window, did not agree to the demonstration of skill. [T]he actor has no right to impose any foreseen risk on him, beyond those associated with the ordinary business of life. He could be given a hot time in the witness-box if he says that in his opinion there was literally no risk.

Question: Would this basis for finding recklessness in the *Shimmen* case be possible under the Model Penal Code's definition of recklessness?

6. Provability of mens rea. Consider the following skeptical observations about the possibility of reliable proof of the various mental states defined by the Model Penal Code. Harold Edgar, Mens Rea, in Encyclopedia of Crime and Justice 1028, 1038-1039 (1983):

> The Model Penal Code . . . gives precise definitions of purpose, knowledge, and recklessness on the supposition that these are provable occurrences. The supposition is very questionable. It is implausible to assume that persons always think of the kind of results they will cause in committing crime. In the typical homicide case growing out of an argument with family or friends, an actor reacts with explosive rage. If he says that he gave absolutely no thought to consequences, is he guilty only of negligent homicide because the thought of "death" or "risk of death" never went through his mind? Moreover, it is not only in cases of intention that the Code asks the jury to decide the unknowable. In a 1975 New York homicide case, the defendant was a religious leader who believed that he could stab fellow believ-

ers without their sustaining injury. The court of appeals held that the jury must be charged with reference to negligent homicide as well as to reckless homicide. If the defendant gave no thought to the possibility of killing, it was said, he is guilty of the former, not the latter (People v. Strong, 37 N.Y.2d 568, 338 N.E.2d 602 (1975)). Yet how can the jury make that determination?

To be sure, the Code, although it makes no use of the common-law presumptions, can rely on juries to determine that people had a "conscious objective," even though their own daily experience shows that this often misdescribes human behavior. Nonetheless, is a body of law seriously flawed if it provides an elaborate set of precise rules whose operability depends upon the jury's willingness to make artificial characterizations?

See also Rebecca Dresser, Culpability and Other Minds, 2 Law and: 41 (1992).

7. *"Specific intent" and "general intent."* Though the Model Penal Code does not use the concepts *specific intent* and *general intent,* they have been used extensively in non-Model Penal Code jurisdictions and in England, and they have been the source of endless confusion in the courts. To provide an introduction to this terminology, this Note gives examples of the usage of these concepts and translates their apparent meanings into their nearest equivalents in the Model Penal Code vocabulary of culpable mental states. The translation has to be rough, however, because "general" and "specific" intent are often used inconsistently or applied loosely to entire crimes (for example, "bigamy is a general intent crime"; "larceny is a specific intent crime"), even though different culpability states ("intents") can and often do apply to different elements of such crimes.

(a) Perhaps the least mysterious and most common usage of specific intent is to identify those actions which must be done with some specified further purpose in mind. The nearest Model Penal Code equivalent would be purpose as to some objective. For example, burglary requires (roughly) that a person break and enter, not simply knowingly or on purpose, but with the further objective of committing a felony inside. Without proof of that further objective, there can be no conviction for burglary. It is therefore common to describe burglary as a "specific intent crime"; the description is accurate in the sense that conviction for burglary requires proof of that further ("specific") purpose to commit a felony inside the building. Similarly, assault with intent to kill requires (roughly) that a person commit a battery upon another with the specific further purpose of killing that person. Without proof of that further purpose, a case of assault with intent to kill must fail. Accordingly, it is likewise common to describe assault with intent to kill as a "specific intent crime."

May the person in the above examples be convicted of some other crime, even without proof of the specified further intention? Yes. He can be convicted of a crime that requires only a "general" intent. But what is that? "General" intent can mean a number of different things, but in this context it generally means that it is sufficient to convict when the defendant did what in ordinary speech we would call simply an intentional action. So in the first example, the actor who broke into a building would be guilty of trespass, a general intent crime; so long as he acted intentionally, in the sense that he knew the nature of the acts he performed, he would be guilty, without proof that he desired any particular further consequence. Similarly, in the second example, the actor would be guilty of simple battery, a general intent crime, regardless of whether he desired any further consequence to follow from his actions.

(b) Another usage of specific intent is to describe a crime that requires actu[al] knowledge (that is, subjective awareness) of some circumstances required by the crime to exist. Take the crime of bigamy, which prohibits a married person from remarrying while having a spouse living. Must it be shown that the defendant knew her husband was still alive? If so, the crime would be called a specific intent crime; if not, it would be called a general intent crime. In the latter case, some lesser mental state than knowledge would suffice — perhaps negligence or recklessness. Statutory rape will serve as another example. The girl must be proven to have been underage. But must the defendant be proven to have actually known that fact? In most jurisdictions today, as we will see, the answer is no — therefore, in language commonly used, statutory rape is a general intent crime. General intent crimes, therefore, include those that do not require actual knowledge of some circumstance required by the definition of the crime to exist. In Model Penal Code parlance, they are crimes that make negligence or recklessness suffice as to a required circumstance.

These usages are just the main ones. There are others. It will be instructive for students as they encounter these terms to consider precisely how they are being used, whether they are in effect equivalent to one of the mens rea concepts used in the Model Penal Code, and whether the court has sound reasons for giving those terms whatever meaning it implicitly or explicitly gives them.

PROBLEM

In United States v. Neiswender, 590 F.2d 1269 (4th Cir. 1979), the defendant was convicted of obstruction of justice under 18 U.S.C. §1503, which provided, "Whoever . . . endeavors to influence, obstruct, or impede the due administration of justice, shall be fined not more than $5,000 or imprisoned not more than five years or both." The prosecution established at the trial that the defendant approached the lawyer defending former Maryland governor Marvin Mandel in a much publicized criminal prosecution and represented that he had contact with a juror sitting on the Mandel case through whom he could ensure that the trial "would come out the right way" for a fee of $2,000. The lawyer promptly informed the United States Attorney and the judge presiding over the Mandel trial. Government agents, posing as associates of Mandel's lawyer, sought to identify the supposedly corrupt juror, but to no avail: The prosecution was unable to establish the truth of defendant's representations to Mandel's counsel. On appeal the defendant contended that the government thus failed to prove an essential element of the statutory crime — the "endeavor," or specific intent, to undermine judicial processes. All it established was a fraudulent attempt to obtain money by deception. *Question:* Should this contention be sustained?

The court summarized the opposing arguments of the parties as follows.

The government concedes that the defendant's primary intent was one to defraud. It urges, however, that every man intends the natural consequences of his acts. Had Neiswender convinced Weiner that he had a juror under his control and induced Weiner to participate in the scheme, the natural consequence would have been to reduce Weiner's efforts in defending his client. This debilitating effect on defense counsel would have altered the normal course of trial and prejudiced the client. This "natural consequence," the government contends, would have obstructed the due administration of justice.

Neiswender has a rejoinder to this argument. In his view, while operation of the time-honored "natural consequences" rule might normally suffice to establish specific intent, it should play no role in this case. Neiswender contends that whatever force a presumed intention has must give way to actual intent. Here Neiswender's motivation was directly at odds with any design to obstruct justice since a guilty verdict would have revealed Neiswender's fraud. It was in his best interest for Weiner to press hard in his efforts to obtain an acquittal. Indeed, the evidence suggests that Neiswender recognized this fact for, during negotiations with Weiner's "associate," he insisted that defense counsel were "not to slouch in their duties" and "were to give it the full effect."

The court upheld the conviction, stating:

> The state-of-mind requirement of §1503 has long confused the courts. Some cases require only that the defendant "intend to do some act which would tend to corruptly impede or influence the administration of justice." . . .
>
> Other cases, however, have imposed the ostensibly more demanding requirement of "a specific intent to obstruct justice." . . .
>
> None of these cases, however, has carefully considered how the specific intent requirement applies to a defendant whose hope is to avoid obstructing justice while the natural consequence of success in his endeavor would be to achieve precisely the opposite result. We see no need to undertake an extended excursion into the subtleties of specific intent. In our view, the defendant need only have had knowledge or notice that success in his fraud would have likely resulted in an obstruction of justice. Notice is provided by the reasonable foreseeability of the natural and probable consequences of one's acts.

The court recognized the "natural-consequences" rule to be a fiction but observed that

> this fiction is grounded upon sound policy, for, as outlined above, a rule focusing on foreseeable, rather than intended, consequences operates in sensible and fair fashion to deter the conduct sought to be avoided and to punish those whose actions are blameworthy, even though undertaken for purposes that may or may not be culpable.

For a critical review of *Neiswender,* see Note (Joseph DeMarco), A Funny Thing Happened on the Way to the Courthouse: Mens Rea, Document Destruction, and the Federal Obstruction of Justice Statute, 67 N.Y.U.L. Rev. 570 (1992).

UNITED STATES v. JEWELL

United States Court of Appeals, 9th Circuit
532 F.2d 697 (1976)

BROWNING, J. [Defendant was convicted of knowingly transporting marijuana in his car from Mexico to the United States.]

It is undisputed that appellant entered the United States driving an automobile in which 110 pounds of marijuana worth $6,250 had been concealed in a secret compartment between the trunk and rear seat. Appellant testified that he did not know the marijuana was present. There was circumstantial evidence from which the jury could infer that appellant had positive knowledge of the presence of the marijuana, and that his contrary testimony was false. On the other hand there was evidence from which the jury could conclude that appellant spoke the truth — that although appellant knew of the presence of the secret compartment and had knowledge of facts indicating that it contained marijuana, he deliberately avoided positive knowledge of the presence of the contraband to avoid responsibility in the event of discovery. If the jury concluded the latter was indeed the situation, and if positive knowledge is required to convict, the jury would have no choice consistent with its oath but to find appellant not guilty even though he deliberately contrived his lack of positive knowledge. Appellant urges this view. . . .

Appellant tendered an instruction that to return a guilty verdict the jury must find that the defendant knew he was in possession of marijuana. The trial judge rejected the instruction because it suggested that "absolutely, positively, he has to know that it's there." . . .

The court told the jury that the government must prove beyond a reasonable doubt that the defendant "knowingly" brought the marijuana into the United States (count 1: 21 U.S.C. §952(a)), and that he "knowingly" possessed the marijuana (count 2: 21 U.S.C. §841(a)(1)). The court continued:

> The Government can complete their burden of proof by proving, beyond a reasonable doubt, that if the defendant was not actually aware that there was marijuana in the vehicle he was driving when he entered the United States his ignorance in that regard was solely and entirely a result of his having made a conscious purpose to disregard the nature of that which was in the vehicle, with a conscious purpose to avoid learning the truth.

The legal premise of these instructions is firmly supported by leading commentators here and in England. . . . The substantive justification for the rule is that deliberate ignorance and positive knowledge are equally culpable. The textual justification is that in common understanding one "knows" facts of which he is less than absolutely certain. To act "knowingly," therefore, is not necessarily to act only with positive knowledge, but also to act with an awareness of the high probability of the existence of the fact in question. When such awareness is present, "positive" knowledge is not required.

This is the analysis adopted in the Model Penal Code. Section 2.02(7) states:

> When knowledge of the existence of a particular fact is an element of an offense, such knowledge is established if a person is aware of a high probability of its existence, unless he actually believes that it does not exist.

As the Comment to this provision explains,

> Paragraph (7) deals with the situation British commentators have denominated "wilful blindness" or "connivance," the case of the actor who is aware of the probable existence of a material fact but does not satisfy himself that it does not in fact exist.

. . . Appellant's narrow interpretation of "knowingly" is inconsistent with the Drug Control Act's general purpose to deal more effectively "with the growing menace of drug abuse in the United States." Holding that this term introduces a requirement of positive knowledge would make deliberate ignorance a defense. It cannot be doubted that those who traffic in drugs would make the most of it. . . .

It is no answer to say that in such cases the fact finder may infer positive knowledge. It is probable that many who performed the transportation function, essential to the drug traffic, can truthfully testify that they have no *positive* knowledge of the load they carry. Under appellant's interpretation of the statute, such persons will be convicted only if the fact finder errs in evaluating the credibility of the witness or deliberately disregards the law. . . .

It is worth emphasizing that the required state of mind differs from positive knowledge only so far as necessary to encompass a calculated effort to avoid the sanctions of the statute while violating its substance. "A court can properly find wilful blindness only where it can almost be said that the defendant actually knew." In the language of the instruction in this case, the government must prove, "beyond a reasonable doubt, that if the defendant was not actually aware . . . his ignorance in that regard was *solely* and *entirely* a result of . . . a conscious purpose to avoid learning the truth."

No legitimate interest of an accused is prejudiced by such a standard, and society's interest in a system of criminal law that is enforceable and that imposes sanctions upon all who are equally culpable requires it.

The conviction is affirmed.

KENNEDY, J., dissenting. The majority opinion justifies the conscious purpose jury instruction as an application of the wilful blindness doctrine recognized primarily by English authorities. . . .

The approach adopted in section 2.02(7) of the Model Penal Code clarifies, and, in important ways restricts, the English doctrine: . . . This provision requires an awareness of a high probability that a fact exists, not merely a reckless disregard, or a suspicion followed by a failure to make further inquiry. It also establishes knowledge as a matter of subjective belief, an important safeguard against diluting the guilty state of mind required for conviction. It is important to note that section 2.02(7) is a *definition* of knowledge, not a substitute for it; as such, it has been cited with approval by the Supreme Court.

In light of the Model Penal Code's definition, the "conscious purpose" jury instruction is defective in three respects. First, it fails to mention the requirement that Jewell have been aware of a high probability that a controlled substance was in the car. It is not culpable to form "a conscious purpose to avoid learning the truth" unless one is aware of facts indicating a high probability of that truth. To illustrate, a child given a gift-wrapped package by his mother while on vacation in Mexico may form a conscious purpose to take it home without learning what is inside; yet his state of mind is totally innocent unless he is aware of a high probability that the package contains a controlled substance. Thus, a conscious purpose instruction is only proper when coupled with a requirement that one be aware of a high probability of the truth.

The second defect in the instruction as given is that it did not alert the jury that Jewell could not be convicted if he "actually believed" there was no controlled substance in the car. The failure to emphasize, as does the Model Penal

Code, that subjective belief is the determinative factor, may allow a jury to convict on an objective theory of knowledge — that a reasonable man should have inspected the car and would have discovered what was hidden inside. . . .

Third, the jury instruction clearly states that Jewell could have been convicted even if found ignorant or "not actually aware" that the car contained a controlled substance. This is unacceptable because true ignorance, no matter how unreasonable, cannot provide a basis for criminal liability when the statute requires knowledge. A proper jury instruction based on the Model Penal Code would be presented as a way of defining knowledge, and not as an alterative to it. . . .

NOTES

1. Willful blindness instructions are commonly used to help the prosecution meet statutory requirements of "knowledge" not only in drug cases but in cases involving theft, securities fraud, environmental pollution, and a wide variety of other common law and regulatory offenses. See United States v. Pacific Hide & Fur Depot, Inc., 768 F.2d 1096 (9th Cir. 1985).

2. Does the *Jewell* court's approach to willful blindness in effect treat recklessness as sufficient to establish "knowledge"? Is a negligent failure to make inquiry sufficient to establish "knowledge"? For studies of these problems see Douglas Husak & Craig Callender, Wilful Ignorance, Knowledge, and the "Equal Culpability Thesis": A Study of the Deeper Significance of the Principle of Legality, [1994] Wis. L. Rev. 26; Note (Jonathan Marcus), Model Penal Code Section 2.02(7) and Willful Blindness, 102 Yale L.J. 2231 (1993); Robin Charlow, Wilful Ignorance and Criminal Culpability, 70 Tex. L. Rev. 1351 (1992); Ira Robbins, The Ostrich Instruction: Deliberate Ignorance as a Criminal Mens Rea, 81 J. Crim. L. & Criminology 191 (1990).

3. In order to avoid the risk that a jury may convict on the basis of mere negligence, some courts hold that willful blindness (or "ostrich") instructions, even if properly formulated, should not be given to the jury unless the evidence establishes both (1) that the defendant was subjectively aware of a high probability of illegal conduct, and (2) that the defendant purposefully contrived to avoid learning of the illegal conduct. See United States v. Farfan-Carreon, 935 F.2d 678, 680 (5th Cir. 1991). Thus, in a bank fraud prosecution, the court held it was error to give a willful blindness instruction, though a bank's owner failed to investigate certain questionable transactions, because the facts available to him "did not suggest that criminal activity was probably afoot." United States v. Barnhart, 979 F.2d 647, 652 (8th Cir. 1992).

With respect to the requirement that the defendant purposely *contrived* to avoid learning the truth, consider United States v. Giovannetti, 919 F.2d 1223 (7th Cir. 1990). Defendant Janis was convicted of aiding and abetting a gambling operation by renting his house to some gamblers, "knowing" that the leasees would use it as a wireroom. There was no direct evidence of Janis's knowledge, but he was a gambler himself, and knowing that his leasees were professional gamblers, he made no inquiries about their intended use of the house. The court (per Posner, J.) reversed the conviction, holding that it was error to give an "ostrich" instruction under these circumstances (id. at 1228-1229):

[Notice] just what it is that real ostriches do (or at least are popularly supposed to do). They do not just fail to follow through on their suspicions of bad things. They are not merely *careless* birds. They bury their heads in the sand so that they will not see or hear bad things. They *deliberately* avoid acquiring unpleasant knowledge. The ostrich instruction is designed for cases in which there is evidence that the defendant, knowing or strongly suspecting that he is involved in shady dealings, takes steps to make sure that he does not acquire full or exact knowledge of the nature and extent of those dealings. . . .

The government points out that the rented house . . . was a short way down a side street from the thoroughfare on which Janis commuted to work daily. It would have been easy for him to drive by the house from time to time to see what was doing, and if he had done so he might have discovered its use as a wireroom. He did not do so. But this is not the active avoidance with which the ostrich doctrine is concerned. . . . Janis failed to display curiosity, but he did nothing to prevent the truth from being communicated to him. He did not *act* to avoid learning the truth.

[T]he deliberate effort to avoid guilty knowledge . . . can be a mental, as well as a physical, effort — a cutting off of one's normal curiosity by an effort of will. There is no evidence of either sort of effort here.

Questions: Is the decision analytically sound? If so, does the result suggest that defendants like Janis should not be convicted, or does it suggest that the statutory mens rea requirement should be relaxed? Why might it be sound to require actual knowledge rather than recklessness as a prerequisite to convicting a defendant like Janis?

PROBLEM

In United States v. Civelli, 883 F.2d 191 (2d Cir. 1989), defendant had received a call from one Diego Bedoya, who asked defendant to drive to Bedoya's home to make a delivery for him. Defendant offered commercial delivery and moving services, and he had moved household items for Bedoya several times before. Defendant left his apartment and drove in his van to Bedoya's home, which was under surveillance as a suspected center of narcotics distribution. Defendant was observed emerging from the house carrying four large tan envelopes. As he drove away, he was followed by two officers from the task force.

After driving some distance, defendant stopped to make a call from a public telephone. The officers from the surveillance team approached defendant and told him that the house he had left was suspected of being a center of drug trafficking. They asked him what was in the packages in the van. Defendant pulled one of the envelopes from the van to show the officers. They discovered 8.5 kilograms of cocaine in the four envelopes. Each envelope was folded shut, not sealed, and each had a name written on the outside. The officers also recovered from defendant a telephone beeper and a list of names. The list was in his handwriting, and the names on the list corresponded to the names on the envelopes. There was a telephone number next to each name on the list, and a circled digit that corresponded to the number of bricks of cocaine in each of the labeled envelopes.

Defendant was indicted for conspiracy to possess cocaine with intent to distribute and possession of more than five kilograms of cocaine with intent to distribute. The key question at trial was whether defendant knew he was carrying narcotics. Defendant testified that he never knew what was inside the packages until they were opened by the officers. He conceded that he had prepared the list of names, but he stated that he had transcribed the list verbatim at Bedoya's direction and that Bedoya was to pay him only $100 to take the packages.

At trial the judge instructed the jury that, in order to find the defendant guilty on either the conspiracy or the substantive count, they had to find that the government had "prove[d] beyond a reasonable doubt that the defendant knew that the packages in the van contained cocaine." During the course of deliberations the jury sent the judge a note asking: "If Oscar Civelli suspected that he was carrying cocaine, but didn't look in the package[,] would that have constituted conspiracy?" In response the judge delivered the following instruction:

> The element of knowledge may be satisfied by inferences drawn from proof that a defendant deliberately closed his eyes to what otherwise would have been obvious to him. A finding beyond a reasonable doubt of a conscious purpose to avoid knowledge would permit an inference of knowledge. Stating that another way, a defendant's knowledge of a fact may be inferred from his willful blindness to the existence of the fact. It is entirely up to you as to whether you find any deliberate closing of the eyes and the inferences to be drawn from any such evidence. A showing of negligence or mistake is not enough to support a finding of willfulness or knowledge.

After resuming deliberations, the jury returned verdicts of guilty on both counts. Defendant was sentenced to 10 years' imprisonment, the mandatory minimum sentence applicable to this offense when the quantity of cocaine possessed exceeds 5 kilograms.

Questions: Was it error to give this willful blindness instruction? On appeal, what should be the result?

b. Mistake of Fact

MODEL PENAL CODE

SECTION 2.04(1)-(2).   IGNORANCE OR MISTAKE

[See Appendix.]

MODEL PENAL CODE AND COMMENTARIES, COMMENT TO §2.04 AT 269-271 (1985):
Subsection (1) states the conventional position under which the significance of ignorance by the defendant of a matter of fact or law, or a mistake as to such matters, is determined by the mental state required for the commission of the offense involved. Thus ignorance or mistake is a defense when it negatives the existence of a state of mind that is essential to the commission of an offense, or when it establishes a state of mind that constitutes a defense under a rule of law relating to defenses. In other words, ignorance or mistake has only evidential import; it is significant whenever it is logically relevant, and it may be logically relevant to negate the required mode of culpability or to establish a special defense.

The critical legislative decisions, therefore, relate to the establishment of the culpability for specific offenses as they are defined in the criminal code. . . .

To put the matter as this subsection does is not to say anything that would not otherwise be true, even if no provision on the subject were made. As Glanville Williams has summarized the matter, the rule relating to mistake "is not a new rule; and the law could be stated equally well without reference to mistake. . . . It is impossible to assert that a crime requiring intention or recklessness can be committed although the accused laboured under a mistake negativing the requisite intention or recklessness. Such an assertion carries its own refutation." This obvious point has, however, sometimes been overlooked in general formulations purporting to require that mistake be reasonable if it is to exculpate, without regard to the mode of culpability required to commit the crime. This is unexceptionable in the case of mistake regarding an element of an offense as to which negligence is the culpability level. There is no justification, however, for requiring that ignorance or mistake be reasonable if the crime or the element of the crime involved requires acting purposely or knowingly for its commission.

It is true, of course, that whether recklessness or negligence suffices as a mode of culpability with respect to a given element of an offense is often raised for the first time in dealing with a question of mistake. That this may happen emphasizes the importance of perceiving that the question relates to the underlying rule as to the kind of culpability required with respect to the particular element of the offense involved. Generalizations about mistake of fact and mistake of law, or about honest and reasonable mistakes as relevant to general and specific intent crimes, tend to obscure rather than clarify that simple point.

NOTE

The Model Penal Code's mistake proposals have had a major influence on recent state penal code revisions. However, states have departed from the Model Penal Code in a number of ways. Consider, for example, the Pennsylvania provision (Pa. Cons. Stat. tit. 18, §304) that makes mistake of fact a defense when it negatives the "intent, knowledge, belief, recklessness, or negligence required" by the offense, but only if the mistake is one "for which there is a reasonable explanation or excuse."

Question: What is the effect of the qualifying clause?

REGINA v. PRINCE

Court of Crown Cases Reserved
L.R. 2 Cr. Cas. Res. 154 (1875)

[Defendant was convicted of taking an unmarried girl under 16 years of age out of the possession and against the will of her father in violation of 24 & 25 Vict., c. 100, §55, providing:

> Whosoever shall unlawfully take or cause to be taken any unmarried girl, being under the age of sixteen years, out of the possession and against the will of her father or mother, or of any person having the lawful care or charge of her, shall be guilty of a misdemeanor. . . .

The jury found that though the girl, Annie Phillips, was 14 at the time, she had told the defendant that she was 18 before he took her away, that the defendant honestly believed that statement, and that his belief was reasonable. On a case stated by Denman, J., the Court for Crown Cases Reserved found that the prisoner was rightly convicted, Brett, J., dissenting.

BRAMWELL, B. [Finding that to sustain the defendant's position it was necessary to read into the statute language requiring that a person not believe the girl he takes is over the age of 16, the opinion continues:] These words are not there, and the question is, whether we are bound to construe the statute as though they were, on account of the rule that the mens rea is necessary to make an act a crime. I am of opinion that we are not, . . . and for the following reasons: The act forbidden is wrong in itself, if without lawful cause; I do not say illegal, but wrong. [W]hat the statute contemplates, and what I say is wrong, is the taking of a female of such tender years that she is properly called a *girl*, can be said to be in another's *possession*, and in that other's *care or charge*. No argument is necessary to prove this; it is enough to state the case. The legislature has enacted that if anyone does this wrong act, he does it at the risk of her turning out to be under sixteen. This opinion gives full scope to the doctrine of the mens rea. If the taker believed he had the father's consent, though wrongly, he would have no mens rea; so if he did not know she was in anyone's possession, nor in the care or charge of anyone. In those cases he would not know he was doing the *act* forbidden by the statute — an act which, if he knew she was in possession and in care or charge of anyone, he would know was a crime or not, according as she was under sixteen or not. He would not know he was doing an act wrong in itself, whatever was his intention, if done without lawful cause. The same principle applies in other cases. A man was held liable for assaulting a police officer in the execution of his duty, though he did not know he was a police officer. Why? Because the act was wrong in itself. So, also, in the case of burglary, could a person charged claim an acquittal on the ground that he believed it was past six when he entered, or in housebreaking, that he did not know the place broken into was a house? It seems to me impossible to say that where a person takes a girl out of her father's possession, not knowing whether she is or is not under sixteen, that he is not guilty; and equally impossible when he believes, but erroneously, that she is old enough for him to do a wrong act with safety. I think the conviction should be affirmed.

BRETT, J., [dissenting]. [I]f the facts had been as the prisoner, according to the findings of the jury, believed them to be, and had reasonable ground for believing them to be, he would have done no act which has ever been a criminal offence in England; he would have done no act in respect of which any civil action could have ever been maintained against him; he would have done no act for which, if done in the absence of the father, and done with the continuing consent of the girl, the father could have had any legal remedy. . . . Upon all the cases I think it is proved that there can be no conviction for crime in England in the absence of a criminal mind or mens rea. Then comes the question, what is the true meaning of the phrase. I do not doubt that it exists where the prisoner knowingly does acts which would constitute a crime if the result were as he anticipated, but in which the result may not improbably end by bringing the offence within a more serious class of crime. As if a man strikes with a dangerous weapon, with intent to do grievous bodily harm, and kills, the result makes the crime murder. The prisoner has run the risk. So, if a prisoner do the prohibited acts, without caring to consider what the truth is as to facts — as if a prisoner were to abduct a girl under sixteen without caring to consider whether she was in truth under sixteen — he runs the risk. So if he without abduction defiles a girl who is in fact under ten years old, with a belief that she is between ten and twelve. If the facts were as he believed he would be committing the lesser crime. Then he runs the risk of his crime resulting in the greater crime. It is clear that ignorance of the law does not excuse. It seems to me to follow that the maxim as to mens rea applies whenever the facts which are present in the prisoner's mind, and which he has reasonable ground to believe, and does believe to be the facts, would, if true, make his acts no criminal offence at all. I come to the conclusion that a mistake of facts, on reasonable grounds, to the extent that if the facts were as believed the acts of the prisoner would make him guilty of no criminal offence at all, is an excuse and that such excuse is implied in every criminal charge and every criminal enactment in England.

NOTES AND QUESTIONS

1. In his book, An Inquiry into Criminal Guilt (1963), Peter Brett stated at pages 148-149, in reference to the various opinions in the *Prince* case:

Which of these minority views is the better? That of Bramwell, B., is to my mind clearly in accord with principle. It reflects the view that we learn our duties, not by studying the statute book, but by living in a community. A defense of mistake rests ultimately on the defendant's being able to say that he has observed the community ethic, and this Prince could not do.

Consider the response of Graham Hughes in Criminal Responsibility, 16 Stan. L. Rev. 470, 480-481 (1964):

[T]his appears as an appallingly dangerous position which comes close to giving the jury a discretion to create new crimes. In *Prince* what the accused was doing that he knew to be wrong was presumably to take away a young girl from the pos- session of her parents without their consent. Let us vary the position slightly and assume that the charge is one of unlawful sexual intercourse with a girl under sixteen. The accused reasonably believed that the girl was over sixteen. Should he be convicted because he knew that he was fornicating and because fornication is wrong according to the community ethic? In the first place this assumes that there is a clear community judgment about the wrongfulness of fornication, which is not so. . . . The truth is that there are many community ethics: the official or Establish- ment ethic which is piously intoned by most of us when making public pronounce- ments, the actual incidence of community behaviour which though of course not synonymous with a judgment about the propriety of conduct is some evidence of it, and the private judgments that we make which may differ significantly from our public utterances. . . . Even though ethical attitudes owe much to culture and environment, there is enough room for individual divergence to make Professor Brett's approach a slippery one.
    But the more serious objection is that there seems no reason why the community ethic concerning some conduct, even though clear, should be relevant to a deter- mination of whether other conduct is criminal. The crime is that of fornicating with girls under sixteen, and it is not obvious that a general judgment about the

morality of fornication should be determinative of guilt. Moral duties should not be identified with criminal duties. If fornication is not a crime in itself, as it is not in England, why should it become one when the defendant makes a reasonable mistake about the age of his partner?

2.   One finds approaches in American cases similar to that taken in *Prince*. For example, in White v. State, 44 Ohio App. 331, 185 N.E. 64 (1933), the defendant was convicted of violating a statute providing that whoever, being the husband of a pregnant woman, leaves with intent to abandon such pregnant woman shall be imprisoned. The trial court had given an instruction to the effect that the defendant was no less guilty because he did not know his wife was pregnant. On appeal, held affirmed.

> The sound doctrine underlying the rule that guilty knowledge is not required to accomplish the crime of rape with consent [statutory rape] is that the act of the accused is at best an immoral one, and that he cannot enter upon the accomplishment of an admittedly immoral act except at his peril, and if in law his act is in fact felony he must suffer the consequences thereof although so far as his actual knowledge was concerned he may not have known the enormity of the offense of which he is guilty. By like reasoning we take the view that a husband abandoning his wife is guilty of wrongdoing. It is a violation of his civil duty. He is charged with her support and protection. If he abandons her, he does so at his peril, and, if she be in fact at the time pregnant, though he may not have known it, he cannot plead that ignorance as a defense. He must make sure of his ground when he commits the simple wrong of leaving her at all.

See also United States v. Collado-Gomez, 834 F.2d 280 (2d Cir. 1987), where the defendant was convicted of possessing crack cocaine with intent to sell. The court held that the defendant was subject to the enhanced penalties applicable to crack under the Anti-Drug Abuse Act of 1986, 21 U.S.C. §841(b)(1), even though he had no reason to know that the drug he possessed was crack. Responding to the argument that conviction without proof of any mens rea with respect to the aggravating element would violate due process, the court said (id. at 280):

> [T]he statute's enhanced penalty provisions did not in any way criminalize otherwise innocent activity or create a trap for the unwary, because the mens rea requirement of proving knowing and intentional possession of a controlled substance remained intact.

3. *Questions.* What are the implications of the views in the *White* case and of the opinions in the *Prince* case? Suppose a different situation obtained: Prince had no interest in the girl but wanted only her father's horse and carriage. He drove the horse and carriage away intending to steal them, totally unaware that the girl was hidden inside the carriage. What result under these cases?

Compare with *Prince* and *White* the cases reprinted earlier, Regina v. Cunningham, page 205 supra, and Regina v. Faulkner, page 207 supra. How would the latter two cases be decided under the theory of the former? How do you account for the differences? Are they reconcilable? If not, on what basis is one or the other set of cases to be preferred?

4. In a portion of Justice Blackburn's address in the *Prince* case, not included above, he makes the following observation in support of the judgment to affirm the conviction:

> Section 50 enacts, that whosoever shall "unlawfully and carnally know and abuse any girl under the age of ten years," shall be guilty of felony. Section 51, whoever shall "unlawfully and carnally know and abuse any girl being above the age of ten years, and under the age of twelve years," shall be guilty of a misdemeanor.
>
> It seems impossible to suppose that the intention of the legislature in those two sections could have been to make the crime depend upon the knowledge of the prisoner of the girl's actual age. It would produce the monstrous result that a man who had carnal connection with a girl, in reality not quite ten years old, but whom he on reasonable grounds believed to be a little more than ten, was to escape altogether. He could not, in that view of the statute, be convicted of the felony, for he did not know her to be under ten. He could not be convicted of the misdemeanor, because she was in fact not above the age of ten.

Model Penal Code §2.04(2) is a response to this kind of situation. See the Comment on this section in Model Penal Code and Commentaries, Comment at 272-273 (1985).

PEOPLE v. OLSEN

Supreme Court of California
36 Cal. 3d 638, 685 P.2d 52 (1984)

BIRD, C. J. Is a reasonable mistake as to the victim's age a defense to a charge of lewd or lascivious conduct with a child under the age of 14 years (Pen. Code, §288, subd. (a)[1])?

In early June 1981, Shawn M. was 13 years and 10 months old. At that time, her parents were entertaining out-of-town guests. Since one of the visitors was using Shawn's bedroom, Shawn suggested that she sleep in her family's camper trailer which was parked in the driveway in front of the house. Shawn's parents agreed to this arrangement on the condition that she keep the windows shut and door locked. . . .

At trial, Shawn testified to the following events. On her third night in the trailer, she locked the door as instructed by her parents. She then fell asleep, but was awakened by appellant Olsen who was knocking on the window and asking to be let in. Shawn said nothing and appellant left. Approximately a half-hour later, Garcia came up to the window and asked if he could enter. Shawn did not respond so he left. . . . After both appellant and Garcia left, Shawn went to sleep.

Shawn was then awakened by the sound of barking dogs and by Garcia, who

---

1. Section 288, subdivision (a) provides in relevant part:

Any person who shall willfully and lewdly commit any lewd or lascivious act . . . upon or with the body, or any part or member thereof, of a child under the age of 14 years, with the intent of arousing, appealing to, or gratifying the lust or passions or sexual desires of such person or of such child, shall be guilty of a felony and shall be imprisoned in the state prison for a term of three, six, or eight years. . . .

had a knife by her side and his hand over her mouth.[2] Garcia called to appellant to come in, and appellant entered the trailer.

Garcia told Shawn to let appellant "make love" to her, or he — Garcia — would stab her. . . .

Appellant proceeded to have sexual intercourse with Shawn. . . . While appellant was still [doing so], her father entered the trailer. Mr. M. grabbed appellant as he was trying to leave, and Garcia stabbed Mr. M. in order to free appellant.

Shawn testified that she knew Garcia "pretty well." . . . She also testified that she was very good friends "off and on" with appellant and that during one three-month period she spent almost every day at appellant's house. At the time of the incident, however, Shawn considered Garcia her boyfriend.[3]

Finally, Shawn admitted that she told both Garcia and appellant that she was over 16 years old. She also conceded that she looked as if she were over 16.[4]

Garcia testified to quite a different set of events. . . . On . . . the day before the offense Shawn invited him to spend the night in the trailer with her so that they could have sex. He and Shawn engaged in sexual intercourse about four times that evening. Shawn invited Garcia to come back the following night at midnight.

The next night, after two unsuccessful attempts to enter the trailer, Garcia and appellant were told by Shawn to return at midnight. . . . Shawn, wearing only a pair of panties, opened the door and invited them in. She told them . . . that she wanted "to make love" with appellant first. When Mr. M. entered the trailer, appellant was on top of Shawn. Garcia denied threatening Shawn with a knife, taking her nightgown off, breaking into the trailer or forcing her to have sex with them.[5]

At the conclusion of the trial, the court found Garcia and appellant guilty of violating section 288, subdivision (a).[7] In reaching its decision, the court rejected defense counsel's argument that a good faith belief as to the age of the victim was a defense to the section 288 charge. Appellant was sentenced to the lower term of three years in state prison. This appeal followed. . . .

The language of section 288 is silent as to whether a good faith, reasonable mistake as to the victim's age constitutes a defense to a charge under that statute. . . .

Twenty years ago, this court in People v. Hernandez [61 Cal. 2d 529, 393 P.2d 673 (1964)] overruled established precedent, and held that an accused's good

---

2. Although Shawn testified she locked the trailer door, she failed to explain how Garcia entered the trailer. A subsequent examination of the trailer revealed that there were no signs of a forced entry.

3. Shawn admitted that she had engaged in intercourse before the night of June 3rd, but denied having any such prior experience with either Garcia or appellant. However, she did admit having had sexual relations, short of intercourse, with both of them in the past.

4. Patricia Alvarez, a police officer, testified that appellant told her that he thought Shawn was 17.

5. Appellant's sister corroborated Shawn's testimony that Shawn made daily visits to the Olsen home during a three-month period. She testified that during these visits Shawn and appellant would go into the latter's bedroom and close the door. On one occasion appellant's sister saw the two in bed together. [Four other witnesses described similar episodes involving Shawn and either appellant or other boys.]

7. Garcia was also found guilty of assault with a deadly weapon with infliction of great bodily injury [in the assault on Mr. M.]. Both Garcia and appellant were found not guilty of burglary, forcible rape, and lewd or lascivious acts upon a child under the age of 14 by use of force. . . .

faith, reasonable belief that a victim was 18 years or more of age was a defense to a charge of statutory rape.[10] . . .

One Court of Appeal has declined to apply *Hernandez* in an analogous context. In People v. Lopez (1969) 271 Cal. App. 2d 754, 77 Cal. Rptr. 59, the court refused to recognize a reasonable mistake of age defense to a charge of offering or furnishing marijuana to a minor. The court noted that the act of furnishing marijuana is criminal regardless of the age of the recipient and that furnishing marijuana to a minor simply yields a greater punishment than when the substance is furnished to an adult. "[A] mistake of fact relating only to the gravity of an offense will not shield a deliberate offender from the full consequences of the wrong actually committed." (Ibid.)

. . . There exists a strong public policy to protect children of tender years. [S]ection 288 was enacted for that very purpose. Furthermore, even the *Hernandez* court recognized this important policy when it made clear that it did not contemplate applying the mistake of age defense in cases where the victim is of "tender years." . . .

This conclusion is supported by the Legislature's enactment of section 1203.066. Subdivision (a)(3) of that statute renders certain individuals convicted of lewd or lascivious conduct who "honestly and reasonably believed the victim was 14 years old or older" eligible for probation. The Legislature's enactment of section 1203.066, subdivision (a)(3). . . . strongly indicates that the Legislature did not intend such a defense to a section 288 charge. To recognize such a defense would render section 1203.066, subdivision (a)(3) a nullity, since the question of probation for individuals who had entertained an honest and reasonable belief in the victim's age would never arise. . . .

Other legislative provisions also support the holding that a reasonable mistake of age is not a defense to a section 288 charge. Time and again, the Legislature has recognized that persons under 14 years of age are in need of special protection. . . .

The Legislature has also determined that persons who commit sexual offenses on children under the age of 14 should be punished more severely than those who commit such offenses on children under the age of 18. . . .

It is significant that a violation of section 288 carries a much harsher penalty than does unlawful sexual intercourse (§261.5), the crime involved in *Hernandez*. Section 261.5 carries a maximum punishment of one year in the county jail or three years in state prison, while section 288 carries a maximum penalty of eight years in state prison. The different penalties for these two offenses further supports the view that there exists a strong public policy to protect children under 14. . . .

The legislative purpose of section 288 would not be served by recognizing a defense of reasonable mistake of age. . . . Accordingly, the judgment of conviction is affirmed.

GRODIN, J., concurring and dissenting. I agree that the enactment of Penal Code section 1203.066, which renders eligible for probation persons convicted

---

10. One commentator believes that *Hernandez* marked a clear break from the "universally accepted view of the courts in this country." (Annot., Mistake or Lack of Information as to Victim's Age as Defense to Statutory Rape (1966) 8 A.L.R.3d 1100, 1102-1105, and cases cited.) The view that mistake of age is not a defense to a charge of statutory rape still prevails in the overwhelming majority of jurisdictions. (See Ibid., and later cases (1983 pocket supp.) pp. 72-73).

of lewd or lascivious conduct who "honestly and reasonably believed the victim was 14 years old or older" is persuasive evidence that in the eyes of the Legislature such a belief is not a defense to the crime.[1] What troubles me is the notion that a person who acted with such belief, and is not otherwise shown to be guilty of any criminal conduct,[2] may not only be convicted but be sentenced to prison notwithstanding his eligibility for probation when it appears that his belief did not accord with reality. To me, that smacks of cruel or unusual punishment.

. . . I recognize . . . that our legal system includes certain "strict liability" crimes, but generally these are confined to the so-called "regulatory" or "public welfare" offenses. . . . (Morissette v. United States (1952) 342 U.S. 246). Moreover, with respect to such crimes, "*The accused, if he does not will the violation, usually is in a position to prevent it with no more care than society might reasonably expect . . . from one who assumed his responsibilities. Also, penalties commonly are relatively small, and conviction does no grave damage to an offender's reputation.*" (Id., at p. 256, emphasis added.)

Even in the regulatory context, "judicial and academic acceptance of liability without fault has not been enthusiastic." (Jeffries & Stephen, Defenses, Presumptions, and Burden of Proof in the Criminal Law (1979) 88 Yale L.J. 1325, 1373.) And "with respect to traditional crimes, it is a widely accepted normative principle that conviction should not be had without proof of fault. At least when the offense carries serious sanctions and the stigma of official condemnation, liability should be reserved for persons whose blameworthiness has been established" (Id., at pp. 1373-1374.)

. . . No doubt the standard of what is reasonable must be set relatively high in order to accomplish the legislative objective of protecting persons under 14 years of age against certain conduct. Perhaps it is not enough that a person "looks" to be more than 14; perhaps there is a duty of reasonable inquiry besides. At some point, however, the belief becomes reasonable by any legitimate standard, so that one would say the defendant is acting in a way which is no different from the way our society would expect a reasonable, careful, and law-abiding citizen to act.

At that point, it seems to me, the imposition of criminal sanctions, particularly imprisonment, simply cannot be tolerated in a civilized society. . . .

NOTE

The Model Penal Code also imposes strict liability as to the age of the victim under certain circumstances. Section 213.6(1) provides that where criminality

---

1. I do not agree that legislative intent to eliminate good faith mistake of fact as a defense can be inferred from the imposition of relatively higher penalties for that crime. On the contrary, as this court has stated in connection with the crime of bigamy: "The severe penalty imposed . . . the serious loss of reputation conviction entails, the infrequency of the offense, and the fact that it has been regarded . . . as a crime involving moral turpitude, make it extremely unlikely that the Legislature meant to include the morally innocent to make sure the guilty did not escape." (People v. Vogel (1956) 46 Cal. 2d 798, 804, 299 P.2d 850.)

2. The People suggest that defendant was at least guilty of "sexual intercourse accomplished with a female not the wife of the perpetrator, where the female is under the age of 18 years." Defendant was neither charged nor convicted of that offense, however, and it is by no means clear from the record that he had sexual intercourse with the victim.

turns on the child's being below the age of 10, the defense of reasonable mistake is not available; but where it turns on the child's being below a critical age other than 10, reasonable mistake is an affirmative defense. What is the theory behind this distinction? Can it be reconciled with §2.04(2) and its supporting commentary, page 225 supra? A defense of the Model Penal Code's position appears in Model Penal Code and Commentaries, Comment to §213.6 at 415-417 (1980).

In most jurisdictions a mistake as to age, even if reasonable, is not a defense to statutory rape. However, a substantial minority of states now allow the defense of reasonable mistake, either by statute or judicial ruling. The authorities are reviewed in Garnett v. State, 332 Md. 571, 582, 632 A.2d 797, 802 (1993), where the court reviewed the recent authorities and concluded that Maryland's statutory rape law imposed strict liability with respect to the age of the female.

NOTE ON THE DISTINCTION BETWEEN MATERIAL AND JURISDICTIONAL ELEMENTS

It is widely accepted that a culpable mental state need not be proved as to those elements of a crime, such as jurisdiction or venue, that have no bearing on the harm that the offense seeks to prevent or on the existence of a justification or excuse. The Model Penal Code, for example, restricts the culpability requirements of §2.02 to what it defines in §1.13(10) as material elements. Because nonmaterial elements have no bearing on the person's culpability, it is logical to dispense with any requirement that the person be shown to have acted culpably with respect to them. A person, for example, charged in State X with shooting another in State X will hardly be heard to say in defense that he had every reason to believe he was in State Y. See Model Penal Code and Commentaries, Comment §1.13 at 211 (1985).

While state jurisdictional requirements are largely based on the locus of the crime, federal crimes often contain jurisdictional elements relating to the method used to commit the crime or the identity of the victim. A good example is 18 U.S.C. §1341, the federal mail fraud statute, which prohibits the use of the mails "for the purpose of executing [any scheme or artifice to defraud]." Section 1341 does not require the use of the mails to be a significant element of the fraudulent scheme; the statute merely requires a showing that the mails were used. Its purpose is to grant federal jurisdiction over what would otherwise be a state offense.

That jurisdictional elements do not require any culpable mental state is universally accepted, but controversies can arise over whether an element that serves jurisdictional purposes also serves purposes that require it to be treated as a "material" element. Consider 18 U.S.C. §111, which prohibits assaults upon federal officers who are engaged in the performance of their duties. In United States v. Feola, 420 U.S. 672 (1975), the defendants attempted to rob several men who had presented themselves as potential drug buyers. The men turned out to be undercover federal drug agents, and the defendants were therefore charged with assaulting federal officers. The United States Supreme Court held that the "federal officer" element of this offense is jurisdictional only, and thus a mistaken belief that the victim was a fellow criminal was no defense:

[I]n order to effectuate the congressional purpose of according maximum protection to federal officers by making prosecutions for assaults upon them cognizable in the federal courts, §111 cannot be construed as embodying an unexpressed requirement that an assailant be aware that his victim is a federal officer. All the statute requires is an intent to assault, not an intent to assault a federal officer.

Justice Stewart, writing in dissent, noted that "[m]any states provide an aggravated penalty for assault upon state law enforcement officers; typically the victim-status element transforms the assault from a misdemeanor to a felony." He argued that §111 was intended to

fil[l] the gap and suppl[y] analogous protection for federal officers. . . . [W]here the assailant reasonably thought his victim a common citizen . . . aggravation is simply out of place, and the case should be tried in the appropriate jurisdiction under the general law of assault, as are unknowing assaults on state officers.

Do you agree with the majority that the victim's status as a federal officer serves only as a way for the federal government to exert jurisdiction, or does it relate to "the harm or evil, incident to conduct, sought to be prevented by the law defining the offense" (Model Penal Code §1.13(10))? The penalty for violations of §111 (fine of up to $50,000 or imprisonment for not more than three years) is similar to that of the felony aggravated assault provisions described by Justice Stewart.

c. Strict Liability

INTRODUCTORY NOTE

In the treatment of mistake of fact in the preceding section we encountered cases of strict liability, that is, cases where liability was imposed without any demonstrated culpability, not even negligence. Here we consider the main problems presented by strict liability legislation — how and why it came to be relied on by legislators as a regulatory device; the role of courts in affecting the extent of strict liability through their authority to interpret statutes; what the virtues and vices of strict liability are; and how far it can be squared with the requirements of just punishment.

UNITED STATES v. BALINT, 258 U.S. 250 (1922). [Defendants were indicted for violating the Narcotic Act of 1914 by selling derivatives of opium and coca leaves without the order form required by the act.[a] The crime was punishable by up to five years in prison. Defendants demurred on the ground that the indictment failed to charge that they knew they were selling prohibited drugs. The Supreme Court held that proof of such knowledge was not required by the statute, stating:]

---

a. "That it shall be unlawful for any person to sell, barter, exchange, or give away any of the aforesaid drugs except in pursuance of a written order of the person to whom such article is sold, bartered, exchanged, or given, on a form to be issued in blank for that purpose by the Commissioner of Internal Revenue. . . ." — EDS.

While the general rule at common law was that the scienter was a necessary element in the indictment and proof of every crime, and this was followed in regard to statutory crimes even where the statutory definition did not in terms include it, there has been a modification of this view in respect to prosecutions under statutes the purpose of which would be obstructed by such a requirement. It is a question of legislative intent to be construed by the court. [I]n the prohibition or punishment of particular acts, the State may in the maintenance of a public policy provide "that he who shall do them shall do them at his peril and will not be heard to plead in defense good faith or ignorance." Many instances of this are to be found in regulatory measures in the exercise of what is called the police power where the emphasis of the statute is evidently upon achievement of some social betterment rather than the punishment of the crimes as in cases of mala in se. . . . [The Act's] manifest purpose is to require every person dealing in drugs to ascertain at his peril whether that which he sells comes within the inhibition of the statute, and if he sells the inhibited drug in ignorance of its character, to penalize him. Congress weighed the possible injustice of subjecting an innocent seller to a penalty against the evil of exposing innocent purchasers to danger from the drug, and concluded that the latter was the result preferably to be avoided. Doubtless considerations as to the opportunity of the seller to find out the fact and the difficulty of proof of knowledge contributed to this conclusion.

UNITED STATES v. DOTTERWEICH, 320 U.S. 277 (1943). [Buffalo Pharmacal Company was a corporation that bought drugs from manufacturers, repackaged them, and shipped them to physicians and others under its own labels, which contained the manufacturer's description of the products. On two occasions the manufacturer's labels, and hence the corporation's labels, were in error, and as a consequence the corporation and Dotterweich, its president and general manager, were prosecuted for shipping misbranded or adulterated products in interstate commerce in violation of the Federal Food, Drug and Cosmetic Act.[b] The jury, remarkably, acquitted the corporation but convicted Dotterweich, who was sentenced to a fine and probation for 60 days, although under the statute he could have been sentenced to imprisonment for a year. The Supreme Court affirmed the conviction, holding that the statute required no mens rea at all with respect to whether those charged knew or should have known the shipment was mislabeled. Justice Frankfurter, writing for the Court, observed:]

The Food and Drugs Act of 1906 was an exertion by Congress of its power to keep impure and adulterated food and drugs out of the channels of commerce. By the Act of 1938, Congress extended the range of its control over illicit and noxious articles and stiffened the penalties for disobedience. The purposes of this legislation thus touch phases of the lives and health of people which, in the circumstances of modern industrialism, are largely beyond self-protection. Regard for these purposes should infuse construction of the legislation if it is to be treated as a working instrument of government and not merely as a collection of English words. The prosecution to which Dotterweich was subjected is based on a now familiar type of legislation whereby penalties serve as effective means

b. Section 301 of the Act prohibits the "Introduction or delivery for introduction into interstate commerce of any . . . drug . . . that is adulterated or misbranded." — Eds.

of regulation. Such legislation dispenses with the conventional requirement for criminal conduct — awareness of some wrongdoing. In the interest of the larger good it puts the burden of acting at hazard upon a person otherwise innocent but standing in responsible relation to a public danger. United States v. Balint, 258 U.S. 250. . . .

Hardship there doubtless may be under a statute which thus penalizes the transaction though consciousness of wrongdoing be totally wanting. Balancing relative hardships, Congress has preferred to place it upon those who have at least the opportunity of informing themselves of the existence of conditions imposed for the protection of consumers before sharing in illicit commerce, rather than to throw the hazard on the innocent public who are wholly helpless.

MORISSETTE v. UNITED STATES

Supreme Court of the United States
342 U.S. 246 (1952)

JUSTICE JACKSON delivered the opinion of the Court.

[Morissette, a junk dealer, openly entered an Air Force practice bombing range and took spent bomb casings that had been lying about for years exposed to the weather and rusting away. He flattened them out and sold them at a city junk market at a profit of $84. He was indicted and convicted of violating 18 U.S.C. §641, which made it a crime to "knowingly convert" government property.[a] There was no question that defendant knew that what he took and sold were Air Force bomb casings. His defense was that he honestly believed that they had been abandoned by the Air Force and that he was therefore violating no one's rights in taking them. The trial judge rejected Morissette's defense and instructed the jury that "[t]he question on intent is whether or not he intended to take the property." The court of appeals affirmed, ruling that the statute created several separate offenses, including stealing and knowing conversion. While the crime of stealing traditionally has required an intent to take another's property without claim of right, the court of appeals held that knowing conversion did not include an element of criminal intent because none was expressly required by the statute. The Supreme Court, in an opinion by Justice Jackson, reversed Morissette's conviction.]

The contention that an injury can amount to a crime only when inflicted by intention is no provincial or transient notion. It is as universal and persistent in mature systems of law as belief in freedom of the human will and a consequent ability and duty of the normal individual to choose between good and evil. A relation between some mental element and punishment for a harmful act is almost as instinctive as the child's familiar exculpatory "But I didn't mean to," and has afforded the rational basis for a tardy and unfinished substitution of

---

a. "Whoever embezzles, steals, purloins, or knowingly converts to his use or the use of another, or without authority, sells, conveys or disposes of any record, voucher, money, or thing of value of the United States or of any department or agency thereof, or any property made or being made under contract for the United States or any department or agency thereof . . . shall be fined not more than $10,000 or imprisoned not more than ten years, or both; but if the value of such property does not exceed the sum of $100, he shall be fined not more than $1,000 or imprisoned not more than one year, or both." — EDS.

deterrence and reformation in place of retaliation and vengeance as the motivation for public prosecution. . . .

Crime, as a compound concept, generally constituted only from concurrence of an evil-meaning mind with an evil-doing hand, was congenial to an intense individualism and took deep and early root in American soil. As the states codified the common law of crimes, even if their enactments were silent on the subject, their courts assumed that the omission did not signify disapproval of the principle but merely recognized that intent was so inherent in the idea of the offense that it required no statutory affirmation. . . .

However, the *Balint* and *Behrman*[b] offenses belong to a category of another character, with very different antecedents and origins. The crimes there involved depend on no mental element but consist only of forbidden acts or omissions. This, while not expressed by the Court, is made clear from examination of a century-old but accelerating tendency, discernible both here and in England, to call into existence new duties and crimes which disregard any ingredient of intent. The industrial revolution multiplied the number of workmen exposed to injury from increasingly powerful and complex mechanisms, driven by freshly discovered sources of energy, requiring higher precautions by employers. Traffic of velocities, volumes and varieties unheard of, came to subject the wayfarer to intolerable casualty risks if owners and drivers were not to observe new cares and uniformities of conduct. Congestion of cities and crowding of quarters called for health and welfare regulations undreamed of in simpler times. Wide distribution of goods became an instrument of wide distribution of harm when those who dispersed food, drink, drugs, and even securities, did not comply with reasonable standards of quality, integrity, disclosure and care. Such dangers have engendered increasingly numerous and detailed regulations which heighten the duties of those in control of particular industries, trades, properties or activities that affect public health, safety or welfare.[20]

While many of these duties are sanctioned by a more strict civil liability, lawmakers, whether wisely or not, have sought to make such regulations more effective by invoking criminal sanctions to be applied by the familiar technique of criminal prosecutions and convictions. This has confronted the courts with a multitude of prosecutions, based on statutes or administrative regulations, for what have been aptly called "public welfare offenses." These cases do not fit neatly into any of such accepted classifications of common-law offenses, such as those against the state, the person, property, or public morals. Many of these offenses are not in the nature of positive aggressions or invasions, with which the common law so often dealt, but are in the nature of neglect where the law requires care, or inaction where it imposes a duty. Many violations of such regulations result in no direct or immediate injury to person or property but merely create the danger or probability of it which the law seeks to minimize. While such offenses do not threaten the security of the state in the manner of treason,

---

b. United States v. Behrman, 258 U.S. 280 (1922), a companion case to *Balint*. — Eds.

20. Sayre, Public Welfare Offenses, 33 Col. L. Rev. 55, 73, 84 (1933), cites and classifies a large number of cases and concludes that they fall roughly into subdivisions of (1) illegal sales of intoxicating liquor, (2) sales of impure or adulterated food or drugs, (3) sales of misbranded articles, (4) violations of antinarcotic Acts, (5) criminal nuisances, (6) violations of traffic regulations, (7) violations of motor-vehicle laws, and (8) violations of general police regulations, passed for the safety, health or well-being of the community.

they may be regarded as offenses against its authority, for their occurrence impairs the efficiency of controls deemed essential to the social order as presently constituted. In this respect, whatever the intent of the violator, the injury is the same, and the consequences are injurious or not according to fortuity. Hence, legislation applicable to such offenses, as a matter of policy, does not specify intent as a necessary element. The accused, if he does not will the violation, usually is in a position to prevent it with no more care than society might reasonably expect and no more exertion than it might reasonably exact from one who assumed his responsibilities. Also, penalties commonly are relatively small, and conviction does no grave damage to an offender's reputation. Under such considerations, courts have turned to construing statutes and regulations which make no mention of intent as dispensing with it and holding that the guilty act alone makes out the crime.[c] This has not, however, been without expressions of misgiving.

The pilot of the movement in this country appears to be a holding that a tavernkeeper could be convicted for selling liquor to an habitual drunkard even if he did not know the buyer to be such. Barnes v. State, 19 Conn. 398 (1849). Later came Massachusetts holdings that convictions for selling adulterated milk in violation of statutes forbidding such sales require no allegation of proof that defendant knew of the adulteration. . . .

After the turn of the Century, a new use for crimes without intent appeared when New York enacted numerous and novel regulations of tenement houses, sanctioned by money penalties. Landlords contended that a guilty intent was essential to establish a violation. Judge Cardozo wrote the answer:

> The defendant asks us to test the meaning of this statute by standards applicable to statutes that govern infamous crimes. The analogy, however, is deceptive. The element of conscious wrongdoing, the guilty mind accompanying the guilty act, is associated with a concept of crimes that are punished as infamous. Even there, it is not an invariable element. But in the prosecution of minor offenses there is a wider range of practice and of power. Prosecutions for petty penalties have always constituted in our law a class by themselves. That is true, though the prosecution is criminal in form.

Tenement House Dept. v. McDevitt, 215 N.Y. 160, 168, 109 N.E. 88, 90, (1915). . . .

Thus, for diverse but reconcilable reasons, state courts converged on the same result, discontinuing inquiry into intent in a limited class of offenses against such statutory regulations. . . .

Before long, similar questions growing out of federal legislation reached this

c. But see Henry M. Hart, The Aims of the Criminal Law, 23 L. & Contemp. Prob. 401, 431 n. 70 (1958): "In relation to offenses of a traditional type, the Court's opinion seems to be saying, we must be much slower to dispense with a basis for genuine blameworthiness in criminal intent than in relation to modern regulatory offenses. But it is precisely in the area of traditional crimes that the nature of the act itself commonly gives some warning that there may be a problem about its propriety and so affords, without more, at least some slight basis of condemnation for doing it. Thus, Morissette knew perfectly well that he was taking property which, at least up to the moment of caption, did not belong to him.

"In the area of regulatory crimes, on the other hand, the moral quality of the act is often neutral; and on occasion, the offense may consist not of any act at all, but simply of an intrinsically innocent omission, so that there is no basis for moral condemnation whatever." — EDS.

Court. Its judgments were in harmony with this consensus of state judicial opinion, the existence of which may have led the Court to overlook the need for full exposition of their rationale in the context of federal law. . . .

It was not until recently [in United States v. Dotterweich, supra] that the Court took occasion more explicitly to relate abandonment of the ingredient of intent . . . with the peculiar nature and quality of the offense. . . .

Neither this Court nor, so far as we are aware, any other has undertaken to delineate a precise line or set forth comprehensive criteria for distinguishing between crimes that require a mental element and crimes that do not. We attempt no closed definition, for the law on the subject is neither settled nor static. The conclusion reached in the *Balint* and *Behrman* Cases has our approval and adherence for the circumstances to which it was there applied. A quite different question here is whether we will expand the doctrine of crimes without intent to include those charged here.

Stealing, larceny, and its variants and equivalents, were among the earliest offenses known to the law that existed before legislation; they are invasions of rights of property which stir a sense of insecurity in the whole community and arouse public demand for retribution, the penalty is high and, when a sufficient amount is involved, the infamy is that of a felony, which, says Maitland, is ". . . as bad a word as you can give to man or thing." State courts of last resort, on whom fall the heaviest burden of interpreting criminal law in this country, have consistently retained the requirement of intent in larceny-type offenses. If any state has deviated, the exception has neither been called to our attention nor disclosed by our research.

Congress, therefore, omitted any express prescription of criminal intent from the enactment before us in the light of an unbroken course of judicial decision in all constituent states of the Union holding intent inherent in this class of offense, even when not expressed in a statute. Congressional silence as to mental elements in an Act merely adopting into federal statutory law a concept of crime already so well defined in common law and statutory interpretation by the states may warrant quite contrary inferences than the same silence in creating an offense new to general law, for whose definition the courts have no guidance except the Act. Because the offenses before this Court in the *Balint* and *Behrman* Cases were of this latter class, we cannot accept them as authority for eliminating intent from offenses incorporated from the common law. . . .

The Government asks us by a feat of construction radically to change the weights and balances in the scales of justice. The purpose and obvious effect of doing away with the requirement of a guilty intent is to ease the prosecution's path to conviction, to strip the defendant of such benefit as he derived at common law from innocence of evil purpose, and to circumscribe the freedom heretofore allowed juries. Such a manifest impairment of the immunities of the individual should not be extended to common-law crimes on judicial initiative. . . .

We hold that the mere omission from §641 of any mention of intent will not be construed as eliminating that element from the crimes denounced. . . .

Of course, the jury, considering Morissette's awareness that these casings were on government property, his failure to seek any permission for their removal and his self-interest as a witness, might have disbelieved his profession of innocent intent and concluded that his assertion of a belief that the casings were abandoned was an after-thought. Had the jury convicted on proper instructions it would be the end of the matter. But juries are not bound by what seems inescapable logic to judges. They might have concluded that the heaps of spent casings left in the hinterland to rust away presented an appearance of unwanted and abandoned junk, and that lack of any conscious deprivation of property or intentional injury was indicated by Morissette's good character, the openness of the taking, crushing and transporting of the casings, and the candor with which it was all admitted. They might have refused to brand Morissette as a thief. Had they done so, that too would have been the end of the matter.

Reversed.

UNITED STATES v. STAPLES

Supreme Court of the United States
114 S. Ct. 1793 (1994)

JUSTICE THOMAS delivered the opinion of the Court.

[Defendant was charged with violating the National Firearms Act, which makes possession of an unregistered firearm punishable by up to 10 years in prison. The rifle found in his possession met the Act's definition of a firearm — a weapon capable of automatically firing more than one shot with a single pull of the trigger. It appears that the rifle originally had a metal piece that precluded automatic firing, but that it had at some time or other been filed down. Defendant testified that the rifle never fired automatically in his possession and that he didn't know it was capable of doing so. He sought an instruction that the government had to prove that he "knew that the gun would fire fully automatically." This was refused, and the jury convicted. On appeal, the Court of Appeals affirmed his conviction, and the Supreme Court granted certiorari.]

. . . Whether or not §5861(d) requires proof that a defendant knew of the characteristics of his weapon that made it a "firearm" under the Act is a question of statutory construction. . . . Section 5861(d) is silent concerning the mens rea required for a violation. It states simply that "[i]t shall be unlawful for any person . . . to receive or possess a firearm which is not registered to him in the National Firearms Registration and Transfer Record." Nevertheless, silence on this point by itself does not necessarily suggest that Congress intended to dispense with a conventional mens rea element, which would require that the defendant know the facts that make his conduct illegal. . . . On the contrary, we must construe the statute in light of the background rules of the common law, in which the requirement of some mens rea for a crime is firmly embedded. . . .

Relying on the strength of the traditional rule, we have stated that offenses that require no mens rea generally are disfavored, and have suggested that some indication of congressional intent, express or implied, is required to dispense with mens rea as an element of a crime.

. . . The Government argues that Congress intended the Act to regulate and restrict the circulation of dangerous weapons. Consequently, in the Government's view, this case fits in a line of precedent concerning what we have termed "public welfare" or "regulatory" offenses, in which we have understood Congress to impose a form of strict criminal liability through statutes that do not require the defendant to know the facts that make his conduct illegal. In construing such statutes, we have inferred from silence that Congress did not intend to require proof of mens rea to establish an offense. . . .

Typically, our cases recognizing such offenses involve statutes that regulate potentially harmful or injurious items. . . . In such situations, we have reasoned that as long as a defendant knows that he is dealing with a dangerous device of a character that places him "in responsible relation to a public danger," [United States v.] Dotterweich, [320 U.S. 277] at 281, he should be alerted to the probability of strict regulation, and we have assumed that in such cases Congress intended to place the burden on the defendant to "ascertain at his peril whether [his conduct] comes within the inhibition of the statute." [United States v.] Balint, [258 U.S. 250] at 254. . . .

The Government argues that §5861(d) defines precisely the sort of regulatory offense described in *Balint*. In this view, all guns, whether or not they are statutory "firearms," are dangerous devices that put gun owners on notice that they must determine at their hazard whether their weapons come within the scope of the Act.

. . . The Government seeks support for its position from our decision in the United States v. Freed, 401 U.S. 601 (1971), which involved a prosecution for possession of unregistered grenades under §5861(d). The defendant knew that the items in his possession were grenades, and we concluded that §5861(d) did not require the Government to prove the defendant also knew that the grenades were unregistered.

. . . [O]ur analysis in *Freed* likening the Act to the public welfare statute in *Balint* rested entirely on the assumption that the defendant knew that he was dealing with hand grenades — that is, that he knew he possessed a particularly dangerous type of weapon (one within the statutory definition of a "firearm"), possession of which was not entirely "innocent" in and of itself. . . .

In glossing over the distinction between grenades and guns, the Government ignores the particular care we have taken to avoid construing a statute to dispense with mens rea where doing so would "criminalize a broad range of apparently innocent conduct." Liparota [v. United States], 471 U.S. [419] at 426 (1985).

[T]here is a long tradition of widespread lawful gun ownership by private individuals in this country. Such a tradition did not apply to the possession of hand grenades in *Freed* or to the selling of dangerous drugs that we considered in *Balint*. . . . Roughly 50 per cent of American homes contain at least one firearm of some sort, and in the vast majority of States, buying a shotgun or rifle is a simple transaction that would not alert a person to regulation any more than would buying a car. . . .

We concur in the Fifth Circuit's conclusion on this point: "It is unthinkable to us that Congress intended to subject such law-abiding, well-intentioned citizens to a possible ten-year term of imprisonment if . . . what they genuinely and reasonably believed was a conventional semiautomatic [weapon] turns out to have worn down into or been secretly modified to be a fully automatic weapon." As we noted in *Morissette*, the "purpose and obvious effect of doing away with the requirement of a guilty intent is to ease the prosecution's path to conviction." We are reluctant to impute that purpose to Congress where, as here, it would mean easing the path to convicting persons whose conduct would not even alert them to the probability of strict regulation in the form of a statute such as §5861(d).

The potentially harsh penalty attached to violation of §5861(d) — up to 10 years' imprisonment — confirms our reading of the Act. Historically, the penalty imposed under a statute has been a significant consideration in determining whether the statute should be construed as dispensing with mens rea. . . . [P]unishing a violation as a felony is simply incompatible with the theory of the public welfare offense. In this view, absent a clear statement from Congress that mens rea is not required, we should not apply the public welfare offense rationale to interpret any statute defining a felony offense as dispensing with mens rea.

[Reversed and remanded.]

JUSTICE GINSBURG, with whom JUSTICE O'CONNOR joins, concurring in the judgment.

. . . Although the word "knowingly" does not appear in the statute's text, courts generally assume that Congress, absent a contrary indication, means to retain a mens rea requirement.[1] Thus, our holding in United States v. Freed, 401 U.S. 601 (1971), that §5861(d) does not require proof of knowledge that the firearm is unregistered, rested on the premise that the defendant indeed knew the items he possessed were hand grenades. Conviction under §5861(d), the Government accordingly concedes, requires proof that Staples "knowingly" possessed the machinegun. The question before us is not whether knowledge of possession is required, but what level of knowledge suffices: (1) knowledge simply of possession of the object; (2) knowledge, in addition, that the object is a dangerous weapon; (3) knowledge, beyond dangerousness, of the characteristics that render the object subject to regulation, for example, awareness that the weapon is a machinegun. . . .

The Nation's legislators chose to place under a registration requirement only a very limited class of firearms, those they considered especially dangerous. The generally "dangerous" character of all guns, the Court therefore observes, did not suffice to give individuals in Staples' situation cause to inquire about the need for registration. Only the third reading . . . suits the purpose of the mens rea requirement — to shield people against punishment for apparently innocent activity. . . .

For these reasons, I conclude that conviction under §5861(d) requires proof that the defendant knew he possessed not simply a gun, but a machinegun. . . . I therefore concur in the Court's judgment.

NOTE ON STRICT LIABILITY AT COMMON LAW

Notwithstanding the common law's commitment to mens rea described in the foregoing opinions, the common law sometimes departed from that commitment before the regulatory era described by Justice Jackson. We have already examined one major departure — the view, still prevailing, that mistake of age is not a defense in sex offenses with minors. Another such departure occurred in the law of homicide. Examples are the felony-murder and misdemeanor-manslaughter rules, according to which a wholly accidental killing — otherwise

---

1. Contrary to the dissent's suggestion, we have not confined the presumption of mens rea to statutes codifying traditional common law offenses, but have also applied the presumption to offenses that are "entirely a creature of statute." . . . [See, e.g., United States v. United States Gypsum Co., 438 U.S. 422 (1978) (specific intent requirement read into antitrust statute prohibiting conspiracies to restrain trade).]

not punishable — became murder if it occurred during the commission of a felony, and manslaughter if it occurred during the commission of a misdemeanor. We will examine these doctrines in Chapter 5, Homicide.

STATE v. GUMINGA

Supreme Court of Minnesota
395 N.W.2d 344 (1986)

YETKA, J. . . . On March 29, 1985, in the course of an undercover operation, two investigators for the City of Hopkins entered Lindee's Restaurant, Hopkins, Minnesota, with a 17-year-old woman. All three ordered alcoholic beverages. The minor had never been in Lindee's before, and the waitress did not ask the minor her age or request identification. When the waitress returned with their orders, the minor paid for all the drinks. After confirming that the drink contained alcohol, the officers arrested the waitress for serving intoxicating liquor to a minor in violation of Minn. Stat. §340.73 (1984). The owner of Lindee's, defendant George Joseph Guminga, was subsequently charged with violation of section 340.73 pursuant to Minn. Stat. §340.941 (1984), which imposes vicarious criminal liability on an employer whose employee serves intoxicating liquor to a minor. The state does not contend that Guminga was aware of or ratified the waitress's actions.

Guminga moved to dismiss the charges on the ground that section 340.941 violates the due process clauses of the federal and state constitutions. . . . After holding a hearing on August 28, 1985, the court denied the motion to dismiss. . . .

The court of appeals . . . requested this court to take jurisdiction over the question, and the request was granted. . . .

The certified question of law before this court is as follows:

> Whether Minn. Stat. §340.941, on its face, violates the defendant's right to due process of law under the Fourteenth Amendment to the United States Constitution and analogous provisions of the Constitution of the State of Minnesota.

We find that the statute in question does violate the due process clauses of the Minnesota and the United States Constitutions and thus answer the question in the affirmative. . . .

Minn. Stat. §340.73 (1984) provides criminal penalties [gross misdemeanor] for any person selling intoxicating liquor to a minor. . . . Minn. Stat. §340.941 (1984) imposes vicarious criminal liability on the employer for an employee's violation of section 340.73:

> Any sale of liquor in or from any public drinking place by any clerk, barkeep, or other employee authorized to sell liquor in such place is the act of the employer as well as that of the person actually making the sale; and every such employer is liable to all the penalties provided by law for such sale, equally with the person actually making the same.

Under Minn. Stat. §609.03 (1984), a defendant who commits a gross misdemeanor may be sentenced to "imprisonment for not more than one year or to payment of a fine of not more than $3,000 or both." In addition, a defendant convicted under section 340.941 may, at the discretion of the licensing authority, have its license suspended, revoked or be unable to obtain a new license. . . .

Since this is not an appeal from a conviction, we do not yet know whether, if found guilty, Guminga would be subjected to imprisonment, a suspended sentence, or a fine. Even if there is no prison sentence imposed, under the new sentencing guidelines, a gross misdemeanor conviction will affect his criminal history score were he to be convicted of a felony in the future. . . .

We find that criminal penalties based on vicarious liability under Minn. Stat. §340.941 are a violation of substantive due process and that only civil penalties would be constitutional. A due process analysis of a statute involves a balancing of the public interest protected against the intrusion on personal liberty while taking into account any alternative means by which to achieve the same end. . . . Section 340.941 serves the public interest by providing additional deterrence to violation of the liquor laws. The private interests affected, however, include liberty, damage to reputation and other future disabilities arising from criminal prosecution for an act which Guminga did not commit or ratify. Not only could Guminga be given a prison sentence or a suspended sentence, but, in the more likely event that he receives only a fine, his liberty could be affected by a longer presumptive sentence in a possible future felony conviction. Such an intrusion on personal liberty is not justified by the public interest protected, especially when there are alternative means by which to achieve the same end, such as civil fines or license suspension, which do not entail the legal and social ramifications of a criminal conviction. See Model Penal Code §1.04 comment (b)(1985).[3]

We decline, however, to rewrite section 340.941 by holding that it can be enforced only by civil penalties. That is more properly a legislative function. . . . Professor Sayre summarize[s] the appropriate legal principle in these terms:

> As the decisions indicate, a sharp line must be drawn between true crimes involving serious punishments and petty misdemeanors involving only light monetary fines. Where the offense is in the nature of a true crime, that is, where it involves moral delinquency or is punishable by imprisonment or a serious penalty, it seems clear that the doctrine of respondeat superior must be repudiated as a

---

3. We agree with the reasoning of the Georgia Supreme Court in Davis v. City of Peachtree City, 251 Ga. 219, 304 S.E.2d 701 (1983). *Davis* involved the criminal conviction of the president of a chain of convenience stores whose employee had sold liquor to a minor. The defendant was prosecuted under a city ordinance holding licensees responsible for the acts of their employees and received a $300 fine and a 60-day suspended sentence. The Georgia Supreme Court reversed the conviction: . . .

> In balancing this burden against the public's interests, we find that it cannot be justified under the due process clauses of the Georgia or United States Constitutions, regardless of Peachtree City's admittedly legitimate interests of deterring employers from allowing their employees to break the law and of facilitating the enforcement of these laws. This is especially true, when, as here, there are other, less onerous alternatives which sufficiently promote these interests. . . .
>
> Although some commentators and courts have found that vicarious criminal liability does not violate due process in misdemeanor cases which involve as punishment only a slight fine and not imprisonment, we decline to so hold. The damage done to an individual's good name and the peril imposed on an individual's future are sufficient reasons to shift the balance in favor of the individual. The imposition of such a burden on an employer "cannot rest on so frail a reed as whether his employee will commit a mistake in judgment," but instead can be justified only by the appropriate prosecuting officials proving some sort of culpability or knowledge by the employer.

foundation for criminal liability. [Criminal Responsibility for the Acts of Another, 43 Harv. L. Rev. 689, 717 (1930).] . . .

The dissent argues that vicarious liability is necessary as a deterrent so that an owner will impress upon employees that they should not sell to minors. However, it does not distinguish between an employer who vigorously lectures his employees and one who does not. According to the dissent, each would be equally guilty. We believe it is a deterrent enough that the employee who sells to the minor can be charged under the statute and that the business is subject to fines or suspension or revocation of license. . . .

We find that, in Minnesota, no one can be convicted of a crime punishable by imprisonment for an act he did not commit, did not have knowledge of, or give expressed or implied consent to the commission thereof.

The certified question is thus answered in the affirmative. . . .

KELLEY, J. (dissenting): . . . The strong public interest in prohibiting the sale of liquor to minors justifies the imposition of vicarious liability on the bar owner — employer for illegal sales to minors made by an employee. I respectfully suggest that in ruling Minn. Stat. §340.941 (1984) unconstitutional, the majority has failed to give adequate weight to the clearly expressed, long-standing public policy of this state as reflected in Section 340.941. Imposition of vicarious liability and criminal punishment for sale of intoxicating liquor to minors has been the law in this state since 1905. . . .

[I]mposition of vicarious liability and the threat of a short jail, not prison, sentence is reasonably related to the legislative purpose: enforcement of laws prohibiting liquor sales to minors. Without the deterrent of possible personal criminal responsibility and a sentence, the legislature could have rationally concluded that liquor establishment owners will be less likely to impress upon employees the need to require identification of age before serving liquor. Limiting punishment to a fine allows bar owners to view their liability for violations as nothing more than an expense of doing business. The gravity of the problems associated with minors who consume alcoholic beverages justifies the importance by the legislature of harsher punishment on those who help contribute to those problems. The state has the right to impose limited criminal vicarious liability on bar proprietors as a reasonable exchange for the state-granted privilege of a liquor license. . . .

The majority's holding today not only fails to give deference to decades of legislative policy, but it is likewise at odds with rulings of the majority of the courts of our sister jurisdictions. It can be stated as a general rule, that statutes imposing vicarious criminal liability upon the "innocent" employer for the illegal conduct of the employee have been generally upheld as constitutional. See Annot., 89 A.L.R.3d 1256 (1979). . . .

NOTES ON VICARIOUS LIABILITY

1. Compare *Guminga* with State v. Beaudry, 123 Wisc. 2d 40, 365 N.W.2d 593 (1985). The defendant and her husband were sole shareholders of a corporation with a license to sell alcohol at the Village Green Tavern. The defendant was the designated agent for the corporate licensee. It appeared that one night the tavern manager remained open past closing time, admittedly against the instructions of the absent owners and for the sole purpose of entertaining his own friends. Nonetheless, the defendant was convicted on the basis of vicarious liability. The court upheld the conviction, even though the statute authorized a 90-day jail sentence, on the ground that the penalty imposed was solely a $200 fine.

2. As the dissent in *Guminga* states, most state decisions have upheld the constitutionality of imprisonment for vicarious liability convictions. Query whether the same approach should apply to vicarious liability imposed on individuals outside the business setting. Consider State v. Akers, 400 A.2d 38 (N.H. 1979). A statute imposed criminal liability on parents of minor children who drive off-highway vehicles on public highways. No evidence of parental culpability (beyond the parental status) was required. The court struck down the statute, stating (id. at 40):

> Without passing upon the validity of statutes that might seek to impose vicarious criminal liability on the part of an employer for acts of his employees, we have no hesitancy in holding that any attempt to impose such liability on parents simply because they occupy the status of parents, without more, offends the due process clause of our State constitution.

In reaching its conclusion the court appeared to invalidate all criminal liability, not just incarceration.

Questions: On what principle can the court strike down vicarious parental liability "without passing upon" vicarious employer liability? What is the distinction between the two situations?

A number of recent state statutes provide for jail sentences for parents whose children are persistently truant. Wall St. J., May 18, 1992, at B7. See generally on criminalizing deficient parenting, T. Weinstein, Visiting the Sins of the Child on the Parent: The Legality of Criminal Parental Liability Statutes, 64 So. Cal. L. Rev. 859 (1991).

STATE v. BAKER

Kansas Court of Appeal
571 P.2d 65 (1977)

SPENCER, J. Defendant has appealed his conviction of driving his motor vehicle at a speed of seventy-seven miles per hour in a fifty-five miles per hour zone in violation of K.S.A. 1976 Supp. 8-1336(a)(3).

Agreed upon facts are that prior to the trial of this matter to the court, the state moved to suppress evidence offered by the defendant that:

1. Defendant's cruise control stuck in the "accelerate" position causing the car to accelerate beyond the posted speed limit.
2. The defendant attempted to deactivate the cruise control by hitting the off button, and the coast button and tapping the brakes.
3. These actions were not immediately successful in deactivating the cruise control.
4. Subsequent to the date of this incident, the defendant had the defective cruise control repaired.

The trial court sustained the motion, thus precluding the defendant from presenting the proffered evidence as a defense. . . . The result was that the defendant was found guilty of driving in excess of the posted speed limit, and, also, that defendant was the "driver" of the car as defined by K.S.A. 8-1416. The sentence of $10 and costs was suspended pending this appeal. . . .

[D]efendant readily concedes that a violation of the speeding statute (K.S.A. 1976 Supp. 8-1336) is an absolute liability offense when read in light of the absolute liability statute (K.S.A. 21-3204), which provides:

> A person may be guilty of an offense without having criminal intent if the crime is a misdemeanor and the statute defining the offense clearly indicates a legislative purpose to impose absolute liability for the conduct described. . . .

Defendant admits that this statute does away with the necessity of proving intent to commit the misdemeanor and, further, that any evidence of the defective cruise control would be inadmissible if introduced merely to negate an intent or culpable state of mind on the part of the motorist. His contention is that the evidence was offered to show that his speeding was not a voluntary act and, therefore, there was no criminal liability. He suggests that the evidence of a defective cruise control goes specifically to whether his speeding was a voluntary act on his part and has nothing to do "with the intent, or state of mind, of the defendant to do the crime to which his act amounted." In sum, the defendant suggests that even though the charge against him was an absolute liability offense per K.S.A. 21-3204, the state must prove that he acted voluntarily. . . .

We have no doubt that if defendant were able to establish that his act of speeding was the result of an unforeseen occurrence or circumstance, which was not caused by him and which he could not prevent, that such would constitute a valid defense to the charge. But, the evidence proffered suggests a malfunction of a device attached to the motor vehicle operated by the defendant over which he had or should have had absolute control. Defendant does not suggest that the operation of the motor vehicle on the day of his arrest was anything but a voluntary act on his part, nor that anyone other than himself activated the cruise control, which may have caused his excessive speed. . . .

In the New York case of People v. Shaughnessy, 66 Misc. 2d 19, 319 N.Y.S.2d 626 (1971), it was held that a defendant could not be found guilty of violating an ordinance prohibiting entry upon private property because the defendant was merely a passenger in the trespassing car and the state's evidence failed to show an overt voluntary act or omission by the defendant. In the case of State v. Kremer, 262 Minn. 190, 114 N.W.2d 88 (1962), the Minnesota Supreme Court held that a defendant could not be guilty of violating a city ordinance requiring all traffic to stop at a flashing red light when the evidence showed that defendant's brakes failed with no prior warning to the defendant. Again, the court found no overt voluntary act on the part of the defendant. . . .

In [State v.] Weller, [230 A.2d 242 (1967),] the Connecticut court stated that the defendant had a valid defense to the speeding charge because the spring which closes the throttle plate broke due to no fault of the defendant. The court reasoned that because "[t]here is not one scintilla of evidence of any intent on the part of the defendant to do the prohibited act . . ." the defendant's conviction should be overturned. . . .

In our view, unexpected brake failure and unexpected malfunction of the throttle on an automobile, both being essential components to the operation of the vehicle, differ significantly from the malfunction of a cruise control device to which the driver has voluntarily delegated partial control of that automobile. We believe it must be said that defendant assumed the full operation of his motor vehicle and when he did so and activated the cruise control attached to that automobile, he clearly was the agent in causing the act of speeding. . . .

Judgment affirmed.

NOTES ON THE INVOLUNTARY-ACT DEFENSE TO ABSOLUTE LIABILITY OFFENSES

1. In Hill v. Baxter, [1958] 1 Q.B. 277, the defendant drove his truck at a fast speed through a halt sign, collided with a car, and overturned. He was charged with dangerous driving under Section 11(1) of the Road Traffic Act and with failing to conform to a traffic sign under Section 49(b). The trial justices dismissed the charges on the basis of some evidence that he had had a blackout. On appeal by the prosecutor, the divisional court reversed on the ground that the defendant had not proved he was in a state of automatism. Lord Goddard observed (at 282-283):

> The first thing to be remembered is that the Road Traffic Act, 1930, contains an absolute prohibition against driving dangerously or ignoring "Halt" signs. No question of mens rea enters into the offence; it is no answer to a charge under those sections to say: "I did not mean to drive dangerously" or "I did not notice the 'Halt' sign." The justices' finding that the respondent was not capable of forming any intention as to the manner of driving is really immaterial. What they evidently mean is that the respondent was in a state of automation. But he was driving and, as the case finds, exercising some skill, and undoubtedly the onus of proving that he was in a state of automation must be on him. . . .[a]
>
> The main contention before us on the part of the appellant was that there was no evidence on which the justices could find that the respondent was in a state of automatism or whatever term may be applied to someone performing acts in a state of unconsciousness. There was in fact no evidence except that of the respondent, and while the justices were entitled to believe him, his evidence shows nothing except that after the accident he cannot remember what took place after he left Preston Circus. This is quite consistent with being overcome with sleep or at least drowsiness. That drivers do fall asleep is a not uncommon cause of serious road accidents, and it would be impossible as well as disastrous to hold that falling asleep at the wheel was any defence to a charge of dangerous driving. If a driver finds that he is getting sleepy he must stop. . . .
>
> I agree that there may be cases where the circumstances are such that the accused could not really be said to be driving at all. Suppose he had a stroke or an epileptic fit, both instances of what may properly be called acts of God; he might well be in the driver's seat even with his hands on the wheel, but in such a state of unconsciousness that he could not be said to be driving. A blow from a stone or an attack by a swarm of bees I think introduces some conception akin to novus actus

a. Would this requirement be possible under American law? Consider Patterson v. New York, page 41 supra. — EDS.

interveniens. In this case, however, I am content to say that the evidence falls far short of what would justify a court holding that this man was in some automatous state.

2. In *Baker* does the court satisfactorily distinguish the cases of the failed brakes and the sticky throttle? If these cases go only to the mens rea (irrelevant in a strict liability offense), why isn't it equally true of the cruise control? Is there any difference between the cruise control and these other cases other than in the degree of risk created?

How should the following hypotheticals be analyzed?

(a) The electric shoulder harness holding the driver suddenly malfunctions and grabs the driver's arms long enough to make the car spin widely back and forth in violation of the traffic laws.

(b) Suppose a child in the back seat lurches over and grabs the driver's arms in a strong show of affection, with the same consequence.

(c) Suppose a tornado picks up the car and deposits it the wrong way on a one-way street.

3. In State v. Miller, 309 Or. 362, 788 P.2d 974 (1990), the Oregon Supreme Court affirmed a driving-while-intoxicated conviction of a defendant who was not permitted to present evidence that unknown to him someone had laced his drink with alcohol. The court declared that the statute created strict liability with respect to the presence of alcohol in the driver's body.

Questions: Could he have successfully argued the defense of absence of a voluntary act? Why not? Suppose his conviction was for driving while in possession of an open container of drinking alcohol, which had been placed in his car without his knowledge. Would he then have a defense of no act? Compare the definition of voluntary act in Model Penal Code §2.01(4), and see Note 2(b), supra.

4. Question: Why should the absence of a voluntary act be a defense to a strict liability offense? See M. Budd & J. Lynch, Voluntariness, Causation and Strict Liability, [1978] Crim. L. Rev. 74, 75 n. 6:

> It is strange . . . that it is thought appropriate for the law to acquit those in a state of automatism of offences of strict liability but to convict those acting voluntarily. It seems to us that there is no sound basis for this difference in treatment. It must certainly be wrong for the law to treat differently those who are both equally free of moral blame and whose conviction would be equally relevant to advancing the purposes of strict liability.

But see Jeffrie Murphy, Involuntary Acts and Criminal Liability, 81 Ethics 332, 340 (1971). See generally Richard Wasserstrom, Strict Liability in the Criminal Law, 12 Stan. L. Rev. 731 742 (1960).

REGINA v. CITY OF SAULT STE. MARIE

Supreme Court of Canada
85 D.L.R.3d 161 (1978)

DICKSON, J. . . . Various arguments are advanced in justification of absolute liability in public welfare offences. Two predominate. Firstly, it is argued that the protection of social interests requires a high standard of care and attention on the part of those who follow certain pursuits and such persons are more likely to be stimulated to maintain those standards if they know that ignorance or mistake will not excuse them. The removal of any possible loophole acts, it is said, is an incentive to take precautionary measures beyond what would otherwise be taken, in order that mistakes and mishaps be avoided. The second main argument is one based on administrative efficiency. Having regard to both the difficulty of proving mental culpability and the number of petty cases which daily come before the Courts, proof of fault is just too great a burden in time and money to place upon the prosecution. To require proof of each person's individual intent would allow almost every violator to escape. This, together with the glut of work entailed in proving mens rea in every case would clutter the docket and impede adequate enforcement as virtually to nullify the regulatory statutes. In short, absolute liability, it is contended, is the most efficient and effective way of ensuring compliance with minor regulatory legislation and the social ends to be achieved are of such importance as to override the unfortunate by-product of punishing those who may be free of moral turpitude. In further justification, it is urged that slight penalties are usually imposed and that conviction for breach of a public welfare offence does not carry the stigma associated with conviction for a criminal offense.

Arguments of greater force are advanced against absolute liability. The most telling is that it violates fundamental principles of penal liability. It also rests upon assumptions which have not been, and cannot be, empirically established. There is no evidence that a higher standard of care results from absolute liability. If a person is already taking every reasonable precautionary measure, is he likely to take additional measures, knowing that however much care he takes, it will not serve as a defence in the event of breach? If he has exercised care and skill, will conviction have a deterrent effect upon him or others? Will the injustice of conviction lead to cynicism and disrespect for the law, on his part and on the part of others? These are among the questions asked. The argument that no stigma attaches does not withstand analysis, for the accused will have suffered loss of time, legal costs, exposure to the processes of the criminal law at trial and, however one may downplay it, the opprobrium of conviction. It is not sufficient to say that the public interest is engaged, and, therefore, liability may be imposed without fault. In serious crimes, the public interest is involved and mens rea must be proven. The administrative argument has little force. . . .

The unfortunate tendency in many past cases has been to see the choice as between two stark alternatives: (i) full mens rea; or (ii) absolute liability. . . . There has, however, been an attempt in Australia, in many Canadian Courts, and indeed in England, to seek a middle position, fulfilling the goals of public welfare offences while still not punishing the entirely blameless. There is an increasing and impressive stream of authority which holds that where an offence does not require full mens rea, it is nevertheless a good defence for the defendant to prove that he was not negligent. . . .

The doctrine proceeds on the assumption that the defendant could have avoided the prima facie offence through the exercise of reasonable care and he is given the opportunity of establishing, if he can, that he did in fact exercise such care. . . . This burden falls upon the defendant as he is the only one who will generally have the means of proof. This would not seem unfair as the alternative is absolute liability which denies an accused any defence whatsoever.

While the prosecution must prove beyond a reasonable doubt that the defendant committed the prohibited act, the defendant must only establish on the balance of probabilities that he has a defence of reasonable care.[a]

I conclude, for the reasons which I have sought to express, that there are compelling grounds for the recognition of three categories of offences rather than the traditional two:

1. Offences in which mens rea, consisting of some positive state of mind such as intent, knowledge, or recklessness, must be proved by the prosecution either as an inference from the nature of the act committed, or by additional evidence.
2. Offences in which there is no necessity for the prosecution to prove the existence of mens rea; the doing of the prohibited act prima facie imports the offence, leaving it open to the accused to avoid liability by proving that he took all reasonable care. . . .
3. Offences of absolute liability where it is not open to the accused to exculpate himself by showing that he was free of fault.

Offences which are criminal in the true sense fall in the first category. Public welfare offences would, prima facie, be in the second category. . . . An offence of this type would fall in the first category only if such words as "wilfully," "with intent," "knowingly," or "intentionally" are contained in the statutory provision creating the offence. . . . Offences of absolute liability would be those in respect of which the Legislature had made it clear that guilt would follow proof merely of the proscribed act. The over-all regulatory pattern adopted by the Legislature, the subject-matter of the legislation, the importance of the penalty, and the precision of the language used will be primary considerations in determining whether the offence falls into the third category.

NOTES

1. In an even more significant move against absolute liability than the *Sault Ste. Marie* case, the Supreme Court of Canada has done what the Supreme Court of the United States has consistently declined to do — it held absolute liability unconstitutional. Specifically, it held that imprisonment for an absolute liability offense is a deprivation of liberty not "in accordance with the precepts of fundamental justice" guaranteed by Section 7 of the Canadian Charter of Rights and Freedoms. Reference Re Section 94(2) of the Motor Vehicle Act, 23 C.C.C3d 289 (1985). The court's reasons were essentially those given in the *Sault Ste. Marie* case.

The Canadian Supreme Court was obliged to confront the qualification in Section 1 of the Charter that makes the protected rights and freedoms subject to "such reasonable limits prescribed by law as can be demonstrably justified in a free and democratic society." The Court held that administrative expediency

---

a. A later (5-4) decision of the Canadian Supreme Court upheld the constitutionality of so shifting the burden of proof. Regina v. Wholesale Travel Group Inc., 67 C.C.C.3d 193, 84 D.L.R. 451 (1991). — EDS.

could justify imprisonment for absolute liability "only in cases arising out of exceptional conditions, such as natural disasters, the outbreak of war, epidemics and the like." (Id. at 313.)

2. In *Sweet v. Parsley, [1970] A.C. 132 (H.L. 1968),* the defendant, who was obliged to live elsewhere, rented her farm house to some people who, unknown to her, smoked cannabis on the premises. She was convicted of violating §5(b) of the Dangerous Drugs Act of 1965. Section 5 provided:

> If a person (a) being the occupier of any premises, permits those premises to be used for the purpose of smoking cannabis or cannabis resin or of dealing in cannabis or cannabis resin (whether by sale or otherwise); or (b) is concerned in the management of any premises used for any such purpose as aforesaid: he shall be guilty of an offence against this Act.

The House of Lords reversed, concluding that in the circumstances the defendant could not be said to be "concerned in the management" of premises used for the purpose of smoking cannabis. Lord Reid approached the issue of whether the statute should be construed to impose absolute liability by trying to put himself in the position of the reasonable legislator. He observed (id. at 149-150):

> When one comes to acts of a truly criminal character, it appears to me that there are at least two . . . factors which any reasonable legislator would have in mind. In the first place a stigma still attaches to any person convicted of a truly criminal offence, and the more serious or more disgraceful the offence the greater the stigma. So he would have to consider whether, in a case of this gravity, the public interest really requires that an innocent person should be prevented from proving his innocence in order that fewer guilty men may escape. And equally important is the fact that fortunately the Press in this country are vigilant to expose injustice and every manifestly unjust conviction made known to the public tends to injure the body politic by undermining public confidence in the justice of the law and of its administration. But I regret to observe that, in some recent cases where serious offences have been held to be absolute offences, the Court has taken into account no more than the wording of the Act and the character and seriousness of the mischief which constitutes the offence. . . .
>
> If this section means what the Court of Appeal have held that it means, then hundreds of thousands of people who sublet part of their premises or take in lodgers or are concerned in the management of residential premises or institutions are daily incurring a risk of being convicted of a serious offence in circumstances where they are in no way to blame. For the greatest vigilance cannot prevent tenants, lodgers or inmates or guests whom they bring in from smoking cannabis cigarettes in their own rooms.

3. United States v. United States District Court (Kantor), 858 F.2d 534 (9th Cir. 1988), involved a prosecution of defendants for producing a pornographic movie featuring 16-year-old Traci Lords. They were charged with violating 18 U.S.C. §2251(a), which prohibits the production of materials depicting a minor engaging in sexually explicit activity. Rebuffed in their attempts to introduce evidence to show the reasonableness of their belief that Ms. Lord was an adult, they sought relief on appeal. The Court of Appeals held that under the terms of the statute, read against the background of the legislative history, culpability as to the age of the minor is not an element of the government's prima facie case. It went on to hold, however, that the defendants have an affirmative defense if they establish by clear and convincing evidence that they did not know, and could not reasonably have learned, that the actor was under 18 years of age. Otherwise, the court concluded, the First Amendment's guarantee of freedom of expression would be impaired because the only way to be safe would be for people not to engage even in lawful expression.

On the issue of whether the court had the authority to engraft a defense of reasonable mistake of age onto a statute interpreted as dispensing with any mens rea requirement as to age, the court stated (id. at 542):

> [T]he statute is silent on whether reasonable mistake of age may serve as an affirmative defense. Moreover, unlike the question whether scienter should be an element of the government's prima facie case, there is no evidence that Congress considered and rejected the possibility of providing for such a defense. . . . Moreover, the federal courts may, in limited circumstances, recognize an affirmative defense where a statute does not expressly provide it. For example, the . . . [Supreme] Court has . . . recognized entrapment as an affirmative defense, reasoning that, so long as Congress has not clearly indicated to the contrary, it "will always . . . be presumed that the legislature intended exceptions to its language which would avoid [injustice, oppression, or an absurd consequence]." Sorrells v. United States, 287 U.S. 435 (1932).

See Laurie L. Levenson, Good Faith Defenses: Reshaping Strict Liability Crimes, 78 Cornell L. Rev. 401 (1993), for a proposal to generalize an affirmative defense of absence of blameworthy conduct to all strict liability crimes.

NOTES ON THE ACADEMIC DEBATE

The great majority of academic writing has opposed absolute liability.[12] In recent years, however, some academics have risen to the defense of the concept.[13] Some idea of the issues in dispute may be gleaned from the following excerpts.

Arthur Goodhart, Possession of Drugs and Absolute Liability, 84 L.Q. Rev. 382, 385-386 (1968): [T]here are certain offences that have a serious effect on the public interest but which it is difficult to prove under the usual procedure. It is then necessary to take other and more stringent steps to wipe out the evil, even at a minimal risk that an innocent man may be convicted. Lord Reid cites, although he does not entirely agree with it, the long-established saying that "it is better that ten guilty men should escape than that one innocent man should be convicted." . . . On the other hand it may be necessary in certain circumstances to alter the strict rules where an act, such as tempting young persons to buy drugs,

---

12. For two frequently cited examples, see Herbert Packer, The Limits of the Criminal Sanction 121-131 (1968); Henry M. Hart, The Aims of the Criminal Law, 23 Law & Contemp. Prob. 401, 422-425 (1958).

13. See, e.g., Michael Davis, Strict Liability: Deserved Conduct for Faultless Conduct, 33 Wayne L. Rev. 1383 (1987); Mark Kelman, Interpretive Construction in the Substantive Criminal Law, 33 Stan. L. Rev. 591, 605-611 (1981); Richard Wasserstrom, Strict Liability in the Criminal Law, 12 Stan. L. Rev. 731 (1960)

is peculiarly harmful, and where it may be difficult to prove the existence of mens rea, although it is almost certain that it does exist. . . . The point here is that the future harm that the ten guilty men who have been acquitted may do, either by repeating their own offences or by encouraging others by showing how easy it is to avoid conviction, far exceeds any injury that the innocent man can suffer by his conviction. The question then becomes: Is it better that ten young persons should be tempted to become drug addicts than that one innocent man should be convicted of being in possession of unauthorized drugs?

Mark Kelman, Strict Liability: An Unorthodox View, in Encyclopedia of Crime and Justice 1512, 1516-1517 (1983): H. L. A. Hart's argument that the defendant convicted of a strict-liability offense "could not have helped" committing the crime depends on the use of a rationally indefensible narrow time frame in focusing on the defendant's conduct. *Whenever* one thinks about criminality, one has available narrow time-frame interpretations of the relevant data — in which one learns all one can about the appropriateness of punishment by looking at some alleged criminal *incident*. One also has available broader time frames in which one incorporates data about the defendant's general personal history (as in the insanity defense), the "history" of the incident (as in the defenses of duress, entrapment, and provocation), or the defendant's conduct subsequent to the incident (as in the defense of abandonment of an attempt). It may well be the case that if one looks only at the precise *moment* at which harm is consummated, the strictly liable actor may seem powerless to avoid criminality, but it is invariably the case that the actor could have avoided liability by taking earlier steps which were hardly impossible. Chief Justice Warren Burger made precisely this point in upholding a strict-liability interpretation of statutes proscribing the shipment of adulterated drugs, on the ground that the parties who were held strictly accountable could refuse to take "responsible" managerial positions if they were afraid they would not be able to prevent violations.

> The requirements of foresight and vigilance imposed on responsible corporate agents are beyond question demanding, and perhaps onerous, *but they are no more stringent than the public has the right to expect of those who voluntarily assume positions of authority* in business enterprises whose services and products affect the health and well-being of the public that supports them. [United States v. Park, 421 U.S. 658, 672-673 (1975).]

It is significant to note that only by constructing the underlying material in the strict-liability situations with a very narrow time frame that the distinction between liability predicated on negligence, and strict liability, maintains its practical import in many critical situations.

An example is the familiar problem of "reasonable" (non-negligent) mistakes as to the victim's age in the statutory rape setting. Is one's view of a "reasonable" belief to be ascertained solely by reference to perceptions available to the defendant during the purportedly illegal seduction (she "*looked*" sixteen or "she told me she was sixteen"), or does one require that some checks prior to seduction be taken, such as checking birth certificates or asking parents? Of course, if one is hostile to statutory rape laws in general, it is perfectly reasonable to negate them by defining negligent perceptions in terms of the girl's physical appearance — that is, in terms of judgments which can be made at the narrow time-framed moment of the allegedly criminal incident. But it is hardly conceivable that a defendant ought to attract serious sympathy as someone unable to avoid crime when he has certainly had the opportunity to check on the legal appropriateness of his companion as an object of sexual desire.[a]

Phillip Johnson, Strict Liability: The Prevalent View, in Encyclopedia of Crime and Justice 1518, 1520-1521 (1983): The objection to strict liability is not that it punishes people who are literally helpless to avoid committing the act, because it is obvious that they could have avoided any possibility of liability by not going into business in the first place. The point is that selling meat or managing a factory is a productive activity which the law means to encourage, not discourage, and we should not punish people who have taken all reasonable steps to comply with the law. Where strict liability is present in the traditional criminal law, as in the felony-murder doctrine or in the rule that mistake of age is no defense to statutory rape, the defendant's underlying conduct (robbery or fornication) is deemed wrongful or socially undesirable in itself. Unless we regard business activity as similarly inherently wrongful, holding business managers up to strict liability is unjustifiable even though they have voluntarily assumed their positions of employment.

Stephen J. Schulhofer, Harm and Punishment: A Critique of Emphasis on the Results of Conduct in the Criminal Law, 122 U. Pa. L. Rev. 1497, 1586-1587 (1974): [Some argue that strict liability can reduce the risk of injury because those who fear liability can avoid areas of activity subject to this stringent form of regulation. Although those] who continue to engage in the activity may be those who believe they can be careful enough, . . . there is no guarantee that these will be the ones who are in fact the most careful. Indeed, there is some reason to suspect that those who are most confident of their ability to avoid causing harm may be just the ones who are most likely to be especially careless.[290] Thus, the strict liability crime may exclude a few accident-prone people from the activity, but it may well fail to select out most of those about whom the law should be most concerned. At the same time, it may exclude from the activity many others who could play a valuable social role but are unwilling to face the risk of suffering criminal penalties for reasons beyond their control. Indeed, if the penalties are serious, those who are careful and make provision for risks may be the most likely to take the sensible precaution of not engaging in this activity at all.
. . . [Thus], the dynamic effect [of strict liability] could be to increase the total harm caused by increasing the proportion of those engaged in the activity who are relatively careless.

Model Penal Code and Commentaries, Comment to §2.05 at 282-283 (1985): This section makes a frontal attack on absolute or strict liability in the penal law,

a. Does this argument imply that there is no practical difference between a strict liability standard and a negligence standard with an expanded time frame? Will the precautions that an actor failed to take at earlier points in time necessarily involve "a gross deviation from the standard of care that a reasonable person would observe" (MPC §2.02(2)(d))? Note that by using a broad time frame, Professor Kelman is able to argue, in effect, that the defendant in his example *was* negligent. But will the defendant have the same opportunity to respond to such an argument if the applicable standard is strict liability rather than negligence? Will the jury's role be the same? — EDS.
290. This confidence may be one reason why such people are dangerous; if they were concerned about the danger, they would not be inadvertent so often. . . .

whenever the offense carries the possibility of criminal conviction, for which a sentence of probation or imprisonment may be imposed. The method used is not to abrogate strict liability completely, but to provide that when conviction rests upon that basis the grade of the offense is reduced to a violation, which is not a "crime" and under Sections 1.04(5) and 6.02(4) may result in no sentence other than a fine, or a fine and forfeiture or other authorized civil penalty.

This position is affirmed not only with respect to offenses defined by the penal code; it is superimposed on the entire corpus of the law so far as penal sanctions are involved. Since most strict liability offenses involve special regulatory legislation, normally found in titles of a code other than the criminal title, this superimposition is essential if the principle of no criminality, probation or imprisonment for strict liability offenses is to be made effective.

. . . It has been argued, and the argument undoubtedly will be repeated, that strict liability is necessary for enforcement in a number of the areas where it obtains. But if practical enforcement precludes litigation of the culpability of alleged deviation from legal requirements, the enforcers cannot rightly demand the use of penal sanctions for the purpose. Crime does and should mean condemnation and no court should have to pass that judgment unless it can declare that the defendant's act was culpable. This is too fundamental to be compromised. The law goes far enough if it permits the imposition of a monetary penalty in cases where strict liability has been imposed.

NOTE ON CULPABILITY AND EXCUSE

The principle of culpability, which we have thus far explored principally in the context of the mens rea elements of crimes, finds expression also in an important body of law having to do with excuses to criminal conduct — the defenses of intoxication and legal insanity; the defense of lack of legal responsibility more generally, such as the defense of alcoholism or narcotics addiction; the defense of duress or compulsion. These defenses are integrally related to the problems of actus reus and mens rea (in its special sense) with which we have so far been dealing; they all respond to fundamental principles in terms of which persons can be justly punished for their wrongful actions. For pedagogical reasons we defer their consideration until Chapter 8, Section B.

d.   Mistake of Law

PEOPLE v. MARRERO

New York Court of Appeals
69 N.Y.2d 382, 507 N.E.2d 1068 (1987)

[Defendant was arrested in a Manhattan social club for unlicensed possession of a loaded .38 caliber automatic pistol, in violation of Penal Law §265.02. A provision of that statute (§265.02 (a)(1)(a)) expressly exempted "peace officers," a term defined in Criminal Procedure Law (CPL) §§1.20 and 2.10 to include "correction officers of any state correctional facility or of any penal correctional institution." At the time of the arrest the defendant protested that he was a Federal corrections officer and therefore exempted from §265.02. He was nonetheless charged with violation of that provision. Thereafter, his pretrial motion to dismiss the indictment was granted on the ground that he was a peace officer within the meaning of the statutory exemption. The People appealed and the Appellate Division reinstated the indictment, holding, by a 3-2 vote, that the defendant was not a "peace officer" within the meaning of CPL §§1.20, 2.10. The defendant was thereupon tried before a jury and convicted, the trial court rejecting his request for a jury instruction that it would be a good defense if he reasonably believed that the statutory exemption for peace officers applied to him as a Federal correctional officer. The Appellate Division affirmed, and the defendant appealed.]

BELLACOSA, J. . . . The central issue is whether defendant's personal misreading or misunderstanding of a statute may excuse criminal conduct in the circumstances of this case.

The common-law rule on mistake of law was clearly articulated in Gardner v. People, (62 N.Y. 299). In *Gardner*, the defendants misread a statute and mistakenly believed that their conduct was legal. The court insisted, however, that the "mistake of law" did not relieve the defendants of criminal liability. . . . This is to be contrasted with People v. Weiss, 276 N.Y. 384, 12 N.E.2d 514 [1938,] where, in a kidnapping case, the trial court precluded testimony that the defendants acted with the honest belief that seizing and confining the [victim] was done with "authority of law." We held it was error to exclude such testimony since a good-faith belief in the legality of the conduct would negate an express and necessary element of the crime of kidnapping, i.e., intent, without authority of law, to confine or imprison another.[a] . . .

The desirability of the *Gardner*-type outcome . . . is underscored by Justice Holmes' statement: "It is no doubt true that there are many cases in which the criminal could not have known that he was breaking the law, but to admit the excuse at all would be to encourage ignorance where the lawmaker has determined to make men know and obey, and justice to the individual is rightly outweighed by the larger interests on the other side of the scales" (Holmes, The Common Law, at 48 [1881]).

The revisors of New York's Penal Law intended no fundamental departure from this common-law rule in Penal Law §15.20, which provides in pertinent part:

> 2. A person is not relieved of criminal liability for conduct because he engaged in such conduct under a mistaken belief that it does not, as a matter of law, constitute an offense, unless such mistaken belief is founded upon an official statement of the law contained in (a) a statute or other enactment . . . (d) an interpretation of the statute or law relating to the offense, officially made or issued by a public servant, agency, or body legally charged or empowered with the responsibility or privilege of administering, enforcing or interpreting such statute or law.

a. In *Weiss*, the defendants were convicted of kidnapping a person suspected of the murder of the Lindbergh child. Kidnapping was defined as follows: "A person who wilfully: 1. Seizes, confines, inveigles, or kidnaps another, with intent to cause him, without authority of law, to be confined or imprisoned within this state, . . . against his will . . . is guilty of kidnapping." The defendants were denied the right to introduce testimony showing that they were led to believe that they had been authorized by a law enforcement officer to seize the victim. The Court of Appeals reversed, on the ground that such belief, if found by the jury to exist, would show that defendants lacked the intent to confine the victim, as the statute required, "without authority of law." — EDS.

The defendant claims as a first prong of his defense that he is entitled to raise the defense of mistake of law under section 15.20(2)(a) because his mistaken belief that his conduct was legal was founded upon an official statement of the law contained in the statute itself. Defendant argues that his mistaken interpretation of the statute was reasonable in view of the alleged ambiguous wording of the peace officer exemption statute, and that his "reasonable" interpretation of an "official statement" is enough to satisfy the requirements of subdivision (2)(a)....

The prosecution . . . counters defendant's argument by asserting that one cannot claim the protection of mistake of law under section 15.20(2)(a) simply by misconstruing the meaning of a statute but must instead establish that the statute relied on actually permitted the conduct in question and was only later found to be erroneous. To buttress that argument, the People analogize New York's official statement defense to the approach taken by the Model Penal Code (MPC). Section 2.04 of the MPC provides:

> (3) A belief that conduct does not legally constitute an offense is a defense to a prosecution for that offense based upon such conduct when . . . (b) he acts in reasonable reliance upon an official statement of the law, *afterward determined to be invalid or erroneous,* contained in (i) a statute or other enactment (emphasis added).[b]

Although the drafters of the New York statute did not adopt the precise language of the Model Penal Code provision with the emphasized clause, it is evident and has long been believed that the Legislature intended the New York statute to be similarly construed....

It was early recognized that the "official statement" mistake of law defense was a statutory protection against prosecution based on reliance on a statute that did *in fact* authorize certain conduct. "It seems obvious that society must rely on some statement of the law, and that conduct which *is in fact* 'authorized' . . . should not be subsequently condemned. The threat of punishment under these circumstances can have no deterrent effect unless the actor doubts the validity of the official pronouncement — *a questioning of authority that is itself undesirable*" (Note, Proposed Penal Law of New York, 64 Colum. L. Rev. 1469, 1486 [emphasis added]). While providing a narrow escape hatch, the idea was simultaneously to encourage the public to read and rely on official statements of the law, not to have individuals conveniently and personally question the validity and interpretation of the law and act on that basis. If later the statute was invalidated, one who mistakenly acted in reliance on the authorizing statute would be relieved of criminal liability. That makes sense and is fair. To go further does not make sense and would create a legal chaos based on individual selectivity....

Strong public policy reasons underlie the legislative mandate and intent which we perceive in rejecting defendant's construction of New York's mistake

---

b. Suppose, for example, that a provision in a state anti-water pollution law exempts nonprofit corporations. Relying on that provision a nonprofit corporation dumps water in a way that would be a violation of the statute were it not for the exemption. In a prosecution of the corporation, the trial court finds this exemption invalid on some ground (perhaps because it conflicts with some federal legislation). The corporation would have a defense under this Model Penal Code provision. — Eds.

of law defense statute. If defendant's argument were accepted, the exception would swallow the rule. Mistakes about the law would be encouraged, rather than respect for and adherence to law. There would be an infinite number of mistake of law defenses which could be devised from a good-faith, perhaps reasonable but mistaken, interpretation of criminal statutes, many of which are concededly complex. Even more troublesome are the opportunities for wrong-minded individuals to contrive in bad faith solely to get an exculpatory notion before the jury. These are not in terrorem arguments disrespectful of appropriate adjudicative procedures; rather, they are the realistic and practical consequences were the dissenters' views to prevail. Our holding comports with a statutory scheme which was not designed to allow false and diversionary strategems. . . . This would not serve the ends of justice but rather would serve game playing and evasion from properly imposed criminal responsibility.

Accordingly, the order of the Appellate Division should be affirmed.

HANCOCK, J. (dissenting). . . . The basic difference which divides the court may be simply put. Suppose the case of a man who has committed an act which is criminal not because it is inherently wrong or immoral but solely because it violates a criminal statute. He has committed the act in complete good faith under the mistaken but entirely reasonable assumption that the act does not constitute an offense because it is permitted by the wording of the statute. Does the law require that this man be punished? The majority says that it does and holds that (1) Penal Law §15.02(2)(a) must be construed so that the man is precluded from offering a defense based on his mistake of law and (2) such construction is compelled by prevailing considerations of public policy and criminal jurisprudence. We take issue with the majority on both propositions.

There can be no question that under the view that the purpose of the criminal justice system is to punish blameworthiness or "choosing freely to do wrong"[1] our supposed man who has acted innocently and without any intent to do wrong should not be punished. . . . Since he has not knowingly committed a wrong there can be no reason for society to exact retribution. Because the man is law-abiding and would not have acted but for his mistaken assumption as to the law, there is no need for punishment to deter him from further unlawful conduct. Traditionally, however, under the ancient rule of Anglo-American common law that ignorance or mistake of law is no excuse, our supposed man would be punished.

The maxim "*ignorantia legis neminem excusat*" finds its roots in Medieval law. . . . Various justifications have been offered for the rule, but all are frankly pragmatic and utilitarian — preferring the interests of society (e.g., in deterring criminal conduct, fostering orderly judicial administration, and preserving the primacy of the rule of law) to the interest of the individual in being free from punishment except for intentionally engaging in conduct which he knows is criminal.

Today there is widespread criticism of the common-law rule mandating categorical preclusion of the mistake of law defense. The utilitarian arguments for retaining the rule have been drawn into serious question but the fundamental

---

1. "Historically, our substantive criminal law is based upon a theory of punishing the vicious will. It postulates a free agent confronted with a choice between doing right and doing wrong and choosing freely to do wrong" (Pound, Introduction to Sayre, Cases on Criminal Law [1927], quoted in Morissette v. United States, 342 U.S. 246, 250, n. 4).

objection is that it is simply wrong to punish someone who, in good-faith reliance on the wording of a statute, believed that what he was doing was lawful. . . . This basic objection to the maxim "*ignorantia legis neminem excusat*" may have had less force in ancient times when most crimes consisted of acts which by their very nature were recognized as evil. In modern times, however, with the profusion of legislation making otherwise lawful conduct criminal (*malum prohibitum*), the "common law fiction that every man is presumed to know the law has become indefensible in fact or logic."

With this background we proceed to a discussion of our disagreement with the majority's construction of Penal Law §15.20(2)(a) and the policy and jurisprudential arguments made in support of that construction. . . .

It is difficult to imagine a case more squarely within the wording of Penal Law §15.20(2)(a) or one more fitted to what appears clearly to be the intended purpose of the statute than the one before us. . . .

Defendant's mistaken belief that, as a Federal corrections officer, he could legally carry a loaded weapon without a license was based on the express exemption from criminal liability under Penal Law §265.02 accorded . . . to "peace officers" as defined in the Criminal Procedure Law and on his reading of the statutory definition for "peace officer" . . . as meaning a correction officer "of *any* penal correctional institution" (emphasis added), including an institution not operated by New York State. Thus, he concluded erroneously that, as a corrections officer in a Federal prison, he was a "peace officer" and, as such, exempt by the express terms of Penal Law §265.02(a)(1)(a). This mistaken belief, based in good faith on the statute defining "peace officer" is, defendant contends, the precise sort of "mistaken belief . . . founded upon an official statement of the law contained in . . . a statute or other enactment" which gives rise to a mistake of law defense under Penal Law §15.20(2)(a). He points out, of course, that when he acted in reliance on his belief he had no way of foreseeing that a court would eventually resolve the question of the statute's meaning against him and rule that his belief had been mistaken, as three of the five-member panel at the Appellate Division ultimately did in the first appeal.

The majority, however, has accepted the People's argument that to have a defense under Penal Law §15.20(2)(a) "a defendant must show that the statute *permitted his conduct*, not merely that he believed it did." . . .

Nothing in the statutory language suggests the interpretation urged by the People and adopted by the majority. . . . It is self-evident that in enacting Penal Law §15.20(2) as part of the revision and modernization of the Penal Law the Legislature intended to effect a needed reform by abolishing what had long been considered the unjust archaic common-law rule totally prohibiting mistake of law as a defense. . . .

The majority construes the statute, however, so as to rule out *any* defense based on mistake of law. In so doing, it defeats the only possible purpose for the statute's enactment and resurrects the very rule which the Legislature rejected in enacting Penal Law §15.20(2)(a) as part of its modernization and reform of the Penal Law. . . .

Instead, the majority bases its decision on an analogous provision in the Model Penal Code and concludes that despite its totally different wording and meaning Penal Law §15.20(2)(a) should be read as if it were Model Penal Code §2.04(3)(b)(i). But New York in revising the Penal Law did not adopt the Model Penal Code. As in New Jersey, which generally adopted the Model Penal Code

but added one section which is substantially more liberal,[10] New York followed
parts of the Model Penal Code provisions and rejected others. . . .

Thus, the precise phrase in the Model Penal Code limiting the defense under
section 2.04(3)(b)(i) to reliance on a statute "afterward determined to be invalid or erroneous" which, if present, would support the majority's narrow construction of the New York statute, is omitted from Penal Law §15.20(2)(a). How
the Legislature can be assumed to have enacted the very language which it has
specifically rejected is not explained. . . .

REGINA v. SMITH (DAVID), [1974] 2 Q.B. 354: [In preparing to leave the
apartment he had been renting, the defendant damaged some wall panels and
floor boards in order to retrieve stereo wiring he had installed with the land-
lord's permission behind wall panels and floor boards of his own construction.
He was charged with violating the Criminal Damage Act, which read: "A person
who without lawful excuse destroys or damages any property belonging to another intending to destroy or damage any such property or being reckless as to
whether any such property would be destroyed or damaged, shall be guilty of an
offence." His defense, in his own words, was: "Look, how can I be done in for
smashing my own property. I put the flooring and that in, so if I want to pull it
down it's a matter for me." He was convicted under an instruction that told the
jury that "belief by the defendant . . . that he had the right to do what he did is
not lawful excuse within the meaning of the Act . . . because in law he had no
right to do what he did." On appeal, the prosecution argued that "the mental
element in the offence relates only to causing damage or to destroying property,
[so] that if in fact the property damaged or destroyed is shown to be another's
property the offence is committed although the defendant did not intend or
foresee damage to another person's property." The Court of Appeal reversed,
finding the jury instruction erroneous and stating:]

Construing the language of section 1(1) we have no doubt that the actus reus
is "destroying or damaging any property belonging to another." It is not possible
to exclude the words "belonging to another" which describes the "property."
Applying the ordinary principles of mens rea, the intention and recklessness and
the absence of lawful excuse required to constitute the offence have reference
to property belonging to another. It follows that in our judgment no offence is
committed under this section if a person destroys or causes damage to property
belonging to another if he does so in the honest though mistaken belief that the
property is his own, and provided that the belief is honestly held it is irrelevant
to consider whether or not it is a justifiable belief.

PROBLEMS

It is important to see why the results in People v. Weiss (discussed in *Marrero*)
and Regina v. Smith (David) are consistent with the basic doctrine that igno-

---

10. In addition to permitting defenses based on ignorance of the law and reasonable reliance
on official statements afterward determined to be invalid or erroneous, the New Jersey statute provides a defense, under the following broad provision, when: "(3) The actor otherwise diligently
pursues all means available to ascertain the meaning and application of the offense to his conduct
and honestly and in good faith concludes his conduct is not an offense in circumstances in which
a law abiding and prudent person would also so conclude." (N.J. Stat. Ann. §2C:2-4[c][3]).

rance of the law is no excuse. Consider Model Penal Code §2.04(1): "Ignorance or mistake as to a matter of fact *or law* is a defense if [it] negatives the purpose, belief, recklessness or negligence required to establish a material element of the offense." (Emphasis added.) Compare §2.02(9): "Neither knowledge nor recklessness or negligence as to whether conduct constitutes an offense or as to the existence, meaning or application of the law determining the elements of an offense is an element of the offense, unless the definition of the offense or the Code so provides." The relationship between these two provisions is articulated in Model Penal Code and Commentaries, Comment to §2.02 at 250 (1985):

> Subsection (9) states the conventional position that knowledge of the existence, meaning or application of the law determining the elements of an offense is not an element of that offense, except in the unusual situations where the law defining the offense or the Code so provides.
>
> It should be noted that the general principle that ignorance or mistake of law is no excuse is greatly overstated; it has no application, for example, when the circumstances made material by the definition of the offense include a legal element. Thus it is immaterial in theft, when claim of right is adduced in defense, that the claim involves a legal judgment as to the right of property. Claim of right is a defense because the property must belong to someone else for the theft to occur and the defendant must have culpable awareness of that fact. Insofar as this point is involved, there is no need to state a special principle; the legal element involved is simply an aspect of the attendant circumstances, with respect to which knowledge, recklessness or negligence, as the case may be, is required for culpability. . . . The law involved is not the law defining the offense; it is some other legal rule that characterizes the attendant circumstances that are material to the offense.
>
> The proper arena for the principle that ignorance or mistake of law does not afford an excuse is thus with respect to the particular law that sets forth the definition of the crime in question. It is knowledge of *that* law that is normally not a part of the crime, and it is ignorance or mistake as to *that* law that is denied defensive significance by this subsection of the Code and by the traditional common law approach to the issue.

On the foregoing analysis, how should the following cases be decided?

1. The defendant was a single woman who traveled with Leo Shuffelt from Vermont to Reno, Nevada, where Shuffelt instituted divorce proceedings against his wife, who was neither a Nevada resident nor present in Nevada. The Nevada judge entered a divorce decree, following which he married the defendant and Shuffelt. Upon return to Vermont, the defendant was prosecuted under a Vermont statute, commonly known as the *Blanket Act,* which provided: "A man with another man's wife, or a woman with another woman's husband, found in bed together, under circumstances affording presumption of an illicit intention, shall each be imprisoned in the state prison not more than three years or fined not more than $1,000." The defendant requested an instruction to the jury that an honest belief in the validity of the Nevada divorce and of her subsequent marriage to Shuffelt would be a defense to the prosecution. Is she entitled to this instruction? Would she be if she had requested an instruction that a *reasonable* belief would be a defense? See State v. Woods, 107 Vt. 354, 179 A. 1 (1935).

2. A physician, attending a patient whom he knows to be brain dead, takes steps to stop his heart, preliminary to removing it for a transplant. He believes the legislature in his jurisdiction has enacted a brain death statute. It hasn't, and the common law definition of death (cessation of heart functions) is in effect. Can the physician be convicted of *intentionally* killing his patient? On the one hand, ignorance of the law is no excuse. On the other hand, how can a person be found to have intentionally killed a person he believed already dead?

NOTE

The basic position of English and American law is, as was seen in *Marrero,* that it is no defense that the defendant mistakenly believed that the law did not prohibit his action. But suppose the defendant mistakenly believed that the law did prohibit his action, when in fact it did not. How should the law treat mistake of law in this situation? Consider the following case.

REGINA v. TAAFFE, [1983] 2 All E.R. 625 (Ct. App.). . . . The appellant drove a car into the green lane of the ferry terminal at Sheerness and told the customs officer who was on duty that he had nothing to declare. The car was searched . . . and inside were found to be five packages containing cannibis resin. Not unnaturally the search then moved to the body of the appellant himself, and strapped to his back and underneath his clothing were discovered three further packages also containing cannibis resin, the total quantity being that stated in the indictment.

The appellant was cautioned by the customs officer and was asked if he knew what the substances in the packages were. He replied, "No, I am waiting to find out, because if it is drugs . . ." and there his reply ended. So the officer then asked him, "What did you think was in the packages?" And to that he replied simply, "Money."

. . . The question is this: on the assumption that the following facts are established, has the alleged offence been committed? . . . (1) the appellant was enlisted by a third party in Holland to import a substance from that country into England in fraudulent evasion of the prohibition upon its importation and he did so import it; (2) that substance was in fact cannibis, the importation of which is prohibited by the Misuse of Drugs Act 1971; (3) the appellant mistakenly believed the substance to be currency; (4) currency is not subject to any such prohibition; (5) the appellant mistakenly believed that currency was the subject of a prohibition against importation. . . .

One starts with the premise that this is not an offense of absolute liability. It is plain, from the use of the word "knowingly" in section 170(2)[a] that the prosecution have the task of proving the existence of mens rea, the mental element of guilt. Mens rea in this context means the mental element required by the particular statute on the part of the defendant before the prosecution can succeed.

What then in this case was the relevant mental element which section 170(2) required to be proved? It seems to us that it was primarily knowledge that the substance which was being imported was a drug, or certainly was a substance of some sort the importation of which was prohibited. . . .

a. Customs and Excise Management Act, 1979, s. 170(2): "If any person is, in relation to any goods, in any way knowingly concerned in any fraudulent evasion . . . (b) of any prohibition . . . in force with respect to the goods . . . he shall be guilty of an offense. . . ." Ed.

What then if the jury in the present case had been asked to decide the matter and had come to the conclusion that the appellant might have believed that what he was importing was currency and not prohibited drugs? He is to be judged against the facts that he believed them to be. Had this indeed been currency and not cannabis, no offence would have been committed. Does it make any difference that the appellant thought wrongly that by clandestinely importing currency he was committing an offence? Mr. Aylwin [for the prosecution] strongly submits that it does. He suggests that a man in this situation has to be judged according to the total mistake that he has made, both the mistake with regard to the fact of what he was carrying and also [the] mistake of law as to the effect of carrying that substance. We think that submission is wrong. It no doubt made his actions morally reprehensible. It did not, in our judgment, turn what he, for the purpose of argument, believed to be the importation of currency into the commission of a criminal offence. His views on the law as to the importation of currency were to that extent, in our judgment, irrelevant. . . .

[F]or the reasons we have endeavoured to give, this appeal must be allowed and the conviction quashed.

Affirmed [1984] A.C. 539 (House of Lords).]

CHEEK v. UNITED STATES

Supreme Court of the United States
498 U.S. 192 (1991)

[Cheek, a professional pilot for American Airlines, was convicted of a number of counts of willfully failing to file a federal income tax return for a number of years in violation of 26 U.S.C. §7201, which provides that any person is guilty of a felony "who willfully attempts in any manner to evade or defeat any tax imposed by this title or the payment thereof." He was also convicted under §7203(1) for the misdemeanor offense of "willfully" failing to make a return required by law. His defense was that based on information he received from a group opposing the institution of taxation, he sincerely believed that under the tax laws he owed no taxes, including taxes on his wages, and that these laws were unconstitutional.

[After the trial judge gave his initial instructions, the jury sent out a note saying that it could not reach a verdict because "[w]e are divided on the issue as to if Mr. Cheek honestly & reasonably believed that he was not required to pay income tax." Thereupon the trial judge further instructed the jury that "[a]n honest but unreasonable belief is not a defense and does not negate willfulness," and that "[a]dvice or research resulting in the conclusion that wages of a privately employed person are not income or that the tax laws are unconstitutional is not objectively reasonable and cannot serve as the basis for a good faith misunderstanding of the law defense." The judge also instructed the jury that "[p]ersistent refusal to acknowledge the law does not constitute a good faith misunderstanding of the law."

[Cheek appealed his convictions, charging the trial judge with error in instructing that only an objectively reasonable misunderstanding of the law negates the statutory willfulness requirement. The Court of Appeals affirmed, and the Supreme Court granted certiorari.]

JUSTICE WHITE delivered the opinion of the Court.

The general rule that ignorance of the law or a mistake of law is no defense to criminal prosecution is deeply rooted in the American legal system. Based on the notion that the law is definite and knowable, the common law presumed that every person knew the law. The common-law rule has been applied by the Court in numerous cases construing criminal statutes.

The proliferation of statutes and regulations has sometimes made it difficult for the average citizen to know and comprehend the extent of the duties and obligations imposed by the tax laws. Congress has accordingly softened the impact of the common-law presumption by making specific intent to violate the law an element of certain federal criminal tax offenses. Thus, the Court almost 60 years ago interpreted the statutory term "willfully" as used in the federal criminal tax statutes as carving out an exception to the traditional rule. This special treatment of criminal tax offenses is largely due to the complexity of the tax laws. In United States v. Murdock, 290 U.S. 389 (1933), the Court recognized that:

> Congress did not intend that a person, by reason of a bona fide misunderstanding as to his liability for the tax, as to his duty to make a return, or as to the adequacy of the records he maintained, should become a criminal by his mere failure to measure up to the prescribed standard of conduct.

Id., at 396. The Court held that the defendant was entitled to an instruction with respect to whether he acted in good faith based on his actual belief. In *Murdock,* the Court interpreted the term "willfully" as used in the criminal tax statutes generally to mean "an act done with a bad purpose," or with "an evil motive."

Subsequent decisions have refined this proposition. . . . Taken together, [these cases] conclusively establish that the standard for the statutory willfulness requirement is the "voluntary, intentional violation of a known legal duty."

Cheek accepts [this] definition of willfulness, but . . . he challenges the ruling that a good-faith misunderstanding of the law or a good-faith belief that one is not violating the law, if it is to negate willfulness, must be objectively reasonable. We agree that the Court of Appeals and the District Court erred in this respect.

Willfulness, as construed by our prior decisions in criminal tax cases, requires the Government to prove that the law imposed a duty on the defendant, that the defendant knew of this duty, and that he voluntarily and intentionally violated that duty. We deal first with the case where the issue is whether the defendant knew of the duty purportedly imposed by the provision of the statute or regulation he is accused of violating, a case in which there is no claim that the provision at issue is invalid. In such a case, if the Government proves actual knowledge of the pertinent legal duty, the prosecution, without more, has satisfied the knowledge component of the willfulness requirement. But carrying this burden requires negating a defendant's claim of ignorance of the law or a claim that because of a misunderstanding of the law, he had a good-faith belief that he was not violating any of the provisions of the tax laws. This is so because one cannot be aware that the law imposes a duty upon him and yet be ignorant of it, misunderstand the law, or believe that the duty does not exist. In the end, the issue is whether, based on all the evidence, the Government has proved that the defendant was aware of the duty at issue, which cannot be true if the jury credits a good-faith misunderstanding and belief submission, whether or not the claimed belief or misunderstanding is objectively reasonable.

In this case, if Cheek asserted that he truly believed that the Internal Revenue Code did not purport to treat wages as income, and the jury believed him, the Government would not have carried its burden to prove willfulness, however unreasonable a court might deem such a belief. . . .

We thus disagree with the Court of Appeals' requirement that a claimed good-faith belief must be objectively reasonable if it is to be considered as possibly negating the Government's evidence purporting to show a defendant's awareness of the legal duty at issue. . . .

It was therefore error to instruct the jury to disregard evidence of Cheek's understanding that, within the meaning of the tax laws, he was not a person required to file a return or to pay income taxes and that wages are not taxable income, as incredible as such misunderstandings of and beliefs about the law might be. Of course, the more unreasonable the asserted beliefs or misunderstandings are, the more likely the jury will consider them to be nothing more than simple disagreement with known legal duties imposed by the tax laws and will find that the Government has carried its burden of providing knowledge.

Cheek asserted in the trial court that he should be acquitted because he believed in good faith that the income tax law is unconstitutional as applied to him and thus could not legally impose any duty upon him of which he should have been aware. Such a submission is unsound, not because Cheek's constitutional arguments are not objectively reasonable or frivolous, which they surely are, but because [*Murdock* and subsequent cases do] not support such a position. Those cases construed the willfulness requirement in the criminal provisions of the Internal Revenue Code to require proof of knowledge of the law. This was because in "our complex tax system, uncertainty often arises even among taxpayers who earnestly wish to follow the law" and " 'it is not the purpose of the law to penalize frank difference of opinion or innocent errors made despite the exercise of reasonable care.' " United State v. Bishop, 412 US. 346, 360-361 (1973).

Claims that some of the provisions of the tax code are unconstitutional are submissions of a different order. They do not arise from innocent mistakes caused by the complexity of the Internal Revenue Code. Rather, they reveal full knowledge of the provisions at issue and a studied conclusion, however wrong, that those provisions are invalid and unenforceable. Thus in this case, Cheek paid his taxes for years, but after attending various seminars and based on his own study, he concluded that the income tax laws could not constitutionally require him to pay a tax.

We do not believe that Congress contemplated that such a taxpayer, without risking criminal prosecution, could ignore the duties imposed upon him by the Internal Revenue Code and refuse to utilize the mechanisms provided by Congress to present his claims of invalidity to the courts and to abide by their decisions. There is no doubt that Cheek, from year to year, was free to pay the tax that the law purported to require, file for a refund and, if denied, present his claims of invalidity, constitutional or otherwise, to the courts. See 26 U.S.C. §7422. Also, without paying the tax, he could have challenged claims of tax deficiencies in the Tax Court, 26 U.S.C. §6213, with the right to appeal to a higher court if unsuccessful. §7482(a)(1). Cheek took neither course in some years, and when he did was unwilling to accept the outcome. . . . Of course, Cheek was free in this very case to present his claims of invalidity and have them adjudicated, but like defendants in criminal cases in other contexts, who "willfully" refuse to comply with the duties placed upon them by the law, he must take the risk of being wrong.

We thus hold that in a case like this, a defendant's views about the validity of the tax statutes are irrelevant to the issue of willfulness, need not be heard by the jury, and if they are, an instruction to disregard them would be proper. For this purpose, it makes no difference whether the claims of invalidity are frivolous or have substance. It was therefore not error in this case for the District Judge to instruct the jury not to consider Cheek's claims that the tax laws were unconstitutional. However, it was error for the court to instruct the jury that petitioner's asserted beliefs that wages are not income and that he was not a taxpayer within the meaning of the Internal Revenue Code should not be considered by the jury in determining whether Cheek had acted willfully.

For the reasons set forth in the opinion above, the judgment of the Court of Appeals is vacated, and the case is remanded for further proceedings consistent with this opinion.

NOTE

Ignorance of the law *is* a defense, obviously it must be, when the crime by its terms requires that a person know of the existence of the prohibition. See Model Penal Code §2.04(1)(b). However, it may be highly problematic whether the terms of a statute do state such a requirement.

For example, federal decisions since *Cheek* have declined to extend its interpretation of "willfully" beyond the context of federal tax crimes. In United States v. Hildebrandt, 961 F.2d 116 (8th Cir. 1992), the defendant was convicted of filing false tax forms in violation of 18 U.S.C. §1001, which prohibits "knowingly and willfully" making a fraudulent statement to a government agency. Defendant argued that under *Cheek* the statute required him to have actual knowledge that it was illegal to file the false form. The court disagreed, holding that *Cheek* applies only to the criminal tax laws, and that under 18 U.S.C. §1001 "the term 'willful' simply means that the defendant did the forbidden act 'deliberately and with knowledge.'" The court observed that *Cheek* was based on the complexity of the tax laws, whereas the defendant in this case "was convicted under a general criminal statute containing a straightforward prohibition against making false, fictitious, or fraudulent statements to the government."

The Supreme Court itself has reached different interpretations in different contexts. For example, in United States v. International Minerals & Chemical Corp., 402 U.S. 558 (1971), the Court considered a statute making it a crime for a person to "knowingly violat[e]" a regulation of the Interstate Commerce Commission regarding the transportation of corrosive liquids. Did that mean that the defendant must be proven to have known of the existence and meaning of the regulation his actions violated, or was it sufficient to prove that the actions he knowingly did violated those regulations? The Court held for the latter by a 6 to 3 vote. But in Liparota v. United States, 471 U.S. 419 (1985), the Court had before it a statute governing food stamp fraud. The statute provided that "whoever knowingly uses, transfers, acquires, alters, or possesses coupons or author-ization cards in any manner not authorized by [the statute] or the regulations [of the Department of Agriculture]" is subject to fine and imprisonment. Does this mean that the defendant must be shown to have known of the regulation that his conduct violated, or only that he was aware of doing the actions that violated the regulation? This time the Court held for the former interpreta-tion, influenced by the concern that "to interpret the statute otherwise would be to criminalize a broad range of apparently innocent conduct." The court continued:

> For instance, §2024(b)(1) declares it criminal to use, transfer, acquire, alter, or possess food stamps in any manner not authorized by statute or regulations. The statute provides further that "[c]oupons issued to eligible households shall be used by them only to purchase food in retail food stores which have been approved for participation in the food stamp program *at prices prevailing in such stores*." 7 U.S.C. §2016(b) (emphasis added). This seems to be the *only* authorized use. A strict reading of the statute with no knowledge-of-illegality requirement would thus render criminal a food stamp recipient who, for example, used stamps to purchase food from a store that, unknown to him, charged higher than normal prices to food stamp program participants.

The dissent was less concerned, replying:

> The Court's opinion . . . provides [the] illustration . . . [of] someone who used food stamps to purchase groceries at inflated prices without realizing he was over-charged. I agree that such a person may not be convicted, but not for the reason given by the majority. The purchaser did not "knowingly" use the stamps in the proscribed manner, for he was unaware of the circumstances of the transaction that made it illegal.
>
> The majority and I would part company in result as well as rationale if the pur-chaser knew he was charged higher than normal prices but not that overcharging is prohibited. In such a case, he would have been aware of the nature of his actions, and therefore the purchase would have been "knowing." I would hold that such a mental state satisfies the statute. Under the Court's holding, as I understand it, that person could not be convicted because he did not know that his conduct was illegal.[3]

In Michael Vitiello, Does Culpability Matter?: Statutory Construction Under 42 U.S.C. §6928, 6 Tulane Env. L.J. 187 (1993), Professor Vitiello critically re-views the efforts of the federal courts to interpret the language of the Resource Conservation and Recovery Act (governing the disposition of hazardous wastes) that prohibits a person from "knowingly" disposing of regulated wastes in speci-fied circumstances. At pages 235-246 he reviews the bearing of *Morissette, Interna-tional Minerals,* and *Liparota* on the question of when the knowledge requirement extends to matters of law.

More recently the Court faced another ambiguous statute and was again influ-enced by wanting to avoid criminalizing otherwise innocent conduct. Ratzlaf v.

---

3. The appropriate prosecutorial target in such a situation would of course be the seller rather than the purchaser. I have no doubt that every prosecutor in the country would agree. The discus-sion of this hypothetical is wholly academic. . . .

United States, 114 S. Ct. 665 (1994). Ratzlaf sought to discharge a large gambling debt owed an importunate Reno casino by presenting it with $100,000 in cash. The casino's cashier explained to Ratzlaf that if it accepted the cash the casino would have to report the transaction to state and federal authorities. However, he told Ratzlaf, the casino could accept a cashier's check for the full amount without triggering any reporting requirements. The casino then placed a limousine at Ratzlaf's disposal and assigned an employee to accompany him to banks in the vicinity. Informed that banks too are required to report cash transactions in excess of $10,000, Ratzlaf purchased cashier's checks, each for less than $10,000 and each from a different bank. The casino was satisfied, but the United States Attorney was not. The prosecutor obtained a conviction against Raztlaf under a federal law making it illegal to "structure" a transaction, that is, to break up a single transaction above the reporting threshold into two or more separate transactions for the purpose of evading a financial institution's reporting requirement. The statute made "a person willfully violating" this antistructuring provision subject to criminal penalties. The Supreme Court reversed the conviction, holding that the prosecution had to prove not only knowledge of the bank's reporting requirement, but also knowledge that the structuring he undertook to evade it constituted a criminal offense. The Court declined to accept the government's argument that currency structuring is so obviously evil that the willfulness requirement is satisfied irrespective of the defendant's knowledge of the illegality of structuring. It offered a number of examples of "innocent" structuring, such as those designed to avoid an audit, to decrease the likelihood of burglary, or to keep a former spouse unaware of the depositor's wealth. More generally, it observed, quoting a lower court, "courts have noted many occasions on which persons, without violating any law, may structure transactions in order to avoid the impact of some regulation or tax."

UNITED STATES v. ALBERTINI

United States Court of Appeals, 9th Circuit
830 F.2d 985 (1987)

[Defendant engaged in a peace demonstration on a naval base in Hawaii after receiving from its commander a "bar letter" which prohibited him from entering the base. His entry constituted a violation of 18 U.S.C. §1832, and he was convicted under that provision. On appeal, the Ninth Circuit (*Albertini I*) reversed the conviction on the ground that the First Amendment protected his right to demonstrate at the base. Thereupon, after consulting with counsel, he demonstrated several more times, in defiance of another bar order, and was again prosecuted. The government petitioned for certiorari from *Albertini I* about this time, but the Supreme Court did not accept review until after the second group of demonstrations. The Supreme Court eventually reversed the Ninth Circuit's decision in *Albertini I* and held that the First Amendment did not preclude convicting him for demonstrating in defiance of a bar order. Thereupon the government pressed its prosecution for the second group of demonstrations (those which occurred after *Albertini I* but before the Supreme Court granted certiorari) and obtained a conviction. Albertini appealed, arguing that due process precluded the retroactive application of the Supreme Court's decision reversing *Albertini I* (which had upheld the legality of his conduct). In its second *Albertini* decision (*Albertini II*) the Ninth Circuit agreed and reversed his conviction for the second group of demonstrations, writing the following opinion:]

GOODWIN, J. . . . The government claims that the litigation in which Albertini's claims were ultimately resolved against him by the Supreme Court was a unitary case or controversy and that this court could create no window of opportunity to engage in challenged conduct while Supreme Court review was still a possibility. Albertini says that after he received a favorable decision from this court, and at least before the petition for certiorari was granted, he was acting within his adjudicated legal rights and had a due process right to rely upon the judgment of this court.

The United States Constitution provides that neither Congress nor any state shall pass any ex post facto law. The prohibition against ex post facto enactments bans "[e]very law that makes an action done before the passing of the law, and which was innocent when done, criminal; and punishes such action."

Although the ex post facto clause applies to the legislature and not to the courts, "the principle on which the Clause is based — the notion that persons have a right to fair warning of that conduct which will give rise to criminal penalties — is fundamental to our concept of constitutional liberty." Marks v. United States, 430 U.S. 188, 191. . . .

In effect, Albertini obtained a declaratory judgment from this court that the actions in which he engaged were lawful. If the due process clause is to mean anything, it should mean that a person who holds the latest controlling court opinion declaring his activities constitutionally protected should be able to depend on that ruling to protect like activities from criminal conviction until that opinion is reversed, or at least until the Supreme Court has granted certiorari.[2] . . .

[T]he government argued that mistake of law is never a defense. There is an exception to the mistake of law doctrine, however, in circumstances where the mistake results from the defendant's reasonable reliance upon an official — but mistaken or later overruled — statement of the law. "It would be an act of 'intolerable injustice' to hold criminally liable a person who had engaged in certain conduct in reasonable reliance upon a judicial opinion instructing that such conduct is legal." Kratz [v. Kratz, 477 F. Supp. 468, 481 (E.D. Pa. 1979)]. As delineated by Section 2.04 of the Model Penal Code, the doctrine may in some circumstances protect a defendant's reasonable reliance on official advisory opinions. . . .

Albertini acted during a window of time when he reasonably believed his acts were protected under *Albertini [I]*. He cannot be convicted for acting in reliance on that opinion at least until the Supreme Court has granted certiorari. To hold otherwise would sanction a kind of "entrapment" by the government — convicting Albertini for acts that the government has told him are protected by the first amendment against prosecution. . . .

"When the 'entrapment' has been caused by a judicial opinion, the argument in favor of recognizing the reliance defense is even more compelling, since

2. We do not . . . reach the issue whether Albertini would have been justified in relying upon *Albertini [I]* in the period after the Supreme Court granted certiorari and before it reversed.

courts are the very entities charged with interpreting the law." *Kratz*, 477 F. Supp. at 482 n. 51. . . .

Reversed.

NOTES

1. Questions: What should be the result if someone not a party to *Albertini I* had participated in the second series of demonstrations, and had relied, as Albertini did, on that decision? Is there any reason why that person should be less entitled to rely on that decision than Albertini himself?

In footnote 2 the court of appeals left open the question of whether a conviction would have been proper for demonstrations that took place after the Supreme Court granted certiorari. Why should it matter whether the Supreme Court has granted certiorari or instead is still considering whether to grant it, so long as the time for review had not lapsed?

Suppose Albertini is president of a company that discharges toxic pollutants into a nearby river. His conviction of violating an environmental regulation is reversed by the court of appeals on the ground that the regulation was not promulgated by the regulatory agency in accordance with required procedures. Albertini thereupon resumes company operations and is prosecuted again, while at about the same time the government petitions for certiorari. If the Supreme Court then grants certiorari and subsequently holds that the regulations were properly promulgated, would the defendant have a good defense to the violations committed after the court of appeals decision but before the grant of certiorari? Could *Albertini II* be distinguished?

2. In Hopkins v. State, 193 Md. 489, 69 A.2d 456 (1950), the defendant was convicted of violating a statute making it unlawful to erect or maintain any sign intended to aid in the solicitation of performance of marriages. He had erected signs that read: "Rev. W. F. Hopkins" and "W. F. Hopkins, Notary Public, Information." On appeal he argued that the trial judge erred in excluding testimony offered to show that the State's Attorney advised him before he erected the signs that they would not violate the law. The Maryland Supreme Court affirmed his conviction, stating:

> It is generally held that the advice of counsel, even though followed in good faith, furnishes no excuse to a person for violating the law and cannot be relied upon as a defense in a criminal action. . . . Moreover, advice given by a public official, even a State's Attorney, that a contemplated act is not criminal will not excuse an offender if, as a matter of law, the act performed did amount to a violation of the law. . . . These rules are founded upon the maxim that ignorance of the law will not excuse its violation. If an accused could be exempted from punishment for crime by reason of the advice of counsel, such advice would become paramount to the law. . . .
>
> In the case at bar defendant did not claim that the State's Attorney misled him regarding any facts of the case, but only that the State's Attorney advised him as to the law based upon the facts. Defendant was aware of the penal statute enacted by the Legislature. He knew what he wanted to do, and he did the thing he intended to do. He claims merely that he was given advice regarding his legal rights. . . . If the right of a person to erect a sign of a certain type and size depends upon the

construction and application of a penal statute, and the right is somewhat doubtful, he erects the sign at his peril. In other words, a person who commits an act
which the law declares to be criminal cannot be excused from punishment upon
the theory that he misconstrued or misapplied the law.

3. In Cox v. Louisiana, 379 U.S. 559 (1965), the defendant was convicted of
violating a Louisiana statute prohibiting "pickets or parades in or near a building housing a court of the State of Louisiana" with intent to interfere with the
administration of justice. The case arose out of defendant's leadership of a civil
rights demonstration protesting the arrest and prosecution of a number of students the previous day. Defendant and a group of 2,000 persons paraded and
demonstrated on the far side of the street from the courthouse, about 100 feet
from the courthouse steps. The Supreme Court reversed the conviction on due
process grounds, relying on the fact that the city officials present, the police
chief and the sheriff, gave permission for the demonstration to take place across
the street from the courthouse.

The Court, noting the lack of specificity in the statutory term "near," stated:

> It is clear that the statute, with respect to the determination of how near the court-
> house a particular demonstration can be, foresees a degree of on-the-spot adminis-
> trative interpretation of how "near" the courthouse a particular demonstration
> might take place. . . . This administrative discretion to construe the term "near"
> concerns a limited control of the streets and other areas in the immediate vicinity
> of the courthouse and is the type of narrow discretion which this Court has recog-
> nized as the proper role of responsible officials in making determinations concern-
> ing the time, place, duration, and manner of demonstrations. . . . Nor does this
> limited administrative regulation of traffic, which the Court has consistently rec-
> ognized as necessary and permissible, constitute a waiver of law which is beyond
> the power of the police. Obviously telling demonstrators how far from the court-
> house steps is "near" the courthouse for purposes of a permissible peaceful dem-
> onstration is a far cry from allowing one to commit, for example, murder, or
> robbery. . . . [A]fter the public officials acted as they did, to sustain appellant's later
> conviction for demonstrating where they told him he could "would be to sanction
> an indefensible sort of entrapment by the State — convicting a citizen for exercis-
> ing a privilege which the State had clearly told him was available to him." [Raley v.
> Ohio,] 360 U.S. at 426. The Due Process Clause does not permit convictions to be
> obtained under such circumstances.

Justice Clark was one of the dissenters. He stated:

> One hardly needed an on-the-spot administrative decision that the demonstration
> was "near" the courthouse with the disturbance being conducted before the eyes
> and ringing in the ears of court officials, police officers and citizens throughout
> the courthouse. . . . Reading the facts in a way most favorable to the appellant
> would, in my opinion, establish only that the Chief of Police consented to the dem-
> onstration at that location. However, if the Chief's action be consent, I never knew
> until today that a law enforcement official — city, state or national — could forgive
> a breach of the criminal laws.

4. The Model Penal Code proposes in §2.04(3) a limited defense based on a
reasonable belief on the part of the defendant that the law is such that his conduct does not constitute an offense:

(3) A belief that conduct does not legally constitute an offense is a defense to a prosecution for that offense based upon such conduct when:

(a) the statute or other enactment defining the offense is not known to the actor and has not been published or otherwise reasonably made available prior to the conduct alleged; or

(b) he acts in reasonable reliance upon an official statement of the law, afterward determined to be invalid or erroneous, contained in (i) a statute or other enactment; (ii) a judicial decision, opinion or judgment; (iii) an administrative order or grant of permission; or (iv) an official interpretation of the public officer or body charged by law with responsibility for the interpretation, administration or enforcement of the law defining the offense.[a]

See Model Penal Code and Commentaries, Comment to §2.04 at 274-275 (1985):

All of the categories dealt with in the formulation involve, for the most part, situations where the act charged is consistent with the entire law-abidingness of the actor, where the possibility of collusion is minimal, and where a judicial determination of the reasonableness of the belief in legality should not present substantial difficulty. It is hard, therefore, to see how any purpose can be served by a conviction. It should be added that in the area of regulatory offenses, where the defense would normally apply, penal sanctions are appropriate in general only for deliberate evasion or defiance. When less than this is involved, lesser sanctions should suffice, for these typically are situations where a single violation works no major public or private injury; it is persistent violations that must be brought to book. And obviously the defense afforded by this section would normally be available to a defendant only once; after a warning he can hardly have a reasonable basis for belief in the legality of his behavior.

Question: Does the Model Penal Code go far enough? Consider Lambert v. California, the decision that follows.

LAMBERT v. CALIFORNIA

Supreme Court of the United States
355 U.S. 225 (1957)

JUSTICE DOUGLAS delivered the opinion of the Court.

Section 52.38(a) of the Los Angeles Municipal Court defines "convicted person" as follows:

Any person who, subsequent to January 1, 1921, has been or hereafter is convicted of an offense punishable as a felony in the State of California, or who has been or who is hereafter convicted of any offense in any place other than the State of Cali-

---

a. A review of the cases from various jurisdictions dealing with what has come to be called the "official statement" mistake of law defense may be found in Annot., Criminal law: "official statement" mistake of law defense, 89 A.L.R.4th 1026 (1991). The principle appears to be widely accepted. For recent applications, see United States v. Levin, 973 F.2d 463, 468 (6th Cir. 1992); Commonwealth v. Twitchell, 416 Mass. 114, 617 N.E.2d 609 (1993). Most of the controversy centers on what constitutes an official statement on which the defendant is entitled to rely. For a recent study, see Note (SueAnn D. Billimack), Reliance on an Official Interpretation of the Law: The Defense's Appropriate Dimensions, 1993 U. Ill. L. Rev. 565 — EDS.

fornia, which offense, if committed in the State of California, would have been punishable as a felony.

Section 52.39 provides that it shall be unlawful for "any convicted person" to be or remain in Los Angeles for a period of more than five days without registering; it requires any person having a place of abode outside the city to register if he comes into the city on five occasions or more during a 30-day period; and it prescribes the information to be furnished the Chief of Police on registering.

Section 52.43(b) makes the failure to register a continuing offense, each day's failure constituting a separate offense.

Appellant, arrested on suspicion of another offense, was charged with a violation of this registration law. . . . The case was tried to a jury which found appellant guilty. The court fined her $250 and placed her on probation for three years. . . .

The registration provision, carrying criminal penalties, applies if a person has been convicted "of an offense punishable as a felony in the State of California" or, in case he has been convicted in another State if the offense "would have been punishable as a felony" had it been committed in California. No element of willfulness is by terms included in the ordinance nor read into it by the California court as a condition necessary for a conviction.

We must assume that appellant had no actual knowledge of the requirement that she register under this ordinance, as she offered proof of this defense which was refused. The question is whether a registration act of this character violates Due Process where it is applied to a person who has no actual knowledge of his duty to register, and where no showing is made of the probability of such knowledge.

. . . There is wide latitude on the lawmakers to declare an offense and to exclude elements of knowledge and diligence from its definition. . . . But we deal here with conduct that is wholly passive — mere failure to register. It is unlike the commission of acts, or the failure to act under circumstances that should alert the doer to the consequences of his deed. Cf. . . . United States v. Balint, 258 U.S. 250; United States v. Dotterweich, 320 U.S. 277, 284. The rule that "ignorance of the law will not excuse" . . . is deep in our law, as is the principle that of all the powers of local government, the police power is "one of the least limitable." . . . On the other hand, Due Process places some limits on its exercise. Engrained in our concept of Due Process is the requirement of notice. Notice is sometimes essential so that the citizen has the chance to defend charges. Notice is required before property interests are disturbed, before assessments are made, before penalties are assessed. Notice is required in a myriad of situations where a penalty or forfeiture might be suffered for mere failure to act. Recent cases illustrating the point . . . involved only property interests in civil litigation. But the principle is equally appropriate where a person, wholly passive and unaware of any wrongdoing, is brought to the bar of justice for condemnation in a criminal case.

Registration laws are common and their range is wide. . . . Many such laws are akin to licensing statutes in that they pertain to the regulation of business activities. But the present ordinance is entirely different. Violation of its provisions is unaccompanied by any activity whatever, mere presence in the city being the test. Moreover, circumstances which might move one to inquire as to the necessity of registration are completely lacking. At most the ordinance is but a law enforcement technique designed for the convenience of law enforcement agencies through which a list of the names and addresses of felons then residing in a given community is compiled. The disclosure is merely a compilation of former convictions already publicly recorded in the jurisdiction where obtained. Nevertheless, this registrant on first becoming aware of her duty to register was given no opportunity to comply with the law and avoid its penalty, even though her default was entirely innocent. She could but suffer the consequences of the ordinance, namely, conviction with the imposition of heavy criminal penalties thereunder. We believe that actual knowledge of the duty to register or proof of the probability of such knowledge and subsequent failure to comply are necessary before a conviction under the ordinance can stand. As Holmes wrote in The Common Law, "A law which punished conduct which would not be blameworthy in the average member of the community would be too severe for that community to bear." Id., at 50. Its severity lies in the absence of an opportunity either to avoid the consequences of the law or to defend any prosecution brought under it. Where a person did not know of the duty to register and where there was no proof of the probability of such knowledge, he may not be convicted consistently with Due Process. Were it otherwise, the evil would be as great as it is when the law is written in print too fine to read or in a language foreign to the community.

Reversed. . . .

JUSTICE FRANKFURTER, whom JUSTICE HARLAN and JUSTICE WHITTAKER join, dissenting.

The present laws of the United States and of the forty-eight States are thick with provisions that command that some things not be done and others be done, although persons convicted under such provisions may have had no awareness of what the law required or that what they did was wrongdoing. The body of decisions sustaining such legislation, including innumerable registration laws, is almost as voluminous as the legislation itself. The matter is summarized in United States v. Balint, 258 U.S. 250, 252: "Many instances of this are to be found in regulatory measures in the exercise of what is called the police power where the emphasis of the statute is evidently upon achievement of some social betterment rather than the punishment of the crimes as in cases of mala in se."

Surely there can hardly be a difference as a matter of fairness, of hardship, or of justice, if one may invoke it, between the case of a person wholly innocent of wrongdoing, in the sense that he was not remotely conscious of violating any law, who is imprisoned for five years for conduct relating to narcotics, and the case of another person who is placed on probation for three years on condition that she pay $250, for failure, as a local resident, convicted under local law of a felony, to register under a law passed as an exercise of the State's "police power." Considerations of hardship often lead courts, naturally enough, to attribute to a statute the requirement of a certain mental element — some consciousness of wrongdoing and knowledge of the law's command — as a matter of statutory construction. Then, too, a cruelly disproportionate relation between what the law requires and the sanction for its disobedience may constitute a violation of the Eighth Amendment as a cruel and unusual punishment, and, in respect to the States, even offend the Due Process Clause of the Fourteenth Amendment.

But what the Court here does is to draw a constitutional line between a State's requirement of doing and not-doing. What is this but a return to Year Book distinctions between feasance and nonfeasance — a distinction that may have significance in the evolution of common law notions of liability, but is inadmissible as a line between constitutionality and unconstitutionality. One can be confident that Mr. Justice Holmes would have been the last to draw such a line. What he wrote about "blameworthiness" is worth quoting in its context:

"It is not intended to deny that criminal liability, as well as civil, is founded on blameworthiness. Such a denial would shock the moral sense of any civilized community; or, to put it another way, a law which punished conduct which would not be blameworthy in the average member of the community would be too severe for that community to bear." (This passage must be read in the setting of the broader discussion of which it is an essential part. Holmes, The Common Law, at 49-50.)

If the generalization that underlies, and alone can justify, this decision were to be given its relevant scope, a whole volume of the United States Reports would be required to document in detail the legislation in this country that would fall or be impaired. I abstain from entering upon a consideration of such legislation, and adjudications upon it, because I feel confident that the present decision will turn out to be an isolated deviation from the strong current of precedents — a derelict on the waters of the law. Accordingly, I content myself with dissenting.

QUESTIONS

What precisely is the "generalization that underlies, and alone can justify" the decision in *Lambert*? That reasonable mistake of law is a defense to all crimes of omission? To some only? Only when the duty to act is triggered by mere presence in a community? Or is the relevant generalization wide enough to cover some cases of affirmative action? For example, suppose the ordinance prohibited "convicted persons" from hiring themselves out as babysitters in the city of Los Angeles.

What precisely is the legislation that would be imperiled by this generalization? All laws imposing absolute liability?

An interesting account of the diplomatic maneuvering among the justices that led to the final form of Justice Douglas's opinion is contained in Note (A. F. Brooke), When Ignorance of the Law Became an Excuse: *Lambert* and Its Progeny, 19 Am. J. Crim. L. 279 (1992). For an exchange of conflicting views on the majority opinion, see Steven B. Duke, Justice Douglas and the Criminal Law, in Stephen L. Wasby, ed., "He Shall Not Pass This Way Again: The Legacy of Justice William O. Douglas 133, 137 (1990), and Sanford H. Kadish, Justice Douglas and the Criminal Law: Another View, id. at 149, 150.

CALIFORNIA JOINT LEGISLATIVE COMMITTEE FOR REVISION OF THE PENAL CODE, PENAL CODE REVISION PROJECT

(Tent. Draft No. 2, 1968)

SECTION 500. IGNORANCE OR MISTAKE . . .

(2) A person's belief that his conduct does not constitute a crime is a defense only if it is reasonable and,

(a) if the person's mistaken belief is due to his ignorance of the existence of the law defining the crime, he exercised all the care which, in the circumstances, a law-abiding and prudent person would exercise to ascertain the law; or

(b) if the person's mistaken belief is due to his misconception of the meaning or application of the law defining the crime to his conduct,

(i) he acts in reasonable reliance upon an official statement of the law, afterward determined to be invalid or erroneous, contained in a statute, judicial decision, administrative order or grant of permission, or an official interpretation of the public officer or body charged by law with the responsibility for interpreting, administering or enforcing the law defining the crime; or,

[(ii) he otherwise diligently pursues all means available to ascertain the meaning and application of the crime to his conduct and honesty and in good faith concludes his conduct is not a crime in circumstances in which a law-abiding and prudent person would also so conclude.]

COMMENTS (64-67) . . .

Subsection (2)(a) is addressed to the situation where the defendant reasonably failed to know of the existence of the criminal prohibition. Where this is so and the jury finds on the preponderance of the evidence adduced by the defendant that he took all the care to ascertain the law which a law-abiding and prudent person would take, the case for exculpation seems to us persuasive. This provision states in general form the essence of the more particular provisions found in Section 2.04(3)(a) of the Model Penal Code and Section 4-8(b)(1) of the Illinois Code to the effect that mistake is a defense where the criminal prohibition was not published or otherwise reasonably made available. Certainly in such cases the language we propose would exculpate. But we think exculpation should be made out in all cases where a law-abiding and prudent person would not have learned of the law's existence. One such case is Lambert v. California, 355 U.S. 225 (1957), where the nature of the offense (visiting Los Angeles and failing to register as a previously convicted felon) itself gave such insufficient notice of the criminal duty that a conviction was found unconstitutional in the absence of circumstances showing probability of the knowledge of the offense by the defendant. Certainly there would not be many cases of this kind. Where the prohibition reaches plainly wrongful conduct, the conduct itself alerts the law-abiding and prudent person to the need for inquiry if there is any doubt. And even in the mala prohibita crimes the circumstances would normally suggest inquiry — engaging in such closely regulated activities as liquor selling, food merchandising, apartment renting, etc. But in the exceptional case, like *Lambert,* where this is not the case only a blind and brutal law would insist on punishment.

Subsection (2)(b) is addressed to the situation where the defendant (still reasonably), although aware of the existence of the crime, was mistaken as to its meaning or its applicability to his conduct. Subsection (i), dealing with situations of reliance on official and responsible interpretations, we have already discussed. As stated, this imports no innovation in present law. Subsection (ii), however, does, insofar as it generalizes the essential quality of the unfairness in holding defendants who are misled by official reliance; i.e., they did all that could be done to learn the nature of the prohibition and in concluding that it was lawful reacted no differently than would any law-abiding and prudent person. The subsection is placed in brackets because some of the Reporters believe it may go too far for reasons that will be stated shortly. The case to be made in favor of this subsection is as follows:

The central point is that it is plainly unjust to hold a defendant criminally liable where a jury is prepared to conclude that the conditions of this subsection are met. A case which illustrates this is Long v. State, 44 Del. 262, 65 A.2d 489 (1949). The court reversed a conviction of bigamy because the court below excluded evidence offered by the defendant to show his reasonable belief that his Arkansas divorce legally severed his prior marriage relationship. The case may be strongly argued to be one where the mistake is not as to the meaning or applicability of the offense (bigamy) but rather to an element of the offense (remarrying while having a spouse) and hence one where the mistake, though of a matter of law, negatived the necessary culpable mental state (negligence) with respect to that element. Be that as it may, the court dealt with the defense as though it were a defense of misconception of the law defining the offense and allowed the defense on the ground that the defendant "before engaging in the conduct made a bona fide, diligent effort, adopting a course and resorting to sources and means at least as appropriate as any afforded under our legal system, to ascertain and abide by the law, and . . . acted in good faith reliance upon the results of such effort." We agree with the Delaware court that in such circumstances the practical difficulties commonly invoked to deny the defense of mistake of law are inapposite. It cannot be said to "encourage ignorance" of the law where the defense requires a showing of diligent and exhaustive effort to comprehend the law. And difficulties of proof are not here substantial since the defendant is required to show affirmative acts of inquiry addressed to an objective standard. We also agree with the conclusion of the Delaware court that punishing in the circumstances would be "unjust and arbitrary. Most of the important reasons which support the prohibition of ex post facto legislation are opposed to such a holding. It is difficult to conceive what more could be reasonably expected of a 'model citizen' than that he guide his conduct by 'the law' ascertained in good faith, not merely by efforts which might seem adequate to a person in his situation, but by efforts as well designed to accomplish ascertainment as any available under our system."

In the *Long* case the steps taken by the defendant included centrally consulting a reputable Delaware lawyer, revealing to him all the relevant circumstances, and being without reason to believe his advice was ill-founded. However, under the proposed draft the defense is not available simply on the ground that an attorney advised the defendant of the noncriminality of the proposed conduct. Still such advice would normally figure in any defense made under this subdivision. But where the defendant's conduct constitutes a diligent pursuit of all means available to comprehend the law and his conclusion that his conduct is not criminal is one which he reaches honestly and in good faith, as opposed to a pretext, and that conclusion is found by the jury to be one which a law-abiding and prudent person would reach, the fact that the evidence leading to this conclusion rested in part on private legal advice should not dissolve the defense. The risk of disingenuous legal advice, which presumably is the main concern in this area, is substantially reduced by the additional requirements stated in the draft.

On the other hand some feel that this provision is subject to abuse. It opens up a new and potentially time-consuming defense in many cases. Further, the defense can be too easily fabricated out of disingenuous advice obtained from lawyers ready to lend themselves to a scheme of evasion through venality or partisanship in their client's cause. Finally, it is believed that the potential injustice is adequately guarded against by the use of the prosecutor's discretion not to prosecute in cases in which the accused acted in good faith, and his conduct was not harmful.

NOTES

1. The California proposal, §2(b)(ii), was adopted in New Jersey. See N.J. Stat. Ann. tit. 2C, §2-4(c)(3).

2. An alternative (or additional) strategy for avoiding the injustice of criminal conviction without fair notice (as a result of understandable ignorance of the law's meaning or validity) is the provision of declaratory relief. This would allow the person to obtain a judicial ruling of the legality of his contemplated conduct before the fact rather than after. The subject is explored in Note, Declaratory Relief in the Criminal Law, 80 Harv. L. Rev. 1490 (1967).

3. For arguments favoring substantial expansion of the mistake-of-law defense on principled grounds of justice, see Douglas Husak & Andrew von Hirsch, Culpability and Mistake of Law, in Action and Value in Criminal Law 157-174 (John Gardner, Jeremy Horder, and Stephen Shute, eds., 1993).

4. The German law treats the defense of mistake of law quite differently from English and American law.

The German Penal Code, 1969, Section 17 (effective 1975, Zweites Gesetz zur Reform des Strafrechts, [1969] Bundesgesetzblatt, Part 1, at 717, 720), provides:

> *Mistake as to the Prohibition.* If in the course of the act the actor lacks the perception that he is acting wrongfully, he acts without culpability if he could not avoid making the mistake. If he could avoid making it the punishment may be mitigated in accordance with §49, subsection 1.

This statutory formulation derives from a famous 1952 decision of the Supreme Court of West Germany (2 BGH St. 194) in which the court, in response to long-standing academic criticism, overturned its past rulings and held that a mistake by the defendant about the criminality of his conduct, whether based on ignorance, on a mistaken interpretation of the statutory prohibition, or on a mistaken interpretation of justificatory privileges, could constitute a legal defense. The court reasoned that blameworthiness is a necessary condition for guilt; hence, where mistake of law is inconsistent with moral blameworthiness, guilt should not be attached. Moral blameworthiness does not exist, the court found, if the defendant was not aware that his conduct was unlawful or wrongful and if a proper application of his moral sensitivities would not have led him to such an awareness:

> As a free and moral agent and as a participant in the legal community, the individual is bound at all times to conform his behavior to law and to avoid doing the wrong thing. He does not fulfill this duty merely by avoiding that which seems to him clearly to be the wrong thing; rather he must attempt to determine whether

that which he plans to do is compatible with the legal imperatives of the system. He must resolve his doubts by reflection or investigation. This requires that he apply his moral sensibility. . . . If despite the moral sensitivity that can fairly be demanded of him, the individual does not perceive the wrongfulness of his contemplated action, then his mistake is to be viewed as ineluctable; the act would be, for him, unavoidable. In a case of this sort, the individual cannot be blamed for his conduct.

The conscientious objector — one who is aware of the criminality of his conduct but rejects the moral judgment of the legislature — was excluded from the reach of this defense, because "The culpability of the morally committed violator consists in his knowing that he substitutes his own system of values for that of the legal community." For discussion of the German approach, see George Fletcher, Rethinking Criminal Law 737-755 (1978). See also Vera Bolgar, The Present Function of the Maxim *Ignorantia Juris Neminem Excusat* — A Comparative Study, 52 Iowa L. Rev. 626 (1967).

PROBLEM: THE "CULTURAL DEFENSE"

Should the law afford an excuse for foreigners who violate the law by actions acceptable in their native cultures? An English court faced this issue in Rex. v. Esop, 7 C. & P. 456 (1836). A sailor who was a native of Bagdad was convicted for sodomy committed aboard an East India ship while it was docked in London harbor. The court sustained the conviction, over the defendant's objection that sodomy was not a crime in his native land. A number of recent incidents reported in the press raise questions about the propriety of applying the traditional *ignoratia legis* rule in arguably analogous situations. A Japanese-American woman killed her children and tried to commit suicide in a ceremony of traditional Japanese culture whereby a wronged wife rids herself of the shame of her husband's infidelity (Sherman, Legal Clash of Cultures, Natl. L.J., Aug. 5, 1985, at 1).[14] A Hmong tribesman, recently arrived from Indo-China, executed his wife for committing adultery, which was his right in his native culture (L.A. Daily J., Nov. 29, 1985, at 15, col. 1). A number of other incidents among the Hmong and Mien tribespeople of Indo-China were reported in the following story from the New York Times (Bishop, Asian Tradition at War with American Laws, N.Y. Times, Feb. 10, 1988, at 10).

> The ancient tradition of Southeast Asia and the laws of 20th-century America are increasingly causing conflicts in the lives of the 30,000 Hmong and Mien tribespeople who settled in the Fresno area after fleeing Laos, Thailand and Vietnam.
>
> Their medicinal use of opium, their "capturing" of young brides, their ritual slaughtering of animals and other practices are resulting in legal problems that bring them confusion and shame. . . .
>
> Many of the legal conflicts do not result in serious charges. . . . More serious legally are charges of opium possession in which conviction can mean jail followed, under Federal law, by mandatory deportation. . . .

14. Apparently the woman's action would also be criminal in Japan, but it would constitute a lesser homicidal offense than the first-degree murder she was charged with in California. See Julia Sams, The Availability of the "Cultural Defense" as an Excuse for Criminal Behavior, 16 Ga. J. Intl. & Comp. L. 335, 342 (1986). — Eds.

"The opium is being used in barter and it's a part of their culture," said Roland Klink of the United States Customs Service in San Francisco. "But what concerns me is the growth. The quantities we're seeing means it isn't being distributed just for medicinal purposes but as an abused drug." . . .

The Hmong practice of marriage by capture has led to charges of kidnapping and rape here. Most cases have been resolved in juvenile courts. One, in 1985, involved adults and was resolved when the clan elders agreed to allow the defendant to plead guilty to a reduced charge of false imprisonment.

Couples meet and carry on a courtship that often begins with the celebration of the New Year, and a ball-tossing game for eligible young people. Eventually the young man "captures" the young woman in the presence of an older relative while the young woman ritually protests that she does not want to go with him.

He takes her to his family home where she is met by relatives for a brief ceremony at the door, and remains for three days in which the marriage is consummated and his relatives visit her family to pay a "bride price" for her.

Mr. Carrington, the defense attorney in the 1985 case, said: "The Hmong have a saying that translates, 'The boy must be strong to the girl. The girl must be shy to the boy.' The girls insist on being captured. It proves their status and virtue."

He said the "capture" occurred at school with the young woman's American friends as witnesses. Upon hearing her ritual protests, they called in the police, who have become increasingly sensitive to both the issue of rape and the cultural practices of the Hmong. Officers interviewed the woman at the man's home to be sure she wanted to stay, Mr. Carrington said. The families negotiated a price for the bride, but she returned to her family and eventually filed charges of kidnapping and rape. He[r] mother refused to agree to the marriage.

The prosecutor, Deputy District Attorney Steven Polacek, said that from the young woman's point of view, "This was a real case of kidnapping and rape," adding, "She is an Americanized woman" who knew her legal rights.

Should there be a mistake-of-law defense for people prosecuted in these circumstances? The issue has been analyzed in two recent studies. Favoring such a defense is Note, The Cultural Defense in the Criminal Law, 99 Harv. L. Rev. 1293 (1986). Opposing the defense is Julia Sams, The Availability of the "Cultural Defense" as an Excuse for Criminal Behavior, 16 Ga. J. Intl. & Comp. L. 335 (1986). See also Note, Cultural Defenses: One Person's Culture is Another Person's Crime, 9 Loy. L.A. Intl. & Comp. L.J. 751 (1987).

C. PROPORTIONALITY

INTRODUCTORY NOTE

The requirement that punishment be proportional to the seriousness of the offense has traditionally been a salient principle of punishment. It is manifested explicitly today in the statement of purpose of various criminal codes. The Model Penal Code (§1.02) includes among the purposes of the definition of crimes the aim "to differentiate on reasonable grounds between serious and minor offenses," and it includes among the purposes of sentencing provisions the aim "to safeguard offenders against excessive, disproportionate or arbitrary punishment." The New York Penal Law includes among the purposes of its pro-

C. Proportionality

visions (§1.05): "To differentiate on reasonable grounds between serious minor offenses and to prescribe proportionate penalties therefor." The Cal nia Penal Code, as amended in 1976, declares in §1170 that punishment is ___ purpose of imprisonment for crimes, which purpose is "best served by terms proportionate to the seriousness of the offense."

What is the justification for this concern with proportionality? If we believe excessive punishment, for whatever reason, is unjust, what constitutes excessive punishment? Is there a precise kind and degree of punishment appropriate to every criminal wrong, as Kant argued? How could it be determined? If this perspective is rejected, we may hold that some general proportion must be maintained between the crime and the amount of punishment in light of the seriousness of the crime. If so, is the point that certain crimes cannot be punished with more than a given quantum of punishment or rather that whatever the scale of punishment meted out in a particular society, whether high or low, less serious crime must be punished less than more serious crimes?

Perhaps the aim is not justice and fairness, whatever they might mean, but strictly utilitarian goals. If we hold this view, must we accept that any amount of punishment, no matter how severe, can be justifiable if, in the circumstances, it yields a desirable balance of utilities?

These are the principal issues addressed in the material that follows. See generally Alan H. Goldman, The Paradox of Punishment, 9 Phil. & Pub. Aff. 42 (1979), Alan Wertheimer, Should Punishment Fit the Crime?, 3 Soc. Theory & Prac. 403 (1975); Michael Clark, The Moral Gradation of Punishment, 21 Phil. Q. 132 (1971).

JEREMY BENTHAM, PRINCIPLES OF PENAL LAW

In 1 J. Bentham's Works, Pt. II, bk. 1 at 399-402 (J. Bowring ed. 1843)

Punishments may be too small or too great; and there are reasons for not making them too small, as well as not making them too great. The terms *minimum* and *maximum* may serve to mark the two extremes of this question, which require equal attention.

With a view of marking out the limits of punishment on the side of the first of these extremes, we may lay it down as a rule —

I. That the value of the punishment must not be less in any case than what is sufficient to outweigh that of the profit of the offence.

By the profit of the crime, must be understood not only pecuniary profit, but every advantage, real or apparent, which has operated as a motive to the commission of the crime.

The profit of the crime is the force which urges a man to delinquency — the pain of the punishment is the force employed to restrain him from it. If the first of these forces be the greater, the crime will be committed;[1] if the second, the crime will not be committed. If then a man, having reaped the profit of a crime, and undergone the punishment, finds the former more than equivalent to the latter, he will go on offending for ever; there is nothing to restrain him. If those,

---

1. That is to say, committed by those who are only restrained by the laws, and not by any other tutelary motives, such as benevolence, religion or honor.

also, who behold him, reckon that the balance of gain is in favour of the delinquent, the punishment will be useless for the purposes of example. . . .

Rule III. *When two offences come in competition, the punishment for the greater offence*
must be sufficient to induce a man to prefer the less.

Two offences may be said to be in competition, when it is in the power of an
individual to commit both. When thieves break into a house, they may execute
their purpose in different manners; by simply stealing, by theft accompanied
with bodily injury, or murder, or incendiarism. If the punishment is the same
for simple theft, as for theft and murder, you give the thieves a motive for committing murder, because this crime adds to the facility of committing the former,
and the chance of impunity when it is committed.

The great inconvenience resulting from the infliction of great punishments
for small offences, is, that the power of increasing them in proportion to the
magnitude of the offence is thereby lost.

Rule IV. *The punishment should be adjusted in such manner to each particular of-*
fence, that for every part of the mischief there may be a motive to restrain the offender from
giving birth to it.

Thus, for example, in adjusting the punishment for stealing a sum of money,
let the magnitude of the punishment be determined by the amount of the sum
stolen. If for stealing ten shillings an offender is punished no more than for
stealing five, the stealing of the remaining five of those ten shillings is an offence
for which there is no punishment at all.

Rule V. *The punishment ought in no case to be more than what is necessary to bring it*
into conformity with the rules here given. . . .

Of the above rules of proportion, the four first may serve to mark the limits of
the minimum side — the limits below which a punishment ought not to be diminished; the fifth will mark out the limits on the maximum side — the limits
above which it ought not to be increased.

The minimum of punishment is more clearly marked than its maximum.
What is *too little* is more clearly observed than what is *too much*. What is not sufficient is easily seen, but it is not possible so exactly to distinguish in excess: an
approximation only can be attained. The irregularities in the force of tempta-
tions compel the legislator to increase his punishments, till they are not merely
sufficient to restrain the ordinary desires of men, but also the violence of their
desires when unusually excited.

The greatest danger lies in an error on the minimum side, because in this case
the punishment is inefficacious; but this error is least likely to occur, a slight
degree of attention sufficing for its escape; and when it does exist, it is at the
same time clear and manifest, and easy to be remedied. An error on the maximum side, on the contrary, is that to which legislators and men in general are
naturally inclined: antipathy, or a want of compassion for individuals who are
represented as dangerous and vile, pushes them onward to an undue severity. It
is on this side, therefore, that we should take the most precautions, as on this
side there has been shown the greatest disposition to err.

By way of supplement and explanation to the first rule, and to make sure of
giving to the punishment the superiority over the offence, the . . . following rules
may be laid down: —

Rule VII. *That the value of the punishment may outweigh the profit of the offence,*
it must be increased in point of magnitude, in proportion as it falls short in point of
certainty.

Rule VIII.   *Punishment must be further increased in point of magnitude, in proportion as it falls short in points of proximity.*

The profit of a crime is commonly more certain than its punishment; or, what amounts to the same thing, appears so to the offender. It is generally more immediate: the temptation to offend is present; the punishment is at a distance. Hence there are two circumstances which weaken the effect of punishment, its *uncertainty* and its *distance*.   swift punishment required

HYMAN GROSS, A THEORY OF CRIMINAL JUSTICE 436 (1979): Th[e] general principle of proportion between crime and punishment is a principle of just desert that serves as the foundation of every criminal sentence that is justifiable. As a principle of criminal justice it is hardly less familiar or less important than the principle that only the guilty ought to be punished. Indeed, the requirement that punishment not be disproportionately great, which is a corollary of just desert, is dictated by the same principle that does not allow punishment of the innocent, for any punishment in excess of what is deserved for the criminal conduct is punishment without guilt.

H. L. A. HART & A. HONORÉ, CAUSATION IN THE LAW 395-396 (2d ed. 1985): On a deterrent theory the rationale of the differential severity of punishments is complex. First, one crime if unchecked may cause greater harm than another, and hence on general utilitarian grounds greater severity may be used in its repression than in the repression of the less harmful crime. Secondly, the temptation to commit one sort of crime may be greater than another and hence a more severe penalty is needed to deter. Thirdly, the commission of one crime may be a sign of a more dangerous character in the criminal needing longer sentence for incapacitation or reform.

A. C. EWING, A STUDY OF PUNISHMENT II: PUNISHMENT AS VIEWED BY THE PHILOSOPHER, 21 Canadian B. Rev. 102, 115-116 (1943): We are now in a position also to give a satisfactory reason why a graver offence should be punished more than a lighter one. To punish a lesser crime more severely than a greater would be either to suggest to men's minds that the former was worse when it was not, or, if they could not accept this, to bring the penal law in some degree into discredit or ridicule. One of the requirements of a good moral code is that there should be a right proportion between values, and, in so far as penal laws affect popular morality, they ought to help and not hinder right judgment in this matter. This is not to fall back on the old retributive conception that a certain amount of pain intrinsically fits a certain degree of moral badness. Granted that a certain degree of punishment is inflicted in a given society, for, e.g., thefts, and that certain other acts, e.g., murders, are morally worse, moral condemnation of the latter can only be suitably expressed by inflicting a severer punishment for them than for the former; but this would not be an objection to lowering the penalty for both, because there is no necessarily fixed scale that we can see by which so much guilt deserves so much pain. There is another bad effect of disproportionate punishments in so far as they involve excessive severity. It is this: if a man is very severely punished for a comparatively slight offence, people will be liable to forget about his crime and think only of his sufferings, so that he appears a victim of cruel laws, and the whole process, instead of reaffirming the law and intensifying men's consciousness that the kind of act punished is wrong, will have the opposite effect of casting discredit on the law and making the action of the lawbreaker appear excusable or even almost heroic. These punishments are specially liable to produce an effect of this sort on their victim. He will be likely to think the penalty excessive in any case, and the great danger of punishment is that this will lead to self-pity and despair, or anger and bitterness, instead of repentance, but if he has really good grounds for complaint, this danger will be doubled. The primary object of punishment is to lead both the offender and others to realize the badness of the act punished; but, if great severity is shown, they are much more likely to realize instead the cruelty of the punishment.

We may then regard punishment as a kind of language intended to express moral disapproval.

JAMES FITZJAMES STEPHEN, LAW, EQUALITY, FRATERNITY 152-154 (R. J. White ed. 1967): If vengeance affects, and ought to affect, the amount of punishment, every circumstance which aggravates or extenuates the wickedness of an act will operate in aggravation or diminution of punishment. If the object of legal punishment is simply the prevention of specific acts, this will not be the case. Circumstances which extenuate the wickedness of the crime will often operate in aggravation of punishment. If, as I maintain, both objects must be kept in view, such circumstances will operate in different ways according to the nature of the case.

A judge has before him two criminals, one of whom appears, from the circumstances of the case, to be ignorant and depraved, and to have given way to very strong temptation, under the influence of the other, who is a man of rank and education, and who committed the offence of which both are convicted under comparatively slight temptation. I will venture to say that if he made any difference between them at all every judge on the English bench would give the first man a lighter sentence than the second.

What should we think of such an address to the prisoners as this? You, *A*, are a most dangerous man. You are ignorant, you are depraved, and you are accordingly peculiarly liable to be led into crime by the solicitations or influence of people like your accomplice *B*. Such influences constitute to men like you a temptation practically all but irresistible. The class to which you belong is a large one, and is accessible only to the coarsest possible motives. For these reasons I must put into the opposite scale as heavy a weight as I can, and the sentence of the court upon you is that you be taken to the place from whence you came and from thence to a place of execution, and that there you be hanged by the neck till you are dead. As to you, *B*, you are undoubtedly an infamous wretch. Between you and your tool *A* there can, morally speaking, be no comparison at all. But I have nothing to do with that. You belong to a small and not a dangerous class. The temptation to which you gave way was slight, and the impression made upon me by your conduct is that you really did not care very much whether you committed this crime or not. From a moral point of view, this may perhaps increase your guilt; but it shows that the motive to be overcome is less powerful in your case than in *A*'s. You belong, moreover, to a class, and occupy a position in society, in which exposure and loss of character are much dreaded. This you will have to undergo. Your case is a very odd one, and it is not likely that you will wish to commit such a crime again, or that others will follow your example.

Upon the whole, I think that what has passed will deter others from such conduct as much as actual punishment. It is, however, necessary to keep a hold over you. You will therefore be discharged on your own recognizances to come up and receive judgment when called upon, and unless you conduct yourself better for the future, you will assuredly be so called upon, and if you do not appear, your recognizances will be inexorably forfeited.

Caricature apart, the logic of such a view is surely unimpeachable. If all that you want of criminal law is the prevention of crime by the direct fear of punishment, the fact that a temptation is strong is a reason why punishment should be severe. In some instances this actually is the case. It shows the reason why political crimes and offences against military discipline are punished so severely. But in most cases the strength of the temptation operates in mitigation of punishment, and the reason of this is that criminal law operates not merely by producing fear, but also indirectly, but very powerfully, by giving distinct shape to the feeling of anger, and a distinct satisfaction to the desire of vengeance which crime excites in a healthy mind.

H. L. A. HART, LAW, LIBERTY AND MORALITY 36-37 (1963): [T]he questions "What sort of conduct may justifiably be punished?" and "How severely should we punish different offenses?" are distinct and independent questions. There are many reasons why we might wish the legal graduation of the seriousness of crimes, expressed in its scale of punishments, not to conflict with common estimates of their comparative wickedness. One reason is that such a conflict is undesirable on simple utilitarian grounds: it might either confuse moral judgments or bring the law into disrepute, or both. Another reason is that principles of justice or fairness between different offenders require morally distinguishable offences to be treated differently and morally similar offences to be treated alike. These principles are still widely respected, although it is also true that there is a growing disinclination to insist on their application where this conflicts with the forward-looking aims of punishment, such as prevention or reform. But those who concede that we should attempt to adjust the severity of punishment to the moral gravity of offences are not thereby committed to the view that punishment merely for immorality is justified. For they can in perfect consistency insist on the one hand that the only justification for having a system of punishment is to prevent harm and only harmful conduct should be punished, and, on the other, agree that when the question of the quantum of punishment for such conduct is raised, we should defer to principles which make relative moral wickedness of different offenders a partial determinant of the severity of punishment.

HARMELIN v. MICHIGAN

Supreme Court of the United States
501 U.S. 957 (1991)

JUSTICE SCALIA announced the judgment of the Court and delivered an opinion in which THE CHIEF JUSTICE joins.

Petitioner was convicted of possessing 672 grams of cocaine and sentenced to a mandatory term of life in prison without possibility of parole. . . .

Petitioner claims that his sentence is unconstitutionally "cruel and unusual" . . . because it is "significantly disproportionate" to the crime he committed. . . .

The Eighth Amendment, which applies against the States by virtue of the Fourteenth Amendment, provides: "Excessive bail shall not be required, nor excessive fines imposed, nor cruel and unusual punishments inflicted." . . .

Solem v. Helm, 463 U.S. 277 (1983), set aside under the Eighth Amendment, because it was disproportionate, a sentence of life imprisonment without possibility of parole, imposed under a South Dakota recidivist statute for successive offenses that included three convictions of third-degree burglary, one of obtaining money by false pretenses, one of grand larceny, one of third-offense driving while intoxicated, and one of writing a "no account" check with intent to defraud. . . . [The Court held in favor of a] "general principle of proportionality," which was "deeply rooted and frequently repeated in common-law jurisprudence," had been embodied in the English Bill of Rights "in language that was later adopted in the Eighth Amendment," and had been "recognized explicitly in this Court for almost a century." . . .

[O]ur 5-to-4 decision eight years ago in *Solem* was scarcely the expression of clear and well accepted constitutional law. . . . Accordingly, we have addressed anew, and in greater detail, the question whether the Eighth Amendment contains a proportionality guarantee — with particular attention to the background of the Eighth Amendment . . . and to the understanding of the Eighth Amendment before the end of the 19th century. . . . We conclude from this examination that *Solem* was simply wrong; the Eighth Amendment contains no proportionality guarantee. . . .

[Justice Scalia discussed the history of the English Bill of Rights, and its influence on the Eighth Amendment. He concluded that the Amendment was adopted to outlaw certain modes of punishment (e.g., drawing and quartering) and to prevent judges from inventing and imposing "unusual" penalties not prescribed by law.]

We think it enough that those who framed and approved the Federal Constitution chose, for whatever reason, not to include within it the guarantee against disproportionate sentences that some State Constitutions contained. It is worth noting, however, that there was good reason for that choice — a reason that reinforces the necessity of overruling *Solem*. While there are relatively clear historical guidelines and accepted practices that enable judges to determine which *modes* of punishment are "cruel and unusual," *proportionality* does not lend itself to such analysis. . . . This is not to say that there are no absolutes; one can imagine extreme examples that no rational person, in no time or place, could accept. But for the same reason these examples are easy to decide, they are certain never to occur. The real function of a constitutional proportionality principle, if it exists, is to enable judges to evaluate a penalty that *some* assemblage of men and women *has* considered proportionate — and to say that it is not. For that real-world enterprise, the standards seem so inadequate that the proportionality principle becomes an invitation to imposition of subjective values.

This becomes clear, we think, from a consideration of the three factors that *Solem* found relevant to the proportionality determination: (1) the inherent gravity of the offense, (2) the sentences imposed for similarly grave offenses in the same jurisdiction, and (3) sentences imposed for the same crime in other jurisdictions. As to the first factor; . . . The difficulty of assessing gravity is demonstrated in the very context of the present case. Petitioner acknowledges that a mandatory life sentence might not be "grossly excessive" for possession of cocaine with intent to distribute. But surely whether it is a "grave" offense merely to possess a significant quantity of drugs — thereby facilitating distribution, subjecting the holder to the temptation of distribution, and raising the possibility of theft by others who might distribute — depends entirely upon how odious and socially threatening one believes drug use to be. Would it be "grossly excessive" to provide life imprisonment for "mere possession" of a certain quantity of heavy weaponry? If not, then the only issue is whether the possible dissemination of drugs can be as "grave" as the possible dissemination of heavy weapons. Who are we to say no? The Members of the Michigan Legislature, and not we, know the situation on the streets of Detroit.

The second factor suggested in *Solem* fails for the same reason. One cannot compare the sentences imposed by the jurisdiction for "similarly grave" offenses if there is no objective standard of gravity. Judges will be comparing what *they* consider comparable. . . . Moreover, even if "similarly grave" crimes could be identified, the penalties for them would not necessarily be comparable, since there are many other justifications for a difference. For example, since deterrent effect depends not only upon the amount of the penalty but upon its certainty, crimes that are less grave but significantly more difficult to detect may warrant substantially higher penalties. Grave crimes of the sort that will not be deterred by penalty may warrant substantially lower penalties, as may grave crimes of the sort that are normally committed once-in-a-lifetime by otherwise law-abiding citizens who will not profit from rehabilitation. Whether these differences will occur, and to what extent, depends, of course, upon the weight the society accords to deterrence and rehabilitation, rather than retribution, as the objective of criminal punishment. . . .

As for the third factor mentioned by *Solem* — the character of the sentences imposed by other States for the same crime — it must be acknowledged that that can be applied with clarity and ease. The only difficulty is that it has no conceivable relevance to the Eighth Amendment. That a State is entitled to treat with stern disapproval an act that other States punish with the mildest of sanctions follows a fortiori from the undoubted fact that a State may criminalize an act that other States do not criminalize *at all*. . . . What greater disproportion could there be than that? . . . Diversity not only in policy, but in the means of implementing policy, is the very *raison d'être* of our federal system. . . .

The first holding of this Court unqualifiedly applying a requirement of proportionality to criminal penalties was . . . Coker v. Georgia [,433 U.S. 584 (1977)], [where] the Court held that, because of the disproportionality, it was a violation of the Cruel and Unusual Punishments Clause to impose capital punishment for rape of an adult woman. . . . Proportionality review is one of several respects in which we have held that "death is different," and have imposed protections that the Constitution nowhere else provides. We would leave it there, but will not extend it further. . . .

The judgment of the Michigan Court of Appeals is affirmed.

JUSTICE KENNEDY, with whom JUSTICE O'CONNOR and JUSTICE SOUTER join, concurring in part and concurring in the judgment.

. . . I write this separate opinion because my approach to the Eighth Amendment proportionality analysis differs from Justice Scalia's. Regardless of whether

Justice Scalia or the dissent has the best of the historical argument, stare decisis counsels our adherence to the narrow proportionality principle that has existed in our Eighth Amendment jurisprudence for 80 years. Although our proportionality decisions have not been clear or consistent in all respects, they can be reconciled, and they require us to uphold petitioner's sentence.

Our decisions recognize that the Cruel and Unusual Punishments Clause encompasses a narrow proportionality principle. We first interpreted the Eighth Amendment to prohibit "'greatly disproportioned'" sentences in Weems v. United States, 217 U.S. 349, 371 (1910). Since *Weems,* we have applied the principle in different Eighth Amendment contexts. Its most extensive application has been in death penalty cases. . . .

The Eighth Amendment proportionality principle also applies to noncapital sentences. In Rummel v. Estelle, 445 U.S. 263 (1980), we acknowledged the existence of the proportionality rule for both capital and noncapital cases, but we refused to strike down a sentence of life imprisonment, with possibility of parole, for recidivism based on three underlying felonies. In *Hutto v. Davis,* 454 U.S. 370 (1982), we recognized the possibility of proportionality review but held it inapplicable to a 40-year prison sentence for possession with intent to distribute nine ounces of marijuana. Our most recent decision discussing the subject is Solem v. Helm, 463 U.S. 277 (1983). There we held that a sentence of life imprisonment without possibility of parole violated the Eighth Amendment because it was "grossly disproportionate" to the crime of recidivism based on seven underlying nonviolent felonies. The dissent in *Solem* disagreed with the Court's application of the proportionality principle but observed that in extreme cases it could apply to invalidate a punishment for a term of years. . . .

[C]lose analysis of our decisions yields some common principles that give content to the uses and limits of proportionality review.

The first of these principles is that the fixing of prison terms for specific crimes involves a substantive penological judgment that, as a general matter, is "properly within the province of legislatures, not courts." . . . Thus, "reviewing courts . . . should grant substantial deference to the broad authority that legislatures necessarily possess in determining the types and limits of punishments for crimes." *Solem,* supra, at 290.

The second principle is that the Eighth Amendment does not mandate adoption of any one penological theory. . . . The federal and state criminal systems have accorded different weights at different times to the penological goals of retribution, deterrence, incapacitation, and rehabilitation. And competing theories of mandatory and discretionary sentencing have been in varying degrees of ascendancy or decline since the beginning of the Republic.

Third, marked divergences both in underlying theories of sentencing and in the length of prescribed prison terms are the inevitable, often beneficial, result of the federal structure. State sentencing schemes may embody different penological assumptions, making interstate comparison of sentences a difficult and imperfect enterprise. And even assuming identical philosophies, differing attitudes and perceptions of local conditions may yield different, yet rational, conclusions regarding the appropriate length of prison terms for particular crimes. Thus, the circumstance that a State has the most severe punishment for a particular crime does not by itself render the punishment grossly disproportionate. . . .

The fourth principle at work in our cases is that proportionality review by "federal courts should be informed by 'objective factors to the maximum possible extent.'" *Rummel,* supra, at 274-275. The most prominent objective factor is the type of punishment imposed. In *Weems,* "the Court could differentiate in an objective fashion between the highly unusual *cadena temporal*[a] and more traditional forms of imprisonment imposed under the Anglo-Saxon system." *Rummel,* 445 U.S., at 275. In a similar fashion, because "'the penalty of death differs from all other forms of criminal punishment,'" id., at 272, the objective line between capital punishment and imprisonment for a term of years finds frequent mention in our Eighth Amendment jurisprudence. By contrast, our decisions recognize that we lack clear objective standards to distinguish between sentences for different terms of years. Although "no penalty is per se constitutional," id., at 290, the relative lack of objective standards concerning terms of imprisonment has meant that "'outside the context of capital punishment, *successful* challenges to the proportionality of particular sentences [are] exceedingly rare.'" Id., at 289-290.

All of these principles — the primacy of the legislature, the variety of legitimate penological schemes, the nature of our federal system, and the requirement that proportionality review be guided by objective factors — inform the final one: the Eighth Amendment does not require strict proportionality between crime and sentence. Rather, it forbids only extreme sentences that are "grossly disproportionate" to the crime. . . .

Petitioner's life sentence without parole is the second most severe penalty permitted by law. It is the same sentence received by the petitioner in *Solem.* Petitioner's crime, however, was far more grave than the crime at issue in *Solem.*

The crime of uttering a no account check at issue in *Solem* was "'one of the most passive felonies a person could commit.'" *Solem,* 463 U.S., at 296. . . .

Petitioner was convicted of possession of more than 650 grams (over 1.5 pounds) of cocaine. This amount of pure cocaine has a potential yield of between 32,500 and 65,000 doses. From any standpoint, this crime falls in a different category from the relatively minor, nonviolent crime at issue in *Solem.* . . .

[F]acts and reports detailing the pernicious effects of the drug epidemic in this country do not establish that Michigan's penalty scheme is correct or the most just in any abstract sense. But they do demonstrate that the Michigan Legislature could with reason conclude that the threat posed to the individual and society by possession of this large an amount of cocaine — in terms of violence, crime, and social displacement — is momentous enough to warrant the deterrence and retribution of a life sentence without parole. . . . [I]ntra- and inter-jurisdictional analyses are appropriate only in the rare case in which a threshold comparison of the crime committed and the sentence imposed leads to an inference of gross disproportionality. . . .

JUSTICE WHITE, with whom JUSTICE BLACKMUN and JUSTICE STEVENS join, dissenting. . . .

The language of the [Eighth] Amendment does not refer to proportionality in so many words, but it does forbid "excessive" fines, a restraint that suggests that a determination of excessiveness should be based at least in part on whether the fine imposed is disproportionate to the crime committed. Nor would it be

---

a. *Cadena temporal* is a punishment based upon the Spanish Penal Code. It calls for incarceration at hard and painful labor with chains fastened to the wrists and ankles at all times. — EDS.

unreasonable to conclude that it would be both cruel and unusual to punish overtime parking by life imprisonment, or, more generally, to impose any punishment that is grossly disproportionate to the offense for which the defendant has been convicted.

. . . Later in his opinion, Justice Scalia backtracks and appears to accept that the Amendment does indeed insist on proportional punishments in a particular class of cases, those that involve sentences of death. His fallback position is that outside the capital cases, proportionality review is not required by the Amendment. . . . This position . . . ignores the generality of the Court's several pronouncements about the Eighth Amendment's proportionality component. And it fails to explain why the words "cruel and unusual" include a proportionality requirement in some cases but not in others. . . .

The Court therefore has recognized that a punishment may violate the Eighth Amendment if it is contrary to the "evolving standards of decency that mark the progress of a maturing society." Trop [v. Dulles], [356 U.S. 86, 101 (1958)]. In evaluating a punishment under this test, "we have looked not to our own conceptions of decency, but to those of modern American society as a whole" in determining what standards have "evolved," and thus have focused not on "the subjective views of individual Justices," but on "objective factors to the maximum possible extent." It is this type of objective factor which forms the basis for the tripartite proportionality analysis set forth in *Solem*.

. . . Application of the *Solem* factors to the statutorily mandated punishment at issue here reveals that the punishment fails muster under Solem and, consequently, under the Eighth Amendment to the Constitution. . . .

The first *Solem* factor requires a reviewing court to assess the gravity of the offense and the harshness of the penalty. . . .

[I]n evaluating the gravity of the offense, it is appropriate to consider "the harm caused or threatened to the victim or society," based on such things as the degree of violence involved in the crime and "the absolute magnitude of the crime," and "the culpability of the offender," including the degree of requisite intent and the offender's motive in committing the crime, [*Solem*,] at 292-293.

Drugs are without doubt a serious societal problem. To justify such a harsh mandatory penalty as that imposed here, however, the offense should be one which will always warrant that punishment. Mere possession of drugs — even in such a large quantity — is not so serious an offense that it will always warrant, much less mandate, life imprisonment without possibility of parole. Unlike crimes directed against the persons and property of others, possession of drugs affects the criminal who uses the drugs most directly. . . .

The "absolute magnitude" of petitioner's crime is not exceptionally serious. . . . Indeed, the presence of a separate statute which reaches manufacture, delivery, or possession with intent to do either, undermines the State's position that the purpose of the *possession* statute was to reach drug dealers. . . . In addition, while there is usually a pecuniary motive when someone possesses a drug with intent to deliver it, such a motive need not exist in the case of mere possession. Finally, this statute applies equally to first-time offenders, such as petitioner, and recidivists. Consequently, the particular concerns reflected in recidivist statutes such as those in *Rummel* and *Solem* are not at issue here. . . .

The second prong of the *Solem* analysis is an examination of "the sentences imposed on other criminals in the same jurisdiction." [T]here is no death penalty in Michigan; consequently, life without parole, the punishment mandated here, is the harshest penalty available. It is reserved for three crimes: first-degree murder; manufacture, distribution, or possession with intent to manufacture or distribute 650 grams or more of narcotics; and possession of 650 grams or more of narcotics. Crimes directed against the persons and property of others — such as second-degree murder, rape, and armed robbery — do not carry such a harsh mandatory sentence, although they do provide for the possibility of a life sentence in the exercise of judicial discretion. It is clear that petitioner "has been treated in the same manner as, or more severely than, criminals who have committed far more serious crimes."

The third factor set forth in *Solem* examines "the sentences imposed for commission of the same crime in other jurisdictions." . . . Of the remaining 49 States, only Alabama provides for a mandatory sentence of life imprisonment without possibility of parole for a first-time drug offender, and then only when a defendant possesses *ten kilograms* or more of cocaine. . . . Thus, "it appears that [petitioner] was treated more severely than he would have been in any other State." *Solem*, supra, at 300. Indeed, the fact that no other jurisdiction provides such a severe, mandatory penalty for possession of this quantity of drugs is enough to establish "the degree of national consensus this Court has previously thought sufficient to label a particular punishment cruel and unusual."

Application of *Solem*'s proportionality analysis leaves no doubt that the Michigan statute . . . violates the Eighth Amendment's prohibition against cruel and unusual punishment. Consequently, I would reverse the decision of the Michigan Court of Appeals.

[Justice Marshall dissented in a separate opinion, agreeing with Justice White, but reiterating his view that the death sentence is unconstitutional.]

NOTES

1. State courts and lower federal courts have tended to interpret *Harmelin* as preserving the proportionality requirement advocated in Justice Kennedy's opinion in *Harmelin*. See State v. Matteson, 851 P.2d 336, 340 (Idaho 1993): "We must first make a threshold comparison of the crime committed and the sentence imposed to determine whether the sentence leads to an inference of gross disproportionality. Intra- and inter-jurisdictional analysis are appropriate only in the rare case in which the threshold comparison . . . leads to [such an] inference." In Thomas v. State, 634 A.2d 1 (Md. 1993), defendant was sentenced to 20 years' imprisonment for slapping his wife. The Maryland Court of Appeals, applying Justice Kennedy's standard, overturned the sentence as "grossly disproportional" to a battery consisting of a single slap. See also State v. Bartlett, 830 P.2d 823, 826 n. 2 (Ariz. 1992) (listing federal and state courts that have adopted Justice Kennedy's test). In *Bartlett* the Arizona Supreme Court, applying the same test, found a mandatory 40-year term of imprisonment for two counts of statutory rape (consensual sex with minors) to violate the Eighth Amendment.

2. Many state constitutions have their own prohibitions of cruel and unusual punishment. Their interpretations are not necessarily dependent on federal interpretation of the Eighth Amendment. In People v. Bullock, 485 N.W.2d 866

(1992), the Michigan Supreme Court overturned the law at issue in *Harmelin* on the ground that it violated the Michigan Constitution. The court emphasized the textual difference between the Eighth Amendment's prohibition of "cruel *and* unusual punishment" and the Michigan Constitution's prohibition of "cruel *or* unusual punishment" (italics added). It also emphasized that the Michigan provision was adopted in 1976 when sensibilities to the excesses of punishment were greater than they were in 1789 when the Eighth Amendment was adopted. The court held, therefore, that under the Michigan Constitution, the courts must apply a three-prong test, identical to that advanced in *Solem,* to determine whether a punishment is "cruel *or* unusual."

Question: Another Michigan law imposes the same punishment (life without possibility of parole) for possession *with intent to distribute.* Is this also unconstitutional under *Bullock?* The opinions leave the answer in doubt. See Mark Hansen, Michigan Drug Law Struck Down, A.B.A. J., Sept. 1992, at 25.

See also In re Lynch, 8 Cal. 3d 410, 503 P.2d 921 (1972), where the California Supreme Court heard a challenge to a sentence based on a state constitutional "cruel or unusual" provision similar to that of the Michigan Constitution. Defendant had been convicted of a second offense of indecent exposure and sentenced to imprisonment in the state prison for the indeterminate period of one year to life, at the discretion of the paroling authority. The court held that the sentence was "so disproportionate to the crime for which it is inflicted that it shocks the conscience and offends fundamental notions of human dignity."

3. A number of state constitutions expressly require that "[a]ll penalties shall be proportioned to the nature of the offense." Ind. Const. art. 1, §16; see also Me. Const. art. I, §9; Neb. Const. art. I, §15; N.H. Const. pt. 1, art. 18; Or. Const. art. I, §16; R.I. Const. art. I, §8; W. Va. Const. art. III, §5.

D. LEGALITY

SHAW v. DIRECTOR OF PUBLIC PROSECUTIONS

House of Lords
[1962] A.C. 220

[Appellant was convicted on an indictment containing three counts that alleged the following offenses: (1) conspiracy to corrupt public morals, (2) living on the earning of prostitution contrary to §30 of the Sexual Offences Act, 1956, and (3) publishing an obscene publication contrary to §2 of the Obscene Publications Act, 1959. The appeal on all three counts was dismissed, and the conviction upheld. Only discussion of the first count is included in the following extracts from several of the addresses.

[The essential facts, as stated by Viscount Simonds, are as follows: "When the Street Offences Act, 1959, came into operation it was no longer possible for prostitutes to ply their trade by soliciting in the streets, and it became necessary for them to find some other means of advertising the service that they were prepared to render. It occurred to the appellant that he could with advantage to himself assist them to this end. The device that he adopted was to publish . . .

a magazine or booklet which was called 'Ladies' Directory.' It contained the names, addresses and telephone numbers of prostitutes with photographs of nude female figures, and in some cases details which conveyed to initiates willingness to indulge not only in ordinary sexual intercourse but also in various perverse practices."

[The first count charged the appellant in the following terms:

> State of offense: Conspiracy to corrupt public morals. Particulars of offence: Frederick Charles Shaw on divers days between the 1st day of October, 1959, and 23rd July, 1960, within the jurisdiction of the Central Criminal Court conspired with certain persons, who inserted advertisements in issues of a magazine entitled "Ladies' Directory" numbered 7, 7 revised, 8, 9, 10 and a supplement thereto, and with certain other persons whose names are unknown, by means of the said magazine and the said advertisements to induce readers thereof to resort to the said advertisers for the purposes of fornication and of taking part in or witnessing other disgusting and immoral acts and exhibitions with intent thereby to debauch and corrupt the morals as well of youth as of divers other liege subjects of Our Lady the Queen and to raise and create in their minds inordinate and lustful desires.]

VISCOUNT SIMONDS. . . . I am concerned only to assert what was vigorously denied by counsel for the appellant, that such an offense is known to the common law, and that it was open to the jury to find on the facts of this case that the appellant was guilty of such an offence. I must say categorically that, if it were not so, Her Majesty's courts would strangely have failed in their duty as servants and guardians of the common law. Need I say, My Lords, that I am no advocate of the right of the judges to create new criminal offences? . . . But I am at a loss to understand how it can be said either that the law does not recognize a conspiracy to corrupt public morals or that, though there may not be an exact precedent for such a conspiracy as this case reveals, it does not fall fairly within the general words by which it is described. . . . In the sphere of criminal law I entertain no doubts that there remains in the courts of law a residual power to enforce the supreme and fundamental purpose of the law, to conserve not only the safety and order but also the moral welfare of the State, and that it is their duty to guard it against attacks which may be the more insidious because they are novel and unprepared for. . . . Such occasions will be rare, for Parliament has not been slow to legislate when attention has been sufficiently aroused. But gaps remain and will always remain since no one can foresee every way in which the wickedness of man may disrupt the order of society. Let me take a single instance. . . . Let it be supposed that at some future, perhaps early, date homosexual practices between adult consenting males are no longer a crime. Would it not be an offense if even without obscenity, such practices were publicly advocated and encouraged by pamphlet and advertisement? Or must we wait until Parliament finds time to deal with such conduct? I say, my Lords, that if the common law is powerless in such an event, then we should no longer do her reverence. . . .

The appeal on both counts should, in my opinion, be dismissed.

LORD MORRIS of Borth-y-Gest. . . . It is said that there is a measure of vagueness in a charge of conspiracy to corrupt public morals, and also that there might be peril of the launching of prosecutions in order to suppress unpopular or unorthodox views. My Lords, I entertain no anxiety on these lines. Even if accepted public standards may to some extent vary from generation to generation, current standards are in the keeping of juries, who can be trusted to maintain the corporate good sense of the community and to discern attacks upon values that must be preserved. If there were prosecutions which were not genuinely and fairly warranted juries would be quick to perceive this. There could be no conviction unless 12 jurors were unanimous in thinking that the accused person or persons had combined to do acts which were calculated to corrupt public morals. . . .

I would dismiss the appeal.

LORD REID. . . . In my opinion there is no such general offence known to the law as conspiracy to corrupt public morals. . . .

I agree with R. S. Wright, J., when he says . . . "There appear to be great theoretical objections to any general rule that agreement may make punishable that which ought not to be punished in the absence of agreement." And I think, or at least I hope, that it is now established, that the courts cannot create new offences by individuals. So far at least I have the authority of Lord Goddard, C. J., in delivering the opinion of the court in *Newland* [[1954] 1 Q.B. 158]: "[The power to create new offenses] would leave it to the judges to declare new crimes and enable them to hold anything which they considered prejudicial to the community to be a misdemeanor. However beneficial that might have been in days when Parliament met seldom or at least only at long intervals it surely is now the province of the legislature and not of the judiciary to create new criminal offenses." Every argument against creating new offences by an individual appears to me to be equally valid against creating new offences by a combination of individuals.

. . . Notoriously, there are wide differences of opinion today as to how far the law ought to punish immoral acts which are not done in the face of the public. . . . Parliament is the proper place, and I am firmly of opinion the only proper place, to settle that. When there is sufficient support from public opinion, Parliament does not hesitate to intervene. Where Parliament fears to tread it is not for the courts to rush in. . . .

Finally I must advert to the consequences of holding that this very general offence exists. It has always been thought to be of primary importance that our law, and particularly our criminal law, should be certain: that a man should be able to know what conduct is and what is not criminal, particularly when heavy penalties are involved. Some suggestion was made that it does not matter if this offence is very wide: no one would ever prosecute and if they did no jury would ever convict if the breach was venial. Indeed, the suggestion goes even further: that the meaning and application of the words. . . . "debauch" and "corrupt" in this indictment ought to be entirely for the jury, so that any conduct of this kind is criminal if in the end a jury think it so. In other words, you cannot tell what is criminal except by guessing what view a jury will take, and juries' views may vary and may change with the passing of time. Normally the meaning of words is a question of law for the court. For example, it is not left to a jury to determine the meaning of negligence: they have to consider on evidence and on their own knowledge a much more specific question — Would a reasonable man have done what this man did? . . . If the trial judge's charge in the present case was right, if a jury is entitled to water down the strong words "deprave," "corrupt" or "debauch" so as merely to mean lead astray morally, then it seems to me that the court has transferred to the jury the whole of its functions as censor morum, the law will be whatever any jury may happen to think it ought to be, and this branch of the law will have lost all the certainty which we rightly prize in other branches of our law.

NOTES

1. There have been a number of critical commentaries on the *Shaw* case. See, e.g., H. L. A. Hart, Law, Liberty and Morality 7-12 (1963); Comment, 75 Harv. L. Rev. 1652 (1962). For a favorable comment, see Arthur Goodhart, 77 Law Q. Rev. 560 (1961).

2. See A. T. Denning, Freedom under the Law 40-42 (1949):

[T]he doctrine that acts done to the public mischief are punishable by law . . . is a doctrine quite unknown to France and the other freedom-loving countries of Western Europe where the law is contained in a written code. They take their stand on the principle that no one shall be punished for anything that is not expressly forbidden by law. *Nullum crimen, nulla poena, sine lege.* They regard that principle as their charter of liberty. In this country, however, the common law has not limited itself in that way. It is not contained in a code but in the breasts of the judges, who enunciate and develop the principles needed to deal with any new situations which arise.

In recent years the judges have been faced with acts such as these: A man may call the fire brigade when there is no fire to attend to: or a woman may go to the police and tell them an invented story about being attacked: and thus these public servants may be diverted from their proper duties. In 1933 the judge declared such conduct to be criminal, even though it had not previously been expressly forbidden by law. No one will doubt that it was criminal, because it was a fraud affecting the public at large. But unfortunately the judges based their decision on a wider and much more questionable ground. They relied on an obiter dictum of a judge in 1801, who said that "all offences of a public nature, that is, such acts or attempts as tend to the prejudice of the community, are indictable."

Now that mode of reasoning is dangerously similar to the reasoning by which the Russian jurists justify the punishment of any acts which are socially dangerous. Starting from the point of view that the interests of the State are paramount, their jurists say that the judges ought to punish any act which is dangerous to the State, even though it is not expressly forbidden. Article 16 of the Soviet Code says that "if the Code has not made provision for any act which is socially dangerous, it is to be dealt with on the basis, and as carrying the same degree of responsibility, as the offences which it most nearly resembles." So the only question for their judges is, Is the Act socially dangerous? That is precisely the same test as was stated by our judges in the public mischief case.

3. The doctrine of common law crimes, under which acts are made criminal if the court (or a court and a jury) regards them as directly tending to injure the public to such an extent as to require the state to punish the wrongdoer, even in the absence of an explicit statutory prohibition, was once recognized in many American jurisdictions. See Note, Common Law Crimes in the United States, 47 Colum. L. Rev. 1332 (1947). An example is Commonwealth v. Mochan, 177 Pa. Super. 454, 110 A.2d 788 (1955), in which this doctrine was successfully invoked to punish the maker of obscene telephone calls. The effect of extensive penal code revisions in the United States has been largely to eliminate common law crimes. Not entirely, however. See Mich. Comp. L. §750.505, making offenses indictable at common law punishable as felonies. See People v. Kevorkian, — N.W.2d — (Mich. 1994). The cognate doctrine that criminalizes a conspiracy to commit acts against the public interest (pages 729-730 infra) has also been rejected in many jurisdictions. At all events, the *Shaw* case represents an extreme instance of the abandonment of the principle of legality. Almost every precept associated with that principle is violated — that judges should not create new crimes, that the criminal law may operate only prospectively, that crimes must be defined with sufficient precision to serve as a guide to lawful conduct and to confine the discretion of police and prosecutors. In the cases that follow we will be concerned with more problematic issues concerning the reach of the principle of legality.

KEELER v. SUPERIOR COURT

Supreme Court of California
2 Cal. 3d 619, 470 P.2d 617 (1970)

[Five months after obtaining an interlocutory decree of divorce, a husband intercepted his wife on a mountain road. She was in an advanced state of pregnancy by another man; fetal movements had already been observed by her and by her obstetrician. Her husband said to her, "I hear you're pregnant," glanced at her body and added, "You sure are. I'm going to stomp it out of you." He shoved his knee into her abdomen and struck her. The fetus was delivered stillborn, its head fractured.]

MOSK, J. . . . An information was filed charging petitioner, in count I, with committing the crime of murder (Pen. Code. §187) in that he did "unlawfully kill a human being, to wit Baby Girl Vogt, with malice aforethought." . . . His motion to set aside the information for lack of probable cause (Pen. Code, §995) was denied, and he now seeks a writ of prohibition. . . .

Penal Code section 187 provides: "Murder is the unlawful killing of a human being, with malice aforethought." The dispositive question is whether the fetus which petitioner is accused of killing was, on February 23, 1969, a "human being" within the meaning of the statute. If it was not, petitioner cannot be charged with its "murder" and prohibition will lie.

Section 187 was enacted as part of the Penal Code of 1872. Inasmuch as the provision has not been amended since that date, we must determine the intent of the legislature at the time of its enactment. But section 187 was, in turn, taken verbatim from the first California statute defining murder, part of the Crimes and Punishments Act of 1850. . . . We begin, accordingly, by inquiring into the intent of the Legislature in 1850 when it first defined murder as the unlawful and malicious killing of a "human being."

It will be presumed, of course, that in enacting a statute the Legislature was familiar with the relevant rules of the common law, and, when it couches its enactment in common law language, that its intent was to continue those rules in statutory form. . . .

We therefore undertake a brief review of the origins and development of the common law of abortional homicide. [Discussion omitted.]

We conclude that in declaring murder to be the unlawful and malicious killing of a "human being" the Legislature of 1850 intended that term to have the settled common law meaning of a person who had been born alive, and did not intend the act of feticide — as distinguished from abortion — to be an offense under the laws of California.

Nothing occurred between the years 1850 and 1872 to suggest that in adopting the new Penal Code on the latter date the Legislature entertained any different intent. The case law of our sister states, for example, remained consonant with the common law. . . .

It is the policy of this state to construe a penal statute as favorably to the defendant as its language and the circumstances of its application may reasonably permit; just as in the case of a question of fact, the defendant is entitled to the benefit of every reasonable doubt as to the true interpretation of words or the construction of language used in a statute. . . . We hold that in adopting the definition of murder in Penal Code section 187 the Legislature intended to exclude from its reach the act of killing an unborn fetus.

The People urge, however, that the sciences of obstetrics and pediatrics have greatly progressed since 1872, to the point where with proper medical care a normally developed fetus prematurely born at 28 weeks or more has an excellent chance of survival, i.e., is "viable"; that the common law requirement of live birth to prove the fetus had become a "human being" who may be the victim of murder is no longer in accord with scientific fact, since an unborn but viable fetus is now fully capable of independent life; and that one who unlawfully and maliciously terminates such a life should therefore be liable to prosecution for murder under section 187. We may grant the premises of this argument. . . . But we cannot join in the conclusion sought to be deduced: we cannot hold this petitioner to answer for murder by reason of his alleged act of killing an unborn — even though viable — fetus. To such a charge there are two insuperable obstacles, one "jurisdictional" and the other constitutional.

Penal Code section 6 declares in relevant part that "No act or omission" accomplished after the code has taken effect "is criminal or punishable, except as prescribed or authorized by this code, or by some of the statutes which it specifies as continuing in force and as not affected by its provisions, or by some ordinance, municipal, county, or township regulation. . . ." This section embodies a fundamental principle of our tripartite form of government, i.e., that subject to the constitutional prohibition against cruel and unusual punishment, the power to define crimes and fix penalties is vested exclusively in the legislative branch. . . . Stated differently, there are no common law crimes in California. . . .

Settled rules of construction implement this principle. Although the Penal Code commands us to construe its provisions "according to the fair import of their terms, with a view to effect its objects and to promote justice" (Pen. Code, §4), it is clear the courts cannot go so far as to create an offense by enlarging a statute, by inserting or deleting words, or by giving the terms used false or unusual meanings. . . . Penal statutes will not be made to reach beyond their plain intent; they include only those offenses coming clearly within the import of their language. . . .

We recognize that the killing of an unborn but viable fetus may be deemed by some to be an offense of similar nature and gravity; but as Chief Justice Marshall warned long ago, "It would be dangerous, indeed, to carry the principle, that a case which is within the reason or mischief of a statute, is within its provisions, so far as to punish a crime not enumerated in the statute, because it is of equal atrocity, or of kindred character, with those which are enumerated." (United States v. Wiltberger (1820) 18 U.S. (5 Wheat.) 76, 96.) Whether to thus extend liability for murder in California is a determination solely within the province of the Legislature. . . .

The second obstacle to the proposed judicial enlargement of section 187 is the guarantee of due process of law. Assuming arguendo that we have the power to adopt the new construction of this statute as the law of California, such a ruling, by constitutional command, could operate only prospectively, and thus could not in any event reach the conduct of petitioner on February 23, 1969.

The first essential of due process is fair warning of the act which is made punishable as a crime. "That the terms of a penal statute creating a new offense must be sufficiently explicit to inform those who are subject to it what conduct on their part will render them liable to its penalties, is a well-recognized requirement, consonant alike with ordinary notions of fair play and the settled rules of law." (Connally v. General Constr. Co. (1926) 269 U.S. 385, 391.) . . .

This requirement of fair warning is reflected in the constitutional prohibition against the enactment of ex post facto laws (U.S. Const., art. I, §§9, 10; Cal. Const. art. I, §16). When a new penal statute is applied retrospectively to make punishable an act which was not criminal at the time it was performed, the defendant has been given no advance notice consistent with due process. And precisely the same effect occurs when such an act is made punishable under a preexisting statute but by means of an unforeseeable *judicial* enlargement thereof. (Bouie v. City of Columbia (1964) 378 U.S. 347.)

In *Bouie* two Negroes took seats in the restaurant section of a South Carolina drugstore; no notices were posted restricting the area to whites only. When the defendants refused to leave upon demand, they were arrested and convicted of violating a criminal trespass statute which prohibited entry on the property of another "after notice" forbidding such conduct. Prior South Carolina decisions had emphasized the necessity of proving such notice to support a conviction under the statute. The South Carolina Supreme Court nevertheless affirmed the convictions, construing the statute to prohibit not only the act of entering after notice not to do so but also the wholly different act of remaining on the property after receiving notice to leave.

The United States Supreme Court reversed the convictions, holding that the South Carolina court's ruling was "unforeseeable" and when an "unforeseeable state-court construction of a criminal statute is applied retroactively to subject a person to criminal liability for past conduct, the effect is to deprive him of due process of law in the sense of fair warning that his contemplated conduct constitutes a crime." Analogizing to the prohibition against retrospective penal legislation, the high court reasoned:

> Indeed, an unforeseeable judicial enlargement of a criminal statute, applied retroactively, operates precisely like an ex post facto law, such as Art. I, §10, of the Constitution forbids. An ex post facto law has been defined by this Court as one "that makes an action done before the passing of the law, and which was *innocent* when done, criminal; and punishes such action," or "that *aggravates* a *crime,* or makes it *greater* than it was, when committed." Calder v. Bull, 3 Dall. 386, 390. If a

state legislature is barred by the Ex Post Facto Clause from passing such a law, it must follow that a State Supreme Court is barred by the Due Process Clause from achieving precisely the same result by judicial construction. The fundamental principle that "the required criminal law must have existed when the conduct in issue occurred," Hall, General Principles of Criminal Law (2d ed. 1960), at 58-59, must apply to bar retroactive criminal prohibitions emanating from courts as well as from legislatures.

The court remarked in conclusion that "Application of this rule is particularly compelling where, as here, the petitioners' conduct cannot be deemed improper or immoral." In the case at bar the conduct with which petitioner is charged is certainly "improper" and "immoral," and it is not contended he was exercising a constitutionally favored right. But the matter is simply one of degree, and it cannot be denied that the guarantee of due process extends to violent as well as peaceful men. The issue remains, would the judicial enlargement of section 187 now proposed have been foreseeable to this petitioner? . . .

Turning to the case law, we find no reported decision of the California courts which should have given petitioner notice that the killing of an unborn but viable fetus was prohibited by section 187. . . .

Properly understood, the often cited case of People v. Chavez (1947) 77 Cal. App. 2d 621, 176 P.2d 92, does not derogate from this rule. . . .

Chavez . . . stands for the proposition — to which we adhere — that a viable fetus "in the process of being born" is a human being within the meaning of the homicide statutes. But it stands for no more; in particular it does not hold that a fetus, however viable, which is *not* "in the process of being born" is nevertheless a "human being" in the law of homicide. On the contrary, the opinion is replete with references to the common law requirement that the child be "born alive," however that term is defined, and must accordingly be deemed to reaffirm that requirement as part of the law of California. . . .

We conclude that the judicial enlargement of section 187 now urged upon us by the People would not have been foreseeable to this petitioner, and hence that its adoption at this time would deny him due process of law. . . .[a]

BURKE, J. The majority hold that "Baby Girl" Vogt, who, according to medical testimony, had reached the 35th week of development, had a 96 percent chance of survival, and was "definitely" alive and viable at the time of her death, nevertheless was not a "human being" under California's homicide statutes. In my view, in so holding, the majority ignore significant common law precedents, frustrate the express intent of the Legislature, and defy reason, logic and common sense. . . .

The majority opinion suggests that we are confined to common law concepts, and to the common law definition of murder or manslaughter. However, the Legislature, in Penal Code sections 187 and 192, has defined those offenses for us: homicide is the unlawful killing of a "human being." Those words need not be frozen in place as of any particular time, but must be fairly and reasonably interpreted by this court to promote justice and to carry out the evident pur-

---

a. Soon after the *Keeler* decision the California legislature amended §187 of its Penal Code to include the killing of a "fetus" in the definition of murder. The Statute excepts voluntary abortion. — EDS.

poses of the Legislature in adopting a homicide statute. Thus, Penal Code section 4, which was enacted in 1872 along with sections 187 and 192, provides:

> The rule of the common law, that penal statutes are to be strictly construed, has no application to this code. All its provisions are to be construed according to the fair import of their terms, with a view to effect its objects and to promote justice. . . .

We commonly conceive of human existence as a spectrum stretching from birth to death. However, if this court properly might expand the definition of "human being" at one end of that spectrum, we may do so at the other end. Consider the following example: All would agree that "Shooting or otherwise damaging a corpse is not homicide. . . ." However, it is readily apparent that our concepts of what constitutes a "corpse" have been and are being continually modified by advances in the field of medicine, including new techniques for life revival, restoration and resuscitation such as artificial respiration, open heart massage, transfusions, transplants and a variety of life-restoring stimulants, drugs and new surgical methods. Would this court ignore these developments and exonerate the killer of an apparently "drowned" child merely because that child would have been pronounced dead in 1648 and 1850? Obviously not. Whether a homicide occurred in that case would be determined by medical testimony regarding the capability of the child to have survived prior to the defendant's act. And that is precisely the test which this court should adopt in the instant case.

The common law reluctance to characterize the killing of a quickened fetus as a homicide was based solely upon a presumption that the fetus would have been born dead. . . . Based upon the state of the medical art in the 17th, 18th and 19th centuries, that presumption may have been well-founded. However, as we approach the 21st century, it has become apparent that "This presumption is not only contrary to common experience and the ordinary course of nature, but it is contrary to the usual rule with respect to presumptions followed in this state." (People v. Chavez, supra, at p. 626. . . .)

The majority suggest that to do so would improperly create some new offense. However, the offense of murder is no new offense. Contrary to the majority opinion, the Legislature has not "defined the crime of murder in California to apply only to the unlawful and malicious killing of one who has been born alive." Instead, the Legislature simply used the broad term "human being" and directed the courts to construe that term according to its "fair import" with a view to effect the objects of the homicide statutes and promote justice. (Pen. Code, §4.) What justice will be promoted, what objects effectuated, by construing "human being" as excluding Baby Girl Vogt and her unfortunate successors? Was defendant's brutal act of stomping her to death any less an act of homicide than the murder of a newly born baby? No one doubts that the term "human being" would include the elderly or dying persons whose potential for life has nearly lapsed; their proximity to death is deemed immaterial. There is no sound reason for denying the viable fetus, with its unbounded potential for life, the same status.

The majority also suggest that such an interpretation of our homicide statutes would deny defendant "fair warning" that his act was punishable as a crime. Aside from the absurdity of the underlying premise that defendant consulted Coke, Blackstone or Hale before kicking Baby Girl Vogt to death, it is clear that defendant had adequate notice that his act could constitute homicide. Due process only precludes prosecution under a new statute insufficiently explicit regarding the specific conduct proscribed, or under a preexisting statute "by means of an unforeseeable *judicial* enlargement thereof."

Our homicide statutes have been in effect in this state since 1850. The fact that the California courts have not been called upon to determine the precise question before us does not render "unforeseeable" a decision which determines that a viable fetus is a "human being" under those statutes. Can defendant really claim surprise that a 5-pound, 18-inch, 34-week-old, living, viable child is considered to be a human being? . . .

NOTES

1. The Supreme Court's decision in Bouie v. City of Columbia has served in subsequent Supreme Court decisions mainly as a case to be distinguished. In Rose v. Locke, 423 U.S. 48 (1975), for example, defendant was convicted of violating a Tennessee statute that proscribed the "crime against nature." He was found to have engaged in the act of cunnilingus. While that act was not within the common law definition of crimes against nature and had never been applied to such acts in Tennessee, the state supreme court in this case, for the first time, construed its statute as extending to such acts. The United States Supreme Court distinguished *Bouie* on the ground that here the defendant could not have been taken by surprise, stating:

> [R]espondent can make no claim that [the statute] afforded no notice that his conduct might be within its scope. Other jurisdictions had already reasonably construed identical statutory language to apply to such acts. And given the Tennessee court's clear pronouncements that its statute was intended to effect broad coverage,[a] there was nothing to indicate, clearly or otherwise, that respondent's acts were outside the scope of [the statute].

2. Are the decisions in the *Keeler* and *Bouie* cases required by the principle of legality? Was Keeler, when he "stomped" his pregnant wife, acting under the view that his conduct was not homicidal because the common law did not treat a developed fetus as a "human being"? (Compare Hughes v. State, 868 P.2d 730 (1994) where the Oklahoma Court of Criminal Appeals abandoned the common law "born alive" doctrine without benefit of statute, but applied its ruling prospectively only.) Were the civil rights protestors in *Bouie* surprised to discover that they were acting in violation of South Carolina law? Or are these questions beside the point?

Consider the comments of Justice Stewart, dissenting, in Parker v. Levy, 417 U.S. 773, 774-775 (1974):

> As many decisions of this Court make clear, vague statutes suffer from at least two fatal constitutional defects. First, by failing to provide fair notice of precisely

---

a. The Tennessee Supreme Court had earlier held that fellatio was included, repudiating jurisdictions that had taken a "narrow restrictive definition of the offense." — EDS.

what acts are forbidden, a vague statute "violates the first essential of due process of law." Connally v. General Construction Co. 269 U.S. 385, 391. As the Court put the matter in Lanzetta v. New Jersey, 306 U.S. 451, 453, "No one may be required at peril of life, liberty or property to speculate as to the meaning of penal statutes. All are entitled to be informed as to what the State commands or forbids." "Words which are vague and fluid . . . may be as much of a trap for the innocent as the ancient laws of Caligula." United States v. Cardiff, 344 U.S. 174, 176.[3]

Secondly, vague statutes offend due process by failing to provide explicit standards for those who enforce them, thus allowing discriminatory and arbitrary enforcement. Papachristou v. City of Jacksonville, 405 U.S. 156, 165-171. "A vague law impermissibly delegates basic policy matters to policemen, judges, and juries for resolution on an ad hoc and subjective basis. . . ." Grayned v. City of Rockford, 408 U.S. 104, 108-109.[4] The absence of specificity in a criminal statute invites abuse on the part of prosecuting officials, who are left free to harass any individuals or groups who may be the object of official displeasure.

3. See John Jeffries, Legality, Vagueness and the Construction of Penal Statutes, 71 Va. L. Rev. 189 (1985), for a helpful treatment of these issues.

NASH v. UNITED STATES

Supreme Court of the United States
229 U.S. 373 (1912)

JUSTICE HOLMES delivered the opinion of the Court.

This is an indictment in two counts, — the first for a conspiracy in restraint of trade, the second for a conspiracy to monopolize trade, contrary to the act of July 2, 1890, . . . commonly known as the Sherman Act. . . .

The two counts before us were demurred to on the grounds that the statute was so vague as to be inoperative on its criminal side; that neither of the counts alleged any overt act; that the contemplated acts and things would not have constituted an offense if they had been done, and that the same acts, etc., were too vaguely charged. The demurrer was overruled and this action of the court raises the important questions of the case. We will deal with them before passing to matters of detail.

The objection to the criminal operation of the statute is thought to be warranted by Standard Oil Co. v. United States, 221 U.S. 1, and United States v. American Tobacco Co., 221 U.S. 106. Those cases may be taken to have established that only such contracts and combinations are within the act as, by reason of intent or the inherent nature of the contemplated acts, prejudice the public

3. See also United States v. Harriss, 347 U.S. 612, 617:

The constitutional requirement of definiteness is violated by a criminal statute that fails to give a person of ordinary intelligence fair notice that his contemplated conduct is forbidden by the statute. The underlying principle is that no man shall be held criminally responsible for conduct which he could not reasonably understand to be proscribed.

4. See also Smith v. Goguen, 415 U.S. 566, 575:

Statutory language of such a standard-less sweep allows policemen, prosecutors, and juries to pursue their personal predilections. Legislatures may not so abdicate their responsibilities for setting the standards of the criminal law.

interests by unduly restricting competition or unduly obstructing the course of trade, 221 U.S. 179. And thereupon it is said that the crime thus defined by the statute contains in its definition an element of degree as to which estimates may differ, with the result that a man might find himself in prison because his honest judgment did not anticipate that of a jury of less competent men. The kindred proposition that "the criminality of an act cannot depend upon whether a jury may think it reasonable or unreasonable. There must be some definiteness and certainty," is cited from the late Mr. Justice Brewer, sitting in the circuit court. Tozer v. United States, 52 Fed. 917, 919.

But apart from the common law as to the restraint of trade thus taken up by the statute, the law is full of instances where a man's fate depends on his estimating rightly, that is, as the jury subsequently estimates it, some matter of degree. If his judgment is wrong, not only may he incur a fine or a short imprisonment, as here; he may incur the penalty of death. "An act causing death may be murder, manslaughter, or misadventure, according to the degree of danger attending it" by common experience in the circumstances known to the actor. "The very meaning of the fiction of implied malice in such cases at common law was, that a man might have to answer with his life for consequences which he neither intended nor foresaw." Com. v. Pierce, 138 Mass. 165, 178. . . . "The criterion in such cases is to examine whether common social duty would, under the circumstances, have suggested a more circumspect conduct." 1 East, P.C. 262. If a man should kill another by driving an automobile furiously into a crowd, he might be convicted of murder, however little he expected the result. . . . If he did no more than drive negligently through a street, he might get off with manslaughter or less. . . . And in the last case he might be held although he himself thought that he was acting as a prudent man should. . . . We are of opinion that there is no constitutional difficulty in the way of enforcing the criminal part of the act. . . .

NOTES

1. Justice Holmes's opinion in Nash v. United States has been widely invoked to justify criminal statutes defining criminal conduct in terms of degree. Statutes imposing criminal liability for negligent, reckless, or careless driving resulting in the death of another have commonly been upheld. In United States v. Ragen, 314 U.S. 513, 523 (1941), the Court sustained a criminal conviction of a defendant for willfully taking a deduction of an unreasonable allowance for salaries on his income tax return, stating: "The mere fact that a penal statute is so framed as to require a jury upon occasion to determine a question of reasonableness is not sufficient to make it too vague to afford a practical guide to permissible conduct." See Ernst Freund, The Use of Indefinite Terms in Statutes, 30 Yale L.J. 437, 443-444 (1921).

In State v. Adams, 180 Neb. 542, 143 N.W.2d 920 (1966), defendant appealed a conviction for violating a statute providing: "Any person or persons who shall operate a vehicle upon any highway in such a manner as to (1) endanger the safety of others or (2) cause immoderate wear or damage to any highway, shall be deemed guilty of a misdemeanor. . . ." Neither in terms or by construction was a showing of negligence required. *Question:* Should the statute be held unconstitutionally vague?

2. Consider the following observations of Lord Simon on legal certainty in Knuller v. Director of Public Prosecutions, [1973] A.C. 435:

> Certainty is a desirable feature of any system of law. But there are some types of conduct desirably the subject matter of legal rule which cannot be satisfactorily regulated by specific statutory enactment, but are better left to the practice of juries and other tribunals of fact. They depend finally for their juridical classification not upon proof of the existence of some particular fact, but upon proof of the attainment of some degree. . . . Has an act been done, or a contract performed, or a duty discharged, within a reasonable time? Are goods reasonably fit for a particular purpose? Are they of merchantable quality? Has the defendant so conducted himself that a reasonable person would assume that he was making a representation of fact meant to be acted on? . . .
>
> The law does not return an answer in advance to any of these questions, which arise both at common law and under statute: all must await the answer of the tribunal. . . .
>
> Nor are such situations limited to the civil law. . . . Whether conduct causing death falls so far short of a proper duty of care as to amount to manslaughter cannot be known until the jury returns its verdict. . . . The driver of a motor vehicle may be accompanied by leading and junior counsel and by his solicitor as well; but he will still not know whether or not he has committed the offence of driving in a manner dangerous to the public or without due care and attention or without reasonable consideration for others or at an excessive speed until jury or justices so find. . . . Similarly with those many offenses which depend on whether admitted conduct was perpetrated dishonestly. Again, did the accused convene an assembly in such a manner as to cause reasonable people to fear a breach of the peace? . . . In none of these cases, which again could be greatly multiplied, can it in advance be said with certainty whether an offence has been committed: and those who choose, in such situations, to sail as close as possible to the wind inevitably run some risk.

3. In Burg v. Municipal Court, 35 Cal. 3d 257, 673 P.2d 732 (1983), the court was presented with a challenge to the constitutionality of a statute making it unlawful "for any person who has 0.10 percent or more, by weight, of alcohol in his or her blood to drive a vehicle." This provision was enacted in response to the difficulties of proof under the more conventional statute that made it criminal to drive while under the influence of alcohol. The new statute was challenged on the ground that it was unconstitutionally vague. The court rejected the challenge, stating:

> Today it is established that due process requires a statute to be definite enough to provide (1) a standard of conduct for those who activities are proscribed and (2) a standard for police enforcement and for ascertainment of guilt. . . .
>
> To begin with the second component, the statute could not be more precise as a standard for law enforcement. . . . It gives no discretion whatever to the police, and thus is not susceptible of arbitrary enforcement. Indeed, the very precision of the standard assures the statute's validity in this respect.
>
> Turning now to the "fair notice" component of the void-for-vagueness doctrine, we observe that the real thrust of defendant's argument is that the statute is in effect "void for preciseness." His complaint is not that the language of the statute is vague or ambiguous, but that it is too exact. His novel theory is that the statute fails to notify potential violators of the condition it proscribes, because it is impos-

sible for a person to determine by means of his senses whether his blood-alcohol level is a "legal" 0.09 percent or an "illegal" 0.10 percent. The latter observation is probably true as a matter of fact, but it does not affect the constitutionality of the statute.

Defendant's theory would render the void-for-vagueness doctrine internally inconsistent: the notice requirement would compete with the need to provide precise standards for law enforcement. When, as in the present case, a statutory standard requires scientific measurement, the very factor that assures due process under the "standards" component would violate due process under the "notice" component.

[Defendant] claims the statute is invalid because it is impossible for ordinary persons actually to know when their blood alcohol reaches the proscribed point. No court, however, has interpreted the notice requirement so strictly; indeed, such a view would invalidate many other criminal laws, violations of which depend on an after-the-fact determination by a judge or jury as to the defendant's state of mind or the reasonableness of his behavior.

"Fair notice" requires only that a violation be described with a "'reasonable degree of certainty'" so that "ordinary people can understand what conduct is prohibited." The notice provided must be such that prosecution does not "trap the innocent" without "fair warning."

One who drives a vehicle after having ingested sufficient alcohol to approach or exceed the level proscribed is neither "innocent" . . . nor is he without "fair warning." . . . It is difficult to sympathize with an "unsuspecting" defendant who did not know if he could take a last sip without crossing the line, but who decided to do so anyway.

4. In International Harvester Co., v. Kentucky, 234 U.S. 216 (1914), the Court invalidated a statute interpreted by the Kentucky Court of Appeals to prohibit certain combinations in restraint of trade, and which forbade the raising or lowering of the price above or below the "real value" of the article, taken to mean its market value under fair competition and under normal market conditions. Justice Holmes, speaking for the Court, stated (at 222):

Value is the effect in exchange of the relative social desire for compared objects expressed in terms of a common denominator. It is a fact, and generally is more or less easy to ascertain. But what it would be with such increase of a never extinguished competition as it might be guessed would have existed had the combination not been made, with exclusion of the actual effect of other abnormal influences, and, it would seem, with exclusion also of any increased efficiency in the machines, but with inclusion of the effect of the combination so far as it was economically beneficial to itself and the community, is a problem that no human ingenuity could solve. The reason is not the general uncertainties of a jury trial, but that the elements necessary to determine the imaginary ideal are uncertain both in nature and degree of effect to the acutest commercial mind. . . . We regard this decision as consistent with Nash v. United States, . . . in which it was held that a criminal law is not unconstitutional merely because it throws upon men the risk of rightly estimating a matter of degree, — what is an undue restraint of trade. That deals with the actual, not with an imaginary condition other than the facts. It goes no further than to recognize that, as with negligence, between the two extremes of the obviously illegal and the plainly lawful there is a gradual approach, and that the complexity of life makes it impossible to draw a line in advance without an artificial simplification that would be unjust. The conditions are as permanent as anything human, and a great body of precedents on the civil side, coupled with familiar practice, make it comparatively easy for common sense to keep to what is safe. But if business is to go on, men must unite to do it and must sell their wares. To compel them to guess, on peril of indictment, what the community would have given for them if the continually changing conditions were other than they are, to an uncertain extent; to divine prophetically what the reaction of only partially determinate facts would be upon the imaginations and desires of purchasers, is to exact gifts that mankind does not possess.

Cf. Justice Frankfurter, dissenting, in Winters v. New York, 333 U.S. 507, 539 (1948):

The teaching of the *Nash* and the *Harvester* Cases is that it is not violative of due process of law for a legislature in framing its criminal law to cast upon the public the duty of care and even of caution, provided that there is sufficient warning to one bent on obedience that he comes near the proscribed area.

PAPACHRISTOU v. CITY OF JACKSONVILLE

Supreme Court of the United States
405 U.S. 156 (1972)

JUSTICE DOUGLAS delivered the opinion of the Court.

This case involves eight defendants who were convicted in a Florida municipal court of violating a Jacksonville, Florida, vagrancy ordinance.[1] . . . For reasons which will appear, we reverse. . . .

The facts are stipulated, Papachristou and Calloway are white females. Melton and Johnson are black males. Papachristou was enrolled in a job-training program sponsored by the State Employment Service at Florida Junior College in Jacksonville. Calloway was a typing and shorthand teacher at a state mental institution located near Jacksonville. She was the owner of the automobile in which the four defendants were arrested. Melton was a Vietnam war veteran who had been released from the Navy after nine months in a veterans' hospital. On the date of his arrest he was a part-time computer helper while attending college as a full-time student in Jacksonville. Johnson was a tow-motor operator in a grocery chain warehouse and was a lifelong resident of Jacksonville.

---

1. Jacksonville Ordinance Code §26-57 provided at the time of these arrests and convictions as follows:

Rogues and vagabonds, or dissolute persons who go about begging, common gamblers, persons who use juggling or unlawful games or plays, common drunkards, common night thieves, pilferers or pickpockets, traders in stolen property, lewd, wanton and lascivious persons, keepers of gambling places, common railers and brawlers, persons wandering or strolling around from place to place without any lawful purpose or object, habitual loafers, disorderly persons, persons neglecting all lawful business and habitually spending their time by frequenting houses of ill fame, gaming houses, or places where alcoholic beverages are sold or served, persons able to work but habitually living upon the earnings of their wives or minor children shall be deemed vagrants and, upon conviction in the Municipal Court shall be punished as provided for Class D offenses.

Class D offenses at the time of these arrests and convictions were punishable by 90 days' imprisonment, $500 fine, or both. . . .

At the time of their arrest the four of them were riding in Calloway's car on the main thoroughfare in Jacksonville. They had left a restaurant owned by Johnson's uncle where they had eaten and were on their way to a night club. The arresting officers denied that the racial mixture in the car played any part in the decision to make the arrest. The arrest, they said, was made because the defendants had stopped near a used-car lot which had been broken into several times. There was, however, no evidence of any breaking and entering on the night in question.

Of these four charged with "prowling by auto" none had been previously arrested except Papachristou who had once been convicted of a municipal offense.

Jimmy Lee Smith and Milton Henry (who is not a petitioner) were arrested between 9 and 10 A.M. on a weekday in downtown Jacksonville, while waiting for a friend who was to lend them a car so they could apply for a job at a produce company. Smith was a part-time produce worker and part-time organizer for a Negro political group. He had a common-law wife and three children supported by him and his wife. He had been arrested several times but convicted only once. Smith's companion, Henry, was an 18-year-old high school student with no previous record of arrest.

This morning it was cold, and Smith had no jacket, so they went briefly into a dry cleaning shop to wait, but left when requested to do so. They thereafter walked back and forth two or three times over a two-block stretch looking for their friend. The store owners, who apparently were wary of Smith and his companion, summoned two police officers who searched the men and found neither had a weapon. But they were arrested because the officers said they had no identification and because the officers did not believe their story.

Heath and codefendant were arrested for "loitering" and for "common thief." Both were residents of Jacksonville, Heath having lived there all his life and being employed at an automobile and body shop. Heath had previously been arrested but his codefendant had no arrest record. Heath and his companion were arrested when they drove up to a residence shared by Heath's girlfriend and some other girls. Some police officers were already there in the process of arresting another man. When Heath and his companion started backing out of the driveway, the officers signaled to them to stop and asked them to get out of the car, which they did. Thereupon they and the automobile were searched. Although no contraband or incriminating evidence was found, they were both arrested. Heath being charged with being a "common thief" because he was reputed to be a thief. The codefendant was charged with "loitering" because he was standing in the driveway, an act which the officers admitted was done only at their command.

Campbell was arrested as he reached his home very early one morning and was charged with "common thief." He was stopped by officers because he was traveling at a high rate of speed, yet no speeding charge was placed against him.

Brown was arrested when he was observed leaving a downtown Jacksonville hotel by a police officer seated in a cruiser. The police testified he was reputed to be a thief, narcotics pusher, and generally opprobrious character. The officer called Brown over to the car, intending at that time to arrest him unless he had a good explanation for being on the street. Brown walked over to the police cruiser, as commanded, and the officer began to search him, apparently preparatory to placing him in the car. In the process of the search he came on two small packets which were later found to contain heroin. When the officer touched the pocket where the packets were, Brown began to resist. He was charged with "disorderly loitering on the street" and "disorderly conduct — resisting arrest with violence." While he was also charged with a narcotics violation, that charge was *nolled*.

Jacksonville's ordinance [was] "derived from early English law," . . . The history is an often-told tale. The breakup of feudal estates in England led to labor shortages which in turn resulted in the Statutes of Laborers, designed to stabilize the labor force by prohibiting increases in wages and prohibiting the movement of workers from their home areas in search of improved conditions. Later vagrancy laws became criminal aspects of the poor laws. The series of laws passed in England on the subject became increasingly severe. But "the theory of the Elizabethan poor laws no longer fits the facts," Edwards v. California, 314 U.S. 160, 174. The conditions which spawned these laws may be gone, but the archaic classifications remain.

This ordinance is void-for-vagueness, both in the sense that it "fails to give a person of ordinary intelligence fair notice that his contemplated conduct is forbidden by the statute," United States v. Harriss, 347 U.S. 612, 617, and because it encourages arbitrary and erratic arrests and convictions. Thornhill v. Alabama, 310 U.S. 88; Herndon v. Lowry, 301 U.S. 242.

Living under a rule of law entails various suppositions, one of which is that "[all persons] are entitled to be informed as to what the State commands or forbids." Lanzetta v. New Jersey, 306 U.S. 451, 453. . . .

The poor among us, the minorities, the average householder are not in business and not alerted to the regulatory schemes of vagrancy laws; and we assume they would have no understanding of their meaning and impact if they read them. Nor are they protected from being caught in the vagrancy net by the necessity of having a specific intent to commit an unlawful act.

The Jacksonville ordinance makes criminal activities which by modern standards are normally innocent. "Nightwalking" is one. Florida construes the ordinance not to make criminal one night's wandering, Johnson v. State, 202 So. 2d, at 855, only the "habitual" wanderer or, as the ordinance describes it, "common night walkers." We know, however, from experience that sleepless people often walk at night, perhaps hopeful that sleep-inducing relaxation will result.

Luis Munoz-Marin, former Governor of Puerto Rico, commented once that "loafing" was a national virtue in his Commonwealth and that it should be encouraged. It is, however, a crime in Jacksonville.

"[P]ersons able to work but habitually living upon the earnings of their wives or minor children" — like habitually living "without visible means of support" — might implicate unemployed pillars of the community who have married rich wives.

"[P]ersons able to work but habitually living upon the earnings of their wives or minor children" may also embrace unemployed people out of the labor market, by reason of a recession or disemployed by reason of technological or so-called structural displacements.

Persons "wandering or strolling" from place to place have been extolled by Walt Whitman and Vachel Lindsay. The qualification "without any lawful purpose or object" may be a trap for innocent acts. Persons "neglecting all lawful business and habitually spending their time by frequenting . . . places where alcoholic beverages are sold or served" would literally embrace many members of golf clubs and city clubs.

Walkers and strollers and wanderers may be going to or coming from a burglary. Loafers or loiterers may be "casing" a place for a holdup. Letting one's wife support him is an intra-family matter, and normally of no concern to the police. Yet it may, of course, be the setting for numerous crimes.

This aspect of the vagrancy ordinance before us is suggested by what this Court said in 1876 about a broad criminal statute enacted by Congress: "It would certainly be dangerous if the legislature could set a net large enough to catch all possible offenders, and leave it to the courts to step inside and say who could be rightfully detained, and who should be set at large." United States v. Reese, 92 U.S. 214, 221.

While that was a federal case, the due process implications are equally applicable to the States and to this vagrancy ordinance. Here the net cast is large, not to give the courts the power to pick and choose but to increase the arsenal of the police. . . .

Another aspect of the ordinance's vagueness appears when we focus, not on the lack of notice given a potential offender, but on the effect of the unfettered discretion it places in the hands of the Jacksonville police. Caleb Foote, an early student of this subject, has called the vagrancy-type law as offering "punishment by analogy." [Foote, Vagrancy Type Law and Its Administration, 104 U. Pa. L. Rev. 603,] 609. Such crimes, though long common in Russia, are not compatible with our constitutional system. We allow our police to make arrests only on "probable cause," a Fourth and Fourteenth Amendment standard applicable to the States as well as to the Federal Government. Arresting a person on suspicion, like arresting a person for investigation, is foreign to our system, even when the arrest is for past criminality. Future criminality, however, is the common justification for the presence of vagrancy statutes. . . .

A direction by a legislature to the police to arrest all "suspicious" persons would not pass constitutional muster. A vagrancy prosecution may be merely the cloak for a conviction which could not be obtained on the real but undisclosed grounds for the arrest. . . .

Those generally implicated by the imprecise terms of the ordinance — poor people, nonconformists, dissenters, idlers — may be required to comport themselves according to the life-style deemed appropriate by the Jacksonville police and the courts. Where, as here, there are no standards governing the exercise of the discretion granted by the ordinance, the scheme permits and encourages an arbitrary and discriminatory enforcement of the law. It furnishes a convenient tool for "harsh and discriminatory enforcement by prosecuting officials, against particular groups deemed to merit their displeasure." Thornhill v. Alabama, 310 U.S. 88, 97-98. It results in a regime in which the poor and the unpopular are permitted to "stand on a public sidewalk . . . only at the whim of any police officer." Shuttlesworth v. Birmingham, 382 U.S. 87, 90. . . .

A presumption that people who might walk or loaf or loiter or stroll or frequent houses where liquor is sold, or who are supported by their wives or who look suspicious to the police are to become future criminals is too precarious for a rule of law. The implicit presumption in these generalized vagrancy standards — that crime is being nipped in the bud — is too extravagant to deserve extended treatment. Of course, vagrancy statutes are useful to the police. Of course they are nets making easy the round-up of so-called undesirables. But the rule of law implies equality and justice in its application. Vagrancy laws of the Jacksonville type teach that the scales of justice are so tipped that even-handed administration of the law is not possible. The rule of law, evenly applied to minorities as well as majorities, to the poor as well as the rich, is the great mucilage that holds society together.

The Jacksonville ordinance cannot be squared with our constitutional standards and is plainly unconstitutional.

Reversed.

MODEL PENAL CODE

SECTION 250.6.   LOITERING OR PROWLING

[See Appendix for text of this section.]

MODEL PENAL CODE AND COMMENTARIES, COMMENT TO §250.6 AT 388-389 (1980):
This provision differs from prior legislation in that it is narrowly designed to reach only alarming loitering. Typical situations covered would be the following: a known professional pickpocket is seen loitering in a crowded railroad station; a person not recognized as a local resident is seen lurking in a doorway and furtively looking up and down the street to see if he is being watched; an unknown man is seen standing for some time in a dark alley where he has no apparent business. Perhaps an even better example comes from the leading New York case of People v. Berck:

> [T]he police had been advised that certain residential premises would be temporarily unoccupied. On patrol, they observed defendant standing behind a tree, at 1:00 A.M., seeming to be examining the unoccupied premises. When questioned by the police, he refused to explain his presence, but more important, even to identify himself. No other person was present and there was, of course, no indication of a tryst.[19]

None of these situations would be covered by the law of attempt, even under the expanded definition of that offense in Section 5.01 of the Model Code. In no case has there been a "substantial step in a course of conduct planned to culminate in [the] commission of the crime." Also, none of these situations involves possession of burglar's tools or other instruments of crime that would sustain a conviction under Section 5.06.

The major issue of policy is what response to make to such situations. At least five courses are open:

19. 32 N.Y.2d 567, 300 N.E.2d 411 (1973). [For another typical example see State v. Ecker, 311 So. 2d 104, 110 (Fla. 1975): The "record reflects that the defendant was hiding among bushes at a private dwelling at 1:20 A.M. When the officer came in response to a call, he saw the defendant jump from the fence surrounding the dwelling and start running. The officer apprehended the defendant and placed him under arrest." — EDS.]

    (i) Loitering or wandering "at unusual hours" or "without lawful business" may be punished as a completed offense. This is the approach characteristic of prior law.

   (ii) The situation giving rise to alarm for persons or property may be treated as an occasion for police inquiry. Failure to explain oneself satisfactorily would constitute an offense.

  (iii) The situation giving rise to alarm may be deemed a proper basis for detention and interrogation but not for criminal prosecution.

  (iv) The situation might be dealt with only as a basis for police orders to "move on" and thus to remove the immediate alarm.

   (v) Finally, the kind of situation described above might be viewed as giving rise to no legal consequence. An officer, of course, could make inquiry of suspicious persons, most of whom would answer voluntarily. Where the responses do not dissipate suspicion, the officer could make such observations as would facilitate later identification of the suspect if a crime did take place.

None of these alternatives is entirely satisfactory. The first authorizes criminal conviction without proof of anti-social behavior or inclination. Additionally, . . . it is difficult to imagine a statute of this sort that could pass constitutional muster under current standards. The second option is no doubt better, but it still imposes liability for failure to identify oneself or to give a credible account of one's behavior without further proof of anti-social purpose. Another trouble with this approach is that the plausible lie about one's identity or purposes will in all probability avoid liability, while an implausible truth at least leaves one open to arrest. Finally, this kind of statute is also not free from constitutional doubt. The third approach involves a controversial and possibly unconstitutional change in the law of arrest rather than the definition of a substantive offense within the scope of the Model Code. The fourth solution, the police order to "move on," hardly solves the problem of the individual who is bent on crime and at the same time confers a disturbingly unbounded discretion on the police. The last option — authorizing no police action other than voluntary questioning and visual observation — is perhaps most consistent with the ideal of the role of police and with general normative principles governing the proper use of penal sanctions. Nonetheless, this total abandonment of the traditional vagrancy concept would lead to a significant loss in effective law enforcement and would encounter justifiably serious political resistance.

Section 250.6 of the Model seeks to provide the least objectionable form of the second alternative discussed above. . . .

As a matter of constitutional policy, abrogation of loitering statutes is arguably sound. There is irreducible indeterminacy in the definition of loitering, as there is necessarily discretion in the police to decide in the first instance what the "public safety demands" or whether the circumstances "justify suspicion" or "warrant alarm." It is worth pointing out, however, that the statutes discussed above are a far cry from the ordinance invalidated in *Papachristou*. If even the Model Code provision is unconstitutionally vague, . . . then it seems likely that no general provision against loitering can be drafted to survive constitutional review. Of course, narrower proscriptions of loitering with specific purpose — e.g., to solicit deviate sexual relations — may continue to be valid, but there would be no provision to deal with the person who is obviously up to no good but whose precise intention cannot be ascertained. Most courts are willing to consider in a void-for-vagueness analysis the need for some provision and the impossibility of achieving greater precision. This factor cuts strongly in favor of the constitutionality of the Model Code provision.

NOTE

Courts have divided on whether the Model Penal Code formulation of the crime of loitering meets the constitutional requirements of *Papachristou*. An Oregon court held a similar ordinance void for vagueness in City of Portland v. White, 9 Or. App. 239, 495 P.2d 778 (1972). However, substantially similar statutes were upheld in State v. Ecker, 311 So. 2d 104 (Fla. 1975); State v. Sparks, 51 Wis. 2d 256, 186 N.W.2d 245 (1971); City of Seattle v. Drew, 70 Wash. 2d 405, 423 P.2d 522 (1967).

In Kolender v. Lawson, 461 U.S. 352 (1983), the Supreme Court held void for vagueness a California statute that required persons who loiter or wander on the streets to provide a "credible and reliable" identification and to account for their presence, when requested to do so by a police officer under circumstances that "indicate to a reasonable man that the public safety demands such identification." Speaking for the Court, Justice O'Connor wrote that the statute, as construed by the California courts, provided no standard for determining what a suspect must do to satisfy its requirements and therefore vested virtually complete discretion in the hands of the police. Justices White and Rehnquist dissented.

Several courts have considered the effect of *Kolender* on loitering statutes closely patterned on the Model Penal Code formulation. In both Watts v. State, 463 So. 2d 205 (Fla. 1985), and Porta v. Mayor, City of Omaha, 593 F. Supp. 863 (D. Neb. 1984), courts distinguished the California provision involved in *Kolender* and upheld statutes comparable to Model Penal Code §250.6. Both courts reasoned that the loitering provisions at issue gave a suspected person the "opportunity" to justify his or her presence but did not require the person to do so and did not make the refusal to answer in itself an element of the offense; rather the refusal to identify is only one of several circumstances that the officer may consider in determining whether the circumstances warrant concern for the public safety. *Question:* Does this reasoning suggest that the Code provision is substantially narrower than the statute involved in *Kolender,* or does the Code provision in effect vest the police officer with even broader discretion?

A new generation of loitering statutes seeks to avoid constitutional obstacles by making it criminal to loiter in circumstances suggesting a specific criminal purpose, such as drug peddling. In City of Akron v. Rowland, 67 Ohio St. 3d 374, 618 N.E.2d 138 (1993) a divided court invalidated such a law on vagueness grounds. The statute made it a crime to loiter in a manner and under circumstances manifesting a purpose to engage in drug-related activity. The majority held there were too many undefined circumstances that might be thought to manifest the proscribed purpose, and found that the statute could not be fairly interpreted to require proof that the defendant actually had the specific purpose to peddle drugs.

CHAPTER
4

RAPE

Few areas of criminal law have attracted as much attention and controversy over the past two decades as the law of rape. Widespread criticism that rape law was unfair to women led to extensive changes in the definition of rape, in the rules of evidence and procedure affecting rape trials, and in the processing of rape complaints.

Is rape law now in accord with prevailing attitudes about the expression of consent in sexual contacts? What are those attitudes (and are they the same for women as for men)? Are the currently prevailing attitudes unfair to women, and if so, should the criminal law move beyond them?

Issues analogous to these rarely present any difficulty in connection with crimes like homicide, burglary, robbery and theft. But because these questions are both difficult to answer and acutely controversial in connection with rape, an understanding of the legal issues requires attention to materials that can elucidate the prevalence of the targeted behavior, the kinds of harm it causes and the social dynamics underlying it. We therefore begin our examination of the issues by considering several contrasting perspectives on the social and behavioral aspects of rape. We then examine the relevant legal doctrines under three headings: mens rea, actus reus, and problems of proof.

A.   PERSPECTIVES

MARGARET T. GORDON & STEPHANIE RIGER, THE FEMALE FEAR: THE SOCIAL COST OF RAPE

2, 26-28, 32-36 (1991)

Most women experience fear of rape as a nagging, gnawing sense that something awful could happen, an angst that keeps them from doing things they want or need to do, or from doing them at the time or in the way they might otherwise do. Women's fear of rape is a sense that one must always be on guard, vigilant and alert, a feeling that causes a woman to tighten with anxiety if someone is walking too closely behind her, especially at night. . . . It is worse than fear of other crimes because women know they are held responsible for avoiding rape, and should they be victimized, they know they are likely to be blamed. . . .

[I]n 1986 there were 90,434 forcible rapes reported by police across the country to the FBI, representing an increase of 3.2 percent over 1985 and a rate of 73 per 100,000 women. . . .

Analyses of how UCR [Uniform Crime Reports] data are gathered and compiled [by the FBI] have indicated errors of omission and commission, most of which lead to the underrepresentation of the actual rate of rape. . . . Some police departments regularly conclude that as many as 50 percent of the charges of forcible rape received are not classifiable as offenses . . .

These findings and others gave rise to the National Crime Surveys (also often referred to as the victimization surveys) now regularly conducted in conjunction with the U.S. Census. [R]apes reported to surveyors in 1986 yield a rate of about 140 per 100,000 women. . . . Thus, the most current victimization surveys indicate a rate [double] that indicated by the UCR data. . . .

Perhaps the greatest source of error in the reported rate of rape is the non-reported incidents. This "doubly dark" figure of crime, which is reported *neither* to the police *nor* to a victimization survey interviewer, remains elusive. Research indicates that rapes by known assailants are particularly likely to go unreported, resulting in a serious underestimation of the extent of violence against women. . . .

When women living in [three] selected cities were asked in telephone interviews if they had ever been raped *or* sexually assaulted *at some time during their lives,* 2 percent said yes. That is a rate of 2,000 per 100,000, much higher than either yearly UCR or survey rates for these cities. But when women were asked the same question in person, the figures were even more startling. Eleven percent (or 11,000 in 100,000) said they had been raped or sexually assaulted. These rates are surprisingly high and help to underscore the problems with any of the figures now available. . . .

While stranger rapes may constitute people's image of what is typical, acquaintance rapes or nonstranger rapes, are an increasingly large proportion of actual rapes and now account for 55 to 60 percent of rapes reported to police. . . .

But the words "nonstranger" or "acquaintance" cover a wide range of types of relationships. [One] type of acquaintance rape is referred to as date rape; this occurs when the victim initially is willing to be in the company of a man who then becomes violent toward her. For several reasons, many of these rapes are not reported. . . . Although the victim may have resisted and been forced, she herself may not recognize it as rape *because* she was on a date. . . . Most important, date-rape victims often feel they won't be believed or will be perceived as having "asked for it" — by the police, the courts, and everyone else and, therefore, there is no point in reporting it. . . .

A special form of date rape is being increasingly reported on college campuses. In what may have become a typical campus rape, a young woman is assaulted by a young man she has met (often the same evening) at a party on campus. She may have danced with him, gone for a walk with him, gone to his room, or allowed him to walk her to her room. Many campus rapes seem to involve the use of excessive amounts of alcohol by one or both persons involved. One victim of campus rape blamed herself because she was drunk. When a faculty member reminded her that it is a crime to rape, but not a crime to get drunk, the coed decided to file charges. Experts in this field say, "Clearly, among college students, sexual aggression is rare among strangers and common among acquaintances." . . .

[R]esearchers argue that campus rape may be so prevalent because of norms in our society that condone sexual violence. People are conditioned to accept sexual roles in which male aggression is an acceptable part of our modern courtship culture. According to this line of reasoning, campus rapists are ordinary males operating in an ordinary social context, not even knowing they are doing something wrong, let alone against the law.

NOTES

1. Attempts to estimate the frequency of rape continue to stir controversy. One major study, led by Professor Mary Koss,[1] found that 27 percent of college women had been victims of at least one rape or attempted rape since age 14. By comparison, the official NCS victim survey discussed by Gordon and Riger reports a victimization rate of about 140 per 100,000 women; this annual rate of 0.14 percent implies that for women aged 24, roughly 1.4 percent would have suffered at least one rape or attempted rape during the 10 years since age 14. Because of the large discrepancy between the 27 percent reported by Koss and the 1.4 percent figure implied by the NCS survey, there has been heated debate over the methods and ideology that underlie these and similar studies. One social scientist dismisses the Koss figures as unrealistic "[a]dvocacy numbers"; he notes that 73 percent of the women counted as rape victims did not label their own experience as "rape" and 42 percent of them subsequently dated and had sex again with their supposed attackers. See Neil Gilbert, The Phantom Epidemic of Sexual Assault, The Public Interest 54, 60, 63 (Spring 1991). Other researchers argue that such behavior on the part of victims — the tendency to blame themselves when their date turns violent and to deny that the experience was rape — is itself a confirmation of the seriousness and prevalence of sexual abuse. See Robin Warshaw, I Never Called It Rape (1988).

To keep this debate in perspective, it is important to stress that even the estimates at the "low" end represent an enormous amount of abuse — almost 150,000 rapes per year. But the debate over the prevalence of rape remains important for understanding the nature of the task that criminal law confronts: Is the law addressing serious but infrequent, aberrational behavior? Or should the law condemn (and does it already condemn) a type of conduct that is commonplace among ordinary, otherwise law-abiding people?

The definitions of rape used in the studies become important here. In the NCS survey, rape is defined as "[c]arnal knowledge through the use of force or the threat of force, including attempts"; the survey does not include statutory rape (consensual sex involving a minor) or sex where the victim is incapacitated

---

1. Mary P. Koss, Christine A. Gidycz & Nadine Wisniewski, The Scope of Rape: Incidence and Prevalence of Sexual Aggression and Victimization in a National Sample of Higher Education Students, 55 J. Consulting & Clinical Psych. 162 (1987).

by drugs or alcohol.[2] In the Koss study, conduct was counted as rape under two circumstances: if the woman "had intercourse when [she] didn't want to because a man threatened or used some degree of physical force" and if she "had intercourse when [she] didn't want to because a man gave [her] alcohol or drugs."[3] Looking only at Koss's most serious category (intercourse because force was used or threatened), the victimization rate (9 percent since age 14) is still many times higher than that reported by NCS (0.14 percent per year, including attempts). What factors could account for this discrepancy?

Most statutes also treat intercourse as rape when the woman was *incapacitated* by drugs or alcohol. Is Koss's second category equivalent to the legal test? If not, should the legal test be expanded to cover all cases where a person "has intercourse when she doesn't want to because a man has given her drugs or alcohol"?

2. In another part of her study, Professor Koss examined cases of "sexual coercion" in which women submitted to sex because of pressures not included in most existing legal definitions of rape. Two percent of the women reported that they had had intercourse "because a man used his position of authority . . . to make [them]"; 25 percent of the women had "given in to sexual intercourse when [they] didn't want to, because [they] were overwhelmed by a man's continual arguments and pressure."[4] Should the law be modified to treat either or both of these situations as rape?

3. One element in the controversy concerns the prevalence of male sexual aggression. Consider this comment (Elizabeth A. Stanko, Intimate Intrusions 9 (1985)):

> To be a woman — in most societies, in most eras — is to experience physical and/ or sexual terrorism at the hands of men. Our everyday behaviour reflects our precautions, the measures we take to protect ourselves. We are wary of going out at night, even in our own neighbourhoods. We are warned by men and other women not to trust strangers. But somehow they forget to warn us about men we know: our fathers, our acquaintances, our co-workers, our lovers, our teachers. Many men familiar to us also terrorize our everyday lives in our homes, our schools, our workplaces.
>
> Women's experiences of incest, battering, rape and sexual harassment become the sources for documenting all women's actual and potential experiences. . . . In each case, a woman endures an invasion of self, the intrusion of inner space, a violation of her sexual and physical autonomy.

Is this an accurate or widely shared perception? Many men clearly do not think so. As Professor Robin West writes (The Difference in Women's Hedonic Lives, 3 Wis. Women's L.J. 81, 95 (1987)), "[T]he claim that women's lives are ruled by fear is heard by these men as wildly implausible. They see no evidence in their own lives to support it." On the other hand, Professor Menachem Amir's study, Patterns in Forcible Rape (1971), reports (p. 130) "general assumptions . . . that

2. U.S. Dept. of Justice Bureau of Justice Statistics, Criminal Victimization in the United States, 1992, at 156 (Mar. 1994).
3. Koss, et al., supra footnote 1, at 167.
4. Id.

there are constant pressures for sexual gratification and experience among all males and that some aggression is an expected part of the male role in sexual encounters." From this perspective, some male aggressiveness may be present, but not noticed as aberrant, in situations ranging from marriage through dates, jobs, and even encounters between strangers. Consider Professor West's comments on "street hassling" (supra, at 106-107):

> Street hassling is not trivial. . . . It is damaging to be pointed at, jeered at, laughed at for one's sexuality. This does not make [us] feel (primarily) "angry," "wronged" or even "assaulted." It makes [us] feel sexually ridiculous, exposed, dirty, vulgar, vulnerable and afraid.

Against this background, the controversy turns in part on what is understood as aggression, and it turns also on perceptions about the extent to which aggression is expected and acceptable (and to whom).

4. What precisely is the nature of the harm in rape? Many think of rape as a crime of violence. On this view the offense appears as a species of aggravated assault, and some would argue that the essential harm is similar to that experienced in any severe beating. Men who view rape in these terms often see the threat of rape as not fundamentally different from the threat of violent assault to which they are also exposed. In contrast, many feminists suggest that the important harm in rape is not violence but unwanted sexual intrusion. They argue that such unwanted sexual intimacy is for practical purposes rarely (outside the prison setting) experienced by men. Taking this view of the essential harm, feminists argue that men often have difficulty understanding when women feel raped and more generally what women fear about male behavior. Feminist law reformers assert that these "male" attitudes lead to inappropriate conceptions about the amount of force necessary to constitute rape. Consider Catharine A. MacKinnon, Feminism Unmodified 86-87 (1987):

> The point of view of men up to this time, called objective, has been to distinguish sharply between rape on the one hand and intercourse on the other; sexual harassment on the one hand and normal, ordinary sexual initiation on the other. . . . What women experience does not so clearly distinguish the normal, everyday things from those abuses from which they have been defined by distinction. . . . What we are saying is that sexuality in exactly these normal forms often *does* violate us. So long as we say that those things are abuses of violence, not sex, we fail to criticize what has been made of sex, what has been done to us *through* sex, because we leave the line between rape and intercourse, sexual harassment and sex roles . . . exactly where it is.

5. One reason that controversy about rape law continues is that underlying attitudes about sexual relationships have become highly controversial and are themselves in a state of flux. Criminal law always reflects, responds to, and acts upon the culture of the community. Nowhere have these interactions become more vivid, and more problematic, than in the law of rape. The nature of these interactions and their impact on the substantive law are among the themes of this chapter.

B. MENS REA

REGINA v. MORGAN

House of Lords
[1976] A.C. 182

[The defendant Morgan and three other defendants were convicted of the forcible rape of Morgan's wife. Morgan's liability rested on his having aided and abetted the three others. The Court of Appeals affirmed all the convictions but certified the following question to the House of Lords:

> Whether in rape the defendant can properly be convicted notwithstanding that he in fact believed that the woman consented, if such a belief was not based on reasonable grounds.

[The applicable statute stated simply: "*Rape* — (1) It is a felony for a man to rape a woman."[a]]

Lord Hailsham of St. Marylebone. . . . The question arises in the following way. The appellant Morgan and his three co-appellants, who were all members of the RAF, spent the evening of 15th August 1973 in one another's company. The appellant Morgan was significantly older than the other three, and considerably senior to them in rank. He was . . . married to the alleged victim, but not, it seems, at the time habitually sleeping in the same bed. [B]y the time the appellants arrived at Morgan's house, Mrs. Morgan was already in bed and asleep, until she was awoken by their presence.

According to the version of the facts which she gave in evidence, and which was evidently accepted by the jury, she was aroused from her sleep, . . . held by each of her limbs, . . . while each of the three young appellants in turn had intercourse with her in the presence of the others. . . .

According to Mrs. Morgan she consented to none of this and made her opposition to what was being done very plain indeed. . . .

All four appellants explained in the witness box that they had spent the evening together in Wolverhampton, and by the time of the alleged offences had had a good deal to drink. Their original intention had been to find some women in the town but, when this failed, Morgan made the surprising suggestion to the others that they should all return to his home and have sexual intercourse with his wife. According to the three younger appellants (but not according to Morgan who described this part of their story as "lying") Morgan told them that they must not be surprised if his wife struggled a bit, since she was "kinky" and this was the only way in which she could get "turned on." However this may be, it is clear that Morgan did invite his three companions home in order that they might have sexual intercourse with his wife and, no doubt, he may well have led them in one way or another to believe that she would consent to their doing so. This, however, would only be matter predisposing them to believe that

---

a. Sexual Offenses Act, 1956, 4 & 5 Eliz. 2 c. 69, §1(1). Common law decisions had defined "rape" as "unlawful carnal knowledge of a woman without her consent by force, fear or fraud." See Regina v. Miller, [1954] 2 All E.R. 529, 530. — Eds.

Mrs. Morgan consented, and would not in any way establish that, at the time, they believed she did consent whilst they were having intercourse.

I need not enter into the details of what the appellants said happened after they had arrived at the house. As I have said they admitted that some degree of struggle took place in the wife's bedroom. But all asserted that after she got into the double bedroom she not merely consented to but actively co-operated with and enjoyed what was being done. . . .

The choice before the jury was thus between two stories each wholly incompatible with the other, and in my opinion it would have been quite sufficient for the judge, after suitable warnings about the burden of proof, corroboration, separate verdicts and the admissibility of the statements only against the makers, to tell the jury that they must really choose between the two versions. . . .

The certified question arises because counsel for the appellants raised the question whether, even if the victim [objected], the appellants may . . . have honestly believed that she did [not]. [I]n the summing-up [to the jury] . . . [t]he learned judge said:

> [T]he prosecution have to prove that each defendant intended to have sexual intercourse with this woman without her consent. Not merely that he intended to have intercourse with her but that he intended to have intercourse without her consent. Therefore if the defendant believed or may have believed that Mrs. Morgan consented to him having sexual intercourse with her, then there would be no such intent in his mind and he would be not guilty of the offence of rape, but such a belief must be honestly held by the defendant in the first place. He must really believe that. And, secondly, his belief must be a reasonable belief; such a belief as a reasonable man would entertain if he applied his mind and thought about the matter. It is not enough for a defendant to rely upon a belief, even though he honestly held it, if it was completely fanciful; contrary to every indication which could be given which would carry some weight with a reasonable man.

It is on the second proposition about the mental element that the appellants concentrate their criticism. An honest belief in consent, they contend, is enough. It matters not whether it be also reasonable. No doubt a defendant will wish to raise argument or lead evidence to show that this belief was reasonable, since this will support its honesty. No doubt the prosecution will seek to cross-examine or raise arguments or adduce evidence to undermine the contention that the belief is reasonable, because, in the nature of the case, the fact that a belief cannot reasonably be held is a strong ground for saying that it was not in fact held honestly at all. Nonetheless, the appellants contend, the crux of the matter, the factum probandum, or rather the fact to be refuted by the prosecution, is honesty and not honesty plus reasonableness. . . .

The beginning of wisdom in all the "mens rea" cases to which our attention was called is, as was pointed out by Stephen, J., in R. v. Tolson, [23 Q.B.D. 168 (1889)], that "mens rea" means a number of quite different things in relation to different crimes. . . .

Once one has accepted, what seems to me abundantly clear, that the prohibited act in rape is non-consensual sexual intercourse, and that the guilty state of mind is an intention to commit it, it seems to me to follow as a matter of inexorable logic that there is no room either for a "defence" of honest belief or mistake, or of a defence of honest and reasonable belief or mistake. Either the prosecution proves that the accused had the requisite intent, or it does not. In the former case it succeeds, and in the latter it fails. Since honest belief clearly negatives intent, the reasonableness or otherwise of that belief can only be evidence for or against the view that the belief and therefore the intent was actually held. . . . Any other view . . . can only have the effect of saying that a man intends something which he does not. . . .

[T]he prohibited act is and always has been intercourse without consent of the victim and the mental element is and always has been the intention to commit that act, or the equivalent intention of having intercourse willy-nilly not caring whether the victim consents or no. A failure to prove this involves an acquittal because the intent, an essential ingredient, is lacking. It matters not why it is lacking if only it is not there, and in particular it matters not that the intention is lacking only because of a belief not based on reasonable grounds. . . .

For the above reasons I would answer the question certified in the negative, but would apply the proviso to the Criminal Appeal Act on the ground that no miscarriage of justice has or conceivably could have occurred.[b] In my view, therefore, these appeals should be dismissed.

NOTE ON THE CONTROVERSY OVER THE MORGAN DECISION

The *Morgan* decision evoked a considerable reaction in the press. An editorial in The Times (London), May 5, 1975, at 15, stated that the decision "does not accord with common sense. Until this decision was given, it had been generally accepted that the belief in the woman's consent had to be reasonable. In ruling otherwise, the law lords have been unduly legalistic."

In a letter to The Times, May 7, 1975, Professor J. C. Smith responded:

> It is surprising that you think that the decision of the majority of the House of Lords in *Morgan,* namely that the crime of rape requires an intention to commit rape, "does not accord with common sense." A man who intends to have sexual intercourse with a consenting woman may have an immoral intention but it is scarcely the kind of criminal mind which should make him liable for an offence carrying a maximum sentence of life imprisonment.
>
> The fact that he *ought* to have known that the woman was not consenting is not a valid ground for imputing to him an intention which he did not possess. . . .
>
> *Morgan* is a victory for common sense so far as intention in the criminal law is concerned. For too long the courts have said, inconsistently, that while the prosecution must prove an intention to do the prohibited act, a mistake negativing the required intention in the accused is not a defence unless it is reasonable. If, as appears likely, *Morgan* authoritatively rejects this fallacy, it is a decision of the greatest importance to the basic principles of criminal liability. . . .

In another letter to The Times, May 8, 1975, Professor Glanville Williams stated:

b. Section 2(1) of the Criminal Appeal Act of 1968 provides that "the Court may, notwithstanding that they are of opinion that the point raised in the appeal might be decided in favour of the appellant, dismiss the appeal if they consider that no miscarriage of justice has actually occurred." The decision to dismiss the appeals reflects a judgment that the jury would have convicted, even if it had been properly instructed. — Eds.

There has been a good deal of misunderstanding of the recent decision of the law lords in the rape case, which merely applied established principles.

(1) With a few exceptions, which need not be considered (and ought not to exist), serious crimes require a mental element (an intention to do the act or to produce the result, and knowledge of the facts, or at least conscious recklessness).

(2) Rape is a serious crime, involving sexual intercourse with a woman without her consent.

(3) Therefore rape requires the mental element that the man must know that the woman does not consent.

This was the simple point decided by their lordships, and the decision is warmly to be welcomed. The opposing view was that a man could be convicted of rape although he honestly believed that the woman was consenting, if he was stupid (unreasonable) in forming that belief. To convict the stupid man would be to convict him for what lawyers call inadvertent negligence — honest conduct which may be the best that this man can do but that does not come up to the standard of the so-called reasonable man. People ought not to be punished for negligence except in some minor offences established by statute. Rape carries a possible sentence of imprisonment for life, and it would be wrong to have a law of negligent rape. . . .

Mr. Jack Ashley, a Labor M.P., joined the debate, writing (May 12, 1975):

[Juries] now have to judge not only whether the woman was forced to submit but whether the man genuinely believed she consented — however irresponsible the grounds for that belief may be.

It is no answer to claim that as juries still have to be convinced the situation is unchanged. Juries are now forbidden to convict on the grounds that a man's belief is unreasonable. . . .

[I]f the three men in [*Morgan*] had claimed that the woman was play acting when she struggled, instead of arguing that she did not struggle, they might have been acquitted. In other words, their mistake was to tell the wrong lie. Future rapists will learn from this error and lie accordingly. . . .

In response to the controversy over the *Morgan* decision, Parliament enacted the Sexual Offences (Amendment) Act (1976), which in §1(1) provided:

A man commits rape if (a) he has unlawful sexual intercourse with a woman who at the time of the intercourse does not consent to it; and (b) at that time he knows that she does not consent to the intercourse or he is reckless as to whether she consents to it.

For further discussion, see Simon Gardner, Reckless and Inconsiderate Rape, [1991] Crim. L. Rev. 172; Celia Wells, Swatting the Subjectivist Bug, [1982] Crim. L. Rev. 209.

COMMONWEALTH v. SHERRY

Supreme Judicial Court of Massachusetts
386 Mass. 682, 437 N.E. 2d 224 (1982)

[Three co-defendants were charged with rape and kidnapping. The jury acquitted on the kidnapping charge and convicted of rape. Each defendant was sentenced to a prison term of not less than three nor more than five years. The judge stipulated that only the first six months of the sentence was to be served, with the balance of the sentence suspended. Defendants appealed.]

LIACOS, J. . . . The victim, a registered nurse, and the defendants, all doctors, were employed at the same hospital in Boston. The defendant Sherry, whom the victim knew professionally, with another doctor was a host at a party in Boston for some of the hospital staff on the evening of September 5, 1980. The victim was not acquainted with the defendants Hussain and Lefkowitz prior to this evening.

According to the victim's testimony, she had a conversation with Hussain at the party, during which he made sexual advances toward her. Later in the evening, Hussain and Sherry pushed her and Lefkowitz into a bathroom together, shut the door, and turned off the light. They did not open the door until Lefkowitz asked them to leave her in peace. At various times, the victim had danced with both Hussain and Sherry.

Some time later, as the victim was walking from one room to the next, Hussain and Sherry grabbed her by the arms and pulled her out of the apartment as Lefkowitz said, "We're going to go up to Rockport." The victim verbally protested but did not physically resist the men because she said she thought that they were just "horsing around" and that they would eventually leave her alone.[3] She further testified that once outside, Hussain carried her over his shoulder to Sherry's car and held her in the front seat as the four drove to Rockport. En route, she engaged in superficial conversation with the defendants. She testified that she was not in fear at this time. When they arrived at Lefkowitz's home in Rockport, she asked to be taken home. Instead, Hussain carried her into the house.

Once in the house, the victim and two of the men smoked some marihuana, and all of them toured the house. Lefkowitz invited them into a bedroom to view an antique bureau, and, once inside, the three men began to disrobe. The victim was frightened. She verbally protested, but the three men proceeded to undress her and . . . attempted intercourse. She told them to stop.[a] At the suggestion of one of the defendants, two of the defendants left the room temporarily. Each defendant separately had intercourse with the victim in the bedroom. The victim testified that she felt physically numbed and could not fight; she felt humiliated and disgusted. After this sequence of events, the victim claimed that she was further sexually harassed and forced to take a bath.

Some time later, Lefkowitz told the victim that they were returning to Boston because Hussain was on call at the hospital. On their way back, the group stopped to view a beach, to eat breakfast, and to get gasoline. The victim was taken back to where she had left her car the prior evening, and she then drove herself to an apartment that she was sharing with another woman.

The defendants testified to a similar sequence of events, although the details of the episode varied significantly. According to their testimony, Lefkowitz invited Sherry to accompany him from the party to a home that his parents owned in Rockport. The victim was present when this invitation was extended and in-

3. The victim testified that she was not physically restrained as they rode down an elevator with an unknown fifth person, or as they walked through the lobby of the apartment building where other persons were present.

a. The victim testified that when she asked the defendants why they were behaving in this manner, one of them replied, "Stop playing games." — EDS.

quired as to whether she could go along. As the three were leaving, Sherry extended an invitation to Hussain. At no time on the way out of the apartment, in the elevator, lobby, or parking lot did the victim indicate her unwillingness to accompany the defendants.

Upon arrival in Rockport, the victim wandered into the bedroom where she inquired about the antique bureau. She sat down on the bed and kicked off her shoes, whereupon Sherry entered the room, dressed only in his underwear. Sherry helped the victim get undressed, and she proceeded to have intercourse with all three men separately and in turn. Each defendant testified that the victim consented to the acts of intercourse.

. . . At the close of the Commonwealth's case, the defendants moved for a required finding of not guilty on each of the indictments. The defendants argued that there was no evidence of force or threat of bodily injury, a required element of the crime of rape. . . . The judge denied their motions. . . .

The evidence was sufficient to permit the jury to find that the defendants had sexual intercourse with the victim by force and against her will. The victim is not required to use physical force to resist; any resistance is enough when it demonstrates that her lack of consent is "honest and real." The jury could well consider the entire sequence of events and acts of all three defendants as it affected the victim's ability to resist. There was no error in the denial of the defendants' motions. . . .

. . . The defendants next contend that because the judge failed to give two instructions exactly as requested, the judge's jury charge, considered as a whole, was inadequate and the cause of prejudicial error. The requested instructions in their entirety are set out in the margin.[8] . . .

[The trial judge refused to give the requested instructions. He stated that the jury "should look at the acts of the defendants, [the victim's] responses to [those] acts, whatever words were used, examining the entire atmosphere, and not look at [the case] from the point of view of the defendant's perceptions. . . . I don't think that's the law."]

To the extent the defendants, at least as to the first requested instruction, appear to have been seeking to raise a defense of good faith mistake on the issue of consent, the defendants' requested instruction would have required the jury to "find beyond a reasonable doubt that the accused had *actual knowledge* of [the victim's] lack of consent" (emphasis added). The defendants, on appeal, argue that mistake of fact negating criminal intent is a defense to the crime of rape. The defense of mistake of fact, however, requires that the accused act in good faith and with reasonableness. Whether a reasonable good faith mistake of fact as to the fact of consent is a defense to the crime of rape has never, to our knowledge, been decided in this Commonwealth. We need not reach the issue whether a reasonable and honest mistake to the fact of consent would be a de-

---

8. "Unless you find beyond a reasonable doubt that [the victim] clearly expressed her lack of consent, or was so overcome by force or threats of bodily injury that she was incapable of consenting, and unless you find beyond a reasonable doubt that the accused had actual knowledge of [the victim's] lack of consent, then you must find them not guilty."

"If you find that [the victim] had a reasonable opportunity to resist being taken to Rockport, Massachusetts, from the apartment . . . , and had a reasonable opportunity to avoid or resist the circumstances that took place in the bedroom at Rockport, but chose not to avail herself of those opportunities, then you must weigh her failure to take such reasonable opportunities on the credibility of her claim that she was kidnapped and raped."

fense, for even if we assume it to be so, the defendants did not request a jury instruction based on a reasonable good faith mistake of fact. We are aware of no American court of last resort that recognizes mistake of fact, without consideration of its reasonableness[,] as a defense; nor do the defendants cite such authority. There was no error.

[In a companion case arising out of the same facts,[b] Justice Brown of the Appeals Court of Massachusetts commented as follows:] It is time to put to rest the societal myth that when a man is about to engage in sexual intercourse with a "nice" woman "a little force is always necessary." . . .

The essence of the offense of rape is lack of consent on the part of the victim. I am prepared to say that when a woman says "no" to someone[,] any implication other than a manifestation of non-consent that might arise in that person's psyche is legally irrelevant, and thus no defense. Any further action is unwarranted and the person proceeds at his peril. In effect, he assumes the risk. In 1985, I find no social utility in establishing a rule defining non-consensual intercourse on the basis of the subjective (and quite likely wishful) view of the more aggressive player in the sexual encounter.

NOTES ON MISTAKE AS TO CONSENT

1. Strict liability? Note that the defendants in *Sherry* did not seek acquittal on the ground that their alleged mistake was both honest and reasonable. In Commonwealth v. Ascolillo, 405 Mass. 456, 541 N.E.2d 570 (1989), the defendant requested a jury instruction that a *reasonable* mistake as to consent would be a defense. The victim was an acquaintance, and the defendant claimed to have had consensual sexual relations with her numerous times in the past. She had come to his home and used cocaine with him just before the alleged rape. The trial judge refused to instruct on a defense of reasonable mistake, and the Supreme Judicial Court affirmed the rape conviction, holding that an honest and reasonable mistake as to consent was not a defense to rape in Massachusetts.

In a subsequent acquaintance rape case, Commonwealth v. Simcock, 31 Mass. App. 184, 575 N.E.2d 1137, 1142-1143 (1991), the trial judge not only refused a defense request for instructions on reasonable mistake but also gave the jury an instruction to the effect that "a belief that the victim consented would not be a defense even if reasonable." The appellate court affirmed the rape conviction, stating that the instruction was "nothing more than a statement of law consistent with Commonwealth v. Ascolillo." The court added (id. at 1142) that the result was "in harmony with the analogous rule that a defendant in a statutory rape case is not entitled to an instruction that a reasonable mistake as to the victim's age is a defense."

Questions: Is the analogy flawed? Or is the court right in suggesting that defendants should be held strictly accountable for the existence of consent by their sexual partners? The weight of American authority now runs strongly against the *Ascolillo* view, but a few states appear to have joined Massachusetts in opting for strict liability on the consent issue. See, e.g., State v. Reed, 479 A.2d 1291 (Me. 1984).

b. Commonwealth v. Lefkowitz, 20 Mass. App. 513, 481 N.E.2d 277, 282 (1985). — Eds.

2. Recklessness or only negligence? Most of the recent American cases permit a mistake defense, but only when the defendant's error as to consent is honest and reasonable. See, e.g., State v. Oliver, 133 N.J. 141, 627 A.2d 144(1993); State v. Smith, 210 Conn. 132, 554 A.2d 713 (1989); People v. Mayberry, 15 Cal. 3d 143, 542 P.2d 1337 (1975). Compare Reynolds v. State, 664 P.2d 621, 624-625 (Alaska App. 1983):

> (R)ecent cases have substantially diluted the requirement of "resistance to the utmost," increasing the risk that a jury might convict a defendant under circumstances where lack of consent was ambiguous. To counteract this risk, some courts . . . have held that the defendant is entitled to an instruction on reasonable mistake of fact. . . .
>
> Alaska has dispensed with any requirement that the victim resist at all. . . . Thus, the legislature has substantially enhanced the risk of conviction in ambiguous circumstances. . . . We are satisfied, however, that the legislature counteracted this risk through its treatment of mens rea. It did this by shifting the focus of the jury's attention from the victim's resistance or actions to the defendant's understanding of the totality of the circumstances. Lack of consent is a "surrounding circumstance" which under the Revised Code, requires a complementary mental state as well as conduct to constitute a crime. No specific mental state is mentioned in AS 11.41.-410(a)(1) governing the surrounding circumstances of "consent." Therefore, the state must prove that the defendant acted "recklessly" regarding his putative victim's lack of consent.[a] This requirement serves to protect the defendant against conviction for first-degree sexual assault where the circumstances regarding consent are ambiguous at the time he has intercourse with the complaining witness.

3. The practical effect of a negligence standard. In what way does it facilitate conviction to shift from a subjective to an objective standard, from requiring proof of recklessness, as in *Morgan*, to permitting conviction on the basis of negligence, as in most American jurisdictions? On the facts of *Sherry*, for example, would a jury be likely to find that the doctors made a reasonable mistake about consent? If not, would a jury nonetheless be likely to acquit, under a *Morgan* standard? Consider Stephen J. Schulhofer, The Gender Question in Criminal Law, 7 Soc. Phil. & Pol. 105, 132-133 (1990):

> Given the [*Sherry*] victim's isolation in an unfamiliar setting, her intimidation by three naked men, and her explicit protests, there could not possibly have been (from the feminist perspective) a reasonable mistake. For the same reasons, however, one would have to say that these defendants actually *knew* that the victim was not consenting. At the very least, they were all aware that she *might* not be consenting; hence, they were reckless. In other words, on any appropriate conception of consent, these defendants were *subjectively* culpable and would be convicted whether or not we insist on a negligence standard.
>
> Against this background, why does it make any difference what the mistake standard is? There is one perspective from which these defendants might have made an honest mistake. That is the perspective that "no" does not really mean "no," that women . . . just want to feign some initial reluctance. On this view of when a

---

a. The court based this conclusion on an Alaska statute providing, as does Model Penal Code §2.02(3), that when a penal prohibition is silent as to the required culpability, then the state must prove recklessness with respect to any specified circumstances or results. — EDS.

woman's behavior signals consent, the defendants probably would not have had an actual awareness of her non-consent, and they could have been acquitted [even if the jury believed the victim's version of the facts]. But if you hold this view of consent (and of women), you might very well consider that the doctors' mistake of fact was not unreasonable. Indeed, on this view of consent, you might even conclude that the victim really *did* consent — that the doctors made no mistake at all. Once one accepts this alternative (hopefully outmoded) conception of what consent means, the defendants could conceivably be acquitted even if they were tried under a strict liability standard.

The point here is not that choice of the mens rea standard can never make a difference. Certainly, conviction becomes progressively easier as we move toward the strict liability approach. But we are working at the fringes of the problem. The [argument for a negligence standard] begs the most important question, or sweeps it under the rug of jury findings about reasonableness. This is really not a debate about mens rea standards. Rather, it is (or ought to be) a debate about what we mean by the construct that we call "consent." In most instances, a juror who comes into court with the conception that "no" means "no" will vote to convict in a case like *Sherry,* no matter what the mistake of fact standard is. Conversely, a juror who comes in with the notion that "no" probably means "yes" will acquit, no matter what the mistake of fact standard is. The debate about mistake of fact standards diverts attention from the question of what it is that you have to be mistaken about. Rather than requiring that the mistake be reasonable, and then leaving the jurors to their own conceptions of what is "reasonable" and what is "consent," we need to spell out what the concept of consent means.

4. *Limiting the reasonable mistake defense.* (a) *Factual basis.* Tyson v. State, 619 N.E.2d 276 (Ind. App. 1993), involved the prosecution of heavyweight boxing champion Mike Tyson for the rape of D.W., a woman who had agreed to accompany him to his hotel room at 2:00 A.M. Tyson testified that D.W. had responded positively to his kissing her in the limousine on the way to his hotel; that "we had both made it clear earlier that day what was going to happen"; and that D.W. cooperated in the act of intercourse. D.W. testified that when Tyson made sexual advances in the room, she was terrified, repeatedly objected and "tried to fight him" without success. The trial court refused to instruct the jury that a reasonable mistake as to consent would be a defense. Tyson was convicted of rape, and the court of appeals affirmed, upholding the refusal to instruct on reasonable mistake of fact (619 N.E.2d at 295):

> Tyson's description is a plain assertion of actual consent. . . . There is no recitation of equivocal conduct by D.W. which reasonably could have led Tyson to believe that D.W. only appeared to consent to the charged sexual conduct; no gray area exists from which Tyson can logically argue that he misunderstood D.W.'s actions. According to Tyson, he exerted no force and D.W. offered no resistance; instead, she was an active and equal participant in the conduct. While this testimony would negate an element of the crime — that Tyson forcibly engaged in sexual conduct with D.W. — and challenges D.W.'s credibility, it does not support the giving of a mistake of fact instruction.

In accord with *Tyson,* see People v. Williams, 4 Cal. 4th 354, 841 P.2d 961 (1992), where the court held that no instructions on reasonable mistake of fact should be given when the victim was either unequivocally resisting (by her account) or unequivocally consenting (by the defendant's account).

Questions: Are these results sound? In cases involving this type of "swearing contest," it seems obvious that once the jury finds one party to be telling the truth and the other party to be lying, there is no possibility for a reasonable mistake. But is it logically inevitable that one of the two competing stories must be completely true? What if the jury believes that *both* parties are exaggerating?

(b) *Burden of proof.* In State v. Camara, 113 Wash. 2d 631, 781 P.2d 483 (1989), Camara met another man, T.D., at a gay bar, and the two returned to Camara's apartment for drinks. T.D. testified that he had agreed to some sexual activity but had explicitly warned Camara that he did not want to engage in intercourse. T.D. testified that he and Camara commenced consensual sexual activities in Camara's bedroom, and that Camara then forcibly penetrated him against his will. Camara testified that T.D. had willingly cooperated and agreed to the act. The trial judge did not require the jury to find nonconsent beyond a reasonable doubt, nor did he require the jury to find beyond a reasonable doubt that Camara's claimed belief in T.D.'s consent was unreasonable. Camara was convicted of rape. The Washington Supreme Court affirmed, reasoning as follows (781 P.2d at 485-487):

[Rape is] defined as "sexual intercourse . . . [b]y forcible compulsion." RCW 9A.44.040, 9A.44.050(1)(a). "Forcible compulsion" in turn is defined as:

> physical force which overcomes resistance, or a threat, express or implied, that places a person in fear of death or physical injury to herself or himself or another person, or in fear that she or he or another person will be kidnapped[.]

Former RCW 9A.44.010(5).

Though the rape statutes no longer expressly mention nonconsent as an element of rape, we believe consent remains a valid defense to a rape charge, for several reasons. First, nonconsent traditionally has been the essence of the crime of rape. Second, the concept of consent has been retained in the new rape statutes in the element of forcible compulsion, its conceptual opposite. . . .

[W]hile there is a conceptual overlap between the consent defense to rape and the rape crime's element of forcible compulsion, we cannot hold that for that reason alone the burden of proof on consent must rest with the State. Rather, we now hold that that burden lies, as we understand the Legislature to have intended, with the defendant.

Questions: Is this an appropriate solution to the mistake problem? Is it a constitutionally permissible one?

5. *Victim consent in other crimes.* Although victim consent is not a defense to homicide and other offenses involving the infliction of serious bodily injury, consent in many other situations can deprive conduct of its criminal character. See generally Model Penal Code §2.11, Appendix. Sexual contact is but one of these situations in which liability may turn on the consequences of a mistake about consent. Consider the following case.

State v. Kelly, 338 S.E.2d 405 (W. Va. 1985): [The defendant, a construction and demolition contractor, removed a number of valuable oak fireplace mantels from two unoccupied houses and sold the mantels to an antique dealer. Despite efforts to board up the houses, they had been frequently vandalized. Evidence suggested that the defendant had broken into the houses and torn locks off the front doors to gain access. He testified that a man named Bradley had called, met him at the houses and discussed tearing them down or salvaging their contents. After the defendant removed and sold the mantels, he paid the $140 proceeds to Bradley and received $40 for his efforts. He also testified that a neighbor told him that Bradley and his wife owned the houses. In fact, the houses were owned by Bradley's estranged wife and her business partner, neither of whom had consented to removal of the mantels. The defendant was convicted of larceny. The appellate court reversed.]

It is . . . fundamental to the definition of larceny that the personal property must be taken without the consent of the owner. . . .

It is also widely recognized that one who takes property in good faith under fair color or claim of title, honestly believing he is the owner and has a right to take it, is not guilty of larceny, even though he is mistaken in such belief, since in such case the felonious intent is lacking. . . .

This general rule has been held to apply to one who sells the property of another with the consent of an agent or a servant of the owner and to one who takes personal property with the honest belief that he has a right to do so under a contract. . . . This matter is summarized in W. LaFave & A. Scott, Handbook on Criminal Law 638 (1972), as follows:

> One may take the property of another honestly but mistakenly believing . . . that the owner has given him permission to take it as he did. In . . . such event, he lacks the intent to steal required for larceny, even though his mistaken but honest belief was unreasonable. . . .

In this case, we believe the evidence when viewed in the light most favorable to the prosecution . . . does not establish beyond a reasonable doubt that the defendant acted with criminal intent because he believed that he had proper authority to remove the mantels. . . . Consequently, we cannot assent to his conviction.

Questions: If actual knowledge of the owner's nonconsent is required for a larceny conviction, why shouldn't actual knowledge of the woman's nonconsent be required for a rape conviction? Does the requirement of some subjective awareness of wrongdoing flow from the essential character of conviction for any serious crime? Or does the need for that requirement depend on the particular kind of harm caused by failing to assure consent? Consider Susan Estrich, Real Rape 97-98 (1987):

> The man who has the inherent capacity to act reasonably but fails to has, through that failure, made a blameworthy choice for which he can justly be punished. The law has long punished unreasonable action which leads to loss of human life as manslaughter. . . . The injury of sexual violation is sufficiently great, the need to provide that additional incentive pressing enough, to justify negligence liability for rape as for killing.

6. Applying a reasonableness standard. What factors should determine whether a man's mistake about consent was "reasonable"? Consider the following comments.

Robin D. Weiner, Shifting the Communication Burden: A Meaningful Consent Standard in Rape, 6 Harv. Women's L.J. 143, 147-149 (1983): [A] gender gap in sexual communications exists. Men and women frequently misinterpret the intent of various dating behaviors and erotic play engaged in by their opposite-sexed partners. . . .

Because both men and women are socialized to accept coercive sexuality as the norm in sexual behavior, men often see extreme forms of this aggressive behavior as seduction, rather than rape. . . . Miscommunication of this sort may create a situation where submission would be reasonable behavior for a woman but would not indicate voluntary consent. A woman may believe she has communicated her unwillingness to have sex — and other women would agree, thus making it a "reasonable" female expression. Her male partner might still believe she is willing — and other men would agree with his interpretation, thus making it a "reasonable" male interpretation. The woman, who believes that she *has* conveyed her lack of consent, may interpret the man's persistence as an indication that he does not care if she objects and plans to have sex despite her lack of consent. She may then feel frightened by the man's persistence, and may submit against her will.

For an analysis of the cultural attitudes that influence conceptions of "consent" in sexual interaction, see Lynne Henderson, Getting to Know: Honoring Women in Law and in Fact, 2 Tex. J. Women & L. 41 (1993). The importance of nonverbal cues in communicating willingness or unwillingness in sexual encounters is discussed in Steven I. Friedland, Date Rape and the Culture of Acceptance, 43 Fla. L. Rev. 487 (1991).

7. *Questions:* How should law respond to the "gender gap"? Should notions of reasonableness be left to evolve in response to changing social mores? Or should legislatures and courts set specific standards, for example, by specifying that "no means no"? In a recent survey of Texas women undergraduates, 39 percent reported that they had said "no" when they meant yes, and 61 percent of the sexually experienced women in the survey said that they had done so. See Charlene L. Muehlenhard & Lisa C. Hollabaugh, Do Women Sometimes Say No When They Mean Yes? The Prevalence and Correlates of Women's Token Resistance to Sex, 54 J. Personality & Soc. Psych. 872, 874 (1988). Ninety percent of these women said that fear of appearing promiscuous was an important reason for their behavior. The authors of the study pointed out that this pattern of communication, though rational for some women, can teach men to disregard women's refusals and thereby increase the incidence of rape. Id., at 878.

Do findings of this sort imply that "no" often *doesn't* mean "no"? Or do such findings suggest an even greater need for legal standards to guarantee that "no" *will be treated as* "no"? Compare the following viewpoints.

Douglas N. Husak & George C. Thomas III, Date Rape, Social Convention and Reasonable Mistakes, 11 Law & Phil. 95, 123, 125 (1992): A single physical rejection (for example, *F* [a woman] moves *M* [a man]'s hand from her leg) following hours of intense foreplay obviously presents a very different picture of nonconsent than repeated physical and verbal rejections, delivered in an emotional and frightened manner. At some point along this spectrum, it is no longer reasonable for *M* to think that *F* has consented.

The reason that *M*'s mistake-of-fact defense fails at this point is not that the word no has a magic, transcendental quality. Rather, *M*'s defense becomes unreasonable because the social convention is that a certain pattern of linguistic and nonlinguistic behavior could not reasonably be understood to mean anything other than no. The social convention wcs[a] provides the vehicle through which *M* interprets the words or actions of *F*. . . .

[T]here is little empirical evidence that the social convention wcs is consistent with the view of men and women entailed by the normative claims of some rape law reformers. Instead, the evidence suggests a convention wcs that might produce somewhat frequent mistakes of fact about a woman's consent. If so, and if the reformers succeed in restricting or eliminating the mistake-of-fact defense, some men will be convicted of rape even though they had reason to believe that consent had been given.

Some might welcome this result. As noted above, one might believe that it is more important to seek to change the social convention or to send a symbolic message than to do justice in an individual case. But if one believes that the criminal law should seek to apply the just result in particular cases, men whose belief in consent is consistent with the social convention seem unlikely candidates for convictions of a serious felony. For this reason, legislatures should proceed slowly when removing some of the common law barriers to rape convictions.

Catharine A. MacKinnon, Feminism, Marxism, Method, and the State: Toward a Feminist Jurisprudence, 8 Signs 635, 652-654 (1983): [M]en are systematically conditioned not even to notice what women want. They may have not a glimmer of women's indifference or revulsion. Rapists typically believe the woman loved it. . . .

Men's pervasive belief that women fabricate rape charges after consenting to sex makes sense in this light. To them, the accusations *are* false because, to them, the facts describe sex. To interpret such events as rapes distorts their experience. . . .

But the deeper problem is the rape law's assumption that a single, objective state of affairs existed, one which merely needs to be determined by evidence, when many (maybe even most) rapes involve honest men and violated women. When the reality is split — a woman is raped but not by a rapist? — the law tends to conclude that a rape *did not happen*. To attempt to solve this by adopting the standard of reasonable belief without asking, on a substantive social basis, to whom the belief is reasonable and why — meaning, what conditions make it reasonable — is one-sided: male-sided.

Wash. Rev. Code Ann. 9A.44.010(6) (1981): "Consent" means that at the time of the act of sexual intercourse there are actual words or conduct indicating freely given agreement to have sexual intercourse.

a. The authors use the term "wcs" as a shorthand to designate the social conventions that women use to express consent to have sex. — Eds.

C. ACTUS REUS

1. Force, Nonconsent, and Resistance

STATE v. RUSK

Court of Appeals of Maryland
289 Md. 230, 424 A.2d 720 (1981)

MURPHY, C.J. Edward Rusk was found guilty by a jury . . . of second degree rape in violation of Maryland Code Art. 27, §463(a)(1), which provides in pertinent part:

> A person is guilty of rape in the second degree if the person engages in vaginal intercourse with another person:
>
> (1) By force or threat of force against the will and without the consent of the other person. . . .[a]

On appeal, the Court of Special Appeals, sitting en banc, reversed the conviction; it concluded by an 8–5 majority that in view of the prevailing law as set forth in Hazel v. State, 221 Md. 464, 157 A.2d 922 (1960), insufficient evidence of Rusk's guilt had been adduced at the trial to permit the case to go to the jury. We granted certiorari to consider whether the Court of Special Appeals properly applied the principles of *Hazel*. . . .

At the trial, the 21-year-old prosecuting witness, Pat, testified that on the evening of September 21, 1977, she attended a high school alumnae meeting where she met a girl friend, Terry. After the meeting, Terry and Pat agreed to drive in their respective cars to Fells Point to have a few drinks. . . . They went to a bar where . . . Rusk approached and said "hello" to Terry. Terry, who was then conversing with another individual, momentarily interrupted her conversation and said "Hi, Eddie." Rusk then began talking with Pat and during their conversation both of them acknowledged being separated from their respective spouses and having a child. Pat told Rusk that she had to go home . . . [and] Rusk requested a ride to his apartment. Although Pat did not know Rusk, she thought that Terry knew him. She thereafter agreed to give him a ride. Pat cautioned Rusk on the way to the car that "I'm just giving a ride home, you know, as a friend, not anything to be, you know, thought of other than a ride." . . .

After a twenty-minute drive, they arrived at Rusk's apartment. . . . Pat testified that she was totally unfamiliar with the neighborhood. She parked the car at the curb . . . but left the engine running. Rusk asked Pat to come in, but she refused. . . . Pat said that Rusk was fully aware that she did not want to accompany him to his room. Notwithstanding her repeated refusals, Pat testified that Rusk reached over and turned off the ignition to her car and took her car keys. He

---

a. The Maryland statute provides that second-degree rape is punishable by imprisonment for a period not to exceed 20 years. First-degree rape is defined to include intercourse by force or threat of force where the defendant uses a deadly weapon, inflicts or threatens "suffocation, strangulation, disfigurement or serious physical injury," or is aided by one or more other persons. First-degree rape is punishable by a maximum of life imprisonment. — EDS.

got out of the car, walked over to her side, opened the door and said, "Now, will you come up?" Pat explained her subsequent actions:

> At that point, because I was scared, because he had my car keys. I didn't know what to do. I was someplace I didn't even know where I was. It was in the city. I didn't know whether to run. I really didn't think at that point, what to do.
>
> Now, I know that I should have blown the horn. I should have run. There were a million things I could have done. I was scared, at that point, and I didn't do any of them.

Pat testified that at this moment she feared that Rusk would rape her. She said: "[I]t was the way he looked at me, and said 'Come on up, come on up'; and when he took the keys, I knew that was wrong."

It was then about 1 A.M. Pat accompanied Rusk across the street into a totally dark house. . . . Rusk unlocked the door to his one-room apartment, and turned on the light. According to Pat, he told her to sit down. She sat in a chair beside the bed. Rusk sat on the bed. After Rusk talked for a few minutes, he left the room for about one to five minutes. Pat remained seated in the chair. She made no noise and did not attempt to leave. She said that she did not notice a telephone in the room. When Rusk returned, he turned off the light and sat down on the bed. Pat asked if she could leave; she told him that she wanted to go home and "didn't want to come up." She said, "Now, [that] I came up, can I go?" Rusk, who was still in possession of her car keys, said he wanted her to stay.

Rusk then asked Pat to get on the bed with him. He pulled her by the arms to the bed and began to undress her. . . . Pat removed the rest of her clothing, and then removed Rusk's pants because "he asked me to do it." After they were both undressed Rusk started kissing Pat as she was lying on her back. Pat explained what happened next:

> I was still begging him to please let, you know, let me leave. I said, "you can get a lot of other girls down there, for what you want," and he just kept saying, "no"; and then I was really scared, because I can't describe, you know, what was said. It was more the look in his eyes; and I said, at that point — I didn't know what to say; and I said, "If I do what you want, will you let me go without killing me?" Because I didn't know, at that point, what he was going to do; and I started to cry; and when I did, he put his hands on my throat, and started lightly to choke me; and I said, "If I do what you want, will you let me go?" And he said, yes, and at that time, I proceeded to do what he wanted me to.

Pat testified that Rusk made her perform oral sex and then vaginal intercourse.

Immediately after the intercourse, Pat asked if she could leave. She testified that Rusk said, "Yes," after which she got up and got dressed and Rusk returned her car keys. She said that Rusk then

> walked me to my car, and asked if he could see me again; and I said, "Yes"; and he asked me for my telephone number; and I said, "No, I'll see you down Fells Point sometime," just so I could leave.

Pat testified that she "had no intention of meeting him again." She asked him for directions out of the neighborhood and left.

. . . As she sat in her car reflecting on the incident, Pat said she began to

> wonder what would happen if I hadn't of done what he wanted me to do. So I thought the right thing to do was to go report it, and I went from there to Hillendale to find a police car.

She reported the incident to the police at about 3:15 A.M. . . .

Rusk and two of his friends, Michael Trimp and David Carroll, testified on his behalf. According to Trimp, they went in Carroll's car to Buggs' bar to dance, drink and "tr[y] to pick up some ladies." Rusk stayed at the bar, while the others went to get something to eat.

Trimp and Carroll next saw Rusk walking down the street arm-in-arm with a lady whom Trimp was unable to identify. . . .

Carroll's testimony corroborated Trimp's. He saw Rusk walking down the street arm-in-arm with a woman. He said "[s]he was kind of like, you know, snuggling up to him like. . . . She was hanging all over him then." Carroll was fairly certain that Pat was the woman who was with Rusk. . . .

According to Rusk, when they arrived in front of his apartment Pat parked the car and turned the engine off. They sat for several minutes "petting each other." . . . Rusk testified that Pat came willingly to his room and that at no time did he make threatening facial expressions. . . . Rusk explained that after the intercourse, Pat "got uptight."

> Well, she started to cry. She said that — she said, "You guys are all alike," she says, "just out for," you know, "one thing." . . . And she said, that she just wanted to leave; and I said, "Well, okay"; and she walked out to the car. I walked out to the car. She got in the car and left.

Rusk denied placing his hands on Pat's throat or attempting to strangle her. He also denied using force or threats of force to get Pat to have intercourse with him.

In reversing Rusk's second degree rape conviction, the Court of Special Appeals quoting from *Hazel*, noted that:

> Force is an essential element of the crime [of rape] and to justify a conviction, the evidence must warrant a conclusion either that the victim resisted and her resistance was overcome by force or that she was prevented from resisting by threats to her safety.

Writing for the majority, Judge Thompson said:

> In all of the victim's testimony we have been unable to see any resistance on her part to the sex acts and certainly can we see no fear as would overcome her attempt to resist or escape as required by *Hazel*. Possession of the keys by the accused may have deterred her vehicular escape but hardly a departure seeking help in the rooming house or in the street. We must say that "the way he looked" fails utterly to support the fear required by *Hazel*.

. . . Of course, due process requirements mandate that a criminal conviction not be obtained if the evidence does not reasonably support a finding of guilt beyond a reasonable doubt. However, as the Supreme Court made clear in Jackson v. Virginia, 443 U.S. 307 (1979), the reviewing court does not ask itself whether *it* believes that the evidence established guilt beyond a reasonable doubt; rather, the applicable standard is "whether, after viewing the evidence in the light most favorable to the prosecution, *any* rational trier of fact could have found the essential elements of the crime beyond a reasonable doubt." (emphasis in original). . . .

The Court [in *Hazel*] noted that lack of consent is generally established through proof of resistance or by proof that the victim failed to resist because of fear. The degree of fear necessary to obviate the need to prove resistance, and thereby establish lack of consent, was defined in the following manner: "The kind of fear which would render resistance by a woman unnecessary to support a conviction of rape includes, but is not necessarily limited to, a fear of death or serious bodily harm, or a fear so extreme as to preclude resistance, or a fear which would well nigh render her mind incapable of continuing to resist, or a fear that so overpowers her that she does not dare resist."

. . . While *Hazel* made it clear that the victim's fear had to be genuine, it did not pass upon whether a real but unreasonable fear of imminent death or serious bodily harm would suffice. The vast majority of jurisdictions have required that the victim's fear be reasonably grounded in order to obviate the need for either proof of actual force on the part of the assailant or physical resistance on the part of the victim. We think that, generally, this is the correct standard. . . .

We think the reversal of Rusk's conviction by the Court of Special Appeals was in error for the fundamental reason so well expressed in the dissenting opinion by Judge Wilner when he observed that the majority had "trampled upon the first principle of appellate restraint [because it had] substituted [its] own view of the evidence (and the inferences that may fairly be drawn from it) for that of the judge and jury [and had thereby] improperly invaded the province allotted to those tribunals." In view of the evidence adduced at the trial, the reasonableness of Pat's apprehension of fear was plainly a question of fact for the jury to determine.[b] . . . Quite obviously, the jury disbelieved Rusk and believed Pat's testimony. From her testimony, the jury could have reasonably concluded that

b. In his opinion in support of this position in the court below, Judge Wilner added this comment: "As a result of the Battelle Study [prepared for the LEAA National Institute of Law Enforcement and Criminal Justice, and published in 1977 and 1978], we now know some things about this crime that we could only guess at before. [A]s in this case, approximately one-third of rape victims had come into contact with their assailants voluntarily, under circumstances other than hitchhiking. *Physical force is absent in over half of reported cases and, in a third of the cases, no weapon is involved.* . . .

"Of particular significance is what was learned about *resistance*. The most common type of resistance offered by victims is *verbal*. Note: verbal resistance *is* resistance! In cases arising in the large cities, only 12.7% of the victims attempted flight, and only 12% offered physical resistance. The reason for this is apparent from the next thing learned: that '[r]*ape victims who resisted were more likely to be injured than ones who did not.*' (Emphasis supplied.) The statistics showed, for rapes in large cities, that, where physical resistance was offered, over 71% of the victims were physically injured in some way, 40% requiring medical treatment or hospitalization. . . .

"Law enforcement agencies throughout the country warn women not to resist an attack haphazardly, not to antagonize a potential attacker, but to protect themselves from more serious injury. The United States Department of Justice, for example, has published a pamphlet warning, among other things: 'If you are confronted by a rapist, stay calm and maximize your chances for escape. *Think* through what you will do. You should not *immediately* try to fight back. Chances are, your attacker has the advantage. Try to stay calm and take stock of the situation.'" — EDS.

the taking of her car keys was intended by Rusk to immobilize her alone, late at night, in a neighborhood with which she was not familiar; that after Pat had repeatedly refused to enter his apartment, Rusk commanded in firm tones that she do so; that Pat was badly frightened and feared that Rusk intended to rape her; . . . that Pat was afraid that Rusk would kill her unless she submitted; that she began to cry and Rusk then put his hands on her throat and began "lightly to choke" her; that Pat asked him if he would let her go without killing her if she complied with his demands; that Rusk gave an affirmative response, after which she finally submitted.

Just where persuasion ends and force begins in cases like the present is essentially a factual issue. . . . Considering all of the evidence in the case, with particular focus upon the actual force applied by Rusk to Pat's neck, we conclude that the jury could rationally find that the essential elements of second degree rape had been established and that Rusk was guilty of that offense beyond a reasonable doubt.[c] . . .

Cole, J., dissenting. [W]hen one of the essential elements of a crime is not sustained by the evidence, the conviction of the defendant cannot stand as a matter of law.

The majority, in applying this standard, concludes that "[i]n view of the evidence adduced at the trial, the reasonableness of Pat's apprehension of fear was plainly a question of fact for the jury to determine." In so concluding, the majority has skipped over the crucial issue. It seems to me that whether the prosecutrix's fear is reasonable becomes a question only after the court determines that the defendant's conduct under the circumstances was reasonably calculated to give rise to a fear on her part to the extent that she was unable to resist. . . .

While courts no longer require a female to resist to the utmost or to resist where resistance would be foolhardy, they do require her acquiescence in the act of intercourse to stem from fear generated by something of substance. She may not simply say, "I was really scared," and thereby transform consent or mere unwillingness into submission by force. These words do not transform a seducer into a rapist. She must follow the natural instinct of every proud female to resist, by more than mere words, the violation of her person by a stranger or an unwelcomed friend. She must make it plain that she regards such sexual acts as abhorrent and repugnant to her natural sense of pride. She must resist unless the defendant has objectively manifested his intent to use physical force to accomplish his purpose. The law regards rape as a crime of violence. The majority today attenuates this proposition. It declares the innocence of an at best distraught young woman. It does not demonstrate the defendant's guilt of the crime of rape.

. . . The majority suggests that "from her testimony the jury could have reasonably concluded that the taking of her keys was intended by Rusk to immobilize her alone, late at night, in a neighborhood with which she was unfamiliar. . . ." But on what facts does the majority so conclude? There is no evidence descriptive of the tone of his voice; her testimony indicates only the bare statement quoted above. . . .

c. Four judges joined the opinion sustaining the conviction. Three judges joined the dissent. —Eds.

She also testified that she was afraid of "the way he looked," and afraid of his statement, "come on up, come on up." But what can the majority conclude from this statement coupled with a "look" that remained undescribed? There is no evidence whatsoever to suggest that this was anything other than a pattern of conduct consistent with the ordinary seduction of a female acquaintance who at first suggests her disinclination. . . .

The majority relies on the trial court's statement that the defendant responded affirmatively to her question "If I do what you want, will you let me go without killing me?" The majority further suggests that the jury could infer the defendant's affirmative response. The facts belie such inference since by the prosecutrix's own testimony the defendant made *no* response. *He said nothing!*

She then testified that she started to cry and he "started lightly to choke" her, whatever that means. Obviously, the choking was not of any persuasive significance. During this "choking" she was able to talk. She said "If I do what you want will you let me go?" It was at this point that the defendant said yes.

I find it incredible for the majority to conclude that on these facts, without more, a woman was *forced* to commit oral sex upon the defendant and then to engage in vaginal intercourse.

[T]here are no acts or conduct on the part of the defendant to suggest that these fears were created by the defendant or that he made any objective, identifiable threats to her which would give rise to this woman's failure to flee, summon help, scream, or make physical resistance. . . .

In my judgment the State failed to prove the essential element of force beyond a reasonable doubt and, therefore, the judgment of conviction should be reversed. . . .

ELIZABETH A. STANKO, INTIMATE INTRUSIONS, 9-11 (1985): [M]any characterise male physical and/or sexual aggression as linked to biological make-up, sparked by an innate, at times uncontrollable, sexual drive. After all, boys will be boys, we sigh. While we acknowledge that not all men publicly display this uncontrollable biological predisposition, we further believe its display is generally aroused by deserving, provoking women. . . . At the same time, though, we recognise that some male aggression is not sparked by provocative women. These, we reassure ourselves, are the rarest of situations. Above all, we retain traditional assumptions about women who experience sexual and/or physical assault; some women are alluring, masochistic and provoke the uncontrollable responses of some men, and some women are pure, proper but unfortunately come across some men who are uncontrollable. When we try to account for women's experience of male violence, explanations of it centre around the naturalness or unnaturalness of male aggression in relation to women's behaviour.

As a result, women's experiences of male violence are filtered through an understanding of *men's* behaviour which is characterised as either typical or aberrant. If it is considered typical, men's physical and sexual aggression toward women is left, to a large extent, unfettered. The sexual advance by a male professor toward a young female student, the 'rough sex,' the slapping of one's wife, the wolf whistle on the street, the comments about women's physicality, the man's brushing up against a female secretary's body in the xerox room (and on and on) are, most people accept, natural expressions of maleness. These expressions are assumed to be non-threatening to women, even, some would say, flattering. The vicious rape, the brutal murder of a woman, the cruel physical torture of a girlfriend are, we feel, the aberrant examples of maleness. These examples, most would agree, are threatening to women. In the abstract we easily draw lines between those aberrant (thus harmful) and those typical (thus unharmful) types of male behaviour. We even label the aberrant behaviour as potentially criminal behaviour.

What becomes lost, though, in this commonsensical separation between 'aberrant' and 'typical' male behaviour is a woman-defined understanding of what is threatening, of what women consider to be potentially violent. Often, women themselves are confused — sometimes defining male behaviour as typical, other times as aberrant — but none the less feel threatened by some displays of either. Women who feel violated or intimidated by typical male behaviour have no way of specifying how or why typical male behaviour feels like aberrant male behaviour. Essentially, the categories *typical* and *aberrant* are not useful for understanding women's feelings about, and thus women's experiences of male intimidation and violence. Confusing though they may be, women's experiences point to a potential for violence in many of women's ordinary encounters with men.

NOTES

1. The force requirement. Statutes typically specify that conviction of rape requires proof of intercourse committed by "force" or by "forcible compulsion." Nonconsensual intercourse in the absence of force ordinarily is criminal only under certain special circumstances. The principal examples are when consent is absent or legally ineffective because the victim is below a given age ("statutory" rape), mentally incompetent, or unconscious. Consent may also be deemed ineffective when it results from certain particularly egregious forms of deception (such as impersonation of the victim's husband). See, e.g., Model Penal Code §§213.1(2)(c), 213.3(1)(d), Appendix. Outside of these special circumstances, intercourse is ordinarily not criminal, even in the absence of consent, unless there is also proof of force or the threat of force. (In a few jurisdictions, recent developments have made nonconsent alone sufficient, at least for the lesser degrees of sexual assault. See State in the Interest of M.T.S., infra page 345, and Note 2, infra page 352).

2. The resistance requirement. (a) In some states, resistance is included among the formal statutory elements, but more often resistance has been read into the statutes as a requirement somehow implicit in the elements of force or nonconsent. The old requirement that the victim resist "to the utmost" has been abandoned by all American jurisdictions, but most courts still require what may be described as "reasonable" resistance. As one court puts it (State v. Lima, 64 Hawaii 470, 643 P.2d 536, 540 (1982)):

[In applying the statutory requirement of "earnest resistance," we have] required a showing that there had been a "genuine physical effort on the part of the complainant to discourage and to prevent her assailant from accomplishing his intended purpose." This does not mean, however, that the complainant must resist to the utmost extent possible. We long ago rejected that view. Instead, we believe a complainant must only exhibit a genuine physical effort to resist as judged by the circumstances of the particular case. Among the factors to be considered are the relative strength of the parties, the age of the complainant, the complainant's mental and physical condition, and the nature and degree of the force used by the assailant.

Question: In light of what is now known about the risks that resistance can pose to the rape victim (see page 336 note b, supra), is "reasonable resistance" really a reasonable requirement?

(b) In New York, objections to a stringent statutory requirement of "earnest resistance" led to numerous revisions of the statute. A 1977 amendment defined "earnest resistance" in the following terms:

> "Earnest resistance" means resistance of a type reasonably expected from a person who genuinely refuses to participate in sexual intercourse, deviate sexual intercourse or sexual contact, under all the attendant circumstances. Earnest resistance does not mean utmost resistance.

The change proved inadequate to meet the concerns about resistance, and in 1982 the resistance requirement was eliminated entirely. As New York law presently stands, "forcible compulsion" is defined as follows (New York Penal Law §130.00(8)):

> "Forcible compulsion" means to compel by either:
> a. use of physical force: or
> b. a threat, express or implied, which places a person in fear of immediate death or physical injury to himself, herself or another person, or in fear that he, she or another person will immediately be kidnapped.

Questions: Have the New York amendments finally solved the problem of resistance? What result if the *Rusk* case had been tried under the current version of the New York statute?

(c) The Model Penal Code, in §213.1, (see Appendix for the text of this section) seeks to shift the focus of attention from the victim's behavior to that of the defendant and also seeks to differentiate, for grading purposes, between different degrees of force. Consider Model Penal Code and Commentaries, Comments to §213.1 at 304-307 (1980):

> Under traditional rape statutes, many courts demanded proof of "utmost resistance" by the victim to demonstrate her non-consent. . . . "Utmost resistance" was not required where precluded by fear of grave harm, and many modern decisions have further moderated the rigor of the doctrine. . . .
>
> To some degree, these variations of the resistance inquiry share common faults. First, resistance may prove an invitation to danger of death or serious bodily harm. Second, it is wrong to excuse the male assailant on the ground that his victim failed to protect herself with the dedication and intensity that a court might expect of a reasonable person in her situation. As a practical matter, juries may require resistance to show that the male compelled her to submit, but there is little reason to encase this generalization in a rule of law. Where the proof establishes that the actor did compel submission to intercourse by force, the failure of a weak or fearful victim to display "utmost" or even "earnest" resistance should not be exculpatory.

The new Michigan statute follows the Model Code on this point, but takes the matter to the opposite extreme by adding the provision that the "victim need not resist."[92] There are contexts, to be sure, where the law should not require resistance, but the Michigan provision seems to imply that the failure to resist is always irrelevant and thus seems to make an overbroad response to the problem. . . . While the Michigan statute seems correct, therefore, in shifting the emphasis away from the preoccupation of much prior law on the victim's resistance, it seems similarly unsound to adopt as a rule of law the judgment that resistance need never be made. . . . By the same token, the lack of resistance on a particular occasion will not preclude a conviction of rape if the jury can be convinced by the context and the degree of force employed by the actor that the submission was by compulsion.

Question: How would the *Rusk* case be decided under the Code?

(*d*) All courts recognize that resistance is unnecessary in at least some situations. That would be the case, for example, if the victim is jumped from behind and thrown to the ground by a stranger pointing a gun at her head. In such a situation the fear aroused by the defendant's conduct could overpower the victim and prevent her from resisting. Thus, the question whether the victim offered "reasonable" resistance is in effect displaced by the question whether the victim "reasonably" feared serious bodily harm — so that the "reasonable" amount of resistance, under the circumstances, was no resistance at all.

3. *The requirement of a "reasonable" apprehension.* In *Rusk* all the judges appeared to accept the rule that the victim's fear must be reasonably grounded; they divided only over the question whether a jury could properly find that it was, on the facts. Many courts seem to agree with that principle, even in the context of encounters between strangers under frightening circumstances. Consider People v. Warren, 113 Ill. App. 3d 1, 446 N.E.2d 591 (1983). The complainant was biking along an isolated reservoir when defendant approached and struck up a conversation. When she attempted to leave, the defendant placed his hand on her shoulder, saying, "This will only take a minute. My girlfriend doesn't meet my needs." He then lifted her off the ground and carried her into the woods, where he performed several sex acts. The complainant was 5'2" tall and weighed about 100 pounds; the defendant was 6'3" and weighed 185 pounds. Because the complainant did not scream, fight back or attempt to flee, the court reversed the conviction:

> Much of the State's case rests upon its contention that complainant's absence of effort in thwarting defendant's advances was motivated by her overwhelming fear. In support of this position, the State offers complainant's statement that she did not attempt to flee because, "it was in the middle of the woods and I didn't feel like I could get away from him and I thought he'd kill me." Moreover, complainant stated that she did not yell or scream because the people she had seen in the area were too far away and that under the circumstances she felt that screaming ". . . would be bad for me."
>
> Despite professing fear for her safety, complainant concedes that defendant did not strike her or threaten to strike her or use a weapon. . . . At no time did complainant tell defendant to leave her alone or put her down. . . . It is well settled that if complainant had the use of her faculties and physical powers, the evidence must

---

92. Mich. §750.520i. Cf. Iowa §709.5; Ohio §2907.02(c); Pa. tit. 18, §3107; Vt. tit. 13, §3254(1). . . .

show such resistance as will demonstrate that the act was against her will. If the circumstances show resistance to be futile or life endangering or if the complainant is overcome by superior strength or paralyzed by fear, useless or foolhardy acts of resistance are not required. We cannot say that any of the above factors are present here. Complainant's failure to resist when it was within her power to do so conveys the impression of consent regardless of her mental state, amounts to consent and removes from the act performed an essential element of the crime. We do not mean to suggest, however, that the complainant did in fact consent; however, she must communicate in some objective manner her lack of consent.

Why should the absence of resistance have to be explained by fears that are objectively "reasonable"? Why should the "reasonableness" of the victim ever be an issue, so long as the trier of fact is persuaded that her fears were genuine? One obvious concern is to assure that the defendant realizes the woman is submitting out of fear rather than desire. But suppose the defendant *knows* that the victim is genuinely afraid. Suppose that he subtly but deliberately reinforces those fears. (Reconsider the facts of *Rusk*.) Shouldn't a conviction be proper regardless of the "reasonableness" of the fears? Conversely, suppose that the victim's fears are reasonable but that the defendant is totally unaware of them. Shouldn't a conviction be *improper,* regardless of whether the fears are "reasonable"? Or is it appropriate to require defendants to know when their conduct arouses fear of bodily harm and to take the initiative in making sure to dispel any apprehension on the part of their partners?

4. *Power vs. "force."* Consider the following discussion of a recent case, State v. Alston, 310 N.C. 399, 312 S.E.2d 470 (1984).

Susan Estrich, Real Rape 60-65, 69 (1987): Mr. Alston and the victim had been involved in a "consensual" relationship for six months. That relationship admittedly involved "some violence" by the defendant and some passivity by the victim. The defendant would strike the victim when she refused to give him money or refused to do what he wanted. As for sex, the court noted that "she often had sex with the defendant just to accommodate him. On those occasions, she would stand still and remain entirely passive while the defendant undressed her and had intercourse with her." This was their "consensual" relationship. It ended when, after being struck by the defendant, the victim left the apartment she shared with him and moved in with her mother.

A month later the defendant came to the school the victim attended, blocked her path, demanded to know where she was living, and, when she refused to tell him, grabbed her arm and stated that she was coming with him. The victim told the defendant she would walk with him if he released her arm. They then walked around the school and talked about their relationship. At one point the defendant told the victim he was going to "fix" her face to show he "was not playing." When told that their relationship was over, the defendant stated that he had a "right" to have intercourse with her again. The two went to the house of a friend of the defendant. The defendant asked her if she was "ready" and the victim told him she did not want to have sexual relations. The defendant pulled her up from the chair, undressed her, pushed her legs apart, and penetrated her. She cried.

The defendant was convicted of rape, and his conviction was affirmed by the intermediate court of appeals. The North Carolina Supreme Court reversed

The state supreme court held that the victim was not required to resist physically to establish nonconsent; it described the victim's testimony that she did not consent as "unequivocal" and held that her testimony provided substantial evidence that the act of sexual intercourse was against her will.

Consent was not the problem. Force was. The North Carolina Supreme Court held that, even viewing the evidence in the light most favorable to the state (as required by law), the element of force had not been established by substantial evidence. The victim did not "resist" — physically, at least. And her failure to resist, in the court's evaluation, was not a result of what the defendant did just before penetration. Therefore, there was no "force." The force used outside the school and the threats made on the walk, "although they may have induced fear" were considered to be "unrelated to the act of sexual intercourse." The court emphasized that the victim testified that it was not what the defendant said that day, but her experience with him in the past, that made her afraid. Such past experience was deemed irrelevant. "Although [the victim's] general fear of the defendant may have been justified by his conduct on prior occasions, absent evidence that the defendant used force or threats to overcome the will of the victim to resist the sexual intercourse alleged to have been rape, such general fear was not sufficient to show that the defendant used the force required to support a conviction of rape." The undressing and the pushing of her legs apart — presumably the "incidental" force — were not even mentioned.

Alston reflects the adoption of the most traditional male notion of a fight as the working definition of "force." In a fight you hit your assailant with your fists or your elbows or your knees. In a fight the person attacked fights back. In these terms there was no fight in *Alston*. Therefore, there was no force.

On its face, the decision creates a paradox. The court explicitly says that the sexual intercourse was without the woman's consent. It also says that there was no force. In other words, the woman was not forced to engage in sex (as proven by her failure to resist), but the sex she engaged in was against her will. I am not at all sure how the judges who decided *Alston* would justify the clear contradiction in their approach. Apparently, they could not understand the woman's reaction. For me, it is not at all difficult to understand that a woman who had been beaten repeatedly, who had been a passive victim of both violence and sex during the "consensual" relationship, who had sought to escape from the man, who is confronted and threatened by him, who summons the courage to tell him their relationship is over only to be answered by his assertion of a "right" to sex, would not fight his advances. She did not fight; she cried. It is the reaction of "sissies" in playground fights. It is the reaction of people who have already been beaten, or never had the power to fight in the first place. It is, from my reading, the most common reaction of women to rape.

To say that there is no "force" in this situation, as the North Carolina court did, is to create a gulf between power and force and to define the latter strictly in schoolboy terms. Alston did not beat his victim — at least not with his fists. He didn't have to. She had been beaten, physically and emotionally, long before. But that beating was one that the court simply refused to recognize.

[T]he "reasonable" woman under [this] view . . . is not a woman at all. [This] version of a reasonable person is one who does not scare easily, one who does not feel vulnerable, one who is not passive, one who fights back, not cries. The reasonable woman, it seems, is not a schoolboy "sissy"; she is a real man.

[Thus,] the force standard . . . ensures broad male freedom to "seduce" women who feel themselves to be powerless, vulnerable, and afraid. It effectively guarantees men freedom to intimidate women and exploit their weakness and passivity, so long as they don't "fight" with them. And it makes clear that the responsibility and blame for such seductions should be placed squarely on the woman.

Compare Vivian Berger, Not So Simple Rape, 7 Crim. Justice Ethics 69, 75-76 (1988):

> I'm certain that Alston is a terrible person and that Cottie should be pitied rather than blamed. But did he *rape* her? I share the doubts of the appellate court that reversed his conviction. Estrich does not. She argues eloquently, indeed angrily, that *Alston* represents yet another instance of schoolboy rules regarding force unjustly applied to defenseless women. . . . I don't quarrel with [Estrich's] overall view that a "no" without an actual fight can turn intercourse into rape. Yet if she means, as the sentence on "beaten" people suggests, that Cottie's global "reaction" to a difficult situation, not just her tears and lack of resistance, is "common" *and* makes what occurred "rape," I find myself somewhat troubled.
>
> . . . I worry that a *too* "understanding" attitude toward the Cotties of the world by the legal system may backfire and ultimately damage the cause of women in general. A good feminist, Estrich wants "to empower women in potentially consensual situations with the weapon of a rape charge." Well and good. But we don't want the law to patronize women; when it did, in a vast number of areas, we fought it and won significant victories. To treat as victims in a legal sense all of the female victims of life is at some point to cheapen, not celebrate, the rights to self-determination, sexual autonomy, and self- and societal respect of women. Naturally, no bright line exists to make the border separating justified use of rape law to safeguard female personhood and choice . . . from abuse of this law to "defend" women who abdicate self and will entirely. Because overprotection risks enfeebling instead of empowering women, the tension between reformist goals . . . seems to me to make cases like *Alston* a close call, not a springboard for moral outrage.
>
> Thus, as to Cottie, I think it acceptable if not ineluctable to regard her as a pitiable woman, involved with an utterly contemptible man in a sick relationship, whose sexual dynamics included a course of conduct involving passivity, submission, and inconsistent response on her part, dominance and occasional violence on his. Had she taken Alston to court when he beat her, he ought to have been convicted of battery: vindicating her right to be free of physical injury would scarcely have amounted to undue solicitude for a weakling or depreciation of women as a group. But "rape" strikes me at least arguably as a misnomer for the event at issue here. Her stated "no," while not a "yes," bore greater resemblance to a mental reservation or a "do what you will" than to a firm and clear rejection, when viewed against the totality of the couple's ongoing interactions.

Does Professor Berger's argument imply that it is "patronizing" to women to treat their silence or ambivalence as equivalent to nonconsent and, therefore, that explicit protests should be a prerequisite to a rape conviction? Compare the following comment (Stephen J. Schulhofer, Taking Sexual Autonomy Seriously: Rape Law and Beyond, 11 Law & Phil. 35, 74-75 (1992)):

> Consider this parable. A hospitalized athlete, suffering from chronic knee problems, consults a surgeon, who recommends an operation. The athlete is not sure. If the operation is successful, he will enjoy a long, fulfilling career with his team.

But there are imponderables. The operation carries a risk of a burdensome infection that can be hard to cure. The procedure may not produce the expected benefits. In any event, it is sure to be stressful in the short run. The athlete hesitates. There are clear advantages, clear disadvantages, and lots of uncertainties. What to do? Maybe he should postpone this big step for a while, see how things go without it. The surgeon is encouraging: "Try it. You'll like it." Still the athlete is unsure.

Now our surgeon becomes impatient. He has spent a lot of time with this case. The athlete's hesitation is becoming tiresome and annoying. So the surgeon signals an anesthesiologist to ready the drugs that will flow through an intravenous tube already in place. One last time the surgeon (a sensitive, modern male) reminds the athlete, "You don't have to go ahead with this. If you really want me to stop, just say so." But the athlete, his brain still clouded with doubts, fears, hopes, and uncertainties, says nothing. So the surgeon starts the anesthesia and just *does it*.

Consent? Of course not. But why not? The athlete was not compelled to submit. Nobody forced him. . . . Surely his silence proves that he was not unwilling. If he really objected, all he had to do was say so!

There are, to be sure, important contextual differences between surgery and sexual intimacy. But even allowing for those differences, it would not be implausible to find "consent" by the patient, provided we could get ourselves to think of illegal surgery as an offense requiring "forcible compulsion," and to think of "nonconsent" in this context as revulsion, aversion, or a clearly crystallized negative attitude.

We do not see matters this way because we are not thinking about a crime of violence. We are thinking about an offense against the patient's autonomy. . . . Nonconsent is simply anything that is not positive consent, anything that is not an affirmative, crystallized expression of willingness. To treat the athlete as a victim is not, of course, to patronize him. It is merely to recognize an obvious violation of the physical autonomy of his person.

5. *Inherent force.* Even in the absence of expressed or implied threats, the act of intercourse itself involves some degree of physical force. Does this kind of force meet the force requirement for a rape conviction? Consider the cases that follow.

STATE IN THE INTEREST OF M.T.S.

New Jersey Supreme Court
129 N.J. 422, 609 A.2d 1266 (1992)

HANDLER, J. Under New Jersey law a person who commits an act of sexual penetration using physical force or coercion is guilty of second-degree sexual assault. The sexual assault statute does not define the words "physical force." The question posed by this appeal is whether the element of "physical force" is met simply by an act of non-consensual penetration involving no more force than necessary to accomplish that result.

That issue is presented in the context of what is often referred to as "acquaintance rape." The record in the case discloses that the juvenile, a seventeen-year-old boy, engaged in consensual kissing and heavy petting with a fifteen-year-old girl and thereafter engaged in actual sexual penetration of the girl to which she had not consented. There was no evidence or suggestion that the juvenile used any unusual or extra force or threats to accomplish the act of penetration.

The trial court determined that the juvenile was delinquent for committing a sexual assault. The Appellate Division reversed the disposition of delinquency, concluding that non-consensual penetration does not constitute sexual assault unless it is accompanied by some level of force more than that necessary to accomplish the penetration. We granted the State's petition for certification. . . .

[F]ifteen-year-old C.G. was living with her mother, her three siblings, and several other people, including M.T.S. and his girlfriend. . . . M.T.S., then age seventeen, was temporarily residing at the home with the permission of C.G.'s mother; he slept downstairs on a couch. C.G. had her own room on the second floor. . . . At trial, C.G. and M.T.S. offered very different accounts concerning the nature of their relationship. . . . The trial court did not credit fully either teenager's testimony.

C.G. stated that [on the day of May 21], M.T.S. had told her three or four times that he "was going to make a surprise visit up in [her] bedroom." [C.G. said she considered the comments a joke because M.T.S. frequently teased her. She testified that M.T.S. had attempted to kiss and fondle her on other occasions, but that she had rejected all of his previous advances. C.G. testified that she awoke that night at approximately 1:30 A.M. and saw M.T.S., fully clothed, standing in her doorway. According to C.G., M.T.S. said "he was going to tease [her] a little bit." C.G. testified that she "didn't think anything of it"; she used the bathroom and returned to bed, falling into a "heavy" sleep within fifteen minutes. The next event C.G. claimed to recall was waking up with M.T.S. on top of her, her underpants and shorts removed.] She said "his penis was into [her] vagina." As soon as C.G. realized what had happened, she said, she immediately slapped M.T.S. once in the face, then "told him to get off [her], and get out." She did not scream or cry out. She testified that M.T.S. complied in less than one minute after being struck. . . .

C.G. said that after M.T.S. left the room, she "fell asleep crying" because "[she] couldn't believe that he did what he did to [her]." She explained that she did not immediately tell her mother or anyone else in the house of the events of that morning because she was "scared and in shock." . . . By her own account, C.G. was not otherwise harmed by M.T.S.

[At about 7:00 A.M., C.G. went downstairs and told her mother about her encounter with M.T.S. and said that they would have to "get [him] out of the house." C.G. and her mother then filed a complaint with the police.]

According to M.T.S., he and C.G. had been good friends for a long time, and their relationship "kept leading on to more and more." He . . . testified that during the three days preceding the incident they had been "kissing and necking" and had discussed having sexual intercourse. . . . He said C.G. repeatedly had encouraged him to "make a surprise visit up in her room."

M.T.S. testified that at exactly 1:15 A.M. on May 22, he entered C.G.'s bedroom as she was walking to the bathroom. He said C.G. soon returned from the bathroom, and the two began "kissing and all," eventually moving to the bed. Once they were in bed, he said, they undressed each other and . . . proceeded to engage in sexual intercourse. According to M.T.S., [he] "did it [thrust] three times, and then the fourth time . . . , that's when [she] pulled [him] off of her." M.T.S. said that as C.G. pushed him off, she said "stop, get off," and he "hopped off right away."

According to M.T.S., after about one minute, he asked C.G. what was wrong; she replied with a back-hand to his face. He recalled asking C.G. what was wrong a second time, and her replying, "how can you take advantage of me or something like that." M.T.S. said that he proceeded to get dressed and told C.G. to calm down, but that she then told him to get away from her and began to cry. Before leaving the room, he told C.G., "I'm leaving. . . . I'm going with my real girlfriend, . . . stay out of my life . . . don't tell anybody about this . . . it would just screw everything up." He then walked downstairs and went to sleep.

. . . M.T.S. was charged with conduct that if engaged in by an adult would constitute second-degree sexual assault. . . . Following a two-day trial . . . , the court concluded that the victim had consented to a session of kissing and heavy petting with M.T.S. The trial court did not find that C.G. had been sleeping at the time of penetration, but nevertheless found that she had not consented to the actual sexual act. Accordingly, the court concluded that the State had proven second-degree sexual assault beyond a reasonable doubt. On appeal, following the imposition of suspended sentences on the [sexual assault] charges,[a] the Appellate Division . . . reversed the juvenile's adjudication of delinquency for that offense.

. . . N.J.S.A. 2C:14-2c(1) defines "sexual assault" as the commission "of sexual penetration" "with another person" with the use of "physical force or coercion."[1] [B]oth the act of "sexual penetration" and the use of "physical force or coercion" are separate and distinct elements of the offense. . . .

The parties offer two alternative understandings of the concept of "physical force" as it is used in the statute. The State would read "physical force" to entail any amount of sexual touching brought about involuntarily. A showing of sexual penetration coupled with a lack of consent would satisfy the elements of the statute. The Public Defender urges an interpretation of "physical force" to mean force "used to overcome lack of consent." That definition equates force with violence and leads to the conclusion that sexual assault requires the application of some amount of force in addition to the act of penetration. . . .

a. In the case of an adult sexual assault offender, the New Jersey sentencing system ordinarily would not permit suspension of the minimum five-year term of imprisonment in the absence of "extraordinary and unanticipated" circumstances. See State v. Johnson, 118 N.J. 10, 570 A.2d 395, 396 (1990). — Eds.

1. The sexual assault statute, N.J.S.A.: 2C:14-2c(1), reads as follows:

c. An actor is guilty of sexual assault if he commits an act of sexual penetration with another person under any one of the following circumstances:

(1) The actor *uses physical force or coercion,* but the victim does not sustain severe personal injury;

(2) The victim is one whom the actor knew or should have known was physically helpless, mentally defective or mentally incapacitated;

(3) The victim is on probation or parole, or is detained in a hospital, prison or other institution and the actor has supervisory or disciplinary power over the victim by virtue of the actor's legal, professional or occupational status;

(4) The victim is at least 16 but less than 18 years old and:

(a) The actor is related to the victim by blood or affinity to the third degree; or

(b) The actor has supervisory or disciplinary power over the victim; or

(c) The actor is a foster parent, a guardian, or stands in loco parentis within the household;

(5) The victim is at least 13 but less than 16 years old and the actor is at least 4 years older than the victim.

Sexual assault is a crime of the second degree [punishable by a minimum of 5 and a maximum of 10 years' imprisonment.]

[When committed with a weapon or when "severe personal injury" is sustained, the offense is aggravated sexual assault, a crime of the first degree, punishable by a minimum of 10 and a maximum of 20 years' imprisonment. — Eds.]

Under traditional rape law, in order to prove that a rape had occurred, the State had to show both that force had been used and that the penetration had been against the woman's will. [T]he traditional definition of rape . . . squarely placed on the victim the burden of proof and of action. Effectively, a woman who was above the age of consent had actively and affirmatively to withdraw that consent for the intercourse to be against her will. . . .

The judicial interpretation of the pre-reform rape law in New Jersey, with its insistence on resistance by the victim, greatly minimized the importance of the forcible and assaultive aspect of the defendant's conduct. . . . Critics of rape law agreed that the focus of the crime should be shifted from the victim's behavior to the defendant's conduct, and particularly to its forceful and assaultive, rather than sexual, character. . . . In dealing with the problem of consent the reform goal was not so much to purge the entire concept of consent from the law as to eliminate the burden that had been placed on victims to prove they had not consented.

Similarly, with regard to force, rape law reform sought . . . to avoid a definition of force that depended on the reaction of the victim. Traditional interpretations of force were strongly criticized for failing to acknowledge that force may be understood simply as the invasion of "bodily integrity." Susan Estrich, Rape, 95 Yale L.J. 1087, 1105 (1986). In urging that the "resistance" requirement be abandoned, reformers sought to break the connection between force and resistance. . . .

[The] Model Penal Code (MPC) proposed provisions did not present a break from traditional rape law. They would have established two principal sexual offenses: aggravated rape [MPC §213.1(1)], a first-degree or second-degree crime involving egregious circumstances; and [gross sexual imposition], a crime of the third-degree . . . defined as sexual intercourse . . . to which [the female] was compelled to submit by any threat that would prevent resistance by a woman of ordinary resolution. The comments to the MPC . . . state that "[c]ompulsion plainly implies non-consent," and that the words "compels to submit" require more than "a token initial resistance." A.L.I., MPC, §213.1, comments at 306 (revised commentary 1980).

The Legislature did not endorse the Model Penal Code approach to rape. Rather, it passed a fundamentally different proposal in 1978. . . . The new statutory provisions covering rape were formulated by a coalition of feminist groups assisted by the National Organization of Women (NOW) National Task Force on Rape. The stated intent of the drafters . . . had been to remove all features found to be contrary to the interests of rape victims. . . .

The reform statute defines sexual assault as penetration accomplished by the use of "physical force" or "coercion," but it does not define either "physical force" or "coercion." . . . The task of defining "physical force" therefore was left to the courts. . . .

The Legislature's concept of sexual assault and the role of force was significantly colored by its understanding of the law of assault and battery. . . . Any "unauthorized touching of another [is] a battery." Perna v. Pirozzi, 92 N.J. 446, 462, 457 A.2d 431 (1983). . . . Sexual contact is criminal under the same circumstances that render an act of sexual penetration a sexual assault, namely, when "physical force" or "coercion" demonstrates that it is unauthorized and offensive. N.J.S.A. 2C:14-3(b). Thus, just as any unauthorized touching is a crime under traditional laws of assault and battery, so is any unauthorized sexual contact a crime under the reformed law of criminal sexual contact, and so is any unauthorized sexual penetration a crime under the reformed law of sexual assault.

The understanding of sexual assault as a criminal battery, albeit one with especially serious consequences, follows necessarily from the Legislature's decision to eliminate non-consent and resistance from the substantive definition of the offense. Under the new law, the victim no longer is required to resist and therefore need not have said or done anything in order for the sexual penetration to be unlawful. . . . [A]n interpretation of the statutory crime of sexual assault to require physical force in addition to that entailed in an act of involuntary or unwanted sexual penetration would be fundamentally inconsistent with the legislative purpose to eliminate any consideration of whether the victim resisted or expressed non-consent.

We note that the contrary interpretation of force — that the element of force need be extrinsic to the sexual act — would not only reintroduce a resistance requirement into the sexual assault law, but also would immunize many acts of criminal sexual contact short of penetration. The characteristics that make a sexual contact unlawful are the same as those that make a sexual penetration unlawful. An actor is guilty of criminal sexual contact if he or she commits an act of sexual contact with another using "physical force" or "coercion." N.J.S.A. 2C:14-3(b). That the Legislature would have wanted to decriminalize unauthorized sexual intrusions on the bodily integrity of a victim by requiring a showing of force in addition to that entailed in the sexual contact itself is hardly possible.

. . . We conclude, therefore, that any act of sexual penetration engaged in by the defendant without the affirmative and freely-given permission of the victim to the specific act of penetration constitutes the offense of sexual assault. . . . The definition of "physical force" is satisfied under N.J.S.A. 2C:14-2c(1) if the defendant applies any amount of force against another person in the absence of what a reasonable person would believe to be affirmative and freely-given permission to the act of sexual penetration. . . . Although it is possible to imagine a set of rules in which persons must demonstrate affirmatively that sexual contact is unwanted or not permitted, such a regime would be inconsistent with modern principles of personal autonomy. The Legislature recast the law of rape as sexual assault to bring that area of law in line with the expectation of privacy and bodily control that long has characterized most of our private and public law. . . .

The decision to engage in sexual relations with another person is one of the most private and intimate decisions a person can make. Each person has the right not only to decide whether to engage in sexual contact with another, but also to control the circumstances and character of that contact. No one, neither a spouse, nor a friend, nor an acquaintance, nor a stranger, has the right or the privilege to force sexual contact. . . .

In a case such as this one, in which the State does not allege violence or force extrinsic to the act of penetration, the factfinder must decide whether the defendant's act of penetration was undertaken in circumstances that led the defendant reasonably to believe that the alleged victim had freely given affirmative permission to the specific act of sexual penetration. Such permission can be indicated either through words or through actions that, when viewed in the light of all the surrounding circumstances, would demonstrate to a reasonable person affirmative and freely-given authorization for the specific act of sexual penetration. [T]he law places no burden on the alleged victim to have expressed non-consent or to have denied permission, and no inquiry is made into what he or she thought or desired or why he or she did not resist or protest. . . . Under the reformed statute, a person's failure to protest or resist cannot be considered or used as justification for bodily invasion.

We acknowledge that cases such as this are inherently fact sensitive and depend on the reasoned judgment and common sense of judges and juries. The trial court concluded that the victim had not expressed consent to the act of intercourse, either through her words or actions. We conclude that the record provides reasonable support for the trial court's disposition. Accordingly, we reverse the judgment of the Appellate Division and reinstate the disposition of juvenile delinquency for the commission of second-degree sexual assault.

COMMONWEALTH v. BERKOWITZ, 641 A.2d 1161 (Pa. 1994): The complainant, a female college student, left her class, went to her dormitory room where she drank a martini, and then went to a lounge to await her boyfriend. When her boyfriend failed to appear, she went to another dormitory to find a friend, Earl Hassel. She knocked on the door, but received no answer. She tried the doorknob and, finding it unlocked, entered the room and discovered a man sleeping on the bed. The complainant originally believed the man to be Hassel, but it turned out to be Hassel's roommate, Appellee. Appellee asked her to stay for a while and she agreed. He requested a back-rub and she declined. He suggested that she sit on the bed, but she declined and sat on the floor.

Appellee then moved to the floor beside her, lifted up her shirt and bra and massaged her breasts. . . . They both stood up, and he locked the door. He returned to push her onto the bed, and removed her undergarments from one leg. He then penetrated her. . . . [Afterward] he stated, "Wow, I guess we just got carried away," to which she responded, "No, we didn't get carried away, you got carried away."

The crime of rape is defined as follows:

§3121. RAPE

> A person commits a felony of the first degree when he engages in sexual intercourse with another person not one's spouse: (1) by forcible compulsion; (2) by threat of forcible compulsion that would prevent resistance by a person of reasonable resolution; (3) who is unconscious; or (4) who is so mentally deranged or deficient that such person is incapable of consent.

The victim of a rape need not resist. "The force necessary to support a conviction of rape . . . need only be such as to establish lack of consent and to induce the [victim] to submit without additional resistance. . . . The degree of force required to constitute rape is relative and depends on the facts and particular circumstance of the case." Commonwealth v. Rhodes, 510 A.2d 1217 (1986).

In regard to the critical issue of forcible compulsion, the complainant's testimony is devoid of any statement which clearly or adequately describes the use of force or the threat of force against her. . . . She testified that "He put me down on the bed. It was kind of like — He didn't throw me on the bed. . . . It was kind of like a push but not — I can't explain what I'm trying to say." . . . She agreed that Appellee's hands were not restraining her in any manner during the actual penetration, and that the weight of his body on top of her was the only force applied. She testified that at no time did Appellee verbally threaten her. The complainant did testify that she sought to leave the room, and said "no" throughout the encounter. As to the complainant's desire to leave the room, the record clearly demonstrates that the door could be unlocked easily from the inside, that she was aware of this fact, but that she never attempted to go to the door or unlock it.

As to the complainant's testimony that she stated "no" throughout the encounter with Appellee, we point out that, while such an allegation of fact would be relevant to the issue of consent, it is not relevant to the issue of force. . . . [W]here there is a lack of consent, but no showing of either physical force, a threat of physical force, or psychological coercion, the "forcible compulsion" requirement under 18 Pa. C.S. §3121 is not met.

Moreover, we find it instructive that in defining the related but distinct crime of "indecent assault" under 18 Pa. C.S. §3126, the Legislature did not employ the phrase "forcible compulsion" but rather chose to define indecent assault as "indecent contact with another . . . without the consent of the other person."[a] . . . The choice by the Legislature to define the crime of indecent assault utilizing the phrase "without the consent of the other" and to not so define the crime of rape indicates a legislative intent that the term "forcible compulsion" under 18 Pa. C.S. §3121, be interpreted as something more than a lack of consent.

[T]he complainant's testimony simply fails to establish that the Appellee forcibly compelled her to engage in sexual intercourse. . . .

The evidence described above is clearly sufficient to support the jury's conviction of indecent assault. "Indecent contact" is defined as "[a]ny touching of the sexual or other intimate parts of the person for the purpose of arousing or gratifying sexual desire, in either person." 18 Pa. C.S. §3101. Appellee himself testified to the "indecent contact." The victim testified that she repeatedly said "no" throughout the encounter. Viewing that testimony in the light most favorable to the Commonwealth as verdict winner, the jury reasonably could have inferred that the victim did not consent to the indecent contact. Thus, the evidence was sufficient to support the jury's verdict finding Appellee guilty of indecent assault.

[T]he order of the Superior Court reversing the rape conviction is affirmed. . . . The conviction and the trial court's sentence on the indecent assault charge are reinstated.

NOTES AND QUESTIONS

1. The meaning of force. Do the differences between the New Jersey and Pennsylvania statutes account for the difference between the holdings of *M.T.S.* and *Berkowitz*? If not, which case presents the better interpretation of the statutory requirement of "force"? Which approach is preferable as a matter of legislative policy?

---

a. 18 Pa. C.S. §3126 provides that indecent assault is a misdemeanor of the second degree, punishable by not more than two years' imprisonment. — EDS.

2. *Statutes eliminating the requirement of force.* Although "force" (or a threat of "force") is a prerequisite to conviction in most jurisdictions, a few states have made nonconsensual intercourse criminal in the absence of force or threat. Under §940.225 of the Wisconsin Criminal Code, first-degree sexual assault includes intercourse without consent by the use or threat of using a dangerous weapon; second-degree sexual assault includes intercourse without consent by other "use or threat of force or violence"; and third-degree sexual assault (punishable by up to five years in prison) is defined in §940.225(3) as "sexual intercourse with a person without the consent of that person." Section 940.225(4) defines "consent" as "words or actions by a person who is competent to give informed consent indicating a freely given agreement to have sexual intercourse. . . ."[5]

Do the Wisconsin statutes provide a satisfactory solution to the problem posed by cases like *M.T.S.* and *Berkowitz?* How does the Wisconsin approach differ, in practice, from the approach produced by the *M.T.S.* interpretation of New Jersey's sexual assault statute?

3. *Nonphysical threats.* Consider the following cases.

State v. Thompson, 792 P.2d 1103 (Mont. 1990): [Defendant, a high school principal, allegedly forced one of his students to submit to sexual intercourse by threatening to prevent her from graduating from high school. The court affirmed the dismissal of sexual assault charges.] Section 45-5-503, MCA, states the following:

> A person who knowingly has sexual intercourse without consent with a person of the opposite sex commits the offense of sexual intercourse without consent. . . .

The phrase "without consent"[,] . . . defined in §45-5-501, [means:]

> the victim is compelled to submit by force or by threat of imminent death, bodily injury, or kidnapping to be inflicted on anyone; . . .

The District Court in its order [dismissing the charges] defined force as follows:

> The word "force" is used in its ordinary and normal connotation: physical compulsion, the use or immediate threat of bodily harm, injury.

. . . [T]he State argues the District Court's definition of force is too limited. . . . [The State] contends that Thompson, in his position of authority as the principal, intimidated Jane Doe into the alleged acts. Furthermore, the State argues the fear and apprehension of Jane Doe show Thompson used force against her. We agree with the State that Thompson intimidated Jane Doe; however, we cannot stretch the definition of force to include intimidation, fear, or apprehension. Rather, we adopt the District Court's definition of force. . . .

The alleged facts, if true, show disgusting acts of taking advantage of a young person by an adult who occupied a position of authority over the young person.

---

5. Similar statutory schemes punishing nonconsensual intercourse in the absence of force or threat include Utah Code Ann. §76-5-402; Wash. Crim. Code §9A.44.060.

If we could rewrite the statutes to define the alleged acts here as sexual intercourse without consent, we would willingly do so. The business of courts, however, is to interpret statutes, not to rewrite them, nor to insert words not put
there by the legislature. With a good deal of reluctance, and with strong condemnation of the alleged acts, we affirm the District Court.

Commonwealth v. Mlinarich, 498 A.2d 395 (Pa. Super. 1985), affirmed by an
equally divided court, *542 A.2d 1335 (Pa. 1988):* [The victim was a 14-year-old
girl who had been committed to a juvenile detention home after stealing from
her brother. Subsequently defendant agreed to assume custody for her, and she
was placed in defendant's home. The victim submitted to defendant's sexual
advances after he had threatened to send her back to the detention home if she
refused his requests. He was convicted of corrupting the morals of a minor and
of committing rape "by threat of forcible compulsion. . . ." 18 Pa. C.S. §3121(2).
The Superior Court reversed the rape conviction:] Our task in this case is made
more difficult because the victim of appellant's sexual advances was a fourteen
year old child. The definition which we adopt, however, will know no age limitation. It is with a view to general application, therefore, that we attempt to define the parameters of the legislative proscription against sexual intercourse by
forcible compulsion or threat of forcible compulsion.

The term "force" and its derivative, "forcible," when used to define the crime
of rape, have historically been understood by the courts and legal scholars to
mean physical force or violence. . . .

To define "forcible compulsion" so as to permit a conviction for rape whenever sexual intercourse is induced by "any threat" or by "physical, moral or
intellectual means or by the exigencies of the circumstances" will undoubtedly
have unfortunate consequences. If a man takes a destitute widow into his home
and provides support for her and her family, such a definition of forcible compulsion will convict him of attempted rape if he threatens to withdraw his support and compel her to leave unless she engages in sexual intercourse. Similarly,
a person may be guilty of rape if he or she extorts sexual favors from another
person upon threat of discharging the other or his or her spouse from a position
of employment, or upon threat of foreclosing the mortgage on the home of the
other's parents, or upon threat of denying a loan application, or upon threat of
disclosing the other's adultery or submission to an abortion. An interpretation
of forcible compulsion which employs an ambiguous, generic definition of force
will create the potential for a veritable parade of threats, express and implied,
in support of accusations of rape and attempted rape. To make it even more
troublesome, such an interpretation of forcible compulsion will place in the
hands of jurors almost unlimited discretion to determine which acts, threats or
promises will transform sexual intercourse into rape. Without intending to condone any of the foregoing, reprehensible acts, our use of them serves to illustrate the intolerable uncertainty which a wholly elastic definition of rape will
create.

. . . We hold that rape, as defined by the legislature . . . requires actual physical
compulsion or violence or a threat of physical compulsion or violence sufficient
to prevent resistance by a person of reasonable resolution. . . .

[Judge Spaeth, dissenting, wrote:] It is frequently said that the words of a
statute are to be "given their plain meaning," or are to be "understood accord-

ing to their common and approved usage." These maxims, however, will not yield the meaning of the phrase, "threat of forcible compulsion," for "force" has more than one plain, or common and approved, meaning. Webster's Third New International Dictionary (1968) provides eleven definitions of "force," some of these being subdivided. . . .

As one considers the range and tone of these several definitions it becomes evident that appellant's threat . . . might, or might not, have been a "threat of forcible compulsion." It was *not* such a threat if "forcible" is to be considered as limited to meaning "to do violence to"; it *might* have been such a threat if "forcible" is to be construed as meaning "to constrain or compel by physical, moral, or intellectual means or by the exigencies of the circumstances," or as meaning "to press, impose, or thrust urgently, importunately, inexorably." . . .

Our problem, therefore, is not to choose *the* "plain meaning" of the phrase, "threat of forcible compulsion," but, rather, to decide *which of several* plain meanings the legislature had in mind when it used the phrase in enacting the Crimes Code. . . .

I have no hesitancy in concluding that the legislature did *not* mean force in the limited sense of "to do violence to," and *did* mean force in the more general sense of "to constrain or compel by physical, moral, or intellectual means or by the exigencies of the circumstances." Only this conclusion is consistent with the legislature's manifested agreement with the Model Penal Code that a "fresh approach" should be taken, and the focus of inquiry shifted away from the victim's consent to the actor's force.

. . . I believe that the jury was entitled to find that the complainant was compelled to submit to appellant's demands by the exigencies of her circumstances, and, further, that in submitting, she acted as a person of reasonable resolution.

4. *Solutions to the problem of nonphysical threats. (a)* Consider the following observations (Comment, Towards a Consent Standard in the Law of Rape, 43 U. Chi. L. Rev. 613, 644-645 (1976)):

> Although the force element has traditionally furthered the policy of physical protection, as well as serving an evidentiary function, . . . freedom of sexual choice rather than physical protection is the primary value served by criminalization of rape. Furthermore, a woman's decision to submit to physical force may be less agonizing than her decision to have intercourse with a person who holds economic or emotional power over her and her family. Although one can argue that a man who obtains intercourse through threats of nonphysical harm should be punished less severely than a violent rapist, the growing legal appreciation of the reality of mental injury and the power of economic duress suggests that he nonetheless should be punished. [T]he freedom of sexual choice which is to be protected by rape law can be as effectively negated by nonphysical as by physical coercion.

(b) Model Penal Code §213.1(2) permits a conviction for "gross sexual imposition" in cases where submission is compelled by threat of force or "by any threat that would prevent resistance by a woman of ordinary resolution." Is this language narrow enough to control jury discretion and give fair warning to potential defendants? Is it broad enough to permit conviction in cases like *Mlinarich* and *Thompson?*

(c) Recall that *M.T.S.* equates "force" with the absence of "affirmative and freely-given permission." How would *Mlinarich* and *Thompson* be decided in New

Jersey? Under the *M.T.S.* approach, what should be the result in the hypothetical posed by the *Mlinarich* court: the destitute widow who submits to sexual intercourse with a benefactor who will otherwise refuse to continue supporting her?

(d) In Commonwealth v. Rhodes, 510 A.2d 1217, 1225 (Pa. 1986), the court, relying on the broad dictionary meanings of force cited in the *Mlinarich* dissent, held: "[T]he phrase 'forcible compulsion' clearly connotes more than the exercise of sheer physical force or violence. . . . The phrase also connotes that act of using superior force — physical, moral, psychological, or intellectual — to compel a person to do a thing against that person's volition. . . ." In light of this test for forcible compulsion, what should be the result on the facts of *Mlinarich* and *Thompson*? How should the case of the destitute widow be decided under this approach?

(e) Several recent articles attempt to develop frameworks for distinguishing legitimate inducements from illegitimate coercion. See Donald A. Dripps, Beyond Rape: An Essay on the Difference Between the Presence of Force and the Absence of Consent, 92 Colum. L. Rev. 1780 (1992); Stephen J. Schulhofer, Taking Sexual Autonomy Seriously: Rape Law and Beyond, 11 Law & Phil. 35, 69-88 (1992); Lois Pineau, Date Rape: A Feminist Analysis, 8 Law & Phil. 217 (1989); Martha Chamallas, Consent, Equality, and the Legal Control of Sexual Conduct, 61 S. Cal. L. Rev. 777 (1988).

2. Deception

PEOPLE v. EVANS

Supreme Court, New York County, Trial Term
85 Misc. 2d 1088, 379 N.Y.S. 2d 912 (1975)

GREENFIELD, J. The question presented in this case is whether the sexual conquest by a predatory male of a resisting female constitutes rape or seduction. . . .

Since a jury has been waived, this Court is called upon to scrutinize the conduct involved and to draw the line between the legally permissible and the impermissible. . . .

Rape is defined in our Penal Law, Section 130.35, subdivision I, as follows: "A male is guilty of rape in the first degree when he engages in sexual intercourse with a female: 1. By forcible compulsion." . . .

Forcible compulsion is defined in Section 130.00 subdivision 8, of the Penal Law as

> physical force that overcomes earnest resistance; or a threat, express or implied, that places a person in fear of immediate death or serious physical injury to himself or another person, or in fear that he or another person will immediately be kidnapped.[a]

[B]ased upon the testimony in this case, the Court first makes the following findings of fact:

---

a. Under the New York statute, first-degree rape is punishable by a maximum of 25 years' imprisonment. Second-degree rape (statutory rape) is punishable by a maximum of 7 years' imprisonment. For the current New York definition of "forcible compulsion," see page 340 supra. — EDS.

   The defendant, a bachelor of approximately thirty-seven years of age, aptly described in the testimony as "glib," on July 15, 1974, met an incoming plane at LaGuardia Airport, from which disembarked L.E.P., of Charlotte, North Carolina, a twenty-year-old petite, attractive second-year student at Wellesley College, an unworldly girl, evidently unacquainted with New York City and the sophisticated city ways, a girl who proved to be, as indicated by the testimony, incredibly gullible, trusting and naive. [The] defendant struck up a conversation with her, posing as a psychologist doing a magazine article and using a name that was not his, inducing Miss P. to answer questions for an interview.

   The evidence further shows that the defendant invited Miss P. to accompany him by automobile to Manhattan, her destination being Grand Central Station. [Then the] defendant and a girl named Bridget took Miss P. to an establishment called Maxwell's Plum, which the defendant explained was for the purpose of conducting a sociological experiment in which he would observe her reactions and the reactions of males towards her in the setting of a singles bar. After several hours there, . . . she was induced to come up to an apartment . . . which the defendant explained was used as one of his five offices or apartments throughout the city. . . .

   She had been there for one to two hours when the defendant made his move and pulled her on to the opened sofa-bed in the living room of that apartment and attempted to disrobe her. She resisted that, and she claims that as articles of clothing were attempted to be removed she would pull them back on and ultimately she was able to ward off these advances and to get herself dressed again. At that point, the defendant's tactics, according to her testimony, appeared to have changed.

   First, he informed her of his disappointment that she had failed the test, that this was all part of his psychological experiment, that, in fact, this was a way in which he was trying to reach her innermost consciousness. . . . Then, after expressing disappointment in the failure of this psychological experiment, he took steps to cause doubt and fear to arise in the mind of Miss P. He said, "Look where you are. You are in the apartment of a strange man. How do you know that I am really who I say I am? How do you know that I am really a psychologist?" Then, he went on and said, "I could kill you. I could rape you. I could hurt you physically."

   Miss P. testified that at that point she became extremely frightened, that she realized, indeed, how vulnerable she was. The defendant did not strike her, did not beat her, he exhibited no weapons at the time, but he made the statement, "I could kill you; I could rape you."

   Then there was . . . an abrupt switch in which the defendant attempted to play on the sympathy of Miss P. by telling her a story about his lost love, how Miss P. had reminded him of her, and the hurt that he had sustained when she had driven her car off a cliff. Obviously, Miss P.'s sympathy was engaged, and at that time acting instinctively, she took a step forward and reached out for him and put her hand on his shoulders, and then he grabbed her and said, "You're mine, you are mine." There thereupon followed an act of sexual intercourse, an act of oral-genital contact; a half-hour later a second act of sexual intercourse, and then, before she left, about seven o'clock that morning, an additional act. . . .

   The testimony indicates that during these various sexual acts Miss P., in fact, offered little resistance. She said that she was pinned down by the defendant's body weight, but in some manner all her clothing was removed, all his clothing was removed, and the acts took place. There was no torn clothing, there were no scratches, there were no bruises. Finally, at approximately seven A.M. Miss P. dressed and left the apartment. . . .

The question is whether having had sexual intercourse by the . . . means described constitutes rape in the first degree. The essential element of rape in the first degree is forcible compulsion. The prevailing view in this country is that there can be no rape which is achieved by fraud, or trick, or stratagem. Provided there is actual consent, the nature of the act being understood, it is not rape, absent a statute, no matter how despicable the fraud, even if a woman has intercourse with a man impersonating her husband or if a fraudulent ceremony leads her to believe she is legally married to a man (contra if an explicit statute to that effect exists) or even if a doctor persuades her that sexual intercourse is necessary for her treatment and return to good health. . . .

It should be noted that seduction, while not considered to be a criminal act at common law, has been made a criminal offense by statute in some jurisdictions. In seduction, unlike rape, the consent of the woman, implied or explicit, has been procured, by artifice, deception, flattery, fraud or promise. The declared public policy of this state looks with disfavor on actions for seduction since the civil action was abolished more than forty years ago. The statute did not repeal any Penal Law provisions, but there are no presently existing penal sanctions against seduction. The law recognizes that there are some crimes where trickery and deceit do constitute the basis for a criminal charge. Since the common law, we have recognized the existence of larceny by trick. But of course, for a larceny there has to be a taking of property of value. I do not mean to imply that a woman's right to her body is not a thing of value, but it is not property in the sense which is defined by the law.

It is clear from the evidence in this case that . . . P. was intimidated; that she was confused; that she had been drowned in a torrent of words and perhaps was terrified. But it is likewise clear from the evidence that the defendant did not resort to actual physical force. . . .

So the question here is not so much the use of force, but whether threats uttered by the defendant had paralyzed her capacity to resist and had, in fact, undermined her will. Now, what was it the defendant said? He said, ". . . I could kill you. I could rape you. I could hurt you physically." Those words, as uttered, are susceptible to two possible and diverse interpretations. The first would be in essence that — you had better do what I say, for you are helpless and I have the power to use ultimate force should you resist. That clearly would be a threat which would induce fear and overcome resistance. The second possible meaning of those words is, in effect, that — you are a foolish girl. You are in the apartment of a strange man. You put yourself in the hands of a stranger, and you are vulnerable and defenseless. The possibility would exist of physical harm to you were you being confronted by someone other than the person who uttered this statement.

Of course, it is entirely possible that Miss P., who heard the statements, construed that as a threat, even though it may not have been intended as such by the person who uttered those words. The question arises as to which is the controlling state of mind — that of a person who hears the words and interprets them as a threat, or the state of mind of the person who utters such words. It appears to the Court that the controlling state of mind must be that of the speaker.* She, the hearer, may, in fact, take the words as a threat and be terrified by them. . . . But this being a criminal trial, it is basic that the criminal intent of the defendant must be shown beyond a reasonable doubt. . . . And so, if he utters words which are taken as a threat by the person who hears them, but are not intended as a threat by the person who utters them, there would be no basis for finding the necessary criminal intent to establish culpability under the law.

So where a statement is ambiguous, where the words and the acts which purport to constitute force or threats are susceptible of diverse interpretations, which may be consistent with either guilt or innocence, the Court, as the trier of the facts, cannot say beyond a reasonable doubt that the guilt of the defendant has been established with respect to the crime of rape. . . . Since the Court, therefore, can find neither forcible compulsion nor threat beyond a reasonable doubt, the defendant is found not guilty on the charges of rape, sodomy and unlawful imprisonment.

Now, acquittal on these charges does not imply that the Court condones the conduct of the defendant. The testimony in the case reveals that the defendant was a predator, and that naive and gullible girls like . . . P. were his natural prey. He posed. He lied. He pretended and he deceived. He used confidences which were innocently bestowed as leverage to effect his will. He used psychological techniques to achieve vulnerability and sympathy, and the erosion of resistance. A young and inexperienced girl like . . . P. was then unable to withstand the practiced onslaught of the defendant. . . . The Court finds his conduct, if not criminal, to be reprehensible. [Nevertheless,] the Court must conclude that the defendant's conduct towards Miss P. cannot be adjudged criminal so as to subject him to the penalty of imprisonment for up to twenty-five years. . . .

BORO v. SUPERIOR COURT, 163 Cal. App. 3d 1224, 210 Cal. Rptr. 122 (1985): Ms. R., the rape victim, . . . received a telephone call from a person who identified himself as "Dr. Stevens" and said that he worked at Peninsula Hospital.

"Dr. Stevens" told Ms. R. that he had the results of her blood test and that she had contracted a dangerous, highly infectious and perhaps fatal disease. . . .

"Dr. Stevens" further explained that there were only two ways to treat the disease. The first was a painful surgical procedure — graphically described — costing $9,000, and requiring her uninsured hospitalization for six weeks. A second alternative, "Dr. Stevens" explained, was to have sexual intercourse with an anonymous donor who had been injected with a serum which would cure the disease. The latter, nonsurgical procedure would only cost $4,500. When the victim replied that she lacked sufficient funds the "doctor" suggested that $1,000 would suffice as a down payment. The victim thereupon agreed to the nonsurgical alternative and consented to intercourse with the mysterious donor, believing "it was the only choice I had."

---

*On the same date as this decision the press reported a decision by the British House of Lords, holding that there could be no conviction of rape if the accused really believed that there was consent, despite the vociferous protest of the woman, when he had been told beforehand that she preferred intercourse to be accomplished over her vehement protest. The principle, of course, is that the subjective state of mind of the defendant controls in determining criminal intent. [The court's footnote appears to be a reference to Regina v. Morgan, pages 320-322 supra. — Eds.]

. . . Ms. R. . . . went to her bank, withdrew $1,000 and, as instructed, checked into [a] hotel. . . . About a half hour later the defendant "donor" arrived at her room [and] had sexual intercourse with her. At the time of penetration, it was Ms. R.'s belief that she would die unless she consented to sexual intercourse with the defendant: as she testified, "My life felt threatened, and for that reason and that reason alone did I do it."

[Defendant was charged with rape "accomplished by means of force or fear of immediate and unlawful bodily injury," Penal Code §261(2), and with rape "[w]here a person is at the time unconscious of the nature of the act and this is known to the accused," Penal Code §261(4). Conviction of either charge would carry a penalty of three, six, or eight years in prison. A pretrial motion to dismiss the former charge was granted by the lower court. Defendant challenged the lower court's failure to set aside the latter charge.[a]]

The People's position is [that] "at the time of the intercourse Ms. R., the victim, was 'unconscious of the nature of the act': because of [petitioner's] misrepresentation she believed it was in the nature of a medical treatment and not a simple, ordinary act of sexual intercourse." Petitioner, on the other hand, stresses that the victim was plainly aware of the *nature* of the act in which she voluntarily engaged, so that her motivation in doing so (since it did not fall within the proscription of section 261, subdivision (2)) is irrelevant.

[A]s a leading authority has written, "if deception causes a misunderstanding as to the fact itself (fraud in the factum) there is no legally-recognized consent because what happened is not that for which consent was given; whereas consent induced by fraud is as effective as any other consent, so far as direct and immediate legal consequences are concerned, if the deception relates not to the thing done but merely to some collateral matter (fraud in the inducement)." (Perkins & Boyce, Criminal Law (3d ed. 1982) p. 1079.) . . .

Another relatively common situation in the literature on this subject—discussed in detail by Perkins[,] is the fraudulent obtaining of intercourse by impersonating a spouse. As Professor Perkins observes, the courts are not in accord as to whether the crime of rape is thereby committed. . . . Some courts have taken the position that such a misdeed is fraud in the inducement on the theory that the woman consents to exactly what is done (sexual intercourse) and hence there is no rape; other courts, with better reason it would seem, hold such a misdeed to be rape on the theory that it involves fraud in the factum since the woman's consent is to an innocent act of marital intercourse while what is actually perpetrated upon her is an act of adultery. . . .

In California, of course, we have by statute[3] adopted the majority view that such fraud is in the factum, not the inducement, and have thus held it to vitiate consent.

[T]he Legislature well understood how to draft a statute to encompass fraud in the factum (§261, subd. (5)) and how to specify certain fraud in the induce-

---

a. The defendant was also charged with attempted grand theft and burglary (entry into the hotel room with intent to commit theft). These charges were not challenged on appeal. A fifth charge was dismissed with the consent of the prosecution. — Eds.

3. Section 261, subdivision (5) reads as follows: "Where a person submits under the belief that the person committing the act is the victim's spouse, and this belief is induced by any artifice, pretense, or concealment practiced by the accused, with intent to induce the belief."

ment as vitiating consent.[4] [A] concurring opinion in Mathews [v. Superior Court, 119 Cal. App. 3d 309 (1981),] specifically decried the lack of a California statutory prohibition against fraudulently induced consent to sexual relations in circumstances other than those specified in section 261, subdivision (5) and then-section 268.

The People, however, direct our attention to Penal Code section 261.6, which in their opinion has changed the rule that fraud in the inducement does not vitiate consent. That provision reads as follows: "In prosecutions under sections 261, 286, 288a or 289, in which consent is at issue, 'consent' shall be defined to mean positive cooperation in act or attitude pursuant to an act of free will. The person must act freely and voluntarily and have knowledge of the nature of the act or transaction involved."

We find little legislative history for this section. . . . [T]he author of a Pacific Law Journal article has concluded that the statute was enacted in response to People v. Mayberry (1975) 15 Cal. 3d 143, in order to provide an explicit definition of consent to be used in prosecutions in which consent was at issue. (Review of 1982 Legislation (1983) 14 Pacific L.J. 357, 547, 548, fn. 8.) . . .

If the Legislature at that time had desired to correct the apparent oversight decried in Mathews, supra,[5] — it could certainly have done so. But the Attorney General's strained reading of section 261.6 would render section 261, subdivision (5) meaningless surplusage; and we are "exceedingly reluctant to attach an interpretation to a particular statute which renders other existing provisions unnecessary." . . .

To so conclude is not to vitiate the heartless cruelty of petitioner's scheme, but to say that it comprised crimes of a different order than a violation of section 261, subdivision (4).

Let a peremptory writ of prohibition issue. . . .

HOLMDAHL, J. . . . The case before us concerns a prosecution under section 261, subd. (4), and "consent is at issue." Consequently, section 261.6, defining "consent" applies in this case.[2] It is apparent from the abundance of appropriate adjectives and adverbs in the statute that the Legislature intended to the point of redundancy to limit "consent" to that which is found to have been truly free and voluntary, truly unrestricted and knowledgeable. . . . Recourse to the Oxford English Dictionary (1978) indicates that the "positive" of "positive cooperation" is that which is "free from qualifications, conditions, or reservations; absolute, unconditional; opposed to *relative* and *comparative*." . . .

"Voluntarily" is defined as "[o]f one's own free will or accord; without compulsion, constraint, or undue influence by others; freely, willingly. . . . Without other determining force than natural character or tendency; naturally, spontaneously."

---

4. Prior to its repeal [in] 1984, section 268 provided that: "Every person who, under promise of marriage, seduces and has sexual intercourse with an unmarried female of previous chaste character, is punishable by imprisonment in the state prison, or by a fine of not more than five thousand dollars [$5,000], or by both such fine and imprisonment."

5. It is not difficult to conceive of reasons why the Legislature may have consciously wished to leave the matter where it lies. Thus, as a matter of degree, where consent to intercourse is obtained by promises of travel, fame, celebrity and the like — ought the liar and seducer to be chargeable as a rapist? Where is the line to be drawn?

2. While the word "consent" appears only in section 261, subd. (1), all the subdivisions concern the victim's state of mind.

[I] conclude that while the Legislature in section 261.6 did not expressly repeal the legalisms distinguishing "fraud in the factum" and "fraud in the inducement," its intention certainly was to restrict "consent" to cases of true, good faith consent, obtained without substantial fraud or deceit.

I believe there is a sufficient basis for prosecution of petitioner pursuant to section 261, subd. (4)....

NOTES ON DECEPTION

1. In apparent response to the result in *Boro,* the California legislature in 1985 enacted the following new provision (Penal Code §266c):

> Every person who induces any other person, except the spouse of the perpetrator, to engage in sexual intercourse, ... when his or her consent is procured by false or fraudulent representation or pretense that is made with the intent to create fear, and which does induce fear, and that would cause a reasonable person in like circumstances to act contrary to the person's free will, and does cause the victim to so act, is punishable by imprisonment in either the county jail for not more than one year or in the state prison for two, three, or four years.
>
> As used in this section, "fear" means the fear of unlawful physical injury or death to the person or to any relative of the person or member of the person's family.

Questions: Why did the legislature adopt such a narrow view of the circumstances under which it should be criminal to obtain consent to intercourse by misrepresentation? Would the new law permit conviction in *Boro* itself?

2. How should *Evans* and *Boro* be decided under the *M.T.S.* standard, which permits a conviction for sexual assault any time there is intercourse in the absence of "affirmative and freely-given permission"? Should use of any deceptive inducement suffice to make the actor guilty of rape?

3. A person who knowingly uses false material representations to obtain tangible personal property is universally held guilty of a criminal offense, usually either theft or fraud. See, e.g., Model Penal Code §223.3, Appendix. Similarly, such a person would be universally held liable for damages in a civil suit. Yet there is generally neither civil nor criminal liability when the false representations are used to obtain sex. Why the distinction? For a detailed argument in favor of reinvigorating tort liability in such cases, see Jane E. Larson, "Women Understand So Little, They Call My Good Nature 'Deceit' ": A Feminist Rethinking of Seduction, 93 Colum. L. Rev. 374 (1993). For a more skeptical view, see Martha Chamallas, Consent, Equality, and the Legal Control of Sexual Conduct, 61 S. Cal. L. Rev. 777, 834-835 (1988). A discussion of criminal liability in these situations appears in Stephen J. Schulhofer, Taking Sexual Autonomy Seriously: Rape Law and Beyond, 11 Law & Phil. 35, 88-93 (1992).

NOTE ON THE IMPACT OF REFORM

There is now a large body of research assessing the effect of rape reform legislation on actual enforcement practices. Though several changes have been observed, most studies find that new laws have had surprisingly little impact on rape reporting, processing of complaints, and conviction rates.

Among the positive effects, there is consistent evidence that justice system officials now treat victims better,[6] and in some cities, victims appear more willing to report their rapes.[7] One study of imprisoned rapists reports that those imprisoned more recently were more likely to know their victims, a finding that suggests that more offenders are now being sent to prison in acquaintance rape cases.[8] Similar conclusions emerge from a study of trends in nationwide data over the period 1973-1990: The reporting rate for rape increased, the probability of imprisonment (given an arrest) increased, and the probability of conviction and imprisonment for acquaintance rape also increased; each of the increases, however, was very small.[9]

Overall, the predominant conclusion is that rape reform legislation has had little effect on either victims' reporting behavior or on criminal justice system practices. Studies of new statutes in California and Washington both find no significant change in reporting, charging practices, or conviction rates.[10] A detailed study of one of the nation's most ambitious reforms, the 1975 Michigan statute (see page 341 supra), concludes that reporting rates increased somewhat, but more because of changed public attitudes than because of the new law, and the statute proved relatively unsuccessful in extending the criminal prohibition to conduct previously thought to be permissible or "borderline"; one law enforcement official dismissed the law's expanded coverage as "messing with the folkways."[11]

The most comprehensive of the recent studies is a 1992 report that analyzes data from six jurisdictions with widely differing approaches to reform, from the far-reaching Michigan effort to relatively minor reforms in Texas and Georgia.[12] Comparing pre-reform and post-reform data, the study found only small improvements in Michigan and virtually none in the other jurisdictions. Only Michigan had an increase in the reporting of rapes, and no jurisdiction experienced an increase in its conviction rate.[13] Reforms had little effect on the way officials evaluated cases, and in all the jurisdictions, officials still considered a

6. Cassia Spohn & Julia Horney, Rape Law Reform 159 (1992). There are also indications that rape reforms have had significant impact on the admissibility of evidence of the complainant's prior sexual history. We explore this topic at pages 372-380 infra.

7. See Mary Ann Largen, Rape-Law Reform: An Analysis, in Rape and Sexual Assault II, 279-281 (Ann W. Burgess ed. 1988); Spohn & Horney, supra note 6, at 86.

8. See Ronet Bachman, Predicting the Reporting of Rape Victimizations: Have Rape Reforms Made a Difference?, 20 Crim. Justice & Behavior 254, 266 (1993).

9. See Ronet Bachman & Raymond Paternoster, A Contemporary Look at the Effects of Rape Law Reform: How Far Have We Really Come?, 84 J. Crim. L. & Criminology 554 (1993).

10. See Kenneth Polk, Rape Reform and Criminal Justice Processing, 31 Crime & Delinquency 191 (1985) (California); Wallace Loh, The Impact of Common Law and Rape Reform Statutes on Prosecution: An Empirical Study, 55 Wash. L. Rev. 543 (1980) (Washington).

11. Jeanne C. Marsh, Alison Geist & Nathan Caplan, Rape and the Limits of Law Reform 25-26, 41-49, 107 (1982).

12. Spohn & Horney, supra note 6.

13. Id. at 86, 160, 173. The finding that Michigan conviction rates (as a percentage of indictments) remained constant can nonetheless be viewed as a modest victory for the reform effort: Reporting rates had increased somewhat, more cases were coming into the system, and more were being indicted. The constant rate of convictions as a percentage of indictments suggests the possibility that the new law facilitated conviction in grey-area cases that might not have been prosecuted before. See id. at 104. An earlier study likewise reports some increase in rape convictions for Michigan. See Marsh, Geist & Caplan, supra note 11.

victim's resistance an important determinant of whether a rape case will result in conviction.[14]

Why have statutory changes had so little impact on actual enforcement practices? If cultural attitudes remain unchanged, is legislative reform bound to be futile? Conversely, when cultural attitudes do change, is legislative reform largely unnecessary? Or is the reform effort important not only because of its direct impact on the legal system but also because of its part in the long-term process of shaping cultural attitudes about the boundaries of permissible behavior?

3. *The Marital Exemption*

1 MATTHEW HALE, THE HISTORY OF THE PLEAS OF THE CROWN 629 (S. Emlyn ed. 1778): [T]he husband cannot be guilty of a rape committed by himself upon his lawful wife, for by their mutual matrimonial consent and contract the wife hath given up herself in this kind unto her husband, which she cannot retract.

PEOPLE v. LIBERTA

New York Court of Appeals
64 N.Y.2d 152, 474 N.E.2d 567 (1984)

WACHTLER, J. . . . Defendant Mario Liberta and Denise Liberta were married in 1978. Shortly after the birth of their son, in October of that year, Mario began to beat Denise. In early 1980 Denise brought a proceeding in the Family Court in Erie County seeking protection from the defendant. On April 30, 1980 a temporary order of protection was issued to her by the Family Court. Under this order, the defendant was to move out and remain away from the family home, and stay away from Denise. The order provided that the defendant could visit with his son once each weekend.

. . . On Tuesday, March 24, 1981 [defendant] called Denise to ask if he could visit his son on that day. Denise [allowed] him to pick up their son and her and take them both back to his motel after being assured that a friend of his would be with them at all times. . . .

When they arrived at the motel the friend left. As soon as only Mario, Denise, and their son were alone in the motel room, Mario attacked Denise, threatened to kill her, and forced her to . . . engage in sexual intercourse with him. The son was in the room during the entire episode, and the defendant forced Denise to tell their son to watch what the defendant was doing to her.

The defendant allowed Denise and their son to leave shortly after the incident. Denise, after going to her parents' home, went to a hospital to be treated for scratches on her neck and bruises on her head and back, all inflicted by her husband. She also went to the police station, and on the next day she swore out a felony complaint. . . .

[The defendant was convicted of rape in the first degree, and the conviction was affirmed by the Appellate Division.]

---

14. Spohn & Horney, supra note 6, at 115, 129, 160.

Section 130.35 of the Penal Law provides in relevant part that "A male is guilty of rape in the first degree when he engages in sexual intercourse with a female . . . by forcible compulsion." "Female," for purposes of the rape statute, is defined as "any female person who is not married to the actor." [D]ue to the "not married" language in the [definition] of "female" . . . , there is a "marital exemption" for [forcible rape]. . . .

Until 1978, the marital exemption applied as long as the marriage still legally existed. In 1978, the Legislature expanded the definition of "not married" to include those cases where the husband and wife were living apart pursuant to either a court order "which by its terms or in its effect requires such living apart" or a decree, judgment, or written agreement of separation (Penal Law, §130.00, subd. 4). [T]he order of protection in the present case falls squarely within the first of these situations. . . .

Accordingly, the defendant was properly found to have been statutorily "not married" to Denise at the time of the rape.

The defendant's constitutional challenges to the rape [statute] are premised on his being considered "not married" to Denise and are the same challenges as could be made by any unmarried male. . . . The defendant's claim is that [the statute violates] equal protection because [it burdens] him, but not others similarly situated. A litigant has standing to raise the claim even though he does not contend that under no circumstances could the burden of the statute be imposed upon him. . . .

The first American case to recognize the marital exemption was decided in 1857 by the Supreme Judicial Court of Massachusetts, which stated in dictum that it would always be a defense to rape to show marriage to the victim (Commonwealth v. Fogerty, 74 Mass. 489). Decisions to the same effect by other courts followed, usually with no rationale or authority cited other than [Matthew Hale's] implied consent view. In New York, a 1922 decision noted the marital exemption in the Penal Law and stated that it existed "on account of the matrimonial consent which [the wife] has given, and which she cannot retract" (People v. Meli, 193 N.Y.S. 365, 366 (Sup. Ct.)).

Presently, over 40 States still retain some form of marital exemption for rape. [T]he equal protection clause does not prohibit a State from making classifications, provided the statute does not arbitrarily burden a particular group of individuals. Where a statute draws a distinction based upon marital status, the classification must be reasonable and must be based upon "some ground of difference that rationally explains the different treatment" (Eisenstadt v. Baird, 405 U.S. 438, 447).

We find that there is no rational basis for distinguishing between marital rape and nonmarital rape. The various rationales which have been asserted in defense of the exemption are either based upon archaic notions about the consent and property rights incident to marriage or are simply unable to withstand even the slightest scrutiny. . . .

Lord Hale's notion of an irrevocable implied consent by a married woman to sexual intercourse has been cited most frequently in support of the marital exemption. Any argument based on a supposed consent, however, is untenable. Rape is not simply a sexual act to which one party does not consent. Rather, it is a degrading, violent act which violates the bodily integrity of the victim and frequently causes severe, long-lasting physical and psychic harm. To ever imply consent to such an act is irrational and absurd. Other than in the context of rape statutes, marriage has never been viewed as giving a husband the right to co-erced intercourse on demand. Certainly, then, a marriage license should not be viewed as a license for a husband to forcibly rape his wife with impunity. . . . If a husband feels "aggrieved" by his wife's refusal to engage in sexual intercourse, he should seek relief in the courts governing domestic relations, not in "violent or forceful self-help."

The other traditional justifications for the marital exemption were the common-law doctrines that a woman was the property of her husband and that the legal existence of the woman was "incorporated and consolidated into that of the husband" (1 Blackstone's Commentaries (1966 ed.), p. 430). Both these doctrines, of course, have long been rejected in this State. Indeed, "[n]owhere in the common-law world — [or] in any modern society — is a woman regarded as chattel or demeaned by denial of a separate legal identity and the dignity associated with recognition as a whole human being" (Trammel v. United States, 445 U.S. 40, 52).

Because the traditional justifications for the marital exemption no longer have any validity, other arguments have been advanced in its defense. . . . While protecting marital privacy and encouraging reconciliation are legitimate State interests, there is no rational relation between allowing a husband to forcibly rape his wife and these interests. . . . Just as a husband cannot invoke a right of marital privacy to escape liability for beating his wife, he cannot justifiably rape his wife under the guise of a right to privacy.

Similarly, it is not tenable to argue that elimination of the marital exemption would disrupt marriages because it would discourage reconciliation. [I]f the marriage has already reached the point where intercourse is accomplished by violent assault it is doubtful that there is anything left to reconcile. This, of course, is particularly true if the wife is willing to bring criminal charges against her husband which could result in a lengthy jail sentence. . . .

The final argument in defense of the marital exemption is that marital rape is not as serious an offense as other rape and is thus adequately dealt with by the possibility of prosecution under criminal statutes, such as assault statutes, which provide for less severe punishment. The fact that rape statutes exist, however, is a recognition that the harm caused by a forcible rape is different, and more severe, than the harm caused by an ordinary assault. [Moreover,] numerous studies have shown that marital rape is frequently quite violent and generally has *more* severe, traumatic effects on the victim than other rape.

Among the recent decisions in this country addressing the marital exemption, only one court has concluded that there is a rational basis for it (see People v. Brown, 632 P.2d 1025 [Sup. Ct. Colo. 1981]). We agree with the other courts which have analyzed the exemption, which have been unable to find any present justification for it. Justice Holmes wrote: "It is revolting to have no better reason for a rule of law than that so it was laid down in the time of Henry IV. It is still more revolting if the grounds upon which it was laid down have vanished long since, and the rule simply persists from blind imitation of the past" (Holmes, The Path of Law, 10 Harv. L. Rev. 457, 469). This statement is an apt character-ization of the marital exemption; it lacks a rational basis, and therefore violates the equal protection clauses of both the Federal and State Constitutions. . . .

Having found [the rape statute] unconstitutionally underinclusive, the re-maining issue is the appropriate remedy for these equal protection violations. When a statute is constitutionally defective because of underinclusion, a court may either strike the statute, and thus make it applicable to nobody, or extend the coverage of the statute to those formerly excluded. . . .

This court's task is to discern what course the Legislature would have chosen to follow if it had foreseen our conclusions as to underinclusiveness. . . . Statutes prohibiting [forcible sexual assaults] are of the utmost importance, and to declare such statutes a nullity would have a disastrous effect on the public interest and safety. The inevitable conclusion is that the Legislature would prefer to eliminate the exemptions and thereby preserve the statutes. Accordingly we choose the remedy of striking the marital exemption . . . from section 130.35 of the Penal Law, so that it is now the law of this State that any person who engages in sexual intercourse . . . by forcible compulsion is guilty of . . . rape in the first degree. . . . Because [the statute] under which the defendant was convicted [is] not being struck down, his conviction is affirmed.

Though our decision does not "create a crime," it does, of course, enlarge the scope of [a criminal statute]. . . . The due process clause of the Fourteenth Amendment requires that an accused have had fair warning at the time of his conduct that such conduct was made criminal by the State. Defendant did not come within any of the exemptions which we have stricken, and thus his conduct was covered by the [statute] at the time of his attack on Denise. . . .

Accordingly, the order of the Appellate Division should be affirmed.

NOTES

1. *The prevalence of marital rape.* Although once assumed to be extremely rare, marital rape is now thought to occur with disturbing frequency. Reliable statistics concerning the percentage of women experiencing any form of rape are difficult to obtain, but one study based on interviews with a random sample of nearly 1000 women found that 14 percent of the women who had been married were the victims of at least one completed or attempted rape by their husbands. See Diana E. H. Russell, Rape in Marriage 57 (2d ed. 1990). The author added that since many of the marital rape victims might have been unwilling to disclose their experience, the 14 percent figure could underestimate the true incidence of marital rape. Another study (Irene Hanson Frieze, Investigating the Causes and Consequences of Marital Rape, 8 Signs 532 (1983)) found that marital rape had been experienced by up to 10 percent of all married women. Statistics on the incidence of nonmarital rape suggest that such rapes may affect 1 percent of women over a 12-month period and up to 20 percent of all women over their lifetime. With nonmarital rape at that general order of magnitude, Professor Frieze concludes (id. at 548) that "marital rape may be one of the most common forms of rape in our society."

2. *The Model Penal Code view.* The Model Penal Code, drafted in the 1950s, chose to preserve the marital exemption. Consider the following effort to justify the Model Penal Code position (Model Penal Code and Commentaries, Comment to §213.1, at 344-346 (1980)):

> First, marriage or equivalent relationship, while not amounting to a legal waiver of the woman's right to say "no," does imply a kind of generalized consent that distinguishes some versions of the crime of rape from parallel behavior by a husband. . . . At a minimum, therefore, husbands must be exempt from those catego-

ries of liability based not on force or coercion but on a presumed incapacity of the woman to consent. For example, a man who has intercourse with his unconscious wife should scarcely be condemned to felony liability on the ground that the woman in such circumstances is incapable of consenting to sex with her own husband, at least unless there are aggravating circumstances. . . . Plainly there must also be some form of spousal exclusion applicable to the crime of statutory rape. . . .

The major context of which those who would abandon the spousal exclusion are thinking, however, is the situation of rape by force or threat. The problem with abandoning the immunity in many such situations is that the law of rape, if applied to spouses, would thrust the prospect of criminal sanctions into the ongoing process of adjustment in the marital relationship. . . . Retaining the spousal exclusion avoids this unwarranted intrusion of the penal law into the life of the family.

Finally, there is the case of intercourse coerced by force or threat of physical harm. Here the law already authorizes a penalty for assault. . . . The issue is whether the still more drastic sanctions of rape should apply. The answer depends on whether the injury caused by forcible intercourse by a husband is equivalent to that inflicted by someone else. The gravity of the crime of forcible rape derives not merely from its violent character but also from its achievement of a particularly degrading kind of unwanted intimacy. Where the attacker stands in an ongoing relation of sexual intimacy, that evil, as distinct from the force used to compel submission, may well be thought qualitatively different. The character of the voluntary association of husband and wife, in other words, may be thought to affect the nature of the harm involved in unwanted intercourse. That, in any event, is the conclusion long endorsed by the law of rape and carried forward in the Model Code provision.

In accord with the Model Penal Code view that rape prosecutions can involve an "unseemly [intrusion upon] the intimacies of the marital relationship," see Michael G. Hilf, Marital Privacy and Spousal Rape, 16 New Eng. L. Rev. 31, 34 (1980). The author argues that the marital exemption remains sound for cohabiting spouses and should terminate only after divorce, legal separation, or a substantial period of living apart. The notion that the harm of marital rape is less serious than that of stranger rape is criticized in Diana E. H. Russell, Rape in Marriage 190-191, 198-199 (2d ed. 1990):

[There are] instances of wife rape that are not particularly traumatic; however, many more cases show wife rape to be extremely traumatic. . . .

[W]ife rape can be as terrifying and life-threatening to the victim as stranger rape. In addition, it often evokes a powerful sense of betrayal, deep disillusionment, and total isolation. Women often receive very poor treatment by friends, relatives, and professional services when they are raped by strangers. This isolation can be even more extreme for victims of wife rape. And just as they are more likely to be blamed, they are more likely to blame themselves.

Much more is at stake for a victim of wife rape than for a woman who is raped by a stranger. When a woman has been raped by her husband she cannot seek comfort and safety at home. She can decide to leave the marriage or to live with what happened. Either choice can be devastating. Leaving involves all the trauma and readjustment of divorce, economically, socially, and psychologically. . . . However, staying usually means being raped again, often repeatedly. [W]ife rape occurred more than once in 69 percent of the marriages [in which any rape had occurred], and in 31 percent of them it occurred more than 20 times. Since the victim of wife rape "accepted" it the first time, why not the second, and the third, and so on? We have seen how this happens with wives who are beaten. Being raped or beaten by a husband is likely to progressively lower a wife's sense of self-worth as the abuse continues. And the lower the self-esteem, the more difficult it is to stop the abuse or leave the marriage. A vicious cycle is set in motion that can lead a wife to suicide or madness.

3. *Legislative developments.* Most of the recently revised penal codes follow the Model Penal Code in preserving some form of spousal exemption. See Model Penal Code and Commentaries, supra Note 2, at 341. But the exemption has been limited in many ways, and no state preserves the exemption in its original, unqualified form. A recent survey shows that 24 states restrict liability by treating marital rape as a lesser offense than other rapes or by permitting prosecution only when aggravated force is used. Five states permit prosecution if the parties are legally separated or if they are living apart and one of them has filed for separation or divorce. Three other states permit prosecution whenever the spouses were "living apart" at the time of the incident. Only 15 states have completely abolished the distinction between marital and nonmarital rape. Conversely, 5 states have actually enlarged the common law marital exemption by affording a "cohabitant" defense to unmarried partners under some circumstances. See Diana E. H. Russell, Rape in Marriage 375-382 (2d ed. 1990); Developments in the Law — Domestic Violence, 106 Harv. L. Rev. 1498, 1533-1534 (1993).

4. *Judicial approaches.* When state statutes do not explicitly require that the rape victim be "a female not his wife," courts have some flexibility in determining whether the common law marital exemption should remain a part of contemporary law. Although defendants have argued that such a change in previously settled understandings should come only from the legislature, several courts have held that a marital exemption should no longer be read into their statutes. See, e.g., Warren v. State, 336 S.E.2d 221 (Ga. 1985) (parties were living together at the time of the incident); State v. Smith, 85 N.J. 193, 426 A.2d 38 (1981) (parties had been living apart for one year). In England the House of Lords has likewise abolished the marital exemption by judicial decision. See R. v. R., [1991] 4 All E.R. 481.

A narrower approach is taken in Weishaupt v. Commonwealth, 227 Va. 389, 315 S.E.2d 847 (1984). The court there held that a husband charged with rape cannot invoke the marital exemption when the wife has "conduct[ed] herself in a manner that establishes a de facto end to the marriage." (In *Weishaupt* the wife had moved out of the common home, and the parties had been separated for 11 months at the time of the offense). But in Kizer v. Commonwealth, 321 S.E.2d 291 (Va. 1984), a rape conviction based on a violent sexual assault was nonetheless reversed. In that case the husband had moved to separate quarters, the parties had not engaged in sexual intercourse for more than six months, and the husband had filed for custody of the child. However, because the wife had at various points made attempts to make the marriage "work" and because she had hesitated to file for divorce, the court found that her "vacillating" conduct was too equivocal to establish that the husband knew or should have known that she considered the marriage at an end.

Does *Weishaupt* provide a workable compromise approach? If not, is a simple "living apart" test preferable? Or is preservation of the marital exemption under any conditions fundamentally unsound?

D.   PROBLEMS OF PROOF

The preceding sections suggest some of the ways in which concerns about un-founded accusations of rape influenced the law relating to the required actus reus and mens rea. The same concerns have also influenced the law of evidence. Their influence has been felt in three important areas: requirements of corroboration, jury instructions relating to the complainant's credibility, and rules relating to cross-examination. The present section examines these three areas, the first two briefly (their interest is now largely historical) and the third, which presents problems of continuing difficulty and importance, in some detail.

1.   *Corroboration and Jury Instructions*

UNITED STATES v. WILEY

United States Court of Appeals, D.C. Circuit
492 F.2d 547 (1974)

[The court held that a complainant's testimony had not been adequately corroborated by independent evidence, as the District of Columbia cases then required. Judge Bazelon's concurring opinion, excerpted here, gives voice to the basic dilemma presented not only by the corroboration issue but by all of the problems of proof examined in this section.]

BAZELON, J. (concurring). The notion that the testimony of a single witness is inadequate to prove a crime is an ancient one. The Code of the Emperor Justinian provided that on any important issue the testimony of one witness was insufficient. Ecclesiastical law refined this approach by requiring, for example, that against the word of a Cardinal, forty-four witnesses were required. But the common law gradually moved toward other modes of inquiry into the truth. Ultimately the common law rejected the requirement of corroboration for all crimes except perjury. Thus there was no common law requirement of corroboration for any sex offense.

Today thirty-five states have similarly rejected the corroboration requirement for rape. Of those jurisdictions that retain the requirement, about half, including the District of Columbia, do so in the absence of legislation. The substance of corroboration requirements varies enormously from state to state, ranging from a requirement of corroboration for force, penetration and identity, to minimal corroboration of any part of the complainant's testimony.

Numerous justifications have been advanced for the requirement of corroboration in sex cases. An examination of these rationales reveals a tangled web of legitimate concerns, out-dated beliefs, and deep-seated prejudices.

The most common basis advanced for the requirement is that false charges of rape are more prevalent than false charges of other crimes. . . .

It is contended that a woman may fabricate a rape accusation because, having consented to intercourse she is ashamed and bitter, or because she is pregnant and feels pressured to create a false explanation, or because she hates the man she accuses or wishes to blackmail him. . . .

There are, however, countervailing reasons not to report a rape. One said to be a victim of rape may be stigmatized by society, there may be humiliating publicity, and the necessity of facing the insinuations of defense counsel may be a deterrent. Moreover, those claiming to have been raped may be treated harshly by the police and by hospitals. One result of all of these obstacles is that rape is one of the most under-reported of all crimes. . . .

In addition to the problem of false charges, the corroboration requirement is justified on the theory that rape is a charge unusually difficult to defend against. In 1680 Lord Chief Justice Hale wrote, in one of the most oft-quoted passages in our jurisprudence, that rape "is an accusation easily to be made and hard to be proved, and harder to be defended by the party accused, tho never so innocent." The same theme has been echoed by modern commentators and courts. . . . Juries are said to be unusually sympathetic to a woman wronged, thus weakening the presumption of innocence.

Again, there is little hard evidence with which to test this theory. What studies are available suggest that . . . juries may be more skeptical of rape accusations than is often supposed. . . .

Still another basis for the corroboration requirement lies in "the sorry history of racism in America." There has been an enormous danger of injustice when a black man accused of raping a white woman is tried before a white jury. Of the 455 men executed for rape since 1930, 405 (89 percent) were black. In the vast majority of these cases the complainant was white.

All of the safeguards that developed in this context should not be automatically applied today. Juries are more integrated than in the past and racial prejudice may be at a somewhat lower level. Numerous rape victims are black and their interests, as well as those of white women, may have been slighted by the concern for black defendants.

A final theory of the corroboration requirement is that it stems from discrimination against women. It is said that traditional sex stereotypes have resulted in rape laws that protect men rather than women. Penalties are high because a "good" woman is a valued possession of a man. Corroboration is required because to a "good" woman rape is "a fate worse than death" and she should fight to the death to resist it. If no such fight is put up, the woman must have consented or at least enticed the rapist, who is therefore blameless. In sum it is said to be the "male desire to 'protect' his 'possession' which results in laws designed to protect the male — both the 'owner' and the assailant — rather than protecting the physical well-being and freedom of movement of women." . . .

Analyzing all of these justifications in order to separate the valid from the invalid is no easy task. . . . But at least for the immediate present, I find that the flexible corroboration rule developed by this Court provides the best accommodation of numerous conflicting considerations. . . . To guard against [the] possible dangers [of fabrication] we retain a corroboration rule which provides that "independent corroborative evidence will be regarded as sufficient when it would permit the jury to conclude beyond a reasonable doubt that the victim's account of the crime was not a fabrication." . . . In cases such as this one where that evidence is lacking the dangers to the defendant outweigh the difficulties created for the prosecution. . . .

Thus I concur in the court's opinion reversing defendant's conviction.

NOTES ON CURRENT LAW

1.   *The corroboration requirement.* By the time of the *Wiley* decision, most American jurisdictions had already abandoned a specific corroboration requirement for rape prosecutions. See Note, The Rape Corroboration Requirement: Repeal Not Reform, 81 Yale L.J. 1365, 1367-1370 (1972). Since then, the remaining jurisdictions have moved in the same direction. See Annot., 31 A.L.R.4th 120 (1982). No American state now requires corroboration in forcible rape cases.[15]

Three years after the *Wiley* decision, the United States Court of Appeals for the District of Columbia Circuit also decided to abandon the corroboration requirement. In United States v. Sheppard, 569 F.2d 114, 118-119 (D.C. Cir. 1977), Judge J. Skelley Wright wrote for the court:[16]

> The corroboration requirement poses a potentially severe obstacle to legitimate convictions for sex offenses. Operation of the rule serves to foreclose jury consideration of cases in which a highly credible complainant prosecutes charges, on the basis of her testimony alone, against a defendant whose account of the events is clearly less credible. . . . Elimination of the corroboration requirement, however, hardly leaves defendants unprotected against unjust convictions. . . . Where the motivation of the complainant in bringing the charge is an issue, as in a case where the defendant contends that she consented to the intercourse, the defense attorney is free to emphasize to the jury the dangers of falsification, and the judge should instruct the jury as to those dangers and the difficulty of establishing consent. Finally, protection against unjust convictions on a case-by-case basis is afforded by the general rule that judgments of acquittal or reversals of convictions must be granted where substantial evidence does not exist to support a guilty verdict, whether or not independent corroboration is technically present.

Questions: Does Judge Wright's emphasis on the "substantial evidence" requirement suggest that appellate courts should not defer heavily to the trier of fact? Or that they should not do so when corroboration is absent? How would Judge Wright have decided the *Rusk* case (page 333 supra) and the *M.T.S.* case (page 345 supra)?

2.   *Special jury instructions.* Many American jurisdictions have long required that in a rape prosecution the jury must be given an instruction like the following (from Cal. Jury Instructions — Criminal No. 10.22 (3d ed. 1970)):

> A charge such as that made against the defendant in this case is one which is easily made and, once made, difficult to defend against, even if the person accused is innocent. Therefore, the law requires that you examine the testimony of the female person named in the information with caution.

The instruction, based on the remarks of Sir Matthew Hale previously quoted (page 370 supra), has fallen into disfavor for essentially the same reasons that have brought the corroboration requirement under attack. In recent years several jurisdictions have barred the instruction, either by statute (e.g., Pa. Stat.

---

15. Nebraska, one of the last states to insist on corroboration, repealed the requirement in 1989. See Neb. Rev. Stat §29-2028.

16. Judge Bazelon, who was also a member of the three-judge panel, joined in the opinion and did not write separately.

Ann. tit. 81, §3106, as amended 1976) or by judicial decision (e.g., People v. Rincon-Pineda, 14 Cal. 3d 864, 538 P.2d 247 (1975)).

3. *The Model Penal Code.* In sex offense prosecutions, the MPC requires both corroboration and a special jury instruction warning the jury to evaluate the complainant's testimony "with special care." See Model Penal Code §213.6(5), Appendix. These proposals, drafted in the 1950s and approved by the American Law Institute in 1962, have largely been superseded by the more recent developments described in Notes 1 and 2 above.

2. *Cross Examination and Shield Laws*

SUSAN ESTRICH, PALM BEACH STORIES, 11 Law & Phil. 5, 14 (1992): Precisely because it is all but impossible these days to argue successfully that no means yes, or that men are privileged to have sex with crying women, or even that stupidity as to consent should serve as a defense, men charged with rape, and those who defend them, have few options but to argue the incredibility of the woman victim. And the argument has appeal, I think, because many people, including many prosecutors and judges, remain ambivalent about the expansion of rape liability: unwilling to continue to afford men the privilege of aggression, but also chary with their sympathy for women who should know better. So the old myths of the lying woman are reasserted, now that the rules of liability will no longer protect male defendants.

Thus, we face a new stage in the changing realities of rape law — a final battle, one hopes, in the effort to expand liability to include date rape and acquaintance rape. The debate is less and less about what counts as force, or what is required to prove nonconsent. Today's debate, on the radio, in the newspaper, and in the courtroom, is about when women should be believed — and about what we need to know about the woman before we can decide whether to believe her.

STATE ex rel. POPE v. SUPERIOR COURT

Supreme Court of Arizona
113 Ariz. 22, 545 P.2d 946 (1976)

GORDON, J. The County Attorney of Mohave County acting on behalf of the State of Arizona brings this special action requesting that this Court reconsider existing law on the admissibility of evidence concerning the unchaste character of a complaining witness in a prosecution for first degree rape. . . .

Almost every jurisdiction [once permitted] the substantive use of evidence concerning the unchastity of a prosecutrix where the defense of consent is raised in a forcible rape prosecution. . . . The leading case in Arizona is State v. Wood, 59 Ariz. 48, 122 P.2d 416 (1942), where we [reasoned]: "If consent be a defense to the charge, then certainly any evidence which reasonably tends to show consent is relevant and material, and common experience teaches us that the woman who has once departed from the paths of virtue is far more apt to consent to another lapse than is the one who has never stepped aside from that path." . . .

The "logic" and "common experience of mankind" upon which we rested our holding in State v. Wood, supra, now clearly dictate that the case be overturned. It is no longer satisfactory to argue that we should "more readily infer assent in the practised [sic] Messalina, in loose attire, than in the reserved and virtuous Lucretia." People v. Abbot, 19 Wend. 192 (N.Y. 1838). The reasoning consistently advanced by this Court to bar most prior bad acts of a witness applies with even greater force in a rape prosecution. Reference to prior unchaste acts of the complaining witness "injects collateral issues into the case which . . . divert the jury's attention from the real issue, the guilt or innocence of the accused." A prosecutrix in a forcible rape prosecution "should not be expected to come prepared to defend every incident of [her] past life." . . .

We recognize there are certain limited situations where evidence of prior unchaste acts has sufficient probative value to outweigh its inflammatory effect and require admission. These would include evidence of prior consensual sexual intercourse with the defendant or testimony which directly refutes physical or scientific evidence, such as the victim's alleged loss of virginity, the origin of semen, disease or pregnancy. . . . [Where] the defendant alleges the prosecutrix actually consented to an act of prostitution, the accused should be permitted to present evidence of her reputation as a prostitute and her prior acts of prostitution to support such a defense. In addition, evidence concerning unchastity would be admissible in conjunction with an effort by the defense to show that the complaining witness has made unsubstantiated charges of rape in the past.

In these and other instances in which the evidence concerning unchastity is alleged to be sufficiently probative to compel its admission despite its inflammatory effect, a hearing should be held by the court outside the presence of the jury prior to the presentation of the evidence. . . . If the defendant alleges that proffered evidence falls into one of the above exceptions, the trial court should allow its admission if it is not too remote and appears credible. . . .

HAYS, J. (specially concurring). I concur with the result reached by the majority opinion, but I cannot approve a procedure which permits evidence of the prosecutrix' reputation as a prostitute even on the limited issue of consent. In advancing to a more reasonable and logical position by overruling State v. Wood, 59 Ariz. 48, 122 P.2d 416 (1942), we should take a full step rather than mincing toward the final goal. . . .

I am also unable to concur with the majority's position which rather vaguely states that the defense may show that "the complaining witness has made unsubstantiated charges of rape in the past." The reason or logic in carving out such an exception to the rule excluding evidence of the unchastity of the complaining witness in a rape case escapes me. . . .

NOTES

1. Did the court go far enough in *Pope?* If the court's assumptions about sexual mores are sound, how can one justify its willingness to admit evidence of prior acts of prostitution? On what basis can one justify an exception even for evidence of prior consensual intercourse with defendant?

2. Did the court go too far in *Pope?* Recall that the general test for the probative value of evidence does not require that the evidence make some fact likely to be true; rather probative value requires only that the fact be somewhat more likely to be true given the evidence than it would be without the evidence. See pages 23-24 supra. By this standard, doesn't evidence of prior sexual activity have at least some probative value? For example, if the complaining witness has often consented to sexual intercourse with men shortly after meeting them in a bar, wouldn't that fact make it at least a little bit more likely that she consented to intercourse with the defendant shortly after meeting him in a bar?

The rationale for excluding evidence of a complainant's prior sexual history presumably is not that such evidence completely lacks probative value. Rather, the principal justification for exclusion is that any probative value is outweighed by the prejudicial effect. (At pages 24-25 supra we discuss this all-important principle of evidence law.) In the present context two kinds of prejudicial effect are especially important. First, such evidence can impair the truth-finding function at trial because its value may be overestimated or because it may lead to confusion of the issues. Second, the very process of airing such evidence can be painful or embarrassing to the victim, aggravating the psychological injury of the original offense and deterring other victims from seeking prosecution. Many rape victims once reported feeling that they had been raped twice — first by their assailant and then a second time in the courtroom. See Vivian D. Berger, Man's Trial, Woman's Tribulation: Rape Cases in the Courtroom, 77 Colum. L. Rev. 1 (1977).

3. Does evidence of a complainant's prior sexual activity *always* have greater prejudicial effect than probative value? Or are there situations where such evidence should be admissible despite its prejudicial effect? In response to the problems posed by *Pope,* nearly all American jurisdictions have enacted "rape shield laws" to limit the admissibility of evidence bearing on a rape complainant's prior sexual behavior. For discussion of the issues posed by these statutes, see J. Alexander Tanford & Anthony Bocchino, Rape Victim Shield Laws and the Sixth Amendment, 128 U. Pa. L. Rev. 544 (1980); Berger, supra Note 2. A recent analysis of the various statutes notes that some are extremely restrictive, admitting evidence of sexual history only when it involves prior incidents with the defendant. Another approach provides a detailed list of specific exceptions to the rule of exclusion. Some states combine a list of specific exceptions with a catch-all exception for any other evidence that has probative value greater than its prejudicial effect. Finally, a few states simply provide a procedure for pretrial hearings while leaving the ultimate decision entirely to the trial judge's discretion. See Harriett R. Galvin, Shielding Rape Victims in the State and Federal Courts: A Proposal for the Second Decade, 70 Minn. L. Rev. 763 (1986).

"Rape shield" statutes are motivated primarily by the need to protect victim-witnesses from serious abuses in the trial process. But to what extent do these statutes interfere with the defendant's right to a fair trial? Consider the cases that follow.

STATE v. DeLAWDER

Maryland Court of Special Appeals
28 Md. App. 212, 344 A.2d 446 (1975)

ORTH, C.J. . . . Lee Franklin DeLawder was found guilty by a jury in the Circuit Court for Montgomery County of carnal knowledge of a female under the age of 14 years. A 15 year sentence was imposed. The judgment was affirmed on direct appeal. [DeLawder then sought postconviction relief.] . . .

In affirming the judgment on direct appeal, we held that the trial court did not err in sustaining objections made to questions attempting to show that the prosecuting witness had sexual intercourse with other men on other occasions. The general rule is that because consent is not an issue in a carnal knowledge prosecution, evidence that the prosecutrix had prior intercourse with men other than the accused, or that her reputation for chastity was bad is immaterial when offered as an excuse or justification, and so is inadmissible for that reason. . . .

The trial judge correctly applied these rules. . . .

As *Davis* [v. Alaska, 415 U.S. 308 (1974)] was decided subsequent to our decision, we must determine whether it affects the validity of DeLawder's conviction. In *Davis,* the Supreme Court of the United States reviewed the reach of the Confrontation Clause of the Sixth Amendment to the federal Constitution. "The . . . right of an accused in a criminal prosecution 'to be confronted with the witnesses against him' . . . is secured for defendants in state as well as federal criminal proceedings. . . . Confrontation means more than being allowed to confront the witness physically. 'Our cases construing the [confrontation] clause hold that a primary interest secured by it is the right of cross-examination.'" "Cross-examination," the Court observed, "is the principal means by which the believability of a witness and the truth of his testimony are tested. . . ." A witness may be discredited by a general attack on his credibility by introducing evidence of a prior criminal conviction of that witness. . . . A witness may also be discredited . . . by means of cross-examination directed toward revealing possible biases, prejudices, or ulterior motives of the witness. . . . The Supreme Court has recognized "that the exposure of a witness's motivation in testifying is a proper and important function of the constitutionally protected right of cross-examination." . . .

We look to see how these rules were applied in *Davis.*

Davis was convicted of burglary and grand larceny in a state court at a trial in which the court on motion of the prosecution issued a protective order prohibiting the questioning of Richard Green, a key prosecution witness, concerning Green's adjudication as a juvenile delinquent relating to a burglary and his probation status at the time of the events as to which he was to testify. The motion was granted in reliance on a state rule and statute which preserved the confidentiality of juvenile adjudications of delinquency. The evidence against Davis was entirely circumstantial. . . . The defense made clear that it did not intend to use Green's juvenile record to impeach his credibility generally, but only as necessary to examine him for any possible bias and prejudice. "Not only might Green have made a hasty and faulty identification of [Davis] to shift suspicion away from himself as one who robbed the Polar Bar, but Green might have been subject to undue pressure from the police and made his identification under fear of possible probation revocation." The trial court rejected even this limited use of Green's adjudication, but defense counsel did his best to expose Green's state of mind at the time he discovered the safe. Green, however, made a flat denial to questions whether he was upset by the fact that the [stolen] safe was found on his property, whether he felt the authorities might suspect him, and whether he felt uncomfortable about it. . . .

The Alaska Supreme Court . . . affirmed the conviction on the grounds that the scope of cross-examination allowed was adequate to develop the issue of bias and convey it to the jury. The Supreme Court did not accept this. It said: "On the basis of the limited cross-examination that was permitted, the jury might well have thought that defense counsel was engaged in a speculative and baseless line of attack on the credibility of an apparently blameless witness. . . . [T]o make any such inquiry effective, defense counsel should have been permitted to expose to the jury the facts from which jurors, as the sole triers of fact and credibility, could appropriately draw inferences relating to the reliability of the witness." It held that disallowance of the defense's attempt to show bias . . . by cross-examination concerning the witness's juvenile record violated Davis's Sixth and Fourteenth Amendment rights.[2] . . .

DeLawder's counsel made clear from the onset of the case that the defense strategy would be to discredit the prosecuting witness. . . . This strategy would be pursued by the tactic of proving that at the time of the alleged incident, she thought she was pregnant by someone else and claimed that DeLawder raped her because she was afraid to tell her mother she voluntarily had sexual intercourse with others. To show that she thought she was pregnant at the time of the alleged encounter with DeLawder, it would be necessary to establish that she had engaged in prior acts of sexual intercourse. . . .

We cannot speculate . . . as to whether the jury . . . would have accepted this line of reasoning had counsel been permitted to present it fully. But [it] seems clear to us, in the light of Davis, that defense counsel should have been permitted to expose to the jury the facts from which jurors, as the sole triers of fact and credibility, could appropriately draw inferences relating to the reliability of the witness. By being prevented from so doing DeLawder was denied the right of effective cross-examination. . . . We conclude, as the Court concluded in Davis, that the desirability that the prosecutrix fulfill her public duty to testify free from embarrassment and with her reputation unblemished must fall before the right of an accused to seek out the truth in the process of defending himself. . . .

NOTES

1. A number of courts have held that highly restrictive rape shield statutes are unconstitutional when they bar use of relevant sexual history evidence. E.g., Commonwealth v. Spiewak, 617 A.2d 696 (Pa. Super. 1992). Statutes with extensive exceptions to the rule of exclusion have also been found unconstitutional in circumstances where the defense was able to show strong probative value for

2. The Court did not challenge the State's interest as a matter of its own policy in the administration of criminal justice to seek to preserve the anonymity of a juvenile offender.

Here, however, petitioner sought to introduce evidence of Green's probation for the purpose of suggesting that Green was biased. . . . Serious damage to the strength of the State's case would have been a real possibility had petitioner been allowed to pursue this line of inquiry. In this setting we conclude that the right of confrontation is paramount to the State's policy of protecting a juvenile offender. Whatever temporary embarrassment might result to Green or his family by disclosure of his juvenile record — if the prosecution insisted on using him to make its case — is outweighed by petitioner's right to probe into the influence of possible bias in the testimony of a crucial identification witness. . . .

sexual history evidence that did not fall within the terms of any statutory exception. E.g., State v. Herndon, 426 N.W.2d 347, 363 (Wis. App. 1988). Some courts have avoided striking down their rape shield statutes by reading in a "catch-all" exception for any evidence needed to preserve the defendant's right to a fair trial. E.g., Neeley v. Commonwealth, 437 S.E.2d 721 (Va. App. 1993).

2. Though "rape shield" statutes have proved much more porous than reformers initially expected, they have nonetheless had a major impact on the administration of rape trials. Empirical studies uniformly report that victims are much better treated in the judicial process and that efforts to limit the admissibility of sexual history evidence are largely successful.[17]

3. Determining the balance between probative value and prejudicial effect can be especially difficult when an incident implicates powerful social prejudices. In Neeley v. Commonwealth, 437 N.E.2d 721 (Va. App. 1993), the facts touched both racial and sexual nerves. The complainant, a 14-year-old white female, alleged that defendant, a young African-American male who lived nearby, climbed through her bedroom window in the middle of the night and forcibly raped her. Defendant denied entering the house that evening. The prosecution introduced expert testimony that a hair fragment found in the complainant's cervix, though not positively identifiable as defendant's, was "characteristic of hair from a person of African-American descent." The defendant offered to prove that shortly before the alleged rape, the complainant had had sexual intercourse with her boyfriend and that the boyfriend was also African-American. A provision of the state's rape shield law permitted the use of sexual history evidence when "offered to provide an alternative explanation for physical evidence of the offense charged which is introduced by the prosecution, limited to evidence designed to explain the presence of semen, pregnancy, disease, or physical injury to the complaining witness's intimate parts. . . ." Because the defendant's evidence was not offered to explain the presence of "semen, pregnancy, disease, or physical injury . . . ," it did not meet the terms of this or any other statutory exception, and the trial court excluded it. On appeal, should the ruling be upheld? Or, as applied to these facts, is the statutory exclusion unconstitutional?

4. *"Public" behavior.* Should prior sexual history evidence be excluded under a rape shield law even when the conduct in question occurred in public? Do concerns about protecting the victim's privacy still apply in that context? Consider State v. Colbath, 130 N.H. 316, 540 A.2d 1212 (1988). Defendant met the complainant at a tavern and later went with her to his trailer, where they had intercourse — forcible according to her testimony, consensual according to his. At trial the tavern owner's daughter described the complainant's behavior at the tavern as "hanging all over everyone and making out with Richard Colbath and a few others." The trial judge instructed the jury to disregard the testimony concerning the complainant's behavior with anyone other than defendant. Defendant argued that the testimony was properly admissible and that the instruction was therefore erroneous. He argued, in particular, that the rape shield law (which excluded evidence of prior sexual conduct with others) was inapplicable

---

17. See Cassia Spohn & Julia Horney, Rape Law Reform: Grassroots Revolution and Its Impact 129 (1992); Mary Ann Largen, Rape-Law Reform: An Analysis, in Rape and Sexual Assault II, 283 (Ann W. Burgess ed. 1988).

because the conduct occurred in public. The court (per Souter, J.) found it unnecessary to decide whether public sexual conduct was, per se, outside the reach of the rape shield law, but held for the defendant on narrower grounds (540 A.2d at 1216-1217):

> Despite the absolute terms of the shield law's prohibition, our cases have consistently reflected the common recognition that such a statute's reach has to be limited by a defendant's State and national constitutional rights to confront the witnesses against him and to present his own exculpatory evidence. . . . [A] rape defendant must be given an opportunity to demonstrate that the "probative value [of the statutorily inadmissible evidence] in the context of that particular case outweighs its prejudicial effect on the prosecutrix." . . .
>
> As soon as we address this process of assigning relative weight to prejudicial and probative force, it becomes apparent that the public character of the complainant's behavior is significant. On the one hand, describing a complainant's open, sexually suggestive conduct in the presence of patrons of a public bar obviously has far less potential for damaging the sensibilities than revealing what the same person may have done in the company of another behind a closed door. On the other hand, evidence of public displays of general interest in sexual activity can be taken to indicate a contemporaneous receptiveness to sexual advances that cannot be inferred from evidence of private behavior with chosen sex partners.
>
> . . . It would, in fact, understate the importance of such evidence in this case to speak of it merely as relevant. We should recall that the fact of intercourse was not denied, and that the evidence of assault was subject to the explanation that the defendant's jealous [live-in] companion [who had discovered him with the complainant in the trailer] had inflicted the visible injuries. The companion's furious behavior had a further bearing on the case, as well, for the jury could have regarded her attack as a reason for the complainant to regret a voluntary liaison with the defendant, and as a motive for the complainant to allege rape as a way to explain her injuries and excuse her undignified predicament. . . . [T]he outcome of the prosecution could well have turned on a very close judgment about the complainant's attitude of resistance or consent.
>
> Because little significance can be assigned here either to the privacy interest or to a fear of misleading the jury, the trial court was bound to recognize the defendant's interest in presenting probably crucial evidence of the complainant's behavior closely preceding the alleged rape. . . . The demand of the Constitution is all the clearer when [the] activities were carried on in a public setting. Because the jury instruction effectively excluded the evidence in question, the conviction must be reversed . . . .

Compare Wood v. Alaska, 957 F.2d 1544 (9th Cir. 1992). Defendant and complainant had been close friends. As in *Colbath*, intercourse was admitted; the defense was consent. Defendant alleged that on occasions prior to the incident, complainant told him that she had posed for *Penthouse*, a sexually explicit men's magazine, had acted in pornographic movies, and had been paid to have sex while people took pictures of her. He also offered to prove that she had shown him her *Penthouse* photographs and that he perceived that "in some respects [her conduct] seemed to be a sexual come-on." The trial judge excluded the evidence under Alaska's rape-shield law, and defendant was convicted of sexual assault. In habeas corpus proceedings asserting the denial of his constitutional rights, the U.S. Court of Appeals (per Rymer, J.) first held that the excluded evidence was relevant on the issue of consent. Nonetheless, the court said, the prejudicial effect outweighed the probative value, even though the behavior had occurred in nationally distributed magazines and films (957 F.2d at 1552-1554):

> Wood argues that the interest in protecting rape victims' privacy does not apply here. . . . We agree. . . . The state cannot claim M.G. has a privacy interest in acts that were fully intended to be public.
> . . . [But] other legitimate interests are implicated as well. The state points out that another purpose of the rape shield statute is to encourage reporting by limiting embarrassing trial inquiry into past sexual conduct. . . .
> This limited interest in encouraging reporting would not in itself outweigh Wood's interest in presenting relevant evidence. . . . [T]he embarrassment to M.G. of having her modeling and acting experiences revealed would be so minor in light of the public nature of the acts that it cannot overcome Wood's right to present relevant evidence.
> But, unlike *Davis* [v. Alaska, page 375 supra], the interests in this case go beyond that of protecting the witness. Of significantly more import are the concerns, intrinsic to the truth-finding process itself, that introducing the evidence would confuse the issues and unduly prejudice the jury. . . . The proffered evidence in this case is particularly prejudicial because it indicates not only that M.G. had extramarital sex, but also that she posed nude and had sex both for money and for the purpose of making pornography. Because many people consider prostitution and pornography to be particularly offensive, there is a significant possibility that jurors would be influenced by their impression of M.G. as an immoral woman. They could also conclude, contrary to the rape law, that a woman with her sexual past cannot be raped, or that she somehow deserved to be raped after engaging in these sexual activities. . . .
> On the other side of the balance, while evidence that M.G. showed Wood sexually provocative pictures of herself and told him about her sexual experiences is probative to some extent of the nature of their relationship, its value is far from substantial. . . .
> Because [the evidence] is not highly probative and the risk of confusion and prejudice is substantial, we conclude that the trial court acted within its discretion when it excluded the evidence.

5. *Prior behavior of the defendant.* In Chapter 1, we considered the principle that evidence of prior misconduct by a defendant is not admissible for purposes of proving a propensity to engage in conduct of a similar nature. See pages 25-34 supra. As we saw there, most jurisdictions apply the prior-misconduct rule just as strictly in rape trials as in other kinds of prosecutions. See especially page 33, Note 2(b) supra.

Is the willingness of courts to admit evidence of some prior sexual acts by a rape complainant inconsistent with the rule that precludes reference to prior misconduct by the defendant? In a recent, highly publicized prosecution, William Kennedy Smith was charged with committing a sexual assault upon a woman who had accompanied him back to his family's vacation home, after drinking and dancing with him at a bar. The case turned on the credibility of the woman's testimony that Smith ignored her protests and forced her to submit to intercourse. Prior to trial, three other women came forward to allege that Smith had sexually assaulted them. The trial judge excluded this evidence, and Smith was acquitted. See N.Y. Times, Dec. 13, 1992, at B14. Was the ruling correct? If not, should the judge admit evidence of the prior sexual conduct of *both* Smith and his accuser? Consider Susan Estrich, Teaching Rape Law, 102 Yale L.J. 509, 519 (1992):

> The [decisive] ruling in the Smith case . . . was the judge's pretrial decision to exclude the testimony of three other women who claimed that they had been sexually abused by the defendant. If the testimony of only one woman cannot be believed[,] . . . is it fair to exclude the testimony of the other women? And if the testimony is not excluded, do we risk convicting a defendant for being a bad man, indeed being a rapist, rather than committing the particular act charged?
>
> One answer is to say that we need symmetry: exclude all the evidence about both of them. That's the approach the judge followed in the William Kennedy Smith case. On the surface, it is neat and appealing. The only problem is that it's a false symmetry. . . . [E]vidence that a man has abused other women is much more probative of rape than evidence that a woman has had consensual sex with other men is probative of consent. Most women have had sexual experiences, and unless those experiences fall into some kind of unusual pattern, the mere fact that a woman has had lovers tells us almost nothing about whether she consented on the particular occasion that she is charging as rape. But won't we all look at a defendant differently if three other women have also come forward to say they were abused? The danger with such evidence is not that it proves so little, but that it may prove too much. Symmetry won't get you out of this hole. . . .
>
> Thus even if most students can agree these days that no means no, and that force can be established if you push a woman down, there's very little agreement about what we need to know about her or him before deciding whether she in fact said yes or no, and whether he actually pushed her down or just lay down with her. The consensus on what counts as rape is more apparent than real.

GOVERNMENT OF THE VIRGIN ISLANDS v. SCUITO

United States Court of Appeals, 3d Circuit
623 F.2d 869 (1980)

ADAMS, J. In this appeal from a conviction for forcible rape, the defendant Louis Scuito asserts . . . [that the] trial judge abused or failed to exercise his discretion in denying the defendant's motion for a psychiatric examination of the complainant. . . .

The complainant worked as a waitress at the Drunken Shrimp restaurant, where the defendant was a frequent patron. When the complainant worked late on the night of July 9, 1978, the owner of the restaurant arranged for Scuito to give the complainant a ride to her apartment. It is undisputed that Scuito took a detour down a beach road, where the two had sexual intercourse, after which he took the complainant home. The crucial issue at trial was solely whether she consented.

According to the complainant, Scuito turned down the beach road to relieve himself, and then continued to a turnaround, stopped the jeep, and began kissing her. She expressed lack of interest, but the defendant then told her he had a knife and would throw her into the ocean if she did not cooperate. She testified that she did not actually see the knife in the dark, but felt "something metal" cut into her neck, after which she ceased resistance and attempted to calm him and avoid harm by cooperating. At trial there was medical and other testimony of a cut on the side of the complainant's neck where she said the knife was held. After taking off her clothes, the defendant raped and sodomized her. During the course of the assault she prayed and recited her "mantra."[2] Upon being dropped off at home, she kissed the defendant on the forehead because, she testified, "I was praying for him" and "it was just kind of like an end to the prayer."

Scuito testified that he casually knew the complainant and her sister and had previously driven them home from the restaurant. He said that on the night of July 9, when he gave the complainant a ride to her apartment, she seemed "a little spaced, not all there." While riding home, she offered him marijuana and he drove off the main road to smoke it with her. He later "came on to her," he said. Although initially she protested, he eventually changed her mind without using or threatening any physical force.

Prior to the first trial there had been a discussion between counsel and the court regarding the admissibility of evidence that Scuito previously had raped another young woman after threatening to shoot her with a flare gun. Defense counsel contended that such evidence would be relevant only if the defendant put his character in issue, which he did not at that time intend to do. The prosecutor agreed not to mention the other alleged rape in the opening statement to the jury, but reserved the right to seek admission of the evidence . . . if the testimony that was adduced created the opportunity. . . .

[The first trial ended in a mistrial after the prosecutor indirectly referred to the previous flare-gun rape by the defendant.]

. . . Scuito moved before the second trial for a psychiatric examination of the complainant. In a supporting affidavit, his attorney made the following specific representations:

> [1] I have been informed by any number of persons in the community that the said complainant appears to be often, if not almost constantly, in a "spaced out" or trancelike state; I have personally observed this; I have been further informed by persons in the community that the said complainant is addicted to, and does continually use, controlled substances, and that she is frequently in altered states of consciousness therefrom; and I have further observed and been told of the said complainant's habit of dressing and being seen publicly in see-through top garments which seem indicative of socially aberrant behavior;
>
> [2] Further, my observation of the said complainant at the first trial herein showed, in my opinion, a rather strange and mysterious countenance on her part, and her testimony appeared strange, not only from the standpoint of her account of not reporting the alleged crimes until the next day, but particularly from her admitted interest and devotion to a certain book, written by a guru devotee of Timothy Leary which contains passages of religious-like worship of LSD and other mind-altering drugs; [and]
>
> [3] That the foregoing observations are highly indicative of a personality which fantasizes to extremes and which indulges in and seeks altered states of consciousness. . . .

Defendant does not press the extreme position, espoused by Wigmore, that a psychiatric examination of a complainant should be required in all sexual of-

---

2. A mantra has been defined as "[a] sound aid used while meditating. Each meditator has his own personal mantra which is never to be revealed to any other person." Malnak v. Yogi, 592 F.2d 197, 198 (3d Cir. 1979). . . .

fense prosecutions.[14] Rather, defendant agrees with the Government that the decision to order an examination is "entrusted to the sound discretion of the trial judge in light of the particular facts." United States v. Benn, 476 F.2d 1127, 1131 (D.C. Cir. 1972) (Bazelon, C.J.). . . .

This discretion is not, of course, unbounded, for there are countervailing considerations weighing heavily against ordering a psychiatric examination of a complainant. As set out by the Court of Appeals for the District of Columbia Circuit, they are that "a psychiatric examination may seriously impinge on a witness' right to privacy; the trauma that attends the role of complainant to sex offense charges is sharply increased by the indignity of a psychiatric examination; the examination itself could serve as a tool of harassment; and the impact of all these considerations may well deter the victim of such a crime from lodging any complaint at all." United States v. Benn, 476 F.2d at 1131. *Benn,* it should be noted, held that the trial judge did not abuse his discretion in declining to order the examination of an admittedly mentally defective complainant.[15]

Fed. R. Evid. 412 is specifically addressed to evidence of a rape victim's prior sexual conduct,[16] whereas defendant's motion was not an attempt to introduce such evidence, but an effort to obtain an expert opinion regarding the complainant's general ability to perceive reality and separate fact from fantasy. Because the rule does not directly apply to his motion, the defendant argues that the court either abused or did not exercise its discretion in denying the motion. The judge's ruling, however, was not based on the letter but on the spirit of Rule 412. The principal purpose of that rule is, as its legislative history demonstrates, quite similar to the countervailing considerations quoted above: "to protect rape victims from the degrading and embarrassing disclosure of intimate details about their private lives." The rationale, according to one commentator, "is to prevent the victim, rather than the defendant, from being put on trial."[19]

We hold that in relying on the *spirit* of Rule 412 the trial judge exercised discretion, and that nothing alleged in defense counsel's affidavit indicates that he abused his discretion. To the extent admissible, and we express no opinion on that matter, evidence that the complainant was thought by members of the

14. See 3A Wigmore on Evidence §924a, at 737 (Chadbourne rev. 1970) ("No judge should let a sex offense charge go to the jury unless the female complainant's social history and mental makeup have been examined and testified to by a qualified physician.") (italics deleted). The Wigmore position does not seem to be accepted in any jurisdiction.

15. . . . The Supreme Court of California has stated that a necessity authorizing the court to order the complainant to undergo such an examination "would generally arise only if little or no corroboration supported the charge and if the defense raised the issue of the effect of the complaining witness' mental or emotional condition on her veracity." Ballard v. Superior Court, 64 Cal. 2d 159, 410 P.2d 838, 849 (1966). In the case sub judice, a key element of the complainant's testimony was corroborated. She testified that the defendant held a knife to her throat, and the medical examiner reported a cut on the side of her throat where the weapon was held. . . .

16. The principal portion of the Rule . . . states: "Notwithstanding any other provision of law, in a criminal case in which a person is accused of rape or of assault with intent to commit rape, reputation or opinion evidence of the past sexual behavior of an alleged victim of such rape or assault is not admissible." [A 1994 amendment to Rule 412 extends the exclusion to "(1) evidence offered to prove that any alleged victim engaged in other sexual behavior; and (2) evidence offered to prove any alleged victim's sexual predisposition." See 55 Crim. L. Rprt. 2345 (Aug. 31, 1994). Even as extended, Rule 412 apparently still would not literally apply to the kind of "mental stability" evidence at issue in *Scuito.* — EDS.]

19. 2 J. Weinstein & M. Berger, Weinstein's Evidence §412[01], at 412-9 (1979). The rule may also be seen as a movement toward making rape prosecutions less special and treating the rape complainant like complainants in other crimes. See Berger, [page 374 supra, Note 2,] at 97

community to indulge in drugs leading to "altered states of consciousness" or to dress in a manner "indicative of socially aberrant behavior" could be introduced by direct rather than expert testimony. If, however, such matters are not relevant or otherwise admissible, there is no justification for letting them into the trial by allowing an expert to give his opinion regarding them. . . .

The judgment of the trial court will be affirmed.

NOTES AND QUESTIONS

1. Suppose that the defendant had sought to present the evidence about the complainant's state of mind through ordinary witnesses rather than through expert testimony. Should such evidence have been admissible under the circumstances? If so, is it really preferable for the matter to be explored through testimony about haphazard observations and "general reputation," rather than through the testimony of experts? Can the disfavoring of expert testimony be justified in terms of the truth-seeking function of the trial or only in terms of the desire to protect the complainant from degrading psychological tests? If the latter explanation is the more satisfactory, is the result in *Scuito* consistent with Davis v. Alaska?

2. Compare *Scuito* with United States v. Lindstrom, 698 F.2d 1154 (11th Cir. 1983). *Lindstrom* was a mail fraud prosecution in which the defendants sought to show that the allegations against them were the product of a vendetta resulting from the mental illness of the prosecution's principal witness. The trial judge, fearing that "the defense would attempt to put the witness herself on trial," permitted only a few narrowly framed questions designed to show that the witness had had mental and emotional problems in the past. The appellate court held that the defendants should have been allowed to cross-examine more extensively and should have been allowed access to the witness's psychiatric records in order to test the perception, credibility and motivation of the witness.

Questions: Should *Lindstrom* have been decided differently if the witness had accused the defendants of rape? If cases of this kind cannot be distinguished in terms of the crime that the complainant charges, should cross-examination about mental problems and access to psychiatric records be barred in both types of cases?

3. In *Scuito* the defendant was denied the right to compel a psychiatric examination of the complainant. Should the result be different if the defendant seeks access to records of psychiatric treatment already provided to the complainant on her initiative, or are the complainant's privacy interests even stronger in the latter situation? Should it matter whether the psychiatric records relate to treatment provided before or after the alleged rape?

Consider Commonwealth v. Stockhammer, 409 Mass. 867, 570 N.E.2d 992 (1991). The defendant and the complainant were college classmates who had become close friends. Prior to April 1988 there was no sexual dimension to their relationship, and the complainant had a boyfriend in another city. The alleged rape occurred in 1988, and the complainant promptly described the incident to a friend but asked the friend not to tell anyone about it. The complainant continued to see the defendant and invited him to visit her at her parents' home later that Spring. In December 1988 the complainant broke up with her boyfriend, and in January 1989 she was hospitalized after an apparent suicide attempt. She reported having a minor problem with her boyfriend but made no mention of having been raped. Shortly thereafter, an anonymous caller told her father that the complainant had been telling others about a sexual assault, and when confronted by her father, she told him that the defendant had raped her. She then reported the incident to the police. She also received extended psychiatric treatment, first as a hospital inpatient and subsequently during four months of counseling from a social worker. Defendant admitted the sexual encounter of April 1988 and claimed that it was consensual. He was convicted of rape, but on appeal the court reversed, holding that defense counsel was entitled to inspect records of the complainant's psychiatric treatment in order to search for evidence to buttress the defendant's claim that the rape charge was fabricated.

Compare Susan Estrich, Palm Beach Stories, 11 Law & Phil. 5, 17-18 (1992):

> *Stockhammer* is precisely the sort of case that probably would not even have been prosecuted ten years ago; it is the sort of conviction that might well have been reversed by an appeals court on the grounds of absence of force as recently as five years ago. In 1991, however, when the Massachusetts Supreme Judicial Court reversed the defendant's conviction (some things don't change), they did so not on culpability grounds such as force or consent, but by holding that the defendant was entitled under the state constitution to review the woman's psychiatric treatment records. . . .
>
> What is striking about *Stockhammer* is that the records in question related to treatment the woman sought after the rape — when many women need psychological help, as the court itself recognized. . . . The bitter irony, of course, is that I can think of few greater deterrents to getting help than the knowledge that one's records may later be viewed not just by a judge, but by defense counsel, the defendant, a jury of strangers, and a bevy of curious newspaper readers.

CHAPTER
5

HOMICIDE

A. INTRODUCTION

There are two principal questions one may ask in considering a particular category of crime. The first is a question of criminality: What distinguishes criminal behavior from noncriminal behavior? The second is a question of punishment grading: What factors warrant greater or lesser punishment within the area of behavior defined as criminal? In the preceding chapter on rape we dealt primarily with questions of the first kind. In this chapter we will deal primarily with questions of the latter kind.

The distinction between criminal and noncriminal homicide usually raises such basic issues as causation, necessity, self-defense, defense of another, insanity, duress, etc. We will deal separately with such general issues later, though there is one problem of criminality we will deal with here — the basis for distinguishing between criminal and noncriminal unintended killings. See Section C1 of this chapter infra.

The questions of the second kind — those of grading — will constitute the principal focus of the materials in this section. Following the introductory historical and statutory materials, we deal in Section B with the factors that influence the categorization of intended killings into homicidal crimes of greater or lesser punishment — murder in the several degrees and voluntary manslaughter. In Section C a similar inquiry is pursued with respect to killings that are unintentional. It will be helpful to bear in mind that virtually all the varieties of behavior dealt with are without question crimes of some sort, the only question being the determination of what crime is involved, which is to say, what punishment is authorized.

REPORT OF THE ROYAL COMMISSION ON CAPITAL PUNISHMENT, 1945-1953
25-28 (1953)

BASIC PRINCIPLES OF THE LAW OF MURDER IN ENGLAND

72. Homicide is the killing of a human being by a human being. Unlawful homicide may be murder, manslaughter, suicide or infanticide. Murder and man-

slaughter are felonies at common law and are not defined by statute. The traditional definition or description of murder derives from that given in the seventeenth century by Coke. "When a man of sound memory and of the age of discretion unlawfully kills any reasonable creature in being, and under the King's peace, with malice aforethought, either express or implied by the law, the death taking place within a year and a day."[a] It is in common practice often more briefly defined as "unlawful killing with 'malice aforethought'"; while manslaughter is defined as "unlawful killing without 'malice aforethought.'" . . .

74. The meaning of "malice aforethought," which is the distinguishing criterion of murder, is certainly not beyond the range of controversy. The first thing that must be said about it is that neither of the two words is used in its ordinary sense: the phrase "malice aforethought" is now a highly technical term of art. "It is now only an arbitrary symbol. For the 'malice' may have in it nothing really malicious; and need never be really 'aforethought,' except in the sense that every desire must necessarily come before — though perhaps only an instant before — the act which is desired. The word 'aforethought,' in the definition, has thus become either false or else superfluous. The word 'malice' is neither; but it is apt to be misleading, for it is not employed in its original (and its popular) meaning." "Malice aforethought" is simply a comprehensive name for a number of different mental attitudes which have been variously defined at different stages in the development of the law, the presence of any one of which in the accused has been held by the courts to render a homicide particularly heinous and therefore to make it murder. These states of mind have been variously expressed by various authorities, but the statement of the modern law most commonly cited as authoritative is that given in 1877 by Sir James Stephen in his Digest of the Criminal Law:

> Malice aforethought means any one or more of the following states of mind preceding or co-existing with the act or omission by which death is caused, and it may exist where that act is unpremeditated.
>
> (a) An intention to cause the death of, or grievous bodily harm to, any person, whether such person is the person actually killed or not;
> (b) knowledge that the act which causes death will probably cause the death of, or grievous bodily harm to, some person, whether such person is the person actually killed or not, although such knowledge is accompanied by indifference whether death or grievous bodily harm is caused or not, or by a wish that it may not be caused;
> (c) an intent to commit any felony whatever;
> (d) an intent to oppose by force any officer of justice on his way to, in, or returning from the execution of the duty of arresting, keeping in custody, or imprisoning any person whom he is lawfully entitled to arrest,

a. The year-and-a-day requirement has been abandoned by legislation in some states. It remains in force in the federal courts, see United States v. Chase, 18 F.3d 1166 (4th Cir. 1994), and in many of the states. See Annot., 60 A.L.R.3d 1323 (1974); cf. Cal. Penal Code §194, replacing the traditional requirement with a limitation of three years and a day. For a critical analysis of the year-and-a-day rule, see State v. Gabehart, 114 N.M. 183, 836 P.2d 102 (1992), and State v. Vance, 328 N.C. 613, 403 S.E.2d 495 (1991). In both *Gabehart* and *Vance,* the courts chose to abrogate the rule, after concluding that it was outmoded in view of modern medical advances. Compare State v. Minster, 302 Md. 240, 486 A.2d 1197 (1985), reaffirming the rule as a useful limit on the reach of proximate causation. In *Minster* the court concluded that the legislature should bear responsibility for any decision to eliminate the rule or replace it with a longer time limit. — EDS.

keep in custody, or imprison, or the duty of keeping the peace or dispersing an unlawful assembly, provided that the offender has notice that the person killed is such an officer so employed. . . .

75. We must now consider how "malice aforethought" came to be the distinctive element of murder and to bear such a meaning as is given to it at the present time. . . . It is sufficient to say here that "murder" originally meant a "secret killing" and only gradually, from the fourteenth century onwards, came to be the name of the worst form of homicide characterised by "malice prepense" or "malice aforethought." The next stage is marked by a series of statutes in the reigns of Henry VII and VIII which largely took away the benefit of clergy from murders "of malice prepensed." It seems clear that at this period and for sometime afterwards "malice prepense" or "malice aforethought" was understood to mean a deliberate, premeditated intent to kill formed some time beforehand, and that no killing "on a sudden," even without provocation or on slight provocation, was considered to be murder. In effect the law regarded unlawful killings as being of only two kinds — killing with malice aforethought and killing on a sudden quarrel. Experience showed, however, that this view was much too simple and the definitions founded upon it inadequate. There were many kinds of killing which should clearly be considered unlawful but which did not fall into either of these categories, and many such cases seemed to deserve the extreme penalty although the offender had no premeditated desire to kill his victim. During the last four centuries the meaning to be given to the term "malice aforethought" has been affected by the changes in the conception of mens rea as a necessary ingredient in criminal liability at common law for all crimes. The courts and the writers of legal textbooks have responded to this change by giving to "malice aforethought" a wider and more technical meaning. As Stephen put it, "the loose term 'malice' was used, and then when a particular state of mind came under their notice, the Judges called it 'malice' or not, according to their view of the propriety of hanging particular people. That is, in two words, the history of the definition of murder." There can be no doubt that the term now covers, and has for long covered, all the most heinous forms of homicide, as well as some cases — those of "constructive murder" — whose inclusion in the category of murder has often been criticised.

76. Thus the following propositions are commonly accepted:

(i) It is murder if one person kills another with intent to do so, without provocation or on slight provocation, although there is no premeditation in the ordinary sense of the word.

(ii) It is murder if one person is killed by an act intended to kill another.

(iii) It is murder if a person is killed by an act intended to kill, although not intended to kill any particular individual, as if a man throws a bomb into a crowd of people.

(iv) It is murder if death results from an act which is intended to do no more than cause grievous bodily harm. An early example may be found in the case of Grey, where a blacksmith, who had had words with an apprentice, struck him on the head with an iron bar and killed him. It was held that it "is all one as if he had run him through with a sword" and he was found guilty of murder.

(v) It is murder if one person kills another by an intentional act which he knows to be likely to kill or to cause grievous bodily harm, although he may not intend to kill or to cause grievous bodily harm and may either be recklessly indifferent as to the results of his act or may even desire that no harm should be caused by it. Two examples may be given. A woman may be guilty of murder if she exposes a helpless infant in circumstances where there is not a reasonable expectation that it will be found and preserved by someone else. A man was convicted of murder when he had killed a number of persons in the street by exploding a barrel of gunpowder against the wall of a prison, although his purpose was only to enable a prisoner to escape. Lord Dockburn, L.C.J., told the jury that such an act was murder, quite apart from the fact that it was committed in the prosecution of a felony.

CALIFORNIA PENAL CODE

SECTION 187.   MURDER DEFINED

(a) Murder is the unlawful killing of a human being, or a fetus,[a] with malice aforethought. . . .

SECTION 188.   MALICE DEFINED: EXPRESS AND IMPLIED MALICE

Such malice may be express or implied. It is expressed when there is manifested a deliberate intention unlawfully to take away the life of a fellow creature. It is implied, when no considerable provocation appears, or when the circumstances attending the killing show an abandoned and malignant heart.

When it is shown that the killing resulted from the intentional doing of an act with express or implied malice as defined above, no other mental state need be shown to establish the mental state of malice aforethought. Neither an awareness of the obligation to act within the general body of laws regulating society nor acting despite such awareness is included within the definition of malice.

SECTION 189.   DEGREES OF MURDER

All murder which is perpetrated by means of a destructive device or explosive, knowing use of ammunition designed primarily to penetrate metal or armor, poison, lying in wait, torture, or by any other kind of willful, deliberate, and premeditated killing, or which is committed in the perpetration or attempt to perpetrate arson, rape, robbery, burglary, mayhem, kidnapping, train wrecking,

a. Except where done in the course of a legal abortion or by a physician pursuant to a medical judgment or where consented to by the mother. Section 187(b). The language was added following Keeler v. Superior Court, page 298 supra, 1970 Cal. Laws ch. 1311, §1. In People v. Davis, 872 P.2d 591 (Cal. 1994), the court held that viability is not an element of the offense of fetal murder; the killing of a fetus can constitute murder, within the meaning of §187(a), as long as the state can show that the fetus has progressed beyond the embryonic stage of seven to eight weeks. — EDS.

or any act punishable under Section 286, 288, 288a, or 289 [prohibiting various forcible sexual acts and certain sexual acts with minors], is murder of the first degree [punishable by death or imprisonment for life without possibility of parole, where special enumerated circumstances exist, or imprisonment for 25 years to life]; and all other kinds of murders are of the second degree [punishable by imprisonment for 15 years to life]. . . .

To prove the killing was "deliberate and premeditated," it shall not be necessary to prove the defendant maturely and meaningfully reflected upon the gravity of his or her act.

Section 192.   Manslaughter . . .

Manslaughter is the unlawful killing of a human being without malice. It is of three kinds:

(a) Voluntary — upon a sudden quarrel or heat of passion. [Punishable by imprisonment for three, six, or eleven years.]

(b) Involuntary — in the commission of an unlawful act, not amounting to felony; or in the commission of a lawful act which might produce death, in an unlawful manner, or without due caution and circumspection. This subdivision shall not apply to acts committed in the driving of a vehicle. [Punishable by imprisonment for two, three, or four years.]

(c) Vehicular —

(1). . . driving a vehicle in the commission of an unlawful act, not amounting to felony, and with gross negligence; or driving a vehicle in the commission of a lawful act which might produce death, in an unlawful manner, and with gross negligence. [Punishable by up to one year in county jail or imprisonment for two, four, or six years.]

(2) . . . driving a vehicle in the commission of an unlawful act, not amounting to felony, but without gross negligence; or driving a vehicle in the commission of a lawful act which might produce death, in an unlawful manner, but without gross negligence. [Punishable by a county jail term not to exceed one year.] . . .

This section shall not be construed as making any homicide in the driving of a vehicle punishable which is not a proximate result of the commission of an unlawful act, not amounting to a felony, or the commission of a lawful act which might produce death, in an unlawful manner.

"Gross negligence," as used in this section, shall not be construed as prohibiting or precluding a charge of murder under Section 188 upon facts exhibiting wantonness and a conscious disregard for life to support a finding of implied malice, or upon facts showing malice. . . .

PENNSYLVANIA CONSOLIDATED STATUTES, TITLE 18

Section 2501.   Criminal Homicide

(a) Offense Defined. — A person is guilty of criminal homicide if he intentionally, knowingly, recklessly or negligently causes the death of another human being.

(b) CLASSSIFICATION. — Criminal homicide shall be classified as murder, voluntary manslaughter, or involuntary manslaughter.

SECTION 2502.   MURDER

(a) MURDER OF THE FIRST DEGREE. — A criminal homicide constitutes murder of the first degree when it is committed by an intentional killing. [Punishable by death or life imprisonment.]

(b) MURDER OF THE SECOND DEGREE. — A criminal homicide constitutes murder of the second degree when it is committed while defendant was engaged as a principal or an accomplice in the perpetration of a felony. [Punishable by life imprisonment.]

(c) MURDER OF THE THIRD DEGREE. — All other kinds of murder shall be murder of the third degree. Murder of the third degree is a felony of the first degree. [Punishable by maximum of 20 years.]

(d) DEFINITIONS. — As used in this section the following words and phrases shall have the meanings given to them in this subsection: . . .

"Intentional killing." Killing by means of poison, or by lying in wait, or by any other kind of willful, deliberate and premeditated killing.

"Perpetration of a felony." The act of the defendant in engaging in or being an accomplice in the commission of, or an attempt to commit, or flight after committing, or attempting to commit robbery, rape, or deviate sexual intercourse by force or threat of force, arson, burglary or kidnapping. . . .

SECTION 2503.   VOLUNTARY MANSLAUGHTER

(a) GENERAL RULE. — A person who kills an individual without lawful justification commits voluntary manslaughter if at the time of the killing he is acting under a sudden and intense passion resulting from serious provocation by:

(1) the individual killed; or

(2) another whom the actor endeavors to kill, but he negligently or accidentally causes the death of the individual killed.

(b) UNREASONABLE BELIEF KILLING JUSTIFIABLE. — A person who intentionally or knowingly kills an individual commits voluntary manslaughter if at the time of the killing he believes the circumstances to be such that, if they existed, would justify the killing under Chapter 5 of this title, but his belief is unreasonable.

(c) GRADING. — Voluntary manslaughter is a felony of the second degree. [Ten-year maximum.]

SECTION 2504.   INVOLUNTARY MANSLAUGHTER

(a) GENERAL RULE — A person is guilty of involuntary manslaughter when as a direct result of the doing of an unlawful act in a reckless or grossly negligent manner, or the doing of a lawful act in a reckless or grossly negligent manner, he causes the death of another person.

(h) GRADING. — Involuntary manslaughter is a misdemeanor of the first degree. [Five-year maximum.]

SECTION 2505.   CAUSING OR AIDING SUICIDE

(a) CAUSING SUICIDE AS CRIMINAL HOMICIDE. — A person may be convicted of criminal homicide for causing another to commit suicide only if he intentionally causes such suicide by force, duress, or deception.

(b) AIDING OR SOLICITING SUICIDE AS AN INDEPENDENT OFFENSE. — A person who intentionally aids or solicits another to commit suicide is guilty of a felony of the second degree if his conduct causes such suicide or an attempted suicide, and otherwise of a misdemeanor of the second degree. [Two-year maximum.]

NEW YORK PENAL LAW

SECTION 125.00.   HOMICIDE DEFINED

Homicide means conduct which causes the death of a person . . . under circumstances constituting murder, manslaughter in the first degree, manslaughter in the second degree, [or] criminally negligent homicide. . . .

SECTION 125.10.   CRIMINALLY NEGLIGENT HOMICIDE

A person is guilty of criminally negligent homicide when, with criminal negligence,[a] he causes the death of another person.

Criminally negligent homicide is a class E felony. [Four-year maximum.]

SECTION 125.15.   MANSLAUGHTER IN THE SECOND DEGREE

A person is guilty of manslaughter in the second degree when:

1. He recklessly[b] causes the death of another person; or . . .
3. He intentionally[c] causes or aids another person to commit suicide.

Manslaughter in the second degree is a class C felony. [15-year maximum.]

SECTION 125.20.   MANSLAUGHTER IN THE FIRST DEGREE

A person is guilty of manslaughter in the first degree when:

1. With intent to cause serious physical injury to another person, he causes the death of such person or of a third person; or

2. With intent to cause the death of another person, he causes the death of such person or of a third person under circumstances which do not constitute

a. Defined similarly to Model Penal Code §2.02(2)(d), Appendix. See N.Y. Penal Law §15.05(4). — EDS.

b. Defined similarly to Model Penal Code §2.02(2)(c), Appendix. See N.Y. Penal Law §15.05(3). — EDS.

c. Defined similarly to "purposely" in Model Penal Code §2.02(2)(a), Appendix. See N.Y. Penal Law §15.05(1). — EDS.

murder because he acts under the influence of extreme emotional disturbance, as defined in paragraph (a) of subdivision one of section 125.25. . . .

Manslaughter in the first degree is a class B felony. [25-year maximum.]

SECTION 125.25.   MURDER IN THE SECOND DEGREE

A person is guilty of murder in the second degree when:

1. With intent to cause the death of another person, he causes the death of such person or of a third person; except that in any prosecution under this subdivision, it is an affirmative defense that:

(a) The defendant acted under the influence of extreme emotional disturbance for which there was a reasonable explanation or excuse, the reasonableness of which is to be determined from the viewpoint of a person in the defendant's situation under the circumstances as the defendant believed them to be. . . . ; or

(b) The defendant's conduct consisted of causing or aiding, without the use of duress or deception, another person to commit suicide. . . . ; or

2. Under circumstances evincing a depraved indifference to human life, he recklessly engages in conduct which creates a grave risk of death to another person, and thereby causes the death of another person; or

3. Acting either alone or with one or more other persons, he commits or attempts to commit robbery, burglary, kidnapping, arson, rape in the first degree, sodomy in the first degree, sexual abuse in the first degree, aggravated sexual abuse, escape in the first degree, or escape in the second degree, and, in the course of and in furtherance of such crime or of immediate flight therefrom, he, or another participant, if there be any, causes the death of a person other than one of the participants; except that in any prosecution under this subdivision, in which the defendant was not the only participant in the underlying crime, it is an affirmative defense that the defendant:

(a) Did not commit the homicidal act or in any way solicit, request, command, importune, cause or aid the commission thereof; and

(b) Was not armed with a deadly weapon, or any instrument, article or substance readily capable of causing death or serious physical injury and of a sort not ordinarily carried in public places by law-abiding persons; and

(c) Had no reasonable ground to believe that any other participant was armed with such a weapon, instrument, article or substance; and

(d) Had no reasonable ground to believe that any other participant intended to engage in conduct likely to result in death or serious physical injury. . . .

Murder in the second degree is a class A-I felony. [Punishable by from 15 years to life imprisonment.]

SECTION 125.27.   MURDER IN THE FIRST DEGREE

[Under this section, those intentional killings that would be second-degree murder under §125.25(1) are raised to first-degree murder when the victim is a police officer or an employee of a state or local correctional institution, or when the crime is committed while a defendant is either in custody under a life sentence or is at large after having escaped from such custody. The statute classifies first-degree murder as a class A-I felony punishable by death. After the New York courts invalidated the statutory death penalty mandated for first-degree murder, the applicable penalty became the same as that provided for second-degree murder.[a]]

MODEL PENAL CODE

SECTION 210.1 TO 210.4

[See Appendix for text of this section.]

THE PENAL CODE OF SWEDEN [1]

SECTION 1

A person who takes the life of another shall be sentenced for *murder* to imprisonment for ten years or for life.

SECTION 2

If, in view of the circumstances that led to the act or for other reasons, the crime mentioned in Section 1 is considered to be less grave, imprisonment for *manslaughter* shall be imposed for at least six and at most ten years. . . .

SECTION 7

A person who through carelessness causes the death of another shall be sentenced for *causing another's death* to imprisonment for at most two years or, if the crime is less grave, to pay a fine.

If the crime is grave, imprisonment shall be imposed for at least six months and at most four years.

B.   LEGISLATIVE GRADING OF INTENDED KILLINGS

1.   *The Premeditation-Deliberation Formula*

INTRODUCTORY NOTE

MODEL PENAL CODE AND COMMENTARIES, Comment to §210.2 at 16 (1980): Prior to the recodification effort begun by the Model Penal Code, most

a. See People v. Smith, 63 N.Y.2d 41, 468 N.E.2d 879 (1984). — EDS.
1. National Council for Crime Prevention (Sweden), The Swedish Penal Code 1990, ch. 3, §§1-7 (1990).

American jurisdictions maintained a law of murder built around [the] common-law [concepts]. The most significant departure was the division of murder into degrees, a change initiated by the Pennsylvania legislation of 1794. [That statute provided that "all murder, which shall be perpetrated by means of poison, or by lying in wait, or by any other kind of willful, deliberate and premeditated killing, or which shall be committed in the perpetration, or attempt to perpetrate any arson, rape, robbery or burglary shall be deemed murder in the first degree; and all other kinds of murder shall be deemed murder in the second degree."] The thrust of this reform was to confine the death penalty, which was then mandatory on conviction of any common-law murder, to homicides judged particularly heinous. Other states followed the Pennsylvania practice until at one time the vast majority of American jurisdictions differentiated degrees of murder and the term "first-degree murder" passed into common parlance.

COMMONWEALTH v. CARROL

Supreme Court of Pennsylvania
412 Pa. 525, 194 A.2d 911 (1963)

BELL, C.J. The defendant, Carrol, pleaded guilty generally to an indictment charging him with the murder of his wife, and was tried by a judge without a jury in the Court of Oyer and Terminer of Allegheny County. The Court found him guilty of first degree murder and sentenced him to life imprisonment. Following argument and denial of motions in arrest of judgment and for a new trial, defendant took this appeal. The only questions involved are thus stated by the appellant:

> [1] Does not the evidence sustain a conviction no higher than murder in the second degree?
> [2] Does not the evidence of defendant's good character, together with the testimony of medical experts, including the psychiatrist for the Behavior Clinic of Allegheny County, that the homicide was not premeditated or intentional, *require* the Court below to fix the degree of guilt of defendant no higher than murder in the second degree?

The defendant married the deceased in 1955, when he was serving in the Army in California. Subsequently he was stationed in Alabama, and later in Greenland. During the latter tour of duty, defendant's wife and two children lived with his parents in New Jersey. Because this arrangement proved incompatible, defendant returned to the United States on emergency leave in order to move his family to their own quarters. On his wife's insistence, defendant was forced first to secure a "compassionate transfer" back to the States, and subsequently to resign from the Army in July of 1960, by which time he had attained the rank of Chief Warrant Officer. Defendant was a hard worker, earned a substantial salary and bore a very good reputation among his neighbors.

In 1958, decedent-wife suffered a fractured skull while attempting to leave defendant's car in the course of an argument. Allegedly this contributed to her mental disorder which was later diagnosed as a schizoid personality type. In 1959 she underwent psychiatric treatment at the Mental Hygiene Clinic in Aberdeen,

Maryland. She complained of nervousness and told the examining doctor "I feel like hurting my children." This sentiment sometimes took the form of sadistic "discipline" toward their very young children. Nevertheless, upon her discharge from the Clinic, the doctors considered her much improved. With this background we come to the immediate events of the crime.

In January, 1962, defendant was selected to attend an electronics school in Winston-Salem, North Carolina, for nine days. His wife greeted this news with violent argument. Immediately prior to his departure for Winston-Salem, at the suggestion and request of his wife, he put a *loaded* .22 calibre pistol on the window sill at the head of their common bed, so that she would feel safe. On the evening of January 16, 1962, defendant returned home and told his wife that he had been temporarily assigned to teach at a school in Chambersburg, which would necessitate his absence from home four nights out of seven for a ten week period. A violent and protracted argument ensued at the dinner table and continued until four o'clock in the morning.

Defendant's own statement after his arrest details the final moments before the crime:

> We went into the bedroom a little before 3 o'clock on Wednesday morning where we continued to argue in short bursts. Generally she laid with her back to me facing the wall in bed and would just talk over her shoulder to me. I became angry and more angry especially what she was saying about my kids and myself, and sometime between 3 and 4 o'clock in the morning I remembered the gun on the window sill over my head. I think she had dozed off. *I reached up and grabbed the pistol and brought it down and shot her twice in the back of the head.*[2]

Defendant's testimony at the trial elaborated this theme. He started to think about the children:

> seeing my older son's feet what happened to them. I could see the bruises on him and Michael's chin was split open, four stitches. I didn't know what to do. I wanted to help my boys. Sometime in there she said something in there, she called me some kind of name. I kept thinking of this. *During this time I either thought or felt — I thought of the gun, just thought of the gun.* I am not sure whether I felt my hand move toward the gun — I saw my hand move, the next thing — the only thing I can recollect after that is right after the shots or right during the shots. I saw the gun in my hand just pointed at my wife's head. She was still lying on her back — I mean her side. I could smell the gunpowder and I could hear something — it sounded like running water. I didn't know what it was at first, didn't realize what I'd done at first. Then I smelled it. I smelled blood before. . . .

> *Q.* At the time you shot her, Donald, were you fully aware and intend to do what you did?
> *A.* I don't know positively. All I remember hearing was two shots and feeling myself go cold all of a sudden.

Shortly thereafter defendant wrapped his wife's body in a blanket, spread and sheets, tied them on with a piece of plastic clothesline and took her down to the

---

2. When pressed on cross-examination defendant approximated that five minutes elapsed between his wife's last remark and the shooting.

cellar. He tried to clean up as well as he could. That night he took his wife's body, wrapped in a blanket with a rug over it to a desolate place near a trash dump. He then took the children to his parents' home in Magnolia, New Jersey. He was arrested the next Monday in Chambersburg where he had gone to his teaching assignment.

Although defendant's brief is voluminous, the narrow and only questions which he raises on this appeal are as hereinbefore quoted. Both are embodied in his contention that the crime amounted only to second degree murder and that his conviction should therefore be reduced to second degree or that a new trial should be granted. . . .

[The court then reviewed the Pennsylvania murder statute, which at the time divided murder into two degrees, in accordance with the formula adopted in 1794. That formula, still in effect for Pennsylvania in 1963 and followed in many states to this day, is quoted above in the excerpt immediately preceding *Carrol*.[a] Then, as now, first-degree murder included killings by poison, lying in wait "or any other kind of willful, deliberate and premeditated killing."]

The specific intent to kill which is necessary to constitute in a nonfelony murder, murder in the first degree, may be found from a defendant's words or conduct or from the attendant circumstances together with all reasonable inferences therefrom, and may be inferred from the intentional use of a deadly weapon on a vital part of the body of another human being. . . .

If we consider only the evidence which is favorable to the Commonwealth, it is without the slightest doubt sufficient in law to prove first degree. However, even if we believe all of defendant's statements and testimony, there is no doubt that this killing constituted murder in the first degree. Defendant first urges that there was insufficient time for premeditation in the light of his good reputation. This is based on an isolated and oft repeated statement in Commonwealth v. Drum, 58 Pa. 9, 16, that " 'no time is too short for a wicked man to frame in his mind the scheme of murder.' " Defendant argues that, conversely, a long time is necessary to find premeditation in a "good man." We find no merit in defendant's analogy or contention. As Chief Justice Maxey appropriately and correctly said in Commonwealth v. Earnest, 342 Pa. 544, 549-550, 21 A.2d 38, 40: "Whether the intention to kill and the killing, that is, the premeditation and the fatal act, were within a brief space of time or a long space of time is immaterial if the killing was in fact intentional, wilful, deliberate and premeditated." . . .

Defendant further contends that the time and place of the crime, the enormous difficulty of removing and concealing the body, and the obvious lack of an escape plan, militate against and make a finding of premeditation legally impossible. This is a "jury argument"; it is clear as crystal that such circumstances do not negate premeditation. This contention of defendant is likewise clearly devoid of merit.

Defendant's most earnestly pressed contention is that the *psychiatrist's opinion of what defendant's state of mind must have been and was at the time of the crime,* clearly establishes not only the lack but also the legal impossibility of premeditation. Dr. Davis, a psychiatrist of the Allegheny County Behavior Clinic, testified that defendant was

---

a. A further refinement adopted by Pennsylvania in 1976 produced three degrees of murder; see the current statute set out at pages 389-390 supra. — Eds.

for a number of years . . . passively going along with a situation which he [was] not controlling and he [was] not making any decisions, and finally a decision [was] forced on him. . . . He had left the military to take this assignment, and he was averaging about nine thousand a year; he had a good job. He knew that if he didn't accept this teaching assignment in all probability he would be dismissed from the Government service, and at his age and his special training he didn't know whether he would be able to find employment. More critical to that was the fact that at this point, as we understand it, his wife issued an ultimatum that if he went and gave this training course she would leave him. . . . He was so dependent upon her he didn't want her to leave. He couldn't make up his mind what to do. He was trapped. . . .

The doctor then gave *his opinion* that "rage," "desperation," and "panic" produced

an impulsive automatic reflex type of homicide, . . . as opposed to an intentional premeditated type of homicide, . . . Our feeling was that if this gun had fallen to the floor he wouldn't have been able to pick it up and consummate that homicide. And I think if he had to load the gun he wouldn't have done it. This is a matter of opinion, but this is our opinion about it.

There are three answers to this contention. First, as we have hereinbefore stated, neither a judge nor a jury has to believe all or any part of the testimony of the defendant or of any witness. Secondly, the opinion of the psychiatrists was based to a large extent upon statements made to them by the defendant, which need not be believed and which are in some instances opposed by the facts themselves. Thirdly, a psychiatrist's opinion of a defendant's impulse or lack of intent or state of mind is, in this class of case, entitled to very little weight, and this is especially so when defendant's own actions, or his testimony or confession, or the facts themselves, belie the opinion. . . .

Defendant's *own statement* after his arrest, upon which his counsel so strongly relies, *as well as his testimony at his trial,* clearly convict him of first degree murder and justify the finding and sentence of the Court below. Defendant himself described his actions at the time he killed his wife. From his own statements and from his own testimony, it is clear that, terribly provoked by his allegedly nagging, belligerent and sadistic wife, *defendant remembered the gun, deliberately took it down, and deliberately fired two shots into the head of his sleeping wife.* There is no doubt that this was a willful, deliberate and premeditated murder.

While defendant makes no contention that he was insane at the commission of the murder or at any time, what this Court said in Commonwealth v. Tyrrell, 405 Pa. 210, 220-221, 174 A.2d 852, 856-57, is equally appropriate here:

Defendant's psychiatrist did not testify that the defendant was insane. What he did say was that because defendant's wife frequently picked on him and just before the killing insulted or goaded him, defendant had an emotional impulse to kill her which he could not resist. . . . [S]*ociety would be almost completely unprotected from criminals if the law permitted a blind or irresistible impulse or inability to control one's self, to excuse or justify a murder or to reduce it from first degree to second degree.* In the times in which we are living, nearly every normal adult human being has moments or hours or days or longer periods when he or she is depressed and disturbed with resultant emotional upset feelings and so-called blind impulses; and the young especially have many uncontrolled emotions every day which are euphemistically called irresistible impulses. *The Courts of Justice should not abdicate their function and duty of determining criminal responsibility to the psychiatrist.* In such event, the test will differ not only with each psychiatrist but also with the prevailing psychiatric winds of the moment. . . .

Just as the Courts cannot abdicate to the psychiatrists the task of determining criminal responsibility in law, so also they cannot remit to psychiatrists the right to determine the intent or the state of mind of an accused at the time of the commission of a homicide. . . .

Judgment and sentence affirmed.

NOTES

1. Many courts follow the *Carrol* approach by suggesting that some premeditation is required, and simultaneously holding that "no time is too short," for the necessary premeditation to occur. Consider Young v. State, 428 So.2d 155, 158 (Ala. Crim. App. 1982). Defendant and his brother were playing cards with several friends when an argument and then a scuffle broke out. Defendant fired several shots, and two of the men were hit; each died from a single .22 caliber shot to the chest. The court upheld defendant's conviction on two counts of first-degree murder. Stressing that "[no] appreciable space of time between the formation of the intention to kill and the act of killing" was required, the court said (428 So.2d at 158) that "[p]remeditation and deliberation may be formed while the killer is 'pressing the trigger that fired the fatal shot.' "

Question: Given decisions like *Carrol* and *Young,* what is the difference between a premeditated intention to kill and an intention to kill without premeditation?

2. Consider Benjamin Cardozo, What Medicine Can Do for Law, in B. Cardozo, Law and Literature and Other Essays and Addresses 99-100 (1931):

> There can be no intent unless there is choice, yet by the hypothesis, the choice without more is enough to justify the inference that the intent was deliberate and premeditated. The presence of a sudden impulse is said to mark the dividing line, but how can an impulse be anything but sudden when the time for its formation is measured by the lapse of seconds? Yet the decisions are to the effect that seconds may be enough. . . . If intent is deliberate and premeditated whenever there is choice, then in truth it is always deliberate and premeditated, since choice is involved in the hypothesis of the intent. What we have is merely a privilege offered to the jury to find the lesser degree when the suddenness of the intent, the vehemence of the passion, seems to call irresistibly for the exercise of mercy. I have no objection to giving them this dispensing power, but it should be given to them directly and not in a mystifying cloud of words.

3. The Pennsylvania Supreme Court clarified *Carrol*'s implications in Commonwealth v. O'Searo, 466 Pa. 224, 352 A.2d 30, 37-38 (1976). The defendant there challenged an instruction that permitted the jury to infer premeditation from the use of a deadly weapon on a vital part of the body. The defendant conceded that such an act would support an inference of intent to kill but argued that it could not support an inference of premeditation. Affirming the conviction, the court responded:

> [Defendant] attempts to support his position by suggesting that the legislative requirement that the act be willful, deliberate and premeditated, requires something more than a conscious intent to bring about the death of the victim. This proposition would introduce a new dimension to the law of homicide within this jurisdiction. It would in effect require the distinction between first and second degree murder to depend upon the degree of reflection from which the plan to kill originated. Our cases have consistently held that the requirement of premeditation and deliberation is met whenever there is a conscious purpose to bring about death. This is emphasized by those decisions which have stated that the design to kill can be formulated in a fraction of a second. [T]he distinction between murder of the first and second degree is the presence of a specific intent to kill. We can find no reason where there is a conscious intent to bring about death to differentiate between the degree of culpability on the basis of the elaborateness of the design to kill.

In accord with *O'Searo*, see State v. Schrader, 172 W. Va. 1, 302 S.E.2d 70 (1982), where the court upheld a jury instruction that permitted a finding of "willful, deliberate and premeditated killing" if the intent to kill came "into existence for the first time at the time of such killing." The court explained (302 S.E.2d at 75): "[W]hat is really meant by the language 'willful, deliberate and premeditated' . . . is that the killing be intentional."

PEOPLE v. ANDERSON

Supreme Court of California
70 Cal. 2d 15, 447 P.2d 942 (1968)

TOBRINER, J. . . . Defendant was indicted for the murder of Victoria Hammond, a 10-year-old girl, in 1962. [T]he jury . . . found defendant guilty of first degree murder, found that he was sane, and fixed the penalty at death. This appeal is automatic. . . .

[W]e conclude that the evidence is insufficient to support a verdict of first degree murder on the theory of . . . premeditated and deliberate murder. . . .

[The defendant had been living for about eight months with Mrs. Hammond and her three children. On the morning of the murder, the defendant did not go to work, and when Mrs. Hammond left for work at 7:30 A.M., she left him at home with one of her children, Victoria, aged 10. He had been home from work the previous two days, during which time he had been drinking heavily. The owner of a nearby liquor store testified that the defendant purchased a quart of whisky between 1 and 2 P.M. that day.

[Victoria's 13-year-old brother Kenneth returned home from school at 3:30 P.M. and found the front door locked, which was not unusual. He went around to the back of the house and down into the basement, where, while working on his microscope, he heard noises coming from upstairs that sounded like objects being moved around "like someone was cleaning up." He also heard shower water running. When Kenneth went upstairs to change clothes, the back-door screen was locked, which also was not unusual, so he jerked on the screen to force the hook to pop out. When he went to the kitchen, he found that door locked also. The defendant answered Kenneth's knock dressed only in slacks. He gave Kenneth $1.00 for a teen dance he was going to attend that night, and when Kenneth noticed blood on the kitchen floor, the defendant told him that he had cut himself. Kenneth then left the house sometime before 4 p.m.

[Mrs. Hammond returned home at 4:45 p.m. and noticed blood on the living room couch. The defendant told her that Kenneth had cut himself. She then went to the grocery store and returned at about 5:30 p.m. Meanwhile, Kenneth discovered at 6:30 p.m. that he had forgotten his wallet and returned home. When his mother found that he had not cut himself, she again asked the defendant about the blood, and defendant told her that Victoria had cut herself, but that the cut was not serious. He also told Mrs. Hammond that Victoria was at a friend's house for dinner. Mrs. Hammond said she wanted to take Kenneth with her to get Victoria. When Kenneth went back to his room to get a jacket, he looked into Victoria's room and found her nude, bloody body under some boxes and blankets on the floor. The last person to see Victoria was a classmate, who had left her in front of the Hammond house at about 3:45 p.m.

[Several witnesses testified that the defendant did not appear intoxicated that night. But Mrs. Hammond testified that he had been drinking when she returned home both times; the officers who talked to defendant smelled alcohol on his breath; a blood test taken at 7:45 p.m. indicated that defendant's blood alcohol content was higher than that necessary to classify an automobile driver as "under the influence."

[Officers found the shades down on all the windows and the doors locked when they came to arrest the defendant, who finally opened the door for them. They also found the defendant's blood-spotted clothing and a knife. Additional evidence included Victoria's bloodstained clothes, which were found throughout the house, and blood in almost every room except the kitchen, which appeared to have been mopped. Over 60 wounds, extending over Victoria's entire body, were found. Several of the wounds were post mortem.]

We must, in the absence of substantial evidence to support the verdict of first degree murder, reduce the conviction to second degree murder. . . .

Recognizing the need to clarify the difference between the two degrees of murder and the bases upon which a reviewing court may find that the evidence is sufficient to support a verdict of first degree murder, we set forth standards, derived from the nature of premeditation and deliberation as employed by the Legislature and interpreted by this court, for the kind of evidence which is sufficient to sustain a finding of premeditation and deliberation. . . .

As we noted in People v. Bender, 27 Cal. 2d 164, 183, we find no indication that the Legislature intended to give the words "deliberate" and "premeditated" other than their ordinary dictionary meanings. Moreover, we have repeatedly pointed out that the legislative classification of murder into two degrees would be meaningless if "deliberation" and "premeditation" were construed as requiring no more reflection than may be involved in the mere formation of a specific intent to kill. . . .

Thus we have held that in order for a killing with malice aforethought to be first rather than second degree murder, " '[t]he intent to kill must be . . . formed upon a *pre-existing* reflection,' [and have] been the subject of actual deliberation or *forethought....*" (People v. Thomas, 25 Cal. 2d at pp. 900-901.) (Italics added.) We have therefore held that "[a] verdict of murder in the first degree [on a theory of a wilful, deliberate, and premeditated killing] is proper only if the slayer killed 'as a result of careful thought and weighing of considerations; as a *deliberate* judgment or plan; carried on coolly and steadily, [especially] according to a *preconceived* design.'" . . . (People v. Caldwell, 43 Cal. 2d 864, at p. 869.)

The type of evidence which this court has found sufficient to sustain a finding of premeditation and deliberation falls into three basic categories: (1) facts about how and what defendant did *prior* to the actual killing which show that the defendant was engaged in activity directed toward, and explicable as intended to result in, the killing — what may be characterized as "planning" activity; (2) facts about the defendant's *prior* relationship and/or conduct with the victim from which the jury could reasonably infer a "motive" to kill the victim, which inference of motive, together with facts of type (1) or (3), would in turn support an inference that the killing was the result of "a pre-existing reflection" and "careful thought and weighing of considerations" rather than "mere unconsidered or rash impulse hastily executed" . . . ; (3) facts about the nature of the killing from which the jury could infer that the *manner* of killing was so particular and exacting that the defendant must have intentionally killed according to a "preconceived design" to take his victim's life in a particular way for a "reason" which the jury can reasonably infer from facts of type (1) or (2).

Analysis of the cases will show that this court sustains verdicts of first degree murder typically when there is evidence of all three types and otherwise requires at least extremely strong evidence of (1) or evidence of (2) in conjunction with either (1) or (3). . . .

In People v. Hillery, 62 Cal. 2d 692, the jury could reasonably infer that the defendant engaged in the following "extended course of conduct": defendant parked his car near the victim's (a 15-year-old girl's) house, entered the house surreptitiously, seized the victim while she was sewing and covered her head with a towel and slip to prevent outcry or identification, cut a length of cord in another room to secure her hands behind her, took the victim's scissors, dragged her to a nearby irrigation ditch where her body was subsequently found, engaged in a struggle with the victim, and then plunged the scissors directly into her chest.

Hillery represents a case of very strong type (1) evidence: the defendant's surreptitious conduct, subjection of his victim to his complete control, and carrying off of his victim to a place where others were unlikely to intrude, can be described as "planning" activity directly related to the killing. Moreover, there is also strong evidence of type (3): directly plunging a lethal weapon into the chest evidences a deliberate intention to kill as opposed to the type of "indiscriminate" multiple attack of both severe and superficial wounds which defendant engaged in in the instant case. . . .

In People v. Kemp (1961) 55 Cal. 2d 458, the defendant entered his victim's apartment through a window after removing the screen, found the victim alone in bed, tied stockings around her neck and hands, gagged her with a washcloth, and then raped and strangled her. In *Kemp,* as in *Hillery,* defendant's surreptitious coming upon the victim and calculated efforts to prevent her from identifying her assailant or crying out for help, together with the deliberate manner of killing — evidence of types (1) and (3) — point to a killing which is the result of "preconceived design" as opposed to "an explosion of violence." . . .

We conclude that a finding of premeditation and deliberation cannot be sustained in the absence of any evidence of (1) defendant's actions prior to the killing, (2) a "motive" or "reason" from which the jury could reasonably infer that defendant intended to kill Victoria, or (3) a manner of killing from which the jury could reasonably infer that the wounds were deliberately calculated to result in death.

[In an omitted portion of the opinion, the court concluded that the prosecution's alternative theory of first-degree murder — felony murder (killing during the perpetration of sexual assault) — could not stand because there was no specific evidence that the defendant intended to commit a sexual act prior to or during the lethal assault.[a]]

The judgment is modified by reducing the degree of the crime to murder of the second degree and, as so modified, is affirmed. . . .

NOTES

1. In People v. Daniels, 52 Cal. 3d 815, 802 P.2d 906, 933 (1991), the court held that the following language, from California Jury Instruction 8.20, provides the appropriate terms in which to explain premeditation and deliberation to the jury:

> The word "deliberate" means formed or arrived at or determined upon as a result of careful thought and weighing of considerations for and against the proposed course of action. The word "premeditated" means considered beforehand. . . .
>
> The true test is not the duration of time, but rather the extent of the reflection. A cold, calculated judgment and decision may be arrived at in a short period of time, but a mere unconsidered and rash impulse, even though it includes an intent to kill, is not such deliberation and premeditation as will fix an unlawful killing as murder of the first degree.
>
> To constitute a deliberate and premeditated killing, the slayer must weigh and consider the question of killing, and the reasons for and against such a choice, and, having in mind the consequences, he decides to and does kill.

2. How would Commonwealth v. Carrol be decided under the approach of People v. Anderson? Which approach is the better one?

3. Most of the recent decisions reject the view that "no time is too short" and instead interpret "premeditation" to require some degree of preexisting reflection. See, e.g., Mills v. United States, 599 A.2d 775 (D.C. App. 1991); Key v. People, 715 P.2d 319 (Colo. 1986). In Bouwkamp v. State, 833 P.2d 486, 494-495 (Wyo. 1992), the court explicitly adopted the three *Anderson* tests as the proper framework for evaluating evidence of premeditation.

In California, however, the courts appear to have softened the strict *Anderson*

---

a. Felony murder is considered in this chapter, Section C2 infra. — EDS.

tests to some extent. In People v. Perez, 2 Cal. 4th 1117, 831 P.2d 1159 (1992), the victim was found in her home, dead from loss of blood due to multiple stab wounds to her head, face, neck, back, and arms. None of the wounds was to a vital organ. Two different knives had been used to inflict the wounds, and one of them was found broken, lying under the victim's body. She was fully clothed and did not appear to have been sexually assaulted. Her purse was found on a table, and nothing of value was missing from the house. The state's theory was that defendant, who had known the victim in high school, entered the house with the intent to assault or rob the victim and then killed her when he realized that she could identify him. The California Supreme Court upheld defendant's conviction of first-degree murder. The court first stated (id. at 1163) that "[t]he *Anderson* factors, while helpful for purposes of review, are not a sine qua non to finding first degree premeditated murder, nor are they exclusive." The court went on to hold, however, that all three of the *Anderson* tests had been met (id. at 1166): "Even if the initial knifing was spontaneous, defendant had time to reflect upon his actions when the knife broke. That he went searching for another knife [in the kitchen] is indicative of a reasoned decision to kill."

4. In jurisdictions that require proof of some degree of prior deliberation, what kinds of evidence should be sufficient to support a first-degree murder conviction? Consider the following situations.

(a) In State v. Bingham, 105 Wash. 2d 820, 719 P.2d 109 (1986), defendant had lured a woman to a secluded spot and strangled her. To establish premeditation, the prosecution presented an expert who testified that to cause death by strangulation, the victim's assailant "would have had to maintain substantial and continuous pressure on her windpipe for 3-5 minutes." A first-degree murder conviction was reversed. The court reasoned (719 P.2d at 113-114) that "[h]olding a hand over someone's mouth or windpipe does not necessarily reflect a decision to kill the person, but possibly only to quiet him or her." The court added:

> [T]o allow a finding of premeditation only because the act takes an appreciable amount of time obliterates the distinction between first and second degree murder. Having the opportunity to deliberate is not evidence the defendant did deliberate, which is necessary for a finding of premeditation. Otherwise any form of killing which took more than a moment could result in a finding of premeditation, without some additional evidence showing reflection. . . . As was recognized in *Austin v. United States,* 382 F.2d 129, 138-39 (D.C. Cir. 1967):
>
>> The facts of a savage murder generate a powerful drive, almost a juggernaut for jurors, and indeed for judges, to crush the crime with the utmost condemnation available, to seize whatever words or terms reflect maximum denunciation, to cry out murder "in the first degree." But it is the task and conscience of a judge to transcend emotional momentum with reflective analysis. The judge is aware that many murders most brutish and bestial are committed in a consuming frenzy or heat of passion, and that these are in law only murder in the second degree. The [State's] evidence suffice[s] to establish an intentional and horrible murder — the kind that could be committed in a frenzy or heat of passion. . . .
>
> Exercising our responsibility, we find manual strangulation alone is insufficient evidence to support a finding of premeditation.

(b) Where death is brought about by repeated shots or blows, courts have sometimes held that the time necessary to effect the killing supports an inference of premeditation. E.g., State v. La Chance, 524 S.W.2d 933 (Tenn. 1975) (parent killed young child by extended period of severe abuse). But in State v. Brown, 836 S.W.2d 530 (Tenn. 1992), another case of repeated and shockingly brutal child abuse, the court overruled *La Chance* and reversed the father's conviction of first-degree murder. The evidence, said the court, showed either that the father intended to abuse rather than kill his son, or showed that his intent, if it was to kill the child, developed during a heated rage while disciplining the child. Neither hypothesis would support a finding of premeditation. The court concluded (836 S.W.2d at 544), "[W]e do not condone the homicide in this case, or the sustained abuse of the defenseless victim, Eddie Brown. We simply hold that in order to sustain the defendant's conviction, the proof must conform to the statute."

(c) In State v. Ollens, 107 Wash. 848, 733 P.2d 984 (1987), defendant robbed and then stabbed a cab driver. The victim died from multiple knife wounds and resulting loss of blood. The forensic evidence indicated that defendant had stabbed the victim numerous times and then, while the victim continued to struggle, slashed his neck, nearly severing the jugular vein. The court held that this evidence was sufficient to support an indictment for first-degree murder, reasoning (733 P.2d at 987) that the "subsequent slashing is an indication that [defendant] did premeditate on his already formed intent to kill." Is the result consistent with *Bingham* (Note 4(a) supra) and *Brown* (Note 4(b), supra)?

5. Should premeditation be not only a quantitative concept (requiring a significant period of deliberation) but also a qualitative concept (requiring a significant mental capacity to deliberate)? A number of jurisdictions permit evidence of mental impairment to rebut an inference of premeditation. Some even allow evidence that the defendant was heavily intoxicated to negate premeditation and deliberation. See, e.g., State v. Mash, 372 S.E.2d 532 (N.C. 1988). The problems of intoxication and diminished mental capacity are explored at pages 913-929 and 999-1008, infra.

6. In State v. Forrest, 321 N.C. 186, 362 S.E.2d 252 (N.C. 1987), the defendant took a pistol with him on a visit to his hospitalized, terminally ill father and, sobbing with emotion, killed his father with a single shot to the head. He was convicted of first-degree murder and sentenced to life imprisonment. The North Carolina Supreme Court upheld the conviction. Wouldn't this killing be classified as first-degree murder in California as well? If so, is premeditation the right criterion for identifying an aggravated murder? Consider Samuel H. Pillsbury, Evil and the Law of Murder, 24 U.C. Davis L. Rev. 437, 455, 459 (1990):

> [T]he [*Anderson*] court took seriously the notion that premeditation requires cool calculation and a carefully reflected-upon decision to kill. The *Anderson* decision was, and remains, controversial because although proof of premeditation was lacking, proof of aggravating circumstances was considerable. The case involved the slaughter of a child by an adult under circumstances which strongly suggested a sexual motivation, a crime that ranks high on an intuitive scale of homicide offenses. . . . [Our ordinary] language of malevolence . . . speaks to important differences in why the offender acted as he did. If we were to speak only in terms of "malice" [in its non-technical sense], . . . we would see a distinction between the killer-rapist and the mercy-killer which traditional mental state analysis ignores.

7. Following the lead of the Model Penal Code, some states have rejected premeditation and deliberation as the basis for identifying murders that deserve the greatest punishment. See, e.g., the New York provisions, page 392 supra. The rationale of this approach is set out in Model Penal Code and Commentaries, Comment to §210.6, at 127-128 (1980):

> [T]his distinction . . . probably rests on the premise that there exists some dependable relation between the duration of reflection and the gravity of the offense. Crudely put, the judgment is that the person who plans ahead is worse than the person who kills on sudden impulse. This generalization does not, however, survive analysis. . . .
>
> [T]he case for a mitigated sentence on conviction of murder does not depend on a distinction between impulse and deliberation. Prior reflection may reveal the uncertainties of a tortured conscience rather than exceptional depravity. The very fact of a long internal struggle may be evidence that the homicidal impulse was deeply aberrational and far more the product of extraordinary circumstances than a true reflection of the actor's normal character. Thus, for example, one suspects that most mercy killings are the consequence of long and careful deliberation, but they are not especially appropriate cases for imposition of capital punishment. The same is likely to be true with respect to suicide pacts, many infanticides, and cases where a provocation gains in its explosive power as the actor broods about his injury.
>
> It also seems clear, moreover, that some purely impulsive murders will present no extenuating circumstances. The suddenness of the killing may simply reveal callousness so complete and depravity so extreme that no hesitation is required.
>
> [T]he argument was advanced by the Home Office in testimony submitted to the Royal Commission on Capital Punishment:
>
> > Among the worst murders are some which are not premeditated, such as murders committed in connection with rape, or murders committed by criminals who are interrupted in some felonious enterprise and use violence without premeditation, but with a reckless disregard of the consequences to human life. . . . There are also many murders where the killing is clearly intentional, unlawful and unaccompanied by any mitigating circumstances, but where there is no evidence to show whether there was or was not premeditation.

In short, the notion that prior reflection should distinguish capital from noncapital murder is fundamentally unsound.

2. *Provocation*

STATE v. THORNTON

Supreme Court of Tennessee
730 S.W.2d 309 (1987)

HARBISON, J. Appellant was convicted of murder in the first degree as a result of shooting his wife's paramour in the home of appellant and his wife on May 3, 1983. Appellant found his wife and the victim, Mark McConkey, engaged in sexual relations in the front bedroom of appellant's home. He fired a single shot which struck McConkey in the left hip. The victim died sixteen days later as a result of a massive infection resulting from the bullet wound. . . .

Appellant and his wife had been married just under four years, and their three-year-old son was in the home in an upstairs bedroom when the shooting occurred in a downstairs bedroom. Appellant and his wife had been separated for about six weeks, but no divorce action had been filed and appellant had been making a serious effort toward reconciliation with his wife. . . . Appellant . . . was thirty-one years of age at the time of the trial of this case. . . . His wife . . . was twenty-seven. . . . Appellant was a second-year law student at Memphis State University. . . . The victim . . . was twenty-five years of age, single, and a third-year student at the University of Tennessee Medical School in Memphis.

[A]ppellant had never met McConkey and did not even know his name. Mrs. Thornton had met him four days before the homicide and had engaged in sexual relations with him in the home belonging to her and appellant every night since that time, including the night of the homicide. She testified that she thought that when she told her husband that she might want to "date" someone else, that this, in modern society, indicated that she intended to have sexual relations. In that manner she sought to mitigate her infidelity and misconduct toward a husband who had never been unfaithful to her insofar as disclosed by the record.

The marriage of the parties was in some difficulty, apparently as a result of dissatisfaction of Mrs. Thornton. She had advised her husband in March 1983 that she wanted to be separated from him for a time, and he had voluntarily taken an apartment about two miles away from their home. He visited the home almost daily, however, and there has been no suggestion that he was ever guilty of violence, physical misconduct or mistreatment toward his wife or son. He was particularly devoted to the child, and frequently kept the child with him at his apartment on weekends or in the evenings.

Appellant . . . was slightly built, being only five feet six inches in height and weighing about 125 to 130 pounds. McConkey was an athlete, a former basketball and football player in high school. He was five feet nine inches in height and weighed about 182 pounds. . . .

Appellant, according to uncontradicted testimony, was deeply disturbed over the separation of the parties. He had sought assistance from a marriage counselor, and had persuaded his wife to go with him to the marriage counselor on several occasions. . . . Appellant testified that the parties had agreed to a separation of six months, and both he and the marriage counselor testified that the parties had agreed that they would not have sexual relations with each other or with anyone else during that period. Mrs. Thornton denied making that agreement. . . .

On the evening of May 3, appellant picked [Mrs. Thornton] and their child up at their home, and the three went to dinner. Again on that occasion Mrs. Thornton reiterated that she thought that the marriage was over, and on this occasion she told appellant that she planned to date someone else whom she had met. . . .

He returned his wife and child to their home at about 7:30 P.M. and then went to his apartment to study for a final examination in the law school. He called two close friends of the parties, however, and discussed his marital situation with them. . . . One of them advised him that his wife apparently did not believe his feelings about a reconciliation were sincere.

Acting on that suggestion, appellant returned to the home of the parties in his automobile, stating that he wanted to try once more to convince his wife that he was indeed sincere. When he arrived at the home he saw an automobile parked in the driveway. He did not recognize the car as being one belonging to any of his wife's friends. Accordingly he parked around the corner and walked back to the house. Observing from the rear of the house, he saw his wife and McConkey in the kitchen with the child. He observed as Mrs. Thornton washed some laundry for McConkey and as they were eating dinner. Thereafter they sat and read. They drank wine and smoked some marijuana, and appellant saw them kissing.

He decided to go home to get his camera, but before doing so he let the air out of one of the tires on McConkey's car. He went to his apartment, and obtained his camera and an old pistol which had belonged to his father. . . . He testified that he intended to take pictures for the purpose of showing them to the marriage counselor on the next day and possibly also for use in evidence if divorce proceedings did ensue.

Appellant spent more than an hour in the backyard of his home observing his wife and McConkey in the den and kitchen. Thereafter they left the den area, but appellant remained behind the house, thinking that McConkey was about to leave. When he went around the house, however, he found that McConkey's car was still in the driveway and saw the drapes in the front guest bedroom downstairs had been closed. He listened near the window and heard unmistakable sounds of sexual intercourse. He then burst through the front door and into the bedroom where he found the nude couple and attempted to take some pictures. At that point he testified that he thought McConkey was attempting to attack him. In all events he drew his pistol and fired a single shot, striking McConkey in the left hip. Appellant . . . assisted in giving directions to enable an ambulance to bring aid to McConkey, and he remained at the house until the police arrived.

Appellant testified that he simply lost control and "exploded" when he found his wife in bed with the victim. He testified that he had armed himself because McConkey was much larger than he, and he felt that he needed protection if there was trouble when he returned to the residence with the camera.

Appellant testified that he did not intend to kill McConkey, but simply to shoot him in order to disable him and also because of his outrage at the situation which he had found. The single shot was not aimed at a vital organ, but the victim ultimately died because of the spread of a massive infection from the wound. . . .

[I]t has long been a well-settled legal principle that the commission of unlawful sexual intercourse with a female relative is an act obviously calculated to arouse ungovernable passion, and that the killing of the seducer or adulterer under the influence or in the heat of that passion constitutes voluntary manslaughter, and not murder, in the absence of evidence of actual malice.[1] . . .

Appellant actually discovered his wife *in flagrante delicto* with a man who was a total stranger to him, and at a time when appellant was trying to save his marriage and was deeply concerned about both his wife and his young child. He did not fire a shot or in any way harm the victim until he actually discovered the victim and his wife engaged in sexual intercourse in appellant's own home. In

---

1. "Manslaughter is the unlawful killing of another without malice, either express or implied, which may be either voluntary upon a sudden heat, or involuntary, but in the commission of some unlawful act." T.C.A. §39-2-221.

our opinion the passions of any reasonable person would have been inflamed and intensely aroused by this sort of discovery, given the factual background of this case. . . . [T]his was a classic case of voluntary manslaughter and no more. . . .

The conviction of murder in the first degree is set aside, and the cause will be remanded to the trial court for sentencing of the defendant for voluntary manslaughter. . . .

[One judge concurred in the reversal of the first-degree murder conviction but argued that "[m]alice is evident on the facts of this case," and that the killing therefore constituted second-degree murder rather than manslaughter.]

NOTES ON THE RATIONALE OF THE PROVOCATION DEFENSE

According to what theory of punishment does it make sense to reduce the penalty for the defendant who kills in response to provocation? Would it make more sense to *increase* the punishment as the temptation to kill increases? Consider the following comments.

1. Stephen J. Morse, Undiminished Confusion in Diminished Capacity, 75 J.Crim.L. & Criminology 1, 33-34 (1984): I would abolish [the provocation defense] and convict all intentional killers of murder. Reasonable people do not kill no matter how much they are provoked, and even enraged people generally retain the capacity to control homicidal or any other kind of aggressive or antisocial desires. We cheapen both life and our conception of responsibility by maintaining the provocation/passion mitigation. This may seem harsh and contrary to the supposedly humanitarian reforms of the evolving criminal law. But this . . . interpretation of criminal law history is morally mistaken. It is humanitarian only if one focuses sympathetically on perpetrators and not on their victims, and views the former as mostly helpless objects of their overwhelming emotions and irrationality. This sympathy is misplaced, however, and is disrespectful to the perpetrator. As virtually every human being knows because we all have been enraged, it is easy not to kill, even when one is enraged.

2. Glanville Williams, Provocation and the Reasonable Man. [1954] Crim. L. Rev. 740, 741-742, 751-752: The reason why provoked homicide is punished is to deter people from committing the offence; and it is curious confession of failure on the part of the law to suppose that, notwithstanding the possibility of heavy punishment, an ordinary person will commit it. If the assertion were correct, it would raise serious doubts whether the offence should continue to be punished.

Surely the true view of provocation is that it is a concession to "the frailty of human nature" in those exceptional cases where the legal prohibition fails of effect. It is a compromise, neither conceding the propriety of the act nor exacting the full penalty for it.

3. Maher v. People, 10 Mich. 212, 81 Am. Dec. 781 (1862): [W]ithin the principle of all the recognized definitions [of murder], the homicide must, in all ordinary cases, have been committed with some degree of coolness and deliberation, or, at least, under circumstances in which ordinary men . . . would not be liable to have their reason clouded or obscured by passion; and the act must be prompted by, or the circumstances indicate that it sprung from, a wicked, depraved or malignant mind — a mind which, even in its habitual condition, and when excited by no provocation which would be liable to give undue control to passion in ordinary men, is cruel, wanton or malignant, reckless of human life, or regardless of social duty.

But if the act of killing, though intentional, be committed under the influence of passion or in heat of blood, produced by an adequate or reasonable provocation, and before a reasonable time has elapsed for the blood to cool and reason to resume its habitual control, . . . then the law, out of indulgence to the frailty of human nature, or rather, in recognition of the laws upon which human nature is constituted, very properly regards the offense as of a less heinous character than murder, and gives it the designation of manslaughter.

To what extent the passions must be aroused and the dominion of reason disturbed to reduce the offense from murder to manslaughter, the cases are by no means agreed. . . .

The principle involved . . . would seem to suggest[,] as the true general rule, that reason should, at the time of the act, be disturbed or obscured by passion to an extent which *might render* ordinary men, of fair average disposition, *liable* to act rashly or without due deliberation or reflection, and from passion, rather than judgment. . . .

[What is required is] not such a provocation as must, by the laws of the human mind, produce such an effect with the *certainty that physical effects follow from physical causes;* for then the individual could hardly be held morally accountable. Nor, on the other hand, must the provocation, in every case, be held sufficient or reasonable, because such a state of excitement has followed from it; for then, by habitual and long continued indulgence of evil passions, a bad man might acquire a claim to mitigation which would not be available to better men, and on account of that very wickedness of heart which, in itself, constitutes an aggravation both in morals and in law.

4. United States v. Roston, 986 F.2d 1287, 1294 (9th Cir. 1993) (Boochever, J., concurring): [T]he standard adopted by our circuit for provocation justifying a voluntary manslaughter instruction is impossibly high. [Our cases require] that the provocation must be such as would "arouse a reasonable and ordinary person to kill someone." I cannot envision such a provocation that would not constitute justification for the crime. "[A] reasonable person does not kill even when provoked. . . ." *Model Penal Code* §210.3 cmt. 5(a), at 56 (1980).

The Model Criminal Jury Instructions for the Ninth Circuit set forth what appears to me to be a more appropriate standard: "Provocation, in order to be adequate, must be such as might naturally cause a reasonable person in the passion of the moment to lose self-control and act on impulse and without reflection." 9th Cir. Crim. Jury Instr. 8.24C (1992). This standard does not imply that reasonable people kill, but rather focuses on the degree of passion sufficient to reduce the actor's ability to control his actions.

5. Provocation as a partial justification? In contrast to the preceding excerpts, which explain the provocation defense as a concession to the "frailty of human nature," some commentators argue that the provocation defense is designed for cases in which the act of killing is partially *justified*. Consider A. J. Ashworth, The Doctrine of Provocation, 35 Camb. L.J. 292, 307-308 (1976):

> [T]he doctrine of provocation as a qualified defence rests just as much on notions of justification as upon the excusing element of loss of self-control. The term "partial justification" will be used for this, but the term does not necessarily imply a connection with the legal concept of justifiable force (*i.e.*, in self-defence): its closest relationship is with the moral notion that the punishment of wrongdoers is justifiable. This is not to argue that it is ever morally right to kill a person who does wrong. Rather, the claim implicit in partial justification is that an individual is *to some extent* morally justified in making a punitive return against someone who intentionally causes him serious offence, and that this serves to differentiate someone who is provoked to lose his self-control and kill from the unprovoked killer. Whereas the paradigmatic case of murder might be an attack on an innocent victim, the paradigm of provocation generally involves moral wrongs by both parties. . . . Ordinary language reflects this approach, with characteristic phrases such as "he brought it on himself," "she asked for it" and "it served him right." Now the court which tries the accused's case is not standing in judgment upon the victim. But [t]he complicity of the victim cannot and should not be ignored, for the blameworthiness of his conduct has a strong bearing on the court's judgment of the seriousness of the provocation and the reasonableness of the accused's failure to control himself.

Compare Joshua Dressler, Rethinking Heat of Passion: A Defense in Search of a Rationale, 73 J. Crim. L. & Criminology 421, 456-458 (1982):

> [T]he theory of comparative moral wrongdoing seems to neatly prove that the provocation defense is a justification. . . . Victim is neither a "good guy," deserving of our full protection, nor a "bad guy," meriting the law's total disinterest. From a moral perspective, the killing involves a gray situation, so the punishment is muted. . . . Nonetheless, a substantial moral problem exists with this approach. It is morally questionable to suggest that there is less societal harm in Victim's death merely because he acted immorally. One must remember that Victim's immoral conduct in no way jeopardized the life of the defendant or anyone else. [H]is immoral conduct should not make his life less deserving of protection by society. . . .
>
> It is here that one must carefully separate justification from excuse. [I]f heat of passion is a partial justification, the injustice, not the passion, is the primary focus. . . . Such a position . . . runs counter to the high value we place on life, as developed in self-defense theory, wherein we only justify killing of deadly aggressors when it is necessary to do so to protect the lives of innocent persons. Similarly, the intentional killing of a misdemeanant in order to prevent his flight, or in order to recapture him, is ordinarily a murder. The misdemeanant's wrongdoing does not even partially justify a homicide. . . . Under a justificatory theory, it is not the defendant's mental state but Victim's conduct, which primarily explains the rule. To be consistent, passion should not be required. . . .
>
> Such a justification rule would also have anomalous results in many cases. For example, suppose Actor walks in and finds his wife in bed with Victim, under circumstances in which it is unclear to the observer whether the intercourse is consensual or not. Actor kills Victim. As a matter of excuse, it may be easy to partially excuse Defendant in either case. But if the issue is Victim's moral right to life, the proper answer might depend on whether Victim's conduct in fact constituted rape, adultery or fornication, and perhaps on whether Victim was, or should have been,

aware of the woman's marital status. It is not plausible to speak of the heat of passion doctrine, at least as we now know it, as being affected by these subtleties.

a. The Nature of the Required Provocation

(i) The Traditional Common Law Limits

GIROUARD v. STATE

Court of Appeals of Maryland
321 Md. 532, 583 A.2d 718 (1991)

COLE, J. In this case we are asked to reconsider whether the types of provocation sufficient to mitigate the crime of murder to manslaughter should be limited to the categories we have heretofore recognized, or whether the sufficiency of the provocation should be decided by the factfinder on a case-by-case basis. . . .

[Defendant Steven Girouard and his wife Joyce had a highly strained marital relationship. One night during an angry argument, Joyce graphically disparaged his sexual ability, said she did not love him, and demanded a divorce. She also said that she had filed charges against him in the Judge Advocate General's Office (both Steven and Joyce were in the Army) and that he would probably be court-martialed. Steven responded by lunging at her with a kitchen knife and stabbing her 19 times. Then, feeling that he wanted to die, he slit his own wrists,] but when he realized that he would not die from his self-inflicted wounds, he . . . called the police, telling the dispatcher that he had just murdered his wife.

When the police arrived they found Steven wandering around outside his apartment building. Steven was despondent and tearful and seemed detached, according to police officers who had been at the scene. He was unconcerned about his own wounds, talking only about how much he loved his wife and how he could not believe what he had done. . . .

Steven Girouard was convicted . . . of second degree murder and was sentenced to 22 years incarceration, 10 of which were suspended. . . .

Petitioner relies primarily on out of state cases to provide support for his argument that the provocation to mitigate murder to manslaughter should not be limited only to the traditional circumstances of: extreme assault or battery upon the defendant; mutual combat; defendant's illegal arrest; injury or serious abuse of a close relative of the defendant's; or the sudden discovery of a spouse's adultery. Petitioner argues that manslaughter is a catchall for homicides which are criminal but that lack the malice essential for a conviction of murder. . . .

Although there are few Maryland cases discussing the issue at bar, those that do hold that words alone are not adequate provocation. . . . Other jurisdictions overwhelmingly agree with our cases. . . . Perkins on Criminal Law, at p. 62, states that it is "with remarkable uniformity that even words generally regarded as 'fighting words' in the community have no recognition as adequate provocation in the eyes of the law." . . .

Thus, with no reservation, we hold that the provocation in this case was not enough to cause a reasonable man to stab his provoker 19 times. . . . "[T]here must be not simply provocation in psychological fact, but one of certain fairly well-defined classes of provocation recognized as being adequate as a matter of law." Tripp v. State, 36 Md. App. at 473, 374 A.2d 384. . . . We cannot in good conscience countenance holding that a verbal domestic argument ending in the death of one spouse can result in a conviction of manslaughter. We agree with the trial judge that social necessity dictates our holding. Domestic arguments easily escalate into furious fights. We perceive no reason for a holding in favor of those who find the easiest way to end a domestic dispute is by killing the offending spouse. . . .

STATE v. SHANE, 63 Ohio St. 3d 630, 590 N.E.2d 272 (1992): [Shane and his fiancée Tina Wagner shared an apartment, together with their infant child. Shane killed Wagner after a bitter argument in which Wagner confirmed that she had been involved with other men and admitted her sexual infidelity. A jury convicted Shane of murder. The question before the court was whether voluntary manslaughter instructions were required under these circumstances.]

[The] rule that mere words cannot be sufficient provocation . . . usually applies even if the spoken words have the effect of informing the defendant of some provocative event that has taken place. It appears, however, that courts are generally more inclined to give a manslaughter instruction when the alleged provocation is a victim-spouse's confession of adultery. This adultery exception has been totally rejected by some courts, unless the situation is where the spouse discovers the other spouse in the act of adultery itself, or immediately thereafter. . . .

While the "mere words" rule is attractive — it has the advantage of offering a bright line test which eliminates an entire class of cases — the rule has been criticized as imposing an "unnecessary limitation on the use of voluntary manslaughter as a mitigating defense." Romero, Sufficiency of Provocation for Voluntary Manslaughter in New Mexico: Problems in Theory and Practice (1982), 12 New Mex. L. Rev. 747, 776. It is argued that such a rule ignores the fact that sometimes words may be even more inflammatory than aggressive actions, and that the rule keeps from the jury some situations that should qualify for a manslaughter instruction. Nevertheless, we do not believe that words alone are generally as inflammatory as aggressive actions. . . .

We disapprove of a rule which does not allow "mere words" to be sufficient provocation to reduce murder to manslaughter generally, but which makes a specific exception when the provocation consists of mere words by one spouse informing the other spouse of infidelity. This exception to the general rule has its foundation in the ancient common-law concept that the wife is the property of the husband. See Regina v. Mawgridge (1707), 84 Eng. Rep. 1107, 1115: "[W]hen a man is taken in adultery with another man's wife, if the husband shall stab the adulterer, or knock out his brains, that is bare manslaughter: for jealousy is the rage of a man, and adultery is the highest invasion of property. . . ." This archaic rule has no place in modern society. Words informing another of infidelity should not be given special treatment by courts trying to determine what provocation is reasonably sufficient provocation. The killing of a spouse (usually a wife) by a spouse (usually a husband) who has just been made aware of the victim spouse's adultery simply is not an acceptable response to the confession of infidelity. See Comment, Provoked Reason in Men and Women: Heat-of-Passion Manslaughter and Imperfect Self-Defense (1986), 33 U.C.L.A.L. Rev. 1679, 1696-1697.

We hold that words alone will not constitute reasonably sufficient provocation to incite the use of deadly force in most situations. Rather, in each case, the trial judge must determine whether evidence of reasonably sufficient provocation occasioned by the victim has been presented to warrant a voluntary manslaughter instruction. The trial judge is required to decide this issue as a matter of law, in view of the specific facts of the individual case. . . .

In this case . . . [we] find that no reasonable jury could have found Shane not guilty of murder, but guilty of voluntary manslaughter. Accordingly, . . . defendant's murder conviction is affirmed.

NOTES

1. *The provoking circumstances. Girouard* and *Shane* reaffirm the long-standing common law rule that permits the jury to find adequate provocation only in a few narrowly defined circumstances. In State v. Starr, 38 Mo. 270, 277 (1886), the court said: "There must be an assault upon the person, as where the provocation was by pulling the nose, purposely jostling the slayer aside on the highway, or other direct actual battery." Most modern courts are only slightly more flexible. See People v. Chevalier, 131 Ill. 2d 66, 544 N.E.2d 942, 944 (1989):

> The only categories of serious provocation which have been recognized are "substantial physical injury or assault, mutual quarrel or combat, illegal arrest, and adultery with the offender's spouse; but not mere words or gestures or trespass to property." The rule that mere words are insufficient provocation applies no matter how aggravated, abusive, opprobrious or indecent the language. A verbal communication that adultery has occurred or will occur falls within the rule that mere words are insufficient provocation.

2. *Sexual infidelity as provocation.* (a) What conception of provocation has led courts to place an act of adultery in the same category as a physical assault? Is the idea that killing is partially justified because adultery, like battery, is (or was) a crime? Is the idea that adultery (but only adultery) is as upsetting as being physically attacked? Or is the idea that an act of adultery is itself a kind of attack on the person (or the masculinity) of the husband?[1] For discussion of the cultural presuppositions of voluntary manslaughter doctrine, see Donna K. Coker, Heat of Passion and Wife Killing: Men Who Batter/Men Who Kill, 2 So. Cal. Rev. L. & Women's Stud. 71 (1992).

Note that women seldom kill their unfaithful male partners. Should this fact have a bearing on the reasonableness of a husband's lethal response to unfaithfulness by his wife? Consider Jeremy Horder, Provocation and Responsibility 193-194 (1992):

---

1. Consider the statement of an English court: "[T]o taunt a man about his lack of sexual inclination or prowess does involve striking at his character and personality at its most vulnerable." Regina v. Mellentin, [1985] 7 Cr. App. Rep. 9, 10.

The use of the provocation defence is dominated by men, for whom the use of violence [to secure] a woman's 'unconditional, unjudgmental attentive acceptance' is all too commonly regarded as natural or understandable — perhaps even appropriate. It is thus largely from a male-centered perspective that the reduction of an intentional killing from murder to manslaughter is capable of being regarded as a compassion to human infirmity. From a feminist perspective the existence of such mitigation simply reinforces in the law that which public institutions ought in fact to be seeking to eradicate, namely, the acceptance that there is something natural, inevitable, and hence in some (legal) sense . . . forgivable about men's violence against women, and their violence in general.

Questions: If Horder's point is valid, what are its implications? Should the provocation defense be abolished entirely? If not, should the courts hold as a matter of law that adultery can never constitute sufficient provocation? Does Horder mean that suddenly discovering a spouse in bed with another person simply would not cause a reasonable, ordinary law-abiding person to lose self-control, or does Horder mean that such a person should be denied mitigation even though the loss of self-control is, in our present culture, understandable for the reasonable person?

(b) Courts interpret the boundaries of the infidelity category very narrowly. In Commonwealth v. McGuirk, 376 Mass. 338, 380 N.E.2d 662 (1978), the court held that no manslaughter instructions were required where the defendant claimed that a jealous rage was triggered by discovering his girlfriend engaged in sexual acts with another man. People v. McDonald, 63 Ill. App. 2d 475, 212 N.E.2d 299 (1965), reached the same result where the defendant and his girlfriend had lived together for 25 years.

3. *Other provocative acts.* (a) It is rare for a man or woman to respond with lethal force when "propositioned" by a member of the opposite sex. In contrast, provocation defenses have been permitted in a number of recent cases in which a defendant killed in response to an unwelcome homosexual advance. See Robert B. Mison, Comment, Homophobia in Manslaughter: The Homosexual Advance as Insufficient Provocation, 80 Cal. L. Rev. 133, 133-136, 167-170 (1992).

Question: Why should a proposal to engage in consensual sexual activity, whether from a member of the same or the opposite sex, ever be sufficient provocation to reduce an intentional killing from murder to manslaughter?

(b) Although domestic tension and sexual jealousy are prominent themes in provoked killings, by no means all "crimes of passion" arise in that context. Consider State v. Madden, 61 N.J. 377, 294 A.2d 609 (1972): During a period of serious racial disturbances, a police officer attempted to arrest a young suspect who had allegedly assaulted some boys with a hammer. When the officer shot and wounded the suspect, a mob indignantly attacked the officer and inflicted a fatal beating. Two members of the mob were convicted of murder. The court held that racial antagonism could not constitute provocation sufficient to require a manslaughter instruction, in the absence of some specific, legitimately provoking act by the officer. The court also held that neither an unlawful arrest nor the use of excessive force could constitute sufficient provocation with respect to bystanders who were not related to the suspect.

4. *Cooling time.* The common law view is that too long a lapse of time between the provocation and the act of killing will render the provocation inadequate "as a matter of law" and therefore deprive the defendant of the right to an

instruction on voluntary manslaughter. For example, in United States v. Bordeaux, 980 F.2d 534 (8th Cir. 1992), defendant was told, during the course of an all-day drinking party, that Shelby White Bear, also at the party, had raped defendant's mother 20 years earlier. Later, about mid-day, defendant's mother confirmed the report. Sometime during the early evening, defendant and some friends severely beat White Bear and left him lying in a bedroom. Defendant returned to the bedroom shortly afterward, saw White Bear lying on the floor bleeding, and slashed his throat. He then told a friend that he had killed White Bear because of the rape and said he would do it again because "[h]e deserved it." The court of appeals upheld the trial judge's refusal to instruct the jury on voluntary manslaughter and affirmed the conviction of murder. The court said that evidence of a prior argument or continuing dispute was insufficient to warrant a voluntary manslaughter instruction in the absence of "some sort of instant incitement." Because the revelation of the rape had occurred much earlier in the day, and because the fatal act was committed "well after" the beating of White Bear had ended, the court found that there would be "no rational basis for the jury to find that Bordeaux killed White Bear in the heat of passion. . . ." See also Stahl v. State, 712 S.W.2d 783 (Tex. App. 1986) (after argument in which defendant's roommate slapped him across the face with a gun, defendant walked away but then, minutes later, he returned to their apartment and shot and killed the roommate; the court found adequate cooling time as a matter of law).

The harsh consequences of the cooling-time limitation could sometimes be avoided by arguing that an event immediately preceding the homicide had rekindled the earlier provocation. But many courts refused to take note of "rekindling." Consider, for example, State v. Gounagias, 88 Wash. 304, 153 P. 9 (1915). The deceased had committed an act of sodomy upon the defendant and then bragged to others about it. Those who heard of the episode repeatedly ridiculed the defendant, and after two weeks he finally lost control and killed the man who had assaulted him. The defendant argued that the cumulative effect of the taunts, reminding him of the previous provocation, led to a sudden heat of passion. But the court held that the legally sufficient provoking event had occurred two weeks before the killing and that the interval constituted adequate cooling time as a matter of law.

5. *Victims other than the provoker.* Should the provocation defense be available when the person killed was not the source of the provocation? The problem arises in several ways.

(a) Suppose that a provoker *P* assaults defendant *D* while *P*'s friend *F* looks on approvingly. *D*, enraged, pulls a gun and shoots both *P* and *F*. Is the provocation defense available in a prosecution for the murder of *F*, whose actions presumably would not, by themselves, constitute sufficient provocation?

(b) In State v. Mauricio, 117 N.J. 402, 568 A.2d 879 (1990), a bouncer forcefully ejected the defendant from a bar; he slammed defendant against a wall, then kicked and pushed him down the stairs, causing the defendant to fall and hit his head sharply on the floor. Expecting the bar to close shortly (it was 2:30 A.M.), defendant waited outside for the bouncer to emerge. About five minutes later, a patron who had not been involved in the fight left the bar. Defendant mistook the patron for the bouncer, followed him, and shot him to death. The New Jersey Supreme Court reversed a murder conviction, holding that the trial judge

had erred in refusing to give voluntary manslaughter instructions. Several states would reach the same result by statute. See, e.g., Pa. Stat. §2503(a)(2), page 390 supra. Are these results sound if the provocation defense is designed to afford mitigation for partially *justified* killings? Or do these results suggest that provocation must be viewed as a partial *excuse*?

(c) Suppose that the person killed is not associated with the provoker and is not the accidental victim of rage directed against the provoker. Should a justifiably enraged defendant be able to claim mitigation to manslaughter when the person he intends to kill is an innocent bystander? In Rex v. Scriva, [1951] Vict. L. R. 298, a father observed an automobile driver knock down and severely injure his daughter. When the father, brandishing a knife, went after the driver, a bystander attempted to restrain him, and the father then fatally stabbed the bystander. In People v. Spurlin, 156 Cal. App. 3d 119, 202 Cal. Rptr. 663 (1984), the defendant killed his wife after an intense argument over their respective sexual escapades, and he then killed his sleeping nine-year-old son.

In cases like *Scriva* and *Spurlin,* are the assaults against the nonprovokers unreasonable as a matter of law? Or does the very fact that the defendant attacked an innocent party reinforce the claim of a total loss of control? In both of the above cases, the courts held that no provocation defense was available with respect to the charges of murdering the nonprovoking relatives or bystanders. On what principle can such results be justified? Compare R. S. O'Regan, Indirect Provocation and Misdirected Retaliation, [1968] Crim. L. Rev. 319, 323: "Once an accused loses his self-control it is unreal to insist that his retaliatory acts be directed only against his provoker. When his reason has been dethroned a man cannot be expected . . . 'to guide his anger with judgment.'"

6. *Defendants who elicit provocation.* In Regina v. Johnson, [1989] 2 All E.R. 839, the defendant had made threatening and insulting remarks to Roberts and his female friend. Roberts and the woman attacked defendant, poured beer over his head, and then pinned him to a wall and punched him. Defendant pulled out a knife and fatally stabbed Roberts. The trial judge refused to instruct the jury on provocation, ruling that "[i]t is rather difficult to see how a man who excites provocative conduct can in turn rely on it as provocation in the criminal law." The appellate court reversed, stating, "[W]e find it impossible to accept that the mere fact that a defendant caused a reaction in others, which in turn led him to lose his self-control, should result in the issue of provocation being kept outside a jury's consideration." Do you agree?

(ii) Departures from the Categorical Approach

MAHER v. PEOPLE

Supreme Court of Michigan
10 Mich. 212, 81 Am. Dec. 781 (1862)

CHRISTIANCY, J. The prisoner was charged with an assault with intent to kill and murder one Patrick Hunt. The evidence on the part of the prosecution was, that the prisoner entered the saloon of one Michael Foley, in the village of Houghton, where said Hunt was standing with several other persons; that prisoner entered through a back door and by a back way leading to it, in his shirt sleeves, in a state of great perspiration, and appearing to be excited; . . . that on entering the saloon, he immediately passed nearly through it to where said Hunt was standing . . . ; that as soon as the prisoner came up to where Hunt was standing, he fired a pistol at Hunt, the charge of which took effect upon the head of Hunt, in and through the left ear, causing a severe wound thereon; by reason of which Hunt in a few moments fell to the floor, was partially deprived of his sense of hearing in that ear, and received a severe shock to his system which caused him to be confined to his bed for about a week, under the care of a physician; that immediately after the firing of the pistol prisoner left the saloon, nothing being said by Hunt or the prisoner. It did not appear how, or with what, the pistol was loaded. The prisoner offered evidence tending to show an adulterous intercourse between his wife and Hunt on the morning of the assault, and within less than half an hour previous; that the prisoner saw them going into the woods together about half an hour before the assault; that on their way out of the woods the prisoner had followed them immediately (evidence having already been given that the prisoner had followed them to the woods); that, on their coming out of the woods, the prisoner followed them and went after said Hunt into the saloon, where, on his arrival, the assault was committed; that the prisoner on his way to the saloon, a few minutes before entering it, was met by a friend who informed him that Hunt and the prisoner's wife had had sexual intercourse the day before in the woods. This evidence was rejected by the court, and the prisoner excepted. Was the evidence properly rejected? This is the main question in the case, and its decision must depend upon the question whether the proposed evidence would have tended to reduce the killing — had death ensued — from murder to manslaughter, or rather, to have given it the character of manslaughter instead of murder? If the homicide — in case death had ensued — would have been but manslaughter, then defendant could not be guilty of the assault *with intent to murder,* but only of a simple assault and battery. The question therefore involves essentially the same principles as where evidence is offered for a similar purpose in a prosecution for murder. . . .

To the question, what shall be considered in law a reasonable or adequate provocation for such state of mind, so as to give to a homicide, committed under its influence, the character of manslaughter? On principle, the answer, as a general rule, must be, anything the natural tendency of which would be to produce such a state of mind in ordinary men, and which the jury are satisfied did produce it in the case before them. . . .

It is doubtless, in one sense, the province of the court to define what, in law, will constitute a reasonable or adequate provocation, but not, I think, in ordinary cases, to determine whether the provocation proved in the particular case is sufficient or reasonable. This is essentially a question of fact, and to be decided with reference to the peculiar facts of each particular case. . . . [J]urors from the mode of their selection, coming from the various classes and occupations of society, and conversant with the practical affairs of life, are, in my opinion, much better qualified to judge of the sufficiency and tendency of a given provocation and much more likely to fix, with some degree of accuracy, the standard of what constitutes the average of ordinary human nature, than the judge whose habits and course of life give him much less experience of the workings of passion in the actual conflicts of life.

The judge, it is true, must, to some extent, assume to decide upon the sufficiency of the alleged provocation, when the question arises upon the admission of testimony, and when it is so clear as to admit of no reasonable doubt upon any theory, that the alleged provocation could not have had any tendency to produce such state of mind, in ordinary men, he may properly exclude the evidence; but, if the alleged provocation be such as to admit of any reasonable doubt, whether it might not have had such tendency, it is much safer, I think, and more in accordance with principle, to let the evidence go to the jury under the proper instructions. . . . The law can not with justice assume by the light of past decision, to catalogue all the various facts and combinations of facts which shall be held to constitute reasonable or adequate provocation. Scarcely two past cases can be found which are identical in all their circumstances; and there is no reason to hope for greater uniformity in future. Provocations will be given without reference to any previous model, and the passions they excite will not consult the precedents.

The same principles which govern, as to the extent to which the passions must be excited and reason disturbed, apply with equal force . . . to the question of cooling time. This, like the provocation itself, must depend upon the nature of man and the laws of the human mind. . . . I am aware there are many cases in which it has been held a question of law, but I can see no principle on which such a rule can rest. The court should, I think, define to the jury the principles upon which the question is to be decided, and leave them to determine whether the time was reasonable under all the circumstances of the particular case. . . .

It remains only to apply these principles to the present case. The proposed evidence, in connection with what had already been given, would have tended strongly to show the commission of adultery by Hunt with the prisoner's wife, within half an hour before the assault. . . . I can not resist the conviction that this would have been sufficient evidence of provocation to go to the jury, and from which, when taken in connection with the excitement and "great perspiration" exhibited on entering the saloon, the hasty manner in which he approached and fired the pistol at Hunt, it would have been competent for the jury to find that the act was committed in consequence of the passion excited by the provocation, and in a state of mind which, within the principle already explained, would have given to the homicide had death ensued, the character of manslaughter only. . . .

The judgment should be reversed and a new trial granted.

MANNING, J. I differ from my brethren in this case. I think the evidence was properly excluded. To make that manslaughter which would otherwise be murder, the provocation — I am not speaking of its sufficiency, but of the provocation itself — must be given in the presence of the person committing the homicide. The cause of the provocation must occur in his presence. . . . Any other rule in an offense so grave as taking the life of a fellow-being, in the heat of passion, I fear would be more humane to the perpetrator than wise in its effects on society. More especially since the abolition of the death penalty for murder, and the division of the crime into murder in the first and second degree there is not now the same reason, namely, the severity of the punishment, for relaxing the rules of law in favor of a party committing homicide as before. It would, it seem to me, be extremely mischievous to let passion engendered by suspicion, or by something one has heard, enter into and determine the nature of a crime committed while under its influence. The innocent as well as the guilty, or those who had not as well as those who had given provocation, might be the sufferers. If it be said that in such cases the giving of the provocation must be proved or it would go for nothing; the answer is, that the law will not, and should not permit the lives of the innocent to be exposed with the guilty in this way, as it would do did it not require the cause of the provocation to occur in the presence of the person committing the homicide.

NOTES

1. Provoking circumstances. Several common law jurisdictions have followed *Maher* in permitting the jury to consider the manslaughter issue whenever the evidence shows *any* circumstances (whether involving conduct or words alone) that might cause a reasonable person to lose self-control. See, e.g., Commonwealth v. Berry, 461 Pa. 233, 336 A.2d 262 (1975); People v. Valentine, 28 Cal. 2d 121, 169 P.2d 1, 11-15 (1946). In England, a House of Lords decision that words alone can never constitute adequate provocation, Holmes v. D.P.P., [1946] A.C. 588, was overruled by statute. The English Homicide Act of 1957, §3, specifies:

> Where on a charge of murder there is evidence on which the jury can find that the person charged was provoked (whether by things done or by things said or by both together) to lose his self-control, the question whether the provocation was enough to make a reasonable man do as he did shall be left to be determined by the jury; and in determining that question the jury shall take into account everything both done and said according to the effect which, in their opinion, it would have on a reasonable man.

The flexible approach adopted in these jurisdictions has nonetheless remained a minority position. What accounts for the resistance to the *Maher* court's view? Why isn't the jury the best judge of whether the circumstances were sufficient to cause a reasonable person to lose self-control?

2. Cooling time. The *Maher* court's flexible position with respect to cooling time proved more influential than its comparable view with respect to the provoking circumstances. Though many modern authorities still permit the trial judge to find adequate cooling time as a matter of law (see Note 4, p. 414 supra), the prevailing view now appears to treat cooling time as an evidentiary consideration to be evaluated by the jury under all the circumstances. Thus, in People v. Berry, 18 Cal. 3d 509, 556 P.2d 777 (1976), the defendant waited for his victim in her apartment for 20 hours before killing her. The court held that the defendant was nevertheless entitled to a manslaughter instruction, because the jury could find that the defendant's heat of passion resulted from a long-smoldering prior course of provocative conduct by the victim, the wait serving to aggravate rather than cool defendant's agitation. See also Ga. Code Ann. §16-5-2 (Michie 1984 & Supp. 1986):

> [I]f there should have been an interval between the provocation and the killing sufficient for the voice of reason and humanity to be heard, of which the jury in all cases shall be the judge, the killing shall be attributed to deliberate revenge and be punished as murder.

3. The Model Penal Code approach. The Model Penal Code (§210.3(1)(b)) rejects the common law provocation formula and adopts a standard that is even more flexible than that of the *Maher* case. The operation of the MPC approach is illustrated in the case that follows.

PEOPLE v. CASASSA

New York Court of Appeals
49 N.Y.2d 668, 404 N.E.2d 1310 (1980)

JASEN, J. . . . On February 28, 1977, Victoria Lo Consolo was brutally murdered. Defendant Victor Casassa and Miss Lo Consolo . . . met in August, 1976 as a result of their residence in the same apartment complex. Shortly thereafter, defendant asked Miss Lo Consolo to accompany him to a social function and she agreed. The two apparently dated casually on other occasions until November, 1976 when Miss Lo Consolo informed defendant that she was not "falling in love" with him. Defendant claims that Miss Lo Consolo's candid statement of her feelings "devastated him."

Miss Lo Consolo's rejection of defendant's advances also precipitated a bizarre series of actions on the part of defendant which, he asserts, demonstrate the existence of extreme emotional disturbance upon which he predicates his affirmative defense. Defendant, aware that Miss Lo Consolo maintained social relationships with others, broke into the apartment below Miss Lo Consolo's on several occasions to eavesdrop. These eavesdropping sessions allegedly caused him to be under great emotional stress. Thereafter, on one occasion, he broke into Miss Lo Consolo's apartment while she was out. Defendant took nothing, but, instead, observed the apartment, disrobed and lay for a time in Miss Lo Consolo's bed. During this break-in, defendant was armed with a knife which, he later told police, he carried "because he knew that he was either going to hurt Victoria or Victoria was going to cause him to commit suicide."

Defendant's final visit to his victim's apartment occurred on February 28, 1977. Defendant brought several bottles of wine and liquor with him to offer as a gift. Upon Miss Lo Consolo's rejection of this offering, defendant produced a steak knife which he had brought with him, stabbed Miss Lo Consolo several times in the throat, dragged her body to the bathroom and submerged it in a bathtub full of water to "make sure she was dead."

The following day the police investigation of Miss Lo Consolo's death began. . . . Police detectives . . . were in the process of questioning several of the residents of the building when defendant . . . volunteered that he had been in the victim's apartment on the night of the murder. While denying any involvement in the murder of Miss Lo Consolo, he professed a willingness to co-operate in the investigation. [After nine and one-half hours of interrogation at police headquarters, defendant made a detailed confession.]

Defendant [was charged with second-degree murder. He] waived a jury and proceeded to trial before the County Court. . . . The defendant did not contest the underlying facts of the crime. Instead, the sole issue presented to the trial court was whether the defendant, at the time of the killing, had acted under the influence of "extreme emotional disturbance." The defense presented only one witness, a psychiatrist, who testified, in essence, that the defendant had become obsessed with Miss Lo Consolo and that the course which their relationship had taken, combined with several personality attributes peculiar to defendant, caused him to be under the influence of extreme emotional disturbance at the time of the killing.

In rebuttal, the People produced several witnesses. Among these witnesses was a psychiatrist who testified that although the defendant was emotionally disturbed, he was not under the influence of "extreme emotional disturbance" within the meaning . . . of the Penal Law, because his disturbed state was not the product of external factors but rather was "a stress he created from within himself, dealing mostly with a fantasy, a refusal to accept the reality of the situation."

The trial court . . . considered the appropriate test to be whether in the totality of the circumstances the finder of fact could understand how a person might have his reason overcome. Concluding that the test was not to be applied solely from the viewpoint of defendant, the court found that defendant's emotional reaction at the time of the commission of the crime was so peculiar to him that it could not be considered reasonable so as to reduce the conviction to manslaughter in the first degree. Accordingly, the trial court found defendant guilty of the crime of murder in the second degree. . . .

On this appeal defendant contends that the trial court erred in failing to afford him the benefit of the affirmative defense of "extreme emotional disturbance". . . .

Section 125.25 (subd. 1, par. [a]) of the Penal Law provides that it is an affirmative defense to the crime of murder in the second degree where "[t]he defendant acted under the influence of extreme emotional disturbance for which there was a reasonable explanation or excuse." . . .

In enacting [this provision], the Legislature adopted the language of the manslaughter provisions of the Model Penal Code. The only substantial distinction between the New York statute and the Model Penal Code is the designation by the Legislature of "extreme emotional disturbance" as an "affirmative defense," thus placing the burden of proof on this issue upon defendant. . . .

The "extreme emotional disturbance" defense is an outgrowth of the "heat of passion" doctrine which had for some time been recognized by New York as a distinguishing factor between the crimes of manslaughter and murder. However, the new formulation is significantly broader in scope than the "heat of passion" doctrine which it replaced. (People v. Patterson, 39 N.Y.2d 288, 347 N.E.2d 898.)

For example, the "heat of passion" doctrine required that a defendant's action be undertaken as a response to some provocation which prevented him from reflecting upon his actions. Moreover, such reaction had to be immediate. The existence of a "cooling off" period completely negated any mitigating effect which the provocation might otherwise have had. In *Patterson*, however, this court recognized that "[a]n action influenced by an extreme emotional disturbance is not one that is necessarily so spontaneously undertaken. Rather, it may be that a significant mental trauma has affected a defendant's mind for a substantial period of time, simmering in the unknowing subconscious and then inexplicably coming to the fore." This distinction between the past and present law of mitigation, enunciated in *Patterson,* was expressly adopted by the trial court and properly applied in this case.

The thrust of defendant's claim, however, concerns a question arising out of another perceived distinction between "heat of passion" and "extreme emotional disturbance" which was not directly addressed in *Patterson,* to wit: whether, assuming that the defense is applicable to a broader range of circumstances, the standard by which the reasonableness of defendant's emotional reaction is to be tested must be an entirely subjective one. Defendant relies principally upon our decision in *Patterson* and upon the language of the statute to support his claim that the reasonableness of his "explanation or excuse" should be determined solely with reference to his own subjective viewpoint. Such reliance is misplaced.

In *Patterson,* . . . we noted that "[t]he purpose of the extreme emotional disturbance defense is to permit the defendant to show that his actions were caused by a mental infirmity not arising to the level of insanity, and that he is less culpable for having committed them." We also noted that "[t]he differences between the present New York statute and its predecessor . . . can be explained by the tremendous advances made in psychology since 1881 and a willingness on the part of the courts, legislators, and the public to reduce the level of responsibility imposed on those whose capacity has been diminished by mental trauma." [But we] did not hold that all mental infirmities not arising to the level of insanity constitute "extreme emotional disturbance" within the meaning of the statute. This . . . is a question that has never been decided by this court. . . .

Consideration of the Comments to the Model Penal Code, from which the New York statute was drawn, are instructive. The defense of "extreme emotional disturbance" has two principal components — (1) the particular defendant must have "acted under the influence of extreme emotional disturbance," and (2) there must have been "a reasonable explanation or excuse" for such extreme emotional disturbance, "the reasonableness of which is to be determined from the viewpoint of a person in the defendant's situation under the circumstances as the defendant believed them to be." The first requirement is wholly subjective — i.e., it involves a determination that the particular defendant did in fact act under extreme emotional disturbance, that the claimed explanation as to the cause of his action is not contrived or sham.

The second component is more difficult to describe — i.e., whether there was a reasonable explanation or excuse for the emotional disturbance. It was designed to sweep away "the rigid rules that have developed with respect to the sufficiency of particular types of provocation, such as the rule that words alone can never be enough. . . . The ultimate test, however, is objective; there must be 'reasonable' explanation or excuse for the actor's disturbance." In light of these comments and the necessity of articulating the defense in terms comprehensible to jurors, we conclude that the determination whether there was reasonable explanation or excuse for a particular emotional disturbance should be made by viewing the subjective, internal situation in which the defendant found himself and the external circumstances as he perceived them at the time, however inaccurate that perception may have been, and assessing from that standpoint whether the explanation or excuse for his emotional disturbance was reasonable, so as to entitle him to a reduction of the crime charged from murder in the second degree to manslaughter in the first degree.[2] We recognize that

2. We emphasize that this test is to be applied to determine whether defendant's emotional disturbance, and not the act of killing, was supported by a reasonable explanation or excuse.

even such a description of the defense provides no precise guidelines and necessarily leaves room for the exercise of judgmental evaluation by the jury. This, however, appears to have been the intent of the draftsmen. "The purpose was explicitly to give full scope to what amounts to a plea in mitigation based upon a mental or emotional trauma of significant dimensions, with the jury asked to show whatever empathy it can." (Wechsler, Codification of Criminal Law in the United States: The Model Penal Code, 68 Col. L. Rev. 1425, 1446.)

By suggesting a standard of evaluation which contains both subjective and objective elements, we believe that the drafters of the code adequately achieved their dual goals of broadening the "heat of passion" doctrine to apply to a wider range of circumstances while retaining some element of objectivity in the process. The result of their draftsmanship is a statute which offers the defendant a fair opportunity to seek mitigation without requiring that the trier of fact find mitigation in each case where an emotional disturbance is shown — or as the drafters put it, to offer "room for argument as to the reasonableness of the explanations or excuses offered." . . .

We conclude that the trial court, in this case, properly applied the statute. The court apparently accepted, as a factual matter, that defendant killed Miss Lo Consolo while under the influence of "extreme emotional disturbance," a threshold question which must be answered in the affirmative before any test of reasonableness is required. The court, however, also recognized that in exercising its function as trier of fact, it must make a further inquiry into the reasonableness of that disturbance. In this regard, the court considered each of the mitigating factors put forward by defendant, including his claimed mental disability, but found that the excuse offered by defendant was so peculiar to him that it was unworthy of mitigation. The court obviously made a sincere effort to understand defendant's "situation" and "the circumstances as defendant believed them to be," but concluded that the murder in this case was the result of defendant's malevolence rather than an understandable human response deserving of mercy. We cannot say, as a matter of law, that the court erred in so concluding. . . .

In our opinion, this statute would not require that the jury or the court as trier of fact find mitigation on any particular set of facts, but, rather, allows the finder of fact the opportunity to do so, such opportunity being conditional only upon a finding of extreme emotional disturbance in the first instance. . . .

[Affirmed.]

NOTES

1. *Influence of the Model Penal Code formulation.* At least 14 states have adopted, in whole or in part, the Model Penal Code's "extreme emotional disturbance" formula for reducing murder to manslaughter. See, e.g., Rainey v. State, 310 Ark. 419, 837 S.W.2d 453 (1992). However, in four of these states (Maine, Ohio, Washington, and Wisconsin) courts or legislatures returned to common law formulations after a brief experience with the Model Penal Code. See Richard Singer, The Resurgence of Mens Rea: I — Provocation, Emotional Disturbance, and the Model Penal Code, 27 B.C.L. Rev. 243, 292-294 (1986). What features of the Model Penal Code approach might account for these reactions?

2. *Distinctive features of the Model Penal Code formulation.* What was the "provocation" in the *Casassa* case? Under the Model Penal Code standard, does emotional disturbance require manslaughter instructions even when the disturbance is not attributable to any provocative behavior at all? In State v. Zdanis, 182 Conn. 388, 438 A.2d 696 (1980), the defendant learned that his eight-year-old niece was dying of cancer. Distraught after several days of brooding about the news, he killed one of the other members of his family. In a prosecution under a Connecticut statute modeled on the Model Penal Code, the defense of extreme emotional disturbance was submitted to the trier of fact but rejected on the evidence. In State v. Elliot, 177 Conn. 1, 411 A.2d 3 (1979), the defendant had for years suffered from an overwhelming fear of his brother. One day, for no apparent reason, he appeared at his brother's house and killed him. The defendant was convicted of murder, but the Connecticut Supreme Court reversed, holding that instructions on extreme emotional disturbance were required. The court said:

> [T]he defense does not require a provoking or triggering event. . . . [T]o establish the "heat of passion" defense a defendant had to prove that the "hot blood" had not had time to "cool off" at the time of the killing. A homicide influenced by an extreme emotional disturbance, in contrast, is not one which is necessarily committed in the "hot blood" stage, but rather one that was brought about by a significant mental trauma that caused the defendant to brood for a long period of time and then react violently, seemingly without provocation.

Question: If the traditional provocation formula and the Model Penal Code approach produce different results in a case like *Elliot,* which approach is preferable?

3. *Boundaries of the Model Penal Code defense.* Under *Casassa* and the Model Penal Code formulation, is the "reasonableness" of a defendant's emotional disturbance *always* a question for the jury? Consider the following situations:

(a) In People v. Mejia, 166 A.D.2d 675, 561 N.Y.S.2d 265 (1990), a co-worker menaced the defendant from a distance with a screwdriver. Defendant pulled out his gun and shot the co-worker without affording him any chance to retreat. The trial court refused to submit manslaughter instructions to the jury. Affirming, the appellate court said:

> Although there may have been sufficient credible evidence to create a question for the jury as to whether the defendant did in fact suffer loss of self control associated with the defense, there was insufficient evidence to support a finding that his emotional state had a reasonable explanation or excuse. Since defendant's reaction to what he perceived to be a threat was not "an understandable human response deserving of mercy" (People v. Casassa), the trial court properly rejected the requested charge.

(b) In People v. Walker, 100 A.D.2d 220, 473 N.Y.S.2d 460 (1984), the defendant, a drug dealer, received a $4,500 consignment of marijuana from his supplier, William Edmunds. He failed to pay Edmunds and claimed that he had been robbed of the marijuana. In spite of the defendant's plea for additional consignments, Edmunds refused to supply him. One evening the defendant encountered Edmunds in a restaurant frequented by drug dealers. A witness heard an angry argument between the two. Edmunds demanded his money, the defen-

dant responded that he did not have any money, and Edmunds then asked how he could afford to eat in the restaurant. The defendant replied that Edmunds should give him money, to which Edmunds responded, "The only dough you're going to get is the dough in that bread." The defendant was then heard to say, "Take your damn hand out of my plate," after which he rose, gun in hand, and fired several shots in rapid succession, killing Edmunds.

At Walker's trial on murder charges, the judge refused to instruct the jury on an extreme emotional disturbance defense. Was this error? The appellate court affirmed,[2] but a dissenting judge commented:

> [The Model Penal Code] explicitly intended to discard the general rule at common law "that words alone, no matter how insulting, could not amount to adequate provocation."
>
> In declining to charge the affirmative defense in this case the trial court may well have applied correctly the traditional rule that had prevailed in the courts of this country. [T]he court failed to appreciate that the rule it was attempting to follow was one of those intended to be discarded in favor of the central principle that where there is evidence of extreme emotional disturbance "it is for the trier of fact to decide, in light of all the circumstances of the case, whether there exists a reasonable explanation or excuse for the actor's mental condition." (See Model Penal Code and Commentaries, §210.3, p. 61.)
>
> [T]he threshold issue clearly is whether there is evidence that the defendant "acted under the influence of extreme emotional disturbance." As we have been instructed by the Court of Appeals in *Casassa,* this requirement "is wholly subjective." From the evidence presented at the trial the jury could reasonably have found that the defendant killed the deceased in a burst of anger, that a smoldering sense of grievance had been ignited by insulting and contemptuous words and actions.
>
> Indeed, I find it difficult to see how a jury could have reasonably reached any other conclusion. . . .
>
> Once it is determined that there was "evidence of extreme emotional disturbance," the controlling rule is clear . . . : "it is for the trier of fact to decide, in light of all the circumstances of the case, whether there exists a reasonable explanation or excuse for the actor's mental condition." (Model Penal Code and Commentaries, §210.3, p. 61.) . . .
>
> This is not a sympathetic case. The plight of a narcotics dealer cut off from his source of supply, and then subjected to insulting and contemptuous words and actions by his former supplier, is not likely to evoke widespread feelings of acute compassion. Nevertheless, it is clear that the controlling statutory sections were carefully designed to permit the essential judgment on the kind of issue presented here to be made by jurors on the basis of all the circumstances, and not by the Trial Judge as a matter of law.

PROBLEM

Lopez v. State, 716 S.W.2d 127 (Tex. Crim. App. 1986): Appellant and his three companions drove to a party in south Odessa. Appellant was apprehensive because of the prospect of encountering members or allies of the Mendoza family

---

2. In a brief memorandum order, the New York Court of Appeals affirmed the decision of the appellate division, 64 N.Y.2d 741, 475 N.E.2d 445 (1984).

with whom his family had been engaged in a protracted conflict. Appellant's mother had been shot and his brother killed the preceding year. In preparation for the party, he placed a loaded .30 caliber carbine in the trunk of the car. A few minutes after they arrived, Appellant was advised that one John Vargas was in a Blazer parked nearby. Appellant had heard that Vargas was responsible for his mother's injury. Vargas too became aware of Appellant's presence and backed out to leave. As he did so, Appellant drew the rifle from the trunk of his vehicle. No threats were made by Vargas and no weapons were observed. Appellant in his confession and testimony stated that he feared being shot at or run over by Vargas:

> I got to thinking about my Mom and my brother and I got mad and started crying. I had been drinking. I looked back and the trunk to Paul's [Appellant's companion, Paul Pequeno] car was open. I went and got my gun out of the trunk. The first shot I took good aim, but the others, about three, I just closed my eyes and shot.

At least three rounds hit the Vargas vehicle. One struck Irineo Duran, Jr. in the head, killing him.

Texas Pen. Code Ann. §19.04 (1974) defines voluntary manslaughter and provides in part:

> (a) A person commits an offense if he causes the death of an individual under circumstances that would constitute murder under Section 19.02 of this code, except that he caused the death under the immediate influence of sudden passion arising from an adequate cause.
>
> (b) "Sudden passion" means passion directly caused by and arising out of provocation by the individual killed or another acting with the person killed which passion arises at the time of the offense and is not solely the result of former provocation.
>
> (c) "Adequate cause" means cause that would commonly produce a degree of anger, rage, resentment, or terror in a person of ordinary temper, sufficient to render the mind incapable of cool reflection.

At trial, a self-defense claim was considered but rejected by the jury. The trial judge refused to instruct the jury on voluntary manslaughter. Lopez was convicted of murder and sentenced to 50 years' imprisonment.

Questions: On appeal, what should be the result under the common law standard? What should be the result under the Texas statute? What should be the result under the New York (Model Penal Code) formulation?

b. The Objectivity of the Standard

In subsection (a) we explored differences between the common law and Model Penal Code approaches to determining when extenuating circumstances may reduce the degree of a homicide from murder to manslaughter. As we saw, the Model Penal Code places many fewer restrictions on the character of the extenuating circumstances that can qualify, and it does not limit such circumstances to provocative acts directed at the defendant. In one respect, however, the common law and Model Penal Code approaches are similar: Both require that the defendant's response to the disturbing external circumstances be "reasonable." The present subsection explores this important restriction common to both approaches.

DIRECTOR OF PUBLIC PROSECUTIONS v. CAMPLIN

House of Lords
[1978] 2 All E.R. 168

LORD DIPLOCK. . . . The respondent, Camplin, who was 15 years of age, killed a middle-aged Pakistani, Mohammed Lal Khan, by splitting his skull with a chapati pan, a heavy kitchen utensil like a rimless frying pan. At the time the two of them were alone together in Khan's flat. At Camplin's trial for murder before Boreham, J., his only defence was that of provocation so as to reduce the offence to manslaughter. According to the story that he told in the witness box but which differed materially from that which he had told to the police, Khan had buggered him in spite of his resistance and had then laughed at him, whereupon Camplin had lost his self-control and attacked Khan fatally with the chapati pan.

In his address to the jury on the defence of provocation, counsel for Camplin had suggested to them that when they addressed their minds to the question whether the provocation relied on was enough to make a reasonable man do as Camplin had done, what they ought to consider was not the reaction of a reasonable adult but the reaction of a reasonable boy of Camplin's age. The judge thought that this was wrong in law. So in this summing-up he took pains to instruct the jury that they must consider whether —

> the provocation was sufficient to make a reasonable man in like circumstances act as the defendant did. Not a reasonable boy, as [counsel for Camplin] would have it, or a reasonable lad; it is an objective test — a reasonable man.

The jury found Camplin guilty of murder. On appeal the Court of Appeal, Criminal Division, allowed the appeal and substituted a conviction for manslaughter on the ground that the passage I have cited from the summing-up was a misdirection. The court held that —

> the proper direction to the jury is to invite the jury to consider whether the provocation was enough to have made a reasonable person of the same age as the appellant in the same circumstances do as he did.

[In the House of Lords, to which the Public Prosecutor had appealed, Lord Diplock surveyed the development of the doctrine of provocation at common law. He then focused on an earlier House of Lords decision in Bedder v. Director of Public Prosecutions, [1954] All E.R. 801:]

. . . The accused had killed a prostitute. He was sexually impotent. According to his evidence he had tried to have sexual intercourse with her and failed. She taunted him with his failure and tried to get away from his grasp. In the course of her attempts to do so she slapped him in the face, punched him in the stomach and kicked him in the groin, whereupon he took a knife out of his pocket and stabbed her twice and caused her death. The struggle that led to her death thus started because the deceased taunted the accused with his physical infirmity; but in the state of the law as it then was, taunts unaccompanied by any physical violence did not constitute provocation. The taunts were followed by violence on the part of the deceased in the course of her attempt to get away from the accused, and it may be that this subsequent violence would have a greater effect on the self-control of an impotent man already enraged by the taunts than it would have had on a person conscious of possessing normal physical attributes. So there might be some justification for the judge to instruct the jury to ignore the fact that the accused was impotent when they were considering whether the deceased's conduct amounted to such provocation as would cause a reasonable or ordinary person to lose his self-control. [But] Lord Simonds, L.C., speaking on behalf of all the members of this House who sat on the appeal . . . also went on to lay down the broader proposition that:

> It would be plainly illogical not to recognize an unusually excitable or pugnacious temperament in the accused as a matter to be taken into account but yet to recognise for that purpose some unusual physical characteristic, be it impotence or another. . . .

[The 1957 Homicide Act] was intended to mitigate in some degree the harshness of the common law of provocation as it had been developed by recent decisions in this House.[a] It recognizes and retains the dual test: the provocation must not only have caused the accused to lose his self-control but also be such as might cause a reasonable man to react to it as the accused did. Nevertheless it brings about two important changes in the law. The first is [that] it abolishes all previous rules of law as to what can or cannot amount to provocation and in particular the rule of law that . . . words unaccompanied by violence could not do so. Secondly it makes it clear that if there was any evidence that the accused himself at the time of the act which caused the death in fact lost his self-control in consequence of some provocation however slight it might appear to the judge, he was bound to leave to the jury the question, which is one of opinion not of law, whether a reasonable man might have reacted to that provocation as the accused did. . . .

The public policy that underlay the adoption of the "reasonable man" test in the common law doctrine of provocation was to reduce the incidence of fatal violence by preventing a person relying on his own exceptional pugnacity or excitability as an excuse for loss of self-control. The rationale of the test may not be easy to reconcile in logic with more universal propositions as to the mental element in crime. Nevertheless it has been preserved by the 1957 Act but falls to be applied now in the context of a law of provocation that is significantly different from what it was before the Act was passed.

Although it is now for the jury to apply the "reasonable man" test, it still remains for the judge to direct them what, in the new context of the section, is the meaning of this apparently inapt expression, since powers of ratiocination bear no obvious relationships to powers of self-control. . . .

[F]or the purposes of the law of provocation the "reasonable man" has never been confined to the adult male. It means an ordinary person of either sex, not

---

a For the text of this statute, see Note 1, page 419 supra. — Eds.

exceptionally excitable or pugnacious, but possessed of such powers of self-control as everyone is entitled to expect that his fellow citizens will exercise in society as it is today. A crucial factor in the defence of provocation from earliest times has been the relationship between the gravity of provocation and the way in which the accused retaliated, both being judged by the social standards of the day. When Hale was writing in the 17th century, pulling a man's nose was thought to justify retaliation with a sword; when *Mancini* [[1942] A.C. 1] was decided by this House, a blow with a fist would not justify retaliation with a deadly weapon. But so long as words unaccompanied by violence could not in common law amount to provocation the relevant proportionality between provocation and retaliation was primarily one of degrees of violence. Words spoken to the accused before the violence started were not normally to be included in the proportion sum. But now that the law has been changed so as to permit of words being treated as provocation, even though unaccompanied by any other acts, the gravity of verbal provocation may well depend on the particular characteristics or circumstances of the person to whom a taunt or insult is addressed. To taunt a person because of his race, his physical infirmities or some shameful incident in his past may well be considered by the jury to be more offensive to the person addressed, however equable his temperament, if the facts on which the taunt is founded are true than it would be if they were not. It would stultify much of the mitigation of the previous harshness of the common law in ruling out verbal provocation as capable of reducing murder to manslaughter if the jury could not take into consideration all those factors which in their opinion would affect the gravity of taunts and insults when applied to the person to whom they are addressed. So to this extent at any rate the unqualified proposition accepted by this House in *Bedder* [[1954] All E.R. 801] that for the purposes of the "reasonable man" test any unusual physical characteristics of the accused must be ignored requires revision as a result of the passing of the 1957 Act.

That he was only 15 years of age at the time of the killing is the relevant characteristic of the accused in the instant case. It is a characteristic which may have its effects on temperament as well as physique. If the jury think that the same power of self-control is not to be expected in an ordinary, average or normal boy of 15 as in an older person, are they to treat the lesser powers of self-control possessed by an ordinary, average or normal boy of 15 as the standard of self-control with which the conduct of the accused is to be compared?

It may be conceded that in strict logic there is a transition between treating age as a characteristic that may be taken into account in assessing the gravity of the provocation addressed to the accused and treating it as a characteristic to be taken into account in determining what is the degree of self-control to be expected of the ordinary person with whom the accused's conduct is to be compared. But to require old heads on young shoulders is inconsistent with the law's compassion of human infirmity to which Sir Michael Foster ascribed the doctrine of provocation more than two centuries ago. The distinction as to the purpose for which it is legitimate to take the age of the accused into account involves considerations of too great nicety to warrant a place in deciding a matter of opinion, which is no longer one to be decided by a judge trained in logical reasoning but by a jury drawing on their experience of how ordinary human beings behave in real life. . . .

In my opinion a proper direction to a jury on the question left to their exclusive determination by S. 3 of the 1957 Act would be on the following lines. The judge should state what the question is, using the very terms of the section. He should then explain to them that the reasonable man referred to in the question is a person having the power of self-control to be expected of an ordinary person of the sex and age of the accused, but in other respects sharing such of the accused's characteristics as they think would affect the gravity of the provocation to him, and that the question is not merely whether such a person would in like circumstances be provoked to lose his self-control but also would react to the provocation as the accused did. . . .

LORD SIMON OF GLAISDALE. . . . The original reasons in this branch of the law were largely reasons of the heart and of common sense, not the reasons of pure juristic logic. . . . But justice and common sense then demanded some limitation: it would be unjust that the drunk man or one exceptionally pugnacious or bad-tempered or over-sensitive should be able to claim that these matters rendered him peculiarly susceptible to the provocation offered, where the sober and even-tempered man would hang for his homicide. Hence . . . the development of the concept of the reaction of a reasonable man to the provocation offered. . . .

The provision that words alone can constitute provocation accentuates the anomalies, inconveniences and injustices liable to follow from the *Bedder* decision. The effect of an insult will often depend entirely on a characteristic of a person to whom the insult is directed. "Dirty nigger" would probably mean little if said to a white man or even if said by one coloured man to another, but is obviously more insulting when said by a white man to a coloured man. Similarly, such an expression as "Your character is as crooked as your back" would have a different connotation to a hunchback on the one hand and to a man with a back like a ramrod on the other. . . .

In my judgment the reference to "a reasonable man" at the end of the section means "a man of ordinary self-control." If this is so, the meaning satisfies what I have ventured to suggest as the reasons for importing into this branch of the law the concept of the reasonable man, namely to avoid the injustice of a man being entitled to rely on his exceptional excitability (whether idiosyncratic or by cultural environment or ethnic origin) or pugnacity or ill-temper or on his drunkenness. . . . [I]n determining whether a person of reasonable self-control would lose it in the circumstances, the entire factual situation which includes the characteristics of the accused, must be considered. . . .

PROBLEMS

1. In Regina v. Newell, 71 Crim. App. 331 (1981), the defendant, a long-time alcoholic, was convicted of the murder of a friend. During a drinking session, after both had become drunk, the friend insulted the defendant's mistress and then made homosexual advances to the defendant. The defendant became enraged and battered his friend to death with an ashtray. The trial judge instructed the jurors that, in applying the objective element of the provocation test, they should apply the standard of the reasonable, sober man. The Court of Appeals upheld the conviction, reasoning that in order for the defendant's alcoholism to be taken into account, there had to be some reference to that factor in the provoking circumstances, such as an insulting comment on his drinking habits. The same conclusion is reached in State v. Heisler, 344 N.W.2d 190 (Wis. App. 1983). Can these results be reconciled with the *Camplin* case? For discussion, see Note, The Provok'd Drunk, 44 Mod. L. Rev. 567 (1981).

2. In Regina v. Raven, *noted*, 1982 Crim. L. Rev. 51, a severely retarded defendant was charged with the murder of a man who, he claimed, had sexually assaulted him. The defendant was 22 years old but had a mental age of 9. In submitting manslaughter instructions to the jury, the trial judge directed the jury to consider the reactions of a "reasonable man" having the mental age of the accused. Was this instruction proper? If the defendant should be treated like a 9-year-old, how can he be held criminally responsible at all?

3. In Gonzales v. State, 689 S.W.2d 900 (Tex. Crim. App. 1985), the defendant was convicted of murder for fatally shooting his common-law wife after a heated argument. The trial judge had instructed on voluntary manslaughter but rejected the defendant's proposed instruction that the situation should be assessed from his own perspective, namely that of "an Hispanic farm worker who was living with a Caucasian woman on a low income." Was this error?

4. Should the defendant's nationality and cultural background be taken into account? Suppose that the defendant recently immigrated from a country where the provoking circumstances (e.g., marital infidelity or a particular insult) are regarded as far more serious than they are in the United States. Suppose that ordinary people in the immigrant's country are far more likely to respond violently to such circumstances. Should the defendant's response be assessed from the perspective of the reasonable person of his cultural background? Or is it more appropriate to hold such a defendant to the standards of self-control that our society expects Americans to exercise?

5. In State v. McClain, 248 N.J. Super. 409, 591 A.2d 652 (1991), defendant shot and killed the man with whom she had lived for nine years in a troubled relationship. Though the man had not physically assaulted the defendant for several years (there had been two beating incidents, several years apart, earlier in the relationship), a psychologist testified that the defendant suffered from battered woman syndrome because a series of psychological humiliations had triggered a mental "breakdown" and led to the killing. The court held that evidence relating to defendant's status as a battered woman was "irrelevant on the question of whether the victim's conduct was adequately provocative because that inquiry requires application of the 'reasonable person' test." Did the court miss the point? For a criticism, see Lawrence S. Lustberg & John V. Jacobi, The Battered Woman as a Reasonable Person: A Critique of the Appellate Division Decision in *State v. McClain*, 22 Seton Hall L. Rev. 365 (1992). See also State v. Felton, 110 Wis. 2d 485, 329 N.W.2d 161, 172-173 (1983): "It is proper in applying the objective test . . . to consider how other persons similarly situated with respect to that type, or that history, of provocation would react. . . . [T]he objective test may be satisfied by considering the situation of the ordinary person who is a battered spouse." The problem of battered spouse syndrome is explored at greater length in Chapter 8, page 814 infra.

6. In State v. Klimas, 94 Wis. 2d 288, 288 N.W.2d 157 (1979), the defendant, after many months of intense conflict with his wife, shot and killed her. He claimed to be distraught over the disintegration of his marriage, his wife's relationship with another man, and her efforts to obtain a divorce. He sought to

introduce psychiatric testimony to the effect that he had been suffering a severe depression, that events on the day preceding the killing had "overwhelmed" him, and that although not legally insane, he was "a desperate man overwhelmed by a psychotic depressive illness." The defendant apparently sought to have his conduct assessed from the perspective of a person in that emotional situation. The trial judge ruled the psychiatric evidence irrelevant and therefore inadmissible. Was this error?

NOTES ON THE OBJECTIVE STANDARD

1. *Reasons for an objective standard.* Why should there be any objective element to the provocation defense? Why not simply ask whether the defendant was in fact provoked to an uncontrollable rage? Consider the following comments.

(a) Royal Commission on Capital Punishment, Report, Cmd. 8932, para. 143 (1953):

> It is a fundamental principle of the criminal law that it should be based on a generally accepted standard of conduct applicable to all citizens alike, and it is important that this principle should not be infringed. Any departure from it might introduce a dangerous latitude into the law. Those idiosyncrasies of individual temperament or mentality that make a man more easily provoked, or more violent in his response to provocation, ought not, therefore, to affect his liability to conviction, although they may justify mitigation of sentence.

(b) Jerome Michael & Herbert Wechsler, A Rationale of the Law of Homicide, 37 Colum. L. Rev. 1261, 1281-1282 (1937):

> Provocation may be greater or less, but it cannot be measured by the intensity of the passions aroused in the actor by the provocative circumstances. It must be estimated by the probability that such circumstances would affect most men in like fashion; although the passions stirred up in the actor were violent, the provocation can be said to be great only if the provocative circumstances would have aroused in most men similar desires of comparable intensity. Other things being equal, the greater the provocation, measured in that way, the more ground there is for attributing the intensity of the actor's passions and his lack of self-control on the homicidal occasion to the extraordinary character of the situation in which he was placed rather than to any extraordinary deficiency in his own character. While it is true, it is also beside the point, that most men do not kill on even the gravest provocation; the point is that the more strongly they would be moved to kill by circumstances of the sort which provoked the actor to the homicidal act, and the more difficulty they would experience in resisting the impulse to which he yielded, the less does his succumbing serve to differentiate his character from theirs. But the slighter the provocation, the more basis there is for ascribing the actor's act to an extraordinary susceptibility to intense passion, to an unusual deficiency in those other desires which counteract in most men the desires which impel them to homicidal acts, or to an extraordinary weakness of reason, and consequent inability to bring such desires into play.

(c) For a review of the development of the law of provocation in England and the United States, and a defense of taking a wholly subjective approach to the issue, see Richard Singer, The Resurgence of Mens Rea: I — Provocation, Emotional Disturbance, and the Model Penal Code, 27 B.C.L. Rev. 243 (1986). For a discussion of the argument that the reasonableness requirement should be eliminated completely, see Dolores A. Donovan & Stephanie M. Wildman, Is the Reasonable Man Obsolete? A Critical Perspective on Self-Defense and Provocation, 14 Loyola L.A.L. Rev. 435 (1981). The authors propose (id. at 467) that murder be reduced to manslaughter when the accused was "honestly and understandably aroused to the heat of passion." The jury would be instructed that "[i]n determining whether [the accused] was understandably aroused to the heat of passion, you must ask yourselves whether she could have been fairly expected to avoid the act of homicide."

2. *Statutory formulations.* Few, if any, states have adopted an entirely subjective standard of provocation. The Model Penal Code retains an objective element but qualifies it by specifying that reasonableness must be assessed "from the viewpoint of a person in the actor's situation." Model Penal Code §210.3(1)(b), Appendix. The Code's reporters explain (Model Penal Code and Commentaries, Comment to §210.3, at 62-63 (1980)):

> The word "situation" is designedly ambiguous. On the one hand, it is clear that personal handicaps and some external circumstances must be taken into account. Thus, blindness, shock from traumatic injury, and extreme grief are all easily read into the term "situation." This result is sound, for it would be morally obtuse to appraise a crime for mitigation of punishment without reference to these factors. On the other hand, it is equally plain that idiosyncratic moral values are not part of the actor's situation. An assassin who kills a political leader because he believes it is right to do so cannot ask that he be judged by the standard of a reasonable extremist. Any other result would undermine the normative message of the criminal law. In between these two extremes, however, there are matters neither as clearly distinct from individual blameworthiness as blindness or handicap nor as integral a part of moral depravity as a belief in the rightness of killing. Perhaps the classic illustration is the unusual sensitivity to the epithet "bastard" of a person born illegitimate. An exceptionally punctilious sense of personal honor or an abnormally fearful temperament may also serve to differentiate an individual actor from the hypothetical reasonable man, yet none of these factors is wholly irrelevant to the ultimate issue of culpability. The proper role of such factors cannot be resolved satisfactorily by abstract definition of what may constitute adequate provocation. The Model Code endorses a formulation that affords sufficient flexibility to differentiate in particular cases between those special aspects of the actor's situation that should be deemed material for purpose of grading and those that should be ignored. There thus will be room for interpretation of the word "situation," and that is precisely the flexibility desired. . . . In the end, the question is whether the actor's loss of self-control can be understood in terms that arouse sympathy in the ordinary citizen. Section 210.3 faces this issue squarely and leaves the ultimate judgment to the ordinary citizen in the function of a juror assigned to resolve the specific case.

Is the ambiguity of the Model Penal Code approach inevitable? Or could a statute be drafted to identify with more precision the appropriate domains of subjectivity and objectivity? Consider the New Zealand Crimes Act of 1961, §169:

> (1) Culpable homicide that would otherwise be murder may be reduced to manslaughter if the person who caused the death did so under provocation. (2) Anything done or said may be provocation if — (a) In the circumstances of the

case it was sufficient to deprive a person having the power of self-control of an
ordinary person, but otherwise having the characteristics of the offender, of the
power of self-control; and (b) It did in fact deprive the offender of the power of
self-control and thereby induced him to commit the act of homicide.

3. Diminished capacity. If external provocation can decrease the "moral depravity" of an act of killing, and thereby warrant reducing the offense to manslaughter, should mental impairment (short of legal insanity) have the same
effect? In People v. Conley, 64 Cal. 2d 310, 411 P.2d 911 (1966), the California
Supreme Court held that the "malice" necessary for a murder conviction required that a defendant have the capacity "to comprehend his duty to govern
his actions in accordance with the duty imposed by law." As a result, malice
could be rebutted not only by provocation that would cause a reasonable person
to lose self-control, but also by evidence of psychological disorder and voluntary
intoxication completely foreign to the "reasonable" mind. After the *Conley* doctrine led to a reduced verdict of manslaughter in a notorious case involving the
assassination of San Francisco Mayor George Moscone and Supervisor Harvey
Milk, the legislature overruled it. Cal. Penal Code §188, amended in 1981, now
specifies that "an awareness of the obligation to act within the general body of
laws regulating society . . . is [not] included within the definition of malice."
Compare the comments of Stephen J. Morse, Undiminished Confusion in Diminished Capacity, 75 J. Crim. L. & Criminology, 1, 30 (1984):

> If one accepts the traditional assumption that the provoked and therefore less
> rational and self-controlled actor is less responsible, how can one deny similar miti-
> gation to an actor whose problems with rationality or self-control are the product
> of mental disorder or defect? Indeed, a powerful argument can be mounted that
> the disordered person deserves mitigation more than his provoked counterpart.
> The provoked actor is presumptively mentally normal and therefore supposedly in
> possession of the capacity to resist the homicidal intention aroused by the provok-
> ing circumstances. Because the truly reasonable person does not kill under even
> highly provoking circumstances, the provoked actor who does kill must have some
> moral or character defect that permits him to yield to his intention to kill. And, of
> course, because we are generally held to be responsible for our characters, it may
> fairly be argued that the provoked killer's lack of rationality or self-control is his
> own fault. By contrast, the irrationality or self-control problems of the disordered
> person are not considered his fault; they are not a product of moral weakness or
> character defect.[a]

Compare Model Penal Code and Commentaries, Comments to Section 210.3
at 71-72 (1980):

> Unlike provocation, diminished responsibility is entirely subjective in character. It
> looks into the actor's mind to see whether he should be judged by a lesser standard
> than that applicable to ordinary men. It recognizes the defendant's own mental
> disorder or emotional instability as a basis for partially excusing his conduct. This
> position undoubtedly achieves a closer relation between criminal liability and

a. Professor Morse goes on to argue that because the reasonable, provoked actor who kills cannot be viewed as less culpable than the mentally abnormal actor who kills, *neither one* should benefit
from a special defense reducing the seriousness of the offense otherwise established by their acts
and their mens rea. — EDS.

moral guilt. Moral condemnation must be founded, at least in part, on some perception of the capacities and limitations of the individual actor. To the extent that the abnormal individual is judged as if he were normal, to the extent that the drunk man is judged as if he were sober, to the extent, in short, that the defective person is judged as if he were someone else, the moral judgment underlying criminal conviction is undermined. The doctrine of diminished responsibility resolves this conflict in favor of an individualistic and subjective determination of criminal liability. But this approach has its costs. By evaluating the abnormal individual on his own terms, it decreases the incentives for him to behave as if he were normal. It blurs the law's message that there are certain minimal standards of conduct to which every member of society must conform. By restricting the extreme condemnation of liability for murder to cases where it is fully warranted in a relativistic sense, diminished responsibility undercuts the social purpose of condemnation. And the factors that call for mitigation under this doctrine are the very aspects of an individual's personality that make us most fearful of his future conduct. In short, diminished responsibility brings formal guilt more closely into line with moral blameworthiness, but only at the cost of driving a wedge between dangerousness and social control.

The subject of diminished capacity is considered further in the context of the overall problem of mental disorder. See Chapter 8, pages 999-1011 infra.

4. *Mental disorder under the "objective" standard.* Even if diminished mental capacity does not automatically negate "malice," can the mentally disordered offender nonetheless argue that his psychological problems are part of the relevant "situation" in which the reactions of a "reasonable" person would have to be judged? Reconsider the implications of *Camplin* and its application to the *Klimas* problem case at page 431 supra.

5. *Mental disorder under the Model Penal Code approach.* The Model Penal Code ostensibly rejects an outright defense of diminished capacity. But the Code's "extreme emotional disturbance" formulation, which stands independent of external provoking events, appears to invite reliance upon subjective mental disability. How are these contrasting positions to be reconciled? The reporters explain (Model Penal Code and Commentaries, Comment to §210.3 at 72-73 (1980)):

> The term "situation," as noted above, is designedly ambiguous and is plainly flexible enough to allow the law to grow in the direction of taking account of mental abnormalities that have been recognized in the developing law of diminished responsibility. . . . [But] the Model Code does not authorize mitigation on the basis of individual abnormality without any measure of the defendant against an objective standard. Mental disorder clearly does not preclude moral depravity, and there surely will be cases where the actor's mental condition, although recognized as disturbed or abnormal, should be regarded as having no just bearing on his liability for intentional homicide. The fact that, given the actor's "situation," the jury will be called upon to determine the "reasonableness" of the actor's conduct will require this factor to be taken into account.
>
> . . . Like blindness or other physical infirmities, perhaps it should be that certain forms of mental abnormality should be regarded as a part of the actor's "situation" that is relevant to the moral assessment of his conduct. Like temperament or unusual excitability, on the other hand, there are surely other forms of abnormality that should not be taken into account for this purpose. It is left to the courts to define "situation" as the cases arise.

Do these comments provide adequate guidance? Consider State v. Raguseo, 225 Conn. 114, 622 A.2d 519 (1993). Defendant, who had a long history of serious emotional and psychiatric problems, including indications of paranoia, stabbed to death a person who had parked in defendant's assigned parking space at his apartment building. At trial the judge instructed the jury on the "extreme emotional disturbance" defense, using the Model Penal Code language adopted in Connecticut, and explained that "[t]he reasonableness of this explanation or excuse is to be determined from the viewpoint of a reasonable person in the defendant's situation under the circumstances as the defendant believes them to be." Struggling to understand, the jury requested further explanation of the defense on three separate occasions. In its final effort, the jury sent the judge a note stating: "[O]nce again, we need the definition of extreme emotional disturbance focusing on ('really stressing on') the following: . . . (2) Definition of 'norm.' Whose 'norm' are we comparing the action/thought process to —, the 'norm' for the defendant or the 'norm' for society? (3) Emphasize a 'reasonable' person's perspective. . . ." The judge responded that "the reasonableness of the explanation for the emotional disturbance must be 'determined from the viewpoint of a reasonable person; that is, a person of ordinary intellect and faculties, who finds him — who would find himself in the defendant's situation under the circumstances as the defendant believed it to be.'" The Connecticut Supreme Court held that this was a correct and adequate answer. Do you agree?

Experience under the Model Penal Code approach is described in Richard Singer, The Resurgence of Mens Rea: I — Provocation, Emotional Disturbance, and the Model Penal Code, 27 B.C.L. Rev. 243, 298-299, 304 (1986):

> Possibly the most striking development under the [MPC] standard is the mounting use of psychiatric testimony in these cases. . . . [P]sychiatric evidence has been admitted, though not always found credible, to explain why a high school counselor killed a student who threatened to expose the counselor's use of marijuana, why a husband shot his estranged wife after the last of many arguments, why a defendant walked into his brother's house one morning and shot him without saying a word, and why a boyfriend stabbed his former girlfriend with a steak knife when she rejected his proffered gift of a bottle of liquor. Perhaps the most notorious instance of psychiatric evidence [under the MPC standard] is the unreported "Yale Murder" case,[298] where Richard Herrin killed his girlfriend, Bonnie Garland, by pummeling her with a hammer while she slept in her house, at which he was a guest. Herrin killed Garland because she had told him that, while she still loved him, she wished to have some [sexual] "freedom" for a time. The case appeared to be nothing more than a typical jilted suitor case, but five psychiatrists turned the trial into a dispute over whether Herrin had suffered from "transient situational reaction."[299] The testimony described in detail Herrin's dependence on women, and his hope that he would find a stable relationship with Garland. When this appeared improbable, according to the psychiatric testimony, despair seized Her-

298. P. Meyer, The Yale Murder (1982); W. Gaylin, The Killing of Bonnie Garland: A Question of Justice (1982).

299. Diagnostic and Statistical Manual of Mental Disorders 300 (1980). Transient situational reaction is defined as "a maladaptive reaction to an identifiable psychological stressor, that occurs within three months of the onset of the stressor [and] . . . is indicated by either of the following: (1) impairment in social or occupational functioning; (2) symptoms that are in excess of a normal and expectable reaction to the stressor." . . .

rin and he acted without self control. . . . Because his action was "in excess of a normal and expectable reaction," it followed that he had a "transient situational reaction." The jury returned a verdict of manslaughter, clearly predicated upon this testimony.

[P]sychiatric evidence threatens to bring total subjectivity to the inquiry, and to allow experts to overwhelm the jury's function of providing a common sense moral judgment to the facts of a provocation pattern.

C. LEGISLATIVE GRADING OF UNINTENDED KILLINGS

1. *The Creation of Homicidal Risk*

The material in this section is organized around the following issues:

Subsection a deals with the criteria for establishing criminal, as opposed to solely civil, liability for unintended homicide.

Subsection b raises the issue whether criminal liability for unintended homicide should rest on a subjective or objective standard.

Subsection c considers the special circumstances that may make an unintended killing murder.

a. Distinguishing Civil and Criminal Liability

COMMONWEALTH v. WELANSKY

Massachusetts Supreme Judicial Court
316 Mass. 383, 55 N.E.2d 902 (1944)

Lummus, J. On November 28, 1942, and for about nine years before that day, a corporation named New Cocoanut Grove, Inc., maintained and operated a "night club" in Boston. . . . The corporation, its officers and employees, and its business, were completely dominated by the defendant Barnett Welansky. . . .

The defendant was accustomed to spend his evenings at the night club, inspecting the premises and superintending the business. On November 16, 1942, he became suddenly ill, and was carried to a hospital, where he was in bed for three weeks and remained until discharged on December 11, 1942. . . . There is no evidence of any act, omission or condition at the night club on November 28, 1942 (apart from the lighting of a match hereinafter described), that was not within the usual and regular practice during the time before the defendant was taken ill when he was at the night club nearly every evening. . . .

The physical arrangement of the night club on November 28, 1942, as well as on November 16, 1942, when the defendant last had personal knowledge of it, was as follows. [The only entrance to the club was through a single revolving door. Various rooms were connected by narrow passageways and corridors to one another and to a small number of exits. Three of the emergency exits were in obscure locations, poorly marked and accessible only to knowledgeable employees. The court observed that an emergency escape "would be difficult for a patron not thoroughly familiar with parts of the premises not ordinarily open to him." Two other emergency exits were marked by "Exit" lights and equipped with panic bars, but one of the two was blocked by a screen and dining tables; the other was regularly kept locked and the court noted that "if that door should be left so that it could be opened by means of the panic bar, a patron might leave through that door without paying his bill."]

. . . A little after ten o'clock on the evening of Saturday, November 28, 1942, the night club was well filled with a crowd of patrons. It was during the busiest season of the year. An important football game in the afternoon had attracted many visitors to Boston. [T]here were from two hundred fifty to four hundred persons in the Melody Lounge, from four hundred to five hundred in the main dining room and the Caricature Bar, and two hundred fifty in the Cocktail Lounge. . . .

A bartender in the Melody Lounge noticed that an electric light bulb which was in or near the cocoanut husks of an artificial palm tree in the corner had been turned off and that the corner was dark. He directed a sixteen year old bar boy who was waiting on customers at the tables to cause the bulb to be lighted. [The bar boy lit a match to see the bulb, turned the bulb in its socket to light it, and blew out the match. The flame of the match ignited a palm tree, which in turn ignited a low cloth ceiling nearby.] The fire spread with great rapidity. . . . The crowd were panic stricken, and rushed and pushed in every direction through the night club, screaming, and overturning tables and chairs in their attempts to escape.

The door at the head of the Melody Lounge stairway was not opened until firemen broke it down from outside with an axe and found it locked by a key lock, so that the panic bar could not operate. . . . The head waiter and another waiter tried to get open the panic doors from the main dining room to Shawmut Street, and succeeded after some difficulty. The other two doors to Shawmut Street were locked, and were opened by force from outside by firemen and others. . . . A considerable number of patrons escaped through the Broadway door, but many died just inside that door. Some employees, and a great number of patrons, died in the fire. . . .

[Defendant was charged with numerous counts of involuntary manslaughter based on overcrowding, installation of flammable decorations, absence of fire doors, and failure to maintain proper means of egress.]

The defendant was found guilty [and sentenced] upon each count for a term of not less than twelve years and not more than fifteen years, the first day of said term to be in solitary confinement and the residue at hard labor, the sentences to run concurrently. . . .

The Commonwealth disclaimed any contention that the defendant intentionally killed or injured the persons named in the indictments as victims. It based its case on involuntary manslaughter through wanton or reckless conduct. The judge instructed the jury correctly with respect to the nature of such conduct.

Usually wanton or reckless conduct consists of an affirmative act, like driving an automobile or discharging a firearm, in disregard of probable harmful consequences to another. But where as in the present case there is a duty of care for the safety of business visitors invited to premises which the defendant controls, wanton or reckless conduct may consist of intentional failure to take such care in disregard of the probable harmful consequences to them or of their right to care.

To define wanton or reckless conduct so as to distinguish it clearly from negligence and gross negligence is not easy. Sometimes the word "wilful" is prefaced to the words "wanton" and "reckless" in expressing the concept. That only blurs it. Wilful means intentional. In the phrase "wilful, wanton or reckless conduct," if "wilful" modifies "conduct" it introduces something different from wanton or reckless conduct, even though the legal result is the same. Wilfully causing harm is a wrong, but a different wrong from wantonly or recklessly causing harm. If "wilful" modifies "wanton or reckless conduct" its use is accurate. What must be intended is the conduct, not the resulting harm. The words "wanton" and "reckless" are practically synonymous in this connection, although the word "wanton" may contain a suggestion of arrogance or insolence or heartlessness that is lacking in the word "reckless." But intentional conduct to which either word applies is followed by the same legal consequences as though both words applied.

The standard of wanton or reckless conduct is at once subjective and objective, as has been recognized ever since Commonwealth v. Pierce, 138 Mass. 165, 52 Am. Rep. 264. Knowing facts that would cause a reasonable man to know the danger is equivalent to knowing the danger. . . . The judge charged the jury correctly when he said, "To constitute wanton or reckless conduct, as distinguished from mere negligence, grave danger to others must have been apparent and the defendant must have chosen to run the risk rather than alter his conduct so as to avoid the act or omission which caused the harm. If the grave danger was in fact realized by the defendant, his subsequent voluntary act or omission which caused the harm amounts to wanton or reckless conduct, no matter whether the ordinary man would have realized the gravity of the danger or not. But even if a particular defendant is so stupid (or) so heedless . . . that in fact he did not realize the grave danger, he cannot escape the imputation of wanton or reckless conduct in his dangerous act or omission, if an ordinary normal man under the same circumstances would have realized the gravity of the danger. A man may be reckless within the meaning of the law although he himself thought he was careful."

The essence of wanton or reckless conduct is intentional conduct, by way either of commission or of omission where there is a duty to act, which conduct involves a high degree of likelihood[a] that substantial harm will result to another. Wanton or reckless conduct amounts to what has been variously described as indifference to or disregard of probable consequences to that other. . . .

The words "wanton" and "reckless" are thus not merely rhetorical, vituperative expressions used instead of negligent or grossly negligent. They express a difference in the degree of risk and in the voluntary taking of risk so marked, as compared with negligence, as to amount substantially and in the eyes of the law to a difference in kind. . . .

Notwithstanding language used commonly in earlier cases, and occasionally in later ones, it is now clear in this Commonwealth that at common law conduct does not become criminal until it passes the borders of negligence and gross negligence and enters into the domain of wanton or reckless conduct. There is in Massachusetts at common law no such thing as "criminal negligence." . . .

---

a. Was there a "high degree of likelihood" that a raging fire would break out in this restaurant at a time when it was filled to capacity? On a statistical basis, is it not improbable that a fire will break out in any particular restaurant? — EDS.

To convict the defendant of manslaughter, the Commonwealth was not required to prove that he caused the fire by some wanton or reckless conduct. Fire in a place of public resort is an ever present danger. It was enough to prove that death resulted from his wanton or reckless disregard of the safety of patrons in the event of fire from any cause.

[A]ffirmed.

NOTES AND QUESTIONS

1. *Questions on* Welansky. Was the defendant aware of the risk to which his conduct had exposed his patrons and employees? Does the fact that the defendant himself spent most of his evenings at the club support or undercut the claim that he was aware of the risk?

Did the trial judge's instructions make actual awareness of the risk a prerequisite to conviction? Does the appellate court's opinion do so? What are the distinctive features of conduct that "passes the borders of negligence and gross negligence and enters into the domain of wanton and reckless conduct"?

How is "wanton and reckless conduct" in Massachusetts different from ordinary civil negligence?

2. *Defining unintended criminal homicide.* A persistent problem faced by the courts and legislatures has been the formulation of the "extra" or "plus" qualities that differentiate unintended homicides that give rise to criminal liability from those that, at most, produce civil liability for negligence. Consider the following comments.

State v. Barnett, 218 S.C. 415, 63 S.E.2d 57, 58-59 (1951): The degree of negligence necessary to establish criminal liability has perplexed the courts of England and America for centuries. The subject has at times been the source of much confusion. In the early development of the criminal law in England it was held that ordinary negligence, that is, the failure to exercise due care, was sufficient. Later it was found that this rule was too harsh. A noted English authority observed that an accident brought about by an act of ordinary negligence "may be the lot of even the wisest and the best of mankind." The English courts finally concluded that more carelessness was required to create criminal liability than civil but they found it difficult to determine "how much more." They use such words as "gross," "reckless" and "culpable," and hold that it is for the jury to decide, in view of all the circumstances, whether the act was of such character as to be worthy of punishment. . . . There was a tendency in the early American decisions to follow the rule first adopted in England to the effect that ordinary negligence was sufficient. That standard was soon repudiated, however, by the great majority of the courts in this country and it is now generally held that the negligence of the accused must be "culpable," "gross," or "reckless," that is, the conduct of the accused must be such a departure from what would be the conduct of an ordinarily prudent or careful man under the same circumstances as to be incompatible with a proper regard for human life, or conduct amounting to an indifference to consequences. Of course, under all the authorities the conduct of the accused must be judged in the light of the potential danger involved in the lawful act being performed. In perhaps a majority of the states, the offense of involuntary manslaughter is now defined by statute. Although variously worded, these statutes, with a few exceptions, have been construed as requiring gross negligence or recklessness.

Andrews v. Director of Public Prosecutions, [1937] A.C. 576, 581-583: My Lords, of all crimes manslaughter appears to afford more difficulties of definition, for it concerns homicide in so many and so varying conditions. From the early days when any homicide involved penalty the law has gradually evolved "through successive differentiations and integrations" until it recognizes murder on the one hand, based mainly, though not exclusively, on an intention to kill, and manslaughter on the other hand, based mainly, though not exclusively, on the absence of intention to kill but with the presence of an element of "unlawfulness" which is the elusive factor. In the present case it is only necessary to consider manslaughter from the point of view of an unintentional killing caused by negligence, that is, the omission of a duty to take care. . . .

Expressions will be found which indicate that to cause death by any lack of due care will amount to manslaughter; but as manners softened and the law became more humane a narrower criterion appeared. After all, manslaughter is a felony, and was capital, and men shrank from attaching the serious consequences of a conviction for felony to results produced by mere inadvertence. The stricter view became apparent in prosecutions of medical men or men who professed medical or surgical skill for manslaughter by reason of negligence. . . . So . . . in Rex v. Bateman [19 Crim. App. 8] a charge of manslaughter was made against a qualified medical practitioner. [T]he Lord Chief Justice, after pointing out that in a civil case once negligence is proved the degree of negligence is irrelevant, said, "In a criminal Court, on the contrary, the amount and degree of negligence are the determining question. There must be mens rea. . . . In explaining to juries the test which they should apply to determine whether the negligence, in the particular case, amounted or did not amount to a crime, judges have used many epithets such as 'culpable,' 'gross,' 'wicked,' 'clear,' 'complete.' But whatever epithet be used and whether an epithet be used or not, in order to establish criminal liability the facts must be such that, in the opinion of the jury, the negligence of the accused went beyond a mere matter of compensation between subjects and showed such disregard for the life and safety of others as to amount to a crime against the State and conduct deserving punishment." . . .

I think with respect that the expressions used are not, indeed they probably were not intended to be, a precise definition of the crime. I do not myself find the connotations of mens rea helpful in distinguishing between degrees of negligence, nor do the ideas of crime and punishment in themselves carry a jury much further in deciding whether in a particular case the degree of negligence shown is a crime and deserves punishment. But the substance of the judgment is most valuable, and in my opinion is correct. In practice it has generally been adopted by judges in charging juries in all cases of manslaughter by negligence, whether in driving vehicles or otherwise.

The principle to be observed is that cases of manslaughter in driving motor cars are but instances of a general rule applicable to all charges of homicide by negligence. Simple lack of care such as will constitute civil liability is not enough: for purposes of the criminal law there are degrees of negligence, and a very high degree of negligence is required to be proved before the felony is established. Probably of all the epithets that can be applied "reckless" most nearly covers the case. It is difficult to visualize a case of death caused by reckless driving in the connotation of that term in ordinary speech which would not justify a conviction for manslaughter: but it is probably not all-embracing, for "reckless" suggests an indifference to risk whereas the accused may have appreciated the risk and intended to avoid it and yet shown such a high degree of negligence in the means adopted to avoid the risk as would justify a conviction. If the principle of *Bateman*'s case is observed it will appear that the law of manslaughter has not changed by the introduction of motor vehicles on the road. Death caused by their negligent driving, though unhappily much more frequent, is to be treated in law as death caused by any other form of negligence, and juries should be directed accordingly.

Model Penal Code and Commentaries, Comment to §2.02 at 240 (1980): [Under traditional] statutes, as at common law, the concept of criminal negligence has been left to judicial definition, and the definitions vary greatly in their terms. As Jerome Hall has put it, the judicial "opinions run in terms of 'wanton and wilful negligence,' 'gross negligence,' and more illuminating yet, 'that degree of negligence that is more than the negligence required to impose tort liability.' The apex of this infelicity is 'wilful, wanton negligence,' which suggests a triple contradiction — 'negligence' implying inadvertence; 'wilful,' intention; and 'wanton,' recklessness." Much of this confusion is dispelled by a clear-cut distinction between recklessness and negligence in terms of the actor's awareness of the risk involved.

3. *The Model Penal Code approach.* Under the Model Penal Code, homicide is manslaughter when it is committed "recklessly," and recklessness is defined to require *conscious* awareness of the risk of death. See Model Penal Code §§2.02(2)(c), 210.3, Appendix. The Code creates a separate, lesser offense of "negligent homicide," and the required negligence is defined as a failure to appreciate a risk of death of which the actor *should be* aware. See Model Penal Code §§2.02(2)(d), 210.4, Appendix. Most modern statutory revisions have followed the Model Penal Code in imposing criminal liability for negligent homicide, limiting the required negligence to some form of *gross* departure from ordinary standards of care, and distinguishing for grading purposes between homicide based on inadvertent negligence and homicide based on conscious awareness of the risk. See Model Penal Code and Commentaries, Comment to §210.4 at 87-88 (1980).

4. *Vehicular homicide.* Although the traditional common law view requires at least gross negligence for a manslaughter conviction, a scattering of cases permit a lower standard in vehicle homicide prosecutions, sometimes on the theory that a motor vehicle is a "dangerous instrumentality" and that ordinary negligence in using it is therefore tantamount to gross negligence. See, e.g., State v. Barnett, 218 S.C. 415, 63 S.E.2d 57 (1951). In some instances statutes have expressly rejected the low standard permitted by cases like *Barnett.* See, e.g., S.C. Code §16-3-60 (1976, 1993) (requiring "criminal negligence" for involuntary manslaughter and defining criminal negligence as "reckless disregard of the safety of others"). The great majority of the common law decisions likewise reject the *Barnett* approach; as the House of Lords noted in *Andrews,* supra Note 2, the prevailing view treats cases of vehicle homicide like other instances of unintentional killing and requires more than ordinary negligence. See, e.g., Commonwealth v. Heck, 517 Pa. 192, 535 A.2d 575 (1987).

A countervailing trend, influenced by concern about large numbers of highway fatalities, has been to enact statutes treating vehicular homicide as a separate form of involuntary manslaughter. These statutes typically dispense with proof of gross negligence and, to reduce jury resistance to conviction, they typically carry lower penalties than those applicable to other types of involuntary manslaughter. See, e.g., Cal. Penal Code §192(c), page 389 supra.

NOTE ON CONTRIBUTORY NEGLIGENCE

In civil cases the deceased's contributory negligence once precluded imposing any liability on the defendant, even when the latter party's lack of care was more serious than that of the deceased. Recent adoption of the comparative negligence doctrine in most jurisdictions has changed this traditional approach in civil damage suits. In criminal cases, the deceased's contributory negligence or other misconduct has never afforded a defense. Consider Dickerson v. State, 441 So. 2d 536 (Miss. 1983). In the early morning hours, the defendant was driving slightly in excess of the speed limit when he suddenly became aware of a vehicle blocking his lane. The defendant applied his brakes, but not in time to avoid a collision that killed the driver of the other car. There was evidence that the deceased was himself quite intoxicated and guilty of gross negligence in parking his vehicle in the middle of the highway with its lights off. The court held such evidence immaterial (id. at 538):

> Contributory negligence is not a defense to manslaughter. All that the state must prove with respect to the victim is that he was prior to the incident a live human being. The homicide laws of this State protect all living beings within the jurisdiction, sinners as well as saints, drunks as well as deacons.

Note, however, that although contributory negligence does not automatically afford a defense, as it would in a civil case, it may have a bearing on the question of whether the defendant's conduct was a proximate cause of the death. See Chapter 6, page 547 infra.

PROBLEMS

1. In Parrish v. State, 97 So. 2d 356 (Fla. Dist. App. 1957), the defendant, in a car with companions, pursued his ex-wife through the city streets of Jacksonville in the early hours of the morning. He was armed with a bayonet and was apparently endeavoring to carry out his threat to kill her. He caught up with her at one point and broke her car window with his bayonet, but she maneuvered her car and eluded him. Continuing her escape she disregarded a stop sign and drove at a high rate of speed into a through street. In so doing she struck another car and subsequently died of the injuries. The defendant was convicted of second-degree murder, on the basis of having killed the deceased by an act "imminently dangerous to another, and evidencing a depraved mind regardless of human life."

Questions: Suppose the deceased had survived but the driver of the car she struck had been killed. Could *she* be held for manslaughter? Was the magnitude of the risk she created any less or the violation of the traffic laws excused because she was fleeing from an attacker? If not, on what basis could her conduct be distinguished from a driver who was simply in a hurry? Is the concept of justification the distinguishing factor? If so, can the creation of risk of death or injury to other innocent persons be justified where it is employed as a means to save oneself from like injury? Would her conduct be noncriminal if she drove through a group of people blocking the street and killed several?

These kinds of issues arise when a person, acting in lawful self-defense against an aggressor, accidentally kills an innocent bystander. See Annot., Unintentional killing of or injury to third person during attempted self-defense, 55 A.L.R.3d 620 (1974). The courts commonly require that the defendant has acted "prudently" in self-defense. But at what point does the risk to innocent persons become so great that the action is not prudent, even though taken in lawful self-defense?

See J. W. Salmond, Jurisprudence 416 (8th ed. 1930):

> What amounts to reasonable care depends entirely on the circumstances of the particular case as known to the person whose conduct is the subject of inquiry. Whether in those circumstances, as so known to him, he used due care — whether he acted as a reasonably prudent man — is in general a mere question of fact as to which no legal rules can be laid down. It would seem clear, however, that for the proper determination of this question of fact there are two chief matters of consideration. The first is the magnitude of the risk to which other persons are exposed, while the second is the importance of the object to be attained by the dangerous form of activity. The reasonableness of any conduct will depend upon the proportion between these two elements. To expose others to danger for a disproportionate object is unreasonable, whereas an equal risk for a better cause may lawfully be run without negligence. By driving trains at the rate of fifty miles an hour, railway companies have caused many fatal accidents which could quite easily have been avoided by reducing the speed to ten miles, but this additional safety would be attained at too great a cost of public convenience, and therefore in neglecting this precaution the companies do not fall below the standard of reasonable care and are not guilty of negligence.

2. A federal panel, appointed by the U.S. Department of Transportation to study the costs and benefits of retaining the national 55 MPH speed limit, estimated that raising the speed limit to 65 MPH would cause an additional 500 deaths per year. The panel also estimated that under the higher speed limit 850,000 hours of travel time would be saved for every life lost. N.Y. Times, Nov. 28, 1984, at A16.

Questions: Is enactment of the higher speed limit justifiable? Should motorists who become involved in fatal accidents while driving at 65 MPH (in violation of a posted speed limit) have a good defense against a charge of criminal homicide?

Subsequent research found that the federal panel's original estimates had been overly optimistic. In April 1987, responding to a perceived easing of the "energy crisis," Congress authorized states to increase their speed limits on rural interstate roads. In a study of 22 states in which speed limits on such roads had been raised to 65 MPH, the National Highway Traffic Safety Administration found that traffic fatalities soared by more than 50 percent, from 296 in the 3-month period May-July, 1986, to 450 in the same 3-month period of 1987. See N.Y. Times, Dec. 18, 1987, at A1. More recent data suggests that raising the speed limit from 55 MPH to 65 MPH increased deaths on rural interstate roads by 20 to 30 percent. See Washington Post, June 29, 1993, at z12. Nationally, there were over 6 million automobile crashes in 1991; 357,000 of these involved severe injuries, including over 39,000 fatalities.[3] By comparison murder and nonnegligent manslaughter took 24,700 lives in the same year.[4] At what point does the saving in driving time justify the additional cost of increased foreign oil consumption? At what point does the saving in driving time justify the additional loss of life?

b.   Objective versus Subjective Standards of Liability

STATE v. WILLIAMS

Washington Court of Appeals
4 Wash. App. 908, 484 P.2d 1167 (1971)

HOROWITZ, C.J. Defendants, husband and wife, were charged by information filed October 3, 1968, with the crime of manslaughter for negligently failing to supply their 17-month child with necessary medical attention, as a result of which he died on September 12, 1968. Upon entry of findings, conclusions and judgment of guilty, sentences were imposed on April 22, 1969. Defendants appeal.

The defendant husband, Walter Williams, is a 24-year-old full-blooded Shoshon[e] Indian with a sixth-grade education. His sole occupation is that of laborer. The defendant wife, Bernice Williams, is a 20-year-old part Indian with an 11th grade education. At the time of the marriage, the wife had two children, the younger of whom was a 14-month-old son. Both parents worked and the children were cared for by the 85-year-old mother of the defendant husband. The defendant husband assumed parental responsibility with the defendant wife to provide clothing, care and medical attention for the child. Both defendants possessed a great deal of love and affection for the defendant wife's young son.

The court expressly found:

> That both defendants were aware that William Joseph Tabafunda was ill during the period September 1, 1968 to September 12, 1968. The defendants were ignorant. They did not realize how sick the baby was. They thought that the baby had a toothache and no layman regards a toothache as dangerous to life. They loved the

3. Bureau of Justice Statistics, Sourcebook of Criminal Justice Statistics — 1992 (U.S. Dept. of Justice 1993), p. 356.
   4. Id. at 357.

baby and gave it aspirin in hopes of improving its condition. They did not take the
baby to a doctor because of fear that the Welfare Department would take the baby
away from them. They knew that medical help was available because of previous
experience. They had no excuse that the law will recognize for not taking the baby
to a doctor.

The defendants Walter L. Williams and Bernice J. Williams were negligent in not
seeking medical attention for William Joseph Tabafunda.

That as a proximate result of this negligence, William Joseph Tabafunda died.

Findings 5, 6, and 7. From these and other findings, the [trial] court concluded
that the defendants were each guilty of the crime of manslaughter as
charged. . . .

[The court of appeals held that both defendants were under a legal duty to
obtain medical assistance for the child.[a]] On the question of the quality or seriousness of breach of the duty, at common law, in the case of involuntary manslaughter, the breach had to amount to more than mere ordinary or simple
negligence — gross negligence was essential. . . . In Washington, however,
R.C.W. 9.48.060[2] (since amended by Laws of 1970, ch. 49, §2) and R.C.W.
9.48.150[3] supersede both voluntary and involuntary manslaughter as those
crimes were defined at common law. Under these statutes the crime is deemed
committed even though the death of the victim is the proximate result of only
simple or ordinary negligence. . . .

The concept of simple or ordinary negligence describes a failure to exercise
the "ordinary caution" necessary to make out the defense of excusable homicide. R.C.W. 9.48.150. Ordinary caution is the kind of caution that a man of
reasonable prudence would exercise under the same or similar conditions. If,
therefore, the conduct of a defendant, regardless of his ignorance, good intentions and good faith, fails to measure up to the conduct required of a man of
reasonable prudence, he is guilty of ordinary negligence because of his failure
to use "ordinary caution." . . . If such negligence proximately causes the death
of the victim, the defendant, as pointed out above, is guilty of statutory
manslaughter. . . .

The remaining issue of proximate cause requires consideration of the question of when the duty to furnish medical care became activated. If the duty to
furnish such care was not activated until after it was too late to save the life of
the child, failure to furnish medical care could not be said to have proximately
caused the child's death. Timeliness in the furnishing of medical care also must

a. In footnote 1, the court observed that the information, in charging the violation of the duty
owed, alleged:

"[T]hey, the said defendants, then and there being the father, mother, guardian and custodian
of one William Joseph Tabafunda, and being then and there under the legal duty of providing
necessary food, clothing, care and medical attention to said William Joseph Tabafunds [sic], a
minor child under the age of sixteen years, to-wit: of the age of seventeen (17) months, did then
and there unlawfully and feloniously fail and neglect, without lawful excuse, to provide said . . .
child . . . with necessary food, clothing, care and medical attention. . . ." — Eds.

2. R.C.W. 9.48.060 provided in part:

"In any case other than those specified in R.C.W. 9.48.030, 9.48.040, and 9.48.050, homicide,
not being excusable or justifiable, is manslaughter."

3. R.C.W. 9.48.150 provides:

"Homicide is excusable when committed by accident or misfortune in doing any lawful act by
lawful means, with ordinary caution and without any unlawful intent."

be considered in terms of "ordinary caution." . . . In our opinion, the duty as formulated in People v. Pierson, 176 N.Y. 201, 68 N.E. 243 (1903) . . . properly defines the duty contemplated by our manslaughter statutes. . . . The court there said: "We quite agree that the Code does not contemplate the necessity of calling a physician for every trifling complaint with which the child may be afflicted, which in most instances may be overcome by the ordinary household nursing by members of the family; that a reasonable amount of discretion is vested in parents, charged with the duty of maintaining and bringing up infant children; and that the standard is at what time would an ordinarily prudent person, solicitous for the welfare of his child and anxious to promote its recovery, deem it necessary to call in the services of a physician."

It remains to apply the law discussed to the facts of the instant case.

Defendants have not assigned error to the findings either on the ground that the evidence is insufficient to prove negligence or proximate cause, or that the state has failed to prove the facts found by failing to apply the required standard of proof beyond a reasonable doubt. . . . They contended below and on appeal that they are not guilty of the crime charged. Because of the serious nature of the charge against the parent and step-parent of a well-loved child, and out of our concern for the protection of the constitutional rights of the defendants, we have made an independent examination of the evidence to determine whether it substantially supports the court's express finding on proximate cause and its implied finding that the duty to furnish medical care became activated in time to prevent death of the child. . . .

Dr. Gale Wilson, the autopsy surgeon and chief pathologist for the King County Coroner, testified that the child died because an abscessed tooth had been allowed to develop into an infection of the mouth and cheeks, eventually becoming gangrenous. This condition, accompanied by the child's inability to eat, brought about malnutrition, lowering the child's resistance and eventually producing pneumonia, causing the death. Dr. Wilson testified that in his opinion the infection had lasted for approximately 2 weeks, and that the odor generally associated with gangrene would have been present for approximately 10 days before death. He also expressed the opinion that had medical care been first obtained in the last week before the baby's death, such care would have been obtained too late to have saved the baby's life. Accordingly, the baby's apparent condition between September 1 and September 5, 1968 became the critical period for the purpose of determining whether in the exercise of ordinary caution defendants should have provided medical care for the minor child.

The testimony concerning the child's apparent condition during the critical period is not crystal clear, but is sufficient to warrant the following statement of the matter. The defendant husband testified that he noticed the baby was sick about 2 weeks before the baby died. The defendant wife testified that she noticed the baby was ill about a week and a half or 2 weeks before the baby died. The evidence showed that in the critical period the baby was fussy; that he could not keep his food down; and that a cheek started swelling up. The swelling went up and down, but did not disappear. In that same period, the cheek turned "a bluish color like." The defendants, not realizing that the baby was as ill as it was or that the baby was in danger of dying, attempted to provide some relief to the baby by giving the baby aspirin during the critical period and continued to do so until the night before the baby died. The defendants thought the swelling would go down and were waiting for it to do so; and defendant husband testified, that from what he had heard, neither doctors nor dentists pull out a tooth "when it's all swollen up like that." There was an additional explanation for not calling a doctor given by each defendant. Defendant husband testified that "the way the cheek looked, . . . and that stuff on his hair, they would think we were neglecting him and take him away from us and not give him back." Defendant wife testified that the defendants were "waiting for the swelling to go down," and also that they were afraid to take the child to a doctor for fear that the doctor would report them to the welfare department, who, in turn, would take the child away. "It's just that I was so scared of losing him." They testified that they had heard that the defendant husband's cousin lost a child that way. The evidence showed that the defendants did not understand the significance or seriousness of the baby's symptoms. However, there is no evidence that the defendants were physically or financially unable to obtain a doctor, or that they did not know an available doctor, or that the symptoms did not continue to be a matter of concern during the critical period. Indeed, the evidence shows that in April 1968 defendant husband had taken the child to a doctor for medical attention.

In our opinion, there is sufficient evidence from which the court could find, as it necessarily did, that applying the standard of ordinary caution, i.e., the caution exercisable by a man of reasonable prudence under the same or similar conditions, defendants were sufficiently put on notice concerning the symptoms of the baby's illness and lack of improvement in the baby's apparent condition in the period from September 1 to September 5, 1968 to have required them to have obtained medical care for the child. The failure so to do in this case is ordinary or simple negligence, and such negligence is sufficient to support a conviction of statutory manslaughter.

The judgment is affirmed.

NOTES AND QUESTIONS

1. The manslaughter statutes involved in *Williams* were repealed in 1975. The current statutes create two degrees of manslaughter: recklessly causing death and causing death by criminal negligence. See Wash. Rev. Code §9A.32.060; Wash. Rev. Code §9A.32.070 (1992). In accord with generally prevailing law, Washington no longer imposes manslaughter liability in cases involving ordinary negligence. See State v. Norman, 61 Wash. App. 16, 808 P.2d 1159, 1162 (1991).

Questions: Would the *Williams* court have reached a different result under the statute in effect today? On the court's view of the facts, wouldn't the behavior of the Williams couple also involve "criminal" negligence?

2. Many will find the conviction of the Williams couple unjust and, perhaps, pointless. Why were the defendants punished?

(a) Note that the court calls attention to the race of the defendants. In what respect, if any, did their race have a bearing on the issues in the case? Was it relevant at all?

(b) Were the defendants punished only because of their ignorance? If the conviction seems unjust, is this because they were unaware of the danger to their child? If so, does it follow that punishment for negligence (where there is no

awareness of the risk) is always unjust? Consider the materials in the following Note in thinking about these questions.

NOTES ON THE CONTROVERSY OVER STANDARDS OF LIABILITY

1. Objective and subjective liability defined. The concepts of objective and subjective standards are subject to a variety of interpretations. See G. Fletcher, Rethinking Criminal Law 504 et seq. (1978). In general, objective or external standards determine liability on the basis of *general norms* of proper and reasonable behavior. Thus, the provocation standard imports an objective standard insofar as the law requires that what provoked the defendant to kill would have severely tested the self-control of a reasonable person. Recklessness and negligence are objective standards insofar as liability turns on whether the action of defendant created a risk of a kind and degree which, in the circumstances, a reasonable person would not have taken. Subjective or internal standards of liability, on the other hand, look to the *individual* characteristics of the actor, and, insofar as they are thoroughgoing in their subjectivity, take "account of the infinite varieties of temperament, intellect and education which make the internal character of a given act so different." O. W. Holmes, The Common Law 108 (1881). Premeditation and deliberation are subjective standards, since they look to what the particular defendant experienced. The same is true of the diminished-capacity defense. Tension between these two kinds of standards runs through the whole of the criminal law.

A standard of negligence is, as we have indicated, substantially objective. Should its objectivity be qualified by requiring that defendant have been aware of the risk his or her action entailed (or, in the Model Penal Code's terminology, by requiring recklessness rather than negligence) before criminal liability may be imposed?

2. In defense of an objective standard. Justice Holmes believed that the direction of legal development was toward objective standards. Consistent with that view, he explained the criminal law's lack of concern with whether the defendant was aware of the risk as follows (The Common Law 53-55, 59 (1881)):

> If the known present state of things is such that the act done will very certainly cause death, and the probability is a matter of common knowledge, one who does the act, knowing the present state of things, is guilty of murder, and the law will not inquire whether he did actually foresee the consequences or not. The test of foresight is not what this very criminal foresaw, but what a man of reasonable prudence would have foreseen.
>
> On the other hand, there must be actual present knowledge of the present facts which make an act dangerous. The act is not enough by itself. . . . A fear of punishment for causing harm cannot work as a motive, unless the possibility of harm may be foreseen. So far, then, as criminal liability is founded upon wrongdoing in any sense, and so far as the threats and punishments of the law are intended to deter men from bringing about various harmful results, they must be confined to cases where circumstances making the conduct dangerous were known.
>
> Still, in a more limited way, the same principle applies to knowledge that applies to foresight. It is enough that such circumstances were actually known as would

have led a man of common understanding to infer from them the rest of the group making up the present state of things. For instance, if a workman on a housetop at mid-day knows that the space below him is a street in a great city, he knows facts from which a man of common understanding would infer that there were people passing below. He is therefore bound to draw that inference, or, in other words, is chargeable with knowledge of that fact also, whether he draws the inference or not. If, then, he throws down a heavy beam into the street, he does an act which a person of ordinary prudence would foresee is likely to cause death, or grievous bodily harm, and he is dealt with as if he foresaw it, whether he does so in fact or not. If a death is caused by the act, he is guilty of murder. . . .

[I]t is to be remembered that the object of the law is to prevent human life being endangered or taken; and that, although it so far considers blameworthiness in punishing as not to hold a man responsible for consequences which no one, or only some exceptional specialist, could have foreseen, still the reason for this limitation is simply to make a rule which is not too hard for the average member of the community. As the purpose is to compel men to abstain from dangerous conduct, and not merely to restrain them from evil inclinations, the law requires them at their peril to know the teachings of common experience, just as it requires them to know the law. Subject to these explanations, it may be said that the test of murder is the degree of danger to life attending the act under the known circumstances of the case. [The difference between murder and manslaughter lies] in the degree of danger attaching to the act in the given state of facts.

A few years after writing the foregoing, Holmes had occasion to apply his views in Commonwealth v. Pierce, 138 Mass. 165, 171-176 (1884). In this case defendant was convicted of manslaughter

on evidence that he publicly practised as a physician, and, being called to attend a sick woman, caused her, with her consent, to be kept in flannels saturated with kerosene for three days, more or less, by reason of which she died. There was evidence that he had made similar applications with favorable results in other cases, but that in one the effect had been to blister and burn the flesh as in the present case.

The alleged errors in the trial court's instructions to the jury turned on its refusal to charge that a finding of recklessness was required for conviction. Holmes formulated the issue as follows (id. at 175-176):

But recklessness in a moral sense means a certain state of consciousness with reference to the consequences of one's acts. No matter whether defined as indifference to what those consequences may be, or as a failure to consider their nature or probability as fully as the party might and ought to have done, it is understood to depend on the actual condition of the individual's mind with regard to consequences, as distinguished from mere knowledge of present or past facts or circumstances from which some one or everybody else might be led to anticipate or apprehend them if the supposed act were done. We have to determine whether recklessness in this sense was necessary to make the defendant guilty of felonious homicide, or whether his acts are to be judged by the external standard of what would be morally reckless, under the circumstances known to him, in a man of reasonable prudence.

More specifically, the questions raised by the foregoing requests and rulings are whether an actual good intent and the expectation of good results are an absolute justification of acts, however foolhardy they may be if judged by the external standard supposed, and whether the defendant's ignorance of the tendencies of kerosene administered as it was will excuse the administration of it.

After reviewing the objective standards applicable in civil cases, Holmes concluded:

If this is the rule adopted in regard to the redistribution of losses, which sound policy allows to rest where they fall in the absence of a clear reason to the contrary, there would seem to be at least equal reason for adopting it in the criminal law, which has for its immediate object and task to establish a general standard, or at least general negative limits, of conduct for the community, in the interest of the safety of all.[a]

3. *Criticism of the objective standard.* Summarizing the arguments against negligence liability, Professor Glanville Williams wrote (Criminal Law: The General Part 122-123 (2d ed. 1961)):

The use of the criminal law to punish negligence has been challenged. An American writer expressed the objection as follows:

If the defendant, being mistaken as to material facts, is to be punished because his mistake is one which an average man would not make, punishment will sometimes be inflicted when the criminal mind does not exist. Such a result is contrary to fundamental principles, and is plainly unjust, for a man should not be held criminal because of lack of intelligence.[b]

The retributive theory of punishment is open to many objections, which are of even greater force when applied to inadvertent negligence than in crimes requiring mens rea. Some people are born feckless, clumsy, thoughtless, inattentive, irresponsible, with a bad memory and a slow "reaction time." With the best will in the world, we all of us at some times in our lives make negligent mistakes. It is hard to see how justice (as distinct from some utilitarian reason) requires mistakes to be punished.

Again, the deterrent theory, which is normally accepted as a justification for criminal punishment, finds itself in some difficulty when applied to negligence. At best the deterrent effect of the legal sanction is a matter of faith rather than of proved scientific fact; but there is no department in which this faith is less firmly grounded than that of negligence. Hardly any motorist but does not firmly believe that if he is involved in an accident it will be the other fellow's fault. It may seem, therefore, that the threat of punishment for negligence must pass him by, because he does not realize that it is addressed to him. Even if a person admits that he occasionally makes a negligent mistake, how, in the nature of things, can punishment for inadvertence serve to deter?

4. *The Model Penal Code position on liability without awareness.* The Model Penal Code takes the position that awareness of the risk (recklessness) is required for manslaughter, but a person who is unaware of the risk may be punished for the

---

a. For a defense of liability for negligence, see A. D. Woozley, Negligence and Ignorance, 53 Phil. 293 (1978). — EDS.

b. For development of the idea that there is no moral difference between strict liability and liability for inadvertent negligence, see Larry Alexander, Reconsidering the Relationship Among Voluntary Acts, Strict Liability, and Negligence in Criminal Law, 7 Soc. Phil. & Pol. 84 (1990). — EDS.

lesser crime of negligent homicide. Compare §§210.3(1)(a) and 210.4, Appendix. In support of retaining negligence as a basis of criminal liability, Model Penal Code and Commentaries, Comment to §2.02 at 243-244 (1980), states:

> When people have knowledge that conviction and sentence, not to speak of punishment, may follow conduct that inadvertently creates improper risk, they are supplied with an additional motive to take care before acting, to use their faculties and draw on their experience in gauging the potentialities of contemplated conduct. To some extent, at least, this motive may promote awareness and thus be effective as a measure of control. Moreover, moral defect can properly be imputed to instances where the defendant acts out of insensitivity to the interests of other people, and not merely out of an intellectual failure to grasp them. In any event legislators act on these assumptions in a host of situations, and it would be dogmatic to assert that they are wholly wrong. Accordingly, negligence, as here defined, should not be wholly rejected as a ground of culpability that may suffice for purposes of penal law, though it should properly not generally be deemed sufficient in the definition of specific crimes and it should often be differentiated from conduct involving higher culpability for the purposes of sentence.

5. *The defendant's ability to conform.* Professor Hart has argued that the difficulty with punishing for negligence does not arise from punishing a person who is unaware of the risk he or she is creating. Rather, the difficulty arises from punishing the person for departing from an external or invariant standard that he or she might have been *unable* to meet. (H. L. A. Hart, Punishment and Responsibility, 152-154 (1968)):

> Excessive distrust of negligence and excessive confidence in the respectability of "foresight of harm" or "having the thought of harm in the mind" as a ground of responsibility have their roots in a common misunderstanding. Both oversimplify the character of the subjective element required in those whom we punish, if it is to be morally tolerable, according to common notions of justice, to punish them. The reason why, according to modern ideas, strict liability is odious, and appears as a sacrifice of a valued principle which we should make, if at all, only for some overriding social good, is not merely because it amounts, as it does, to punishing those who did not at the time of acting "have in their minds" the elements of foresight or desire for muscular movement. . . . What is crucial is that those whom we punish should have had, when they acted, the normal capacities, physical and mental, for doing what the law requires and abstaining from what it forbids, and a fair opportunity to exercise these capacities. Where these capacities and opportunities are absent, as they are in different ways in the varied cases of accident, mistake, paralysis, reflex action, coercion, insanity, etc., the moral protest is that it is morally wrong to punish because "he could not have helped it" or "he could not have done otherwise" or "he had no real choice." But . . . there is no reason . . . *always* to make this protest when someone who "just didn't think" is punished for carelessness. For in some cases at least we may say "he could have thought about what he was doing" with just as much rational confidence as one can say of any intentional wrongdoing "he could have done otherwise." . . .
>
> The most important compromise which legal systems make over the subjective element consists in its adoption of what has been unhappily termed the "objective standard." This may lead to an individual being treated for the purposes of conviction and punishment as if he possessed capacities for control of his conduct which he did not possess, but which an ordinary or reasonable man possesses and would

have exercised. The expression "objective" and its partner "subjective" are un-happy because, as far as negligence is concerned, they obscure the real issue. . . . For, when negligence is made criminally punishable, this itself leaves open the question: whether, before we punish, both or only the first of the following two questions must be answered affirmatively:

> (i) Did the accused fail to take those precautions which any reasonable man with normal capacities would in the circumstances have taken?
> (ii) Could the accused, given his mental and physical capacities, have taken those precautions?

One use of the dangerous expressions "objective" and "subjective" is to make the distinction between these two questions: given the ambiguities of those expres-sions, the distinction would have been more happily expressed by the expressions "invariant" standard of care, and "individualized conditions of liability." It may well be that, even if the "standard of care" is pitched very low so that individuals are held liable only if they fail to take very elementary precautions against harm, there will still be some unfortunate individuals who, through lack of intelligence, powers of concentration or memory, or through clumsiness, could not attain even this low standard. If our conditions of liability are invariant and not flexible, i.e., if they are not adjusted to the capacities of the accused, then some individuals will be held liable for negligence though they could not have helped their failure to comply with the standard. In *such* cases, indeed, criminal responsibility will be made independent of any "subjective element," since the accused could not have conformed to the required standard. But this result [has] nothing to do with neg-ligence being taken as a basis for criminal liability. . . . "Absolute liability" results, not from the admission of the principle that one who has been grossly negligent is criminally responsible for the consequent harm even if "he had no idea in his mind of harm to anyone," but from the refusal in the application of this principle to consider the capacities of an individual who has fallen below the standard of care.

The kind of individualization Hart defends would result in legal guilt and moral blameworthiness being made more nearly the same. What are the prob-lems with this approach? Consider Sanford H. Kadish, Blame and Punishment 96-97 (1987):

[State v. Williams] vividly illustrates [the force of Hart's position]. Nonetheless, . . . [i]f we excuse parents for ignorance of the medical needs of their child on the ground that they are ignorant people, must we not also excuse a person for yield-ing to a trivial threat of future harm on the ground that he is a cowardly person? If it is a defense to a crime of negligence that the defendant couldn't have known and taken care because that's the kind of person he is, why would it not also be a defense to a crime of intention that the defendant could not help choosing to act as he did because that is the kind of person *he* is: aggressive, self-centered, brutal, and so on?

6. A foreign law solution. German law defines negligence in accord with Hart's analysis. The view announced in a leading 1922 case was as follows (The Case of the Gable-Wall (Giebelmauer), 56 RGSt 343, 349 (1922)):

A harm caused by defendants can be said to be caused by negligence only when it is established that they disregarded the care which they were obliged to exercise and of which they were capable under the circumstances and according to their personal knowledge and abilities. . . .

For discussion of this approach see George Fletcher, The Theory of Criminal Negligence: A Comparative Analysis, 119 U. Pa. L. Rev. 401 (1971).

7. *The Model Penal Code on individualization.* In contrast to the German approach, the Model Penal Code's definition of negligence (see §2.02(2)(d), Appendix) rejects a fully individualized standard. However, some elements of an individualized standard are invited by its reference to "the care that would be exercised by a reasonable person in his [the actor's] situation." Model Penal Code and Commentaries, Comment to §2.02 at 242 (1985) states:

> There is an inevitable ambiguity in "situation." If the actor were blind or if he had just suffered a blow or experienced a heart attack, these would certainly be facts to be considered in a judgment involving criminal liability, as they would be under traditional law. But the heredity, intelligence or temperament of the actor would not be held material in judging negligence, and could not be without depriving the criterion of all its objectivity. The Code is not intended to displace discriminations of this kind, but rather to leave the issue to the courts.

Recall that the Model Penal Code took a similar approach in its formulation of provocation, where the objectivity of the standard is qualified by the sentence (§210.3): "The reasonableness of such explanation or excuse shall be determined from the viewpoint of a person *in the actor's situation* under the circumstances as he believes them to be." [Italics added.] See page 433 supra.

Question: How would the *Williams* case be decided under the Code?

8. *The case law on individualization.* Although the Model Penal Code leaves to the courts the problem of determining the appropriate degree of individualization, the courts remain ambivalent or in conflict. In State v. Everhart, 291 N.C. 700, 231 S.E.2d 604 (1977), the defendant, a young girl with an IQ of 72, gave birth in her own bedroom and, thinking that the baby had been born dead, wrapped it from head to foot in a blanket. The baby smothered to death. The court reversed a conviction for involuntary manslaughter, holding that because of the defendant's low IQ and the admittedly accidental nature of the death, the state had not proved culpable negligence. Compare Edgmon v. State, 702 P.2d 643, 645 (Alaska App. 1985). The court there held that individual capabilities would have to be considered in assessing recklessness (necessary in Alaska for a manslaughter conviction) but that "[i]n contrast, peculiarities of a given individual — his or her intelligence, experience, and physical capabilities — are irrelevant in determining criminal negligence [necessary for the lesser negligent homicide offense] since the standard is one of a reasonably prudent person."

PROBLEM

In Walker v. Superior Court, 47 Cal. 3d 112, 763 P.2d 852 (1988), defendant's four-year-old daughter fell ill with flu-like symptoms, and four days later she developed a stiff neck. In accord with the tenets of her religion, defendant, a member of the Church of Christ Scientist, elected to treat her daughter with prayer rather than medicine.[5] An "accredited Christian Scientist prayer practitioner" was summoned to supervise the child's treatment. Over a 17-day period, the child's condition worsened. She lost weight, grew disoriented, and eventually died of meningitis.

Questions: Is the mother guilty of involuntary manslaughter? In what respects are the arguments for conviction stronger or weaker than those in the *Williams* case? Prevailing interpretations of the First Amendment right to free exercise of religion make clear that there is no constitutional defense in such cases.[6] But consider the following additional issues:

(a) Religious accommodation statutes. About half the states have enacted statutes providing that a parent who chooses not to provide medical care to a minor child and instead treats the child by prayer, in accord with the practices of a recognized religion, may not be found guilty of abuse or neglect "for that reason alone." See Hermanson v. State, 604 So. 2d 775, 776 n. 1 (Fla. 1992). These statutes are generally interpreted as affording a limited defense in child custody and abuse and neglect proceedings; most courts have held that they do not pose a bar to an involuntary manslaughter prosecution when the parent has failed to provide medical treatment for a life-threatening illness. See, e.g., Commonwealth v. Twitchell, 416 Mass. 114, 617 N.E.2d 609 (1993). Under these conditions, does the involuntary manslaughter prohibition give adequate notice of the difference between privileged and prohibited conduct? In *Walker,* supra, the California court rejected the "void-for-vagueness" argument, but in *Hermanson,* supra, the Florida Supreme Court upheld a vagueness challenge to a manslaughter prosecution. Which is the better view? Is extreme vagueness inherent in any statute punishing "criminal negligence"?

(b) The meaning of the objective standard. How should the parents' religious beliefs be treated in considering whether, in a case like *Walker,* their conduct is criminally negligent? Should those beliefs, and the special deference owed to religious conviction in our society, count among the justifications that can be

---

5. The court explained (763 P.2d at 855 n. 1):

Members of the Church "believe that disease is a physical manifestation of errors of the mind." (Comment, Religious Beliefs and the Criminal Justice System: Some Problems of the Faith Healer, (1975) 8 Loyola L.A.L. Rev. 396, 397, fn. 7.) The use of medicine is believed to perpetuate such error and is therefore discouraged. Nonetheless, "the Church sets up no abstract criteria for determining what diseases or injuries should be treated by prayer or other methods but, rather, leaves such questions to individual decision in concrete instances. . . . If some turn in what they think is an urgent time of need to medical treatment for themselves or their children, they are *not* — contrary to some recent charges — stigmatized by their church." (Talbot, The Position of the Christian Science Church, (1983) 26 N.E. Med. J. 1641, 1642, italics in original.)

6. In Commonwealth v. Barnhart, 497 A.2d 616, 624-625 (Pa. Super. 1985), the court upheld a manslaughter conviction on facts comparable to those in the *Walker* case. On the First Amendment issue, the court explained:

We recognize that our decision today directly penalizes appellants in the practice of their religion. We emphasize that the liability attaches not to appellants' decisions for themselves but rather to their decision effectively to forfeit their child's life. Accord Prince v. Massachusetts, 321 U.S. [158, 170 (1944)] ("Parents may be free to become martyrs themselves. But it does not follow they are free, in identical circumstances, to make martyrs of their children before they (the children) have reached the age of full and legal discretion when they can make that choice for themselves").

weighed against the degree of the risk? Are the parents' religious beliefs part of their "situation," so that the proper standard would be to consider the actions expected of a reasonable person of the defendant's religion? In *Walker,* the court sustained the manslaughter indictment, holding (763 P.2d at 868) that "criminal negligence must be evaluated objectively" and that the controlling question was whether "a reasonable person in defendant's position would have been aware of the risk involved." Would this be the proper approach under the Model Penal Code? For discussion of the issues, see Edward Smith, Note, The Criminalization of Belief: When Free Exercise Isn't, 42 Hastings L.J. 1491 (1991).

c. The Line Between Murder and Manslaughter

COMMONWEALTH v. MALONE

Supreme Court of Pennsylvania
354 Pa. 180, 47 A.2d 445 (1946)

Maxey, C.J. This is an appeal from the judgment and sentence under a conviction of murder in the second degree.[a] William H. Long, age 13 years, was killed by a shot from a 32-caliber revolver held against his right side by the defendant, then aged 17 years. These youths were on friendly terms at the time of the homicide. The defendant and his mother while his father and brother were in the U.S. Armed Forces, were residing in Lancaster, Pa., with the family of William H. Long, whose son was the victim of the shooting.

On the evening of February 26th, 1945, when the defendant went to a moving picture theater, he carried in the pocket of his raincoat a revolver which he had obtained at the home of his uncle on the preceding day. In the afternoon preceding the shooting, the decedent procured a cartridge from his father's room and he and the defendant placed it in the revolver.

After leaving the theater, the defendant went to a dairy store and there met the decedent. Both youths sat in the rear of the store ten minutes, during which period the defendant took the gun out of his pocket and loaded the chamber to the right of the firing pin and then closed the gun. A few minutes later, both youths sat on stools in front of the lunch counter and ate some food. The defendant suggested to the decedent that they play "Russian Poker."[1] Long replied, "I don't care; go ahead." The defendant then placed the revolver against the right side of Long and pulled the trigger three times. The third pull resulted in a fatal wound to Long. The latter jumped off the stool and cried: "Oh! Oh! Oh!" and Malone said: "Did I hit you, Billy? Gee, Kid, I'm sorry." Long died from the wounds two days later.

---

a. The Pennsylvania homicide statute in effect at the time divided murder into two degrees, in accordance with the formula adopted in 1794. After classifying certain especially heinous murders as murders of the first degree, the statute provided simply that "[a]ll other kinds of murder shall be murder in the second degree." See page 394 supra. Comparable statutory language continues to define second-degree murder in many jurisdictions and what is now called "third-degree murder" in Pennsylvania. See 18 Pa. Stat. Ann. §2502 (c), reproduced at page 390 supra. — Eds.

1. It has been explained that "Russian Poker" is a game in which the participants, in turn, place a single cartridge in one of the five chambers of a revolver cylinder, give the latter a quick twirl, place the muzzle of the gun against the temple and pull the trigger, leaving it to chance whether or not death results to the trigger puller.

The defendant testified that the gun chamber he loaded was the first one to the right of the firing chamber and that when he pulled the trigger he did not "expect to have the gun go off." He declared he had no intention of harming Long, who was his friend and companion. The defendant was indicted for murder, tried and found guilty of murder in the second degree and sentenced to a term in the penitentiary for a period not less than five years and not exceeding ten years. A new trial was refused and after sentence was imposed, an appeal was taken.

Appellant alleges certain errors in the charge of the court and also contends that the facts did not justify a conviction for any form of homicide except involuntary manslaughter. This contention we overrule. A specific intent to take life is, under our law, an essential ingredient of murder in the first degree. At common law, the "grand criterion" which "distinguished murder from other killing" was malice on the part of the killer and this malice was not necessarily "malevolent to the deceased particularly" but "any evil design in general; the dictate of a wicked, depraved and malignant heart"; 4 Blackstone 199. . . .

When an individual commits an act of gross recklessness for which he must reasonably anticipate that death to another is likely to result, he exhibits that "wickedness of disposition, hardness of heart, cruelty, recklessness of consequences, and a mind regardless of social duty" which proved that there was at that time in him "the state or frame of mind termed malice." This court has declared that if a driver "wantonly, recklessly, and in disregard of consequences" hurls "his car against another, or into a crowd" and death results from that act "he ought . . . to face the same consequences that would be meted out to him if he had accomplished death by wantonly and wickedly firing a gun": Com. v. Mayberry, 290 Pa. 195, 199, 138 A. 686, 688, citing cases from four jurisdictions. . . .

The killing of William H. Long by this defendant resulted from an act intentionally done by the latter, in reckless and wanton disregard of the consequences which were at least sixty percent certain from his thrice attempted discharge of a gun known to contain one bullet and aimed at a vital part of Long's body. This killing was, therefore, murder, for malice in the sense of a wicked disposition is evidenced by the intentional doing of an uncalled-for act in callous disregard of its likely harmful effects on others. The fact that there was no motive for this homicide does not exculpate the accused. In a trial for murder proof of motive is always relevant but never necessary.

All the assignments of error are overruled and the judgment is affirmed.

NOTES

1. The facts in Malone. In concluding that there was a 60 percent chance of the gun's discharging, the court apparently assumed that the defendant twirled the revolver cylinder once before beginning to pull the trigger (see footnote 1 of the opinion), contrary to the implication of the defendant's testimony that he loaded the chamber to the right of the firing pin and fired without spinning the cylinder. On the court's assumption, pulling the trigger of a five-chambered gun three consecutive times creates, as the court said, a three-out-of-five chance of the gun's discharging. Some, however, might want to argue that the relevant risk is that of the gun's discharging on the third pull, which is one out of three. Which is the appropriate way to characterize the defendant's course of conduct? Would it make any difference to the defendant's liability? Suppose the gun discharged at the very first pull, when the chance of that happening would have been one out of five? Would that have made a difference?

If, in fact, the defendant did just what he testified he did — loaded the chamber to the right of the firing pin and then fired without twirling the chamber — how is it that the gun discharged? There are several possibilities. Conceivably the gun misfired in some fashion. Or conceivably there was *more than one* bullet in the gun. (Recall the testimony about how the gun was handled during the afternoon preceding the shooting.) If the court had accepted the defendant's version of the facts, would the result have been different? If a defendant pulls the trigger of a gun believed to be empty, forgetting that it had been loaded the previous day, and death results, should he or she be guilty of murder rather than manslaughter?

2. *Definitions of unintentional murder.* The common law formulations of the circumstances under which an unintentional killing constituted murder rather than manslaughter have been incorporated into many American statutes either directly or by reference to such common law terms as *malice.* The formulas have tended to carry more flavor than meaning — "the dictate of a wicked, depraved and malignant heart"; when the circumstances show "an abandoned and malignant heart"; where the circumstances show "a depraved heart regardless of human life." The *Malone* case is an example of circumstances in which the criteria have been held to have been met. Many states continue to adhere to these formulations, although others have altered them in ways suggested by the Model Penal Code. The Code treats an unintended killing as murder when it is committed recklessly (as defined in §2.02(2)(c)) and "under circumstances manifesting extreme indifference to the value of human life." (§210.2, Appendix.) The Comment supporting §210.2 explains (Model Penal Code and Commentaries, Comment to §210.2 at 21-22 (1980)):

Recklessness, as defined in Section 2.02(2)(c), presupposes an awareness of the creation of substantial homicidal risk, a risk too great to be deemed justifiable by any valid purpose that the actor's conduct serves. Since risk, however, is a matter of degree and the motives for risk creation may be infinite in variation, some formula is needed to identify the case [1] where recklessness may be found and [2] where it should be assimilated to purpose or knowledge for purposes of grading. Under the Model Code, [the first] judgment must be made in terms of whether the actor's conscious disregard of the risk, given the circumstances of the case, so far departs from acceptable behavior that it constitutes a "gross deviation from the standard of conduct that a law-abiding person would observe in the actor's situation." Ordinary recklessness in this sense is made sufficient for a conviction of manslaughter under Section 210.3(1)(a). In a prosecution for murder, however, the Code calls for the further judgment whether the actor's conscious disregard of the risk, under the circumstances, manifests extreme indifference to the value of human life. The significance of purpose or knowledge as a standard of culpability is that, cases of provocation or other mitigation apart, purposeful or knowing homicide demonstrates precisely such indifference to the value of human life. Whether recklessness is so extreme that it demonstrates similar indifference is not a question, it is submitted, that can be further clarified. It must be left directly to the trier of fact under instructions which make it clear that recklessness that can fairly be assimilated to purpose or knowledge should be treated as murder and that less extreme recklessness should be punished as manslaughter.

Insofar as Subsection (1)(b) includes within the murder category cases of homicide caused by extreme recklessness, though without purpose to kill, it reflects both the common law and much pre-existing statutory treatment usually cast in terms of conduct evidencing a "depraved heart regardless of human life" or some similar words.

3. Problem. Would Malone have been guilty of murder under the Model Penal Code? Consider People v. Roe, 74 N.Y.2d 20, 542 N.E.2d 610 (1989). The New York homicide statute, patterned closely on the Model Penal Code formula, makes a killing murder when it is committed recklessly "[u]nder circumstances evincing a depraved indifference to human life." Defendant, a 15-year-old high school student, loaded a mix of live and dummy shells into a 12-gauge shotgun. He pumped a shell into the firing chamber, not knowing whether it was a "dummy" or a live round. He then pointed the gun at a 13-year-old friend and said, "Let's play Polish roulette. Who is first?" He pulled the trigger and discharged a live round that struck and killed the friend. The court, finding that these facts met the requirements of recklessness and extreme indifference, upheld the murder conviction. Judge Bellacosa, dissenting, commented (543 N.E.2d at 616-620):

> In this case, a 15-year-old person stands convicted of the tragic and senseless killing of the 13-year-old brother of his best friend. . . . [When he pulled the trigger, the] gun fired a live shell which hit Darrin's right chest and shoulder area, knocking him to the floor. Defendant dropped the shotgun and ran over to Darrin, screaming, "Don't die. I killed my best friend's brother." He quickly directed [a friend] to go downstairs to call an ambulance, which was done. . . . When the police arrived shortly thereafter, they observed the defendant pounding his fists against the wall, crying, "I can't believe I shot him. I can't believe I shot my best friend. Help, please, oh my God, help." The ambulance arrived and Darrin was taken to the hospital where he was pronounced dead on arrival.
>
> The testimony of the only other eyewitness, Dennis Bleakley, established that defendant was shaken and distraught immediately upon realizing that he had shot their companion. . . . [T]he neighbor testified that when she arrived on the scene, seconds after hearing the shot, defendant was kneeling over his friend's body and crying. Similarly, the police officer who arrived on the scene testified that defendant was extremely distraught and overcome with grief. This is not evidence beyond a reasonable doubt of that hardness of heart or that malignancy of attitude qualifying as "depraved indifference." Frankly, the evidence proves the opposite. . . .
>
> By . . . catapulting the defendant's admittedly reckless criminal act to one "evincing depraved indifference to human life," the court . . . discards and disregards the legislatively drawn distinction between manslaughter and murder.

4. Murder by omission. We have seen that the death of an infant through its parents' neglect may constitute manslaughter. State v. Williams, page 445 supra. May such neglect constitute murder? A California court upheld a second-degree murder conviction of a father for his conscious and callous failure to feed his child resulting in death through malnutrition and dehydration. The evidence showed that the father was aware during the last two weeks of the baby's life that it was starving to death, that he did not remember anyone's having fed the baby in that period, and that he did nothing himself to feed the baby, although he could have if he had really wanted to, because he "just didn't care." The court stated: "The omission of a duty is in law the equivalent of an act and when death results, the standard for determination of the degree of homicide is identical." People v. Burden, 72 Cal. App. 3d 603, 616 (Dist. App. 1977). In accord, see Simpkins v. State, 88 Md. App. 607, 596 A.2d 655 (1991).

UNITED STATES v. FLEMING

United States Court of Appeals, 4th Circuit
739 F.2d 945 (1984)

WINTER, C.J.: . . . Defendant David Earl Fleming was convicted of second-degree murder, in violation of 18 U.S.C. §1111,[1] in the death of Margaret Jacobsen Haley. . . .

Fleming's car was observed at about 3:00 P.M. on June 15, 1983, traveling southbound on the George Washington Memorial Parkway in northern Virginia [a park within federal jurisdiction] at speeds variously estimated by witnesses as between 70 and 100 miles per hour. The speed limit on the Parkway is, at most points, 45 miles per hour. Fleming several times directed his southbound car into the northbound lanes of the Parkway in order to avoid traffic congestion in the southbound lanes. Northbound traffic had to move out of his way in order to avoid a head-on collision. At one point, a pursuing police officer observed Fleming steer his car into the northbound lanes, which were separated from the southbound lanes at that point and for a distance of three-tenths of a mile by a raised concrete median, and drive in the northbound lanes, still at a high rate of speed, for the entire length of the median. At two other points, Fleming traveled in northbound lanes that were separated from the southbound lanes by medians.

Approximately six miles from where his car was first observed traveling at excessive speed, Fleming lost control of it on a sharp curve. The car slid across the northbound lanes, striking the curb on the opposite side of the highway. After striking the curb, Fleming's car straightened out and at that moment struck the car driven by Mrs. Haley that was coming in the opposite direction. Fleming's car at the moment of impact was estimated by witnesses to have been traveling 70 to 80 miles per hour; the speed limit at that point on the Parkway was 30 miles per hour. Mrs. Haley received multiple severe injuries and died before she could be extricated from her car.

Fleming was pulled from the wreckage of his car and transported to a Washington hospital for treatment. His blood alcohol level was there tested at .315 percent.

Fleming was indicted by a grand jury on a charge of second-degree murder. . . . He was tried before a jury and convicted.

---

1. 18 U.S.C. §1111(a) provides:

> Murder is the unlawful killing of a human being with malice aforethought. Every murder perpetrated by poison, lying in wait, or any other kind of willful, deliberate, malicious, and premeditated killing; or committed in the perpetration of [designated felonies] is murder in the first degree.
> Any other murder is murder in the second degree.

Defendant maintains that the facts of the case cannot support a verdict of murder. Particularly, defendant contends that the facts are inadequate to establish the existence of malice aforethought, and thus that he should have been convicted of manslaughter at most.

Malice aforethought, as provided in 18 U.S.C. §1111(a), is the distinguishing characteristic which, when present, makes a homicide murder rather than manslaughter.[2] . . . Proof of the existence of malice does not require a showing that the accused harbored hatred or ill will against the victim or others. Neither does it require proof of an intent to kill or injure. Malice may be established by evidence of conduct which is "reckless and wanton and a gross deviation from a reasonable standard of care, of such a nature that a jury is warranted in inferring that defendant was aware of a serious risk of death or serious bodily harm." To support a conviction for murder, the government need only have proved that defendant intended to operate his car in the manner in which he did with a heart that was without regard for the life and safety of others.[3]

We conclude that the evidence regarding defendant's conduct was adequate to sustain a finding by the jury that defendant acted with malice aforethought. It is urged upon us, however, that a verdict of murder in this case should be precluded by the existence of a statute defining and proscribing involuntary manslaughter, 18 U.S.C. §1112(a).[4] Defendant maintains that vehicular homicide where no purpose on the part of the accused to have caused death or injury has been shown should result only in conviction of involuntary manslaughter. Otherwise, defendant argues, all drunk driving homicides and many reckless driving ones will be prosecutable as murder. We are not persuaded by the argument.

The difference between malice, which will support conviction for murder, and gross negligence, which will permit of conviction only for manslaughter, is one of degree rather than kind. See, e.g., United States v. Dixon, 419 F.2d 288, 292-293 (D.C. Cir. 1969) (Leventhal, J., concurring) (difference between murder and manslaughter lies in the quality of the accused's awareness of the risk). See also Holmes, The Common Law 59 (1881) (The difference between murder and manslaughter lies "in the degree of danger attaching to the act in the given state of facts.") . . . [In the present case,] . . . the facts show a deviation from

2. Malice aforethought is a concept that originated with the common law and is used in 18 U.S.C. §1111(a) in its common law sense. . . .

Accordingly, we do not confine our consideration of the precedents to decisions of federal courts interpreting the federal statute, but rather consider other sources which may shed light on the issues of this case.

3. We note that, even assuming that subjective awareness of the risk is required to establish murder where the killing resulted from reckless conduct, an exception to the requirement of subjective awareness of risk is made where lack of such awareness is attributable solely to voluntary drunkenness. See, e.g., Model Penal Code §2.08(2) ("When recklessness establishes an element of the offense, if the actor, due to self-induced intoxication, is unaware of a risk of which he would have been aware had he been sober, such unawareness is immaterial.") Defendant's state of voluntary intoxication thus would not have been relevant to whether the jury could have inferred from the circumstances of the crime that he was aware of the risk created by his conduct.

4. 18 U.S.C. §1112(a) provides:

Manslaughter is the unlawful killing of a human being without malice. It is of two kinds:

Voluntary — Upon a sudden quarrel or heat of passion.

Involuntary — In the commission of an unlawful act not amounting to a felony, or in the commission in an unlawful manner, or without due caution and circumspection, of a lawful act which might produce death.

established standards of regard for life and the safety of others that is markedly different in degree from that found in most vehicular homicides. In the average drunk driving homicide, there is no proof that the driver has acted while intoxicated with the purpose of wantonly and intentionally putting the lives of others in danger. Rather, his driving abilities were so impaired that he recklessly put others in danger simply by being on the road and attempting to do the things that any driver would do. In the present case, however, danger did not arise only by defendant's determining to drive while drunk. Rather, in addition to being intoxicated while driving, defendant drove in a manner that could be taken to indicate depraved disregard of human life, *particularly* in light of the fact that *because he was drunk* his reckless behavior was all the more dangerous.

Defendant also contends that the district court's response to the jury's request for reinstruction as to the distinction between murder and manslaughter confused the two crimes and now requires reversal. After a close reading of the challenged portion of the instructions, we are far from convinced that there was any failure of the district court in its definition of the crimes.[5] In any event, however, we must read the district court's instructions as a whole. Any confusion . . . was not misleading "in the context of the overall charge."

Affirmed.

NOTES AND QUESTIONS

1. *The murder/manslaughter distinction.* What is the difference between dangerous conduct that should lead to a murder conviction and dangerous conduct that should lead to conviction for manslaughter only? In *Fleming*, the court says that the difference is "one of degree," but a degree of what? Is the crucial factor the probability of harm, the defendant's awareness of that probability, both of these factors, or neither one? What distinguishing factor was the jury required to find in *Fleming?*

2. *Murder by vehicle.* In accord with *Fleming*, the great majority of American courts hold that extreme carelessness in the operation of an automobile can support a conviction of murder. See David Luria, Death on the Highway: Reckless Driving as Murder, 67 Or. L. Rev. 799 (1988).[7] Usually the theory is that the

5. The district court stated that the negligence necessary to establish manslaughter "must amount to gross negligence, that is conduct which is a *wanton and reckless disregard for human life.*" A few words later, the court told the jury that the distinguishing mark of manslaughter was that "there is nothing about [the killing] that shows you that there was intent in the mind to do acts that amount to *wanton and reckless disregard for human life.*" (Emphasis added in both quotations.) Though judges have suggested that clarity of the definitions of murder and manslaughter is best maintained by restricting use of the term "wanton" to the former and avoiding any reference to "negligence" with regard to the latter, use of the phrase "wanton and reckless disregard for human life" in the definition of both murder and manslaughter has been common in modern jurisprudence. . . . The key point is that malice requires that the circumstances have been such that the jury could conclude that defendant's entering into the risk created by his conduct evidenced a depraved mind without regard for human life. The district court's instruction suggested, albeit with some lack of clarity, this characteristic of murder. The jury was told that if there was "nothing about [the killing] that shows . . . *that there was intent* in the mind [of the accused] *to do acts that* amount to wanton and reckless *disregard* for *human life*" (emphasis added), then the killing could not be murder but at most manslaughter.

7. For a contrary view, see Essex v. Commonwealth, 322 S.E.2d 216, 222 (Va. 1984). In that case the court found that the defendant was "guilty of an appalling degree of reckless driving" which

defendant had an actual awareness of a great risk of fatal harm. See, e.g., Pears v. State, 672 P.2d 903 (Alaska App. 1983): Despite warnings by two police officers and by a companion that he was too drunk to drive, the defendant returned to his truck and drove at high speed through several stop signs and red lights until he collided with a car at an intersection. Two people in the car were killed. The appellate court affirmed a murder conviction, holding that the statutory requirement of "extreme indifference to the value of human life" was satisfied because the warnings Pears had received made him "abundantly aware of the dangerous nature of his driving. . . ." (672 P.2d at 910), and his actions therefore were not merely inadvertent.

Compare People v. Watson, 30 Cal. 3d 290, 637 P.2d 279 (1981). Here the court found sufficient evidence of an actual awareness of the danger merely because the defendant "had driven his car to the establishment where he had been drinking, and he must have known that he would have to drive it later. It also may be presumed that defendant was aware of the hazards of driving while intoxicated." 637 P.2d at 285-286. In dissent, Chief Justice Bird observed (id. at 288):

> [I]t cannot be found that respondent committed an act likely to kill. The act of speeding through a green light at 55 or 60 miles per hour in a 35-mile-per-hour zone was dangerous, but was not an act likely to result in the death of another. It was 1 o'clock in the morning. The person whose car respondent nearly collided with testified that he saw no other cars around. . . .
>
> The fact that respondent was under the influence of alcohol made his driving more dangerous. . . . No one holds a brief for this type of activity. However, [d]eath or injury is not the probable result of driving while under the influence of alcohol. "Thousands, perhaps hundreds of thousands, of Californians each week reach home without accident despite their driving intoxicated."
>
> The majority also fail to demonstrate that it is reasonable to infer that respondent had a conscious disregard for life. Can a conscious disregard for life be established by the fact that several hours *before* the accident respondent drove his car to a bar? The majority hold as a matter of law that he "must have known" he would have to drive his car later and that he wilfully drank alcohol until he was under its influence.
>
> How does respondent's state of mind at the time he drove to the bar and began drinking justify an inference that he had a reckless state of mind at the time of the accident? This meager evidence does not justify the inference that by drinking alcohol he harbored a conscious disregard for life when he later drove his car! I submit that the majority's reasoning that such an inference may be drawn to support a finding of implied malice will be used to establish second degree murder in every case in which a person drives a car to a bar, a friend's home, or a party, drinks alcohol so that he is under its influence, drives away and is involved in a fatal accident.

3. *Sentencing in vehicle murder cases.* The punishment of drivers convicted of murder by vehicle can be quite severe. In Simmons v. State, 215 S.E.2d 883 (S.C. 1975), the court upheld a sentence of life imprisonment imposed on a reckless

---

resulted in three deaths, but held that the common law malice requirement was not satisfied in the absence of proof that the defendant "embarked on his ill-fated course of conduct wilfully and with a malicious purpose."

driver who fatally injured two people. In Pears v. State (summarized in the preceding note) the intermediate appellate court upheld a sentence of 20 years' imprisonment imposed on a 19-year-old driver who had no prior record of alcohol-related driving offenses. On a further appeal, the Alaska Supreme Court set aside the sentence. 698 P.2d 1198 (1985). The court noted that the defendant's conduct was not comparable to the behavior involved in convictions for second-degree murder by knives or guns (where sentences ranging from 30 to 99 years had been upheld). The court ruled that Pears' sentence should be in line with those imposed on other drunken drivers who had recklessly caused death, even when such drivers had been convicted only of manslaughter. In such cases, Alaska sentences had ranged from 8 to 12 years' imprisonment, for drivers with several (in one case 6) prior drunk driving convictions. The court therefore ruled Pears's 20-year sentence excessive and remanded for resentencing.

Questions: Why did the court treat it as irrelevant that Pears (unlike the other drunk drivers) had been convicted of murder rather than manslaughter? What *is* the appropriate punishment for a defendant like Pears?

4. *Inadvertent murder?* Can a defendant be convicted of murder even if she was *not* consciously aware of the risk of fatal harm? Vehicle murder cases such as *Pears* and *Watson* appear to assume that conscious awareness is required. Justice Holmes was of the view, however (see page 450 supra), that an unintended killing could be murder, even without advertence to the risk, if the danger to life was great enough. How can this approach be reconciled with the traditional common law formulations of malice ("depraved heart," etc.)? What becomes of the distinction between murder and involuntary manslaughter if neither one requires conscious awareness of the risk?

These issues may be considered in the context of Hamilton v. Commonwealth, 560 S.W.2d 539 (Ky. 1978). The defendant was convicted of murder under a statute that provided:

> A person is guilty of murder when . . . under circumstances manifesting extreme indifference to human life, he wantonly engages in conduct which creates a grave risk of death to another person and thereby causes the death of another person.

The record showed that while in a heavily intoxicated condition the defendant drove his truck substantially over the speed limit through an intersection where another car was crossing. The defendant ignored the stop light, collided with the other car, and killed its driver.

A majority of the Kentucky Supreme Court affirmed, stating (560 S.W.2d at 543-544):

> Hamilton's conduct surpasses the usual vehicle manslaughter case and demonstrates "wanton" conduct and extreme indifference to human life. The jury was instructed on murder, second degree manslaughter and reckless homicide. It found that Hamilton should have known of the plain and obvious likelihood that death or great bodily injury could have resulted from operating his truck, while in a drunken condition, through an intersection where a red light demanded that he stop.
>
> This is a "hurry-up" world of people on the go, with heavy traffic by high-powered vehicles on all types of roads and at all times of the day or night. Such a situation coupled with a driver's inclination to take "one or more [drinks] for the

road," increases the vehicular death rate on the highways of this Commonwealth. A majority of the members of this court is of the opinion that the legislature enacted K.R.S. 507.020(1)(b) to deter such conduct. The legislature is commended for taking a giant step forward. Its action in enacting this statute will do much to decrease vehicular highway deaths by persons operating an automobile while under the influence of intoxicants.

The dissent stated (id. at 544):

I do not believe that either the drafters of the Kentucky Penal Code or the members of the General Assembly that enacted it had any intention of placing the reckless act of an automobile driver, whether drunk or sober, in the same category as that of a deliberate murderer. I concede that fatal carelessness in the operation of a motor vehicle calls for stern punishment, but murder is something else. There simply is a difference in culpability between committing an act that endangers people whose presence is known and an act that endangers people whose presence *should be* anticipated but *in fact* is not known.

5. *The Model Penal Code approach.* What is the Model Penal Code position on the issue of liability for inadvertent murder? Note that under §210.2(1)(b), murder requires proof that the defendant acted "recklessly under circumstances manifesting extreme indifference to the value of human life." According to the official Comment (Model Penal Code and Commentaries, Comment to §210.2 at 27-28 (1980)):

The Model Code provision makes clear that inadvertent risk creation, however extravagant and unjustified, cannot be punished as murder. . . . This result is consistent with the general conception of the Model Code that serious felony sanctions should be grounded securely in the subjective culpability of the actor. To the extent that inadvertent risk creation, or negligence, should be recognized as a form of criminal homicide, that question should be faced separately from the offense of murder. . . . At the least it seems clear that negligent homicide should not be assimilated to the most serious forms of criminal homicide catalogued under the offense of murder.

Questions: Does the Commentary accurately describe the standard mandated by the Code's text? Note that the choice between a subjective and an objective standard seldom has much practical bite, because defendants cannot easily persuade a jury that they honestly failed to perceive a risk that the reasonable person would perceive. Such a claim can be quite plausible, however, if the defendant was intoxicated. Situations involving intoxication (for example, drunk driving) are therefore the primary ones in which the choice between a subjective and an objective standard is likely to make a difference. How are such situations treated under the Code? Reconsider Model Penal Code §2.08(2) and the *Fleming* case, especially page 461, footnote 3 supra. Is the Model Penal Code Commentary accurate in asserting that "inadvertent risk creation . . . cannot be punished as murder"?

These issues confronted the Supreme Court of New Hampshire under a statute, derived from the Model Penal Code, which makes a killing murder when the defendant acted "recklessly under circumstances manifesting an extreme indifference to the value of human life." N.H. Rev. Stat. Ann. §630:1-b, I(b). In

State v. Dufield, 549 A.2d 1205 (N.H. 1988), the trial court refused to allow expert testimony offered to prove that the defendant, who was intoxicated, could not have formed the requisite conscious indifference to human life. A unanimous court upheld the murder conviction. Relying on the approach of Model Penal Code §2.08(2), Justice Souter (then a justice of the state supreme court) said (549 A.2d at 1208):

> [T]he statutory definition of reckless conduct . . . precludes the recognition of voluntary intoxication as an excuse, and thus "postulate[s] a general equivalence between the risks created by the conduct of the drunken actor and the risks created . . . in becoming drunk." . . . [C]onsistent policy demands the same treatment of socially deviant conduct [with regard to the additional statutory requirement of] circumstances manifesting an extreme indifference to the value of human life. The law in each case invests an adult defendant with responsibility to know what sort of person he is, and to stay sober if his intoxication will jeopardize the lives and safety of others.

A closely divided New York Court of Appeals came to the same conclusion in People v. Register, 60 N.Y.2d 270, 457 N.E.2d 704 (1983). In a dissenting opinion, Judge Jasen commented (457 N.E.2d at 711-712):

> The rule announced by the majority today effectively eviscerates the distinction between manslaughter in the second degree (Penal Law, §125.15, subd. 1) and murder in the second degree (Penal Law, §125.25, subd. 2) with respect to the accused's state of mind. . . .
>
> It is a deep-rooted part of our jurisprudence that, in the ordinary case, only those offenders who consciously choose to do evil rather than good will be punished. Under the majority's rule, however, a person who possessed only a reckless state of mind when he caused the death of another could be convicted of depraved mind murder (Penal Law, §125.25, subd. 2) and sentenced to a term of 15 years to life imprisonment simply because objective circumstances surrounding the killing presented a "grave risk" of death even though the actor, due to intoxication, was unaware of those circumstances and could not appreciate the risks. The majority would also hold that another person who is fully aware of a "substantial and unjustifiable risk" and consciously disregards that risk can only be found guilty of manslaughter in the second degree and sentenced to as little as one and one-half years in jail. (Penal Law, §125.15, subd. 1; §15.05, subd. 3.) While there may be a technical distinction between a "grave" risk and a "substantial" one, the only real difference is about 15 years in prison. To accept this distinction as justification for the disparate penalties which the respective crimes carry defies basic principles of fairness and logic. I simply cannot agree that the Legislature intended that convictions for murder as opposed to manslaughter would turn upon the nature of the objective surrounding circumstances regardless of whether or not the accused was aware of those circumstances or could appreciate the consequences of his conduct.[a]

6. Intent to inflict great bodily harm. In a case of unintended killing, what legal effect should be given to facts suggesting that the defendant intended to inflict serious injury short of death? Obviously, such facts have evidentiary significance

---

a. For a useful discussion of recent cases involving the "depraved indifference" formula, see Bernard Gegan, More Cases of Depraved Mind Murder: The Problem of Mens Rea, 64 St. John's L. Rev. 429 (1990). — Eds on the question whether the defendant recklessly or negligently created a risk of death. But the common law went further, by giving such facts independent substantive significance. The malice required for murder was established by the intent of the defendant to do great bodily harm to the victim. See G. Williams, Textbook of Criminal Law 210 (1978). The intent-to-inflict-grievous-harm formula is followed in many American jurisdictions. See Wayne R. LaFave & Austin W. Scott, Jr., Criminal Law 616-617 (2d ed. 1986). In some states, the doctrine survives as a consequence of statutes retaining the common law definition of murder (that is, "malice aforethought"). In a few states, homicide statutes adopt the "great bodily harm" formula explicitly.[8]

What is the justification for treating an intent to inflict grievous harm as independently sufficient to support a murder conviction whenever death happens to result? Is there, in practice, any significant difference between this standard and the normal mens rea requirement (an intention, or recklessness, with respect to the risk of *death*)? Consider the comments of Patrick Devlin, Criminal Responsibility and Punishment: Functions of Judge and Jury, [1954] Crim. L. Rev. 661, 668-670:

> Most cases of murder which come before the courts are cases of death by sudden violence manifestly done by the accused: in many of them the only really debatable point is whether he intended death to result. Under the existing law the jury is properly directed to ignore that question, and that it need only be satisfied that there was an intent to cause grievous bodily harm. On that, the facts generally speak for themselves, and if considered dispassionately would lead almost automatically to a verdict of murder; in an attempt to avert this the defence resorts to suggestions of accident, provocation, or mental blackout. Thus, what many people would take to be the fundamental question, and the one which ought to be answered by the jury if the nature of the crime and the degree of gravity is to be determined by the appropriate tribunal, is not put to the jury at all. . . .
>
> The other side of the argument is that a man ought to know that if he deliberately commits an act of grievous bodily harm, he runs the risk that death may result. If he chooses to run the risk of endangering life, ought he not to be held liable for the consequences? The answer, I think, is that he is in any event held liable for the consequences, that is to say, he may be found guilty either of manslaughter or causing grievous bodily harm with intent, and for either offence may be sentenced to imprisonment for life. The question is not whether he should be exempt from the consequences, but whether his degree of guilt should be equated with that of a man who deliberately intended the consequences.

The Model Penal Code did not include the grievous harm doctrine on the ground that the "reckless indifference to human life" formula for murder made it unnecessary. See Model Penal Code and Commentaries, Comment to §210.2 at 28-29 (1980).

---

8. See, e.g., Ill. Ann. Stat. ch. 720, §5/9-1(a):

A person who kills an individual without lawful justification commits first degree murder if, in performing the acts which cause death:
    (1) he either intends to kill or do great bodily harm to that individual or another, or knows that such acts will cause death to that individual or another; or
    (2) he knows that such acts create a strong probability of death or great bodily harm to that individual or another. . . .

Where the "grievous bodily harm" formula is followed, how serious must the intended injuries be? In Commonwealth v. Dorazio, 365 Pa. 291, 74 A.2d 125 (1950), the defendant (who had once been a professional fighter) beat up a co-worker. The latter died from a brain hemorrhage caused either by a blow to the head or by a fall that occurred in the course of his attempt to flee from the defendant. In upholding a conviction for murder, the court said (74 A.2d at 130) that the kind of "enormous" bodily harm involved in a case like Commonwealth v. Malone (page 456 supra) did not establish the minimum level necessary for a showing of malice. Rather, the court continued, "it is not necessary that the injury be intended to be permanent or dangerous to life, it is malicious to intend injury such as to seriously interfere with health and comfort...." Many courts have required more. See, e.g., People v. Crenshaw, 298 Ill. 412, 416, 131 N.E. 576, 577 (1921) (injury "likely to be attended with dangerous or fatal consequences").

2. The Felony-Murder Rule

a. The Basic Doctrine

REGINA v. SERNÉ

Central Criminal Court
16 Cox Crim. Cas. 311 (1887)

The prisoners Leon Serné and John Henry Goldfinch were indicted for the murder of a boy, Sjaak Serné, the son of the prisoner Leon Serné, it being alleged that they wilfully set on fire a house and shop, No. 274 Strand, London, by which act the death of the boy had been caused.

It appeared that the prisoner Serné with his wife, two daughters, and two sons were living at the house in question; and that Serné, at the time he was living there, in Midsummer, 1887, was in a state of pecuniary embarrassment, and had put into the premises furniture and other goods of but very little value, which at the time of the fire were not of greater value than £30. It also appeared that previously to the fire the prisoner Serné had insured the life of the boy Sjaak Serné, who was imbecile, and on the first day of September, 1887, had insured his stock at 274 Strand, for £500, his furniture for £100, and his rent for another £100; and that on the 17th of the same month the premises were burnt down.

Evidence was given on behalf of the prosecution that fires were seen breaking out in several parts of the premises at the same time, soon after the prisoners had been seen in the shop together, two fires being in the lower part of the house and two above, on the floor whence escape could be made on the roof of the adjoining house, and in which part were the prisoners, and the wife, and two daughters of Serné, who escaped. That on the premises were a quantity of tissue transparencies for advertising purposes, which were of a most inflammable character; and that on the site of one of the fires was found a great quantity of these transparencies close to other inflammable materials. That the prisoner Serné, his wife and daughters, were rescued from the roof of the adjoining house, the other prisoner being rescued from a window in the front of the house, but that the boys were burnt to death, the body of the one being found on the floor near the window from which the prisoner Serné, his wife, and daughters had escaped, the body of the other being found at the basement of the premises.

STEPHEN, J. Gentlemen, it is now my duty to direct your attention to the law and the facts into which you have to inquire. The two prisoners are indicted for the wilful murder of the boy Sjaak Serné, a lad of about fourteen years of age; and it is necessary that I should explain to you, to a certain extent, the law of England with regard to the crime of wilful murder, inasmuch as you have heard something said about constructive murder. Now that phrase, gentlemen, has no legal meaning whatever. There was wilful murder according to the plain meaning of the term, or there was no murder at all in the present case. The definition of murder is unlawful homicide with malice aforethought, and the words malice aforethought are technical. You must not, therefore, construe them or suppose that they can be construed by ordinary rules of language. The words have to be construed according to a long series of decided cases, which have given them meanings different from those which might be supposed. One of those meanings is, the killing of another person by an act done with an intent to commit a felony. Another meaning is, an act done with the knowledge that the act will probably cause the death of some person. Now it is such an act as the last which is alleged to have been done in this case; and if you think that either or both of these men in the dock killed this boy, either by an act done with intent to commit a felony, that is to say, the setting of the house on fire in order to cheat the insurance company, or by conduct which to their knowledge was likely to cause death and was therefore eminently dangerous in itself — in either of these cases the prisoners are guilty of wilful murder in the plain meaning of the word. I will say a word or two upon one part of this definition, because it is capable of being applied very harshly in certain cases, and also because, though I take the law as I find it, I very much doubt whether the definition which I have given, although it is the common definition, is not somewhat too wide. Now when it is said that murder means killing a man by an act done in the commission of a felony, the mere words cover a case like this, that is to say, a case where a man gives another a push with an intention of stealing his watch, and the person so pushed, having a weak heart or some other internal disorder, dies. To take another very old illustration, it was said that if a man shot a fowl with intent to steal it and accidentally killed a man, he was to be accounted guilty of murder, because the act was done in the commission of a felony.[a] I very much doubt, however, whether that is really the law, or whether the Court for the Consideration of Crown Cases Reserved would hold it to be so. The present case, however, is not such as I have cited, nor anything like them. In my opinion the definition of the law which makes it murder to kill by an act done in the commission of a felony might and ought to be narrowed, while that part of the law under which the Crown in this

---

a. Coke, 3d Institute 56 (1644): "If the act be unlawful it is murder. As if *A* meaning to steale a deer in the park of *B*, shooteth at the deer, and by the glance of the arrow killeth a boy that is hidden in a bush; this is murder, for that the act was unlawful, although *A* had no intent to hurt the boy, nor knew not of him. But if *B* the owner of the park had shot at his own deer, and without any ill intent had killed the boy by the glance of his arrow, this had been homicide by misadventure, and no felony.

"So if one shoot at any wild fowle upon a tree, and the arrow killeth any reasonable creature afar off, without any evill intent in him, this is per infortunium: for it was not unlawful to shoot at the wilde fowle: but if he had shot at a cock or hen, or any tame fowle of another mans, and the arrow by mischance had killed a man, this had been murder, for the act was unlawfull." — EDS.

case claim to have proved a case of murder is maintained. I think that, instead of saying that any act done with intent to commit a felony and which causes death amounts to murder, it would be reasonable to say that any act known to be dangerous to life and likely in itself to cause death, done for the purpose of committing a felony which causes death, should be murder. As an illustration of this, suppose that a man, intending to commit a rape upon a woman, but without the least wish to kill her, squeezed her by the throat to overpower her, and in so doing killed her, that would be murder. I think that every one would say in a case like that, that when a person began doing wicked acts for his own base purposes, he risked his own life as well as that of others. That kind of crime does not differ in any serious degree from one committed by using a deadly weapon, such as a bludgeon, a pistol, or a knife. If a man once begins attacking the human body in such a way, he must take the consequences if he goes further than he intended when he began. That I take to be the true meaning of the law in the subject. In the present case, gentlemen, you have a man sleeping in a house with his wife, his two daughters, his two sons, and a servant, and you are asked to believe that this man, with all these people under his protection, deliberately set fire to the house in three or four different places and thereby burnt two of them to death. It is alleged that he arranged matters in such a way that any person of the most common intelligence must have known perfectly well that he was placing all those people in deadly risk. It appears to me that if that were really done, it matters very little indeed whether the prisoners hoped the people would escape or whether they did not. If a person chose, for some wicked purpose of his own to sink a boat at sea, and thereby caused the deaths of the occupants, it matters nothing whether at the time of committing the act he hoped that the people would be picked up by a passing vessel. He is as much guilty of murder if the people are drowned, as if he had flung every person into the water with his own hand. Therefore, gentlemen, if Serné and Goldfinch set fire to this house when the family were in it, and if the boys were by that act stifled or burnt to death, then the prisoners are as much guilty of murder as if they had stabbed the children. I will also add, for my own part, that I think, in so saying, the law of England lays down a rule of broad, plain common-sense. Treat a murderer how you will, award him what punishment you choose, it is your duty, gentlemen, if you think him really guilty of murder, to say so. That is the law of the land, and I have no doubt in my mind with regard to it. There was a case tried in this court which you will no doubt remember, and which will illustrate my meaning. It was the Clerkenwell explosion case in 1868, when a man named Barrett was charged with causing the death of several persons by an explosion which was intended to release one or two men from custody; and I am sure that no one can say truly that Barrett was not justly hanged. With regard to the facts in the present case, the very horror of the crime, if crime it was, the abomination of it, is a reason for your taking the most extreme care in the case, and for not imputing to the prisoners anything which is not clearly proved. God forbid that I should, by what I say, produce on your minds, even in the smallest degree any feeling against the prisoners. You must see, gentlemen, that the evidence leaves no reasonable doubt upon your minds; but you will fail in the performance of your duty if, being satisfied with the evidence, you do not convict one or both the prisoners of wilful murder, and it is wilful murder of which they are accused.

[Verdict, not guilty.]

PEOPLE v. STAMP, 2 Cal. App. 3d 203, 82 Cal. Rptr. 598 (1969): [Defendant burglarized the business premises of one Carl Honeyman and robbed him at gunpoint. During the robbery, Honeyman had been led from his office by the elbow and required to lie on the floor for about ten minutes, until the defendant had fled. Shortly thereafter, Honeyman began suffering chest pains, collapsed and died of a heart attack. He was described as "an obese 60-year-old man, with a history of heart disease, who was under a great deal of pressure due to the intensely competitive nature of his business. Additionally, he did not take good care of his heart." Doctors testified that "[t]he fright induced by the robbery was too much of a shock to Honeyman's system." Defendant's conviction of first-degree murder was upheld. The court stated:] The [felony-murder] doctrine is not limited to those deaths which are foreseeable. Rather a felon is held strictly liable for *all* killings committed by him or his accomplices in the course of the felony. As long as the homicide is the direct causal result of the robbery the felony-murder rule applies whether or not the death was a natural or probable consequence of the robbery. So long as a victim's predisposing physical condition, regardless of its cause, is not the *only* substantial factor bringing about his death, that condition and the robber's ignorance of it, in no way destroys the robber's criminal responsibility for the death. So long as life is shortened as a result of the felonious act it does not matter that the victim might have died soon anyway. In this respect, the robber takes his victim as he finds him.

NOTE ON THE CAUSATION REQUIREMENT

Although a defendant can be held liable under the felony-murder rule in the absence of fault (i.e., mens rea) with respect to the death, the prosecution still must establish that the defendant's conduct "caused" the death, under the normal standards of causation. As we shall see in Chapter 6, page 547 infra, these standards require the defendant's criminal acts to be both the "but for" cause of the harm and the "proximate" cause of the harm. "Proximity" usually means that the harm was the natural and probable consequence, or the foreseeable consequence, of the criminal act. *Stamp* illustrates one situation in which the "proximity" requirement can be met even though the harm may be unforeseeable. Heart attack fatalities induced by the fright of experiencing a robbery or burglary are very unlikely events, but the recent decisions continue to hold, in accord with *Stamp,* that defendants in such cases are guilty of murder under a felony-murder theory. See, e.g., State v. Dixon, 222 Neb. 787, 387 N.W.2d 682 (1986). These results are consistent with ordinary principles of proximate cause, under which the defendant must "take his victim as he finds him." See Chapter 6, especially the Note on vulnerability of the victim, page 555 infra.

Compare King v. Commonwealth, 6 Va. App. 351, 368 S.E.2d 704 (1988). Defendant King and his co-pilot were transporting 500 pounds of marijuana in a light plane when they became lost in fog and crashed into a mountainside. King survived the crash, but his co-pilot did not, and as a result King was charged and convicted of felony murder. The appellate court reversed, holding that the drug-distribution crime was not the proximate cause of the death. Although the "but for" requirement was met, the crash was not a foreseeable result of the crime and was not made more likely by the fact that the plane's cargo was contraband.

The court noted that, in contrast, a finding of proximate causation might have been possible if the crash had resulted from flying the plane at low altitude to avoid detection.

Note that the result in *King* contrasts with the broader application of the felony-murder rule advanced in several of Coke's hypotheticals, page 469 supra. The *King* case's more restricted approach to felony-murder has become standard in contemporary American law.

NOTES ON THE RATIONALE OF THE FELONY-MURDER RULE

We have previously examined the proposition sometimes asserted that the mens rea of a lesser offense may substitute for the mens rea of a greater offense. Reconsider Regina v. Cunningham, page 205 supra, and Regina v. Faulkner, page 207 supra, where that proposition was rejected. Yet in connection with felony-murder, precisely that proposition serves as the basis of liability. Does the proposition have any greater justification in homicidal crimes than in other crimes? If the law is sound in requiring a particular mens rea to establish murder, is it, by definition, unsound to require less solely because the actor is guilty of another crime? The offense accompanying the killing has its own punishment. In what sense does the offense also add to the criminality of the killing (as by making an otherwise noncriminal killing criminal) or to the grade of the criminal killing (as by making murder what otherwise would be manslaughter)?

Consider the following comments on the felony-murder rule.

1. People v. Washington, 62 Cal. 2d 777, 402 P.2d 130, 133 (1965): The purpose of the felony-murder rule is to deter felons from killing negligently or accidentally by holding them strictly responsible for killings they commit.

2. T. B. Macaulay, A Penal Code Prepared by the Indian Law Commissioners, Note M, 64-65 (1837): It will be admitted that, when an act is in itself innocent, to punish the person who does it because bad consequences which no human wisdom could have foreseen have followed from it would be in the highest degree barbarous and absurd. . . . [T]o pronounce [that person] guilty of one offence because a misfortune befell him while he was committing another offence . . . is surely to confound all the boundaries of crime. . . .

To punish as a murderer every man who, while committing a heinous offence, causes death by pure misadventure, is a course which evidently adds nothing to the security of human life. No man can so conduct himself as to make it absolutely certain that he shall not be so unfortunate as to cause the death of a fellow creature. The utmost that he can do is to abstain from every thing which is at all likely to cause death. No fear of punishment can make him do more than this: and therefore to punish a man who has done this can add nothing to the security of human life. The only good effect which such punishment can produce will be to deter people from committing any of those offences which turn into murders what are in themselves mere accidents. It is in fact an addition to the punishment of those offences, and it is an addition in the very worst way. For example, hundreds of persons in some great cities are in the habit of picking pockets. They know that they are guilty of a great offence. But it has never occurred to one of them, nor would it occur to any rational man, that they are guilty of an offence which endangers life. Unhappily one of these hundreds attempts to take the purse of a gentleman who has a loaded pistol in his pocket. The thief touches the trigger: the pistol goes off: the gentleman is shot dead. To treat the case of this pick-pocket differently from that of the numerous pick-pockets who steal under exactly the same circumstances, with exactly the same intentions, with no less risk of causing death, with no greater care to avoid causing death, — to send them to the house of correction as thieves, and him to the gallows as a murderer, — appears to us an unreasonable course. If the punishment for stealing from a person be too light, let it be increased, and let the increase fall alike on all the offenders. Surely the worst mode of increasing the punishment of an offence is to provide that, besides the ordinary punishment, every offender shall run an exceedingly small risk of being hanged. The more nearly the amount of punishment can be reduced to a certainty the better. But if chance is to be admitted there are better ways of admitting it. It would be a less capricious, and therefore a more salutary course, to provide that every fiftieth or every hundredth thief selected by lot should be hanged, than to provide that every thief should be hanged who, while engaged in stealing, should meet with an unforeseen misfortune such as might have befallen the most virtuous man while performing the most virtuous action.

3. *George P. Fletcher, Reflections on Felony-Murder, 12 Sw. U. L. Rev. 413, 427-429 (1981):* [One] unrefined mode of thought behind the [felony-murder] rule begins not with the deadly outcome, but with the felonious background. That someone engages in a felony lowers the threshold of moral responsibility for the resulting death. If there is a principle behind this way of thinking, it is that a wrongdoer must run the risk that things will turn out worse than she expects. The same principle has motivated common law courts and legislatures to reject the claim of mistake in cases of abducting infants, statutory rape, and assaulting a police officer. If the act is wrong, even as the defendant conceives the facts to be, then she presumably has no grounds for complaining if the facts turn out to be worse than she expects. . . .

[This mode of thought violates] a basic principle of just punishment. Punishment must be proportional to wrongdoing. When the felony-murder rule converts an accidental death into first-degree murder, then punishment is rendered disproportionate to the wrong for which the offender is personally responsible. [T]he principle that the wrongdoer must run the risk explicitly obscures the question of actual responsibility for the harmful result.

There may be an apology for the felony-murder rule, but it is one that could easily excuse too much injustice in our substantive criminal law. If we compare our combined system of substantive law and procedural rights with the total system that prevails in a Continental jurisdiction, say, in West Germany, we could hazard the following generalization. American law achieves a balance of advantage between defense and prosecution by bestowing extraordinary procedural protections on the accused and yet compensating the prosecution with rules of strict liability, felony-murder, conspiracy, and vicarious liability. German law, in contrast, offers fewer procedural protections — no jury, no exclusionary rule in our sense, fewer restrictions on hearsay evidence — yet the German substantive law is more refined and more consistent with principles of individual responsibility. . . . What the [American] law of procedure grants the accused, the law of substance takes away.

4. *Model Penal Code and Commentaries, Comment to §210.2 at 37-39 (1980):* [The American Law Institute recommended eliminating the felony-murder rule. However, it provided that for the purpose of establishing murder by an act "committed recklessly under circumstances manifesting extreme indifference to the value of human life," the fact that the actor is "engaged, or is an accomplice in the commission of, or an attempt to commit, or flight after committing or attempting to commit robbery, rape or deviate sexual intercourse by force or threat of force, arson, burglary, kidnapping or felonious escape" creates a rebuttable presumption (defined in §1.12(5))that the required indifference and recklessness existed.

[In support of this proposal, the Comment states:] Principled argument in favor of the felony-murder doctrine is hard to find. The defense reduces to the explanation that Holmes gave for finding the law "intelligible as it stands":

> [I]f experience shows, or is deemed by the law-maker to show, that somehow or other deaths which the evidence makes accidental happen disproportionately often in connection with other felonies, or with resistance to officers, or if on any other ground of policy it is deemed desirable to make special efforts for the prevention of such deaths, the law-maker may consistently treat acts which, under the known circumstances, are felonious, or constitute resistance to officers, as having a sufficiently dangerous tendency to be put under a special ban. The law may, therefore, throw on the actor the peril, not only of the consequences foreseen by him, but also of consequences which, although not predicted by common experience, the legislator apprehends.[95]

The answer to such arguments is twofold. First, there is no basis in experience for thinking that homicides *which the evidence makes accidental* occur with disproportionate frequency in connection with specified felonies. Second, it remains indefensible in principle to use the sanctions that the law employs to deal with murder unless there is at least a finding that the actor's conduct manifested an extreme indifference to the value of human life. The fact that the actor was engaged in a crime of the kind that is included in the usual first-degree felony-murder enumeration or was an accomplice in such crime, as has been observed, will frequently justify such a finding. Indeed, the probability that such a finding will be justified seems high enough to warrant the presumption of extreme indifference that Subsection (1)(b) creates.[a] But liability depends, as plainly it should, upon the crucial finding. The result may not differ often under such a formulation from that which would be reached under some form of the felony-murder rule. But what is more important is that a conviction on this basis rests solidly upon principle.

95. O. Holmes, The Common Law 49 (1881).
a. Does this sentence square with the point made at the beginning of the same paragraph? — Eds.

5. *David Crump & Susan W. Crump, In Defense of the Felony Murder Doctrine, 8 Harv. J. L. & Pub. Poly. 359, 362-363, 370-371 (1985):* Differences in result must be taken into account as part of actus reus if classification and grading are to be rational. For example, murder and attempted murder may require similar mental states (indeed, attempted murder generally requires proof of a higher mental element), but no common law jurisdiction treats the two offenses as one, and certainly none treats attempted murder more severely. The only difference justifying this classification is that death results in one offense but not in the other. Similarly, it is a misdemeanor for a person to operate a motor vehicle while impaired by drugs or alcohol, but if this conduct causes the death of a human being, the offense in some jurisdictions is elevated to the status of homicide. Most jurisdictions treat vehicular homicide more severely than the misdemeanor of alcohol-impaired driving, even though the actions and mental states of the defendant may be equivalent or identical.

These classifications are the result of a concern for grading offenses so as to reflect societal notions of proportionality. . . . The felony murder doctrine serves this goal, just as do the distinctions inherent in the separate offenses of attempted murder and murder, or impaired driving and vehicular homicide. Felony murder reflects a societal judgment that an intentionally committed robbery that causes the death of a human being is qualitatively more serious than an identical robbery that does not. . . . There is impressive empirical evidence that this classification does indeed reflect widely shared societal attitudes. . . .

Deterrence is the [felony-murder] policy most often recognized in the cases. Scholars, however, tend to dismiss this rationale . . . The trouble with these criticisms is that they underestimate the complexity of deterrence. . . . The felony murder rule is just the sort of simple, commonsense, readily enforceable, and widely known principle that is likely to result in deterrence. . . .

The argument against deterrence often proceeds on the . . . assumption that felony murder is addressed only to accidental killings and cannot result in their deterrence.[45] By facilitating proof and simplifying the concept of liability, however, felony murder may deter intentional killings as well. The robber who kills intentionally, but who might claim under oath to have acted accidentally, is thus told that he will be deprived of the benefit of this claim. . . . Furthermore, the . . . proposition that accidental killings cannot be deterred is inconsistent with the widespread belief that the penalizing of negligence, and even the imposition of strict liability, may have deterrent consequences.

6. For further development of the argument for the potential deterrent value of the felony-murder rule, see Kevin Cole, Killings During Crime: Toward a Discriminating Theory of Strict Liability, 28 Am. Crim. L. Rev. 73 (1990). With respect to the frequency with which death occurs during the commission of serious felonies, consider Model Penal Code and Commentaries, Comment to §210.2 at 38 n. 96:

> In fact, the number of all homicides which occur in the commission of such crimes as robbery, burglary, or rape is lower than might be expected. For example, comparison of the figures for solved and unsolved homicides from M. Wolfgang,

---

45. The Model Penal Code provision is based upon this erroneous assumption.

Criminal Homicide (1958), with statistics on basic felonies taken from the FBI Uniform Crime Reports reveals the following for Philadelphia from 1948-1952:

Relation of Total Felonies to Homicides Occurring during the Felony
Philadelphia 1948-1952

Offense	No. of Crimes Reported	No. Accompanied by Homicide	%	No. per 1000
Robbery	6,432	38	0.59	5.9
Rape	1,133	4	0.35	3.5
Burglary	27,669	1	0.0036	[.036]
Auto Theft	10,315	2	0.019	[.19]

Similar figures are found in Cook County, Illinois, robbery statistics from 1926-1930. . . . More recent statistics derived from N.J. State Police, Crime in New Jersey: Uniform Crime Reports 42-45 (1975) reveal strikingly similar percentages. In 1975, 16,273 robberies were committed in New Jersey, and 66 homicides resulted from these robberies, only .41 per cent, a figure even lower than the earlier statistics from Cook County and Philadelphia. When other violent felonies are taken into account, this percentage drops even lower.

On a national basis, the fatality rate from major felonies appears even lower than these data from urban areas suggest. One study indicates that out of 1.5 million robberies and robbery attempts annually, there are roughly 2,090 robbery-related homicides, a fatality rate of .14 percent. See Phillip J. Cook, Robbery Violence, 78 J. Crim. L. & Criminology 357, 358-359, 362-363 (1987). But in response to data of this sort, Professor Cole observes (Cole, supra, at 105):

The statistics have struck some as indicating that felonies are not particularly dangerous to life. For example, only about .6 percent of all armed robberies end in death. But just because this rate is lower than we might have thought does not mean that robberies are safe relative to the normal range of human activities governed by the laws relating to simple killings. If the average robbery takes an hour (probably a high estimate), that means one homicide occurs every 166 hours of robbery. If everyday activities were as dangerous as robbery, and if the average person is awake 16 hours a day, then the average person would kill one person every eleven days.

NOTES ON THE MISDEMEANOR-MANSLAUGHTER RULE

1. The basic doctrine. Just as a felony resulting in death can provide a basis for a murder conviction without proof of malice, in many states a misdemeanor resulting in death can provide a basis for an involuntary manslaughter conviction without proof of recklessness or negligence. The misdemeanor-manslaughter rule, also known as the "unlawful-act doctrine," was reflected in the traditional common law definition of involuntary manslaughter. The language of Cal. Penal Code §192(b), drawn from Blackstone's formulation, is typical: Involuntary manslaughter is a killing "in the commission of an unlawful act, not amounting to a felony; or in the commission of a lawful act which might produce death, in an unlawful manner, or without due caution and circumspection "

In states that retain the traditional common law formula, the prosecution thus has two distinct theories available to establish involuntary manslaughter. If a defendant, after driving through a red light, has killed a pedestrian, the prosecution can argue for involuntary manslaughter on the basis that the defendant's conduct amounted to criminal negligence under the circumstances. See page 437 supra. In the alternative, however, in states that recognize the unlawful-act doctrine, the prosecution need only show that the defendant's unlawful act caused the death; proof of criminal negligence becomes unnecessary. See State v. Hupf, 48 Del. 254, 101 A.2d 355 (1953)).

2. *Criticism of the unlawful-act doctrine.* The Model Penal Code rejects the unlawful-act doctrine, regarding it as a species of strict liability (Model Penal Code and Commentaries, Comment to §210.3 at 77 (1980)):

> It dispenses with proof of culpability and imposes liability for serious crime without reference to the actor's state of mind. This result is not only morally unjustified, but it also operates quite inequitably among individuals.

Questions: Is the argument sound? Why is the requirement of culpability for the misdemeanor insufficient to meet the criticism?

3. *Limitations on the unlawful-act doctrine.* In states that retain the unlawful-act doctrine, some of its harshest effects have been moderated by a variety of limitations. Most of these limitations are similar to the ones that apply to the felony-murder rule.

(a) Proximate cause. As indicated in the Note on the Causation Requirement, page 471 supra, the felony-murder rule applies only when the crime committed is the proximate cause of the death. Nearly all jurisdictions impose a similar limitation on the misdemeanor-manslaughter rule. Thus, in Commonwealth v. Williams, 133 Pa. Super. 104, 1 A.2d 812 (1938), the defendant had been convicted of manslaughter by vehicle on the basis of his unlawful act of failing to renew his driver's license. The court reversed, holding that the expiration of the license had no causal connection to the accident, which had resulted from the carelessness of another driver. In Todd v. State, 594 So. 2d 802 (Fla. Dist. App. 1992), defendant grabbed $110 from a church collection plate and fled. One of the congregants, Voegltin, took off in his car in pursuit of the defendant, but Voegltin, who had a serious heart condition, lost control of his car, collided with a tree at low speed and died of cardiac arrest. Because the defendant had committed the misdemeanor of petty theft, Florida's unlawful-act doctrine was applicable, but the court nonetheless reversed the manslaughter conviction, stating (594 So. 2d at 806):

> [I]t cannot be said that the petty theft was the legal cause of Mr. Voegltin's death. The crime itself was a minor property offense. There is no suggestion of any touching or any threat to anyone's person. . . . Although the petty theft did trigger a series of events that concluded in the death of Mr. Voegltin and was, in that sense, a "cause" of the death, the petty theft did not encompass the kind of direct, foreseeable risk of physical harm that would support a conviction of manslaughter.

(b) Regulatory offenses. Some courts restrict the unlawful-act doctrine to malum in se as opposed to malum prohibitum misdemeanors. E.g., Mills v. State, 13 Md. App. 196, 282 A.2d 147 (1971). Many other courts, however, have explicitly re-

jected that limitation. See, e.g., State v. Hose, 187 W. Va. 429, 419 S.E.2d 690 (1992) (truck driver convicted of involuntary manslaughter for fatal accident that occurred after he violated federal and state laws by remaining on duty for more than 15 hours).

(c) *Dangerousness.* Another approach is to require that the misdemeanor (whether malum in se or malum prohibitum) be inherently dangerous or "evince a marked disregard for the safety of others." State v. Lingman, 97 Utah 180, 91 P.2d 457 (1939). In State v. Powell, 426 S.E.2d 91 (N.C. App. 1993), a 20-year-old jogger was killed when he was attacked by two Rottweiler dogs belonging to the defendant. The dogs apparently had escaped from defendant's fenced yard, as they had done frequently in the past, in violation of a local ordinance requiring dogs to be restrained by a secure fence or leash at all times. The court found that the ordinance was a "safety" ordinance, because it was designed to protect persons as well as property, and held that the violation of the ordinance therefore would support the defendant's conviction for involuntary manslaughter (426 S.E.2d at 96): "[Because] defendant intentionally violated an ordinance requiring all unattended dogs to be confined or restrained on the owner's property, the State is not required to prove that defendant's dogs had vicious propensities of which defendant had knowledge."

In the District of Columbia, the unlawful-act doctrine applies only if the misdemeanor is "dangerous in itself." Consider United States v. Walker, 380 A.2d 1388 (D.C. App. 1977). The defendant, who was carrying a pistol without a license, dropped it. The gun went off, fatally injuring a bystander. Although there was no allegation of criminal negligence in handling the weapon, the court held that Walker could be convicted of involuntary manslaughter under the unlawful-act doctrine. Is carrying a weapon without a license inherently dangerous? If so, is the illegal aspect of the conduct (the lack of a license) the proximate cause of death? Compare Commonwealth v. Williams, discussed in Note 3(a) supra.

Some courts hold that the unlawful-act doctrine can come into play only when the unlawful conduct rises to the level of criminal negligence. See, e.g., State v. Stanislaw, 153 Vt. 517, 573 A.2d 286 (1990); State v. Burrell, 699 P.2d 499 (Kan. 1985). Some statutory revisions also limit the doctrine in this fashion. See, e.g., 18 Pa. Stat. §2504(a), set out at page 390 supra. Once the unlawful-act doctrine is qualified in this way, does it add anything to the possibilities for a manslaughter conviction that would exist in the absence of such a doctrine?

4. *Statutory reform.* Under the influence of the Model Penal Code, many states have abolished the unlawful-act doctrine, but a fair number have preserved it, and of course the doctrine continues in force in most jurisdictions that have not recodified their law. See Model Penal Code and Commentaries, Comment to §210.3 at 77 (1980).

NOTES ON STATUTORY REFORM OF THE FELONY-MURDER RULE

England, whose judges created the felony-murder rule through the common law process, abolished it by statute in 1957 (Homicide Act of 1957, 5 & 6 Eliz. 2, ch. 11, §1):

Where a person kills another in the course or furtherance of some other offence, the killing shall not amount to murder unless done with the same malice aforethought (express or implied) as is required for a killing to amount to murder when not done in the course or furtherance of another offence.

In this country the felony-murder rule has proven of greater durability. Despite the substantial influence of the Model Penal Code in other areas, it has had a smaller measure of success here: Only New Hampshire adopted the Model Penal Code's formulation (N.H. Rev. Stat. Ann. tit. 62, §630:1-b); very few legislatures went further and abolished the doctrine (e.g., Haw. Rev. Stat. tit. 37, §707-701; Ky. Rev. Stat. Ann. tit. 50, §507.020). In Ohio, a death resulting from any felony is involuntary manslaughter rather than murder (unless actual malice is proved). Ohio Rev. Code §2903.04.

However, statutes over the years have qualified the severity of the common law rule in a variety of ways.

1. When common law murder was divided into two degrees by the Pennsylvania statute of 1794 (see page 394 above), certain particularly dangerous felonies—arson, rape, robbery, and burglary—were designated as the only felonies on which a first-degree felony-murder conviction could be obtained. Where this approach is followed (see, e.g., 18 U.S.C. §1111; Cal. Penal Code §189, page 388 supra), a killing in the course of a nondesignated felony still triggers the felony-murder rule, but (in the absence of deliberation and premeditation) the offense will only be murder in the second degree.

2. Some states have designated particular felonies (such as rape, arson, burglary, kidnapping, and robbery) as the only felonies on which a felony-murder conviction may be obtained; other felonies serve only as the possible basis of a manslaughter conviction (Ind. Code §35-42-1-4; La. Rev. Stat. tit. 14, §31) or cannot by themselves serve as the basis for conviction of any form of culpable homicide (N.Y. Pen. Law §125.25(3), page 392 supra).

3. Another approach is to require that a killing in the course of the felony be otherwise culpable before it may constitute murder—for example, that the defendant has "recklessly" caused the death of another (Del. Code Ann. tit. 11, §636) or that the defendant has caused another's death by "an act clearly dangerous to human life" (Tex. Pen. Code §19.02).

Question: To what extent do these various qualifications meet the criticisms of the felony-murder rule made by Macaulay and the Model Penal Code?

People v. Aaron, 409 Mich. 672, 299 N.W.2d 304 (1980): [Defendants in several unrelated cases were convicted of first-degree murder for deaths that occurred in the course of robbery or arson. In each case the jury instructions permitted conviction on the basis of the felony, without other evidence of malice. The Michigan Supreme Court held that the convictions should be reversed:] Felony murder has never been a static, well-defined rule at common law, but throughout its history has been characterized by judicial reinterpretation to limit the harshness of the application of the rule. Historians and commentators have concluded that the rule is of questionable origin and that the reasons for the rule no longer exist, making it an anachronistic remnant. . . .

Michigan does not have a statutory felony-murder doctrine which designates as murder any *death* occurring in the course of a felony without regard to whether it was the result of accident, negligence, recklessness or willfulness. Rather, Michigan has a statute which makes a *murder* occurring in the course of one of the enumerated felonies a first-degree murder:

Murder which is perpetrated by means of poison, lying in wait, or other wilful, deliberate, and premeditated killing, or which is committed in the perpetration, or attempt to perpetrate [designated felonies] is murder of the first degree, and shall be punished by imprisonment for life. M.S.A. §28.548.

The Michigan Legislature adopted verbatim the first-degree murder statute of Pennsylvania, the statute we have today. . . . In Commonwealth ex rel. Smith v. Myers, 438 Pa. 224, 261, A.2d 550, the Pennsylvania Supreme Court stated: "Clearly this statutory felony-murder rule merely serves to raise the degree of certain murders to first degree; it gives no aid to the determination of what constitutes murder in the first place." . . . This Court has not been faced previously with a decision as to whether it should abolish the felony-murder doctrine. Thus, the common-law doctrine remains the law in Michigan. . . .

We believe that it is no longer acceptable to equate the intent to commit a felony with the intent to kill, intent to do great bodily harm, or wanton and willful disregard of the likelihood that the natural tendency of a person's behavior is to cause death or great bodily harm. Today we exercise our role in the development of the common law by abrogating the common-law felony-murder rule. We hold that in order to convict a defendant of murder, as that term is defined by Michigan case law, it must be shown that he acted with intent to kill or to inflict great bodily harm or with a wanton and willful disregard of the likelihood that the natural tendency of his behavior is to cause death or great bodily harm. We further hold that the issue of malice must always be submitted to the jury.

The first-degree murder statute will continue to operate in that all *murder* committed in the perpetration or attempted perpetration of the enumerated felonies will be elevated to first-degree murder.

NOTES ON JUDICIAL REFORM

1. Statutory interpretation. The *Aaron* decision has influenced judicial interpretation of homicide statutes in several other states. In State v. Ortega, 112 N.M. 554, 817 P.2d 1196 (1991), a case of homicide in the course of a kidnapping and robbery, the court read into New Mexico's first-degree felony-murder statute a requirement that the state prove intent to kill or conscious disregard for life. Similarly, in Commonwealth v. Matchett, 386 Mass. 492, 436 N.E.2d 400 (1982), the court held that before prosecutors can invoke that state's second-degree felony-murder rule for nonenumerated felonies, the jury must find that the defendant demonstrated a conscious disregard for the risk to human life. Such decisions in effect abolish the felony-murder rule as a distinctive way to establish malice.

The great majority of courts, however, have not felt free to reinterpret their homicide statutes in the way that *Aaron* does, even when the judges disapprove of the felony-murder rule on the merits. In People v. Dillon, 34 Cal. 3d 441, 668 P.2d 697 (1983), the court declined to follow *Aaron,* even though the wording of California's statute is identical to Michigan's and even though both statutes were explicitly based on the 1794 Pennsylvania model. The *Dillon* court held that subsequent reenactments by the California legislature demonstrated an intent to codify the felony-murder rule in that state. To date, most other courts have likewise refused to use their powers of common law interpretation to abolish the felony-murder rule outright.

2. *Constitutional issues.* If the felony-murder rule is required by statute, then to what extent is its application to nonintentional killings unconstitutional? In *Dillon,* supra Note 1, the court read California's felony-murder statute as imposing first-degree murder liability for a wide range of robbery killings — from accidental to premeditated homicides — and held that in order to comply with the constitutional prohibition on cruel and unusual punishment (see page 287 supra), the sentencing court would have to consider whether the first-degree penalty, life imprisonment, was disproportionate to the culpability of the defendant in the particular case.

A related approach is developed in Nelson E. Roth & Scott E. Sundby, The Felony-Murder Rule: A Doctrine at Constitutional Crossroads, 70 Cornell L. Rev. 446 (1985). The authors argue that courts should hold the felony-murder rule unconstitutional because its effect is either to conclusively presume malice (thus violating the requirement of proof beyond a reasonable doubt) or to eliminate malice (thus violating the Eighth Amendment requirement that severe punishments be proportional to culpability). Although no United States court has, to our knowledge, adopted this position to date,[8] the Roth and Sundby arguments played a large role in influencing the New Mexico Supreme Court to read an intent requirement into that state's felony-murder statute, in order to avoid serious constitutional questions. See *Ortega,* supra Note 1. And in The Queen v. Vaillancourt, [1987] S.C.R. 636, the Canadian Supreme Court held that the felony-murder rule provisions of that country's Criminal Code, by permitting conviction in the absence of mens rea, violate the Canadian Charter of Rights and Freedoms, in particular §7 (requiring respect for "principles of fundamental justice") and §11(d) (guaranteeing the presumption of innocence).

These important countercurrents aside, the great majority of American jurisdictions retain the felony-murder rule in principle. But all those jurisdictions qualify the rule in some fashion or confine it through one or more doctrinal limitations. The remaining materials in this section consider the issues that arise in administering the felony-murder rule.

b. The "Inherently Dangerous-Felony" Limitation

PEOPLE v. PHILLIPS

Supreme Court of California
64 Cal. 2d 574, 414 P.2d 353 (1966)

TOBRINER, J. Defendant, a doctor of chiropractic, appeals from a judgment of the Superior Court of Los Angeles County convicting him of second degree murder in connection with the death from cancer of one of his patients. We reverse solely on the ground that the trial court erred in giving a felony-murder instruction. . . .

---

8. See, e.g., State v. Crump, 232 Kan. 265, 654 P.2d 922 (1982), upholding the constitutionality of the Kansas felony-murder rule.

[Deceased was an eight-year-old child with a fast-growing cancer of the eye. Her parents were advised at a medical center to consent to immediate removal of the eye as the only means of saving or prolonging her life. However, defendant induced them not to do so by representing that he could cure her without surgery by treatment designed "to build up her resistance." Defendant charged the parents $700 for his treatment and medicine. The child died in about six months.]

Defendant challenges the propriety of the trial court's instructions to the jury. The court gave the following tripartite instruction on murder in the second degree:[4]

> [T]he unlawful killing of a human being with malice aforethought, but without a deliberately formed and premeditated intent to kill, is murder of the second degree:
> (1) If the killing proximately results from an unlawful act, the natural consequences of which are dangerous to life, which act is deliberately performed by a person who knows that his conduct endangers the life of another, or
> (2) If the circumstances proximately causing the killing show an abandoned and malignant heart, or
> (3) If the killing is done in the perpetration or attempt to perpetrate a felony such as Grand Theft. If a death occurs in the perpetration of a course of conduct amounting to Grand Theft, which course of conduct is a proximate cause of the unlawful killing of a human being, such course of conduct constitutes murder in the second degree, even though the death was not intended.

The third part of this instruction rests upon the felony-murder rule and reflects the prosecution's theory that defendant's conduct amounted to grand theft by false pretenses in violation of Penal Code section 484. . . .

Despite defendant's contention that the Penal Code does not expressly set forth any provision for second degree felony murder and that, therefore, we should not follow any such doctrine here, the concept lies imbedded in our law. [T]he perpetration of some felonies, exclusive of those enumerated in Penal Code section 189, may provide the basis for a murder conviction under the felony-murder rule.

We have held, however, that only such felonies as are in themselves "inherently dangerous to human life" can support the application of the felony-murder rule. We have ruled that in assessing such peril to human life inherent in any given felony "we look to the elements of the felony in the abstract, not the particular 'facts' of the case." (People v. Williams, 63 Cal. 2d 452, 458, fn. 5).

We have thus recognized that the felony-murder doctrine expresses a highly artificial concept that deserves no extension beyond its required application.

---

4. The record suggests that the evidence would have supported a finding of involuntary manslaughter. The jury might, for example, have found that defendant sincerely, though *unreasonably*, believed that the removal of Linda from the hospital and treatment according to the principles of chiropractic would be in her best interests. Having so found, the jury could have concluded that in causing Linda's removal from the hospital and so endangering her life defendant acted "without due caution and circumspection." (Pen. Code, §192, subd. 2.) Accordingly, the trial court should have given a manslaughter instruction. The record reveals, however, that defendant's counsel strongly opposed the manslaughter instruction and indicated to the trial court that he considered it "tactically" to defendant's advantage to confront the jury with the limited choice between murder and acquittal. Thus the failure of the trial court to instruct on manslaughter, though erroneous, was invited error; defendant may not properly complain of such error on appeal.

Indeed, the rule itself has been abandoned by the courts of England, where it had its inception. It has been subjected to severe and sweeping criticism. No case to our knowledge in any jurisdiction has held that because death results from a course of conduct involving a felonious perpetration of a fraud, the felony-murder doctrine can be invoked.

Admitting that grand theft is not inherently dangerous to life, the prosecution asks us to encompass the entire course of defendant's conduct so that we may incorporate such elements as would make his crime inherently dangerous. In so framing the definition of a given felony for the purpose of assessing its inherent peril to life the prosecution would abandon the statutory definition of the felony as such and substitute the factual elements of defendant's actual conduct. In the present case the Attorney General would characterize that conduct as "grand theft medical fraud," and this newly created "felony," he urges, clearly involves danger to human life and supports an application of the felony-murder rule.

To fragmentize the "course of conduct" of defendant so that the felony-murder rule applies if any segment of that conduct may be considered dangerous to life would widen the rule beyond calculation. It would then apply not only to the commission of specific felonies, which are themselves dangerous to life, but to the perpetration of *any* felony during which defendant may have acted in such a manner as to endanger life.

The proposed approach would entail the rejection of our holding in *Williams.* That case limited the felony-murder doctrine to such felonies as were themselves inherently dangerous to life. That decision eschews the prosecution's present sweeping concept because, once the Legislature's own definition is discarded, the number or nature of the contextual elements which could be incorporated into an expanded felony terminology would be limitless. We have been, and remain, unwilling to embark on such an uncharted sea of felony murder.

The felony-murder instruction should not, then, have been given; its rendition, further, worked prejudice upon defendant. It withdrew from the jury the issue of malice, permitting a conviction upon the bare showing that Linda's death proximately resulted from conduct of defendant amounting to grand theft. The instruction as rendered did not require the jury to find either express malice or the implied malice which is manifested in an "intent with conscious disregard for life to commit acts likely to kill." (People v. Washington, 62 Cal. 2d 777, 780.) . . .

The prosecution does not deny that the giving of a felony-murder instruction engendered the possibility of a conviction of murder in the absence of a finding of malice. It contends, however, that even if the jury acted on the erroneous instruction it must necessarily have found facts which establish, as a matter of law, that defendant acted with conscious disregard for life and hence with malice. . . . The prosecution urges that the jury could not have convicted defendant under the felony-murder instruction without having found that he made representations to the Eppings which he knew to be false or which he recklessly rendered without information which would justify a reasonable belief in their truth. Such a finding does not, however, establish as a matter of law the existence of an "intent with conscious disregard for life to commit acts likely to kill." (People v. Washington, supra.) In the absence of a finding that defendant subjectively appreciated the peril to which his conduct exposed the girl, we cannot determine that he acted with conscious disregard for life. The record contains evidence from which a trier of fact could reasonably have concluded that although defendant made false representations concerning his ability to cure, he nevertheless believed that the treatment which he proposed to give would be as efficacious in relieving pain and prolonging life as the scheduled surgery.

Of course the jury could have concluded from some of the evidence that defendant did *not* entertain any such belief in the relative efficacy of his proposed treatment. We cannot, however, undertake to resolve this evidentiary conflict without invading the province of the trier of fact. We cannot predicate a finding of conscious disregard of life upon a record that would as conclusively afford a basis for the opposite conclusion. . . .

The judgment is reversed.[a]

PEOPLE v. SATCHELL, 6 Cal. 3d 28, 489 P.2d 1361 (1972): Defendant, an ex-felon with four prior felony convictions, was convicted of second-degree murder arising out of a street fight. Defendant shot and killed the deceased with a sawed-off shotgun he obtained from his car. Section 12021 of the Penal Code made it a felony for an ex-felon to possess such a weapon. The trial judge gave the following second-degree felony-murder instruction:

> The unlawful killing of a human being, whether intentional, unintentional or accidental, which occurs as a direct causal result of the commission of or attempt to commit a felony inherently dangerous to human life, namely, the crime of possession of a concealable firearm by a felon, and where there was in the mind of the perpetrator the specific intent to commit such crime, is murder of the second degree.

The supreme court held this instruction erroneous and reversed the conviction, concluding that the felony of possession of a concealable weapon by an ex-felon was not a "felony inherently dangerous to human life."

[The court started by recalling the approach to felony murder established by several recent California decisions; namely that, "Although it is the law in this state, it should not be extended beyond any rational function that it is designed to serve," and that the "highly artificial concept of strict criminal liability incorporated in the felony-murder doctrine [must] be given the narrowest possible application consistent with its ostensible purpose — which is to deter those engaged in felonies from killing negligently or accidentally." The court then continued:]

It bears emphasis that, in determining whether a felony is inherently dangerous for purposes of the felony-murder rule we assess that felony *in the abstract*. The felony here in question is possession of a concealable firearm by one who has previously been convicted of a (i.e., another) felony. We do *not* look to the specific facts of the case before us in order to determine whether, in light of the nature of the particular felony of which defendant was previously convicted, his possession of a concealable firearm was inherently dangerous. Rather, we direct our attention to the genus of crimes known as felonies and determine whether

---

a. On retrial Phillips was convicted of second-degree murder. The theory of the prosecution this time was that defendant had exhibited actual malice by causing the deceased to terminate a surgical treatment that would have prolonged her life. The court of appeal affirmed the conviction. People v. Phillips, 270 Cal. App. 2d 381, 75 Cal. Rptr. 720 (1969). — Eds.

the possession of a concealable firearm by one who has been convicted of *any crime within that genus* is an act inherently dangerous to human life which, as such, justifies the extreme consequence (i.e., imputed malice) which the felony-murder doctrine demands.

. . .[T]he range of antisocial activities which are criminally punishable as felonies in this state is very wide indeed. Some of these felonies . . . distinctly manifest a propensity for acts dangerous to human life on the part of the perpetrator. Others, of which a random sampling is set forth in the margin,[19] just as distinctly fail to manifest such a propensity. Surely it cannot be said that a person who has committed a crime in this latter category, when he arms himself with a concealable weapon, presents a danger to human life so significantly more extreme than that presented by a nonfelon similarly armed as to justify the imputation of malice to him if a homicide should result. Accordingly, because we can conceive of such a vast number of situations wherein it would be grossly illogical to impute malice, we must conclude that the violation of section 12021 by one previously convicted of a felony is not itself a felony *inherently* dangerous to human life which will support a second-degree felony-murder instruction.

NOTES AND QUESTIONS

1. Question. What would be the result if §12021 had made it a felony for a person who had been convicted of a felony of personal violence to possess a concealable firearm?

2. In a comparable case, the Kansas Supreme Court reached a conclusion contrary to that reached in the *Satchell* case. State v. Goodseal, 220 Kan. 487, 553 P.2d 279 (1977). The court stated (553 P.2d at 285):

> [W]here doubt may exist, we see nothing wrong in considering both the nature of the offense in the abstract and the circumstances of its commission in determining whether a particular felony was inherently dangerous to human life. Some felonies, such as aggravated robbery, viewed in the abstract alone, are of such nature as to be inherently dangerous to human life,[a] while another which seems of itself not to involve any element of human risk may be committed in such a dangerous manner as to be of the same character. Hence we hold that the nature of the felony and, where necessary for determination, the circumstances of its commission are relevant factors in considering whether the particular felony was inherently and foreseeably dangerous to human life so as to support a conviction of felony murder. These are questions for the trial court and jury to decide in appropriate cases.

However, in State v. Underwood, 615 P.2d 153 (Kan. 1980), which also involved firearm possession by an ex-felon, the Kansas Supreme Court overruled

---

19. See, for example, Corporations Code (fraudulent and deceptive acts relating to corporations); Elections Code, (elections offenses); Financial Code, (unauthorized sale of investment certificates); Government Code, (interference with the legislative process); Insurance Code, (false or fraudulent insurance claim). . . .

The Penal Code, of course, renders felonious many activities which do not indicate a propensity for dangerous acts.

a. But compare Commonwealth v. Moran, 387 Mass. 644, 442 N.E.2d 399 (1982), holding that *unarmed* robbery is not inherently dangerous to human life. — EDS.

the *Goodseal* case and brought the Kansas law into line with the California law as announced in *Satchell.*

3. Was the Kansas Supreme Court right the first time or the second? Or neither time? What is the justification for the inherently dangerous-felony limitation developed by the courts? What considerations favor interpreting that limitation in terms of the definition of the felony in the abstract, apart from the circumstances of its actual commission?

4. In Ford v. State, 262 Ga. 602, 423 S.E.2d 255 (1992), defendant, a previously convicted felon, was cleaning a pistol at his girlfriend's house when the weapon accidentally discharged, sending a bullet through the floor and into the basement, where it killed a tenant living in a basement apartment. There was no evidence the defendant knew that the basement apartment existed or that the tenant was present there. The court chose to follow the *Goodseal* approach but held that the felony — possession of a firearm by a convicted felon — was *not* inherently dangerous in the particular circumstances of this case.

Question: When courts follow this approach, how does prosecution on a felony-murder theory differ from an ordinary second-degree murder prosecution on a theory of implied malice under the circumstances?

5. In People v. Henderson, 19 Cal. 3d 86, 560 P.2d 1180 (1977), the California Supreme Court reversed a second-degree felony-murder conviction based on the felony of "false imprisonment . . . effected by violence, menace, fraud or deceit." Defendant held the victim hostage by holding a gun to his head. When the victim ducked and attempted to deflect the barrel of the gun from his head, the gun went off and killed a bystander. The court found that unlawful restraint of another does not necessarily involve the requisite danger to human life for a felony-murder conviction and that the factors elevating the offense to a felony — violence, menace, fraud, or deceit — do not all involve conduct that is life endangering. While the factors of violence or menace may involve such danger, the others do not. Therefore, viewing the offense as a whole and in the abstract, it is not an offense inherently dangerous to human life. The prosecution argued that the matter would not differ in substance if the legislature had created two separate false imprisonment felonies, one by violence or menace, the other by fraud or deceit. The court disagreed, finding this formal difference to be crucial (19 Cal. 3d at 95):

> The Legislature has not evinced a particular concern for violent as opposed to nonviolent acts of false imprisonment by separate statutory treatment, proscription, or punishment. Accordingly, we cannot conclude that the cause of deterring homicide during the commission of false imprisonment is better served by imputing malice to one who kills in the course of committing false imprisonment rather than allowing the jury to determine directly the question of the presence of malice aforethought.

Is there something to be said for the court's reasoning, other than the result? Is that enough?

Compare People v. Patterson, 49 Cal. 3d 615, 778 P.2d 549 (1989). Defendant was charged with the felony murder of a woman who overdosed on cocaine that the defendant had "furnished" in violation of §11352 of the Health and Safety Code. The trial judge dismissed the murder count, and the Court of Appeals affirmed, holding that "section 11352 could be violated in various nonhazardous ways, such as transporting or offering to transport controlled substances. . . . [V]iewing the statute 'in the abstract,' a violation of section 11352 could not be characterized as an inherently dangerous felony." (49 Cal. 3d at 620.) The California Supreme Court reversed (49 Cal. 3d at 624-625):

> In [People v. Henderson,] we observed that the offense in question had a "primary element[,]" . . . "the unlawful restraint of another's liberty." . . . In contrast, Health and Safety Code section 11352 . . . has no primary element. For instance, the elements of the crime of transporting a controlled substance bear no resemblance to those underlying the offense of administering such a substance; yet the two offenses are included in the same statute.
>
> The fact that the Legislature has included a variety of offenses in Health and Safety Code section 11352 does not require that we treat them as a unitary entity. Rather, we must decide whether in "[r]eading and considering the statute as a whole to determine the true legislative intent . . . we find [a] basis for severing" the various types of conduct it forbids. (People v. Henderson.) There are more than 100 different controlled substances that fall within the confines of Health and Safety Code section 11352. To create statutes separately proscribing the importation, sale, furnishing, administration, etc., of each of these drugs, would require the enactment of hundreds of individual statutes. It thus appears that for the sake of convenience the Legislature has included the various offenses in one statute.
>
> The determination whether a defendant who furnished cocaine commits an inherently dangerous felony should not turn on the dangerousness of other drugs included in the same statute, such as heroin and peyote; nor should it turn on the danger to life, if any, inherent in the transportation or administering of cocaine. Rather, each offense set forth in the statute should be examined separately to determine its inherent dangerousness.

Questions: Is the *Patterson* court's effort to distinguish *Henderson* persuasive? If not, which case provides the better way to determine whether the felony is dangerous "in the abstract"?

In People v. Burroughs, 35 Cal. 3d 824, 678 P.2d 894 (1984), defendant provided advice and treatment to a man suffering from leukemia. He gave the man massages and instructed him to consume nothing but lemonade, salt water, and herb tea. The man's condition rapidly deteriorated, and he died from a hemorrhage caused by the massages. Defendant was convicted of felony murder, based on the underlying offense of "felonious unlicensed practice of medicine," defined to proscribe unauthorized medical practice under "conditions which cause or create a risk of great bodily harm, serious physical or mental illness, or death." Does this felony meet the inherent dangerousness requirement as interpreted in *Henderson* and *Patterson?*

6. *Drug distribution as a dangerous felony.* Although the California courts have not yet resolved the question whether cocaine distribution meets the inherent dangerousness requirement, as interpreted in *Patterson,* the court in People v. Taylor, 6 Cal. App. 4th 1084, 8 Cal. Rptr. 2d 439 (1992), held that the felony of furnishing PCP does not carry a "high probability" of death and therefore cannot support conviction on a felony-murder theory. In Heacock v. Commonwealth, 323 S.E.2d 90 (Va. 1984), the court held that felony distribution of cocaine met the inherent dangerousness requirement and noted that cocaine had been classified as a controlled substance because of its "high potential for abuse." For contrary conclusions, see State v. Wesson, 802 P.2d 574 (Kan. 1990);

State v. Aarsvold, 376 N.W.2d 518, 522 (Minn. 1985) ("use of cocaine, even when injected, does not generally cause death").

Distribution of heroin was held insufficient to trigger the felony-murder rule in Commonwealth v. Bowden, 456 Pa. 278, 309 A.2d 714 (1973), and State v. Randolph, 676 S.W.2d 943 (Tenn. 1984). In *Randolph,* the court said:

> We decline to adopt a general rule that death occurring during or resulting from the commission of any felony shall automatically be deemed murder in the second degree regardless of the nature of the offense proscribed. . . . [D]eath is neither the inevitable nor necessarily the most probable result of the injection of a controlled substance. . . . However, when all the circumstances shown in this record are taken into account [defendant had been warned that the heroin was dangerous and should not be sold until it had been "cut"], we are of the opinion that, if competently established beyond a reasonable doubt, they could justify a conclusion by the trier of fact that appellant and his co-defendants acted with such conscious indifference to the consequences . . . as to evince malice.

The question arose in somewhat different form in State v. Amaro, 436 So. 2d 1056 (Fla. App. 1983). In this case, the drug dealers were surprised by police. After Amaro had been placed under arrest, one of his co-felons (who was hiding in a bedroom) shot and killed an officer. Rejecting the argument that the arrest had terminated Amaro's responsibility (see page 501 infra), the court held that Amaro could be convicted of felony-murder on the basis of the underlying felony, which in this case was the possession and distribution of marijuana.[9] The court never considered whether this underlying felony meets the inherent dangerousness requirement. Does it? Some statutes deal with the question explicitly. Under Ariz. Rev. Stat. §13-1105, homicide resulting from the unlawful sale of controlled substances is a capital offense.[10]

c.   The Limitation to Felonies "Independent" of the Homicide

PEOPLE v. SMITH

California Supreme Court
35 Cal. 3d 798, 678 P.2d 886 (1984)

Mosk, J. Defendant appeals from a judgment convicting her of second degree murder (Pen. Code §187), felony child abuse (§273a, subd. (1)), and child beating (§273d). The court sentenced her to imprisonment for 15 years to life on the murder count and stayed service of sentence on the 2 remaining counts to avoid double punishment. The principal issue on appeal is whether felony child abuse may serve as the underlying felony to support a conviction of second degree murder on a felony-murder theory. . . .

---

9. The statute applicable at the time stated (Fla. Stat. Ann. §782.04 (1975)): "The unlawful killing of a human being, when perpetrated without any design to effect death, by a person engaged in . . . any felony other than any arson, involuntary sexual battery, robbery, [or] burglary . . . shall be murder in the third degree."

10. The application of the death penalty provision of such statutes, in a case not involving an intent to kill or conscious recklessness, is restricted by Eighth Amendment principles reflected in Enmund v. Florida and Tison v. Arizona, pages 532-534 infra.

Defendant and her two daughters, three-and-a-half-year-old Bethany (Beth) and two-year-old Amy, lived with David Foster. On the day Amy died, she refused to sit on the couch instead of the floor to eat a snack. Defendant became angry, took Amy into the children's bedroom, spanked her and slapped her in the face. Amy then went towards the corner of the bedroom which was often used for discipline; defendant hit her repeatedly, knocking her to the floor. Foster then apparently joined defendant to "assist" in Amy's discipline. Both testified that both Foster and defendant were striking Amy, who at that point had been at least partially undressed by defendant. Defendant and Foster used both their hands and a paddle on the child, and were also biting her. In addition, Beth testified that Foster put a wastebasket on Amy's head and hit her on the head with his fist. Eventually, defendant knocked the child backwards and she fell, hitting her head on the closet door.

Amy stiffened and went into respiratory arrest. Defendant and Foster took her to the hospital, where defendant admitted that she "beat her too hard." . . . Amy died that evening. Her injuries were consistent with compressive force caused by numerous blows by hands, fists, and a paddle. The severe head injury that was the direct cause of death occurred within an hour before the child was brought to the hospital. . . .

The court gave the jury the standard instructions defining murder, malice aforethought, second degree murder, second degree felony murder, and manslaughter. The second degree felony-murder instruction informed the jury that an unlawful killing, whether intentional, unintentional, or accidental, is second degree murder if it occurs during the commission of a felony inherently dangerous to human life, and that felony child abuse is such a crime. Defendant contends that on the facts of this case the crime of felony child abuse was an integral part of and included in fact within the homicide, and hence that it merged into the latter under the rule of People v. Ireland (1969) 70 Cal. 2d 522, 538-540. We agree.

Our opinions have repeatedly emphasized that felony murder, although the law of this state, is a disfavored doctrine: "We have recognized that the rule is much censured 'because it anachronistically resurrects from a bygone age a "barbaric" concept that has been discarded in the place of its origin' and because 'in almost all cases in which it is applied it is unnecessary' and 'it erodes the relation between criminal liability and moral culpability.'" (People v. Dillon (1983) 34 Cal. 3d 441, 463.) . . .

In accord with this policy, we restricted the scope of the felony-murder rule in *Ireland* by holding it inapplicable to felonies that are an integral part of and included in fact within the homicide. In that case the defendant and his wife were experiencing serious marital difficulties which eventually culminated in defendant's drawing a gun and killing his wife. The jury was instructed that it could find the defendant guilty of second degree felony murder if it determined that the homicide occurred during the commission of the underlying felony of assault with a deadly weapon. Like all felony-murder instructions, this instruction had the "effect of 'reliev[ing] the jury of the necessity of finding one of the elements of the crime of murder' to wit, malice aforethought." (People v. Ireland, supra, 70 Cal. 2d at p. 538.) We reasoned that "the utilization of the felony-murder rule in circumstances such as those before us extends the operation of that rule 'beyond any rational function that it is designed to serve.' To allow such use of the felony-murder rule would effectively preclude the jury from considering the issue of malice aforethought in all cases wherein homicide has been committed as a result of a felonious assault — a category which includes the great majority of all homicides. This kind of bootstrapping finds support neither in logic nor in law. We therefore hold that *a second degree felony-murder instruction may not properly be given when it is based upon a felony which is an integral part of the homicide and which the evidence produced by the prosecution shows to be an offense included in fact within the offense charged.*" (Italics added.)

Very soon after *Ireland* we again had occasion to consider the question of merger in People v. Wilson (1969) 1 Cal. 3d 431. There the defendant forcibly entered his estranged wife's apartment carrying a shotgun. Once inside the apartment, he fatally shot a man in the living room and proceeded to break into the bathroom where he killed his wife. The jury was instructed on second degree felony murder based on the underlying felony of assault with a deadly weapon, and convicted the defendant of second degree murder of the man. We determined that the predicate felony was a "necessary ingredient of the homicide" and reversed under *Ireland*, which explicitly prohibited use of the felony-murder rule in such circumstances.

The defendant was also convicted of the first degree murder of his wife, and we reversed that conviction on similar grounds. The jury was instructed on first degree murder on the theory that the homicide was committed in the course of a burglary because the defendant had entered the premises with intent to commit a felony, i.e., assault with a deadly weapon.[a] We held that the felony-murder rule cannot apply to burglary-murder cases in which "the entry would be non-felonious but for the intent to commit the assault, and the assault is an integral part of the homicide and is included in fact in the offense charged. . . ." We reasoned that "Where a person enters a building with an intent to assault his victim with a deadly weapon, he is not deterred by the felony-murder rule. That doctrine can serve its purpose only when applied to a felony independent of the homicide." We concluded that an instruction telling the jury that "the intent to assault makes the entry burglary and that the burglary raises the homicide resulting from the assault to first degree murder without proof of malice aforethought and premeditation" used the same bootstrap reasoning we condemned in *Ireland*.

In People v. Sears (1970) 2 Cal. 3d 180, we followed *Wilson* in a slightly different factual situation. There the defendant entered a cottage with the intent to assault his estranged wife. In the course of the assault, her daughter intervened and was killed by the defendant. The People argued that this situation was distinguishable on the ground that the felony of burglary with intent to assault the wife was "independent of the homicide" of the daughter and therefore the felony-murder rule could apply. We rejected the theory, holding that "It would be anomalous to place the person who intends to attack one person and in the course of the assault kills another inadvertently or in the heat of battle in a worse

a. *Wilson* involved two separate entries, one into the apartment through the front door and one into the bathroom. However, the crucial entry, for purposes of the first degree felony-murder instruction, was the defendant's entry into the bathroom for the purpose of inflicting violent injury upon his wife. Section 459 of the Cal. Penal Code provides that "Every person who enters any house, room, apartment [and other defined structures] . . . with intent to commit . . . any felony is guilty of burglary." Eds.

position than the person who from the outset intended to attack both persons and killed one or both." . . .

Cases in which the second degree felony-murder doctrine has withstood an *Ireland* attack include those in which the underlying felony was furnishing narcotics; driving under the influence of narcotics; poisoning food, drink or medicine (People v. Mattison (1971) 4 Cal. 3d 177); armed robbery (People v. Burton (1971) 6 Cal. 3d 375); kidnapping; and finally, felony child abuse by malnutrition and dehydration (§273a, subd. (1); People v. Shockley (1978) 79 Cal. App. 3d 669). . . .

In People v. Burton, supra, we refined the *Ireland* rule. [In *Burton* the defendant was charged with felony-murder on the basis of a killing in the course of an armed robbery. He argued that the armed robbery was not independent of the homicide, within the meaning of *Ireland*. Because robbery is defined as the felonious taking of property "accomplished by force or fear" (Penal Code §211), the defendant noted that robbery necessarily includes an assault and that armed robbery necessarily includes an assault with a deadly weapon. Thus, he claimed, armed robbery met the *Ireland* test, in that the underlying offense was "an integral part of the homicide and . . . an offense included in fact within the [homicide] charged." The *Burton* court rejected this reasoning and held that armed robbery was sufficiently independent to support a felony-murder conviction.]

[We held in *Burton* that even] if the felony was included within the facts of the homicide and was integral thereto, a further inquiry is required to determine if the homicide resulted "from conduct for an independent felonious purpose" as opposed to a "single course of conduct with a single purpose." In cases like *Ireland,* the "purpose of the conduct was the very assault which resulted in death"; on the other hand, "in the case of armed robbery, as well as the other felonies enumerated in section 189 of the Penal Code, there is an independent felonious purpose, namely in the case of robbery to acquire money or property belonging to another." [b]

Our task is to apply the foregoing rules to the offense at issue here — felony child abuse defined by section 273a, subdivision (1). [4] We recognize that a violation of its terms can occur in a wide variety of situations: the definition broadly includes both active and passive conduct, i.e., child abuse by direct assault and child endangering by extreme neglect. Two threshold considerations, however, govern all types of conduct prohibited by this law: first, the conduct must be willful; second, it must be committed "under circumstances or conditions likely to produce great bodily harm or death." Absent either of these elements, there can be no violation of the statute.

---

b. In *Burton,* the court elaborated as follows (6 Cal. 3d at 387): "[T]here is a very significant difference between deaths resulting from assaults with a deadly weapon, when the purpose of the conduct was the very assault which resulted in death, and deaths resulting from conduct for an independent felonious purpose, such as robbery or rape, which happened to be accomplished by a deadly weapon and technically includes assault with a deadly weapon. Our inquiry cannot stop with the fact that death resulted from the use of a deadly weapon and, therefore, technically included an assault with a deadly weapon, but must extend to an investigation of the purpose of the conduct." — Eds.

4. Section 273a, subdivision (1), provided: "Any person who, under circumstances or conditions likely to produce great bodily harm or death, willfully causes or permits any child to suffer, or inflicts thereon unjustifiable physical pain or mental suffering, . . . is punishable by imprisonment in the county jail not exceeding 1 year, or in the state prison for not less than 1 year nor more than 10."

The language of *Ireland, Wilson* and *Burton* bars the application of the felony-murder rule "where the purpose of the conduct was the very assault which resulted in death." In cases in which the violation of section 273a, subdivision (1), is a direct assault on a child that results in death (i.e., causing or permitting a child to suffer or inflicting thereon unjustifiable physical pain), it is plain that the purpose of the child abuse was the "very assault which resulted in death." It would be wholly illogical to allow this kind of assaultive child abuse to be bootstrapped into felony murder merely because the victim was a child rather than an adult, as in *Ireland.*

In the present case the homicide was the result of child abuse of the assaultive variety. Thus, the underlying felony was unquestionably an "integral part of" and "included in fact" in the homicide within the meaning of *Ireland.* . . . Accordingly, despite our deep abhorrence of the crime of child abuse, we see no escape from our duty to apply the merger doctrine we carefully enunciated in *Ireland* and its progeny. . . .

The People argue that the present case is controlled by People v. Shockley, supra, but that decision is distinguishable on its facts. In *Shockley,* the death followed from malnutrition and dehydration; by contrast, the cause of death here was unquestionably a severe beating. The *Shockley* court envisaged this very distinction when it stated that "Where the underlying felony is based on an independent felony *not related to the assault causing the murder,* a different result follows." (Italics added.) Here the death of the child was directly caused by an assault that in turn was the basis of the charge of felony child abuse; on these facts, *Ireland* compels application of the merger rule.[7]

It was therefore error to give a felony-murder instruction in this case.

[Reversed.]

NOTES AND QUESTIONS

1. Merger and child abuse. (a) In State v. Brown, 236 Kan. 800, 696 P.2d 954 (1985), a six-week-old baby had died from a combination of repeated beatings and continued neglect. The Kansas Supreme Court held that the charge of felony child abuse did not merge under these circumstances and that the mother could be convicted of felony murder, but the court left open the question whether the merger doctrine would have to apply if the child's death had resulted from a single assault. Subsequently, in State v. Lucas, 243 Kan. 462, 759 P.2d 90 (1988), the court found that the merger doctrine did apply to child abuse involving a single assaultive incident, that a distinction between such cases and cases of repeated abuse was untenable, and therefore that *neither* sort of child abuse could support conviction on a felony-murder theory; *Brown* was overruled.

(b) What should be the result under *Smith* if the child abuse is inflicted by neglect rather than by a direct assault? Suppose, for example, that a parent deliberately abandons a young child in an unheated apartment and the child freezes to death. If felony child abuse merges in the case of a violent assault, why

---

7. Because of this factual distinction we need not address the question whether the merger doctrine applies when the defendant is guilty of felony child abuse of the nonassaultive variety, e.g., by extreme neglect — as in *Shockley* — or by failure to intervene when a child in his care or custody is placed in a life-endangering situation.

should the result be any different when the parent chooses to abuse the child by deliberate, life-threatening neglect? Compare the *Shockley* case, discussed in *Smith* at page 492 supra.

(c) What should be the result under *Smith* if the abuse consists of a direct assault, but the prosecution alleges that there was an "independent purpose" for the child abuse. In People v. Jackson, 218 Cal. Rptr. 637 (Cal. App. 1985), a father set out to punish his two-year-old son because the latter had refused to undress as instructed; the father brutally beat the child, inflicting fatal injuries. Jackson was convicted of inflicting cruel or inhuman corporal punishment on a child, a felony under Cal. Penal Code §273d, which is a *lesser* included offense of the §273a charge at issue in *Smith*.[11] Jackson was also convicted of second degree felony murder on the basis of the §273d charge. The court held that the child-abuse charge did not merge and that the felony-murder conviction accordingly was proper. The court explained the result on the grounds that a different statutory offense was involved and that Jackson, unlike Smith, had "an independent, collateral purpose separate from the intent to inflict bodily harm," namely an intention "to bend the child's actions into conformity with his father's ideas of propriety, and to impress upon him the virtue of obedience" (218 Cal. Rptr. at 641). Is either reason persuasive? Is the court's premise that a parent who inflicts a brutal beating with intent to kill sometimes should not be guilty of murder (perhaps because of provocation or diminished capacity), but that a parent who improperly disciplines a child by a brutal beating *without* intent to kill should *always* be guilty of murder (under the felony-murder rule)? How could the merger doctrine be restructured to avoid such results?

2. Problem. In People v. Hansen, 24 Cal. Rptr. 2d 242 (Cal. App. 1993), defendant gave Echaves money to buy methamphetamine for him. When Echaves did not return with the drugs, defendant obtained a gun in order to either get back his money or beat up Echaves. He then drove past Echaves' apartment, firing repeatedly into the building. A 13-year-old child living in Echaves' apartment was killed by the shots. Defendant was charged with the felony of discharging a firearm at an inhabited dwelling house (Cal. Penal Code §246) and with felony murder. Does the merger doctrine apply here?

3. Merger and burglary. (a) In People v. Miller, 32 N.Y.2d 157, 297 N.E.2d 85 (1973), the New York Court of Appeals rejected the California approach to burglary discussed in the *Smith* case at page 490 supra. In *Miller,* the defendant entered the apartment of another, Fennell, intending to assault him with a deadly weapon. When another occupant, Aleem, attempted to help Fennell, the defendant killed Aleem. The court held that because the defendant committed the crime of burglary by knowingly and unlawfully entering Fennell's apartment with intent to assault him, and the defendant killed Aleem in the course of and in furtherance of his commission of that burglary, the requirements of the felony-murder statute were satisfied. The court stated (297 N.E.2d at 87-88):

> Defendant would have us extend the merger doctrine to the facts of this case with the result that neither the assault on Fennell, nor the assault on Aleem, could,

---

11. Section 273d provides: "Any person who willfully inflicts upon any child any cruel or inhuman corporal punishment or injury resulting in a traumatic condition is guilty of a felony, and upon conviction thereof shall be punished by imprisonment in the state prison for 2, 3 or 4 years, or in the county jail for not more than one year."

for the purposes of the felony-murder statute, be used as the intended crime ele-ment of burglary. The considerations which prompted our court to announce the merger doctrine do not justify its extension here. We developed this doctrine to remedy a fundamental defect in the old felony-murder statute (Penal Law of 1909, §1044). Under that statute, any felony, including assault, could be the predicate for a felony murder. Since, a fortiori, every homicide, not excusable or justifiable, occurs during the commission of assault, every homicide would constitute a felony murder.

This defect was remedied by the Legislature in 1965 by including in the revised Penal Law a list of specified felonies — all involving violence or substantial risk of physical injury — as the only felonies forming a basis for felony murder. The leg-islative purpose for this limitation was "to exclude from felony murder, cases of accidental or not reasonably foreseeable fatality occurring in an unlikely manner in the course of a non-violent felony." (Denzer and McQuillan, Practice Commen-tary, McKinney's Cons. Laws of N.Y., vol. 39, p. 236.)

It should be apparent that the Legislature, in including burglary as one of the enumerated felonies as a basis for felony murder, recognized that persons within domiciles are in greater peril from those entering the domicile with criminal in-tent, than persons on the street who are being subjected to the same criminal in-tent. Thus, the burglary statutes prescribe greater punishment for a criminal act committed within the domicile than for the same act committed on the street. Where, as here, the criminal act underlying the burglary is an assault with a dan-gerous weapon, the likelihood that the assault will culminate in a homicide is sig-nificantly increased by the situs of the assault. When the assault takes place within the domicile, the victim may be more likely to resist the assault; the victim is also less likely to be able to avoid the consequences of the assault, since his paths of retreat and escape may be barred or severely restricted by furniture, walls and other obstructions incidental to buildings. Further, it is also more likely that when the assault occurs in the victim's domicile, there will be present family or close friends who will come to the victim's aid and be killed. Since the purpose of the felony-murder statute is to reduce the disproportionate number of accidental homicides which occur during the commission of the enumerated predicate felonies by punishing the party responsible for the homicide not merely for manslaughter, but for murder, the Legislature, in enacting the burglary and felony-murder statutes, did not exclude from the definition of burglary, a burglary based upon the intent to assault, but intended that the definition be "satisfied if the intruder's intent, existing at the time of the unlawful entry or remaining, is to commit any crime." (Denzer and McQuillan [supra at] 355.)

(b) In accord with the California view that the merger doctrine applies when burglary is committed in order to carry out an assault, see Sellers v. State, 295 Ark. 489, 749 S.W.2d 669 (1988). But most of the recent decisions side with the New York view that burglary based on an intent to assault will support a felony-murder conviction (usually first-degree felony murder), even though a similar assault will not support a felony-murder charge in the absence of "entry" into a building or room. See, e.g., United States v. Loonsfoot, 905 F.2d 116 (6th Cir. 1990); State v. Lucas, 794 P.2d 1353 (Ariz. App. 1990); Smith v. State, 499 So. 2d 750 (Miss. 1986). Is the key point here that indoor assaults tend to be more dangerous than outdoor assaults? Why should differences in dangerousness be the basis for determining when the merger doctrine applies? Is an outdoor rob-bery (which clearly triggers the felony-murder rule) more dangerous than an outdoor assault with intent to kill (which clearly does not)?

4. Although the great majority of jurisdictions adopt some version of the merger doctrine, several states reject it entirely.[12] Have such states, in effect, abolished the provocation defense as a means of reducing murder to manslaughter? Or does the absence of a merger doctrine simply mean that provocation remains a viable defense when the prosecution chooses to permit it (by withholding felony-murder charges)? For discussion of the merger doctrine, see Note, Merger and the California Felony-Murder Rule, 20 U.C.L.A.L. Rev. 250 (1972).

d. Killings Not "in Furtherance" of the Felony

STATE v. CANOLA

Supreme Court of New Jersey
73 N.J. 206, 374 A.2d 20 (1977)

CONFORD, J. Defendant, along with three confederates, was in the process of robbing a store when a victim of the robbery, attempting to resist the perpetration of the crime, fatally shot one of the co-felons. The sole issue for our resolution is whether, under N.J.S.A. 2A:113-1, defendant may be held liable for felony murder. . . .

The facts of this case . . . may be summarized as follows. The owner of a jewelry store and his employee, in an attempt to resist an armed robbery, engaged in a physical skirmish with one of the four robbers. A second conspirator, called upon for assistance, began shooting, and the store owner returned the gunfire. Both the owner and the felon, one Lloredo, were fatally shot in the exchange, the latter by the firearm of the owner.

Defendant and two others were indicted on two counts of murder, one count of robbery and one count of having been armed during the robbery. The murder counts were based on the deaths, respectively, of the robbery victim and the co-felon. After trial on the murder counts defendant was found guilty on both and was sentenced to concurrent terms of life imprisonment. The Appellate Division unanimously affirmed the conviction for the murder of the robbery victim, and this court denied a petition for certification addressed thereto. However, when the Appellate Division majority upheld the trial court's denial of a motion to dismiss the count addressed to the homicide of the co-felon, Judge Handler dissented, [and we granted a petition for certification addressed to this count.]

Conventional formulations of the felony murder rule would not seem to encompass liability in this case. [T]he early formulations of the felony murder rule by such authorities as Lord Coke, Foster and Blackstone and of later ones by Judge Stephen and Justice Holmes . . . were concerned solely with situations where the felon or a confederate did the actual killing. [T]he English courts never applied the felony murder rule to hold a felon guilty of the death of his co-felon at the hands of the intended victim. . . .

---

12. See, e.g., State v. Jackson, 346 N.W.2d 634 (Minn. 1984) (assault with knife); State v. Beeman, 315 N.W.2d 770 (Iowa 1982) ("willful injury" by stabbing); State v. Thompson, 88 Wash. 2d 13, 558 P.2d 202 (1977) (assault).

It is clearly the majority view throughout the country that, at least in theory, the doctrine of felony murder does not extend to a killing, although growing out of the commission of the felony, if directly attributable to the act of one other than the defendant or those associated with him in the unlawful enterprise. . . . This rule is sometimes rationalized on the "agency" theory of felony murder.[2]

A contrary view, which would attach liability under the felony murder rule for *any* death proximately resulting from the unlawful activity — even the death of a co-felon — notwithstanding the killing was by one resisting the crime, does not seem to have the present allegiance of any court. . . .

At one time the proximate cause theory was espoused by the Pennsylvania Supreme Court. . . . Commonwealth v. Almeida, 362 Pa. 596, 68 A.2d 595 (1949). The reasoning of the *Almeida* decision, involving the killing of a policeman shot by other police attempting to apprehend robbers, was distinctly circumvented when the question later arose whether it should be applied to an effort to inculpate a defendant for the killing of his co-felon at the hands of the victim of the crime. Commonwealth v. Redline, 391 Pa. 486, 137 A.2d 472 (1958). The court there held against liability. Examining the common-law authorities relied upon by the *Almeida* majority, the *Redline* court concluded: "As already indicated, *Almeida* was, itself, an extension of the felony-murder doctrine by judicial decision and is not to be extended in its application beyond facts such as those to which it was applied." The court then held that "in order to convict for felony-murder, *the killing must have been done by the defendant or by an accomplice or confederate or by one acting in furtherance of the felonious undertaking.*" The court refused, however, actually to overrule the *Almeida* decision, thereby creating a distinction . . . between the situation in which the victim was an innocent party and the killing therefore merely "excusable" and that in which the deceased was a felon and the killing thus "justifiable." Twelve years later the Pennsylvania court did overrule *Almeida* in a case involving Almeida's companion, Smith. (Commonwealth ex rel. Smith v. Myers, 438 Pa. 218, 261 A.2d 550 (1970).) The court noted, inter alia, the harsh criticism leveled against the common-law felony rule, its doubtful deterrent effect, the failure of the cases cited in *Almeida* to support the conclusions reached therein, the inappropriateness of tort proximate-cause principles to homicide prosecution, and the "will-of-the-wisp" distinction drawn by the *Almeida* court between justifiable and excusable homicides. . . .

The course of the decisions in Michigan illustrates the influence of the Pennsylvania cases in the development of the felony murder rule in other jurisdictions. In People v. Podolski, 332 Mich. 508, 52 N.W.2d 201 (1952), the bullet killing the deceased officer came from the revolver of a fellow officer attempting to stop defendant's armed robbery of a bank. In affirming the murder conviction, the court adopted both the language and reasoning of the Pennsylvania court . . . , to the effect that if a robber sets in motion a chain of events which should have been within his contemplation, he is liable for any death which results.

---

2. The classic statement of the theory is found in an early case applying it in a context pertinent to the case at bar, Commonwealth v. Campbell, 89 Mass. (7 Allen) 541, 544 (Sup. Jud. Ct. 1863), as follows: "No person can be held guilty of homicide unless the act is either actually or constructively his, and it cannot be his act in either sense unless committed by his own hand or by someone acting in concert with him or in furtherance of a common object or purpose."

After the Pennsylvania court changed course in *Redline*, supra, the Michigan court followed suit in People v. Austin, 370 Mich. 12, 129 N.W.2d 766 (1963), where defendants' indictments for the slaying of their accomplice by the robbery victim were quashed. Relying heavily on Pennsylvania's curtailment of the expansion of the felony murder rule, the court, while not overruling *Podolski*, nonetheless refused to extend liability to instances where the deceased was a co-felon. . . .

The Pennsylvania developments were also influential in Illinois. Prior to any of the Pennsylvania cases cited above, Illinois had adopted a rule of proximate causation in People v. Payne, 359 Ill. 246, 194 N.E. 539 (1935), where a felon's conviction of murder for the death of a bystander was affirmed despite the absence of any proof of who fired the fatal shot. The court found this fact immaterial: "It reasonably might be anticipated that an attempted robbery would meet with resistance, during which the victim might be shot either by himself or some one else in attempting to prevent the robbery, and those attempting to perpetrate the robbery would be guilty of murder."

Nevertheless, following the Pennsylvania *Redline* decision, the Illinois courts refused to apply the proximate causation test where the decedent was an accomplice of the defendant killed by a victim of the felony. People v. Morris, 1 Ill. App. 3d 566, 274 N.E.2d 898 (1971). The rationale, quite inconsistent with that applied in *Payne*, supra, was that the lethal act was not done in furtherance of the common design to commit a felony.

In the most recent Illinois case, People v. Hickman, 12 Ill. App. 3d 412, 297 N.E.2d 582 (1973), *aff'd*, 59 Ill. 2d 89, 319 N.E.2d 511 (1974), where an officer chasing burglars mistakenly shot and killed a fellow officer, and liability was imposed pursuant to *Payne*, supra, yet another theory of differentiation of the co-felon killing cases was advanced — the dubious assumption-of-risk concept that the co-felon "assisted in setting in motion a chain of events which was the proximate cause of his death and therefore in the criminal law as in the civil law there is no redress for the victim." 297 N.E.2d at 586. . . .

To be distinguished from the situation before us here, and from the generality of the cases discussed above, are the so-called "shield" cases. The first of these were the companion cases of Taylor v. State, 55 S.W. 961 (Tex. Cr. App. 1900), and Keaton v. State, 57 S.W. 1125 (Tex. Cr. App. 1900). In attempting to escape after robbing a train, defendants thrust the brakeman in front of them as a shield, as a result of which he was fatally shot by law officers. The court had no difficulty in finding defendants guilty of murder. The court in *Taylor* noted the correctness of the *Campbell* case doctrine that a person could not be held liable for homicide unless the act is either actually or constructively committed by him, but indicated it was inapplicable to a case where defendants forced deceased to occupy a place of danger in order that they might carry out the crime. In *Keaton*, the court said defendant would be responsible for the "reasonable, natural and probable result of his act" of placing deceased in danger of his life. The conduct of the defendants in cases such as these is said to reflect "express malice," justifying a murder conviction.

This review of the development in this country of the felony murder rule in relation to culpability for lethal acts of non-felons shows that, despite its early limitation to deadly acts of the felons themselves or their accomplices, the rule has undergone several transformations and can no longer be stated in terms of universal application. . . . [T]he trend since [*Redline*] has been towards nonliability.

Reverting to our immediate task here, it is to determine whether our own statute necessarily mandates the proximate cause concept of felony murder, as thought by the Appellate Division majority. . . . [T]he view of the Appellate Division was that the "ensues clause" of N.J.S.A. 2A:113-1[a] must be deemed to have expanded the culpability of the felon to killings by others not confederated with him, if proximately related to the felonious enterprise, else the clause would be meaningless surplusage in the act. . . .

[A]ssuming the statute is facially susceptible to the interpretation here advocated by the State, it is appropriate to consider the public policy implications of the proposed doctrine as an extension of prior assumptions in this State as to the proper limitations of the felony murder rule.

Most modern progressive thought in criminal jurisprudence favors restriction rather than expansion of the felony murder rule. A leading text states: "The felony murder rule is somewhat in disfavor at the present time. The courts apply it when the law requires, but they do so grudgingly and tend to restrict its application where the circumstances permit." Perkins on Criminal Law (2d ed. 1969) 44. It has frequently been observed that although the rule was logical at its inception, when all felonies were punishable by death, its survival to modern times when other felonies are not thought to be as blameworthy as premeditated killings is discordant with rational and enlightened views of criminal culpability and liability. . . .

In view of all of the foregoing, it appears to us regressive to extend the application of the felony murder rule beyond its classic common-law limitation to acts by the felon and his accomplices, to lethal acts of third persons not in furtherance of the felonious scheme. The language of the statute does not compel it, and, as indicated above, is entirely compatible with the traditional limitations of the rule. Tort concepts of foreseeability and proximate cause have shallow relevance to culpability for murder in the first degree. Gradations of criminal liability should accord with [the] degree of moral culpability for the actor's conduct. . . .

The judgment of the Appellate Division is modified so as to strike the conviction and sentencing of defendant for murder of the co-felon Lloredo.

SULLIVAN, J. (concurring in result only). The practical result of the majority holding is that even though some innocent person or a police officer be killed during the commission of an armed robbery, the felon would bear no criminal responsibility of any kind for that killing as long as it was not at the hand of the felon or a confederate. The legislative intent, as I see it, is otherwise.

The thrust of our felony murder statute, N.J.S.A. 2A:113-1, is to hold the criminal liable for any killing which ensues during the commission of a felony, even though the felon, or a confederate, did not commit the actual killing. The only exception I would recognize would be the death of a co-felon, which could be classified as a justifiable homicide and not within the purview of the statute. . . .

---

a. That statute, the felony-murder provision in effect at the time of the *Canola* decision, provided as follows: "If any person, in committing or attempting to commit arson, burglary, kidnapping, rape, robbery, sodomy or any unlawful act against the peace of this state, of which the probable consequences may be bloodshed, kills another, *or if the death of anyone ensues from the committing or attempting to commit any such crime or act; . . . then such person so killing is guilty of murder.*" (Emphasis added.) — EDS.

NOTES

As *Canola* indicates, courts have often drawn distinctions that depend on who does the killing and who is killed. Consider to what extent liability for felony-murder does and should depend on the identity of the actual killer or victim.

1. *Who does the killing?* Under the agency theory, the identity of the actual killer becomes a central issue; only if the act of killing is done by a cofelon or someone acting in concert with a cofelon will the felony-murder rule be applicable. Under the proximate-cause theory, in contrast, the central issue is whether the killing, no matter by whose hand, is within the foreseeable risk of the commission of the felony.

(*a*) The great majority of the recent decisions follow *Canola* in adopting the agency theory. See State v. Branson 487 N.W.2d 880 (Minn. 1992); State v. Bonner, 330 N.C. 536, 411 S.E.2d 598 (1992); State v. Hoang, 243 Kan. 40, 755 P.2d 7 (1988); Annot., 89 A.L.R.4th 683 (1991). Thus, when the act of killing is committed by a police officer or bystander, the felony-murder rule is not applicable. Conversely, the felony-murder rule *is* applicable when a felon performs the lethal act, even when one of the cofelons is the victim, as in *Hoang,* supra.

(*b*) Although the trend of judicial interpretation strongly favors the agency theory, statutory revisions often complicate the picture by using language that arguably introduces proximate-cause concepts. For example, New York law (Penal Law §125.25, page 392 supra) provides that a person is guilty of murder if, "in the course of and in furtherance of [designated felonies,] he, or another participant . . . causes the death of a person other than one of the participants." The statute affords an affirmative defense for felons who can show that they had no reason to anticipate the use of lethal force. See N.Y. Penal Law §125.25(3)(a)-(d), page 392 supra. Several other states follow the New York model. See, e.g., Conn. Gen. Stat. §53A-54(c); Or. Rev. Stat. §163.115.

Questions: Does the New York statute's "in furtherance" requirement imply adoption of the agency approach, or does its "he . . . causes" language require adoption of the proximate-cause theory? The New York Court of Appeals chose the latter interpretation and upheld a felony-murder conviction where a policeman was fatally shot by a fellow officer in the course of a gun battle with several armed robbers. See People v. Hernandez, 82 N.Y. 309, 624 N.E.2d 661 (1993). Do you agree with that reading of the statute?

The Wisconsin statute is among the broadest; it imposes felony-murder liability upon any person who "causes the death of another human being while committing or attempting to commit [designated felonies]." Wis. Stat. §940.03. In State v. Oimen, 516 N.W.2d 399 (Wis. 1994), a robbery victim had fired upon his assailants and killed one of them. The Wisconsin Supreme Court held that the surviving felon could be convicted of felony murder. The court interpreted the statute as rejecting any limitation based on the identity of either the person shooting or the person killed.

In New Jersey, the legislature responded to *Canola* by adopting a new statute modeled closely on that of New York. Under N.J. Stat. §2C:11-3a(3), a person is now guilty of murder whenever he commits or attempts to commit a designated felony, and "in the course of and in furtherance of [the crime] . . . *any person causes* the death of any person other than one of the participants." (emphasis added). The New Jersey statute, like that of New York, affords an affirmative defense for felons who can show that they had no reason to anticipate the use of deadly force. N.J. Stat. §2C:11-3a(3)(a)-(d). The New Jersey Supreme Court held that this statute was intended to adopt the position that Justice Sullivan had advanced, concurring in *Canola:* a proximate-cause approach, coupled with an exception precluding liability when the victim is a cofelon. See State v. Martin, 119 N.J. 2, 573 A.2d 1359 (1990). Thus, although the *Canola* decision remains influential in guiding judicial interpretation of the felony-murder rule outside New Jersey, the decision has been superseded by legislation in its home state.

What accounts for the tendency of many legislatures to expand the felony-murder rule by adopting the proximate-cause approach? Consider People v. Hernandez, supra, 624 N.E.2d at 665-666:

> [W]e believe New York's . . . proximate cause theory to be consistent with funda-mental principles of criminal law. Advocates of the agency theory suggest that no culpable party has the requisite mens rea when a nonparticipant is the shooter. We disagree. The basic tenet of felony murder liability is that the mens rea of the un-derlying felony is imputed to the participant responsible for the killing. . . . Whether the death is an immediate result or an attenuated one, the necessary mens rea is present if the causal act is part of the felonious conduct.
>
> No more persuasive is the argument that the proximate cause view will extend criminal liability unreasonably. First, New York law is clear that felony murder does not embrace any killing that is coincidental with the felony but instead is limited to those deaths caused by one of the felons in furtherance of their crime. More than civil tort liability must be established; criminal liability will adhere only when the felons' acts are a sufficiently direct cause of the death.
>
> When the intervening acts of another party are supervening or unforeseeable, the necessary causal chain is broken, and there is no liability for the felons. . . . Second, the New York felony murder statute spells out the affirmative defense available to the accomplice who does not cause the death. . . .
>
> In short, our established common-law rules governing determinations of causal-ity and the availability of the statutory defense provide adequate boundaries to felony murder liability.

2. *Killings not in furtherance of the felony.* We have been considering killings com-mitted by persons other than the felons. If one of the felons commits the killing, does it always follow that the other felons are guilty of felony murder? In United States v. Heinlein, 490 F.2d 725 (D.C. Cir. 1973), three defendants participated in a rape. In defending herself, the woman slapped Heinlein, who, enraged at the blow, stabbed and killed her. On these facts Heinlein could, of course, be held for felony murder. But what of the other two? Is it enough that Heinlein killed in the course of a felony they were helping him commit? Or is the killing by Heinlein outside their common purpose, unplanned and unexpected by them, and therefore not attributable to them? Insofar as a jurisdiction adopts an agency theory in dealing with the liability of a felon for killings committed by another, as the court did in *Canola,* it would appear that the unanticipated ac-tions of a felon not in furtherance of the common purpose could no more be attributed to other felons than the actions of a policeman or victim could be attributed to them. The court so held in the *Heinlein* case.

Consider the following problems in applying the "in furtherance" require-ment when one of the felons is the actual killer.

(a) In People v. Cabaltero, 31 Cal. App. 2d 52, 87 P.2d 364 (1939), a look-out during a robbery panicked at the approach of a car and fired shots at the occu-

pants. The leader of the group, angered by his cofelon's stupidity, shot and killed him. The leader could, of course, be convicted of first-degree murder. Could the other members of the group be convicted of murder as well?

(b) Suppose that police officers enter a house to arrest marijuana dealers making a sale. After the principals are arrested, a police officer searching the house is shot and killed by a cofelon attempting to evade arrest. Are the dealers who had already been arrested responsible for the killing on a felony-murder theory, or are they relieved of liability on the ground that the arrest terminated their participation? In State v. Amaro, 436 So. 2d 1056 (Fla. App. 1983), the court upheld the convictions, finding that the cofelon's act was foreseeable and in furtherance of the common design. What should be the result if some of the felons had been taken to jail before the shooting took place?

(c) Commonwealth v. Waters, 418 A.2d 312 (Pa. 1980), involved the following facts:

> Allen and Waters . . . proceeded to the Williamsport apartment of Diane Buck[,] who was known to Allen. Allen suggested they go in "and maybe get a piece of ass and little bit of money." When Allen was unable to break in the door, Waters opened it with a karate kick. Once inside, the men proceeded to a bedroom where they found Diane Buck and Terry Brennan in bed nude. Allen fired a shot between the couple, took Diane Buck from the bed, and, for the next one and one-half hours, pushed, beat, and shoved her around the apartment while attempting, unsuccessfully, to rape her. During this time, Waters kept guard over Brennan and took his cash and watch. At some point, when Waters left the room to get a cigarette, Allen entered the bedroom and shot Brennan in the neck with the pistol. Later, [Waters returned to the room, and Allen departed,] leaving Waters in the room with Brennan.
>
> Waters whispered to Brennan he would get him help and would try to mislead Allen by saying in a loud voice that he was going to finish Brennan off. He did so and shot his weapon into the air. He exited the room, told Allen he had killed Brennan, and encouraged him to leave. Allen went to check whether Brennan was really dead. By Diane Buck's account, Allen threatened to kill both her and Waters if Brennan was not, in fact, dead. As Allen entered the bedroom, Waters shot him from behind. Allen died instantly.
>
> Waters advised Diane Buck to call an ambulance, but, when she could not compose herself sufficiently to complete the call, Waters himself called the police. He remained at the apartment until the police arrived and, later that night, gave a statement to the police concerning the evening's events. . . .
>
> On April 14, 1976, Waters was charged with the murder of Allen, but this charge was later withdrawn by the district attorney who concluded this killing was justifiable homicide. . . . However, when Brennan died on May 29 from the gunshot wound inflicted by Allen, Waters was rearrested and charged with the murder of Brennan.

At trial Waters was found guilty of the murder of Brennan and sentenced to life imprisonment. On appeal, the Pennsylvania Supreme Court reversed the conviction because the trial judge had refused to instruct the jury that the act of killing by Allen had to be done in furtherance of the felonies to which Waters was an accomplice. Was this killing "in furtherance"? How should the issue be resolved at the retrial?

3. *Who is killed?* The *Canola* case discusses a number of decisions that exclude the death of one of the felons as a basis for felony murder regardless of who

actually does the killing. The same pattern is revealed in recent statutes (including those quoted in Note 1 above). What is the appeal of this distinction?

(a) Agency and proximate cause theories. Under the agency theory, it is, of course, essential that one of the felons do the killing, but as long as that requirement is met and the killing is committed in furtherance of the felony, why does it matter who the victim is? A case in which a felon kills another felon in furtherance of the felony is readily conceivable. Suppose, for example, that one robber accidentally shoots and kills a cofelon while firing at a policeman. Does the act of shooting cease to be "in furtherance of the felony" when we discover whom the bullet strikes?

Under the proximate-cause theory, the central issue is the foreseeable risk of death. On what ground can such a death be excluded simply because the victim happens to be another felon? Consider the situation in State v. Chambers, 373 N.E.2d 393 (Ohio App. 1977). Ohio has long been one of the rare states without a felony-murder rule. However, under the Ohio Revised Code §2903.04, it is involuntary manslaughter for a person to "cause the death of another as a proximate result of the offender's committing or attempting to commit" a felony or misdemeanor. In *Chambers,* the defendant and his partner, apparently unarmed, were surprised by the return of the owner of the home they were burglarizing. While the owner was holding them at gunpoint, the partner knocked the owner aside, and both he and the defendant ran to make an escape. The owner shot and killed the retreating partner. The court read the statute as squarely adopting the proximate-cause theory rather than the agency theory. It upheld a conviction of the defendant, concluding that the end result in this case was a foreseeable consequence of the burglary: "The risk of actual serious physical harm to a victim or wrongdoer, the threat of surprise of one by the other, the natural inclination of the victim, if present, to defend his abode and his family are all factors too clear to discuss further." Was the court in error in failing to accord any significance to the fact that it was one of the felons who was killed?

(b) Justifiable homicide? One argument for special treatment of cases in which a felon is killed was advanced in the *Redline* case, discussed in *Canola:*

> The victim of the homicide was one of the robbers who, while resisting apprehension in his effort to escape was shot and killed by a policeman in the performance of his duty. Thus, the homicide was justifiable and, obviously, could not be availed of, on any rational legal theory, to support a charge of murder. How can anyone, no matter how much of an outlaw he may be, have a criminal charge lodged against him for the consequences of the lawful conduct of another person?

How cogent is the reasoning? Suppose two felons are holed up in a house and engaged in a gun battle with police officers surrounding the house. Felon *A* tells felon *B* to run out the back door where, he says, the coast is clear. He says this because he wants felon *B* dead and he knows that the police have the back door well covered. As felon *B* dashes out, gun in hand, he is shot dead by police. Is it self-evident that felon *A* is not criminally liable for the police officer's killing of felon *B*?

(c) Protecting the innocent? Another argument for the exemption of the death of felons was stated as follows in State v. Williams, 254 So. 2d 548, 550-551 (Fla. Dist. App. 1971):

The test we suggest is predicated upon the obvious ultimate purpose of the felony-murder statute itself which is, we think, to prevent the death of innocent persons likely to occur during the commission of certain inherently dangerous and particularly grievous felonies. [T]he statute is primarily designed to protect the *innocent public;* and it would be incongruous to reach a conclusion having the effect of placing the perpetrators themselves beneath its mantle. . . .

We hold, therefore, that the felony-murder statute is applicable only when an innocent person is killed as a sequential result of events or circumstances set in motion by one or more persons acting in furtherance of an intent or attempt to commit one of the felonies specified in such statute. . . .

This does not mean to say however, that co-conspirators acting in furtherance of their conspiracy, even to commit the high crimes contemplated by the felony-murder statute, can kill or murder each other with impunity. . . . Certainly, one conspirator may be guilty of the murder of a co-conspirator if the facts support premeditated murder or a lesser degree of unlawful homicide. But this is quite apart from the felony-murder concept with which we are here concerned.

Compare United States v. Martinez, 16 F.3d 202 (7th Cir. 1994). In this case Martinez, along with Mahn and Mares, planned to bomb several of Chicago's adult bookstores whose owners had refused to pay them "protection" money. Mares built six pipe bombs that could be detonated by remote-control electronic devices. He and Mahn then drove through downtown Chicago, placed one of the bombs and headed for a second destination along one of Chicago's main streets, "traversing an area dense with electro-magnetic signals" (id. at 208). One of their bombs exploded, killing Mares. The court held that Martinez and Mahn could be sentenced for felony murder, on the basis of the death of their cofelon. Judge Posner wrote for the Court (16 F.3d at 207):

The lives of criminals are not completely worthless, so their deaths should not be considered nonevents for sentencing purposes; and lest that seem an amorphous and even mawkish ground for an expansive interpretation of felony murder, we add that liability for felony murder in a case such as the present serves the practical function of deterring felons from using lethal weaponry, more broadly from committing the kind of felony in which someone is likely to be shot or run down or otherwise injured (and hence possibly killed), by punishing them severely should death result — to anyone. . . . The doctrine creates marginal deterrence of dangerous felonies even when the principal danger is to the felons themselves. One who commits a crime of violence is more likely to be shot by a victim or a police officer than one who commits a nonviolent crime. Even within the class of violent felonies, a felon is more likely to be shot by a victim or a police officer if he is armed — and if he is not shot but his cofelon is, he stands to receive a heavier punishment. If we must have felons, at least let them be peaceable felons.

TAYLOR v. SUPERIOR COURT

Supreme Court of California
3 Cal. 3d 578, 477 P.2d 131 (1970)

BURKE, J. Petitioner and his codefendant Daniels were charged by information with the murder of John H. Smith, robbery, assault with a deadly weapon against Linda West, and assault with a deadly weapon against Jack West. The superior court denied petitioner's motion to set aside the information as to the murder count, and we issued an alternative writ of prohibition.

At the preliminary hearing, the following facts were adduced regarding the murder count: On the evening of January 12, 1969, two men attempted to rob Jax Liquor Store which was operated by Mrs. Linda Lee West and her husband Jack. Mrs. West testified that James Daniels entered the store first and asked Mr. West, who was behind the counter, for a package of cigarettes. While Mr. West was getting the cigarettes, John Smith entered the store and approached the counter. Mrs. West, who was on a ladder at the time the two men entered the store, then heard her husband say something about money. Turning her attention to the counter, she heard Daniels repeatedly saying, "Put the money in the bag," and observed her husband complying with the order.

While Mr. West was putting the money from the register in the bag, Daniels repeatedly referred to the fact that he and Smith were armed. According to Mrs. West, Daniels "chattered insanely" during this time, telling Mr. West "Put the money in the bag. Put the money in the bag. Put the money in the bag. Don't move or I'll blow your head off. He's got a gun. He's got a gun. Don't move or we'll have an execution right here. Get down on the floor. I said on your stomach, on your stomach." Throughout this period, Smith's gun was pointed at Mr. West. Mrs. West testified that Smith looked "intent" and "apprehensive" as if "waiting for something big to happen." She indicated that Smith's apparent apprehension and nervousness was manifested by the way he was staring at Mr. West.

While Daniels was forcing Mr. West to the floor, Mrs. West drew a pistol from under her clothing and fired at Smith, who was standing closest to her. Smith was struck on the right side of the chest. Mrs. West fired four more shots in rapid succession, and observed "sparks" coming from Smith's gun, which was pointed in her direction. A bullet hole was subsequently discovered in the wall behind the place Mrs. West had been standing, approximately eight or nine feet above the floor. During this period, Mr. West had seized a pistol and fired two shots at Smith. Mrs. West's last shot was fired at Daniels as he was going out of the door. He "lurched violently and almost went down, [but] picked himself up and kept going." Smith died as the result of multiple gunshot wounds.

The evidence at the preliminary examination indicated that petitioner [Taylor] was waiting outside the liquor store in a getaway car. He was apprehended later and connected with the crime through bills in his possession and through the automobile which was seen by a witness leaving the scene of the robbery.

Under Penal Code section 995, an information must be set aside if the defendant has been committed without "reasonable or probable cause." Of course, the probable cause test is not identical with the test which controls a jury in a murder case. The jury must be convinced to a moral certainty and beyond a reasonable doubt of the existence of . . . every essential element of that crime. But a magistrate conducting a preliminary examination must be convinced of only such a state of facts as would lead a man of ordinary caution or prudence to believe, and conscientiously entertain a strong suspicion of the guilt of the accused. . . .

"Except when the common-law-felony-murder doctrine is applicable, an essential element of murder is an intent to kill or an intent with conscious disregard for life to commit acts likely to kill." (People v. Washington, 62 Cal. 2d 777,

780, 402 P.2d 130, 133). Petitioner correctly contends that he cannot be convicted under the felony-murder doctrine, since

> When a killing is not committed by a robber or his accomplice but by his victim,
> malice aforethought is not attributable to the robber, for the killing is not com-
> mitted by him in the perpetration or attempt to perpetrate robbery.

(People v. Washington, supra).[a] However, apart from the felony-murder doctrine, petitioner could be found guilty of murder on a theory of vicarious
liability.

As stated in People v. Gilbert, 63 Cal. 2d 690, 408 P.2d 365, *rev. on other grounds,*
388 U.S. 263,

> When the defendant or his accomplice, with a conscious disregard for life, inten-
> tionally commits an act that is likely to cause death, and his victim or a police
> officer kills in reasonable response to such act, the defendant is guilty of murder.
> In such a case, the killing is attributable, not merely to the commission of a felony,
> but to the intentional act of the defendant or his accomplice committed with con-
> scious disregard for life. Thus, the victim's self-defensive killing or the police offi-
> cer's killing in the performance of his duty cannot be considered an independent
> intervening cause for which the defendant is not liable, for it is a reasonable re-
> sponse to the dilemma thrust upon the victim or the policeman by the intentional
> act of the defendant or his accomplice.

Therefore, if petitioner were an accomplice to the robbery, he would be vicariously responsible[1] for any killing attributable to the intentional acts of his
associates committed with conscious disregard for life, and likely to result in
death. We must determine whether the committing magistrate had any rational
ground for believing that Smith's death was attributable to intentional acts of
Smith and Daniels meeting those criteria.

Petitioner relies upon the following language in *Washington,* wherein defendant's accomplice merely pointed a gun at the robbery victim who, without further provocation, shot and killed him: "In every robbery there is a possibility
that the victim will resist and kill. The robber has little control over such a killing
once the robbery is undertaken as this case demonstrates. To impose an additional penalty for the killing would discriminate between robbers, *not on the basis
of any difference in their own conduct,* but solely on the basis of the response by
others that the robber's conduct happened to induce."

---

a. In *Washington,* where the victim shot and killed the defendant's cofelon in resistance to their
armed robbery, the California court held, in accord with *Canola* (page 495 supra), that agency
rather than proximate cause was the proper basis for attributing liability to the surviving felon. The
opinion in *Washington,* following the excerpt quoted in the text, continues: "It is not enough that
the killing was a risk reasonably to be foreseen and that the robbery might therefore be regarded
as a proximate cause of the killing. Section 189 requires that the felon or his accomplice commit
the killing, for if he does not, the killing is not committed to perpetrate the felony. Indeed, in the
present case the killing was committed to thwart a felony." — Eds.

1. "Under the rules defining principals and criminal conspiracies, the defendant may be guilty
of murder for a killing attributable to the act of his accomplice. To be so guilty, however, the accomplice must cause the death of another human being by an act committed in furtherance of the
common design." (People v. Gilbert, supra.) Petitioner does not dispute that the conduct of his
confederates set forth above was in furtherance of the robbery.

As indicated by the italicized words in the foregoing quotation, the central inquiry in determining criminal liability for a killing committed by a resisting victim or police officer is whether the *conduct* of a defendant or his accomplices was sufficiently provocative of lethal resistance to support a finding of implied malice. If the trier of fact concludes that under the particular circumstances of the instant case Smith's death proximately resulted from acts of petitioner's accomplices done with conscious disregard for human life, the natural consequences of which were dangerous to life, then petitioner may be convicted of first degree murder.[2]

For example, we pointed out in *Washington* that "Defendants who initiate gun battles may also be found guilty of murder if their victims resist and kill. Under such circumstances, 'the defendant for a base, anti-social motive and with wanton disregard for human life, does an act that involves a high degree of probability that it will result in death,' and it is unnecessary to imply malice by invoking the felony-murder doctrine."

Petitioner contends that since neither Daniels nor Smith fired the first shot, they did not "initiate" the gun battle which led to Smith's death. However, depending upon the circumstances, a gun battle can be initiated by acts of provocation falling short of firing the first shot. Thus, in People v. Reed, 270 Cal. App. 2d 37, defendant resisted the officers' commands to "put up your hands," and pointed his gun toward the officers and toward the kidnap-robbery victim. The officers commenced firing, wounding defendant and killing the victim. Although defendant did not fire a single shot, his murder conviction was upheld on the theory that his "aggressive actions" were sufficient evidence of implied malice, and that "under these circumstances it may be said that defendant initiated the gunplay. . . ." . . .

In the instant case, the evidence at the preliminary hearing set forth above discloses acts of provocation on the part of Daniels and Smith from which the trier of fact could infer malice, including Daniels' coercive conduct toward Mr. West and his repeated threats of "execution," and Smith's intent and nervous apprehension as he held Mr. West at gunpoint. The foregoing conduct was sufficiently provocative of lethal resistance to lead a man of ordinary caution and prudence to conclude that Daniels and Smith "initiated" the gun battle, or that such conduct was done with conscious disregard for human life and with natural consequences dangerous to life.[3] Accordingly, we conclude that the evidence supported the magistrate's finding that reasonable and probable cause existed to charge petitioner with first degree murder. . . .

PETERS, J. (dissenting). . . . In *Washington,* two robbers held up a service station. The owner, Carpenter, was in the office totaling up the receipts and disburse-

---

2. . . . When murder has been established pursuant to the foregoing principles, Penal Code section 189 may be invoked to determine its degree. (People v. Gilbert, supra.)

3. Petitioner contends that we should ignore evidence regarding Smith's conduct, on the theory that Smith could not have been held responsible for his own death. We rejected a similar contention in *Washington,* stating that "A distinction based on the person killed, however, would make the defendant's criminal liability turn upon the marksmanship of victims and policemen. A rule of law cannot reasonably be based on such a fortuitous circumstance. . . ." Therefore, the trier of fact may find that Smith set into motion, through the intentional commission of acts constituting implied malice and in furtherance of the robbery, a gun battle resulting in his own death. Since petitioner may be held vicariously responsible for *any* killing legally attributable to his accomplices, he may be charged with Smith's death.

ments while an employee was depositing the money in a vault in an adjoining room. Upon hearing someone yell "robbery," Carpenter opened his desk and took out a revolver. A few moments later one of the robbers, Ball, entered the office and pointed a revolver at Carpenter. Carpenter fired immediately, mortally wounding Ball. Washington, the accomplice, was convicted of the murder of Ball. We reversed the murder conviction. We held that the felony-murder doctrine could not be invoked to convict Washington of murder because the killing was not committed by Washington or his accomplice. . . .

In *Washington* the decedent-accomplice pointed a gun directly at the victim. If this court was of the opinion that a defendant in such a situation could properly be convicted of murder for the killing committed by the victim, it would have so stated and would have held that Washington could be so convicted of murder. Instead, it held that Washington could not be convicted of murder and mentioned only one case where defendants could properly be convicted of murder for a killing committed by the victim: the case where the defendants initiate the gun battle. Therefore, *Washington* stands for the proposition that the act of pointing a gun at the victim, unlike the act of initiating a gun battle, is *not* an act done "with wanton disregard for human life," involving "a high degree of probability that it will result in death" from which malice can be implied. . . .

The majority . . . purport to distinguish [*Washington*] simply by characterizing it as a case "wherein defendant's accomplice *merely* pointed a gun at the robbery victim who, *without further provocation,* shot and killed him." (Italics added.) . . . The majority are making the incredible statement that because the robber in *Washington* did not articulate his obvious threat — because, in the majority's words, he "merely" pointed a gun at the victim — it cannot be said that he committed an act with conscious disregard for life and likely to result in death, whereas if he articulated his threat — as did the robbers in the instant case — his act could be found to have met such criteria.

To me, it is too obvious to dispute that inherent in the brandishing of a gun in a robbery is the conditional threat of the robber that he will use the gun if his demands are not complied with. . . . It is unreasonable to assume that, just because the robber in *Washington* did not articulate his threat, the victim in that case had less reason to fear for his safety or, as the majority assert, less "provocation" for shooting the robber than did the victims in the instant case. It is absurd to suggest that the robber's acts in *Washington* were, as a matter of law, not "sufficiently provocative of lethal resistance to support a finding of implied malice," whereas the robbers' acts in the instant case could be so considered. . . . The difference between an implied and an express threat furnishes no significant basis for discrimination between robbers. . . .

[T]he majority's purported distinction of *Washington* . . . simply demonstrates a desire on the part of the majority to overrule *Washington* sub silento. . . .

NOTES

1. Developments in other jurisdictions. Courts in at least two other states have expressed agreement with the principle adopted in *Taylor* — namely that, apart from the felony-murder rule, the doctrine of malice based on recklessness can be invoked to hold a felon responsible for a killing committed by a victim in response to provocative behavior by one of the felons. See Dowden v. State, 758 S.W.2d 264, 272-273 (Tex. Crim. App. 1988); People v. Guraj, 431 N.Y.S.2d 925 (Sup. Ct. 1980).

Of course, as the *Canola* case indicates, all jurisdictions will hold a felon for murder, under a theory of malice based on recklessness, in a "shield" situation — that is, where a hostage is shot by someone acting in opposition to the felony. Is there some reason why this result should be less controversial than the result in *Taylor*? On what basis can the two situations be distinguished?

2. *Recklessness of the person killed.* In *Taylor* the finding of recklessness was based on the behavior of cofelons Smith and Daniels. This presented a potential problem because it was Smith himself who was killed, but the court rejected the argument that Taylor should not be held liable for Smith's recklessness in provoking his own death. See page 506 footnote 3 supra.

That aspect of the *Taylor* holding was subsequently modified by People v. Antick, 15 Cal. 3d 79, 539 P.2d 43 (1975). Following a residential burglary, during which a variety of household goods was stolen, police observed a moving car, packed with household goods, occupied by a driver and one passenger. Shortly, they came upon the car, parked beside the road. Only the driver, Bose, was in it. As Bose was being frisked, he pulled a gun from his waist and fired at one of the officers, who returned the fire. Bose then broke away and sought to escape, but another officer brought him down with gunfire. Bose died from the wounds. Subsequently, the police uncovered evidence that the defendant was the other man in the car when it was first spotted and that he had participated with Bose in the burglary. Defendant was charged with murder under both the felony-murder and vicarious-liability theories, and the jury convicted. The court ruled that the conviction could not be upheld under either theory. The felony-murder theory was inapplicable inasmuch as the killing was not committed by a felon or a confederate acting in furtherance of the felony. Turning to the vicarious-liability theory, the court said:

> In order to predicate defendant's guilt upon the theory [of vicarious liability], it is necessary to prove that Bose committed a murder, in other words, that he caused the death of another human being and that he acted with malice.
>
> It is well settled that Bose's conduct in initiating a shootout with police officers may establish the requisite malice. . . . However, Bose's malicious conduct did not result in the unlawful killing of *another* human being, but rather in Bose's own death. The only homicide which occurred was the justifiable killing of Bose by the police officer. Defendant's criminal liability certainly cannot be predicated upon the actions of the officer. As Bose could not be found guilty of murder in connection with his own death, it is impossible to base defendant's liability for this offense upon his vicarious responsibility for the crime of his accomplice. . . .
>
> [D]efendant in the instant case may not be held vicariously liable for a crime which his accomplice did not commit.

Question: Suppose a case with identical facts except that the police officer's bullet struck and killed someone other than the confederate who initiated the gun battle — another confederate, say, or a bystander. Presumably, in this event, the defendant could have been held for murder, but would there be any difference whatsoever in the defendant's culpability?

3. *Problem.* In United States v. Martinez, 16 F.3d 202 (7th Cir. 1994), page 503 supra, Martinez, Mahn, and Mares planned to bomb several adult bookstores, and Mares built the bombs. While Mares and Mahn were in a car, with Mahn driving, on their way to place one of the bombs, a bomb exploded, killing Mares. Are Mahn and Martinez guilty of felony-murder? Under *Antick,* is Mares's death a homicide or a suicide?

4. *What degree of murder?* Note the *Taylor* court's holding that when robbers recklessly provoke a killing, they are liable for murder in the *first degree.* Does this holding make sense? The California Supreme Court reaffirmed this aspect of *Taylor* in Pizano v. Superior Court, 21 Cal. 3d 128, 577 P.2d 659 (1978). Writing for the majority, Justice Clark said:

Section 189 of the Penal Code provides in pertinent part: "All murder . . . which is committed in the perpetration of, or attempt to perpetrate . . . robbery . . . is murder of the first degree. . . ."

In People v. Washington, 62 Cal. 2d 777, 781, this court held that "[w]hen a killing is not committed by a robber or by his accomplice but by his victim, malice aforethought is not attributable to the robber [under the felony-murder rule], for the killing is not committed by him in the perpetration or attempt to perpetrate robbery."

Reading section 189 in light of the quoted passage from *Washington,* the dissent concludes that the *Gilbert* court [63 Cal. 2d 690 (1965)] erred insofar as it held that section 189 may be invoked to determine the degree of a murder established under the implied malice/vicarious liability doctrine. . . .

The killing itself, having been committed by the policeman to thwart the robbery, cannot be said to have been committed in perpetration of it. *But the act which made the killing a murder attributable to the robber — initiating the gun battle — was committed in the perpetration of the robbery.* Therefore, as *Gilbert* held, section 189 may properly be invoked to determine that the murder is of the first degree.

Chief Justice Bird, in dissent, wrote:

While conceding that the *killing* of Vaca was *not* "committed in the perpetration of . . . robbery . . . ," the majority assert that the *murder* of Vaca was, because Esquivel's *act* of using Vaca as a shield was committed in the perpetration of robbery. . . .

Assuming, arguendo, the conceptual possibility of the majority's analysis, their goal can be achieved only by writing into section 189 a third "kind" of first degree murder not provided for by the Legislature, i.e., a murder in which "the act which made the killing a murder attributable to the robber . . . was committed in the perpetration of the robbery." To do so, however, expressly contradicts the Legislature's provision that "all other [nonenumerated] kinds of murder are of the second degree."

D. THE DEATH PENALTY

The preceding materials suggest the variety of homicidal behavior and the importance of classifying such behavior in degrees of seriousness, by reference to the dangerousness of the conduct and the moral turpitude of the offender. What penalty should be authorized for the most serious homicidal offenses? Are there situations in which capital punishment is an appropriate or even a necessary response to a criminal offense? In this section we explore the case for and against the death penalty, in terms of principles applicable to criminal punishments generally and in terms of the special requirements of constitutional law flowing from the Eighth Amendment prohibition of "cruel and unusual punishments." Of course, the two perspectives are closely intertwined. We believe it preferable to put constitutional problems to one side, for a moment, and to consider first the factors that might motivate a state legislator or a concerned citizen in supporting or opposing capital punishment as a policy matter.

1. *Policy Considerations*

Suppose that a bill pending in the legislature of your state proposes to abolish the death penalty. Would you support or oppose such a bill? Or would you support it only with certain amendments or exceptions? (Which ones?) What reasons would you advance in support of your position?

In the familiar public debate about capital punishment, principles that traditionally are central to the study of criminal law seldom inform the discussion. In Chapter 2 we examined a variety of materials bearing on the justification for criminal punishments. One concern throughout that chapter was to identify the extent to which punishment serves various utilitarian goals. Another was to consider whether utilitarian benefits are necessary to justify punishment. In other words, is there an *obligation* to punish wrongdoers in proportion to their desert, regardless of the social utility (or disutility) of doing so? These issues, which Chapter 2 explores with reference to the justification of punishments in general, can provide a framework for examining the justification of the ultimate punishment. Consider the following materials as they bear on these questions.

a. Deterrence

THORSTEN SELLIN, THE DEATH PENALTY

A Report for the Model Penal Code Project of the American Law Institute
21-22, 34, 63 (1959)

It seems reasonable to assume that if the death penalty exercises a deterrent or preventive effect on prospective murderers, the following propositions would be true:

(a) Murders should be less frequent in states that have the death penalty than in those that have abolished it, other factors being equal. . . .
(b) Murders should increase when the death penalty is abolished and should decline when it is restored.
(c) The deterrent effect should be greatest and should therefore affect murder rates most powerfully in those communities where the crime occurred and its consequences are most strongly brought home to the population.
(d) Law enforcement officers would be safer from murderous attacks in states that have the death penalty than in those without it.

. . . The data examined reveal that

1. The *level* of the homicide death rates varies in different groups of states. It is lowest in the New England areas and in the northern states of the middle west and lies somewhat higher in Michigan, Indiana and Ohio.
2. Within each group of states having similar social and economic conditions and populations, it is impossible to distinguish the abolition state from the others.
3. The *trends* of the homicide rates of comparable states with or without the death penalty are similar. . . .

Any one who carefully examines the above data is bound to arrive at the conclusion that the death penalty, as we use it, exercises no influence on the extent or fluctuating rates of capital crimes. It has failed as a deterrent. If it has utilitarian value, it must rest in some other attribute than its power to influence the future conduct of people.

ERNEST VAN DEN HAAG, ON DETERRENCE AND THE DEATH PENALTY, 60 J. Crim. L., Criminology & Pol. Sci. 141, 145-146 (1969): In some fairly infrequent but important circumstances the death penalty is the only possible deterrent. Thus, in case of acute coups d'état, or of acute substantial attempts to overthrow the government, prospective rebels would altogether discount the threat of any prison sentence. . . . Execution would be the only deterrent because, unlike prison sentences, it cannot be revoked by victorious rebels. The same reasoning applies to deterring spies or traitors in wartime. Finally, men who, by virtue of past acts, are already serving, or are threatened, by a life sentence, could be deterred from further offenses only by the threat of the death penalty.

What about criminals who do not fall into any of these (often ignored) classes? Prof. Thorsten Sellin has made a careful study of the available statistics: he concluded that they do not yield evidence for the deterring effect of the death penalty. Somewhat surprisingly, Prof. Sellin seems to think that this lack of evidence for deterrence is evidence for the lack of deterrence. It is not. It means that deterrence has not been demonstrated statistically — not that non-deterrence has been.

It is entirely possible, indeed likely (as Prof. Sellin appears willing to concede), that the statistics used, though the best available, are nonetheless too slender a reed to rest conclusions on. They indicate that the homicide rate does not vary greatly between similar areas with or without the death penalty, and in the same area before and after abolition. However, the similar areas are not similar enough; the periods are not long enough; many social differences and changes, other than the abolition of the death penalty, may account for the variation (or lack of) in homicide rates with and without, before and after abolition; some of these social differences and changes are likely to have affected homicide rates. . . . Therefore variation or constancy cannot be attributed to variations or constancy of the penalties, unless we know that no other factor influencing the homicide rate has changed. Usually we don't. . . .

Contrary to what Prof. Sellin et al. seem to presume, I doubt that offenders are aware of the absence or presence of the death penalty state by state or period by period. Such unawareness argues against the assumption of a calculating murderer. However, unawareness does not argue against the death penalty if by deterrence we mean a preconscious, general response to a severe, but not necessarily specifically and explicitly apprehended, or calculated threat . . . : people remain deterred for a lengthy interval by the severity of the penalty in the past, or by the severity of penalties used in similar circumstances nearby.

I do not argue for a version of deterrence which would require me to believe that an individual shuns murder while in North Dakota, because of the death penalty, and merrily goes to it in South Dakota since it has been abolished there; or that he will start the murderous career from which he had hitherto refrained, after abolition. I hold that the generalized threat of the death penalty may be a deterrent, and the more so, the more generally applied. Deterrence will not cease in the particular areas of abolition or at the particular times of abolition. Rather, general deterrence will be somewhat weakened, through local (partial) abolition. Even such weakening will be hard to detect owing to changes in many offsetting, or reinforcing, factors.

HUGO BEDAU, THE COURTS, THE CONSTITUTION, AND CAPITAL PUNISHMENT 55-57 (1957): Van den Haag rests considerable weight on the claims that "the added severity of the death penalty adds to deterrence, or may do so"; and that "the generalized threat of the death penalty may be a deterrent, and the more so, the more generally applied." [T]he abolitionist . . . of course, can play the same game. He has his own equally plausible first principle: *the greater the severity of punishment the greater the brutality provoked throughout society.* When at last, frustrated and exhausted by mere plausibilities, we once again turn to study the evidence, we will find that the current literature on deterrence in criminology does not encourage us to believe in van den Haag's principle.

. . . Van den Haag has not given any reason why, in the quest for deterrent efficacy, one should fasten (as he does) on the severity of the punishments in question, rather than, as Bentham long ago counseled, on all the relevant factors, notably the facility, celerity, and reliability with which the punishment can be inflicted. Van den Haag cannot hope to convince anyone who has studied the matter that the death penalty and "life" imprisonment differ only in their severity, and that in all other respects affecting deterrent efficacy they are equivalent. . . .

NOTE ON THE EHRLICH STUDY

Whatever the weakness of studies suggesting the absence of a deterrent effect, those who would abolish the death penalty long drew comfort from the fact that no empirical study had ever succeeded in detecting the *presence* of a deterrent effect. The abolitionist position was dealt a significant blow, therefore, when economist Isaac Ehrlich, using complex techniques pioneered in econometric analysis, did find a significant correlation between capital punishment and the deterrence of homicide. See Isaac Ehrlich, The Deterrent Effect of Capital Punishment: A Question of Life and Death, 65 Am. Econ. Rev. 397 (1975). Ehrlich examined the relationship over time between the national homicide rate and the national "execution risk" (actual executions as a percentage of total murder convictions). Focusing on the years 1933 to 1969, Ehrlich found that increases in execution risk were associated with *increases* in the homicide rate. He then used the technique of multivariate regression analysis to control for the influence of other variables that presumably have an impact on the homicide rate. These variables included the unemployment rate, population characteristics, the probability of arrest for homicide, and the probability of conviction given arrest. Controlling for such factors, he found that increases in execution risk were indeed associated with decreases in the homicide rate. His much-publicized conclusion was that for the period 1933 to 1967 each additional execution might have saved eight lives.

Ehrlich's research, and a similar econometric study by Stephen K. Layson, prompted an enormous outpouring of commentary, most of it critical.[13] The next excerpt discusses some of the more important issues that have been raised.

RICHARD O. LEMPERT, DETERRENCE AND DESERT: AN ASSESSMENT OF THE MORAL BASES FOR CAPITAL PUNISHMENT, 79 Mich. L. Rev. 1177, 1210-1212, 1222-1224 (1981): In Ehrlich's model, the deterrent effects of the probability of execution given conviction are dwarfed by the deterrent effects of the probability of conviction given arrest. It is commonly thought that the possibility of capital punishment makes it more difficult to convict, and there is evidence that supports this view.[99] If the presence of the death penalty were to reduce the conviction rate for homicide by seventeen percent, Ehrlich's own findings indicate that executing would be counterproductive. My intuition is that the presence of the death penalty would not reduce convictions this far, but it might well reduce them to the point where the tradeoff between executions and lives saved would have vitally different policy implications. . . .

A second difficulty with Ehrlich's study, which he himself recognizes, is its failure to include any measure of the length of prison sentences in general and the probability of life sentences in particular. This is not a mere technical deficiency; it is fundamental. Without some measure of the probability of life sen-

---

13. E.g., David C. Baldus & James W. L. Cole, A Comparison of the Work of Thorsten Sellin & Isaac Ehrlich on the Deterrent Effect of Capital Punishment, 85 Yale L.J. 170 (1975); William J. Bowers & Glenn L. Pierce, The Illusion of Deterrence in Isaac Ehrlich's Research on Capital Punishment, 85 Yale L.J. 187 (1975); Peter Passell & John B. Taylor, The Deterrent Effect of Capital Punishment: Another View, 67 Am. Econ. Rev. 445 (1977). Studies critical of Professor Layson's research are collected in Hugo A. Bedau & Michael L. Radelet, The Myth of Infallibility: A Reply to Markman and Cassell, 41 Stan. L. Rev. 161, 168 n. 49 (1988).

For responses to these critics, see Isaac Ehrlich, Deterrence: Evidence and Inference, 85 Yale L.J. 209 (1975); Isaac Ehrlich, The Deterrent Effect of Capital Punishment: A Reply, 67 Am. Econ. Rev. 452 (1977).

99. [I]n North Carolina when a mandatory death sentence for first-degree burglary replaced a discretionary one convictions for this offense went from an annual average of 40 to an average of three. . . . Among [California] proponents of the death penalty, 60% claimed that if they sat on a jury in a murder trial they would require "much more" or "somewhat more" evidence to vote guilty if the relevant penalty were death. Forty percent of those opposed to capital punishment said they could never vote guilty in these circumstances. However, where the death penalty is not mandatory it might be easier to convict because jury holdouts for acquittal might compromise on a verdict that saves the defendant from death. Also the possibility of the death penalty, whether or not mandatory, may make it easier for prosecutors to secure convictions by plea bargains.

tences, Ehrlich's research does not address the fundamental issue in the debate. That issue is not whether executions deter, but *whether they deter more than prison sentences for life*. . . . [T]he same factors which lead a state to cease executing may lead it to shorten its sentences so that the perceived penalty for even serious homicide becomes considerably less than life imprisonment. Thus, aspects of the sentencing structure other than the death penalty may entirely explain effects that Ehrlich would attribute to death.

[Third,] replication of Ehrlich's research consistently reveals that when data from the years 1965 through 1969 are eliminated from the analysis the impact of the conditional probability of execution on the homicide rate is no longer statistically significant. Indeed, excluding years after 1962 and treating variables in their natural rather than logarithmic forms produces insignificantly *positive* associations between the probability of execution and the homicide rate; that is, the data fit Ehrlich's model so as to suggest, although not at conventional levels of statistical reliability, that higher likelihoods of executions are associated with higher homicide rates.

[N]othing about the theory of economic man suggests that people ought to respond to incentives one way during the period 1933-1962 or 1935-1964, and another way during the period 1933-1969 or 1941-1969. Thus, the sensitivity of Ehrlich's results to time destroys the theoretical underpinnings of his approach.

[Professor Lempert then summarizes the results of statistical studies subsequent to Ehrlich's. He concludes:] As it is, the body of econometric research overwhelmingly favors the conclusion that executions do not deter.[a] This evidence, together with the simpler but more revealing work of Sellin and others and our initial theoretical perspective, is sufficient to justify the conclusion that capital punishment, as administered historically in the United States, does not prevent more homicides than it may cause. Do we have absolute proof that capital punishment, as historically administered, does not save lives? No; we can never have such proof. . . . It may never be possible for social scientists to be certain that the death penalty does not deter homicide, but there is now enough research that fails to reveal deterrence that for purposes of moral argument one must proceed as if the death penalty does not deter. At some point possibilities become so mere that they cannot serve as a moral basis for action.

NOTES

1. The burden of proof. If neither retentionists nor abolitionists can make a definitive case on the deterrence question, which side offers the more persuasive evidence? The more plausible intuitive arguments? If the debate simply seems inconclusive, which side should bear the burden of proof? Compare Ernest van den Haag, On Deterrence and the Death Penalty, 60 J. Crim. L.C. & P.S. 141, 146-147 (1969), with Hugo Bedau, The Courts, the Constitution, and Capital

a. For a recent empirical study in accord with Lempert's assessment, see Ruth D. Peterson & William C. Bailey, Felony Murder and Capital Punishment: An Examination of the Deterrence Question, 29 Criminology 367 (1991). — Eds.

Punishment 57-58 (1977), and H. L. A. Hart, Punishment and Responsibility 88-89 (1968).

2. Special cases. Even if deterrence remains unproved as a general proposition, is van den Haag correct in arguing that there are some situations in which the death penalty provides the only available deterrent? If so, is the death penalty justified under such special circumstances, or do the basic objections remain? Consider the following facts arising under federal law, which did not then provide a death penalty for murder (United States v. Fountain, 768 F.2d 790, 793 (7th Cir. 1985) (Posner, J.)):

> We have consolidated the appeals in two closely related cases of murder of prison guards in the Control Unit of the federal penitentiary at Marion, Illinois — the maximum-security cell block in the nation's maximum-security federal prison — by past masters of prison murder, Clayton Fountain and Thomas Silverstein.
>
> Shortly before these crimes, Fountain and Silverstein, both of whom were already serving life sentences for murder, had together murdered an inmate in the Control Unit of Marion, and had again been sentenced to life imprisonment. After that, Silverstein killed another inmate, pleaded guilty to that murder, and received his third life sentence. At this point Fountain and Silverstein had each killed three people. . . . The prison authorities — belatedly, and as it turned out ineffectually — decided to take additional security measures. Three guards would escort Fountain and Silverstein (separately), handcuffed, every time they left their cells to go to or from the recreation room, the law library, or the shower. . . . But the guards would not be armed; nowadays guards do not carry weapons in the presence of prisoners, who might seize the weapons.
>
> The two murders involved in these appeals took place on the same October day in 1983. In the morning, Silverstein, while being escorted from the shower to his cell, stopped next to Randy Gometz's cell; and while two of the escorting officers were for some reason at a distance from him, reached his handcuffed hands into the cell. The third officer, who was closer to him, heard the click of the handcuffs being released and saw Gometz raise his shirt to reveal a homemade knife ("shank") — which had been fashioned from the iron leg of a bed — protruding from his waistband. Silverstein drew the knife and attacked one of the guards, Clutts, stabbing him 29 times and killing him. While pacing the corridor after the killing, Silverstein explained that "this is no cop thing. This is a personal thing between me and Clutts. The man disrespected me and I had to get him for it." Having gotten this off his chest he returned to his cell.
>
> Fountain was less discriminating. While being escorted that evening back to his cell from the recreation room, he stopped alongside the cell of another inmate . . . and reached his handcuffed hands into the cell, and when he brought them out he was out of the handcuffs and holding a shank. He attacked all three guards, killing one (Hoffman) with multiple stab wounds (some inflicted after the guard had already fallen), injuring another gravely (Ditterline, who survived but is permanently disabled), and inflicting lesser though still serious injuries on the third (Powles). After the wounded guards had been dragged to safety by other guards, Fountain threw up his arms in the boxer's gesture of victory, and laughing walked back to his cell.

3. For a helpful review of the literature on deterrence, see Franklin E. Zimring & Gordon Hawkins, Capital Punishment and the American Agenda 167-186 (1986).

b.   Error and Irrevocability

HUGO A. BEDAU & MICHAEL L. RADELET, MISCARRIAGES OF JUSTICE IN POTENTIALLY CAPITAL CASES

40 Stan. L. Rev. 21, 22-24, 35-39, 71-72, 83-85 (1987)

Few errors made by government officials can compare with the horror of executing a person wrongly convicted of a capital crime. . . . Yet the risk of executing the innocent is largely unknown. [This article presents research on] 350 cases in which [American] defendants convicted of capital or potentially capital crimes in this century, and in many cases sentenced to death, have later been found to be innocent. . . .

[The authors considered a defendant "innocent" only if the alleged crime never occurred or if the defendant had no involvement (physically or as an accomplice) in the crime. They thus excluded cases in which the defendants had strong claims of "legal" innocence (such as a valid claim of self-defense) and focused solely on cases in which the "wrong person," someone not factually involved at all, was convicted.

[Various kinds of evidence were used to support the authors' conclusions as to innocence. In some instances, investigators established that the defendant had an ironclad alibi, or someone else was incontrovertibly guilty, or the homicide "victim" turned up alive. In most cases the evidence leaves some room for debate. In 309 of the 350 cases, however, the authors' conclusions about innocence were based on official state decisions (such as pardons or indemnities) indicating that factual error had occurred. In the remaining cases the judgment about innocence was based on such factors as semi-official conclusions or strong evidence implicating another person.]

The final dispositions by the trial court after the erroneous convictions for the 350 defendants are reported in Table 2. . . . Only in five cases was the error discovered prior to sentencing. In 40 percent of the cases an innocent person was sentenced to death. This is . . . an average rate of three such errors every two years. In twenty-three of these cases, the execution was carried out.

[I]n virtually every year in this century, in some jurisdiction or other, at least one person has been under death sentence who was later proved to be innocent. Based on this evidence, it is virtually certain that at least some of the nearly two thousand men and women currently under sentence of death in this country are

Table 2
Final Disposition by Type of Sentence (N = 350)

Type of sentence	Number of cases
Error corrected before sentencing	5
Prison term less than life	67
Life term (25 years or more)	139
Death	139
Not executed	116
Executed	23

innocent. . . . In more than half the cases, the error was corrected within five years of the conviction. But in . . . another thirty-one cases, the error was not corrected before the defendant's death: Twenty-three defendants were erroneously executed and eight died in prison. . . .

Does the paucity of known and documented cases in which an innocent defendant was executed show that the criminal justice system, at least where the death penalty is concerned, works satisfactorily? . . . In 1983, the Senate Judiciary Committee reported favorably on a bill that would have restored the federal death penalty. In its report, the Committee noted that "the procedural safeguards for criminal defendants mandated by the Supreme Court in recent years . . . have all but reduced the danger of error in . . . [capital] cases to that of a mere theoretical possibility." . . .

The Committee's confidence on the issue of risk is both excessive and misleading. . . . Although we point only to a small number of what we believe to be erroneous executions, and although further research could undoubtedly increase that number, an estimate of the *risk* of [erroneous execution] cannot be determined merely by establishing the *proportion* of known cases of error among all capital convictions or all death sentences. . . . Our total of twenty-three wrongful executions is not an estimate, and it cannot serve as a basis for a reasonable estimate, of the total number of wrongful executions in the United States during this century. . . . The full story of all cases disposed of by execution must be examined before such an estimate would be possible. . . .

Our results lead us to believe that the small number of cases in our catalogue in which major doubts remain about the guilt of the executed is an indication not of the reliability and fairness of the system, but rather of its power and finality. For a variety of reasons, very few cases in this century have managed to attract the sustained interest of persons in a position to undertake the research necessary to challenge successfully a guilty verdict meted out to a defendant later executed. Once the defendant is dead, the best source of evidence is gone, as is the main motive to reinvestigate.

ERNEST VAN DEN HAAG, PUNISHING CRIMINALS 219-220 (1975): Errors would not justify the abolition of the death penalty for retributionists. Many social policies have unintended effects that are statistically certain, irrevocable, unjust, and deadly. Automobile traffic unintentionally kills innocent victims; so does surgery (and most medicines); so does the death penalty. These activities are justified, nevertheless, because benefits (including justice) are felt to outweigh the statistical certainty of unintentionally killing innocents. The certain death of innocents argues for abolishing the death penalty no more than for abolishing surgery or automobiles. Injustice justifies abolition only if the losses to justice outweigh the gains — if more innocents are lost than saved by imposing the penalty compared to whatever net result alternatives (such as no punishment or life imprisonment) would produce. If innocent victims of future murderers are saved by virtue of the death penalty imposed on convicted murderers, it must be retained, just as surgery is, even though some innocents will be lost through miscarriages of justice — as long as more innocent lives are saved than lost. More justice is done with than without the death penalty. . . .

NOTE

The question whether our criminal justice process permits the conviction and execution of an innocent person remains intensely disputed. One major issue in the debate involves the system for appointing counsel to represent indigents at trial. Although big-city public defenders are often dedicated and experienced, there remains great concern that many lawyers appointed to handle capital trials, especially those selected by judges in small rural counties, are often insufficiently competent or committed.[14] A related question is whether the system of post-conviction review, including federal habeas corpus proceedings, is adequate to identify error and miscarriages of justice that might occur through substandard lawyering at the original trial. See Welsh S. White, Capital Punishment's Future, 91 Mich. L. Rev. 1429, 1435-1438 (1993).

With respect to specific examples of erroneous conviction, the conclusions of Bedau and Radelet are challenged in Stephen J. Markman & Paul G. Cassell, Protecting the Innocent: A Response to the Bedau-Radelet Study, 41 Stan. L. Rev. 121 (1988). The authors present evidence that, in their view, confirms guilt in many of the cases detailed by Bedau and Radelet; they also contend (id. at 152-156) that even if 23 innocent persons have been executed in this century, the death penalty has saved more innocent lives than it has cost. Bedau and Radelet respond that the cases of erroneous conviction they have identified represent only the tip of an iceberg, and that few cases of possibly erroneous conviction are ever investigated sufficiently to bring potential miscarriages of justice to light. See Bedau & Radelet, The Myth of Infallibility: A Reply to Markman and Cassell, 41 Stan. L. Rev. 161 (1988). For subsequent research detailing more than 400 allegedly erroneous convictions in capital or potentially capital cases from 1900 through 1991, see Michael L. Radelet, Hugo A. Bedau & Constance E. Putnam, In Spite of Innocence: Erroneous Convictions in Capital Cases (1993).

c. Discriminatory Administration

CHARLES BLACK, CAPITAL PUNISHMENT: THE INEVITABILITY OF CAPRICE AND MISTAKE

29, 96-101 (2d ed. augmented, 1981)

[I]n one way or another, the official choices — by prosecutors, judges, juries, and governors — that divide those who are to die from those who are to live are on the whole not made, and cannot be made, under standards that are consistently meaningful and clear[;] they are often made, and in the foreseeable future will continue often to be made, under no standards at all or under pseudo-standards without discoverable meaning. . . .

[I]f a defense cannot be presented in the best possible manner, the chances of even a valid defense's being rejected are obviously increased. . . . But we are

14. See ABA, Criminal Justice Section, Task Force on Death Penalty Habeas Corpus, Toward a More Just and Effective System of Review in State Death Penalty Cases 55 (Ira P. Robbins, reporter, 1990).

not ready to furnish poor defendants with really adequate resources for the development of a defense, by investigation at early stages while the trail is still warm. . . . This is, of course, just another way of saying that both conviction and conviction by mistake are from the beginning made much more likely for the poor. . . .

Now what about blackness? Why are more than half of the people on death row black in a country with about eleven percent blacks? . . . What is *your* explanation? And can you go on living with such a system?

ERNEST VAN DEN HAAG, PUNISHING CRIMINALS 220-221 (1975): Now, since abolitionists remain opposed to capital punishment even where it is distributed without discrimination, e.g., where populations are nearly racially homogeneous, as in England or Sweden, it appears that the discrimination argument is used to screen objections to the death penalty that do not depend on that argument. At any rate, objections to unwarranted discrimination are relevant to the discriminatory distribution of penalties, not to the penalties distributed. . . . The vice must be corrected by correcting the distributive process that produces it. . . . Nor can much be accomplished by abolishing any penalty, since all penalties can be meted out discriminatorily. The defect to be corrected is in the courts.[a]

NOTES

1. Arbitrariness. A recent empirical study of the charging process in San Francisco found that prosecutorial decisions to seek the death penalty appeared to be largely random or capricious, much like the output of a lottery, but the data is complex and subject to conflicting interpretations. See Richard A. Berk, Robert Weiss & Jack Boger, Chance and the Death Penalty, 27 Law & Socy. Rev. 89 (1993).

2. Race discrimination. Detailed empirical studies designed to document racial discrimination have been the basis for extensive litigation that we consider at pages 536-544 infra, in connection with the constitutional limits on capital punishment.

d.   The Sanctity of Human Life

RAMSEY CLARK, STATEMENT, Hearings on S. 1760 ("To Abolish the Death Penalty") before the Subcommittee on Criminal Laws and Procedures, Senate Judiciary Committee, 90th Cong. 2d Sess. (July 2, 1968): In the midst of anxiety and fear, complexity and doubt, perhaps our greatest need is reverence for life — mere life: our lives, the lives of others, all life. Life is an end in itself. A humane and generous concern for every individual, for his safety, his health and

---

a. Van den Haag adds (at 219 n. *): "[T]o insist that only the total elimination of 'capriciousness' — which [Professor Black] knows to be impossible in the prosecution of any crime and generally in human affairs — would make the death penalty legally or morally justifiable is a counsel of perfection meant to exclude a disliked policy, and not a serious argument." — Eds.

his fulfillment, will do more to soothe the savage heart than the fear of state-inflicted death which chiefly serves to remind us how close we remain to the jungle.

"Murder and capital punishment are not opposites that cancel one another, but similars that breed their kind," Shaw advises. When the state itself kills, the mandate "thou shalt not kill" loses the force of the absolute.

Surely the abolition of the death penalty is a major milestone in the long road up from barbarism. There was a time when self preservation necessitated its imposition. . . . Our civilization has no such excuse. . . .

Our emotions may cry vengeance in the wake of a horrible crime. But reason and experience tell us that killing the criminal will not undo the crime, prevent other crimes, or bring justice to the victim, the criminal, or society. Executions cheapen life. We must cherish life. . . .

ERNEST VAN DEN HAAG, PUNISHING CRIMINALS 213 (1975): No matter what can be said for abolition of the death penalty, it will be perceived symbolically as a loss of nerve: social authority no longer is willing to pass an irrevocable judgment on anyone. Murder is no longer thought grave enough to take the murderer's life, no longer horrendous enough to deserve so fearfully irrevocable a punishment. When murder no longer forfeits the murderer's life (though it will interfere with his freedom), respect for life itself is diminished, as the price for taking it is. Life becomes cheaper as we become kinder to those who wantonly take it. The responsibility we avoid is indeed hard to bear. Can we sit in judgment and find that anyone is so irredeemably wicked that he does not deserve to live? Many of us no longer believe in evil, only in error or accident. How can one execute a murderer if one believes that he became one only by error or accident and is not to blame? Yet if life is to be valued and secured, it must be known that anyone who takes the life of another forfeits his own.

NOTE

For further development of the argument that respect for the sanctity of life *requires* the death penalty, see Walter Berns, For Capital Punishment 153-176 (1979).

Ethical arguments based on the sanctity of life are closely related to concepts derived from specifically religious sources. Although we cannot present here an adequate sampling of arguments advanced from the viewpoint of the principal religious faiths, that perspective is of considerable importance for this aspect of the capital punishment debate. In Punishing Criminals, Professor van den Haag comments (id. at 225):

> [I]t is not easy to see what "sanctity" [of life] could mean outside of its religious context other than the assertion, disguised as proof, that it is wrong to put criminals to death. . . . Unless one resorts to a religiously or, in some other way, revealed source, one cannot show that society, unlike the murderer, must hold life unconditionally inviolate; and the fact that the nonreligious urge it so religiously cannot commend this precept to believers. The death penalty has been part of all major religious traditions: Graeco-Roman, Judaic, Islamic, and Christian.

Note, however, that many American religious denominations have officially condemned capital punishment on religious grounds. For discussion of the religious issues by several leading theologians, see The Death Penalty in America 123-130, 171-182 (H. Bedau ed. 1964).

JACQUES BARZUN, IN FAVOR OF CAPITAL PUNISHMENT
31 Am. Scholar 181 (Spring 1962)

. . . The propaganda for abolition speaks in hushed tones of the sanctity of human life, as if the mere statement of it should silence all opponents who have any moral sense. . . . [I]s the movement then campaigning also against the principle of self-defense? Absolute sanctity means letting the cutthroat have his sweet will of you, even if you have a poker handy to bash him with, for you might kill. And again, do we hear any protest against the police firing at criminals on the street — mere bank robbers usually — and doing this, often enough, with an excited marksmanship that misses the artist and hits the bystander? The absolute sanctity of human life is, for the abolitionist, a slogan rather than a considered proposition.

[T]here are hundreds and indeed thousands whom, in our concern with the horrors of execution, we forget: on the one hand, the victims of violence; on the other, the prisoners in our jails. . . .

[T]here is one form of barbarity in our law that I want to see mitigated before any other. I mean imprisonment. The enemies of capital punishment . . . speak of the sanctity of life, but have no concern with its quality. . . . They do not see and suffer the cell, the drill, the clothes, the stench, the food; they do not feel the sexual racking of young and old bodies, the hateful promiscuity, the insane monotony, the mass degradation, the impotent hatred. . . .

Nothing is revocable here below, imprisonment least of all. . . . What we accept, and what the abolitionist will clamp upon us all the more firmly if he succeeds, is an incoherence which is not remedied by the belief that second-degree murder merits a kind of second-degree death; that a doubt as to the identity of a killer is resolved by commuting real death into intolerable life. . . .

HUGO BEDAU: DEATH AS A PUNISHMENT, in The Death Penalty in America 216-219 (H. Bedau ed. 1964): [O]ne distinction of importance, neglected by Professor Barzun, is between a man's killing someone else when there is a clear and present danger that he will otherwise be the victim of some violent act, and the state's killing a man as a punishment, i.e., between a man's right to defend himself and society's right to punish criminals. . . . [R]espect for human life has never been an obstacle to the use of force in self-defense; indeed, it has always been thought to be its justification. It has, however, obligated anyone who pleads self-defense in justification of a killing to satisfy society that the force he used really was necessary in the circumstances and was motivated solely by a desire to ward off imminent harm to himself. . . . Were it to be shown that there is a threat to society, or to any of its members, in allowing a criminal in prison to remain there, comparable to the danger a man invites in a dark alley if he turns his back on a thug who has a weapon in his hand and violence on his mind, then — but

only then — would it be inconsistent for the abolitionist to tolerate force sufficient to kill the thug in the alley but to refuse to kill the prisoner. . . .

On the issue of whether abolition of the death penalty would improve the lot
of persons unjustly convicted, I think . . . Professor Barzun [is] misled and confusing. Barzun is unquestionably right when he points to cases where men have
been exonerated after years in prison, only to find that their lives have been
destroyed. Of course, abolishing the death penalty is no remedy for the injustice
of convicting and punishing an innocent man. . . . But I should have thought it
. . . *worse* for him to be killed than for him to be imprisoned. This point must not
be blurred by speculating whether it is worse from the convict's point of view to
be dead than to be imprisoned and perhaps never vindicated or released. If an
innocent convict thinks he is better off dead than alive, this is for *him* to determine, not us. . . .

[W]e ought to consider allowing our penal authorities, under proper judicial
and medical supervision, to cooperate with any long-term prisoner who is too
dangerous to be released and who would honestly and soberly prefer to be dead
rather than endure further imprisonment. That there are such convicts I am
willing to concede. The question here is this: is it wisest for the state to allow a
convict to take his own life if he decides that it would be better for him to be
dead than to suffer any more imprisonment? . . . Does not civilized society always
have a fundamental interest, if not an obligation, to try to provide even for
its most incompetent members in that most oppressive of environments, a
prison, some opportunity to make their lives worth living? Wouldn't a policy that
amounts to euthanasia for certain convicts run counter to this interest and sap
the motive to satisfy it?

These questions are not new, for they arise whenever "mercy killing" as a
social policy is advocated. [W]e are asking whether we ought to allow a convict,
if he so wishes, to be painlessly put to death for no other reason than so that his
imprisonment and his despair may come to an end — as if there were no better
alternatives! . . .

2. *Constitutional Limitations*

INTRODUCTORY NOTE

Until the 1950s, opponents of the death penalty had largely devoted their
efforts to legislative reform, but thereafter abolitionists began a concentrated
assault on the constitutionality of capital punishment.[15] Recall that at common
law all murder had been punishable by death. Gradually, the scope of capital
punishment had been narrowed, first by the division of murder into two degrees, so that only the more serious was subject to mandatory capital punishment, and then by the introduction of discretion in sentencing even for the
highest category of criminal homicides. By the beginning of the twentieth century, 23 American jurisdictions made capital punishment discretionary in first-

---

15. The development of a detailed strategy for litigation against the death penalty is recounted
in Michael Meltsner, Cruel and Unusual: The Supreme Court and Capital Punishment (1973).

degree murder cases, and by 1962 all the remaining jurisdictions had adopted this approach.[16]

Litigation challenging this punishment scheme focused on two issues:

(1) Procedural due process. All the states committed the death penalty decision to the discretion of judge or jury, but none provided any standards to guide the exercise of that discretion. The reliance on unguided discretion was prevalent in sentencing decisions generally, but many thought that when a choice between life and death was to be made, due process required some explicit criteria of decision. The Court rejected that view in McGautha v. California, 402 U.S. 183, 207-208 (1971), holding that "committing to the untrammelled discretion of the jury the power to pronounce life or death is [not] offensive to anything in the Constitution." The Court reasoned that

> [an] attempt to catalog the appropriate factors in this elusive area could inhibit rather than expand the scope of consideration. . . . The infinite variety of cases . . . would make general standards either meaningless "boiler plate" or a statement of the obvious that no jury would need.

McGautha proved to be less significant than it seemed, however, because the same concerns about unguided discretion soon surfaced in attacks based on the cruel-and-unusual-punishment clause.

(2) Cruel and unusual punishment. Only a year after *McGautha,* a 5–4 majority of the Court held in Furman v. Georgia, 408 U.S. 238 (1972), that capital punishment, as then administered, violated the Eighth Amendment's prohibition of "cruel and unusual punishments." The Court's holding was stated in a brief per curiam opinion that made no attempt to set forth the majority's reasoning. Each of the justices filed a separate concurring or dissenting opinion explaining his own approach to the Eighth Amendment issue.

Justices Brennan and Marshall concluded that all capital punishment was unconstitutional. The other three concurring justices put their objections to capital punishment on narrower grounds. Justice Douglas stressed the potential for discriminatory administration of the death penalty. Justice Stewart said (id. at 309-310), in a passage that reflects Justice White's position as well:

> These death sentences are cruel and unusual in the same way that being struck by lightning is cruel and unusual. [I]f any basis can be discerned for the selection of these few to be sentenced to die, it is the constitutionally impermissible basis of race. But racial discrimination has not been proved, and I put it to one side. I simply conclude that the Eighth and Fourteenth Amendments cannot tolerate the infliction of a sentence of death under legal systems that permit this unique penalty to be so wantonly and so freakishly imposed.

The Chief Justice and Justices Blackmun, Powell and Rehnquist dissented. The dissenters stressed the long tradition and continued acceptance of capital punishment and argued that the majority's position involved an unwarranted intrusion into the legislative process.

---

16. The history is detailed in Model Penal Code and Commentaries, Comment to §210.6 at 120-132 (1980).

Because a clear majority of the justices had neither rejected capital punishment outright nor indicated under what conditions it might be preserved, *Furman* created considerable confusion for states that desired to retain the death penalty. Two alternatives appeared viable: (1) enacting legislation to make capital punishment mandatory in certain cases and (2) establishing guidelines to determine who would be subjected to capital punishment. By 1976, at least 35 states and the United States Congress had enacted new capital punishment legislation; half of these jurisdictions had adopted provisions for a mandatory death penalty, while the remainder opted for schemes under which the sentencing authority would be required to consider specified aggravating and mitigating circumstances.[17] The Court soon confronted challenges to the new legislation.

GREGG v. GEORGIA

Supreme Court of the United States
428 U.S. 153 (1976)

[Gregg was convicted by a jury on two counts of armed robbery and two counts of murder. After the guilty verdicts, a penalty hearing was held before the same jury, under guidelines enacted in response to the *Furman* decision. The jury imposed the death sentence on each count. The Georgia Supreme Court set aside the death sentences for armed robbery, on the ground that capital punishment had rarely been imposed for that crime, but the court affirmed the convictions on all counts and upheld the death sentences on the murder counts. The United States Supreme Court granted certiorari.]

Justice Stewart, Justice Powell, and Justice Stevens announced the judgment of the Court and filed an opinion delivered by Justice Stewart. . . .

We address initially the basic contention that the punishment of death for the crime of murder is, under all circumstances, "cruel and unusual" in violation of the Eighth and Fourteenth Amendments of the Constitution. . . . We now hold that the punishment of death does not invariably violate the Constitution. . . .

It is clear from the . . . precedents that the Eighth Amendment has not been regarded as a static concept. As Chief Justice Warren said, in an oft-quoted phrase, "[t]he Amendment must draw its meaning from the evolving standards of decency that mark the progress of a maturing society." Trop v. Dulles, 356 U.S. 86, 101 (1958). Thus, an assessment of contemporary values concerning the infliction of a challenged sanction is relevant to the application of the Eighth Amendment. . . .

But our cases also make clear that public perceptions of standards of decency with respect to criminal sanctions are not conclusive. A penalty also must accord with "the dignity of man," which is the "basic concept underlying the Eighth Amendment." Trop v. Dulles, supra, 356 U.S., at 100. This means, at least, that the punishment not be "excessive." [T]he inquiry into "excessiveness" has two aspects. First, the punishment must not involve the unnecessary and wanton

---

17. For details concerning these enactments, see Samuel R. Gross, The Romance of Revenge: Capital Punishment in America, 13 Stud. L., Pol. & Socy. 71, 84-92 (1993); Model Penal Code and Commentaries, Comment to §210.6 at 156-157 & nn. 144-148 (1980).

infliction of pain. Second, the punishment must not be grossly out of proportion to the severity of the crime.

Of course, the requirements of the Eighth Amendment must be applied with an awareness of the limited role to be played by the courts. [W]hile we have an obligation to insure that constitutional bounds are not overreached, we may not act as judges as we might as legislators. . . .

Therefore, in assessing a punishment selected by a democratically elected legislature against the constitutional measure, we presume its validity. We may not require the legislature to select the least severe penalty possible so long as the penalty selected is not cruelly inhumane or disproportionate to the crime involved. And a heavy burden rests on those who would attack the judgment of the representatives of the people.

. . . We now consider specifically whether the sentence of death for the crime of murder is a per se violation of the Eighth and Fourteenth Amendments to the Constitution. We note first that history and precedent strongly support a negative answer to this question. It is apparent from the text of the Constitution itself that the existence of capital punishment was accepted by the Framers. . . . For nearly two centuries, this Court, repeatedly and often expressly, has recognized that capital punishment is not invalid per se. . . .

Four years ago, the petitioners in *Furman* and its companion cases predicated their argument primarily upon the asserted proposition that standards of decency had evolved to the point where capital punishment no longer could be tolerated. . . . The petitioners in the capital cases before the Court today renew the "standards of decency" argument, but developments during the four years since *Furman* have undercut substantially the assumptions upon which their argument rested. Despite the continuing debate, dating back to the 19th century, over the morality and utility of capital punishment, it is now evident that a large proportion of American society continues to regard it as an appropriate and necessary criminal sanction.

The most marked indication of society's endorsement of the death penalty for murder is the legislative response to *Furman*. The legislatures of at least 35 States have enacted new statutes that provide for the death penalty for at least some crimes that result in the death of another person. And the Congress of the United States, in 1974, enacted a statute providing the death penalty for aircraft piracy that results in death. . . . [T]he relative infrequency of jury verdicts imposing the death sentence does not indicate rejection of capital punishment per se. Rather, the reluctance of juries in many cases to impose the sentence may well reflect the humane feeling that this most irrevocable of sanctions should be reserved for a small number of extreme cases. . . .

As we have seen, however, the Eighth Amendment demands more than that a challenged punishment be acceptable to contemporary society. The Court also must ask whether it comports with the basic concept of human dignity at the core of the Amendment. Although we cannot "invalidate a category of penalties because we deem less severe penalties adequate to serve the ends of penology," the sanction imposed cannot be so totally without penological justification that it results in the gratuitous infliction of suffering.

The death penalty is said to serve two principal social purposes: retribution and deterrence of capital crimes by prospective offenders.

In part, capital punishment is an expression of society's moral outrage at particularly offensive conduct. This function may be unappealing to many, but it is essential in an ordered society that asks its citizens to rely on legal processes rather than self-help to vindicate their wrongs. "The instinct for retribution is part of the nature of man, and channeling that instinct in the administration of criminal justice serves an important purpose in promoting the stability of a society governed by law. When people begin to believe that organized society is unwilling or unable to impose upon criminal offenders the punishment they 'deserve,' then there are sown the seeds of anarchy — of self-help, vigilante justice, and lynch law." Furman v. Georgia, 408 U.S., at 308 (Stewart, J., concurring). . . .

Statistical attempts to evaluate the worth of the death penalty as a deterrent to crimes by potential offenders have occasioned a great deal of debate. The results simply have been inconclusive. . . .

The value of capital punishment as a deterrent of crime is a complex factual issue the resolution of which properly rests with the legislatures, which can evaluate the results of statistical studies in terms of their own local conditions and with a flexibility of approach that is not available to the courts. . . .

Finally, we must consider whether the punishment of death is disproportionate in relation to the crime for which it is imposed. There is no question that death as a punishment is unique in its severity and irrevocability. . . . But we are concerned here only with the imposition of capital punishment for the crime of murder, and when a life has been taken deliberately by the offender, we cannot say that the punishment is invariably disproportionate to the crime. It is an extreme sanction, suitable to the most extreme of crimes.

We hold that the death penalty is not a form of punishment that may never be imposed, . . . regardless of the procedure followed in reaching the decision to impose it. . . . Because of the uniqueness of the death penalty, *Furman* held that it could not be imposed under sentencing procedures that created a substantial risk that it would be inflicted in an arbitrary and capricious manner. . . .

Jury sentencing has been considered desirable in capital cases in order "to maintain a link between contemporary community values and the penal system — a link without which the determination of punishment could hardly reflect 'the evolving standards of decency that mark the progress of a maturing society.'" But it creates special problems. Much of the information that is relevant to the sentencing decision may have no relevance to the question of guilt, or may even be extremely prejudicial to a fair determination of that question. This problem, however, is scarcely insurmountable. Those who have studied the question suggest that a bifurcated procedure — one in which the question of sentence is not considered until the determination of guilt has been made — is . . . likely to ensure elimination of the constitutional deficiencies in *Furman*.

But the provision of relevant information under fair procedural rules is not alone sufficient to guarantee that the information will be properly used. . . . Since the members of a jury will have had little, if any, previous experience in sentencing, they are unlikely to be skilled in dealing with the information they are given. . . . It seems clear, however, that the problem will be alleviated if the jury is given guidance regarding the factors about the crime and the defendant that the State, representing organized society, deems particularly relevant to the sentencing decision. . . .

While some have suggested that standards to guide a capital jury's sentencing deliberations are impossible to formulate, the fact is that such standards have been developed. [The Court here referred to the Model Penal Code proposals. See §210.6, Appendix.] While such standards are by necessity somewhat general, they do provide guidance to the sentencing authority and thereby reduce the likelihood that it will impose a sentence that fairly can be called capricious or arbitrary. . . .

In summary, the concerns expressed in *Furman* that the penalty of death not be imposed in an arbitrary or capricious manner can be met by a carefully drafted statute that ensures that the sentencing authority is given adequate information and guidance. As a general proposition these concerns are best met by a system that provides for a bifurcated proceeding at which the sentencing authority is apprised of the information relevant to the imposition of sentence and provided with standards to guide its use of the information. . . .

We now turn to consideration of the constitutionality of Georgia's capital-sentencing procedures. In the wake of *Furman*, Georgia amended its capital punishment statute, but chose not to narrow the scope of its murder provisions. Thus, now as before *Furman*, in Georgia "[a] person commits murder when he unlawfully and with malice aforethought, either express or implied, causes the death of another human being." Ga. Code Ann. §26-1101(a) (1972). All persons convicted of murder "shall be punished by death or by imprisonment for life." §26-1101(c) (1972).

Georgia did act, however, to narrow the class of murderers subject to capital punishment by specifying 10 statutory aggravating circumstances, one of which must be found by the jury to exist beyond a reasonable doubt before a death sentence can ever be imposed.[48] In addition, the jury is authorized to consider

---

48. The text of the statute enumerating the various aggravating circumstances is [as follows:

(1) The offense of murder, rape, armed robbery, or kidnapping was committed by a person with a prior record of conviction for a capital felony, or the offense of murder was committed by a person who has a substantial history of serious assaultive criminal convictions.

(2) The offense of murder, rape, armed robbery, or kidnapping was committed while the offender was engaged in the commission of another capital felony, or aggravated battery, or the offense of murder was committed while the offender was engaged in the commission of burglary or arson in the first degree.

(3) The offender by his act of murder, armed robbery, or kidnapping knowingly created a great risk of death to more than one person in a public place by means of a weapon or device which would normally be hazardous to the lives of more than one person.

(4) The offender committed the offense of murder for himself or another, for the purpose of receiving money or any other thing of monetary value.

(5) The murder of a judicial officer, former judicial officer, district attorney or solicitor or former district attorney or solicitor during or because of the exercise of his official duty.

(6) The offender caused or directed another to commit murder or committed murder as an agent or employee of another person.

(7) The offense of murder, rape, armed robbery, or kidnapping was outrageously or wantonly vile, horrible or inhuman in that it involved torture, depravity of mind, or an aggravated battery to the victim.

(8) The offense of murder was committed against any peace officer, corrections employee or fireman while engaged in the performance of his official duties.

(9) The offense of murder was committed by a person in, or who has escaped from, the lawful custody of a peace officer or place of lawful confinement.

(10) The murder was committed for the purpose of avoiding, interfering with, or preventing a lawful arrest or custody in a place of lawful confinement, of himself or another.]

any other appropriate aggravating or mitigating circumstances. The jury is not required to find any mitigating circumstance in order to make a recommendation of mercy that is binding on the trial court, but it must find a *statutory* aggravating circumstance before recommending a sentence of death. . . .

As an important additional safeguard against arbitrariness and caprice, the Georgia statutory scheme provides for automatic appeal of all death sentences to the State's supreme court. That court is required by statute to review each sentence of death and determine whether it was imposed under the influence of passion or prejudice, whether the evidence supports the jury's finding of a statutory aggravating circumstance, and whether the sentence is disproportionate compared to those sentences imposed in similar cases.

. . . On their face these procedures seem to satisfy the concerns of *Furman*. No longer should there be "no meaningful basis for distinguishing the few cases in which [the death penalty] is imposed from the many cases in which it is not."

The petitioner contends, however, that the changes in the Georgia sentencing procedures are only cosmetic, that the arbitrariness and capriciousness condemned by *Furman* continue to exist. . . . First, the petitioner focuses on the opportunities for discretionary action that are inherent in the processing of any murder case under Georgia law. He notes that the state prosecutor has unfettered authority to select those persons whom he wishes to prosecute for a capital offense and to plea bargain with them. Further, at the trial the jury may choose to convict a defendant of a lesser included offense rather than find him guilty of a crime punishable by death, even if the evidence would support a capital verdict. And finally, a defendant who is convicted and sentenced to die may have his sentence commuted by the Governor of the State and the Georgia Board of Pardons and Paroles.

The existence of these discretionary stages is not determinative of the issues before us. At each of these stages an actor in the criminal justice system makes a decision which may remove a defendant from consideration as a candidate for the death penalty. *Furman*, in contrast, dealt with the decision to impose the death sentence on a specific individual who had been convicted of a capital offense. Nothing in any of our cases suggests that the decision to afford an individual defendant mercy violates the Constitution. *Furman* held only that, in order to minimize the risk that the death penalty would be imposed on a capriciously selected group of offenders, the decision to impose it had to be guided by standards so that the sentencing authority would focus on the particularized circumstances of the crime and the defendant.

The petitioner further contends that . . . the statute is so broad and vague as to leave juries free to act as arbitrarily and capriciously as they wish. . . . In light of the decisions of the Supreme Court of Georgia we must disagree. [That court held §1 of the statute] to be impermissibly vague . . . because it did not provide the jury with "sufficiently 'clear and objective standards.'" . . .

For the reasons expressed in this opinion, we hold that the statutory system under which Gregg was sentenced to death does not violate the Constitution. Accordingly, the judgment of the Georgia Supreme Court is affirmed. . . .

[The concurring opinion of Justice White, joined by the Chief Justice and Justice Rehnquist, the concurring opinion of Justice Blackmun, and the dissenting opinion of Justice Brennan are omitted.]

JUSTICE MARSHALL, dissenting. . . .

I would be less than candid if I did not acknowledge that [legislative] developments [since *Furman*] have a significant bearing on a realistic assessment of the moral acceptability of the death penalty to the American people. But if the constitutionality of the death penalty turns, as I have urged, on the opinion of an *informed* citizenry, then even the enactment of new death statutes cannot be viewed as conclusive. In *Furman*, I observed that the American people are largely unaware of the information critical to a judgment on the morality of the death penalty, and concluded that if they were better informed they would consider it shocking, unjust, and unacceptable....

The two purposes that sustain the death penalty as nonexcessive in the Court's view are general deterrence and retribution.... The evidence I reviewed in *Furman* remains convincing, in my view, that "capital punishment is not necessary as a deterrent to crime in our society."...

The other principal purpose said to be served by the death penalty is retribution.... As my Brother Brennan stated in *Furman*, "[t]here is no evidence whatever that utilization of imprisonment rather than death encourages private blood feuds and other disorders." It simply defies belief to suggest that the death penalty is necessary to prevent the American people from taking the law into their own hands....

NOTES

1. Mandatory death penalty statutes. (a) In Woodson v. North Carolina, 428 U.S. 280 (1976), the Court held that a mandatory death sentence for any first-degree murder violates the Eighth Amendment. Justice Stewart, joined by Justices Powell and Stevens, gave three reasons for this conclusion:

(i) Mandatory capital punishment is inconsistent with contemporary standards of decency. He noted that the recent enactment of mandatory-sentence statutes was not a reversal of the historical trend of popular rejection of mandatory sentences but was only an effort to retain the death penalty in light of *Furman*.

(ii) Mandatory sentences fail to provide standards that will effectively guide the jury. Justice Stewart noted experience with earlier mandatory schemes, under which "[j]uries continued to find the death penalty inappropriate in a significant number of first-degree murder cases and refused to return guilty verdicts for that crime." Id. at 291. He therefore concluded that "mandatory statutes enacted in response to *Furman* have simply papered over the problem of unguided and unchecked jury discretion." Id. at 302. (Do you find this point convincing? If so, does it not apply with virtually equal force to the statute upheld in *Gregg*?)

(iii) Most important, Justice Stewart reasoned that the fundamental respect for individual dignity underlying the Eighth Amendment requires (id. at 303-304)

the particularized consideration of relevant aspects of the character and record of each convicted defendant [and the circumstances of the offense] before the imposition upon him of a sentence of death.... A process that [fails to provide such consideration] ... treats all persons convicted of a designated offense not as uniquely individual human beings, but as members of a faceless, undifferentiated mass to be subjected to the blind infliction of the penalty of death.

(b) Shuman killed a fellow prisoner while serving a sentence of life imprisonment without possibility of parole. He was convicted of murder, and under the applicable Nevada statute the offense carried a mandatory penalty of death. Despite intimations in the earlier cases that mandatory capital punishment might be permissible in these narrow circumstances, the Court held Shuman's death sentence unconstitutional. Sumner v. Shuman, 483 U.S. 66 (1987). Writing for the Court, Justice Blackmun stressed that "the fundamental respect for humanity underlying the Eighth Amendment . . . requires consideration of the character and record of the offender and the circumstances of the particular offense" (id. at 75). The Court noted that prior conviction of an offense carrying a life sentence provided insufficient information about the seriousness of the present killing, the defendant's leadership role in its commission, or mitigating circumstances that might fall short of a complete defense. The Court also noted that a mandatory capital sentence was not essential for deterrence because life prisoners who kill would still face the death penalty under a regime of guided discretion.

2. *Other guided-discretion statutes.* (a) In Jurek v. Texas, 428 U.S. 262 (1976), the Court considered a post-*Furman* statute that limits capital punishment to five categories of intentional homicide[17] and then provides the following procedure for determining whether to impose the death penalty in any such case. The jury is directed to answer three questions: (1) whether the conduct was done deliberately and with a reasonable expectation of causing death; (2) whether "there is a probability that the defendant would commit criminal acts of violence that would constitute a continuing threat to society" (id. at 269); and (3) if raised by the evidence, whether the defendant's conduct was an unreasonable response to provocation by the deceased. If the jury gives a negative answer to any question, life imprisonment is imposed, but if the jury finds beyond a reasonable doubt that the answer to all three questions is affirmative, then the death sentence must be imposed. Although this approach is quasi-mandatory in directing capital punishment under specified conditions, the Court treated the case as closer to *Gregg* than to *Woodson* and sustained the statutory scheme. The plurality opinion (by Justices Stewart, Powell, and Stevens) reasoned that the five categories of capital murder were equivalent to aggravating circumstances and noted that Texas courts had read the second question put to the jury, the probability of future violence, as permitting the defense to place before the jury whatever mitigating circumstances might exist. The plurality did not, however, clarify how a jury, unaided by further guidelines, could make a rational response to the broad and ambiguously worded second question. The plurality simply concluded that "[b]ecause this system serves to assure that sentences of death will not be 'wantonly' or 'freakishly' imposed, it does not violate the Constitution." Id. at 276.

(b) Lockett v. Ohio, 438 U.S. 586 (1978), involved a post-*Furman* statute that specified that once any of seven aggravating circumstances was found, the death

---

17. The categories are murder of a peace officer or firefighter, intentional murder in the course of specified felonies, murder committed for remuneration, murder committed while escaping from prison, or murder of a prison employee by an inmate.

penalty must be imposed unless it is found that (1) the victim had induced or facilitated the offense, (2) it was unlikely that the defendant would have committed the offense but for the fact that he or she was under duress, coercion, or strong provocation, or (3) the offense was primarily the product of the defendant's psychosis or mental deficiency. The Court struck down this statute by a 7–1 vote, but the Court was widely split in its reasoning. Chief Justice Burger, writing for himself and Justices Stewart, Powell, and Stevens, found the narrow range of permissible mitigating circumstances to be a fatal flaw. "[T]he sentencer, in all but the rarest kind of capital case, [must] not be precluded from considering *as a mitigating factor,* any aspect of a defendant's character or record and any of the circumstances of the offense that the defendant proffers as a basis for a sentence less than death." Id. at 604.

Questions: Chief Justice Burger's view seems to flow naturally from *Woodson,* but is it compatible with the goals of confining and structuring the jury's decision? Is it consistent with the principles implicit in *Furman* and *Gregg?*

(c) Cases subsequent to *Lockett* reaffirmed and extended the principle espoused by the plurality in that case. In Eddings v. Oklahoma, 455 U.S. 104 (1982), the defense offered in mitigation the fact that the defendant, who was 16 years old at the time of the offense, had a history of beatings by a harsh father and serious emotional disturbance. The state statute permitted consideration of "any mitigating circumstances," but the sentencing judge ruled that while the defendant's youth was relevant in mitigation, the troubled family background and emotional disturbance were not relevant as a matter of law. Justice Powell, in an opinion for five members of the Court, held this approach impermissible. He ruled that the evidence of Eddings' background could not be ruled irrelevant and that the sentencer must give some consideration to it. The Court held that "a consistency produced by ignoring individual differences is a false consistency." (455 U.S. at 112.)

In Skipper v. South Carolina, 476 U.S. 1 (1986), Justice White, writing for six members of the Court, held it impermissible to exclude evidence regarding the defendant's good behavior in jail *while awaiting trial.* Justice Powell, for the three dissenters, argued that such evidence had little probative value given the special incentives for good behavior under the circumstances.

A different aspect of the *Lockett* principle was considered in Penry v. Lynaugh, 492 U.S. 302 (1989). In *Penry* there was evidence that the defendant suffered from organic brain damage and significant mental retardation that left him with the mental age of a $6\frac{1}{2}$-year-old; there was also evidence that, in his childhood, he had suffered serious beatings and other abuse. This potentially mitigating evidence was admitted at his trial, as *Lockett* clearly requires, but under the Texas death penalty scheme (see page 530 supra), the judge was in effect required to impose the death penalty if the jury answered affirmatively to the question whether "there is a probability that the defendant would commit criminal acts of violence that would constitute a continuing threat to society." The Supreme Court held (5–4) that the narrow focus of the jury's inquiry under the Texas scheme violated *Lockett* by preventing the jury from considering the defendant's mental retardation and abused background as *mitigating* factors and by precluding a "reasoned moral response" to the mitigating evidence. (Id. at 328.)

The scope of *Penry* was limited by Graham v. Collins, 113 S. Ct. 892 (1993). In *Graham* the defendant relied for mitigation on evidence of his youth (he was 17 at the time of the offense), unstable family background, and positive character traits. The evidence was admitted at trial, but, as in *Penry,* the jury was able to consider the evidence only within the narrow framework of the question whether he would pose a "continuing threat to society." This time the Court held (5–4) that *Lockett* was *not* violated, reasoning that the defendant had been permitted to place his mitigating evidence before the jury and that his evidence, unlike Penry's, did have some mitigating relevance on the "continuing threat" issue. *Penry,* the Court said, "does *not* broadly suggest the invalidity of the [Texas] special issues framework." (Id. at 901, emphasis in original.) In *Graham* Justice White, who had dissented in *Penry,* wrote the majority opinion, and Justice O'Connor, who had written the majority opinion in *Penry,* was now one of the four dissenters.

   3. *Crimes other than intentional murder. (a)* In Coker v. Georgia, 433 U.S. 584, 592 (1977), the Court held that the death penalty "is grossly disproportionate and excessive punishment for the crime of rape and is therefore forbidden by the Eighth Amendment. . . ." Justice White, in an opinion joined by Justices Stewart, Blackmun, and Stevens, said (id. at 597-598):

> We do not discount the seriousness of rape as a crime. It is highly reprehensible, both in a moral sense and in its almost total contempt for the personal integrity and autonomy of the female victim. . . . Short of homicide, it is "the ultimate violation of self."
>
> Rape is without doubt deserving of serious punishment; but in terms of moral depravity and of the injury to the person and to the public, it does not compare with murder. . . . Although it may be accompanied by another crime, rape by definition does not include the death of or even the serious injury to another person. . . . We have the abiding conviction that the death penalty, which "is unique in its severity and revocability," . . . is an excessive penalty for the rapist who, as such, does not take human life.

Justices Brennan, Marshall, and Powell concurred in the result. Chief Justice Burger and Justice Rehnquist dissented.

   (b) The Court has not yet considered the constitutionality of capital punishment for such crimes as espionage or aircraft hijacking. Of course, these crimes may create a risk of death, perhaps to many persons, but given *Coker,* should the death penalty be permissible when death does not actually occur? For that matter, given *Coker,* should death be an impermissible penalty for such a crime even if death does occur? The hijacker, like the rapist, may simultaneously commit another crime, but the hijacker, "as such, does not take human life."

   (c) When is it constitutional to impose capital punishment on someone guilty of first-degree murder who did not actually intend to take life? Consider the situations of this kind that we have explored in previous sections of this chapter: an offender who causes death accidentally or even recklessly in the course of committing rape; an accomplice, not intending to kill, who is held for a homicide perpetrated accidentally, recklessly, or even intentionally by his cofelon. Given *Coker,* should capital punishment be permissible in such cases? For Eighth Amendment purposes, should the proportionality analysis focus on the injury caused or on the injury intended?

   In Enmund v. Florida, 458 U.S. 782 (1982), the evidence suggested that the defendant had waited in a getaway car while two accomplices approached a rural farmhouse and then robbed and murdered the elderly couple who lived there. The defendant was convicted of capital murder and sentenced to death, on the theory that the felony-murder rule and the Florida law of aiding and abetting made Enmund responsible for the lethal acts of his cofelons. The Supreme Court held (5–4) that the Eighth Amendment prohibits imposition of the death penalty on a defendant "who does not himself kill, attempt to kill, or intend that a killing take place or that lethal force will be employed." Id. at 797. In an opinion by Justice White, the Court stressed that Enmund's culpability was "plainly different from that of the robbers who killed" and that it is "fundamental that 'causing harm intentionally must be punished more severely than causing the same harm unintentionally.'" Id. at 798, quoting H. L. A. Hart, Punishment and Responsibility 162 (1968).

Tison v. Arizona, 481 U.S. 137 (1987), involved two brothers, Raymond and Ricky Tison, who helped their father Gary escape from prison, where he was serving time on a murder conviction for killing a guard in a prior prison escape attempt. The Arizona court found that Raymond and Ricky supplied weapons and a getaway car to their father, knowing his willingness to use lethal force to effect his escape. They helped him lock up the guards and fled with him into the desert. During the course of the escape, the Tisons decided to flag down a passing motorist in order to steal another car. After they had succeeded in stopping a car carrying a family of four, Gary Tison guarded the group and sent his two sons away to get water; while Raymond and Ricky were some distance away, their father murdered all four of the captives (including a two-year-old child). Gary Tison subsequently escaped into the desert but died there of exposure. Raymond and Ricky were apprehended, convicted of capital murder for the four killings committed by their father, and sentenced to death.

Do the death sentences in *Tison* violate the Eighth Amendment proportionality requirement as developed in *Enmund*? A 5–4 majority of the Supreme Court did not think so. Recognizing that the defendants neither committed the killing nor had an actual intent to kill, the Court held that "major participation in the felony committed, combined with reckless indifference to human life, is sufficient to satisfy the *Enmund* culpability requirement" (id. at 158). Justice O'Connor, writing for the majority, explained (id. at 157):

> [S]ome nonintentional murderers may be among the most dangerous and inhumane of all — the person who tortures another not caring whether the victim lives or dies, or the robber who shoots someone in the course of the robbery, utterly indifferent to the fact that the desire to rob may have the unintended consequence of killing the victim as well as taking the victim's property. This reckless indifference to the value of human life may be every bit as shocking to the moral sense as an "intent to kill." Indeed it is for this very reason that the common law and modern criminal codes alike have classified behavior such as occurred in this case along with intentional murders. See, e.g., G. Fletcher, Rethinking Criminal Law §6.5, pp. 447-448 (1978) (". . . [T]he Model Penal Code treats reckless killing, 'manifesting extreme indifference to the value of human life,' as equivalent to purposeful and knowing killing.")

What should be the result if the killing is neither intentional nor reckless? Suppose, for example, that a robber inflicts no violent injuries but that a robbery victim dies of a heart attack induced by fright. (Reconsider the facts of People v.

Stamp, page 471 supra). Or suppose that a robber pushes the victim away and that the latter trips, falls and suffers a fatal cranial injury. Does the *Enmund-Tison* requirement — that reckless indifference to human life is a prerequisite to capital punishment — apply only when the defendant is not the actual killer? In *Tison*, Justice O'Connor implied that a felony murderer who "actually killed" could be executed even when the killing was purely accidental (481 U.S. at 150), and the California Supreme Court has so held, People v. Anderson, 742 P.2d 1306 (Cal. 1987). Is this defensible? As a matter of Eighth Amendment proportionality analysis, how does a defendant's role as the "actual" killer substitute for the *culpability* requirement of a murderous mens rea? The issue is examined in Welsh S. White, Life in the Balance 92-96 (1984).

For a careful critique of *Tison* and the indeterminacy of its test for applying the Eighth Amendment proportionality requirement, see Richard A. Rosen, Felony Murder and the Eighth Amendment Jurisprudence of Death, 31 B.C.L. Rev. 1103, 1146-1163 (1990).

4. In Callins v. Collins, 114 S. Ct. 1127 (1994), Justice Blackmun, dissenting from the Supreme Court's refusal to review Callins's death sentence, offered the following comments on the law of capital punishment (id. at 1129-1135):

> Experience has taught us that the constitutional goal of eliminating arbitrariness and discrimination from the administration of death, see Furman v. Georgia, can never be achieved without compromising an equally essential component of fundamental fairness — individualized sentencing. See Lockett v. Ohio, 438 U.S. 586 (1978).
>
> It is tempting, when faced with conflicting constitutional commands, to sacrifice one for the other or to assume that an acceptable balance between them already has been struck. In the context of the death penalty, however, such jurisprudential maneuvers are wholly inappropriate. The death penalty must be imposed "fairly, and with reasonable consistency, or not at all." Eddings v. Oklahoma, 455 U.S. 104, 112 (1982). . . .
>
> From this day forward, I no longer shall tinker with the machinery of death. For more than 20 years I have endeavored — indeed, I have struggled — along with a majority of this Court, to develop procedural and substantive rules that would lend more than the mere appearance of fairness to the death penalty endeavor. Rather than continue to coddle the Court's delusion that the desired level of fairness has been achieved, . . . I feel morally and intellectually obligated simply to concede that the death penalty experiment has failed. It is virtually self-evident to me now that no combination of procedural rules or substantive regulations ever can save the death penalty from its inherent constitutional deficiencies. . . . The problem is that the inevitability of factual, legal, and moral error gives us a system that we know must wrongly kill some defendants, a system that fails to deliver the fair, consistent, and reliable sentences of death required by the Constitution. . . .
>
> Although most of the public seems to desire, and the Constitution appears to permit, the penalty of death, it surely is beyond dispute that if the death penalty cannot be administered consistently and rationally, it may not be administered at all. . . .
>
> There is a heightened need for fairness in the administration of death. This unique level of fairness is born of the appreciation that death truly is different from all other punishments a society inflicts upon its citizens. . . . Because of the qualitative difference of the death penalty, "there is a corresponding difference in the need for reliability in the determination that death is the appropriate punishment in a specific case." [*Woodson*, 428 U.S. at 305.] In *Woodson*, a decision striking down

mandatory death penalty statutes as unconstitutional, a plurality of the Court explained: "A process that accords no significance to relevant facets of the character and record of the individual offender or the circumstances of the particular offense excludes from consideration in fixing the ultimate punishment of death the possibility of compassionate or mitigating factors stemming from the diverse frailties of humankind." Id., at 304.

While the risk of mistake in the determination of the appropriate penalty may be tolerated in other areas of the criminal law, "in capital cases the fundamental respect for humanity underlying the Eighth Amendment . . . requires consideration of the character and record of the individual offender and the circumstances of the particular offense as a constitutionally indispensable part of the process of inflicting the penalty of death." Ibid. Thus, although individualized sentencing in capital cases was not considered essential at the time the Constitution was adopted, *Woodson* recognized that American standards of decency could no longer tolerate a capital sentencing process that failed to afford a defendant individualized consideration in the determination whether he or she should live or die. Id. at 301. . . .

I believe the *Woodson-Lockett* line of cases to be fundamentally sound and rooted in American standards of decency that have evolved over time. The notion of prohibiting a sentencer from exercising its discretion "to dispense mercy on the basis of factors too intangible to write into a statute," *Gregg*, 428 U.S., at 222 (White, J., concurring), is offensive to our sense of fundamental fairness and respect for the uniqueness of the individual. . . .

Yet, as several Members of the Court have recognized, there is real "tension" between the need for fairness to the individual and the consistency promised in *Furman*. On the one hand, discretion in capital sentencing must be " 'controlled by clear and objective standards so as to produce non-discriminatory [and reasoned] application.' " *Gregg*, 428 U.S. at 198 (opinion of Stewart, Powell, and Stevens, JJ.). On the other hand, the Constitution also requires that the sentencer be able to consider "any relevant mitigating evidence regarding the defendant's character or background, and the circumstances of the particular offense." The power to consider mitigating evidence that would warrant a sentence less than death is meaningless unless the sentencer has the discretion and authority to dispense mercy based on that evidence. Thus, the Constitution, by requiring a heightened degree of fairness to the individual, and also a greater degree of equality and rationality in the administration of death, demands sentencer discretion that is at once generously expanded and severely restricted.

The theory underlying . . . *Lockett* is that an appropriate balance can be struck between the *Furman* promise of consistency and the *Lockett* requirement of individualized sentencing. . . . While one might hope that providing the sentencer with as much relevant mitigating evidence as possible will lead to more rational and consistent sentences, experience has taught otherwise. It seems that the decision whether a human being should live or die is so inherently subjective — rife with all of life's understandings, experiences, prejudices, and passions — that it inevitably defies the rationality and consistency required by the Constitution.

Justice Scalia, concurring in the Court's denial of review, responded to Justice Blackmun as follows (id. at 1127-1128):

The Fifth Amendment provides that "[n]o person shall be held to answer for a capital . . . crime, unless on a presentment or indictment of a Grand Jury, . . . nor be deprived of life . . . without due process of law." This clearly permits the death penalty to be imposed, and establishes beyond doubt that the death penalty is not one of the "cruel and unusual punishments" prohibited by the Eighth Amendment. . . .

Though Justice Blackmun joins those of us who have acknowledged the incompatibility of the Court's *Furman* and *Lockett-Eddings* lines of jurisprudence, he unfortunately draws the wrong conclusion.... Surely ... at least one of these judicially announced irreconcilable commands which cause the Constitution to prohibit what its text explicitly permits must be wrong.

5. Questions. (a) Interpreting the constitutional text. A clause of the Fifth Amendment omitted from Justice Scalia's quotation provides: "[N]or shall any person be subject for the same offense to be twice put in jeopardy of life or limb." Does this provision of the Constitution permit imposition of severe corporal punishment and "establish beyond doubt that [such a] penalty is not one of the 'cruel and unusual punishments' prohibited by the Eighth Amendment" (*Callins*, supra at 1127)? If not, then is it plausible to read the Constitution's "due process," "equal protection," and "cruel and unusual punishments" clauses as limiting the circumstances in which government is permitted to subject offenders to loss of life or limb?

(b) Reconciling the requirements of consistency and individualization. For a close examination of the tension between *Furman* and *Lockett*, see Scott E. Sunby, The *Lockett* Paradox: Reconciling Guided Discretion and Unguided Mitigation in Capital Sentencing, 38 U.C.L.A.L. Rev. 1147 (1991). Professor Sunby argues (id. at 1207) that death penalty administration does not pose an "all-or-nothing [choice] between discretion or no discretion," and that the Court can continue to seek a middle ground between the position of Justice Scalia (which entails overruling *Lockett*) and that of Justice Blackmun (which entails overruling *Gregg*).

McCLESKEY v. KEMP

Supreme Court of the United States
481 U.S. 279 (1987)

JUSTICE POWELL delivered the opinion of the Court.

This case presents the question whether a complex statistical study that indicates a risk that racial considerations enter into capital sentencing determinations proves that petitioner McCleskey's capital sentence is unconstitutional under the Eighth or Fourteenth Amendment.

I

McCleskey, a black man, was convicted of two counts of armed robbery and one count of murder in the Superior Court of Fulton County, Georgia, on October 12, 1978. McCleskey's convictions arose out of the robbery of a furniture store and the killing of a white police officer during the course of the robbery. The evidence at trial indicated that McCleskey and three accomplices planned and carried out the robbery. All four were armed. . . . During the course of the robbery, a police officer, answering a silent alarm, entered the store through the front door. [Two shots] struck the officer. One hit him in the face and killed him. At trial, the State introduced evidence that at least one of the bullets that struck the officer was fired [by McCleskey].

The jury convicted McCleskey of murder. . . . Under Georgia law, the jury could not consider imposing the death penalty unless it found beyond a reasonable doubt that the murder was accompanied by one of the statutory aggravating circumstances.[a] The jury in this case found two aggravating circumstances to exist beyond a reasonable doubt: the murder was commited during the course of an armed robbery, and the murder was committed upon a peace officer engaged in the performance of his duties. . . . McCleskey offered no mitigating evidence. The jury recommended that he be sentenced to death on the murder charge and to consecutive life sentences on the armed robbery charges. The court followed the jury's recommendation and sentenced McCleskey to death.

On appeal, the Supreme Court of Georgia affirmed the convictions and the sentences. . . .

[After state court challenges, McCleskey] filed a petition for a writ of habeas corpus in the federal District Court for the Northern District of Georgia. His petition raised 18 claims, one of which was that the Georgia capital sentencing process is administered in a racially discriminatory manner in violation of the Eighth and Fourteenth Amendments to the United States Constitution. In support of his claim, McCleskey proffered a statistical study performed by Professors David C. Baldus, George Woodworth, and Charles Pulaski (the Baldus study) that purports to show a disparity in the imposition of the death sentence in Georgia based on the race of the murder victim and, to a lesser extent, the race of the defendant. The Baldus study is actually two sophisticated statistical studies that examine over 2,000 murder cases that occurred in Georgia during the 1970s. The raw numbers collected by Professor Baldus indicate that defendants charged with killing white persons received the death penalty in 11% of the cases, but defendants charged with killing blacks received the death penalty in only 1% of the cases. The raw numbers also indicate a reverse racial disparity according to the race of the defendant: 4% of the black defendants received the death penalty, as opposed to 7% of the white defendants.

Baldus also divided the cases according to the combination of the race of the defendant and the race of the victim. He found that the death penalty was assessed in 22% of the cases involving black defendants and white victims; 8% of the cases involving white defendants and white victims; 1% of the cases involving black defendants and black victims; and 3% of the cases involving white defendants and black victims. . . .

Baldus subjected his data to an extensive analysis, taking account of 230 variables that could have explained the disparities on nonracial grounds. One of his models concludes that, even after taking account of 39 nonracial variables, defendants charged with killing white victims were 4.3 times as likely to receive a death sentence as defendants charged with killing blacks. [T]he Baldus study indicates that black defendants, such as McCleskey, who kill white victims have the greatest likelihood of receiving the death penalty.[5]

---

a. For the text of the Georgia statute, see Gregg v. Georgia, page 527 footnote 48 supra. — Eds.

5. Baldus's 230-variable model divided cases into eight different ranges, according to the estimated aggravation level of the offense. Baldus argued in his testimony to the District Court that the effects of racial bias were most striking in the mid-range cases. "[W]hen the cases become tremendously aggravated so that everybody would agree that if we're going to have a death sentence, these are the cases that should get it, the race effects go away. It's only in the mid-range of cases where the decision makers have a real choice as to what to do. If there's room for the exercise of discretion, then the [racial] factors begin to play a role." Under this model, Baldus found that 14.4% of the black-victim mid-range cases received the death penalty, and 34.4% of the white-victim cases

The District Court . . . found that the methodology of the Baldus study was flawed in several respects. . . . Accordingly, the Court dismissed the petition. The Court of Appeals affirmed. . . .

II

McCleskey's first claim is that the Georgia capital punishment statute violates the Equal Protection Clause of the Fourteenth Amendment.[7] . . . As a black defendant who killed a white victim, McCleskey claims that the Baldus study demonstrates that he was discriminated against because of his race and because of the race of his victim. . . .

Our analysis begins with the basic principle that a defendant who alleges an equal protection violation has the burden of proving "the existence of purposeful discrimination." . . . [T]o prevail under the Equal Protection Clause, McCleskey must prove that the decision-makers in *his* case acted with discriminatory purpose. He offers no evidence specific to his own case that would support an inference that racial considerations played a part in his sentence. Instead, he relies solely on the Baldus study. . . . McCleskey's claim that these statistics are sufficient proof of discrimination, without regard to the facts of a particular case, would extend to all capital cases in Georgia, at least where the victim was white and the defendant is black.

. . . McCleskey challenges decisions at the heart of the State's criminal justice system. . . . Because discretion is essential to the criminal justice process, we would demand exceptionally clear proof before we would infer that the discretion had been abused. . . . Accordingly, we hold that the Baldus study is clearly insufficient to support an inference that any of the decisionmakers in McCleskey's case acted with discriminatory purpose.

McCleskey also suggests that the Baldus study proves that the State as a whole has acted with a discriminatory purpose. He appears to argue that the State has violated the Equal Protection Clause by adopting the capital punishment statute and allowing it to remain in force despite its allegedly discriminatory application. But " '[d]iscriminatory purpose' . . . implies more than intent as volition or intent as awareness of consequences. It implies that the decisionmaker, in this case a state legislature, selected or reaffirmed a particular course of action at least in part 'because of,' not merely 'in spite of,' its adverse effects upon an identifiable group." For this claim to prevail, McCleskey would have to prove that the Georgia Legislature enacted or maintained the death penalty statute

---

received the death penalty. According to Baldus, the facts of McCleskey's case placed it within the mid-range.

7. Although the District Court rejected the findings of the Baldus study as flawed, the Court of Appeals assumed that the study is valid and reached the constitutional issues. Accordingly, those issues are before us. As did the Court of Appeals, we assume the study is valid statistically without reviewing the factual findings of the District Court. Our assumption that the Baldus study is statistically valid does not include the assumption that the study shows that racial considerations actually enter into any sentencing decisions in Georgia. Even a sophisticated multiple regression analysis such as the Baldus study can only demonstrate a *risk* that the factor of race entered into some capital sentencing decisions and a necessarily lesser risk that race entered into any particular sentencing decision.

because of an anticipated racially discriminatory effect. In Gregg v. Georgia, 428 U.S. 153 (1976), this Court found that the Georgia capital sentencing system could operate in a fair and neutral manner. There was no evidence then, and there is none now, that the Georgia Legislature enacted the capital punishment statute to further a racially discriminatory purpose. . . .

[IV]

McCleskey also argues that the Baldus study demonstrates that the Georgia capital sentencing system violates the Eighth Amendment. . . .

To evaluate McCleskey's challenge, we must examine exactly what the Baldus study may show. Even Professor Baldus does not contend that his statistics *prove* that race enters into any capital sentencing decisions or that race was a factor in McCleskey's particular case.[29] . . . There is, of course, some risk of racial prejudice influencing a jury's decision in a criminal case. . . . The question "is at what point that risk becomes constitutionally unacceptable."

McCleskey's argument that the Constitution condemns the discretion allowed decisionmakers in the Georgia capital sentencing system is antithetical to the fundamental role of discretion in our criminal justice system. Discretion in the criminal justice system offers substantial benefits to the criminal defendant. Not only can a jury decline to impose the death sentence, it can decline to convict, or choose to convict of a lesser offense. . . . Similarly, . . . a prosecutor can decline to charge, offer a plea bargain,[34] or decline to seek a death sentence in any particular case. Of course, "the power to be lenient [also] is the power to discriminate," K. Davis, Discretionary Justice 170 (1973), but a capital-punishment system that did not allow for discretionary acts of leniency "would be totally alien to our notions of criminal justice." Gregg v. Georgia, 428 U.S., at 200, n. 50.

. . . The discrepancy indicated by the Baldus study is "a far cry from the major systemic defects identified in *Furman.*"[36] Where the discretion that is fundamental to our criminal process is involved, we decline to assume that what is unexplained is invidious.[b] In light of the safeguards designed to minimize racial bias in the process, the fundamental value of jury trial in our criminal justice system, and the benefits that discretion provides to criminal defendants, we hold

29. According to Professor Baldus: "McCleskey's case falls in [a] grey area where . . . you would find the greatest likelihood that some inappropriate consideration may have come to bear on the decision. In an analysis of this type, obviously one cannot say that we can say to a moral certainty what it was that influenced the decision. We can't do that."

[*Questions:* Is the Court saying that in order to "prove" a proposition for purposes of constitutional litigation, a party must establish that proposition "to a moral certainty"? Is this the proper burden of persuasion? — EDS.]

34. In this case, for example, McCleskey declined to enter a guilty plea. According to his trial attorney: "[T]he Prosecutor was indicating that we might be able to work out a life sentence if he were willing to enter a plea. But we never reached any concrete stage on that because Mr. McCleskey's attitude was that he didn't want to enter a plea. So it never got any further than just talking about it."

36. The Baldus study in fact confirms that the Georgia system results in a reasonable level of proportionality among the class of murderers eligible for the death penalty. As Professor Baldus confirmed, the system sorts out cases where the sentence of death is highly likely and highly unlikely, leaving a mid-range of cases where the imposition of the death penalty in any particular case is less predictable.

b. Is the pattern in this case "unexplained"? — EDS.

that the Baldus study does not demonstrate a constitutionally significant risk of racial bias affecting the Georgia capital-sentencing process.[37]

V

Two additional concerns inform our decision in this case. First, McCleskey's claim, taken to its logical conclusion, throws into serious question the principles that underlie our entire criminal justice system. The Eighth Amendment is not limited in application to capital punishment, but applies to all penalties. Thus, if we accepted McCleskey's claim that racial bias has impermissibly tainted the capital sentencing decision, we could soon be faced with similar claims as to other types of penalty. Moreover, the claim that his sentence rests on the irrelevant factor of race easily could be extended to apply to claims based on unexplained discrepancies that correlate to membership in other minority groups, and even to gender. . . . Also, there is no logical reason that such a claim need be limited to racial or sexual bias. If arbitrary and capricious punishment is the touchstone under the Eighth Amendment, such a claim could — at least in theory — be based upon any arbitrary variable, such as the defendant's facial characteristics, or the physical attractiveness of the defendant or the victim,[44] that some statistical study indicates may be influential in jury decisionmaking. As these examples illustrate, there is no limiting principle to the type of challenge brought by McCleskey. . . .

Second, McCleskey's arguments are best presented to the legislative bodies. . . . Legislatures also are better qualified to weigh and "evaluate the results of statistical studies in terms of their own local conditions and with a flexibility of approach that is not available to the courts," Gregg v. Georgia, supra. . . . Despite McCleskey's wide ranging arguments that basically challenge the validity of capital punishment in our multi-racial society, the only question before us is whether in his case the law of Georgia was properly applied. We agree with the District Court and the Court of Appeals for the Eleventh Circuit that this was carefully and correctly done in this case.

Accordingly, we affirm. . . .

Justice Brennan, [with whom Justices Marshall, Blackmun, and Stevens join], dissenting. . . .

It is important to emphasize at the outset that the Court's observation that McCleskey cannot prove the influence of race on any particular sentencing decision is irrelevant in evaluating his Eighth Amendment claim. Since Furman v. Georgia, 408 U.S. 238 (1972), the Court has been concerned with the *risk* of the imposition of an arbitrary sentence, rather than the proven fact of one. . . . As Justice O'Connor observed in Caldwell v. Mississippi, 472 U.S. 320, 343 (1985), a death sentence must be struck down when the circumstances under which it

37. . . . The dissent repeatedly emphasizes the need for "a uniquely high degree of rationality in imposing the death penalty." [Yet,] no suggestion is made as to how greater "rationality" could be achieved under any type of statute that authorizes capital punishment. [T]he dissent's call for greater rationality is no less than a claim that a capital-punishment system cannot be administered in accord with the Constitution. . . .

44. Some studies indicate that physically attractive defendants receive greater leniency in sentencing than unattractive defendants, and that offenders whose victims are physically attractive receive harsher sentences than defendants with less attractive victims.

has been imposed "creat[e] an unacceptable *risk* that 'the death penalty [may have been] meted out arbitrarily or capriciously' or through 'whim or mistake'" (emphasis added). This emphasis on risk . . . reflects the fact that concern for arbitrariness focuses on the rationality of the system as a whole, and that a system that features a significant probability that sentencing decisions are influenced by impermissible considerations cannot be regarded as rational. . . . McCleskey's claim does differ, however, in one respect from these earlier cases: it is the first to base a challenge not on speculation about how a system *might* operate, but on empirical documentation on how it *does* operate. . . .

The Baldus study . . . distinguishes between those cases in which (1) the jury exercises virtually no discretion because the strength or weakness of aggravating factors usually suggests that only one outcome is appropriate; and (2) cases reflecting an "intermediate" level of aggravation, in which the jury has considerable discretion in choosing a sentence. McCleskey's case falls into the intermediate range. In such cases, . . . just under 59% — almost 6 in 10 — defendants comparable to McCleskey would not have received the death penalty if their victims had been black. . . .

The statistical evidence in this case . . . relentlessly documents the risk that McCleskey's sentence was influenced by racial considerations. This evidence shows that there is a better than even chance in Georgia that race will influence the decision to impose the death penalty: a majority of defendants in white-victim crimes would not have been sentenced to die if their victims had been black. . . . In determining the guilt of a defendant, a state must prove its case beyond a reasonable doubt. That is, we refuse to convict if the chance of error is simply less likely than not. Surely, we should not be willing to take a person's life if the chance that his death sentence was irrationally imposed is *more* likely than not. . . .

Georgia's legacy of a race-conscious criminal justice system . . . indicate[s] that McCleskey's claim is not a fanciful product of mere statistical artifice. For many years, Georgia operated openly and formally precisely the type of dual system the evidence shows is still effectively in place. . . . By the time of the Civil War, a dual system of crime and punishment was well established in Georgia. The state criminal code contained separate sections for "Slaves and Free Persons of Color" and for all other persons. [Justice Brennan here cited numerous instances in which the Georgia Penal Code had provided more severe punishments for crimes committed by blacks and for crimes (especially rape) committed against white victims.]

. . . Citation of past practices does not justify the automatic condemnation of current ones. But it would be unrealistic to ignore the influence of history in assessing the plausible implications of McCleskey's evidence. "[A]mericans share a historical experience that has resulted in individuals within the culture ubiquitously attaching a significance to race that is irrational and often outside their awareness." Lawrence, The Id, The Ego, and Equal Protection: Reckoning With Unconscious Racism, 39 Stan. L. Rev. 327 (1987). As we said in Rose v. Mitchell:

> [W]e . . . cannot deny that, 114 years after the close of the War Between the States and nearly 100 years after *Strauder*, racial and other forms of discrimination still remain a fact of life, in the administration of justice as in our society as a whole.

Perhaps today that discrimination takes a form more subtle than before. But it is not less real or pernicious. 443 U.S. 545, 558-559 (1979).

. . . The Court . . . declines to find McCleskey's evidence sufficient in view of "the safeguards designed to minimize racial bias in the [capital sentencing] process." In Gregg v. Georgia, 428 U.S., at 226, the Court rejected a facial challenge to the Georgia capital sentencing statute, describing such a challenge as based on "simply an assertion of lack of faith" that the system could operate in a fair manner (White, J., concurring). Justice White observed that the claim that prosecutors might act in an arbitrary fashion was "unsupported by any facts." . . . It is clear that *Gregg* bestowed no permanent approval on the Georgia system. It simply held that the State's statutory safeguards were assumed sufficient to channel discretion without evidence otherwise. . . .

The Court next states [its] fear that recognition of McCleskey's claim would open the door to widespread challenges to all aspects of criminal sentencing. [T]o reject McCleskey's powerful evidence on this basis is to ignore both the qualitatively different character of the death penalty and the particular repugnance of racial discrimination. . . .

Finally, the Court justifies its rejection of McCleskey's claim by cautioning against usurpation of the legislatures' role in devising and monitoring criminal punishment. . . . Those whom we would banish from society or from the human community itself often speak in too faint a voice to be heard above society's demand for punishment. It is the particular role of courts to hear these voices, for the Constitution declares that the majoritarian chorus may not alone dictate the conditions of social life. . . .

. . . [I]t has been scarcely a generation since this Court's first decision striking down racial segregation, and barely two decades since the legislative prohibition of racial discrimination in major domains of national life. These have been honorable steps, but we cannot pretend that in three decades we have completely escaped the grip of an historical legacy spanning centuries. Warren McCleskey's evidence confronts us with the subtle and persistent influence of the past. His message is a disturbing one to a society that has formally repudiated racism, and a frustrating one to a Nation accustomed to regarding its destiny as the product of its own will. Nonetheless, we ignore him at our peril, for we remain imprisoned by the past as long as we deny its influence in the present. . . .

JUSTICE BLACKMUN, [with whom JUSTICES MARSHALL, BRENNAN, and STEVENS join], dissenting. . . .

The Court today seems to give a new meaning to our recognition that death is different. Rather than requiring "a correspondingly greater degree of scrutiny of the capital sentencing determination," California v. Ramos, 463 U.S. 992, 998-999 (1983), the Court relies on the very fact that this is a case involving capital punishment to apply a *lesser* standard of scrutiny under the Equal Protection Clause. . . .

A criminal defendant alleging an equal protection violation must prove the existence of purposeful discrimination. Washington v. Davis, 426 U.S. 229 (1976). He may establish a prima facie case of purposeful discrimination "by showing that the totality of the relevant facts gives rise to an inference of discriminatory purpose." Batson v. Kentucky, 106 S. Ct., at 1721. Once the defendant establishes a prima facie case, the burden shifts to the prosecution to rebut that case. "The State cannot meet his burden on mere general assertions that its officials did not discriminate or that they properly performed their official duties." Ibid. The State must demonstrate that the challenged effect was due to "'permissible racially neutral selection criteria.'" Ibid. . . .

McCleskey . . . demonstrated that it was more likely than not that the fact that the victim he was charged with killing was white determined that he received a sentence of death — 20 out of every 34 defendants in McCleskey's midrange category would not have been sentenced to be executed if their victims had been black. [T]he race of the victim is more important in explaining the imposition of a death sentence than is the factor whether the defendant was a prime mover in the homicide.[9] Similarly, the race-of-victim factor is nearly as crucial as the statutory aggravating circumstance whether the defendant had a prior record of a conviction for a capital crime.[10] . . . In sum, McCleskey has demonstrated a clear pattern of differential treatment according to race that is "unexplainable on grounds other than race."

The Court's explanations for its failure to apply this well-established equal protection analysis to this case are not persuasive. . . . I do not believe acceptance of McCleskey's claim would eliminate capital punishment in Georgia. [I]n extremely aggravated murders the risk of discriminatory enforcement of the death penalty is minimized. . . . Moreover, the establishment of guidelines for Assistant District Attorneys as to the appropriate basis for exercising their discretion at the various steps in the prosecution of a case would provide at least a measure of consistency. The Court's emphasis on the procedural safeguards in the system ignores the fact that there are none whatsoever during the crucial process leading up to trial. As Justice White stated for the plurality in Turner v. Murray, I find "the risk that racial prejudice may have infected petitioner's capital sentencing unacceptable in light of the ease with which that risk could have been minimized." 106 S. Ct., at 1688. I dissent.

JUSTICE STEVENS, with whom JUSTICE BLACKMUN joins, dissenting.

. . . This sort of disparity is constitutionally intolerable. It flagrantly violates the Court's prior "insistence that capital punishment be imposed fairly, and with reasonable consistency, or not at all." Eddings v. Oklahoma, 455 U.S. 104, 112 (1982).

The Court's decision appears to be based on a fear that the acceptance of McCleskey's claim would sound the death knell for capital punishment in Georgia. If society were indeed forced to choose between a racially discriminatory death penalty (one that provides heightened protection against murder "for whites only") and no death penalty at all, the choice mandated by the Constitution would be plain. But the Court's fear is unfounded. One of the lessons of the Baldus study is that there exist certain categories of extremely serious crimes for which prosecutors consistently seek, and juries consistently impose, the death penalty without regard to the race of the victim or the race of the offender. If Georgia were to narrow the class of death-eligible defendants to those categories, the danger of arbitrary and discriminatory imposition of the death penalty

---

9. A defendant's chances of receiving a death sentence increase by a factor of 4.3 if the victim is white, but only by 2.3 if the defendant was the prime mover behind the homicide.

10. A prior record of a conviction for murder, armed robbery, rape, or kidnapping with bodily injury increases the chances of a defendant's receiving a death sentence by a factor of 4.9.

would be significantly decreased, if not eradicated.... [S]uch a restructuring of the sentencing scheme is surely not too high a price to pay....

NOTES

1. *Racial discrimination.* For helpful discussions of the issues posed by the *McCleskey* case, see David C. Baldus, George G. Woodworth & Charles A. Pulaski, Equal Justice and the Death Penalty (1990); Welsh S. White, The Death Penalty in the Eighties, 113-139 (1987); Randall Kennedy, *McCleskey v. Kemp:* Race, Capital Punishment, and the Supreme Court, 101 Harv. L. Rev. 1388 (1988); Samuel R. Gross, Race and Death: The Judicial Evaluation of Evidence of Discrimination in Capital Sentencing, 18 U.C. Davis L. Rev. 1275 (1985).

For several years, critics of the result in *McCleskey* have sought to overturn the decision by enacting national legislation requiring states to demonstrate that their enforcement of the death penalty is racially neutral. A provision to this effect was passed by the United States House of Representatives as part of the Crime Control Act of 1994, but the House-Senate conference committee deleted it from the bill. See N.Y. Times, July 29, 1994, at A1, A9.

2. *Gender discrimination with respect to defendants?* Consider Elizabeth Rapaport, The Death Penalty and Gender Discrimination, 25 Law & Socy. Rev. 367, 367-368 (1991):

> A gross comparison of the death-sentencing rates for men and women suggests that women convicted of murder are underrepresented on death row. Two percent of men but only one tenth of 1 percent of women convicted of murder are condemned to die.
>
> For a feminist to raise the issue of gender discrimination and capital punishment is not an altogether comfortable undertaking. At worst, it suggests a campaign to exterminate a few more wretched sisters. In my view, however, the issue is worth confronting. The reputed leniency that women receive with respect to death sentencing supports the view widely held in our society that women are incapable of achieving, nor are they in fact held to, the same standards of personal responsibility as are men. Although there may well be fields of endeavor in which the most profound forms of equality call for recognition of difference, equal democratic citizenship can proceed from no other premise than that of equal personal responsibility for decisions and actions. The chivalry from which women supposedly benefit is too costly: In ideological coin it is supposed to be repaid with tacit recognition of the moral inferiority of females and our lack of aptitude for full citizenship. As a matter of both logic and political necessity, then, feminists must embrace either gender-neutral evenhandedness or abolitionism.

Professor Rapaport goes on to examine data on the characteristics of male and female murderers. She concludes that a woman offender's low likelihood of receiving a death sentence is primarily the result of legitimate sentencing variables (less serious crimes or less serious prior records), but that women's "underrepresentation" on death row may also be due in part to the continued hold of the "chivalry" notion. (Id. at 374.)

3. *Gender discrimination with respect to victims?* The types of murder classified as "aggravated," and therefore eligible for the death penalty, typically include felony murders and other "stranger" homicides. See, for example, the Georgia statute quoted at page 527 n. 48 supra. Conversely, killings of spouses or acquaintances, which are often killings of a woman by a man, are much less likely to be punished by the death penalty. Does this mean that there is a "*McCleskey*" problem of inadequate protection for one class of potential victims? Consider Rapaport, supra Note 2, at 377-382:

> Domestic crimes may . . . become capital cases if they are regarded as especially brutal crimes or if they are also pecuniary crimes. But the paradigmatic domestic killing, arising out of hot anger at someone who is capable, as it were by definition, of calling out painful and sudden emotion in his or her killer, is virtually the antithesis of a capital murder. Yet there are features of domestic homicides that could plausibly be regarded as among the most reprehensible crimes: They involve the betrayal of familial trust and responsibility. . . . They also have characteristics that could be read as inherent extreme brutality. The victims of family murders are typically especially vulnerable to their killers because of physical weakness and psychological dependency. Often the victims have been the objects of prior and habitual violence by their killers.
>
> . . . [T]here is, from a feminist point of view, an invidious subordination of the interests of women involved in the failure of the statutes to attach our society's most profound condemnation to crimes that destroy the domestic peace. . . . The supposition that predatory violence is more reprehensible than domestic violence is a symptom or effect of the ancient family privacy doctrine that has supported male domestic authority, and the parental authority of both sexes, at the price of tolerating if not encouraging a culture of domestic violence.
>
> One piece of evidence that on the surface suggests social valuing of female victims is the finding that murderers of women are more likely to be death sentenced than murderers of men. We cannot, however, infer from this finding that the higher likelihood of a death sentence reflects a societal judgment that murders of female victims are in all circumstances more serious than murders of male victims. . . . It is congruent with patriarchal values, and offensive to feminist values, that violence against women belonging to others be more heavily sanctioned than violence against your own women.
>
> . . . [T]he criminal law is not being mobilized to sufficiently discredit, discourage, and sanction crimes of domestic oppression from which women and children suffer disproportionately.

CHAPTER
6

THE SIGNIFICANCE OF
RESULTING HARM

A. CAUSATION

Where a crime is defined without regard to any result of the defendant's conduct (for example, attempt, conspiracy, burglary), there is no need to face the issue of causation. But where a particular result of a defendant's conduct is a necessary element of the crime charged, a perplexing problem sometimes arises as to whether the defendant's act caused the result. Homicide cases are the most fertile source of causation problems. When the actor kills the very person he meant to kill (or knew he would kill), in precisely the way he intended, no causation difficulty arises. Nor is there difficulty in the case of unintended killings when the death occurs in precisely the way that the defendant's risky conduct made likely. But when the intended death occurs in a way not intended or the unintended death occurs in an unlikely way, the law must distinguish variations (between the actual result and the result intended or risked) that preclude liability from variations that do not preclude liability. The following hypotheticals will suggest the scope of the problem.

(1) Accused places poison by the bedside of his sick wife intending that she drink it. During the night she dies of a heart attack without having consumed the drink.
(2) Same as above, except that the wife sips the poison and is repelled by the taste; to wash it away, she goes to the bathroom for water, slips and injures herself fatally.
(3) Accused attempts to shoot her husband, but she misses. He thereupon boards a train for his mother's home and is killed in a train wreck.
(4) Accused shoots at deceased intending to kill him. The bullet misses but deceased dies of fright.
(5) While thoroughly intoxicated, accused No. 1 drives his car containing sleeping children at a speed greatly in excess of the speed limit. He crashes into the rear of a truck stalled in the middle of the road around a bend, the truck's driver, accused No. 2, having failed to

leave his lights on or otherwise give warning to approaching cars. The children of accused No. 1 are killed in the crash.

(6) Accused administers a vicious blow to victim's head with a black-jack. The victim is taken to a hospital for treatment where (a) due to negligent medical treatment of the wound he dies of meningitis, (b) he dies of scarlet fever communicated by a nurse, (c) he is mortally wounded by a knife-wielding maniac, (d) he is decapitated by a maniac, (e) he deliberately takes a fatal dose of sleeping pills to end his misery, or (f) he is seized with an attack of appendicitis from which he dies.

(7) Accused No. 1 throws a live hand grenade into the room of accused No. 2 intending to kill him. The latter seizes it and throws it out his window where it falls to the crowded street below, exploding and killing several persons.

(8) Accused and deceased engage in an armed robbery. Deceased is killed in an exchange of bullets with the police.

1. Foreseeability and Coincidence

PEOPLE v. ACOSTA

Court of Appeal of California, 4th Appellate District
284 Cal. Rptr. 117 (1991)

WALLIN, J. Vincent William Acosta appeals his conviction on three counts of second degree murder . . . contending: (1) there was insufficient evidence his conduct was the proximate cause of the deaths; (2) there was insufficient evidence of malice. . . .

At 10 P.M. on March 10, 1987, Officers Salceda and Francis of the Santa Ana Police Department's automobile theft detail saw Acosta in Elvira Salazar's stolen Nissan Pulsar parked on the street. The officers approached Acosta and identified themselves. Acosta inched the Pulsar forward, then accelerated rapidly. He led Salceda, Francis and officers from other agencies on a 48-mile chase along numerous surface streets and freeways throughout Orange County. The chase ended near Acosta's residence in Anaheim.

During the chase, Acosta engaged in some of the most egregious driving tactics imaginable. He ran stop signs and red lights, and drove on the wrong side of streets, causing oncoming traffic to scatter or swerve to avoid colliding with him. . . .

Police helicopters from Anaheim, Costa Mesa, Huntington Beach, and Newport Beach assisted in the chase by tracking Acosta. During the early part of the pursuit, the Costa Mesa and Newport Beach craft were used, pinpointing Acosta's location with their high beam spotlights. The Costa Mesa helicopter was leading the pursuit, in front of and below the Newport Beach helicopter. As they flew into Newport Beach, the pilots agreed the Newport Beach craft should take the lead. . . .

At the direction of the Costa Mesa pilot, the Newport Beach helicopter moved forward and descended while the Costa Mesa helicopter banked to the right. Shortly after commencing this procedure, the Costa Mesa helicopter, having terminated radio communication, came up under the Newport Beach helicopter from the right rear and collided with it. Both helicopters fell to the ground. Three occupants in the Costa Mesa helicopter died as a result of the crash.

Menzies Turner, a retired Federal Aviation Administration (FAA) investigator, testified as an expert and concluded the accident occurred because the Costa Mesa helicopter, the faster of the two aircraft, made a 360-degree turn and closed too rapidly on the Newport Beach helicopter. He opined the Costa Mesa helicopter's pilot violated an FAA regulation prohibiting careless and reckless operation of an aircraft by failing to properly clear the area, not maintaining communication with the Newport Beach helicopter, failing to keep the other aircraft in view at all times, and not changing his altitude. He also testified the Costa Mesa pilot violated another FAA regulation prohibiting operation of one aircraft so close to another as to create a collision hazard.

Turner could not think of any reason for the Costa Mesa helicopter's erratic movement. The maneuver was not a difficult one, and was not affected by the ground activity at the time. He had never heard of a midair collision between two police helicopters involved in tracking a ground pursuit, and had never investigated a midair collision involving helicopters.[3] . . .

Acosta claims there was insufficient evidence . . . that he proximately caused the deaths of the victims. . . .

Acosta argues that although a collision between ground vehicles was a foreseeable result of his conduct, one between airborne helicopters was not, noting his expert had never heard of a similar incident. He also contends the Costa Mesa helicopter pilot's violation of FAA regulations was a superseding cause. Because the deaths here were unusual, to say the least, the issue deserves special scrutiny. . . .

"Proximate cause" is the term historically used[6] to separate those results for which an actor will be held responsible from those not carrying such responsibility. The term is, in a sense, artificial, serving matters of policy surrounding tort and criminal law and based partly on expediency and partly on concerns of fairness and justice. Because such concerns are sometimes more a matter of "common sense" than pure logic, the line of demarcation is flexible, and attempts to lay down uniform tests which apply evenly in all situations have failed. That does not mean general guidelines and approaches to analysis cannot be constructed.

The threshold question in examining causation is whether the defendant's act was an "actual cause" of the victim's injury. It is a sine qua non test: But for the defendant's act would the injury have occurred? Unless an act is an actual cause of the injury, it will not be considered a proximate cause.

[The court then reviewed the various verbal tests used by courts and concluded that in this case the issue was whether the death of the helicopter pilots was foreseeable.]

Prosser and Keeton, in an in-depth discussion of the dynamics of foresight, conclude that although it is desirable to exclude extremely remarkable and unusual results from the purview of proximate cause, it is virtually impossible to

---

3. Our research yielded no published civil or criminal case nationwide which involved a two-helicopter collision.

6. The American Law Institute has urged the use of "legal cause" instead. Although there is some merit to its arguments, I abide with the traditional term, "proximate cause."

express a logical verbal formula which will produce uniform results. (Prosser & Keeton, [Torts] 300 [(5th ed. 1984)].) I agree. The standard should be simply stated, exclude extraordinary results, and allow the trier of fact to determine the issue on the particular facts of the case using "the common sense of the common man as to common things." As with other ultimate issues, appellate courts must review that determination, giving due deference to the trier of fact.

The "highly extraordinary result" standard serves that purpose. It is consistent with the definition of foreseeability used in California. It does not involve the defendant's state of mind, but focuses upon the objective conditions present when he acts.[19] . . .

Here, but for Acosta's conduct of fleeing the police, the helicopters would never have been in position for the crash. . . .

The result was not highly extraordinary. Although a two-helicopter collision was unknown to expert witness Turner and no reported cases describe one, it was "a possible consequence which reasonably might have been contemplated." Given the emotional dynamics of any police pursuit, there is an "appreciable probability" that one of the pursuers, in the heat of the chase, may act negligently or recklessly to catch the quarry. That no pursuits have ever before resulted in a helicopter crash or midair collision is more a comment on police flying skill and technology than upon the innate probabilities involved. . . .

[T]he concurring opinion offers [no] case law "on all fours," suggesting this case is unique and presents a close question. Partly because this is so, it is appropriate to rely on two compelling factors: the jury found proximate cause based on proper instructions, and the dearth of case law to support a rejection of that finding. Given these circumstances, a finding of proximate cause is appropriate. . . .

[On the other issue in the case, whether there was sufficient evidence of malice, the court found in the negative because there was not enough evidence to show that Acosta consciously disregarded the risk to the helicopter pilots: "In the absence of more evidence, no reasonable juror could find a conscious disregard for a risk which is barely objectively cognizable."]

The judgment is reversed. . . .

CROSBY, J., . . . Whether the defendant may be held criminally culpable for the tragic deaths in this case is the key issue before us. Justice Wallin says yes, but not for murder. . . . I disagree . . . because the law does not assign blame to an otherwise blameworthy actor when neither the intervening negligent conduct nor the risk of harm was foreseeable.

Or, as Justice Cardozo put it,

We are told that one who drives at reckless speed through a crowded city street is guilty of a negligent act and, therefore, of a wrongful one irrespective of the consequences. Negligent the act is, and wrongful in the sense that it is unsocial, but wrongful and unsocial in relation to other travelers, only because the eye of vigilance perceives the risk of damage. . . . [R]isk imports relation; it is risk to another or to others within the range of apprehension.

19. The Model Penal Code takes a similar approach, focusing on whether the result is "too remote or accidental in its occurrence to have a [just] bearing on the actor's liability or on the gravity of his offense." (Model Pen. Code, §2.03(2)(b).) . . .

(Palsgraf v. Long Island R. Co. (1928) 248 N.Y. 339.) The occupants of these helicopters were surely not "within the range of apprehension" of a fleeing criminal on the ground.

To be sure, defendant represented a threat to everyone traveling the same roads and would have been responsible for any injury directly or indirectly caused by his actions in those environs; but to extend that responsibility to persons in the air, whose role was merely to observe his movements, a simple enough task in far speedier helicopters, defies common sense. . . . They were not in the zone of danger in this case by any stretch of the imagination, and the manner and circumstances of the collision could hardly have reasonably been foreseen. . . . Although less remote than a dispatcher suffering a coronary, perhaps, this was a "highly extraordinary result" by any measure and, properly viewed, beyond the long arm of the criminal law. . . .

PEOPLE v. ARZON

Supreme Court, New York County
92 Misc. 2d 739, 401 N.Y.S.2d 156 (1978)

MILONAS, J. The defendant was indicted on September 28, 1977 for two counts of murder in the second degree and arson in the third degree after he allegedly intentionally set fire to a couch, thus causing a serious fire on the fifth floor of an abandoned building at 358 East 8th Street in New York County. The New York City Fire Department, in responding to the conflagration, arrived to find the rear portion of the fifth and sixth floors burning. The firemen attempted to bring the situation under control, but making no progress and there being no additional assistance available, they decided to withdraw from the building. At that point, they were suddenly enveloped by a dense smoke, which was later discovered to have arisen from another independent fire that had broken out on the second floor.

Although this fire was also determined to have originated in arson, there is virtually no evidence implicating the defendant in its responsibility. However, the combination of the thick smoke and the fifth floor fire made evacuation from the premises extremely hazardous, and, in the process, Fireman Martin Celic sustained injuries from which he subsequently died. Accordingly, the defendant was accused of murder in the second degree for having, "Under circumstances evincing a depraved indifference to human life, recklessly engaged in conduct which created a grave risk of death to another person," thereby causing the death of Martin Celic, and with felony murder. The third charge of the indictment, arson, is not at issue for purposes of the instant application.

It is the defendant's contention that the evidence before the grand jury is insufficient to support the first two counts. He argues that . . . murder requires a causal link between the underlying crime and the death, a connection which, in the defendant's view, is here lacking.

There is remarkably little authority on precisely what sort of behavior constitutes "depraved indifference to human life." In the leading case on the subject, People v. Kibbe, 35 N.Y.2d 407, 321 N.E.2d 773 (1974), the Court of Appeals affirmed the [murder] conviction of defendants who had abandoned their helplessly intoxicated robbery victim by the side of a dark road in subfreezing temperature, one-half mile from the nearest structure, without shoes or eye-glasses, with his trousers at his ankles, his shirt pulled up and his outer clothing removed. The court held that while the deceased was actually killed by a passing truck, the defendants' conduct was a sufficiently direct cause of the ensuing death to warrant criminal liability and that "it is not necessary that the ultimate harm be intended by the actor. It will suffice if it can be said beyond a reasonable doubt, as indeed it can here be said, that the ultimate harm is something which should have been foreseen as being reasonably related to the acts of the accused."

Clearly, an obscure or merely probable connection between the defendant's conduct and another person's death is not enough to support a charge of homicide. People v. Stewart, [40 N.Y.2d 692, 358 N.E.2d 487 (1976)]. In *Stewart,* the victim had been operated upon for a stab wound in the stomach inflicted by the defendant. Afterwards, the surgeon performed an entirely unrelated hernia procedure on him, and he died. According to the court, "the prosecutor must, at least, prove that the defendant's conduct was an actual cause of death, in the sense that it forged a link in the chain of causes which actually brought about the death. . . ." In this instance, the possibility that death resulted from a factor not attributable to the defendant could not be ruled out beyond a reasonable doubt, since the patient would, in all likelihood, have survived except for the hernia operation. . . .

[T]he defendant's conduct need not be the sole and exclusive factor in the victim's death. In the standard established by People v. Kibbe, supra, and People v. Stewart, supra, an individual is criminally liable if his conduct was a sufficiently direct cause of the death, and the ultimate harm is something which should have been foreseen as being reasonably related to his acts. It is irrelevant that, in this instance the fire which had erupted on the second floor intervened, thus contributing to the conditions that culminated in the death of Fireman Celic. In *Kibbe,* the victim was killed when he was struck by a truck. This did not relieve the defendants in that case from criminal responsibility for his murder, as it does not absolve the defendant here. Certainly, it was foreseeable that firemen would respond to the situation, thus exposing them, along with the persons already present in the vicinity, to a life-threatening danger. The fire set by the defendant was an indispensable link in the chain of events that resulted in the death. It continued to burn out of control, greatly adding to the problem of evacuating the building by blocking off one of the access routes. At the very least, the defendant's act, as was the case in *Kibbe,* placed the deceased in a position where he was particularly vulnerable to the separate and independent force, in this instance, the fire on the second floor.

Consequently, the defendant's motion to dismiss the [murder counts] of the indictment is denied.

PEOPLE v. WARNER-LAMBERT CO., 51 N.Y.2d 295, 414 N.E.2d 660 (1980): [Defendant corporation and several of its officers and employees were indicted for second-degree manslaughter (N.Y. Penal Law §125.15, page 391 supra) and criminally negligent homicide (N.Y. Penal Law §125.10, page 391 supra). Several of the corporation's employees were killed (and many more injured) in a massive explosion at one of its chewing-gum factories. Evidence before the grand jury showed that the corporation used two potentially explosive substances in its manufacturing process, magnesium stearate (MS) and liquid nitrogen; that defendants had earlier been warned by their insurance carrier that the high concentrations of MS dust, combined with other conditions, created an explosion hazard; and that these hazards were not eliminated by the time of the accident. On the issue of what triggered the explosion there was apparently no hard proof, only speculations by experts that it could have been caused by mechanical sparking in the machines or by the liquid nitrogen dripping onto a concentration of MS and igniting under the impact of a moving metal part. The court held that the evidence before the grand jury was not legally sufficient to establish the foreseeability of the immediate, triggering cause of the explosion and therefore dismissed the indictment. The court stated:]

It has been the position of the People that but-for causation is all that is required for the imposition of criminal liability. Thus, it is their submission, reduced to its simplest form, that there was evidence of a foreseeable and indeed foreseen risk of explosion of MS dust and that in consequence of defendants' failure to remove the dust a fatal explosion occurred. The chain of physical events by which the explosion was set off, i.e., its particular cause, is to them a matter of total indifference. On oral argument the People contended that liability could be imposed if the cause of the explosion were the lighting of a match by an uninvited intruder or the striking of a bolt of lightning. In effect they would hold defendants to the status of guarantors until the ambient dust was removed. It thus appears that the People would invoke an expanded application of proximate cause principles lifted from the civil law of torts.

We have rejected the application of any such sweeping theory of culpability under our criminal law, however. . . . [In People v. Kibbe (discussed in the *Arzon* case, supra)] the critical issue was whether the defendants should be held criminally liable for murder when the particular cause of death was vehicular impact rather than freezing. Under the theory now advanced by the People it would have been irrelevant that death had been the consequence of one particular chain of causation rather than another; it would have been enough that the defendants exposed their victim to the risk of death and that he died. That, of course, was not the analysis of culpability that we adopted. [W]e held that . . . "We subscribe to the requirement that the defendants' actions must be a *sufficiently direct cause* of the ensuing death before there can be any imposition of criminal liability, and recognize, of course, that this standard is greater than that required to serve as a basis for tort liability." Thus, we were concerned for the nature of the chain of particularized events which in fact led to the victim's death; it was not enough that death had occurred as the result of the defendants' abandonment of their helpless victim. To analogize the factual situation in the case now before us to that in *Kibbe* it might be hypothesized that the abandoned victim in *Kibbe* instead of being either frozen to death or killed when struck by a passing motor vehicle was killed when struck by an airplane making an emergency landing on the highway or when hit by a stray bullet from a hunter's rifle — occasions of death not reasonably to have been foreseen when the defendants abandoned their victim.

NOTES ON FORESEEABILITY

1. The specific causal mechanism. Is *Warner-Lambert* correct in requiring that the defendant foresee the specific triggering cause of an explosion? Or should it be sufficient that a defendant foresee enhanced danger *in the event* of a spark or other precipitating cause? Consider the following variations.

(*a*) In Commonwealth v. Welansky, page 437 supra, several hundred night-club patrons died in a fire caused when a busboy carelessly struck a match; the defendant, who was responsible for the lack of adequate safety exits in the club, was held liable for involuntary manslaughter. Is the result consistent with *Warner-Lambert*? Suppose there had been no evidence of how the fire in *Welansky* had started?

(*b*) In a much-publicized prosecution, the director of the film "Twilight Zone — The Movie" was charged with involuntary manslaughter when actor Vic Morrow and two children were killed by a helicopter that crashed on top of them during the filming of a Vietnam War scene. Some of the evidence suggested that the crash was caused by special effects explosions during the scene. Prosecutors initially argued that the crash resulted when flying debris from the explosions dented the helicopter's tail rotor blade, a development that they argued was foreseeable. Defense attorneys claimed that the crash occurred because heat from the explosions removed the aluminum skin from the rotor blade, rendering the aircraft uncontrollable; they also argued that this development, unprecedented in aviation history, was unforeseeable. The judge ruled that the precise cause of the crash was irrelevant and that the defendants would be liable as long as the risk of death in the situation was "reasonably foreseeable." See N.Y. Times, Mar. 5, 1987, at 22. Was this the correct approach, or does it confuse the causation requirement with the requirement of a culpable mens rea?

(*c*) People v. Deitsch, 97 A.D.2d 327, 470 N.Y.S.2d 158 (1983), involved a warehouse fire that killed an employee who was trapped on the sixth floor when the flames broke out. Evidence before the grand jury suggested that bales of material stored in the building blocked the fire escape and that signs indicating the escape route might have been inadequate. However, the cause of the fire was never determined. The defendants controlled the building, and there was evidence that they were aware of its conditions. Can they properly be charged with manslaughter? The court upheld the indictment. Distinguishing *Warner-Lambert*, the court said (470 N.Y.S.2d at 164):

> In the instant case the theory of the prosecution is not that the defendants caused the fire which resulted in Logan's death. Rather, the prosecution is predicated upon the theory that defendants created conditions in the warehouse which they should have foreseen could result in death in the event of a fire. This case bears more of a resemblance to People v. Kibbe than it does to *Warner-Lambert*. In *Kibbe* . . . the court held that by creating the circumstances that led to death by a foreseeable intervening event, the defendants caused death in a sufficiently direct manner to warrant imposing criminal liability. Similarly, in the instant case, the Grand Jury might well have concluded that defendants created unsafe conditions in the warehouse which led to Logan's death by a foreseeable intervening cause — the fire.

Question: Why can't the same be said of *Warner-Lambert*?

2. Might the decision in *Warner-Lambert* have been influenced by the fact that the homicides occurred in the course of manufacturing operations? In a footnote (414 N.E.2d at 664 n. 1) the court observed:

Inasmuch as we find the causation issue hereafter discussed to be decisive of this appeal, we assume for purposes of this decision, without deciding, that sections 125.10 and 125.15 of the Penal Law are broad enough to cover deaths occurring in the course of manufacturing operations. We note, however, that no case applying these sections or the predecessor sections to such operations has been found; that no legislative history which mandates that conclusion has been found, either by the parties from whom we solicited submissions on that subject prior to reargument or by our independent research; and that tenable arguments for and against it can be made.

Question: What might those arguments be?

3. Vulnerability of the victim. In People v. Stamp, page 471 supra, a robbery victim who suffered from severe coronary disease died of a heart attack triggered by fright experienced during the offense. The court held the defendant guilty of felony-murder, stating that liability was "not limited to those deaths which are foreseeable. [T]he robber takes his victim as he finds him."

Consider the following: In February 1993, Jose Alonso Garcia was indicted for sexually assaulting a 79-year-old woman. When the woman died of congestive heart failure a month after the attack, he was also indicted for first-degree felony murder. Prosecutors argued that the woman died because Garcia "destroyed her will to live," and pointed to testimony that the deceased cried daily after the incident and ceased talking about her future. Prosecutors analogized this case to one where a victim collapses of a heart attack during or shortly after the crime. A rape prosecutor from New York expressed doubts about this theory: "I think they'll have a huge causation problem. I mean, how many of my victims, down the road, die of drug or alcohol abuse because of rape?" Wall St. J., Aug. 23, 1993, at B6.

In People v. Brackett, 117 Ill. 2d 170, 510 N.E.2d 877 (1987), the defendant inflicted a severe beating on an 85-year-old woman. After three weeks of hospitalization the woman was transferred to a nursing home. Although her wounds continued to heal, she became depressed and often refused to eat. Doctors were unable to insert a nasal feeding tube because her nasal passages were too small and her facial injuries made the procedure painful. About a month after the attack, she died of asphyxiation when she aspirated a small quantity of pureed food. Apparently, her inability to clear her throat was due to a combination of her advanced age and limited air in her lungs because the pain associated with a broken rib (suffered in defendant's assault) had prevented normally deep breathing. The court upheld a conviction for murder. While recognizing that "a person can accidentally choke to death while eating," and that such an accidental death "could be the type of intervening cause which would relieve a defendant of criminal responsibility for death," the court said (117 Ill. 2d at 176, 178-179, 181):

> [T]his is precisely the kind of case where the defendant takes his victim as he finds him. [A] person's advanced age is as significant a part of his existing health condition as diabetes or hardening of the arteries. [T]he defendant did not have to foresee that this victim would die from asphyxiation. . . ."

Questions: If death results from an unusual disease unforeseeably contracted by the victim after an assault, the defendant presumably is relieved of liability.

This remains true even when the victim would not have contracted the disease, but for the situation created by the injuries. Why should the result be different when the disease producing death was contracted by the victim *before* the defendant's assault? Why should it be the case that the defendant always "takes his victim as he finds him"?

4. Is medical maltreatment foreseeable? Consider the following.

(a) 1 M. Hale, Pleas of the Crown 428: If a man give another a stroke, which it may be, is not in itself so mortal, but that with good care he might be cured, yet if he die of this wound within the year and day, it is homicide or murder, as the case is, and so it hath been always ruled. 3 Inst. 47.

But if the wound or hurt be not mortal, but with ill applications by the party, or those about him, of unwholesome salves or medicines the party dies, if it can clearly appear, that this medicine, and not the wound, was the cause of his death, it seems it is not homicide, but then that must appear clearly and certainly to be so.

But if a man receives a wound, which is not in itself mortal, but either for want of helpful applications, or neglect thereof, it turns to a gangrene, or a fever, and that gangrene or fever be the immediate cause of his death, yet, this is murder or manslaughter in him that gave the stroke or wound, for that wound, tho it were not the immediate cause of his death, yet, if it were the mediate cause thereof, and the fever or gangrene was the immediate cause of his death, yet the wound was the cause of the gangrene or fever, and so consequently is causa causati.

If a man be sick of some such disease, which possibly by course of nature would end his life in half a year, and another gives him a wound or hurt, which hastens his end by irritating and provoking the disease to operate more violently or speedily, this hastening of his death sooner than it would have been is homicide or murder, as the case happens, in him, that gives the wound or hurt, for he doth not die simply ex visitatione Dei, but the hurt that he receives hastens it, and an offender of such a nature shall not apportion his own wrong, and thus I have often heard that learned and wise judge Justice Rolle frequently direct.

(b) Hall v. State, 199 Ind. 592, 159 N.E. 420 (1927): [During the course of a robbery, defendant struck several blows to the head of deceased, using an instrument and fracturing deceased's skull. Deceased died some 10 days later. The cause of death was given by the state's witnesses as blood poisoning following a fractured skull (meningitis). Defendant appealed from a conviction of first-degree murder alleging error in the trial court's sustaining objections to the questions asked on cross-examination of the coroner designed to show that the deceased's "wound in the head received improper or incompetent medical treatment and that the cause of his death was the doctor's treatment, or a disease brought on by the wound or by the treatment, and not the act of the appellant." The court sustained the conviction finding that even entirely favorable answers to the questions put would not have authorized the jury to return a different verdict, in view of the principles stated in Hale's Pleas of the Crown, supra. Citing many cases, the court asserted the following propositions (159 N.E. at 425-426):] (A) It is not indispensable to a conviction that a wound be necessarily fatal and the direct cause of death. If the wound caused death indirectly through

a chain of natural effects and causes unchanged by human action, such as the consequential development of septicaemia or blood poisoning, he who inflicted the wound or injury is responsible.[a] (B) A person who inflicts a serious wound upon another, calculated to destroy or endanger his life, will not be relieved of responsibility, even though unskilled or improper medical treatment aggravates the wound and contributes to the death. Every person is held to contemplate and be responsible for the natural consequences of his own acts, and the criminality of an act is not altered or diminished by the fact that other causes cooperated in producing the fatal result.

(c) Regina v. Cheshire, [1991] 3 All E.R. 670: Treatment which falls short of the standard expected of the competent medical practitioner is unfortunately only too frequent in human experience for it to be considered abnormal in the sense of extraordinary. Acts or omissions of a doctor treating the victim for injuries he has received at the hands of an accused may conceivably be so extraordinary as to be capable of being regarded as acts independent of the conduct of the accused but it is most unlikely that they will be. . . . [I]f at the time of death the original wound is still an operating cause and a substantial cause, then the death can properly be said to be the result of the wound, albeit that some other cause of death is also operating. Only if it can be said that the original wounding is merely the setting in which another cause operates can it be said that the death does not result from the wound.

(d) A rare case where incompetent medical treatment was found to have broken the chain of causation between defendant's knife assault and the victim's death is Regina v. Jordan, 40 Crim. App. 152 (1956). Two medical witnesses testified to two egregious departures from proper medical treatment. (1) The stab wound had penetrated the intestine in two places but was mainly healed at the time of death. In order to prevent infection an antibiotic, Terramycin, was administered. This was proper. However, subsequently the deceased manifested symptoms indicating he was intolerant to Terramycin. In recognition of this fact the administration of the drug was stopped, but the next day its resumption was ordered by another doctor. The witnesses agreed that to introduce a poisonous substance after the intolerance of the patient was shown was palpably wrong. (2) The attending health workers intravenously fed wholly abnormal quantities of liquid far exceeding the output. This caused waterlogging of the lungs, pulmonary edema, and finally bronchopneumonia, from which the deceased died.

NOTE ON OMISSIONS AS CAUSES

The principle that conduct is a legal or proximate cause of a result only when it is a necessary condition of the result (that is, a condition but for which the result would not have happened) is sometimes said to raise difficulties where the

a. In a footnote the court observed: "Where, however, the wound is not in its nature mortal, and death results solely from an entirely independent cause not traceable in any way to the wound, the person inflicting the wound cannot be held responsible for the death. Bush v. Com. (1880) 78 Ky. 268" — Eds.

conduct consists only of a failure to act. See discussion in Jerome Hall, Principles of Criminal Law 190 (2d ed. 1960); Graham Hughes, Criminal Omissions, 67 Yale L.J. 590, 627 (1958). For example, consider a case where a baby-sitter deliberately fails to rescue a small child who has been pushed into a shallow pool by a stranger. It is sometimes argued that only the stranger's action, not the failure of the sitter to avert the harm, is the necessary condition for the result to happen.

Questions: Is the argument convincing? Why must it be that the stranger's action is the *only* (but-for) cause of the drowning? It's clear enough that the sitter's inaction is not a sufficient condition for the child's drowning. But since the result would not have happened had the baby-sitter acted to prevent it, why isn't the latter's failure to act a necessary condition for the result? It is true that the child would have drowned even if the sitter had not been present to save it. And is it also true that strangers passing by who failed to rescue the child can also be said to be but-for causes of the drowning on the same argument? See J. C. Smith & Brian Hogan, Criminal Law 46 (7th ed. 1992). Yet what singles out the sitter's failure to act from the inactivity of strangers or of those not present is that the sitter was under a duty and was able to act. In other words, the failure of anyone to prevent the harm was a necessary condition of its happening, but only the sitter's failure is the legal cause. For an exploration of the subject see Arthur Leavens, A Causation Approach to Criminal Omissions, 76 Cal. L. Rev. 547 (1988). An article by Alison McIntyre, Guilty Bystanders? On the Legitimacy of Duty to Rescue Statutes, 23 Phil. & Pub. Aff. 157 (1994), develops an interesting critique of the concept of causation by omission.

At all events, whatever the metaphysical difficulties of the concept of causation by omission (see Michael Moore, Act and Crime — The Philosophy of Action and its Implications for Criminal Law 78 et seq. (1993)), the law is settled that omissions can be legal causes of results — courts have not found it difficult to find a person's failure to act (in the presence of a duty and an ability to act) to be the legal cause of a prohibited result, like the death of another. See, e.g., Palmer v. State, 223 Md. 341, 164 A.2d 467 (1960), and Jones v. State, page 191 supra, and Notes following.

MODEL PENAL CODE

Section 2.03.   Causal Relationship Between Conduct and Result; Divergence Between Result Designed or Contemplated and Actual Result or Between Probable and Actual Result

[See Appendix for text of this section.]

NOTES ON STATUTORY STANDARDS

1. Most state codes include no explicit rules for determining causation, and even among jurisdictions that have recently revised their codes, the majority have not adopted causation provisions. In these jurisdictions, the courts are left to resolve causation issues entirely on the basis of evolving common law prin ciples. Roughly a dozen states have adopted causation provisions based in whole or in part on the Model Penal Code formulation. See Model Penal Code and Commentaries, Comment to §2.03, at 264-265 (1985).

2. In evaluating any of the causation standards that might be proposed, consider two questions. First, *what difference will it make,* in terms of whether the defendant's conduct is punishable at all or in terms of the severity of the punishment, if the defendant's conduct is held to be the "cause" of the result. This question should be asked with respect to each of the cases and hypotheticals in this chapter. Second, what is the *reason* for that difference in liability or in the severity of punishment. In other words, why should the result of conduct ever make a difference? Consider the following.

Meir Dan-Cohen, Causation, in 1 Encyclopoedia of Crime and Justice 165-166 (1983): A functional analysis of causation would derive the legal meaning and contours of this concept from the answer to the question, What purpose is served by linking the harmful event to the accused's conduct? . . .

The functional analysis of causation is . . . greatly impeded by discovering that there is considerable difficulty in establishing the relevance of the occurrence of actual harm to criminal liability or severity of punishment. . . . The rational and moral grounds for punishment, it has been argued, should lead one to focus on the defendant's conduct and state of mind or degree of culpability, not on whether some harmful result actually followed from that conduct. . . .

Imagine two cases, in both of which the respective defendants shoot their victim with intent to kill. In both cases the bullets lodge in the respective victim's chest. Both victims undergo surgery. The cases are identical in all respects but one: in the first case the victim dies of the wound, and in the second, he is saved by the operation. Rationally, what does this difference in outcome have to do with the proper criminal disposition of the two defendants? Both have demonstrated precisely the same degree of dangerousness and culpability. . . . Neither considerations of deterrence nor calculations of the two defendants' just deserts can support differential legal treatment. Consequently, any attempt to base the analysis of causation on grounds of policy must fail: if the fact of the first victim's death is irrelevant to the policies served by the criminal law, the same must be true of the causal relation between that death and the defendant's shooting. We can, therefore, entertain little hope for deriving guidelines for . . . causation from its function in serving the criminal law's goals.

That the actual death of the victim is somehow relevant to determining the accused's criminal liability is nonetheless a widely shared and deeply entrenched intuition. . . . The legal concept of causation may accordingly be seen as a corollary of this intuition. Although the intuition itself resists rationalization by reference to the goals of the criminal law, it can still be demonstrated that the *fact* of its existence and pervasiveness is relevant to the criminal law's ability to discharge its main functions. . . .

One may condemn [retribution] by characterizing it as a crude urge for vengeance, or dignify it with a loftier image according to which punishment is needed to expunge the "tainting" effect of crime or to restore a social equilibrium disturbed by the crime's commission. But it is hard to deny both the pervasiveness of that underlying sentiment and the influence it actually exerts on the criminal law, even in the absence of compelling rational arguments to support it. . . . Posed in connection with the retributive goal of punishment, the question of causation (namely, "Is there a causal relation between A's conduct and B's death?") amounts to asking whether punishing A is necessary to satisfy the retributive urge aroused by the fact of B's death.

Two conclusions about the investigation of the legal concept of causation are implied by these comments. First, to the extent that causation plays a role in serving the retributive goal of punishment, its elucidation compels us to investigate the ordinary use of causal notions in the context of blaming others for harm done. Second, in conducting this investigation it is likely to become apparent that, as an element of the retributive urge, the concept of causation is inextricably bound up, in ordinary usage, with the entire complex of blaming. [T]he statement that A caused B's death may, in ordinary speech, be as much a conclusory statement, based on the prior tacit judgment that A deserves to be punished for B's death, as it is an independent statement of fact which leads to that conclusion. Put differently, in ordinary usage the concepts of causation and blame or deserts often reverse the idealized roles usually assigned to them in moral and legal theory. [O]ne would expect the conclusion that A should be punished for B's death to be based, in part, on the judgment that A caused B's death. In fact, the conclusion that A deserves to be punished may be directly and intuitively generated by the retributive urge, preceding and merely rationalized by the finding of a sufficient causal relationship between A's acts and B's death.

NOTES ON TRANSFERRED INTENT

1. D shoots at X with the intention of killing him. The bullet strikes and kills Y, perhaps because D missed her target and the bullet unaccountably ricocheted. Is D guilty of murdering Y, regardless of how accidental the killing of Y was? The law is clear in all jurisdictions — the answer is yes. The doctrinal justification is the doctrine of transferred intent, according to which D's intent to kill X is transferred to her action of killing Y.

How compelling is this analysis? Isn't it a mere fiction to say that D intended to kill Y, when in fact she killed Y by accident while trying to kill X? Why isn't the reality that D is guilty of the attempted murder of X and of the involuntary manslaughter of Y (assuming the required level of negligence or recklessness could be established)? Or are there sound policy reasons for punishing D more seriously than other would-be murderers whose attempts miscarry?

The Model Penal Code appears to believe so because it would convict D of murder, though under a provision of its causation section rather than under a fictional notion of transferred intent. Section 2.03(2)(a) provides that where the crime requires that a defendant intentionally cause a particular result (killing someone, say), that element of the crime will be satisfied where the defendant accidentally causes that result to one person while intentionally trying to cause it to another.

2. Problem. In People v. Roberts, 2 Cal. 4th 271, 826 P.2d 274 (1992), defendant, a prison inmate, stabbed X, another inmate, many times, in execution of a premeditated design to kill him, while Y, a third inmate, held X. X, dazed and out of his mind with pain and shock, broke free, picked up the knife, and tried to stab Y. When a prison guard attempted to subdue X, X stabbed and killed the guard. The court held that *X*'s action of killing the officer was a kind of reflexive act, the natural and probable consequence of the wounds inflicted by defendant, and therefore that a jury could find that defendant's acts were the proximate cause of the death of the officer, or, in other words, that defendant killed the guard. It therefore upheld defendant's liability for murder of the guard. But it drew the line at holding defendant liable for first-degree murder of the guard, because there was no evidence that he premeditated and deliberated the killing of the guard.

Questions: Why must there be such evidence, so long as there is evidence that he premeditated and deliberated the killing of the inmate? Suppose that defendant, with premeditation and deliberation, shot at the inmate but missed and killed the guard by accident. Under the doctrine of transferred intent, shouldn't he be guilty of the first-degree murder of the guard? Is the situation in *Roberts* distinguishable?

3. Note that the problem of transferred intent is not confined to homicidal crimes. See, e.g., State v. Contua-Ramirez, 149 Ariz. 377, 718 P.2d 1030 (1986), where the defendant, in attempting to strike his wife, accidentally hit their baby, whom she was holding in her arms. The court upheld a conviction for intentionally injuring the child. Intentional assault upon an adult was a class 1 misdemeanor, but intentional injury of a child was a class 4 felony. The court held that the defendant could be convicted of the more serious offense. Is this sound?

2. Subsequent Human Actions

PEOPLE v. CAMPBELL

Court of Appeals of Michigan
124 Mich. App. 333, 335 N.W.2d 271 (1983)

HOEHN, J. [Defendant was charged with murder in connection with the suicide death of Kevin Patrick Basnaw. He moved to quash the information and dismiss, on the ground that providing a weapon to a person, who subsequently uses it to commit suicide, does not constitute the crime of murder. The motion to quash was denied by the circuit court, and this court granted leave to appeal.

[Campbell and deceased were drinking heavily and conversing. At one point, Campbell, aggrieved at deceased for having had sex with his wife, encouraged the deceased to kill himself. When deceased told him had no weapon, Campbell offered to sell him his own for any price. Eventually he gave deceased his gun and five shells and left. Deceased shortly thereafter shot himself.]

The prosecutor and the trial court relied on People v. Roberts, 211 Mich. 187, 178 N.W. 690 (1920), to justify trying defendant for open murder. In that case, Mr. Roberts' wife had terminal multiple sclerosis. She was in great pain. In the past, she had unsuccessfully attempted suicide by ingesting carbolic acid. At his wife's request, Mr. Roberts made a potion of water and poison and placed it within her reach. Defendant Roberts was convicted of murder in the first degree. . . . We now consider whether the *Roberts* case still represents the law of

Michigan, and we find that it does not. Recent cases of our Supreme Court cast doubt on the vitality of the 1920 *Roberts* decision.[a]

The prosecutor argues that inciting to suicide, coupled with the overt act of furnishing a gun to an intoxicated person, in a state of depression, falls within the prohibition, "or other wilful, deliberate and premeditated killing." There exists no statutory definition of the term "murder." That crime is defined in the common law. "Homicide is the killing of one human being by another." . . . The term suicide excludes by definition a homicide. Simply put, the defendant here did not kill another person.

A second ground militates against requiring the defendant to stand trial for murder. Defendant had no present intention to kill. He provided the weapon and departed. Defendant hoped Basnaw would kill himself but hope alone is not the degree of intention requisite to a charge of murder. . . .

A number of legislatures have considered the problem and have enacted legislation which may be accepted as evidence of present-day social values in this area. A number of states have made, or proposed making, incitement to suicide a crime. The penalties imposed by some of these states include: 15 years (Florida, Minnesota, Missouri); ten years (Arkansas, Oregon, Michigan); 5 years (Wisconsin); 1 year (Maine); Manslaughter (Colorado).

Incitement to suicide has not been held to be a crime in two-thirds of the states of the United States. . . . While we find the conduct of the defendant morally reprehensible, we do not find it to be criminal under the present state of the law. The remedy for this situation is in the Legislature.[b]

The trial court is reversed and the case is remanded with instructions to quash the information and warrant and discharge the defendant.

NOTE

The *Campbell* case is fairly representative of American law — one who successfully urges or assist another to commit suicide is not guilty of murder or manslaughter, so long, at least, as the deceased was mentally responsible and was not forced or deceived. But a substantial number of states now have statutes that make it criminal to assist a suicide. Many are modeled on §210.5 of the Model Penal Code, which makes it criminal for a person to purposely aid or solicit another to commit suicide. If as a consequence the person solicited or aided commits suicide or attempts to do so, the crime is punishable as a felony. Otherwise it is a misdemeanor.

NOTE ON INTERVENING HUMAN ACTIONS[1]

It is plain that Basnaw's suicide was a readily foreseeable consequence of Campbell's actions. Indeed, he meant his actions to have precisely the effect they

a. The Michigan Supreme Court has now overruled the *Roberts* case. People v. Kevorkian, — N.W.2d — (1994) — Eds.

b. In 1992 Michigan adopted a statute making it criminal to assist a suicide. The prosecution of Dr. Kevorkian under this law has focused attention on the constitutionality of criminalizing consensual euthanasia. The subject is explored infra page 804 — Eds.

had. If the causation doctrines we studied in the preceding section were applicable, Campbell would surely be found to have caused Basnaw's death, in short, to have killed him. But the foreseeability doctrine is not applicable in cases like *Campbell,* and it is important to see why.

Putting aside whether the perception is philosophically sound, the fact is that there is a powerful strain of thought in our culture that leads us to perceive human actions as differing from other events. Events seem to us to happen regularly and necessarily in accordance with the laws of nature, and we express this perception in the language of causation. But our perceptions of human action is different. We tend to regard a person's acts as the products of his or her choice, not as inevitable, natural results of a chain of events governed by the laws of nature. How accurate these perceptions are is another matter. The point is that by and large this is the way most people, in Western cultures, at least, respond to happenings and actions, and not unnaturally the law tends to respond in the same way.

As a result the law treats natural events that follow the defendant's actions differently from the subsequent actions of others that follow. The law treats the events that follow upon the defendant's action as caused by the defendant (subject, of course, to requirements of foreseeability, proximity, and the other elements of legal cause). But the subsequent actions of others the law, except in certain situations, does not treat as having been caused. Nothing *causes* another person to act; the person *chooses* to act of his or her own free will. Therefore the results the second person produces are caused by him alone and not by the first actor. As it is sometimes put, there has been a *novus actus interveniens,* a new action by another party that becomes the new foundation of causal responsibility. As we shall see later when we reach Chapter 7, Section A, these conceptions create the need for the special law governing the responsibility of one person for the actions of another, for if the law of causation is not applicable, some other doctrine must be created to deal with the need to hold responsible those who instigate or help another to do a criminal act.

But not all subsequent human actions are treated as outside the laws of causation. Only those that have all the earmarks of having been freely chosen (what H. L. A. Hart and Tony Honoré, in their classic study of causation, Causation in the Law, 2d ed., 1985, call "voluntary" actions) are treated this way. Actions that are truly involuntary in the traditional sense, see supra page 171, can of course be caused. But there are other exceptions as well, even where the subsequent action is volitional in the traditional sense of involving some choice. For example, actions taken without full knowledge of the circumstances are often held to be not a sufficiently free choice to require that they be treated as chosen rather than caused. Other kinds of action that may be caused are those thought of as "constrained" by such factors as compulsion of duty or by excusable conditions, such as understandable excitement of the moment or duress, even when the actions are informed and intentional. We saw examples in the case of the negligent helicopter pilot, *Acosta,* supra page 548, the case of the fire fighter who enters the burning building, *Arzon,* supra page 551, and in the cases of

---

1. Drawn from Sanford H. Kadish, Blame and Punishment: Essays in the Criminal Law 140-145 (1987).

subsequent medical maltreatment, supra page 556. We will see further examples in the materials in this section.

When do subsequent human actions tend to be viewed as chosen rather than as caused? The principal situation is where the subsequent actor has acted intentionally, with full knowledge and without constraint to produce the result. The *Campbell* case is an example. We will focus on this situation in Subsection a in the material that follows. Another situation is where the subsequent actor did not intentionally cause the result. This is considered in Subsection b in the material that follows. But, as we shall see, the *novus actus* doctrine is much less consistently adhered to in this second situation. Indeed, the cases make it more accurate to think of this doctrine generally less as a hard rule than as a principle that tends to pull the law in the ways indicated, but not always pulling it all the way.

A helpful analysis of the doctrine may be found in Glanville Williams, *Finis* for *Novus Actus?* 48 Camb. L.J. 391 (1989). He observes therein:

> The legal attitude, in general, rests on what is known to philosophers as the principle of autonomy, which enters deeply into our traditional moral perceptions, reinforced by language. . . . The autonomy doctrine, expressing itself through its corollary, the doctrine of *novus actus interveniens,* teaches that the individual's will is the autonomous (self-regulating) prime cause of behavior. . . .
>
> We do not mean to suggest that the foregoing analysis invariably accounts for the decisions of the courts. Here as elsewhere in the law one finds decisions that do not conform to the pattern apparently underlying what most courts do. We only suggest that the foregoing considerations seem to be a powerful, if not always a determining, factor in the development of law in this area.

a.   Subsequent Actions Intended to Produce the Result

STEPHENSON v. STATE

Supreme Court of Indiana
205 Ind. 141, 179 N.E. 633 (1932)

[Defendant, with the aid of several of his associates, abducted the deceased, a woman he had known socially for several months, and in the ensuing days subjected her to various forms of sexual perversion, including the infliction of bite wounds on her body. Deceased seized an opportunity secretly to buy and take six tablets of bichloride of mercury in an effort to commit suicide. She became violently ill. Defendant had her drink a bottle of milk and suggested that he take her to a hospital; she refused. Defendant thereupon proceeded to drive her to her home. On the way deceased's pain grew worse, and she screamed for a doctor. Defendant, however, did not stop until he reached his home. Soon thereafter she was taken to her parents. They summoned a doctor who treated her for poisoning. In the ensuing 10 days, all her wounds healed normally except one which became infected. She grew worse and died, although the infected wound had healed at the time of her death. The medical cause of death was apparently a combination of shock, loss of food and rest, action of the poison and the infection, and lack of early treatment, probably none of which, taken singly, would have been sufficient to result in death.

[The indictment against defendant was in four counts. The first count charged him with murder arising from the following: that on March 16 he kidnapped the deceased from her home in Indianapolis, where she had been visiting, detained her on a railroad train en route to Chicago, struck, beat, bit, and grievously wounded her with intent to rape in a drawing room on the train, and forced her to get off at Hammond and to occupy a hotel bed with him; that on March 17 deceased, "distracted with the pain and shame so inflicted upon her," swallowed poison; that defendant neither administered an antidote nor called for medical help although able to do so; that the same day he forced her into a car and drove her back to Indianapolis where he kept her in his garage without administering an antidote or calling for medical help until March 18; and that finally she died on April 14 "from the effects of her wounds inflicted as aforesaid and said poison taken as aforesaid."

[The jury found defendant guilty of second-degree murder under this first count of the indictment, and the supreme court affirmed.]

PER CURIAM. . . . Appellant very earnestly argues that the evidence does not show appellant guilty of murder. He points out in his brief that, after they reached the hotel, Madge Oberholtzer left the hotel and purchased a hat and the poison, and voluntarily returned to his room, and at the time she took the poison she was in an adjoining room to him, and that she swallowed the poison without his knowledge, and at a time when he was not present. From these facts he contends that she took her life by committing suicide; that her own act in taking poison was [the act of] an intervening responsible agent which broke the causal connection between his acts and the death; that his acts were not the proximate cause of her death, but the taking of the poison was the proximate cause of death. In support of his contention, he cites State v. Preslar (1856) 48 N.C. 421; . . . Bush v. Com. (1880) 78 Ky. 268 . . . and other cases from other jurisdictions.

In the case of State v. Preslar, supra, the defendant in the nighttime fought with his wife, and she left to go in the house of her father. When she reached a point about two hundred yards from her father's home, she, for some reason, did not want to go in the house till morning, laid down on a bed cover, which she had wrapped around her, till daylight. The weather was cold and the next morning she could not walk, but made herself known. She afterwards died. The court held that the wife without necessity exposed herself, and the defendant was not guilty. In Bush v. Com., 78 Ky. 268, defendant wounded one V. who was taken to the hospital and treated by a physician who communicated to her scarlet fever from which disease she died. The court held in that case, that if the wound is not dangerous, and when in the natural course of events a new and intervening cause appears and causes the death, there is no guilt. If death was not connected with the wound in the regular chain of cause and consequence, there ought not to be any responsibility. If a new and wholly independent instrumentality interposed and produced death, the wound is not the proximate cause. The principle laid down in the last case is well supported by decided cases and text-book writers, and we agree that the reasoning is sound and that it was properly applied in those cases. It is quite clear that in the *Bush* Case there was no causal connection between the wound inflicted and the death. But we do not believe that the rule stated in the above case is controlling here. . . .

In the case of Rex. v. Beech [23 Cox Crim. Cas. 181 (1912)] the prosecutrix was the village nurse and lived alone. At 11:45 P.M. on an evening in November, the appellant came to her house when she was in bed. He entered the house by breaking a window and went upstairs to the bedroom occupied by the prosecutrix. The door was locked, and the appellant threatened to break it open if the prosecutrix would not let him in. She refused, and the appellant then tried to burst open the door. The prosecutrix called out that if he got in he would not find her in the room, and, as the appellant continued his attack upon the door, the prosecutrix jumped out of the window sustaining injuries. The prosecutrix also testified that the appellant had attempted to interfere with her on a previous occasion when she had threatened to take poison if he touched her. The court approved the proposition as stated by the lower court as follows: "Whether the conduct of the prisoner amounted to a threat of causing injury to the young woman; was the act of jumping the natural consequence of the conduct of the prisoner and was the grievous bodily harm the result of the conduct of the prisoner." The court held that, if these questions were answered in the affirmative, he would be guilty. In Rex v. Valade (Que.) 22 Rev. de Jur. 524, 26 Can. Cr. Cas. 233, where the accused induced a young girl under the age of consent to go along with him to a secluded apartment, and there had criminal sexual intercourse with her, following which she jumped from a window to the street to get away from him, and was killed by the fall, the accused was held guilty of murder. Bishop in his work on Criminal Law, vol. 2 (9th Ed.), page 484, says: "When suicide follows a wound inflicted by the defendant his act is homicidal, if deceased was rendered irresponsible by the wound and as a natural result of it."

We do not understand that by the rule laid down by Bishop, supra, that the wound which renders the deceased mentally irresponsible is necessarily limited to a physical wound. We should think the same rule would apply if a defendant engaged in the commission of a felony such as rape or attempted rape, and inflicts upon his victim both physical and mental injuries, the natural and probable result of which would render the deceased mentally irresponsible and suicide followed, we think he would be guilty of murder. In the case at bar, appellant is charged with having caused the death of Madge Oberholtzer while engaged in the crime of attempted rape. The evidence shows that appellant, together with Earl Gentry and the deceased, left their compartment on the train and went to a hotel about a block from the depot, and there appellant registered as husband and wife, and immediately went to the room assigned to them. This change from their room on the train to a room in the hotel is of no consequence, for appellant's control and dominion over the deceased was absolute and complete in both cases. The evidence further shows that the deceased asked for money with which to purchase a hat, and it was supplied her by "Shorty," at the direction of appellant, and that she did leave the room and was taken by Shorty to a shop and purchased a hat and then, at her request, to a drug store where she purchased the bichloride of mercury tablets, and then she was taken back to the room in the hotel, where about 10 o'clock A.M. she swallowed the poison. Appellant argues that the deceased was a free agent on this trip to purchase a hat, etc., and that she voluntarily returned to the room in the hotel. This was a question for the jury, and the evidence would justify them in reaching a contrary conclusion. Appellant's chauffeur accompanied her on this trip, and the deceased had, before she left appellant's home in Indianapolis, attempted to get away, and also made two unsuccessful attempts to use the telephone to call help. She was justified in concluding that any attempt she might make, while purchasing a hat or while in the drug store to escape or secure assistance, would be no more successful in Hammond than it was in Indianapolis. We think the evidence shows that the deceased was at all times from the time she was entrapped by the appellant at his home on the evening of March 15th till she returned to her home two days later, in the custody and absolute control of appellant. Neither do we think the fact that the deceased took the poison some four hours after they left the drawing-room on the train or after the crime of attempted rape had been committed necessarily prevents it from being a part of the attempted rape. . . . At the very moment Madge Oberholtzer swallowed the poison she was subject to the passion, desire, and will of appellant. She knew not what moment she would be subjected to the same demands that she was while in the drawing-room on the train. What would have prevented appellant from compelling her to submit to him at any moment? The same forces, the same impulses, that would impel her to shoot herself during the actual attack or throw herself out of the car window after the attack had ceased, [were] pressing and overwhelming her at the time she swallowed the poison. The evidence shows that she was so weak that she staggered as she left the elevator to go to the room in the hotel, and was assisted by appellant and Gentry; that she was very ill, so much that she could not eat, all of which was the direct and proximate result of the treatment accorded to her by appellant.

We think the situation no different here than we find in the *Beech* Case or the *Valade* Case, supra. To say that there is no causal connection between the acts of appellant and the death of Madge Oberholtzer, and that the treatment accorded her by appellant had no causal connection with the death of Madge Oberholtzer would be a travesty on justice. The whole criminal program was so closely connected that we think it should be treated as one transaction, and should be governed by the same principles of law as was applied in the case of Rex v. Beech and Rex v. Valade, supra. We therefore conclude that the evidence was sufficient and justified the jury in finding that appellant by his acts and conduct rendered the deceased distracted and mentally irresponsible, and that such was the natural and probable consequence of such unlawful and criminal treatment, and that the appellant was guilty of murder in the second degree as charged in the first count of the indictment.

COMMENT ON *STEPHENSON,* 31 Mich. L. Rev. 659, 668-674 (1933): At the outset it is clear that homicide cannot be committed by the defendant unless the intervening actor who strikes the fatal blow has been rendered irresponsible by defendant's unlawful act. This act may provide another with the opportunity, the instrument, or the motive for striking, but if it leaves him sane, the courts will not look behind the last responsible, self-determining actor. . . . Suppose a man commits suicide after losing all his money to a criminal swindler; is the swindler guilty of homicide? . . . Our common law, whatever may be said of divine law, does not hold him responsible for the death.

A new element enters the situation when the intervening actor is insane. . . . Where a policeman was grappling with a lunatic to arrest him, and defendant by freeing his hand enabled the lunatic to shoot the policeman, defendant was held guilty of homicide. From this case we may derive the principle that an insane intervening actor will not break the causal connection between defendant's act and the death.

We have been assuming, however, that the intervening actor is already insane at the time of defendant's act. The facts of Stephenson v. State put a further strain on the causal connection. To convict of homicide there, it was necessary to prove, not only that deceased was irresponsible when she took the poison, but also that defendant's unlawful acts caused her irresponsibility. For such a conviction no square precedent is to be found. Indeed the cases reveal, if anything, a marked reluctance to permit proof of any purely mental link in the causal chain. . . .

It is true that certain psychological phenomena have been admitted to proof when they have been induced by physical violence. The mentally paralyzing effect of fear and the mentally unbalancing effect of pain and fever are sufficiently familiar to the average man so that he can pass a sound judgment upon their causal relation. . . . Where a dangerous wound has been inflicted, which unseats the mind of deceased through pain or fever and so causes him to kill himself, the courts are . . . ready to hold defendant for homicide.

These last cases come nearest to supporting the majority opinion in Stephenson v. State, but they are not squarely in point. The prosecution did not seriously contend, nor did the court think, that deceased was rendered irresponsible by the physical injuries, the bruises and bites, inflicted by defendant. It was rather the shame and humiliation of having been raped. . . .

We have noted above that all prior unlawful actors in the causal chain are insulated from liability if the person who strikes the fatal blow is a responsible, self-determining actor. The law recognizes a number of situations, however, in which a man who takes his own life or another's is not responsible. Insanity destroys his responsibility, as we have seen, and criminal liability for the death may then be cast on the next previous actor. So also the actual killer's responsibility will be destroyed if he acts innocently in ignorance of fact, or in necessary self-defense, or instinctively as a result of fear, or in pursuance of public duty. Here, human nature being what it is, the law excuses the homicidal act because it represents the average man's natural and instinctive reaction to a situation in which he finds himself; and conversely because the reaction is natural and instinctive, the law holds for homicide the previous actor who unlawfully created the situation. . . .

Such liability of an antecedent actor is best illustrated where he has created a situation in which another's mortal blow is motivated by the powerful instinct of self-preservation. At the point of a gun A commands B to jump from a moving train, and B is killed in the jump; by violence and threats of death A drives his wife poorly-clad from the house, and she dies of exposure; A shoots at a boat to frighten its occupants, B jumps overboard upsetting the boat, and C is drowned. In these cases desperate measures of escape are warranted; the imminence of deadly peril prompts B to act first and think afterwards. . . .

When a situation arises in which the law makes the performance of a homicidal act a duty, and prescribes penalties for disobedience, we feel without hesitation that the unlawful creator of that situation is criminally guilty of the death. Where A obtains C's conviction of a capital offense by perjured testimony, and executioner *B* hangs *C,* the proximity of causation between *A's* unlawful act and the death seems amply clear. So the master of a vessel is guilty of homicide if he sends a sailor into the rigging, knowing or chargeable with knowledge that he is not fit to go aloft, and the sailor falls to his death. . . .

It is difficult to fit Stephenson v. State into this picture of liability. True, the law justifies the taking of life when necessary to prevent the commission of rape. And had deceased been helpless in the manual grasp of defendant at the time of her suicidal act, or had a third-party defender, bursting upon the scene, shot her to death through faulty aim, then defendant might have been liable for her death within the principles developed above. But one can scarcely overlook the fact that deceased was alone and unmolested, and in a position to summon help, at the time she took the poison. The predominant motive for her suicide, clearly, was not to escape further assault but to escape the shame of what had already been done to her. The case represents a new and doubtful departure in so far as it suggests that the unlawful infliction of shame and disgrace may lead so naturally to suicide as to amount to a killing by him who inflicted it.

NOTES AND QUESTIONS

1. An article in the N.Y. Times, Feb. 7, 1968, stated:

PHOENIX, Ariz., Feb. 6 (AP) — Linda Marie Ault killed herself, policemen said today, rather than make her dog Beauty pay for her night with a married man.

"I killed her. I killed her. It's just like I killed her myself," a detective quoted her grief-stricken father as saying.

"I handed her the gun. I didn't think she would do anything like that."

The 21-year-old Arizona State University coed died in a hospital yesterday of a gunshot wound in the head.

The police quoted her parents, Mr. and Mrs. Joseph Ault, as giving this account:

Linda failed to return home from a dance in Tempe Friday night. On Saturday she admitted she had spent the night with an Air Force lieutenant.

The Aults decided on a punishment that would "wake Linda up." They ordered her to shoot the dog she had owned about two years.

On Sunday, the Aults and Linda took the dog into the desert near their home. They had the girl dig a shallow grave. Then Mrs. Ault grasped the dog between her hands, and Mr. Ault gave his daughter a .22-caliber pistol and told her to shoot the dog.

Instead, the girl put the pistol to her right temple and shot herself.

The police said there were no charges that could be filed against the parents except possibly cruelty to animals.

Question: Were the police correct?

2. Consider the story of Uriah the Hittite, as told in the Bible, 2 Samuel 11, 12. Uriah was a captain in King David's army. David ordered his General to place Uriah in the "forefront of the hardest fighting, and then draw back from him, that he may be struck down and die." David's motive was to be rid of Uriah so he could marry Uriah's widow, Bath-sheba. David's plan worked: Uriah was killed in the battle with the Ammonites and David married Bath-sheba. The judgment of the Lord upon King David as reported by Nathan the Prophet was: "You have struck down Uriah the Hittite with a sword, the man himself you murdered by the sword of the Ammonites." Would it be proper for a court to so hold under American law? Is the decision in *Campbell* consistent with the Biblical judgment?

Consider also the following hypothetical discussed in Glanville Williams, *Finis for Novus Actus?* 48 Camb. L.J. 391 (1989):

> A distinguished writer recently raised the question whether a general who orders his troops to battle intentionally kills those of his men who fall in action. He was considering this as a problem on intention. There may be some argument on intentionality, but none on the subject of killing. Obviously, it is the enemy, not the general, who kills the men. The reason why the general cannot be said to kill them is not because he does not want to kill them; not because he does not expect the deaths of many of them to follow from obedience to his command; and not because he is justified in issuing the command; it is simply that he has not committed or helped the act of killing, or influenced anybody to do the deed.
>
> A person is primarily responsible for what he himself does. He is not responsible, not blameworthy, for what other people do. The fact that his own conduct, rightful or wrongful, provided the background for a subsequent voluntary and wrong act by another does not make him responsible for it. What he does may be a but-for cause of the injurious act, but he did not do it. His conduct is not an imputable cause of it. Only the later actor, the doer of the act that intervenes between the first act and the result, the final wielder of human autonomy in the matter, bears responsibility (along with his accomplices) for the result that ensues.

Question: Is Professor Williams' analysis of the hypothetical he discusses inconsistent with the Biblical judgment in the case of Uriah the Hittite, or are the situations distinguishable?

3. In Bailey v. Commonwealth, 229 Va. 258, 329 S.E.2d 37 (1985), an appeal from a conviction of involuntary manslaughter, the court summarized the facts as follows.

> The death of the victim, Gordon E. Murdock, occurred during the late evening of May 21, 1983, in the aftermath of an extended and vituperative conversation between Bailey and Murdock over their citizens' band radios. During the conversation, which was to be the last in a series of such violent incidents, Bailey and Murdock cursed and threatened each other repeatedly.
>
> Bailey and Murdock lived about two miles apart in the Roanoke area. On the evening in question, each was intoxicated. Bailey had consumed a "twelve-pack" of beer and a "fifth of liquor" since mid-afternoon; a test of Murdock's blood made during an autopsy showed alcoholic content of ".271% . . . by weight." Murdock was also "legally blind," with vision of only 3/200 in the right eye and 2/200 in the left. Bailey knew that Murdock had "a problem with vision" and that he was intoxicated on the night in question.
>
> Bailey also knew that Murdock owned a handgun and had boasted "about how he would use it and shoot it and scare people off with it." Bailey knew further that Murdock was easily agitated and that he became especially angry if anyone disparaged his war hero, General George S. Patton. During the conversation in question, Bailey implied that General Patton and Murdock himself were homosexuals.
>
> Also during the conversation, Bailey persistently demanded that Murdock arm himself with his handgun and wait on his front porch for Bailey to come and injure or kill him. Murdock responded by saying he would be waiting on his front porch, and he told Bailey to "kiss [his] mother or [his] wife and children good-bye because [he would] never go back home."

Bailey then made two anonymous telephone calls to the Roanoke City Police Department. In the first, Bailey reported "a man . . . out on the porch [at Murdock's address] waving a gun around." A police car was dispatched to the address, but the officers reported they did not "see anything."

Bailey called Murdock back on the radio and chided him for not "going out on the porch." More epithets and threats were exchanged. Bailey told Murdock he was "going to come up there in a blue and white car" [the court here notes that both Bailey and the police drove blue and white cars] and demanded that Murdock "step out there on the . . . porch" with his gun "in [his] hands" because he, Bailey, would "be there in just a minute."

Bailey telephoned the police again. This time, Bailey identified Murdock by name and told the dispatcher that Murdock had "a gun on the porch," had "threatened to shoot up the neighborhood," and was "talking about shooting anything that moves." Bailey insisted that the police "come out here and straighten this man out." Bailey refused to identify himself, explaining that he was "right next to [Murdock] out here" and feared revealing his identity.

Three uniformed police officers, Chambers, Beavers, and Turner, were dispatched to Murdock's home. None of the officers knew that Murdock was intoxicated or that he was in an agitated state of mind. Only Officer Beavers knew that Murdock's eyesight was bad, and he did not know "exactly how bad it was."

When the officers arrived on the scene, they found that Murdock's "porch light was on" but observed no one on the porch. After several minutes had elapsed, the officers observed Murdock come out of his house with "something shiny in his hand." Murdock sat down on the top step of the porch and placed the shiny object beside him.

Officer Chambers approached Murdock from the side of the porch and told him to "[l]eave the gun alone and walk down the stairs away from it." Murdock "just sat there." When Chambers repeated his command, Murdock cursed him. Murdock then reached for the gun, stood up, advanced in Chambers' direction, and opened fire. Chambers retreated and was not struck.

All three officers returned fire, and Murdock was struck. Lying wounded on the porch, he said several times, "I didn't know you was the police." He died from "a gunshot wound of the left side of the chest." In the investigation which followed, Bailey stated that he was "the hoss that caused the loss."

Questions: Was he? How would you analyze the liability of Bailey for the death of Murdock? Can he be said to have killed him?

4. The notion of contributing cause is sometimes invoked in cases of subsequent actions by or upon a person already wounded by defendant. In People v. Lewis, 124 Cal. 551, 57 P. 470 (1889), for example, the defendant shot the victim in the abdomen, inflicting a mortal wound, a severing of the mesenteric artery, which would produce death in an hour, according to medical testimony. Deceased was put to bed and, upon procuring a knife, cut his own throat and died shortly thereafter. Defendant was convicted of manslaughter and appealed, alleging that the facts showed a case where one languishing from a mortal wound is killed by an intervening cause taken in the sense of an act which shortens the life of deceased for any period whatever. The court conceded that if the knife wound was an intervening cause the conviction could not stand unless it were established that the knife wound itself could be attributed to defendant, either by his wielding the knife or because of the causal connection between the gunshot and the knife wound, that is, self-inflicted because of grief and pain or through desire to shield the first actor. The court held that the conviction

should stand in any event, since "when the throat was cut, Farrell was not merely languishing from a mortal wound. He was actually dying; and after the throat was cut he continued to languish from both wounds. Drop by drop the life current went out from both wounds, and at the very instant of death the gunshot wound was contributing to the event."

5. Can the actor ever be an intervening and superseding cause of a result initiated by the actor's original conduct? For example, in Thabo Meli v. Regina, [1954] 1 All E.R. 373 (P.C.), the defendants attacked the deceased with the intent to kill him. Believing he was dead, when in fact he was alive, they rolled him over a cliff where he subsequently died from exposure rather than from the original attack. Presumably the defendants might be found guilty of manslaughter in their reckless treatment of a body that might have been alive. Could they have been found guilty of murder on the basis of their initial assault? Another example is Regina v. Church, [1965] 49 Crim. App. 206, where the defendant, after assaulting and injuring the deceased, threw her body into the Thames in panic, believing he had killed her. In fact, she was then alive and died from drowning. Was this murder? See discussion in Ian D. Elliott, Australian Letter, [1969] Crim. L. Rev. 511; Geoffrey Marston, Contemporaneity of Act and Intention in Crimes, 86 L.Q. Rev. 208 (1970).

PROBLEM: OMISSIONS AS SUPERSEDING CAUSES

Earlier, page 558 supra, we considered the hypothetical of a baby-sitter who deliberately fails to rescue a small child drowning in a shallow pool where a stranger had pushed her. The point was to raise the issue of whether a failure to act can be said to have caused a death. We concluded that it could and that the hypothetical sitter could be held for criminal homicide. But now consider the liability of the stranger. In the earlier discussion it was assumed that he too was liable. But is that conclusion unproblematical? Contrast the case where the sitter does an affirmative action calculated to kill. Suppose, for example, the sitter, seeing the child floundering in the water and wishing to avoid the possibility of someone rescuing it, shoots the child dead. The sitter's action would probably be regarded as a superseding cause, making *his* action the cause of the child's death and not the action of the stranger, who could be held only for attempted murder. The question now is this: Is it possible for a failure to act to amount to a superseding cause, just like an affirmative action?

Consider this case: A robber shoots and injures a victim. The injury is readily treatable if the victim is given prompt medical attention. An ambulance is called, but the driver, who has her own reasons for wanting the victim to die, intentionally delays taking the victim to the hospital until he expires — say she stops at a bar for a leisurely beer and talk with some friends. When she finally reaches the hospital the attendants find the victim dead. The driver could be held for having caused the death of the victim, as we said. But could her failure to act amount to a superseding cause, analogous to the shooting of the child in the pool in our previous hypothetical, so that the person who shot the victim could only be held for attempted murder? If an omission can be a legal cause of a death, why can't it also be a superseding cause? On the other hand, how can actions that kill as intended not be the legal cause of the death just because someone else failed to save the victim? See generally People v. McGee, 31 Cal. 2d 229, 243, 187, P.2d 706 (1947) (wrongful failure to provide proper medical treatment not intervening, superseding cause).

b. Subsequent Actions That Recklessly Risk the Result

COMMONWEALTH v. ROOT

Supreme Court of Pennsylvania
403 Pa. 571, 170 A.2d 310 (1961)

JONES, C.J. The appellant was found guilty of involuntary manslaughter for the death of his competitor in the course of an automobile race between them on a highway. . . .

The testimony, which is uncontradicted in material part, discloses that, on the night of the fatal accident, the defendant accepted the deceased's challenge to engage in an automobile race; that the racing took place on a rural 3-lane highway; that the night was clear and dry, and traffic light; that the speed limit on the highway was 50 miles per hour; that, immediately prior to the accident, the two automobiles were being operated at varying speeds of from 70 to 90 miles per hour; that the accident occurred in a no-passing zone on the approach to a bridge where the highway narrowed to two directionally-opposite lanes; that, at the time of the accident, the defendant was in the lead and was proceeding in his right hand lane of travel; that the deceased, in an attempt to pass the defendant's automobile, when a truck was closely approaching from the opposite direction, swerved his car to the left, crossed the highway's white dividing line and drove his automobile on the wrong side of the highway head-on into the oncoming truck with resultant fatal effect to himself.

This evidence would of course amply support a conviction of the defendant for speeding, reckless driving and, perhaps, other violations of The Vehicle Code. [But] unlawful or reckless conduct is only one ingredient of the crime of involuntary manslaughter. Another essential and distinctly separate element of the crime is that the unlawful or reckless conduct charged to the defendant was the *direct* cause of the death in issue. The first ingredient is obviously present in this case but, just as plainly, the second is not.

While precedent is to be found for application of the tort law concept of "proximate cause" in fixing responsibility for criminal homicide, the want of any rational basis for its use in determining criminal liability can no longer be properly disregarded. When proximate cause was first borrowed from the field of tort law and applied to homicide prosecutions in Pennsylvania, the concept connoted a much more direct causal relation in producing the alleged culpable result than it does today. Proximate cause, as an essential element of a tort founded in negligence, has undergone in recent times, and is still undergoing, a marked extension. More specifically, this area of civil law has been progressively liberalized in favor of claims for damages for personal injuries to which careless conduct of others can in some way be associated. To persist in applying the tort liability concept of proximate cause to prosecutions for criminal homicide after the marked expansion of *civil* liability of defendants in tort actions for negligence would be to extend possible *criminal* liability to persons chargeable with unlawful or reckless conduct in circumstances not generally considered to present the likelihood of a resultant death. . . .

Here, the action of the deceased driver in recklessly and suicidally swerving his car to the left lane of a 2-lane highway into the path of an oncoming truck was not forced upon him by any act of the defendant; it was done by the deceased and by him alone, who thus directly brought about his own demise. . . .

Legal theory which makes guilt or innocence of criminal homicide depend upon such accidental and fortuitous circumstances as are now embraced by modern tort law's encompassing concept of proximate cause is too harsh to be just. . . .

In the case now before us, the deceased was aware of the dangerous condition created by the defendant's reckless conduct in driving his automobile at an excessive rate of speed along the highway but, despite such knowledge, he recklessly chose to swerve his car to the left and into the path of an oncoming truck, thereby bringing about the head-on collision which caused his own death. [T]he defendant's reckless conduct was not a sufficiently direct cause of the competing driver's death to make him criminally liable therefor.

[Reversed.]

EAGEN, J., dissenting. . . . If the defendant did not engage in the unlawful race and so operate his automobile in such a reckless manner, this accident would never have occurred. He helped create the dangerous event. He was a vital part of it. The victim's acts were a natural reaction to the stimulus of the situation. The race, the attempt to pass the other car and forge ahead, the reckless speed, all of these factors the defendant himself helped create. He was part and parcel of them. That the victim's response was normal under the circumstances, that his reaction should have been expected and was clearly foreseeable, is to me beyond argument. That the defendant's recklessness was a substantial factor is obvious. All of this, in my opinion, makes his unlawful conduct a direct cause of the resulting collision. . . .

PEOPLE v. KERN, 545 N.Y.S.2d 4 (App. Div. 1989): [This case arose from the infamous "Howard Beach incident," in which a group of white youths assaulted several black men who were walking in the neighborhood after their car had broken down. The teenagers chased the men, while wielding bats, screaming racial epithets, and threatening to kill them. One of the men, Griffith, tried to escape by running across a highway; he was struck by a car and killed. The defendants were convicted of second-degree manslaughter and appealed, arguing that there was insufficient evidence of causation, and furthermore that the driver (Blum) who struck Griffith had been negligent, and therefore his actions constituted an intervening act that broke the chain of causation. Upholding the convictions the court stated:] [U]nder these circumstances, the defendants' actions were a "sufficiently direct cause" of Griffith's ensuing death so as to warrant the imposition of criminal liability. . . . [T]he only reasonable alternative left open to Griffith while being persistently chased and threatened by the defendants and their friends, several of whom were carrying weapons, was to seek safety by crossing the parkway where he unfortunately met his death. Clearly, on the basis of these facts, it cannot be said that the defendants' despicable conduct was not a sufficiently direct cause of Griffith's death. The defendants will not be heard to complain that, in desperately fleeing their murderous assault, Griffith chose the wrong escape route.

The defendants' further assertion that Blum's alleged negligent operation of his vehicle was an intervening proximate cause of Griffith's death is also without merit. Based on the circumstances surrounding the incident, including the dark early morning hour, it cannot be said that an intervening wrongful act occurred to relieve the defendants from the directly foreseeable consequences of their actions. Moreover, even if we assume that Blum was less than cautious in the operation of his vehicle, the facts demonstrate that his actions were not the sole cause of Griffith's ensuing death since it was the defendants' wrongful conduct which forced Griffith to seek refuge from his assailants by crossing the highway.

QUESTIONS

1. Is the *Kern* case inconsistent with the *Root* case or is it distinguishable?

2. In Commonwealth v. Berggren, 496 N.E.2d 660 (Mass. 1986), a motorcyclist ignored a patrolman's signal to pull over and attempted to out-distance the officer. After a high-speed chase over six miles of narrow, winding roads, the police officer lost control of his vehicle and was killed in the resulting crash. Although the motorcyclist was one hundred yards ahead of the officer at the time of the accident and was unaware of the crash, his conviction for negligent homicide was upheld.

In People v. Matos, 83 N.Y.2d 509 (1994), the defendant, running from the scene of an armed robbery he had just committed, climbed a ladder to the roof of a building and fled in the dark across the Manhattan rooftops. The police officer pursuing him fell down an air shaft and plunged 25 feet to his death. The New York Court of Appeals upheld a conviction for felony murder on the ground that the officer's death was a foreseeable result of the defendant's burglary and his flight therefrom.

Are these cases inconsistent with *Root* or are they distinguishable?

STATE v. McFADDEN

Supreme Court of Iowa
320 N.W.2d 608 (1982)

ALLBEE, J. This case stems from a drag race between defendant Michael Dwayne McFadden and another driver, Matthew Sulgrove, which occurred on a Des Moines city street in April 1980. During the course of the two vehicles' southbound progression, Sulgrove lost control of his automobile and swerved into a lane of oncoming traffic, where he struck a lawfully operated northbound vehicle. This third vehicle contained a six-year-old passenger, Faith Ellis, who was killed in the collision along with Sulgrove. Defendant's automobile did not physically contact either of the two colliding vehicles.

Defendant was charged with two counts of involuntary manslaughter, a violation of section 707.5(1), The Code 1979. Having waived a jury, defendant was tried to the court and convicted and sentenced on both counts. In this appeal, he challenged the validity of his convictions and the sentences imposed. . . . [D]efendant does not argue that the evidence was insufficient for trial court to find that both he and Sulgrove recklessly committed those public offenses prior to the accident. Rather, defendant's main contention is that proof of the causation element . . . was lacking.

Trial court found that defendant was guilty of involuntary manslaughter under each of three separate theories: (1) that defendant aided and abetted Sulgrove in Sulgrove's commission of involuntary manslaughter; (2) that defendant was vicariously responsible for Sulgrove's commission of involuntary manslaughter by reason of their joint participation in the public offense of drag racing; and (3) that defendant himself committed the crime of involuntary manslaughter by recklessly engaging in a drag race so as to proximately cause the Sulgrove-Ellis collision.

We note that aiding and abetting and joint criminal conduct are theories of vicarious liability, based on Sulgrove's commission of involuntary manslaughter. Although a vicarious liability theory may be sufficient to convict defendant for the death of Faith Ellis,[a] the same is not true with regard to the death of Sulgrove. This is because the involuntary manslaughter statute requires proof that the perpetrator caused the death of "another person." Obviously, Sulgrove could not have committed involuntary manslaughter with respect to his own death. Therefore, a theory under which defendant is only vicariously liable for Sulgrove's crime would be inadequate to convict defendant for Sulgrove's death. We turn, then, to consideration of the third theory of liability, i.e., that defendant's reckless commission of the public offense of drag racing was a proximate cause of the Sulgrove and Ellis deaths. . . .

Defendant asserts that because Sulgrove was a competitor in the drag race, he assumed the risk of his own death, and therefore defendant could not be convicted or sentenced for that death. . . . We quote with approval the following discussion from [Commonwealth v. Peak, 12 Pa. D.&C. 379, 382 (1961)] which is pertinent to the issue at hand:

> Defendants by participating in the unlawful racing initiated a series of events resulting in the death of Young. Under these circumstances, decedent's own unlawful conduct does not absolve defendants from their guilt. The acts of defendants were contributing and substantial factors in bringing about the death of Young. The acts and omissions of two or more persons may work concurrently as the efficient cause of an injury and in such case each of the participating acts or omissions is regarded in law as a proximate cause.

We hold that the fact of Sulgrove's voluntary and reckless participation in the drag race does not of itself bar defendant from being convicted of involuntary manslaughter for Sulgrove's death.

Next, defendant contends trial court erred in applying the civil standard of proximate cause in a criminal prosecution, rather than adopting the more stringent standard of "direct causal connection" used by the Pennsylvania court in Commonwealth v. Root, 403 Pa. 571, 580, 170 A.2d 310, 314 (1961). In *Root*, the court held that "the tort liability concept of proximate cause has no proper

---

a. The possibility of an aiding-and-abetting theory in cases of this kind is considered infra page 662.

place in prosecutions for criminal homicide and more direct causal connection is required for conviction." . . . We had occasion to consider a similar standard-of-causation issue in State v. Marti, 290 N.W.2d 570, 584-585 (Iowa 1980), which upheld the involuntary manslaughter conviction of a man who provided an obviously intoxicated, suicidal woman with the means to shoot herself by loading a gun for her and placing it within her reach. As here, the defendant in *Marti* argued that the trial court "inappropriately adopted the standards of proximate cause applied in civil cases." Unlike the Pennsylvania court in *Root*, however, we said in *Marti* that we were "unwilling to hold as a blanket rule of law that instructions used in civil trials regarding proximate cause are inappropriate for criminal trials." Id. We explained: One reason for this is the similar functions that the requirement of proximate cause plays in both sorts of trials. The element of proximate cause in criminal prosecutions serves as a requirement that there be a sufficient causal relationship between the defendant's conduct and a proscribed harm to hold him criminally responsible. Similarly, in the law of torts it is the element that requires there to be a sufficient causal relationship between the defendant's conduct and the plaintiff's damage to hold the defendant civilly liable. . . .

[D]efendant has suggested no specific policy differences, nor can we think of any, that would justify a different standard of proximate causation under our involuntary manslaughter statute than under our tort law. The *Root* court opined that "[l]egal theory which makes guilt or innocence of criminal homicide depend upon such accidental and fortuitous circumstances as are now embraced by modern tort law's encompassing concept of proximate cause is too harsh to be just." We do not agree. Proximate cause is based on the concept of foreseeability. We believe the foreseeability requirement, coupled with the requirement of recklessness . . . will prevent the possibility of harsh or unjust results in involuntary manslaughter cases. . . .

Accordingly, we hold that trial court did not err in applying ordinary proximate cause principles to determine whether the causation element . . . had been met, and in declining to adopt the more stringent "direct causal connection" standard of *Root*.

[Convictions affirmed.]

COMMONWEALTH v. ATENCIO

Supreme Judicial Court of Massachusetts
345 Mass. 627, 189 N.E.2d (1963)

WILKINS, C.J. Each defendant has been convicted upon an indictment for manslaughter in the death of Stewart E. Britch. . . . The defendants argue assignments of error in the denial of motions for directed verdicts. . . .

Facts which the jury could have found are these. On Sunday, October 22, 1961, the deceased, his brother Ronald, and the defendants spent the day drinking wine in the deceased's room in a rooming house in Boston. At some time in the afternoon, with reference to nothing specific so far as the record discloses, Marshall said, "I will settle this," went out, and in a few minutes returned clicking a gun, from which he removed one bullet. Early in the evening Ronald left, and the conversation turned to "Russian roulette." . . .

[T]he "game" was played. The deceased and Atencio were seated on a bed, and Marshall was seated on a couch. First, Marshall examined the gun, saw that it contained one cartridge, and after spinning it on his arm, pointed it at his head, and pulled the trigger. Nothing happened. He handed the gun to Atencio, who repeated the process, again without result. Atencio passed the gun to the deceased, who spun it, put it to his head, then pulled the trigger. The cartridge exploded, and he fell over dead. . . .

We are of opinion that the defendants could properly have been found guilty of manslaughter. This is not a civil action against the defendants by the personal representatives of Stewart Britch. In such a case his voluntary act, we assume, would be a bar. Here the Commonwealth had an interest that the deceased should not be killed by the wanton or reckless conduct of himself and others. . . . Such conduct could be found in the concerted action and cooperation of the defendants in helping to bring about the deceased's foolish act. . . .

The defendants argue as if it should have been ruled, as matter of law, that there were three "games" of solitaire and not one "game" of "Russian roulette." That the defendants participated could be found to be a cause and not a mere condition of Stewart Britch's death. It is not correct to say that his act could not be found to have been caused by anything which Marshall and Atencio did, nor that he would have died when the gun went off in his hand no matter whether they had done the same. The testimony does not require a ruling that when the deceased took the gun from Atencio it was an independent or intervening act not standing in any relation to the defendants' acts which would render what he did imputable to them. It is an oversimplification to contend that each participated in something that only one could do at a time. There could be found to be mutual encouragement in a joint enterprise. In the abstract, there may have been no duty on the defendants to prevent the deceased from playing. But there was a duty on their part not to cooperate or join with him in the "game." Nor, if the facts presented such a case, would we have to agree that if the deceased, and not the defendants, had played first that they could not have been found guilty of manslaughter. The defendants were much more than merely present at a crime. It would not be necessary that the defendants force the deceased to play or suggest that he play.

We are referred in both briefs to cases of manslaughter arising out of automobiles racing upon the public highway. . . .

Whatever may be thought of those . . . decisions, there is a very real distinction between drag racing and "Russian roulette." In the former much is left to the skill, or lack of it, on the competitor. In "Russian roulette" it is a matter of luck as to the location of the one bullet, and except for a misfire (of which there was evidence in the case at bar) the outcome is a certainty if the chamber under the hammer happens to be the one containing the bullet. . . .

The judgments on the indictments for manslaughter are affirmed. . . .

NOTES AND QUESTIONS

1. In Lewis v. State, 474 So. 2d 766 (Ala. Crim. App. 1985), the defendant introduced Damon Sanders (a 15-year-old boy) to the game of Russian roulette and played it with him on several occasions without incident. (It was unclear

whether the gun had been loaded on those occasions.) After one such game the defendant put the gun away and went into the next room to make a phone call. While he was on the phone, other witnesses outside the house observed Sanders spin the chamber, point the gun at his head and pull the trigger; the gun fired, killing Sanders instantly. The court accepted the state's premise that Sanders would not have died if the defendant had not "directed, instructed and influenced" Sanders to play the game, and that the defendant would have been liable if he had been in the room or otherwise playing the game at the time. The court nonetheless held that liability was precluded because "the free will of the victim is seen as an intervening cause which . . . breaks the chain of causation." Id. at 771, quoting Susan W. Brenner, Undue Influence in the Criminal Law: A Proposed Analysis of "Causing Suicide," 47 Alb. L. Rev. 62, 83 (1982).

Question: Is this situation distinguishable from that in *Atencio?*

2. In Commonwealth v. Feinberg, 433 Pa. 558, 253 A.2d 636 (1969), the defendant was a proprietor of a cigar store in a skid-row area of Philadelphia. One of the items he had regularly stocked and sold was sterno, a canned heat containing methanol. Late in 1963 he received a single shipment of a new kind of sterno called "industrial" sterno, which contained a much higher percentage of methanol. This made it far more dangerous for persons to consume internally. Imprinted on the lids of the new sterno was the legend: "Institutional sterno. Danger. Poison. For use only as a fuel. Not for consumer use. For industrial and commercial use." The defendant sold approximately 400 cans of the new industrial sterno before returning the remainder of the shipment to the manufacturer. About 32 persons in the skid-row area died as a result of methanol poisoning caused by drinking the cans of industrial sterno sold by defendant. Defendant was subsequently tried and convicted of manslaughter. The record showed that the defendant was aware of the proclivity of some of his customers to consume the sterno for its intoxicating effect. There was also sufficient evidence to warrant the conclusion that the defendant was aware or should have been aware that the sterno he was selling was toxic if consumed. On appeal the Supreme Court of Pennsylvania affirmed the conviction. In explaining why *Root* was inapplicable, the court said:

> Defendant contends that the drinking of liquor by deceased was his voluntary act and served as an intervening cause, breaking the causal connection between the giving of the liquor by defendant and the resulting death. The drinking of the liquor, in consequence of defendant's act, was, however, what the defendant contemplated. Deceased, it is true, may have been negligent in drinking, but, where the defendant was negligent, then the contributory negligence of the deceased will be no defense in a criminal action.

3. Suppose Livia provides Augustus with a controlled substance, a dangerous drug, at Augustus' request. If her purpose is to help Augustus commit suicide and he does so, as we have seen (People v. Campbell, supra page 561), Livia cannot be held for killing him (although she might be guilty of a statutory offense of assisting another to commit suicide). But suppose her purpose was to indulge Augustus' desire to experiment with a new drug, and in doing so Augustus took an overdose and died. Could she then be held to have caused his death and hence be liable for manslaughter or perhaps murder under a felony-murder

theory? Many cases have so held. See, e.g., Heacock v. Commonwealth, 323 S.E.2d 90 (Va. 1984). See also Ramirez, Homicide Liability for the Furnishing of Dangerous Narcotics, 6 St. Louis U. Pub. L. Rev. 161 (1987). How can we account for the apparent paradox that if Livia only intends to help Augustus enjoy the drug she may be held for killing him, but if she intends for Augustus to die she could not be?

c.   A Statutory Solution

CALIFORNIA JOINT LEGISLATIVE COMMITTEE FOR REVISION OF THE PENAL CODE, PENAL CODE REVISION PROJECT
(Tent. Draft No. 2, 1968)

SECTION 408.   CAUSATION: RESPONSIBILITY FOR CAUSING A RESULT

(1) An element of an offense which requires that the defendant have caused a particular result is established when his conduct is an antecedent but for which the result would not have occurred, and,

(a) if the offense requires that the defendant intentionally or knowingly cause the result, that the actual result, as it occurred,

(i) is within the purpose or contemplation of the defendant, whether the purpose or contemplation extends to natural events or to the conduct of another, or, if not,

(ii) involves the same kind of injury or harm as that designed or contemplated and is not too remote, accidental in its occurrence or dependent on another's volitional act to have a just bearing on the defendant's liability or on the gravity of his offense;

(b) if the offense requires that the defendant recklessly or negligently cause the result, that the actual result, as it occurred,

(i) is within the risk of which the defendant was or should have been aware, whether that risk extends to natural events or to the conduct of another, or, if not,

(ii) involves the same kind of injury or harm as that recklessly or negligently risked and is not too remote, accidental in its occurrence or dependent on another's volitional act to have a just bearing on the defendant's liability or on the gravity of his offense;

(c) if the offense imposes strict liability, that the actual result, as it occurred, is a probable consequence of the actor's conduct.

QUESTIONS

The foregoing California draft builds upon the Model Penal Code's formulation but makes several changes in substance as well as arrangement. What are those changes, and how significant are they?

Consider the comments of H. L. A. Hart & A. Honoré, Causation in the Law 398 (2d ed. 1985). Referring to the Model Penal Code formulation, they observe that it is open to the criticism that:

it does not provide *specifically* for those cases where causal problems arise because, although the accused did not intend it, another human action besides accused's is involved in the production of the proscribed harm. These are treated merely as one kind of case where harm may or may not be "too accidental" in its manner or occurrence. This is surely a weakness in a scheme which is designed to reproduce, and to allow the jury to express, the convictions of common sense that, even if harm would not have occurred without the act of accused, it is still necessary to distinguish, for purposes of punishment, one manner of upshot from another. For whatever else may be vague or disputable about common sense in regard to causation and responsibility, it is surely clear that the primary case where it is reluctant to treat a person as having caused harm which would not have occurred without his act is that where another voluntary human action has intervened.

Are these appropriate suggestions in drafting a causation provision? Does the California draft meet them? For example, do you agree with the drafters that the formulation in paragraphs (a)(ii) and (b)(ii) ("too . . . dependent on another's volitional act," etc.)[2] provides the right framework for dealing with intervening but unexpected acts?[3]

B. ATTEMPT

1. Introduction

Statutory definitions of the crime of attempt are usually minimal. Consider some representative examples: "A person is guilty of an attempt to commit a crime when, with the intent to commit a crime, he engages in conduct which tends to effect the commission of such crime" (N.Y. Penal Law §110.00); "Every person who attempts to commit any crime, but fails, or is prevented or intercepted in the perpetration thereof is punishable . . ." (Cal. Penal Code §664); "A person commits an attempt when, with intent to commit a specific offense, he does any act which constitutes a substantial step toward the commission of that offense" (Ill. Stat. Ch. 720, §5/8-4(a)); "[W]hoever, within the special maritime and territorial jurisdiction of the United States, attempts to commit murder or manslaughter shall be [punishable]" (18 U.S.C. §113).

At common law attempts were misdemeanors. Today the usual punishment grading system for attempt involves making it punishable by a reduced factor of the punishment for the completed crime. In California (Cal. Penal Code §664) attempt carries a maximum term of not more than one-half of the highest maximum term authorized for the completed offense. Under the New York Penal Law, which uses punishment classification of offenses, the sentence for an attempt is one classification below that for the completed crime (§110.05), ex-

---

2. Some states have adopted this formulation. See Del. Code Ann. tit. 11, §702-216; Hawaii Rev. Stat. §§702-215(2) & 702-216(2); N.J. Stat. Ann. tit. 2C, §2C:2-3.

3. Compare Model Penal Code and Commentaries, Comment to §2.03 at 262 (1985): "The language of Subsection (2)(b) [of the MPC] does not accept the view that volitional human intervention should be treated differently from other intervening causes, but neither does it mandate a contrary position. It is up to the trier of fact to give weight to such variables if it is persuaded that these considerations are significant. . . ."

cept for certain offenses, notably drug offenses, where the punishment is the same. Since the Model Penal Code proposals, however, a substantial minority of states have departed from the predominant scheme by making the punishment the same for the attempt as for the crime attempted, except for crimes punishable by death or life imprisonment. See, e.g., Conn. Gen. Stat. Ann. §53a-51; Del. Code Ann. tit. 11, §531; Ill. Ann. Stat. Ch. 720, §5/8-4(c); Pa. Stat. Ann. tit. 18, §905.

What is the justification for the traditional approach to the punishment grading of attempt? The relationship of harm to the proper degree of punishment is a pervasive problem in criminal law. The issue is implicit in several topics we have already considered. Thus, all the cases on causation in effect require us to consider the reasons why conduct that causes harm should ever be treated differently from identical conduct that does not. A similar issue is implicit in the Chapter 5 materials dealing with homicidal risk creation. An actor whose recklessness or criminal negligence creates a substantial risk of death can be convicted of manslaughter and sometimes even of murder, provided that death actually results. But what crime has the actor committed if the person he endangers suffers only nonlethal injuries or escapes with no injuries at all? Because such an actor is not "attempting" to kill anyone, he normally cannot be convicted of any form of attempted homicide. (We explore this point in connection with the mens rea of attempt at page 585 infra.) Absent some statutory risk-creation offense (such as Model Penal Code §211.2), such an actor may have committed no crime at all. But even if there is a criminal offense that applies to his conduct, its penalties will be far lower than those applicable under homicide statutes when a death occurs. The law of attempts poses the same issue in its starkest form. The actor who intentionally seeks to cause a harm (the death of another person, for example) is traditionally punished much less severely if his attempt proves unsuccessful. Is there sufficient justification for attributing so much importance in punishment to the actual result of a defendant's conduct? Consider the following comments.

JAMES FITZJAMES STEPHEN, A HISTORY OF THE CRIMINAL LAW (VOL. 3) 311 (1883): If two persons are guilty of the very same act of negligence, and if one of them causes thereby a railway accident, involving the death and mutilation of many persons, whereas the other does no injury to anyone, it seems to me that it would be rather pedantic than rational to say that each had committed the same offence, and should be subjected to the same punishment. In one sense, each has committed an offence, but the one has had the *bad luck* to cause a horrible misfortune, and to attract public attention to it, and the other the good *fortune* to do no harm. Both certainly deserve punishment, but it gratifies a natural public feeling to choose out for punishment the one who actually has caused great harm, and the effect in the way of preventing a repetition of the offence is much the same as if both were punished.

H. L. A. HART, THE MORALITY OF THE CRIMINAL LAW 52-53 (1965): [Professor Hart, after quoting the above extract from Stephen, observes:] This doctrine allocating to "public feeling" so important a place in the determination of punishment reflects the element of populism which, as we have seen, is often prominent in English judicial conceptions of the morality of punishment. But it conflicts with important principles of justice as between different offenders which would prima facie preclude treating two persons, guilty of "the very same act" of negligence, differently because of a fortuitous difference in the outcome of these acts. No doubt there is often an inclination to treat punishment like compensation and measure it by the outcome alone. There may even be at times a public demand that this should be done. And no doubt if the machinery of justice were nullified or could not proceed unless the demand were gratified we might have to gratify it and hope to educate people out of this misassimilation of the principles of punishment to those of compensation. But there seems no good reason for adopting this misassimilation as a principle or to stigmatise as pedantic the refusal to recognise that the difference made by "bad fortune" and "good luck" to the outcome of the very same acts justifies punishing the one and not the other.

STEPHEN J. SCHULHOFER, ATTEMPT, in 1 Encyclopedia of Crime and Justice 97 (1983): [T]he most plausible explanation for more lenient treatment of attempts is that the community's resentment and demand for punishment are not aroused to the same degree when serious harm has been averted. This explanation, however, raises further questions. Can severe punishment (in the case of completed crime, for example) be justified simply by reference to the fact that society "demands" or at least desires this? To what extent should the structure of penalties serve to express intuitive societal judgments that cannot be rationalized in terms of such instrumental goals as deterrence, isolation, rehabilitation, and even retribution — that is, condemnation reflecting the moral culpability of the act? Conversely, to what extent should the criminal justice system see its mission as one not of expressing the intuitive social demand for punishment, but rather as one of restraining that demand and of protecting *from* punishment the offender who, rationally speaking, deserves a less severe penalty?

MODEL PENAL CODE: *Section 5.05(1).* Except as otherwise provided in this Section, attempt, solicitation and conspiracy are crimes of the same grade and degree as the most serious offense which is attempted or solicited or is an object of the conspiracy. An attempt, solicitation or conspiracy to commit a [capital crime or a] felony of the first degree is a felony of the second degree. [Under §6.06, a felony of the first degree is punishable by imprisonment for a term whose minimum is between 1 and 10 years and whose maximum is life. A felony of the second degree is punishable by imprisonment for a term whose minimum is between one and three years and whose maximum is 10 years.]

MODEL PENAL CODE AND COMMENTARIES, Comment to §5.05 at 490 (1985): The theory of this grading system may be stated simply. To the extent that sentencing depends upon the antisocial disposition of the actor and the demonstrated need for a corrective sanction, there is likely to be little difference in the gravity of the required measures depending on the consummation or the failure of the plan. It is only when and insofar as the severity of sentence is designed for general deterrent purposes that a distinction on this ground is likely to have reasonable force. It is doubtful, however, that the threat of punishment for the inchoate crime can add significantly to the net deterrent efficacy of the sanction threatened for the substantive offense that is the actor's object, which he, by hypothesis, ignores. Hence, there is a basis for economizing in use of the heaviest and most afflictive sanctions by removing them from the inchoate crimes.

H. L. A. HART, PUNISHMENT AND RESPONSIBILITY 129-131 (1968): It is perfectly true that those who commit crimes intend to succeed, but this does not show that punishing a man for an unsuccessful attempt will not increase the efficacy of the law's threats, or that failure to punish him would not often diminish their efficacy. This is so for two reasons: first, there must be many who are not completely confident that they will succeed in their criminal objective, but will be prepared to run the risk of punishment if they can be assured that they have to pay nothing for attempts which fail; whereas if unsuccessful attempts were also punished the price might appear to them to be too high. Again, there must be many cases where men might with good or bad reason believe that if they succeed in committing some crime they will escape, but if they fail they may be caught. Treason is only the most obvious of such cases, and unless attempts were punished, there would, in such cases, be no deterrent force in the law's threat attached to the main crime.

[A] retributive theory in which severity of punishment is proportioned to the allegedly evil intentions of the criminal is in grave difficulty; for there seems to be no difference in wickedness, though there may be in skill, between the successful and the unsuccessful attempt in this respect. Very often an unsuccessful attempt is merely the accidental failure to commit the crime because somebody unexpectedly intervenes and frustrates the attempt. As far as I can see a deterrent theory, except in relation to a very specialized class of crimes, is in similar difficulties. The exceptions, which have been mooted since Beccaria first discussed them, are those crimes whose consummation occupies a considerable space of time so that the criminal may have time between the attempt and its consummation to think again. [I]f he is already involved in the full penalty by virtue of merely having attempted to commit the crime, he may have no motive for desisting. . . . Such cases are, of course, realities; but they are surely very rare, if only because in the law of most systems in order to be guilty of an attempt one has to get very near to the completion of the full offence. . . . Yet apart from this, there seems no reason on any form of deterrent theory, whether we consider the general deterrent or the individual deterrent, for punishing the unsuccessful attempt less severely than the completed crime. The individual who has tried but failed to carry out the planned crime may need just as much punishment to keep him straight in the future as the successful criminal. He may be as much disposed to repeat his crime.

The almost universal tendency in punishing to discriminate between attempts and completed crimes rests, I think, on a version of the retributive theory which has permeated certain branches of English law, and yet has on occasion been stigmatized even by English judges as illogical. This is the simple theory that it is a perfectly legitimate ground to grade punishments according to the amount of harm actually done, whether this was intended or not; "if he has done the harm he must pay for it, but if he has not done it he should pay less." To many people such a theory of punishment seems to confuse punishment with compensation, the amount of which should indeed be fixed in relation to harm done. Even if punishment and compensation were not distinguished in primitive law, many think that this is no excuse for confusing them now. Why should the accidental fact that an intended harmful outcome has not occurred be a ground for punishing less a criminal who may be equally dangerous and equally wicked? I may be wrong in thinking that there is so little to be said for this form of retributive theory. It is certainly popular, and the nearest to a rational defence that I know of it is the following. It is pointed out that in some cases the successful completion of a crime may be a source of gratification, and, in the case of theft, of actual gain, and in such cases to punish the successful criminal more severely may be one way of depriving him of these illicit satisfactions which the unsuccessful have never had. This argument, which certainly has some attraction where the successful criminal has hidden loot to enjoy on emerging from prison, would be an interesting addition to theories of punishment of the principle that the wicked should not be allowed to profit by their crimes.

My own belief is that this form of retributive theory appeals to something with deeper instinctive roots than the last mentioned principle. Certainly the resentment felt by a victim actually injured is normally much greater than that felt by the intended victim who has escaped harm because an attempted crime has failed. Bishop Butler, in his sermon on resentment explains on this ground the distinction men draw between 'an injury done' and one 'which, though designed, was prevented, in cases where the guilt is perhaps the same.' But again the question arises, if this form of retributive theory depends on the connection between blame and resentment, whether the law should give effect to such a theory. Can we not control resentment, however natural, in the interests of some deliberate forward-looking policy, much as we control our natural fears in the interest of forward-looking prudential aims? And if we can do this, should we not do so? And might not this require us in some cases to punish attempts as severely as the completed offence?

NOTE

For further exploration of these issues, see Sanford H. Kadish, The Criminal Law and the Luck of the Draw, 84 J. Crim. L. & Criminology 679 (1994); Stephen J. Schulhofer, Harm and Punishment: A Critique of Emphasis on the Results of Conduct in the Criminal Law, 122 U. Pa. L. Rev. 1497 (1974). For discussion of the grading issue from the perspective of the economic analysis of law, see Steven Shavell, Deterrence and the Punishment of Attempts, 19 J. Legal Stud. 435 (1990).

2. Mens Rea

PEOPLE v. KRAFT

Appellate Court of Illinois, 1st District
133 Ill. App. 3d 294, 478 N.E.2d 1154 (1985)

BUCKLEY, J.: Following a jury trial, defendant Paul Kraft was found guilty on two counts of attempted murder. [D]efendant was sentenced to 10 years imprisonment on each count, the sentences to run concurrently. . . .

Evidence produced by the State reveals that Mr. and Mrs. Roderick Grossi, aged 71 and 62 years respectively, were on their way home from a Sunday drive on July 24, 1982, at about 7:40 p.m. [When Mr. Grossi attempted to pass a truck (driven by defendant), the truck accelerated and forced the Grossi vehicle off the road. Shortly thereafter Mr. Grossi saw the truck parked on the road ahead of him. He] decided he wanted to talk to the driver and pulled up very close to the truck. . . . Before Mr. Grossi had a chance to say anything, defendant fired a shot, over the Grossi's car, which was within four feet of defendant's truck. . . . Mr. Grossi stepped on the accelerator and heard two or three more shots. . . . A bullet hole was later discovered in the right rear tail lens of the Grossi's car. The bullet was recovered from the trunk of the car.

[Mr. Grossi hailed a police car. Officer Lancaster turned his squad car around and drove up to defendant's truck. As the officer started to get out of his car, defendant pointed a gun at him.] Officer Lancaster crouched behind the open door of his squad car and ordered defendant to drop the gun. He repeated the order a second time at which time defendant fired [two shots.] Lancaster shot back and moved to the back of his car to reload. As he did, defendant turned his truck and proceeded southbound on Western Avenue. [After police succeeded in blocking the road and shooting out the truck's tires, defendant repeatedly fired at Lancaster and other officers. Some of the shots were fired from very close range.] Defendant subsequently threw out his gun and was removed from the truck. He had been wounded in the face and neck. . . .

Defendant testified that when the Grossis' car pulled up next to him after they had swerved off the road, . . . he became very afraid and pulled out a gun and fired it over their car. Defendant admitted firing a few more shots in the "general direction" of the Grossis' car as they drove away. Defendant claimed he only intended to scare them away and he thought they might have had a gun "or something." Defendant stated that when he thought about what he had done, he was in shock. He claimed he fired at Officer Lancaster because "he just wanted to die" after he realized what he had done to Mr. and Mrs. Grossi. . . .

Defendant also presented expert testimony on his mental condition. Dr. Albert Stipes testified that he had examined defendant on two occasions and diagnosed him as having a schizotypal personality disorder with depression and a history of drug abuse. . . .

Dr. Stipes further testified that during these interviews defendant related some details of the shooting incident. Defendant indicated that he had been drinking and smoking marijuana and that he was "high but not drunk." He . . . said he felt the [Grossis] were harassing him. Defendant told Dr. Stipes that he pursued and fired at the occupants of the car to scare them but then became fearful that they would tell the police and he would be arrested. He became so depressed at this prospect that he decided to commit suicide by letting the police shoot him. Defendant further stated that when he was confronted by the police, he shot in various areas, not intending to shoot or harm anyone. Based upon these statements and other available information, Dr. Stipes testified that he was of the opinion that defendant was sane at the time of the incident and that he had full knowledge and was aware of what he was doing. . . .

From the foregoing, it is clear that defendant's entire defense was predicated on the theory that he never intended to kill anyone and therefore he lacked the required mental state for attempted murder. . . . Accordingly, the question of jury instructions on the required mental state for attempted murder is of critical importance.

The record reveals that the following instructions were given to the jury:

> A person commits the offense of murder when he kills an individual if, in performing the acts which cause the death, he intends to kill that individual; or he knows that such acts will cause death to that individual; or he knows that such acts create a strong probability of death to that individual. . . .
>
> A person commits the offense of attempted murder when he, with intent to commit the offense of murder, does any act which constitutes a substantial step toward the commission of the offense of murder.
>
> The offense attempted need not have been committed.

Judging from the number of decisions addressing this issue, the proper jury instructions for attempted murder has served as a continuing source of confusion and uncertainty among members of the bar. All authorities agree that the crime of attempt is a specific intent crime and "an instruction must make it clear that to convict for attempted murder nothing less than a criminal intent to kill must be shown." However, problems have arisen in the past from the fact that in an attempted murder trial the jurors must be instructed not only on the crime of attempt but also on the target crime attempted, here murder.

The crime of murder is defined in our statute as follows:

> (a) A person who kills an individual without lawful justification commits murder if, in performing the acts which cause the death:
>
> (1) He either intends to kill or do great bodily harm to that individual or another, or knows that such acts will cause death to that individual or another; or
>
> (2) He knows that such acts create a strong probability of death or great bodily harm to that individual or another; or
>
> (3) He is attempting or committing a forcible felony other than voluntary manslaughter. Ill. Rev. Stat. 1983, ch. 38, par. 9-1(a).

The crime of attempt has been statutorily defined as follows:

> A person commits an attempt when, with intent to commit a specific offense, he does any act which constitutes a substantial step toward the commission of that offense. Ill. Rev. Stat. 1983, ch. 38, par. 8-4.

From the above, it is clear that a discrepancy exists between the culpable mental state for attempt which requires an intent to commit the offense and the alternative culpable mental states for murder which include not only intent to kill another, but also intent to do great bodily harm, or knowledge that one's acts create a strong probability of death or great bodily harm. . . .

In People v. Morano (1979), 69 Ill. App. 3d 580, 387 N.E.2d 816, the court reviewed an attempted murder conviction where the jury was given an instruction which stated that one commits murder if "he knows that such acts will cause death to that individual or he knows that such acts create a strong probability of death to that individual." The court held that knowledge that one's actions create a strong probability of death sufficiently satisfied the intent to kill requirement for attempted murder and upheld the conviction. . . .

The validity of *Morano* has been called into question by the recent Illinois Supreme Court opinion in People v. Jones (1979), 81 Ill. 2d 1, 405 N.E.2d 343. There, the court . . . commented broadly on the required mental state for attempted murder, noting:

> The offense of attempted murder requires the mental state of specific intent to commit murder, to kill someone. Section 8-4(a) of the Criminal Code of 1961 clearly sets this out: 'A person commits an attempt when, with intent to commit a specific offense, he does any act which constitutes a substantial step toward the commission of that offense.' *Knowledge* that the consequences of an accused's act may result in death (or grave bodily injury), or intent to do bodily harm, is not enough; specific intent to kill is required. . . .

The court went on to contrast the mental state requirements of attempted murder and murder:

> The offense of murder, on the other hand, does not always require specific intent to kill. Specific intent to do grave bodily harm or knowledge that one's actions will cause or could cause death or bodily harm are also sufficient mental states for murder.

From the above quoted language it would appear that *knowledge* that the consequences of one's act may result in death does not satisfy the specific intent requirement for attempted murder. . . .

The instructions given in the case at bar are virtually identical to those found proper in *Morano* and its progeny. However, we believe the rule espoused in *Jones* . . . to be the better approach. The *Morano* court acknowledged that the crime of attempted murder requires that the defendant act with "intent to kill." Yet, the court went on to erroneously conclude that knowledge that one's conduct creates a strong probability of death will satisfy the specific intent to kill requirement imposed by our attempt statute. . . .

Our criminal code contains separate statutory definitions for the four culpable mental states of intent, knowledge, recklessness, and negligence, with knowledge encompassing a distinct and less purposeful state of mind than intent. In so doing, our state legislature manifested a desire to treat intent and knowledge as distinct mental states when imposing criminal liability for conduct. . . .

Based on the foregoing, we must reverse and remand for a new trial. The instructions given in the case at bar would have permitted a conviction upon finding that defendant acted with knowledge that his actions created a strong probability of death even if the jury believed defendant did not intend to kill anyone. . . .

Reversed and remanded.

NOTES AND QUESTIONS

1. Both the common law and the majority of American statutory formulations are in accord with the result in *Kraft* — an attempt requires a purpose or "specific intent" to produce the proscribed result, even when recklessness or some lesser mens rea would suffice for conviction of the completed offense. See, e.g.,

People v. Campbell, 72 N.Y.2d 602, 532 N.E.2d 86 (1988); Keys v. State, 766 P.2d 270 (Nev. 1988); Model Penal Code §5.01(1)(b), Appendix.

2. Assume that a defendant, in order to destroy a competitor's experimental aircraft, plants a bomb on the plane and sets it to explode in midair, knowing that the test pilot will be killed. The bomb fails to explode. May the defendant be convicted of attempted murder? Does he have a "purpose" or "specific intent" to kill? Note the solution to this problem in Model Penal Code §5.01(1)(b): The required mens rea is satisfied if the defendant acts "with the purpose of causing or with the belief that [his conduct] will cause" the prohibited result.

3. Suppose that two robbers fire shots at a bank guard in the course of their escape. The guard is wounded but survives. The evidence suggests that the robbers intended to frighten the guard but did not intend to kill him. Is this situation distinguishable from *Kraft*? Can the robbers be convicted of attempted felony murder on the ground that they had a specific intent to commit the felony? Most states do not recognize a crime of attempted felony murder. See Bruce v. State, 317 Md. 642, 566 A.2d 103 (1989); State v. Bell, 785 P.2d 390 (Utah 1989); Criminal Law Survey, 49 Md. L. Rev. 604, 656-670 (1990). But a few courts have held otherwise, e.g., White v. State, 166 Ark. 499, 585 S.W.2d 952 (1979); Amlotte v. State, 456 So. 2d 448 (Fla. 1984). In the latter case, the court said (id. at 450): "Because the attempt occurs during the commission of a felony, the law, as under the felony-murder doctrine, presumes the existence of the specific intent required to prove attempt."

Questions: On this reasoning, is an unarmed robber guilty of attempted felony murder if a robbery victim suffers a nonfatal heart attack brought on by fright? Is every robber and burglar guilty of attempted felony murder, even if shots are never fired and none of the victims suffers any physical injury?

4. What reasons underlie the traditional requirement of a "specific intent" or "purpose" in the law of attempt? How can it be unsound to convict for an attempted crime if the defendant, though he lacked "purpose," had the mental state sufficient for conviction of the substantive offense? One explanation may be that we can consider the act sufficiently dangerous only if it is either accompanied by intent or followed by a harmful result. As Justice Holmes put it in The Common Law 68 (1881): "The importance of the intent is not to show that the act was wicked but that it was likely to be followed by hurtful consequences."

How satisfactory is this explanation? Consider Thacker v. Commonwealth, 134 Va. 767, 114 S.E. 504 (1922). A drunk, angered by the refusal of a woman in a tent to admit him, walked down the road a way, turned, and shot at the light shining through the canvas. If the bullet had accidentally killed the woman, the defendant could be convicted of murder. But in *Thacker*, the bullet fortunately missed the woman. The court held that defendant, lacking intent to kill, could not be convicted of attempted murder. Is the result sound? If the defendant is not guilty of attempt, for what crime (if any) *could* he be convicted? Do the penalties provided for an offense such as Model Penal Code §211.2 (reckless endangerment) afford adequate punishment for a case of this kind?

Consider another observation of Justice Holmes in The Common Law at 66:

It may be true in the region of attempts, as elsewhere, the law began with cases of actual intent, as those cases are the most obvious ones. But it cannot stop with them, unless it attaches more importance to the etymological meaning of the word *attempt* than to the general principles of punishment. Accordingly there is at least color of authority for the proposition that an act is punishable as an attempt, if, supposing it to have produced its natural and probable effect, it would have amounted to a substantive crime.

Compare J. C. Smith, The Elements of Chance in Criminal Liability, [1971] Crim. L. Rev. 63, 72-73:

> You will recall my example of the man who threw the stone through the window, being reckless whether it injured anyone. He could not be convicted of attempted wounding because he was not trying to wound anyone. I had assumed that it was impossible to deal with this sort of case as an attempt until I found that this is exactly what has been done in South Africa. What I have called recklessness is there regarded simply as a variety of intention; the thrower of the stone is regarded as having intended injury to the person and, therefore, he may be convicted of an attempt. He was not, of course, "attempting" to cause injury within the ordinary natural meaning of the word "attempt" but it is perfectly possible for the law to use words in a different sense from that which they bear in ordinary usage. I would say, however, that I think this course is to be avoided as far as possible in the criminal law, where it is particularly important that the layman should understand what the lawyer is talking about. It did moreover occur to me that the South African rule about intention if generally applied would lead to some rather odd results. Suppose that a driver, X, overtakes on the brow of a hill when he cannot see whether anything is coming in the opposite direction. If anything were coming, there would certainly be a crash and, obviously, someone might be killed. But nothing is coming and no harm is done. Certainly X ought to be convicted of dangerous driving; but to convict him of attempted murder would be rather startling. Yet there is evidence that he was reckless whether he caused death and if recklessness is indistinguishable in law from intention, there is equally evidence that he was guilty of attempted murder.

5. A few jurisdictions have rejected the traditional position and upheld attempt convictions in the absence of an intent to achieve the prohibited harm. See, e.g., Gentry v. State, 437 So. 2d 1097 (Fla. 1983) (voluntary intoxication no defense to second-degree murder and therefore no defense to *attempted* second-degree murder, even though intoxication would negate specific intent to kill).

In People v. Thomas, 729 P.2d 972 (Colo. 1986), the defendant fired three shots at a man he believed to be a fleeing rapist. Two of the shots struck the man. The defendant claimed that one of the shots had been fired accidentally and that the other two were warning shots. At trial, he was convicted of attempted reckless manslaughter under Colo. Rev. Stat. §18-2-101(1), which provides:

> A person commits criminal attempt if, acting with the kind of culpability otherwise required for commission of an offense, he engages in conduct constituting a substantial step toward the commission of the offense.

Questions: On appeal from the conviction in *Thomas,* what should be the result? Note how the Colorado statute differs from Model Penal Code §5.01. The language of the Colorado statute, if read literally, seems sufficient to permit an attempt conviction on the facts of *Thomas.* But is it plausible to read that language literally? Would the statutory language permit a conviction for attempted felony murder in every Colorado robbery case? Prior to *Thomas,* in People v.

Krovarz, 697 P.2d 378 (Colo. 1985), the Colorado Supreme Court held that knowledge would suffice for attempt liability, but it implied that recklessness would not suffice (id. at 381-382 n. 9):

> [C]onscious disregard does not imply that one chooses the result in the same way that one chooses a result he knows to be a practical certainty. Thus, the Model Penal Code, while permitting attempt liability for results obtained knowingly, explicitly excludes results obtained recklessly. In addition, every state court that has considered this question has declined to extend attempt liability to reckless crimes, on the ground that one cannot intend to commit a crime defined as having an unintended result.

In *Thomas* the court reconsidered its opposition to reckless attempts and upheld the conviction for attempted reckless manslaughter. The court reasoned that the traditional requirement of intent served to identify cases where conduct was likely to produce harmful consequences. The court found that the necessary potential for future harm is present not only in cases of intentional conduct but also when the defendant knows that the prohibited result is practically certain to occur or when he recklessly disregards a substantial risk. The court again declined to rest its result solely on the language of the attempt statute. Do you see why? Are all Colorado motorists who commit highly negligent acts while driving guilty of attempted negligent homicide?

6. Since almost all jurisdictions hold that an intention to achieve the prohibited result is required for an attempt conviction, does it follow that intention is also required with respect to attendant circumstances that may be necessary elements of the crime attempted? Consider the following situations.

(a) In Regina v. Khan, [1990] 1 W.L.R. 813, the defendant was charged with attempted rape. The judge instructed the jury that the completed offense of rape requires proof that the defendant had intercourse and either knew that the woman did not consent or "was reckless as to whether [she] was consenting or not." The judge then explained the law applicable to attempts and added, "As in the case of rape the principles relevant to consent apply in exactly the same way in attempted rape. I do not suppose you need me to go through it again. Apply the same principles as to rape." Defendant was convicted of attempted rape. The Court of Appeal affirmed, stating:

> The only difference between the two offences is that in rape sexual intercourse takes place whereas in attempted rape it does not, although there has to be some act which is more than preparatory to sexual intercourse. Considered in that way, the intent of the defendant is precisely the same in rape and in attempted rape and the mens rea is identical, namely, an intention to have intercourse plus a knowledge of or recklessness as to the woman's absence of consent. . . .
>
> If this is the true analysis, as we believe it is, the attempt does not require any different intention on the part of the accused from that for the full offence of rape. We believe this to be a desirable result which in the instant case did not require the jury to be burdened with different directions as to the accused's state of mind, dependent upon whether the individual achieved or failed to achieve sexual intercourse.

Questions: Is the court's result consistent with the principle that attempt requires the specific intent to commit the object crime? If not, which is wrong — the result or the principle?

(b) In Commonwealth v. Dunne, 394 Mass. 10, 474 N.E.2d 538 (1985), the defendant was convicted of assault with intent to commit statutory rape, an offense that the court referred to as "attempted statutory rape." The statutory age of consent was sixteen, and the victim was fifteen years and four months old on the date of the offense. There was no allegation that the defendant knew (or should have known) that the victim was underage. Affirming the conviction, the court said:

> [In] Commonwealth v. Miller, 385 Mass. 521, 522, 432 N.E.2d 463 (1982) . . . we held that in a prosecution for statutory rape "it is immaterial that the defendant reasonably believed that the victim was sixteen years of age or older." This is the rule in most jurisdictions. Similarly, in a prosecution for an assault with intent to commit statutory rape, this court has held that whether or not the defendant is aware of the victim's age is irrelevant. . . . Indeed, it would be incongruous for us to posit one rule for the completed act and another for the attempt.

Questions: Is the result sound? How can a person be convicted of attempting (trying) to do what he is unaware of doing?

7. How would the situations in the preceding Note be resolved under the Model Penal Code? Consider carefully the text of §5.01(1), Appendix. If §5.01(1)(b) applies, the defendants in *Khan* and *Dunne* would seem to be liable. But if §5.01(1)(b) is not available, then these defendants might not be liable, because they do not meet the requirements of §5.01(1)(a) (their conduct would not "constitute the crime if the attendant circumstances were as [they believe] them to be"), and §5.01(1)(c) arguably is not met either (their conduct was not "planned to culminate in . . . the commission of the crime").

In what situations does §5.01(1)(b) apply? The Code specifies in §1.13(9) that the elements of a crime may concern either "conduct," "attendant circumstances," or "a result of conduct." To apply §5.01(1), the Model Penal Code apparently requires courts to determine whether the crime has a "result" element; only when it does can §5.01(1)(b) be invoked. But how can we tell whether the element of intercourse in a statutory rape case is a "conduct" element or a "result of conduct" element? The Model Penal Code position on this issue is not crystal clear from the text of §5.01, but the commentary does make clear the outcome that the Code's drafters intended to reach. See Model Penal Code and Commentaries, Comments to §5.01 at 301-304 (1985):

> The requirement of purpose extends to the conduct of the actor and to the results that his conduct causes, but his purpose need not encompass all of the circumstances included in the formal definition of the substantive offense. As to them, it is sufficient that he acts with the culpability that is required for commission of the completed crime.
>
> Several illustrations may serve to clarify the point. Assume, for example, a statute that provides that sexual intercourse with a female under a prescribed age is an offense, and that a mistake as to age will not afford a defense no matter how reasonable its foundation. The policy of the substantive offense as to age, therefore, is one of strict liability. . . . Suppose, however, that [the actor] is arrested before he engages in the proscribed conduct, and that the charge is an attempt to commit the offense. Should he then be entitled to rely on a mistake as to age as a defense? . . . Or, assume a statute that makes it a federal offense to murder an FBI agent and treats the agent's status as a member of the FBI as a jurisdictional ingre-

dient, with no culpability required in respect to that element. The question again is whether the policy of the substantive crime should control the same issue when it arises on a charge of attempt. . . .

Under the formulation in Subsection (1)(c), the proffered defense would not succeed in either case. In the statutory rape example, the actor must have a purpose to engage in sexual intercourse with a female in order to be charged with the attempt, and must engage in a substantial step in a course of conduct planned to culminate in his commission of that act.[a] With respect to the age of the victim, however, it is sufficient if he acts "with the kind of culpability otherwise required for the commission of the crime," which in the case supposed is none at all. Since, therefore, mistake as to age is irrelevant with respect to the substantive offense, it is likewise irrelevant with respect to the attempt. The same result would obtain in the murder illustration. The actor must, in the case supposed, engage in a substantial step in a course of conduct planned to culminate in the death of his victim. But with respect to his awareness of the status of his victim as an FBI agent, a mistake would not be relevant since the policy of the substantive offense controls on such matters and that policy is one of strict liability.[13]

The judgment is thus that if the defendant manifests a purpose to engage in the type of conduct or to cause the type of result that is forbidden by the criminal law, he has sufficiently exhibited his dangerousness to justify the imposition of criminal sanctions, so long as he otherwise acts with the kind of culpability that is sufficient for the completed offense.

Question: If the mens rea required with respect to "attendant circumstances" should be the same for attempted and completed crimes, why not apply the same principle with respect to the "result"? For helpful discussions, see R. A. Duff, The Circumstances of an Attempt, 50 Camb. L.J. 100-119 (1991); Richard Buxton, Circumstances, Consequences and Attempted Rape, [1984] Crim. L. Rev. 25.

3.   Preparation

a.   The Traditional "Proximity" Approach

COMMONWEALTH v. PEASLEE

Supreme Judicial Court of Massachusetts
177 Mass. 267, 59 N.E. 55 (1901)

HOLMES, C.J. This is an indictment for an attempt to burn a building and certain goods therein, with intent to injure the insurers of the same. The defense is that the overt acts alleged and proved do not amount to an offense. . . .

The evidence was that the defendant had constructed and arranged combustibles in the building in such a way that they were ready to be lighted, and if lighted would have set fire to the building and its contents. To be exact, the plan would have required a candle which was standing on a shelf six feet away to be

---

a. Does this analysis reflect an accurate reading of §5.01(1)(c)? — EDS.

13. It should be noted that while offenses involving strict liability were chosen for clarity of illustration, the analysis would be the same for circumstance elements where the culpability level is set at recklessness or negligence. For example, if negligence as to age or the status of the FBI agent were required and sufficient for the substantive offense, the same would hold true for the attempt.

placed on a piece of wood in a pan of turpentine and lighted. The defendant offered to pay a younger man in his employment if he would go to the building, seemingly some miles from the place of the dialogue, and carry out the plan. This was refused. Later the defendant and the young man drove towards the building, but when within a quarter of a mile the defendant said that he had changed his mind, and drove away. This is as near as he ever came to accomplishing what he had in contemplation.

The question on the evidence, more precisely stated, is whether the defendant's acts come near enough to the accomplishment of the substantive offense to be punishable. The statute does not punish every act done towards the commission of a crime, but only such acts done in an attempt to commit it. The most common types of an attempt are either an act which is intended to bring about the substantive crime, and which sets in motion natural forces that would bring it about in the expected course of events, but for the unforeseen interruption, as, in this case, if the candle had been put out by the police, or an act which is intended to bring about the substantive crime, and would bring it about but for a mistake of judgment in a matter of nice estimate or experiment, as when a pistol is fired at a man, but misses him, or when one tries to pick a pocket which turns out to be empty. In either case the would-be criminal has done his last act.

Obviously new considerations come in when further acts on the part of the person who has taken the first steps are necessary before the substantive crime can come to pass. In this class of cases there is still a chance that the would-be criminal may change his mind. In strictness, such first steps cannot be described as an attempt, because that word suggests an act seemingly sufficient to accomplish the end, and has been supposed to have no other meaning. That an overt act, although coupled with an intent to commit the crime, commonly is not punishable if further acts are contemplated as needful, is expressed in the familiar rule that preparation is not an attempt. But some preparations may amount to an attempt. It is a question of degree. If the preparation comes very near to the accomplishment of the act, the intent to complete it renders the crime so probable that the act will be a misdemeanor, although there is still a locus poenitentiae, in the need of a further exertion of the will to complete the crime.[a] As was observed in a recent case, the degree of proximity held sufficient may vary with circumstances, including, among other things, the apprehension which the particular crime is calculated to excite. Com. v. Kennedy, 170 Mass. 18, 22, 48 N.E. 770.[b]

[The court suggested, but declined to decide, that on the evidence a conviction of attempt was proper. The conviction was reversed on the procedural ground that the indictment failed to allege the solicitation of the employee to set the fire as one of the overt acts.]

THE KING v. BARKER, [1924] N.Z.L.R. 865 (Salmond, J.): That the common law has recognized the distinction between acts of attempt and acts of prepara-

a. "Combination, intent and overt act may all be present without amounting to a criminal attempt — as if all that were done should be an agreement to murder a man fifty miles away and the purchase of a pistol for the purpose. There must be a dangerous proximity to success." Holmes, J., disssenting in Hyde v. United States, 225 U.S. 347, 387 (1912). — Eds.

h. Justice Holmes observed in that case: "As the aim of the law is not to punish sins, but is to prevent certain external results, the act done must come pretty near to accomplishing that result before the law will notice it." 48 N.E. at 770. — Eds.

tion — between acts which are, and acts which are not, too remote to constitute a criminal attempt — is undoubted. Thus, in R. v. Eagleton [169 E.R. 826 (1855)] it is said by Parke, B.: "The mere intention to commit a misdemeanor is not criminal; some act is required; and we do not think that all acts towards committing a misdemeanor are indictable. Acts remotely leading towards the commission of the offence are not to be considered as attempts to commit it, but acts immediately connected with it are."

If, however, we proceed to inquire as to the precise nature of the distinction thus recognised and indicated, we find that the common law authorities are almost as silent as the Crimes Act itself. . . . The rule so suggested in R. v. Eagleton was that in order to constitute a criminal attempt, as opposed to mere preparation, the accused must have taken the last step which he was able to take along the road of his criminal intent. He must have done all that he intended to do and was able to do for the purpose of effectuating his criminal purpose. When he has stopped short of this, whether because he has repented, or because he has been prevented, or because the time or occasion for going further has not arrived, or for any other reason, he still has a locus penitentiae and still remains within the region of innocent preparation. Until he has done his best to complete his guilty purpose, he has not attempted to complete it. On this principle the act of firing a pistol at a man would be attempted murder, although the bullet missed him. So would the act of pulling the trigger, although the pistol missed fire. But the prior and preliminary acts of procuring and loading the pistol, and of going with it to look for his enemy, and of lying in wait for him, and even of presenting the pistol at him, would not constitute criminal attempts, none of these being the proximate and final step towards the fulfillment of his criminal purpose. . . .[c]

Subsequent authorities make it clear that the [*Eagleton*] test is not the true one. [I]n R. v. White, [1910] 2 K.B. 124; 4 Cr. App. R. 257, it was held that the first administration of poison in a case of intended slow poisoning by repeated doses amounted in itself to attempted murder. It is said by the Court: "The completion [or attempted completion] of one of a series of acts intended by a man to result in killing is an attempt to murder, even though the completed act would not, unless followed by other acts, result in killing. It might be the beginning of an attempt but would none the less be an attempt."

Although the test adopted by Parke, B., has been rejected, no definite substitute for it has been formulated. All that can be definitely gathered from the authorities is that to constitute a criminal attempt, the first step along the way of criminal intent is not necessarily sufficient and the final step is not necessarily required. The dividing line between preparation and attempt is to be found somewhere between these two extremes; but as to the method by which it is to be determined the authorities give no clear guidance. . . .

NOTES ON PROXIMITY

1. In People v. Rizzo, 246 N.Y. 334, 335, 338-339, 158 N.E. 888, 889-890 (1927), the defendant and his confederates, all armed, were driving through the

---

c. A recent defense of the "last act" test appears in Lawrence Crocker, Justice in Criminal Liability: Decriminalizing Harmless Attempts, 53 Ohio St. L.J. 1057 (1992). — Eds.

streets of an area in New York searching for Rao, a payroll clerk, whom they planned to rob of about $1,200. Their efforts to find their victim attracted the attention of the police, who apprehended them after a period of surveillance. The court of appeals reversed a conviction of attempted robbery on the ground that the defendants' acts constituted mere preparation, stating:

> To constitute the crime of robbery, the money must have been taken from Rao by means of force or violence, or through fear. The crime of attempt to commit robbery was committed, if these defendants did an act tending to the commission of this robbery. Did the acts above described come dangerously near to the taking of Rao's property? Did the acts come so near the commission of robbery that there was reasonable likelihood of its accomplishment but for the interference? Rao was not found; the defendants were still looking for him; no attempt to rob him could be made, at least until he came in sight; he was not in the building [where he was expected to be]. There was no man there with the pay roll for the United Lathing Company whom these defendants could rob. Apparently no money had been drawn from the bank for the pay roll by anybody at the time of the arrest. In a word, these defendants had planned to commit a crime, and were looking around the city for an opportunity to commit it, but the opportunity fortunately never came. Men would not be guilty of an attempt at burglary if they had planned to break into a building and were arrested while they were hunting about the streets for the building not knowing where it was. Neither would a man be guilty of an attempt to commit murder if he armed himself and started out to find the person whom he had planned to kill but could not find him. So here these defendants were not guilty of an attempt to commit robbery in the first degree when they had not found or reached the presence of the person they intended to rob.

However, the court commented that,

> The police of the city of New York did excellent work in this case by preventing the commission of a serious crime. It is a great satisfaction to realize that we have such wide-awake guardians of our peace.

Subsequently the New York attempt statute was amended to require that the defendant engage in conduct "which tends to effect the commission" of the crime. N.Y. Pen. Law §110. The New York Court of Appeals held that "in this State we have adhered to *Rizzo*'s 'very near' or 'dangerously near' requirement, despite the later enactment." People v. Acosta, 80 N.Y.2d 665, 609 N.E.2d 518, 521 (1993).

2. In Commonwealth v. Ortiz, 408 Mass. 463, 560 N.E.2d 698 (1990), defendant got into his car with a loaded shotgun and went looking for Rodriguez, a man with whom his family had a longstanding feud. Defendant drove to Rodriguez's neighborhood and drove the car around the block six times, hoping to find him. When Rodriguez could not be found, defendant returned home. He was convicted of an attempt to assault with a dangerous weapon, but the appellate court reversed; it held, relying on *Peaslee* and *Rizzo*, that despite clear evidence of intent, there was insufficient evidence of the necessary act.

3. In United States v. Schoof, 34 Mil. J. Rptr. 811 (Court of Military Review 1992), defendant, a sailor who was having financial problems, induced a shipmate to obtain for him classified documents from the safe of the USS Fairfax County. Defendant hid the documents in his locker on board ship and made

several calls to the Soviet Embassy in Washington, D.C., in an unsuccessful effort to arrange for someone to pick up the material from him in Norfolk. The court described the subsequent events as follows:

> In mid-November 1989, the appellant borrowed a motorcycle and began driving toward Washington with the intent to deliver the classified material to the Soviet Embassy. Upon reaching a point between Williamsburg and Richmond, he changed his mind, decided that he could not go through with it, and returned to Norfolk. Upon his return, he stopped at a bar and was drinking heavily when he encountered a friend who was on terminal leave. He explained, in sufficient detail for his friend to surmise what he was up to, how he planned to make some money and solicited his friend to drive him up to Washington. After stalling for a few days, the friend ultimately refused. A short time later, the microfiches in the possession of the appellant were discovered missing from the ship's safe, and a search for them was ordered. The appellant was apprehended on 1 December 1989 while leaving the ship. When it was clear that he would be searched, he surrendered the microfiches to a Naval Investigative Service agent.

In court-martial proceedings, defendant was convicted of attempted espionage by attempting to deliver the documents to a foreign power. The Court of Military Review reversed the conviction:

> [T]he appellant made vague, preliminary unreported contacts from Norfolk by telephone with the Soviet Embassy in Washington, conspired with OS3 Haeger to obtain the classified material in question and did obtain it, borrowed a motorcycle, and headed off in the direction of Washington, where the Soviet Embassy is located, to an uncertain reception. He had no appointment with anyone in the embassy; in fact, no one in the embassy was even aware that he was coming. The Soviets had no idea who he was or what he had, and no terms of payment or delivery had even been mentioned, much less agreed upon. In this regard, it should be remembered that the appellant's ultimate objective was not to commit espionage for political reasons but to obtain money, and that the delivery of classified material was intended solely as a means to that end. Thus, it may be inferred that any intent to deliver the material to the Soviets was probably only conditional upon reaching a satisfactory agreement with the Soviets on price and terms of payment. . . . At the time he turned back, more than a hundred miles of locus poenitentiae lay between him and the Soviet Embassy. Had the appellant ever reached Washington, he would still have been confronted with the daunting choice of whether or not to take the fateful step of entering the curtilage of the Soviet Embassy, not to mention the embassy building, itself — steps not dependent upon external circumstances but requiring the further exercise of the appellant's will. The charge is that he did "attempt to deliver microfiche . . . to a foreign government[.]" As a matter of law, no reasonable trier of fact could have found the appellant guilty of an attempt to deliver on such evidence.

A dissenting judge commented:

> While the microfiche was in his locker, appellant, during 29 and 30 October, 1989, made at least three phone calls to the Soviet Embassy in Washington D.C. to arrange the sale of the microfiche. Appellant was told to bring the microfiche to the embassy in Washington, D.C. Appellant then removed the microfiche from his locker aboard USS Fairfax County, put the microfiche in his coat pocket and started toward Washington D.C. on a borrowed motorcycle. . . . Appellant testified

that he changed his mind. In view of his continued efforts to get transportation by car from another person when he stopped on the trip, I find the logical inference to be that appellant changed his mind about riding a motorcycle to Washington D.C. . . . I find that the criminal acts of removing the microfiche from the safe, putting the microfiche in his locker, calling the Soviet Embassy to make a deal, reaching what appellant believed to be a deal, taking the microfiche from his locker, getting on the motorcycle and heading toward Washington D.C. amounted to more than mere preparation. Indeed, I find appellant's acts to be substantial steps toward commission of the crime, strongly corroborative of the firmness of appellant's criminal intent.

The U.S. Court of Military Appeals granted a petition to review the foregoing decision and reinstated the conviction. 37 Mil. J. Rptr. 96 (1993).

Questions: Is that result consistent with *Rizzo?* How would *Schoof* be decided under the New York law of attempts? How *should* Schoof be decided?

4. The foregoing cases indicate that commission of the "last act" is not always necessary for attempt liability. But it is safe to say that ordinarily commission of the last act will be sufficient — in other words, when the defendant *does* commit the last act necessary on his part for completion of the offense, it will ordinarily be obvious that he has gone beyond "mere preparation."[4] But does commission of the last act always satisfy the concerns about firmness of purpose, opportunity to repent and so on? What if the defendant lights a very long, very slow fuse? Consider the following cases.

(a) Hope v. Brown, [1954] 1 All E.R. 330, 332. The defendant was employed as manager at a butcher's shop. He prepared tags showing prices in excess of those permitted by law and placed them in a drawer, expecting that in due course a sales clerk would affix them to packages of meat, as instructed. The court held that the defendant could not be convicted of an attempt to sell meat in excess of the maximum price:

> [W]hat remained to be done before there would be an attempt was the affixing to the meat of the false tickets. . . . The [clerk] would have affixed the ticket, no doubt, because she was delivering the meat on behalf of the respondent on his instructions, . . . but, until she had done that, one cannot say that an offence had been committed. The preparation of the false tickets and putting them in the drawer is too remote from the actual transaction which would be necessary to constitute the attempt. There might be a sudden change of heart, or an intervention by the [storeowner], which would have prevented any attempt being made to sell this meat to the customers. In all these cases where it has been held that there has been an attempt the court has always found that the crime would have been committed but for the intervention of someone. The crime here would not have been committed until, at any rate, the meat had got the false ticket on it and it had been sold with that false ticket on it to the customer. Therefore, the mere fact that the respondent prepared a false ticket is not enough.

(b) Director of Public Prosecutions v. Stonehouse, [1977] 2 All E.R. 909. The defendant, a well-known politician, found himself in financial and other diffi-

---

4. An important exception to this generalization is discussed at pages 617-623 infra, in connection with solicitation and incitement.

culties. Seeking to make a fresh start for himself and provision for his wife, he insured his life, naming his wife as beneficiary, feigned his own death in a staged drowning incident in Miami, and secretly traveled to Australia under a false passport and a new identity. He was later discovered in Australia and his plot revealed — before his wife, who was not a party to his scheme, had applied for the insurance benefits. The House of Lords upheld a conviction of attempting dishonestly to obtain money from the insurance company by deception.

Question: Was the conviction consistent with Hope v. Brown?

5. Bearing in mind the cases in the foregoing Notes, consider the following observations of Professor Glanville Williams (Police Control of Intending Criminals, [1955] Crim. L. Rev. 66, 69):

> In a rational system of justice the police would be given every encouragement to intervene early where a suspect is clearly bent on crime. Yet in England, if the police come on the scene too early they may find that they can do nothing with the intending offender except admonish him. This is largely because of the rule that an attempt, to be indictable, must be sufficiently "proximate" to the crime intended. . . . One is led to ask whether there is any real need for the requirement of proximity in the law of attempt. Quite apart from this requirement, it must be proved beyond reasonable doubt that the accused intended to commit the crime . . . and that he did some act towards committing it. If only a remote act of preparation is alleged against him, that will weigh with the court in deciding whether he had the firm criminal intention alleged against him. If, however, the court finds that this intention existed, is there any reason why the would-be criminal should not be dealt with by the police and by the criminal courts?

Compare Robert L. Misner, The New Attempt Laws: An Unsuspected Threat to the Fourth Amendment, 33 Stan. L. Rev. 201 (1981). Professor Misner argues that recent expansion of the law of attempts results in greatly increased police powers to arrest and thus to conduct thorough searches incident to the arrest. In contrast, because traditional attempt doctrine often would not permit arrest under comparable circumstances, police would be allowed, at most, only a limited "stop and frisk" of a suspicious person.

NOTES ON ABANDONMENT

1. The interaction between proximity and abandonment doctrines. One reason for judicial reluctance to move the threshold of criminality to an earlier point in time has been the desire to preserve for the defendant a "locus penitentiae" — an opportunity to repent. It is important to see how that "opportunity to repent" is lost once the defendant crosses the threshold of criminality. First, a defendant may be arrested before she has the chance to take the steps remaining to complete the crime. Such a defendant will be liable for attempt even though we can never be sure that she would have taken those steps. Second, a defendant may not be arrested until after she has "repented" and fully abandoned the criminal plan. (Recall the facts of *Peaslee,* page 593 supra.) Here the appearance of unfairness is even more striking: The defendant could be held liable for committing an attempt (by crossing the threshold of criminality), even though she later did everything in her power to turn back and even though she successfully prevented any actual harm.

Could one argue that a defendant's actions in abandoning the criminal purpose serve to defeat liability for the attempt? If inchoate crimes are to be treated like other offenses, the answer would have to be negative: Remorse and restitution may affect the sentence, but they cannot erase liability once the elements necessary for conviction are complete. Applying this reasoning, the common law traditionally denied any defense of abandonment, and many modern courts continue to adhere to that view. See, e.g., State v. Stewart, 143 Wis. 2d 28, 420 N.W.2d 44 (1988); People v. Steele, 156 Ill. App. 3d 508, 509 N.E.2d 719 (1987); People v. Dillon, 34 Cal. 3d 441, 668 P.2d 697 (1983). To minimize the resulting potential for unfairness, courts may therefore insist that the threshold of criminality be placed very close to the last act, even when this approach means freeing some defendants who almost certainly would *not* have repented. (Recall the facts of *Rizzo*, page 595 supra.)

2. *Reform.* One way of mitigating the dilemma described in the preceding Note is simply to recognize abandonment as a complete defense. A number of states have done so, either by statute or judicial decision. A typical requirement is that the abandonment occur "under circumstances manifesting a voluntary and complete renunciation of [the] criminal purpose." N.Y. Penal Code §4.10. Model Penal Code §5.01(4), upon which the New York provision is based, is similar. For the definition of when the renunciation is considered "voluntary" and "complete," see Model Penal Code §5.01(4), Appendix. Most of the recently revised codes adopt a renunciation defense substantially similar to that of the Model Penal Code. For a canvas of the recent cases and statutes, see Daniel G. Moriarty, Extending the Defense of Renunciation, 62 Temple L. Rev. 1, 7-11 (1989).

3. *Problems.* (a) In People v. Johnston, 87 A.D.2d 703, 448 N.Y.S.2d 902, 902-903 (1982), defendant entered a gas station, pulled a gun, and demanded money. When the station attendant produced only $50 and said that this was all the cash available, defendant departed, stating, "I was just kidding, forget it ever happened." The court denied a renunciation defense, but several commentators favor a defense in these circumstances. See George P. Fletcher, Rethinking Criminal Law 191-192 (1978); Paul R. Hoeber, The Abandonment Defense to Criminal Attempt and Other Problems of Temporary Individuation, 74 Cal. L. Rev. 377, 411-412 (1986). Which is the better view?

(*b*) In People v. McNeal, 152 Mich. App. 404, 393 N.W.2d 907 (1986), defendant accosted a girl who had been waiting at a bus stop and forced her at knife point to accompany him to a house, with the intent to rape her. After an extended conversation in which the girl pleaded with him to let her go, defendant released the girl, saying that he was sorry and would never engage in such behavior again. The court affirmed a conviction for attempted sexual assault, upholding a finding that because of the victim's "unexpected resistance," the defendant's renunciation was not voluntary. On similar facts, the court in Ross v. State, 601 So. 2d 872, 875 (Miss. 1992), found abandonment as a matter of law and reversed a conviction for attempted rape, stating: "[Defendant] did not fail in his attack. No one prevented him from completing it. [The victim] did not sound an alarm. She successfully persuaded Ross, of his own free will, to abandon his attempt."

b. Alternatives to the "Proximity" Approach

STATE v. YOUNG

Supreme Court of New Jersey
57 N.J. 240, 271 A.2d 569 (1970)

WEINTRAUB, C.J. A jury found defendant guilty on an indictment charging that he entered Trenton High School with the intent to disrupt classes therein and otherwise to interfere with the peace and good order of that school. He was fined $500. We certified his appeal before the Appellate Division acted upon it.

The statute, N.J.S.A. 2A:149A-2, reads:

> Any person, other than a bona fide student therein or parent or legal guardian of such student or a teacher, administrator, or other school employee while in the performance of his duties, who enters any building structure or place used for any educational purpose with the intent to disrupting classes or of otherwise interfering with the peace and good order of the place shall be guilty of a misdemeanor.

[There was evidence that the defendant, a lay minister, was active in organizing student protests initially over suspension of a student for refusing to stand for a flag salute. On the day in question he was present at the school and took a leadership role in a student sit-in, although he had been asked to leave by the superintendent of schools.]

[D]efendant contends that the act of entering a public school is in itself "blameless" and that it is beyond the power of the State to punish an innocent act merely because of a forbidden purpose. We think the police power of the State is not thus restricted. . . .

There are a host of statutes, federal and State, which condemn acts, themselves innocent, if done with a forbidden intent. We will summarize them in approximate terms, sufficient for our immediate purpose.

The possession of certain counterfeit obligations is made criminal but only if the obligation is possessed "with intent to defraud," 18 U.S.C.A. §480. There is nothing necessarily wrong in teaching or demonstrating the use, application or making of a firearm or explosive or incendiary device or a technique capable of causing injury or death, but 18 U.S.C.A. §231(a)(1) makes it a crime to do so "intending that the same will be unlawfully employed for use in, or in furtherance of, a civil disorder which may in any way or degree obstruct, delay, or adversely affect commerce" or the performance of any federally protected function. . . .

There are a number of statutes which make possession criminal if there is an intent to do some hostile act. See N.J.S.A. 2A:94-3 relating to possession of burglar tools; and see N.J.S.A. 2A:109-2 subds. a and b, relating to possession of counterfeits. As to weapons and explosives, see N.J.S.A. 2A:151-56, 59 and 60. It is a disorderly persons offense to possess certain implements if the intent is to break and enter, or to have on one's person an offensive or dangerous weapon with intent to assault another, or to be in any place of public resort or assemblage for business, travel, worship, amusement or other lawful place, with intent to steal, N.J.S.A. 2A:170-3.

We refer to this array of statutes solely to evidence the widely held legislative view that such measures are within the legislative power, and to reveal the impact upon public safety and order if it should be held that government, in seeking to anticipate and prevent criminal events, may punish only if a step taken in pursuit of a criminal objective itself bespeaks criminality. . . .

Generally a line is sought to be drawn between an "attempt" and mere "preparation," preparation itself not being punishable as an attempt. Nonetheless some conduct short of an attempt was punishable at common law. So a solicitation to commit a crime, though not equalling an attempt, was dealt with as a crime. The most conspicuous proscription of the common law in anticipation of actual injury or an attempt thereat was the crime of conspiracy, for that crime required no more than an agreement for an unlawful end. . . .

To meet the added dangers of a complex and congested society, legislatures have gone beyond the common law in punishing conduct which by common law standards might fall short of an attempt. . . . [T]he many statutes we recounted above have the common feature of punishing an act only because of the evil purpose it pursues, without regard to whether the act would constitute an attempt to commit the offense the statutes seek to head off, and even though the act, absent such purpose, may be one protected by the Constitution.

We see no serious challenge to the power of a legislature to make it an offense to take a step, otherwise lawful, in furtherance of a hostile end. . . .

Affirmed.

NOTE ON SUBSTANTIVE CRIMES OF PREPARATION

As the *Young* case makes clear, the need for early police intervention was often frustrated by traditional limitations on the law of attempt. New substantive crimes were developed, by statute and by common law decisions, to reach conduct that otherwise would be considered "merely preparatory." There are important instances of this, in addition to those discussed in *Young*.

One such instance is represented by measures to deal with suspicious persons in circumstances that arouse fear that the person may soon try to commit a crime. In light of the invalidation of traditional vagrancy-type statutes (see Papachristou v. City of Jacksonville, page 302 supra), two principal approaches have been used. One is procedural, allowing police to stop and detain a suspect in circumstances short of those justifying an arrest on probable cause under the Fourth Amendment. See Terry v. Ohio, 392 U.S. 1 (1968). The other approach is substantive, making it a crime, in effect, to loiter or prowl in circumstances giving rise to alarm that a crime will be attempted. See Model Penal Code §250.6, Appendix, and the supporting commentary reprinted at pages 312-314 supra.

Two traditional instances of making preparatory behavior criminal as substantive crimes are the crimes of burglary and assault.

1. Burglary. Common law burglary consisted of breaking and entering a dwelling of another at night with the intent to commit a felony inside. Cases and statutes gradually enlarged the offense: Under some statutes an entry is all that is required, in day as well as at night, into any structure, with intent to commit any crime. For example, in People v. Salemme, 3 Cal. App. 4th 775, 3 Cal. Rptr. 2d 398 (1992), the court held that the defendant had committed burglary when he entered a person's home with the intent to perpetrate a fraudulent sale of securities.

The relationship between burglary and the crime of attempt is developed in the Model Penal Code and Commentaries, Comment to §221.1 at 62-63 (1980):

> The common law of attempt ordinarily did not reach a person who embarked on a course of criminal behavior unless he came very close to his goal. . . . Under that view of the law of attempt, a person apprehended while breaking into a dwelling with intent to commit a felony therein would not have committed an attempt, for he would not have arrived at the scene of his projected theft, rape, or murder. Moreover, even when the actor's conduct reached the stage where an attempt was committed, penalties for attempt were disproportionately low as compared to the penalties for the completed offense.
>
> The development and expansion of the offense of burglary provided a partial solution to these problems. Making entry with criminal intent an independent substantive offense carrying serious sanctions moved back the moment when the law could intervene in a criminal design and authorized penalties more nearly in accord with the seriousness of the actor's conduct.

A further difficulty with the law of attempt that is overcome with the crime of burglary is pointed out in the above comments (id. at 67-68):

> It is not uncommon for surreptitious entry to occur under circumstances where law enforcement officials are hard pressed to establish precisely what crime the actor contemplated within the premises. A serious penalty may be justified whether it is assault or theft that is the object of the entry, though the facts of the case may make it difficult to establish beyond a reasonable doubt that it was the one rather than the other. An attempt prosecution would require just such specific proof, whereas prosecution under a burglary statute requires only that it be established that the intrusion was made as a conscious step toward the accomplishment of one of a number of possible criminal objectives.

The line separating innocence from criminality in the steps leading up to the commission of a substantive offense has been pushed back even further than the definition of burglary itself implies. First, courts have often upheld convictions of attempted burglary. Typical instances are as follows: The defendant entered a store yard at night carrying a ladder and bag of tools and wearing gloves, People v. Gibson, 94 Cal. App. 2d 468, 210 P.2d 747 (1949); the defendant was apprehended in the early morning hours climbing the stairs to a second-floor store and carrying a bolt cutter, State v. Kleier, 69 Idaho 491, 210 P.2d 388 (1949). Second, many legislatures have enacted statutes making criminal the manufacture, repair, or possession of burglars' tools with intent to commit a felony, most often burglary. See, e.g., Cal. Penal Code §466.

2. *Assault.* Assault is another substantive crime that is essentially a kind of attempt. It is generally defined as an attempt to commit a battery on another. See, e.g., Cal. Penal Code §240: "An assault is an unlawful attempt, coupled with a present ability, to commit a violent injury on the person of another." Note that the crime of assault is typically defined more narrowly than the tort of assault. A person who deliberately places another in fear of a battery, but does not actually intend to carry out the attack, normally would not be guilty of assault under traditional criminal law definitions, although the person might be

liable for damages in tort. Some modern statutes extend the definition of assault to cover such conduct under some circumstances. See Model Penal Code §211.1(1)(c), Appendix.

May the point of criminality be pushed back by convicting a person of an attempt to commit an assault? Some courts have held not. See Wilson v. State, 53 Ga. 205, 206 (1874):

> As an assault is itself an attempt to commit a crime, an attempt to make an assault can only be an attempt to attempt to do it, or to state the matter still more definitely, it is to do any act towards doing an act towards the commission of the offense. This is simply absurd. As soon as any act is done towards committing a violent injury on the person of another, the party doing the act is guilty of an assault, and he is not guilty until he has done the act. Yet it is claimed that [defendant] may be guilty of an attempt to make an assault, when, under the law, he must do an act before the attempt is complete. The refinement and metaphysical acumen that can see a tangible idea in the words an attempt to attempt to act is too great for practical use. It is like conceiving of the beginning of eternity or the starting place of infinity.

Other courts have held to the contrary. See, e.g., State v. Wilson, 218 Or. 575, 346 P.2d 115 (1959) (defendant came looking for his wife at her place of work carrying a shotgun and intending to shoot her, but her fellow workers hid her and he was unable to find her). For an analysis of these issues, see Ira P. Robbins, Double Inchoate Crimes, 26 Harv. J. Legis. 1 (1989). Professor Robbins finds (id. at 39) that "[a]lthough no jurisdiction recognizes the crime of attempted *simple* assault, an increasing number of state courts have convicted defendants of attempted aggravated assaults." Consider Thurmond Arnold, Criminal Attempts — The Rise and Fall of an Abstraction, 40 Yale L.J. 53, 65 (1930):

> [It is said that] there can be no attempt at a direct attempt. But the query immediately arises. Why not? We do not punish attempts at ordinary assaults which carry light penalties. But suppose the accused is guilty of conduct tending toward an aggravated assault but which does not seem to require the heavier penalty. The court is confronted with the alternative of either discharging the accused or modifying the penalty to make it more nearly fit his conduct. An easy way to accomplish this is by making attempts at aggravated assaults punishable, and this is frequently done. It is academic to call such cases "wrong" because assault is in the nature of an attempt and hence cannot be attempted, particularly when a common sense result is reached. In short the generalization that there can be no attempt tells us nothing and tends merely to divert the court's mind from the real issue.

McQUIRTER v. STATE

Alabama Court of Appeals
36 Ala. App. 707, 63 So. 2d 388 (1953)

PRICE, J. Appellant, a Negro man, was found guilty of an attempt to commit an assault with intent to rape, under an indictment charging an assault with intent to rape. The jury assessed a fine of $500.

About 8:00 o'clock on the night of June 29, 1951, Mrs. Ted Allen, a white woman, with her two children and a neighbor's little girl, were drinking Coca-

Cola at the "Tiny Diner" in Atmore. When they started in the direction of Mrs. Allen's home she noticed appellant sitting in the cab of a parked truck. As she passed the truck appellant said something unintelligible, opened the truck door and placed his foot on the running board.

Mrs. Allen testified appellant followed her down the street and when she reached Suell Lufkin's house she stopped. As she turned into the Lufkin house appellant was within two or three feet of her. She waited ten minutes for appellant to pass. When she proceeded on her way, appellant came toward her from behind a telephone pole. She told the children to run to Mr. Simmons' house and tell him to come and meet her. When appellant saw Mr. Simmons he turned and went back down the street to the intersection and leaned on a stop sign just across the street from Mrs. Allen's home. Mrs. Allen watched him at the sign from Mr. Simmons' porch for about thirty minutes, after which time he came back down the street and appellant went on home. . . .

Mr. W. E. Strickland, Chief of Police of Atmore, testified that appellant stated in the Atmore jail he didn't know what was the matter with him; that he was drinking a little; that he and his partner had been to Pensacola; that his partner went to the "Front" to see a colored woman; that he didn't have any money and he sat in the truck and made up his mind he was going to get the first woman that came by and that this was the first woman that came by. He said he got out of the truck, came around the gas tank and watched the lady and when she started off he started off behind her; that he was going to carry her in the cotton patch and if she hollered he was going to kill her. He testified appellant made the same statement in the Brewton jail. . . .

Appellant, as a witness in his own behalf, testified he and Bill Page, another Negro, carried a load of junk-iron from Monroeville to Pensacola; on their way back to Monroeville they stopped in Atmore. They parked the truck near the "Tiny Diner" and rode to the "Front," the colored section, in a cab. Appellant came back to the truck around 8:00 o'clock and sat in the truck cab for about thirty minutes. He decided to go back to the "Front" to look for Bill Page. As he started up the street he saw prosecutrix and her children. He turned around and waited until he decided they had gone, then he walked up the street toward the "Front." When he reached the intersection at the street telegraph pole he decided he didn't want to go to the "Front" and sat around there a few minutes, then went on to the "Front" and stayed about 25 to 30 minutes, and came back to the truck.

He denied that he followed Mrs. Allen or made any gesture toward molesting her or the children. He denied making the statements testified to by the officers. . . .

Appellant insists the trial court erred in refusing the general affirmative charge and in denying the motion for a new trial on the ground the verdict was contrary to the evidence.

" 'An attempt to commit an assault with intent to rape,' . . . means an attempt to rape which has not proceeded far enough to amount to an assault." Burton v. State, 8 Ala. App. 295, 62 So. 394, 396.

Under the authorities in this state, to justify a conviction for an attempt to commit an assault with intent to rape the jury must be satisfied beyond a reasonable doubt that defendant intended to have sexual intercourse with prosecutrix against her will, by force or by putting her in fear.

Intent is a question to be determined by the jury from the facts and circumstances adduced on the trial, and if there is evidence from which it may be inferred that at the time of the attempt defendant intended to gratify his lustful desires against the resistance of the female a jury question is presented.

In determining the question of intention the jury may consider social conditions and customs founded upon racial differences, such as that the prosecutrix was a white woman and defendant was a Negro man.

After considering the evidence in this case we are of the opinion it was sufficient to warrant the submission of the question of defendant's guilt to the jury, and was ample to sustain the judgment of conviction. . . .

Affirmed.

NOTES AND QUESTIONS

1. McQuirter. What is troublesome about the conviction in this case? The racial context certainly is, as is the evidence of intent, which came solely from the sheriff's testimony about what the defendant said in jail. A modern appellate court might well be troubled by these circumstances, but what doctrinal grounds would be available to the court as a basis for reversal? Is it troublesome to regard the defendant's conduct as sufficient to constitute a criminal attempt? If there had been some corroborating evidence of the defendant's intent and if the defendant and the woman had been of the same race, would a conviction still be troublesome? For what reason?

2. Equivocality. Can the actus reus requirements for attempt be formulated in a way that would avoid problems like that presented by the conviction in *McQuirter*? Consider the following efforts to develop an "equivocality" test to separate mere preparation from a punishable attempt.

The King v. Barker, [1924] N.Z.L.R. 865, 874-876: A criminal attempt is an act which shows criminal intent on the face of it. The case must be one in which Res ipsa loquitur. An act, on the other hand, which is in its own nature and on the face of it innocent is not a criminal attempt. It cannot be brought within the scope of criminal attempt by evidence aliunde as to the criminal purpose with which it is done. . . . The law does not punish men for their guilty intentions or resolutions in themselves. Nor does it commonly punish them even for the expression, declaration, or confession of such intentions or resolutions. That a man's unfulfilled criminal purposes should be punishable they must be manifested not by his words merely, or by acts which are in themselves of innocent or ambiguous significance, but by overt acts which are sufficient in themselves to declare and proclaim the guilty purpose with which they are done. . . .

To buy a box of matches with intent to use them in burning a haystack is not an attempt to commit arson, for it is in itself and in appearance an innocent act, there being many other reasons than arson for buying matches. The act does not speak for itself of any guilty design. . . . But he who takes matches to a haystack and there lights one of them and blows it out on finding that he is observed, has done an act which speaks for itself, and he is guilty of criminal attempt accordingly. . . . The purchaser of matches would not be guilty of attempted arson even if he declared to the vendor or to any other person the guilty purpose with which he bought them. Such evidence is relevant for the purpose of satisfying the jury that the requisite criminal intent existed, but it is not relevant in determining the prior question of law whether the act charged amounts in law to an attempt or is too remote for that purpose. . . .

People v. Miller, 2 Cal. 2d 527, 531-532, 42 P.2d 308 (1935): [Defendant, who had threatened to kill Jeans, entered a field where Jeans and the local constable were planting hops. Defendant was carrying a rifle, and he walked straight toward them. He stopped once to load his rifle, but at no time did he lift it to take aim. Jeans fled, and the constable disarmed the defendant. A conviction of attempted murder was reversed:] The reason for requiring evidence of a direct act, however slight, toward consummation of the intended crime, is . . . that in the majority of cases up to that time the conduct of the defendant, consisting merely of acts of preparation, has never ceased to be equivocal; and this is necessarily so, irrespective of his declared intent. It is that quality of being equivocal that must be lacking before the act becomes one which may be said to be a commencement of the commission of the crime, or an overt act, or before any fragment of the crime itself has been committed, and this is so for the reason that, so long as the equivocal quality remains, no one can say with certainty what the intent of the defendant is. . . . In the present case, up to the moment the gun was taken from defendant, no one could say with certainty whether defendant had come into the field to carry out his threat to kill Jeans or merely to demand his arrest by the constable.

Wis. Stat. Ann. tit. 45, §939.32(2): An attempt to commit a crime requires that the actor have an intent to perform acts and attain a result which, if accomplished, would constitute such crime and that he does acts toward the commission of the crime which demonstrate unequivocally, under all the circumstances, that he formed that intent and would commit the crime except for the intervention of another person or some other extraneous factor.

Question: How does this formulation of the equivocality test differ from that in the *Barker* and *Miller* cases? Is it an improvement?

3. Does the equivocality test provide a workable approach to the preparation-attempt problem, or does it set *too high* a barrier to conviction? Consider Glanville Williams, Criminal Law: The General Part 630 (2d ed. 1961):

D goes up to a haystack, fills his pipe, and lights a match. The act of lighting the match, even to a suspicious-minded person, is ambiguous. It may indicate only that *D* is going to light his pipe; but perhaps, on the other hand, the pipe is only a 'blind' and *D* is really bent on setting fire to the stack. We do not know. Therefore, on the equivocality test, the act is not proximate. But suppose that as a matter of actual fact *D*, after his arrest, confesses to the guilty intent, and suppose that that confession is believed. We are now certain of the intent and the only question is as to proximity. It becomes clear that the act satisfies all the requirements for a criminal attempt. Since it is practically the last act that *D* intended to do in order to commit the crime (the very last being setting the match to the stack), it is almost necessarily proximate. That the act is ambiguous, which in itself might have created a doubt as to the mens rea, no longer matters, for the mens rea has been proved by the confession.

NOTES ON STALKING STATUTES

1. *The background.* The strict requirements of the law of attempts have fueled perceptions that traditional criminal laws are inadequate to reach the conduct of "stalkers," who follow or harass others, often as a prelude to a violent attack. One recent news report (Tamar Lewin, New Laws Address Old Problem, N.Y. Times, Feb. 8, 1993, at A1) notes:

> For more than a month, a young woman in Stratford, N.J., was hounded by a man she had briefly dated. He followed her to work and to the hairdresser. He left repeated messages on her answering machine. She talked to the police several times and filed a harassment complaint, but there was little the police could do except ask the man to stop.
>
> "Our hands were tied," said Jay Wilkins, a detective in the Stratford Police Department. "We were in the position of waiting for a crime to happen."

Consider Matthew J. Gilligan, Note, Stalking the Stalker: Developing New Laws to Thwart Those Who Terrorize Others, 27 Ga. L. Rev. 285, 285-286, 295-299 (1992):

> For over two years, Robert Bardo maintained a deranged obsession for the young, popular actress Rebecca Schaeffer, co-star of the television sitcom *My Sister Sam*. He sent her letters threatening to hurt her, followed her on several occasions, and was restrained by security guards after trying to enter her television studio. . . . Finally, . . . [o]n the morning of July 18, 1989, he gunned down Schaeffer in the doorway of her apartment, killing her instantly.
>
> The highly publicized murder of Rebecca Schaeffer focused national attention on a problem confronted by men and women who are repeatedly followed, harassed, or physically threatened by other persons. . . . Until the enactment of stalking statutes, law enforcement officers could do little to ensure the privacy and safety of stalking victims, since existing civil and criminal remedies often fail to deter stalkers' abusive, and sometimes fatal, conduct. . . .
>
> Many jurisdictions have statutorily extended the scope of criminal assault statutes to include intentional scaring, which occurs when a perpetrator commits an act with the intent to cause another a reasonable apprehension of immediate bodily harm. . . .
>
> The overt act requirement makes the crime of intentional scaring inapplicable in many stalking cases, since it forces prosecutors to show that a stalker's conduct was of the type that would arouse apprehension of *immediate* bodily harm in an ordinary, reasonable person. . . . Threatening looks and words, however, without an overt act portending to carry out the threat, do not constitute intentional scaring. Yet, a typical stalker may consistently follow and harass a person, intentionally causing that person to fear for his or her safety, but never commit an overt act sufficient to raise a fear of *immediate* bodily harm. . . .
>
> Harassment statutes, as alternative criminal remedies, seek to deter conduct that causes alarm in others and serves no legitimate purpose.[80]
>
> These statutes, however, provide minimal penalties for punishing stalkers, classifying harassment as a petty misdemeanor or an even less serious crime. The primary concern of the legislatures that enacted these statutes was the protection of

---

80. Several states have patterned harassment statutes after . . . Model Penal Code §250.4 [Appendix].

individuals from unwanted invasions of their privacy interests. . . . While these statutes may be employed against stalkers who repeatedly engage in "annoying" and "alarming" conduct, they are not designed to deter the more serious conduct of the stalker who obsessively and maliciously follows and harasses a victim, intending to place the victim in fear for his or her physical safety.

Currently available criminal remedies, therefore, provide insufficient solutions to the stalking problem. To provide victims with adequate protection, states must develop stricter laws specifically aimed at curtailing the threatening conduct of stalkers.

2. Statutory solutions. California enacted the nation's first stalking statute in 1990, and at the most recent count, 30 other states had similar laws. See Lewin, supra Note 1, at B10. Consider the representative examples that follow.

Cal. Penal Code §646.9 (Supp. 1994): Stalking

(a) Any person who willfully, maliciously, and repeatedly follows or harasses another person and who makes a credible threat with the intent to place that person in reasonable fear for his or her safety, or the safety of his or her immediate family, is guilty of the crime of stalking, punishable by imprisonment in a county jail for not more than one year or by a fine of not more than one thousand dollars ($1,000), or by both that fine and imprisonment, or by imprisonment in the state prison.

(b) Any person who violates subdivision (a) when there is a temporary restraining order, injunction, or any other court order in effect prohibiting the behavior described in subdivision (a) against the same party, shall be punished by imprisonment in the state prison for two, three, or four years. . . .

(d) For the purposes of this section, "harasses" means a knowing and willful course of conduct directed at a specific person which seriously alarms, annoys, torments, or terrorizes the person, and which serves no legitimate purpose. The course of conduct must be such as would cause a reasonable person to suffer substantial emotional distress, and must actually cause substantial emotional distress to the person. "Course of conduct" means a pattern of conduct composed of a series of acts over a period of time, however short, evidencing a continuity of purpose. Constitutionally protected activity is not included within the meaning of "course of conduct."

(e) For the purposes of this section, "credible threat" means a verbal or written threat or a threat implied by a pattern of conduct or a combination of verbal or written statements and conduct made with the intent and the apparent ability to carry out the threat so as to cause the person who is the target of the threat to reasonably fear for his or her safety or the safety of his or her immediate family.

(f) This section shall not apply to conduct which occurs during labor picketing. . . .

Fla. Stat. ch. 784.048 (1994): Stalking; definitions; penalties

(1) As used in this section:

(a) "Harasses" means to engage in a course of conduct directed at a specific person that causes substantial emotional distress in such person and serves no legitimate purpose.

(b) "Course of conduct" means a pattern of conduct composed of a series of acts over a period of time, however short, evidencing a continuity of purpose. Constitutionally protected activity is not included within the meaning of "course of conduct." Such constitutionally protected activity includes picketing or other organized protests.

(c) "Credible threat" means a threat made with the intent to cause the person who is the target of the threat to reasonably fear for his or her safety. The threat must be against the life of, or a threat to cause bodily injury to, a person.

(2) Any person who willfully, maliciously, and repeatedly follows or harasses another person commits the offense of stalking, a misdemeanor of the first degree. . . .

(3) Any person who willfully, maliciously, and repeatedly follows or harasses another person, and makes a credible threat with the intent to place that person in reasonable fear of death or bodily injury, commits the offense of aggravated stalking, a felony of the third degree. . . .

(4) Any person who, after an injunction for protection against repeat violence . . . or after any other court-imposed prohibition of conduct toward the subject person or that person's property, knowingly, willfully, maliciously, and repeatedly follows or harasses another person commits the offense of aggravated stalking, a felony of the third degree. . . .

3. Questions. Does the California statute represent an adequate response to the problem of "stalking?" How does the Florida approach differ, and what concerns account for the differences? Does either of the statutes pose a danger of criminalizing conduct that should not be subject to punishment? The arguments in support of antistalking statutes are developed in Gilligan, supra Note 1. For a more critical view, suggesting that statutes such as those of Florida and California violate constitutional prohibitions against vagueness and overbreadth, see Robert P. Faulkner & Douglas H. Hsiao, And Where You Go I'll Follow: The Constitutionality of Antistalking Laws and Proposed Model Legislation, 31 Harv. J. Legis. 1, 21-29 (1994).

4. Anti-loitering laws represent an earlier but related statutory response to the problem of conduct that arouses fear of impending criminal acts but may not rise to the level of a punishable attempt. For analysis of these statutes and the constitutional problems they pose, see page 308 supra.

c. The Model Penal Code Approach

UNITED STATES v. JACKSON

United States Court of Appeals, 2d Circuit
560 F.2d 112 (1977)

FREDERICK VAN PELT BRYAN, J.: Robert Jackson, William Scott, and Martin Allen appeal from judgments of conviction entered . . . after a trial before Chief Judge Jacob Mishler without a jury.

Count one of the indictment alleged that between June 11 and June 21, 1976 the appellants conspired to commit an armed robbery of the Manufacturers Hanover Trust . . . Counts two and three each charged appellants with an attempted robbery of the branch on June 14 and on June 21, 1976, respectively . . . Chief Judge Mishler filed a memorandum of decision finding each defendant guilty on all . . . counts.

Appellants' principal contention is that the court below erred in finding them guilty on counts two and three. While they concede that the evidence supported the conspiracy convictions on count one, they assert that, as a matter of law, their conduct never crossed the elusive line which separates "mere preparation" from "attempt."[a] . . .

The Government's evidence at trial consisted largely of the testimony of Vanessa Hodges, an unindicted co-conspirator, and of various FBI agents who surveilled the Manufacturers Hanover branch on June 21, 1976. . . .

On June 11, 1976, Vanessa Hodges was introduced to appellant Martin Allen by Pia Longhorne, another unindicted co-conspirator. Hodges wanted to meet someone who would help her carry out a plan to rob the Manufacturers Hanover branch located at 210 Flushing Avenue in Brooklyn, and she invited Allen to join her. Hodges proposed that the bank be robbed the next Monday, June 14th, at about 7:30 A.M. She hoped that they could enter with the bank manager at that time, grab the weekend deposits, and leave. Allen agreed to rob the bank with Hodges, and told her he had access to a car, two sawed-off shotguns, and a .38 caliber revolver.

The following Monday, June 14, Allen arrived at Longhorne's house about 7:30 A.M. in a car driven by appellant Robert Jackson. A suitcase in the back seat of the car contained a sawed-off shotgun, shells, materials intended as masks, and handcuffs to bind the bank manager. While Allen picked up Hodges at Longhorne's, Jackson filled the car with gas. The trio then left for the bank.

When they arrived, it was almost 8:00 A.M. It was thus too late to effect the first step of the plan, *viz.*, entering the bank as the manager opened the door. They rode around for a while longer, and then . . . drove back to the bank. . . . but decided it was too risky to rob the bank without an extra man.

Consequently, Jackson, Hodges, and Allen drove to Coney Island in search of another accomplice. In front of a housing project on 33rd Street they found appellant William Scott, who promptly joined the team. Allen added to the arsenal another sawed-off shotgun obtained from one of the buildings in the project, and the group drove back to the bank.

When they arrived again, Allen entered the bank to check the location of any surveillance cameras, while Jackson placed a piece of cardboard with a false license number over the authentic license plate of the car. . . . After further discussion, Scott left the car and entered the bank. He came back and informed the group that the tellers were separating the weekend deposits and that a number of patrons were now in the bank. Hodges then suggested that they drop the plans for the robbery that day, and reschedule it for the following Monday, June 21. Accordingly, they left. . . .

---

a. Since the defendants conceded the validity of their conspiracy convictions, why did it matter whether they could also be convicted of attempt? Note that the federal conspiracy statute, 18 U.S.C. §371, carries a maximum sentence of five years' imprisonment, while 18 U.S.C. §2113(a) provides that attempted bank robbery is punishable by a maximum of twenty years' imprisonment. In the present case, the defendant Jackson received a two-year sentence on the conspiracy count and a suspended sentence on the other counts; Scott received a five-year sentence on the conspiracy count and concurrent seven-year terms on the attempt counts; Allen received a five-year sentence on the conspiracy count and concurrent ten-year terms on the attempt counts. — EDS.

Hodges was arrested on Friday, June 18, 1976 on an unrelated bank robbery charge, and immediately began cooperating with the Government. After relating the events on June 14, she told FBI agents that a robbery of the Manufacturers branch at 210 Flushing Avenue was now scheduled for the following Monday, June 21. [Hodges also provided a detailed physical description of the three robbers.]

At the request of the agents, Hodges called Allen on Saturday, June 19, and asked if he were still planning to do the job. He said that he was ready. On Sunday she called him again. This time Allen said that he was not going to rob the bank that Monday because he had learned that Hodges had been arrested and he feared that federal agents might be watching. Hodges nevertheless advised the agents that she thought the robbery might still take place as planned with the three men proceeding without her.

At about 7:00 A.M. on Monday, June 21, 1976, some ten FBI agents took various surveilling positions in the area of the bank. At about 7:39 A.M. the agents observed a brown four-door Lincoln, with a New York license plate on the front and a cardboard facsimile of a license plate on the rear, moving in an easterly direction on Flushing Avenue past the bank. . . . [The car, which was occupied by three men fitting the description Hodges had provided, stopped near the bank. One of the men got out, stood for a while on a corner in front of the bank and then returned to the car. The Lincoln drove up and down the streets near the bank, then stopped for several minutes a few blocks away. When it returned and parked near the bank, agents noticed that its front license plate was now missing. After parking for thirty minutes, the car began moving in the direction of the bank.]

At some point near the bank as they passed down Flushing Avenue, the appellants detected the presence of the surveillance agents. The Lincoln . . . was overtaken by FBI agents who ordered the appellants out of the car and arrested them. The agents then observed a black and red plaid suitcase in the rear of the car. The zipper of the suitcase was partially open and exposed two loaded sawed-off shotguns, a toy nickel-plated revolver, a pair of handcuffs, and masks. A New York license plate was seen lying on the front floor of the car. All of these items were seized.

In his memorandum of decision, Chief Judge Mishler concluded that the evidence against Jackson, Scott, and Allen was "overwhelming" on [the conspiracy count]. In contrast, he characterized the question of whether the defendants had attempted a bank robbery as charged in counts two and three or were merely engaged in preparations as "a close one." After canvassing the authorities . . . Chief Judge Mishler applied the following two-tiered inquiry formulated in United States v. Mandujano, 499 F.2d 370, 376 (5th Cir. 1974):

> First, the defendant must have been acting with the kind of culpability otherwise required for the commission of the crime which he is charged with attempting. . . .
> Second, the defendant must have engaged in conduct which constitutes a substantial step toward commission of the crime. A substantial step must be conduct strongly corroborative of the firmness of the defendant's criminal intent.

He concluded that on June 14 and again on June 21, the defendants took substantial steps, strongly corroborative of the firmness of their criminal intent, toward commission of the crime of bank robbery and found the defendants guilty on each of the two attempt counts. These appeals followed.

[T]here is no comprehensive statutory definition of attempt in federal law. . . .

Chief Judge Kaufman, writing for [this court in United States v. Stallworth, 543 F.2d 1038 (2d Cir. 1976),] selected the two-tiered inquiry of United States v. Mandujano, supra, as stating the proper test for determining whether . . . conduct constituted an attempt. He observed that this analysis "conforms closely to the sensible definition of an attempt proffered by the American Law Institute's Model Penal Code [§5.01]."

The draftsmen of the Model Penal Code recognized the difficulty of arriving at a general standard for distinguishing acts of preparation from acts constituting an attempt. . . .

The formulation upon which the draftsmen ultimately agreed required, in addition to criminal purpose, that an act be a substantial step in a course of conduct designed to accomplish a criminal result, and that it be strongly corroborative of criminal purpose in order for it to constitute such a substantial step. The following differences between this test and previous approaches to the preparation-attempt problem were noted:

> First, this formulation shifts the emphasis from what remains to be done — the chief concern of the proximity tests — to what the actor *has already done.* The fact that further major steps must be taken before the crime can be completed does not preclude a finding that the steps already undertaken are substantial. It is expected, in the normal case, that this approach will broaden the scope of attempt liability.
>
> Second, although it is intended that the requirement of a substantial step will result in the imposition of attempt liability only in those instances in which some firmness of criminal purpose is shown, no finding is required as to whether the actor would probably have desisted prior to completing the crime. . . .
>
> Finally, the requirement of proving a substantial step generally will prove less of a hurdle for the prosecution than the *res ipsa loquitur* approach, which requires that the actor's conduct must itself manifest the criminal purpose. . . .

Model Penal Code §5.01, Comment at 47 (Tent. Draft No. 10, 1960).

The draftsmen concluded that, in addition to assuring firmness of criminal design, the requirement of a substantial step would preclude attempt liability, with its accompanying harsh penalties, for relatively remote preparatory acts. At the same time, however, by not requiring a "last proximate act" or one of its various analogues it would permit the apprehension of dangerous persons at an earlier stage than the other approaches without immunizing them from attempt liability. . . .

In the case at bar, Chief Judge Mishler [concluded that on both June 14 and June 21] these men were seriously dedicated to the commission of a crime, had passed beyond the stage of preparation, and would have assaulted the bank had they not been dissuaded by certain external factors, *viz.*, the breaking up of the weekend deposits and crowd of patrons in the bank on June 14 and the detection of the FBI surveillance on June 21.

We cannot say that these conclusions . . . were erroneous. On two separate occasions, appellants reconnoitered the place contemplated for the commission of the crime and possessed the paraphernalia to be employed in the commission of the crime — loaded sawed-off shotguns, extra shells, a toy revolver, hand-cuffs, and masks — which was specially designed for such unlawful use and which could serve no lawful purpose under the circumstances. Under the Model Penal Code formulation, either type of conduct, standing alone, was sufficient as a matter of law to constitute a "substantial step" if it strongly corroborated their criminal purpose. Here both types of conduct coincided on both June 14 and June 21, along with numerous other elements strongly corroborative of the firmness of appellants' criminal intent. [We] thus affirm the convictions for attempted bank robbery on counts two and three.[9]

NOTE ON STATUTORY REFORM

The Model Penal Code draws on elements of both the proximity and the equivocality tests. As *Jackson* indicates, the Model Penal Code approach has proved influential with many courts. And in a number of jurisdictions, statutory provisions reflect the Model Penal Code. E.g., N.J. Stat. Ann. §2C:5-1. Altogether, roughly half the states and two-thirds of the federal circuits now use a "substantial step" test comparable to that of the Model Penal Code. See Young v. State, 439 A.2d 352, 361 (Md. 1985). Some states have adopted the Model Penal Code's substantial step formulation without the requirement that the actor's conduct strongly corroborate the intent. E.g., Ga. Code §16-4-1; Ill. Stat. ch. 720, §5/8-4; 18 Pa. Stat. Ann §901.

Several of the statutory formulations include significant variations on the Model Penal Code approach:

(a) Colo Rev. Stat., §18-2-101 defines a "substantial step" as one which is "strongly corroborative of the firmness of the actor's purpose." *Question:* What is the intention behind this change in wording?

(b) 11 Del. Code Ann. §532 defines a substantial step as "an act or omission which leaves no reasonable doubt as to the defendant's intention to commit the crime. . . ." *Question:* How does this language alter the effect of the normal requirement of proof beyond a reasonable doubt? Is the change a desirable one?

PROBLEMS

1. United States v. Buffington, 815 F.2d 1292 (9th Cir. 1987): An informant told the Sacramento Police Department that appellants planned to rob a bank[1] in the shopping center at Florin Road and Franklin Boulevard, and that appellant Cabrellis would be dressed as a woman. [O]n December 22, about 4:20 P.M., two men, later identified as Buffington and Cook, and a third person appearing to be a woman, later identified as appellant Cabrellis, driving a white Pontiac, entered the shopping center.

---

9. Since Chief Judge Mishler was justified on the facts of this case in construing the June 14 and June 21 attempts as distinct criminal transactions or episodes, rather than simultaneous violations, the concurrent sentences on counts two and three were not improper. We feel impelled here, however, to remind the Government that it may face valid double jeopardy claims if it tries to fragment what is in fact a single crime into its components and punish each separately.

1. Two institutions are located in the shopping center: The Bay View Federal Savings and Loan Association (Bay View) and the Farmers and Merchants Bank (Farmers Bank), a state bank.

The Pontiac proceeded down one aisle of parking and slowly went past Bay View Federal Savings, toward which the occupants of the vehicle seemed to be looking. . . . After a U-turn, the car slowly returned down another aisle of parking past the bank, and the occupants again looked toward Bay View Federal. The driver, Buffington, parked the vehicle about one hundred fifty feet from a Pay-less Store, which was about the same distance from the bank. Buffington left the car, entered Payless, and walked to a window which overlooked Bay View Federal. He did not purchase, inspect goods, or shop, but after three minutes, walked over and stood in a cashier line.

About two minutes after Buffington left the vehicle, Cook also emerged and stood by the car door. . . . The person dressed in women's clothes, Cabrellis, also exited the car and stood by the door. Both persons were facing Bay View.

By sheer coincidence, a major power outage then occurred affecting the shopping center area. Shortly afterwards, Margaret Morningstar, a Bay View Federal teller, walked to the front door of the bank and locked the door, at which time she noticed Cook wrapping the scarf over his face so that only his glasses showed. She mentioned to a security guard that the man would be unable to rob the bank because she had just locked the door. Buffington, meanwhile, returned to the car, which he, Cabrellis and Cook reentered. . . . Police officers . . . stopped the vehicle, ordered the appellants to exit the car at gunpoint, and forced them to lie face down on the pavement. Police found a revolver on Cook's person and a revolver on the left rear floorboard of the vehicle. Appellants were then arrested [and all three were subsequently convicted of attempted bank robbery.]

[Applying the Model Penal Code approach, the Ninth Circuit reversed the convictions. *Question:* Is the result consistent with *Jackson*? The court commented:]

[T]he circumstances fall short of showing the intent to rob a federal bank. If intent to rob existed at all, it could easily have been directed against the Payless market, or the nearby state bank. . . .

Moreover, even if sufficient intent to rob were shown, the conduct fell short of constituting a substantial step toward the commission of a robbery. [We] could well believe that the defendants intended to do what the informant claimed they had planned; but their actual conduct did not cross the boundary between preparation and attempt. . . . Not only did appellants not take a single step toward the bank, they displayed no weapons and no indication that they were about to make an entry. Standing alone, their conduct did not constitute that requisite "appreciable fragment" of a bank robbery, nor a step toward commission of the crime of such substantiality that, unless frustrated, the crime would have occurred.

2. *United States v. Mandujano, 499 F.2d 370 (5th Cir. 1974):* Alfonso H. Cavalier, Jr., [was] a San Antonio police officer assigned to the Office of Drug Abuse Law Enforcement. Agent Cavalier testified that, at the time the case arose, he was working in an undercover capacity and represented himself as a narcotics trafficker. . . . [P]ursuant to information Cavalier had received, he and a government informer went to the Tally-Ho Lounge. . . . Once inside the bar, the informant introduced Cavalier to Roy Mandujano. After some general conversation Mandujano asked the informant if he was looking for "stuff." Cavalier said, "Yes" . . . and told Mandujano he was looking for an ounce sample of heroin to determine the quality of the material. Mandujano replied that he had good brown Mexican heroin for $650.00 an ounce, but that if Cavalier wanted any of it he would have to wait until later in the afternoon when the regular man made his deliveries.

Cavalier said that he was from out of town and did not want to wait that long. Mandujano offered to locate another source, and made four telephone calls in an apparent effort to do so. The phone calls appeared to be unsuccessful, for Mandujano told Cavalier he wasn't having any luck contacting anybody. Cavalier stated that he could not wait any longer. Then Mandujano said he had a good contact, a man who kept narcotics around his home, but that if he went to see this man, he would need the money "out front." . . . Cavalier counted out $650.00 to Mandujano, and Mandujano left the premises of the Tally-Ho Lounge at about 3:30 P.M. About an hour later, he returned and explained that he had been unable to locate his contact. He gave back the $650.00 and told Cavalier he could still wait until the regular man came around. Cavalier left, but arranged to call back at 6:00 P.M. When Cavalier called at 6:00 and again at 6:30, he was told that Mandujano was not available. Cavalier testified that he did not later attempt to contact Mandujano because, "based on the information that I had received, it would be unsafe for either my informant or myself to return to this area."

Question: On these facts, defendant Mandujano was convicted of attempting to distribute heroin. The Fifth Circuit affirmed. Is the result proper under the Model Penal Code test?

3. *United States v. Joyce, 693 F.2d 838 (8th Cir. 1982):* [Government informant James Gebbie called Joyce and informed him that cocaine] was available for purchase in St. Louis. Joyce indicated that he had twenty-two thousand dollars and would be in St. Louis the following day, October 21, 1980. Gebbie and Joyce agreed that twenty-two thousand dollars would be more than sufficient to purchase a pound of cocaine.

On October 21, 1980, Joyce flew from Oklahoma City, Oklahoma to St. Louis, Missouri, where he met Gebbie and undercover officer Robert Jones, who was posing as a cocaine seller. Jones and Gebbie took Joyce to a room in a local St. Louis hotel, where Joyce immediately asked to see the cocaine. Jones told Joyce that the cocaine was not in the hotel room, but could be easily obtained by Jones if Joyce was interested in dealing rather than merely talking. After Joyce professed his interest in dealing, Jones recited prices for various quantities of cocaine and Joyce said that he could "handle" a pound of cocaine for twenty thousand dollars. Officer Jones then went to his office and obtained the cocaine.

When officer Jones returned to the hotel room, he handed Joyce a duct-tape wrapped plastic package said to contain a kilogram of cocaine. Without unwrapping the tape, Joyce immediately returned the package, stating that he could not see the cocaine. Jones then unwrapped about half of the tape covering the plastic package and handed the package back to Joyce. Joyce again returned the package to Jones and asked Jones to open up the package so that Joyce could examine the cocaine more closely. Jones answered that he would only open the plastic package if and when Joyce showed the money that he intended to use to purchase the cocaine.[a] Joyce then replied that he would not produce his money until Jones first opened up the plastic package. After Jones persisted in asking Joyce to produce his money, Joyce again refused, stating that he would not deal

a. Elsewhere in its opinion, the court stated that "Jones was acting in compliance with DEA guidelines which prohibit illegal drugs from going into the physical possession of persons under investigation." — EDS.

with officer Jones no matter how good the cocaine was. Realizing that Joyce was not going to show his money or purchase the cocaine, Jones told Joyce to leave and Joyce left, with no apparent intention of returning at a later time to purchase any cocaine.

As Joyce left the hotel, he was arrested by DEA agents. A search warrant was thereafter obtained and used to search Joyce's luggage revealing twenty-two thousand dollars in cash.

[Joyce was convicted of attempting to purchase cocaine with intent to distribute, but the Eighth Circuit, applying the Model Penal Code formulation, reversed. The court explained:]

. . . Whatever intention Joyce had to procure cocaine was abandoned prior to the commission of a necessary and substantial step to effectuate the purchase of cocaine. . . . While Joyce professed a desire to purchase cocaine during his preliminary discussions with Jones, Joyce never attempted to carry through with that desire by producing the money necessary to purchase and hence ultimately possess the cocaine. And, although Jones gave Joyce the sealed and wrapped package said to contain a kilogram of cocaine, Joyce did not open the package but immediately returned the package to Jones who in turn refused to open the package because Joyce refused to produce the money necessary to effectuate the purchase of a pound of cocaine. Thus, all we have here is a preliminary discussion regarding the purchase of cocaine which broke down. . . .

We also find unpersuasive the government's claim that Joyce would have purchased the cocaine had it not been for Jones's refusal to open the package of cocaine. We simply fail to see why Joyce's motive for refusing to commit a "substantial step" toward possession of the cocaine is particularly relevant. Joyce's motive for refusing to purchase the cocaine here is no different than had he refused to purchase because he disagreed with Jones as to the price for which the cocaine was offered. And, while we may agree with the government's suggestion that Joyce, who was presumably "street-wise," may have been tipped off that Jones was a DEA undercover agent when Jones refused to open the package, we fail to see how an increased awareness of the risk of apprehension converts what would otherwise be "mere preparation" into an attempt.

Question: Is the result sound? Compare People v. Acosta, 80 N.Y.2d 665, 671, 609 N.E.2d 518, 521 (1993):

A person who orders illegal narcotics from a supplier, admits a courier into his or her home and examines the quality of the goods has unquestionably passed beyond mere preparation and come "very near" to possessing those drugs. Indeed, the only remaining step between the attempt and the completed crime is the person's acceptance of the proffered merchandise, an act entirely within his or her control.

d. Solicitation

STATE v. DAVIS

Supreme Court of Missouri
319 Mo. 1222, 6 S.W.2d 609 (1928)

Davis, C. [Defendant was convicted of attempted murder in the first degree on the following facts. He and Alberdina Lourie planned to have the latter's husband, Edmon Lourie, killed in order to collect the insurance and live together. He sought the help of Earl Leverton in obtaining an ex-convict to do the job, but Leverton disclosed the plot to Dill, a police officer, who decided to pose as the ex-convict. Defendant paid Dill $600 to carry out plans he had devised for killing Lourie. After several conferences and one aborted plan, a scheme was arranged whereby Dill was to appear at the Lourie home, kill Edmon, and feign a robbery by "mussing up" Alberdina and taking her jewels. At the appointed hour Dill appeared at the Lourie home but at this point revealed his identity. He then proceeded to defendant's home where he made an arrest.]

The sufficiency of the evidence to sustain the conviction is raised. The defining of an attempt to commit a crime and the ascertaining of its essential elements is necessary in the consideration of the question. . . .

The elements of an attempt are stated in 16 Corpus Juris, p. 113, thus: "An attempt to commit a crime consists of three elements: (1) The intention to commit the crime; (2) performance of some act toward the commission of the crime; and (3) the failure to consummate its commission."

The proof adduced advises us that the only debatable question is the presence of sufficient facts to demonstrate the second element. . . .

The physical overt act, which with intent and failure to consummate brings the crime of attempt into existence, is distinguishable from solicitation and preparation. An attempt to commit a crime involves an act on the part of the defendant moving directly toward the commission of the offense. . . .

While a few of the courts have treated solicitation to commit a crime as an attempt, the great weight of authority warrants the assertion that mere solicitation, unaccompanied by an act moving directly toward the commission of the intended crime, is not an overt act constituting an element of the crime of attempt. Solicitation of itself is a distinct offense when declared so by law. Therefore, in conformity with the weight of authority, we hold that merely soliciting one to commit a crime does not constitute an attempt.

The state contends that the arrangement of a plan for the accomplishment of the murder of Lourie and the selecting and hiring of the means or instrumentality by which the murder was to be consummated were demonstrated. We take it that the state means by the foregoing declarations that overt acts were shown. To that we do not agree. The evidence goes no further than developing a verbal arrangement with Dill, the selection of Dill as the one to kill Lourie, the delivery of a certain drawing and two photographs of Lourie to Dill, and the payment of a portion of the agreed consideration. These things were mere acts of preparation, failing to lead directly or proximately to the consummation of the intended crime.

. . . The contract of hiring entered into between defendant and Dill also fails to extend beyond mere preparation. In regard to the hiring, the trial court instructed the jury that the payment of money by defendant to Dill to commit the intended crime did not constitute such an overt act as was tantamount to an attempt. The ruling of the court we think was right, for the payment of money was not an act moving directly toward the consummation of the intended crime. . . .

The employment of Dill as agent to murder Lourie was not tantamount to an attempt. Dill not only had no intention of carrying out the expressed purpose of defendant, but was guilty of no act directly or indirectly moving toward the consummation of the intended crime. He did nothing more than listen to the plans and solicitations of defendant without intending to act upon them. It was not shown that Dill committed an act that could be construed as an attempt.

Whether it is necessary to make an actual assault before the crime of attempt can be said to come into existence, we need not decide, for the solicitations and preparations upon the part of defendant were not equivalent to an overt act which must take place before the crime of attempt comes into existence. . . .

It follows from what we have said that the judgment must be reversed, and the defendant discharged. It is so ordered.

UNITED STATES v. CHURCH, 29 Mil. J. Rptr. 679 (Ct. Milit. Rev. 1989): [Appellant] was found guilty of the attempted premeditated murder of his wife. . . . His sentence, as adjudged and approved, extends to a dishonorable discharge, confinement for ten years, [and] forfeiture of all pay and allowances. . . . [On appeal] defense counsel conceded that the appellant is guilty of soliciting another to commit murder, but argued forcefully that he was not guilty of attempted murder because no act beyond mere preparation was proven.[3] To resolve this matter, it will be necessary to review the evidence of record in some detail.

[Appellant, an airman stationed in North Dakota, had separated from his wife after two years of marriage. The wife won custody of their son and moved with the child to Michigan. Appellant hoped to regain custody of his son but realized that he was unlikely to succeed in doing so through the courts. At that point he began talking about finding a "hit man" to kill his wife. Eventually some of appellant's associates began to take him seriously, and they reported the matter to the Office of Special Investigations (OSI). Shortly thereafter, an undercover OSI agent was presented as a "hit man."

[In a motel room meeting, appellant provided the agent with a partial payment; expense money for the round trip flight to Michigan; street maps of Mrs. Church's neighborhood; photographs of Mrs. Church and their son; and descriptions of all the people in the house, including where they slept and what their work schedules were. Appellant also approved use of the weapon the agent presented, a .22-caliber pistol with silencer, and he expressed a preference for where on the victim he wanted the shots placed. The job was to be done while appellant was conspicuously on duty in North Dakota. Unbeknownst to appellant, the entire conversation was videotaped. Several days later appellant was notified through command channels that his wife had been murdered. Appellant put on "a Class A act" of grief. That same day, he was notified by the undercover agent to meet him at the North Dakota motel. Appellant arrived, expressed satisfaction with the job done, paid the agent, and identified his wife's "body" from a staged photograph. This meeting also was videotaped. Appellant was then arrested.]

In various factual situations involving "contracting out" for crimes, [many courts have] held that the evidence only established mere acts of preparation

---

3. Among other punishments, confinement for 20 years is authorized for attempted murder, whereas the period of confinement authorized for soliciting another to commit murder is 5 years. . . .

not leading directly or proximately to consummation of the intended crime. . . . Typical, and perhaps closest factually to the present appellant's case, [is State v. Davis, supra]. . . . The Supreme Court of Missouri concluded: "The employment of Dill as agent to murder Lourie was not tantamount to an attempt. Dill not only had no intention of carrying out the expressed purpose of defendant, but was guilty of no act directly or indirectly moving toward the consummation of the intended crime." . . .

Not all authority favors the defense position. A few state courts have upheld attempt convictions in cases involving crimes for hire. . . . Appellate defense counsel urge that it would be inappropriate to adopt this minority view under military law. . . . We are not convinced, however, that military law should extend so far as to hold that a factual situation such as that present in the *Davis* [case] will not constitute an attempt to commit a crime. . . . The appellant's conduct in obtaining the services of Nicholas Karnezis to murder his wife, his detailed participation in planning the intended crime, up to advising the agent exactly how he wanted his wife shot, and his payment of the agreed upon consideration, . . . constitutes "a substantial step toward commission of the crime," and establishes the requisite overt act amounting to more than mere preparation. We can envision nothing else the appellant could possibly have done to effect what he believed would be his wife's murder, short of committing the act himself (which is precisely what he did not want to do). As characterized by appellate government counsel during oral argument, the appellant armed a missile (Nick) and fired it off, fully believing it was aimed directly at his intended victim.

NOTE

On review of the decision in *Church*, the U.S. Court of Military Appeals noted (32 Mil. J. Rptr. 70, 70-71 n. 1, 74 n. 7 (1991)):

> The real stake in this appeal is the sentence. If, as appellant contends, he is merely guilty of soliciting murder, the most he can be confined is 5 years. If, however, he is guilty of attempted murder, the maximum confinement is 20 years, with the result that his approved sentence would stand.
>
> Of course, if the facts stood as appellant believed and hoped them to be, he would be guilty as a principal to premeditated murder — and conspiracy as well. Under those circumstances, the *minimum* term he could have received would have been confinement for life. Fortuitously for all concerned, appellant's efforts were frustrated by law enforcement personnel. Thus, murder is not applicable because the intended victim is not dead. Conspiracy is also arguably not available because the *agent* did not actually agree to kill Mrs. Church. . . .
>
> These vast distinctions in punishment ceilings among solicitations, attempts, and completed offenses — at least when the crimes are very serious — reflect the traditional view that the punishment should be commensurate with the *resulting harm*, irrespective of the badness of the actor or the seriousness of the threat. The modern approach, on the other hand, . . . is to make the punishment levels generally the same or nearly the same for solicitations, attempts, and completed offenses — based upon the badness of the actor, not upon the fortuitousness of the results. *See, e.g.,* §5.05, Model Penal Code; §2X1.1, Federal Sentencing Guidelines; §§12-32(a) and 15.03(d), Vernon's Code of Texas Annotated, Penal Code. Narrowing these vast discrepancies in punishment ceilings would lessen the premium put

on factfinder hair-splitting as the evidence proceeds down the continuum of solicitation, conspiratorial agreement, overt act in furtherance of the conspiracy, act beyond mere preparation tending to effect commission of a crime, etc. It would also remove the illogical consequence that the punishment for soliciting premeditated murder can be no greater than that for soliciting the making of a check of $101 without sufficient funds.

Affirming the conviction, the court held:

It is clear that appellant did everything he thought not only necessary but possible to make the enterprise successful — before, during, and after the supposed crime. Looking to his conduct only, we agree the evidence was sufficient for a rational factfinder to find, beyond a reasonable doubt, that his actions exceeded mere preparation.

NOTES ON SOLICITATION

1. Solicitation as an attempt. Near the end of its opinion in the *Davis* case, the court states: "It was not shown that Dill committed an act that could be construed as an attempt." What difference would it have made if Dill *had* gone further than he had? Would the prosecution's difficulties have been resolved if Dill had been instructed by the district attorney to play the scene to the hilt, as, for example, by leveling his pistol at the husband's chest? Could this feigned overt act of attempt be attributed to the defendant as his, the defendant's, genuine overt act of attempt? Since Dill was only a feigned participant, can the defendant's guilt be made to rest in any way on the acts of Dill? See State v. Hayes, page 671 infra.

Courts differ sharply over the question whether solicitation constitutes an attempt. In accord with *Church*, the recent federal cases hold that a solicitation can constitute a punishable attempt if it represents a "substantial step" under the circumstances. See United States v. American Airlines, Inc., 743 F.2d 1114, 1121 (5th Cir. 1984); United States v. May, 625 F.2d 186, 194 (8th Cir. 1980). But many states adhere to the view that "no matter what acts the solicitor commits, he cannot be guilty of an attempt because it is not his purpose to commit the offense personally." Model Penal Code and Commentaries, Comment to §5.02 at 369 (1985).

2. Solicitation as an independent crime. At common law, inciting or soliciting another to commit a crime was a crime itself, independent of any other offense that either party might commit. For a long time, American codes by and large did not contain provisions incorporating this offense but rather made criminal the solicitation of particular crimes. However, a substantial number of states now have general solicitation statutes. They are usually patterned after Model Penal Code §5.02. The commentary defends that formulation as follows (Model Penal Code and Commentaries, Comment to §5.02 at 365-366, 375-378 (1985)):

It has been argued [that the solicitor's] conduct is not dangerous because the resisting will of an independent moral agent is interposed between the solicitor and the commission of the crime that is his object. By the same token it is urged that the solicitor, manifesting his reluctance to commit the crime himself, is not a significant menace. The opposing view is that a solicitation is, if anything, more dangerous than a direct attempt, because it may give rise to the special hazard of cooperation among criminals. Solicitation may, indeed, be thought of as an attempt to conspire. . . .

There should be no doubt on this issue. Purposeful solicitation presents dangers calling for preventive intervention and is sufficiently indicative of a disposition towards criminal activity to call for liability. Moreover, the fortuity that the person solicited does not agree to commit or attempt to commit the incited crime plainly should not relieve the solicitor of liability, when otherwise he would be a conspirator or an accomplice. . . .

When this section was considered by the Institute, it appeared that solicitation of another to commit a crime was not protected by the first amendment. . . . [O]ne who uses words as a means to crime, who intends that his words should cause a criminal result, does not make a contribution to community discussion that is worthy of protection. But the main problem [is] how to prevent legitimate agitation of an extreme or inflammatory nature from being misinterpreted as solicitation to crime. It would not be difficult to convince a jury that inflammatory rhetoric in behalf of an unpopular cause is in reality an invitation to violate the law rather than an effort to seek its change through legitimate criticism. Minority criticism has to be extreme in order to be politically audible, and if it employs the typical device of lauding a martyr, who is likely to have been a lawbreaker, the eulogy runs the risk of being characterized as a request for emulation.

. . . [Section 5.02(1)] makes an effort to protect legitimate agitation by requiring that the speaker solicit "specific conduct" that would constitute the crime that he is charged with [trying] to promote. It is . . . necessary under this formulation that, in the context of the knowledge and position of the intended recipient, the solicitation carry meaning in terms of some concrete course of conduct that it is the actor's object to incite. . . .

In 1969 the Supreme Court in a per curiam opinion in Brandenburg v. Ohio[44] used language indicating that solicitation of crime was, on some occasions, constitutionally protected. [The Court said that] "the constitutional guarantees of free speech and free press do not permit a State to forbid or proscribe advocacy of the use of force or of law violation except where such advocacy is directed to inciting or producing imminent lawless action and is likely to incite or produce such action."[45]

It is difficult to know how broadly to read *Brandenburg*. . . . Apparently the Supreme Court does believe that even direct incitement of specific illegal acts enjoys some constitutional protection, perhaps because such incitement expresses most eloquently the intensity of opposition to hated laws or policies. . . . It would be difficult to make similar arguments about private solicitations to commit ordinary crimes made on wholly nonpolitical grounds and it seems unlikely that the Supreme Court meant to afford protection in such cases. But the precise bounds of application of the *Brandenburg* test are still uncertain.

In NAACP v. Claiborne Hardware Co. 458 U.S. 886, 927-928 (1982), the Supreme Court reaffirmed the *Brandenburg* rule that public advocacy of violent acts may be constitutionally protected when the advocacy is not intended or likely to produce *imminent* lawless action. But the Court suggested that public speeches may lose any such constitutional protection if there is evidence, other than the

44. 395 U.S. 444 (1969).
45. Id. at 447.

speeches themselves, that the speaker authorized, ratified, or directly threatened specific acts of violence. 458 U.S. at 929. For a revealing examination of these issues, see Kent Greenawalt, Speech and Crime, [1980] Am. B. Found. Res. J. 645, 655-670.

3. *Soliciting to solicit?* In the normal solicitation situation, *D* solicits *E* to commit the crime. But in the *Davis* case, the defendants solicited Leverton to solicit another person to kill Edmon Lourie, that is, *D* solicits *E* to solicit *F* to commit the crime. Although the court makes nothing of this difference and suggests that defendants would be guilty of the crime of solicitation, can it be argued to the contrary? There have often been objections to making it criminal to attempt to attempt. Should there be similar objections to punishing a solicitation to solicit? Would this conduct be made criminal under Model Penal Code §5.02?

PROBLEM

A hypothetical put by Professor Kent Greenawalt, Speech and Crime, [1980] Am. B. Found. Res. J. 645, 662, is as follows:

A knows that his neighbor *B* is an important figure in organized crime, but *A* conceals his knowledge of this fact from *B*. Wishing that *C*, one of *B*'s employees, might be killed, *A* lets the fact that *C* is a police informer "slip out" in a conversation with *B*.

Questions: Is *A* guilty of solicitation? What should be the result under Model Penal Code §5.02?

4. Impossibility

PEOPLE v. JAFFE

New York Court of Appeals
185 N.Y. 497, 78 N.E. 169 (1906)

BARTLETT, J. The indictment charged that the defendant on the 6th day of October, 1902, in the county of New York, feloniously received 20 yards of cloth, of the value of 25 cents a yard, belonging to the copartnership of J. W. Goddard & Son, knowing that the said property had been feloniously stolen, taken, and carried away from the owners. It was found under section 550 of the Penal Code, which provides that a person who buys or receives any stolen property knowing the same to have been stolen is guilty of criminally receiving such property. The defendant was convicted of an attempt to commit the crime charged in the indictment. The proof clearly showed, and the district attorney conceded upon the trial, that the goods which the defendant attempted to purchase on October 6, 1902, had lost their character as stolen goods at the time when they were offered to the defendant and when he sought to buy them. In fact the property had been restored to the owners and was wholly within their control and was offered to the defendant by their authority and through their agency. The question presented by this appeal, therefore, is whether upon an indictment for receiving goods, knowing them to have been stolen, the defendant may be convicted of an attempt to commit the crime where it appears without dispute that the property which he sought to receive was not in fact stolen property.

The conviction was sustained by the Appellate Division chiefly upon the authority of the numerous cases in which it has been held that one may be convicted of an attempt to commit a crime notwithstanding the existence of facts unknown to him which would have rendered the complete perpetration of the crime itself impossible. Notably among these are what may be called the "Pickpocket Cases," where, in prosecutions for attempts to commit larceny from the person by pocketpicking, it is held not to be necessary to allege or prove that there was anything in the pocket which could be the subject of larceny. Much reliance was also placed in the opinion of the learned Appellate Division upon the case of People v. Gardner, 144 N.Y. 119, 38 N.E. 1003, where a conviction of an attempt to commit the crime of extortion was upheld, although the woman from whom the defendant sought to obtain money by a threat to accuse her of a crime was not induced to pay the money by fear, but was acting at the time as a decoy for the police, and hence could not have been subjected to the influence of fear. In passing upon the question here presented for our determination, it is important to bear in mind precisely what it was that the defendant attempted to do. He simply made an effort to purchase certain specific pieces of cloth. He believed the cloth to be stolen property, but it was not such in fact. The purchase, therefore, if it had been completely effected, could not constitute the crime of receiving stolen property, knowing it to be stolen, since there could be no such thing as knowledge on the part of the defendant of a nonexistent fact, although there might be a belief on his part that the fact existed. As Mr. Bishop well says, it is a mere truism *that there can be no receiving of stolen goods which have not been stolen.* 2. Bishop's New Crim. Law, §1140. It is equally difficult to perceive how there can be an attempt to receive stolen goods, knowing them to have been stolen, when they have not been stolen in fact.

The crucial distinction between the case before us and the pickpocket cases, and others involving the same principle, lies not in the possibility or impossibility of the commission of the crime, but in the fact that, in the present case, the act, which it was doubtless the intent of the defendant to commit, would not have been a crime if it had been consummated. If he had actually paid for the goods which he desired to buy and received them into his possession, he would have committed no offense under section 550 of the Penal Code, because the very definition in that section of the offense of criminally receiving property makes it an essential element of the crime that the accused shall have known the property to have been stolen or wrongfully appropriated in such a manner as to constitute larceny. . . . No man can know that to be so which is not so in truth and in fact. He may believe it to be so but belief is not enough under this statute. In the present case . . . the goods which the defendant intended to purchase had lost their character as stolen goods at the time of the proposed transaction. Hence, no matter what was the motive of the defendant, and no matter what he supposed, he could do no act which was intrinsically adapted to the then present successful perpetration of the crime denounced by this section of the Penal Code, because neither he nor any one in the world could know that the property was stolen property inasmuch as it was not, in fact, stolen property. In the pickpocket cases the immediate act which the defendant had in contemplation was an act which, if it could have been carried out, would have been criminal, whereas in the present case the immediate act which the defendant had in contemplation (to wit, the purchase of the goods which were brought to his place for sale) could not have been criminal under the statute even if the purchase had been completed. . . .

If all which an accused person intends to do would, if done, constitute no crime, it cannot be a crime to attempt to do with the same purpose a part of the thing intended. The crime of which the defendant was convicted necessarily consists of three elements: First, the act; second, the intent; and third, the knowledge of an existing condition. There was proof tending to establish two of these elements, the first and second, but none to establish the existence of the third. This was knowledge of the stolen character of the property sought to be acquired. There could be no such knowledge. The defendant could not know that the property possessed the character of stolen property when it had not in fact been acquired by theft. . . . A particular belief cannot make that a crime which is not so in the absence of such belief. Take, for example, the case of a young man who attempts to vote, and succeeds in casting his vote under the belief that he is but 20 years of age, when he is in fact over 21 and a qualified voter. His intent to commit a crime, and his belief that he was committing a crime, would not make him guilty of any offense under these circumstances, although the moral turpitude of the transaction, on his part, would be just as great as it would if he were in fact under age. So also, in the case of a prosecution under the statute of this state, which makes it rape in the second degree for a man to perpetrate an act of sexual intercourse with a female not his wife under the age of 18 years. There could be no conviction if it was established upon the trial that the female was in fact over the age of 18 years, although the defendant believed her to be younger and intended to commit the crime. No matter how reprehensible would be his act in morals, it would not be the act forbidden by this particular statute. "If what a man contemplates doing would not be in law a crime, he could not be said, in point of law, to intend to commit the crime. If he thinks his act will be a crime, this is a mere mistake of his understanding where the law holds it not to be such, his real intent being to do a particular thing. If the thing is not a crime, he does not intend to commit one whatever he may erroneously suppose." 1 Bishop's Crim. Law (7th Ed.) §742.

The judgment of the Appellate Division and of the Court of General Sessions must be reversed, and the defendant discharged upon this indictment. . . .

PEOPLE v. DLUGASH

New York Court of Appeals
41 N.Y.2d 725, 363 N.E.2d 1155 (1977)

JASEN, J. . . . For years, serious studies have been made on the subject in an effort to resolve the continuing controversy when, if at all, the impossibility of successfully completing the criminal act should preclude liability for even making the futile attempt. The 1967 revision of the Penal Law approached the impossibility defense to the inchoate crime of attempt in a novel fashion. The statute provides that, if a person engaged in conduct which would otherwise constitute an attempt to commit a crime,

> it is no defense to a prosecution for such attempt that the crime charged to have been attempted was, under the attendant circumstances, factually or legally impossible of commission, if such crime could have been committed had the attendant circumstances been as such person believed them to be.

(Penal Law, §110.10.) This appeal presents to us, for the first time, a case involving the application of the modern statute. We hold that, under the proof presented by the People at trial, defendant Melvin Dlugash may be held for attempted murder, though the target of the attempt may have already been slain, by the hand of another [Bush], when Dlugash made his felonious attempt.

On December 22, 1973, Michael Geller, 25 years old, was found shot to death in the bedroom of his Brooklyn apartment. The body, which had literally been riddled by bullets, was found lying face up on the floor. An autopsy revealed that the victim had been shot in the face and head no less than seven times. Powder burns on the face indicated that the shots had been fired from within one foot of the victim. Four small caliber bullets were recovered from the victim's skull. The victim had also been critically wounded in the chest. . . . Subsequent ballistics examination established that the four bullets recovered from the victim's head were .25 caliber bullets and that the heart-piercing bullet was of .38 caliber. . . .

Defendant stated [to police] that, on the night of December 21, 1973, he, Bush and Geller had been out drinking. Bush had been staying at Geller's apartment and, during the course of the evening, Geller several times demanded that Bush pay $100 towards the rent on the apartment. According to defendant, Bush rejected these demands, telling Geller that "you better shut up or you're going to get a bullet." All three returned to Geller's apartment at approximately midnight, took seats in the bedroom, and continued to drink until sometime between 3:00 and 3:30 in the morning. When Geller again pressed his demand for rent money, Bush drew his .38 caliber pistol, aimed it at Geller and fired three times. Geller fell to the floor. After the passage of a few minutes, perhaps two, perhaps as much as five, defendant walked over to the fallen Geller, drew his .25 caliber pistol, and fired approximately five shots in the victim's head and face. Defendant contended that, by the time he fired the shots, "it looked like Mike Geller was already dead." . . .

After [Officer] Carrasquillo had taken the bulk of the statement, he asked the defendant why he would do such a thing. According to Carrasquillo, the defendant said, "gee, I really don't know." Carrasquillo repeated the question 10 minutes later, but received the same response. After a while, Carrasquillo asked the question for a third time and defendant replied, "well, gee, I guess it must have been because I was afraid of Joe Bush."

. . . At the trial . . . the prosecution sought to establish that Geller was still alive at the time defendant shot at him. Both physicians testified that each of the two chest wounds, for which defendant alleged Bush to be responsible, would have caused death without prompt medical attention. Moreover, the victim would have remained alive until such time as his chest cavity became fully filled with blood. Depending on the circumstances, it might take 5 to 10 minutes for the chest cavity to fill. Neither prosecution witness could state, with medical certainty, that the victim was still alive when, perhaps five minutes after the initial chest wounds were inflicted, the defendant fired at the victim's head.

The defense produced but a single witness, the former Chief Medical Examiner of New York City. This expert said that, in his view, Geller might have died of the chest wounds "very rapidly" since, in addition to the bleeding, a large bullet going through a lung and the heart would have other adverse medical effects. . . .

The trial court declined to charge the jury, as requested by the prosecution, that defendant could be guilty of murder on the theory that he had aided and abetted the killing of Geller by Bush. Instead, the court submitted only two theories to the jury: that defendant had either intentionally murdered Geller or had attempted to murder Geller.

The jury found the defendant guilty of murder. . . .

On appeal, the Appellate Division reversed the judgment of conviction on the law and dismissed the indictment. The court ruled that "the People failed to prove beyond a reasonable doubt that Geller had been alive at the time he was shot by defendant; defendant's conviction of murder thus cannot stand." . . .

Further, the court held that the judgment could not be modified to reflect a conviction for attempted murder because "the uncontradicted evidence is that the defendant, at the time that he fired the five shots into the body of the decedent, believed him to be dead, and . . . there is not a scintilla of evidence to contradict his assertion in that regard." . . .

Preliminarily, we state our agreement with the Appellate Division that the evidence did not establish, beyond a reasonable doubt, that Geller was alive at the time defendant fired into his body. To sustain a homicide conviction, it must be established, beyond a reasonable doubt, that the defendant caused the death of another person. . . . While the defendant admitted firing five shots at the victim approximately two to five minutes after Bush had fired three times, all three medical expert witnesses testified that they could not, with any degree of medical certainty, state whether the victim had been alive at the time the latter shots were fired by the defendant. Thus, the People failed to prove beyond a reasonable doubt that the victim had been alive at the time he was shot by the defendant. Whatever else it may be, it is not murder to shoot a dead body. . . .

[W]e must now decide whether, under the evidence presented, the defendant may be held for attempted murder, though someone else perhaps succeeded in killing the victim. . . .

The most intriguing attempt cases are those where the attempt to commit a crime was unsuccessful due to mistakes of fact or law on the part of the would-be criminal. A general rule developed in most American jurisdictions that legal impossibility is a good defense but factual impossibility is not. . . . Thus, for example, it was held that defendants who shot at a stuffed deer did not attempt to take a deer out of season, even though they believed the dummy to be a live animal. The court stated that there was no criminal attempt because it was no crime to "take" a stuffed deer, and it is no crime to attempt to do that which is legal. (State v. Guffey, 262 S.W.2d 152 [Mo. App.]; see, also, State v. Taylor, 345 Mo. 325, 133 S.W.2d 336 [no liability for attempt to bribe a juror where person bribed was not, in fact, a juror].) These cases are illustrative of legal impossibility. . . .

On the other hand, factual impossibility was no defense. For example, a man was held liable for attempted murder when he shot into the room in which his target usually slept and, fortuitously, the target was sleeping elsewhere in the house that night. (State v. Mitchell, 170 Mo. 633, 71 S.W. 175.) Although one bullet struck the target's customary pillow, attainment of the criminal objective was factually impossible. . . . On the same view, it was held that men who had sexual intercourse with a woman, with the belief that she was alive and did not consent to the intercourse, could be charged for attempted rape when the woman had, in fact, died from an unrelated ailment prior to the acts of intercourse. (United States v. Thomas, 13 U.S.C.M.A. 278.)[a]

The New York cases can be parsed out along similar lines. One of the leading cases on legal impossibility is People v. Jaffe, 185 N.Y. 497, 78 N.E. 169, in which we held that there was no liability for the attempted receipt of stolen property when the property received by the defendant in the belief that it was stolen was, in fact under the control of the true owner. . . . Similarly, in People v. Teal, 196 N.Y. 372, 89 N.E. 1086, a conviction for attempted subornation of perjury was overturned on the theory that the testimony attempted to be suborned was irrelevant to the merits of the case. Since it was not subornation of perjury to solicit false, but irrelevant, testimony, "the person through whose procuration the testimony is given cannot be guilty of subornation of perjury and, by the same rule, an unsuccessful attempt to that which is not a crime when effectuated, cannot be held to be an attempt to commit the crime specified." Factual impossibility, however, was no defense. Thus, a man could be held for attempted grand larceny when he picked an empty pocket. (People v. Moran, 123 N.Y. 254, 25 N.E. 412.) . . .

As can be seen from even this abbreviated discussion, the distinction between "factual" and "legal" impossibility was a nice one indeed and the courts tended to place a greater value on legal form than on any substantive danger the defendant's actions posed for society. The approach of the draftsmen of the Model Penal Code was to eliminate the defense of impossibility in virtually all situations. [See §5.01(1), Appendix.] Under the code provision, to constitute an attempt, it is still necessary that the result intended or desired by the actor constitute a crime. However, the code suggested a fundamental change to shift the locus of analysis to the actor's mental frame of reference and away from undue dependence upon external considerations. The basic premise of the code provision is that what was in the actor's own mind should be the standard for determining his dangerousness to society and, hence, his liability for attempted criminal conduct. . . . In the belief that neither of the two branches of the traditional impossibility arguments detracts from the offender's moral culpability . . . the Legislature substantially carried the [Model Penal] code's treatment of impossibility into the 1967 revision of the Penal Law. . . . Thus, a person is guilty of an attempt when, with intent to commit a crime, he engages in conduct which tends to effect the commission of such crime. (Penal Law, §110.00.) It is no defense that, under the attendant circumstances, the crime was factually or legally impossible of commission, "if such crime could have been committed had the attendant circumstances been as such person believed them to be." (Penal

---

a. Accord, People v. Thompson, 15 Cal. Rptr. 2d 333 (Ct. App. 1993). — Eds.

Law, §110.10). Thus, if defendant believed the victim to be alive at the time of the shooting, it is no defense to the charge of attempted murder that the victim may have been dead.

Turning to the facts of the case before us, we believe that there is sufficient evidence in the record from which the jury could conclude that the defendant believed Geller to be alive at the time defendant fired shots into Geller's head. . . .

The jury convicted the defendant of murder. Necessarily, they found that defendant intended to kill a live human being.[b] Subsumed within this finding is the conclusion that defendant acted in the belief that Geller was alive. Thus, there is no need for additional fact findings by a jury. Although it was not established beyond a reasonable doubt that Geller was, in fact, alive, such is no defense to attempted murder since a murder would have been committed "had the attendant circumstances been as [defendant] believed them to be." The jury necessarily found that defendant believed Geller to be alive when defendant shot at him.

The Appellate Division erred in not modifying the judgment to reflect a conviction for the lesser included offense of attempted murder. . . .

NOTES ON IMPOSSIBILITY

1. Factual impossibility. When attempts misfire because of poor aim or the use of a defective or inadequate weapon, such as an unloaded gun, courts have traditionally classified the situation as one of mere factual impossibility and denied a defense. In State v. Smith, 262 N.J. Super. 487, 621 A.2d 493 (1993), defendant was a county jail inmate who had tested positive for HIV, the virus that causes AIDS. During an altercation with several guards, defendant spat in one officer's face, bit his hand and said, "[N]ow die you pig, die from what I have." At his trial for attempted murder of the officer, defendant offered evidence that it was medically impossible to transmit HIV by spitting or biting, but the court held, affirming the conviction, that such evidence was irrelevant so long as the defendant himself had believed it possible to infect the officer and had intended to kill him.

2. Legal impossibility. Prior to the enactment of statutes addressed to the issue of impossibility, courts had taken a variety of positions. All courts agreed that there is a defense of legal impossibility when, unknown to the actor, what the actor planned to do had not been made criminal. There was dispute, however, over whether "legal impossibility" could be a defense in other situations, and if so, how was it distinguished from "factual impossibility," which was not a defense.

The California Supreme Court, in a case virtually identical to *Jaffe*, reached the opposite result. People v. Rojas, 55 Cal. 2d 252, 358 P.2d 921 (1961). As in New York at the time *Jaffe* was decided, the California cases had upheld convictions of attempted larceny where a pickpocket picked an empty pocket and of

---

b. Does this follow? Note the definition of murder under New York Penal Law §125.25, page 392 supra, and reconsider People v. Kraft, page 585 supra. For subsequent litigation focused on this aspect of the attempt conviction, see Dlugash v. New York, 476 F. Supp. 921 (E.D.N.Y. 1979) — Eds.

attempted theft by deception where the intended victim had not been deceived. The California court saw no distinction between such cases and a case of attempted receipt of stolen property. The applicable principle, it reasoned, was the same as that involved in the false pretenses situation, where the court had stated:[5]

> One of the purposes of the criminal law is to protect society from those who intend to injure it. When it is established that the defendant intended to commit a specific crime and that in carrying out this intention he committed an act that caused harm or sufficient danger of harm, it is immaterial that for some collateral reason he could not complete the intended crime. Although the law does not impose punishment for guilty intent alone, it does impose punishment when guilty intent is coupled with action that would result in a crime but for the intervention of some fact or circumstance unknown to the defendant. . . . In the present case there was not a legal but only a factual impossibility of consummating the intended offense, i.e., the intended victim was not deceived.

The Model Penal Code has had a major influence on this debate. About two-thirds of the states have revised their codes since the Model Penal Code proposals were formulated. Nearly all of them have rejected the impossibility defense entirely. See Model Penal Code and Commentaries, Comment to §5.01 at 317 (1985).

The debate continues, however, where the legislature has not unambiguously resolved it. Where no statutory language governs (as in federal prosecutions), many American decisions continue to reflect the *Jaffe* view or variations on it. Thus, in State v. Collins, 54 Ohio App. 3d 134, 561 N.E.2d 954 (1988), defendant was convicted of attempting to receive stolen goods, on facts similar to those in *Jaffe*. The relevant Ohio statute, Rev. Code §2923.02(B), provided "It is no defense to a charge under this section that, in retrospect, commission of the offense which was the object of the attempt was impossible under the circumstances." The court nonetheless reversed the conviction. The court held that the Ohio provision precluded a defense of factual impossibility but that the defense of *legal* impossibility should remain available in the absence of unambiguous statutory language to the contrary.

What is the appeal of this view? In Glanville Williams, Textbook of Criminal Law 392 (1978), a discussion of the problem begins with a newspaper article headlined "Equine to Asinine": "A man who bought an ounce of horse manure from a hippie in the West End, thinking it was cannabis, was fined £5 at North London court yesterday for attempting to procure cannabis." Consider the following cases.

UNITED STATES v. BERRIGAN, 482 F.2d 171 (3d Cir. 1973): [Father Berrigan, an imprisoned Vietnam War resister, was convicted of an attempt to violate a federal statute making it criminal to take anything into or out of a federal prison

---

5. People v. Camodeca, 52 Cal. 2d 142, 338 P.2d 903, 906 (1959). In this case, defendant tried to exact money from a bar owner on the false representation that he needed it to bribe a state official to clear up some difficulty with the bar owner's license. The bar owner learned that defendant was lying and arranged for police to overhear and record a meeting at which these representations were renewed. The court upheld a conviction of attempted grand larceny by false pretenses.

contrary to regulations of the Attorney General. The latter had promulgated a regulation prohibiting such traffic "without the knowledge and consent" of the prison warden. The conviction was based on evidence that Berrigan had smuggled letters into and out of a prison through a courier, believing that the warden was ignorant of what was going on. In fact the warden had prior knowledge of the arrangement and had agreed to let the courier pretend cooperation in the plan. The court reversed the conviction:] Generally speaking factual impossibility is said to occur when extraneous circumstances unknown to the actor or beyond his control prevent consummation of the intended crime. The classic example is the man who puts his hand in the coat pocket of another with the intent to steal his wallet and finds the pocket empty. . . . Legal impossibility is said to occur where the intended acts, even if completed, would not amount to a crime. Thus, legal impossibility would apply to those circumstances where (1) the motive, desire and expectation is to perform an act in violation of the law; (2) there is intention to perform a physical act; (3) there is a performance of the intended physical act; and (4) the consequence resulting from the intended act does not amount to a crime.[35]

Were intent to break the law the sole criterion to be considered in determining criminal responsibility . . . we could sustain the conviction. . . . Clearly, it can be said that Father Berrigan intended to send letters to Sister McAlister. . . . Normally, of course, the exchange of letters is not a federal offense. Where one of the senders is in prison, however, the sending may or may not be a criminal offense. If the letter is sent within normal channels with the consent and knowledge of the warden it is not a criminal offense. Therefore, an attempt to send a letter through normal channels cannot be considered an attempt to violate the law because none of the intended consequences is in fact criminal. If the letter is sent without the knowledge and consent of the warden, it is a criminal offense and so is the attempt because both the intended consequence and the actual consequence are in fact criminal. Here, we are faced with a third situation where there is a motivation, desire and expectation of sending a letter without the knowledge and consent, and the intended act is performed, but unknown to the sender, the transmittal is accomplished with the knowledge and consent of the warden.

Applying the principles of the law of attempt to the instant case, the writing of the letters, and their copying and transmittal by the courier . . . constituted the *Act*. This much the government proved. What the government did not prove — and could not prove because it was a legal impossibility — was the "external, objective situation which the substantive law may require to be present," to-wit, absence of knowledge and consent of the warden. Thus, the government failed to prove the "*Circumstances or attendant circumstances*" vital to the offense. Without such proof, the *Consequence* or *Result* did not constitute an offense that

---

35. Intent as used in this connection must be distinguished from motive, desire, and expectation. If *C* by reason of his hatred of *A* plans to kill him, but mistaking *B* for *A* shoots *B*, his motive desire and expectation are to kill *A* but his intent is to kill *B* . . . If *A* takes an umbrella which he believes to belong to *B*, but which in fact is his own, he does not have the intent to steal, his intent being to take the umbrella he grasps in his hand, which is his own umbrella. . . . If a man mistakes a stump for his enemy and shoots at it, notwithstanding his desire and expectation to shoot his enemy, his intent is to shoot the object aimed at, which is the stump. Keedy, Criminal Attempts at Common Law, 102 U. of Pa. L. Rev. 464, 466-467 (1954). . . .

violated the federal statute. . . . Simply stated, attempting to do that which is not a crime is not attempting to commit a crime.[a]

UNITED STATES v. OVIEDO, 525 F.2d 881 (5th Cir. 1976): [An undercover agent contacted defendant and asked to buy heroin. Defendant agreed and appeared at an arranged time and place with what he claimed was heroin. The agent then performed a field test with positive result and arrested defendant. However, a later laboratory test of the substance revealed it was not in fact heroin but procaine hydrochloride (not a controlled substance), which happens to give a positive reaction to the usual field test. The prosecution therefore charged defendant with attempted distribution of heroin, and a jury convicted, apparently rejecting defendant's testimony that he knew the substance was not heroin and was only trying to "rip off" the agent. On appeal, the Fifth Circuit reversed the conviction.

[The court rejected the traditional distinction between legal and factual impossibility, saying:] These definitions are not particularly helpful here, for they do nothing more than provide a different focus for the analysis. In one sense, the impossibility involved here might be deemed legal, for those *acts* which Oviedo set in motion, the transfer of the substance in his possession, were not a crime. In another sense, the impossibility is factual, for the *objective* of Oviedo, the sale of heroin, was proscribed by law, and failed only because of a circumstance unknown to Oviedo.

[However, the court also rejected an approach that would find an attempt because the objective of defendant was criminal, since "It would allow us to punish one's thoughts, desires, or motives, through indirect evidence, without reference to any objective fact." The court concluded:] We reject the notion . . . , adopted by the district court, that the conviction in the present case can be sustained since there is sufficient proof of intent, not because of any doubt as to the sufficiency of the evidence in that regard, but because of the inherent dangers such a precedent would pose in the future. . . .

When the defendant sells a substance which is actually heroin, it is reasonable to infer that he knew the physical nature of the substance, and to place on him the burden of dispelling that inference. . . . However, if we convict the defendant of attempting to sell heroin for the sale of a non-narcotic substance, we eliminate an objective element that has major evidentiary significance and we increase the risk of mistaken conclusions that the defendant believed the goods were narcotics.

a. Compare United States v. Everett, 700 F.2d 900 (3d Cir. 1983), where the court held that impossibility was *not* a defense to a charge of attempted distribution of a controlled substance under 21 U.S.C. §846. Everett was suspected of dealing in P-2-P, a controlled substance used in the manufacture of methamphetamines. An undercover DEA agent obtained from Everett a pint of liquid that field tested as P-2-P. After his arrest Everett identified the substance as P-2-P and named the source of his illicit supply. Subsequent testing determined that the liquid was not P-2-P or any other controlled substance. The jury found beyond a reasonable doubt that Everett believed the liquid to be P-2-P, and his conviction of attempting to distribute a controlled substance was affirmed. The Third Circuit held that the analysis of its earlier decision in *Berrigan* was not controlling because 21 U.S.C. §846, enacted after the *Berrigan* decision, was "part of an all-out effort to reach all acts and activities related to the drug traffic." 700 F.2d at 907. The court concluded that Congress would not have wanted that effort to become mired in the complexities of the impossibility defense. — Eds.

Thus, we demand that in order for a defendant to be guilty of a criminal attempt, the objective acts performed, without any reliance on the accompanying mens rea, mark the defendant's conduct as criminal in nature. . . .

. . . We cannot conclude that the objective acts of Oviedo apart from any indirect evidence of intent mark his conduct as criminal in nature. Rather, those acts are consistent with a noncriminal enterprise. Therefore, we will not allow the jury's determination of Oviedo's intent to form the sole basis of a criminal offense.[b]

THE CASE OF LADY ELDON'S FRENCH LACE

A hypothetical decision on a hypothetical state of facts, by the editors

A perennial in the crop of attempt hypotheticals was suggested by Dr. Wharton.[1] "Lady Eldon, when traveling with her husband on the Continent, bought what she supposed to be a quantity of French lace, which she hid, concealing it from Lord Eldon in one of the pockets of the coach. The package was brought to light by a customs officer at Dover. The lace turned out to be an English manufactured article, of little value, and of course, not subject to duty. Lady Eldon had bought it at a price vastly above its value, believing it to be genuine, intending to smuggle it into England." Dr. Wharton, supra, and Professor Sayre[2] conclude that she could be found guilty of an attempt since she intended to smuggle dutiable lace into England. Professor Keedy disagrees, finding the fallacy of the argument in the failure to recognize "that the particular lace which Lady Eldon intended to bring into England was not subject to duty and therefore, although there was the wish to smuggle, there was not the intent to do so."[3]

Keedy was employing the distinction he has advanced between intent, on the one hand, and motive, desire, and expectation, on the other,[4] a distinction that served as the linchpin of the decision in People v. Jaffe, supra, and United States v. Berrigan, supra. As he sees it, what people intend to do on a particular occasion is to be determined by what they do in fact, rather than by what they thought they were doing. The lace was in fact not dutiable; thus, there was no intent on the part of Lady Eldon to smuggle dutiable French lace into the country, and there could be no conviction of the crime of attempt to do so, since what she intended to do on this view was not a crime — a straightforward case of legal impossibility. Professor Perkins has not, so far as we can tell, addressed himself to this particular case. But from what he has written it is clear that he would concur with Keedy. Presumably his analysis would rest on his distinction between primary and secondary intent.[5] Only the former may be considered in determin-

b. *Question:* Should the court's insistence on evidence from "the objective acts performed . . . apart from any indirect evidence of intent" apply even if the defendant confesses that he *knew* (i.e., incorrectly thought) the material sold was a controlled substance? Reconsider United States v. Everett, footnote a above, and see United States v. Hough, 561 F.2d 594, 595-596 (5th Cir. 1977). — Eds.

1. 1 Criminal Law 304 n. 9 (12th ed. 1932).
2. Criminal Attempts, 41 Harv. L. Rev. 821, 852 (1928).
3. Criminal Attempts at Common Law, 102 U. Pa. L. Rev. 464, 477 n. 85 (1954).
4. Id. at 466-468.
5. Rollin M. Perkins, Criminal Attempt and Related Problems, 2 U.C.L.A.L. Rev. 319, 330-332 (1955).

ing the existence of the necessary intent to establish an attempt. It, like Keedy's term *intent*, is determined by what the actor objectively and in fact did. What the actor believed he was doing, on the level of the facts as the actor took them to be, constitutes secondary intent. Apparently the latter is basically the same in description and function as what Keedy refers to as the motive, desire, or expectation.

We concur with Wharton and Sayre.

We submit, with respect, that Keedy and Perkins, and the courts that follow their reasoning, have been guilty of some plain silliness in supporting their position. Their conclusion that Lady Eldon must be acquitted rests on the premise that what a person intends to do is what he actually does, even if that was the furthest thing from the person's mind:

"You're eating my salad."

"Sorry, I didn't mean to; I thought it was mine."

"You might have *thought* it was yours. But in fact it was mine. So it was my salad you intended to eat. You should be ashamed!"

Surely this is an extraordinary way of regarding what a person intended, quite at odds with common sense and common language. Where a circumstance is not known to the actor, there is no way consistent with straight thought that his act can be regarded as intentional as to that circumstance.

Of course, it is hardly unknown for courts to adopt strained and artificial reasoning to support a sound result. Is that the case here? Is it sound to conclude that the type of conduct engaged in by Lady Eldon should not be made criminal? Let us consider if it is.

Suppose Lady Eldon believed she had purchased an inexpensive English lace but in fact had purchased an expensive French lace. Certainly she could not be found guilty of smuggling if she got past the customs inspector or of an attempt if she failed. The reason is that the intent to smuggle French lace, necessary to establish either offense, does not exist. (We are assuming this is not a crime of absolute liability). And it does not exist because her intent is judged by what she believed she was doing and not by what she in fact did. Now why should it make any more difference in Wharton's hypothetical that her act was objectively lawful than it does in our variation that her act was objectively unlawful? Why in both cases should not the intent be judged by the same standard, what she believed she was doing, rather than what she did in fact?

It may be answered that while an innocent mind can exculpate, a criminal mind simpliciter cannot inculpate. The reasoning might be as follows: There is no legitimate purpose to be served by punishing those who mean to act blamelessly; and while a purpose could be served by punishing a person who decides to commit a crime (to the extent that all must first decide to commit an intentional crime before actually committing it, some will thereby be prevented from committing it, at this or another occasion) other considerations make it inexpedient and undesirable to do so. What are those considerations? They are those, presumably, which underlie the principle which forbids punishing people for their thoughts alone, i.e., that thinking evil is not a reliable indication that a person will do evil and the criminal law may properly concern itself only with acts. See pages 180-181 supra.

But can this be said of Lady Eldon? Has she merely *thought* to smuggle French lace? No. She has *done* everything in her power and all she thought necessary to smuggle French lace. Has she shown herself to be less eligible for the imposition of criminal sanctions because, through no fault of her own, she failed? Surely not.

From the basic postulate that the law concerns itself with acts and not thoughts, it may be argued that the law is concerned not with what a person *may* do but with what he in fact *does*. But the conclusion is erroneous. There are many crimes that may be established without proof that acts have occurred that actually invade the interest sought to be protected. The law of attempts and conspiracy are prime examples. The reason for punishing in such cases is based not on what the actor has already done but rather on what is apprehended he is likely to do subsequently. As Holmes has pointed out, even larceny may be viewed in this way, since there is no requirement that the possessor be permanently deprived of his property, only that the actor intend to deprive him of it.[6] Looked at objectively, apart from intent, the acts done may be wholly innocuous — like striking a match or having a quiet conversation. The innocuous acts are made criminal because, combined with the requisite intent of that actor, they demonstrate him to be likely to commit the injury that the law seeks to prevent.

Perhaps it may be argued that there is a different policy supporting exculpation in cases like Lady Eldon's — namely, that in real cases, as opposed to hypotheticals, intention must be proved rather than supposed, and it is too dangerous to the innocent to permit juries to speculate on a defendant's intent in the absence of actions that strongly evidence that intent. One may fully agree with this, however, without concluding that Lady Eldon should be acquitted. Of course it would be evidentiary of Lady Eldon's intent to smuggle if she had been found with dutiable French lace at the border. (But only evidentiary — after all, she might have thought it was English lace, or it might have been put with her things by her maid without her knowledge.) But why should it be held, as it was in United States v. Oviedo, supra, that, since the lace was nondutiable in fact, a finding of intent will necessarily be suspect, regardless of the strength of the evidence? Suppose, for example, that the lace were carefully secreted in a specially tailored, concealed pocket of the coach; that the coachman testified to incriminating statements Lady Eldon made to Lord Eldon; that a letter from her to her sister, which described her newly bought "French lace" in exquisite and appreciative detail, had been introduced; that her receipt showed she paid a price appropriate for French lace rather than for the vastly less expensive English lace. There would seem little danger to the innocent in allowing a jury to find an attempt to smuggle French lace on these facts. Indeed, in cases like *Jaffe* and *Berrigan,* "attempt" is charged only because of the involvement of an undercover agent, whose participation prevents completion of the intended crime. Whatever else one may say about such investigatory tactics, they do not necessarily render suspect the evidence of the defendant's intent; indeed, in practice, they usually render that evidence far *less* speculative than it otherwise would be. The proper remedy for speculative and unreliable jury findings of intent is a court alert to preclude such findings in particular cases where the evidence is insufficient.

---

6. The Common Law 72 (1881).

In the end, then, the arguments in favor of Lady Eldon (and those which have been used to reverse convictions in cases like *Jaffe, Oviedo,* and *Berrigan*) are founded on unpersuasive policy considerations rationalized by a peculiar and Pickwickian interpretation of what it means to intend to do an act, one that is utterly at odds both with the common usage of our language and its usage elsewhere in the criminal law.[7] *We conclude that the innocuous character of the action actually done (innocuous in the sense that it could not constitute a crime under the actual circumstances) will not save her from an attempt conviction if she believed that the circumstances were otherwise, and, had her belief been correct, what she set out to do would constitute a crime.* This is the principle that has found favor in virtually every serious statutory effort to deal with the problem, and in numerous decisions reached without benefit of a specific statute to tell the court that a person intends to do what he thinks he intends to do.

We must say a few words more about the final qualification to the principle just asserted; namely, that "had her belief (in the circumstances) been correct, what she set out to do would constitute a crime." The point can best be made by altering the hypothetical. Suppose the lace that Lady Eldon had purchased was in fact the expensive French lace she meant to buy. The customs officer at Dover brings it to light. He then says to Lady Eldon: "Lucky for you you returned to England today rather than yesterday. I just received word this morning that the government has removed French lace from the duty list." Could Lady Eldon be held for attempt to smuggle in these circumstances?[8] Certainly what she did and what she intended to do were not different simply because she acted one day later, when French lace was removed from the duty list. But there is this important difference: that at the time she acted, *what* she intended to do (always judged, of course, from her own perspective) was not a violation of the criminal law, even though she thought it was.

It is true that under the Canon Law of the Medieval Church, a person who committed a permissible action in the belief it was forbidden was considered guilty and subject to the same penance as that required of one who had actually done a forbidden action. Stephan Kuttner, Kanonistische Schuldlehre 209-213 (1935). But that was a reflection of the Church's concern with the state of a person's soul, a concern that is foreign to secular law.

Of course, in the case of Lady Eldon, her action showed her to be a person who would break some law under some circumstances. But what law? The law against smuggling French lace? There no longer was such a law. The criminal laws generally? Fortunately our law has not gone so far in accepting that *any*

---

7. Consider the Missouri court's justification for reversing the conviction of a hunter for attempting to take a deer out of season where the evidence showed that the defendant, believing that he had a live deer in his sights, shot at a stuffed deer, placed in the woods by a game warden: "If the state's evidence showed an attempt to take the dummy, it fell far short of proving an attempt to take a deer." State v. Guffey, 262 S.W.2d 152 (Mo. App. 1953).

8. For an actual prosecution presenting just this problem, see Regina v. Taaffe, page 264 supra. Consider also a news story that appeared during the 1974 sugar shortage in England: "Travellers trying to beat Britain's sugar shortage are smuggling more and more of it into this country. They do not know that importing sugar is legal. A woman filled a shoebox with sugar and wrapped it like a gift, with fancy ribbons and bright paper. Another woman had sugar in a can marked 'face powder.' Customs officials chuckled at the reaction of sugar smugglers when they found out there was nothing wrong in what they were doing." N.Y. Herald Tribune, Oct. 22, 1974, reprinted in Glanville Williams, Textbook of Criminal Law 998 (1978).

antisocial attitude is sufficient to justify criminal punishment. A mere disposition to engage in conduct thought to be criminal is much too speculative a basis for inferring that the actor will engage in some other kind of conduct that *is* illegal. And, as Professor Williams has pointed out, "if the legislature has not seen fit to prohibit the consummated act, a mere approach to consummation should a fortiori be guiltless. Any other view would offend against the principle of legality; in effect the law of attempt would be used to manufacture a new crime, when the legislature has left the situation outside the ambit of the law." Glanville Williams, Criminal Law: The General Part 633-634 (2d ed. 1961). Had the criminal law been changed as supposed in our variation of the Lady Eldon hypothetical, therefore, it would be just as wrong to convict her as to convict an abortionist of attempted abortion where the abortion was committed, unknown to the defendant, after the abortion law was repealed or held invalid. These are the true cases of legal impossibility.[9]

But, it should be noted, these situations are totally different from cases like *Jaffe* and *Berrigan,* even though the courts in each case made it seem otherwise, by asserting that what the defendants intended to do could not have constituted a crime. What the abortionist intended to do (and did) could not constitute a crime because there was no such crime. What Jaffe and Berrigan intended to do (and thought they did) was indeed a crime. It is only through a perverse use of intent that we can say that Jaffe intended to receive honestly obtained property or that Berrigan intended to send out a letter the warden knew about, and that therefore they intended to do what was no crime at all.

Lady Eldon, in the actual hypothetical, in contrast to the hypothetical hypothetical, presents no more a case of genuine legal impossibility than do *Jaffe* and *Berrigan.* She will be convicted of attempt to smuggle French lace.

COMMENT, 6 Hypothetical L. Rev. 1, 3-4 (1962-1995): The hypothetical *Lady Eldon* decision is a good effort, but it doesn't quite work.

First: Consider a safecracker who tries to open a safe with magic incantations. Under the Lady Eldon analysis, the safecracker would merely have made a mistake of fact, and he could be convicted of attempt. Or consider the case of Leroy Ivy and John Henry Ivy, two brothers who tried to use voodoo to kill a judge who had sentenced one of them to prison for robbery.[1] The brothers paid the judge's housekeeper $100 for his photo and a lock of his hair, which they planned to mail to a voodoo practitioner in Jamaica. Police officers in Tupelo, Mississippi

---

9. The same principle applies when the chronology is reversed. In United States v. Schwartz, 924 F.2d 410, 419 (2d Cir. 1991), defendants had fraudulently obtained export licenses from the U.S. Commerce Department. At the time of their conduct, all the circuits had held that such a fraud was covered by the federal mail fraud statute, and the defendants apparently believed that their conduct was illegal. Subsequently, the Supreme Court held to the contrary, but Congress had the last word and passed a law adopting the more expansive view of the mail fraud statute's reach. Prosecutors then attempted to apply the new law retroactively and obtained convictions for conduct that had occurred prior to the new law's enactment. The Second Circuit reversed: "[W]e are not aware of any [authority] for the proposition that a defendant's subjective belief that his actions might violate then existing law, though in fact they did not, allows application of an ex post facto law to his case."

1. For accounts of the case, see Fred Grimm, Man Charged in Plot to Kill Judge By Hex, Miami Herald, Mar. 31, 1989, at 1, 10; R. J. Smith, Conspiracy to Commit Voodoo, Village Voice, Sept. 26, 1989, at 37-41.

foiled the plot by arresting Leroy Ivy before he could send off the items needed to cast the spell. Charged with attempting to kill the judge, the brothers pleaded guilty and were sentenced to five and ten years respectively. But these defendants, like the safecracker, are more pathetic than dangerous. The convictions in these cases are as absurd as the defendants' own actions.

The Model Penal Code, in recognition of this problem, gives a court the power to dismiss a prosecution or decrease the penalty if "the particular conduct charged to constitute a criminal attempt . . . is so inherently unlikely to result or culminate in the commission of a crime that neither such conduct nor the actor presents a public danger." Section 5.05(2). But this is to commend the matter to the discretion of the judge; it is not a statement of a rule of law. A better approach is that taken by the revised Minnesota Criminal Code which states an exception to its rule that impossibility is no defense where the "impossibility would have been clearly evident to a person of normal understanding." Minn. Stat. Ann. §609.17.2. A similar solution has been developed by Professor Robbins, who proposes that a person be guilty of attempt only when "he purposely does or omits to do anything that, *under the circumstances as a reasonable person would believe them to be*," is a substantial step in a course of conduct planned to culminate in commission of the crime.[2]

Second: The effort to deal with the so-called "true legal impossibility" problem comes off more smoothly than convincingly. Consider the following case. Two friends, Mr. Fact and Mr. Law, go hunting in the morning of October 15 in the fields of the state of Dakota, whose law makes it a misdemeanor to hunt any time other than from October 1 to November 30. Both kill deer on the first day out, October 15. Mr. Fact, however, was under the erroneous belief that the date was September 15, and Mr. Law was under the erroneous belief that the hunting season was confined to the month of November, as it was the previous year. Under the *Lady Eldon* formulation, Mr. Fact could be convicted of an attempt to hunt out of season, but Mr. Law could not be. We fail to see how any rational system of criminal law could justify convicting one and acquitting the other on the fragile and unpersuasive distinction that one was suffering under a mistake of fact, and the other under a mistake of law. Certainly if the ultimate test is the dangerousness of the actor (i.e., readiness to violate the law), as *Lady Eldon* would have it, no distinction is warranted — Mr. Law has indicated himself to be no less "dangerous" than Mr. Fact.[a]

---

2. Ira P. Robbins, Attempting the Impossible: The Emerging Consensus, 23 Harv. J. Legisl. 377, 441 (1986) (emphasis added). See also N.J. Stat. Ann. §2C:5-1a(1).

a. For analyses of the problems posed by this hypothetical, see Kenneth W. Simons, Mistake and Impossibility, Law and Fact, and Culpability: A Speculative Essay, 81 J. Crim. L. & Criminology 447, 467-469 (1990); Graham Hughes, One Further Footnote on Attempting the Impossible, 42 N.Y.U.L. Rev. 1005, 1012-1013, 1033 (1967); and Fernand N. Dutile & Harold F. Moore, Mistake and Impossibility: Arranging a Marriage Between Two Difficult Partners, 74 Nw. U.L. Rev. 166, 166-167 (1979). The last article disagrees with the reasoning of the Hypothetical Law Review comment on this point: "[We argue] that Mr. Law in the Kadish and [Schulhofer] example would be acquitted, since he contemplated it, was not within the statute, while Mr. Fact would not [be acquitted]. From the standpoint of symmetry, or the dangerous propensities of the defendant, there is no way to justify the result. From a 'moral' standpoint they are equally culpable.

"The key to finding the result anomalous, however, is the tacit assumption that there are not other relevant concerns. From the standpoint of the criminal law, no *socially protected* value is violated by the 'attempt' in a 'Mr. Law' case of genuine legal impossibility. In such a case, it need not

The same point can be made with the very example that the Editors use to support their *Lady Eldon* opinion — the case in which, unbeknownst to Lady Eldon, French lace has just been removed from the duty list. The Editors ask, in effect, *What law* did she show her readiness to break? Not smuggling French lace, they say, because there's no longer such a law. Correct. Not criminal laws generally, they say, because that would be going too far toward resting criminality on speculative proclivity. Correct again. But how about the law against smuggling? Has she shown herself to be less a smuggler, just because she arrived right after French lace had been removed from the duty list? The Editors err in treating the case as if duties had been repealed on all goods, whereas it was just one item that was removed from the duty list.

Third: In formulating a rule that would eliminate the defense of factual impossibility in all cases, the opinion overlooks the strong case for retaining the defense in one class of cases. These are the cases in which the acts done by the defendant are as consistent with an innocent as with a culpable state of mind. Take for example the old saw about the professor who takes his own umbrella thinking it belongs to his colleague. The act is utterly neutral. A man taking his own umbrella conveys no evidence of guilt. Now of course the matter changes if it can be *proven* that he believed it was his colleague's umbrella. But proof of state of mind where there are only ambiguous acts to support the inference is inherently unreliable.

Consider how the Model Penal Code deals with this very concern when it addresses itself to a different problem, i.e., drawing the line between preparation and attempt. This is typically the situation in which the actor has not yet completed all he set out to do. In Section 5.01, the Model Penal Code not only reflects existing law in requiring some substantial step toward commission of the crime. It also requires that the step at the same time be "strongly corroborative of the actor's criminal purpose." Why is this required? It may be supposed that the primary function of this requirement is to avoid the risk of false convictions; the animating idea is that where the evidence of intent falls below a certain level we are not willing to allow the jury to speculate.

Now both the *Lady Eldon* opinion and the Model Penal Code are short-sighted for not seeing that the same concern may exist in the class of impossibility cases under discussion. In this respect the court in *Oviedo* [page 632 supra], and cases that have followed its lead,[3] are on very solid ground. If apprehension of false convictions calls for the requirement that the acts strongly corroborate the intent in those cases where the acts fall short of what was intended by the actor, then the same concern calls for the same requirement where the actor has done all he meant to do. If it is answered that in the latter cases the completed pattern of conduct carries the criminal intent on its face, the response must be that while this is generally so, it need not be so. The professor taking his own umbrella surely is such a case.

---

be claimed that the actor is harmless. He may be extremely dangerous, yet what precisely is he guilty of? What penalty should he receive? . . . It is totally unclear how any system based on liability for intending to violate the law, as opposed to intending *conduct* that *is* in violation of the law, could function as a properly justified system of criminal law. Such a system provides neither appropriate deterrence to crime nor proper retribution for crime." — Eds.

3. E.g., United States v. Bagnariol, 665 F.2d 877 (9th Cir. 1981).

To put the suggestion in statutory form, we suggest the following amendment to the Model Penal Code's Section 5.01:

"A person is guilty of an attempt to commit a crime if, acting with the kind of culpability otherwise required for commission of the crime, he: (a) purposely engages in conduct that *strongly corroborates the required culpability and* would constitute the crime if the attendant circumstances were as he believes them to be. . . ."[4]

4. On the issues raised by this statutory proposal, see Robbins, footnote 2 supra at 400-12; Hughes, supra footnote a; Thomas Weigend, Why Lady Eldon Should Be Acquitted: The Social Harm in Attempting the Impossible, 27 De Paul L. Rev. 231 (1979). A related proposal has been developed by Professor Fletcher, who suggests that attempts be punishable only when two conditions are satisfied: "the actor must attempt an act punishable under the law, and, further, this attempt must be *dangerous on its face.*" George P. Fletcher, Constructing a Theory of Impossible Attempts, 5 Crim. J. Ethics 53, 67 (1986) (emphasis added). Professor Fletcher locates his proposal in "a theory that stresses the individual's right to an autonomous sphere free of state intrusion. Being suspected of dangerous propensities does not in itself justify the state's incursions into our private sphere. The minimal demand is that the actor's dangerousness express itself in an objectively dangerous act that treads upon the rights of others." Id.

CHAPTER
7

GROUP CRIMINALITY

A. ACCOUNTABILITY FOR THE ACTS OF OTHERS

INTRODUCTORY NOTES

1. From common law to statute. At the common law there were distinct categories of circumstances that rendered a person a participant in a course of criminal conduct. These distinctions had consequences for both procedure and punishment. The following excerpts from 4 Blackstone, Commentaries, ch. 3, *34-39, broadly describe those categories:

> A man may be *principal* in an offence in two degrees. A principal, in the first degree, is he that is the actor, or absolute perpetrator of the crime; and, in the second degree, he is who is present, aiding, and abetting the fact to be done. Which presence need not always be an actual immediate standing by, within sight or hearing of the fact; but there may be also a constructive presence, as when one commits a robbery or murder, and another keeps watch or guard at some convenient distance. . . .
>
> An *accessory* is he who is not the chief actor in the offence, nor present at its performance, but is some way concerned therein, either before or after the fact committed. . . .
>
> As to . . . who may be an accessory *before* the fact, Sir Matthew Hale defines him to be one, who being absent at the time of the crime committed, doth yet procure, counsel, or command another to commit a crime. Herein absence is necessary to make him an accessory; for if such procurer, or the like, be present, he is guilty of the crime as principal. . . .
>
> An accessory *after* the fact may be, where a person, knowing a felony to have been committed, receives, relieves, comforts, or assists the felon. . . .

Modern statutes have largely eliminated the significance of these discrete modes of criminal participation: (1) Apart from the accessory after the fact, who is still generally subject to a lesser punishment, the punishment is the same for the three main modes of complicity. (2) It is no longer the case that accessories to crime cannot be convicted until their principal is convicted (although, of course, it must be proved that a crime was committed). (3) It is no longer necessary in most states for a defendant to be charged with a particular form of complicity. The defendant may simply be charged with the substantive crime committed by the person the defendant aided or encouraged.

These changes are the result of statutes antedating the wave of legislative reform initiated by the Model Penal Code. These older statutes abolish all distinctions between principals and accessories before the fact, requiring that all be treated as principals. The California Penal Code is representative:

SECTION 31

All persons concerned in the commission of a crime, whether it be felony or misdemeanor, and whether they directly commit the act constituting the offense, or aid and abet in its commission, or, not being present, have advised and encouraged its commission, and all persons counseling, advising or encouraging children under the age of fourteen years, lunatics or idiots to commit any crime, or who, by fraud, contrivance, or force, occasion the drunkenness of another for the purpose of causing him to commit any crime, or who, by threats, menaces, command, or coercion, compel another to commit any crime, are principals in any crime so committed.

SECTION 32

Every person who, after a felony has been committed, harbors, conceals or aids a principal in such felony, with the intent that said principal may avoid or escape from arrest, trial, conviction or punishment, having knowledge that said principal has committed such felony or has been charged with such felony or convicted thereof, is an accessory to such felony.

SECTION 33

Except in cases where a different punishment is prescribed, an accessory is punishable by imprisonment in the state prison not exceeding five years, or in a county jail not exceeding two years, or by fine not exceeding five thousand dollars.

SECTION 971

The distinction between an accessory before the fact and a principal, and between principals in the first and second degree is abrogated; and all persons concerned in the commission of a crime, who by the operation of other provisions of this code are principals therein, shall hereafter be prosecuted, tried, and punished as principals, and no other facts need be alleged in any accusatory pleading against any such person than are required in an accusatory pleading against a principal.

SECTION 972

An accessory to the commission of a felony may be prosecuted, tried, and punished, though the principal may be neither prosecuted nor tried, and though the principal may have been acquitted.

See also the federal complicity statute, 18 U.S.C. §2:

(a) Whoever commits an offense against the United States or aids, abets, counsels, commands, induces or procures its commission, is punishable as a principal.

(b) Whoever willfully causes an act to be done which if directly performed by him or another would be an offense against the United States, is punishable as a principal.

The statutes of more recent vintage, influenced by the Model Penal Code proposals (see §2.06, Appendix), typically make people who are accomplices of another person accountable for that person's conduct and define people as accomplices in the other person's offense if they solicit that person to commit such an offense or aid that person in planning or committing it. See, e.g., N.J. Stat. Ann. tit. 2C, §2C:2-6.

2. Conspiracy as a doctrine of complicity. An additional basis for holding one person liable for the crimes of another derives from the doctrine of conspiracy. In general terms, a criminal conspiracy is an agreement or combination by two or more persons to commit a crime. Conspiracy is a substantive crime in itself, but it has the further consequence of making each of the coconspirators criminally responsible for the criminal acts of fellow conspirators committed in furtherance of the planned criminal enterprise, whether or not those particular criminal acts were planned, so long as they were reasonably foreseeable. A coconspirator, therefore, may be liable for the criminal acts of fellow conspirators even though strictly under the law of principals and accessories (requiring aiding, abetting, encouraging, etc.) the person might not be liable. This problem is explored in the conspiracy section, in connection with Pinkerton v. United States, page 732 infra and the materials following.

3. Punishment. American law punishes accomplices the same as principals. This is in contrast to the approach in other legal systems. For example, the German Penal Code (§25) provides different punishments for the perpetrator, the instigator and the aider, and the law is rich in doctrine for distinguishing between these classifications of participants. See C. Roxin, Täterschaft und Tatherrschaft (1984). Judge Posner comments on the American approach in United States v. Ambrose, 740 F.2d 505, 508-509 (7th Cir. 1985):

The aiding and abetting statute states: "Whoever commits an offense against the United States or aids, abets, counsels, commands, induces or procures its commission, is punishable as a principal." 18 U.S.C. §2(a). Although th[e] language [of 18 U.S.C. §2(a)] makes clear that an aider and abettor can be punished as severely as the principal, it does not make clear that he must always be punished so severely. History is against such an interpretation. The distinction between "principal" and "aider and abettor" goes back to the time when all felonies carried the same sanction — death. By enabling the courts to punish a class of less culpable offenders — aiders and abettors as distinct from principals — less severely, the distinction introduced a welcome element of gradation into the sentencing of felons. But as judges acquired more and more sentencing discretion, the need to distinguish between principals and aiders and abettors diminished, and since it was sometimes a difficult decision to make there was a movement to abolish it with regard to determining criminal liability. This movement culminated in 18 U.S.C. §2(a). But the purpose was not to make sure that aiders and abettors were always punished as severely as principals. Indeed, in passing the statute Congress must have realized that judges would use their sentencing discretion to proportion the severity of the sentence to the aider and abettor's fault. The history suggests that, rather than being intended to limit sentencing discretion, the abolition of the distinction between principals and aiders and abettors presupposed such discretion.

For a review of the variety of factors governing the sentencing of aiders and abettors see U.S. Sentencing Comm., Federal Sentencing Guidelines Manual Sections 3.E.1.1 and 1.2 (1992).

4. *The theory of complicity.* The relationship between the doctrine of complicity and other doctrines of criminal liability is explored in the following excerpt.

Sanford H. Kadish, A Theory of Complicity, in Issues in Contemporary Legal Philosophy: The Influence of H. L. A. Hart 288 (Ruth Gavison ed. 1987):[1] [We] regard a person's acts as the products of his choice, not of regularities of nature which require that certain happenings will occur whenever certain conditions are present. Therefore, antecedent events do not cause a person to act in the same way they cause things to happen, and neither do the antecedent acts of others. To treat the acts of others as causing a person's actions would be inconsistent with the premise on which we hold a person responsible. . . .[a]

The . . . implication [of this] is that when we seek to determine the responsibility of one person for the volitional actions of another the concept of physical cause is not available to determine the answer, for whatever the relation of one person's acts to those of another, it cannot be described in terms of that sense of cause and effect appropriate to the occurrence of natural events without doing violence to our concept of a human action as freely chosen. . . .

How, then, can the law reach those whose conduct makes it appropriate to punish for the criminal actions of others — a person, for example, who persuades or helps another to commit a crime? . . . If it were not for the very special way in which we conceive of human actions, causation doctrine might serve this purpose, on the view that one who intentionally causes another to commit certain actions falls under the prohibition against committing those actions. But our conception of human actions as controlled by choice will not allow that to work. . . . Some alternative doctrine is needed, therefore, which imposes liability on the actor who is to blame for the conduct of another, but which does so upon principles that comport with our perception of human actions. This is the office of the doctrine of complicity.

1. Mens Rea

a. Mens Rea as to Actions of the Principal

HICKS v. UNITED STATES

Supreme Court of the United States
150 U.S. 442 (1893)

JUSTICE SHIRAS delivered the opinion of the Court.

In the Circuit Court of the United States for the Western District of Arkansas, John Hicks, an Indian, was jointly indicted with Stand Rowe, also an Indian, for the murder of Andrew J. Colvard, a white man, by shooting him with a gun on

---

1. For further discussion of the theoretical issues see Joshua Dressler, Reassessing the Theoretical Underpinnings of Accomplice Liability: New Solutions to an Old Problem, 37 Hastings L. Rev. 91 (1985).

a. See the material in the Causation chapter, page 561 supra. — EDS.

the 13th of February, 1892. Rowe was killed by the officers in the attempt to arrest him, and Hicks was tried separately and found guilty in March, 1893. We adopt the statement of the facts in the case made in the brief for the government as correct and as sufficient for our purposes:

> It appears that on the night of the 12th of February, 1892, there was a dance at the house of Jim Rowe, in the Cherokee Nation; that Jim Rowe was a brother to Stand Rowe, who was indicted jointly with the defendant; . . . that Stand Rowe and the defendant were engaged in what was called "scouting," viz., eluding the United States marshals who were in search of them with warrants for their arrest, and were armed for the purpose of resisting arrest; they appeared at the dance, each armed with a Winchester rifle; they were both Cherokee Indians. The deceased, Andrew J. Colvard, was a white man who had married a Cherokee woman; he [was also at] the dance on . . . on the evening of the 12th. A good deal of whiskey was drank [sic] during the night by the persons present, and Colvard appears to have been drunk at some time during the night. Colvard spoke Cherokee fluently, and appears to have been very friendly with Stand Rowe and the defendant Hicks. . . .
>
> Some time after sunrise on the morning of the 13th, about 7 o'clock, [four witnesses] saw Stand Rowe, coming on horseback in a moderate walk, with his Winchester rifle lying down in front of him. . . . Stand Rowe halted within five or six feet of the main road, and the men on the porch saw Mr. Colvard and the defendant Hicks riding together down the main road from the direction of Jim Rowe's house.
>
> As Colvard and Hicks approached the point where Stand Rowe was sitting on his horse, Stand Rowe rode out into the road and halted. Colvard then rode up to him in a lope or canter, leaving Hicks, the defendant, some 30 or 40 feet in his rear. The point where the three men were together on their horses was about 100 yards from where the four witnesses stood on the porch. The conversation between the three men on horseback was not fully heard by the four men on the porch, and all that was heard was not understood, because part of it was carried on in the Cherokee tongue; but some part of this conversation was distinctly heard and clearly understood by these witnesses; they saw Stand Rowe twice raise his rifle and aim it at Colvard, and twice he lowered it; they heard Colvard say, "I am a friend to both of you"; they saw and heard the defendant Hicks laugh aloud when Rowe directed his rifle toward Colvard; they saw Hicks take off his hat and hit his horse on the neck or shoulder with it; they heard Hicks say to Colvard, "Take off your hat and die like a man"; they saw Stand Rowe raise his rifle for the third time, point it at Colvard, fire it; . . . they saw Colvard fall from his horse; they went to where he was lying in the road and found him dead; they saw Stand Rowe and John Hicks ride off together after the shooting.

Hicks testified in his own behalf, denying that he had encouraged Rowe to shoot Colvard, and alleging that he had endeavored to persuade Rowe not to shoot. . . .

The language attributed to Hicks, and which he denied having used, cannot be said to have been entirely free from ambiguity. It was addressed not to Rowe, but to Colvard. Hicks testified that Rowe was in a dangerous mood, and that he did not know whether he would shoot Colvard or Hicks. The remark made — if made — accompanied with the gesture of taking off his own hat, may have been an utterance of desperation, occasioned by his belief that Rowe would shoot one or both of them. That Hicks and Rowe rode off together after seeing Colvard fall was used as a fact against Hicks, pointing to a conspiracy between them.

Hicks testified that he did it in fear of his life; that Rowe had demanded that he should show him the road which he wished to travel. Hicks further testified, and in this he was not contradicted, that he separated from Rowe a few minutes afterwards, on the first opportunity, and that he never afterwards had any intercourse with him, nor had he been in the company of Rowe for several weeks before the night of the fatal occurrence.

Two of the assignments of error are especially relied on by the counsel of the accused. One arises out of that portion of the charge wherein the judge sought to instruct the jury as to the evidence relied on as showing that Hicks aided and abetted Rowe in the commission of the crime. . . .

We agree with the counsel for the plaintiff in error in thinking that this instruction was erroneous in two particulars. It omitted to instruct the jury that the acts or words of encouragement and abetting must have been used by the accused with the intention of encouraging and abetting Rowe. So far as the instruction goes, the words may have been used for a different purpose, and yet have had the actual effect of inciting Rowe to commit the murderous act. Hicks, indeed, testified that the expressions used by him were intended to dissuade Rowe from shooting. But the jury were left to find Hicks guilty as a principal because the effect of his words may have had the result of encouraging Rowe to shoot, regardless of Hicks' intention. In another part of the charge the learned judge did make an observation as to the question of intention in the use of the words, saying:

> If the deliberate and intentional use of words has the effect to encourage one man to kill another, he who uttered these words is presumed by the law to have intended that effect, and is responsible therefor.

This statement is itself defective in confounding the intentional use of the words with the intention as respects the effect to be produced. Hicks no doubt, *intended* to use the words he did use, but did he thereby *intend* that they were to be understood by Rowe as an encouragement to act? However this may be, we do not think this expression of the learned judge availed to cure the defect already noticed in his charge, that the mere use of certain words would suffice to warrant the jury in finding Hicks guilty, regardless of the intention with which they were used.

Another error is contained in that portion of the charge now under review, and that is the statement:

> that if Hicks was actually present at that place at the time of the firing by Stand Rowe, and he was there for the purpose of either aiding, abetting, advising, or encouraging the shooting of Andrew J. Colvard by Stand Rowe, and that, as a matter of fact, he did not do it, but was present for the purpose of aiding or abetting or advising or encouraging his shooting, but he did not do it because it was not necessary, it was done without his assistance, the law says there is a third condition where guilt is fastened to his act in that regard.

We understand this language to mean that where an accomplice is present for the purpose of aiding and abetting in a murder, but refrains from so aiding and abetting because it turned out not to be necessary for the accomplishment of the common purpose, he is equally guilty as if he had actively participated by words or acts of encouragement. Thus understood, the statement might, in some instances, be a correct instruction. Thus, if there had been evidence sufficient to show that there had been a previous conspiracy between Rowe and Hicks to waylay and kill Colvard, Hicks, if present at the time of the killing, would be guilty, even if it was found unnecessary for him to act. But the error of such an instruction, in the present case, is in the fact that there was no evidence on which to base it. The evidence, so far as we are permitted to notice it, as contained in the bills of exception, and set forth in the charge, shows no facts from which the jury could have properly found that the encounter was the result of any previous conspiracy or arrangement. The jury might well, therefore, have thought that they were following the court's instructions, in finding the accused guilty because he was present at the time and place of the murder, although he contributed neither by word or action to the crime, and although there was no substantial evidence of any conspiracy or prior arrangement between him and Rowe. . . .

The judgment of the court below is reversed and the cause remanded, with directions to set aside the verdict and award a new trial.

NOTES

1. Variations on Hicks. Consider the responsibility of Hicks for the killing by Rowe in the following hypothetical situations.

   (i) Hicks hears that Rowe has set out to kill his old enemy, Colvard, and goes along to enjoy the spectacle.

  (ii) Same situation as in (i), except that while watching Rowe's assault on Colvard with satisfaction, Hicks shouts such words of encouragement to Rowe as "Go get him!" and "Attaboy!"

 (iii) Same situation as in (i), except that Hicks resolves to make certain Rowe succeeds — by helping him if necessary.

 (iv) Same situation as in (iii), except that Hicks tells Rowe on the way that he will help him if it seems necessary.

2. Departures from the common scheme: Often the issue of the required intention of the accomplice arises where there is genuine concert between the secondary and primary parties, but the latter commits a criminal action that is not part of the common scheme. An example is Regina v. Anderson and Morris, [1966] 2 W.L.R. 1195, where Anderson armed himself with a knife and went looking for Welch. Anderson's friend, Morris, went along to help Anderson. When they found Welch, a fight broke out, during which Anderson used his knife to kill Welch. Morris' conviction of manslaughter was reversed because the trial court gave the following instruction, found to be erroneous:

> If you think there was a common design to attack Welch but it is not proved, in the case of Morris, that he had any intention to kill or cause grievous bodily harm, but that Anderson, without the knowledge of Morris, had a knife, took it from the flat and at some time formed the intention to kill or cause grievous bodily harm to Welch and did kill him — an act outside the common design to which Morris is proved to have been a party — then you would or could on the evidence find it

proved that Anderson committed murder and Morris would be liable to be convicted of manslaughter provided you are satisfied that he took part in the attack or fight with Welch. . . .

The appellate court held that "where two persons embark on a joint enterprise, each is liable for the acts done in pursuance of that joint enterprise, [but] if one of the adventurers goes beyond what has been tacitly agreed as part of the common enterprise, his co-adventurer is not liable for the consequences of that unauthorized act."

The Model Penal Code is in accord. See §2.06(3), which provides: "A person is an accomplice of another person in the commission of an offense if: (a) with the purpose of promoting or facilitating the commission of the offense, he . . ." In its commentary the Model Penal Code defends its position that the secondary party is not an accomplice even if he should (or did) realize that the primary party would act as he did, stating (Model Penal Code and Commentaries, Comment to §2.06 at 310-313 (1985)):

> Subsection (3)(a) requires that the actor have the purpose of promoting or facilitating the commission of the offense. [H]e must have the purpose to promote or facilitate the particular conduct that forms the basis for the charge, and thus he will not be liable for conduct that does not fall within this purpose.
>
> This does not mean, of course, that the precise means used in the commission of the crime must have been fixed or contemplated or, when they have been, that liability is limited to their employment. One who solicits an end, or aids or agrees to aid in its achievement, is an accomplice in whatever means may be employed, insofar as they constitute an offense fairly envisaged in the purposes of the association.[a] But when a wholly different crime has been committed, thus involving conduct not within the conscious objectives of the accomplice, he is not liable for it unless the case falls within the specific terms of Subsection (4).
>
> Whatever may have been the law on the point, . . . it is submitted that the liability of an accomplice ought not to be extended beyond the purposes that he shares. Probabilities have an important evidential bearing on these issues; to make them independently sufficient is to predicate the liability on negligence when, for good reason, more is normally required before liability is found.

In a footnote at this point (footnote 4), the commentary goes on to point out:

> The culpability required to be shown of the principal actor, of course, is normally higher than negligence. See Section 2.02(3). To say that the accomplice is liable if the offense committed is "reasonably foreseeable" or the "probable con-

---

a. In Regina v. Bainbridge, [1960] 1 Q.B. 129, the defendant procured oxyacetylene equipment for another, believing it was to be used for cutting up stolen property. Contrary to his expectation, it was used to break into a bank. The court held that he was an accomplice in the bank robbery because he knew that the principal intended a crime of the same type as that actually committed.

In Director of Public Prosecutions for Northern Ireland v. Maxwell, [1978] 3 All E.R. 1140, defendant, a member of a terrorist organization, used his car to lead another car containing a group of fellow terrorists to a designated place. After he left, the others exploded a bomb in a public place. He knew the others intended a military operation of some sort but did not know that they planned to explode a bomb or that they had a bomb with them. Did he have the mens rea to be considered an accomplice to this bombing? The House of Lords held that he did, on the ground that the crime actually committed was one that defendant had in contemplation as an obvious possibility among those crimes likely to be committed by the people he helped.

For a discussion of these cases, see Buxton, Note, 42 Mod. L. Rev. 315 (1979). — EDS.

sequence" of another crime is to make him liable for negligence, even though more is required in order to convict the principal actor. This is both incongruous and unjust; if anything, the culpability level for the accomplice should be higher than that of the principal actor, because there is generally more ambiguity in the overt conduct engaged in by the accomplice, and thus a higher risk of convicting the innocent.

3. *Problem of the agent provocateur.* Wilson and Pierce spent an evening drinking together. At one point Wilson discovered his watch missing and accused Pierce of stealing it. Pierce adamantly denied the accusation. The subject of their conversation turned to feats of crime. They decided to burglarize a drugstore. Later that evening Wilson boosted Pierce through a transom. While Pierce was inside, Wilson telephoned the police and returned to receive bottles of whiskey that Pierce handed to him through the transom. When the police arrived Wilson told them that Pierce was inside the store. Pierce escaped through the back door, and Wilson led police to Pierce's hotel room, where he identified Pierce as the burglar. Shortly after Pierce's arrest Wilson told the police that his connection with the burglary was for the purpose of getting even with Pierce for taking his watch, which he hoped in this way to recover. Nevertheless, Wilson was convicted of aiding in the commission of the burglary. On appeal, the defendant contended the trial court committed error in charging:

> One may not participate in the commission of a felony and then obtain immunity from punishment on the ground that he was a mere detective or spy. One who attempts to detect the commission of crime in others must himself stop short of lending assistance, or participation in the commission of the crime.

The Colorado Supreme Court reversed. Wilson v. People, 103 Colo. 441, 87 P.2d 5 (1939). Agreeing that the instruction was erroneous, the court quoted 1 F. Wharton, Criminal Law §271 (12th ed. 1932):

> A detective entering apparently into a criminal conspiracy already formed for the purpose of exploding it is not an accessory before the fact. For it should be remembered that while detectives, when acting as decoys, may apparently provoke the crime, the essential element of dolus, or malicious determination to violate the law, is wanting in their case. And it is only the formal, and not the substantive, part of the crime that they provoke. They provoke, for instance, in larceny, the asportation of the goods, but not the ultimate loss by the owner. They may be actuated by the most unworthy of motives, but the animus furandi in larceny is not imputable to them; and it is in larcenous cases or cheats that they are chiefly employed.

Questions: Can the result in the *Wilson* case be explained on the ground that Wilson lacked the mens rea of burglary (breaking and entry with intent to steal), since he did not intend that Pierce should succeed in stealing the bottles of whiskey? The problem with this reasoning is that even though Wilson did not intend that Pierce should succeed in stealing, he did intend for Pierce to commit the crime of burglary and, in fact, intentionally helped him to do so.

Then how can we account for the result that Wilson is not guilty of the crime he intentionally helped Pierce to commit? Perhaps the following hypothetical will help: Suppose Wilson, in order to secure the conviction of Pierce of attempted murder, gives Pierce a gun with which to kill X. Though he assures

Pierce the gun is loaded, in fact he deliberately unloaded it before giving it to Pierce. Pierce shoots X with the intention of killing him. Pierce is surely guilty of attempted murder. But would Wilson also be guilty of attempted murder, on the ground that he intentionally helped Pierce to commit that crime? How could he be, since he had no intention that X should be killed?

4. A variation on these scenarios is where the provocateur induces the defendant to help him, the provocateur, commit the crime. For example, suppose the same facts as in the *Wilson* case, except that Pierce hoisted Wilson through the transom. Wilson would, of course, have the same defense. But how about Pierce? Could he be convicted of being an accomplice to Wilson's "burglary"? These situations are further explored in State v. Hayes and the notes following, infra page 671.

STATE v. GLADSTONE

Supreme Court of Washington
78 Wash. 2d 306, 474 P.2d 274 (1980)

HALE, J. A jury found defendant Bruce Gladstone guilty of aiding and abetting one Robert Kent in the unlawful sale of marijuana. . . .

Gladstone's guilt as an aider and abettor in this case rests solely on evidence of a conversation between him and one Douglas MacArthur Thompson concerning the possible purchase of marijuana from one Robert Kent. There is no other evidence to connect the accused with Kent who ultimately sold some marijuana to Thompson. . . .

[Thompson, Kent, and defendant, Gladstone, were all students at the University of Puget Sound. Thompson was hired by the Tacoma Police Department to attempt a purchase of marijuana from Gladstone. Thompson visited defendant at his home and asked to buy marijuana. Defendant replied that he did not have enough to sell him any but volunteered the name of Kent as someone who did have enough and who was willing to sell. He then gave Thompson Kent's address and, at Thompson's request, drew a map to direct him to Kent's residence. Thompson went there and bought marijuana from Kent. There was no evidence of any communication between defendant and Kent concerning marijuana, but only, the court said, of "a possible accommodation to someone who said he wanted to buy marijuana."]

If all reasonable inferences favorable to the state are accorded the evidence, it does not, in our opinion, establish the commission of the crime charged. That vital element — a nexus between the accused and the party whom he is charged with aiding and abetting in the commission of a crime — is missing. The record contains no evidence whatever that Gladstone had any communication by word, gesture or sign, before or after he drew the map, from which it could be inferred that he counseled, encouraged, hired, commanded, induced or procured Kent to sell marijuana to Douglas Thompson as charged, or took any steps to further the commission of the crime charged. He was not charged with aiding and abetting Thompson in the purchase of marijuana, but with Kent's sale of it. . . .

[E]ven without prior agreement, arrangement or understanding, a bystander to a robbery could be guilty of aiding and abetting its commission if he came to the aid of a robber and knowingly assisted him in perpetrating the crime. But . . . there is no aiding and abetting unless one " 'in some sort associate himself with the venture, that he participate in it as in something that he wishes to bring about, that he seek by his action to make it succeed.' " Nye & Nissen v. United States, 336 U.S. 613, 619 (1949).

Gladstone's culpability, if at all, must be brought within R.C.W. 9.01.030, which makes a principal of one who aids and abets another in the commission of the crime. Although an aider and abettor need not be physically present at the commission of the crime to be held guilty as a principal, his conviction depends on proof that he did something in association or connection with the principal to accomplish the crime. Learned Hand, J., we think, hit the nail squarely when, in United States v. Peoni, 100 F.2d 401, 402 (2d Cir. 1938), he wrote that, in order to aid and abet another to commit a crime, it is necessary that a defendant "in some sort associate himself with the venture, that he participate in it as in something that he wishes to bring about, that he seek by his action to make it succeed. All the words used — even the most colorless, "abet" — carry an implication of purposive attitude towards it." . . .

It would be a dangerous precedent indeed to hold that mere communications to the effect that another might or probably would commit a criminal offense amount to an aiding and abetting of the offense should it ultimately be committed.

There being no evidence whatever that the defendant ever communicated to Kent the idea that he would in any way aid him in the sale of any marijuana, or said anything to Kent to encourage or induce him or direct him to do so, or counseled Kent in the sale of marijuana, or did anything more than describe Kent to another person as an individual who might sell some marijuana, or would derive any benefit, consideration or reward from such a sale, there was no proof of an aiding and abetting, and the conviction should, therefore, be reversed as a matter of law. Remanded with directions to dismiss.

HAMILTON, J. (dissenting). . . . I am satisfied that the jury was fully warranted in concluding that appellant, when he affirmatively recommended Kent as a source and purveyor of marijuana, entertained the requisite conscious design and intent that his action would instigate, induce, procure or encourage perpetration of Kent's subsequent crime of selling marijuana to Thompson. . . .

NOTES AND QUESTIONS

1. Questions on Gladstone. The court emphasizes that defendant was "not charged with aiding and abetting Thompson in the purchase of marijuana, but with Kent's sale of it." Could he have been charged and convicted of aiding and abetting Thompson's purchase? What difficulties would be presented? Cf. Model Penal Code §§2.06(3) and 5.01(3). Would the reasoning of the majority, finding the defendant not liable as an aider and abettor of Kent's sale, be equally applicable to preclude his liability as an aider and abettor (or an attempted aider and abettor) of Thompson's purchase? Why should it not? Why should it matter that Thompson asked for and received the aid? Would the defendant's state of mind as to the purchase by Thompson be any different than it was as to the sale by Kent?

2. Model Penal Code and Commentaries, Comment to §2.06 at 315-316 (1985), states the issue as follows:

[Should] knowingly facilitating the commission of a crime . . . be sufficient for complicity, absent a true purpose to advance the criminal end[?] The problem, to be sure, is narrow in its focus: often, if not usually, aid rendered with guilty knowledge implies purpose since it has no other motivation. But there are many and important cases where this is the central question in determining liability. A lessor rents with knowledge that the premises will be used to establish a bordello. A vendor sells with knowledge that the subject of the sale will be used in the commission of a crime. A doctor counsels against an abortion during the third trimester but, at the patient's insistence, refers her to a competent abortionist. A utility provides telephone or telegraph service, knowing it is used for bookmaking. An employee puts through a shipment in the course of his employment though he knows the shipment is illegal. A farm boy clears the ground for setting up a still, knowing that the venture is illicit. Such cases can be multiplied indefinitely; they have given courts much difficulty when they have been brought, whether as prosecutions for conspiracy or for the substantive offense involved.

The solution originally proposed by the Model Penal Code was contained in §2.04(3)(b) (Tent. Draft No. 1 1953):

A person is an accomplice of another person in the commission of a crime if . . . acting with knowledge that such other person was committing or had the purpose of committing the crime, he knowingly, substantially facilitated its commission.

In defense of this proposal the Commentary observed (id., Comment at 27-32):

The problem has had most attention in the federal courts where there is division of opinion as to the criterion that measures liability. The Second Circuit, speaking through Judge Learned Hand, has taken the position that the traditional definitions of complicity (aiding, abetting, counseling, procuring, etc.) "have nothing whatever to do with the probability that the forbidden result would follow upon the accessory's conduct; and that they all demand that he in some sort associate himself with the venture, that he participate in it as in something that he wishes to bring about, that he seek by his action to make it succeed. All the words used — even the most colorless, 'abet' — carry an implication of purposive attitude towards it." [United States v. Peoni, 100 F.2d 401, 402 (1938).] . . .
   Strong disagreement has, however, been expressed. Judge Parker, for example, has declared that guilt "as an accessory depends, not on 'having a stake' in the outcome of the crime . . . but on aiding and assisting the perpetrators. . . . The seller may not ignore the purpose for which the purchase is made if he is advised of that purpose, or wash his hands of the aid that he has given the perpetrator of a felony by the plea that he has merely made a sale of merchandise. One who sells a gun to another knowing that he is buying it to commit a murder, would hardly escape conviction as an accessory to the murder by showing that he received full price for the gun." [Backun v. United States, 112 F.2d 635, 637 (4th Cir. 1940)] . . .
   The draft, it is submitted, should not embrace the *Peoni* limitation. Conduct which knowingly facilitates the commission of crimes is by hypothesis a proper object of preventive effort by the penal law, unless, of course, it is affirmatively justifi-

able. It is important in that effort to safeguard the innocent but the requirement of guilty knowledge adequately serves this end — knowledge both that there is a purpose to commit a crime and that one's own behavior renders aid. There are, however, infinite degrees of aid to be considered. This is the point, we think, at which distinctions should be drawn. Accordingly, when a true purpose to further the crime is lacking, the draft requires that the accessorial behavior substantially facilitate commission of the crime and that it do so to the knowledge of the actor. This qualification provides a basis for discrimination that should satisfy the common sense of justice. A vendor who supplies materials readily available upon the market arguably does not make substantial contribution to commission of the crime since the materials could have as easily been gotten elsewhere. The minor employee may win exemption on this ground, though he minded his own business to preserve his job. What is required is to give the courts and juries a criterion for drawing lines that must be drawn. The formula proposed accomplishes this purpose by a standard that is relevant, it is submitted, to all the legal ends involved. There will, of course, be arguable cases; they should, we think, be argued in these terms. . . .

We also agree that a problem of conflicting interests is presented but submit that, absent special grounds that constitute legal justification, it ought to be resolved in favor of a principle that regards crime prevention as the prior value to be served. . . . [W]hen the only interest of the actor is his wish for freedom to forego concern about the criminal purposes of others, though he knowingly facilitates in a substantial measure the achievement of such purposes, it is an interest that, we think, is properly subordinated generally to the larger interest of preventing crime. It should be added that the issue here is that of liability, not that of treatment on conviction; discriminations among parties with respect to punishment or treatment is, of course, in order; the basis for them will be furnished by the draft.

The Model Penal Code's 1953 proposals were rejected by the American Law Institute. The Code now requires that the actor have "the purpose of promoting or facilitating" the commission of the crime. Section 2.06(3)(a), Appendix.

Question: What are the inadequacies, if any, in the reporter's arguments that led to its rejection? Consider Glanville Williams, Criminal Law: The General Part 369-370 (2d ed. 1961):

From the point of view of policy the question is one of some complexity. On the one side are the policy of repressing crime, and the difficulty of distinguishing between the merchant who knowingly assists a crime and the ordinary accessory before the fact. On the other side stand the undesirability of giving too great an extension to the criminal law, and the inconvenience to legitimate trade of requiring a merchant to concern himself with the affairs of his customers. The difficulty is increased by the number of different modes in which the question may arise. The merchant may desire the crime, or he may foresee it as certain if he sells the commodity, or he may foresee it as belonging to one of many degrees of probability. The sale may be completely in the ordinary course of business, or the order may in some way be a special one — as when a tailor makes a suit with secret pockets for poaching or smuggling. The merchant may charge the usual price or an extra price on account of the legal risk. The commodity may be appropriate only to a single crime (as with poison that is consumed only once), or may enable the purchaser to engage in a life of crime. The crime in contemplation may be a serious or a trivial one.

See also George Fletcher, Rethinking Criminal Law 676 (1978):

> From the standpoint of the supplier, the problem of refusing services to known criminals closely resembles the problem of intervening to prevent impending harm. The grocery store, the gas station, the physician, the answering service all provide routine services. Does the business-person have a duty to make an exception just because he or she knows that the purchaser is engaged in illegal activity? That question of duty corresponds to the problem of the motorist who must decide whether to stop his car and render aid to an accident victim. The assumption underlying both fields is that people are entitled to carry on their lives without deviating every time doing so might help a person in distress or hamper the execution of a criminal plan.

The case against imposing liability for knowing aid is made in R. A. Duff, "Can I Help You?" Accessorial Liability and the Intention to Assist, 10 Legal Stud. 167 (1990).

3. *Criminal facilitation.* One response to these contending considerations is compromise: Make aid without a true purpose a separate crime with a lesser penalty than the crime aided. New York has pioneered this approach with a new crime called "criminal facilitation."[2] N.Y. Penal Code §115 provides:

> A person is guilty of criminal facilitation in the second degree when, believing it probable that he is rendering aid to a person who intends to commit a crime, he engages in conduct which provides such person with means or opportunity for the commission thereof and which in fact aids such person to commit a felony. Criminal facilitation in the second degree is a class A misdemeanor.[3]

Note that the formula of liability is wider than that originally proposed by the Model Penal Code, which would have required "knowing" aid as a basis of accomplice liability. It is enough under the New York formulation that the aider believes it "probable" that the person aided will commit a crime.

Question: Would the defendant in the *Gladstone* case be guilty of criminal facilitation under the New York statute? See People v. Gordon, 32 N.Y.2d 62, 295 N.E.2d 777 (1973), holding in the negative. Do you agree?

4. In United States v. Fountain, 768 F.2d 790 (7th Cir. 1985) (page 515 supra), a prison inmate (Gometz) was convicted of aiding and abetting another inmate (Silverstein) to murder a guard. The evidence disclosed that Silverstein, in handcuffs, was being led down the corridor by some guards. When he reached Gometz's cell he thrust his manacled hands through the bars. Gometz came close and pulled up his shirt to reveal a knife in his waistband. Somehow Silverstein got free of the handcuffs, seized the knife, and stabbed the guard with it. Judge Posner held that to convict Gometz it was not necessary to prove that it was Gometz's purpose that Silverstein should kill the guard; it was enough that he knew when he helped Silverstein obtain the knife that Silverstein would use it to attack the guards. In holding that knowledge was enough, the court bor-

---

2. Several jurisdictions have followed New York's lead. Ariz. Rev. Stat. Ann. tit. 13, §13-1004; Ky. Rev. Stat. Ann. §506.080; N.D. Cent. Code §12.1-06-02.

3. Section 115.05 makes such conduct first-degree criminal facilitation when the crime committed is a class A felony (such crimes as murder, for example) and subjects it to punishment as a class C felony (maximum 15 years of imprisonment).

rowed the approach of a California conspiracy case (People v. Lauria, reported page 753 infra) that held that *purpose* was required to convict of lesser offenses, but that *knowledge* sufficed to convict of major crimes. Judge Posner stated (id. at 798):

> In People v. Lauria, — not a federal case, but illustrative of the general point — the court, en route to holding that knowledge of the principal's purpose would not suffice for aiding and abetting of just any crime, said it would suffice for "the seller of gasoline who knew the buyer was using his product to make Molotov cocktails for terroristic use." Compare the following hypothetical cases. In the first, a shopkeeper sells dresses to a woman whom he knows to be a prostitute. The shopkeeper would not be guilty of aiding and abetting prostitution unless the prosecution could establish the elements of Judge Hand's test. Little would be gained by imposing criminal liability in such a case. Prostitution, anyway a minor crime, would be but trivially deterred, since the prostitute could easily get her clothes from a shopkeeper ignorant of her occupation. In the second case, a man buys a gun from a gun dealer after telling the dealer that he wants it in order to kill his mother-in-law, and he does kill her. The dealer would be guilty of aiding and abetting the murder. This liability would help to deter — and perhaps not trivially given public regulation of the sale of guns — a most serious crime. We hold that aiding and abetting murder is established by proof beyond a reasonable doubt that the supplier of the murder weapon knew the purpose for which it would be used.

5. The material presented up to this point on the required mens rea of the accomplice as to the principal's criminal action rests on the premise that an actual intention of some kind must exist. This is the Model Penal Code view and perhaps was also once the majority view. There are now, however, a number of cases and statutes that depart from that strict requirement. They are the subject of the material that follows.

PEOPLE v. LUPARELLO

California Court of Appeal, 4th District
187 Cal. App. 3d 410, 231 Cal. Rptr. 832 (1987)

KREMER, J. [Defendant Luparello wanted to locate Terri, his former lover who had deserted him to marry another. He thought he could discover her whereabouts from Mark Martin, a good friend of her current husband. To that end he enlisted the help of several friends, telling them that he wanted the information at any cost. His friends visited Martin but failed to get what they sought. They returned the next evening armed with gun and sword, but without Luparello apparently, and lured Martin outside. Thereupon one of their group, waiting in a car, shot and killed Martin. Luparello was charged and convicted of murder.]

The trial court charged the jury with several different theories by which Luparello's guilt for first degree murder could be affixed; among these were . . . aiding and abetting. On appeal . . . Luparello . . . attacks the theoretical underpinnings of . . . aiding-and-abetting liability, and specifically argues the murder here was the unplanned and unintended act of a coconspirator and therefore not chargeable to Luparello under complicity theory.

Luparello first faults [the] theor[y] for "imposing" the mens rea of the perpetrator upon him. As Luparello views it, [the] theor[y] work[s] to presume conclusively the accomplice shares the perpetrator's intent. . . . Luparello errs when he concludes the perpetrator and accomplice must "share" an identical intent to be found criminally responsible for the same crime. Technically, only the perpetrator can (and must) manifest the mens rea of the crime committed. Accomplice liability is premised on a different or, more appropriately, an equivalent mens rea. This equivalence is found in intentionally encouraging or assisting or influencing the nefarious act. . . . Thus, to be a principal to a crime . . . the aider and abettor must intend to commit the offense or to encourage or facilitate its commission. Liability is extended to reach the actual crime committed, rather than the planned or "intended" crime, on the policy [that] aiders and abettors should be responsible for the criminal harms they have naturally, probably and foreseeably put in motion. And it is precisely this policy which Luparello next challenges. . . .

The California Supreme Court [stated] in the recent case of People v. Croy, 41 Cal. 3d 1, 710 P.2d 392:

> The requirement that the jury determine the intent with which a person tried as an aider and abettor has acted is not designed to ensure that his conduct constitutes the offense with which he is charged. His liability is vicarious. . . . [H]e is guilty not only of the offense he intended to facilitate or encourage, but also of any reasonably foreseeable offense committed by the person he aids and abets. . . .

Adopting the reasoning of the Supreme Court, we find the . . . aiding and abetting theor[y] proffered here do[es] not suffer the theoretical infirmities of which Luparello complains. In the circumstances of this case, [it] provides a sound basis to derive Luparello's criminal responsibility for first degree murder. . . .

Judgments affirmed.

WIENER, J., concurring:

I concur . . . in the result reached by the majority under the compulsion of . . . People v. Croy (1985) 41 Cal. 3d 1, 12, footnote 5, 710 P.2d 392. [That case] require[s] a holding that an aider and abettor or co-conspirator is liable not only for those crimes committed by a co-felon which he intended or agreed to facilitate but also for any additional crimes which are "reasonably foreseeable."[2] . . . The fact that the Supreme Court has announced a principle of law certainly requires that as an intermediate appellate court we follow it. This does not mean, however, that the announced principle is either logically consistent or theoretically sound.

. . . The major fallacy I see in the "foreseeable consequence" doctrine is not so much that it attributes an unintended act to the accomplice/co-conspirator but rather that it assesses the degree of his culpability for that act not by his own

2. Henceforth I refer to this principle as the "foreseeable consequence" doctrine because that is the terminology used in *Croy*. I am concerned, however, about how a principle which was originally phrased in terms of "probable and natural consequences" was slightly modified to become the "natural and reasonable consequences" and has now been saddled with a monicker traditionally associated with theories of expanding tort liability. If we were to return to strict interpretation of the "natural and probable" standard, I would argue that liability could not be imposed here on Luparello because in no sense can it be said that Mark Martin's death was the "probable" result of a conspiracy to assault him in order to obtain information.

mental state but rather by the mental state of the perpetrator and/or the circumstances of the crime. The present case provides an appropriate example. The assault on Mark Martin contemplated by the conspiracy involved a foreseeable risk of death or serious injury. We can assume (although there was no jury finding on the issue) that Luparello was criminally negligent in failing to appreciate the degree of risk. Under usual circumstances, a person negligently causing the death of another is guilty, at most, of involuntary manslaughter. Here, however, Luparello's liability is not based on his individual mental state but instead turns on the jury's finding that the unidentified shooter intentionally killed Martin while lying in wait. Thus, Luparello is guilty of first degree murder. If the circumstances of Luparello's participation were exactly the same but the shooter did not "lie in wait," Luparello could only be convicted of second degree murder. I am intrigued by the notion that if unknown to Luparello, the shooter ingested drugs and/or alcohol to the point where he did not in fact harbor the requisite malice, Luparello would presumably be guilty only of voluntary manslaughter. . . . I find such fortuity of result irrational. So too, apparently, do Professors LaFave and Scott in their treatise [Handbook on Criminal Law (1972) p. 516:]

> The "natural and probable consequence" rule of accomplice liability, if viewed as a broad generalization, is inconsistent with more fundamental principles of our system of criminal law. It would permit liability to be predicated upon negligence even when the crime involved requires a different state of mind. Such is not possible as to one who has personally committed a crime, and should likewise not be the case as to those who have given aid or counsel.

The drafters of the Model Penal Code reached a similar conclusion. . . .

In contrast to the majority, which seeks to distinguish the "foreseeable consequence" doctrine from the "disfavored" felony-murder rule, I view both as being founded on the same outmoded and logically indefensible proposition that if a person exhibits some intent to violate the law, we need not be terribly concerned that the contemplated crime was far less serious than the crime which actually took place. . . .

The artificial imputation of stepped-up intent, inherent in both the felony-murder rule and the "foreseeable consequence" doctrine, is inconsistent with the "universal and persistent" notion that criminal punishment must be proportional to the defendant's culpable mental state. Justice Mosk's dissent in Taylor v. Superior Court (1970) 3 Cal. 3d 578, 593, 477 P.2d 131 expressed it well: "Fundamental principles of criminal responsibility dictate that the defendant be subject to a greater penalty only when he has demonstrated a greater degree of culpability." The fact that the accomplice or co-conspirator intended to facilitate some less serious criminal act does not render these fundamental principles inapplicable.

NOTES

1. The reasonable foreseeability test applied in *Luparello* stands in sharp contrast to the Model Penal Code position, which requires that it be the purpose of the secondary actor to help or encourage the very crime of the principal for which the secondary party is to be held, supra page 652. That position, however, is now probably the minority view, even among states that have otherwise modeled their revised codes on the Model Penal Code model. See Model Penal Code and Commentaries, Comment to §2.06 at 313 n. 43 (1985). For a description of the various approaches American jurisdictions take in comparison with that of the Model Penal Code, see Note (Grace Mueller), The Mens Rea of Accomplice Liability, 61 S. Cal. L. Rev. 2169 (1988).

2. A more extreme interpretation of the test of natural and probable (or foreseeable) consequence was applied by a divided court in People v. Brigham, 216 Cal. App. 3d 1039, 265 Cal. Rptr. 486 (1990). There defendant and Bluitt went looking for a man named Chuckie, intending to kill him. When they came upon Barfield, Bluitt, believing he was Chuckie, made preparations to shoot him. Defendant protested that it was not Chuckie and that Bluitt should not shoot. The latter disregarded defendant's command and shot and killed Barfield. Defendant was charged and convicted of the murder of Barfield on the theory that he aided and abetted Bluitt's murder of him. Because of Bluitt's "hard-headed and erratic nature," the prosecution argued and the jury found that the defendant could "reasonably foresee" that Bluitt, once set in motion, might knowingly kill someone other than his assigned target. A majority upheld the conviction, stating:

> The major issue we must decide here is this: [I]s the aider and abettor relieved of derivative criminal liability as a matter of law if [the] criminal act of the perpetrator is an "independent product" of his mind, and is outside and not in furtherance of the criminal offense the aider and abettor originally agreed to aid or facilitate?
>
> We will hold that in such circumstances the aider and abettor is not relieved of liability as a matter of law, because his derivative criminal liability continues to be factually determined by the test of whether the criminal act committed by the principal was a natural and probable (or foreseeable) consequence of an act the aider and abettor knowingly aided, encouraged, or facilitated.

3. In a case comparable to People v. Brigham an English court affirmed a conviction of murder. Regina v. Hyde, [1990] 3 W.L.R. 1115. Professor John C. Smith has defended this result. Commentary, [1991] Crim. L. Rev. 134. Though recognizing that it leaves the secondary party liable to conviction for murder despite the fact that he is only reckless, Prof. Smith argues that:

> there is a difference between (i) recklessness whether death be caused (which is sufficient for manslaughter but not for murder) and (ii) recklessness whether murder be committed. The accessory's recklessness must extend to the principal's mens rea of murder. The person who embarks on a joint enterprise knowing that his confederate may intentionally kill is taking a deliberate risk of assisting or encouraging not merely killing but murder.

Questions: How convincing is the distinction between the person who recklessly risks killing another and the person who recklessly risks that another will kill intentionally? Suppose two cases. In the first, *defendant 1* engages in target practice in an area close to a pedestrian walk, though aware of an "n percent" risk of accidentally shooting someone. His bullet kills a pedestrian. In the second case, *defendant 2* lends X a gun for target practice, though aware that X is a violent person who has threatened to kill *V* and that there is an "n percent" risk that he might use the gun to do so. *X* uses the gun to murder *V.* Why should *defendant 2* be treated more severely than *defendant 1?* So long as the magnitude of the risk is the same, why should it matter whether the risk is of someone receiving a bullet accidentally or of someone receiving it intentionally? Finally, even assuming a difference in culpability between *defendant 1* and *defendant 2,* does it follow that *defendant 2*'s culpability is as great as that of *X,* the actual murderer? Does *defendant 2* have the mens rea for murder?

4. In United States v. Powell, 929 F.2d 724 (D.C. Cir. 1991), the court interpreted the "natural and probable consequence" test of accomplice liability to mean that one party to a drug sale may not be charged with aiding and abetting the possession of a gun by his confederate unless it is proven that he knew the other carried a gun (or "perhaps should have known" that "as a matter of practical certainty the principal would be carrying the gun"). The court discussed the disarray in the cases on what the "natural and probable consequence" meant and made the following observation (id. at 727):

> It is common to state that liability as an accomplice encompasses acts of the principal that are a "natural and probable consequence" of the criminal scheme the accomplice encouraged or aided. . . . The phrase "natural and probable consequences" by no means communicates just how likely the forbidden act must have appeared to the accomplice. It could signify any position within a broad range: for example, all acts with a substantial probability of occurrence (e.g., one chance in five); acts that are more probable than not to occur; acts of very high probability (e.g., 90%); and acts so likely that their occurrence is a practical certainty. Given the imperfection of human knowledge, the latter is the equivalent of knowledge; an accomplice "knows" an act will happen if he is "practically certain" it will. See Model Penal Code §2.02 (1985). Our review of the cases suggests that no court uses one of these degrees of probability for all contexts; each varies the requirement with the circumstances.

b. Mens Rea as to Attendant Circumstances

JOHNSON v. YOUDEN, [1950] 1 K.B. 544: [Defendant solicitors were charged with aiding and abetting a builder in selling a house at a price in excess of that permitted by law, in violation of a criminal statute. On appeal from a dismissal of the information, the prosecutor argued that the lack of knowledge by the solicitors that their client was charging an unlawful price was no defense, since the crime they were charged with aiding and abetting was a crime of absolute liability. He argued:

> The justices formed the view that the offence of aiding and abetting involved mens rea, and that the burden of proving mens rea was on the prosecution. They were clearly wrong: mens rea is irrelevant. Mens rea is not an essential ingredient of the offence of aiding and abetting the commission of a substantive offence of which mens rea is not an essential ingredient.

The court affirmed the dismissal of the informations, stating:] Before a person can be convicted of aiding and abetting the commission of an offence, he must at least know the essential matters which constitute that offence. He need not actually know that an offence has been committed, because he may not know that the facts constitute an offence and ignorance of the law is not a defence. If a person knows all the facts and is assisting another person to do certain things, and it turns out that the doing of those things constitutes an offence, the person who is assisting is guilty of aiding and abetting that offence, because to allow him to say, "I knew of all those facts but I did not know that an offence was committed," would be allowing him to set up ignorance of the law as a defence. The reason why, in our opinion, the justices were right in dismissing the informations against the first two defendants is that they found, and found on good grounds, that they did not know of the matters which in fact constituted the offence; and, as they did not know of those matters, it follows that they cannot be guilty of aiding and abetting the commission of the offence.

NOTES

1. See also Giorgianni v. The Queen, 156 C.L.R. 473 (High Court of Australia 1985): "[N]o one may be convicted of aiding, abetting, counselling or procuring the commission of an offense unless, knowing all the essential facts which made what was done a crime, he intentionally aided, abetted, counselled or procured the acts of the principal offender. Wilful blindness . . . is treated as equivalent to knowledge but neither negligence nor recklessness is sufficient."

2. As we saw, the Model Penal Code takes the position that for complicity liability, purpose (as distinguished from mere knowledge) is required as to the "commission of the offense." §2.06(3)(a). But does this mens rea requirement apply to the *attendant-circumstance* elements of the contemplated offense? The Comment states (Model Penal Code and Commentaries, Comment to §2.06 at page 311 n. 37 (1985)):

> There is deliberate ambiguity as to whether the purpose requirement extends to circumstance elements of the contemplated offense or whether, as in the case of attempts, the policy of the substantive offense on this point should control. The result, therefore, is that the actor must have a purpose with respect to the proscribed conduct, with his attitude towards the circumstances to be left to resolution by the courts. . . .

How should the courts resolve this issue? Consider this hypothetical: *A* encourages *B* to have sexual relations with a female who is underage. If the crime of statutory rape only requires that the primary actor be negligent as to her age, is the secondary actor liable as an accomplice if he too was negligent as to her age, or must he have *known* she was underage? If the state imposes strict liability as to the age of the female, should that suffice for the accomplice?

What would be the result under Johnson v. Youden? Is it a sensible solution? Recall that where a defendant is charged with an *attempt* to commit some crime the Model Penal Code holds that the mens rea of the substantive crime governs the liability of the defendant. So, in the hypothetical given, supra page 592, the person who tries but fails to have sex with a female who is underage would be guilty of attempted statutory rape even if the defendant had no grounds to suspect she might be underage. Why doesn't the Model Penal Code take the same position in the case of complicity? If the requirement of purpose is qualified for attendant circumstances in the case of complicity, why should it not be similarly qualified in the case of attempt?

c. Mens Rea as to Result

STATE v. McVAY

Supreme Court of Rhode Island
47 R.I. 292, 132 A. 436 (1926)

BARROWS, J. Heard on a certification of a question of law before trial. Three indictments for manslaughter, each containing four counts, were brought against the captain and engineer of the steamer Mackinac, as principals, and against Kelley, as accessory before the fact. The steamer carried several hundred passengers from Pawtucket to Newport via Narragansett Bay. The boiler producing the steam by which the vessel was propelled burst near Newport and many lives were lost. The present indictments are for causing the deaths of three persons killed by escaping steam after the explosion of the boiler. . . .

The same question is raised upon each indictment. That question is:

> May a defendant be indicted and convicted of being an accessory before the fact to the crime of manslaughter arising through criminal negligence as set forth in the indictment?

. . . The charge against Kelley as accessory is that "before said felony and manslaughter was committed," he did, at Pawtucket, "feloniously and maliciously aid, assist, abet, counsel, hire, command and procure the said George W. McVay and John A. Grant [the captain and engineer, respectively], the said felony and manslaughter in manner and form aforesaid to do and commit." . . .

Because the manslaughter charge is "without malice" and "involuntary," Kelley contends that he cannot be indicted legally as an accessory before the fact. The argument is that manslaughter, being a sudden and unpremeditated crime, inadvertent and unintentional by its very nature, cannot be "maliciously" incited before the crime is committed. . . .

While every one must agree that there can be no accessory before the fact when a killing results from a sudden and unpremeditated blow, we do not think it can be broadly stated that premeditation is inconsistent with every charge of manslaughter. Manslaughter may consist, among other things, of doing an unlawful act resulting in unintentional killing, such as violation of motor vehicle laws or administration of drugs to procure an abortion. Manslaughter is likewise committed if an unintentional killing is occasioned by gross negligence in the doing of an act lawful in itself. There is no inherent reason why, prior to the commission of such a crime, one may not aid, abet, counsel, command, or procure the doing of the unlawful act or of the lawful act in a negligent manner. A premeditated act may be involved in such unlawful homicides.

[T]he present indictment for involuntary manslaughter is not self-contradictory when it charges Kelley to be an accessory before the fact. It was possible for him at Pawtucket to intentionally direct and counsel the grossly neg-

ligent act which the indictment charges resulted in the crime. Involuntary manslaughter, as set forth in this indictment, means that defendants exercised no
conscious volition to take life, but their negligence was of such a character that
criminal intention can be presumed. The crime was consummated when the
explosion occurred. The volition of the principals was exercised when they
chose negligently to create steam which the boiler could not carry. The doing of
the act charged or failure to perform the duty charged was voluntary and intentional in the sense that defendants exercised a choice among courses of conduct. It is obvious that Kelley could participate and is charged with participating
in procuring defendants to act in a grossly negligent manner prior to the explosion. . . . Specific duties are stated to have been laid upon the captain and engineer. Defendant is charged with full knowledge of those duties and of the fact
that the boiler was unsafe. He is charged with counseling and procuring the
principals at Pawtucket to disregard their duties and negligently create steam.
. . . The facts set forth in these indictments, if existent, are such that a jury might
find that defendant Kelley, with full knowledge of the possible danger to human
life, recklessly and willfully advised, counseled, and commanded the captain and
engineer to take a chance by negligent action or failure to act.

We therefore answer the question certified on each indictment in the
affirmative. . . .

PEOPLE v. ABBOTT

New York Supreme Court, Appellate Division
84 A.D.2d 11, 445 N.Y.S.2d 344 (1981)

SCHNEPP, J. [A]t approximately 1:00 A.M. on January 19, 1980 defendant Paul T.
Moon was traveling alone in his car in an easterly direction on Maple Road . . .
when he became involved in a "drag race" with an automobile driven by
Abbott. Maple Road, which traverses a residential area, is a four-lane highway with designated speed limits, controlled by traffic signals, and separated
by double yellow lines into two eastbound and two westbound lanes. Moon
and Abbott were seen racing at very high rates of speeds. [At one point Moon,
in seeking to overtake Abbott, crossed over the double yellow lines into the opposing lanes of traffic at an intersection. Abbott's vehicle struck a car driven by
Patricia Hammond, which had just entered the intersection, and killed her and
her two passengers.]

Moon and Abbott were jointly indicted for . . . three counts of criminally negligent homicide in that they, "each being intentionally aided by the other, . . .
with criminal negligence, caused the death of another person," and other accident related offenses. Both defendants were . . . convicted of three counts of
criminally negligent homicide. . . .

The theory of the prosecution against Moon was that he intentionally aided
Abbott to engage in the criminally negligent conduct which resulted in the
deaths of the three victims. Moon claims that such a theory is "not logical" and
that one must be liable by "one's own acts as a principal for criminally negligent
homicide or not at all." . . .

Section 20.00 of the Penal Law provides that when one person engages in
conduct which constitutes an offense "another person is criminally liable for

such conduct when, acting with the mental culpability required for the commission thereof, he . . . intentionally aids such a person to engage in such conduct." . . .

A "drag race" involves two or more drivers engaged in a contest of speed with the use of their automobiles. When this activity occurs on a public highway there is an inherent danger of increasing the death-dealing potential of the automobile. . . . It necessarily evinces a "failure to perceive a substantial and unjustifiable risk, constituting a 'gross deviation from the standard of care that a reasonable person would observe in the situation'" and it is "sufficient to sustain the conviction for criminally negligent homicide." (People v. Soto, 44 N.Y.2d 683, 684.)

The statutory scheme permits accessorial liability to attach for criminally negligent homicide provided that the accessory shares the requisite culpable mental state for the crime and intentionally aids in its commission. While Moon did not personally control Abbott's vehicle which struck and killed the three victims, it could reasonably be found that he "intentionally" aided Abbott in the unlawful use of the vehicle by participating in a high-speed race, weaving in and out of traffic, and thus shared Abbott's culpability. Skid marks and other evidence at the scene of the accident permitted expert testimony that the pre-braking speed of Moon's automobile was 80 to 85 miles per hour and that the speed of Abbott's automobile immediately prior to the collision was 93.5 miles per hour. Moon associated himself with the high-speed race on a busy highway and took a part in it for nearly two minutes over a distance in excess of one mile. Actually his conduct made the race possible. He accepted Abbott's challenge and shared in the venture. Without Moon's aid Abbott could not have engaged in the high-speed race which culminated in the tragedy. The accident was "the culmination of a continuum of events" in which both defendant and Abbott participated. . . .

The evidence was, therefore, sufficient for the trier of fact to conclude beyond a reasonable doubt that Moon while acting with the culpable mental state of criminal negligence gave assistance or encouragement to Abbott to engage in conduct dangerous to life. This is sufficient to impose criminal liability. . . .

NOTES

1. Compare Model Penal Code §2.06, Appendix. Subsection 3 provides that one who aids or solicits another person to commit an offense is an accomplice of that person only if he or she acts "with the purpose of promoting or facilitating the commission of the offense." Subsection 4, however, provides:

> When causing a particular result is an element of an offense, an accomplice in the conduct causing such result is an accomplice in the commission of that offense, if he acts with the kind of culpability, if any, with respect to that result that is sufficient for the commission of the offense.

Questions: How would this provision resolve the issues in the *McVay* and *Abbott* cases? In *McVay* it seems clear that Kelley would be regarded as an accomplice in the conduct of the captain and the engineer because, knowing as well as they the dangerous condition of the boiler, he ordered them to fire the boilers, the very reckless act that caused the explosion and the deaths. What considerations might have led the Model Penal Code drafters to depart from the requirement of purpose for results?

There has been some resistance to the Model Penal Code approach. Consider, for example, People v. Wheeler, 772 P.2d 101 (Colo. 1989). Wheeler's boyfriend got into a fight with Bothun; in the course of the struggle, the boyfriend — with Wheeler's encouragement — stabbed Bothun. The jury found Wheeler guilty of criminally negligent homicide on an aiding and abetting theory. The Colorado Supreme Court upheld the verdict. While the majority accepted the Model Penal Code approach, a dissenting judge did not, stating (id. at 104):

> The critical factor in imputing criminal responsibility under the complicity doctrine is the defendant's intent to promote or facilitate the commission of the unlawful act. §18-1-603. I share the trial judge's view that it is not logical to hold that an accused complicitor intended to promote or facilitate unintentional conduct such as criminally negligent homicide. It is incongruous to say that one person intended to facilitate an act when the actor himself did not intend to commit that act. To hold otherwise bestows upon the accused complicitor prescient qualities, inasmuch as it implies that a complicitor can know and intend to assist a principal in unlawful conduct when the principal himself does not know he will engage in that conduct.

Does this argument have merit?

Turning to the *Abbott* case, would §2.06(4) justify the result in that case as well? Can it be said of Moon, as it could of Kelley, that he encouraged Abbott to do the very act that caused the death? Did he intend that Abbott should drive over the double line and into deceased's car at the intersection?

2. *Abbott* revisits the drag race problem, which we considered in the Causation section in connection with Commonwealth v. Root, supra page 573, and State v. McFadden, supra page 575. While those cases dealt with the liability of the race survivor in terms of causation, *Abbott* deals with it in terms of complicity; that is, not whether the survivor caused the deaths, but whether he is an accomplice of the driver who did. Which of these doctrinal approaches is the more satisfactory?

PROBLEM

In State v. Ayers, 478 N.W.2d 606 (Iowa 1991), the Iowa Supreme Court reversed an involuntary manslaughter conviction arising out of the sale of a stolen handgun by the defendant to a 16-year-old who did not possess a handgun permit. Shortly after purchasing the gun, the minor showed it off at a party with some friends, one of whom pushed his arm, resulting in the discharge of the gun and the killing of one of his friends. Defendant was not present and not involved with the party. Reversing his conviction, the court stated:

> It is not enough that Ayers' conduct was outrageous and criminal. [W]here the criminal liability arises from the act of another, it must appear that the act was done in furtherance of the common design, or in prosecution of the common purpose for which the parties were assembled or combined together.

Two years later, in State v. Travis, 497 N.W.2d 905 (Iowa App. 1993), the Iowa Court of Appeals reviewed an involuntary manslaughter conviction arising out of the following situation. Travis, though aware that his motorcycle was defective and that there were children playing in the area, drove the motorcycle around in a reckless manner, with his 15-year-old friend, Engler, on the back pillion. Thereafter, though aware that Engler had no experience driving motorcycles, Travis offered to permit him to drive. He gave Engler some basic instructions — where the brakes and accelerator were, how to shift gears — and then sat on the pillion behind his young friend while the latter drove. Although it was almost dark, the headlights were not on. They did not see the victim, a 6-year-old child, until they were 4 feet away from her. "Engler did not attempt to swerve or brake and testified Travis did not instruct him likewise. The motorcycle hit [the child], sending her approximately seventy feet and killing her." Engler pleaded guilty to involuntary manslaughter, and Travis was convicted by a jury as an aider and abettor in involuntary manslaughter. The court affirmed, stating (id. at 909):

> To support a conviction on a theory of aiding and abetting, the record must contain substantial evidence to show the defendant assented to or lent countenance and approval to the criminal act either by an act of participation in it or in some manner encouraging it prior to or at the time of commission.
> Although the defendant's mere presence is insufficient to support a conviction on a theory of aiding and abetting, the requisite participation can be inferred from circumstantial evidence including presence, companionship and conduct before and after the offense is committed.
> Travis did not merely assent to Engler's driving his motorcycle, he initiated it. While riding as passenger, he failed to provide sufficient instruction; nor did he tell Engler to slow down or drive with caution. In addition, while Travis was earlier driving the vehicle and Engler accompanied him as a passenger, he role-modeled driving the vehicle in a reckless manner. We find the evidence of Travis's conduct sufficient to support the charge of aiding and abetting.

The court distinguished *Ayers* on the grounds that Ayers was nowhere near the accident at the time it occurred (absence of "proximity to harm," the court stated) and that Ayers had no subsequent involvement with the the principal after he sold him the gun.

QUESTIONS

1. Is *Travis* governed by the same principle that governed the conviction of Kelley in State v. McVay, supra page 661? Could it be said of Travis, as it was of Kelley, that he "intentionally direct[ed] and counsel[ed] the grossly negligent act which the indictment charges resulted in the crime"?

2. Is *Ayers* properly distinguishable from *Travis*? Why should it make any difference that Ayers was not present at the party when the gun went off? Should the case have been decided differently if he had been present? Should *Travis* have come out differently if, instead of riding on the back pillion of the motorcycle, he went off somewhere? In State v. McVay should the court have held that Kelley was not liable as an aider and abettor because he was in port at Pawtucket when the ship's boiler exploded at sea en route to Newport?

2. *Actus Reus*

WILCOX v. JEFFERY
King's Bench Division
[1951] 1 All E.R. 464

LORD GODDARD, C.J. This is a Case stated by the metropolitan magistrate at Bow Street Magistrate's Court before whom the appellant, Herbert William Wilcox, the proprietor of a periodical called "Jazz Illustrated," was charged on an information that

> on Dec. 11, 1949, he did unlawfully aid and abet one Coleman Hawkins in contravening art. 1(4) of the Aliens Order, 1920, by failing to comply with a condition attached to a grant of leave to land, to wit, that the said Coleman Hawkins should take no employment paid or unpaid while in the United Kingdom, contrary to art. 18(2) of the Aliens Order, 1920. . . .

The case is concerned with the visit of a celebrated professor of the saxophone, a gentleman by the name of Hawkins who was a citizen of the United States. He came here at the invitation of two gentlemen of the name of Curtis and Hughes, connected with a jazz club which enlivens the neighbourhood of Willesden. . . . Mr. Hawkins . . . arrived with four French musicians. When they came to the airport, among the people who were there to greet them was the appellant. He had not arranged their visit, but he knew they were coming and he was there to report the arrival of these important musicians for his magazine. So, evidently, he was regarding the visit of Mr. Hawkins as a matter which would be of interest to himself and the magazine which he was editing and selling for profit. Messrs. Curtis and Hughes arranged a concert at the Princes Theatre, London. The appellant attended that concert as a spectator. He paid for his ticket. Mr. Hawkins went on the stage and delighted the audience by playing the saxophone. The appellant did not get up and protest in the name of the musicians of England that Mr. Hawkins ought not to be here competing with them and taking the bread out of their mouths or the wind out of their instruments. It is not found that he actually applauded, but he was there having paid to go in, and, no doubt, enjoying the performance, and then, lo and behold out comes his magazine with a most laudatory description, fully illustrated, of this concert. On those facts the magistrate has found that he aided and abetted.

Reliance is placed by the prosecution on R. v. Coney ((1882), 8 Q.B.D. 534) which dealt with a prize fight. This case relates to a jazz band concert, but the particular nature of the entertainment provided, whether by fighting with bare fists or playing on saxophones, does not seem to me to make any difference to the question which we have to decide. The fact is that a man is charged with aiding and abetting an illegal act, and I can find no authority for saying that it matters what that illegal act is, provided that the aider and abettor knows the facts sufficiently well to know that they would constitute an offence in the principal. In R. v. Coney the prize fight took place in the neighbourhood of Ascot, and four or five men were convicted of aiding and abetting the fight. The conviction was quashed on the ground that the chairman had not given a correct direction to the jury when he told them that, as the prisoners were physically present at the fight, they must be held to have aided and abetted. That direction, the court held, was wrong, it being too wide. The matter was very concisely put by Cave, J., whose judgment was fully concurred in by that great master of the criminal law, Stephen, J. Cave, J., said (8 Q.B.D. 540): "Where presence may be entirely accidental, it is not even evidence of aiding and abetting. Where presence is prima facie not accidental it is evidence, but no more than evidence, for the jury."

There was not accidental presence in this case. The appellant paid to go to the concert and he went there because he wanted to report it. He must, therefore, be held to have been present, taking part, concurring, or encouraging, whichever word you like to use for expressing this conception. It was an illegal act on the part of Hawkins to play the saxophone or any other instrument at this concert. The appellant clearly knew that it was an unlawful act for him to play. He had gone there to hear him, and his presence and his payment to go there was an encouragement. He went there to make use of the performance, because he went there, as the magistrate finds and was justified in finding, to get "copy" for his newspaper. It might have been entirely different, as I say, if he had gone there and protested, saying: "The musicians' union do not like you foreigners coming here and playing and you ought to get off the stage." If he had booed, it might have been some evidence that he was not aiding and abetting. If he had gone as a member of a claque to try to drown the noise of the saxophone, he might very likely be found not guilty of aiding and abetting. In this case it seems clear that he was there, not only to approve and encourage what was done, but to take advantage of it by getting "copy" for his paper. In those circumstances there was evidence on which the magistrate could find that the appellant aided and abetted, and for these reasons I am of opinion that the appeal fails. . . .

Appeal dismissed with costs.

STATE ex rel. ATTORNEY GENERAL v. TALLY, JUDGE, 102 Ala. 25, 69, 15 So. 722, 739 (1894): [On an impeachment proceeding against Judge Tally, it was established as follows: Ross had seduced Judge Tally's sister-in-law. Her brothers, the Skeltons, followed Ross to the nearby town of Stevenson, in order to kill him. Judge Tally went to the local telegraph office at Scottsboro and while there learned that one of Ross's relatives had sent Ross a telegram warning, "Four men on horseback with guns following. Look out." Judge Tally then sent his own telegram to the telegraph operator at Stevenson (whom he knew), telling him not to deliver the warning telegram to Ross. The operator received both telegrams and failed to deliver the message to Ross. The Skelton brothers caught up with Ross and killed him. On these facts, the court held that the judge was an accomplice of the Skelton brothers in the killing:]

We are therefore clear to the conclusion that before Judge Tally can be found guilty of aiding and abetting the Skeltons to kill Ross, it must appear that his vigil at Scottsboro to prevent Ross from being warned of his danger was by preconcert with them, or at least known to them, whereby they would naturally be incited, encouraged and emboldened, "given confidence" to the deed, or that he aided them to kill Ross, contributed to Ross's death in point of physical fact by means of the telegram he sent to Huddleston [the telegraph operator.] . . .

The assistance given, however, need not contribute to the criminal result in the sense that but for it the result would not have ensued. It is quite sufficient if it facilitated a result that would have transpired without it. It is quite enough if the aid merely renders it easier for the principal actor to accomplish the end intended by him and the aider and abettor, though in all human probability the end would have been attained without it. If the aid in homicide can be shown to have put the deceased at a disadvantage, to have deprived him of a single chance of life, which but for it he would have had, he who furnishes such aid is guilty though it can not be known or shown that the dead man, in the absence thereof, would have availed himself of that chance. As where one counsels murder he is guilty as an accessory before the fact, though it appears to be probable that murder would have been done without his counsel, and as where one being present by concert to aid if necessary is guilty as a principal in the second degree, though had he been absent murder would have been committed, so where he who facilitates murder, even by so much as destroying a single chance of life the assailed might otherwise have had, he thereby supplements the efforts of the perpetrator, and he is guilty as principal in the second degree at common law, and is principal in the first degree under our statute, notwithstanding it may be found that in all human probability the chance would not have been availed of, and death would have resulted anyway.

PROBLEMS ON THE MATERIALITY OF THE AID OR ENCOURAGEMENT GIVEN

1. *Causation and complicity.* Consider the contrast between causation and accessorial liability. In both kinds of liability, the issue is whether the defendant is liable for an event that takes place through intermediate occurrences. For the defendant to be held to have caused the event, the prosecution must establish — as a minimum — that, but for the defendant's action, the event would not have occurred. On the other hand, for the defendant to be held accessorially liable for an event through the intermediate action of another person, as the *Tally* case and Wilcox v. Jeffery make clear, it is not necessary to establish a but-for relation between the defendant's action and the criminal conduct of another. Even if the same result might have occurred without the defendant's contribution, he can be liable as an accomplice if he acted with the required mens rea.

How should we account for this difference between causation and accessorial liability? See Sanford H. Kadish, Blame and Punishment 158-165 (1987).

2. *Attempted complicity?* We just noted that even a minimal possibility of actual aid or encouragement suffices for accessorial liability. *Question:* Need there be any actual aid or encouragement at all? Consider these variations on cases we have just read.

In *Hicks,* suppose the defendant deliberately shouted encouragement to Rowe to spur him on to kill Colvard, but it is shown at the trial that Rowe was completely deaf and was, moreover, totally unaware of Hicks's presence.

In *Tally,* what would have been result:

   (a) if the telegraph operator had disregarded the judge's instructions and had tried, though in vain, to deliver the warning telegram?

(b) if the telegraph operator followed the judge's instructions and did not deliver the warning, but the pursuers never succeeded in catching up with their intended victim?

(c) if the pursuers did catch up, but were effectively resisted by their victim?

In the *Hicks* and the first *Tally* hypothetical, there is attempted encouragement or aid to the person who commits the crime, but none in fact rendered. What should be the liability of the defendants? Under the law before the Model Penal Code, there would be no liability. See J. C. Smith, Aid, Abet, Counsel or Procure, in Reshaping the Criminal Law 132-133 (P. R. Glazebrook ed. 1978): "An attempt to counsel . . . does not amount to counselling. Advice or encouragement proffered at the scene of the crime but not communicated to the mind of the principal offender does not amount to aiding and abetting."

These difficulties are avoided by the Model Penal Code, §2.06(3), and the jurisdictions that follow its lead.[4] Defendants in the first and third of the above *Tally* hypotheticals would be accomplices because a person acting with the required mens rea is an accomplice whether the person aids or "attempts to aid" another person in planning or committing the offense. Moreover, §2.06(3)(a)(i) makes solicitation the basis for accomplice liability, and §5.02(2) provides that solicitation is established even if the actor fails to communicate with the person he solicits to commit the crime. In support of its position the Comment to the Model Penal Code observes (Model Penal Code and Commentaries, Comment to §2.06 at 314 (1985)):

> The inclusion of attempts to aid may go in part beyond present law, but attempted complicity ought to be criminal, and to distinguish it from effective complicity appears unnecessary where the crime has been committed. Where complicity is based upon agreement or solicitation, one does not ask for evidence that they were actually operative psychologically on the person who committed the offense; there ought to be no difference in the case of aid.

Note the difficulty introduced in the second *Tally* hypothetical. Here the crime the defendant tried to aid is not committed. Does §2.06(3) cover the situation? How should it be dealt with? As an attempt to be an accomplice (by attempting to aid in the commission of a crime)? The Model Penal Code solution to this problem is sketched in the Comment to §2.06 supra, at 314 n. 46:

> Section 2.06(3) of the Model Code is predicated . . . on the actual commission of an offense by the person aided. Assuming the requisite culpability, one who aids, or attempts to aid, or agrees to aid, is thus liable under this section only if the principal actor actually commits an offense. If the principal actor completes the offense, then a charge for the substantive crime can be made against both him and the accomplice; if the principal actor attempts to commit the offense, then again both may be charged with the attempt.

---

4. See, e.g., Ky. Rev. Stat. Ann. ch. 500, §502.020; N.J. Stat. Ann. §2C:2-6(c); 18 Pa. Cons. Stat. Ann. §306(c); Tex. Pen. Code Ann. §7.02.

Where the principal actor commits neither the completed offense nor an attempt, however, a different situation is presented. The purported accomplice in that situation would not be liable under Section 2.06 because he did not aid in the commission of a crime. His conduct designed to render aid may be criminal, however, either as an attempt (Section 5.01(3)) or, in the case of preconcert, as criminal conspiracy (Section 5.03(1)(b)). In both situations liability for the abortive effort plainly seems appropriate.

3. Complicity by omission. Can a person become an accomplice by failing to act to prevent another from committing a crime? Consistent with the general approach to determining criminal liability for omissions, the Model Penal Code provides that a person can be an accomplice if he has a legal duty to prevent the offense and he fails to do so with the purpose of promoting or facilitating the crime. §2.06(3)(a)(iii). In support of its position the commentary states (p. 320):

> The policeman or the watchman who closes his eyes to a burglary fails to present an obstacle to its commission that he is obliged to interpose. If his purpose is to promote or facilitate its perpetration, a fact that normally can be proved only by preconcert with the criminals, no reason can be offered for denying his complicity. But if the dereliction is not purposeful in that respect, as when it rests upon timidity or inefficiency, it is unduly harsh to view it as participation in the crime.

In what kinds of situations might complicity by omission be found in the absence of preconcert? Consider State v. Davis, 182 W. Va. 482, 388 S.E.2d 506 (1989). The victim, a friend of the Davis family, went to defendant's home to pick up her laundry. When defendant's son attempted to drag her into his bedroom, the victim pleaded with defendant to help her. Defendant told her that he could not help and then stepped out of the way while his son dragged her into the bedroom. Defendant followed and lay down next to her on the bed while his son raped her. The court found that defendant was not a mere bystander: the attack occurred in his home, the perpetrator was his son, and the victim was a family friend. The court held that in these circumstances the defendant's refusal to help, and his presence during the rape, "facilitated and encouraged" the perpetrator's actions. 388 S.E.2d at 512.

Questions: Would the result be the same under the Model Penal Code formulation? Did the father have a legal duty to prevent the rape? Is this a case where silence gives encouragement, as well as consent? For a discussion of these issues in another context, see David Lanham, Drivers, Control and Accomplices, [1982] Crim. L. Rev. 419.

Consider also People v. Stanciel, 606 N.E.2d 1201 (Ill. 1992). Violetta Burgos was charged as an accomplice to murder when her boyfriend, Stanciel, beat her three-year-old daughter to death. Burgos had violated a court order to keep Stanciel away from the child and had authorized Stanciel to discipline the child despite his past and ongoing abusive behavior. Though Burgos did not perform any of the acts that led to her daughter's death, the court ruled that her failure to protect her child from Stanciel rendered Burgos an accomplice to her daughter's murder.

Questions: Would the result be the same under the Model Penal Code? Plainly the mother was here under a legal duty, but is there enough evidence on these facts to support a finding that she acted with the purpose that Stanciel should beat the child to death? Suppose she had not authorized him to discipline the child and had stood by out of fear?

Many cases have held, in accord with *Stanciel,* that a mother can be convicted as an aider and abettor of child abuse for failing to protect a child from abuse by a third party. See State v. Walden, 293 S.E.2d 780 (N.C. 1982); Dorothy E. Roberts, Motherhood and Crime, 79 Iowa L. Rev. 95 (1993). In cases such as these, if a parent's failure to intervene satisfies the actus reus requirement, should she become liable as an accomplice regardless of what her mens rea was? In *Walden,* the court adverted to the mens rea issue, but resolved it as follows (293 S.E.2d at 787):

> [There must be] something showing [her] consent to the criminal purpose and contribution to its execution. But [we] hold that the failure of a parent who is present to take all steps reasonably possible to protect the parent's child from an attack by another person constitutes an act of omission by the parent showing the parent's consent and contribution to the crime being committed.

Question: Is this an adequate resolution of the mens rea problem?

4. Causation by omission compared. In situations like *Stanciel* where a mother fails to save her child from a foreseeable, possibly deadly, beating by her paramour (for example, by keeping the child away from him or by intervening or seeking help), some courts hold her guilty of manslaughter as a principal, rather than as an accomplice of the man. See Palmer v. State, 223 Md. 341, 164 A.2d 467 (1960). The theory is that her reckless failure to discharge her duty to protect her child caused the death, notwithstanding the novus actus interveniens doctrine, which is commonly not invoked in cases of causation by omission. In such jurisdictions, does it make any difference whether the mother is charged as an accessory, as in *Stanciel,* or as a principal, as in *Palmer?* Suppose Stanciel intentionally and cooly killed the child, but that Burgos was only reckless in failing to protect her child from him. Could she be convicted as a principal of first-degree murder on the theory of cases like *Palmer?* Presumably not, because she would lack the mens rea for first-degree murder. But then why doesn't the same objection apply if she is charged as an accomplice to the man's deadly beating of the child, as in *Stanciel?*

3. The Relationship Between the Liability of the Parties

STATE v. HAYES

Supreme Court of Missouri
105 Mo. 76, 16 S.W. 514 (1891)

THOMAS, J. The defendant appeals from a sentence of five years' imprisonment in the penitentiary for burglary and larceny. [Defendant proposed to one Hill that he join him in the burglary of a general store. Hill, actually a relative of the store owners, feigned acquiescence in order to obtain the arrest of defendant and advised the store owners of the plan. On the night of the planned burglary, defendant and Hill arrived at the store together. Defendant raised the window and assisted Hill in climbing through into the building. Hill handed out a side of bacon. Shortly thereafter they were apprehended.] It will be seen the trial court told the jury in [its] instruction that defendant was guilty of burglary if he, with a felonious intent, assisted and aided Hill to enter the building, notwithstanding Hill himself may have had no such intent. In this we think the court erred. One cannot read this record without being convinced beyond a reasonable doubt that Hill did not enter the warehouse with intent to steal. . . . We may assume, then, for the sake of the argument, that Hill committed no crime in entering the wareroom. The act of Hill, however, was by the instruction of the court imputed to defendant. This act, according to the theory of the instructions, so far as Hill was concerned, was not a criminal act, but when it was imputed to defendant it became criminal because of the latter's felonious intent. This would probably be true if Hill had acted under the control and compulsion of defendant, and as his passive and submissive agent. But he was not a passive agent in this transaction. He was an active one. He acted of his own volition. He did not raise the window and enter the building with intent to commit crime, but simply to entrap defendant in the commission of crime, and have him captured.

Judge Brewer sets this idea in a very clear light in State v. Jansen, 22 Kan. 498. He says: "The act of a detective may perhaps be not imputable to the defendant, as there is a want of community of motive. The one has a criminal intent, while the other is seeking the discovery and punishment of crime." Where the owner learns that his property is to be stolen, he may employ detectives and decoys to catch the thief. And we can do no better than to quote again from Judge Brewer in the case above cited, as to the relation of the acts of detectives and the thief when a crime is alleged to have been committed by the two. He says: "Where each of the overt acts going to make up the crime charged is personally done by the defendant, and with criminal intent, his guilt is complete, no matter what motives may prompt or what acts be done by the party who is with him, and apparently assisting him. Counsel have cited and commented upon several cases in which detectives figured, and in which defendants were adjudged guiltless of the crimes charged. But this feature distinguishes them: that some act essential to the crime charged was in fact done by the detective, and not by the defendant, and, this act not being imputable to the defendant, the latter's guilt was not made out. The intent and act must combine, and all the elements of the act must exist and be imputable to the defendant." Applying the principle here announced to the case at bar, we find that defendant did not commit every overt act that went to make up the crime. He did not enter the warehouse, either actually or constructively, and hence he did not commit the crime of burglary, no matter what his intent was, it clearly appearing that Hill was guilty of no crime. To make defendant responsible for the acts of Hill, they must have had a common motive and common design. The design and the motives of the two men were not only distinct, but dissimilar, even antagonistic. . . . The court should instruct the jury that if Hill broke into and entered the wareroom with a felonious intent, and defendant was present, aiding him with the same intent, then he is guilty; but if Hill entered the room with no design to steal, but simply to entrap defendant, and capture him in the commission of crime, and defendant did not enter the room himself, then he is not guilty of burglary and larceny as charged. He may be found guilty, however, of petit larceny, in taking and removing the bacon after it was handed to him. This overt act he did in fact commit. . . . The judgment is reversed, and the cause remanded for new trial.

All concur.

VADEN v. STATE, 768 P.2d 1102 (Alaska 1989): [Fish and Wildlife Protection officers received a tip that Vaden, a local guide, was promoting illegal hunting practices by his customers. They assigned one of their undercover agents, John Snell, to pose as a hunter and to commission Vaden's services. On the hunt Vaden piloted the aircraft and maneuvered it to facilitate Snell's shooting game from the plane with a shotgun Vaden had lent him for the purpose. Snell shot and killed four foxes. Vaden was convicted, as Snell's accomplice, of taking foxes from an aircraft and hunting during closed season, in violation of Alaskan law. On appeal, the Supreme Court affirmed the convictions, rejecting Vaden's argument that because Snell's action was justified in light of the needs of law enforcement (the "public authority justification defense"), no criminal action occurred for which he could be convicted of being an accomplice. The court reasoned that the action of Snell was not justified, but that even if it were, it would not avail Vaden, because the justification would be personal to the agent.[a] The majority also found that no entrapment had been shown and that the actions of Snell, while unlawful, were not so outrageous as to constitute a denial of due process. The dissenting opinion disagreed that the agent's actions were not outrageous, stating:] Here, the state seeks to obtain convictions because of the illegal conduct of its own agents, rather than in spite of such conduct. The state does not ask this court merely to close its eyes to the officers' illegal acts. On the contrary, it asks that we recognize such acts as an acceptable means of providing an element essential to conviction of these defendants. . . .

The accomplice liability charges should fail on another ground as well: the long-standing common law rule that the act of a feigned accomplice may never be imputed to the targeted defendant for purposes of obtaining a conviction. In State v. Neely, 90 Mont. 199, 300 P. 561 (1931), the Montana Supreme Court applied this principle under circumstances akin to those in the case at bar. In *Neely*, a cattle owner employed a detective, Harrington, to "get in" with suspected cattle thieves during an act of cattle rustling. Harrington associated himself with the criminal enterprise, and the crime was carried out. Harrington himself, however, committed the principal offense of purloining the cattle, while the targeted suspect merely stood watch outside the premises and offered various other forms of assistance before and after commission of the offense. The court reversed Neely's conviction as an accomplice to the crime. . . .[5]

The principle enunciated in *Neely*, which has been repeated by numerous courts under a variety of factual circumstances . . . is based in sound reason. It is the general rule that one who aids and abets another in criminal activity is liable

a. See infra page 677. — EDS.
5. Notably, this was not a case in which the court found that the owner's consent to Harrington's taking vitiated the unlawfulness of his acts. Like the majority today, the court in *Neely* concluded that Harrington had exceeded his rightful authority in taking and butchering the cattle. Id. 300 P. at 565. Nonetheless, the court concluded that Harrington's acts, as a feigned accomplice, could not be imputed to Neely.

for all of the "natural and probable consequences" of his accomplice's criminal acts. Thus, the potential for abuse inherent in law enforcement methods such as those employed in the case at bar is substantial. Once an agent has succeeded in persuading an individual to take some substantial act in furtherance of his general criminal scheme, the ultimate liability of the targeted defendant, if any, will depend upon which foreseeable crimes the agent chooses to commit in order to secure convictions against his criminal "accomplice."

In this case, Officer Snell shot four foxes. Vaden, as pilot of the plane from which they were shot, was charged with four separate criminal counts of taking foxes from the air out of season. Had Snell opted to shoot a fifth fox, one more count could have been added to Vaden's indictment. In my view, it is clearly inconsistent with due process principles, and manifestly unjust, that the ultimate criminal liability of a defendant should be made to depend upon the good aim and/or the good intentions of the police officer charged with securing his arrest.

NOTES

1. *Questions.* The dissent invokes the rule that acts of a feigned accomplice may not be imputed to the targeted defendant for purpose of obtaining a conviction against him. This appears to be what underlay the decision to reverse the conviction of the *Hayes* case. But is the situation in the *Vaden* case distinguishable? Snell did shoot the foxes in violation of law, and Vaden did help him do so. How can it be that Snell's motive in violating the hunting laws (to secure a conviction against Vaden) could render Vaden not guilty? In the *Vaden* case there are plausible answers, turning on the public policy of discouraging law enforcement practices that either entrap persons who otherwise would not commit the crime or that are otherwise unconscionable. But the dissent in *Vaden* relies on a principle that applies to all feigned accomplices, not only to law enforcement personnel. If Snell were a private individual with a grudge against Vaden, would the dissent's argument hold up? If not, does that show that the decision in *Hayes* was necessarily wrong? Was Snell a "feigned" principal?

2. *Entrapment.* The requirements of the defense of entrapment by a law enforcement person vary in different jurisdictions. For the Model Penal Code's proposed formulation, see §2.13, Appendix. A review of the law of entrapment may be found in Model Penal Code and Commentaries, Comment to §2.13 at 405-413 (1985).

3. *Public authority justification defense.* Police and other law enforcement personnel enjoy some degree of authority to break the law in the interests of law enforcement. How much is often not clear. Consider the following attempts to formulate this defense.

Section 35.05 of the N.Y. Penal Code provides,

> Unless otherwise limited by the ensuing provisions of this article defining justifiable use of physical force, conduct which would otherwise constitute an offense is justifiable and not criminal when . . . [the] conduct is required or authorized by law or by a judicial decree, or is performed by a public servant in the reasonable exercise of his official powers, duties or functions. . . .

See also Utah Code Ann. §76-2-401:

> The defense of justification may be claimed . . . when the actor's conduct is reasonable and in fulfillment of his duties as a governmental officer or employee.

Questions: Do you perceive any difficulties with these provisions? Would you make them wider or narrower? Compare the materials on Choice of the Lesser Evil, page 860 infra.

NOTES AND PROBLEMS ON THE DERIVATIVE NATURE OF ACCOMPLICE LIABILITY

The derivative nature of accomplice liability is an axiom in the doctrine of complicity: "It is hornbook law that a defendant charged with aiding and abetting the commission of a crime by another cannot be convicted in the absence of proof that the crime was actually committed." United States v. Ruffin, 613 F.2d 408, 412 (2d Cir. 1979); "There must be a guilty principal before there can be an aider and abettor." United States v. Jones, 425 F.2d 1048, 1056 (9th Cir. 1970).

It is important, however, not to construe derivative liability as implying vicarious liability. Accomplice liability does not involve imposing liability on one party for the wrongs of another solely because of the relationship between the parties. Liability requires conduct by the secondary actor — intentional conduct designed to persuade or help — that makes it appropriate to blame him for what the primary actor does. The term "derivative" merely means that his liability is dependent on the principal violating the law. What is at issue is the responsibility of the secondary actor for the principal actor's violation of law. Unless the latter occurs there can be no accomplice liability.

This axiom of accessorial liability has given rise to many problems. To a large extent these problems can be solved by making a failed accomplice guilty of attempt. As we saw, this is done in the attempt provision of the Model Penal Code Section 5.01(3) provides: "A person who engages in conduct designed to aid another to commit a crime which would establish his complicity under Section 2.06 if the crime were committed by such other person, is guilty of an attempt to commit the crime, although the crime is not committed or attempted by such other person." But traditionally (and under the present law of many jurisdictions) this option has not been available, so that the problems persist.

1. The excused principal. In State v. Hayes, suppose that the absence of a "common motive and common design" on the part of Hill was not due to his motive to catch Hayes but to the fact that he was being coerced at gunpoint by Hayes. Would Hayes still not be guilty of burglary?

See Model Penal Code §2.06(2)(a): "A person is legally accountable for the conduct of another person when . . . acting with the kind of culpability that is sufficient for the commission of the offense, he causes an innocent or irresponsible person to engage in such conduct." The drafter's comment states (Model Penal Code and Commentaries, Comment to §206 at 300 (1985)):

> Subsection (2)(a) is based upon the universally acknowledged principle that one is no less guilty of the commission of a crime because he uses the overt conduct of

an innocent or irresponsible agent. He is accountable in such cases as if the conduct were his own. At common law he was considered a principal for such behavior.[a]

2. *Limits of the innocent agent doctrine.* There may be difficulties in employing an innocent agent doctrine even where the mens rea of the defendant and the innocence of the agent are established. These difficulties derive from two sources: Either the statute defines the crime so that it can only be committed by designated classes of persons, or the action prohibited is such that it can only be performed by the person himself and not through the acts of another, what we may call "nonproxyable" actions. These problems are described and illustrated in the following excerpt (Sanford H. Kadish, Blame and Punishment 172 (1987).

It is easy to see the difficulties in applying the innocent-agency doctrine to crimes so defined that they can only be committed by designated classes of persons. If a statute prohibits an officer or employee of a bank from entering false records of transactions, then one who is not an officer or an employee cannot commit the offense. If he helps or encourages a culpable officer or employee to do so, he can be held as an accomplice. As such, his liability is derived from that of the culpable officer or employee. If, however, he dupes an innocent officer or employee into doing so, the absence of a guilty principal precludes accomplice liability. The usual recourse, therefore, is to apply the innocent-agency doctrine on the theory that the instigator has done the prohibited act, using the officer or employee as his instrument. But because the instigator is not an officer or employee, he cannot violate the statute. Thus, in this case, the innocent-agency doctrine would not serve to make him liable.

A second, more elusive difficulty derives not from a legislative judgment to limit the proscribed action to defined classes of persons, but from the nature of the action proscribed. Most criminal actions can readily be committed through the instrumentality of another person: breaking and entering (burglary), taking another's property (larceny), obtaining property by deception (false pretenses), or making and uttering (forgery). But some actions can be done by the actor only with his own body and never through the action of another. I will call these nonproxyable actions. A sober defendant may cause an insensate and disorderly drunk to appear in a public place by physically depositing him there. But we could hardly say that the sober person has, through the instrumentality of the drunk, himself committed the criminal action of being drunk and disorderly in a public place. A defendant may cause a married person to marry another by falsely leading the married person to believe his prior marriage was legally terminated. But the defendant could hardly be held liable for the crime of bigamy, since one does not marry simply by causing another person to marry. A defendant may cause a man to have intercourse with a nonconsenting woman, perhaps by duress or by inducing him to misinterpret the resistance of the woman. But we cannot properly say that the defendant (who might in fact be a woman) has, through the agency of another man, committed rape by having sexual intercourse with a woman against her will. Or, to take a final example, a visitor to a prison who abducts a prisoner could not be said to have committed the crime of escaping from prison by forcing a prisoner to do so.

a. Compare Bailey v. Commonwealth, 229 Va. 258, 329 S.E.2d 37 (1985).

Question: Is perjury a "proxyable" offense? Consider United States v. Walser, 3 F.3d 380 (11th Cir. 1993). Walser was on trial for defrauding the Federal Crop Insurance Corporation (FCIC). As part of her defense, she called Morrow, an FCIC claims specialist who testified about two documents Walser had sent him in her attempt to recover for crop losses insured by FCIC. Partly as a result of Morrow's testimony about the documents, Walser was acquitted on the fraud charges. Subsequently, a federal agent discovered that Walser had backdated one of the documents, so that Morrow's testimony was materially false, as Walser knew, though Morrow did not. Walser was thereupon indicted and convicted of perjury under 18 U.S.C. §1623, which provides:

> Whoever under oath . . . in any proceeding before or ancillary to any court or grand jury of the United States knowingly makes any false material declaration . . . shall be fined not more than $10,000, or imprisoned not more than five years, or both.

Was the conviction proper? Note that Walser could not be convicted on an aiding and abetting theory because Morrow lacked the knowledge necessary to convict him of perjury as a principal. The U.S. Court of Appeals upheld Walser's conviction on the theory that she had violated §1623 as a principal, using Morrow as an innocent intermediary. Is the result sound? Did the defendant make the false declarations under oath?

Federal courts, including this court, have solved the difficulty by interpreting the federal aiding and abetting statute to mean that one is criminally liable as a principal for causing another to commit criminal acts where the other, even though innocent, has the capacity to do so and the defendant does not. See United States v. Ruffin, 613 F.2d 408 (2d Cir. 1979). The federal statute, 12 U.S.C. §2(b) reads: "Whoever willfully causes an act to be done which if directly performed by him *or another* would be an offense against the United States, is punishable as a principal." (Emphasis added.)

3. *The culpable-but-unconvictable principal.* Another class of cases raising questions for the traditional doctrine that the liability of the accomplice follows that of the principal are those in which the principal would be guilty except for a policy-based defense that makes him unconvictable. Consider, for example:

(a) The defendant conspired with and aided another in the commission of espionage, but the latter could not be convicted because of diplomatic immunity. See Farnsworth v. Zerbst, 98 F.2d 541 (5th Cir. 1938).

(b) The defendant aided a principal who has been acquitted on grounds of entrapment. See United States v. Azadian, 436 F.2d 81 (9th Cir. 1971).

There seems little reason to grant the accomplice a defense in these cases just because the principal has a defense, because the grounds of granting the principal a defense are reasons of policy that are inapplicable to the accomplice. But how can convicting the accomplice be squared with the rule that makes the liability of the accomplice turn on the liability of the principal? Consider People v. Eberhardt, 169 Cal. App. 3d 292, 215 Cal. Rptr. 161 (1985). The defendant was convicted of conspiring with his Native American wife to violate the California Fish and Game Code, which prohibited the sale of fish taken from the Klamath River and of salmon taken in California waters by gill net. The defendant's wife was immune from prosecution by the state because federal law preempted the state from enforcing these laws against Native Americans. Over the objection that it takes two guilty persons to conspire, the court upheld the conviction, stating (at 300): "Mrs. Eberhardt['s . . .] immunity from prosecution by the state is not inconsistent with her culpability as a coconspirator, and the fact that she cannot be prosecuted by the state does not amount to a declaration of her innocence."

See Douglas Husak, Justifications and the Criminal Liability of Accessories, 80 J. Crim. L. & Criminology 491 (1989).

4. *Problem.* A number of cases have involved fathers abducting their children from the custody of their mothers with the aid of third persons. The general rule appears to be that absent a custody award, a parent does not commit the crime of kidnapping by taking exclusive possession of his or her child because each parent has an equal right to custody. Assume that in a jurisdiction following this rule a father abducts his child from its mother with the assistance of a third person. What would be the liability of the person who assists the father? Does the answer depend on the rationale for the defense afforded to the parent? If the father's defense is like diplomatic immunity and entrapment, the person aiding him would seem to have no defense. But if the father's defense is treated as a justification, would there be any basis for holding the aider liable?

Consider two kinds of cases. In one, the father does the abduction, with the other person assisting him. In the other case, the other person does the abducting, upon the father's request and acting for him. Should these cases be treated differently? See the various approaches discussed in Stave v. Stocksdale, 138 N.J. Super. 312, 350 A.2d 312 (1975); Wilborn v. Superior Court, 51 Cal. 2d 828, 337 Cal. Rptr. 787 (1959).

5. *The acquitted principal.* We have seen that there can be no guilty aider and abettor without a guilty principal; the situations in the above Notes are possible exceptions to that rule. What happens when the principal has been acquitted? May the accomplice who is subsequently tried raise that acquittal as a defense?

In United States v. Standefer, 447 U.S. 10 (1980), the defendant, the head of Gulf Oil Company's tax department, was prosecuted for providing five separate vacations, at company expense, to one Niederberger, an Internal Revenue Service agent in charge of the audit of Gulf's tax returns. In an indictment involving separate counts for each of the various vacations, defendant and Gulf Oil were charged both with violating 18 U.S.C. §201(f) (making gifts to a public official) and with aiding and abetting Niederberger in violating 26 U.S.C. §7214(a)(2) (acceptance of unauthorized compensation by a government employee). Another multicount indictment charged Niederberger with violations of related statutory provisions in connection with each of the various vacations. Gulf Oil pled guilty to all counts. Prior to the defendant's trial, Niederberger was tried and convicted on some counts but acquitted on counts relating to certain of the vacations. The defendant moved for dismissal of the charges corresponding to those on which Niederberger had been acquitted, but the motion was denied, and defendant was convicted on all counts.

The Supreme Court upheld the defendant's convictions for aiding and abetting Niederberger in the commission of the very crimes for which Niederberger had been acquitted. The Court noted that, under the doctrine of "nonmutual collateral estoppel," a party who has had a fair opportunity to litigate a question of fact in a civil suit sometimes can be precluded from relitigating that fact in a subsequent civil suit. But the Court reasoned that the special rules of procedure and evidence applicable in criminal cases sometimes deny the prosecution a fair opportunity to litigate and prevent correction of an erroneous acquittal. Accordingly, the Court held that the acquittal of Niederberger at his trial should not be given preclusive effect (447 U.S. at 25-26):

> In denying preclusive effect to Niederberger's acquittal, we do not deviate from the sound teaching that "justice must satisfy the appearance of justice." Offutt v. United States, 348 U.S. 11, 14 (1954). This case does no more than manifest the simple, if discomforting, reality that "different juries may reach different results under any criminal statute. That is one of the consequences we accept under our jury system." Roth v. United States, 354 U.S. 476, 492 (1957). While symmetry of results may be intellectually satisfying, it is not required.
>
> Here, [defendant] received a fair trial at which the Government bore the burden of proving beyond reasonable doubt that Niederberger violated 26 U.S.C. §7214(a)(2) and that petitioner aided and abetted him in that venture. He was entitled to no less — and to no more.

Most states now take the same position. See Note, 15 Baltimore L. Rev. 344 (1986).

NOTE ON DIFFERENCES IN THE DEGREE OF CULPABILITY

Does it follow from the derivative nature of accomplice liability that the secondary party cannot be convicted of a crime more serious or less serious than the one committed by the principal actor? Consider the following situations.

1. Regina v. Richards, [1974] Q.B. 776. The defendant, Isabelle Richards, hired two men to beat up her husband. She told them she "wanted them to beat him up bad enough to put him in the hospital for a month." The men accosted Mr. Richards and struggled with him, but he escaped without suffering any serious injuries. Mrs. Richards and the two men were tried on charges of felonious assault, requiring proof of wounding with intent to cause grievous bodily harm, and misdemeanor assault, requiring proof of intent to cause harm, but not necessarily serious harm. The two men were acquitted on the felony charges and convicted on the misdemeanor count. Mrs. Richards, tried as their accomplice, was convicted of felonious assault. On appeal, she argued that her conviction on the felony charge was inconsistent with principles of accomplice liability.

> Mr. Purvis [for the prosecution] has [argued] that a person who did no physical act herself by way of assault should nevertheless be guilty of the graver crime of wounding with intent if it is established that she had that specific intent, although persons who were acting at her counselling and command did not have the specific intent that she had and therefore are not themselves guilty of the graver offence. . . .
>
> Mr. Purvis invites our attention to Smith and Hogan, Criminal Law, 2nd ed. (1969): . . . "The true principle . . . is that where the principal has caused an actus reus, the liability of each of the secondary parties should be assessed according to his own mens rea. If there is no actus reus, then certainly no one can be convicted." [p. 93] . . .

Mr. Purvis says that here one can properly look at the actus reus, that is the physical blows struck upon Mr. Richards, and separately the intention with which the blows were struck. The defendant, he says, is responsible for the blows being struck, the actus reus, because they were struck at her request by the co-accused. If, as Mr. Purvis says is the case, the specific intention of the defendant was different from the specific intention of any proved to be entertained on the part of the co-accused, then it is proper that the defendant should be convicted of the [felony] offence if that specific intention goes so far as to amount to intent to cause grievous bodily harm, although that intention was never in the minds of the persons who committed the acts at her request. We do not take that view. . . .

There is proved on the evidence in this case one offence and one offence only, namely, the offence of unlawful wounding without the element of specific intent. . . . That is the short point in the case as we see it. If there is only one offence committed, and that is the offence of unlawful wounding, then the person who has requested that offence to be committed, or advised that that offence be committed, cannot be guilty of a graver offence than that in fact which was committed.

For those reasons we think that this conviction cannot stand. On the other hand it is quite clear that the defendant was guilty of the offence which was in fact committed, namely, an offence of unlawful wounding. . . . [S]o what this court will do is to quash the conviction that was sustained and substitute a conviction for unlawful wounding.

The House of Lords has said in dicta that *Richards* was in error. Regina v. Howe, [1987] 1 All E.R. 771, 799. For an argument in defense of *Richards,* see Sanford H. Kadish, Blame and Punishment 181-186 (1987). Professor J. C. Smith rejects that argument in Comment, [1987] Crim. L. Rev. 480, 484, but later finds some merit in *Richards* in J. C. Smith & B. Hogan, Criminal Law 150-151 (7th ed. 1992).

2. Suppose that Mrs. Jones, seeking the death of her husband, and knowing he has a weak heart, hires two men and instructs them to assault him and give him a good fright, though not to hurt him badly. They do so, and Mr. Jones dies of heart failure as Mrs. Jones had planned. Because the hired assailants had no reason to believe that their attack was life-threatening, presumably they could be convicted of no more than manslaughter. Would it follow from the *Richards* decision that Mrs. Jones too could be convicted of no more than manslaughter? Is there any analytically sound way to support a conviction for murder? Mrs. Richards' confederates were not innocent agents. Is this also true of Mrs. Jones' confederates?

3. Consider Shakespeare's *Othello*: Iago calmly and maliciously drives Othello into a blind rage and incites him to kill his wife Desdemona, by making Othello believe (falsely) that Desdemona has been unfaithful to him. If Othello would be guilty of no more than manslaughter, should it follow that Iago cannot be convicted of first-degree murder?

Professor Glanville Williams has offered the following argument for permitting the accessory to be held liable for a greater offense than the principal's in a case like *Othello*: "In effect the primary party is an innocent agent in respect of part of the responsibility of the secondary party."[5] He also stated: "If a person can act through a completely innocent agent, there is no reason why he should

5. Glanville Williams, Criminal Law: The General Part 391 (2d ed. 1961).

not act through a semi-innocent agent. It is wholly unreasonable that the partial guilt of the agent should operate as a defence to the instigator."[6] An alternative argument[7] is that the actions of the principal perpetrator (Othello in our example) are not fully volitional. As a result, those actions cannot pose a barrier to our treating the actions of an instigator (such as Iago) as the *cause* of the resulting death. When that is so, there is no difficulty in making the crime each party commits dependent on his own mens rea.

4. How should the responsibilities of the parties be sorted out when the accomplice has a *less* culpable mens rea than that of the principal actor? For example, suppose that an enraged Othello had hired someone else to kill Desdemona. The hired killer, presumably, would be guilty of murder. Does it follow that Othello is also guilty of murder?

In Moore v. Lowe, 116 W. Va. 165, 168, 180 S.E. 1, 2 (1935), a hired killer murdered the defendant's husband at her instigation. The court held that, as an accessory to the murder, the defendant could be convicted of manslaughter. In support of its position, the court quoted 1 Wharton, Criminal Law 363-364 (12th ed. 1932):

> [T]he offense of the instigator is not necessarily of the same grade as that of the perpetrator. The instigator may act in hot blood, in which case he will be guilty only of manslaughter, while the perpetrator may act coolly, and thus be guilty of murder. The converse, also, may be true; the instigation may be cool and deliberate, the execution in hot blood by a person whom the instigator finds in a condition of unreasoning frenzy.... Hence an accessory before the fact ... may be guilty of murder, while the principal (or perpetrator) may be guilty of manslaughter; or the accessory before the fact (instigator), acting in hot blood, may be guilty of manslaughter, while the perpetrator (principal), acting with deliberate malice, may be guilty of murder.

NOTE: MUST THE SECONDARY PARTY BE GUILTY IF THE PRIMARY PARTY IS?

We have been examining cases in which the principal party for various reasons is not guilty of the same crime that the secondary party is charged with helping or encouraging the principal party to commit. We have seen that the secondary party can sometimes be guilty of a different crime in this situation. Consider now cases in which the principal party has committed the crime that the secondary party, acting with the required mens rea, helped or encouraged the principal party to commit. Should the secondary party always be liable where this is so?

1. In The Queen v. Tyrell, [1894] 1 Q.B. 710, a conviction of a minor for aiding, abetting and encouraging statutory rape upon her by an adult was reversed on the ground that the statutory rape law was designed for the protection and not for the prosecution of young girls. The court stated:

> [I]t is impossible to say that the Act, which is absolutely silent about aiding or abetting, or soliciting or inciting, can have intended that the girls for whose protection

6. Glanville Williams, Textbook on Criminal Law 374 (2d ed. 1983).
7. Sanford H. Kadish, Blame and Punishment 183 (1987).

it was passed should be punishable under it for the offences committed upon themselves.

The same reasoning has been applied to victims charged with conspiracy to commit an offense. See Gebardi v. United States, page 774 infra. For further discussion of the victim rule see Glanville Williams, Victims and Other Exempt Parties in Crime, 10 Legal Stud. 245 (1990); Brian Hogan, Victims as Parties to Crime, [1962] Crim. L. Rev. 683.

2. The Model Penal Code contains a provision, followed in a number of states, that a person is not an accomplice in an offense committed by another either if he is victim of that offense or if the offense is so defined that his conduct is inevitably incident to its commission. §2.06(6)(a), (b). The Comment on this provision states (Model Penal Code and Commentaries, Comment to §2.06 at 324-325 (1985)):

> Exclusion of the victim does not wholly meet the problems that arise. Should a woman be deemed an accomplice when a criminal abortion is performed upon her? Should the man who has intercourse with a prostitute be viewed as an accomplice in the act of prostitution, the purchaser an accomplice in the unlawful sale, the unmarried party to a bigamous marriage an accomplice of the bigamist, the bribe-giver an accomplice of the taker? . . .
>
> To seek a systematic legislative resolution of these issues seems a hopeless effort; the problem must be faced and weighed as it arises in each situation. What is common to these cases, however, is that the question is before the legislature when it defines the individual offense involved. No one can draft a prohibition of adultery without awareness that two parties to the conduct necessarily will be involved. The provision, therefore, is that the general section on complicity is inapplicable, leaving to the definition of the crime itself the selective judgment that must be made. If legislators know that buyers will not be viewed as accomplices in sales unless the statute indicates that this behavior is included in the prohibition, they will focus on the problem as they frame the definition of the crime. And since the exception is confined to conduct "inevitably incident to" the commission of the crime, the problem inescapably presents itself in defining the crime.

3. Consider United States v. Doig, 950 F.2d 411 (7th Cir. 1991): Three workers were killed in Milwaukee when a sewage tunnel they were building exploded. Their employer, S. A. Healy Company (Healy), was charged with 12 counts of violating the Occupational Safety and Health Act (OSHA), 29 U.S.C. §666(e) (imposing criminal liability on any "employer" whose willful violation of OSHA causes the death of an employee), by failing to provide the men with adequate ventilation, training, and safety equipment. The tunnel project manager, Patrick Doig, was charged with aiding and abetting Healy's violations by using unsafe electrical equipment on the project, rather than the "explosion-proof" equipment required by OSHA standards. The trial court dismissed the charges against Doig and the appellate court affirmed, noting that OSHA is intended to make employers, not their agents, responsible for workplace safety: "[W]e believe that the affirmative legislative policy placing the onus of workplace safety upon employers precludes finding that an employee may aid and abet his employer's criminal OSHA violation." 950 F.2d at 413. The court also noted that Doig was charged, in essence, with "assist[ing] himself in violating the relevant OSHA standards, because no other individual or natural person was indicted for the offense. . . . [I]t is logically inconsistent to hold a corporation criminally liable because of the acts of its agent, and, at the same time to hold the agent liable of aiding and abetting the corporation." 950 F.2d at 415.

The court noted that the stated purpose of OSHA places the "onus" of safety on the employer: Is this a way of saying that employees are "victims" of safety violations in the same way a young girl is a "victim" of statutory rape? Does this make sense when the employee is managing the site where the violations occur? Is some employee action "inevitably incident" to violations of OSHA standards, as the court suggests Doig's was here?

4. Suppose that the complicity of the secondary party ends before the offense is committed. The law prior to the Model Penal Code proposals was unclear about what circumstances, if any, sufficed to insulate the secondary party from liability. Section 2.06 of the Model Penal Code, followed in many states, requires that the defendant "terminate his complicity prior to the commission of the offense" and either (1) wholly deprive it of effectiveness or (2) give timely warning to law enforcement authorities or otherwise make proper effort to prevent the crime.

Compare N.Y. Penal Code §40.10(1), which requires (in addition to acts of withdrawal and substantial efforts to prevent the crime) that the defendant have acted under circumstances manifesting a "voluntary and complete renunciation" of his or her criminal purpose. These requirements are substantially those proposed by the Model Penal Code for the defense of abandonment of an attempt. See §5.01(4). *Questions:* Are they equally apposite for terminating liability as an accomplice? What situations would be treated differently under the Model Penal Code and New York provisions?

B.   LIABILITY WITHIN THE CORPORATE FRAMEWORK

The two main problems of corporate criminality with which these materials deal are: (1) For whose acts is the corporation responsible? (2) On what ground may corporate officials be held liable for acts of lesser employees?

The first problem involves the rationale of corporate punishment as a supplement or substitute for punishment of the individual actors; it also involves the legal criteria for determining which actions, of which employees and officials, render the corporation criminally liable.

The second problem deals with the *personal* criminal liability of individual employees and officials who act for the corporation. The lesser employees present no special issue; the normal legal doctrines of personal and accomplice liability suffice. The major issue is the individual liability of high officials of corporations who may be accountable in some sense for the actions of lower-echelon employees but may not be liable under the rigorous requirements of purpose or knowledge imposed by the usual doctrines of accomplice liability.

A useful overview of these subjects is John Coffee, Corporate Criminal Responsibility, in Encyclopedia of Crime and Justice 253-264 (1983). There is now a comprehensive, three-volume treatment of the subject by Kathleen Brickey,

Corporate Criminal Liability: A Treatise on the Criminal Liability of Corporations, Their Officers and Agents (2d ed. 1992).

1. Liability of the Corporate Entity

NEW YORK CENTRAL & HUDSON RIVER RAILROAD CO. v. UNITED STATES

United States Supreme Court
212 U.S. 481 (1909)

Justice Day delivered the opinion of the court.

This is a writ of error to the Circuit Court of the United States for the Southern District of New York, sued out by the New York Central and Hudson River Railroad Company, plaintiff in error. In the Circuit Court the railroad company and Fred L. Pomeroy, its assistant traffic manager, were convicted for the payment of rebates to the American Sugar Refining Company and others, upon shipments of sugar from the city of New York to the city of Detroit, Michigan. . . .

The facts are practically undisputed. . . . It was shown that the established, filed and published rate between New York and Detroit was 23 cents per 100 pounds on sugar, except during the month of June, 1904, when it was 21 cents per 100 pounds.

The sugar refining companies were engaged in selling and shipping their products in Brooklyn and Jersey City, and W. H. Edgar & Son were engaged in business in Detroit, Michigan, where they were dealers in sugar. By letters between Palmer, in charge of the traffic of the sugar refining companies and of procuring rates for the shipment of sugar, and the general and assistant traffic managers of the railroad company, it was agreed that Edgar & Son should receive a rate of 18 cents per 100 pounds from New York to Detroit. It is unnecessary to quote from these letters, from which it is abundantly established that this concession was given to Edgar & Son to prevent them from resorting to transportation by the water route between New York and Detroit, thereby depriving the roads interested of the business, and to assist Edgar & Son in meeting the severe competition with other shippers and dealers. . . .

The principal attack in this court is upon the constitutional validity of certain features of the Elkins act. 32 Stat. 847. That act, among other things, provides:

> (1) That anything done or omitted to be done by a corporation common carrier subject to the act to regulate commerce, and the acts amendatory thereof, which, if done or omitted to be done by any director or officer thereof, or any receiver, trustee, lessee, agent or person acting for or employed by such corporation, would constitute a misdemeanor under said acts, or under this act, shall also be held to be a misdemeanor committed by such corporation, and upon conviction thereof it shall be subject to like penalties as are prescribed in said acts, or by this act, with reference to such persons, except as such penalties are herein changed. . . .
> In construing and enforcing the provisions of this section, the act, omission or failure of any officer, agent or other person acting for or employed by any common carrier, acting within the scope of his employment, shall in every case be also deemed to be the act, omission or failure of such carrier, as well as of that person.

It is contended that these provisions of the law are unconstitutional because Congress has no authority to impute to a corporation the commission of criminal offenses, or to subject a corporation to a criminal prosecution by reason of the things charged. The argument is that to thus punish the corporation is in reality to punish the innocent stockholders, and to deprive them of their property without opportunity to be heard, consequently without due process of law. . . . As no action of the board of directors could legally authorize a crime, and as indeed the stockholders could not do so, the arguments come to this: that owing to the nature and character of its organization and the extent of its power and authority, a corporation cannot commit a crime of the nature charged in this case.

Some of the earlier writers on common law held the law to be that a corporation could not commit a crime. . . . In Blackstone's Commentaries, chapter 18, §12, we find it stated: "A corporation cannot commit treason, or felony, or other crime in its corporate capacity, though its members may in their distinct individual capacities." The modern authority, universally, so far as we know, is the other way. In considering the subject, Bishop's New Criminal Law, §417, devotes a chapter to the capacity of corporations to commit crime, and states the law to be: "Since a corporation acts by its officers and agents their purposes, motives, and intent are just as much those of the corporation as are the things done. If, for example, the invisible, intangible essence of air, which we term a corporation, can level mountains, fill up valleys, lay down iron tracks, and run railroad cars on them, it can intend to do it, and can act therein as well viciously as virtuously." . . .

It is now well established that in actions for tort the corporation may be held responsible for damages for the acts of its agent within the scope of his employment.

And this is the rule when the act is done by the agent in the course of his employment, although done wantonly or recklessly or against the express orders of the principal. In such cases the liability is not imputed because the principal actually participates in the malice or fraud, but because the act is done for the benefit of the principal, while the agent is acting within the scope of his employment in the business of the principal, and justice requires that the latter shall be held responsible for damages to the individual who has suffered by such conduct. . . .

It is true that there are some crimes, which in their nature cannot be committed by corporations. But there is a large class of offenses, of which rebating under the Federal statutes is one, wherein the crime consists in purposely doing the things prohibited by statute. In that class of crimes we see no good reason why corporations may not be held responsible for and charged with the knowledge and purposes of their agents, acting within the authority conferred upon them. . . .

It is a part of the public history of the times that statutes against rebates could not be effectually enforced so long as individuals only were subject to punishment for violation of the law, when the giving of rebates or concessions inured to the benefit of the corporations of which the individuals were but the instruments. This situation, developed in more than one report of the Interstate Commerce Commission, was no doubt influential in bringing about the enactment of the Elkins Law, making corporations criminally liable. . . .

We see no valid objection in law, and every reason in public policy, why the corporation, which profits by the transaction, and can only act through its agents and officers, shall be held punishable by fine because of the knowledge and intent of its agents to whom it has intrusted authority to act in the subject-matter of making and fixing rates of transportation, and whose knowledge and purposes may well be attributed to the corporation for which the agents act. [T]he law . . . cannot shut its eyes to the fact that the great majority of business transactions in modern times are conducted through [corporations], and particularly that interstate commerce is almost entirely in their hands, and to give them immunity from all punishment because of the old and exploded doctrine that a corporation cannot commit a crime would virtually take away the only means of effectually controlling the subject-matter and correcting the abuses aimed at. . . .

UNITED STATES v. HILTON HOTELS CORP.

United States Court of Appeals, 9th Circuit
467 F.2d 1000 (1972)

BROWNING, J. This is an appeal from a conviction under an indictment charging a violation of section 1 of the Sherman Act, 15 U.S.C. §1.

Operators of hotels, restaurants, hotel and restaurant supply companies, and other businesses in Portland, Oregon, organized an association to attract conventions to their city. To finance the association, members were asked to make contributions in predetermined amounts. Companies selling supplies to hotels were asked to contribute an amount equal to one per cent of their sales to hotel members. To aid collections, hotel members, including appellant, agreed to give preferential treatment to suppliers who paid their assessments, and to curtail purchases from those who did not.

The jury was instructed that such an agreement by the hotel members, if proven, would be a per se violation of the Sherman Act. Appellant argues that this was error.

We need not explore the outer limits of the doctrine that joint refusals to deal constitute per se violations of the Act, for the conduct involved here was of the kind long held to be forbidden without more. . . . [The court's discussion of substantive antitrust law under the Sherman Act is omitted.]

Appellant's president testified that it would be contrary to the policy of the corporation for the manager of one of its hotels to condition purchases upon payment of a contribution to a local association by the supplier. The manager of appellant's Portland hotel and his assistant testified that it was the hotel's policy to purchase supplies solely on the basis of price, quality, and service. They also testified that on two occasions they told the hotel's purchasing agent that he was to take no part in the boycott. The purchasing agent confirmed the receipt of these instructions, but admitted that, despite them, he had threatened a supplier with loss of the hotel's business unless the supplier paid the association assessment. He testified that he violated his instructions because of anger and personal pique toward the individual representing the supplier.

Based upon this testimony, appellant requested certain instructions bearing upon the criminal liability of a corporation for the unauthorized acts of its agents. These requests were rejected by the trial court. The court instructed the jury that a corporation is liable for the acts and statements of its agents "within the scope of their employment," defined to mean "in the corporation's behalf in performance of the agent's general line of work," including "not only that which has been authorized by the corporation, but also that which outsiders could reasonably assume the agent would have authority to do." The court added:

> A corporation is responsible for acts and statements of its agents, done or made within the scope of their employment, even though their conduct may be contrary to their actual instructions or contrary to the corporation's stated policies.

Appellant objects only to the court's concluding statement.

Congress may constitutionally impose criminal liability upon a business entity for acts or omissions of its agents within the scope of their employment. Such liability may attach without proof that the conduct was within the agent's actual authority, and even though it may have been contrary to express instructions.

The intention to impose such liability is sometimes express, New York Central & Hudson R.R. Co. v. United States, 212 U.S. 481, but it may also be implied. The text of the Sherman Act does not expressly resolve the issue. For the reasons that follow, however, we think the construction of the Act that best achieves its purpose is that a corporation is liable for acts of its agents within the scope of their authority even when done against company orders. . . .

Legal commentators have argued forcefully that it is inappropriate and ineffective to impose criminal liability upon a corporation, as distinguished from the human agents who actually perform the unlawful acts. . . . But it is the legislative judgment that controls, and "the great mass of legislation calling for corporate criminal liability suggests a widespread belief on the part of legislators that such liability is necessary to effectuate regulatory policy." ALI Model Penal Code, Comment on §2.07, Tentative Draft No. 4, p. 149 (1956). Moreover, the strenuous efforts of corporate defendants to avoid conviction, particularly under the Sherman Act, strongly suggest that Congress is justified in its judgment that exposure of the corporate entity to potential conviction may provide a substantial spur to corporate action to prevent violations by employees.

Because of the nature of Sherman Act offenses and the context in which they normally occur, the factors that militate against allowing a corporation to disown the criminal acts of its agents apply with special force to Sherman Act violations.

Sherman Act violations are commercial offenses. They are usually motivated by a desire to enhance profits.[4] They commonly involve large, complex, and highly decentralized corporate business enterprises, and intricate business processes, practices, and arrangements. More often than not they also involve basic policy decisions, and must be implemented over an extended period of time.

Complex business structures, characterized by decentralization and delegation of authority, commonly adopted by corporations for business purposes, make it difficult to identify the particular corporate agents responsible for Sher-

---

4. A purpose to benefit the corporation is necessary to bring the agent's acts within the scope of his employment. Standard Oil Co. v. United States, 307 F.2d 120, 128-129 (5th Cir. 1962).

man Act violations. At the same time, it is generally true that high management officials, for whose conduct the corporate directors and stockholders are the most clearly responsible, are likely to have participated in the policy decisions underlying Sherman Act violations, or at least to have become aware of them.

Violations of the Sherman Act are a likely consequence of the pressure to maximize profits that is commonly imposed by corporate owners upon managing agents and, in turn, upon lesser employees. In the face of that pressure, generalized directions to obey the Sherman Act, with the probable effect of foregoing profits, are the least likely to be taken seriously. And if a violation of the Sherman Act occurs, the corporation, and not the individual agents, will have realized the profits from the illegal activity.

In sum, identification of the particular agents responsible for a Sherman Act violation is especially difficult, and their conviction and punishment is peculiarly ineffective as a deterrent. At the same time, conviction and punishment of the business entity itself is likely to be both appropriate and effective.

For these reasons we conclude that as a general rule a corporation is liable under the Sherman Act for the acts of its agents in the scope of their employment, even though contrary to general corporate policy and express instructions to the agent.

Thus the general policy statements of appellant's president were no defense. Nor was it enough that appellant's manager told the purchasing agent that he was not to participate in the boycott. The purchasing agent was authorized to buy all of appellant's supplies. Purchases were made on the basis of specifications, but the purchasing agent exercised complete authority as to source. He was in a unique position to add the corporation's buying power to the force of the boycott. Appellant could not gain exculpation by issuing general instructions without undertaking to enforce those instructions by means commensurate with the obvious risks. . . . Affirmed.

NOTES

1. The respondeat superior approach. The use of the tort doctrine of respondeat superior announced in the *New York Central* case and developed in the *Hilton Hotels* case is one of the two main approaches to corporate liability in the United States. (The other is the more restrictive doctrine of the Model Penal Code, which is discussed subsequently.) The requirements of liability under the respondeat superior approach have been summarized as follows in Note, Developments in the Law — Corporate Crime: Regulating Corporate Behavior through Criminal Sanctions, 92 Harv. L. Rev. 1227, 1247-1251 (1979):

> Under the doctrine of respondeat superior, a corporation may be held criminally liable for the acts of any of its agents if an agent (1) commits a crime (2) within the scope of employment (3) with the intent to benefit the corporation.
>
> First, it must be proved that an illegal act was committed by an agent of the corporation, and that the agent acted with the specific intent required by the governing statute. Proving specific intent should be the same for a corporation as for an individual defendant, because under respondeat superior, the intent of the offending agent is imputed directly to the corporation. However, since the corporation is perceived as an aggregation of its agents, it is not necessary to prove that a

specific person acted illegally, only that *some* agent of the corporation committed the crime. Thus, proving that a corporate defendant committed the illegal act is in practice substantially easier than an individual prosecution. . . .

Second, to establish corporate liability under the doctrine of respondeat superior, the prosecution must show that the illegal act was committed within the agent's scope of employment. The traditional agency definition limits scope of employment to conduct that is authorized, explicitly or implicitly, by the principal or that is similar or incidental to authorized conduct. However, courts generally find conduct to fall within the scope of employment even if it was specifically forbidden by a superior and occurred despite good faith efforts on the part of the corporation to prevent the crime. Thus, scope of employment in practice means little more than that the act occurred while the offending employee was carrying out a job-related activity. . . .

Third, it must be proved that the agent committed the crime with the intent to benefit the corporation. The corporation may be held criminally liable even if it received no actual benefit from the offense, although the existence or absence of benefit is relevant as evidence of an intent to benefit.[a]

The requirements of scope of employment and intent to benefit the corporation can also be met through ratification. When an employee commits a crime with no intent to benefit the corporation, or while acting outside the scope of his employment, subsequent approval of the act by his supervisor will be sufficient to hold the corporation liable for the employee's criminal act. In a sense, under the doctrine of ratification, a corporation is culpable for approving the criminal act, rather than committing it.[38]

2. *Relationship to tort standards.* *(a)* Is the test of respondeat superior applied in criminal cases the same as that applied in tort suits for compensatory damages? Should it be stricter?

(b) What test of respondeat superior should apply in civil suits against corporations where punitive (exemplary) damages are sought, in addition to compensatory ones? (Courts usually require a showing of outrageous intentional misconduct or at least reckless or wanton disregard of the rights of others for a punitive-damage award.) Some courts apply the same respondeat superior standards for both compensatory and punitive damages. See Clarence Morris, Punitive Damages in Personal Injury Cases, 21 Ohio St. L.J. 216, 220 (1960). A large number, however, apply a stricter standard and require that superior corporate officers either order or ratify the misconduct (id. at 221). See Restatement (Second) of Torts §909 (1965).

On what grounds can a distinction be made between criminal liability and punitive liability in a civil suit? Does it matter that while a criminal penalty is imposed just once, punitive damages may be awarded to a multiplicity of injured

a. "But while benefit is not essential in terms of result, the purpose to benefit the corporation is decisive in terms of equating the agent's action with that of the corporation. For it is an elementary principle of agency that 'an act of a servant is not within the scope of employment if it is done with no intention to perform it as a part of or incident to a service on account of which he is employed.' Restatement of the Law of Agency (2d) §235. . . . Thus the taking in or paying out of money by a bank teller, while certainly one of his regular functions, would hardly cast the corporation for criminal liability if in such 'handling' the faithless employee was pocketing the funds as an embezzler or handing them over to a confederate under some ruse." Standard Oil Co. of Texas v. United States, 307 F.2d 120, 128 (5th Cir. 1962). — EDS.

38. This notion conflicts with the traditional criminal law principle that one is generally not criminally liable for an act merely because he approved of it after the fact. See generally Francis Sayre, Criminal Responsibility for the Acts of Another, 43 Harv. L. Rev. 689, 708 (1930).

plaintiffs, as, for example, in a products-liability case? See the opinion of Judge Friendly in Roginsky v. Richardson-Merrell, Inc., 378 F.2d 832 (2d Cir. 1967). See Annot., 29 A.L.R.3d 1021 (1968).

3. *The case for corporate liability.* Is corporate criminal liability fair, in view of the fact that the loss (that is, the fine and other adverse consequences of conviction) is suffered by shareholders? Is corporate criminal liability useful? Can punishing the corporation add to the deterrent effect of punishing the individual corporate actors? Consider the following observations in Model Penal Code and Commentaries, Comment to §2.07 at 335-339 (1985):

[T]he imposing of criminal penalties on corporate bodies results in a species of vicarious liability. . . . In most cases, the shareholders have not participated in the criminal conduct and lack the practical means of supervision of corporate management to prevent misconduct by corporate agents. This is not to say, of course, that all the policy considerations at issue in imposing vicarious responsibility on a human principal are present to the same degree in the corporate cases. Two fundamental distinctions should be noted. First, the fact that the corporation is the party nominally convicted means that the individual shareholders escape the opprobrium and incidental disabilities that normally follow a personal conviction or even indictment. Second, the shareholder's loss is limited to his equity in the corporation. His personal assets are not ordinarily subject to levy and the conviction of the corporation will not result in loss of liberty to the stockholders. Nevertheless, the fact that the direct impact of corporate fines is felt by a group ordinarily innocent of criminal conduct underscores the point that such fines ought not to be authorized except where they clearly may be expected to accomplish desirable social purposes. To the extent that shareholders participate in criminal conduct, or to the extent that there are unlawful transactions involving the shareholders' holdings, they may be reached directly through application of the ordinary principles of criminal liability.

It would seem that the ultimate justification of corporate criminal responsibility must rest in large measure on an evaluation of the deterrent effects of corporate fines on the conduct of corporate agents. Is there a reason for anticipating a substantially higher degree of deterrence from fines levied on corporate bodies than . . . from proceeding directly against the guilty officer or agent or from other feasible sanctions of a noncriminal character?

. . . If the agent cannot be prevented from committing an offense by the prospect of personal liability, he ordinarily will not be prevented by the prospect of corporate liability.

Yet . . . there are probably cases in which the economic pressures within the corporate body are sufficiently potent to tempt individuals to hazard personal liability for the sake of company gain, especially where the penalties threatened are moderate and where the offense does not involve behavior condemned as highly immoral by the individual's associates. This tendency may be particularly strong where the individual knows that his guilt may be difficult to prove or where a favorable reaction to his position by a jury may be anticipated even where proof of guilt is strong. A number of . . . juries have held the corporate defendant criminally liable while acquitting the obviously guilty agents who committed the criminal acts.

This may reflect more than faulty or capricious judgment on the part of the juries. It may represent a recognition that the social consequences of a criminal conviction may fall with a disproportionately heavy impact on the individual defendants where the conduct involved is not of a highly immoral character. It may also reflect a shrewd belief that the violation may have been produced by pressures on the subordinates created by corporate managerial officials even though the latter may not have intended or desired the criminal behavior and even though the pressures can only be sensed rather than demonstrated. . . .

The case so made out, however, does not demonstrate the wisdom of corporate fines generally. Rather, it tends to suggest that such liability can best be justified in cases in which penalties directed to the individual are moderate and where the criminal conviction is least likely to be interpreted as a form of social moral condemnation. This indicates a general line of distinction between the "malum prohibitum" regulatory offenses, on the one hand, and more serious offenses on the other. The same distinction is suggested in dealing with the problem of jury behavior. The cases cited above involving situations in which individual defendants were acquitted are all cases of economic regulations. It may be doubted that such results would have followed had the offenses involved a more obvious moral element. In any event, it is not clear just what conclusions are to be drawn from the cited cases. In each, the jury had corporate liability available as an alternative to acquittal of all of the defendants. Conceivably, if that alternative had not been available, verdicts against the individuals in some of the cases might have been returned. Thus, it is at least possible that corporate liability encourages erratic jury behavior. It may be true that the complexities of organization characteristic of large corporate enterprise at times present real problems of identifying the guilty individual and establishing his criminal liability. It would be hoped, however, that more could be pointed to in justification of placing the pecuniary burdens of criminal fines on the innocent than the difficulties of proving the guilt of the culpable individual. Where there is concrete evidence that the difficulties are real, however, the effectuation of regulatory policy may be thought to justify the means.

For further discussion of the merits of imposing criminal liability upon corporations, see Jennifer Arlen, The Potentially Perverse Effects of Corporate Criminal Liability, 23 J. Legal Stud. 833 (1994); Brent Fisse, Reconstructing Corporate Criminal Law: Deterrence, Retribution, Fault, and Sanctions, 56 S. Cal. L. Rev. 1141 (1983); John Coffee, "No Soul to Damn: No Body to Kick": An Unscandalized Inquiry into the Problem of Corporate Punishment, 79 Mich. L. Rev. 386 (1981); Note, Economic Inefficiency of Corporate Criminal Liability, 73 J. Crim. L. & Criminology 582 (1982).

4. The Model Penal Code alternative. The Model Penal Code provisions have influenced some state reform. See Model Penal Code and Commentaries, Comment to §2.07 at 340 n. 18 (1985). They represent an attempt to cut back on the traditional scope of corporate liability based on respondeat superior. (Consider whether the *Hilton Hotels* case would be decided the same way under the Model Penal Code.) A critique of the Model Penal Code proposals may be found in Kathleen F. Brickey, Rethinking Corporate Liability Under the Model Penal Code, 19 Rutgers L.J. 593 (1988). Professor Brickey summarizes the Model Penal Code proposals as follows (id. at 596-598):

The Code adopts a trifurcated scheme of corporate liability that draws intersecting lines between acts and omissions, between true crimes and regulatory offenses, and between the operatives who are the "hands" of the corporation and the policy makers who constitute its "mind."

Among the most expansive of the three rules is section 2.07(1)(a), which adopts a broad respondeat superior theory of liability. Under this rule, a corporation may incur liability for minor infractions and for non-Code penal offenses when a legislative purpose to impose liability on corporations "plainly appears," provided that the conduct constituting the offense is performed by a corporate agent acting within the scope of his employment and on behalf of the corporation.

The potential reach of the (1)(a) liability rule is limited, however, by the availability of a due diligence defense. Proof that "the high managerial agent having supervisory responsibility over the subject matter of the offense employed due diligence to prevent its commission" exonerates the corporation from criminal liability.

The second rule of corporate liability pertains to omissions as opposed to acts. Subsection (1)(b) provides that a corporation is accountable for failure to discharge specific duties imposed on corporations by law. Neither the text of this provision nor the comments address the question of whose omission may lead to liability.

The third rule of liability is by far the most restrictive. Under subsection (1)(c), a corporation will incur liability for true crimes — that is, for an offense defined in the Penal Code — only if the conduct constituting the offense is authorized, commanded, solicited, performed, or recklessly tolerated by the board of directors or a "high managerial agent" whose acquiescence to the wrongdoing — by virtue of his position of authority — may fairly be regarded as reflecting corporate policy.

COMMONWEALTH v. BENEFICIAL FINANCE CO.

Supreme Judicial Court of Massachusetts
360 Mass. 188, 275 N.E.2d 33 (1971)

SPIEGEL, J. [Individual and corporate defendants, including Beneficial Finance Co., were convicted of bribing, and conspiring to bribe, state banking officials in order to obtain favorable treatment from the state Small Loans Regulatory Board. The corporate convictions were based on acts committed by employees of the corporation who were neither officers nor directors of the corporation. One of the employees, Farrell, was an officer and director of Beneficial Management Co., a wholly owned subsidiary of BFC. Another, Glynn, reported to Farrell but was on the payroll of Industrial Bankers, another wholly owned BFC subsidiary. Glynn had direct contact with the state officials who were bribed. Farrell supervised Glynn's activities and also chaired an intercorporate meeting at which the bribery plan was adopted.]

The defendants and the Commonwealth have proposed differing standards upon which the criminal responsibility of a corporation should be predicated. The defendants argue that a corporation should not be held criminally liable for the conduct of its servants or agents unless such conduct was performed, authorized, ratified, adopted or tolerated by the corporations' directors, officers or other "high managerial agents" who are sufficiently high in the corporate hierarchy to warrant the assumption that their acts in some substantial sense reflect corporate policy. This standard is that adopted by the American Law Institute Model Penal Code. . . . Section 2.07 of the Code provides that, except in the case of regulatory offences and offences consisting of the omission of a duty imposed on corporations by law, a corporation may be convicted of a crime if "the commission of the offence was authorized, requested, commanded, performed or recklessly tolerated by the board of directors or by a high managerial agent acting in behalf of the corporation within the scope of his office or employment." The section proceeds to define "high managerial agent" as "an officer of a corporation . . . or any other agent . . . having duties of such responsibility that his conduct may fairly be assumed to represent the policy of the corporation."

The Commonwealth, on the other hand, argues that the standard applied by the judge in his instructions to the jury was correct. These instructions, which prescribe a somewhat more flexible standard than that delineated in the Model Penal Code, state in part, as follows:

> [T]he Commonwealth does not have to prove that the individual who acted criminally was expressly requested or authorized in advance by the corporation to do so, nor must the Commonwealth prove that the corporation expressly ratified or adopted that criminal conduct on the part of that individual or those individuals. It does not mean that the Commonwealth must prove that the individual who acted criminally was a member of the corporation's board of directors, or that he was a high officer in the corporation, or that he held any office at all. If the Commonwealth did prove that an individual for whose act it seeks to hold a corporation criminally liable was an officer of the corporation, the jury should consider that. But more important than that, it should consider what the authority of that person was as such officer in relation to the corporation. The mere fact that he has a title is not enough to make the corporation liable for his criminal conduct. The Commonwealth must prove that the individual for whose conduct it seeks to charge the corporation criminally was placed in a position by the corporation where he had enough power, duty, responsibility and authority to act for and in behalf of the corporation to handle the particular business or operation or project of the corporation in which he was engaged at the time that he committed the criminal act, with power of decision as to what he would or would not do while acting for the corporation, and that he was acting for and in behalf of the corporation in the accomplishment of that particular business or operation or project, and that he committed a criminal act while so acting. . . .

The difference between the judge's instructions to the jury and the Model Penal Code lies largely in the latter's reference to a "high managerial agent" and in the Code requirement that to impose corporate criminal liability, it at least must appear that its directors or high managerial agent "authorized . . . or recklessly tolerated" the allegedly criminal acts. The judge's instructions focus on the authority of the corporate agent in relation to the particular corporate business in which the agent was engaged. The Code seems to require that there be authorization or reckless inaction by a corporate representative having some relation to framing corporate policy, or one "having duties of such responsibility that his conduct may fairly be assumed to represent the policy of the corporation." Close examination of the judge's instructions reveals that they preserve the underlying "corporate policy" rationale of the Code by allowing the jury to infer "corporate policy" from the position in which the corporation placed the agent in commissioning him to handle the particular corporate affairs in which he was engaged at the time of the criminal act. We need not deal with the Model Penal Code in greater detail. . . .

[The court then analyzed prior Massachusetts cases concerning vicarious criminal liability and found "a long line of decisions in this Commonwealth holding that before criminal responsibility can be imposed on the master, based on a master-servant relationship under the doctrine of respondeat superior, actual participation in, or approval of, the servant's criminal act must be shown."

The court also noted that this rule was applied in both mala in se and mala prohibita offenses.]

The thrust of each of the cases cited above involving a human principal is that it is fundamental to our criminal jurisprudence that for more serious offences guilt is personal and not vicarious. . . . [But] the very nature of a corporation as a "person" before the law renders it impossible to equate the imposition of vicarious liability on a human principal with the imposition of vicarious liability on a corporate principal. "A corporation can act only through its agents. . . . [C]orporate criminal liability is necessarily vicarious." Note, Criminal Liability of Corporations for Acts of Their Agents, 60 Harv. L. Rev. 283. . . . Thus, the issue is not whether vicarious liability should be imposed on a corporation under the "direct participation and assent rule" of the master-servant cases cited above, but rather, whether the acts and intent of natural persons, be they officers, directors or employees, can be treated as the acts and intent of the corporation itself. For the foregoing reasons, despite the strenuous urging of the defendants, we are unconvinced that the standard for imposing criminal responsibility on a human principal adequately deals with the evidentiary problems which are inherent in ascribing the acts of individuals to a corporate entity. . . .

[The court examined several federal cases, including *New York Central*, 212 U.S. 481, supra page 684, where corporations were held criminally liable for the acts of their employees. Defendants had argued that all the federal cases imposing criminal liability on corporations either involved regulatory crimes in which intent was not an element or, when the crimes charged did require intent, presented situations in which someone high in the corporate heirarchy had directed, approved or acquiesced in the agent's criminal act. The court concluded that the precedents supported corporate liability for intentional crimes even when a minor employee, such as a salesman, had performed the critical acts. The court then addressed one defendant's objection that applying such a rule imposes criminal liability based upon a civil law standard.]

It may be that the theoretical principles underlying this standard are, in general, the same as embodied in the rule of respondeat superior. Nevertheless, as we observed at the outset, the judge's instructions, as a whole and in context, required a greater quantum of proof in the practical application of this standard than is required in a civil case. In focusing on the "kinship" between the authority of an individual and the act he committed, the judge emphasized that the jury must be satisfied "beyond a reasonable doubt" that the act of the individual "*constituted*" the act of the corporation. Juxtaposition of the traditional criminal law requirement of ascertaining guilt beyond a reasonable doubt (as opposed to the civil law standard of the preponderance of the evidence), with the rule of respondeat superior, fully justifies application of the standard enunciated by the judge to a criminal prosecution against a corporation for a crime requiring specific intent.

The foregoing is especially true in view of the particular circumstances of this case. In order to commit the crimes charged in these indictments, the defendant corporations either had to offer to pay money to a public official or conspire to do so. The disbursal of funds is an act peculiarly within the ambit of corporate activity. These corporations by the very nature of their business are constantly dealing with the expenditure and collection of moneys. It could hardly be expected that any of the individual defendants would conspire to pay, or would pay, the substantial amount of money here involved, namely $25,000, out of his own pocket. The jury would be warranted in finding that the disbursal of such an amount of money would come from the corporate treasury. A reasonable inference could therefore be drawn that the payment of such money by the corporations was done as a matter of corporate policy and as a reflection of corporate intent, thus comporting with the underlying rationale of the Model Penal Code, and probably with its specific requirements.

Moreover, we do not think that the Model Penal Code standard really purports to deal with the evidentiary problems which are inherent in establishing the quantum of proof necessary to show that the directors or officers of a corporation authorize, ratify, tolerate, or participate in the criminal acts of an agent when such acts are apparently performed on behalf of the corporation. Evidence of such authorization or ratification is too easily susceptible of concealment. As is so trenchantly stated by the judge: "Criminal acts are not usually made the subject of votes of authorization or ratification by corporate Boards of Directors; and the lack of such votes does not prevent the act from being the act of the corporation." . . .

Additional factors of importance are the size and complexity of many large modern corporations which necessitate the delegation of more authority to lesser corporate agents and employees. As the judge pointed out: "There are not enough seats on the Board of Directors, nor enough offices in a corporation, to permit the corporation engaged in widespread operations to give such a title or office to every person in whom it places the power, authority, and responsibility for decision and action." This latter consideration lends credence to the view that the title or position of an individual in a corporation should not be conclusively determinative in ascribing criminal responsibility. In a large corporation, with many numerous and distinct departments, a high ranking corporate officer or agent may have no authority or involvement in a particular sphere of corporate activity, whereas a lower ranking corporate executive might have much broader power in dealing with a matter peculiarly within the scope of his authority. Employees who are in the lower echelon of the corporate hierarchy often exercise more responsibility in the *everyday operations* of the corporation than the directors or officers. Assuredly, the title or office that the person holds may be considered, but it should not be the decisive criterion upon which to predicate corporate responsibility. . . .

Considering everything we have said above, we are of opinion that the quantum of proof necessary to sustain the conviction of a corporation for the acts of its agents is sufficiently met if it is shown that the corporation has placed the agent in a position where he has enough authority and responsibility to act for and in behalf of the corporation in handling the *particular* corporate business, operation or project in which he was engaged at the time he committed the criminal act. The judge properly instructed the jury to this effect and correctly stated that this standard does not depend upon the responsibility or authority which the agent has with respect to the entire corporate business, but only to his position with relation to the particular business in which he was serving the corporation. Some of the factors that the jury were entitled to consider in applying the above test, although perhaps not in themselves decisive, are the following:

(1) the extent of control and authority exercised by the individual over and within the corporation;[62] (2) the extent and manner to which corporate funds were used in the crime; (3) a repeated pattern of criminal conduct tending to indicate corporate toleration or ratification of the agent's acts. . . .

[The court then considered whether, under the legal standards it enunciated, the conduct of Farrell and Glynn and their relationship to Beneficial sufficed to support the conviction of Beneficial. The conduct of these two individuals presented a problem because neither was formally an employee of Beneficial. The court, after examining the interlocking relationships and the functional identity of the corporate operations (Beneficial and its subsidiaries were all part of the "Beneficial Finance System," a term used by Beneficial to describe its overall operations) concluded that there was "sufficient evidence to support a finding that there existed between defendants Farrell and Glynn and the corporation Beneficial Management a relationship of agency with the corporation Beneficial which empowered Farrell and Glynn to act on behalf of Beneficial in dealing with" the state officials who were bribed.]

NOTES

1. The Supreme Court of Minnesota has upheld the conviction of a corporation for theft and forgery based on the fraudulent activities of its employees in retaining for the corporation rebates intended for the purchaser. State v. Christy Pontiac-GMC, 354 N.W.2d 17 (1984). Stating that it was not "troubled by any anthropomorphic implications in assigning specific intent to a corporation for theft or forgery," it dealt with the evidentiary basis for corporate criminal responsibility as follows (id. at 19-20):

> Criminal liability, especially for more serious crimes, is thought of as a matter of personal, not vicarious, guilt. One should not be convicted for something one does not do. In what sense, then, does a corporation "do" something for which it can be convicted of a crime? . . . If a corporation is to be criminally liable, it is clear that the crime must not be a personal aberration of an employee acting on his own; the criminal activity must, in some sense, reflect corporate policy so that it is fair to say that the activity was the activity of the corporation. . . .
>
> [W]e hold that a corporation may be guilty of a specific intent crime committed by its agent if: (1) the agent was acting within the course and scope of his or her employment, having the authority to act for the corporation with respect to the particular corporate business which was conducted criminally; (2) the agent was acting, at least in part, in furtherance of the corporation's business interests; and (3) the criminal acts were authorized, tolerated, or ratified by corporate management.
>
> This test is not quite the same as the test for corporate vicarious liability for a civil tort of an agent. The burden of proof is different, and, unlike civil liability, criminal guilt requires that the agent be acting at least in part in furtherance of the corporation's business interests. Moreover, it must be shown that corporate management authorized, tolerated, or ratified the criminal activity. Ordinarily, this will

---

62. With regard to a small closely held corporation, in which the individual is the corporation, this factor may be considered somewhat decisive.

be shown by circumstantial evidence, for it is not to be expected that management authorization of illegality would be expressly or openly stated. Indeed, there may be instances where the corporation is criminally liable even though the criminal activity has been expressly forbidden. What must be shown is that from all the facts and circumstances, those in positions of managerial authority or responsibility acted or failed to act in such a manner that the criminal activity reflects corporate policy, and it can be said, therefore, that the criminal act was authorized or tolerated or ratified by the corporation.

2. Commentators have floated a number of alternatives to the Model Penal Code and respondeat superior approaches for dealing with corporate criminality. These alternatives usually involve strategies to influence the internal functioning of the corporation. See, e.g., Christopher Stone, Where the Law Ends 124 (1975) (proposing legally mandated requirements on the way the corporation does its business); John Coffee, "No Soul to Damn: No Body to Kick": An Unscandalized Inquiry into the Problem of Corporate Punishment, 79 Mich. L. Rev. 386 (1981) (proposing that judges impose internal controls on convicted corporations as a condition of probation).

A related group of proposals bases corporate fault on systemic conditions of corporate operation that encourage criminal actions by employees. In a recent study, Jennifer Moore, Corporate Culpability and the Federal Sentencing Guidelines, 34 Ariz. L. Rev. 743 (1992), the theory of these proposals is called "the corporate character theory." In this article the theory is described as follows (id. at 767-768):

> This theory builds on the findings of organizational research by recognizing that corporations shape and control the behavior of their agents not only through direct supervision by high managerial officials, but also through the use of such devices as standard operating procedures, hierarchical structures, decision rules and disciplinary sanctions. . . . [R]ules, structures, policies and procedures are appropriate loci of corporate fault because they are intended to replace agents' decisional autonomy with an organizational decision-making process. Their effect is to create a corporate "culture" or "character" which endures over time and which channels behavior in ways that are in the interest of the corporation. . . . Under the corporate character theory, a corporation is culpable when its policies, structures, or procedures — features of the corporate character — cause its agents to commit illegal acts on its behalf.

An interesting proposal along these lines is described in Pamela H. Bucy, Corporate Ethos: A Standard for Imposing Corporate Criminal Liability, 75 Minn. L. Rev. 1095, 1099-1101, 1145 (1991):

> This Article proposes a standard of corporate criminal liability that uses a new conceptual paradigm for identifying and proving corporate intent. This standard assumes that each corporate entity has a distinct and identifiable personality or "ethos." The government can convict a corporation under this standard only if it proves that the corporate ethos encouraged agents of the corporation to commit the criminal act. Central to this approach is the assumption that organizations possess an identity that is independent of specific individuals who control or work for the organization.
>
> Most of the factfinders' work . . . will occur in the analysis of whether there existed a corporate ethos that encouraged the criminal conduct. The factfinders

should examine the corporation's internal structure to make this finding. Beginning with the corporate hierarchy, the factfinders should determine whether the directors' supervision of officers, or management's supervision of employees was dilatory. Next, factfinders should examine the corporate goals, as communicated to the employees, to determine whether these goals could be achieved only by disregarding the law. The third and fourth factors focus on the corporation's affirmative steps to educate and monitor employees and are more relevant in some fields than others. In highly technical fields where corporate employees daily decide issues involving legal compliance or violation, the factfinders should view the corporation's failure to educate its employees as encouraging criminal acts. In other fields where few corporate employees deal in issues affected by law and regulations, the corporation has a minimal duty to educate its employees and its failure to do so is less relevant. . . . The factfinders should [also] assess . . . how the corporation has reacted to past violations, to further evaluate whether the corporation encourages or discourages illegal behavior. . . .

The . . . corporate ethos standard . . . rewards those corporations that make efforts to educate and motivate their employees to follow the letter and spirit of the law. This encourages responsible corporate behavior. This advantage is in sharp contrast to the Model Penal Code's standard of liability that discourages higher echelon employees from properly supervising lower echelon employees. This advantage also contrasts with the minimal deterrence achieved by imposing criminal liability on individuals within the corporation. Convicting individual agents and employees of a corporation does not stop other corporate employees from committing future criminal acts if sufficient internal corporate pressure to violate the law continues to exist. In such an environment, the agents are cogs in a wheel. Those convicted are simply replaced by others whose original propensity to obey the law is similarly overcome by a corporate ethos that encourages illegal acts. Unless inside or outside forces change the lawless ethos, it will corrupt each generation of corporate agents. The proposed standard of liability addresses this problem by punishing any corporation that establishes a lawless ethos which overcomes its employees' propensity to obey the law.

STATE v. FORD MOTOR CO.

Indiana Superior Court, Elkhart County, No. 5324 (1979)

THE INDICTMENT

IN THE ELKHART SUPERIOR COURT

INDICTMENT IN FOUR COUNTS CHARGING THREE COUNTS OF RECKLESS HOMICIDE, A CLASS D FELONY AND ONE COUNT OF CRIMINAL RECKLESSNESS, A CLASS A MISDEMEANOR

The Grand Jurors of Elkhart County, State of Indiana, being first duly sworn upon their oaths do present and say:

COUNT I

That Ford Motor Company, a corporation, on or about the 10th day of August, 1978, in the County of Elkhart, State of Indiana, did then and there through the acts and omissions of its agents and employees acting within the scope of their authority with said corporation recklessly cause the death of Judy Ann Ulrich, a human being, to-wit: that the Ford Motor Company, a corporation, did recklessly authorize and approve the design, and did recklessly design and manufacture a certain 1973 Pinto automobile, Serial Number F3T10X298722F, in such a manner as would likely cause said automobile to flame and burn upon rear-end impact; and the said Ford Motor Company permitted said Pinto automobile to remain upon the highways and roadways of Elkhart County, State of Indiana, to-wit: U.S. Highway Number 33, in said County and State; and the said Ford Motor Company did fail to repair and modify said Pinto automobile; and thereafter on said date as a proximate contributing cause of said reckless disregard for the safety of other persons within said automobile, including, the said Judy Ann Ulrich, a rear-end impact involving said Pinto automobile did occur creating fire and flame which did then and there and thereby inflict mortal injuries upon the said Judy Ann Ulrich, and the said Judy Ann Ulrich did then languish and die by incineration in Allen County, State of Indiana, on or about the 11th day of August, 1978.

And so the Grand Jurors aforesaid, upon their oaths aforesaid, do say and charge that the said Ford Motor Company, a corporation, did recklessly cause the death of the said Judy Ann Ulrich, a human being, in the manner and form aforesaid, and contrary to the form of the statutes in such cases made and provided, to-wit: Burns Indiana Statutes, Indiana Code Section 35-42-1-5;[a] and against the peace and dignity of the State of Indiana.

[Counts II and III repeat the above allegations in connection with the deaths of Donna M. Ulrich and Lynn M. Ulrich, respectively.]

COUNT IV

That Ford Motor Company, a corporation, on or about the 10th day of August, 1978, and diverse days prior thereto, in the County of Elkhart, State of Indiana, did through the acts and omissions of its agents and employees acting within the scope of their authority with said corporation, recklessly create a substantial risk of bodily injury to the persons of Judy Ann Ulrich, Donna M. Ulrich and Lynn M. Ulrich, human beings, and each of them, to-wit: that the Ford Motor Company, a corporation, did recklessly permit a certain 1973 Pinto automobile, Serial Number F3T10X298722F, designed and manufactured by the said Ford Motor Company to remain upon the highways and roadways of Elkhart County, State of Indiana, to-wit: U.S. Highway Number 33 in said County and State; and said Pinto automobile being recklessly designed and manufactured in such a manner as would likely cause said automobile to flame and burn upon rear-end impact; and that the said Ford Motor Company had a legal duty to warn the general public and certain occupants of said Pinto automobile, namely: Judy Ann Ulrich, Donna M. Ulrich and Lynn M. Ulrich of the dangerous tendency of said Pinto automobile to flame and burn upon rear-end impact; and the said Ford Motor Company did fail to repair and modify said Pinto automobile; and

---

a. This section provides: "A person who recklessly kills another human being commits reckless homicide, a Class C felony. However, if the killing results from the operation of a vehicle, the offense is a Class D felony." Section 35-40-2-2(c) defines *recklessly* as follows: "A person engages in conduct 'recklessly' if he engages in the conduct in plain, conscious, and unjustifiable disregard of harm that might result and the disregard involves a substantial deviation from acceptable standards of conduct." — EDS.

that as a proximate contributing cause of said Ford Motor Company's acts, omissions and reckless disregard for the safety of other persons within said Pinto automobile, including the said Judy Ann Ulrich, Donna M. Ulrich and Lynn M. Ulrich, a rear-end impact involving said Pinto automobile did occur on or about August 10, 1978, in Elkhart County, Indiana, creating fire and flame which did then and there and thereby inflict bodily injury upon the persons of the said Judy Ann Ulrich, Donna M. Ulrich and Lynn M. Ulrich, human beings, and each of them.

And so the Grand Jurors aforesaid, upon their oaths aforesaid, do say and charge that the said Ford Motor Company, a corporation, did recklessly create a substantial risk of bodily injury to the persons of Judy Ann Ulrich, Donna M. Ulrich and Lynn M. Ulrich, human beings, and each of them, in the manner and form aforesaid, and contrary to the form of the Statutes in such cases made and provided, to-wit: Burns Indiana Statutes, Indiana Code Section 35-42-2-2,[b] and against the peace and dignity of the State of Indiana.

A True Bill

The Trial (N.Y. Times, Feb. 17, 1980, §4, at 9)

The Ford Pinto trial may go down as a spirited, but defective prototype for trying a new hybrid in American courtrooms — a case in which a manufacturer is tried on criminal charges for an allegedly defective product. . . .

The state, with the help of volunteer lawyers and law school students, is pursuing its case on a bargain basement budget of $20,000. Ford is spending approximately $1 million on its defense.

Judge Harold R. Staffeldt has insisted from the outset that since this is a criminal case, he would apply "strict construction" rules of evidence. Thus, he will admit only evidence concerning the 1973 Pinto, unless the State lays a "proper foundation" (demonstrating their relevancy) to justify admitting such items as a history of the vehicle's development.

State prosecutors, however, have assumed that [they must] prove recklessness. . . . Critical in this context is what the company knew or should have known before the date of the incident, in addition to information about dates of design and sale.

The 1973 Pinto was the same design as the Pinto sold in 1971 and 1972, prosecutors assert. They argue that crash test results for those models would help demonstrate that their fuel tanks, and thus the 1973 fuel tank, were unsafe and Ford officials knew it.

The State would also like to adduce as evidence hundreds of company documents, from 1960 through 1972, in which the Pinto fuel tank system is discussed. Ford will not authenticate these. But with 20 motions on record to limit admissible evidence, its lawyers have applauded the judge's continued rulings against

---

b. This section provides: "(a) A person who recklessly, knowingly, or intentionally performs an act that creates a substantial risk of bodily injury to another person commits criminal recklessness, a Class B misdemeanor. However, the offense is a Class A misdemeanor if the conduct includes the use of a vehicle or deadly weapon. (b) A person who recklessly, knowingly, or intentionally inflicts serious bodily injury on another person commits criminal recklessness, a Class D felony." — Eds.

the State. Its presentation now completed, the prosecution has been barred from introducing 40 percent of its case into the court record. . . .

THE VERDICT (N.Y. TIMES, MAR. 14, 1980, AT 1:A1)

WINAMAC, Ind., March 13 — An Indiana jury today found the Ford Motor Company not guilty on three charges of reckless homicide in connection with the deaths of three young women in a fiery crash in August 1978 involving its Pinto passenger car.

The verdict, delivered just after noon, came after 25 hours of deliberations over a four-day period. It included a session lasting over 14 hours that ended at 3 A.M. today, with the jury foreman reporting to the court that the group of seven men and five women was hopelessly deadlocked. In a session that began at 10 A.M., the jury reached a consensus of not guilty, ending the 10-week trial.

The state charges against Ford led to the first criminal prosecution of an American corporation in a case involving alleged product defects that led to a death. Only monetary penalties were involved, but nonetheless the case was closely watched nationally because of its implications for the enforcement of criminal as well as civil laws against companies accused of manufacturing and selling defective products that subsequently result in death.

The charges arose after the women were killed when their 1973 Pinto burst into flames after it was struck from the rear by a van north of Winamac. The prosecution charged that Ford and its officials knew that gasoline tanks on the once-popular subcompact Pinto model tended to explode when struck from behind, but did nothing to correct the defect after manufacture. Ford denied the charges, arguing that its vehicles are as safe as its competitors'.

There was conflicting testimony about whether the car was moving when it was struck. Prosecution witnesses, including the driver of the van, said the car was moving at about 50 miles per hour, but a hospital attendant testified for the defense that one of the three women, as she was dying, told him that the car was not moving.

After the verdict was announced, jurors discussed their deliberations, and several said that, while they were convinced that the Pinto fuel tank could not withstand a puncture in a rear-end crash at highway speed and was thus unsafe, they had heard insufficient evidence based on the charges in this case.

[For a study of this case, see L. Strobel, Reckless Homicide? Ford's Pinto Trial (1980).]

NOTE, CORPORATE HOMICIDE: A NEW ASSAULT ON CORPORATE DECISION-MAKING
54 Notre Dame Law. 911, 922-924 (1979)

State v. Ford Motor Co. presents issues which transcend those of existing precedents. Prior indictments of corporations for homicide resulted from acts of corporate agents performed within the scope of employment. The engineer recklessly operating the train or a repairman recklessly installing a gas pipe are examples of the norm. The prosecution of Ford, however, occurs in a completely different setting. Ford's alleged illegal conduct [comprises] three acts: (1) defectively designing the vehicle, (2) defectively manufacturing the vehicle, and (3) allowing the vehicle to remain on the public highways. Each of these acts is the product of a complex business decision. Both the design and manufacture of automobiles are subject to extensive federal regulation. Rigorous testing precedes marketing. Defects discovered after sale to the public may involve recalls, either voluntary or compulsory. Therefore, the Pinto which exploded on August 10, 1978, was the product of many substantial business decisions occurring at various levels of the corporate hierarchy. The deterrent effect of corporate liability for criminal homicide, therefore, must be assessed by the effect of conviction on this decision-making process.

The maximum penalty which can be imposed on a corporation convicted under the Indiana reckless homicide statute is a $10,000 fine. The effectiveness of this sanction as a deterrent to a large, profitable corporation is questionable. . . . Thus, superficially, such indictments appear as futile attempts to impede corporate recklessness when deterrence is the standard of evaluation and "small" fines are the sanction.

The inherent flaw in this analysis is the assumption that the $10,000 fine is the only consequence of conviction. The negative publicity of a criminal conviction is the consequence most likely to deter reckless corporate conduct. A guilty verdict could threaten the fate of a corporation's entire product line by inspiring public mistrust and thereby jeopardizing future revenues. . . . Therefore, the imposition of corporate criminal penalties should deter the instigation of corporate policies that produce incidents such as the Pinto explosion of August 10, 1978, by stimulating greater managerial scrutiny of the design and manufacture of products. . . .

Absent potential criminal responsibility for marketing a defective product, the value of human life is reduced to mere cost analysis. Probability distributions estimating potential consumer deaths and resulting civil liabilities pitted against the cost of adequate safety precautions threaten to become the standard of corporate decision-making. Thus, potential criminal liability provides a prophylactic variable likely to weigh heavily in contemporary decision-making models, thereby enhancing corporate responsibility to consumers.

MALCOLM E. WHEELER, PRODUCTS LIABILITY: MANUFACTURERS, WRONG TARGETS FOR THREAT OF CRIMINAL SANCTIONS? [a]

Natl. L.J. (Dec. 22, 1980)

Even absent the threat of criminal sanctions, manufacturers, in deciding whether to implement any modification affecting product safety, must consider several costs they might incur by producing and selling products that could be made safer. These potential costs include amounts awarded in civil lawsuits for compensatory damages. . . . In any one lawsuit these can total several millions of dollars. . . .

[O]ne might contend that even more deterrence is socially desirable and that the additional deterrence can be efficiently achieved by the use of criminal sanctions. . . .

a. The author was one of the counsel for the defense in the Pinto prosecution. — Eds.

[O]ne might contend that criminal sanctions are needed to deter manufacturers from quantifying the indisputably necessary cost-benefit analysis — that is, from assigning some dollar value to the societal cost of physical injuries and premature deaths.[63] . . . But both the purpose of trying to provide the public with the mix that it wants and the purpose of enabling courts, juries and regulatory agencies to review the decision-making processes of manufacturers will be better served by encouraging — not deterring — a cost-benefit approach that seeks:

(1) to identify, not lump together, all of the relevant factors;
(2) to ascertain the weight the public would attach to them if the public could be as informed as the scientists, engineers and managers responsible for making the products; and
(3) to design and manufacture products that reflect the public's desires ex ante. . . .

Alternatively, therefore, one might contend that criminal sanctions are needed to deter manufacturers from marketing any product that could be made safer by using current technology, irrespective of the cost consumers might have to pay for the added safety. Costs of additional safety might include higher price, lower reliability, shorter useful life, reduced efficiency, higher maintenance or service costs and many others.

[T]his contention, however, ignores the indisputable fact that the public does not want all technologically feasible safety at any cost. Rather, individual citizens constantly choose to risk their own personal safety and the safety of others, including their loved ones, for a variety of reasons, including price, function, convenience, aesthetics, vanity and pleasure. . . .

Thus, if criminal sanctions were to be applied to product manufacturers for marketing products that are somewhat less safe, but somewhat cheaper, more reliable, more durable or better in some other respect, criminal sanctions should be applied with equal vigor to Congress for not lowering the speed limit below 55 mph. . . .

Alternatively, therefore, one might contend that criminal sanctions are needed to deter manufacturers from marketing products that are less safe than the public wants them to be, all factors considered ex ante. This seems to be the proper, non-paternalistic basis on which to try to justify the application of criminal sanctions under a deterrence theory. . . .

In short, the use of criminal sanctions based on a deterrence theory may be desirable where . . . a manufacturer is not sufficiently likely to calculate and internalize accurately the full social costs of manufacturing a particular product.

That, however, serves only to state a theoretical justification for using criminal sanctions to regulate product safety. Several additional questions must be answered before it can sensibly be concluded that such a use of the criminal law is desirable. . . .

---

63. It must be emphasized that the relevant cost that society wishes to cause manufacturers to internalize and use in their cost-benefit analyses is the societal cost of human injury, not the "value of human life" as calculated by a particular person whose life is in issue or by a friend or relative of that person. Many, if not most, persons undoubtedly would refuse to give up their own lives or the lives of their loved ones for any sum of money; but society obviously attaches some finite dollar value to human life by allocating only limited resources to police, fire and health programs, among others.

[I]n most instances in which lay juries historically have been called upon to pronounce conduct to be criminally reckless or not, jurors have been able to draw upon their own wealth of first-hand experience to decide whether the conduct substantially deviates from an accepted societal norm. . . .

But in deciding whether a manufacturer acted in a criminally reckless fashion by, for example, making a car more fuel efficient at the cost of a minuscule increase in the risk of whiplash injuries, lay jurors will have neither common experience nor statutory guidance to assist them in judging the propriety of that conduct under general criminal statutes.

Jurors are more likely, therefore, to be influenced in a product case by a gut-level antipathy — inconsistent with their own daily conduct — to the use of cost-benefit safety analysis. Subjecting manufacturers to that irrational antipathy in a civil suit for compensation is one thing; doing it in a criminal proceeding is quite another. . . .

[T]he deterrent effect of applying general criminal recklessness or criminal negligence laws to product manufacturers is a complete unknown. . . .

Applying criminal sanctions may therefore result in much more deterrence than is socially desirable. Again, to paint an extreme picture, the result may be that manufacturers will produce ugly, fuel-guzzling, expensive, uncomfortable, slow, cumbersome, inconvenient, short-lived automobiles that are difficult to service.

The public's recent mass move to small, fuel-efficient, more dangerous cars designed to deal better with the world oil situation dramatically demonstrates that maximum safety is not the foremost consideration in product purchases.

NOTE

Mr. Wheeler develops his argument further and makes the following observations concerning the costs of the criminal stigma.

Malcolm E. Wheeler, The Use of Criminal Statutes to Regulate Product Safety, 13 J. Legal Stud. 593, 616-618 (1984): The effectiveness of the criminal sanction against corporations depends on the deterrent force of two elements: the fine and the social stigma attending a criminal conviction. Fines themselves usually are small, especially in comparison to multimillion dollar awards available in civil actions, both compensatory and punitive. Fines alone can hardly justify the costs of introducing a novel system of social control. . . .

The criminal sanction therefore must be justified by the stigma it creates. But stigma is a poor way to obtain optimal deterrence. One problem with relying on the criminal stigma to achieve optimal deterrence is that a sentencing judge cannot vary the magnitude of the stigma to meet the demands of the individual case with anything close to the precision with which he can vary the monetary fine. . . .

The impact of stigma is especially difficult to trace in the corporate context, because the firm as such can "feel" only a loss of financial assets or a reduced financial income, whether that loss is imposed directly (as through a civil damages award or a civil penalty) or indirectly (as through sales lost because of customer antipathy resulting from a criminal stigma). Therefore, the desired deterrent effect of the stigma must be to stigmatize indirectly the employees, directors, and shareholders of the manufacturer, and thereby to deter them and persons in parallel positions in all other manufacturing corporations. . . . This intentional indiscriminate sanction against all employees dramatizes one of the most heavily criticized concepts of an instrumentalist theory of punishment: the idea that any number of wholly innocent moral agents can properly be punished for the benefit of society as a whole.

Phillip Cook, The Use of Criminal Sanctions to Regulate Product Safety: Comment on Wheeler, 13 J. Legal Stud. 619 (1984): [Cook replies to Mr. Wheeler's article and makes the following point concerning Wheeler's argument that compensatory remedies provide all the deterrence that is needed (id. at 621):] A well-functioning tort system will force manufacturers to take account of the expected costs to victims of defective products and to adjust their designs and operating procedures accordingly. In the case of manufacturer error, the victims will sue and receive full compensation. The liability rule serves to protect the consumers' entitlement to be free from hazardous products. But there is a different perspective, frequently expressed in political rhetoric and written into health and safety legislation, from which the liability rule is not sufficient protection. Indeed, any legislation or regulation ordering that a product meet certain minimum safety standards is in effect denying consumers the right to "sell" their entitlement to be free from hazardous products (in exchange for, say, a lower product price). This entitlement is thus protected by an inalienability rule. The manufacture and sale of a defective product not only harms the immediate victim, but also damages society at large by violating (and hence weakening) the system of rules for protecting entitlements, and in particular the inalienable right to be free from defective products. Posner asserts that a liability rule is an inadequate protection against theft, even in a world where all thieves were easily caught and possessed adequate assets to compensate the victim, because we would prefer the transfer price to be set by mutual voluntary agreement rather than by court order; the theft is a violation of the rules protecting property. Similarly, some may assert that a liability rule is an inadequate protection against defective products because there is *no* appropriate transfer price for personal safety.

Corporate liability for homicidal crimes is further explored in the following: Celia Wells, Corporations and Criminal Responsibility (1993); Michael B. Bixby, Workplace Homicide: Trends, Issues, and Policy, 70 Or. L. Rev. 333 (1991); Comment (Donald J. Miester, Jr.), Criminal Liability for Corporations That Kill, 64 Tul. L. Rev. 919 (1990); Kathleen Brickey, Death in the Workplace: Corporate Liability for Criminal Homicide, 2 Notre Dame J. L. Ethics & Pub. Pol. 753 (1987).

On the *Pinto* case in particular, see F. Cullen, Corporate Crime Under Attack: The Ford Pinto Case and Beyond (1987).

2.   *Liability of Corporate Agents*

INTRODUCTORY NOTE

Personal liability of corporate officers and agents has not been much affected by the conceptual concerns that hindered development of criminal liability of the corporate entity. One argument against criminal liability was that corporate agents should not be criminally liable for their actions when they acted for the corporation in a representative capacity. But this argument never drew much support in the case law. See 3A W. Fletcher, Encyclopedia of the Law of Private Corporations §1348, at 630 (1975); Note, Individual Liability of Agents for Corporate Crime under the Proposed Federal Criminal Code, 31 Vand. L. Rev. 965, 971 (1978). The prevailing view is reflected in §2.07(6) of the Model Penal Code:

> (a) A person is legally accountable for any conduct he performs or causes to be performed in the name of the corporation or an unincorporated association or in its behalf to the same extent as if it were performed in his own name or behalf.
> (b) Whenever a duty to act is imposed by law upon a corporation or an unincorporated association, any agent of the corporation or association having primary responsibility for the discharge of the duty is legally accountable for reckless omission to perform the required act to the same extent as if the duty were imposed by law directly upon himself.

A major problem in seeking to impose criminal liability on individual corporate actors derives from the bureaucratic arrangement of corporate activities, with lower employees responsible to higher-level employees in a hierarchy leading up to the highest officers. This arrangement often makes it difficult to fasten liability upon the upper-echelon employees and officers under the prevailing standards of accomplice liability requiring intentional aiding or encouraging criminal conduct of another, for these doctrines are designed for personal rather than bureaucratic relationships. The doctrine of vicarious liability would be one solution, but its use entails potential unfairness and injustice. The materials that follow explore these problems.

GORDON v. UNITED STATES

United States Court of Appeals, 10th Circuit
203 F.2d 248 (1953), rev'd, *347 U.S. 909 (1954)*

[Defendant partners in a sewing-machine and appliance business were convicted of violating the Defense Production Act by selling sewing machines on credit terms prohibited by that act and regulations issued thereunder. Section 601 provided that any person who "willfully" violated its provisions or any regulation or order issued thereunder should upon conviction be punished as therein specified. The case was not submitted to the jury on the question whether the partners had actual notice of the transactions. Instead, it was tried and submitted on the theory that knowledge of one partner regarding the transactions was "imputable, attributable and chargeable" to the other and that the knowledge and acts of the salespeople who made the sales and kept the records while acting in the course of their employment were imputable and chargeable to the employing partners. On the "very perplexing question whether the partners can be held criminally responsible for the knowledge and acts of their agents and employees, who the evidence shows, while acting in the course of their employment, actually made the sales without having collected the required down payment," the court, per MURRAH, J., answered in the affirmative, stating:]

Deeply rooted in our criminal jurisprudence is the notion that criminal guilt is personal to the accused; that wilfulness or a guilty mind is an essential ingredient of a punishable offense, and that one cannot intend an act in which he did not consciously participate, acquiesce, or have guilty knowledge. Morissette v. United States, 342 U.S. 246.

Amenable to this notion, the courts have been reluctant to hold the master or the employer criminally responsible for the acts of his agent or employee which he did not authorize, counsel, advise, approve or ratify.

It is only in the so-called public welfare offenses usually involving police regulation of food, drink and drugs that the courts have relaxed the necessity for proof of a wilful intent.

In our case wilfulness is specifically made a prerequisite to guilt. Indeed it is the gist of the offenses charged in all of the counts in the information. And the trial court instructed the jury that in every crime or public offense there must be a "union or joint operation of act and intent" but "that the intent or intention is manifest by the circumstances connected with the offense as well as by direct testimony."

What the court did in effect was to make wilfulness an essential element of the offenses charged in the information, and to charge the employers with the guilty knowledge and acts of the employees in determining the question of wilfulness. . . .

The effect of this is not to dispense with wilfulness or guilty knowledge as an element of the offense. It is to charge the employer with knowledge of records he is required to keep and acts he is required or forbidden to do, and which he necessarily keeps, does or omits to do by and through his agents and employees. To be sure, the knowledge with which he is charged is not direct; it is constructive. If it be called vicarious responsibility, it is nevertheless a responsibility of him on whom the law places the duty. It is permissible proof of a wilfulness which in its proper context denotes more than mere negligence but less than bad purpose or evil motive. It connotes a course of conduct which may be construed by the triers of facts as deliberate and voluntary, hence intentional; or it may be construed as negligent, inadvertent and excusable. The act or omission itself is not inexorably penalized. The ultimate question of guilt is left to the ameliorating influence of those who sit in judgment. Considered in this light, we do not think the instructions of the court fall short of the traditional standards for guilt.

Huxman, J. dissenting: . . . The partners denied intent to violate the law or any knowledge that their employees were violating it. They were entitled to have their testimony weighed and evaluated under proper instructions by the court together with all other relevant evidence. They were entitled to have the jury told that they were not criminally liable for the acts of their employees, although committed within the scope of their employment, unless they directed such activities or had guilty knowledge thereof. It is a principle embedded in the English law from time immemorial that the sins of the father shall not be visited upon the son merely because the father is the agent of the son and his unlawful acts were committed within the scope of his employment, under a criminal statute making wilfulness an element of the offense when the son had no knowledge of or part in such violations.

Strong reliance is placed upon Inland Freight Lines v. United States, 191 F.2d 313, by this court. But that case is clearly distinguishable. There the sole defendant was the corporation charged with keeping false records and it was held that the knowledge of its agents was the knowledge of the corporation. That is the well established principle of criminal law as applied in the case of a corporation. It is, as the law recognizes, the only way a corporation can be held criminally responsible for violations of penal statutes. While a corporation is recognized as a separate legal entity, such separate entity is a pure fiction of the law. As a separate entity and aside from its agents and employees a corporation can do nothing. It has no conscience, will, or power of thought. It acts only through its agents. Their acts are the only acts it can commit and their knowledge of necessity is the only knowledge it can have.

The only cases in which a principal without actual intent or knowledge of criminal acts of wrong-doing by his employees has been held criminally responsible for such acts arose under welfare statutes such as the Pure Food and Drug Laws, Liquor Laws and Weight and Measure Acts. But under all of these acts where a principal was held guilty because of the acts of his agents without knowledge or intent on his part wilfulness was not an element of the offense and the statute made the doing of the act the offense.

NOTE

The United States Supreme Court granted certiorari and reversed the Tenth Circuit's decision in *Gordon* in the following per curiam opinion (347 U.S. 909, 909 (1954)):

> Petitioners are business partners in the sale of appliances. They were convicted under Section 603 of the Defense Production Act of 1950 . . . which provides that "Any person who willfully violates" regulations promulgated under the Act shall be guilty of crime. The jury was instructed that the knowledge of petitioners' employees was chargeable to petitioners in determining petitioners' willfulness. Because of the instruction, the government has confessed error. We agree, and accordingly reverse the judgment and remand the case to the district court for retrial.

Four years later, the Supreme Court held a partnership liable for the "knowing and willful" violation of the Motor Carrier Act, 18 U.S.C. §835, 49 U.S.C. §332(a), based on the conduct of an employee, and distinguished *Gordon* by explaining, "here the government does not seek to hold the individual partners, but only the partnership as an entity." United States v. A & P Trucking Co., 358 U.S. 121, 126 (1958).

UNITED STATES v. PARK

Supreme Court of the United States
421 U.S. 658 (1975)

CHIEF JUSTICE BURGER delivered the opinion of the Court. . . .

Acme Markets, Inc., is a national retail food chain with approximately 36,000 employees, 874 retail outlets, 12 general warehouses, and four special ware houses. Its headquarters, including the office of the president, respondent Park, who is chief executive officer of the corporation, are located in Philadelphia, Pa. In a five-count information filed in the United States District Court for the District of Maryland, the Government charged Acme and respondent with violations of the Federal Food, Drug, and Cosmetic Act. Each count of the information alleged that the defendants had received food that had been shipped in interstate commerce and that, while the food was being held for sale in Acme's Baltimore warehouse following shipment in interstate commerce, they caused it to be held in a building accessible to rodents and to be exposed to contamination by rodents. These acts were alleged to have resulted in the food's being adulterated within the meaning of 21 U.S.C. §§342(a)(3) and (4),[1] in violation of 21 U.S.C. §331(k).[2]

Acme pleaded guilty to each count of the information. Respondent pleaded not guilty. The evidence at trial demonstrated that in April 1970 the Food and Drug Administration (FDA) advised respondent by letter of insanitary conditions in Acme's Philadelphia warehouse. In 1971 the FDA found that similar conditions existed in the firm's Baltimore warehouse. An FDA consumer safety officer testified concerning evidence of rodent infestation and other insanitary conditions discovered during a 12-day inspection of the Baltimore warehouse in November and December 1971. He also related that a second inspection of the warehouse had been conducted in March 1972. On that occasion the inspectors found that there had been improvement in the sanitary conditions, but that "there was still evidence of rodent activity in the building and in the warehouses and we found some rodent-contaminated lots of food items."

The Government also presented testimony by the Chief of Compliance of the FDA's Baltimore office, who informed respondent by letter of the conditions at the Baltimore warehouse after the first inspection.[6] There was testimony by

---

1. Section 402 of the Act, 21 U.S.C. §342, provides in pertinent part:

A food shall be deemed to be adulterated —
(a) . . . (3) if it consists in whole or in part of any filthy, putrid, or decomposed substance, or if it is otherwise unfit for food; or (4) if it has been prepared, packed, or held under insanitary conditions whereby it may have become contaminated with filth, or whereby it may have been rendered injurious to health. . . .

2. Section 301 of the Act, 21 U.S.C. §331, provides in pertinent part:

The following acts and the causing thereof are prohibited: . . .
(k) The alteration, mutilation, destruction, obliteration, or removal of the whole or any part of the labeling of, or the doing of any other act with respect to, a food, drug, device, or cosmetic, if such act is done while such article is held for sale (whether or not the first sale) after shipment in interstate commerce and results in such article being adulterated or misbranded.

6. The letter, dated January 27, 1972, included the following:

We note with much concern that the old and new warehouse areas used for food storage were actively and extensively inhabited by live rodents. Of even more concern was the observation that such reprehensible conditions obviously existed for a prolonged period of time without any detection, or were completely ignored. . . .
  We trust this letter will serve to direct your attention to the seriousness of the problem and formally advise you of the urgent need to initiate whatever measures are necessary to prevent recurrence and ensure compliance with the law.

Acme's Baltimore division vice president, who had responded to the letter on behalf of Acme and respondent and who described the steps taken to remedy the insanitary conditions discovered by both inspections. The Government's final witness, Acme's vice president for legal affairs and assistant secretary, identified respondent as the president and chief executive officer of the company and read a bylaw prescribing the duties of the chief executive officer.[7] He testified that respondent functioned by delegating "normal operating duties," including sanitation, but that he retained "certain things, which are the big, broad, principles of the operation of the company," and had "the responsibility of seeing that they all work together." . . .

Respondent was the only defense witness. He testified that, although all of Acme's employees were in a sense under his general direction, the company had an "organizational structure for responsibilities for certain functions" according to which different phases of its operation were "assigned to individuals who, in turn, have staff and departments under them." He identified those individuals responsible for sanitation, and related that upon receipt of the January 1972 FDA letter, he had conferred with the vice president for legal affairs, who informed him that the Baltimore division vice president "was investigating the situation immediately and would be taking corrective action and would be preparing a summary of the corrective action to reply to the letter." Respondent stated that he did not "believe there was anything [he] could have done more constructively than what [he] found was being done."

On cross-examination, respondent conceded that providing sanitary conditions for food offered for sale to the public was something that he was "responsible for in the entire operation of the company," and he stated that it was one of many phases of the company that he assigned to "dependable subordinates." Respondent was asked about and, over the objections of his counsel, admitted receiving, the April 1970 letter addressed to him from the FDA regarding insanitary conditions at Acme's Philadelphia warehouse. He acknowledged that, with the exception of the division vice president, the same individuals had responsibility for sanitation in both Baltimore and Philadelphia. Finally, in response to questions concerning the Philadelphia and Baltimore incidents, respondent admitted that the Baltimore problem indicated the system for handling sanitation "wasn't working perfectly" and that as Acme's chief executive officer he was responsible for "any result which occurs in our company."

At the close of the evidence, respondent's renewed motion for a judgment of acquittal was denied. The relevant portion of the trial judge's instructions to the jury challenged by respondent is set out in the margin.[9] Respondent's counsel

7. The bylaw provided in pertinent part:

   The Chairman of the board of directors or the president shall be the chief executive officer of the company as the board of directors may from time to time determine. He shall, subject to the board of directors, have general and active supervision of the affairs, business, offices and employees of the company. . . .
   He shall, from time to time, in his discretion or at the order of the board, report the operations and affairs of the company. He shall also perform such other duties and have such other powers as may be assigned to him from time to time by the board of directors.

9. "In order to find the Defendant guilty on any count of the Information, you must find beyond a reasonable doubt on each count. . . .
   "Thirdly, that John R. Park held a position of authority in the operation of the business of Acme Markets, Incorporated.

objected to the instructions on the ground that they failed fairly to reflect our decision in United States v. Dotterweich, [320 U.S. 277 (1943)], and to define "'responsible relationship.'" The trial judge overruled the objection. The jury found respondent guilty on all counts of the information, and he was subsequently sentenced to pay a fine of $50 on each count.[10]

The Court of Appeals reversed the conviction and remanded for a new trial. That court viewed the Government as arguing "that the conviction may be predicated solely upon a showing that [respondent] was the President of the offending corporation," and it stated that as "a general proposition, some act of commission or omission is an essential element of every crime." It reasoned that, although our decision in United States v. Dotterweich had construed the statutory provisions under which respondent was tried to dispense with the traditional element of "'awareness of some wrongdoing,'" the Court had not construed them as dispensing with the element of "wrongful action." The Court of Appeals concluded that the trial judge's instructions "might well have left the jury with the erroneous impression that Park could be found guilty in the absence of 'wrongful action' on his part," and that proof of this element was required by due process. It . . . directed that on retrial the jury be instructed as to "wrongful action," which might be "gross negligence and inattention in discharging . . . corporate duties and obligations or any of a host of other acts of commission or omission which would 'cause' the contamination of food." . . .

The question presented by the Government's petition for certiorari in United States v. Dotterweich, supra, and the focus of this Court's opinion, was whether "the manager of a corporation, as well as the corporation itself, may be prosecuted under the Federal Food, Drug, and Cosmetic Act of 1938 for the introduction of misbranded and adulterated articles into interstate commerce." In Dotterweich, a jury had disagreed as to the corporation, a jobber purchasing drugs from manufacturers and shipping them in interstate commerce under its own label, but had convicted Dotterweich, the corporation's president and general manager. The Court of Appeals reversed the conviction on the ground that only the drug dealer, whether corporation or individual, was subject to the criminal provisions of the Act, and that where the dealer was a corporation, an individual connected therewith might be held personally only if he was operating the corporation "as his 'alter ego.'"

"However, you need not concern yourselves with the first two elements of the case. The main issue for your determination is only with the third element, whether the Defendant held a position of authority and responsibility in the business of Acme Markets. . . .

"The statute makes individuals, as well as corporations, liable for violations. An individual is liable if it is clear, beyond a reasonable doubt, that the elements of the adulteration of the food as to travel in interstate commerce are present. As I have instructed you in this case, they are, and that the individual had a responsible relation to the situation, even though he may not have participated personally.

"The individual is or could be liable under the statute, even if he did not consciously do wrong. However, the fact that the Defendant is pres[id]ent and is a chief executive officer of the Acme Markets does not require a finding of guilt. Though, he need not have personally participated in the situation, he must have had a responsible relationship to the issue. The issue is, in this case, whether the Defendant, John R. Park, by virtue of his position in the company, had a position of authority and responsibility in the situation out of which these charges arose."

10. Sections 303(a) and (b) of the Act, 21 U.S.C. §§333(a) and (b), provide:

(a) Any person who violates a provision of section 331 of this title shall be imprisoned for not more than one year or fined not more than $1,000, or both. . . .

In reversing the judgment of the Court of Appeals and reinstating Dotterweich's conviction, this Court looked to the purposes of the Act and noted that
they "touch phases of the lives and health of people which, in the circumstances
of modern industrialism, are largely beyond self-protection." It observed that
the Act is of "a now familiar type" which "dispenses with the conventional requirement for criminal conduct — awareness of some wrongdoing. In the interest of the larger good it puts the burden of acting as hazard upon a person
otherwise innocent but standing in responsible relation to a public danger."

Central to the Court's conclusion that individuals other than proprietors are
subject to the criminal provisions of the Act was the reality that "the only way in
which a corporation can act is through the individuals who act on its behalf." . . .

At the same time, however, the Court was aware of the concern which was the
motivating factor in the Court of Appeals' decision, that literal enforcement
"might operate too harshly by sweeping within its condemnation any person
however remotely entangled in the proscribed shipment." A limiting principle,
in the form of "settled doctrines of criminal law" defining those who "are responsible for the commission of a misdemeanor," was available. In this context,
the Court concluded, those doctrines dictated that the offense was committed
"by all who . . . have . . . a responsible share in the furtherance of the transaction
which the statute outlaws."

The Court recognized that, because the Act dispenses with the need to prove
"consciousness of wrongdoing," it may result in hardship even as applied to
those who share "responsibility in the business process resulting in" a violation.
It regarded as "too treacherous" an attempt "to define or even to indicate by
way of illustration the class of employees which stands in such a responsible
relation." The question of responsibility, the Court said, depends "on the
evidence produced at the trial and its submission — assuming the evidence warrants it — to the jury under appropriate guidance." The Court added: "In such
matters the good sense of prosecutors, the wise guidance of trial judges, and the
ultimate judgment must be trusted." . . .

Dotterweich and the cases which have followed reveal that in providing sanctions which reach and touch the individuals who execute the corporate mission
— and this is by no means necessarily confined to a single corporate agent
or employee — the Act imposes not only a positive duty to seek out and remedy violations when they occur but also, and primarily, a duty to implement measures that will insure that violations will not occur. The requirements of foresight
and vigilance imposed on responsible corporate agents are beyond question demanding, and perhaps onerous, but they are no more stringent than the public
has a right to expect of those who voluntarily assume positions of authority in
business enterprises whose services and products affect the health and well-
being of the public that supports them. Cf. Wasserstrom, Strict Liability in the
Criminal Law, 12 Stan. L. Rev. 731, 741-745 (1960).

The Act does not, as we observed in *Dotterweich*, make criminal liability turn
on "awareness of some wrongdoing" or "conscious fraud." The duty imposed
by Congress on responsible corporate agents is, we emphasize, one that requires
the highest standard of foresight and vigilance, but the Act, in its criminal aspect, does not require that which is objectively impossible. The theory upon
which responsible corporate agents are held criminally accountable for "causing" violations of the Act permits a claim that a defendant was "powerless" to

prevent or correct the violation to "be raised defensively at a trial on the merits." United States v. Wiesenfeld Warehouse Co., 376 U.S. 86, 91 (1964). If such a claim is made, the defendant has the burden of coming forward with evidence, but this does not alter the Government's ultimate burden of proving beyond a reasonable doubt the defendant's guilt, including his power, in light of the duty imposed by the Act, to prevent or correct the prohibited condition. Congress has seen fit to enforce the accountability of responsible corporate agents dealing with products which may affect the health of consumers by penal sanctions cast in rigorous terms, and the obligation of the courts is to give them effect so long as they do not violate the Constitution.

We cannot agree with the Court of Appeals that it was incumbent upon the District court to instruct the jury that the Government had the burden of establishing "wrongful action" in the sense in which the Court of Appeals used that phrase. The concept of a "reasonable relationship" to, or a "reasonable share" in, a violation of the Act indeed imports some measure of blameworthiness; but it is equally clear that the Government establishes a prima facie case when it introduces evidence sufficient to warrant a finding by the trier of the facts that the defendant had, by reason of his position in the corporation, responsibility and authority either to prevent in the first instance, or promptly to correct, the violation complained of, and that he failed to do so. . . .

Reading the entire charge satisfies us that the jury's attention was adequately focused on the issue of respondent's authority with respect to the conditions that formed the basis of the alleged violations. Viewed as a whole, the charge did not permit the jury to find guilt solely on the basis of respondent's position in the corporation. . . .

Reversed.

Justice Stewart, with whom Justice Marshall and Justice Powell join, dissenting.

Although agreeing with much of what is said in the Court's opinion, I dissent from the opinion and judgment, because the jury instructions in this case were not consistent with the law as the Court today expounds it.

As I understand the Court's opinion, it holds that in order to sustain a conviction under §301(k) of the Federal Food, Drug, and Cosmetic Act the prosecution must at least show that by reason of an individual's corporate position and responsibilities, he had a duty to use care to maintain the physical integrity of the corporation's food products. A jury may then draw the inference that when the food is found to be in such condition as to violate the statute's prohibitions, that condition was "caused" by a breach of the standard of care imposed upon the responsible official. This is the language of negligence, and I agree with it.

To affirm this conviction, however, the Court must approve the instructions given to the members of the jury who were entrusted with determining whether the respondent was innocent or guilty. Those instructions did not conform to the standards that the Court itself sets out today.

The trial judge instructed the jury to find Park guilty if it found beyond a reasonable doubt that Park "had a responsible relation to the situation. . . . The issue is, in this case, whether the Defendant, John R. Park, by virtue of his position in the company, had a position of authority and responsibility in the situation out of which these charges arose." Requiring, as it did, a verdict of guilty upon a finding of "responsibility," this instruction standing alone could have been construed as a direction to convict if the jury found Park "responsible" for the condition in the sense that his position as chief executive officer gave him formal responsibility within the structure of the corporation. But the trial judge went on specifically to caution the jury not to attach such a meaning to his instruction, saying that "the fact that the Defendant is pres[id]ent and is a chief executive officer of the Acme Markets does not require a finding of guilt." "Responsibility" as used by the trial judge therefore had whatever meaning the jury in its unguided discretion chose to give it.

The instructions, therefore, expressed nothing more than a tautology. They told the jury: "You must find the defendant guilty if you find that he is to be held accountable for this adulterated food." In other words: "You must find the defendant guilty if you conclude that he is guilty." . . .

To be sure, "the day [is] long past when [courts] . . . parsed instructions and engaged in nice semantic distinctions," Cool v. United States, 409 U.S. 100, 107 (Rehnquist, J., dissenting). But this Court has never before abandoned the view that jury instructions must contain a statement of the applicable law sufficiently precise to enable the jury to be guided by something other than its rough notions of social justice. And while it might be argued that the issue before the jury in this case was a "mixed" question of both law and fact, this has never meant that a jury is to be left wholly at sea, without any guidance as to the standard of conduct the law requires. . . .

The *Dotterweich* case stands for two propositions, and I accept them both. First, "any person" within the meaning of 21 U.S.C. §333 may include any corporate officer or employee "standing in responsible relation" to a condition or transaction forbidden by the Act. 320 U.S., at 281. Second, a person may be convicted of a criminal offense under the Act even in the absence of "the conventional requirement for criminal conduct — awareness of some wrongdoing." Ibid.

But before a person can be convicted of a criminal violation of this Act, a jury must find — and must be clearly instructed that it must find — evidence beyond a reasonable doubt that he engaged in wrongful conduct amounting at least to common-law negligence. There were no such instructions, and clearly, therefore, no such finding in this case. . . .

NOTES

1. The Park *"impossibility" defense.* The federal courts have been slow to recognize situations in which the corporate agents found it "objectively impossible" to avoid the harm. See United States v. Gel Spice Co., 773 F.2d 427 (2d Cir. 1985); United States v. Y. Heta Ltd., 535 F.2d 508 (9th Cir. 1976). In United States v. New England Grocers Supply Co., 488 F. Supp. 230 (D. Mass 1980), the court offered the following reflections on the problem (id. at 235):

> It is not easy to ascertain from [the language of *Park*] the exact nature and scope of the impossibility defense. . . .
>
> An . . . interpretation of the impossibility defense is that it is satisfied by evidence that the corporate officer exercised "extraordinary care" and was still unable to prevent the violations. Under this interpretation, the impossibility defense would serve as an affirmative defense, incorporating an objective element — use of extraordinary care   into a strict liability offense. That this interpretation is what the

Park Court intended is suggested by the Court's insistence that "the Act, in its criminal aspect, does not require that which is objectively impossible." This interpretation is also suggested by the Court's repeated emphasis that corporate officers must exercise the "highest standard of foresight and vigilance," and the "highest standard of care." . . .

In light of the severe penalties which may be imposed for a second conviction under the Act,[4] I am inclined to adopt this more lenient interpretation of the impossibility defense.

In sum, the impossibility defense allows the corporate officer to introduce evidence to establish an affirmative defense that he exercised extraordinary care and still could not prevent violations of the Act. The defense is raised when the defendant introduces a sufficient quantum of evidence as to his exercise of "extraordinary care" so as to justify placing an additional burden on the government. At this point, the government must prove beyond a reasonable doubt that the defendant, by the use of extraordinary care, was not without the power or capacity to correct or prevent the violations of the Act.

2. A useful exchange on the issues raised by the *Park* case may be found in Kathleen Brickey, Criminal Liability of Corporate Officers for Strict Liability — Another View, 35 Vand. L. Rev. 1337 (1982); Norman Abrams, Criminal Liability of Corporate Officers for Strict Liability Offenses — A Comment on *Dotterweich* and *Park,* 28 U.C.L.A. L. Rev. 463 (1981). See also Steven Zipperman, The Park Doctrine — Application of Strict Criminal Liability to Corporate Individuals for Violation of Environmental Crimes, 10 U.C.L.A. J. Environ. L. 123 (1991).

3. Reconsider the *Guminga* case, supra page 244. Guminga's objection was to the kind of vicarious liability exemplified in the tort doctrine of respondeat superior; namely, where the liability of *A* for the acts of *B* is based solely on some relationship between them rather than on any culpable conduct of *A.* Is the liability of Park (and Dotterweich) of this nature? Consider Note, Developments in the Law — Corporate Crime: Regulating Corporate Behavior through Criminal Sanctions, 92 Harv. L. Rev. 1227, 1262 n. 102 (1979):

It should be stressed that holding corporate officials criminally responsible for causing strict liability violations is not imposing vicarious liability. In *Park* and *Dotterweich,* corporate executives were culpable for their own failure to exercise the quality of care needed to prevent violations within the realms of their own authority; their guilt was not vicariously imputed from the guilt of their subordinates.

UNITED STATES v. MacDONALD & WATSON WASTE OIL CO.

United States Court of Appeals, 1st Circuit
933 F.2d 35 (1991)

CAMPBELL, C.J. [MacDonald & Watson Waste Oil Co., a corporation engaged in the business of transporting and disposing of contaminated wastes, operated a disposal facility at the Poe Street Lot, a facility leased from the Narragansett

---

4. Section 303 of the Act, 21 U.S.C. §333, provides in relevant part:

(b) Notwithstanding the provisions of subsection (a) of this section, if any person commits such a violation after a conviction of him under this section has become final, or commits such a violation with the intent to defraud or mislead, such person shall be imprisoned for not more than three years or fined not more than $10,000, or both.

Improvement Company (NIC). Neither MacDonald nor NIC held a permit authorizing them to dispose of solid hazardous wastes in that site, although NIC did have a permit to dispose of *liquid* wastes there.

[MacDonald was hired to remove solid waste (toluene-contaminated soil) from the grounds of the Master Chemical Company. An employee of MacDonald supervised the transportation of the contaminated soil from Master Chemical to the Poe Street Lot. Subsequently Eugene K. D'Allesandro, president of MacDonald, was convicted of knowingly transporting and causing the transportation of hazardous waste to a facility that did not have a permit, in violation of the Resource Conservation and Recovery Act (RCRA), §3008(d)(1). The company was also convicted, but discussion of its liability is omitted.]

D'Allesandro . . . contends that his conviction . . . must be vacated because the district court incorrectly charged the jury regarding the element of knowledge in the case of a corporate officer. Section 3008(d)(1) penalizes "Any person who . . . (1) knowingly transports or causes to be transported any hazardous waste identified or listed under this subchapter . . . to a facility which does not have a permit. . . ." In his closing, the prosecutor conceded that the government had "no direct evidence that Eugene D'Allesandro actually knew that the Master Chemical shipments were coming in," i.e., were being transported to the Poe Street Lot under contract with his company. The prosecution did present evidence, however, that D'Allesandro was not only the President and owner of MacDonald & Watson but was a "hands-on" manager of that relatively small firm. There was also proof that . . . D'Allesandro's subordinates had contracted for and transported the Master Chemical waste for disposal at [the Poe Street] site. The government argued that D'Allesandro was guilty of violating §3008(d)(1) because, as the responsible corporate officer, he was in a position to ensure compliance with RCRA and had failed to do so even after being warned by a consultant on two earlier occasions that other shipments of toluene-contaminated soil had been received from other customers, and that such material violated NIC's permit. In the government's view, any failure to prove D'Allesandro's actual knowledge of the Master Chemical contract and shipments was irrelevant to his criminal responsibility under §3008(d)(1) for those shipments.

The court apparently accepted the government's theory. It instructed the jury as follows:

> When an individual Defendant is also a corporate officer, the Government may prove that individual's knowledge in either of two ways. The first way is to demonstrate that the defendant had actual knowledge of the act in question. The second way is to establish that the defendant was what is called a responsible officer of the corporation committing the act. In order to prove that a person is a responsible corporate officer three things must be shown.
>
> First, it must be shown that the person is an officer of the corporation, not merely an employee.
>
> Second, it must be shown that the officer had direct responsibility for the activities that are alleged to be illegal. Simply being an officer or even the president of a corporation is not enough. The Government must prove that the person had a responsibility to supervise the activities in question.
>
> And the third requirement is that the officer must have known or believed that the illegal activity of the type alleged occurred. . . .

D'Allesandro challenges this instruction, contending that the use of the "responsible corporate officer" doctrine is improper under §3008(d)(1) which expressly calls for proof of knowledge, i.e., requires *scienter*. The government responds that the district court properly adapted the responsible corporate officer doctrine traditionally applied to strict liability offenses to this case, instructing the jury to find knowledge "that the illegal activity of the *type alleged* occurred," — a finding that, together with the first two, made it reasonable to infer knowledge of the particular violation. We agree with D'Allesandro that the jury instructions improperly allowed the jury to find him guilty without finding he had actual knowledge of the alleged transportation of hazardous waste on July 30 and 31, 1986, from Master Chemical Company, Boston, Massachusetts, to NIC's site, knowledge being an element the statute requires. We must, therefore, reverse his conviction.

The seminal cases regarding the responsible corporate officer doctrine are United States v. Dotterweich, 320 U.S. 277 (1943), and United States v. Park, 421 U.S. 658 (1975). These cases concerned misdemeanor charges . . . [that] dispensed with a scienter requirement, placing "the burden of acting at hazard upon a person otherwise innocent but standing in responsible relation to a public danger." *Dotterweich*, 320 U.S. at 277. . . . But while *Dotterweich* and *Park* thus reflect what is now clear and well-established law in respect to public welfare statutes and regulations lacking an express knowledge or other *scienter* requirement, we know of no precedent for failing to give effect to a knowledge requirement that Congress has expressly included in a criminal statute. Especially is that so where, as here, the crime is a felony carrying possible imprisonment of five years and, for a second offense, ten. . . .

Contrary to the government's assertions, [the court's] instruction did more than simply permit the jury, if it wished, to infer knowledge of the Master Chemical shipments from relevant circumstantial evidence including D'Allesandro's responsibilities and activities as a corporate executive. With respect to circumstantial evidence, the district court properly instructed elsewhere that knowledge did not have to be proven by direct evidence but could be inferred from the defendant's conduct and other facts and circumstances. The court also instructed that the element of knowledge could be satisfied by proof of willful blindness. . . . These [instructions] would have sufficed had it merely been the court's purpose to point out that knowledge could be established by circumstantial evidence. . . .

Instead, the district court charged, in effect, that proof that D'Allesandro was a responsible corporate officer would conclusively prove the element of his knowledge of the Master Chemical shipments. . . . Under the district court's instruction, the jury's belief that the responsible corporate officer lacked actual knowledge of, and had not willfully blinded himself to, the criminal transportation alleged would be insufficient for acquittal so long as the officer knew or even erroneously believed that illegal activity of the same type had occurred on another occasion. . . .

Simply because a responsible corporate officer believed that on a prior occasion illegal transportation occurred, he did not necessarily possess knowledge of the violation charged. In a crime having knowledge as an express element, a mere showing of official responsibility under *Dotterweich* and *Park* is not an adequate substitute for direct or circumstantial proof of knowledge. . . .

We vacate the conviction of Eugene D'Allesandro . . . and remand for a new trial or such other action as may be consistent herewith.

NOTES

1. If the responsible officer doctrine suffices to hold the officer criminally accountable for the acts of a corporate employee, as it does in strict liability offenses, why should it not also suffice to hold the officer accountable as well for the mens rea with which the employee acted?

Comment (Jeremy D. Heep), Adapting the Responsible Corporate Officer Doctrine in Light of *United States v. MacDonald & Watson Waste Oil Co.,* 78 Minn. L. Rev. 699 (1994), critically appraises the application of the responsible corporate officer doctrine in the federal courts.

2. In evaluating the reasoning and conclusion of this case consider the following discussion and proposal.

National Commission on Reform of Federal Criminal Laws, Working Papers, Vol. 1, 200-201, 185-188 (1970): [C]ompany policy with respect to compliance with regulatory standards or requirements is usually set not at the level of actual compliance or noncompliance, but rather at the highest managerial or supervisory level. There seems to be a general belief that many individual employees who violate these regulatory statutes do so because they are under pressure, although not necessarily stated pressure, from higher levels to increase profits in any way possible. In such cases, it seems distasteful to prosecute inferior officials or employees "who are the tools rather than the responsible originators of the violative conduct." . . . In addition, it has been noted that in many cases violation by a lower echelon employee "may have been produced by pressures on the subordinates created by corporate managerial officials even though the latter may not have intended or even desired the criminal behavior and even though the pressures can only be sensed rather than demonstrated."[112] In either case the problem is essentially one involving the difficulties of locating and proving participation in the offense by such high-level policy formulators. . . .

There are two possibilities with respect to the corporation's managers. First, the managers of the corporation could be held vicariously responsible for the criminal conduct of the employees of the corporation. The most extreme application of this possibility would be to authorize a fine and/or jail term for the directors for all types of offenses committed by all employees of the corporation: the directors would be held responsible (a) even though they have no direct means of controlling the conduct of the employees, and (b) regardless of (i) whether they had knowledge of the fact the conduct was taking place, or (ii) whether the officers appointed by them were involved in the conduct; each of the executive officers could be held similarly responsible without regard to whether the offense occurred within his particular line of duty or was committed

---

112. Model Penal Code, §2.07, Comment at 149 (Tent. Draft No. 4, 1955).

by an employee under his supervision. A more limited application of the vicarious responsibility possibility would be to restrict managerial responsibility on a line of duty basis — the directors would be responsible only for offenses occurring in connection with corporate activities requiring board approval and offenses in which elected officers were involved; and each of the executive officers would be held for offenses occurring within his sphere of authority and for offenses committed by employees under his supervision. Vicarious responsibility could be further restricted by eliminating directorial liability and limiting responsibility of the officers to those offenses within their jurisdiction over which no other person had the final signoff power. Finally, vicarious liability of the officers and directors could be limited to strict liability offenses.

The second possibility with respect to the officers and directors would be to pin their responsibility upon their own fault; they could be held responsible for offenses which they could have prevented had they properly performed their duties of management and supervision. . . .

Finally, it has been suggested that such a duty could be imposed generally upon all corporate executives with respect to all types of criminal conduct occurring on behalf of their corporations. Liability for failure to perform the duty (i.e., to exercise one's authority to prevent the offense) . . . would probably have to depend upon negligence, or perhaps recklessness. The imposition of such a duty, enforced through criminal sanctions directed to the managers, would tend to decrease the incidence of conduct constituting the actual offense by applying a threat to those actually having control over the actors (compulsory self-policing), as well as by stepping up the deterrent impact upon the actor — he is now threatened not only with detection and prosecution by law enforcement officials but with an increased possibility of detection and punishment administered within the corporation for which he works.

Criminal Code Reform Bill, S. 1437, 95th Cong., 2d Sess. (1978): Section 403.
(a) CONDUCT ON BEHALF OF AN ORGANIZATION. — Except as otherwise expressly provided, a person is criminally liable for an offense based upon conduct that he engages in or causes in the name of an organization or on behalf of an organization to the same extent as if he engaged in or caused the conduct in his own name or on his own behalf.

(b) OMISSION TO PERFORM A DUTY OF AN ORGANIZATION. — Except as otherwise expressly provided, whenever a duty to act is imposed upon an organization by a statute, or by a regulation, rule, or order issued pursuant thereto, an agent of the organization having significant responsibility for the subject matter to which the duty relates is criminally liable for an offense based upon an omission to perform the duty, if he has the state of mind required for the commission of the offense, to the same extent as if the duty were imposed upon him directly.

(c) RECKLESS FAILURE TO SUPERVISE CONDUCT OF AN ORGANIZATION. — Except as otherwise expressly provided, a person responsible for supervising particular activities on behalf of an organization who, by his reckless failure to supervise adequately those activities, permits or contributes to the commission of an offense by the organization is criminally liable for the offense, except that if the offense committed by the organization is a felony the person is liable under this subsection only for a Class A misdemeanor.

C. CONSPIRACY

CLARENCE DARROW, THE STORY OF MY LIFE 64 (1932): If there are still any citizens interested in protecting human liberty, let them study the conspiracy laws of the United States.

MODEL PENAL CODE AND COMMENTARIES, Comment to §5.03 at 387 (1985): [C]onspiracy as an offense has two different aspects, reflecting the different functions it serves in the legal system. In the first place, conspiracy is an inchoate crime, complementing the provisions dealing with attempt and solicitation in reaching preparatory conduct before it has matured into commission of a substantive offense. Second, it is a means of striking against the special danger incident to group activity, facilitating prosecution of the group, and yielding a basis for imposing added penalties when combination is involved.

INTRODUCTORY NOTE

Conspiracy is an offense carrying its own penalty, and a conspiracy charge also has collateral effects on the rules of procedure, evidence, and criminal liability for other offenses. Before considering the elements of conspiracy as a substantive crime, we examine the most important of these collateral consequences. The collateral effects are crucial for understanding the implications of a prosecution for conspiracy.

1. An Overview: The Consequences of a Conspiracy Charge

KRULEWITCH v. UNITED STATES

Supreme Court of the United States
336 U.S. 440 (1949)

JUSTICE BLACK delivered the opinion of the Court.

A federal district court indictment charged in three counts that petitioner and a woman defendant had (1) induced and persuaded another woman to go on October 20, 1941, from New York City to Miami, Florida for the purpose of prostitution, in violation of 18 U.S.C.A. §399 [now §2422]; (2) transported or caused her to be transported from New York to Miami for that purpose, in violation of 18 U.S.C.A. §398 [now §2421]; and (3) conspired to commit those offenses in violation of 18 U.S.C.A. §88 [now §371]. Tried alone, the petitioner was convicted on all three counts of the indictment. The Court of Appeals affirmed. We granted certiorari limiting our review to consideration of alleged error in admission of certain hearsay testimony against petitioner over his timely and repeated objections.

The challenged testimony was elicited by the Government from its complaining witness, the person whom petitioner and the woman defendant allegedly induced to go from New York to Florida for the purpose of prostitution. The testimony narrated the following purported conversation between the complaining witness and petitioner's alleged co conspirator, the woman defendant.

She asked me, she says, "You didn't talk yet?" And I says, "No." And she says, "Well, don't," she says, "until we get you a lawyer." And then she says, "Be very careful what you say." And I can't put it in exact words. But she said, "It would be better for us two girls to take the blame than Kay (the defendant) because he couldn't stand it, he couldn't stand to take it."

The time of the alleged conversation was more than a month and a half after October 20, 1941, the date the complaining witness had gone to Miami. Whatever original conspiracy may have existed between petitioner and his alleged co-conspirator to cause the complaining witness to go to Florida in October, 1941, no longer existed when the reported conversation took place in December, 1941. For on this latter date the trip to Florida had not only been made — the complaining witness had left Florida, had returned to New York, and had resumed her residence there. Furthermore, at the time the conversation took place, the complaining witness, the alleged co-conspirator, and the petitioner had been arrested. They apparently were charged in a United States District Court of Florida with the offense of which petitioner was here convicted.

It is beyond doubt that the central aim of the alleged conspiracy — transportation of the complaining witness to Florida for prostitution — had either never existed or had long since ended in success or failure when and if the alleged co-conspirator made the statement attributed to her. The statement plainly implied that petitioner was guilty of the crime for which he was on trial. It was made in petitioner's absence and the Government made no effort whatever to show that it was made with his authority. The testimony thus stands as an unsworn, out-of-court declaration of petitioner's guilt. This hearsay declaration, attributed to a co-conspirator, was not made pursuant to and in furtherance of objectives of the conspiracy charged in the indictment, because if made, it was after those objectives either had failed or had been achieved. Under these circumstances, the hearsay declaration attributed to the alleged co-conspirator was not admissible on the theory that it was made in furtherance of the alleged criminal transportation undertaking. . . .

Although the Government recognizes that the chief objective of the conspiracy — transportation for prostitution purposes — had ended in success or failure before the reported conversation took place, it nevertheless argues for admissibility of the hearsay declaration as one in furtherance of a continuing subsidiary objective of the conspiracy. Its argument runs this way. Conspirators about to commit crimes always expressly or implicitly agree to collaborate with each other to conceal facts in order to prevent detection, conviction and punishment. Thus the argument is that even after the central criminal objectives of a conspiracy have succeeded or failed, an implicit subsidiary phase of the conspiracy always survives, the phase which has concealment as its sole objective. The Court of Appeals adopted this view. It viewed the alleged hearsay declaration as one in furtherance of this continuing subsidiary phase of the conspiracy, as part of "the implied agreement to conceal." It consequently held the declaration properly admitted.

We cannot accept the Government's contention. There are many logical and practical reasons that could be advanced against a special evidentiary rule that permits out-of-court statements of one conspirator to be used against another. But however cogent these reasons, it is firmly established that where made in furtherance of the objectives of a going conspiracy, such statements are admissible as exceptions to the hearsay rule. This prerequisite to admissibility, that hearsay statements by some conspirators to be admissible against others must be made in furtherance of the conspiracy charged, has been scrupulously observed by federal courts. The Government now asks us to expand this narrow exception to the hearsay rule and hold admissible a declaration, not made in furtherance of the alleged criminal transportation conspiracy charged, but made in furtherance of an alleged implied but uncharged conspiracy aimed at preventing detection and punishment. The rule contended for by the Government could have far-reaching results. For under this rule plausible arguments could generally be made in conspiracy cases that most out-of-court statements offered in evidence tended to shield co-conspirators. We are not persuaded to adopt the Government's implicit conspiracy theory which in all criminal conspiracy cases would create automatically a further breach of the general rule against the admission of hearsay evidence. . . .

Reversed.

JUSTICE JACKSON, concurring in the judgment and opinion of the Court.

This case illustrates a present drift in the federal law of conspiracy which warrants some further comment because it is characteristic of the long evolution of that elastic, sprawling and pervasive offense. Its history exemplifies the "tendency of a principle to expand itself to the limit of its logic."[1] The unavailing protest of courts against the growing habit to indict for conspiracy in lieu of prosecuting for the substantive offense itself, or in addition thereto, suggests that loose practice as to this offense constitutes a serious threat to fairness in our administration of justice.

The modern crime of conspiracy is so vague that it almost defies definition. Despite certain elementary and essential elements,[4] it also, chameleon-like, takes on a special coloration from each of the many independent offenses on which it may be overlaid. It is always "predominantly mental in composition" because it consists primarily of a meeting of minds and an intent.

. . . It is not intended to question that the basic conspiracy principle has some place in modern criminal law, because to unite, back of a criminal purpose, the strength, opportunities and resources of many is obviously more dangerous and more difficult to police than the efforts of a lone wrongdoer. It also may be trivialized, as here, where the conspiracy consists of the concert of a loathsome panderer and a prostitute to go from New York to Florida to ply their trade and it would appear that a simple Mann Act prosecution would vindicate the majesty of federal law. However, even when appropriately invoked, the looseness and pliability of the doctrine present inherent dangers which should be in the back-

1. The phrase is Judge Cardozo's — Nature of Judicial Process, p. 51. [See Justice Holmes in Hudson County Water Co. v. McCarter, 209 U.S. 349, 355 (1908): "All rights tend to declare themselves absolute to their logical extreme. Yet all in fact are limited by the neighborhood of principles of policy which are other than those on which the particular right is founded, and which become strong enough to hold their own when a certain point is reached." — EDS.]

4. Justice Holmes supplied an oversimplified working definition in United States v. Kissel, 218 U.S. 601, 608: "A conspiracy is a partnership in criminal purposes." This was recently restated "A conspiracy is a partnership in crime." Pinkerton v. United States, 328 U.S. 640, 644. The latter is inaccurate, since concert in criminal purposes, rather than concert in crime, establishes the conspiracy. . . .

ground of judicial thought wherever it is sought to extend the doctrine to meet the exigencies of a particular case.

Conspiracy in federal law aggravates the degree of crime over that of unconcerted offending. The act of confederating to commit a misdemeanor, followed by even an innocent overt act in its execution, is a felony and is such even if the misdemeanor is never consummated. The more radical proposition also is well-established that at common law and under some statutes a combination may be a criminal conspiracy even if it contemplates only acts which are not crimes at all when perpetrated by an individual or by many acting severally.

Thus, the conspiracy doctrine will incriminate persons on the fringe of offending who would not be guilty of aiding and abetting or of becoming an accessory, for those charges only lie when an act which is a crime has actually been committed.

Attribution of criminality to a confederation which contemplates no act that would be criminal if carried out by any one of the conspirators is a practice peculiar to Anglo-American law. . . . The doctrine does not commend itself to jurists of civil law countries, despite universal recognition that an organized society must have legal weapons for combatting organized criminality. Most other countries have devised what they consider more discriminating principles upon which to prosecute criminal gangs, secret associations, and subversive syndicates. . . .

Doctrines of conspiracy are not only invoked for criminal prosecution, but also in civil proceedings for damages or for injunction, and in administrative proceedings to apply regulatory statutes. . . .

The interchangeable use of conspiracy doctrine in civil as well as penal proceedings opens it to the danger, absent in the case of many crimes, that a court having in mind only the civil sanctions will approve lax practices which later are imported into criminal proceedings. In civil proceedings this Court frankly has made the end a test of the means, saying, "To require a greater showing would cripple the Act," United States v. Griffith, 334 U.S. 100, in dispensing with the necessity for specific intent to produce a result violative of the statute. Further, the Court has dispensed with even the necessity to infer any definite agreement, although that is the gist of the offense. . . . One might go on from the reports of this and lower courts . . . to demonstrate that the minimum of proof required to establish conspiracy is extremely low, and we may expect our pronouncements in civil cases to be followed in criminal ones also.

Of course, it is for prosecutors rather than courts to determine when to use a scatter gun to bring down the defendant, but there are procedural advantages from using it which add to the danger of unguarded extension of the concept.

An accused, under the Sixth Amendment, has the right to trial "by an impartial jury of the state and district wherein the crime shall have been committed." The leverage of a conspiracy charge lifts this limitation from the prosecution and reduces its protection to a phantom, for the crime is considered so vagrant as to have been committed in any district where any one of the conspirators did any one of the acts, however innocent, intended to accomplish its object. The Government may, and often does, compel one to defend at a great distance from any place he ever did any act because some accused confederate did some trivial and by itself innocent act in the chosen district. . . .

When the trial starts, the accused feels the full impact of the conspiracy strategy. Strictly, the prosecution should first establish prima facie the conspiracy and identify the conspirators, after which evidence of acts and declarations of each in the course of its execution are admissible against all. But the order of proof of so sprawling a charge is difficult for a judge to control. As a practical matter, the accused often is confronted with a hodgepodge of acts and statements by others which he may never have authorized or intended or even known about, but which help to persuade the jury of existence of the conspiracy itself. In other words, a conspiracy often is proved by evidence that is admissible only upon assumption that conspiracy existed. The naive assumption that prejudicial effects can be overcome by instructions to the jury all practicing lawyers know to be unmitigated fiction.

The trial of a conspiracy charge doubtless imposes a heavy burden on the prosecution, but it is an especially difficult situation for the defendant. . . .

A co-defendant in a conspiracy trial occupies an uneasy seat. There generally will be evidence of wrongdoing by somebody. It is difficult for the individual to make his own case stand on its own merits in the minds of jurors who are ready to believe that birds of a feather are flocked together. If he is silent, he is taken to admit it and if, as often happens, co-defendants can be prodded into accusing or contradicting each other, they convict each other. . . .

Against this inadequately sketched background, I think the decision of this case in the court below introduced an ominous expansion of the accepted law of conspiracy. . . .

It is difficult to see any logical limit to the [Government's theory of] "implied conspiracy," either as to duration or means. . . . On the theory that the law will impute to the confederates a continuing conspiracy to defeat justice, one conceivably could be bound by another's unauthorized and unknown commission of perjury, bribery of a juror or witness, or even putting an incorrigible witness with damaging information out of the way.

Moreover, the assumption of an indefinitely continuing offense would result in an indeterminate extension of the statute of limitations. If the law implies an agreement to cooperate in defeating prosecution, it must imply that it continues as long as prosecution is a possibility, and prosecution is a possibility as long as the conspiracy to defeat it is implied to continue. . . .

There is, of course, strong temptation to relax rigid standards when it seems the only way to sustain convictions of evildoers. But statutes authorize prosecution for substantive crimes for most evil-doing without the dangers to the liberty of the individual and the integrity of the judicial process that are inherent in conspiracy charges. We should disapprove the doctrine of implied or constructive crime in its entirety and in every manifestation. And I think there should be no straining to uphold any conspiracy conviction where prosecution for the substantive offense is adequate and the purpose served by adding the conspiracy charge seems chiefly to get procedural advantages to ease the way to conviction. . . .

PAUL MARCUS, CRIMINAL CONSPIRACY LAW: TIME TO TURN BACK FROM AN EVER EXPANDING, EVER MORE TROUBLING AREA, 1 Wm. & Mary Bill of Rights J. 1, 8-11 (1992): Perhaps the most striking change in the conspiracy area during the past two decades has been the enormous number of cases involving many defendants, complex evidentiary issues, and dozens and dozens of complicated charges. While it was not highly unusual twenty years ago to see such big and cumbersome cases, today it is absolutely commonplace. Consider, for instance, this handful of recent and somewhat typical cases:

- United States v. Casamento,[42] with twenty-one defendants, 275 witnesses, thousands of exhibits, and 40,000 pages of transcripts; the trial lasted seventeen months.
- United States v. Ianniello,[43] lasted more than thirteen months at the trial level; involved eleven defendants.
- United States v. Accetturo,[44] twenty-six-defendant trial; lasted fifteen months.
- United States v. Kopituk,[45] involved a seven-month trial with twelve defendants, seventy counts, 130 witnesses, and more than 22,000 pages of transcript.
- United States v. Martino,[46] with twenty defendants and thirty-five counts; produced a record of almost 100 volumes holding more than 11,000 pages of the testimony of over 200 witnesses, along with five boxes of exhibits.

It is difficult to imagine how a jury goes about sorting the testimony of hundreds of witnesses, or considering evidence it heard more than a year earlier. Indeed, how does a jury begin to apply the reasonable doubt standard when there are more than fifty counts charging more than a dozen different individuals? In today's world of conspiracy prosecution, however, such a situation — while perhaps not the norm — occurs with great frequency.

NOTES ON THE CO-CONSPIRATOR EXCEPTION TO THE HEARSAY RULE

1. What is hearsay? Rule 801 of the Federal Rules of Evidence defines hearsay as "a statement, other than one made by the declarant [the person testifying] while testifying at the trial or hearing, offered in evidence to prove the truth of the matter asserted." Thus, in *Krulewitch*, if witness *A* had testified at trial, "Kay was the brains behind all this, the guy who arranged it," *A*'s statement would not be hearsay. But if witness *B* testified at trial that *A* had told her out of court, "Kay was the brains behind all this, the guy who arranged it," then *A*'s statement would be hearsay.

What out-of-court statement was recounted at the *Krulewitch* trial? Why was it relevant at all? And why was it hearsay?

2. The hearsay rule and its exceptions. Because hearsay assertions are not subject to cross-examination, they are normally inadmissible. But there are many excep-

---

42. 887 F.2d 1141 (2d Cir. 1989).
43. 866 F.2d 540 (2d Cir. 1989).
44. 842 F.2d 1408 (3d Cir. 1988).
45. 690 F.2d 1289 (11th Cir. 1982).
46. 648 F.2d 367 (5th Cir. 1981).

tions to this rule. Typically, the exceptions come into play when the person making the statement is unavailable as a witness and circumstances surrounding the statement afford some assurance of its reliability. Illustrative are "dying declarations" and "admissions against penal interest." Both kinds of statements are admissible as exceptions to the hearsay rule.

3. *The co-conspirator exception.* The *Krulewitch* decision excluded the particular statement at issue in that case but reaffirmed the general doctrine permitting introduction against one co-conspirator of out-of-court statements made by another. The doctrine applies whether or not the parties have been formally indicted or convicted of conspiracy, provided that the statement is in furtherance of a conspiratorial agreement between them. This doctrine is widely followed in state courts. For federal prosecutions it is now codified in Rule 801(d)(2)(E) of the Federal Rules of Evidence. What is the rationale of this doctrine? Consider United States v. Trowery, 542 F.2d 623 (3d Cir. 1976):

> The co-conspirator exception to the hearsay rule [is] a rule of evidence founded, to some extent, on concepts of agency law. It may be applied in both civil and criminal cases. . . . Its rationale is the common sense appreciation that a person who has authorized another to speak or to act to some joint end will be held responsible for what is later said or done by his agent, whether in his presence or not. . . .

See also United States v. Gil, 604 F.2d 546, 549 (7th Cir. 1979):

> The evidentiary principle . . . is a limited application of agency principles, viewing a conspiracy as a "partnership in crime." It is justified in part because of the assurances of accuracy traditionally associated with statements against interest and the community of interest among the conspirators. It has also been candidly proposed by commentators . . . that the exception is largely a result of necessity, since it is most often invoked in conspiracy cases in which the proof would otherwise be very difficult and the evidence largely circumstantial.

Compare Phillip Johnson, The Unnecessary Crime of Conspiracy, 61 Cal. L. Rev. 1137, 1183 (1973):

> This exception to the hearsay rule is a particular application of the more general principle that statements of an agent concerning matters within the scope of the agency relationship and made during the existence of that relationship are admissible against the principal.
>
> The justification for admitting these "vicarious admissions" is not altogether easy to grasp. Some authorities have found the analogy to the substantive liability of the principal for his agent's acts compelling. Because the employer is liable for the torts of his servant committed within the scope of the employment, and the conspirator for the crimes of his co-conspirator committed in furtherance of the common objective, these authorities have reasoned that the principal should bear the risk of what his agents say as well as the risk of what they do. It does not seem that hearsay statements of agents are admitted because they are regarded as carrying some particular guarantee of trustworthiness. Although there are some suggestions in the literature that an agent is not likely to make statements against his principal's interest unless they are true, the authorities agree that admissions of the agent, like those of the principal himself, are admissible whether or not he

thought the statements to be against his or his principal's interest at the time he made them.

4. For further discussion, see Stephen Whitzman, Proof of Conspiracy: The Co-Conspirator's Exception to the Hearsay Rule, 28 Crim. L.Q. 203 (1986).

5. Bootstrapping? In United States v. Glasser, 315 U.S. 60 (1942), the Court held that the hearsay declarations of an alleged co-conspirator become admissible only if there is independent proof that the conspiracy exists and that the defendant was connected with it. "Otherwise," the Court said, "hearsay would lift itself by its own bootstraps to the level of competent evidence." But this limit on the co-conspirator exception was later discarded. In Bourjaily v. United States, 483 U.S. 171 (1987), the Court held that co-conspirator hearsay becomes admissible under the Federal Rules of Evidence whenever the judge determines by a preponderance of the evidence that the defendant was a member of the conspiracy. The Court also held that the judge may consider the hearsay statement itself, along with other evidence, in making this determination. This usually means, of course, that the jury hears this evidence before its admissibility is determined. If the evidence is later held inadmissible, the jury is told to disregard it.[8] A few state courts have rejected the *Bourjaily* approach and insisted that the conspiracy be proved by evidence independent of the conspiracy. See, e.g., People v. Hardy, 5 Cal. Rptr. 796, 824 (Cal. 1992); Romani v. State, 542 So. 2d 984 (Fla. 1989). In the latter case, the court noted (542 So. 2d at 986): "We are apprehensive that adopting the *Bourjaily* rule would frequently lead to the admission of statements which are not reliable. Our present rule of disallowing the statement itself in determining its admissibility helps assure that a defendant is convicted only on credible evidence."

NOTES ON THE DURATION OF A CONSPIRACY

Conspiracy traditionally has been viewed as a continuing offense. The basic rule is that once formed, a conspiracy remains in effect until its objectives have either been achieved or abandoned. See United States v. Kissel, 218 U.S. 601 (1910). Thus, unlike most criminal offenses, the statute of limitations for conspiracy begins to run not when the offense is committed (that is, when the agreement is made), but when the conspiracy terminates. One effect of this concept is that a conspiracy often can remain subject to prosecution long after the initial agreement was made and long after some of its members have ceased any active participation in the activities. In addition, because the various collateral consequences of conspiracy come into play only with respect to the period when the conspiracy is in existence, it may be crucial for defendants to try to shorten that period or for prosecutors to try to extend it. Consider the following problems.

1. The breadth of the conspiratorial objectives. In accord with *Krulewitch,* most of the recent decisions have refused to infer that an implicit agreement to cover

---

8. One court has said that this is a bit like throwing a skunk into the jury box and telling the jury not to smell it. See United States v. Dunn, 307 F.2d 883, 886 (5th Cir. 1962). The effectiveness of cautionary jury instructions is a problem that pervades criminal law and procedure. We examine it in detail starting at page 35 supra.

up the crime is inherent in every conspiracy. See State v. Rivenbark, 533 A.2d 271 (Md. Ct. App. 1987). And in Grunewald v. United States, 353 U.S. 391, 404 (1957), the Court held that a particular conspiracy cannot be treated as including a cover-up agreement unless there is "direct evidence [of] an express original agreement among the conspirators to continue to act in concert in order to cover up . . . traces of the crime. . . ." Thus, the Court explained (id. at 402):

> [A] subsidiary conspiracy to conceal may not be implied from circumstantial evidence showing merely that the conspiracy was kept a secret and that the conspirators took care to cover up their crime. . . . Acts of covering up, even though done in the context of a mutually understood need for secrecy, cannot themselves constitute proof that concealment of the crime after its commission was part of the initial agreement. . . .

What would be the result in a case like *Krulewitch*, if the prosecution alleges that the conspirators did agree to help each other cover up the crime? When would the objective of such a conspiracy be achieved? When would the statute of limitations begin to run?

For an example of prosecutorial creativity in broadening the objectives of the alleged conspiratorial agreement, consider Forman v. United States, 361 U.S. 416 (1960). The defendants there had conspired to evade income taxes by filing false returns. Although *Krulewitch* and *Grunewald* prevented the government from inferring an implicit agreement to conceal the false return, the Court in *Forman* permitted prosecution on the theory that the objective of the conspiracy (tax evasion) would be achieved not when the false returns were filed but only when government action to recover the taxes was barred. Thus, the statute of limitations on the conspiracy would *begin* to run only after the statute of limitations on the underlying tax offense had *finished* running.

2. *Abandonment.* A conspiracy is generally considered to be abandoned when none of the conspirators is engaging in any action to further the conspiratorial objectives. If such inactivity continues for a period equal to the statute of limitations, prosecution will be barred. See Model Penal Code §5.03(7)(b). But what if a particular defendant "wants out" of an ongoing conspiracy? Can a conspirator cut off his responsibility for later acts and statements of his co-conspirators by terminating his own participation? When should withdrawal by a particular defendant start the statute of limitations running as to him? Courts traditionally have required that a defendant take "affirmative action" to announce his withdrawal to all the other conspirators. Hyde v. United States, 225 U.S. 347, 369 (1912). Is this requirement realistic? How are the co-conspirators likely to react to such an announcement? So long as the evidence of a defendant's withdrawal is persuasive, why should the defendant have to announce it to his confederates? Some courts have gone even further, requiring that a defendant not only announce his withdrawal but thwart the success of the conspiracy. These courts compare an ongoing conspiracy to a ticking time bomb. On this view, a defendant should not be able to disassociate himself merely by walking away while the bomb continues to tick; he must prove that he "defused the bomb" by reporting the conspirators to police or otherwise thwarting the plot. See Eldredge v. United States, 62 F.2d 449, 451-452 (10th Cir. 1932). But this stringent requirement no longer applies in the federal courts. See United States v. United States Gypsum Co., 438 U.S. 422, 464-465 (1978):

> Affirmative acts inconsistent with the object of the conspiracy and communicated in a manner reasonably calculated to reach co-conspirators have generally been regarded as sufficient to establish withdrawal or abandonment.

The Model Penal Code approach is in accord with the flexible *U.S. Gypsum* standard. See Model Penal Code §5.03(7)(c), Appendix. The recent authorities are discussed in Roger C. Spaeder & Gary D. Weinfeld, Effective Withdrawal from a Business Conspiracy, 9 Crim. Just. 8 (ABA), (Spring 1994).

3. Renunciation as a complete defense. Should a defendant's change of heart and withdrawal from the conspiracy ever be sufficient to afford a defense to the conspiracy charge itself? As in the case of abandoned attempts, the common law answer was no. See page 600 supra. The theory was that once the crime was committed, it could not be "uncommitted." Post-offense conduct was considered relevant only to sentencing. Today most states, following the lead of the Model Penal Code, allow a complete defense for renunciation under some circumstances. See Note, 75 Colum. L. Rev. 1122, 1169 (1975). The Code allows the defense only if the circumstances manifest renunciation of the actor's criminal purpose *and* the actor succeeds in preventing commission of the criminal objectives. Model Penal Code §5.03(6). Some states have found this latter requirement too severe and therefore require only that the actor make a substantial effort to prevent the crime. See, e.g., Ark. Code Ann. §5-3-405(2)(B) (Michie 1987); Hawaii Rev. Stat. tit. 37, §705-530(3).

NOTES ON OTHER CONSEQUENCES OF A CONSPIRACY CHARGE

1. Criminalizing noncriminal objectives. As Justice Jackson indicates, concurring in *Krulewitch*, "at common law and under some statutes a combination may be a criminal conspiracy even if it contemplates only acts which are not crimes at all when perpetrated by an individual." Traditionally, an agreement became punishable as a conspiracy if the objectives were criminal or "unlawful," or if the agreement contemplated pursuing a lawful objective by criminal or "unlawful" means. See Commonwealth v. Hunt, 45 Mass. 111 (1842). The broadest and most troublesome reach of this common law rule occurs when conspiracy doctrine is invoked to punish conduct deemed offensive to "public morals." The common law rule can also be troublesome when it is applied to criminalize conduct that may be inconsistent with civil law regulations or precedents.

(a) Public morals. In Shaw v. Director of Public Prosecutions, [1962] A.C. 220, page 294 supra, the House of Lords upheld a conviction for "conspiracy to corrupt public morals," on the basis of a defendant's agreement to publish a directory listing prostitutes and their services. In the United States, most of the recently enacted Codes reject this common law doctrine and confine criminal conspiracy to those agreements whose objectives are otherwise criminal. See Note, Conspiracy: Statutory Reform Since the Model Penal Code, 75 Colum. L. Rev. 1122, 1129 (1975). But in many jurisdictions an agreement to pursue non-

ɹinal objectives can be a criminal conspiracy. For example, Cal. Penal Code ;2(a) makes it a punishable conspiracy for two or more persons to agree:

(1) To commit any crime.

(2) Falsely and maliciously to indict another for any crime, or to procure another to be charged or arrested for any crime.

(3) Falsely to move or maintain any suit, action or proceeding.

(4) To cheat and defraud any person of any property, by any means which are in themselves criminal, or to obtain money or property by false pretenses or by false promises with fraudulent intent not to perform such promises.

(5) To commit any act injurious to the public health, to public morals, or to pervert or obstruct justice, or the due administration of the laws. . . .

Question: Can a prosecution under §182(a)(5) survive a challenge for unconstitutional vagueness? Reconsider Papachristou v. City of Jacksonville, page 308 supra. In Musser v. Utah, 333 U.S. 95 (1948), the Court held that a statute punishing conspiracy to commit acts injurious to public morals would be unconstitutionally vague unless narrowed by the state supreme court. On remand the state court held the provision unconstitutional in the context of a prosecution for preaching and practicing polygamy. State v. Musser, 118 Utah 537, 223 P.2d 193 (1950).

(b) Other noncriminal objectives. Even where the "public morals" doctrine is not directly invoked, statutes may use the conspiracy concept to punish those who agree to pursue objectives that are improper or unlawful, but not necessarily criminal. Consider Cal. Penal Code §182(a)(2)-(3) supra. Similarly, the federal conspiracy statute, 18 U.S.C. §371, provides:

If two or more persons conspire either to commit any offense against the United States, or to defraud the United States, or any agency thereof in any manner or for any purpose, and one or more of such persons do any act to effect the object of the conspiracy, each shall be fined not more than $10,000 or imprisoned not more than five years, or both. If, however, the offense, the commission of which is the object of the conspiracy, is a misdemeanor only, the punishment for such conspiracy shall not exceed the maximum punishment provided for such misdemeanor.

The term "defraud the United States" has been construed to reach not only conduct that subjects the Government to monetary loss, but any act that interferes with a governmental interest. United States v. Hutto, 256 U.S. 524 (1921). Consider United States v. Hay, 527 F.2d 990 (10th Cir. 1975): Defendant was an engineer employed by a private firm that contracted with the South Vietnamese government to assist in building a water system for the city of Saigon, a project partially financed by the U.S. Agency for International Development. Defendant helped a French subcontractor obtain reimbursement for fraudulent cost-overrun claims submitted to the South Vietnamese. Because the U.S. loan funds had been exhausted before the claims were submitted, the financial loss fell entirely on the government of South Vietnam. Was defendant properly convicted of conspiracy to defraud the United States? The court held in the affirmative, stating (527 F.2d at 998): "[The U.S.] interest is not limited strictly to accounting for United States Government funds . . . but extends to seeing that the entire project is administered honestly and efficiently. . . ."

Question: Does this approach avoid the vagueness problems raised by prosecutions for conspiracy to corrupt "public morals"?

(c) Problem. The so-called Boland Amendment, a rider to an appropriations statute, provided that no federal funds were to be used by the Defense Department or the Central Intelligence Agency to support the "Contra" rebels who were then opposing the Nicaraguan government. No criminal or civil penalties were specified for failure to adhere to this proviso. Defendant, a staff member at the National Security Counsel, allegedly agreed with other government officials on a plan to divert federal funds to the CIA for use in supporting the Contras. On such facts would the defendant be subject to criminal punishment under 18 U.S.C. §371? Cf. United States v. North, 920 F.2d 940 (D.C. Cir. 1990) (reversing conviction on other grounds).

2. *The level of punishment.* The traditional approach to grading is to treat conspiracy as a generic offense and to prescribe a punishment range unrelated to those authorized for the object crimes. Thus, 18 U.S.C. §371 provides that the punishment for conspiracy is up to five years' imprisonment, regardless of the seriousness of the object offense. One perverse result of this approach, described by Justice Jackson, has now been eliminated: The current federal statute specifies that when the object crime is a misdemeanor, punishment for the conspiracy shall not exceed that authorized for the misdemeanor. Nonetheless, there are surviving traces of the common law doctrine that made it a felony to conspire to commit a misdemeanor. Under Cal. Penal Code §182, a conspiracy to commit a crime against certain federal or state officials is a felony punishable by imprisonment for five, seven, or nine years; an agreement to throw a tomato at such an official would call for a *minimum* sentence of five years, though actually throwing the tomato, without a prior agreement, would be a misdemeanor assault carrying a *maximum* sentence of one year. Under 18 U.S.C. §371 an agreement to commit murder carries the same five-year maximum sentence as an agreement to commit a minor theft or embezzlement, and an agreement to commit a felony carrying a two-year maximum subjects the conspirators to a five-year sentence, while an individual who commits the object offense by himself faces only the two-year maximum.

Though this approach to grading survives in a number of jurisdictions, the majority of states now reject it. Most fix the punishment for conspiracy at some term less than that provided for the object crime. See Note, 75 Colum. L. Rev. 1122, 1183-1188 (1975). Roughly a third of the states, following the lead of the Model Penal Code, make the punishment for conspiracy the same as that authorized for the object crime, except in the case of the most serious felonies. See Model Penal Code §5.05(1), Appendix. Recall that this is the same approach that the Model Penal Code uses in the case of attempts. But are the two offenses really comparable for grading purposes? Note that an attempt is not punishable under the Code until the defendant has taken a "substantial step" that is "strongly corroborative" of the criminal purpose. In such a case, punishment is permitted up to the level authorized for the object crime. But a conspiracy may be punishable from the moment that an agreement is made. (We will explore this problem in detail when we take up the actus reus of conspiracy. See page 743 infra.) When defendants have not taken significant steps to put their plan into action, is it appropriate to impose the same punishment authorized for successful commission of the object crime?

What should be the appropriate level of punishment in the opposite situation, when the conspirators have actually committed the object crimes? Inchoate offenses such as attempt and solicitation are said to "merge" with their object crimes, so that a defendant charged with both the completed crime and an attempt cannot be punished for both. But the same approach is not always followed in the case of conspiracy. Instead, the traditional view permits separate punishments, with consecutive sentences, for the object crime and the conspiracy to commit it. Consider Callanan v. United States, 364 U.S. 587 (1961). In that case, the defendant was convicted of obstructing interstate commerce by extortion and of conspiring to obstruct commerce by that same extortion. The maximum punishment provided for obstructing commerce by any means, including extortion, was 20 years. The trial court imposed a sentence of 12 years on the extortion count and another 12 years to run consecutively on the conspiracy count. The defendant alleged that Congress did not intend to authorize punishment for both the extortion conspiracy and the extortion itself. Justice Frankfurter, for the Court, rejected the claim, stating (id. at 593-594):

"It has been long and consistently recognized by the Court that the commission of the substantive offense and a conspiracy to commit it are separate and distinct offenses." Pinkerton v. United States, 328 U.S. 640, 643. Over the years this distinction has been applied in various situations. For example, in Clune v. United States, 159 U.S. 590, the Court upheld a two-year sentence for conspiracy over the objection that the crime which was the object of the unlawful agreement could only be punished by a $100 fine. In Carter v. McClaughry, 183 U.S. 365, cumulative sentences for conspiracy to defraud and fraud were upheld. . . .

This settled principle derives from the reason of things in dealing with socially reprehensible conduct: collective criminal agreement — partnership in crime — presents a greater potential threat to the public than individual delicts. Concerted action both increases the likelihood that the criminal object will be successfully attained and decreases the probability that the individuals involved will depart from their path of criminality. Group association for criminal purposes often, if not normally, makes possible the attainment of ends more complex than those which one criminal could accomplish. Nor is the danger of a conspiratorial group limited to the particular end toward which it has embarked. Combination in crime makes more likely the commission of crimes unrelated to the original purpose for which the group was formed. In sum, the danger which a conspiracy generates is not confined to the substantive offense which is the immediate aim of the enterprise.

Compare Model Penal Code and Commentaries, Comment to §5.03, at 390 (1985):

When a conspiracy is declared criminal because its object is a crime, it is entirely meaningless to say that the preliminary combination is more dangerous than the forbidden consummation; the measure of its danger is the risk of such a culmination. On the other hand, the combination may and often does have criminal objectives that transcend any particular offenses that have been committed in pursuance of its goals. In the latter case, cumulative sentences for conspiracy and substantive offenses ought to be permissible, subject to the general limits on cumulation that the Code prescribes. In the former case, when the preliminary agreement does not go beyond the consummation, double conviction and sentence are barred.

For analysis of the practice of stacking conspiracy charges and substantive counts, and the resulting "compound liability" in which a single act can sustain liability for multiple offenses, see Susan W. Brenner, RICO, CCE, and Other Complex Crimes: The Transformation of American Criminal Law, 2 Wm. & Mary Bill of Rights J. 239 (1993).

3. Liability for substantive offenses. One of the most important collateral consequences of conspiracy is that in many jurisdictions a party can sometimes be held liable for crimes committed by co-conspirators during the course of the conspiracy, even when he could not be held accountable for those crimes under traditional principles of accomplice liability. We examine this doctrine in detail in connection with Pinkerton v. United States, infra Section C2.

4. Assessing the collateral consequences of conspiracy. Consider the observations of Professor Phillip Johnson in The Unnecessary Crime of Conspiracy, 61 Cal. L. Rev. 1137, 1139-1140 (1973):

The law of criminal conspiracy is not basically sound. It should be abolished, not reformed.

The central fault of conspiracy law and the reason why any limited reform is bound to be inadequate can be briefly stated. What conspiracy adds to the law is simply confusion, and the confusion is inherent in the nature of the doctrine. The confusion stems from the fact that conspiracy is not only a substantive inchoate crime in itself, but the touchstone for invoking several independent procedural and substantive doctrines. We ask whether a defendant agreed with another person to commit a crime initially for the purpose of determining whether he may be convicted of the offense of conspiracy even when the crime itself has not yet been committed. If the answer to that question is in the affirmative, however, we find that we have also answered a number of other questions that would otherwise have to be considered independently. Where there is evidence of conspiracy, the defendant may be tried jointly with his criminal partners and possibly with many other persons whom he has never met or seen, the joint trial may be held in a place he may never have visited, and hearsay statements of other alleged members of the conspiracy may be used to prove his guilt. Furthermore, a defendant who is found guilty of conspiracy is subject to enhanced punishment and may also be found guilty of any crime committed in furtherance of the conspiracy, whether or not he knew about the crime or aided in its commission.

Each of these issues involves a separate substantive or procedural area of the criminal law of considerable importance and complexity. The essential vice of conspiracy is that it inevitably distracts the courts from the policy questions or balancing of interests that ought to govern the decision of specific legal issues and leads them instead to decide those issues by reference to the conceptual framework of conspiracy. Instead of asking whether public policy or the interests of the parties require a particular holding, the courts are led instead to consider whether the theory of conspiracy is broad enough to permit it. What is wrong with conspiracy, in other words, is much more basic than the overbreadth of a few rules. The problem is not with particular results, but with the use of a single abstract concept to decide numerous questions that deserve separate consideration in light of the various interests and policies they involve.

2.   Conspiracy as a Form of Accessorial Liability

PINKERTON v. UNITED STATES

Supreme Court of the United States
328 U.S. 640 (1946)

Justice Douglas delivered the opinion of the Court.

Walter and Daniel Pinkerton are brothers who live a short distance from each other on Daniel's farm. They were indicted for violations of the Internal Revenue Code. The indictment contained ten substantive counts and one conspiracy count. The jury found Walter guilty on nine of the substantive counts and on the conspiracy count. It found Daniel guilty on six of the substantive counts and on the conspiracy count. Walter was fined $500 and sentenced generally on the substantive counts to imprisonment for thirty months. On the conspiracy count he was given a two year sentence to run concurrently with the other sentence. Daniel was fined $1,000 and sentenced generally on the substantive counts to imprisonment for thirty months. On the conspiracy count he was fined $500 and given a two year sentence to run concurrently with the other sentence. The judgments of conviction were affirmed by the Circuit Court of Appeals. . . .

It is contended that there was insufficient evidence to implicate Daniel in the conspiracy. But we think there was enough evidence for submission of the issue to the jury.

There is, however, no evidence to show that Daniel participated directly in the commission of the substantive offenses on which his conviction has been sustained, although there was evidence to show that these substantive offenses were in fact committed by Walter in furtherance of the unlawful agreement or conspiracy existing between the brothers. The question was submitted to the jury on the theory that each petitioner could be found guilty of the substantive offenses, if it was found at the time those offenses were committed petitioners were parties to an unlawful conspiracy and the substantive offenses charged were in fact committed in furtherance of it.[6]

Daniel relies on United States v. Sall (C.C.A. 3d) 116 F.2d 745. That case held that participation in the conspiracy was not itself enough to sustain a conviction for the substantive offense even though it was committed in furtherance of the conspiracy. The court held that, in addition to evidence that the offense was in fact committed in furtherance of the conspiracy, evidence of direct participation in the commission of the substantive offense or other evidence from which participation might fairly be inferred was necessary.

We take a different view. We have here a continuous conspiracy. There is here no evidence of the affirmative action on the part of Daniel which is necessary to establish his withdrawal from it. Hyde v. United States, 225 U.S. 347, 369. As stated in that case, "Having joined in an unlawful scheme, having constituted agents for its performance, scheme and agency to be continuous until full fruition be secured, until he does some act to disavow or defeat the purpose he is in no situation to claim the delay of the law. As the offense has not been terminated or accomplished, he is still offending. And we think, consciously of-

---

6. . . . Daniel was not indicted as an aider or abetter (see Criminal Code, §332, 18 U.S.C.A. 550), nor was his case submitted to the jury on that theory.

fending, offending as certainly, as we have said, as at the first moment of his confederation, and consciously through every moment of its existence." And so long as the partnership in crime continues the partners act for each other in carrying it forward. It is settled that "an overt act of one partner may be the act of all without any new agreement specifically directed to that act." Motive or intent may be proved by the acts or declarations of some of the conspirators in furtherance of the common objective. The governing principle is the same when the substantive offense is committed by one of the conspirators in furtherance of the unlawful project. The criminal intent to do the act is established by the formation of the conspiracy. Each conspirator instigated the commission of the crime. The unlawful agreement contemplated precisely what was done. It was formed for the purpose. The act done was in execution of the enterprise. The rule which holds responsible one who counsels, procures, or commands another to commit a crime is founded on the same principle. That principle is recognized in the law of conspiracy when the overt act of one partner in crime is attributable to all. An overt act is an essential ingredient of the crime of conspiracy under §37 of the Criminal Code, 18 U.S.C.A. §88 [now §371]. If that can be supplied by the act of one conspirator, we fail to see why the same or other acts in furtherance of the conspiracy are likewise not attributable to the others for the purpose of holding them responsible for the substantive offense.

A different case would arise if the substantive offense committed by one of the conspirators was not in fact done in furtherance of the conspiracy, did not fall within the scope of the unlawful project, or was merely a part of the ramifications of the plan which could not be reasonably foreseen as a necessary or natural consequence of the unlawful agreement. But as we read this record, that is not this case.

Affirmed.

JUSTICE RUTLEDGE, dissenting in part.

The judgment concerning Daniel Pinkerton should be reversed. In my opinion it is without precedent here and is a dangerous precedent to establish.

Daniel and Walter, who were brothers living near each other, were charged in several counts with substantive offenses, and then a conspiracy count was added naming those offenses as overt acts. The proof showed that Walter alone committed the substantive crimes. There was none to establish that Daniel participated in them, aided and abetted Walter in committing them, or knew that he had done so. Daniel in fact was in the penitentiary, under sentence for other crimes, when some of Walter's crimes were done.

There was evidence, however, to show that over several years Daniel and Walter had confederated to commit similar crimes concerned with unlawful possession, transportation, and dealing in whiskey, in fraud of the federal revenues. On this evidence both were convicted of conspiracy. Walter also was convicted on the substantive counts on the proof of his committing the crimes charged. Then, on that evidence without more than the proof of Daniel's criminal agreement with Walter and the latter's overt acts, which were also the substantive offenses charged, the court told the jury they could find Daniel guilty of those substantive offenses. They did so. . . .

Daniel has been held guilty of the substantive crimes committed only by Walter on proof that he did no more than conspire with him to commit offenses of the same general character. There was no evidence that he counseled, advised or had knowledge of those particular acts or offenses. There was, therefore, none that he aided, abetted or took part in them. There was only evidence sufficient to show that he had agreed with Walter at some past time to engage in such transactions generally. As to Daniel this was only evidence of conspiracy, not of substantive crime.

The Court's theory seems to be that Daniel and Walter became general partners in crime by virtue of their agreement and because of that agreement without more on his part Daniel became criminally responsible as a principal for everything Walter did thereafter in the nature of a criminal offense of the general sort the agreement contemplated, so long as there was not clear evidence that Daniel had withdrawn from or revoked the agreement. Whether or not his commitment to the penitentiary had that effect, the result is a vicarious criminal responsibility as broad as, or broader than, the vicarious civil liability of a partner for acts done by a co-partner in the course of the firm's business. . . .

STATE v. BRIDGES, 133 N.J. 447, 628 A.2d 270 (1993) (Handler, J.): [At a birthday party for a 16-year-old friend, defendant got into a heated argument with another guest, Andy Strickland. Defendant left, yelling that he would return with help. He recruited two acquaintances, Bing and Rolle, to accompany him back to the party, where he expected a confrontation. On the way back, they stopped at Bing's house and picked up guns, to be used to hold Strickland's supporters at bay while defendant fought it out with him. When they returned to the party, defendant began fighting with a friend of Strickland's, while Bing and Rolle stood by. A member of the crowd hit Bing in the face, whereupon Bing and Rolle drew their guns and began firing — first into the air and then into the crowd, as onlookers tried to flee. One of the onlookers was fatally wounded. At trial defendant was convicted of conspiracy to commit aggravated assault and of several substantive crimes including murder. On the murder count defendant was sentenced to life imprisonment, with parole ineligibility for a minimum of 30 years. The intermediate appellate court held that defendant was not responsible for the murder committed by Rolle and Bing in the course of the conspiracy. The prosecution appealed to the New Jersey Supreme Court.]

The Appellate Division majority determined that the Code of Criminal Justice, which provides that the involvement in a conspiracy can be the basis for criminal liability for the commission of substantive crimes, N.J.S.A. 2C:2-6b(4), requires a level of culpability and state of mind that is identical to that required of accomplice liability. The Appellate Division therefore ruled that a conspirator is vicariously liable for the substantive crimes committed by co-conspirators only when the conspirator had the same intent and purpose as the co-conspirator who committed the crimes.

The provision of the New Jersey Code of Criminal Justice . . . that posits criminal liability on the basis of participation in a conspiracy is silent with respect to its culpability requirement. It provides:

> A person is legally accountable for the conduct of another person when: . . . He
> is engaged in a conspiracy with such other person.

The majority below concluded that the Code contemplated "complete congruity" between accomplice and vicarious conspirator liability. . . . The Appellate

Division majority reasoned that *Pinkerton* . . . mandates that a crime "must have been within [a co-conspirator's] contemplation when he entered into the agreement and reasonably comprehended by his purpose and intention in entering into the agreement."

. . . That understanding of *Pinkerton* is not supported. . . . [I]t has not been disputed that [*Pinkerton*] purported to impose vicarious liability on each conspirator for the acts of others based on an objective standard of reasonable foreseeability. . . . [I]t was understood that the liability of a co-conspirator under the objective standard of reasonable foreseeability would be broader than that of an accomplice, where the defendant must actually foresee and intend the result of his or her acts.

That understanding of *Pinkerton* is also widely accepted by commentators and treatises, whether they are critical of its rule, or only expounding the existing law. . . .

We appreciate the concern of the concurring opinion that such a standard of vicarious liability for conspirators differs from that of accomplices. Although conspirator liability is circumscribed by the requirement of a close causal connection between the conspiracy and the substantive crime, that standard concededly is less strict than that defining accomplice accountability. It is, however, evident that the Legislature chose to address the special dangers inherent in group activity and therefore intended to include the crime of conspiracy as a distinctive basis for vicarious criminal liability.[a] . . .

Accordingly, we conclude, and now hold, that a co-conspirator may be liable for the commission of substantive criminal acts that are not within the scope of the conspiracy if they are reasonably foreseeable as the necessary or natural consequences of the conspiracy. . . .

The conspiracy [here] did not have as its objective the purposeful killing of another person. Nevertheless, the evidence discloses that the conspiratorial plan contemplated bringing loaded guns to keep a large contingent of young hostile partygoers back from a beating of one of their friends, and that it could be anticipated that the weapon might be fired at the crowd. . . .

From that evidence a jury could conclude that a reasonably foreseeable risk and a probable and natural consequence of carrying out a plan to intimidate the crowd by using loaded guns would be that one of the gunslingers would intentionally fire at somebody, and, under the circumstances, that act would be sufficiently connected to the original conspirational plan to provide a just basis for a determination of guilt for that substantive crime.

[Reversed.]

---

a. N.J. Stat. §2C:2-6 provides as follows:

    b. A person is legally accountable for the conduct of another person when: . . .
        (3) He is an accomplice of such other person in the commission of an offense; or
        (4) He is engaged in a conspiracy with such other person.
    c. A person is an accomplice of another person in the commission of an offense if:
        (1) With the purpose of promoting or facilitating the commission of the offense; he
            (a) Solicits such other person to commit it;
            (b) Aids or agrees or attempts to aid such other person in planning or committing it; or
            (c) Having a legal duty to prevent the commission of the offense, fails to make proper effort so to do; or
        (2) His conduct is expressly declared by law to establish his complicity. — Eds.

O'HERN, J., concurring in part and dissenting in part. An interpretation of the provisions of the Code of Criminal Justice that would allow a sentence of life imprisonment to be imposed on the basis of the negligent appraisal of a risk that another would commit a homicide, conflicts with the internal structure of the Code. . . . If we assume, as the majority does, that Bridges did not intend that Shawn Lockley be killed, he could not have been convicted of attempted murder.

Nor could defendant have been convicted as an accomplice to the murder. . . .

And finally, defendant could not even have been found guilty of conspiracy to commit murder. A person is guilty of a conspiracy to commit an offense only if "*with the purpose* of promoting or facilitating its commission he" or she agrees with another person that they will "engage in conduct which constitutes such crime" or agrees to aid such person "in the planning or commission of such crime." N.J.S.A. 2C:5-2a (emphasis added).

The Code establishes a carefully-measured grid of criminal responsibility. . . . Thus, one who causes the death of another with the knowledge or purpose to kill will be guilty of murder and can be sentenced to death in certain circumstances or to life imprisonment with a minimum of thirty years without parole. . . .

The manslaughter offenses require a finding that an actor causing death has exhibited a reckless disregard for human life. When that recklessness is in disregard of a *probability* that death may occur, the offense is aggravated manslaughter and carries a penalty of up to thirty years in prison. When the proof shows reckless disregard of a possibility of causing death, the offense is reckless manslaughter and carries the penalty of a first-degree crime, up to twenty years in prison. Except for one form of vehicular homicide, N.J.S.A. 2C:11-4b(3), *no negligent homicide* exists under New Jersey law, much less a crime of negligent murder.

. . . This case is an example of the most extreme sort — life imprisonment with no possibility of parole for thirty years on the basis of a negligent mental state. . . . The most reasonable construction of N.J.S.A. 2C:2-6b(4) is that the Legislature intended that the conspirator to the commission of an offense, like an accomplice to the commission of an offense, be punished as a principal. . . . No liability is foreseen [under the statute] other than for the crime or crimes that were the object of the conspiracy.

NOTES AND PROBLEMS

1. Liability of a new conspirator for prior acts of co-conspirators. It is often said that upon joining an ongoing conspiracy, a person becomes liable for all acts committed by co-conspirators in furtherance of the conspiracy, including acts committed prior to his joining. See, e.g., 16 Am. Jur. 2d Conspiracy §20 (1979). Such statements are sometimes misinterpreted to suggest that a defendant is liable under *Pinkerton* for *substantive crimes* that co-conspirators committed before he joined the conspiracy. But *Pinkerton* liability is not retroactive. As explained in United States v. Blackmon, 839 F.2d 900, 908-909 (2d Cir. 1988):

The confusion here is that with regard to liability for *conspiracy*, a defendant may be legally responsible for acts of co-conspirators prior to that defendant's entry into the conspiracy [in the sense that such acts may be used as evidence against him in the prosecution for the crime of conspiracy], whereas, with regard to *substantive offenses*, a defendant cannot be retroactively liable for offenses committed prior to his joining the conspiracy.

See also Levine v. United States, 383 U.S. 265, 266 (1965), where the Court vacated a conviction after the Solicitor General conceded that "an individual cannot be held criminally liable for substantive offenses committed . . . before that individual had joined . . . the conspiracy."

2. *Conspiracy and complicity compared.* As we saw in the section on complicity, pages 657-658 supra, some jurisdictions now use an objective foreseeability test to determine the liability of an accomplice for originally unintended crimes committed by the principal in the course of the criminal endeavor. In these jurisdictions, the *Pinkerton* theory of conspiratorial liability and the objective theory of accomplice liability produce similar results. Under the more traditional view, illustrated by the *Bridges* case, liability as an *accomplice* requires proof that the secondary party intended to promote or facilitate the specific offense for which the prosecution seeks to hold him accountable. In jurisdictions adhering to this view, liability as a co-conspirator under a *Pinkerton* theory represents a considerable expansion of the liability that the co-conspirator would face under the normal rules of accomplice liability.

3. *Problems.* (a) In the following hypothetical case, consider the liability of each of the parties for the crimes committed by the others under (1) the normal doctrines of complicity and (2) the doctrine of vicarious conspiratorial accessorial liability (Note, Developments in the Law — Criminal Conspiracy, 72 Harv. L. Rev. 920, 996 (1959)):

> A is the organizer and ringleader of a conspiracy to rob banks. He hires B and C to rob banks *1* and *2* respectively. Although B and C do not meet face-to-face, both know that they are members of a large conspiracy and each knows of the other's assignment. At A's instigation, D, knowing of the conspiracy, steals a car for use in the robberies. B and C perform their robberies, the former using D's car.

(b) In People v. Luparello, 187 Cal. App. 3d 410, 231 Cal. Rptr. 832 (1987), supra page 655, defendant, who was attempting to locate his former girlfriend Terri, agreed with several friends to beat up a man named Martin, in order to force Martin to disclose Terri's whereabouts. When one of the conspirators lured Martin outside of his house, another conspirator, who was waiting in a parked car, fired six shots at Martin and killed him. Luparello, who was not present at the scene, was convicted of first-degree murder. Is the conviction proper under the *Pinkerton* doctrine? Under any other doctrine?

(c) In People v. Brigham, 216 Cal. App. 3d 1039, 265 Cal. Rptr. 486 (1989), supra page 658, defendant and one Bluitt set out to kill a man named "Chuckie." They saw a teenager on the street, defendant said, "That is Chuckie," and the two men walked toward the teenager, carrying their weapons. When they got closer, defendant said to Bluitt, "[T]hat is not Chuckie. . . . Don't do it. . . . That's not the dude." Bluitt rejected defendant's advice, saying that he wanted to let people "know we [are] serious." Bluitt fired twice, killing the teen-ager. Because of Bluitt's "hardheaded and erratic nature," the prosecution ar-gued and the jury found that defendant could "reasonably foresee" that Bluitt, once set in motion, might knowingly kill someone other than his assigned target. On this basis defendant was convicted of first-degree murder. Is the conviction proper under the *Pinkerton* doctrine? Under any other doctrine?

(d) Garcia negotiated the sale of 17 kilograms of cocaine to an undercover agent, and sat in the back seat of the car that co-defendant Soto drove to the meeting where they delivered the drugs. Garcia and Soto were arrested, and the next day, in a search of Soto's car, agents found a loaded handgun under the front floormat near the driver's seat. Under *Pinkerton*, is Garcia chargeable with Soto's weapons possession offense? See United States v. Garcia, 909 F.2d 1346, 1350 (9th Cir. 1990):

> [I]t does not appear from the record that Garcia had actual knowledge of Soto's possession of the gun, which was hidden under the floormat. Nor can we tell from the record how well Garcia and Soto knew each other. . . . While this court has "stop(ped) short of holding that there is a presumption as to the presence of a firearm in illicit narcotics transactions," we have noted that "trafficking in narcot-ics is very often related to the carrying and use of firearms." In light of the large amount of drugs involved in this case, Soto's possession of the gun was reasonably foreseeable.

Compare United States v. Johnson, 886 F.2d 1120 (9th Cir. 1989): Defendant was convicted as the co-conspirator of two men who were selling cocaine from a "crack" house. In a search of the house police found 15 grams of cocaine base, 480 grams of cocaine, and a gun. Though there was no evidence that defendant knew about the gun, she was convicted of the weapons offense under a *Pinkerton* theory, with the result of raising her sentence from five to ten years' imprison-ment. Was the weapons conviction proper? The court said (id. at 1123):

> When an individual conspires to sell cocaine in a "crack house" operation, it is reasonable to assume that a weapon of some kind would be carried.

UNITED STATES v. ALVAREZ, 755 F.2d 830 (11th Cir. 1985) (Kravitch, J.): [A run-down motel in Miami, Florida was the scene of a drug "buy" that had been arranged after long negotiation. Undercover agents from the Bureau of Alco-hol, Tobacco, and Firearms (BATF) were in the motel room with the drug deal-ers, waiting for another dealer to return with a quantity of cocaine that the agents had agreed to buy for $147,000. On the arrival of the cocaine other agents outside began to converge on the motel and a shoot-out started in the motel room. One of the BATF agents was killed and the other agent, along with two of the cocaine dealers, was seriously wounded. All the dealers were convicted of conspiracy to commit and commission of various drug offenses. Two of them, Alvarez and Simon, who shot the agents, were also convicted of first-degree mur-der of a federal agent. Three of the dealers, Portal, Concepcion, and Hernan-dez, were convicted of second-degree murder, though they played no part in the shooting.] Appellants Portal, Concepcion, and Hernandez contend that their murder convictions . . . were based on an unprecedented and improper exten-sion of Pinkerton v. United States, 328 U.S. 640 (1946), . . . The[y] argue that murder is not a reasonably foreseeable consequence of a drug conspiracy, and that their murder convictions therefore should be reversed. We conclude that, although the murder convictions of the three appellants may represent an unprecedented application of *Pinkerton*, such an application is not improper. . . .

Upon reviewing the record, we find ample evidence to support the jury's conclusion that the murder was a reasonably foreseeable consequence of the drug conspiracy alleged in the indictment. In making this determination, we rely on two critical factors. First, the evidence clearly established that the drug conspiracy was designed to effectuate the sale of a large quantity of cocaine. . . .

Second, based on the amount of drugs and money involved, the jury was entitled to infer that, at the time the cocaine sale was arranged, the conspirators must have been aware of the likelihood (1) that at least some of their number would be carrying weapons, and (2) that deadly force would be used, if necessary, to protect the conspirators' interests. . . . In our opinion, these two critical factors provided ample support for the jury's conclusion that the murder was a reasonably foreseeable consequence of the drug conspiracy alleged in the indictment. . . .

The three appellants also contend that, even if the murder was reasonably foreseeable, their murder convictions nevertheless should be reversed. The appellants argue that the murder was sufficiently distinct from the intended purposes of the drug conspiracy, and that their individual roles in the conspiracy were sufficiently minor, that they should not be held responsible for the murder. We are not persuaded. . . .

We acknowledge that the instant case is not a typical *Pinkerton* case. Here, the murder of Agent Rios was not within the originally intended scope of the conspiracy, but instead occurred as a result of an unintended turn of events. We have not found, nor has the government cited, any authority for the proposition that all conspirators, regardless of individual culpability, may be held responsible under *Pinkerton* for reasonably foreseeable but originally unintended substantive crimes.[25] Furthermore, we are mindful of the potential due process limitations on the *Pinkerton* doctrine in cases involving attenuated relationships between the conspirator and the substantive crime.

Nevertheless, these considerations do not require us to reverse the murder convictions of Portal, Concepcion, and Hernandez. . . . All three were more than "minor" participants in the drug conspiracy. Portal served as a lookout in front of the Hurricane Motel during part of the negotiations that led to the shoot-out, and the evidence indicated that he was armed. Concepcion introduced the agents to Alvarez, the apparent leader of the conspiracy, and was present when

---

25. The imposition of *Pinkerton* liability for such crimes is not wholly unprecedented. See, e.g., Government of Virgin Islands v. Dowling, 633 F.2d 660, 666 (3d cir.) (1980) (conspiracy to commit bank robbery; substantive crime of assault with deadly weapons against police officers, committed during escape attempt); Park v. Huff, 506 F.2d 849, 859 (5th Cir.) (1975) (liquor conspiracy; substantive crime of first degree murder of local district attorney, committed in attempt to stop investigation of illegal liquor sales). In each of the aforementioned cases, however, vicarious liability was imposed only on "major" participants in the conspiracy.

At trial in the instant case, the government's attorney argued that *Pinkerton* liability for Agent Rios' murder properly could be imposed on all of the conspirators, and expressed the view that prosecutorial discretion would protect truly "minor" participants, such as appellants Rios and Raymond, from liability for the far more serious crimes committed by their co-conspirators. We do not find this argument persuasive. In our view, the liability of such "minor" participants must rest on a more substantial foundation than the mere whim of the prosecutor.

the shoot-out started. Finally, Hernandez, the manager of the motel, allowed the drug transactions to take place on the premises and acted as a translator during part of the negotiations that led to the shoot-out.

In addition, all three appellants had actual knowledge of at least some of the circumstances and events leading up to the murder. The evidence that Portal was carrying a weapon demonstrated that he anticipated the possible use of deadly force to protect the conspirators' interests. Moreover, both Concepcion and Hernandez were present when Alvarez stated that he would rather be dead than go back to prison, indicating that they, too, were aware that deadly force might be used to prevent apprehension by Federal agents.

. . . We therefore hold that *Pinkerton* liability for the murder of Agent Rios properly was imposed on the three appellants. . . .[27]

NOTE ON THE MERITS OF PINKERTON

1. In support of the *Pinkerton* rule, see the statement of Deputy Assistant Attorney General Kenney to a Senate subcommittee considering this issue in the context of a revision of the federal criminal law (quoted in Note, 75 Colum. L. Rev. 1122, 1152 (1975)):

> The ever-increasing sophistication of organized crime presents a compelling reason against abandonment of *Pinkerton*. Complicated and highly refined stock frauds . . . and narcotics conspiracies represent a substantial and ever-increasing threat to society justifying retention of the *Pinkerton* doctrine. Empirical evidence has repeatedly demonstrated that those who form and control illegal enterprises are generally well insulated from prosecutions, with the exception of prosecutions predicated upon the theory of conspiracy. To preclude uniformly their exposure to additional sanctions, regardless of the circumstances, for the very crimes which sustain their illegal ventures, would have the most unfortunate and inequitable consequences.

2. Compare People v. McGee, 49 N.Y.2d 48, 399 N.E.2d 1177, 1181-1182 (1979), where the court observed, in rejecting the *Pinkerton* doctrine:

> The crime of conspiracy is an offense separate from the crime that is the object of the conspiracy. Once an illicit agreement is shown, the overt act of any conspirator may be attributed to other conspirators to establish the offense of conspiracy. . . . It is not offensive to permit a conviction of conspiracy to stand on the overt act committed by another, for the act merely provides corroboration of the existence of the agreement and indicates that the agreement has reached a point where it poses a sufficient threat to society to impose sanctions. . . . But it is repugnant to our system of jurisprudence, where guilt is generally personal to the defendant, . . . to impose punishment, not for the socially harmful agreement to which the defendant is a party, but for substantive offenses in which he did not participate. . . .

---

27. Although our decision today extends the *Pinkerton* doctrine to cases involving reasonably foreseeable but originally unintended substantive crimes, we emphasize that we do so only within narrow confines. Our holding is limited to conspirators who played more than a "minor" role in the conspiracy, or who had actual knowledge of at least some of the circumstances and events culminating in the reasonably foreseeable but originally unintended substantive crime.

3. The Model Penal Code, as well as many of the reformed state codes, have rejected the *Pinkerton* doctrine. See State ex rel. Woods v. Cohen, 173 Ariz. 497, 844 P.2d 1147 (1992); Note, 75 Colum. L. Rev. 1122, 1151 (1975). Supporting that position, the drafters of the Model Penal Code stated as follows (Model Penal Code and Commentaries, Comment to §2.06(3) at 307 (1985)):

> The Model Code . . . does not make "conspiracy" as such a basis of complicity in substantive offenses committed in furtherance of its aims. It asks, instead, more specific questions about the behavior charged to constitute complicity, such as whether the defendant solicited commission of the particular offense or whether he aided, or agreed or attempted to aid, in its commission.
>
> The reason for this treatment is that there appears to be no better way to confine within reasonable limits the scope of liability to which conspiracy may theoretically give rise. In People v. Luciano [277 N.Y. 348, 14 N.E.2d 433 (1938)], for example, Luciano and others were convicted of sixty-two counts of compulsory prostitution, each count involving a specific instance of placing a girl in a house of prostitution, receiving money for so doing or receiving money from the earnings of a prostitute — acts proved to have been committed pursuant to a combination to control commercialized vice in New York City.
>
> Liability was properly imposed with respect to these defendants, who directed and controlled the combination. They solicited and aided the commission of numberless specific crimes, including the ones for which they were held. But would so extensive a liability be just for each of the prostitutes or runners involved in the plan? They have, of course, committed their own crimes; they may actually have assisted in others but they exerted no substantial influence on the behavior of a hundred other prostitutes or runners, each pursuing his own ends within the shelter of the combination. A court would and should hold that they are parties to a conspiracy. . . . And they should also be held for those crimes they actually committed, or . . . for those to which they were accomplices. However, law would lose all sense of just proportion if simply because of the conspiracy itself each were held accountable for thousands of additional offenses of which he was completely unaware and which he did not influence at all. . . .
>
> Conspiracy may prove solicitation, aid or agreement to aid, etc.; it is evidentially important and may be sufficient for that purpose. But whether it suffices ought to be decided by the jurors; they should not be told that it establishes complicity as a matter of law. . . .

3. The Actus Reus of Conspiracy

INTRODUCTORY NOTE

As we have seen, conspiracy is typically defined as an agreement by two or more persons to commit a crime. The actus reus of the offense, therefore, is the agreement itself. As the Supreme Court stated in Ianelli v. United States, 420 U.S. 770, 777 n. 10 (1975), "agreement remains the essential element of the crime." But agreements to commit crime are rarely reduced to writing and even oral agreements are unlikely to make clear or explicit all the terms and conditions of the joint undertaking. How then can the necessary agreement be described and proved? For a representative statement of the applicable standard, consider United States v. James, 528 F.2d 999, 1011 (5th Cir. 1976):

lish the common plan element of a conspiracy, it is not necessary for the
ent to prove an express agreement between the alleged conspirators to go
d violate law. . . . "A conspiracy is seldom born of open covenants openly
t. The proof, by the very nature of the crime, must be circumstantial and
tneretore inferential to an extent varying with the conditions under which the
crime may be consummated." Direct Sales Co. v. United States, 319 U.S. 703, 714.
Knowledge by a defendant of all details or phases of a conspiracy is not required.
It is enough that he knows the essential nature of it. "And, it is black letter law that
all participants in a conspiracy need not know each other; all that is necessary is
that each know that it has a scope and that for its success it requires an organization
wider than may be disclosed by his personal participation."

INTERSTATE CIRCUIT, INC. v. UNITED STATES

Supreme Court of the United States
306 U.S. 208 (1939)

JUSTICE STONE delivered the opinion of the Court.
. . . This case is here on appeal . . . from a final decree of the District Court for
northern Texas restraining appellants from continuing in a combination and
conspiracy condemned by the court as a violation of Section 1 of the Sherman
Anti-Trust Act. . . .
[The case involved two related movie theater chains, Interstate Circuit and
Texas Consolidated Theaters, which together dominated the market for exhibiting films in the cities where their theaters were located. The other members of
the alleged conspiracy were eight independent corporations that distributed
films to theaters; together the eight distributed 75 percent of all first-run films
exhibited in the United States. Interstate and Consolidated admittedly had entered contractual agreements with each of the eight distributors, specifying the
terms on which the theaters would exhibit their films, but each individual contract between the exhibitor and a distributor could not by itself constitute an
unlawful conspiracy. In order to prove the Sherman Act violation, the Government had to establish that the eight distributors had an agreement with one
another.
[The centerpiece of the Government's case was a letter written by O'Donnell,
Interstate's manager, to each distributor, in which he asked compliance with two
demands as a condition of Interstate's continued exhibition of that distributor's
films. One demand was that the distributor agree that on subsequent runs it
would not permit its films to be shown in theaters charging an admission price
of less than 25 cents. (At the time, 1934-1935, admission tickets to see second-
run films in Texas theaters sold for as little as 10 or 15 cents!) Interstate's second
demand was that the distributor agree not to permit its first-run motion pictures
to be shown on a double-bill with another feature film.
[The letter addressed to each distributor identified all eight distributors as
addressees of the proposal, and subsequently each distributor agreed with Interstate to accept the proposed restrictions. On this basis the trial court found that
the distributors had agreed and conspired *with one another* to take uniform action on the Interstate proposals and to impose the demanded restrictions, in
violation of the Sherman Act.]

As is usual in cases of alleged unlawful agreements to restrain commerce, the Government is without the aid of direct testimony that the distributors entered into any agreement with each other to impose the restrictions upon subsequent-run exhibitors. In order to establish agreement it is compelled to rely on inferences drawn from the course of conduct of the alleged conspirators.

The trial court drew the inference of agreement from the nature of the proposals made on behalf of Interstate and Consolidated; from the manner in which they were made; from the substantial unanimity of action taken upon them by the distributors; and from the fact that appellants did not call as witnesses any of the superior officials who negotiated the contracts with Interstate or any official who, in the normal course of business, would have had knowledge of the existence or non-existence of such an agreement among the distributors. This conclusion is challenged by appellants because not supported by subsidiary findings or by the evidence. We think this inference of the trial court was rightly drawn from the evidence. . . .

The O'Donnell letter named on its face as addressees the eight local representatives of the distributors, and so from the beginning each of the distributors knew that the proposals were under consideration by the others. Each was aware that all were in active competition and that without substantially unanimous action with respect to the restrictions for any given territory there was risk of a substantial loss of the business and good will of the subsequent-run and independent exhibitors, but that with it there was the prospect of increased profits. There was, therefore, strong motive for concerted action, full advantage of which was taken by Interstate and Consolidated in presenting their demands to all in a single document.

There was risk, too, that without agreement diversity of action would follow. Compliance with the proposals involved a radical departure from the previous business practices of the industry and a drastic increase in admission prices of most of the subsequent-run theatres. . . .

It taxes credulity to believe that the several distributors would, in the circumstances, have accepted and put into operation with substantial unanimity such far-reaching changes in their business methods without some understanding that all were to join, and we reject as beyond the range of probability that it was the result of mere chance. . . .

While the District Court's finding of an agreement of the distributors among themselves is supported by the evidence, we think that in the circumstances of this case such agreement for the imposition of the restrictions upon subsequent-run exhibitors was not a prerequisite to an unlawful conspiracy. It was enough that, knowing that concerted action was contemplated and invited, the distributors gave their adherence to the scheme and participated in it. Each distributor was advised that the others were asked to participate; each knew that cooperation was essential to successful operation of the plan. They knew that the plan, if carried out, would result in a restraint of commerce, which, we will presently point out, was unreasonable within the meaning of the Sherman Act, and knowing it, all participated in the plan. The evidence is persuasive that each distributor early became aware that the others had joined. With that knowledge they renewed the arrangement and carried it into effect for the two successive years.

It is elementary that an unlawful conspiracy may be and often is formed without simultaneous action or agreement on the part of the conspirators. . . .

We think the conclusion is unavoidable that the conspiracy and each contract between Interstate and the distributors by which those consequences were effected are violations of the Sherman Act and that the District Court rightly enjoined the conspiracy among the distributors. Affirmed.

NOTES ON THE REQUIRED AGREEMENT

1. *Parallel action or common action? Interstate Circuit* is a landmark in the law of conspiracy, not only for antitrust cases but for the general problem of establishing the existence of a conspiratorial relationship. Consider the Court's statement that "in the circumstances of this case [an] agreement for the imposition of the restrictions . . . was not a prerequisite to an unlawful conspiracy. . . . It is elementary that an unlawful conspiracy may be and often is formed without simultaneous action or agreement on the part of the conspirators." How can this "elementary" proposition be reconciled with the definition of conspiracy? Without an agreement, what would the "conspiracy" be? Note that the evidence in *Interstate Circuit* could support an inference that the distributors actually spoke to one another and agreed to act in common. In other words, there might have been an express agreement, but its existence must be inferred from circumstantial evidence. Presumably, the Court meant that it was not necessary to establish *this kind* of agreement. Even if one were convinced that the distributors never communicated with one another at all, there would be a conspiracy because "each knew that cooperation was essential" and acted accordingly. In other words, a conspiracy may exist if there is no communication and no *express* agreement, provided that there is a tacit agreement reached without communication. But then what is the difference between parallel action that occurs because of a tacit agreement (that is, a conspiracy) and parallel action that occurs without any agreement at all?

2. *Problems.* (a) During an urban riot, one teenager shouts to three of his friends, "There's great stuff in that store, and the owner's a cheat. Let's go get it!" All four run into the store and start grabbing goods. Seeing the looting, two passersby, strangers to each other, enter the store and join in the looting. Are the four teenagers guilty of conspiracy? Are the two passersby guilty of conspiracy with each other? Are they guilty of conspiracy with the four teenagers?

Note that the answer can be important for several reasons. A conspiracy charge could permit a substantial increase in punishment. And if looter *X* assaults or kills the store owner while making his escape, his co-conspirator *Y* could be held liable for the assault or homicide. Has any of the looters conspired with any of the others? Are all of them guilty of conspiring with all the others?

(b) Motorist *M* loudly protests the action of an officer who stops him for a traffic violation, and a crowd gathers. When the officer attempts to make an arrest, *M* pushes the officer to the ground and various members of the crowd then assault the officer. Is *M* guilty of conspiracy? Griffin v. State, 455 S.W.2d 882 (Ala. 1970), finds a conspiracy on similar facts. Is this a correct result under the *Interstate Circuit* principle?

3. *The Coleridge Instruction.* In Rex v. Murphy, 173 Eng. Rep. 502, 508 (1837), Coleridge, J., directed the jury as follows:

You have been properly told that this being a charge of conspiracy, if you are of opinion that the acts, though done, were done without common concert and design between these two parties, the present charge cannot be supported. On the other hand, I am bound to tell you, that although the common design is the root of the charge, it is not necessary to prove that these two parties came together and actually agreed in terms to have this common design, and to pursue it by common means, and so to carry it into execution. This is not necessary, because in many cases of the most clearly-established conspiracies there are no means of proving any such thing, and neither law nor common sense requires that it should be proved. If you find that these two persons pursued by their acts the same object, often by the same means, one performing one part of an act and the other another part of the same act, so as to complete it, with a view to the attainment of the object which they were pursuing, you will be at liberty to draw the conclusion that they have been engaged in a conspiracy to effect that object. The question you have to ask yourselves is, "Had they this common design, and did they pursue it by these common means — the design being unlawful."

See Theodore W. Cousens, Agreement as an Element of Conspiracy, 23 Va. L. Rev. 898 (1937), describing the importation of the Coleridge instruction into the United States and its widespread acceptance by American courts. Commenting on this instruction, Glanville Williams observed (Criminal Law: The General Part 667 (2d ed. 1961)):

Properly read, this direction is a valuable statement of a principle of the law of evidence; but it is capable of dangerous misinterpretation. . . . A conspiracy is not merely a concurrence of wills but a concurrence resulting from agreement. Of course, if . . . two burglars actually executed their respective plans and were both caught in the house, they would be under a heavy suspicion of having acted in concert, and would be fortunate to convince a jury that they had not. . . . Nevertheless, if the jury are satisfied that the concurrence of the defendants' acts was accidental, the conspiracy charge must fail, for the concurrence of acts is only evidence of conspiracy, not equivalent to conspiracy. It is submitted that Coleridge, J., did not mean anything other than this; his direction meant only that agreement could be implied from acts in the absence of evidence that the concurrence was accidental.

UNITED STATES v. ALVAREZ

United States Court of Appeals, 5th Circuit
625 F.2d 1196 (1981)

[An indictment named Cifarelli, Cruz, and Peterson as co-conspirators in a plan to import marijuana into the United States. Alvarez was convicted of joining with the three others in a conspiracy to import 110,000 pounds of marijuana from Colombia by air. The government's evidence portrayed Alvarez as an underling who loaded electrical appliances aboard a plane that was to fly from the United States to Colombia, and who had stated he would unload a cargo of marijuana upon its return.

[Pursuant to arrangements with an undercover DEA agent (Martinez), Cifarelli came to meet the agent at the Opa-Locka airport. Alvarez drove a pickup truck in which Cruz and Cifarelli were riding. The truck was loaded with some household appliances, including a washer and dryer; the DEA agent asked Cifa-relli who Alvarez was and Cifarelli said Alvarez "would be at the off-loading site in the United States." The agent then spoke to Alvarez in Spanish and asked him if he planned to be at the unloading site. Alvarez nodded his head, signify-ing "yes," smiled, and asked the DEA agent if he was going on the plane. The agent said he was. After the conversation, Alvarez unloaded the household ap-pliances from the truck. The agent then spoke with Cruz, and, after Cruz out-lined his plans for arrival of the plane and its unloading, all were arrested.

[On appeal, a three-judge panel reversed Alvarez's conviction. The panel stated:

> A defendant does not join a conspiracy merely by participating in a substantive offense, or by associating with persons who are members of a conspiracy. . . . There-fore, even if a conspiracy between two parties is established, not every act of a third person that assists in the accomplishment of the objective of the conspiracy is a sufficient basis to demonstrate his concurrence in that agreement. . . .
>
> When we consider all the evidence in the case, we find that, at most, the govern-ment proved that Alvarez was a menial who intended to lend his pickup truck and his strong back to a plot confected by the mind of others. . . . Whatever his subjec-tive transgressions, he was not shown to have been a conspirator or to have adopted or joined in the scheme contrived by others.

[The Fifth Circuit granted a rehearing en banc.]

REAVLEY, J. . . . A panel of this court . . . concluded that the government had failed to produce sufficient evidence that Alvarez had joined in the agreement to engage in illegal activity. Sitting en banc we now reach a different conclusion; the evidence was sufficient to convict.

The government was not required to prove that Alvarez had knowledge of all the details of the conspiracy or each of its members, provided that [the] prose-cution established his knowledge of the essential of the conspiracy. Nor can a defendant escape criminal responsibility on the grounds that he did not join the conspiracy until well after its inception, or because he plays only a minor role in the total scheme.

We agree with the panel that the aggregate of the evidence is sufficient to infer that Alvarez knew that criminal activity was afoot. It must also have been obvious to him that there was conspiracy to import the contraband because prior planning and concerted action would be required to load the marijuana in Colombia, fly it into this country, and unload it upon its arrival. Alvarez' join-der in the illicit compact is inferable on two fronts. First, there is direct evidence that Alvarez intended to be at the off-loading site. A jury may well conclude that his intended presence manifested a prior agreement to assist in the unloading. Alternatively, the nodded head may be viewed as assurance to Martinez, then thought to be one in confederacy with Cifarelli and Cruz, that Alvarez would be at the unloading site to insure that the aircraft was unloaded rapidly. That such assurances to assuage jittery accomplices can constitute conduct in furtherance of the conspiracy, indicating joinder, [has also been] recognized. . . .

The evidence would have been insufficient to support the conviction without the proof that Cifarelli and Alvarez assured agent Martinez that Alvarez would be on hand at the place and time of the airplane's return to Florida. That proof, combined with all of the other evidence, clearly warranted the verdict of guilt.

A reasonable jury could very well conclude that only one with knowledge of the marijuana, and who had agreed to participate in the scheme to accomplish its importation, would promise to be on hand at a remote and unlikely area for the unloading of cargo. . . .

[J]udgment of conviction is affirmed.

Vance, J., with whom Fay, Rubin, Kravitch, Henderson, Politz, Hatchett, Tate, and Thomas A. Clark, JJ., join, dissenting. Alvarez nodded his head and smiled. For this he will go to the penitentiary.

In another case a smile and the nod of the head may be sufficient to establish guilt. Here it clearly was not.

This is not a case where an alleged conspirator was engaged in an illegal act or in the presence of a large quantity of contraband so that it reasonably may be inferred that he knew what was afoot. . . . Alvarez was engaged in a completely legal act. He was loading a washing machine onto an airplane. He was asked whether he was going to be there at the unloading site when the plane got back. It was in response to this innocuous inquiry that he smiled and nodded his head. This is all the admissible evidence to which we are cited to show that Alvarez knew of the unlawful conspiracy and agreed to join in it. . . .

Alvarez may have been a guilty co-conspirator or he may have been a humble workman performing a lawful act totally unrelated to any conspiracy, who simply indicated that he would report back to work as instructed. To my mind the majority opinion suggests no way that a jury reasonably could accept one hypothesis to the exclusion of the other.

The conspiracy statutes are vitally important to the protection of society. Yet the potential for injustice in conspiracy cases is enormous. The prosecutor's net may well ensnare the innocent as well as the guilty. The presentation of evidence in such cases is sometimes almost chaotic. We should use particular care to ensure that the prosecution actually proved that the defendant was a participant in the conspiracy before he is sent to prison. Our concept of justice rests on the basic notion that it is only for personal guilt that punishment is justified. . . . I would reverse.

NOTE, DEVELOPMENTS IN THE LAW — CRIMINAL CONSPIRACY, 72 Harv. L. Rev. 920, 933-935 (1959): The basic principle that a conspiracy is not established without proof of an agreement has been weakened, or at least obscured, by three factors. The first is the courts' unfortunate tendency to overemphasize a rule of evidence at the expense of a rule of law. Conspiracy is by nature a clandestine offense. It is improbable that the parties will enter into their illegal agreement openly; it is not necessary, in fact, that all the parties ever have direct contact with one another, or know one another's identity, or even communicate verbally their intention to agree. It is therefore unlikely that the prosecution will be able to prove the formation of the agreement by direct evidence, and the jury must usually infer its existence from the clear co-operation among the parties. But in their zeal to emphasize that the agreement need not be proved directly, the courts sometimes neglect to say that it need be proved at all. The second factor tending to undermine the strict rule that agreement must be proved is the existence of what are perhaps more liberal requirements in antitrust cases, which, although they may be justified in that area, are ever likely to be extended to the general law of conspiracy.

The third, and perhaps the most important, factor is another result of the verbal ambiguity which leads courts to deal with the crime of conspiracy as though it were a group rather than an act. If a "conspiracy" consists of the people who are working towards a proscribed object, and if one who aids and abets a substantive offense becomes liable as a principal thereto, then it follows that one who aids and abets these men in the attainment of their object becomes liable as a conspirator. It is this reasoning from a faulty premise — a premise difficult to discover since it is assumed rather than articulated — which leads an appellate court to say: "The (lower) court clearly instructed the jury that, if defendant had knowledge that Jensen and Clark were in a conspiracy . . . and . . . assisted and aided Jensen and Clark by selling and delivering the materials to be used, thus making it possible to carry out the unlawful object of the conspiracy, defendant was a coconspirator. This is a correct statement of the law." But to aid and abet a crime it is necessary not merely to help the criminal, but to help him in the commission of the particular criminal offense. A person does not aid and abet a conspiracy by helping the "conspiracy" to commit a substantive offense, for the crime of conspiracy is separate from the offense which is its object. . . . [T]o convict the defendant of conspiracy it is necessary to prove not only knowledge on his part that he was helping a wrongful enterprise, but also knowledge on another's part that he intended to do so, and at least a tacit agreement to give and accept such help.

PROBLEM

The COWBOY, a large shrimping boat fully equipped with shrimping gear, left a Florida port with its captain and a crew of four, including Freeman, who was the cook. After several hours of sailing, the captain diverted the ship from its original course and proceeded to a point off the coast of Nicaragua, where the crew of another vessel loaded 20 tons of marijuana into the shrimping boat's ice hold while the COWBOY's crew looked on. The COWBOY then sailed toward the United States, but it was intercepted by the U.S. Coast Guard. The captain and his four crew members were convicted of conspiracy to import marijuana. Did the crew members join in the conspiratorial agreement? Does the reasoning of the majority in *Alvarez* support a finding of conspiracy here? In United States v. Freeman, 660 F.2d 1030, 1036 (5th Cir. 1981), the court, upholding the convictions of all four crew members, stated:

> Appellants contend that mere presence and association is insufficient to convict them of conspiracy. The simple response to this argument is that a ten day voyage on a vessel that was bulging with 41,000 pounds of marijuana constitutes much more than "mere presence" or "mere association." . . . [T]he probable length of the voyage, . . . the large quantity of marijuana on board, which made it indisputable that [defendants] had knowledge of the marijuana, and the necessarily close relationship between the captain of the trawler and his . . . crew were factors from which the jury could reasonably find guilt beyond a reasonable doubt.

Judge Godbold, dissenting on this point, commented (id. at 1038-1040):

> [Under the majority's approach,] every officer and every crewman on every fishing and shrimping boat that makes a "long voyage" . . . is now prima facie a

conspirator if a large quantity of contraband is found aboard. . . . [T]here is evidence from which it can be inferred that [the crew] had knowledge of a conspiracy in progress on the vessel. But knowledge is not participation in the conspiracy. . . . [Nor is] the crew's usual performance of duty and their failure to mutiny, take to lifeboats, or radio the Coast Guard.

NOTES ON THE OVERT ACT REQUIREMENT

Both at common law and under statutory formulations, conduct can be punishable as a conspiracy at points much farther back in the stages of preparation than the point where liability begins to attach for attempt. In some instances conspiracy is punishable without any overt act at all. In other situations an overt act must be proved, but the act may fall well short of the kind of conduct sufficient to constitute an attempt.

1. *Liability without an overt act.* At common law, the sole actus reus of conspiracy was the agreement itself; no "overt act" was required in addition. Does this mean that the offense becomes purely mental? Consider Mulcahy v. The Queen, L.R. 3 E. & I. App. 306, 316-317 (H.L. Ire. 1868). Defendants were indicted for conspiracy to foment the Irish rebellion. They argued that the indictment was defective for failing to charge some overt act, such as publishing writings or procuring arms. The court rejected the argument, stating:

A conspiracy consists not merely in the intention of two or more, but in the agreement of two or more to do an unlawful act, or to do a lawful act by unlawful means. So long as such a design rests in intention only, it is not indictable. When two agree to carry it into effect, the very plot is an act in itself, and the act of each of the parties, promise against promise, actus contra actum, capable of being enforced, if lawful, punishable if for a criminal object or for the use of criminal means. And so far as proof goes, conspiracy . . . is generally a matter of inference deduced from certain criminal acts of the parties accused, done in pursuance of an apparent criminal purpose in common between them. The number and the compact give weight and cause danger, and this is more especially the case in a conspiracy like those charged in this indictment. Indeed, it seems a reduction to absurdity, that procuring a single stand of arms should be a sufficient overt act to make the disloyal design indictable, and that conspiring with a thousand men to enlist should not.

2. *Statutes requiring an overt act.* American conspiracy statutes have typically added an overt-act requirement. Note, for example, the wording of 18 U.S.C. §371, quoted in Note 1(b), page 730 supra. But it is not unusual for statutes to dispense with this overt-act requirement in the case of conspiracies to commit the most serious offenses. See, e.g., Model Penal Code §5.03(5), Appendix. See also 21 U.S.C. §846, which makes no mention of an overt-act requirement for conspiracies to distribute illegal drugs.[9]

The usual reason for requiring proof of an overt act is explained in Yates v. United States, 354 U.S. 298, 334 (1957): "The function of the overt act in a conspiracy prosecution is simply to manifest 'that the conspiracy is at work' . . .

9. The Supreme Court has refused to read an overt-act limitation into §846. See United States v. Shabani, 115 S. Ct. 382 (1994).

and is neither a project still resting solely in the minds of the conspirators nor a fully completed operation no longer in existence." Thus, even when an overt-act requirement applies, it generally can be satisfied by acts that would be considered equivocal or merely preparatory in the law of attempts. See Holmes, J., dissenting in Hyde v. United States, 225 U.S. 347, 387-388 (1912):

> An attempt, in the strictest sense, is an act expected to bring about a substantive wrong by the forces of nature. With it is classed the kindred offence where the act and the natural conditions present or supposed to be present are not enough to do the harm without a further act, but where it is so near to the result that if coupled with an intent to produce that result, the danger is very great. But combination, intention and overt act may all be present without amounting to a criminal attempt — as if all that were done should be an agreement to murder a man fifty miles away and the purchase of a pistol for the purpose. There must be dangerous proximity to success. . . . On the other hand, the essence of the conspiracy is being combined for an unlawful purpose — and if an overt act is required, it does not matter how remote the act may be from accomplishing the purpose, if done to effect it; that is, I suppose, in furtherance of it in any degree.

By contrast, some states have required a more substantial overt act. Ohio, for example, provides that an overt act is sufficient only "when it is of such character as to manifest a purpose on the part of the actor that the object of the conspiracy should be completed." Ohio Rev. Code Ann. tit. 29, §2923.01(B). Maine goes further toward bringing together the points at which liability begins for attempt and for conspiracy: The statute requires a "substantial step," which it defines as "conduct which, under the circumstances in which it occurs is strongly corroborative of the firmness of the actor's intent to complete commission of the crime"; it further provides that "speech alone may not constitute a substantial step." Maine Rev. Stat. Ann. tit. 17, §151.4.

3. Justifications for the traditional approach. Unlike the Maine and Ohio statutes just mentioned, the traditional view is that any "overt act" (or sometimes the act of agreement alone) suffices to render conduct punishable as a conspiracy. But what is there about an agreement to commit a crime that justifies dispensing with the normal requirement of substantial preparatory conduct? Consider Note, 14 U. Toronto Fac. L. Rev. 56, 61-62 (1956):

> Since we are fettered by an unrealistic law of criminal attempts, overbalanced in favour of external acts, awaiting the lit match or the cocked and aimed pistol, the law of criminal conspiracy has been employed to fill the gap. If there are two persons involved, legal sanctions can be applied to the actor's intentions; this can seldom be done if only one person is involved and if he is wise in the ways of the law but acts unsuccessfully alone.

Does this argument remain valid under modern codes that eliminate unrealistically rigid requirements from the law of attempt? For another defense of the traditional position, consider Model Penal Code and Commentaries, Comment to §5.03 at 388 (1985):

> *First:* The act of agreeing with another to commit a crime, like the act of soliciting, is concrete and unambiguous; it does not present the infinite degrees and

variations possible in the general category of attempts. The danger that truly equivocal behavior may be misinterpreted as preparation to commit a crime is minimized; purpose must be relatively firm before the commitment involved in agreement is assumed.

Second: If the agreement was to aid another to commit a crime or if it otherwise encouraged the crime's commission, complicity would be established in the commission of the substantive offense. It would be anomalous to hold that conduct that would suffice to establish criminality, if something else is done by someone else, is insufficient if the crime is never consummated. Although this reason covers less than all the cases of conspiracy, it is significant that it covers many others.

Third: In the course of preparation to commit a crime, the act of combining with another is significant both psychologically and practically, the former because it crosses a clear threshold in arousing expectations, the latter because it increases the likelihood that the offense will be committed. Sharing lends fortitude to purpose. The actor knows, moreover, that the future is no longer governed by his will alone; others may complete what he has had a hand in starting, even if he has a change of heart.

4. Questions. In *Alvarez,* page 747 supra, would the defendant's actions be punishable as an attempt? If not, what does the fact of agreement (even if there was one) add to his actions? In light of the policies against treating mere preparatory conduct as criminal, how does Alvarez's expressed willingness to help unload a future shipment suffice to justify treating his conduct as criminal?

4. The Mens Rea of Conspiracy

PEOPLE v. LAURIA

California District Court of Appeal
251 Cal. App. 2d 471, 59 Cal. Rptr. 628 (1967)

FLEMING, J. In an investigation of call-girl activity the police focused their attention on three prostitutes actively plying their trade on call, each of whom was using Lauria's telephone answering service, presumably for business purposes.

On January 8, 1965, Stella Weeks, a policewoman, signed up for telephone service with Lauria's answering service. Mrs. Weeks, in the course of her conversation with Lauria's officer manager, hinted broadly that she was a prostitute concerned with the secrecy of her activities and their concealment from the police. She was assured that the operation of the service was discreet and "about as safe as you can get." It was arranged that Mrs. Weeks need not leave her address with the answering service, but could pick up her calls and pay her bills in person.

On February 11, Mrs. Weeks talked to Lauria on the telephone and told him her business was modeling and she had been referred to the answering service by Terry, one of the three prostitutes under investigation. She complained that because of the operation of the service she had lost two valuable customers, referred to as tricks. Lauria defended his service and said that her friends had probably lied to her about having left calls for her. But he did not respond to Mrs. Weeks' hints that she needed customers in order to make money, other than to invite her to his house for a personal visit in order to get better acquainted. In the course of his talk he said "his business was taking messages."

On February 15, Mrs. Weeks talked on the telephone to Lauria's office manager and again complained of two lost calls, which she described as a $50 and a $100 trick. On investigation the office manager could find nothing wrong, but she said she would alert the switchboard operators about slip-ups on calls.

On April 1, Lauria and the three prostitutes were arrested. Lauria complained to the police that this attention was undeserved, stating that Hollywood Call Board had 60 to 70 prostitutes on its board while his own service had only 9 or 10, that he kept separate records for known or suspected prostitutes for the convenience of himself and the police. When asked if his records were available to police who might come to the office to investigate call girls, Lauria replied that they were whenever the police had a specific name. However, his service didn't "arbitrarily tell the police about prostitutes on our board. As long as they pay their bills we tolerate them." In a subsequent voluntary appearance before the Grand Jury Lauria testified he had always cooperated with the police. But he admitted he knew some of his customers were prostitutes, and he knew Terry was a prostitute because he had personally used her services, and he knew she was paying for 500 calls a month.

Lauria and the three prostitutes were indicted for conspiracy to commit prostitution, and nine overt acts were specified. Subsequently the trial court set aside the indictment as having been brought without reasonable or probable cause. The People have appealed, claiming that a sufficient showing of an unlawful agreement to further prostitution was made.

To establish agreement, the People need show no more than a tacit, mutual understanding between co-conspirators to accomplish an unlawful act. . . . Here the People attempted to establish a conspiracy by showing that Lauria, well aware that his codefendants were prostitutes who received business calls from customers through his telephone answering service, continued to furnish them with such service. This approach attempts to equate knowledge of another's criminal activity with conspiracy to further such criminal activity, and poses the question of the criminal responsibility of a furnisher of goods or services who knows his product is being used to assist the operation of an illegal business. Under what circumstances does a supplier become a part of a conspiracy to further an illegal enterprise by furnishing goods or services which he knows are to be used by the buyer for criminal purposes?

The two leading cases on this point face in opposite directions. In United States v. Falcone, 311 U.S. 205, the sellers of large quantities of sugar, yeast, and cans were absolved from participation in a moonshining conspiracy among distillers who bought from them, while in Direct Sales Co. v. United States, 319 U.S. 703, a wholesaler of drugs was convicted of conspiracy to violate the federal narcotic laws by selling drugs in quantity to a codefendant physician who was supplying them to addicts. The distinction between these two cases appears primarily based on the proposition that distributors of such dangerous products as drugs are required to exercise greater discrimination in the conduct of their business than are distributors of innocuous substances like sugar and yeast.

In the earlier case, *Falcone,* the sellers' knowledge of the illegal use of the goods was insufficient by itself to make the sellers participants in a conspiracy with the distillers who bought from them. Such knowledge fell short of proof of a conspiracy, and evidence on the volume of sales was too vague to support a jury finding that respondents knew of the conspiracy [with others] from the size of the sales alone.

In the later case of *Direct Sales,* the conviction of a drug wholesaler for conspiracy to violate federal narcotic laws was affirmed on a showing that it had actively promoted the sale of morphine sulphate in quantity and had sold codefendant physician, who practiced in a small town in South Carolina, more than 300 times his normal requirements of the drug, even though it had been repeatedly warned of the dangers of unrestricted sales of the drug. The court contrasted the restricted goods involved in *Direct Sales* with the articles of free commerce involved in *Falcone:* "All articles of commerce may be put to illegal ends," said the court. "But all do not have inherently the same susceptibility to harmful and illegal use. . . . This difference is important for two purposes. One is for making certain that the seller knows the buyer's intended illegal use. The other is to show that by the sale he intends to further, promote and cooperate in it. This intent, when given effect by overt act, is the gist of conspiracy. While it is not identical with mere knowledge that another proposes unlawful action, it is not unrelated to such knowledge. . . . The step from knowledge to intent and agreement may be taken. There is more than suspicion, more than knowledge, acquiescence, carelessness, indifference, lack of concern. There is informed and interested cooperation, stimulation, instigation. And there is also a 'stake in the venture' which, even if it may not be essential, is not irrelevant to the question of conspiracy." (319 U.S. at 710-713.)

While *Falcone* and *Direct Sales* may not be entirely consistent with each other in their full implications, they do provide us with a framework for the criminal liability of a supplier of lawful goods or services put to unlawful use. Both the element of *knowledge* of the illegal use of the goods or services and the element of *intent* to further that use must be present in order to make the supplier a participant in a criminal conspiracy.

Proof of *knowledge* is ordinarily a question of fact and requires no extended discussion in the present case. The knowledge of the supplier was sufficiently established when Lauria admitted he knew some of his customers were prostitutes and admitted he knew that Terry, an active subscriber to his service, was a prostitute. In the face of these admissions he could scarcely claim to have relied on the normal assumption an operator of a business or service is entitled to make, that his customers are behaving themselves in the eyes of the law. Because Lauria knew in fact that some of his customers were prostitutes, it is a legitimate inference he knew they were subscribing to his answering service for illegal business purposes and were using his service to make assignations for prostitution. On this record we think the prosecution is entitled to claim positive knowledge by Lauria of the use of his service to facilitate the business of prostitution.

The more perplexing issue in the case is the sufficiency of proof of *intent* to further the criminal enterprise. The element of intent may be proved either by direct evidence, or by evidence of circumstances from which an intent to further a criminal enterprise by supplying lawful goods or services may be inferred. Direct evidence of participation, such as advice from the supplier of legal goods or services to the user of those goods or services on their use for illegal purpose, such evidence as appeared in a companion case we decide today, People v. Roy, 59 Cal. Rptr. 636, provides the simplest case.[a] . . . But in cases where direct proof of complicity is lacking, intent to further the conspiracy must be derived from the sale itself and its surrounding circumstances in order to establish the supplier's express or tacit agreement to join the conspiracy.

In the case at bench the prosecution argues that since Lauria knew his customers were using his service for illegal purposes but nevertheless continued to furnish it to them, he must have intended to assist them in carrying out their illegal activities. Thus through a union of knowledge and intent he became a participant in a criminal conspiracy. Essentially, the People argue that knowledge alone of the continuing use of his telephone facilities for criminal purposes provided a sufficient basis from which his intent to participate in those criminal activities could be inferred.

1. Intent may be inferred from knowledge, when the purveyor of legal goods for illegal use has acquired a stake in the venture. (United States v. Falcone, 2 Cir. 109 F.2d 579, 581.)[b] For example, in Regina v. Thomas, (1957), 2 All E.R. 181, 342, a prosecution for living off the earnings of prostitution, the evidence showed that the accused, knowing the woman to be a convicted prostitute, agreed to let her have the use of his room between the hours of 9 P.M. and 2 A.M. for a charge of £3 a night. The Court of Criminal Appeal refused an appeal from the conviction, holding that when the accused rented a room at a grossly inflated rent to a prostitute for the purpose of carrying on her trade, a jury could find he was living on the earnings of prostitution.

In the present case, no proof was offered of inflated charges for the telephone answering services furnished the codefendants.

2. Intent may be inferred from knowledge, when no legitimate use for the goods or services exists. The leading California case is People v. McLaughlin, 111 Cal. App. 2d 781, 245 P.2d 1076, in which the court upheld a conviction of the suppliers of horse-racing information by wire for conspiracy to promote bookmaking, when it had been established that wire service information had no other use than to supply information needed by bookmakers to conduct illegal gambling operations. . . .

---

a. In this case the court upheld liability. The facts were very similar, but there was evidence that the answering service operator actively participated in the business of prostitution by making arrangements for the sharing of customers between two supposed prostitutes who used the service. The court said, speaking of the operator, "Perhaps she was motivated solely by a desire to further the welfare and serve the interests of her customers and acted without thought of added profit for herself. But disinterested loyalty and devotion to the patrons of her service provide no excuse for the promotion of a criminal enterprise." 59 Cal. Rptr. at 641. — EDS.

b. In United States v. Falcone, Judge Learned Hand wrote the opinion of the Second Circuit Court of Appeals. He stated: "Civilly, a man's liability extends to any injuries which he should have apprehended to be likely to follow from his acts. . . . There are indeed instances of criminal liability of the same kind, where the law imposes punishment merely because the accused did not forbear to do that from which the wrong was likely to follow; but in prosecutions for conspiracy or abetting, his attitude towards the forbidden undertaking must be more positive. It is not enough that he does not forego a normally lawful activity, of the fruits of which he knows that others will make an unlawful use; he must in some sense promote their venture himself, make it his own, have a stake in its outcome. The distinction is especially important today when so many prosecutors seek to sweep within the drag-net of conspiracy all those who have been associated in any degree whatever with the main offenders. We may agree that morally the defendants at bar should have refused to sell to illicit distillers; but, both morally and legally, to do so was toto coelo different from joining with them in running the stills." — EDS.

In Shaw v. Director of Public Prosecutions, [1962] A.C. 220, the defendant was convicted of conspiracy to corrupt public morals and of living on the earnings of prostitution, when he published a directory consisting almost entirely of advertisements of the names, addresses, and specialized talents of prostitutes. Publication of such a directory, said the court, could have no legitimate use and serve no other purpose than to advertise the professional services of the prostitutes whose advertisements appeared in the directory. The publisher could be deemed a participant in the profits from the business activities of his principal advertisers. . . .

However, there is nothing in the furnishing of telephone answering service which would necessarily imply assistance in the performance of illegal activities. Nor is any inference to be derived from the use of an answering service by women, either in any particular volume of calls, or outside normal working hours. Nightclub entertainers, registered nurses, faith healers, public stenographers, photographic models, and free lance substitute employees, provide examples of women in legitimate occupations whose employment might cause them to receive a volume of telephone calls at irregular hours.

3. Intent may be inferred from knowledge, when the volume of business with the buyer is grossly disproportionate to any legitimate demand, or when sales for illegal use amount to a high proportion of the seller's total business. In such cases an intent to participate in the illegal enterprise may be inferred from the quantity of the business done. For example, in *Direct Sales,* supra, the sale of narcotics to a rural physician in quantities 300 times greater than he would have normal use for provided potent evidence of an intent to further the illegal activity.[c] In the same case the court also found significant the fact that the wholesaler had attracted as customers a disproportionately large group of physicians who had been convicted of violating the Harrison Act. In Shaw v. Director of Public Prosecutions, [1962] A.C. 220, almost the entire business of the directory came from prostitutes.

No evidence of any unusual volume of business with prostitutes was presented by the prosecution against Lauria.

Inflated charges, the sale of goods with no legitimate use, sales in inflated amounts, each may provide a fact of sufficient moment from which the intent of the seller to participate in the criminal enterprise may be inferred. In such instances participation by the supplier of legal goods to the illegal enterprise may be inferred because in one way or another the supplier has acquired a special interest in the operation of the illegal enterprise. His intent to participate in the crime of which he has knowledge may be inferred from the existence of his special interest.

Yet there are cases in which it cannot reasonably be said that the supplier has a stake in the venture or has acquired a special interest in the enterprise, but in which he has been held liable as a participant on the basis of knowledge alone. Some suggestion of this appears in *Direct Sales,* supra, where both the knowledge of the illegal use of the drugs and the intent of the supplier to aid that use were inferred. In Regina v. Bainbridge (1959), 3 W.L.R. 656 (CCA 6), a supplier of oxygen-cutting equipment to one known to intend to use it to break into a bank

---

c. The court in *Direct Sales* also emphasized the quantity discounts the defendant offered to the physician. — Eds.

was convicted as an accessory to the crime. . . . It seems apparent from these cases that a supplier who furnishes equipment which he *knows* will be used to commit a serious crime may be deemed from that knowledge alone to have intended to produce the result. Such proof may justify an inference that the furnisher intended to aid the execution of the crime and that he thereby became a participant. For instance, we think the operator of a telephone answering service with positive knowledge that his service was being used to facilitate the extortion of ransom, the distribution of heroin, or the passing of counterfeit money who continued to furnish the service with knowledge of its use, might be chargeable on knowledge alone with participation in a scheme to extort money, to distribute narcotics, or to pass counterfeit money. The same result would follow the seller of gasoline who knew the buyer was using his product to make Molotov cocktails for terroristic use.

Logically, the same reasoning could be extended to crimes of every description. Yet we do not believe an inference of intent drawn from knowledge of criminal use properly applies to the less serious crimes classified as misdemeanors. The duty to take positive action to dissociate oneself from activities helpful to violations of the criminal law is far stronger and more compelling for felonies than it is for misdemeanors or petty offenses. . . . We believe the distinction between the obligations arising from knowledge of a felony and those arising from knowledge of a misdemeanor continues to reflect basic human feelings about the duties owed by individuals to society. Heinous crime must be stamped out, and its suppression is the responsibility of all. Venial crime and crime not evil in itself present less of a danger to society, and perhaps the benefits of their suppression through the modern equivalent of the posse, the hue and cry, the informant, and the citizen's arrest, are outweighed by the disruption to everyday life brought about by amateur law enforcement and private officiousness in relatively inconsequential delicts which do not threaten our basic security. . . .

With respect to misdemeanors, we conclude that positive knowledge of the supplier that his products or services are being used for criminal purposes does not, without more, establish an intent of the supplier to participate in the misdemeanors. With respect to felonies, we do not decide the converse, viz. that in all cases of felony knowledge of criminal use alone may justify an inference of the supplier's intent to participate in the crime. The implications of *Falcone* make the matter uncertain with respect to those felonies which are merely prohibited wrongs. . . . But decision on this point is not compelled, and we leave the matter open.

From this analysis of precedent we deduce the following rule: the intent of a supplier who knows of the criminal use to which his supplies are put to participate in the criminal activity connected with the use of his supplies may be established by (1) direct evidence that he intends to participate, or (2) through an inference that he intends to participate based on, (a) his special interest in the activity, or (b) the aggravated nature of the crime itself.

When we review Lauria's activities in the light of this analysis, we find no proof that Lauria took any direct action to further, encourage, or direct the call-girl activities of his codefendants and we find an absence of circumstances from which his special interest in their activities could be inferred. Neither excessive charges for standardized services, nor the furnishing of services without a legitimate use, nor an unusual quantity of business with call girls, are present. The offense which he is charged with furthering is a misdemeanor, a category of crime which has never been made a required subject of positive disclosure to public authority. Under these circumstances, although proof of Lauria's knowledge of the criminal activities of his patrons was sufficient to charge him with that fact, there was insufficient evidence that he intended to further their criminal activities, and hence insufficient proof of his participation in a criminal conspiracy with his codefendants to further prostitution. Since the conspiracy centered around the activities of Lauria's telephone answering service, the charges against his codefendants likewise fail for want of proof.

In absolving Lauria of complicity in a criminal conspiracy we do not wish to imply that the public authorities are without remedies to combat modern manifestations of the world's oldest profession. Licensing of telephone answering services under the police power, together with the revocation of licenses for the toleration of prostitution, is a possible civil remedy. The furnishing of telephone answering service in aid of prostitution could be made a crime. (Cf. Pen. Code, §316, which makes it a misdemeanor to let an apartment with knowledge of its use for prostitution.) Other solutions will doubtless occur to vigilant public authorities if the problem of call-girl activity needs further suppression.

The order is affirmed.

NOTES ON MENS REA

1. Purpose or knowledge in felony cases. Does the *Lauria* court's analysis imply that knowledge alone is a sufficient mens rea for conspiracy when the object crime is a felony? If there was no "agreement" between Lauria and the prostitutes in California, in what sense would such an "agreement" exist, on identical facts, in a state that declared prostitution a felony?

What should be the result when the object offense is a very serious crime? Recall that in United States v. Fountain, page 654 supra, the court held (relying on *Lauria*) that Gometz, who supplied a knife knowing that it would be used to kill, could be an accomplice in the murder. Should the same facts be sufficient to hold Gometz for conspiracy to commit murder? Even if knowledge alone is considered sufficient for aiding and abetting liability, might it make sense to hold that more is required to make the supplier and his customer "partners in crime"? In this regard, consider how accomplice liability differs from conspiracy liability. What is Supplier's liability, under each theory, if he provides a stolen car for use in a bank robbery but Customer never attempts the crime? What is Supplier's liability if Customer kidnaps a teller and holds her hostage in order to facilitate his escape?

The Model Penal Code solution to these problems is to require purpose for *both* conspiracy and accomplice liability. See §§2.06(3)(a); 5.03(1). For the commentary relevant to these provisions, see the Model Penal Code discussion of accomplice mens rea, set out at pages 652-653 supra. The majority of the states likewise require purpose in conspiracy cases, either by statute or judicial precedent. See Comment, Whose Head Is in the Sand? Problems with the Use of the Ostrich Instruction in Conspiracy Cases, 13 W. New Eng. L. Rev. 35, 41 n. 42 (1991).

2. Problems. (a) Zahm wanted to use Lawrence's house trailer as a site for

manufacturing methamphetamine. The chemicals used to "cook" methamphetamine can soil or damage the work area, and there is a risk of explosion
when the volatile ingredients are heated to high temperatures. Lawrence agreed
to accept $1,000 for leasing the trailer to Zahm for one day. Zahm was unable to
find all the necessary equipment, and the "cook" was never carried out. Is Lawrence guilty of conspiracy to manufacture methamphetamine? See United
States v. Blankenship, 970 F.2d 283 (7th Cir. 1992).

(b) Viera wanted to fly cocaine from Colombia into Puerto Rico, and he asked
Volmar if he could use an airstrip on Volmar's farm as a landing site. Volmar
demanded half the profits in exchange for use of his land, and Viera refused.
Volmar then referred Viera to another landowner who had access to a suitable
airstrip. Viera paid that landowner $15,000 and used his airstrip as a clandestine
landing site for smuggling cocaine from Colombia. Is Volmar guilty of conspiracy to import cocaine? See United States v. Aponte-Suarez, 905 F.2d 483 (1st
Cir. 1990).

(c) Morse owned a Beechcraft light plane that had no passenger seats, leaving
more room for cargo. Though witnesses testified that the plane was worth
$50,000 to $70,000, he asked two young buyers to pay $80,000 for it and then
raised his price to $115,000, to be paid in cash installments. The buyers agreed,
took possession of the plane, and used it to smuggle marijuana from Mexico to
Texas. Is Morse guilty of conspiracy to import marijuana? In United States v.
Morse, 851 F.2d 1317, 1319-1320 (11th Cir. 1988), the court held:

> The circumstantial evidence in this case adequately supports Morse's conspiracy
> convictions. First, the plane in Florida that Morse sold to Colding was particularly
> suited for smuggling: there were no passenger seats in the plane, leaving more
> room for hauling marijuana; one witness — a customs agent — testified that "a
> Beechcraft Queen Aire happens to be one of the profile aircraft that is involved in
> narcotic smuggling." Second, Morse sold the plane for $115,000, almost twice its
> market value; he had raised the price from $80,000 after meeting with Cauthen
> and Colding. Third, all payments were made in cash of low denominations. Fourth,
> Morse sold the plane to Colding, a twenty-three year old, without any contract or
> receipt to evidence the transaction. Fifth, Morse, who never had registered his pur-
> chase of the plane with the Federal Aviation Administration (FAA), sold the plane
> without providing the FAA with an aircraft registration application or bill of sale
> as required by law. Sixth, Morse was informed that the plane had been used to
> smuggle marijuana; yet he made no attempt to contact law enforcement officials.
> Seventh, when Colding failed to pay the balance of the agreed purchase price,
> Morse did not threaten to file suit to recover the money.

Question: Is this analysis consistent with the reasoning of *Lauria, Direct Sales,*
and *Falcone*?

3. Corrupt motive. In a leading common law precedent, People v. Powell, 63
N.Y. 88 (1875), the court held that to be criminal, a conspiracy must be animated
by a "corrupt" motive or an intention to engage in conduct known to be wrongful. The effect of the *Powell* doctrine is illustrated by Commonwealth v. Gormley,
77 Pa. Super. 298, 301-303 (1921). The defendant, an election officer, was indicted for conspiracy to violate the election law by entering the votes cast in the
official tally sheets before the time set by law and for the substantive offense of
entering false figures on the sheets. The jury acquitted him on the substantive
charge but found him guilty of the conspiracy. The court reversed on appeal,

finding error in the trial judge's refusal to allow testimony of the defendant's good faith (there was apparently no opposition candidate) and ignorance of the criminality of his act. The court said:

> The reason for the court's refusal . . . was that a defendant having violated the plain provisions of a statute, he cannot give his reasons why he did so. That a violation of the act subjects the defendant to the penalties prescribed whether he is conscious that he is violating the law or not. This view is no doubt correct as applied to the second count of the indictment charging a violation of the election laws. The legislature can declare an act a crime regardless of intent. As to the charge of conspiracy, we think the testimony was admissible. This is the pivotal question in the case. May a defendant when charged with conspiracy show that he had no intention to violate the law; that there was no corrupt motive? . . .
>
> [In] People v. Powell, 63 N.Y. 88, . . . it was said, "To make an agreement between two or more persons to do an act innocent in itself a criminal conspiracy, it is not enough that it appears that the act which was the object of the agreement was prohibited. The confederation must be corrupt. The agreement must have been entered into with an evil purpose, as distinguished from a purpose simply to do the act prohibited, in ignorance of the prohibition. This is implied in the meaning of the word conspiracy." And later on it was said: "It was open to the jury to find upon the evidence that no criminal intention existed; and if this had been found to have acquitted the defendants." . . .
>
> It follows that if a material part of the crime is the intention, the defendant may introduce any testimony that throws light on it. On the charge of making fraudulent entries on the tally sheet, the defendants had no right to show their intention and ignorance of the law was no answer to the charge, but the trial being had upon two counts, one charging conspiracy, the testimony should not have been excluded and defendants should have been allowed to explain their action and their motives.

Question: Doesn't this approach in effect make mistake of law a defense in a conspiracy prosecution? The *Powell* doctrine has been widely criticized. See Model Penal Code and Commentaries, Comment to §503, at 417-418 (1985):

> The *Powell* rule, and many of the decisions that rely on it, may be viewed as a judicial endeavor to import fair mens rea requirements into statutes creating regulatory offenses that do not rest on traditional concepts of personal fault and culpability. This should, however, be the function of the statutes defining such offenses. Section 2.04(3) specifies the limited situations when ignorance of the criminality of one's conduct is a defense in general. There is no good reason why the fortuity of concert should be used as a device for limiting criminality in this area. . . .

The *Powell* doctrine has been rejected in England, see Churchill v. Walton, [1967] 2 A.C. 224, and in most of the state codifications enacted in the wake of the Model Penal Code. See Note, Conspiracy: State Statutory Reform Since the Model Penal Code, 75 Colum. L. Rev. 1122, 1131 n. 48 (1975).

4. Attendant circumstances. In cases like Commonwealth v. Gormley and People v. Powell (see Note 3 supra), the "corrupt motive" defense amounts to a claim of ignorance of the law. As the preceding Note indicates, the current trend is toward parity between the requirements for conspiracy and the substantive offense on this issue: If ignorance of the law is no defense with respect to the substantive offense, it is likewise no defense to a conspiracy charge. Should the result be different where the defendant claims a mistake of *fact* as to some attendant circumstance; that is, should mistake of fact be a defense to a conspiracy charge even if it would not be a defense in a prosecution for the substantive offense? Consider the following situations.

(a) Jurisdictional facts. In United States v. Feola, 420 U.S. 672 (1975), defendants, planning to steal substantial sums from a group they believed to be prospective drug buyers, drew guns on their victims, who were in fact undercover federal agents. The defendants were then charged with assaulting, and conspiring to assault, federal officers. The Supreme Court held that defendants' ignorance that their victims were federal officers was not a defense to the substantive charge of assaulting a federal officer; it was enough that they knew they were assaulting someone. Should ignorance of the status of the victims nonetheless be a defense to the conspiracy charge? How can it be said that defendants conspired (that is, "agreed") to assault a federal officer? The Court upheld the conspiracy convictions, but on narrow grounds. The Court took care to distinguish Judge Learned Hand's "traffic light analogy," a famous argument *against* parity between the mens rea requirements for conspiracy and the object crime. Judge Hand wrote in United States v. Cummins, 123 F.2d 271, 273:

> While one may, for instance, be guilty of running past a traffic light of whose existence one is ignorant, one cannot be guilty of conspiring to run past such a light, for one cannot agree to run past a light unless one supposes that there is a light to run past.

In *Feola,* the Court noted that "[t]he problem posed by the traffic light analogy is not before us," and said it would "save for another day" the question whether a party can be punished for conspiracy on the basis of an agreement to engage in apparently innocent conduct where the unintended result of engaging in that conduct is the violation of a criminal statute. The Court ruled the "traffic light analogy" inapt because in *Feola* the defendants' mistake concerned a fact that was not relevant to guilt or innocence but was "jurisdictional only" (420 U.S. at 677 n. 9). The Court explained (id at 694):

> [W]e fail to see how the agreement is any less blameworthy or constitutes less of a danger to society solely because the participants are unaware of which body of law they intend to violate. . . . [I]mposition of a requirement of knowledge of those facts that serve only to establish federal jurisdiction would render it more difficult to serve the policy behind the law of conspiracy without serving any other apparent social policy. . . .

(b) Facts that increase the gravity of the offense. Suppose that Supplier and Dealer meet with Buyer and negotiate terms for a large purchase of drugs. At Buyer's request, they agree to deliver the drugs to him at Seedy's Bar, at the corner of Fourth and Elm. Before the delivery is made, Supplier and Dealer are arrested. Buyer turns out to be an undercover agent, and (unknown to Dealer and Supplier) Seedy's Bar turns out to be directly across the street from a public school. State law imposes much higher penalties for drug sales that occur within 1,000 feet of a school. Can Dealer and Supplier be convicted of conspiracy to distribute

drugs within 1,000 feet of a school? Consider United States v. Freed, 401 U.S. 601 (1971). In that case, the Supreme Court upheld an indictment charging both possession and conspiracy to possess unregistered hand grenades, despite its failure to allege that the defendant knew the grenades were unregistered. The Court treated the substantive offense of possessing unregistered hand grenades as imposing strict liability so far as the fact of registration was concerned. The Court disposed of the conspiracy charge as follows (id. at n. 14):

> We need not decide whether a criminal conspiracy to do an act "innocent in itself" and not known by the alleged conspirators to be prohibited must be actuated by some corrupt motive other than the intention to do the act which is prohibited and which is the object of the conspiracy. An agreement to acquire hand grenades is hardly an agreement innocent in itself. Therefore what we have said of the substantive offense satisfies on these special facts the requirements for a conspiracy.

Questions: Is this holding sound? So far as the conspiracy count was concerned, was the defendant's argument simply that he did not know it was possibly a crime to possess grenades or that he did not agree to possess unregistered hand grenades? Did the Court confuse two separate mens rea defenses, namely, the defense of ignorance of the criminality or immorality of the agreement and the defense of lack of agreement to do the act that was criminal?

(c) Facts essential to criminality. Suppose that, in contrast to United States v. Freed, supra, the alleged conspiracy involves an act "innocent in itself." For example, suppose that Alan and Mary, after spending an evening together, decide to go to a motel where they will have consensual sexual relations. Bill agrees to drive them there, knowing their intentions, but just before they leave, Mary's parents arrive on the scene and foil the plan. Though neither Alan nor Bill could have known it, Mary is underage. Can Alan and Bill be convicted of conspiracy to commit statutory rape?

We considered variations on this hypothetical at two earlier points above. With respect to attempt liability, the Model Penal Code Commentary states that a person in Alan's position would be guilty of attempted statutory rape. See page 592 supra. With respect to Bill's liability as an accomplice, §2.06(3)(a) appears to preclude conviction, but in this instance the Commentary argues that the Code is ambiguous and states that the issue was left for the courts to decide. See page 660 supra. The Code and its Commentary reflect a similar ambivalence with respect to the mens rea for conspiracy. The Commentary states that the Code is ambiguous and that the issue was left to the courts. See Model Penal Code and Commentaries, Comment to §5.03 at 413 (1985). Yet §5.03(1) provides that a person is guilty of conspiracy to commit a crime only if he acts "with the purpose of promoting or facilitating its commission." How can it be said that either Alan or Bill has "the purpose of promoting or facilitating [the] commission" of the crime of statutory rape?

Apart from the question of textual interpretation, what is the sensible way to resolve this problem? Should the policies that determine the mens rea for the object crime logically govern the matter on the conspiracy charge as well? Or, given the very early point at which conspiracy liability can attach, is it important to require subjective culpability? Whatever may be the right solution to this problem for complicity and attempts, how can a mens rea that is less than purpose or knowledge ever suffice for conspiracy, which — by definition — consists of an *agreement* to engage in the prohibited conduct?

The English approach acknowledges these concerns. The English Criminal Law Act, 1977, ch. 45, §1 (2) states:

> Where liability for any offence may be incurred without knowledge on the part of the person committing it of any particular fact or circumstance necessary for the commission of the offence, a person shall nevertheless not be guilty of conspiracy to commit that offence by virtue of subsection (1) above unless he and at least one other party to the agreement intend or know that that fact or circumstance shall or will exist at the time when the conduct constituting the offence is to take place.

5.   Scope of the Agreement — Single or Multiple Conspiracies

MODEL PENAL CODE AND COMMENTARIES, Comment to §5.03 at 422-423 (1985): Much of the most perplexing litigation in conspiracy has been concerned less with the essential elements of the offense than with the scope to be accorded to a combination, i.e., the singleness or multiplicity of the conspiratorial relationships typical in a large, complex and sprawling network of crime.... [I]n most of these cases it is clear that each defendant has committed or conspired to commit one or more crimes; the question now is, to what extent is he a conspirator with each of the persons involved in the larger criminal network to commit the crimes that are its objects....

The inquiry may be crucial for a number of purposes. These include not only defining each defendant's liability but also the propriety of joint prosecution, admissibility against a defendant of the hearsay acts and declarations of others, questions of multiple prosecution or conviction and double jeopardy, satisfaction of the overt act requirement or statutes of limitation or rules of jurisdiction and venue, and possibly liability for substantive crimes executed pursuant to the conspiracy. The scope problem is thus central to the present concern of courts and commentators about the use of conspiracy, a concern based on the conflict between the need for effective means of prosecuting large criminal organizations, and the dangers of prejudice to individual defendants.

KOTTEAKOS v. UNITED STATES

Supreme Court of the United States
328 U.S. 750 (1946)

JUSTICE RUTLEDGE delivered the opinion of the Court.

The only question is whether petitioners have suffered substantial prejudice from being convicted of a single general conspiracy by evidence which the Government admits proved not one conspiracy but some eight or more different ones of the same sort executed through a common key figure, Simon Brown. Petitioners were convicted under the general conspiracy section of the Criminal Code, 18 U.S.C.A. §88 [now §371], of conspiring to violate the provisions of the

National Housing Act. The judgments were affirmed by the Circuit Court of Appeals. . . .

The indictment named thirty-two defendants, including the petitioners. The gist of the conspiracy, as alleged, was that the defendants had sought to induce various financial institutions to grant credit, with the intent that the loans for advances would then be offered to the Federal Housing Administration for insurance upon applications containing false and fraudulent information.

Of the thirty-two persons named in the indictment nineteen were brought to trial and the names of thirteen were submitted to the jury. Two were acquitted; the jury disagreed as to four; and the remaining seven, including petitioners, were found guilty.

The government's evidence may be summarized briefly, for the petitioners have not contended that it was insufficient, if considered apart from the alleged errors relating to the proof and the instructions at the trial.

Simon Brown, who pleaded guilty, was the common and key figure in all of the transactions proven. He was president of the Brownie Lumber Company. Having had experience in obtaining loans under the National Housing Act, he undertook to act as broker in placing for others loans for modernization and renovation, charging a five per cent commission for his services. Brown knew, when he obtained the loans, that the proceeds were not to be used for the purposes stated in the applications. [The Court then summarized the evidence against several defendants.]

The evidence against the other defendants whose cases were submitted to the jury was similar in character. They too had transacted business with Brown relating to National Housing Act loans. But no connection was shown between them and petitioners, other than that Brown had been the instrument in each instance for obtaining the loans. In many cases the other defendants did not have any relationship with one another, other than Brown's connection with each transaction. As the Circuit Court of Appeals said, there were "at least eight, and perhaps more, separate and independent groups, none of which had any connection with any other, though all dealt independently with Brown as their agent." As the Government puts it, the pattern was "that of separate spokes meeting at a common center," though we may add without the rim of the wheel to enclose the spokes.

The proof therefore admittedly made out a case, not of a single conspiracy, but of several, notwithstanding only one was charged in the indictment. The Court of Appeals aptly drew analogy in the comment, "Thieves who dispose of their loot to a single receiver — a single 'fence' — do not by that fact alone become confederates; they may, but it takes more than knowledge that he is a 'fence' to make them such." It stated that the trial judge "was plainly wrong in supposing that upon the evidence there could be a single conspiracy; and in the view which he took of the law, he should have dismissed the indictment."[a] Nev-

a. Judge Learned Hand wrote the opinion for the court of appeals. The sentences quoted are part of the following paragraph in which he stated, in reference to the view of the trial judge (151 F.2d at 172): "He was apparently misled by an erroneous understanding of the rule that, when anyone joins an existing conspiracy, he takes it over as it is, and becomes a party to it in its earlier phases, and that the declarations of other conspirators, even though made before he has entered, are competent against him. What he failed to remember was that to bring this rule into operation ertheless the appellate court held the error not prejudicial, saying among other things that "especially since guilt was so manifest, it was 'proper' to join the conspiracies," and "to reverse the conviction would be a miscarriage of justice." This is indeed the Government's entire position. . . .

[T]he trial court itself was confused in the charge which it gave to guide the jury in deliberation. The court instructed:

> The indictment charges but one conspiracy, and to convict each of the defendants of a conspiracy the Government would have to prove, and you would have to find, that each of the defendants was a member of that conspiracy. You cannot divide it up. It is one conspiracy, and the question is whether or not each of the defendants or which of the defendants, are members of that conspiracy.

On its face, as the Court of Appeals said, this portion of the charge was plainly wrong in application to the proof made; and the error pervaded the entire charge, not merely the portion quoted. The jury could not possibly have found, upon the evidence, that there was only one conspiracy. The trial court was of the view that one conspiracy was made out by showing that each defendant was linked to Brown in one or more transactions, and that it was possible on the evidence for the jury to conclude that all were in a common adventure because of this fact and the similarity of purpose presented in the various applications for loans.

The view, specifically embodied throughout the instructions, obviously confuses the common purpose of a single enterprise with the several, though similar purposes of numerous separate adventures of like character. It may be that, notwithstanding the misdirection, the jury actually understood correctly the purport of the evidence, as the Government now concedes it to have been, and came to the conclusion that the petitioners were guilty only of the separate conspiracies in which the proof shows they respectively participated. But, in the face of the misdirection and in the circumstances of this case, we cannot assume that the lay triers of fact were so well informed upon the law or that they disregarded the permission expressly given to ignore that vital difference.

As we have said, the error permeated the entire charge, indeed the entire trial. Not only did it permit the jury to find each defendant guilty of conspiring with thirty-five other potential co-conspirators, . . . when none of the evidence would support such a conviction. . . . It had other effects. . . . Carrying forward his premise that the jury could find one conspiracy on the evidence, the trial judge further charged that, if the jury found a conspiracy,

---

it is not enough that, when one joins with another in a criminal venture, he knows that his confederate is engaged in other criminal undertakings with other persons, even though they may be of the same general nature. The acts and declarations of confederates, past or future, are never competent against a party except in so far as they are steps in furtherance of a purpose common to him and them. . . . In the case at bar, we assume that Lekacos and Kotteakos and Regenbogen knew that Brown was for the time being acting as a broker for a number of other persons, who were getting loans in fraud of the Act, and who were making false representations to the bank like those which they themselves were making. But that was not enough to make them confederates with the other applicants; it did not give them any interest in the success of any loans but their own; there was no interest, no venture, common to them and anyone else but Brown himself. Thieves who dispose of their loot to a single receiver — a single 'fence' — do not by that fact alone become confederates: they may, but it takes more than knowledge that he is a 'fence' to make them such. United States v. Falcone, 311 U.S. 205; United States v. Peoni, 2 Cir., 10 F.2d 401." — Eds.

then the acts or the statements of *any* of those whom you so find to be conspirators between the two dates that I have mentioned, may be considered by you in evidence as against *all* of the defendants whom you so find to be members of *the* conspiracy.

(Emphasis added.) . . .

On those instructions it was competent not only for the jury to find that all of the defendants were parties to a single common plan, design and scheme, where none was shown by the proof, but also for them to impute to each defendant the acts and statements of the others without reference to whether they related to one of the schemes proven or another, and to find an overt act affecting all in conduct which admittedly could only have affected some. . . .

Here toleration went too far. . . .

Reversed.

BLUMENTHAL v. UNITED STATES, 332 U.S. 539, 557-559 (1947): [Defendants Weiss and Goldsmith were, respectively, owner and sales manager of the Francisco Distributing Company, a licensed wholesale liquor dealing agency. Defendants Feigenbaum, Blumenthal, and Abel were local businesspeople with no connection with the company except as hereafter stated. Weiss and Goldsmith, acting in the name of Francisco, received shipment of two carloads of whiskey from an unidentified person or persons with whom they agreed to distribute the shipment under the Francisco name in such a way as to conceal the fact that they were selling the whiskey at prices above those legally permitted at the time. Accordingly, Weiss and Goldsmith arranged with Feigenbaum, Blumenthal, and Abel, all unknown to one another, for them to negotiate sales of portions of the shipment to various taverns. The sales were made at prices above the maximum prices prescribed by law to the knowledge of all defendants. There was no evidence that the salesmen knew of the unknown owner's existence or part in the plan. Defendants were charged and convicted of a single conspiracy in a single count holding they had conspired together and with the unidentified owner to sell the shipment of whiskey at prices over the ceiling set by regulations of the Office of Price Administration in violation of the Emergency Price Control Act. On appeal it was contended that there was not one but two conspiracies — one between the unidentified owner and Weiss and Goldsmith; the other between Weiss and Goldsmith, on the one hand, and Feigenbaum and Blumenthal, on the other. The Supreme Court affirmed, upholding the finding of one large conspiracy:]

We think that in the special circumstances of this case the two agreements were merely steps in the formation of the larger and ultimately more general conspiracy. In that view it would be perversion of justice to regard the salesmen's ignorance of the unknown owner's participation as furnishing adequate ground for reversal of their convictions. Nor does anything in the *Kotteakos* decision require this. The scheme was in fact the same scheme; the salesmen knew or must have known that others unknown to them were sharing in so large a project; and it hardly can be sufficient to relieve them that they did not know, when they joined the scheme, who those people were or exactly the parts they were playing in carrying out the common design and object of all. By their separate agreements, if such they were, they became parties to the larger common plan, joined together by their knowledge of its essential features and broad scope, though not of its exact limits, and by their common single goal.

The case therefore is very different from the facts admitted to exist in the *Kotteakos* case. Apart from the much larger number of agreements there involved, no two of those agreements were tied together as stages in the formation of a larger all-inclusive combination, all directed to achieving a single unlawful end or result. On the contrary each separate agreement had its own distinct, illegal end. Each loan was an end in itself, separate from all others, although all were alike in having similar illegal objects. Except for Brown, the common figure, no conspirator was interested in whether any loan except his own went through. And none aided in any way, by agreement or otherwise, in procuring another's loan. The conspiracies therefore were distinct and disconnected, not parts of a larger general scheme, both in the phase of agreement with Brown and also in the absence of any aid given to others as well as in specific object and result. There was no drawing of all together in a single, over-all, comprehensive plan.

Here the contrary is true. All knew of and joined in the overriding scheme. All intended to aid the owner, whether Francisco or another, to sell the whiskey unlawfully, though the two groups of defendants differed on the proof in knowledge and belief concerning the owner's identity. All by reason of their knowledge of the plan's general scope, if not its exact limits, sought a common end, to aid in disposing of the whiskey. True, each salesman aided in selling only his part. But he knew the lot to be sold was larger and thus that he was aiding in a larger plan. He thus became a party to it and not merely to the integrating agreement with Weiss and Goldsmith.

ANDERSON v. SUPERIOR COURT, 78 Cal. App. 2d 22, 24-25, 177 P.2d 315, 317 (1947): [Petitioner sought a writ of prohibition to prevent her prosecution under an indictment returned by the grand jury. Evidence before the grand jury revealed that one Stern was engaged in the commission of abortions as a regular business. He had made arrangements with many persons for them to refer to him women desiring abortions. Such persons were paid a fee for this service. Petitioner was one of these people. She had referred several women to Stern. She was indicted for conspiring to commit abortions, the conspiracy embracing not only Stern and herself but the greater enterprise among Stern and the others who referred women to him. She was also indicted for the substantive offenses of several abortions performed on women she had referred to Stern and abortions committed by Stern upon women who had been referred by others. Denying the writ, the court stated:] The inference is almost compelled, if the evidence is believed, that this petitioner knew that Stern was engaged in the commission of abortions not casually but as a regular business and that others, like herself, had conspired with him to further his operations. If the grand jury concluded that, with this knowledge, she saw fit to join with him and those others, even though unknown to her, in furthering the unlawful activities of the group we cannot say that the grand jury did not have substantial evidence upon which to find the indictment.

If she did join the conspiracy she is responsible for the substantive offenses later committed as a part of the conspiracy.

UNITED STATES v. BRUNO

United States Court of Appeals, 2d Circuit
105 F.2d 921, rev'd on other grounds, *308 U.S. 287 (1939)*

PER CURIAM. Bruno and Iacono were indicted along with 86 others for a conspiracy to import, sell and possess narcotics; some were acquitted; others, besides these two, were convicted, but they alone appealed. They complain . . . that if the evidence proved anything, it proved a series of separate conspiracies, and not a single one, as alleged in the indictment. . . .

The evidence allowed the jury to find that there had existed over a substantial period of time a conspiracy embracing a great number of persons, whose object was to smuggle narcotics into the Port of New York and distribute them to addicts both in this city and in Texas and Louisiana. This required the cooperation of four groups of persons: the smugglers who imported the drugs; the middlemen who paid the smugglers and distributed to retailers; and two groups of retailers — one in New York and one in Texas and Louisiana — who supplied the addicts. The defendants assert that there were, therefore, at least three separate conspiracies: one between the smugglers and the middlemen, and one between the middlemen and each group of retailers. The evidence did not disclose any cooperation or communication between the smugglers and either group of retailers, or between the two groups of retailers themselves; however, the smugglers knew that the middlemen must sell to retailers, and the retailers knew that the middlemen must buy from importers of one sort or another. Thus the conspirators at one end of the chain knew that the unlawful business would not, and could not, stop with their buyers; and those at the other end knew that it had not begun with their sellers. That being true, a jury might have found that all the accused were embarked upon a venture, in all parts of which each was a participant, and an abettor in the sense that the success of that part with which he was immediately concerned, was dependent upon the success of the whole. . . . It might still be argued that there were two conspiracies; one including the smugglers, the middlemen and the New York group, and the other, the smugglers, the middlemen and the Texas & Louisiana group, for there was apparently no privity between the two groups of retailers. That too would be fallacious. Clearly, quoad the smugglers, there was but one conspiracy, for it was of no moment to them whether the middlemen sold to one or more groups of retailers, provided they had a market somewhere. So too of any retailer; he knew that he was a necessary link in a scheme of distribution, and the others, whom he knew to be convenient to its execution, were as much parts of a single undertaking or enterprise as two salesmen in the same shop. We think therefore that there was only one conspiracy.

UNITED STATES v. BORELLI, 336 F.2d 376 (2d Cir. 1964): [In this case, dealing with an elaborate heroin importing and distributing operation extending over a long period of time and involving numerous participants, Judge Friendly wrote:] As applied to the long term operation of an illegal business, the common pictorial distinction between "chain" and "spoke" conspiracies can obscure as much as it clarifies. The chain metaphor is indeed apt in that the links of a narcotics conspiracy are inextricably related to one another, from grower, through exporter and importer, to wholesaler, middleman, and retailer, each depending for his own success on the performance of all the others. But this simple picture tends to obscure that the links at either end are likely to consist of a number of persons who may have no reason to know that others are performing a role similar to theirs — in other words the extreme links of a chain conspiracy may have elements of the spoke conspiracy.[2] Moreover, whatever the value of the chain concept where the problem is to trace a single operation from the start through its various phases to its successful conclusion, it becomes confusing when, over a long period of time, certain links continue to play the same role but with new counterparts, as where importers who regard their partnership as a single continuing one, having successfully distributed one cargo through X distributing organization, turn, years later, to moving another cargo obtained from a different source through Y. . . .

The basic difficulty arises in applying the seventeenth century notion of conspiracy, where the gravamen of the offense was the making of an *agreement* to commit a readily identifiable crime or series of crimes, such as murder or robbery, to what in substance is the conduct of an illegal business over a period of years. . . . Although it is usual and often necessary in conspiracy cases for the agreement to be proved by inference from acts, the gist of the offense remains the agreement, and it is therefore essential to determine what kind of agreement or understanding existed as to each defendant. It is a great deal harder to tell just *what* agreement can reasonably be inferred from the purchase, even the repeated purchase, of contraband, than from the furnishing of dynamite to prospective bank robbers or the exchange of worthless property for securities to be subsequently distributed. Purchase or sale of contraband may, of course, warrant the inference of an agreement going well beyond the particular transaction. A seller of narcotics in bulk surely knows that the purchasers will undertake to resell the goods over an uncertain period of time, and the circumstances may also warrant the inference that a supplier or a purchaser indicated a willingness to repeat. But a sale or a purchase scarcely constitutes a sufficient basis for inferring agreement to cooperate with the opposite parties for whatever period they continue to deal in this type of contraband, unless some such understanding is evidenced by other conduct which accompanies or supplements the transaction.

PROBLEM

What degree of interdependence between parties should be necessary to show that they are part of the same "agreement"? When should antagonism or indifference between two parties be considered inconsistent with their membership in a single "conspiracy"? Suppose that a shoe store owner hires two salespeople to work on commission, and that the salespeople compete for the attention of customers entering the store, because each one wants to serve as many custom-

---

2. Thus, in the oft-cited *Bruno* case, although it is clear enough that "quoad the smugglers, there was but one conspiracy, for it was of no moment to them whether the middlemen sold to one or more groups of retailers, provided they had a market somewhere," it is not so clear why the New York and Texas groups of retailers were not in a "spoke" relation with the smugglers and the middleman, so that there would be two conspiracies unless the evidence permitted the inference that each group of retailers must have known the operation to be so large as to require the other as an outlet.

ers as possible. Are the owner and salespeople parties to a single agreement or are there separate agreements between the owner and each salesperson? Consider the following case.

United States v. Townsend, 924 F.2d 1385 (7th Cir. 1991): The government charged that the defendants conspired together and with others to possess and distribute heroin, cocaine, and marijuana between December 1986 and February 1988. The evidence against each of the defendants was gathered during the course of an undercover investigation that focused on the drug trafficking activities of Apolinar Marquez. . . . The government set up drug buys from Marquez and tapped his home phone, along with the business phone of codefendant Luis Diaz; anyone who discussed drugs on these two phone lines was indicted as a member of the conspiracy. The indictment charged nineteen defendants as members of the conspiracy. . . . On appeal, the defendants argue jointly that the government's proof failed to establish the existence of a single, ongoing conspiracy, as charged in its indictment.

. . . The fact that we can squeeze a group into a hypothetical organizational chart says little about whether a single agreement exists between the members of the group. [W]hen dealer *A* sells drugs to dealer *B*, we don't presume that *A* has agreed to work for the benefit of everyone else with whom *B* deals, or that *A* benefits from *B*'s other deals. . . .

Granted, one crime might aid the commission of another, but the point is that we cannot infer that both parties agreed to work together to achieve that result from the fact that they engaged together in some other crime. . . . In fact, any inference should probably run in the other direction. There is — hard though it may be to believe — a finite supply of drugs. Those in the market to sell or buy large quantities (for distribution) are just as likely, if not more, to be competitors as collaborators. . . .

[As between a buyer and a seller, moreover, the] buy-sell transaction is simply not probative of an agreement to join together to accomplish a criminal objective beyond that already being accomplished by the transaction. As we explained long ago in United States v. Ford, 324 F.2d 950, 952 (7th Cir. 1963), . . . ["the] buyer's purpose is to buy; the seller's purpose is to sell. There is no joint objective." . . .

The government presented abundant evidence demonstrating that Apolinar Marquez frequently purchased drugs from defendant Luis Diaz. . . . Diaz had no interest in Marquez's activities, however, beyond occasionally obtaining drugs for Marquez. He knew that Marquez had extensive drug dealings beyond those in which he was involved (and he had separate dealings as well), but that knowledge alone did not make him a coconspirator with those involved in Marquez's other deals. The evidence does not suggest that Diaz was in league with Marquez's other suppliers, for example; rather, it shows that he was competing with them. Their gain was his loss. Marquez frequently threatened to take his business elsewhere, a prospect Diaz did not view with the equanimity of a partner. Instead, Diaz protested emphatically. . . . Partnership implies a joint stake in the success of an enterprise, and it is clear that Diaz's interest in Marquez did not extend to Marquez's future or his other confederates.

. . . Joseph Angel Claudio was Diaz's primary, if not exclusive, source of drugs. Claudio was part of a chain of supply that ultimately extended to Marquez and his customers, but that chain hardly fits the picture of the ongoing distribution chain that gave rise to the paradigm of chain liability. . . .

Claudio obviously knew that Diaz was reselling the drugs in bulk, but the government presented no evidence indicating that he had any stake in the subsequent distribution of those drugs. As with Diaz, the government's evidence proved only that Claudio knew that the drugs he sold to Diaz were going to continue on in the stream of commerce; it does not establish that he had any interest in whether those with whom Diaz dealt — principally Marquez — were successful or not.

. . . Our review in this case convinces us that the evidence was insufficient to prove that defendants Diaz [and] Claudio . . . joined the conspiracy charged in count 1 of the indictment.

NOTE ON MULTIPLE OBJECTIVES

In all of the foregoing cases, prosecutors sought to establish a single, inclusive conspiracy, while defendants attempted to break up the alleged relationship into smaller conspiracies. In United States v. Braverman, 317 U.S. 49 (1942), the positions were reversed: The Government indicted a group of defendants on seven counts, each charging a conspiracy to violate a separate provision of the internal revenue laws. The applicable statute carried a maximum penalty of two years on each count. Defendants were convicted on all seven counts and each defendant was sentenced to eight years' imprisonment. The Supreme Court reversed:

> The gist of the crime of conspiracy as defined by the statute is the agreement to commit one or more unlawful acts. . . . Whether the object of a single agreement is to commit one or many crimes, it is in either case that agreement which constitutes the conspiracy which the statute punishes. The one agreement cannot be taken to be several agreements and hence several conspiracies because it envisages the violation of several statutes rather than one. . . . For such a violation, only the single penalty prescribed by the statute can be imposed.[a]

Question: If conspiracy is regarded as an inchoate offense, punishing combinations that threaten a substantive harm, does it make sense to treat an agreement to commit seven different crimes as only a single offense?

---

a. In Albernaz v. United States, 450 U.S. 333 (1981), the Supreme Court adopted an exception to the *Braverman* rule. In *Albernaz,* the defendant had conspired with others to import and distribute marijuana. He was convicted on two counts, one charging conspiracy to import and the other conspiracy to distribute. Accepting the premise that there was only a single agreement, the Court nonetheless upheld the two convictions, emphasizing that separate statutes proscribed conspiracy to import and conspiracy to distribute. The Court held that by enacting two statutes, each with its own penalties, Congress had manifested its intention to authorize separate convictions and punishments. The Court distinguished *Braverman* on the ground that "the conspiratorial agreement in *Braverman,* although it had many objectives, violated but a single statute." Id. at 339. See also United States v. Morehead, 959 F.2d 1489 (10th Cir. 1992): Applying *Albernaz,* the court held that a single agreement to distribute drugs, using firearms to do so, constituted two conspiracies — a drug distribution conspiracy (in violation of 21 U.S.C. §846) and a conspiracy to use firearms in committing a federal crime (in violation of 18 U.S.C. §371). — Eds.

NOTE ON THE MODEL PENAL CODE APPROACH

The Model Penal Code proposes an innovative solution to the problems of defining the scope of a conspiratorial relationship:

Model Penal Code and Commentaries, Comment to §5.03 at 425-431 (1985): The combined operation of Subsections (1), (2) and (3) is relied upon to delineate the identity and scope of a conspiracy. All three provisions focus on the culpability of the individual actor. Subsections (1) and (2) limit the scope of his conspiracy both in terms of its criminal objectives, to those crimes that he had the purpose of promoting or facilitating, and in terms of parties, to those with whom he agreed, except when the same crime that he conspired to commit is, to his knowledge, also the object of a conspiracy between one of his co-conspirators and another person or persons. Subsection (3) provides that his conspiracy is a single one despite a multiplicity of criminal objectives, as long as such crimes are the object of the same agreement or continuous conspiratorial relationship. . . .

The Model Code provision would require a different approach to a case such as *Bruno* and might produce different results. Since the overall operation involved the separate crimes of importing by the smugglers and possession and sale by each group [smugglers, distributors, and retailers], the question as to each defendant would be whether and with whom he conspired to commit *each* of these crimes, under the criteria set forth in Subsections (1) and (2). The conspiratorial objective for the purpose of this inquiry could not be characterized in the manner of the *Bruno* court, as "to smuggle narcotics into the Port of New York and distribute them to addicts both in [New York] and in Texas and Louisiana." This is indeed the overall objective of the entire operation. It also may be true that *some* of the participants conspired to commit all of the crimes involved in the operation; under Subsection (3), as under prevailing law, they would be guilty of only one conspiracy if all these crimes were the object of the same agreement or continuing conspiratorial relationship, and the objective of *that* conspiracy or relationship could fairly be phrased in terms of the overall operation. But this multiplicity of criminal objectives affords a poor referent for testing the culpability of each individual who is in any manner involved in the operation.

With the conspiratorial objectives characterized as the particular crimes and the culpability of each participant tested separately, it would be possible to find in a case such as *Bruno,* considering for the moment only each separate chain of distribution, that the smugglers conspired to commit the illegal sales of the retailers, but that the retailers did not conspire to commit the importing of the smugglers. Factual situations warranting such a finding may easily be conceived. For example, the smugglers might depend upon and seek to foster their retail markets, while the retailers might have many suppliers and be indifferent to the success of any single source. The court's approach in *Bruno* does not admit of such a finding, for treating the conspiratorial objective as the entire series of crimes involved in smuggling, distributing, and retailing requires a finding either of no conspiracy or of a single conspiracy in which all three links in the chain conspired to commit all of each other's crimes.

It also would be possible to find, with the inquiry focused on each individual's culpability as to each criminal objective, that some of the parties in a chain conspired to commit the entire series of crimes while others conspired to commit only some of these crimes. Thus the smugglers and the middlemen in *Bruno* may have conspired to commit, promote, or facilitate the importing and the possession and sales of all of the parties down to the final retail sale; the retailers might have conspired with them as to their own possession and sales, but might be indifferent to all the steps prior to their receipt of the narcotics. In this situation, a smuggler or a middleman might have conspired with all three groups to commit the entire series of crimes, while a retailer might have conspired with the same parties but to achieve fewer criminal objectives. Such results are conceptually difficult to reach under existing doctrine not only because of the frequent failure to focus separately on the different criminal objectives, but also because of the traditional view of the agreement as a bilateral relationship between each of the parties, congruent in scope both as to its party and its objective dimensions.

6. Parties

INTRODUCTORY NOTE

Because conspiracy liability shares with accomplice liability the need for the participation of another party, both doctrines pose similar issues concerning the nature of the required relationship. We considered in the section on accomplices whether, for example, a secondary party S can be liable for aiding the principal when S is in effect a victim of the principal's conduct. We also considered whether a secondary party may be liable even when the party who commits the proscribed act is not liable — for example, when the principal party was a feigned participant, had a personal immunity, or was acquitted of the charge. Here we consider similar issues in connection with the crime of conspiracy. Attention should be given to the parallels and differences in the legal treatment of these issues in the two kinds of liability.

GEBARDI v. UNITED STATES

Supreme Court of the United States
287 U.S. 112 (1932)

JUSTICE STONE delivered the opinion of the Court.

This case is here on certiorari to review a judgment of conviction for conspiracy to violate the Mann Act. Petitioners, a man and a woman, not then husband and wife, were indicted in the District Court for Northern Illinois, for conspiring together, and with others not named, to transport the woman from one state to another for the purpose of engaging in sexual intercourse with the man. At the trial without a jury there was evidence from which the court could have found that the petitioners had engaged in illicit sexual relations in the course of each of the journeys alleged; that the man purchased the railway tickets for both petitioners for at least one journey, and that in each instance the woman, in advance of the purchase of the tickets, consented to go on the jour ney and did go on it voluntarily for the specified immoral purpose. There was no evidence supporting the allegation that any other person had conspired. The trial court . . . gave judgment of conviction, which the Court of Appeals . . . affirmed.

Congress set out in the Mann Act to deal with cases which frequently, if not normally, involve consent and agreement on the part of the woman to the forbidden transportation. In every case in which she is not intimidated or forced into the transportation, the statute necessarily contemplates her acquiescence. Yet this acquiescence, though an incident of a type of transportation specifically dealt with by the statute, was not made a crime under the Mann Act itself. Of this class of cases we say that the substantive offense contemplated by the statute itself involves the same combination or community of purpose of two persons only which is prosecuted here as conspiracy. If this were the only case covered by the Act, it would be within those decisions which hold, consistently with the theory upon which conspiracies are punished, that where it is impossible under any circumstances to commit the substantive offense without cooperative action, the preliminary agreement between the same parties to commit the offense is not an indictable conspiracy either at common law or under the federal statute. . . . But criminal transportation under the Mann Act may be effected without the woman's consent as in cases of intimidation or force (with which we are not now concerned). We assume, therefore, . . . that the decisions last mentioned do not in all strictness apply. We do not rest our decision upon the theory of those cases. . . . We place it rather upon the ground that we perceive in the failure of the Mann Act to condemn the woman's participation in those transportations which are effected with her mere consent, evidence of an affirmative legislative policy to leave her acquiescence unpunished. . . . It would contravene that policy to hold that the very passage of the Mann Act effected a withdrawal by the conspiracy statute of that immunity which the Mann Act itself confers.

It is not to be supposed that the consent of an unmarried person to adultery with a married person, where the latter alone is guilty of the substantive offense, would render the former an abettor or a conspirator, or that the acquiescence of a woman under the age of consent would make her a co-conspirator with the man to commit statutory rape upon herself. The principle, determinative of this case, is the same.

On the evidence before us the woman petitioner has not violated the Mann Act and, we hold, is not guilty of a conspiracy to do so. . . .

As there is no proof that the man conspired with anyone else to bring about the transportation, the convictions of both petitioners must be reversed.

NOTES

1. The Gebardi *rule.* The general principle reflected in *Gebardi* is widely accepted. See Glanville Williams, Criminal Law: The General Part 673 (2d ed. 1961): "One may submit with some confidence that a person cannot be convicted of conspiracy when there is a recognized rule of justice or policy exempting him from prosecution from the substantive crime." For a statutory statement of a similar principle, see Model Penal Code §5.04(2), Appendix. See also Ill. Ann. Stat. ch. 720, §5/8-3 (1993): "It is a defense to a charge of solicitation or conspiracy that if the criminal object were achieved the accused would not be guilty of an offense."

2. *The Wharton rule.* Justice Stone notes that the *Gebardi* case was not governed by the line of precedent holding that "where it is impossible under any circumstances to commit the substantive offense without cooperative action, the preliminary agreement between the same parties to commit the offense is not an indictable conspiracy." That line of precedent exemplifies what has become known as the "Wharton rule." It was explained as follows (2 F. Wharton, Criminal Law §1604 at 1862 (12th ed. 1932)):

> When to the idea of an offense plurality of agents is logically necessary, conspiracy, which assumes the voluntary accession of a person to a crime of such a character that it is aggravated by a plurality of agents, cannot be maintained. . . . In other words, when the law says, "a combination between two persons to effect a particular end shall be called, if the end be effected, by a certain name," it is not lawful for the prosecution to call it by some other name; and when the law says, such an offense — e.g., adultery — shall have a certain punishment, it is not lawful for the prosecution to evade this limitation by indicting the offense as conspiracy.

Compare Model Penal Code and Commentaries, Comment to §5.04 at 482-483 (1985):

> The classic Wharton's rule cases involve crimes such as dueling, bigamy, adultery, and incest, but it has also been said to apply to gambling, the giving and receiving of bribes, and the buying and selling of contraband goods. The rule has been unevenly applied and has been subject to a number of exceptions and limitations.
>
> It seems clear that Wharton's rule as generally stated and the rationale that conspiracy "assumes . . . a crime of such a nature that it is aggravated by a plurality of agents" completely overlook the functions of conspiracy as an inchoate crime. That an offense inevitably requires concert is no reason to immunize criminal preparation to commit it. Further, the rule operates to immunize from a conspiracy prosecution *both* parties to *any* offense that inevitably requires concert, thus disregarding the legislative judgment that at least one should be punishable and taking no account of the varying policies that ought to determine whether the other should be. The rule is supportable only insofar as it avoids cumulative punishment for conspiracy and the completed substantive crime, for it is clear that the legislature would have taken the factor of concert into account in grading a crime that inevitably requires concert. This consideration is of course irrelevant under the Model Code, which precludes cumulative punishment in any case for a conspiracy with a single criminal objective and the completed substantive crime.

In Ianelli v. United States, 420 U.S. 770 (1975), eight defendants were convicted and punished for violating 18 U.S.C. §1955, which makes it a crime for five or more persons to conduct a gambling business in violation of state law. They were also convicted and punished for conspiring to violate §1955 by conducting that same gambling business. The Supreme Court rejected a Wharton rule challenge to that latter conviction. The Court held that the ultimate issue was whether the legislature intended separate punishments for conspiracy and for the substantive offense, and that when the substantive offense requires concert, Wharton's rule creates only a presumption against separate punishments, in the absence of legislative intent to the contrary. With respect to §1955, the

Court concluded that the statute's requirement of concerted activity by five or more people reflected only a concern to avoid federal jurisdiction over small-scale gambling operations that pose a limited threat to federal interests and that Congress did not intend to bar separate punishments. Thus, the Court sustained the convictions for both conspiracy and the substantive §1955 offense, even though the only way that the latter crime could be committed was by concerted activity. See Note, An Analysis of Wharton's Rule, 71 Nw. U.L. Rev. 547 (1976).

3. *Problems.* (a) 21 U.S.C. §861 makes it a crime "for any person at least 18 years of age to knowingly and intentionally [employ] a person under 18 years of age" to sell or distribute drugs. Palmer and Harris organized a group of juveniles to sell cocaine. They both knew that the youngsters working for them were under 18. The prosecution proved that Palmer was over 18, and he was therefore liable under §861. But because the prosecution did not prove Harris's age, Harris could not be convicted of violating §861 personally. Can Harris be convicted of conspiring with Palmer to violate §861? Cf. United States v. Harris, 959 F.2d 246, 262-264 (D.C. Cir. 1992).

(b) The Foreign Corrupt Practices Act makes it a crime for any U.S. citizen to bribe a foreign government official, but it does not make it an offense for such an official to accept the bribe. Can Canadian officials who took bribes from U.S. citizens be convicted of conspiracy to violate the FCPA? See United States v. Castle, 925 F.2d 831 (5th Cir. 1991).

GARCIA v. STATE

Supreme Court of Indiana
71 Ind. 366, 394 N.E.2d 106 (1979)

PRENTICE, J. Defendant was convicted in a trial by jury of conspiracy to commit murder, a class A felony. . . . On appeal she raises the . . . issue . . . whether the defendant can be convicted of conspiracy when the only person with whom the defendant conspired was a police informant who only feigned his acquiescence in the scheme. . . .

The evidence introduced at trial consisted of the following: On September 30, 1977, State's witness, Allen Young, was first contacted by the defendant with regard to certain marital problems that she was having. She stated that her husband constantly beat her and her children and that she "couldn't take it any longer" — that she wanted her husband killed. [After several subsequent conversations with defendant] Young went to the Whiting Police Department and discussed the matter with two detectives. He offered to call the defendant and let them listen and record the conversation, which they did. During the conversation, Young again asked the defendant if she wanted him to help her find someone to kill her husband, and she responded affirmatively. Young replied that he would try to find someone. Several more conversations took place. . . . At their final meeting, Young, accompanied by a plain-clothed detective, introduced the defendant to the detective, stating that here was a man who might be willing to do the job. The defendant then produced $200, a picture of her husband, and a record of his daily habits and gave them to the detective. She agreed to pay the balance of the contract price when the "job" was completed. Defendant was subsequently arrested.

At trial, Young testified that he only feigned his acquiescence in the plan and at no time did he intend to actually carry it out.

The issue is whether the conspiracy section of our new penal code adopts the Model Penal Code's "unilateral" concept or whether it retains the traditional "bilateral" concept.

The bilateral concept is the traditional view of conspiracy as derived from common law. It is formulated in terms of two or more persons agreeing to commit a crime, each with intent to do so. In cases where the person or persons with whom the defendant conspired only feigned his acquiescence in the plan, the courts have generally held that neither person could be convicted of conspiracy because there was no "conspiratorial agreement." . . .

Reacting to criticism of this viewpoint, the drafters of the Model Penal Code, though not without internal disagreement, adopted a "unilateral" concept, as follows: [The court then quoted Model Penal Code §§5.03(1) and 5.04(1). See Appendix.]

In explanation of their new approach, the Drafters of the Model Penal Code commented:

> . . . The definition of the Draft departs from the traditional view of conspiracy as an entirely bilateral or multilateral relationship. . . . Attention is directed instead to each individual's culpability by framing the definition in terms of the conduct which suffices to establish the liability of any given actor, rather than the conduct of a group of which he is charged to be a part — an approach which in this comment we have designated "unilateral."
>
> One consequence of this approach is to make it immaterial to the guilt of a conspirator whose culpability has been established that the person or all of the persons with whom he conspired have not been or cannot be convicted. . . . Under the unilateral approach of the Draft, the culpable party's guilt would not be affected by the fact that the other party's agreement was feigned. . . . True enough, the project's chances of success have not been increased by the agreement; indeed, its doom may have been sealed by this turn of events. But the major basis of conspiratorial liability — the unequivocal evidence of a firm purpose to commit a crime — remains the same. . . .

M.P.C. §5.03 [Tent. Draft No. 10,] Comments at pp. 104-105. . . .

This concept has been adopted, in whole or in part, in at least 26 states and is under consideration in most of the remaining states. See Note, Conspiracy: Statutory Reform Since the Model Penal Code, 75 Col. L. R. 1122, 1125 (1975).

In 1976, our Indiana Legislature repealed the existing conspiracy statute[2] and adopted Ind. Code §35-41-5-2 . . . which reads as follows:

2. The repealed conspiracy statute read as follows:

35-1-111-1 [10-1101]. Conspiracy to commit a felony. — Any person or persons who shall unite or combine with any other person or persons for the purpose of committing a felony, within or without this state; or any person or persons who shall knowingly unite with any other person or persons, body, association or combination of persons, whose object is the commission of a felony or felonies, within or without this state, shall, on conviction, be [punished.]"

[Sec. 2.] (a) A person conspires to commit a felony when, with intent to commit the felony, he agrees with another person to commit the felony. . . .

(c) It is no defense that the person with whom the accused person is alleged to have conspired:

(1) has not been prosecuted;

(2) has not been convicted;

(3) has been acquitted;

(4) has been convicted of a different crime;

(5) cannot be prosecuted for any reason; or

(6) lacked the capacity to commit the crime.

. . . [I]t is clear upon the face of the act that defenses available under the multilateral concept were to be eliminated. The inclusion of the "catch-all" sub-proviso (5) can leave no doubt. Clearly "any reason," as recited therein, includes the absence of criminal culpability on the part of a co-conspirator — including a sole co-conspirator. The words "agrees" and "agreement" have not been used as words of art denoting a "meeting of the minds" and "contract." Rather, the former is descriptive of the defendant's state of mind at the time he communicated with another in furtherance of the felony; and the latter refers to the defendant's understanding.

Defendant has cited us to numerous cases supporting the bilateral concept requiring "concurrence of sentiment and cooperative conduct in the unlawful and criminal enterprise"; however, those cases were not decided under statutes remotely similar to our own. . . . Her argument that, by definition, an agreement requires the concurrence of sentiment of at least two individuals . . . is not persuasive in the light of the express wording of the entire enactment. . . .

The judgment of the trial court is affirmed.

NOTES

1. *The traditional offense of conspiracy.* In jurisdictions that have not reformulated their definition of conspiracy, the requirement of bilateral agreement remains, and conspiracy charges will not lie when the defendant's only collaborators are undercover informants or other feigned participants. See, e.g., United States v. Schmidt, 947 F.2d 362, 367 (9th Cir. 1991); Fortune v. Commonwealth, 406 S.E.2d 47 (Va. App. 1991).

2. *Modern conspiracy statutes.* In jurisdictions that have adopted definitions of conspiracy similar to that proposed by the Model Penal Code, most courts have held, in accord with *Garcia,* that a defendant can be guilty of conspiracy if he agrees to commit a crime with a feigned accomplice. E.g., State v. Rambousek, 479 N.W.2d 832 (N.D. 1992). But in Connecticut and Illinois, two states with conspiracy statutes patterned on the Model Penal Code, courts have held that the requirement of bilateral agreement survives. See State v. Grullon, 212 Conn. 195, 562 A.2d 481 (1989); People v. Foster, 99 Ill. 2d 48, 457 N.E.2d 405, 407 (1983). The Illinois statute states that a "person commits conspiracy when, with intent that an offense be committed, he agrees with another to the commission of that offense." Ill. Rev. Stat. ch. 720, §5/8-2(a). In *Foster,* the Illinois Supreme Court held that the required "agree[ment]" could not exist unless at least two

parties genuinely intended to carry out the plan. Rejecting the reasoning of the *Garcia* case, the court said (457 N.E.2d at 407): "We doubt . . . that the drafters could have intended what represents a rather profound change in the law of conspiracy without mentioning it in the comments to section 8-2." The court noted, however, that the Illinois solicitation statute would (like the corresponding Model Penal Code provision) "embrace virtually every situation in which one could be convicted of conspiracy under the unilateral theory." Id., 457 N.E.2d at 408.

3. The case in favor of the traditional view is stated as follows in United States v. Escobar De Bright, 742 F.2d 1196, 1198-1200 (9th Cir. 1984):

> Criminal conspiracy is an offense separate from the actual criminal act because of the perception "that collective action toward an antisocial end involves a greater risk to society than individual action toward the same end." In part, this view is based on the perception that group activity increases the likelihood of success of the criminal act and of future criminal activity by members of the group, and is difficult for law enforcement officers to detect. . . .
>
> Such dangers, however, are non-existent when a person "conspires" only with a government agent. There is no continuing criminal enterprise and ordinarily no inculcation of criminal knowledge and practices. Preventive intervention by law enforcement officers also is not a significant problem in such circumstances. The agent, as part of the "conspiracy," is quite capable of monitoring the situation in order to prevent the completion of the contemplated criminal plan; in short, no cloak of secrecy surrounds any agreement to commit the criminal acts.
>
> Finally, the [traditional] rule responds to the same concern that underlies the entrapment defense: the legitimate law enforcement function of crime prevention "does not include the manufacturing of crime." Allowing a government agent to form a conspiracy with only one other party would create the potential for law enforcement officers to "manufacture" conspiracies when none would exist absent the government's presence.

See also Dierdre A. Burgman, Unilateral Conspiracy: Three Critical Perspectives, 29 DePaul L. Rev. 75 (1979); Paul Marcus, Conspiracy: The Criminal Agreement in Theory and Practice, 65 Geo. L.J. 925, 927 (1977).

4. *Attempted conspiracy?* In states that adhere to the bilateral approach, can a defendant who "agrees" to commit a crime with an undercover agent or pretended "hit man" be convicted of attempted conspiracy? In State v. Kihnel, 488 So. 2d 1238, 1241 (La. App. 1986), the court held in the negative:

> Attempt and conspiracy are both inchoate crimes. Just as there can be no attempt to commit an attempt, such as "attempted assault" . . . we conclude that under the bilateral formulation of conspiracy there can be no "attempted conspiracy."
>
> As part of the very foundation of criminal law, crimes include both a criminal act (or omission) and a criminal intent. "Attempted conspiracy" suggests a crime formed only of criminal intent, as it is the agreement which constitutes the act. We are not prepared to judicially legislate such a crime.

For thorough discussion of the problem, see Ira Robbins, Double Inchoate Crimes, 26 Harv. J. Legis. 1, 54-58, 80-83, 91-94 (1989).

7. *Criminal Enterprises and RICO*

INTRODUCTORY NOTE

The preceding materials illustrate some of the difficulties of prosecuting complex, ongoing criminal organizations and some of the dangers that conspiracy doctrines pose to innocent individuals and petty offenders who find themselves in contact with the activities of such organizations. In response to a perception that traditional conspiracy law provided inadequate tools for combatting sophisticated criminal enterprises, Congress in 1970 passed the Racketeer Influenced and Corrupt Organizations Act, popularly known as RICO. The growing body of RICO law and its importance in modern law enforcement have made RICO a distinctive branch of conspiracy law that is worth careful study in its own right. In examining the RICO statute, reprinted below, consider to what extent its provisions reach activities that could not be punished under traditional conspiracy doctrines, and to what extent its provisions change the treatment of activities that remain punishable under the traditional doctrines.

RACKETEER INFLUENCED AND CORRUPT ORGANIZATIONS ACT

18 U.S.C. ch. 96

§1961. DEFINITIONS

As used in this chapter —

(1) "racketeering activity" means (A) any act or threat involving murder, kidnaping, gambling, arson, robbery, bribery, extortion, dealing in obscene matter, or dealing in narcotic or other dangerous drugs, which is chargeable under State law and punishable by imprisonment for more than one year; (B) any act which is indictable under any of the following provisions of title 18, United States Code: [References are to sections relating to bribery, counterfeiting, theft from interstate shipment, embezzlement from pension and welfare funds, extortionate credit transactions, the transmission of gambling information, mail fraud, wire fraud, obstruction of justice, obstruction of criminal investigations, obstruction of State or local law enforcement, interference with commerce, robbery, or extortion, racketeering, interstate transportation of wagering paraphernalia, unlawful welfare fund payments, prohibition of illegal gambling businesses, interstate transportation of stolen property]; (C) any act which is indictable under title 29, United States Code, section 186 (dealing with restrictions on payments and loans to labor organizations) or section 501(c) (relating to embezzlement from union funds), [or] (D) any offense involving [bankruptcy fraud], fraud in the sale of securities, or the felonious manufacture, importation, receiving, concealment, buying, selling, or otherwise dealing in narcotic or other dangerous drugs, punishable under any law of the United States. . . .

(4) "enterprise" includes any individual, partnership, corporation, association, or other legal entity, and any union or group of individuals associated in fact although not a legal entity;

(5) "pattern of racketeering activity" requires at least two acts of racketeering activity, one of which occurred after the effective date of this chapter [Oct. 15, 1970] and the last of which occurred within ten years (excluding any period of imprisonment) after the commission of a prior act of racketeering activity. . . .

§1962. Prohibited Activities

(a) It shall be unlawful for any person who has received any income derived, directly or indirectly, from a pattern of racketeering activity or through collection of an unlawful debt . . . to use or invest [any part of such income in acquisition of] any enterprise . . . the activities of which affect interstate or foreign commerce. . . .

(b) It shall be unlawful for any person through a pattern of racketeering activity or through collection of an unlawful debt to acquire or maintain [any interest in any enterprise the activities of which affect] interstate or foreign commerce.

(c) It shall be unlawful for any person employed by or associated with any enterprise engaged in, or the activities of which affect, interstate or foreign commerce, to conduct or participate, directly or indirectly, in the conduct of such enterprise's affairs through a pattern of racketeering activity or collection of unlawful debt.

(d) It shall be unlawful for any person to conspire to violate any of the provisions of subsection (a), (b), or (c) of this section.

§1963. Criminal Penalties

(a) Whoever violates any provision of section 1962 of this chapter shall be fined under this title or imprisoned not more than 20 years (or for life if the violation is based on a racketeering activity for which the maximum penalty includes life imprisonment), or both. . . .

NOTES

The RICO statute has become one of the most controversial provisions in the federal criminal code. RICO bases criminal liability on new, potentially elastic concepts such as the "enterprise" and "racketeering activity." The penalties imposed for a violation of RICO can be far higher than those that would apply when the underlying criminal acts are not part of a "pattern" of "racketeering activity," and the statute provides powerful prosecutorial tools to compel forfeiture of assets derived from racketeering. In addition, RICO permits individuals harmed by racketeering to bring civil suits, and it awards treble damages for injuries resulting from RICO violations. By including a provision for treble damage lawsuits, the statute creates a fertile field for civil litigation, and expansive interpretations of RICO in civil suits open the door in turn to wider criminal liability. This note sets out the most important decisions governing the elements of a RICO violation.

1. The "enterprise." Because much of RICO's original focus was on preventing organized crime from infiltrating and capturing control of legitimate businesses, some courts held that the "enterprise" must be an organization engaged in some legal activities. In contrast, these courts reasoned, an ordinary criminal conspiracy, in which individuals associate for the sole and specific purpose of committing criminal acts, could not by itself constitute the kind of "enterprise" with which RICO was concerned. But in United States v. Turkette, 452 U.S. 576 (1981), the Supreme Court held that an "enterprise" for RICO purposes can include an exclusively criminal organization. In response to the argument that this approach would make the required "enterprise" synonymous with the required "pattern of racketeering activity," the court said (452 U.S. at 583):

> The enterprise is an entity, for present purposes a group of persons associated together for a common purpose of engaging in a course of conduct. The pattern of racketeering activity is, on the other hand, a series of criminal acts as defined by the statute. The former is proved by evidence of an ongoing organization, formal or informal, and by evidence that the various associates function as a continuing unit. The latter is proved by evidence of the requisite number of acts of racketeering committed by the participants in the enterprise. While the proof used to establish these separate elements may in particular cases coalesce, proof of one does not necessarily establish the other. The "enterprise" is not the "pattern of racketeering activity"; it is an entity separate and apart from the pattern of activity in which it engages. The existence of an enterprise at all times remains a separate element which must be proved by the Government.

Elaborating on *Turkette*, the court in United States v. Bledsoe, 674 F.2d 647, 665 (8th Cir. 1982), held that a RICO "enterprise" must have "continuity of both structure and personality" and "an 'ascertainable structure' distinct from that inherent in the conduct of a pattern of racketeering activity."

2. The "pattern." In H.J. Inc. v. Northwestern Bell Telephone Co., 492 U.S. 229 (1989), phone company customers sued for treble damages, alleging that Northwestern and several of its employees had violated RICO by bribing members of the Minnesota Public Utilities Commission (MPUC) to approve excessive rates. The court of appeals upheld the dismissal of the case, on the ground that the acts of alleged bribery did not constitute a "pattern" because they were all part of a "single scheme" to influence the MPUC. The Supreme Court reversed. the Court held that a RICO "pattern" must involve something more than just two predicate acts, but that a pattern need not involve separate illegal schemes and need not involve conduct indicative of organized crime activity in the traditional sense. Drawing on RICO's legislative history, the Court interpreted the "pattern" element to require proof "that the racketeering predicates are related, *and* that they . . . pose a threat of continued criminal activity." 492 U.S. at 239. The Court also held that Congress intended courts to define "relatedness" by referring to 18 U.S.C. §3575(e), which specifies that criminal conduct is related

> if it embraces criminal acts that have the same or similar purposes, results, participants, victims, or methods of commission, or otherwise are interrelated by distinguishing characteristics and are not isolated events.

In an opinion concurring only in the judgment, Justice Scalia, joined by the Chief Justice and Justices O'Connor and Kennedy, commented (492 U.S. at 252-256):

> Elevating to the level of statutory text a phrase taken from the legislative history, the Court counsels the lower courts: "continuity plus relationship." This seems to me about as helpful to the conduct of their affairs as "life is a fountain." . . . It hardly closes in on the target to know that "relatedness" refers to acts that are related by "purposes, results, participants, victims, . . . methods of commission, *or* [just in case that is not vague enough] *otherwise.*" Is the fact that the victims of both predicate acts were women enough? Or that both acts had the purpose of enriching the defendant? Or that the different coparticipants of the defendant in both acts were his co-employees? I doubt that the lower courts will find the Court's instructions much more helpful than telling them to look for a "pattern" — which is what the statute already says.
>
> The Court finds "continuity" more difficult to define precisely. "Continuity," it says, "is both a closed- and open-ended concept, referring either to a closed period of repeated conduct, or to past conduct that by its nature projects into the future with a threat of repetition." I have no idea what this concept of a "closed period of repeated conduct" means. Virtually all allegations of racketeering activity, in both civil and criminal suits, will relate to past periods that are "closed" (unless one expects plaintiff or the prosecutor to establish that the defendant not only committed the crimes he did, but is still committing them), and all of them *must* relate to conduct that is "repeated," because of RICO's multiple-act requirement. . . .
>
> It is clear to me . . . that the word "pattern" in the phrase "pattern of racketeering activity" was meant to import some requirement beyond the mere existence of multiple predicate acts. . . . But what that something more is, is beyond me. As I have suggested, it is also beyond the Court. Today's opinion has added nothing to improve our prior guidance, which has created a kaleidoscope of circuit positions, except to clarify that RICO may in addition be violated when there is a "threat of continuity." It seems to me this increases rather than removes the vagueness. . . .
>
> No constitutional challenge to this law has been raised in the present case, and so that issue is not before us. That the highest Court in the land has been unable to derive from this statute anything more than today's meager guidance bodes ill for the day when that challenge is presented.

3. *"Conduct" and "participation."* Reves v. Ernst & Young, 113 S. Ct. 1163 (1993), involved a civil suit growing out of the insolvency of an Arkansas farmers' cooperative. In auditing the co-op's books, the Arthur Young accounting firm (which later merged into Ernst & Young) permitted one of the co-op's major assets to be carried at its original cost of $4.5 million rather than its market value of $1.5 million, and failed to disclose the problematic nature of the $4.5 million valuation. When the co-op became insolvent in 1984, the trustee in bankruptcy sued Arthur Young and several individual accountants, alleging that the co-op's noteholders had been defrauded by misrepresentations that violated various securities laws and RICO. The Supreme Court held that Arthur Young and its accountants had not violated §1962(c) because, in order to "conduct or participate directly or indirectly in the conduct of [an] enterprise's affairs," an individual must have some role in directing or managing the business of the enterprise (which in this case was the co-op). Justice Blackmun wrote for the Court (113 S. Ct. at 1170, 1173):

In order to "participate, directly or indirectly, in the conduct of such enterprise's affairs," one must have some part in directing those affairs. Of course, the word "participate" makes clear that RICO liability is not limited to those with primary responsibility for the enterprise's affairs, . . . but *some* part in directing the enterprise's affairs is required. The "operation or management" test expresses this requirement in a formulation that is easy to apply.

. . . We agree that liability under §1962(c) is not limited to upper management, but we disagree that the "operation or management" test is inconsistent with this proposition. An enterprise is "operated" not just by upper management but also by lower-rung participants in the enterprise who are under the direction of upper management. An enterprise also might be "operated" or "managed" by others "associated with" the enterprise who exert control over it as, for example, by bribery.

Question: Does the "operation or management" test protect low-level employees and outside professionals from conviction of racketeering offenses under RICO? Consider Daniel R. Fischel & Alan O. Sykes, Civil RICO After *Reves:* An Economic Commentary, [1993] Sup. Ct. Rev. 157, 190-194:

On first reading, the [*Reves*] opinion provides considerable comfort to professionals. . . . Only those who have "some part in directing the enterprise's affairs" can be liable. . . . [But] there is sufficient contradictory language in *Reves* to make the issue murky at best. . . . The Court [stated] that: "An enterprise is 'operated' not just by upper management but also by lower-rung participants in the enterprise who are under the direction of upper management." With this one sentence, the Court undercut much of its earlier emphasis on the importance of "directing" an enterprise's affairs. Now the "direction" requirement includes both those who direct, as well as those who take direction. For a Court that prides itself on the importance of the plain language of its statute, this contorted interpretation of the words "operated" and "direction" is, at the very least, paradoxical. . . .

Why was it "clear" that Arthur Young was not acting "under the direction" of the Co-op's management? Presumably the Court was referring to the absence of any direct evidence [that] Co-op management instruct[ed] Arthur Young to use fraudulent numbers. For Arthur Young's liability to turn on this point, however, is to exalt form over substance. The sale of the Co-op notes at inflated prices benefited the Co-op, not Arthur Young. Why else would Arthur Young knowingly participate and assist in the Co-op's fraud except at the behest of management? And even if Arthur Young somehow decided to participate in the fraud independently as opposed to being directed to do so by management, why should this be exonerating? The more the fraud can be attributed to Arthur Young and management as opposed to just management, the stronger the case for imposing liability on both. . . .

To determine whether a defendant played a role in directing an enterprise's affairs also requires a definition of "enterprise." In *Reves,* the enterprise was the Co-op but this is not the only possibility. . . . What if the plaintiff in *Reves* had alleged that an association in fact consisting of Arthur Young, Jack White [Co-op's general manager], and the Co-op constituted the racketeering enterprise and that Arthur Young directed the affairs of this "enterprise"?

Such an allegation might be sufficient if the plaintiff could demonstrate that the alleged association in fact was, as *Turkette* requires, "ongoing" and functioned "as a continuing unit." . . . In future cases, courts' attitude toward association in fact enterprises will be critical in light of the obvious incentives of plaintiffs to allege such associations in fact to satisfy *Reves*'s "operation or management" test.

4. *RICO conspiracies.* Section 1962(c) can be viewed as a kind of conspiracy statute: by imposing criminal liability on those who "participate . . . in the conduct of [an] enterprise's affairs through a pattern of racketeering activity," §1962(c) reaches what is inherently a type of group crime. But the RICO statute also includes a provision, §1962(d), that punishes conspiracies to violate §1962(c). See page 782 supra. Does this provision in effect prohibit conspiring to engage in a conspiracy? What are the effects of §1962(d), and how does it change the traditional law of conspiracy? Consider the case that follows.

UNITED STATES v. ELLIOTT

United States Court of Appeals, 5th Circuit
571 F.2d 880 (1978)

SIMPSON, J. In this case we deal with the question of whether and, if so, how a free society can protect itself when groups of people, through division of labor, specialization, diversification, complexity of organization, and the accumulation of capital, turn crime into an ongoing business. Congress fired a telling shot at organized crime when it passed the Racketeer Influenced and Corrupt Organizations Act of 1970. . . . Since the enactment of RICO, the federal courts, guided by constitutional and legislative dictates, have been responsible for perfecting the weapons in society's arsenal against criminal confederacies.

Today we review the convictions of six persons accused of conspiring to violate the RICO statute, two of whom were also accused and convicted of substantive RICO violations. The government admits that in this prosecution it has attempted to achieve a broader application of RICO than has heretofore been sanctioned. Predictably, the government and the defendants differ as to what this case is about. According to the defendants, what we are dealing with is a leg, a tail, a trunk, an ear — separate entities unaffected by RICO proscriptions. The government, on the other hand, asserts that we have come eyeball to eyeball with a single creature of behemoth proportions, securely within RICO's grasp. After a careful, if laborious study of the facts and the law, we accept, with minor exceptions, the government's view. . . .

[All six defendants were indicted and convicted of conspiracy to violate 18 U.S.C. §1962(c), in violation of 18 U.S.C. §1962(d). The essence of the conspiracy charge was that the defendants agreed to participate in the conduct of the affairs of an enterprise whose purposes were to commit thefts, fence stolen property, illegally traffic in narcotics, obstruct justice, and engage in other criminal activities. Thirty-seven unindicted co-conspirators were named, and 25 overt acts were listed.

[The Court of Appeals described the facts as falling into ten specific episodes. Each defendant was involved in one or several of these episodes, but never in concert with more than two other defendants. Only J. C. Hawkins was involved in every episode.

[In 1970 defendant Foster defrauded a group of investors in a nursing home, built by his construction company and leased to the investor group by a corporation set up by Foster. The day before the nursing home was to open Foster paid J. C. Hawkins and Recea Hawkins to burn it down.

[Between 1971 and 1974 defendants J. C. Hawkins, Delph, and Taylor furnished counterfeit titles to and sold cars stolen by a major car theft ring.

[In 1972 and 1973 defendant J. C. Hawkins masterminded several thefts. In 1972 he and defendants Elliott and Recea Hawkins stole and fenced a truckload of Hormel meat. When a friend of J. C. Hawkins who had stored the stolen meat in his grocery store was indicted for possession of stolen goods, J. C. influenced the outcome of the trial by tampering with a juror.

[In 1973 J. C. Hawkins stole two trucks and attempted to sell them to another man, Jimmy Reeves. Suspecting that Reeves was informing to the police, J. C. had Reeves killed by Recea Hawkins.

[Later in 1973, defendants J. C. Hawkins and Foster were involved in two thefts, J. C. committing the thefts and Foster providing storage for the stolen goods. A third theft in late 1973 involved defendant Recea Hawkins as well. Defendants Delph and Taylor were not involved in any of the thefts committed in 1972 and 1973.

[Between 1971 and 1976 a number of drug transactions took place. One involved defendant Taylor alone, another defendant Elliott alone, and another, defendant J. C. Hawkins alone. Another transaction involved defendants Delph and Taylor together, and another J. C. Hawkins and Recea Hawkins.

[Finally, in 1976, defendant J. C. Hawkins planned to steal fungicide from a chemical company. None of the other defendants was involved.

[Following conviction, the trial court imposed these sentences: J. C. Hawkins, 80 years' imprisonment; Recea Hawkins, 50 years' imprisonment; Delph and Taylor, each 10 years' imprisonment; Foster, 1 year in prison and 5 years of probation; Elliott, 5 years' probation.]

. . . In this appeal, all defendants, with the exception of Foster, argue that while the indictment alleged but one conspiracy, the government's evidence at trial proved the existence of several conspiracies, resulting in a variance which substantially prejudiced their rights and requires reversal, citing Kotteakos v. United States, 328 U.S. 750 (1946). Prior to the enactment of the RICO statute, this argument would have been more persuasive. However, as we explain below, RICO has displaced many of the legal precepts traditionally applied to concerted criminal activity. Its effect in this case is to free the government from the strictures of the multiple conspiracy doctrine and to allow the joint trial of many persons accused of diversified crimes.

A. PRIOR LAW: WHEELS AND CHAINS

1. *Kotteakos* and the Wheel Conspiracy Rationale: The Court in *Kotteakos* held that proof of multiple conspiracies under an indictment alleging a single conspiracy constituted a material variance requiring reversal where a defendant's substantial rights had been affected. At issue was "the right not to be tried en masse for the conglomeration of distinct and separate offenses committed by others." 328 U.S. at 775. *Kotteakos* thus protects against the "spill-over effect," the transference of guilt from members of one conspiracy to members of another. . . .

[The] facts in *Kotteakos* led the Court to speak in terms of a "wheel conspiracy," in which one person, the "hub" of the wheel, was accused of conspiring with several others, the "spokes" of the wheel. As we explained in United States v. Levine, 546 F.2d 658, 663 (5th Cir. 1977): "For a [single] wheel conspiracy to exist those people who form the wheel's spokes must have been aware of each other and must do something in furtherance of some single, illegal enterprise. Otherwise the conspiracy lacks 'the rim of the wheel to enclose the spokes.'" ...

2. *Blumenthal* and the Chain Conspiracy Rationale: The impact of *Kotteakos* was soon limited by the Court in Blumenthal v. United States, 332 U.S. 539 (1947), where the indictment charged a single conspiracy to sell whiskey at prices above the ceiling set by the Office of Price Administration. The owner of the whiskey, through a series of middlemen, had devised an intricate scheme to conceal the true amount he was charging for the whiskey. Although some of the middlemen had no contact with each other and did not know the identity of the owner, they had to have realized that they were indispensable cogs in the machinery through which this illegal scheme was effectuated. The Court concluded that "in every practical sense the unique facts of this case reveal a single conspiracy of which the several agreements were essential and integral steps." Thus the "chain conspiracy" rationale evolved.

The essential element of a chain conspiracy — allowing persons unknown to each other and never before in contact to be jointly prosecuted as coconspirators — is interdependence. The scheme which is the object of the conspiracy must depend on the successful operation of each link in the chain. ... "Thus, in a 'chain' conspiracy prosecution, the requisite element — knowledge of the existence of remote links — may be inferred solely from the nature of the enterprise." United States v. Perez, 489 F.2d at 59 n. 10.[24]

3. Limits of the Chain Conspiracy Rationale: The rationale of *Blumenthal* applies only insofar as the alleged agreement has "a common end or single unified purpose." ... Generally, where the government has shown that a number of otherwise diverse activities were performed to achieve a simple goal, courts have been willing to find a single conspiracy. This "common objective" test has most often been used to connect the many facets of drug importation and distribution schemes. The rationale falls apart, however, where the remote members of the alleged conspiracy are not truly interdependent or where the various activities sought to be tied together cannot reasonably be said to constitute a unified scheme. ...

Applying pre-RICO conspiracy concepts to the facts of this case, we doubt that a single conspiracy could be demonstrated. Foster had no contact with Delph and Taylor during the life of the alleged conspiracy. Delph and Taylor, so far as the evidence revealed, had no contact with Recea Hawkins. The activities allegedly embraced by the illegal agreement in this case are simply too diverse to be tied together on the theory that participation in one activity necessarily implied awareness of others. Even viewing the "common objective" of the conspiracy as the raising of revenue through criminal activity, we could not say, for example, that Foster, when he helped to conceal stolen meat, had to know that J. C. was selling drugs to persons unknown to Foster, or that Delph and Taylor, when they

---

24. Although *Perez* was a hybrid case, involving a wheel conspiracy in which each spoke was itself a chain conspiracy, we applied the interdependence rationale to find a single, overall conspiracy. *Perez* involved a series of fraudulent insurance claims based on several staged car accidents involving different groups of people, with minimal overlap among the groups. The scheme could not be described as a "chain" in the ordinary sense, but we noted that each participant had to realize that the single fraudulent claim in which he or she was involved could not be profitable unless it was one of multiple claims and that, in turn, multiple claims could not be successfully made unless they involved many different people and accidents in different locations across the state.

furnished counterfeit titles to a car theft ring, had to know that the man supplying the titles was also stealing goods out of interstate commerce. The enterprise involved in this case probably could not have been successfully prosecuted as a single conspiracy under the general federal conspiracy statute, 18 U.S.C. §371.

B. RICO TO THE RESCUE: THE ENTERPRISE CONSPIRACY

In enacting RICO, Congress found that "organized crime continues to grow" in part "because the sanctions and remedies available to the Government are unnecessarily limited in scope and impact." Thus, one of the express purposes of the Act was "to seek the eradication of organized crime . . . by establishing new penal prohibitions, and by providing enhanced sanctions and new remedies to deal with the unlawful activities of those engaged in organized crime." Pub. L. 91-452, §1, 84 Stat. 922 (1970). Against this background, we are convinced that, through RICO, Congress intended to authorize the single prosecution of a multi-faceted, diversified conspiracy by replacing the inadequate "wheel" and "chain" rationales with a new statutory concept: the enterprise.

To achieve this result, Congress acted against the backdrop of hornbook conspiracy law. Under the general federal conspiracy statute, "the precise nature and extent of the conspiracy must be determined by reference to the agreement which embraces and defines its objects. Whether the object of a single agreement is to commit one or many crimes, it is in either case that agreement which constitutes the conspiracy which the statute punishes." Braverman v. United States, 317 U.S. 49, 53. In the context of organized crime, this principle inhibited mass prosecutions because a single agreement or "common objective" cannot be inferred from the commission of highly diverse crimes by apparently unrelated individuals. RICO helps to eliminate this problem by creating a substantive offense which ties together these diverse parties and crimes. Thus, the object of a RICO conspiracy is to violate a substantive RICO provision — here, to conduct or participate in the affairs of an enterprise through a pattern of racketeering activity — and not merely to commit each of the predicate crimes necessary to demonstrate a pattern of racketeering activity. The gravamen of the conspiracy charge in this case is not that each defendant agreed to commit arson, to steal goods from interstate commerce, to obstruct justice, and to sell narcotics; rather, it is that each agreed to participate, directly and indirectly, in the affairs of the enterprise by committing two or more predicate crimes. Under the statute, it is irrelevant that each defendant participated in the enterprise's affairs through different, even unrelated crimes, so long as we may reasonably infer that each crime was intended to further the enterprise's affairs. To find a single conspiracy, we still must look for agreement on an overall objective. What Congress did was to define that objective through the substantive provisions of the Act.

C. CONSTITUTIONAL CONSIDERATIONS

The "enterprise conspiracy" is a legislative innovation in the realm of individual liability for group crime. We need to consider whether this innovation comports with the fundamental demand of due process that guilt remain "individual and personal." *Kotteakos,* supra, 328 U.S. at 772.

The substantive proscriptions of the RICO statute apply to insiders *and outsiders* — those merely "associated with" an enterprise — who participate directly *and indirectly* in the enterprise's affairs through a pattern of racketeering activity. Thus, the RICO net is woven tightly to trap even the smallest fish, those peripherally involved with the enterprise. This effect is enhanced by principles of conspiracy law also developed to facilitate prosecution of conspirators at all levels. Direct evidence of agreement is unnecessary: "proof of such an agreement may rest upon inferences drawn from relevant and competent circumstantial evidence — ordinarily the acts and conduct of the alleged conspirators themselves." United States v. Morado, 454 F.2d at 174. . . .

Undeniably, then, under the RICO conspiracy provision, remote associates of an enterprise may be convicted as conspirators on the basis of purely circumstantial evidence. We cannot say, however, that this section of the statute . . . offends the rule that guilt be individual and personal. The Act does not authorize that individuals "be tried en masse for the conglomeration of distinct and separate offenses committed by others." *Kotteakos,* supra. Nor does it punish mere association with conspirators or knowledge of illegal activity; its proscriptions are directed against conduct, not status. To be convicted as a member of an enterprise conspiracy, an individual, by his words or actions, must have objectively manifested an agreement to participate, directly or indirectly, in the affairs of an enterprise *through the commission of two or more predicate crimes.* One whose agreement with the members of an enterprise did not include this vital element cannot be convicted under the Act. Where, as here, the evidence establishes that each defendant, over a period of years, committed several acts of racketeering activity in furtherance of the enterprise's affairs, the inference of an agreement to do so is unmistakable.

It is well established that "[t]he government is not required to prove that a conspirator had full knowledge of all the details of the conspiracy; knowledge of the essential nature of the plan is sufficient." United States v. Brasseaux, 509 F.2d 157, 160 n. 3 (5th Cir. 1975). . . .

In the instant case, it is clear that "the essential nature of the plan" was to associate for the purpose of making money from repeated criminal activity. Defendant Foster, for example, hired J. C. Hawkins to commit arson, helped him to conceal large quantities of meat and shirts stolen from interstate commerce, and bought a stolen forklift from him. . . . Foster knew he was directly involved in an enterprise whose purpose was to profit from crime. As we noted in United States v. Gonzalez, 491 F.2d 1202, 1206 (5th Cir. 1974), "persons so associating and forming organizations for furthering such illicit purposes do not normally conceive of the associations as engaging in one unlawful transaction and then disbanding. Rather the nature of such organizations seems to be an ongoing operation. . . ." Foster also had to know that the enterprise was bigger than his role in it, and that others unknown to him were participating in its affairs. He may have been unaware that others who had agreed to participate in the enterprise's affairs did so by selling drugs and murdering a key witness. That, however, is irrelevant to his own liability, for he is charged with agreeing *to participate* in the enterprise through his own crimes, not with agreeing *to commit* each of the crimes through which the overall affairs of the enterprise were conducted. We perceive in this no significant extension of a co-conspirator's liability. When a person "embarks upon a criminal venture of indefinite outline, he takes his chances as to its content and membership, so be it that they fall within the common purposes as he understands them." United States v. Andolschek, 142 F.2d [503, 507 (2d Cir. 1944)].[31]

Our society disdains mass prosecutions because we abhor the totalitarian doctrine of mass guilt. We nevertheless punish conspiracy as a distinct offense because we recognize that collective action toward an illegal end involves a greater risk to society than individual action toward the same end. That risk is greatly compounded when the conspirators contemplate not a single crime but a career of crime. "There are times when of necessity, because of the nature and scope of the particular federation, large numbers of persons taking part must be tried together or perhaps not at all. . . . When many conspire, they invite mass trial by their conduct." Kotteakos, supra, 328 U.S. at 773.

We do not lightly dismiss the fact that under this statute four defendants who did not commit murder have been forced to stand trial jointly with, and as confederates of, two others who did. Prejudice inheres in such a trial; . . . But the Constitution does not guarantee a trial free from the prejudice that inevitably accompanies any charge of heinous group crime; it demands only that the potential for transference of guilt be minimized to the extent possible under the circumstances. . . . The RICO statute does not offend this principle. Congress, in a proper exercise of its legislative power, has decided that murder, like thefts from interstate commerce and the counterfeiting of securities, qualifies as racketeering activity. This, of course, ups the ante for RICO violators who personally

---

31. . . . A close look at the modus operandi of the enterprise reveals a pattern of interdependence which bolsters our conclusion that the functions of each "department" directly contributed to the success of the overall operation. Many of the enterprise's practices were analogous to those common in legitimate businesses:

— *Investment Capital:* Most of the enterprise's activities depended upon the ready availability of investment capital, or "front money," to finance the purchase of stolen goods and narcotics for eventual resale at a profit. In this sense, money brought in from one project could be used to purchase goods in another unrelated project.

— *"Good Will":* Part of the value of a business is the reputation it has established in the community, its "good will." The enterprise here benefited from a negative form of "good will." For example, Foster and J. C. exploited their cooperation in the Sparta nursing home arson to gain the confidence of James Gunnells when they needed his help in concealing stolen meat; that earlier endeavor furnished proof that Foster and J. C. could be trusted in criminal pursuits. Similarly, J. C.'s threats of physical harm to many of those involved with the enterprise helped to build a fear in the community which deterred potential witnesses from going to the police. In this way, each successful criminal act and each threat contributed to the success of the enterprise as a whole.

— *Arrangements to Limit Liability:* Like most large business organizations, this enterprise conducted its affairs in a manner calculated to limit its liability for the acts of its agents. J. C. erroneously believed that he could limit each person's liability by keeping him as isolated from the others as possible — in other words, that it would be safer to have the affairs of the enterprise conducted through chains composed of many persons playing limited roles than through a small circle of individuals performing many functions. Where overlap was unavoidable, the enterprise's ongoing operations depended upon each member's confidence that the others would remain silent. When J. C. spoke to Joe Fuchs in January, 1976, for example, he expressed confidence that the government could never make a case against his enterprise. He was certain that James Elliott would not talk because "James is scared." He also assured Fuchs that he, J. C., and Scooter Herring would say nothing; as for Recea, "that's plum out of the question, you can eliminate that." Thus, he concluded, the only other persons who might implicate Fuchs could provide only uncorroborated accounts which would "mean nothing" in court.

would not contemplate taking a human life. Whether there is a moral imbalance in the equation of thieves and counterfeiters with murderers is a question whose answer lies in the halls of Congress, not in the judicial conscience. . . .

[The court affirmed all the conspiracy convictions except Elliott's. The court found the evidence insufficient to support a reasonable inference of his guilt:]

Viewed in a light most favorable to the government, the evidence against Elliott proved the following:

(1) Early in the spring of 1971, Joe Fuchs gave Elliott a bottle of 500 amphetamine capsules without a prescription.

(2) Shortly thereafter, Elliott negotiated a deal with Fuchs for Joe Breland to build an enclosed porch and for Fuchs to repay Elliott and Breland with amphetamine pills. During the next year, Fuchs delivered the pills in installments of 400.

(3) In April, 1972, Elliott, apparently as a favor for J. C., either sold or gave to Fuchs a 50 pound piece of stolen Hormel meat.

(4) In May, 1973, Elliott, serving as a juror in the trial of Rudolph Flanders for possession of meat from the same stolen shipment, held out for acquittal, causing a mistrial. No evidence was presented that Elliott had been contacted in advance about how he would vote in the Flanders case, although J. C. had told others that he felt Elliott would cooperate.

(5) In January, 1976, Elliott encouraged Fuchs to lie to a federal grand jury about how he acquired the stolen meat given to him by Elliott in 1972.

This evidence could not be taken to support, to the exclusion of all other reasonable hypotheses, a conclusion by the jury that Elliott agreed to participate, directly or indirectly, in the affairs of an enterprise through a pattern of racketeering activity. At best, this evidence discloses that Elliott used a close friend, Joe Fuchs, as a personal source of amphetamines and that he became peripherally involved in a stolen meat deal, an involvement he later attempted to conceal. The government failed to prove that Elliott's amphetamine transactions with Fuchs were in any way connected with the affairs of the enterprise. The Hormel meat, on the other hand, undeniably was acquired as a result of enterprise activity, but Elliott's cooperation with J. C. Hawkins in disposing of a small portion of the meat is insufficient to prove beyond a reasonable doubt that Elliott knowingly and intentionally joined the broad conspiracy to violate RICO. Elliott's acts are equally consistent with the hypothesis that he conspired with J. C. and Fuchs for the limited purpose of aiding in the distribution of stolen meat, an offense with which he was not charged in this case. Under this hypothesis, Elliott agreed to participate in the affairs of the enterprise, but not through a *pattern* of racketeering activity, hence, not in violation of the Act. Similarly, Elliott's two subsequent attempts to cover up the facts in the Hormel meat case are subject to two interpretations: (1) as possible overt acts in furtherance of an agreement to participate in the enterprise's affairs through a pattern of racketeering activity, or (2) as efforts at concealment undertaken after the object of his more limited conspiracy with J. C. and Fuchs had been accomplished, on the theory that "every conspiracy will inevitably be followed by actions taken to cover the conspirators' traces." Grunewald v. United States, 353 U.S. 391 (1957). To allow these predictable acts of concealment to be construed as independent evidence that Elliott agreed to conduct a pattern of racketeering activity would unjustifiably broaden the already pervasive scope of the RICO statute. We hold, then, that the more reasonable conclusion dictated by these facts is that, while Elliott may have conspired to distribute stolen meat, the jury could not reasonably conclude that he conspired to violate RICO.

NOTES

1. Comparing RICO conspiracy with ordinary conspiracy. If under pre-RICO law there would be insufficient proof in *Elliott* to tie Foster, Delph, and Taylor together with J. C. Hawkins in a single agreement, how does passage of the RICO statute create a single agreement between them? Conversely, if — as the *Elliott* court holds — these conspirators agreed "to associate for the purpose of making money from repeated criminal activity," then why would pre-RICO law pose any barrier to finding a single agreement? Consider Michael Goldsmith, RICO and Enterprise Criminality: A Response to Gerard E. Lynch, 88 Colum. L. Rev. 774, 798 (1988):

> The answer [to this question] is that the enterprise itself is an important link in the evidentiary chain: a defendant's knowledge of the enterprise's existence is probative of a central purpose. Thus, upon proof that such an enterprise exists, the enterprise itself provides the basis for inferring one large conspiracy instead of many smaller ones. The objective of this conspiracy, which potentially encompasses many crimes, is to conduct enterprise affairs through a pattern of racketeering activity. In contrast, because ordinary conspiracy cases do not involve proof of enterprise, this unifying function is absent.

2. The "enterprise." One of the many criticisms of the *Elliott* case was expressed as follows in Barry Tarlow, RICO: The New Darling of the Prosecutor's Nursery, 49 Ford. L. Rev. 165, 243, 251-252 (1980):

> The primary flaw in the *Elliott* view is the court's assumption that the scope of a RICO substantive offense or a RICO conspiracy is defined by the enterprise. The court believed that, although the defendants must agree to commit a pattern of racketeering activity, they need not agree to commit the same pattern as long as the defendants' patterns involve the same enterprise. Applying *Elliott* to a legitimate enterprise, however, it is apparent that the enterprise does not always supply a substantial connection between the activities of the defendants.
>
> The following hypothetical illustrates this defect in *Elliott*. Assume that five police officers are charged with operating the same police department through the following patterns: (1) Officer A makes illegal payments in 1971 to a legislator to obtain a salary increase; (2) Officer B receives bribes in 1973 in exchange for protecting prostitution; (3) Officer C murders two minority citizens while arresting them in 1975; (4) Officer D removes cocaine from the evidence locker in 1977 and sells it with the aid of individuals he is supposedly investigating; and (5) Officer E embezzles money from the police pension benefit plan in 1979. All of the police officers know of, but are not involved in, the activities of the other officers.

Under a literal application of *Elliott,* these parties would be part of a single chargeable 1962(c) or 1962(d) RICO offense solely because their acts occurred in the conduct of the same enterprise.

This flaw in *Elliott* was largely corrected by United States v. Sutherland, 656 F.2d 1181 (5th Cir. 1981). In *Sutherland* one defendant was a traffic court judge, and each of the other two (Walker and Maynard) was a person allegedly involved with the judge in a scheme to fix traffic tickets. The government conceded that neither Walker nor Maynard knew of the other's activities; under pre-RICO law there would have been two separate conspiracies — a "wheel" without a "rim." But the government claimed that the affairs of the traffic court constituted the RICO "enterprise" and that the three defendants could be charged with a single "enterprise conspiracy" under RICO. In essence, the government argued that "so long as the object of each conspiracy is participation in the same enterprise in violation of RICO, it matters not that the different conspiracies are otherwise unrelated." Id. at 1191. The Fifth Circuit conceded that some of the language in *Elliott* lent support to this argument, but noted that *Elliott* was addressed primarily to the problem that under prior law, it was difficult to infer a single agreement from the commission of highly diverse crimes. *Elliott* explained that "RICO helps to eliminate this problem by creating a substantive offense which ties together these diverse parties and crimes." The court then clarified the holding in *Elliott* (id. at 1192-1194):

> *Elliott* does indeed hold that on the facts of that case a series of agreements that under pre-RICO law would constitute multiple conspiracies could under RICO be tried as a single "enterprise" conspiracy. But the language of *Elliott* explains that what ties these conspiracies together is not the mere fact that they involve the same enterprise, but is instead — as in any other conspiracy — an "agreement on an overall objective." What RICO does is to provide a new criminal objective by defining a new substantive crime. In *Elliott,* as here, that crime consists of participation in an enterprise through a pattern of racketeering activity. . . .
>
> To be sure, the government did not prove in *Elliott* that each of the conspirators had explicitly agreed with all of the others to violate the substantive RICO provision at issue. However, the government did prove that, as in a traditional "chain" conspiracy, the nature of the scheme was such that each defendant must necessarily have known that others were also conspiring to participate in the same enterprise through a pattern of racketeering activity. . . .
>
> *Elliott* does not stand for the proposition that multiple conspiracies may be tried on a single "enterprise conspiracy" count under RICO merely because the various conspiracies involve the same enterprise. What *Elliott* does state is two-fold: (1) a pattern of agreements that absent RICO would constitute multiple conspiracies may be joined under a single RICO conspiracy count if the defendants have agreed to commit a substantive RICO offense; and (2) such an agreement to violate RICO may, as in the case of a traditional "chain" or "wheel" conspiracy, be established on circumstantial evidence, i.e., evidence that the nature of the conspiracy is such that each defendant must necessarily have known that others were also conspiring to violate RICO.
>
> In this case the government has not attempted to prove that Walker and Maynard agreed with each other to participate in a bribery scheme with Sutherland, nor has it contended that the nature of each defendant's agreement with Sutherland was such that he or she must necessarily have known that others were also

conspiring to commit racketeering offenses in the conduct of the Municipal Court. We must conclude, therefore, that the multiple conspiracy doctrine precluded the joint trial of the two multiple conspiracies involved in this case on a single RICO conspiracy count. . . .

NOTE ON THE CONTROVERSY OVER RICO

The RICO statute has remained extremely controversial. Some of the principal issues concern its potential for unduly promoting or distorting civil litigation; also prominent in the debate are concerns about RICO's provisions for pretrial seizure of a defendant's assets, forfeiture of assets connected to the "enterprise," and related procedural matters. These strands in the RICO debate cannot be pursued in depth here, but many of the most important themes in the debate raise problems of substantive criminal law — the breadth and potential vagueness of the RICO offense, the risk of guilt by association, and the possibility for criminal liability greatly disproportionate to personal fault. These issues are central to conspiracy law in general and to other topics that pervade the subject of criminal law. Consider the comments that follow.

DAVID SENTELLE,[11] RICO: THE MONSTER THAT ATE JURISPRUDENCE

Lecture to the CATO Institute, Oct. 18, 1989, pp. 5-13

The [RICO] monster is . . . hungrily devouring traditional concepts of American jurisprudence. Among the traditional concepts the monster is eating, I would include federalism, the separation of powers, . . . repose of actions and perhaps even the basic concept of government of laws, not of men.

As to federalism: . . . look back to the language of section 1961(1) defining "racketeering activity." Within the incredible compass of that definition, Section (1)(A) adopts wholesale great areas of State criminal law encompassing "any act or threat involving murder, kidnapping, gambling, arson, robbery, bribery, extortion, dealing in obscene matter, or dealing in narcotic or other dangerous drugs, which is chargeable under *State* law and punishable by imprisonment for more than one year." (Emphasis added.)

. . . The almost boundless breadth of RICO, invites, perhaps requires, the Article II Executive in the form of the prosecutor and the Judiciary in the form of Article III Judges to undertake the Article I Legislative role of defining federal crimes. . . .

[D]efenders of RICO . . . tell us that we should rely on prosecutorial discretion to protect against the overbreadth of RICO. Even some of those who seek to reform RICO by the repeal of its civil remedy would retain criminal RICO because they are willing to rely on the discretion of prosecutors despite their distrust of civil plaintiff's attorneys. But we are not given angels in the form of men to make prosecutorial decisions. If we can rely on the discretion of Executive

---

11. David Sentelle is a U.S. Circuit Judge on the U.S. Court of Appeals for the D.C. Circuit.

Branch officials to protect our liberties, why did we need a Constitution creating a limited government and a Bill of Rights protecting our liberties in the first place? . . .

Finally, we see the RICO monster violently attacking traditional principles of repose of actions. . . . The definition of "pattern of racketeering activity" permits the use of "at least two acts of racketeering activity, one of which occurred after the effective date of this chapter and the last of which occurred within ten years (excluding any period of imprisonment) after the commission of a prior act of racketeering activity." . . .

In other words, RICO creates an essentially perpetual cause of action alien to our traditional jurisprudence. . . . Congress, of course, has the power to make determinations as to the period of limitations. Nonetheless, one must wonder if Congress in the RICO statute really made a conscious decision to create a perpetual cause of action or simply unwittingly unleashed a monster. . . .

GERARD E. LYNCH, RICO: THE CRIME OF BEING A CRIMINAL
87 Colum. L. Rev. 661, 920, 932-955, 967-970 (1987)

Fundamental to our traditional law of crimes, criminal procedure and evidence is a conception of crime that is transaction-bound. [T]he core of any definition of crime is a particular act or omission. That act or omission is conceived as taking place in an instant of time so precise that it can be associated with a particular mental state of intention, awareness of risk, or neglect of due care. . . . Even the crime of conspiracy, which in practice may permit an examination of an extended course of conduct by one or more individuals, does so in the guise of using that course of conduct as evidence from which to infer that a particular act of "agreement" occurred, presumably at a specific, if not precisely ascertainable, moment in time. . . .

The focus on particular events in defining crimes is not merely a linguistic convention. The requirement that criminal punishment be based on a specific act has deep roots. The very nature of criminal punishment, as distinct from other uses of the compulsive power of the state (such as mandatory treatment for physical or mental illness), requires that a person not be punished for bad character, tendency to commit crime, or even a specifically formulated intention to commit some particular prohibited act. Before the state can deprive a citizen of liberty in a *punitive* way, the individual must manifest that character or tendency by the commission of some concrete prohibited act.

In significant part, the purpose of this limitation is the protection of an individual from punishment for thoughts or traits not yet exemplified by actual harmful conduct. But the moral basis of the focus on particular acts extends beyond this problem. Even for those accused of committing what is unquestionably a concrete, particular offense, we are careful to guard against the possibility that a defendant may be convicted and punished for bad character rather than for the particular act charged. The insistence on incident-based liability thus has important consequences for our rules of procedure and evidence. . . .

RICO prosecutions of criminal enterprises present a serious challenge to the substantive and procedural implications of this transaction-based model of crime. . . . The very words of the statute reveal an intent to prohibit not any particular, time-bound action, but a course of conduct extending over a potentially lengthy period of time. Although the predicate acts of racketeering are conventional crimes, defined in terms of specific conduct, the actual RICO violation is not identifiable by the physical contours of a particular action or effect. Rather, the defining characteristic of the "pattern of racketeering" is the relationship of certain conduct to other conduct and to the "enterprise," which itself is an abstract construct of certain interpersonal relationships. . . .

[T]he fact that RICO define[s] a crime entails some of its most dramatic procedural and evidentiary consequences. . . . Suppose, for example, the authorities develop evidence that the same defendant from whom they have recently made an undercover purchase of narcotics is a member of an organized crime family who committed a contract killing three years earlier. Under our ordinary, transaction-bound rules of procedure and evidence, the defendant would have to be tried separately for each offense. . . . In a trial on the narcotics charge alone, moreover, the evidence of a prior homicide committed by the defendant would likely be excluded as irrelevant and highly prejudicial. . . . And the prosecutor presumably would not even think about trying to elicit evidence of crimes that some *other* member of the same crime family had committed, in which this particular defendant was not personally involved. Evidence of the defendant's involvement in organized crime or of the murder he may have committed might finally surface after the defendant's conviction, as part of an argument for a severe sentence.

If the case could be indicted and tried under RICO, however, all of the evidence regarding this defendant's activities could easily be presented in the same trial. Since the government would have to allege and prove a pattern of racketeering activity, the murder and the narcotics offense could be alleged as elements of the same crime, the violation of section 1962(c). The rules precluding admission of evidence of other crimes, consequently, would simply have no application — evidence of the homicide would not be evidence of a *prior* crime, but evidence of the very offense charged in the indictment. . . .

One value served by the transaction model of crime is its preclusion of punishment in the absence of behavior manifesting a concrete threat of harm to legitimate social interests. . . . "Character" or "predicted danger" are flexible and unpredictable standards of decision, too easily used as tools of oppression.

These substantive concerns, however, are not directly violated by RICO. Although the distinguishing features of RICO are its somewhat amorphous associational and course of conduct elements, a fundamental prerequisite of a substantive RICO violation is the commission of particular criminal acts. These predicate racketeering acts are themselves conventional, transactionally defined crimes. . . .

[Other objections to RICO are procedural. More] lenient rules of admissibility or joinder [can] distract the jury from [accurately determining] the likelihood that the defendant committed a particular act. . . . But . . . RICO insists that the whole is more than the sum of its parts. If jurors react differently to the prosecution of a bookmaker when he is tried alone for illegal gambling than they do to the same evidence presented as part of an illicit association case in which the bookmaker is charged with participating through a pattern of gambling offenses in the conduct of a violent crime "family," it can be argued that they are not being overwhelmed by prejudice, but that they are responding to a genuine difference in the facts presented. The additional evidence . . . is an essential part of what makes the defendant's actions particularly threatening to society. Only if the jury is permitted to see the fuller story — the pattern that links this particular defendant's acts to social harm — can a judgment about his guilt be made. . . .

Recognizing the importance of context to the gravity of individual criminal acts, increasing the possibility of convicting racketeers who might otherwise slip through the cracks in a transaction-based model of procedure, and utilizing the dramatic context of the criminal trial to educate the public to models of criminal activity more significant than the isolated derelictions of particular individuals are important and appropriate goals for criminal law. . . .

Such arguments are tenable, however, only if the RICO trial affords due process. . . . [I]s it within the physical and mental capacity of a jury to recall accurately the separate evidence relating to so many different individuals and so many separate incidents? What is the effect on a jury pool of the elimination of all potential jurors who cannot serve in a trial that may last over a year? . . . The threat of substantive injustice in RICO cases may come far more from such practical concerns than from the conceptual issues discussed above.

NOTES ON ENTERPRISE LIABILITY UNDER STATE LAW

1. *State RICO.* One recent analysis finds that 33 states have enacted antiracketeering statutes closely tracking the structure and terminology of federal RICO. See Susan W. Brenner, RICO, CCE, and Other Complex Crimes: The Transformation of American Criminal Law?, 2 Wm. & Mary Bill of Rights J. 239, 273 (1992). Because these statutes are so similar to the federal model, state courts often look to federal RICO precedent in interpreting them. In some jurisdictions, however, state statutes have been interpreted to reach even more broadly than federal RICO. An example is State v. Ball, 268 N.J. Super. 72, 632 A.2d 1222 (1993), where the court held that, despite similarities between the New Jersey and federal statutes, New Jersey RICO did not require that the "enterprise" have any ascertainable structure (632 A.2d at 1240):

> [I]n our view, all that is required to satisfy the New Jersey RICO enterprise element is a group of people, however loosely associated, whose existence provides the common purpose of committing two or more predicate acts.
>   . . . In the present case, we are presented with a somewhat disorganized group of individuals. They had no real "leader" as that term is commonly understood; there was no one to whom all members owed allegiance, or to whom all members are required to report. In fact, the group's members did not even seem to like each other, and were often engaged in double-dealing and back-stabbing. However, they deliberately associated themselves with one another in order to make money from illegal dumping [of solid wastes]. To accomplish this objective, they collectively agreed to take part in a number of criminal activities, including money laundering, forgery, theft of services, and bribery.
>   This group's corrupting influence is no less a threat to society, and its members no less deserving of heightened RICO punishment, than any slick "organized" crime group of the traditional "command system of a Mafia family. . . ." Its members should not be allowed to escape harsher RICO penalties simply because they

lacked the management skills or ambition to raise the group to a higher and more organized realm of criminality. Nor should internal friction caused by individual greed be a bar to the Statute's application.

2. State antigang statutes. Nearly a dozen states have recently enacted statutes that make it an offense to aid or conspire to aid crimes intended to further the activities of a "criminal street gang." See Brenner, supra Note 1, at 275-276. In Lanzetta v. New Jersey, 306 U.S. 451 (1939), the Supreme Court held void for vagueness a New Jersey statute that made it a crime for any person with a criminal record, not engaged in a lawful occupation, "to be a member of any gang consisting of two or more persons." "Gang" was not defined in the statute, and the Court held that it was impossible to derive concrete meaning for it from history, sociology, or the common law. The new antigang statutes are more specific, but their definitions of "street gang" and "gang participation" can be broad. Their grading provisions can make felony sanctions applicable to acts that would otherwise be classified as simple misdemeanors or even minor violations like petty vandalism. In addition, because young urban gang members often organize themselves along explicit ethnic or racial lines, antigang prosecutions and penalty enhancements can be used to target particular minority groups. Consider Iowa Code Ann. §723A (1993):

723A.1. DEFINITIONS . . .

2. "Criminal street gang" means any ongoing organization, association, or group of three or more persons, whether formal or informal, having as one of its primary activities the commission of one or more criminal acts, which has an identifiable name or identifying sign or symbol, and whose members individually or collectively engage in or have engaged in a pattern of criminal gang activity.

3. "Pattern of criminal gang activity" means the commission, attempt to commit, conspiring to commit, or solicitation of two or more criminal acts, provided the criminal acts were committed on separate dates or by two or more persons who are members of, or belong to, the same criminal street gang.

723A.2. CRIMINAL GANG PARTICIPATION

A person who actively participates in or is a member of a criminal street gang and who willfully aids and abets any criminal act committed for the benefit of, at the direction of, or in association with any criminal street gang, commits a class "D" felony.

Questions: Do the modern antigang statutes fill an important gap in existing criminal law? Do they adequately respond to the concerns that underlie *Lanzetta?*

CHAPTER

8

EXCULPATION

A. PRINCIPLES OF JUSTIFICATION

1. *Protection of Life and Person*

UNITED STATES v. PETERSON

United States Court of Appeals, District of Columbia Circuit
483 F.2d 1222 (1973)

ROBINSON, J. . . . Self-defense, as a doctrine legally exonerating the taking of human life, is as viable now as it was in Blackstone's time, . . . But "[t]he law of self-defense is a law of necessity"; the right of self-defense arises only when the necessity begins, and equally ends with the necessity; and never must the necessity be greater than when the force employed defensively is deadly. The "necessity must bear all semblance of reality, and appear to admit of no other alternative, before taking life will be justifiable as excusable." Hinged on the exigencies of self-preservation, the doctrine of homicidal self-defense emerges from the body of the criminal law as a limited though important exception to legal outlawry of the arena of self-help in the settlement of potentially fatal personal conflicts.

So it is that necessity is the pervasive theme of the well defined conditions which the law imposes on the right to kill or maim in self-defense. There must have been a threat, actual or apparent, of the use of deadly force against the defender. The threat must have been unlawful and immediate. The defender must have believed that he was in imminent peril of death or serious bodily harm, and that his response was necessary to save himself therefrom. These beliefs must not only have been honestly entertained, but also objectively reasonable in light of the surrounding circumstances. It is clear that no less than a concurrence of these elements will suffice.

PEOPLE v. GOETZ

New York Court of Appeals
68 N.Y.2d 96, 497 N.E.2d 41 (1986)

WACHTLER, C.J. A Grand Jury has indicted defendant on attempted murder, assault, and other charges for having shot and wounded four youths on a New

York City subway train after one or two of the youths approached him and asked for $5. The lower courts, concluding that the prosecutor's charge to the Grand Jury on the defense of justification was erroneous, have dismissed the attempted murder, assault and weapons possession charges. We now reverse and reinstate all counts of the indictment.

The precise circumstances of the incident giving rise to the charges against defendant are disputed, and ultimately it will be for a trial jury to determine what occurred. We feel it necessary, however, to provide some factual background to properly frame the legal issues before us. Accordingly, we have summarized the facts as they appear from the evidence before the Grand Jury. We stress, however, that we do not purport to reach any conclusions or holding as to exactly what transpired or whether defendant is blameworthy. The credibility of witnesses and the reasonableness of defendant's conduct are to be resolved by the trial jury.

On Saturday afternoon, December 22, 1984, Troy Canty, Darryl Cabey, James Ramseur, and Barry Allen boarded an IRT express subway train in The Bronx and headed south toward lower Manhattan. The four youths rode together in the rear portion of the seventh car of the train. Two of the four, Ramseur and Cabey, had screwdrivers inside their coats, which they said were to be used to break into the coin boxes of video machines.

Defendant Bernhard Goetz boarded this subway train at 14th Street in Manhattan and sat down on a bench towards the rear section of the same car occupied by the four youths. Goetz was carrying an unlicensed .38 caliber pistol loaded with five rounds of ammunition in a waistband holster. The train left the 14th Street station and headed towards Chambers Street.

It appears from the evidence before the Grand Jury that Canty approached Goetz, possibly with Allen beside him, and stated "give me five dollars." Neither Canty nor any of the other youths displayed a weapon. Goetz responded by standing up, pulling out his handgun and firing four shots in rapid succession. The first shot hit Canty in the chest; the second struck Allen in the back; the third went through Ramseur's arm and into his left side; the fourth was fired at Cabey, who apparently was then standing in the corner of the car, but missed, deflecting instead off of a wall of the conductor's cab. After Goetz briefly surveyed the scene around him, he fired another shot at Cabey, who then was sitting on the end bench of the car. The bullet entered the rear of Cabey's side and severed his spinal cord.

All but two of the other passengers fled the car when, or immediately after, the shots were fired. The conductor, who had been in the next car, heard the shots and instructed the motorman to radio for emergency assistance. The conductor then went into the car where the shooting occurred and saw Goetz sitting on a bench, the injured youths lying on the floor or slumped against a seat, and two women who had apparently taken cover, also lying on the floor. Goetz told the conductor that the four youths had tried to rob him.

While the conductor was aiding the youths, Goetz headed towards the front of the car. The train had stopped just before the Chambers Street station and Goetz went between two of the cars, jumped onto the tracks and fled. Police and ambulance crews arrived at the scene shortly thereafter. Ramseur and Canty, initially listed in critical condition, have fully recovered. Cabey remains paralyzed, and has suffered some degree of brain damage.

On December 31, 1984, Goetz surrendered to police in Concord, New Hampshire. . . . [A]fter receiving *Miranda* warnings, he made two lengthy statements, both of which were tape recorded with his permission. In the statements . . . Goetz admitted that he had been illegally carrying a handgun in New York City for three years. He stated that he had first purchased a gun in 1981 after he had been injured in a mugging. Goetz also revealed that twice between 1981 and 1984 he had successfully warded off assailants simply by displaying the pistol.

According to Goetz's statement, the first contact he had with the four youths came when Canty, sitting or lying on the bench across from him, asked "how are you," to which he replied "fine." Shortly thereafter, Canty, followed by one of the other youths, walked over to the defendant and stood to his left, while the other two youths remained to his right, in the corner of the subway car. Canty then said "give me five dollars." Goetz stated that he knew from the smile on Canty's face that they wanted to "play with me." Although he was certain that none of the youths had a gun, he had a fear, based on prior experiences, of being "maimed."

Goetz then established "a pattern of fire," deciding specifically to fire from left to right. His stated intention at that point was to "murder [the four youths], to hurt them, to make them suffer as much as possible." When Canty again requested money, Goetz stood up, drew his weapon, and began firing, aiming for the center of the body of each of the four. Goetz recalled that the first two he shot "tried to run through the crowd [but] they had nowhere to run." Goetz then turned to his right to "go after the other two." One of these two "tried to run through the wall of the train, but . . . he had nowhere to go." The other youth (Cabey) "tried pretending that he wasn't with [the others]" by standing still, holding on to one of the subway hand straps, and not looking at Goetz. Goetz nonetheless fired his fourth shot at him. He then ran back to the first two youths to make sure they had been "taken care of." Seeing that they had both been shot, he spun back to check on the latter two. Goetz noticed that the youth who had been standing still was now sitting on a bench and seemed unhurt. As Goetz told the police, "I said '[y]ou seem to be all right, here's another,'" and he then fired the shot which severed Cabey's spinal cord. Goetz added that "if I was a little more under self-control . . . I would have put the barrel against his forehead and fired." He also admitted that "if I had had more [bullets], I would have shot them again, and again, and again." . . .

Penal Law article 35 recognizes the defense of justification, which "permits the use of force under certain circumstances." One such set of circumstances pertains to the use of force in defense of a person, encompassing both self-defense and defense of a third person. Penal Law §35.15 (1) sets forth the general principles governing all such uses of force: "[a] person may . . . use physical force upon another person when and to the extent he *reasonably believes* such to be necessary to defend himself or a third person from what he *reasonably believes* to be the use or imminent use of unlawful physical force by such other person" (emphasis added).

Section 35.15 (2) sets forth further limitations on these general principles with respect to the use of "deadly physical force": "A person may not use deadly physical force upon another person under circumstances specified in subdivision one unless (a) He *reasonably believes* that such other person is using or about to use deadly physical force . . . or (b) He *reasonably believes* that such other person is committing or attempting to commit a kidnapping, forcible rape, forcible sodomy or robbery" (emphasis added). . . .

Because the evidence before the second Grand Jury included statements by Goetz that he acted to protect himself from being maimed or to avert a robbery, the prosecutor correctly chose to charge the justification defense in section 35.15 to the Grand Jury. The prosecutor properly instructed the grand jurors to consider whether the use of deadly physical force was justified to prevent either serious physical injury or a robbery, and, in doing so, to separately analyze the defense with respect to each of the charges. He elaborated upon the prerequisites for the use of deadly physical force essentially by reading or paraphrasing the language in Penal Law §35.15. The defense does not contend that he committed any error in this portion of the charge.

When the prosecutor had completed his charge, one of the grand jurors asked for clarification of the term "reasonably believes." The prosecutor responded by instructing the grand jurors that they were to consider the circumstances of the incident and determine "whether the defendant's conduct was that of a reasonable man in the defendant's situation." It is this response by the prosecutor — and specifically his use of "a reasonable man" — which is the basis for the dismissal of the charges by the lower courts. As expressed repeatedly in the Appellate Division's plurality opinion, because section 35.15 uses the term "*he* reasonably believes," the appropriate test, according to that court, is whether a defendant's beliefs and reactions were "reasonable to *him*." Under that reading of the statute, a jury which believed a defendant's testimony that he felt that his own actions were warranted and were reasonable would have to acquit him, regardless of what anyone else in defendant's situation might have concluded. Such an interpretation defies the ordinary meaning and significance of the term "reasonably" in a statute, and misconstrues the clear intent of the Legislature, in enacting section 35.15, to retain an objective element as part of any provision authorizing the use of deadly physical force.

Penal statutes in New York have long codified the right recognized at common law to use deadly physical force, under appropriate circumstances, in self-defense. These provisions have never required that an actor's belief as to the intention of another person to inflict serious injury be correct in order for the use of deadly force to be justified, but they have uniformly required that the belief comport with an objective notion of reasonableness. . . .

In 1961 the Legislature established a Commission to undertake a complete revision of the Penal Law and the Criminal Code. The impetus for the decision to update the Penal Law came in part from the drafting of the Model Penal Code by the American Law Institute, as well as from the fact that the existing law was poorly organized and in many aspects antiquated. . . . While using the Model Penal Code provisions on justification as general guidelines . . . the drafters of the new Penal Law did not simply adopt them verbatim.

The provisions of the Model Penal Code with respect to the use of deadly force in self-defense reflect the position of its drafters that any culpability which arises from a mistaken belief in the need to use such force should be no greater than the culpability such a mistake would give rise to if it were made with respect to an element of a crime. Accordingly, under Model Penal Code §3.04 (2) (b), a defendant charged with murder (or attempted murder) need only show that he "*believe[d]* that [the use of deadly force] was necessary to protect himself against death, serious bodily injury, kidnapping or [forcible] sexual intercourse" to prevail on a self-defense claim (emphasis added). If the defendant's belief was wrong, and was recklessly, or negligently formed, however, he may be convicted of the type of homicide charge requiring only a reckless or negligent, as the case may be, criminal intent (see, Model Penal Code §3.09 . . .).

New York did not follow the Model Penal Code's equation of a mistake as to the need to use deadly force with a mistake negating an element of a crime, choosing instead to use a single statutory section which would provide either a complete defense or no defense at all to a defendant charged with any crime involving the use of deadly force. The drafters of the new Penal Law adopted in large part the structure and content of Model Penal Code §3.04, but, crucially, inserted the word "reasonably" before "believes."

The plurality below agreed with defendant's argument that the change in the statutory language from "reasonable ground," used prior to 1965, to "he reasonably believes" in Penal Law §35.15 evinced a legislative intent to conform to the subjective standard contained in Model Penal Code §3.04. This argument, however, ignores the plain significance of the insertion of "reasonably." Had the drafters of section 35.15 wanted to adopt a subjective standard, they could have simply used the language of section 3.04. "Believes" by itself requires an honest or genuine belief by a defendant as to the need to use deadly force. Interpreting the statute to require only that the defendant's belief was "reasonable to *him*," as done by the plurality below, would hardly be different from requiring only a genuine belief; in either case, the defendant's own perceptions could completely exonerate him from any criminal liability.

We cannot lightly impute to the Legislature an intent to fundamentally alter the principles of justification to allow the perpetrator of a serious crime to go free simply because that person believed his actions were reasonable and necessary to prevent some perceived harm. To completely exonerate such an individual, no matter how aberrational or bizarre his thought patterns, would allow citizens to set their own standards for the permissible use of force. . . .

We can only conclude that the Legislature retained a reasonableness requirement to avoid giving license for such actions. . . .

Goetz also argues that the introduction of an objective element will preclude a jury from considering factors such as the prior experiences of a given actor and thus, require it to make a determination of "reasonableness" without regard to the actual circumstances of a particular incident. This argument, however, falsely presupposes that an objective standard means that the background and other relevant characteristics of a particular actor must be ignored. To the contrary, we have frequently noted that a determination of reasonableness must be based on the "circumstances" facing a defendant or his "situation." Such terms encompass more than the physical movements of the potential assailant. [T]hese terms include any relevant knowledge the defendant had about that person. They also necessarily bring in the physical attributes of all persons involved, including the defendant. Furthermore, the defendant's circumstances encompass any prior experiences he had which could provide a reasonable basis for a belief that another person's intentions were to injure or rob him or that the use of deadly force was necessary under the circumstances. . . .

The prosecutor's instruction to the second Grand Jury that it had to determine whether, under the circumstances, Goetz's conduct was that of a reasonable man in his situation was thus essentially an accurate charge. . . .

Accordingly, the order of the Appellate Division should be reversed, and the dismissed counts of the indictment reinstated.

NOTES ON THE GOETZ *CASE*

The jury subsequently convicted Goetz on the charge of carrying an unlicensed concealed weapon, but acquitted him on all other counts. N.Y. Times, June 18, 1987, at B6. He was sentenced on the weapons count to one year in jail, with the possibility of release after 60 days. N.Y. Times, Jan. 14, 1989, at 1.

The *Goetz* case became a cause célèbre. Two book-length studies appeared. George Fletcher, A Crime of Self-Defense: Bernhard Goetz and the Law on Trial (1988); Lilian Rubin, Quiet Rage: Bernie Goetz in a Time of Madness (1988). See also the reflections of Prof. Stephen L. Carter on racism and victimhood in the context of the *Goetz* case, When Victims Happen to be Black, 97 Yale L.J. 420 (1988). Consider the following reactions.

Joseph Berger, Goetz Case: Commentary on Nature of Urban Life, *N.Y. Times, June 18, 1987, at B6:* The jury's decision in the Bernhard Goetz case seemed to be a verdict on the nature of contemporary urban life, churning up issues of vulnerability, rage and racial tensions that lie just beneath the surface.

The acquittal of Mr. Goetz on charges of attempted murder broke no dramatic new legal ground, in the opinion of legal experts. But in the context of the national debate on the balance between self-defense and social order, it appeared to widen the circumstances that justify the use of deadly force. . . .

There was almost no evidence presented that any of the four youths who approached Mr. Goetz had actually tried to rob him before he shot them. Thus the jury, by rejecting the charge of attempted murder, seemed to be saying that in the nervousness that courses through much of urban experience, from riding the subway at night to walking a darkened street, such evidence may not matter all that much. Perceptions, the jury suggested, can attain the power of facts.

"The jury decided that no man is reasonable when he's surrounded by four thugs," said Alan Dershowitz, professor of law at Harvard Law School. "It's hard to pay attention to lines drawn by academics in a classroom."

Mr. Dershowitz, noting that jurors often nullify self-defense standards set by the law, said he believed that what Mr. Goetz did was by definition illegal in New York State and every other state. It is illegal, he said, to shoot a person after the immediate danger has passed. "It doesn't change the law," he said of the verdict. "It may show the law is somewhat out of line with people's passions today."

The jury's decision also seemed to be a back-handed commentary on the effectiveness of the police and the courts. Burt Neuborne, a professor at New York University Law School, said, "The jurors had so little faith in the criminal justice system, both to protect us and to bring the guilty to justice, that they were willing to tolerate a degree of vigilante behavior that I think rationally cannot be justified." . . .

Crime has become such a daily feature of urban life that several of the jurors had themselves been victims. It is often on people's minds, determining where they live, how and when they travel, and how they spend their time.

The jury seemed to be saying that the fear of crime, in someone who has been a previous mugging victim like Mr. Goetz, can weigh so heavily on one's emotions that it can lead to conduct that might normally be considered wrongful. The jury in the Goetz case apparently believed there was not enough evidence to show that Mr. Goetz acted out of any motive other than fear. . . .

Underlying the issue of crime in this case was the issue of race. Scholars such as Dr. Kenneth B. Clark, professor emeritus of psychology at the City University of New York, have expressed doubt that Mr. Goetz would have shot four white youths asking him for money.

However, Marvin E. Wolfgang, a criminologist at the University of Pennsylvania, said that perceptions about who is more likely to commit a crime have some statistical basis. The rates of crime for four violent offenses — homicide, rape, robbery and aggravated assault — are at least ten times as high for blacks as they are for whites, he said.

"The expectation that four young black males are going to do you harm is indeed greater than four young whites," he said. "I can understand the black position that this is a racist attitude, but it's not unrealistic."

It is possible that jurors have absorbed such racially based perceptions about who is going to commit a crime. Elijah Anderson, a black sociologist at the University of Pennsylvania who spent three years studying street-corner life in a tough, black neighborhood in Philadelphia, said law-abiding people, black and white, have a distinctive way of relating "to people they assume to be members of the black underclass."

People, he said, "can be very intimidated by young black males or people who seem to represent this so-called underclass by their dress or comportment, very intimidated." . . .

Because it raises such issues, the jury verdict may pose some hard questions for the American public to deal with. Will some New Yorkers come to feel that they can now make hair-trigger assumptions about the character of people who somehow threaten them, and if they have a gun, use it in self-defense? Will blacks have to fear that if they look at someone the wrong way or dress too casually they may be mistaken for criminals? . . .

William Raspberry, In the Goetz *Case, Whites and Blacks Are Both Wrong, Chicago Tribune, June 22, 1987, Sec. 1, at 9:* I wish white people would stop pretending they believe race was no factor in the Bernhard Goetz case: in the shooting, in the jury's verdict or in the public reaction.

And I wish black people would stop pretending they believe Goetz saw only four young black men who, for all he knew, might have been on their way home from choir practice.

It does not make sense to blacks when we hear Goetz's lawyer, or the jury foreman, or any number of white people insist that race was absolutely no factor. We simply cannot imagine a black man being exonerated of shooting down four white youths who had not directly threatened him.

It makes no sense to whites when they hear New York ministers and civil rights leaders contend that the character of the victims of the subway shootings was not a factor, that Goetz learned only after the fact that they were thugs.

In subtle ways, you learn (in the big cities) to distinguish among casually dressed black college students, boisterous black teenagers and black thugs. Goetz knew his assailants were thugs. And, yes, they were assailants, even though they never raised a hand against him. They were at least prospective robbers. Goetz was right to be afraid.

But was he right to shoot them? The jury verdict notwithstanding, I say no. He could have used his illegal weapon to hold them at bay until he managed his escape. Goetz might not have been the "subway vigilante" he has been painted as being; he might not have been looking for an excuse to use the gun he had taken to carrying after an earlier mugging. But, as his subsequent taped "confession" made clear, the multiple shootings were far more than mere self-defense. He was making a statement.

And now a number of well-respected blacks are saying the jury verdict was also a statement: a message to whites that it is open season on black hoodlums. One group of New York blacks is even talking of riding the subways in defense of the likes of Goetz's assailants.

The first is, I suspect, overreaction. To begin with, Goetz was convicted of carrying an illegal weapon and stands to serve at least a year for that offense. But even if he is given probation, it doesn't follow that white people will now arm themselves against black thugs and start blasting away at the first sign of trouble. There may be widespread belief among whites (and among many blacks as well) and even a degree of pleasure in the fact that Goetz beat the attempted-murder rap. But don't expect wholesale carnage on the streets and subways of New York.

The second strikes me as merely silly. People like Goetz, as sick and trigger-happy as he might have been, are far less a threat to the public safety than people like the youths who saw him as an easy mark.

Too many whites are behaving as though race was no factor at all in the tragic affair. Too many blacks are behaving as though race was the only factor.

They're both wrong.

Jody D. Armour, Race Ipsa Loquitur: Of Reasonable Racists, Intelligent Beyesians, and Involuntary Negrophobes, 46 Stan. L. Rev. 781, 787-788, 790, 792, 794, 795 (1994): The Reasonable Racist asserts that, even if his belief that blacks are "prone to violence" stems from pure prejudice, he should be excused for considering the victim's race before using force because most similarly situated Americans would have done so as well. For inasmuch as the criminal justice system operates on the assumption that "blame is reserved for the (statistically) deviant,"[18] an individual racist in a racist society cannot be condemned for an expression of human frailty as ubiquitous as racism. . . .

The flaw in the Reasonable Racist's self-defense claim lies in his primary assumption that the sole objective of criminal law is to punish those who deviate from statistically defined norms. For even if the "typical" American believes that blacks' "propensity" toward violence justifies a quicker and more forceful response when a suspected assailant is black, this fact is legally significant only if the law defines *reasonable* beliefs as *typical* beliefs. The reasonableness inquiry, however, extends beyond typicality to consider the social interests implicated in a given situation. Hence not all "typical" beliefs are per se reasonable. . . . If we

18. Mark Kelman, Reasonable Evidence of Reasonableness, 17 Critical Inquiry 798, 801 (1991).

accept that racial discrimination violates contemporary social morality, then an actor's failure to overcome his racism for the sake of another's health, safety, and personal dignity is blameworthy and thus unreasonable, independent of whether or not it is "typical." . . .

A second argument which a defendant may advance to justify acting on race-based assumptions is that, given statistics demonstrating blacks' disproportionate involvement in crime, it is reasonable to perceive a greater threat from a black person than a white person. . . .

Although biases in the criminal justice system exaggerate the differences in rates of violent crime by race, it may, tragically, still be true that blacks commit a disproportionate number of crimes. Given that the blight of institutional racism continues to disproportionately limit the life chances of African-Americans, and that desperate circumstances increase the likelihood that individuals caught in this web may turn to desperate undertakings, such a disparity, if it exists, should sadden but not surprise us. . . .

To the extent that socioeconomic status explains the overinvolvement of blacks in robbery and assault (assuming that there is, in fact, such overinvolvement), race serves merely as a proxy for socioeconomic status. But if race is a proxy for socioeconomic factors, then race loses its predictive value when one controls for those factors. . . .

The use of race-based generalizations in the self-defense context has an especially grievous effect: . . . Ultimately, race-based evidence of reasonableness impairs the capacity of jurors to rationally and fairly strike a balance between the costs of waiting (increased risk for the person who perceives imminent attack) and the costs of not waiting (injury or death to the immediate victim, exclusion of blacks from core community activities, and, ultimately, reduction of individuals to predictable objects). In fact, such evidence may be so effective at tapping the racism — conscious or unconscious — which has been proven to infect jury deliberations, that it should arguably be excluded under the "more prejudicial than probative" standard of most states' evidence codes, of which the provisions in section 403 of the Federal Rules of Evidence are illustrative.[55]

NOTES ON REASONABLE BELIEF

1. A subjective test? Is the conventional position requiring that the defendant's defensive action must be reasonable preferable to a wholly subjective rule? Professor Glanville Williams advanced the following argument in behalf of a subjective view (quoted in Model Penal Code and Commentaries, Comment to §3.09 at 152, n. 10 (1985)):

> The criminal law of negligence works best when it gives effect to the large number of rules of prudence which are commonly observed though not directly incorporated into the law. Such rules include the rule against pulling out on a blind corner, the rule against carrying a gun in such a way that it is pointing at another

---

55. See Fed. R. Evid. 403. Rule 403 reads, in relevant part: "Although relevant, evidence may be excluded if its probative value is substantially outweighed by the danger of unfair prejudice, confusion of the issues, or misleading the jury."

person, the rule against deliberately pointing a gun at another person, even in play, and so on. These rules are not part either of enacted or of common law, but as customary standards of behavior they become binding via the law of negligence. Are there any similar rules of behavior applicable when a person acts in self-defense or in making an arrest? It must be recollected that the injury he inflicts on the other is in itself intentional, so that the usual rules of prudence in respect to the handling of weapons are not in question. The only question is whether the defendant was negligent in arriving at the conclusion that the use of the force in question was called for. It is hard to imagine what rules of prudence could normally serve in this situation. Either the defendant is capable of drawing the inferences that a reasonable man would draw or he is not. If he is not, and he is a peace officer, his tendency to make miscalculations would certainly justify his dismissal from the police force. But there is no obvious case for the intervention of the criminal courts.

The only common situation in which a person makes an unreasonable mistake in what he believes to be self-defense is when he is drunk or otherwise in an abnormal mental state. For example, a drunken person may misconstrue a gesture as an attempt to kill, and, acting under this misconception, he may take a knife and kill or nearly kill the person whom he mistakenly supposes to be an assailant. It is submitted that the solution of this problem lies in provisions directed specifically to it. There should be a specific offense of being drunk and dangerous. . . . Where the defendant is insane or feeble-minded, the problem of treatment belongs to the wider problem of insanity and feeblemindedness in the criminal law.

Consider the following critique of the reasonableness requirement. R. Restak, The Fiction of the "Reasonable Man," The Washington Post, Sunday, May 17, 1987, at C3:

As a neurologist and neuropsychiatrist with over a decade of experience in conducting pretrial interviews of individuals who have acted violently, the "reasonable person" argument seems an illogical and outdated approach to fully understanding events such as occurred on the New York subway in December of 1984 when Bernhard Goetz shot and injured four teenagers.

On the basis of what I know about the human brain I'm convinced that there are no reasonable people under conditions in which death or severe bodily harm are believed imminent.

Deep within the brain of every reasonable person resides the limbic system: an ancient interconnected network of structures that anatomically and chemically haven't changed much over hundreds of thousands of years. We share these structures with jungle animals as well as animals that many reasonable people keep as pets. Moreover, the limbic system is capable under conditions of extreme duress of overwhelming the cerebral cortex wherein are formulated many of the reasonable person's most reasonable attributes, like interpretation, judgment and restraint.

. . . Emotions are not incidental and subsidiary to rational processes. Instead, the reasonable person, even at his or her most reasonable moments, is influenced by emotional processes. . . .

In view of what we now know of such cases, the logic of the "reasonable man" standard — in the Bernhard Goetz case or similar cases in the future — may be inherently flawed.

"We don't contend that the defendant had no cause for apprehension" said Assistant District Attorney Gregory Waples on the first day of the trial. He went on to argue that Goetz, once aroused, should have been capable of stopping himself at some point. The firing of a second shot into Darrell Cabey — after, as the prose cution has contended, the immediate threat was over — is crucial to the state's argument. "When he fired that last shot," Waples said, "beyond the slightest doubt, Cabey was seated helpless doing nothing to threaten or menace Bernhard Goetz." . . .

The prosecutor's logic is this: Once Goetz coolly discerned that he was out of danger, he should have calmed down, put away his gun and awaited the arrival of the police.

[S]uch expectations are neurologically unrealistic. Once aroused, the limbic system can become a directive force for hours, sometimes days, and can rarely be shut off like flipping a switch. The heart keeps pounding, the breathing — harsh and labored — burns in the throat; the thoughts keep churning as fear is replaced by anger and finally, murderous rage. . . .

Consider Goetz' response to the question "Did you just shoot each one of these people just once?"

Goetz: "Well, you see that's why I, that's, that's one of the things that puzzles me. . . . Because you know what you're doing, you cannot do something and not know it. I mean, how could I do it and not know it? But if you can accept this, I was out of control, and that's, you know, but that's, that's, it's true, maybe you should always be in control, but if you, if you put people in a situation where they're threatened with mayhem, several times, and then if, then if something happens, and if a person acts, turns into a vicious animal. . . . That's not the end of the shooting. That's what. . . . It's not the end. I ran back to the first two, to make sure."

Is that what a reasonable person would do under such circumstances?

Although lawyers and judges love to explore such questions, . . . I'm convinced that they're . . . products of an outmoded mentality that places an overemphasis on empty intellectualization to the exclusion of those deep and powerful emotional currents of fear, self-preservation or territoriality that can surface in any one of us and overpower the cogitations of reason.

Granted that this isn't a pretty or elegant arrangement. But as long as our brain is put together the way it is, no one should be too confident that he or she would remain completely reasonable under conditions where their life is perceived to be in imminent danger. Moreover, this critical perception of threat isn't based on rationality. It's fueled by those limbic derived emotions that have promoted the survival of our species.

Isn't it preferable therefore to face up courageously to these sometimes frightening and unpleasant realities instead of pretending that questions such as those being asked about Bernhard Goetz can be answered by courtroom speculations about how a reasonable person would have responded in his place?

To expect reasonable behavior in the face of perceived threat, terror and rage is itself a most unreasonable expectation.

Questions: (1) What would it mean for the law "to face up courageously to these . . . realities"? Is it Restak's point that the law should allow a complete defense whenever the defendant subjectively fears for his life, regardless of the circumstances?

(2) Consider Justice Holmes' oft-quoted epigram: "Detached reflection cannot be demanded in the presence of an uplifted knife." Brown v. United States, 256 U.S. 335, 343 (1921). Does the evidence of the operation of the limbic system say something different from that? Reconsider the arguments for and against criminal liability for negligence, page 449 supra.

2. Qualifications to the objective rule. As in other instances in which the law employs an objective standard, there is always the question of just how objective the standard is to be — that is, how far should features of defendant's particular situation be taken into account in determining whether the choice of defensive force was reasonable? Compare the discussion of the reasonable-provocation standard, page 426 supra, and the discussion of the definition of negligence and recklessness, page 449 supra. Recall the Model Penal Code standards (§2.02), calling for a judgment (in the case of recklessness) whether the risk is of a nature and degree that "its disregard involves a gross deviation from the standard of conduct that a law-abiding person would observe *in the actor's situation*" and (in the case of negligence) whether that risk "involves a gross deviation from the standard of care that a reasonable person would observe *in the actor's situation*." (Italics added.) The Model Penal Code's position represents a partial subjectivizing of the objective standard of the reasonable person. See page 451 supra, where this issue is discussed in connection with the definition of criminal negligence. Was the jury's verdict in the *Goetz* case defensible under the Model Penal Code approach?

3. *A grading problem.* Where reasonableness is required for total exculpation, how should the law deal with a person who holds an honest but unreasonable belief in the need to use lethal force? Assume such a person kills because she genuinely believes it is the only way to save her life, but she comes to her conclusion on grossly unreasonable grounds. She has killed intentionally and, under the prevailing objective test, she has no defense of self-defense. Thus in some states, she would be guilty of murder, just like the person who kills for revenge or gain. In other states this logical consequence of the objective test has been avoided through various doctrinal approaches:

(*a*) *Imperfect self-defense.* When a person has killed another in honest but unreasonable belief in the need to kill, or when she uses more force than is reasonably necessary, many courts treat this as "imperfect self-defense" and classify the crime as voluntary manslaughter on the view that "malice" is not present. In Commonwealth v. Colandro, 231 Pa. 343, 80 A. 571, 574 (1911), the court, reversing a conviction for murder, held:

> [I]f the act is committed under the influence of an uncontrollable fear of death or great bodily harm, caused by the circumstances, but without the presence of all the ingredients necessary to excuse the act on the ground of self-defense, the killing is manslaughter.

This approach is common in American jurisdictions. See, e.g., Faulkner v. State, 54 Md. App. 113, 458 A.2d 81 (1983); People v. Flannel, 25 Cal. 3d 668, 603 P.2d 1 (1979). Some state statutes require this result. See Ill. Comp. Stat. ch. 720, §5/9-2(b); Pa. Cons. Stat. tit. 18, §2503(b), supra page 390.

A different doctrinal basis for imperfect self-defense leads to involuntary rather than voluntary manslaughter — the killing is treated like a criminally negligent or reckless killing. A problem for this theory is that involuntary manslaughter assumes an unintentional killing, while an unreasonable self-defense killing by definition involves an intentional act of killing. The Supreme Court of Kentucky wrestled with this problem through two overrulings, finally coming to rest on the following rationale, Shannon v. Commonwealth, 767 S.W.2d 548, 550 (1988):

> An act cannot be classified as both intentional and wanton or reckless at the same time. But an intentional act may be accompanied by a wanton or reckless belief,

and, indeed, this specifically characterizes the circumstances that exist when a person kills in self-defense, but is wanton or reckless in the belief that his action was justified. . . . By classifying a killing in self-defense with Manslaughter II or Reckless Homicide, we do not label the act both intentional and wanton or reckless at the same time. We simply say that an intentional killing precipitated by a wanton or reckless belief in the need to kill is less culpable than murder, and shall be classified for punishment as either Manslaughter II or Reckless Homicide, depending on whether the belief was wantonly or recklessly formed.

(*b*) *The Model Penal Code approach.* The Model Penal Code rests on a rationale similar to that expressed in the *Shannon* case but proposes an innovative formulation. Section 2.02(10) provides:

When the grade or degree of an offense depends on whether the offense is committed purposely, knowingly, recklessly or negligently, its grade or degree shall be the lowest for which the determinative kind of culpability is established with respect to any material element of the offense.

Model Penal Code and Commentaries, Comment to §2.02 at 251-252 (1985) explains:

[T]he grade or degree of a conviction ought to be the lowest for which the determinative kind of culpability is established with respect to *any* material element of the offense. The theory is, of course, that when the kinds of culpability involved vary with respect to different material elements, it is the lowest common denominator that indicates the quality of the defendant's conduct.

The best illustration is afforded by the case of homicide, where a killing done purposefully or knowingly is normally treated as an offense of a higher degree than negligent homicide. Even though the actor meant to kill, he may have acted only negligently with respect to another material element of the offense, e.g., he may have deemed the homicide to be necessary in self-defense or necessary to prevent a felony or to effect arrest, without sufficient ground for such belief. For purposes of sentence, the position of the Code is that such a homicide ought to be viewed as reckless or as negligent, as the case may be, since recklessness or negligence is all that is established with respect to justifying elements as integral to the offense as the killing itself. A person who believes that justifying facts exist, but has been reckless or negligent in so concluding, presents, from the point of view of sentence, the same type of problem as a person who acts recklessly or negligently with respect to the creation of a risk of death.

The drafting device through which the Model Penal Code achieves this result is to specify in the various justification provisions the circumstances that the actor must believe to exist in order for his or her action to be justified[1] and to employ the following general provision (§3.09(2)) to deal with mistaken belief in those circumstances:

When the actor believes that the use of force upon or toward the person of another is necessary for any of the purposes for which such belief would establish a justification under §§3.03 to 3.08 but the actor is reckless or negligent in having such

---

1. Section 3.04(2) explicitly provides that "a person employing protective force may estimate the necessity thereof under the circumstances as he believes them to be when the force is used."

belief on in acquiring or failing to acquire any knowledge or belief which is material to the justifiability of his use of force, the justification afforded by those Sections is unavailable in a prosecution for an offense for which recklessness or negligence, as the case may be, suffices to establish culpability.

The approach has not been influential in state statutory reform. See Note, Justification: The Impact of the Model Penal Code on State Law Reform, 75 Colum. L. Rev. 914, 920 (1975).

4. Problem. As we have seen, the Model Penal Code and the New York self-defense formulations differ in the way they deal with the reasonableness requirement. Consider how the following hypothetical should be analyzed under each formulation: The defendant shoots to kill Z in the honest but unreasonable belief that it is necessary to do so to save the defendant's life. He misses, and Z escapes unharmed. Is the defendant guilty of attempted murder? Of attempt to commit manslaughter?

STATE v. KELLY

Supreme Court of New Jersey
91 N.J. 178, 478 A.2d 364 (1984)

WILENTZ, C.J. . . . On May 24, 1980, defendant, Gladys Kelly, stabbed her husband, Ernest, with a pair of scissors. He died shortly thereafter at a nearby hospital. . . .

Ms. Kelly was indicted for murder. At trial, she did not deny stabbing her husband, but asserted that her action was in self-defense. To establish the requisite state of mind for her self-defense claim, Ms. Kelly called Dr. Lois Veronen as an expert witness to testify about the battered-woman's syndrome. After hearing a lengthy voir dire examination of Dr. Veronen, the trial court ruled that expert testimony concerning the syndrome was inadmissible on the self-defense issue. . . .

Ms. Kelly was convicted of reckless manslaughter. [We] reverse.

The Kellys had a stormy marriage. Some of the details of their relationship, especially the stabbing, are disputed. The following is Ms. Kelly's version of what happened — a version that the jury could have accepted and, if they had, a version that would make the proffered expert testimony not only relevant, but critical.

The day after the marriage, Mr. Kelly got drunk and knocked Ms. Kelly down. Although a period of calm followed the initial attack, the next seven years were accompanied by periodic and frequent beatings, sometimes as often as once a week. During the attacks, which generally occurred when Mr. Kelly was drunk, he threatened to kill Ms. Kelly and to cut off parts of her body if she tried to leave him. Mr. Kelly often moved out of the house after an attack, later returning with a promise that he would change his ways. Until the day of the homicide, only one of the attacks had taken place in public.

The day before the stabbing, Gladys and Ernest went shopping. They did not have enough money to buy food for the entire week, so Ernest said he would give his wife more money the next day.

The following morning he left for work. Ms. Kelly next saw her husband late that afternoon at a friend's house. She had gone there with her daughter,

Annette, to ask Ernest for money to buy food. He told her to wait until they got home, and shortly thereafter the Kellys left. After walking past several houses, Mr. Kelly, who was drunk, angrily asked "What the hell did you come around here for?" He then grabbed the collar of her dress, and the two fell to the ground. He choked her by pushing his fingers against her throat, punched or hit her face, and bit her leg.

A crowd gathered on the street. Two men from the crowd separated them, just as Gladys felt that she was "passing out" from being choked. Fearing that Annette had been pushed around in the crowd, Gladys then left to look for her. . . .

After finding her daughter, Ms. Kelly then observed Mr. Kelly running toward her with his hands raised. Within seconds he was right next to her. Unsure of whether he had armed himself while she was looking for their daughter, and thinking that he had come back to kill her, she grabbed a pair of scissors from her pocketbook. She tried to scare him away, but instead stabbed him.[1]

The central question in this case is whether the trial court erred in its exclusion of expert testimony on the battered-woman's syndrome. That testimony was intended to explain defendant's state of mind and bolster her claim of self-defense. We shall first examine the nature of the battered-woman's syndrome and then consider the expert testimony proffered in this case and its relevance. . . .

As the problem of battered women has begun to receive more attention, sociologists and psychologists have begun to focus on the effects a sustained pattern of physical and psychological abuse can have on a woman. The effects of such abuse are what some scientific observers have termed "the battered-woman's syndrome," a series of common characteristics that appear in women who are abused physically and psychologically over an extended period of time by the dominant male figure in their lives. Dr. Lenore Walker, a prominent writer on the battered-woman's syndrome, defines the battered woman as one

> who is repeatedly subjected to any forceful physical or psychological behavior by a man in order to coerce her to do something he wants her to do without concern for her rights. Battered women include wives or women in any form of intimate relationships with men. Furthermore, in order to be classified as a battered woman, the couple must go through the battering cycle at least twice. Any woman may find herself in an abusive relationship with a man once. If it occurs a second time, and she remains in the situation, she is defined as a battered woman. [L. Walker, The Battered Woman (1979) at xv.]

According to Dr. Walker, relationships characterized by physical abuse tend to develop battering cycles. Violent behavior directed at the woman occurs in three distinct and repetitive stages that vary both in duration and intensity depending on the individuals involved.

Phase one of the battering cycle is referred to as the "tension-building stage," during which the battering male engages in minor battering incidents and ver-

---

1. This version of the homicide — with a drunk Mr. Kelly as the aggressor both in pushing Ms. Kelly to the ground and again in rushing at her with his hands in a threatening position after the two had been separated — is sharply disputed by the State. The prosecution presented testimony intended to show that the initial scuffle was started by Gladys; that upon disentanglement, while she was restrained by bystanders, she stated that she intended to kill Ernest; that she then chased after him, and upon catching up with him stabbed him with a pair of scissors taken from her pocketbook.

bal abuse while the woman, beset by fear and tension, attempts to be as placating and passive as possible in order to stave off more serious violence.

Phase two of the battering cycle is the "acute battering incident." At some point during phase one, the tension between the battered woman and the batterer becomes intolerable and more serious violence inevitable. The triggering event that initiates phase two is most often an internal or external event in the life of the battering male, but provocation for more severe violence is sometimes provided by the woman who can no longer tolerate or control her phase-one anger and anxiety.

Phase three of the battering cycle is characterized by extreme contrition and loving behavior on the part of the battering male. During this period the man will often mix his pleas for forgiveness and protestations of devotion with promises to seek professional help, to stop drinking, and to refrain from further violence. For some couples, this period of relative calm may last as long as several months, but in a battering relationship the affection and contrition of the man will eventually fade and phase one of the cycle will start anew.

The cyclical nature of battering behavior helps explain why more women simply do not leave their abusers. The loving behavior demonstrated by the batterer during phase three reinforces whatever hopes these women might have for their mate's reform and keeps them bound to the relationship. R. Langley & R. Levy, Wife Beating: The Silent Crisis 112-14 (1977).

Some women may even perceive the battering cycle as normal, especially if they grew up in a violent household. . . . Other women, however, become so demoralized and degraded by the fact that they cannot predict or control the violence that they sink into a state of psychological paralysis and become unable to take any action at all to improve or alter the situation. There is a tendency in battered women to believe in the omnipotence or strength of their battering husbands and thus to feel that any attempt to resist them is hopeless.

In addition to these psychological impacts, external social and economic factors often make it difficult for some women to extricate themselves from battering relationships. A woman without independent financial resources who wishes to leave her husband often finds it difficult to do so because of a lack of material and social resources. . . . Thus, in a violent confrontation where the first reaction might be to flee, women realize soon that there may be no place to go. Moreover, the stigma that attaches to a woman who leaves the family unit without her children undoubtedly acts as a further deterrent to moving out.

In addition, battered women, when they want to leave the relationship, are typically unwilling to reach out and confide in their friends, family, or the police, either out of shame and humiliation, fear of reprisal by their husband, or the feeling they will not be believed.

Dr. Walker and other commentators have identified several common personality traits of the battered woman: low self-esteem, traditional beliefs about the home, the family, and the female sex role, tremendous feelings of guilt that their marriages are failing, and the tendency to accept responsibility for the batterer's actions.

Finally, battered women are often hesitant to leave a battering relationship because, in addition to their hope of reform on the part of their spouse, they harbor a deep concern about the possible response leaving might provoke in their mates. They literally become trapped by their own fear. Case histories are replete with instances in which a battered wife left her husband only to have him pursue her and subject her to an even more brutal attack.

The combination of all these symptoms — resulting from sustained psychological and physical trauma compounded by aggravating social and economic factors — constitutes the battered-woman's syndrome. Only by understanding these unique pressures that force battered women to remain with their mates, despite their long-standing and reasonable fear of severe bodily harm and the isolation that being a battered woman creates, can a battered woman's state of mind be accurately and fairly understood.

The voir dire testimony of Dr. Veronen, sought to be introduced by defendant Gladys Kelly, conformed essentially to this outline of the battered-woman's syndrome. . . .

In addition, Dr. Veronen was prepared to testify as to how, as a battered woman, Gladys Kelly perceived her situation at the time of the stabbing, and why, in her opinion, defendant did not leave her husband despite the constant beatings she endured.

Whether expert testimony on the battered-woman's syndrome should be admitted in this case depends on whether it is relevant to defendant's claim of self-defense, and, in any event, on whether the proffer meets the standards for admission of expert testimony in this state. We examine first the law of self-defense and consider whether the expert testimony is relevant.

. . . The use of force against another in self-defense is justifiable "when the actor reasonably believes that such force is immediately necessary for the purpose of protecting himself against the use of unlawful force by such other person on the present occasion." N.J.S.A. 2C:3-4(a). Further limitations exist when deadly force is used in self-defense. The use of such deadly force is not justifiable

> unless the actor reasonably believes that such force is necessary to protect himself against death or serious bodily harm. . . . [N.J.S.A. 2C:3-4(b)(2).]

Gladys Kelly claims that she stabbed her husband in self-defense, believing he was about to kill her. The gist of the State's case was that Gladys Kelly was the aggressor, that she consciously intended to kill her husband, and that she certainly was not acting in self-defense.

The credibility of Gladys Kelly is a critical issue in this case. If the jury does not believe Gladys Kelly's account, it cannot find she acted in self-defense. The expert testimony offered was directly relevant to one of the critical elements of that account, namely, what Gladys Kelly believed at the time of the stabbing, and was thus material to establish the honesty of her stated belief that she was in imminent danger of death. . . .

As can be seen from our discussion of the expert testimony, Dr. Veronen would have bolstered Gladys Kelly's credibility. Specifically, by showing that her experience, although concededly difficult to comprehend, was common to that of other women who had been in similarly abusive relationships, Dr. Veronen would have helped the jury understand that Gladys Kelly could have honestly feared that she would suffer serious bodily harm from her husband's attacks, yet still remain with him. This, in turn, would support Ms. Kelly's testimony about her state of mind (that is, that she honestly feared serious bodily harm) at the time of the stabbing.

On the facts of this case, we find that the expert testimony was relevant to Gladys Kelly's state of mind, namely, it was admissible to show she *honestly* believed she was in imminent danger of death. . . .

We also find the expert testimony relevant to the reasonableness of defendant's belief that she was in imminent danger of death or serious injury. We do not mean that the expert's testimony could be used to show that it was understandable that a battered woman might believe that her life was in danger when indeed it was not and when a reasonable person would not have so believed. . . . Expert testimony in that direction would be relevant solely to the honesty of defendant's belief, not its objective reasonableness. Rather, our conclusion is that the expert's testimony, if accepted by the jury, would have aided it in determining whether, under the circumstances, a reasonable person would have believed there was imminent danger to her life.

At the heart of the claim of self-defense was defendant's story that she had been repeatedly subjected to "beatings" over the course of her marriage. . . . When that regular pattern of serious physical abuse is combined with defendant's claim that the decedent sometimes threatened to kill her, defendant's statement that on this occasion she thought she might be killed when she saw Mr. Kelly running toward her could be found to reflect a reasonable fear; that is, it could so be found if the jury believed Gladys Kelly's story of the prior beatings, if it believed her story of the prior threats, and, of course, if it believed her story of the events of that particular day.

The crucial issue of fact on which this expert's testimony would bear is why, given such allegedly severe and constant beatings, combined with threats to kill, defendant had not long ago left decedent. Whether raised by the prosecutor as a factual issue or not, our own common knowledge tells us that most of us, including the ordinary juror, would ask himself or herself just such a question. [O]ne of the common myths, apparently believed by most people, is that battered wives are free to leave. To some, this misconception is followed by the observation that the battered wife is masochistic, proven by her refusal to leave despite the severe beatings; to others, however, the fact that the battered wife stays on unquestionably suggests that the "beatings" could not have been too bad for if they had been, she certainly would have left. The expert could clear up these myths, by explaining that one of the common characteristics of a battered wife is her *inability* to leave despite such constant beatings; her "learned helplessness"; her lack of anywhere to go; her feeling that if she tried to leave, she would be subjected to even more merciless treatment; her belief in the omnipotence of her battering husband; and sometimes her hope that her husband will change his ways. . . .

The difficulty with the expert's testimony is that it *sounds* as if an expert is giving knowledge to a jury about something the jury knows as well as anyone else, namely, the reasonableness of a person's fear of imminent serious danger. That is not at all, however, what this testimony is *directly* aimed at. It is aimed at an area where the purported common knowledge of the jury may be very much mistaken, an area where jurors' logic, drawn from their own experience, may lead to a wholly incorrect conclusion. . . . After hearing the expert, instead of saying Gladys Kelly could not have been beaten up so badly for if she had, she certainly would have left, the jury could conclude that her failure to leave was very much part and parcel of her life as a battered wife. The jury could conclude that instead of casting doubt on the accuracy of her testimony about the severity and frequency of prior beatings, her failure to leave actually reinforced her credibility.

Since a retrial is necessary, we think it advisable to indicate the limit of the expert's testimony on this issue of reasonableness. It would not be proper for the expert to express the opinion that defendant's belief on that day was reasonable, not because this is the ultimate issue, but because the area of *expert* knowledge relates, in this regard, to the reasons for defendant's failure to leave her husband. Either the jury accepts or rejects that explanation and, based on that, credits defendant's stories about the beatings she suffered. No expert is needed, however, once the jury has made up its mind on those issues, to tell the jury the logical conclusion, namely, that a person who has in fact been severely and continuously beaten might very well reasonably fear that the imminent beating she was about to suffer could be either life-threatening or pose a risk of serious injury. What the expert could state was that defendant had the battered-woman's syndrome, and could explain that syndrome in detail, relating its characteristics to defendant, but only to enable the jury better to determine the honesty and reasonableness of defendant's belief. Depending on its content, the expert's testimony might also enable the jury to find that the battered wife, because of the prior beatings, numerous beatings, as often as once a week, for seven years, from the day they were married to the day he died, is particularly able to predict accurately the likely extent of violence in any attack on her. That conclusion could significantly affect the jury's evaluation of the reasonableness of defendant's fear for her life.

Having determined that testimony about the battered-woman's syndrome is relevant, we now consider whether Dr. Veronen's testimony satisfies the limitations placed on expert testimony by Evidence Rule 56(2) and by applicable case law. . . . In effect, this Rule imposes three basic requirements for the admission of expert testimony: (1) the intended testimony must concern a subject matter that is beyond the ken of the average juror; (2) the field testified to must be at a state of the art such that an expert's testimony could be sufficiently reliable; and (3) the witness must have sufficient expertise to offer the intended testimony.

[The court remanded for a hearing on these issues.[a]]

NOTES ON THE BATTERED WOMAN'S SYNDROME

The defense of the battered woman's syndrome has attracted a great deal of attention. Many jurisdictions have by now pronounced its relevance and upheld the admissibility of expert evidence designed to establish it, and a large litera-

a. On remand, the prosecution did not challenge the admissibility of the expert's evidence on the battered woman's syndrome. Instead it offered its own experts to support the conclusion that the defendant did not meet the criteria of a battered woman. Apparently the strategy was successful because at the second trial the jury convicted her of murder. See Elizabeth Schneider, Describing and Changing: Women's Self-Defense Work and the Problem of Expert Testimony on Battering, 9 Women's Rights L. Rptr. 195, 211-212 (1986). — Eds.

ture has developed on the subject. The material that follows presents some of the principal elements of the controversy.[2]

Note that we are only considering here the issue of justified self-defense. Whether evidence of the battered woman's syndrome establishes an excuse — for example, heat-of-passion manslaughter or diminished capacity — is another issue. See supra page 405 on whether a battered woman would be entitled to a manslaughter instruction.

1. The issue of reasonableness. How is evidence of the battered woman's syndrome relevant to whether the defendant acted reasonably? Is it relevant because the standard is that of the reasonable battered woman? The *Kelly* case appears to have said no. Consider the following views on this issue.

(*a*) Elizabeth Schneider, Describing and Changing: Women's Self-Defense Work and the Problem of Expert Testimony on Battering, 9 Women's Right L. Rptr. 195, 211-212 (1986): Certainly the court [in the *Kelly* case] is correct that the question of why the battered woman did not leave (so as to avoid the possibility of death) is a threshold issue in the jury's mind. Her failure to leave raises the question of whether the woman was really battered (for if she was, why did she stay?), as well as the question of whether, by staying, she had in a sense "assumed the risk" of death. However, these questions only present the first issue for the jury. The second issue (and the more pressing one in many cases) is the reasonableness of the battered woman's belief that she was in particular jeopardy at the time that she responded in self-defense. A battered woman who has been the victim of abuse for many years and has survived it before must credibly explain why it was necessary to act on that occasion. Expert testimony, admitted for the purpose of explaining why the battered woman did not leave, does not help the jury answer the question whether she was reasonable in acting violently in order to save her life. It thus does not address the basic defense problem that the battered woman faces. Indeed, if the testimony is limited, or perceived as limited to the issue of why the woman does not leave, it highlights a contradiction implicit in the message of battered woman syndrome — if the battered woman was so helpless and passive, why did she kill the batterer?

In fairness to the Supreme Court, the *Kelly* opinion does mention that "the expert's testimony might also enable the jury to find that the battered wife, because of the prior beatings . . . is particularly able to predict accurately the likely extent of violence in any attack on her" and "that conclusion could significantly affect the jury's evaluation of the reasonableness of defendant's fear for her life." This is a crucial point, indeed in most cases this is the real importance of the testimony. Yet the court seems to minimize the importance of this broader and more central understanding of relevance by its statement that the expert

---

2. See Regina A. Schuller & Neil Vidmar, BWS Evidence in the Courtroom: A Review of the Literature, 16 Law & Hum. Behav. 273 (1992). For some recent writing see Cynthia Gillespie, Justifiable Homicide: Battered Women, Self-Defense and the Law (1989); Hugh Breyer, The Battered Woman Syndrome and the Admissibility of Expert Testimony, 28 Crim. L. Bull. 99 (1992); Lenore Walker, Battered Women Syndrome and Self-Defense, 6 N.D.J.L. Ethics & Pub. Poly. 321 (1992); B. S. Byrd, Till Death Do Us Part: A Comparative Law Approach to Justifying Lethal Self-Defense by Battered Women, 1991 Duke J. Comp. & Intl. L. 169; Holly Maguigan, Battered Women and Self-Defense: Myths and Misconceptions in Court Reform Proposals, 140 U. Pa. L. Rev. 379 (1991); Walter W. Steele, Jr. & Christine W. Sigman, Reexamining the Doctrine of Self-Defense to Accommodate Battered Women, 18 Am. J. Crim. L. 169 (1991).

testimony is not relevant to the jury's determination of the reasonableness of a person's fear of imminent severe danger because this is "something the jury knows as well as anyone else."

. . . In this sense, the opinion only focuses on part of the problem. The reasonableness of the woman's fear and the reasonableness of her act are *not* issues which the jury knows as well as anyone else. The jury needs expert testimony on reasonableness precisely because the jury may not understand that the battered woman's prediction of the likely extent and imminence of violence is particularly acute and accurate.

(*b*) People v. Aris, 215 Cal. App. 3d 1178, 1195-1196, 264 Cal. Rptr. 167 (1989): To answer the question of the admissibility of BWS on the issue of self-defense, we must determine the relevance of BWS testimony to self-defense. The precise question we must first answer is whether an expert opinion that defendant acted reasonably in self-defense is relevant to the reasonableness requirement for perfect self-defense. The answer is determined by the nature of perfect self-defense as a criminal defense.

A homicide committed in self-defense is classified by the California Penal Code as a "justifiable homicide" as opposed to an "excusable homicide." Excuses for homicide include accident and sufficient provocation as well as insanity and provocation and a genuine, but unreasonable, belief in the need for self-defense. Thus, reasonable self-defense is a defense of justification rather than of excuse under current California law.

Justification declares the allegedly criminal act legal; excuse admits the act's criminality but declares the allegedly criminal actor not to be worthy of blame. Therefore justification requires an objective evaluation of the allegedly criminal act; excuse requires only a subjective evaluation of the allegedly criminal state of mind.

Thus, the questions of the reasonableness of a defendant's belief that self-defense is necessary and of the reasonableness of the actions taken in self-defense do not call for an evaluation of the defendant's subjective state of mind, but for an objective evaluation of the defendant's assertedly defensive acts. California law expresses the criterion for this evaluation in the objective terms of whether a reasonable person, as opposed to the defendant, would have believed and acted as the defendant did. We hold that expert testimony about a defendant's state of mind is not relevant to the reasonableness of the defendant's self-defense. . . . [S]elf-defense is not concerned with the reasonableness of the defendant's mental processes, but with what the hypothetical reasonable person would have done. . . .

Although BWS testimony is admissible . . . trial courts should recognize the possibility that the jury in a particular case may misuse such evidence to establish the reasonableness requirement for perfect self-defense, for which purpose it is irrelevant as previously discussed. Therefore, upon request whenever the jury is instructed on perfect self-defense, trial courts should instruct that such testimony is relevant only to prove the honest belief requirement for both perfect and imperfect self-defense, not to prove the reasonableness requirement for perfect self-defense.

(*c*) Susan Estrich, Defending Women (Book Review, Cynthia Gillespie, Justifiable Homicide: Battered Women, Self-Defense and the Law (1989)), 88 Mich.

L. Rev. 1430, 1434-1437 (1990): The problem here, as always in the criminal law, is striking the balance between the defender's subjective perceptions and those of the hypothetical reasonable person. To apply a purely objective standard is unduly harsh because it ignores the characteristics which inevitably and justifiably shape the defender's perspective, thus holding him (or her) to a standard he simply cannot meet. If the defender is young or crippled or blind, we should not expect him to behave like a strapping, sighted adult. On the other hand, if the reasonable person has all of the defender's characteristics, the standard loses any normative component and becomes entirely subjective. Applying a purely subjective standard in all cases would give free rein to the short-tempered, the pugnacious, and the foolhardy who see threats of harm where the rest of us would not and who blind themselves to opportunities for escape that seem plainly available. These unreasonable people may not be as wicked as (although perhaps more dangerous than) cold-blooded murderers — imperfect self-defense generally reduces murder to man-slaughter — but neither are they, in practical or legal terms, justified in causing death.

As applied to the cases Gillespie presents, the question is whether the reasonable person is a woman of a certain age and height and weight — or a battered woman. . . .

The hard . . . question is whether [BWS] evidence is . . . relevant to and probative of the determination of the "reasonableness" of [her] belief [in the need to kill].

In this context, "reasonableness" can have two possible meanings. First, a woman's choice may be "reasonable," even if it conflicts with our own (or a mythical other's) assessment of the situation, if the woman is indeed right, or probably right, or at least more likely right than us, in her assessment. To the extent that her experience as a battered woman, and the syndrome from which she suffers, makes her a better judge than us of the seriousness of the situation she actually faces, there should be no question that such evidence is not only relevant, but also highly probative. . . .

But what of the woman who shoots her husband while he is sound asleep, and not, by anyone's account, about to do anything? What of the woman who faces a beating, but not — even within her own or her expert's description of the cycles of violence — serious bodily harm? Put aside the woman who has tried to escape in the past and been beaten for it, or who has called the police and been rebuffed, or who would be leaving her young children defenseless if she left. In these cases, properly applied, the retreat requirement cannot be met with the necessary "complete safety." But what of the woman who has never tried any of these alternatives? What of the woman who could walk out the back door and into a neighbor's house?

In such cases, the "reasonableness" inquiry, and the evidence of battered woman's syndrome, does not really go to the rightness of the woman's belief in the need for deadly force. It is, instead, a request to abandon the limits on self-defense out of empathy for the circumstances of the defender and disgust for the acts of her abuser. We can find her belief in the imminence of danger "reasonable" only by deciding that these standards mean less in the home than outside it, mean less when applied to cruel husbands who torment defenseless wives than to others.

On its face, that is a very uncomfortable request — at least for those of us who see in the rules of self-defense a laudable recognition of the value of human life and a desirable effort to articulate a normative standard which protects even aggressors and wrongdoers from instant execution or vigilante justice.

2. *The issue of scientific reliability.* (*a*) At the time *Kelly* was decided courts were divided over whether the experts' testimony on the battered woman's syndrome was sufficiently reliable to allow it to go to the jury. Today its admissibility is overwhelmingly accepted by courts and legislatures. See Rogers v. State, 616 So. 2d 1098, 1100 (Fla. Ct. App. 1993). In some jurisdictions the issue is resolved by statute. See, e.g., Cal. Evid. Code §1107(b) (1991) ("Expert opinion testimony on battered women's syndrome shall not be considered a new scientific technique whose reliability is unproven"); Mo. Rev. Stat. §563.033 (Supp. 1988) ("Evidence the actor was suffering from the battered spouse syndrome shall be admissible upon the issue of whether the actor lawfully acted in self-defense or defense of another"); Ohio Rev. Code Ann. §2901.06 (1991 Supp.) (". . . expert testimony of the 'battered woman syndrome' and expert testimony that the person suffered from that syndrome can be introduced as evidence to establish the requisite belief of an imminent danger of death or great bodily harm. . . ."). Texas has the broadest provision inasmuch as it is not restricted to battered woman's cases. Tex. Pen. Code §19.06 (Vernon Supp. 1992):

> In a prosecution for murder or manslaughter . . . the defendant, in order to establish the defendant's reasonable belief that use of force or deadly force was immediately necessary, shall be permitted to offer: (1) relevant evidence that the defendant had been the victim of acts of family violence committed by the deceased, . . . and (2) relevant expert testimony regarding the condition of the mind of the defendant at the time of the offense, including those relevant facts and circumstances relating to family violence that are the basis of the expert's opinion.

(*b*) Concerns about the methodology and reliability of establishing the battered woman's syndrome have been raised. See Note (David L. Faigman), The Battered Woman Syndrome and Self-Defense: A Legal and Empirical Dissent, 72 Va. L. Rev. 619 (1986). The author points to several empirical problems underlying the theory that a syndrome afflicts battered women. He notes, for example, that the pivotal research of Lenore Walker leaves unclear the nature of the "loving contrition" phase in the "cycle of violence" and does not indicate whether battered women felt powerless or unable to leave during the periods when intimidation was in abeyance. In addition, he suggests that the Walker research does not specify which groups of women experienced which phases of the cycle of violence, and her data implies that at most only 58 percent of those considered battered women experienced all three phases of the cycle (id. at 639-640). As a result, he argues, several of the claims that become central in self-defense cases — that is, that battered women develop "learned helplessness" and believe themselves unable to flee — lack verifiable empirical support. Professor Faigman concludes (id. at 647):

> The prevailing theories of battered woman syndrome have little evidentiary value in self-defense cases. The work of Lenore Walker, the leading researcher on battered woman syndrome, is unsound and largely irrelevant to the central issues

in such cases. The Walker cycle theory suffers from significant methodological and interpretive flaws that render it incapable of explaining why an abused woman strikes out at her mate when she does. Similarly, Walker's application of learned helplessness to the situation of battered women does not account for the actual behavior of many women who remain in battering relationships.

A recent reassessment of the Walker research (as well as many subsequent studies) expresses similar misgivings. See Robert F. Schopp, Barbara J. Sturgis & Megan Sullivan, Battered Woman Syndrome, Expert Testimony, and the Distinction Between Justification and Excuse, [1994] U. Ill. L. Rev. 45. The authors find that "Walker's data . . . are inconsistent with the notion that learned helplessness determines whether a battered woman leaves the relationship," and that "[o]ther available research . . . provides no strong support for the proposition that the battered woman syndrome is an accurate description of a syndrome that regularly results from battering relationships" (id. at 58-59). The authors conclude (id. at 63-64):

> [T]he currently available data do not justify the claim that the battered woman syndrome, as usually formulated, provides a general portrait of those who have suffered battering relationships. . . .
> Perhaps most importantly from the perspective of the criminal courts, learned helplessness has been the aspect of the battered woman syndrome most frequently cited as central to cases of self-defense by battered women, yet it draws very little support from the available data. The complete body of work provides neither any clear conception of learned helplessness nor any good reason to believe that it regularly occurs in battered women. . . . Collectively, the data reviewed supports the proposition that battered women do not suffer learned helplessness, at least as well as it supports the claim that they do. Finally, it would be more consistent with the theoretical and empirical foundations of learned helplessness to contend that battered women who kill their batterers differ from those who remain in the battering relationships without killing their batterers precisely because those who kill do *not* manifest learned helplessness.

(c) Do the objections to a battered woman syndrome defense, if valid, render evidence of battering irrelevant to a claim of self-defense? Consider the case of Karen Straw (N.Y. Times, Oct. 1, 1987, at 18). After suffering several years of harassment and beatings by her husband, Straw consulted a Legal Aid attorney about a divorce but was told the divorce would cost $200, money she did not have. Later, she separated from her husband and obtained an order of protection from the family court. When he continued to pursue and attack her, she filed assault charges against him, but her repeated calls for police assistance brought little response. One night he appeared at her apartment, beat her and raped her at knifepoint in front of her two children. The next morning during a further violent argument, she stabbed and killed him. Even if Straw was not suffering from battered woman's *syndrome*, doesn't her situation as a battered woman nonetheless remain relevant to her claim of justified self-defense? The prosecutor's argument that Straw could have fled down the stairwell or the elevator evidently did not persuade the jury, which acquitted her on all charges. For a thorough analysis of the dimensions of self-defense litigation in behalf of battered women and the possibilities for bringing the context of a battering relationship into the framework of traditional self-defense doctrine, see Holly

Maguigan, Battered Women and Self-Defense: Myths and Misconceptions in Current Reform Proposals, 140 U. Pa. L. Rev. 379 (1991).

3. *Feminist perspectives.* Much feminist writing tends to be strongly supportive of the battered woman's defense. There is, however, a growing feminist reaction against it. See, e.g., Anne M. Coughlin, Excusing Women, 82 Cal. L. Rev. 1 (1994). The author states (at 4-6):

> While many feminist scholars conclude that the courts cannot justly blame an accused woman without considering abuse that she endured at the hands of her husband, several others have expressed uneasiness with the battered woman syndrome defense because it institutionalizes within the criminal law negative stereotypes of women. I agree with this criticism; in particular, the defense is objectionable because it relieves the accused woman of the stigma and pain of criminal punishment only if she embraces another kind of stigma and pain: she must advance an interpretation of her own activity that labels it the irrational product of a "mental health disorder."
>
> However, this criticism leaves off precisely where the most profound feminist objection to the defense should begin. [T]he negative implications for women go far beyond the reinforcement of particular aspects of stereotyped gender roles that some of us may wish to shed. None of those who advocate, or, for that matter, criticize, adoption of the battered woman syndrome defense has noticed that, for many centuries, the criminal law has been content to excuse women for criminal misconduct on the ground that they cannot be expected to, and, indeed, should not, resist the influence exerted by their husbands. No similar excuse has ever been afforded to men; to the contrary, the criminal law consistently has demanded that men withstand any pressures in their lives that compel them to commit crimes, including pressures exerted by their spouses. In this way, the theory of criminal responsibility has participated in the construction of marriage and, indeed, of gender, as a hierarchical relationship. By construing wives as incapable of choosing lawful conduct when faced with unlawful influence from their spouses, the theory invests men with the authority to govern both themselves and their irresponsible wives.
>
> The battered woman syndrome defense rests on and reaffirms this invidious understanding of women's incapacity for rational self-control.

4. *Other syndrome evidence.* In Werner v. State, 711 S.W.2d 639 (Tex. Crim. App. 1986), the defendant appealed his conviction of murder, complaining that the trial court erred in refusing to permit the jury to hear the testimony of his expert witness. He had raised the issue of self-defense, and the witness would have testified that the defendant, as the son of a Nazi concentration camp survivor, was a victim of a so-called "Holocaust Syndrome," which causes people to be unusually assertive in confrontational settings, as a reaction to the memory of Jewish concentration camp victims who did not fight back. The court rejected his argument, stating: "The evidence excluded only tended to show that possibly appellant was not an ordinary and prudent man with respect to self-defense. This did not entitle appellant to an enlargement of the statutory defense on account of his psychological peculiarities" (id. at 646). The dissent made the following observations:

> Dr. Roden's testimony was highly relevant on the issue of the condition of the appellant's state of mind at the time he fired the fatal shot, and would have aided the

jury, all of whom were probably totally unfamiliar with this type syndrome, in better deciding . . . how his suffering from "The Holocaust Syndrome" affected the condition of his mind at that time. . . .

When a relatively large number of persons, having the same symptoms, exhibit a combination or variation of functional psychiatric disorders that lead to purely emotional stress that causes intense mental anguish or emotional trauma, . . . the psychiatrists put those persons under one or more labels. Today, we have the following labels: "The Battered Wife Syndrome"; "The Battered Child Syndrome"; "The Battered Husband Syndrome"; "The Battered Parent Syndrome"; "The Battle Fatigue Syndrome"; "The Policeman's Syndrome"; and "The Holocaust Syndrome." Tomorrow, there will probably be additions to the list, such as "The Appellate Court Judge Syndrome." . . .

If scientific, technical, or other specialized knowledge will assist the trier of fact to better understand the evidence or determine a fact in issue, a witness . . . qualified as an expert by knowledge, skill, experience, training, or education, . . . should be able to testify in the form of opinion evidence.

In this instance, I find that the subject "The Holocaust Syndrome" was beyond the ken of the average lay person. The jury was entitled to know that when the appellant fired the fatal shot [his] state of mind . . . was affected, not only by that which he visually saw on the night in question, but also [by] his belief that it was necessary for him to defend himself because he comes from a family who did not defend themselves, thus causing them to perish in the Holocaust.

STATE v. NORMAN

Supreme Court of North Carolina
324 N.C. 253, 378 S.E.2d 8 (1989)

MITCHELL, J. The defendant was tried [for] the first degree murder of her husband. The jury found the defendant guilty of voluntary manslaughter. The defendant appealed from the trial court's judgment sentencing her to six years imprisonment.

The Court of Appeals granted a new trial, citing as error the trial court's refusal to submit a possible verdict of acquittal by reason of perfect self-defense.

[The defendant's evidence tended to show the following: The 39-year-old defendant was badly abused by her husband during most of their 25-year marriage. He frequently punched and kicked her, threw beer bottles and other objects at her, and burned her with cigarettes or hot coffee. He forced her into prostitution at a local truck stop and then humiliated her in public and at home by calling her "dog," "bitch," or "whore" and forcing her to eat pet food from a bowl on the floor. He frequently forced her to sleep on the floor. For years he threatened to maim her and to kill her.

[The day before she killed him, defendant's husband beat her so badly that she called the police. When they arrived, however, they would not arrest him unless she filed a complaint, which she was afraid to do. An hour later she tried to kill herself. When paramedics came to assist her, her husband tried to interfere, insisting that they let her die. He was chased back into the house by a sheriff's deputy but was not arrested.

[The next morning she went to the local mental health center to talk about filing charges and possibly having her husband committed. When she confronted him with this possibility, he threatened to cut her throat before he was taken away. Later, defendant went to the social services office to sign up for welfare so that she would no longer have to prostitute herself to feed her children. Her husband followed her to the office, and dragged her from the interview, forcing her to return home. There he beat her and burned her with cigarettes. He refused to let her eat and forced her to sleep on the floor. When her grandchild began to cry, defendant crept out of the house, and took the baby to her mother's home so that it would not wake up defendant's husband. She returned with a pistol, went to the bedroom, and tried to shoot her husband in the back of the head. The gun jammed, but she fixed it and shot him. After she determined that he was still moving, she fired two more shots into the back of his head.]

Based on the evidence that the defendant exhibited battered wife syndrome, that she believed she could not escape her husband nor expect help from others, that her husband had threatened her, and that her husband's abuse of her had worsened in the two days preceding his death, the Court of Appeals concluded that a jury reasonably could have found that her killing of her husband was justified as an act of perfect self-defense. The Court of Appeals reasoned that the nature of battered wife syndrome is such that a jury could not be precluded from finding the defendant killed her husband lawfully in perfect self-defense, even though he was asleep when she killed him. We disagree. . . .

In North Carolina, a defendant is entitled to have the jury consider acquittal by reason of *perfect* self-defense when the evidence, viewed in the light most favorable to the defendant, tends to show that at the time of the killing it appeared to the defendant and she believed it to be necessary to kill the decedent to save herself from imminent death or great bodily harm. That belief must be reasonable, however, in that the circumstances as they appeared to the defendant would create such a belief in the mind of a person of ordinary firmness. Further, the defendant must not have been the initial aggressor provoking the fatal confrontation. A killing in the proper exercise of the right of *perfect* self-defense is always completely justified in law and constitutes no legal wrong.

Our law also recognizes an *imperfect* right of self-defense in certain circumstances, including, for example, when the defendant is the initial aggressor, but without intent to kill or to seriously injure the decedent, and the decedent escalates the confrontation to a point where it reasonably appears to the defendant to be necessary to kill the decedent to save herself from imminent death or great bodily harm.[a] Although the culpability of a defendant who kills in the exercise of *imperfect* self-defense is reduced, such a defendant is *not justified* in the killing so as to be entitled to acquittal, but is guilty at least of voluntary manslaughter.

The defendant in the present case was not entitled to a jury instruction on either perfect or imperfect self-defense. . . .

The killing of another human being is the most extreme recourse to our inherent right of self-preservation and can be justified in law only by the utmost

---

a. Imperfect self-defense, as we have seen, supra page 812, is more commonly made out in American jurisdictions when the jury concludes that the defendant truly believed she had to kill to avoid an imminent threat to her life, but that her belief was not reasonable. — Eds.

real or apparent necessity brought about by the decedent. . . . Only [where it is shown that defendant] killed due to a reasonable belief that death or great bodily harm was imminent can the justification for homicide remain clearly and firmly rooted in necessity. . . .

The term "imminent," as used to describe such perceived threats of death or great bodily harm as will justify a homicide by reason of perfect self-defense, has been defined as "immediate danger, such as must be instantly met, such as cannot be guarded against by calling for the assistance of others or the protection of the law." Black's Law Dictionary 676 (5th ed. 1979). Our cases have sometimes used the phrase "about to suffer" interchangeably with "imminent" to describe the immediacy of threat that is required to justify killing in self-defense.

The evidence in this case did not tend to show that the defendant reasonably believed that she was confronted by a threat of imminent death or great bodily harm. The evidence tended to show that no harm was "imminent" or about to happen to the defendant when she shot her husband. The uncontroverted evidence was that her husband had been asleep for some time when she . . . shot her husband three times in the back of the head. The defendant was not faced with an instantaneous choice between killing her husband or being killed or seriously injured. Instead, all of the evidence tended to show that the defendant had ample time and opportunity to resort to other means of preventing further abuse by her husband. There was no action underway by the decedent from which the jury could have found that the defendant had reasonable grounds to believe either that a felonious assault was imminent or that it might result in her death or great bodily injury. Additionally, no such action by the decedent had been underway immediately prior to his falling asleep. . . .

[T]he lack of any belief by the defendant — reasonable or otherwise — that she faced a threat of imminent death or great bodily harm from the drunk and sleeping victim in the present case was illustrated by the defendant and her own expert witnesses when testifying about her subjective assessment of her situation at the time of the killing. . . .

Dr. Tyson . . . testified that the defendant "believed herself to be doomed . . . to a life of the worst kind of torture and abuse, degradation that she had experienced over the years in a progressive way; that it would only get worse, and that death was inevitable." Such evidence of the defendant's speculative beliefs concerning her remote and indefinite future, while indicating she had felt generally threatened, did not tend to show that she killed in the belief — reasonable or otherwise — that her husband presented a threat of imminent death or great bodily harm. Under our law of self-defense, a defendant's subjective belief of what might be "inevitable" at some indefinite point in the future does not equate to what she believes to be "imminent." Dr. Tyson's opinion that the defendant believed it was necessary to kill her husband for "the protection of herself and her family" was similarly indefinite and devoid of time frame and did not tend to show a threat or fear of *imminent* harm.

The defendant testified that, "I knowed when he woke up, it was going to be the same thing, and I was scared when he took me to the truck stop that night it was going to be worse than he had ever been." She also testified, when asked if she believed her husband's threats: "Yes. . . . [H]e would kill me if he got a chance. If he thought he wouldn't a had to went to jail, he would a done it." Testimony about such indefinite fears concerning what her sleeping husband might do at some time in the future did not tend to establish a fear — reasonable or otherwise — of *imminent death or great bodily harm* at the time of the killing.

We are not persuaded by the reasoning of our Court of Appeals in this case that when there is evidence of battered wife syndrome, neither an actual attack nor threat of attack by the husband at the moment the wife uses deadly force is required to justify the wife's killing of him in perfect self-defense. The Court of Appeals concluded that to impose such requirements would ignore the "learned helplessness," meekness and other realities of battered wife syndrome and would effectively preclude such women from exercising their right of self-defense. . . .

The reasoning of our Court of Appeals in this case proposes to change the established law of self-defense by giving the term "imminent" a meaning substantially more indefinite and all-encompassing than its present meaning. This would result in a substantial relaxation of the requirement of real or apparent necessity to justify homicide. Such reasoning proposes justifying the taking of human life not upon the reasonable belief it is necessary to prevent death or great bodily harm — which the imminence requirement ensures — but upon purely subjective speculation that the decedent probably would present a threat of life at a future time and that the defendant would not be able to avoid the predicted threat.

The Court of Appeals suggests that such speculation would have been particularly reliable in the present case because the jury, based on the evidence of the decedent's intensified abuse during the thirty-six hours preceding his death, could have found that the decedent's passive state at the time of his death was "but a momentary hiatus in a continuous reign of terror by the decedent [and] the defendant merely took advantage of her first opportunity to protect herself." Requiring jury instructions on perfect self-defense in such situations, however, would still tend to make opportune homicide lawful as a result of mere subjective predictions of indefinite future assaults and circumstances. Such predictions of future assaults to justify the defendant's use of deadly force in this case would be entirely speculative, because there was no evidence that her husband had ever inflicted any harm upon her that approached life-threatening injury, even during the "reign of terror." It is far from clear in the defendant's poignant evidence that any abuse by the decedent had ever involved the degree of physical threat required to justify the defendant in using deadly force, even when those threats were imminent. The use of deadly force in self-defense to prevent harm other than death or great bodily harm is excessive as a matter of law.

. . . The relaxed requirements for perfect self-defense proposed by our Court of Appeals would tend to categorically legalize the opportune killing of abusive husbands by their wives solely on the basis of the wives' testimony concerning their subjective speculation as to the probability of future felonious assaults by their husbands. Homicidal self-help would then become a lawful solution, and perhaps the easiest and most effective solution, to this problem. . . . It has even been suggested that the relaxed requirements of self-defense found in what is often called the "battered woman's defense" could be extended in principle to any type of case in which a defendant testified that he or she subjectively believed that killing was necessary and proportionate to any perceived threat. . . .

[The court also ruled that the defendant was not entitled to instructions on *imperfect* self-defense. It held that the imminence requirement applied to both perfect and imperfect self-defense and that the defendant did not meet the requirements for imperfect self-defense because there was no evidence that she actually believed the use of deadly force against her was imminent. The court also noted, however, that the failure to instruct on imperfect self-defense, even if error, was harmless because the defendant was convicted only of voluntary manslaughter; an instruction on imperfect self-defense would have given her nothing more, because in North Carolina killings in cases of imperfect self-defense are treated as voluntary manslaughter.]

[W]e conclude that the defendant's conviction for voluntary manslaughter and the trial court's judgment sentencing her to a six-year term of imprisonment were without error. Therefore, we must reverse the decision of the Court of Appeals which awarded the defendant a new trial.

MARTIN, J., dissenting. . . . Defendant does not seek to expand or relax the requirements of self-defense and thereby "legalize the opportune killing of allegedly abusive husbands by their wives," as the majority overstates. Rather, defendant contends that the evidence as gauged by the existing laws of self-defense is sufficient to require the submission of a self-defense instruction to the jury. . . . I conclude that it was. . . .

Evidence presented by defendant described a twenty-year history of beatings and other dehumanizing and degrading treatment by her husband. In his expert testimony a clinical psychologist concluded that defendant fit "and exceed[ed]" the profile of an abused or battered spouse. . . . The psychologist described the defendant as a woman incarcerated by abuse, by fear, and by her conviction that her husband was invincible and inescapable:

> Mrs. Norman didn't leave because she believed, fully believed that escape was totally impossible. There was no place to go. He, she had left before; he had come and gotten her. She had gone to the Department of Social Services. He had come and gotten her. The law, she believed the law could not protect her; no one could protect her, and I must admit, looking over the records, that there was nothing done that would contradict that belief. . . .

Evidence presented in the case sub judice revealed no letup of tension or fear, no moment in which the defendant felt released from impending serious harm, even while the decedent slept. . . . For the battered wife, if there is no escape, if there is no window of relief or momentary sense of safety, then the next attack, which could be the fatal one, is imminent. . . . Properly stated, the . . . [question] is not whether the threat was *in fact* imminent, but whether defendant's belief in the impending nature of the threat, given the circumstances as she saw them, was reasonable in the mind of a person of ordinary firmness.

Defendant's intense fear, based on her belief that her husband intended not only to maim or deface her, as he had in the past, but to kill her, was evident in the testimony of witnesses who recounted events of the last three days of the decedent's life. This testimony could have led a juror to conclude that defendant reasonably perceived a threat to her life as "imminent," even while her husband slept. . . .

From this evidence of the exacerbated nature of the last three days of twenty years of provocation, a juror could conclude that defendant believed that her husband's threats to her life were viable, that serious bodily harm was imminent, and that it was necessary to kill her husband to escape that harm. And from this evidence a juror could find defendant's belief in the necessity to kill her husband not merely reasonable but compelling.

DAVID McCORD & SANDRA K. LYONS, MORAL REASONING AND THE CRIMINAL LAW: THE EXAMPLE OF SELF-DEFENSE, 30 Am. Crim. L. Rev. 97, 110 (1992): [Reviewing the *Norman* decision, the authors conclude that it is in accord with traditional law but not with what is morally required. They say:] There are at least ten significant facts which our common sense and life experience tell us are highly significant in this case but which seem not to be considered by the traditional law. In no particular order these ten are: (1) J. T. and Judy [Norman] were not equally matched in terms of physical prowess, as J. T. apparently was significantly more powerful; (2) Judy was distraught because of the actions of J. T.; (3) Judy's mental state was colored not merely by one single incident of abuse, but by the culmination of twenty years of abuse; (4) Because J. T. lived in the same house as Judy, he had virtually constant access to her to inflict abuse on her; (5) Having Judy at his disposal in this manner, J. T. thus was able to decide when, where, and how to inflict the abuse — he took advantage of the option which the law apparently ceded to him to launch nondeadly attacks on her at his whim, without fear of a justifiable deadly response; (6) Judy's future was bleak — there was no basis for her to believe that J. T. would be content to live without her or that he had any intent to stop abusing her; (7) Judy apparently had no viable alternative but to stay in the vicinity — she had no job skills to support herself elsewhere, and her support network was in that community; (8) Judy had no reasonable prospect of being able to stay in that community outside the presence of J. T., since he would find her anywhere in the vicinity; (9) The governmental authorities failed to take any action to protect Judy despite having been contacted by her; and (10) J. T.'s actions prevented Judy from doing anything further to invoke the help of the governmental authorities.

These ignored facts have no place in the moral reasoning mandated by the traditional law of self-defense, yet they cause us to suffer moral disquiet with the result.

Questions: How could the rules of the law of self-defense be formulated to take account of these morally relevant factors? Would it be desirable to add to the traditional rules allowing self-defense in designated circumstances: "or in any other circumstance in which the defendant's killing of the victim was morally justified"?

NOTES ON THE IMMINENT DANGER REQUIREMENT

1. Would the arguments favoring a self-defense instruction for a battered woman who kills her abuser while he sleeps extend to a woman who hires another to kill him for her? The few cases that have faced the question of third-person killings have rejected the defense. See People v. Yaklich, 833 P.2d 758 (Colo. App. 1991); State v. Anderson, 785 S.W.2d 596 (Mo. App. 1990); State v.

Leaphart, 673 S.W.2d 870 (Tenn. Crim. App. 1983). In the *Yaklich* case the defendant argued that "in the context of a battered woman situation in which the woman kills her abuser, 'imminent' should be defined as: impending, not immediate. Thus, according to the defendant, a woman who kills her abuser or, as here, who hires another to kill her abuser is nevertheless entitled to a self-defense instruction even though she was not threatened with harm contemporaneously with the killing." The court rejected the argument.

Questions: Was the court correct? If the basic rationale of the defense of the battered woman syndrome is sound, why doesn't it extend to the case where the woman hires someone to kill her abuser for her? See Stephen J. Schulhofer, The Gender Question in Criminal Law, 7 Soc. Phil. & Pol. 105, 119-20 (1990):

> [I]n thinking about non-confrontational cases . . . the Walker approach turns traditional intuitions inside out. In traditional terms, the strongest . . . of the non-confrontational cases [is] that of the woman who filed for divorce, fled, and sought outside help. But such behavior does not fit the typical pattern of learned helplessness. Expert testimony about battered spouse syndrome could be ruled inadmissible, or prosecution experts could testify that the defendant, even if abused, did not display the battered wife *syndrome,* and therefore could be expected to avoid resort to deadly force.
>
> Conversely, . . . the contract killing begins to look like the strongest case of all. The utter passivity, the inability to act even when the abuser is sleeping, the apparent dependence on the intervention of a male support figure, all reinforce a diagnosis of battered wife syndrome. In fact, Lenore Walker is very explicit in challenging traditional assumptions about contract killing. She writes with irritation that under the traditional approach, "hiring someone else to kill an abusive mate is seen as evidence of premeditation, even though many women, because of sex role conditioning or other factors, cannot use sufficient force to protect themselves."[47] Walker concludes that this traditional view is just evidence of the criminal law's "[b]iases . . . against women."[48]

Does this argument imply that self-defense should be available both to the battered woman who herself kills and to the one who hires another to do so? Or that, in the absence of an imminent threat of great bodily harm, it should be available to neither?

2. The opinion of the court in the *Norman* case states the traditional and generally prevailing requirement of the law of self-defense that the danger be imminent, in the sense of about to happen right then and there.

In pondering the pros and cons of this requirement, consider the following.

(*a*) In an English motion picture, a cuckolded husband imprisons and chains his wife's latest lover in an abandoned cellar with the announced intention of killing him after the passage of sufficient time for the stir over his disappearance to quiet down, probably several months. Must the intended victim wait until the final moment when the husband is about to commit the fatal act, or may he kill the husband in self-defense at any time during the period of imprisonment that he can succeed in laying hands on him?

---

47. Lenore E. Walker, A Response to Elizabeth M. Schneider's Describing and Changing, 9 Women's Rights L. Rptr. 223 (1986).
48. Ibid.

(*b*) In State v. Schroeder, 199 Neb. 822, 261 N.W.2d 759 (1978), a 19-year-old inmate stabbed his older cell-mate at 1 A.M. while the latter was asleep. He was convicted of assault with intent to inflict great bodily harm. The evidence was that the deceased had a reputation for sex and violence, that the defendant had incurred a large gambling debt to the deceased who threatened to make a "punk" out of him by selling his debt to another prisoner, that before going to bed the morning of the incident the deceased said he might walk in his sleep and "collect" some of the money owed.

The majority found no error in the trial court's failure to give any instruction on self-defense. The court said (261 N.W.2d at 761):

> The problem in this case is that there was no evidence to sustain a finding that the defendant could believe an assault was imminent except the threat that Riggs had made before he went to bed. The general rule is that words alone are not sufficient justification for an assault. . . . There is a very real danger in a rule which would legalize preventive assaults involving the use of deadly force where there has been nothing more than threats. We conclude that the trial court did not err in refusing to instruct the jury as requested.

The dissent stated (id. at 761, 762):

> In this case the defendant was faced with a threat by Riggs that he would "collect some of this money I got owed to me tonight." The defendant could not be expected to remain awake all night, every night, waiting for the attack that Riggs had threatened to make. The defendant's evidence here was such that the jury could have found the defendant was justified in believing the use of force was necessary to protect himself against an attack by Riggs "on the present occasion."

3. The Model Penal Code has proposed a modest relaxation of the imminence requirement, providing that it is sufficient if the actor reasonably believed that the use of defensive force was "immediately necessary . . . on the present occasion." §3.04(1). Several states have adopted similar language. E.g., Del. tit. 11, §464; N.J. §2C:3-4a; Pa. tit. 18, §505. Some courts have loosened the imminence requirement on their own authority. In State v. Janes, 121 Wash. 2d 220, 850 P.2d 495 (1993), for example, a battered child case, the court interpreted the statutory imminence requirement as follows (id. at 241-242):

> Imminence does not require an actual physical assault. A threat, or its equivalent, can support self-defense when there is a reasonable belief that the threat will be carried out. Especially in abusive relationships, patterns of behavior become apparent which can signal the next abusive episode. . . . That the triggering behavior and the abusive episode are divided by time does not necessarily negate the reasonableness of the defendant's perception of imminent harm. Even an otherwise innocuous comment which occurred days before the homicide could be highly relevant when the evidence shows that such a comment inevitably signaled the beginning of an abusive episode.

Question: Would a self-defense instruction have been required in *Norman* if North Carolina had adopted these qualifications of the imminency requirement?

4. For a critique of both the traditional imminence requirement and the more flexible Model Penal Code standard of immediacy, see Richard A. Rosen, On Self-Defense, Imminence, and Women Who Kill Their Batterers, 71 N.C.L. Rev. 371 (1993). After criticizing the result in the *Norman* case, Professor Rosen argues that neither imminence nor "immediacy" should be required when a killing is necessary, under all the circumstances, to avoid a nonimminent danger.

5. Jahnke v. State, 682 P.2d 991 (Wyo. 1984), involved a 16-year-old boy who waited with his shotgun for an hour and a half for his parents to return from dinner and then shot his father dead as he entered the house. For 14 years the father apparently had subjected the boy to extreme physical and psychological abuse. The boy was rebuffed in his effort to support a self-defense claim with testimony regarding the "battered person syndrome." The Supreme Court found no error and upheld a verdict of voluntary manslaughter. The majority opinion observed:

> Although many people, and the public media, seem to be prepared to espouse the notion that a victim of abuse is entitled to kill the abuser[,] that special justification defense is antithetical to the mores of modern civilized society. It is difficult enough to justify capital punishment as an appropriate response of society to criminal acts even after the circumstances have been carefully evaluated by a number of people. To permit capital punishment to be imposed upon the subjective conclusion of the individual that prior acts and conduct of the deceased justified the killing would amount to a leap into the abyss of anarchy.
>
> . . . It is clear that if [battered person] evidence has any role at all it is in assisting the jury to evaluate the reasonableness of the defendant's fear in a case involving the recognized circumstances of self-defense which include a confrontation or conflict with the deceased not of the defendant's instigation.

A concurring judging commented:

> This is a textbook case of first-degree murder. . . . In his defense, appellant employed the oldest, most common and most successful tactic in homicide cases. He put the deceased on trial. . . . There was no one to speak for the deceased. . . . [But by] no stretch of the imagination was this a case of self-defense.

A dissenting opinion stated:

> This case concerns itself with what happens — or can happen — and did happen when a cruel, ill-tempered, insensitive man roams, gun in hand, through his years of family life as a battering bully — a bully who, since his two children were babies, beat both of them and his wife regularly and unmercifully. Particularly, this appeal has to do with a 16-year-old boy who could stand his father's abuse no longer — who could not find solace or friendship in the public services which had been established for the purpose of providing aid, comfort and advice to abused family members — and who had no place to go or friends to help either him or his sister for whose protection he felt responsible and so — in fear and fright, and with fragmented emotion, Richard Jahnke shot and killed his father. . . .
>
> It is my conception that Richard Jahnke properly came to the courts of Wyoming asking — not that he be judged as one who, at the time and place in question, was *insanely unreasonable* — but that his 14 years of beatings and uncivilized emotional

abuse be explained by a qualified expert in order that judgment be passed on the question which asks whether or not his behavior was *sanely reasonable*. . . .

[W]hen the beatings of 14 years have — or may have — caused the accused to harbor types of fear, anxiety and apprehension with which the nonbrutalized juror is unfamiliar and which result in the taking of unusual defensive measures which, in the ordinary circumstances, might be thought about as premature [or] excessive . . .then expert testimony is necessary to explain the battered-person syndrome and the way these people respond to what they understand to be the imminence of danger. . . .

A number of courts that have approved the use of battered woman's syndrome evidence to support claims of self-defense have extended their approval to cases of battered and abused children. E.g., State v. Janes, 121 Wash. 2d 220, 850 P.2d 495 (1993). But some, like *Jahnke*, have not. For a discussion and review of the authorities see Joelle Anne Moreno, Killing Daddy: Developing a Self-Defense Strategy for the Abused Child, 137 U. Pa. L. Rev. 1281 (1989); Comment (Jamie Heather Sacks), A New Age of Understanding: Allowing Self-Defense Claims for Battered Children Who Kill Their Abusers, 10 J. Contemp. Health L. & Poly. 349 (1994).

NOTES AND QUESTIONS ON OTHER ISSUES OF SELF-DEFENSE

1. Limits on the use of deadly force. Against what kind of threats may deadly force be used? The recent tendency has been to confine its use to narrow bounds. See, e.g., State v. Clay, 297 N.C. 555, 256 S.E.2d 176, 182 (1979):

We define deadly force as force likely to cause death or great bodily harm.[a] . . . In so holding, we expressly reject defendant's contention, and any implication in our cases in support thereof, that a defendant would be justified by the principles of self-defense in employing deadly force to protect against bodily injury or offensive physical contact. Our decision says, in effect, that where the assault being made upon defendant is insufficient to give rise to a reasonable apprehension of death or great bodily harm, then the use of deadly force by defendant to protect himself from bodily injury or offensive physical contact is excessive force as a matter of law. Although we may hear protestations to the contrary, this decision will not compel anyone "to submit in meekness to indignities or violence to his person merely because such indignities or violence stop short of threatening him with death or great bodily harm." In such cases, a person so accosted may use such force, short of deadly force, as reasonably appears to him to be necessary under the circumstances to prevent bodily injury or offensive physical contact. This decision precludes the use of deadly force to prevent bodily injury or offensive physical contact and in so doing recognizes the premium we place on human life.

The Model Penal Code §3.04(2)(b) limits the use of deadly force to cases where the threatened danger is "death, serious bodily harm, kidnapping or

a. The Model Penal Code defines deadly force as "force which the actor uses with the purpose of causing or which he knows to create a substantial risk of causing death or serious bodily harm." §3.11(2). — Eds.

sexual intercourse compelled by force or threat." *Question:* On what theory were the latter two dangers included?

In John Q. La Fond, The Case for Liberalizing the Use of Deadly Force in Self-Defense, 6 U. Puget Sound L. Rev. 237 (1983), the author criticizes the rule that deadly force can be used only to counter a threat of death or great bodily harm or rape. Because this rule leaves many law-abiding citizens (including most female victims) without a practically effective means of defense against an unlawful, nondeadly assault by an unpredictable or much stronger attacker, the author proposes that resort to deadly force be permissible whenever it is "necessary to protect [the defendant] effectively" against a threat of unlawful physical violence (id. at 280).

In considering the significance of this issue for the battered woman's defense, recall the language of the *Norman* decision that even apart from the absence of an imminent danger, the assaults the defendant suffered during her married life were not deadly, so that she had no ground for fearing a deadly attack at the time she shot her husband.

2. Defense of another. Though the universal view in this country makes justification turn on the reasonableness of the judgment of the defendant in appraising the need to use the defensive force he used, a special problem has arisen when the actor acted in the defense of another person. The problem is often put in terms of whether the defendant should be regarded as "standing in his own shoes," or "in the shoes" of the person in whose defense he acted. Is the defendant exculpated if he reasonably believed he had to attack in order to save the person he reasonably took to be the victim? Or is the defendant exculpated only if that other person in fact had a right to use defensive force?

The issue was clearly presented in People v. Young, 12 A.D.2d 262, 210 N.Y.S.2d 358 (1st Dept. 1961), *rev'd,* 11 N.Y.2d 274, 183 N.E.2d 319 (1962). In this case a 40-year-old Western Union messenger came upon two middle-aged men beating and struggling with a youth of 18. Believing the youth was being unlawfully assaulted, he entered the affray, in the course of which his leg locked with that of one of the older men, who suffered a broken leg. It turned out the older men were detectives in plain clothes making a lawful arrest. The Appellate Division reversed an assault conviction and, in reliance on Model Penal Code §3.05, rejected the "other person's shoes" doctrine, stating (210 N.Y.S.2d at 365):

> It is a sterile and desolate legal system that would exact punishment for an intentional assault from one like this defendant, who acted [reasonably] from the most commendable motives and without excessive force. Had the facts been as he thought them, he would have been a hero and not condemned as a criminal actor.

The New York Court of Appeals reversed, stating (183 N.E.2d at 319-320):

> [O]ne who goes to the aid of a third person does so at his own peril. While the doctrine espoused by the . . . court below may have support in some States, we feel that such a policy would not be conducive to an orderly society. [T]he right of a person to defend another ordinarily should not be greater than such person's right to defend himself.

The New York legislature had the last word. N.Y. Penal Law §35.15 now provides:

> A person may . . . use physical force upon another person when and to the extent he reasonably believes such to be necessary to defend himself or a third person from what he reasonably believes to be the use of imminent use of unlawful physical force by such other person.

States are divided on the issue raised by the *Young* case. In most jurisdictions the law is probably in accord with that of the Appellate Division and the New York statute. See, e.g., Fersner v. United States, 482 A.2d 387 (D.C. App. 1984); United States v. Ochoa, 526 F.2d 1278 (5th Cir. 1976). Other jurisdictions hold in accord with the New York Court of Appeals. See, e.g., State v. Gelinas, 417 A.2d 1381 (R.I. 1980); State v. Weniger, 55 Ohio St. 2d 336, 390 N.E.2d 801 (1979).

3. *The risk of injury to others.* To what extent is a person who is privileged to use deadly force against an aggressor criminally responsible if his defensive actions cause injury to innocent persons?

In People v. Adams, 9 Ill. App. 3d 61, 291 N.E.2d 54, 55-56 (1972), the defendant, acting in self-defense, shot and killed his assailant, Robinson, who was threatening his life. The deceased, Mary Davis, was at the time sitting in a car with some friends, including Robinson. One of the defendant's bullets passed through Robinson's body and struck and killed Mary Davis, who was sitting next to him. The defendant was convicted of manslaughter of the woman. On appeal, the prosecution contended that:

> [S]elf-defense does not necessarily protect an individual from criminal responsibility for all his acts performed in defending his life against a felonious assault, and that even though defendant's conduct here may have been justified as to Robinson nonetheless it constituted a reckless disregard for the consequences towards Mary Davis, and, as such, supported his conviction for involuntary manslaughter.

The court rejected these arguments and reversed the conviction, stating:

> [I]f the circumstances are such that they would excuse the killing of an assailant in self-defense, the emergency will be held to excuse the person assailed from culpability, if in attempting to defend himself he unintentionally kills or injures a third person. . . .
>
> We are aware that the above rule is not absolute and that . . . , it may be subject to modification depending on the circumstances involved. But we do not believe such circumstances present themselves in the case before us. There were other persons present in the car with defendant's assailant, but it was dark and defendant was being fired on at close range. He had very little time to think or assess the situation. He had to act immediately to protect himself from a man who had been drinking all day and who was not just threatening him but was shooting at him. Even under such circumstances defendant did not shoot wildly or carelessly. From the record it can be inferred that he hit his assailant with every shot and that the innocent victim was killed only as a result of a bullet passing through the body of the assailant. We conclude that under the circumstances of this case the killing of Mary Davis constituted no crime.

Suppose that the defendant knew or should have known that there was a substantial possibility that in shooting at his assailant in self-defense one of the innocent persons in the car would be killed. For example, suppose he were armed only with a shotgun. Would the decision then have been otherwise? Or consider a more extreme situation in which the defendant knew there was a high probability or a virtual certainty that in killing his assailant one or more of the others would also be killed. See the material on choice of evils, page 860 infra and Sanford H. Kadish, Blame and Punishment 122-126 (1987).

Compare §3.09(3) of the Model Penal Code:

> When the actor is justified under Sections 3.03 to 3.08 in using force upon or toward the person of another but he recklessly or negligently injures or creates a risk to injury to innocent persons, the justification afforded by these Sections is unavailable in a prosecution for such recklessness or negligence towards innocent persons.

See Ann E. Barlow, Self-Defense and Reckless Crimes Against Third Parties, 22 Colum. J.L. & Soc. Probs. 417 (1989).

4. *Burden of proof.* Most jurisdictions place the burden on the prosecution to disprove self-defense beyond a reasonable doubt, once the issue is raised by the evidence. Ohio, however, requires the defendant to prove self-defense by a preponderance of the evidence. In Martin v. Ohio, 480 U.S. 228 (1987), the Supreme Court upheld the constitutionality of this practice, on the ground that the absence of the conditions of self-defense was not among the elements of the crime charged (aggravated murder) as defined by the Ohio statute.

Does this mean that a state could abolish the plea of self-defense completely? Would it be constitutional to punish as a murderer someone who had killed when it was immediately necessary to save herself from an unlawful aggressor? See page 51 supra.

5. *Exceptions to the right of self-defense.* In a number of situations, the law disallows the use of defensive force, even though the defendant faces an imminent threat of injury or death from the unlawful action of another. These situations are explored in the cases that follow.

STATE v. ABBOTT

Supreme Court of New Jersey
36 N.J. 63, 174 A.2d 881 (1961)

WEINTRAUB, C.J. . . . Abbott shared a common driveway with his neighbors, Michael and Mary Scarano. The Scaranos engaged a contractor to pave their portion. Abbott obtained some asphalt from the contractor and made a doorstop to keep his garage door from swinging onto the Scaranos' property. Nicholas Scarano, who was visiting with the Scaranos, his parents, objected to Abbott's innovation. After some words between them a fist fight ensued.

Although Abbott managed to land the first punch, with which he sent Nicholas to the ground, a jury could find Nicholas was the aggressor. At this point Michael Scarano came at Abbott with a hatchet. Michael said the tool had just been returned to him by the contractor, and denied he meant to use it as a weapon. According to Abbott, Mary Scarano followed, armed with a carving knife and large fork. The actors gave varying versions of what happened, but the end result was that all of the Scaranos were hit by the hatchet. Nicholas received severe head injuries. Abbott claimed he too suffered a laceration.

Abbott admitted he finally wrested the hatchet from Michael but denied he wielded it at all. Rather he insisted that the Scaranos were injured during a common struggle for the instrument. A jury could, however, find Abbott intentionally inflicted the blows.

Abbott was separately indicted for atrocious assault and battery upon each of the Scaranos. There was a common trial of these indictments. The jury acquitted Abbott of the charges relating to Michael and Mary, but found him guilty as to Nicholas.

The principal question is whether the trial court properly instructed the jury upon . . . the subject of retreat. . . .

The question whether one who is neither the aggressor nor a party to a mutual combat must retreat has divided the authorities. Self-defense is measured against necessity. . . . From that premise one could readily say there was no necessity to kill in self-defense if the use of deadly force could have been avoided by retreat. The critics of the retreat rule do not quarrel with the theoretical validity of this conclusion, but rather condemn it as unrealistic. The law of course should not denounce conduct as criminal when it accords with the behavior of reasonable men. Upon this level, the advocates of no-retreat say the manly thing is to hold one's ground and hence society should not demand what smacks of cowardice. Adherents of the retreat rule reply it is better that the assailed shall retreat than that the life of another be needlessly spent. They add that not only do right-thinking men agree, but further a rule so requiring may well induce others to adhere to that worthy standard of behavior. . . .

Other justifications are closely divided upon the retreat doctrine. It is said the preponderant view rejects it.[a] . . . Our Court of Errors and Appeals deliberately adopted the retreat rule with an awareness of the contending views. . . . The Model Penal Code embraces the retreat rule while acknowledging that on numerical balance a majority of the precedents oppose it.

We are not persuaded to depart from the principle of retreat. We think it salutary if reasonably limited. Much of the criticism goes not to its inherent validity but rather to unwarranted applications of the rule. For example, it is correctly observed that one can hardly retreat from a rifle shot at close range. But if the weapon were a knife, a lead of a city block might well be enough. Again, the rule cannot be stated baldly, with indifference to the excitement of the occasion. As Mr. Justice Holmes cryptically put it, "Detached reflection cannot be demanded in the presence of an uplifted knife." Brown v. United States, 256 U.S. 335, 343 (1921). Such considerations, however, do not demand that a man should have the absolute right to stand his ground and kill in any and all situations. Rather they call for a fair and guarded statement of appropriate principles. . . .

We believe the following principles are found:

1. The issue of retreat arises only if the defendant resorted to a deadly force. It is a deadly force which is not justifiable when an opportunity to retreat is at

---

a. But a number of states have adopted the retreat rule in the course of recent statutory revisions. They all tend to build upon the Model Penal Code's formulation. — Eds.

hand. Model Penal Code §3.04(2)(b)(ii). As defined in §3.11(2) a deadly force means "force which the actor uses with the purpose of causing or which he knows to create a substantial risk of causing death or serious bodily harm."

Hence it is not the nature of the force defended against which raises the issue of retreat, but rather the nature of the force which the accused employed in his defense. If he does not resort to a deadly force, one who is assailed may hold his ground whether the attack upon him be of a deadly or some lesser character. Although it might be argued that a safe retreat should be taken if thereby the use of *any* force could be avoided, yet, as the comment in the Model Penal Code observes, "The logic of this position never has been accepted when moderate force is used in self-defense; here all agree that the actor may stand his ground and estimate necessity upon that basis." . . . Hence, in a case like the present one, the jury should be instructed that Abbott could hold his ground when Nicholas came at him with his fists, and also when Michael and Mary came at him with the several instruments mentioned, and that the question of retreat could arise only if Abbott intended to use a deadly force.

2. What constitutes an opportunity to retreat which will defeat the right of self-defense? As §3.04(2)(b)(ii) of the Model Penal Code states, deadly force is not justifiable "if the actor *knows* that he can avoid the necessity of using such force *with complete safety* by retreating. . . ." We emphasize "knows" and "with complete safety." One who is wrongfully attacked need not risk injury by retreating, even though he could escape with something less than serious bodily injury. It would be unreal to require nice calculations as to the amount of hurt, or to ask him to endure any at all. And the issue is not whether in retrospect it can be found the defendant could have retreated unharmed. Rather the question is whether he knew the opportunity was there, and of course in that inquiry the total circumstances including the attendant excitement must be considered. . . .

[The court reversed the conviction because it found that the trial court's instructions were ambiguous and confusing to a jury.]

PROBLEMS

1. In jurisdictions adhering to the duty of retreat before deadly force may be used, an exception is commonly made when the defendant is attacked in his own home. Thus, in People v. Tomlins, 213 N.Y. 240, 243, 107 N.E. 496, 497 (1914). Judge Cardozo, in reversing a conviction of a father for killing his son in his own home, stated:

> It is not now and never has been the law that a man assailed in his own dwelling is bound to retreat. If assailed there, he may stand his ground and resist the attack. He is under no duty to take to the fields and the highways, a fugitive from his own home. More than 200 years ago it was said by Lord Chief Justice Hale (1 Hale's Pleas of the Crown, 486): In case a man "is assailed in his own house, he need not flee as far as he can, as in other cases of se defendendo, for he hath the protection of his house to excuse him from flying, as that would be to give up the protection of his house to his adversary by flight." Flight is for sanctuary and shelter, and shelter, if not sanctuary, is in the home. That there is, in such a situation, no duty to retreat is, we think, the settled law in the United States as in England. It was so held by the United States Supreme Court in Beard v. United States, 158 U.S. 550.

In evaluating the rationale of this exception, consider further whether it should matter that the deceased-aggressor is another occupant or an intruder. Some cases hold that the homeowner can stand his ground only when the threat comes from an intruder. See, e.g., State v. Bobbitt, 415 So. 2d 724 (Fla. 1982). Other courts permit the homeowner to kill rather than retreat, even when the party killed is another lawful occupant. See People v. Tomlins, supra (father can kill son rather than retreat). The Model Penal Code also follows the latter view. Is the position sound? In State v. Shaw, 441 A.2d 561 (Conn. 1981), the court declined to accept the homeowner's privilege to stand his ground. The statute in *Shaw,* patterned after the Model Penal Code, stated: "[T]he actor shall not be required to retreat if he is in his dwelling . . . and was not the initial aggressor. . . ." Nevertheless, the court, noting the overriding policy favoring human life and stressing that in the great majority of homicides the killer and victim are relatives or close acquaintances, chose to read into the statute a requirement of retreat from co-occupants. The court stated: "We cannot conclude that the Connecticut legislature intended to sanction the reenactment of the climactic scene from 'High Noon' in the familial kitchens of this state."

Questions: In jurisdictions that require retreat from one's home when the aggressor is also a lawful occupant, can a battered woman's defense succeed? How could the defendant show that the retreat duty is inapplicable in her situation?

Two in-depth studies of the retreat issue are Richard M. Brown, No Duty to Retreat: Violence and Values in American History and Society (1991); Garrett Epps, Any Which Way But Loose: Interpretive Strategies and Attitudes Toward Violence in the Evolution of the Anglo-American "Retreat Rule," 55 Law & Contemp. Prob. 303 (1992).

2. In jurisdictions following the retreat rule, when does the duty to retreat arise? Suppose a friend warns *D,* who is on duty picketing a struck supermarket, that *V* has just set out with a knife to kill *D.* (1) *D* remains where he is. (2) Ten minutes later *D* sees *V* a block away hobbling in his direction with the aid of a crutch. *D* still remains where he is. (3) *D* watches *V* carefully and as *V* gets within 20 feet of *D,* he pulls out a knife and screams he is going to kill *D. D* still remains where he is. (4) As *V* gets within reach, he raises his knife to strike, and *D* shoots him dead.

Questions: At what point was *D* obliged to retreat in order to maintain his right to kill in self-defense? Cf. Regina v. Field, [1972] Crim. L. Rev. 435. The court reversed a conviction because the instruction indicated that if the defendant could reasonably have left the place where he was before his attackers arrived, he had a duty to do so and he should not have stayed to defend himself. The report summarizes the court's reasoning as follows ([1972] Crim. L. Rev. 435-436):

> It was not the law that a man could be driven off the streets and compelled not to go to a place where he might lawfully be because he had reason to believe that he would be confronted by people intending to attack him. No duty to retreat could arise until the parties were at any rate within sight of each other and the threat to the person relying on self-defence so imminent that he was able to demonstrate that he did not mean to fight. Although it was a matter of degree, no one was obliged to get out of the way of possible attackers. The relevance of [defendant's] conduct was that it was a factor for the jury to consider when deciding whether it was reasonable for him to use force, and to use a knife.

Is this the right approach to the question? Or is it rather that the duty to retreat arises only at the point where killing in self-defense is otherwise justified?

3. There is another situation in which it is problematic whether a person may kill in self-defense, even when threatened with imminent death by an aggressor. This is the case where the defendant is unaware of his predicament and kills his aggressor for some illicit reason. In his Justification and Excuse in the Criminal Law 38-39 (1989), Professor J. C. Smith puts the following case:

> Peter is now a notorious practical joker. One day, he enters the office of his colleague, Dan, points at Dan what Dan supposes to be a toy pistol and says, "You have got to die." Dan, who has been irritated beyond endurance by Peter's merry japes, responds by throwing his heavy inkstand which hits Peter on the head and kills him. Full of remorse, Dan phones the police and tells them that he has killed a man simply for playing a practical joke on him. But when the police examine the pistol they find that it is a real one and loaded. Further, they find a note in Peter's room, stating that he is going to kill Dan, whom he detests, and then commit suicide. If Dan had not thrown the inkstand, it appears likely that he would have been shot dead. If Dan is charged with murder or manslaughter, can he successfully claim that he was acting in self-defence? Can he rely on unknown circumstances of justification or excuse?

Under the Model Penal Code (and probably under existing American law) a necessary condition for claiming self-defense is that the defendant actually believed in the necessity to use defensive force. See Wayne LaFave & Austin Scott, Criminal Law 458 (2d ed. 1986). Is that a sound position? If the theory of self-defense is excuse, that is, that a reasonable person who believes that his life is about to be taken by another can't be expected simply to permit it to happen, then obviously he should not be permitted to claim self-defense because the condition for the excuse, his belief, is not present. But if the theory of self-defense is that it is right to do as the defendant did under the circumstances, why should it be thought less right because he was unaware of his right? Wasn't it still a good thing that the aggressor should be stopped from killing an innocent person? And isn't that just what the defendant did? For discussion of these issues see the exchange of views in Paul Robinson, A Theory of Justification: Societal Harm as a Prerequisite for Criminal Liability, 23 U.C.L.A.L. Rev. 266 (1975), and George Fletcher, The Right Deed for the Wrong Reason: A Reply to Mr. Robinson, 23 U.C.L.A.L. Rev. 293 (1975). See also G. R. Sullivan, Bad Thoughts and Bad Acts, [1990] Crim. L. Rev. 559; Glanville Williams, Offences and Defences, 2 Leg. Stud.: J. Socy. Pub. Teach L. 233 (1982).

UNITED STATES v. PETERSON

United States Court of Appeals, District of Columbia Circuit
483 F.2d 1222 (1973)

ROBINSON, J. Indicted for second-degree murder, and convicted by a jury of manslaughter as a lesser included offense, Bennie L. Peterson urges . . . reversal. . . . He complains . . . that the judge . . . erred in the instructions given the jury in relation to his claim that the homicide was committed in self-defense.

[The] error alleged was an instruction that the jury might consider whether Peterson was the aggressor in the altercation that immediately foreran the homicide. . . . After careful study of these arguments in light of the trial record, we affirm Peterson's conviction.

The events immediately preceding the homicide are not seriously in dispute. The version presented by the Government's evidence follows. Charles Keitt, the deceased, and two friends drove in Keitt's car to the alley in the rear of Peterson's house to remove the windshield wipers from the latter's wrecked car. While Keitt was doing so, Peterson came out of the house into the back yard to protest. After a verbal exchange, Peterson went back into the house, obtained a pistol, and returned to the yard. In the meantime, Keitt had reseated himself in his car, and he and his companions were about to leave.

Upon his reappearance in the yard, Peterson paused briefly to load the pistol. "If you move," he shouted to Keitt, "I will shoot." He walked to a point in the yard slightly inside a gate in the rear fence and, pistol in hand, said, "If you come in here I will kill you." Keitt alighted from his car, took a few steps toward Peterson and exclaimed, "What the hell do you think you are going to do with that?" Keitt then made an about-face, walked back to his car and got a lug wrench. With the wrench in a raised position, Keitt advanced toward Peterson, who stood with the pistol pointed toward him. Peterson warned Keitt not to "take another step" and, when Keitt continued onward shot him in the face from a distance of about ten feet. Death was apparently instantaneous. . . .

Peterson's complaint centers upon an instruction that the right to use deadly force in self-defense is not ordinarily available to one who provokes a conflict or is the aggressor in it. Mere words, the judge explained, do not constitute provocation or aggression; and if Peterson precipitated the altercation but thereafter withdrew from it in good faith and so informed Keitt by words or acts, he was justified in using deadly force to save himself from imminent danger or death or grave bodily harm. And, the judge added, even if Keitt was the aggressor and Peterson was justified in defending himself, he was not entitled to use any greater force than he had reasonable ground to believe and actually believed to be necessary for that purpose. Peterson contends that there was no evidence that he either caused or contributed to the conflict, and that the instructions on the topic could only [have] misled the jury.

It has long been accepted that one cannot support a claim of self-defense by a self-generated necessity to kill. The right of homicidal self-defense is granted only to those free from fault in the difficulty; it is denied to slayers who incite the fatal attack, encourage the fatal quarrel or otherwise promote the necessitous occasion for taking life. The fact that the deceased struck the first blow, fired the first shot or made the first menacing gesture does not legalize the self-defense claim if in fact the claimant was the actual provoker. In sum, one who is the aggressor in a conflict culminating in death cannot invoke the necessities of self-preservation. Only in the event that he communicates to his adversary his intent to withdraw and in good faith attempts to do so is he restored to his right of self-defense.

This body of doctrine traces its origin to the fundamental principle that a killing in self-defense is excusable only as a matter of genuine necessity. Quite obviously, a defensive killing is unnecessary if the occasion for it could have been averted, and the roots of that consideration run deep with us. . . .

In the case at bar, the trial judge's charge fully comported with these governing principles. The remaining question, then, is whether there was evidence to make them applicable to the case. A recapitulation of the proofs shows beyond peradventure that there was. . . .

The evidence is uncontradicted that when Peterson reappeared in the yard with his pistol, Keitt was about to depart the scene. . . . The uncontroverted fact that Keitt was leaving shows plainly that so far as he was concerned the confrontation was ended. It demonstrates just as plainly that even if he had previously been the aggressor, he no longer was.

Not so with Peterson, however, as the undisputed evidence made clear. Emerging from the house with the pistol, he paused in the yard to load it, and to command Keitt not to move. He then walked through the yard to the rear gate and, displaying his pistol, dared Keitt to come in, and threatened to kill him if he did. While there appears to be no fixed rule on the subject, the cases hold, and we agree, that an affirmative unlawful act reasonably calculated to produce an affray foreboding injurious or fatal consequences is an aggression which, unless renounced, nullifies the right of homicidal self-defense. We cannot escape the abiding conviction that the jury could readily find Peterson's challenge to be a transgression of that character.

The situation at bar is not unlike that presented in *Laney*. [294 Fed. 412 (1923)] There the accused, chased along the street by a mob threatening his life, managed to escape through an areaway between two houses. In the back yard of one of the houses, he checked a gun he was carrying and then returned to the areaway. The mob beset him again, and during an exchange of shots one of its members was killed by a bullet from the accused's gun. In affirming a conviction of manslaughter, the court reasoned: "It is clearly apparent . . . that, when defendant escaped from the mob into the back yard . . . he was in a place of comparative safety, from which, if he desired to go home, he could have gone by the back way, as he subsequently did. The mob had turned its attention to a house on the opposite side of the street. According to Laney's testimony, there was shooting going on in the street. His appearance on the street at that juncture could mean nothing but trouble for him. Hence, when he adjusted his gun and stepped out into the areaway, he had every reason to believe that his presence there would provoke trouble. We think his conduct in adjusting his revolver and going into the areaway was such as to deprive him of any right to invoke the plea of self-defense."

Similarly, in Rowe v. United States, 370 F.2d 240 (D.C. Cir. 1966)] the accused was in the home of friends when an argument, to which the friends became participants, developed in the street in front. He left, went to his nearby apartment for a loaded pistol and returned. There was testimony that he then made an insulting comment, drew the pistol and fired a shot into the ground. In any event, when a group of five men began to move toward him, he began to shoot at them, killing two, and wounding a third. We observed that the accused "left an apparently safe haven to arm himself and return to the scene," and that "he inflamed the situation with his words to the men gathered there, even though he could have returned silently to the safety of the [friends'] porch." We held that "[t]hese facts could have led the jury to conclude that [the accused] returned to the scene to stir up further trouble, if not actually to kill anyone, and that his actions instigated the men into rushing him. Self-defense may not be claimed by one who deliberately places himself in a position where he has reason to believe "his presence . . . would provoke trouble." We noted the argument "that a defendant may claim self-defense if he arms himself in order to proceed upon his normal activities, even if he realizes that danger may await him"; we responded by pointing out "that the jury could have found that the course of action defendant here followed was for an unlawful purpose." We accordingly affirmed his conviction of manslaughter over his objection that an acquittal should have been directed.

We are brought much the readier to the same conclusion here. We think the evidence plainly presented an issue of fact as to whether Peterson's conduct was an invitation to and provocation of the encounter which ended in the fatal shot. We sustain the trial judge's action in remitting that issue for the jury's determination.

NOTES AND QUESTIONS

1. How far should the doctrine that fault forfeits self-defense be extended? Suppose Uriah catches David in flagrante delicto with Uriah's wife. Uriah, enraged, tries to kill David. Can David defend himself with deadly force, or has David lost his right of self-defense, having become, in a way, the aggressor by offering this provocation to Uriah? The traditional answer was that David could not use deadly force. See Dabney v. State, 21 So. 211 (1897). However, recent cases addressing the issue have rejected this view. See Atkins v. State, 339 S.E.2d 782 (Ga. 1986); Annot., 9 A.L.R.3d 93 (1966).

2. The traditional common law approach reflected in *Peterson* differs from the approach of the Model Penal Code, §3.04. The Comments to this provision, Model Penal Code and Commentaries, Comment to §3.04 at 49-51 (1985), state:

Use of Protective Force by Initial Aggressor. Subsection (2)(b)(i) denies justification for the use of deadly force if the actor, with the purpose of causing death or serious bodily harm, provoked the use of force against himself in the same encounter. This is a narrower forfeiture of the privilege of self-defense than commonly obtains in cases where a justification is claimed by an initial aggressor or after an agreement to fight. It was believed, however, that it is sufficient to resolve the problem, in view of the adoption in Subsection (2)(b)(ii) of a general duty to retreat before resorting to deadly force.

The typical case to be imagined is this: *A* attacks *B* with his fists; *B* defends himself, and manages to subdue *A* to the extent of pinning him to the floor. *B* then starts to batter *A*'s head savagely against the floor. *A* manages to rise, and since *B* is still attacking him and *A* now fears that if he is thrown again to the floor he will be killed, *A* uses a knife. *B* is killed or seriously wounded.

The solution to this situation under the provisions of this section is as follows: *B* is entitled to defend himself against *A*'s attack, but only to the extent of using moderate, nondeadly force. He is given this privilege by Subsection (1). *B* exceeds the bounds of "necessary" force under that provision, however, when, after reducing *A* to helplessness, he batters *A*'s head on the floor. Since this excessive force is, in its turn, unlawful, under Subsection (1) *A* is entitled to defend himself against it and, if he believes that he is then in danger of death or serious bodily harm without apparent opportunity for safe retreat, *A* is also entitled to use his knife in self-protection. *A* of course is criminally liable for his initial battery on *B*, but would have a justifying defense that he could raise against prosecution for the ultimate homicide or wounding. Subsection (2)(b)(i), depriving *A* of his justification on the ground of initial aggression, would not become operative unless *A* entered the encounter with the purpose of causing death or serious bodily harm. . . .

So long as the assailant's victim employs moderate force in self-protection, it is not unlawful; the original assailant cannot, therefore, claim a privilege for a response in kind. The problem arises only when the victim goes beyond the necessity by answering moderate force with deadly force. If in such a case there is no opportunity for withdrawal and safe retreat, the fact of the original minor aggression does not warrant the denial of a privilege to defend against deadly force; the initial aggressor can and ought to be convicted of assault.

2.   *Protection of Property and Law Enforcement*

PEOPLE v. CEBALLOS

Supreme Court of California
12 Cal. 3d 470, 526 P.2d 241 (1974)

BURKE, J. Don Ceballos was found guilty by a jury of assault with a deadly weapon (Pen. Code, §245). Imposition of sentence was suspended and he was placed on probation. . . .

Defendant lived alone in a home in San Anselmo. The regular living quarters were above the garage, but defendant sometimes slept in the garage and had about $2,000 worth of property there.

In March 1970 some tools were stolen from defendant's home. On May 12, 1970, he noticed the lock on his garage doors was bent and pry marks were on one of the doors. The next day he mounted a loaded .22 caliber pistol in the garage. The pistol was aimed at the center of the garage doors and was connected by a wire to one of the doors so that the pistol would discharge if the door was opened several inches.

The damage to defendant's lock had been done by a 16-year-old boy named Stephen and a 15-year-old boy named Robert. On the afternoon of May 15, 1970, the boys returned to defendant's house while he was away. Neither boy was armed with a gun or knife. After looking in the windows and seeing no one, Stephen succeeded in removing the lock on the garage doors with a crowbar, and, as he pulled the door outward, he was hit in the face with a bullet from the pistol.

Stephen testified: He intended to go into the garage "[f]or musical equipment" because he had a debt to pay to a friend. His "way of paying that debt would be to take [defendant's] property and sell it" and use the proceeds to pay the debt. He "wasn't going to do it [i.e., steal] for sure, necessarily." He was there "to look around," and "getting in, I don't know if I would have actually stolen."

Defendant, testifying in his own behalf, admitted having set up the trap gun. He stated that after noticing the pry marks on his garage door on May 12, he felt he should "set up some kind of a trap, something to keep the burglar out of my home." When asked why he was trying to keep the burglar out, he replied, ". . . Because somebody was trying to steal my property . . . and I don't want to come home some night and have the thief in there . . . usually a thief is pretty desperate . . . and . . . they just pick up a weapon . . . if they don't have one . . . and do the best they can."

When asked by the police shortly after the shooting why he assembled the trap gun, defendant stated that "he didn't have much and he wanted to protect what he did have."

[T]he jury found defendant guilty of assault with a deadly weapon. An assault is "an unlawful attempt, coupled with a present ability, to commit a violent injury on the person of another." (Pen. Code, §240.)

Defendant contends that had he been present he would have been justified in shooting Stephen since Stephen was attempting to commit burglary, that under cases such as United States v. Gilliam, 25 Fed. Cas. p. 1319, No. 15, 205a, defendant had a right to do indirectly what he could have done directly, and that therefore any attempt by him to commit a violent injury upon Stephen was not "unlawful" and hence not an assault. The People argue that the rule in *Gilliam* is unsound, that as a matter of law a trap gun constitutes excessive force, and that in any event the circumstances were not in fact such as to warrant the use of deadly force. . . .

In the United States, courts have concluded that a person may be held criminally liable under statutes proscribing homicides and shooting with intent to injure, or civilly liable, if he sets upon his premises a deadly mechanical device and that device kills or injures another. . . . However, an exception to the rule that there may be criminal and civil liability for death or injuries caused by such a device has been recognized where the intrusion is, in fact, such that the person, were he present, would be justified in taking the life or inflicting the bodily harm with his own hands. . . .

Allowing persons, at their own risk, to employ deadly mechanical devices imperils the lives of children, firemen and policemen acting within the scope of their employment, and others. Where the actor is present, there is always the possibility he will realize that deadly force is not necessary, but deadly mechanical devices are without mercy or discretion. Such devices "are silent instrumentalities of death. They deal death and destruction to the innocent as well as the criminal intruder without the slightest warning. The taking of human life [or infliction of great bodily injury] by such means is brutally savage and inhuman." (See State v. Plumlee, . . . 149 So. 425, 430).

It seems clear that the use of such devices should not be encouraged. Moreover, whatever may be thought in torts, the foregoing rule setting forth an exception to liability for death or injuries inflicted by such devices "is inappropriate in penal law for it is obvious that it does not prescribe a workable standard of conduct; liability depends upon fortuitous results." (See Model Penal Code (Tent. Draft No. 8), §3.06, com. 15.) We therefore decline to adopt that rule in criminal cases.

Furthermore, even if that rule were applied here, as we shall see, defendant was not justified in shooting Stephen. Penal Code section 197 provides:

> Homicide is . . . justifiable . . . 1. When resisting any attempt to murder any person, or to commit a felony, or to do some great bodily injury upon any person; or, 2. When committed in defense of habitation, property, or person, against one who manifestly intends or endeavors, by violence or surprise, to commit a felony. . . .

Since a homicide is justifiable under the circumstances specified in section 197, a fortiori an attempt to commit a violent injury upon another under those circumstances is justifiable.

By its terms subdivision 1 of Penal Code section 197 appears to permit killing to prevent any "felony," but in view of the large number of felonies today and the inclusion of many that do not involve a danger of serious bodily harm, a literal reading of the section is undesirable. People v. Jones, 191 Cal. App. 2d 478, 481, in rejecting the defendant's theory that her husband was about to commit the felony of beating her (Pen. Code §273d) [a] and that therefore her killing him to prevent him from doing so was justifiable, stated that Penal Code section 197 "does no more than codify the common law and should be read in light of it." *Jones* read into section 197, subdivision 1, the limitation that the felony be "some atrocious crime attempted to be committed by force." *Jones* further stated, "the punishment provided by a statute is not necessarily an adequate test as to whether life may be taken for in some situations it is too artificial and unrealistic. We must look further into the character of the crime and the manner of its perpetration. . . . *When these do not reasonably create a fear of great bodily harm,* as they could not if defendant apprehended only a misdemeanor assault, *there is no cause for the exaction of a human life.*" (Italics added. . . .)

Jones involved subdivision 1 of Penal Code section 197, but subdivision 2 of that section is likewise so limited. The term "violence or surprise" in subdivision 2 is found in common law authorities . . . and, whatever may have been the very early common law . . . the rule developed at common law that killing or use of deadly force to prevent a felony was justified only if the offense was a forcible and atrocious crime. . . . "Surprise" means an unexpected attack — which includes force and violence . . . and the word thus appears redundant.

Examples of forcible and atrocious crimes are murder, mayhem, rape and robbery. . . . In such crimes "from their atrocity and violence human life [or personal safety from great harm] either is, or is presumed to be, in peril" (see United States v. Gilliam, supra, 25 Fed. Cas. pp. 1319, 1320 . . .).

Burglary has been included in the list of such crimes. . . . However, in view of the wide scope of burglary under Penal Code section 459, as compared with the common law definition of that offense, in our opinion it cannot be said that under all circumstances burglary under section 459 constitutes a forcible and atrocious crime.[2]

Where the character and manner of the burglary do not reasonably create a fear of great bodily harm, there is no cause for exaction of human life . . . or for the use of deadly force. The character and manner of the burglary could not reasonably create such a fear unless the burglary threatened, or was reasonably believed to threaten, death or serious bodily harm.

---

a. She relied on a statutory amendment that raised a simple assault from a misdemeanor to a felony where committed by a husband upon his wife. — EDS.

2. A common law burglary was the breaking and entering of a mansion house in the night with the intent to commit a felony. . . . Burglary under Penal Code section 459 differs from common law burglary in that the entry may be in the daytime and of numerous places other than a mansion house . . . and breaking is not required. . . . For example, under section 459 a person who enters a store with the intent of committing theft is guilty of burglary. . . . It would seem absurd to hold that a store detective could kill that person if necessary to prevent him from committing that offense. . . .

In the instant case the asserted burglary did not threaten death or serious bodily harm, since no one but Stephen and Robert was then on the premises. A defendant is not protected from liability merely by the fact that the intruder's conduct is such as would justify the defendant, were he present, in believing that the intrusion threatened death or serious bodily injury. . . .

We thus conclude that defendant was not justified under Penal Code section 197, subdivisions 1 or 2, in shooting Stephen to prevent him from committing burglary. . . .

We recognize that our position regarding justification for killing under Penal Code section 197, subdivisions 1 and 2, differs from the position of section 143, subdivision (2), of the Restatement Second of Torts, regarding the use of deadly force to prevent a "felony . . . of a type . . . involving the breaking and entry of a dwelling place" . . . but in view of the supreme value of human life, we do not believe deadly force can be justified to prevent all felonies of the foregoing type, including ones in which no person is, or is reasonably believed to be, on the premises except the would-be burglar.

Defendant also argues that had he been present he would have been justified in shooting Stephen under subdivision 4 of Penal Code section 197, which provides, "Homicide is . . . justifiable . . . 4. When necessarily committed in *attempting*, by lawful ways and means, to *apprehend* any person for any felony committed. . . ." (Italics added.) The argument cannot be upheld. The words "attempting . . . to apprehend" contain the idea of acting for the purpose of apprehending. . . . Here no showing was made that defendant's intent in shooting was to apprehend a felon. Rather it appears from his testimony and extra-judicial statement heretofore recited that his intent was to prevent a burglary, to protect his property, and to avoid the possibility that a thief might get into defendant's house and injure him upon his return. . . .

Defendant also does not, and could not properly, contend that the intrusion was in fact such that, were he present, he would be justified under Civil Code section 50 in using deadly force. That section provides, "Any necessary force may be used to protect from wrongful injury the person or property of oneself. . . ." This section also should be read in the light of the common law, and at common law in general deadly force could not be used solely for the protection of property. . . . "The preservation of human life and limb from grievous harm is of more importance to society than the protection of property." (Commonwealth v. Emmons, 157 Pa. Super. 495, 43 A.2d 568, 569.) Thus defendant was not warranted under Civil Code section 50 in using deadly force to protect his personal property. . . .

At common law an exception to the foregoing principle that deadly force could not be used solely for the protection of property was recognized where the property was a dwelling house in some circumstances. "According to the older interpretation of the common law, even extreme force may be used to prevent dispossession [of the dwelling house]." (Model Penal Code, Tent. Draft No. 8 (1958), Comment at pp. 48-51.) Also at common law if another attempted to burn a dwelling the owner was privileged to use deadly force if this seemed necessary to defend his "castle" against the threatened harm. Further, deadly force was privileged if it was, or reasonably seemed, necessary to protect the dwelling against a burglar.

Here we are not concerned with dispossession or burning of a dwelling, and, as heretofore concluded, the asserted burglary in this case was not of such a character as to warrant the use of deadly force.

We conclude that as a matter of law the exception to the rule of liability for injuries inflicted by a deadly mechanical device does not apply under the circumstances here appearing. . . .

The judgment is affirmed.

NOTE: TWO STATUTORY SCHEMES

Compare the following Model Penal Code and New York provisions governing the use of deadly force in the protection of property and habitation and the prevention of crime.

Model Penal Code: Section 3.04(2)(b). Use of Force in Self-Protection [see Appendix for text of this section].

Section 3.05(1). Use of Force for the Protection of Other Persons [see Appendix for text of this section].

Section 3.06(3)(d). Use of Force for the Protection of Property [see Appendix for text of this section].

Section 307(5). Use of Force in Law Enforcement [see Appendix for text of this section].

New York Penal Law: Section 35.15. Justification; Use of Physical Force in Defense of a Person. 1. A person may, subject to the provisions of subdivision two, use physical force upon another person when and to the extent he reasonably believes such to be necessary to defend himself or a third person from what he reasonably believes to be the use or imminent use of unlawful physical force by such other person, unless: . . .

2. A person may not use deadly physical force upon another person under circumstances specified in subdivision one unless:

(a) He reasonably believes that such other person is using or about to use deadly physical force. . . .[a]

(b) He reasonably believes that such other person is committing or attempting to commit a kidnapping, forcible rape, forcible sodomy[b] or robbery; or

(c) He reasonably believes that such other person is committing or attempting to commit a burglary, and the circumstances are such that the use of deadly physical force is authorized by subdivision three of section 35.20.

Section 35.20. Justification; Use of Physical Force in Defense of Premises and in Defense of a Person in the Course of Burglary. 1. . . .

---

a. Subject to a duty to retreat modeled on the Model Penal Code §3.04(2)(b). — Eds.

b. A similar Maine statute uses the term *forcible sex offense.* In State v. Philbrick, 402 A.2d 59 (1979), the Maine Supreme Court held that this statute justified defendant in killing in order to prevent a person who forcibly fondled defendant's crotch from doing so again, so long as defendant reasonably believed his action was necessary to prevent a repetition of that offense.

Question: Who was at fault, the legislature or the court? — Eds.

2. A person in possession or control of any premises, or a person licensed or privileged to be thereon or therein, may use physical force upon another person when he reasonably believes such to be necessary to prevent or terminate what he reasonably believes to be the commission or attempted commission by such other person of a criminal trespass upon such premises. He may use any degree of physical force, other than deadly physical force, which he reasonably believes to be necessary for such purpose, and he may use deadly physical force in order to prevent or terminate the commission or attempted commission of arson, as prescribed in subdivision one, or in the course of a burglary or attempted burglary, as prescribed in subdivision three.

3. A person in possession or control of, or licensed or privileged to be in, a dwelling or an occupied building, who reasonably believes that another person is committing or attempting to commit a burglary of such dwelling or building, may use deadly physical force upon such other person when he reasonably believes such to be necessary to prevent or terminate the commission or attempted commission of such burglary.

Section 35.25. Justification; Use of Physical Force to Prevent or Terminate Larceny or Criminal Mischief. A person may use physical force, other than deadly physical force, upon another person when and to the extent that he reasonably believes such to be necessary to prevent or terminate what he reasonably believes to be the commission or attempted commission by such other person of larceny or of criminal mischief with respect to property other than premises.

PROBLEM

Consider the statutes presented above in light of the story of the shooting of Yoshihiro Hattori, widely covered by the press. See, e.g., N.Y. Times, May 23, 1993, at A1, and May 20, 1993, at A10.

On the night of October 17, 1992, Rodney Peairs, a manager at a Baton Rouge meat market, killed Yoshihiro Hattori, a 16-year-old Japanese exchange student. He and a friend were looking for a Halloween party, and he was dressed in a "Saturday Night Fever" costume. He mistakenly rang Mr. Peairs' doorbell, and when Mrs. Peairs came to the door and saw them, she became frightened and screamed. Apparently neither Hattori nor his friend could speak enough English to reassure her. At this point Peairs grabbed his laser-scoped .44-magnum handgun from his bedroom and went to the carport door. The two boys had retreated to the sidewalk, but when the carport door opened, Hattori began walking towards Peairs, waving his arms as he often did when trying to communicate. Peairs yelled "freeze," but Hattori did not understand him. Hattori continued forward; he had recently lost a contact lens and presumably did not see the gun. When Hattori was less than five feet away Mr. Peairs fired one shot into his chest. Only a few minutes had passed between the time the doorbell rang, and the time Peairs shot Hattori.

Rodney Peairs was indicted for manslaughter, but he claimed that the shooting, though mistaken, was justified under La. Rev. Stat. Ann. §14:20(3), which allows the use of deadly force based on a reasonable belief that an intruder is "likely to use any unlawful force against a person [in the dwelling] while committing . . . a burglary of that dwelling. . . ." Peairs' lawyer argued that Peairs saw an intruder who was grinning, and who kept advancing "with absolutely no respect for [Peairs'] home, his gun, or his warning." During closing arguments, Peairs' lawyer proclaimed "You have the absolute legal right in this country to answer your door with a gun. In your house, if you want to do it, you have the legal right to answer everybody that comes to your door with a gun." The prosecutor emphasized the fact that Peairs acted without investigating why his wife screamed; Peairs' alleged negligence was "his conduct in going to the closet and getting the biggest handgun made by human beings and never ever asking what it's for." After a seven-day trial and three hours of deliberation, Peairs was acquitted. The acquittal sparked outrage in Japan where owning a handgun is illegal (with minor exceptions), but many people in Peairs' community supported his actions.

In a subsequent development a judge in a civil case found "no justification whatsoever" for the shooting and awarded the estate of Mr. Hattori $650,000 in damages against Mr. Peairs. N.Y. Times, Sept. 16, 1994, at A7.

DURHAM v. STATE

Supreme Court of Indiana
199 Ind. 567, 159 N.E. 145 (1927)

[Defendant, a deputy game warden, arrested one Long for illegal fishing. Long jumped into his boat in an attempt to escape. Defendant pursued him, grabbing first the gunwale and then the anchor chain. While Long was beating defendant about the head with an oar, defendant shot him in the arm. Defendant was convicted of assault and battery and appealed.]

MARTIN, J. . . . Instruction 12 was to the effect that, if Long resisted arrest, appellant would not be authorized to use such force and instrumentalities as would imperil the life of Long in order to overcome his resistance; that human life is too precious to be imperiled by the arrest of one who is only guilty of a misdemeanor; that, if appellant, in order to overcome Long's resistance, used a dangerous and deadly weapon, and in such manner as to endanger his life, and thereby inflict serious wounds, then the appellant would be guilty of assault and battery, at least. This instruction, standing alone, or considered in conjunction with instruction 15 and the other instructions, did not correctly state the law, and the court erred in giving it.

Our general statutes concerning arrests, and applicable to all classes of criminal cases, provide that:

"The defendant shall not be subject to any more restraint than is necessary for his arrest and detention." Section 2157, Burns' 1926.

"If, after notice of the intention to arrest the defendant, he either flees or forcibly resists, the officer may use all necessary means to effect the arrest." Section 2159, Burns' 1926.

In Plummer v. State (1893) 135 Ind. 308, 34 N.E. 968, the court said:

"The law does not allow a peace officer to use more force than is necessary to effect an arrest. And if he does use such unnecessary force, he . . . may be lawfully resisted. If the officer is resisted before he had used needless force and violence, he may then press forward and overcome such resistance, even to the taking of the life of the person arrested, if absolutely necessary."

The degree or limit of force that lawfully may be employed by an officer in arresting one charged with a misdemeanor (as distinguished from a felony) has been considered in a large number of cases in other jurisdictions. . . .

The general rules deduced therefrom may be stated to be: (a) That an officer having the right to arrest a misdemeanant may use all the force that is reasonably necessary to accomplish the arrest, except (b) that he may not, merely for the purpose of effecting the arrest, kill or inflict great bodily harm, endangering the life of the misdemeanant. Thus an officer may not kill or shed blood in attempting to arrest a misdemeanant who is fleeing, but not resisting.[2] (c) That, if the defendant physically resists, the officer need not retreat but may press forward and repel the resistance with such force, short of taking life, as is necessary to effect the arrest; and, if in so doing the officer is absolutely obliged to seriously wound or take the life of the accused, in order to prevent the accused from seriously wounding, or killing him, he will be justified.[3] . . .

To adopt the rule contended for by the prosecution in the trial below, and stated by the court in instruction 12, would be to paralyze the strong arm of the law, and render the state powerless to use extreme force when extreme resistance is offered, and would permit misdemeanants to stay the power of the state by unlawful resistance.

"To say to a defendant, 'You may measure strength with the arresting officer, and avoid being taken if you are the stronger or after your arrest you may break away unless he can prevail over you in a wrestle,' is to elevate mere brute force to a position of command over the wheels of justice." 1 Bishop's Cr. Proc. (2d Ed.) §16. . . .

The judgment is reversed, with directions to sustain appellant's motion for a new trial, and for further proceedings not inconsistent herewith.

TENNESSEE v. GARNER

Supreme Court of the United States
471 U.S. 1 (1985)

WHITE, J., delivered the opinion of the Court.

This case requires us to determine the constitutionality of the use of deadly force to prevent the escape of an apparently unarmed suspected felon. We conclude that such force may not be used unless it is necessary to prevent the escape and the officer has probable cause to believe that the suspect poses a significant threat of death or serious physical injury to the officer or others.

At about 10:45 P.M. on October 3, 1974, Memphis Police Officers Elton Hymon and Leslie Wright were dispatched to answer a "prowler inside call." Upon arriving at the scene they saw a woman standing on her porch and gesturing

---

2. The most common examples of this class of cases are those where officers shoot at misdemeanants, their mounts, or their automobile tires, and wound or kill the misdemeanants. "To permit the life of one charged with a mere misdemeanor to be taken when fleeing from the officer would, aside from its inhumanity, be productive of more abuse than good. The law need not go unenforced. The officer can summon his posse, and take the offender." Head v. Martin (1887) 85 Ky. 480, 3 S.W. 622.

3. [T]he protection which an officer is entitled to receive in making an arrest is a different thing from self-defense, for it is his duty to push forward and make the arrest and to secure and retain custody of the prisoner. . . .

toward the adjacent house. She told them she had heard glass breaking and that "they" or "someone" was breaking in next door. While Wright radioed the dispatcher to say that they were on the scene, Hymon went behind the house. He heard a door slam and saw someone run across the back yard. The fleeing suspect, who was appellee-respondent's decedent, Edward Garner, stopped at a 6-feet-high chain link fence at the edge of the yard. With the aid of a flashlight, Hymon was able to see Garner's face and hands. He saw no sign of a weapon, and, though not certain, was "reasonably sure" and "figured" that Garner was unarmed. He thought Garner was 17 or 18 years old and about 5'5" or 5'7" tall.[2] While Garner was crouched at the base of the fence, Hymon called out "police, halt" and took a few steps toward him. Garner then began to climb over the fence. Convinced that if Garner made it over the fence he would elude capture,[3] Hymon shot him. The bullet hit Garner in the back of the head. Garner was taken by ambulance to a hospital, where he died on the operating table. Ten dollars and a purse taken from the house were found on his body.

In using deadly force to prevent the escape, Hymon was acting under the authority of a Tennessee statute and pursuant to Police Department policy. The statute provides that "[i]f, after notice of the intention to arrest the defendant, he either flee or forcibly resist, the officer may use all the necessary means to effect the arrest." Tenn. Code Ann. §40-7-108 (1982).[5] The Department policy was slightly more restrictive than the statute, but still allowed the use of deadly force in cases of burglary. The incident was reviewed by the Memphis Police Firearm's Review Board and presented to a grand jury. Neither took any action.

Garner's father then brought this action in the Federal District Court for the Western District of Tennessee, seeking damages under 42 U.S.C. §1983 for asserted violations of Garner's constitutional rights. . . . [T]he district court entered judgment for all defendants. . . . The Court of Appeals reversed and remanded. It reasoned that the killing of a fleeing suspect is a "seizure" under the Fourth Amendment,[6] and is therefore constitutional only if "reasonable." . . .[7] The State of Tennessee, which had intervened to defend the statute, appealed to this Court. . . .

---

2. In fact, Garner, an eighth-grader, was 15. He was 5'4" tall and weighed somewhere around 100 or 110 pounds.

3. When asked at trial why he fired, Hymon stated:

Well, first of all it was apparent to me from the little bit that I knew about the area at the time that he was going to get away because, number 1, I couldn't get to him. My partner then couldn't find where he was because, you know, he was late coming around. He didn't know where I was talking about. I couldn't get to him because of the fence here, I couldn't have jumped this fence and come up, consequently jumped this fence and caught him before he got away because he was already up on the fence, just one leap and he was already over the fence, and so there is no way that I could have caught him.

He also stated that the area beyond the fence was dark, that he could not have gotten over the fence easily because he was carrying a lot of equipment and wearing heavy boots, and that Garner, being younger and more energetic, could have outrun him.

5. Although the statute does not say so explicitly, Tennessee law forbids the use of deadly force in the arrest of a misdemeanant.

6. "The right of the people to be secure in their persons . . . against unreasonable searches and seizures, shall not be violated. . . . " U.S. Const., Amdt. 4.

7. The Court of Appeals concluded that the rule set out in the Model Penal Code "accurately states Fourth Amendment limitations on the use of deadly force against fleeing felons." . . .

Whenever an officer restrains the freedom of a person to walk away, he has seized that person. While it is not always clear just when minimal police interference becomes a seizure, there can be no question that apprehension by the use of deadly force is a seizure subject to the reasonableness requirement of the Fourth Amendment.

A police officer may arrest a person if he has probable cause to believe that person committed a crime. Petitioners and appellant argue that if this requirement is satisfied the Fourth Amendment has nothing to say about *how* that seizure is made. This submission ignores the many cases in which this Court, by balancing the extent of the intrusion against the need for it, has examined the reasonableness of the manner in which a search or seizure is conducted. . . .

[N]otwithstanding probable cause to seize a suspect, an officer may not always do so by killing him. The intrusiveness of a seizure by means of deadly force is unmatched. The suspect's fundamental interest in his own life need not be elaborated upon. The use of deadly force also frustrates the interest of the individual, and of society, in judicial determination of guilt and punishment. Against these interests are ranged governmental interests in effective law enforcement. It is argued that overall violence will be reduced by encouraging the peaceful submission of suspects who know that they may be shot if they flee. . . . "Being able to arrest such individuals is a condition precedent to the state's entire system of law enforcement."

Without in any way disparaging the importance of these goals, we are not convinced that the use of deadly force is a sufficiently productive means of accomplishing them to justify the killing of nonviolent suspects. . . . [W]hile the meaningful threat of deadly force might be thought to lead to the arrest of more live suspects by discouraging escape attempts, the presently available evidence does not support this thesis. The fact is that a majority of police departments in this country have forbidden the use of deadly force against nonviolent suspects. If those charged with the enforcement of the criminal law have abjured the use of deadly force in arresting nondangerous felons, there is a substantial basis for doubting that the use of such force is an essential attribute of the arrest power in all felony cases. . . .

The use of deadly force to prevent the escape of all felony suspects, whatever the circumstances, is constitutionally unreasonable. It is not better that all felony suspects die than that they escape. It is no doubt unfortunate when a suspect who is in sight escapes, but the fact that the police arrive a little late or are a little slower afoot does not always justify killing the suspect. A police officer may not seize an unarmed, nondangerous suspect by shooting him dead. The Tennessee statute is unconstitutional insofar as it authorizes the use of deadly force against such fleeing suspects.

It is not, however, unconstitutional on its face. Where the officer has probable cause to believe that the suspect poses a threat of serious physical harm, either to the officer or to others, it is not constitutionally unreasonable to prevent escape by using deadly force. Thus, if the suspect threatens the officer with a weapon or there is probable cause to believe that he has committed a crime involving the infliction or threatened infliction of serious physical harm, deadly force may be used if necessary to prevent escape, and if, where feasible, some warning has been given. As applied in such circumstances, the Tennessee statute would pass constitutional muster.

It is insisted that the Fourth Amendment must be construed in light of the common-law rule, which allowed the use of whatever force was necessary to effect the arrest of a fleeing felon, though not a misdemeanant. . . . Because of sweeping change in the legal and technological context, reliance on the common-law rule in this case would be a mistaken literalism that ignores the purposes of a historical inquiry.

It has been pointed out many times that the common-law rule is best understood in light of the fact that it arose at a time when virtually all felonies were punishable by death. . . . Courts have also justified the common-law rule by emphasizing the relative dangerousness of felons.

Neither of these justifications makes sense today. Almost all crimes formerly punishable by death no longer are or can be. . . . Many crimes classified as misdemeanors . . . at common law are now felonies. These changes have . . . made the assumption that a "felon" is more dangerous than a misdemeanant untenable. Indeed, numerous misdemeanors involve conduct more dangerous than many felonies. . . .

In reversing, the Court of Appeals accepted the District Court's factual conclusions and held that "the facts, as found, did not justify the use of deadly force." We agree. Officer Hymon could not reasonably have believed that Garner — young, slight, and unarmed — posed any threat. Indeed, Hymon never attempted to justify his actions on any basis other than the need to prevent an escape. . . .

The dissent argues that the shooting was justified by the fact that Officer Hymon had probable cause to believe that Garner had committed a nighttime burglary. While we agree that burglary is a serious crime, we cannot agree that it is so dangerous as automatically to justify the use of deadly force. . . . Although the armed burglar would present a different situation, the fact that an unarmed suspect has broken into a dwelling at night does not automatically mean he is physically dangerous. This case demonstrates as much. In fact, the available statistics demonstrate that burglaries only rarely involve physical violence. During the 10-year period from 1973-1982, only 3.8 percent of all burglaries involved violent crime. Bureau of Justice Statistics, Household Burglary, p. 4 (1985). . . .

The judgment of the Court of Appeals is affirmed. . . .

O'CONNOR, J., with whom THE CHIEF JUSTICE and REHNQUIST, J., join, dissenting. . . .

The clarity of hindsight cannot provide the standard for judging the reasonableness of police decisions made in uncertain and often dangerous circumstances. . . .

The public interest involved in the use of deadly force as a last resort to apprehend a fleeing burglary suspect relates primarily to the serious nature of the crime. Household burglaries represent not only the illegal entry into a person's home, but also "pos[e] real risk of serious harm to others." Solem v. Helm, 463 U.S. 277, 315-316 (1983) (Burger, C.J., dissenting). . . . Victims of a forcible intrusion into their home by a nighttime prowler will find little consolation in the majority's confident assertion that "burglaries only rarely involve physical violence." Moreover, even if a particular burglary, when viewed in retrospect, does not involve physical harm to others, the "harsh potentialities for violence" inherent in the forced entry into a home preclude characterization of the crime as "innocuous, inconsequential, minor, or 'nonviolent.'" Solem v. Helm, supra, at 316 (Burger, C.J., dissenting).

Because burglary is a serious and dangerous felony, the public interest in the prevention and detection of the crime is of compelling importance. Where a police officer has probable cause to arrest a suspected burglar, the use of deadly force as a last resort might well be the only means of apprehending the suspect. . . . Although some law enforcement agencies may choose to assume the risk that a criminal will remain at large, the Tennessee statute reflects a legislative determination that the use of deadly force in prescribed circumstances will serve generally to protect the public. . . .

The majority declares that "[t]he suspect's fundamental interest in his own life need not be elaborated upon." . . . Without questioning the importance of a person's interest in his life, I do not think this interest encompasses a right to flee unimpeded from the scene of a burglary. . . . The legitimate interests of the suspect in these circumstances are adequately accommodated by the Tennessee statute: to avoid the use of deadly force and the consequent risk to his life, the suspect need merely obey the valid order to halt. . . .

The Court's silence on critical factors in the decision to use deadly force invites second-guessing of difficult police . . . decisions that must be made quickly in the most trying of circumstances. Police are given no guidance for determining which objects, among an array of potentially lethal weapons ranging from guns to knives to baseball bats to rope, will justify the use of deadly force. The Court also declines to outline the additional factors necessary to provide "probable cause" for believing that a suspect "poses a significant threat of death or serious physical injury." . . .

Whatever the constitutional limits on police use of deadly force in order to apprehend a fleeing felon, I do not believe they are exceeded in a case in which a police officer has probable cause to arrest a suspect at the scene of a residential burglary, orders the suspect to halt, and then fires his weapon as a last resort to prevent the suspect's escape into the night. I respectfully dissent.

UNITED STATES v. HILLSMAN

United States Court of Appeals, 7th Circuit
522 F.2d 454 (1975)

PELL, J. The defendants James Hillsman and Clinton Bush were convicted by a jury of assaulting a federal officer, in violation of 18 U.S.C. §111. On appeal, the defendants contend that . . . the district court erred in refusing to instruct the jury that if the defendants reasonably believed the federal officer to be a fleeing felon, the defendants should be acquitted. . . .

On February 8, 1974, the defendants, along with two to three hundred other persons, attended a funeral in Gary, Indiana. Several agents of the Drug Enforcement Administration were conducting undercover surveillance at the funeral home for the purpose of observing and identifying suspected narcotics dealers. All of the agents involved in the surveillance wore ordinary "street" clothes and drove unmarked cars.

Agent David Munson, who was equipped with a video tape camera, stationed himself outside the funeral home alongside photographers from a Gary newspaper and began filming the mourners as they left the funeral home. Most of the several hundred mourners at the funeral home (including the defendants) were black and a group of the black mourners demanded that Munson, who is white, cease taking pictures and leave the area. One member of the crowd, William Hanyard, began shoving and hitting Munson when he continued to film the mourners. The defendants Hillsman and Bush were not identified as being in any way involved in the verbal or physical exchange with Munson.

Agent Kenneth Rhodes, the acting agent in charge of the DEA in the area, was approximately six feet from Munson at this time and observed Hanyard's attack on the agent. Intending to shoot Hanyard, Rhodes, who is black, drew his revolver and began to assume the "combat position." However, before he was able to get into this position, Rhodes either stepped back or was pushed from the rear and his gun discharged prematurely. The bullet merely grazed Hanyard but struck and killed Albert Griffin, an innocent bystander.

Immediately after the shot was fired, Rhodes announced that he was a federal agent and told Munson, "Let's get out of here." Although Munson heard the later statement, he did not hear Rhodes announce that he was a federal officer. Rhodes and Munson then moved to their cars. . . .

As Rhodes was moving toward his car, a woman in the crowd pointed at him and said, "He is the one; there he goes." A group of the mourners then began running after Rhodes. As Rhodes drove away, shots were fired at his car. One bullet struck the car but Rhodes himself was not injured.

Hillsman and Bush were identified as being members of the group that chased Rhodes and were observed firing weapons at Rhodes' car. . . .

With respect to the defendants' claim that they were only seeking to stop a person they believed to be a fleeing felon, the district court gave a lengthy instruction concerning the right of a private citizen to make an arrest. The court however, refused to give a defense instruction which provided: . . .

> If you find from the evidence that the Defendants . . . acted out of reasonable belief that Kenneth Rhodes was not a Federal Agent but instead was a private citizen who the Defendants . . . had reasonable cause to believe had committed a felony and was fleeing the scene in order to avoid apprehension, and that the Defendants . . . chased Kenneth Rhodes in order to stop his flight and detain him then you must find the Defendants . . . not guilty. . . .

[W]here a defendant charged with violating §111 claims that he was unaware that the victim was a federal officer, the question becomes: would the defendant have been justified, because of the agent's actions, in using force against the agent had the latter, in fact, been a "civilian." . . .

Since the incident would have been governed by Indiana law if Rhodes had been a private citizen, we look to the law of that state in making this determination.

Indiana follows the general common law rule that "a private citizen has the right to arrest one who has committed a felony in his presence, and may even arrest one he reasonably believes to have committed a felony, so long as the felony was in fact committed." . . .

The private citizen's right to make an arrest . . . is limited by the fact that he, unlike a police officer, acts at his own peril. . . . Hillsman and Bush would have been justified in making a citizen's arrest only if they reasonably believed that Rhodes had committed a felony *and* a felony had in fact been committed.

The instructions actually given to the jury . . . did adequately inform the jury of the requirements of a valid defense. . . . The trial court . . . accurately stated that although deadly force could be used to effect such an arrest in an appropriate case, no citizen's arrest would be valid unless a felony had in fact been committed. . . .

In addition, the district court instructed the jury with respect to the question of whether a felony had occurred when Rhodes shot Hanyard and Griffin. The jury was expressly told that if they found that a felony had occurred, then they could apply the law of citizen's arrest. The court admittedly instructed the jury with respect to only one type of felony, voluntary manslaughter.[7] This, however, was the only felony for which the defense requested an instruction and the defense does not contend on appeal that instructions on other felonies were necessary. Although it may be argued that a jury could have found that Rhodes committed a felony other than voluntary manslaughter, we cannot say that the district court's failure to instruct on other felonies, in the absence of any request by the defendant, was plain error requiring reversal. . . .

TONE, J. (concurring). . . . I am uncomfortable in holding a defendant criminally accountable for conduct which, we hypothesize for present purposes, he thought was not only lawful but socially desirable. . . . The defendants here were each sentenced to nine years' imprisonment. The severity of the sentences indicates that the judge did not believe that they were merely trying to apprehend a felon, but the jury might have found otherwise. . . . I concur . . . only because I believe [precedent] requires that result. If I were free to do so, I would hold otherwise.

MODEL PENAL CODE

SECTION 3.07(2)(b). USE OF FORCE IN LAW ENFORCEMENT

[See Appendix.]

MODEL PENAL CODE AND COMMENTARIES, COMMENT TO §3.07 AT 111-120 (1985):
The common law approach to the problem of deadly force in arrest was based on the distinction between felony and misdemeanor. Deadly force was authorized where necessary to prevent the escape of one fleeing from arrest for felony, but not for misdemeanor. . . .

The extreme breadth of the privilege apparently induced some courts and legislatures to limit its application in the very worst way — by imposing a rule of strict liability. Thus, the privilege was at times said to attach only when the deceased had in fact committed a felony, apart from all considerations of good faith and reasonable belief on the part of the arresting officer. In other jurisdictions, the rule appears to have required that a felony must in fact have been

---

7. The instruction stated:

The Crime of voluntary manslaughter is defined by statute in the State of Indiana as follows:
    "Whoever voluntarily kills any human being without malice, express or implied, in a sudden heat, is guilty of voluntary manslaughter."
    If, from the evidence, in this case you find that Kenneth Rhodes committed the crime of manslaughter in the presence of the defendants and was fleeing from the scene of the commission of said crime in order to avoid arrest and apprehension, then you may apply the law that a private individual may make a citizen's arrest of the fleeing felon.

committed, though the deceased need not have committed it if the officer reasonably believed that he did. Such a rule also creates the possibility of an absolute liability. Still other jurisdictions appeared to adhere to a rule of reasonable belief, but the law was in a state of considerable ambiguity and uncertainty on this vital point. . . .

Like the common law rule, Paragraph (i) of Subsection (2)(b) restricts the use of extreme force to arrests for felonies. . . . But unlike the common law rule, Subsection (2)(b) imposes certain additional qualifications on the privilege.

> First, the use of deadly force is restricted by Paragraph (ii) of Subsection (2)(b) to those who, under the law of the jurisdiction, are authorized to act as peace officers and to those who are assisting persons whom they believe are authorized to act as peace officers. Where the purpose to be served is the apprehension of persons to answer criminal charges, it has seemed important, in an age of firearms, to restrict the use of deadly force to situations where official personnel are involved, or at least are believed to be involved. . . .
>
> . . . Another difference between the common law and these provisions is stated in Paragraph (iii) of Subsection (2). It is there recognized that the public interest is poorly served if the use of deadly force creates a substantial risk of injury to innocent bystanders. The privilege is accordingly withheld unless the actor believes that there is no such risk. . . .
>
> The third way in which these provisions differ from the common law is contained in Paragraph (iv) of Subsection (2)(b), which is based on the principle that the character of the offender as it can be inferred from the available information, rather than from an abstract classification of the offense he is thought to have committed, should be determinative as to the use of deadly force. Specifically, the judgment is that the use of deadly force should be sanctioned only in cases where the offender is thought to pose such a danger to life or limb that his immediate apprehension overrides competing considerations.

3.   Choice of the Lesser Evil — The Residual Principle of Justification

PEOPLE v. UNGER

Supreme Court of Illinois
66 Ill. 2d 333, 362 N.E.2d 319 (1977)

Ryan, J. Defendant, Francis Unger, was charged with the crime of escape and was convicted following a jury trial before the circuit court of Will County. Defendant was sentenced to a term of three to nine years to be served consecutively to the remainder of the sentence for which he was imprisoned at the time of the escape. The conviction was reversed upon appeal and the cause was remanded for a new trial. . . . We granted leave to appeal and now affirm the judgment of the appellate court.

At the time of the present offense, the defendant was confined at the Illinois State Penitentiary in Joliet, Illinois. Defendant was serving a one- to three-year term as a consequence of a conviction for auto theft. . . . On February 23, 1972, the defendant was transferred to the prison's minimum security, honor farm. It is undisputed that on March 7, 1972, the defendant walked off the honor farm. Defendant was apprehended two days later in a motel room in St. Charles, Illinois.

At trial, defendant testified that prior to his transfer to the honor farm he had been threatened by a fellow inmate. This inmate allegedly brandished a six-inch knife in an attempt to force defendant to engage in homosexual activities. Defendant was 22 years old and weighed approximately 155 pounds. He testified that he did not report the incident to the proper authorities due to fear of retaliation. Defendant also testified that he is not a particularly good fighter.

Defendant stated that after his transfer to the honor farm he was assaulted and sexually molested by three inmates, and he named the assailants at trial. The attack allegedly occurred on March 2, 1972, and from that date until his escape defendant received additional threats from inmates he did not know. On March 7, 1972, the date of the escape, defendant testified that he received a call on an institution telephone. Defendant testified that the caller, whose voice he did not recognize, threatened him with death because the caller had heard that defendant had reported the assault to prison authorities. Defendant said that he left the honor farm to save his life and that he planned to return once he found someone who could help him. None of these incidents were reported to the prison officials. As mentioned, defendant was apprehended two days later still dressed in his prison clothes. . . .

Defendant's first trial for escape resulted in a hung jury. The jury in the second trial returned its verdict after a five-hour deliberation. The following instruction (People's Instruction No. 9) was given by the trial court over defendant's objection. "The reasons, if any, given for the alleged escape are immaterial and not to be considered by you as in any way justifying or excusing, if there were in fact such reasons." The appellate court majority found that the giving of People's Instruction No. 9 was reversible error. . . . Two instructions which were tendered by defendant but refused by the trial court are also germane to this appeal. Defendant's instructions Nos. 1 and 3 were predicated upon the affirmative defenses of compulsion and necessity. (Ill. Rev. Stat. 1971, ch. 38, pars 7-11 (compulsion), 7-13 (necessity.) Defendant's instructions Nos. 1 and 3 read as follows:

> It is a defense to the charge made against the Defendant that he left the Honor Farm of the Illinois State Penitentiary by reason of necessity if the accused was without blame in occasioning or developing the situation and reasonably believed such conduct was necessary to avoid a public or private injury greater than the injury which might reasonably result from his own conduct.
>
> It is a defense to the charge made against the Defendant that he acted under the compulsion of threat or menace of the imminent infliction of death or great bodily harm, if he reasonably believed death or great bodily harm would be inflicted upon him if he did not perform the conduct with which he is charged.

The principal issue in the present appeal is whether it was error for the court to instruct the jury that it must disregard the reasons given for defendant's escape and to conversely refuse to instruct the jury on the statutory defenses of compulsion and necessity. . . . The State contends that, under the facts and circumstances of this case, the defenses of compulsion and necessity are, as a matter of law, unavailable to defendant. . . .

Traditionally, the courts have been reluctant to permit the defenses of compulsion and necessity to be relied upon by escapees. This reluctance appears to have been primarily grounded upon considerations of public policy. Several recent decisions, however, have recognized the applicability of the compulsion and necessity defenses to prison escapes. In People v. Harmon (1974), 53 Mich. App. 482, 220 N.W.2d 212, the defense of duress was held to apply in a case where the defendant alleged that he escaped in order to avoid repeated homosexual attacks from fellow inmates. In People v. Lovercamp (1974), 43 Cal. App. 3d 823, 118 Cal. Rptr. 110, a limited defense of necessity was held to be available to two defendants whose escapes were allegedly motivated by fear of homosexual attacks.

As illustrated by *Harmon* and *Lovercamp*, different courts have reached similar results in escape cases involving sexual abuse, though the question was analyzed under different defense theories. A certain degree of confusion has resulted from the recurring practice on the part of the courts to use the terms "compulsion" (duress) and "necessity" interchangeably, though the defenses are theoretically distinct. . . .

In our view, the defense of necessity, as defined by our statute (Ill. Rev. Stat. 1971, ch. 38, par. 7-13), is the appropriate defense in the present case. In a very real sense, the defendant here was not deprived of his free will by the threat of imminent physical harm which, according to the Committee Comments, appears to be the intended interpretation of the defense of compulsion as set out in section 7-11 of the Criminal Code. . . . Rather, if defendant's testimony is believed, he was forced to choose between two admitted evils by the situation which arose from actual and threatened homosexual assaults and fears of reprisal. Though the defense of compulsion would be applicable in the unlikely event that a prisoner was coerced by the threat of imminent physical harm to perform the specific act of escape, no such situation is involved in the present appeal. . . .

The defendant's testimony was clearly sufficient to raise the affirmative defense of necessity. That defense is defined by statute (Ill. Rev. Stat. 1971, ch. 38, par. 7-13):

> Conduct which would otherwise be an offense is justifiable by reason of necessity if the accused was without blame in occasioning or developing the situation and reasonably believed such conduct was necessary to avoid a public or private injury greater than the injury which might reasonably result from his own conduct.

Defendant testified that he was subjected to threats of forced homosexual activity and that, on one occasion, the threatened abuse was carried out. He also testified that he was physically incapable of defending himself and that he feared greater harm would result from a report to the authorities. Defendant further testified that just prior to his escape he was told that he was going to be killed, and that he therefore fled the honor farm in order to save his life. Though the State's evidence cast a doubt upon the defendant's motives for escape and upon the reasonableness of defendant's assertion that such conduct was necessary, the defendant was entitled to have the jury consider the defense on the basis of his testimony. . . .

The State, however, would have us apply a more stringent test to prison escape situations. The State refers to the *Lovercamp* decision, where only a limited necessity defense was recognized. In *Lovercamp*, it was held that the defense of necessity need be submitted to the jury only where five conditions had been met. Those conditions are: "(1) The prisoner is faced with a specific threat of death, forcible sexual attack or substantial bodily injury in the immediate future; (2) There is no time for a complaint to the authorities or there exists a history of futile complaints which make any result from such complaints illusory; (3) There is no time or opportunity to resort to the courts; (4) There is no evidence of force or violence used towards prison personnel or other 'innocent' persons in the escape; and (5) The prisoner immediately reports to the proper authorities when he has attained a position of safety from the immediate threat."

The State correctly points out that the defendant never informed the authorities of his situation and failed to report immediately after securing a position of safety. Therefore, it is contended that, under the authority of *Lovercamp,* defendant is not entitled to a necessity instruction. We agree with the State and with the court in *Lovercamp* that the above conditions are relevant factors to be used in assessing claims of necessity. We cannot say, however, that the existence of each condition is, as a matter of law, necessary to establish a meritorious necessity defense.

The preconditions set forth in *Lovercamp* are, in our view, matters which go to the weight and credibility of the defendant's testimony. . . . The absence of one or more of the elements listed in *Lovercamp* would not necessarily mandate a finding that the defendant could not assert the defense of necessity.

By way of example, in the present case defendant did not report to the authorities immediately after securing his safety. In fact, defendant never voluntarily turned himself in to the proper officials. However, defendant testified that he intended to return to the prison upon obtaining legal advice from an attorney and claimed that he was attempting to get money from friends to pay for such counsel. Regardless of our opinion as to the believability of defendant's tale, this testimony, if accepted by the jury, would have negated any negative inference which would arise from defendant's failure to report to proper authorities after the escape. The absence of one of the *Lovercamp* preconditions does not alone disprove the claim of necessity and should not, therefore, automatically preclude an instruction on the defense. We therefore reject the contention that the availability of the necessity defense be expressly conditioned upon the elements set forth in *Lovercamp.*

In conclusion, we hold that under the facts and circumstances of the present case the defendant was entitled to submit his defense of necessity to the jury. It was, therefore, reversible error to give People's Instruction No. 9 to the jury and to refuse to give an appropriate instruction defining the defense of necessity, such as the instruction tendered by the defendant. . . .

UNDERWOOD, J., dissenting: My disagreement with my colleagues stems from an uneasy feeling that their unconditional recognition of necessity as a defense to the charge of escape carries with it the seeds of future troubles. Unless narrowly circumscribed, the availability of that defense could encourage potential escapes, disrupt prison discipline, and could even result in injury to prison guards, police or private citizens. For these reasons courts have been quite reluctant to honor the defenses of duress, necessity or compulsion in prison escapes, and, until recent years, they were uniformly held insufficient to justify escapes. . . .

I am not totally insensitive to the sometimes brutal and unwholesome problems faced by prison inmates, and the frequency of sexually motivated assaults. Prisoner complaints to unconcerned or understaffed prison administrations may produce little real help to a prisoner or may actually increase the hazard from fellow inmates of whose conduct complaint has been made. Consequently, and until adequate prison personnel and facilities are realities, I agree that a necessity defense should be recognized. The interests of society are better served, however, if the use of that defense in prison-escape cases is confined within well-defined boundaries such as those in *Lovercamp*. In that form it will be available, but with limitations precluding its wholesale use.

It is undisputed that defendant here did not meet those conditions. . . . Rather, he stole a truck some nine hours after his escape, drove to Chicago, and later drove to St. Charles, using the telephone to call friends in Canada. This conduct, coupled with his admitted intent to leave in order to gain publicity for what he considered an unfair sentence, severely strain the credibility of his testimony regarding his intention to return to the prison.

NOTES

1. In United States v. Bailey, 444 U.S. 394 (1980), the Supreme Court held, contrary to *Unger,* but in accord with *Lovercamp,* that a prerequisite for invoking the necessity defense in a prison escape case is that the defendant make a bona fide effort to surrender or return "as soon as the duress or necessity had lost its coercive force."

2. Consider the bearing of the following comment on the task of weighing the evils in a prison escape case (Model Penal Code and Commentaries, Comments to §3.02 at 12, n. 5 (1985):

The harm sought to be prevented by the law defining the offense may be viewed broadly enough to permit judicial attention to the effects on law enforcement of allowing the defense in the particular circumstances involved. For example, a court could consider whether recognition of the defense when a prisoner has escaped to avoid assault would have the effect of substantially encouraging unjustified escapes.

Question: Under this approach could a court deny a §3.02 defense in an otherwise justified circumstance, on the ground that other defendants might abuse the defense by invoking it when their conduct was *not* justified?

3. The *Unger* case treats the prison escape defense as an issue of justification. The possibility of a defense based on excuse is raised page 904 infra. In considering what difference it might make, consider United States v. Lopez, 662 F. Supp. 1083 (N.D. Cal. 1987). Defendant McIntosh landed a helicopter in the recreation yard of a federal prison and then flew off with Lopez, who had been prisoner there. Prosecuted for escape, Lopez asserted the defenses of duress and necessity, on the basis of her fear that she would have been killed or seriously injured if she had not escaped. McIntosh was charged with aiding and abetting Lopez in her escape. Does he have a good justification defense so long as Lopez does? Does he have a good duress defense so long as Lopez does?

4. For commentaries on the prison escape problem, see Martin Gardner, The Defense of Necessity and the Right to Escape from Prison, 49 S. Cal. L. Rev. 110 (1975); Comment, Intolerable Conditions as a Defense to Prison Escapes, 26

U.C.L.A.L. Rev. 1126 (1979); Note, The Necessity Defense to Prison Escape after *United States v. Bailey,* 65 Va. L. Rev. 359. (1979).

BOROUGH OF SOUTHWARK v. WILLIAMS, [1971] 2 All E.R. 175: [Defendants were homeless families in dire straits, several among many in London at the time, which was suffering an extreme housing shortage. Obtaining no help from local government, they made an orderly entry into some empty houses belonging to the Borough and became squatters there. The Borough brought an action to oust them. The squatters resisted by raising the defense of necessity. Lord Denning rejected the defense:] There is authority for saying that in case of great and imminent danger, in order to preserve life, the law will permit of an encroachment on private property. . . . The doctrine so enunciated must, however, be carefully circumscribed. Else necessity would open the door to many an excuse. . . . If homelessness were once admitted as a defence to trespass, no one's house could be safe. Necessity would open a door which no man could shut. It would not only be those in extreme need who would enter. . . . There would be others who would imagine that they were in need, or would invent a need, so as to gain entry. Each man would say his need was greater than the next man's. The plea would be an excuse for all sorts of wrongdoing. So the courts must, for the sake of law and order, take a firm stand. They must refuse to admit the plea of necessity to the hungry and the homeless; and trust that their distress will be relieved by the charitable and the good. Applying these principles, it seems to me [the] circumstances of these squatters are not such as to afford any justification or excuse in law for their entry into these houses. We can sympathise with the plight in which they find themselves. We can recognise the orderly way in which they made their entry. But we can go no further. They must make their appeal for help to others, not to us. . . . But, so far as these courts are concerned, we must, in the interest of law and order itself, uphold the title to these properties. . . . The court must exercise its summary jurisdiction and order the defendants to go out.

COMMONWEALTH v. LENO, 415 Mass. 835, 616 N.E.2d 453 (1993): Massachusetts is one of ten States that prohibit distribution of hypodermic needles without a prescription. In the face of those statutes the defendants operated a needle exchange program in an effort to combat the spread of acquired immuno-deficiency syndrome (AIDS). As a result, the defendants were charged with and convicted of (1) unauthorized possession of instruments to administer controlled substances, and (2) unlawful distribution of an instrument to administer controlled substances, . . . On appeal, the defendants challenge the judge's refusal to instruct the jury on the defense of necessity. . . . We affirm. . . . The defendants did not show that the danger they sought to avoid was clear and imminent, rather than debatable or speculative. . . . That some States prohibit the distribution of hypodermic needles without a prescription, and others do not, merely indicates that the best course to take to address the long-term hazard of the spread of AIDS remains a matter of debate. The defendants' argument is that, in their view, the prescription requirement for possession and distribution of hypodermic needles and syringes is both ineffective and dangerous. The Legislature, however, has determined that it wants to control the distribution of drug-related paraphernalia and their use in the consumption of illicit drugs.

That public policy is entitled to deference by courts. Whether a statute is wise or effective is not within the province of courts. . . . Our deference to legislative judgments reflects neither an abdication of nor unwillingness to perform the judicial role; but rather a recognition of the separation of powers and the undesirability of the judiciary substituting its notions of correct policy for that of a popularly elected Legislature. . . . The defendants argue that the increasing number of AIDS cases constitutes a societal problem of great proportions, and that their actions were an effective means of reducing the magnitude of that problem; they assert that their possession, transportation and distribution of hypodermic needles eventually will produce an over-all reduction in the spread of HIV and in the future incidence of AIDS. The defendants' argument raises the issue of jury nullification, not the defense of necessity. . . . We do not accept the premise that jurors have a right to nullify the law on which they are instructed by the judge, or that the judge must inform them of their power.

[For a thoughtful opinion to the contrary, See People v. Berkowitz, 588 N.Y.S.2d 507 (N.Y. Crim. Ct. 1991).]

COMMONWEALTH v. HUTCHINS, 410 Mass. 726, 575 N.E.2d 741 (1991): [Defendant was charged with illegal possession and cultivation of marijuana. At trial defendant made an offer of proof, supported by affidavits and other material, to show that he was a victim of progressive systemic sclerosis, a serious and sometimes fatal disease with frightful symptoms for which no cure exists, and that ingestion of marijuana had produced a remarkable remission. The judge denied the offer of proof on the ground that the proof offered would not support a necessity defense. The defendant was convicted, and he appealed. The majority of the Supreme Judicial Court of Massachusetts affirmed, stating:] The defendant's proffered evidence does not raise the defense of necessity. In our view, the alleviation of the defendant's medical symptoms, the importance to the defendant of which we do not underestimate, would not clearly and significantly outweigh the potential harm to the public were we to declare that the defendant's cultivation of marihuana and its use for his medicinal purposes may not be punishable. We cannot dismiss the reasonably possible negative impact of such a judicial declaration on the enforcement of our drug laws, including but not limited to those dealing with marihuana, nor can we ignore the government's overriding interest in the regulation of such substances.

[Liacos, C. J., dissenting, stated:] [T]he court . . . fails to give sufficient consideration to the rationale behind the common law defense of necessity. That rationale is based on the recognition that, under very limited circumstances, "the value protected by the law is, as a matter of public policy, eclipsed by a superseding value which makes it inappropriate and unjust to apply the usual criminal rule." Commonwealth v. Brugmann, 13 Mass. App. Ct. 373, 377, 433 N.E.2d 457 (1982). The superseding value in a case such as the present one is the humanitarian and compassionate value in allowing an individual to seek relief from agonizing symptoms caused by a progressive and incurable illness in circumstances which risk no harm to any other individual. In my view, the harm to an individual in having to endure such symptoms may well outweigh society's generalized interest in prohibiting him or her from using the marihuana in such circumstances. On a proper offer of proof I would recognize the availability of a necessity defense when marihuana is used for medical purposes.

[The dissent added in footnote 1:] There is no reason to believe, as the court suggests, that allowing a defendant to present evidence of medical necessity to a jury will have a negative impact on the enforcement of drug laws. I am confident that juries would apply their wisdom and common sense in making sure that the necessity defense is not successfully utilized by defendants who use marihuana for purposes other than to alleviate agonizing and painful medical symptoms.

NOTE

A story in N.Y. Times, Oct. 11, 1993, §B, at 1, reports the arrest and conviction of Mildred Katz, a 79-year-old grandmother, for growing marijuana in the backyard of her Monticello home in the Catskills. The account states that she did it so that her son would eat properly. It appeared that the son was a victim of chronic multiple sclerosis, and that his failing appetite was restored by ingesting the marijuana. Asked by the police if she would rob a bank if her son needed an operation, she replied, "If it would cure his sickness, I would absolutely. I'd go to jail for life." The local magistrate placed her on probation with an admonition to stay out of trouble.

MODEL PENAL CODE

SECTION 3.02. JUSTIFICATION GENERALLY: CHOICE OF EVILS

(1) Conduct which the actor believes to be necessary to avoid a harm or evil to himself or to another is justifiable, provided that:

(a) the harm or evil sought to be avoided by such conduct is greater than that sought to be prevented by the law defining the offense charged; and

(b) neither the Code nor other law defining the offense provides exceptions or defenses dealing with the specific situation involved; and

(c) a legislative purpose to exclude the justification claimed does not otherwise plainly appear.

(2) When the actor was reckless or negligent in bringing about the situation requiring a choice of harms or evils or in appraising the necessity for his conduct, the justification afforded by this Section is unavailable in a prosecution for any offense for which recklessness or negligence, as the case may be, suffices to establish culpability.

MODEL PENAL CODE AND COMMENTARIES, COMMENT TO §3.02 AT 9-14 (1985):
This section accepts the view that a principle of necessity, properly conceived, affords a general justification for conduct that would otherwise constitute an offense. It reflects the judgment that such a qualification on criminal liability, like the general requirements of culpability, is essential to the rationality and justice of the criminal law, and is appropriately addressed in a penal code. Under this section, property may be destroyed to prevent the spread of a fire. . . . An ambulance may pass a traffic light. Mountain climbers lost in a storm may take refuge in a house or may appropriate provisions. Cargo may be jettisoned or an embargo violated to preserve the vessel. . . . A druggist may dispense a drug with-

out the requisite prescription to alleviate grave distress in an emergency. A developed legal system must have better ways of dealing with such problems than to refer only to the letter of particular prohibitions, framed without reference to cases of this kind. . . .[3]

The Code's principle of necessity is subject to a number of limitations. First, the actor must actually believe that his conduct is necessary to avoid an evil. . . . It is not enough that the actor believes that his behavior possibly may be conducive to ameliorating certain evils; he must believe it is "necessary" to avoid the evils.[4]

Second, the necessity must arise from an attempt by the actor to avoid an evil or harm that is greater than the evil or harm sought to be avoided by the law defining the offense charged. . . .

Third, the balancing of evils is not committed to the private judgment of the actor; it is an issue for determination at the trial. . . . Subsection (1)(a) . . . requires that the harm or evil sought to be avoided be greater than that which would be caused by the commission of the offense, not that the defendant believe it to be so. What is involved may be described as an interpretation of the law of the offense, in light of the submission that the special situation calls for an exception to the criminal prohibition that the legislature could not reasonably have intended to exclude, given the competing values to be weighed. The Code does not resolve the question of how far the balancing of values should be determined by the court as a matter of law or submitted to the jury. . . .

Fourth, under Subsections (1)(b) and (1)(c), the general choice of evils defense cannot succeed if the issue of competing values has been previously foreclosed by a deliberate legislative choice, as when some provision of the law deals explicitly with the specific situation that presents the choice of evils or a legislative purpose to exclude the claimed justification otherwise appears. . . .

NEW YORK PENAL LAW

Section 35.05   Justification; Generally

Unless otherwise limited by the ensuing provisions of this article defining justifiable use of physical force, or with some other provision of law, conduct which would otherwise constitute an offense is justifiable and not criminal when: . . .

2. Such conduct is necessary as an emergency measure to avoid an imminent public or private injury which is about to occur by reason of a situation occasioned or developed through no fault of the actor, and which is of such gravity that, according to ordinary standards of intelligence and morality, the desir-

---

3. A contrary view is expressed in Brown Commn. Final Report §601 Comment, which suggests that any general "choice of evils" codification would be "a potential source of unwarranted difficulty in ordinary cases," and that case by case prosecutive discretion is preferable. But reliance on prosecutorial discretion alone leaves the matter to be decided in the absence of governing principles and by an executive official who must act without legislative guidance or judicial check. . . .

4. This requirement would pose a significant barrier to assertion of the defense both in cases of illegal political protest, see, e.g., United States v. Kroncke, 459 F.2d 697 (8th Cir. 1972), and in cases of illegal governmental action claimed to protect the national security, see, e.g., United States v. Ehrlichman, 546 F.2d 910 (D.C. Cir. 1976).

ability and urgency of avoiding such injury clearly outweigh the desirability of avoiding the injury sought to be prevented by the statute defining the offense in issue. The necessity and justifiability of such conduct may not rest upon considerations pertaining only to the morality and advisability of the statute, either in its general application or with respect to its application to a particular class of cases arising thereunder. Whenever evidence relating to the defense of justification under this subdivision is offered by the defendant, the court shall rule as a matter of law whether the claimed facts and circumstances would, if established, constitute a defense.

NOTES

1. *New York and Model Penal Code approaches compared.* Consider Model Penal Code and Commentaries, Comment to §3.02 at 17, 19-21 (1985):

[The New York law differs from the Model Code in requiring that the conduct be an "emergency measure to avoid an imminent . . . injury."] Such a requirement unduly emphasizes one ingredient in the judgment that is called for at the expense of others just as important. It is true that genuine necessity rests on the unavailability of alternatives that would avoid both evils, and that typically when the evil is not imminent some such alternative will be available; but it is a mistake to erect imminence as an absolute requirement, since there may be situations in which an otherwise illegal act is necessary to avoid an evil that may occur in the future. . . .

A more important variation from the Model Code is the requirement in the New York provision that the situation that gives rise to the necessity for action be occasioned or developed "through no fault of the actor." Thus, an actor who negligently starts a fire is deprived of any defense for destroying property or breaking traffic regulations in an effort to prevent its spread or to notify the proper authorities. . . .

By contrast, [under] the Code resolution of this matter . . . the actor who negligently starts a fire creating the need for him then to act to stop its spread may be prosecuted for offenses for which negligence would suffice, but would not be deprived of the choice of evils defense for offenses committed in the attempt to put out the fire that require a higher culpability level. . . .

Question: Consider how the previous cases would be decided under the Model Penal Code and New York formulations.

2. Lawrence Tiffany & Carl Anderson, Legislating the Necessity Defense in Criminal Law, 52 Den. L.J. 839, 861-862 (1975), write:

A question which needs to be clarified is posed by LaFave and Scott: "*A*, driving a car, suddenly finds himself in a predicament where he must either run down *B* or hit *C*'s house and he reasonably chooses the latter, unfortunately killing two people in the house who by bad luck happened to be just at that place inside the house where *A*'s car struck. . . ."

Of course, the defendant in this case is guilty of no crime to begin with. Were defendant charged with manslaughter (reckless homicide), the difficulty would be that recklessness means a conscious disregard of a risk that is "substantial and unjustifiable." The same is true of crimes defined in terms of negligence. Defendant needs no general justification defense when charged with a crime based on recklessness or negligence since it is implicit in the charge itself that the defendant's conduct was not justified; unjustifiability of conduct becomes an element of the charge itself and must be proved by the state.

Cf. Problem, page 443 supra.

3. What perils are created by the inevitable uncertainty and elasticity of the defense of necessity? We saw earlier, in the section on the principle of legality, page 294 supra, that vagueness is regarded as a serious evil in the criminal law. Is vagueness less offensive when it affects defenses to, rather than definitions of, criminal conduct? Consider the views of James Fitzjames Stephen on this question. Defending a proposal to eliminate judicial authority to create new crimes while retaining another authorizing judges to develop new defenses, he stated (quoted in Glanville Williams, (2) Necessity, [1978] Crim. L. Rev. 128, 130):

> [T]he reason why the common law definitions of offences should be taken away, whilst the common law principles as to justification and excuse are kept alive, is like the reason why the benefit of a doubt should be given to a prisoner. The worst result that could arise from the abolition of the common law offences would be the occasional escape of a person morally guilty. The only result which can follow from preserving the common law as to justification and excuse is, that a man morally innocent, not otherwise protected, may avoid punishment. In the one case you remove rusty spring-guns and man-traps from unfrequented plantations, in the other you decline to issue an order for the destruction of every old-fashioned drag or life-buoy which may be found on the banks of a dangerous river, but is not in the inventory of the Royal Humane Society.

A modern-day version of the proposals defended by Stephen is represented in the New Jersey Code of Criminal Justice. N.J. Stat. Ann. tit. 2C, §1-5 provides: "Common law crimes are abolished and no conduct constitutes an offense unless the offense is defined by this code or another statute of this State." But §3-2 provides: "a. *Necessity.* Conduct which would otherwise be an offense is justifiable by reason of necessity to the extent permitted by law and as to which neither the code nor other statutory law defining the offense provides exceptions or defenses dealing with the specific situation involved and a legislative purpose to exclude the justification claimed does not otherwise plainly appear." The drafters' commentary states: "The Commission believes it more appropriate to leave the issue to the Judiciary. The rarity of the defense and the imponderables of the particulars of specific cases convince us that the Courts can better define and apply this defense than can be done through legislation." 2 N.J. Crim. Law Rev. Commn., Final Report, The New Jersey Penal Code, Commentary 80 (1971).

Compare Louis B. Schwartz, Reform of the Federal Criminal Laws, [1977] Duke L.J. 171, 217. Responding to a proposal to allow courts to develop new defenses and justifications "in the light of reason and experience," Professor Schwartz observed:

> The open-ended invitation to judges to *add* to the listed defenses is a civil liberties monster. It was earlier urged on the Brown Commission . . . in order to retain all sorts of bad things — for example, the right of police to kill in suppressing riots and the right of a householder to shoot to kill a supposedly burglarious intruder

whether or not he is perceived as a threat to life (as where the burglar is shot leaving the house). To leave the judges free to define defenses is virtually to abandon the effort to define crimes, since an offense is defined by the combination of what it prohibits and what is declared to be justified.

UNITED STATES v. SCHOON

United States Court of Appeals, 9th Circuit
971 F.2d 193 (1992)

BOOCHEVER, J.: Gregory Schoon, Raymond Kennon, Jr., and Patricia Manning appeal their convictions for obstructing activities of the Internal Revenue Service Office in Tucson, Arizona, and failing to comply with an order of a federal police officer. Both charges stem from their activities in protest of United States involvement in El Salvador. They claim the district court improperly denied them a necessity defense. Because we hold the necessity defense inapplicable in cases like this, we affirm.

On December 4, 1989, thirty people, including appellants, gained admittance to the IRS office in Tucson, where they chanted "keep America's tax dollars out of El Salvador," splashed simulated blood on the counters, walls, and carpeting, and generally obstructed the office's operation. After a federal police officer ordered the group, on several occasions, to disperse or face arrest, appellants were arrested.

At a bench trial, appellants proffered testimony about conditions in El Salvador as the motivation for their conduct. They attempted to assert a necessity defense, essentially contending that their acts in protest of American involvement in El Salvador were necessary to avoid further bloodshed in that country. While finding appellants motivated solely by humanitarian concerns, the court nonetheless precluded the defense as a matter of law. . . .

To invoke the necessity defense . . . the defendants colorably must have shown that: (1) they were faced with a choice of evils and chose the lesser evil; (2) they acted to prevent imminent harm; (3) they reasonably anticipated a direct causal relationship between their conduct and the harm to be averted; and (4) they had no legal alternatives to violating the law. The district court denied the necessity defense on the grounds that (1) the requisite immediacy was lacking; (2) the actions taken would not abate the evil; and (3) other legal alternatives existed. Because the threshold test for admissibility of a necessity defense is a conjunctive one, a court may preclude invocation of the defense if "proof is deficient with regard to any of the four elements."

While we could affirm substantially on those grounds relied upon by the district court, we find a deeper, systemic reason for the complete absence of federal case law recognizing a necessity defense in an indirect civil disobedience case. As used in this opinion, "civil disobedience" is the wilful violation of a law, undertaken for the purpose of social or political protest. Indirect civil disobedience involves violating a law or interfering with a government policy that is not, itself, the object of protest. Direct civil disobedience, on the other hand, involves protesting the existence of a law by breaking that law or by preventing the execution of that law in a specific instance in which a particularized harm would otherwise follow. This case involves indirect civil disobedience because these protestors were not challenging the laws under which they were charged. In contrast, the civil rights lunch counter sit-ins, for example, constituted direct civil disobedience because the protestors were challenging the rule that prevented them from sitting at lunch counters. . . . Today, we conclude, for the reasons stated below, that the necessity defense is inapplicable to cases involving indirect civil disobedience.

Necessity is, essentially, a utilitarian defense. It therefore justifies criminal acts taken to avert a greater harm, maximizing social welfare by allowing a crime to be committed where the social benefits of the crime outweigh the social costs of failing to commit the crime. Pursuant to the defense, prisoners could escape a burning prison; a person lost in the woods could steal food from a cabin to survive; . . . a crew could mutiny where their ship was thought to be unseaworthy; and property could be destroyed to prevent the spread of fire.

What all the traditional necessity cases have in common is that the commission of the "crime" averted the occurrence of an even greater "harm." In some sense, the necessity defense allows us to act as individual legislatures, amending a particular criminal provision or crafting a one-time exception to it, subject to court review, when a real legislature would formally do the same under those circumstances. For example, by allowing prisoners who escape a burning jail to claim the justification of necessity, we assume the lawmaker, confronting this problem, would have allowed for an exception to the law proscribing prison escapes.

Because the necessity doctrine is utilitarian, however, strict requirements contain its exercise so as to prevent nonbeneficial criminal conduct. . . .

Analysis of three of the necessity defense's four elements leads us to the conclusion that necessity can never be proved in a case of indirect civil disobedience. We do not rely upon the imminent harm prong of the defense because we believe there can be indirect civil disobedience cases in which the protested harm is imminent.

. . . Indirect civil disobedience seeks first and foremost to bring about the repeal of a law or a change of governmental policy, attempting to mobilize public opinion through typically symbolic action. These protestors violate a law, not because it is unconstitutional or otherwise improper, but because doing so calls public attention to their objectives. Thus, the most immediate "harm" this form of protest targets is the existence of the law or policy. However, the mere existence of a constitutional law or governmental policy cannot constitute a legally cognizable harm. See Comment, Political Protest and the Illinois Defense of Necessity, 54 U. Chi. L. Rev. 1070, 1083 (1987) ("In a society based on democratic decision making, this is how values are ranked — a protester cannot simply assert that her view of what is best should trump the decision of the majority of elected representatives."). . . . If there is no cognizable harm to prevent, the harm resulting from criminal action taken for the purpose of securing the repeal of the law or policy necessarily outweighs any benefit of the action.

This inquiry requires a court to judge the likelihood that an alleged harm will be abated by the taking of illegal action. In the sense that the likelihood of abatement is required in the traditional necessity cases, there will never be such likelihood in cases of indirect political protest. In the traditional cases, a prisoner flees a burning cell and averts death, or someone demolishes a home to create a firebreak and prevents the conflagration of an entire community. The nexus between the act undertaken and the result sought is a close one. Ordinarily it is the volitional illegal act alone which, once taken, abates the evil.

In political necessity cases involving indirect civil disobedience against congressional acts, however, the act alone is unlikely to abate the evil precisely because the action is indirect. Here, the IRS obstruction, or the refusal to comply with a federal officer's order, are unlikely to abate the killings in El Salvador, or immediately change Congress's policy; instead, it takes another volitional actor not controlled by the protestor to take a further step; Congress must change its mind.

A final reason the necessity defense does not apply to these indirect civil disobedience cases is that legal alternatives will never be deemed exhausted when the harm can be mitigated by congressional action. As noted above, the harm indirect civil disobedience aims to prevent is the continued existence of a law or policy. Because congressional action can always mitigate this "harm," lawful political activity to spur such action will always be a legal alternative. . . .

[T]he "possibility" that Congress will change its mind is sufficient in the context of the democratic process to make lawful political action a reasonable alternative to indirect civil disobedience. . . . [P]etitioning Congress to change a policy is always a legal alternative in such cases, regardless of the likelihood of the plea's success. Thus, indirect civil disobedience can never meet the necessity defense requirement that there be a lack of legal alternatives. . . .

Thus, we see the failure of any federal court to recognize a defense of necessity in a case like ours not as coincidental, but rather as the natural consequence of the historic limitation of the doctrine. Indirect protests of congressional policies can never meet all the requirements of the necessity doctrine. Therefore, we hold that the necessity defense is not available in such cases.

Affirmed.

NOTES

1. The necessity defense has been raised in many sit-in, vandalism, trespass, and related prosecutions in recent years. The causes have ranged from nuclear power and missile protests to anti-abortion protests. See Matthew Lippman, The Necessity Defense and Political Protest, 26 Crim. L. Bull. 317 (1990); Note (Laura Schulkind), Applying the Necessity Defense, 64 N.Y.U.L. Rev. 79 (1989); Note, The State Made Me Do It: The Applicability of the Necessity Defense to Civil Disobedience, 39 Stan. L. Rev. 1173 (1987). An Annotation, "Necessity, Choice of Evils, or Similar Defense to Charges Stemming from Public Protest," reviewing the cases appears in 3 A.L.R.5th 521 (1992). Though the defense has sometimes prevailed with juries and magistrates, it has been notably unsuccessful on the appellate level, where courts have overwhelmingly refused necessity instructions or barred defendants from introducing evidence on the issue, or both. See Note, Political Protest and the Illinois Defense of Necessity, 54 U. Chi. L. Rev. 1070 (1987). The *Schoon* case, however, is unusual in flatly denying the necessity defense in any indirect civil disobedience case. See Casenote (James Cavallaro), The Demise of the Political Necessity Defense: Indirect Civil Disobedience and *United States v. Schoon,* 81 Cal. L. Rev. 351 (1993).

Consider the availability of the lesser-evil doctrine as a defense for the perpetrators of the appalling mass kidnapping in the Bisbee Deportation case (State v. Wootton), a famous prosecution rising out of developments in Arizona during World War I. The following summary of the facts is taken from Comment, The Law of Necessity as Applied in the Bisbee Deportation Case, 13 Ariz. L. Rev. 264 (1961):

> On April 26, 1917, hard on the heels of our declaration of war against Germany, a strike of copper miners in the Warren District of Cochise County, Arizona, was ordered by the Industrial Workers of the World — the I.W.W. On July 12th an armed posse, organized by the sheriff and numbering more than 1000, rounded up some 1100 to 1200 of the strikers and their associates, including practically every member of the I.W.W. in the district, put them aboard a special freight train, and transported them under guard to Hermanas, near Columbus, New Mexico, where they were left to be cared for by federal troops. Eventually, about 200 of the possemen were charged with kidnapping, and one of them, H. E. Wootton, was selected to be brought to trial.
>
> At the close of the state's case in chief, the defendant offered to prove that the I.W.W. had been organized about 1908 as an anarchistic conspiracy to overthrow the government and the capitalistic system by force; that these strikes in the Warren District and elsewhere were designed to obstruct the successful prosecution of the war; that at the time of the alleged kidnapping the conspirators were present in the Warren District in great numbers, to destroy the lives and property of its inhabitants; that they had assaulted and threatened its citizens and had accumulated quantities of dynamite, firearms, and ammunition to be used for their purposes; that the day before the deportation a leader of the conspirators had told the sheriff that he would no longer be responsible for the acts of his men; that the sheriff and possemen reasonably believed that the conspirators intended to commit many felonies in the district, including riot, treason, assault, murder, and the destruction of property; and that protection by the state and federal troops had been sought without avail; that the jails of the county were inadequate to confine the conspirators, and that as prudent men the defendant and his associates had reasonably believed that the deportation was imminently necessary for the preservation of life and property in the district.

The judge instructed the jury as follows (id. at 277):

> Laying aside for the moment the offer of proof with respect to a conspiracy existing long prior to the acts complained of, the offer of proof as to conditions existing in the Warren District at the time of the so-called deportation, the purpose and intent of the persons deported, the contemplated destruction of lives and property within that district, the preparations to carry out that intent and the acts and conduct as well as the statements of the persons deported, present a situation where it cannot be said as a matter of law that the rule of necessity cannot be applicable, but rather leaves the question of the existence of such necessity to be determined by the jury as a question of fact under proper instructions. If such were the conditions and the citizens of Bisbee had called in vain upon state and federal authorities for protection against a threatened calamity such as is set forth in the offer of proof, it cannot be said as a matter of law that they must sit supinely by and await the destruction of their lives and property without having the right to take steps to protect themselves.

The jury deliberated for 15 minutes and reached a verdict of "not guilty" on the first ballot.

For discussion of this case see also Edward Arnolds & Norman Garland, The Defense of Necessity in Criminal Law, 65 J. Crim. L. & Criminology 289, 292 (1974).

The facts of the Bisbee Deportations were investigated by a Commission appointed by the President of the United States, with Felix Frankfurter as Counsel to the Commission. Its report to the President, written by Frankfurter, made a number of findings, including the following (Dept. of Labor, Office of the Secretary, Report on the Bisbee Deportations, made by the President's Mediation Commission to the President of the United States (Nov. 6, 1917):

> 7. The deportation was carried out under the sheriff of Cochise County. It was formally decided upon at a meeting of citizens on the night of July 11 participated in by the managers and other officials of the Copper Queen Consolidated Mining Co. . . . and the Calumet & Arizona Mining Co. Those who planned and directed the deportation purposely abstained from consulting about their plans either with the United States attorney in Arizona, or the law officers of the State or county, or their own legal advisers.
>
> 8. In order to carry the plans for the deportation into successful execution, the leaders in the enterprise . . . attempted to exercise a censorship over parts of interstate connections of both the telephone and telegraph lines in order to prevent any knowledge of the deportation reaching the outside world.
>
> 9. The plans for the deportation and its execution are attributable to the belief in the minds of those who engineered it that violence was contemplated by the strikers and sympathizers with the strikers who had come into the district from without, that life and property would be insecure unless such deportation was undertaken, and that the State was without the necessary armed force to prevent such anticipated violence and to safeguard life and property within the district. This belief has no justification in the evidence in support of it presented by the parties who harbored it.
>
> 10. Neither such fear on the part of the leaders of the deportation as to anticipated violence nor evidence justifying such fear was ever communicated to the governor of the State of Arizona with a view to renewing the request for Federal troops, based upon changing conditions, nor were the Federal authorities in fact ever apprised that a change of conditions had taken place in the district from that found by the investigating Army officer to call for or warrant the interposition of Federal troops.
>
> 11. The deportation was wholly illegal and without authority in law, either State or Federal.

Among the recommendations of the Commission were the following:

> 2. In so far as the deportation of July 12 and the events following constitute violations of the laws of Arizona, we join in the recommendation of Gov. Campbell that the responsible law officers of the State and county pursue appropriate remedies for the vindication of such laws. . . .
>
> 5. In so far as deportations such as we have set forth has not yet been made a Federal offense, it is our duty to report to the President the wisdom of recommending to the Congress that such occurrences hereafter be made criminal under the Federal law to the full extent of the constitutional authority of the Federal Government.

The subsequent Arizona prosecution, described above, was apparently initiated in response to the Commission's recommendation.

REGINA v. DUDLEY AND STEPHENS

Queen's Bench Division
14 Q.B.D. 273 (1884)

[For the opinion in this case, see page 131 supra.]

NOTES

1. James Fitzjames Stephen, Digest of the Criminal Law 25 n. 1 (5th ed. 1894):

I can discover no principle in the judgment in R. v. Dudley. It depends entirely on its peculiar facts. The boy was deliberately put to death with a knife in order that his body might be used for food. This is quite different from any of the following cases — (1) The two men on a plank. Here the successful man does no direct bodily harm to the other. He leaves him the chance of getting another plank. (2) Several men are roped together on the Alps. They slip, and the weight of the whole party is thrown on one, who cuts the rope in order to save himself. Here the question is not whether some shall die, but whether one shall live. (3) The choice of evils. The captain of a ship runs down a boat, as the only means of avoiding shipwreck. A surgeon kills a child in the act of birth, as the only way to save the mother. A boat being too full of passengers to float, some are thrown overboard. Such cases are best decided as they arise.

Professor Glanville Williams offers a critical analysis of *Dudley and Stephens* in A Commentary on *R. v. Dudley and Stephens,* 8 Cambrian L. Rev. 94 (1977).

2. The American case referred to in Lord Coleridge's opinion was United States v. Holmes, 26 F. Cas. 360, 1 Wall Jr. 1 (C.C.E.D. Pa. 1842). The first mate, 8 seamen and 32 passengers were cast adrift on a life boat following a shipwreck on the high seas. The boat was grossly overcrowded and sprang a leak making it necessary to bail constantly in order to stay afloat. After a day and a half bailing became difficult because of the rough seas and the overcrowding, and the passengers panicked. The first mate ordered all male passengers whose wives were not in the boat to be thrown overboard. Eighteen passengers were jettisoned before a rescue ship arrived. Subsequently Holmes, one of the crew who assisted in ejecting the passengers, was charged with manslaughter, after the grand jury declined to return an indictment for murder. In charging the jury the judge made these points: that generally if two persons face a situation in which only one can survive "neither is bound to save the other's life by sacrificing his own, nor would either commit a crime in saving his own life for the only means of safety"; that while this principle prevailed between sailor and sailor it did not prevail between sailor and passenger because of the special duty owed the latter by the former; that absent this special relationship the choice of who should be sacrificed must be made by lot, since, "In no other way than this or some like way are those having equal rights put on an equal footing, and in no other way is it possible to guard against partiality and oppression, violence and conflict. . . ." Holmes was convicted and sentenced to six months' imprisonment and a fine of $20. Shortly thereafter the penalty was remitted.

For accounts of this case see F. Hicks, Human Jettison (1927); Benjamin Cardozo, Law and Literature 110-114 (1930). The latter observes (at 113):

Where two or more are overtaken by a common disaster, there is no right on the part of one to save the lives of some by the killing of another. There is no rule of human jettison. Men there will often be who, when told that their going will be the salvation of the remnant, will choose the nobler part and make the plunge into the water. In that supreme moment the darkness for them will be illumined by the thought that those behind will ride to safety. If none of such mold are found aboard the boat, or too few to save the others, the human freight must be left to meet the chances of the waters. Who shall choose in such an hour between the victims and the saved? Who shall know when masts and sails of rescue may emerge out of the fog?

3. In his opinion in *Dudley and Stephens* Lord Coleridge argues that it was not certain the defendants had to kill Parker, that the jury's verdict speaks only in terms of probability, that "they might possibly have been picked up next day by a passing ship; they might possibly not have been picked up at all; in either case it is obvious that the killing of the boy would have been an unnecessary and profitless act." But suppose there had been the level of certainty Lord Coleridge was looking for? Professor Glanville Williams supposes the following case in his Textbook of Criminal Law 606 (2d ed. 1983):

[L]et us suppose that the boat was equipped with an experimental radio transmitter, although radio-telephony was not in general use. The crew were able to make contact with Whitehall, which arranged for a ship to go to the rescue, but it could not arrive for seven days. The boat was lying off the trade routes, so it was unlikely that any other vessel would effect a rescue. The crew had reached such a stage of exhaustion that very soon none of them would be able to wield a knife. In these circumstances they asked to speak to the Home Secretary. They put the question to him: should they all accept death, or may they draw lots, kill the one with the unlucky number, and live on his body? In this way all but one will be saved. What should the Home Secretary reply? What would you reply, if you were Home Secretary?

For a tour de force of hypothetical opinions in a fictional case putting something like the scenario Professor Williams imagines, see Lon Fuller, The Case of the Speluncean Explorers, 62 Harv. L. Rev. 616 (1949).

NOTE ON TAKING LIFE TO SAVE LIFE

May the choice-of-evils principle ever justify the intentional killing of an innocent person who is not an aggressor? The Model Penal Code plainly anticipates an affirmative answer. In the commentary on the necessity proposal, the drafters state (Model Penal Code and Commentaries, Comment to §3.02 at 14-15 (1985)):

It would be particularly unfortunate to exclude homicidal conduct from the scope of the defense. For, recognizing that the sanctity of life has a supreme place in the hierarchy of values, it is nonetheless true that conduct that results in taking life may promote the very value sought to be protected by the law of homicide. Suppose, for example, that the actor makes a breach in a dike, knowing that this will inundate a farm, but taking the only course available to save a whole town. If he is charged with homicide of the inhabitants of the farm house, he can rightly point out that the object of the law of homicide is to save life, and that by his conduct he has effected a net saving of innocent lives. The life of every individual must be taken in such a case to be of equal value and the numerical preponderance in the lives saved compared to those sacrificed surely should establish legal justification for the act. So too, a mountaineer, roped to a companion who has fallen over a precipice, who holds on as long as possible but eventually cuts the rope, must certainly be granted the defense that he accelerated one death slightly but avoided the only alternative, the certain death of both. Although the view is not universally held that it is ethically preferable to take one innocent life than to have many lives lost,[15] most persons probably think a net saving of lives is ethically warranted if the choice among lives to be saved is not unfair. Certainly the law should permit such a choice.

How sound is the use of a numerical calculus to justify the intentional killing of an innocent, nonthreatening person? Resistance to such a position is evident in its explicit rejection by statutes and commentators.[3] Professor Andenaes, for example, has observed (Johannes Andenaes, The General Part of the Criminal Law of Norway 169 (1965)): "Even though many lives could be saved by the sacrifice of one, this would hardly be justifiable. It would conflict with the general attitude toward the inviolability of human life to interfere in this way with the course of events." But if it is better, when accidents happen, that fewer lives be lost, why is it wrong for a person to bring this about by his action? How can it be wrong to make things better?[4]

NOTE ON RIGHTS AND LIVES[5]

The one circumstance in which the Model Penal Code (and perhaps the law also, to some indeterminate extent) arguably justifies killing an innocent, non-

---

15. Roman Catholic moralists have generally taken the position that one should not cause effects that are directly evil even if they are thought to be a necessary means to a greater good. . . . Thus, it is considered wrong to terminate the life of a fetus even if that is the only way the mother can be saved and even if the fetus will die in any event. On the other hand, an ordinary operation designed directly to protect the mother's health is permissible, even if an inevitable effect is the death of the fetus, under the so-called principle of "double effect" that death is only permitted, not intended, and is not itself a means to saving the mother's life.

Many acts justifiable under this section would also be justifiable under the principle of "double effect." Diverting a flood to destroy a farmhouse instead of a town would be acceptable since the destruction of the farmhouse is not intended and is not a means of saving the town. Suppose, however, the citizens of a town receive a credible threat, say from a foreign invader, that everyone in the town will be killed unless the townspeople themselves kill their mayor, who is hiding. If the townspeople accede, they would have a substantial argument against criminal liability under this section but their act would be immoral under the double effect analysis, since they have intended to kill the mayor and it is his death that is the means to their safety.

3. See John M. Taurek, Should the Numbers Count?, 6 Phil. & Pub. Aff. 293 (1977); Jeffrie G. Murphy, The Killing of the Innocent, 57 Monist 527 (1973); Note, Justification: The Impact of the Model Penal Code on Statutory Reform, 75 Colum. L. Rev. 914, 923 (1975).

4. Professor Philippa Foot addresses the question of how it can ever be right to prefer a worse state of affairs to a better in Utilitarianism and the Virtues, 94 MIND 196 (1985). For critical comments see Samuel Scheffler, Agent Centered Restrictions, Rationality, and the Virtues, 94 MIND 406 (1985).

5. Drawn from Sanford H. Kadish, Blame and Punishment 122-123 (1987).

threatening bystander is that in which killing him is necessary to avoid the death of several. This result is produced by the lesser-evil principle, under which killing one person is deemed a lesser evil than the death of more than one. To use the example of the Model Penal Code, it is justifiable to deflect flood waters to a farm, even if a family there would be killed, to avert flooding the whole town, which would result in many more deaths. It does not matter that the farm family members are wholly innocent and nonthreatening bystanders, or that deflecting the flood waters to them is itself an act of aggression that violates their rights.

But this maximizing-lives principle is not applicable to a case where a person is being threatened by an attacker, even multiple attackers. The privilege of self-defense justifies the person attacked in taking the life of his attacker to save his own life, no matter how many attackers there are. So maximizing lives here yields to the person's right to resist aggression and save himself. Moreover that right exists even if the attackers are innocent — that they would have a defense of absence of intent, negligence or mental capacity, or a defense of duress or youth would not qualify the right of the victim to kill them if necessary to save his life. See Model Penal Code §3.11.

But stories, even farfetched ones, tell more than propositions. Suppose a terrorist and her insane husband and eight-year-old son are operating a machine gun emplacement from a flat in an apartment building. They are about to shoot down a member of the diplomatic corps, whose headquarters the terrorist band is attacking. His only chance is to throw a hand grenade (which he earlier picked up from a fallen terrorist) through his assailants' window. Under the Model Penal Code and American law he will be legally justified in doing so. His right to resist the aggressors' threat is determinative. The value of preserving even the lives of the terrorist, her legally insane husband and their infant son carry no weight on the scale of rights.

Add to the facts that the victim knows there is one person in an adjoining flat who will surely be killed by the blast. Now the diplomat would *not* be legally justified in throwing the grenade (though he might be excused), for his action will not result in a net saving of nonaggressor lives. The right of the person in the adjoining flat (who is no part of the threat against him) not to be subjected to his aggression is, therefore, determinative.

Finally, assume in addition that the terrorists are directing the machine gun against a companion as well as himself. Under the lesser-evil doctrine the victim will be legally justified in throwing the grenade. The right of the person in the adjoining flat is the same, but that person's claim of right yields to the social valuation that the two other lives are to be preferred over his one life.

This last case reveals the anomaly in the law: that rights prevail over lives in the aggression cases, even multiple or innocent lives, but that lives prevail over rights in the bystander cases like this one or the flood deflection case. We must conclude that, to the extent this is the law, a bystander's right against aggression yields to a utilitarian assessment in terms of net saving of lives. Yet, it should be added, this is not always so, for there are some killings fairly within the net-saving-of-lives, lesser-evil doctrine that we can be sure courts would not sanction — for example, killing a person to obtain his organs to save the lives of several other people, or even removing them for that purpose against his will without killing him. This evidences an acute moral unease with reliance on a utilitarian calculus for assessing the justification of intended killings, even when a net savings of lives is achieved.

PROBLEM

Can the innocent victim of a lesser-evil choice use force to protect himself? For example, *A*'s house stands just outside the main village. A storm of unusual intensity threatens to break the levee protecting the village from flooding by a nearby river. *B*, seeking to avert the danger to the village and its occupants, prepares to explode a hole in the levee at a point calculated to cause the flood to miss the town but to inundate *A*'s house, which has been evacuated. *A* holds *B* off with a loaded gun, preventing *B* from setting the explosion. The village is flooded, with loss of life and property. Is *A* guilty of assault with a deadly weapon? Of murder or manslaughter of the dead villagers? See Glanville Williams, Criminal Law: The General Part 745 (2d ed. 1961); Peter Glazebrook, The Necessity Plea in English Criminal Law, 30 Camb. L.J. 87, 93 (1972).

Professor Johannes Andenaes puts the following problem:

> An immediate blood transfusion must be made in order to save an injured person: the only one who has the same blood type as the injured refuses to give blood. Can he be overpowered and the blood taken from him?

The General Part of the Criminal Law of Norway 169 (1965).

Consider 2 James Fitzjames Stephen, History of the Criminal Law of England 108-109 (1883):

> In an American case in which sailors threw passengers overboard to lighten a boat it was held that the sailors ought to have been thrown overboard first unless they were required to work the boat, and that at all events the particular persons to be sacrificed ought to have been decided on by ballot. (Comm. v. Holmes, 1 Wall. Jr. 1.) Such a view appears to me to be over refined. Self-sacrifice may or may not be a moral duty, but it seems hard to make it a legal duty, and it is impossible to state its limits or the principle on which they can be determined. Suppose one of the party in the boat had a revolver and was able to use it, and refused either to draw lots or to allow himself or his wife or daughter to be made to do so or to be thrown overboard, could any one deny that he was acting in self-defence and the defence of his nearest relations, and would he violate any legal duty in so doing?

4.   Euthanasia

INTRODUCTORY NOTE

In the material on omissions, supra page 197, we considered the use of the omission doctrine to avoid criminal liability for physicians who withhold life-sustaining medical measures or withhold treatment from terminal patients or those in a permanent vegetative state. Here we revisit the subject of what may loosely be called "euthanasia" to consider how far courts have gone in making legally justified the actions of those who directly take the life of a person who consents, or who help another person take his own life.

CRUZAN v. DIRECTOR, MISSOURI DEPT. OF HEALTH

Supreme Court of the United States
497 U.S. 261 (1989)

CHIEF JUSTICE REHNQUIST delivered the opinion of the Court.

On the night of January 11, 1983, Nancy Cruzan lost control of her car as she traveled down Elm Road in Jasper County, Missouri. The vehicle overturned, and Cruzan was discovered lying face down in a ditch without detectable respiratory or cardiac function. . . . She now lies in a Missouri state hospital in what is commonly referred to as a persistent vegetative state: generally, a condition in which a person exhibits motor reflexes but evinces no indications of significant cognitive function. The State of Missouri is bearing the cost of her care.

After it had become apparent that Nancy Cruzan had virtually no chance of regaining her mental faculties, her parents asked hospital employees to terminate the artificial nutrition and hydration procedures. All agree that such a removal would cause her death. The employees refused to honor the request without court approval. The parents then sought and received authorization from the state trial court for termination. The court found that a person in Nancy's condition had a fundamental right under the State and Federal Constitutions to refuse or direct the withdrawal of "death prolonging procedures." The court also found that Nancy's "expressed thoughts at age twenty-five in somewhat serious conversation with a housemate friend that if sick or injured she would not wish to continue her life unless she could live at least halfway normally suggests that given her present condition she would not wish to continue on with her nutrition and hydration."

The Supreme Court of Missouri reversed by a divided vote. . . . The court found that Cruzan's statements to her roommate regarding her desire to live or die under certain conditions were "unreliable for the purpose of determining her intent," "and thus insufficient to support the co-guardians['] claim to exercise substituted judgment on Nancy's behalf." . . .

We granted certiorari to consider the question whether Cruzan has a right under the United States Constitution which would require the hospital to withdraw life-sustaining treatment from her under these circumstances.

. . . Before the turn of the century, this Court observed that "[n]o right is held more sacred, or is more carefully guarded, by the common law, than the right of every individual to the possession and control of his own person, free from all restraint or interference of others, unless by clear and unquestionable authority of law." Union Pacific R. Co. v. Botsford, 141 U.S. 250, 251 (1891). This notion of bodily integrity has been embodied in the requirement that informed consent is generally required for medical treatment. Justice Cardozo, while on the Court of Appeals of New York, aptly described this doctrine: "Every human being of adult years and sound mind has a right to determine what shall be done with his own body; and a surgeon who performs an operation without his patient's consent commits an assault, for which he is liable in damages." Schloendorff v. Society of New York Hospital, 211 N.Y. 125, 129-130, 105 N.E. 92, 93 (1914). The informed consent doctrine has become firmly entrenched in American tort law . . .

The logical corollary of the doctrine of informed consent is that the patient generally possesses the right not to consent, that is, to refuse treatment. . . .

In [In re Quinlan, 70 N.J. 10, 355 A.2d 647 (1976)], young Karen Quinlan suffered severe brain damage as the result of anoxia and entered a persistent vegetative state. Karen's father sought judicial approval to disconnect his daughter's respirator. The New Jersey Supreme Court granted the relief, holding that Karen had a right of privacy grounded in the Federal Constitution to terminate treatment. . . .

After *Quinlan* . . . most courts have based a right to refuse treatment either solely on the common-law right to informed consent or on both the common-law right and a constitutional privacy right. [The Court then reviewed the state case law developments that followed *Quinlan*.]

As these cases demonstrate, the common-law doctrine of informed consent is viewed as generally encompassing the right of a competent individual to refuse medical treatment. . . . This is the first case in which we have been squarely presented with the issue whether the United States Constitution grants what is in common parlance referred to as a "right to die." . . .

The Fourteenth Amendment provides that no State shall "deprive any person of life, liberty, or property, without due process of law." The principle that a competent person has a constitutionally protected liberty interest in refusing unwanted medical treatment may be inferred from our prior decisions. . . .

But determining that a person has a "liberty interest" under the Due Process Clause does not end the inquiry; "whether respondent's constitutional rights have been violated must be determined by balancing his liberty interests against the relevant state interests." Youngberg v. Romeo, 457 U.S. 307, 321 (1982).

Petitioners insist that under the general holdings of our cases, the forced administration of life-sustaining medical treatment, and even of artificially delivered food and water essential to life, would implicate a competent person's liberty interest. Although we think the logic of the cases discussed above would embrace such a liberty interest, the dramatic consequences involved in refusal of such treatment would inform the inquiry as to whether the deprivation of that interest is constitutionally permissible. But for purposes of this case, we assume that the United States Constitution would grant a competent person a constitutionally protected right to refuse lifesaving hydration and nutrition.

Petitioners go on to assert that an incompetent person should possess the same right in this respect as is possessed by a competent person. . . .

The difficulty with petitioners' claim is that in a sense it begs the question: An incompetent person is not able to make an informed and voluntary choice to exercise a hypothetical right to refuse treatment or any other right. Such a "right" must be exercised for her, if at all, by some sort of surrogate. Here, Missouri has in effect recognized that under certain circumstances a surrogate may act for the patient in electing to have hydration and nutrition withdrawn in such a way as to cause death, but it has established a procedural safeguard to assure that the action of the surrogate conforms as best it may to the wishes expressed by the patient while competent. Missouri requires that evidence of the incompetent's wishes as to the withdrawal of treatment be proved by clear and convincing evidence. The question, then, is whether the United States Constitution forbids the establishment of this procedural requirement by the State. We hold that it does not.

Whether or not Missouri's clear and convincing evidence requirement comports with the United States Constitution depends in part on what interests the State may properly seek to protect in this situation. Missouri relies on its interest in the protection and preservation of human life, and there can be no gainsaying this interest. . . .

We cannot say that the Supreme Court of Missouri committed constitutional error in reaching the conclusion that it did.

The judgment of the Supreme Court of Missouri is affirmed.

JUSTICE SCALIA, concurring. . . .

[F]ederal courts have no business in this field; . . . American law has always accorded the State the power to prevent, by force if necessary, suicide — including suicide by refusing to take appropriate measures necessary to preserve one's life. . . .

The test of the Due Process Clause does not protect individuals against deprivations of liberty simpliciter. It protects them against deprivations of liberty "without due process of law." To determine that such a deprivation would not occur if Nancy Cruzan were forced to take nourishment against her will, it is unnecessary to reopen the historically recurrent debate over whether "due process" includes substantive restrictions. It is at least true that no "substantive due process" claim can be maintained unless the claimant demonstrates that the State has deprived him of a right historically and traditionally protected against state interference. That cannot possibly be established here.

At common law in England, a suicide — defined as one who "deliberately puts an end to his own existence, or commits any unlawful malicious act, the consequence of which is his own death," 4 W. Blackstone, Commentaries *189 — was criminally liable. Ibid. Although the States abolished the penalties imposed by the common law (i.e., forfeiture and ignominious burial), they did so to spare the innocent family and not to legitimize the act. Case law at the time of the adoption of the Fourteenth Amendment generally held that assisting suicide was a criminal offense. . . .

Petitioners rely on three distinctions to separate Nancy Cruzan's case from ordinary suicide: (1) that she is permanently incapacitated and in pain; (2) that she would bring on her death not by any affirmative act but by merely declining treatment that provides nourishment; and (3) that preventing her from effectuating her presumed wish to die requires violation of her bodily integrity. None of these suffices. Suicide was not excused even when committed "to avoid those ills which [persons] had not the fortitude to endure." 4 Blackstone, supra, at *189. . . .

The second asserted distinction . . . relies on the dichotomy between action and inaction. Suicide, it is said, consists of an affirmative act to end one's life; refusing treatment is not an affirmative act "causing" death, but merely a passive acceptance of the natural process of dying. I readily acknowledge that the distinction between action and inaction has some bearing upon the legislative judgment of what ought to be prevented as suicide — though even there it would seem to me unreasonable to draw the line precisely between action and inaction, rather than between various forms of inaction. It would not make much sense to say that one may not kill oneself by walking into the sea, but may sit on the beach until submerged by the incoming tide; or that one may not intentionally lock oneself into a cold storage locker, but may refrain from coming indoors when the temperature drops below freezing. . . . Starving oneself to death is no different from putting a gun to one's temple as far as the common-law definition of suicide is concerned; the cause of death in both cases is the suicide's conscious decision to "pu[t] an end to his own existence." 4 Blackstone, supra, at *189. . . .

The third asserted basis of distinction — that frustrating Nancy Cruzan's wish to die in the present case requires interference with her bodily integrity — is likewise inadequate, because such interference is impermissible only if one begs the question whether her refusal to undergo the treatment on her own is suicide. It has always been lawful not only for the State, but even for private citizens, to interfere with bodily integrity to prevent a felony. That general rule has of course been applied to suicide. . . .

PEOPLE v. KEVORKIAN

Supreme Court of Michigan
— N.W.2d — (1994)

[Dr. Jack Kevorkian was prosecuted under Mich. Comp. L. §752.1027 for intentionally assisting several persons to commit suicide by providing them with the physical means of doing so.[a] Dr. Kevorkian raised a number of defenses, including the unconstitutionality of the statute under the due process clause of the United States Constitution. The Michigan Supreme Court upheld the statute against this challenge in the following opinion.]

CAVANAGH, C. J., and BRICKLEY and GRIFFIN, JJ. [BOYLE and RILEY, JJ., concurring.] [T]he threshold question in this case is whether the [due process] clause encompasses a fundamental right to commit suicide and, if so, whether it includes a right to assistance. Those who assert that there is such a right rely heavily on decisions of the United States Supreme Court in abortion and so-called "right to die" cases. Focusing especially on Planned Parenthood of South-

---

a. The statute reads as follows:
(1) A person who has knowledge that another person intends to commit or attempt to commit suicide and who intentionally does either of the following is guilty of criminal assistance to suicide, a felony punishable by imprisonment for not more than 4 years or by a fine of not more than $2,000.00, or both:
(a) Provides the physical means by which the other person attempts or commits suicide.
(b) Participates in a physical act by which the other person attempts or commits suicide.
(2) Subsection (1) shall not apply to withholding or withdrawing medical treatment.
(3) Subsection (1) does not apply to prescribing, dispensing, or administering medications or procedures if the intent is to relieve pain or discomfort and not to cause death, even if the medication or procedure may hasten or increase the risk of death. — EDS.

eastern Pennsylvania v. Casey, 112 S. Ct. 2791 (1992), and Cruzan v. Director, Missouri Dep't of Health, 497 U.S. 261 (1990), these advocates argue that the right to end one's own life is a fundamental liberty interest, grounded in the notion of personal autonomy and springing from common-law concepts of bodily integrity and informed consent. They further contend that an integral part of this protected interest is the right to assistance, hence the term "assisted suicide." . . .

The advocates of assisted suicide ask us to adopt the reasoning of a recent federal decision that invalidated the State of Washington's criminal prohibition against assisted suicide. The court held in Compassion in Dying v. Washington, 850 F. Supp. 1454, 1461 (W.D. Wash. 1994), that the right of a terminally ill person to the assistance of a physician in committing suicide is analogous to the right of abortion because both fall within the 'realm of personal liberty which the government may not enter.'"

The federal court found that the rationale in *Casey* was "almost prescriptive" of the right to end one's life. The court held that, under *Casey,* the state cannot proscribe assisted suicide if such a ban would unduly burden the right to commit suicide, i.e., if the purpose of the ban is to place a substantial obstacle in the path of the person seeking to exercise the right.

The federal court also found that the right of a terminally ill person to commit suicide with assistance does not differ in a constitutional sense from the right recognized in *Cruzan* to refuse life-sustaining medical treatment. The essential premise of the court's holding was that, in each instance, the liberty interest is "the freedom to make choices according to one's individual conscience about those matters which are essential to personal autonomy and basic human dignity."

We disagree. . . . In *Cruzan,* the Court was able to "assume" a protected liberty interest in the withdrawal of life-sustaining medical treatment because it was able to distinguish between acts that artifically sustain life and acts that artificially curtail life. Although some suggest that this is a distinction without constitutional significance — a meaningless exercise in semantic gymnastics — the Cruzan majority disagreed and so do we.

Indeed, the notion that there is a difference between action and inaction is not unfamiliar to the law. . . . [W]hereas suicide involves an affirmative act to end a life, the refusal or cessation of life-sustaining medical treatment simply permits life to run its course, unencumbered by contrived intervention. Put another way, suicide frustrates the natural course by introducing an outside agent to accelerate death, whereas the refusal or withdrawal of life-sustaining medical treatment allows nature to proceed, i.e., death occurs because of the underlying condition. . . .

We agree that persons who opt to discontinue life-sustaining medical treatment are not, in effect, committing suicide. There is a difference between choosing a natural death summoned by an uninvited illness or calamity, and deliberately seeking to terminate one's life by resorting to death-inducing measures unrelated to the natural process of dying. . . . *Cruzan* does not portend that the United States Supreme Court would find a fundamental liberty interest in suicide, let alone assisted suicide, that is protected by the Due Process Clause of the Fourteenth Amendment.

Neither does *Casey* provide support for the position that the Due Process Clause encompasses a fundamental right to commit suicide. . . .

Although acts of suicide are documented throughout the recorded history of England and this nation, we find no indication of widespread societal approval. To the contrary, suicide was a criminal offense, with significant stigmatizing consequences. As a policy matter, and for practical reasons, suicide was not criminalized in most states. Lawmakers recognized the futility of punishment and the harshness of property forfeiture and other consequences. . . . One who assisted a suicide was accorded no such concession, however. At the time the Fourteenth Amendment was ratified, at least twenty-one of the thirty-seven existing states (including eighteen of the thirty ratifying states) proscribed assisted suicide either by statute or as a common-law offense. . . . Presently, a substantial number of jurisdictions have specific statutes that criminalize assisted suicide, and the Model Penal Code also provides for criminal penalties. . . .

On the basis of the foregoing analysis, we . . . hold that the right to commit suicide is neither implicit in the concept of ordered liberty nor deeply rooted in this nation's history and tradition. . . . We . . . hold that the Due Process Clause of the federal constitution does not encompass a fundamental right to commit suicide, with or without assistance, and regardless of whether the would-be assistant is a physician. . . .

LEVIN, J. [dissenting.]

The real issue facing the Court is not whether suicide or assisting suicide can be proscribed by law, but whether the Due Process Clause bars a state from depriving a competent, terminally ill person, facing imminent death, and increasing agony, from obtaining medical assistance to avoid suffering such a bitter end of life.

The lead opinion distinguishes at length the instant cases from *Cruzan* and *Casey*, and stresses the obvious: there is a long history of laws outlawing suicide. Abortion and withdrawal of life-sustaining measures are indeed different from assisted suicide. Nevertheless, a reasoned application of the principles stated in *Casey* and *Cruzan* persuades me that state law restrictions on a person's ability to end his life implicate the interest in personal liberty. Whether a competent, terminally ill person has a right to medical assistance to commit suicide cannot be decided without balancing the state's interest against the person's interest. . . .

A rule allowing a person to have his respirator disconnected, but to take no other steps to end his life, condemns him to choke to death on his own sputum. Similarly, if the law bars a person who can only take nourishment through a feeding tube from taking steps in addition to ordering the tube removed to end his life, he is required to suffer death by starvation and dehydration. Barring such persons from taking other steps to end their lives would, I think, constitute an undue burden on the right implicitly recognized in *Cruzan*. *Cruzan* should not be read as limiting a person to a half step when that would result in greater suffering. The legitimate concerns about involuntary euthanasia apply with at least as much force to the withdrawal of life support where the person is incompetent, yet the United States Supreme Court in *Cruzan* held that a state statute permitting the withdrawal of life support on proof of the incompetent's wishes by clear and convincing evidence was consistent with due process. . . .

Where an otherwise healthy person is depressed or mentally disturbed, the personal liberty interest is weak, and the state has a strong interest in protecting the person's interests in life. In contrast, where the person involved is competent, terminally ill, and facing imminent, agonizing death, the interest of the state in preserving life is weak, and the interest of the terminally ill person in ending suffering is strong. . . .

MALLETT, J. [dissenting.]

The lead opinion . . . contend[s] that liberty interests exist only where conduct is " 'deeply rooted in this Nation's history and tradition' " or " 'implicit in the concept of order liberty.'. . ." They argue that because there is a common background making suicide and assisted suicide crimes, physician-assisted suicide cannot be a fundamental right. They also argue that such a right cannot be found anywhere in the constitution or its amendments. However, to recognize only fundamental rights according to such a test is unsuitable for the vast and fast-moving progressions of the modern world. Earlier laws or traditions are not the "source" of liberty or privacy interests. If this were so, our nation's Supreme Court would have been unable to recognize the rights that many of us now understand to be inherent in our very being. . . .

[S]ome decisions remain so personal in nature that society is not in a position to make judgments about their appropriateness. It is difficult to imagine a more personal or intimate choice than determining the nature or extent of one's suffering during a terminal illness. A person's conscience, coupled with the advice of an informed and personally chosen physician, is the appropriate decision-making method. Therefore, . . . [a] complete ban on physician-assisted suicide represents an "undue burden" on the right of the terminally ill to end their suffering through physician-prescribed medications. As in *Casey*, an infringement of a fundamental right by the state that completely bars the exercise of that right cannot pass constitutional muster. . . .[10]

While it is arguable that each of us possesses the right to commit suicide because suicide is no longer criminally punishable, such a right, if it exists, is not absolute when a third party is involved. . . . Accordingly, I do not embrace the suggestion that because a person may have the right to commit suicide, he also has an unconditional constitutional right to physician-assisted suicide. Rather, the right to physician-assisted suicide must be balanced against the countervailing interests of the state and society. . . . [A]uthorities have uniformly maintained that a "state's interest in the preservation of life has been held to be insufficient to outweigh the individual right where the life which would be preserved would be one in a merely vegetative state or one enduring only a

10. In the only other case directly addressing the constitutionality of an assisted suicide law, Compassion in Dying v. Washington, supra, the court was asked to rule on the constitutionality of the State of Washington's assisted suicide law. The court stated that abortion raises even more difficult questions about competing interests than does suicide by the terminally ill. "In reproductive rights cases, there is not only the interest of the pregnant woman seeking an abortion, but also the potential life interest which cannot speak for itself. By contrast, in the case of assisted suicide involving a competent person, only one life is involved and that individual can voice his or her wishes." Id. at 1460. . . . The court concluded: "[T]he suffering of a terminally ill person cannot be deemed any less intimate or personal, or any less deserving of protection from unwarranted governmental interference, than that of a pregnant woman. Thus, consonant with the reasoning in *Casey*, such an intimate personal decision *falls within the realm of the liberties constitutionally protected under the Fourteenth Amendment*." [Id. at 1460 (emphasis added).]

prolonged process of dying. . . ." Similarly, there does not exist a sufficiently compelling justification for the infringement of the right of a competent, terminally ill person suffering from great pain to hasten death through physician-prescribed medications.

NOTE

Public referenda to legalize assisted suicide (and active euthanasia as well) were voted on in Washington in 1991 and California in 1992. While both were defeated, the voting reflected a deep split in public opinion. More recently an Oregon initiative petition was passed by a majority at the November 8, 1994, election, resulting in the enactment of the Oregon Death with Dignity Act, 1995 Or. Laws ch. 3, the first such legislation in the United States. The ballot description of the act reads as follows:

> This measure would allow an informed and capable adult resident of Oregon, who is terminally ill and within six months of death, to voluntarily request a prescription for medication to take his or her life. The measure allows a physician to prescribe a lethal dose of medication when conditions of the measure are met. . . .
>
> The process begins when the patient makes the request of his or her physician, who shall:
>
> - Determine if the patient is terminally ill, is capable of making health care decisions, and has made the request voluntarily.
> - Inform the patient of his or her diagnosis and prognosis; the risks and results of taking the medication; and alternatives, including comfort care, hospice care, and pain control. . . .
> - Ask that the patient notify next of kin. . . .
> - Refer the patient for counseling, if appropriate.
> - Refer the patient to a consulting physician.
>
> A consulting physician, who is qualified by specialty or experience, must confirm the diagnosis and determine that the patient is capable and acting voluntarily. If either physician believes that the patient might be suffering from a psychiatric or psychological disorder, or from depression causing impaired judgment, the physician must refer the patient to a licensed psychiatrist or psychologist for counseling. The psychiatrist or psychologist must determine that the patient does not suffer from such a disorder before medication may be prescribed. . . .
>
> At least fifteen days must pass from the time of the initial oral request and 48 hours must pass from the time of the written request before the prescription may be written. Before writing the prescription, the attending physician must again verify the patient is making a voluntary and informed request, and offer the patient the opportunity to rescind the request. . . . Those who comply with the requirements of the measure are protected from prosecution and professional discipline. . . . The measure does not authorize lethal injection, mercy killing or active euthanasia. Actions taken in accordance with this measure shall not constitute suicide, assisted suicide, mercy killing or homicide, under the law.

For various views on the issues see Ronald Dworkin, Life's Dominion 179 (1993); Note, Physician-Assisted Suicide and the Right to Die with Assistance,

105 Harv. L. Rev. 2031 (1992); Comment (E. A. Gifford), *Artes Moriendi:* Active Euthanasia and the Art of Dying, 40 U.C.L.A. L. Rev. 1545 (1993). See also what has become a classic exchange on legalizing euthanasia: Glanville Williams, the Sanctity of Life and the Criminal Law (1956); Yale Kamisar, Some Non-Religous Views Against Proposed "Mercy-Killing" Legislation, 42 Minn. L. Rev. 969 (1958); Glanville Williams, "Mercy-Killing" Legislation — A Rejoinder, 43 Minn. L. Rev. 1 (1958).

Consider the following points of view.

Sanford H. Kadish, Letting Patients Die: Legal and Moral Reflections, 80 Cal. L. Rev. 857, 867-868 (1992): One ground on which courts have sought to distinguish letting-die situations from conventional suicide is that the latter requires affirmative life-taking actions. On this view a patient refusing to be attached to an apparatus necessary for his survival is not taking his life, but is simply letting nature take its course. Hence death is caused by the disease, not by the person himself, nor by the physician who respects his wishes. [This] distinction between intentionally killing oneself and intentionally submitting to an avoidable death is suspect. There is disagreement over the general moral significance of the distinction between doing and letting happen, but the intuitive appeal of the distinction is less in some cases than in others, and its appeal seems particularly weak in cases of treatment refusal.

Consider a patient who finds himself attached against his will to some life-sustaining apparatus he had earlier explicitly rejected. He removes it for the same reason he earlier rejected it — he prefers death to living attached to a machine — and dies moments later. Presumably this would constitute suicide, since he achieved his death by positive actions. But could we justifiably say that if the doctors had followed his instructions and he had died, this would not be suicide because his death would then not have been caused by the patient's actions? Or consider an analogous case: a paralyzed man, sitting on a beach threatened by an incoming tide, deliberately, in order to end his life, declines to allow a lifeguard to move him out of harm's way, and drowns in consequence. (To make the analogy closer, assume he took no action to place himself in danger from the tide — say, for example, he was initially placed there against his will.) Would it not be correct to see this as a suicide? Yet the person dying of a disease who chooses not to permit some medical intervention that would save him is in no different a situation.

We might have good reasons to think that in certain circumstances intentionally achieving one's death is justifiable, or that it is less blameworthy in some circumstances than in others. Moreover, we may for these reasons, or indeed for other reasons of a more practical and prudential character, want to call it something else. But as a matter of principle, that a person achieves his goal by refusing necessary medical intervention hardly seems a better reason to treat his action differently than that a person achieves his goal by letting the tide come to him rather than going to it. . . .

Consider the basic argument courts and commentators make on behalf of the right to refuse treatment. The argument is that the choice between medical treatment and death is so fundamental that it is protected against state control by a constitutional right of autonomy. That being the case, however, there is no principled basis for denying the same freedom of choice to those not dependent on medical treatment for survival. The failure of efforts to distinguish suicide from refusal of treatment is attributable not simply to usage and definition, but to the equivalence between the two. The moral case for autonomy extends to both if it extends to one.

It isn't hard to surmise why courts have drawn back from the conclusion that there is no difference between suicide and refusal of treatment. To accept it would be to acknowledge a radical break with the received tradition and open the door to positions the courts are not yet willing to adopt: for example, that the state may not act to prevent suicide (except perhaps temporarily to assure competent consent), or to prevent a person from assisting another's suicide, or conceivably even to prevent one person from killing another who competently consents to being killed. By "open the door" I do not mean that courts would be compelled by consistency to adopt these positions. There might well be compelling practical considerations for not doing so, such as fear of abuse and difficulties of administering controls to prevent such abuse. I mean only that, by not distinguishing suicide and consensual euthanasia, the courts would by implication be endorsing these positions in principle. Yet this would be the greatest affront to the moral tradition. The courts, therefore, have chosen to improvise lines of distinction, even at the cost of some coherence. The distinctions permit results that courts regard as right in the medical context while giving at least the appearance of continuity with the established tradition and avoiding positions that may be either impractical or premature. As I have suggested, it is not unusual for common law courts to adopt lines of distinction out of unspoken considerations of strategy rather than of logic and principle. This is such a case.

New York State Task Force on Life and the Law, When Death Is Sought — Assisted Suicide in the Medical Context ix, xiii-xiv (1994): Recent proposals to legalize assisted suicide and euthanasia in some states would transform the right to decide about medical treatment into a far broader right to control the timing and manner of death. After lengthy deliberations, the Task Force unanimously concluded that the dangers of such a dramatic change in public policy would far outweigh any possible benefits. In light of the pervasive failure of our health care system to treat pain and diagnose and treat depression, legalizing assisted suicide and euthanasia would be profoundly dangerous for many individuals who are ill and vulnerable. The risks would be most severe for those who are elderly, poor, socially disadvantaged, or without access to good medical care. . . .

The Task Force members unanimously concluded that legalizing assisted suicide and euthanasia would pose profound risks to many patients. . . .

No matter how carefully any guidelines are framed, assisted suicide and euthanasia will be practiced through the prism of social inequality and bias that characterizes the delivery of services in all segments of our society, including health care. The practices will pose the greatest risks to those who are poor, elderly, members of a minority group, or without access to good medical care.

The growing concern about health care costs increases the risks presented by legalizing assisted suicide and euthanasia. This cost consciousness will not be diminished, and may well be exacerbated, by health care reform.

The clinical safeguards that have been proposed to prevent abuse and errors would not be realized in many cases. For example, most doctors do not have a long-standing relationship with their patients or information about the complex personal factors relevant to evaluating a request for suicide assistance or a lethal injection. In addition, neither treatment for pain nor the diagnosis of and treatment for depression is widely available in clinical practice.

The Task Force members feel deep compassion for patients in those rare cases when pain cannot be alleviated even with aggressive palliative care. They also recognize that the desire for control at life's end is widely shared and deeply felt. As a society, however, we have better ways to give people greater control and relief from suffering than by legalizing assisted suicide and euthanasia.

Depression accompanied by feelings of hopelessness is the strongest predictor of suicide for both individuals who are terminally ill and those who are not. Most doctors, however, are not trained to diagnose depression, especially in complex cases such as patients who are terminally ill. Even if diagnosed, depression is often not treated. In elderly patients as well as the terminally and chronically ill, depression is grossly underdiagnosed and undertreated.

The presence of unrelieved pain also increases susceptibility to suicide. The undertreatment of pain is a widespread failure of current medical practice, with far-reaching implications for proposals to legalize assisted suicide and euthanasia.

If assisted suicide and euthanasia are legalized, it will blunt our perception of what it means for one individual to assist another to commit suicide or to take another person's life. Over time, as the practices are incorporated into the standard arsenal of medical treatments, the sense of gravity about the practices would dissipate.

The criteria and safeguards that have been proposed for assisted suicide and euthanasia would prove elastic in clinical practice and in law. Policies limiting suicide to the terminally ill, for example, would be inconsistent with the notion that suicide is a compassionate choice for patients who are in pain or suffering. As long as the policies hinge on notions of pain or suffering, they are uncontainable; neither pain nor suffering can be gauged objectively, nor are they subject to the kind of judgments needed to fashion coherent public policy. Euthanasia to cover those who are incapable of consenting would also be a likely, if not inevitable, extension of any policy permitting the practice for those who can consent.

These concerns are heightened by experience in the Netherlands, where the practices have been legally sanctioned. Although Dutch law requires an explicit request for euthanasia by the patient, a national study in the Netherlands found that of approximately 3300 deaths annually resulting from mercy killing, 1,000 deaths from euthanasia occurred without an explicit request. Moreover, in some cases, doctors have provided assisted suicide in response to suffering caused solely by psychiatric illness, including severe depression.

Yale Kamisar, A Law to Stay the Cold Hand of "Dr. Death," Legal Times, Mar. 8, 1993, at 2: The argument for assisted suicide (and for active euthanasia as well) has a certain logical appeal. After all, if one can bring about death by declining medical treatment, why can't one achieve the same result by enlisting the aid of others in committing suicide? Isn't that the next logical step?

But why stop there? Doctor-assisted suicide is not quite active euthanasia, for the final act is performed by the patient herself, not by another. And there is always the possibility that the patient may not carry out the final act. Suppose that a person cannot swallow sleeping pills or trigger a suicide machine or is otherwise unable to perform the final act by herself? Isn't the next logical step, and a short step at that, the right to authorize others to engage in euthanasia?

Of course, doctor-administered euthanasia is the direct, intentional killing of an innocent person. The criminal laws of every state prohibit that — regardless of the consent of the person killed or the motive of the killer. Are all these laws to be struck down, too, insofar as they violate the right to die?

The right to die is a sound principle in certain settings. But it is also a vague, unruly concept. If there really is a broad right to die, why should it be limited to the terminally ill or even the seriously ill? Why should we set any limits on the right to decide the time and manner of one's death?

. . . The right-to-die principle should not be carried to the point where it collides with other principles rubbing against it from other directions — such as the principle that the law protects all human life regardless of the worth or value of a person. . . . .

That is why the right to die should be confined to the right to decline or to terminate life-sustaining treatment. A state that so limits the right may be said by some to be acting illogically, but, given our history and our culture, it is not acting unconstitutionally.

Joel Feinberg, Overlooking the Merits of the Individual Case: An Unpromising Approach to the Right to Die, 4 Ratio Juris. 131, 150-151 (1991): [M]ost of the arguments against the legalization of voluntary euthanasia (or in favour of creating legal impediments to it) are indirect arguments. They don't argue that individual cases judged internally, that is on their own merits, do not warrant euthanasia. Indeed, some of these arguments candidly concede that judged on the merits, many individual cases do deserve euthanasia. Rather, these arguments favour deliberately overlooking the merits of individual cases, and cite extraneous considerations in favour of a blanket prohibition. The most plausible of these arguments is the argument from abusable discretion, which maintains that if legally competent individuals are granted the discretion to decide on their own whether in certain circumstances to continue or to terminate life-sustaining treatment, the inevitability of honest mistakes and not-so-honest abuses will create evils that outweigh the evils of sustaining the comatose and the pain-wracked against their presumed wills. Convincing as the argument from abusable discretion may be in some contexts, . . . it fails in its application to the euthanasia situation, because it cannot be shown that the likely number of mistakenly killed individuals would constitute a greater evil than the likely number of mistakenly sustained individuals. The philosophical problem of voluntary euthanasia is in large part a matter of comparing real risks. The enemy of voluntary euthanasia errs in minimizing the evils of human suffering and overrating the value of merely biological life in the absence of a human person, or in the presence of a human person whose sufferings are too severe for him to have a human life, even though his heart beats on.

B. PRINCIPLES OF EXCUSE

1. Introduction

We pointed out earlier (Note on Culpability and Excuse, page 257 supra), the close relation between the mens rea doctrines there explored (mens rea in its special sense) and the general principles of excuse (mens rea in its general sense). The materials that follow are designed to explore that relationship.

J. L. AUSTIN, A PLEA FOR EXCUSES
57 Proceedings Aristotelian Soc. 1 (1956-1957)

One way of [defending conduct] is to admit flatly that he, *X*, did do that very thing, *A*, but to argue that it was a good thing, or the right or sensible thing, or a permissible thing to do, either in general or at least in the special circumstances of the occasion. To take this line is to *justify* the action, to give reasons for doing it . . .

A different way of going about it is to admit that it wasn't a good thing to have done, but to argue that it is not quite fair or correct to say *baldly* "*X* did *A*." We may say it isn't fair just to say *X* did it; perhaps he was under somebody's influence, or was nudged. Or, it isn't fair to say baldly he *did A;* it may have been partly accidental or an unintentional slip. Or, it isn't fair to say he did simply *A* — he was really doing something quite different and *A* was only incidental, or he was looking at the whole thing quite differently. Naturally these arguments can be combined or overlap or run into each other.

In the one defence, briefly, we accept responsibility but deny that it was bad: in the other, we admit that it was bad but don't accept full, or even any, responsibility.

By and large, justifications can be kept distinct from excuses. . . . But the two certainly can be confused, and can *seem* to go very near to each other, even if they do not perhaps actually do so. [W]hen we plead, say, provocation, there is genuine uncertainty or ambiguity as to what we mean — is *he* partly responsible, because he roused a violent impulse or passion in me, so that it wasn't truly or merely me acting "of my own accord" (excuse)? Or is it rather that, he having done me such injury, I was entitled to retaliate (justification)? . . . But that the defences I have for convenience labelled "justification" and "excuse" are in principle distinct can scarcely be doubted.

A NOTE ON THE VARIETY OF EXCUSES[6]

As a prelude to examining the subject of legal excuses it will be useful to have an overview of the several kinds of excuses the law allows, particularly inasmuch as excuses don't always come bearing that label. Indeed, a number of them we have already examined under other guises, for example, the defense of involuntary action, and certain mens rea defenses. The classifications we present here

---

6. Adapted from Sanford H. Kadish, Excusing Crime, 75 Calif. L. Rev. 257 (1987).

are not the only way to classify legal excuses (see, for example, Michael Moore's classification in Causation and Excuses, 73 Cal. L. Rev. 201 (1985)), but they are one way and they are offered to help students perceive the similarities and differences among various defenses.

As Austin suggests, excuses occur when the law allows a defense (either total or partial, though we will here emphasize total defenses) to a wrongful action because the actor has displayed some disability in capacity to know or to choose, which renders the person either free of blame or subject to less blame. The disabilities that ground excuse in our law seem to fall into one of three groups: those disabilities that produce involuntary actions; those that produce deficient but reasonable actions; and those that render all actions irresponsible.

1. *Involuntary actions.* We have already studied this group of excuses under the label of the defense of the involuntary act. They include situations in which in the most literal sense the person had no control over his bodily movements. Cases of physical compulsion are obvious examples. Others are tumbling downstairs or being pushed. These are easy to deal with because we can see the external force being applied. But the law recognizes some excuses as belonging to this category even when the source of the lack of control is internal, as in the case of reflex movements or epileptic seizures.

Such extreme instances of involuntariness may be viewed as raising a bar to liability more fundamental even than excuse; namely, that there is no *action* at all, only bodily movement, so that there is nothing to excuse. Under this view, which represents the conventional characterization of the involuntary act defense, the defense comes to an "I-didn't-do-it" defense, a failure of the prima facie case. Alternatively, involuntariness may be viewed as the basis of an affirmative defense serving to excuse bodily movements of the defendant that did the harm, on the ground that the defendant was not responsible for them. Whichever way the involuntary act exculpation is classified, however, the reason it exculpates is the same — the defendant had no choice in the matter.

2. *Deficient but reasonable actions.* In the second group of excusing conditions there is power to choose in a literal sense — nothing prevents the person from making a choice — but the choice is so constrained that an ordinary law-abiding person could not be expected to choose otherwise. The constraining circumstances are of two kinds. In the first, the constraint arises from defect of knowledge; in the second, from defect of will.

(*a*) *Cognitive deficiency.* We have already studied the law's excuses based on lack of knowledge earlier in the sections on mens rea, particularly the section on Mistake of Fact, supra page 225. To constitute an excuse it is not enough that the person lacked knowledge of some relevant feature of his action — his lack of knowledge must itself be excusable, in the sense that he was not reckless, or perhaps, negligent in making the mistake.

For example, if you shoot at an object in the forest reasonably thinking it is a game animal, when in fact it is a person dressed in animal costume, you have killed by mistake. Of course, you could have chosen not to shoot at all. But once it is accepted that shooting in the circumstances, are you reasonably took them to be, was a proper action, the mistaken killing was an accident effectively beyond your control.

Explaining mistake or the related concept of accident as excuse is today some-what unconventional. Like the involuntary-act defense, accident and mistake are more likely to be viewed as precluding liability not because of excuse, but because the elements of the crime have not been proven, thus resulting in failure of the prima facie case. After all, homicidal crimes are defined to require a mens rea of at least culpable negligence. Why, then, in my example, isn't reasonable mistake or accident a defense, not because either one excuses what otherwise would be a crime, but simply because each negates the required culpable mens rea, without which there is no crime to excuse? The answer requires a brief explanation.

Some mens rea requirements are essential elements in the definition of the crime. Take loitering with criminal intent or reckless driving. Without the intent in the first case or recklessness in the second, there is only standing around or driving a car. There is nothing to excuse because we would not expect the person to have acted otherwise. This is the case with all crimes whose definitions, like that of loitering with intent and reckless driving, do not require occurrence of the ultimate harm the crimes seek to prevent. The concern of such crimes is the danger that the harm may occur. The mens rea serves to identify the presence of the danger. This is true of all inchoate crimes.

Other mens rea requirements, on the other hand, are excuses in mens rea clothing. They are excusing conditions because they serve to deny blame for a harm done. That they are cast in the form of mens rea requirements does not change their character. The reasons these particular mental states are required are the very reasons for excusing conditions — if a person could not reasonably be expected to know of some circumstance that made his action harmful, he could not reasonably be said to have effective power of choice to avoid the harm. This is why the defense of reasonable mistake functions as an excuse. True, its presence negates a required element of the crime, but the reason why that element (viz., that the person have acted at least negligently) is included in the definition of the crime is because a reasonable mistake is excusable. This was how mistake and accident were traditionally thought of before the Model Penal Code.[7]

(b) *Volitional deficiency.* The law's excuses based on defect of will (short of a total loss of will, as in the defense of involuntary action) are not as well developed as those based on defect of knowledge. Duress is the best established defense of this kind, and even its status is not free of doubt, as we shall shortly see. It is generally established when a person commits a crime under such threats of physical injury that even a person of reasonable fortitude would have yielded to the threat.

---

7. The dual character of accident and mistake defenses may be seen in Cal. Penal Code §26 (West 1993), enacted in 1872:

   All persons are capable of committing crimes except those belonging to the following classes: . . .
   Three — Persons who committed the act or made the omission charged under an ignorance or mistake of fact, which disproves any criminal intent. . . .
   Five — Persons who committed the act or made the omission charged through misfortune or by accident, when it appears that there was no evil design, intention, or negligence.

3. Irresponsible actions. The excuses in our third category, unlike those in the first, do not involve involuntary actions. And unlike those in the second, they do not rest on circumstances that would lead a person of normal capacities to make the choice the defendant made. The grounds for excuse are simply that this person could not have been expected to act otherwise, given the person's inadequate capacities for making rational judgments.

Our law is grudging with excuses of this kind. The individual's difficulty in complying with the law is a common ground for sentencing mitigation, but it is rarely a ground for a total excuse. Infancy and legal insanity are the only two excuses of this kind the law allows, and because the juvenile court laws have preempted the defense of infancy in practice, legal insanity is the only significant defense remaining in this category.

While the basis for excuses in the second category is that the actor has shown herself no different from the rest of us, the basis of the insanity excuse is that she has shown herself *very* different from the rest of us. But how different, and in what respects? After all, those who commit atrocious crimes are certainly very different from the rest of us. That fact alone scarcely excuses them. We will examine these issues in the section on legal insanity.

The three categories of legal excuses just described suggest the common rationale behind them both in the law and in everyday moral judgments; namely, that justice precludes blame where none is deserved. In the first category, people are not to blame because they have no control over their movements; in the second, because they acted in circumstances so constraining that most people would have done the same; in the third, because they suffer from a fundamental deficiency of mind and are therefore not responsible moral agents.

Of course, one might escape excuses altogether by withdrawing the element of blame from a finding of criminality. Indeed there are some who would prefer that the criminal law reject all backward-looking judgments of punishment, blame, and responsibility and concern itself exclusively with identifying and treating those who constitute a social danger. We will examine this challenge later in connection with the proposals of Lady Barbara Wootton, infra page 1034.

2. Duress

STATE v. TOSCANO

Supreme Court of New Jersey
74 N.J. 421, 378 A.2d 755 (1977)

PASHMAN, J. Defendant Joseph Toscano was convicted of conspiring to obtain money by false pretenses in violation of N.J.S.A. 2A:98-1. Although admitting that he had aided in the preparation of a fraudulent insurance claim by making out a false medical report, he argued that he had acted under duress. The trial judge ruled that the threatened harm was not sufficiently imminent to justify charging the jury on the defense of duress. After the jury returned a verdict of guilty, the defendant was fined $500.

The Appellate Division affirmed the conviction. . . . We granted certification to consider the status of duress as an affirmative defense to a crime. . . .

On April 20, 1972, the Essex County Grand Jury returned a 48-count indictment alleging that eleven named defendants and two unindicted co-conspirators had defrauded various insurance companies by staging accidents in public places and obtaining payments in settlement of fictitious injuries. . . .

Dr. Joseph Toscano, a chiropractor, was named as a defendant in the First Count and in two counts alleging a conspiracy to defraud the Kemper Insurance Company (Kemper). Prior to trial, seven of the eleven defendants pleaded guilty to various charges, leaving defendant as the sole remaining defendant charged with the conspiracy to defraud Kemper. Among those who pleaded guilty was William Leonardo, the architect of the alleged general conspiracy and the organizer of each of the separate incidents. . . .

The State attempted to show that Toscano agreed to fill out the false medical report because he owed money to Richard Leonardo [William's brother] for gambling debts. It also suggested that Toscano subsequently sought to cover up the crime by fabricating office records of non-existent office visits by Hanaway.[a] Defendant sharply disputed these assertions and maintained that he capitulated to William Leonardo's demands only because he was fearful for his wife's and his own bodily safety. Since it is not our function here to assess these conflicting versions, we shall summarize only those facts which, if believed by the jury, would support defendant's claim of duress. . . .

[The court recited a number of overtures made by William Leonardo to defendant, which defendant refused, to prepare a false medical report for submission to a claims adjuster.]

The third and final call occurred on Friday evening. Leonardo was "boisterous and loud" repeating, "You're going to make this bill out for me." Then he said: "Remember, you just moved into a place that has a very dark entrance and you leave there with your wife. . . . You and your wife are going to jump at shadows when you leave that dark entrance." Leonardo sounded "vicious" and "desperate" and defendant felt that he "just had to do it" to protect himself and his wife. He thought about calling the police, but failed to do so in the hope that "it would go away and wouldn't bother me any more."

In accordance with Leonardo's instructions, defendant left a form in his mailbox on Saturday morning for Leonardo to fill in with the necessary information about the fictitious injuries. It was returned that evening and defendant completed it. On Sunday morning he met Hanaway at a prearranged spot and delivered a medical bill and the completed medical report. He received no compensation for his services, either in the form of cash from William Leonardo or forgiven gambling debts from Richard Leonardo. He heard nothing more from Leonardo after that Sunday.

Shortly thereafter, still frightened by the entire episode, defendant moved to a new address and had his telephone number changed to an unlisted number in an effort to avoid future contacts with Leonardo. He also applied for a gun permit but was unsuccessful. His superior at his daytime job with the Newark Housing Authority confirmed that the quality of defendant's work dropped so markedly that he was forced to question defendant about his attitude. After

---

a. Hanaway was an unindicted coconspirator who acted as the victim in a number of staged accidents. — EDS.

some conversation, defendant explained that he had been upset by threats against him and his wife. He also revealed the threats to a co-worker at the Newark Housing Authority.

After defendant testified, the trial judge granted the State's motion to exclude any further testimony in connection with defendant's claim of duress, and announced his decision not to charge the jury on that defense. . . .

After stating that the defense of duress is applicable only where there is an allegation that an act was committed in response to a threat of present, imminent and impending death or serious bodily harm, the trial judge charged the jury:

> Now, one who is standing and receiving instructions from someone at the point of a gun is, of course, in such peril. . . .
> Now, where the peril is not imminent, present and pending to the extent that the defendant has the opportunity to seek police assistance for himself and his wife as well, the law places upon such a person the duty not to acquiesce in the unlawful demand and any criminal conduct in which he may thereafter engage may not be excused. Now, this principle prevails regardless of the subjective estimate he may have made as to the degree of danger with which he or his wife may have been confronted. Under the facts of this case, I instruct you, as members of the jury, that the circumstances described by Dr. Toscano leading to his implication in whatever criminal activities in which you may find he participated are not sufficient to constitute the defense of duress.

. . . Since New Jersey has no applicable statute defining the defense of duress,[b] we are guided only by common law principles which conform to the purposes of our criminal justice system and reflect contemporary notions of justice and fairness.

At common law the defense of duress was recognized only when the alleged coercion involved a use or threat of harm which is "present, imminent and pending" and "of such a nature as to induce a well grounded apprehension of death or serious bodily harm if the act is not done."

It was commonly said that duress does not excuse the killing of an innocent person even if the accused acted in response to immediate threats. Aside from this exception, however, duress was permitted as a defense to prosecution for a range of serious offenses. . . .

To excuse a crime, the threatened injury must induce "such a fear as a man of ordinary fortitude and courage might justly yield to." Although there are scattered suggestions in early cases that only a fear of death meets this test, . . .[8] an apprehension of immediate serious bodily harm has been considered sufficient to excuse capitulation to threats. Thus, the courts have assumed as a matter of law that neither threats of slight injury nor threats of destruction to property are coercive enough to overcome the will of a person of ordinary courage. [The

---

b. New Jersey does have such a statute at the present time, the legislature having enacted in the meantime the draft proposal referred to subsequently in the court's opinion. — EDS.

8. Several states, by statute, continue to require that the actor have reasonable cause to believe that his life was in danger. . . . Minnesota limits the defense to situations in which "instant death" is threatened. Minn. Stat. 609.08 (1965).

court then referred to cases in which threats of loss of job, denial of food rations, economic need, and prospect of financial ruin were held inadequate.] . . . When the alleged source of coercion is a threat of "future" harm, courts have generally found that the defendant had a duty to escape from the control of the threatening person or to seek assistance from law enforcement authorities.

Assuming a "present, imminent and impending" danger, however, there is no requirement that the threatened person be the accused. [C]oncern for the well-being of another, particularly a near relative, can support a defense of duress if the other requirements are satisfied. . . .

The insistence under the common law on a danger of immediate force causing death or serious bodily injury may be ascribed to . . . judicial fears of perjury and fabrication of baseless defenses. We do not discount [this] concern as a reason for caution in modifying this accepted rule, but we are concerned by its obvious shortcomings and potential for injustice. Under some circumstances, the commission of a minor criminal offense should be excusable even if the coercive agent does not use or threaten force which is likely to result in death or "serious" bodily injury. Similarly, it is possible that authorities might not be able to prevent a threat of future harm from eventually being carried out. . . .

[S]ome commentators have advocated a flexible rule which would allow a jury to consider whether the accused actually lost his capacity to act in accordance with "his own desire, or motivation, or will" under the pressure of real or imagined forces. See Newman & Weitzer, "Duress, Free Will and the Criminal Law," 30 S. Cal. L. Rev. 313, 331 (1957); Fletcher, "The Individualization of Excusing Conditions," 47 S. Cal. L. Rev. 1269, 1288-93 (1974). The inquiry here would focus on the weaknesses and strengths of a particular defendant, and his subjective reaction to unlawful demands. Thus, the "standard of heroism" of the common law would give way, not to a "reasonable person" standard, but to a set of expectations based on the defendant's character and situation.

The drafters of the Model Penal code and the New Jersey Penal Code . . . focus[ed] on whether the standard imposed upon the accused was one with which "normal members of the community will be able to comply." . . .

They substantially departed from the existing statutory and common law limitations requiring that the result be death or serious bodily harm, that the threat be immediate and aimed at the accused, or that the crime committed be a noncapital offense. While these factors would be given evidential weight, the failure to satisfy one or more of these conditions would not justify the trial judge's withholding the defense from the jury. . . .

Although they are not entirely identical, under both model codes defendant would have had his claim of duress submitted to the jury.[12] Defendant's testimony provided a factual basis for a finding that Leonardo threatened him and his wife with physical violence if he refused to assist in the fraudulent scheme. Moreover, a jury might have found from other testimony adduced at trial that Leonardo's threats induced a reasonable fear in the defendant. Since he asserted that he agreed to complete the false documents only because of this ap-

---

12. The most significant difference between the two provisions is the treatment of duress as a defense to murder. The Model Penal Code permits it as an affirmative defense, while the New Jersey Penal Code allows it only to reduce a crime from murder to manslaughter.

prehension, the requisite elements of the defense were established. Under the model code provisions, it would have been solely for the jury to determine whether a "person of reasonable firmness in his situation" would have failed to seek police assistance or refused to cooperate, or whether such a person would have been, unlike defendant, able to resist.

Exercising our authority to revise the common law, we have decided to adopt this approach as the law of New Jersey. Henceforth, duress shall be a defense to a crime other than murder if the defendant engaged in conduct because he was coerced to do so by the use of, or threat to use, unlawful force against his person or the person of another, which a person of reasonable firmness in his situation would have been unable to resist. . . .

Defendant's conviction of conspiracy to obtain money by false pretenses is hereby reversed and remanded for a new trial.

PEOPLE v. ROMERO, 10 Cal. App. 4th 1150, 13 Cal. Rptr. 2d 332 (1992): [Defendant, Debra Romero, and the man she lived with, Terrance Romero, were convicted of robbery and attempted robbery. Her defense was duress, based on her fear that Terrance would kill her if she did not help him commit the robberies. Following her conviction, she petitioned for habeas corpus, arguing that the failure of her counsel to introduce expert evidence that she suffered from battered woman's syndrome (BWS) violated her constitutional right to effective assistance of counsel. The court agreed and ordered a new trial, stating:] If BWS testimony is relevant to credibility when a woman kills her batterer, it is a fortiori relevant to her credibility when she participates in robberies at her batterer's insistence. . . . As relevant to this case, the defense of duress is the same as self-defense — in both, the key issue is whether the defendant reasonably and honestly believed she was in imminent danger of great bodily harm or death. . . . With the two defenses thus juxtaposed, it is clear that a rule permitting expert testimony about BWS in a self-defense case must necessarily permit it in a case where duress is claimed as a defense. In both cases, the evidence is relevant to the woman's credibility and to support her testimony that she entertained a good faith objectively reasonable and honest belief that her act was necessary to prevent an imminent threat of greater harm. . . .

We agree with Debra that there is a reasonable probability that presentation of expert testimony about BWS would have bolstered her credibility and persuaded the jury to accept the defense of duress. . . . Although substantial evidence established that Debra was frequently and severely beaten by Terrance and that he threatened her with further harm and even death if she left or did not do what he wanted her to do, there was no mention at all of BWS. There was no explanation for Debra's failure simply to walk away from Terrance or for her continued participation in the robberies or for her apparently inconsistent behavior after they were arrested, when she wrote loving letters to him while he was still incarcerated.

MODEL PENAL CODE

Section 2.09.   Duress

[See Appendix for text of this section.]

Model penal code and commentaries, comment to §2.09 at 372-375 (1985):
The problem of how far duress should exculpate conduct that otherwise would constitute a crime is much debated in the literature of the penal law. The positions taken cover a wide range of possibilities.

Stephen argued, for example, that "compulsion by threats ought in no case whatever to be admitted as an excuse for crime, though it may and ought to operate in mitigation of punishment in most though not in all cases." His reason was, in substance, that "it is at the moment when temptation to crime is strongest that the law should speak most clearly and emphatically to the contrary."[29]

Jerome Hall is less hostile to allowing the defense, but he would limit it with rigor to the situation where the actor rightly chose the lesser of two evils; and even then he gives such weight to the moral duty to resist the evil-doing author of the duress that he does not commit himself beyond the proposition that "coercion should not exculpate in the most serious crimes but . . . should be a defense where, e.g., it is a question of imminent death or the commission of relatively minor harm."[30]

Much of the issue posed by these competing views is resolved . . . in Section 3.02, which provides a general defense in cases where the actor believed his conduct necessary to avoid an evil to himself or to another and the evil sought to be avoided is greater than that sought to be prevented by the law defining the offense charged. The Institute saw no reason why this principle should be denied full application when the evil apprehended has its source in the action or the threatened action of another person, rather than the forces and perils of the physical world. The only basis offered for drawing this distinction, that the agent of coercion is an evil-doer who should be resisted, was thought to bear on the necessity of the actor's conduct, rather than the rightness of his choice when the necessity obtains. Surely there are cases where the actor may correctly think resistance on his part to be impossible or doomed to failure. . . . Section 2.09(4) provides, therefore, that Section 3.02 is not superseded by the present section in cases that may seem to give rise to both defenses. . . .

The problem of Section 2.09, then, reduces to the question of whether there are cases where the actor cannot justify his conduct under Section 3.02, as when his choice involves an equal or greater evil than that threatened, but where he nonetheless should be excused because he was subjected to coercion. If he is so far overwhelmed by force that his behavior is involuntary, as when his arm is physically moved by someone else, Section 2.01(1) stands as a barrier to liability, following in this respect the long tradition of the penal law. The case of concern here is that in which the actor makes a choice, but claims in his defense that he

---

29. 2 J. Stephen, History of the Criminal Law of England 108 (1883).
30. General Principles of Criminal Law 448 (2d ed. 1960).

was so intimidated that he was unable to choose otherwise. Should such psychological incapacity be given the same exculpative force as the physical incapacity that may afford a defense under Section 2.01? . . .

In favor of allowing the defense, it may be argued that the legal sanction cannot be effective in the case supposed and that the actor may not properly be blamed for doing what he had to choose to do. It seems clear, however, that the argument in its full force must be rejected. The crucial reason is the same as that which elsewhere leads to an unwillingness to vary legal norms with the individual's capacity to meet the standards they prescribe, absent a disability that is both gross and verifiable, such as the mental disease or defect that may establish irresponsibility. The most that it is feasible to do with lesser disabilities is to accord them proper weight in sentencing. To make liability depend upon the fortitude of any given actor would be no less impractical or otherwise impolitic than to permit it to depend upon such other variables as intelligence or clarity of judgment, suggestibility or moral insight.

Moreover, the legal standard may gain in its effectiveness by being unconditional in this respect. It cannot be known what choices might be different if the actor thought he had a chance of exculpation on the ground of his peculiar disabilities instead of knowing that he does not. No less important, legal norms and sanctions operate not only at the moment of climactic choice, but also in the fashioning of values and of character.

Though, for the foregoing reasons, the submission that the actor lacked the fortitude to make the moral choice should not be entertained as a defense, a different situation is presented if the claimed excuse is based upon the incapacity of men in general to resist the coercive pressures to which the individual succumbed. . . . [L]aw is ineffective in the deepest sense, indeed . . . it is hypocritical, if it imposes on the actor who has the misfortune to confront a dilemmatic choice, a standard that his judges are not prepared to affirm that they should and could comply with if their turn to face the problem should arise. Condemnation in such a case is bound to be an ineffective threat; what is, however, more significant is that it is divorced from any moral base and is unjust. . . .

The Model Code accordingly provides for the defense in cases where the actor was coerced by force or threats of force "that a person of reasonable firmness in his situation would have been unable to resist." The standard is not, however, wholly external in its reference; account is taken of the actor's "situation," a term that should here be given the same scope it is accorded in appraising recklessness and negligence. Stark, tangible factors that differentiate the actor from another, like his size, strength, age, or health, would be considered in making the exculpatory judgment. Matters of temperament would not.

NOTES

1. Questions. Does the rationale for the defense of duress given by the Model Penal Code apply as well to the defense of provocation in the law of homicide? If so, why should provocation only reduce the crime from murder to manslaughter, while duress, where applicable, excuses altogether? For analysis of these and related questions, see Jeremy Horder, Autonomy, Provocation and Duress, [1992] Crim. L. Rev. 70.

2. As will be seen from the foregoing excerpt from the commentary, the Model Penal Code takes a strong position against individualizing the defense, concluding that "the submission that the actor lacked fortitude to make the moral choice should not be entertained as a defense." A recent proposal from the English Law Commission takes a different position. The Law Commission, Consultation Paper No. 122, Legislating the Criminal Code, Offences Against the Person and General Principles (1992). They propose in §26(2)(b) of their Draft Bill to allow a defense when the threat made against the defendant "is one which in all the circumstances (including any of his personal characteristics that affect its gravity) he cannot reasonably be expected to resist." In support of their position they state (id. at 55):

> We said in our 1977 report: "Threats directed against a weak, immature or disabled person may well be much more compelling than the same threats directed against a normal healthy person." The Court of Appeal in *Graham* accepted this approach in part when stating that the resistance to be expected was that of one "sharing the characteristics of the defendant." But the court added the requirement that the resistance match that of "a sober person of reasonable firmness," seeking in this way to "limit the defence . . . by means of an objective criterion formulated in terms of reasonableness." We continue to think, however, that the test should simply be whether in all the circumstances the person in question could reasonably be expected to have resisted the threat. We take it to go without saying that a person could not under this test rely upon his insobriety as a relevant circumstance. At the same time we are not convinced that a person's "characteristics" can be distinguished in the way that the *Graham* test appears to contemplate. Relative timidity, for example, may be an inseparable aspect of a total personality that is in turn part cause and part product of its possessor's life situation; and thus may itself be one of the "circumstances" in the light of which the pressure represented by the duress is to be assessed.

In a subsequent report, The Law Commission (Law Commn. No. 218), the Commission adhered to this view, adding (id. at 52):

> On consultation, there was strong support for our view that the defense should apply where *the particular defendant in question* could not reasonably have been expected to resist the threat. We do not accept the contrary view, for which there was very little support, that the defence should be withheld from the "objectively weak." First, such an approach would be ineffectual as a means of law enforcement. If a person is in a condition that makes it unreasonable to expect him to resist, then he will not resist, and the fact that a different person in those circumstances might have resisted will not affect the matter. Second, the purpose of the defence is not to enforce unrealistically high standards of behaviour. Rather, the defence acknowledges that where the defendant could not reasonably have been expected to act otherwise he should not be convicted of a crime.

NOTE: NECESSITY AND DURESS COMPARED

The relationship between the defenses of necessity and duress can be confusing. Partly the reason is terminological: Courts and writers don't always use the terms the same way. But, more significantly, the confusion is analytical. See generally Miriam Gur-Arye, Should the Criminal Law Distinguish Between Necessity as a Justification and Necessity as an Excuse?, 102 L.Q. Rev. 71 (1986); George Fletcher, Should Intolerable Conditions Generate a Justification or an Excuse for Escape?, 26 U.C.L.A.L. Rev. 1355 (1979).

There are two separate concepts at work here. What is usually called necessity refers to a defense resting on the rationale of justification. One can see this most clearly in the Model Penal Code defense of the choice of evils (§3.02), which we explored in the preceding section: The defendant violated a criminal prohibition, but in the circumstances it was a good thing she did, for to do so was the lesser evil. The other concept rests on the rationale of excuse. The defendant is accorded a defense not because it was right to violate the law, but because the circumstances were so urgent and compelling that otherwise law-abiding people might well have done the same in the circumstances. This is the spirit behind the Model Penal Code formulation of the defense of duress. See Joshua Dressler, Understanding Criminal Law 264 (1987), who also locates the rationale of duress in excuse, not justification.

But the lines between these two distinguishable concepts are often blurred in the way the law is formulated and talked about. Note the New York defense of justification, §35.05 of the N.Y. Penal code, supra page 868. While that section is unmistakably a justification provision, the first sentence of the statute requires that the choice be made "as an emergency measure," which is an appropriate consideration for an excuse but not for a justification. The same blurring sometimes occurs in the way duress is defined. See, for example, Wayne LaFave & Austin Scott, Criminal Law 432 (2d ed. 1986), which summarizes the law of duress as requiring not only that the defendant be threatened by another with imminent serious unlawful harm, but that the defendant's choice to break the law was the lesser evil in the circumstances.

In those jurisdictions where the law of duress is as LaFave and Scott summarize it, duress becomes a species of justification. But why is it needed? Wouldn't the defense of justification (necessity) cover all the cases duress covers? The answer might well be no because of the peculiarity that the law in some jurisdictions came to accord significance to the source of the peril the defendant sought to avoid. Under this view, if the source of the peril was the "do-it-or-else" command of another person, the only possible defense is that of duress, not necessity; but if the source of the peril is anything else, necessity may be available as a defense, but not duress. Recall, for example, the dictum in People v. Unger, supra page 860, that the defense of compulsion (duress) would be available only if someone commanded the prisoner to escape by threatening him with serious harm if he did not; because the peril the defendant sought to avoid was the threat of one who was not ordering him to escape, the relevant defense was necessity, not duress.

These ways of formulating the defense of duress and necessity — that they are both justification defenses and that only a do-it-or-else command of another could establish a defense of duress — are problematical. The Model Penal Code, which has been influential in shaping the law in many jurisdictions, proposes some important changes. Duress is defined in §2.09 purely as an excuse. What establishes the defense is that the defendant acted under a threat a person of reasonable firmness would have been unable to resist; it is not required that he chose the lesser evil. Of course, the circumstances that would make out a defense under this formulation might also be a case where the defendant's act was the lesser evil. Indeed, this may often be the case. Where this is so the Model Penal Code permits the justification defense as well. As the Commentary to §3.02 states: "The Institute saw no reason why the [choice-of-evils] principle should be denied full application when the evil apprehended has its source in the action or the threatened action of another person, rather than the forces and perils of the physical world."

But while the Model Penal Code allows the choice-of-evils justification regardless of the source of the peril, it is interesting that it does not allow the duress excuse regardless of the source of the peril. It makes the duress excuse available only when the peril confronting the defendant arises from the do-it-or-else command of another person, not when it arises from some other source, such as a natural condition or another's aggression. To this extent the Model Penal Code adheres to the tradition of differentiating the availability of defenses depending on the source of the peril. Why this should be is explored in the first of the following notes, which are devoted to a sampling of the major issues in the law of duress.

NOTES ON DURESS

1. *Source of the threat.* What is the basis for the Model Penal Code's distinction depending on the source of the threat? If the peril is great enough that a person of reasonable firmness would be unable to resist, why should it matter whether the peril is from the do-it-or-else command of another or from some other source? Consider the following cases.

(*a*) X is unwillingly driving a car along a narrow and precipitous mountain road which drops off sharply on both sides, under the command of Y, an armed escaping felon. The headlights pick out two drunken persons lying across the road in such a position as to make passage impossible without running them over. X is prevented from stopping by the threat of Y to shoot him dead if he declines to drive straight on. If X does go on and kills the drunks in order to save himself, he would not be justified under the lesser evil principle of §3.02, but he will be excused under §2.09 if the jury should find that "a person of reasonable firmness in his situation would have been unable to resist."

(*b*) The same situation as above except that X is prevented from stopping by suddenly inoperative brakes. His alternatives are either to run down the drunks or to run off the road and down the mountainside. If X chooses the first alternative to save his own life and kills the drunks, he will not be excused under §2.09 even if a jury should find that a person of reasonable firmness would have been unable to do otherwise.

Can the difference between these two cases be defended? Does the logic of the matter necessarily push to a formulation that would excuse an actor whenever she commits a criminal act in such circumstances that people in general would lack the fortitude to do otherwise? If so, it would be open in every criminal case for the accused to present evidence to show that reasonable people in the defendant's situation would lack the will to act otherwise than as defendant acted. Would such a defense be too easily abused? If so, how could the "person of reasonable firmness" formula be narrowed? Consider the following models.

Section 25 of the Criminal Codes of Queensland and Western Australia provide:

> [A] person is not criminally responsible for an act or omission done or made under such circumstances of sudden or extraordinary emergency that an ordinary person possessing ordinary power of self-control could not reasonably be expected to act otherwise.

California Joint Legislative Committee for Revision of the Penal Code, Penal Code Revision Project §520 (Tent. Draft No. 1, 1967):

> In a prosecution for any offense: (1) it is an affirmative defense that the defendant engaged in the conduct otherwise constituting the offense because he was coerced into doing so by the threatened use of unlawful force against his person or the person of another in circumstances where a person of reasonable firmness in his situation would not have done otherwise; (2) it is an affirmative defense that the defendant engaged in the conduct otherwise constituting the offense in order to avoid death or great bodily harm to himself or another in circumstances where a person of reasonable firmness in his situation would not have done otherwise.[a]

The Model Penal Code, in its final commentary (Model Penal Code and Commentaries, Comment to §2.09 at 378-379 (1985)), justifies its position on hypotheticals (a) and (b) found at the beginning of this Note. Taking note of a Wisconsin statute[8] that would allow a defense in those cases, it states:

> The judgment of the Institute . . . was that such a defense should not be included. The general justification defense of Section 3.02 does apply to choices of evils required by natural causes. It will be an extraordinarily rare case in which a person will not be able to claim successfully that a response to natural causes was a choice of a lesser evil but could successfully claim that the choice was one a person of reasonable firmness would make. And there is a significant difference between the situations in which an actor makes the choice of an equal or greater evil under the threat of unlawful human force and when he does so because of a natural event. In the former situation, the basic interests of the law may be satisfied by prosecution of the agent of unlawful force; in the latter circumstance, if the actor is excused, no one is subject to the law's application.

a. The Brown Commission, in its proposals for reform of the federal criminal code, adopted this suggestion and influenced a number of states to enact it. See Model Penal Code and Commentaries, Comment to §2.09 at 383 n. 59 (1985). — Eds.

8. Wisc. Stat. §939.47:

> Pressure of natural physical forces which causes the actor reasonably to believe that his act is the only means of preventing imminent public disaster, or imminent death or great bodily harm to himself or another and which causes him so to act, is a defense to a prosecution for any crime based on that act except that if the prosecution is for murder the degree of the crime is reduced to manslaughter.

The English courts have developed a similar defense under the rubric "duress of circumstances." See Smith & Hogan, Criminal Law 232, 242 (7th Ed. 1992); K. J. M. Smith, Must Heroes Behave Heroically?, [1989] Crim. L. Rev. 622.

What are the "basic interests of the law" that the Model Penal Code has in mind? If in principle the defendant in the latter case should be excused, why should it matter that there is no one else to prosecute?

Is it true that only in "an extraordinarily rare case" will a defendant who is precluded from a duress defense by the Model Penal Code formulation be unable to succeed with a necessity defense? Consider the following scenario based on the *Unger* case, supra page 860: Defendant is charged with escaping from prison. His defense is that he had no other way to avoid an imminent gang rape by fellow inmates. In this jurisdiction the courts hold that the defense of necessity is not available in prison escape cases because, considering the danger to prison administration throughout the state if such a defense was allowed, escape from prison is not a lesser evil. What defense does the defendant have under the Model Penal Code?

2. *Imminence of the threat.* Both the *Toscano* decision and Model Penal Code §2.09 treat the imminence of the threatened harm as one factor to be weighed by the jury in determining whether the defendant's conduct was that of "a person of reasonable firmness in his situation." In contrast, many common law decisions treated imminence as an absolute prerequisite to the availability of a duress defense, and some statutes expressly limited the defense to situations involving threats of "instant" death. The great majority of the recent statutory revisions have rejected the Model Penal Code's flexible approach and preserved some requirement that the threatened harm be "immediate," "imminent" or "instant." See Model Penal Code and Commentaries, Comments to §2.09 at 369, 382 (1985). What is the reason for this limitation? Consider its application to the following cases.

United States v. Fleming, 23 C.M.R. 7 (1957): [Defendant, an Army officer, was court-martialed for violating the Uniform Code of Military Justice while a prisoner of war in Korea. The charges against him rested on his having allegedly collaborated with the enemy by helping prepare propaganda recordings designed to promote disaffection among U.S. troops, and by making numerous English language broadcasts criticizing American war objectives and calling upon U.S. authorities to withdraw or surrender. In describing the circumstances leading up to the acts of collaboration, the court noted that after being captured, defendant suffered numerous interrogations, forced marches, physical abuse and extended deprivation of food and water. It characterized the prison camp conditions as "extremely bad." The court then described specific threats that occurred in response to defendant's initial refusals to cooperate (*id.* at 15-16):]

[T]he accused testified that he was constantly harangued and pressured by Colonel Kim. According to Kim, there were two kinds of people: those for peace and those against peace. Those against peace were war criminals and not fit to live. If the accused fitted into that category he would be put in a "hole" and would never come out. But if he were for peace, he was a friend. . . . When the accused initially refused to do the acts to prove his "friendliness," he was asked if he wanted to return to the previous camp up north. The accused replied in the affirmative and Kim informed him that he could start walking the 150-200 mile distance. It was midwinter, the accused's shoes had been stolen, and he was wearing rags wrapped around his feet. These factors, plus his greatly weakened physical condition, led the accused to the conclusion that he would never reach the north camp alive. Thereafter, on each occasion when the accused objected to Kim's propaganda efforts, he was threatened with the walk north. . . .

Major Allen [a defense witness] also testified to numerous threats to march the prisoners north to the Yalu River. In his opinion, none could have survived the march. . . .

Also Kim's subsequent threat of the caves made to the accused and the other prisoners of war unless they cooperated undoubtedly affected prisoner cooperation. [The caves] were recesses in the hillside. They were wet and muddy with little or no heating facilities. The prisoners lived in the muck and mire like animals. . . . The mortality rate in the indescribable filth and privation of these holes in the ground was extremely high. The prisoners felt that a sentence to the caves was almost tantamount to a sentence of death. Of the prisoner group with whom the accused was associated at least eight were punished by being sent to the caves. Fortunately these eight survived, except that one officer died shortly after being taken out of the caves because of his weakened condition. Almost all who testified were of the opinion that had their confinement in the caves lasted much longer, they would have died. Major MacGhee, one of the officers sentenced to the caves, testified that all twenty-three Americans already there when he arrived died. . . . According to the accused, whenever he balked on the propaganda, Kim reminded him of the Americans in the caves and again took him to see them.

[At the court-martial the trier of fact was instructed that defendant's acts could be excused on grounds of duress only if he had "a well-grounded apprehension of immediate and impending death or of immediate, serious, bodily harm." Defense counsel argued that the insistence on a fear of *immediate* death was error under the circumstances, that fear of "a delayed, or a wasting death from starvation, deprivation or other like conditions can just as well spell coercion and compulsion as the fear of immediate death." Rejecting this argument, the court upheld the conviction (id. at 24-25):]

We are not unmindful of the hardships or the pressures to which the accused and his fellow prisoners were subjected prior to the time of his collaboration with the enemy. . . . It could hardly be argued that the accused was not under great pressure. However, it is important to note that, at the times accused committed the acts alleged, the food ration, though scarcely abundant, was considerably improved over the ration in Camp Five. Furthermore, we cannot overlook the fact that accused cooperated with his captors upon the mere assertion of the threats. . . . It was not at all certain at the time the threat was made that walking north to Pyoktong would cause death at all, much less immediately. By way of comparison, if, for example, accused's captors had actually made him start on foot for Camp Five, and it then became evident that he could not survive the march, a valid defense of duress might have arisen for capitulation at that point. . . . Here the danger of death was problematical and remote.

Even more damaging to the cause of the accused was the instance of the 'surrender appeal.' Accused 'voice-signed' this monstrous item of propaganda apparently upon the threat of having the food rations cut off or curtailed, and of being sent to the 'Caves.' The junior officers and enlisted men present refused en masse, although they were subject to substantially the same pressures as accused. Despite the example of capitulation set by the accused, a field grade officer and their leader, they at least were willing to determine whether their captors would send them to the Caves or cut off the food if they refused to collaborate. Accused was not. As the court stated in D'Aquino v. United States. 'The person claiming the defense of coercion and duress must be a person whose resistance has brought him to the last ditch' (182 F.2d at 359). Accused's resistance had not 'brought him to the last ditch'; the danger of death or great bodily harm was not *immediate*. Accused can not now avail himself of the defense of duress.

United States v. Contento-Pachon, 723 F.2d 691 (9th Cir. 1984): [Defendant, a native of Bogota, Colombia, was employed there as a taxicab driver. One of his passengers, Jorge, proposed] that Contento-Pachon swallow cocaine-filled balloons and transport them to the United States. Contento-Pachon agreed to consider the proposition. He was told not to mention the proposition to anyone, otherwise he would "get into serious trouble." Contento-Pachon testified that he did not contact the police because he believes that the Bogota police are corrupt and that they are paid off by drug traffickers.

Approximately one week later, Contento-Pachon told Jorge that he would not carry the cocaine. In response, . . . Jorge told Contento-Pachon that his failure to cooperate would result in the death of his wife and three-year-old child.

The following day the pair met again. Contento-Pachon's life and the lives of his family were again threatened. At this point, Contento-Pachon agreed to take the cocaine into the United States.

The pair met two more times. At the last meeting, Contento-Pachon swallowed 129 balloons of cocaine. He was informed that he would be watched at all times during the trip, and that if he failed to follow Jorge's instruction he and his family would be killed.

After leaving Bogota, Contento-Pachon's plane landed in Panama. Contento-Pachon asserts that he did not notify the authorities there because he felt that the Panamanian police were as corrupt as those in Bogota. Also, he felt that any such action on his part would place his family in jeopardy.

When he arrived at the customs inspection point in Los Angeles, Contento-Pachon consented to have his stomach x-rayed. The x-rays revealed a foreign substance which was later determined to be cocaine.

[At trial, the government's motion to exclude the duress defense was granted. The District Court held that two necessary elements of the defense are the immediacy and the inescapability of the threat. It concluded that neither element was satisfied:]

> The first threat made to defendant and his family about three weeks before the flight was not immediate; the threat was conditioned upon defendant's failure to cooperate in the future and did not place the defendant and his family in immediate danger or harm. Moreover, after the initial threat and until he went to the house where he ingested the balloons containing cocaine, defendant and his family were not physically restrained and could have sought help from the police or fled. No such efforts were attempted by defendant. Thus, defendant's own offer of proof negates two necessary elements of the defense of duress.

[The court of appeals reversed:] [T]he defendant was dealing with a man who was deeply involved in the exportation of illegal substances. Large sums of money were at stake and, consequently, Contento-Pachon had reason to believe that Jorge would carry out his threats. . . . These were not vague threats of possible future harm. According to the defendant, if he had refused to cooperate, the consequences would have been immediate and harsh. . . . Contento-Pachon's contention that he was operating under the threat of immediate harm was supported by sufficient evidence to present a triable issue of fact.

The defendant must show that he had no reasonable opportunity to escape. . . . The trier of fact should decide whether one in Contento-Pachon's position might believe that some of the Bogota police were paid informants for drug traffickers and that reporting the matter to the police did not represent a reasonable opportunity of escape.

If he chose not to go to the police, Contento-Pachon's alternative was to flee. We reiterate that the opportunity to escape must be reasonable. To flee, Contento-Pachon, along with his wife and three year-old child, would have been forced to pack his possessions, leave his job, and travel to a place beyond the reaches of the drug traffickers. A juror might find that this was not a reasonable avenue of escape. Thus, Contento-Pachon presented a triable issue on the element of escapability.

3. Duress as a defense to murder. Prior to the Model Penal Code proposals, most jurisdictions held the duress defense inapplicable in prosecutions for murder (and sometimes for other very serious crimes) even when the stringent requirements of an imminent, inescapable lethal threat were otherwise satisfied. The Model Penal Code rejected this exclusion of murder cases, but the great majority of recent statutory revisions continue to adhere to it. See Model Penal Code and Commentaries, Comment to §2.09 at 381 (1985). In England, the House of Lords has likewise held the defense unavailable in murder cases. See Regina v. Howe, [1987] 2 W.L.R. 568. It has also held duress to be no defense to attempted murder. Regina v. Gotts, [1991] 2 All. E.R. 1.

The argument in favor of granting the defense, even to murder, is that the law should not demand a degree of heroism of which the ordinary person is, by definition, incapable. On the other hand, consider the comments of Lord Salmon explaining the English position that denies the defense (Abbott v. The Queen, [1976] 3 All E.R. 140, 146):

> In the trials of those responsible for wartime atrocities such as mass killings of men, women or children, inhuman experiments on human beings, often resulting in death, and like crimes, it was invariably argued for the defence that these atrocities should be excused on the ground that they resulted from superior orders and duress; if the accused had refused to do these dreadful things, they would have been shot and therefore they should be acquitted and allowed to go free. This argument has always been universally rejected. Their Lordships would be sorry indeed to see it accepted by the common law of England.
>
> . . . A terrorist of notorious violence might, e.g., threaten death to A and his family unless A obeys his instructions to put a bomb with a time fuse set by A in a certain passenger aircraft and/or in a thronged market, railway station or the like. . . . Is there any limit to the number of people you may kill to save your own life and that of your family?

Question: Suppose that a defendant is compelled to participate in a robbery, and during the course of that crime a bystander is shot and killed by one of the other robbers. If duress is available in a prosecution for robbery but not in a murder prosecution, should the defendant be able to invoke the duress defense in a prosecution for felony murder?[9]

4. *The defendant's role in a homicidal offense.* Where, as in most jurisdictions, duress cannot be a defense to a murder charge, should the defense nonetheless remain available if the coerced defendant's participation in the crime was relatively minor? Consider the observations of Bray, C.J., dissenting in Regina v. Brown, [1968] S.A.S.R. 467, 494:

> The reasoning generally used to support the proposition that duress is no defence to a charge of murder is, to use the words of Blackstone cited above, that "he ought rather to die himself, than escape by the murder of an innocent." Generally speaking I am prepared to accept this position. Its force is obviously considerably less where the act of the threatened man is not the direct act of killing but only the rendering of some minor form of assistance, particularly when it is by no means certain that if he refuses the death of the victim will be averted, or conversely when it is by no means certain that if he complies the death will be a necessary consequence. It would seem hard, for example, if an innocent passer-by seized in the street by a gang of criminals visibly engaged in robbery and murder in a shop and compelled at the point of a gun to issue misleading comments to the public, or an innocent driver compelled at the point of a gun to convey the murderer to the victim, were to have no defence. . . .

When is a defendant's role sufficiently limited to justify the availability of a duress defense to homicide?

Consider the following case reported in an article in the San Francisco Chronicle (Dec. 24, 1985, at 1): A young man, despairing over his father's suffering from cancer and distraught because the father had said he did not want a lingering death, allegedly strode into the hospital's intensive care unit, held a pistol to a nurse's head, and threatened to kill her unless she allowed his father to "die with dignity." The nurse disconnected a mechanical respirator and the father, who had been in a coma, died a few minutes later. If the son has no defense to a murder charge, should the nurse nonetheless have a duress defense? On what theory? Should it matter whether the nurse is characterized as the "actual killer" or instead merely as a person guilty of an omission — namely the failure to continue rendering aid?

5. *Nature of the threat.* At common law the threat had to be one of death or serious bodily harm before it could ground a duress defense. The Model Penal Code requires a threat of unlawful force against the person. What is the reason for these limitations? Do they represent a view that only such threats could lead a person of reasonable firmness to take any part at all in the commission of any crime? Is it plausible that a threat of economic harm or a threat to damage one's reputation could never constitute overwhelming pressure? Consider the com-

---

9. Courts are divided. Compare State v. Hunter, 241 Kan. 629, 740 P.2d 559 (1987) (duress available); Tully v. State, 730 P.2d 1206 (Okla. 1986) (same); with State v. Rumble, 680 S.W.2d 939 (Mo. 1984) (duress not available); State v. Berndt, 138 Ariz. 41, 672 P.2d 1311 (1983) (same).

ment of Lord Simon dissenting in D. P. P. for Northern Ireland v. Lynch, [1975] A.C. 653, 686:

> But a threat to property may, in certain circumstances, be as potent in overbearing the actor's wish not to perform the prohibited act as a threat of physical harm. For example, the threat may be to burn down his house unless the householder merely keeps watch against interruption while a crime is committed. Or a fugitive from justice may say, "I have it in my power to make your son bankrupt. You can avoid that merely by driving me to the airport." Would not many ordinary people yield to such threats, and act contrary to their wish not to perform an action prohibited by law?

6. *Contributory fault.* Should it make any difference whether the defendant is in some way to blame for being in a position that leads to duress? Consider the following situations.

(*a*) *Gang membership.* The defendant joins a gang engaged in petty thefts. When the leader decides to rob a bank, the defendant refuses to go along, but is threatened with death if he fails to cooperate. If the defendant participates in the robbery, should he have a duress defense? A common approach is to hold that where a defendant "voluntarily, and with knowledge of its nature, joined a criminal organization or gang which he knew might bring pressure on him to commit an offense and was an active member when he was put under such pressure, he cannot avail himself of the defense of duress." Regina v. Sharp, [1987] 3 W.L.R. 1, 8-9. If, however, the nature of the criminal enterprise is such that the defendant has no reason to suspect he will be forcibly prevented from withdrawing, and if trouble materializes unexpectedly, the defense remains available. Regina v. Shepherd, 86 Cr. App. R. 47 (1988). See also Model Penal Code §2.09(2), withdrawing the defense where the defendant "recklessly placed himself in a situation in which it is probable that he would be subjected to duress."

Questions: Is the Model Penal Code exception too narrow? Is it fair for the defense to remain available, as it does under the Model Penal Code, even though the defendant has negligently run an unreasonable risk of incurring duress? Conversely, is the Model Penal Code exception overly broad in relation to crimes that require a culpability level higher than recklessness? For example, suppose that a defendant was aware that his conduct and his involvement with others exposed him to a vague risk that he might be pressured to participate in various unspecified crimes. If in the future the defendant is threatened with death if he does not help in a bank robbery plan, is it appropriate to deny him the duress defense to a bank robbery charge?

(*b*) *Mistaken threats.* The defendant drives a couple of would-be bank robbers to a bank and serves as lookout, believing they will beat him up badly if he refuses. In fact, the robbers never actually made any such threat, either explicitly or implicitly; defendant is just an abnormally timid soul with a lively imagination. Does the defendant qualify for the duress defense even though he was unreasonable in believing he was being threatened? The language of Model Penal Code §2.09(1) is not clear, although the Commentary states that the drafters intended in such a case that he would have a defense to robbery, although not to a crime of recklessness or negligence. Model Penal Code and Commentaries, Comment to §2.09 at 380 (1985). Most jurisdictions today appear to follow the common law rule requiring the defendant to have not just a fear of harm, but a "well-grounded" fear, Wayne LaFave & Austin Scott, Criminal Law 439 (2d ed. 1986), so that in our hypothetical the defendant would not have a duress defense to the robbery.

Which position is sounder? Recall that the provocation defense to murder contains an objective standard. Does it follow that an objective standard should also apply to the duress defense? Can duress be argued to be an a fortiori case for requiring an objective standard, on the ground that duress is a complete defense while provocation only reduces the crime to manslaughter?

7. *"Brainwashing."* The prosecution of Patty Hearst for bank robbery generated considerable discussion of the possible defense of "brainwashing" as an extension of traditional exculpatory defenses. Ms. Hearst was kidnapped and held in confinement for months by members of the Symbionese Liberation Army. During that period, she participated with her abductors in a bank robbery, with great willingness, to judge by the testimony of witnesses and the bank's television tapes. On her subsequent apprehension, she was charged with bank robbery. An issue in the case was not only whether she was forced to participate by threats of death, principally a factual question, but also whether, even if that were not the case, her actions should be regarded as excusable because they resulted from the inculcation of beliefs by her captors through pressures of psychological indoctrination while she was held in captivity and complete subservience. As one article put it, "The jury in the Hearst case was faced with the question of when coerced behavior ends and truly voluntary action begins for persons who appear to have changed their loyalties and values while held in captivity." Donald T. Lunde & Thomas E. Wilson, Brainwashing as a Defense to Criminal Liability: Patty Hearst Revisited, 13 Crim. L. Bull. 341, 342 (1977).

Consider what possible defenses might be plausibly argued for Ms. Hearst, what changes in existing doctrine, if any, would be needed to cover the case, and whether it would be sound to make those changes.

See, in addition to the article by Lunde and Wilson, Richard Delgado, Ascription of Criminal States of Mind: Toward a Defense Theory for the Coercively Persuaded ("Brainwashed") Defendant, 63 Minn. L. Rev. 1 (1978), as well as an exchange generated by this article between Professors Dressler and Delgado in 63 Minn. L. Rev. 335, 361 (1979).

3. Intoxication

REGINA v. KINGSTON

Court of Appeal, Criminal Division
[1993] 4 All E.R. 373,
rev'd,
House of Lords
[1994] 3 All E.R. 353

LORD TAYLOR OF GOSFORTH, C.J. (for the Court of Appeal): [In order to obtain material with which to blackmail defendant, Penn lured a 15-year-old boy to his (Penn's) flat, doped him, and then invited defendant over to abuse the boy sexually. Penn then photographed and audiotaped defendant committing the act. At trial for indecent assault, defendant could not remember drinking anything before going to the bedroom, but stated that he sometimes drank coffee at Penn's flat. In addition defendant could be heard to say on the tape "I don't know why, am I falling asleep?" and "Have you put something in my coffee?"

[Prior to trial defendant's counsel asked the judge to give an affirmative answer to the question: "If the jury find that Mr. Kingston assaulted [the boy] pursuant to an intent induced by the influence of drugs administered to him secretly by Kevin Penn, is it open to them to find Mr. Kingston not guilty?" The judge declined and instead instructed the jury it should acquit the defendant only if it found that because of the drug he did not intend to commit an indecent assault upon the boy, but so long as he did have that intent, it is irrelevant that he had been drugged, because "a drugged intent is still an intent." The jury convicted.

[Defendant's counsel argued on appeal that "the law recognizes that, exceptionally, an accused person may be entitled to be acquitted if there is a possibility that although his act was intentional, the intent itself arose out of circumstances for which he bears no blame." After reviewing such scanty authority as there was for this proposition, the court observed that the question of when involuntary intoxication negatives mens rea can be answered by turning to first principles, and continued:]

[T]he purpose of the criminal law is to inhibit, by proscription and by penal sanction, anti-social acts which individuals may otherwise commit. . . . Having paedophiliac inclinations and desires is not proscribed; putting them into practice is. If the sole reason why the threshold between the two has been crossed is or may have been that the inhibition which the law requires has been removed by the clandestine act of a third party, the purposes of the criminal law are not served by nevertheless holding that the person performing the act is guilty of an offence. A man is not responsible for a condition produced "by stratagem, or the fraud of another." If therefore drink or drug, surreptitiously administered, causes a person to lose his self-control and for that reason to form an intent which he would not otherwise have formed, it is consistent with the principle that the law should exculpate him because the operative fault is not his. The law permits a finding that the intent formed was not a criminal intent or, in other words, that the involuntary intoxication negatives the mens rea. . . .

By answering . . . the question put to him at the beginning of the trial in the negative, the judge may have inhibited a sufficient ventilation of this issue at a later stage. Further, by summing up as he did, the judge effectively withdrew the issue from the jury. In our judgment, that amounted to a material misdirection. . . . [Conviction set aside and appellant discharged.]

LORD MUSTILL (for the House of Lords): [T]he general nature of the case is clear enough. In ordinary circumstances the respondent's paedophiliac tendencies would have been kept under control, even in the presence of the sleeping or unconscious boy on the bed. The ingestion of the drug (whatever it was) brought about a temporary change in the mentality or personality of the respondent which lowered his ability to resist temptation so far that his desires overrode his ability to control them. Thus we are concerned here with a case of disinhibition. The drug is not alleged to have created the desire to which the respondent gave way, but rather to have enabled it to be released.

. . . The decision [below] was explicitly founded on [the] general principle . . . that if blame is absent the necessary mens rea must also be absent.

My Lords, with every respect I must suggest that no such principle exists or, until the present case, had ever in modern times been thought to exist. . . . [T]o assume that contemporary moral judgments affect the criminality of the act, as distinct from the punishment appropriate to the crime once proved, is to be misled by the expression "mens rea," the ambiguity of which has been the subject of complaint for more than a century. Certainly, the "mens" of the defendant must usually be involved in the offence; but the epithet "rea" refers to the criminality of the act in which the mind is engaged, not to its moral character. . . .

I would therefore reject . . . the respondent's argument which treats the absence of moral fault on the part of the appellant as sufficient in itself to negative the necessary mental element of the offence. . . .

To recognize a new defense of this type would be a bold step. . . . So one must turn to consider just what defence is now to be created. The judgment under appeal implies five characteristics.

1. The defence applies to all offences, except perhaps to absolute offences. It therefore differs from other defences such as provocation and diminished responsibility.

2. The defence is a complete answer to a criminal charge. If not rebutted it leads to an outright acquittal, and unlike provocation and diminished responsibility leaves no room for conviction and punishment for a lesser offence. The underlying assumption must be that the defendant is entirely free from culpability. . . .

5. The defence is subjective in nature. Whereas provocation and self-defence are judged by the reactions of the reasonable person in the situation of the defendant, here the only question is whether this particular defendant's inhibitions were overcome by the effect of the drug. The more susceptible the defendant to the kind of temptation presented, the easier the defence is to establish.

[T]he defence appears to run into difficulties at every turn. . . . Before the jury could form an opinion on whether the drug might have turned the scale witnesses would have to give a picture of the defendant's personality and susceptibilities, for without it the crucial effect of the drug could not be assessed; pharmacologists would be required to describe the potentially disinhibiting effect of a range of drugs whose identity would, if the present case is anything to go by, be unknown; psychologists and psychiatrists would express opinions, not on the matters of psychopathology familiar to those working within the framework of the Mental Health Acts but on altogether more elusive concepts. No doubt as time passed those concerned could work out techniques to deal with these questions. Much more significant would be the opportunities for a spurious defence. Even in the field of road traffic the "spiked" drink as a special reason for not disqualifying from driving is a regular feature. Transferring this to the entire range of criminal offences is a disturbing prospect. The defendant would only have to assert, and support by the evidence of well-wishers, that he was not the sort of person to have done this kind of thing, and to suggest an occasion when by some means a drug might have been administered to him for the jury to be sent straight to the question of a possible disinhibition. The judge would direct the jurors that if they felt any legitimate doubt on the matter — and by its nature the defence would be one which the prosecution would often have no means to rebut — they must acquit outright, all questions of intent, mental capacity and the like being at this stage irrelevant.

My Lords, the fact that a new doctrine may require adjustment of existing principles to accommodate it, and may require those involved in criminal trials to learn new techniques, is not of course a ground for refusing to adopt it, if that is what the interests of justice require. Here, however, justice makes no such demands, for the interplay between the wrong done to the victim, the individual characteristics and frailties of the defendant, and the pharmacological effects of whatever drug may be potentially involved can be far better recognised by a tailored choice from the continuum of sentences available to the judge than by the application of a single Yea-or-Nay jury decision. [Court of Appeal reversed.]

NOTE ON INTOXICATION AND RESPONSIBILITY

American law, including the Model Penal Code, is in accord with the position announced by the House of Lords. The Model Penal Code allows involuntary intoxication to be a defense (beyond its possible role in negating mens rea elements of the offense) only if it creates in the defendant at the time of the crime a condition that meets the test of legal insanity, that is, a substantial incapacity either to appreciate the criminality of the actor's conduct or to conform to the law. See Model Penal Code §2.08. The Commentaries to this section state (at 363): "The actor whose personality is altered by intoxication to a lesser degree is treated like others who may have difficulty in conforming to the law and yet are held responsible for violation."

Intoxication that is voluntary is treated even more restrictively. Again, apart from its possible role in negating the mens rea elements of the offense, the only circumstance in which voluntary intoxication is generally recognized as a defense is summarized as follows in State v. Booth, 169 N.W.2d 869, 873 (Iowa 1989):

> Voluntary temporary intoxication does not excuse one for the criminal consequences of his conduct. . . . A distinction is made when prolonged extensive use of alcohol damages the brain and "settled or established" insanity results therefrom. This is treated the same as insanity from any other cause. However, a temporary condition caused by voluntary intoxication . . . does not excuse one from responsibility for his conduct.

Compare the criticism of prevailing law in situations of voluntary as well as involuntary intoxication:

Glanville Williams, Criminal Law: The General Part 564 (2d ed. 1961): If a man is punished for doing something when drunk that he would not have done when sober, is he not in plain truth punished for getting drunk?

Thomas Babbington Macaulay, A Penal Code Prepared by the Indian Law Commissioners, Clause 68 (1837): Nothing is an offence which a person does in consequence of being in a state of intoxication, provided that either the substance which intoxicated him was administered to him without his knowledge, or against his will, or that he was ignorant that it possessed any intoxicating quality.

Jerome Hall, General Principles of Criminal Law 556 (1960): The principle of mens rea limits penal liability to normal persons who intentionally or recklessly commit harms forbidden by penal law. But since drinking is not usually followed by intoxication, and intoxication does not usually lead to the commission of such harms, it follows that normal persons who commit harms while grossly intoxicated, should not be punished unless, at the time of sobriety and the voluntary drinking, they had such prior experience as to anticipate their intoxication and that they would become dangerous in that condition.

ROBERTS v. PEOPLE

Supreme Court of Michigan
19 Mich. 401 (1870)

CHRISTIANCY, J. The defendant was tried in the Circuit Court for the County of Calhoun, upon an information charging him with assaulting, with intent to murder, one Charles E. Greble, by shooting at him with a loaded pistol. . . .

The . . . question raised by the exceptions is whether the voluntary drunkenness of the defendant, immediately prior to and at the time of the assault, to a degree that would render him incapable of entertaining, in fact, the intent charged, would constitute a valid defense, so far as related to the intent, and leave the defendant liable only for what he actually did — the assault, without the aggravation of the intent. . . .

In determining the question whether the assault was committed with the intent charged, it was therefore material to inquire whether the defendant's mental faculties were so far overcome by the effect of intoxication, as to render him incapable of entertaining the intent. And for this purpose, it was the right and duty of the jury — as upon the question of intent of which this forms a part — to take into consideration the nature and circumstances of the assault, the actions, conduct and demeanor of the defendant, and his declaration before, at the time, and after the assault; and especially to consider the nature of the intent and what degree of mental capacity was necessary to enable him to entertain the simple intent to kill, under circumstances of this case. . . . And as a matter of law, I think the jury should have been instructed, that if his mental faculties were so far overcome by intoxication, that he was not conscious of what he was doing, or if he did know what he was doing, but did not know why he was doing it, or that his actions and the means he was using were naturally adapted or calculated to endanger life or produce death; that he had not sufficient capacity to entertain the intent, and in that event they could not infer that intent from his acts. But if he knew what he was doing, why he was doing it, and that his actions with the means he was using were naturally adapted or likely to kill, then the intent to kill should be inferred from his acts in the same manner and to the same extent as if he was sober. But that on the other hand, to be capable of entertaining the intent, it was not necessary that he should so far have the possession of his mental faculties as to be capable of appreciating the moral qualities of his actions, or of any intended results, as being right or wrong. He must have presumed to have intended the obscuration and perversion of his faculties which followed from his voluntary intoxication. He must be held to have purposely blinded his moral perceptions, and set his will free from the control of reason — to have suppressed the guards and invited the mutiny. . . .

But he is not to be held responsible for the intent, if he was too drunk for a conscious exercise of the will to the particular end, or, in other words, too drunk to entertain the intent, and did not entertain it in fact. If he did entertain it in fact, though but for the intoxication he would not have done so, he is responsible for the intent as well as the acts. . . .

But the Circuit Court held, in effect, that no extent of intoxication could have the effect to disprove the intent, treating the intent as an inference of law for the Court, rather than a question of fact for the jury. In this we think there was error. . . .

PEOPLE v. HOOD

Supreme Court of California
1 Cal. 3d 444, 462 P.2d 370 (1969)

TRAYNOR, C.J. [The evidence showed that defendant, who had been drinking heavily, resisted an effort by a police officer to subdue and arrest him and in the course of the struggle seized the officer's gun and shot him in the legs. He was convicted on count 1 of assault with a deadly weapon upon a peace officer. The California Supreme Court reversed because of the failure of the trial court to instruct on the lesser-included offense of simple assault. He was also convicted on count 3 of assault with intent to murder the officer. The Supreme Court reversed this conviction because the trial court gave "hopelessly conflicting instructions on the effect of intoxication." In order to guide the trial court on retrial, the supreme court proceeded to consider the effect of intoxication on the crime of assault with a deadly weapon. The Supreme Court noted that the California courts of appeal were in conflict on whether simple assault and assault with a deadly weapon were "specific intent" or "general intent" crimes. It then continued:]

The distinction between specific and general intent crimes evolved as a judicial response to the problem of the intoxicated offender. That problem is to reconcile two competing theories of what is just in the treatment of those who commit crimes while intoxicated. On the one hand, the moral culpability of a drunken criminal is frequently less than that of a sober person effecting a like injury. On the other hand, it is commonly felt that a person who voluntarily gets drunk and while in that state commits a crime should not escape the consequences.

Before the nineteenth century, the common law refused to give any effect to the fact that an accused committed a crime while intoxicated. The judges were apparently troubled by this rigid traditional rule, however, for there were a number of attempts during the early part of the nineteenth century to arrive at a more humane, yet workable, doctrine. The theory that these judges explored was that evidence of intoxication could be considered to negate intent, whenever intent was an element of the crime charged. . . . To limit the operation of the doctrine and achieve a compromise between the conflicting feelings of sympathy and reprobation for the intoxicated offender, later courts both in England and this country drew a distinction between so-called specific intent and general intent crimes.

Specific and general intent have been notoriously difficult terms to define and apply, and a number of text writers recommended that they be abandoned altogether. Too often the characterization of a particular crime as one of specific or general intent is determined solely by the presence or absence of words describing psychological phenomena — "intent" or "malice," for example — in the statutory language defining the crime. When the definition of a crime consists of only the description of a particular act, without reference to intent to do a further act or achieve a future consequence, we ask whether the defendant intended to do the proscribed act. This intention is deemed to be a general criminal intent. When the definition refers to defendant's intent to do some further act or achieve some additional consequence, the crime is deemed to be one of specific intent. There is no real difference, however, only a linguistic one, between an intent to do an act already performed and an intent to do that same act in the future.

The language of Penal Code section 22, drafted in 1872 when "specific" and "general" intent were not yet terms of art, is somewhat broader than those terms:

> No act committed by a person while in a state of voluntary intoxication is less criminal by reason of his having been in such condition. But whenever the actual existence of any particular purpose, motive, or intent is a necessary element to constitute any particular species or degree of crime, the jury may take into consideration the fact that the accused was intoxicated at the time, in determining the purpose, motive, or intent with which he committed the act.

Even this statement of the relevant policy is no easier to apply to particular crimes. We are still confronted with the difficulty of characterizing the mental element of a given crime as a particular purpose, motive, or intent necessary to constitute the offense, or as something less than that to which evidence of intoxication is not pertinent.

Even if we assume that the presence or absence of words clearly denoting mental activity is a valid criterion for determining the significance of intoxication, our present problem is not resolved. The difficulty with applying such a test to the crime of assault or assault with a deadly weapon is that no word in the relevant code provisions unambiguously denotes a particular mental element, yet the word "attempt" in Penal Code section 240 strongly suggests goal-directed, intentional behavior.[6] This uncertainty accounts for the conflict over whether assault is a crime only of intention or also of recklessness.

We need not reconsider our position in *Carmen* [footnote 6 supra] that an assault cannot be predicated merely on reckless conduct. Even if assault requires

---

6. Penal Code, section 240 provides: "An assault is an unlawful attempt, coupled with a present ability, to commit a violent injury on the person of another."

It was the strong suggestion of intent in the ordinary usage of the word "attempt" that was at the basis of this court's remark in People v. Carmen, 36 Cal. 2d 768, 775 [228 P.2d 281], that "[o]ne could not very well 'attempt' or try to 'commit' an injury on the person of another if he had no intent to cause any injury to such other person."

an intent to commit a battery on the victim, it does not follow that the crime is one in which evidence of intoxication ought to be considered in determining whether the defendant had that intent. It is true that in most cases specific intent has come to mean an intention to do a future act or achieve a particular result, and that assault is appropriately characterized as a specific intent crime under this definition. An assault, however, is equally well characterized as a general intent crime under the definition of general intent as an intent merely to do a violent act. Therefore, whatever reality the distinction between specific and general intent may have in other contexts, the difference is chimerical in the case of assault with a deadly weapon or simple assault. Since the definitions of both specific intent and general intent cover the requisite intent to commit a battery, the decision whether or not to give effect to evidence of intoxication must rest on other considerations.

A compelling consideration is the effect of alcohol on human behavior. A significant effect of alcohol is to distort judgment and relax the controls on aggressive and anti-social impulses. Alcohol apparently has less effect on the ability to engage in simple goal-directed behavior, although it may impair the efficiency of that behavior. In other words, a drunk man is capable of forming an intent to do something simple, such as strike another, unless he is so drunk that he has reached the stage of unconsciousness. What he is not as capable as a sober man of doing is exercising judgment about the social consequences of his acts or controlling his impulses toward anti-social acts. He is more likely to act rashly and impulsively and to be susceptible to passion and anger. It would therefore be anomalous to allow evidence of intoxication to relieve a man of responsibility for the crimes of assault with a deadly weapon or simple assault, which are so frequently committed in just such a manner. As the court said in Parker v. United States (D.C. Cir. 1966) 359 F.2d 1009, 1012-1013, "Whatever ambiguities there may be in distinguishing between specific and general intent to determine whether drunkenness constitutes a defense, an offense of this nature is not one which requires an intent that is susceptible to negation through a showing of voluntary intoxication."

Those crimes that have traditionally been characterized as crimes of specific intent are not affected by our holding here. The difference in mental activity between formulating an intent to commit a battery and formulating an intent to commit a battery for the purpose of raping or killing may be slight, but it is sufficient to justify drawing a line between them and considering evidence of intoxication in the one case and disregarding it in the other. Accordingly, on retrial the court should not instruct the jury to consider evidence of defendant's intoxication in determining whether he committed assault with a deadly weapon on a peace officer or any of the lesser assaults included therein. . . .

NOTES

1. *The association of crime and alcohol.* Some of the reluctance to give the defendant's intoxication its normal evidentiary significance in rebutting the definitional mens rea elements of the crime charged is explained by the following data in Robert A. Moore, Legal Responsibility and Chronic Alcoholism, 122 Am. J. Psychiatry 748, 753 (1966):

To demonstrate that the association of crime and alcohol is not insignificant, a sampling of a few statistics is enlightening. Of 882 felons arrested in a two-year period in Cincinnati, 64 percent had a urine alcohol level of 0.10 percent or higher. In crimes of violence, the incidence varied from 67 to 88 percent. A four-year study of 588 homicide cases in Philadelphia revealed that one or both parties had been drinking in 64 percent of the cases. In 44 percent of these cases, both parties had been drinking; in 9 percent, the victim only had been drinking and in 11 percent, the offender only had been drinking. In Cincinnati, 84 percent of 225 homicide victims had been drinking and 44 percent had a blood alcohol level of 0.15 percent or higher. So that we are not misled into thinking that the association is between crime and alcohol but not crime and alcoholism, we should consider another study which showed that 43 percent of 223 consecutively admitted male criminals were alcoholics.

This is not an American phenomenon. In Yugoslavia, 60 to 80 percent of all crimes involve intoxication to some degree, with over half of the homicides committed during a state of pathological intoxication. The association of alcohol and crime was lower but not insignificant in Sweden: 39 percent of male offenders but only 4.2 percent of women offenders were intoxicated at the time of the offense. In Japan, it was found that 36 percent of arsonists, 27 percent of murderers and 18 percent of assaulters had been intoxicated at the time of the crime, and 17.6 percent of all prisoners were intoxicated offenders.

2. The holding in *Hood* may have been affected by subsequent statutory amendments to California Penal Code §22, which provide that evidence of voluntary intoxication is not admissible to prove that a defendant lacked the *capacity* to form a required mental state, but that such evidence is admissible, and only admissible, on the issue of whether the defendant "actually formed a required specific intent, premeditated, deliberated, or harbored malice aforethought, when a specific intent crime is charged."

Question: Under these amendments is evidence of intoxication admissible more or less broadly than under the *Hood* case? For exploration of the meaning and possible significance of the statutory distinction between the *capacity* to form an intent and the *actual* formation of that intent, see the discussion of the same issue as it arises in connection with evidence of mental impairment, page 1006 infra.

3. The common law approach. Prior to the advent of the Model Penal Code proposals, the prevailing approach permitted intoxication evidence to be considered as potentially negating the mens rea of a "specific intent" crime, but excluded any consideration of self-induced intoxication, even when it was logically relevant to the required state of mind, in a "general intent" crime. This remains the governing rule in many American jurisdictions, as well as in England. See Model Penal Code and Commentaries, Comment to §2.08 at 353-354 (1985); Director of Public Prosecutions v. Majewski, [1976] 2 All E.R. 142; D. McCord, The English and American History of Voluntary Intoxication to Negate Mens Rea, 11 J. Legal Hist. 372 (1990).

4. Identifying "general intent" crimes. If assault were defined as an act that recklessly creates a risk of injury, all courts would classify the offense as a "general intent" crime, and it would then follow, under the common law rule set out in Note 3 supra, that intoxication evidence would not be admissible to negate the required mens rea. But because statutes in California (and many other states) define assault as a kind of attempt and require proof of an *intent* to inflict injury (not just recklessness), see People v. Carmen, cited in *Hood* at page 919 n. 6 supra, how can assault be classified as a general intent crime? Because assault, like any other attempt, requires proof of a purpose to accomplish a particular result, the offense seems to meet one of the classic definitions of a *specific intent* crime. See the Note on General Intent and Specific Intent, Chapter 3, page 218 supra. Did the court in *Hood* decide that assault nonetheless was *not* a specific intent crime, or did it decide that intoxication evidence should be inadmissible even though assault *is* a specific intent crime? Which approach is analytically preferable?

In People v. Rocha, 3 Cal. 3d 893, 479 P.2d 372 (1971), the California Supreme Court noted the confusion generated by *Hood* and announced flatly that assault with a deadly weapon is a "general intent" crime as to which intoxication evidence is inadmissible. This approach preserves the traditional "general intent"-"specific intent" test for determining the admissibility of intoxication evidence, but only at the cost of confounding the traditional test for determining what is a general intent crime. Pursuing the same approach of using policy considerations relating to intoxication to guide its classification of "general intent" crimes, the California Supreme Court held in People v. Whitfield, 7 Cal. 4th 437, 868 P.2d 272 (1994), that a charge of second-degree murder based on a theory of implied malice (i.e., recklessness) is a *specific* intent crime for which intoxication evidence *is* admissible. Thus, in California, assault is considered a general intent crime even though recklessness is insufficient and intention to injure must be proved, but second-degree murder is considered a specific intent crime even though recklessness is sufficient and intent to kill or injure need *not* be proved.

Do the concepts of general and specific intent really aid the analysis, or are they simply labels used to announce conclusions reached on other grounds? Why shouldn't a court focus directly on the question whether intoxication evidence *should* be admissible, without attempting to determine whether the crime is properly classified as one of "general intent"?[10]

The Model Penal Code, and many of the recent court decisions, reject the controlling significance of the general intent-specific intent distinction and instead focus directly on the question of when intoxication evidence should be admissible. Yet there remain wide variations in the conclusions reached. The remaining materials in this section consider the principal approaches and their rationales.

STATE v. STASIO, 78 N.J. 467, 396 A.2d 1129 (1979): [The defendant was convicted of assault with intent to rob. Conceding that this was a "specific intent"

---

10. In California, the court could not simply bypass the general intent-specific intent test because the admissibility of intoxication evidence was controlled by Cal. Penal Code §22(b), enacted in 1982, which provides as follows:

> Evidence of voluntary intoxication is admissible solely on the issue of whether or not the defendant actually formed a required specific intent, premeditated, deliberated, or harbored malice aforethought, when a specific intent crime is charged.

In *Whitfield*, the court held (868 P.2d at 275-276) that the statute's reference to "malice aforethought" was intended to encompass both the mental states of express malice (i.e., intent to kill) and implied malice (i.e., recklessness), and that "the Legislature considered murder to be a 'specific intent crime' within the meaning of [the statute] whether the prosecution's theory is that malice is express or implied" (id. at 277).

crime, the court nonetheless ruled that evidence of voluntary intoxication was inadmissible:[11] [D]istinguishing between specific and general intent gives rise to incongruous results by irrationally allowing intoxication to excuse some crimes but not others. In some instances if the defendant is found incapable of formulating the specific intent necessary for the crime charged, such as assault with intent to rob, he may be convicted of a lesser included general intent crime, such as assault with a deadly weapon. In other cases there may be no related general intent offense so that intoxication would lead to acquittal. Thus, a defendant acquitted for breaking and entering with intent to steal because of intoxication would not be guilty of any crime — breaking and entering being at most under certain circumstances the disorderly persons offense of trespass. . . .

Finally, where the more serious offense requires only a general intent, such as rape, . . . intoxication provides no defense, whereas it would be a defense to an attempt to rape, specific intent being an element of that offense. Yet the same logic and reasoning which impels exculpation due to the failure of specific intent to commit an offense would equally compel the same result when a general intent is an element of the offense.

The [traditional] approach may free defendants of specific intent offenses even though the harm caused may be greater than in an offense held to require only general intent. This course thus undermines the criminal law's primary function of protecting society from the results of behavior that endangers the public safety. This should be our guide rather than concern with logical consistency in terms of any single theory of culpability, particularly in view of the fact that alcohol is significantly involved in a substantial number of offenses. The demands of public safety and the harm done are identical irrespective of the offender's reduced ability to restrain himself due to his drinking. . . .

Our holding today does not mean that voluntary intoxication is always irrelevant in criminal proceedings. Evidence of intoxication may be introduced to demonstrate that premeditation and deliberation have not been proven so that a second degree murder cannot be raised to first degree murder or to show that the intoxication led to a fixed state of insanity. Intoxication may be shown to prove that a defendant never participated in a crime. Thus it might be proven that a defendant was in such a drunken stupor and unconscious state that he was not a part of a robbery. . . . His mental faculties may be so prostrated as to preclude the commission of the criminal act. Under some circumstances intoxication may be relevant to demonstrate mistake. However, in the absence of any basis for the defense, a trial court should not in its charge introduce that element. A trial court, of course, may consider intoxication as a mitigating circumstance when sentencing a defendant.

[Judge Pashman, dissenting, commented:] [T]he majority rules that a person may be convicted of the crimes of assault *with intent* to rob and breaking and entering *with intent* to steal even though he never, in fact, intended to rob anyone or steal anything. The majority arrives at this anomalous result by holding that voluntary intoxication can never constitute a defense to any crime other than first-degree murder even though, due to intoxication, the accused may not

---

11. *Stasio* was superseded by New Jersey legislation based on the Model Penal Code, but the approach it followed — excluding intoxication evidence for *both* general intent and specific intent crimes — has been adopted by statute or judicial decision in a substantial number of jurisdictions. See, e.g., McDaniel v. State, 356 So. 2d 1151 (Miss. 1978); 18 Pa. Stat. Ann. §308; Ark. Stat. Ann. §41-207.

have possessed the mental state specifically required as an element of the offense. This holding . . . defies logic and sound public policy. . . .

A person who intentionally commits a bad act is more culpable than one who engages in the same conduct without any evil design. The intentional wrongdoer is also more likely to repeat his offense, and hence constitutes a greater threat to societal repose. A sufficiently intoxicated defendant is thus subject to less severe sanctions not because the law "excuses" his conduct but because the circumstances surrounding his acts have been deemed by the Legislature to be less deserving of punishment. . . .

Just as the lack of premeditation, willfulness, or deliberation precludes a conviction for first-degree murder, so should the lack of intent to rob or steal be a defense to assault and battery with intent to rob, or breaking and entering with intent to steal. The principle is the same in both situations. If voluntary intoxication negates an element of the offense, the defendant has not engaged in the conduct proscribed by the criminal statute, and hence should not be subject to the sanctions imposed by that statute.

The majority ultimately grounds its conclusions on public policy considerations. It professes to be concerned with protecting society from drunken offenders. There are several problems with this approach. First, the majority's opinion is not even internally consistent. Although intoxication is not to be given the status of a defense, the majority states that it can be considered to "buttress the affirmative defense of reasonable mistake." It is difficult to comprehend why the public would be less endangered by persons who become intoxicated and, as a result, commit alcohol-induced "mistakes" which would otherwise be criminal offenses, than by persons who get so intoxicated that they commit the same acts without any evil intent. In fact, it appears highly likely that the first group would encompass a larger number of persons and hence constitute a greater menace to society. . . .

The most important consideration, however, is that the standards for establishing the defense are extremely difficult to meet. Contrary to the implications contained in the majority opinion, it is not the case that every defendant who has had a few drinks may successfully urge the defense. The mere intake of even large quantities of alcohol will not suffice. Moreover, the defense cannot be established solely by showing that the defendant might not have committed the offense had he been sober. What is required is a showing of such a great prostration of the faculties that the requisite mental state was totally lacking. That is, to successfully invoke the defense, an accused must show that he was so intoxicated that he did not have the intent to commit an offense. Such a state of affairs will likely exist in very few cases. I am confident that our judges and juries will be able to distinguish such unusual instances. . . .

MODEL PENAL CODE

SECTION 2.08.   INTOXICATION

[See Appendix for text of this section.]

MODEL PENAL CODE AND COMMENTARIES, COMMENT TO §2.08 AT 357-359 (1985):
Two major issues are . . . presented by the Model Code's provisions. The first,

which seems more readily disposed of, is the question of whether intoxication ought to be accorded a significance that is entirely coextensive with its relevance to disprove purpose or knowledge when they are the requisite mental elements of a specific crime. The answer ought to be affirmative, that when the definition of a crime or a degree thereof requires proof of such a state of mind, the legal policy involved will almost certainly obtain whether or not the absence of purpose or knowledge is due to the actor's self-induced intoxication or to some other cause. For when purpose or knowledge, as distinguished from recklessness, is made essential for conviction, the reason very surely is that in the absence of such states of mind the conduct involved does not present a comparable danger, as in burglary or theft; or that the actor is not deemed to present as significant a threat, as in treason and perhaps in the first degree of murder; or, finally, that the ends of legal policy are served by bringing to book or subjecting to graver sanctions those who consciously defy the legal norm. If the mental state that is the basis of the law's concern does not exist, the reason for its nonexistence is usually immaterial. So it is that in the case of crimes of violence against the person, purpose or knowledge rarely is required to establish liability, though their presence may have weight in aggravating the degree of the offense or in sentencing; recklessness or even negligence is ordinarily sufficient.

The second and more difficult question relates to recklessness, where awareness of the risk created by the actor's conduct ordinarily is requisite for liability under Section 2.02. The problem is whether intoxication ought to be accorded a significance coextensive with its relevance to disprove such awareness, as in the case of purpose or knowledge that has previously been discussed. . . .

Those who oppose a special rule for drunkenness in relation to awareness of the risk in recklessness draw strength initially from the presumptive disfavor of any special rules of liability. . . . The protagonists of this position draw further strength from the proposition that it is precisely the awareness of the risk in recklessness that is the essence of its moral culpability — a culpability dependent upon the magnitude of the specific risk knowingly created. When that risk is greater in degree than that which the actor perceives at the time of getting drunk, as is frequently the case, the result of a special rule is bound to be a liability disproportionate to culpability. Hence the solution urged is to dispense with any special rule, relying rather on the possibility of proving foresight at the time of drinking and, when this cannot be proved, upon a generalized prohibition of being drunk and dangerous, with sanctions appropriate for such behavior. This approach would also permit prosecution for negligence if negligent commission of the act in question was sufficient to establish criminal liability. With respect to negligence, the essence of the culpability is the failure to perceive a risk that the actor should have perceived. The actor's culpability in failing to perceive a risk would be judged against the standard of a man in normal possession of his faculties. Thus, the fact that the defendant was drunk will not exculpate him from a charge of negligence. . . .

The case thus made is worthy of respect, but there are strong considerations on the other side. There is first the weight of the antecedent law which here, more clearly than in England, has tended toward a special rule for drunkenness in this context. Beyond this, there is the fundamental point that awareness of the potential consequences of excessive drinking on the capacity of human beings to gauge the risks incident to their conduct is by now so dispersed in our culture that it is not unfair to postulate a general equivalence between the risks created by the conduct of the drunken actor and the risks created by his conduct in becoming drunk. Becoming so drunk as to destroy temporarily the actor's powers of perception and judgment is conduct that plainly has no affirmative social value to counterbalance the potential danger. The actor's moral culpability lies in engaging in such conduct. Added to this are the impressive difficulties posed in litigating the foresight of any particular actor at the time when he imbibes and the relative rarity of cases where intoxication really does engender unawareness as distinguished from imprudence. These considerations led to the conclusion, on balance, that the Model Code should declare that unawareness of a risk, of which the actor would have been aware had he been sober, is immaterial. Most states with revised codes have taken a similar position.

NOTES

1. *Degree of intoxication:* Some cases allow evidence only of a particularly high level of intoxication even when intoxication is admissible to negate a required mens rea. Consider the following case.

State v. Cameron, 104 N.J. 42, 514 A.2d 1302 (1986): Defendant, Michele Cameron, age 22 at the time of trial, was indicted for second degree aggravated assault; possession of a weapon, a broken bottle, with a purpose to use it unlawfully; and fourth degree resisting arrest. A jury convicted defendant of all charges.

The charges arose out of an incident of June 6, 1981, on a vacant lot in Trenton. The unreported opinion of the Appellate Division depicts the following tableau of significant events:

> The victim, Joseph McKinney, was playing cards with four other men. Defendant approached and disrupted the game with her conduct. The participants moved their card table to a new location within the lot. Defendant followed them, however, and overturned the table. The table was righted and the game resumed. Shortly thereafter, defendant attacked McKinney with a broken bottle. As a result of that attack he sustained an injury to his hand, which necessitated 36 stitches and caused permanent injury.
>
> Defendant reacted with violence to the arrival of the police. She threw a bottle at their vehicle, shouted obscenities, and tried to fight them off. She had to be restrained and handcuffed in the police wagon.

[We are] in accord with the determinations of the court below that all three of the charges of which this defendant was convicted — aggravated assault, the possession offense, and resisting arrest — have purposeful conduct as an element of the offense. . . . We part company with the Appellate Division, however, in its conclusion that the circumstances disclosed by the evidence in this case required that the issue of defendant's intoxication be submitted to the jury.[a] . . .

Justice Depue's instruction to a jury over a century ago . . . remains good law:

---

a. The applicable statute, N.J. Stat Ann. §2C:2-8, was in all relevant respects identical to Model Penal Code §2.08. — Eds.

You should carefully discriminate between that excitable condition of the mind produced by drink, which is not incapable of forming an intent, but determines to act on a slight provocation, and such prostration of the faculties by intoxication as puts the accused in such a state that he is incapable of forming an intention from which he shall act.

. . . In order to satisfy the statutory condition that . . . intoxication must negative an element of the offense, the intoxication must be of an extremely high level. [T]he standard [must] be "prostration of faculties." Less certain is how that standard is to be satisfied. . . .

[S]ome of the factors pertinent to the determination of intoxication sufficient to satisfy the test of "prostration of faculties" — a shorthand expression used here to indicate a condition of intoxication that renders the actor incapable of purposeful or knowing conduct — are the following: the quantity of intoxicant consumed, the period of time involved, the actor's conduct as perceived by others (what he said, how he said it, how he appeared, how he acted, how his coordination or lack thereof manifested itself), any odor of alcohol or other intoxicating substance, the results of any tests to determine blood-alcohol content, and the actor's ability to recall significant events.

Measured by the foregoing standard and evidence relevant thereto, it is apparent that the record in this case is insufficient to have required the trial court to grant defendant's request to charge intoxication. . . .

True, the victim testified that defendant was drunk, and defendant herself said she felt "pretty intoxicated," "pretty bad," and "very intoxicated." But these are no more than conclusory labels. . . . Defendant's conduct was violent, abusive, and threatening. But with it all there is not the slightest suggestion that she did not know what she was doing or that her faculties were so beclouded by the wine that she was incapable of engaging in purposeful conduct. That the purpose of the conduct may have been bizarre, even violent, is not the test. The critical question is whether defendant was capable of forming that bizarre or violent purpose, and we do not find sufficient evidence to permit a jury to say she was not. . . .

Ordinarily, of course, the question of whether a defendant's asserted intoxication satisfies the standards enunciated in this opinion should be resolved by the jury. But here, viewing the evidence and the legitimate inferences to be drawn therefrom in the light most favorable to defendant, the best that can be made of the proof of intoxication is that defendant may have been extremely agitated and distraught. . . . [T]here is no suggestion in the evidence that defendant's faculties were so prostrated by her consumption of something less than a pint of wine as to render her incapable of purposeful or knowing conduct. The trial court correctly refused defendant's request.

2. Crimes where intoxication inadmissible. Most of the states with recently revised codes follow the Model Penal Code in holding intoxication evidence inadmissible to negate recklessness, even when such evidence would otherwise be "relevant" under ordinary standards. But a significant minority reject the Model Penal Code approach and allow intoxication its normal evidentiary effect even in crimes of recklessness.[12]

12. The statutes are collected in Model Penal Code and Commentaries, Comment to §2.08 at 359-360 n. 29 (1985).

On the other hand, some states restrict intoxication evidence even more than the Model Penal Code does. See, e.g., Chittun v. Commonwealth, 211 Va. 12, 174 S.E.2d 779 (1970) (intoxication evidence need not be considered in deciding whether defendant had the specific intent required on charges of kidnapping and statutory rape); 18 Pa. Stat. Ann. §308 ("evidence of voluntary intoxication may [not] be introduced to negative the element of intent," except when relevant "to reduce murder from a higher degree to a lower degree"; Tex. Pen. Code §8.04 (voluntary intoxication no defense to any criminal charge).

3. *Constitutional problems.* Once a state decides to require a particular mens rea (for example, knowledge or recklessness) as an element of an offense, can it legitimately deny a defendant the opportunity to present relevant evidence (for example, testimony that the defendant was highly intoxicated) that bears on the existence of the required element? Most courts have upheld the constitutionality of statutes and common law rules excluding intoxication evidence. See, e.g., Wyant v. State, 519 A.2d 649 (Del. 1986). Compare Terry v. State, 465 N.E.2d 1085 (Ind. 1984). *Terry* arose under a statute providing that "[v]oluntary intoxication is a defense only to the extent that it negatives an element of an offense referred to by the phrase 'with intent' or 'with intention to.'" In an attempted murder case, the prosecution argued that voluntary intoxication was not a defense with respect to this offense, traditionally one of specific intent, because the attempt statute did not contain the precise phrase "with intent" or "with an intention to." The Indiana Supreme Court declined to construe the statutory phrases as extending to crimes interpreted to require a specific intent. Rather, that court held evidence of voluntary intoxication admissible without regard to the nature of the offense charged and ruled the Indiana statute unconstitutional. The court said (id. at 1088):

> Any factor which serves as a denial of the existence of mens rea must be considered by a trier of fact before a guilty finding is entered. Historically, facts such as age, mental condition, mistake or intoxication have been offered to negate the capacity to formulate intent. The attempt by the legislature to remove the factor of voluntary intoxication, except in limited situations, goes against this firmly ingrained principle. We thus hold Ind. Code §35-41-3-5(b) is void and without effect.

4. *A separate offense?* One argument for the fairness of punishing a defendant even though intoxication may have negated a required mens rea is that the defendant's culpability lies in his having knowingly incurred the risk of dangerous conduct by voluntarily drinking to excess. Does this argument confuse the particular kind of culpability required for a given crime (for example, for robbery — forcibly taking property with intent to steal; for murder — consciously creating a substantial risk of death) with the vaguer and usually less serious culpability involved in choosing to get drunk? Would it be more logical to acquit on charges related to the specific harm caused, but convict for a more general offense akin to reckless endangerment?

Such a proposal was made by an English Committee in 1975. Report of the Committee on Mentally Abnormal Offenders 235 (1975) (the Butler Committee). It has been revived in different form in Law Commission Consultation Paper No. 127 (1993), Intoxication and Criminal Liability. Under the proposal, anyone who causes the harm proscribed by a "listed offense" while "deliberately" intoxicated is guilty of "criminal intoxication." The listed offenses are those which cause substantial harm to persons, public order, or the physical safety of property. To be culpable, the defendant must have voluntarily taken a substance, knowing that the quantity he took might cause his awareness, understanding, or control to be substantially impaired. The suggested punishment for criminal intoxication is based on the underlying offense: two-thirds of the possible sentence, with a maximum of ten years' imprisonment for nonhomicide offenses. Does linking the punishment to the harm caused make sense given that defendant's culpability is based on choosing to become intoxicated? The Butler Committee had suggested a standard punishment for the offense, regardless of the underlying harm.

4. Mental Disorder

INTRODUCTORY NOTE

Insanity can become an important legal issue in a variety of circumstances. A contract may be unenforceable if one of the parties was insane when the contract was made. A will may be held void if the testator was insane. In the criminal process, insanity can be relevant at several different stages. Of greatest importance to the substantive criminal law, insanity at the time of the offense is usually a defense to a criminal charge. In addition, a person who is insane may not be tried, convicted, or sentenced. Neither may such a person be executed if convicted of a capital offense. Further, under many state statutes, a person who becomes insane while in prison must be transferred to a mental hospital.

Question: Should the definition of insanity for these varied purposes be the same? Consider the following issues.

1. Competency to stand trial. (*a*) Model Penal Code §4.04 states the generally accepted test of insanity for purposes of determining whether an accused may be tried and sentenced: "No person who as a result of mental disease or defect lacks capacity to understand the proceedings against him or to assist in his own defense shall be tried, convicted or sentenced for the commission of an offense so long as such incapacity endures." In Dusky v. United States, 362 U.S. 402 (1960), the Court stated: "[T]he test must be whether [the defendant] has sufficient present ability to consult with his lawyer with a reasonable degree of rational understanding — and whether he has a rational as well as factual understanding of the proceedings against him."

(*b*) Some courts have permitted forcible medication of defendants in order to render them competent to stand trial. E.g., Khiem v. United States, 612 A.2d 160, 168-169 (D.C. 1992). Yet antipsychotic drugs used for this purpose often affect the defendant's demeanor at trial. Does involuntary medication under these circumstances violate a defendant's right to a fair trial? In Riggins v. Nevada, 112 S. Ct. 1810, 1814-1815 (1992), the Court declined to rule that forcible medication was impermissible per se but held that forcible medication in that case was a violation of due process, because the state had not shown that other means to render the defendant competent to stand trial were unavailable.

(*c*) If a judge finds that the defendant is suffering from total amnesia concerning the alleged crime but is otherwise in full command of her faculties, most courts hold that the defendant is competent to stand trial. See State v. Wynn, 490 A.2d 605 (Del. Super. 1985); People v. Francobandera, 33 N.Y.2d 429, 310 N.E.2d 292, 295 (1974). What is the basis for this view? Doesn't an inability to recall the events charged seriously impede a defendant's ability to mount a defense? Compare State v. McClendon, 101 Ariz. 285, 419 P.2d 69 (1966) (improper to hold trial if continuance might enable amnesiac to recover).

2. *Execution.* All states bar execution of a condemned prisoner who becomes insane. But how should insanity be defined in this context?

(*a*) The 1951 Pennsylvania Mental Health Act provided for the transfer to a mental hospital of any person detained in a penal institution who is mentally ill, and defined mental illness as "an illness which so lessens the capacity of a person to use his customary self-control, judgment and discretion in the conduct of his affairs and social relations as to make it necessary or advisable for him to be under care." In Commonwealth v. Moon, 383 Pa. 18, 117 A.2d 96 (1955), the court held this test applicable to determine whether to stay execution of a convicted murderer, because such a person is "detained" in a penal institution (pending execution) within the meaning of the act. Is the result sound? Why should execution of a person be stayed until the person is able to take proper care of himself while alive?

(*b*) In Ford v. Wainwright, 477 U.S. 399 (1986), the Supreme Court held that the Eighth Amendment's proscription of "cruel and unusual punishment" bars execution of the insane, but the Court offered no definition of what constitutes insanity for purposes of the Eighth Amendment requirement. Nor did the Court pinpoint the specific reasons *why* execution of the "insane" would be cruel and unusual. Justice Marshall, speaking for five members of the Court, concluded:

> Unanimity of rationale . . . we do not find. "But whatever the reason of the law is, it is plain the law is so." Hawles, [Remarks on the Trial of Mr. Charles Bateman, [1685] 11 HOW. St. Tr. *477 (1816)]. We know of virtually no authority condoning the execution of the insane at English common law. . . . And the intuition that such an execution simply offends humanity is evidently shared across this Nation. Faced with such widespread evidence of a restriction upon sovereign power, this Court is compelled to conclude that the Eighth Amendment prohibits a State from carrying out a sentence of death upon a prisoner who is insane. Whether its aim be to protect the condemned from fear and pain without comfort of understanding, or to protect the dignity of society itself from the barbarity of exacting mindless vengeance, the restriction finds enforcement in the Eighth Amendment.

Justice Powell, in a concurring opinion, commented as follows:

> [S]ome authorities contended that the prohibition against executing the insane was justified as a way of preserving the defendant's ability to make arguments on his own behalf. Other authorities suggest, however, that the prohibition derives from more straightforward humanitarian concerns. . . .
>
> The first of these justifications has slight merit today. Modern practice provides far more extensive review of convictions and sentences than did the common law, including not only direct appeal but ordinarily both state and federal collateral review. . . . It is thus unlikely indeed that a defendant today could go to his death with knowledge of undiscovered trial error that might set him free. . . .
>
> The more general concern of the common law — that executions of the insane are simply cruel — retains its vitality. It is as true today as when Coke lived that most men and women value the opportunity to prepare, mentally and spiritually,

for their death. Moreover, today as at common law, one of the death penalty's critical justifications, its retributive force, depends on the defendant's awareness of the penalty's existence and purpose. . . .[a] For precisely these reasons, Florida requires the Governor to stay executions of those who "d[o] not have the mental capacity to understand the nature of the death penalty and why it was imposed" on them. Fla. Stat. §922.07 (1985). A number of States have more rigorous standards, but none disputes the need to require that those who are executed know the fact of their impending execution and the reason for it.

Such a standard appropriately defines the kind of mental deficiency that should trigger the Eighth Amendment prohibition.

(c) Most jurisdictions now define insanity for purposes of execution along the lines endorsed by Justice Powell in *Ford*. See, e.g., Ill. Stat. ch. 730, §5/5-2-3 (1993). In Penry v. Lynaugh, 492 U.S. 302, 333 (1989), a majority of the Supreme Court assumed that the Powell test stated the correct standard under the Eighth Amendment but held that the test was met in the case of a mentally retarded prisoner described as having a mental age of seven. A few states have adopted stricter tests. The Washington and South Carolina Supreme Courts have declared that sanity for purposes of execution requires that the prisoner not only understand the nature of the death penalty and why it is being imposed, but also have the ability to communicate rationally with defense counsel. See Singleton v. State, 437 S.E.2d 53 (S.C. 1993); State v. Harris, 789 P.2d 60, 64-65 (Wash. 1990). And subsequent to *Penry*, seven states enacted legislation barring execution of offenders who are "seriously mentally retarded." See Vincent J. Aprile, Criminal Justice Matters: Executing the Mentally Retarded, 9 Crim. J. 38, 38-39 (Spring 1994).

(d) At least one court has held that the state may not subject an insane death-row prisoner to antipsychotic medication, against his will, in order to restore his sanity so that he may be executed. See State v. Perry, 610 So. 2d 746 (La. 1992). The problem is a recurrent one, because antipsychotic drugs are an increasingly popular means of treating mental disorder, and up to 70 percent of death-row inmates are estimated to suffer some form of mental illness. See Robert Johnson, Death Work 50 (1990). Does the *Perry* approach mean that the incompetent prisoner (or someone acting on his behalf) must choose between continued insanity and death by execution? Is there any way to escape this dilemma? For a useful discussion of the problem, see Kristen Wenstrup Crosby, Comment, *State v. Perry*, 77 Minn. L. Rev. 1193 (1993).

(e) What *procedures* should be used to determine whether a condemned prisoner has become insane? Under the California Penal Code, a sentenced prisoner may not be executed if a specially impanelled jury of 12 persons finds that he is presently insane. Under the same code, a woman may not be executed while pregnant, but the determination of her pregnancy is to be made by three physicians. §§3705, 3706.

Questions: How can one account for the difference in procedure? Would it make sense to do the reverse — that is, to have 12 jurors determine whether a woman is pregnant and 3 physicians determine whether a person is too insane to be executed? Why not?

---

a. For a detailed development of this theme, see R. A. Duff, Trials and Punishments 16-35 (1986). — Eds.

Fla. Stat. §922.07 (1985) provides that when the governor is informed that a condemned inmate may be insane, he must appoint a commission of three psychiatrists who shall examine the prisoner "with all three psychiatrists present at the same time." Each psychiatrist prepares a report for the governor, who then determines whether the convicted person is insane. In Ford v. Wainwright, Note 2(b) supra, the statutory procedure was initiated after Ford exhibited acute symptoms of mental disorder, including extreme delusions and virtually total incoherence of thought and speech. The three psychiatrists concluded that Ford, though severely disturbed, knew he faced the death penalty and understood its implications. The governor considered the three reports, refused to accept oral or written argument or to consider psychiatric evidence proffered by the defense, and found Ford to be sane.

The Supreme Court held this procedure constitutionally inadequate. A majority of the Court concluded that full-scale adversary procedures were not required but that the prisoner must be afforded an opportunity to present evidence and argument before an impartial officer or board independent of the executive branch. Florida subsequently revised its procedures to permit de novo judicial review of the sanity question, with consideration of experts' reports and any other written or oral submissions from the parties, whenever the Governor determines the prisoner to be sane.[13]

a. The Traditional Test of Legal Insanity

M'NAGHTEN'S CASE

House of Lords
10 Cl. & F. 200, 8 Eng. Rep. 718 (1843)

[Defendant was indicted for the murder of Edward Drummond, secretary to the prime minister, Sir Robert Peel. Apparently M'Naghten had mistaken Drummond for Peel and had shot Drummond by mistake. Upon his arrest he told police that he had come to London to murder the Prime Minister because "[t]he tories in my city follow and persecute me wherever I go, and have entirely destroyed my peace of mind. [T]hey do everything in their power to harass and persecute me; in fact they wish to murder me." The defense introduced extensive expert and lay testimony indicating that M'Naghten was obsessed with delusions and suffered from acute insanity.[a] The presiding judge, Lord Chief Justice Tindal, in his charge to the jury stated:

> The question to be determined is whether at the time the act in question was committed, the prisoner had or had not the use of his understanding, so as to know that he was doing a wrong or wicked act. If the jurors should be of opinion that the

_____

13. Fla. R. Crim. P. 3.811, 3.812 (1987). See Joy B. Shearer, Insanity of the Condemned: Florida's Response to *Ford*, Fla. Bar. J., Mar. 1988, at 39-41.

a. At the time of his arrest, M'Naghten was found in possession of £750, and as a result he "probably had the best-financed defense in the history of the Old Bailey." He had the assistance of "four of the most able barristers in Britain [and] nine prominent medical experts." No expert witnesses appeared for the prosecution. See Richard Moran, Knowing Right from Wrong 90 (1981), which provides a fascinating, detailed account of M'Naghten's Case. — Eds.

prisoner was not sensible, at the time he committed it, that he was violating the laws both of God and man, then he would be entitled to a verdict in his favour: but if, on the contrary, they were of opinion that when he committed the act he was in a sound state of mind, then their verdict must be against him.

[The jury returned a verdict of "not guilty, on the ground of insanity." The verdict attracted great public attention and aroused considerable alarm. The press suggested that the insanity defense left madmen free to kill with impunity. Queen Victoria was particularly concerned: she herself had been the object of three recent assassination attempts, and one of her attackers had also benefited from an insanity acquittal. Both the *M'Naghten* verdict and the general problem of the insanity defense were debated in the House of Lords. As a result, the English judiciary (there were some 15 judges at the time) were invited to attend the House of Lords for the purpose of delivering answers to certain questions propounded to them. The famous *M'Naghten* Rule is found in the answer to the second and third questions delivered by Lord Chief Justice Tindal.]

Your Lordships are pleased to inquire of us, secondly, "What are the proper questions to be submitted to the jury, where a person alleged to be afflicted with insane delusion respecting one or more particular subjects or persons, is charged with the commission of a crime (murder, for example), and insanity is set up as a defence?" And, thirdly, "In what terms ought the question to be left to the jury as to the prisoner's state of mind at the time when the act was committed?" And as these two questions appear to us to be more conveniently answered together, we have to submit our opinion to be, that the jurors ought to be told in all cases that every man is to be presumed to be sane, and to possess a sufficient degree of reason to be responsible for his crimes, until the contrary be proved to their satisfaction; and that to establish a defence on the ground of insanity, it must be clearly proved that, at the time of the committing of the act, the party accused was labouring under such a defect of reason, from disease of the mind, as not to know the nature and quality of the act he was doing; or, if he did know it, that he did not know he was doing what was wrong. The mode of putting the latter part of the question to the jury on these occasions has generally been, whether the accused at the time of doing the act knew the difference between right and wrong: which mode, though rarely, if ever, leading to any mistake with the jury, is not, as we conceive, so accurate when put generally and in the abstract, as when put with reference to the party's knowledge of right and wrong in respect to the very act with which he is charged. If the question were to be put as to the knowledge of the accused solely and exclusively with reference to the law of the land, it might tend to confound the jury, by inducing them to believe that an actual knowledge of the law of the land was essential in order to lead to a conviction; whereas the law is administered upon the principle that every one must be taken conclusively to know it, without proof that he does know it. If the accused was conscious that the act was one which he ought not to do, and if the act was at the same time contrary to the law of the land, he is punishable; and the usual course therefore has been to leave the question to the jury, whether the party accused had a sufficient degree of reason to know that he was doing an act that was wrong: and this course we think is correct, accompanied with such observations and explanations as the circumstances of each particular case may require.

THE KING v. PORTER, 55 Commw. L.R. 182, 186-188 (1933): [Presiding at the trial, Justice Dixon explained the *M'Naghten* Rule in his charge to the jury:] There is a legal standard of disorder of mind which is sufficient to afford a ground of irresponsibility for crime, and a ground for your finding such a verdict as I have indicated [that is, not guilty on the ground of insanity].

Before explaining what that standard actually is, I wish to draw your attention to some general considerations affecting the question of insanity in the criminal law in the hope that by so doing you may be helped to grasp what the law prescribes. The purpose of the law in punishing people is to prevent others from committing a like crime or crimes. Its prime purpose is to deter people from committing offences. It may be that there is an element of retribution in the criminal law, so that when people have committed offences the law considers that they merit punishment, but its prime purpose is to preserve society from the depredations of dangerous and vicious people. Now, it is perfectly useless for the law to attempt, by threatening punishment, to deter people from committing crimes if their mental condition is such that they cannot be in the least influenced by the possibility or probability of subsequent punishment; if they cannot understand what they are doing or cannot understand the ground upon which the law proceeds. The law is not directed, as medical science is, to curing mental infirmities. The criminal law is not directed, as the civil law of lunacy is, to the care and custody of people of weak mind whose personal property may be in jeopardy through someone else taking a hand in the conduct of their affairs and their lives. This is quite a different thing from the question, what utility there is in the punishment of people who, at a moment, would commit acts which, if done when they were in sane minds, would be crimes. What is the utility of punishing people if they be beyond the control of the law for reasons of mental health? In considering that, it will not perhaps, if you have ever reflected upon the matter, have escaped your attention that a great number of people who come into a Criminal Court are abnormal. They would not be there if they were the normal type of average everyday people. Many of them are very peculiar in their dispositions and peculiarly tempered. That is markedly the case in sexual offences. Nevertheless, they are mentally quite able to appreciate what they are doing and quite able to appreciate the threatened punishment of the law and the wrongness of their acts, and they are held in check by the prospect of punishment. It would be very absurd if the law were to withdraw that check on the ground that they were somewhat different from their fellow creatures in mental make-up or texture at the very moment when the check is most needed. You will therefore see that the law, in laying down a standard of mental disorder sufficient to justify a jury in finding a prisoner not guilty on the ground of insanity at the moment of offence, is addressing itself to a somewhat difficult task. It is attempting to define what are the classes of people who should not be punished although they have done actual things which in others would amount to crime. . . . With that explanation I shall tell you what that standard is.

The first thing which I want you to notice is that you are only concerned with the condition of the mind at the time the act complained of was done. . . .

The next thing which I wish to emphasize is that his state of mind must have been one of disease, disorder or disturbance. Mere excitability of a normal man, passion, even stupidity, obtuseness, lack of self-control, and impulsiveness, are quite different things from what I have attempted to describe as a state of disease or disorder or mental disturbance arising from some infirmity, temporary or of long standing. If that existed it must then have been of such a character as to prevent him from knowing the physical nature of the act he was doing or of knowing that what he was doing was wrong. . . .

NOTES ON ADMINISTERING THE INSANITY DEFENSE

1. Who may raise the defense? There has been disagreement about whether the prosecutor or trial judge should be able to force an insanity defense on an unwilling defendant. Whalem v. United States, 346 F.2d 812 (D.C. Cir. 1965), held that the trial judge had authority to impose the defense over the defendant's objection. The court thought that the interests of justice preclude conviction of a defendant who obviously is mentally irresponsible. But subsequent decisions in most other jurisdictions held that the decision to raise the insanity issue must be left entirely within the defendant's control. These courts stressed that a properly counseled defendant may prefer to be found guilty rather than not guilty by reason of insanity, because the latter verdict can lead to longer confinement, more intrusive treatment or greater stigma. See, e.g., Frendak v. United States, 408 A.2d 364 (D.C. App. 1979). Recently, the U.S. Court of Appeals overruled *Whalem* and aligned itself with the prevailing view that bars imposition of the insanity defense on an unwilling defendant. See United States v. Marble, 940 F.2d 1543 (D.C. Cir. 1991). Compare Lord Denning in Bratty v. Attorney-General, [1963] A.C. 386, 411: "The old notion that only the defence can raise a defence of insanity is now gone. The prosecution are entitled to raise it and it is their duty to do so rather than allow a dangerous person to be at large."

2. Instructing the jury on the consequences of an insanity acquittal. In jurisdictions that provide for mandatory commitment following an insanity acquittal, defendants have pressed to have the jury informed of that fact because the jury may otherwise assume that an insanity acquittal will lead to the release of a dangerous, mentally unstable individual. Yet most courts have held that the jury should not be instructed on the procedures that follow an insanity verdict, on the ground that what will happen to the defendant is not relevant to whether the defendant met the test of legal insanity. See, e.g., People v. Goad, 421 Mich. 20, 364 N.W.2d 584 (1984). For federal prosecutions, the Supreme Court has held that juries should not be informed of the mandatory commitment provisions applicable under federal law. Shannon v. United States, 114 S. Ct. 2419 (1994). The Court said (id. at 2424) that "the principle that juries are not to consider the consequences of their verdicts is a reflection of the basic division of labor in our legal system between judge [as sentencer] and jury [as fact-finder]"; the Court also noted (id. at 2427) that "[even if] some jurors will harbor the mistaken belief that defendants found [not guilty by reason of insanity] will be released into society immediately . . . [there is] no reason to depart from 'the almost invariable assumption of the law that jurors follow their instructions.'" However, a number of courts have taken a less formalistic view. For example, in Commonwealth v. Mutina, 366 Mass. 810, 323 N.E.2d 294 (1975), the court stated (323 N.E.2d at 301-302):

> If jurors can be entrusted with responsibility for a defendant's life and liberty in such cases as this, they are entitled to know what protection they and their fellow

citizens will have if they conscientiously apply the law to the evidence and arrive at a verdict of not guilty by reason of insanity. . . .

The instant case represents a classic example of the injustice which may occur when such information is withheld from the jury. The jury could have had no doubt that the defendant killed Miss Achorn. The jury also heard overwhelmingly persuasive evidence that the defendant was insane at the time of the killing and that, for a long time into the future, he will remain a menace to himself and to society. . . .

Implicit in the jury's guilty verdict was a determination that the Commonwealth had proven the defendant's sanity beyond a reasonable doubt. On the record before us, we have found no rational justification or basis for such a finding, except the jury's understandable concern for the need to confine an insane and still dangerous killer for the protection of society. The jury, lacking knowledge of the commitment necessarily flowing from a verdict of not guilty by reason of insanity, applied their own standards of justice in arriving at a verdict designed to ensure the confinement of the defendant for his own safety and that of the community.

A substantial minority of the state courts now hold, in accord with *Mutina,* that where commitment is mandatory, the jury should be informed that a defendant found not guilty by reason of insanity must be detained until it is determined that she is no longer mentally ill and dangerous. See, e.g., Erdman v. State, 315 Md. 46, 553 A.2d 244 (1989); State v. Shickles, 760 P.2d 291 (Utah 1988).

Question: If commitment is *not* mandatory, should the jury be informed of that fact?

3. *Burden of proof.* (*a*) *State law.* All jurisdictions create a presumption of legal sanity at the trial. The effect of this presumption is that, in the absence of evidence on the issue, the sanity of the accused is presumed for all legal purposes. American jurisdictions, however, differ on two issues: (1) How much evidence need be presented before the effect of the presumption disappears and the question of the defendant's insanity becomes an issue that must be established by the evidence? (2) Where the issue must be established by the evidence, who bears the burden of persuasion, and how is that burden defined?

As to the first question, some states require only "some evidence" of legal insanity in order to eliminate the presumption of sanity. Others require more; this is usually that the evidence raise a reasonable doubt about the sanity of the accused. For discussion see Abraham S. Goldstein, The Insanity Defense ch. 8 (1967); Julian Eule, The Presumption of Sanity: Bursting the Bubble, 25 U.C.L.A.L. Rev. 637 (1978).

As to the second question, once insanity becomes an issue, many states require the prosecution to prove the sanity of the defendant beyond a reasonable doubt. See Annot., 17 A.L.R.3d 146, 159 (1968). This was once the rule in the federal courts as well. See Davis v. United States, 160 U.S. 469 (1895). However, as part of the reaction to the *Hinckley* verdict, see page 948 infra, there has been a change in recent years. In more than half the states, the defendant now must prove insanity by a preponderance of the evidence. See H.R. Rep. No. 98-577, 98th Cong., 1st Sess. 14 (1983). For the federal courts, the question is governed by 18 U.S.C. §17(b): "The defendant has the burden of proving the defense of insanity by clear and convincing evidence."

(*b*) *Constitutional requirements.* The constitutionality of requiring the defendant to carry the burden of proving insanity has been the subject of some controversy. In Leland v. Oregon, 343 U.S. 790 (1952), an Oregon statute requiring that defendant establish insanity beyond a reasonable doubt was upheld, over a forceful dissent by Justices Frankfurter and Black. In Patterson v. New York, 432 U.S. 197 (1977), the Court reaffirmed the constitutionality of requiring the defendant to bear the burden of persuasion on the sanity issue. The federal courts have also upheld the constitutionality of the heightened "clear and convincing evidence" burden now imposed on defendants in federal criminal prosecutions. See, e.g., United States v. Freeman, 804 F.2d 1574 (11th Cir. 1986). Most state courts have likewise held that statutes imposing the burden of persuasion on the defendant do not violate the due process requirements of state constitutions. See, e.g., State v. Joyner, 225 Conn. 450, 625 A.2d 791, 796-803 (1993); People v. Kohl, 72 N.Y.2d 191, 527 N.E.2d 1182 (1988).

For exploration of the issues of constitutionality and fairness arising from such shifts in the burden of proof, see page 41 supra.

STATE v. CRENSHAW

Washington Supreme Court
98 Wash. 2d 789, 659 P.2d 488 (1983)

BRACHTENBACH, J. . . . While defendant and his wife were on their honeymoon in Canada, petitioner was deported as a result of his participation in a brawl. He secured a motel room in Blaine, Washington and waited for his wife to join him. When she arrived 2 days later, he immediately thought she had been unfaithful — he sensed "it wasn't the same Karen . . . she'd been with someone else."

Petitioner did not mention his suspicions to his wife, instead he took her to the motel room and beat her unconscious. He then went to a nearby store, stole a knife, and returned to stab his wife 24 times, inflicting a fatal wound. He left again, drove to a nearby farm where he had been employed and borrowed an ax. Upon returning to the motel room, he decapitated his wife with such force that the ax marks cut into the concrete floor under the carpet and splattered blood throughout the room.

Petitioner then proceeded to conceal his actions. He placed the body in a blanket, the head in a pillowcase, and put both in his wife's car. Next, he went to a service station, borrowed a bucket and sponge, and cleaned the room of blood and fingerprints. Before leaving, petitioner also spoke with the motel manager about a phone bill, then chatted with him for a while over a beer.

When Crenshaw left the motel he drove to a remote area 25 miles away where he hid the two parts of the body in thick brush. He then fled, driving to the Hoquiam area, about 200 miles from the scene of the crime. There he picked up two hitchhikers, told them of his crime, and enlisted their aid in disposing of his wife's car in a river. The hitchhikers contacted the police and Crenshaw was apprehended shortly thereafter. He voluntarily confessed to the crime.

The defense of not guilty by reason of insanity was a major issue at trial. Crenshaw testified that he followed the Moscovite religious faith, and that it would be improper for a Moscovite not to kill his wife if she committed adultery. Crenshaw also has a history of mental problems, for which he has been hospitalized in the past. The jury, however, rejected petitioner's insanity defense, and found him guilty of murder in the first degree. . . .

Petitioner assigned error to insanity defense instruction 10 which reads: . . .

> For a defendant to be found not guilty by reason of insanity you must find that, as a result of mental disease or defect, the defendant's mind was affected to such an extent that the defendant was unable to perceive the nature and quality of the acts with which the defendant is charged or was unable to tell right from wrong with reference to the particular acts with which defendant is charged.
>
> What is meant by the terms "right and wrong" refers to knowledge of a person at the time of committing an act that he was acting contrary to the law.

But for the last paragraph, this instruction tracks the language of . . . the *M'Naghten* test as codified in RCW 9A.12.-010. Petitioner contends, however, that the trial court erred in defining "right and wrong" as legal right and wrong rather than in the moral sense. . . .

The definition of the term "wrong" in the *M'Naghten* test has been considered and disputed by many legal scholars. See, e.g., A. Goldstein, The Insanity Defense 51-53 (1967); H. Fingarette, The Meaning of Criminal Insanity 153-157 (1972). . . . Courts from other jurisdictions are divided on the issue. . . .

This court's view has been that "when *M'Naghten* is used, all who might possibly be deterred from the commission of criminal acts are included within the sanctions of the criminal law." State v. White, 60 Wash. 2d 551, 592, 374 P.2d 942 (1962).

> [O]nly those persons "who have lost contact with reality so completely that they are beyond any of the influences of the criminal law," may have the benefit of the insanity defense in a criminal case.

State v. McDonald, 89 Wash. 2d 256, 272, 571 P.2d 930 (1977). Given this perspective, the trial court could assume that one who knew the illegality of his act was not necessarily "beyond any of the influences of the criminal law," thus finding support for the statement in instruction 10.

Alternatively, the statement in instruction 10 may be approved because, in this case, legal wrong is synonymous with moral wrong. [I]t is important to note that it is society's morals, and not the individual's morals, that are the standard for judging moral wrong under *M'Naghten*. If wrong meant moral wrong judged by the individual's own conscience, this would seriously undermine the criminal law, for it would allow one who violated the law to be excused from criminal responsibility solely because, in his own conscience, his act was not morally wrong. . . .

There is evidence on the record that Crenshaw knew his actions were wrong according to society's standards, as well as legally wrong. Dr. Belden testified:

> I think Mr. Crenshaw is quite aware on one level that he is in conflict with the law *and with people.* However, this is not something that he personally invests his emotions in.

We conclude that Crenshaw knew his acts were morally wrong from society's viewpoint and also knew his acts were illegal.[a] His personal belief that it was his duty to kill his wife for her alleged infidelity cannot serve to exculpate him from legal responsibility for his acts.

A narrow exception to the societal standard of moral wrong has been drawn for instances wherein a party performs a criminal act, knowing it is morally and legally wrong, but believing, because of a mental defect, that the act is ordained by God: such would be the situation with a mother who kills her infant child to whom she is devotedly attached, believing that God has spoken to her and decreed the act. Although the woman knows that the law and society condemn the act, it would be unrealistic to hold her responsible for the crime, since her free will has been subsumed by her belief in the deific decree.

This exception is not available to Crenshaw, however. Crenshaw argued only that he followed the Moscovite faith and that Moscovites believe it is their duty to kill an unfaithful wife. This is not the same as acting under a deific command. Instead, it is akin to "[t]he devotee of a religious cult that enjoins . . . human sacrifice as a duty [and] is *not* thereby relieved from responsibility before the law." (Italics ours.) [People v. Schmidt, 216 N.Y. 324, 340, 110 N.E. 945, 950 (1915).] Crenshaw's personal "Moscovite" beliefs are not equivalent to a deific decree and do not relieve him from responsibility for his acts. . . .

NOTES AND QUESTIONS

1. In People v. Schmidt, cited in *Crenshaw,* the trial judge had instructed that "wrong" within the meaning of the *M'Naghten* test meant "contrary to the law of this state." Judge Cardozo's opinion, which held this instruction erroneous, is worth quoting in context (110 N.E. at 949-950):

> [T]here are times and circumstances in which the word "wrong," as used in the statutory test of responsibility, ought not to be limited to legal wrong. . . . Knowledge that an act is forbidden by law will in most cases permit the inference of knowledge that, according to the accepted standards of mankind, it is also condemned as an offense against good morals. . . . If, however, there is an insane delusion that God has appeared to the defendant and ordained the commission of a crime, we think it cannot be said of the offender that he knows the act to be wrong.
>
> It is not enough, to relieve from criminal liability, that the prisoner is morally depraved. It is not enough that he has views of right and wrong at variance with those that find expression in the law. The variance must have its origin in some disease of the mind. The anarchist is not at liberty to break the law because he reasons that all government is wrong. The devotee of a religious cult that enjoins polygamy or human sacrifice as a duty is not thereby relieved from responsibility before the law. In such cases the belief, however false according to our own standards, is not the product of disease. Cases will doubtless arise where criminals will take shelter behind a professed belief that their crime was ordained by God, just as

a. How does the court's conclusion on this point defeat Crenshaw's objection? Did the instructions at trial permit conviction only if the jury found that Crenshaw knew his acts were morally wrong? — Eds.

this defendant attempted to shelter himself behind that belief. We can safely leave such fabrications to the common sense of juries.

2. *Legal vs. moral wrong.* American courts appear sharply divided on the issue presented in *Crenshaw*. Several jurisdictions hold, in accord with *Crenshaw*, that an insanity acquittal requires the defendant to be unaware that his conduct was *legally* wrong. Although ignorance of the law is not, of course, a defense, *knowledge* of the law will be sufficient in these jurisdictions to defeat any claim under *M'Naghten*. See, e.g., State v. Hollis, 731 P.2d 260 (Kan. 1987); State v. Hamann, 285 N.W.2d 180 (Iowa 1979). In contrast, a number of recent decisions hold that "wrong" means "morally wrong." E.g., People v. Serravo, 823 P.2d 128 (Colo. 1992); State v. Worlock, 117 N.J. 596, 569 A.2d 1314 (1990); People v. Skinner 39 Cal. 3d 765, 704 P.2d 752 (1985).

Which approach to the *Crenshaw* issue is more consistent with the purposes of an insanity defense? If a defendant has sufficient awareness to realize the illegality of his conduct and to attempt to conceal his crime, doesn't he fall, by definition, among those whose behavior is potentially deterrable? Compare James F. Stephen, 2 History of the Criminal Law of England 167 (1883):

> [T]he question whether "wrong" means "morally wrong," or only "illegal," may be important. In Hadfield's case, for instance, knowledge of the illegality of his act was the very reason why he did it. He wanted to be hung for it. He no doubt knew it to be wrong in the sense that he knew that other people would disapprove of it, but he would also have thought, had he thought at all, that if they knew all the facts (as he understood them) they would approve of him, and see that he was sacrificing his own interest for the common good. I could not say that such a person knew that such an act was wrong. His delusion would prevent anything like an act of calm judgment in the character of the act.

Consider also Justice Dixon's instructions to the jury in The King v. Porter, 55 Commw. L.R. 182, 188-190 (1933):

> We are not dealing with right or wrong in the abstract. The question is whether [the defendant] was able to appreciate the wrongness of the particular act he was doing at the particular time. . . . If through the disordered condition of the mind he could not reason about the matter with a moderate degree of sense and composure it may be said that he could not know that what he was doing was wrong. What is meant by "wrong"? What is meant by wrong is wrong having regard to the everyday standards of reasonable people. If you think that at the time when he administered the poison to the child he had such a mental disorder or disturbance or derangement that he was incapable of reasoning about the right or wrongness, according to ordinary standards, of the thing which he was doing, not that he reasoned wrongly, or that being a responsible person he had queer or unsound ideas, but that he was quite incapable of taking into account the considerations which go to make right or wrong, then you should find him not guilty upon the ground that he was insane at the time he committed the acts charged.

In *Serravo*, supra, expert testimony established that due to either brain damage or paranoid schizophrenia, defendant suffered from the delusion that God had told him to construct a multimillion dollar sports facility to teach people the path to perfection and that he believed he had to stab his wife to achieve that goal. At his trial for her murder, psychiatric experts for both the state and the defense agreed that Serravo was unable to distinguish moral right from wrong, though he probably knew that his act was illegal. Holding that knowledge of the act's illegality will not defeat a defense under *M'Naghten,* the court said (823 P.2d at 135-137):

> We acknowledge that some cases subsequent to *M'Naghten* have interpreted the right-wrong test as limiting the insanity defense to a cognitive inability to distinguish legal right from legal wrong, with the result that a person's simple awareness that an act is illegal is a sufficient basis for finding criminal responsibility. We believe, however, that such an analysis injects a formalistic legalism into the insanity equation to the disregard of the psychological underpinnings of legal insanity. A person in an extremely psychotic state, for example, might be aware that an act is prohibited by law, but due to the overbearing effect of the psychosis may be utterly without the capacity to comprehend that the act is inherently immoral. A standard of legal wrong would render such a person legally responsible and subject to imprisonment for the conduct in question notwithstanding the patent injustice of such a disposition. Conversely, a person who, although mentally ill, has the cognitive capacity to distinguish right from wrong and is aware that an act is morally wrong, but does not realize that it is illegal, should nonetheless be held responsible for the act, as ignorance of the law is no excuse.

3. *The "deific decree" exception.* Why does the court in *Crenshaw* suggest that the result would be different if the defendant had said that his acts were "ordained by God" rather than merely by his "Moscovite" religious tenets? Consider the following case.

State v. Cameron, 100 Wash. 2d 520, 674, P.2d 650 (1983): [O]n the morning of June 9, 1980, petitioner stabbed Marie Cameron in excess of 70 times, leaving the knife sticking in her heart. The body was left in the bathtub with no apparent attempt to conceal it. Later that day a police officer saw petitioner in downtown Shelton wearing only a pair of women's stretch pants, a woman's housecoat, a shirt and no shoes. He was stopped and questioned. After first giving a false name, he corrected it and explained he was dressed that way because "I just grabbed what I could. . . . My [stepmother] turned vicious." He also stated he was headed for California. Having no known reason to detain petitioner, the officer released him to continue hitchhiking.

The next day petitioner was detained by the Oregon State Police as he wandered along the shoulder of Interstate 5 near Salem. Since he was wearing only the stretch pants and one shoe he was thought to be an escapee from a nearby mental hospital. A check revealed petitioner was wanted in Shelton for the death of Marie Cameron.

[In a tape-recorded confession, petitioner stated that he] left home dressed as he was because his stepmother had become violent. "[S]he's into different types of sorcery. She's just strictly a very evil person . . . and she became very violent with me, with a knife in her hand, and so, uh, I don't deny that I'm the one that did what went on out there." . . .

Concerning his feelings about the incident petitioner said: "I felt confused. . . .

I felt no different from the beginning than the end there was no difference . . .
legally I know, that it is against the law, but as far as right and wrong in the eye
of God, I would say I felt no particular wrong." . . .

When petitioner subsequently gave the written confession he added: "My attack wasn't a vicious attack the first time. I was trying to stop the spirit that was
moving in her. She kept saying, 'Gary, Gary, Gary,' as if she was enjoying it."
When she stopped moving he washed himself, changed his clothes and then
"My stepmother started moving again as if a spirit was in her. I took the knife
and started stabbing her again. When I realized there was something in her that
wouldn't stop moving, I started stabbing her in the head and heart. I wanted to
kill the spirit that seemed to be attacking my spirit." Once again he changed his
clothes but again found her moving and again stabbed her numerous times until
all movement stopped. He then changed clothes once more and left. . . .

Prior to trial, petitioner made a motion to acquit on the ground of insanity. . . .
Three psychiatrists [and a psychologist] were called to testify. They agreed petitioner suffered from paranoid schizophrenia both at the time of the killing and
at the time of trial. . . .

While expressing their views in slightly different ways, they agreed petitioner
understood that, as a mechanical thing, he was killing his stepmother and knew
it was against the laws of man. They stressed, however, that at the time, he was
preoccupied with the delusional belief that his stepmother was an agent of satan
who was persecuting him, as were others like Yasser Arafat and the Ayatollah
Khomeini. He believed he was being directed by God to kill satan's angel and
that by so doing, he was obeying God's higher directive or law. At this time he
believed himself to be a messiah and in fact compared himself with Jesus Christ.

The doctors pointed out, in different ways, that because of his delusional beliefs, petitioner felt God had directed him to send her from this life to another.
He had no remorse over the killing. He felt it was justified by God and that he
was merely doing a service. "He felt he would generally be protected from any
difficulties . . . because 'God would not allow it to happen'." . . .

Concerning petitioner's insanity defense the trial court gave standard WPIC
pattern jury instruction 20.01, but, over petitioner's exception, added a last paragraph which defines "right and wrong" . . . [:]

> What is meant by the terms "right and wrong" refers to knowledge of a person
> at the time of committing an act that he was acting contrary to the law. . . .

[A]s we held in *Crenshaw,* one who believes that he is acting under the direct
command of God is no less insane because he nevertheless knows murder is
prohibited by the laws of man. Indeed, it may actually emphasize his insanity.

In the instant case there is considerable evidence (although not unanimous)
from which the jury could have concluded that petitioner suffered from a mental disease; that he believed his stepmother was satan's angel or a sorceress; that
he believed God directed him to kill his stepmother; that because of the mental
disease it was impossible for him to understand that what he was doing was
wrong; and, as stated in *Crenshaw,* that his free will had "been subsumed by [his]
belief in the deific decree." The last paragraph of the trial court's challenged
instruction precluded the jury's consideration of these factors and thus runs
afoul of the *Crenshaw* exception. . . .

[Reversed.]

[In a concurring opinion, Justice Dore objected to the majority's effort to preserve a distinction between *Crenshaw* and *Cameron:*] Both *Crenshaw* and the subject case were almost factually identical; both involved outrageous, vicious, messy murders. . . . I frankly don't see much or any distinction, however, in carrying out or executing a murder under the direction of God or Crenshaw's Moscovite religious beliefs, or under the beliefs of a prophet, Buddha, etc. . . .

4. The irresistible impulse test. Many *M'Naghten* jurisdictions have supplemented the right/wrong test with an additional defense if the defendant is "unable to adhere to the right as a result of irresistible impulse." Typically, the test has been formulated in stringent terms. For example, a common jury instruction explains that "[a]n inability to adhere to the right does not exist unless the act is committed under an irresistible impulse which completely deprives the person of the power of choice or volition." See United States v. Kunak, 17 C.M.R. 346 (Ct. Mil. App. 1954). In addition, some jurisdictions accepting the irresistible impulse defense add a further qualification known as the "policeman at the elbow" test: the jury will be instructed that "[i]f the accused would not have committed the act had there been a . . . policeman present, he cannot be said to have acted under an irresistible impulse." Id.

Questions: Why should a person's ability to resist (or at least postpone) acting on a powerful inner compulsion at the moment when a police officer is at his elbow be decisive in determining his responsibility for actions committed under more normal circumstances? Does a defendant's ability to desist from a criminal act when a police officer is present show that he also could desist in other circumstances if he really wanted to?

5. Questions on the M'Naghten *formulation.* Consider, in light of the facts of *Crenshaw* and *Cameron,* the question of how an insanity defense should be formulated. Should the defense be broad enough so that either (or both) of these defendants would be eligible for acquittal, and if so under what circumstances? A related issue, considered at page 966 infra, is whether the insanity defense should be abolished completely. In cases involving defendants like *Cameron* and *Crenshaw,* would it be acceptable to have no insanity defense available at all?

NOTE ON CRITICISM OF THE M'NAGHTEN TEST

Dissatisfaction with the *M'Naghten* test of insanity led a number of jurisdictions to consider entirely different ways to formulate the insanity defense. United States v. Freeman, 357 F.2d 606, 618-622 (2d Cir. 1966), summarizes the background:

[*M'Naghten*] has several serious deficiencies which stem in the main from its narrow scope. Because *M'Naghten* focuses only on the cognitive aspect of the personality, i.e., the ability to know right from wrong, we are told by eminent medical scholars that it does not permit the jury to identify those who can distinguish between good and evil but who cannot control their behavior. The result is that instead of being treated at appropriate mental institutions for a sufficiently long period to bring about a cure or sufficient improvement so that the accused may return with relative safety to . . . the community, he is ordinarily sentenced to a prison term as if criminally responsible and then released as a potential recidivist with society at his mercy. To the extent that these individuals continue to be released from prison because of the narrow scope of *M'Naghten*, that test poses a serious danger to society's welfare. . . .

A further fatal defect of the *M'Naghten* Rules stems from the unrealistically tight shackles which they place upon expert psychiatric testimony. When the law limits a testifying psychiatrist to stating his opinion whether the accused is capable of knowing right from wrong, the expert is thereby compelled to test guilt or innocence by a concept which bears little relationship to reality. He is required thus to consider one aspect of the mind as a "logic-tight compartment in which the delusion holds sway leaving the balance of the mind intact. . . . "

Prominent psychiatrists have expressed their frustration when confronted with such requirements. . . . Dr. Lawrence Kolb, Director of the New York Psychiatric Institute . . . declared that "answers supplied by a psychiatrist in regard to questions of rightness or wrongness of an act or 'knowing' its nature constitute a professional perjury." . . .

The tremendous growth of psychiatric knowledge since the Victorian origins of *M'Naghten* and even the near-universal disdain in which it is held by present-day psychiatrists are not by themselves sufficient reasons for abandoning the test. At bottom, the determination whether a man is or is not held responsible for his conduct is not a medical but a legal, social or moral judgment. Ideally, psychiatrists — much like experts in other fields — should provide grist for the legal mill, should furnish the raw data upon which the legal judgment is based. . . .

The true vice of *M'Naghten* is not, therefore, that psychiatrists will feel constricted in artificially structuring their testimony but rather that the ultimate deciders — the judge or the jury — will be deprived of information vital to their final judgment.[a] . . .

Efforts to supplement or replace the *M'Naghten* Rules with a more meaningful and workable test have persisted for generations, with varying degrees of success. . . . [W]e find the "irresistible impulse" test to be inherently inadequate and unsatisfactory. [It appears applicable only if the crime was] perpetrated in a sudden and explosive fit. Thus, the "irresistible impulse" test is unduly restrictive because it excludes the far more numerous instances of crimes committed after excessive brooding and melancholy by one who is unable to resist sustained psychic compulsion or to make any real attempt to control his conduct. . . .

Judge Bazelon's opinion for the District of Columbia Circuit in Durham v. United States,[48] [recognized] that disease or defect of the mind may impair the whole mind and not a subdivided portion of it. . . . A defendant is not criminally responsible, wrote Judge Bazelon, "if his unlawful act was the product of mental disease or mental defect." . . .

The [*Durham*] test entirely eliminated the "right-wrong" dichotomy, and hence interred the overriding emphasis on the cognitive element of the personality which had for so long plagued *M'Naghten*. The fetters upon expert testimony were removed and psychiatrists were permitted and indeed encouraged to provide all

---

a. In practice, courts in *M'Naghten* jurisdictions tend to admit a broad range of psychiatric testimony. See Abraham S. Goldstein, The Insanity Defense 53-54 (1967). Thus, it is seldom true that the *M'Naghten* standard completely deprives the jury of exposure to a psychiatric picture of a defendant's mental illness. But the *M'Naghten* standard nonetheless has an indirect effect on the flow of information. See People v. Drew, 22 Cal. 3d 333, 583 P.2d 1318, 1323 (1978): "Even if the psychiatrist is able to place before the trier of fact a complete picture of the defendant's mental incapacity, that testimony reaches the trier of fact weakened by cross-examination designed to show that defendant knew right from wrong and limited by the *M'Naghten* instruction. As a result, conscientious juries have often returned verdicts of sanity despite plain evidence of serious mental illness and unanimous expert testimony that the defendant was insane." — Eds.

48. 214 F.2d 862 (1954).

relevant medical information for the common sense application of judge or jury. Finally, *Durham* ended to a large degree the "professional perjury" decried by psychiatrists — the "juggling" of legal standards made inevitable by *M'Naghten*. . . .

The most significant criticism of *Durham,* however, is that it fails to give the factfinder any standard by which to measure the competency of the accused. As a result, psychiatrists when testifying that a defendant suffered from a "mental disease or defect" in effect usurped the jury's function. This problem was strikingly illustrated in 1957, when a staff conference at Washington's St. Elizabeth's Hospital reversed its previous determination and reclassified "psychopathic personality" as a "mental disease." Because this single hospital provides most of the psychiatric witnesses in the District of Columbia courts, juries were abruptly informed that certain defendants who had previously been considered responsible were now to be acquitted.[b] . . . [A] test which permits all to stand or fall upon the labels or classifications employed by testifying psychiatrists hardly affords the court the opportunity to perform its function of rendering an independent legal and social judgment.

This history of dissatisfaction with the *M'Naghten,* irresistible impulse, and *Durham* tests led the American Law Institute to formulate a new approach in Model Penal Code §4.01.

b.   The Model Penal Code Approach

MODEL PENAL CODE

SECTION 4.01.   Mental Disease or Defect Excluding Responsibility

(1) A person is not responsible for criminal conduct if at the time of such conduct as a result of mental disease or defect he lacks substantial capacity either to appreciate the criminality [wrongfulness] of his conduct or to conform his conduct to the requirements of law. . . .

COMMENT TO §4.01 AT 156-160 (TENTATIVE DRAFT No. 4, 1955)
1. No problem in the drafting of a penal code presents larger intrinsic difficulty than that of determining when individuals whose conduct would otherwise be criminal ought to be exculpated on the ground that they were suffering from mental disease or defect when they acted. . . . [T]he problem is to discriminate between the cases where a punitive-correctional disposition is appropriate and those in which a medical-custodial disposition is the only kind that the law should allow.

2. The traditional *M'Naghten* rule resolves the problem solely in regard to the capacity of the individual to know what he was doing and to know that it was

b. This problem was dramatically illustrated in what came to be known as the "weekend flip-flop case," In re Rosenfield, 157 F. Supp. 18 (D.D.C. 1957). On Friday afternoon, a St. Elizabeth's psychiatrist testified that the defendant, diagnosed as a psychopath, was not suffering from a mental disease. The following Monday morning the St. Elizabeth's staff decided to classify psychopathic personality as a mental disease. Returning to the stand Monday afternoon, the psychiatrist changed his testimony and declared that the defendant was suffering from a mental disease. See United States v. Brawner, 471 F.2d 969, 978 (D.C. Cir. 1972). — EDS.

wrong. Absent these minimal elements of rationality, condemnation and punishment are obviously both unjust and futile. They are unjust because the individual could not, by hypothesis, have employed reason to restrain the act; he did not and he could not know the facts essential to bring reason into play. On the same ground, they are futile. A madman who believes that he is squeezing lemons when he chokes his wife or thinks that homicide is the command of God is plainly beyond reach of the restraining influence of law; he needs restraint but condemnation is entirely meaningless and ineffective. Thus the attacks on the *M'Naghten* rule as an inept definition of insanity or as an arbitrary definition in terms of special symptoms are entirely misconceived. The *rationale* of the position is that these are cases in which reason cannot operate and in which it is totally impossible for individuals to be deterred. Moreover, the category defined by the rule is so extreme that to the ordinary man the exculpation of the persons it encompasses bespeaks no weakness in the law. He does not identify such persons and himself; they are a world apart.

Jurisdictions in which the *M'Naghten* test has been expanded to include the case where mental disease produces an "irresistible impulse" proceed on the same *rationale*. They recognize, however, that cognitive factors are not the only ones that preclude inhibition; that even though cognition still obtains, mental disorder may produce a total incapacity for self-control. The same result is sometimes reached under *M'Naghten* proper, in the view, strongly put forth by Stephen, that "knowledge" requires more than the capacity to verbalize right answers to a question, it implies capacity to function in the light of knowledge. Stephen, History of English Criminal Law, vol. 2, p. 171. In modern psychiatric terms, the "fundamental difference between verbal or purely intellectual knowledge and the mysterious other kind of knowledge is familiar to every clinical psychiatrist; it is the difference between knowledge divorced from affect and knowledge so fused with affect that it becomes a human reality." Zilboorg, Misconceptions of Legal Insanity, 9 Am. J. Orthopsychiatry 540, 552. The application of *M'Naghten* has been mitigated somewhat, especially in England, by accepting evidence couched in these terms.

3. The draft accepts the view that any effort to exclude the non-deterrables from strictly penal sanctions must take account of the impairment of volitional capacity no less than of impairment of cognition; and that this result should be achieved directly in the formulation of the test, rather than left to mitigation in the application of *M'Naghten*. It also accepts the criticism of the "irresistible impulse" formulation as inept in so far as it may be impliedly restricted to sudden, spontaneous acts as distinguished from insane propulsions that are accompanied by brooding or reflection. . . . The application of the principle will call, of course, for a distinction between incapacity, upon the one hand, and mere indisposition on the other. Such a distinction is inevitable in the application of a standard addressed to impairment of volition. We believe that the distinction can be made. . . .

4. One further problem must be faced. In addressing itself to impairment of the cognitive capacity, *M'Naghten* demands that impairment be complete: the actor must *not* know. So, too, the irresistible impulse criterion presupposes a complete impairment of capacity for self-control. The extremity of these conceptions is, we think, the point that poses largest difficulty to psychiatrists when called upon to aid in their administration. The schizophrenic, for example, is

disoriented from reality; the disorientation is extreme; but it is rarely total. Most psychotics will respond to a command of someone in authority within the mental hospital; they thus have some capacity to conform to a norm. But this is very different from the question whether they have the capacity to conform to requirements that are not thus immediately symbolized by an attendant or policeman at the elbow. Nothing makes the inquiry into responsibility more unreal for the psychiatrist than limitation of the issue to some ultimate extreme of total incapacity, when clinical experience reveals only a graded scale with marks along the way.

. . . The law must recognize that when there is no black and white it must content itself with different shades of gray. The draft, accordingly, does not demand *complete* impairment of capacity. It asks instead for *substantial* impairment. This is all, we think, that candid witnesses, called on to infer the nature of the situation at a time that they did not observe, can ever confidently say, even when they know that a disorder was extreme.

NOTES

1. Knowledge and appreciation. In choosing to require for conviction that a defendant "appreciate" the wrongfulness of his conduct, the Model Penal Code broadened *M'Naghten*'s "knowledge" test, which was sometimes held to be satisfied merely by a capacity to verbalize socially acceptable answers to questions. Some courts had avoided that result, even under *M'Naghten,* by interpreting "knowledge" to mean a genuine appreciation or understanding. See, e.g., People v. Wolff, 61 Cal. 2d 795, 800-801, 394 P.2d 959 (1964). Zilboorg's discussion of the difference between the two kinds of knowledge (cited in the Model Penal Code Commentary, page 946 supra) sheds light on a significant distinction between the Model Penal Code and the narrower versions of *M'Naghten.* Zilboorg elaborates on the concept of knowledge "fused with affect" as follows (Zilboorg, supra, at 552-553):

> The law automatically assumes that a child committing a felony does not know the nature and quality of the act and does not know that it is wrong. Yet a child of moderate brightness will say that he hit his sister in the head, that she bled and then she fell; he will even admit that she died or that he killed her and will perhaps say that he was wrong to kill his sister. The criminal code does not accept this knowledge as valid; without knowing it the law itself recognizes here a fundamental medico-psychological distinction between the purely verbal knowledge which characterizes the child and the other type of knowledge which characterizes the adult. This fundamental difference between verbal or purely intellectual knowledge and the mysterious other kind of knowledge is familiar to every clinical psychiatrist; it is the difference between knowledge divorced from affect and knowledge so fused with affect that it becomes a human reality. . . . To conceive that reason is an independent power, springing from reason only, and that it is fortified by nothing more than memory means to conceive of the human being as a combination of separate and autonomous mechanisms which act independently, all by themselves; it is almost as if we conceive of the individual as a phonograph record which may repeat time and again that it is wrong to kill and that killing means murdering. To accept this type of phonographic explanation as knowledge means to disregard everything that is human.

Therefore, "defect of reason" which the law stresses may not and, with the exception of cases of mental defectives, does not lie within the field of reason at all, but within the field of emotional appreciation. This emotional appreciation is a very complex phenomenon. It is based on a series of intricate psychological mechanisms, the most potent of which is that of identification. What makes it possible for a civilized, mentally healthy human being to resist a murderous impulse is not the cold detached reasoning that it is wrong and dangerous but the automatic emotional, mostly unconscious identification with the prospective victim, an identification which automatically inhibits the impulse to kill and causes anxiety ("It is dangerous") which in turn produces the reflection: "It is wrong, the same may and should happen to me." Unless this identification is present the impulse breaks through and fear of the law and the sense of wrong is paled, devoid of its affective component: It becomes a verbal, coldly intellectual, formal, childish, infantile psychological presentation.

2. *Trends in prevailing law.* During the 1960s and 1970s a few courts explicitly rejected the Model Penal Code formulation in favor of *M'Naghten.* See, e.g., State v. Smith, 223 Kan. 203, 574 P.2d 548 (1977). Nonetheless, the trend of statutory developments and judicial decisions during this period strongly favored the Model Penal Code approach. By 1980, the Model Penal Code test had been adopted by roughly half the states and by all but one of the federal circuit courts of appeal.

The trend in favor of the Model Penal Code approach was abruptly reversed following the 1982 trial of John W. Hinckley, Jr., who shot and wounded President Reagan (and several people accompanying the President) in an abortive assassination attempt. When the jury, applying the Model Penal Code test, found Hinckley not guilty by reason of insanity, there were widespread expressions of concern about the insanity defense and an outpouring of outraged reactions to the verdict. See Valerie P. Hans & Dan Slater, John W. Hinckley, Jr. & the Insanity Defense: The Public's Verdict, 47 Pub. Op. Q. 202 (1983). Lawyers and psychiatrists were not slow in responding to this occasion for reconsidering the insanity tests, and a number of jurisdictions either reinstituted the *M'Naghten* formulation or adopted an even more restrictive test. These developments are explored in detail at pages 953-959 infra.

c. Common Concerns

In this section we explore a number of concerns that are present, directly or indirectly, in connection with all of the prevailing tests of legal insanity. First, in subsection (i), we consider the question of volitional impairment, a problem to which the Model Penal Code and the *M'Naghten* test appear to give quite different responses. Subsection (ii) probes the similarities and differences among the various insanity tests by considering their application to a concrete situation of serious mental disorder. Following that material, subsection (iii) takes up an issue that lies at the core of the controversies, the question whether the insanity defense should be abolished completely. Subsection (iv) returns to issues in the administration of an insanity defense, focusing on the meaning of the disease concept that determines the boundaries of the defense under both *M'Naghten* and the Model Penal Code. Finally, subsection (v) explores the important practical problem of determining the appropriate disposition of a defendant who is acquitted by reason of insanity.

(i)   *Volitional Impairment*   •

UNITED STATES v. LYONS

United States Court of Appeals, 5th Circuit, en banc
731 F.2d 243, 739 F.2d 994 (1984)

GEE, J. Defendant Robert Lyons was indicted on twelve counts of knowingly and intentionally securing controlled narcotics. . . . Lyons proffered evidence that in 1978 he began to suffer from several painful ailments, that various narcotics were prescribed to be taken as needed for his pain, and that he became addicted to these drugs. He also offered to present expert witnesses who would testify that his drug addiction affected his brain both physiologically and psychologically and that as a result he lacked substantial capacity to conform his conduct to the requirements of the law. . . .

[The trial court excluded the proffered evidence, and Lyons was convicted.]

Today the great weight of legal authority clearly supports the view that evidence of mere narcotics addiction, standing alone and without other physiological or psychological involvement, raises no issue of such a mental defect or disease as can serve as a basis for the insanity defense. . . . [a]

We do not doubt that actual physical damage to the brain itself falls within the ambit of "mental disease or defect." . . . Because the proffer offers evidence tending to suggest such damage, that evidence should have been submitted to the jury. And although we today withdraw our recognition of the volitional prong of [the insanity defense] — that as to which such evidence has usually been advanced — we also conclude that should Lyons wish to offer such evidence in an attempt to satisfy the remaining cognitive prong, fairness demands that we afford him an opportunity to do so.

. . . We last examined the insanity defense in Blake v. United Sates, 407 F.2d 908 (5th Cir. 1969) (en banc), where we adopted the ALI Model Penal Code definition of insanity. [W]e concluded that then current knowledge in the field of behavioral science supported such a result. Unfortunately, it now appears our conclusion was premature. . . .

Reexamining the *Blake* standard today, we conclude that the volitional prong of the insanity defense — a lack of capacity to conform one's conduct to the requirements of the law — does not comport with current medical and scientific knowledge, which has retreated from its earlier, sanguine expectations. Consequently, we now hold that a person is not responsible for criminal conduct on the grounds of insanity only if at the time of that conduct, as a result of a mental disease or defect, he is unable to appreciate the wrongfulness of that conduct.

We do so for several reasons. First, as we have mentioned, a majority of psychiatrists now believe that they do not possess sufficient accurate scientific bases for measuring a person's capacity for self-control or for calibrating the impair-

a. See pages 1023-1029 infra. — EDS.

ment of that capacity. Bonnie, The Moral Basis of the Insanity Defense, 69 A.B.A.J. 194, 196 (1983). "The line between an irresistible impulse and an impulse not resisted is probably no sharper than between twilight and dusk." American Psychiatric Association Statement on the Insanity Defense, 11 (1982) [APA Statement]. Indeed, Professor Bonnie [supra] states:

> There is, in short, no objective basis for distinguishing between offenders who were undeterrable and those who were merely undeterred, between the impulse that was irresistible and the impulse not resisted, or between substantial impairment of capacity and some lesser impairment.[b]

In addition, the risks of fabrication and "moral mistakes" in administering the insanity defense are greatest "when the experts and the jury are asked to speculate whether the defendant had the capacity to 'control' himself or whether he could have 'resisted' the criminal impulse." Bonnie, supra, at 196. Moreover, psychiatric testimony about volition is more likely to produce confusion for jurors than is psychiatric testimony concerning a defendant's appreciation of the wrongfulness of his act. It appears, moreover, that there is considerable overlap between a psychotic person's inability to understand and his ability to control his behavior. Most psychotic persons who fail a volitional test would also fail a cognitive test, thus rendering the volitional test superfluous for them. Finally, [case law currently] requires that such proof be made by the federal prosecutor beyond a reasonable doubt, an all but impossible task in view of the present murky state of medical knowledge.[13]

[W]e see no prudent course for the law to follow but to treat all criminal impulses — including those not resisted — as resistible. To do otherwise in the present state of medical knowledge would be to cast the insanity defense adrift upon a sea of unfounded scientific speculation, with the palm awarded case by case to the most convincing advocate of that which is presently unknown — and may remain so, because unknowable. . . .

RUBIN, J., with whom TATE, J., joins, dissenting. . . . An adjudication of guilt is more than a factual determination that the defendant pulled a trigger, took a bicycle, or sold heroin. It is a moral judgment that the individual is blameworthy. "Our collective conscience does not allow punishment where it cannot impose blame." . . . "[H]istorically, our substantive criminal law is based on a theory of

---

b. In accord with this view, a recent analysis of irresistible impulse and related claims about loss of self-control concludes: "No established metric exists to determine the magnitude of impulses, desires, or feelings. . . . [The psychological] studies do not address, and folk psychology does not know, whether and to what degree people are *unable* to refrain from acting. Neither in psychology [nor in] philosophy . . . is there a reasonably uncontroversial understanding of these matters. . . . The strongest contrary claims in the literature fail both conceptually and empirically." Stephen J. Morse, Culpability and Control, 142 U. Pa. L. Rev. 1587, 1657-1658 (1994). — EDS.

13. [Phillip E. Johnson, Book Review, 50 U. Chi. L. Rev. 1534, 1536 (1983) (reviewing Norval Morris, Madness and the Criminal Law (1982)):] " . . . If taken literally, the instruction [requiring proof of sanity beyond a reasonable doubt in the John Hinckley prosecution] amounted to a directed verdict of not guilty, considering the deadlock of expert opinion and the difficulty of certifying the sanity of a young man who shot the President to impress a movie star. Juries usually ignore such unpopular legal standards, but the *Hinckley* jury surprised everybody by taking the law seriously and finding him not guilty. Hinckley will now be confined to a mental hospital indefinitely because he is "dangerous," although there is no reliable way to predict what he would do if released and no reliable test to determine if he has been "cured."

[For recent changes in the law governing the burden of proof, see Note 5, page 936 supra.]

punishing the [vicious] will. It postulates a free agent confronted with a choice between doing right and wrong, and choosing freely to do wrong."[3] . . . An acquittal by reason of insanity is a judgment that the defendant is not *guilty* because, as a result of his mental condition, he is unable to make an effective choice regarding his behavior.

The majority does not controvert these fundamental principles; indeed it accepts them as the basis for the defense when the accused suffers from a disease that impairs cognition. It rests its decision to redefine insanity and to narrow the defense on "new policy considerations." . . .

The first is the potential threat to society created by the volitional prong of the insanity defense. Public opposition to any insanity-grounded defense is often based, either explicitly or implicitly, on the view that the plea is frequently invoked by violent criminals who fraudulently use it to evade just punishment. . . . This perception depicts an insanity trial as a "circus" of conflicting expert testimony that confuses a naive and sympathetic jury. And it fears insanity acquittees as offenders who, after manipulating the criminal justice system, are soon set free to prey once again on the community.

Despite the prodigious volume of writing devoted to the plea, the empirical data that are available provide little or no support for these fearsome perceptions and in many respects directly refute them. Both the frequency and the success rate of insanity pleas are grossly overestimated by professionals and lay persons alike; the plea is rarely made, and even more rarely successful.[8] The number of insanity pleas based on control defects, as compared to those based on lack of cognition, must have been almost negligible.

The perception that the defendant who successfully pleads insanity is quickly released from custody is also based only on assumption. . . . "The truth is that in almost every case, the acquittee is immediately hospitalized and evaluated for dangerousness. Usually, the acquittee remains hospitalized for an extended time."[9]

Another set of objections to the plea is based on the thesis that factfinders — especially juries — are confused and manipulated by the vagueness of the legal standards of insanity and the notorious "battle of the experts" who present conclusory, superficial, and misleading testimony. These conditions, the argument runs, conspire to produce inconsistent and "inaccurate" verdicts.

---

3. Morissette v. United States, 342 U.S. 246, 250 n. 4 (1952) (quoting Pound, Introduction to Sayre, Cases on Criminal Law (1927)).

8. For example, one extensive study examined the opinions held by college students, the general public, state legislators, law enforcement officers, and mental health personnel in Wyoming. Estimates of the frequency with which [felony] defendants entered the plea ranged from 13% to 57%. During the time period considered, however, the actual frequency was only 0.47%: one case in 200. Similarly, although estimates of its success rate varied from 19% to 44%, during the relevant period only one of the 102 defendants who entered the plea was acquitted by reason of insanity. . . .

[Data from the more populous jurisdictions reveal a similar picture. In New York the insanity defense is raised about once in every 600 to 700 cases and is successful in about 25 percent of the cases in which it is raised; in 1982 the New Jersey Public Defenders office entered insanity pleas once in every 600 cases and was successful in about 28 percent of these. Nationally, insanity acquittals probably represent no more than 0.2 percent of terminated felony prosecutions. See National Commission on the Insanity Defense, Myths and Realities 14-15 (1983); Richard A. Pasewark, Insanity Plea: A Review of the Research Literature, 9 J. Psychiatry & L. 357 (1981). — EDS.]

9. Rappeport, The Insanity Plea Scapegoating the Mentally Ill — Much Ado about Nothing?, 24 So. Tex. L.J. 687, 698 (1983). . . .

Let us first put these objections in perspective. Most cases involving an insanity plea do not go to trial; instead, like most other criminal cases, they are settled by a plea bargain. In many of the cases that do go to trial, psychiatric testimony is presented by deposition, without disagreement among experts, and without opposition by the prosecution. And in the few cases in which a contest does develop, the defendant is usually convicted. . . .

The manipulated-jury argument is supported largely by declamation, not data. [N]o source has been cited to the court to support the conclusion that, as an empirical matter, pleas based upon the volitional prong present an especially problematic task for the jury.

Indeed, the majority opinion does not assert that the insanity defense, particularly the control test, *doesn't* work; it contends that the defense *can't* work. The principal basis for this contention is the belief, held by "a majority of psychiatrists," that they lack "sufficient accurate scientific bases for measuring a person's capacity for self-control or for calibrating the impairment of that capacity." . . . [B]ut the absence of useful expert evidence, if indeed there is none, does not obviate the need for resolving the question whether the defendant ought to be held accountable for his criminal behavior. . . .

Our concept of responsibility in this sense is not limited to observable behavior: it embraces *meaningful* choice, and necessarily requires inferences and assumptions regarding the defendant's unobservable mental state. . . . The difference between the concepts of excusing circumstances such as coercion and the insanity defense is that the former is based on objective assumptions about human behavior and is tested against hypothetical-objective standards such as "the reasonable person." "The insanity defense [on the other hand] marks the transition from the adequate man the law demands to the inadequate man he may be."[17]

The relevant inquiry under either branch of the insanity test is a subjective one that focuses on the defendant's actual state of mind. Our duty to undertake that inquiry is not based on confidence in the testimony of expert witnesses, but on the ethical precept that the defendant's mental state is a crucial aspect of his blameworthiness. . . . The availability of expert testimony and the probative value of such testimony are basically evidentiary problems that can be accommodated within the existing test. . . .

Even the few cases in which the trial develops into a battle of experts provide no basis for the majority's conclusion that the prosecution faces an "all but impossible task." [A] defendant pleading insanity typically faces both a judge and a jury who are skeptical about psychiatry in general and the insanity plea in particular. Sharply adversarial presentation of conflicting psychiatric testimony may increase this skepticism, and thus make acquittal more unlikely. Usually the defendant will have been adjudicated sane enough to understand the proceedings against him and to assist in his defense: otherwise he would be incompetent to stand trial. The formal allocation of the persuasion burden notwithstanding, the defendant to prevail must convince the doubting factfinder that, despite present outward appearances, he was insane at the time he committed the crime.

17. A. Goldstein, The Insanity Defense 18 (1967).

The majority's fear that the present test invites "moral mistakes" is difficult to understand. The majority opinion concedes that some individuals cannot conform their conduct to the law's requirements. . . . [T]he majority embraces a rule certain to result in the conviction of at least some who are not morally responsible and the punishment of those for whom retributive, deterrent, and rehabilitative penal goals are inappropriate. A decision that virtually ensures undeserved, and therefore unjust, punishment in the name of avoiding moral mistakes rests on a peculiar notion of morality. . . .

Judges are not, and should not be, immune to popular outrage over this nation's crime rate. Like everyone else, judges watch television, read newspapers and magazines, listen to gossip, and are sometimes themselves victims. They receive the message trenchantly described in a recent book criticizing the insanity defense: "Perhaps the bottom line of all these complaints is that *guilty people go free*. . . . These are not cases in which the defendant is *alleged* to have committed a crime. *Everyone knows he did it.*"[25] Although understandable as an expression of uninformed popular opinion, such a viewpoint ought not to serve as the basis for judicial decisionmaking; for it misapprehends the very meaning of guilt.

. . . By definition, guilt cannot be attributed to an individual unable to refrain from violating the law. When a defendant is properly acquitted by reason of insanity under the control test, the guilty does not go free. . . .

NOTES ON THE HINCKLEY *AFTERMATH*

Responses to the *Hinckley* verdict (see Note 2, page 948 supra) assumed a variety of distinct doctrinal forms. Efforts to restrict defenses based on mental illness included adjustments in the burden of proof, changes in the disposition of insanity acquittees, introduction of a separate verdict of "guilty but mentally ill" and complete abolition of the insanity defense. The choice of which approach (if any) to take involves a complex mixture of substantive and tactical judgments. For helpful discussions see Donald H. J. Hermann, Assault on the Insanity Defense, 14 Rutgers L.J. 241 (1983); Ralph Slovenko, The Insanity Defense in the Wake of the *Hinckley* Trial, 14 Rutgers L.J. 373 (1983); Peter Arenella, Reflections on Current Proposals to Abolish or Reform the Insanity Defense, 8 Am. J.L. & Med. 271 (1982).

Developments in each of the areas just mentioned are explored in the appropriate places in this chapter. The present Note, like *Lyons*, focuses on the formulation of the insanity test itself.

1. State law. Although a substantial minority of the states still adhere to the Model Penal Code test, recent years have seen several important jurisdictions return to the *M'Naghten* rule. California adopted the Model Penal Code formulation by judicial decision in 1978 but returned to *M'Naghten* as a result of a voter initiative approved in 1982. See People v. Skinner, 39 Cal. 3d 765, 704 P.2d 752 (1985). At least seven other states, including Texas and Indiana, likewise dropped the Model Penal Code test in the wake of the *Hinckley* verdict and adopted *M'Naghten* in its place. See John Q. LaFond & Mary L. Durham, Back to the

---

25. W. Winslade & J. Ross, The Insanity Plea 2-3 (1983) (emphasis added).

Asylum 64 (1992). By one recent count, 21 states now adhere to some form of the *M'Naghten* rule, and 22 states currently use the Model Penal Code test. See John Ogloff, A Comparison of Insanity Defense Standards on Juror Decision Making, 15 L. & Human Behavior 509, 510 (1991).

2. *Federal law.* As part of the Comprehensive Crime Control Act of 1984, Congress enacted a provision that supercedes the *Lyons* decision and narrows the insanity test even further. 18 U.S.C. §17(a) provides:

§17.   INSANITY DEFENSE

(a) *Affirmative Defense.* It is an affirmative defense to a prosecution under any Federal statute that, at the time of the commission of the acts constituting the offense, the defendant, as a result of a severe mental disease or defect, was unable to appreciate the nature and quality or the wrongfulness of his acts. Mental disease or defect does not otherwise constitute a defense.

3. *Legislative proposals.* Three influential bodies have, in very similar language, proposed retention of the cognitive branch of the Model Penal Code test and rejection of the control branch. See American Bar Association, Criminal Justice Mental Health Standards §7-6.1(a) (approved Feb. 9, 1983); American Psychiatric Association, Statement on the Insanity Defense, 140 Am. J. Psychiatry 6 (1983); National Conf. of Commissioners on Uniform State Laws, Model Insanity Defense and Post-Trial Disposition Act §201 (1984). The ABA standard provides:

A person is not responsible for criminal conduct if, at the time of such conduct, and as a result of mental disease or defect, that person was unable to appreciate the wrongfulness of such conduct.

With respect to the important problem of defining what constitutes a "mental disease or defect," the ABA standard provides that this concept:

refers to impairments of mind, whether enduring or transitory, or to mental retardation which substantially affected the mental or emotional processes of the defendant at the time of the alleged offense.

The Commentary to the ABA standards explains that this definition "attempts to clarify the meaning of the term 'mental disease or defect.'"

Question: Is the ABA's attempt at clarification successful? One observer comments, "One wonders what the drafters would have written had their intent been to allow the term to remain obscure."[14]

The American Psychiatric Association standard, based on a formulation proposed by Professor Bonnie,[15] provides:

A person charged with a criminal offense should be found not guilty by reason of insanity if it is shown that as a result of mental disease or mental retardation he was unable to appreciate the wrongfulness of his conduct at the time of the offense.

14. Phillip E. Johnson, The Turnabout on the Insanity Defense, in 6 Crime & Justice 221, 227 (Michael Tonry & Norval Morris eds., 1905).

15. Richard J. Bonnie, The Moral Basis of the Insanity Defense, 69 A.B.A.J. 194, 197 (1983).

As used in this standard, the terms mental disease or mental retardation include only those severely abnormal mental conditions that grossly and demonstrably impair a person's perception or understanding of reality and that are not attributable primarily to the voluntary ingestion of alcohol or other psychoactive substances.

4. Practical concerns. (a) The impact of the insanity defense. As noted in Judge Rubin's dissenting opinion in *Lyons,* supra, the frequency and success rate of insanity pleas are often overestimated. The actual use of the insanity defense varies markedly from jurisdiction to jurisdiction. Colorado had an average of one insanity plea for every 5,000 arrests, while the rate was one in 480 arrests for Michigan and one in 200 arrests for Wyoming. As might be expected, success rates for insanity pleas tend to be higher where the plea is infrequently used. Success rates ranged from 44 percent of all insanity pleas tendered in Colorado to 7 percent in Michigan and 2 percent in Wyoming. The two largest states, California and New York, had only 63 and 88 successful insanity pleas per year, a ratio of one for every 27,000 arrests in California and one for every 11,000 arrests in New York. See Hugh McGinley & Richard A. Pasewark, National Survey of the Frequency and Success of the Insanity Plea and Alternate Pleas, 17 J. Psychiatry & L. 205, 208-214 (1989). Nationally, insanity acquittals probably represent no more than 0.25 percent of terminated felony prosecutions. See Andrew Blum, Debunking Myths of the Insanity Plea, Natl. L.J., Apr. 20, 1992, at 9, reporting a 1992 study by the American Academy of Psychiatry and the Law. The overall figures have varied very little over time; the overall success rate for the insanity plea was virtually identical in the early 1980s, before the post-*Hinckley* reforms took effect. See National Commission on the Insanity Defense, Myths and Realities 14-15 (1983).

(b) The effect of different versions of the insanity defense. There is little evidence that different formulations of the insanity defense produce different results in practice. In one attempt to study this question empirically,[16] Professor Rita J. Simon assembled roughly 100 experimental jury panels from actual jury pools in Chicago, St. Louis, and Minneapolis. The juries listened to the transcript of an actual insanity defense case, then deliberated until they reached a unanimous verdict. Two different cases (housebreaking and incest) were used. Among juries listening to the identical case, one-third received *M'Naghten* instructions, one-third received *Durham* instructions, and one-third were simply told to find the defendant not guilty by reason of insanity "[i]f you believe the defendant was insane" at the time of the offense. In the housebreaking case (where there was strong evidence of cognitive impairment), there was no significant difference in the rate of jury acquittals between juries receiving the *M'Naghten* instruction and those receiving no insanity definition at all; the *Durham* instruction actually produced the lowest rate of insanity acquittals. In the incest case (where the evidence of insanity was much closer and more problematic), both the *Durham* juries and the uninstructed juries acquitted about 20 percent of the time, while none of the *M'Naghten* juries acquitted.

Although the Simon study appears to confirm the assumption that *M'Naghten* is a "stricter" test, at least in some contexts, differences among the insanity tests were sometimes dwarfed by differences among the juries. For example, in the

---

16. Rita James Simon, The Jury and the Defense of Insanity (1967).

housebreaking case, there was little difference in the average acquittal rate produced by each of the three tests, but among ten juries that heard identical testimony under an identical *M'Naghten* instruction, two juries convicted, seven acquitted and one failed to reach agreement.

Other researchers have reached similar conclusions. One series of studies relied on mock jurors (usually college undergraduates who read a case summary and vote without benefit of deliberation) to compare acquittal rates under *M'Naghten* and various alternative tests, including *Durham,* irresistible impulse, the Model Penal Code formula, and the so-called no test test, in which jurors are told to render a verdict using "their own best lights." No significant differences among the tests were found.[17] A similar mock juror study compared the highly restrictive federal test adopted in 1984 (see Note 2 supra) to the relatively expansive Model Penal Code test; again no significant differences in acquittal rates were found.[18]

Another approach relies on before-and-after comparisons in jurisdictions that have enacted statutory changes. In Wyoming, legislation replaced *M'Naghten*-plus-irresistible-impulse with the Model Penal Code test; the change had no significant effect on the rate of insanity pleas tendered, the rate of insanity acquittals, or in the characteristics of defendants invoking the defense.[19] California moved in the opposite direction, replacing the MPC test with *M'Naghten;* again, there was no significant change in the rate of insanity pleas and acquittals or in the types of defendants invoking the defense.[20]

One reason why different insanity defenses do not seem to produce substantially different results may be that none of the tests gives significant guidance to jurors or that jurors often respond to considerations other than those that are legally relevant. Another factor may be that the same essential problems are inherent in all the tests. In this regard, consider Dr. Alan Stone's comments in the excerpt that follows. Dr. Stone, a member of the unanimous "Insanity Defense Work Group" that prepared the American Psychiatric Association's Statement on the Insanity Defense (set forth Note 3 supra), uses the *Hinckley* trial to illustrate some shortcomings of the APA proposal.

ALAN A. STONE, LAW, PSYCHIATRY, AND MORALITY
83-91, 94-96 (1984)

The DSM-III diagnoses[a] offered by the three psychiatrists for the defense included schizophrenia, schizotypal personality disorder with psychosis, and borderline and paranoid personality disorder with psychosis. . . .

---

17. See Norman J. Finkel, The Insanity Defense: A Comparison of Verdict Schemas, 15 L. & Human Behavior 533, 534 (1991).

18. See Norman J. Finkel, The Insanity Defense Reform Act of 1984: Much Ado About Nothing, 7 Behavioral Sciences & L. 403 (1989).

19. See Richard A. Pasewark, R. Randolph & B. Bieber, Insanity Plea: Statutory Language and Trial Procedure, 12 J. Psychiatry & L. 399 (1984).

20. Margaret A. McGreevy, Henry J. Steadman & Lisa A. Callahan, The Negligible Effects of California's 1982 Reform of the Insanity Defense Test, 148 Am. J. Psychiatry 744 (1991).

a. DSM-III is the Diagnostic and Statistical Manual of Mental Disorders (3d ed. 1980), published by the American Psychiatric Association to promote greater accuracy and uniformity in diagnosis and in the use of diagnostic terminology. A fourth edition (1994) is now available. — Eds.

The defense psychiatrists also mentioned as appropriate diagnoses, even though not included in DSM-III, schizophrenic spectrum disorder, process schizophrenia, simple schizophrenia, pseudoneurotic schizophrenia, and ambulatory schizophrenia. The psychiatrists for the prosecution confined themselves to the DSM-III classification, but they diagnosed narcissistic personality disorder, schizoid personality disorder, mixed personality disorder with borderline and passive/aggressive features, and dysthymic disorder. One can only sympathize with the jurors. They would have needed to be sequestered for a week with Robert Spitzer (Chairman of the APA's DSM-III task force) just to digest the nosological jargon.

. . . The core of the diagnostic dispute comes down to whether Hinckley had a thought disorder, a perfect test for the APA's new proposal. All of the defense psychiatrists said he did. But the prosecution found no thought disorder and they rejected even those DSM-III personality disorders which are most suggestive of thought disorder — schizotypal and paranoid personality. . . .

The first psychiatrist for the defense, Doctor Researcher, . . . described a pattern of growing social isolation, failure, unhappiness, and suicidal ideation. Against this background, Hinckley created a fantasy world of unrealistic, bizarre, and grandiose expectation. He began to have ideas of reference and magical thinking. He travelled all over the country: to Hollywood to become a song writer, to Yale to rescue Jodie Foster, to Memphis to assassinate President Carter. Having failed at everything, he went home and made a suicide attempt. This is what led to his therapy with Doctor Defendant. During therapy Hinckley's condition further deteriorated. Doctor Defendant apparently was concerned that Hinckley's parents were reinforcing dependency and failure. Based on this conception, he advised the family not to take Hinckley back into their home after another cross-country excursion that led to failure. The father took this advice and refused to be supportive. Hinckley left Colorado. He alternated between suicidal thoughts and grandiose identification with the hero of the movie "Taxi Driver," Travis Bickle, and with John Lennon and with his assassin. He ended up in Washington where he tried to assassinate President Reagan — a grandiose historic deed that would make him famous and unite him perhaps in death with the delusional love object, Jodie Foster.

For those of us who have tried to understand the subjective, psychodynamic experience of schizophrenia, Doctor Researcher's testimony was compelling. Doctor Researcher was convinced that Hinckley demonstrated features that are [characteristic] of schizophrenia. He described Hinckley's condition as process schizophrenia and concluded that Hinckley could neither appreciate the wrongfulness of his actions nor conform. . . .

Doctor Forensics, the first prosecution psychiatrist, set about recasting the history. He brought out four main themes: advantages, entitlement, premeditation, and manipulation. In place of psychological hardship and painful isolation, he saw advantages, luxurious surroundings, and a spoiled rich kid. Where the defense psychiatrists saw failure and frustration, he saw entitlement and easy living. Where they saw a suicide attempt he saw a suicidal gesture. Where they saw acting out of a delusional fantasy, he saw premeditation. Finally, where they saw isolation and inability to deal with others, he saw deception, dishonesty, and clever manipulation to get what Hinckley wanted. . . .

Doctor Forensics carefully applied the "statute law" of DSM-III and concluded that Hinckley could be diagnosed in at least four personality disorder categories, but he was not psychotic and he was certainly responsible for his actions. . . .

How are we to understand these radical discrepancies between the defense and prosecution psychiatrists' diagnoses? The defense experts seem to have adopted the traditional nonconfrontational interviewing style with Hinckley that most of us would use when dealing with ordinary patients. They believed the patient, and they looked for psychopathology the way we psychiatrists usually do. Perhaps they were conned by Hinckley. The prosecution experts, in contrast, challenged Hinckley's assertions, confronted contradictions, and checked the objective evidence against his statements. They assumed he might be trying to con them. Perhaps they made him defensive. They combined ordinary psychiatric skills and police investigation techniques. There must have been radical differences in the emotional climate of the interviews. The different emotional climates may well have influenced the perceptions of pathology. For example, where the defense saw flattened and inappropriate affect, the prosecution saw a demanding manipulative person who was aware of what was going on, wanted special treatment, and had only a little blunting of affect. . . .

None of this conflicting testimony, which was the result of psychiatrists doing psychiatry in the courtroom, would have been eliminated by the APA's new restrictive test. Nor would it be eliminated by barring psychiatric diagnosis. The only way to eliminate such conflicts would be to eliminate psychiatric testimony. . . .

Despite the endless attempts of law to define precise tests of criminal responsibility, the ordinary psychiatrist typically asks: Is the person psychotic? If the diagnosis is psychosis, particularly schizophrenia, the person is insane. If a personality disorder is diagnosed, the person is sane. The new APA proposal[b] has gone back to that time-honored clinical distinction, noting that we now have 80 percent reliability as to the DSM-III diagnosis of psychosis. But this new threshold question would have had no impact on the Hinckley testimony since the defense diagnosed schizophrenia and the prosecution diagnosed personality disorder. Hinckley apparently fell into the 20 percent nonreliability category. We should not be surprised by that. Rather, we should expect that in most cases where the prosecution would want to contest an insanity defense, the defendant will not be obviously psychotic. The obviously psychotic defendant can be readily identified even by a prosecutor. Thus it may be that contested cases raising the insanity defense will be those about which we can expect diagnostic disagreement by psychiatrists. . . .

[The] APA proposal involves going back to an essentially cognitive test — again in part because psychiatric testimony relevant to cognitive matters such as appreciation and understanding "is more reliable, and has a stronger scientific base" than testimony relevant to volition. Here again the hopes of the APA proposal fail. The defense found ample evidence of thought disorder, including ideas of reference, magical thinking, bizarre ideas, and a break with reality. The prosecution found none of this. Thus testimony limited to the cognitive issue did not prove reliable in the courtroom. . . .

. . . The APA's new restrictive test would have made little difference in either the testimony or the verdict. . . . The basic goal of the APA's proposal was to try to limit psychiatrists to what they do best: evaluating the mental status and condition of the defendant psychiatrically and medically.

b. See Note 3, page 954 supra. — Eds.

The APA hoped that psychiatric testimony limited to what psychiatrists do best would be more exact, more reliable, and less controversial. The Hinckley transcript dashes those hopes. Most of the testimony was devoted to just those considerations, and yet the experts disagreed on every significant aspect of clinical evaluation: history, symptoms, mental status, and reliability of the informant.

The APA's narrowing of the insanity defense to the cognitive test would also have failed because the experts disagreed about whether Hinckley had a thought disorder. Cognitive evaluation did not prove more reliable. . . .

Changing the insanity defense is like chipping away at the tip of the iceberg. . . . An exchange between defense and prosecution psychiatrists will illustrate one aspect of these deeper and more basic theoretical problems. Doctor Biological Psychiatry said that the Valium Hinckley took may well have produced "paradoxical rage," thus causing him to be unable to control himself. Doctor Corrections said it was "appropriate" for Hinckley to take Valium if he was anxious about assassinating the President. Put aside the fact that these are both conjectures. They are conjectures which are part of two quite different kinds of discourse.

The theory of paradoxical rage is part of a discourse about organisms with brains, enzymes, and physical chemical reactions. The theory of appropriate behavior is part of a discourse about persons with minds, intentions, and motivated actions. In the discourse about organisms, the self disappears and paradoxical rage is *caused* by the chemical release of the inhibitory neural system. In the discourse about persons, the self is the agent who chooses, who intends, and who assumes a firing position and pulls the trigger. Morality does not enter the discourse of organisms because free will and choice are not part of that language. To say that a *person* had a paradoxical rage reaction is to confuse the two discourses. The correct statement is that the organism was subject to a paradoxical rage reaction. (Even then the word rage is suspect.)

Psychiatry has not yet found a unified discourse about organisms and persons. That is the giant iceberg against which the insanity defense inevitably is wrecked. Neither psychiatry nor law nor moral philosophy has found a sure way past this barrier. It does no good to pretend the barrier does not exist or to ask the jury to deal with it. These are not questions for which common sense has an answer.

(ii)   Applying the Tests: When Is a Person "Crazy"?

STATE v. GREEN

Tennessee Court of Appeals
643 S.W.2d 902 (1982)

DAUGHTREY, J. . . . On the evening of January 18, 1979, Chattanooga police found the body of Officer Harry Wilcox in a restroom at Warner Park. The corpse, clothed in a blue park police uniform, was lying face down in a pool of blood. The victim had been shot twice in the head, and his police revolver was missing. On the victim's back officers found a plastic bag containing a note. The note, addressed to Agent Ray Hanrahan of the FBI, contained a meaningless string of words and phrases, including reference to an "ousiograph." . . .

Police were led to Green by contacting FBI agent Hanrahan. . . . At trial Hanrahan testified that Green had come to the FBI office . . . and told the agent that some people in New York were talking to him, sending messages to his brain, and "directing" him. Green told Hanrahan that a doctor in New York had invented a machine called an "oustograph" or "ousiograph" that could detect these matters. He asked Hanrahan to find out about the oustograph for him. Hanrahan looked up the word in a dictionary and contacted a radio technician, but could not learn anything about such a machine. Hanrahan said he thought the defendant "had [mental] problems," and he suggested to Green at the time that he go to Erlanger Hospital to seek help.

Hanrahan's perception of the precariousness of Green's mental health was indeed accurate. Green had first received psychiatric treatment at the age of seven when as a child in New York City he was suspended from school for picking fights with other children "for no reason at all. . . . , beat[ing] them up really viciously." At that time he began seeing a psychiatrist who diagnosed his problem as paranoia. After treating the defendant for over two years, the psychiatrist pronounced Green "all right" but warned that the condition could recur during his teenage years. At age twelve, Green attacked his mother with a knife and again received psychiatric treatment.

By the time Green was sixteen, he had become a loner. He refused to go to school, remained in bed all day, and stayed out all night. He refused to bathe. He would not talk to anyone, and when spoken to, he would not respond or would laugh hysterically. Green carried a bag around with him, explaining to his parents that the bag "kept him company." He complained that the television talked back at him. At first Green insisted there was nothing wrong with him, but he eventually agreed to accept psychiatric treatment. After he was hospitalized for more than a month in 1978, his family reached the limits of their insurance coverage, and Green was transferred to an out-patient clinic. During this period he was heavily medicated and "was just like a zombie." Because the medication made Green so drowsy he could not study, he stopped taking the medicine and refused to visit the out-patient clinic.

Green enrolled in a Navy reserve program, returned to school, and managed to graduate from high school in June 1978. Immediately after graduation, he reported for Navy training, but a few weeks later the Navy discharged him for failure to adapt to regulations. When he returned home from the Navy, Green resumed his old behavior patterns. He stayed in bed during the day and walked the streets at night. He had a fight with his brother and cut him on the leg with a knife. He said that other people in the apartment building had a machine that tampered with his brain. . . . Toward the end of August 1978, he stole the family's household money and left home.

. . . Green stayed with his uncle in Memphis for six to seven weeks. At trial Noah Green described his nephew's bizarre behavior during that time. . . . The defendant would stay in his room all day and only went outside when his uncle insisted. . . . Sometimes he locked himself in the bathroom, but ran the shower without bathing. Green laughed at inappropriate times, and he would stare into space and move his mouth without saying anything. Twice the defendant visited a mental health clinic, but each time he refused to cooperate with the doctors. The medical staff told his family that because Green had not yet exhibited violent tendencies, he could not be hospitalized involuntarily. By November 1978, Green's behavior had become so bizarre that Noah Green feared for the safety of his young children and asked his nephew to leave. Green then went to stay with an aunt, Julia McNair, who also lived in Memphis.

Green lived in McNair's home for two weeks. She testified that during that time he never went out, he kept her apartment in darkness, and he refused to bathe. He would not talk to other people but laughed and talked to himself constantly.

When a psychologist at the local mental health center told McNair that the defendant needed to be hospitalized and that he might "go off at any time" and "do anything," she became frightened. She told her nephew that he would have to leave her home if he did not seek medical help immediately. When he refused, she called her brother, the defendant's father, and told him to come get Green and take him back to New York City. When Green's father arrived in Memphis, the defendant insisted that he did not need treatment and refused to return to New York. His father bought him a pair of shoes, paid for a hotel room for him, and gave him some money. . . .

Some two months later, in January 1979, the defendant was arrested and charged with the Wilcox murder. [In July 1979 Green was found incompetent to stand trial and committed to the Middle Tennessee Mental Health Institute, where the staff also found him "insane at the time of the offense, . . . committable and in need of maximum security." After intensive drug therapy, Green's ability to think coherently gradually improved and he was found competent to stand trial. At the trial in November 1980, Green offered both lay and expert testimony to establish insanity, his sole defense. The case was tried under the Model Penal Code test. The jury found Green guilty of first-degree murder. On appeal, Green argued that there was "overwhelming proof" of insanity. The appellate court summarized the evidence:]

The medical experts [testified] that they and all the other professional staff members who came in contact with Green after his arrest agreed unanimously that he was insane at the time of the offense. . . .

After months of treatment, Green was finally able to recall and communicate to the staff what occurred on the day Wilcox was killed. Although his various recollections of the event were not entirely consistent, the defendant told the staff in effect that he had acted in response to voices telling him that if he killed, he would be Adolf Hitler.

Shanks [a nurse-clinician at the hospital] described Green as initially talking only in "gibberish." (When asked by one hospital staff member what language he was using, Green replied that it was Chinese; however, a Chinese-speaking staff member knew otherwise.) Gradually, under medication, Green's gibberish gave way to coherent language and there was a lessening of both his inappropriate laughter and his tendency to talk to the ceiling. This improvement, Shanks said, was mainly attributable to the medication Green was receiving; the other factor was his presence in a highly structured environment. She said Green showed no signs of "faking," and she concluded that he had been insane at the time of the offense.

The State's rebuttal evidence, offered to establish the defendant's sanity at the time of the offense, consisted of testimony by five Chattanooga police officers and a former county employee. The first of these witnesses was Terry Slaughter, the detective who arrested Green on January 20, [1979], for the Wilcox killing. He described Green as "cooperative," "coherent," and "intelligent," but said that Green did not want to discuss the shooting. In the two hours he spent with Green, Slaughter noticed no bizarre behavior nor any sign that Green was "under delusion." . . . Asked if he had also told Green's lawyer that this would be an "easy case" for him because the accused was "crazy as a loon," the detective responded, "I don't remember expressing it in that way. . . . I remember expressing the thought to you that I thought the party [Green] needed help."

Officer Janus Marlin, a Warner Park patrolman and a colleague of the victim's, found Green huddled in a phone booth in the park on December 27, [1978]. Green had taken refuge there to get out of the cold and told Marlin he had "no place to go." The officer took him to a nearby rescue mission. Asked if there was "anything out of the ordinary" about Green at the time, Marlin said no, but also testified that "he was dirty and he smelled."

[Three other police officers presented testimony similar to that of Officer Marlin. They described incidents in December 1978 and January 1979 when they had found Green loitering in the park or other public places. Green had told them he had no place to go and was "trying to find someplace to stay warm." In these incidents the officers either arrested Green for vagrancy or simply told him to move on. They described him as "coherent," "fairly quiet," and "very polite" but "unkempt and dirty."]

Finally, the State offered testimony by a former county employee, William Cox, who gave Green a ride [on] the day Officer Wilcox was killed. . . . [Green] was carrying what was apparently his only possession at that time, a pair of shiny black shoes. During the 45 minutes they were in the van together, Cox said, they engaged in "small talk." In response to a question by the prosecution, the witness agreed that he noticed nothing out of the ordinary about Green.

From this testimony, the State took the position that Green was "not insane and crazy and bizarre at the time [the Wilcox killing] happened," but was just "a little bit different." However, the testimony of the various State witnesses, all of whom had had only brief contact with Green over a period of several weeks and described him as "normal," is not inconsistent with a determination that Green was insane at the time of the offense. The medical experts testified, and their testimony is unrefuted, that a paranoid schizophrenic can operate in a *seemingly* normal way. . . . Dr. Pieper [noted:]

> Paranoid schizophrenic people have a characteristic of what we call encapsulated delusions. That is they may have some abnormal thoughts that are about a very particular area. . . . When the person is functioning in areas which don't require any thinking about that particular problem, they can look pretty normal. They can get on a bus and ride the bus and no problem. But if somebody asks them a question or says something or makes a movement that they regard as threatening, suddenly all of this bizarre thinking takes charge and at that point they may react in any sort of way that's totally unexpected and totally irrational. . . .

To undercut the weight of the medical testimony, the State tried to establish that Green was faking his symptoms, or, in the alternative, that his psychosis was the result of the Wilcox killing and not its cause. The record clearly and eloquently refutes these theories. . . . [I]t is difficult if not impossible to believe that Green was able to fake the symptoms outlined above successfully enough to fool the highly trained and experienced medical personnel who both evaluated and treated him in this case. Moreover, the extensive history of Green's mental illness, going back over a decade and evidenced by medical and hospital records, as well as the cogent testimony of his family and the experts who diagnosed and treated him, wholly refutes the idea that Green dropped into a sudden psychotic condition upon shooting Officer Wilcox. The disease from which he suffered is a progressive one, and as Dr. Speal [a court-appointed psychologist] noted, . . . "he has been psychotic for most of his life, if not all of his life." . . .

Given the nature of the evidence offered by the defendant, the burden of proof in this case fell squarely on the State to establish the defendant's sanity beyond a reasonable doubt. Graham v. State, 547 S.W.2d at 544. Under the *Graham* standard, it was incumbent upon the State to prove (1) that at the time of the offense the defendant was not suffering from a mental disease or defect, *or* (2) if he was, that his illness was not such as to prevent him from knowing the wrongfulness of his conduct *and* from conforming his conduct to the requirements of the law. . . .

The State sought to discharge its burden of proof at trial by proving . . . that Green was not suffering from mental incapacity at the time of the offense, a theory which was totally demolished by the strength of the defendant's insanity proof at trial.

[B]efore this Court . . . the State argues that the nature of the defendant's condition was not sufficient to meet the remaining two-prong test of *Graham*. First, the State says, evidence that the defendant fled from the scene of the crime and hid the weapon involved in the shooting proves that he knew the wrongfulness of his act. The most obvious response to this argument is that the record shows only that the defendant left the scene at some point after the shooting and that Officer Wilcox's revolver was never recovered; neither of these facts establishes beyond a reasonable doubt that the defendant was attempting to conceal his identity or complicity from police, or that he otherwise was able to appreciate the wrongfulness of what he had done. . . .

But even if it were conceded that by his post-event behavior Green evidenced some appreciation of the wrongfulness of his conduct, the record is wholly devoid of any evidence that at the time he shot Wilcox, Green was able to conform his conduct to the dictates of law. The State's only argument in response to overwhelming evidence of Green's incapacity in this respect is that his failure to react violently toward *other* police officers with whom he came into contact proves that he was able to conform his conduct to the law with respect to Officer Wilcox. . . . This argument, of course, not only begs the question (that is, whether under this analysis any initial violent behavior could ever be the product of insanity), but it also ignores the nature of paranoid schizophrenia, as described by experts in this and other cases. . . .

The State correctly points out that a jury is not bound by expert testimony, even when it is non-conflicting. However, the Tennessee Supreme Court has clearly delineated what proof the State must produce to meet and overcome evidence of insanity:

> Th[e] burden can be met by the state through the introduction of expert testimony on the issue [of insanity], or through lay testimony where a proper foundation for the expressing of an opinion is laid, or through the showing of acts or statements of the petitioner, at or very near the time of the commission of the crime, which are consistent with sanity *and inconsistent with insanity*.

Edwards v. State, 540 S.W.2d 641, 646 (Tenn. 1976) (emphasis added). In this case, although the acts of the defendant at or near the time of the killing were arguably "consistent with sanity," quite obviously they were not also "inconsistent with insanity." Under the *Edwards* rule, the State has failed to meet its burden of establishing sanity, and thus "the evidence is insufficient to support the findings by the trier of fact of guilt beyond a reasonable doubt." . . . [W]e have no choice but to set aside Green's conviction. . . .

NOTES AND QUESTIONS

1. Beyond criminal law. Was the killing of Officer Wilcox preventable? If Green is not to be blamed for the death, who is? Were his parents or relatives at fault? The health insurance system? The lack of a warm place for him to sleep? Or is Agent Hanrahan responsible? (Note that the great majority of severely disturbed schizophrenics remain nonviolent.) Should Green have been subject to involuntary hospitalization because of his incoherent thinking and delusions about mind control and the "ousiograph"? What is the "moral" of the *Green* case?

2. Applying the legal standard. On the procedural issue presented in *Green,* was the court correct in holding that the prosecution's evidence was insufficient to support a finding of sanity? Why wasn't this a question for the jury? Insanity defense cases often involve evidentiary conflicts similar to that in *Green;* some courts are willing to find testimony about episodes of "normal" behavior sufficient to overcome extensive evidence of profound mental disorder. See, e.g., State v. Lawton, 734 P.2d 1138 (Kan. 1987); People v. Weber, 170 Cal. App. 3d 139, 215 Cal. Rptr. 827 (1985). Does the difference between such decisions and *Green* reflect different attitudes about the proper degree of deference to the jury? Or do such decisions reflect a different conception of what it means to be "crazy"? What conception of insanity could have led the jury to conclude that Green was *not* insane? Consider the comments of Professor Fingarette in the excerpt that follows.

Herbert Fingarette, The Meaning of Criminal Insanity 137-142 (1972): [The familiar criteria of insanity are] unsatisfactory on their face . . . when straightforwardly applied to several paradigm types of insanity. . . .

M'Naghten held the delusionary belief that there was widespread Tory plotting aimed at his ultimate destruction. In "self-defense," M'Naghten attempted to assassinate the Tory leader, Prime Minister [Peel]. [I]f we take the language in its direct and plain meaning, we should say that the defendant knew he was attempting the assassination of a high government official and knew this was treason, a crime prohibited by law and by the moral views of his fellows; and M'Naghten did this because of his irrational belief, but without being coerced or otherwise caused to act nonvoluntarily. In the language of the Model Penal Code, we must say (I believe) that he did have the capacity to conform to law and to refrain from the killing. In fact he generally did conform to law; but in this case, for his own insane reasons, he did not want to conform to law but wanted, quite consciously, to "take the law into his own hands."

We are familiar with the attempt by many courts, legal commentators, and psychiatrists to "save" one or another of the criteria mentioned by arguing that . . . M'Naghten did not *really* know what [he was] doing, did not appreciate fully and properly or did not understand the nature or the wrongness of [his] acts; or by arguing that such persons could not *really* be considered to be acting freely or voluntarily or could not have criminal intent. But such tactics . . . amount to a confession that we cannot take this language at its face value but must give it a special or unusual — and unclear — meaning, whether we call this a "deeper" meaning or not.

[Prof. Fingarette notes that a similar problem arises in cases of "psychotic depressive states" and other extreme forms of psychosis. He focuses on two cases in which mothers not suffering from delusions or hallucinations killed their children in an acute phase of psychotic depression].

It is a manifestation of their psychoses that both these mothers made their plans, took appropriate precautions, and then deliberately executed those plans. They knew that what they were doing was morally and legally condemned by society. True, they based their conduct on irrational beliefs, moods, or attitudes, just as the paranoid bases his conduct on an irrational belief. The irrational mood leads to views on life very different from what a rational person would accept. But given this dark mood, the person then acts purposefully, voluntarily, knowingly.

Here, again, the temptation is strong to "deepen" (that is, alter) the meaning of the words in order to get the result one intuitively knows to be right: The person in a state of depression does not really know the wrongness of what he's doing; he does not appreciate it truly; or he cannot really be said to act voluntarily for his mood is so strong that it is irresistible; or he cannot justly be said to have criminal intent because he's insane.

This felt need to deepen or amplify the meaning of the phrases derives from the feeling that these phrases must be saved and an awareness that in their plain sense they do not apply. . . .

My conclusion, however, is that insanity is in this respect like childhood; both are conditions that exculpate in a more radical way than the ignorance or involuntariness of the otherwise responsible person. . . . Of a small child, for example, it is in certain respects beside the point to say that he knew what he was doing, just as it would be beside the point to say that he didn't. . . . Our inclination is to say, "Of course he knew (in the way a child does) what he was doing, but he's just a child! What can you expect?" . . .

I believe the point of characterizing someone as insane is essentially the same in this respect. It is somehow beside the point that M'Naghten knew he was attempting to murder [Peel] and that he did it of his own will. What is at issue when we call him insane is something else. And this something else, among other things, renders him nonresponsible. It infects his will and his knowledge and his conduct, just as childishness qualifies a child's will and knowledge and conduct. Some further dimension of mind is absent, a dimension that makes mere absence of compulsion or mere knowledge of what one is doing insufficient for establishing responsibility.

[Professor Fingarette goes on to argue that the unarticulated "something else" that is at the heart of our judgments about insanity — the "further dimension of mind [that] is absent" — is a "capacity for rational conduct" (id. at 240), a capacity to respond to the morally and legally relevant circumstances of a situation. See id. at 186-187, 239-241.]

3. The Prerequisites of Moral Accountability. For detailed development of the view that a capacity for rational action is an essential prerequisite to being a moral agent, that is, a freely choosing person who can be held criminally responsible, see Michael S. Moore, Law and Psychiatry: Rethinking the Relationship (1984), and Robert Schopp, Automatism, Insanity and the Psychology of Criminal Responsibility (1991). See also Peter Arenella, Convicting the Morally Blameless: Reassessing the Relationship Between Legal and Moral Accountability, 39 U.C.L.A.L. Rev. 1511 (1992). Professor Arenella argues that moral agency requires not only a capacity for rational action but also particular traits of character, and he develops a detailed account of the character attributes necessary for a person to be able to take account of moral norms in making practical judgments. See id. at 1609-1610.

(iii)   Abolition of the Insanity Defense?

STATE v. STRASBURG

Supreme Court of Washington
60 Wash. 106, 110 P. 1020 (1910)

PARKER, J. The prosecuting attorney for King county by information charged the defendant with the crime of assault in the first degree. . . . The trial resulted in a verdict of guilty. . . . [On appeal, defendant argued] that the trial court erred in refusing to admit evidence tending to prove that the defendant . . . was insane [at the time of the offense,] and also that the court erred in instructing the jury

> that, under the laws of this state, it is no defense to a criminal charge that the person charged was at the time of the commission of the offense unable, by reason of his insanity, idiocy or imbecility to comprehend the nature and quality of the act committed, or to understand that it was wrong.

In support of these rulings of the learned trial court, counsel for the state rely upon the provisions of section 7 of our New Criminal Code, providing as follows:

> It shall be no defense to a person charged with the commission of a crime that at the time of its commission he was unable, by reason of his insanity, idiocy or imbecility, to comprehend the nature and quality of the act committed, or to understand that it was wrong; or that he was afflicted with a morbid propensity to commit prohibited acts; nor shall any testimony or other proof thereof be admitted in evidence.[a]

It is contended by learned counsel for appellant that this statute withholds from him rights guaranteed by our state Constitution, and particularly those rights guaranteed by the following provisions thereof: Article 1, §3: "No person shall be deprived of life, liberty, or property without due process of law." Article 1, §21: "The right of trial by jury shall remain inviolate." . . .

[T]he sanity of the accused at the time of committing the act charged against him has always been regarded as much a substantive fact, going to make up his

---

a. The statute further provided that the trial judge could, after verdict of guilty, order the defendant committed to a state hospital for the insane or confined in the insane ward of the penitentiary, if of the view that the defendant, by virtue of her insanity, was unable to comprehend the nature and quality of her act or to understand that such act was wrong. — EDS guilt, as the fact of his physical commission of the act. . . . If he was insane at the time to the extent that he could not comprehend the nature and quality of the act — in other words, if he had no will to control the physical act of his physical body — how can it in truth be said that the act was his act? To take from the accused the opportunity to offer evidence tending to prove this fact is in our opinion as much a violation of his constitutional right of trial by jury as to take from him the right to offer evidence before the jury tending to show that he did not physically commit the act or physically set in motion a train of events resulting in the act. . . .

[C]ounsel for the state [argues] that the modern humane treatment of those convicted of crime practically removes them from the realm of punishment, and places them in a position but little different from those other unfortunate members of society which the state is obliged to care for and restrain of their liberty, not because they have committed wrong, but because of their menace to society and themselves without fault of their own — the insane. . . . Learned counsel's premise suggests a noble conception, and may give promise of a condition of things towards which the humanitarian spirit of the age is tending; yet the stern and awful fact still remains, and is patent to all men, that the status and condition in the eyes of the world, and under the law, of one convicted of crime, is vastly different from that of one simply adjudged insane. We cannot shut our eyes to the fact that the element of punishment is still in our criminal laws. . . . As long as this is the spirit of our laws, though it may be much mellowed in the treatment of the convicted, as compared with former times, the constitutional rights here invoked must be given full force and effect when an accused person is put upon trial to determine the question of his guilt of crime. . . .

The judgment of the learned trial court is reversed, with direction to grant appellant a new trial.

STATE v. KORELL

Supreme Court of Montana
213 Mont. 316, 690 P.2d 992 (1984)

[Defendant was a Vietnam veteran who had several traumatic experiences during his tour of duty. Upon his return to the United States, he experienced severe psychological problems, including periods of paranoia, and he was twice admitted to VA hospitals for psychiatric treatment. Subsequently, he set fire to a laundromat because he lost nine quarters in a machine and set fire to his wife's former home because she had bad feelings about it. While on bail pending trial in these incidents, Korell developed the belief that Gregg Lockwood, his former job supervisor, was trying to kill him. He broke into Lockwood's home and fired several shots at Lockwood before Lockwood managed to subdue him.

[At trial for the attack on Lockwood, experts testified on Korell's mental condition, but the jury was charged that it could consider mental disease or defect only insofar as it negated the mental state required for the offenses charged. Korell was convicted of attempted murder and sentenced to 35 years in prison. On appeal, he challenged the state's failure to allow insanity as an independent defense.]

In 1979 . . . the Montana Legislature . . . abolished use of the traditional insanity defense . . . and substituted alternative procedures for considering a criminal defendant's mental condition. . . .

During trial, evidence of mental disease or defect is admissible when relevant to prove that, at the time of the offense charged, the defendant did not have the state of mind that is an element of the crime charged, e.g., that the defendant did not act purposely or knowingly. The State retains the burden of proving each element of the offense beyond a reasonable doubt. Defendant may, of course, present evidence to contradict the State's proof that he committed the offense and that he had the requisite state of mind at that time.

Whenever the jury finds that the State has failed to prove beyond a reasonable doubt that the defendant had the requisite state of mind at the time he committed the offense, it is instructed to return a special verdict of not guilty "for the reason that due to a mental disease or defect he could not have a particular state of mind that is an essential element of the offense charged. . . . " Section 46-14-201(2), MCA.

Finally at the dispositional stage following the trial and conviction, the sentencing judge must consider any relevant evidence presented at the trial, plus any additional evidence presented at the sentencing hearing, to determine whether the defendant was able to appreciate the criminality of his acts or to conform his conduct to the law at the time he committed the offense for which he was convicted. Section 46-14-311, MCA.

Whenever the sentencing court finds the defendant was suffering from mental disease or defect which rendered him unable to appreciate the criminality of his conduct or to conform his conduct to the requirements of law, mandatory minimum sentences are waived. The defendant is committed to the custody of the director of institutions and placed in an appropriate institution for custody, care and treatment not to exceed the maximum possible sentence. . . . The institutionalized defendant may later petition the District Court for release from the hospital upon a showing that the individual has been cured of the mental disease or defect. If the petition is granted, the court must transfer the defendant to the state prison or place the defendant under alternative confinement or supervision. The length of this confinement or supervision must equal the original sentence. Section 46-14-312(3), MCA.

In summary, while Montana has abolished the traditional use of insanity as a defense, alternative procedures have been enacted to deal with insane individuals who commit criminal acts.

. . . Appellant contends that the insanity defense is so embedded in our legal history that it should be afforded status as a fundamental right. . . .

Three older state court decisions have found state statutes abolishing the insanity defense to be unconstitutional. State v. Lange (1929), 168 La. 958, 123 So. 639; Sinclair v. State (1931), 161 Miss. 142, 132 So. 581; State v. Strasburg (1910), 60 Wash. 106, 110 P. 1020. These decisions are distinguishable in that they interpret statutes that precluded *any* trial testimony of mental condition, including that which would cast doubt on the defendant's state of mind at the time he committed the charged offense. The Montana statutes in question expressly allow evidence of mental disease or defect to be introduced to rebut proof of defendant's state of mind.

... Korell argues that individuals may be clearly insane yet also be capable of forming the requisite intent to commit a crime.... Illustrations include the assassin acting under instructions of God, the mother drowning her demonically-possessed child, and the man charging up Montana Avenue on a shooting spree believing he is Teddy Roosevelt on San Juan Hill. Defendant contends that these people could properly be found guilty by a jury under current Montana law....

It is further argued that subjecting the insane to the stigma of a criminal conviction violates fundamental principles of justice. We cannot agree. The legislature has made a conscious decision to hold individuals who act with a proven criminal state of mind accountable for their acts, regardless of motivation or mental condition. Arguably, this policy does not further criminal justice goals of deterrence and prevention in cases where an accused suffers from a mental disease that renders him incapable of appreciating the criminality of his conduct. However, the policy does further goals of protection of society and education. One State Supreme Court Justice who wrestled with this dilemma observed: "In a very real sense, the confinement of the insane is the punishment of the innocent; the release of the insane is the punishment of society." State v. Stacy (Tenn. 1980), 601 S.W.2d 696, 704 (Henry, J., dissenting)....

NOTES

1. Two other states have abolished the insanity defense. See Idaho Code §18-207 (1982); Utah Code Ann. §76-2-305 (1990). In State v. Searcy, 188 Idaho 632, 798 P.2d 914 (1990), the Idaho Supreme Court, relying on *Korell,* upheld the constitutionality of the Idaho statute.

2. A study of experience in Montana for the three years before and the three years after the 1979 reform found that acquittals by reason of insanity dropped sharply but did not disappear altogether, because the new statute permits "acquittal by reason of insanity" when evidence of mental disorder negates mens rea. See Henry J. Steadman, et al., Maintenance of an Insanity Defense Under Montana's "Abolition" of the Insanity Defense, 146 Am. J. Psychiatry 357 (1989). The total number of insanity pleas tendered by defendants actually increased, and there were 5 insanity acquittals in the post-reform period, compared to 61 in the pre-reform period. Of greatest interest, the drop in acquittals by reason of insanity did not produce a corresponding increase in the proportion of insanity pleas ending in conviction. Rather, there was a sharp increase in *dismissals.* In the pre-reform period, 64 percent of defendants found incompetent to stand trial were eventually tried and acquitted by reason of insanity. Post-reform, 75 percent of the defendants found incompetent were never tried, charges against them were dropped, and they were civilly committed. The study concluded that dismissal based on incompetency to stand trial became a substitute for acquittal by reason of insanity and noted (id. at 357):

[T]here is still a system of detention that retains persons indefinitely in a maximum security ward at the state mental hospital under criminal mental health detentions just as there was before 1979.

INSANITY AS A DEFENSE: A PANEL DISCUSSION

Annual Judicial Conference, Second Judicial Circuit of the United States
37 F.R.D. 365, 369-372, 381-383 (1964)

JOSEPH WEINTRAUB, C.J. [N.J. Supreme Court]: . . . My thesis is that insanity should have nothing to do with the adjudication of guilt but rather should bear upon the disposition of the offender after conviction, and that the contest among *M'Naghten* and its competitive concepts which you have on a paper before you is simply a struggle over an irrelevancy. . . .

I think we all agree that society must be protected from hostile acts and when a forbidden act is done, it must be adjudged that the accused committed it before he may be deprived of his liberty. [A]s long as we have two processes which may be employed to deal custodially with anti-social conduct, one criminal and the other civil, the test for their application must be blameworthiness or the non-existence of blameworthiness in a very personal sense. And that distinction is supposed to be between the bad and the sick. Now, in separating the bad from the sick, the common law deemed it indisputable that every man has the ability to adhere to the right; psychiatry challenges this basis for a finding of personal blameworthiness. Psychiatry does recognize a volitional apparatus but conceives it to be integrated with the intellect and the emotions, and from its objective view no man can be said to have selected the dimensions of these faculties and hence to be the author of the inadequacy of any of them. And, indeed, the unconscious is deemed to mock and play havoc with the conscious. On that approach, the sick and the wicked must be equally free of blame in a personal sense and there can be no denominator which in terms of justice to the individual will separate one from the other. . . . Upon the psychiatric view the distinction between the sick and the bad is I think an illusion. . . . The thrust of the psychiatric thesis must be to reject insanity as a defense and to deal with all transgressors as unfortunate mortals. In other words, if we could think of the adjudication of guilt as nothing more than a finding that this mortal has demonstrated his capacity to do harm, the need for segregating him or otherwise treating him or dealing with him, I think half the battle would be decided. We then would get to the question of what can we do? How can we best redeem him; recapture whatever there is that can be salvaged? The difficulty I think is that the psychiatry-based critics of *M'Naghten* will not accept the inevitable answer, which, I think, psychiatry gives but rather they urge that *M'Naghten* be abandoned in favor of some other concept of insanity which will excuse and then debate whether the test will be *Durham* . . . or the model code . . . or some refinement of them. And I think that debate just has to be fruitless. It's a quixotic attempt to draw a line that just doesn't exist. No definition of criminal responsibility and hence of legal insanity can be valid unless it truthfully separates the man who is personally blameworthy for his makeup from the man who is not, and I submit to you that there is just no basis in psychiatry to make a differentiation between the two. I would think that if there is anything that would be an anathema to a psychiatrist, it's the concept of blame. I don't think he's interested in that at all and I doubt very much that a psychiatrist would contend that he has any expert information which can give us insight into that real riddle.

PROFESSOR HERBERT WECHSLER: . . . Chief Justice Weintraub has . . . ventured the suggestion that the whole effort to develop a criterion for determining criminal responsibility as affected by mental disease or defect is a misguided effort. . . . I think it is not a misguided effort. It rests not only on the universal experience of all modern legal systems but I'm tempted to say of all civilized legal systems, though I don't want to beg the question by an epithet. I think, moreover, that there is a solid basis for this phenomenon. I suggest that you think about it not in terms of the effort to do absolute justice to individuals (we must agree with the Chief Justice, this is for God and not for man) but rather in terms of asking ourselves this question: how would you feel about living in a society in which a differentiation of this sort were not attempted?

For example, your elderly father in an advanced arteriosclerotic state is taken to the hospital and while in the hospital experiences a tantrum, a delusion, delusional phase, and knocks over a lamp, with the result that an attendant is killed. Now, would you be satisfied with a legal system in which he could be indicted and convicted of a homicidal crime and his condition regarded as relevant only on the question of what to do with him. Everybody would say no to this. That is why the criterion of responsibility as affected by disease or a defect parallels the traditional mens rea rules in requiring a determination of blameworthiness in the ordinary moral sense, in the sense of working morality, not in the sense of man's responsibility for his nature or his nurture but in the sense that the afflictive sanctions of the law will not be visited on anyone unless he does something which is the product of a choice, unless in traditional jurisprudential terms he performs a juridical act. Now, general confidence that this is so seems to me quite central to the sense of security that is one of the greatest values in a law abiding society. It is a very important thing for all of us to know that if we should be afflicted and in the course of affliction should be the physical agent of harm to others, that the legal system will conduct an inquiry in which the nature of that affliction can be adduced for an estimate of its bearing on blameworthiness in the ordinary sense. We're dealing thus with a proposition which is directly akin to the legal point that accident is not a crime, not punishable, and indeed even to the hesitance of the system to impose criminal liability for negligence, for mere negligence and to the general effort to require at least recklessness and, for ordinary purposes, purposeful wrongdoing. . . .

This brings me to the second part of Chief Justice Weintraub's theme. He spoke of drawing a distinction between civil and criminal roads to commitment, and that of course is what's involved here. But, again, you must face the question, do you believe in that distinction? And I put it to you that it is vital to believe in that distinction, vital to a healthy society which will use its criminal law to build and buttress self-reliant action on the part of citizens affected by it. And, also, for another reason, namely that an awful lot of sick people in this world have to go to mental institutions who have not engaged in hostile acts of the kind that would ordinarily be crimes. About the toughest problem in dealing with that mental health problem, I should say, is the problem of protecting those people from a deep and scarring stigma, the more so at a time when such commitments seem happily to be relatively brief on the whole and release safe within a short time largely due to the new drugs. Now, how can you safeguard these people from stigma if you merge the process by which they may be committed to a mental institution and the process of dealing with people who have done what the social order condemns . . . ? So I don't think that it's just a question of whether you get sent away and for how long. I rather think that the distinctive feature of the entire criminal process is the element of condemnation that it marshals, of social condemnation. And, indeed, is it not the mark of a healthy society that the criminal law marshal an appropriate moral condemnation?

NORVAL MORRIS, PSYCHIATRY AND THE DANGEROUS CRIMINAL, 41 S. Cal. L. Rev. 514, 519-521 (1968): Overwhelmingly, criminal matters are disposed of by pleas of guilty and by bench trials. Only the exceptional case goes to trial by jury. And of these exceptional cases, in only two of every hundred is this defense raised. Does anyone believe that this percentage measures the actual significance of gross psychopathology to crime? Let him visit the nearest criminal court or penitentiary if he does. Clearly this defense is a sop to our conscience, a comfort for our failure to address the difficult arena of psychopathology and crime.

. . . It too often is overlooked that one group's exculpation from criminal responsibility confirms the inculpation of other groups. . . . You argue that insanity destroys, undermines, diminishes man's capacity to reject what is wrong and to adhere to what is right. So does the ghetto — more so. But surely, you reply, I would not have us punish the sick. Indeed I would, if you insist on punishing the grossly deprived. To the extent that criminal sanctions serve punitive purposes, I fail to see the difference between these two defenses. To the extent that they serve rehabilitative, treatment, and curative purposes I fail to see the need for the difference. . . .

In a few cases moral non-responsibility is so clear that it would be purposeless to invoke the criminal process . . . , [for example, when] a person did not know what he was doing at the time of the alleged crime. But in these situations there is no need for the *M'Naghten* or *Durham* rules, because they clearly fall within general criminal law exculpatory rules. The actor simply lacks the mens rea of the crime. It thus seems to me that, within the area of criminal responsibility and psychological disturbance, all that we need is already achieved with existing, long-established rules of intent. . . .

MODEL PENAL CODE AND COMMENTARIES, Comment to §4.01, at 182-186 (1985): A variety of reasons for abolition have been advanced from quite different ideological perspectives. . . . The first position is perhaps epitomized by President Nixon's support of abolition, which he said was "the most significant feature" of the codification of general defenses in the Administration's proposed criminal code and was designed to curb "unconscionable abuse" of the insanity defense. . . . This position . . . has little empirical support. The insanity defense is in fact infrequently invoked and then only for very serious crimes. When it has been invoked, jurors have not shown themselves ready to accept attenuated claims. Those who do successfully claim the defense are often committed for long periods of time. Unfounded fears of "abuse" are hardly a sufficient reason for abolishing a defense that has properly come to be viewed as fundamental.

The other attack on the insanity defense is more complex and it goes to the roots of the criminal law. It shares with the first position a skepticism that distinctions can sensibly be made between those who are responsible and those who are not. Critics taking this view cite the rarity of the employment of the defense as evidence that most mentally ill defendants are being convicted despite the availability of the defense. They doubt that the stigma of those convicted and subsequently treated as mentally disturbed is any worse than the stigma of those who commit criminal acts and are committed to high security institutions for the mentally ill without undergoing trial or after being acquitted on grounds of insanity. They argue that there is little basis for withholding condemnation of those whose mental illness causes them to act criminally when those whose deprived economic and social background causes them to act criminally are condemned. They regard the adversarial debate over the responsibility of particular defendants as wasteful, confusing for the jury, and possibly harmful for those defendants who are mentally disturbed. They think psychiatric diagnosis should be employed primarily after conviction to determine what sort of correctional treatment is appropriate instead of prior to conviction to determine criminal responsibility. Ideally, in the view of some of these critics, criminal convictions generally should not be regarded as stigmatizing, but as determinants of dangerousness to which the community must respond.

When properly understood, this attack is a challenge to the basic notion that a criminal conviction properly reflects moral condemnation by the community of the act performed. Yet those who advance the attack do not provide persuasive reasons for believing it would benefit society if the association between moral wrongdoing and criminal conviction were dissipated. Nor do they give reasons for supposing that the association will be dissipated in the near future. Yet they propose labeling as criminal many persons whom society at large would clearly not regard as morally blameworthy.

NOTE

For an overview of the arguments for abolishing the insanity defense and a cogent criticism of them, see Stephen J. Morse, Excusing the Crazy: The Insanity Defense Reconsidered, 58 So. Cal. L. Rev. 777 (1985). For further debate on the proposal to abolish the insanity defense and to defer inquiry into the mental condition of the defendant until after conviction, compare Barbara Wootton, Crime and the Criminal Law, chs. 2 & 3 (1963), with H. L. A. Hart, The Morality of the Criminal Law 12-29 (1964); and Norval Morris, Psychiatry and the Dangerous Criminal, 41 S. Cal. L. Rev. 514 (1968), with Sanford H. Kadish, The Decline of Innocence, 26 Camb. L.J. 273 (1968). See also John Monahan, Abolish the Insanity Defense? — Not Yet, 26 Rutgers L. Rev. 719 (1973).

(iv)   The Definition of "Disease"

STATE v. GUIDO

New Jersey Supreme Court
40 N.J. 191, 191 A.2d 45 (1963)

WEINTRAUB, C.J. Adele Guido was convicted of murder in the second degree and sentenced to imprisonment for a minimum of 24 years and a maximum of 27 years. She appeals directly to this Court. . . .

The victim was defendant's husband. When they first met, she was a young girl and he a professional fighter of some success. . . .

All the details of the marital discord need not be stated. [Defendant] wanted a divorce, while decedent insisted upon holding on to her notwithstanding he would not or could not end his extra marital romance and assume the role of a responsible husband and parent. . . . In the early morning of April 17, 1961, after deceased fell asleep on a couch in the living room while watching television, defendant, according to her testimony, took the gun and went into her room, intending to end her life. Deciding that suicide would be no solution, she returned to the living room to put the weapon back in the suitcase, but when her eyes fell upon Guido, she raised the weapon and fired until it was empty.

With respect to physical abuse, the jury could find that although there were only a few incidents of actual injury, there was the constant threat of it from a man who had to have his way and who would not let go of a woman who had had her fill. It appears that on several occasions shortly before the homicide defendant called the local police to express her fear of harm. . . .

Defendant claimed "temporary" insanity. She was examined by two court-appointed psychiatrists. [Their] report contained sundry medical findings and ultimately the opinion that defendant was "legally" sane at the time of the shooting. Mr. Saltzman [defense counsel] met with the psychiatrists, and after some three hours of debate the psychiatrists changed their opinion as to "legal" insanity although their underlying medical findings remained the same. They then retyped the last page of their report.

On cross-examination of the first defense psychiatrist, it was developed that the original report had been revised. We do not know how the prosecutor learned of the change. The record shows that on its own initiative the court immediately directed that "Counsel shall produce the original report to the prosecutor." . . . What followed was some high drama that the occasion did not warrant.

Mr. Saltzman . . . returned from his office with the original report. The court undertook to interrogate him [out of the presence of the jury] with respect to the receipt of the changed last page. . . . With much formality the trial court . . . elicited step by step the receipt and transmittal of the papers. . . . The trial then resumed before the jury. . . .

Defense counsel and defense psychiatrists were thus subjected to a humiliating experience. Later the prosecutor berated them in his summation. He said "the defense in this case — I am sorry to say this — has been concocted"; . . . that Mr. Saltzman was "in cahoots with Doctors Galen and Chodosh and perpetrated a fraud on this Court"; and "how, how can you believe a woman who lends herself to the deception that was practiced on the Court, on this Court by the doctors and her attorney? Certainly she knew about it."

The trial judge did not stop this unjustifiable attack. On the contrary he intervened in a way that tended to sustain it. . . .

When the basis of the change in the experts' opinion was explored, it quickly appeared that the change was thoroughly consistent with honesty however mistaken it might be. In the minds of the witnesses the change involved no alteration whatever in their medical findings. Rather it stemmed from an altered understanding of the law's concept of insanity. Specifically, the doctors originally understood that the "disease of the mind" required by the *M'Naghten* concept of legal insanity to which we adhere, means a *psychosis* and not some lesser illness or functional aberration. As the result of their pretrial debate with Mr. Saltzman, the doctors concluded they had had too narrow a view of *M'Naghten* and that the "anxiety neurosis" they had found did qualify as a "disease" within the legal rule, and hence when the anxiety reached a "panic" state, "meaning simply a severe disorganizing degree of anxiety," defendant did not know right from wrong and she did not know what she was doing was wrong because of that "disease." . . .

The change in the opinions of the defense psychiatrists simply focuses attention upon an area of undeniable obscurity. As we have said, the *M'Naghten* rule requires a "disease of the mind." The competing concepts of legal insanity also require a disease (or defect) of the mind. . . . But the hard question under any concept of legal insanity is, What constitutes a "disease"? . . . The postulate is that some wrongdoers are sick while others are bad, and that it is against good morals to stigmatize the sick. Who then are the sick whose illness shows they are free of moral blame? We cannot turn to the psychiatrist for a list of illnesses which have that quality because, for all his insight into the dynamics of behavior, he has not solved the riddle of blame. The question remains an ethical one, the answer to which lies beyond scientific truth.

The *M'Naghten* rule does not identify the disease which will excuse, but rather stresses a specific effect of disease, i.e., that at the time of the committing of the act the accused was laboring under a defect of reason such as not to know the nature and quality of the act he was doing, or, if he did know it, that he did not know what he was doing was wrong. But although emphasis is thus upon a state of mind, it is nonetheless required that that state be due to "disease" and not something else. So our cases contrast that concept of insanity with "emotional insanity" or "moral insanity" which, upon the dichotomy mentioned above, is attributed to moral depravity or weakness and hence will not excuse the offender even if his rage was so blinding that he did not really appreciate what he was doing or that it was wrong. . . . Yet the traditional charge of the *M'Naghten* rule to the jury does not attempt to say what is meant by "disease," and [there is a] rather universal reluctance to assay a definition. . . .

We have described the problem, not to resolve it, but simply to reveal the room for disputation, to the end of demonstrating the unfairness of charging defendant, her attorney, and her witnesses with a fraud when the change in the experts' opinion, however frivolous it may be in law, involved no departure from prior medical findings but rather a change in the witnesses' understanding of what the law means by "disease." . . .

The judgment is reversed. . . .

NOTES AND QUESTIONS

1. Questions on Guido. Is "mental disease" a medical or a legal concept? If the former, why was it legitimate for defense counsel to tell the psychiatrists what it meant? But if the latter, why were the psychiatrists allowed to express their conclusions about it at all? In what sense were they "experts" in the meaning of a legal concept?

2. A legal definition of "disease." Most courts seem to assume that "mental disease" for purposes of the insanity defense is a legal, not a medical concept. But then how should the legal concept of disease be defined? Few courts have supplied a definition, or even indicated the general criteria that help determine when this legal element is present. Consider whether the following formulation is helpful (McDonald v. United States, 312 F.2d 847, 850-851 (D.C. Cir. 1962)):

> What psychiatrists may consider a "mental disease or defect" for clinical purposes, where their concern is treatment, may or may not be the same as mental disease or defect for the jury's purpose in determining criminal responsibility. Consequently, for that purpose the jury should be told that a mental disease or defect includes any abnormal condition of the mind which substantially affects mental or emotional processes and substantially impairs behavior controls.

Compare the definition proposed by the American Psychiatric Association, supra pages 954-955:

> [T]he terms mental disease or mental retardation include only those severely abnormal mental conditions that grossly and demonstrably impair a person's perception or understanding of reality and that are not attributable primarily to the voluntary ingestion of alcohol or other psychoactive substances.

Another attempt at definition, offered by the American Bar Association, supra page 954, states that mental disease

> refers to impairments of mind, whether enduring or transitory, or to mental retardation which substantially affected the mental or emotional processes of the defendant at the time of the alleged offense.

3. Problem. Suppose that psychiatric examination indicates that the defendant, because of "explosive personality disorder," lacks the capacity to "appreciate" the wrongfulness of his aggressive, violent reactions. Does he qualify for the insanity defense? Should the answer depend on whether the psychiatric profession classifies this abnormality as a "personality disorder" rather than as a psychosis? Consider whether the *McDonald* definition helps resolve the difficulties. The defendant's situation presumably is "abnormal," but is it a "condition of the mind" within the meaning of *McDonald*? Is this a legal or a medical question? Apart from the *McDonald* formulation, what is the "right" result in a case like this one?

4. Battered spouse syndrome. Defendants usually offer evidence of battered spouse syndrome to support a claim of self-defense, but sometimes the defense may find it useful to present as an alternative theory that the battered woman was not guilty by reason of insanity. Trial courts often admit battered spouse evidence for that purpose, see, e.g., People v. Gindorf, 512 N.E.2d 770, 773 (Ill. App. 1987), but many of the appellate decisions assume that battered spouse syndrome is not a mental disease for purposes of the insanity defense. E.g., Bechtel v. State, 840 P.2d 1, 7 (Okla. Cr. App. 1992); State v. Myers, 570 A.2d 1260, 1266 (N.J. Super. 1990). What is the basis for this view? Should battered wife syndrome be classified as a mental disease under the definitions of "disease" considered in Note 2 supra?

5. Compulsive gambling disorder. In several cases defendants have offered testimony to the effect that they suffer from "pathological gambling," an impulse control disorder recognized in the Diagnostic and Statistical Manual of the

American Psychiatric Association.[21] Such defendants have also offered to prove that this disorder renders them unable to refrain from gambling and unable to avoid criminal activities to raise funds to gamble or to meet gambling debts. Most courts to date have excluded the expert testimony on the ground that there is not yet a sufficient scientific consensus that pathological gambling disorder substantially affects capacity to refrain from the specific criminal acts charged. See, e.g., United States v. Gould, 741 F.2d 45 (4th Cir. 1984) (attempted bank robbery); United States v. Torniero, 735 F.2d 725 (2d. Cir. 1984) (interstate transportation of stolen jewelry); United States v. Lewellyn, 723 F.2d 615 (8th Cir. 1983) (embezzlement of over $17 million from two Iowa banks). Compare State v. Lafferty, 189 Conn. 360, 456 A.2d 272 (1983), where the testimony was admitted and a defendant charged with embezzling $300,000 was acquitted at trial.

Should a compulsion to gamble be treated as a "mental disease" for purposes of the insanity defense? Should the answer depend on whether (or how) this disorder can be treated?

6. *Premenstrual syndrome.* Some medical researchers believe that hormone fluctuations and other bodily changes during the menstrual cycle can produce extreme alteration of normal emotional processes and behavioral controls in some women. Once recognized, the condition sometimes can be treated successfully with regular injections of progesterone. See especially Katharina Dalton, The Premenstrual Syndrome and Progesterone Therapy (2d ed. 1984). In two highly publicized English cases, women who killed while reportedly suffering from premenstrual syndrome (PMS) avoided murder convictions. The evidence was considered admissible under the English doctrine of diminished responsibility (see page 1009 infra), and after conviction on the lesser charge of manslaughter, both women avoided imprisonment and received probation or a suspended sentence. Many physicians and attorneys welcomed this development as giving deserved attention to a severe but long-neglected medical problem. A number of writers have suggested that PMS might sometimes afford a basis for a complete acquittal on grounds of insanity. See, e.g., A. Wallach & L. Rubin, The Premenstrual Syndrome and Criminal Responsibility, 19 U.C.L.A.L. Rev. 209 (1971). There has been little litigation on this issue in the United States, but two trial-level dispositions illustrate the possibilities. In a 1991 Virginia case, a woman charged with drunk driving was acquitted on the basis of evidence that PMS had caused her erratic driving behavior. See Note, Has the PMS Defense Gained a Legitimate Toehold in Virginia Criminal Law?, 14 Geo. Mason L. Rev. 427 (1991). In a 1981 New York case, Shirley Santos, charged with two felony counts for severely beating her four-year-old daughter, sought dismissal on the ground that she had been in a state of unconsciousness due to PMS. After the presiding judge indicated some sympathy for the claim, prosecutors permitted Santos to plead guilty to a misdemeanor, and she received a suspended sentence.[22] Consider Elizabeth Holtzman, Premenstrual Symptoms: No Legal Defense, 60 St. Johns L. Rev. 712, 714-715 (1986):

_____

21. See Am. Psychiatric Assn., Diagnostic and Statistical Manual of Mental Disorders: DSM-IV, 615-618 (4th ed. 1994).

22. Santos later lost custody of her daughter, apparently in part because of her susceptibility to PMS.

Because diagnosis of "premenstrual syndrome" relies solely on information from the presumed sufferer or one who has observed her, there is no way of proving its presence scientifically — or disproving its presence. Thus, its diagnosis may be easily feigned. Just as bad, a woman wrongfully charged with having "premenstrual syndrome" would have no medical or scientific way of disproving it. For example, a woman charged with suffering from premenstrual syndrome by her husband seeking custody of their children would have no scientific way of refuting his claim. . . .

The mistaken notion of premenstrual symptoms as a cause of violence by women could seriously undermine women's progress in the workplace and elsewhere. For example, employers could claim their female employees suffered from premenstrual syndrome, and become violent once a month and therefore fire or refuse to promote them. What an expedient way to end the employment gains women have made.

Certainly, the women who experience discomfort or pain in connection with their menstrual cycle deserve to have these symptoms studied in a serious, scientific way so that the symptoms may be alleviated. For far too long the discomfort, pain, or other symptoms triggered by the onset of the menses have been ignored as medically unimportant or trivial. We need much more research so that women can get the effective help they need.

Should evidence relating to PMS be admissible in the case of a woman who kills while suffering its symptoms? Should such a defendant be entitled to jury instructions on the insanity defense? For a helpful examination of the PMS issue, see Christopher Boorse, Premenstrual Syndrome and Criminal Responsibility, in Premenstrual Syndrome 81-124 (B. E. Ginsburg & B. F. Carter eds. 1987).

7. *Postpartum disorders.* Psychologists estimate that 50-80 percent of new mothers experience at least a mild form of "the blues" following childbirth, and 10-20 percent of new mothers suffer a serious form of clinical depression, including feelings of great despondency, fatigue, anxiety, and inadequacy. The depressive state can be quite severe, and women suffering from this condition often experience thoughts of suicide or infanticide. In a limited number of cases (1 to 2 in 10,000) new mothers suffer from postpartum psychosis, an extreme form of the condition, characterized by inability to distinguish fantasy from reality, visual or auditory hallucinations, and other severe psychiatric symptoms. Women who kill their newborns often plead mental disorder, and in one survey of 20 recent cases, half the women were acquitted by reason of insanity, one-quarter received light sentences such as probation, and one-quarter received severe sentences ranging from 8 to 20 years in prison. See Laura E. Reece, Comment, Mothers Who Kill: Postpartum Disorders and Criminal Infanticide, 38 U.C.L.A.L. Rev. 699, 701-702, 711-712 (1991). See also R. D. Mackay, The Consequences of Killing Very Young Children, [1993] Crim. L. Rev. 21.

There is no doubt that postpartum psychosis, which involves severe cognitive disturbance, can qualify as a mental disease for purposes of the insanity defense. Courts are less clear, however, about how to classify the less severe postpartum disorders, and whether to afford a defense to a mother who kills her baby because of the severe mood changes triggered by childbirth. What considerations should determine the result?

8. *Multiple personality disorder.* Defendant Denny-Shaffer was charged with kidnapping as a result of her abducting an infant from a hospital and attempting to keep it as her own. Government and defense psychiatrists agreed that Denny-

Shaffer suffered from "multiple personality disorder" (MPD): Defendant's dominant personality ("Gidget") did not participate in the kidnapping, while one or both of her alter-personalities ("Rina" and "Bridget") controlled her conduct at the time. The defense's expert witness could not determine whether either Rina or Bridget was "unable to appreciate the nature and quality or the wrongfulness of [the] acts." The government's expert testified that "[e]ach of the personalities taken alone knew, or was very capable of knowing, what she was doing and of making moral judgments." Is MPD a "mental disease"? Even if it is, does the defendant qualify for an insanity defense? If "Rina" and "Bridget" are "guilty," can "Gidget" be sent to prison? See United States v. Denny-Shaffer, 2 F.3d 999 (10th Cir. 1993).

9. *Post-traumatic stress disorder.* A recognized psychiatric abnormality, post-traumatic stress disorder (PTSD) applies to individuals who have experienced an extraordinarily traumatic event (such as an earthquake, bombing, plane accident, or military combat) and suffer recurrent, vivid recollections of it, together with a variety of associated emotional problems. Such individuals can have unpredictable and inappropriately violent reactions to seemingly ordinary encounters that in some small detail recall for them the traumatic experience. Sometimes called the "Vietnam Vet Syndrome," PTSD has become quite important to the medical and legal problems of combat veterans, and one authority estimates that from 500,000 to 1,500,000 Vietnam veterans may suffer from PTSD. See C. Peter Erlinder, Paying the Price for Vietnam: Post-Traumatic Stress Disorder and Criminal Behavior, 25 B.C.L. Rev. 305 (1984). The PTSD defense is now frequent in cases of veterans accused of both violent and nonviolent offenses. Consider Erlinder, supra at 321-326:

> In . . . a 1982 case in Chicago, Illinois, the defendant was charged with attempted murder in the shooting of his foreman after a dispute at work. Jearl Wood was accused of drinking on the job by his foreman and was given a breathalyzer test by a nurse that apparently confirmed the foreman's charge. As a result, he was sent out of the plant. Mr. Wood then went to his car in the parking lot, returned to the plant and, in front of several dozen witnesses, fired twice, severely wounding the foreman. . . .
>
> Mr. Wood was a veteran who had no criminal record. He was married, had a family and possessed a good work record. . . .
>
> [At trial] Mr. Wood's service records and those of his unit were read into evidence . . . in order to verify his combat service and to illustrate the conditions in Vietnam; . . .
>
> . . . Dr. Bennett Braun, a former army captain and a psychiatrist, who had treated the defendant, testified that he had toured the plant and that the sights and sounds of the plant were much like combat. Tape recordings of loud plant sounds and photographs of physical conditions were made by the psychiatrist to illustrate his testimony. . . . Dr. John Wilson . . . testified that Mr. Wood's attempts to get psychiatric treatment in 1979, his bouts with alcohol, his strange behavior at the plant the night of the shooting, and the shooting incident itself all grew out of his reactions to Vietnam. In Mr. Wood's case, the precipitating incidents that caused the PTSD reaction were the death of a brother, also a Vietnam veteran, with whom he was very close and the threat of the loss of his job.
>
> The testimony at trial tended to establish that Mr. Wood entered a "survivor mode" of behavior before and during the shooting. . . . For a brief time Mr. Wood was once again the frightened eighteen-year-old Marine who carried his .45 caliber

automatic pistol everywhere and who survived his traumatic Vietnam experiences by learning to react without thinking.

Because Illinois had adopted the Model Penal Code test for insanity, the jury was asked to decide whether Mr. Wood could "substantially appreciate the criminality of his acts" or "conform his conduct to the law." The general verdict [was] "not guilty by reason of insanity." . . . In a separate commitment hearing after the trial, a psychiatrist for the Illinois Department of Mental Health confirmed the PTSD diagnosis. He also explained that the unique episode that precipitated the PTSD reaction which led to the shooting did not indicate that Mr. Wood was dangerous at the time of the hearing, nor that he would be dangerous in the future. As a result, Mr. Wood was released to receive court-supervised outpatient care. . . .

10. *Alcohol and drug addiction.* Medical opinion has differed sharply on the question whether alcoholics and drug addicts suffer from a "disease" (or from a "mental" disease). The underlying issues, which can affect substantial numbers of criminal defendants, are explored in depth beginning at page 1011 infra.

11. *Questions on the disease concept.* If a defendant suffers from an impairment of cognition or control sufficiently serious to satisfy the prevailing insanity test, why should it matter that the impairment results not from disease but only from a "personality disorder"? Isn't blame inappropriate (and deterrence unlikely) in either case? In other words, why *bother* to define disease? This issue can be considered with respect to the problems posed in each of the preceding Notes. In addition, consider the problem of the "psychopath," explored in the Notes that follow.

NOTES ON THE PSYCHOPATH

A major issue of policy for the insanity defense concerns its application to the psychopath — the offender with a long history of antisocial conduct. Many persistent offenders "know" (in a purely verbal way) that their conduct is illegal, but they experience little or no empathy and have no apparent capacity to "understand" (at the "affective," emotional level) the rights of others. Their behavior brings them repeatedly into conflict with others and with the law. Often psychiatrists diagnose them as suffering from "psychopathic personality" or "sociopathic personality," now more commonly designated "antisocial personality disorder," and many mental health professionals regard the disorder as a "mental disease." Is such an offender legally insane?

1. *The Model Penal Code approach.* Section 4.01(2) of the Code, commonly referred to as the "caveat paragraph," states that "the terms 'mental disease or defect' do not include an abnormality manifested only by repeated criminal or otherwise antisocial conduct." The Reporter's Comment states (Tent. Draft No. 4, 1955, at 160) that this section "is designed to exclude from the concept of 'mental disease or defect' the case of the so-called 'psychopathic personality.'"

Consider State v. Werlein, 401 N.W.2d 848 (Wis. Ct. App. 1987). The defendant, who was armed with a semiautomatic rifle, opened fire on another man (for reasons not fully explained). He fired 25 to 30 shots, inflicting serious injury. He was convicted of attempted first-degree murder. At trial he had called

Dr. Albert Lorenz, who diagnosed him as suffering from antisocial personality disorder:

> Lorenz testified that Werlein's [symptoms] included an inability to handle work, squandering money, lack of attachment to people or groups, and reckless behavior. Lorenz stated that Werlein has no personality of his own, cannot plan for the future, and follows others much like a little child would. Lorenz concluded that as a result of Werlein's illness, he could not conform his conduct to the requirements of law.

The trial court struck Dr. Lorenz's testimony and precluded the jury from considering whether Werlein was mentally irresponsible. The court of appeals reversed, holding that Wis. Stat. §971.15(2) (identical to the Model Penal Code "caveat paragraph") was inapplicable: "[Dr. Lorenz's] diagnosis goes far beyond that of an abnormality manifested only by repeated criminal or otherwise antisocial conduct." A dissenting judge objected:

> Lorenz describes the common symptoms of the antisocial personality disorder as people who seldom hold a job, are not loyal to any person, group, code or religion. They basically have an undeveloped conscience and they have no super ego. This is all founded on the theory that the "disorder" started early in life and remained uncorrected. Consequently, the sufferer becomes a product of his or her environment.
>
> The result is that persons such as Werlein are able, but fail to accept the social norms with respect to legal behavior. I suspect that a "spoiled brat" who turns to crime as an adult would fit Lorenz's description of a person with an antisocial personality disorder unable to conform his conduct to the requirements of law. Also, a person who is raised in a criminal environment would probably fall within a similar diagnosis. . . .
>
> Wisconsin has not, and should not, recognize this type of "disorder" as a legal defense under sec. 971.15. . . .

Questions: Does Model Penal Code §4.01(2) achieve its intended purpose? Consider Wade v. United States, 426 F.2d 64, 73 (9th Cir. 1970): "[I]t is practically inconceivable that a mental disease or defect would, in the terms of paragraph (2), be 'manifested *only* by repeated criminal or otherwise antisocial conduct' (emphasis added)." If the Model Penal Code text is inadequate to achieve the broad exclusion intended by its drafters, should it be amended? How?

2. The merits of the issue. As a matter of policy, should a defendant like Werlein qualify for the insanity defense? Such individuals appear to have very limited capacity to identify with others, to experience guilt (or other emotions) and to learn from experience. Can the psychopath be deterred? Or blamed? On the other hand, the dangerous psychopath presumably should not simply be released. Where should such a person be confined and for how long? Consider United States v. Currens, 290 F.2d 751, 761-763 (3d Cir. 1961):

> We are aware that some jurists and legal scholars are of the view that, as a matter of law, a psychopath is not "insane." This view seems to be based on a fear that [any other] rule . . . would open the door to the acquittal of persons accused of crime solely on the basis of a history of recurrent antisocial conduct. It is readily

apparent that this objection . . . assumes a particular definition of psychopathy; viz., that the term psychopathy comprehends a person who is a habitual criminal but whose mind is functioning normally. [But] as the majority of experts use the term, a psychopath is very distinguishable from one who merely demonstrates recurrent criminal behavior. . . .

One of the most respected, perhaps the leading, modern work on psychopathy is The Mask of Sanity by Hervey Cleckley, M.D. (1941). Dr. Cleckley's findings are best summarized in Professor Robert W. White's, The Abnormal Personality (1948) at p. 401 as follows: "He [Cleckley] rules out those cases in which social standards are rejected only in respect to some one particular kind of behavior: for example, alcoholism or deviant sexual behavior in a person otherwise adapted to social demands. He also rules out those cases in which delinquency and crime have been adopted as a positive way of life — in which the person is an enemy of society but is capable of being a loyal and stable member of a delinquent gang. There remains a group characterized by a diffuse and chronic incapacity for persistent, ordered living of any kind. These are, in Cleckley's view, the true psychopathic personalities. . . . It is clear that we are dealing with a fairly serious disorder. . . . Although the patient outwardly presents a 'convincing mask of sanity' and a 'mimicry of human life,' he has lost contact with the deeper emotional accompaniments of experience and with its purposiveness. To this extent he may be said to have an incomplete contact with reality, and it is certainly very hard to approach him and influence him therapeutically."[a]

Thus, it can be seen that in many cases the adjective "psychopathic" will be applied by experts to persons who are very ill indeed. It would not be proper for this court in this case to deprive a large heterogeneous group of offenders of the defense of insanity by holding blindly and indiscriminately that a person described as psychopathic is always criminally responsible.

[A]ll the pertinent symptoms of the accused should be put before the court and jury and the accused's criminal responsibility should be developed from the totality of his symptoms. A court of law is not an appropriate forum for a debate as to the meaning of abstract psychiatric classifications.

A different view is indicated in a leading psychiatric treatment manual. The authors discuss their recommendations for "Tom," a patient who presents the classic symptoms of an antisocial (psychopathic) personality disorder (Samuel Perry, Allen Frances & John Clarkin, A DSM-III Casebook of Differential Therapeutics 304-305 (1985)):

> This 21-year-old man . . . has already been arrested 50 times and been in scrapes with the law on another 150 occasions. He is a barroom brawler, a thief, and a runaway who has never formed meaningful attachments to anyone. . . .
>
> His behavioral problems have a long and consistent history. In childhood he couldn't or wouldn't tell the truth. He was truant from school and stole from both his family and others. He set fires, killed animals needlessly, and frequently vandalized property, always covering his tracks with alibis. Throughout his childhood and during his entire adolescence, multiple attempts have been made to alter his behavior by psychiatric treatment or confinement. All these efforts have failed.

---

a. For discussion of psychopathic behavior and current psychiatric views concerning the diagnosis of the condition, see Comment, The Psychopath and the Definition of "Mental Disease or Defect" Under the Model Penal Code Test of Insanity: A Question of Psychology or a Question of Law?, 69 Neb. L. Rev. 190 (1990). — EDS.

. . . Because Tom has limited control of his behavior, the consultant might understandably wish to protect him from legal action and to help him overcome rather than be punished for emotional problems. At present, however, there is no treatment for Tom's disorder that is very effective — and the provision of an ineffective treatment will make it even worse. Once Tom is offered the opportunity to become a psychiatric patient as a refuge from legal responsibility, he will have even less reason to apply whatever controls are within his power. In addition, if Tom is sent to a hospital instead of a jail, he is likely to become a wolf, preying on the weaknesses of mental patients who are especially unable to protect themselves. He might also study the other patients to learn the particular signs and symptoms of mental illness that will provide him with even more convincing excuses in the future and enable him to be transferred to a hospital and avoid going to jail.

Rather than offering Tom psychiatric treatment instead of imprisonment, the consultant might suggest psychiatric treatment only if he still needs it after he is placed in a highly controlled and structured correctional setting. He might then be more receptive to a behavioral or an exploratory psychotherapy program. The consultant's best contribution in this case is to make clear to the legal and correctional authorities that our capacity to treat antisocial personality disorders is extremely limited and that these individuals should not avoid punishment by being referred for a treatment that does not exist.

(v) Disposition after Acquittal

JONES v. UNITED STATES

Supreme Court of the United States
463 U.S. 354 (1983)

JUSTICE POWELL delivered the opinion of the Court.

The question presented is whether petitioner, who was committed to a mental hospital upon being acquitted of a criminal offense by reason of insanity, must be released because he has been hospitalized for a period longer than he might have served in prison had he been convicted.

In the District of Columbia a criminal defendant may be acquitted by reason of insanity if his insanity is "affirmatively established by a preponderance of the evidence." D.C. Code §24-301(j) (1981). If he successfully invokes the insanity defense, he is committed to a mental hospital. §24-301(d)(1). The statute provides several ways of obtaining release. Within 50 days of commitment the acquittee is entitled to a judicial hearing to determine his eligibility for release, at which he has the burden of proving by a preponderance of the evidence either that he is no longer mentally ill or that he is no longer dangerous. §24-301(d)(2). If he fails to meet this burden at the 50-day hearing, the committed acquittee subsequently may be released, with court approval, upon certification of his recovery by the hospital chief of service. Alternatively, the acquittee is entitled to a judicial hearing every six months at which he may establish by a preponderance of the evidence that he is entitled to release.

Independent of its provision for the commitment of insanity acquittees, the District of Columbia also has adopted a civil-commitment procedure, under which an individual may be committed upon clear and convincing proof by the Government that he is mentally ill and likely to injure himself or others. The individual may demand a jury in the civil-commitment proceeding. Once committed, a patient may be released at any time upon certification of recovery by the hospital chief of service. Alternatively, the patient is entitled after the first 90 days, and subsequently at 6-month intervals, to request a judicial hearing at which he may gain his release by proving by a preponderance of the evidence that he is no longer mentally ill or dangerous.

On September 19, 1975, petitioner was arrested for attempting to steal a jacket from a department store. The next day he was arraigned in the District of Columbia Superior Court on a charge of attempted petit larceny, a misdemeanor punishable by a maximum prison sentence of one year. The court ordered petitioner committed to St. Elizabeths, a public hospital for the mentally ill, for a determination of his competency to stand trial. . . . The court ruled that petitioner was competent to stand trial. Petitioner subsequently decided to plead not guilty by reason of insanity. The Government did not contest the plea, and [on] March 12, 1976, the Superior Court found petitioner not guilty by reason of insanity and committed him to St. Elizabeths pursuant to §24-301(d)(1).

On May 25, 1976, the court held the 50-day hearing required by §24-301(d)(2)(A). A psychologist from St. Elizabeths testified on behalf of the Government that, in the opinion of the staff, petitioner continued to suffer from paranoid schizophrenia and that "because his illness is still quite active, he is still a danger to himself and to others." . . . The court then found that "the defendant-patient is mentally ill and as a result of his mental illness, at this time, he constitutes a danger to himself or others." Petitioner was returned to St. Elizabeths. . . . [A] second release hearing was held on February 22, 1977. By that date petitioner had been hospitalized for more than one year, the maximum period he could have spent in prison if he had been convicted. On [this] basis he demanded that he be released unconditionally or recommitted pursuant to the civil-commitment standards in §21-545(b), including a jury trial and proof by clear and convincing evidence of his mental illness and dangerousness. The Superior Court denied petitioner's request . . . and continued petitioner's commitment to St. Elizabeths. [The court of appeals affirmed, and the Supreme Court granted certiorari.]

It is clear that "commitment for any purpose constitutes a significant deprivation of liberty that requires due process protection." Addington v. Texas, 441 U.S. 418, 425 (1979). Therefore, a State must have "a constitutionally adequate purpose for the confinement." O'Connor v. Donaldson, 422 U.S. 563, 574 (1975). . . . Petitioner does not contest the Government's authority to commit a mentally ill and dangerous person indefinitely to a mental institution, but rather contends that "the petitioner's trial was not a constitutionally adequate hearing to justify an indefinite commitment."

Petitioner's argument rests principally on Addington v. Texas, supra, in which the Court held that the Due Process Clause requires the Government in a civil-commitment proceeding to demonstrate by clear and convincing evidence that the individual is mentally ill and dangerous. Petitioner contends that these due process standards were not met in his case because the judgment of not guilty by reason of insanity did not constitute a finding of present mental illness and dangerousness and because it was established only by a preponderance of the evidence. Petitioner then concludes that the Government's only conceivably legitimate justification for automatic commitment is to ensure that insanity acquittees do not escape confinement entirely, and that this interest can justify commitment at most for a period equal to the maximum prison sentence the acquittee could have received if convicted. Because petitioner has been hospitalized for longer than the one year he might have served in prison, he asserts that he should be released unconditionally or recommitted under the District's civil-commitment procedures.

We turn first to the question whether the finding of insanity at the criminal trial is sufficiently probative of mental illness and dangerousness to justify commitment. . . .

The fact that a person has been found, beyond a reasonable doubt, to have committed a criminal act certainly indicates dangerousness. . . . We do not agree with petitioner's suggestion that the requisite dangerousness is not established by proof that a person committed a non-violent crime against property. This Court never has held that "violence," however that term might be defined, is a prerequisite for a constitutional commitment.[14]

Nor can we say that it was unreasonable for Congress to determine that the insanity acquittal supports an inference of continuing mental illness. It comports with common sense to conclude that someone whose mental illness was sufficient to lead him to commit a criminal act is likely to remain ill and in need to treatment. . . . Because a hearing is provided within 50 days of the commitment, there is assurance that every acquittee has prompt opportunity to obtain release if he has recovered.

Petitioner also argues that, whatever the evidentiary value of the insanity acquittal, the Government lacks a legitimate reason for committing insanity acquittees automatically because it can introduce the insanity acquittal as evidence in a subsequent civil proceeding. This argument fails to consider the Government's strong interest in avoiding the need to conduct a de novo commitment hearing following every insanity acquittal — a hearing at which a jury trial may be demanded, and at which the Government bears the burden of proof by clear and convincing evidence. . . . We therefore conclude that a finding of not guilty by reason of insanity is a sufficient foundation for commitment of an insanity acquittee for the purposes of treatment and the protection of society.

Petitioner next contends that his indefinite commitment is unconstitutional because the proof of his insanity was based only on a preponderance of the evidence, as compared to *Addington*'s civil-commitment requirement of proof by clear and convincing evidence. In equating these situations, petitioner ignores important differences between the class of potential civil-commitment candidates and the class of insanity acquittees that justify differing standards of proof. The *Addington* Court expressed particular concern that members of the public could be confined on the basis of "some abnormal behavior which might be perceived by some as symptomatic of a mental or emotional disorder, but which is in fact within a range of conduct that is generally acceptable." In view of this concern, the Court deemed it inappropriate to ask the individual "to share

14. See Overholser v. O'Beirne, 302 F.2d 852, 861 (1961) (Burger, J.) ("[T]o describe the theft of watches and jewelry as 'non-dangerous' is to confuse danger with violence. Larceny is usually less violent than murder or assault, but in terms of public policy the purpose of the statute is the same as to both."). It also may be noted that crimes of theft frequently may result in violence from the efforts of the criminal to escape or the victim to protect property or the police to apprehend the fleeing criminal. . . .

equally with society the risk of error." But since automatic commitment under §24-301(d)(1) follows only if the *acquittee himself* advances insanity as a defense and proves that his criminal act was a product of his mental illness, [such proof] eliminates the risk that he is being committed for mere "idiosyncratic behavior," *Addington,* 441 U.S., at 427. A criminal act by definition is not "within a range of conduct that is generally acceptable."

We therefore conclude that concerns critical to our decision in *Addington* are diminished or absent in the case of insanity acquittees. Accordingly, there is no reason for adopting the same standard of proof in both cases. . . . The preponderance of the evidence standard comports with due process for commitment of insanity acquittees.[17]

The remaining question is whether petitioner nonetheless is entitled to his release because he has been hospitalized for a period longer than he could have been incarcerated if convicted. . . . The purpose of commitment following an insanity acquittal, like that of civil commitment, is to treat the individual's mental illness and protect him and society from his potential dangerousness. . . .

[W]e think petitioner clearly errs in contending that an acquittee's hypothetical maximum sentence provides the constitutional limit for his commitment. . . . As he was not convicted, he may not be punished. His confinement rests on his continuing illness and dangerousness. Thus, under the District of Columbia statute, no matter how serious the act committed by the acquittee, he may be released within 50 days of his acquittal if he has recovered. In contrast, one who committed a less serious act may be confined for a longer period if he remains ill and dangerous. There simply is no necessary correlation between severity of the offense and length of time necessary for recovery. The length of the acquittee's hypothetical criminal sentence therefore is irrelevant to the purposes of his commitment.

[Our] holding accords with the widely and reasonably held view that insanity acquittees constitute a special class that should be treated differently from other candidates for commitment. . . .

The judgment of the District of Columbia Court of Appeals is affirmed.

JUSTICE BRENNAN, with whom JUSTICES MARSHALL and BLACKMUN join, dissenting.

The Court begins by posing the wrong question. The issue in this case is not whether petitioner must be released because he has been hospitalized for longer than the prison sentence he might have served had he been convicted. . . . The question before us is whether the fact that an individual has been found "not guilty by reason of insanity," by itself, provides a constitutionally adequate basis for involuntary, indefinite commitment to psychiatric hospitalization. . . .

Commentators and researchers have long acknowledged that even the best attempts to identify dangerous individuals on the basis of specified facts have been inaccurate roughly two-thirds of the time, almost always on the side of overprediction. . . . Research is practically nonexistent on the relationship of *non-*

---

17. A defendant could be required to prove his insanity by a higher standard than a preponderance of the evidence. See Leland v. Oregon, 343 U.S. 790 (1952). Such an additional requirement hardly would benefit a criminal defendant who wants to raise the insanity defense, yet imposition of a higher standard would be a likely legislative response to a holding that an insanity acquittal could support automatic commitment only if the verdict were supported by clear and convincing evidence.

violent criminal behavior, such as petitioner's attempt to shoplift, to future dangerousness. We do not even know whether it is even statistically valid as a predictor of similar non-violent behavior, much less of behavior posing more serious risks to self and others. . . .

Today's decision. . . . relies on a *connection* between mental condition and criminal conduct that is unique to verdicts of "not guilty by reason of insanity." Yet the relevance of that connection, as opposed to each of its separate components, is far from a matter of obvious "common sense." None of the available evidence that criminal behavior of the mentally ill is likely to repeat itself distinguishes between behaviors that were "the product" of mental illness and those that were not. It is completely unlikely that persons acquitted by reason of insanity display a rate of future "dangerous" activity higher than civil committees with similar arrest records, or than persons convicted of crimes who are later found to be mentally ill. . . .

Given the close similarity of the governmental interests at issue in this case and those at issue in *Addington,* and the highly imperfect "fit" between the findings required for an insanity acquittal and those required . . . to support an indefinite commitment, I cannot agree that the Government should be excused from the burden that *Addington* held was required by due process. . . .

Justice Stevens, dissenting.

. . . What Justice Powell has written lends support to the view that the *initial* confinement of the acquittee is permissible, but provides no support for the conclusion that he has the burden of proving his entitlement to freedom after he has served the maximum sentence authorized by law. I respectfully dissent because I believe this shoplifter was presumptively entitled to his freedom after he had been incarcerated for a period of one year.

NOTES AND QUESTIONS

1. Questions on Jones. *(a) The presumption of insanity.* The argument for upholding automatic initial commitment rests in large part on the presumption of continuing insanity. Since *Jones* authorizes automatic commitment without a hearing, isn't the presumption in effect *conclusive?*

(b) The opportunity to seek release. Are doubts about the adequacy of the initial commitment hearing allayed by the 50-day release hearing and the right to petition for release thereafter? Note that the 50-day release hearing may be "waived." Thus an insanity acquittee, who is "presumed" to suffer continuing mental illness and who is receiving involuntary treatment (which may include psychotropic drugs), is permitted to waive a hearing. Does this make sense? Arguably, the right to petition later for release provides some reassurance, but consider Fasulo v. Arafeh, 173 Conn. 473, 378 A.2d 553, 557 (1977):

> [T]hough the Statute provides for annual notice to patients of their right to a hearing, the burden of requesting and, therefore, initiating review remains with the patient. The state seeks to justify this procedure by arguing that allowing the patient to choose whether to have a hearing will avoid unnecessary judicial proceedings. We doubt whether this rationale is adequate since it ignores the practical difficulties of requiring a mental patient to overcome the effects of his confine-

ment, his closed environment, his possible incompetence and the debilitating effects of drugs or other treatment on his ability to make a decision which may amount to the waiver of his constitutional right to a review of his status.

The potential consequences of this approach were brought to light by litigation involving the mental hospital population in New York (United States ex rel. Schuster v. Herold, 410 F.2d 1071, 1079 (2d Cir. 1969)):

> Matteawan has 119 inmates who have been confined there since 1935, 29 since 1925, and 4 patients who have been there since at least 1915 — over half a century. . . . [A]s of November 1, 1965, one inmate, then 83 years old, had been at Matteawan since 1901. . . . [A]nother individual was accused of stealing a horse and buggy in 1905 . . . [and] was released 59 years later at the age of 89 because he was no longer a menace to society or other patients. . . . [Another patient] wrongfully [spent] 24 years in Dannemora because he had stolen candy valued at $5.00 at the age of 16.

(c) *The burden of proof at the criminal trial.* In *Jones* insanity had been established by a preponderance of the evidence at the criminal trial. Are the presumption of continuing insanity and policy of automatic commitment justified if state law requires acquittal on the basis of only a reasonable doubt about sanity? One answer may be that the defendant himself *pleaded* insanity. But should the plea be interpreted as asserting only that there is a reasonable doubt about sanity? If so, automatic commitment would appear difficult to justify under the reasoning of *Jones.* If, however, a case presents serious doubts about whether the defendant's place of confinement should be a prison or a hospital, would it make sense to conclude that he cannot be confined at all?

2. *Constitutional requirements governing release. Jones* deals with the validity of the automatic initial commitment but does not address the standards and procedures governing release. Consider the following problems.

(a) Arizona statutes provide that in cases involving physical injury, a person acquitted by reason of insanity shall be automatically committed and shall not be entitled to a release hearing for at least 230 days. Should it be permissible to hold an acquittee during this period if he can prove that he has recovered his sanity? See State ex rel. Collins v. Superior Court, 150 Ariz. 295, 723 P.2d 644 (1986), holding the statute unconstitutional on the ground that acquittees have a due process right to a prompt opportunity to establish their recovery. If 230 days is too long, what period should be permissible? What is the justification for the 50-day delay apparently permitted by *Jones?*

(b) 18 U.S.C. §4243 provides for hospitalization of federal insanity acquittees. After an initial commitment for observation and examination, the statute requires a hearing to determine whether the acquittee should be released. Section 4243(d) provides that at such a hearing:

> a person found not guilty only by reason of insanity of an offense involving bodily injury to, or serious damage to the property of, another person, or involving a substantial risk of such injury or damage, has the burden of proving by clear and convincing evidence that his release would not create a substantial risk of bodily injury to another person or serious damage of property of another due to a present

mental disease or defect. With respect to any other offense, the person has the burden of such proof by a preponderance of the evidence.

If the acquittee is committed after the initial hearing, then in any subsequent proceeding he must satisfy the burden of proof specified in §4243(d) in order to obtain his release. See §4243(f).

Questions: Are these burden of proof provisions constitutional? Are they justified by the Court's reasoning in *Jones?*

(c) Prosecuted for burglary, Foucha was found not guilty by reason of insanity and committed to a psychiatric hospital. Four years later, a doctor at the hospital determined that Foucha was no longer mentally ill, but the doctor also reported that Foucha was an untreatable "antisocial personality" and that while in the hospital, Foucha had committed several assaults against other inmates. The doctor therefore refused to certify that Foucha was no longer a danger to himself or others. The Louisiana statute provided that, to obtain release, an insanity acquittee must prove both that he is no longer mentally ill and that he is no longer dangerous. Accordingly, the state courts ordered Foucha's continued incarceration.

In Foucha v. Louisiana, 112 S. Ct. 1780 (1992), the Supreme Court reversed and held the Louisiana scheme unconstitutional. The Court first noted that because Foucha was not suffering from a mental disease, it was irrational (and hence a violation of due process) to hold him in a mental hospital as a mentally ill person. In addition, the Court held, Foucha's alleged dangerousness did not warrant confining him for the protection of others. The court acknowledged that prior precedent, notably United States v. Salerno, 481 U.S. 739 (1987), had permitted preventive detention of dangerous defendants prior to trial and in a few other limited circumstances. But the Court refused to extend *Salerno* to permit approval of Louisiana's statutory scheme, stating (112 S. Ct. at 1786-1787):

> Unlike the sharply focused scheme at issue in *Salerno,* the Louisiana scheme of confinement is not carefully limited. Under the state statute, Foucha is not now entitled to an adversary hearing at which the State must prove by clear and convincing evidence that he is demonstrably dangerous to the community. Indeed, the State need prove nothing to justify continued detention, for the statute places the burden on the detainee to prove that he is not dangerous. . . .
>
> Furthermore, if Foucha committed criminal acts while at [the state hospital], such as assault, the State does not explain why its interest would not be vindicated by . . . the normal means of dealing with persistent criminal conduct. Had they been employed against Foucha when he assaulted other inmates, there is little doubt that if then sane he could have been convicted and incarcerated in the usual way.
>
> It was emphasized in *Salerno* that the [pretrial] detention we found constitutionally permissible was strictly limited in duration. Here, in contrast, the State asserts that because Foucha once committed a criminal act and now has an antisocial personality that sometimes leads to aggressive conduct, a disorder for which there is no effective treatment, he may be held indefinitely. This rationale would permit the State to hold indefinitely any other insanity acquittee not mentally ill who could be shown to have a personality disorder that may lead to criminal conduct. The same would be true of any convicted criminal, even though he has completed his prison term. It would also be only a step away from substituting confinements

for dangerousness for our present system which, with only narrow exceptions and aside from permissible confinements for mental illness, incarcerates only those who are proved beyond reasonable doubt to have violated a criminal law.

Questions: Why doesn't the principle that justifies confining mental patients against their will also justify the confinement of those who have recovered their sanity but remain dangerous? Is the theory that we confine the mentally ill for their own benefit? Or is it that we consider predictions of dangerousness more reliable when the person is mentally ill? (Note that available data provide scant support for the latter hypothesis.) Alternatively, does the objection to a general power of preventive detention rest on respect for the autonomy of persons who have ordinary powers of rationality and self-determination? The sane individual may be very dangerous, but he presumably remains subject to the deterrent effect of criminal sanctions, and if he does commit an offense, he can be convicted and incarcerated. If the dangerous insane offender were not subject to preventive detention, how else could he be controlled?

(d) For a helpful discussion of the issues posed by *Jones* and *Foucha*, see Samuel Jan Brakel, After the Verdict: Dispositional Decisions Regarding Criminal Defendants Acquitted by Reason of Insanity, 37 DePaul L. Rev. 181 (1988); James W. Ellis, The Consequences of the Insanity Defense: Proposals to Reform Post-Acquittal Commitment Laws, 35 Cath. U.L. Rev. 961 (1986).

3. *State law restrictions on commitment and release.* Although *Jones* holds that automatic commitment without a hearing is constitutionally permissible, most states have chosen to impose some limitations on commitment following a verdict of not guilty by reason of insanity. At the time of the *Jones* decision, only 14 jurisdictions provided for automatic commitment, while most others used some form of discretionary procedure; 19 states permitted the commitment of insanity acquittees only under the same procedures used for civil commitment. See *Jones,* 463 U.S. at 370 n. 20. The Court's holding in *Jones* apparently has not encouraged more states to follow the automatic commitment route. One survey finds that several states repealed their automatic commitment laws in the wake of *Jones* and that only 10 states currently authorize automatic commitment. See Samuel Jan Brakel, After the Verdict: Dispositional Decisions Regarding Criminal Defendants Acquitted by Reason of Insanity, 37 DePaul L. Rev. 181, 184 n. 11 (1988). In addition, several states permit automatic commitment but limit its duration. Consider the following issues.

(a) *The duration of commitment.* At least 11 states limit the commitment of an insanity acquittee to the maximum prison sentence the defendant could have received if convicted. See Brakel, supra at 196. In such cases, once the "cap" is reached, the insanity acquittee must be released unless the authorities can obtain a commitment order under strict civil commitment standards.

(b) *Commitment procedures.* Many states permit the initial commitment of insanity acquittees only in compliance with the procedures applicable for civil commitment. As a result, insanity acquittees in such jurisdictions are in effect treated exactly like any other mentally disturbed citizen facing civil commitment, not only after expiration of a commitment "cap," but from the very outset. What risks are inherent in this approach?

(c) *Substantive criteria for commitment.* Many jurisdictions permit involuntary commitment of the mentally ill only to prevent violence or serious personal injury. Some of these jurisdictions have no separate procedures for commitment of insanity acquittees and accordingly, the same restrictive substantive criteria limit the grounds for commitment after an insanity acquittal. In Pennsylvania, for example, involuntary treatment of insanity acquittees may be ordered only under the state's general civil commitment statutes. See 50 Pa. Stat. Ann. §7406. Those statutes, moreover, permit commitment only upon showing a clear and present danger of harm to self or others. Harm to self is limited to suicide, self-mutilation or "a reasonable probability [of] death, serious bodily injury or serious physical debilitation." Harm to others is limited to the infliction of "serious bodily harm," and the clear-and-present-danger requirement can be met only by showing behavior actually attempting to inflict the relevant harm in the recent past, together with "a reasonable probability that such conduct will be repeated." 50 Pa. Stat. Ann. §§7301, 7304.

Consider the application of the Pennsylvania regime to a mentally disabled individual like the defendant in *Jones*. If such an individual repeatedly engages in shoplifting, can he be civilly committed? Why do jurisdictions like Pennsylvania in effect bar both punitive and nonpunitive regimes of incapacitation in such cases? Consider State v. Krol, 68 N.J. 236, 344 A.2d 289, 295-296 (1975):

> Dangerous conduct involves not merely violation of social norms enforced by criminal sanctions, but significant physical or psychological injury to persons or substantial destruction of property. . . . Personal liberty and autonomy are of too great value to be sacrificed to protect society against the possibility of future behavior which some may find odd, disagreeable, or offensive, or even against the possibility of future non-dangerous acts which would be ground for criminal prosecution if actually committed. Unlike inanimate objects, people cannot be suppressed simply because they may become public nuisances. . . . It is not sufficient that the state establish a possibility that defendant might commit some dangerous acts at some time in the indefinite future. The risk of danger, a product of the likelihood of such conduct and the degree of harm which may ensue, must be substantial within the reasonably foreseeable future. On the other hand, certainty of prediction is not required and cannot reasonably be expected. . . .

NOTES ON THE VERDICT OF GUILTY BUT MENTALLY ILL

1. Origins. The verdict of "guilty but mentally ill" grew out of Michigan developments that are described in Sharon M. Brown & Nicholas J. Wittner, Criminal Law (1978 Annual Survey of Michigan Law), 25 Wayne L. Rev. 335, 355-358 (1979):

> In 1974, the supreme court decided [in] People v. McQuillan [112] . . . that the statute mandating automatic commitment of a defendant found not guilty by reason of insanity violated due process and equal protection. The court found objectionable that such defendants, unlike persons civilly committed, were not afforded a hearing to determine their mental condition at the time of commitment. . . .
>
> The court made clear that defendants must be released from temporary detention absent a determination that they are mentally ill and dangerous. Finally, the

---

112. 392 Mich. 511, 221 N.W.2d 569 (1974).

court ruled that the release procedures for defendants who are committed after temporary detention must be similar to those for persons civilly committed. . . .

In practice, these procedures have led to horrifying results. Once a patient's symptoms are brought under control by powerful tranquilizing drugs, the Department of Mental Health no longer considers the patient mentally ill for purposes of continued hospitalization. Thus, the patient is prescribed medicine and released. Problems occur when the patient simply decides to discontinue medication. In many such cases, individuals become "time bombs ready to explode."

The danger is best exemplified by the highly publicized cases of John McGee and Ronald Manlen. Both had been committed following verdicts of not guilty by reason of insanity. While institutionalized, McGee claimed to have previously committed some twenty-five other murders. Both men were released from mental institutions after the center for forensic psychiatry determined that they were no longer mentally ill and dangerous. One month after his release, McGee kicked his wife to death. Manlen raped two women shortly after his release.

Apparently in response to public outrage over these incidents, the state legislature enacted a statute authorizing the verdict of "guilty but mentally ill" when a defendant raised an insanity defense. The verdict is appropriate when the judge or jury determines that the defendant (1) is guilty of the offense; (2) was mentally ill at the time of the offense; and (3) was not legally insane at the time of the offense. A judge retains the same sentencing powers as in the case of a general guilty verdict. If, however, the court sentences the defendant to prison, treatment "as is psychiatrically indicated for his mental illness" must be given. . . .

The "guilty but mentally ill" verdict has been assailed by members of the defense bar as well as by mental health personnel in the Department of Corrections. Defense lawyers contend that the intended effect of the verdict is to eviscerate the insanity defense. The argument, in essence, is that in those cases where the jurors are afraid that an insane defendant may be set free under the *McQuillan* procedures, they will view the "guilty but mentally ill" verdict as an acceptable compromise. In the eyes of the jurors, the verdict will be "a vehicle for protecting the public's need for security while simultaneously providing for the defendant's individualized treatment." To defense lawyers, of course, the verdict is merely an illegitimate end run of *McQuillan* and an abolition of the mens rea requirement. Mental health practitioners express concern that neither the Department of Corrections nor the Department of Mental Health can provide the "individualized treatment" envisioned by jurors.

2. *Developments in other jurisdictions.* At least 14 states have followed Michigan's lead in enacting "guilty but mentally ill" (GBMI) legislation.[23] To date, all state courts have upheld the constitutionality of the GBMI verdict. See, e.g., State v. Neely, 112 N.M. 702, 819 P.2d 249 (1991); People v. Ramsey, 422 Mich. 500, 375 N.W.2d 297 (1985).

3. *Administering the GBMI verdict.* One of the ostensible purposes of the GBMI legislation is to afford more suitable treatment to mentally disturbed defendants who are convicted. But the actual disposition of GBMI cases is not necessarily different from that which follows an unqualified conviction. Psychiatric treatment is ordinarily available to convicted offenders not classified GBMI, and conversely, GBMI statutes typically provide that a GBMI offender may receive any sentence available after an ordinary guilty verdict. As a result, there is ordinarily

23. See Hugh McGinley & Richard A. Pasewark, National Survey of the Frequency and Success of the Insanity Plea and Alternate Pleas, J. Psychiatry & L. 205, 214 (Summer 1989).

no *requirement* that a GBMI offender receive psychiatric treatment; courts have held that the GBMI offender, like any other offender, may be incarcerated without treatment, so long as essential medical care is available when needed. See Robinson v. Solem, 432 N.W.2d 246 (S.D. 1988). Applying the same logic, courts in GBMI states have generally held that murder defendants found "guilty but mentally ill" may be sentenced to death. See, e.g., State v. Wilson, 413 S.E.2d 19 (S.C. 1992); People v. Crews, 122 Ill. 2d 266, 522 N.E.2d 1167 (1988).

Should these implications of the GBMI verdict be explained to the jury? Should the defendant have the right to ensure that jurors understand how the consequences of this verdict differ from the consequences of finding the defendant guilty or not guilty by reason of insanity? The question is related to the issue, discussed at page 935 above, of whether the jury should be informed of the consequences of an insanity acquittal. The GBMI verdict arguably poses a stronger case for explanatory instructions because the jurors' decision could so easily be influenced by incorrect assumptions about the verdict's effect. In State v. Shickles, 760 P.2d 290 (Utah 1988), the court held that explanatory instructions were required. But in State v. Neely, 112 N.M. 702, 819 P.2d 249, 256-257 (1991), the court held that the jury's function is confined to factfinding and that an instruction on the consequences of various verdicts would inject an irrelevant issue into its deliberations. A dissenting judge observed (819 P.2d at 262-263):

> To instruct the jury . . . — as was done in this case — that it is not to concern itself with the consequences of its verdict, and at the same time to rely on the jury's ability to send "signals" to the sentencing court and the Corrections Department as an objective legitimating this statute, strikes me as fundamentally unfair.
>
> In point of fact, what the jury *really* needs are instructions telling it that a defendant found guilty but mentally ill will have precisely the same opportunities for mental treatment as all other prison inmates — no more, no less — and will probably receive the same sentence as any other person convicted of the same crime, mentally ill or not. Likewise, to put such an instruction into perspective, the jury needs to be told that a finding of not guilty by reason of insanity may, and probably will, result in the involuntary commitment of the defendant to the state hospital for an indefinite time and at least until the defendant is "cured." The absence of any requirement that the court give such consequential instructions . . . in my view render[s] the statutes unconstitutional on their face and as applied.

4. *The impact on acquittal and conviction rates.* In Michigan, the worst fears of defense attorneys apparently have not materialized. The number of insanity acquittals in Michigan did not decline after enactment of the GBMI statute,[24] and in recent years both the number of insanity pleas and the rate of insanity acquittals has risen somewhat.[25] But Professor Linda Fentiman notes that Michigan broadened its insanity defense by adopting the Model Penal Code formulation in the same year that the GBMI legislation was passed, and many more defendants then sought to invoke the insanity defense.[26] The failure to observe any net change in the number of acquittals thus suggests that the availability of the

---

24. G. A. Smith & J. A. Hall, Evaluating Michigan's Guilty But Mentally Ill Verdict, 16 J.L. Reform 75 (1982).

25. McGinley & Pasewark, supra footnote 23, at 208, 211.

26. Linda C. Fentiman, "Guilty But Mentally Ill": The Real Verdict Is Guilty, 26 B.C.L. Rev. 601, 614-615 (1985).

GBMI verdict may have substantially reduced the number of insanity acquittals that otherwise might have occurred.

In contrast to the Michigan experience, Georgia's GBMI statute, enacted in 1982, apparently did decrease the likelihood of an insanity acquittal, and the recent research also finds that defendants who plead insanity in that state and are found GBMI tend to receive harsher sentences than otherwise similar defendants who are found guilty.[27]

5. *The implications of* Jones. GBMI statutes were originally motivated by concern that due process and equal protection principles would enable dangerous insanity acquittees to avoid needed periods of incapacitation. See Note 1 supra. But after *Jones,* do the GBMI statutes remain necessary?

The GBMI experiment also suggests a broader problem — the pervasive perception that public safety considerations make some dilution of the insanity defense a practical necessity. Of course, many would dispute this view. But if public opinion in effect insists on some such dilution, what is the best way to achieve it? Is it preferable to dilute the insanity defense in the way that the GBMI verdict does (by encouraging juries not to vote an insanity acquittal) or in the way that *Jones* does (by depriving insanity acquittees of the full benefits of an ordinary acquittal)?

NOTES ON AUTOMATISM — SANE AND INSANE

We have already examined the requirement that criminal liability be based upon a voluntary act. See pages 171-178 supra. As we saw, this requirement prevents conviction for conduct committed in a state of "automatism" — that is, in a state of unconsciousness or spasmodic reflex reactions. What is the relationship between "automatism" and "insanity"? Does one defense supersede or preclude the other? Does the *reason* for a defendant's being in a state of automatism ever matter? The questions are important because the defendant who successfully pleads automatism will win a complete acquittal and discharge, while a defendant who successfully pleads insanity will face some form of optional or mandatory commitment. When the automatism results from a mental disorder, should the defendant retain the option of relying on the involuntary act defense, or should he be restricted to a plea of not guilty by reason of insanity?

1. *Defendant's option?* Most American courts hold that the defendant may elect to plead either insanity, involuntariness, or both. See, e.g., State v. Massey, 747 P.2d 802 (Kan. 1987); People v. Grant, 71 Ill. 2d 551, 377 N.E.2d 4, 8 (1978) ("[T]he defense of involuntary conduct and the insanity defense are alternative theories at the disposal of the defendant whose volition to control or prevent his conduct is at issue."). The English rule, in contrast, holds that when automatism results from a mental disease or defect, the only defense available is the plea of not guilty by reason of insanity. See Bratty v. Attorney-General for Northern Ireland, [1963] A.C. 386. A few American jurisdictions follow the English approach. See, e.g., Wyo. Stat. §7-11-304(c) (1977):

---

27. Lisa A. Callahan, Margaret A. McGreevy, Carmen Cirincione & Henry J. Steadman, Measuring the Effects of the Guilty But Mentally Ill (GMBI) Verdict, 16 L. & Human Behavior 447 (1992).

Evidence that a person is not responsible for criminal conduct by reason of mental illness or deficiency is not admissible at the trial of the defendant unless a plea of "not guilty by reason of mental illness or deficiency" is made.

2. *Distinguishing sane from insane automatisms.* Where insanity and automatism are mutually exclusive defenses, courts must decide whether the claimed automatism results from a mental disorder. Consider the following treatments of the issue.

(a) In Wyoming, the insanity defense is available for impairments resulting from "mental illness or deficiency." "Mental deficiency" is defined as "a defect attributable to mental retardation, brain damage and learning disabilities." Wyo. Stat. §7-11-301(a)(iii) (1977). In Fulcher v. State, 633 P.2d 142 (Wyo. 1981), the defendant was charged with aggravated assault. With the support of expert medical testimony, he claimed that his actions were committed in a state of automatism resulting from traumatic head injuries inflicted in a brawl shortly before the alleged offense. Should such injuries be regarded as a form of "brain damage," which Wyoming law would require to be raised solely in terms of the insanity defense? The Wyoming Supreme Court held that the defendant's injuries did not represent "brain damage" within the meaning of the statute and accordingly that the automatism defense remained available. The court said (id. at 146):

It is our view that the "brain damage" contemplated in the statute is some serious and irreversible condition having an impact upon the ability of the person to function. It is undoubtedly something far more significant than a temporary and transitory condition.

A dissenting judge commented (id. at 155, 162-163):

[A] blow to the head causing unconsciousness creates a mental deficiency and is to be treated as any other mental deficiency. A pretrial examination by an unbiased medical expert is indicated, and that is the procedure which should have been followed in this case with all of its ramifications. . . .

There is no basis whatsoever that supports the proposition the majority espouses that, . . . "the 'brain damage' contemplated in the statute is some serious and irreversible condition . . . " To the contrary, the only material condition is that which exists at the moment of the crime. How long should the condition exist before it comes within the cloak of the statute — a minute, an hour, a day, a week, two weeks, a month, a year, five years, a lifetime? The statute says nothing about a temporary condition or one that is "serious and irreversible." . . .

[W]e do not know the full extent of the appellant's brain damage. The majority takes a big leap when they say, "The commitment of an automatistic individual to a mental institution for rehabilitation has absolutely no value. Mental hospitals generally treat people with psychiatric or psychological problems. This form of treatment is not suited to unconscious behavior resulting from a bump on the head." That is pure conjecture. . . . One of the purposes of the required pretrial commitment and examination [in insanity defense cases] is to determine the nature of the claimed defect or deficiency and the period covered by the alleged disability. . . .

(b) The problem of distinguishing sane from insane automatisms has generated extensive litigation in England. In *Bratty*, supra Note 1, a defendant accused
of murder claimed that his act was committed in a state of automatism resulting
from an attack of psychomotor epilepsy. The House of Lords held that this defense could be raised only through a plea of insanity. In explaining why epilepsy
should be classified as a mental disease, Lord Denning suggested the following
approach:

> The major mental diseases, which the doctors call psychoses, such as
> schizophrenia, are clearly disease of the mind. But in Reg. v. Charlson [1955] 1
> W.L.R. 317, Barry, J., seems to have assumed that other diseases such as epilepsy or
> cerebral tumour are not diseases of the mind, even when they are such as to mani-
> fest themselves in violence. I do not agree with this. It seems to me that any mental
> disorder which has manifested itself in violence and is prone to recur is a disease
> of the mind. At any rate it is the sort of disease for which a person should be de-
> tained in hospital rather than be given an unqualified acquittal.

Subsequent cases suggested anomalies in Lord Denning's approach. In Regina v. Quick, [1973] 3 W.L.R. 26, defendant was a diabetic who committed
an assault during a state of unconsciousness due to hypoglycaemia (low blood
sugar), a condition that resulted from his taking either too much insulin or too
little food just prior to the attack. The court recognized that by Lord Denning's
test, Quick would be restricted to a defense of legal insanity because his condition "manifested itself in violence and [was] prone to recur." The court rejected
that approach and held that Quick was entitled to rely on the involuntary act
defense, explaining:

> No mental hospital would admit a diabetic merely because he had a low blood
> sugar reaction; and common sense is affronted by the prospect of a diabetic being
> [detained in] such a hospital, when in most cases the disordered mental condition
> can be rectified quickly by pushing a lump of sugar or a teaspoonful of glucose into
> the patient's mouth.
>   . . . A malfunctioning of the mind of transitory effect caused by the application
> to the body of some external factor such as violence, drugs, including anaesthetics,
> alcohol and hypnotic influences cannot fairly be said to be due to disease. . . .
>   In this case Quick's alleged mental condition, if it ever existed, was not caused
> by his diabetes but by his use of the insulin prescribed by his doctor. Such malfunc-
> tioning of his mind as there was, was caused by an external factor and not by a
> bodily disorder in the nature of a disease which disturbed the working of his mind.
> It follows in our judgment that Quick was entitled to have his defence of automa-
> tism left to the jury. . . .

In Regina v. T., noted [1990] Crim. L. Rev. 256, defendant claimed that while
participating with two men in a robbery, she was in an unconscious fugue state,
the result of a post-traumatic stress disorder brought on by a rape she had
suffered three days prior to the robbery incident. Applying *Quick*'s "internal-
external" test, the court held that her post-traumatic stress condition did not
constitute a "disease of the mind" because it was the result of a violent injury,
and therefore that the defense of noninsane automatism was available. In Regina v. Hennessy, [1989] 1 W.L.R. 287, defendant, a diabetic charged with auto

theft, claimed that he had taken the car in an unconscious fugue state brought on by hyperglycaemia (high blood sugar) resulting from his failure to take his regular dosages of insulin. Again applying the "internal-external" test, the court reasoned that hypoglycaemia (as in *Quick*) was not a mental disease because it results from an excessive intake of insulin, but that hyperglycaemia (as in *Hennessy*) *was* a mental disease because it results from an internal condition that the defendant failed to treat. Thus, the court held, Hennessy's defense could be raised only by a plea of insanity.

(c) *People v. Grant, 46 Ill. App. 3d 125, 360 N.E.2d 809 (1977).* Grant spent several hours at a bar and had consumed four drinks when the owner got into an argument with another patron. The police were called and forcibly escorted the other patron out of the bar while a large crowd gathered to protest the arrest. Suddenly Grant burst through the crowd; using a parking meter for leverage, he leaped into the air and struck Officer Vonderahe twice in the face. Grant was arrested and charged with aggravated battery. An hour after the arrest, a jailer found Grant lying on his cot gasping for breath; his eyes were fixed and his back formed a rigid arch, typical symptoms of a grand mal epileptic seizure.

Grant's medical history included a number of violent attacks on other persons. Several were serious. One, a knife assault in a hospital, was of such violence that officers seeking to restrain him were forced to use a weapon. His past history was replete with emotional outbursts, and he had been convicted on separate occasions of involuntary manslaughter and aggravated assault.

At trial a defense expert testified that, in his opinion, at the time the offense was committed, Grant was suffering from a psychomotor seizure that prevented his conscious mind from controlling his actions. The trial judge instructed the jury on the insanity defense but did not instruct on the requirement of a voluntary act. Grant was convicted of aggravated battery and sentenced to 3 to 9 years' imprisonment. The appellate court reversed:

> [The insanity] instruction . . . fails to distinguish behavior by a person lacking ". . . substantial capacity either to appreciate the criminality of his conduct or to conform his conduct to the requirements of the law . . ." from automatic behavior by an individual who possesses the requisite capacity. . . . [N]o Illinois court has [previously] determined [whether] a person's actions during a psychomotor epileptic seizure are the actions of an insane person or merely the involuntary or automatic actions of a sane person. . . .
>
> The term automatism is defined as the state of a person who, though capable of action, is not conscious of what he is doing. Automatism is not insanity. . . .
>
> Although a voluntary act is an absolute requirement for criminal liability under section 4-1 of our Code, there is no requirement that every act preceding the actual commission of the offense be voluntary. Thus, the jury may, on remand, determine that the defendant attacked Officer Vonderahe while in a state of automatism, but that he nevertheless committed an offense for which he is criminally responsible if he had prior notice of his susceptibility to engage in violent involuntary conduct brought on by drinking alcoholic beverages or by some other conscious causal behavior.
>
> We are not troubled by the decision of the British House of Lords affirming a murder conviction in which the trial judge refused to instruct on the defense of automatism despite the presence of evidence tending to establish that the defendant was suffering a psychomotor epileptic seizure at the time the offense was

committed. (Bratty v. Attorney-General for Northern Ireland (1961), 3 All E.R. 535.) . . . Lord Denning . . . felt that any mental disorder manifesting itself in a form of violence that is prone to recur is a disease of the mind. He stated that it is the sort of disease requiring detention rather than an unqualified acquittal.

. . . Our legislature has provided that a person found not guilty of an offense by reason of insanity can be committed to a mental health facility for treatment, although no such provision applies to an alleged offender who commits an involuntary act. . . . If the jury finds that the defendant was sane but not responsible for the attack on Officer Vonderahe, then he cannot be committed for the offenses. We find this course to be mandated by our legislature which only provided for the commitment of persons who are criminally insane.[a]

3. *Disposition after a successful automatism defense.* Rupert Cross, Reflections on *Bratty's Case,* 78 Law Q. Rev. 236, 239 (1962), writes:

Is it right that someone who has been acquitted on the ground of non-insane automatism should inevitably go free? In R. v. Charlson [39 Crim. App. 37 (1955)] the accused was acquitted on various charges of causing grievous bodily harm to his son because he had acted in a state of automatism which may have been due to a cerebral tumour. It is only natural to feel the deepest sympathy for the accused in such a case, but it is equally natural to question the propriety of an unqualified acquittal. One way of dealing with such problems would be to give the judge power in all cases of a successful plea of automatism, insane or non-insane, to order the detention of the accused pending a medical inquiry, after which the appropriate order could be made. The absence of any such power in cases of non-insane automatism has no doubt contributed to the recent tendencies to define a disease of the mind in broad terms, and to encourage the prosecution to ask for a verdict of "guilty but insane."

4. Relatively few cases have dealt with criminal conduct during various states of sleep. The courts appear to be divided on the question whether the defendant in such a case is entitled to outright acquittal due to the absence of a volitional act, or whether the defendant must plead insanity and face commitment to a mental hospital.

In Regina v. Burgess, [1991] 2 All E.R. 769, defendant fell asleep while watching a videotape with his neighbor. He awoke to find himself hitting her on the head with a bottle and attempting to strangle her. He quickly came to his senses and called an ambulance for her, but he was charged with assault. He had no history of mental illness and had been on completely friendly terms with the victim. Applying the "internal-external" test used in England to determine whether an involuntary act is the result of "mental disease," the court held that the defendant could not raise of a defense of noninsane automatism, and he was found not guilty by reason of insanity. For a trenchant criticism of the result, see Irene Mackay, The Sleepwalker is Not Insane, 55 Mod. L. Rev. 714 (1992).

a. The appellate court's decision in *Grant* was reversed on other grounds, namely that the trial judge's instructions had given the jury a fair opportunity to rule in defendant's favor on the automatism claim. 71 Ill. 2d 551, 377 N.E.2d 4 (1978). — Eds.

Under the Model Penal Code a defendant charged with conduct during a somnambulistic state would be entitled to an outright acquittal for lack of a voluntary act. See §2.01(2)(b), Appendix. In this connection reconsider the *Cogden* case, page 177 supra. Is an outright acquittal appropriate in such a case?

d. Diminished Capacity

UNITED STATES v. BRAWNER

United States Court of Appeals, District of Columbia Circuit
471 F.2d 969 (1972)

LEVENTHAL, J. [After examining the test of legal insanity as a complete defense, the court considered whether mental health evidence should be admissible apart from its bearing on the insanity issue.] [E]xpert testimony as to a defendant's abnormal mental condition may be received and considered, as tending to show, in a responsible way, that defendant did not have the specific mental state required for a particular crime or degree of crime — even though he was aware that his act was wrongful and was able to control it, and hence was not entitled to complete exoneration.

Some of the cases following this doctrine use the term "diminished responsibility," but we prefer the example of the cases that avoid this term, for its convenience is outweighed by its confusion: Our doctrine has nothing to do with "diminishing" responsibility of a defendant because of his impaired mental condition, but rather with determining whether the defendant had the mental state that must be proved as to all defendants.

Procedurally, the issue of abnormal mental condition negativing a person's intent may arise in different ways: For example, the defendant may offer evidence of mental condition not qualifying as mental disease. . . . Or he may tender evidence that qualifies [as a mental disease], yet the jury may conclude from all the evidence that defendant has knowledge and control capacity sufficient for responsibility. . . .

The issue often arises with respect to mental condition tendered as negativing the element of premeditation in a charge of first degree premeditated murder. . . . An offense like deliberated and premeditated murder requires a specific intent that cannot be satisfied merely by showing that defendant failed to conform to an objective standard. This is plainly established by the defense of voluntary intoxication. In Hopt v. Utah, 104 U.S. 631 (1881), the Court, after stating the familiar rule that voluntary intoxication is no excuse for crime, said: "[W]hen a statute establishing different degrees of murder requires deliberate premeditation in order to constitute murder in the first degree, the question of whether the accused is in such a condition of mind, by reason of drunkenness or otherwise, as to be capable of deliberate premeditation, necessarily becomes a material subject of consideration by the jury. . . . "

Neither logic nor justice can tolerate a jurisprudence . . . such that one defendant can properly argue that his voluntary drunkenness removed his capacity to form the specific intent but another defendant is inhibited from a submission of his contention that an abnormal mental condition, for which he was in no way responsible, negated his capacity to form a particular specific intent, even though the condition did not exonerate him from all criminal responsibility. . . .

The pertinent reasoning was succinctly stated by the Colorado Supreme Court as follows [Battalino v. People, 118 Colo. 587, 199 P.2d 897, 901 (1948)]:

> The question to be determined is not whether defendant was insane, but whether the homicidal act was committed with deliberation and premeditation. The evidence offered as to insanity may or may not be relevant to that issue. . . . "A claim of insanity cannot be used for the purpose of reducing a crime of murder in the first degree to murder in the second degree or from murder to manslaughter. If the perpetrator is responsible at all in this respect, he is responsible in the same degree as a sane man; and if he is not responsible at all, he is entitled to an acquittal in both degrees. However, . . . *evidence of the condition of the mind* of the accused at the time of the crime, together with the surrounding circumstances, may be introduced, not for the purpose of establishing insanity, but to prove that the situation was such that a specific intent was not entertained — that is, *to show absence of any deliberate or premeditated design.*" (Emphasis in original.) . . .

[D]evelopments within our own jurisdiction underscore the soundness of a doctrine for consideration of abnormal mental condition on the issue of specific intent. . . . In 1964, after extensive hearings, Congress enacted the Hospitalization of the Mentally Ill Act, which provides civil commitment for the "mentally ill" who are dangerous to themselves or others. . . . These statutory provisions provide a shield against danger from persons with abnormal mental conditions. . . .

Our rule permits the introduction of expert testimony as to abnormal condition if it is relevant to negative, or establish, the specific mental condition that is an element of the crime. The receipt of this expert testimony to negative the mental condition of specific intent requires careful administration by the trial judge. . . . The judge will . . . determine whether the testimony is grounded in sufficient scientific support to warrant use in the courtroom, and whether it would aid the jury in reaching a decision on the ultimate issues. . . .

STATE v. WILCOX

Supreme Court of Ohio
70 Ohio St. 182, 436 N.E.2d 523 (1982)

[Defendant participated in a burglary in which the victim was shot and killed. He was charged with aggravated felony murder, a charge requiring a purpose to kill, and aggravated burglary, a charge requiring a purpose to commit a felony. Before trial, a court-appointed psychiatrist found defendant to be borderline retarded, schizophrenic, dyslexic, and to be suffering from organic brain syndrome. At trial he was permitted to introduce some psychiatric testimony to support his insanity defense, but the trial judge excluded other psychiatric testimony and refused to charge the jury that defendant's mental condition could negate the specific intents required for aggravated murder and aggravated burglary. Defendant was convicted on both counts and sentenced to life imprisonment. The intermediate court of appeals reversed, and the prosecution appealed.]

SWEENEY, J. The question before the court in the instant appeal is whether appellee is entitled to a new trial at which he may present expert psychiatric testimony relating to his alleged incapacity to form the requisite specific intent to commit aggravated murder and aggravated burglary. . . .

If the *Brawner* rule [see page 999 supra] were applied to the case at bar, then appellee, even though legally sane, could present psychiatric testimony as to his abnormal mental condition (diminished capacity) to show that he did not have the specific mental state — in this instance, the purpose — required to commit the crimes with which he stands charged. However, our review of the history and policies underlying the diminished capacity concept and the experience of jurisdictions that have attempted to apply the doctrine militate against the adoption of a *Brawner*-type rule in Ohio.

. . . [I]t appears that enthusiasm for the diminished capacity defense is on the wane and that there is, if anything, a developing movement away from diminished capacity although the authorities at this point are still quite mixed in their views.

The diminished capacity defense developed as a covert judicial response to perceived inequities in the criminal law. The purported justifications for the doctrine include the following:

(1) it ameliorates defects in a jurisdiction's insanity test criteria; (2) it permits the jury to avoid imposing the death penalty on mentally disabled killers who are criminally responsible for their acts; and (3) it permits the jury to make more accurate individualized culpability judgments.

[Peter Arenella, The Diminished Capacity and Diminished Responsibility Defenses: Two Children of a Doomed Marriage, 77 Colum. L. Rev. 827 (1977)] at page 853. . . .

Upon examination, however, we find none of the foregoing justifications for the defense of diminished capacity sufficiently compelling as to warrant its adoption, particularly in light of the problems posed by the doctrine, problems even its proponents acknowledge.

The diminished capacity defense does serve to ameliorate the limitations of the traditional, *M'Naghten*, right from wrong test for insanity. It is no coincidence that California, which pioneered the diminished capacity defense, for many years adhered to a strict *M'Naghten* standard. . . .

The ameliorative argument loses much of its force, however, in jurisdictions that have abandoned or expanded upon the narrow *M'Naghten* standard. The test for insanity in Ohio is . . . as follows:

One accused of criminal conduct is not responsible for such criminal conduct if, at the time of such conduct, as a result of mental disease or defect, he does not have the capacity either to know the wrongfulness of his conduct or to conform his conduct to the requirements of law. . . .

While this standard is arguably less expansive than that espoused by the drafters of the Model Penal Code, see Section 4.01, it is considerably more flexible than the *M'Naghten* rule. . . . Thus we see no reason to fashion a halfway measure, e.g., diminished capacity, when an accused may present a meaningful insanity defense in a proper case.

The interplay between the diminished capacity doctrine and the insanity defense, moreover, is not limited to the supposed ameliorative effect of the former on the latter. Rather, as Dr. Diamond, among others, has observed, . . . "this defense does not just supplement the insanity defense, but tends to supersede it. . . ." . . .

Professor Arenella notes that "[s]eriously disturbed defendants can avoid an indefinite commitment to a mental hospital for the criminally insane by relying on the diminished responsibility defense which frequently leads to a reduced term in prison." Arenella, supra, at page 854. According to this view, the principal practical effect of the diminished capacity defense is to enable mentally ill offenders to receive shorter and more certain sentences than they would receive if they were adjudged insane. Having satisfied ourselves that Ohio's test for criminal responsibility adequately safeguards the rights of the insane, we are disinclined to adopt an alternative defense that could swallow up the insanity defense and its attendant commitment provisions.

We can quickly dispose of the argument that the diminished capacity defense alleviates the harshness of the death penalty when mentally ill but nonetheless sane defendants are convicted of capital crimes. . . . Mental capacity is a formal mitigating factor in capital cases under current Ohio law at the punishment stage of the now bifurcated proceedings. Thus the ameliorative purpose served by the diminished capacity defense in capital cases has largely been accomplished by other means.

The justifications for diminished capacity . . . are based largely on analogies to the insanity defense and the defense of intoxication, respectively. . . .

As Professor Arenella notes, at page 860,

> [t]he analogy to the insanity defense is misleading because the diminished responsibility doctrine asks the expert witness and the jury to make a far more subtle distinction. The insanity defense asks both to distinguish between a large group of offenders who are punishable for their acts despite their mental deficiencies, and a small class of offenders who are so mentally disabled that they cannot be held accountable because they lack the minimal capacity to act voluntarily. The diminished responsibility doctrine attempts to divide the first large group of responsible sane offenders into two subgroups: a group of "normal" fully culpable criminal offenders, and a group of mentally abnormal but sane offenders with reduced culpability.

In light of the line-drawing difficulties courts and juries face when assessing expert evidence to make the "bright line" insanity determination, we are not at all confident that similar evidence will enable juries, or the judges who must instruct them, to bring the blurred lines of diminished capacity into proper focus so as to facilitate principled and consistent decision-making in criminal cases. In short, the fact that psychiatric evidence is admissible to prove or disprove insanity does not necessarily dictate the conclusion that it is admissible for purposes unrelated to the insanity defense.

The *Brawner* court emphasized the apparent illogic of permitting evidence of voluntary intoxication to be introduced to negate specific intent while precluding the introduction of evidence of an abnormal mental condition not amounting to insanity for the same purpose. While we concede that there is a superficial attractiveness to the intoxication-diminished capacity analogy, upon closer examination we . . . find the concepts to be quite disparate. . . .

It takes no great expertise for jurors to determine whether an accused was "so intoxicated as to be mentally unable to intend anything (unconscious)," whereas the ability to assimilate and apply the finely differentiated psychiatric concepts associated with diminished capacity demands a sophistication (or as critics would maintain a sophistic bent) that jurors (and officers of the court) ordinarily have not developed. We are convinced . . . that these "significant evidentiary distinctions" preclude treating diminished capacity and voluntary intoxication as functional equivalents for purposes of partial exculpation from criminal responsibility. . . .

The open-endedness of the diminished capacity doctrine troubles us as well. Under the California rule evidence of diminished capacity could only be introduced to negate the mental element in crimes requiring specific intent. The specific intent limitation imposed by the California courts did not, however, flow from the theory underlying the diminished capacity doctrine and, indeed, may have been in direct conflict therewith. The *Bethea* court [Bethea v. United States, 365 A.2d 64 (D.C. App. 1976)] acknowledged this theoretical incongruity in its discussion of *Brawner:*

> . . . Assuming the competency of experts to testify as to an accused's capacity for specific intent we see no logical bar to their observations as to the possible existence or lack of malice or general intent. . . .

If however, in the interests of doctrinal purity, evidence of diminished capacity were admitted to disprove the mental element in general intent crimes, then "successful application of the diminished capacity doctrine . . . would create the anomalous result of a 'partial defense' leading to outright acquittal of the defendant because of the absence of a lesser included offense." Arenella, supra, at page 832, fn. 25. [T]he potential applicability of diminished capacity as a complete defense to crimes of general intent dramatically highlights the paradox inhering in the doctrine. . . .

> While there may be superficial appeal to the idea that the standards of criminal responsibility should be applied as subjectively as possible, the overriding danger of the disputed doctrine is that it would discard the traditional presumptions concerning mens rea without providing for a corresponding adjustment in the means whereby society is enabled to protect itself from those who cannot or will not conform their conduct to the requirements of the law.

Bethea supra, at page 90. . . .

We hold, therefore, that the partial defense of diminished capacity is not recognized in Ohio and consequently, a defendant may not offer expert psychiatric testimony, unrelated to the insanity defense, to show that the defendant lacked the mental capacity to form the specific mental state required for a particular crime or degree of crime.

[Conviction affirmed.]

NOTES ON USE OF MENTAL DISORDER TO NEGATE MENS REA

1. *Contemporary trends.* The issue that divides *Brawner* and *Wilcox* continues to provoke wide disagreement in the courts and legislatures. Many of the recent decisions hold, in accord with *Bethea* and *Wilcox,* that expert psychiatric evidence is never admissible for purposes of proving that the defendant lacked a required mental state, even when the objective is solely to reduce first-degree to second-degree murder. See, e.g., State v. Provost, 490 N.W.2d 93 (Minn. 1992); Chestnut v. State, 538 So. 2d 820 (Fla. 1989). In contrast, the federal courts and about half the states continue to favor the *Brawner* view that expert psychiatric evidence should be admissible whenever relevant to negate the mens rea of a specific intent crime. See, e.g., United States v. Cameron, 907 F.2d 1051 (10th Cir. 1990); People v. Saille, 54 Cal. 3d 1103, 820 P.2d 588, 595-596 (1991). In a few instances, courts or legislatures have gone even further than *Brawner* and have held such evidence admissible to negate the mens rea of *any* crime, e.g., Hendershott v. People, 653 P.2d 385 (Colo. 1985); N.J. Stat. Ann. §2C:4-2. The Model Penal Code adopts this last approach. See §4.02, Appendix. See Model Penal Code and Commentaries, Comment to §4.02 at 219 (1985):

> The Institute perceived no justification for a limitation on evidence that may bear significantly on a determination of the mental state of the defendant at the time of the commission of the crime. If states of mind are accorded legal significance, psychiatric evidence should be admissible when relevant to prove or disprove their existence to the same extent as any other relevant evidence. It is true that when a claim is successfully made that the defendant did not have the state of mind necessary for an offense, there is no provision for automatic commitment, as there is under Section 4.08 for those who successfully claim the defense of irresponsibility of Section 4.01. But procedures for civil commitment remain available, and often the defendant who lacks the state of mind for a more serious offense will still be guilty of a lesser offense based on recklessness or negligence.

2. *Problem.* Defendant barricaded himself in his home. His wife called the police and when they arrived, he fired several shots at them before eventually surrendering. At his trial for attempted murder of the officers, he offered the testimony of a psychiatrist to support his claim that he had been suffering from severe depression, that he wanted to commit suicide but lacked the strength to do so, and that he had shot at the police not to harm them but solely to goad them into returning his fire and killing him. Applying Minnesota cases that hold, in accord with *Wilcox,* that expert evidence is inadmissible for purposes of negating specific intent, the court ruled the psychiatrist's testimony inadmissible. State v. Brink, 500 N.W.2d 799 (Minn. App. 1993). Is the result sound? Is the problem posed by the attempted use of psychiatric evidence in *Brink* the same as the problem posed in *Wilcox*?

3. *Mitigation versus exoneration.* In McCarthy v. State, 372 A.2d 180, 183 (Del. 1977), the Delaware Supreme Court held that an instruction on diminished capacity was not appropriate in a prosecution for kidnapping and attempted rape. The court stated:

> [T]he salient aspect of the diminished responsibility doctrine is that it does not relieve the defendant of criminal responsibility. . . . In practice under the doctrine,

while conviction for an offense requiring a specific intent was foreclosed, conviction for a lesser-included crime, requiring only a general criminal intent, was not. This specific intent — general intent dichotomy explains not only the application of the doctrine in the first degree murder cases wherein the specific intent element of premeditation and deliberation are negated, . . . but also the seemingly more liberal application of the doctrine in such cases as assault and battery with intent to kill; first degree forgery, requiring specific intent to defraud; . . . and entering a building with intent to commit theft. In each of these instances, the requisite specific intent constituted an aggravating factor to an otherwise general mens rea offense and the doctrine was applied to permit a finding of the lesser offense.

As the above cases illustrate, acceptance of the doctrine requires that there be some lesser-included offense which lacks the requisite specific intent of the greater offense charged. Otherwise, the doctrine of diminished responsibility becomes an impermissible substitute test of criminal responsibility. . . .

In the instant case, there are no such lesser-included offenses within those for which the defendant was charged and tried. The acceptance of the doctrine in this case, therefore, would be inconsistent with the theory's basic purpose.

Compare People v. Wetmore, 22 Cal. 3d 318, 583 P.2d 1308, 1315 (1978):

[A] defense of diminished capacity arising from mental disease or defects extends to all specific intent crimes, whether or not they encompass lesser included offenses. Clearly, if a crime requires specific intent, a defendant who, because of mental disease or defect lacks that intent, cannot commit that crime. The presence or absence of a lesser included offense within the charged crime cannot affect the result. The prosecution must prove all elements of the crime beyond a reasonable doubt; we do not perceive how a defendant who has in his possession evidence which rebuts an element of the crime can logically be denied the right to present that evidence merely because it will result in his acquittal.

The court recognized the practical danger of the defense so interpreted — namely, that mentally disordered persons acquitted on a diminished-capacity defense would be set free, since only persons acquitted on a legal insanity defense are subject to the state's confinement and treatment provisions. It responded (id. at 1315):

The solution to this problem . . . does not lie in barring the defense of diminished capacity when the charged crime lacks a lesser included offense, but in providing [legislation] for the confinement and treatment of defendants with diminished capacity arising from mental disease or defect.

4. *The nature of the evidence.* Some jurisdictions have attempted to limit the kinds of mental impairment evidence that can be admitted for purposes other than the insanity defense. Consider the following provisions of the California Penal Code:

28. (a) Evidence of mental disease, mental defect, or mental disorder shall not be admitted to show or negate the capacity to form any mental state, including, but not limited to, purpose, intent, knowledge, premeditation, deliberation, or malice aforethought, with which the accused committed the act. Evidence of mental disease, mental defect, or mental disorder is admissible solely on the issue of whether or not the accused actually formed a required specific intent, premeditated, deliberated, or harbored malice aforethought, when a specific intent crime is charged.

(b) As a matter of public policy there shall be no defense of diminished capacity, diminished responsibility, or irresistible impulse in a criminal action. . . .

29. In the guilt phase of a criminal action, any expert testifying about a defendant's mental illness, mental disorder, or mental defect shall not testify as to whether the defendant had or did not have the required mental states, which include, but are not limited to, purpose, intent, knowledge, or malice aforethought, for the crimes charged. The question as to whether the defendant had or did not have the required mental states shall be decided by the trier of fact.

Note that the California statute "abolishes" the diminished capacity defense, but only in the sense that evidence of mental disorder cannot be introduced to negate a defendant's "capacity" to form a required mental state; such evidence is still admissible on the question whether the accused actually formed the required mental state. See People v. Saille, 54 Cal. 3d 1103, 820 P.2d 588, 595-596 (1991); Miguel A. Mendez, Diminished Capacity in California: Premature Reports of Its Demise, 3 Stan. L. & Pol. Rev. 216 (1991). But what, precisely, is the distinction between *capacity* to form the mens rea and *actually* forming the mens rea? Consider Stephen J. Morse, Undiminished Confusion in Diminished Capacity, 75 J. Crim. L. & Criminology 1, 42-43 (1984):

> [One] cause of trouble with expert testimony . . . is the conceptualization of the issue in terms of the defendant's *capacity* to form a mens rea, rather than whether he formed it *in fact*. In California, this distinction is colloquially referred to as the difference between "capacity" and "actuality" evidence. On the face of it, the capacity conceptualization appears to make sense. Although the law requires proof of whether a defendant formed a mens rea in fact, if he lacked the capacity to form it, he could not have formed it in fact. . . .
>
> [But] mental disorder . . . seldom negates the capacity to form [mens rea]. A mens rea is a relatively simple mental state; it requires little cognitive capacity to intend to do something or to know legally relevant facts, such as that the car one is driving across the border contains contraband in a hidden compartment. A mentally abnormal person may not form a requisite intent or have the required knowledge, but it will rarely be because he lacked the capacity to form the mens rea. For example, suppose a mentally disordered person abroad in the streets becomes disorganized and lost in a deserted part of town on a cold evening. Lacking the resources to find his way to proper shelter, he breaks into a building to get out of the cold. Caught by the police while doing so, he is charged with burglary on the theory that he intended to steal. Our poor defendant is innocent of burglary because he lacks the mens rea for theft — he only wanted to stay warm, not to steal — but he does not lack mens rea because he did not have the capacity to form it. He was perfectly capable of intending to steal; it is simply the case, however, that he did not intend to do so on this occasion. The defendant's mental disorder is relevant to proving that he lacked mens rea, for it is the reason he became disorganized, got lost, and needed to get warm, but his mental disorder did not affect his capacity to form the mens rea. Once again, the capacity to form mens rea will virtually never be obliterated by mental disorder. In the very few cases where this might occur, the person would be wildly and obviously out of touch with reality.

5. *Problem.* In United States v. Busic, 592 F.2d 13 (2d Cir. 1978), the defendant was convicted of aircraft piracy, defined in 49 U.S.C. §1472(i) to mean "any seizure or exercise of control, by force or violence or threat of force or violence, or by any other form of intimidation, and with wrongful intent, of an aircraft within the special aircraft jurisdiction of the United States."

On appeal, the defendant contended that the trial court had improperly excluded psychiatric testimony offered to show that he was incapable of forming the requisite intent to commit the offense. His counsel had offered the testimony of Dr. Bernard L. Diamond, who was prepared to testify as follows (id. at 21):

> Zvanko Busic was in an abnormal mental state on September 10, 1976 when he is alleged to have committed air piracy, homicide, and other criminal acts. . . . It is also my opinion that this abnormal mental state was of such a quality and degree that it prevented the defendant from exercising the ordinary, reasonable and rational powers of free will, choice and decision that constitute the intent required by the definitions of the crimes of which he is charged. Hence, I conclude that Zvanko Busic lacked the capacity for such criminal intent.
>
> I am of the opinion that this abnormal mental state was not caused by mental disease, illness or defect. I do not find the defendant insane or mentally ill in any sense of those terms. . . .
>
> He did what he did out of psychological necessity, not free choice.

The court upheld the exclusion of the testimony on the ground that the availability of such a defense as defendant tendered (id. at 21)

> turns upon whether the offense in question, like deliberated and premeditated murder, requires a specific intent that cannot be satisfied merely by showing that defendant failed to conform to an objective standard. The offense of aircraft piracy, however, requires a showing of general criminal intent, not a showing of specific criminal intent.

Questions: Is the court's reason convincing? Suppose that Dr. Diamond was prepared to testify that the defendant's abnormal mental state prevented him from intending to seize the aircraft because he was under a delusion that the aircraft was his own car. Would the psychiatric testimony still be inadmissible? In *Busic* itself, is the difficulty with the defendant's position the fact that the crime charged was a general-intent rather than a specific-intent crime, or does the difficulty lie in the relevance of the proffered testimony? Would Dr. Diamond's testimony be admissible in jurisdictions that permit the use of diminished capacity evidence in prosecutions for both general-intent and specific-intent crimes?

6. State v. Sikora, 44 N.J. 453, 210 A.2d 193 (1965), illustrates the kind of psychiatric testimony that contributed to the revolt against diminished capacity evidence. Defendant was convicted of the first-degree murder of Douglas Hooey, a casual acquaintance. He had overheard Hooey making nasty remarks about Sikora's separation from the woman with whom Sikora had been living. An altercation arose and Hooey, with several others, beat up Sikora and threw him out of the tavern. Sikora went home, obtained his gun, test-fired it and returned to the tavern, where he shot and killed Hooey. On appeal, he sought reversal on the ground that the trial court had excluded the psychiatric testimony of Dr. Galen relative to defendant's capacity to premeditate. The supreme court summarized Dr. Galen's proposed testimony as follows:

> In short the doctor opined that the circumstances to which Sikora had been subjected imposed on his personality disorder a stress that impaired or removed his ability consciously to premeditate or weigh a design to kill. The tension was so

great that he could handle it only by an automatic reaction motivated by the pre-determined influence of his unconscious. Plainly the doctor meant that Sikora's response was not a voluntary exercise of his free will. . . . During the various actions Sikora took leading up to the killing, which so clearly indicated conception, deliberation and execution of a plan to kill, he was thinking but the thinking was automatic; it was simply subconscious thinking or reaction; it was not conscious thinking. The doctor said Sikora's anxieties at the time were of such a nature that conceivably, his reaction in that automatic way and the commission of the homicide, actually prevented a further disorganization of his personality. The killing, said the doctor, was "a rational murder" but "everything this man did was irrational," and engaged in when he could not conceive the design to kill. . . .

The court referred to the statement of Dr. Galen concerning a physician friend of his who, while driving on a highway, was cut off by another motorist. In Dr. Galen's words: "This man who is a professional knows clearly, in a general way, right from wrong, good from evil . . . but this man chased the car who cut him off and finally cut the car off that cut him off. Now, at this particular time, when he was behaving in this way, which was really endangering his life, endangering the lives of other people, although he was sane at the time, he was acting in an irrational manner with a disturbance of his consciousness. . . ."

The court upheld the exclusion of this psychiatric testimony and affirmed the conviction. Weintraub, C. J., concurring, observed:

> Under this psychiatric concept no man could be convicted of anything if the law were to accept the impulses of the unconscious as an excuse for conscious misbehavior. Although the specific question put to Dr. Galen was whether the defendant was capable of premeditating the murder, his answer would have to be the same if he were asked whether defendant was able to form an intent to do grievous bodily harm or any harm at all. His answer would have to be that the unconscious directed the killing in response to the stimulus of the events preceding the killing. The same explanation would account for the misbehavior of Dr. Galen's motoring friend if he were charged with a violation of the motor vehicle act. . . .
>
> To grant a role in our existing structure to the theme that the conscious is just the innocent puppet of a nonculpable unconscious is to make a mishmash of the criminal law, permitting — indeed requiring — each trier of the facts to choose between the automation thesis and the law's existing concept of criminal accountability. It would be absurd to decide criminal blameworthiness upon a psychiatric thesis which can find no basis for personal blame. So long as we adhere to criminal blameworthiness, mens rea must be sought and decided at the level of conscious behavior.

NOTE ON DIMINISHED RESPONSIBILITY AS GROUNDS FOR MITIGATION

The diminished capacity doctrine at issue in cases like *Brawner* and *Wilcox* involves the use of evidence of mental disorder to negate a required mens rea. That doctrine therefore must be distinguished from what has sometimes been called "diminished responsibility" or "partial responsibility." According to the latter doctrine, the fact that the defendant was mentally disturbed has the effect of entitling him to a reduction in the severity of the sentence, even though the prosecution has proved all the legal elements technically required for conviction. Such a doctrine has been recognized by some European countries. For example, the German Criminal Code provides in §21 that if a defendant's capacity to appreciate the wrongfulness of his or her act or to act in accordance with such understanding was severely impaired at the time of the act as a result of mental illness or serious mental abnormality, the defendant is subject to a lesser punishment. In the United Kingdom, a partial-responsibility doctrine has been adopted, applicable solely to murder. The English Homicide Act, 1957, 5 & 6 Eliz. II, ch. II, §2(1) provides:

> Where a person kills or is a party to the killing of another, he shall not be convicted of murder if he was suffering from such abnormality of mind (whether arising from a condition of arrested or retarded development of mind or any inherent causes or induced by disease or injury) as substantially impaired the mental responsibility for acts and omissions in doing or being a party to the killing. . . . A person who but for this section would be liable . . . to be convicted of murder shall be liable instead to be convicted of manslaughter.

For a helpful discussion of the English experience, see Suzanne Dell, Diminished Responsibility Reconsidered, [1982] Crim. L. Rev. 809.

Is there a case for adopting such an approach in the United States? Since the American doctrine tends to serve some of the same purposes as the less technical German and English approaches, would it be more straightforward to create an explicit affirmative defense for cases in which mens rea requirements are technically present but mental disorder is sufficient to suggest greatly reduced culpability? Consider the following.

Stephen J. Morse, Undiminished Confusion in Diminished Capacity, 75 J. Crim. L. & Criminology 1, 30-32 (1984): [A]ctors who commit the same acts with the same mens rea should, on moral grounds, be convicted of the same crime and punished alike without regard to differences in background, mental or emotional condition, or other factors often thought to necessitate mitigation. Thus, there should be no affirmative defense of partial responsibility. . . .

Analysis of responsibility usually begins by asking about all the difficulties, burdens, problems, and misfortunes suffered by the perpetrator, all the criminogenic reasons why obeying the law seemed so hard, why offending seemed so inevitable. But suppose we start with a different question: How hard is it not to offend the law? . . .

The substantive criminal law sets minimal ethical and legal standards that ask very little of us and are easy to meet. Even if an actor has rationality or self-control problems, it is not hard for a legally responsible person to avoid offending. [T]he differences that exist between offenders convicted of the same crime are morally insignificant compared to the similarities. The great value of this position . . . is that it treats people with greater respect and dignity than the opposing view, which treats them as helpless puppets buffeted by forces that rob them of responsibility for their deeds. Moreover, I do not believe it is a harshly unrealistic view. Rather, it goes to the heart of what it means to be a responsible person in a world that cannot exist without vast amounts of restraint and forbearance towards our fellows.

As long as the function of conviction and sentencing is to punish the actor for what he has done, rather than for who he is, there is no injustice in treating alike actors whose behavior satisfies the elements of the same crime and meets the low threshold standard for legal responsibility. So little self-control and rationality are necessary to obey the law that [t]he culpability of those who satisfy the prima facie case is fundamentally equivalent.

Peter Arenella, The Diminished Capacity and Diminished Responsibility Defenses: Two Children of a Doomed Marriage, 77 Colum. L. Rev. 827, 850-853 (1977): [In the case of a mentally disabled offender] the sentencing judge retains the authority to consider other mitigating and aggravating factors, including the offender's continuing dangerousness to society, before passing sentence. Contrast this process with that engendered by treating his mental abnormality as a formal mitigating factor. The diminished responsibility defense transfers partial sentencing authority from the judge to the jury. Under a theory of formal mitigation, the jury *must* reduce the grade of the offense if it finds diminished responsibility regardless of aggravating factors such as the offender's dangerousness. . . . Although the jury may still covertly consider other factors before returning a verdict, its *sub rosa* evaluation will be speculative at best. . . .

Admittedly, the transfer of partial sentencing authority to the jury is inherent in any process of formal mitigation. For example, the accepted defenses of voluntary intoxication and provocation also give the jury such partial sentencing power. [But the] analogy to voluntary intoxication is faulty because those courts which admit evidence of intoxication do so for the limited purpose of permitting the jury to consider whether defendant's intoxication prevented him from entertaining the requisite specific intent. [E]vidence of inebriation which merely shows that the defendant had special difficulty in controlling himself should not be considered. . . .

The analogy to provocation [is also] misleading. The provocation defense is qualified by objective criteria. . . . The defendant must introduce evidence to show not only that he was provoked, but that a reasonable person would have been provoked by the victim's actions and would not have had sufficient time to "cool off" before committing the criminal act. . . . Thus, the criminal law's recognition of provocation as a formal mitigating factor does not weaken its social control function because liability is reduced only in those cases in which objective factors suggest that the offender is not only less culpable but less dangerous than the unprovoked killer. In contrast, the diminished responsibility doctrine relies on a purely subjective theory of liability which reduces the actor's punishment solely on grounds of decreased culpability even though the offender's mental abnormality reveals a character deficiency that might make him dangerous in the future.

For further discussion of these issues see Stephen J. Morse, Diminished Capacity, in Stephen Shute, et al., eds., Action and Value in Criminal Law 239-278 (1993); Joshua Dressler, Reaffirming the Moral Legitimacy of the Doctrine of Diminished Capacity: A Brief Reply to Professor Morse, 75 J. Crim. L. & Criminology 953 (1984); Stephen J. Morse, Failed Explanations and Criminal Responsibility: Experts and the Unconscious, 68 Va. L. Rev. 971 (1982); Richard J.

Bonnie & Christopher Slobogin, The Role of Mental Health Professionals in the Criminal Process: The Case for Informed Speculation, 66 Va. L. Rev. 427 (1980).

5.   Changing Patterns of Excuse

ROBINSON v. CALIFORNIA
Supreme Court of the United States
370 U.S. 660 (1962)

JUSTICE STEWART delivered the opinion of the Court.

A California statute makes it a criminal offense for a person to "be addicted to the use of narcotics." This appeal draws into question the constitutionality of that provision of the state law, as construed by the California courts in the present case. . . .

[The prosecution's evidence was principally the testimony of policemen that defendant had scar tissue, discoloration and needle marks which indicated his frequent use of narcotics.]

The judge . . . instructed the jury that the appellant could be convicted under a general verdict if the jury agreed *either* that he was of the "status" *or* had committed the "act" denounced by the statute. "All that the People must show is either that the defendant did use a narcotic in Los Angeles County, or that while in the City of Los Angeles he was addicted to the use of narcotics. . . ."

Under these instructions the jury returned a verdict finding appellant "guilty of the offense charged." . . .

The broad power of a State to regulate the narcotic drugs traffic within its borders is not here in issue. . . . This statute is not one which punishes a person for the use of narcotics, for their purchase, sale or possession, or for antisocial or disorderly behavior resulting from their administration. It is not a law which even purports to provide or require medical treatment. Rather, we deal with a statute which makes the "status" of narcotic addiction a criminal offense, for which the offender may be prosecuted "at any time before he reforms." California has said that a person can be continuously guilty of this offense, whether or not he has ever used or possessed any narcotics within the State, and whether or not he has been guilty of any antisocial behavior there.

It is unlikely that any State at this moment in history would attempt to make it a criminal offense for a person to be mentally ill, or a leper, or to be afflicted with a venereal disease. A State might determine that the general health and welfare require that the victims of these and other human afflictions be dealt with by compulsory treatment, involving quarantine, confinement, or sequestration. But, in the light of contemporary human knowledge, a law which made a criminal offense of such a disease would doubtless be universally thought to be an infliction of cruel and unusual punishment in violation of the Eighth and Fourteenth Amendments.

We cannot but consider the statute before us as of the same category. In this Court counsel for the State recognized that narcotic addiction is an illness. Indeed, it is apparently an illness which may be contracted innocently or involuntarily.[9] We hold that a state law which imprisons a person thus afflicted as a criminal, even though he has never touched any narcotic drug within the State or been guilty of any irregular behavior there, inflicts a cruel and unusual punishment in violation of the Fourteenth Amendment. To be sure, imprisonment for ninety days is not, in the abstract, a punishment which is either cruel or unusual. But the question cannot be considered in the abstract. Even one day in prison would be a cruel and unusual punishment for the "crime" of having a common cold. . . .

Reversed.

JUSTICE DOUGLAS, concurring. . . .

The addict is a sick person. He may, of course, be confined for treatment or for the protection of society. Cruel and unusual punishment results not from confinement, but from convicting the addict of a crime. . . . A prosecution for addiction, with its resulting stigma and irreparable damage to the good name of the accused, cannot be justified as a means of protecting society, where a civil commitment would do as well. . . . We would forget the teachings of the Eighth Amendment if we allowed sickness to be made a crime and permitted sick people to be punished for being sick. The age of enlightenment cannot tolerate such barbarous action.

JUSTICE HARLAN, concurring.

I am not prepared to hold that on the present state of medical knowledge it is completely irrational and hence unconstitutional for a State to conclude that narcotics addiction is something other than an illness, nor that it amounts to cruel and unusual punishment for the State to subject narcotics addicts to its criminal law. . . . But in this case the trial court's instructions permitted the jury to find the appellant guilty on no more proof than that he was present in California while he was addicted to narcotics. Since addiction alone cannot reasonably be thought to amount to more than a compelling propensity to use narcotics, the effect of this instruction was to authorize criminal punishment for a bare desire to commit a criminal act. . . .

JUSTICE WHITE, dissenting. . . .

The Court clearly does not rest its decision upon the narrow ground that the jury was not expressly instructed not to convict if it believed appellant's use of narcotics was beyond his control. The Court recognizes no degrees of addiction. The Fourteenth Amendment is today held to bar any prosecution for addiction regardless of the degree of frequency of use, and the Court's opinion bristles with indications of further consequences. If it is "cruel and unusual punishment" to convict appellant for addiction, it is difficult to understand why it would be any less offensive to the Fourteenth Amendment to convict him for use on the same evidence of use which proved he was an addict. . . .

The Court has not merely tidied up California's law by removing some irritating vestige of an outmoded approach to the control of narcotics. At the very least, it has effectively removed California's power to deal effectively with the recurring case under the statute where there is ample evidence of use but no evidence of the precise location of use. Beyond this it has cast serious doubt upon the power of any State to forbid the use of narcotics under threat of crimi-

9. Not only may addiction innocently result from the use of medically prescribed narcotics, but a person may even be a narcotics addict from the moment of his birth. . . .

nal punishment. I cannot believe that the Court would forbid the application of the criminal laws to the use of narcotics under any circumstances. But the States, as well as the Federal Government, are now on notice. They will have to await a final answer in another case. . . .

POWELL v. TEXAS
Supreme Court of the United States
392 U.S. 514 (1968)

JUSTICE MARSHALL announced the judgment of the Court and delivered an opinion in which THE CHIEF JUSTICE, JUSTICE BLACK, and JUSTICE HARLAN join.

In late December 1966, appellant was arrested and charged with being found in a state of intoxication in a public place, in violation of Texas Penal Code, Art. 477 (1952), which reads as follows: "Whoever shall get drunk or be found in a state of intoxication in any public place, or at any private house except his own, shall be fined not exceeding one hundred dollars." . . .

The trial judge in the county court, sitting without a jury, made certain findings of fact, . . . but ruled as a matter of law that chronic alcoholism was not a defense to the charge. He found appellant guilty, and fined him $50. There being no further right to appeal within the Texas judicial system, appellant appealed to this Court. . . .

The principal testimony was that of Dr. Davis Wade, a Fellow of the American Medical Association, duly certified in psychiatry. . . . Dr. Wade sketched the outlines of the "disease" concept of alcoholism; noted that there is no generally accepted definition of "alcoholism"; alluded to the ongoing debate within the medical profession over whether alcohol is actually physically "addicting" or merely psychologically "habituating"; and concluded that in either case a "chronic alcoholic" is an "involuntary drinker," who is "powerless not to drink," and who "loses his self-control over his drinking." He testified that he had examined appellant, and that appellant is a "chronic alcoholic," who "by the time he has reached [the state of intoxication] is not able to control his behavior, and [who] has reached this point because he has an uncontrollable compulsion to drink." . . . He added that in his opinion jailing appellant without medical attention would operate neither to rehabilitate him or lessen his desire for alcohol.

On cross-examination, Dr. Wade admitted that when appellant was sober he knew the difference between right and wrong, and he responded affirmatively to the question whether appellant's act of taking the first drink in any given instance when he was sober was a "voluntary exercise of his will." Qualifying his answer, Dr. Wade stated that

> these individuals have a compulsion, and this compulsion, while not completely overpowering, is a very strong influence, an exceedingly strong influence, and this compulsion, coupled with the firm belief in their mind that they are going to be able to handle it from now on causes their judgment to be somewhat clouded.

Appellant testified concerning the history of his drinking problem. He reviewed his many arrests for drunkenness; testified that he was unable to stop drinking; stated that when he was intoxicated he had no control over his actions and could not remember them later, but that he did not become violent; and admitted that he did not remember his arrest on the occasion for which he was being tried. On cross-examination, appellant admitted that he had had one drink on the morning of the trial and had been able to discontinue drinking. . . .

Evidence in the case then closed. The State made no effort to obtain expert psychiatric testimony of its own, or even to explore with appellant's witness the question of appellant's power to control the frequency, timing, and location of his drinking bouts, or the substantial disagreement within the medical profession concerning the nature of the disease, the efficacy of treatment and the prerequisites for effective treatment. . . . Instead, the State concerned itself with a brief argument that appellant had no defense to the charge because he "is legally sane and knows the difference between right and wrong."

Following this abbreviated exposition of the problem before it, the trial court indicated its intention to disallow appellant's claimed defense of "chronic alcoholism." Thereupon defense counsel submitted, and the trial court entered, the following "findings of fact":

> (1) That chronic alcoholism is a disease which destroys the afflicted person's will power to resist the constant, excessive consumption of alcohol.
> (2) That a chronic alcoholic does not appear in public by his own volition but under a compulsion symptomatic of the disease of chronic alcoholism.
> (3) That Leroy Powell, a defendant herein, is a chronic alcoholic who is afflicted with the disease of chronic alcoholism.

Whatever else may be said of them, those are not "findings of fact" in any recognizable, traditional sense in which that term has been used in a court of law; they are the premises of a syllogism transparently designed to bring this case within the scope of this Court's opinion in Robinson v. California, 370 U.S. 660 (1962). Nonetheless, the dissent would have us adopt these "findings" without critical examination; it would use them as the basis for a constitutional holding that "a person may not be punished if the condition essential to constitute the defined crime is part of the pattern of his disease and is occasioned by a compulsion symptomatic of the disease."

The difficulty with that position, as we shall show, is that it goes much too far on the basis of too little knowledge. In the first place, the record in this case is utterly inadequate to permit the sort of informed and responsible adjudication which alone can support the announcement of an important and wide-ranging new constitutional principle. We know very little about the circumstances surrounding the drinking bout which resulted in this conviction, or about Leroy Powell's drinking problem, or indeed about alcoholism itself. . . .

Furthermore, the inescapable fact is that there is no agreement among members of the medical profession about what it means to say that "alcoholism" is a "disease." One of the principal works in this field states that the major difficulty in articulating a "disease concept of alcoholism" is that "alcoholism has too many definitions and disease has practically none." This same author concludes that "*a disease is what the medical profession recognizes as such.*" In other words, there is widespread agreement today that "alcoholism" is a "disease," for the simple reason that the medical profession has concluded that it should attempt to treat those who have drinking problems. There the agreement stops. Debate rages within the medical profession as to whether "alcoholism" is a separate "disease" in any meaningful biochemical, physiological or psychological sense, or whether it represents one peculiar manifestation in some individuals of underlying psychiatric disorders. . . .

The trial court's "finding" that Powell "is afflicted with the disease of chronic alcoholism, which destroys the afflicted person's will power to resist the constant, excessive consumption of alcohol" covers a multitude of sins. Dr. Wade's testimony that appellant suffered from a compulsion which was an "exceedingly strong influence," but which was "not completely overpowering" is at least more carefully stated, if no less mystifying. Jellinek insists that conceptual clarity can only be achieved by distinguishing carefully between "loss of control" once an individual has commenced to drink and "inability to abstain" from drinking in the first place. Presumably a person would have to display both characteristics in order to make out a constitutional defense, should one be recognized. Yet the "findings" of the trial court utterly fail to make this crucial distinction, and there is serious question whether the record can be read to support a finding of either loss of control or inability to abstain.

Dr. Wade did testify that once appellant began drinking he appeared to have no control over the amount of alcohol he finally ingested. Appellant's own testimony concerning his drinking on the day of the trial would certainly appear, however, to cast doubt upon the conclusion that he was without control over his consumption of alcohol when he had sufficiently important reasons to exercise such control. . . . Dr. Wade testified that when appellant was sober, the act of taking the first drink was a "voluntary exercise of his will," but that this exercise of will was undertaken under the "exceedingly strong influence" of a "compulsion" which was "not completely overpowering." Such concepts, when juxtaposed in this fashion, have little meaning. . . .

It is one thing to say that if a man is deprived of alcohol his hands will begin to shake, he will suffer agonizing pains and ultimately he will have hallucinations; it is quite another to say that a man has a "compulsion" to take a drink, but that he also retains a certain amount of "free will" with which to resist. It is simply impossible, in the present state of our knowledge, to ascribe a useful meaning to the latter statement. This definitional confusion reflects, of course, not merely the undeveloped state of the psychiatric art but also the conceptual difficulties inevitably attendant upon the importation of scientific and medical models into a legal system generally predicated upon a different set of assumptions. . . .

Despite the comparatively primitive state of our knowledge on the subject, it cannot be denied that the destructive use of alcoholic beverages is one of our principal social and public health problems. . . .

There is as yet no known generally effective method for treating the vast number of alcoholics in our society. . . . [I]t is entirely possibly that, even were the manpower and facilities available for a full-scale attack upon chronic alcoholism, we would find ourselves unable to help the vast bulk of our "visible" — let alone our "invisible" — alcoholic population. . . . The medical profession cannot, and does not, tell us with any assurance that, even if the buildings, equipment and trained personnel were made available, it could provide anything more than slightly higher-class jails for our indigent habitual inebriates. Thus we run the grave risk that nothing will be accomplished beyond the hanging of a new sign — reading "hospital" — over one wing of the jailhouse.

One virtue of the criminal process is, at least, that the duration of penal incarceration typically has some outside statutory limit; this is universally true in the case of petty offenses, such as public drunkenness, where jail terms are quite short on the whole. "Therapeutic civil commitment" lacks this feature; one is typically committed until one is "cured." Thus, to do otherwise than affirm might subject indigent alcoholics to the risk that they may be locked up for an indefinite period of time under the same conditions as before, with no more hope than before of receiving effective treatment and no prospect of periodic "freedom."

Faced with this unpleasant reality, we are unable to assert that the use of the criminal process as a means of dealing with the public aspects of problem drinking can never be defended as rational. . . .

Appellant claims that his conviction on the facts of this case would violate the Cruel and Unusual Punishment Clause of the Eighth Amendment as applied to the States through the Fourteenth Amendment. [He] seeks to come within the application of the Cruel and Unusual Punishment Clause announced in Robinson v. California, 370 U.S. 660 (1962), which involved a state statute making it a crime to "be addicted to the use of narcotics." . . .

On its face the present case does not fall within that holding, since appellant was convicted, not for being a chronic alcoholic, but for being in public while drunk on a particular occasion. The State of Texas thus has not sought to punish a mere status, as California did in *Robinson;* nor has it attempted to regulate appellant's behavior in the privacy of his own home. Rather, it has imposed upon appellant a criminal sanction for public behavior which may create substantial health and safety hazards, both for appellant and for members of the general public, and which offends the moral and aesthetic sensibilities of a large segment of the community. This seems a far cry from convicting one for being an addict, being a chronic alcoholic, being "mentally ill or a leper. . . ."

Robinson so viewed brings this Court but a very small way into the substantive criminal law. And unless *Robinson* is so viewed it is difficult to see any limiting principle that would serve to prevent this Court from becoming, under the aegis of the Cruel and Unusual Punishment Clause, the ultimate arbiter of the standards of criminal responsibility, in diverse areas of the criminal law, throughout the country.

It is suggested in dissent that *Robinson* stands for the "simple" but "subtle" principle that "[c]riminal penalties may not be inflicted on a person for being in a condition he is powerless to change." . . . In that view, appellant's "condition" of public intoxication was "occasioned by a compulsion symptomatic of the disease" of chronic alcoholism, and thus, apparently, his behavior lacked the critical element of mens rea. Whatever may be the merits of such a doctrine of criminal responsibility, it surely cannot be said to follow from *Robinson.* The entire thrust of *Robinson*'s interpretation of the Cruel and Unusual Punishment Clause is that criminal penalties may be inflicted only if the accused has committed some act, has engaged in some behavior, which society has an interest in preventing, or perhaps in historical common law terms, has committed some actus reus. It thus does not deal with the question of whether certain conduct cannot constitutionally be punished because it is, in some sense, "involuntary" or "occasioned by a compulsion." . . . The only relevance of *Robinson* to this issue is that because the Court interpreted the statute there involved as making a "status" criminal, it was able to suggest that the statute would cover even a situation in which addiction had been acquired involuntarily. 370 U.S., at 667, n. 9. That this factor was not determinative in the case is shown by the fact that there was no indication of how *Robinson* himself had become an addict.

Ultimately, then, the most troubling aspects of this case, were *Robinson* to be extended to meet it, would be the scope and content of what could only be a constitutional doctrine of criminal responsibility. In dissent it is urged that the decision could be limited to conduct which is "a characteristic and involuntary part of the pattern of the disease as it afflicts" the particular individual, and that "it is not foreseeable" that it would be applied "in the case of offenses such as driving a car while intoxicated, assault, theft, or robbery." That is limitation by fiat. . . . If Leroy Powell cannot be convicted of public intoxication, it is difficult to see how a State can convict an individual for murder, if that individual, while exhibiting normal behavior in all other respects, suffers from a "compulsion" to kill, which is an "exceedingly strong influence," but "not completely overpowering." Even if we limit our consideration to chronic alcoholics, it would seem impossible to confine the principle within the arbitrary bounds which the dissent seems to envision. . . .

Traditional common-law concepts of personal accountability and essential considerations of federalism lead us to disagree with appellant. We are unable to conclude, on the state of this record or on the current state of medical knowledge, that chronic alcoholics in general, and Leroy Powell in particular, suffer from such an irresistible compulsion to drink and to get drunk in public that they are utterly unable to control their performance of either or both of these acts and thus cannot be deterred at all from public intoxication. And in any event this Court has never articulated a general constitutional doctrine of mens rea.

We cannot cast aside the centuries-long evolution of the collection of interlocking and overlapping concepts which the common law has utilized to assess the moral accountability of an individual for his antisocial deeds. The doctrines of actus reus, mens rea, insanity, mistake, justification, and duress have historically provided the tools for a constantly shifting adjustment of the tension between the evolving aims of the criminal law and changing religious, moral, philosophical, and medical views of the nature of man. This process of adjustment has always been thought to be the province of the States.

Nothing could be less fruitful than for this Court to be impelled into defining some sort of insanity test in constitutional terms. Yet, that task would seem to follow inexorably from an extension of *Robinson* in this case. If a person in the "condition" of being a chronic alcoholic cannot be criminally punished as a constitutional matter for being drunk in public, it would seem to follow that a person who contends that, in terms of one test, "his unlawful act was the product of mental disease or mental defect," Durham v. United States, 214 F.2d 862, 875 (C.A.D.C. Cir. 1954), would state an issue of constitutional dimension with regard to his criminal responsibility had he been tried under some different and perhaps lesser standard, e.g., the right-wrong test of *M'Naghten*'s Case. . . . But formulating a constitutional rule would reduce, if not eliminate, that fruitful experimentation, and freeze the developing productive dialogue between law and psychiatry into a rigid constitutional mold. It is simply not yet the time to write into the Constitution formulas cast in terms whose meaning, let alone relevance, are not yet clear either to doctors or to lawyers.

Affirmed.

JUSTICE BLACK, whom JUSTICE HARLAN joins, concurring. . . .

I agree with Justice Marshall that the findings of fact in this case are inadequate to justify the sweeping constitutional rule urged upon us. I could not, however, consider any findings that could be made with respect to "voluntariness" or "compulsion" controlling on the question whether a specific instance of human behavior should be immune from punishment as a constitutional matter. When we say that appellant's appearance in public is caused not by "his own" volition but rather by some other force, we are clearly thinking of a force that is nevertheless "his" except in some special sense.[1] The accused undoubtedly commits the proscribed act and the only question is whether the act can be attributed to a part of "his" personality that should not be regarded as criminally responsible. Almost all of the traditional purposes of the criminal law can be significantly served by punishing the person who in fact committed the proscribed act, without regard to whether his action was "compelled" by some elusive "irresponsible" aspect of his personality. [P]unishment of such a defendant can clearly be justified in terms of deterrence, isolation, and treatment. On the other hand, medical decisions concerning the use of a term such as "disease" or "volition," based as they are on the clinical problems of diagnosis and treatment, bear no necessary correspondence to the legal decision whether the overall objectives of the criminal law can be furthered by imposing punishment. For these reasons, much as I think that criminal sanctions should in many situations be applied only to those whose conduct is morally blameworthy, see Morissette v. United States, 342 U.S. 246 (1951), I cannot think the States should be held constitutionally required to make the inquiry as to what part of a defendant's personality is responsible for his actions and to excuse anyone whose action was, in some complex, psychological sense, the result of a "compulsion." . . .

The rule of constitutional law urged by appellant is not required by Robinson v. California, 370 U.S. 660 (1962). In that case we held that a person could not be punished for the mere status of being a narcotics addict. We explicitly limited our holding to the situation where no conduct of any kind is involved. . . .

Punishment for a status is particularly obnoxious, and in many instances can reasonably be called cruel and unusual, because it involves punishment for a mere propensity, a desire to commit an offense; the mental element is not simply one part of the crime but may constitute all of it. This is a situation universally sought to be avoided in our criminal law; the fundamental requirement that some action be proved is solidly established even for offenses most heavily based on propensity, such as attempt, conspiracy, and recidivist crimes. . . .

The rule of constitutional law urged upon us by appellant would have a revolutionary impact on the criminal law. . . . If the original boundaries of Robinson are to be discarded, any new limits too would soon fall by the wayside and the Court would be forced to hold the States powerless to punish any conduct that could be shown to result from a "compulsion," in the complex, psychological

---

1. If an intoxicated person is actually carried into the street by someone else, "he" does not do the act at all, and of course he is entitled to acquittal. E.g., Martin v. State, 31 Ala. App. 334, 17 So. 2d 427 (1944) [page 171 supra].

meaning of that term. The result, to choose just one illustration, would be to require recognition of "irresistible impulse" as a complete defense to any crime; this is probably contrary to present law in most American jurisdictions.

The real reach of any such decision, however, would be broader still, for the basic premise underlying the argument is that it is cruel and unusual to punish a person who is not morally blameworthy. I state the proposition in this sympathetic way because I feel there is much to be said for avoiding the use of criminal sanctions in many such situations. See Morissette v. United States [, 342 U.S. 246 (1952), reprinted at page 237 supra.] But the question here is one of constitutional law. The legislatures have always been allowed wide freedom to determine the extent to which moral culpability should be a prerequisite to conviction of a crime. E.g., United States v. Dotterweich, 320 U.S. 277 (1943). The criminal law is a social tool that is employed in seeking a wide variety of goals, and I cannot say the Eighth Amendment's limits on the use of criminal sanctions extend as far as this viewpoint would inevitably carry them. . . .

JUSTICE WHITE, concurring in the result.

If it cannot be a crime to have an irresistible compulsion to use narcotics, Robinson v. California, 370 U.S. 660, I do not see how it can constitutionally be a crime to yield to such a compulsion. Punishing an addict for using drugs convicts for addiction under a different name. Distinguishing between the two crimes is like forbidding criminal conviction for being sick with flu or epilepsy but permitting punishment for running a fever or having a convulsion. Unless *Robinson* is to be abandoned, the use of narcotics by an addict must be beyond the reach of the criminal law. Similarly, the chronic alcoholic with an irresistible urge to consume alcohol should not be punishable for drinking or for being drunk.

Powell's conviction was for the different crime of being drunk in a public place. Thus even if Powell was compelled to drink, and so could not constitutionally be convicted for drinking, his conviction in this case can be invalidated only if there is a constitutional basis for saying that he may not be punished for being in public while drunk. . . .

The trial court said that Powell was a chronic alcoholic with a compulsion not only to drink to excess but also to frequent public places when intoxicated. Nothing in the record before the trial court supports the latter conclusion, which is contrary to common sense and to common knowledge. . . . Before and after taking the first drink, and until he becomes so drunk that he loses the power to know where he is or to direct his movements, the chronic alcoholic with a home or financial resources is as capable as the nonchronic drinker of doing his drinking in private, of removing himself from public places and, since he knows or ought to know that he will become intoxicated, of making plans to avoid his being found drunk in public. For these reasons, I cannot say that the chronic who proves his disease and a compulsion to drink is shielded from conviction when he has knowingly failed to take feasible precautions against committing a criminal act, here the act of going to or remaining in a public place. On such facts the alcoholic is like a person with smallpox, who could be convicted for being on the street but not for being ill, or like the epileptic, punishable for driving a car but not for his disease.

The fact remains that some chronic alcoholics must drink and hence must drink *somewhere*. Although many chronics have homes, many others do not. For all practical purposes the public streets may be home for these unfortunates, not because their disease compels them to be there, but because, drunk or sober, they have no place else to go and no place else to be when they are drinking. . . . For some of these alcoholics I would think a showing could be made that resisting drunkenness is impossible and that avoiding public places when intoxicated is also impossible. As applied to them this statute is in effect a law which bans a single act for which they may not be convicted under the Eighth Amendment — the act of getting drunk. . . .

It is unnecessary to pursue at this point the further definition of the circumstances or the state of intoxication which might bar conviction of a chronic alcoholic for being drunk in a public place. [Powell] made no showing that he was unable to stay off the streets on the night in question. . . .

JUSTICE FORTAS, with whom JUSTICE DOUGLAS, JUSTICE BRENNAN, and JUSTICE STEWART join, dissenting. . . .

The sole question presented is whether a criminal penalty may be imposed upon a person suffering the disease of "chronic alcoholism" for a condition — being "in a state of intoxication" in public — which is a characteristic part of the pattern of his disease and which, the trial court found, was not the consequence of appellant's volition but of "a compulsion symptomatic of the disease of chronic alcoholism." . . . This case does not . . . concern the responsibility of an alcoholic for criminal *acts*. We deal here with the mere *condition* of being intoxicated in public.

. . . [C]onsideration of the Eighth Amendment issue in this case requires an understanding of "the disease of chronic alcoholism." . . . Although there is some problem in defining the concept, its core meaning, as agreed by authorities, is that alcoholism is caused and maintained by something other than the moral fault of the alcoholic, something that, to a greater or lesser extent depending upon the physiological or psychological makeup and history of the individual, cannot be controlled by him. . . .

Authorities have recognized that a number of factors may contribute to alcoholism. Some studies have pointed to physiological influences, such as vitamin deficiency, hormone imbalance, abnormal metabolism, and hereditary proclivity. Other researchers have found more convincing a psychological approach, emphasizing early environment and underlying conflicts and tensions. Numerous studies have indicated the influence of sociocultural factors. It has been shown, for example, that the incidence of alcoholism among certain ethnic groups is far higher than among others.

The manifestations of alcoholism are reasonably well identified. . . . It is well established that alcohol may be habituating and "can be physically addicting." It has been said that "the main point for the nonprofessional is that alcoholism is not within the control of the person involved. He is not willfully drinking." . . .

Robinson stands upon a principle which, despite its subtlety, must be simply stated and respectfully applied because it is the foundation of individual liberty and the cornerstone of the relations between a civilized state and its citizens: Criminal penalties may not be inflicted upon a person for being in a condition he is powerless to change. In all probability, Robinson at some time before his conviction elected to take narcotics. But the crime as defined did not punish this conduct. The statute imposed a penalty for the offense of "addiction" — a condition which Robinson could not control. Once Robinson had become an addict, he was utterly powerless to avoid criminal guilt. He was powerless to choose not to violate the law.

In the present case, appellant is charged with a crime comprised of two elements — being intoxicated and being found in a public place while in that condition. The crime, so defined, differs from that in *Robinson*. The statute covers more than a mere status. But the essential constitutional defect here is the same as in *Robinson*, for in both cases the particular defendant was accused of being in a condition which he had no capacity to change or avoid. The trial judge sitting as trier of fact found, upon the medical and other relevant testimony, that Powell is a "chronic alcoholic." He defined appellant's "chronic alcoholism" as "a disease which destroys the afflicted person's will power to resist the constant, excessive consumption of alcohol." He also found that " a chronic alcoholic does not appear in public by his own volition but under a compulsion symptomatic of the disease of chronic alcoholism." I read these findings to mean that appellant was powerless to avoid drinking; that having taken his first drink, he had "an uncontrollable compulsion to drink" to the point of intoxication; and that, once intoxicated, he could not prevent himself from appearing in public places. . . .

The findings in this case, read against the background of the medical and sociological data to which I have referred, compel the conclusion that the infliction upon appellant of a criminal penalty for being intoxicated in a public place would be "cruel and inhuman punishment." . . .

I would reverse the judgment below.

STATE EX REL. HARPER v. ZEGEER, 296 S.E.2d 873 (W. Va. 1982): Medical experts and professional groups have concluded that alcoholism is a disease. We agree. . . . We also believe that criminally punishing alcoholics for being publicly intoxicated violates the prohibition against cruel and unusual punishment. W. Va. Const. art. III, §5.

In Powell v. Texas, 392 U.S. 514 (1968), five Justices agreed that alcoholism was a disease, but because of a confusing trial court record the majority was unwilling to extend *Robinson*'s rationale to public intoxication. . . . Since *Powell*, no state court has held that alcoholics could not be punished criminally for public intoxication, except Minnesota. [State v. Fearon, 283 Minn. 90, 166 N.W.2d 720 (1969).]

Most states have adopted the Uniform Alcoholism and Intoxication Treatment Act that deals with alcoholism as a disease. Others stopped short of decriminalization, and instead developed diversionary systems for both alcoholics and public drunks. . . . We urge our Legislature to enact a comprehensive plan for dealing with alcoholics in a humane and beneficial manner.

Criminal punishment of chronic alcoholics violates constitutional prohibitions against cruel and unusual punishment. However, their public presence is a potential threat to their own and others' well-being, is often offensive, even obnoxious to other people, and the State has a legitimate right to get them off the streets or out of whatever public area in which they may be gamboling.[10] . . .

If the arresting officer has knowledge that the accused has a previous history of arrests for public intoxication, he has a duty to bring these facts to the attention of the judicial officer, or to make application for involuntary hospitalization

---

10. The State has a right and duty to prosecute people who, while drunk, commit crimes: drunken drivers, for example, and peace breachers, assaulters, and such. This opinion is about people who are charged solely with public intoxication. . . .

for examination of an accused who, because of his inebriated state, is likely to harm himself or others if allowed to remain at liberty. . . . Upon a showing that an accused is a chronic alcoholic, he is to be accorded all of the procedural safeguards that surround those with mental disabilities who are accused of crime.

NOTES

1. The medical and scientific premises of the defense position in *Powell* are questioned in Herbert Fingarette, Heavy Drinking (1988). Professor Fingarette characterizes the disease concept of alcoholism as a "myth" that attained ever wider public acceptance just at the time that its empirical foundations were being discredited by researchers. He notes that E. M. Jellinek's early articles and his influential 1960 book, The Disease Concept of Alcoholism, upon which Justice Fortas relied heavily in *Powell*, drew on preliminary data subject to limitations that Jellinek himself acknowledged. The research of the next two-and-a-half decades consistently contradicted Jellinek's hypotheses, and Fingarette states (id. at 3) that today "*no* leading research authorities accept the classic disease concept."

The notion that alcoholics cannot "control" their drinking similarly has gained wide acceptance, and Fingarette observes (id. at 32) that "[a]nyone who has ever observed the behavior of a chronic heavy drinker cannot help feeling a sense of powerful momentum at work." Nonetheless, Fingarette notes (id. at 34), researchers have published "decisive evidence disproving the myth." The studies show that on any particular occasion heavy drinkers, including those labeled chronic alcoholics, may drink heavily, moderately, or not at all, and the choice depends on a wide variety of situational factors including the rewards or penalties the drinker believes likely to follow.

For studies more sympathetic to the view of alcoholism as a disease, see George E. Vaillant, The Natural History of Alcoholism (1983); L. Tiffany & M. Tiffany, Nosologic Objection to the Criminal Defense of Pathological Intoxication: What Do the Doubters Doubt?, 13 Intl. J.L. & Psych. 49 (1990).

For further consideration of these issues, see Herbert Fingarette, The Perils of *Powell:* In Search of a Factual Foundation for the "Disease Concept of Alcoholism," 83 Harv. L. Rev. 793 (1970); Kent Greenawalt, "Uncontrollable" Actions and the Eighth Amendment: Implications of *Powell v. Texas,* 69 Colum. L. Rev. 927 (1969).

2. In Bowers v. Hardwick, 478 U.S. 186 (1986), a 5-4 majority of the Supreme Court rejected a due process challenge to the application of a Georgia anti-sodomy law to private, consenting homosexual acts. See page 155 supra. The Court did not consider objections based on the Eighth Amendment. Does the enforcement of statutes like that in *Bowers* raise Eighth Amendment problems? Consider the observations of Justice Blackmun, writing for the four dissenters (id. at 203 n. 2):

> Despite historical views of homosexuality, it is no longer viewed by mental health professionals as a "disease" or disorder. But, obviously, neither is it simply a matter of deliberate personal election. Homosexual orientation may well form part of the very fiber of an individual's personality. Consequently, under Justice White's analy-

sis in *Powell,* the Eighth Amendment may pose a constitutional barrier to sending an individual to prison for acting on that attraction regardless of the circumstances. An individual's ability to make constitutionally protected "decisions concerning sexual relations" is rendered empty indeed if he or she is given no real choice but a life without any physical intimacy.

UNITED STATES v. MOORE

United States Court of Appeals, District of Columbia Circuit
486 F. 2d 1139 (1973)

WILKEY, J. . . . Appellant contends that his conviction [for possession of heroin] was improper because he is a heroin addict with an overpowering need to use heroin and should not, therefore, be held responsible for being in possession of the drug. After careful consideration, we must reject appellant's contention. . . .

[The prosecution conceded that Moore was an addict. The evidence was in conflict as to whether he was a trafficking addict. The trial court refused to permit defendant's expert witnesses to testify on the nature of defendant's heroin addiction, and declined to instruct the jury that a nontrafficking addict could not be convicted under the statutes charged.]

We believe it is clear from the evidence that Moore was not a mere nontrafficking addict but was in fact engaged in the drug trade. Yet even if we were to assume that appellant was a simple addict and nothing more, we believe that his conviction must be sustained. . . .

According to appellant this case has one central issue:

Is the proffered evidence of Appellant's long and intensive dependence on (addiction to) injected heroin, resulting in substantial impairment of his behavior controls and a loss of self-control over the use of heroin, relevant to his criminal responsibility for unlawful possession . . . ?

In other words, is appellant's addiction a defense to the crimes, involving only possession, with which he is charged? Arguing that he has lost the power of self-control with regard to his addiction, appellant maintains that by applying "the broad principles of common law criminal responsibility" we must decide that he is entitled to dismissal of the indictment or a jury trial on this issue. The gist of appellant's argument here is that "the common law has long held that the capacity to control behavior is a prerequisite for criminal responsibility." . . .

Drug addiction of varying degrees may or may not result in loss of self-control, depending on the strength of character opposed to the drug craving. Under appellant's theory, adopted by the dissenters, only if there is a resulting loss of self-control can there be an absence of *free will* which, under the extension of the common law theory, would provide a valid defense to the addict. If there is a demonstrable absence of free will (loss of self-control), the illegal acts of possession and acquisition cannot be charged to the user of the drugs.

But if it is absence of free will which excuses the mere possessor-acquirer, the more desperate bank robber for drug money has an even more demonstrable lack of free will and derived from precisely the same factors as appellant argues should excuse the mere possessor.

. . . [T]he peculiar nature of the problem of the heroin traffic makes certain policies necessary that should not be weakened by the creation of this defense. There is no compelling policy requiring us to intervene here. . . .

Robinson is no authority for the proposition that the Eighth Amendment prevents punishment of an addict for acts he is "compelled" to do by his addiction. . . . *Robinson* simply illustrates repugnance at the prospect of punishing one for his status as an addict.. . . .

The Eighth Amendment defense for chronic alcoholics advanced by some members of the Court in Powell v. Texas, that is, the interpretation that *Robinson* held that it was not criminal to give in to the irresistible compulsions of a "disease," weaves in and out of the *Powell* opinions, but there is definitely no Supreme Court holding to this effect. . . .

[Conviction affirmed.]

LEVENTHAL, J., with whom McGOWAN, J., concurs. . . . Appellant's key defense concepts are impairment of behavioral control and loss of self-control. These have been considered by this court most fully in discussion of the insanity defense, and the philosophy of those opinions is invoked, although appellant disclaims the insanity defense as such. . . .

Apellant's presentation rests, in essence, on the premise that the "mental disease or defect" requirement of [the insanity defense] is superfluous. He discerns a broad principle that excuses from criminal responsibility when conduct results from a condition that impairs behavior control. . . . The broad assertion is that in general the mens rea element of criminal responsibility requires freedom of will, which is negatived by an impairment of behavioral control and loss of self-control. . . .

It does not follow that because one condition (mental disease) yields an exculpatory defense if it results in impairment of and lack of behavioral controls the same result follows when some other condition impairs behavior controls.

. . . By long tradition of the penal law, an actor's behavior is "involuntary" and there is no criminal responsibility, when he is overwhelmed by force, as when his arm is physically moved by someone else. By long tradition, too, the criminal law reaches only acts that are not only voluntary but also accompanied by a mental element, a "mens rea" (Law latin for guilty mind). . . . The elements that our basic jurisprudence requires for criminal responsibility — a voluntary act, and a mental state — are plainly fulfilled by an offense of knowing possession of a prohibited article.

The legal conception of criminal capacity cannot be limited to those of unusual endowment or even average powers. A few may be recognized as so far from normal as to be entirely beyond the reach of criminal justice, but in general the criminal law is a means of social control that must be potentially capable of reaching the vast bulk of the population. Criminal responsibility is a concept that not only extends to the bulk of those below the median line of responsibility, but specifically extends to those who have a realistic problem of substantial impairment and lack of capacity due, say, to weakness of intellect that establishes susceptibility to suggestion; or to a loss of control of the mind as a result of passion, whether the passion is of an amorous nature or the result of hate, prejudice or vengeance; or to a depravity that blocks out conscience as an influence on conduct.

The criminal law cannot "vary legal norms with the individual's capacity to meet the standards they prescribe, absent a disability that is both gross and verifiable, such as the mental disease or defect that may establish irresponsibility. The most that it is feasible to do with lesser disabilities is to accord them proper weight in sentencing."[65]

Only in limited areas have the courts recognized a defense to criminal responsibility, on the basis that a described condition establishes a psychic incapacity negativing free will in the broader sense. These are areas where the courts have been able to respond to a deep call on elemental justice, and to discern a demarcation of doctrine that keeps the defense within verifiable bounds that do not tear the fabric of the criminal law as an instrument of social control.

. . . The subject of mental disease, though subject to some indeterminacy, and difficulty of diagnosis when extended to volitional impairment as well as cognitive incapacity, has long been the subject of systematic study, and in that framework it is considered manageable to ask psychiatrists to address the distinction, all-important and crucial to the law, between incapacity and indisposition, between those who can't and those who won't, between the impulse irresistible and the impulse not resisted. These are matters as to which the court has accepted the analysis of medicine, medical conditions and symptoms, and on the premise that they can be considered on a verifiable basis, and with reasonable dispatch, the courts have recognized a defense even in conditions not as obvious and verifiable as those covered in the older and limited test of capacity to know right from wrong.

As to the subject of drug dependence and psychic incapacity to refrain from narcotics, even the 1970 Study Draft of the Staff of the National Commission on Reform of Federal Criminal Laws, which favors on balance a drug dependence defense to the crime of possession, for incapacity to refrain from use, candidly recognizes the problems involved. One is "the paradox of jail for the least dangerous possessors (non-addict experimenters and the like) while addicts go free." More important, for present purposes, is the Staff's caution first, that even physical symptoms might "be successfully feigned," and, more broadly, that there is considerable difficulty of verification of the claim of a drug user that he is unable to refrain from use. . . .

The difficulty is sharpened by the appreciable number of narcotic "addicts" who do abandon their habits permanently, and much larger number who reflect their capacity to refrain by ceasing use for varying periods of time. The reasons are not clear but the phenomenon is indisputable. . . .

Our analysis has revealed that there is no broad common law principle of exculpation on ground of lack of control, but rather a series of particular defenses staked out in manageable areas, with the call for justice to the individual confined to ascertainable and verifiable conditions, and limited by the interest of society in control of conduct. . . .

WRIGHT, J., dissenting: . . . I suggest that the development of the common law of mens rea has reached the point where it should embrace a new principle: a drug addict who, by reason of his use of drugs, lacks substantial capacity to con-

---

65. ALI Model Penal Code §2.09, Comment (Tent. Draft No. 10, 1960), at 6.

form his conduct to the requirements of the law may not be held criminally responsible for mere possession of drugs for his own use. . . .

The concept of criminal responsibility is, by its very nature, "an expression of the moral sense of the community." United States v. Freeman, 2 Cir., 357 F.2d 606, 615 (1966). In western society, the concept has been shaped by two dominant value judgments — that punishment must be morally legitimate, and that it must not unduly threaten the liberties and dignity of the individual in his relationship to society. As a result, there has historically been a strong conviction in our jurisprudence that to hold a man criminally responsible his actions must have been the product of a "free will." . . . Thus criminal responsibility is assessed only when through "free will" a man elects to do evil, and if he is not a free agent, or is unable to choose or to act voluntarily, or to avoid the conduct which constitutes the crime, he is outside the postulate of the law of punishment.[182]

Despite this general principle, however, it is clear that our legal system does not exculpate all persons whose capacity for control is impaired, for whatever cause or reason. Rather, in determining responsibility for crime, the law assumes "free will" and then recognizes known deviations "where there is a broad consensus that free will does not exist" with respect to the particular condition at issue. . . . The evolving nature of this process is amply demonstrated in the gradual development of such defenses as infancy, duress, insanity, somnambulism and other forms of automatism, epilepsy and unconsciousness, involuntary intoxication, delirium tremens, and chronic alcoholism.

A similar consensus exists today in the area of narcotics addiction. [I]t can no longer seriously be questioned that for at least some addicts the "overpowering" psychological and physiological need to possess and inject narcotics cannot be overcome by mere exercise of "free will."

Moreover, recognition of a defense of "addiction" for crimes such as possession of narcotics is consistent . . . with the traditional goals of penology — retribution, deterrence, isolation and rehabilitation. . . . Revenge, if it is ever to be legitimate, must be premised on moral blameworthiness, and what segment of our society would feel its need for retribution satisfied when it wreaks vengeance upon those who are diseased because of their disease? It is of course true that there may have been a time in the past before the addict lost control when he made a conscious decision to use drugs. But imposition of punishment on this basis would violate the longstanding rule that "[t]he law looks to the immediate, and not to the remote cause; to the actual state of the party, and not to the causes, which remotely produced it." . . .

The most widely employed argument in favor of punishing addicts for crimes such as possession of narcotics is that such punishment or threat of punishment

---

182. [T]he courts are willing to allow strict liability [under regulatory statutes] insofar as mistake of fact is concerned for the accused under such statutes ordinarily is capable of preventing the violation "with no more care than society might reasonably expect and no more exertion than it might reasonably exact from one who has assumed his responsibility." Morisette v. United States, 342 U.S. 246, 256 (1952). . . .

The situation is quite different, however, where the defendant's ability to control his behavior is impaired by some legally recognized disability such as duress, insanity, chronic alcoholism or addiction. Since these persons are *incapable* of conforming to the law no matter what standard of care is required, they cannot be held responsible for violation of even "regulatory statutes."

has a substantial deterrent effect. Given our present knowledge, however, the merits of this argument appear doubtful. Deterrence presupposes rationality — it proceeds on the assumption that the detriments which would inure to the prospective criminal upon apprehension can be made so severe that he will be dissuaded from undertaking the criminal act. In the case of the narcotic addict, however, the normal sense of reason, which is so essential to effective functioning of deterrence, is overcome by the psychological and physiological compulsions of the disease. As a result, it is widely agreed that the threat of even harsh prison sentences cannot deter the addict from using and possessing the drug.

A similar situation prevails insofar as deterrence of *potential* addicts is concerned. [N]othing in this opinion would in any way affect the criminal responsibility of non-addict users for crimes they may commit — including illegal possession of narcotics. . . .

Shifting our focus now to the goal of isolating the offender, we arrive here at not only a justifiable basis for action but one which, in some cases at least, may be vital to the interests of society. . . . This does not mean, however, that the goal of isolation justifies infliction of criminal punishment upon the addict. On the contrary, this interest may be fully vindicated through a program of civil commitment with treatment as well as by criminal incarceration. . . .

This, then, brings us to the final and most important goal of modern penology — to rehabilitate the offender. In this age of enlightened correctional philosophy, we now recognize that society has a responsibility to both the individual and the community to treat the offender so that upon his release he may function as a productive, law-abiding citizen. . . .

Perhaps the most troublesome question arising out of recognition of the addiction defense I suggest is whether it should be limited only to those acts — such as mere possession for use — which are inherent in the disease itself. It can hardly be doubted that, in at least some instances, an addict may in fact be "compelled" to engage in other types of criminal activity in order to obtain sufficient funds to purchase his necessary supply of narcotics. . . . Nevertheless, I am convinced that Congress has manifested a clear intent to preclude common law extension of the defense beyond those crimes which, like the act of possession, cause direct harm only to the addict himself. . . .

The basic question of criminal responsibility under the addiction defense is a legal, and not a purely medical, determination. Not all drug users are "addicts" and, as with any compulsion, the degree of dependence may vary among different individuals and, indeed, even in a given individual at different stages of his addiction. Thus what we are concerned with here is not an abstract medical or psychiatric definition of addiction which sets forth a clinical checklist of relevant symptoms but, rather, a behavioral model, based upon traditional legal and moral principles, which tests the ability of the defendant to control his behavior. The essential inquiry, then, is simply whether, at the time of the offense, the defendant, as a result of his repeated use of narcotics, lacked substantial capacity to conform his conduct to the requirements of the law.

BAZELON, C.J. (concurring in part and dissenting in part): . . . On the issue of guilt or innocence, Judge Wright's views are closest to my own. I cannot, however, accept his view that the addiction/responsibility defense should be limited to the offense of possession. I would also permit a jury to consider addiction as a defense to a charge of, for example, armed robbery or trafficking in drugs, to determine whether the defendant was under such duress or compulsion, because of his addiction, that he was unable to conform his conduct to the requirements of the law. . . .

MEIR DAN-COHEN, ACTUS REUS, in Encyclopedia of Criminal Justice 15, 18-19 (1983): The criminal law, echoing common beliefs and pervasive ordinary practices, . . . postulates that, by and large, people are capable of choosing their course of conduct. . . . Only in the exceptional case where, because of some special circumstances, the defendant completely lacks control over his bodily movements in a way that makes the legally mandated conduct impossible, does the claim of involuntariness become a legal issue.

However, keeping the claim of involuntariness within such narrow bounds is [not easy]. For punishment to serve as an effective deterrent, the law must preserve a sufficiently wide range of cases where punishment can be imposed. The law, therefore, can and does recognize involuntariness only when the defendant's determinist account of the criminal event is both of a rare kind and is generally perceived to be clearly convincing. By insisting on these two conditions, the law affirms its commitment to fairness (or justice) without significantly diminishing its effectiveness.

From this perspective, the compromise struck by the law is extremely precarious. There is no escaping the recognition that the requirement of voluntariness is locked in a deadly, and possibly losing, battle with determinism. Scientific (psychological, biological, or medical) explanations, it is argued, almost invariably increase the deterministic element in our view of human conduct. An epileptic seizure supports a claim of involuntariness because the acts in question are accounted for by a determinist medical theory. The more such accounts we possess, the greater the encroachment on the presupposition of voluntariness that underlies the criminal law. Any recognition of a case of involuntariness is bound to take us down a slippery slope, at the end of which we would have nullified the entire criminal law. On the other hand, a refusal to go down the slope, or any attempt to stop somewhere along the way, is bound to be arbitrary and unfair. . . .

NOTES

1. For a detailed analysis of the opinions in the *Moore* case, see Richard Boldt, The Construction of Responsibility in the Criminal Law, 140 U. Pa. L. Rev. 2245 (1992), especially 2285-2294. The author observes:

> In the nearly two decades since *Moore*, other state courts have considered the question referred to them in general terms by Justice Marshall in the *Powell* case. With few significant exceptions, they have declined to recognize any version of the involuntariness or lack-of-choice defense pressed by alcoholic or drug-addicted defendants. The relative paucity of cases in which defendants have pressed a loss-of-control defense, together with the near universal hostility accorded such arguments by the few courts to reach the issue, is significant evidence that a judicially created involution doctrine is unlikely to emerge in the foreseeable future.

A review of the cases is contained in Phillip Hassman, Annot., Drug Addiction or Related Mental State as Defense to Criminal Charge, 73 A.L.R.3d 16 (1991).

2. In Commonwealth v. Sheehan, 383 N.E.2d 1115 (Mass. 1978), the defendant appealed his conviction of robbery of a registered pharmacist on the ground that the trial judge excluded his proffer of expert testimony to show that because of his drug addiction he was not criminally responsible under the Massachusetts test of legal insanity (modeled after the Model Penal Code test). The court affirmed, stating (id. at 1118-1119):

> We reject the defendant's argument that drug addiction itself may qualify as a mental disease or defect which, along with other necessary elements, would warrant a finding of not guilty by reason of insanity. . . .
> If the normal consequences of drug addiction are to be accepted as a ground for avoidance of responsibility for criminal conduct, the Legislature is the appropriate body to make that determination. Although the Legislature has dealt with drug dependency and drug addiction in relation to criminal proceedings, it has not adopted the view that drug addiction absolves a defendant of responsibility for his criminal conduct. Indeed, for all crimes other than drug offenses, the Legislature has adopted a procedure which calls for the sentencing of a drug dependent person in the normal course, with the possibility of drug treatment on the order of the judge and with the consent of the defendant. With this expression of public policy by the Legislature, we decline to adopt a general rule of law which absolves one from responsibility for criminal conduct based solely on the consequences of the voluntary use of drugs.

For commentary on these issues see Herbert Fingarette, Addiction and Criminal Responsibility, 84 Yale L.J. 413 (1975); Patricia M. Wald, Alcohol, Drugs, and Criminal Responsibility, 63 Geo. L.J. 69 (1974); Annot., 73 A.L.R.3d 16 (1976).

3. An informative discussion of the complexity of addiction appears in John Kaplan, The Hardest Drug 15-51 (1983). Professor Kaplan argues that the physical symptoms of heroin withdrawal are roughly comparable to those of a bad case of a one-week flu. Thus, even a severely addicted user apparently can manage withdrawal without medical assistance when he is motivated to do so. In addition, the high price and low purity of heroin now available on the street means that the majority of users are addicted at low levels; today few, if any, experience the dramatic symptoms of classic heroin withdrawal. Although our understanding of the process of addiction and re-addiction remains incomplete, the evidence suggests that heroin use is strongly influenced by social setting and a variety of related factors affecting the motivation of the user. Addiction need not be permanent, and many addicts voluntarily abstain for temporary or extended periods. The capacity to control heroin use and avoid re-addiction appears weakest among addicts who have few other sources of personal gratification, limited opportunities for nonmenial employment (or for any employment at all) and restricted ability to escape the social and environmental stimuli that "cue" the conditioned desire for the drug.

4. Consider Richard Delgado, "Rotten Social Background": Should the Criminal Law Recognize a Defense of Severe Environmental Deprivation?, 3 Law & Inequality 9, 20-23 (1985):

> Judge Bazelon first raised the possibility that extreme poverty might give rise to an RSB [Rotten Social Background] defense in United States v. Alexander.[73] . . . In

---

73. 471 F.2d 923, 957-65 (D.C. Cir. 1973) (Bazelon, C.J., dissenting).

Alexander, one of the defendants shot and killed a marine in a tavern after the marine called him a "black bastard." The defense attempted to show that the youth's action stemmed from an irresistible impulse to shoot, which they, in turn, traced to an emotionally and economically deprived childhood in Watts, California. The defendant reported that when he was young, his father deserted the family and the boy grew up with little money or attention. He was subjected to racist treatment and learned to fear and hate white persons.

A psychiatrist testified that the defendant suffered from impaired behavior controls rooted in his "rotten social background." The psychiatrist refused to label the defendant insane, however. The trial judge instructed the jury to disregard the testimony about the defendant's deprived background and to consider only whether or not his mental condition met the legal standard of insanity. The jury found him sane and the defendant was sentenced to twenty years to life.

The court of appeals affirmed. In a lengthy, troubled opinion that concurred in part and dissented in part, Judge Bazelon laid out his early thoughts on the RSB defense. For Bazelon, the trial judge erred in instructing the jury to disregard the testimony about defendant's social and economic background. That testimony might well have persuaded the jury that the defendant's behavioral controls were so impaired as to require acquittal, even though that impairment might not render him clinically insane. Apart from this, exposure to the testimony would benefit society. As a result of learning about the wretched conditions in which some of its members live, society would presumably decide to do something about them.[82]

Nevertheless, Bazelon was not prepared to abandon all the trappings of the "disease" model. Among other things, that model provides a rationale for detaining dangerous persons following acquittal. Bazelon reviewed other possible dispositions for the RSB defendant — outright release, preventive detention, and psychological reprogramming — finding each unacceptable. According to Bazelon, the ultimate solution to the problem of violent crime in our society is some form of income redistribution coupled with other social reform measures. The current narrow insanity test conceals the need for such reform and thus should be broadened, although disposition of offenders not "sick" in any classic sense remained a problem for Bazelon.

Judge Bazelon further developed his views on an RSB defense in his Hoover lecture[87] and in a reply article.[88] . . .

In a response to Judge Bazelon[95] and a short rejoinder,[96] Professor Stephen Morse argued against Judge Bazelon's position. For Morse, all environments affect choice, making some choices easy and others hard. Rarely, however, will environmental adversity completely eliminate a person's power of choice. Poor persons are free to choose or not choose to commit crimes, and the criminal law may justifiably punish them when they give in to temptation and break the law. Although he conceded a statistical correlation between poverty and crime, Morse denied that poverty causes crime. He pointed out that some poor persons are law-abiding, while

---

82. Some may contend that there are better forums for educating the public about the effect of RSB than the courtroom. . . . Educating the public is not the *primary* goal of an RSB defense, nor should it be. In the context of an actual trial, however, the lesson society learns and its determination to alter the social conditions which breed crime are uniquely and conspicuously urgent.

87. David Bazelon, The Morality of the Criminal Law, 49 S. Cal. L. Rev. 385 (1976).

88. David Bazelon, The Morality of the Criminal Law: A Rejoinder to Professor Morse, 49 S. Cal. L. Rev. 1269 (1976).

95. Stephen Morse, The Twilight of Welfare Criminology: A Reply to Judge Bazelon, 49 S. Cal. L. Rev. 1247 (1976).

96. Stephen Morse, The Twilight of Welfare Criminology: A Final Word, 49 S. Cal. L. Rev. 1275 (1976).

some wealthy persons break the law, and that economic improvements often result in more, not less, crime. Moreover, Bazelon's social-welfare suggestions would be impractical because there is not enough money to eradicate all poverty; giving money to the poor would entail higher taxation, thus endangering such goals as free accumulation and disposition of wealth; and though eradicating poverty may eliminate some crime, it is a wasteful way to do it. Consequently, Bazelon's broadened inquiry into culpability could exonerate dangerous criminals without generating socially useful knowledge or experience. Indeed, Bazelon's defense skirts paternalism. When an individual has freely broken the law, respect for that individual's personhood *demands* punishment; any other treatment demeans the defendant, and treats him or her as something less than an autonomous individual.

The Bazelon-Morse debate thus raises, but does not answer, a number of key questions concerning a "rotten social background" defense. Does economic and cultural disadvantage impair controls or otherwise cause crime, and if so, how? If severe impairment can be shown in a particular case, what effect should this have on criminal responsibility? What should be done with the successful RSB defendant?

In R. George Wright, The Progressive Logic of Criminal Responsibility and the Circumstances of the Most Deprived, 43 Cath. U.L. Rev. 459 (1994), the author develops the argument that in failing to make allowances for the dire economic and social circumstances of the most deprived elements of the population, the criminal law is departing from its professed principle that only the morally responsible may be punished for their acts. On the related question whether it is just to blame and punish an individual who commits criminal acts because his genes or his upbringing, or both, have conspired to inflict on him a bad character, see Sanford H. Kadish, Blame and Punishment 102-103 (1987); Peter Arenella, Convicting the Morally Blameless: Reassessing the Relationship Between Legal and Moral Accountability, 39 U.C.L.A.L. Rev. 1511 (1992); Samuel H. Pillsbury, The Meaning of Deserved Punishment: An Essay on Choice, Character, and Responsibility, 67 Ind. L.J. 719 (1992).

5. In the section on Mental Disorder, supra page 966, we considered proposals to eliminate the defense of legal insanity. We also considered proposals to enlarge the defense by expansive interpretations of the requirement of a "mental disease" to include such conditions as the battered woman's syndrome, compulsive gambling disorder, premenstrual syndrome, postpartum disorder, multiple personality disorder, and post-traumatic stress disorder, supra pages 976-980. Those materials should be reconsidered at this point as further manifestations of changes in thought about the proper contours of legal responsibility. Further proposals to expand legal irresponsibility include those to exculpate defendants experiencing the effects of Halcion sleeping pills (Todd Paul Myers, Halcion Made Me Do It: New Liability and a New Defense — Fear and Loathing in the Halcion Paper Chase, 62 U. Cin. L. Rev. 603 (1993)), victims of lead poisoning (Deborah Denno, Considering Lead Poisoning as a Criminal Defense, 20 Ford. Urb. L.J. 377 (1993)), adopted children suffering from "adoption trauma" (N.Y. Times, Natl. Ed., July 27, 1994, at A14) and others (see the remarks of the dissenting opinion in Werner v. State, supra page 825. A review of much of this literature and a critical assessment of it appears in Joshua Dressler, Reflections on Excusing Wrongdoers: Moral Theory, New Excuses and the Model Penal Code, 19 Rutgers L.J. 671 (1988).

For a popular book by a noted defense lawyer critical of these trends, see Alan M. Dershowitz, The Abuse Excuse (1994).

6. *H. L. A. Hart, Punishment and Responsibility 31-33 (1968):* [N]o legal system in practice admits without qualification the principle that *all* criminal responsibility is excluded by *any* of the excusing conditions. . . . This is so for a variety of reasons.

For one thing, it is clear that not only lawyers but scientists and plain men differ as to the relevance of some excusing conditions, and this lack of agreement is usually expressed as a difference of view regarding what kind of factor limits the human *capacity* to control behaviour. Views so expressed have indeed changed with the advance of knowledge about the human mind. Perhaps most people are now persuaded that it is possible for a man to have volitional control of his muscles and also to know the physical character of his movements and their consequences for himself and others, and yet be *unable* to resist the urge or temptation to perform a certain act; yet many think this incapacity exists only if it is associated with well-marked physiological or neurological symptoms or independently definable psychological disturbances. . . .

Another reason limiting the scope of the excusing conditions is difficulty of *proof.* Some of the mental elements involved are much easier to prove than others. It is relatively simple to show that an agent lacked, either generally or on a particular occasion, volitional muscular control; it is somewhat more difficult to show that he did not know certain facts . . . ; it is much more difficult to establish whether or not a person was deprived of "self-control" by passion provoked by others, or by partial mental disease. As we consider these different cases not only do we reach much vaguer concepts, but we become progressively more dependent on the agent's own statements about himself, buttressed by inferences from "common-sense" generalizations about human nature, such as that men are capable of self-control when confronted with an open till but not when confronted with a wife in adultery. The law is accordingly much more cautious in admitting "defects of the will" than "defect in knowledge" as qualifying or excluding criminal responsibility. Further difficulties of proof may cause a legal system to limit its inquiry into the agent's "subjective condition" by asking what a "reasonable man" would in the circumstances have known or foreseen, or by asking whether "a reasonable man" in the circumstances would have been deprived (say, by provocation) of self-control; and the system may then impute to the agent such knowledge or foresight or control.

For these practical reasons, no simple identification of the necessary mental subjective elements in responsibility with the full list of excusing conditions can be made; and in all systems far greater prominence is given to the more easily provable elements of volitional control of muscular movement and knowledge of circumstances or consequences than to the other more elusive elements.

7. *Clarence Thomas, Crime and Punishment — and Personal Responsibility, The Natl. Times, Sept. 1994, at 31:* We can see . . . how the intellectual currents of the legal revolution in individual rights affected the management of community institutions such as schools and the civility of our streets, parks and other common spaces. But how did the ideas underlying this revolution affect the functioning of the criminal justice system?

Many began questioning whether the poor and minorities could be blamed for the crimes they committed. Our legal institutions and popular culture began identifying those accused of wrongdoing as victims of upbringing and circumstances. The point was made that human actions and choices, like events in the natural world, are often caused by factors outside of one's control. No longer was an individual identified as the cause of a harmful act. Rather, societal conditions or the actions of institutions and others in society became the responsible causes of harm. These external causes might be poverty, poor education, a faltering family structure, systemic racism or other forms of bigotry, and spousal or child abuse, just to name a few. The consequence of this new way of thinking about accountability and responsibility — or lack thereof — was that a large part of our society could escape being held accountable for the consequences of harmful conduct. The law punishes only those who are responsible for their actions: and in a world of countless uncontrollable causes of aggression or lawlessness, few will have to account for their behavior.

As a further extension of these ideas, some began challenging society's moral authority to hold many of our less fortunate citizens responsible for their harmful acts. Punishment is an expression of society's disapproval or reprobation. In other words, punishment is a way of directing society's moral indignation toward persons responsible for violating its rules. Critics insisted, though, that an individual's harmful conduct is not the only relevant factor in determining whether punishment is morally justified. The individual's conduct must be judged in relation to how society has acted toward that individual in the past. In this regard, many began appearing hesitant to hold responsible those individuals whose conduct might be explained as a response to societal injustice. How can we hold the poor responsible for their actions, some asked, when our society does little to remedy the social conditions of the ill-educated and unemployed in our urban areas? In a similar vein, others questioned how we could tell blacks in our inner cities to face the consequences for breaking the law when the very legal system and society which will judge their conduct perpetuated years of racism and unequal treatment under the law.

Once our legal system accepted the general premise that social conditions and upbringing could be excuses for harmful conduct, the range of cases that might prevent society from holding anyone accountable for his actions became potentially limitless. Do we punish a drunk driver who has a family history of alcoholism? A bigoted employer reared in a segregationist environment, who was taught that blacks are inferior? A thief or drug pusher who was raised in a dysfunctional family and who received a poor education? A violent gang member, rioter or murderer who attributes his rage, aggression and lack of respect for authority to a racist society that has oppressed him since birth? Which of these individuals, if any, should be excused for their conduct? Can we really distinguish among them in a principled way?

An effective criminal justice system — one that holds people accountable for harmful conduct — simply cannot be sustained under conditions where there are boundless excuses for violent behavior and no moral authority for the state to punish. If people know that they are not going to be held accountable because of a myriad of excuses, how will our society be able to influence behavior and provide incentives to follow the law? How can we teach future generations right from wrong if the idea of criminal responsibility is riddled with exceptions and our governing institutions and courts lack the moral self-confidence? A society that does not hold someone accountable for harmful behavior can be viewed as condoning — or even worse, endorsing — such conduct. In the long run, a society that abandons personal responsibility will lose its moral sense. And it is the urban poor whose lives are being destroyed the most by this loss of moral sense.

This is not surprising. A system that does not hold individuals accountable for their harmful acts treats them as less than full citizens. In such a world, people are reduced to the status of children or, even worse, treated as though they are animals without a soul. There may be a hard lesson here: In the fact of injustice on the part of society, it is natural and easy to demand recompense or a dispensation from conventional norms. But all too often, doing so involves the individual accepting diminished responsibility for his future. Does the acceptance of diminished responsibility assure that the human spirit will not rise above the tragedies of one's existence? When we demand something from our oppressors — more lenient standards of conduct, for example — are we merely going from a state of slavery to a more deceptive, but equally destructive, state of dependency?

It also bears noting that contemporary efforts to rehabilitate criminals will never work in a system that often neglects to assign blame to individuals for their harmful acts. How can we encourage criminals not to return to crime if our justice system fosters the idea that it is society that has perpetuated racism and poverty — not the individuals who engaged in harmful conduct — that is to blame for aggression and crime, and thus, in greatest need of rehabilitation and reform.

The transformation of the criminal justice system has had and will continue to have its greatest impact in our urban areas. It is there that modern excuses for criminal behavior abound — poverty, substandard education, faltering families, unemployment, a lack of respect for authority because of deep feelings of oppression.

I have no doubt that the rights revolution had a noble purpose: to stop society from threatening blacks, the poor and others, many of whom today occupy our urban areas — as if they were invisible, not worthy of attention. But the revolution missed a larger point by merely changing their status from invisible to victimized. Minorities and the poor are humans — capable of dignity as well as shame, folly as well as success. [They] should be treated as such.

NOTE ON THE ELIMINATION OF MENS REA FOR ALL CRIMES

The debate over strict criminal liability is usually cast in terms of the justification of eliminating mens rea requirements for particular categories of undesirable conduct. A more far-reaching debate has followed from proposals to extend the principle of strict liability throughout the substantive criminal law by eliminating the requirement of mens rea from the definition of all offenses. See, e.g., James Marshall, Intention — in Law and Society (1968); Barbara Wootton, Crime and the Criminal Law (1963); Jay Campbell, A Strict Accountability Approach to Criminal Responsibility, 29 Fed. Prob. 333 (1965).

Lady Wootton has been the most articulate exponent of these proposals. Her scheme[28] would require two separate stages in the case of a person accused of crime. At the first stage there would be decided only whether the defendant committed the act prohibited by the criminal law, without regard to whether he acted intentionally, knowingly, recklessly, and even negligently, or whether he had the capacity to conform to the law under the circumstances. His mental state would be altogether irrelevant. The second stage would arise if it were found that he committed the prohibited act. Now the issue would be to decide what ought to be done with the defendant considering all we know and can find out about him — from psychiatrists, from social workers or from any other source — including, but not limited to, his mental and emotional state at the time he acted. The choice of the disposition would be governed by whatever is desirable to protect the public from his further criminality, whether what is required be medical or psychiatric treatment, training, a permissive or a rigorous environment, punishment or incarceration. Presumably if the offender did not pose a danger he would be released immediately. If he did, he would be held whether he was culpable or not, and for as long as he continued to pose the danger. Thus, according to Lady Wootton, a forward looking approach would be substituted for a backward one we now use, a preventive system for a punitive one.

This proposal could have important implications for the whole body of substantive criminal law. Plainly it would not do to leave the criminal law as it is with only the mental element removed because under our present law (strict liability apart) mens rea is crucial to the description of the behavior we want to prevent. Perjury without knowledge of the lie is simply making an incorrect statement under oath. An unlawful assembly without the intent to do unlawful acts is simply joining a group of people in a public place. An attempt to commit a crime without the intent to do so would be incoherent. It would follow under Lady Wootton's proposal that the substantive law of crimes might ultimately have to be rewritten to consist entirely in the specification of harms, somewhat on the order of the following hypothetical provision dealing with crimes against the person:

"A person commits a crime who engages in conduct (in the sense only of bodily movements) as a factual consequence of which:

"(1) another person's life is lost; or,

"(2) another person is physically injured; or

"(3) another person's life or physical well-being is imperilled."

In the course of her argument, Lady Wootton observes (Crime and the Criminal Law 51-53 (1963)):

> If . . . the primary function of the courts is conceived as the prevention of forbidden acts, there is little cause to be disturbed by the multiplication of offences of strict liability. If the law says that certain things are not to be done, it is illogical to confine this prohibition to occasions on which they are done from malice aforethought; for at least the material consequences of an action, and the reasons for prohibiting it, are the same whether it is the result of sinister malicious plotting, of

---

28. This description is adapted from Sanford H. Kadish, The Decline of Innocence, 26 Camb. L.J. 273, 285 (1968).

negligence or of sheer accident. A man is equally dead and his relatives equally bereaved whether he was stabbed or run over by a drunken motorist or by an incompetent one; and the inconvenience caused by the loss of your bicycle is unaffected by the question whether or not the youth who removed it had the intention of putting it back, if in fact he had not done so at the time of his arrest. . . .

The conclusion to which this argument leads is, I think, not that the presence or absence of the guilty mind is unimportant, but that mens rea has, so to speak — and this is the crux of the matter — got into the wrong place. Traditionally, the requirement of the guilty mind is written into the actual definition of a crime. No guilty intention, no crime, is the rule. Obviously this makes sense if the law's concern is with wickedness: where there is no guilty intention, there can be no wickedness. But it is equally obvious, on the other hand, that an action does not become innocuous merely because whoever performed it meant no harm. If the object of the criminal law is to prevent the occurrence of socially damaging actions, it would be absurd to turn a blind eye to those which were due to carelessness, negligence or even accident. The question of motivation is in the first instance irrelevant.

But only in the first instance. At a later stage, that is to say, after what is now known as a conviction, the presence or absence of guilty intention is all-important for its effect on the appropriate measures to be taken to prevent a recurrence of the forbidden act. The prevention of accidental deaths presents different problems from those involved in the prevention of wilful murders. The results of the actions of the careless, the mistaken, the wicked and the merely unfortunate may be indistinguishable from one another, but each case calls for a different treatment. Tradition, however, is very strong, and the notion that these differences are relevant only after the fact has been established that the accused committed the forbidden act seems still to be deeply abhorrent to the legal mind.

Consider the following comments on Lady Wootton's thesis in Professor Hart's book review of Wootton, Crime and the Criminal Law (1963) in 74 Yale L.J. 1325, 1328-1330 (1965):

[Lady Wootton argues] that if the aim of the criminal law is "the prevention of socially damaging actions" and not retribution for past wickedness, the doctrine of mens rea puts the investigation of the offender's mind "into the wrong place." Such investigation on a preventive theory of punishment can be relevant only after conviction as a guide to the measures to be taken to prevent a repetition of the crime. It is therefore "illogical" to make mens rea part of the definition of the crime and a necessary condition of the offender's liability to compulsory measures. The conventional doctrine of mens rea can only make sense or be "logical" within the framework of a retributive theory according to which punishment is used and justified as an "appropriate" return for past wickedness and not merely as a prevention of anti-social conduct.

This argument is I think mistaken though many writers besides Lady Wootton have used it, sometimes for purposes quite alien to hers. It rests I think on the illusory idea that our only interest in asking whether those whom we punish could at the time of their offence have conformed to the law is to determine whether they were "wicked" in doing what they did. This altogether ignores an outlook on punishment which is surely common, intelligible and, except perhaps for determinists (among whom Lady Wootton does not number herself) perfectly defensible. According to this outlook we should restrict even punishment designed as "preventive" to those who at the time of their offence had the capacity and a fair opportunity or chance to obey the law: and we should do this out of consideration of fairness or justice to those whom we punish. This is an intelligible ideal of justice to the individual and remains intelligible even when we punish to protect society from harm in the future and not to "pay back" the harm that those whom we punish have done. Viewed in this way as a restriction imposed on preventive punishment by considerations of fairness or justice to individuals the doctrine of mens rea presents an aspect neglect of which renders Lady Wootton's argument inconclusive. For such a restriction on punishment has a perfectly "logical" place even within a preventive theory.

CHAPTER
9

THEFT OFFENSES

A. THE MEANS OF ACQUISITION

MODEL PENAL CODE AND COMMENTARIES

Comment to §223.1 at 127-132 (1980)

Distinctions among larceny, embezzlement, obtaining by false pretenses, extortion, and the other closely related theft offenses are explicable in terms of a long history of expansion of the role of the criminal law in protecting property. That history begins with a concern for crimes of violence — in the present context, the taking of property by force from the possession of another, i.e., robbery. The criminal law then expanded, by means of the ancient quasi-criminal writ of trespass, to cover all taking of another's property from his possession without his consent, even though no force was used. This misconduct was punished as larceny. The law then expanded once more, through some famous judicial manipulation of the concept of possession, to embrace misappropriation by a person who with the consent of the owner already had physical control over the property, as in the case of servants and even bailees in certain particularly defined situations.

At this point in the chronology of the law of theft, about the end of the 18th century, a combination of circumstances caused the initiative in the further development of the criminal law to pass from the courts to the legislature. . . .

The earliest statutes dealt with embezzlement by such narrowly defined groups as bank clerks. Subsequent laws extended coverage to agents, attorneys, bailees, fiduciaries, public officers, partners, mortgagors in possession, etc., until at last a few American legislatures enacted fraudulent-conversion statutes penalizing misappropriation by anyone who received or had in his possession or control the property of another or property which someone else "is entitled to receive and have." Indeed, some modern embezzlement statutes go so far as to penalize breach of faith without regard to whether anything is misappropriated. Thus, the fiduciary who makes forbidden investments, the official who deposits public funds in an unauthorized depository, the financial advisor who betrays his client into paying more for a property than the market value, may be designated an embezzler. Although this kind of coverage is relatively new for Anglo-American penal law, certain foreign codes have long recognized criminal "breach of trust" as a distinct entity.

1039

The fraud aspects of theft, never regarded with such abhorrence as larceny, begin with the common-law misdemeanor of cheat. This offense required use of false weights or similar "tokens," thus limiting criminal deception to certain special techniques conceived as directed against the public generally. One may suspect that this development was an outgrowth of guild regulation of unfair competition as much as it reflected a desire to protect the buying public. At any rate, the use of false tokens was a technique against which it would be difficult for even a cautious yeoman to guard himself. A mere lie for the purpose of deceiving another in a business transaction did not become criminal until the Statute of 30 Geo. 2, ch. 24 (1757), created the misdemeanor of obtaining property by false pretenses. Even this statute was not at first believed to make mere misrepresentation criminal. Instead, it was thought to require some more elaborate swindling stratagem, such as French law to this day requires. Eventually it was settled in Anglo-American law that false representations of "fact," if "material," would suffice. Today's battleground is over such matters as misrepresentation of "opinion," "law," or "value," as well as "misleading omissions" and "false promises." . . .

If history were the whole explanation of the existence of distinctive theft crimes, there would be little reason to preserve differentiations whose subtleties have occasioned serious procedural difficulties. The problem is not so simple. History has its own logic. The criminal law reached larceny first and embezzlement later because of real distinctions between theft by a stranger and the peculations of a trusted agent. If the move to punish embezzlement was a natural one, it was nevertheless a momentous step when the exceptional liability of servants for stealing from their masters was generalized into fraudulent conversion by anyone who had goods of another in his possession. The ordinary trespass-theft was committed by a stranger, an intruder with no semblance of right even to touch the object taken. The offender was easily recognized by the very taking, surreptitious or forceful, and so set apart from the law-abiding community. No bond of association in joint endeavor linked criminal and victim. In contrast, the embezzler stands always in a lawful as well as in an unlawful relation to the victim and the property. He is respectable; indeed, some tend to identify with him rather than with the bank or insurance company from which he embezzles. The line between lawful and unlawful activity is for the embezzler a question of the scope of his authority, which may be ill-defined. Not every deviation from the authority conferred will be civilly actionable, much less a basis for criminal liability. Sometimes the scope of the authority may be so broad, e.g., as in the case of a revocable inter-vivos trust where the grantor is trustee, as to be hardly distinguishable from ownership. The agent or bailee may actually be part of a co-proprietorship, being entitled to a commission or satisfaction of a lien out of funds in his hands. A man who is psychologically the absolute "owner" may be in the legal position of a bailee with extremely circumscribed freedom to deal with the property, as a result of modern methods of selling consumer goods on credit arrangements involving retention of title by the seller.

The embezzlement problem is complicated further by the necessity of distinguishing between defalcation by one who has "property of another" and failure of a debtor to pay his debts. Modern society is opposed to imprisonment for debt, however committed it may be to punishment for betrayal of trust. Yet when property is entrusted to a dealer for sale, with the expectation that he will receive the proceeds, deduct his commission, and remit the balance, the dealer's criminal liability if he fails to remit may turn on refinements of the civil law of contracts, agency, sales, or trusts. Such refinements, designed to allocate financial risks or to determine priorities among creditors of an insolvent, are hardly a relevant index to the harm done the owner or to the character of the defaulting dealer and thus may be entirely inappropriate as a measure of criminal liability.

It may nevertheless be true that theft by a stranger and a suitably delimited offense of theft by a fiduciary represent similar dangers requiring approximately the same treatment and characterization. . . . To that extent, at least, consolidation conforms to the common understanding of what is substantially the same kind of undesirable conduct. Consolidation also has advantages in the administration of the criminal law if it eliminates procedural problems arising from nice distinctions between closely related types of misbehavior. Differences in the treatment of thieves can be determined on an individual basis by taking into account many factors which are at least as significant as whether fraud or stealth was the means employed to deprive another of his property.

NOTE

Professor George Fletcher has presented a different view of the traditional common law distinctions and technicalities in the law of theft. Fletcher, The Metamorphosis of Larceny, 89 Harv. L. Rev. 469 (1976). His article is worth consulting in connection with the various categories of theft discussed in the following portions of this chapter.

1. Trespassory Takings

COMMONWEALTH v. TLUCHAK

Superior Court of Pennsylvania
166 Pa. Super. 16, 70 A.2d 657 (1950)

RENO, J. Appellants, husband and wife, separately appealed from convictions for larceny. The court below overruled their motions for new trials and arrest of judgment. The husband was sentenced to pay a fine of $50 and make restitution. Sentence was suspended in the wife's case.

The case arose out of a real estate transaction. By a written instrument appellants agreed to sell their farm to the prosecutor and his wife. The agreement did not include any personal property but it did cover: "All buildings, plumbing, heating, lighting fixtures, screens, storm sash, shades, blinds, awnings, shrubbery and plants." The purchasers took possession on June 14, 1946, and discovered that certain articles which had been on the premises at the time the agreement of sale was executed were missing. They were a commode which had never been attached and lay on the back porch in its shipping crate, an unattached washstand which had been stored in a bedroom, a hay carriage used in the barn, an electric stove cord extending from the switch box in the cellar to the kitchen, and 30 or 35 peach trees. These articles were charged in the indictment as subjects of the larceny.

The Commonwealth contended that the articles which were not covered by the written contract had been sold by an oral agreement between the parties. Appellants denied the oral agreement; denied the sale of the personal property; denied taking the trees; admitted they took the hay carriage; and as to all the articles which they took they contended that they were taken under a claim of right and therefore not feloniously. The jury found against them and, although they contend that the evidence is not sufficient in law to sustain a conviction, we shall assume, for the purpose of this decision, that the testimony established a *sale* of the personal property by appellants to the prosecutor and his wife. That is, that appellants sold but failed or refused to deliver the goods to the purchasers. Are sellers who refuse or fail to deliver goods sold to their purchasers guilty of larceny?

. . . Appellants had possession of the goods, not mere custody of them. The evidence indicates that they were allowed to retain possession without trick or artifice and without fraudulent intent to convert them. Presumably title passed upon payment of the purchase price; nevertheless appellants had lawful possession thereafter. "One who is in lawful possession of the goods or money of another cannot commit larceny by feloniously converting them to his own use, for the reason that larceny, being a criminal trespass on the right of possession, . . . cannot be committed by one who, being invested with that right, is consequently incapable of trespassing on it." 52 C.J.S., Larceny, §31; and see §1.

An extensive research failed to uncover a Pennsylvania case in which the rule was applied to a factual situation similar to that at bar. But the principle has been recognized; e.g., in Com. v. Quinn, 144 Pa. Super. 400, 408, 19 A.2d 526, 530, this Court approved instructions to a jury wherein it was said:

> But a person may come into possession of somebody else's property in a legal way and if he, being so in possession of the property in a legal way converts it to his own use or withholds it from the owner so that the owner is deprived of the use thereof which he should have, then, though the defendant could not be guilty of larceny because he received it legally, he may be guilty of fraudulent conversion because after having received it he has deprived the owner of his use of it. . . .

As suggested, appellants may have been guilty of fraudulent conversion, or of larceny by bailee *if* the theory is accepted that a vendor retaining possession of goods sold by him becomes constructively a bailee of the purchaser, and criminally culpable for a failure to deliver them to his purchaser. Appellants were indicted for larceny only, and of that they clearly were not guilty. . . .

Judgments and sentences reversed and appellants discharged without delay.

NOTES

1. *Traditional asportation and its statutory variants.* Larceny, both at common law and under statutory formulations, requires a carrying away (asportation) as well as a trespassory taking. While courts have substantially minimized the significance of this requirement by holding that any movement of the thing, no matter how slight, is sufficient, problems still may arise. Consider State v. Patton, 364 Mo. 1044, 271 S.W.2d 560 (1954). The defendant purported to sell concrete building blocks, not his own, to an innocent purchaser, who himself carried the blocks away. May the defendant be held for larceny? A few courts would answer in the negative because of the absence of an asportation. See, e.g., State v. Laborde, 202 La. 59, 11 So. 2d 404 (1942); Ridgell v. State, 110 Ark. 606, 162 S.W. 773 (1914). The majority, however, as in State v. Patton, supra, turn the trick by finding the purchaser to be the innocent agent of the seller and imputing his acts to defendant. See Annot., 144 A.L.R. 1383 (1942). Can this be analytically defended?

The New York Court of Appeals in People v. Alamo, 34 N.Y.2d 453, 358 N.Y.S.2d 375 (1974), dispensed with the requirement of an actual movement of the object in a case where defendant entered a stranger's car, turned on the lights and started the engine. The court upheld the trial court's instruction that the jury might find theft of the car in these circumstances even if defendant had not moved the vehicle (assuming, of course, they found the requisite intent to steal it). The court read the traditional doctrine requiring an asportation as reflecting a concern that the crucial elements of possession and control were established. Comparing pickpocket cases where some movement of the seized object had been held to be required, the court stated (358 N.Y.S.2d at 379, 381):

> The actions needed to gain possession and control over a wallet, including movement of the wallet which, in itself, is merely an element tending to show possession and control, are not necessarily the actions needed to gain possession and control of an automobile. A wallet, or a diamond ring, or a safe are totally inert objects susceptible of movement only by physical lifting or shoving by the thief. An automobile, however, is itself an instrument of transportation and when activated comes within the total possession and control of the operator. In this situation movement or motion is not essential to control. Absent any evidence that the vehicle is somehow fastened or immovable because of a mechanical defect, the thief has taken command of the object of the larceny. He has, in the words of subdivision 1 of section 155.05 of the Penal Law, wrongfully "taken" the property from its owner surely as much so as had the thief in [the pickpocket case]. . . .

The Model Penal Code eliminates the requirement of an asportation and substitutes the requirement that the defendant "exercise unlawful control" over the movable property. Section 223.2(1). Model Penal Code and Commentaries, Comment to §223.2(1), at 164 (1980) states:

> Since larceny was generally a felony and attempt a misdemeanor, important differences in procedure and punishment turned on the criminologically insignificant fact of slight movement of the object of the theft. Under §5.01 of the Model Code, and in modern criminal law generally, differences in penal consequences between attempt and completed crime are minimized, so that it becomes less important where the line is drawn between them. It is clear, moreover, that similar penalties for the attempt and the completed offense make obsolete any reference to the concept of "asportation"; the same penal consequences follow whether or not an "asportation" has occurred.

Most revised codes follow this lead. Id. at 165.

2. *Problems.* The defendant removed a price label for £2.73 from a piece of meat in a supermarket and affixed the label to a piece of meat that should have cost £6.91. His act was detected at the checkout counter before he paid for the second piece of meat. Could the defendant be convicted of larceny? This situ-

ation was presented in Regina v. Morris, [1983] 3 All E.R. 288 (H.L. 1983). The English Theft Act of 1968 defines theft as "dishonestly appropriating" another's property (§1(1)); appropriation is defined as, "Any assumption of the rights of an owner" (§3(1)). The House held that appropriation takes place when the defendant does an act that adversely interferes with or usurps the right of the owner, and that the switching of the price labels was such an appropriation, since it usurped the right of the owner to ensure that the goods were sold and paid for at the greater price. By contrast, removing articles from the shelves, unlike switching labels, would not amount to an appropriation, since a supermarket consents to that much handling of its merchandise. The decision is criticized in J. C. Smith, The Law of Theft, para. 34 (5th ed. 1984); L. H. Leigh, Some Remarks on Appropriation in the Law of Theft after *Morris*, 48 Mod. L. Rev. 167 (1985).

An American counterpart is People v. Olivo, 52 N.Y.2d 309, 420 N.E.2d 40 (1981). The case involved a consolidated appeal from several petit larceny convictions for shoplifting from department stores and a bookstore. In one case the defendant took objects on display and secreted them in his clothing, while furtively looking around. In another case the defendant removed a sensor device from a jacket, put the jacket on, and leaving his own jacket on the table, walked toward the exit. In a third case the defendant furtively concealed a book in his case while appearing to browse. N.Y. Pen. Code §155.05 provides that one commits larceny when "he wrongfully takes" another's property, with the intent to steal. The defendant argued that a customer cannot "wrongfully take" an article in a self-service store so long as he remains in the store. The court disagreed and affirmed all the convictions, holding that these defendants could be held for larceny even though they were apprehended before leaving the store. The court stated (52 N.Y.2d at 317-318):

> [I]n modern self-service stores customers are impliedly invited to examine, try on, and carry about the merchandise on display. Thus in a sense, the owner has consented to the customer's possession of the goods for a limited purpose. That the owner has consented to that possession does not, however, preclude a conviction for larceny. If the customer exercises dominion and control wholly inconsistent with the continued rights of the owner, and the other elements of the crime are present, a larceny has occurred. Such conduct on the part of a customer satisfies the "taking" element of the crime.

TOPOLEWSKI v. STATE

Supreme Court of Wisconsin
130 Wis. 244, 109 N.W. 1037 (1906)

[The accused arranged with Dolan, who owed him money and was an employee of the Plankinton Packing Company, to place three barrels of the company's meat on the loading platform, the plan being that accused would load the barrels on his wagon and drive away as if he were a customer. Dolan carried out his end of the plan after informing the company's representatives and receiving their instructions to feign cooperation. Accused took the barrels as planned and was arrested, charged, and convicted of stealing the barrels of meat.]

MARSHALL, J. [after stating the facts.] . . . Did the agreement in legal effect with the accused to place the property of the packing company on the loading platform, where it could be appropriated by the accused, if he was so disposed and was not interfered with in so doing, though his movements in that regard were known to the packing company, and his taking of the property, his efforts to that end being facilitated as suggested, constitute consent to such appropriation?

The case is very near the border line, if not across it, between consent and nonconsent to the taking of the property. [In] Reg. v. Lawrence, 4 Cox C.C. 438, it was held that if the property was delivered by a servant to the defendant by the master's direction the offense cannot be larceny, regardless of the purpose of the defendant. In this case the property was not only placed on the loading platform, as was usual in delivering such goods to customers, with knowledge that the accused would soon arrive, having a formed design to take it, but the packing company's employé in charge of the platform, Ernst Klotz, was instructed that the property was placed there for a man who would call for it. Klotz from such statement had every reason to infer, when the accused arrived and claimed the right to take the property, that he was the one referred to and that it was proper to make delivery to him and he acted accordingly. While he did not physically place the property, or assist in doing so, in the wagon, his standing by, witnessing such placing by the accused, and then assisting him in arranging the wagon, as the evidence shows he did, and taking the order, in the usual way, from the accused as to the disposition of the fourth barrel, and his conduct in respect thereto amounted, practically, to a delivery of the three barrels to the accused.

In Rex v. Egginton, 2 P. & P. 508, we have a very instructive case on the subject under discussion here. A servant informed his master that he had been solicited to aid in robbing the latter's house. By the master's direction the servant opened the house, gave the would-be thieves access thereto and took them to the place where the intended subject of the larceny had been laid in order that they might take it. All this was done with a view to the apprehension of the guilty parties after the accomplishment of their purpose. The servant by direction of the master not only gave access to the house but afforded the would-be thieves every facility for taking the property, and yet the court held that the crime of larceny was complete, because there was no direction to the servant to deliver the property to the intruders or consent to their taking it. They were left free to commit the larceny, as they had purposed doing, and the way was made easy for them to do so, but they were neither induced to commit the crime, nor was any act essential to the offense done by any one but themselves.

. . . We cannot well escape the conclusion that this case falls under the condemnation of the rule that where the owner of property by himself or his agent, actually or constructively, aids in the commission of the offense, as intended by the wrongdoer, by performing or rendering unnecessary some act in the transaction essential to the offense, the would-be criminal is not guilty of all the elements of the offense. . . .

The logical basis for the doctrine above discussed is that there can be no larceny without a trespass. So if one procures his property to be taken by another intending to commit larceny, or delivers his property to such other, the latter purposing to commit such crime, the element of trespass is wanting and the crime not fully consummated however plain may be the guilty purpose of the one possessing himself of such property. That does not militate against a person's being free to set a trap to catch one whom he suspects of an intention to commit the crime of larceny, but the setting of such trap must not go further than to afford the would-be thief the amplest opportunity to carry out his purpose, formed without such inducement on the part of the owner of the property, as to put him in the position of having consented to the taking. If I induce one to come and take my property and then place it before him to be taken, and he takes it with criminal intent, or if knowing that one intends to take my property I deliver it to him and he takes it with such intent, the essential element of trespass involving nonconsent requisite to a completed offense of larceny does not characterize the transaction, regardless of the fact that the moral turpitude involved is no less than it would be if such essential were present. Some writers in treating this subject give so much attention to condemning the deception practiced to facilitate and encourage the commission of a crime by one supposed to have such a purpose in view, that the condemnation is liable to be viewed as if the deception were sufficient to excuse the would-be criminal, or to preclude his being prosecuted; that there is a question of good morals involved as to both parties to the transaction and that the wrongful participation of the owner of the property renders him and the public incapable of being heard to charge the person he has entrapped with the offense of larceny. That is wrong. It is the removal from the completed transaction, which from the mental attitude of the would-be criminal may have all the ingredients of larceny, from the standpoint of the owner of the property of the element of trespass or nonconsent. When such element does not characterize a transaction involving the full offense of larceny so far as concerns the mental purpose of such would-be criminal is concerned, is often not free from difficulty and courts of review should incline quite strongly to support the decision of the trial judge in respect to the matter and not disturb it except in a clear case. It seems that there is such a case before us.

The judgment is reversed, and the cause remanded for a new trial.

NOTES

1. The police had been troubled by a large number of car thefts in a particular locality. An informer approached a police officer and told him that the defendant, Jarrott, proposed that he join him in the theft and sale of automobiles. The informer was instructed to play along. Later the informer informed the police officer that Jarrott stated he wanted to get a 1925 coupé and indicated the general time and place that Jarrott, with his ostensible help, planned to steal a car. The police officer thereupon arranged for his own coupé to be present at that time and place. He left it with its parking lights on and with the key in the ignition, concealing himself in the back end. This was known to the informer. Jarrott and the informer later appeared. Jarrott saw the car and proposed they steal it. They entered and drove the car to a car lot, the informer doing the driving on Jarrott's protestation that he could not drive. While Jarrott and the buyer were haggling over the price, the policeman climbed out from the car and made his arrest. Defendant appealed a conviction of larceny on the grounds (1) that the car was never taken from the personal possession of the owner and (2) that the taking occurred with the consent of the owner. What should be the result? Jarrott v. State, 108 Tex. Crim. 427, 1 S.W.2d 619 (1927). Could the defendant have also argued that since the informer drove the car it was he who took it and not the defendant because the acts of the informer, as a feigned accomplice, could not be attributed to the defendant? See State v. Hayes, page 671 supra.

Concerning the defense of entrapment by police agents, which is raised in this Note, see Model Penal Code §2.13, Appendix; Annot., Larceny: entrapment or consent, 10 A.L.R.3d 1121 (1966).

2. In United States v. Bryan, 483 F.2d 88 (3d Cir. 1973), the U.S. Lines, on the instruction of the FBI, permitted its agents to deliver a shipment of whiskey to Echols, who was believed to be posing as an agent of the consignee. The court rejected the argument that Echols committed no crime because the U.S. Lines consented to the taking, stating (at 90-92):

> The crime alleged here is violation of 18 U.S.C. §659, which provides penalties for, inter alia, "[w]hoever embezzles, steals, or unlawfully takes, carries away, or conceals . . . from any . . . platform or depot . . . with intent to convert to his own use any goods . . . which constitute an interstate . . . shipment of freight." The crime of stealing under 18 U.S.C. §659 has been given a broad construction, free from the technical requirements of common law larceny. United States v. De-Normand, 149 F.2d 622, 624 (2d Cir. 1945).[1] A trial court instruction that the jury need only find "an unlawful taking of the goods by the defendants," was found sufficient in *DeNormand*. The consent to the removal of the goods by U.S. Lines personnel in this case does not demonstrate the absence of an unlawful taking. In reviewing the record to determine if there was an unlawful taking, the relevant question involves not the state of mind of personnel of U.S. Lines, but rather the state of mind of defendants.
>
> We therefore find no difficulty in reconciling our conclusion that a crime was committed here with the statements in United States v. Cohen, 274 F. 596, 597 (3d Cir. 1921):

> > To constitute "stealing" there must be an unlawful taking . . . with intent to convert to the use of the taker and permanently deprive the owner.

> and in Vaughn v. United States, 272 F. 451, 452 (9th Cir. 1921), that in a case of larceny, the corpus delicti consists of two elements:

> > First, that the property was lost by the owner; and, second, that it was lost by a felonious taking.

> Both formulations of the elements of stealing concentrate on the state of mind of the criminal, not upon that of the possessor of the goods taken. In cases where the lawful possessor indicated to the taker that permission was granted for the taking, a finding of commission of a crime would be unlikely. That, however, is not the case sub judice. There is no proof that U.S. Lines led defendants to believe they had permission to take the goods.

---

1. The crime detailed in 18 U.S.C. §659 is therefore different from that detailed in 18 U.S.C. §2113(b), stealing from a bank. The latter statute describes common law larceny and thus requires a "trespassory taking," a taking without consent. Bennett v. United States, 399 F.2d 740, 742 (9th Cir. 1968). While conviction for violation of 18 U.S.C. §2113(b) would be impossible under the consensual circumstances found in the present case, the limitations of the common law do not prevent conviction for violation of 18 U.S.C. §659. See also United States v. Patton, 120 F.2d 73 (3d Cir. 1941).

3. In the *Topolewski* case, would it have been possible to convict the defendant of an attempt to commit larceny? See Regina v. Miller and Page, 49 Crim. App. 241 (1965), holding affirmatively. See The Case of Lady Eldon's French Lace, page 633 supra.

4. See George Fletcher, The Metamorphosis of Larceny, 89 Harv. L. Rev. 469, 491-498 (1976), for an interpretation of the *Topolewski* case as a modern survival of the common law commitment to the requirement of "manifest criminality" ("acting like a thief"). The problem in *Topolewski* is also illuminatingly discussed in Glanville Williams, Theft, Consent and Illegality: Some Problems, [1977] Crim. L. Rev. 327, 330 et seq.

NOTE ON ROBBERY AND EXTORTION

Note, A Rationale of the Law of Aggravated Theft, 54 Colum. L. Rev. 84-86 (1954): Obviously, larceny may be perpetrated in many ways: a pocket may be picked or a man may be killed to obtain a bankroll. In the former situation, the sole evil is the misappropriation of property; in the latter, bodily injury also results. Consequently, to protect not only against misappropriation but also against injuries which may result from peculiarly dangerous means devised for accomplishing misappropriation, there developed the law of aggravated theft. At common law the only substantive crime embodied within this law was robbery, a larceny accomplished by violence or threat of immediate violence to the person of the victim. In time it was acknowledged that men may be intimidated by threats other than those foreboding bodily harm. As a result, modern legislation has extended the substantive content of aggravated theft, complementing robbery with the crime of extortion. . . .

Entirely a creature of legislative enactment, extortion now exists as a substantive crime in forty-seven states, and in each there is also a robbery statute. The first inquiry, then, concerns the manner in which these crimes differ. The statutory definitions of robbery restate in essence the common law definition: the felonious and forcible taking of property from the person of another or in his presence, against his will, by violence or putting in fear. Extortion statutes are generally of two types. The majority of jurisdictions treat as the substantive crime of extortion the making of certain specified threats for the purpose of obtaining property, but a substantial number require an actual misappropriation with the owner's consent. The differences between the robbery and extortion statutes, therefore, depend to a certain extent on the particular jurisdiction. In jurisdictions following either extortion pattern, robbery requires a taking from the person or in his presence, while for extortion the intimidation is crucial and the place of the taking immaterial. In states which do not require more than the threat for extortion, the fact of misappropriation is relevant only to robbery. In those states where misappropriation is essential to extortion, there is a distinction based on the factor of consent. The robbery statutes speak of the absence of consent; the extortion statutes require its presence. However, the willingness to surrender the property in any case is only an apparent willingness since in both instances the victim must choose between alternative evils, namely, the surrender of his property or the execution of the threat. Only if the taking is accomplished by violence to the person of the victim is this apparent consent precluded, for then the victim is presented with no choice. Thus the definitional distinctions between robbery and extortion are extremely tenuous.[15] . . .

California Penal Code: Section 211. Definition. Robbery Defined. Robbery is the felonious taking of personal property in the possession of another, from his person or immediate presence, and against his will, accomplished by means of force or fear.

Section 212. Fear Defined. The fear mentioned in Section 211 may be either:

1. The fear of an unlawful injury to the person or property of the person robbed, or of any relative of his or member of his family; or,

2. The fear of an immediate and unlawful injury to the person or property of anyone in the company of the person robbed at the time of the robbery.

Section 518. Definition. Extortion is the obtaining of property from another, with his consent, or the obtaining of an official act of a public officer, induced by a wrongful use of force or fear, or under color of official right.

Section 519. Fear Used to Extort: Threats Inducing. Fear, such as will constitute extortion, may be induced by a threat, either:

1. To do an unlawful injury to the person or property of the individual threatened or of a third person; or,

2. To accuse the individual threatened, or any relative of his, or member of his family, of any crime; or,

3. To expose, or to impute to him or them any deformity, disgrace or crime; or,

4. To expose any secret affecting him or them.

Model Penal Code: Section 222.1. Robbery. [See Appendix.]

Model Penal Code: Section 223.4. Theft by Extortion.[a] [See Appendix.]

Further on extortion (also called blackmail), see page 1079, infra.

2. Misappropriation

NOLAN v. STATE

Maryland Court of Appeals
213 Md. 298, 131 A.2d 851 (1957)

[Defendant was convicted of embezzlement on the following facts. He was the office manager of the Federal Discount Corporation, a finance company en-

---

15. Often the conviction is for extortion where seemingly the facts constitute robbery. See People v. Jacobsen, 11 Cal. App. 2d 728, 54 P.2d 748 (1936).

a. Model Penal Code and Commentaries, Comment to §223.4 at 202 n. 1 (1980), observes: "At common law, robbery included taking not only by force but also by threat of force or even by threat of certain other serious harms. To be guilty of robbery under the Model Penal Code, the defendant must threaten immediate and serious harm. Other coercive deprivation falls under §223.4." — EDS.

See also id. at 208: "There is no requirement in Section 223.4 that the threatened harm be 'unlawful.' The actor may be privileged or even obligated to inflict the harm threatened; yet, if he employs the threat to coerce a transfer of property for his own benefit, he clearly belongs among those who should be subject to punishment for theft. The case of the policeman who has a duty to arrest illustrates the point. His threat to arrest unless the proposed subject of the arrest pays him money should be treated as extortionate even though the failure to arrest would be dereliction of duty." — EDS.

gaged in the business of making loans and collections. The evidence showed that he appropriated money from his employer as follows: As payments were received from customers, the payments would be placed in the cash drawer. At the end of the day, an accomplice would prepare a report showing the daily cash receipts. Defendant would then appropriate some of the cash from the drawer, and his accomplice would recompute the adding tapes to equal the remaining cash.]

COLLINS, J. . . . The appellant . . . contends that . . . the evidence produced made the crime larceny and not embezzlement, as charged in the indictment.

. . . It is stated in 2 Wharton's Criminal Law, 12th Ed., pgs. 1589, 1590, that, if the case is larceny at common law because the money was taken from the prosecutor's possession, the charge for embezzlement fails. The embezzlement statutes were passed, not to cover any cause within the common law range of larceny, but to cover new cases outside of that range. If the goods were taken from the owner's possession, the crime is larceny, not embezzlement. Goods which have reached their destination are constructively in the owner's possession although he may not yet have touched them and, hence, after such termination of transit, the servant who converts them is guilty of larceny, not of embezzlement. It is there stated at page 1591: "No inconvenience can arise from the maintenance of this distinction, since it is allowable *as well as prudent* to join a count for larceny to that for embezzlement. But great inconvenience would follow from the acceptance of the principle that the embezzlement statutes absorb all cases of larceny by servants." (Italics supplied.) . . .

From the testimony offered by the State, Federal had provided a cash drawer in which the money was deposited as received. Mr. Abrams and Mr. Wolk, officers of the company, also accepted payments and had access to the money drawer in which all the money was placed. The money was not taken by Mr. Nolan until it had been placed in the cash drawer and balanced at the end of the day. When taken by appellant, as alleged, the cash was in the possession of Federal. We must therefore conclude that under the authorities cited and under the testimony in this case there was not sufficient evidence to find the defendant guilty of embezzlement. The case will be remanded for further proceedings in order that the State, if it deems proper, may try the defendant on an indictment for embezzlement and larceny, if such an indictment is returned against the defendant.

PRESCOTT, J. (concurring). It is unfortunate not to be able to concur fully in such an able and carefully prepared opinion as that filed by a majority of this Court. However, as it seems to me that it reestablishes many of the tenuous niceties between larceny and embezzlement with which the early English cases are replete, and that it unnecessarily will embarrass many future prosecutions although the accused palpably may be guilty, I have decided to state the reasons that prevent my complete concurrence.

It seems as though the present case properly can be decided by reference to our present statute on embezzlement alone, without the necessity of the citation of other authorities. . . . Our statute, Art. 27, §154 of the Maryland Code 1951, reads:

> Whosoever being a . . . servant . . . shall fraudulently embezzle any money . . . which . . . shall be . . . taken into possession by him, for . . . his master or employer, shall be deemed to have feloniously stolen the same from his master or em-

ployer, although such money . . . was not received into the possession of such master . . . otherwise than by the actual possession of his . . . servant. . . .

A simple down-to-earth application of the facts presented in the record discloses that every element required in the statute is fully and completely covered. It is conceded that the nature of his employment is within the terms of the statute, and the evidence established to the satisfaction of the jury that the money was taken into his possession for and on behalf of his employer, and that he fraudulently appropriated it to his own use. The statute seems to require no more.

But the majority of the Court feel that the English decisions and other authorities (although apparently there is no Maryland case so ruling) require a holding that because the money went into the drawers before its fraudulent conversion, the offense was larceny and not embezzlement. If this be so, it seems to place the law in an unfortunate and somewhat indefensible position. When a man is in complete charge and control of an office and the law says to him: "If you steal your employer's money before it is placed in a drawer (under your charge and control) you are guilty of embezzlement, but, if you or someone under you places the money in that drawer (still under your charge and control) and then you steal it, you are guilty of larceny, and larceny alone," does it seem right? Could not it be said with just as much reason, logic and justification that if you steal money and place it in your left pocket, you are guilty of embezzlement, but, if you place it in your right pocket, you are guilty of larceny and larceny alone? Would it not be a sounder policy to follow the example of such cases as Calkins v. State, 18 Ohio St. 366. [T]he Ohio Court was requested to make a rather tenuous holding under its embezzlement statute as to whether or not certain property was "under (the) care" of the defendant, but the Court refused to do so, and said: "There is no more reason why courts should allow themselves to be misled by mere names and shadows in the administration of justice in criminal, than in civil cases." . . .

The apprehension that I have concerning the ruling in this case is aptly stated in Komito v. State, 90 Ohio St. 352, 107 N.E. 762, 763, where it is said:

"Courts sometimes indulge in an *ethereal refinement* between larceny and embezzlement that in practical operation very often nullifies these statutes. The only benefit accruing from such a policy results in the rather doubtful advantage of the *criminal escaping his just punishment.*" (Emphasis supplied.)

Thus, we find ourselves in the peculiar position of following the subtle reasoning developed in the English decisions for the purpose of bringing the guilty to the bar of justice; but, in so doing, we directly come to their aid and comfort. Probably the solution of this rather difficult problem lies in the course followed by several of our sister States (and as was done in England) where the legislative power has provided that under an indictment for larceny, or for larceny in one count and embezzlement in another, there may be a conviction of either offense.

NOTE ON EMBEZZLEMENT

The very early conception of larceny as a *vi et armis* (with force and arms) trespassory taking from the possession of the owner *invito domino* (against the will of the owner) was thought to preclude conviction of persons who physically and lawfully held property of the owner, as, for example, servants, guests, and employees. Since they themselves had "possession" of the owner's goods, their making off with them could not constitute larceny.

This was changed through the course of adjudication by development of the concept of "legal" (or "constructive") possession as distinguished from mere custody. The development was gradual, and there was considerable disputation as to whether, for example, a servant had mere custody or possession when the master entrusted property to him to be taken a distance from the house, as to a market, or when certain property, perhaps jewels, were expressly entrusted to a servant. See Holmes, J., in Commonwealth v. Ryan, 155 Mass. 523, 528, 30 N.E. 364, 365 (1892). Such doubts were resolved by statute in 1529 (21 Hen. VIII, ch. 7) and by later cases so that it soon became established that "a servant, whether at the master's home or elsewhere, never has legal possession of such property of his master as he controls in his capacity as servant." 2 W. O. Russell, Crime 1035 (11th ed., Turner, 1958). A servant, therefore, who made off with his master's goods, committed larceny from the possession of the master. By analogous reasoning, similar results were reached with guests.

What of the case in which the servant is given goods by a third party for delivery to his master? Could it be said that here as well, when a servant misappropriated the goods, he was taking them from the possession of the master and was hence guilty of larceny? The answer was no, since the master did not have possession and the third party voluntarily gave up possession. See 1 M. Hale, Pleas of the Crown 667.

A distinction was soon developed where the servant deposited the goods or money so received in a place provided by the master and subject to the master's control prior to the act of misappropriation. In such a case, the possession passed to the master, and the servant retained only custody; hence a dishonest appropriation was larceny. There was again much disputation as to precisely what manner and place of deposit sufficed to justify such a conclusion. In Nolan v. State, supra, for example, defendant's placement of the receipts in the cash drawer was held to transfer "possession" to the employer. Holmes, J., in Commonwealth v. Ryan, supra, reached a contrary result on similar facts (except that the money was picked up by defendant just a few minutes after he deposited it) and sustained an embezzlement conviction, stating (30 N.E. at 364):

> [T]he judge was right in charging the jury that, if the defendant, before he placed the money in the drawer, intended to appropriate it, and with that intent simply put it in the drawer for his own convenience in keeping it for himself, that would not make his appropriation of it just afterwards larceny. The distinction may be arbitrary, but, as it does not affect the defendant otherwise than by giving him an opportunity, whichever offense he was convicted of, to contend that he should have been convicted of the other, we have the less uneasiness in applying it.

A subsequent statutory development of great importance was precipitated by the decision in Bazeley's Case, 168 Eng. Rep. 517 (1799). Bazeley was a bank teller who pocketed a £1000 note received from a customer for deposit. The court found no larceny since the employer did not acquire possession of the note but only a right to possess it; at the time of the conversion, it was in the legal possession of the teller. It would have been otherwise, it was said, if Bazeley had first deposited the note in a drawer kept for this purpose by the employer. Largely to fill the gap in the law dramatized by this case, the first embezzlement statute was passed in 1799 (39 Geo. III, ch. 85) providing:

> if any servant or clerk, or any person employed for the purpose in the capacity of a servant or clerk, to any person or persons whomsoever, or to any body corporate or politick, shall, by virtue, of such employment, receive or take into his possession any money, goods, bond, bill, note, banker's draft, or other valuable security, or effects, for or in the name or on the account of his master or masters, or employer or employers, and shall fraudulently embezzle, secrete, or make away with the same, or any part thereof, every such offender shall be deemed to have feloniously stolen the same.

Modern cases, such as Nolan v. State, supra, are products of and explicable in terms of, if not justified by, this history.

Additional enactments following the original embezzlement statute gradually extended the categories of persons capable of embezzling to others than servants or clerks: brokers, merchants, bankers, attorneys, and other agents in 1812; factors in 1827; trustees under express trusts in 1857; etc. American embezzlement statutes still bear the mark of this piecemeal legislative development. See State v. Riggins, page 1059 infra.

BURNS v. STATE

Supreme Court of Wisconsin
145 Wis. 373, 128 N.W. 987 (1911)

[A constable upon taking an insane man in charge after pursuit received from another of the pursuers a roll of money that had been thrown away by the man in his flight. The jury, having heard evidence supporting the accusation that the constable had misappropriated the funds, convicted him of larceny by bailee under a Wisconsin statute, which is reproduced in the text of the opinion.]

MARSHALL, J. . . . . Error is assigned because the court instructed the jury to the effect that, if the accused converted to his own use any of Adamsky's money, he did so as bailee. It is suggested that the court should have defined the term "bailee," as used in the statute, and left it to the jury to find the fact as to whether the circumstances satisfied such statute or not.

A court may properly instruct a jury in a criminal case, as well as any other, respecting any fact, or facts, established by the evidence beyond any room for reasonable controversy, and when such evidentiary facts exist establishing, beyond any room for reasonable controversy, an essential of any ultimate conclusion sought, it is not harmful error, if error at all, to treat such essential as having been proven, as the court here did in saying that the accused was a bailee of whatever of Adamsky's money came to his possession.

It seems to be thought that a bailment was not established by the evidence because some sort of contract inter partes was essential thereto. No particular ceremony or actual meeting of minds is necessary to the creation of a bailment. If one, without the trespass which characterizes ordinary larceny, comes into possession of any personalty of another and is in duty bound to exercise some degree of care to preserve and restore the thing to such other or to some person for that other, or otherwise account for the property as that of such other, according to circumstances, — he is a bailee. It is the element of lawful possession, however created, and duty to account for the thing as the property of another, that creates the bailment, regardless of whether such possession is based on contract in the ordinary sense or not.

It is said, generally, in the books, that a bailment is created by delivery of the personalty to one person by another to be dealt with in specie as the property of such other person under a contract, express or implied, but the word "contract" is used in a broad sense. The mutuality essential to the contractual feature may be created by operation of law as well as by the acts of the parties with intention to contract.

So it makes no difference whether the thing be intrusted to a person by the owner, or another, or by some one for the owner or by the law to the same end. Taking possession without present intent to appropriate raises all the contractual elements essential to a bailment. So the person who bona fide recovers the property of another which has been lost, or irresponsibly cast away by an insane man, as in this case, is a bailee as much as if the same property were intrusted to such person by contract inter partes. In the latter case the contract creates the duty. In the former the law creates it. Such a situation is to be distinguished from that where one knowingly receives money paid him by mistake and fraudulently retains it. There the element of bona fide possession may be said not to exist and so the duty accompanied by such possession essential to a bailment not to have been created. . . .

The finder of property who voluntarily bona fide takes it into his possession, immediately, thereupon, has imposed upon him by law the duties of a depositary, the mildest type, as regards degree of duty, of bailee.

So the finder here of the cast-away money was clearly a bailee, and when his duties were voluntarily assumed by the accused he became such, and as there was no controversy in respect to such finding and assumption, the court's reference to the matter was proper.

The next suggestion in behalf of plaintiff in error is that, if the accused was guilty of any offense, it was that of having broken the package and extracted therefrom part of the contents for the purpose of appropriating it to his own use, and executed such purpose, thus committing the offense of larceny, not of conversion by a bailee. It is a sufficient answer thereto that the purpose of the statute [containing provisions on traditional larceny and on takings by bailees] was to abolish the distinction between conversion by a bailee of an entire thing, as a quantity of property in a package of some kind, and the unlawful breaking of the package and conversion of part or all of the contents — whether preceded by the element of breaking bulk with intent to permanently deprive the owner of the thing appropriated or not, — making the latter a statutory class of larcenies, differing only from ordinary larcenies, by absence in the former of the element of trespass in gaining original possession, which is essential to the latter. The meaning of the statute, as indicated, seems very plain:

> Whoever being a bailee of any chattel, money or valuable security shall fraudulently take or fraudulently convert the same to his own use or to the use of any person other than the owner thereof, although he shall not break bulk or otherwise determine the bailment, shall be guilty of larceny

It follows that acquittal of the accused of the offense of larceny is not inconsistent with his conviction of the statute offense of larceny as bailee. . . .

NOTE ON THE MISAPPROPRIATING BAILEE

In the Note following Nolan v. State, supra, we briefly described the development of the possession-custody distinction as a means whereby certain kinds of misappropriation by persons lawfully holding the property of another came to be treated as larceny prior to the enactment of the embezzlement statutes, which eliminated the need for such judicial gap-filling. However, just as this distinction proved inadequate to deal with the servant who received goods for his master from a third person, it proved inadequate to deal with the bailee who misappropriated his bailor's property, because the crucial significance of a bailment relation was the transfer of possession and not mere custody. See 5 Words and Phrases, Bailment, 48 (perm. ed.); 2 W. O. Russell, Crime 916 (12th ed., Turner, 1964). The resources of the early common law, however, were up to the task of bringing at least some bailee misappropriations within the scope of larceny. In the Carrier's Case, decided in 1473 (Y.B. 13 Edw. IV, f. 9, pl. 5), a carrier to whom a foreign merchant delivered a shipment for delivery to a consignee broke into the bales and decamped with the contents. The judges of the Star Chamber produced a variety of opinions but apparently reached no conclusion. The case was again argued before the judges in the Exchequer Chamber, who expressed several opinions as to the theory to govern the case. The majority apparently agreed that if the bailment has terminated, the former bailee who then takes the goods may be guilty of larceny. What was unclear was the theory on which the defendant should be said to have terminated the bailment. Finally the judges, without stating their reasons, reported that a majority found that in the circumstances defendant committed larceny (2 W. O. Russell, Crime 917-918 (12th ed., Turner, 1964)). As Russell observes (at 918),

> Much later we find accepted by the courts the proposition that by breaking bulk the bailee determined [terminated] the bailment and having ceased thereby to be a bailee, in some strange manner lost possession of the property which had been bailed to him and so became a trespasser when he took any portion of the contents.

Stephen observed:

> This has always appeared an extraordinary decision, as, to all common apprehension, theft of the whole thing bailed must determine the bailment quite as much as a theft of part of it. I think it obvious from the report that the decision was a compromise intended to propitiate the chancellor and perhaps the King. This required a deviation from the common law, which was accordingly made, but was as slight as the judges could make it.

3 James Fitzjames Stephen, History of the Criminal Law 139 (1883). The pragmatic basis for the decision suggested by Stephen was further developed by Professor Jerome Hall in his classic study of the case in Theft, Law and Society (2d

ed. 1952), where the political, social and economic interests are explored. Hall concludes (at 93):

> On the one hand, the criminal law at the time is clear. On the other hand, the whole complex aggregate of political and economic conditions described above thrusts itself upon the court. The more powerful forces prevailed — that happened which in due course must have happened under the circumstances. The most powerful forces of the time were interrelated very intimately and at many points: the New Monarchy and the nouveau riche — the mercantile class; the business interests of both and the consequent need for a secure carrying trade; the wool and textile industry, the most valuable, by far, in all the realm; wool and cloth, the most important exports; these exports and the foreign trade; this trade and Southampton, chief trading city with the Latin countries for centuries; the numerous and very influential Italian merchants who bought English wool and cloth inland and shipped them from Southampton. The great forces of an emerging modern world, represented in the above phenomena, necessitated the elimination of a formula which had outgrown its usefulness. A new set of major institutions required a new rule. The law, lagging behind the needs of the times, was brought into more harmonious relationship with the other institutions by the decision rendered in the Carrier's Case.

At all events, the breaking-bulk device proved only a stopgap. It left without criminal sanction appropriations without breaking bulk as well as cases where the requirement of breaking was difficult to establish, as where the shipment consisted of separable units.[1] The remedy was again statutory, an act of 1857 (20 & 21 Vict., ch. 54, §4) creating the new crime of larceny by bailee, which placed the dishonest bailee on a par with the dishonest servant. American statutes today either retain similar provisions as a separate crime of larceny by bailee or include misappropriation by a bailee as an instance of embezzlement.

NOTES ON APPROPRIATION OF LOST PROPERTY AND PROPERTY TRANSFERRED BY MISTAKE

Where property dishonestly appropriated by a defendant comes into his or her possession through a mistake of the transferor, as by a mistake in the identity of the transferee, the character of the property, or the quantity being delivered, or through the defendant's finding property which the owner has lost, there is apparently no trespassory interference with possession required for larceny. Neither is there the employee or fiduciary relationship or the element of "entrusting" required by the usual embezzlement statute.[2] Of what crime, then, may the dishonest accused be convicted?

1. As for lost property, an early partial solution was the distinction between lost property (that property unintentionally placed where found) and mislaid

---

1. The breaking-bulk doctrine was supplemented as a means of dealing with dishonest bailees by the larceny-by-trick doctrine, whereby larceny could be established if the bailee used fraud in obtaining the goods. This is considered in the next section.

2. But in the case of finding, at least, the finder may be held for larceny by bailee or fraudulent conversion under statutes making the misappropriating bailee guilty of crime even where the property was not entrusted to him or her.

property (that property deliberately placed where found, the owner forgetting where he or she put it). In the latter case, the courts often found that "possession" never left the owner, so that when the finder appropriated it, the finder "took" it from the owner's possession. Regina v. Pierce, 6 Cox Crim. Cas. 117 (1852); State v. Courtsol, 89 Conn. 564, 94 A. 973 (1915). Even as to the former, however, it was eventually determined that the finder took from the constructive possession of the owner, and if at the time the finder appropriated the lost property he or she intended to convert it, knowing or having reason to believe he or she might discover the owner's identity, the finder was guilty of larceny. Penny v. State, 109 Ark. 343, 159 S.W. 1127 (1913); State v. Levy, 23 Minn. 104 (1876). It is generally held, however, that the felonious intent (to appropriate in the face of knowledge or means of knowing the owner's identity) must accompany the original finding and appropriation — otherwise there is no felonious taking. Long v. State, 33 Ala. App. 334, 33 So. 2d 382 (1948); State v. Belt, 125 S.C. 473, 119 S.E. 576 (1923).

Consider the solution to this problem proposed by the Model Penal Code and now adopted by many states. Section 223.5 provides:

> A person who comes into control of property of another that he knows to have been lost, mislaid, or delivered under a mistake as to the nature or amount of the property or the identity of the recipient is guilty of theft if, with purpose to deprive the owner thereof, he fails to take reasonable measures to restore the property to a person entitled to have it.

See Model Penal Code and Commentaries, Comment to §223.5 at 228 (1980):

> The common-law view of larceny as an infringement of the possession of another required a determination of the actor's state of mind at the moment of finding. . . . The search for an initial fraudulent intent appears to be largely fictional, and in any event poses the wrong question. The realistic objective in this area is not to prevent initial appropriation but to compel subsequent acts to restore to the owner. The section therefore permits conviction even where the original taking was honest in the sense that the actor then intended to restore; if he subsequently changes his mind and determines to keep the property, he will then be guilty of theft.

2. In the case of dishonest appropriation of property delivered by mistake, there is again a twofold problem: first, finding the necessary taking from possession and second, finding a felonious intent coincident with the taking. The solution of the Model Penal Code, also now followed in many states, is §223.5, just quoted. The supporting Commentary states as follows (Model Penal Code and Commentaries, Comment to §223.5 at 225-226 (1980)):

> [O]ne who accepts a $10 bill knowing that the other person thinks he is handing over a $1 bill acquires it without trespass or false pretense. Moreover, he may not be in any of the employee or fiduciary relations that were enumerated in the typical older embezzlement statutes. Consequently, special legislation or judicial sleight-of-hand was required to reach persons taking advantage of such mistakes. Similarly, if the owner or his agent voluntarily hands the property over to the accused while laboring under a misapprehension as to the identity of the recipient, it requires

strenuous manipulation of concepts to disregard the apparent transfer of title as well as possession and to hold that the accused is guilty of larceny because he committed a trespass against the transferor's possession. A prosecution for false pretenses may also be frustrated because the actor may not have created or reinforced the misimpression. Yet the recipient, knowing that the transfer to him is inadvertent, is in a moral and physical situation with respect to the property much like that of the finder of lost property. Moreover, he knows who is rightfully entitled to the property and can easily take steps to restore the property. Accordingly, Section 223.5 imposes theft sanctions against one in this situation who fails to take reasonable measures to restore. Most recent codes and proposals also specifically cover theft of misdelivered property. Some, however, are restricted to theft of lost or mislaid property.

It is necessary to limit the reach of Section 223.5, on the other hand, in order to avoid impinging on certain types of tolerated sharp trading. For example, it is not proposed to punish the purchase of another's property at a bargain price on a mere showing that the buyer was aware that the seller was misinformed regarding the value of what he sold. The language of Section 223.5 is accordingly limited to situations where the mistake is as to "the nature or amount of the property or the identity of the recipient."

PROBLEM

S.F. Chronicle, Nov. 14, 1964, at 4, contained the following story:

MONTGOMERY, Ala. — A man who withdrew $43,000 mistakenly credited to his bank account and refused to give it back was convicted yesterday by a jury in Federal Court.

T. L. (Cotton) Thaggard of Montgomery faces a possible maximum sentence of 10 years in prison and a $5,000 fine. He will be sentenced Friday.

It was Thaggard's second trial. The first ended with a deadlocked jury.

Thaggard was tried under a Federal law which prohibits taking anything worth more than $100 from a bank "with intent to steal or purloin."

In his argument to the jury Thursday, defense attorney Calvin Whitesell contended that as far as the defendant knew, the balance in his account was just what the bank told him it was.

"You can't steal what is yours," Whitesell argued.

The dispute began in March 1963 when the Union Bank & Trust Co. erroneously credited a $43,000 deposit to the account of Alabama Motors, a used car business operated by Thaggard. The money belonged to Alabama Power Co.

On March 6, Thaggard asked for his balance, then drew out the $43,000 after the teller had three times verified the amount, at his request.

He finally signed a withdrawal slip and tellers spent 30 minutes counting out the bills and putting them in a brown paper sack.

In the first trial, Thaggard's lawyer, Ira De Ment, contended his client was not guilty of larceny since the money was voluntarily handed over. "I'm not saying he did right. I'm saying he's not guilty of larceny," De Ment said.

U.S. Attorney Ben Hardeman said, "Cotton Thaggard entered that bank with a heart full of larceny and left there with a sack full of money."

Thaggard has spent the time since carrying the bag of money from the bank in and out of jail and court.

He was locked up by a circuit judge on contempt charges when he refused to tell where he put the money, saying he would incriminate himself by answering.

Thaggard was first arrested on a state charge of false pretense. But that charge was dropped when the State Supreme Court ruled that it wasn't false pretense to get the money after three times asking the bank to recheck his balance.

Later, a Federal grand jury indicted Thaggard on a larceny charge involving a bank whose funds were insured by the Federal Deposit Insurance Corporation.

The bank has won a civil judgment against Thaggard in state court and some $10,575 worth of property belonging to him has been sold to satisfy the judgment.

STATE v. RIGGINS

Supreme Court of Illinois
8 Ill. 2d 78, 132 N.E.2d 519 (1956)

HERSHEY, C.J. The defendant, Marven E. Riggins, was indicted in the circuit court of Winnebago County for embezzlement. After a verdict of guilty by a jury, the court sentenced him to a term in the penitentiary of not less than two nor more than seven years. . . .

At the time of the indictment (January, 1955), the defendant was the owner and operator of a collection agency in Rockford, called the Creditors Collection Service, and had been so engaged for about five years. He maintained an office, had both full- and part-time employees, and during 1953 and 1954 had a clientele of some 500 persons and firms for whom he collected delinquent accounts.

In February, 1953, he called on the complaining witness, Dorothy Tarrant, who operated a firm known as Cooper's Music and Jewelry. He said he was in the collection business and asked to collect the firm's delinquent accounts. As a result, they reached an oral agreement whereby the defendant was to undertake the collections.

By this agreement, the defendant was to receive one third on city accounts and one half on out-of-city accounts. It was further agreed that he need not account for the amounts collected until a bill was paid in full, at which time he was to remit by check.

There is a conflict in the evidence as to whether the defendant was to give a check for the whole amount collected and then receive his commission, or whether he was authorized to deduct his commission and account only for the net amount due.

It was further agreed that the defendant would be liable for court costs in the event he chose to file suit on any of the accounts, but the first money collected was to be applied to those costs. If no collection was made, however, the defendant was to stand the loss.

The parties operated under this agreement for almost two years. During that time the complaining witness exercised no control over the defendant as to the time or manner of collecting the accounts, and with her knowledge he commingled funds collected for all his clients in a single bank account. He also used this as a personal account, from which he drew for business, family and personal expenses.

In October, 1954, the complaining witness became aware that the defendant had collected several accounts for her in full, but had not accounted to her. . . . Thereafter, the complaining witness preferred the charges against the defendant which resulted in his indictment and conviction for embezzlement.

To decide whether the defendant, a collection agent, can be guilty of embezzlement in Illinois, it is helpful to consider our embezzlement statutes in the historical context of this crime.

Embezzlement, unknown at common law, is established by statute, and its scope, therefore, is limited to those persons designated therein. . . .

Viewed in their entirety, our laws relating to embezzlement are broad and comprehensive. The following persons are included in those statutes making the crime of embezzlement a felony: "Whoever embezzles or fraudulently converts to his own use" (Ill. Rev. Stat. 1953, chap. 38, par. 207); "a clerk, agent, servant or apprentice of any person" (par. 208); "any banker or broker, or his agent or servant, or any officer, agent or servant of any banking company, or incorporated bank" (par. 209); "any clerk, agent, servant, solicitor, broker, apprentice or officer . . . receiving any money . . . in his fiduciary capacity" (par. 210); "public officers" (par. 214); "administrators, guardians, conservators and other fiduciaries" (par. 216); and certain members and officers of fraternal societies (par. 218). . . .

In this instance we are particularly interested in the general embezzlement statute (par. 208), and the special statute under which defendant was indicted (par. 210). The former, applying to any "clerk, agent, servant or apprentice of any person," was originally enacted in 1827, and has existed in its present form since 1874. The latter, however, refers to "any clerk, agent, servant, solicitor, broker, apprentice or officer . . . receiving any money, . . . in his fiduciary capacity" and was not passed until 1919. For present purposes, this latter enactment is very significant, for it also provides as follows: such person

> shall be punished as provided by the criminal statutes of this state for the punishment of larceny, *irrespective of whether any such* officer, agent, clerk, servant, solicitor, broker or apprentice *has or claims to have any commission or interest in such money,* substitute for money, or thing of value so received by him.

(Italics added.)

In Commonwealth v. Libbey, 11 Metc., Mass., 64 decided in 1846, it was held that a collecting agent, who followed that as an independent business and who had the right to commingle funds, could not be convicted as an "agent" under a general embezzlement statute. This was predicated on the idea that he had a joint interest in the property said to be embezzled.

Similarly, a 1903 decision of this court reversed the conviction of an agent who was employed to solicit subscriptions on commission and who was authorized to deduct her commissions from the amounts collected, for the reason that she was joint owner with the principal in the amounts collected. McElroy v. People, 202 Ill. 473, 66 N.E. 1058. . . .

Briefly, then, this was the status of the law in 1919 when the special statute (par. 210) . . . expressly abrogated the doctrine enunciated in the foregoing cases and relied upon by the defendant here.[a] . . .

---

a. Many cases have taken the view (contrary to that of the cases cited by the court) that, even absent such a specific statutory provision, the fact that a collector is entitled to deduct a commission out of the funds collected does not preclude an embezzlement conviction for appropriation of the entire proceeds. See, e.g., Commonwealth v. Hutchins, 232 Mass. 285, 122 N.E. 275 (1919); Smith v. State, 74 Fla. 44, 76 So. 334 (1917). — Eds.

[I]t can hardly be disputed but that the defendant acted as agent for the complaining witness in collecting her accounts. He undertook the collections on her behalf by virtue of authority which she delegated to him. He had no right to collect from anyone except as authorized by her and was required to render a full account of all matters entrusted to him, the same as any agent. . . . The prevailing view of the courts in construing embezzlement statutes is succinctly expressed in 18 Am. Jur., Embezzlement, §30, as follows: "The term 'agent' as used in embezzlement statutes is construed in its popular sense as meaning a person who undertakes to transact some business or to manage some affair for another by the latter's authority and to render an account of such business or affair. . . ."

We conclude that the defendant was an "agent" of the complaining witness, receiving money in a "fiduciary capacity" and, therefore, within the purview of said embezzlement statute. . . .

Reversed and remanded.

SCHAEFER, J., dissenting. . . . The critical question is whether the defendant was the agent of the complaining witness. Upon the record it seems to me that he was not. He maintained his own office, had his own employees, and collected accounts for approximately 500 other individuals and firms. He was subject to no control whatsoever by any of his customers in making his collections. His customers knew that he kept all of his collections in a single account. That the defendant was not an agent would be clear, I think, if vicarious liability was sought to be asserted against Dorothy Tarrant on account of the defendant's conduct in the course of his collection activities.

The conclusion of the majority that the defendant was an agent rests upon the assertion that "[t]he term 'agent' as used in embezzlement statutes is construed in its popular sense. . . ." That generalization runs counter to the basic rule that criminal statutes are strictly construed.

More important than generalized statements as to the proper approach to the problem of construction, however, is the language to be construed. The statute under which the defendant was indicted (Ill. Rev. Stat. 1953, chap. 38, par. 210), refers to "any clerk, agent, servant, solicitor, broker, apprentice, or officer." If "agent" has the broad meaning which the majority gives it, each of the other terms is superfluous because all are embraced within the single term "agent." Many of the specific enumerations in the other statutes referred to by the majority likewise become largely, if not entirely, meaningless, for the particular relationships they seek to reach are also swallowed up in the expanded definition of the term "agent."

It is arguable of course that the conduct of the defendant in this case should be regarded as criminal. The General Assembly might wish to make it so. But it might not. It might regard the collection agency as a desirable service enterprise which should not be made unduly perilous. If the defendant in this case, with his little agency, is guilty of one embezzlement, he is guilty of 500. The General Assembly might not want to make the enterprise so hazardous. It has not done so, in my opinion, by the statute before us.[b]

---

b. The various statutes relevant to embezzlement at issue in these opinions have all been replaced by §16-1 (Theft and Related Offenses) of the Illinois Revised Criminal Code of 1961, reprinted at page 1089 infra. How should this case be decided under the new provisions? — EDS.

MODEL PENAL CODE

SECTION 223.8.   THEFT BY FAILURE TO MAKE REQUIRED DISPOSITIONS OF FUNDS RECEIVED

[See Appendix.]

MODEL PENAL CODE AND COMMENTARIES, COMMENT TO §223.8 AT 255-262 (1980):
The challenge is to distinguish default that should be assimilated to theft from
non-performance that should be left to the traditional remedies for breach of
contract.

The difficulty that has troubled courts in the past may be illustrated by the
decisions in Commonwealth v. Mitchneck[1] and State v. Polzin.[2] The *Mitchneck*
case involved a mine operator whose employees signed written authorizations
for him to deduct from their wages the amounts of their grocery bills. Mitchneck made the deductions but failed to pay the grocer. He was convicted under
the Pennsylvania fraudulent-conversion statute, which at the time covered anyone who

> having received or having possession, in any capacity or by any means or manner
> whatever, of any money or property, of any kind whatsoever, of or belonging to any
> other person, firm, or coporation, or which any other person, firm, or corporation
> is entitled to receive and have, who fraudulently withholds, converts, or applies the
> same, or any part thereof, . . . to and for his own use and benefit, or to and for the
> use and benefit of any other person.

The conviction was reversed on the ground that Mitchneck did not have in his
possession

> any money *belonging* to his employees. True he owed them money. . . . Defendant's
> liability for the unpaid wages due his employees was, and remained, civil, not crimi-
> nal. His liability for the amount due Vagnoni after his agreement to accept or
> honor the assignments of his employees' wages was likewise civil and not criminal.

If the miners in the *Mitchneck* case had drawn their pay at one window and
passed part of it back to Mitchneck's cashier at the next window, conviction for
embezzlement or fraudulent conversion could have been obtained. The premise of Section 223.8 is that liability should also follow on the facts of the case as
they occurred. The bookkeeping shortcut actually used hardly serves as a rational basis for exculpating Mitchneck from criminal liability.

The *Polzin* case presents a more complex variation of the same situation. Polzin was a money lender who took a note from a Mrs. Braseth under an arrangement by which, instead of paying the cash to her, he agreed to pay off certain of
her creditors. Instead of doing so, he made out a check to a collection agency
which he owned. He then approached the creditors with a proposal to act for
them in collecting their claim from Mrs. Braseth for a 33 percent collection fee.

1. 130 Pa. Super. 433, 198 A. 463 (1938).
2. 197 Wash. 612, 85 P.2d 1057 (1939).

They accepted the arrangement, after which Polzin paid the creditors and withheld $19 as his agreed-upon collection fee.

Polzin was convicted of petty larceny, the jury having evidently taken the view that what was stolen was the $19 fee which Polzin had withheld. The Supreme Court of Washington reversed the conviction. The court held first that there could be no misappropriation of any "property" belonging to Mrs. Braseth, because she never gave Polzin anything other than her note. Since Polzin held no "property" belonging to Mrs. Braseth but had merely promised to make certain payments, he was her debtor rather than her trustee. Second, with respect to the $19 withheld from the creditors, Mrs. Braseth "lost nothing"; the bills had been completely discharged and Polzin had therefore performed his agreement as far as she was concerned.

Section 223.8 was designed in part to provide a theory for reaching cases like *Mitchneck* and *Polzin*. Both were thought to illustrate situations that properly should be assimilated to theft rather than treated as mere breach of contract. . . .

There is a long tradition, deriving to some extent from the harsh days of the debtors' prison and to some extent enshrined in constitutional provisions, against enforcing individual consensual obligations by criminal sanctions. . . . Among the valid objections to the employment of criminal sanctions to enforce debts, as distinct from protecting "ownership" of "property," may be included the following: . . . a feeling that it is up to the contract maker to select his risks and that the invocation of criminal sanctions in cases of non-performance involves the impairment of the incentive to make wise risk selections and thus impairment of the social functions of contract-making . . . ; the unlikelihood of deterring honest insolvency by criminal threats, since insolvency is so often a result of factors beyond the control of the individual; the dangers, in attempting to punish insolvency for which the actor may properly be viewed as at fault, of discouraging the kind of speculation that is properly a part of a free-enterprise system and of securing unjust convictions by hindsight; and the futility, from the creditors' standpoint, of imprisoning a debtor who is unable to pay.

None of the foregoing considerations was thought applicable to cases such as *Mitchneck* and *Polzin*. In neither of those cases was there an ordinary credit transaction or an understanding that involves an assessment of risks at some future date. Mitchneck and Polzin were not supposed to use the funds in any way for their own purposes nor even to retain them for any substantial period. They were merely conduits for the transmission of money to persons designated by the real owner of the money. [A] proprietary use of the money should properly be regarded as theft, much as a guardian may be guilty of embezzlement when he commingles fiduciary funds with his own and reduces the account below the level of his fiduciary obligation in order to satisfy his personal financial needs. . . .

It should be noted, however, that the *Mitchneck* and *Polzin* situations are not free from difficulty even under such a formulation as Section 223.8. The text of the offense requires that the actor "obtain" property from another. The term "obtain" is defined in Section 223.0(5) to mean, in relation to property, "to bring about a transfer or purported transfer of a legal interest in the property, whether to the obtainer or another." The problem in both *Mitchneck* and *Polzin* was that the defendant was not perceived as having "obtained" anything from the victim in this sense, and that perception might be no less applicable to Section 223.8. Indeed, if the property were regarded as having been "obtained" as that term is defined, Section 223.2(1) would be an adequate basis for prosecution. If Mitchneck and Polzin obtained property of another under an understanding and then "exercised unlawful control over" that property, there would seem to be no bar to an ordinary embezzlement prosecution. Even if this is true, however, there may be an important value in addressing a specific formulation to situations of this kind. Convictions of embezzlement are not easily obtained under the broader standards embodied in the general definition of theft.

It is important, nevertheless, to emphasize the point that Section 223.8 must not be construed so broadly that a bright line between theft and breach of contract is obscured. [Consider] credit-card purchases, a practice that has assumed enormous proportions in today's economy. Typically, the purchaser of goods "obtains" property by becoming the drawee-acceptor of a draft, drawn by the merchant in favor of the credit-card company as payee. If unauthorized use of the card is involved, or if forged or stolen cards are used, Section 224.6 is adequate to handle the problem. If the actor intended from the beginning not to pay, Section 223.3 covers the situation. But if the actor is engaged in authorized use and simply cannot pay his bills, it is inappropriate to make him a thief; the risk that he cannot pay is a cost of doing business that credit-card companies should assume. . . .

The path to avoiding such undue extensions of Section 223.8 is to accord proper weight to the limitation embodied in the words "to be reserved," so that Section 223.8 is deemed applicable only in cases of a promise to turn over property actually received in kind or an equivalent sum of money specifically reserved in the sense that a trustee reserves a fiduciary account. It is true that such a construction would seem to limit Section 223.8 to classic instances of embezzlement. [T]here may be some cases beyond ordinary embezzlement to which the provision could be applied by a broad construction of "obtains" to deal with situations where property was not physically exchanged. But in order to eliminate application of the section to cases where civil remedies alone should be permitted, something approaching an explicit agreement to "reserve" would seem to be required.

NOTE

Only some nine states followed the Model Penal Code's lead in this section. See Model Penal Code and Commentaries, Comment to §223.8 at 266 (1980). What might have been the reasons for the reluctance?

3. Fraud

INTRODUCTORY NOTE

The deposit of history is no less substantial in crimes dealing with the use of fraud to acquire another's property than in crimes dealing with misappropriation by one in lawful possession, previously discussed. In both situations, the common law judges through some remarkable reasoning brought certain species of these nontrespassory takings within the scope of the basic common law crime of larceny, while in parallel developments Parliament expressly dealt with these nontrespassory situations by creating new statutory crimes to cover them. This uncoordinated judicial and legislative development left parallel crimes to cover fundamentally similar kinds of theft. The necessity to distinguish which of these kinds of theft were within the stretched judicial definition of larceny and which within the statutory definitions of new crimes is the legacy of this history.

The early common law, influenced by the ethic of caveat emptor, declined to treat as criminal, situations in which a person acquired another's property through simple deception. The classic justification was given by Holt, C.J., in 1703: "[W]e are not to indict one for making a fool of another." Regina v. Jones, 91 Eng. Rep. 330.[3] But through the development of common law "cheats," the principle was modified as to certain kinds of fraud, which were aimed indiscriminately at any member of the public rather than at a particular person and which were thought to be such that ordinary prudence was an insufficient protection: for example, using a false token, false weights or measures, etc. See Rex. v. Wheatley, 97 Eng. Rep. 746, 748 (1761). This common law development was supplemented and amplified by a statute in 1541 that made criminal the acquisition of another's property by deceit in situations doubtfully reached by common law cheats: where accomplished "by colour and means of any [privy] false token or counterfeit letter made in any other man's name." 33 Hen. VIII, ch. 1.

A more far-reaching legislative innovation came in 1757 with the enactment of what subsequently became the prototype false pretense statute, 30 Geo. II, ch. 24, making it a misdemeanor to obtain "money, goods, wares or merchandizes" from any person by false pretenses with intent to cheat or defraud. There originally appeared to be some doubt whether the false pretense statute reached any and all misrepresentations or was to be narrowly read in the light of the common law of cheats and the earlier cheating statutes. It was not until 1789 that the broader meaning was established in Young v. The King, 100 Eng. Rep. 475. See Jerome Hall, Theft, Law and Society 45-52 (2d ed. 1952); R. Pearce, Theft by False Promises, 101 U. Pa. L. Rev. 967 (1953). In the meantime the landmark case of The King v. Pear had been decided in 1779, I Leach 211, 168 Eng. Rep. 208, creating the crime of what came to be known as "larceny by trick" as a distinct form of common law larceny. The following report of the case is taken from 168 Eng. Rep. 208:

> The prisoner was indicted for stealing a black horse, the property of Samuel Finch. It appeared in evidence that Samuel Finch was a Livery-Stablekeeper in the Borough; and that the prisoner, on the 2d of July 1779, hired the horse of him to go to Sutton, in the county of Surry, and back again, saying on being asked where he lived, that he lodged at No. 25 in King-street, and should return about eight o'clock the same evening. He did not return; and it was proved that he had sold the horse on the very day he had hired it, to one William Hollist, in Smithfield Market; and that he had no lodging at the place to which he had given the Prosecutor directions.
>
> The learned Judge said: There had been different opinions on the law of this class of cases; that the general doctrine then was that if a horse be let for a particu-

---

3. Cf. 1 W. Hawkins, Pleas of the Crown 344 (6th ed. 1788): "[It is] needless to provide severe laws for such mischiefs, against which common prudence and caution may be a sufficient security."

lar portion of time, and after that time is expired, the party hiring, instead of returning the horse to its owner, sell it and convert the money to his own use, it is
felony, because there is then no privity of contract subsisting between the parties;
that in the present case the horse was hired to take a journey into Surry, and the
prisoner sold him the same day, without taking any such journey; that there were
also other circumstances which imported that at the time of the hiring the prisoner
had it in intention to sell the horse, as his saying that he lodged at a place where in
fact he was not known. He therefore left it with the Jury to consider, Whether the
prisoner meant at the time of the hiring to take such journey, but was afterwards
tempted to sell the horse? for if so he must be acquitted; but that if they were of
opinion that at the time of the hiring the journey was a mere pretense to get the
horse into his possession, and he had no intention to take such journey but intended to sell the horse, they would find that fact specially for the opinion of the
Judges.

The Jury found that the facts above stated were true; and also that the prisoner
had hired the horse with a fraudulent view and intention of selling it immediately.

The question was referred to the Judges, Whether the delivery of the horse by
the prosecutor to the prisoner, had so far changed the possession of the property,
as to render the subsequent conversion of it a mere breach of trust, or whether the
conversion was felonious?

The Judges differed greatly in opinion on this case; and delivered their opinions
seriatim upon it at Lord Chief Justice De Gray's house on 4th February 1780 and
on the 22nd of the same month Mr. Barron Perryn delivered their opinion on it.
The majority of them thought, That the question, as to the original intention of
the prisoner in hiring the horse, had been properly left to the jury; and as they had
found, that his view in so doing was fraudulent, the parting with the property had
not changed the nature of the possession, but that it remained unaltered in the
prosecutor at the time of the conversion; and that the prisoner was therefore guilty
of felony.

The reason the judges thought the false pretense statute, 30 Geo. II, was inapplicable to *Pear* appears in the report of the case in 2 E. H. East, Pleas of the
Crown 685, 688-689 (1806):

[T]he next question was, Whether this offence were within or at all affected by the
statutes of Hen. 8 and Geo. 2. Seven of the Judges were of the opinion, that it was
not. That the statute of Hen. 8 was confined to the cases of obtaining goods in
other men's names, by false tokens or counterfeit letters, made in any other man's
name. The statute of Geo. 2 extended that law to all cases where goods were obtained by false pretenses of any kind. But both these statutes were confined to cases
where credit was obtained in the name of a third person; and did not extend to
cases where a man, on his own account, got goods with an intention to steal them.

Use was made, therefore, of the singular notion that possession never passes to
a fraudulent bailee to stretch the concept of larceny to include a species of act
thought otherwise unamenable to proper criminal sanction. "Fraud in securing
possession joined breaking bulk and custody in servants to extend the definition
of larceny far beyond its original traditional meaning." Jerome Hall, Theft, Law
and Society 42 (2d ed. 1952).

When the false pretense statute was subsequently extended to all misrepresentations of fact, regardless of the technique of deception, there were two crimes,
larceny by trick (a felony) and statutory false pretenses (only a misdemeanor),
covering very much the same kind of criminal conduct. Perhaps the first hint of

the theory on which the crimes would be distinguished appears in the *Pear* case itself, as reported in 2 E. H. East, Pleas of the Crown 685, 689 n. (a) (1806):

> On the debate in this case Eyre, B., adverting to these statutes, said he doubted if there was a distinction in this respect between the owner's parting with the possession and with the property in the thing delivered. That where goods were delivered upon a false token, and the owner meant to part with the property absolutely and never expected to have the goods returned again, it might be difficult to reach the case otherwise than through the statutes; aliter, where he parted with the possession only: for there if the possession were obtained by fraud, and not taken according to the agreement; it was on the whole a taking against the will of the owner; and if done animo furandi, it was felony.

Question: Is there any logical reason why "the deceit which eliminated the consent which the owner intended to give when he regarded himself as parting with merely the possession of his chattel would not have the same effect when he regarded himself as parting with something greater, namely, the ownership of it?" 2 W. O. Russell, Crime 1089 (10th ed. 1950).

HUFSTETLER v. STATE

Alabama Court of Appeals
37 Ala. App. 71, 63 So. 2d 730 (1953)

CARR, J. The accused was convicted by the court without a jury on a charge of petit larceny. The property involved was 6½ gallons of gasoline.

The defendant did not testify nor offer any evidence.

The undisputed facts are narrated by a witness [Peter Whorton] as follows.

> . . . I own and operate a store and service station at Forney, Alabama. On March 29, 1952, the defendant drove an automobile up to my gasoline tanks. There were some two or three other men in the car with him, and a man in the back seat got out and started in the store and asked if I had a telephone. When I told him I did not have a telephone, he said he wanted some gasoline and went back and got in the car. I asked him how much and he said "fill it up." I put 6½ gallons of gasoline in the car and this man said to get a quart of oil, and when I went for the oil, the defendant drove off in the automobile together with the man who ordered the gas and the others in the car without paying for the gasoline. This 6½ gallons of gas belonged to me and was of the value of $1.94. . . .

The only question of critical concern is whether, on the basis of the above proof, the judgment of conviction can be sustained.

Appellant's attorney in brief urges that Whorton voluntarily parted with the possession and ownership of the gasoline.

Confusion sometimes arises in an effort to distinguish the kindred criminal offenses of larceny, false pretenses, and embezzlement.

The Massachusetts Supreme Court in Commonwealth v. Barry, 124 Mass. 325, gave a distinction that is clear and comprehensive:

> If a person honestly receives the possession of the goods, chattels or money of another upon any trust, express or implied, and, after receiving them, fraudulently

converts them to his own use, he may be guilty of the crime of embezzlement, but cannot be of that of larceny, except as embezzlement is by statute made larceny. If the possession of such property is obtained by fraud, and the owner of it intends to part with his title as well as his possession, the offence is that of obtaining property by false pretenses, provided the means by which they are acquired are such as, in law, are false pretenses. If the possession is fraudulently obtained, with intent on the part of the person obtaining it, at the time he received it, to convert the same to his own use, and the person parting with it intends to part with his possession merely, and not with his title to the property, the offence is larceny.

In the case at bar the circumstances disclose that by the application of the well-known doctrine of aid and abet the appellant secured the possession of the gasoline by a trick or fraud. The obtaining of the property by the consent of the owner under such conditions will not necessarily prevent the taking from being larceny. In other words, an actual trespass is not always required to be proven. The trick or fraud vitiates the transaction, and it will be deemed that the owner still retained the constructive possession.

What we have said related to the possession. It is certainly a logical conclusion that Whorton had no intention of parting with the ownership of the property until he had received pay therefor.

The element of the intent of the appellant is inferable from the factual background. . . .

Affirmed. Remanded for proper sentence.

GRAHAM v. UNITED STATES

United States Court of Appeals, District of Columbia Circuit
187 F. 2d 87 (1950)

WASHINGTON, J. The appellant, an attorney, was indicted in two counts for grand larceny under section 2201 of Title 22 of the District of Columbia Code (1940 ed.). He was charged with having stolen money from Francisco Gal in the amounts of $100 and $1,900. He appeals from a judgment and conviction entered upon a verdict of guilty.

The complaining witness, Francisco Gal, consulted appellant in his professional capacity. Gal had been arrested and charged with disorderly conduct, and had forfeited $25 as collateral. He was seeking American citizenship and was apprehensive that the arrest would impede or bar his attainment of that goal. An immigrant employed as a cook, his command of the English language was far from complete. He testified that appellant Graham told him that he wasn't sure what he could do, that Graham would "have to talk to the policeman. You have to pay money for that, because the money is talk." He further testified that Graham told him he would charge him $200 for a fee; that he would have to pay an additional $2,000 for the police; that Graham said "don't mention the money for nobody and for the police either." As a result, Gal testified that he paid the appellant $300 on February 2, 1950 (of which, he said, $200 was paid as a legal fee), and $1,900 on February 3, 1950. The police officer who originally had arrested Gal testified that he came to appellant's office, and after talking with Graham, told Gal that he wasn't in any trouble. Gal testified to substantially the same effect. The officer testified that Graham did not then or at any other time offer or give him money. The appellant testified that the entire payment was intended as a fee for legal services; that he had never mentioned money for the police; that no part of the money was in fact paid to the police or anyone else, but was kept by the appellant.

Appellant's principal contentions are: First, that the evidence supports the proposition that Gal voluntarily gave Graham complete title to the money and therefore appellant is entitled to a directed verdict; and, second, that the trial court's charge to the jury was erroneous in not sufficiently distinguishing between the situation where one obtains complete title to another's property by fraud or trick and the case where possession only is obtained.

Section 2201 of Title 22 of the District of Columbia Code provides as follows:

> Whoever shall feloniously take and carry away anything of value of the amount or value of $50 or upward, including things savoring of the realty, shall suffer imprisonment of not less than one nor more than ten years.

Interpreting this statute, this court has held that "one who obtains money from another upon the representation that he will perform certain service therewith for the latter, intending at the time to convert the money, and actually converting it, to his own use, is guilty of larceny." In classic terminology, "the distinction drawn by the common law is between the case of one who gives up possession of a chattel for a special purpose to another who by converting it to his own use is held to have committed a trespass, and the case of one who, although induced by fraud or trick, nevertheless actually intends that title to the chattel shall pass to the wrongdoer." United States v. Patton, 3 Cir., 1941, 120 F.2d 73, 76.

We now turn to appellant's first contention, that under the evidence in the case the court should have directed a verdict for the defendant. We think this contention without merit. If the jury believed Gal's testimony, and did not believe that of the defendant, it was possible for the jury to conclude beyond a reasonable doubt that the defendant fraudulently induced Gal to give him $2,000 to be used for a special purpose, i.e., to bribe the police, that the defendant did not intend so to use the money, and converted it to his own use. Under the rule stated above, this would be larceny by trick.

Thus, in the *Means* case [Means v. United States, 65 F.2d 206], the defendant was convicted of the crime of larceny under the following circumstances: After the kidnapping of the infant son of Charles Lindbergh, the defendant in an interview with Mrs. McLean persuaded her that he could assist in locating and recovering the kidnapped baby, stating that if Mrs. McLean would give him $100,000 he would use that sum to pay the ransom and secure the return of the child. On the basis of these representations he secured the money from Mrs. McLean. His representations were fraudulent and he intended at the time to convert the money to his own use, and actually so converted it. People v. Edwards, 72 Cal. App. 102, 236 P. 944, provides an even closer precedent. There the defendant took money from the complainant, representing to her that it would be used to bribe officers investigating criminal activities by her husband. The complainant did not know exactly how the defendant was going to use the money but understood that it was going to be used in some manner to corrupt the police. The court, in sustaining a conviction for larceny, held that under these circumstances "title would remain in [the complainant] until the accomplishment of the purpose for which she gave [the defendant] the money, i.e., until its final delivery by [him] to the officers whom she was led to believe were to be bribed." . . .

The judgment of the District Court is affirmed.

NOTES AND QUESTIONS

1. Because on Gal's testimony the money was handed to the defendant to be given to the police officer as a bribe, how can the court defend its decision that Gal did not intend to pass his whole interest in the money to the defendant, title and all? On the other hand, if the court had held otherwise, thus precluding a larceny-by-trick conviction, could the defendant have been convicted of obtaining money by false pretenses? Note that a false promise is often regarded as inadequate to sustain a false pretense conviction, although it suffices for larceny by trick. See People v. Ashley, page 1071 infra.

2. In Bourbonnaise v. State, 96 Okla. Crim. 28, 248 P.2d 640 (1952), the defendant bootlegger obtained money from Bean as payment for a bottle of whiskey; he stated he would return with the bottle within 30 minutes after purchasing same from another bootlegger. He never returned. Affirming a conviction of larceny, the court stated (248 P.2d at 642):

> This money was not given the defendant to consummate a purchase of liquor represented by defendant to be in his possession. . . . If such had been the case, then the money would have become defendant's money, and if the defendant had failed to turn over the liquor, then supposed to be in his possession either on his person or somewhere outside, such facts would have supported a charge of obtaining money under false pretense. But here defendant . . . merely agreed to take Bean's money and go purchase the liquor from another bootlegger. The money was not his. He was to pay it over for Bean. It was Bean's money until paid over, and then the whiskey would be Bean's.

3. R. Pearce, Theft by False Promises, 101 U. Pa. L. Rev. 967, 987-989 (1953), writes:

> Although some legal scholars have treated larceny by trick as closely related functionally to false pretenses, or even as completely engulfing it, the offenses are respectively aimed at quite different acquisitive techniques. False pretenses is theft by deceit. The misappropriation it punishes must be effected by communication to the owner. Larceny by trick is theft by stealth. It punishes misappropriation effected by unauthorized disposition of the owner's property. The former focuses on defendant's behavior while face to face with the owner: did it amount to a false pretense? The focus of the latter is upon defendant's behavior behind the owner's back: did it amount to an unauthorized appropriation?
>
> One cause of confusion of the offenses is that larceny by trick requires some deceit in addition to the unauthorized disposition of property which is its gravamen. It is thus thought of as a type of theft by fraud. However, the requirement of deceit in larceny by trick stems from its history rather than its function and plays a minor role. . . .
>
> It should be apparent that deceit had little to do with the offensiveness of Pear's

behavior. It can hardly be said that being a servant is offensive, yet being a servant plays the same role in larceny by servants as deceit plays in larceny by trick. Each permits a circumvention of the requirement of a "trespassory taking" in order to reach a misappropriation by a person in possession as common law larceny. Fraud for this highly technical purpose need not be subjected to close scrutiny or held to an exacting standard, for there is adequate external evidence of the defendant's antisocial bent in his subsequent misappropriation. Indeed it is true generally, as it was in Pear's Case, that the only substantial evidence of the initial fraud is found in the subsequent unauthorized appropriation.

In contrast, the antisocial act defined by the crime of false pretenses consists entirely of deceit. It consists of so deceiving the owner of the property that he is induced to consent to the defendant's treating the property as his own. This being so, it is unnecessary as well as impossible for the defendant to subsequently misappropriate property which he has stolen by false pretenses. If the behavior by which he induced consent amounts to a false pretense, he has completed his form of theft at the moment the bargain is struck. . . .

Thus it is said that a defendant cannot be convicted of larceny if his deceit induces the owner to transfer his entire interest in the property, whereas he can be if it induces consent merely to his possession or use of the property. This creates the often troublesome paradox that larceny punishes the lesser fraud and exempts the greater. The apparent contradiction disappears with the realization that larceny by trick does not punish *deceit* — it punishes unauthorized appropriation. This functional distinction between larceny and false pretenses suggests a simple test by which specific fact situations can be distributed between the two offenses. If the deceit be eliminated from the transaction by which the property initially came into the defendant's hands, would his subsequent behavior with respect to the property constitute a conversion? If so, the offense may be larceny by trick; it cannot be false pretenses. If not, the offense may be false pretenses; it cannot be larceny by trick.

4. Problem. Defendant went to an auto dealership, took a vehicle for a test drive, and failed to return it. He was convicted of larceny by false pretenses. Should the conviction be affirmed? See Baker v. Commonwealth, 300 S.E.2d 788 (Va. 1983).

PEOPLE v. ASHLEY

Supreme Court of California
42 Cal. 2d 246, 267 P.2d 271 (1954)

TRAYNOR, J. . . . [Defendant, the business manager of a corporation chartered for the purpose of "introducing people," was charged with feloniously taking money from two women and convicted of grand theft under §404 of the California Penal Code. The evidence revealed that defendant obtained a loan of $7,200 from a Mrs. Russ, a woman 70 years of age, by promising that the loan would be secured by a first mortgage on certain improved property of the corporation and that the money would be used to build a theater on other property owned by the corporation. In fact the corporation leased but did not own the improved property, and no theater was ever built, the money having been used to meet the corporation's operating expenses. After defendant received the money, Mrs. Russ frequently quarreled with him over his failure to deliver the promised first mortgage. She finally received a note of the corporation secured by a second trust deed on some unimproved property owned by the corporation. She testified that she accepted this security because defendant had told her to "take that or nothing." She subsequently received four postdated checks in payment of the loan. After it became apparent that these checks would not be paid, defendant requested an extension. Mrs. Russ granted the extension after defendant had threatened to destroy himself if she refused so that she might be paid from the proceeds of his life insurance policies.

[Defendant obtained $13,590 from a Mrs. Neal representing that the corporation intended to use the money to buy the El Patio Theatre. She was initially told that the loan would be secured by a trust deed on the theater building and that she would have good security for her loan because the corporation was worth a half million dollars. However, after obtaining the money, defendant issued Mrs. Neal a note of the corporation for $13,500. Subsequently, she loaned the corporation an additional $4,470 receiving a note for $17,500 in exchange for the previous note. Mrs. Neal testified that when she hesitated in making the additional loan, defendant placed a gun on his desk and said: "Now look here, Mrs. Neal, I don't want no monkey business out of you. Do you understand that?" The corporation did not buy the theater; Mrs. Neal never received the trust deed; and the money was deposited to the corporation's account.

[Evidence was introduced indicating that the corporation was in a strained financial condition and was worth nothing like a half million dollars. There was also evidence showing that the defendant received no salary from the corporation, but that he drove an expensive automobile paid for by the corporation, and that he had drawn numerous checks on corporation funds for the payment of expenses.]

. . . The case went to the jury with instructions relating to larceny by trick and device and obtaining property by false pretenses. The jurors were instructed that all would have to agree on the type of theft, if any, that was committed. . . .

Although the crimes of larceny by trick and device and obtaining property by false pretenses are much alike, they are aimed at different criminal acquisitive techniques. Larceny by trick and device is the appropriation of property, the possession of which was fraudulently acquired; obtaining property by false pretenses is the fraudulent or deceitful acquisition of both title and possession. In this state, these two offenses, with other larcenous crimes, have been consolidated into the single crime of theft (Pen. Code, §484), but their elements have not been changed thereby. The purpose of the consolidation was to remove the technicalities that existed in the pleading and proof of these crimes at common law. Indictments and informations charging the crime of "theft" can now simply allege an "unlawful taking." Pen. Code, §§951, 952. Juries need no longer be concerned with the technical differences between the several types of theft, and can return a general verdict of guilty if they find that an "unlawful taking" has been proved. The elements of the several types of theft included within section 484 have not been changed, however, and a judgment of conviction of theft, based on a general verdict of guilty, can be sustained only if the evidence discloses the elements of one of the consolidated offenses. In the present case, it is clear from the record that each of the prosecuting witnesses intended to pass both title and possession, and that the type of theft, if any, in each case, was that of obtaining property by false pretenses. [Defendant's] defense was not based on distinctions between title and possession, but rather he contends that there was no unlawful taking of any sort.

To support a conviction of theft for obtaining property by false pretenses, it must be shown that the defendant made a false pretense or representation with intent to defraud the owner of his property, and that the owner was in fact defrauded. It is unnecessary to prove that the defendant benefited personally from the fraudulent acquisition. People v. Jones, 36 Cal. 2d 373, 377, 381, 224 P.2d 353. The false pretense or representation must have materially influenced the owner to part with his property, but the false pretense need not be the sole inducing cause. If the conviction rests primarily on the testimony of a single witness that the false pretense was made, the making of the pretense must be corroborated. Pen. Code, §1110.

The crime of obtaining property by false pretenses was unknown in the early common law, and our statute, like those of most American states, is directly traceable to 30 Geo. 11, ch. 24, section 1. In an early Crown Case Reserved, Rex v. Goodhall, Russ. & Ry. 461 (1821), the defendant obtained a quantity of meat from a merchant by promising to pay at a future day. The jury found that the promise was made without intention to perform. The judges concluded, however, that the defendant's conviction was erroneous because the pretense "was merely a promise of future conduct, and common prudence and caution would have prevented any injury arising from it." Russ. & Ry. at 463. . . . By stating that the "promise of future conduct" was such that "common prudence and caution" could prevent any injury arising therefrom, the new offense was confused with the old common law "cheat." The decision also seems contrary to the plain meaning of the statute, and was so interpreted by two English writers on the law of crimes. Archbold, Pleading and Evidence in Criminal Cases 183 [3d ed. 1828]; Roscoe, Digest of the Law of Evidence in Criminal Cases 418 [2d Amer. ed. 1840]. The opinion of Rex v. Goodhall, supra, was completely misinterpreted in the case of Commonwealth v. Drew, 1837, 19 Pick. 179, 185, 36 Mass. 179, 185, in which the Supreme Judicial Court of Massachusetts declared by way of dictum, that under the statute "naked lies" could not be regarded as "false pretenses." On the basis of these two questionable decisions, Wharton formulated the following generalization: ". . . the false pretense to be within the statute, must relate to a state of things averred to be at the time existing, and not to a state of things thereafter to exist." Wharton, American Criminal Law 542 [1st ed. 1846]. This generalization has been followed in the majority of American cases, almost all of which can be traced to reliance on Wharton or the two cases mentioned above. The rule has not been followed in all jurisdictions, however. Some courts have avoided the problems created by the rule by blurring the distinctions between larceny by trick and device and obtaining property by false pretenses. See generally, Pearce, "Theft by False Promises," 101 U. of Pa. L. Rev. 967.[a] . . . Other courts have repudiated the majority rule. . . .[3]

---

a. "The technique is to throw the crime of larceny by trick into the breach in the law of theft by fraud which is opened by the promissory fraud rule." Pearce, Theft by False Promises, 101 U. Pa. L. Rev. 967, 987 (1953). See, e.g., Graham v. United States, page 1068 supra. — Eds.

3. The majority rule was also rejected by the United States Supreme Court in the construction of the federal mail fraud statute, 17 Stat. 283, 323. See Durland v. United States, 161 U.S. 306, 313. On the basis of the *Durland* case, the statute was amended to include specifically false promises, 35 Stat. 1130, 18 U.S.C. §1341 (1946).

The Court of Appeals for the District of Columbia has however, advanced the following reasons in defense of the majority rule: "It is of course true that then [at the time of the early English cases cited by Wharton, supra], as now, the intention to commit certain crimes was ascertained by looking backward from the act and finding that the accused intended to do what he did do. However, where, as here, the act complained of — namely, failure to repay money or use it as specified at the time of borrowing — is as consonant with ordinary commercial default as with criminal conduct, the danger of applying this technique to prove the crime is quite apparent. Business affairs would be materially incumbered by the ever present threat that a debtor might be subjected to criminal penalties if the prosecutor and jury were of the view that at the time of borrowing he was mentally a cheat. The risk of prosecuting one who is guilty of nothing more than a failure or inability to pay his debts is a very real consideration. . . ." Chaplin v. United States, 157 F.2d 697, 698-699.

. . . We do not find this reasoning persuasive. In this state, and in the majority of American states as well as in England, false promises can provide the foundation of a civil action for deceit. In such actions something more than nonperformance is required to prove the defendant's intent not to perform his promise. Nor is proof of nonperformance alone sufficient in criminal prosecutions based on false promises. In such prosecutions the People must, as in all criminal prosecutions, prove their case beyond a reasonable doubt. Any danger, through the instigation of criminal proceedings by disgruntled creditors, to those who have blamelessly encountered "commercial defaults" must, therefore, be predicated upon the idea that trial juries are incapable of weighing the evidence and understanding the instruction that they must be convinced of the defendant's fraudulent intent beyond a reasonable doubt, or that appellate courts will be derelict in discharging their duty to ascertain that there is sufficient evidence to support a conviction. . . .

Moreover, in cases of obtaining property by false pretenses, it must be proved that any misrepresentations of fact alleged by the People were made knowingly and with intent to deceive. If such misrepresentations are made innocently or inadvertently, they can no more form the basis for a prosecution for obtaining property by false pretenses than can an innocent breach of contract. . . .

If false promises were not false pretenses, the legally sophisticated, without fear of punishment, could perpetrate on the unwary fraudulent schemes like that divulged by the record in this case. . . . The inclusion of false promises within sections 484 and 532 of the Penal Code will not "materially encumber" business affairs. . . .

The judgment and the order denying the motion for a new trial are affirmed.

SCHAUER, J. I concur in the judgment solely on the ground that the evidence establishes, with ample corroboration, the making by the defendant of false representations as to existing facts. On that evidence the convictions should be sustained pursuant to long accepted theories of law. . . . Accordingly, I dissent from all that portion of the opinion which discusses and pronounces upon the theories which in my view are extraneous to the proper disposition of any issue actually before us. . . .

In a prosecution for obtaining property by the making of a false promise, knowingly and with intent to deceive, the matter to be proved, as to its criminality, is purely subjective. It is not, like the specific intent in such a crime as burglary, a mere element of the crime; it is, in any significant sense, all of the crime. The proof will necessarily be of objective acts, entirely legal in themselves, from which inferences as to the ultimate illegal subjective fact will be drawn. But, whereas in burglary the proof of the subjective element is normally as strong and reliable as the proof of any objective element, in this type of activity the proof of such vital element can almost never be reliable; it must inevitably (in the absence of confession or something tantamount thereto) depend on inferences drawn by creditors, prosecutors, jurors, and judges from facts and circumstances which by reason of their nature cannot possibly exclude innocence with any certainty. . . . Such inferences as proof of the alleged crime have long been recognized as so unreliable that they have been excluded from the category of acceptable proof.

. . . I am unwilling to accept as a premise the scholastic redaction of the majority that rules of proof may be set aside because appellate judges will always know when a jury has been misled and the proof is not sufficient. . . .

The suggestion in the majority opinion that it is inconceivable "that trial juries are incapable of weighing the evidence [impliedly, with omniscient accuracy however inconclusive it be] and understanding the instruction that they must be convinced of the defendant's fraudulent intent beyond a reasonable doubt, or that appellate courts will be derelict [less than omniscient] in discharging their duty" affords no substantial basis for striking down a rule of proof. . . .

With the rule that the majority opinion now enunciates, no man, no matter how innocent his intention, can sign a promise to pay in the future, or to perform an act at a future date, without subjecting himself to the risk that at some later date others, in the light of differing perspectives, philosophies and subsequent events, may conclude that, after all, the accused *should* have known that at the future date he could not perform as he promised — and if he, as a "reasonable" man from the point of view of the creditor, district attorney and a grand or trial jury — *should* have known, then, it may be inferred, he did know. And if it can be inferred that he knew, then this court and other appellate courts will be bound to affirm a conviction. . . .

NOTE

In accord with *Ashley*, see Commonwealth v. Parker, 564 A.2d 46 (Pa. Super. 1989); Kennedy v. State, 342 S.E.2d 251 (W. Va. 1986). In contrast, some courts continue to hold that a false promise cannot constitute false pretenses. E.g., State v. Allen, 505 So. 2d 1024 (Miss. 1987); People v. Cage, 301 N.W.2d 819 (Mich. 1981). See Annot., 19 A.L.R.4th 959 (Supp. 1993).

NEW YORK PENAL LAW

SECTION 155.05(2)(d)

A person obtains property by false promise when, pursuant to a scheme to defraud, he obtains property of another by means of a representation, express or implied, that he or a third person will in the future engage in particular conduct, and when he does not intend to engage in such conduct or, as the case may be, does not believe that the third person intends to engage in such conduct.

In any prosecution for larceny based upon a false promise, the defendant's intention or belief that the promise would not be performed may not be established by or inferred from the fact alone that such promise was not performed. Such a finding may be based only upon evidence establishing that the facts and circumstances of the case are wholly consistent with guilty intent or belief and wholly inconsistent with innocent intent or belief, and excluding to a moral certainty every hypothesis except that of the defendant's intention or belief that the promise would not be performed. . . .

MODEL PENAL CODE

SECTION 223.3.   THEFT BY DECEPTION

[See Appendix.]

NELSON v. UNITED STATES

United States Court of Appeals, District of Columbia Circuit
227 F.2d 21 (1955)

DANAHER, J. This is an appeal from a conviction for obtaining goods by false pretenses in violation of D.C. Code §22-1301 (1951). The trial court entered judgment of acquittal on a second count charging grand larceny. Evidence was offered to show that appellant from time to time over a period of months, for purposes of resale, had purchased merchandise from Potomac Distributors of Washington, D.C., Inc. (hereinafter referred to as Potomac Distributors). By September 18, 1952, his account was said to be in arrears more than thirty days. Late that afternoon, appellant sought immediate possession of two television sets and a washing machine, displayed his customers' purchase contracts to support his statement that he had already sold such merchandise and had taken payment therefor, and told one Schneider, secretary-treasurer of Potomac Distributors, "I promised delivery tonight." Appellant was told no further credit could be extended to him because of his overdue indebtedness in excess of $1800, whereupon appellant offered to give security for the desired items as well as for the delinquent account. He represented himself as the owner of a Packard car for which he had paid $4,260.50, but failed to disclose an outstanding prior indebtedness on the car of $3,028.08 secured by a chattel mortgage in favor of City Bank. Instead, he represented that he owed only one payment of some $55, not then due. Relying upon such representations, Potomac Distributors delivered to appellant two television sets each worth $136, taking in return a demand note for the entire indebtedness, past and present, in the total, $2,047.37, secured by a chattel mortgage on the Packard and the television sets. Appellant promised to make a cash payment on the note within a few days for default of which the holder was entitled to demand full payment. When the promised payment was not forthcoming, Schneider, by telephone calls and a personal visit to appellant's home, sought to locate appellant but learned he had left town. The

Packard about that time was in a collision, incurring damage of about $1,000, and was thereupon repossessed in behalf of the bank which held the prior lien for appellant's car purchase indebtedness. . . .

Appellant argues that Potomac Distributors could not have been defrauded for the car on September 18, 1952, "had an equity of between $900 and $1000 and roughly five times the value of the two television sets." That fact is immaterial. . . .

This appellant has sold two television sets, and apparently had taken payment therefor although he had no television sets to deliver to his customers. He could not get the sets from Potomac Distributors without offering security for his past due account as well as for his present purchase. In order to get them he lied. He represented that his car acquired at a cost of more than $4000 required only one further payment of $55. He now complains because his victim believed him when he lied. He argues that the misrepresentations were not material although the victim testified, and the jury could properly find, that he would not have parted with his goods except in reliance upon appellant's statements. . . .

He argues that there was no proof of an intent upon his part to defraud his victim.

> Wrongful acts knowingly or intentionally committed can neither be justified nor excused on the ground of innocent intent. The intent to injure or defraud is presumed when the unlawful act, which results in loss or injury, is proved to have been knowingly committed. It is a well-settled rule, which the law applies in both criminal and civil cases, that the intent is presumed and inferred from the result of the action.

This quotation from a challenged charge was found by the Supreme Court to be "unexceptionable as matter of law" in Agnew v. United States, 1897, 165 U.S. 36, 53. . . .

Affirmed.

MILLER, J. (dissenting). . . . Nelson did make a false representation; but the question is whether there was evidence from which the jury could properly be permitted to infer that he intended to defraud, and to conclude that Potomac was thereby defrauded. . . .

Differing definitions of the word "defraud" probably cause the difference in opinion between the majority and me. They seem to think it means, in connection with a purchase, to make a false pretense in the process of obtaining goods even though the purchase price is well secured. I think the word means, in connection with a purchase, to make a false pretense as a result of which the seller is deprived of his goods or of the purchase price. The difference is particularly important in a case like this one where a purchaser is charged with defrauding a seller. A purchaser can be said to have defrauded the seller of his goods only if he intended to defraud him of the purchase price for which the seller was willing to exchange them. It seems to me to follow that a purchaser who makes a false statement in buying on credit has not defrauded the seller of his goods if he nevertheless amply secures the debt. . . .

In considering the criminality vel non of the false statement, it must be remembered that the past due indebtedness of $1,697.87 is to play no part. That credit had already been extended generally, and with respect to it Potomac parted with nothing on September 18. Nelson was only charged with defrauding

Potomac by obtaining through false pretense the articles then delivered, which had a total value of only $349.50.

What was the actual value on September 18 of the property upon which Potomac took a lien, on the strength of which it parted with property worth $349.50? The bank collection manager, testifying for the Government, said that although on September 18 Nelson still owed the bank $3,028.08, he had on that day an equity in the car worth from $900 to $1,000. The mortgaged television sets were, I suppose, worth their price of $272. Adding to this the minimum equity in the automobile proved by the prosecution, it appears that Potomac had a lien on property worth at least $1,172 to protect a debt of $349.50. The proportion was more than three to one.

Such is the evidence as to what happened September 18, from which the jury was permitted to infer that Nelson then intended to defraud, and to conclude that he then did fraudulently obtain from Potomac the three articles purchased. As to intent, I suggest that it is wholly irrational to presume or infer that one intends to defraud when he buys goods on credit and safeguards that credit by giving more than triple security for it — no matter if he does falsely pretend that the security is even greater. It is equally illogical to conclude that the creditor was thereby defrauded. For that reason, my opinion is that the proof I have outlined — which was the only pertinent proof — did not warrant the trial court in submitting the case to the jury. . . .

As I have said, Nelson was guilty of a moral wrong in falsely and grossly misrepresenting his debt to the bank, but in the circumstances he should not have been indicted and convicted because of it. The District of Columbia statute under which he was prosecuted does not make mere falsehood felonious; it only denounces as criminal a false pretense which was intended to defraud and which in fact had that result. Even a liar is entitled to the full protection of the law. I am afraid a grave injustice has been done in this case.

NOTES AND QUESTIONS

1. The defendant contractor applied to the owner of the house he was in the process of constructing for an advance to meet the weekly payroll. Periodic advances were provided for in the construction contract. Since the owner had just been notified that the defendant was indebted to a material-man and requested not to make further advancements, he informed the defendant he would make no further payments until the debt was paid. The defendant then assured him that he had that morning discharged the debt (in fact, he had not done so), whereupon the owner paid over the requested advance and defendant paid the employees their wages. May the defendant be convicted of obtaining money by false pretenses? See Sanson v. Commonwealth, 313 Ky. 631, 233 S.W.2d 258 (1950); Annot., Obtaining payment by debtor on valid indebtedness by false representation as criminal false pretenses, 20 A.L.R.2d 1266 (1951). Would the prosecutor's case be stronger if the defendant's false representation had been that he needed the money to obtain from a carrier a recently arrived shipment of materials for the house? See the material on mens rea, page 1114 infra.

2. Cf. Rex v. Clucas, [1949] 2 All E.R. 40, 41-42, per Lord Goddard, C.J.:

The evidence showed that these two men, who obviously were dishonest, induced bookmakers to bet with them by representing that they were commission agents acting on behalf of a large number of workmen who were making small bets on various races, whereas, in fact, they were making bets in considerable sums of money for themselves alone. The main question which arises . . . can be stated in this way. Does a man who induces a bookmaker to bet with him by making false pretences as to his identity or as to the capacity in which he is making the bets obtain money by false pretences if he is fortunate enough to back a winning horse and so receives money from the bookmaker? In the opinion of the court it is impossible to say that there was here an obtaining of the money by the false pretences which were alleged, because the money was obtained, not by reason of the fact that the accused persons falsely pretended that they were somebody or acting in some capacity which they were not, but because they backed a winning horse as a result of which the bookmaker paid them the sums obtained. No doubt, the bookmaker might never have opened an account with these men if he had known the true facts, but we must distinguish between a contributing cause and the effective cause which led the bookmaker to pay the money, namely, the fact that these men had backed a winning horse.

4.   Blackmail

STATE v. HARRINGTON

Supreme Court of Vermont
128 Vt. 242, 260 A.2d 692 (1969)

HOLDEN, C.J. [The respondent, John B. Harrington, was a Vermont attorney retained by Mrs. Norma Morin to obtain a divorce from her husband, Mr. Armand Morin. As Mrs. Morin was without funds, respondent agreed to work on a contingent fee basis. The couple owned assets worth approximately $50,000, including a motel in New Hampshire where the two had previously lived.

[Together with his client, Harrington arranged to obtain evidence of Mr. Morin's infidelity by hiring a woman, armed with a tape recorder, to entice him into having sex with her in one of his motel rooms. She succeeded, and at the appropriate moment Harrington and his associates entered the room and took pictures of Mr. Morin and the woman naked in bed.

[Several days later Harrington, in the presence of Mrs. Morin, dictated a letter to Mr. Morin proposing a settlement of the divorce action in which Mrs. Morin would receive her divorce, give up her interest in the marital assets, waive alimony, and receive a lump sum of $175,000. The letter also provided that

> any such settlement would include the return to you of all tape recordings, all negatives, all photographs and copies of photographs that might in any way, bring discredit upon yourself. Finally, there would be an absolute undertaking on the part of your wife not to divulge any information of any kind or nature which might be embarrassing to you in your business life, your personal life, your financial life, or your life as it might be affected by the Internal Revenue Service, the United States Customs Service, or any other governmental agency.

The letter stressed Mrs. Morin's current state of insolvency, and requested a prompt reply. The letter went on to say that]

> Unless the writer has heard from you on or before March 22, we will have no alternative but to withdraw the offer and bring immediate divorce proceedings in Grafton County. This will, of course, require the participation by the writer's cor-

respondent attorneys in New Hampshire. If we were to proceed under New Hampshire laws, without any stipulation, it would be necessary to allege, in detail, all of the grounds that Mrs. Morin has in seeking the divorce. The writer is, at present, undecided as to advising Mrs. Morin whether or not to file for "informer fees" with respect to the Internal Revenue Service and the United States Customs Service. In any event, we would file, alleging adultery, including affidavits, alleging extreme cruelty and beatings, and asking for a court order enjoining you from disposing of any property, including your stock interests, during the pendency of the proceeding. . . . With absolutely no other purpose than to prove to you that we have all of the proof necessary to prove adultery beyond a reasonable doubt, we are enclosing a photograph taken by one of my investigators on the early morning of March 8. The purpose of enclosing the photograph as previously stated, is simply to show you that cameras and equipment were in full operating order.

13 V.S.A. §1701 provides: "A person who maliciously threatens to accuse another of a crime or offense, or with an injury to his person or property, with intent to extort money or other pecuniary advantage, or with intent to compel the person so threatened to do an act against his will, shall be imprisoned in the state prison not more than two years or fined not more than $500.00." . . .

[T]he respondent maintains his letter does not constitute a threat to accuse Morin of the crime of adultery. He argues the implicit threats contained in the communication were "not to accuse of the CRIME of adultery but to bring an embarrassing, reputation-ruining divorce proceeding in Mr. Morin's county of residence unless a stipulation could be negotiated."

In dealing with a parallel contention in State v. Louanis, 79 Vt. 463, 467, 65 A. 532, 533, the Court answered the argument in an opinion by Chief Judge Rowell. "The statute is aimed at blackmailing, and a threat of any public accusation is as much within the reason of the statute as a threat of a formal complaint, and is much easier made, and may be quite as likely to accomplish its purpose. There is nothing in the statute that requires such a restricted meaning of the word 'accuse'; and to restrict it thus, would well nigh destroy the efficacy of the act."

The letter, marked "personal and confidential," makes a private accusation of adultery in support of a demand for a cash settlement. An incriminating photograph was enclosed for the avowed purpose of demonstrating "we have all of the proof necessary to prove adultery beyond a reasonable doubt." According to the writing itself, cost of refusal will be public exposure of incriminating conduct in the courts of New Hampshire where the event took place.

In further support of motion for acquittal, the respondent urges that the totality of the evidence does not exclude the inference that he acted merely as an attorney, attempting to secure a divorce for his client on the most favorable terms possible. This, of course, was the theory of the defense. . . .

At the time of the writing, the respondent was undecided whether to advise his client to seek "informer fees." One of the advantages tendered to Morin for a "quiet" and "undamaging" divorce is an "absolute undertaking" on the part of the respondent's client not to inform against him in any way. The Internal Revenue Service, the United States Customs Service and other governmental agencies are suggested as being interested in such information. Quite clearly, these veiled threats exceeded the limits of the respondent's representation of his client in the divorce action. Although these matters were not specified in the indictment, they have a competent bearing on the question of intent.

Apart from this, the advancement of his client's claim to the marital property, however well founded, does not afford legal cause for the trial court to direct a verdict of acquittal in the background and context of his letter to Morin. A demand for settlement of a civil action, accompanied by a malicious threat to expose the wrongdoer's criminal conduct, if made with intent to extort payment, against his will, constitutes the crime alleged in the indictment.

The evidence at hand establishes beyond dispute the respondent's participation was done with preconceived design. The incriminating evidence which his letter threatens to expose was wilfully contrived and procured by a temptress hired for that purpose. These factors in the proof are sufficient to sustain a finding that the respondent acted maliciously and without just cause, within the meaning of our criminal statutes. The sum of the evidence supports the further inference that the act was done with intent to extort a substantial contingent fee to the respondent's personal advantage. . . . The evidence of guilt is ample to support the verdict and the trial was free from errors in law.

Judgment affirmed.

NOTES AND QUESTIONS

1. Consider whether the Vermont statute quoted in the principal case makes criminal the following threats.

(a) Employee, who has been directing a crucial project for employer, to employer: "Give me a raise, or I will quit." Without employee the project will likely fail, possibly placing employer in bankruptcy.

(b) A to his lover B: "If you stop having sexual relations with me, I will require that you leave my house and sue you for all of that money you owe me." See Lovely v. Cunningham, 796 F.2d 1 (1st Cir. 1986).

(c) Storeowner to shoplifter: "I saw you steal that radio last week. Pay me the $50 it costs, or I'll report you to the police." See People v. Fichtner, 118 N.Y.S.2d 392 (1952), reprinted infra page 1083.

(d) Customer to garage mechanic: "Every time you fix my car it breaks within two weeks. Now my car has broken down so many times it's worthless. Buy me a new one, or I'll write to the newspapers about your lousy practices, and you'll never see another customer."

2. *Model Penal Code.* Consider how the foregoing hypotheticals and the *Harrington* case would come out under Model Penal Code §223.4, Appendix, and the California Penal Code, supra page 1049.

3. Consider the following criticism of the decision in *Harrington:*

Taking the opinion at face value, very serious problems are created for every lawyer. Any time a cause of action involves behavior that is either criminal or embarrassing, a threat to bring the action would be extortionate. Obviously this would effectively preclude many lawyer demand letters. Anomalously, it would be permissible to destroy reputation by bringing suit but not to allow the defendant to avoid that destruction by paying the claim. Not only would this mean a net loss to the privacy that the extortion statute is, in part, aimed at protecting, but it would also involve significantly expanded litigation costs and burdens on efficient utilization of judicial resources. So read, the *Harrington* rule is obviously absurd.

Joseph M. Livermore, Lawyer Extortion, 20 Ariz. L. Rev. 403, 406 (1978).

Question: How else could that decision be read?

4. *Lawyers threatening lawsuits.* Should what John Harrington did be considered a crime, or merely aggressive advancement of his client's interests? Consider Rex v. Dymond, [1920] 2 K.B. 260, where defendant, who had been sexually assaulted, demanded that her attacker pay her reparations upon threat of "let[ting] the town knowed all about your going on." Glanville Williams criticized her conviction for blackmail:

> The matter assumes a somewhat surprising aspect when it is realised how fine is the line dividing proper from improper threats. Dymond was an illiterate girl, trying to obtain what she may have believed to be her rights without legal aid. Had she the [money] . . . with which to consult a solicitor, instead of writing herself, he would have written a letter to the [attacker] on her behalf in something like the following terms. "Dear Sir, We have been consulted by . . . who states that . . . Our client claims the sum of _____ as compensation for the wrong committed against her, and unless we have your cheque for this amount we are instructed to commence legal proceedings against you." Such a letter would not constitute a criminal offense.

Glanville Williams, Blackmail, [1954] Crim. L. Rev. 162, 165-166.

5. If it is problematic to find extortion in the threat to sue for divorce on the basis of adultery, can the same be said of Harrington's threats to reveal Morin's tax evasion to the Internal Revenue Service and the Customs Service? We are told that for some reason these allegations were not included in the indictment. If they were, should they be regarded as not extortionate because made by a lawyer in the course of representing the interests of his client?

6. American blackmail (often termed extortion) statutes vary a great deal. A useful review may be found in the Commentaries to Model Penal Code §223.4 at 201-224 (1980). There are important variations in the types of threats required. Threats of personal and property injury or to accuse of crime are always enough. Common also are threats to make disclosures that would defame the victim. But how about threats to expose matters that are not defamatory? Some statutes include threats of this nature. See, e.g., Cal. Penal Code §519 (threats to expose any secret affecting the victim); Ill. ch. 38, §15-5 (threats to reveal any information sought to be concealed by the victim). Others, like New York, apparently do not. See N.Y. Pen. Code §155.05(2)(e). The Model Penal Code would seem also to exclude such threats, unless they are picked up in the catch-all provision that includes "any other harm which would not benefit the actor."

Statutes also vary in how they define what the blackmailer seeks to obtain by his threats. Many statutes, like the Model Penal Code, limit the purpose of the threats to obtaining property or other things of value and rely on other code provisions to deal with the use of coercive threats to obtain other benefits for the threatener. See, e.g., Model Penal Code §212.5 (Criminal Coercion). Some statutes, on the other hand, define the object of the threat more comprehensively; e.g., Fla. Penal Code §836.05 (threats made to compel person to do any act or refrain from doing any act against his will); Minn. Penal Code §609.27 (threats that cause another against his will to do any act or forbear doing a lawful act).

PEOPLE v. FICHTNER

New York Supreme Court, Appellate Division, Second Department
281 A.D. 159, 118 N.Y.S.2d 392, aff'd without opinion,
305 N.Y. 864, 114 N.E.2d 212 (1952)

JOHNSTON, J. Section 850 of the Penal Law provides: "Extortion is the obtaining of property from another . . . , with his consent, induced by a wrongful use of . . . fear. . . ."

Section 851 of the Penal Law provides:

Fear, such as will constitute extortion, may be induced by an oral or written threat: . . . 2. To accuse him, or any relative of his or any member of his family, of any crime; or, 3. To expose, or impute to him, or any of them, any . . . disgrace. . . .

Defendant Fichtner is the manager, and defendant McGuinness the assistant manager, of the Hill Supermarket in Freeport, Nassau County. On January 30, 1951, an indictment was filed against both defendants, charging them in two counts with the crime of extortion in that on January 18, 1951, defendants, aiding and abetting each other, obtained $25 from one Smith, with his consent, which consent defendants induced by a wrongful use of fear by threatening to accuse Smith of the crime of petit larceny, and to expose and impute to him a disgrace unless Smith paid them $25.

Smith testified that on January 18, 1951, he purchased a number of articles in the Hill store for a total of about $12, but left the store without paying for a fifty-three-cent jar of coffee, which he had concealed in his pocket. After Smith left the store he returned at defendant Fichtner's request. Defendants then threatened to call a policeman, to arrest Smith for petit larceny, with resulting publicity in the newspapers and over the radio, unless he paid $75 and signed a paper admitting that during the course of several months he had unlawfully taken merchandise from the store in that amount. Although Smith admitted he had shopped in Hill's Freeport store about sixteen times and in Hill's Merrick store for about two years, he insisted that the only merchandise he had ever stolen was the fifty-three-cent jar of coffee on the evening in question, and a sixty-five-cent roll of bologna one week previously. However, he finally signed the paper admitting that he had unlawfully taken $50 worth of merchandise from the store during a period of four months. That evening Smith paid $25 in cash and promised to pay the balance in weekly installments of $5. He testified he was induced to sign the paper and make the payment because defendants threatened to accuse him of petit larceny and to expose him to the disgrace of the criminal charge and the resulting publicity. It is not disputed that the $25 taken from Smith was "rung up" on the store register; that the money went into the company funds and that defendants received no part of the money. During the following week Smith reported the incident to the police, and defendants were arrested on January 25, 1951, when Smith, accompanied by a detective, returned to the store and paid the first $5 installment.

Defendants testified that over the course of several weeks, they saw Smith steal merchandise amounting to $5.61, and they honestly believed that during the several months that Smith had been shopping, he had stolen merchandise of the value of $75; that on January 18, 1951, Smith freely admitted that during the four-month period he stole merchandise of the value of $50, and that he voluntarily signed the paper admitting thefts in that amount; that on that date he paid $25 on account and promised to pay the balance in weekly installments.

That the Smith incident was not an isolated one, but rather part of a course of conduct pursued by defendants, even after warning by the police to discontinue the practice, was not only clearly established but admitted by defendant Fichtner. . . .

In my opinion, the verdict is amply supported by the evidence. Implicit in the verdict is a finding that Smith stole only $1.18 in merchandise as he admitted, or at most the $5.61 which defendants claimed they actually saw him steal, and that he was induced to pay the $25 on January 18, 1951, by defendants' threats to accuse him of crime and to expose him to disgrace. By its verdict, the jury rejected defendants' contention that Smith voluntarily admitted having stolen $50 worth of merchandise and that they demanded from Smith only what was rightfully due.

Defendants requested the court to charge that

> if in the judgment of the jury the defendants honestly believed that the amount which the complainant paid or agreed to pay represented the approximate amount of the merchandise which he or they had previously stolen from the Hill Supermarket, then the defendants must be acquitted.

The court refused the request "except as already charged." Although two members of the court are of the opinion that for the reason stated the trial court was justified in refusing to charge as requested, four members of the court are of the further opinion that the request was legally incorrect and, therefore, should have been refused. In other words, we believe that the portion of the main charge to the effect that, under the circumstances of this case, extortion is committed only when one obtains property from another by inducing fear in that other by threatening to accuse him of crime unless he pays an amount over and above what was rightfully due was more favorable to defendants than that which they were entitled to receive. In our opinion, the extortion statutes were intended to prevent the collection of money by the use of fear induced by means of threats to accuse a debtor of crime, and it makes no difference whether the debtor stole any goods, nor how much he stole, and that defendants may properly be convicted even though they believed that the complainant was guilty of the theft of their employer's goods in an amount either equal to or less, or greater than any sum of money obtained from the complainant. Nor is defendants' good faith in thus enforcing payment of the money alleged to be due to their employer a defense. . . .

The law does not authorize the collection of just debts by threatening to accuse the debtor of crime, even though the complainant is in fact guilty of the crime. In my opinion, it makes no difference whether the indebtedness for which a defendant demands repayment is one arising out of the crime for the prosecution of which he threatens the complainant, or is entirely independent and having no connection with the crime which forms the basis of the accusation. The result in both cases is the concealment and compounding of a felony to the injury of the State. It is that result which the extortion statutes were intended to prevent.

[Conviction affirmed.]

WENZEL, J. (dissenting). [T]he jury was permitted to convict defendants of the crime of extortion on proof that they had induced complainant, by the threats alleged, to pay to defendants more than he rightfully owed for goods which he had stolen, even though defendants might have honestly believed that the amount demanded from complainant was the amount which he rightfully owed. In my opinion, although the question is one as to which there is a conflict of authority, if defendants, acting without malice and in good faith, made an honest mistake, they were not guilty of the crime charged. There would then be no criminal intent. The defendants were not acting in their own behalf but in that of their employer, in recovering what they believed to be rightfully due it. . . .

NOTE

Under the New York Penal Law enacted subsequent to *Fichtner,* extortion remains excluded from the class of larceny-type crimes for which a claim of right is a defense. See People v. Reid, page 1123 infra. However, a special provision applicable to extortion, N.Y. Pen. Law §155.15(2) provides:

> In any prosecution for larceny by extortion committed by instilling in the victim a fear that he or another person would be charged with a crime, it is an affirmative defense that the defendant reasonably believed the threatened charge to be true and that his sole purpose was to compel or induce the victim to take reasonable action to make good the wrong which was the subject of such threatened charge.

Section 215.45 provides:

> 1. A person is guilty of compounding a crime when: (a) He solicits, accepts or agrees to accept any benefit upon an agreement or understanding that he will refrain from initiating a prosecution for a crime; or (b) He confers, or offers or agrees to confer, any benefit upon another person upon an agreement or understanding that such other person will refrain from initiating a prosecution for a crime.
> 2. In any prosecution under this section, it is an affirmative defense that the benefit did not exceed an amount which the defendant reasonably believed to be due as restitution or indemnification for harm caused by the crime.

NOTE ON THE RATIONALE OF BLACKMAIL

In Unraveling the Paradox of Blackmail, 84 Colum. L. Rev. 670 (1984), James Lindgren identifies the puzzle about blackmail:

> Most crimes do not need theories to explain why the behavior is criminal. The wrongdoing is self-evident. But blackmail is unique among major crimes: no one has yet figured out why it ought to be illegal. Recognizing the magnitude of the problem, one theorist wondered whether we can find a principled distinction (or indeed any interesting distinction) between blackmail and permissible behavior that is not blackmail.

In blackmail, the heart of the problem is that two separate acts, each of which is a moral and legal right, can combine to make a moral and legal wrong. For example, if I threaten to expose a criminal act unless I am paid money, I have committed blackmail. Or if I threaten to expose a sexual affair unless I am given a job, once again I have committed blackmail. I have a legal right to expose or threaten to expose the crime or affair, and I have a legal right to seek a job or money, but if I combine these rights it is blackmail. If both a person's ends — seeking a job or money — and his means — threatening to expose — are otherwise legal, why is it illegal to combine them? Therein lies what has been called the "paradox of blackmail."[7]

Following is a sampling of the attempts that have been made to deal with this apparent paradox.

James Lindgren, Unraveling the Paradox of Blackmail, 84 Colum. L. Rev. 670, 692 (1984): [T]he key to the wrongfulness of the blackmail transaction is its triangular structure. The transaction implicitly involves not only the blackmailer and his victim but always a third party as well. This third party may be, for example, the victim's spouse or employer, the authorities or even the public at large. When a blackmailer tries to use his right to release damaging information, he is threatening to tell others. If the blackmail victim pays the blackmailer, it is to avoid the harm that those others would inflict. Thus blackmail is a way that one person requests something in return for suppressing the actual or potential interests of others. To get what he wants, the blackmailer uses leverage that is less his than someone else's. Selling the right to go to the police involves suppressing the state's interests. Selling the right to tell a tort victim who committed the tort involves suppressing the tort victim's interests. And selling the right to inform others of embarrassing (but legal) behavior involves suppressing the interests of those other people.

Noninformational blackmail involves the same misuse of a third party's leverage for the blackmailer's own benefit. For example, when a labor leader threatens to call a strike unless he is given a personal payoff, he is using the leverage of third parties to bargain for his own benefit. Thus the criminalization of informational and noninformational blackmail represents a principled decision that advantages may not be gained by extra leverage belonging more to a third party than to the threatener. Recognizing the triangular structure of the blackmail transaction makes clear the parasitic nature of the blackmailer's conduct. Once this structure is understood, it becomes easier to find in blackmail the kind of behavior that concerns the other theorists: immorality, invasiveness, and economic waste.

---

7. Most of the blackmail theorists have centered their theories on the paradoxical case, where the blackmailer has the right to do what he threatens to do. But there is another kind of blackmail, one that is neither paradoxical nor particularly troubling to theorists. Where what the blackmailer threatens to do is itself criminal, the criminality of blackmail is fairly easily justified. . . .

For example, assume a person threatens to damage a victim's house unless the victim pays the threatener money. Because generally no one has the right to destroy another's property, no one should be allowed to profit by selling a right the law prohibits. Conversely, no person should have to pay a potential wrongdoer to avoid being the victim of such a crime, since the law already protects victims from having their property destroyed. Here the blackmailer is selling something the law disallows and the blackmail victim is buying something that the law says should be his by right. . . .

George P. Fletcher, Blackmail: The Paradigmatic Crime, 141 U. Pa. L. Rev. 1617, 1626, 1635 (1993): The proper test, I submit, is whether the transaction with the suspected blackmailer generates a relationship of dominance and subordination. If *V*'s paying money or rendering a service to *D* creates a situation in which *D* can or does dominate *V*, then the action crosses the line from permissible commerce to criminal wrongdoing. The essence of *D*'s dominance over *V* is the prospect of repeated demands. . . . Blackmail occurs when, by virtue of the demand and the action satisfying the demands, the blackmailer knows that she can repeat the demand in the future. Living with that knowledge puts the victim of blackmail in a permanently subordinate position. . . .

In order to counteract the power of the criminal over the victim, the state must intervene by exercising power over the criminal. It is not enough to make the offender pay damages or a fine, for all this means is that she purchases her ongoing status exempt from the prohibitions that apply to others. The state must dominate the criminal's freedom, lest the criminal continue her domination of the victim. The deprivation of liberty and the stigmatization of the offense and the offender — these means counteract the criminal's dominance by reducing his capacity to exercise power over others and symbolically lowering his status.

Douglas H. Ginsburg & Paul Shechtman, Blackmail: An Economic Analysis of the Law, 141 U. Pa. L. Rev. 1849, 1873-1874 (1993): [T]he apparent paradox of blackmail, that one may not threaten to do what one has a lawful right to do, is an economically rational rule. If such threats were lawful, there would be an incentive for people to expend resources to develop embarrassing information about others in the hope of then selling their silence. In that case, some people would be deterred from engaging in embarrassing (but lawful) conduct, while some others who were undeterred would find that their business or social acquaintances or family were informed of their activity. Neither such deterrence nor such information can be counted as a good in many situations, however. These particularly include social and family relations in which the concern of one individual for another is altruistic rather than self-interested; i.e., where one might be distressed to learn another's secret, but was not harmed by ignorance of it. It is precisely these relationships that are threatened with disruption by the prototypical blackmail threat, and that would be protected by an economically rational law. The general principle of the Model Penal Code closely approximates this result by prohibiting threats that it would not benefit the actor to carry out.

Wendy J. Gordon, Truth and Consequences: The Force of Blackmail's Central Case, 141 U. Pa. L. Rev. 1741, 1758, 1770, 1775, 1776, 1777 (1993):

[P]olicymakers prohibit blackmail less because of economic waste or inefficiency than because of they perceive the act of blackmail to be wrong in itself. . . . One person deliberately seeks to harm another to serve her own ends — to exact money or other advantage — and does so in a context where she has no conceivable justification for her act. . . .

Libertarians who recommend the legalization of blackmail, sometimes claim that there is no way to distinguish blackmail from an ordinary commercial transaction. . . . I suggest [these] distinctions . . . : first, that the blackmailer intends to harm; and second, that regardless of intent, the buyer of silence in an extortion transaction suffers a net harm, while the buyer in an ordinary commercial transaction is benefitted. [The author follows this with a lengthy discussion of how to define harm and benefit in this context.]

The question still remains whether blackmail is the kind of act that should be criminalized. . . . As a wrongful harm, its criminalization is consistent with the liberal view that only the presence of harm toward others justifies criminal prohibition. . . .

It is important to note that criminalization also has an impact on blackmail victims, providing them with . . . tools to encourage and assist them in resisting the blackmailer's demands. . . . By threatening to go to the authorities if and only if disclosure is made, victims can discourage blackmailers from disclosing the contested information. This is what Joel Feinberg terms "counterblackmail."

5. Consolidation

INTRODUCTORY NOTE

Insofar as the pattern of discrete theft offenses covering fundamentally similar kinds of acquisitive conduct has left gaps in the law — for example, where deliberately false promises are employed to induce another to transfer his property — only legislative or judicial revision of the definitions of criminal conduct can supply an effective remedy. Another and more direct consequence of this condition of the law of theft is procedural in character. A defendant convicted of one of these theft offenses, embezzlement, say, may be able to obtain a reversal on appeal through the curious device of proving that the evidence technically established another offense, say, larceny. See, e.g., Nolan v. State, page 1049 supra. There are some dramatic examples of this tactic succeeding altogether in frustrating conviction of acknowledged thieves. See, e.g., Commonwealth v. O'Malley, 97 Mass. 584 (1867); Nichols v. People, 17 N.Y. 114 (1858). In all cases the possibility is a constant threat to the efficient administration of criminal justice. The problem is not with the general principles that a person may not be convicted of a crime with which he has not been charged or that a conviction may not stand on appeal where the proof shows the commission of a different crime than the one charged. It is rather that the distinctions between many of the discrete theft offenses (1) are without criminological significance, (2) are so indefinite and intangible that it is often anybody's guess into which theft category some conduct falls in any particular jurisdiction, and (3) turn on highly technical legal characterizations of basically similar fact situations rather than real differences in conduct, so that in these cases a defendant is not likely to be prejudiced (though, of course, he may be) by a variance between charge and proof.

The principal means of reform, which has gained widespread acceptance, is to consolidate the variety of common law forms of wrongful acquisition of another's property into one single crime, which might be called "theft" or "larceny," and to deprive the differences in modes of acquisition of any legal significance. Some examples follow.

MODEL PENAL CODE: *Section 223.1. Consolidation of Theft Offenses; Grading; Provisions Applicable to Theft Generally. [See Appendix.]*

NEW YORK PENAL LAW: *Section 155.05.* Larceny; Defined. 1. A person steals property and commits larceny when, with intent to deprive another of property or to appropriate the same to himself or to a third person, he wrongfully takes, obtains or withholds such property from an owner thereof.

2. Larceny includes a wrongful taking, obtaining or withholding of another's property, with the intent prescribed in subdivision one of this section, committed in any of the following ways:

    (a) By conduct heretofore defined or known as common law larceny by trespassory taking, common law larceny by trick, embezzlement, or obtaining property by false pretenses;

    (b) By acquiring lost property. . . .

    (c) By committing the crime of issuing a bad check. . . .

    (d) By false promise. . . .

    (e) By extortion. . . .

Section 155.45. Larceny; Pleading and Proof. 1. Where it is an element of the crime charged that property was taken from the person or obtained by extortion, an indictment for larceny must so specify. In all other cases, an indictment, information or complaint for larceny is sufficient if it alleges that the defendant stole property of the nature or value required for the commission of the crime charged without designating the particular way or manner in which such property was stolen or the particular theory of larceny involved.

2. Proof that the defendant engaged in any conduct constituting larceny as defined in section 155.05 is sufficient to support any indictment, information or complaint for larceny other than one charging larceny by extortion. An indictment charging larceny by extortion must be supported by proof establishing larceny by extortion.

ILLINOIS ANNOTATED STATUTES chapter 720: *Section 16 — 1.* Theft. (a) A person commits theft when he knowingly:

    (1) Obtains or exerts unauthorized control over property of the owner; or

    (2) Obtains by deception control over property of the owner; or

    (3) Obtains by threat control over property of the owner; or

    (4) Obtains control over stolen property knowing the property to have been stolen, or under such circumstances as would reasonably induce him to believe that the property was stolen, and

        (A) Intends to deprive the owner permanently of the use or benefit of the property; or

        (B) Knowingly uses, conceals or abandons the property in such manner as to deprive the owner permanently of such use or benefit; or

        (C) Uses, conceals, or abandons the property knowing such use, concealment or abandonment probably will deprive the owner permanently of such use or benefit. . . .

CALIFORNIA PENAL CODE: *Section 484.* Every person who shall feloniously steal, take, carry, lead, or drive away the personal property of another, or who shall fraudulently appropriate property which has been entrusted to him, or who shall knowingly and designedly, by any false or fraudulent representation or pretense, defraud any other person of money, labor or real or personal property, . . . is guilty of theft.

Section 952. In charging an offense, each count shall contain, and shall be sufficient if it contains in substance, a statement that the accused has committed some public offense therein specified. . . . In charging theft it shall be sufficient to allege that the defendant unlawfully took the labor or property of another.

B.   THE PROPERTY SUBJECT TO THEFT

1.   *Traditional Theft*

STATE v. MILLER

Supreme Court of Oregon
192 Or. 188, 233 P.2d 786 (1951)

Lusk, J. [Defendant induced complaining witness to agree to guarantee his indebtedness to another on his false representation that he owned a tractor free of encumbrance and on his executing a chattel mortgage thereto as security. In fact defendant was purchasing the tractor under a conditional sales contract. He was convicted of obtaining property by false pretenses.]

The statute under which this prosecution is attempted to be maintained is §23-537, O.C.L.A., and, so far as in any way material, reads:

> If any person shall, by any false pretenses or by any privity [sic] or false token, and with intent to defraud, obtain or attempt to obtain, from any other person any money or property whatsoever, or shall obtain or attempt to obtain with the like intent the signature of any person to any writing, the false making whereof would be punishable as forgery, such person, upon conviction thereof, shall be punished by imprisonment. . . . The making of a bill of sale, or assignment, or mortgage of personal property, by any person not the owner thereof, for the purpose of obtaining money or credit, or to secure an existing indebtedness, shall be deemed a false pretense within the meaning of this section.

. . . Reduced to its simplest terms, this indictment means that by false pretenses the defendant induced the Hub Lumber Company to agree to pay his indebtedness to the Howard Cooper Corporation if he should fail to pay it. The question is whether this amounts to an allegation that, in the sense of the statute, the defendant obtained "any property" from the Hub Lumber Company. If not, then the indictment does not charge a crime. . . . There is no claim that the case falls within the provision of the statute which denounces the making of a bill of sale or assignment or mortgage of personal property by any person not the owner thereof for the purpose of obtaining money or credit or securing an existing indebtedness. Under this latter provision the person in whose favor the false instrument is made must also be the person from whom the money or credit is sought to be obtained or to whom the existing indebtedness is owing. So much is not disputed. . . .

The source of the false pretenses statute in this country is the common law and the statute law of England. The English courts hold that the thing obtained must be the subject of larceny at common law, and accordingly a conviction for obtaining two dogs by false pretenses was quashed because at common law dog stealing is not larceny; so likewise of an indictment for obtaining food and lodging by false pretenses. Under statutes like ours many of the courts of this country take the same view of the law. The California statute covers "money or property." Pen. Code, §532. The court in People v. Cummings, 114 Cal. 437, 46 P. 284, in holding that the word "property" did not include real property, said: "And the offense of false pretenses, under the English statutes, has always been construed as largely analogous to, and closely bordering upon, that of larceny, and as applying only to personal property, which was capable of manual delivery. . . . Real property under the English law was never the subject of the offense either of cheating or of false pretenses." . . .

It should be observed at this point that our statute in respect of the present question is not as broad as those in some of the other states. It reads "any money or property whatsoever." In some of the states, as stated in Burdick [Law of Crime], 481, §640, the statutes, "after enumerating various classes of personal property, conclude the list with what is apparently intended as an all inclusive term, such as 'other things of value,' 'any other valuable thing,' or 'any other valuable thing or effects whatsoever.'" The Kansas statute includes "any money, personal property, right in action, or any other valuable thing or effects whatsoever." G.S. 1949, 21-551. Notwithstanding the comprehensiveness of this provision, the [Kansas] court held, in the light of the origin and history of the crime of false pretenses, that obtaining an extension of time in which to pay a matured debt was not a "valuable thing" within the meaning of the section. [State v. Tower, 251 Pac. 401.] The term "personal property" was said "to denote personal movable things generally." "Mere pecuniary advantage, devoid of any physical attribute of money, chattel, or valuable security, in the sense of the English statute, was not included."

The Louisiana statute refers to "money or any property." In State v. Eicher, 174 La. 344, 140 So. 498, 499, the defendant was charged with obtaining credit from a bank by falsely representing that a certain note had value and was secured by a chattel mortgage. The indictment was held bad, the court saying that "The privilege of having a note renewed or the time of its payment extended may be and frequently is a valuable one to the debtor. But such privilege or advantage is neither money nor property in the sense those terms are ordinarily used and understood." The court further said: "'Property,' as that term is used in this statute, means worldly goods or possessions, tangible things, and things which have an exchangeable or commercial value."

These are not isolated holdings, but in their conception of the meaning of the word "property," as used in statutes of this sort, represent the current of authority. . . .

The provisions of the statute which make unlawful the obtaining of the signature of any person with intent to defraud, and the making of a bill of sale or assignment or mortgage of personal property for the purpose of obtaining money or credit or to secure an existing indebtedness, rather definitely indicate that such an intangible thing as credit was not considered by the legislature to be property.

Moreover, this court [has] recognized that "property" under the statute must be something capable of being possessed and the title to which can be transferred. . . . It need hardly be said that the thing which the defendant is charged with obtaining in the present indictment, the guaranty, or, to be more accurate,

the benefit of the guaranty which the Hub Lumber Company gave to the Howard Cooper Corporation, could not be possessed, and that there could be no
such thing as holding title to it.

Had the indictment alleged that the defendant obtained the signature of the
Hub Lumber Company or its agent to a guaranty of the defendant's indebtedness, we would have had an entirely different question. The failure so to allege
was not due to an oversight of the pleader but to the facts themselves, for the
proof is that no written guaranty was ever executed but merely an oral one. . . .

Even though our statute included "a thing in action," it would avail the prosecution nothing, for the guaranty was not, so far as the defendant was concerned,
a "thing in action." It is doubtless true, as the state's brief asserts, that "a guaranty is a chose in action, a right to indemnity from the guarantor," but it is the
right of the creditor who extends credit on the faith of the guaranty, not of the
debtor to whom credit is given. The defendant did not receive even a chose in
action from the Hub Lumber Company. . . .

The state argues that by the weight of authority the obtaining of a loan by
fraud is a violation of the statute and asserts that this is a similar case. But in the
loan cases, as the state's brief itself points out, the victim parts with his money.
And, while it is true (although not alleged in the indictment) that, just as in the
loan cases, the accused obtained credit, he obtained it, not from the victim of
his false representations, but from another.

The state's argument of "policy" that the public are entitled to the protection
of the law against immoral and reprehensible conduct such as that with which
the accused was charged, and of which, no doubt, he was guilty, is appealing, but
should be addressed to the legislature, not to the courts. The legislature has not
undertaken to make every fraud a crime, but has set boundaries around the
crime of false pretenses which the courts must respect and have no authority
to pass.

The indictment, in our opinion, does not allege a crime, and the judgment
must therefore be reversed and the action dismissed.

NOTES

1. What result under these later formulations? Model Penal Code, §223.0(6):

"Property" means anything of value, including real estate, tangible and intangible
personal property, contract rights, choses-in-action and other interests in or claims
to wealth, admission or transportation tickets, captured or domestic animals, food
and drink, electric or other power.

Or. Rev. Stat. §164.005(5):

"Property" any article, substance or thing of value, including, but not limited to,
money, tangible and intangible personal property, real property, choses-in-action,
evidence of debt or of contract.

2. Theft of services. In Chappell v. United States, 270 F.2d 274 (9th Cir. 1959),
the defendant, an Air Force sergeant, was convicted of knowingly converting

property of the United States by making use of the services and labor of an air-man to paint his own private dwellings during the airman's on-duty hours. The statute, 18 U.S.C. §641, making it criminal to knowingly convert to one's own use anything of value of the United States (the same statute involved in Morissette v. United States, 342 U.S. 246 (1952), page 237 supra), was construed as intending no such revolutionary change in the common law as would be entailed, in the court's view, in holding that an employee's services were property which could be stolen. The conviction was reversed.

The Seventh Circuit reached a contrary conclusion in a case involving a pro-fessor who used the services of a research assistant, hired and paid for out of his grant from the Environmental Protection Agency, to perform work for him on a private research contract unrelated to his E.P.A. grant. United States v. Croft, 750 F.2d 1354 (7th Cir. 1984). Affirming his conviction under 18 U.S.C. §641, the court held that the section is designed to punish "intentional conduct by which a person either misappropriates or obtains a wrongful advantage from government property," and that the defendant "obtained a wrongful advantage by converting and misappropriating the services of [the assistant] for his per-sonal research project while allowing those services to be paid for by the E.P.A."

In accord, see Commonwealth v. Matty, 619 A.2d 1383 (Pa. Super. 1993), where the court affirmed the theft-of-services conviction of a prison warden who had used an inmate to perform work at a friend's home during time when the inmate should have been working at the prison. For a criticism of such results as an unwarranted judicial extension of a statute concerned with traditional prop-erty offenses, see Note, Theft of Employee Services Under the United States Pe-nal Code, 23 San Diego L. Rev. 897 (1986).

With respect to theft of services, see Model Penal Code §223.7, Appendix; cf. Ill. Cons. Stat. ch. 720, §5/16-3; N.Y. Penal Law §165.15; Or. Rev. Stat. §164.125.

Under the Illinois provision, a person commits theft of services when he ob-tains "labor or services of another which are available only for hire, by means of threat or deception or knowing that such use is without the consent of the per-son providing the . . . labor or services." In People v. Davis, 203 Ill.App.3d 838, 561 N.E.2d 165 (1990), defendants were city officials who were supervising a construction project being performed for the city by an independent contrac-tor. They were responsible for giving job assignments to the contractor's em-ployees daily when the employees reported for work. Defendants asked several of the employees to participate in political campaigning instead of working on the construction project. The employees willingly agreed to do so, but their em-ployer was not aware of the arrangement and lost the value of their services. Are the defendants guilty of theft under the Illinois statute? The court held in the negative. Was there any way, under this statute, to support the opposite result?

3. *Theft of use of property.* In State v. McGraw, 480 N.E.2d 552 (Ind. 1985), a city employee used a city computer and services for his personal business and was convicted of theft under Ind. Code §35-43-4-2: "A person who knowingly or in-tentionally exerts unauthorized control over property of another person with intent to deprive the other of its value or use, commits theft. . . ." It appeared that the defendant's unauthorized use cost the city nothing, since the computer service was leased at a fixed charge and the tapes and discs he had used could be erased and reused. The court held that these facts could not support a con-viction, even assuming arguendo that the use of the computer was "property"

under the theft statute. The court reasoned that the city was not deprived of any part of the value or use of the property. The court said (id. at 554):

> We find no distinction between Defendant's use of the City's computer and the use, by a mechanic, of the employer's hammer or a stenographer's use of the employer's typewriter, for other than the employer's purposes. Under traditional concepts, the transgression is in the nature of a trespass, a civil matter — and a de minimis one, at that. Defendant has likened his conduct to the use of an employer's vacant bookshelf, for the temporary storage of one's personal items, and to the use of an employer's telephone facilities for toll-free calls. The analogies appear to us to be appropriate.

The court noted a conversion statute, Ind. Code §35-43-4-3: "A person who knowingly or intentionally exerts unauthorized control over property of another person commits criminal conversion, a class A misdemeanor." The evidence might have supported a conviction under this statute, in the court's view. Cf. People v. Ashworth, 220 A.D. 498, 222 N.Y.S. 24 (1927) (unauthorized use of another's property not larceny).

Question: What should be the result under the Model Penal Code?

UNITED STATES v. GIRARD

United States Court of Appeals, 2d Circuit
601 F.2d 69 (1969)

VAN GRAAFEILAND, J. Appellants have appealed from judgments convicting them of the unauthorized sale of government property (18 U.S.C. §641) and of conspiring to accomplish the sale (18 U.S.C. §371). . . .

In May 1977, appellant Lambert was an agent of the Drug Enforcement Administration, and Girard was a former agent. During that month, Girard and one James Bond began to discuss a proposed illegal venture that involved smuggling a planeload of marijuana from Mexico into the United States. Girard told Bond that for $500 per name he could, through an inside source, secure reports from the DEA files that would show whether any participant in the proposed operation was a government informant. Unfortunately for Mr. Girard, Bond himself became an informant and disclosed his conversations with Girard to the DEA. Thereafter, dealings between Bond and Girard were conducted under the watchful eye of the DEA. Bond asked Girard to secure reports on four men whose names were furnished him by DEA agents. DEA records are kept in computerized files, and the DEA hoped to identify the inside source by monitoring access to the four names in the computer bank. In this manner, the DEA learned that Girard's informant was Lambert, who obtained the reports through a computer terminal located in his office. The convictions on Counts One and Two are based on the sale of this information.

Section 641, so far as pertinent, provides that whoever without authority sells any "record . . . or thing of value" of the United States or who "receives . . . the same with intent to convert it to his use or gain, knowing it to have been embezzled, stolen, purloined or converted," shall be guilty of a crime.[a] Appellants contend that the statute covers only tangible property or documents and therefore is not violated by the sale of information. This contention was rejected by District Judge Daly. . . . We agree with the District Judge's decision. . . .

Like the District Judge, we are impressed by Congress' repeated use of the phrase "thing of value" in section 641 and its predecessors. These words are found in so many criminal statutes throughout the United States that they have in a sense become words of art. The word "thing" notwithstanding, the phrase is generally construed to cover intangibles as well as tangibles. For example, amusement is held to be a thing of value under gambling statutes. . . . Sexual intercourse, or the promise of sexual intercourse, is a thing of value under a bribery statute. . . . So also are a promise to reinstate an employee . . . and an agreement not to run in a primary election. . . . The testimony of a witness is a thing of value under 18 U.S.C. §876, which prohibits threats made through the mails with the intent to extort money or any other "thing of value." . . .

Although the content of a writing is an intangible, it is nonetheless a thing of value. The existence of a property in the contents of unpublished writings was judicially recognized long before the advent of copyright laws. . . . Although we are not concerned here with the laws of copyright, we are satisfied, nonetheless, that the Government has a property interest in certain of its private records which it may protect by statute as a thing of value. It has done this by the enactment of section 641. . . . If, as the Court said in [Morissette v. United States, 342 U.S. 246, 269 n. 28 (1952)], conversion is the "misuse or abuse of property" or its use "in an unauthorized manner," the defendants herein could properly be found to have converted DEA's computerized records.

The District Judge also rejected appellants' constitutional challenge to section 641 based upon alleged vagueness and overbreadth, and again we agree with his ruling. Appellants, at the time of the crime a current and a former employee of the DEA, must have known that the sale of DEA confidential law enforcement records was prohibited. The DEA's own rules and regulations forbidding such disclosure may be considered as both a delimitation and clarification of the conduct proscribed by the statute. . . . Where, as here, we are not dealing with defendants' exercise of a First Amendment freedom, we should not search for statutory vagueness that did not exist for the defendants themselves. . . . Neither should we find a constitutional infirmity simply because the statute might conceivably trespass upon the First Amendment rights of others. In view of the statute's plainly legitimate sweep in regulating conduct, it is not so substantially

---

a. The full text of 18 U.S.C. §641 reads as follows: "Whoever embezzles, steals, purloins, or knowingly converts to his use or the use of another, or without authority, sells, conveys or disposes of any record, voucher, money, or thing of value of the United States or of any department or agency thereof, or any property made or being made under contract for the United States or any department or agency thereof, or

"Whoever receives, conceals, or retains the same with intent to convert it to his use or gain, knowing it to have been embezzled, stolen, purloined or converted —

"Shall be fined not more than $10,000 or imprisoned not more than ten years, or both; but if the value of such property does not exceed the sum of $100, he shall be fined not more than $1,000 or imprisoned no more than one year, or both.

"The word 'value' means face, par, or market value, or cost price, either wholesale or retail, whichever is greater." — Eds.

overbroad that any overbreadth that may exist cannot be cured on a case by case basis.

The judgments . . . are affirmed.

NOTES

1. Mr. Anthony Lewis, of the New York Times, had some harsh things to say about such an interpretation of §641. Speaking about the same theory sanctioned by a federal trial court in another case, he said (N.Y. Times, June 19, 1978, at 19, col. 1):

> The two men were charged — and convicted — under Section 641 of the federal criminal code, which makes it a crime to steal government property. What was the property? The Justice Department said it was information, and Judge Albert V. Bryan Jr. followed that view of the law when he charged the jury.
>
> "Information may be government property," the judge said, "apart from the document or the sheets of paper themselves." Thus it does not matter if the original government document remains in the files. Anyone who copies it or makes notes from it without official approval has still stolen "property."
>
> For advocates of secrecy, the beauty of that legal theory is that it applies to no matter what kind of government information is involved. National security need not have a thing to do with it. The price of food in the White House mess, the Amtrak deficit — any fact that leaked could be the subject of a criminal prosecution.
>
> In short, the government-property theory of information would give this country an Official Secrets Act. It would be potentially as devastating to the press and public knowledge as Britain's secrecy law, which Americans and a good many Britons have for years condemned.

See Harold Edgar & Benno C. Schmidt, Jr., *Curtiss-Wright* Comes Home: Executive Power and National Security Secrecy, 21 Harv. Civ. Rts.-Civ. Lib. L. Rev. 349, 401-406 (1986); Melvin Nimmer, National Secrets v. Free Speech: The Issues Left Undecided in the *Ellsberg* Case, 28 Stan. L. Rev. 311 (1974).

2. Jones was visiting the United States Attorney's office when he overheard conversations between government personnel concerning an ongoing criminal investigation of an employee at Barclays Bank. The conversations took place in a reception area and in an individual office. Jones subsequently told officials at Barclays that he had information relating to a criminal investigation and offered to sell it to them for $100; ultimately he received $60 for revealing what he knew. The court held that these facts were sufficient to support an indictment for larceny under 18 U.S.C. §641. United States v. Jones, 677 F. Supp. 238 (S.D.N.Y. 1988). Do you agree?

3. Dreiman repeatedly called and harassed his ex-girlfriend. In defense she obtained an unlisted telephone number. Dreiman then broke into her trailer, so that he could copy down the unlisted number. He was convicted of burglary, on the theory that he had entered with the intent to commit a crime (larceny). The court held that copying the unlisted number constituted larceny, and it therefore upheld the burglary conviction. Dreiman v. State, 825 P.2d 758

(Wyo. 1992). Is the result sound? If so, does the same principle justify the results in *Girard* and in the *Jones* case (Note 2 supra), or are those situations distinguishable?

4. In United States v. Bottone, 365 F.2d 389, 393-394 (2d Cir. 1966), the defendants purchased documents, for ultimate exportation to Europe, from several former employees of Lederle Laboratories, knowing that the employees had temporarily removed and copied the documents. The documents described secret processes for manufacturing antibiotics. The court, per Friendly, J., upheld their conviction of a federal receiving charge, stating (at 393-394):

> The only serious point of law raised by appellants is whether the transportation of papers describing the Lederle processes constituted the transportation in interstate or foreign commerce of "any goods, wares, merchandise, securities or money, of the value of $5,000 or more, knowing the same to have been stolen, converted or taken by fraud." 18 U.S.C. §2314. The problem is not any doubt on our part that papers describing manufacturing procedures are goods, wares, or merchandise, as was held with respect to geophysical maps in United States v. Seagraves, 265 F.2d 876 (3d Cir. 1959), and United States v. Lester, 282 F.2d 750 (3d Cir. 1960). Neither do we have any concern over the value of these papers, since we dismiss out of hand the contentions that secret processes for which European drug manufacturers were willing to pay five and six figures and in whose illicit exploitation appellants eagerly invested a large portion of their time and an appreciable amount of their fortunes were not worth the $5,000 required to subject them to federal prosecution. . . . The serious question is whether, on the facts of this case, the papers showing Lederle processes that were transported in interstate or foreign commerce were "goods" which had been "stolen, converted or taken by fraud" in view of the lack of proof that any of the physical materials so transported came from Lederle's possession. The standard procedure was for Fox and Cancelarich to remove documents from Lederle's files at Pearl River, N.Y., take these to Fox' home within New York state, make photocopies, microfilms or notes, and then restore the purloined papers to the files; only the copies and notes moved or were intended to move in interstate or foreign commerce. The case differs in this respect from the Third Circuit cases of *Seagraves* and *Lester* where, as the records on appeal show, the photostats and tracings delivered by the Gulf Oil geologist were the property of the company, having been made in the company's office, on its paper and with its equipment.
>
> We are not persuaded, however, that a different result should obtain simply because the intangible information that was the purpose of the theft was transformed and embodied in a different physical object. To be sure, where no tangible objects were ever taken or transported, a court would be hard pressed to conclude that "goods" had been stolen and transported within the meaning of §2314; the statute would presumably not extend to the case where a carefully guarded secret formula was memorized, carried away in the recesses of a thievish mind and placed in writing only after a boundary had been crossed. The situation, however, is quite different where tangible goods are stolen and transported and the only obstacle to condemnation is a clever intermediate transcription or use of a photocopy machine. In such a case, when the physical form of the stolen goods is secondary in every respect to the matter recorded in them, the transformation of the information in the stolen papers into a tangible object never possessed by the original owner should be deemed immaterial. It would offend common sense to hold that these defendants fall outside the statute simply because, in efforts to avoid detec-

tion, their confederates were at pains to restore the original papers to Lederle's files and transport only copies or notes, although an oversight would have brought them within it.

REGINA v. STEWART

Supreme Court of Canada, 1988
50 D.L.R. 4th 1, 41 C.C.C.3d 481

LAMER, J.: . . . A union attempting to organize the approximately 600 employees of the Constellation Hotel, in Toronto, was unable to obtain the names, addresses and telephone numbers of the employees because of a hotel policy that such information be treated as confidential. . . . The appellant, Wayne John Stewart, a self-employed consultant, was hired by somebody he assumed to be acting for the union to obtain the names and addresses of the employees. Stewart offered a security guard [Hart] at the hotel a fee to obtain this information. . . . The security guard reported the offer to his security chief and the police; as a result, a subsequent telephone conversation between Hart and Stewart was recorded, and Stewart was indicted for, [inter alia, counselling the offense of theft, defined in s.283 of the Criminal Code as the taking of "anything whether animate or inanimate" with the required intention. The accused was acquitted by a single judge court, but on appeal[a] the Ontario Court of Appeal reversed and entered a verdict of conviction. The defendant then appealed to the Supreme Court of Canada.]

We are here dealing not with the theft of a list or any other tangible object containing confidential information, but with the theft of confidential information per se, a pure intangible. . . . [T]he assumption that no tangible object would have been taken was part of the agreed statement of facts, and the case was argued throughout on that basis. The word "anything" is not in itself a bar to including any intangible, whatever its nature. However, its meaning must be determined within the context of s.283 of the Code. . . .

[I]t is clear that to be the object of theft, "anything" must be property in the sense that to be stolen, it has to belong in some way to someone. For instance, no conviction for theft would arise out of a taking or converting of the air that we breathe, because air is not property. . . .

It is possible that, with time, confidential information will come to be considered as property in the civil law or even be granted special legal protection by statutory enactment. Even if confidential information were to be considered as property under civil law, it does not, however, automatically follow that it qualifies as property for the purposes of criminal law. Conversely, the fact that something is not property under civil law is likewise not conclusive for the purpose of criminal law. Whether or not confidential information is property under the Criminal Code should be decided in the perspective of the criminal law. . . .

[T]he qualification of confidential information as property must be done in each case by examining the purposes and context of the civil and criminal law.

---

a. In Canada, unlike the United States, a prosecutor may apeal an acquittal. — ED.

It is understandable that one who possesses valuable information would want to protect it from unauthorized use and reproduction. In civil litigation, this protection can be afforded by the courts because they simply have to balance the interests of the parties involved. However, criminal law is designed to prevent wrongs against society as a whole. From a social point of view, whether confidential information should be protected requires a weighing of interests much broader than those of the parties involved. As opposed to the alleged owner of the information, society's best advantage may well be to favour the free flow of information and greater accessibility by all. Would society be willing to prosecute the person who discloses to the public a cure for cancer, although its discoverer wanted to keep it confidential?

The criminalization of certain types of conduct should not be done lightly. If the unauthorized appropriation of confidential information becomes a criminal offence, there would be far-reaching consequences that the courts are not in a position to contemplate. For instance, the existence of such an offence would have serious implications with respect to the mobility of labour. . . .

Moreover, because of the inherent nature of information, treating confidential information as property simpliciter for the purposes of the law of theft would create a host of practical problems. For instance, what is the precise definition of "confidential information"? Is confidentiality based on the alleged owner's intent or on some objective criteria? At what point does information cease to be confidential and would it therefore fall outside the scope of the criminal law? Should only confidential information be protected under the criminal law, or any type of information deemed to be of some commercial value? I am of the view that, given recent technological developments, confidential information, and in some instances, information of a commercial value, is in need of some protection through our criminal law. Be that as it may, in my opinion, the extent to which this should be done and the manner in which it should be done are best left to be determined by Parliament rather than by the courts.

Indeed, the realm of information must be approached in a comprehensive way, taking into account the competing interests in the free flow of information and in one's right to confidentiality or again, one's economic interests in certain kinds of information. The choices to be made rest upon political judgments that, in my view, are matters of legislative action and not of judicial decision. . . .

Appeal allowed; acquittal restored.

NOTES AND QUESTIONS

1. Intangible property. In Oxford v. Moss, 68 Crim. App. 183 (Eng. Div. Ct. 1978), the defendant, an engineering student, managed to obtain the page proof to the Civil Engineering exam to be given at his university the following month. He was caught and charged with theft. It was stipulated that the defendant intended only to "borrow" the proofs and hoped to return them undetected after acquiring advance knowledge of the questions to be asked. Section 1(1) of the English Theft Act of 1968 provided that "[a] person is guilty of theft if he dishonestly appropriates property belonging to another with the intention of permanently depriving the other of it." Section 4(1) defined "property" to include "money and all other property, real or personal, including things in action and other intangible property." The court held that the confidential information contained in the exam paper was not "intangible property" within the meaning of the statute.

Questions. Are Oxford v. Moss and the *Stewart* cases distinguishable? Consider whether the following defendants should be found guilty of theft: (1) Defendant 1 "borrows" *A*'s season pass to the ice hockey rink and returns it after the season is over. (2) Defendant 2 "borrows" *B*'s car battery and returns it after the battery's power is exhausted.

Model Penal Code §223.0(1) provides that temporarily withholding property from its owner can be treated as a permanent deprivation when the effect is "to appropriate a major portion of [the property's] economic value." This provision would probably suffice to permit conviction of defendants 1 and 2 above. Under the Model Penal Code approach, what would be the result in Oxford v. Moss?

2. *Jointly owned property.* Can a partner be convicted of larceny or embezzlement for appropriating partnership funds to her personal use? The common law answer was no, although today courts are divided. The New York Court of Appeals recently reaffirmed its negative answer to that question, People v. Zinke, 76 N.Y.2d 8, 555 N.E.2d 263 (1990), stating:

> At common law, no less than today, the requirement that the victim of a theft be an "owner" of the stolen property was an indispensable element of the crime of larceny. . . . From this principle emerged the rule that if property was owned by two or more persons, none of the owners could commit larceny from the others.
>
> Consistent with this principle was the common-law view that a partner could not be convicted of larceny for the misappropriation of partnership assets; because each partner held title to an undivided interest in the partnership, the theory was that partners could not misappropriate what was already theirs. . . . As in other States, the courts of this State consistently regarded the common-law definition of owner as controlling, concluding that partners could not be prosecuted for stealing firm property. . . .
>
> The Model Penal Code, completed in 1962, had rejected the common-law view by defining larceny as stealing "property of another," which was in turn defined as property "in which any person other than the actor has an interest . . . regardless of the fact that the actor also has an interest in the property." (Model Penal Code §223.0[7].) The purpose of this provision was to permit "a person ordinarily considered the owner of a property . . . [to] be convicted of theft. . . . Thus, a partner may be convicted of theft of partnership property." (Model Penal Code §223.2, revised comment, at 169 [1980].) In enacting the present Penal Law in 1965, however, the New York Legislature chose to reject the Model Penal Code approach and instead codified its own existing rule. . . . [T]he Legislature was concerned both about the effects of criminalizing conduct arising out of legitimate business activities — where there can often be close questions as to intent — and the effects of offering defeated litigants in civil suits the opportunity to seek retaliation by criminal actions. Allowing larceny prosecutions against partners is, of course, contrary to those legislative concerns.

Theft from a spouse raises related problems. In this area, the traditional common law dogmas have disappeared. See, e.g., Stewart v. Commonwealth, 252 S.E.2d 329 (Va. 1979); People v. Morton, 308 N.Y. 96, 123 N.E.2d 790 (1954).

Are there valid reasons for continuing to treat interspousal theft as an exceptional situation? Cf. Model Penal Code §223.1(4):

> It is no defense that theft was from the actor's spouse, except that misappropriation of household and personal effects, or other property normally accessible to both spouses, is theft only if it occurs after the parties have ceased living together.

3. *Secured property.* In cases where the actual owner of property wrongfully takes it from the possession of another who has a special interest therein, such as a lienor, e.g., People v. Travis, 275 A.D. 444, 90 N.Y.S.2d 848 (1949), or a pledgee, e.g., Rose v. Matt, [1951] 1 All E.R. 361, the prevailing view is that such action constitutes theft. What is the difference between these cases and the partnership and spouse cases?

A somewhat different problem is presented if a person rightfully in possession of goods transfers them with intent to defeat the interests of a secured creditor. For example, someone who purchases an electrical appliance under a conditional sales contract may default on the payments due, but conceal the appliance or transfer it to a friend to avoid repossession. Some states have enacted statutes that specifically treat such conduct as theft, at least when certain kinds of security interests are involved. See, e.g., Cal. Penal Code §504a.[4] The Model Penal Code chose to treat these situations not as theft but rather as a separate misdemeanor of defrauding secured creditors. See §§223.0(7), 224.10, Appendix. The reason for separate treatment of those who impair security interests is stated to be that such conduct "deviates less from social norms than does the conduct of thieves who take property to which they have no claim. Moreover, sellers can guard against this kind of fraud by caution in extending credit." Model Penal Code and Commentaries, Comment to §224.10 at 347-348 (1980).

Question: Is the rationale persuasive? Compare the treatment of theft by deception. Section 223.3, Appendix.

4. *Unsecured property.* Does it follow from the decision to criminalize the defrauding of secured creditors that defrauding unsecured creditors should also be made criminal? See, e.g., Cal. Penal Code §154: "Every debtor who fraudulently removes his property or effects out of this state, or fraudulently sells, conveys, assigns or conceals his property with intent to defraud, hinder or delay his creditors of their rights, claims or demands, is" guilty of a misdemeanor. The Model Penal Code rejected such provisions on the ground that they present a

> problem of punishing conduct that is not itself indicative of any criminal purpose. This problem is analogous to the distinction between preparation and attempt. Section 5.01(2) provides that conduct shall not be held to constitute a substantial step toward completion of the crime, as is required for conviction for attempt, "unless it is strongly corroborative of the actor's criminal purpose." The sale of one's own unencumbered property is itself a neutral and entirely legal act, distin-

---

4. The section reads: "Every person who shall fraudulently remove, conceal or dispose of any goods, chattels or effects, leased or let to him by any instrument in writing, or any personal property or effects of another in his possession, under a contract of purchase not yet fulfilled, and any person in possession of such goods, chattels, or effects knowing them to be subject to such lease or contract of purchase who shall so remove, conceal or dispose of the same with intent to injure or defraud the lessor or owner thereof, is guilty of embezzlement."

guishable from legitimate business transactions only if intent to defraud creditors can be shown. It is not conduct "strongly corroborative" of any intent to defraud. To permit such interest to be shown in the absence of some corroboration from the act itself comes dangerously close to punishing evil intention alone.

Model Penal Code and Commentaries, Comment to §224.10 at 346-347 (1980).

2. Mail and Wire Fraud

UNITED STATES v. SIEGEL

United States Court of Appeals, 2d Circuit
717 F.2d 9 (1983)

GEORGE C. PRATT, J. . . . [Abrams and Siegel were officers and directors of Mego International, a publicly held manufacturer and distributor of toys and games. They were charged with and convicted of violating the wire fraud statute by engaging in a scheme to defraud Mego and its stockholders by violating their fiduciary duties to act honestly and faithfully in the best interest of the corporation and to account for the sale of all Mego property entrusted to them. The fraudulent scheme involved the creation of a hidden cash fund derived from cash sales of merchandise that had been closed out, marked down for clearance, or returned as damaged. These "off the books" sales all together generated in excess of $100,000 in cash. The indictment charged that the defendants used the cash for bribery and self-enrichment. There was much evidence of use of the cash for pay-offs to union officials and to other persons dealing with the corporation. Whether there was evidence of self-enrichment was an issue on appeal, which dealt generally with the sufficiency of the evidence to prove violations of the wire fraud statute.]

The wire fraud statute, 18 U.S.C. §1343 (1976), provides:

> Whoever, having devised or intending to devise any scheme or artifice to defraud, or for obtaining money or property by means of false or fraudulent pretenses, representations, or promises, transmits or causes to be transmitted by means of wire, radio, or television communication in interstate or foreign commerce, any writings, signs, signals, pictures, or sounds for the purpose of executing such scheme or artifice, shall be fined not more than $1,000 or imprisoned not more than five years, or both.

While we have described this provision, as well as the mail fraud statute, 18 U.S.C. §1341 (1976), which has been identically construed with respect to the issues before us, as "seemingly limitless," United States v. Von Barta, 635 F.2d at 1001, we have also recognized that "a mere breach of fiduciary duty, standing alone, may not necessarily constitute a mail fraud," United States v. Bronston, 658 F.2d 920, 926 (2d Cir. 1981).

However, we have held that the statute is violated when a fiduciary fails to disclose material information "which he is under a duty to disclose to another under circumstances where the non-disclosure could or does result in harm to the other." United States v. Newman, 664 F.2d 12, 19 (2d Cir. 1981). While the prosecution must show that some harm or injury was contemplated by the scheme, it need not show that direct, tangible economic loss resulted to the scheme's intended victims. In this record there is sufficient evidence from which the jury could reasonably have concluded that defendants received the cash proceeds and used them for non-corporate purposes in breach of their fiduciary duties to act in the best interest of the corporation and to disclose material information to Mego and its stockholders. . . .

Defendants do not seriously contend that the wire fraud statute is not violated when a corporate officer or employee breaches his fiduciary duty to the corporation by taking the proceeds from unrecorded cash sales and using them for his own benefit. Rather, they argue that even if they did participate in the unrecorded cash sales, the record is devoid of any evidence that the money was used for other than corporate purposes and thus fails to support a finding of a breach of fiduciary duty. Defendants claim that at best the evidence merely shows that Abrams and Siegel received the proceeds from the cash sales and that Siegel periodically placed the money in the corporate safe deposit box. While neither Abrams nor Siegel testified, they argue that they received none of it for personal use and that any use of the proceeds for labor payoffs served a legitimate corporate purpose and was not in violation of any fiduciary duty.

While there is little, if any, direct evidence to show that Siegel and Abrams used the cash proceeds for other than corporate purposes, we conclude that the record as a whole does support the determination that Abrams and Siegel used the money for their own enrichment. We reach this conclusion by considering several factors. . . .

[T]here was testimony which showed that Abrams and Siegel personally received the proceeds from the cash sales and either pocketed them or placed them in the corporate safe deposit box. Further, although the cash sales generated in excess of $100,000, the testimony concerning the use to which the money was put accounted for approximately $31,000, used mainly for illicit payoffs. The reasonable mind can think of several destinations for the more than $69,000 that was missing, and, since we have rejected the view that a jury may not rely upon an inference to support an essential allegation unless no opposite inference may be drawn from the proof, we conclude that the jury could have inferred that Abrams and Siegel used some or all of the remainder of the proceeds for their own benefit, and could have fairly concluded beyond a reasonable doubt that theirs was a scheme to misappropriate the proceeds from the sale of Mego assets for self-enrichment. . . .

We do not need to consider whether use of the cash for bribery on behalf of the corporation breached defendants' fiduciary duties, for . . . the jury's verdict establishes that it found beyond a reasonable doubt that the funds were misappropriated for both bribery and self-enrichment. . . .

In affirming defendants' convictions on the wire fraud counts, we in no way wish to encourage the type of indictment prosecuted here. Twenty counts were brought against five defendants, all but two of whom were acquitted of all charges. Siegel and Abrams, although convicted of the wire fraud charges (which might more properly have been redressed in a shareholder's derivative suit or in a state criminal prosecution), were acquitted on several other counts. . . . While we applaud the government's concentration on unrecorded cash sales, a particularly common form of criminal activity, we nevertheless urge the government to think carefully before instituting other massive prosecutions having such slender foundations as this one.

Defendants' convictions on counts one through fifteen are affirmed. . . .

WINTER, J., dissenting. . . .

Once again sailing against the wind in mail or wire fraud cases (or so they are called), I dissent.

In United States v. Margiotta, 688 F.2d 108 (2d Cir. 1982), we read the mail fraud statute to create a regulatory code subjecting public officials, candidates and party leaders to criminal prosecution for allegedly deceptive political speech. Today we read the wire fraud statute to create a federal law of fiduciary obligations imposed on corporate directors and officers, thereby setting the stage for the development of an expandable body of criminal law regulating intracorporate affairs.

The majority's legal theory is that wire fraud occurred because some of Mego's funds were diverted "for noncorporate purposes in breach of [the defendants'] fiduciary duties to act in the best interest of the corporation and to disclose material information to Mego and its stockholders." The evidence is that Mego, a corporation with sales ranging between $30 million and $109 million, during the relevant period, had off-book transactions engineered by the defendants averaging slightly over $11,000 per year. There is no evidence — *none* — that any of the money was diverted to the personal use of either Siegel or Abrams. The government's *prima facie* case is thus made out solely by a showing of improper corporate record keeping. . . .

There is nothing in the language or legislative history of the wire fraud statute remotely suggesting that it was intended as a vehicle for the enforcement of fiduciary duties imposed upon corporate directors or officers by state law. To allow it to be so used would thus be a grave error. However, what the majority does is infinitely worse, for it holds that the wire fraud statute creates a *federal* law of fiduciary obligations. There is no pretense that the source of the fiduciary duty at issue in this case was anything but federal law. There is no reference in the majority opinion to state law or even to Mego's state of incorporation. The jury simply was told that it was up to it to decide whether, as part of the obligation "to act in the best interest of the corporation," the defendants were under a duty to disclose the off-book transactions to shareholders.

The creation of this federal fiduciary duty is no minor step. The relationship of federal and state law in the governance of corporations is a matter of great debate, in which the proponents of federal regulation have strenuously argued that state law governing the conduct of corporate directors and officers is too lax. Over the years, Congress has responded by mandating disclosure through the various securities laws, but has generally declined to enact substantive regulation of corporate transactions.

Notwithstanding the lack of even a hint of relevant Congressional intent in enacting the wire fraud laws, notwithstanding Congress' repeated rejection of pleas to strengthen the fiduciary obligations imposed on corporate directors and officers by state law, and notwithstanding the existence of precise federal legislation requiring disclosure of particular corporate matters, we read the wire fraud statute to embody a federal law of fiduciary obligations, including an undefined duty of yet further disclosure, enforceable by the sanctions of the criminal law.

It will be up to later juries and later panels to define what actions by corporate directors and officers are or are not "in the best interest of the corporation." The elasticity of the concept and the potential for infinite expansion, however, are foreshadowed by the facts of the present case. The "material" information not disclosed to shareholders in the instant case is a series of transactions of roughly $11,000 annually over nine years, a wholly trivial sum in light of Mego's sales. In holding that these transactions "would be important to a Mego stockholder," the majority simply closes its eyes to investment realities, for there is not a shred of evidence that such a sum would affect share price in the slightest. It requires little imagination to foresee future application of the theory of this case to the use of corporate airplanes, the size of executive salaries, expense accounts, etc.

Moreover, there is no evidence — again, *none* — that the transactions in question harmed the corporation. By allowing an inference of diversion to personal use to be drawn solely from the lack of proper records, the majority has in effect dropped the element of a scheme to defraud from the offense. Courts long ago eliminated the need to show a substantial connection between the scheme to defraud and the use of the mails or wires. Now we are eliminating the need to show fraud. In effect, a new crime — corporate improprieties — which entails neither fraud nor even a victim, has been created.

Other aspects of the majority decision also trouble me. Adequate notice to those affected by such elastic concepts is simply not possible, for even the wisest counsel cannot foresee what corporate acts may after the fact attract a prosecutor's suspicion (or ire) and a judicial stamp of impropriety. The key act of the defendants here was the arousal of prosecutorial suspicions. The government's argument brims with innuendo of other crimes: embezzlement, bribery of a union official, commercial bribery, tax evasion, and securities law violations, all of which go to prove only that the criminal charges in issue are a surrogate for ones which the prosecutor lacked either evidence or jurisdiction to make. The overtones of the majority opinion suggest that the defendants here have been convicted essentially of stealing or embezzling funds from Mego. Had those been the crimes actually charged, however, verdicts would likely have been directed in their favor, for there is no evidence that the cash in question was diverted to any purpose other than increasing the profits of the corporation.

Finally, as in *Margiotta*, a crime is created which by its nature will be prosecuted infrequently and in a highly selective manner. If judges perceive a need for a catch-all federal common law crime, the issue should be addressed explicitly with some recognition of the dangers, rather than continue an inexorable expansion of the mail and wire fraud statutes under the pretense of merely discharging Congress' will.

Quite apart from the self-evident danger in creating vast areas of discretion for prosecutors to single out individuals for improper reasons, there is a real question as to whether the costs in resources equal the benefits achieved. The trial here, involving five defendants, each with his own counsel, lasted seven weeks, consuming substantial prosecutorial, private and judicial resources. Only two of the five defendants were convicted, and total jail sentences amounted to only seven months. In truth, the law enforcement results from society's point of view are as trivial as the off-book transactions were to Mego. Even had the government been more successful, however, there is reason to doubt that much would have been gained. Ill-defined crimes which are necessarily prosecuted on an infrequent and selective basis probably have little deterrent value. Were we to restrict the mail and wire fraud statutes to swindling and fraud, as originally intended, rather than extend them to perceived political or corporate improprieties, we would not only perform the judicial function correctly but probably also make a sensible policy judgment in terms of costs and benefits.

NOTES

1. What was the real controversy between the majority and the dissent? Was it solely a difference over whether the facts supported an inference of personal enrichment, or was it a disagreement about the proper reach of the statute, that is, about whether under the statute personal enrichment was required? The Second Circuit decided another "cash fund" case two years later and pronounced further on the issue of the import of personal enrichment by the defendant. United States v. Weiss, 752 F.2d 777 (2d Cir. 1985). Weiss, an officer of Warner Communications Inc., created a secret cash fund for the corporation from cash refunds on stock purchases, concealing these transactions and the existence of the fund by creating false documents. He was convicted of mail fraud.[5] The circuit court affirmed, stating:

> Appellant's argument that he did not violate the mail fraud statute because his creation of the cash fund was not illegal, was not intended to harm Warner or its shareholders, and did not lead to any personal gain presents a close question. . . .
> In *Siegel* defendants defrauded the corporation and its shareholders by deliberately concealing and by failing to account for the sales of all corporate property and merchandise. The government theorized that such acts by top corporate officers defrauded the corporation and its shareholders, and violated the executives' fiduciary duty to act honestly and faithfully. . . .
> Our case is within the ambit of the holding in *Siegel.* There is no requirement that the government prove that the misappropriated funds were used by Weiss for his own enrichment. Rather, evidence of a non-corporate purpose, explicitly or implicitly derived, will satisfy the requirements of *Siegel.* There was no direct evidence offered concerning the final destination of the misappropriated funds. However the jury could reasonably have concluded that the disbursement of corporate funds for fake feasibility studies and fake invoices for non-rendered services established non-corporate use of the funds. Indeed the record here, as in *Siegel,* allowed the jury to "have drawn a justifiable inference that defendants used the scheme for their own benefit." With the evidence presented here, a jury could, at the very least, infer that the diversion of corporate funds by Weiss was for a non-corporate purpose. This is sufficient to bring the case within the holding in *Siegel.*

2. Note, Peter R. Ezersky, Intra-Corporate Mail and Wire Fraud: Criminal Liability for Fiduciary Breach, 94 Yale L.J. 1427 (1985), makes a critical assault on the *Siegel* and *Weiss* cases, along the lines of Judge Winter's dissent in *Siegel.* The opening paragraphs of the Note state its conclusions:

5. Section 1341 prohibits use of the mails in "any scheme or artifice to defraud, or for obtaining money or property by means of false or fraudulent pretense or promises." 18 U.S.C. §1341 (1976).

Mail/wire fraud law has evolved from its origins as an antidote to "lottery swindles" into a vehicle for attacking a wide range of conduct. Recently, a national standard of fiduciary liability, developed by federal courts in mail/wire fraud cases, has been held to govern the obligations of corporate directors and officers to their shareholders. Public, criminal enforcement under mail/wire fraud thus overlaps the private, civil enforcement of corporate fiduciary obligations. . . . [T]his use of the criminal law to police corporate fiduciary obligations is injurious to corporate shareholders — the supposed beneficiaries, contrary to principles of federalism that apply with special force in the corporate law context, and inconsistent with the principle that criminal proscriptions should be certain and knowable in advance.

This recent use of mail/wire fraud law to enforce fiduciary duties has little to do with fraud. The new corporate fiduciary standard is untenable on theoretical grounds, as is the use of criminal sanctions to enforce essentially contractual duties. Furthermore, this development in mail/wire fraud clashes with the congressional and judicial policy of minimizing federal involvement in intra-corporate affairs. . . . [C]ontrary to accepted notions of legality, courts have used mail/wire fraud law to create a virtual common law crime.

3. A penetrating assessment of the expansion of mail fraud as a threat to rule-of-law values may be found in two articles by Professor John Coffee: From Tort to Crime: Some Reflections on the Criminalization of Fiduciary Breaches and the Problematic Line Between Law and Ethics, 19 Am. Crim. L. Rev. 117 (1981), and The Metastasis of Mail Fraud: The Continuing Story of the "Evolution" of a White-Collar Crime, 21 Am. Crim. L. Rev. 1 (1983).

McNALLY v. UNITED STATES

Supreme Court of the United States
483 U.S. 350 (1987)

JUSTICE WHITE delivered the opinion of the Court.

This action involves the prosecution of petitioner Gray, a former public official of the Commonwealth of Kentucky, and petitioner McNally, a private individual, for alleged violation of the federal mail fraud statute, 18 U.S.C. §1341.[1] The prosecution's principal theory of the case, which was accepted by the courts below, was that petitioners' participation in a self-dealing patronage scheme defrauded the citizens and government of Kentucky of certain "intangible rights," such as the right to have the Commonwealth's affairs conducted honestly. We must consider whether the jury charge permitted a conviction for conduct not within the scope of the mail fraud statute.

We accept for the sake of argument the government's view of the evidence, as follows. The petitioners and a third individual, Howard P. "Sonny" Hunt, were

---

1. Section 1341 provides in pertinent part:

Whoever, having devised or intending to devise any scheme or artifice to defraud, or for obtaining money or property by means of false or fraudulent pretenses, representations, or promises, . . . for the purpose of executing such scheme or artifice or attempting so to do [uses the mails or causes them to be used,] shall be fined not more than $1,000 or imprisoned not more than five years, or both.

politically active in the Democratic Party in the Commonwealth of Kentucky during the 1970's. After Democrat Julian Carroll was elected Governor of Kentucky in 1974, Hunt was made chairman of the state Democratic Party and given de facto control over selecting the insurance agencies from which the State would purchase its policies. In 1975, the Wombwell Insurance Company of Lexington, Kentucky (Wombwell), which since 1971 had acted as the Commonwealth's agent for securing a workmen's compensation policy, agreed with Hunt that in exchange for a continued agency relationship it would share any resulting commissions in excess of $50,000 a year with other insurance agencies specified by him. The commissions in question were paid to Wombwell by the large insurance companies from which it secured coverage for the State.

From 1975 to 1979, Wombwell funneled $851,000 in commissions to 21 separate insurance agencies designated by Hunt. Among the recipients of these payments was Seton Investments, Inc. (Seton), a company controlled by Hunt and petitioner Gray and nominally owned and operated by petitioner McNally.

Gray served as Secretary of Public Protection and Regulation from 1976 to 1978 and also as Secretary of the Governor's Cabinet from 1977 to 1979. Prior to his 1976 appointment, he and Hunt established Seton for the sole purpose of sharing in the commissions distributed by Wombwell. Wombwell paid some $200,000 to Seton between 1975 and 1979, and the money was used to benefit Gray and Hunt. Pursuant to Hunt's direction, Wombwell also made excess commission payments to the Snodgrass Insurance Agency, which in turn gave the money to McNally.

On account of the foregoing activities, Hunt was charged with and pleaded guilty to mail and tax fraud and was sentenced to three years' imprisonment. The petitioners were charged with one count of conspiracy and seven counts of mail fraud, six of which were dismissed before trial. The remaining mail fraud count was based on the mailing of a commission check to Wombwell by the insurance company from which it had secured coverage for the State. This count alleged that petitioners had devised a scheme (1) to defraud the citizens and government of Kentucky of their right to have the Commonwealth's affairs conducted honestly, and (2) to obtain, directly and indirectly, money and other things of value by means of false pretenses and the concealment of material facts. The conspiracy count alleged that petitioners had . . . conspired to violate the mail fraud statute through the scheme just described. . . .

The jury convicted petitioners on both the mail fraud and conspiracy counts, and the Court of Appeals affirmed the convictions. In affirming the substantive mail fraud conviction, the court relied on a line of decisions from the Court of Appeals holding that the mail fraud statute proscribes schemes to defraud citizens of their intangible rights to honest and impartial government. See, e.g., United States v. Mandel, 591 F.2d 1347 (CA4 1979). Under these cases, a public official owes a fiduciary duty to the public, and misuse of his office for private gain is a fraud. Also, an individual without formal office may be held to be a public fiduciary if others rely on him, " 'because of a special relationship in the government' " and he in fact makes governmental decisions. The Court of Appeals held that Hunt was such a fiduciary because he "substantially participated in governmental affairs and exercised significant, if not exclusive, control over awarding the workmen's compensation insurance contract to Wombwell and the payment of monetary kickbacks to Seton."

We granted certiorari, and now reverse.

The mail fraud statute clearly protects property rights, but does not refer to the intangible right of the citizenry to good government. As first enacted in 1872, as part of a recodification of the postal laws, the statute contained a general proscription against using the mails to initiate correspondence in furtherance of "any scheme or artifice to defraud." . . . Insofar as the sparse legislative history reveals anything, it indicates that the original impetus behind the mail fraud statute was to protect the people from schemes to deprive them of their money or property.

Durland v. United States, 161 U.S. 306 (1896), the first case in which this Court construed the meaning of the phrase "any scheme or artifice to defraud," held that the phrase is to be interpreted broadly insofar as property rights are concerned, but did not indicate that the statute had a more extensive reach. The Court rejected the argument that "the statute reaches only such cases as, at common law, would come within the definition of 'false pretenses,' in order to make out which there must be a misrepresentation as to some existing fact and not a mere promise as to the future." Instead, it construed the statute to "includ[e] everything designed to defraud by representations as to the past or present, or suggestions and promises as to the future." Id., at 313. Accordingly, the defendant's use of the mails to sell bonds which he did not intend to honor was within the statute. The Court explained that "[i]t was with the purpose of protecting the public against all such intentional efforts to despoil, and to prevent the post office from being used to carry them into effect, that this statute was passed. . . ."

Congress codified the holding of *Durland* in 1909, and in doing so gave further indication that the statute's purpose is protecting property rights. The amendment added the words "or for obtaining money or property by means of false or fraudulent pretenses, representations, or promises" after the original phrase "any scheme or artifice to defraud." The new language is based on the statement in *Durland* that the statute reaches "everything designed to defraud by representations as to the past or present, or suggestions and promises as to the future." However, instead of the phrase "everything designed to defraud" Congress used the words "[any scheme or artifice] for obtaining money or property."

After 1909, therefore, the mail fraud statute criminalized schemes or artifices "to defraud" or "for obtaining money or property by means of false or fraudulent pretenses, representation, or promises. . . ." Because the two phrases identifying the proscribed schemes appear in the disjunctive, it is arguable that they are to be construed independently and that the money-or-property requirement of the latter phrase does not limit schemes to defraud to those aimed at causing deprivation of money or property. This is the approach that has been taken by each of the Courts of Appeals that has addressed the issue: schemes to defraud include those designed to deprive individuals, the people or the government of intangible rights, such as the right to have public officials perform their duties honestly.

As the Court long ago stated, however, the words "to defraud" commonly refer "to wronging one in his property rights by dishonest methods or schemes," and "usually signify the deprivation of something of value by trick, deceit, chicane or overreaching." Hammerschmidt v. United States, 265 U.S. 182, 188

(1924). The codification of the holding in *Durland* in 1909 does not indicate that Congress was departing from this common understanding. As we see it, adding the second phrase simply made it unmistakable that the statute reached false promises and misrepresentations as to the future as well as other frauds involving money or property. . . .

Rather than construe the statute in a manner that leaves its outer boundaries ambiguous and involves the Federal Government in setting standards of disclosure and good government for local and state officials, we read §1341 as limited in scope to the protection of property rights. If Congress desires to go further, it must speak more clearly than it has.

For purposes of this action, we assume that Hunt, as well as Gray, was a state officer. The issue is thus whether a state officer violates the mail fraud statute if he chooses an insurance agent to provide insurance for the State but specifies that the agent must share its commissions with other named insurance agencies, in one of which the officer has an ownership interest and hence profits when his agency receives part of the commissions. We note that as the action comes to us, there was no charge and the jury was not required to find that the Commonwealth itself was defrauded of any money or property. It was not charged that in the absence of the alleged scheme the Commonwealth would have paid a lower premium or secured better insurance. Hunt and Gray received part of the commissions but those commissions were not the Commonwealth's money. Nor was the jury charged that to convict it must find that the Commonwealth was deprived of control over how its money was spent. Indeed, the premium for insurance would have been paid to some agency, and what Hunt and Gray did was to assert control that the Commonwealth might not otherwise have made over the commissions paid by the insurance company to its agent. Although the Government now relies in part on the assertion that the petitioners obtained property by means of false representations to Wombwell, there was nothing in the jury charge that required such a finding. We hold, therefore, that the jury instruction on the substantive mail fraud count permitted a conviction for conduct not within the reach of §1341.

The Government concedes that if petitioners' substantive mail fraud convictions are reversed their conspiracy convictions should also be reversed.

The judgment of the Court of Appeals is reversed and the case remanded for proceedings consistent with this opinion.

JUSTICE STEVENS, with whom JUSTICE O'CONNOR joins . . . dissenting.

Congress has broadly prohibited the use of the United States mails to carry out "any scheme or artifice to defraud." 18 U.S.C. §1341. The question presented is whether that prohibition is restricted to fraudulent schemes to deprive others of money or property, or whether it also includes fraudulent schemes to deprive individuals of other rights to which they are entitled. . . .

The same question of statutory construction has arisen in a variety of contexts over the past few decades. In the public sector, judges, state Governors, chairmen of state political parties, state cabinet officers, city aldermen, congressmen and many other state and federal officials have been convicted of defrauding citizens of their right to the honest services of their governmental officials. In most of these cases, the officials have secretly made governmental decisions with the objective of benefiting themselves or promoting their own interests, instead of fulfilling their legal commitment to provide the citizens of the State or local government with their loyal service and honest government. Similarly, many elected officials and their campaign workers have been convicted of mail fraud when they have used the mails to falsify votes, thus defrauding the citizenry of its right to an honest election. In the private sector, purchasing agents, brokers, union leaders, and others with clear fiduciary duties to their employers or unions have been found guilty of defrauding their employers or unions by accepting kickbacks or selling confidential information. In other cases, defendants have been found guilty of using the mails to defraud individuals of their rights to privacy, and other nonmonetary rights. All of these cases have something in common — they involved what the Court now refers to as "intangible rights." They also share something else in common. The many federal courts that have confronted the question whether these sorts of schemes constitute a "scheme or artifice to defraud" have uniformly and consistently read the statute in the same, sensible way. They have realized that nothing in the words "any scheme or artifice to defraud," or in the purpose of the statute, justifies limiting its application to schemes intended to deprive victims of money or property. . . .

In considering the scope of the mail fraud statute it is essential to remember Congress' purpose in enacting it. Congress sought to protect the integrity of the United States mails by not allowing them to be used as "instruments of crime." United States v. Brewer, 528 F.2d 492, 498 (CA4 1975). . . . Once this purpose is considered, it becomes clear that the construction the Court adopts today is senseless. Can it be that Congress sought to purge the mails of schemes to defraud citizens of money but was willing to tolerate schemes to defraud citizens of their right to an honest government, or to unbiased public officials? Is it at all rational to assume that Congress wanted to ensure that the mails not be used for petty crimes, but did not prohibit election fraud accomplished through . . . mailing fictitious ballots? . . .

Even if there were historical evidence of a limited definition of "fraud," the Court's holding would reflect a strange interpretation of legislation enacted by the Congress in the 19th Century. Statutes like the Sherman Act, the civil rights legislation, and the mail fraud statute were written in broad general language on the understanding that the courts would have wide latitude in construing them to achieve the remedial purposes that Congress had identified. The wide open spaces in statutes such as these are most appropriately interpreted as implicit delegations of authority to the courts to fill in the gaps in the common-law tradition of case by case adjudication. The notion that the meaning of the words "any scheme or artifice to defraud" was frozen by a special conception of the term recognized by Congress in 1872 is manifestly untenable. . . .

To support its crabbed construction of the Act, the Court makes a straightforward but unpersuasive argument. Since there is no explicit, unambiguous evidence that Congress actually contemplated "intangible rights" when it enacted the mail fraud statute in 1872, the Court explains, any ambiguity in the meaning of the criminal statute should be resolved in favor of lenity. The doctrine of lenity is, of course, sound, for the citizen is entitled to fair notice of what sort of conduct may give rise to punishment. But the Court's reliance on that doctrine in this case is misplaced. [The] asserted ambiguity in the meaning of the word "defraud," if it ever existed, was removed by judicial construction long ago. [T]he series of Court of Appeals' opinions applying this very statute to schemes to defraud a State and its citizens of their intangible right to honest and faithful government, notwithstanding the absence of evidence of tangible loss, removed any relevant ambiguity in this statute. Surely these petitioners knew that it would be unlawful to place Kentucky's insurance coverage with an agent who would secretly make hundreds of thousands of dollars available for the private use of petitioners, their relatives, and their paramours. This is, indeed, a strange application of the doctrine of lenity.[9]

I recognize that there may have been some overly expansive applications of §1341 in the past. With no guidance from this Court, the Courts of Appeals have struggled to define just when conduct which is clearly unethical is also criminal. In some instances, however, such as voting fraud cases, the criminality of the scheme and the fraudulent use of the mails could not be clearer. It is sometimes difficult to define when there has been a scheme to defraud someone of intangible rights. But it is also sometimes difficult to decide when a tangible loss was caused by fraud. The fact that the exercise of judgment is sometimes difficult is no excuse for rejecting an entire doctrine that is both sound and faithful to the intent of Congress. . . .

In the long run, it is not clear how grave the ramifications of today's decision will be. Congress can, of course, negate it by amending the statute. Even without Congressional action, prosecutions of corrupt officials who use the mails to further their schemes may continue since it will frequently be possible to prove some loss of money or property.[10] But many other types of fraudulent use of the mail will now be immune from prosecution. The possibilities that the decision's impact will be mitigated do not moderate my conviction that the Court has made a serious mistake. Nor do they erase my lingering questions about why a Court that has not been particularly receptive to the rights of criminal defendants in recent years has acted so dramatically to protect the elite class of powerful individuals who will benefit from this decision.

I respectfully dissent.

NOTE

Congress had the last word in this dispute. In 1988 it amended Title 18 of the U.S. Code by adding Section 1346, which reads: "For the purposes of this chapter, the term 'scheme or artifice to defraud' includes a scheme or artifice to deprive another of the intangible right of honest services." The issue of policy remains open, however. Was Congress well advised to overrule *McNally*? Consider the observations of Professor Francis A. Allen in The Erosion of Legality in

9. When considering how much weight to accord to the doctrine of lenity, it is appropriate to identify the class of litigants that will benefit from the Court's ruling today. They are not uneducated, or even average, citizens. They are the most sophisticated practitioners of the art of government among us. There is an element of fiction in the presumption that every citizen is charged with a responsibility to know what the law is. But the array of government executives, judges, and legislators who have been accused, and convicted, of mail fraud under the well-settled construction of the statute that the Court renounces today are people who unquestionably knew that their conduct was unlawful.

10. When a person is being paid a salary for his loyal services, any breach of that loyalty would appear to carry with it some loss of money to the employer — who is not getting what he paid for. Additionally, "[i]f an agent receives anything as a result of his violation of a duty of loyalty to the principal, he is subject to a liability to deliver it, its value, or its proceeds, to the principal." Restatement (Second) of Agency §403 (1958). This duty may fulfill the Court's "money or property" requirement in most kickback schemes.

American Criminal Justice: Some Latter-Day Adventures of the *Nulla Poena* Principle, 29 Ariz. L. Rev. 387, 410-411 (1987):

> [T]he expansion of judicial doctrine in these [mail fraud] cases has at times ignored the restraints of the *nulla poena* principle in the area of its most basic application: that of requiring the criminal law to give fair notice to potential offenders of the threat of criminal punishment. It can hardly be supposed that the lawyer Bronston,[a] aware as he was of his involvement in an unprofessional conflict of interests and presumably of possible professional discipline, could, nevertheless, have contemplated his behavior risked conviction for a federal felony. Nor can it be doubted that the conviction, when it occurred, engendered a powerful sense of injustice in the accused and in those bound to him by ties of family and friendship. . . .
>
> The expansion of coverage of the Mail Fraud Act by the courts assaults the values of legality in another way: it exacerbates the problems of prosecutorial discretion, an area of power surely among the most resistent to regulation by authoritative norms within the range of criminal justice administration. These problems are particularly troublesome, as some dissenting judges have observed, in cases involving immoral and corrupt behavior by persons engaged in state and local governments. The incidents of serious improprieties in these areas are so numerous and ubiquitous that federal prosecution is incapable of responding to more than a small fraction of the total. Because choosing cases for prosecution must necessarily be highly selective, there is the ever-present danger of choices being made that promise the greatest political advantage to the national administration or to political and economic groups at the local level. Almost equally serious, suspicions of politicizing the processes of justice are engendered, whether or not justified in the particular case.
>
> The last category of costs to be mentioned involves definition of the proper judicial role in these cases. What is at issue is more than the structural question of separation of powers in the American governmental system. A basic element in the legitimacy of law is the perception that in making law, the law-giver acted within the limits of its designated authority. The recent decisions under the Mail Fraud Act surely strain at the limits and may, indeed, exceed them. Apart from questions of legitimacy, it may also be seen that before the law intrudes into areas as sensitive as those entered by the courts in the mail fraud cases, the political judgment of the legislature should be obtained. Converting the federal district courts into a national tribunal to test the political morality of local officials, or precipitately enlarging the fiduciary obligations of corporate managers in their relations with the corporation, may be sound courses for public policy to pursue, but confidence in that conclusion is seriously weakened by the absence of legislative consideration and contribution.

Professor Allen has revisited these and related themes in A Crisis of Legality in the Criminal Law? Reflections on the Rule of Law, 42 Mercer L. Rev. 811, 836

---

a. At 407, the author states "In Bronston v. United States, [658 F.2d 920 (2d Cir. 1981)] the accused, a state senator and member of a large New York law firm, gave secret assistance to a personal client who was competing for a franchise from the city with a company already being represented by defendant's law firm. Bronston thus wrongfully created and concealed a serious conflict of interest. On the other hand, there is no evidence the accused made use of confidential information supplied by the firm's client to advance the interests of his own client. Nevertheless, the accused's conviction under the Mail Fraud Act was affirmed in the Court of Appeals, principally on the ground that, as a partner, he breached a fiduciary obligation of loyalty owed by him to the firm's clients." — Eds.

(1991). Professor Coffee has also revisited these issues. In his Does "Unlawful" Mean "Criminal"?: Reflections on the Disappearing Tort/Crime Distinction in American Law, 71 B.U.L. Rev. 193 (1993), he makes the case against the expansion of the criminal sanction into the areas traditionally remitted to the civil law.

See generally on the issues canvassed in this subsection, Geraldine Moohr, Mail Fraud and the Intangible Rights Doctrine, 31 Harv. J. Leg. 153 (1994).

C. MENS REA

PEOPLE v. BROWN

Supreme Court of California
105 Cal. 66, 38 P. 518 (1894)

GAROUTE, J. [Appellant, a 17-year-old boy, was convicted of burglary on an information charging that he entered a house with intent to commit larceny. The facts revealed that he entered an acquaintance's house and took a bicycle. He testified: "I took the wheel to get even with the boy, and, of course, I didn't intend to keep it. I just wanted to get even with him. The boy was throwing oranges at me in the evening, and he would not stop when I told him to, and it made me mad. I intended to take it back Sunday night; but, before I got back, they caught me."]

Upon the foregoing state of facts, the court gave the jury the following instruction:

> I think it is not necessary to say very much to you in this case. I may say, generally, that I think counsel for the defense here stated to you in his argument very fairly the principles of law governing this case, except in one particular. In defining to you the crime of grand larceny, he says it is essential that the taking of it must be felonious. That is true; the taking with the intent to deprive the owner of it; but he adds the conclusion that you must find that the taker intended to deprive him of it permanently. I do not think that is the law. I think in this case, for example, if the defendant took this bicycle, we will say for the purpose of riding twenty-five miles, for the purpose of enabling him to get away, and then left it for another to get it, and intended to do nothing else except to help himself away for a certain distance, it would be larceny, just as much as though he intended to take it all the while. A man may take a horse, for instance, not with the intent to convert it wholly and permanently to his own use, but to ride it to a certain distance, for a certain purpose he may have, and then leave it. He converts it to that extent to his own use and purpose feloniously.

This instruction is erroneous, and demands a reversal of the judgment. If the boy's story be true, he is not guilty of larceny in taking the machine; yet, under the instruction of the court, the words from his own mouth convicted him. The court told the jury that larceny may be committed, even though it was only the intent of the party taking the property to deprive the owner of it temporarily. We think the authorities form an unbroken line to the effect that the felonious intent must be to deprive the owner of the property permanently. The illustration contained in the instruction as to the man taking the horse is too broad in its terms as stating a correct principle of law. Under the circumstances depicted by the illustration, the man might, and again he might not, be guilty of larceny. It would be a pure question of fact for the jury, and dependent for its true solution upon all the circumstances surrounding the transaction. But the test of law to be applied in these circumstances for the purpose of determining the ultimate fact as to the man's guilt or innocence is, did he intend to permanently deprive the owner of his property? If he did not intend so to do, there is no felonious intent, and his acts constitute but a trespass. While the felonious intent of the party taking need not necessarily be an intention to convert the property to his own use, still it must in all cases be an intent to wholly and permanently deprive the owner thereof.

For the foregoing reasons, it is ordered that the judgment and order be reversed, and the cause remanded for a new trial.

NOTE

Some limited exceptions to the requirement of an intent to take permanently have been made judicially and by statute. The courts early found that, where the thing taken was abandoned or recklessly exposed to loss by the taker, this fact was not only evidentiary of an intent to effect a permanent deprivation but would sustain larceny even if a permanent taking was not the object of the defendant's acts. State v. Davis, 38 N.J.L. 176 (1875). See N.Y. Penal Law §155.00(3): "To 'deprive' another of property means . . . (b) to dispose of the property in such manner or under such circumstances as to render it unlikely that an owner will recover such property." Likewise, where the intent to return the thing taken is conditional, as upon receipt of a reward, the requisite mens rea has been found. State v. Hauptman, 115 N.J.L. 412, 426, 180 A. 809, 819 (1935); Slaughter v. State, 113 Ga. 284, 38 S.E. 854 (1901). The risk of loss rationale has also supported larceny convictions where the defendant intends to pledge, though ultimately to redeem and return, the property taken. Regina v. Phetheon, 9 Car. & P. 552, 173 Eng. Rep. 952 (1840); but cf. Blackburn v. Commonwealth, 28 Ky. 96, 89 S.W. 160 (1905). Many states have long enacted "joy ride" statutes which make criminal the temporary taking of an automobile, and sometimes other vehicles. See, e.g., Cal. Penal Code §499(b).

Question: Why should the law of theft confine itself to cases where the intent of the taker is to effect a permanent deprivation? As Holmes observed (The Common Law 71 (1881)): "A momentary loss of possession is not what has been guarded against with such severe penalties. What the law means to prevent is the loss of it wholly and forever. . . ." But should interference with possession which is more than momentary, though less than permanent, be protected against by the law of theft? Following Model Penal Code §223.0(1), N.Y. Penal Law §155.00(3) now provides: "To 'deprive' another of property means (a) to withhold it or cause it to be withheld . . . for so extended a period or under such circumstances that the major portion of its economic value or benefit is lost to him. . . ." §155.00(4) provides: "To 'appropriate' property of another to oneself or a third person means (a) to exercise control over it . . . permanently or for so extended a period or under such circumstances as to acquire the major portion of its economic value or benefit, . . ." These provisions were construed in the following case.

People v. Jennings, 69 N.Y.2d 103, 504 N.E.2d 1079 (1986). [Defendants, Sentry Armored Courier Corp. and its officers, had an agreement with its client, Chemical Bank, to pick up, "fine count" and deliver Chemical's bulk deposits to Chemical's account at the Federal Reserve Bank within 72 hours. Since it took only 24 hours to count the money, defendants used the extra 48 hours to obtain interest on the money by arrangement with the Hudson Valley Bank. The scheme involved little risk, since a "loan," which was a key element in the arrangement, was secured by A-rated bonds. The majority found these facts not to constitute a deprivation or appropriation of Chemical's money under the New York larceny provisions.]

. . . While Sentry's conduct may have provided a basis for civil liability in some form, that conduct did not constitute criminal larceny. . . . What is lacking here from the People's proof is evidence demonstrating an "intent to deprive . . . or to appropriate."

The gist of the People's claim is that by investing Chemical's money for periods up to 48 hours, defendants evinced an intent to deprive its true owner of the money's "economic value or benefit," that is, the interest that the money was capable of generating. The mens rea element of larceny, however, is simply not satisfied by an intent temporarily to use property without the owner's permission, or even an intent to appropriate outright the benefits of the property's short-term use.

The problem presented in this case is similar to that presented in "joy-riding" cases, in which it was held that the intent merely to borrow and use an automobile without the owner's permission cannot support a conviction for larceny. An analysis of the evidence before the Grand Jury in this case indicates only that defendants exercised control over Chemical's money to the extent of using it to make short-term, profitable investments and, as a result, appropriated some portion of its economic benefit for themselves. However, in light of the fact that their unauthorized use of Chemical's money extended over no more than a series of discrete 48-hour periods, the proof was insufficient to show that they intended to use Chemical's money "for so extended a period or under such circumstances as to acquire the *major portion* of its economic value or benefit" (emphasis supplied).[5]

Moreover, the "economic value or benefit" to be derived from the money was the interest or other financial leverage that could be gained by the party who possessed it. Inasmuch as Chemical had ceded possession of its money to Sentry for various 72-hour periods, it had no legal rights during those periods to the money's "economic value or benefit," which is an incident of possession. Thus,

5. Although a person who "borrows" a vehicle without the owner's consent unquestionably appropriates its *entire* economic benefit during the time he is using it, our case law does not recognize such conduct as larceny if it was accompanied by an intention to return the vehicle to its true owner. Thus, contrary to the dissent's view, we do not deem defendants' conduct larcenous because they "acquired *all* the economic benefit of [Chemical's money] for the time they held it." Indeed, if that proposition were true, there would be no distinction between the crime of larceny and the crime of misapplication of property under Penal Law §165.00.

to the extent that defendants intended to appropriate to themselves the "economic value or benefit" of Chemical's money, it cannot be said that their intentions were unlawful or even inconsistent with the terms of the bailment. . . .

For similar reasons it cannot be said that defendants committed larceny by intentionally and permanently stealing the interest earned on Chemical's money, as distinguished from the money itself. First, absent proof of an agreement to the contrary, Chemical cannot be deemed the true owner of the interest earned while its money was in defendants' custody pursuant to the parties' "fine counting" agreement. Indeed, there is really no practical difference between the contention that defendants stole the interest on Chemical's money and the contention that they stole the money itself by intentionally appropriating its "economic value or benefit."

Second, it would be inconsistent with the statutory design to treat defendants' concededly permanent taking of the interest earned on Chemical's funds as a larceny within the meaning of Penal Law §§155.00, 155.05 and 155.35. It is clear that an individual who "joy-rides" and thereby deprives the automobile's owner of the value arising from its temporary use is not liable in larceny for stealing that intangible "value" under article 155 of the Penal Law. By parity of reasoning, an individual who temporarily invests another's money and thereby gains interest or profit cannot be deemed guilty of larceny for appropriating that interest or profit. Consistent with our long-held view that criminal liability "cannot be extended beyond the fair scope of the statutory mandate," we hold that in these circumstances the statute must be read to apply only to a taking of the property itself and not to a permanent taking of what is, in essence, only the economic value of its use during the short time the property has been withheld. . . .

Finally, we note that neither Sentry's patently false response to Chemical's inquiry concerning the rerouting of its money through Hudson nor Sentry's disobedience when ordered by Chemical to deliver the money directly are sufficient to establish that Sentry was acting with the larcenous intent required by Penal Law §155.05(3), (4) and §155.05(1). At worst, Sentry's conduct demonstrates its unwillingness to relinquish what was obviously a profitable short-term use of Chemical's money. It does not, however, alter the inescapable and uncontradicted inference that Sentry was merely emulating the behavior of many reputable financial institutions by taking advantage of the "float" on the temporarily idle money in its possession.

Having determined that the People's proof did not establish a larceny, we turn now to the question whether it was sufficient to establish the lesser crime of misapplication of property, which is defined in Penal Law §165.00(1) as follows: "A person is guilty of misapplication of property when, knowingly possessing personal property of another pursuant to an agreement that the same will be returned to the owner at a future time, he loans, leases, pledges, pawns or otherwise encumbers such property without the consent of the owner thereof in such manner as to create a risk that the owner will not be able to recover it or will suffer pecuniary loss."

The obvious thrust of this statute, which we have not previously construed, is to make it a crime to alienate in any way property belonging to another under circumstances creating a risk of loss. While the created risk of loss need not rise to the level of "likelihood" or even mere "probability," the statute does require proof of a risk that is more than a far-fetched or wholly speculative possibility. . . .

There was no actual risk here that the money would not be repaid, since even in the unlikely event of a default by Hudson, the "loans" to Hudson were secured by A-rated bonds held in Hudson's Federal Reserve Bank vault. . . .

In short, however unethical defendants' conduct may have been, it did not constitute the crimes of larceny or misapplication of property. Accordingly, the indictments charging those crimes were properly dismissed.

REGINA v. FEELY
Court of Appeal
[1973] 2 W.L.R. 201

LAWTON, L.J. . . . The appeal raises an important point of law, namely, can it be a defence *in law* for a man charged with theft and proved to have taken money to say that when he took the money he intended to repay it and had reasonable grounds for believing and did believe that he would be able to do so.

[The facts were as follows: Defendant was a branch manager for a firm of bookmakers. In September 1971 the firm sent a circular to all branch managers that the practice of borrowing from tills was to stop. Defendant nevertheless took about £30 from a branch safe on October 4. On October 8 he was transferred to another branch. His successor discovered a cash shortage of about £40, and defendant gave him an IOU for that amount. Though his successor did not report the deficiency, a member of the firm's security staff did and asked defendant for an explanation. Defendant accounted for about £10 by reference to some bets he had paid out, but as to the balance he said that he had taken it because he was "stuck for cash." Defendant stated he borrowed the £30 intending to pay it back and that his employers owed him about £70 from which he wanted them to deduct the money. Trial testimony showed that the firm did owe him that amount. He was convicted of theft of the £30.

[The trial judge directed the jury] that if the defendant had taken the money from either the safe or the till — and it was the prosecution's case and the defendant's own case to start with, that he had taken it from the safe — it was no defence for him to say that he had intended to repay it and that his employers owed him more than enough to cover what he had taken. The trial judge put his direction in stark terms: . . .

> As a matter of law, members of the jury, I am bound to direct you, even if he were prepared to pay back the following day and even if he were a millionaire, it makes no defence in law to this offence. If he took the money, that is the essential matter for you to decide.

At no stage of his summing up did he leave the jury to decide whether the prosecution had proved that the defendant had taken the money dishonestly. This was because he seems to have thought that he had to decide as a matter of law what amounted to dishonesty and he expressed his concept of dishonesty as follows: ". . . if someone does something deliberately knowing that his employers are not prepared to tolerate it, is that not dishonest?"

Should the jury have been left to decide whether the defendant had acted dishonestly? The search for an answer must start with the Theft Act 1968, under section 1 of which the defendant had been indicted. . . . The design of the new Act is clear; nearly all the old legal terms to describe offences of dishonesty have been left behind; larceny, embezzlement and fraudulent conversion have become theft; receiving stolen goods has become handling stolen goods; obtaining by false pretences has become pecuniary advantage by deception. Words in everyday use have replaced legal jargon in many parts of the Act. That is particularly noticeable in the series of sections (1 to 6) defining theft.

"Theft" itself is a word known and used by all and is defined . . . as follows: "A person is guilty of theft if he dishonestly appropriates property belonging to another with the intention of permanently depriving the other of it. . . ."

In section 1(1) of the Act of 1968, the word "dishonestly" can only relate to the state of mind of the person who does the act which amounts to appropriation. . . . The Crown did not dispute this proposition, but it was submitted that in some cases (and this, it was said, was such a one) it was necessary for the trial judge to define "dishonestly." . . .

We do not agree that judges should define what "dishonestly" means. This word is in common use whereas the word "fraudulently" which was used in section 1(1) of the Larceny Act 1916 had acquired as a result of case law a special meaning. Jurors, when deciding whether an appropriation was dishonest can be reasonably expected to, and should, apply the current standards of ordinary decent people. . . .

[T]he jury should have been left to decide whether the defendant's alleged taking of the money had been dishonest. They were not, with the result that a verdict of guilty was returned without their having given thought to what was probably the most important issue in the case.

This would suffice for the appeal were it not for . . . two decisions. . . . In Reg. v. Williams [1953] 1 Q.B. 660, the two appellants, who were husband and wife, carried on a general shop, part of which was a sub-post office. The wife was the sub-postmistress. The business of the shop got into difficulties and in order to get out of them the wife, with the knowledge of her husband, took money from the Post Office till to discharge some of the debts of the business. In her evidence, which was supported by that of her husband, she said that she thought she would be able to repay the money out of her salary from the Post Office and from sales from the business. The husband said that he knew it was wrong to do what they had done, but he thought that it would all come right in the end. They were found guilty on a number of counts and in respect of two the jury added a rider that the appellants had intended to repay the money and honestly believed that they would be able to do so, but in respect of three counts, although they intended to repay, they had no honest belief that they would be able to do so. The main ground of the appeal was that the jury had been misdirected as to the word "fraudulently" in section 1(1) of the Larceny Act 1916.

. . . The question in the case which is relevant for the purposes of this appeal was whether the facts found by the jury and recorded in their riders afforded any defence. [The court held they did not, stating]: "They knew that they had no right to take the money which they knew was not their money. The fact that they may have had a hope or expectation in the future of repaying that money is a matter which at most can go to mitigation and does not amount to a defence."

It is possible to imagine a case of taking by an employee in breach of instructions to which no one would, or could reasonably, attach moral obloquy; for example, that of a manager of a shop, who having been told that under no circumstances was he to take money from the till for his own purposes, took 40p from it, having no small change himself, to pay for a taxi hired by his wife who had arrived at the shop saying that she only had a £5 note which the cabby could not change. . . .

If the law drifted off course in Reg. v. Williams [1953] 1 Q.B. 660 because of the strong inference of fraud arising on the facts of that case, it got on to the wrong tack in Reg. v. Cockburn [1968] 1 W.L.R. 281 in which the manager of a shop took money from the till on a Saturday intending, so he said, to replace it with a cheque drawn by his daughter. Before he did so he was dismissed, and when the deficiency of cash was discovered and he was asked by telephone about it, he did not then put forward the explanation which was his defence to a charge of larceny as a servant. At his trial the jury were not directed that it would be a good defence to the charge if the accused were to satisfy them that he intended to replace the money with its currency equivalent. . . . Winn, L.J. delivered the judgment of the court [finding no error and stating] . . . "If coins, half a crown, a 10s. note, a £5 note, whatever it may be, are taken in all the circumstances which I have already indicated with the intention of spending or putting away somewhere those particular coins or notes, albeit not only hoping but intending and expecting reasonably to be able to replace them with their equivalent, nevertheless larceny has been committed because with full appreciation of what is being done, the larcenous person, the person who commits the offence, has taken something which he was not entitled to take, had no claim of right to take, without the consent of the owner, and is in effect trying to force upon the owner a substitution to which the owner has not consented."

We find it impossible to accept that a conviction for stealing, whether it be called larceny or theft, can reveal no moral obloquy. A man so convicted would have difficulty in persuading his friends and neighbours that his reputation had not been gravely damaged. He would be found to be lowered in the estimation of right thinking people. . . .

If the principle enunciated in Reg. v. Cockburn [1968] 1 W.L.R. 281 was right, there would be a strange divergence between the position of a man who obtains cash by passing a cheque on an account which has no funds to meet it and one who takes money from a till. The man who passes the cheque is deemed in law not to act dishonestly if he genuinely believes on reasonable grounds that when it is presented to the paying bank there will be funds to meet it. . . . But, according to the decision in Reg. v. Cockburn, the man who takes money from a till intending to put it back and genuinely believing on reasonable grounds that he will be able to do so should be convicted of theft. Lawyers may be able to appreciate why one man should be adjudged to be a criminal and the other not; but we doubt whether anyone else would. People who take money from tills and the like without permission are usually thieves, but if they do not admit that they are by pleading guilty, it is for the jury, not the judge, to decide whether they have acted dishonestly. . . .

For these reasons we allowed the appeal.

PROBLEM

Section 2 of the Theft Act of 1968 deals as follows with the concept of dishonesty:

(1) A person's appropriation of property belonging to another is not to be regarded as dishonest —
    (a) if he appropriates the property in the belief that he has in law the right to deprive the other of it, on behalf of himself or a third person; or
    (b) if he appropriates the property in the belief that he would have the other's consent if the other knew of the appropriation and the circumstances of it; or
    (c) (except where the property came to him as trustee or personal representative) if he appropriates the property in the belief that the person to whom the property belongs cannot be discovered by taking reasonable steps
(2) A person's appropriation of property belonging to another may be dishonest notwithstanding that he is willing to pay for the property.

Questions: Should the court in the *Feely* case have considered these provisions? What effect should they have on the resolution of the issue?

See the discussion of the *Feely* case in Glanville Williams, Textbook of Criminal Law 725-727 (2d ed. 1983).

NOTES AND QUESTIONS ON INTENT TO RESTORE OR PAY

1. In State v. Pratt, 114 Kan. 660, 220 P. 505, 506, 507 (1923), the defendant was convicted of embezzlement on the following facts:

[T]he Building & Loan Association purchased $10,000 worth, face value, of the Second Liberty Loan bonds of the United States, which passed into the custody of the appellant as secretary-treasurer of the association. Without any authority to do so, and without the knowledge of the directors and other officers of the association, appellant sold these bonds in January, 1920, in Kansas City. The money was not used for the benefit of the association. In fact, appellant concealed his disposition of these bonds from the association until some time in May or June, 1921. At two or three of the meetings of the board of directors of the association held in the meantime, in which they were checking up the assets of the association, appellant substituted other bonds, which he had taken without authority from the envelopes of private boxes of depositors of the bank of which he was president, and counted those at the board meeting as the bonds of the association.

On appeal the defendant contended "that before he could be convicted of the crime of embezzlement the state must prove beyond a reasonable doubt that at the time he wrongfully converted the bonds he had the intent to deprive the owner, not temporarily, but permanently, of its property," and that error was committed in refusing evidence of his intent to restore the bonds or their equivalent and in failing to instruct that such an intent was a good defense. The court affirmed, resting on the weight of authority that "While to constitute . . . embezzlement it is necessary that there be a criminal intent, yet where the money of the principal is knowingly used by the agent in violation of his duty, it is none the less embezzlement because at the time he intended to restore it." Cf. Cal. Penal Code §512 (intent to restore no defense or mitigation in embezzlement if property not restored before indictment or information); §513 (restoration prior to indictment or information mitigates punishment for embezzlement).

Questions: Does the holding and reasoning of the court mean that defendant could also have been convicted of embezzlement of the depositors' bonds, which he removed temporarily from the bank of which he was president to cover his misappropriation of the savings and loan association bonds? Why not, if intent to restore is not a defense to embezzlement?

2. The intent to restore is likewise held to be no defense to a false pretense charge. See People v. Weiger, 100 Cal. 352, 34 P. 826 (1893). The defendant obtained goods on credit from the complaining witness on false representations concerning his financial position. The court affirmed a conviction of obtaining by false pretenses, holding immaterial that defendant intended to pay for the goods which he purchased, stating (34 P. at 827):

> In the assumption that it must be held that defendant did not intend to defraud the Sharpless firm if he intended at the time to pay for the goods according to the contract of sale, and truly believed that he was able to do so, I think counsel is in error. Deception, deliberately practiced, for the purpose of gaining an unfair advantage of another, is fraud. Goods obtained by such practices are obtained by fraud. One deprived of his property by such means is defrauded.

Questions: Suppose the goods defendant obtained in the *Weiger* case were a set of law books and that her defense was as follows: The defendant was a young attorney, expecting a visit from a potential client of substance whom she wanted to impress. She obtained the books for this purpose, fully intending to ship them back to the seller after the client's visit. Would it follow from the principle stated in *Weiger* that she would be guilty of obtaining by false pretenses? If so, consider the liability of the young attorney if she took the books from another attorney's office for the same purpose and with the same intent to return them after the client's visit. Would this not be a clear temporary taking inconsistent with larceny? Why is the same defense not available whether she obtained the books by a false representation or by a taking?

3. In connection with the various issues raised in this Note, consider the following observations in Model Penal Code §206.1(2)(c), Comment at 72-73 (Tent. Draft No. 1, 1953):

> As under present law, it is no defense that the actor intends to reimburse the owner later for property presently misappropriated. . . . Deprivation accompanied by an intent to make good later, by payment of money or by the actor's repurchasing an equivalent article for restoration to the owner, is quite different in effect from the taking of a thing for temporary use of the taker. In the latter situation, the actor's retention of the property offers some assurance of his ability to restore, beyond his general credit. In the former situation, the man who takes money intending to repay or the broker who sells his client's bonds meaning to repurchase and restore the bonds later, substitutes his own credit for the owner's property in hand. Even if the actor carries out his intent to restore, he is simply paying off a liability from his own assets, rather than restoring property which has continued to belong to the owner during the interval of deprivation.

PEOPLE v. REID

New York Court of Appeals
69 N.Y.2d 469, 508 N.E.2d 661 (1987)

SIMONS, J. . . . [Appellants Reid and Riddles were convicted of armed robberies of money from their victims, despite evidence that they were only trying to recover money owed to them. In one case, the trial court, conducting a trial without a jury, stated that it credited the testimony of defendant that he had taken the money to satisfy a debt, but the court denied him the defense of claim of right because he used force.]

The common issue presented by these two appeals is whether a good-faith claim of right, which negates larcenous intent in certain thefts (see, Penal Law §155.15[1]), also negates the intent to commit robbery by a defendant who uses force to recover cash allegedly owed him. We hold that it does not. Accordingly, we affirm the order of the Appellate Division in each case. . . .

A person "commits robbery when, in the course of committing a larceny, he uses or threatens the immediate use of physical force."[1] The larceny statute, in turn, provides that an assertion that "property was appropriated under a claim of right made in good faith" is a defense to larceny.[a] Since a good-faith claim of right is a defense to larceny, and because robbery is defined as forcible larceny, defendants contend that claim of right is also a defense to robbery. They concede the culpability of their forcible conduct, but maintain that because they acted under a claim of right to recover their own property, they were not guilty of robbery, but only some lesser crime, such as assault or unlawful possession of a weapon.

Defendants' general contention is not without support. Several jurisdictions have held that one who acts under a claim of right lacks the intent to steal and should not be convicted of robbery (see generally, Annotation, Robbery, Attempted Robbery, or Assault to Commit Robbery, as Affected by the Intent to Collect or Secure Debt or Claim, 88 A.L.R. 3d 1309). That logic is tenable when a person seeks to recover a specific chattel: it is less so when asserted under the circumstances presented in these two cases: in *Reid* to recover the proceeds of crime, and in *Riddles,* to recover cash to satisfy a debt.

We have not had occasion to address the issue but the Appellate Divisions to which it has been presented have uniformly ruled that claim of right is not a defense to robbery. Their determinations have been based upon the interpretation of the applicable statutes and a policy decision to discourage self-help and

---

1. Penal Law §160.00 provides:

Robbery; defined
Robbery is forcible stealing. A person forcibly steals property and commits robbery when, in the course of committing a larceny, he uses or threatens the immediate use of physical force upon another person for the purpose of:
1. Preventing or overcoming resistance to the taking of the property or to the retention thereof immediately after the taking; or
2. Compelling the owner of such property or another person to deliver up the property or to engage in other conduct which aids in the commission of the larceny.

a. N.Y. Penal Law §155.15 provides: "1. In any prosecution for larceny committed by trespassory taking or embezzlement, it is an affirmative defense that the property was appropriated under a claim of right made in good faith." — EDS.

they are consistent with what appears to be the emerging trend of similar appellate court decisions from other jurisdictions. For similar reasons, we conclude that the claim of right defense is not available in these cases. We need not decide the quite different question of whether an individual who uses force to recover a specific chattel which he owns may be convicted of robbery. It should be noted, however, that because taking property "from an owner thereof" is an element of robbery, a person who recovers property which is his own (as compared to the fungible cash taken to satisfy a claimed debt in the cases before us) may not be guilty of robbery. . . .

The claim of right defense is found in the larceny article of the Penal Law, which provides that a good-faith claim of right is a defense to trespassory larceny or embezzlement (see, Penal Law §155.15[1]). The defense does not apply to all forms of larceny. For example, extortion is a form of larceny, but the Legislature, consistent with a prior decision of this court, has not authorized a claim of right defense to extortion (see, People v. Fichtner, 281 App. Div. 159, 118 N.Y.S.2d 159 affd. 305 N.Y. 864, 114 N.E.2d 212. The exception is significant for extortion entails the threat of actual or potential force or some form of coercion. Thus, the inference may reasonably be drawn that in failing to authorize a claim of right defense for extortion in Penal Law §155.15(1), and by failing to incorporate it in article 160 of the statute, which governs robbery, the Legislature recognized that an accused should not be permitted to invoke it in crimes involving force. We assume that if the Legislature intended to excuse forcible taking, it would have said so.

Our decision also rests upon policy considerations against expanding the area of permissible self-help. Manifestly, a larceny, in which the accused reacquires property belonging to him without using force, differs from a robbery in which the defendant obtains money allegedly owed to him by threatening or using force. "The former is an instance of mistake, not subjected to penal sanctions because the threat to private property is not so serious as to warrant intervention by the criminal law. The latter is a species of self help and whether or not the exponent of force or threats is correct in estimating his rights, he is resorting to extra-judicial means in order to protect a property interest" (Note, A Rationale of the Law of Aggravated Theft, 54 Colum. L. Rev. 84, 98 [1954]). Since such forcible conduct is not merely a transgression against property, but also entails the risk of physical or mental injury to individuals, it should be subjected to criminal sanctions. Consequently, we find the courts in both [cases] correctly denied defendants' requests to assert claim of right defenses.

NOTE ON MODEL PENAL CODE TREATMENT OF CLAIM OF RIGHT

Section 223.1(3) of the Model Penal Code provides:

> It is an affirmative defense to prosecution for theft that the actor (a) was unaware that the property or service was that of another; or (b) acted under an honest claim of right to the property or service involved or that he had a right to acquire or dispose of it as he did; or (c) took property exposed for sale, intending to purchase and pay for it promptly, or reasonably believing that the owner, if present, would have consented.

Model Penal Code and Commentaries, Comment to §223.1(3) at 155-157 (1980):

Subsection (3)(b) deals with situations where the defendant may know that the property belongs to another but where he believes that he is nevertheless entitled to behave as he does. . . .

There is debate in the cases over several situations to which the defense provided in Subsection (3)(b) will apply. One occurs where the actor believes himself privileged to appropriate the property of another in satisfaction of a debt, without any special claim to the particular property appropriated. . . .

Even more doubt as to the defense of claim of right exists in a second situation, namely that of an agent or a fiduciary who profits from dealing with his principal but who believes himself entitled to the profit because, ignorantly or mistakenly, he supposed that he was under no legal obligation to refrain from such dealing or to turn over such profits to his principal. The defense was recognized in one case, where an agent was given $1,450 to buy some land, bought it for $1,150, and kept the difference. On the other hand, the Supreme Court of Indiana affirmed the conviction of a fiduciary who bought bonds for $430 and resold them the same day to the estate for $2,000, the trial court having refused to instruct that the defendant might be acquitted if he had a *bona fide* belief that he was entitled to make a profit in dealing with the estate. . . .

Subsection (3)(b) would permit a defense of claim of right in all of these situations, as well as others. The general principle is that the actor should have a defense where, although he is not in a position to claim that the property belongs to him, he honestly believes that he is entitled to acquire it and that his privilege extends to the use of force or other unlawful method of acquisition. A further example might be where an employee threatens his employer in some way covered by Section 223.4 on theft by extortion, but only for the purpose of compelling the employer to pay wages which the employee believes to be due. If the employee acted with the prescribed belief in his right to acquire the property "as he did," he would not be guilty of theft although he might be punishable under other sections of the Code for assault or coercion.

. . . Subsection (3)(b) provides a defense . . . premised on the view that a genuine belief in one's legal right should in all cases be a defense to theft. Persons who take only property to which they believe themselves entitled constitute no significant threat to the property system and manifest no character trait worse than ignorance.[99]

---

99. Again, it should be emphasized that the provisions of Article 211 dealing with assault and Section 212.5 dealing with criminal coercion would be fully applicable to such conduct. The point is closely related to the Model Code provision rejecting strict liability in the enforcement of the criminal law. . . . It ought to be the objective of the criminal law to describe the character deficiencies of those subjected to it in accord with the propensities that they actually manifest. One who is prepared to use violence to regain what he regards as his own property is, properly viewed, one who should be subjected to the laws designed to regulate violence and not to the laws designed to regulate the misappropriation of property of another.

APPENDIX

AMERICAN LAW INSTITUTE
MODEL PENAL CODE
OFFICIAL DRAFT, 1962

PART I.   GENERAL PROVISIONS

PART I.   GENERAL PROVISIONS

Article 1.   Preliminary

SECTION 1.01.   TITLE AND EFFECTIVE DATE [omitted]

SECTION 1.02.   PURPOSES; PRINCIPLES OF CONSTRUCTION

(1) The general purposes of the provisions governing the definition of offenses are:
    (a) to forbid and prevent conduct that unjustifiably and inexcusably inflicts or threatens substantial harm to individual or public interests;

(b) to subject to public control persons whose conduct indicates that they are disposed to commit crimes;

(c) to safeguard conduct that is without fault from condemnation as criminal;

(d) to give fair warning of the nature of the conduct declared to constitute an offense;

(e) to differentiate on reasonable grounds between serious and minor offenses.

(2) The general purposes of the provisions governing the sentencing and treatment of offenders are:

(a) to prevent the commission of offenses;

(b) to promote the correction and rehabilitation of offenders;

(c) to safeguard offenders against excessive, disproportionate or arbitrary punishment;

(d) to give fair warning of the nature of the sentences that may be imposed on conviction of an offense;

(e) to differentiate among offenders with a view to a just individualization in their treatment;

(f) to define, coordinate and harmonize the powers, duties and functions of the courts and of administrative officers and agencies responsible for dealing with offenders;

(g) to advance the use of generally accepted scientific methods and knowledge in the sentencing and treatment of offenders;

(h) to integrate responsibility for the administration of the correctional system in a State Department of Correction [or other single department or agency].

(3) The provisions of the Code shall be construed according to the fair import of their terms but when the language is susceptible of differing constructions it shall be interpreted to further the general purposes stated in this Section and the special purposes of the particular provision involved. The discretionary powers conferred by the Code shall be exercised in accordance with the criteria stated in the Code and, insofar as such criteria are not decisive, to further the general purposes stated in this Section.

SECTION 1.03.   TERRITORIAL APPLICABILITY

(1) Except as otherwise provided in this Section, a person may be convicted under the law of this State of an offense committed by his own conduct or the conduct of another for which he is legally accountable if:

(a) either the conduct which is an element of the offense or the result which is such an element occurs within this State; or

(b) conduct occurring outside the State is sufficient under the law of this State to constitute an attempt to commit an offense within the State; or

(c) conduct occurring outside the State is sufficient under the law of this State to constitute a conspiracy to commit an offense within the State and an overt act in furtherance of such conspiracy occurs within the State; or

(d) conduct occurring within the State establishes complicity in the commission of, or an attempt, solicitation or conspiracy to commit, an offense in another jurisdiction which also is an offense under the law of this State; or

(e) the offense consists of the omission to perform a legal duty imposed by the law of this State with respect to domicile, residence or a relationship to a person, thing or transaction in the State; or

(f) the offense is based on a statute of this State which expressly prohibits conduct outside the State, when the conduct bears a reasonable relation to a legitimate interest of this State and the actor knows or should know that his conduct is likely to affect that interest.

(2) Subsection (1)(a) does not apply when either causing a specified result or a purpose to cause or danger of causing such a result is an element of an offense and the result occurs or is designed or likely to occur only in another jurisdiction where the conduct charged would not constitute an offense, unless a legislative purpose plainly appears to declare the conduct criminal regardless of the place of the result.

(3) Subsection (1)(a) does not apply when causing a particular result is an element of an offense and the result is caused by conduct occurring outside the State which would not constitute an offense if the result had occurred there, unless the actor purposely or knowingly caused the result within the State.

(4) When the offense is homicide, either the death of the victim or the bodily impact causing the death constitutes a "result," within the meaning of Subsection (1)(a) and if the body of the homicide victim is found within the State, it is presumed that such result occurred within the State.

(5) This State includes the land and water and the air space above such land and water with respect to which the State has legislative jurisdiction.

SECTION 1.04.   CLASSES OF CRIMES; VIOLATIONS

(1) An offense defined by this Code or by any other statute of this State, for which a sentence of [death or of] imprisonment is authorized, constitutes a crime. Crimes are classified as felonies, misdemeanors or petty misdemeanors.

(2) A crime is a felony if it is so designated in this Code or if persons convicted thereof may be sentenced [to death or] to imprisonment for a term which, apart from an extended term, is in excess of one year.

(3) A crime is a misdemeanor if it is so designated in this Code or in a statute other than this Code enacted subsequent thereto.

(4) A crime is a petty misdemeanor if it is so designated in this Code or in a statute other than this Code enacted subsequent thereto or if it is defined by a statute other than this Code which now provides that persons convicted thereof may be sentenced to imprisonment for a term of which the maximum is less than one year.

(5) An offense defined by this Code or by any other statute of this State constitutes a violation if it is so designated in this Code or in the law defining the offense or if no other sentence than a fine, or fine and forfeiture or other civil penalty is authorized upon conviction or if it is defined by a statute other than this Code which now provides that the offense shall not constitute a crime. A violation does not constitute a crime and conviction of a violation shall not give rise to any disability or legal disadvantage based on conviction of a criminal offense.

(6) Any offense declared by law to constitute a crime, without specification of the grade thereof or of the sentence authorized upon conviction, is a misdemeanor.

(7) An offense defined by any statute of this State other than this Code shall be classified as provided in this Section and the sentence that may be imposed upon conviction thereof shall hereafter be governed by this Code.

SECTION 1.05.   ALL OFFENSES DEFINED BY STATUTE: APPLICATION OF GENERAL PROVISIONS
                 OF THE CODE

(1) No conduct constitutes an offense unless it is a crime or violation under this Code or another statute of this State.

(2) The provisions of Part I of the Code are applicable to offenses defined by other statutes, unless the Code otherwise provides.

(3) This Section does not affect the power of a court to punish for contempt or to

employ any sanction authorized by law for the enforcement of an order or a civil judgment or decree.

SECTION 1.06.   TIME LIMITATIONS

(1) A prosecution for murder may be commenced at any time.

(2) Except as otherwise provided in this Section, prosecutions for other offenses are subject to the following periods of limitation:

(a) a prosecution for a felony of the first degree must be commenced within six years after it is committed;

(b) a prosecution for any other felony must be commenced within three years after it is committed;

(c) a prosecution for a misdemeanor must be commenced within two years after it is committed;

(d) a prosecution for a petty misdemeanor or a violation must be commenced within six months after it is committed.

(3) If the period prescribed in Subsection (2) has expired, a prosecution may nevertheless be commenced for:

(a) any offense a material element of which is either fraud or a breach of fiduciary obligation within one year after discovery of the offense by an aggrieved party or by a person who has legal duty to represent an aggrieved party and who is himself not a party to the offense, but in no case shall this provision extend the period of limitation otherwise applicable by more than three years; and

(b) any offense based upon misconduct in office by a public officer or employee at any time when the defendant is in public office or employment or within two years thereafter, but in no case shall this provision extend the period of limitation otherwise applicable by more than three years.

(4) An offense is committed either when every element occurs, or, if a legislative purpose to prohibit a continuing course of conduct plainly appears, at the time when the course of conduct or the defendant's complicity therein is terminated. Time starts to run on the day after the offense is committed.

(5) A prosecution is commenced either when an indictment is found [or an information filed] or when a warrant or other process is issued, provided that such warrant or process is executed without unreasonable delay.

(6) The period of limitation does not run:

(a) during any time when the accused is continuously absent from the State or has no reasonably ascertainable place of abode or work within the State, but in no case shall this provision extend the period of limitation otherwise applicable by more than three years; or

(b) during any time when a prosecution against the accused for the same conduct is pending in this State.

SECTION 1.07.   METHOD OF PROSECUTION WHEN CONDUCT CONSTITUTES MORE THAN
              ONE OFFENSE

(1) *Prosecution for Multiple Offenses; Limitation on Convictions.* When the same conduct of a defendant may establish the commission of more than one offense, the defendant may be prosecuted for each such offense. He may not, however, be convicted of more than one offense if:

(a) one offense is included in the other, as defined in Subsection (4) of this Section; or

(b) one offense consists only of a conspiracy or other form of preparation to commit the other; or

(c) inconsistent findings of fact are required to establish the commission of the offenses; or

(d) the offenses differ only in that one is defined to prohibit a designated kind of conduct generally and the other to prohibit a specific instance of such conduct; or

(e) the offense is defined as a continuing course of conduct and the defendant's course of conduct was uninterrupted, unless the law provides that specific periods of such conduct constitute separate offenses.

(2) *Limitation on Separate Trials for Multiple Offenses.* Except as provided in Subsection (3) of this Section, a defendant shall not be subject to separate trials for multiple offenses based on the same conduct or arising from the same criminal episode, if such offenses are known to the appropriate prosecuting officer at the time of the commencement of the first trial and are within the jurisdiction of a single court.

(3) *Authority of Court to Order Separate Trials.* When a defendant is charged with two or more offenses based on the same conduct or arising from the same criminal episode, the Court, on application of the prosecuting attorney or of the defendant, may order any such charge to be tried separately, if it is satisfied that justice so requires.

(4) *Conviction of Included Offense Permitted.* A defendant may be convicted of an offense included in an offense charged in the indictment [or the information]. An offense is so included when:

(a) it is established by proof of the same or less than all the facts required to establish the commission of the offense charged; or

(b) it consists of an attempt or solicitation to commit the offense charged or to commit an offense otherwise included therein; or

(c) it differs from the offense charged only in the respect that a less serious injury or risk of injury to the same person, property or public interest or a lesser kind of culpability suffices to establish its commission.

(5) *Submission of Included Offense to Jury.* The Court shall not be obligated to charge the jury with respect to an included offense unless there is a rational basis for a verdict acquitting the defendant of the offense charged and convicting him of the included offense.

SECTION 1.08.   WHEN PROSECUTION BARRED BY FORMER PROSECUTION FOR THE SAME OFFENSE [OMITTED]

SECTION 1.09.   WHEN PROSECUTION BARRED BY FORMER PROSECUTION FOR DIFFERENT OFFENSE [OMITTED]

SECTION 1.10.   FORMER PROSECUTION IN ANOTHER JURISDICTION: WHEN A BAR [OMITTED]

SECTION 1.11.   FORMER PROSECUTION BEFORE COURT LACKING JURISDICTION OR WHEN FRAUDULENTLY PROCURED BY THE DEFENDANT [OMITTED]

SECTION 1.12.   PROOF BEYOND A REASONABLE DOUBT; AFFIRMATIVE DEFENSES; BURDEN OF PROVING FACT WHEN NOT AN ELEMENT OF AN OFFENSE; PRESUMPTIONS

(1) No person may be convicted of an offense unless each element of such offense is proved beyond a reasonable doubt. In the absence of such proof, the innocence of the defendant is assumed.

(2) Subsection (1) of this Section does not:

(a) require the disproof of an affirmative defense unless and until there is evidence supporting such defense; or

(b) apply to any defense which the Code or another statute plainly requires the defendant to prove by a preponderance of evidence.

(3) A ground of defense is affirmative, within the meaning of Subsection (2)(a) of this Section, when:

(a) it arises under a section of the Code which so provides; or

(b) it relates to an offense defined by a statute other than the Code and such statute so provides; or

(c) it involves a matter of excuse or justification peculiarly within the knowledge of the defendant on which he can fairly be required to adduce supporting evidence.

(4) When the application of the Code depends upon the finding of a fact which is not an element of an offense, unless the Code otherwise provides:

(a) the burden of proving the fact is on the prosecution or defendant, depending on whose interest or contention will be furthered if the finding should be made; and

(b) the fact must be proved to the satisfaction of the Court or jury, as the case may be.

(5) When the Code establishes a presumption with respect to any fact which is an element of an offense, it has the following consequences:

(a) when there is evidence of the facts which give rise to the presumption, the issue of the existence of the presumed fact must be submitted to the jury, unless the Court is satisfied that the evidence as a whole clearly negatives the presumed fact; and

(b) when the issue of the existence of the presumed fact is submitted to the jury, the Court shall charge that while the presumed fact must, on all the evidence, be proved beyond a reasonable doubt, the law declares that the jury may regard the facts giving rise to the presumption as sufficient evidence of the presumed fact.

(6) A presumption not established by the Code or inconsistent with it has the consequences otherwise accorded it by law.

SECTION 1.13.   GENERAL DEFINITIONS

In this Code, unless a different meaning plainly is required:

(1) "statute" includes the Constitution and a local law or ordinance of a political subdivision of the State;

(2) "act" or "action" means a bodily movement whether voluntary or involuntary;

(3) "voluntary" has the meaning specified in Section 2.01;

(4) "omission" means a failure to act;

(5) "conduct" means an action or omission and its accompanying state of mind, or, where relevant, a series of acts and omissions;

(6) "actor" includes, where relevant, a person guilty of an omission;

(7) "acted" includes, where relevant, "omitted to act";

(8) "person," "he" and "actor" include any natural person and, where relevant, a corporation or an unincorporated association;

(9) "element of an offense" means (i) such conduct or (ii) such attendant circumstances or (iii) such a result of conduct as

(a) is included in the description of the forbidden conduct in the definition of the offense; or

(b) establishes the required kind of culpability; or

(c) negatives an excuse or justification for such conduct; or

(d) negatives a defense under the statute of limitations; or

(e) establishes jurisdiction or venue;

(10) "material element of an offense" means an element that does not relate exclusively to the statute of limitations, jurisdiction, venue or to any other matter similarly unconnected with (i) the harm or evil, incident to conduct, sought to be prevented by the law defining the offense, or (ii) the existence of a justification or excuse for such conduct;

(11) "purposely" has the meaning specified in Section 2.02 and equivalent terms such as "with purpose," "designed" or "with design" have the same meaning;

(12) "intentionally" or "with intent" means purposely;

(13) "knowingly" has the meaning specified in Section 2.02 and equivalent terms such as "knowing" or "with knowledge" have the same meaning;

(14) "recklessly" has the meaning specified in Section 2.02 and equivalent terms such as "recklessness" or "with recklessness" have the same meaning;

(15) "negligently" has the meaning specified in Section 2.02 and equivalent terms such as "negligence" or "with negligence" have the same meaning;

(16) "reasonably believes" or "reasonable belief" designates a belief which the actor is not reckless or negligent in holding.

Article 2.   General Principles of Liability

SECTION 2.01.   REQUIREMENT OF VOLUNTARY ACT; OMISSION AS BASIS OF LIABILITY; POSSESSION AS AN ACT

(1) A person is not guilty of an offense unless his liability is based on conduct which includes a voluntary act or the omission to perform an act of which he is physically capable.

(2) The following are not voluntary acts within the meaning of this Section:

(a) a reflex or convulsion;

(b) a bodily movement during unconsciousness or sleep;

(c) conduct during hypnosis or resulting from hypnotic suggestion;

(d) a bodily movement that otherwise is not a product of the effort or determination of the actor, either conscious or habitual.

(3) Liability for the commission of an offense may not be based on an omission unaccompanied by action unless:

(a) the omission is expressly made sufficient by the law defining the offense; or

(b) a duty to perform the omitted act is otherwise imposed by law.

(4) Possession is an act, within the meaning of this Section, if the possessor knowingly procured or received the thing possessed or was aware of his control thereof for a sufficient period to have been able to terminate his possession.

SECTION 2.02.   GENERAL REQUIREMENTS OF CULPABILITY

(1) *Minimum Requirements of Culpability.* Except as provided in Section 2.05, a person is not guilty of an offense unless he acted purposely, knowingly, recklessly or negligently, as the law may require, with respect to each material element of the offense.

(2) *Kinds of Culpability Defined.*

(a) *Purposely.* A person acts purposely with respect to a material element of an offense when:

(i) if the element involves the nature of his conduct or a result thereof, it is his conscious object to engage in conduct of that nature or to cause such a result; and

(ii) if the element involves the attendant circumstances, he is aware of the existence of such circumstances or he believes or hopes that they exist.

(b) *Knowingly.* A person acts knowingly with respect to a material element of an offense when:

(i) if the element involves the nature of his conduct or the attendant circumstances, he is aware that his conduct is of that nature or that such circumstances exist; and

(ii) if the element involves a result of his conduct, he is aware that it is practically certain that his conduct will cause such a result.

(c) *Recklessly.* A person acts recklessly with respect to a material element of an offense when he consciously disregards a substantial and unjustifiable risk that the material element exists or will result from his conduct. The risk must be of such a nature and degree that, considering the nature and purpose of the actor's conduct and the circumstances known to him, its disregard involves a gross deviation from the standard of conduct that a law-abiding person would observe in the actor's situation.

(d) *Negligently.* A person acts negligently with respect to a material element of an offense when he should be aware of a substantial and unjustifiable risk that the material element exists or will result from his conduct. The risk must be of such a nature and degree that the actor's failure to perceive it, considering the nature and purpose of his conduct and the circumstances known to him, involves a gross deviation from the standard of care that a reasonable person would observe in the actor's situation.

(3) *Culpability Required Unless Otherwise Provided.* When the culpability sufficient to establish a material element of an offense is not prescribed by law, such element is established if a person acts purposely, knowingly or recklessly with respect thereto.

(4) *Prescribed Culpability Requirement Applies to All Material Elements.* When the law defining an offense prescribes the kind of culpability that is sufficient for the commission of an offense, without distinguishing among the material elements thereof, such provision shall apply to all the material elements of the offense, unless a contrary purpose plainly appears.

(5) *Substitutes for Negligence, Recklessness and Knowledge.* When the law provides that negligence suffices to establish an element of an offense, such element also is established if a person acts purposely, knowingly or recklessly. When recklessness suffices to establish an element, such element also is established if a person acts purposely or knowingly. When acting knowingly suffices to establish an element, such element also is established if a person acts purposely.

(6) *Requirement of Purpose Satisfied if Purpose Is Conditional.* When a particular purpose is an element of an offense, the element is established although such purpose is conditional, unless the condition negatives the harm or evil sought to be prevented by the law defining the offense.

(7) *Requirement of Knowledge Satisfied by Knowledge of High Probability.* When knowledge of the existence of a particular fact is an element of an offense, such knowledge is established if a person is aware of a high probability of its existence, unless he actually believes that it does not exist.

(8) *Requirement of Wilfulness Satisfied by Acting Knowingly.* A requirement that an offense be committed wilfully is satisfied if a person acts knowingly with respect to the material elements of the offense, unless a purpose to impose further requirements appears.

(9) *Culpability as to Illegality of Conduct.* Neither knowledge nor recklessness or negligence as to whether conduct constitutes an offense or as to the existence, meaning or application of the law determining the elements of an offense is an element of such offense, unless the definition of the offense or the Code so provides.

(10) *Culpability as Determinant of Grade of Offense.* When the grade or degree of an offense depends on whether the offense is committed purposely, knowingly, recklessly or negligently, its grade or degree shall be the lowest for which the determinative kind of culpability is established with respect to any material element of the offense.

SECTION 2.03.   CAUSAL RELATIONSHIP BETWEEN CONDUCT AND RESULT; DIVERGENCE
          BETWEEN RESULT DESIGNED OR CONTEMPLATED AND ACTUAL RESULT
          OR BETWEEN PROBABLE AND ACTUAL RESULT

(1) Conduct is the cause of a result when:
   (a) it is an antecedent but for which the result in question would not have occurred; and

(b) the relationship between the conduct and result satisfies any additional causal requirements imposed by the Code or by the law defining the offense.

(2) When purposely or knowingly causing a particular result is an element of an offense, the element is not established if the actual result is not within the purpose or the contemplation of the actor unless:

(a) the actual result differs from that designed or contemplated, as the case may be, only in the respect that a different person or different property is injured or affected or that the injury or harm designed or contemplated would have been more serious or more extensive than that caused; or

(b) the actual result involves the same kind of injury or harm as that designed or contemplated and is not too remote or accidental in its occurrence to have a [just] bearing on the actor's liability or on the gravity of his offense.

(3) When recklessly or negligently causing a particular result is an element of an offense, the element is not established if the actual result is not within the risk of which the actor is aware or, in the case of negligence, of which he should be aware unless:

(a) the actual result differs from the probable result only in the respect that a different person or different property is injured or affected or that the probable injury or harm would have been more serious or more extensive than that caused; or

(b) the actual result involves the same kind of injury or harm as the probable result and is not too remote or accidental in its occurrence to have a [just] bearing on the actor's liability or on the gravity of his offense.

(4) When causing a particular result is a material element of an offense for which absolute liability is imposed by law, the element is not established unless the actual result is a probable consequence of the actor's conduct.

SECTION 2.04.   IGNORANCE OR MISTAKE

(1) Ignorance or mistake as to a matter of fact or law is a defense if:

(a) the ignorance or mistake negatives the purpose, knowledge, belief, recklessness or negligence required to establish a material element of the offense; or

(b) the law provides that the state of mind established by such ignorance or mistake constitutes a defense.

(2) Although ignorance or mistake would otherwise afford a defense to the offense charged, the defense is not available if the defendant would be guilty of another offense had the situation been as he supposed. In such case, however, the ignorance or mistake of the defendant shall reduce the grade and degree of the offense of which he may be convicted to those of the offense of which he would be guilty had the situation been as he supposed.

(3) A belief that conduct does not legally constitute an offense is a defense to a prosecution for that offense based upon such conduct when:

(a) the statute or other enactment defining the offense is not known to the actor and has not been published or otherwise reasonably made available prior to the conduct alleged; or

(b) he acts in reasonable reliance upon an official statement of the law, afterward determined to be invalid or erroneous, contained in (i) a statute or other enactment; (ii) a judicial decision, opinion or judgment; (iii) an administrative order or grant of permission; or (iv) an official interpretation of the public officer or body charged by law with responsibility for the interpretation, administration or enforcement of the law defining the offense.

(4) The defendant must prove a defense arising under Subsection (3) of this Section by a preponderance of evidence.

SECTION 2.05.   WHEN CULPABILITY REQUIREMENTS ARE INAPPLICABLE TO VIOLATIONS AND
                  TO OFFENSES DEFINED BY OTHER STATUTES; EFFECT OF ABSOLUTE LIABILITY
                  IN REDUCING GRADE OF OFFENSE TO VIOLATION

(1) The requirements of culpability prescribed by Sections 2.01 and 2.02 do not
apply to:
     (a) offenses which constitute violations, unless the requirement involved is in-
cluded in the definition of the offense or the Court determines that its application is
consistent with effective enforcement of the law defining the offense; or
     (b) offenses defined by statutes other than the Code, insofar as a legislative purpose
to impose absolute liability for such offenses or with respect to any material element
thereof plainly appears.
(2) Notwithstanding any other provision of existing law and unless a subsequent statute otherwise provides:
     (a) when absolute liability is imposed with respect to any material element of an
offense defined by a statute other than the Code and a conviction is based upon such
liability, the offense constitutes a violation; and
     (b) although absolute liability is imposed by law with respect to one or more of the
material elements of an offense defined by a statute other than the Code, the culpable
commission of the offense may be charged and proved, in which event negligence with
respect to such elements constitutes sufficient culpability and the classification of the
offense and the sentence that may be imposed therefor upon conviction are determined by Section 1.04 and Article 6 of the Code.

SECTION 2.06.   LIABILITY FOR CONDUCT OF ANOTHER; COMPLICITY

(1) A person is guilty of an offense if it is committed by his own conduct or by the
conduct of another person for which he is legally accountable, or both.
(2) A person is legally accountable for the conduct of another person when:
     (a) acting with the kind of culpability that is sufficient for the commission of the
offense, he causes an innocent or irresponsible person to engage in such conduct; or
     (b) he is made accountable for the conduct of such other person by the Code or by
the law defining the offense; or
     (c) he is an accomplice of such other person in the commission of the offense.
(3) A person is an accomplice of another person in the commission of an offense if:
     (a) with the purpose of promoting or facilitating the commission of the offense, he
          (i) solicits such other person to commit it; or
          (ii) aids or agrees or attempts to aid such other person in planning or commit-
     ting it; or
          (iii) having a legal duty to prevent the commission of the offense, fails to make
     proper effort so to do; or
     (b) his conduct is expressly declared by law to establish his complicity.
(4) When causing a particular result is an element of an offense, an accomplice in the
conduct causing such result is an accomplice in the commission of that offense, if he acts
with the kind of culpability, if any, with respect to that result that is sufficient for the
commission of the offense.
(5) A person who is legally incapable of committing a particular offense himself may
be guilty thereof if it is committed by the conduct of another person for which he is
legally accountable, unless such liability is inconsistent with the purpose of the provision
establishing his incapacity.
(6) Unless otherwise provided by the Code or by the law defining the offense, a person is not an accomplice in an offense committed by another person if:

(a) he is a victim of that offense; or

(b) the offense is so defined that his conduct is inevitably incident to its commission; or

(c) he terminates his complicity prior to the commission of the offense and

(i) wholly deprives it of effectiveness in the commission of the offense; or

(ii) gives timely warning to the law enforcement authorities or otherwise makes proper effort to prevent the commission of the offense.

(7) An accomplice may be convicted on proof of the commission of the offense and of his complicity therein, though the person claimed to have committed the offense has not been prosecuted or convicted or has been convicted of a different offense or degree of offense or has an immunity to prosecution or conviction or has been acquitted.

SECTION 2.07.   LIABILITY OF CORPORATIONS, UNINCORPORATED ASSOCIATIONS AND PERSONS ACTING, OR UNDER A DUTY TO ACT, IN THEIR BEHALF

(1) A corporation may be convicted of the commission of an offense if:

(a) the offense is a violation or the offense is defined by a statute other than the Code in which a legislative purpose to impose liability on corporations plainly appears and the conduct is performed by an agent of the corporation acting in behalf of the corporation within the scope of his office or employment, except that if the law defining the offense designates the agents for whose conduct the corporation is accountable or the circumstances under which it is accountable, such provisions shall apply; or

(b) the offense consists of an omission to discharge a specific duty of affirmative performance imposed on corporations by law; or

(c) the commission of the offense was authorized, requested, commanded, performed or recklessly tolerated by the board of directors or by a high managerial agent acting in behalf of the corporation within the scope of his office or employment.

(2) When absolute liability is imposed for the commission of an offense, a legislative purpose to impose liability on a corporation shall be assumed, unless the contrary plainly appears.

(3) An unincorporated association may be convicted of the commission of an offense if:

(a) the offense is defined by a statute other than the Code which expressly provides for the liability of such an association and the conduct is performed by an agent of the association acting in behalf of the association within the scope of his office or employment, except that if the law defining the offense designates the agents for whose conduct the association is accountable or the circumstances under which it is accountable, such provisions shall apply; or

(b) the offense consists of an omission to discharge a specific duty of affirmative performance imposed on associations by law.

(4) As used in this Section:

(a) "corporation" does not include an entity organized as or by a governmental agency for the execution of a governmental program;

(b) "agent" means any director, officer, servant, employee or other person authorized to act in behalf of the corporation or association and, in the case of an unincorporated association, a member of such association;

(c) "high managerial agent" means an officer of a corporation or an unincorporated association, or, in the case of a partnership, a partner, or any other agent of a corporation or association having duties of such responsibility that his conduct may fairly be assumed to represent the policy of the corporation or association.

(5) In any prosecution of a corporation or an unincorporated association for the commission of an offense included within the terms of Subsection (1)(a) or Subsection

(3) (a) of this Section, other than an offense for which absolute liability has been imposed, it shall be a defense if the defendant proves by a preponderance of evidence that the high managerial agent having supervisory responsibility over the subject matter of the offense employed due diligence to prevent its commission. This paragraph shall not apply if it is plainly inconsistent with the legislative purpose in defining the particular offense.

(6) (a) A person is legally accountable for any conduct he performs or causes to be performed in the name of the corporation or an unincorporated association or in its behalf to the same extent as if it were performed in his own name or behalf.

(b) Whenever a duty to act is imposed by law upon a corporation or an unincorporated association, any agent of the corporation or association having primary responsibility for the discharge of the duty is legally accountable for a reckless omission to perform the required act to the same extent as if the duty were imposed by law directly upon himself.

(c) When a person is convicted of an offense by reason of his legal accountability for the conduct of a corporation or an unincorporated association, he is subject to the sentence authorized by law when a natural person is convicted of an offense of the grade and the degree involved.

SECTION 2.08.   INTOXICATION

(1) Except as provided in Subsection (4) of this Section, intoxication of the actor is not a defense unless it negatives an element of the offense.

(2) When recklessness establishes an element of the offense, if the actor, due to self-induced intoxication, is unaware of a risk of which he would have been aware had he been sober, such unawareness is immaterial.

(3) Intoxication does not, in itself, constitute mental disease within the meaning of Section 4.01.

(4) Intoxication which (a) is not self-induced or (b) is pathological is an affirmative defense if by reason of such intoxication the actor at the time of his conduct lacks substantial capacity either to appreciate its criminality [wrongfulness] or to conform his conduct to the requirements of law.

(5) *Definitions.* In this Section unless a different meaning plainly is required:

(a) "intoxication" means a disturbance of mental or physical capacities resulting from the introduction of substances into the body;

(b) "self-induced intoxication" means intoxication caused by substances which the actor knowingly introduces into his body, the tendency of which to cause intoxication he knows or ought to know, unless he introduces them pursuant to medical advice or under such circumstances as would afford a defense to a charge of crime;

(c) "pathological intoxication" means intoxication grossly excessive in degree, given the amount of the intoxicant, to which the actor does not know he is susceptible.

SECTION 2.09.   DURESS

(1) It is an affirmative defense that the actor engaged in the conduct charged to constitute an offense because he was coerced to do so by the use of, or a threat to use, unlawful force against his person or the person of another, which a person of reasonable firmness in his situation would have been unable to resist.

(2) The defense provided by this Section is unavailable if the actor recklessly placed himself in a situation in which it was probable that he would be subjected to duress. The defense is also unavailable if he was negligent in placing himself in such a situation, whenever negligence suffices to establish culpability for the offense charged.

(3) It is not a defense that a woman acted on the command of her husband, unless she acted under such coercion as would establish a defense under this Section. [The presumption that a woman, acting in the presence of her husband, is coerced is abolished.]

(4) When the conduct of the actor would otherwise be justifiable under Section 3.02, this Section does not preclude such defense.

SECTION 2.10. MILITARY ORDERS

It is an affirmative defense that the actor, in engaging in the conduct charged to constitute an offense, does no more than execute an order of his superior in the armed services which he does not know to be unlawful.

SECTION 2.11. CONSENT

(1) *In General.* The consent of the victim to conduct charged to constitute an offense or to the result thereof is a defense if such consent negatives an element of the offense or precludes the infliction of the harm or evil sought to be prevented by the law defining the offense.

(2) *Consent to Bodily Harm.* When conduct is charged to constitute an offense because it causes or threatens bodily harm, consent to such conduct or to the infliction of such harm is a defense if:

(a) the bodily harm consented to or threatened by the conduct consented to is not serious; or

(b) the conduct and the harm are reasonably foreseeable hazards of joint participation in a lawful athletic contest or competitive sport; or

(c) the consent establishes a justification for the conduct under Article 3 of the Code.

(3) *Ineffective Consent.* Unless otherwise provided by the Code or by the law defining the offense, assent does not constitute consent if:

(a) it is given by a person who is legally incompetent to authorize the conduct charged to constitute the offense; or

(b) it is given by a person who by reason of youth, mental disease or defect or intoxication is manifestly unable or known by the actor to be unable to make a reasonable judgment as to the nature or harmfulness of the conduct charged to constitute the offense; or

(c) it is given by a person whose improvident consent is sought to be prevented by the law defining the offense; or

(d) it is induced by force, duress or deception of a kind sought to be prevented by the law defining the offense.

SECTION 2.12. DE MINIMIS INFRACTIONS

The Court shall dismiss a prosecution if, having regard to the nature of the conduct charged to constitute an offense and the nature of the attendant circumstances, it finds that the defendant's conduct:

(1) was within a customary license or tolerance, neither expressly negatived by the person whose interest was infringed nor inconsistent with the purpose of the law defining the offense; or

(2) did not actually cause or threaten the harm or evil sought to be prevented by the

law defining the offense or did so only to an extent too trivial to warrant the condemnation of conviction; or

(3) presents such other extenuations that it cannot reasonably be regarded as envisaged by the legislature in forbidding the offense.

The Court shall not dismiss a prosecution under Subsection (3) of this Section without filing a written statement of its reasons.

SECTION 2.13.   ENTRAPMENT

(1) A public law enforcement official or a person acting in cooperation with such an official perpetrates an entrapment if for the purpose of obtaining evidence of the commission of an offense, he induces or encourages another person to engage in conduct constituting such offense by either:

(a) making knowingly false representations designed to induce the belief that such conduct is not prohibited; or

(b) employing methods of persuasion or inducement which create a substantial risk that such an offense will be committed by persons other than those who are ready to commit it.

(2) Except as provided in Subsection (3) of this Section, a person prosecuted for an offense shall be acquitted if he proves by a preponderance of evidence that his conduct occurred in response to an entrapment. The issue of entrapment shall be tried by the Court in the absence of the jury.

(3) The defense afforded by this Section is unavailable when causing or threatening bodily injury is an element of the offense charged and the prosecution is based on conduct causing or threatening such injury to a person other than the person perpetrating the entrapment.

Article 3.   General Principles of Justification

SECTION 3.01.   JUSTIFICATION AN AFFIRMATIVE DEFENSE; CIVIL REMEDIES UNAFFECTED

(1) In any prosecution based on conduct which is justifiable under this Article, justification is an affirmative defense.

(2) The fact that conduct is justifiable under this Article does not abolish or impair any remedy for such conduct which is available in any civil action.

SECTION 3.02.   JUSTIFICATION GENERALLY: CHOICE OF EVILS

(1) Conduct which the actor believes to be necessary to avoid a harm or evil to himself or to another is justifiable, provided that:

(a) the harm or evil sought to be avoided by such conduct is greater than that sought to be prevented by the law defining the offense charged; and

(b) neither the Code nor other law defining the offense provides exceptions or defenses dealing with the specific situation involved; and

(c) a legislative purpose to exclude the justification claimed does not otherwise plainly appear.

(2) When the actor was reckless or negligent in bringing about the situation requiring a choice of harms or evils or in appraising the necessity for his conduct, the justification afforded by this section is unavailable in a prosecution for any offense for which recklessness or negligence, as the case may be, suffices to establish culpability.

SECTION 3.03.   EXECUTION OF PUBLIC DUTY

(1) Except as provided in Subsection (2) of this Section, conduct is justifiable when it is required or authorized by:

(a) the law defining the duties or functions of a public officer or the assistance to be rendered to such officer in the performance of his duties; or

(b) the law governing the execution of legal process; or

(c) the judgment or order of a competent court or tribunal; or

(d) the law governing the armed services or the lawful conduct of war; or

(e) any other provision of law imposing a public duty.

(2) The other sections of this Article apply to:

(a) the use of force upon or toward the person of another for any of the purposes dealt with in such sections; and

(b) the use of deadly force for any purpose, unless the use of such force is otherwise expressly authorized by law or occurs in the lawful conduct of war.

(3) The justification afforded by Subsection (1) of this Section applies:

(a) when the actor believes his conduct to be required or authorized by the judgment or direction of a competent court or tribunal or in the lawful execution of legal process, notwithstanding lack of jurisdiction of the court or defect in the legal process; and

(b) when the actor believes his conduct to be required or authorized to assist a public officer in the performance of his duties, notwithstanding that the officer exceeded his legal authority.

SECTION 3.04.   USE OF FORCE IN SELF-PROTECTION

(1) *Use of Force Justifiable for Protection of the Person.* Subject to the provisions of this Section and of Section 3.09, the use of force upon or toward another person is justifiable when the actor believes that such force is immediately necessary for the purpose of protecting himself against the use of unlawful force by such other person on the present occasion.

(2) *Limitations on Justifying Necessity for Use of Force.*

(a) The use of force is not justifiable under this Section:

(i) to resist an arrest which the actor knows is being made by a peace officer, although the arrest is unlawful; or

(ii) to resist force used by the occupier or possessor of property or by another person on his behalf, where the actor knows that the person using the force is doing so under a claim of right to protect the property, except that this limitation shall not apply if:

(1) the actor is a public officer acting in the performance of his duties or a person lawfully assisting him therein or a person making or assisting in a lawful arrest; or

(2) the actor has been unlawfully dispossessed of the property and is making a re-entry or recaption justified by Section 3.06; or

(3) the actor believes that such force is necessary to protect himself against death or serious bodily harm.

(b) The use of deadly force is not justifiable under this Section unless the actor believes that such force is necessary to protect himself against death, serious bodily harm, kidnapping or sexual intercourse compelled by force or threat; nor is it justifiable if:

(i) the actor, with the purpose of causing death or serious bodily harm, provoked the use of force against himself in the same encounter; or

(ii) the actor knows that he can avoid the necessity of using such force with complete safety by retreating or by surrendering possession of a thing to a person asserting a claim of right thereto or by complying with a demand that he abstain from any action which he has no duty to take, except that:

(1) the actor is not obliged to retreat from his dwelling or place of work, unless he was the initial aggressor or is assailed in his place of work by another person whose place of work the actor knows it to be; and

(2) a public officer justified in using force in the performance of his duties or a person justified in using force in his assistance or a person justified in using force in making an arrest or preventing an escape is not obliged to desist from efforts to perform such duty, effect such arrest or prevent such escape because of resistance or threatened resistance by or on behalf of the person against whom such action is directed.

(c) Except as required by paragraphs (a) and (b) of this Subsection, a person employing protective force may estimate the necessity thereof under the circumstances as he believes them to be when the force is used, without retreating, surrendering possession, doing any other act which he has no legal duty to do or abstaining from any lawful action.

(3) *Use of Confinement as Protective Force.* The justification afforded by this Section extends to the use of confinement as protective force only if the actor takes all reasonable measures to terminate the confinement as soon as he knows that he safely can, unless the person confined has been arrested on a charge of crime.

SECTION 3.05.   USE OF FORCE FOR THE PROTECTION OF OTHER PERSONS

(1) Subject to the provisions of this Section and of Section 3.09, the use of force upon or toward the person of another is justifiable to protect a third person when:

(a) the actor would be justified under Section 3.04 in using such force to protect himself against the injury he believes to be threatened to the person whom he seeks to protect; and

(b) under the circumstances as the actor believes them to be, the person whom he seeks to protect would be justified in using such protective force; and

(c) the actor believes that his intervention is necessary for the protection of such other person.

(2) Notwithstanding Subsection (1) of this Section:

(a) when the actor would be obliged under Section 3.04 to retreat, to surrender the possession of a thing or to comply with a demand before using force in self-protection, he is not obliged to do so before using force for the protection of another person, unless he knows that he can thereby secure the complete safety of such other person; and

(b) when the person whom the actor seeks to protect would be obliged under Section 3.04 to retreat, to surrender the possession of a thing or to comply with a demand if he knew that he could obtain complete safety by so doing, the actor is obliged to try to cause him to do so before using force in his protection if the actor knows that he can obtain complete safety in that way; and

(c) neither the actor nor the person whom he seeks to protect is obliged to retreat when in the other's dwelling or place of work to any greater extent than in his own.

SECTION 3.06.   USE OF FORCE FOR THE PROTECTION OF PROPERTY

(1) *Use of Force Justifiable for Protection of Property.* Subject to the provisions of this Section and of Section 3.09, the use of force upon or toward the person of another is justifiable when the actor believes that such force is immediately necessary:

(a) to prevent or terminate an unlawful entry or other trespass upon land or a trespass against or the unlawful carrying away of tangible, movable property, provided that such land or movable property is, or is believed by the actor to be, in his possession or in the possession of another person for whose protection he acts; or

(b) to effect an entry or re-entry upon land or to retake tangible movable property, provided that the actor believes that he or the person by whose authority he acts or a person from whom he or such other person derives title was unlawfully dispossessed of such land or movable property and is entitled to possession, and provided, further, that:

(i) the force is used immediately or on fresh pursuit after such dispossession; or

(ii) the actor believes that the person against whom he uses force has no claim of right to the possession of the property and, in the case of land, the circumstances, as the actor believes them to be, are of such urgency that it would be an exceptional hardship to postpone the entry or re-entry until a court order is obtained.

(2) *Meaning of Possession.* For the purposes of Subsection (1) of this Section:

(a) a person who has parted with the custody of property to another who refuses to restore it to him is no longer in possession, unless the property is movable and was and still is located on land in his possession;

(b) a person who has been dispossessed of land does not regain possession thereof merely by setting foot thereon;

(c) a person who has a license to use or occupy real property is deemed to be in possession thereof except against the licensor acting under claim of right.

(3) *Limitations on Justifiable Use of Force.*

(a) *Request to Desist.* The use of force is justifiable under this Section only if the actor first requests the person against whom such force is used to desist from his interference with the property, unless the actor believes that:

(i) such request would be useless; or

(ii) it would be dangerous to himself or another person to make the request; or

(iii) substantial harm will be done to the physical condition of the property which is sought to be protected before the request can effectively be made.

(b) *Exclusion of Trespasser.* The use of force to prevent or terminate a trespass is not justifiable under this Section if the actor knows that the exclusion of the trespasser will expose him to substantial danger of serious bodily harm.

(c) *Resistance of Lawful Re-entry or Recaption.* The use of force to prevent an entry or re-entry upon land or the recaption of movable property is not justifiable under this Section, although the actor believes that such re-entry or recaption is unlawful, if:

(i) the re-entry or recaption is made by or on behalf of a person who was actually dispossessed of the property; and

(ii) it is otherwise justifiable under paragraph (1)(b) of this Section.

(d) *Use of Deadly Force.* The use of deadly force is not justifiable under this Section unless the actor believes that:

(i) the person against whom the force is used is attempting to dispossess him of his dwelling otherwise than under a claim of right to its possession; or

(ii) the person against whom the force is used is attempting to commit or consummate arson, burglary, robbery or other felonious theft or property destruction and either:

(1) has employed or threatened deadly force against or in the presence of the actor; or

(2) the use of force other than deadly force to prevent the commission or the consummation of the crime would expose the actor or another in his presence to substantial danger of serious bodily harm.

(4) *Use of Confinement as Protective Force.* The justification afforded by this Section extends to the use of confinement as protective force only if the actor takes all reasonable

measures to terminate the confinement as soon as he knows that he can do so with safety to the property, unless the person confined has been arrested on a charge of crime.

(5) *Use of Device to Protect Property.* The justification afforded by this Section extends to the use of a device for the purpose of protecting property only if:

(a) the device is not designed to cause or known to create a substantial risk of causing death or serious bodily harm; and

(b) the use of the particular device to protect the property from entry or trespass is reasonable under the circumstances, as the actor believes them to be; and

(c) the device is one customarily used for such a purpose or reasonable care is taken to make known to probable intruders the fact that it is used.

(6) *Use of Force to Pass Wrongful Obstructor.* The use of force to pass a person whom the actor believes to be purposely or knowingly and unjustifiably obstructing the actor from going to a place to which he may lawfully go is justifiable, provided that:

(a) the actor believes that the person against whom he uses force has no claim of right to obstruct the actor; and

(b) the actor is not being obstructed from entry or movement on land which he knows to be in the possession or custody of the person obstructing him, or in the possession or custody of another person by whose authority the obstructor acts, unless the circumstances, as the actor believes them to be, are of such urgency that it would not be reasonable to postpone the entry or movement on such land until a court order is obtained; and

(c) the force used is not greater than would be justifiable if the person obstructing the actor were using force against him to prevent his passage.

SECTION 3.07.   USE OF FORCE IN LAW ENFORCEMENT

(1) *Use of Force Justifiable to Effect an Arrest.* Subject to the provisions of this Section and of Section 3.09, the use of force upon or toward the person of another is justifiable when the actor is making or assisting in making an arrest and the actor believes that such force is immediately necessary to effect a lawful arrest.

(2) *Limitations on the Use of Force.*

(a) The use of force is not justifiable under this Section unless:

(i) the actor makes known the purpose of the arrest or believes that it is otherwise known by or cannot reasonably be made known to the person to be arrested; and

(ii) when the arrest is made under a warrant, the warrant is valid or believed by the actor to be valid.

(b) The use of deadly force is not justifiable under this Section unless:

(i) the arrest is for a felony; and

(ii) the person effecting the arrest is authorized to act as a peace officer or is assisting a person whom he believes to be authorized to act as a peace officer; and

(iii) the actor believes that the force employed creates no substantial risk of injury to innocent persons; and

(iv) the actor believes that:

(1) the crime for which the arrest is made involved conduct including the use or threatened use of deadly force; or

(2) there is a substantial risk that the person to be arrested will cause death or serious bodily harm if his apprehension is delayed.

(3) *Use of Force to Prevent Escape from Custody.* The use of force to prevent the escape of an arrested person from custody is justifiable when the force could justifiably have been employed to effect the arrest under which the person is in custody, except that a guard or other person authorized to act as a peace officer is justified in using any force, including deadly force, which he believes to be immediately necessary to prevent the escape of

a person from a jail, prison, or other institution for the detention of persons charged with or convicted of a crime.

(4)   *Use of Force by Private Person Assisting an Unlawful Arrest.*

(a)   A private person who is summoned by a peace officer to assist in effecting an unlawful arrest, is justified in using any force which he would be justified in using if the arrest were lawful, provided that he does not believe the arrest is unlawful.

(b)   A private person who assists another private person in effecting an unlawful arrest, or who, not being summoned, assists a peace officer in effecting an unlawful arrest, is justified in using any force which he would be justified in using if the arrest were lawful, provided that (i) he believes the arrest is lawful, and (ii) the arrest would be lawful if the facts were as he believes them to be.

(5)   *Use of Force to Prevent Suicide or the Commission of a Crime.*

(a)   The use of force upon or toward the person of another is justifiable when the actor believes that such force is immediately necessary to prevent such other person from committing suicide, inflicting serious bodily harm upon himself, committing or consummating the commission of a crime involving or threatening bodily harm, damage to or loss of property or a breach of the peace, except that:

(i)   any limitations imposed by the other provisions of this Article on the justifiable use of force in self-protection, for the protection of others, the protection of property, the effectuation of an arrest or the prevention of an escape from custody shall apply notwithstanding the criminality of the conduct against which such force is used; and

(ii)   the use of deadly force is not in any event justifiable under this Subsection unless:

(1)   the actor believes that there is a substantial risk that the person whom he seeks to prevent from committing a crime will cause death or serious bodily harm to another unless the commission or the consummation of the crime is prevented and that the use of such force presents no substantial risk of injury to innocent persons; or

(2)   the actor believes that the use of such force is necessary to suppress a riot or mutiny after the rioters or mutineers have been ordered to disperse and warned, in any particular manner that the law may require, that such force will be used if they do not obey.

(b)   The jurisdiction afforded by this Subsection extends to the use of confinement as preventive force only if the actor takes all reasonable measures to terminate the confinement as soon as he knows that he safely can, unless the person confined has been arrested on a charge of crime.

Section 3.08.   Use of Force by Persons with Special Responsibility
              for Care, Discipline or Safety of Others

The use of force upon or toward the person of another is justifiable if:

(1)   the actor is the parent or guardian or other person similarly responsible for the general care and supervision of a minor or a person acting at the request of such parent, guardian or other responsible person and:

(a)   the force is used for the purpose of safeguarding or promoting the welfare of the minor, including the prevention or punishment of his misconduct; and

(b)   the force used is not designed to cause or known to create a substantial risk of causing death, serious bodily harm, disfigurement, extreme pain or mental distress or gross degradation; or

(2)   the actor is a teacher or a person otherwise entrusted with the care or supervision for a special purpose of a minor and:

(a) the actor believes that the force used is necessary to further such special purpose, including the maintenance of reasonable discipline in a school, class or other group, and that the use of such force is consistent with the welfare of the minor; and

(b) the degree of force, if it had been used by the parent or guardian of the minor, would not be unjustifiable under Subsection (1)(b) of this Section; or

(3) the actor is the guardian or other person similarly responsible for the general care and supervision of an incompetent person; and:

(a) the force is used for the purpose of safeguarding or promoting the welfare of the incompetent person, including the prevention of his misconduct, or, when such incompetent person is in a hospital or other institution for his care and custody, for the maintenance of reasonable discipline in such institution; and

(b) the force used is not designed to cause or known to create a substantial risk of causing death, serious bodily harm, disfigurement, extreme or unnecessary pain, mental distress, or humiliation; or

(4) the actor is a doctor or other therapist or a person assisting him at his direction, and:

(a) the force is used for the purpose of administering a recognized form of treatment which the actor believes to be adapted to promoting the physical or mental health of the patient; and

(b) the treatment is administered with the consent of the patient or, if the patient is a minor or an incompetent person, with the consent of his parent or guardian or other person legally competent to consent in his behalf, or the treatment is administered in an emergency when the actor believes that no one competent to consent can be consulted and that a reasonable person, wishing to safeguard the welfare of the patient, would consent; or

(5) the actor is a warden or other authorized official of a correctional institution, and:

(a) he believes that the force used is necessary for the purpose of enforcing the lawful rules or procedures of the institution, unless his belief in the lawfulness of the rule or procedure sought to be enforced is erroneous and his error is due to ignorance or mistake as to the provisions of the Code, any other provision of the criminal law or the law governing the administration of the institution; and

(b) the nature or degree of force used is not forbidden by Article 303 or 304 of the Code; and

(c) if deadly force is used, its use is otherwise justifiable under this Article; or

(6) the actor is a person responsible for the safety of a vessel or an aircraft or a person acting at his direction, and

(a) he believes that the force used is necessary to prevent interference with the operation of the vessel or aircraft or obstruction of the execution of a lawful order, unless his belief in the lawfulness of the order is erroneous and his error is due to ignorance or mistake as to the law defining his authority; and

(b) if deadly force is used, its use is otherwise justifiable under this Article; or

(7) the actor is a person who is authorized or required by law to maintain order or decorum in a vehicle, train or other carrier or in a place where others are assembled, and:

(a) he believes that the force used is necessary for such purpose; and

(b) the force used is not designed to cause or known to create a substantial risk of causing death, bodily harm, or extreme mental distress.

SECTION 3.09.   MISTAKE OF LAW AS TO UNLAWFULNESS OF FORCE OR LEGALITY OF ARREST;
RECKLESS OR NEGLIGENT USE OF OTHERWISE JUSTIFIABLE FORCE;
RECKLESS OR NEGLIGENT INJURY OR RISK OF INJURY TO INNOCENT PERSONS

(1) The justification afforded by Sections 3.04 to 3.07, inclusive, is unavailable when:

(a) the actor's belief in the unlawfulness of the force or conduct against which he employs protective force or his belief in the lawfulness of an arrest which he endeavors to effect by force is erroneous; and

   (b) his error is due to ignorance or mistake as to the provisions of the Code, any other provision of the criminal law or the law governing the legality of an arrest or search.

   (2) When the actor believes that the use of force upon or toward the person of another is necessary for any of the purposes for which such belief would establish a justification under Sections 3.03 to 3.08 but the actor is reckless or negligent in having such belief or in acquiring or failing to acquire any knowledge or belief which is material to the justifiability of his use of force, the justification afforded by those Sections is unavailable in a prosecution for an offense for which recklessness or negligence, as the case may be, suffices to establish culpability.

   (3) When the actor is justified under Sections 3.03 to 3.08 in using force upon or toward the person of another but he recklessly or negligently injures or creates a risk of injury to innocent persons, the justification afforded by those Sections is unavailable in a prosecution for such recklessness or negligence towards innocent persons.

SECTION 3.10.   JUSTIFICATION IN PROPERTY CRIMES

   Conduct involving the appropriation, seizure or destruction of, damage to, intrusion on or interference with property is justifiable under circumstances which would establish a defense of privilege in a civil action based thereon, unless:

   (1) the Code or the law defining the offense deals with the specific situation involved; or

   (2) a legislative purpose to exclude the justification claimed otherwise plainly appears.

SECTION 3.11.   DEFINITIONS

   In this Article, unless a different meaning plainly is required:

   (1) "unlawful force" means force, including confinement, which is employed without the consent of the person against whom it is directed and the employment of which constitutes an offense or actionable tort or would constitute such offense or tort except for a defense (such as the absence of intent, negligence, or mental capacity; duress; youth; or diplomatic status) not amounting to a privilege to use the force. Assent constitutes consent, within the meaning of this Section, whether or not it otherwise is legally effective, except assent to the infliction of death or serious bodily harm.

   (2) "deadly force" means force which the actor uses with the purpose of causing or which he knows to create a substantial risk of causing death or serious bodily harm. Purposely firing a firearm in the direction of another person or at a vehicle in which another person is believed to be constitutes deadly force. A threat to cause death or serious bodily harm, by the production of a weapon or otherwise, so long as the actor's purpose is limited to creating an apprehension that he will use deadly force if necessary, does not constitute deadly force.

   (3) "dwelling" means any building or structure, though movable or temporary, or a portion thereof, which is for the time being the actor's home or place of lodging.

Article 4.   Responsibility

SECTION 4.01.   MENTAL DISEASE OR DEFECT EXCLUDING RESPONSIBILITY

   (1) A person is not responsible for criminal conduct if at the time of such conduct as a result of mental disease or defect he lacks substantial capacity either to appreciate the

criminality [wrongfulness] of his conduct or to conform his conduct to the requirements of law.

(2) As used in this Article, the terms "mental disease or defect" do not include an abnormality manifested only by repeated criminal or otherwise anti-social conduct.

SECTION 4.02.   EVIDENCE OF MENTAL DISEASE OR DEFECT ADMISSIBLE WHEN RELEVANT TO
            ELEMENT OF THE OFFENSE; [MENTAL DISEASE OR DEFECT IMPAIRING CAPACITY
            AS GROUND FOR MITIGATION OF PUNISHMENT IN CAPITAL CASES]

(1) Evidence that the defendant suffered from a mental disease or defect is admissible whenever it is relevant to prove that the defendant did or did not have a state of mind which is an element of the offense.

[(2) Whenever the jury or the Court is authorized to determine or to recommend whether or not the defendant shall be sentenced to death or imprisonment upon conviction, evidence that the capacity of the defendant to appreciate the criminality [wrongfulness] of his conduct or to conform his conduct to the requirements of law was impaired as a result of mental disease or defect is admissible in favor of sentence of imprisonment.]

SECTION 4.03.   MENTAL DISEASE OR DEFECT EXCLUDING RESPONSIBILITY IS AFFIRMATIVE
            DEFENSE; REQUIREMENT OF NOTICE; FORM OF VERDICT AND JUDGMENT
            WHEN FINDING OF IRRESPONSIBILITY IS MADE

(1) Mental disease or defect excluding responsibility is an affirmative defense.

(2) Evidence of mental disease or defect excluding responsibility is not admissible unless the defendant, at the time of entering his plea of not guilty or within ten days thereafter or at such later time as the Court may for good cause permit, files a written notice of his purpose to rely on such defense.

(3) When the defendant is acquitted on the ground of mental disease or defect excluding responsibility, the verdict and the judgment shall so state.

SECTION 4.04.   MENTAL DISEASE OR DEFECT EXCLUDING FITNESS TO PROCEED

No person who as a result of mental disease or defect lacks capacity to understand the proceedings against him or to assist in his own defense shall be tried, convicted or sentenced for the commission of an offense so long as such incapacity endures.

SECTION 4.05.   PSYCHIATRIC EXAMINATION OF DEFENDANT WITH RESPECT TO MENTAL DISEASE
            OR DEFECT

(1) Whenever the defendant has filed a notice of intention to rely on the defense of mental disease or defect excluding responsibility, or there is reason to doubt his fitness to proceed, or reason to believe that mental disease or defect of the defendant will otherwise become an issue in the cause, the Court shall appoint at least one qualified psychiatrist or shall request the Superintendent of the _____ Hospital to designate at least one qualified psychiatrist, which designation may be or include himself, to examine and report upon the mental condition of the defendant. The Court may order the defendant to be committed to a hospital or other suitable facility for the purpose of the examination for a period of not exceeding sixty days or such longer period as the Court deter-

mines to be necessary for the purpose and may direct that a qualified psychiatrist retained by the defendant be permitted to witness and participate in the examination.

(2) In such examination any method may be employed which is accepted by the medical profession for the examination of those alleged to be suffering from mental disease or defect.

(3) The report of the examination shall include the following: (a) a description of the nature of the examination; (b) a diagnosis of the mental condition of the defendant; (c) if the defendant suffers from a mental disease or defect, an opinion as to his capacity to understand the proceedings against him and to assist in his own defense; (d) when a notice of intention to rely on the defense of irresponsibility has been filed, an opinion as to the extent, if any, to which the capacity of the defendant to appreciate the criminality [wrongfulness] of his conduct or to conform his conduct to the requirements of law was impaired at the time of the criminal conduct charged; and (e) when directed by the Court, an opinion as to the capacity of the defendant to have a particular state of mind which is an element of the offense charged.

If the examination can not be conducted by reason of the unwillingness of the defendant to participate therein, the report shall so state and shall include, if possible, an opinion as to whether such unwillingness of the defendant was the result of mental disease or defect.

The report of the examination shall be filed [in triplicate] with the clerk of the Court, who shall cause copies to be delivered to the district attorney and to counsel for the defendant.

SECTION 4.06.   DETERMINATION OF FITNESS TO PROCEED; EFFECT OF FINDING OF UNFITNESS; PROCEEDINGS IF FITNESS IS REGAINED[; POST-COMMITMENT HEARING]

(1) When the defendant's fitness to proceed is drawn in question, the issue shall be determined by the Court. If neither the prosecuting attorney nor counsel for the defendant contests the finding of the report filed pursuant to Section 4.05, the Court may make the determination on the basis of such report. If the finding is contested, the Court shall hold a hearing on the issue. If the report is received in evidence upon such hearing, the party who contests the finding thereof shall have the right to summon and to cross-examine the psychiatrists who joined in the report and to offer evidence upon the issue.

(2) If the Court determines that the defendant lacks fitness to proceed, the proceeding against him shall be suspended, except as provided in Subsection (3) [Subsections (3) and (4)] of this Section, and the Court shall commit him to the custody of the Commissioner of Mental Hygiene [Public Health or Correction] to be placed in an appropriate institution of the Department of Mental Hygiene [Public Health or Correction] for so long as such unfitness shall endure. When the Court, on its own motion or upon the application of the Commissioner of Mental Hygiene [Public Health or Correction] or the prosecuting attorney, determines, after a hearing if a hearing is requested, that the defendant has regained fitness to proceed, the proceeding shall be resumed. If, however, the Court is of the view that so much time has elapsed since the commitment of the defendant that it would be unjust to resume the criminal proceeding, the Court may dismiss the charge and may order the defendant to be discharged or, subject to the law governing the civil commitment of persons suffering from mental disease or defect, order the defendant to be committed to an appropriate institution of the Department of Mental Hygiene [Public Health].

(3) The fact that the defendant is unfit to proceed does not preclude any legal objection to the prosecution which is susceptible of fair determination prior to trial and without the personal participation of the defendant.

[Alternative: (3) At any time within ninety days after commitment as provided in Subsection (2) of this Section, or at any later time with permission of the Court granted for good cause, the defendant or his counsel or the Commissioner of Mental Hygiene [Public Health or Correction] may apply for a special post-commitment hearing. If the application is made by or on behalf of a defendant not represented by counsel, he shall be afforded a reasonable opportunity to obtain counsel, and if he lacks funds to do so, counsel shall be assigned by the Court. The application shall be granted only if the counsel for the defendant satisfies the Court by affidavit or otherwise that as an attorney he has reasonable grounds for a good faith belief that his client has, on the facts and the law, a defense to the charge other than mental disease or defect excluding responsibility.

[(4) If the motion for a special post-commitment hearing is granted, the hearing shall be by the Court without a jury. No evidence shall be offered at the hearing by either party on the issue of mental disease or defect as a defense to, or in mitigation of, the crime charged. After hearing, the Court may in an appropriate case quash the indictment or other charge, or find it to be defective or insufficient, or determine that it is not proved beyond a reasonable doubt by the evidence, or otherwise terminate the proceedings on the evidence or the law. In any such case, unless all defects in the proceedings are promptly cured, the Court shall terminate the commitment ordered under Subsection (2) of this Section and order the defendant to be discharged or, subject to the law governing the civil commitment of persons suffering from mental disease or defect, order the defendant to be committed to an appropriate institution of the Department of Mental Hygiene [Public Health].]

SECTION 4.07.   DETERMINATION OF IRRESPONSIBILITY ON BASIS OF REPORT; ACCESS TO DEFENDANT BY PSYCHIATRIST OF HIS OWN CHOICE; FORM OF EXPERT TESTIMONY WHEN ISSUE OF RESPONSIBILITY IS TRIED

(1) If the report filed pursuant to Section 4.05 finds that the defendant at the time of the criminal conduct charged suffered from a mental disease or defect which substantially impaired his capacity to appreciate the criminality [wrongfulness] of his conduct or to conform his conduct to the requirements of law, and the Court, after a hearing if a hearing is requested by the prosecuting attorney or the defendant, is satisfied that such impairment was sufficient to exclude responsibility, the Court on motion of the defendant shall enter judgment of acquittal on the ground of mental disease or defect excluding responsibility.

(2) When, notwithstanding the report filed pursuant to Section 4.05, the defendant wishes to be examined by a qualified psychiatrist or other expert of his own choice, such examiner shall be permitted to have reasonable access to the defendant for the purposes of such examination.

(3) Upon the trial, the psychiatrists who reported pursuant to Section 4.05 may be called as witnesses by the prosecution, the defendant or the Court. If the issue is being tried before a jury, the jury may be informed that the psychiatrists were designated by the Court or by the Superintendent of the _____ Hospital at the request of the Court, as the case may be. If called by the Court, the witness shall be subject to cross-examination by the prosecution and by the defendant. Both the prosecution and the defendant may summon any other qualified psychiatrist or other expert to testify, but no one who has not examined the defendant shall be competent to testify to an expert opinion with respect to the mental condition or responsibility of the defendant, as distinguished from the validity of the procedure followed by, or the general scientific propositions stated by, another witness.

(4) When a psychiatrist or other expert who has examined the defendant testifies concerning his mental condition, he shall be permitted to make a statement as to the nature of his examination, his diagnosis of the mental condition of the defendant at the time of the commission of the offense charged and his opinion as to the extent, if any,

to which the capacity of the defendant to appreciate the criminality [wrongfulness] of his conduct or to conform his conduct to the requirements of law or to have a particular state of mind which is an element of the offense charged was impaired as a result of mental disease or defect at that time. He shall be permitted to make any explanation reasonably serving to clarify his diagnosis and opinion and may be cross-examined as to any matter bearing on his competency or credibility or the validity of his diagnosis or opinion.

SECTION 4.08.   LEGAL EFFECT OF ACQUITTAL ON THE GROUND OF MENTAL DISEASE OR DEFECT EXCLUDING RESPONSIBILITY; COMMITMENT; RELEASE OR DISCHARGE

(1) When a defendant is acquitted on the ground of mental disease or defect excluding responsibility, the Court shall order him to be committed to the custody of the Commissioner of Mental Hygiene [Public Health] to be placed in an appropriate institution for custody, care and treatment.

(2) If the Commissioner of Mental Hygiene [Public Health] is of the view that a person committed to his custody, pursuant to paragraph (1) of this Section, may be discharged or released on condition without danger to himself or to others, he shall make application for the discharge or release of such person in a report to the Court by which such person was committed and shall transmit a copy of such application and report to the prosecuting attorney of the county [parish] from which the defendant was committed. The Court shall thereupon appoint at least two qualified psychiatrists to examine such person and to report within sixty days, or such longer period as the Court determines to be necessary for the purpose, their opinion as to his mental condition. To facilitate such examination and the proceedings thereon, the Court may cause such person to be confined in any institution located near the place where the Court sits, which may hereafter be designated by the Commissioner of Mental Hygiene [Public Health] as suitable for the temporary detention of irresponsible persons.

(3) If the Court is satisfied by the report filed pursuant to paragraph (2) of this Section and such testimony of the reporting psychiatrists as the Court deems necessary that the committed person may be discharged or released on condition without danger to himself or others, the Court shall order his discharge or his release on such conditions as the Court determines to be necessary. If the Court is not so satisfied, it shall promptly order a hearing to determine whether such person may safely be discharged or released. Any such hearing shall be deemed a civil proceeding and the burden shall be upon the committed person to prove that he may safely be discharged or released. According to the determination of the Court upon the hearing, the committed person shall thereupon be discharged or released on such conditions as the Court determines to be necessary, or shall be recommitted to the custody of the Commissioner of Mental Hygiene [Public Health], subject to discharge or release only in accordance with the procedure prescribed above for a first hearing.

(4) If, within [five] years after the conditional release of a committed person, the Court shall determine, after hearing evidence, that the conditions of release have not been fulfilled and that for the safety of such person or for the safety of others his conditional release should be revoked, the Court shall forthwith order him to be recommitted to the Commissioner of Mental Hygiene [Public Health], subject to discharge or release only in accordance with the procedure prescribed above for a first hearing.

(5) A committed person may make application for his discharge or release to the Court by which he was committed, and the procedure to be followed upon such application shall be the same as that prescribed above in the case of an application by the Commissioner of Mental Hygiene [Public Health]. However, no such application by a committed person need be considered until he has been confined for a period of not less than [six months] from the date of the order of commitment, and if the determina-

tion of the Court be adverse to the application, such person shall not be permitted to file a further application until [one year] has elapsed from the date of any preceding hearing on an application for his release or discharge.

SECTION 4.09.   STATEMENTS FOR PURPOSES OF EXAMINATION OR TREATMENT INADMISSIBLE
                 EXCEPT ON ISSUE OF MENTAL CONDITION

A statement made by a person subjected to psychiatric examination or treatment pursuant to Sections 4.05, 4.06 or 4.08 for the purposes of such examination or treatment shall not be admissible in evidence against him in any criminal proceeding on any issue other than that of his mental condition but it shall be admissible upon that issue, whether or not it would otherwise be deemed a privileged communication [, unless such statement constitutes an admission of guilt of the crime charged].

SECTION 4.10.   IMMATURITY EXCLUDING CRIMINAL CONVICTION; TRANSFER OF PROCEEDINGS
                 TO JUVENILE COURT

(1) A person shall not be tried for or convicted of an offense if:
(a) at the time of the conduct charged to constitute the offense he was less than sixteen years of age [, in which case the Juvenile Court shall have exclusive jurisdiction]; or
(b) at the time of the conduct charged to constitute the offense he was sixteen or seventeen years of age, unless:
(i) the Juvenile Court has no jurisdiction over him, or,
(ii) the Juvenile Court has entered an order waiving jurisdiction and consenting to the institution of criminal proceedings against him.
(2) No court shall have jurisdiction to try or convict a person of an offense if criminal proceedings against him are barred by Subsection (1) of this Section. When it appears that a person charged with the commission of an offense may be of such an age that criminal proceedings may be barred under Subsection (1) of this Section, the Court shall hold a hearing thereon, and the burden shall be on the prosecution to establish to the satisfaction of the Court that the criminal proceeding is not barred upon such grounds. If the Court determines that the proceeding is barred, custody of the person charged shall be surrendered to the Juvenile Court, and the case, including all papers and processes relating thereto, shall be transferred.

Article 5.   Inchoate Crimes

SECTION 5.01.   CRIMINAL ATTEMPT

(1) *Definition of Attempt.* A person is guilty of an attempt to commit a crime if, acting with the kind of culpability otherwise required for commission of the crime, he:
(a) purposely engages in conduct which would constitute the crime if the attendant circumstances were as he believes them to be; or
(b) when causing a particular result is an element of the crime, does or omits to do anything with the purpose of causing or with the belief that it will cause such result without further conduct on his part; or
(c) purposely does or omits to do anything which, under the circumstances as he believes them to be, is an act or omission constituting a substantial step in a course of conduct planned to culminate in his commission of the crime.

(2) *Conduct Which May Be Held Substantial Step Under Subsection (1)(c).* Conduct shall not be held to constitute a substantial step under Subsection (1)(c) of this Section unless it is strongly corroborative of the actor's criminal purpose. Without negativing the sufficiency of other conduct, the following, if strongly corroborative of the actor's criminal purpose, shall not be held insufficient as a matter of law:

(a) lying in wait, searching for or following the contemplated victim of the crime;

(b) enticing or seeking to entice the contemplated victim of the crime to go to the place contemplated for its commission;

(c) reconnoitering the place contemplated for the commission of the crime;

(d) unlawful entry of a structure, vehicle or enclosure in which it is contemplated that the crime will be committed;

(e) possession of materials to be employed in the commission of the crime, which are specially designed for such unlawful use or which can serve no lawful purpose of the actor under the circumstances;

(f) possession, collection or fabrication of materials to be employed in the commission of the crime, at or near the place contemplated for its commission, where such possession, collection or fabrication serves no lawful purpose of the actor under the circumstances;

(g) soliciting an innocent agent to engage in conduct constituting an element of the crime.

(3) *Conduct Designed to Aid Another in Commission of a Crime.* A person who engages in conduct designed to aid another to commit a crime which would establish his complicity under Section 2.06 if the crime were committed by such other person, is guilty of an attempt to commit the crime, although the crime is not committed or attempted by such other person.

(4) *Renunciation of Criminal Purpose.* When the actor's conduct would otherwise constitute an attempt under Subsection (1)(b) or (1)(c) of this Section, it is an affirmative defense that he abandoned his effort to commit the crime or otherwise prevented its commission, under circumstances manifesting a complete and voluntary renunciation of his criminal purpose. The establishment of such defense does not, however, affect the liability of an accomplice who did not join in such abandonment or prevention.

Within the meaning of this Article, renunciation of criminal purpose is not voluntary if it is motivated, in whole or in part, by circumstances, not present or apparent at the inception of the actor's course of conduct, which increase the probability of detection or apprehension or which make more difficult the accomplishment of the criminal purpose. Renunciation is not complete if it is motivated by a decision to postpone the criminal conduct until a more advantageous time or to transfer the criminal effort to another but similar objective or victim.

Section 5.02.   Criminal Solicitation

(1) *Definition of Solicitation.* A person is guilty of solicitation to commit a crime if with the purpose of promoting or facilitating its commission he commands, encourages or requests another person to engage in specific conduct which would constitute such crime or an attempt to commit such crime or which would establish his complicity in its commission or attempted commission.

(2) *Uncommunicated Solicitation.* It is immaterial under Subsection (1) of this Section that the actor fails to communicate with the person he solicits to commit a crime if his conduct was designed to effect such communication.

(3) *Renunciation of Criminal Purpose.* It is an affirmative defense that the actor, after soliciting another person to commit a crime, persuaded him not to do so or otherwise prevented the commission of the crime, under circumstances manifesting a complete and voluntary renunciation of his criminal purpose.

SECTION 5.03.   CRIMINAL CONSPIRACY

(1) *Definition of Conspiracy.* A person is guilty of conspiracy with another person or persons to commit a crime if with the purpose of promoting or facilitating its commission he:

(a) agrees with such other person or persons that they or one or more of them will engage in conduct which constitutes such crime or an attempt or solicitation to commit such crime; or

(b) agrees to aid such other person or persons in the planning or commission of such crime or of an attempt or solicitation to commit such crime.

(2) *Scope of Conspiratorial Relationship.* If a person guilty of conspiracy, as defined by Subsection (1) of this Section, knows that a person with whom he conspires to commit a crime has conspired with another person or persons to commit the same crime, he is guilty of conspiring with such other person or persons, whether or not he knows their identity, to commit such crime.

(3) *Conspiracy With Multiple Criminal Objectives.* If a person conspires to commit a number of crimes, he is guilty of only one conspiracy so long as such multiple crimes are the object of the same agreement or continuous conspiratorial relationship.

(4) *Joinder and Venue in Conspiracy Prosecutions.*

(a) Subject to the provisions of paragraph (b) of this Subsection, two or more persons charged with criminal conspiracy may be prosecuted jointly if:

(i) they are charged with conspiring with one another; or

(ii) the conspiracies alleged, whether they have the same or different parties, are so related that they constitute different aspects of a scheme of organized criminal conduct.

(b) In any joint prosecution under paragraph (a) of this Subsection:

(i) no defendant shall be charged with a conspiracy in any county [parish or district] other than one in which he entered into such conspiracy or in which an overt act pursuant to such conspiracy was done by him or by a person with whom he conspired; and

(ii) neither the liability of any defendant nor the admissibility against him of evidence of acts or declarations of another shall be enlarged by such joinder; and

(iii) the Court shall order a severance or take a special verdict as to any defendant who so requests, if it deems it necessary or appropriate to promote the fair determination of his guilt or innocence, and shall take any other proper measures to protect the fairness of the trial.

(5) *Overt Act.* No person may be convicted of conspiracy to commit a crime, other than a felony of the first or second degree, unless an overt act in pursuance of such conspiracy is alleged and proved to have been done by him or by a person with whom he conspired.

(6) *Renunciation of Criminal Purpose.* It is an affirmative defense that the actor, after conspiring to commit a crime, thwarted the success of the conspiracy, under circumstances manifesting a complete and voluntary renunciation of his criminal purpose.

(7) *Duration of Conspiracy.* For purposes of Section 1.06(4):

(a) conspiracy is a continuing course of conduct which terminates when the crime or crimes which are its object are committed or the agreement that they be committed is abandoned by the defendant and by those with whom he conspired; and

(b) such abandonment is presumed if neither the defendant nor anyone with whom he conspired does any overt act in pursuance of the conspiracy during the applicable period of limitation; and

(c) if an individual abandons the agreement, the conspiracy is terminated as to him only if and when he advises those with whom he conspired of his abandonment or he informs the law enforcement authorities of the existence of the conspiracy and of his participation therein.

Section 5.04. Incapacity, Irresponsibility or Immunity of Party to Solicitation
or Conspiracy

(1) Except as provided in Subsection (2) of this Section, it is immaterial to the liability
of a person who solicits or conspires with another to commit a crime that:

(a) he or the person whom he solicits or with whom he conspires does not occupy
a particular position or have a particular characteristic which is an element of such
crime, if he believes that one of them does; or

(b) the person whom he solicits or with whom he conspires is irresponsible or has
an immunity to prosecution or conviction for the commission of the crime.

(2) It is a defense to a charge of solicitation or conspiracy to commit a crime that if
the criminal object were achieved, the actor would not be guilty of a crime under the law
defining the offense or as an accomplice under Section 2.06(5) or 2.06(6)(a) or (b).

Section 5.05. Grading of Criminal Attempt, Solicitation and Conspiracy; Mitigation
in Cases of Lesser Danger; Multiple Convictions Barred

(1) *Grading.* Except as otherwise provided in this Section, attempt, solicitation and
conspiracy are crimes of the same grade and degree as the most serious offense which is
attempted or solicited or is an object of the conspiracy. An attempt, solicitation or conspiracy to commit a [capital crime or a] felony of the first degree is a felony of the second
degree.

(2) *Mitigation.* If the particular conduct charged to constitute a criminal attempt, solicitation or conspiracy is so inherently unlikely to result or culminate in the commission
of a crime that neither such conduct nor the actor presents a public danger warranting
the grading of such offense under this Section, the Court shall exercise its power under
Section 6.12 to enter judgment and impose sentence for a crime of lower grade or degree or, in extreme cases, may dismiss the prosecution.

(3) *Multiple Convictions.* A person may not be convicted of more than one offense
defined by this Article for conduct designed to commit or to culminate in the commission of the same crime.

Section 5.06. Possessing Instruments of Crime; Weapons

(1) *Criminal Instruments Generally.* A person commits a misdemeanor if he possesses
any instrument of crime with purpose to employ it criminally. "Instrument of crime"
means:

(a) anything specially made or specially adapted for criminal use; or

(b) anything commonly used for criminal purposes and possessed by the actor under circumstances which do not negative unlawful purpose.

(2) *Presumption of Criminal Purpose from Possession of Weapon.* If a person possesses a
firearm or other weapon on or about his person, in a vehicle occupied by him, or otherwise readily available for use, it shall be presumed that he had the purpose to employ
it criminally, unless:

(a) the weapon is possessed in the actor's home or place of business;

(b) the actor is licensed or otherwise authorized by law to possess such weapon; or

(c) the weapon is of a type commonly used in lawful sport.

"Weapon" means anything readily capable of lethal use and possessed under circumstances not manifestly appropriate for lawful uses which it may have; the term
includes a firearm which is not loaded or lacks a clip or other component to render
it immediately operable, and components which can readily be assembled into a
weapon.

(3) *Presumptions as to Possession of Criminal Instruments in Automobiles.* Where a weapon or other instrument of crime is found in an automobile, it is presumed to be in the possession of the occupant if there is but one. If there is more than one occupant, it shall be presumed to be in the possession of all, except under the following circumstances:

(a) where it is found upon the person of one of the occupants;

(b) where the automobile is not a stolen one and the weapon or instrument is found out of view in a glove compartment, car trunk, or other enclosed customary depository, in which case it shall be presumed to be in the possession of the occupant or occupants who own or have authority to operate the automobile;

(c) in the case of a taxicab, a weapon or instrument found in the passengers' portion of the vehicle shall be presumed to be in the possession of all the passengers, if there are any, and, if not, in the possession of the driver.

SECTION 5.07. PROHIBITED OFFENSIVE WEAPONS

A person commits a misdemeanor if, except as authorized by law, he makes, repairs, sells, or otherwise deals in, uses or possesses any offensive weapon. "Offensive weapon" means any bomb, machine gun, sawed-off shotgun, firearm specially made or specially adapted for concealment or silent discharge, any blackjack, sandbag, metal knuckles, dagger, or other implement for the infliction of serious bodily injury which serves no common lawful purpose. It is a defense under this Section for the defendant to prove by a preponderance of evidence that he possessed or dealt with the weapon solely as a curio or in a dramatic performance, or that he possessed it briefly in consequence of having found it or taken it from an aggressor, or under circumstances similarly negativing any purpose or likelihood that the weapon would be used unlawfully. The presumptions provided in Section 5.06(3) are applicable to prosecutions under this Section.

Article 6. Authorized Disposition of Offenders

SECTION 6.01. DEGREES OF FELONIES

(1) Felonies defined by this Code are classified, for the purpose of sentence, into three degrees, as follows:

(a) felonies of the first degree;

(b) felonies of the second degree;

(c) felonies of the third degree.

A felony is of the first or second degree when it is so designated by the Code. A crime declared to be a felony, without specification of degree, is of the third degree.

(2) Notwithstanding any other provision of law, a felony defined by any statute of this State other than this Code shall constitute for the purpose of sentence a felony of the third degree.

SECTION 6.02. SENTENCE IN ACCORDANCE WITH CODE; AUTHORIZED DISPOSITIONS

(1) No person convicted of an offense shall be sentenced otherwise than in accordance with this Article.

[(2) The Court shall sentence a person who has been convicted of murder to death or imprisonment, in accordance with Section 210.6.]

(3) Except as provided in Subsection (2) of this Section and subject to the applicable provisions of the Code, the Court may suspend the imposition of sentence on a person

who has been convicted of a crime, may order him to be committed in lieu of sentence, in accordance with Section 6.13, or may sentence him as follows:

(a) to pay a fine authorized by Section 6.03; or

(b) to be placed on probation [, and, in the case of a person convicted of a felony or misdemeanor to imprisonment for a term fixed by the Court not exceeding thirty days to be served as a condition of probation]; or

(c) to imprisonment for a term authorized by Sections 6.05, 6.06, 6.07, 6.08, 6.09, or 7.06; or

(d) to fine and probation or fine and imprisonment, but not to probation and imprisonment [, except as authorized in paragraph (b) of this Subsection].

(4) The Court may suspend the imposition of sentence on a person who has been convicted of a violation or may sentence him to pay a fine authorized by Section 6.03.

(5) This Article does not deprive the Court of any authority conferred by law to decree a forfeiture of property, suspend or cancel a license, remove a person from office, or impose any other civil penalty. Such a judgment or order may be included in the sentence.

SECTION 6.03.   FINES

A person who has been convicted of an offense may be sentenced to pay a fine not exceeding:

(1) $10,000, when the conviction is of a felony of the first or second degree;

(2) $5,000, when the conviction is of a felony of the third degree;

(3) $1,000, when the conviction is of a misdemeanor;

(4) $500, when the conviction is of a petty misdemeanor or a violation;

(5) any higher amount equal to double the pecuniary gain derived from the offense by the offender;

(6) any higher amount specifically authorized by statute.

SECTION 6.04.   PENALTIES AGAINST CORPORATIONS AND UNINCORPORATED ASSOCIATIONS;
FORFEITURE OF CORPORATE CHARTER OR REVOCATION OF CERTIFICATE
AUTHORIZING FOREIGN CORPORATION TO DO BUSINESS IN THE STATE

(1) The Court may suspend the sentence of a corporation or an unincorporated association which has been convicted of an offense or may sentence it to pay a fine authorized by Section 6.03.

(2) (a) The [prosecuting attorney] is authorized to institute civil proceedings in the appropriate court of general jurisdiction to forfeit the charter of a corporation organized under the laws of this State or to revoke the certificate authorizing a foreign corporation to conduct business in this State. The Court may order the charter forfeited or the certificate revoked upon finding (i) that the board of directors or a high managerial agent acting in behalf of the corporation has, in conducting the corporation's affairs, purposely engaged in a persistent course of criminal conduct and (ii) that for the prevention of future criminal conduct of the same character, the public interest requires the charter of the corporation to be forfeited and the corporation to be dissolved or the certificate to be revoked.

(b) When a corporation is convicted of a crime or a high managerial agent of a corporation, as defined in Section 2.07, is convicted of a crime committed in the conduct of the affairs of the corporation, the Court, in sentencing the corporation or the agent, may direct the [prosecuting attorney] to institute proceedings authorized by paragraph (a) of this Subsection.

(c) The proceedings authorized by paragraph (a) of this Subsection shall be conducted in accordance with the procedures authorized by law for the involuntary dissolution of a corporation or the revocation of the certificate authorizing a foreign corporation to conduct business in this State. Such proceedings shall be deemed additional to any other proceedings authorized by law for the purpose of forfeiting the charter of a corporation or revoking the certificate of a foreign corporation.

SECTION 6.05.   YOUNG ADULT OFFENDERS

(1) *Specialized Correctional Treatment.* A young adult offender is a person convicted of a crime who, at the time of sentencing, is sixteen but less than twenty-two years of age. A young adult offender who is sentenced to a term of imprisonment which may exceed thirty days [alternatives: (1) ninety days; (2) one year] shall be committed to the custody of the Division of Young Adult Correction of the Department of Correction, and shall receive, as far as practicable, such special and individualized correctional and rehabilitative treatment as may be appropriate to his needs.

(2) *Special Term.* A young adult offender convicted of a felony may, in lieu of any other sentence of imprisonment authorized by this Article, be sentenced to a special term of imprisonment without a minimum and with a maximum of four years, regardless of the degree of the felony involved, if the Court is of the opinion that such special term is adequate for his correction and rehabilitation and will not jeopardize the protection of the public.

[(3) *Removal of Disabilities; Vacation of Conviction.*

(a) In sentencing a young adult offender to the special term provided by this Section or to any sentence other than one of imprisonment, the Court may order that so long as he is not convicted of another felony, the judgment shall not constitute a conviction for the purposes of any disqualification or disability imposed by law upon conviction of a crime.

(b) When any young adult offender is unconditionally discharged from probation or parole before the expiration of the maximum term thereof, the Court may enter an order vacating the judgment of conviction.]

[(4) *Commitment for Observation.* If, after pre-sentence investigation, the Court desires additional information concerning a young adult offender before imposing sentence, it may order that he be committed, for a period not exceeding ninety days, to the custody of the Division of Young Adult Correction of the Department of Correction for observation and study at an appropriate reception or classification center. Such Division of the Department of Correction and the [Young Adult Division of the] Board of Parole shall advise the Court of their findings and recommendations on or before the expiration of such ninety-day period.]

SECTION 6.06.   SENTENCE OF IMPRISONMENT FOR FELONY; ORDINARY TERMS

A person who has been convicted of a felony may be sentenced to imprisonment, as follows:

(1) in the case of a felony of the first degree, for a term the minimum of which shall be fixed by the Court at not less than one year nor more than ten years, and the maximum of which shall be life imprisonment;

(2) in the case of a felony of the second degree, for a term the minimum of which shall be fixed by the Court at not less than one year nor more than three years, and the maximum of which shall be ten years;

(3) in the case of a felony of the third degree, for a term the minimum of which shall

be fixed by the Court at not less than one year nor more than two years, and the maximum of which shall be five years.

ALTERNATE SECTION 6.06.   SENTENCE OF IMPRISONMENT FOR FELONY; ORDINARY TERMS

A person who has been convicted of a felony may be sentenced to imprisonment, as follows:

(1) in the case of a felony of the first degree, for a term the minimum of which shall be fixed by the Court at not less than one year nor more than ten years, and the maximum at not more than twenty years or at life imprisonment;

(2) in the case of a felony of the second degree, for a term the minimum of which shall be fixed by the Court at not less than one year nor more than three years, and the maximum at not more than ten years;

(3) in the case of a felony of the third degree, for a term the minimum of which shall be fixed by the Court at not less than one year nor more than two years, and the maximum at not more than five years.

No sentence shall be imposed under this Section of which the minimum is longer than one-half the maximum, or, when the maximum is life imprisonment, longer than ten years.

SECTION 6.07.   SENTENCE OF IMPRISONMENT FOR FELONY; EXTENDED TERMS

In the cases designated in Section 7.03, a person who has been convicted of a felony may be sentenced to an extended term of imprisonment, as follows:

(1) in the case of a felony of the first degree, for a term the minimum of which shall be fixed by the Court at not less than five years nor more than ten years, and the maximum of which shall be life imprisonment;

(2) in the case of a felony of the second degree, for a term the minimum of which shall be fixed by the Court at not less than one year nor more than five years, and the maximum of which shall be fixed by the Court at not less than ten nor more than twenty years;

(3) in the case of a felony of the third degree, for a term the minimum of which shall be fixed by the Court at not less than one year nor more than three years, and the maximum of which shall be fixed by the Court at not less than five nor more than ten years.

SECTION 6.08.   SENTENCE OF IMPRISONMENT FOR MISDEMEANORS AND PETTY MISDEMEANORS;
                ORDINARY TERMS

A person who has been convicted of a misdemeanor or a petty misdemeanor may be sentenced to imprisonment for a definite term which shall be fixed by the Court and shall not exceed one year in the case of a misdemeanor or thirty days in the case of a petty misdemeanor.

SECTION 6.09.   SENTENCE OF IMPRISONMENT FOR MISDEMEANORS AND PETTY MISDEMEANORS;
                EXTENDED TERMS

(1) In the cases designated in Section 7.04, a person who has been convicted of a misdemeanor or a petty misdemeanor may be sentenced to an extended term of imprisonment, as follows:

(a) in the case of a misdemeanor, for a term the minimum of which shall be fixed by the Court at not more than one year and the maximum of which shall be three years;

(b) in the case of a petty misdemeanor, for a term the minimum of which shall be fixed by the Court at not more than six months and the maximum of which shall be two years.

(2) No such sentence for an extended term shall be imposed unless:

(a) the Director of Correction has certified that there is an institution in the Department of Correction, or in a county, city [or other appropriate political subdivision of the State] which is appropriate for the detention and correctional treatment of such misdemeanants or petty misdemeanants, and that such institution is available to receive such commitments; and

(b) the [Board of Parole] [Parole Administrator] has certified that the Board of Parole is able to visit such institution and to assume responsibility for the release of such prisoners on parole and for their parole supervision.

SECTION 6.10.   FIRST RELEASE OF ALL OFFENDERS ON PAROLE; SENTENCE OF IMPRISONMENT
                  INCLUDES SEPARATE PAROLE TERM; LENGTH OF PAROLE TERM; LENGTH
                  OF RECOMMITMENT AND REPAROLE AFTER REVOCATION OF PAROLE;
                  FINAL UNCONDITIONAL RELEASE

(1) *First Release of All Offenders on Parole.* An offender sentenced to an indefinite term of imprisonment in excess of one year under Section 6.05, 6.06, 6.07, 6.09 or 7.06 shall be released conditionally on parole at or before the expiration of the maximum of such term, in accordance with Article 305.

(2) *Sentence of Imprisonment Includes Separate Parole Term; Length of Parole Term.* A sentence to an indefinite term of imprisonment in excess of one year under Section 6.05, 6.06, 6.07, 6.09 or 7.06 includes as a separate portion of the sentence a term of parole or of recommitment for violation of the conditions of parole which governs the duration of parole or recommitment after the offender's first conditional release on parole. The minimum of such term is one year and the maximum is five years, unless the sentence was imposed under Section 6.05(2) or Section 6.09, in which case the maximum is two years.

(3) *Length of Recommitment and Reparole After Revocation of Parole.* If an offender is recommitted upon revocation of his parole, the term of further imprisonment upon such recommitment and of any subsequent reparole or recommitment under the same sentence shall be fixed by the Board of Parole but shall not exceed in aggregate length the unserved balance of the maximum parole term provided by Subsection (2) of this Section.

(4) *Final Unconditional Release.* When the maximum of his parole term has expired or he has been sooner discharged from parole under Section 305.12, an offender shall be deemed to have served his sentence and shall be released unconditionally.

SECTION 6.11.   PLACE OF IMPRISONMENT

(1) When a person is sentenced to imprisonment for an indefinite term with a maximum in excess of one year, the Court shall commit him to the custody of the Department of Correction [or other single department or agency] for the term of his sentence and until release in accordance with law.

(2) When a person is sentenced to imprisonment for a definite term, the Court shall designate the institution or agency to which he is committed for the term of his sentence and until released in accordance with law.

SECTION 6.12.   REDUCTION OF CONVICTION BY COURT TO LESSER DEGREE OF FELONY
                OR TO MISDEMEANOR

If, when a person has been convicted of a felony, the Court, having regard to the nature and circumstances of the crime and to the history and character of the defendant, is of the view that it would be unduly harsh to sentence the offender in accordance with the Code, the Court may enter judgment of conviction for a lesser degree of felony or for a misdemeanor and impose sentence accordingly.

SECTION 6.13.   CIVIL COMMITMENT IN LIEU OF PROSECUTION OR OF SENTENCE

(1) When a person prosecuted for a [felony of the third degree,] misdemeanor or petty misdemeanor is a chronic alcoholic, narcotic addict [or prostitute] or person suffering from mental abnormality and the Court is authorized by law to order the civil commitment of such person to a hospital or other institution for medical, psychiatric or other rehabilitative treatment, the Court may order such commitment and dismiss the prosecution. The order of commitment may be made after conviction, in which event the Court may set aside the verdict or judgment of conviction and dismiss the prosecution.

(2) The Court shall not make an order under Subsection (1) of this Section unless it is of the view that it will substantially further the rehabilitation of the defendant and will not jeopardize the protection of the public.

Article 7.   Authority of Court in Sentencing

SECTION 7.01.   CRITERIA FOR WITHHOLDING SENTENCE OF IMPRISONMENT AND
                FOR PLACING DEFENDANT ON PROBATION

(1) The Court shall deal with a person who has been convicted of a crime without imposing sentence of imprisonment unless, having regard to the nature and circumstances of the crime and the history, character and condition of the defendant, it is of the opinion that his imprisonment is necessary for protection of the public because:

(a) there is undue risk that during the period of a suspended sentence or probation the defendant will commit another crime; or

(b) the defendant is in need of correctional treatment that can be provided most effectively by his commitment to an institution; or

(c) a lesser sentence will depreciate the seriousness of the defendant's crime.

(2) The following grounds, while not controlling the discretion of the Court, shall be accorded weight in favor of withholding sentence of imprisonment:

(a) the defendant's criminal conduct neither caused nor threatened serious harm;

(b) the defendant did not contemplate that his criminal conduct would cause or threaten serious harm;

(c) the defendant acted under a strong provocation;

(d) there were substantial grounds tending to excuse or justify the defendant's criminal conduct, though failing to establish a defense;

(e) the victim of the defendant's criminal conduct induced or facilitated its commission;

(f) the defendant has compensated or will compensate the victim of his criminal conduct for the damage or injury that he sustained;

(g) the defendant has no history of prior delinquency or criminal activity or has led a law-abiding life for a substantial period of time before the commission of the present crime;

(h) the defendant's criminal conduct was the result of circumstances unlikely to recur;

(i) the character and attitudes of the defendant indicate that he is unlikely to commit another crime;

(j) the defendant is particularly likely to respond affirmatively to probationary treatment;

(k) the imprisonment of the defendant would entail excessive hardship to himself or his dependents.

(3) When a person who has been convicted of a crime is not sentenced to imprisonment, the Court shall place him on probation if he is in need of the supervision, guidance, assistance or direction that the probation service can provide.

SECTION 7.02.   CRITERIA FOR IMPOSING FINES

(1) The Court shall not sentence a defendant only to pay a fine, when any other disposition is authorized by law, unless having regard to the nature and circumstances of the crime and to the history and character of the defendant, it is of the opinion that the fine alone suffices for protection of the public.

(2) The Court shall not sentence a defendant to pay a fine in addition to a sentence of imprisonment or probation unless:

(a) the defendant has derived a pecuniary gain from the crime; or

(b) the Court is of opinion that a fine is specially adapted to deterrence of the crime involved or to the correction of the offender.

(3) The Court shall not sentence a defendant to pay a fine unless:

(a) the defendant is or will be able to pay the fine; and

(b) the fine will not prevent the defendant from making restitution or reparation to the victim of the crime.

(4) In determining the amount and method of payment of a fine, the Court shall take into account the financial resources of the defendant and the nature of the burden that its payment will impose.

SECTION 7.03.   CRITERIA FOR SENTENCE OF EXTENDED TERM OF IMPRISONMENT; FELONIES

The Court may sentence a person who has been convicted of a felony to an extended term of imprisonment if it finds one or more of the grounds specified in this Section. The finding of the Court shall be incorporated in the record.

(1) The defendant is a persistent offender whose commitment for an extended term is necessary for protection of the public.

The Court shall not make such a finding unless the defendant is over twenty-one years of age and has previously been convicted of two felonies or of one felony and two misdemeanors, committed at different times when he was over [insert Juvenile Court age] years of age.

(2) The defendant is a professional criminal whose commitment for an extended term is necessary for protection of the public.

The Court shall not make such a finding unless the defendant is over twenty-one years of age and:

(a) the circumstances of the crime show that the defendant has knowingly devoted himself to criminal activity as a major source of livelihood; or

(b) the defendant has substantial income or resources not explained to be derived from a source other than criminal activity.

(3) The defendant is a dangerous, mentally abnormal person whose commitment for an extended term is necessary for protection of the public.

The Court shall not make such a finding unless the defendant has been subjected to a psychiatric examination resulting in the conclusions that his mental condition is gravely abnormal; that his criminal conduct has been characterized by a pattern of repetitive or compulsive behavior or by persistent aggressive behavior with heedless indifference to consequences; and that such condition makes him a serious danger to others.

(4) The defendant is a multiple offender whose criminality was so extensive that a sentence of imprisonment for an extended term is warranted.

The court shall not make such a finding unless:

(a) the defendant is being sentenced for two or more felonies, or is already under sentence of imprisonment for felony, and the sentences of imprisonment involved will run concurrently under Section 7.06; or

(b) the defendant admits in open court the commission of one or more other felonies and asks that they be taken into account when he is sentenced; and

(c) the longest sentences of imprisonment authorized for each of the defendant's crimes, including admitted crimes taken into account, if made to run consecutively would exceed in length the minimum and maximum of the extended term imposed.

SECTION 7.04. CRITERIA FOR SENTENCE OF EXTENDED TERM OF IMPRISONMENT; MISDEMEANORS AND PETTY MISDEMEANORS

The Court may sentence a person who has been convicted of a misdemeanor or petty misdemeanor to an extended term of imprisonment if it finds one or more of the grounds specified in this Section. The finding of the Court shall be incorporated in the record.

(1) The defendant is a persistent offender whose commitment for an extended term is necessary for protection of the public.

The Court shall not make such a finding unless the defendant has previously been convicted of two crimes, committed at different times when he was over [insert Juvenile Court age] years of age.

(2) The defendant is a professional criminal whose commitment for an extended term is necessary for protection of the public.

The Court shall not make such a finding unless:

(a) the circumstances of the crime show that the defendant has knowingly devoted himself to criminal activity as a major source of livelihood; or

(b) the defendant has substantial income or resources not explained to be derived from a source other than criminal activity.

(3) The defendant is a chronic alcoholic, narcotic addict, prostitute or person of abnormal mental condition who requires rehabilitative treatment for a substantial period of time.

The Court shall not make such a finding unless, with respect to the particular category to which the defendant belongs, the Director of Correction has certified that there is a specialized institution or facility which is satisfactory for the rehabilitative treatment of such persons and which otherwise meets the requirements of Section 6.09, Subsection (2).

(4) The defendant is a multiple offender whose criminality was so extensive that a sentence of imprisonment for an extended term is warranted.

The Court shall not make such a finding unless:

(a) the defendant is being sentenced for a number of misdemeanors or petty misdemeanors or is already under sentence of imprisonment for crimes of such grades, or admits in open court the commission of one or more such crimes and asks that they be taken into account when he is sentenced; and

(b) maximum fixed sentences of imprisonment for each of the defendant's crimes, including admitted crimes taken into account, if made to run consecutively, would exceed in length the maximum period of the extended term imposed.

SECTION 7.05.   FORMER CONVICTION IN ANOTHER JURISDICTION; DEFINITION AND PROOF
OF CONVICTION; SENTENCE TAKING INTO ACCOUNT ADMITTED CRIMES
BARS SUBSEQUENT CONVICTION FOR SUCH CRIMES

(1) For purposes of paragraph (1) of Section 7.03 or 7.04, a conviction of the commission of a crime in another jurisdiction shall constitute a previous conviction. Such conviction shall be deemed to have been of a felony if sentence of death or of imprisonment in excess of one year was authorized under the law of such other jurisdiction, of a misdemeanor if sentence of imprisonment in excess of thirty days but not in excess of a year was authorized and of a petty misdemeanor if sentence of imprisonment for not more than thirty days was authorized.

(2) An adjudication by a court of competent jurisdiction that the defendant committed a crime constitutes a conviction for purposes of Sections 7.03 to 7.05 inclusive, although sentence or the execution thereof was suspended, provided that the time to appeal has expired and that the defendant was not pardoned on the ground of innocence.

(3) Prior conviction may be proved by any evidence, including fingerprint records made in connection with arrest, conviction or imprisonment, that reasonably satisfies the Court that the defendant was convicted.

(4) When the defendant has asked that other crimes admitted in open court be taken into account when he is sentenced and the Court has not rejected such request, the sentence shall bar the prosecution or conviction of the defendant in this State for any such admitted crime.

SECTION 7.06.   MULTIPLE SENTENCES; CONCURRENT AND CONSECUTIVE TERMS

(1) *Sentences of Imprisonment for More Than One Crime.* When multiple sentences of imprisonment are imposed on a defendant for more than one crime, including a crime for which a previous suspended sentence or sentence of probation has been revoked, such multiple sentences shall run concurrently or consecutively as the Court determines at the time of sentence, except that:

(a) a definite and an indefinite term shall run concurrently and both sentences shall be satisfied by service of the indefinite term; and

(b) the aggregate of consecutive definite terms shall not exceed one year; and

(c) the aggregate of consecutive indefinite terms shall not exceed in minimum or maximum length the longest extended term authorized for the highest grade and degree of crime for which any of the sentences was imposed; and

(d) not more than one sentence for an extended term shall be imposed.

(2) *Sentences of Imprisonment Imposed at Different Times.* When a defendant who has previously been sentenced to imprisonment is subsequently sentenced to another term for a crime committed prior to the former sentence, other than a crime committed while in custody:

(a) the multiple sentences imposed shall so far as possible conform to Subsection (1) of this Section; and

(b) whether the Court determines that the terms shall run concurrently or consecutively, the defendant shall be credited with time served in imprisonment on the prior sentence in determining the permissible aggregate length of the term or terms remaining to be served; and

(c) when a new sentence is imposed on a prisoner who is on parole, the balance of the parole term on the former sentence shall be deemed to run during the period of the new imprisonment.

(3) *Sentence of Imprisonment for Crime Committed While on Parole.* When a defendant is sentenced to imprisonment for a crime committed while on parole in this State, such

term of imprisonment and any period of reimprisonment that the Board of Parole may require the defendant to serve upon the revocation of his parole shall run concurrently, unless the Court orders them to run consecutively.

(4) *Multiple Sentences of Imprisonment in Other Cases.* Except as otherwise provided in this Section, multiple terms of imprisonment shall run concurrently or consecutively as the Court determines when the second or subsequent sentence is imposed.

(5) *Calculation of Concurrent and Consecutive Terms of Imprisonment.*

(a) When indefinite terms run concurrently, the shorter minimum terms merge in and are satisfied by serving the longest minimum term and the shorter maximum terms merge in and are satisfied by discharge of the longest maximum term.

(b) When indefinite terms run consecutively, the minimum terms are added to arrive at an aggregate minimum to be served equal to the sum of all minimum terms and the maximum terms are added to arrive at an aggregate maximum equal to the sum of all maximum terms.

(c) When a definite and an indefinite term run consecutively, the period of the definite term is added to both the minimum and maximum of the indefinite term and both sentences are satisfied by serving the indefinite term.

(6) *Suspension of Sentence or Probation and Imprisonment; Multiple Terms of Suspension and Probation.* When a defendant is sentenced for more than one offense or a defendant already under sentence is sentenced for another offense committed prior to the former sentence:

(a) the Court shall not sentence to probation a defendant who is under sentence of imprisonment [with more than thirty days to run] or impose a sentence of probation and a sentence of imprisonment [, except as authorized by Section 6.02(3)(b)]; and

(b) multiple periods of suspension or probation shall run concurrently from the date of the first such disposition; and

(c) when a sentence of imprisonment is imposed for an indefinite term, the service of such sentence shall satisfy a suspended sentence on another count or a prior suspended sentence or sentence to probation; and

(d) when a sentence of imprisonment is imposed for a definite term, the period of a suspended sentence on another count or a prior suspended sentence or sentence to probation shall run during the period of such imprisonment.

(7) *Offense Committed While Under Suspension of Sentence or Probation.* When a defendant is convicted of an offense committed while under suspension of sentence or on probation and such suspension or probation is not revoked:

(a) if the defendant is sentenced to imprisonment for an indefinite term, the service of such sentence shall satisfy the prior suspended sentence or sentence to probation; and

(b) if the defendant is sentenced to imprisonment for a definite term, the period of the suspension or probation shall not run during the period of such imprisonment; and

(c) if sentence is suspended or the defendant is sentenced to probation, the period of such suspension or probation shall run concurrently with or consecutively to the remainder of the prior periods, as the Court determines at the time of sentence.

SECTION 7.07.   PROCEDURE ON SENTENCE; PRE-SENTENCE INVESTIGATION AND REPORT; REMAND FOR PSYCHIATRIC EXAMINATION; TRANSMISSION OF RECORDS TO DEPARTMENT OF CORRECTION

(1) The Court shall not impose sentence without first ordering a pre-sentence investigation of the defendant and according due consideration to a written report of such investigation where:

(a) the defendant has been convicted of a felony; or

(b) the defendant is less than twenty-two years of age and has been convicted of a crime; or

(c) the defendant will be [placed on probation or] sentenced to imprisonment for an extended term.

(2) The Court may order a pre-sentence investigation in any other case.

(3) The pre-sentence investigation shall include an analysis of the circumstances attending the commission of the crime, the defendant's history of delinquency or criminality, physical and mental condition, family situation and background, economic status, education, occupation and personal habits and any other matters that the probation officer deems relevant or the Court directs to be included.

(4) Before imposing sentence, the Court may order the defendant to submit to psychiatric observation and examination for a period of not exceeding sixty days or such longer period as the Court determines to be necessary for the purpose. The defendant may be remanded for this purpose to any available clinic or mental hospital or the Court may appoint a qualified psychiatrist to make the examination. The report of the examination shall be submitted to the Court.

(5) Before imposing sentence, the Court shall advise the defendant or his counsel of the factual contents and the conclusions of any pre-sentence investigation or psychiatric examination and afford fair opportunity, if the defendant so requests, to controvert them. The sources of confidential information need not, however, be disclosed.

(6) The Court shall not impose a sentence of imprisonment for an extended term unless the ground therefor has been established at a hearing after the conviction of the defendant and on written notice to him of the ground proposed. Subject to the limitation of Subsection (5) of this Section, the defendant shall have the right to hear and controvert the evidence against him and to offer evidence upon the issue.

(7) If the defendant is sentenced to imprisonment, a copy of the report of any pre-sentence investigation or psychiatric examination shall be transmitted forthwith to the Department of Correction [or other state department or agency] or, when the defendant is committed to the custody of a specific institution, to such institution.

SECTION 7.08.   COMMITMENT FOR OBSERVATION; SENTENCE OF IMPRISONMENT FOR FELONY DEEMED TENTATIVE FOR PERIOD OF ONE YEAR; RE-SENTENCE ON PETITION OF COMMISSIONER OF CORRECTION

(1) If, after pre-sentence investigation, the Court desires additional information concerning an offender convicted of a felony or misdemeanor before imposing sentence, it may order that he be committed, for a period not exceeding ninety days, to the custody of the Department of Correction, or, in the case of a young adult offender, to the custody of the Division of Young Adult Correction, for observation and study at an appropriate reception or classification center. The Department and the Board of Parole, or the Young Adult Divisions thereof, shall advise the Court of their findings and recommendations on or before the expiration of such ninety-day period. If the offender is thereafter sentenced to imprisonment, the period of such commitment for observation shall be deducted from the maximum term and from the minimum, if any, of such sentence.

(2) When a person has been sentenced to imprisonment upon conviction of a felony, whether for an ordinary or extended term, the sentence shall be deemed tentative, to the extent provided in this Section, for the period of one year following the date when the offender is received in custody by the Department of Correction [or other state department or agency].

(3) If, as a result of the examination and classification by the Department of Correction [or other state department or agency] of a person under sentence of imprisonment upon conviction of a felony, the Commissioner of Correction [or other department head] is satisfied that the sentence of the Court may have been based upon a misappre-

hension as to the history, character or physical or mental condition of the offender, the Commissioner, during the period when the offender's sentence is deemed tentative under Subsection (2) of this Section shall file in the sentencing Court a petition to resentence the offender. The petition shall set forth the information as to the offender that is deemed to warrant his re-sentence and may include a recommendation as to the sentence to be imposed.

(4) The Court may dismiss a petition filed under Subsection (3) of this Section without a hearing if it deems the information set forth insufficient to warrant reconsideration of the sentence. If the Court is of the view that the petition warrants such reconsideration, a copy of the petition shall be served on the offender, who shall have the right to be heard on the issue and to be represented by counsel.

(5) When the Court grants a petition filed under Subsection (3) of this Section, it shall re-sentence the offender and may impose any sentence that might have been imposed originally for the felony of which the defendant was convicted. The period of his imprisonment prior to re-sentence and any reduction for good behavior to which he is entitled shall be applied in satisfaction of the final sentence.

(6) For all purposes other than this Section, a sentence of imprisonment has the same finality when it is imposed that it would have if this Section were not in force.

(7) Nothing in this Section shall alter the remedies provided by law for vacating or correcting an illegal sentence.

SECTION 7.09.   CREDIT FOR TIME OF DETENTION PRIOR TO SENTENCE; CREDIT FOR
                IMPRISONMENT UNDER EARLIER SENTENCE FOR THE SAME CRIME

(1) When a defendant who is sentenced to imprisonment has previously been detained in any state or local correctional or other institution following his [conviction of] [arrest for] the crime for which such sentence is imposed, such period of detention following his [conviction] [arrest] shall be deducted from the maximum term, and from the minimum, if any, of such sentence. The officer having custody of the defendant shall furnish a certificate to the Court at the time of sentence, showing the length of such detention of the defendant prior to sentence in any state or local correctional or other institution, and the certificate shall be annexed to the official records of the defendant's commitment.

(2) When a judgment of conviction is vacated and a new sentence is thereafter imposed upon the defendant for the same crime, the period of detention and imprisonment theretofore served shall be deducted from the maximum term, and from the minimum, if any, of the new sentence. The officer having custody of the defendant shall furnish a certificate to the Court at the time of sentence, showing the period of imprisonment served under the original sentence, and the certificate shall be annexed to the official records of the defendant's new commitment.

PART II.   DEFINITION OF SPECIFIC CRIMES

Offenses Involving Danger to the Person

Article 210.   Criminal Homicide

SECTION 210.0.   DEFINITIONS

In Articles 210-213, unless a different meaning plainly is required:
(1) "human being" means a person who has been born and is alive;

(2) "bodily injury" means physical pain, illness or any impairment of physical condition;

(3) "serious bodily injury" means bodily injury which creates a substantial risk of death or which causes serious, permanent disfigurement, or protracted loss or impairment of the function of any bodily member or organ;

(4) "deadly weapon" means any firearm, or other weapon, device, instrument, material or substance, whether animate or inanimate, which in the manner it is used or is intended to be used is known to be capable of producing death or serious bodily injury.

SECTION 210.1.   CRIMINAL HOMICIDE

(1) A person is guilty of criminal homicide if he purposely, knowingly, recklessly or negligently causes the death of another human being.

(2) Criminal homicide is murder, manslaughter or negligent homicide.

SECTION 210.2.   MURDER

(1) Except as provided in Section 210.3(1)(b), criminal homicide constitutes murder when:

(a) it is committed purposely or knowingly; or

(b) it is committed recklessly under circumstances manifesting extreme indifference to the value of human life. Such recklessness and indifference are presumed if the actor is engaged or is an accomplice in the commission of, or an attempt to commit, or flight after committing or attempting to commit robbery, rape or deviate sexual intercourse by force or threat of force, arson, burglary, kidnapping or felonious escape.

(2) Murder is a felony of the first degree [but a person convicted of murder may be sentenced to death, as provided in Section 210.6.].

SECTION 210.3.   MANSLAUGHTER

(1) Criminal homicide constitutes manslaughter when:

(a) it is committed recklessly; or

(b) a homicide which would otherwise be murder is committed under the influence of extreme mental or emotional disturbance for which there is reasonable explanation or excuse. The reasonableness of such explanation or excuse shall be determined from the viewpoint of a person in the actor's situation under the circumstances as he believes them to be.

(2) Manslaughter is a felony of the second degree.

SECTION 210.4.   NEGLIGENT HOMICIDE

(1) Criminal homicide constitutes negligent homicide when it is committed negligently.

(2) Negligent homicide is a felony of the third degree.

SECTION 210.5.   CAUSING OR AIDING SUICIDE

(1) *Causing Suicide as Criminal Homicide.* A person may be convicted of criminal homicide for causing another to commit suicide only if he purposely causes such suicide by force, duress or deception.

(2) *Aiding or Soliciting Suicide as an Independent Offense.* A person who purposely aids or solicits another to commit suicide is guilty of a felony of the second degree if his conduct causes such suicide or an attempted suicide, and otherwise of a misdemeanor.

[Section 210.6.   Sentence of Death for Murder; Further Proceedings
                  to Determine Sentence *

(1) *Death Sentence Excluded.* When a defendant is found guilty of murder, the Court shall impose sentence for a felony of the first degree if it is satisfied that:

(a) none of the aggravating circumstances enumerated in Subsection (3) of this Section was established by the evidence at the trial or will be established if further proceedings are initiated under Subsection (2) of this Section; or

(b) substantial mitigating circumstances, established by the evidence at the trial, call for leniency; or

(c) the defendant, with the consent of the prosecuting attorney and the approval of the Court, pleaded guilty to murder as a felony of the first degree; or

(d) the defendant was under 18 years of age at the time of the commission of the crime; or

(e) the defendant's physical or mental condition calls for leniency; or

(f) although the evidence suffices to sustain the verdict, it does not foreclose all doubt respecting the defendant's guilt.

(2) *Determination by Court or by Court and Jury.* Unless the Court imposes sentence under Subsection (1) of this Section, it shall conduct a separate proceeding to determine whether the defendant should be sentenced for a felony of the first degree or sentenced to death. The proceeding shall be conducted before the Court alone if the defendant was convicted by a Court sitting without a jury or upon his plea of guilty or if the prosecuting attorney and the defendant waive a jury with respect to sentence. In other cases it shall be conducted before the Court sitting with the jury which determined the defendant's guilt or, if the Court for good cause shown discharges that jury, with a new jury empanelled for the purpose.

In the proceeding, evidence may be presented as to any matter that the Court deems relevant to sentence, including but not limited to the nature and circumstances of the crime, the defendant's character, background, history, mental and physical condition and any of the aggravating or mitigating circumstances enumerated in Subsections (3) and (4) of this Section. Any such evidence not legally privileged, which the Court deems to have probative force, may be received, regardless of its admissibility under the exclusionary rules of evidence, provided that the defendant's counsel is accorded a fair opportunity to rebut any hearsay statements. The prosecuting attorney and the defendant or his counsel shall be permitted to present argument for or against sentence of death.

The determination whether sentence of death shall be imposed shall be in the discretion of the Court, except that when the proceeding is conducted before the Court sitting with a jury, the Court shall not impose sentence of death unless it submits to the jury the issue whether the defendant should be sentenced to death or to imprisonment and the jury returns a verdict that the sentence should be death. If the jury is unable to reach a unanimous verdict, the Court shall dismiss the jury and impose sentence for a felony of the first degree.

The Court, in exercising its discretion as to sentence, and the jury, in determining upon its verdict, shall take into account the aggravating and mitigating circumstances enumerated in Subsections (3) and (4) and any other facts that it deems relevant, but it shall not impose or recommend sentence of death unless it finds one of the aggravating circumstances enumerated in Subsection (3) and further finds that there are no mitigat-

---

*. . . The brackets are meant to reflect the fact that the Institute took no position on the desirability of the death penalty. . . .

ing circumstances sufficiently substantial to call for leniency. When the issue is submitted to the jury, the Court shall so instruct and also shall inform the jury of the nature of the sentence of imprisonment that may be imposed, including its implication with respect to possible release upon parole, if the jury verdict is against sentence of death.

Alternative formulation of Subsection (2):

(2) *Determination by Court.* Unless the Court imposes sentence under Subsection (1) of this Section, it shall conduct a separate proceeding to determine whether the defendant should be sentenced for a felony of the first degree or sentenced to death. In the proceeding, the Court, in accordance with Section 7.07, shall consider the report of the pre-sentence investigation and, if a psychiatric examination has been ordered, the report of such examination. In addition, evidence may be presented as to any matter that the Court deems relevant to sentence, including but not limited to the nature and circumstances of the crime, the defendant's character, background, history, mental and physical condition and any of the aggravating or mitigating circumstances enumerated in Subsections (3) and (4) of this Section. Any such evidence not legally privileged, which the Court deems to have probative force, may be received, regardless of its admissibility under the exclusionary rules of evidence, provided that the defendant's counsel is accorded a fair opportunity to rebut any hearsay statements. The prosecuting attorney and the defendant or his counsel shall be permitted to present argument for or against sentence of death.

The determination whether sentence of death shall be imposed shall be in the discretion of the Court. In exercising such discretion, the Court shall take into account the aggravating and mitigating circumstances enumerated in Subsections (3) and (4) and any other facts that it deems relevant but shall not impose sentence of death unless it finds one of the aggravating circumstances enumerated in Subsection (3) and further finds that there are no mitigating circumstances sufficiently substantial to call for leniency.

(3) *Aggravating Circumstances.*

(a) The murder was committed by a convict under sentence of imprisonment.

(b) The defendant was previously convicted of another murder or of a felony involving the use or threat of violence to the person.

(c) At the time the murder was committed the defendant also committed another murder.

(d) The defendant knowingly created a great risk of death to many persons.

(e) The murder was committed while the defendant was engaged or was an accomplice in the commission of, or an attempt to commit, or flight after committing or attempting to commit robbery, rape or deviate sexual intercourse by force or threat of force, arson, burglary or kidnapping.

(f) The murder was committed for the purpose of avoiding or preventing a lawful arrest or effecting an escape from lawful custody.

(g) The murder was committed for pecuniary gain.

(h) The murder was especially heinous, atrocious or cruel, manifesting exceptional depravity.

(4) *Mitigating Circumstances.*

(a) The defendant has no significant history of prior criminal activity.

(b) The murder was committed while the defendant was under the influence of extreme mental or emotional disturbance.

(c) The victim was a participant in the defendant's homicidal conduct or consented to the homicidal act.

(d) The murder was committed under circumstances which the defendant believed to provide a moral justification or extenuation for his conduct.

(e) The defendant was an accomplice in a murder committed by another person and his participation in the homicidal act was relatively minor.

(f) The defendant acted under duress or under the domination of another person.

(g) At the time of the murder, the capacity of the defendant to appreciate the criminality [wrongfulness] of his conduct or to conform his conduct to the requirements of law was impaired as a result of mental disease or defect or intoxication.

(h) The youth of the defendant at the time of the crime.]

Article 211.   Assault; Reckless Endangering; Threats

SECTION 211.0.   DEFINITIONS

In this Article, the definitions given in Section 210.0 apply unless a different meaning plainly is required.

SECTION 211.1.   ASSAULT

(1) *Simple Assault.* A person is guilty of assault if he:

(a) attempts to cause or purposely, knowingly or recklessly causes bodily injury to another; or

(b) negligently causes bodily injury to another with a deadly weapon; or

(c) attempts by physical menace to put another in fear of imminent serious bodily injury.

Simple assault is a misdemeanor unless committed in a fight or scuffle entered into by mutual consent, in which case it is a petty misdemeanor.

(2) *Aggravated Assault.* A person is guilty of aggravated assault if he:

(a) attempts to cause serious bodily injury to another, or causes such injury purposely, knowingly or recklessly under circumstances manifesting extreme indifference to the value of human life; or

(b) attempts to cause or purposely or knowingly causes bodily injury to another with a deadly weapon.

Aggravated assault under paragraph (a) is a felony of the second degree; aggravated assault under paragraph (b) is a felony of the third degree.

SECTION 211.2.   RECKLESSLY ENDANGERING ANOTHER PERSON

A person commits a misdemeanor if he recklessly engages in conduct which places or may place another person in danger of death or serious bodily injury. Recklessness and danger shall be presumed where a person knowingly points a firearm at or in the direction of another, whether or not the actor believed the firearm to be loaded.

SECTION 211.3.   TERRORISTIC THREATS

A person is guilty of a felony of the third degree if he threatens to commit any crime of violence with purpose to terrorize another or to cause evacuation of a building, place of assembly, or facility of public transportation, or otherwise to cause serious public inconvenience, or in reckless disregard of the risk of causing such terror or inconvenience.

Article 212.   Kidnapping and Related Offenses; Coercion

SECTION 212.0.   DEFINITIONS

In this Article, the definitions given in Section 210.0 apply unless a different meaning plainly is required.

SECTION 212.1.   KIDNAPPING

A person is guilty of kidnapping if he unlawfully removes another from his place of residence or business, or a substantial distance from the vicinity where he is found, or if he unlawfully confines another for a substantial period in a place of isolation, with any of the following purposes:

(a) to hold for ransom or reward, or as a shield or hostage; or

(b) to facilitate commission of any felony or flight thereafter; or

(c) to inflict bodily injury on or to terrorize the victim or another; or

(d) to interfere with the performance of any governmental or political function.

Kidnapping is a felony of the first degree unless the actor voluntarily releases the victim alive and in a safe place prior to trial, in which case it is a felony of the second degree. A removal or confinement is unlawful within the meaning of this Section if it is accomplished by force, threat or deception, or, in the case of a person who is under the age of 14 or incompetent, if it is accomplished without the consent of a parent, guardian or other person responsible for general supervision of his welfare.

SECTION 212.2.   FELONIOUS RESTRAINT

A person commits a felony of the third degree if he knowingly:

(a) restrains another unlawfully in circumstances exposing him to risk of serious bodily injury; or

(b) holds another in a condition of involuntary servitude.

SECTION 212.3.   FALSE IMPRISONMENT

A person commits a misdemeanor if he knowingly restrains another unlawfully so as to interfere substantially with his liberty.

SECTION 212.4.   INTERFERENCE WITH CUSTODY

(1) *Custody of Children.* A person commits an offense if he knowingly or recklessly takes or entices any child under the age of 18 from the custody of its parent, guardian or other lawful custodian, when he has no privilege to do so. It is an affirmative defense that:

(a) the actor believed that his action was necessary to preserve the child from danger to its welfare; or

(b) the child, being at the time not less than 14 years old, was taken away at its own instigation without enticement and without purpose to commit a criminal offense with or against the child.

Proof that the child was below the critical age gives rise to a presumption that the actor knew the child's age or acted in reckless disregard thereof. The offense is a misdemeanor unless the actor, not being a parent or person in equivalent relation to the child, acted with knowledge that his conduct would cause serious alarm for the child's safety, or in reckless disregard of a likelihood of causing such alarm, in which case the offense is a felony of the third degree.

(2) *Custody of Committed Persons.* A person is guilty of a misdemeanor if he knowingly or recklessly takes or entices any committed person away from lawful custody when he is not privileged to do so. "Committed person" means, in addition to anyone committed under judicial warrant, any orphan, neglected or delinquent child, mentally defective or insane person, or other dependent or incompetent person entrusted to another's custody by or through a recognized social agency or otherwise by authority of law.

SECTION 212.5.   CRIMINAL COERCION

(1) *Offense Defined.* A person is guilty of criminal coercion if, with purpose unlawfully to restrict another's freedom of action to his detriment, he threatens to:
   (a) commit any criminal offense; or
   (b) accuse anyone of a criminal offense; or
   (c) expose any secret tending to subject any person to hatred, contempt or ridicule, or to impair his credit or business repute; or
   (d) take or withhold action as an official, or cause an official to take or withhold action.
It is an affirmative defense to prosecution based on paragraphs (b), (c) or (d) that the actor believed the accusation or secret to be true or the proposed official action justified and that his purpose was limited to compelling the other to behave in a way reasonably related to the circumstances which were the subject of the accusation, exposure or proposed official action, as by desisting from further misbehavior, making good a wrong done, refraining from taking any action or responsibility for which the actor believes the other disqualified.
(2) *Grading.* Criminal coercion is a misdemeanor unless the threat is to commit a felony or the actor's purpose is felonious, in which cases the offense is a felony of the third degree.

Article 213.   Sexual Offenses

SECTION 213.0.   DEFINITIONS

In this Article, unless a different meaning plainly is required:
(1) the definitions given in Section 210.0 apply;
(2) "Sexual intercourse" includes intercourse per os or per anum, with some penetration however slight; emission is not required;
(3) "Deviate sexual intercourse" means sexual intercourse per os or per anum between human beings who are not husband and wife, and any form of sexual intercourse with an animal.

SECTION 213.1.   RAPE AND RELATED OFFENSES

(1) *Rape.* A male who has sexual intercourse with a female not his wife is guilty of rape if:
   (a) he compels her to submit by force or by threat of imminent death, serious bodily injury, extreme pain or kidnapping, to be inflicted on anyone; or
   (b) he has substantially impaired her power to appraise or control her conduct by administering or employing without her knowledge drugs, intoxicants or other means for the purpose of preventing resistance; or
   (c) the female is unconscious; or
   (d) the female is less than 10 years old.
Rape is a felony of the second degree unless (i) in the course thereof the actor inflicts serious bodily injury upon anyone, or (ii) the victim was not a voluntary social companion of the actor upon the occasion of the crime and had not previously permitted him sexual liberties, in which cases the offense is a felony of the first degree. Sexual intercourse includes intercourse per os or per anum, with some penetration however slight; emission is not required.
(2) *Gross Sexual Imposition.* A male who has sexual intercourse with a female not his wife commits a felony of the third degree if:

(a) he compels her to submit by any threat that would prevent resistance by a woman of ordinary resolution; or

(b) he knows that she suffers from a mental disease or defect which renders her incapable of appraising the nature of her conduct; or

(c) he knows that she is unaware that a sexual act is being committed upon her or that she submits because she mistakenly supposes that he is her husband.

SECTION 213.2.   DEVIATE SEXUAL INTERCOURSE BY FORCE OR IMPOSITION

(1) *By Force or Its Equivalent.* A person who engages in deviate sexual intercourse with another person, or who causes another to engage in deviate sexual intercourse, commits a felony of the second degree if:

(a) he compels the other person to participate by force or by threat of imminent death, serious bodily injury, extreme pain or kidnapping, to be inflicted on anyone; or

(b) he has substantially impaired the other person's power to appraise or control his conduct, by administering or employing without the knowledge of the other person drugs, intoxicants or other means for the purpose of preventing resistance; or

(c) the other person is unconscious; or

(d) the other person is less than 10 years old.

Deviate sexual intercourse means sexual intercourse per os or per anum between human beings who are not husband and wife, and any form of sexual intercourse with an animal.

(2) *By Other Imposition.* A person who engages in deviate sexual intercourse with another person, or who causes another to engage in deviate sexual intercourse, commits a felony of the third degree if:

(a) he compels the other person to participate by any threat that would prevent resistance by a person of ordinary resolution; or

(b) he knows that the other person suffers from a mental disease or defect which renders him incapable of appraising the nature of his conduct; or

(c) he knows that the other person submits because he is unaware that a sexual act is being committed upon him.

SECTION 213.3.   CORRUPTION OF MINORS AND SEDUCTION

(1) *Offense Defined.* A male who has sexual intercourse with a female not his wife, or any person who engages in deviate sexual intercourse or causes another to engage in deviate sexual intercourse, is guilty of an offense if:

(a) the other person is less than [16] years old and the actor is at least [4] years older than the other person; or

(b) the other person is less than 21 years old and the actor is his guardian or otherwise responsible for general supervision of his welfare; or

(c) the other person is in custody of law or detained in a hospital or other institution and the actor has supervisory or disciplinary authority over him; or

(d) the other person is a female who is induced to participate by a promise of marriage which the actor does not mean to perform.

(2) *Grading.* An offense under paragraph (a) of Subsection (1) is a felony of the third degree. Otherwise an offense under this section is a misdemeanor.

SECTION 213.4.   SEXUAL ASSAULT

A person who has sexual contact with another not his spouse, or causes such other to have sexual conduct with him, is guilty of sexual assault, a misdemeanor, if:

(1) he knows that the contact is offensive to the other person; or

(2) he knows that the other person suffers from a mental disease or defect which renders him or her incapable of appraising the nature of his or her conduct; or

(3) he knows that the other person is unaware that a sexual act is being committed; or

(4) the other person is less than 10 years old; or

(5) he has substantially impaired the other person's power to appraise or control his or her conduct, by administering or employing without the other's knowledge drugs, intoxicants or other means for the purpose of preventing resistance; or

(6) the other person is less than [16] years old and the actor is at least [four] years older than the other person; or

(7) the other person is less than 21 years old and the actor is his guardian or otherwise responsible for general supervision of his welfare; or

(8) the other person is in custody of law or detained in a hospital or other institution and the actor has supervisory or disciplinary authority over him.

Sexual contact is any touching of the sexual or other intimate parts of the person for the purpose of arousing or gratifying sexual desire.

SECTION 213.5. INDECENT EXPOSURE

A person commits a misdemeanor if, for the purpose of arousing or gratifying sexual desire of himself or of any person other than his spouse, he exposes his genitals under circumstances in which he knows his conduct is likely to cause affront or alarm.

SECTION 213.6. PROVISIONS GENERALLY APPLICABLE TO ARTICLE 213

(1) *Mistake as to Age.* Whenever in this Article the criminality of conduct depends on a child's being below the age of 10, it is no defense that the actor did not know the child's age, or reasonably believed the child to be older than 10. When criminality depends on the child's being below a critical age other than 10, it is a defense for the actor to prove by a preponderance of the evidence that he reasonably believed the child to be above the critical age.

(2) *Spouse Relationships.* Whenever in this Article the definition of an offense excludes conduct with a spouse, the exclusion shall be deemed to extend to persons living as man and wife, regardless of the legal status of their relationship. The exclusion shall be inoperative as respects spouses living apart under a decree of judicial separation. Where the definition of an offense excludes conduct with a spouse or conduct by a woman, this shall not preclude conviction of a spouse or woman as accomplice in a sexual act in which he or she causes another person, not within the exclusion, to perform.

(3) *Sexually Promiscuous Complainants.* It is a defense to prosecution under Section 213.3. and paragraphs (6), (7) and (8) of Section 213.4 for the actor to prove by a preponderance of the evidence that the alleged victim had, prior to the time of the offense charged, engaged promiscuously in sexual relations with others.

(4) *Prompt Complaint.* No prosecution may be instituted or maintained under this Article unless the alleged offense was brought to the notice of public authority within [3] months of its occurrence or, where the alleged victim was less than [16] years old or otherwise incompetent to make complaint, within [3] months after a parent, guardian or other competent person specially interested in the victim learns of the offense.

(5) *Testimony of Complainants.* No person shall be convicted of any felony under this Article upon the uncorroborated testimony of the alleged victim. Corroboration may be circumstantial. In any prosecution before a jury for an offense under this Article, the jury shall be instructed to evaluate the testimony of a victim or complaining witness with special care in view of the emotional involvement of the witness and the difficulty of determining the truth with respect to alleged sexual activities carried out in private.

Offenses Against Property

Article 220.   Arson, Criminal Mischief, and Other Property Destruction

SECTION 220.1.   ARSON AND RELATED OFFENSES

(1) *Arson.* A person is guilty of arson, a felony of the second degree, if he starts a fire or causes an explosion with the purpose of:

(a) destroying a building or occupied structure of another; or

(b) destroying or damaging any property, whether his own or another's, to collect insurance for such loss. It shall be an affirmative defense to prosecution under this paragraph that the actor's conduct did not recklessly endanger any building or occupied structure of another or place any other person in danger of death or bodily injury.

(2) *Reckless Burning or Exploding.* A person commits a felony of the third degree if he purposely starts a fire or causes an explosion, whether on his own property or another's, and thereby recklessly:

(a) places another person in danger of death or bodily injury; or

(b) places a building or occupied structure of another in danger of damage or destruction.

(3) *Failure to Control or Report Dangerous Fire.* A person who knows that a fire is endangering life or a substantial amount of property of another and fails to take reasonable measures to put out or control the fire, when he can do so without substantial risk to himself, or to give a prompt fire alarm, commits a misdemeanor if:

(a) he knows that he is under an official, contractual, or other legal duty to prevent or combat the fire; or

(b) the fire was started, albeit lawfully, by him or with his assent, or on property in his custody or control.

(4) *Definitions.* "Occupied structure" means any structure, vehicle or place adapted for overnight accommodation of persons, or for carrying on business therein, whether or not a person is actually present. Property is that of another, for the purposes of this section, if anyone other than the actor has a possessory or proprietory interest therein. If a building or structure is divided into separately occupied units, any unit not occupied by the actor is an occupied structure of another.

SECTION 220.2.   CAUSING OR RISKING CATASTROPHE

(1) *Causing Catastrophe.* A person who causes a catastrophe by explosion, fire, flood, avalanche, collapse of building, release of poison gas, radioactive material or other harmful or destructive force or substance, or by any other means of causing potentially widespread injury or damage, commits a felony of the second degree if he does so purposely or knowingly, or a felony of the third degree if he does so recklessly.

(2) *Risking Catastrophe.* A person is guilty of a misdemeanor if he recklessly creates a risk of catastrophe in the employment of fire, explosives or other dangerous means listed in Subsection (1).

(3) *Failure to Prevent Catastrophe.* A person who knowingly or recklessly fails to take reasonable measures to prevent or mitigate a catastrophe commits a misdemeanor if:

(a) he knows that he is under an official, contractual or other legal duty to take such measures; or

(b) he did or assented to the act causing or threatening the catastrophe.

SECTION 220.3. CRIMINAL MISCHIEF

(1) *Offense Defined.* A person is guilty of criminal mischief if he:

(a) damages tangible property of another purposely, recklessly, or by negligence in the employment of fire, explosives, or other dangerous means listed in Section 220.2(1); or

(b) purposely or recklessly tampers with tangible property of another so as to endanger person or property; or

(c) purposely or recklessly causes another to suffer pecuniary loss by deception or threat.

(2) *Grading.* Criminal mischief is a felony of the third degree if the actor purposely causes pecuniary loss in excess of $5,000, or a substantial interruption or impairment of public communication, transportation, supply of water, gas or power, or other public service. It is a misdemeanor if the actor purposely causes pecuniary loss in excess of $100, or a petty misdemeanor if he purposely or recklessly causes pecuniary loss in excess of $25. Otherwise criminal mischief is a violation.

Article 221. Burglary and Other Criminal Intrusion

SECTION 221.0. DEFINITIONS

In this Article, unless a different meaning plainly is required:

(1) "occupied structure" means any structure, vehicle or place adapted for overnight accommodation of persons, or for carrying on business therein, whether or not a person is actually present.

(2) "night" means the period between thirty minutes past sunset and thirty minutes before sunrise.

SECTION 221.1. BURGLARY

(1) *Burglary Defined.* A person is guilty of burglary if he enters a building or occupied structure, or separately secured or occupied portion thereof, with purpose to commit a crime therein, unless the premises are at the time open to the public or the actor is licensed or privileged to enter. It is an affirmative defense to prosecution for burglary that the building or structure was abandoned.

(2) *Grading.* Burglary is a felony of the second degree if it is perpetrated in the dwelling of another at night, or if, in the course of committing the offense, the actor:

(a) purposely, knowingly or recklessly inflicts or attempts to inflict bodily injury on anyone; or

(b) is armed with explosives or a deadly weapon.

Otherwise burglary is a felony of the third degree. An act shall be deemed "in the course of committing" an offense if it occurs in an attempt to commit the offense or in flight after the attempt or commission.

(3) *Multiple Convictions.* A person may not be convicted both for burglary and for the offense which it was his purpose to commit after the burglarious entry or for an attempt to commit that offense, unless the additional offense constitutes a felony of the first or second degree.

SECTION 221.2.   CRIMINAL TRESPASS

(1) *Buildings and Occupied Structures.* A person commits an offense if, knowing that he is not licensed or privileged to do so, he enters or surreptitiously remains in any building or occupied structure, or separately secured or occupied portion thereof. An offense under this Subsection is a misdemeanor if it is committed in a dwelling at night. Otherwise it is a petty misdemeanor.

(2) *Defiant Trespasser.* A person commits an offense if, knowing that he is not licensed or privileged to do so, he enters or remains in any place as to which notice against trespass is given by:

(a) actual communication to the actor; or

(b) posting in a manner prescribed by law or reasonably likely to come to the attention of intruders; or

(c) fencing or other enclosure manifestly designed to exclude intruders.

An offense under this Subsection constitutes a petty misdemeanor if the offender defies an order to leave personally communicated to him by the owner of the premises or other authorized person. Otherwise it is a violation.

(3) *Defenses.* It is an affirmative defense to prosecution under this Section that:

(a) a building or occupied structure involved in an offense under Subsection (1) was abandoned; or

(b) the premises were at the time open to members of the public and the actor complied with all lawful conditions imposed on access to or remaining in the premises; or

(c) the actor reasonably believed that the owner of the premises, or other person empowered to license access thereto, would have licensed him to enter or remain.

Article 222.   Robbery

SECTION 222.1.   ROBBERY

(1) *Robbery Defined.* A person is guilty of robbery if, in the course of committing a theft, he:

(a) inflicts serious bodily injury upon another; or

(b) threatens another with or purposely puts him in fear of immediate serious bodily injury; or

(c) commits or threatens immediately to commit any felony of the first or second degree.

An act shall be deemed "in the course of committing a theft" if it occurs in an attempt to commit theft or in flight after the attempt or commission.

(2) *Grading.* Robbery is a felony of the second degree, except that it is a felony of the first degree if in the course of committing the theft the actor attempts to kill anyone, or purposely inflicts or attempts to inflict serious bodily injury.

Article 223.   Theft and Related Offenses

SECTION 223.0.   DEFINITIONS

In this Article, unless a different meaning plainly is required:

(1) "deprive" means: (a) to withhold property of another permanently or for so extended a period as to appropriate a major portion of its economic value, or with intent

to restore only upon payment of reward or other compensation; or (b) to dispose of the property so as to make it unlikely that the owner will recover it.

(2) "financial institution" means a bank, insurance company, credit union, building and loan association, investment trust or other organization held out to the public as a place of deposit of funds or medium of savings or collective investment.

(3) "government" means the United States, any State, county, municipality, or other political unit, or any department, agency or subdivision of any of the foregoing, or any corporation or other association carrying out the functions of government.

(4) "movable property" means property the location of which can be changed, including things growing on, affixed to, or found in land, and documents although the rights represented thereby have no physical location. "Immovable property" is all other property.

(5) "obtain" means: (a) in relation to property, to bring about a transfer or purported transfer of a legal interest in the property, whether to the obtainer or another; or (b) in relation to labor or service, to secure performance thereof.

(6) "property" means anything of value, including real estate, tangible and intangible personal property, contract rights, choses-in-action and other interests in or claims to wealth, admission or transportation tickets, captured or domestic animals, food and drink, electric or other power.

(7) "property of another" includes property in which any person other than the actor has an interest which the actor is not privileged to infringe, regardless of the fact that the actor also has an interest in the property and regardless of the fact that the other person might be precluded from civil recovery because the property was used in an unlawful transaction or was subject to forfeiture as contraband. Property in possession of the actor shall not be deemed property of another who has only a security interest therein, even if legal title is in the creditor pursuant to a conditional sales contract or other security agreement.

SECTION 223.1.   CONSOLIDATION OF THEFT OFFENSES; GRADING; PROVISIONS APPLICABLE
                 TO THEFT GENERALLY

(1) *Consolidation of Theft Offenses.* Conduct denominated theft in this Article constitutes a single offense. An accusation of theft may be supported by evidence that it was committed in any manner that would be theft under this Article, notwithstanding the specification of a different manner in the indictment or information, subject only to the power of the Court to ensure fair trial by granting a continuance or other appropriate relief where the conduct of the defense would be prejudiced by lack of fair notice or by surprise.

(2) *Grading of Theft Offenses.*

(a) Theft constitutes a felony of the third degree if the amount involved exceeds $500, or if the property stolen is a firearm, automobile, airplane, motorcycle, motorboat or other motor-propelled vehicle, or in the case of theft by receiving stolen property, if the receiver is in the business of buying or selling stolen property.

(b) Theft not within the preceding paragraph constitutes a misdemeanor, except that if the property was not taken from the person or by threat, or in breach of a fiduciary obligation, and the actor proves by a preponderance of the evidence that the amount involved was less than $50, the offense constitutes a petty misdemeanor.

(c) The amount involved in a theft shall be deemed to be the highest value, by any reasonable standard, of the property or services which the actor stole or attempted to steal. Amounts involved in thefts committed pursuant to one scheme or course of conduct, whether from the same person or several persons, may be aggregated in determining the grade of the offense.

(3) *Claim of Right.* It is an affirmative defense to prosecution for theft that the actor:

(a) was unaware that the property or service was that of another; or

(b) acted under an honest claim of right to the property or service involved or that he had a right to acquire or dispose of it as he did; or

(c) took property exposed for sale, intending to purchase and pay for it promptly, or reasonably believing that the owner, if present, would have consented.

(4) *Theft from Spouse.* It is no defense that theft was from the actor's spouse, except that misappropriation of household and personal effects, or other property normally accessible to both spouses, is theft only if it occurs after the parties have ceased living together.

SECTION 223.2.   THEFT BY UNLAWFUL TAKING OR DISPOSITION

(1) *Movable Property.* A person is guilty of theft if he unlawfully takes, or exercises unlawful control over, movable property of another with purpose to deprive him thereof.

(2) *Immovable Property.* A person is guilty of theft if he unlawfully transfers immovable property of another or any interest therein with purpose to benefit himself or another not entitled thereto.

SECTION 223.3.   THEFT BY DECEPTION

A person is guilty of theft if he purposely obtains property of another by deception. A person deceives if he purposely:

(1) creates or reinforces a false impression, including false impressions as to law, value, intention or other state of mind; but deception as to a person's intention to perform a promise shall not be inferred from the fact alone that he did not subsequently perform the promise; or

(2) prevents another from acquiring information which would affect his judgment of a transaction; or

(3) fails to correct a false impression which the deceiver previously created or reinforced, or which the deceiver knows to be influencing another to whom he stands in a fiduciary or confidential relationship; or

(4) fails to disclose a known lien, adverse claim or other legal impediment to the enjoyment of property which he transfers or encumbers in consideration for the property obtained, whether such impediment is or is not valid, or is or is not a matter of official record.

The term "deceive" does not, however, include falsity as to matters having no pecuniary significance, or puffing by statements unlikely to deceive ordinary persons in the group addressed.

SECTION 223.4.   THEFT BY EXTORTION

A person is guilty of theft if he obtains property of another by threatening to:

(1) inflict bodily injury on anyone or commit any other criminal offense; or

(2) accuse anyone of a criminal offense; or

(3) expose any secret tending to subject any person to hatred, contempt or ridicule, or to impair his credit or business repute; or

(4) take or withhold action as an official, or cause an official to take or withhold action; or

(5) bring about or continue a strike, boycott or other collective unofficial action, if the property is not demanded or received for the benefit of the group in whose interest the actor purports to act; or

(6) testify or provide information or withhold testimony or information with respect to another's legal claim or defense; or

(7) inflict any other harm which would not benefit the actor.

It is an affirmative defense to prosecution based on paragraphs (2), (3) or (4) that the property obtained by threat of accusation, exposure, lawsuit or other invocation of official action was honestly claimed as restitution or indemnification for harm done in the circumstances to which such accusation, exposure, lawsuit or other official action relates, or as compensation for property or lawful services.

SECTION 223.5.   THEFT OF PROPERTY LOST, MISLAID, OR DELIVERED BY MISTAKE

A person who comes into control of property of another that he knows to have been lost, mislaid, or delivered under a mistake as to the nature or amount of the property or the identity of the recipient is guilty of theft if, with purpose to deprive the owner thereof, he fails to take reasonable measures to restore the property to a person entitled to have it.

SECTION 223.6.   RECEIVING STOLEN PROPERTY

(1) *Receiving.* A person is guilty of theft if he purposely receives, retains, or disposes of movable property of another knowing that it has been stolen, or believing that it has probably been stolen, unless the property is received, retained, or disposed with purpose to restore it to the owner. "Receiving" means acquiring possession, control or title, or lending on the security of the property.

(2) *Presumption of Knowledge.* The requisite knowledge or belief is presumed in the case of a dealer who:

(a) is found in possession or control of property stolen from two or more persons on separate occasions; or

(b) has received stolen property in another transaction within the year preceding the transaction charged; or

(c) being a dealer in property of the sort received, acquires it for a consideration which he knows is far below its reasonable value.

"Dealer" means a person in the business of buying or selling goods including a pawnbroker.

SECTION 223.7.   THEFT OF SERVICES

(1) A person is guilty of theft if he purposely obtains services which he knows are available only for compensation, by deception or threat, or by false token or other means to avoid payment for the service. "Services" includes labor, professional service, transportation, telephone or other public service, accommodation in hotels, restaurants or elsewhere, admission to exhibitions, use of vehicles or other movable property. Where compensation for service is ordinarily paid immediately upon the rendering for such service, as is the case of hotels and restaurants, refusal to pay or absconding without payment or offer to pay gives rise to a presumption that the service was obtained by deception as to intention to pay.

(2) A person commits theft if, having control over the disposition of services of others,

to which he is not entitled, he knowingly diverts such services to his own benefit or to the benefit of another not entitled thereto.

SECTION 223.8.   THEFT BY FAILURE TO MAKE REQUIRED DISPOSITION OF FUNDS RECEIVED

A person who purposely obtains property upon agreement, or subject to a known legal obligation, to make specified payment or other disposition, whether from such property or its proceeds or from his own property to be reserved in equivalent amount, is guilty of theft if he deals with the property obtained as his own and fails to make the required payment or disposition. The foregoing applies notwithstanding that it may be impossible to identify particular property as belonging to the victim at the time of the actor's failure to make the required payment or disposition. An officer or employee of the government or of a financial institution is presumed: (i) to know any legal obligation relevant to his criminal liability under this Section, and (ii) to have dealt with the property as his own if he fails to pay or account upon lawful demand, or if an audit reveals a shortage or falsification of accounts.

SECTION 223.9.   UNAUTHORIZED USE OF AUTOMOBILES AND OTHER VEHICLES

A person commits a misdemeanor if he operates another's automobile, airplane, motorcycle, motorboat, or other motor-propelled vehicle without consent of the owner. It is an affirmative defense to prosecution under this Section that the actor reasonably believed that the owner would have consented to the operation had he known of it.

Article 224.   Forgery and Fraudulent Practices

SECTION 224.0.   DEFINITIONS

In this Article, the definitions given in Section 223.0 apply unless a different meaning plainly is required.

SECTION 224.1.   FORGERY

(1) *Definition.* A person is guilty of forgery if, with purpose to defraud or injure anyone, or with knowledge that he is facilitating a fraud or injury to be perpetrated by anyone, the actor:

(a) alters any writing of another without his authority; or

(b) makes, completes, executes, authenticates, issues or transfers any writing so that it purports to be the act of another who did not authorize that act, or to have been executed at a time or place or in a numbered sequence other than was in fact the case, or to be a copy of an original when no such original existed; or

(c) utters any writing which he knows to be forged in a manner specified in paragraphs (a) or (b).

"Writing" includes printing or any other method of recording information, money, coins, tokens, stamps, seals, credit cards, badges, trade-marks, and other symbols of value, right, privilege, or identification.

(2) *Grading.* Forgery is a felony of the second degree if the writing is or purports to be part of an issue of money, securities, postage or revenue stamps, or other instruments

issued by the government, or part of an issue of stock, bonds or other instruments representing interests in or claims against any property or enterprise. Forgery is a felony of the third degree if the writing is or purports to be a will, deed, contract, release, commercial instrument, or other document evidencing, creating, transferring, altering, terminating, or otherwise affecting legal relations. Otherwise forgery is a misdemeanor.

SECTION 224.2.   SIMULATING OBJECTS OF ANTIQUITY, RARITY, ETC.

A person commits a misdemeanor if, with purpose to defraud anyone or with knowledge that he is facilitating a fraud to be perpetrated by anyone, he makes, alters or utters any object so that it appears to have value because of antiquity, rarity, source, or authorship which it does not possess.

SECTION 224.3.   FRAUDULENT DESTRUCTION, REMOVAL OR CONCEALMENT
              OF RECORDABLE INSTRUMENTS

A person commits a felony of the third degree if, with purpose to deceive or injure anyone, he destroys, removes or conceals any will, deed, mortgage, security instrument or other writing for which the law provides public recording.

SECTION 224.4.   TAMPERING WITH RECORDS

A person commits a misdemeanor if, knowing that he has no privilege to do so, he falsifies, destroys, removes or conceals any writing or record, with purpose to deceive or injure anyone or to conceal any wrongdoing.

SECTION 224.5.   BAD CHECKS

A person who issues or passes a check or similar sight order for the payment of money, knowing that it will not be honored by the drawee, commits a misdemeanor. For the purposes of this Section as well as in any prosecution for theft committed by means of a bad check, an issuer is presumed to know that the check or order (other than a post-dated check or order) would not be paid, if:

(1) the issuer had no account with the drawee at the time the check or order was issued; or

(2) payment was refused by the drawee for lack of funds, upon presentation within 30 days after issue, and the issuer failed to make good within 10 days after receiving notice of that refusal.

SECTION 224.6.   CREDIT CARDS

A person commits an offense if he uses a credit card for the purpose of obtaining property or services with knowledge that:

(1) the card is stolen or forged; or

(2) the card has been revoked or cancelled; or

(3) for any other reason his use of the card is unauthorized by the issuer.

It is an affirmative defense to prosecution under paragraph (3) if the actor proves by a preponderance of the evidence that he had the purpose and ability to meet all obligations to the issuer arising out of his use of the card. "Credit card" means a writing, or other evidence of an undertaking to pay for property or services delivered or rendered to or upon the order of a designated person or bearer. An offense under this Section is a felony of the third degree if the value of the property or services secured or sought to be secured by means of the credit card exceeds $500; otherwise it is a misdemeanor.

SECTION 224.7.   DECEPTIVE BUSINESS PRACTICES

A person commits a misdemeanor if in the course of business he:

(1) uses or possesses for use a false weight or measure, or any other device for falsely determining or recording any quality or quantity; or

(2) sells, offers or exposes for sale, or delivers less than the represented quantity of any commodity or service; or

(3) takes or attempts to take more than the represented quantity of any commodity or service when as buyer he furnishes the weight or measure; or

(4) sells, offers or exposes for sale adulterated or mislabeled commodities. "Adulterated" means varying from the standard of composition or quality prescribed by or pursuant to any statute providing criminal penalties for such variance, or set by established commercial usage. "Mislabeled" means varying from the standard of truth or disclosure in labeling prescribed by or pursuant to any statute providing criminal penalties for such variance, or set by established commercial usage; or

(5) makes a false or misleading statement in any advertisement addressed to the public or to a substantial segment thereof for the purpose of promoting the purchase or sale of property or services; or

(6) makes a false or misleading written statement for the purpose of obtaining property or credit; or

(7) makes a false or misleading written statement for the purpose of promoting the sale of securities, or omits information required by law to be disclosed in written documents relating to securities.

It is an affirmative defense to prosecution under this Section if the defendant proves by a preponderance of the evidence that his conduct was not knowingly or recklessly deceptive.

SECTION 224.8.   COMMERCIAL BRIBERY AND BREACH OF DUTY TO ACT DISINTERESTEDLY

(1) A person commits a misdemeanor if he solicits, accepts or agrees to accept any benefit as consideration for knowingly violating or agreeing to violate a duty of fidelity to which he is subject as:

(a) partner, agent, or employee of another;

(b) trustee, guardian, or other fiduciary;

(c) lawyer, physician, accountant, appraiser, or other professional adviser or informant;

(d) officer, director, manager or other participant in the direction of the affairs of an incorporated or unincorporated association; or

(e) arbitrator or other purportedly disinterested adjudicator or referee.

(2) A person who holds himself out to the public as being engaged in the business of making disinterested selection, appraisal, or criticism of commodities or services commits a misdemeanor if he solicits, accepts or agrees to accept any benefit to influence his selection, appraisal or criticism.

(3) A person commits a misdemeanor if he confers, or offers or agrees to confer, any benefit the acceptance of which would be criminal under this Section.

SECTION 224.9.   RIGGING PUBLICLY EXHIBITED CONTEST

(1) A person commits a misdemeanor if, with purpose to prevent a publicly exhibited contest from being conducted in accordance with the rules and usages purporting to govern it, he:
    (a) confers or offers or agrees to confer any benefit upon, or threatens any injury to a participant, official or other person associated with the contest or exhibition; or
    (b) tampers with any person, animal or thing.
(2) *Soliciting or Accepting Benefit for Rigging.* A person commits a misdemeanor if he knowingly solicits, accepts or agrees to accept any benefit the giving of which would be criminal under Subsection (1).
(3) *Participation in Rigged Contest.* A person commits a misdemeanor if he knowingly engages in, sponsors, produces, judges, or otherwise participates in a publicly exhibited contest knowing that the contest is not being conducted in compliance with the rules and usages purporting to govern it, by reason of conduct which would be criminal under this Section.

SECTION 224.10.   DEFRAUDING SECURED CREDITORS

A person commits a misdemeanor if he destroys, removes, conceals, encumbers, transfers or otherwise deals with property subject to a security interest with purpose to hinder enforcement of that interest.

SECTION 224.11.   FRAUD IN INSOLVENCY

A person commits a misdemeanor if, knowing that proceedings have been or are about to be instituted for the appointment of a receiver or other person entitled to administer property for the benefit of creditors, or that any other composition or liquidation for the benefit of creditors has been or is about to be made, he:
    (a) destroys, removes, conceals, encumbers, transfers, or otherwise deals with any property with purpose to defeat or obstruct the claim of any creditor, or otherwise to obstruct the operation of any law relating to administration of property for the benefit of creditors; or
    (b) knowingly falsifies any writing or record relating to the property; or
    (c) knowingly misrepresents or refuses to disclose to a receiver or other person entitled to administer property for the benefit of creditors, the existence, amount or location of the property, or any other information which the actor could be legally required to furnish in relation to such administration.

SECTION 224.12.   RECEIVING DEPOSITS IN A FAILING FINANCIAL INSTITUTION

An officer, manager or other person directing or participating in the direction of a financial institution commits a misdemeanor if he receives or permits the receipt of a deposit, premium payment or other investment in the institution knowing that:
(1) due to financial difficulties the institution is about to suspend operations or go into receivership or reorganization; and
(2) the person making the deposit or other payment is unaware of the precarious situation of the institution.

SECTION 224.13.   MISAPPLICATION OF ENTRUSTED PROPERTY AND PROPERTY OF GOVERNMENT
        OR FINANCIAL INSTITUTION

A person commits an offense if he applies or disposes of property that has been entrusted to him as a fiduciary, or property of the government or of a financial institution,
in a manner which he knows is unlawful and involves substantial risk of loss or detriment
to the owner of the property or to a person for whose benefit the property was entrusted.
The offense is a misdemeanor if the amount involved exceeds $50; otherwise it is a petty
misdemeanor. "Fiduciary" includes trustee, guardian, executor, administrator, receiver
and any person carrying on fiduciary functions on behalf of a corporation or other organization which is a fiduciary.

SECTION 224.14.   SECURING EXECUTION OF DOCUMENTS BY DECEPTION

A person commits a misdemeanor if by deception he causes another to execute any
instrument affecting, purporting to affect, or likely to affect the pecuniary interest of any
person.

Offenses Against the Family

Article 230.   Offenses Against the Family

SECTION 230.1.   BIGAMY AND POLYGAMY

(1) *Bigamy.* A married person is guilty of bigamy, a misdemeanor, if he contracts or
purports to contract another marriage, unless at the time of the subsequent marriage:
   (a) the actor believes that the prior spouse is dead; or
   (b) the actor and the prior spouse have been living apart for five consecutive years
throughout which the prior spouse was not known by the actor to be alive; or
   (c) a Court has entered a judgment purporting to terminate or annul any prior
disqualifying marriage, and the actor does not know that judgment to be invalid; or
   (d) the actor reasonably believes that he is legally eligible to remarry.
(2) *Polygamy.* A person is guilty of polygamy, a felony of the third degree, if he marries
or cohabits with more than one spouse at a time in purported exercise of the right of
plural marriage. The offense is a continuing one until all cohabitation and claim of marriage with more than one spouse terminates. This section does not apply to parties to a
polygamous marriage, lawful in the country of which they are residents or nationals,
while they are in transit through or temporarily visiting this State.
(3) *Other Party to Bigamous or Polygamous Marriage.* A person is guilty of bigamy or polygamy, as the case may be, if he contracts or purports to contract marriage with another
knowing that the other is thereby committing bigamy or polygamy.

SECTION 230.2.   INCEST

A person is guilty of incest, a felony of the third degree, if he knowingly marries or
cohabits or has sexual intercourse with an ancestor or descendant, a brother or sister of
the whole or half blood [or an uncle, aunt, nephew or niece of the whole blood]. "Co-
habit" means to live together under the representation or appearance of being married.

The relationships referred to herein include blood relationships without regard to legitimacy, and relationship of parent and child by adoption.

SECTION 230.3.   ABORTION [OMITTED]

SECTION 230.4.   ENDANGERING WELFARE OF CHILDREN

A parent, guardian, or other person supervising the welfare of a child under 18 commits a misdemeanor if he knowingly endangers the child's welfare by violating a duty of care, protection or support.

SECTION 230.5.   PERSISTENT NON-SUPPORT

A person commits a misdemeanor if he persistently fails to provide support which he can provide and which he knows he is legally obliged to provide to a spouse, child or other dependent.

Offenses Against Public Administration

Article 240.   **Bribery and Corrupt Influence** [omitted]

Article 241.   **Perjury and Other Falsification in Official Matters** [omitted]

Article 242.   **Obstructing Governmental Operations; Escapes** [omitted]

Article 243.   **Abuse of Office** [omitted]

Offenses Against Public Order and Decency

Article 250.   **Riot, Disorderly Conduct, and Related Offenses**

SECTION 250.1.   RIOT; FAILURE TO DISPERSE

(1) *Riot.* A person is guilty of riot, a felony of the third degree, if he participates with [two] or more others in a course of disorderly conduct:
    (a) with purpose to commit or facilitate the commission of a felony or misdemeanor;
    (b) with purpose to prevent or coerce official action; or
    (c) when the actor or any other participant to the knowledge of the actor uses or plans to use a firearm or any other deadly weapon.
(2) *Failure of Disorderly Persons to Disperse Upon Official Order.* Where [three] or more persons are participating in a course of disorderly conduct likely to cause substantial harm or serious inconvenience, annoyance or alarm, a peace officer or other public servant engaged in executing or enforcing the law may order the participants and others in the immediate vicinity to disperse. A person who refuses or knowingly fails to obey such an order commits a misdemeanor.

SECTION 250.2. DISORDERLY CONDUCT

(1) *Offense Defined.* A person is guilty of disorderly conduct if, with purpose to cause public inconvenience, annoyance or alarm, or recklessly creating a risk thereof, he:

(a) engages in fighting or threatening, or in violent or tumultuous behavior; or

(b) makes unreasonable noise or offensively coarse utterance, gesture or display, or addresses abusive language to any person present; or

(c) creates a hazardous or physically offensive condition by any act which serves no legitimate purpose of the actor.

"Public" means affecting or likely to affect persons in a place to which the public or a substantial group has access; among the places included are highways, transport facilities, schools, prisons, apartment houses, places of business or amusement, or any neighborhood.

(2) *Grading.* An offense under this section is a petty misdemeanor if the actor's purpose is to cause substantial harm or serious inconvenience, or if he persists in disorderly conduct after reasonable warning or request to desist. Otherwise disorderly conduct is a violation.

SECTION 250.3. FALSE PUBLIC ALARMS

A person is guilty of a misdemeanor if he initiates or circulates a report or warning of an impending bombing or other crime or catastrophe, knowing that the report or warning is false or baseless and that it is likely to cause evacuation of a building, place of assembly, or facility of public transport, or to cause public inconvenience or alarm.

SECTION 250.4. HARASSMENT

A person commits a petty misdemeanor if, with purpose to harass another, he:

(1) makes a telephone call without purpose of legitimate communication; or

(2) insults, taunts or challenges another in a manner likely to provoke violent or disorderly response; or

(3) makes repeated communications anonymously or at extremely inconvenient hours, or in offensively coarse language; or

(4) subjects another to an offensive touching; or

(5) engages in any other course of alarming conduct serving no legitimate purpose of the actor.

SECTION 250.5. PUBLIC DRUNKENNESS; DRUG INCAPACITATION

A person is guilty of an offense if he appears in any public place manifestly under the influence of alcohol, narcotics or other drugs, not therapeutically administered, to the degree that he may endanger himself or other persons or property, or annoy persons in his vicinity. An offense under this Section constitutes a petty misdemeanor if the actor has been convicted hereunder twice before within a period of one year. Otherwise the offense constitutes a violation.

SECTION 250.6. LOITERING OR PROWLING

A person commits a violation if he loiters or prowls in a place, at a time, or in a manner not usual for law abiding individuals under circumstances that warrant alarm for the safety of persons or property in the vicinity. Among the circumstances which may be considered in determining whether such alarm is warranted is the fact that the actor takes flight upon appearance of a peace officer, refuses to identify himself, or manifestly endeavors to conceal himself or any object. Unless flight by the actor or other circumstances makes it impracticable, a peace officer shall prior to any arrest for an offense under this section afford the actor an opportunity to dispel any alarm which would otherwise be warranted, by requesting him to identify himself and explain his presence and conduct. No person shall be convicted of an offense under this Section if the peace officer did not comply with the preceding sentence, or if it appears at trial that the explanation given by the actor was true and, if believed by the peace officer at the time, would have dispelled the alarm.

SECTION 250.7.   OBSTRUCTING HIGHWAYS AND OTHER PUBLIC PASSAGES

(1) A person, who, having no legal privilege to do so, purposely or recklessly obstructs any highway or other public passage, whether alone or with others, commits a violation, or, in case he persists after warning by a law officer, a petty misdemeanor. "Obstructs" means renders impassable without unreasonable inconvenience or hazard. No person shall be deemed guilty of recklessly obstructing in violation of this Subsection solely because of a gathering of persons to hear him speak or otherwise communicate, or solely because of being a member of such a gathering.

(2) A person in a gathering commits a violation if he refuses to obey a reasonable official request or order to move:
(a) to prevent obstruction of a highway or other public passage; or
(b) to maintain public safety by dispersing those gathered in dangerous proximity to a fire or other hazard.
An order to move, addressed to a person whose speech or other lawful behavior attracts an obstructing audience, shall not be deemed reasonable if the obstruction can be readily remedied by police control of the size or location of the gathering.

SECTION 250.8.   DISRUPTING MEETINGS AND PROCESSIONS

A person commits a misdemeanor if, with purpose to prevent or disrupt a lawful meeting, procession or gathering, he does any act tending to obstruct or interfere with it physically, or makes any utterance, gesture or display designed to outrage the sensibilities of the group.

SECTION 250.9.   DESECRATION OF VENERATED OBJECTS [OMITTED]

SECTION 250.10.   ABUSE OF CORPSE [OMITTED]

SECTION 250.11.   CRUELTY TO ANIMALS [OMITTED]

SECTION 250.12.   VIOLATION OF PRIVACY [OMITTED]

Article 251.   Public Indecency

SECTION 251.1.   OPEN LEWDNESS

A person commits a petty misdemeanor if he does any lewd act which he knows is likely to be observed by others who would be affronted or alarmed.

SECTION 251.2.   PROSTITUTION AND RELATED OFFENSES

(1) *Prostitution.* A person is guilty of prostitution, a petty misdemeanor, if he or she:

(a) is an inmate of a house of prostitution or otherwise engages in sexual activity as a business; or

(b) loiters in or within view of any public place for the purpose of being hired to engage in sexual activity.

"Sexual activity" includes homosexual and other deviate sexual relations. A "house of prostitution" is any place where prostitution or promotion of prostitution is regularly carried on by one person under the control, management or supervision of another. An "inmate" is a person who engages in prostitution in or through the agency of a house of prostitution. "Public place" means any place to which the public or any substantial group thereof has access.

(2) *Promoting Prostitution.* A person who knowingly promotes prostitution of another commits a misdemeanor or felony as provided in Subsection (3). The following acts shall, without limitation of the foregoing, constitute promoting prostitution:

(a) owning, controlling, managing, supervising or otherwise keeping, alone or in association with others, a house of prostitution or a prostitution business; or

(b) procuring an inmate for a house of prostitution or a place in a house of prostitution for one who would be an inmate; or

(c) encouraging, inducing, or otherwise purposely causing another to become or remain a prostitute; or

(d) soliciting a person to patronize a prostitute; or

(e) procuring a prostitute for a patron; or

(f) transporting a person into or within this state with purpose to promote that person's engaging in prostitution, or procuring or paying for transportation with that purpose; or

(g) leasing or otherwise permitting a place controlled by the actor, alone or in association with others, to be regularly used for prostitution or the promotion of prostitution, or failure to make reasonable effort to abate such use by ejecting the tenant, notifying law enforcement authorities, or other legally available means; or

(h) soliciting, receiving, or agreeing to receive any benefit for doing or agreeing to do anything forbidden by this Subsection.

(3) *Grading of Offenses Under Subsection (2).* An offense under Subsection (2) constitutes a felony of the third degree if:

(a) the offense falls within paragraph (a), (b) or (c) of Subsection (2); or

(b) the actor compels another to engage in or promote prostitution; or

(c) the actor promotes prostitution of a child under 16, whether or not he is aware of the child's age; or

(d) the actor promotes prostitution of his wife, child, ward or any person for whose care, protection or support he is responsible.

Otherwise the offense is a misdemeanor.

(4) *Presumption from Living off Prostitutes.* A person, other than the prostitute or the prostitute's minor child or other legal dependent incapable of self-support, who is supported in whole or substantial part by the proceeds of prostitution is presumed to be knowingly promoting prostitution in violation of Subsection (2).

(5) *Patronizing Prostitutes.* A person commits a violation if he hires a prostitute to engage in sexual activity with him, or if he enters or remains in a house of prostitution for the purpose of engaging in sexual activity.

(6) *Evidence.* On the issue whether a place is a house of prostitution the following shall be admissible evidence: its general repute; the repute of the persons who reside in or frequent the place; the frequency, timing and duration of visits by non-residents. Testimony of a person against his spouse shall be admissible to prove offenses under this Section.

Section 251.3.   Loitering to Solicit Deviate Sexual Relations

A person is guilty of a petty misdemeanor if he loiters in or near any public place for the purpose of soliciting or being solicited to engage in deviate sexual relations.

Section 251.4.   Obscenity [omitted]

PART III.   TREATMENT AND CORRECTION [omitted]

PART IV.   ORGANIZATION OF CORRECTION [omitted]

TABLE OF CASES

Italics indicate principal cases or cases otherwise prominently treated.

BIBLIOGRAPHIC REFERENCES

This table lists books, articles, reports and other secondary authorities extracted or referred to in the casebook. Anonymous student notes and comments follow alphabetical listing by author.

Materials of General Import

American Law Institute, Model Penal Code and Commentaries (1980-1985).
J. Dressler, Understanding Criminal Law (1987).
Encyclopedia of Crime and Justice (S. H. Kadish ed. 1983)
G. Fletcher, Rethinking Criminal Law (1978).
J. Hall, General Principles of the Criminal Law (1960).
H. L. A. Hart, The Morality of the Criminal Law (1964).
H. L. A. Hart, Punishment and Responsibility (1968).
O. W. Holmes, The Common Law (1881).
S. H. Kadish, Blame and Punishment (1987).
W. LaFave & A. Scott, Criminal Law (2d ed. 1986).
National Commission on Reform of Federal Criminal Laws, Working Papers (1970).
H. Packer, The Limits of the Criminal Sanction (1968).
President's Commission on Law Enforcement and the Administration of Justice, The Challenge of Crime in a Free Society (1967).
J. F. Stephen, A History of the Criminal Law of England (1883).
G. Williams, Criminal Law: The General Part (2d ed. 1961).
G. Williams, Textbook of Criminal Law (2d ed. 1983).

Chapter 1
How Guilt Is Established

R. Allen, The Restoration of In re Winship: A Comment on Burdens of Persuasion in Criminal Cases After Patterson v. New York, 76 Mich. L. Rev. 30 (1977).
A. Alschuler, Courtroom Misconduct by Prosecutors and Trial Judges, 50 Tex. L. Rev. 629 (1972).
A. Alschuler, The Prosecutor's Role in Plea Bargaining, 36 U. Chi. L. Rev. 50 (1968).
American Bar Association, Annotated Model Rules of Professional Conduct (2d ed. 1992).
American Bar Association, Model Code of Professional Responsibility.
M. Angel, Substantive Due Process and the Criminal Law, 9 Loy. U. Chi. L.J. 61 (1977).

H. Ashford & D. Risinger, Presumptions, Assumptions, and Due Process in Criminal Cases: A Theoretical Overview, 79 Yale L.J. 165 (1969).

S. Beale, Prior Similar Acts in Prosecutions for Rape and Child Sex Abuse, 4 Crim. L. Forum 307 (1993).

D. Bress, Professional Ethics in Criminal Trials: A View of Defense Counsel's Responsibility, 64 Mich. L. Rev. 1493 (1966).

D. Broeder, The Functions of the Jury — Facts or Fictions?, 21 U. Chi. L. Rev. 386 (1947).

D. Bryden & R. C. Park, "Other Crimes" Evidence in Sex Offense Cases, 78 Minn. L. Rev. 529 (1994).

W. Burger, Standards of Conduct for Prosecution and Defense Personnel: A Judge's Viewpoint, 5 Am. Crim. L.Q. 11 (1966).

R. Charrow & V. Charrow, Making Legal Language Understandable: A Psycholinguistic Study of Jury Instructions, 79 Colum. L. Rev. 1306 (1979).

J. Conley, W. O'Barr, & E. Lind, The Power of Language: Presentational Style in the Courtroom, [1978] Duke L.J. 1375.

W. Cornish & A. Sealy, Juries and the Rules of Evidence, [1973] Crim. L. Rev. 208.

E. Dauer & A. Leff, Correspondence: The Lawyer as Friend, 86 Yale L.J. 573 (1977).

F. Dutile, The Burden of Proof in Criminal Cases: A Comment on the *Mullaney-Patterson* Doctrine, 55 Notre Dame Law. 380 (1980).

A. Elwork, B. Sales, & J. Alfini, Making Jury Instructions Understandable (1982).

A. Enker, Perspectives on Plea Bargaining, in President's Commission on Law Enforcement and the Administration of Justice, Task Force Report: The Courts (1967).

G. Fletcher, Two Kinds of Legal Rules: A Comparative Study of Burden-of-Persuasion Practices in Criminal Cases, 77 Yale L.J. 880 (1968).

M. Freedman, The Aftermath of Nix v. Whiteside, 23 Crim. L. Bull. 25 (1987).

M. Freedman, Lawyers' Ethics in an Adversary System (1975).

M. Freedman, Professional Responsibility of the Criminal Defense Lawyer: The Three Hardest Questions, 64 Mich. L. Rev. 1469 (1966).

C. Fried, The Lawyer as Friend: The Moral Foundations of the Lawyer-Client Relation, 85 Yale L.J. 1060 (1976).

M. Friedland, Double Jeopardy (1969).

A. Goldman, The Moral Foundations of Professional Ethics (1980).

G. Hazard, Jr., Criminal Justice System: Overview, in 2 Encyclopedia of Crime and Justice 450 (1983).

J. Jeffries & P. Stephan, Defenses, Presumptions and Burdens of Proof in the Criminal Law, 88 Yale L.J. 1325 (1979).

M. Kadish & S. Kadish, Discretion to Disobey (1973).

M. Kadish & S. Kadish, On Justified Rule Departures by Officials, 59 Calif. L. Rev. 905, 914 (1971).

H. Kalven & H. Zeisel, The American Jury (1966).

J. Kaplan & J. Waltz, The Trial of Jack Ruby (1965).

S. Kassin & S. Wrightsman, Coerced Confessions, Judicial Instruction and Mock Juror Verdicts, 11 J. Applied Soc. Psych. 489 (1981).

N. Lefstein, The Criminal Defendant Who Proposes Perjury, 6 Hofstra L. Rev. 665 (1978).

N. Lefstein, Legal Ethics, 1 Crim. Justice 27 (ABA 1986).

L. Levin & H. Cohen, The Exclusionary Rules in Nonjury Criminal Cases, 119 U. Pa. L. Rev. 905 (1971).

P. Low & J. Jeffries, DICTA: Constitutionalizing the Criminal Law?, 29 Va. L. Weekly, No. 18, p.1 (1977).

D. Luban, Are Criminal Defenders Different?, 91 Mich. L. Rev. 1729 (1993).

G. Lynch, RICO: The Crime of Being a Criminal, Parts III & IV, 87 Colum. L. Rev. 920 (1987).

R. Markus, A Theory of Trial Advocacy, 56 Tulane L. Rev. 95 (1981).

M. McLane, The Burden of Proof in Criminal Cases: *Mullaney* and *Patterson* Compared, 15 Crim. L. Bull. 346 (1979).

M. Mendez, California's New Law on Character Evidence: Evidence Code Section 352 and the Impact of Recent Psychological Studies, 31 U.C.L.A.L. Rev. 1003 (1984).

D. Newman, Conviction 216 (1966).

C. J. Ogletree, Jr., Beyond Justifications: Seeking Motivations to Sustain Public Defenders, 106 Harv. L. Rev. 1239 (1993).

M. Orkin, Defence of One Known to Be Guilty, 1 Crim. L.Q. 170 (1958).

R. Reed, Jury Simulation: The Impact of Judge's Instructions and Attorney Tactics on Decisionmaking, 71 J. Crim. L. & Criminology 68 (1980).

C. Rieger, Client Perjury: A Proposed Resolution of the Constitutional and Ethical Issues, 70 Minn. L. Rev. 121 (1985).

S. Saltzburg, Burdens of Persuasion in Criminal Cases, 20 Am. Crim. L. Rev. 393 (1983).

S. Saltzburg, The Unnecessarily Expanding Role of the American Trial Judge, 64 Va. L. Rev. 1 (1978).

A. Scheflin, Jury Nullification: The Right to Say "No," 45 S. Cal. L. Rev. 168 (1972).

A. Scheflin & J. Van Dyke, Jury Nullification: The Contours of a Controversy, 43 L. & Contemp. Prob. 51 (1980).

W. Schwartzer, Communicating with Juries: Problems and Remedies, 69 Calif. L. Rev. 731 (1981).

L. Severance, E. Greene, & E. Loftus, Toward Criminal Jury Instructions That Jurors Can Understand, 75 J. Crim. L. & Criminology 198 (1984).

R. Simon, The Effects of Newspapers on the Verdicts of Potential Jurors, in R. Simon, The Sociology of Law (1968).

R. Simon & L. Mahan, Quantifying Burdens of Proof, 5 L. & Socy. Rev. 319 (1971).

W. Simon, The Ethics of Criminal Defense, 91 Mich. L. Rev. 1703 (1993).

W. Simon, Homo Psychologicus: Notes on a New Legal Formalism, 32 Stan. L. Rev. 487 (1980).

W. Simon, The Ideology of Advocacy, [1978] Wis. L. Rev. 29.

G. Simpson, Jury Nullification in the American System: A Skeptical View, 54 Tex. L. Rev. 488 (1976).

D. Strawn & R. Buchanan, Jury Confusion: A Threat to Justice, 59 Jud. 478 (1976).

S. Stuart, Evidentiary Use of Other Crime Evidence: A Survey of Recent Trends in Criminal Procedure, 20 Ind. L. Rev. 183 (1987).

S. Sue, R. Smith, & C. Caldwell, Effects of Inadmissible Evidence on the Decisions of Simulated Jurors: A Moral Dilemma, 3 J. Applied Soc. Psych. 345 (1973).

S. E. Sunby, The Reasonable Doubt Rule and the Meaning of Innocence, 40 Hastings L.J. 457 (1989).

S. Tanford & S. Penrod, Social Inference Processes in Juror Judgments of Multiple Offense Trials, 47 J. Personality & Soc. Psych. 749 (1984).

B. Underwood, The Thumb on the Scales of Justice: Burdens of Persuasion in Criminal Cases, 86 Yale L.J. 1299 (1977).

R. Uviller, Evidence of Character to Prove Conduct: Illusion, Illogic and Injustice in the Courtroom, 130 U. Pa. L. Rev. 845 (1982).

J. Van Dyke, The Jury as a Political Institution, The Center Magazine 17 (Mar.-Apr. 1970).

M. Vitiello, Reconsidering Rehabilitation, 65 Tulane L. Rev. 1011 (1991).

M. Walsh, The American Jury: A Reassessment, 79 Yale L.J. 142 (1969).

R. Wasserstrom, Lawyers as Professionals: Some Moral Issues, 5 Human Rights 1 (1975).

S. Wax, Inconsistent and Repugnant Verdicts in Criminal Trials, 24 N.Y.L. Sch. L. Rev. 713 (1979).

G. Williams, The Proof of Guilt (3d ed. 1963).

I. Younger, The Facts of a Case, 3 Ark. L. Rev. 345 (1980).

Comment, Inconsistent Verdicts in a Federal Criminal Trial, 60 Colum. L. Rev. 999 (1960).

Comment, Jury Nullification in Historical Perspective: Massachusetts as a Case Study, 12 Suffolk U.L. Rev. 968 (1978).

Note, Improper Evidence in Nonjury Trials: Basis for Reversal?, 79 Harv. L. Rev. 407 (1965).

Note, Winship on Rough Waters, The Erosion of the Reasonable Doubt Standard, 106 Harv. L. Rev. 1093 (1993).

President's Commission on Law Enforcement and the Administration of Justice, The Challenge of Crime in a Free Society (1967).

Chapter 2
The Justification of Punishment

H. Acton, ed., The Philosophy of Punishment (1969).

F. Allen, The Decline of the Rehabilitative Ideal — Penal Policy and Social Policy (1981).

J. Andenaes, General Prevention, 43 J. Crim. L. & Criminology 176 (1952).

J. Andenaes, The General Preventive Effects of Punishment, 114 U. Pa. L. Rev. 949 (1960).

K. Armstrong, The Retributivist Hits Back, 70 Mind 471 (1961).

T. Baker & F. Baldwin, Eighth Amendment Challenges to the Length of a Criminal Sentence: "From Precedent to Precedent," 27 Ariz. L. Rev. 25 (1985).

J. Bentham, An Introduction to the Principles of Morals and Legislation, in Bentham & Mill, The Utilitarians 162 (Dolphin Books 1961).

J. Bentham, Principles of Penal Law, in 1 J. Bentham's Works, pt. II (J. Bowring ed. 1843).

A. Blumstein & J. Cohen, Estimation of Individual Crime Rates from Arrest Records, 70 J. Crim. L. & Criminology 561 (1979).

J. Cederblom and W. Blizek, eds., Justice and Punishment (1977).

M. Clark, The Moral Gradation of Punishment, 21 Phil. Q. 132 (1971).

J. Cohen, Incapacitating Criminals: Recent Research Findings, U.S. Department of Justice, National Institute of Justice, Research in Brief (Dec. 1983).

J. Cohen, Selective Incapacitation: An Assessment, [1984] U. Ill. L. Rev. 253.

J. Cohen & J. A. Canela-Cacho, Incapacitation and Violent Crime (Natl. Academy of Sciences 1994).

M. Cohen, Moral Aspects of the Criminal Law, 49 Yale L.J. 987 (1940).

A. Denning, Freedom Under the Law (1949).

P. Devlin, The Enforcement of Morals (1965).

E. Durkheim, The Division of Labor in Society (Simpson trans. 1933).

R. Dworkin, Lord Devlin and the Enforcement of Morals, 75 Yale L.J. 986 (1966).

A. Ewing, The Morality of Punishment (1929).

A. Ewing, A Study of Punishment II: Punishment as Viewed by the Philosopher, 21 Canadian B. Rev. 102 (1943).

G. Ezorsky, ed., Philosophical Perspectives on Punishment (1972).

J. Feinberg, The Moral Limits of the Criminal Law (1984).

L. Ferrajoli & D. Zolo, Marxism and the Criminal Question, 4 L. & Phil. 71 (1985).

M. Frankel, Criminal Sentences: Law Without Order (1973).

D. Galligan, The Return to Retribution in Penal Theory, in Crime, Proof, and Punishment 144 (C. Tapper ed. 1981).

R. Gerber & P. McAnany, eds., Contemporary Punishment: Views, Explanations and Justifications (1972).

R. Gerber & P. McAnany, Punishment: Current Survey of Philosophy and Law, 11 St. Louis U.L.J. 491 (1967).

K. Greenawalt, Punishment, in Encyclopedia of Crime and Justice 1336 (1983).

P. Greenwood, with A. Abrahams, Selective Incapacitation: Report to the National Institute of Justice (1982).

S. Grupp, ed., Theories of Punishment (1971).

J. Gussfield, On Legislating Morals: The Symbolic Process of Designating Deviancy, 56 Calif. L. Rev. 54 (1968).

H. L. A. Hart, The Aims of the Criminal Law, 23 L. & Contemp. Prob. 401 (1958).

H. L. A. Hart, Law, Liberty, and Morality (1963).

H. L. A. Hart, Review of Wootton, Crime and the Criminal Law (1963), 74 Yale L.J. 1325 (1965).

H. L. A. Hart, Social Solidarity and the Enforcement of Morality, 35 U. Chi. L. Rev. 1 (1967).

D. Hoekema, Punishment, the Criminal Law, and Christian Social Ethics, 5 Crim. Just. Ethics 31 (1986).

O. W. Holmes, The Path of the Law, 10 Harv. L. Rev. 457 (1897).

G. Hughes, Criminal Responsibility, 16 Stan. L. Rev. 470 (1964).

G. Hughes, Morals and the Criminal Law, 71 Yale L.J. 662 (1962).

J. Junker, Criminalization and Criminogenesis, 19 U.C.L.A.L. Rev. 697 (1972).

S. Kadish, More on Overcriminalization: A Reply to Professor Junker, 19 U.C.L.A.L. Rev. 719 (1972).

I. Kant, The Philosophy of Law (W. Hastie trans. 1887).

L. J. Long, Rethinking Selective Incapacitation: More at Stake than Controlling Violent Crime, 62 U.M.K.C.L. Rev. 107 (1993).

J. L. Mackie, Retribution: A Test Case For Ethical Objectivity, in J. Feinberg & Hyman Gross, eds., Philosophy of Law 677 (1991).

R. Martinson, New Findings, New Views: A Note of Caution Regarding Sentencing Reform, 7 Hofstra L. Rev. 243 (1979).

R. Martinson, What Works? — Questions and Answers About Prison Reform, 36 Pub. Interest (1974).

M. Moore, Law and Psychiatry (1984).

M. Moore, The Moral Worth of Retribution, in Character, Emotions and Responsibility (F. Schoeman ed. 1988).

H. Morris, ed., Freedom and Responsibility 546 (1961).

H. Morris, On Guilt and Innocence (1976).

H. Morris, Persons and Punishment, 52 Monist 475 (1968).

N. Morris & G. Hawkins, The Honest Politician's Guide to Crime Control 4 (1970).

J. Murphy, Marxism and Retribution, 2 Phil. & Pub. Aff. 217 (1973).

K. Pecarovich, Bibliography of Responsibility, 49 L. & Contemp. Prob. 277 (1986).

E. Pincoffs, The Rationale of Legal Punishment (1966).

R. Posner, An Economic Theory of the Criminal Law, 85 Colum. L. Rev. 1193 (1985).

L. Radzinowicz & J. Turner, A Study of Punishment I: Introductory Essay, 21 Canadian B. Rev. 91 (1943).

M. Raeder, Gender and Sentencing: Single Moms, Battered Women and Other Sex-Based Anomalies in the Gender-Free World of the Federal Sentencing Guidelines, 20 Pepp. L. Rev. 905 (1993).

N. Rafter, Partial Justice: Women, Prisons, and Social Control (2d ed. 1990).

J. Reiman, The Marxian Critique of Criminal Justice, 6 Crim. Just. Ethics 30 (1987).

D. E. Roberts, Punishing Drug Addicts Who Have Babies: Women of Color, Equality, and the Right of Privacy, 104 Harv. L. Rev. 1419 (1991).

S. Schulhofer, Due Process of Sentencing, 128 U. Pa. L. Rev. 733 (1980).

L. Seidman, Soldiers, Martyrs, and Criminals: Utilitarian Theory and the Problem of Crime Control, 94 Yale L.J. 315 (1984).

T. Sellin, The Law and Some Aspects of Criminal Conduct, in Aims and Methods of Legal Research (A. Conard ed. 1955).

S. Shavell, Criminal Law and the Optimal Use of Nonmonetary Sanctions as a Deterrent, 85 Colum. L. Rev. 1232 (1985).

J. Skolnick, Criminalization and Criminogenesis: A Reply to Professor Junker, 19 U.C.L.A.L. Rev. 715 (1972).

Steinberger, Hegel on Crime and Punishment, 77 Am. Pol. Sci. Rev. 858 (1983).

J. Stephen, Liberty, Equality, Fraternity (R. J. White ed. 1967).

G. Sykes, The Society of Captives (1971).

M. Tonry, Sentencing Reform Impacts (1987).

A. Von Hirsch, K. Knapp, & M. Tonry, The Sentencing Commission and Its Guidelines (1987).

N. Walker, The Efficacy and Morality of Deterrents, [1979] Crim. L. Rev. 129.

N. Walker, Punishment, Danger and Stigma: The Morality of Criminal Justice (1980).

R. Wasserstrom, Philosophy and Social Issues (1980).

A. Wertheimer, Should Punishment Fit the Crime?, 3 Soc. Theory & Prac. 403 (1975).

F. Zimring, Making the Punishment Fit the Crime: A Consumer's Guide to Sentencing Reform, Hastings Center Rep. (Dec. 1976).

F. Zimring & G. Hawkins, Deterrence: The Legal Threat in Crime Control (1973).

F. Zimring & G. Hawkins, Incapacitation: Penal Confinement and the Restraint of Crime (1995).

California Assembly Committee on Criminal Procedure, Progress Report, Deterrent Effects of Criminal Sanctions (May 1968).

Home Office Scottish Home Department, Report of the Committee on Homosexual Offenses and Prostitution (Wolfenden Report 1957).

Note, Selective Incapacitation: Reducing Crime Through Prediction of Recidivism, 96 Harv. L. Rev. 511 (1982).

Note, Survey on the Constitutional Right to Privacy in the Context of Homosexual Activity, 40 Miami U.L. Rev. 521 (1986).

Royal Commission on Capital Punishment, Minutes of Evidence (1949).

Chapter 3
Defining Criminal Conduct

N. Abrams, Criminal Liability of Corporate Officers for Strict Liability Offenses — A Comment on *Dotterweich* and *Park,* 28 U.C.L.A.L. Rev. 463 (1981).

A. Ashworth & E. Steiner, Criminal Omissions and Public Duties: The French Experience, 10 Leg. Stud. 153 (1990).

J. Beale, Consent in the Criminal Law, 8 Harv. L. Rev. 317 (1895).

J. C. Blue, High Noon Revisited: Commands of Assistance by Peace Officers in the Age of the Fourth Amendment, 101 Yale L.J. 1475 (1992).

V. Bolgar, the Present Function of the Maxim Ignorantia Juris Neminem Excusat — A Comparative Study, 52 Iowa L. Rev. 626 (1967).

J. Brady, Strict Liability Offenses: A Justification, 8 Crim. L. Bull. 217 (1973).

P. Brett, An Inquiry into Criminal Guilt (1963).

P. Brett, Mistake of Law as a Criminal Defense, 5 Melb. U.L. Rev. 179 (1966).

K. Brickey, Criminal Liability of Corporate Officers for Strict Liability — Another View, 35 Vand. L. Rev. 1337 (1982).

K. Brickey, Developments in the Law — Corporate Crime: Regulating Corporate Behavior Through Criminal Sanctions, 92 Harv. L. Rev. 1227 (1979).

M. Budd & J. Lynch, Voluntariness, Causation and Strict Liability, [1978] Crim. L. Rev. 74.

J. Campbell, A Strict Accountability Approach to Criminal Responsibility, 29 Fed. Prob. 333 (1965).

R. Charlow, Wilful Ignorance and Criminal Culpability, 70 Tex. L. Rev. 1351 (1992).

D. Cowley, The Retreat from *Morgan,* [1982] Crim. L. Rev. 200.

E. Curley, Excusing Rape, 5 Phil. & Pub. Aff. 325 (1976).

M. Davis, Strict Liability: Deserved Conduct for Faultless Conduct, 33 Wayne L. Rev. 1393 (1987).

F. R. Denton, The Case Against a Duty to Rescue, 4 Can. J. L. & Juris. 101 (1991).

R. Dresser, Culpability and Other Minds, 2 Law and: 41 (1992).

G. Dworkin & G. Blumenfeld, Punishment for Intentions, 75 Mind 396 (1966).

S. Estrich, Real Rape (1987).

F. Feldbrugge, Good and Bad Samaritans — A Comparative Survey of Criminal Law Provisions Concerning Failure to Rescue, 14 Am. J. Comp. L. 630 (1966).

P. Foot, Life and Death, Lond. Rev. of Books, Aug. 7, 1986.

M. Gardner, The Mens Rea Enigma: Observations on the Role of Motive in the Criminal Law Past and Present, 1993 Utah L. Rev. 635.

A. Goldstein, Conspiracy to Defraud the United States, 68 Yale L.J. 405 (1959).

A. Goodhart, Possession of Drugs and Absolute Liability, 84 L.Q. Rev. 382 (1968).

H. L. A. Hart & A. Honoré, Causation in the Law (2d ed. 1985).

S. J. Heyman, Foundations of the Duty to Rescue, 47 Vand. L. Rev. 673 (1994).

L. Houlgate, Ignorantia Juris: A Plea for Justice, 78 Ethics 32 (1967).

D. Husak, Motive and Criminal Liability, 8 Crim. Just. Ethics 3 (1989).

D. Husak & C. Callender, Wilful Ignorance, Knowledge, and the "Equal Culpability Thesis": A Study of the Deeper Significance of the Principle of Legality, 1994 Wis. L. Rev. 26.

D. Husak & A. von Hirsch, Culpability and Mistake of Law, in Action and Value in Criminal Law 157-174 (J. Gardner, J. Horder, and S. Shute, eds., 1993).

J. Jeffries, Legality, Vagueness and the Construction of Penal Statutes, 71 Va. L. Rev. 189 (1985).

J. Jeffries & P. Stephan, Defenses, Presumptions, and Burden of Proof in the Criminal Law, 88 Yale L.J. 1325 (1979).

P. Johnson, Strict Liability: The Prevalent View, in Encyclopedia of Crime and Justice 1518 (1983).

S. Kadish, The Decline of Innocence, 26 Cambridge L.J. 273 (1968).

M. Kelman, Interpretive Construction in the Substantive Criminal Law, 33 Stan. L. Rev. 591 (1981).

M. Kelman, Strict Liability: An Unorthodox View, in Encyclopedia of Crime and Justice 1512 (1983).

D. Kiesel, Who Saw This Happen — States Move to Make Crime Bystanders Responsible, 69 A.B.A.J. 1208 (1983).

J. Kleinig, Good Samaritanism, 5 Phil. & Pub. Aff. 382 (1975).

R. Leng, Death and the Criminal Law, 45 Mod. L. Rev. 206 (1982).

L. L. Levenson, Good Faith Defenses: Reshaping Strict Liability Crimes, 78 Cornell L. Rev. 401 (1993).

J. Lindgren, Death by Default, 56 Law & Contemp. Prob. 185 (1993).

J. Marshall, Intention — in Law and Society (1968).

J. Michael & H. Wechsler, A Rationale of the Law of Homicide, 37 Colum. L. Rev. 701 (1937).

B. Mitchell, Law, Morality and Religion in a Secular Society (1967).

M. S. Moore, Act and Crime — The Philosophy of Action and Its Implications for the Criminal Law (1993).

N. Morris, Somnambulistic Homicide: Ghosts, Spiders, and North Koreans, 5 Res Judicatae 29 (1951).

J. Murphy, Involuntary Acts and Criminal Liability, 81 Ethics 332 (1971).

M. Orne, Review of Reiter, Antisocial or Criminal Acts and Hypnosis: A Case Study, 46 A.B.A.J. 81 (1960).

E. Puttkammer, Consent in Criminal Assault, 19 Ill. L. Rev. 617 (1925).

J. Rachels, Active and Passive Euthanasia, 292 New Eng. J. Med. 78 (1975).

I. Robbins, The Ostrich Instruction: Deliberate Ignorance as a Criminal Mens Rea, 81 J. Crim. L. & Criminology 191 (1990).

D. E. Roberts, Motherhood and Crime, 79 Iowa L. Rev. 95 (1993).

P. Robinson, A Brief History of Distinctions in Criminal Culpability, 31 Hastings L. Rev. 815 (1980).

P. Robinson, Criminal Liability for Omissions: A Brief Summary and Critique of the Law in the United States, 29 N.Y.L. Sch. L. Rev. 101 (1984).

P. Robinson, Hate Crimes: Crimes of Motive, Character, or Group Terror?, 1992/1993 Annual Survey of American Law 605.

P. Robinson & J. Grall, Element Analysis in Defining Criminal Liability: The Model Penal Code and Beyond, 35 Stan. L. Rev. 681 (1983).

J. Sams, The Availability of the "Cultural Defense" as an Excuse for Criminal Behavior, 16 Ga. J. Intl. & Comp. L. 335 (1986).

F. Sayre, Public Welfare Offenses, 33 Colum. L. Rev. 55 (1933).

S. Schulhofer, Harm and Punishment: A Critique of Emphasis on the Results of Conduct in the Criminal Law, 122 U. Pa. L. Rev. 1497 (1974).

L. Schwartz, Reform of the Federal Criminal Laws: Issues, Tactics and Prospects, [1977] Duke L.J. 171.

K. W. Simons, Rethinking Mental States, 72 B.U.L. Rev. 463 (1992).

J. Smith, Liability for Omissions in Criminal Law, 14 Leg. Stud. 88 (1984).

M. Thornton, Intention in Criminal Law, 5 Can. J.L. & Juris. 177 (1992).

M. Vitiello, Does Culpability Matter?: Statutory Construction Under 42 U.S.C. §6928, 6 Tulane Env. L.J. 187 (1993).

R. Wasserstrom, Strict Liability in the Criminal Law, 12 Stan. L. Rev. 731 (1960).

T. Weinstein, Visiting the Sins of the Child on the Parent: The Legality of Criminal Parental Liability Statutes, 64 S. Cal. L. Rev. 859 (1991).

G. Williams, Consent and Public Policy, [1962] Crim. L. Rev. 74.

G. Williams, Euthanasia, 41 Med.-Leg. J. 14 (1973).

G. Williams, The Mental Element in Crime (1965).

G. Williams, Oblique Intention, 46 Camb. L.J. 417 (1987).

G. Williams, The Unresolved Problem of Recklessness, 8 Leg. Studies 74 (1988).

B. Wootton, Crime and the Criminal Law (1963).

D. B. Yaeger, A Radical Community of Aid: A Rejoinder to Opponents of Affirmative Duties to Help Strangers, 71 Wash. U.L.Q. 1, 15 (1993).

Annot., Consent as defense to charge of mayhem, 86 A.L.R.2d 268 (1962).

Annot., Homicide: Physician's withdrawal of life supports from comatose patient, 47 A.L.R.4th 19 (1986).

California Joint Legislative Committee for Revision of the Penal Code, Penal Code Revision Project (Tent. Draft No. 2, 1968).

Comment, United States v. Barker: Misapplication of the Reliance on an Official Interpretation of the Law Defense, 66 Calif. L. Rev. 809 (1978).

Note, Common Law Crimes in the United States, 47 Colum. L. Rev. 1332 (1947).

Note, Criminal Liability Without Fault: A Philosophical Perspective, 75 Colum. L. Rev. 1517 (1975).

Note, Cultural Defenses: One Person's Culture Is Another Person's Crime, 9 Loy. L.A. Intl. & Comp. L.J. 751 (1987).

Note, The Cultural Defense in the Criminal Law, 99 Harv. L. Rev. 1293 (1986).

Note, Declaratory Relief in the Criminal Law, 80 Harv. L. Rev. 1490 (1967).

Note, Developments in the Law — Corporate Crime: Regulating Corporate Behavior Through Criminal Sanctions, 92 Harv. L. Rev. 1227 (1979).

Note (J. DeMarco), A Funny Thing Happened on the Way to the Courthouse: Mens Rea, Document Destruction, and the Federal Obstruction of Justice Statute, 67 N.Y.U.L. Rev. 570 (1992).

Note, Hypnotism and the Law, 14 Vand. L. Rev. 1509 (1961).

Note (J. Marcus), Model Penal Code Section 2.02(7) and Willful Blindness, 102 Yale L.J. 2231 (1993).

Note, Sports Violence as Criminal Assault: Development of the Doctrine by Canadian Courts, [1986] Duke L.J. 1030.

Note, The Tragic Choice: Termination of Care for Patients in a Permanent Vegetative State, 51 N.Y.U.L. Rev. 285 (1976).

Note (A. F. Brooke), When Ignorance of the Law Became an Excuse: *Lambert* and Its Progeny, 19 Am. J. Crim. L. 279 (1992).

A Symposium on Punishment: Critique and Justification, 33 Rutgers L. Rev. 607 (1981).

Chapter 4
Rape

M. Amir, Patterns in Forcible Rape (1971).

V. Berger, Man's Trial, Woman's Tribulation: Rape Cases in the Courtroom, 77 Colum. L. Rev. 1 (1977).

V. Berger, Not So Simple Rape, 7 Crim. J. Ethics 69 (1988).

M. Chamallas, Consent, Equality and the Legal Control of Sexual Conduct, 61 S. Cal. L. Rev. 777 (1988).

Developments in the Law—Domestic Violence, 106 Harv. L. Rev. 1498 (1993).

D. A. Dripps, Beyond Rape: An Essay on the Difference Between the Presence of Force and the Absence of Consent, 92 Colum. L. Rev. 1780 (1992).

S. Estrich, Palm Beach Stories, 11 Law & Phil. 5 (1992).

S. Estrich, Real Rape (1987).

S. Estrich, Teaching Rape Law, 102 Yale L.J. 509 (1992).

S. Friedland, Date Rape and the Culture of Acceptance, 43 Fla. L. Rev. 487 (1991).

I. Frieze, Investigating the Causes and Consequences of Marital Rape (1983).

N. Gilbert, The Phantom Epidemic of Sexual Assault, The Public Interest 54 (Spring 1991).

S. Gordon, Reckless and Inconsiderate Rape, [1991] Crim. L. Rev. 172.

M. Gordon & S. Riger, The Female Fear: The Social Cost of Rape (1991).

V. Hans & N. Vidmar, Judging the Jury (1986).

L. Henderson, Getting to Know: Honoring Women in Law and in Fact, 2 Tex. J. Women & L. 41 (1993).

M. Hilf, Marital Privacy and Spousal Rape, 16 New Eng. L. Rev. 31 (1980).

D. Husak & G. C. Thomas III, Date Rape, Social Convention and Reasonable Mistakes, 11 Law & Phil. 95 (1992).

M. Koss, et al., The Scope of Rape, 55 J. Consulting & Clinical Psych. 162 (1987).

J. Larson, "Women Understand So Little, They Call My Good Nature 'Deceit'": A Feminist Rethinking of Seduction, 93 Colum. L. Rev. 374 (1993).

W. Loh, The Impact of Common Law and Reform Rape Statutes on Prosecution: An Empirical Study, 55 Wash. L. Rev. 543 (1980).

C. MacKinnon, Feminism, Marxism, Method, and the State: Toward a Feminist Jurisprudence, 8 Signs 635 (1983).

C. MacKinnon, Feminism Unmodified (1987).

J. Marsh, A. Geist & N. Caplan, Rape and the Limits of Law Reform (1982).

L. Pineau, Date Rape: A Feminist Analysis, 8 Law & Phil. 217 (1989).

D. Russell, Rape in Marriage (2d ed. 1990).

S. Schulhofer, The Gender Question in Criminal Law, 7 Soc. Phil. & Pol. 105 (1990).

S. Schulhofer, Taking Sexual Autonomy Seriously: Rape Law and Beyond, 11 Law & Phil. 35 (1992).

E. Stanko, Intimate Intrusions (1985).

J. Tanford & A. Bocchino, Rape Victim Shield Laws and the Sixth Amendment, 128 U. Pa. L. Rev. 544 (1980).

R. Weiner, Shifting the Communication Burden: A Meaningful Consent Standard in Rape, 6 Harv. Women's L.J. 143 (1983).

C. Wells, Swatting the Subjectivist Bug, [1982] Crim. L. Rev. 209.

R. West, The Difference in Women's Hedonic Lives, 3 Wis. Women's L.J. 81 (1987).

Comment, Towards a Consent Standard in the Law of Rape, 43 U. Chi. L. Rev. 613 (1976).

Chapter 5
Homicide

A. J. Ashworth, The Doctrine of Provocation, 35 Camb. L.J. 292 (1976).

D. C. Baldus, G. G. Woodworth & C. A. Pulaski, Equal Justice and the Death Penalty (1990).

J. Barzun, In Favor of Capital Punishment, 31 Am. Scholar 181 (Spring 1962).

H. Bedau, The Case Against the Death Penalty (1977).

H. Bedau, The Courts, the Constitution, and Capital Punishment (1977).

H. Bedau, Death as Punishment (1964).

H. Bedau, ed., The Death Penalty in America (1964).

H. Bedau & M. Radelet, Miscarriages of Justice in Potentially Capital Cases, 40 Stan. L. Rev. 21 (1987).

R. A. Berk, R. Weiss & J. Boger, Chance and the Death Penalty, 27 Law & Socy. Rev. 89 (1993).

W. Berns, For Capital Punishment (1979).

C. Black, Capital Punishment: The Inevitability of Caprice and Mistake 29 (2d ed. 1981).

B. Cardozo, What Medicine Can Do for Law, in Law and Literature and Other Essays and Addresses (1931).

D. K. Coker, Heat of Passion and Wife Killing: Men Who Batter / Men Who Kill, 2 S. Cal. Rev. L. & Women's Stud. 71 (1992).

K. Cole, Killings During Crime: Toward a Discriminating Theory of Strict Liability, 28 Am. Crim. L. Rev. 73 (1990).

R. A. Collings, Jr., Negligent Murder — Some Stateside Footnotes to D.P.P. v. Smith, 49 Calif. L. Rev. 254 (1961).

D. Crump & S. W. Crump, In Defense of the Felony-Murder Doctrine, 8 Harv. J.L. & Pub. Pol. 359 (1985).

D. A. Donovan & S. Wildman, Is the Reasonable Man Obsolete? A Critical Perspective on Self-Defense and Provocation, 14 Loy. L.A.L. Rev. 435 (1981).

J. Dressler, Rethinking Heat of Passion: A Defense in Search of a Rationale, 73 J. Crim. L. & Criminology 421 (1982).

I. Ehrlich, The Deterrent Effect of Capital Punishment: A Question of Life and Death, 65 Am. Econ. Rev. 397 (1975).

G. Fletcher, Reflections on Felony-Murder, 12 Sw. U.L. Rev. 413 (1981).

G. Fletcher, The Theory of Criminal Negligence: A Comparative Analysis, 119 U. Pa. L. Rev. 401 (1971).

S. Gross, Race and Death: The Judicial Evaluation of Evidence of Discrimination in Capital Sentencing, 18 U.C. Davis L. Rev. 1275 (1985).

J. Horder, Provocation and Responsibility (1992).

P. E. Johnson, Foreword: The Accidental Decision and How It Happens, 65 Calif. L. Rev. 231 (1977).

R. Lempert, Deterrence and Desert: An Assessment of the Moral Bases for Capital Punishment, 79 Mich. L. Rev. 1177 (1981).

L. S. Lustberg & J. V. Jacobi, The Battered Woman as a Reasonable Person: A Critique of the Appellate Division Decision in *State v. McClain*, 22 Seton Hall L. Rev. 365 (1992).

T. B. Macaulay, A Penal Code Prepared by the Indian Law Commissioners (1837).

M. Meltsner, Cruel and Unusual: The Supreme Court and Capital Punishment (1973).

J. Michael & H. Wechsler, A Rationale of the Law of Homicide, 37 Colum. L. Rev. 1261 (1937).

S. J. Morse, Diminished Capacity: A Moral and Legal Conundrum, 2 Intl. J.L. & Psych. 271 (1979).

S. J. Morse, Undiminished Confusion in Diminished Capacity, 75 J. Crim. L. & Criminology 1 (1984).

S. H. Pillsbury, Evil and the Law of Murder, 24 U.C. Davis L. Rev. 437 (1990).

M. L. Radelet, H. A. Bedau & C. E. Putnam, In Spite of Innocence: Erroneous Convictions in Capital Cases (1993).

E. Rapaport, The Death Penalty and Gender Discrimination, 25 Law & Socy. Rev. 367 (1991).

R. A. Rosen, Felony Murder and the Eighth Amendment Jurisprudence of Death, 31 B.C.L. Rev. 1103 (1990).

N. E. Roth & S. E. Sunby, The Felony-Murder Rule: A Doctrine at Constitutional Crossroads, 70 Cornell L. Rev. 446 (1985).

J. W. Salmond, Jurisprudence (8th ed. 1930).

S. Schulhofer, Harm and Punishment: A Critique of Emphasis on the Results of Conduct in the Criminal Law, 122 U. Pa. L. Rev. 1497 (1974).

T. Sellin, The Death Penalty, A Report for the Model Penal Code Project of the American Law Institute (1959).

R. Singer, The Resurgence of Mens Rea: I - Provocation, Emotional Disturbance, and the Model Penal Code, 27 B.C.L. Rev. 243 (1986).

J. C. Smith, The Element of Chance in Criminal Liability, [1971] Crim. L. Rev. 63.

J. F. Stephen, A History of the Criminal Law (Vol. 3) (1883).

S. E. Sunby, The Lockett Paradox: Reconciling Guided Discretion and Unguided Mitigation in Capital Sentencing, 38 U.C.L.A.L. Rev. 1147 (1991).

E. Van Den Haag, On Deterrence and the Death Penalty, 60 J. Crim. L. & Criminology 141 (1969).

E. Van Den Haag, Punishing Criminals (1975).

H. Wechsler, The Challenge of a Model Penal Code, 65 Harv. L. Rev. 1097 (1952).

W. White, Capital Punishment's Future, 91 Mich. L. Rev. 1429 (1993).

W. White, The Death Penalty in the Eighties (1987).

W. White, Life in the Balance (1984).

G. Williams, Provocation and the Reasonable Man, [1954] Crim. L. Rev. 740.

F. Zimring & G. Hawkins, Capital Punishment and the American Agenda (1986).

Annot., Unintentional killing of or injury to third person during attempted self-defense, 55 A.L.R.3d 620 (1974).

Comment (R. Mison), Homophobia in Manslaughter: The Homosexual Advance as Insufficient Provocation, 80 Cal. L. Rev. 133 (1992).

Note, Merger and the California Felony-Murder Rule, 20 U.C.L.A.L. Rev. 250 (1972).

Note, The California Supreme Court Assaults the Felony-Murder Rule, 22 Stan. L. Rev. 1059 (1970).

Report of the Royal Commission on Capital Punishment, 1949-1953, 25-28 (1953).

Chapter 6
The Significance of Resulting Harm

T. Arnold, Criminal Attempts — The Rise and Fall of an Abstraction, 40 Yale L.J. 53 (1930).

S. Brenner, Undue Influence in the Criminal Law: A Proposed Analysis of the Criminal Offense of Causing Suicide, 47 Albany L. Rev. 62 (1982).

R. Buxton, Circumstances, Consequences and Attempted Rape, [1984] Crim. L. Rev. 25.

M. Dan-Cohen, Causation, in 1 Encyclopedia of Crime and Justice 165 (1983).

R. A. Duff, The Circumstances of an Attempt, 50 Camb. L.J. 100 (1991).

F. Dutile & H. Moore, Mistake and Impossibility: Arranging a Marriage Between Two Difficult Partners, 74 Nw. U.L. Rev. 166 (1979).

I. Elliott, Australian Letter, [1969] Crim. L. Rev. 511.

A. Enker, Mens Rea and Criminal Attempt, [1977] Am. B. Found. Res. J. 845.

R. P. Faulkner & D. H. Hsiao, And Where You Go I'll Follow: The Constitutionality of Antistalking Laws and Proposed Model Legislation, 31 Harv. J. Legis. 1 (1994).

G. Fletcher, Constructing a Theory of Impossible Attempts, 5 Crim. J. Ethics 53 (1986).

K. Greenawalt, Speech and Crime, [1980] Am. B. Found. Res. J. 645.

H. L. A. Hart & A. Honoré, Causation in the Law (1958).

P. Hasset, Absolutism in Causation, 38 Syracuse L. Rev. 683 (1987).

G. Hughes, One Further Footnote on Attempting the Impossible, 42 N.Y.U.L. Rev. 1005 (1967).

S. H. Kadish, The Criminal Law and the Luck of the Draw, 84 J. Crim. L. & Criminology 679 (1994).

M. Kelman, Interpretive Construction in the Substantive Criminal Law, 33 Stan. L. Rev. 591 (1981).

D. Lanham, Murder by Instigating Suicide, [1980] Crim. L. Rev. 213.

G. Marston, Contemporaneity of Act and Intention in Crimes, 86 L.Q. Rev. 208 (1970).

A. McIntyre, Guilty Bystanders? On the Legitimacy of Duty to Rescue Statutes, 23 Phil. & Pub. Aff. 157 (1994).

R. Misner, The New Attempt Laws: An Unsuspected Threat to the Fourth Amendment, 33 Stan. L. Rev. 201 (1981).

M. Moore, Act and Crime — The Philosophy of Action and Its Implications for Criminal Law (1993).

D. G. Moriarty, Extending the Defense of Renunciation, 62 Temple L. Rev. 1 (1989).

R. Perkins, An Analysis of Assault and Attempts to Assault, 47 Minn. L. Rev. 71 (1962).

R. Perkins, Criminal Attempt and Related Problems, 2 U.C.L.A.L. Rev. 319 (1955).

I. Robbins, Attempting the Impossible: The Emerging Consensus, 23 Harv. J. Legisl. 377 (1986).

I. Robbins, Double Inchoate Crimes, 26 Harv. J. Legis. 1 (1989).

P. Robinson, Imputed Criminal Liability, 93 Yale L.J. 609 (1984).

S. Schulhofer, Attempt, in 1 Encyclopedia of Crime and Justice 97 (1983).

S. Schulhofer, Harm and Punishment: A Critique of Emphasis on the Results of Conduct in the Criminal Law, 122 U. Pa. L. Rev. 1497 (1974).

S. Shavell, Deterrence and the Punishment of Attempts, 19 J. Legal Stud. 435 (1990).

J. Smith, The Element of Chance in Criminal Liability, [1971] Crim. L. Rev. 63.

J. C. Smith & B. Hogan, Criminal Law 46 (7th ed. 1992).

J. Waite, The Prevention of Repeated Crime (1943).

T. Weigend, Why Lady Eldon Should be Acquitted: The Social Harm in Attempting the Impossible, 27 De Paul L. Rev. 231 (1979).

G. Williams, *Finis* for *Novus Actus,* 48 Camb. L.J. 391 (1989).
G. Williams, Police Control of Intending Criminals, [1955] Crim. L. Rev. 66.
G. Williams, The Problem of Reckless Attempts, [1983] Crim. L. Rev. 365.

Comment on *Stephenson,* 31 Mich. L. Rev. 659 (1933).
Note (M. J. Gilligan), Stalking the Stalker: Developing New Laws to Thwart Those Who Terrorize Others, 27 Ga. L. Rev. 285 (1992).

Chapter 7
Group Criminality

J. Arlen, The Potentially Perverse Effects of Corporate Criminal Liability, 23 J. Legal Stud. 833 (1994).
M. B. Bixby, Workplace Homicide: Trends, Issues, and Policy, 70 Or. L. Rev. 333 (1991).
S. W. Brenner, RICO, CCE, and Other Complex Crimes: The Transformation of American Criminal Law?, 2 Wm. & Mary Bill of Rights J. 239 (1993).
K. Brickey, Corporate Criminal Liability, A Primer for Corporate Counsel, 40 Bus. Law. 129 (1984).
K. Brickey, Corporate Criminal Liability: A Treatise on the Criminal Liability of Corporations, Their Officers and Agents (2d ed. 1992).
K. Brickey, Death in the Workplace: Corporate Liability for Criminal Homicide, 2 Notre Dame J. L., Ethics & Pub. Pol. 753 (1987).
P. H. Bucy, Corporate Ethos: A Standard for Imposing Corporate Criminal Liability, 75 Minn. L. Rev. 1095 (1991).
D. Burgman, Unilateral Conspiracy: Three Critical Perspectives, 29 De Paul L. Rev. 75 (1979).
S. Burke, RICO, 24 Am. Crim. L. Rev. 651 (1987).
J. Coffee, Corporate Criminal Responsibility, in Encyclopedia of Crime and Justice 253 (1983).
P. Cook, The Use of Criminal Sanctions to Regulate Product Safety: Comment on Wheeler, 13 J. Leg. Stud. 619 (1984).
T. Cousens, Agreement as an Element of Conspiracy, 23 Va. L. Rev. 898 (1937).
F. Cullen, Corporate Crime Under Attack: The Ford Pinto Case and Beyond (1987).
J. Dressler, Reassessing the Theoretical Underpinnings of Accomplice Liability: New Solutions to an Old Problem, 37 Hastings L. Rev. 91 (1985).
R. A. Duff, "Can I Help You?" Accessorial Liability and the Intention to Assist, 10 Legal Stud. 167 (1990).
R. Farrell & V. Swigert, Corporate Homicide: Definitional Processes in the Creation of Deviance, 15 L. & Socy. Rev. 161 (1980).
D. Fischel & A. Sykes, Civil RICO after *Reves:* An Economic Commentary, [1993] Sup. Ct. Rev. 157.
B. Fisse, Reconstructing Corporate Criminal Law: Deterrence, Retribution, Fault and Sanctions, 56 S. Cal. L. Rev. 114 (1983).
M. Goldsmith, RICO and Enterprise Criminality: A Response to Gerard E. Lynch, 88 Colum. L. Rev. 774 (1988).
A. Goldstein, Conspiracy to Defraud the United States, 68 Yale L.J. 405 (1959).

J. F. Holderman, Reconciling RICO's Conspiracy and "Group" Enterprise Concepts with Traditional Conspiracy Doctrine, 52 U. Cin. L.R. 385 (1983).

D. Husak, Justifications and the Criminal Liability of Accessories, 80 J. Crim. L. & Criminology 491 (1989).

P. Johnson, The Unnecessary Crime of Conspiracy, 61 Calif. L. Rev. 1137 (1973).

S. Kadish, Some Observations on the Use of Criminal Sanctions in Enforcing Economic Regulations, 30 U. Chi. L. Rev. 423 (1963).

S. Kadish, A Theory of Complicity, in Issues in Contemporary Legal Philosophy: The Influence of H. L. A. Hart 288 (Ruth Gavison ed. 1987).

D. Lanham, Drivers, Control and Accomplices, [1982] Crim. L. Rev. 419.

E. Lederman, Criminal Law, Perpetrator and Corporations: Rethinking a Complex Triangle, 76 J. Crim. L. & Criminology 285 (1985).

G. Lynch, RICO: The Crime of Being a Criminal, 87 Colum. L. Rev. 920 (1987).

G. E. Lynch, A Reply to Michael Goldsmith, 88 Colum. L. Rev. 802 (1988).

P. Marcus, Criminal Conspiracy Law: Time to Turn Back from an Ever Expanding, Ever More Troubling Area, 1 Wm. & Mary Bill of Rights J. 1 (1992).

J. Moore, Corporate Culpability and the Federal Sentencing Guidelines, 34 Ariz. L. Rev. 743 (1992).

C. Morris, Punitive Damages in Personal Injury Cases, 21 Ohio St. L.J. 216 (1960).

R. Posner, Retribution and Related Concepts of Punishment, 9 J. Leg. Stud. 71 (1980).

I. Robbins, Double Inchoate Crimes, 26 Harv. J. Legis. 1 (1989).

D. E. Roberts, Motherhood and Crime, 79 Iowa L. Rev. 95 (1993).

F. Sayre, Criminal Responsibility for the Acts of Another, 43 Harv. L. Rev. 689 (1930).

D. Sentelle, RICO: The Monster That Ate Jurisprudence (1989).

J. C. Smith, Commentary, [1991] Crim. L. Rev. 134.

J. C. Smith & B. Hogan, Criminal Law (7th ed. 1992).

W. Spurgeon & T. Fagan, Criminal Liability for Life-Endangering Corporate Conduct, 72 J. Crim. L. & Criminology 400 (1981).

B. Tarlow, RICO: The New Darling of the Prosecutor's Nursery, 49 Fordham L. Rev. 165 (1980).

B. Tarlow, RICO Revisited, 17 Ga. L. Rev. 291 (1983).

C. Wells, Corporations and Criminal Responsibility (1993).

M. Wheeler, Products Liability: Manufacturers, Wrong Targets for Threat of Criminal Sanctions?, Natl. L.J. (Dec. 22, 1980).

M. Wheeler, The Use of Criminal Statutes to Regulate Product Safety, 13 J. Leg. Stud. 593 (1984).

S. Whitzman, Proof of Conspiracy: The Co-Conspirator's Exception to the Hearsay Rule, 28 Crim. L.Q. 203 (1986).

G. Williams, Victims and Other Exempt Parties in Crime, 10 Legal Stud. 245 (1990).

S. Zipperman, The Park Doctrine—Application of Strict Criminal Liability to Corporate Individuals for Violation of Environmental Crimes, 10 U.C.L.A.J. Environ. L. 123 (1991).

Comment (J. D. Heep), Adapting the Responsible Corporate Officer Doctrine in Light of United States v. MacDonald & Watson Waste Oil Co., 78 Minn. L. Rev. 699 (1994).

Comment, Corporate Homicide: Will Michigan Follow Suit?, 62 U. Det. L. Rev. 65 (1984).

Comment (D. J. Miester, Jr.), Criminal Liability for Corporations That Kill, 64 Tul. L. Rev. 919 (1990).

Comment, Whose Head Is in the Sand? Problems with the Use of the Ostrich Instruction in Conspiracy Cases, 13 W. New Eng. L. Rev. 35 (1991).

National Commission on Reform of Federal Criminal Laws, Working Papers, Vol. 1 (1970).

Note, An Analysis of Wharton's Rule, 71 Nw. U.L. Rev. 547 (1976).

Note, Conspiracy: Statutory Reform Since the Model Penal Code, 75 Colum. L.R. 1122 (1975).

Note, Conspiracy to Violate RICO: Expanding Traditional Conspiracy Law, 58 Notre Dame Law 587 (1983).

Note, Corporate Criminal Liability for Homicide, 17 Cal. West. L. Rev. 465 (1981).

Note, Corporate Homicide: A New Assault on Corporate Decision-Making, 54 Notre Dame Law. 911 (1979).

Note, Corporate Homicide: The Stark Realities of Artificial Beings and Legal Fictions, 8 Pepperdine L. Rev. 367 (1981).

Note, Developments in the Law — Corporate Crime: Regulating Corporate Behavior Through Criminal Sanctions, 92 Harv. L. Rev. 1227 (1979).

Note, Developments in the Law — Criminal Conspiracy, 72 Harv. L. Rev. 920 (1959).

Note, Economic Inefficiency of Corporate Criminal Liability, 73 J. Crim. L. & Criminology 582 (1982).

Note, The Unnecessary Rule of Consistency in Conspiracy Trials, 135 U. Pa. L. Rev. 246 (1986).

Note, The Withdrawal Defense to Criminal Conspiracy: An Unconstitutional Allocation of the Burden of Proof, 51 Geo. Wash. L. Rev. 420 (1981).

Chapter 8
Exculpation

R. Aldridge & B. Stark, Nuclear War, Citizen Intervention, and the Necessity Defense, 26 Santa Clara L. Rev. 299 (1986).

V. J. Aprile, Criminal Justice Matters: Executing the Mentally Retarded, 9 Crim. L.J. 38 (Spring 1994).

P. Arenella, Convicting the Morally Blameless: Reassessing the Relationship Between Legal and Moral Accountability, 39 U.C.L.A.L. Rev. 1511 (1992).

P. Arenella, The Diminished Capacity and Diminished Responsibility Defenses: Two Children of a Doomed Marriage, 77 Colum. L. Rev. 827 (1977).

P. Arenella, Reflections on Current Proposals to Abolish or Reform the Insanity Defense, 8 Am. J.L. & Med. 271 (1982).

J. D. Armour, Race Ipsa Loquitur: Of Reasonable Racists, Intelligent Beyesians, and Involuntary Negrophobes, 46 Stan. L. Rev. 781 (1994).

E. Arnolds & N. Garland, The Defense of Necessity in Criminal Law, 65 J. Crim. L. & Criminology 289 (1974).

R. Aronson, Should the Privilege Against Self-Incrimination Apply to Compelled Psychiatric Examinations?, 26 Stan. L. Rev. 55 (1973).

J. Austin, A Plea for Excuses, 57 Proceedings Aristotelian Socy. 1 (1956-1957).

A. E. Barlow, Self-Defense and Reckless Crimes Against Third Parties, 22 Colum. J.L. & Soc. Probs. 417 (1989).

J. Blackman, Potential Uses for Expert Testimony: Ideas Toward the Representation of Battered Women Who Kill, 9 Women's Rights L. Rptr. 227 (1986).

A. Blum, Debunking Myths of the Insanity Plea, Natl. L. J., Apr. 20, 1992, at 9.

R. Boldt, The Construction of Responsibility in the Criminal Law, 140 U. Pa. L. Rev. 2245 (1992).

R. Bonnie, The Moral Basis of the Insanity Defense, 69 A.B.A.J. 194 (1983).

R. Bonnie & C. Slobogin, The Role of Mental Health Professionals in the Criminal Process: The Case for Informed Speculation, 66 Va. L. Rev. 427 (1980).

C. Boorse & R. Sorensen, Ducking Harm, 85 J. Phil. 115 (1988).

C. Boorse, Premenstrual Syndrome and Criminal Responsibility, in Premenstrual Syndrome (B. Ginsburg & B. Carter eds. 1987).

R. M. Brown, No Duty to Retreat: Violence and Values in American History and Society (1991).

B. Cardozo, Law and Literature (1930).

S. Carter, When Victims Happen to Be Black, 97 Yale L.J. 420 (1988).

R. Cipparone, The Defense of Battered Women Who Kill, 135 U. Pa. L. Rev. 427 (1987).

A. M. Coughlin, Excusing Women, 82 Cal. L. Rev. 1 (1994).

D. Creach, Partially Determined Imperfect Self-Defense, 34 Stan. L. Rev. 615 (1982).

P. L. Crocker, The Meaning of Equality for Battered Women Who Kill in Self-Defense, 8 Harv. Women's L.J. 121 (1985).

R. Cross, Reflections on *Bratty*'s Case, 78 L.Q. Rev. 236 (1962).

M. Dan-Cohen, Actus Reus, in Encyclopedia of Crime and Justice 15 (1983).

R. Delgado, Ascription of Criminal States of Mind: Toward a Defense Theory for the Coercively Persuaded ("Brainwashed") Defendant, 63 Minn. L. Rev. 1 (1978).

R. Delgado, "Rotten Social Background": Should the Criminal Law Recognize a Defense of Severe Environmental Deprivation?, 3 L. & Inequality 9 (1985).

S. Dell, Diminished Responsibility Reconsidered, [1982] Crim. L. Rev. 809.

D. Denno, Considering Lead Poisoning as a Criminal Defense, 20 Ford. Urb. L.J. 377 (1993).

A. Dershowitz, The Abuse Excuse (1994).

G. Dix, Psychological Abnormality as a Factor in Grading Criminal Liability: Diminished Capacity, Diminished Responsibility, and the Like, 62 J. Crim. L., Criminology & P.S. 313 (1971).

J. Dressler, Reaffirming the Moral Legitimacy of the Doctrine of Diminished Capacity: A Brief Reply to Professor Morse, 75 J. Crim. L. & Criminology 953 (1984).

R. Dworkin, Life's Dominion 179 (1993).

J. Ellis, The Consequences of the Insanity Defense: Proposals to Reform Post-Acquittal Commitment Laws, 35 Catholic U.L. Rev. 961 (1986).

G. Epps, Any Which Way But Loose: Interpretive Strategies and Attitudes Toward Violence in the Evolution of the Anglo-American "Retreat Rule," 55 Law & Contemp. Prob. 303 (1992).

C. Erlinder, Paying the Price for Vietnam: Post-Traumatic Stress Disorder and Criminal Behavior, 25 B.C.L. Rev. 305 (1984).

S. Estrich, Defending Women (Book Review, Cynthia Gillespie, Justifiable Homicide: Battered Women, Self-Defense and the Law (1989)), 88 Mich. L. Rev. 1430 (1990).

J. Eule, The Presumption of Sanity: Bursting the Bubble, 25 U.C.L.A.L. Rev. 637 (1978).

C. P. Ewing, Battered Women Who Kill: Psychological Self-Defense as Legal Justification (1987).

D. L. Faigman, Discerning Justice When Battered Women Kill, 39 Hastings L.J. 207 (1987).

J. Feinberg, Overlooking the Merits of the Individual Case: An Unpromising Approach to the Right to Die, 4 Ratio Juris. 131 (1991).

L. Fentiman, "Guilty But Mentally Ill": The Real Verdict Is Guilty, 26 B.C.L. Rev. 601 (1985).

H. Fingarette, Addiction and Criminal Responsibility, 84 Yale L.J. 413 (1975).

H. Fingarette, Heavy Drinking (1988).

H. Fingarette, The Meaning of Criminal Insanity (1972).

H. Fingarette, The Perils of *Powell:* In Search of a Factual Foundation for the "Disease Concept of Alcoholism," 83 Harv. L. Rev. 793 (1970).

G. Fletcher, A Crime of Self Defense: Bernhard Goetz and the Law on Trial (1988).

G. Fletcher, The Individualization of Excusing Conditions, 47 S. Cal. L. Rev. 1269 (1974).

G. Fletcher, Proportionality and the Psychotic Aggressor: A Vignette in Comparative Criminal Theory, 8 Israel L. Rev. 367 (1973).

G. Fletcher, Should Intolerable Conditions Generate a Justification or an Excuse for Escape?, 26 U.C.L.A.L. Rev. 1355 (1979).

S. Fox, Physical Disorder, Consciousness, and Criminal Liability, 63 Colum. L. Rev. 645 (1963).

L. Fuller, The Case of the Speluncean Explorers, 62 Harv. L. Rev. 616 (1949).

M. Gardner, The Defense of Necessity and the Right to Escape from Prison, 49 S. Cal. L. Rev. 110 (1975).

P. Glazebrook, The Necessity Plea in English Criminal Law, 30 Camb. L.J. 87 (1972).

K. Greenawalt, "Uncontrollable" Actions and the Eighth Amendment: Impiications of Powell v. Texas, 69 Colum. L. Rev. 927 (1969).

M. Gur-Arye, Should the Criminal Law Distinguish Between Necessity as a Justification and Necessity as an Excuse?, 102 L.Q. Rev. 71 (1986).

V. Hans & D. Slater, John W. Hinckley, Jr. & the Insanity Defense: The Public's Verdict, 47 Public Opinion Q. 202 (1983).

P. Hassman, Annot., Drug Addiction or Related Mental State as Defense to Criminal Charge, 73 A.L.R.3d 16 (1991).

D. Hermann, Assault on the Insanity Defense, 14 Rutgers L.J. 241 (1983).

F. Hicks, Human Jettison (1927).

E. Holtzman, Premenstrual Symptoms: No Legal Defense, 60 St. John's L. Rev. 712 (1986).

J. Horder, Autonomy, Provocation and Duress, [1992] Crim. L. Rev. 70.

P. Johnson, The Turnabout in the Insanity Defense, in 6 Crime and Justice 221 (M. Tonry & N. Morris eds. 1985).

R. Johnson, Death Work 50 (1990).

M. Kadish & S. Kadish, Discretion to Disobey (1973).

S. Kadish, The Decline of Innocence, 26 Camb. L.J. 273 (1968).

S. Kadish, Letting Patients Die: Legal and Moral Reflections, 80 Cal. L. Rev. 857 (1992).

Y. Kamisar, A Law to Stay the Cold Hand of "Dr. Death," Legal Times, Mar. 8, 1993.

J. Kaplan, The Hardest Drug (1983).

J. Q. La Fond, The Case for Liberalizing the Use of Deadly Force in Self-Defense, 6 U. Puget Sound L. Rev. 237 (1983).

M. Lippman, The Necessity Defense and Political Protest, 26 Crim. L. Bull. 317 (1990).

D. Lunde & R. Wilson, Brainwashing as a Defense to Criminal Liability: Patty Hearst Revisited, 13 Crim. L. Bull. 341 (1977).

I. Mackay, The Sleepwalker Is Not Insane, 55 Mod. L. Rev. 714 (1992).

R. D. Mackay, The Consequences of Killing Very Young Children, [1993] Crim. L. Rev. 21.

C. MacKinnon, Toward Feminist Jurisprudence, 34 Stan. L. Rev. 703 (1982).

H. Maguigan, Battered Women and Self-Defense: Myths and Misconceptions in Current Reform Proposals, 140 U. Pa. L. Rev. 379 (1991).

V. M. Mather, The Skeleton in the Closet: The Battered Woman Syndrome, Self-Defense and Expert Testimony, 39 Mercer L. Rev. 545 (1988).

D. McCord, The English and American History of Voluntary Intoxication to Negate Mens Rea, 11 J. Legal Hist. 372 (1990).

D. McCord & S. K. Lyons, Moral Reasoning and the Criminal Law: The Example of Self-Defense, 30 Am. Crim. L. Rev. 97 (1992).

H. McGinley & R. A. Pasewark, National Survey of the Frequency and Success of the Insanity Pleas and Alternate Pleas, 17 J. Psychiatry & L. 205 (1989).

M. Mihajlovich, Does Plight Make Right: The Battered Woman Syndrome, Expert Testimony and the Law of Self-Defense, 62 Ind. L.J. 1253 (1987).

S. Milgram, Obedience to Authority (1974).

M. H. Mitchell, Does Wife Abuse Justify Homicide?, 24 Wayne L. Rev. 1705 (1978).

J. Monahan, Abolish the Insanity Defense? — Not Yet, 26 Rutgers L. Rev. 719 (1973).

M. Moore, Law and Psychiatry: Rethinking the Relationship (1984).

R. Moore, Legal Responsibility and Chronic Alcoholism, 122 Am. J. Psych. 748 (1966).

J. A. Moreno, Killing Daddy: Developing a Self-Defense Strategy for the Abused Child, 137 U. Pa. L. Rev. 1281 (1989).

N. Morris, Madness and the Criminal Law (1982).

N. Morris, Psychiatry and the Dangerous Criminal, 41 S. Cal. L. Rev. 514 (1968).

S. Morse, Diminished Capacity: A Moral and Legal Conundrum, 2 Intl. J. L. & Psych. 271 (1979).

S. Morse, Diminished Capacity, in S. Shute et al., eds., Action and Value in Criminal Law 239 (1993).

S. Morse, Failed Explanations and Criminal Responsibility: Experts and the Unconscious, 68 Va. L. Rev. 971 (1982).

S. Morse, Undiminished Confusion in Diminished Capacity, 75 J. Crim. L. & Criminology 1 (1984).

T. P. Myers, Halcion Made Me Do It: New Liability and a New Defense — Fear and Loathing in the Halcion Paper Chase, 62 U. Cin. L. Rev. 603 (1993).

D. Neely, Legal Necessity and Civil Disobedience, 74 Ill. B.J. 596 (1986).

R. Nozick, Anarchy, State and Utopia (1974).

J. Ogloff, A Comparison of Insanity Defense Standards on Juror Decision Making, 15 Law & Human Behavior 509 (1991).

R. Pasework, Insanity Plea: A Review of the Research Literature, 9 J. Psych. & L. 357 (1981).

S. H. Pillsbury, The Meaning of Deserved Punishment: An Essay on Choice, Character, and Responsibility, 67 Ind. L.J. 719 (1992).

L. E. Reece, Comment, Mothers Who Kill: Postpartum Disorders and Criminal Infanticide, 38 U.C.L.A.L. Rev. 699 (1991).

R. A. Rosen, On Self-Defense, Imminence, and Women Who Kill Their Batterers, 71 N.C.L. Rev. 371 (1993).

W. Roth, General Versus Specific Intent: A Time for Terminological Understanding in California, 7 Pepperdine L. Rev. 67 (1979).

L. Rubin, Quiet Rage: Bernie Goetz in a Time of Madness (1988).

E. M. Schneider, Describing and Changing: Women's Self-Defense Work and the Problem of Expert Testimony on Battering, 9 Women's Rights L. Rptr. 195 (1986).

R. F. Schopp, Automatism, Insanity and the Psychology of Criminal Responsibility (1991).

R. F. Schopp, B. J. Sturgis & M. Sullivan, Battered Woman Syndrome, Expert Testimony, and the Distinction Between Justification and Excuse, [1994] U. Ill. L. Rev. 45.

S. J. Schulhofer, The Gender Question in Criminal Law, 7 Soc. Phil. & Pol. 105 (1990).

L. Schwartz, Reform of the Federal Criminal Laws, [1977] Duke L.J. 171.

R. Simon, The Jury and the Defense of Insanity (1967).

A. Singer, The Imposition of the Insanity Defense on an Unwilling Defendant, 41 Ohio St. L.J. 637 (1980).

R. Slovenko, The Insanity Defense in the Wake of the *Hinckley* Trial, 14 Rutgers L.J. 373 (1983).

J. C. Smith, Justification and Excuse in the Criminal Law (1989).

H. J. Steadman, et al., Maintenance of an Insanity Defense Under Montana's "Abolition" of the Insanity Defense, 146 Am. J. Psychiatry 357 (1989).

A. Stone, Law, Psychiatry, and Morality (1984).

G. R. Sullivan, Bad Thoughts and Bad Acts, [1990] Crim. L. Rev. 559.

L. Taylor, Provoked Reason in Men and Women: Heat-of-Passion Manslaughter and Imperfect Self-Defense, 33 U.C.L.A.L. Rev. 1679 (1986).

C. Thomas, Crime and Punishment—and Personal Responsibility, The National Times, Sept. 1994, at 31.

L. Tiffany & C. Anderson, Legislating the Necessity Defense in Criminal Law, 52 Den. L.J. 839 (1975).

L. Tiffany & M. Tiffany, Nosologic Objection to the Criminal Defense of Pathological Intoxication: What Do the Doubters Doubt?, 13 Intl. J.L. & Psych. 49 (1990).

P. Wald, Alcohol, Drugs, and Criminal Responsibility, 63 Geo. L.J. 69 (1974).

H. Wales, An Analysis of the Proposal to "Abolish" the Insanity Defense in S. 1: Squeezing a Lemon, 124 U. Pa. L. Rev. 687 (1976).

A. Wallach & L. Rubin, The Premenstrual Syndrome and Criminal Responsi-
    bility, 19 U.C.L.A.L. Rev. 209 (1971).
D. Wasserman, Justifying Self-Defense, 16 Phil. & Pub. Aff. 356 (1987).
D. Wexler, An Offense-Victim Approach to Insanity Defense Reform, 26 Ariz. L.
    Rev. 17 (1984).
G. Williams, A Commentary on Regina v. Dudley and Stephens, 8 Cambrian L.
    Rev. 94 (1977).
W. Winslade & J. Ross, The Insanity Plea (1983).
B. Wootton, Crime and the Criminal Law (1963).

California Special Commission on Insanity and Criminal Offenders, First Report
    30 (1962).
Casenote (James Cavallaro), The Demise of the Political Necessity Defense: In-
    direct Civil Disobedience and United States v. Schoon, 81 Cal. L. Rev. 351
    (1993).
Comment (E. A. Gifford), Artes Moriendi: Active Euthanasia and the Art of Dying,
    40 U.C.L.A.L. Rev. 1545 (1993).
Comment, The Battered Wife's Dilemma: To Kill or To Be Killed, 32 Hastings
    L.J. 895 (1981).
Comment, From Duress to Intent: Shifting the Burden in Prison-Escape Prose-
    cutions, 127 U. Pa. L. Rev. 1142 (1979).
Comment, Intolerable Conditions as a Defense to Prison Escapes, 26 U.C.L.A.L.
    Rev. 1126 (1979).
Comment, The Law of Necessity as Applied in the Bisbee Deportation Case, 13
    Ariz. L. Rev. 264 (1961).
Insanity as a Defense: A Panel Discussion, Annual Judicial Conference, Second
    Judicial Circuit of the United States, 37 F.R.D. 365 (1964).
The Law Commission Consultation Paper No. 127, Intoxication and Criminal
    Liability (1993).
The Law Commission, Consultation Paper No. 122, Legislating the Criminal
    Code, Offenses Against the Person and General Principles (1992).
New York State Task Force on Life and the Law, When Death Is Sought—As-
    sisted Suicide in the Medical Context (1994).
Note, Amnesia, A Case Study in the Limits of Particular Justice, 71 Yale L.J. 109
    (1961).
Note, Antinuclear Demonstrations and the Necessity Defense, 5 Vt. L. Rev. 103
    (1980).
Note (Laura Schulkind), Applying the Necessity Defense, 64 N.Y.U.L. Rev. 79
    (1989).
Note, The Battered Woman Syndrome and Self-Defense: A Legal and Empirical
    Dissent, 72 Va. L. Rev. 619 (1986).
Note, Does Plight Make Right: The Battered Woman Syndrome, Expert Testi-
    mony and the Law of Self-Defense, 62 Ind. L.J. 1263 (1987).
Note, Has the PMS Defense Gained a Legitimate Toehold in Virginia Criminal
    Law?, 14 Geo. Mason L. Rev. 427 (1991).
Note, Justification: The Impact of the Model Penal Code on Statutory Reform,
    75 Colum. L. Rev. 914 (1975).
Note, Limits on the Use of Defensive Force to Prevent Intramarital Assaults, 10
    Rut.-Cam. L.J. 643 (1979).

Note, Medical Necessity as a Defense to Criminal Liability: United States v. Randall, 46 Geo. Wash. L. Rev. 273 (1978).

Note, Necessity as a Defense to a Charge of Criminal Trespass in an Abortion Clinic, 48 Cin. L. Rev. 509 (1979).

Note, The Necessity Defense to Prison Escape After United States v. Bailey, 65 Va. L. Rev. 359 (1979).

Note, Physician-Assisted Suicide and the Right to Die with Assistance, 105 Harv. L. Rev. 2031 (1992).

Note, Political Protest and the Illinois Defense of Necessity, 54 U. Chi. L. Rev. 1070 (1987).

Chapter 9
Theft Offenses

F. Allen, A Crisis of Legality in the Criminal Law? Reflections on the Rule of Law, 42 Mercer L. Rev. 811 (1991).

F. Allen, The Erosion of Legality in American Criminal Justice: Some Latter-Day Adventures of the *Nulla Poena* Principle, 29 Ariz. L. Rev. 387 (1987).

J. Coffee, Does "Unlawful" Mean "Criminal"?: Reflections on the Disappearing Tort/Crime Distinction in American Law, 71 B.U.L. Rev. 193 (1993).

J. Coffee, From Tort to Crime: Some Reflections on the Criminalization of Fiduciary Breaches and the Problematic Line Between Law and Ethics, 19 Am. Crim. L. Rev. 117 (1981).

J. Coffee, The Metastasis of Mail Fraud: The Continuing Story of the "Evolution" of a White-Collar Crime, 21 Am. Crim. L. Rev. 1 (1983).

P. R. Ezersky, Intra-Corporate Mail and Wire Fraud: Criminal Liability for Fiduciary Breach, 94 Yale L.J. 1427 (1985).

G. Fletcher, Blackmail: The Paradigmatic Crime, 141 U. Pa. L. Rev. 1617 (1993).

G. Fletcher, The Metamorphosis of Larceny, 89 Harv. L. Rev. 469 (1976).

D. H. Ginsburg & P. Shechtman, Blackmail: An Economic Analysis of the Law, 141 U. Pa. L. Rev. 1849, 1873-1874 (1993).

W. J. Gordon, Truth and Consequences: The Force of Blackmail's Central Case, 141 U. Pa. L. Rev. 1741 (1993).

J. Hall, Theft, Law and Society (2d ed. 1952).

R. Hammond, Theft of Information, 100 L.Q. Rev. 252 (1984).

J. Lindgren, Unraveling the Paradox of Blackmail, 84 Colum. L. Rev. 670 (1984).

J. M. Livermore, Lawyer Extortion, 20 Ariz. L. Rev. 403 (1978).

G. Moohr, Mail Fraud and Intangible Rights Doctrine, 31 Harv. J. Leg. 153 (1994).

M. Nimmer, National Secrets v. Free Speech: The Issues Left Undecided in the *Ellsberg* Case, 28 Stan. L. Rev. 311 (1974).

R. Pearce, Theft by False Promises, 101 U. Pa. L. Rev. 967 (1953).

G. Williams, Forgery and Falsity, [1974] Crim. L. Rev. 71.

G. Williams, Theft, Consent and Illegality: Some Problems, [1977] Crim. L. Rev. 327.

Note, A Rationale of the Law of Aggravated Theft, 54 Colum. L. Rev. 84 (1954).

INDEX